The Pocket Oxford–Duden rman Dictionary

Second Edition

German ·····> English
English ·····> German

Edited by
the Dudenredaktion
and the German Section of
the Oxford University Press
Dictionary Department

Chief Editors
M. Clark
O. Thyen

TED SMART

OXFORD
UNIVERSITY PRESS

This edition produced for

The Book People Ltd
Hall Wood Avenue
Haydock
St Helens
WA11 9UL

OXFORD
UNIVERSITY PRESS

Great Clarendon Street, Oxford OX2 6DP

Oxford University Press is a department of the University of Oxford.
It furthers the University's objective of excellence in research, scholarship,
and education by publishing worldwide in

Oxford New York

Athens Auckland Bangkok Bogotá Buenos Aires Calcutta
Cape Town Chennai Dar es Salaam Delhi Florence Hong Kong Istanbul
Karachi Kuala Lumpur Madrid Melbourne Mexico City Mumbai
Nairobi Paris São Paulo Singapore Taipei Tokyo Toronto Warsaw

with associated companies in Berlin Ibadan

Oxford is a registered trade mark of Oxford University Press
in the UK and in certain other countries

Published in the United States
by Oxford University Press Inc., New York

British Library Cataloguing in Publication Data
Data available

Library of Congress Cataloging in Publication Data
Data available
ISBN 0–19–860280–4

10 9 8 7 6 5 4

Designed by Information Design Unit, Newport Pagnell
Typeset in Nimrod, Arial and Meta by Tradespools
Printed in Great Britain by Mackays of Chatham, Kent

Erläuterungen zum deutsch-englischen Text / Key to German-English Entries

Stichwort •——————— **Bịld·schirm** *der* (Ferns., Informationst.) screen
Headword

     Bịldschirm-: ~**gerät** *das* VDU; visual ——— • **Kompositablock.**
     display unit; ~**schoner** *der;* ~~s, ~~   **Eine Tilde ersetzt**
     (DV) screen saver   **jeweils den**
        gemeinsamen
Die Aussprache- •——— **Blues** /bluːs/ *der;* ~, ~: blues *pl.*   **ersten Bestandteil**
angaben (in IPA-   **der Komposita**
Lautschrift) stehen   Compound block
unmittelbar hinter   with a swung dash
dem Stichwort   representing the
(s.S.xi)   first element of
Pronunciation is   each compound
shown in IPA
immediately after the **dar|bieten** (geh.) *unr. tr. V.* (aufführen, ——— • **Ein senkrechter**
headword (see p. xi)   vortragen) perform; ...   **Strich nach dem**
        ersten Bestandteil
        eines zusammen-
Ein unter einen •——— **darüber** *Adv.* (a) over it/them; ~ stehen **gesetzten Verbs**
Vokal gesetzter   (fig.) be above such things   **zeigt an, dass es**
waagerechter Strich   **sich um eine**
zeigt die Länge des   **unfeste Zusam-**
Vokals und in   **mensetzung handelt**
mehrsilbigen   A vertical bar
Wörtern zugleich   indicates that a
die Betonung der   compound verb is
betreffenden Silbe   separable
an
An underline indicates **darụm** *Adv.* (a) [a]round it/them; ... ——— • **Ein unter einen**
a long vowel, stressed   **Vokal gesetzter**
in words of more than   **Punkt zeigt die**
one syllable   **Kürze des Vokals**
        und in mehrsilbigen
        Wörtern zugleich
Ein hochgestellter •——— **dạss, *dạß** *Konj.* (a) that; ...   **die Betonung**
Stern vor einem   **der betreffenden**
Stichwort zeigt an,   **Silbe an**
dass es sich um   An underdot
eine alte, künftig   indicates a short
nicht mehr gültige   vowel, stressed in
Schreibung handelt   words of more than
An asterisk indicates   one syllable
an old spelling

     Erst·aufführung *die* première ——————— • **Kompositionsfuge**
        Dot marking the
Grammatische •——— **erstklassig** **1** *Adj.* first-class   junction of the
Gliederungspunkte   **2** *adv.* superbly   elements of a
und Wortartangaben   compound
Grammatical
categories
and parts of speech

• •

Die Formen des •——— Falter der; ~s, ~ ⟨Nacht~⟩ moth; ⟨Tag~⟩
Genitivs und des butterfly
Plurals eines
Substantivs **fliehen** /ˈfliːən/ unr. itr. V.; mit sein flee ———• **Der Hinweis** *mit sein*
Genitive and plural ⟨vor + Dat. from⟩; ... **zeigt an, dass das**
forms of a noun **betreffende Verb die**
Perfekttempora mit
dem Hilfsverb *sein*
bildet
Unregelmäßige •——— fromm; ~er od. frömmer, ~st... od. *mit sein* indicates that
Steigerungsformen **frömmst...** [1] *Adj.* pious, devout ⟨person⟩; a verb is conjugated
eines Adjektivs with the auxiliary verb
Irregular comparative *sein* in its perfect
and superlative forms tenses
of an adjective

Gehässigkeit die; ~, ~en **(a)** (Wesen) ———• **Semantische**
spitefulness; **Gliederungspunkte**
(b) (Äußerung) spiteful remark **und Bedeutungs-**
indikatoren
Stilistische •——— happig *Adj.* (ugs.) ~e Preise fancy prices Sense categories and
Kennzeichnungen (coll.) indicators
Style labels
Haube die; ~, ~n **(a)** bonnet; (einer
Krankenschwester) cap;
(b) (Kfz-W.) bonnet (Brit.); hood (Amer.) ———• **Angaben zur**
heuer *Adv.* (südd., österr., schweiz.) this year **räumlichen**
Zuordnung
Bereichsangaben •——— Icon /ˈaikən/ das; ~s, ~s (DV) icon Regional labels
Subject labels **Immun·schwäche** die (Med.)
immunodeficiency; immune deficiency

knallen [1] *itr. V.* **(a)** ⟨shot⟩ ring out; ———• **Kollokatoren**
⟨firework⟩ go bang; ⟨cork⟩ pop; ⟨door⟩ slam; **(Wörter, mit denen**
⟨whip, rifle⟩ crack; **zusammen das**
knapp [1] *Adj.* **(a)** meagre; narrow ⟨victory, **Stichwort häufig**
lead⟩; narrow, bare ⟨majority⟩; **vorkommt) als Hilfe**
zur Auswahl der für
den jeweiligen
Beispiele (jeweils •——— machen [1] *tr. V.* **(a)** make; aus Plastik/ **Kontext passenden**
mit einer Tilde an Holz usw. **gemacht** made of plastic/wood etc.; **Übersetzung**
Stelle des sich ⟨Dat.⟩ etw. ~ lassen have sth. made; ... Collocators—words
Stichworts) often used with the
Examples (with headword, shown to
a swung dash help select the correct
representing the translation for each
headword) context

Omi die; ~, ~s ▶ OMA ———• **Ein Pfeil verweist**
auf ein bedeutungs-
Mit *s. auch* **wird •——— Samstag** der; ~[e]s, ~e Saturday; *s. auch* **gleiches anderes**
auf ein Stichwort DIENSTAG **Stichwort**
verwiesen, unter An arrow directs the
dem noch user to another
zusätzliche headword with the
Informationen same meaning
zu finden sind
s. auch directs the
user to another
headword where
additional information
can be found

ix

Key to English-German Entries / Erläuterungen zum englisch-deutschen Text

Headword •
Stichwort

barber /ˈbɑːbə(r)/ *n.* [Herren]friseur, *der;*
~'s shop (Brit.) Friseursalon, *der*
barbiturate /bɑːˈbɪtjʊrət/ *n.* (Chem.)
Barbiturat, *das*

bar: ~**chart** *n.* Stabdiagramm, *das;*
~**code** *n.* Strichcode, *der*

Compound block •
with a swung dash
representing the
first element of each
compound
Kompositablock. Eine
Tilde ersetzt jeweils
den gemeinsamen
ersten Bestandteil der
Komposita

bear[2] [1] *v.t.,* bore /bɔː(r)/, borne /bɔːn/ ...
■ **bear 'out** *v.t.* (fig.) bestätigen ⟨Bericht,
Erklärung⟩; ~ sb. out jmdm. Recht geben.
■ **'bear with** *v.t.* Nachsicht haben mit

Each phrasal verb •
is entered on a new
line immediately
following the entry
for the first element
Die *Phrasal Verbs*
folgen, jedes auf einer
neuen Zeile, direkt auf
den Eintrag zu ihrem
Grundverb

bemused /brˈmjuːzd/ *adj.* verwirrt

Pronunciation •
shown in IPA
(see p. xiii).
Aussspracheangaben
(in IPA-Lautschrift) (s.
S. xiii)

Stress mark, •
showing stress on
the following
syllable
Betonungszeichen vor
der betonten Silbe

'bin liner *n.* Müllbeutel, *der*

cart /kɑːt/ [1] *n.* Wagen, *der*
[2] *v.t.* (coll.) schleppen

Grammatical •
categories
and parts of speech
Grammatische
Gliederungspunkte
und Wortartangaben

Irregular tenses •
of a verb (see also
table on p. 927)
Unregelmäßige
Verbformen (siehe
auch die Liste auf S.
927)

choose /tʃuːz/ [1] *v.t.,* chose /tʃəʊz/,
chosen /ˈtʃəʊzn/ (a) wählen

dub /dʌb/ *v.t.,* -bb- (Cinemat.) synchronisieren

Doubling of a final •
consonant of a verb
before -ed *or* -ing
Verdoppelung des
Endkonsonanten
eines Verbs vor -ed
oder -ing

Irregular •
comparative and
superlative forms
of an adjective
Unregelmäßige
Steigerungsformen
eines Adjektivs

good /gʊd/ [1] *adj.,* better /ˈbetə(r)/, best
/best/ (a) gut; günstig ⟨Gelegenheit,
Angebot⟩; ...

groom /gruːm, grʊm/ [1] *n.* (a) (stable boy)
Stallbursche, *der*
(b) (bride~) Bräutigam, *der*

Sense categories •
and sense
indicators
Semantische
Gliederungspunkte
und Bedeutungs-
indikatoren

Subject labels •
Bereichsangaben

HTML *abbr.* (Comp.) **hypertext markup
language** HTML
immobilizer /rˈməʊbɪlaɪzə(r)/ *n.* (Motor Veh.)
Wegfahrsperre, *die*

Key to English-German entries

• •

Style labels •————— **jam-packed** *adj.* (coll.) knallvoll (ugs.),
Stilistische   proppenvoll (ugs.) (with von)
Kennzeichnungen

loch /lɒx, lɒk/ *n.* (Scot.) See, *der*
Medicare /'mediːkeə(r)/ *n.* (Amer.)   •————— **Regional labels**
[bundes]staatliches   Angaben zur
Krankenversicherungssystem für Personen   räumlichen
über 65 Jahre   Zuordnung

Collocators •————— **oppress** /ə'pres/ *v.t.* unterdrücken; (fig.)
—words often used   ⟨*Gefühl:*⟩ bedrücken
with the headword,   **oppressive** /ə'presɪv/ *adj.* repressiv; (fig.)
shown to help select   bedrückend ⟨*Ängste, Atmosphäre*⟩; (hot and
the correct transla-   close) drückend ⟨*Wetter, Klima, Tag*⟩
tion for each context.
Kollokatoren (Wörter,
mit denen zusammen   **price** /praɪs/ *n.* (lit. or fig.) Preis, *der;* **at a**   •————— **Examples (with a
das Stichwort häufig   ~ **of** zum Preis von; **what is the ~ of this?**   swung dash
vorkommt) als Hilfe   was kostet das?; **at/not at any ~:** um jeden/   representing the
zur Auswahl der für   keinen Preis   headword)**
den jeweiligen Kontext   Beispiele (jeweils mit
passenden   einer Tilde an Stelle
Übersetzung   des Stichworts)

An arrow directs •————— **sitcom** /'sɪtkɒm/ (coll.) ▶ SITUATION COMEDY
the user to another
headword with the
same meaning
Ein Pfeil verweist auf **Sunday** /'sʌndeɪ, 'sʌndɪ/ *n.* Sonntag, *der;*
ein bedeutungsglei-   ~ **opening** die sonntägliche Öffnung;
ches anderes   ~ **trading** sonntägliche Ladenöffnung; *see*   •————— **see also directs the
Stichwort   *also* FRIDAY   user to another
                                                                               headword where
                                                                               additional
                                                                               information can be
                                                                               found**
                                                                               Mit *see also* wird auf
                                                                               ein Stichwort
                                                                               verwiesen, unter dem
                                                                               noch zusätzliche
                                                                               Informationen zu
                                                                               finden sind

Phonetic symbols used in transcriptions of German words

Phonetic information given in the German-English section

The pronunciation of German is largely regular, and phonetic transcriptions have only been given where additional help is needed. In all other cases only the position of the stressed syllable and the length of the vowel in that syllable are shown: a long vowel is indicated by an underline, e.g. **Maß**, a short vowel by a dot placed underneath, e.g. **Masse**.

a	*h**a**t*	hat
aː	*B**a**hn*	baːn
ɐ	*Ob**er***	'oːbɐ
ɐ̯	*Uhr*	uːɐ̯
ã	*Ensemble*	ã'sãːbl̩
ãː	*Abonnement*	abɔnə'mãː
ai̯	*w**ei**t*	vai̯t
au̯	*H**au**t*	hau̯t
b	*B**a**ll*	bal
ç	*i**ch**	ıç
d	*d**a**nn*	dan
dʒ	*G**i**n*	dʒın
e	*eg**a**l*	e'gaːl
eː	*B**ee**t*	beːt
ɛ	*m**ä**sten*	'mɛstn̩
ɛː	*w**ä**hlen*	'vɛːlən
ɛ̃	*M**a**nnequin*	'manəkɛ̃
ɛ̃ː	*Cousin*	ku'zɛ̃ː
ə	*N**a**se*	'naːzə
f	*F**a**ß*	fas
g	*G**a**st*	gast
h	*h**a**t*	hat
i	*vit**a**l*	vi'taːl
iː	*v**ie**l*	fiːl
i̯	*Stud**ie***	'ʃtuːdi̯ə
ı	*B**i**rke*	'bırkə
j	*j**a***	jaː
k	*k**a**lt*	kalt
l	*L**a**st*	last
l̩	*N**a**bel*	'naːbl̩

Phonetics used in transcriptions of German

m	*Mast*	mast
n	*Naht*	naːt
ņ	*baden*	'baːdņ
ŋ	*lang*	laŋ
o	*Moral*	moˈraːl
oː	*Boot*	boːt
ọ	*loyal*	lọaˈjaːl
õ	*Fondue*	fõˈdyː
õː	*Fond*	fõː
ɔ	*Post*	pɔst
ø	*Ökonom*	økoˈnoːm
øː	*Öl*	øːl
œ	*göttlich*	'gœtlɪç
œ̃	*Parfum*	parˈfœ̃ː
ɔy	*Heu*	hɔy
p	*Pakt*	pakt
pf	*Pfahl*	pfaːl
r	*Rast*	rast
s	*Hast*	hast
ʃ	*schal*	ʃaːl
t	*Tal*	taːl
ts	*Zahl*	tsaːl
tʃ	*Matsch*	matʃ
u	*kulant*	kuˈlant
uː	*Hut*	huːt
ụ	*aktuell*	akˈtụɛl
ʊ	*Pult*	pʊlt
v	*was*	vas
x	*Bach*	bax
y	*Physik*	fyˈziːk
yː	*Rübe*	'ryːbə
y̆	*Nuance*	'ny̆ãːsə
ʏ	*Fülle*	'fʏlə
z	*Hase*	'haːzə
ʒ	*Genie*	ʒeˈniː

ǀ	Glottal stop, e.g. beachten /bəǀaxtņ/
ː	Length sign, indicating that the preceding vowel is long, e.g. Chrom /kroːm/
˜	Indicates a nasal vowel, e.g. Fond /fõː/
'	Stress mark, immediately preceding a stressed syllable, e.g. Ballon /baˈlɔn/

Die für das Englische verwendeten Zeichen der Lautschrift

ɑ	*barb*	bɑːb		p	*pet*	pet
ãː	*séance*	ˈseɪ ãs		r	*rat*	ræt
æ	*fat*	fæt		s	*sip*	sɪp
ǽ	*lingerie*	ˈlæ̃ʒərɪ		ʃ	*ship*	ʃɪp
aɪ	*fine*	faɪn		t	*tip*	tɪp
aʊ	*now*	naʊ		tʃ	*chin*	tʃɪn
b	*bat*	bæt		θ	*thin*	θɪn
d	*dog*	dɒg		ð	*the*	ðə
dʒ	*jam*	dʒæm		uː	*boot*	buːt
e	*met*	met		ʊ	*book*	bʊk
eɪ	*fate*	feɪt		ʊə	*tourist*	ˈtʊərɪst
eə	*fairy*	ˈfeərɪ		ʌ	*dug*	dʌg
əʊ	*goat*	gəʊt		v	*van*	væn
ə	*ago*	əˈgəʊ		w	*win*	wɪn
ɜː	*fur*	fɜː(r)		x	*loch*	lɒx
f	*fat*	fæt		z	*zip*	zɪp
g	*good*	gʊd		ʒ	*vision*	ˈvɪʒn
h	*hat*	hæt		:	Längezeichen, bezeichnet Länge des unmittelbar davor stehenden Vokals, z. B. boot /buːt/	
ɪ	*bit, lately*	bɪt, ˈleɪtlɪ				
ɪə	*nearly*	ˈnɪəlɪ				
iː	*meet*	miːt		'	Betonung, steht unmittelbar vor einer betonten Silbe, z. B. ago /əˈgəʊ/	
j	*yet*	jet				
k	*kit*	kɪt				
l	*lot*	lɒt		(r)	Ein „r" in runden Klammern wird nur gesprochen, wenn im Textzusammenhang ein Vokal unmittelbar folgt, z. B. pare /peə(r)/; pare away /peər əˈweɪ/	
m	*mat*	mæt				
n	*not*	nɒt				
ŋ	*sing*	sɪŋ				
ɒ	*got*	gɒt				
ɔː	*paw*	pɔː				
ɔɪ	*boil*	bɔɪl				

German spellings in this dictionary

German spellings in this dictionary are in accordance with the reforms ratified by the governments of Germany, Austria, and Switzerland in July 1996 and in force since August 1998. Key points of the reforms are summarized below. In cases of doubt the editors have followed *Duden—Rechtschreibung der deutschen Sprache*, twenty-first edition, 1996.

To help the user who may not yet be familiar with the reforms, the German-English section of the dictionary gives both the new spellings and the old versions which will become 'invalid' in 2005 after a transition period during which both spellings are 'valid'. The old spellings are marked with an asterisk and are cross-referred where necessary to the new. For example, the translations of the compound verb *wiedererkennen* will no longer be found at this headword, since under the new spelling rules the word will vanish from the language. Instead they are covered by two phrases at the entry for *wieder: jemanden/etwas wieder erkennen* (in the form *jmdn./etw. ~ erkennen*) and *er war kaum wieder zu erkennen* (in the form *er war kaum ~ zu erkennen*). Similarly, the translations of the adjective previously written *belemmert* will be found at the new entry for the headword *belämmert*.

In a number of cases, however, implementing the new spelling rules has meant that just some, but not all, uses of a word have had to be transferred from one entry to another. In these cases the headword is not marked with an asterisk, but the entry is provided with a cross-reference to where the transferred information is now to be found. So, for example, the user who consults the entry for *leid* looking for a translation of the phrase previously written *jemandem leid tun* will find a cross-reference to the entry for the noun *Leid*, since according to the new spelling rules the word is written with a capital *L* in this expression. The headword *leid* itself is not marked with an asterisk, since it continues to exist in its own right as an adjective.

The following summary lists the most important changes:

1 The ß character The ß character, which is generally replaced in Switzerland by a double s, will be retained in Germany and Austria, but will only be written after a long vowel (as in Fuß, Füße) and after a diphthong (as in Strauß, Sträuße). *Fluß, Baß, keß, läßt, Nußknacker* become in future: *Fluss, Bass, kess, lässt, Nussknacker*

. . . .

2 Nominalized adjectives

Nominalized adjectives will be written with a capital even in set phrases.

sein Schäfchen ins trockene bringen, im trüben fischen, im allgemeinen become in future: *sein Schäfchen ins Trockene bringen, im Trüben fischen, im Allgemeinen*

3 Words from the same word family

In certain cases the spelling of words belonging to the same family will be made uniform.

numerieren, überschwenglich become in future: *nummerieren* (like Nummer), *überschwänglich* (being related to Überschwang)

4 The same consonant repeated three times

When the same consonant repeated three times occurs in compounds, all three will be written even when a vowel follows.

Brennessel, Schiffahrt become in future: *Brennnessel, Schifffahrt* (exceptions are dennoch, Drittel, Mittag)

5 Verb, adjective and participle compounds

Verb, adjective and participle compounds will be written more frequently than previously in two words.

spazierengehen, radfahren, ernstgemeint, erdölexportierend become in future: *spazieren gehen, Rad fahren, ernst gemeint, Erdöl exportierend*

6 Compounds containing numbers in figures

Compounds containing numbers in figures will in future be written with a hyphen.

24karätig, 8pfünder become in future: *24-karätig, 8-Pfünder*

7 The division of words containing st

st will be treated like a normal combination of consonants and no longer be indivisible.

Ha-stig, Ki-ste become in future: *has-tig, Kis-te*

8 The division of words containing ck

The combination ck will not be divided and will go on to the next line.

Bäk-ker, schik-ken become in future: *Bä-cker, schi-cken*

9 The division of foreign words

Compound foreign words which are hardly recognized as such today may be divided by syllables, without regard to their original components.

He-li-ko-pter (from the Greek helix and pteron) may also become in future: *He-li-kop-ter*

10 The comma before und

Where two complete clauses are connected by *und* a comma will not be obligatory.

Karl war in Schwierigkeiten, und niemand konnte ihm helfen. may also in future be written: *Karl war in Schwierigkeiten und niemand konnte ihm helfen.*

11 The comma with infinitives and participles

Even longer clauses containing an infinitive or participle will not have to be divided off with a comma.

Er begann sofort, das neue Buch zu lesen. Ungläubig den Kopf schüttelnd, verließ er das Zimmer. may also in future be written: *Er begann sofort das neue Buch zu lesen. Ungläubig den Kopf schüttelnd verließ er das Zimmer.*

Abkürzungen / Abbreviations

anderes, andere	a.	other, others
ähnliches, ähnliche	ä.	similar
Abkürzung	abbr.	abbreviation
Abkürzung	Abk.	abbreviation
absolut	abs.	absolute
adjektivisch	adj.	adjective, adjectival
Adjektiv	Adj.	adjective
Verwaltungssprache	Admin.	Administration, Administrative
adverbial	adv.	adverb, adverbial
Adverb	Adv.	adverb
Flugwesen	Aeronaut.	Aeronautics
Landwirtschaft	Agric.	Agriculture
Akkusativ	Akk.	accusative
Amerika	Amer.	American, America
amerikanisch	amerik.	American
Amtssprache	Amtsspr.	official language
Anatomie	Anat.	Anatomy
Anthropologie	Anthrop.	Anthropology
veraltet	arch.	archaic
Archäologie	Archaeol.	Archaeology
Architektur	Archit.	Architecture
Artikel	art.	article
Astrologie	Astrol.	Astrology
Astronomie	Astron.	Astronomy
Raumfahrt	Astronaut.	Astronautics
Altes Testament	A. T.	Old Testament
attributiv	attr., attrib.	attributive
Australien	Austral.	Australian, Australia
Bauwesen	Bauw.	Construction
Bergmannssprache	Bergmannsspr.	Mining terminology
besonders	bes.	especially
Bezeichnung	Bez.	name
biblisch	bibl.	biblical
Biologie	Biol.	Biology
Buchführung	Bookk.	Bookkeeping
Börsenwesen	Börsenw.	Stock Market
Botanik	Bot.	Botany
Bundesrepublik Deutschland	BRD	Federal Republic of Germany
britisch, Großbritannien	Brit.	British, Britain
britisch	brit.	British
Bruchzahl	Bruchz.	fraction
Buchführung	Buchf.	Bookkeeping
Buchwesen	Buchw.	Book Trade
Chemie	Chem.	Chemistry
chemisch	chem.	chemical
Kindersprache	child lang.	child language
christlich	christl.	Christian
Kinematographie	Cinemat.	Cinematography
umgangssprachlich	coll.	colloquial
Kollektivum	collect.	collective
Kombination	comb.	combination
Handel, Handels-	Commerc.	Commerce, Commercial
elektronische Datenverarbeitung	Comp.	Computing
Komparativ, komparativ	compar.	comparative
Konditional, konditional	condit.	conditional
Konjunktion	conj.	conjunction
Dativ	Dat.	dative
Deutsche Demokratische Republik	DDR	German Democratic Republic
bestimmt	def.	definite
Deklination	Dekl.	declension
Demonstrativpronomen	Demonstrativpron.	demonstrative pronoun
Zahnmedizin	Dent.	Dentistry
abwertend	derog.	derogatory
das heißt	d. h.	that is [to say]
Dialekt	dial.	dialect
dichterisch	dichter.	poetic
Damenschneiderei	Dressm.	Dressmaking
Druckwesen	Druckw.	Printing
deutsch	dt.	German
Datenverarbeitung	DV	Data Processing
kirchlich	Eccl.	Ecclesiastical
Ökologie	Ecol.	Ecology
Ökonomik	Econ.	Economics
Bildungswesen	Educ.	Education
ehemals, ehemalig	ehem.	former
Eisenbahn	Eisenb.	Railways
Elektrizität	Electr.	Electricity
Elektrotechnik	Elektrot.	Electrical Engineering
elektrisch	elektr.	electrical
elliptisch	ellipt.	elliptical
emphatisch	emphat.	emphatic
besonders	esp.	especially
etwas	etw.	something
euphemistisch	euphem.	euphemistic
evangelisch	ev.	Evangelical
ausdrückend	expr.	expressing

fachsprachlich	fachspr.	technical
familiär	fam.	familiar
feminin	fem.	feminine
Fernsehen	Ferns.	Television
Fernsprechwesen	Fernspr.	Telephony
figurativ	fig.	figurative
Finanzwesen	Finanzw.	Finance
Flugwesen	Flugw.	Aeronautics
Fußball	Footb.	Football
Forstwesen	Forstw.	Forestry
Fotografie	Fot.	Photography
Gastronomie	Gastr.	Gastronomy
gehoben	geh.	elevated
Genitiv	Gen.	genitive
Geographie	Geog.	Geography
Geologie	Geol.	Geology
Geometrie	Geom.	Geometry
Handarbeit	Handarb.	Handicraft
Heraldik	Her.	Heraldry
Hilfsverb	Hilfsv.	auxiliary verb
historisch	hist.	historical
Geschichte, historisch	Hist.	History, historical
Hochschulwesen	Hochschulw.	Higher Education
Gartenbau	Hort.	Horticultural
Imperativ, imperativisch	imper.	imperative
unpersönlich	impers.	impersonal
unbestimmt	indef.	indefinite
Indefinitpronomen	Indefinit-pron.	indefinite pronoun
Indeklinabel	Indekl.	indeclinable
Indikativ	Indik.	indicative
Infinitiv	Inf.	infinitive
Interjektion	Interj., int.	interjection
interrogativ	interrog.	interrogative
intransitiv	intr.	intransitive
irisch, Irland	Ir.	Irish, Ireland
ironisch	iron.	ironical
Jägersprache	Jägerspr.	hunting language
jemand	jmd.	somebody
jemandem	jmdm.	somebody
jemanden	jmdn.	somebody
jemandes	jmds.	somebody
scherzhaft	joc.	jocular
Journalismus	Journ.	Journalism
Jugendsprache	Jugendspr.	young people's language
juristisch	jur.	legal
Kardinalzahl	Kardinalz.	cardinal number
katholisch	kath.	Catholic
Kaufmannssprache	Kaufmannsspr.	business language
Kraftfahrzeugwesen	Kfz-W.	Motor Vehicles

Kindersprache	Kinderspr.	child language
Kochkunst	Kochk.	Cookery
Komparativ	Komp.	Comparative
Konjunktion	Konj.	conjunction
landschaftlich	landsch.	regional
Landwirtschaft	Landw.	Agriculture
Linguistik	Ling.	Linguistics
wortwörtlich	lit.	literal
Literatur	Lit.	Literature
Literaturwissenschaft	Literaturw.	Literary Studies
Luftfahrt	Luftf.	Aeronautics
mittelalterlich	ma.	medieval
Mittelalter	MA.	Middle Ages
marxistisch	marx.	Marxist
maskulin	masc.	masculine
Mathematik	Math.	Mathematics
Maschinenbau	Mech. Engin.	Mechanical Engineering
Medizin	Med.	Medicine
Meereskunde	Meeresk.	oceanography
Meteorologie	Met.	Meteorology
Metallurgie	Metall.	Metallurgy
Metallbearbeitung	Metallbearb.	Metalwork
Metallbearbeitung	Metalw.	Metalwork
Meterologie	Meteorol.	Meteorology
Militär	Mil., Milit.	Military
modifizierend	mod.	modifying
Modalverb	Modalv.	modal verb
Kraftfahrzeugwesen	Motor Veh.	Motor Vehicles
Musik	Mus.	Music
Mythologie	Mythol.	Mythology
Substantiv	n.	noun
seemännisch	Naut.	Nautical
negativ	neg.	negative
Nominativ	Nom.	nominative
norddeutsch	nordd.	North German
nordostdeutsch	nordostd.	North-East German
Substantive	ns. (English)	nouns
nationalsozialistisch	ns. (Deutsch)	National Socialist
Neues Testament	N. T.	New Testament
Kernphysik	Nucl. Phys.	Nuclear Physics
ohne; oben	o.	without; above
Objekt	obj.	object
oder	od.	or
Ordinalzahl	Ordinalz.	ordinal number
Ornithologie	Ornith.	Ornithology
österreichisch	österr.	Austrian
Papierdeutsch	Papierdt.	officialese
Parlament	Parl.	Parliament
Partizip	Part.	participle

Abkürzungen / Abbreviations

Passiv	pass.	passive	Wissenschaft	Sci.	Science
Perfekt	Perf.	perfect	schottisch	Scot.	Scottish, Scotland
Person	Pers.	person	Schulwesen	Schulw.	School System
Philosophie	Philos.	Philosophy	Seemannssprache	Seemanns-spr.	Nautical
Fotografie	Photog.	Photography			
Phrase(n)	phr(s).	Phrase(s)	Seewesen	Seew.	maritime affairs
Physik	Phys.	Physics	Singular	Sg., sing.	singular
Physiologie	Physiol.	Physiology	salopp	sl.	slang
Plural	Pl., pl.	plural	siehe oben	s. o.	see above
Plusquamperfekt	Plusq.	pluperfect	Soziologie	Sociol.	Sociology
dichterisch	poet.	poetical	Soldatensprache	Soldaten-spr.	army slang
Politik	Polit.	Politics			
possessiv, Possessiv-	poss.	possessive	Soziologie	Soziol.	Sociology
nachgestellt	postpos.	postpositive	spöttisch	spött.	derisive
Postwesen	Postw.	Post Office	Sprichwort	Spr.	proverb
zweites Partizip	p.p.	past participle	Sprach-wissenschaft	Sprachw.	Linguistics
prädikativ	präd.	predicative			
Präposition	Präp.	preposition	Börsenwesen	St. Exch.	Stock Exchange
Präsens	Präs.	present	Steuerwesen	Steuerw.	Taxation
Präteritum	Prät.	preterite	etwas	sth.	something
prädikativ	pred.	predicative	Studentensprache	Studen-tenspr.	student slang
Präfix	pref.	prefix			
Präposition	prep.	preposition	siehe unten	s. u.	see below
Präsens	pres.	present	Subjekt	Subj.	subject
erstes Partizip	pres. p.	present participle	substantivisch; substantiviert	subst.	nominal; nominalized
Eigenname	pr. n.	proper noun			
Pronomen	Pron., pron.	pronoun	Substantiv	Subst.	noun
			süddeutsch	südd.	South German
sprichwörtlich	prov.	proverbial	südwestdeutsch	südwestd.	South-West German
Psychologie	Psych.	Psychology			
Präteritum	p.t.	past tense	Suffix	suf.	suffix
Warenzeichen	®	Registered Trade Mark	Superlativ	Sup., superl.	superlative
Eisenbahn	Railw.	Railways	Landvermessung	Surv.	Surveying
Raumfahrt	Raumf.	Space Travel	Symbol	symb.	symbol
römisch-katholische Kirche	RC Ch.	Roman Catholic Church	fachsprachlich	tech.	technical
			Fernsprechwesen	Teleph.	Telephony
Rechtssprache	Rechtsspr.	legal terminology	Fernsehen	Telev.	Television
Rechtswesen	Rechtsw.	Law	Textilwesen	Textilw.	Textiles
reflexiv	refl.	reflexive	Theologie	Theol.	Theology
regelmäßig	regelm.	regular	Tiermedizin	Tiermed.	Veterinary Medicine
relativ	rel.	relative			
Religion	Rel.	Religion	transitiv	tr.	transitive
Relativpronomen	Relativ-pron.	relative pronoun	Trennung	Trenn.	division
			und	u.	and
römisch	röm.	Roman	und Ähnliches	u. Ä.	and similar
römisch-katholisch	röm-kath.	Roman Catholic	umgangssprachlich	ugs.	colloquial
Rundfunk	Rundf.	Radio	unbestimmt	unbest.	indefinite
siehe	s.	see	Universität	Univ.	University
Seite	S.	page	unpersönlich	unpers.	impersonal
jemand	sb.	somebody	unregelmäßig	unr.	irregular
Schule	Sch.	School	gewöhnlich	usu.	usually
scherzhaft	scherzh.	jocular	und so weiter	usw.	et cetera
Schülersprache	Schüler-spr.	school slang	von	v.	of
			Verb	V.	verb
schweizerisch	schweiz.	Swiss	Hilfsverb	v. aux.	auxiliary verb

veraltet; veraltend	**veralt.**	obsolete; obsolescent
Verhaltensfor- schung	**Verhal- tensf.**	Behavioural Research
verhüllend	**verhüll.**	euphemistic
Verkehrswesen	**Verkehrsw.**	Transport
Versicherungs- wesen	**Versicher- ungsw.**	Insurance
Tiermedizin	**Vet. Med.**	Veterinary Medicine
vergleiche	**vgl.**	compare
intransitives Verb	**v. i.**	intransitive verb
Verkleinerungs- form	**Vkl.**	diminutive
Völkerkunde	**Völkerk.**	Ethnology
volkstümlich	**volkst.**	popular, vernacular
reflexives Verb	**v. refl.**	reflexive verb
transitives Verb	**v. t.**	transitive verb
transitives und in- transitives Verb	**v. t. & i.**	transitive and intransitive verb
vulgär	**vulg.**	vulgar
Werbesprache	**Werbespr.**	advertising jargon
westdeutsch	**westd.**	western German
Wirtschaft	**Wirtsch.**	Commerce and Industry
Wissenschaft	**Wissensch.**	Science
Warenzeichen	**Wz.**	Registered Trade Mark
Zahnmedizin	**Zahnmed.**	Dentistry
zum Beispiel	**z. B.**	for example
Zeitungswesen	**Zeitungsw.**	Newspaper Industry
Zoologie	**Zool.**	Zoology
Zusammensetzung	**Zus.**	compound
Zusammen- schreibung	**Zusschr.**	writing as one word

a, A /a:/ *das;* ~, ~ **(a)** (Buchstabe) a/A; **das A und O** (fig.) the essential thing/things ⟨*Gen.* for⟩; **von A bis Z** (fig. ugs.) from beginning to end

(b) (Musik) [key of] A

a *Abk.* = **Ar**

à /a/ *Präp. mit Nom., Akk.* (Kaufmannsspr.) **zehn Marken à 50 Pfennig** ten stamps at 50 pfennigs each

A *Abk.* = **Autobahn** ≈ M

Aal *der;* ~[e]s, ~e eel; ~ **grün** (Kochk.) green eels; stewed eels

aalen *refl. V.* (ugs.) stretch out

aal·glatt (abwertend) ⟦1⟧ *Adj.* slippery; ~ **sein** be as slippery as an eel
⟦2⟧ *adv.* smoothly

Aas *das;* ~es, ~e *od.* Äser **(a)** *Pl.* ~e carrion *no art.;* (Kadaver) [rotting] carcass

(b) *Pl.* Äser (salopp abwertend) swine; (anerkennend) devil

ab ⟦1⟧ *Präp. mit Dat.* **(a)** from; **ab 1980** as from 1980; **ab Werk** (Kaufmannsspr.) ex works; **ab Frankfurt fliegen** fly from Frankfurt

(b) ([Rang]folge) from … on[wards]; **ab 20 DM** from 20 DM [upwards]

⟦2⟧ *Adv.* **(a)** (weg) off; away; **[an etw.** *(Dat.)*] **ab sein** (ugs.: sich [von etw.] gelöst haben) have come off [sth.]

(b) (ugs.: Aufforderung) off; away; **ab nach Hause** get off home

(c) Gewehr ab! (milit. Kommando) order arms!

(d) ab und zu *od.* **an** now and then

ab|ändern *tr. V.* alter; amend ⟨*text*⟩

Ab-änderung *die* alteration; (eines Textes) amendment

ab|arbeiten *tr. V.* work for ⟨*meal*⟩; work off ⟨*debt, amount*⟩

Ab-art *die* variety

ab-artig *Adj.* deviant; abnormal

Ab-artigkeit *die;* ~, ~en abnormality; deviancy

Abb. *Abk.* = **Abbildung** Fig.

Ab-bau *der* **(a)** dismantling; (von Zelten, Lagern) striking

(b) ▶ ABBAUEN C: cutback ⟨*Gen.* in⟩; pruning; reduction

(c) (Bergbau) mining; (von Stein) quarrying

ab|bauen *tr. V.* **(a)** dismantle; strike ⟨*tent, camp*⟩

(b) (beseitigen) gradually remove; break down ⟨*prejudices, inhibitions*⟩

(c) (verringern) cut back ⟨*staff*⟩; prune ⟨*jobs*⟩; reduce ⟨*wages*⟩

(d) (Bergbau) mine; quarry ⟨*stone*⟩

ab|beißen ⟦1⟧ *unr. tr. V.* bite off
⟦2⟧ *unr. itr. V.* have a bite

ab|bekommen *unr. tr. V.* **(a)** get

(b) einen Schlag/ein paar Kratzer ~: get hit/get a few scratches; **etwas** ~ (getroffen werden) be hit; (verletzt werden) be hurt

(c) (los-, herunterbekommen) get ⟨*paint, lid, chain*⟩ off

ab|berufen *unr. tr. V.* recall ⟨*ambassador, envoy*⟩ ⟨aus, von from⟩

ab|bestellen *tr. V.* cancel

ab|bezahlen *tr. V.* pay off

ab|biegen *unr. itr. V.; mit sein* turn off; **links/rechts** ~: turn [off] left/right

Abbieger *der;* ~s, ~, **Abbiegerin** *die;* ~, ~nen (Verkehrsw.) motorist/cyclist/car *etc.* turning off

Ab-bild *das* (eines Menschen) likeness; (eines Gegenstandes) copy; (fig.) portrayal

ab|bilden *tr. V.* copy; reproduce ⟨*object, picture*⟩; depict ⟨*person, landscape*⟩; (fig.) portray

Abbildung *die* illustration

ab|binden *unr. tr. V.* **(a)** (losbinden) untie; undo

(b) (abschnüren) put a tourniquet on ⟨*artery, arm, leg, etc.*⟩; tie ⟨*umbilical cord*⟩

ab|blasen *unr. tr. V.* (ugs.) call off

ab|blättern *itr. V.; mit sein* flake off

ab|blenden *tr., itr. V.* black out; dip (Brit.), dim (Amer.) ⟨*headlights*⟩; **bei Gegenverkehr frühzeitig** ~: dip *or* (Amer.) dim one's headlights promptly when there is oncoming traffic

ab|blitzen *itr. V.; mit sein* (ugs.) **sie ließ alle Verehrer** ~: she gave all her admirers the brush-off

ab|brausen *tr. V.* ▶ ABDUSCHEN

ab|brechen ⟦1⟧ *unr. tr. V.* **(a)** break off; break ⟨*needle, pencil*⟩

(b) (zerlegen) strike ⟨*tent, camp*⟩

(c) (abreißen) demolish; pull down ⟨*building*⟩

(d) (beenden) break off ⟨*negotiations, [diplomatic] relations, discussion, activity*⟩; (vorzeitig) cut short ⟨*conversation, holiday, activity*⟩

(e) (DV) cancel
⟦2⟧ *unr. itr. V.* **(a)** *mit sein* break [off]

(b) (aufhören) break off

ab|bremsen ⟦1⟧ *tr. V.* **(a)** brake

(b) retard ⟨*motion*⟩
⟦2⟧ *itr. V.* brake

ab|brennen ⟦1⟧ *unr. itr. V.; mit sein* **(a)** be burned down; **das Haus ist abgebrannt** the house has burned down

(b) ⟨*fuse*⟩ burn away; ⟨*candle*⟩ burn down
⟦2⟧ *unr. itr. V.* **(a)** let off ⟨*firework*⟩

(b) burn down ⟨*building*⟩

ạb|bringen *unr. tr. V.* jmdn. davon ∼, etw. zu tun dissuade sb. from doing sth; jmdn. vom Kurs ∼: make sb. change course

ạb|bröckeln *itr. V.; mit sein* (auch fig.) crumble away

Ạb-bruch *der* **(a)** (Abriss) demolition; pulling down
(b) (Beendigung) breaking-off; (einer Schwangerschaft) termination
(c) einer Sache (*Dat.*) [keinen] ∼ tun do [no] harm to sth.

ạb|buchen *tr. V.* ⟨bank⟩ debit (von to); ⟨creditor⟩ claim by direct debit (von to); etw. ∼ lassen (durch die Bank) pay sth. by standing order; (durch Gläubiger) pay sth. by direct debit

ạb|bügeln *tr. V.* (ugs.) reject, brush aside ⟨warning, question, criticism⟩; rebuff ⟨person⟩

ạb|bürsten *tr. V.* **(a)** brush off
(b) (säubern) brush ⟨garment⟩

ạb|büßen *tr. V.* serve [out] ⟨prison sentence⟩

Abc /aː(ː)beː(ː)'tseː/ *das;* ∼ (auch fig.) ABC

Abc-Schütze *der,* **Abc-Schützin** *die* child just starting school

ạb|dampfen *itr. V.; mit sein* (ugs.: abfahren) set off

ạb|danken *itr. V.* ⟨ruler⟩ abdicate; ⟨government, minister⟩ resign

Ạbdankung *die;* ∼, ∼**en** ▶ ABDANKEN: abdication; resignation

ạb|decken *tr. V.* **(a)** open up; ⟨gale⟩ take the roof/roofs off ⟨house⟩, take the tiles off ⟨roof⟩
(b) (herunternehmen, -reißen) take off
(c) (abräumen) clear ⟨table⟩; clear away ⟨dishes⟩
(d) (schützen) cover ⟨person⟩

ạb|dichten *tr. V.* seal

ạb|drängen *tr. V.* push away

ạb|drehen ⬚1 *tr. V.* **(a)** (ausschalten) turn off; den Hahn ∼ (fig.) turn off the supply
(b) (abtrennen) twist off
⬚2 *itr. V.; meist mit sein* turn off

Ạb-druck *der; Pl.* Abdrücke (Fuß∼) footprint; (Wachs∼) impression; (Gips∼) cast

ạb|drücken ⬚1 *itr. V.* pull the trigger; shoot
⬚2 *tr. V.* (zudrücken) constrict

ạb|dunkeln *tr. V.* darken ⟨room⟩; dim ⟨light⟩

ạb|duschen *tr. V.* sich/jmdn. [warm] ∼: take/give sb. a [hot] shower

ạb|düsen *itr. V.* (ugs.) zoom off

*abend ▶ ABEND A

Ạbend *der;* ∼**s,** ∼**e** evening; guten ∼! good evening; am [frühen/späten] ∼: [early/late] in the evening; heute/morgen/gestern ∼: this/tomorrow/yesterday evening; zu ∼ essen have one's; (allgemeiner) have one's evening meal; ein bunter ∼: a social [evening]

abend-, Abend-: ∼**akademie** *die*

*old spelling - see note on page xiv

evening school; ∼**anzug** *der* evening suit; ∼**blatt** *das* evening [news]paper; ∼**brot** *das* supper; ∼**dämmerung** *die* [evening] twilight; ∼**essen** *das* dinner; ∼**füllend** *Adj.* occupying a whole evening *postpos., not pred.;* ein ∼füllendes Programm a full evening's programme; ∼**gymnasium** *das* night school, evening classes *pl.* (leading to the 'Abitur'); ∼**kasse** *die* box office (open on the evening of the performance); ∼**kleid** *das* evening dress; ∼**kurs[us]** *der* evening class

Ạbend-land *das;* ∼[e]s West

ạbendlich *Adj.* evening; ⟨quiet, coolness⟩ of the evening

Ạbend-: ∼**mahl** *das* (Rel.) Communion; (N.T.) Last Supper; ∼**programm** *das* evening programmes *pl.;* ∼**rot** *das* red glow of the sunset sky

ạbends *Adv.* in the evenings; um sechs Uhr ∼: at six o'clock in the evening

Ạbend-: ∼**schule** *die* night school; ∼**sonne** *die* evening sun; ∼**stern** *der* evening star; ∼**stunde** *die* evening hour; in den frühen/späten ∼stunden early/late in the evening; ∼**vorstellung** *die* evening performance; ∼**zeitung** *die* ▶ ∼BLATT

Abenteuer *das;* ∼**s,** ∼ **(a)** (auch fig.) adventure
(b) (Unternehmen) venture
(c) (Liebesaffäre) affair

abenteuerlich *Adj.* **(a)** (riskant) risky
(b) (bizarr) bizarre

Abenteuer-: ∼**lust** *die* thirst for adventure; ∼**roman** *der* adventure novel

Abenteurer *der;* ∼**s,** ∼: adventurer

Abenteurerin *die;* ∼, ∼**nen** adventuress

aber ⬚1 *Konj.* but
⬚2 *Partikel* ∼ ja/nein! why, yes/no! ∼ natürlich! but of course!; du bist ∼ groß! aren't you tall!

Ạber-glaube[n] *der* superstition

ạber-gläubisch *Adj.* superstitious

abermals *Adv.* once again; once more

Ạbf. *Abk.* = **Abfahrt** dep.

ạb|fahren ⬚1 *unr. itr. V.; mit sein* **(a)** (wegfahren) leave; wo fährt der Zug nach Paris ab? where does the Paris train leave from?
(b) (hinunterfahren) drive down; (Skisport) ski down
(c) (salopp: sich begeistern) auf jmdn./etw. [voll] ∼: be mad about sb./sth.
(d) (salopp: abgewiesen werden) jmdn. ∼ lassen tell sb. where he/she can go (sl.)
⬚2 *unr. tr. V.* **(a)** (abtransportieren) take away
(b) (abnutzen) wear out; abgefahrene Reifen worn tyres

Ạb-fahrt *die* **(a)** departure
(b) (Skisport) descent; (Strecke) run

Ạbfahrts-: ∼**lauf** *der* (Skisport) downhill [racing]; ∼**läufer** *der,* ∼**läuferin** *die*

(Skisport) downhill racer; ~**rennen** *das* (Skisport) downhill [racing]; ~**zeit** *die* time of departure; departure time

Ab·fall *der* (Küchen~ o Ä.) rubbish, (Amer.) trash *no indef. art., no pl.*; (Fleisch~) offal *no indef. art., no pl.*; (Industrie~) waste *no indef. art.*; (auf der Straße) litter *no indef. art., no pl.*

Abfall: ~**beseitigung** *die* refuse disposal; (industriell) waste disposal; ~**eimer** *der* rubbish bin; trash can (Amer.); (auf der Straße) litter bin; trash can (Amer.)

ab|fallen *unr. itr. V.; mit sein* **(a)** fall off **(b)** (abschüssig sein) ⟨land, road, etc.⟩ drop away, slope **(c)** (übrigbleiben) be left [over]; **für dich wird [dabei] auch etwas** ~: you'll get something out of it too **(d) von jmdm.** ~: leave sb.; **vom Glauben** ~: desert the faith

ab·fällig ① *Adj.* disparaging ② *adv.* **sich** ~ **über jmdn. äußern** make disparaging remarks about sb.

Abfall-: ~**produkt** *das* (auch fig.) by-product; (Sekundärstoff) secondary product; ~**vermeidung** *die* waste avoidance

ab|fangen *unr. tr. V.* **(a)** catch; intercept ⟨agent, message, aircraft⟩ **(b)** repel ⟨charge, assault⟩; ward off ⟨blow, attack⟩

ab|färben *itr. V.* **(a)** ⟨colour, garment, etc.⟩ run **(b) auf jmdn./etw.** ~ (fig.) rub off on sb./sth.

ab|fassen *tr. V.* write ⟨report, letter, etc.⟩; draw up ⟨will⟩

ab|fegen *tr. V.* **(a)** brush off; **etw. von etw.** ~: brush sth. off sth. **(b)** (säubern) **etw.** ~: brush sth. clean

ab|feiern *tr. V.* use up ⟨excess hours worked⟩ (by taking time off)

ab|fertigen *tr. V.* dispatch ⟨mail⟩; deal with ⟨applicant⟩; handle ⟨passengers⟩; serve ⟨customer⟩; clear ⟨ship⟩ for sailing; clear ⟨aircraft⟩ for take-off; clear ⟨lorry⟩ for departure

ab|feuern *tr. V.* fire

ab|finden ① *unr. tr. V.* **jmdn. mit etw.** ~: compensate sb. with sth.; **seine Gläubiger** ~: settle with one's creditors ② *unr. refl. V.* **sich** ~: resign oneself; **sich** ~ **mit** come to terms with; learn to live with ⟨noise, heat⟩

Abfindung *die;* ~, ~**en** settlement; **eine** ~ **in Höhe von … zahlen** make a settlement of …

Abfindungs·summe *die* ▶ ABFINDUNG

ab|flauen *itr. V.; mit sein* die down; subside; ⟨interest, conversation⟩ flag; ⟨business⟩ become slack; ⟨noise⟩ abate

ab|fliegen *unr. itr. V.; mit sein* leave

ab|fließen *unr. itr. V.; mit sein* flow off

Ab·flug *der* departure

Abflug·zeit *die* departure time

Ab·fluss, *****Ab·fluß** *der* drain; (Rohr) drainpipe; (für Abwasser) waste pipe

Ab·folge *die* sequence; **die** ~ **der Jahreszeiten** the cycle of the seasons

ab|fotografieren *tr. V.* take pictures of

ab|fragen *tr. V.* test; **jmdn. od. jmdm. die Vokabeln** ~: test sb. on his/her vocabulary

Abfuhr *die;* ~, ~**en (a)** removal **(b) jmdm. eine** ~ **erteilen** (fig. ugs.) rebuff sb.

ab|führen ① *tr. V.* **(a)** (nach Festnahme) take away **(b)** (zahlen) pay out **(c)** (abbringen) take away ② *itr. V.* (für Stuhlgang sorgen) be a laxative

Abführ·mittel *das* laxative

ab|füllen *tr. V.* (in Flaschen) bottle; (in Dosen) can

Ab·gabe *die* **(a)** handing in; (eines Briefes, Pakets, Telegramms) delivery; (eines Gesuchs, Antrags) submission **(b)** (Steuer, Gebühr) tax; (auf Produkte) duty **(c)** (Ausstrahlung) release; emission **(d)** (Sport: Abspiel) pass

Ab·gang *der* **(a)** leaving; departure; (Abfahrt) departure; (Theater) exit **(b)** (jmd., der ausscheidet) departure; (Schule) leaver **(c)** (bes. Amtsspr.: Todesfall) death **(d)** (Turnen) dismount

Ab·gas *das* exhaust

Abgas·katalysator *der* (Kfz-W.) catalytic converter

abgearbeitet *Adj.* work-worn ⟨hands⟩

ab|geben ① *unr. tr. V.* **(a)** (aushändigen) hand over; deliver ⟨letter, parcel, telegram⟩; hand in, submit ⟨application⟩; hand in ⟨school work⟩; **den Mantel in der Garderobe** ~: leave one's coat in the cloakroom **(b)** *auch itr.* **jmdm. [etwas] von etw.** ~: let sb. have some of sth. **(c)** (abfeuern) fire ② *unr. refl. V.* **sich mit jmdm./etw.** ~: spend time on sb./sth.; (geringschätzig) waste one's time on sb./sth.

ab·gebrannt *Adj.* (ugs.) broke (coll.)

abgebrüht *Adj.* (ugs.) hardened

ab·gedroschen *Adj.* (ugs.) hackneyed

ab·gegriffen *Adj.* battered

ab|gehen *unr. itr. V.; mit sein* **(a)** (sich entfernen) leave; (Theater) exit **(b)** (ausscheiden) leave **(c)** (abfahren) ⟨train, ship, bus⟩ leave, depart **(d)** (abgeschickt werden) ⟨message, letter⟩ be sent [off] **(e)** (abzweigen) branch off **(f)** (sich lösen) come off

abgehetzt *Adj.* exhausted

ab·gelegen *Adj.* remote; (einsam) isolated; out-of-the-way ⟨district⟩

abgemagert *Adj.* emaciated; wasted

ab·geneigt *Adj.* averse (*Dat.* to); [**nicht**] ~ **sein, etw. zu tun** [not] be averse to doing sth.

Abgeordnete der/die; adj. Dekl. member [of parliament]; (z.B. in Frankreich) deputy

ab·gerissen Adj. ragged

ab·geschieden Adj. secluded; (abgelegen) isolated

ab·geschlagen Adj. (Sport) [well] beaten

ab·geschlossen Adj. secluded

ab·geschnitten Adj. isolated; **von der Außenwelt ~:** cut off from the outside world

ab·gesehen Adv. **~ von** apart from; **~ davon, dass ...** apart from the fact that ...

ab·gespannt Adj. weary; exhausted

ab·gestanden Adj. flat

ab·gestorben Adj. dead ⟨branch, tree⟩; numb ⟨fingers, legs, etc.⟩

ab·getreten Adj. worn down

abgewetzt Adj. well-worn; battered ⟨case etc.⟩

ab|gewöhnen tr. V.: **jmdm. etw. ~:** make sb. give up sth.; **sich** (Dat.) **etw. ~:** give up sth.

ab|gießen unr. tr. V. pour away ⟨liquid⟩; drain ⟨potatoes⟩

abgöttisch Adj. idolatrous

ab|grenzen tr. V. **(a)** bound; **etw. gegen** od. **von etw. ~:** separate sth. from sth. **(b)** (unterscheiden) distinguish

Ab·grund der abyss; chasm; (Abhang) precipice

ab|hacken tr. V. chop off; **jmdm. die Hand** usw. **~:** chop sb.'s hand etc. off

ab|haken tr. V. tick off; check off (Amer.)

ab|halten unr. tr. V. **(a)** jmdn./etw. [von jmdm./etw.] **~:** keep sb./sth. off [sb./sth.] **(b)** jmdn. davon **~,** etw. zu tun stop sb. doing sth. **(c)** (durchführen) hold ⟨elections, meeting, referendum⟩

ab|handeln tr. V. **(a)** jmdm. etw. **~:** do a deal with sb. for sth. **(b)** (darstellen) deal with

abhanden Adv. **~ kommen** get lost; go astray; **etw. kommt jmdm. ~:** sb. loses sth.

Ab·handlung die treatise (über + Akk. on)

Ab·hang der slope; incline

ab|hängen[1] unr. tr. itr. V. **von jmdm./etw. ~:** depend on sb./sth.

ab|hängen[2] [1] tr. V. **(a)** take down **(b)** (abkuppeln) uncouple **(c)** (ugs.) shake off ⟨pursuer, competitor⟩ [2] itr. V. (den Hörer auflegen) hang up

abhängig Adj. dependent **(von on)**; (süchtig) addicted **(von to);** **von jmdm./etw. ~ sein** depend on sb./sth.

Abhängige der/die; adj. Dekl. (Rechtspr.) dependant; (Untergebene) subordinate

Abhängigkeit die; **~, ~en** dependence; (Sucht) addiction

Abhängigkeits·verhältnis das relationship of dependence (zu on)

─────────────

*alte Schreibung - vgl. Hinweis auf S. xiv

ab|härten tr. V. harden

ab|hauen [1] unr. tr. V. **(a)** Prät. haute ab knock off **(b)** Prät. hieb (geh.) od. haute ab (mit Schwert, Axt usw.) chop off [2] unr. itr. V.; mit sein; Prät. haute ab (salopp) beat it (coll.)

ab|heben [1] unr. tr. V. **(a)** lift off ⟨lid, cover, etc.⟩; [den Hörer] **~:** answer [the telephone] **(b)** (von einem Konto) withdraw ⟨money⟩ [2] unr. itr. V. ⟨balloon⟩ rise; ⟨aircraft, bird⟩ take off; ⟨rocket⟩ lift off [3] unr. refl. V. stand out **(von** against)

ab|heften tr. V. file

ab|hetzen refl. V. rush [around]; s. auch ABGEHETZT

Ab·hilfe die action to improve matters; **~ schaffen** put things right

ab|holen tr. V. collect, pick up ⟨parcel, book, tickets, etc.⟩; pick up ⟨person⟩

ab|hören tr. V. **(a)** jmdm. od. jmdn. Vokabeln **~:** test sb.'s vocabulary [orally]; **das Einmaleins ~:** ask questions on the multiplication tables **(b)** tap ⟨telephone conversation, telephone⟩; bug (coll.) ⟨conversation, premises⟩; jmdn. **~:** tap sb.'s telephone

abhör·sicher Adj. bug-proof (coll.); tap-proof ⟨telephone⟩

Abi das; **~s, ~s** (Schülerspr.), **Abitur** das; **~s, ~e** Abitur ⟨school-leaving examination at grammar school needed for entry to higher education⟩; ≈ A levels (Brit.)

Abiturient der; **~en, ~en, Abiturientin** die; **~, ~nen** sb. who is taking/has passed the 'Abitur'

ab|jagen tr. V. jmdm. etw. **~:** finally get sth. away from sb.

Abk. Abk. = **Abkürzung** abbr.

ab|kapseln tr. V. encapsulate; **sich gegen die Umwelt ~** (fig.) isolate oneself from one's surroundings

ab|kaufen tr. V. jmdm. etw. **~:** buy sth. from sb.

Ab·klatsch der (abwertend) pale imitation; poor copy

ab|klopfen tr. V. **(a)** knock off **(b)** (säubern) knock the dirt/snow/crumbs etc. off **(c)** (untersuchen) tap

ab|knallen tr. V. (salopp) shoot down; gun down

ab|knicken [1] tr. V. snap off [2] itr. V.; mit sein snap

ab|kochen tr. V. boil

ab|kommen unr. itr. V.; mit sein **(a)** vom Weg **~:** lose one's way; **vom Kurs ~:** go off course; **von der Fahrbahn ~:** leave the road; **vom Thema ~:** stray from the topic **(b)** von einem Plan **~:** abandon a plan

Ab·kommen das; **~s, ~:** agreement

abkömmlich Adj. free; available

ạb|können *unr. tr. V.* (nordd.: mögen) stand; (vertragen) take

ạb|kratzen ① *tr. V.* **(a)** (mit den Fingern) scratch off; (mit einem Werkzeug) scrape off **(b)** (säubern) scrape [clean] ② *itr. V.; mit sein* (derb) snuff it (sl.)

ạb|kriegen *tr. V.* (ugs.) ▶ ABBEKOMMEN

ạb|kühlen ① *tr. V.* cool down ② *itr., refl. V.; itr. meist mit sein* cool down

Ạb·kühlung *die* cooling

ạb|kupfern *tr. V.* (ugs.) copy mechanically (bei from)

ạb|kürzen *tr., itr. V.* **(a)** (räumlich) shorten; **den Weg ∼:** take a shorter route **(b)** (zeitlich) cut short **(c)** (kürzer schreiben) abbreviate (mit to)

Ạbkürzung *die* **(a)** (Weg) short cut **(b)** (Wort) abbreviation

ạb|küssen *tr. V.* cover with kisses

ạb|laden *unr. tr., itr. V.* unload

Ạb·lage *die* **(a)** storage place **(b)** (Raum) storage room **(c)** (Bürow.) filing

ạb|lagern *tr. V.* deposit

ạb|lassen ① *unr. tr. V.* let out (**aus** of); let off ⟨steam⟩ ② *unr. itr. V.* **(a) von jmdm./etw. ∼:** leave sb./sth. alone **(b) von etw. ∼** ⟨etw. aufgeben⟩ give sth. up

Ạb·lauf *der* **(a)** (Verlauf) course; (einer Veranstaltung) passing off **(b)** (Ende) **nach ∼ eines Jahres** after a year; **nach ∼ einer Frist** at the end of a period of time

ạb|laufen *unr. itr. V.; mit sein* **(a)** flow away; (aus einem Behälter) run out **(b)** (verlaufen) pass off **(c)** ⟨alarm clock⟩ run down; ⟨parking meter⟩ expire **(d)** ⟨period, contract, passport⟩ expire

ạb|lecken *tr. V.* **(a)** lick off **(b)** (säubern) lick clean

ạb|legen ① *tr. V.* **(a)** lay *or* put down **(b)** (Bürow.) file **(c)** stop wearing ⟨clothes⟩ **(d)** give up ⟨habit⟩; lose ⟨shyness⟩ **(e)** swear ⟨oath⟩; sit ⟨examination⟩; make ⟨confession⟩ ② *tr., itr. V.* take off; **möchten Sie ∼?** would you like to take your coat off? ③ *itr. V.* **[vom Kai] ∼:** cast off

Ạbleger *der; ∼s, ∼:* layer; (Steckling) cutting

ạb|lehnen *tr. V.* **(a)** decline; decline, turn down ⟨money, invitation, position⟩; reject ⟨suggestion, applicant⟩ **(b)** (missbilligen) disapprove of

Ạblehnung *die; ∼, ∼en* **(a)** rejection **(b)** (Missbilligung) disapproval

ạb|leiten *tr. V.* **(a)** divert **(b)** (herleiten) **etw. aus/von etw. ∼:** derive sth. from sth.

Ạb·leitung *die* derivation

ạb|lenken *tr. V.* **(a)** deflect **(b) jmdn. von etw. ∼:** distract sb. from sth. **(c)** (zerstreuen) divert; **sich ∼:** amuse oneself

Ạb·lenkung *die* ▶ ABLENKEN: deflection; distraction; diversion

Ạblenkungs-manöver *das* diversion[ary tactic]

ạb|lesen *unr. tr. V.* **(a)** read ⟨speech, lecture⟩; **werden Sie frei sprechen oder ∼?** will you be talking from notes or reading your speech? **(b)** read ⟨gas meter, thermometer, etc.⟩; check ⟨time, speed, temperature⟩ **(c)** (erkennen) see

ạb|lichten *tr. V.* **(a)** (fotokopieren) photocopy **(b)** (fotografieren) take a photograph of

Ạb·lichtung *die* **(a)** (das Fotografieren) photographing; (das Fotokopieren) photocopying **(b)** (Fotokopie) photocopy

ạb|liefern *tr., itr. V.* hand in; deliver ⟨goods⟩

ạb|lösen ① *tr. V.* **(a) etw. [von etw.] ∼:** get sth. off [sth.] **(b) jmdn. ∼:** relieve sb.; **sich od. einander ∼:** take turns ② *refl. V.* **sich [von etw.] ∼:** come off [sth.]

Ạb·lösung *die* (eines Postens) changing; **ich schicke Ihnen jemanden zur ∼:** I'll send someone to relieve you

ạb|machen *tr. V.* **(a)** (ugs.) take off; take down ⟨sign, rope⟩ **(b)** (vereinbaren) agree

Ạbmachung *die; ∼, ∼en* agreement

ạb|magern *itr. V.; mit sein* become thin; (absichtlich) slim

Ạbmagerungs-kur *die* reducing diet

ạb|marschieren *itr. V.; mit sein* depart; (Milit.) march off

ạb|melden *tr. V.* **(a) sich/jmdn. ∼:** report that one/sb. is leaving **(b)** (Umzug melden) notify the authorities that one is moving from an address; **(c) ein Auto ∼:** cancel a car's registration **(d)** (DV) ▶ AUSLOGGEN

Ạb·meldung *die* **(a)** (beim Weggehen) report that one is leaving **(b)** (beim Umzug) registration of a move with the authorities at one's old address; **(c) ∼ eines Autos** cancellation of a car's registration

Ạb·messung *die* (Dimension) dimension; measurement

ạb|montieren *tr. V.* take off ⟨part⟩; dismantle ⟨machine, equipment⟩

ạb|mühen *refl. V.* toil; **sie mühte sich mit dem schweren Koffer ab** she struggled with the heavy suitcase

ạb|murksen *tr. V.* (salopp) do in (sl.)

Ạbnahme *die; ∼, ∼n* **(a)** (das Entfernen) removal **(b)** (Verminderung) decrease

ab|nehmen [1] *unr. tr. V.* **(a)** (entfernen)
take off; take down ⟨*picture, curtain, lamp*⟩
(b) jmdm. den Koffer ∼: take sb.'s suitcase;
jmdm. eine Arbeit ∼: save sb. a job
(c) jmdm. ein Versprechen/einen Eid ∼:
make sb. give a promise/swear an oath
(d) (prüfen) inspect and approve; test and
pass ⟨*vehicle*⟩
(e) jmdm. etw. ∼ (wegnehmen) take sth. off sb.
(f) (beim Telefon) answer ⟨*telephone*⟩; pick up
⟨*receiver*⟩
(g) (Handarb.) decrease
(h) das nehme ich dir/ihm *usw.* nicht ab I
won't buy that (coll.)
[2] *unr. itr. V.* **(a)** (Gewicht verlieren) lose
weight
(b) (sich verringern) decrease; drop; ⟨*attention,
interest*⟩ flag; ⟨*brightness*⟩ diminish; wir
haben ∼den Mond there is a waning moon
(c) (beim Telefon) answer the telephone

Ab·neigung *die* dislike (gegen for)

ab|nutzen, (landsch.:) **ab|nützen** *tr., refl.
V.* wear out; abgenutzt worn

Abonnement /abonə'mã:/ *das;* ∼s, ∼s
subscription (*Gen.* to)

Abonnent *der;* ∼en, ∼en, **Abonnentin**
die; ∼, ∼nen subscriber (+ *Gen.* to); (Theater,
Oper) season ticket holder

abonnieren *tr. V.* subscribe to

Ab·ordnung *die* delegation

ab|packen *tr. V.* pack; wrap ⟨*bread*⟩;
abgepacktes Obst/abgepackte
Fleischportionen packaged fruit/pieces of
meat

ab|passen *tr. V.* **(a)** (abwarten) wait for
(b) (aufhalten) catch

ab|pausen *tr. V.* trace

ab|pfeifen (Sport) [1] *itr. V.* blow the whistle
[2] *tr. V.* [blow the whistle to] stop

Ab·pfiff *der* (Sport) final whistle; (Halbzeit∼)
half-time whistle

ab|pflücken *tr. V.* pick

ab|plagen *refl. V.* slave away

ab|prallen *itr. V.; mit sein* rebound; ⟨*bullet,
missile*⟩ ricochet

Ab·produkt *das* waste product

ab|putzen *tr. V.* (ugs.); **(a)** wipe off
(b) (säubern) wipe; jmdm./sich das Gesicht ∼:
clean sb.'s/one's face

ab|quälen *refl. V.* sich [mit etw.] ∼:
struggle [with sth.]

ab|rackern *refl. V.* (ugs.) flog oneself to
death (coll.)

ab|rasieren *tr. V.* shave off

ab|raten *unr. itr. V.* jmdm. von etw. ∼:
advise sb. against sth.

ab|räumen *tr. V.* **(a)** clear away
(b) (leer machen) clear ⟨*table*⟩

ab|rechnen [1] *itr. V.* cash up; mit jmdm.
∼ (fig.) call sb. to account

[2] *tr. V.* die Kasse ∼: reckon up the till;
seine Spesen ∼: claim one's expenses

Ab·rechnung *die* **(a)** cashing up *no art.;*
(Aufstellung) statement
(b) (fig.: Vergeltung) reckoning

Ab·rede *die* **(a)** arrangement; agreement
(b) etw. in ∼ stellen deny sth.

ab|regen *refl. V.* (ugs.) calm down; reg dich
ab! cool it! (coll.); calm down!

ab|reiben *unr. tr. V.* **(a)** rub off
(b) (säubern) rub

Ab·reise *die* departure (nach for); bei
meiner ∼: when I left/leave

ab|reisen *itr. V.; mit sein* leave (nach for)

ab|reißen [1] *unr. tr. V.* **(a)** tear off; tear
down ⟨*poster, notice*⟩; pull off ⟨*button*⟩
(b) (niederreißen) demolish, pull down
⟨*building*⟩
[2] *unr. itr. V.; mit sein* **(a)** fly off; ⟨*shoelace*⟩
break off
(b) (aufhören) come to an end; ⟨*connection,
contact*⟩ be broken off

ab|richten *tr. V.* train

Ab·riss, ****Ab·riß** *der* **(a)** ▶ ABREISSEN 1B:
demolition; pulling down
(b) (knappe Darstellung) outline

ab|rollen [1] *tr. V.* unwind
[2] *itr. V.; mit sein* unwind [itself]

ab|rücken [1] *unr. tr. V.* (wegschieben) move
away
[2] *itr. V.; mit sein* move away

Ab·ruf *der:* auf ∼: on call; (DV) in
retrievable form

ab|rufen *unr. tr. V.* summon; call

ab|runden *tr. V.* (auch fig.) round off
(b) round ⟨*figure*⟩ up/down (auf + Akk. to);
etw. nach oben/unten ∼: round sth. up/down

abrupt [1] *Adj.* abrupt
[2] *adv.* abruptly

ab|rüsten *itr., tr. V.* disarm

Ab·rüstung *die;* ∼: disarmament

ab|rutschen *itr. V.; mit sein* **(a)** slip
(b) (nach unten rutschen) slide down

Abs. *Abk.* **(a)** = **Absender;**
(b) = **Absatz**

ABS *Abk.* = **Antiblockiersystem** ABS

Ab·sage *die* (auf eine Einladung) refusal; (auf
eine Bewerbung) rejection

ab|sagen [1] *tr. V.* cancel; withdraw
⟨*participation*⟩
[2] *itr. V.* jmdm. ∼: tell sb. one cannot come

ab|sägen *tr. V.* saw off

Ab·satz *der* **(a)** (am Schuh) heel
(b) (Textunterbrechung) break
(c) (Textabschnitt) paragraph
(d) (Kaufmannsspr.) sales *pl.*

Absatz-: ∼chance *die* (Kaufmannsspr.)
sales prospect; ∼förderung *die*
(Kaufmannsspr.) sales promotion; ∼markt *der*
(Kaufmannsspr.) market; ∼steigerung *die*
(Kaufmannsspr.) increase in sales

**old spelling - see note on page xiv

ab|saufen *unr. itr. V.; mit sein* (ugs.) ⟨*engine, car*⟩ flood

ab|saugen *tr. V.* **(a)** suck away **(b)** (säubern) hoover (Brit.)

ab|schaben *tr. V.* **(a)** scrape off **(b)** (säubern) scrape [clean]

ab|schaffen *tr. V.* **(a)** (beseitigen) abolish ⟨*capital punishment, regulation, customs duty, institution*⟩; repeal ⟨*law*⟩; put an end to ⟨*injustice, abuse*⟩ **(b)** (weggeben) get rid of

Ab·schaffung *die* abolition; (von Gesetzen) repeal; (von Unrecht, Missstand) ending

ab|schalten *tr., itr. V.* switch off; shut down ⟨*power station*⟩

abschätzig **1** *Adj.* derogatory **2** *adv.* derogatorily

Ab·scheu *der;* ∼s detestation; abhorrence

abscheulich **1** *Adj.* **(a)** disgusting ⟨*smell, taste*⟩; repulsive ⟨*sight*⟩ **(b)** (verwerflich) disgraceful ⟨*behaviour*⟩; abominable ⟨*crime*⟩ **2** *adv.* disgracefully

ab|schicken *tr. V.* send [off]

ab|schieben *unr. tr. V.* **(a)** push away **(b)** (abwälzen) shift ⟨*responsibility, blame*⟩ **(c)** (außer Landes bringen) deport

Ab·schiebung *die* (Rechtsw.) deportation

Abschiebungs·haft *die* (Rechtsw.) detention prior to deportation

Abschied *der;* ∼[e]s, ∼e parting (von from); farewell (von to); ∼ nehmen take one's leave (von of)

Abschieds-: ∼**brief** *der* farewell letter; ∼**geschenk** *das* parting gift; ∼**gruß** *der* goodbye; farewell

ab|schießen *unr. tr. V.* **(a)** shoot down ⟨*aeroplane*⟩ **(b)** fire ⟨*arrow*⟩; launch ⟨*spacecraft*⟩ **(c)** (töten) take

ab|schirmen *tr. V.* **(a)** (schützen) shield **(b)** (fernhalten) screen off ⟨*light, radiation*⟩

ab|schlachten *tr. V.* slaughter

Ab·schlag *der* **(a)** (Kaufmannsspr.) discount **(b)** (Teilzahlung) interim payment; (Vorschuss) advance **(c)** (Fußball) goalkeeper's kick out

ab|schlagen **1** *unr. tr. V.* **(a)** knock off; (mit dem Beil, Schwert usw.) chop off **(b)** (ablehnen) refuse **(c)** (abwehren) beat off **2** *unr. itr. V.* (Fußball) kick the ball out

ab|schleifen *unr. tr. V.* (von Holz) sand off; (von Metall, Glas usw.) grind off

Abschlepp·dienst *der* breakdown recovery service; tow[ing] service (Amer.)

ab|schleppen tow away; take ⟨*ship*⟩ in tow; **ein Auto zur Werkstatt** ∼: tow a car to the garage

Abschlepp: ∼**seil** *das* tow rope; (aus Draht) towing cable; ∼**stange** *die* tow bar; ∼**wagen** *der* breakdown vehicle; tow truck (Amer.); (der Polizei) tow-away vehicle

ab|schließen **1** *unr. tr. V.* **(a)** auch itr. (zuschließen) lock ⟨*door, gate, cupboard*⟩; lock [up] ⟨*house, flat, room, park*⟩ **(b)** (verschließen) seal; **etw. luftdicht** ∼: seal sth. hermetically **(c)** (begrenzen) border **(d)** (zum Abschluss bringen) conclude; **sein Studium** ∼: finish one's studies; **Bewerber mit abgeschlossenem Universitätsstudium** applicants with a degree **(e)** (vereinbaren) strike ⟨*bargain, deal*⟩; make ⟨*purchase*⟩; enter into ⟨*agreement*⟩ **2** *unr. itr. V.* (aufhören, enden) end; ∼**d sagte er ...:** in conclusion he said ...

Ab·schluss, *Ab·schluß *der* **(a)** (Verschluss) seal **(b)** (Beendigung) conclusion; end **(c)** (eines Geschäfts, Vertrags) conclusion

Abschluss-, *Abschluß-: ∼**ball** *der* final dance; ∼**prüfung** *die* **(a)** (Schulw.) leaving *or* (Amer.) final examination; (Hochschulw.) final examination; finals *pl.;* **(b)** (Wirtsch.) audit

ab|schmecken *tr. V.* **(a)** (kosten) taste; try **(b)** (würzen) season

ab|schmieren *tr. V.* (Technik) grease

ab|schminken *tr. V.* jmdn./sich ∼: remove sb.'s/one's make-up

ab|schmirgeln *tr. V.* rub off with emery; (mit Sandpapier) sand off

ab|schnallen *tr. V.* unfasten

ab|schneiden **1** *unr. tr. V.* **(a)** (auch fig.: isolieren) cut off; cut down ⟨*sth. hanging*⟩; **etw. von etw.** ∼: cut sth. off sth.; **sich** *(Dat.)* **eine Scheibe Brot** ∼: cut oneself a slice of bread **(b)** (kürzer schneiden) cut **(c)** **jmdm. den Weg** ∼: take a short cut to get ahead of sb. **2** *unr. itr. V.* **bei etw. gut/schlecht** ∼: do well/badly in sth.

Ab·schnitt *der* **(a)** (Kapitel) section **(b)** (Zeitspanne) phase **(c)** (Teil eines Formulars) [detachable] portion

ab|schrauben *tr. V.* unscrew [and remove]

ab|schrecken *tr. V.* **(a)** deter **(b)** (fernhalten) scare off **(c)** (Kochk.) pour cold water over

Abschreckung *die;* ∼, ∼en deterrence; (Mittel zur Abschreckung) deterrent

ab|schreiben **1** *unr. tr. V.* **(a)** copy out; **etw. bei** *od.* **von jmdm.** ∼ (in der Schule) copy sth. off sb.; (als Plagiator) plagiarize sth. from sb. **(b)** (Wirtsch.) amortize **2** *unr. itr. V.* **bei** *od.* **von jmdm.** ∼ (in der Schule) copy off sb.; (als Plagiator) copy from sb.

Ab·schreibung *die* (Wirtsch.) amortization

Ab·schrift *die* copy

ab|schürfen *tr. V.* graze

Ab·schuss, *Ab·schuß *der* **(a)** (eines Flugzeugs) shooting down ⋯⊹

(b) (von Geschossen) firing; (eines Raumschiffs) launching

abschüssig *Adj.* downward sloping ⟨*land*⟩

ab|schütteln *tr. V.* shake off; (herunterschütteln) shake down

ab|schwächen ① *tr. V.* **(a)** (mildern) tone down ⟨*statement, criticism*⟩
(b) (verringern) lessen ⟨*effect, impression*⟩; cushion ⟨*blow, impact*⟩
② *refl. V.* ⟨*interest, demand*⟩ wane

Abschwächung *die;* ~ **(a)** (Milderung) toning down
(b) (eines Aufpralls, Stoßes usw.) cushioning

ab|schweifen *itr. V.; mit sein* digress

Abschweifung *die;* ~, ~en digression

ab|schwören *unr. itr. V.* **dem Teufel/ seinem Glauben** ~: renounce the Devil/one's faith; **dem Alkohol/Laster** ~: forswear alcohol/vice

absehbar *Adj.* foreseeable; **in** ~**er Zeit** within the foreseeable future

ab|sehen ① *unr. tr. V.* **(a)** (voraussehen) predict; foresee ⟨*event*⟩
(b) es auf etw. (*Akk.*) **abgesehen haben** be after sth.; **er hat es darauf abgesehen, uns zu ärgern** he's out to annoy us; **der Chef hat es auf ihn abgesehen** the boss has got it in for him
② *unr. itr. V.* **(a) von etw.** ~ (etw. nicht beachten) leave aside sth.; *s. auch* ABGESEHEN;
(b) von etw. ~ (auf etw. verzichten) refrain from sth

ab|seilen ① *tr. V.* lower [with a rope]
② *refl. V.* (Bergsteigen) abseil

*ab|sein ▶ AB 2A

abseits ① *Präp. mit Gen.* away from
② *Adv.* **(a)** (far away
(b) (Ballspiele) ~ **sein** *od.* **stehen** be offside

Abseits *das;* ~, ~: **das war ein klares** ~: that was clearly offside

ab|senden *unr. od. regelm. tr. V.* dispatch

Ab·sender *der,* **Ab·senderin** *die;* ~, ~nen sender; (Anschrift) sender's address

ab|setzen ① *tr. V.* **(a)** take off ⟨*hat, glasses, etc.*⟩
(b) (hinstellen) put down ⟨*bag, suitcase*⟩
(c) (aussteigen lassen) jmdn. ~ (im öffentlichen Verkehr) put sb. down; let sb. out (Amer.); (im privaten Verkehr) drop sb. [off]
(d) (entfernen) remove ⟨*chancellor, judge*⟩ from office; depose ⟨*king, emperor*⟩
② *refl. V.* **(a)** (sich ablagern) be deposited
(b) (flüchten) get away

Absetzung *die;* ~, ~en ▶ ABSETZEN 1D: removal; deposition

ab|sichern ① *tr. V.* make safe
② *refl. V.* safeguard oneself

Ab·sicht *die* intention; **etw. mit** ~ **tun** do sth. intentionally; **etw. ohne** *od.* **nicht mit** ~ **tun** do sth. unintentionally

ab·sichtlich ① *Adj.* intentional; deliberate

② *adv.* intentionally; deliberately

ab|sinken *unr. itr. V.; mit sein* sink

absolut *Adj.* absolute

Absolutismus *der;* ~ (hist.) absolutism *no art.*

Absolvent /...'vɛnt/ *der;* ~en, ~en, **Absolventin** *die;* ~, ~nen (einer Schule) one who has taken the leaving *or* (Amer.) final examination; (einer Akademie) graduate

absolvieren *tr. V.* complete

Absolvierung *die;* ~: completion

ab·sonderlich *Adj.* strange; odd

ab|sondern ① *tr. V.* exude; (Physiol.) secrete
② *refl. V.* isolate oneself

absorbieren *tr. V.* absorb

ab|speisen *tr. V.* **jmdn. mit etw.** ~: fob sb. off with sth.

abspenstig *Adj.* **jmdm. etw.** ~ **machen** get sb. to part with sth.

ab|sperren *tr. V.* seal off; close off

Ab·spiel *das* (Ballspiele) passing

ab|spielen ① *tr. V.* **(a)** play ⟨*record, tape*⟩
(b) vom Blatt ~: ⟨*piece of music*⟩ play at sight
(c) (Ballspiele) pass
② *refl. V.* take place

Ab·sprache *die* arrangement; **eine** ~ **treffen** make an arrangement

ab|sprechen *unr. tr. V.* **(a) jmdm. etw.** ~: deny that sb. has sth.
(b) (vereinbaren) arrange

ab|springen *unr. itr. V.; mit sein* jump off; (herunterspringen) jump down; **vom Fahrrad** ~: jump off one's bicycle

Ab·sprung *der* take-off; (das Herunterspringen) jump

ab|spülen ① *tr. V.* **(a)** wash off
(b) (reinigen) rinse off; **sich** (*Dat.*) **die Hände** usw. ~: rinse one's hands *etc.*; **das Geschirr** ~ (bes. südd.) wash the dishes
② *itr. V.* (bes. südd.) wash up

ab|stammen *itr. V.* be descended (von from)

Abstammung *die;* ~, ~en descent

Ab·stand *der* **(a)** distance; **in 20 Meter** ~: at a distance of 20 metres
(b) (Unterschied) gap

ab|stauben *tr., itr. V.* dust

Abstecher *der;* ~s, ~: side trip

ab|stehen *unr. itr. V.* ⟨*hair*⟩ stand up; ⟨*pigtail[s]*⟩ stick out; ~**de Ohren** protruding ears

Ab·steige *die;* ~, ~n (ugs. abwertend) cheap and crummy hotel (coll. derog.)

ab|steigen *unr. itr. V.; mit sein* **(a)** [vom Pferd/Fahrrad] ~: get off [one's horse/ bicycle]
(b) (abwärts gehen) go down

ab|stellen *tr. V.* **(a)** put down
(b) (unterbringen) put; (parken) park
(c) (ausschalten, abdrehen) turn off

---

*alte Schreibung - vgl. Hinweis auf S. xiv

(d) (unterbinden) put a stop to
Abstell-: ~**kammer** die, ~**raum** der
lumber room
ab|stempeln tr. V. **(a)** frank ⟨letter⟩;
cancel ⟨stamp⟩
(b) (fig.) label, brand (**zu, als** as)
ab|sterben unr. itr. V.; mit sein **(a)**
[gradually] die
(b) (gefühllos werden) go numb
Abstieg der; ~[e]s, ~e **(a)** descent
(b) (Niedergang) decline
ab|stimmen ① itr. V. vote (**über** + Akk.
on)
② tr. V. etw. mit jmdm. ~: discuss and agree
on sth. with sb.
Ab·stimmung die **(a)** vote; **während der**
~: during the voting
(b) (Absprache) agreement
abstinent /apsti'nɛnt/ Adj. teetotal; ~
sein be a teetotaller
Abstinenz die; ~: teetotalism
Abstinenzler der; ~s, ~,
Abstinenzlerin die; ~, ~**nen** teetotaller
ab|stoppen ① tr. V. halt; stop; check
⟨advance⟩
② itr. V. come to a halt; ⟨person⟩ stop
Ab·stoß der (Fußball) goal kick
ab|stoßen unr. tr. V. **(a)** push off
(b) (beschädigen) chip ⟨crockery, paintwork,
plaster⟩
(c) (verkaufen) sell off
(d) (anwidern) repel; put off
abstoßend Adj. repulsive
abstrakt /ap'strakt/ Adj. abstract
ab|streifen tr. V. pull off; strip off
⟨berries⟩; **die Asche [von der Zigarette/
Zigarre]** ~: remove the ash [from one's
cigarette/cigar]
ab|streiten unr. tr. V. deny
Ab·strich der **(a)** (Med.) swab; **einen** ~
machen take a swab
(b) (Streichung, Kürzung) cut; ~**e machen** make
cuts (**an** + Dat. in)
ab|stumpfen itr. V.; mit sein **jmd. stumpft
ab** (wird unsensibel) sb.'s mind becomes
deadened
Ab·sturz der fall; (eines Flugzeugs) crash
ab|stürzen itr. V.; mit sein fall; ⟨aircraft,
pilot, passenger⟩ crash
Absturz·ursache die cause of the crash
ab|stützen ① refl. V. support oneself (**mit**
on, **an** + Dat. against)
② tr. V. support
ab|suchen tr. V. search (**nach** for)
absurd Adj. absurd
absurderweise Adv. absurdly enough
Absurdität die; ~, ~**en** absurdity;
(Ungereimtheit) inconsistency
Abszess, *Abszeß der; Abszesses,
Abszesse **(a)** (Med.) abscess
(b) (Geschwür) ulcer
Abszisse die; ~, ~**n** (Math.) abscissa

Abt der; ~[e]s, **Äbte** abbot
Abt. Abk. = **Abteilung**
ab|tasten tr. V. etw. ~: feel sth. all over
ab|tauen ① itr. V.; mit sein (eis-/schneefrei
werden) become clear of ice/snow;
⟨refrigerator⟩ defrost
② tr. V. melt; thaw; defrost ⟨refrigerator⟩
Abtei die; ~, ~**en** abbey
Abteil das; ~[e]s, ~**e** compartment
Ab·teilung die department
Abteilungs·leiter der,
Abteilungs·leiterin die head of
department
ab|tippen tr. V. (ugs.) type out
Äbtissin die; ~, ~**nen** abbess
ab|tönen tr. V. tint
ab|töten tr. V. destroy ⟨parasites, germs⟩;
deaden ⟨nerve, feeling⟩
ab|tragen unr. tr. V. (abnutzen) wear out;
abgetragen well worn
abträglich Adj. (geh.) **einer Sache** (Dat.) ~
sein be detrimental to sth.
Ab·transport der ▶ ABTRANSPORTIEREN:
taking away; removal
ab|transportieren tr. V. take away;
remove ⟨dead, injured⟩
ab|treiben ① unr. tr. V. **(a)** carry away;
jmdn./ein Schiff vom Kurs ~: drive sb./a
ship off course
(b) abort ⟨foetus⟩; **ein Kind** ~ **lassen** have an
abortion
② unr. itr. V.; mit sein be carried away;
⟨ship⟩ be driven off course
Abtreibung die; ~, ~**en** abortion
ab|trennen tr. V. detach
ab|treten ① unr. tr. V. **(a) sich** (Dat.) **die
Füße/Schuhe** ~: wipe one's feet
(b) jmdm. etw. ~: let sb. have sth.
② unr. itr. V.; mit sein **(a)** (Theater) exit; (fig.)
make one's exit
(b) (zurücktreten) step down; ⟨monarch⟩
abdicate
Abtreter der; ~s, ~: doormat
ab|trocknen tr. V. dry; **sich** (Dat.) **die
Hände/die Tränen** ~: dry one's hands/tears
ab|tropfen itr. V.; mit sein drip off
abtrünnig Adj. (einer Partei) renegade; (einer
Religion, Sekte) apostate; **der Kirche/dem
Glauben** ~ **werden** desert the Church/the
faith
ab|tun unr. tr. V. dismiss
ab|wägen unr. od. regelm. tr., itr. V. weigh
up; **abgewogen** carefully weighted; balanced
⟨judgement⟩
ab|wählen tr. V. vote out; drop ⟨school
subject⟩
ab|wandeln tr. V. adapt
ab|wandern itr. V.; mit sein migrate; (in
ein anderes Land) emigrate
Abwanderung die migration; (in ein
anderes Land) emigration
Ab·wandlung die adaptation

Ab·wärme *die* (Technik) waste heat

ab|warten ① *itr. V.* wait; **sie warteten ab** they awaited events; **warte ab!** wait and see; (als Drohung) just you wait! ② *tr. V.* wait for

abwärts *Adv.* downwards; (bergab) downhill; **den Fluss ~:** downstream

Abwärts·trend *der* downward trend

Abwasch *der;* ~[e]s washing-up (Brit.); washing dishes (Amer.); **den ~ machen** do the washing-up/wash the dishes

abwaschbar *Adj.* washable

ab|waschen ① *unr. tr. V.* (a) wash off (b) (reinigen) wash down; wash [up] ⟨*dishes*⟩ ② *unr. itr. V.* wash up (Brit.); wash the dishes (Amer.)

Ab·wasser *das; Pl.* Abwässer sewage

Abwasser: ~aufbereitung *die;* ~~: sewage treatment; **~kanal** *der* sewer

ab|watschen *tr. V.* (ugs.) lambaste (coll.)

ab|wechseln *refl., itr. V.* alternate; **wir wechselten uns ab** we took turns

abwechselnd *Adv.* alternately

Abwechslung *die;* ~, ~en variety; (Wechsel) change; **zur ~:** for a change

Ab·weg *der:* **auf ~e kommen** *od.* **geraten** go astray

abwegig erroneous; false ⟨*suspicion*⟩

Ab·wehr *die;* ~ (a) repulsion; (von Schlägen) fending off; (Sport) clearance; clearing (Amer.) (b) (Sport: Hintermannschaft) defence

ab|wehren *tr. V.* (a) repulse; fend off ⟨*blow*⟩; (Sport) clear ⟨*ball, shot*⟩ (b) avert ⟨*danger, consequences*⟩

Abwehr: ~kraft *die* power of resistance; **~spieler** *der,* **~spielerin** *die* (Sport) defender

ab|weichen *unr. itr. V.; mit sein* (a) deviate (b) (sich unterscheiden) differ

Abweichung *die;* ~, ~en (a) deviation (b) (Unterschied) difference

ab|weisen *unr. tr. V.* turn away; turn down ⟨*applicant, suitor*⟩

abweisend *Adj.* cold ⟨*look, tone of voice*⟩; **in ~em Ton** coldly

Ab·weisung *die;* ▶ ABWEISEN: turning away; turning down

ab|wenden ① *unr. od. regelm. tr. V.* (a) turn away (b) *nur regelm.* (verhindern) avert ② *unr. od. regelm. refl. V.* turn away

ab|werben *unr. tr. V.* lure away

ab|werfen ① *unr. tr. V.* (a) drop; throw off ⟨*clothing*⟩; jettison ⟨*ballast*⟩; throw ⟨*rider*⟩ (b) (ins Spielfeld werfen) throw out ⟨*ball*⟩ (c) (einbringen) bring in; **Profit ~:** make a profit ② *unr. itr. V.* (Sport) throw the ball out

ab|werten *tr., itr. V.* devalue

abwertend *Adj.* derogatory ⟨*term*⟩

Ab·wertung *die* devaluation

abwesend *Adj.* absent

Abwesenheit *die;* ~: absence

ab|wickeln *tr. V.* (a) unwind (b) (erledigen) deal with ⟨*case*⟩; do ⟨*business*⟩

Abwicklung *die;* ~, ~en ▶ ABWICKELN 1B: dealing (Gen. with); doing

ab|wiegen *unr. tr. V.* weigh out; weigh ⟨*single item*⟩

ab|wimmeln *tr. V.* (ugs.) get rid of

ab|winken *itr. V.* uninteressiert ~: wave it/ them aside uninterestedly; **Skat dreschen bis zum Abwinken** (ugs.) play skat till you can't stand any more (coll.); **Champagner bis zum Abwinken** (ugs.) more champagne than you can drink

ab|wischen *tr. V.* (a) wipe away (b) (säubern) wipe

Ab·wurf *der* (a) dropping; (von Ballast) jettisoning (b) **beim ~ stolperte der Torwart** the goalkeeper stumbled as he threw the ball out

ab|zahlen *tr. V.* pay off ⟨*debt, loan*⟩

ab|zählen *tr. V.* count

Ab·zahlung *die* paying off; **etw. auf ~ kaufen/verkaufen** buy/sell sth. on easy terms

Ab·zeichen *das* emblem; (Anstecknadel, Plakette) badge

ab|zeichnen ① *tr. V.* (a) (kopieren) copy (b) (signieren) initial ② *refl. V.* stand out; (fig.) begin to emerge

Abzieh·bild *das* transfer

ab|ziehen ① *unr. tr. V.* (a) pull off; peel off ⟨*skin*⟩; strip ⟨*bed*⟩ (b) (Fot.) make a print/prints of (c) (Milit., auch fig.) withdraw (d) (subtrahieren) subtract; take away; (abrechnen) deduct ② *unr. itr. V.; mit sein* (a) (sich verflüchtigen) escape (b) (Milit.) withdraw

Ab·zug *der* (a) (an einer Schusswaffe) trigger (b) (Fot.) print (c) (Verminderung) deduction

abzüglich *Präp. mit Gen.* (Kaufmannsspr.) less

ab|zweigen ① *itr. V.; mit sein* branch off ② *tr. V.* put aside

Abzweigung *die;* ~, ~en turn-off; (Gabelung) fork

ach *Interj.* (a) (betroffen, mitleidig) oh [dear] (b) (bedauernd, unwirsch) oh (c) (klagend) ah (d) (erstaunt) oh; **~, wirklich?** no, really?; **~, der!** oh, him! (e) **~ so!** oh, I see; **~ was** *od.* **wo!** of course not

Achat *der;* ~[e]s, ~e (Min.) agate

Achse *die;* ~, ~n (a) (Rad~) axle (b) (Dreh~, Math., Astron.) axis

Achsel _die;_ ~, ~n (Schulter) shoulder; (~höhle) armpit

Achsel-: ~**haare** _Pl._ armpit hair _sing.;_ ~**höhle** _die_ armpit

acht[1] _Kardinalz._ eight; um ~ [Uhr] at eight [o'clock]; um halb ~: at half past seven; drei viertel ~, Viertel vor ~: [a] quarter to eight; es steht ~ zu ~/~ zu zwei (Sport) the score is eight all/eight to two

acht[2]**:** sie waren zu ~: there were eight of them

acht... _Ordinalz._ eighth; der ~**e September** the eighth of September; **München, [den] 8. Mai 1984** Munich, 8 May 1984

Acht[1] _die;_ ~, ~**en** (a) eight (b) (Figur) figure eight (c) (Verbiegung) buckle; **mein Rad hat eine** ~: my wheel is buckled

Acht[2] _etw._ außer ~ lassen disregard sth.; sich in ~ nehmen be careful; sich vor jmdm./etw. in ~ nehmen be wary of sb./sth.; auf jmdn./etw. ~ geben take care of sb./sth.; ~ **geben** be careful

Achte _der/die; adj. Dekl._ eighth

acht-, Acht-: ~**eck** _das_ octagon; ~**eckig** _Adj._ octagonal; ~**einhalb** _Bruchz._ eight and a half

achtel _Bruchz._ eighth

Achtel _das_ (schweiz. meist _der_); ~**s,** ~: eighth

Achtel·note _die_ (Musik) quaver

achten ⨂1⨂ _tr. V._ respect ⨂2⨂ _itr. V._ auf etw. (_Akk._) ~: pay heed to sth.

achtens _Adv._ eighthly

Achterbahn _die_ roller coaster

acht·fach _Vervielfältigungsz._ eightfold; **die** ~**fache Menge** eight times the quantity; ~**fach vergrößert/verkleinert** magnified/reduced eight times; **das Achtfache kosten** cost eight times as much

*****acht|geben** ▶ ACHT[2]

acht-: ~**hundert** _Kardinalz._ eight hundred; ~**jährig** _Adj._ (8 Jahre alt) eight-year-old _attrib.;_ eight years old _pred.;_ (8 Jahre dauernd) eight-year _attrib.;_ ~**köpfig** _Adj._ ⟨family, committee⟩ of eight

acht·los ⨂1⨂ _Adj._ heedless ⨂2⨂ _adv._ heedlessly

Achtlosigkeit _die;_ ~: heedlessness

acht-: ~**mal** _Adv._ eight times; ~**spurig** _Adj._ eight-lane ⟨road⟩; eight-track ⟨cassette⟩; ~**stellig** _Adj._ eight-figure _attrib.;_ ~**stellig sein** have eight figures; ~**stimmig** ⨂1⨂ _Adj._ eight-part _attrib.;_ ⨂2⨂ _adv._ in eight parts; ~**stöckig** _Adj._ eight-storey _attrib.;_ ~**tägig** _Adj._ (8 Tage alt) eight-day-old _attrib.;_ (8 Tage dauernd) eight-day[-long] _attrib.;_ ~**tausend** _Kardinalz._ eight thousand; ~**teilig** _Adj._ eight-piece ⟨tea service, tool set, etc.⟩; eight-part ⟨series, serial⟩

Achtung _die;_ ~ (a) respect (vor + _Dat.,_ _Gen._ for)

(b) ~**!** watch out!; ~, **fertig, los!** on your marks, get set, go!

acht·zehn _Kardinalz._ eighteen; **18 Uhr 33** 6.33p.m.; (auf der 24-Stunden-Uhr) 1833

achtzehn-jährig _Adj._ (18 Jahre alt) eighteen-year-old _attrib.;_ eighteen years old _pred.;_ (18 Jahre dauernd) eighteen-year _attrib._

achtzig _Kardinalz._ eighty; [mit] ~ [km/h] **fahren** drive at _or_ (coll.) do eighty [k.p.h.]; **über/etwa** ~ [Jahre alt] **sein** be over/about eighty [years old]; **mit** ~ [Jahren] at eighty [years of age]

achtzig-jährig _Adj._ (80 Jahre alt) eighty-year-old _attrib.;_ eighty years old _pred.;_ (80 Jahre dauernd) eighty-year _attrib._

ächzen _itr. V._ groan

Acker _der;_ ~**s,** Äcker field

Acker-: ~**bau** _der_ arable farming; ~**land** _das_ farmland

A.D. _Abk._ = **Anno Domini** AD

ADAC _Abk._ = **Allgemeiner Deutscher Automobilclub**

Adams-apfel _der_ (ugs.) Adam's apple

adäquat /at|ɛ'kvaːt/ _Adj._ appropriate (_Dat._ to); suitable (_Dat._ for)

addieren ⨂1⨂ _tr. V._ add [up] ⨂2⨂ _itr. V._ add

Addition _die;_ ~, ~**en** addition

ade _Interj._ (veralt., landsch.) farewell (dated); bye (coll.); **jmdm.** ~ _od._ **Ade sagen** bid farewell to sb.

Adel _der;_ ~**s** nobility; **der niedere/hohe** ~: the lesser nobility/the aristocracy

adelig ▶ ADLIG

Adelige ▶ ADLIGE

adeln _tr. V._ jmdn. ~: give sb. a title; (in den hohen Adel erheben) raise sb. to the peerage

Adels-: ~**geschlecht** _das_ noble family; ~**stand** _der_ nobility; (hoher Adel) nobility; ~**titel** _der_ title of nobility

Ader _die;_ ~, ~**n** (a) blood vessel (b) (Anlage, Begabung) streak (c) (Bot., Geol.) vein (d) (Elektrot.) core

adieu /a'djøː/ _Interj._ (veralt.) adieu

Adjektiv _das;_ ~**s,** ~**e** (Sprachw.) adjective

Adjutant _der;_ ~**en,** ~**en, Adjutantin** _die;_ ~, ~**nen** adjutant

Adler _der;_ ~**s,** ~: eagle

adlig _Adj._ noble; ~ **sein** be a noble [man/woman]

Adlige _der/die; adj. Dekl._ noble [man/woman]

Admiral _der;_ ~**s,** ~**e** _od._ **Admiräle** admiral

adoptieren _tr. V._ adopt

Adoption _die;_ ~, ~**en** adoption

Adoptiv-: ~**eltern** _Pl._ adoptive parents; ~**kind** _das_ adopted child; ~**mutter** _die;_ _Pl._ ~**mütter** adoptive mother; ~**sohn** _der_ adoptive _or_ adopted son; ~**tochter** _die_ adoptive _or_ adopted daughter; ~**vater** _der_ adoptive father

Adressat *der;* ~en, ~en, **Adressatin** *die;* ~, ~nen addressee

Adress-buch, **Adreß-buch das* directory

Adresse *die;* ~, ~n address; **bei jmdm. an die falsche ~ kommen** *od.* **geraten** (fig. ugs.) come to the wrong address (fig.)

adressieren *tr. V.* address

adrett ① *Adj.* smart
② *adv.* smartly

Advent /at'vɛnt/ *der;* ~s **(a)** Advent
(b) (Adventssonntag) Sunday in Advent

Advents-: ~**kalender** *der* Advent calendar; ~**kranz** *der: garland of evergreens with four candles for the Sundays in Advent*

Adverb /at'vɛrp/ *das;* ~s, ~ien (Sprachw.) adverb

adverbial (Sprachw.) ① *Adj.* adverbial
② *adv.* adverbially

Advokat /atvo'ka:t/ *der;* ~en, ~en, **Advokatin** *die;* ~, ~nen (österr., schweiz., sonst veralt.) lawyer; advocate (arch.)

Aero- /aero- *od.* ɛːro-/: ~**gramm** *das* air[mail] letter; ~**sol** *das;* ~~s, ~~e aerosol

Affäre *die;* ~, ~n affair; **sich aus der ~ ziehen** (ugs.) get out of it

Affe *der;* ~n, ~n **(a)** monkey; (Menschen~) ape
(b) (salopp) (dummer Kerl) oaf; clot (Brit. coll.); (Geck) dandy

Affekt *der;* ~[e]s, ~e emotion; **im ~:** in the heat of the moment

affektiert (abwertend) ① *Adj.* affected
② *adv.* affectedly

Affen-theater *das* (salopp) farce

Afghane /afˈgaːnə/ *der;* ~n, ~n **(a)** Afghan
(b) (Hund) Afghan hound

Afghanin *die;* ~, ~nen Afghan

afghanisch *Adj.* Afghan

Afghanistan /afˈgaːnɪstaːn/ *(das);* ~s Afghanistan

Afrika *(das);* ~s Africa

Afrikaner *der;* ~s, ~, **Afrikanerin** *die;* ~, ~nen African

afrikanisch *Adj.* African

After *der;* ~s, ~: anus

AG *Abk.* **(a)** = **Aktiengesellschaft** PLC (Brit.); Ltd. (*private company*) (Brit.); Inc. (Amer.)
(b) = **Arbeitsgemeinschaft**

Agent *der;* ~en, ~en, **Agentin** *die;* ~, ~nen agent

Agentur *die;* ~, ~en agency

Agentur-bericht *der,* **Agentur-meldung** *die* agency report

Aggregat *das;* ~[e]s, ~e (Technik) unit; (Elektrot.) set

Aggregat-zustand *der* (Chemie) state

Aggression *die;* ~, ~en aggression

aggressiv ① *Adj.* aggressive
② *adv.* aggressively

Aggressivität *die;* ~: aggressiveness

Aggressor *der;* ~s, ~en, **Aggressorin** *die;* ~, ~nen aggressor

Agitation *die;* ~: agitation

agitieren *itr. V.* agitate

Agrar-land *das* agrarian country

Ägypten *(das);* ~s Egypt

Ägypter *der;* ~s, ~, **Ägypterin** *die;* ~, ~nen Egyptian

ägyptisch *Adj.* Egyptian

ah *Interj.* (verwundert) oh; (freudig, genießerisch) ah; (verstehend) oh; ah

äh /ɛ(ː)/ *Interj.* **(a)** (angeekelt) ugh
(b) (stotternd) er; hum

aha /aˈha(ː)/ *Interj.* (verstehend) oh[, I see]; (triumphierend) aha

Ahn *der;* ~[e]s, *od.* ~en, ~en (geh.), **Ahne** *der;* ~n, ~n forebear; ancestor

ähneln *itr. V.* jmdm. ~: resemble *or* be like sb.; **jmdm. sehr/wenig ~:** strongly resemble *or* be very like sb./bear little resemblance to sb.; **einer Sache** *(Dat.)* **~:** be similar to sth.; be like sth.; **sich** *(Dat.)* **~:** resemble one another; be alike

ahnen *tr. V.* **(a)** (im Voraus fühlen) have a premonition of
(b) (vermuten) suspect; **das konnte ich doch nicht ~!** I had no way of knowing that

Ahnin *die;* ~, ~nen ▸ AHN

ähnlich ① *Adj.* similar; **jmdm. ~ sein** be like sb.; **~ wie** like
② *adv.* similarly; ⟨answer, react⟩ in a similar way
③ *Präp. mit Dat.* like

Ähnlichkeit *die;* ~, ~en similarity; **mit jmdm. ~ haben** be like sb.

Ahnung *die;* ~, ~en **(a)** (Vorgefühl) premonition
(b) (ugs.: Kenntnisse) knowledge; **von etw.** [**viel**] **~ haben** know [a lot] about sth.; **keine ~!** [I've] no idea

ahnungs-los *Adj.* (nichts ahnend) unsuspecting; (naiv, unwissend) naïve

Ahnungslosigkeit *die;* ~ (Naivität, Unschuld) naïvety; innocence; (Unwissenheit) naïvety

ahoi *Interj.* (Seemannsspr.) ahoy

Ahorn /ˈaːhɔrn/ *der;* ~s, ~e maple

Ähre *die;* ~, ~n ear

Aids /eːts/ *das;* ~: Aids

Aids-: ~**kranke** *der/die* person suffering from Aids; ~**test** *der* Aids test

Airbag /ˈɛːɐbɛk/ *der;* ~s, ~s (Kfz.-W.) air bag

Akademie *die;* ~, ~n academy; (Bergbau, Forstw., Bauw.) school; college

Akademiker *der;* ~s, ~, **Akademikerin** *die;* ~, ~nen [university/college] graduate

akademisch ① *Adj.* academic

|2| *adv.* academically

Akazie /aˈkaːtsːjə/ *die;* ~, ~n acacia

akklimatisieren *refl. V.* become *or* get acclimatized

Akkord *der;* ~[e]s, ~e (a) (Musik) chord (b) (Wirtsch.) (Arbeit) piecework; (Lohn) piecework pay *no indef. art., no pl.;* (Satz) piece rate

Akkordeon *das;* ~s, ~s accordion

Akku *der;* ~s, ~s (ugs.), **Akkumulator** *der;* ~s, ~en accumulator (Brit.); storage battery

akkurat |1| *Adj.* meticulous
  |2| *adv.* meticulously

Akkusativ *der;* ~s, ~e (Sprachw.) accusative [case]

Akkusativ-objekt *das* (Sprachw.) accusative *or* direct object

Akne *die;* ~, ~n (Med.) acne

Akribie /akriˈbiː/ *die;* ~ (geh.) meticulousness; meticulous precision

akribisch /aˈkriːbɪʃ/|1| *Adj.* meticulous; meticulously precise
  |2| *adv.* meticulously; with meticulous precision

Akrobat *der;* ~en, ~en acrobat

Akrobatik *die;* ~: acrobatics *pl.*

Akrobatin *die;* ~, ~nen acrobat

akrobatisch *Adj.* acrobatic

Akt *der;* ~[e]s, ~e (a) (auch Theater, Zirkus-, Varieteeakt) act
  (b) (Zeremonie) ceremony
  (c) (Geschlechtsakt) sexual act
  (d) (Kunst) nude

Akt-: ~**aufnahme** *die* nude photograph; ~**bild** *das* nude [picture]

Akte *die;* ~, ~n file

Akten-: ~**deckel** *der* folder; ~**koffer** *der* attaché case; ~**mappe** *die* briefcase; ~**notiz** *die* note [for the files]; ~**ordner** *der* file; ~**tasche** *die* briefcase; ~**zeichen** *das* reference

Akteur /akˈtøːɐ̯/ *der;* ~s, ~e, **Akteurin** *die;* ~, ~nen person involved

Akt-foto *das* nude photo

Aktie /ˈaktsːjə/ *die;* ~, ~n (Wirtsch.) share; ~n shares (Brit.); stock (Amer.); **die ~n fallen/ steigen** share *or* stock prices are falling/ rising

Aktien-: ~**gesellschaft** *die* joint stock company; ~**kapital** *das* share capital; ~**mehrheit** *die* majority shareholding (Gen. in); ~**paket** *das* block of shares

Aktion *die;* ~, ~en (a) action *no indef. art.;* (militärisch) operation
  (b) (Kampagne) campaign

Aktionär *der;* ~s, ~e, **Aktionärin** *die;* ~, ~nen shareholder

aktiv |1| *Adj.* (a) active
  (b) (Milit.) serving *attrib.* ⟨officer, soldier⟩
  |2| *adv.* actively

Aktiv *das;* ~s, ~e (Sprachw.) active

Aktive *der/die; adj. Dekl.* (Sport) participant

aktivieren *tr. V.* (a) mobilize ⟨party members, group, class, etc.⟩; **den Kreislauf** ~: stimulate the circulation
  (b) (DV) activate

Aktivität *die;* ~, ~en activity

Akt-modell *das* nude model

aktualisieren *tr. V.* update

Aktualität *die;* ~, ~en (a) (Gegenwartsbezug) relevance [to the present]
  (b) (von Nachrichten usw.) topicality

aktuell *Adj.* topical; (gegenwärtig) current; (neu) up-to-the-minute; **eine** ~**e Sendung** (Ferns., Rundf.) a [news and] current affairs programme

Akupunktur *die;* ~, ~en (Med.) acupuncture

Akustik *die;* ~ (a) (Lehre vom Schall) acoustics *sing., no art.;*
  (b) (Schallverhältnisse) acoustics *pl.*

akustisch |1| *Adj.* acoustic
  |2| *adv.* acoustically

akut *Adj.* (auch Med.) acute; pressing, urgent ⟨question, issue⟩

AKW *Abk.* = **Atomkraftwerk**

Akzent *der;* ~[e]s, ~e (a) (Sprachw.) (Betonung) stress; (Betonungszeichen) accent
  (b) (Sprachmelodie, Aussprache) accent

akzeptabel |1| *Adj.* acceptable
  |2| *adv.* acceptably

akzeptieren *tr. V.* accept

à la /ala/ (Gastr., ugs.) à la

Alabaster *der;* ~s, ~: alabaster

à la carte /alaˈkart/ (Gastr.) à la carte

Alarm *der;* ~[e]s, ~e alarm; (Flieger~) air-raid warning; ~ **geben**/(fig. ugs.) **schlagen** raise the alarm; **blinder** ~: false alarm

alarm-, Alarm-: ~**anlage** *die* alarm system; ~**bereit** *Adj.* on alert *postpos.;* ~**bereitschaft** *die* alert

alarmieren *tr. V.* (a) alarm
  (b) (zu Hilfe rufen) call [out] ⟨doctor, police, fire brigade, etc.⟩

Alarm-: ~**sirene** *die* warning siren; ~**stufe** *die* alert stage

Albaner *der;* ~s, ~, **Albanerin** *die;* ~, ~nen Albanian

Albanien /alˈbaːnjən/ (das) ~s Albania

albanisch *Adj.* Albanian

Albatros *der;* ~, ~se (Zool.) albatross

Alben ▶ ALBUM

albern *Adj.* (a) silly; **sich** ~ **benehmen** act silly
  (b) (ugs.: nebensächlich) silly; stupid

Albernheit *die;* ~, ~en silliness

Albino *der;* ~s, ~s albino

Alb-traum *der* nightmare

Album *das;* ~s, **Alben** album

Alge *die;* ~, ~n alga

Algebra /österr.: alˈgeːbra/ *die;* ~: algebra

Algerien /alˈgeːrjən/ (das) ~s Algeria

a

Algerier der; ~s, ~, **Algerierin** die; ~, ~nen Algerian

algerisch Adj. Algerian

alias Adv. alias

Alibi das; ~s, ~s alibi

Alkohol der; ~s, ~e alcohol

alkohol-, Alkohol-: ~**abhängig** Adj. dependent on alcohol postpos.; ~**abhängigkeit** die dependence on alcohol; alcohol dependence; ~**ein·fluss,** *~**ein·fluß** der, ~**ein·wirkung** die influence of alcohol or drink; unter ~einfluss od. ~einwirkung [stehen] [be] under the influence of alcohol or drink; ~**fahne** die smell of alcohol [on one's breath]; eine ~fahne haben smell of alcohol; ~**frei** Adj. non-alcoholic

Alkoholiker der; ~s, ~, **Alkoholikerin** die; ~, ~nen alcoholic

alkoholisch Adj. alcoholic

Alkoholismus der; ~: alcoholism no art.

alkohol-, Alkohol-: ~**konsum** der consumption of alcohol; ~**missbrauch,** *~**mißbrauch** der alcohol abuse; ~**sucht** die alcohol addiction; alcoholism; ~**süchtig** Adj. addicted to alcohol postpos.; alcoholic; ~**süchtige** der/die; adj. Dekl. alcoholic; ~**sünder** der, ~**sünderin** die (ugs.) drunk[en] driver; ~**vergiftung** die alcohol[ic] poisoning

all Indefinitpron. u. unbest. Zahlw. **1** attr. (ganz, gesamt...) all; ~es andere/Weitere/Übrige everything else; ~es Schöne everything or all that is beautiful; ~es Gute! all the best!; wir/ihr/sie ~e all of us/you/them; ~e Anwesenden all those present; ~e Bewohner der Stadt all the inhabitants of the town; ~e Jahre wieder every year; ~e fünf Minuten/Meter every five minutes/metres; Bücher ~er Art all kinds of books; in ~er Ruhe in peace and quiet

2 allein stehend **(a)** ~e all; ~e, die ...: all those who ... **(b)** ~es (auf Sachen bezogen) everything; (auf Personen bezogen) everybody; das ~es all that; trotz ~em in spite of everything; ~es in ~em all in all; vor ~em above all; das ist ~es that's all or (coll.) it; ist das ~es? is that all or (coll.) it?; ~es mal herhören! (ugs.) listen everybody!; ~es aussteigen! (ugs.) everyone out!; (vom Schaffner gesagt) all change!

All das; ~s ▶ WELTALL

alle Adj. ~ sein be all gone; ~ werden run out

alle·dem Pron. trotz ~: in spite of or despite all that

Allee die; ~, ~n avenue

allein 1 Adj. **(a)** (für sich) alone; on one's/its own; by oneself/itself; ganz ~: all on one's/its own **(b)** (einsam) alone

2 adv. (ohne Hilfe) by oneself/itself; on one's/its own; etw. ~ tun do sth. oneself; von ~ (ugs.) by oneself/itself

3 Adv. **(a)** (geh.: ausschließlich) alone **(b)** [schon] ~ der Gedanke, [schon] der Gedanke ~: the mere thought [of it]

alleine (ugs.) ▶ ALLEIN 1A, 2, 3B

allein-, Allein-: *~**erziehend** Adj. single ⟨mother, father, parent⟩; ~**erziehende** der/die; adj. Dekl. single parent; ~**gang** der (fig.) independent initiative; im ~gang off one's own bat

alleinig Adj. sole

*****allein·stehend** Adj. ⟨person⟩ living alone; (ledig) single ⟨person⟩

Alleinstehende der/die; adj. Dekl. person living alone; (Ledige[r]) single person

alle·mal Adv. (ugs.) any time (coll.); was der kann, das kann ich doch ~: anything he can do, I can too; s. auch EIN¹ 1

allen·falls Adv. **(a)** (höchstens) at [the] most **(b)** (bestenfalls) at best

aller-: ~**dings** Adv. **(a)** (einschränkend) though; es stimmt ~dings, dass ...: it's true though that ...; **(b)** (zustimmend) [yes,] certainly; das war ~dings Pech that was bad luck, to be sure; ~**erst...** Adj. **(a)** very first; der/die/das ~erste the very first; **(b)** (best...) very best

Allergie die; ~, ~n (Med.) allergy

allergisch 1 Adj. (Med.) allergic (gegen to) **2** adv. auf etw. (Akk.) ~ reagieren have an allergic reaction to sth.

aller-, Aller-: ~**größt...** Adj. utmost ⟨trouble, care, etc.⟩; biggest ⟨car, house, town, etc.⟩ of all; tallest ⟨person⟩ of all; am ~größten sein be [the] biggest/tallest of all; ~**hand** indekl. Adj. (ugs.) **(a)** attr. all kinds or sorts of; **(b)** allein stehend all kinds or sorts of things; das ist ~hand (viel) that's a lot; das ist ja ~hand! that's just not on! (Brit. coll.); ~**heiligen** das; ~~s (bes. kath. Kirche) All Saints' Day; ~**herzlichst 1** Adj. warmest ⟨thanks, greetings, congratulations⟩; most cordial ⟨reception, welcome, invitation⟩; **2** most warmly; ~**höchst... 1** Adj. highest ⟨building, tree, etc.⟩ of all; **2** adv. am ~höchsten ⟨fly, jump, etc.⟩ the highest of all; ~**höchstens** Adv. at the very most

allerlei indekl. Adj. all kinds or sorts of; allein stehend all kinds or sorts of things

Allerlei das; ~s, ~s (Gemisch) pot-pourri; (Durcheinander) jumble

aller-: ~**letzt...** Adj. **(a)** very last; **(b)** (ugs. abwertend) most dreadful (coll.); das ist das Allerletzte that's the absolute limit; ~**liebst... 1** Adj. most favourite; es wäre mir am ~liebsten od. das Allerliebste, wenn ...: I should like it best of all if ...; **2** adv. etw. am ~liebsten tun like doing sth. best of all; ~**meist... 1** Indefinitpron. u. unbest. Zahlw. by far the most attrib.; das ~meiste am ~meisten most of all/by far the most; **2** Adv. am ~meisten most of all;

~**mindest...** *Adj.* slightest; least; **das ~mindeste** the very least; ~**nächst...** [1] *Adj.* very nearest *attrib.*; (Reihenfolge ausdrückend) very next *attrib.*; [2] *adv.* am ~**nächsten** nearest of all; ~**neu[e]st...** *Adj.* very latest *attrib.*; **das Allerneu[e]ste** the very latest; ~**schlimmst...** *Adj.* very worst *attrib.*; ~**schönst...** [1] *Adj.* most beautiful *attrib.*; loveliest *attrib.*; (angenehmst...) very nicest *attrib.*; [2] *adv.* er singt am ~**schönsten** his singing is the most beautiful of all; ~**seits** *Adv.* guten Morgen ~**seits**! good morning everyone

Allerwelts-: ~**gesicht** *das* nondescript face; ~**wort** *das* hackneyed word

allerwenigst... [1] *Adj.* lest ... of all; *Pl.* fewest ... of all [2] *adv.* am ~**wenigsten** least of all

alle·samt *Indefinitpron. u. unbest. Zahlw.* (ugs.) all [of you/us/them]; **wir ~:** we all

Alles·kleber *der* all-purpose adhesive

all·gemein [1] *Adj.* general; universal ⟨conscription, suffrage⟩; **im ~en Interesse** in the common interest; **im Allgemein,** ***~**en** in general [2] *adv.* **(a)** generally; (ausnahmslos) universally; **es ist ~ bekannt, dass ...:** it is common knowledge that ... **(b)** (unverbindlich) ⟨write, talk, discuss⟩ in general terms

Allgemein-: ~**befinden** *das* (Med.) general state of health; ~**bildung** *die* general education

Allgemeinheit *die;* ~ **(a)** generality **(b) die ~:** the general public

Allgemein-: ~**medizin** *die* general medicine; ~**wohl** *das* public good

All·heilmittel *das* (auch fig.) cure-all; panacea

Alligator *der;* ~**s,** ~**en** alligator

Alliierte *der; adj. Dekl.* ally; **die** ~**n** the Allies

all-: ~**jährlich** [1] *Adj.* annual; yearly; [2] *adv.* annually; every year; ~**mächtig** *Adj.* all-powerful

all-mählich [1] *Adj.* gradual [2] *adv.* gradually; [3] *Adv.* **wir sollten ~ gehen** it's time we got going

all-, All-: ~**morgendlich** [1] *Adj.* regular morning; [2] *adv.* every morning; ~**seitig** [1] *Adj.* general; all-round, (Amer.) all-around *attrib.*; [2] *adv.* generally; ~**seits** *Adv.* on all sides; ~**tag** *der* **(a)** (Werktag) weekday; **(b)** (Einerlei) daily routine; **der graue ~:** the dull routine of everyday life; ~**täglich** *Adj.* ordinary ⟨face, person, appearance, etc.⟩; everyday ⟨topic, event, sight⟩; commonplace ⟨remark⟩; **ein nicht ~täglicher Anblick** a sight one doesn't see every day; ~**tags** *Adv.* [on] weekdays; ~**zu** *Adv.* all too; ~**zu bald/früh** all too

soon/early; ~**zu lange/oft/sehr** too long/often/much; ~**zu viel** too much; **nicht ~zu viele** not too many

****allzu·bald** *usw.* ▶ ALLZU

Alm *die;* ~, ~**en** mountain pasture; Alpine pasture

Alm·hütte *die* Alpine hut

Almosen *das;* ~**s,** ~: alms *pl.*

Alp *die;* ~, ~**en** (bes. schweiz.) ▶ ALM

Alpaka *das;* ~**s,** ~**s** alpaca

Alpen *Pl.* **die** ~: the Alps

Alpen-: ~**rose** *die* rhododendron; ~**veilchen** *das* cyclamen

Alpha *das;* ~[s], ~[s] alpha

Alphabet *das;* ~[e]s, ~e alphabet

alphabetisch [1] *Adj.* alphabetical [2] *adv.* alphabetically

Alp·horn *das* alpenhorn

alpin *Adj.* Alpine

Alpinist *der;* ~**en,** ~**en, Alpinistin** *die;* ~, ~**nen** Alpinist

Alp·traum ▶ ALBTRAUM

als *Konj.* **(a)** (zeitlich) when; **damals,** ~: [in the days] when; **gerade** ~: just as **(b)** (kausal) **um so mehr,** ~: all the more **since** *or* in that **(c)** *Vergleichspartikel* **größer/älter/mehr/weniger** ~: bigger/older/more/less than; **anders ~ wir sein/leben** be different/live differently from us; **so viel/so weit ~ möglich** as much/as far as possible; **so bald/schnell ~ möglich** as soon/as quickly as possible; ~ [wenn od. ob] (+ *Konjunktiv II*) as if; as though; ~ **ob ich das nicht wüsste!** as if I didn't know **(d)** ~ **Rentner/Arzt** as a pensioner/a doctor; **sich ~ wahr/Lüge erweisen** prove to be true/a lie

also [1] *Adv.* so; therefore [2] *Partikel* **(a)** (das heißt) that is **(b)** (nach Unterbrechung) well [then] **(c)** (verstärkend) **na ~!** there you are[, you see]; ~ **schön** well all right then

alt, älter, ältest... *Adj.* **(a)** old; **Alt und Jung** old and young; **seine ~en Eltern** his aged parents; **wie ~ bist du?** how old are you?; **mein älterer/ältester Bruder** my elder/eldest brother **(b)** (nicht mehr frisch) old; ~**es Brot** stale bread **(c)** (vom letzten Jahr) old; ~**e Äpfel/Kartoffeln** last year's apples/potatoes **(d)** (langjährig) long-standing ⟨acquaintance⟩ **(e)** (antik, klassisch) ancient **(f)** (vertraut) old familiar ⟨streets, sights, etc.⟩; **ganz der/die Alte sein** be just the same

Alt¹ *der;* ~**s,** ~**e** (Musik) alto; (Frauenstimme) contralto; (im Chor) contraltos *pl.*

Alt² *das;* ~[s], ~: top fermented, dark beer

Altar *der;* ~[e]s, Altäre altar

alt-, Alt-: ~**bau-wohnung** *die* flat (Brit.) *or* (Amer.) apartment in an old building; ~**bekannt** *Adj.* well-known; ~**bier** *das* ▶ ALT²

Alte *der/die; adj. Dekl.* **(a)** (alter Mensch) old man/woman; *Pl.* old people
(b) (salopp) (Vater, Ehemann) old man (coll.); (Mutter, Ehefrau) old woman (coll.); (Chef) governor (coll.); (Chefin) boss (coll.); **die** ∼**n** (Eltern) my/his *etc.* old man and old woman (coll.)
(c) *Pl.* (Tiereltern) parents
alt·ehrwürdig *Adj.* (geh.) venerable; time-honoured ⟨*customs*⟩
Alt·englisch *das* Old English
Alten-: ∼**pfleger** *der*, ∼**pflegerin** *die* geriatric nurse; ∼**tages·stätte** *die* old people's day centre
Alter *das;* ∼**s**, ∼: age; (hohes ∼) old age; **im** ∼: in one's old age; **im** ∼ **von** at the age of
älter [1] ▶ ALT
[2] *Adj.* (nicht mehr jung) elderly
altern *itr. V.; mit sein* age
alters-, Alters-: ∼**beschwerden** *Pl.* complaints of old age; ∼**genosse** *der*, ∼**genossin** *die* contemporary; person/child of the same age; **meine** ∼**genossen** my contemporaries; people of my age; ∼**gruppe** *die* age group; ∼**heim** *das* old people's home; old-age home (Amer.); ∼**rente** *die* old-age pension; ∼**ruhe·geld** *das* retirement pension; ∼**schwach** *Adj.* old and infirm ⟨*person*⟩; old and weak ⟨*animal*⟩; ∼**schwäche** *die* (bei Menschen) [old] age and infirmity; (bei Tieren) [old] age and weakness; ∼**starrsinn** *der* obstinacy of old age; ∼**stufe** *die* age; ∼**unterschied** *der* age difference; ∼**versorgung** *die* provision for one's old age; (System) pension scheme
Altertum *das;* ∼**s** antiquity *no art.*
Älteste *der/die; adj. Dekl.* **(a)** (Dorf-, Vereins-, Kirchenälteste usw.) elder
(b) (Sohn, Tochter) eldest
alt-, Alt-: ∼**glas·behälter** *der* bottle bank; ∼**griechisch** *das* classical or ancient Greek; ∼**hochdeutsch** *das* Old High German; ∼**klug;** ∼**kluger,** ∼**klugst...** [1] *Adj.* precocious; [2] *adv.* precociously; ∼**last** *die* (Ökologie) old, improperly disposed of harmful waste; (fig.) inherited problem
ältlich *Adj.* rather elderly
alt-, Alt-: ∼**metall** *das* scrap metal; ∼**modisch** [1] *Adj.* old-fashioned; [2] *adv.* in an old-fashioned way; ∼**papier** *das* waste paper; ∼**rosa** *Adj.* old rose; ∼**stadt** *die* old [part of the] town; ∼**waren·händler** *der*, ∼**waren·händlerin** *die* second-hand dealer
Alu *das;* ∼**s** (ugs.) aluminium
Alu·folie *die* aluminium foil
Aluminium *das;* ∼**s** aluminium; aluminum (Amer.)
am *Präp. + Art.* **(a)** = **an dem;**
(b) Frankfurt am Main Frankfurt on [the]

Main; **am Marktplatz** on the market square; **am Meer/Fluss** by the sea/on *or* by the river; **am Anfang/Ende** at the beginning/end; **am 19. November** on 19 November; **am schnellsten laufen** run [the] fastest; **am Verwelken sein** be wilting
Amalgam *das;* ∼**s**, ∼**e** (Chemie, auch fig.) amalgam
Amalgam·füllung *die* (Zahnmed.) amalgam filling
Amateur /ama'tøːɐ̯/ *der;* ∼**s**, ∼**e**, **Amateurin** *die;* ∼, ∼**nen** amateur
Amazonas *der;* ∼: Amazon
Amboss, *****Amboß** *der;* Ambosses, Ambosse anvil
ambulant (Med.) [1] *Adj.* outpatient *attrib.;* [2] *adv.* **jmdn.** ∼ **behandeln** give sb. outpatient treatment
Ambulanz *die;* ∼, ∼**en** **(a)** (in Kliniken) outpatient[s'] department
(b) (Krankenwagen) ambulance
Ameise *die;* ∼, ∼**n** ant
Ameisen-: ∼**bär** *der* anteater; ∼**haufen** *der* anthill
amen *Adv.* amen
Amen *das;* ∼**s**, ∼: Amen
Amerika (*das*); ∼**s** America
Amerikaner *der;* ∼**s**, ∼ **(a)** American
(b) (Gebäck) *small, flat iced cake*
Amerikanerin *die;* ∼, ∼**nen** American
amerikanisch *Adj.* American
Amino·säure *die* (Chemie) amino acid
Ammann *der;* ∼**[e]s, Ammänner** (schweiz.) (Gemeinde-, Bezirksamman) ≈ mayor; (Landamman) cantonal president
Amme *die;* ∼, ∼**n** wet nurse
Amnestie /amnɛs'tiː/ *die;* ∼, ∼**n** amnesty
amnestieren *tr. V.* grant an amnesty to
Amöbe *die;* ∼, ∼**n** (Biol.) amoeba
Amok *der;* ∼ **laufen** run amok
Amok·läufer *der* madman
Amok·läuferin *die* madwoman
Ampel *die;* ∼, ∼**n** **(a)** traffic lights *pl.;*
(b) (für Pflanzen) hanging flowerpot
Amphibie /am'fiːbi̯ə/ *die;* ∼, ∼**n** (Zool.) amphibian
Amphibien·fahrzeug *das* amphibious vehicle
Amphi·theater *das* amphitheatre
Ampulle *die;* ∼, ∼**n** (Med.) ampoule
Amputation *die;* ∼, ∼**en** (Med.) amputation
amputieren *tr. V.* amputate
Amsel *die;* ∼, ∼**n** blackbird
Amt *das;* ∼**[e]s, Ämter (a)** (Stellung) post; position; (hohes politisches od. kirchliches ∼) office; **im** ∼ **sein** be in office
(b) (Aufgabe) task; job
(c) (Behörde) office
(d) (Fernsprechvermittlung) exchange
amtieren *itr. V.* **(a)** hold office

*****alte Schreibung - vgl. Hinweis auf S. xiv

(b) (vorübergehend) act (**als** as)

amtlich ⓵ *Adj.* official; (ugs.: sicher) definite
⓶ *adv.* officially

Amt·mann *der; Pl.* ...**männer** *od.* ...**leute,**
Amt·männin *die;* ~, ~**nen** senior civil
servant

Amts-: ~**anmaßung** *die* (Rechtsw.)
unauthorized assumption of authority;
~**arzt** *der,* ~**ärztin** *die* medical officer;
~**eid** *der* oath of office; ~**gericht** *das*
local or district court; ~**geschäfte** *Pl.*
official duties; ~**handlung** *die* official act
or duty; ~**leitung** *die* (Fernspr.) exchange
line

Amulett *das;* ~[e]s, ~e amulet; charm

amüsant ⓵ *Adj.* entertaining; amusing
⓶ *adv.* in an entertaining or amusing way

amüsieren ⓵ *refl. V.* **(a)** (sich vergnügen)
enjoy oneself; **sich mit jmdm.** ~: have fun or
a good time with sb.
(b) (belustigt sein) be amused; **sich über jmdn./**
etw. ~: find sb./sth. funny
⓶ *tr. V.* amuse

an ⓵ *Präp. mit Dat.* **(a)** (räumlich) at; (auf) on;
Frankfurt an der Oder Frankfurt on [the]
Oder; **Tür an Tür** next door to one another;
an ... vorbei past
(b) (zeitlich) on; **an jedem Sonntag** every
Sunday; **an Ostern** (bes. südd.) at Easter
(c) arm/reich **an Vitaminen** low/rich in
vitamins; **jmdn. an etw. erkennen** recognize
sb. by sth.; **an etw. leiden** suffer from sth.;
an einer Krankheit sterben die of a disease
(d) an [und für] sich actually
⓶ *Präp. mit Akk.* **(a)** to; (auf, gegen) on
(b) an etw./jmdn. glauben believe in sth./sb.;
an etw. denken think of sth.; **sich an etw.**
erinnern remember sth.
⓷ *Adv.* **(a)** (Verkehrsw.) **Köln an: 9.15** arriving
Cologne 09.15
(b) (ugs.: in Betrieb) on; **die Waschmaschine/**
der Fernseher/das Licht/das Gas ist an the
washing machine/television/light/gas is on
(c) (ugs.: ungefähr) around; about; **an [die]**
20 000 DM around or about 20,000 DM

Anabolikum *das;* ~s, **Anabolika** (Med.)
anabolic steroid

analog ⓵ *Adj.* **(a)** (gleichartig) analogous; ~
[zu] diesem Fall analogous to this case
(b) (Technik, DV) analogue
⓶ *adv.* **(a)** (gleichartig) analogously
(b) (Technik, DV) ⟨display, reproduce⟩ in
analogue form

Analog-: ~**rechner** *der* (DV) analogue
computer; ~**uhr** *die* analogue clock;
(Armbanduhr) analogue watch

Analphabet *der;* ~en, ~en,
Analphabetin *die;* ~, ~**nen** illiterate
[person]; ~ **sein** be illiterate

Analyse *die;* ~, ~**n** analysis

analysieren *tr. V.* analyse

Analyst *der;* ~en, ~en, **Analystin,** *die;*
~, ~**nen** (Börsenw.) analyst

analytisch ⓵ *Adj.* analytical

⓶ *adv.* analytically

Ananas *die;* ~, ~ *od.* ~**se** pineapple

Anarchie *die;* ~, ~**n** anarchy

Anarchist *der;* ~**en,** ~**en, Anarchistin**
die; ~, ~**nen** anarchist

Anästhesie *die;* ~, ~**n** (Med.) anaesthesia

anästhesieren *tr. V.* (Med.) anaesthetize

Anästhesist *der;* ~**en,** ~**en,**
Anästhesistin *die;* ~, ~**nen** (Med.)
anaesthetist

Anatomie *die;* ~, ~**n** anatomy

anatomisch *Adj.* anatomical

an|bahnen ⓵ *tr. V.* initiate ⟨*negotiations,*
talks, process, etc.⟩; develop ⟨*relationship,*
connection⟩
⓶ *refl. V.* ⟨*development*⟩ be in the offing;
⟨*friendship, relationship*⟩ start to develop

an|bändeln *itr. V.* **mit jmdm.** ~ (ugs.) get
off with sb. (Brit. coll.); pick sb. up

An·bau *der; Pl.* ~**ten (a)** building
(b) (Gebäude) extension
(c) (das Anpflanzen) growing

an|bauen ⓵ *tr. V.* **(a)** build on
(b) (anpflanzen) grow
⓶ *itr. V.* (das Haus vergrößern) build an
extension

an-bei *Adv.* (Amtsspr.) herewith; **Rückporto**
~: return postage enclosed

an|beißen ⓵ *unr. tr. V.* bite into; take a
bite of
⓶ *unr. itr. V.* (auch fig. ugs.) bite

an|belangen *tr. V.* **was mich/dies** *usw.*
anbelangt as far as I am/this matter is *etc.*
concerned

an|beten *tr. V.* (auch fig.) worship

An-betracht *der:* **in** ~ **einer Sache** (*Gen.*)
in view of sth.

an|betreffen *unr. tr. V.* ▶ ANBELANGEN

an|betteln *tr. V.* **jmdn.** ~: beg from sb.;
jmdn. um etw. ~: beg sb. for sth.

Anbetung *die;* ~, ~**en** (auch fig.) worship

an|biedern *refl. V.* **sich [bei jmdm.]** ~:
curry favour [with sb.]

an|bieten ⓵ *unr. tr. V.* offer; **jmdm. etw.**
~: offer sb. sth.
⓶ *unr. refl. V.* **(a)** offer one's services; **sich**
~, **etw. zu tun** offer to do sth.
(b) (fig.) ⟨*possibility, solution*⟩ suggest itself

An·bieter *der,* **An·bieterin** *die* (Wirtsch.)
supplier

an|binden *unr. tr. V.* tie [up] (**an** + *Dat. od.*
Akk. to); tie up, moor ⟨*boat*⟩ (**an** + *Dat. od.*
Akk. to); tether ⟨*animal*⟩ (**an** + *Dat. od. Akk.*
to)

an|blasen *unr. tr. V.* **(a)** blow at
(b) (anfachen) blow on

An·blick *der* sight

an|blicken *tr. V.* look at

an|blinzeln *tr. V.* **(a)** blink at
(b) (zuzwinkern) wink at

an|brechen ⓵ *unr. tr. V.* **(a)** crack
(b) (öffnen) open

                                 ···⟡

(c) (zu verbrauchen beginnen) break into ⟨supplies, reserves⟩ ② unr. itr. V.; mit sein (geh.: beginnen) ⟨dawn, day⟩ break; ⟨age, epoch⟩ dawn

an|brennen ① unr. tr. V. (anzünden) light ② unr. itr. V.; mit sein burn

an|bringen unr. tr. V. **(a)** (befestigen) put up ⟨sign, aerial, curtain, plaque⟩ (an + Dat. on) **(b)** (äußern) make ⟨request, complaint, comment⟩ **(c)** (zeigen) demonstrate ⟨knowledge, experience⟩ **(d)** (ugs.: herbeibringen) bring

An-bruch der (geh.: Beginn) dawn[ing]; der ~ des Tages daybreak

an|brüllen tr. V. (ugs.) bellow at

Andacht die; ~, ~en **(a)** (Sammlung) rapt attention; (im Gebet) silent worship or prayer **(b)** (Gottesdienst) prayers pl.

andächtig ① Adj. rapt; (ins Gebet versunken) devout ② adv. with rapt attention; (ins Gebet versunken) devoutly

an|dauern itr. V. ⟨negotiations⟩ continue, go on; ⟨weather, rain⟩ last

andauernd ① Adj. continual; constant ② adv. continually; constantly

Anden Pl. die ~: the Andes

An-denken das; ~s, ~ **(a)** memory; zum ~ an jmdn./etw. to remind you/us etc. of sb./sth. **(b)** (Erinnerungsstück) memento; (Reise~) souvenir

ander... Indefinitpron. ① attr. **(a)** other; ein ~er/eine ~e/ein ~es another; das Kleid gefällt mir nicht, haben Sie noch ~e/ein ~es? I don't like that dress, do you have any others/another?; jemand ~er od. ~es someone else; (in Fragen) anyone else; niemand ~er od. ~es nobody else; etwas ~es something else; (in Fragen) anything else; nichts ~es nothing else; not anything else **(b)** (verschieden) different ② allein stehend ein ~r/eine ~e: another [one]; nicht drängeln, einer nach dem ~n don't push, one after the other; ein ~er/eine ~e/ein ~es another [one]; ein[e]s nach dem ~[e]n first things first; ich will weder das eine noch das ~e I don't want either

anderen·falls Adv. otherwise

anderer·seits Adv. on the other hand

ander·mal Adv. ein ~: another time

ändern ① tr. V. change; alter; alter ⟨garment⟩; change ⟨person⟩ ② refl. V. change

ändern·falls Adv. otherwise

anders Adv. **(a)** (verschieden) ⟨think, act, feel, do⟩ differently (als from or (esp. Brit) to); ⟨be, look, sound, taste⟩ different (als from or (esp. Brit.) to); es war alles ganz ~: it was all quite different

(b) (sonst) else; niemand ~: nobody else; jemand ~: someone else; (in Fragen) anyone else

anders-, Anders-: ~artig Adj. different; ~farbig Adj. different-coloured attrib.; of a different colour postpos.; ~gläubige der/die person of a different religion; ~herum Adv. the other way round or (Amer.) around; ~herum gehen/fahren go/drive round or (Amer.) around the other way; ~wo Adv. (ugs.) elsewhere; ~woher Adv. (ugs.) from somewhere else; ~wohin Adv. (ugs.) somewhere else

andert·halb Bruchz. one and a half; ~ Stunden an hour and a half

Änderung die; ~, ~en change (Gen. in); alteration (Gen. to)

Änderungs·schneiderei die tailor's [that does alterations]

anderweitig ① Adj. other ② adv. in another way

an|deuten ① tr. V. **(a)** (zu verstehen geben) hint **(b)** (nicht vollständig ausführen) outline; (kurz erwähnen) indicate ② refl. V. be indicated

An-deutung die hint

An-drang der crowd; (Gedränge) crush

andre... ▶ ANDER...

an|drehen tr. V. **(a)** (einschalten) turn on **(b)** jmdm. etw. ~ (ugs.) palm sb. off with sth.

andrer·seits Adv. on the other hand

an|drohen tr. V. jmdm. etw. ~: threaten sb. with sth

An-drohung die threat

an|drücken tr. V. press down

an|ecken itr. V.; mit sein bei jmdm. ~ (fig. ugs.) rub sb. [up (Brit.)] the wrong way

an|eignen refl. V. **(a)** appropriate **(b)** (lernen) acquire; learn

an-einander Adv. (zusammen) together; (nebeneinander) next to each other; next to one another; ~ denken think of each other or one another; ~ vorbeigehen pass each other or one another

*****aneinander|binden** usw. ▶ ANEINANDER

Anekdote die; ~, ~n anecdote

an|ekeln tr. V. disgust

Anemone die; ~, ~n anemone

an|erkennen unr. tr. V. **(a)** recognize ⟨country, record, verdict, qualification, document⟩; acknowledge ⟨debt⟩; accept ⟨demand, bill, conditions, rules⟩; allow ⟨claim, goal⟩ **(b)** (nicht leugnen) acknowledge **(c)** (würdigen) appreciate; respect ⟨viewpoint, opinion⟩; ein ~der Blick an appreciative look

anerkennens·wert Adj. commendable

Anerkennung die; ~, ~en ▶ ANERKENNEN: **(a)** recognition; acknowledgement; acceptance; allowance **(b)** acknowledgement **(c)** appreciation; respect (Gen. for)

---

*old spelling - see note on page xiv

an|fachen *tr. V.* fan; (fig.) arouse ⟨*anger, curiosity, enthusiasm*⟩; inflame ⟨*passion*⟩; stir up ⟨*hatred*⟩; inspire ⟨*hope*⟩; ferment ⟨*discord, war*⟩

an|fahren ☐ *unr. tr. V.* (a) run into; hit
(b) (herbeifahren) deliver
(c) (ansteuern) stop at ⟨*village etc.*⟩; ⟨*ship*⟩ put in at ⟨*port*⟩
(d) (zurechtweisen) shout at
☐ *unr. itr. V.; mit sein* (a) (starten) start off
(b) **angefahren kommen** come driving/riding up

An·fahrt *die* (a) (das Anfahren) journey
(b) (Weg) approach

Anfahrts·skizze *die* map showing directions

An·fall *der* attack; (epileptischer ∼, fig.) fit; **einen ∼ bekommen** *od.* (ugs.) **kriegen** have an attack/a fit

an|fallen ☐ *unr. tr. V.* attack
☐ *unr. itr V.; mit sein* ⟨*costs*⟩ be incurred; ⟨*interest*⟩ accrue; ⟨*work*⟩ come up

an·fällig *Adj.* ⟨*person*⟩ with a delicate constitution; ⟨*machine*⟩ susceptible to faults; **gegen** *od.* **für etw. ∼ sein** be susceptible to sth.

An·fang *der* beginning; start; (erster Abschnitt) beginning; **am** *od.* **zu ∼:** at first; **von ∼ an** from the outset; **∼ 1984/der Woche** *usw.* at the beginning of 1984/of the week *etc.*

an·fangen ☐ *unr. itr. V.* (a) begin; start; **mit etw. ∼:** start [on] sth.; **∼, etw. zu tun** start to do sth.
(b) (zu sprechen anfangen) begin; **von etw. ∼:** start on about sth.
(c) (eine Stelle antreten) start
☐ *unr. tr. V.* (a) begin; start; (anbrechen) start
(b) (machen) do

An·fänger *der;* ∼s, ∼, **An·fängerin** *die;* ∼, ∼nen beginner

anfänglich *Adj.* initial

anfangs *Adv.* at first; initially

Anfangs-: ∼**buchstabe** *der* initial [letter]; ∼**stadium** *das* initial stage

an|fassen ☐ *tr. V.* (a) (fassen, halten) take hold of
(b) (berühren) touch
(c) **jmdn. ∼** (an der Hand nehmen) take sb.'s hand
(d) (angehen) tackle ⟨*problem, task, etc.*⟩
(e) (behandeln) treat ⟨*person*⟩
☐ *itr. V.* [mit] ∼**:** lend a hand

anfechtbar *Adj.:* ▶ ANFECHTEN A: disputable; contestable; challengeable

an|fechten *unr. tr. V.* (a) dispute ⟨*statement, contract*⟩; contest ⟨*will*⟩; challenge ⟨*decision, law, opinion*⟩
(b) (beunruhigen) trouble

an|fertigen *tr. V.* make

an|feuchten *tr. V.* moisten ⟨*lips, stamp*⟩; dampen ⟨*ironing, cloth, etc.*⟩

an|feuern *tr. V.* spur on

an|fixen *tr. V.* (Drogenjargon) **jmdn. ∼:** get sb. shooting up for the first time (sl.); **von etw. angefixt sein** (fig.) be hooked on sth. (coll.)

an|flehen *tr. V.* beseech; implore

an|fliegen ☐ *unr. tr. V.; mit sein* fly in; **angeflogen kommen** come flying in; **gegen den Wind ∼:** fly into the wind
☐ *unr. tr. V.* fly to ⟨*city, country, airport*⟩

An·flug *der* (a) approach
(b) (Hauch) hint
(c) (Anwandlung) fit; **in einem ∼ von Großzügigkeit** in a fit of generosity

an|fordern *tr. V.* ask for; order ⟨*goods, materials*⟩; send for ⟨*ambulance*⟩

An·forderung *die* (a) (das Anfordern) request (*Gen.* for)
(b) (Anspruch) demand

An·frage *die* inquiry; (Parl.) question

an|fragen *itr. V.* inquire; ask

an|freunden *refl. V.* become friends

an|fügen *tr. V.* add

an|fühlen *refl. V.* feel

an|führen *tr. V.* (a) lead
(b) (zitieren) quote
(c) (nennen) give ⟨*example, reason, details, proof*⟩
(d) (ugs.: hereinlegen) have on (Brit. coll.); dupe

An·führer *der,* **An·führerin** *die* leader; (Rädelsführer) ringleader

An·führung *die* (a) (das Zitieren, Zitat) quotation
(b) (Nennung) giving

Anführungs-: ∼**strich** *der,* ∼**zeichen** *das* quotation mark

An·gabe *die* (a) (das Mitteilen) giving
(b) (Information) piece of information; ∼**n** information *sing.;*
(c) (Ballspiele) service; serve

an|geben ☐ *unr. tr. V.* (a) give ⟨*reason*⟩; declare ⟨*income, dutiable goods*⟩; name ⟨*witness*⟩
(b) (bestimmen) set ⟨*course, direction*⟩; **den Takt ∼:** keep time
☐ *unr. tr. V.* (a) (prahlen) boast; brag; (sich angeberisch benehmen) show off
(b) (Ballspiele) serve

Angeber *der;* ∼s, ∼: braggart

Angeberei *die;* ∼: showing-off

Angeberin *die;* ∼, ∼nen ▶ ANGEBER

angeblich ☐ *Adj.* alleged
☐ *adv.* supposedly; allegedly

an·geboren *Adj.* innate ⟨*characteristic*⟩; congenital ⟨*disease*⟩

An·gebot *das* (a) offer
(b) (Wirtsch.) supply; (Sortiment) range; **∼ und Nachfrage** supply and demand
(c) (Kaufmannsspr.: Sonder∼) [special] offer; **im ∼:** on [special] offer; **∼ der Woche** bargain of the week

an·gebracht *Adj.* appropriate

an-gegriffen Adj. weakened ⟨health, stomach⟩; strained ⟨nerves, voice⟩

angeheitert Adj. tipsy

an|gehen ① unr. itr. V.; mit sein (a) ⟨radio, light, heating⟩ come on; ⟨fire⟩ catch (b) (anwachsen, wachsen) ⟨plant⟩ take root (c) es mag noch ∼: it's [just about] acceptable (d) gegen etw./jmdn. ∼: fight sth./sb. ② unr. tr. V. (a) (angreifen) attack (b) (in Angriff nehmen) tackle ⟨problem, difficulty⟩; take ⟨fence, bend⟩ (c) (bitten) ask (**um** for) (d) (betreffen) concern; **das geht dich nichts an** it's none of your business

angehend Adj. budding; (zukünftig) prospective

an|gehören itr. V. jmdm./einer Sache ∼: belong to sb./sth.; **der Regierung/einer Familie** ∼: be a member of the government/a family

an-gehörig Adj. belonging (Dat. to)

Angehörige der/die; adj. Dekl. (a) (Verwandte) relative; relation (b) (Mitglied) member

Angeklagte der/die; adj. Dekl. accused; defendant

Angel die; ∼, ∼n (a) fishing rod (b) (Tür∼, Fenster∼ usw.) hinge; **etw. aus den** ∼n **heben** (fig.) turn sth. upside down

An-gelegenheit die matter; (Aufgabe, Problem) affair

Angel-haken der fish hook

angeln ① tr. V. (zu fangen suchen) fish for; (fangen) catch ② itr. V. angle; fish

Angel-rute die fishing rod

Angel-sachse der, **Angel-sächsin** die Anglo-Saxon

Angel-schnur die fishing line

an-gemessen Adj. appropriate; reasonable, fair ⟨price, fee⟩

an-genehm ① Adj. pleasant; ∼**e Reise/ Ruhe!** [have a] pleasant journey/have a good rest; **[sehr]** ∼! delighted to meet you ② adv. pleasantly

an-gesehen Adj. respected

angesichts Präp. mit Gen. (geh.) (a) in the face of (b) (fig.: in Anbetracht) in view of

angespannt Adj. (a) close ⟨attention⟩; taut ⟨nerves⟩ (b) tense ⟨situation⟩; tight ⟨market, economic situation⟩

angestellt Adj. **bei jmdm.** ∼ **sein** be employed by sb.; work for sb.

Angestellte der/die; adj. Dekl. [salaried] employee

Angestellten-gewerkschaft die white-collar union

*alte Schreibung - vgl. Hinweis auf S. xiv

an-getan Adj. **von jmdm./etw.** ∼ **sein** be taken with sb./sth.

an-getrunken Adj. [slightly] drunk

an-gewiesen Adj. **auf jmdn./etw.** ∼ **sein** have to rely on sb./sth.

an|gewöhnen tr. V. jmdm. etw. ∼: get sb. used to sth.; **jmdm.** ∼, **etw. zu tun** get sb. used to doing sth.; **sich** (Dat.) **etw.** ∼: get into the habit of sth.; **[es] sich** (Dat.) ∼, **etw. zu tun** get into the habit of doing sth.

An-gewohnheit die habit

an|gleichen ① unr. tr. V. **etw. einer Sache** (Dat.) od. **an etw.** (Akk.) ∼: bring sth. into line with sth. ② unr. refl. V. **sich jmdm./einer Sache** od. **an jmdn./etw.** ∼: become like sb./sth.

An-gleichung die: **die** ∼ **der Löhne an die Preise** bringing wages into line with prices

Angler der; ∼s, ∼, **Anglerin** die; ∼, ∼nen angler

Anglikaner der; ∼s, ∼, **Anglikanerin** die; ∼, ∼nen Anglican

anglikanisch Adj. Anglican

Anglistik die; ∼: English studies pl., no art.

Angola (das); ∼s Angola

Angora-: ∼**katze** die angora cat; ∼**wolle** die angora [wool]

an|greifen ① unr. tr. V. (a) (auch fig.) attack (b) (schwächen) affect ⟨health, heart, stomach, intestine, voice⟩; weaken ⟨person⟩ ② unr. itr. V. (auch fig.) attack

Angreifer der; ∼s, ∼, **Angreiferin** die; ∼, ∼nen (auch fig.) attacker

An-griff der (a) attack; **zum** ∼ **blasen** (auch fig.) sound the attack (b) **etw. in** ∼ **nehmen** tackle sth.

angst Adj. **jmdm. ist/wird [es]** ∼ **[und bange]** sb. is/becomes frightened

Angst die; ∼, **Ängste** (a) (Furcht) fear; ∼ **bekommen** od. (ugs.) **kriegen** become frightened; ∼ **haben** be frightened (**vor** + Dat. of) (b) (Sorge) anxiety; ∼ **haben** be anxious (**um** about); **keine** ∼, **ich vergesse es schon nicht!** don't worry, I won't forget [it]!

ängstigen ① tr. V. frighten; (beunruhigen) worry ② refl. V. be frightened; (sich sorgen) worry

ängstlich ① Adj. anxious ② adv. anxiously

Ängstlichkeit die; ∼: timidity

an|gucken tr. V. (ugs.) look at; **sich** (Dat.) **etw./jmdn.** ∼: have a look at sth./sb.

an|gurten tr. V. strap in; **sich** ∼: put on one's seat belt

an|haben unr. tr. V. (a) (ugs.: am Körper tragen) have on (b) **jmdm./einer Sache etwas** ∼ **können** be able to harm sb./sth.

an|halten ① unr. tr. V. (a) stop (b) (auffordern) urge

21

2 *unr. itr. V.* (a) stop
(b) (andauern) go on; last
anhaltend 1 *Adj.* constant; continuous
2 *adv.* constantly; continuously
An·halter *der* hitch-hiker; **per** ~ **fahren**
hitch[-hike]
An·halterin *die* hitch-hiker
Anhalts·punkt *der* clue (**für** to); (für eine
Vermutung) grounds *pl.*
an·hand 1 *Präp. mit Gen.* with the help of
2 *Adv.* ~ **von** with the help of
An·hang *der* (a) (Buchw.) appendix
(b) (Anhängerschaft) following
(c) (Verwandtschaft) family
an|hängen 1 *tr. V.* (a) hang up (**an** +
Akk. on)
(b) (ankuppeln) couple on (**an** + *Akk.* to); hitch
up ⟨*trailer*⟩ (**an** + *Akk.* to)
(c) (anfügen) add (**an** + *Akk.* to)
(d) (ugs.: zuschreiben, anlasten) **jmdm. etw.** ~
blame sb. for sth.; blame sth. on sb.; **er will
mir nur was** ~ he just wants to pin
something on me
2 *refl. V.* (a) hang on (**an** + *Akk.* to)
(b) (ugs.: sich anschließen) **sich [an jmdn.** *od.*
bei jmdm.] ~: tag along [with sb.]
An·hänger *der* (a) (Mensch) supporter
(b) (Wagen) trailer
(c) (Schmuckstück) pendant
(d) (Schildchen) tag
Anhängerin *die;* ~, ~nen ▶ ANHÄNGER A
Anhängerschaft *die;* ~, ~en supporters
pl.
anhänglich *Adj.* devoted ⟨*dog, friend*⟩
Anhänglichkeit *die;* ~: devotion
an|hauchen *tr. V.* breathe on ⟨*mirror,
glasses*⟩; blow on ⟨*fingers, hands*⟩
an|häufen *tr. V.* accumulate
Anhäufung *die* accumulation
an|heben *unr. tr. V.* (a) lift [up]
(b) (erhöhen) raise ⟨*prices, wages, etc.*⟩
an|heften *tr. V.* attach ⟨*label, list*⟩; put up
⟨*sign, notice*⟩
anheim (geh.): **[es] jmdm.** ~ **stellen, etw. zu
tun** leave it to sb. to do sth.
***anheim|stellen** ▶ ANHEIM
An·hieb *der:* **auf** ~ (ugs.) straight off
an|himmeln *tr. V.* worship
An·höhe *die* rise
an|hören 1 *tr. V.* listen to; **sich** (*Dat.*)
jmdn./etw. ~: listen to sb./sth.
2 *refl. V.* sound
animieren *tr. V.* encourage
Anis *der;* ~es aniseed
Ank. *Abk.* = **Ankunft** arr.
An·kauf *der* purchase
an|kaufen *tr. V.* purchase; buy
Anker *der;* ~s, ~ anchor; **vor** ~ **gehen/
liegen** drop anchor/lie at anchor; ~ **werfen**
drop anchor
ankern *itr. V.* (a) anchor
(b) (vor Anker liegen) be anchored

Anker·platz *der* anchorage
An·klage *die* (a) charge; **unter** ~ **stehen**
have been charged (**wegen** with)
(b) (~vertretung) prosecution
Anklage·bank *die; Pl.* Anklagebänke
dock; **auf der** ~ **sitzen** (auch fig.) be in the
dock
an|klagen *tr. V.* (a) (Rechtsw.) charge (*Gen.,*
wegen with); accuse
(b) (geh.: beschuldigen) accuse
An·kläger *der,* **An·klägerin** *die*
prosecutor
an|klammern 1 *tr. V.* peg (Brit.), pin
(Amer.) ⟨*clothes, washing*⟩ up; clip ⟨*sheet etc.*⟩;
(mit Heftklammern) staple ⟨*sheet etc.*⟩
2 *refl. V.* **sich an jmdn./etw.** ~: cling to sb./
sth.
An·klang *der:* **[bei jmdm.]** ~ **finden** meet
with [sb.'s] approval
an|kleben 1 *tr. V.* stick up ⟨*poster, etc.*⟩
2 *itr. V.; mit sein* stick
an|kleiden *tr. V.* (geh.) dress; **sich** ~: dress
an|klicken *tr. V.* (DV) click on
an|klopfen *itr. V.* knock
an|knüpfen 1 *tr. V.* (a) tie on (**an** + *Akk.*
to)
(b) (beginnen) start up ⟨*conversation*⟩;
establish ⟨*relations, business links*⟩; form
⟨*relationship*⟩
2 *itr. V.* **an etw.** (*Akk.*) ~: take sth. up; **ich
knüpfe dort an, wo** ... I'll pick up where ...
an|kommen *unr. itr. V.; mit sein* (a)
(eintreffen) arrive; **seid ihr gut angekommen?**
did you arrive safely?
(b) **[bei jmdm.] [gut]** ~ (fig. ugs.) go down
[very] well [with sb.]
(c) **gegen jmdn./etw.** ~: be able to deal with
sb./fight sb.
(d) *unpers.* **es kommt auf jmdn./etw. an**
(jmd./etw. ist ausschlaggebend) it depends on
sb./sth.; **es kommt auf etw.** (*Akk.*) **an** (etw. ist
wichtig) sth. matters (*Dat.* to); **es kommt
[ganz] darauf** *od.* **drauf an** (ugs.) it [all]
depends
(e) *unpers.* **es darauf** *od.* **drauf** ~ **lassen**
(ugs.) chance it; **es auf etw.** (*Akk.*) ~ **lassen**
[be prepared to] risk sth.
an|koppeln 1 *tr. V.* couple ⟨*carriage*⟩ up;
hitch ⟨*trailer*⟩ up; dock ⟨*spacecraft*⟩
2 *itr. V.* ⟨*spacecraft*⟩ dock
an|kreuzen *tr. V.* mark with a cross
an|kündigen 1 *tr. V.* announce
2 *refl. V.* announce itself
An·kündigung *die* announcement
Ankunft *die;* ~, Ankünfte arrival; „~"
'arrivals'
Ankunfts-: ~halle *die* arrival[s] hall;
~tafel *die* arrivals board
an|kuppeln *tr. V.* ▶ ANKOPPELN 1
an|kurbeln *tr. V.* (a) crank [up]
(b) (fig.) boost ⟨*economy, production, etc.*⟩
Anl. *Abk.* = **Anlage** encl.
an|lächeln *tr. V.* smile at

an|lachen 1 *tr. V.* smile at
2 *refl. V.* **sich** (*Dat.*) jmdn. ∼ (ugs.) get off
with sb. (Brit. coll.); pick sb. up

An·lage *die* (a) (das Anlegen) (einer Kartei)
establishment; (eines Parks, Gartens usw.) laying
out; (eines Parkplatzes, Stausees) construction
(b) (Grünanlage) park; (um ein Schloss usw.
herum) grounds *pl.*;
(c) (Einrichtung) facilities *pl.*; **militärische** ∼**n**
military installations
(d) (Werk) plant
(e) (Musikanlage usw.) system
(f) (Geldanlage) investment
(g) (Konzeption) conception; (Struktur) structure
(h) (Veranlagung) aptitude; (Neigung) tendency
(i) (Beilage zu einem Brief) enclosure

Anlage-: ∼**berater** *der,* ∼**beraterin**
die investment advisor; ∼**kapital** *das*
investment capital

Anlass, *Anlaß *der;* Anlasses, Anlässe (a)
cause (**zu** for); **etw. zum** ∼ **nehmen, etw. zu**
tun take sth. as an opportunity to do sth.;
aus aktuellem ∼: because of current events
(b) (Gelegenheit) occasion

an|lassen 1 *unr. tr. V.* (a) leave ⟨light,
radio, heating, etc.⟩ on; leave ⟨engine⟩
running; leave ⟨candle⟩ burning
(b) keep ⟨coat, gloves, etc.⟩ on
(c) (in Gang setzen) start [up]
2 *unr. refl. V.* **sich gut/schlecht** ∼: get off to
a good/bad start

Anlasser *der;* ∼**s,** ∼: starter

an-lässlich, *an-läßlich *Präp. mit Gen.*
on the occasion of

An-lauf *der* (a) run-up; [**mehr**] ∼ **nehmen**
take [more of] a run-up
(b) (Versuch) attempt; **beim** *od.* **im ersten/**
dritten ∼: at the first/third attempt

an|laufen 1 *unr. itr. V.; mit sein* (a)
angelaufen kommen come running along; (auf
einen zu) come running up
(b) **gegen jmdn./etw.** ∼: run at sb./sth.
(c) (Anlauf nehmen) take a run-up
(d) (zu laufen beginnen) ⟨engine⟩ start [up]; (fig.)
⟨film⟩ open; ⟨production, campaign, search⟩
start
(e) **rot/dunkel** usw. ∼: go *or* turn red/dark
etc.;
(f) (beschlagen) mist up
2 *unr. tr. V.* put in at ⟨port⟩

an|legen 1 *tr. V.* (a) put *or* lay ⟨domino,
card⟩ [down] (**an** + *Akk.* next to); place,
position ⟨ruler, protractor⟩ (**an** + *Akk.* on);
put ⟨ladder⟩ up (**an** + *Akk.* against)
(b) **die Flügel/Ohren** ∼: close its wings/lay
its ears back; **die Arme** ∼: put one's arms to
one's sides
(c) (geh.: anziehen, umlegen) don
(d) (schaffen, erstellen) lay out ⟨town, garden,
plantation, street⟩; start ⟨file, album⟩;
compile ⟨statistics, index⟩
(e) (investieren) invest
(f) (ausgeben) spend (**für** on)

(g) **es darauf** ∼, **etw. zu tun** be determined to
do sth.
2 *itr. V.* (a) (landen) moor
(b) (Kartenspiele) lay a card/cards
(c) (Domino) play [a domino/dominoes]
(d) (zielen) aim (**auf** + *Akk.* at)
3 *refl. V.* **sich mit jmdm.** ∼: pick an
argument with sb

Anlege-: ∼**platz** *der* berth; ∼**steg** *der*
jetty

an|lehnen 1 *tr. V.* (a) lean (**an** + *Akk. od.*
Dat. against)
(b) leave ⟨door, window⟩ slightly open
2 *refl. V.* **sich** [**an** jmdn. *od.* jmdm./etw.] ∼:
lean [on sb./against sth.]

Anlehnung *die:* **in** ∼ **an** (+ *Akk.*) in
imitation of; following

Anleihe *die;* ∼, ∼**n** (Finanzw.) bond

an|leiten *tr. V.* instruct

An-leitung *die* instructions *pl.*

an|lernen *tr. V.* train

an|liegen *unr. itr. V.* (a) ⟨pullover etc.⟩ fit
tightly
(b) (ugs.: vorliegen) be on

An-liegen *das;* ∼**s,** ∼ (Bitte) request;
(Angelegenheit) matter

anliegend *Adj.* (a) (angrenzend) adjacent
(b) (beiliegend) enclosed

Anlieger *der;* ∼**s,** ∼, **Anliegerin** *die;* ∼,
∼**nen** resident; „∼ **frei**" 'access only'

an|locken *tr. V.* attract ⟨customers, tourists,
etc.⟩; lure ⟨bird, animal⟩

an|lügen *tr. V.* lie to

an|machen *tr. V.* (a) put ⟨light, radio,
heating⟩ on; light ⟨fire⟩
(b) mix ⟨cement, plaster, paint, etc.⟩; dress
⟨salad⟩
(c) (ugs.: ansprechen) ⟨woman, girl⟩ give ⟨man,
boy⟩ the come-on (coll.); ⟨man, boy⟩ chat
⟨woman, girl⟩ up (Brit. coll.)
(d) (ugs.: begeistern, erregen) get ⟨audience etc.⟩
going; **das macht mich ungeheuer/nicht an** it
really turns me on (coll.)/does nothing for me
(coll.)
(e) (provozieren) **mach mich nicht an!** leave me
alone!

an|malen *tr. V.* paint

an|maßen *refl. V.* **sich** (*Dat.*) etw. ∼: claim
sth. [for oneself]

an-maßend 1 *Adj.* presumptuous;
(arrogant) arrogant
2 *adv.* presumptuously; (arrogant) arrogantly

Anmaßung *die;* ∼, ∼**en** presumption;
(Arroganz) arrogance

Anmelde-formular *das* (a) application
form
(b) (einer Meldebehörde) registration form

an|melden 1 *tr. V.* (a) (als Teilnehmer)
enrol (**zu** for); **sich** ∼: enrol (**zu** for)
(b) (melden, anzeigen) license ⟨radio,
television⟩; apply for ⟨patent⟩; register
⟨domicile, change of address, car, trade
mark⟩; **sich** ∼: register one's new address

(c) (ankündigen) announce; **sind Sie angemeldet?** do you have an appointment?; **sich beim Arzt ~:** make an appointment to see the doctor
(d) (geltend machen) express ⟨*reservation, doubt, wish*⟩; put forward ⟨*demand*⟩
2 *refl V.* (DV) log on

An·meldung *die* **(a)** (zur Teilnahme) enrolment
(b) ▶ ANMELDEN B: licensing; application (*Gen.* for); registration
(c) (Ankündigung) announcement; (beim Arzt, Rechtsanwalt usw.) making an appointment

an|merken *tr. V.* **(a)** jmdm. seinen Ärger/ seine Verlegenheit *usw.* **~:** notice that sb. is annoyed/embarrassed *etc.;* **man merkt ihm [nicht] an, dass er krank ist** you can[not] tell that he is ill; **sich nichts ~ lassen** not let it show
(b) (geh.: bemerken) note

Anmerkung *die;* **~, ~en (a)** (Fußnote) note
(b) (geh.: Bemerkung) comment

an|motzen *tr. V.* (ugs.) swear at

Anmut *die;* **~** (geh.) grace

an·mutig (geh.) **1** *Adj.* graceful ⟨*girl, movement, dance*⟩; charming, delightful ⟨*girl, smile, picture, landscape*⟩
2 *adv.* ⟨*move, dance*⟩ gracefully; ⟨*smile, greet*⟩ charmingly

an|nähen *tr. V.* sew on

an|nähern **1** *refl. V.* get closer (*Dat.* to sth)
2 *tr. V.* bring closer (*Dat.* to)

annähernd **1** *Adv.* almost; (ungefähr) approximately
2 *adj.* approximate

Annahme *die;* **~, ~n (a)** (das Annehmen) acceptance
(b) (Vermutung) assumption; **in der ~, dass ...:** on the assumption that ...

annehmbar **1** *Adj.* **(a)** acceptable
(b) (recht gut) reasonable
2 *adv.* reasonably [well]

an|nehmen **1** *unr. tr. V.* **(a)** accept; take; accept ⟨*alms, invitation, condition, help*⟩; take ⟨*food, telephone call*⟩; accept, take up ⟨*offer, challenge*⟩
(b) (Sport) take ⟨*ball, pass, etc.*⟩
(c) (billigen) approve
(d) (aufnehmen) take on ⟨*worker, patient, pupil*⟩
(e) (hinnehmen) accept ⟨*fate, verdict, punishment*⟩
(f) (adoptieren) adopt
(g) (haften lassen) take ⟨*dye, ink*⟩
(h) (sich aneignen) adopt ⟨*habit, mannerism, name, attitude*⟩
(i) (bekommen) take on ⟨*look, appearance, form, dimension*⟩
(j) (vermuten, voraussetzen) assume; **angenommen, [dass] ...:** assuming [that] ...
2 *unr. refl. V.* (geh.) **sich jmds./einer Sache ~:** look after sb./sth.

Annehmlichkeit *die;* **~, ~en** comfort; (Vorteil) advantage

annektieren *tr. V.* annex

Annektierung *die;* **~, ~en, Annexion** *die;* **~, ~en** annexation

Annonce /a'nõːsə/ *die;* **~, ~n** advertisement; advert (Brit. coll.)

annoncieren *itr. V.* advertise

annullieren *tr. V.* annul

Annullierung *die;* **~, ~en** annulment

anonym **1** *Adj.* anonymous
2 *adv.* anonymously

Anonymität *die;* **~:** anonymity

Anorak *der;* **~s, ~s** anorak

an|ordnen *tr. V.* **(a)** (arrangieren) arrange
(b) (befehlen) order

An·ordnung *die* ▶ ANORDNEN: **(a)** arrangement
(b) order

an·organisch *Adj.* inorganic

an|packen **1** *tr. V.* **(a)** (ugs.: anfassen) grab hold of
(b) (angehen) tackle
2 *itr. V.* [mit] **~** (ugs.: mithelfen) lend a hand

an|passen **1** *tr. V.* **(a)** (passend machen) fit
(b) (abstimmen) suit (*Dat.* to)
2 *refl. V.* adapt [oneself] (*Dat.* to); ⟨*animal*⟩ adapt

Anpassung *die;* **~, ~en** adaptation (**an** + *Akk.* to)

anpassungs·fähig *Adj.* adaptable

an|pfeifen **1** *unr. tr. V.* **das Spiel/die zweite Halbzeit ~:** blow the whistle to start the game/the second half
2 *unr. itr. V.* blow the whistle

An·pfiff *der* **(a)** (Sport) whistle for the start of play
(b) (salopp: Zurechtweisung) bawling-out (coll.)

an|pflanzen *tr. V.* **(a)** plant
(b) (anbauen) grow

an|pöbeln *tr. V.* (ugs.) abuse

an|prangern *tr. V.* denounce (**als** as)

an|preisen *unr. tr. V.* extol

An·probe *die* fitting

an|probieren *tr. V.* try on

an|rechnen *tr. V.* **(a)** count
(b) jmdm. etw. **~** (in Rechnung stellen) charge sb. for sth.

An·recht *das* right; **ein ~ auf etw.** (*Akk.*) **haben** be entitled to sth.

An·rede *die* form of address

an|reden *tr. V.* address

an|regen *tr. V.* **(a)** stimulate ⟨*imagination, digestion*⟩; whet ⟨*appetite*⟩
(b) (ermuntern) prompt; (vorschlagen) propose

anregend *Adj.* stimulating

An·regung *die* **(a)** ▶ ANREGEN A: stimulation; whetting
(b) (Denkanstoß) stimulus
(c) (Vorschlag) proposal

an|reichern **1** *tr. V.* enrich   ⋯⋰

2 *refl. V.* accumulate

An·reise *die* journey [there/here]

an|reisen *itr. V.; mit sein* travel there/here;
mit der Bahn ~: go/come by train

An·reiz *der* incentive

an|rempeln *tr. V.* barge into; (absichtlich)
jostle

Anrichte *die;* ~, ~n sideboard

an|richten *tr. V.* (a) arrange ⟨*food*⟩;
(servieren) serve
(b) cause ⟨*disaster, confusion, devastation,
etc.*⟩

anrüchig *Adj.* (a) disreputable
(b) (unanständig) indecent

an|rücken *itr. V.; mit sein* ⟨*troops*⟩
advance; ⟨*firemen, police*⟩ move in

An·ruf *der* call

Anruf·beantworter *der;* ~s, ~:
[telephone] answering machine

an|rufen *unr. tr. V.* (a) call *or* shout to
⟨*friend, passer-by*⟩; call ⟨*sleeping person*⟩
(b) (geh.: angehen, bitten) appeal to ⟨*person,
court*⟩; call upon ⟨*God*⟩
(c) *auch itr.* (telefonisch ~) call

Anrufer *der;* ~s, ~, **Anruferin** *die;* ~,
~nen caller

an|rühren *tr. V.* (a) touch
(b) (bereiten) mix

ans *Präp. + Art.* (a) = an das;
(b) sich ~ Arbeiten machen set to work

An·sage *die* announcement

an|sagen *tr. V.* (a) announce
(b) (Kartenspiele) bid

Ansager *der;* ~s, ~, **Ansagerin** *die;* ~,
~nen (Radio, Fernsehen) announcer

an|sammeln **1** *tr. V.* accumulate; amass
⟨*riches, treasure*⟩
2 *refl. V.* accumulate; (fig.) ⟨*anger,
excitement*⟩ build up

An·sammlung *die* (a) collection
(b) (Auflauf) crowd

ansässig *Adj.* resident

An·satz *der* (erstes Zeichen, Beginn) beginnings
pl.

an|schaffen *tr. V.* (sich ⟨*Dat.*⟩) etw. ~ get
[oneself] sth.

An·schaffung *die* purchase

an|schalten *tr. V.* switch on

an|schauen *tr. V.* (bes. südd., österr., schweiz.)
▶ ANSEHEN

anschaulich **1** *Adj.* vivid
2 *adv.* vividly

Anschauung *die;* ~, ~en (a) (Wahrnehmung)
experience
(b) (Auffassung) view

An·schein *der* appearance; allem *od.* dem
~ nach to all appearances

an·scheinend *Adv.* apparently

an|schieben *unr. tr. V.* push ⟨*vehicle*⟩

an|schießen *unr. tr. V.* shoot and wound

An·schlag *der* (a) (Bekanntmachung) notice;
(Plakat) poster
(b) (Attentat) assassination attempt; (auf ein
Gebäude, einen Zug usw.) attack
(c) (Texterfassung) keystroke
(d) mit dem Gewehr im ~: with rifle/rifles
levelled

an|schlagen *unr. tr. V.* (a) put up, ⟨*notice,
announcement, message*⟩ (an + Akk. on)
(b) (beschädigen) chip

an|schließen **1** *unr. tr. V.* (a) connect (an
+ Akk. od. Dat. to); connect up ⟨*electrical
device*⟩
(b) (festschließen) lock, secure (an + Dat. od.
Akk. to)
2 *unr. refl. V.* sich jmdm./einer Sache ~:
join sb./sth.

An·schluss, *An·schluß *der* connection;
kein ~ unter dieser Nummer number
unobtainable

Anschluss-, *Anschluß-: ~kabel *das*
connecting cable *or* (esp. Brit.) lead; ~zug
der connecting train

an|schnallen *tr. V.* put on ⟨*skis, skates*⟩;
sich ~ (im Auto) put on one's seat belt; (im
Flugzeug) fasten one's seat belt

an|schrauben *tr. V.* screw on (an + Akk.
to)

An·schreiben *das* covering letter

an|schreien *unr. tr. V.* shout at

An·schrift *die* address

Anschuldigung *die;* ~, ~en accusation

an|schwärzen *tr. V.* (ugs.) jmdn. ~ (in
Misskredit bringen) blacken sb.'s name; (schlecht
machen) run sb. down (**bei** to); (denunzieren)
inform *or* (Brit. sl.) grass on sb. (**bei** to)

an|schwellen *unr. itr. V.; mit sein* (a)
swell [up]; (fig.) swell; ⟨*water, river*⟩ rise
(b) (lauter werden) grow louder; ⟨*noise*⟩ rise

an|schwemmen *tr. V.* wash ashore

an|sehen *unr. tr. V.* (a) look at; watch
⟨*television programme*⟩; see ⟨*play, film*⟩;
jmdn. groß/böse ~: stare at sb./give sb. an
angry look; hübsch *usw.* anzusehen sein be
pretty *etc.* to look at; sieh [mal] [einer] an!
(ugs.) well, I never! (coll.)
(b) (erkennen) man sieht ihm sein Alter nicht
an he does not look his age; man sieht ihr die
Strapazen an she's showing the strain
(c) (zusehen bei) etw. [mit] ~: watch sth.; das
kann man doch nicht [mit] ~: I/you can't just
stand by and watch that

Ansehen *das;* ~s [high] standing

an·sehnlich *Adj.* (a) (beträchtlich)
considerable
(b) (gut aussehend, stattlich) handsome

*an|sein ▶ AN 3B

an|setzen *tr. V.* (a) (in die richtige Stellung
bringen) position ⟨*ladder, jack, drill, saw*⟩
(b) (anfügen) attach, put on (an + Akk. od.
Dat. to)
(c) (festlegen) fix ⟨*meeting etc.*⟩ (für, auf + Akk.
for); fix, set ⟨*deadline, date, price*⟩

(d) (veranschlagen) estimate
(e) (anrühren) mix

An·sicht *die* (a) (Meinung) opinion; view; **meiner** ~ **nach** in my opinion *or* view (b) (Bild) view

Ansichts·karte *die* picture postcard

an|spannen *tr. V.* (a) harness ⟨*horse etc.*⟩ (**an** + *Akk.* to); yoke up ⟨*oxen*⟩ (**an** + *Akk.* to); hitch up ⟨*carriage, cart, etc.*⟩ (**an** + *Akk.* to)
(b) (anstrengen) strain

An·spannung *die* strain

an|spielen *itr. V.* **auf jmdn./etw.** ~: allude to sb./sth.

Anspielung *die;* ~, ~en allusion (**auf** + *Akk.* to); (verächtlich, böse) insinuation (**auf** + *Akk.* about)

Ansporn *der;* ~[e]s, ~e incentive

an|spornen *tr. V.* spur on

An·sprache *die* speech; address

an|sprechen 1 *unr. tr. V.* (a) speak to
(b) (gefallen) appeal to
2 *unr. itr. V.* (reagieren) respond (**auf** + *Akk.* to)

ansprechend 1 *Adj.* attractive; attractive, appealing ⟨*personality*⟩
2 *adv.* attractively

Ansprech·partner *der,*
Ansprech·partnerin *die* contact

an|springen 1 *unr. itr. V.; mit sein* ⟨*car, engine*⟩ start
2 *unr. tr. V.* jump up at

An·spruch *der* (a) claim; (Forderung) demand; [keine] Ansprüche stellen make [no] demands; in ~ nehmen take advantage of ⟨*offer*⟩; exercise ⟨*right*⟩; take up ⟨*time*⟩; [einen] ~/keinen ~ auf etw. (*Akk.*) haben be/not be entitled to sth.
(b) (Anrecht) right

an·spruchs-: ~**los** 1 *Adj.* (a) (genügsam) undemanding; (b) (schlicht) unpretentious; 2 *adv.* (a) (genügsam) undemandingly; ⟨*live*⟩ modestly; (b) (schlicht) unpretentiously; ~**voll** *Adj.* discriminating ⟨*reader, audience, gourmet*⟩; (schwierig) demanding; ambitious ⟨*subject*⟩

an|spucken *tr. V.* spit at

Anstalt *die;* ~, ~en institution

An·stand *der* decency

anständig 1 *Adj.* decent; (ehrbar) respectable
2 *adv.* decently; (ordentlich) properly

an|starren *tr. V.* stare at

an·statt *Konj.* ~ **zu arbeiten/**~**, dass er arbeitet** instead of working

an|stecken 1 *tr. V.* (a) pin on ⟨*badge, brooch*⟩; put on ⟨*ring*⟩
(b) (infizieren, auch fig.) infect
2 *itr. V.* be infectious

ansteckend *Adj.* infectious; (durch Berührung) contagious

Ansteckung *die;* ~, ~en infection; (durch Berührung) contagion

Ansteckungs·gefahr *die* risk *or* danger of infection

an|stehen *unr. itr. V.* (Schlange stehen) queue [up], (Amer.) stand in line (**nach** for)

an·stelle 1 *Präp. mit Gen.* instead of
2 *Adv.* ~ **von** instead of

an|stellen 1 *refl. V.* queue [up], (Amer.) stand in line (**nach** for)
2 *tr. V.* (a) (aufdrehen) turn on
(b) (einschalten) switch on
(c) (einstellen) employ

An·stellung *die* (a) employment
(b) (Stellung) job

Anstieg *der;* ~[e]s rise, increase (+ *Gen.* in)

an|stiften *tr. V.* incite

An·stifter *der,* **An·stifterin** *die* instigator

An·stiftung *die* incitement

an|stimmen *tr. V.* start singing ⟨*song*⟩; start playing ⟨*piece of music*⟩; ein Geschrei ~: start shouting

An·stoß *der* (a) stimulus (**zu** for); den [ersten] ~ **zu etw. geben** initiate sth.
(b) ~ **erregen** cause offence (**bei** to); [keinen] ~ **an etw.** (*Dat.*) **nehmen** [not] object to sth.

an|stoßen 1 *unr. itr. V.* (a) **mit sein an etw.** (*Akk.*) ~: bump into sth.
(b) [mit den Gläsern] ~: clink glasses; auf jmdn./etw. ~: drink to sb./sth.
2 *unr. tr. V.* jmdn./etw. ~: give sb./sth. a push; jmdn. aus Versehen ~: knock into sb. inadvertently

anstößig 1 *Adj.* offensive
2 *adv.* offensively

an|strahlen *tr. V.* (a) illuminate; (mit Scheinwerfer) floodlight
(b) (anblicken) beam at

an|streben *tr. V.* (geh.) aspire to; (mit großer Anstrengung) strive for

an|streichen *unr. tr. V.* (a) paint
(b) (markieren) mark

an|strengen 1 *refl. V.* make an effort; **sich mehr/sehr** ~: make more of an effort/a great effort
2 *tr. V.* strain ⟨*eyes, ears, voice*⟩; be a strain on ⟨*person*⟩; seine Fantasie ~: exercise one's imagination

anstrengend *Adj.* (körperlich) strenuous; (geistig) demanding

Anstrengung *die;* ~, ~en (a) effort; große ~en machen, etw. zu tun make every effort to do sth.
(b) (Strapaze) strain

An·strich *der* paint

An·sturm *der* rush (**auf** + *Akk.* to); (auf Banken, Waren) run (**auf** + *Akk.* on)

Antarktika (*das*); ~s Antarctica

Antarktis *die;* ~: Antarctic

antarktisch *Adj.* Antarctic

An·teil *der* share (**an** + *Dat.* of); ~ **an etw.** (*Dat.*) **nehmen** take an interest in sth.

An·teilnahme *die;* ~ **(a)** interest (an + *Dat.* in)
(b) (Mitgefühl) sympathy (an + *Dat.* with)
Antenne *die;* ~, ~n aerial; antenna (Amer.)
anthrazit *Adj.* anthracite[-grey]
anthrazit-grau *Adj.* anthracite-grey
anti-, Anti- anti-
Anti-alkoholiker *der,*
Anti-alkoholikerin *die* teetotaller
Antibiotikum *das;* ~s, **Antibiotika** (Med.) antibiotic
anti-, Anti-: ~**blockier-system** *das* (Kfz-W.) anti-lock braking system;
~**faschist** *der,* ~**faschistin** *die* anti-fascist;
~**faschistisch** *Adj.* anti-fascist
antik *Adj.* **(a)** classical
(b) (aus vergangenen Zeiten) antique ⟨*furniture, fittings, etc.*⟩
Antike *die;* ~: classical antiquity *no art.*
Antilope *die;* ~, ~n antelope
Antipathie *die;* ~, ~n antipathy
Antiquariat antiquarian bookshop/ department; (mit neueren gebrauchten Büchern) second-hand bookshop/department
Antiquität *die;* ~, ~en antique
Antlitz *das;* ~es, ~e (dichter., geh.) countenance (literary); face
Antrag *der;* ~[e]s, **Anträge (a)** application (auf + *Akk.* for); **einen** ~ **stellen** make an application
(b) (Formular) application form
Antrags-formular *das* application form
an|treffen *unr. tr. V.* find; (zufällig) come across
an|treiben *unr. tr. V.* **(a)** drive ⟨*animals, column of prisoners*⟩ on *or* along; (fig.) urge
(b) (in Bewegung setzen) drive; power ⟨*ship, aircraft*⟩
an|treten [1] *unr. itr. V.; mit sein* **(a)** form up; (in Linie) line up; (Milit.) fall in
(b) (sich stellen) meet one's opponent; (als Mannschaft) line up; **gegen jmdn.** ~: meet sb./ line up against sb.
[2] *unr. tr. V.* start ⟨*job, apprenticeship*⟩; take up ⟨*position, appointment*⟩; set out on ⟨*journey*⟩; begin ⟨*prison sentence*⟩; come into ⟨*inheritance*⟩
An·trieb *der* drive
An·tritt *der:* **vor** ~ **Ihres Urlaubs** before you go on holiday (Brit.) *or* (Amer.) vacation; **vor** ~ **der Reise** before setting out on the journey
an|tun *unr. tr. V.* **(a)** **jmdm. ein Leid** ~: hurt sb.; **jmdm. etwas Böses/ein Unrecht** ~: do sb. harm/an injustice
(b) **jmd./etw. hat es jmdm. angetan** sb. was taken with sb./sth.; *s. auch* ANGETAN
Antwort *die;* ~, ~en **(a)** answer; reply; **er gab mir keine** ~: he didn't answer [me] *or* reply
(b) (Reaktion) response

antworten *itr. V.* **(a)** answer; reply; **auf etw.** (*Akk.*) ~: answer sth.; reply to sth.; **jmdm.** ~: answer sb.; reply to sb.
(b) (reagieren) respond (**auf** + *Akk.* to)
an|vertrauen [1] *tr. V.* **jmdm. etw.** ~: entrust sb. with sth.; (fig.: mitteilen) confide sth. to sb.
[2] *refl. V.* **sich jmdm./einer Sache** ~: put one's trust in sb./sth.; **sich jmdm.** ~ (fig.: sich jmdm. mitteilen) confide in sb.
an|wachsen *unr. itr. V.; mit sein* **(a)** grow on
(b) (Wurzeln schlagen) take root
(c) (zunehmen) grow
Anwalt *der;* ~[e]s, **Anwälte, Anwältin** *die;* ~, ~nen **(a)** (Rechtsanwalt, -anwältin) lawyer; solicitor (Brit.); attorney (Amer.); (vor Gericht) barrister (Brit.); attorney[-at-law] (Amer.); advocate (Scot.)
(b) (Fürsprecher) advocate
An·wärter *der,* **An·wärterin** *die* candidate (**auf** + *Akk.* for); (Sport) contender (**auf** + *Akk.* for)
an|weisen *unr. tr. V.* instruct
An·weisung *die* instruction
an|wenden *unr.* (*auch regelm.*) *tr. V.* use, employ ⟨*process, trick, method, violence, force*⟩; use ⟨*medicine, money, time*⟩; apply ⟨*rule, paragraph, proverb, etc.*⟩ (**auf** + *Akk.* to)
Anwender *der;* ~s, ~ (DV) user
anwender-freundlich *Adj.* (bes. DV) user-friendly
Anwenderin *die;* ~, ~nen (DV) user
An·wendung *die* **(a)** ▶ ANWENDEN: use; employment; application
(b) (DV) application
An·wesen *das* property
anwesend *Adj.* present (**bei** at); **die Anwesenden** those present
Anwesenheit *die;* ~: presence
an|widern *tr. V.* nauseate
Anwohner *der;* ~s, ~, **Anwohnerin** *die;* ~, ~nen resident; **Parken nur für** ~ residents-only parking
An·zahl *die;* ~: number; **eine ganze** ~: a whole lot
an|zahlen *tr. V.* put down ⟨*sum*⟩ as a deposit (**auf** + *Akk.* on); (bei Ratenzahlung) make a down payment of ⟨*sum*⟩ (**auf** + *Akk.* on)
An·zahlung *die* deposit; (bei Ratenzahlung) down payment
An·zeichen *das* sign; indication
Anzeige *die;* ~, ~n **(a)** (Straf~) report
(b) (Inserat) advertisement
(c) (eines Instruments) display
an|zeigen *tr. V.* **(a)** (Strafanzeige erstatten) **jmdn./etw.** ~: report sb./sth. to the police/the authorities
(b) (zeigen) show; indicate; show ⟨*time, date*⟩
(c) (DV) display

---

*old spelling - see note on page xiv

Anzeigen-: ∼**blatt** *das* advertiser; ∼**teil** *der* advertisement section *or* pages *pl.*

an|ziehen *unr. tr. V.* **(a)** (auch fig.) attract **(b)** draw up ⟨*knees, feet, etc.*⟩ **(c)** tighten ⟨*rope, wire, screw, knot, belt, etc.*⟩; put on ⟨*handbrake*⟩ **(d)** (ankleiden) dress; **sich** ∼: get dressed **(e)** (anlegen) put on ⟨*clothes*⟩

anziehend *Adj.* attractive

An·ziehung *die* attraction

Anziehungs·kraft *die* attractive force; (fig.) attraction

An·zug *der* **(a)** suit **(b) im** ∼ **sein** ⟨*storm*⟩ be approaching; ⟨*fever, illness*⟩ be coming on; ⟨*enemy*⟩ be advancing

anzüglich [1] *Adj.* insinuating ⟨*remark, question*⟩ [2] *adv.* in an insinuating way

Anzüglichkeit *die;* ∼, ∼**en** **(a)** (Art) insinuating nature **(b)** (Bemerkung) insinuating remark

an|zünden *tr. V.* light; set fire to ⟨*building etc.*⟩

an|zweifeln *tr. V.* doubt; question

apart [1] *Adj.* individual *attrib.;* [2] *adv.* in an individual style

Apartheid *die;* ∼: apartheid *no art.*

Apartheit *die;* ∼: individuality

Apartment *das;* ∼**s,** ∼**s** studio flat (Brit.); studio apartment (Amer.)

Apartment·haus *das* block of studio flats (Brit.) *or* (Amer.) studio apartments

Apathie *die;* ∼, ∼**n** apathy

apathisch [1] *Adj.* apathetic [2] *adv.* apathetically

Aperitif /aperi'ti:f/ *der;* ∼**s,** ∼**s** aperitif

Apfel *der;* ∼**s,** Äpfel apple

Apfel-: ∼**baum** *der* apple tree; ∼**kuchen** *der* apple cake; (mit Äpfeln belegt) apple flan; ∼**mus** *das* apple purée; ∼**saft** *der* apple juice

Apfelsine *die;* ∼, ∼**n** orange

Apfel-: ∼**strudel** *der* apfelstrudel; ∼**wein** *der* cider

Apostel *der;* ∼**s,** ∼: apostle

Apotheke *die;* ∼, ∼**n** **(a)** chemist's [shop] (Brit.); drugstore (Amer.) **(b)** (Hausapotheke) medicine cabinet; (Reise-, Bordapotheke) first-aid kit

Apotheker *der;* ∼**s,** ∼, **Apothekerin** *die;* ∼, ∼**nen** [dispensing] chemist (Brit.); druggist

App. *Abk.* = **Apparat** ext.

Apparat *der;* ∼**[e]s,** ∼**e** **(a)** apparatus *no pl.;* (Haushaltsgerät) appliance; (kleiner) gadget **(b)** (Radio) radio; (Fernseher) television; (Kamera) camera **(c)** (Telefon) telephone; (Nebenstelle) extension; **am** ∼**!** speaking! **(d)** (Personen und Hilfsmittel) organization; (Verwaltungsapparat) system

Apparate·medizin *die* (oft abwertend) high-technology medicine

Appartement /apartə'mã:, (schweiz. auch:) -'ment/ *das;* ∼**s,** ∼**s** (schweiz. auch: ∼e) **(a)** ▶ APARTMENT; **(b)** (Hotelsuite) suite

Appell *der;* ∼**s,** ∼**e** **(a)** appeal (**zu** for, **an** + *Akk.* to) **(b)** (Milit.) muster; (Anwesenheits∼) roll-call

appellieren *itr. V.* appeal (**an** + *Akk.* to)

Appetit *der;* ∼**[e]s,** ∼**e** appetite (**auf** + *Akk.* for); **guten** ∼**!** enjoy your meal!

appetitlich *Adj.* **(a)** appetizing **(b)** (sauber, ansprechend) attractive and hygienic

Appetit·losigkeit *die;* ∼: lack of appetite

applaudieren *itr. V.* applaud

Applaus *der;* ∼**es,** ∼**e** applause

Aprikose *die;* ∼, ∼**n** apricot

April *der;* ∼**[s],** ∼**e** April; **der** ∼: April

apropos /apro'po:/ *Adv.* apropos; by the way; incidentally

Aquädukt *der od. das;* ∼**[e]s,** ∼**e** aqueduct

Aquarell *das;* ∼**s,** ∼**e** watercolour [painting]

Aquarium *das;* ∼**s,** **Aquarien** aquarium

Äquator *der;* ∼**s** equator

Ar *das od. der;* ∼**s,** ∼**e** are

Ära *die;* ∼, **Ären** era

Araber *der;* ∼**s,** ∼, **Araberin** *die;* ∼, ∼**nen** Arab

Arabien /a'ra:biən/ (*das*) ∼**s** Arabia

arabisch *Adj.* Arabian; Arabic ⟨*language, numeral, literature, etc.*⟩

Arbeit *die;* ∼, ∼**en** **(a)** work *no indef. art.;* **vor/nach der** ∼ (ugs.) before/after work **(b)** (Produkt, Werk) work **(c)** (Aufgabe) job **(d)** (Klassenarbeit) test

arbeiten [1] *itr. V.* work [2] *tr. V.* (herstellen) make

Arbeiter *der;* ∼**s,** ∼, **Arbeiterin** *die;* ∼, ∼**nen** worker; (Bau∼, Land∼) labourer

Arbeiter-: ∼**kind** *das* working-class child; ∼**klasse** *die* working class[es *pl.*]

Arbeiterschaft *die;* ∼: workers *pl.*

Arbeit·geber *der;* ∼**s,** ∼: employer

Arbeitgeber·anteil *der* employer's contribution

Arbeit·geberin *die;* ∼, ∼**nen** employer

Arbeitgeber·verband *der* employers' association *or* organization

Arbeitnehmer *der;* ∼**s,** ∼ employee

Arbeitnehmer·anteil *der* employee's contribution

Arbeitnehmerin *die;* ∼, ∼**nen** employee

arbeits-, Arbeits-: ∼**amt** *das* job centre (Brit.); ∼**anfang** *der* starting time [at work]; ∼**bedingungen** *Pl.* working conditions; ∼**beginn** *der* ▶ ∼ANFANG; ∼**belastung** *die* workload; ····⟩

~**beschaffungs·maßnahme** die job-creation measure; ~**erlaubnis** die work permit; ~**fähig** Adj. fit for work postpos.; (grundsätzlich) able to work postpos.; ~**gang** der operation; ~**genehmigung** die work permit; ~**gericht** das industrial tribunal; ~**kollege** der, ~**kollegin** die (bei Arbeitern) workmate (Brit.); fellow worker; (bei Angestellten, Beamten) colleague; ~**kraft** die (a) capacity for work; (b) (Mensch) worker; ~**last** die burden of work; ~**leben** das (a) (Berufstätigkeit) working life; (b) (Arbeitswelt) world of work; working life no art.; ~**los** Adj. unemployed; sich ~los melden sign on [for the dole] (coll.); ~**lose** der/die; adj. Dekl. unemployed person/man/woman etc.; die ~losen the unemployed; ~**losengeld** das (full-rate) earnings-related unemployment benefit; ~**losenhilfe** die (a) (Geld) reduced-rate unemployment benefit; (b) (Institution) reduced-rate unemployment benefit system; ~**losigkeit** die; ~~: unemployment no indef. art.; ~**mangel** der lack of work; ~**markt** der labour market; ~**platz** der (a) (Platz im Betrieb) workplace; am ~platz at one's workplace; (b) (~stätte) place of work; den ~platz wechseln change one's place of work; (c) (~verhältnis) job; ~**scheu** Adj. work-shy; ~**suchende** der/die; adj. Dekl. person/man/woman looking for work; die ~suchenden those looking for work; ~**tag** der working day; ~**teilung** die division of labour; ~**unfähig** Adj. unfit for work postpos.; (grundsätzlich) unable to work postpos.; ~**unfähigkeit** die ▶ ~UNFÄHIG: inability to work; unfitness for work; ~**unfall** der industrial accident; er hatte einen ~unfall he had an accident at work; ~**vermittlung** die (a) (Tätigkeit) arranging employment; (b) (Stelle) employment exchange; job centre (Brit.); (Firma) employment agency; ~**vertrag** der contract of employment; ~**zeit** die working hours pl.; die tägliche ~zeit the working day; ~**zeit·konto** das flexitime work record; ~**zimmer** das study

Archäologe der; ~n, ~n archaeologist

Archäologie die; ~: archaeology no art.

Archäologin die; ~, ~nen archaeologist

archäologisch Adj. archaeological

Arche die; ~, ~n ark; die ~ Noah Noah's Ark

Architekt der; ~en, ~en, **Architektin** die; ~, ~nen architect

Architektur die; ~ architecture

Archiv das; ~s, ~e archives pl.; archive

Ären ▶ ÄRA

Arena die; ~, Arenen arena; (Stierkampf~, Manege) ring

---

arg, ärger, ärgst... (geh., landsch.) **1** Adj. (a) (schlimm) bad; im Argen liegen be in a sorry state (b) (unangenehm groß, stark) severe ⟨pain, hunger, shock, disappointment⟩; serious ⟨error, dilemma⟩; extreme ⟨embarrassment⟩; gross ⟨exaggeration, injustice⟩ **2** adv. (äußerst, sehr) extremely

Ärger der; ~s (a) annoyance (b) (Unannehmlichkeiten) trouble; ~ bekommen get into trouble

ärgerlich **1** Adj. (a) annoyed (b) (Ärger erregend) annoying **2** adv. (a) with annoyance (b) (Ärger erregend) annoyingly

ärgern **1** tr. V. (a) annoy (b) (reizen) tease **2** refl. V. sich [über jmdn./etw.] ~: be/get annoyed [at sb./about sth.]

Ärgernis das; ~ses, ~se annoyance; (etw. Anstößiges) nuisance

arg-, Arg-: ~**list** die deceit; (Heimtücke) malice; ~**listig** Adj. deceitful; (heimtückisch) malicious; ~**los** **1** Adj. unsuspecting; **2** adv. unsuspectingly; ~**losigkeit** die; ~~: unsuspecting nature

ärgst... ▶ ARG

Argument das; ~[e]s, ~e argument

Argumentation die; ~, ~en argumentation

argumentieren itr. V. argue

Argwohn der; ~[e]s suspicion

argwöhnisch (geh.) **1** Adj. suspicious **2** adv. suspiciously

Arie /'aːri̯ə/ die; ~, ~n aria

arisch Adj. (Völkerk., Sprachw., ns.) Aryan

Aristokrat der; ~en, ~en aristocrat

Aristokratie die; ~, ~n aristocracy

Aristokratin die; ~, ~nen aristocrat

aristokratisch **1** Adj. aristocratic **2** adv. aristocratically

arithmetisch **1** Adj. arithmetical **2** adv. arithmetically

Arkade die; ~, ~n arcade

Arktis die; ~: Arctic

arktisch Adj. Arctic; (fig.) arctic

arm, ärmer, ärmst... Adj. poor; Arm und Reich (veralt.) rich and poor [alike]; ~ an Nährstoffen poor in nutrients; der/die Ärmste od. Arme the poor man/boy/woman/girl

Arm der; ~[e]s, ~e arm; jmdm. [mit etw.] unter die ~e greifen help sb. out [with sth.]; ein Hemd mit halbem ~: a short-sleeved shirt

Armaturen·brett das instrument panel; (im Kfz) dashboard

Arm-: ~**band** das bracelet; (Uhr~) strap; ~**band·uhr** die wristwatch

Armee die; ~, ~n (auch fig.) army

Ärmel der; ~s, ~: sleeve; [sich (Dat.)] etw. aus dem ~ schütteln (ugs.) produce sth. just like that

Ärmel·kanal der; ~s [English] Channel

ärmer ▶ ARM

ärmlich 1 *Adj.* cheap *‹clothing›*; shabby *‹flat, office›*; meagre *‹meal›*
2 *adv.* cheaply *‹furnished, dressed›*

Arm-reif *der* armlet

arm·selig *Adj.* (a) miserable; pathetic *‹result, figure›*; meagre *‹meal, food›*; paltry *‹return, salary, sum, fee›*
(b) (abwertend: erbärmlich) miserable

ärmst... ▶ ARM

Armut *die;* ∼: poverty

Aroma *das;* ∼s, Aromen (Duft) aroma; (Geschmack) flavour

aromatisch *Adj.* aromatic; distinctive *‹taste›*; ∼ **duften** give off an aromatic fragrance

arrangieren /arãˈziːrən/ 1 *tr. V.* (geh., Musik) arrange
2 *refl. V.* sich ∼: adapt; sich mit jmdm. ∼: come to an accommodation with sb.

Arrest *der;* ∼[e]s, ∼e detention

arrogant 1 *Adj.* arrogant
2 *adv.* arrogantly

Arroganz *die;* ∼ arrogance

Arsch *der;* ∼[e]s, Ärsche (derb) (a) arse (Brit. coarse); ass (Amer. sl.); **leck mich am** ∼**!** (fig.) piss off (sl.); **im** ∼ **sein** (fig.) be buggered (coarse)
(b) (widerlicher Mensch) arsehole (Brit. coarse); asshole (Amer. coarse.)

Arsch·loch *das* (derb) ▶ ARSCH B

Art *die;* ∼, ∼en (a) kind; sort; **Bücher aller** ∼: all kinds *or* sorts of books; **[so] eine** ∼ **...**: a sort of ...; **aus der** ∼ **schlagen** not be true to type; (in einer Familie) be different from all the rest of the family
(b) (Biol.) species
(c) (Wesen) nature; (Verhaltensweise) way; (gutes Benehmen) behaviour; **die feine englische** ∼ (ugs.) the proper way to behave
(d) (Weise) way; **auf diese** ∼: in this way; ∼ **und Weise** way; (Kochk.) **nach** ∼ **des Hauses** à la maison; **nach Schweizer** ∼: Swiss style

arten-, Arten-: ∼**reich** *Adj.* (Biol.) species-rich; ∼**reichtum** *der* (Biol.) species-richness; ∼**schutz** *der* protection of species; species protection

Arterie /arˈteːriə/ *die;* ∼, ∼n artery

artig *Adj.* well-behaved; **sei** ∼: be a good boy/girl/dog *etc.*

Artikel *der;* ∼s, ∼ (a) article
(b) (Ware) item

Artillerie *die;* ∼, ∼n artillery

Artischocke *die;* ∼, ∼n artichoke

Artist *der;* ∼en, ∼en, **Artistin** *die;* ∼, ∼nen [variety/circus] performer

Arznei *die;* ∼, ∼en (veralt.), **Arznei·mittel** *das* medicine

Arzt *der;* ∼es, Ärzte, **Ärztin** *die;* ∼, ∼nen doctor

Arzthelferin *die* doctor's receptionist

ärztlich 1 *Adj.* medical; **auf** ∼**e Verordnung** on doctor's orders
2 *adv.* **sich** ∼ **behandeln lassen** have medical treatment

***As** ▶ ASS

Asbest *der;* ∼[e]s, ∼e asbestos

Asche *die;* ∼, ∼n ash[es *pl.*]; (sterbliche Reste) ashes *pl.*

Aschen-: ∼**becher** *der* ashtray; ∼**brödel** *das;* ∼∼s, ∼∼ (auch fig.) Cinderella

Ascher·mittwoch *der* Ash Wednesday

Äser ▶ AAS

Asiat *der;* ∼en, ∼en, **Asiatin** *die;* ∼, ∼nen Asian

asiatisch *Adj.* Asian

Asien /ˈaːziən/ (*das*) ∼s Asia

Askese *die;* ∼: asceticism

Asket *der;* ∼en, ∼en, **Asketin** *die;* ∼, ∼nen ascetic

asketisch 1 *Adj.* ascetic
2 *adv.* ascetically

asozial 1 *Adj.* asocial; (gegen die Gesellschaft gerichtet) antisocial
2 *adv.* asocially

Aspekt *der;* ∼[e]s, ∼e aspect

Asphalt *der;* ∼[e]s, ∼e asphalt

Aspik *der* (österr. auch das); ∼s, ∼e aspic

aß *1. u. 3. Pers. Sg. Prät. v.* ESSEN

Ass *das;* ∼es, ∼e ace

Assistent *der;* ∼en, ∼en, **Assistentin** *die;* ∼, ∼nen assistant

Ast *der;* ∼[e]s, Äste branch; **sich** (*Dat.*) **einen** ∼ **lachen** (ugs.) split one's sides [with laughter]

Aster *die;* ∼, ∼n aster; (Herbstaster) Michaelmas daisy

ästhetisch 1 *Adj.* aesthetic
2 *adv.* aesthetically

Asthma *das;* ∼s asthma

ast·rein 1 *Adj.* (ugs.) (in Ordnung) on the level (coll.); (echt) genuine; (salopp: prima, toll) fantastic (coll.); (salopp: prima, toll) great (coll.)
2 *adv.* (salopp: prima) fantastically (coll.)

Astrologe *der;* ∼n, ∼n astrologer

Astrologie *die;* ∼: astrology *no art.*

Astrologin *die;* ∼, ∼nen astrologer

Astronaut *der;* ∼en, ∼en, **Astronautin** *die;* ∼, ∼nen astronaut

Astronom *der;* ∼en, ∼en astronomer

Astronomie *die;* ∼: astronomy *no art.*

Astronomin *die;* ∼, ∼nen astronomer

astronomisch *Adj.* astronomical

Asyl *das;* ∼s, ∼e (a) asylum
(b) (Obdachlosenheim) hostel

Asylant *der;* ∼en, ∼en, **Asylantin** *die;* ∼, ∼nen asylum seeker

Asylanten·heim *das* asylum seekers' hostel

Asyl-: ∼**antrag** *der* application for asylum; ∼**bewerber** *der,* **bewerberin** ···✦

die person seeking [political] asylum;
~bewerber·heim *das* ▶ ASYLANTENHEIM;
~gesetz *das* asylum law[s *pl.*];
~missbrauch, *****~mißbrauch** *der*
misuse of asylum; **~recht** *das* (Rechtsw.) **(a)**
right of [political] asylum; **(b)** (eines Staates)
right to grant [political] asylum; **~werber**
der; ~~s, ~~, **~werberin** *die;* ~~,
~~nen (österr.) ▶ ~BEWERBER

Atelier /atə'lie:/ *das;* ~s, ~s studio

Atem *der;* ~s breath; außer ~ sein/geraten
be/get out of breath

atem-, Atem-: **~beraubend** [1] *Adj.*
breathtaking; [2] *adv.* breathtakingly; **~los**
[1] *Adj.* breathless; [2] *adv.* breathlessly;
~pause *die* breathing space; **~zug** *der*
breath

Atheismus *der;* ~: atheism *no art.*

Atheist *der;* ~en, ~en, **Atheistin** *die;* ~,
~nen atheist

atheistisch [1] *Adj.* atheistic
[2] *adv.* atheistically

Athen (*das*) ~s Athens

Äther *der;* ~s, ~: ether

Äthiopien /ɛ'tio:piən/ (*das*) ~s Ethiopia

Athlet *der;* ~en, ~en **(a)** (Sportler) athlete
(b) (ugs.: kräftiger Mann) muscleman

Athletin *die;* ~, ~nen athlete

athletisch *Adj.* athletic

Atlanten ▶ ATLAS[1]

Atlantik *der;* ~s Atlantic

atlantisch *Adj.* Atlantic; **der Atlantische
Ozean** the Atlantic Ocean

Atlas *der;* ~ *od.* ~ses, **Atlanten** *od.* ~se
atlas

atmen *itr., tr. V.* breathe

Atmosphäre /atmo'sfɛ:rə/ *die;* ~, ~n (auch
fig.) atmosphere

Atmung *die;* ~: breathing

Atom *das;* ~s, ~e atom

atomar *Adj.* atomic; (Atomwaffen betreffend)
nuclear

atom-, Atom-: **~ausstieg** *der*
abandonment of nuclear power; **~bombe**
die atom bomb; **~energie** *die* nuclear
energy *no indef. art.;* **~kern** *der* atomic
nucleus; **~kraft** *die* nuclear power *no indef.
art.;* **~kraftwerk** *das* nuclear power
station; **~krieg** *der* nuclear war; **~müll**
der nuclear waste; **~physik** *die* nuclear
physics *sing., no art.;* **~pilz** *der* mushroom
cloud; **~reaktor** *der* nuclear reactor;
~strom *der* (ugs.) electricity generated by
nuclear power; **~waffe** *die* nuclear
weapon; **~waffen-frei** *Adj.* nuclear-free;
~waffen·test *der* nuclear [weapons] test;
~zeit·alter *das* nuclear age

Attacke *die;* ~, ~n (auch Med.) attack **(auf +
Akk. on)

---

*old spelling - see note on page xiv

Attentat *das;* ~[e]s, ~e assassination
attempt; (erfolgreich) assassination

Attentäter *der;* ~s, ~, **Attentäterin**
die; ~, ~nen would-be assassin; (erfolgreich)
assassin

Attest *das;* ~[e]s, ~e medical certificate

Attraktion *die;* ~, ~en attraction

attraktiv [1] *Adj.* attractive
[2] *adv.* attractively

Attraktivität *die;* ~: attractiveness

Attrappe *die;* ~, ~n dummy

Attribut *das;* ~[e]s, ~e attribute

ätzen [1] *tr. V.* etch
[2] *itr. V.* corrode

ätzend [1] *Adj.* corrosive; (fig.) caustic ⟨*wit,
remark, criticism*⟩; pungent ⟨*smell*⟩
[2] *adv.* caustically ⟨*ironic, critical*⟩

au *Interj.* **(a)** (bei Schmerz) ouch
(b) (bei Überraschung, Begeisterung) oh

Aubergine /obɛr'ʒi:nə/ *die;* ~, ~n
aubergine (Brit.); eggplant

auch [1] *Adv.* **(a)** as well; too; also; **Klaus
war ~ dabei** Klaus was there as well *or* too;
Klaus was also there; **Ich gehe jetzt. – Ich ~:**
I'm going now – So am I; **Mir ist warm. – Mir
~:** I feel warm – So do I; **das weiß ich ~**
nicht I don't know either
(b) (sogar, selbst) even; **~ wenn, wenn ~:** even
if
[2] *Partikel* **(a)** etwas anderes habe ich ~
nicht erwartet I never expected anything else;
nun hör aber ~ zu! now listen!
**(b) bist du dir ~ im Klaren, was das
bedeutet?** are you sure you understand what
that means?; **bist du ~ glücklich?** are you
truly happy?; **lügst du ~ nicht?** you're not
lying, are you?
(c) wo .../wer .../was ... *usw.* ~: wherever/
whoever/whatever *etc.* ...; **wie dem ~ sei**
however that may be
(d) mag er ~ noch so klug sein no matter
how clever he is

Audienz *die;* ~, ~en audience

Auditorium *das;* ~s, **Auditorien (a)**
(Hörsaal) auditorium
(b) (Zuhörerschaft) audience

auf [1] *Präp. mit Dat.* **(a)** on; **~ See** at sea;
~ dem Baum in the tree; **~ der Erde** on
earth; **~ der Welt** in the world; **~ der Straße**
in the street
(b) at ⟨*post office, town, hall, police station*⟩;
~ seinem Zimmer (ugs.) in his room; **Geld ~
der Bank haben** have money in the bank; **~
der Schule/Uni** at school/university
(c) at ⟨*party, wedding*⟩; on ⟨*course, trip,
walk, holiday, tour*⟩
[2] *Präp. mit Akk.* **(a)** on; **~ einen Berg
steigen** climb up a mountain; **~ die Straße
gehen** go [out] into the street
(b) ~ die Schule/Uni gehen go to school/
university; **~ einen Lehrgang gehen** go on a
course
(c) ~ 10 km [Entfernung] for [a distance of]

10 km; **wir näherten uns der Hütte [bis]** ~
30 m we approached to within 30m of the
hut

(d) ~ **Jahre [hinaus]** for years [to come];
etw. ~ nächsten Mittwoch verschieben
postpone sth. until next Wednesday; **die
Nacht von Sonntag ~ Montag** Sunday night;
das fällt ~ einen Montag it falls on a
Monday

(e) ~ **diese Art und Weise** in this way; ~
Deutsch in German; ~ **das Sorgfältigste**
(geh.) most carefully

(f) ~ **Wunsch** on request; ~ **meine Bitte** at
my request; ~ **Befehl** on command

(g) **ein Teelöffel** ~ **einen Liter Wasser** one
teaspoon to one litre of water; ~ **die
Sekunde/den Millimeter [genau]** [precise] to
the second/millimetre; ~ **deine Gesundheit!**
your health; ~ **bald/morgen!** (bes. südd.) see
you soon/tomorrow

③ *Adv.* (a) (aufgerichtet, aufgestanden) up; ~**!**
(steh/steht auf!) up you get!

(b) **sie waren längst ~ und davon** they had
made off long before

(c) ~**!** (bes. südd.: los) come on; ~ **gehts** off
we go; ~ **ins Schwimmbad!** come on, off to
the swimming pool!

(d) ~ **und ab** (hin und her) up and down; to
and fro

(e) **Helm/Hut/Brille** ~**!** helmet/hat/glasses
on!

(f) (ugs.: geöffnet, offen) open; **Fenster/Mund** ~**!**
open the window/your mouth!

auf|atmen *itr. V.* breathe a sigh of relief

auf|bahren *tr. V.* lay out; **aufgebahrt sein**
lie in state

Auf·bau *der;* ~**[e]s,** ~**ten (a)** building

(b) (Struktur) structure

(c) *Pl.* (Schiffbau) superstructure *sing.*

auf|bauen *tr. V.* (a) erect ⟨*hut, kiosk,
podium*⟩; set up ⟨*equipment, train set*⟩; build
⟨*house, bridge*⟩; put up ⟨*tent*⟩

(b) (hinstellen, arrangieren) lay *or* set out ⟨*food,
presents, etc.*⟩

(c) (fig.: schaffen) build ⟨*state, economy, etc.*⟩;
build up ⟨*business, organization, army, spy
network*⟩

(d) (fig.: strukturieren) structure

auf|bäumen *refl. V.* rear up; **sich gegen
jmdn./etw.** ~ (fig.) rise up against sb./sth.

auf|bessern *tr. V.* improve; increase
⟨*pension, wages, etc.*⟩

auf|bewahren *tr. V.* keep; **etw. kühl** ~**:**
store sth. in a cool place

Auf·bewahrung *die* keeping

auf|bieten *unr. tr. V.* exert ⟨*strength,
energy, will power, influence, authority*⟩; call
on ⟨*skill, wit, powers of persuasion or
eloquence*⟩

auf|blasen *unr. tr. V.* blow up; inflate

auf|bleiben *unr. itr. V.; mit sein* (a)
(geöffnet bleiben) stay open

(b) (nicht zu Bett gehen) stay up

auf|blenden *itr. V.* switch to full beam

auf|blicken *itr. V.* (a) look up; (kurz)
glance up

(b) **zu jmdm.** ~ (fig.) look up to sb.

auf|blühen *itr. V.; mit sein* (a) come into
bloom; ⟨*bud*⟩ open

(b) (fig.: aufleben) blossom [out]

auf|brauchen *tr. V.* use up

auf|brechen ① *unr. tr. V.* break open
⟨*lock, safe, box, crate, etc.*⟩; break into ⟨*car*⟩;
force [open] ⟨*door*⟩

② *unr. itr. V.; mit sein* (a) ⟨*bud*⟩ open; ⟨*ice
[sheet], surface, ground*⟩ break up; ⟨*wound*⟩
open

(b) (losgehen, -fahren) set off

auf|bringen *unr. tr. V.* (a) find; raise
⟨*money*⟩; (fig.) summon [up] ⟨*strength, energy,
courage*⟩; find ⟨*patience*⟩

(b) (kreieren) start ⟨*fashion, custom, rumour*⟩;
introduce ⟨*slogan, theory*⟩

(c) jmdn. ~**:** make sb. angry

(d) jmdn. gegen jmdn./etw. ~**:** set sb.
against sb./sth.

Auf·bruch *der* departure

auf|brühen *tr. V.* brew [up]

auf|decken *tr. V.* (a) uncover

(b) (Kartenspiele) show

(c) (fig.) reveal; uncover; (enthüllen) expose

auf|drängen ① *tr. V.* jmdm. etw. ~**:** force
sth. on sb.

② *refl.* **sich jmdm.** ~**:** force oneself on sb.

auf|drehen *tr. V.* (a) unscrew ⟨*bottle cap,
nut*⟩; undo ⟨*screw*⟩; turn on ⟨*tap, gas, water*⟩;
open ⟨*valve, bottle, vice*⟩

(b) (ugs.) turn up ⟨*radio, record player, etc.*⟩

auf·dringlich ① *Adj.* pushy (coll.)
⟨*person*⟩; (fig.) insistent ⟨*music,
advertisement*⟩; pungent ⟨*perfume, smell*⟩;
loud ⟨*colour, wallpaper*⟩

② *adv.* ⟨*behave*⟩ pushily (coll.)

Aufdringlichkeit *die;* ~ ▶ AUFDRINGLICH:
pushiness (coll.); insistent manner; pungency

auf·einander *Adv.* (a) on top of one
another; ~ **prallen** crash into one another;
collide; (fig.) ⟨*opinions*⟩ clash; ~ **treffen** (fig.)
meet

(b) ~ **folgen** follow one another; ~**folgend**
successive

Aufeinander·folge *die* sequence; **in
rascher** ~ in rapid *or* quick succession

***aufeinander|folgen** *usw.*
▶ AUFEINANDER

Aufenthalt *der;* ~**[e]s,** ~**e (a)** stay

(b) (Fahrtunterbrechung) stop

Aufenthalts-: ~**erlaubnis** *die*
residence permit; ~**raum** *der* (in einer Schule
o. Ä.) common room (Brit.); (in einer
Jugendherberge) day room; (in einem Betrieb o. Ä.)
recreation room

auf|essen *unr. tr. V.* (*auch itr.*) *V.* eat up

auf|fahren ① *unr. itr. V.; mit sein* (a) **auf
ein anderes Fahrzeug** ~ (aufprallen) drive into
the back of another vehicle ···⊹

(b) auf den Vordermann zu dicht ~: drive too close to the car in front
(c) (vorfahren) drive up
(d) (in Stellung gehen) move up [into position] ② *unr. tr. V.* **(a)** (in Stellung bringen) move up
(b) (ugs.: auftischen) serve up

Auf·fahrt *die* **(a)** drive up
(b) (Weg) drive
(c) (Autobahnauffahrt) slip road (Brit.); access road (Amer.)
(d) (schweiz.) ▶ HIMMELFAHRT

Auffahr·unfall *der* rear-end collision

auf|fallen *unr. itr. V.; mit sein* stand out; jmdm. **fällt etw. auf** sb. notices sth.

auffallend ① *Adj.* conspicuous; (eindrucksvoll, bemerkenswert) striking
② *adv.* conspicuously; (eindrucksvoll, bemerkenswert) strikingly

auf·fällig ① *Adj.* conspicuous; garish ⟨*colour*⟩
② *adv.* conspicuously

auf|fangen *unr. tr. V.* **(a)** catch
(b) (aufnehmen, sammeln) collect

Auffang·lager *das* reception camp

auf|fassen *tr. V.* grasp; **etw. als etw. ~:** regard sth. as sth.; **etw. persönlich/falsch ~:** take sth. personally/misunderstand sth.

Auf·fassung *die* (Ansicht) view; (Begriff) conception; **der ~ sein, dass ...:** take the view that ...

auffindbar *Adj.* findable

auf|finden *unr. tr. V.* find

auf|fordern *tr. V.* **jmdn. ~, etw. zu tun** call upon sb. to do sth.; (einladen, ermuntern) ask sb. to do sth.; **jmdn. [zum Tanz] ~:** ask sb. to dance

Auf·forderung *die* request; (nachdrücklicher) demand; (Einladung, Ermunterung) invitation

auf|forsten ① *tr. V.* afforest; (wieder ~) reforest; **einen Wald ~:** restock a forest
② *itr. V.* establish woods; (wieder ~) reestablish the woods

Aufforstung *die;* **~, ~en** afforestation; (Wieder~) reforestation; **die ~ der Wälder** restocking the forests

auf|fressen *unr. tr. V.* (auch fig.) eat up

auf|frischen ① *tr. V.* freshen up; brighten up ⟨*colour, paintwork*⟩; renovate ⟨*polish, furniture*⟩; (restaurieren) restore ⟨*tapestry, fresco, etc.*⟩; (fig.) revive ⟨*old memories*⟩; renew ⟨*acquaintance, friendship*⟩; **seine Englischkenntnisse ~:** brush up one's [knowledge of] English
② *itr. V.; auch mit sein* ⟨*wind*⟩ freshen

auf|führen ① *tr. V.* **(a)** put on ⟨*film*⟩; stage ⟨*play, ballet, opera*⟩; perform ⟨*piece of music*⟩
(b) (auflisten) list
② *refl. V.* behave

Auf·führung *die* performance

Auf·gabe *die* **(a)** task
(b) (fig.: Zweck, Funktion) function

(c) (Schulw.) (Übung) exercise; (Prüfungs~) question; (Haus~) ▶ HAUSAUFGABE
(d) (Rechen~, Mathematik~) problem
(e) (Kapitulation) retirement; (im Schach) resignation; **jmdn. zur ~ zwingen** force sb. to retire/resign
(f) (das Aufgeben a) giving up
(g) (einer Postsendung) posting (Brit.); mailing (Amer.); (eines Telegramms) handing in; (einer Bestellung, einer Annonce) placing
(h) (von Gepäck) checking in

Aufgaben-: **~bereich** *der,* **~gebiet** *das* area of responsibility

Auf·gang *der* **(a)** (eines Gestirns) rising
(b) (Treppe) stairs *pl.;* staircase; stairway; (in einem Bahnhof, zu einer Galerie, einer Tribüne) steps *pl.*

auf|geben ① *unr. tr. V.* **(a)** give up; (Sport) retire from ⟨*race, competition*⟩
(b) (übergeben, übermitteln) post (Brit.), mail ⟨*letter, parcel*⟩; hand in, (telefonisch) phone in ⟨*telegram*⟩; place ⟨*advertisement, order*⟩; check ⟨*luggage, baggage*⟩ in
(c) (Schulw.: als Hausaufgabe) set (Brit.); assign (Amer.)
(d) jmdm. ein Rätsel ~: set (Brit.) *or* (Amer.) assign sb. a puzzle
② *unr. itr. V.* give up; (im Sport) retire; (im Schach) resign

Auf·gebot *das* **(a)** contingent; **ein gewaltiges ~ an Polizisten/Fahrzeugen/ Material** a huge force of police/array of vehicles/materials
(b) (zur Heirat) notice of an/the intended marriage; (kirchlich) banns *pl.*

auf|gehen *unr. itr. V.; mit sein* **(a)** rise
(b) (sich öffnen [lassen]) ⟨*door, parachute, wound*⟩ open; ⟨*stage curtain*⟩ go up; ⟨*knot, button, zip, bandage, shoelace, stitching*⟩ come undone; ⟨*boil, pimple, blister*⟩ burst; ⟨*flower, bud*⟩ open [up]
(c) (keimen) come up
(d) (aufgetrieben werden) ⟨*dough, cake*⟩ rise
(e) (Math.) ⟨*calculation*⟩ work out; ⟨*equation*⟩ come out
(f) etw. geht jmdm. auf sb. realizes sth.

auf|geilen *tr. V.* (salopp) jmdn. [mit/durch etw.] ~: get sb. randy [with sth.]; sich [an etw. (*Dat.*)] ~: get randy [with sth.]; (fig.) get worked up [about sth.]

aufgeklärt *Adj.* enlightened; **~ sein** (sexualkundlich) know the facts of life

auf·gelegt *Adj.* gut/schlecht *usw.* **~ sein** be in a good/bad *etc.* mood; **zu etw. ~ sein** be in the mood for sth.

auf·gelöst *Adj.* distraught ⟨*person*⟩

aufgeregt ① *Adj.* excited; (nervös, beunruhigt) agitated
② *adv.* excitedly; (nervös, beunruhigt) agitatedly

auf·geschlossen *Adj.* open-minded (gegenüber as regards, about); (interessiert, empfänglich) receptive (*Dat.,* für to); (zugänglich) approachable

---

Auf·geschlossenheit *die*
▶ AUFGESCHLOSSEN: open-mindedness; receptiveness; approachableness

aufgeweckt *Adj.* bright

Aufgewecktheit *die;* ∼: brightness

auf|gießen *unr. tr. V.* make ⟨coffee, tea⟩

auf|gliedern *tr. V.* subdivide, break down (in + *Akk.* into)

Auf·gliederung *die* subdivision; breakdown

auf|greifen *unr. tr. V.* pick up

aufgrund ① *Präp. mit Gen.* on the basis or strength of; (wegen) because of

auf|haben (ugs.) ① *unr. tr. V.* (a) (aufgesetzt haben) have on
(b) (geöffnet haben) have ⟨zip⟩ undone; have ⟨door, window, jacket, blouse⟩ open
② *unr. itr. V.* ⟨shop, office⟩ be open

auf|halsen *tr. V.* (ugs.) jmdm./sich etw. ∼: saddle sb./oneself with sth.; sich (*Dat.*) etw. ∼ lassen get oneself saddled with sth.

auf|halten ① *unr. tr. V.* (a) halt
(b) (stören) hold up
(c) (ugs.: geöffnet halten) hold ⟨sack, door, etc.⟩ open; die Augen [und Ohren] ∼: keep one's eyes [and ears] open
② *unr. refl. V.* (a) stay
(b) sich mit jmdm./etw. ∼: spend [a long] time on sth./sb.

auf|hängen ① *tr. V.* (a) hang up; hang ⟨picture, curtains⟩
(b) (erhängen) hang
② *refl. V.* hang oneself

Aufhänger *der;* ∼s, ∼: loop

auf|heben *unr. tr. V.* (a) pick up
(b) (aufbewahren) keep
(c) (abschaffen) abolish; repeal ⟨law⟩; rescind ⟨order, instruction⟩; cancel ⟨contract⟩; lift ⟨ban, prohibition⟩
(d) (ausgleichen) cancel out; neutralize ⟨effect⟩

Aufheben *das;* ∼s: viel ∼[s]/kein ∼ von jmdm./etw. machen make a great fuss/not make any fuss about sb./sth.

Aufhebungs·vertrag *der* agreement to terminate a/the contract

auf|heitern ① *tr. V.* cheer up
② *refl. V.* ⟨weather⟩ brighten up

Aufheiterung *die;* ∼, ∼en (a) (des Wetters) bright period
(b) (Erheiterung) cheering up

auf|hetzen *tr. V.* incite

auf|holen ① *tr. V.* make up ⟨time, delay⟩; pull back ⟨lead⟩
② *itr. V.* catch up; ⟨athlete, competitor⟩ make up ground

auf|horchen *itr. V.* prick up one's ears

auf|hören *itr. V.* stop; [damit] ∼, etw. zu tun stop doing sth.

auf|kaufen *tr. V.* buy up

auf|klappen *tr. V.* open, fold open ⟨chair, table⟩; open [up] ⟨suitcase, trunk⟩; open ⟨book, knife⟩

auf|klären ① *tr. V.* (a) clear up ⟨matter,

mystery, question, misunderstanding, error, confusion⟩; solve ⟨crime, problem⟩; explain ⟨event, incident, cause⟩; resolve ⟨contradiction, disagreement⟩
(b) (unterrichten) enlighten; ein Kind ∼ (sexualkundlich) tell a child the facts of life
② *refl. V.* (a) ⟨misunderstanding, mystery⟩ be cleared up
(b) ⟨weather⟩ brighten [up]; ⟨sky⟩ brighten

Auf·klärung *die* ▶ AUFKLÄREN 1: (a) clearing up; solution; explanation; resolution
(b) enlightenment; die ∼ der Kinder (über Sexualität) telling the children the facts of life

auf|kleben *tr. V.* stick on; (mit Kleister) paste on

Auf·kleber *der* sticker

auf|knöpfen *tr. V.* unbutton; undo

auf|kochen ① *tr. V.* bring to the boil
② *itr. V.; mit sein* come to the boil

auf|kommen *unr. itr. V.; mit sein* (a) ⟨wind⟩ spring up; ⟨storm, gale⟩ blow up; ⟨fog⟩ come down; ⟨rumour⟩ start; ⟨suspicion, doubt, feeling⟩ arise; ⟨fashion, style, invention⟩ come in; ⟨boredom⟩ set in; ⟨mood, atmosphere⟩ develop
(b) ∼ für (bezahlen) bear ⟨costs⟩; pay for ⟨damage⟩; pay ⟨expenses⟩; be liable for ⟨debts⟩; stand ⟨loss⟩
(c) ∼ für (Verantwortung tragen für) be responsible for

auf|krempeln *tr. V.* roll up

auf|laden ① *unr. tr. V.* (a) load (auf + *Akk.* on [to])
(b) jmdm. etw. ∼ (ugs.) load sb. with sth.; (fig.) saddle sb. with sth.
(c) charge [up] ⟨battery⟩
② *unr. refl. V.* ⟨battery⟩ charge

Auf·lage *die* (a) (Buchw.) edition
(b) (Verpflichtung) condition

auflagen·stark *Adj.* high-circulation ⟨newspaper, magazine⟩

auf|lassen *unr. tr. V.* (ugs.) (a) leave ⟨door, window, jacket, etc.⟩ open
(b) keep on ⟨hat, glasses, etc.⟩

auf|lauern *itr. V.* jmdm. ∼: lie in wait for sb.

Auf·lauf *der* (a) (Menschen∼) crowd
(b) (Speise) soufflé

auf|leben *itr. V.; mit sein* revive; (fig.: wieder munter werden) come to life

auf|legen ① *tr. V.* (a) put on; den Hörer ∼: put down the receiver
(b) (Buchw.) publish
② *itr. V.* (den Hörer auflegen) hang up

auf|lehnen *refl. V.* rebel

Auflehnung *die;* ∼, ∼en rebellion

auf|leuchten *itr. V.; auch mit sein* light up; (für kurze Zeit) flash

auf|lockern *tr. V.* (a) loosen; break up ⟨soil⟩
(b) (fig.) introduce some variety into ····❯

⟨landscape, lesson, lecture⟩; relieve ⟨pattern, façade⟩; make ⟨mood, atmosphere, evening⟩ more relaxed

Auf·lockerung die (a) ▶ AUFLOCKERN A: loosening; breaking up
(b) zur ∼ der Stimmung/des Abends to make the mood/evening more relaxed

auf|lösen ① tr. V. dissolve; resolve ⟨difficulty, contradiction⟩; solve ⟨puzzle, equation⟩; break off ⟨engagement⟩; cancel ⟨arrangement, contract, agreement⟩; dissolve ⟨organization⟩
② refl. V. dissolve (in + Akk. into); ⟨parliament⟩ dissolve itself; ⟨crowd, demonstration⟩ break up; ⟨fog, mist⟩ lift; (fig.) ⟨empire, social order⟩ disintegrate

Auf·lösung die (a) ▶ AUFLÖSEN 1: dissolving; resolution; solution; breaking off; cancellation; dissolution
(b) ▶ AUFLÖSEN 2: dissolving; breaking up lifting; disintegration

auf|machen ① tr. V. (a) open; undo ⟨button, knot⟩
(b) (ugs.: eröffnen) open [up] ⟨shop, business, etc.⟩
② itr. V. (a) ⟨shop, office, etc.⟩ open
(b) (ugs.: die Tür öffnen) open the door; jmdm. ∼: open the door to sb.
(c) (ugs.: eröffnet werden) ⟨shop, business⟩ open [up]

Aufmachung die; ∼, ∼en presentation; (Kleidung) get-up

Aufmarsch·gebiet das (Milit.) deployment area

auf|marschieren itr. V.; mit sein assemble; (heranmarschieren) march up; **Truppen sind an der Grenze aufmarschiert** troops were deployed along the border

aufmerksam ① Adj. (a) attentive; sharp ⟨eyes⟩; jmdn. auf jmdn./etw. ∼ machen draw sb.'s attention to sb./sth.; auf jmdn./etw. ∼ werden become aware of sb./sth.; ∼ werden notice
(b) (höflich) attentive
② adv. attentively

Aufmerksamkeit die; ∼, ∼en (a) attention
(b) (Höflichkeit) attentiveness
(c) (Geschenk) small gift

auf|motzen tr. V. (ugs.) tart up (Brit. coll.); doll up (coll.)

auf|muntern tr. V. (a) cheer up
(b) (beleben) liven up
(c) (ermutigen) encourage

Aufmunterung die; ∼, ∼ ▶ AUFMUNTERN: cheering up; livening up; encouragement

Aufnahme die; ∼, ∼n (a) ▶ AUFNEHMEN B: opening; establishment; taking up
(b) (Empfang) reception
(c) ▶ AUFNEHMEN D: admission (in + Akk. into)
(d) (Einschließung) inclusion

(e) (Finanzw.) raising
(f) (Aufzeichnung) taking down; (von Personalien, eines Diktats) taking [down]
(g) ▶ AUFNEHMEN K: taking: photographing; filming
(h) (Bild) shot
(i) (das Aufnehmen auf Tonträger, das Aufgenommene) recording
(j) (Anklang) reception; response (Gen. to)
(k) (Einverleibung, Absorption) absorption

aufnahme-, Aufnahme-: ∼antrag der application for membership; ∼fähig Adj. receptive (für to); ich bin nicht mehr ∼fähig I can't take any more in; ∼fähigkeit die receptivity (für to); ability to take things in; ∼land das host country

auf|nehmen unr. tr. V. (a) (aufheben) pick up; (fig.) take up ⟨idea, theme, etc.⟩; es mit jmdm./etw. ∼/nicht ∼ können (fig.) be a/no match for sb./sth.
(b) (beginnen mit) open ⟨negotiations, talks⟩; establish ⟨relations, contacts⟩; take up ⟨studies, activity, occupation⟩; start ⟨production, investigation⟩
(c) (empfangen) receive; (beherbergen) take in
(d) (beitreten lassen) admit (in + Akk. to)
(e) (einschließen, verzeichnen) include
(f) (erfassen) take in ⟨impressions, information, etc.⟩
(g) (absorbieren) absorb
(h) (Finanzw.) raise ⟨mortgage, money, loan⟩
(i) (reagieren auf) receive
(j) (aufschreiben) take down; take [down] ⟨dictation, particulars⟩
(k) (fotografieren) take ⟨picture⟩; photograph, take a photograph of ⟨scene, subject⟩; (filmen) film
(l) (auf Tonträger) record
(m) (auf Videoband) videotape; video

auf|opfern refl. V. devote oneself sacrificingly (für to)

aufopfernd ① Adj. self-sacrificing
② adv. self-sacrificingly

auf|passen itr. V. (a) watch out; (konzentriert sein) pay attention; **pass mal auf!** (ugs.: hör mal zu!) now listen
(b) auf jmdn./etw. ∼: keep an eye on sb./sth.

auf|platzen itr. V.; mit sein burst open; ⟨seam, cushion⟩ split open; ⟨wound⟩ open up

Auf·prall der; ∼[e]s, ∼e impact

auf|prallen itr. V.; mit sein auf etw. (Akk.) ∼: hit sth.

Auf·preis der additional charge

auf|pumpen tr. V. pump up

auf|putschen tr. V. stimulate; arouse ⟨passions, urge⟩

Aufputsch·mittel das stimulant

auf|räumen tr., itr. V. clear up

Aufräumungs·arbeiten Pl. clearance work sing.

auf·recht ① Adj. (auch fig.) upright
② adv. ⟨walk, sit, hold oneself⟩ straight

aufrecht|erhalten unr. tr. V. maintain; keep up ⟨deception, fiction, contact, custom⟩

---

*old spelling - see note on page xiv

auf|regen ⟨1⟩ *tr. V.* excite; (ärgern) annoy; irritate; (beunruhigen) agitate
⟨2⟩ *refl. V.* get worked up (**über** + *Akk.* about)

Auf·regung *die* excitement *no pl.;* (Beunruhigung) agitation *no pl.;* **jmdn. in ~ versetzen** make sb. excited/agitated

auf|reißen ⟨1⟩ *unr. tr. V.* (a) (öffnen) tear open; wrench open ⟨*drawer*⟩; fling open ⟨*door, window*⟩; **die Augen/den Mund ~:** open one's eyes/mouth wide
(b) (beschädigen) tear open; tear ⟨*clothes*⟩; break up ⟨*road, soil*⟩
⟨2⟩ *itr. V.;* mit sein ⟨*clothes*⟩ tear; ⟨*seam*⟩ split; ⟨*wound*⟩ open; ⟨*cloud*⟩ break up

auf|reizen *tr. V.* excite

auf·reizend ⟨1⟩ *Adj.* provocative
⟨2⟩ *adv.* provocatively

auf|richten ⟨1⟩ *tr. V.* erect; put up; **den Oberkörper ~:** raise one's upper body; **jmdn.** [**wieder**] **~** (fig.) give fresh heart to sb.
⟨2⟩ *refl. V.* stand up [straight]; **sich an jmdm./ etw.** [**wieder**] **~** (fig.) take heart from sb./sth.

auf·richtig ⟨1⟩ *Adj.* sincere
⟨2⟩ *adv.* sincerely

Auf·richtigkeit *die* sincerity

auf|rücken *itr. V.;* mit sein move up

Auf·ruf *der* (a) call
(b) (Appell) appeal (**an** + *Akk.* to)

auf|rufen *unr. tr. V.* (a) call
(b) **jmdn. ~, etw. zu tun** call upon sb. to do sth.
(c) (Rechtsw.) appeal for ⟨*witnesses*⟩

Aufruhr *der;* ~s, ~e (a) (Widerstand) rebellion
(b) (Erregung) turmoil

aufrührerisch *Adj.* inflammatory

auf|rüsten *tr., itr. V.* (a) arm; **wieder ~:** rearm
(b) (DV) upgrade

Auf·rüstung *die* armament

aufs *Präp.* + *Art.* = **auf das**

auf|sagen *tr. V.* recite

auf|sammeln *tr. V.* gather up

aufsässig ⟨1⟩ *Adj.* recalcitrant
⟨2⟩ *adv.* recalcitrantly

Aufsässigkeit *die;* ~, ~en (a) recalcitrance
(b) (Handlung) piece of recalcitrance

Auf·satz *der* (Text) essay

auf|saugen *unr.* (*auch regelm.*) *tr. V.* soak up; (fig.) absorb

auf|schieben *unr. tr. V.* postpone

Auf·schlag *der* (a) (Aufprall) impact
(b) (Preis~) surcharge
(c) (Ärmel~) cuff; (Hosen~) turn-up; (Revers) lapel
(d) (Tennis usw.) serve

auf|schlagen ⟨1⟩ *unr. itr. V.* (a) mit sein **auf etw.** (*Dat. od. Akk.*) **~:** hit sth.
(b) (teurer werden) ⟨*price, rent, costs*⟩ go up
(c) (Tennis usw.) serve

⟨2⟩ *unr. tr. V.* (a) (öffnen) crack ⟨*nut, egg*⟩ [open]; knock a hole in ⟨*ice*⟩; **sich** (*Dat.*) **das Knie/den Kopf ~:** cut one's knee/head
(b) open ⟨*book, newspaper, one's eyes*⟩; **schlagt Seite 15 auf!** turn to page 15
(c) turn up ⟨*collar, sleeve, trouser leg*⟩
(d) (aufbauen) set up ⟨*camp*⟩; pitch ⟨*tent*⟩; put up ⟨*bed, hut, scaffolding*⟩
(e) **5 % auf etw.** (*Akk.*) **~:** put 5% on sth.

auf|schließen ⟨1⟩ *unr. tr. V.* unlock
⟨2⟩ *unr. itr. V.* [jmdm.] **~:** unlock the door/ gate *etc.* [for sb.]

Auf·schluss, *Auf·schluß *der* information *no pl.*

auf|schneiden ⟨1⟩ *unr. tr. V.* (a) cut open
(b) (zerteilen) cut
⟨2⟩ *unr. tr. V.* (ugs.: prahlen) boast (**mit** about)

Auf·schneider *der,* **Auf·schneiderin** *die* (ugs. abwertend) boaster; braggart

Auf·schnitt *der* [assorted] cold meats *pl./* cheeses *pl.*

auf|schnüren *tr. V.* undo

auf|schrauben *tr. V.* unscrew; unscrew the top of ⟨*bottle, jar, etc.*⟩

Auf·schrei *der* cry; (stärker) yell; (schriller) scream; **ein ~ der Empörung** *od.* **Entrüstung** (fig.) an outcry

auf|schreiben *unr. tr. V.* write down; [**sich** (*Dat.*)] **etw. ~:** make a note of sth.

auf|schreien *unr. itr. V.* cry out; (stärker) yell out; (schrill) scream

Auf·schrift *die* inscription

Auf·schub *der* postponement; **die Sache duldet keinen ~:** the matter brooks no delay

Auf·schwung *der* upturn (*Gen.* in)

Aufsehen *das;* ~s stir; [**großes**] **~ erregen** cause a [great] stir

Auf·seher *der,* **Auf·seherin** *die;* ~, ~nen (im Gefängnis) warder (Brit.); [prison] guard (Amer.); (im Park) park-keeper; (im Museum, auf dem Parkplatz) attendant; (auf einem Gut, Sklavenaufseher) overseer

*auf|sein ▸ AUF 3A, F

auf|setzen ⟨1⟩ *tr. V.* (a) put on
(b) (verfassen) draw up ⟨*text*⟩
⟨2⟩ *refl. V.* sit up

Auf·sicht *die* supervision; (bei Prüfungen) invigilation (Brit.); proctoring (Amer.)

auf|spielen ⟨1⟩ *refl. V.* (ugs. abwertend) angeben) put on airs; **sich vor jmdm. ~:** show off in front of sb.
⟨2⟩ *itr. V.* (a) (musizieren) play; **zum Tanz ~:** play dance music
(b) (Sport) **groß/eindrucksvoll ~:** give a fine/ impressive display

auf|springen *unr. itr. V.;* mit sein (a) jump up
(b) (hinaufspringen) jump on (**auf** + *Akk.* to)
(c) (rissig werden) crack

auf|stacheln *tr. V.* incite

Auf·stand *der* rebellion

auf·ständisch *Adj.* rebellious

auf|stehen *unr. itr. V.; mit sein* stand up; (aus dem Liegen) get up

auf|steigen *unr. itr. V.; mit sein* **(a)** (auf ein Fahrzeug) get on; **auf etw.** (*Akk.*) ~: get on [to] sth.
(b) (bergan steigen) climb
(c) (hochsteigen) ‹sap, smoke, mist› rise
(d) (beruflich, gesellschaftlich) rise (**zu** to); **zum Direktor** ~: rise to be manager

auf|stellen ⊡ *tr. V.* **(a)** put up (**auf** + *Akk.* on); set up ‹skittles›; (postieren) post
(b) (aufrecht hinstellen) stand up
(c) (Sport) select, pick ‹team, player›
(d) (bilden) put together ‹team of experts›; raise ‹army›
(e) (nominieren) nominate; put up
⊡ *refl. V.* position oneself

Auf·stellung *die* **(a)** ▶ AUFSTELLEN 1A: putting up; setting up; posting
(b) ▶ AUFSTELLEN B: standing up
(c) ▶ AUFSTELLEN C: selection; picking
(d) ▶ AUFSTELLEN D: putting together; raising
(e) (Nominierung) nomination

Aufstieg *der;* ~[e]s, ~e **(a)** climb
(b) ▶ AUFSTEIGEN D: rise

auf|stoßen ⊡ *unr. tr. V.* push open
⊡ *unr. itr. V.* belch; ‹baby› bring up wind

Auf·strich *der* spread

auf|stützen ⊡ *tr. V.* rest ‹one's arms etc.›
⊡ *refl. V.* support oneself; **die Arme auf etw.** (*Akk. od. Dat.*) ~: rest one's arms on sth.

auf|suchen *tr. V.* call on; go to ‹doctor›

Auf·takt *der* **(a)** (fig.) start
(b) (Musik) upbeat

auf|tauchen *itr. V.; mit sein* **(a)** surface
(b) (sichtbar werden) appear

auf|tauen ⊡ *tr. V.* thaw
⊡ *itr. V.; mit sein* (auch fig.) thaw

auf|teilen *tr. V.* **(a)** divide [up]
(b) (verteilen) share out

Auftrag *der;* ~[e]s, **Aufträge (a)** instructions *pl.;* **in jmds.** ~ (*Dat.*) on sb.'s instructions; (für jmdn.) on behalf of sb
(b) (Bestellung) order; (bei Künstlern, Architekten usw.) commission
(c) (Mission) task; (Aufgabe) job

auf|tragen *unr. tr. V.* **(a)** **jmdm.** ~, **etw. zu tun** instruct sb. to do sth.
(b) (aufstreichen) put on ‹paint, make-up, etc.›

Auftrag·geber *der;* ~s, ~, **Auftrag·geberin** *die;* ~, ~**nen** client

Auftrags·buch *das* (Kaufmannsspr.) order book

auf|treten *unr. itr. V.; mit sein* **(a)** tread
(b) (sich benehmen) behave
(c) (eine Vorstellung geben) appear; **als Zeuge/Kläger** ~: appear as a witness/a plaintiff
(d) (auftauchen) ‹problem, difficulty, difference of opinion› arise; ‹symptom, danger, pest› appear

Auftreten *das;* ~s (Benehmen) manner

Auf·trieb *der* **(a)** (Physik) (statischer ~) buoyancy; (dynamischer ~) lift
(b) (fig.) impetus; **das hat ihm** ~/**neuen** ~ **gegeben** that has given him a lift/given him new impetus

Auf·tritt *der* **(a)** (Vorstellung) appearance
(b) (Theater: das Auftreten) entrance; (Szene) scene

auf|tun *unr. refl. V.* (geh.) open; (fig.) open up

auf|wachen *itr. V.; mit sein* wake up, awaken (**aus** from); (aus Ohnmacht, Narkose) come round (**aus** from)

auf|wachsen *unr. itr. V.; mit sein* grow up

Auf·wand *der;* ~[e]s cost; expense

aufwändig ▶ AUFWENDIG

Aufwands·entschädigung *die* expense allowance

auf|wärmen ⊡ *tr. V.* heat *or* warm up ‹food›
⊡ *refl. V.* warm oneself up

aufwärts *Adv.* upwards

Aufwärts·trend *der* upward trend

auf|wecken *tr. V.* wake [up]; waken

auf|weichen ⊡ *tr. V.* soften
⊡ *itr. V.; mit sein* become soft; soften up

auf|wenden *unr. (auch regelm.) tr. V.* use ‹skill, influence›; expend ‹energy, resources›; spend ‹money, time›; **viel Geld/seine ganze Freizeit für etw.** ~ spend a great deal of money/all one's spare time on sth.

auf·wendig ⊡ *Adj.* lavish; (kostspielig) costly; expensive
⊡ *adv.* lavishly; (kostspielig) expensively

Auf·wendung *die* **(a)** ▶ AUFWENDEN: using; expenditure; spending; **unter** ~ **von etw.** by using/expending/spending sth.
(b) *Pl.* (Kosten) expenditure *sing.*

auf|wiegeln *tr. V.* incite; stir up

auf|wirbeln *tr. V.* swirl up

auf|wischen *tr. V.* **(a)** wipe *or* mop up
(b) (säubern) wipe ‹floor›; (mit Wasser) wash ‹floor›

auf|zählen *tr. V.* list

Auf·zählung *die* **(a)** listing
(b) (Liste) list

auf|zeichnen *tr. V.* **(a)** record
(b) (zeichnen) draw

Auf·zeichnung *die* record; (Film-, Tonaufzeichnung) recording; ~**en** (Notizen) notes

auf|ziehen ⊡ *unr. tr. V.* **(a)** pull open ‹drawer›; open, draw [back] ‹curtains›; undo ‹zip›
(b) wind up ‹clock, toy, etc.›
⊡ *unr. itr. V.; mit sein* come up; ‹clouds, storm› gather

Auf·zucht *die* raising; rearing

Auf·zug *der* **(a)** (Lift) lift (Brit.); elevator (Amer.)
(b) (abwertend: Aufmachung) get-up
(c) (Theater: Akt) act

Aug·apfel *der* eyeball

Auge *das;* ~s, ~n eye; **gute/schlechte** ~n

haben have good/poor eyesight; **auf einem** ∼ **blind** blind in one eye; **da wird er** ∼**n machen** (fig. ugs.) his eyes will pop out of his head; **ich traute meinen** ∼**n nicht** (ugs.) I couldn't believe my eyes; **ein** ∼ *od.* **beide** ∼**n zudrücken** (fig.) turn a blind eye; **jmdn./ etw. nicht aus den** ∼**n lassen** not take one's eyes off sb./sth.; **ins** ∼ **gehen** (fig. ugs.) end in disaster; **unter vier** ∼**n** (fig.) in private

augen; Augen-: ∼**arzt** *der,* ∼**ärztin** *die* eye specialist; ∼**blick** */auch: --'-/ der* ▶ MOMENT[1]; ∼**blicklich** */auch: --'--/* ⓵ *Adj.* **(a)** (sofortig) immediate; **(b)** (gegenwärtig) present; ⓶ *adv.* **(a)** (sofort) at once; **(b)** (zurzeit) at the moment; ∼**braue** *die* eyebrow; ∼**farbe** *die* colour of one's eyes; ∼**klinik** *die* eye hospital; ∼**lid** *das* eyelid; ∼**maß** *das:* **ein gutes/schlechtes** ∼**maß haben** have a good eye/no eye for distances; ∼**merk** *das:* **sein** ∼**merk auf jmdn./etw. richten** *od.* **lenken** give one's attention to sb./sth.; ∼**optiker** *der,* ∼**optikerin** *die* ophthalmic optician

Augen-schein *der* (geh.) **(a)** (Eindruck) appearance; **dem** ∼ **nach** by all appearances **(b)** (Betrachtung) inspection; **jmdn./etw. in** ∼ **nehmen** have a close look at sb./sth.; give sb./sth. a close inspection

augen-scheinlich (geh.) ⓵ *Adj.* (scheinbar) apparent; evident; (sichtbar) obvious; evident ⓶ *adv.* (scheinbar) apparently; evidently; (sichtbar) obviously; evidently

augen-, Augen-: ∼**weide** *die* feast for the eyes; ∼**zeuge** *der,* ∼**zeugin** *die* eyewitness; ∼**zwinkernd** ⓵ *Adj.* tacit ⟨agreement⟩; ⓶ *adv.* with a wink

August *der;* ∼[e]s *od.* ∼, ∼e August

Auktion *die;* ∼, ∼en auction

Aula *die;* ∼, Aulen *od.* ∼s hall

aus ⓵ *Präp. mit Dat.* **(a)** (aus dem Inneren von) out of **(b)** (Herkunft, Quelle, Ausgangspunkt angebend, auch zeitlich) from; ∼ **Spanien/Köln** *usw.* from Spain/Cologne *etc.;* **(c)** ∼ **der Mode/Übung sein** be out of fashion/training **(d)** (Grund, Ursache angebend) out of; **etw.** ∼ **Erfahrung wissen** know sth. from experience; ∼ **Versehen** by mistake **(e)** (bestehend ∼) of; (hergestellt ∼) made of; ∼ **etw. bestehen** consist of sth. **(f)** ∼ **ihm ist ein guter Arzt geworden** he made a good doctor ⓶ *Adv.* **(a)** (vorbei) over; **wann ist die Vorstellung** ∼? what time does the performance end?; **die Schule ist** ∼ school is out; ∼ **jetzt!** that's enough **(b)** (ausgeschaltet) off; (erloschen) out **(c) vom Fenster/obersten Stockwerk** ∼: from the window/top storey; **von mir** ∼ (ugs.) if you like; **von sich** (*Dat.*) ∼: of one's own accord

aus|atmen *itr., tr. V.* breathe out

aus|baden *tr. V.* (ugs.) carry *or* take the can for (Brit. coll.); take the rap for (coll.)

Aus-bau *der;* ∼[e]s **(a)** (Erweiterung) extension **(b)** (Ausgestaltung) conversion (zu into)

aus|bauen *tr. V.* **(a)** (demontieren) remove (aus from) **(b)** (erweitern) extend

Aus-beute *die* yield

aus|beuten *tr. V.* exploit

Ausbeutung *die;* ∼, ∼en exploitation

aus|bilden *tr. V.* **(a)** train **(b)** (entwickeln) develop

Aus-bildung *die* **(a)** training **(b)** (Entwicklung) development

Aus-blick *der* view (auf + *Akk.* of)

aus|brechen *unr. itr. V.; mit sein* **(a)** break out (aus of); (fig.) break free (aus from) **(b) jmdm. bricht der Schweiß aus** sb. breaks into a sweat **(c)** ⟨volcano⟩ erupt **(d)** (beginnen) break out; ⟨crisis⟩ break **(e) in Gelächter/Weinen** ∼: burst out laughing/crying; **in Beifall/Tränen** ∼: burst into applause/tears

aus|breiten ⓵ *tr. V.* spread; spread [out] ⟨map, cloth, sheet, etc.⟩; open out ⟨fan, newspaper⟩; (nebeneinander legen) spread out ⓶ *refl. V.* spread

Aus-bruch *der* **(a)** (Flucht) escape (aus from) **(b)** (Beginn) outbreak **(c)** (Gefühlsausbruch) outburst **(d)** (eines Vulkans) eruption

aus|brüten *tr. V.* hatch out; (im Brutkasten) incubate

aus|bürsten *tr. V.* brush out ⟨dust, dirt⟩ (aus of); brush ⟨clothes, upholstery, etc.⟩

Aus-dauer *die* stamina

aus-dauernd *Adj.* with stamina *postpos.*

Ausdauer-training *das* stamina training

aus|dehnen ⓵ *tr. V.* **(a)** stretch; (fig.) extend (auf + *Akk.* to) **(b)** (zeitlich) prolong ⓶ *refl. V.* expand; (zeitlich) go on

Aus-dehnung *die* expansion; (fig.) extension; (zeitlich) prolongation

aus|denken *unr. refl. V.* **sich** (*Dat.*) **etw.** ∼: think sth. up

aus|diskutieren *tr. V.* **etw.** ∼: discuss sth. fully *or* thoroughly

Aus-druck *der; Pl.* **Ausdrücke** expression; (Terminus) term; **etw. zum** ∼ **bringen** express sth.

aus|drucken *tr. V.* (Nachrichtenw., DV) print out

aus|drücken ⓵ *tr. V.* **(a)** (auspressen) squeeze ⟨juice⟩ out; squeeze [out] ⟨lemon, grape, orange, etc.⟩; squeeze out ⟨sponge⟩; squeeze ⟨boil, pimple⟩ **(b)** stub out ⟨cigarette⟩ **(c)** (mitteilen) express ⋯❖

2 *refl. V.* **(a)** express oneself
(b) (offenbar werden) be expressed

ausdrücklich */od. -'--/* 1 *Adj.* express
attrib. ⟨command, wish, etc.⟩; explicit
⟨reservation⟩
2 *adv.* expressly; ⟨mention⟩ explicitly

ausdrucks-: ~**los** 1 *Adj.* expressionless;
2 *adv.* expressionlessly; ~**voll** 1 *Adj.*
expressive; 2 *adv.* expressively

aus-einander *Adv.* **(a)** (voneinander getrennt)
apart; etw. ~ **schreiben** write sth. as
separate words; ~ **brechen** break up; etw. ~
brechen break sth. up; ~ **gehen** part; ⟨
crowd⟩ disperse; ⟨opinions, views⟩ differ;
zwei Dinge ~ **halten** (unterscheiden) distinguish
between two things; **ich kann die beiden**
Brüder nicht ~ **halten** I cannot tell the two
brothers apart; etw. ~ **nehmen** take sth.
apart
(b) jmdm. etw. ~ **setzen** explain sth. to sb.;
sich mit jmdm. ~ **setzen** have it out with sb.;
sich mit etw. ~ **setzen** concern oneself with
sth.

*auseinander|brechen *usw.*
▶ AUSEINANDER

Auseinandersetzung *die;* ~, ~**en** **(a)**
(Streit) argument
(b) (Kampfhandlung) clash

Aus-fahrt *die* exit

Aus-fall *der* **(a)** (das Nichtstattfinden)
cancellation
(b) (Einbuße, Verlust) loss
(c) (eines Motors) failure; (einer Maschine, eines
Autos) breakdown

aus|fallen *unr. itr. V.; mit sein* **(a)** fall out
(b) (nicht stattfinden) be cancelled; etw. ~
lassen cancel sth.
(c) (ausscheiden) drop out
(d) (nicht mehr funktionieren) ⟨engine, brakes,
signal⟩ fail; ⟨machine, car⟩ break down
(e) (ein bestimmtes Ergebnis zeigen) turn out

ausfallend *Adj.* **[gegen jmdn.]** ~ **sein/**
werden be/become abusive [towards sb.]

Ausfall-straße *die* main road out of the/a
town/city

aus-findig *Adv.* jmdn./etw. ~ **machen** find
sb./sth.

Aus-flug *der* outing

Ausflügler *der;* ~**s,** ~**, Ausflüglerin**
die; ~, ~**nen** day tripper; excursionist
(Amer.)

Ausflugs-: ~**dampfer** *der* pleasure
steamer; ~**lokal** *das* restaurant/café
catering for [day] trippers; ~**verkehr** *der*
(am Wochenende) weekend holiday traffic; (an
Feiertagen) holiday traffic

aus|fragen *tr. V.* jmdn. ~: question sb.,
ask sb. questions (**nach, über** + *Akk.* about)

aus|fransen *itr. V.; mit sein* fray

Aus-fuhr *die;* ~, ~**en** ▶ EXPORT

aus|führen *tr. V.* **(a)** (ausgehen mit) take
⟨person⟩ out
(b) (spazieren führen) take ⟨person, animal⟩ for
a walk
(c) (exportieren) export
(d) (durchführen) carry out; (Sport) take
⟨penalty, free kick, corner⟩

ausführlich */auch: -'--/* 1 *Adj.* detailed;
full
2 *adv.* in detail

Ausfuhr-sperre *die* ▶ AUSFUHRVERBOT

Aus-führung *die* (Durchführung) carrying out;
(Sport) taking

Ausfuhr-verbot *das* (Wirtsch.) export
embargo

aus|füllen *tr. V.* **(a)** fill; fill in ⟨form,
crossword puzzle⟩
(b) (beanspruchen, einnehmen) take up ⟨space⟩

Aus-gabe *die* **(a)** giving out; (von Essen)
serving
(b) (Geldausgabe) item of expenditure; ~**n**
expenditure *sing.* (**für** on)
(c) (Edition) edition
(d) (DV) output

Ausgabe-gerät *das* (DV) output device

Aus-gang *der* **(a)** (Erlaubnis zum Ausgehen)
time off; (von Soldaten) leave
(b) (Tür ins Freie) exit (*Gen.* from)
(c) (Anat.) outlet
(d) (Ende) end; (eines Romans, Films usw.)
ending
(e) (Ergebnis) outcome; (eines Wettbewerbs)
result; **ein Unfall mit tödlichem** ~: an
accident with fatal consequences

Ausgangs-: ~**punkt** *der* starting point;
~**sperre** *die* (bes. Milit.) (für Zivilisten) curfew;
(für Soldaten) confinement to barracks; **[eine]**
~**sperre verhängen** impose a curfew/confine
the soldiers/regiment *etc.* to barracks

aus|geben *unr. tr. V.* **(a)** give out; serve
⟨food, drinks⟩
(b) (verbrauchen) spend ⟨money⟩ (**für** on)

ausgebucht *Adj.* booked up

ausgedehnt *Adj.* extensive

aus-gefallen *Adj.* unusual

Ausgeflippte *der/die; adj. Dekl.* (salopp)
dropout (coll.)

ausgeglichen *Adj.* balanced; well-
balanced ⟨person⟩; equable ⟨climate⟩

aus|gehen *unr. itr. V.; mit sein* **(a)** go out
(b) (fast aufgebraucht sein) run out
(c) (enden) end; **gut/schlecht** ~: turn out
well/badly; ⟨story, film⟩ end happily/
unhappily
(d) von jmdm./etw. ~: come from sb./sth.
(e) von etw. ~ (etw. zugrunde legen) take sth. as
one's starting point; (etw. annehmen) assume
sth.

aus-gelassen 1 *Adj.* exuberant ⟨mood,
person⟩; lively ⟨party, celebration⟩; (wild)
boisterous
2 *adv.* exuberantly; (wild) boisterously

---

*old spelling - see note on page xiv

aus·gemacht *Adj.* (a) (beschlossen) agreed; **es ist [eine] ∼e Sache, dass ...** it is an accepted fact that ... (b) (vollkommen) complete; utter ⟨*nonsense*⟩; **eine ∼e Dummheit** downright stupidity

aus·genommen *Konj.* except

ausgeprägt *Adj.* marked

ausgerechnet *Adv.* (ugs.) **∼ heute/ morgen** today/tomorrow of all days; **∼ hier** here of all places; **∼ Sie** you of all people

aus·geschlossen *Adj.* **das ist ∼:** that is out of the question

aus·geschnitten *Adj.* low-cut ⟨*dress, blouse, etc.*⟩

aus·gesprochen 1 *Adj.* definite, marked ⟨*preference, inclination, resemblance*⟩; pronounced ⟨*dislike*⟩; marked ⟨*contrast*⟩; **∼es Pech/Glück haben** be decidedly unlucky/lucky; **ein ∼es Talent für etw.** a definite talent for sth.; **ein ∼er Gegner von etw. sein** be a strong opponent of sth.
2 *adv.* (besonders) decidedly; downright ⟨*stupid, ridiculous, ugly*⟩

aus·gestorben *Adj.* [wie] **∼:** deserted

aus·gewogen *Adj.* (ausgeglichen) balanced; [well-]balanced ⟨*personality*⟩

Aus·gewogenheit *die;* **∼:** balance

ausgezeichnet */od.* '--'--/ 1 *Adj.* excellent; outstanding ⟨*expert*⟩
2 *adv.* excellently

ausgiebig 1 *Adj.* substantial ⟨*meal*⟩
2 *adv.* ⟨*profit*⟩ handsomely; ⟨*read*⟩ extensively; **von etw. ∼ Gebrauch machen** make full use of sth.

aus·gießen *unr. tr. V.* (a) pour out (aus of) (b) (leeren) empty

Aus·gleich *der;* **∼[e]s, ∼e** (a) ▶ AUSGLEICHEN A: evening out; reconciliation (b) (Schadensersatz) compensation; **als** *od.* **zum ∼ für etw.** to make up for sth.

aus·gleichen *unr. tr. V.* (a) even out; reconcile ⟨*differences of opinions, contradictions*⟩ (b) compensate for ⟨*damage*⟩; make up for ⟨*misfortune, lack*⟩; **etw. durch etw. ∼:** make up for sth. with sth.; **sich ∼:** balance out; (sich gegenseitig aufheben) cancel each other out

aus·graben *unr. tr. V.* dig up; (Archäol.) excavate

Aus·grabung *die* (Archäol.) excavation

Aus·guss, *Aus·guß *der* sink

aus·halten *unr. tr. V.* stand; bear; endure; withstand ⟨*attack, load, pressure, test, wear and tear*⟩; **er konnte es zu Hause nicht mehr ∼:** he couldn't stand it at home any more; **es ist nicht zum Aushalten** it is unbearable

aus·handeln *tr. V.* negotiate

aus·händigen *tr. V.* hand over

Aus·hang *der* notice; **einen ∼ machen** put up a notice

aus|heben *unr. tr. V.* dig out ⟨*earth etc.*⟩; dig ⟨*trench, grave, etc.*⟩

aus|helfen *unr. itr. V.* help out; **jmdm. ∼:** help sb. out (mit, bei with)

Aus·hilfe *die* (a) (das Aushelfen) help (b) ▶ AUSHILFSKRAFT

aushilfs-, Aushilfs-: **∼kraft** *die* temporary worker; (in Läden, Gaststätten) temporary assistant; (Sekretärin) temporary secretary; temp (coll.); **∼lehrer** *der,* **∼lehrerin,** *die* supply teacher; **∼weise** *adv.* on a temporary basis

aus|holen *itr. V.* [mit dem Arm] **∼:** draw back one's arm; (zum Schlag) raise one's arm

aus|kennen *unr. refl. V.* (an einem Ort usw.) know one's way around; (in einem Fach, einer Angelegenheit usw.) know what's what; **sie kennt sich in dieser Stadt aus** she knows her way around the town; **sich [gut] mit/in etw.** (*Dat.*) **∼:** know [a lot] about sth.

Aus·klang *der* (geh.) end; **zum ∼ des Festes** to end *or* close the festival

aus|kleiden *tr. V.* (geh.) undress; **sich ∼:** undress

aus|klingen *unr. itr. V.; mit sein* end

aus|klopfen *tr. V.* (a) beat out (aus + *Dat.* of) (b) (säubern) beat ⟨*carpet*⟩; knock ⟨*pipe*⟩ out

aus|kochen *tr. V.* boil; (keimfrei machen) sterilize ⟨*instruments etc.*⟩ [in boiling water]

aus|kommen *unr. itr. V.; mit sein* (a) manage (mit on) (b) **mit jmdm. [gut] ∼:** get on [well] with sb.

Auskommen *das;* **∼s** livelihood

Auskunft *die;* **∼, Auskünfte** (a) piece of information; Auskünfte information *sing.;* [jmdm. über etw. (*Akk.*)] **∼ geben** give [sb.] information [about sth.] (b) (Stelle) information desk/counter/office/ centre *etc.;* (Fernspr.) directory enquiries *no art.* (Brit.); directory information *no art.* (Amer.)

Auskunftei *die;* **∼, ∼en** private detective agency; (Kredit∼) credit reference agency

Auskunfts-: **∼büro** *das* information office; enquiry office (Brit.); **∼schalter** *der* information counter; **∼stelle** *die* information office

aus|kungeln *tr. V.* (ugs.) reach by wheeling and dealing

aus|kurieren *tr. V.* heal ⟨*wound*⟩ [completely]

aus|lachen *tr. V.* laugh at

aus|laden *unr. tr. V.* unload ⟨*goods etc.*⟩

Aus·lage *die* (a) *Pl.* (Unkosten) expenses (b) (ausgestellte Ware) item on display; **∼n** goods on display

aus|lagern *tr. V.* (a) remove ⟨*art treasures*⟩ for safe-keeping (b) relocate ⟨*firm, activity*⟩ (nach to); (an einen externen Dienstleister) outsource ⟨*function, activity*⟩

Aus·land das foreign countries pl.; im/ins ∼: abroad; aus dem ∼: from abroad

Ausländer der; ∼s, ∼, **Ausländerin** die; ∼, ∼nen foreigner

ausländer·feindlich Adj. hostile to foreigners postpos.

ausländisch Adj. foreign

Auslands-: ∼aufenthalt der stay abroad; ∼gespräch das (Fernspr.) international call; ∼korrespondent der, ∼korrespondentin die foreign correspondent; ∼reise die trip abroad

aus|lassen unr. tr. V. (a) (weglassen) leave out
(b) (versäumen) miss ⟨opportunity, chance, etc.⟩

Auslauf der (a) keinen/zu wenig ∼ haben have no/too little chance to run around outside
(b) (Raum) space to run around in

aus|laufen unr. itr. V.; mit sein (a) run out (aus of)
(b) (leer laufen) empty; ⟨egg⟩ run out
(c) (in See stechen) sail (nach for)
(d) (erlöschen) ⟨contract, agreement, etc.⟩ run out

Aus·läufer der (a) (Geogr.) foothill usu. in pl.;
(b) (Met.) (eines Hochs) ridge; (eines Tiefs) trough

aus|legen tr. V. (a) (hinlegen) lay out; display ⟨goods, exhibits⟩
(b) etw. mit Fliesen/Teppichboden ∼: tile/carpet sth.
(c) (leihen) lend
(d) (interpretieren) interpret; etw. falsch ∼: misinterpret sth.

Auslegung die; ∼, ∼en interpretation

aus|leihen unr. tr. V. ▶ LEIHEN

aus|liefern tr. V. (a) jmdm. etw. od. etw. an jmdn. ∼: hand sth. over to sb.
(b) auch itr. (Kaufmannsspr.: liefern) deliver

Aus·lieferung die (a) (Übergabe) handing over; (an ein Land) extradition; jmds. ∼ fordern demand that sb. be handed over/extradited
(b) (Kaufmannsspr.: Lieferung) delivery

Auslieferungs-: ∼antrag der application for extradition; ∼lager das (Wirtsch.) distribution centre

aus|loggen refl. V. (DV) log off or out

aus|löschen tr. V. (a) extinguish
(b) (beseitigen) erase ⟨drawing, writing⟩

aus|losen tr. V. etw. ∼: draw lots for sth.

aus|lösen tr. V. (a) trigger ⟨mechanism, device, alarm, etc.⟩; release ⟨camera shutter⟩
(b) provoke ⟨discussion, anger, laughter, reaction, outrage, heart attack⟩; cause ⟨sorrow, horror, surprise, disappointment, panic, war⟩; excite, arouse ⟨interest, enthusiasm⟩

Auslöser der; ∼s, ∼ (Fot.) shutter release

*alte Schreibung - vgl. Hinweis auf S. xiv

aus|machen tr. V. (a) (ugs.) put out ⟨light, fire, cigarette, candle⟩; switch off ⟨television, radio, hi-fi⟩; turn off ⟨gas⟩
(b) (vereinbaren) agree [on]; ∼, dass ...: agree that ...
(c) (auszeichnen, kennzeichnen) make up
(d) wenig/nichts/viel ∼: make little/no/a great difference
(e) das macht mir nichts aus I don't mind

Aus·maß das (a) (Größe) size
(b) (Grad) extent

aus|messen unr. tr. V. measure up

Aus·nahme die; ∼, ∼n exception; mit ∼ von with the exception of; bei jmdm. eine ∼ machen make an exception in sb.'s case

Ausnahme-: ∼erscheinung die exceptional phenomenon; ∼zustand der state of emergency

ausnahms-: ∼los ① Adj. unanimous ⟨approval, agreement⟩; ② adv. without exception; ∼weise Adv. by way of an exception; Dürfen wir mitkommen? – Ausnahmsweise [ja] May we come too? – Yes, just this once

aus|nehmen unr. tr. V. (a) gut ⟨fish, rabbit, chicken⟩
(b) (ausschließen von) exclude; (gesondert behandeln) make an exception of

aus|nüchtern tr., itr., refl. V. sober up

Ausnüchterung die; ∼, ∼en sobering up; jmdn. zur ∼ auf die Wache bringen take sb. to the [police] station to sober up

Ausnüchterungs·zelle die drying-out cell

aus|nutzen, (bes. südd., österr.) **aus|nützen** tr. V. (a) take advantage of
(b) (ausbeuten) exploit

Aus·nutzung die, (bes. südd., österr.) **Ausnützung** die; ∼: use; (Ausbeutung) exploitation; unter voller ∼ einer Sache (Gen.) making full use of sth.

aus|packen ① tr., itr. V. unpack; (auswickeln) unwrap
② itr. V. (ugs.) (Geheimnisse verraten) talk (coll.); squeal (sl.)

aus|pressen tr. V. squeeze out ⟨juice⟩; squeeze ⟨orange, lemon⟩; (keltern) press ⟨grapes etc.⟩

aus|probieren tr. V. try out

Aus·puff der exhaust

Auspuffgase Pl. exhaust fumes pl.

aus|radieren tr. V. rub out; erase

aus|rangieren tr. V. (ugs.) throw out; discard; scrap ⟨vehicle, machine⟩; ausrangierte Fahrzeuge scrap vehicles

aus|rasten itr. V.; mit sein (Technik) disengage; er rastete aus, es rastete bei ihm aus (fig. salopp) something snapped in him

aus|rauben tr. V. rob

aus|räuchern tr. V. (auch fig.) smoke out; fumigate ⟨room⟩

aus|räumen ① tr. V. (a) clear out (aus of)

(b) (fig.) clear up; dispel ⟨prejudice, suspicion, misgivings⟩
2 itr. V. clear everything out

aus|rechnen tr. V. work out; **das kannst du dir leicht ~** (ugs.) you can easily work that out [for yourself]

Aus·rede die excuse

aus|reden 1 itr. V. finish [speaking]
2 tr. V. **jmdm. etw. ~**: talk sb. out of sth.

aus|reichen itr. V. be enough or sufficient (**zu** for)

ausreichend 1 Adj. sufficient; enough; (als Note) fair
2 adv. sufficiently

Aus·reise die: **jmdm. die ~ verweigern** refuse sb. permission to leave [the/a country]; **vor/bei der ~:** before/when leaving the country

Ausreise·antrag der application to leave the country; application for an exit visa

aus|reißen 1 unr. tr. V. tear out; pull out ⟨plants, weeds⟩
2 unr. itr. V.; mit sein **(a)** (sich lösen) come off
(b) (ugs.: weglaufen) run away (Dat. from)

aus|renken tr. V. dislocate

aus|richten tr. V. **(a) jmdm. etw. ~:** tell sb. sth.
(b) (einheitlich anordnen) line up
(c) (erreichen) achieve

aus|rollen tr. V. roll out

aus|rotten tr. V. eradicate

Aus·ruf der cry

aus|rufen unr. tr. V. **(a)** call out; **„Schön!", rief er aus** 'Lovely', he exclaimed
(b) (offiziell verkünden) proclaim; declare ⟨state of emergency⟩
(c) (zum Kauf anbieten) cry

Ausrufe·zeichen das exclamation mark

aus|ruhen refl., itr. V. have a rest; **[sich] ein wenig/richtig ~:** rest a little/have a good rest; **ausgeruht sein** be rested

aus|rüsten tr. V. equip

Aus·rüstung die **(a)** equipping
(b) (Gegenstände) equipment no pl.

Ausrüstungs·gegenstand der item of equipment

aus|rutschen itr. V.; mit sein slip

aus|säen tr. (auch itr.) V. (auch fig.) sow

Aus·sage die statement

aussage-, Aussage-: ~kraft die meaningfulness; (Ausdruckskraft) expressiveness; **~kräftig** Adj. meaningful; (ausdruckskräftig) expressive

aus|sagen 1 tr. V. **(a)** say
(b) (vor Gericht, vor der Polizei) state; (unter Eid) testify
2 itr. V. make a statement; (unter Eid) testify

aus|saugen regelm. (geh. auch unr.) tr. V. **(a)** suck out (**aus** of); (leer saugen) suck dry

(b) (fig.: ausbeuten) **jmdn./etw. ~:** bleed sb./sth. [white]; **jmdn. bis aufs Blut** od. **Mark ~:** bleed sb. white

aus|schaben tr. V. **(a)** scrape out
(b) (Med.) remove; (mit der Kürette) curette

aus|schalten tr. V. **(a)** switch or turn off
(b) (fig.) eliminate; exclude ⟨emotion, influence⟩; dismiss ⟨doubt, objection⟩; shut out ⟨feeling, thought⟩

Aus·schank der; **~[e]s** serving

Aus·schau die: **nach jmdm./etw. ~ halten** keep a lookout for sb./sth.

aus|schauen itr. V. **nach jmdm./etw. ~:** look out for sb./sth.

aus|scheiden 1 unr. itr. V.; mit sein **(a) aus etw. ~:** leave sth.; **aus dem Amt ~:** leave office
(b) (Sport) be eliminated
(c) diese Möglichkeit/dieser Kandidat scheidet aus this possibility/candidate has to be ruled out
2 unr. tr. V. (Physiol.) excrete ⟨waste⟩; eliminate, expel ⟨poison⟩; exude ⟨sweat⟩

Aus·scheidung die **(a)** (Physiol.)
▶ AUSSCHEIDEN 2: excretion; elimination; expulsion; exudation; **~en** (Ausgeschiedenes) excreta
(b) (Sport) qualifier

aus|schenken tr. V. serve

aus|scheren itr. V.; mit sein pull out

aus|schildern tr. V. signpost

aus|schimpfen tr. V. **jmdn. ~:** tell sb. off

aus|schlachten tr. V. **(a)** (ugs.: brauchbare Teile ausbauen aus) cannibalize ⟨machine, vehicle⟩; break ⟨vehicle⟩ for spares
(b) (ugs. abwertend: ausnutzen) exploit; **etw. politisch ~:** make political capital out of sth.

aus|schlafen 1 unr. itr., refl. V. have a good sleep
2 unr. tr. V. **seinen Rausch ~:** sleep off the effects of alcohol

Aus·schlag der **(a)** (Hautausschlag) rash
(b) (eines Zeigers, einer Waage) deflection; (eines Pendels) swing; **den ~ geben** (fig.) tip the scales (fig.)

aus|schlagen 1 unr. tr. V. **(a)** knock out
(b) (ablehnen) turn down
2 unr. itr. V. **(a)** ⟨horse⟩ kick
(b) ⟨needle, pointer⟩ be deflected, swing
(c) (sprießen) come out [in bud]

ausschlag·gebend Adj. decisive

aus|schließen unr. tr. V. **(a)** (ausstoßen) expel (**aus** from)
(b) (nicht teilnehmen lassen) exclude (**aus** from)
(c) (fig.) rule out ⟨possibility⟩; **jeden Irrtum ~:** rule out all possibility of error
(d) (aussperren) lock out

aus·schließlich /od. '·'--, '·'--/ 1 Adj. exclusive
2 Adv. exclusively
3 Präp. mit Gen. excluding

Ausschließlichkeit *die;* ~:
exclusiveness

Aus·schluss, *Aus·schluß *der*
exclusion (**von** from); (aus einer Gemeinschaft)
expulsion (**aus** from); **unter** ~ **der**
Öffentlichkeit with the public excluded;
(Rechtsw.) in camera

aus|schmücken *tr. V.* deck out

aus|schneiden *unr. tr. V.* cut out; (DV)
cut

Aus·schnitt *der* (a) (Zeitungsausschnitt)
cutting; clipping
(b) (Halsausschnitt) neck; **ein tiefer** ~: a
plunging neckline
(c) (Teil) part; (eines Textes) excerpt; (eines
Films) clip; (Bildausschnitt) detail

aus|schreiben *unr. tr. V.* (a) (nicht
abgekürzt schreiben) **etw.** ~: write sth. out in
full
(b) (ausstellen) make out ⟨*cheque, invoice,
receipt*⟩
(c) (bekannt geben) call ⟨*election, meeting*⟩;
advertise ⟨*flat, job*⟩; put ⟨*supply order etc.*⟩
out to tender

Aus·schreibung *die* ▶ AUSSCHREIBEN C:
calling; advertisement; invitation to tender

Ausschreitungen *Pl.* acts of violence

Aus·schuss, *Aus·schuß *der*
committee

aus|schütten *tr. V.* tip out ⟨*water, sand,
coal, etc.*⟩; (ausleeren) empty ⟨*bucket, bowl,
container*⟩

ausschweifend [1] *Adj.* wild
⟨*imagination, emotion, hope, desire, orgy*⟩;
extravagant ⟨*idea*⟩; riotous, wild ⟨*enjoyment*⟩;
dissolute ⟨*life, person*⟩
[2] *adv.* ~ **leben** lead a dissolute life

Ausschweifung *die;* ~, ~**en** (im Genießen)
dissolution

aus|sehen *unr. itr. V.* look (**wie** like); **so**
siehst du aus! (ugs.) that's what you think!

Aussehen *das;* ~**s** appearance

*aus|sein *unr. itr. V.; mit sein; nur im Inf.*
und Part. zusammengeschrieben (a) ⟨*play,
film, war*⟩ be over; **wann ist die Vorstellung**
aus? what time does the performance end?;
die Schule ist aus school is out
(b) ⟨*fire, candle, etc.*⟩ be out
(c) ⟨*radio, light, etc.*⟩ be off

außen *Adv.* outside; **die Vase ist** ~ **bemalt**
the vase is painted on the outside; **das**
Fenster geht nach ~ **auf** the window opens
outwards; **von** ~: from the outside

außen-, Außen-: ~**dienst** *der:* **im**
~**dienst sein** *od.* **arbeiten,** ~**dienst machen**
od. **haben** be working out of the office;
⟨*salesman*⟩ be on the road; ~**handel** *der*
foreign trade *no art.;* ~**handels·bilanz**
die balance of trade; ~**minister** *der,*
~**ministerin** *die* Foreign Minister;
~**ministerium** *das* Foreign Ministry;
~**politik** *die* foreign politics *sing.;*

~**politisch** [1] *Adj.* ⟨*question*⟩ relating to
foreign policy; [2] *adv.* as regards foreign
policy; ~**seite** *die* outside

Außenseiter *der;* ~**s,** ~,
Außenseiterin *die;* ~, ~**nen** outsider

Außen: ~**spiegel** *der* exterior mirror;
~**stände** *Pl.* outstanding debts *or*
accounts; ~**wand** *die* external *or* outside
wall; ~**welt** *die* outside world

außer [1] *Präp. mit Dat.* (a) (abgesehen von)
apart from; aside from (Amer.)
(b) (außerhalb von) out of; ~ **sich sein** be
beside oneself (**vor** + *Dat.* with)
(c) (zusätzlich zu) in addition to
[2] *Präp. mit Akk.* ~ **sich geraten** become
beside oneself (**vor** + *Dat.* with)
[3] *Konj.* except

äußer... *Adj.* outer; outside ⟨*pocket*⟩;
outlying ⟨*district, area*⟩; external ⟨*injury,
form, circumstances, cause, force*⟩; outward
⟨*appearance, similarity, effect, etc.*⟩; foreign
⟨*affairs*⟩

außer·dem /auch: --'--/ *Adv.* as well;
(überdies) besides

Äußere *das; adj. Dekl.* [outward]
appearance

außer-: ~**ehelich** [1] *Adj.* extra-marital;
illegitimate ⟨*child, birth*⟩; [2] *adv.* outside
marriage; ~**gewöhnlich** [1] *Adj.* (a)
unusual; (b) (das Gewohnte übertreffend)
exceptional; [2] *adv.* (a) unusually; (b) (sehr)
exceptionally; ~**halb** *Präp. mit Gen.*
outside

äußerlich [1] *Adj.* external ⟨*use, injury*⟩;
outward ⟨*appearance, calm, similarity, etc.*⟩
[2] *adv.: s. Adj.:* externally; outwardly

Äußerlichkeit *die;* ~, ~**en** formality;
(Unwesentliches) minor point

äußern [1] *tr. V.* express, voice ⟨*opinion,
view, criticism, reservations, disapproval,
doubt*⟩; express ⟨*wish*⟩; voice ⟨*suspicion*⟩
[2] *refl. V.* (a) **sich über etw.** (*Akk.*) ~: give
one's view on sth.
(b) ⟨*illness*⟩ manifest itself (**in** + *Dat.,* **durch**
in)

außer-: ~**ordentlich** [1] *Adj.* (a)
extraordinary; (b) (das Gewohnte übertreffend)
exceptional; [2] *adv.* (sehr) exceptionally;
extremely ⟨*pleased, relieved*⟩; ~**schulisch**
Adj. outside the school *postpos.*

äußerst *Adv.* extremely

äußerst... *Adj.* (a) extreme ⟨*date,
deadline*⟩; (höchst...) highest ⟨*price*⟩; (niedrigst...)
lowest ⟨*price*⟩
(c) (schlimmst...) worst

außerstande *Adv.* ~ **sein, etw. zu tun**
(nicht befähigt) be unable to do sth.; (nicht in der
Lage) not be in a position to do sth.

Äußerung *die;* ~, ~**en** comment

aus|setzen [1] *tr. V.* (a) expose (*Dat.* to);
Belastungen ausgesetzt sein be subject to
strains

(b) (sich selbst überlassen) abandon ⟨baby, animal⟩; (auf einer einsamen Insel) maroon
(c) an jmdm./etw. etwas auszusetzen haben find fault with sb./sth.
2 itr. V. **(a)** (aufhören) stop; ⟨engine, machine⟩ cut out
(b) (pausieren) ⟨player⟩ miss a turn; **mit der Arbeit/dem Training [ein paar Wochen] ~:** stop work/training [for a few weeks]
Aus·sicht die **(a)** view (auf + Akk. of)
(b) (fig.) prospect; **~ auf etw. (Akk.) haben, etw. in ~ haben** have the prospect of sth.

aussichts-, Aussichts-: ~los 1 Adj. hopeless; 2 adv. hopelessly; **~losigkeit** die; ~~: hopelessness; **~punkt** der vantage point; **~reich** Adj. promising; **~turm** der lookout tower

Aus·siedler der (Auswanderer) emigrant; (Evakuierter) evacuee; (Umsiedler) resettled person

Aussiedler·heim das resettlement hostel (for German nationals and ethnic Germans from Eastern europe)
Aussiedlerin die ▶ AUSSIEDLER
aus|sortieren tr. V. sort out
aus|spannen tr. V. take or have a break
aus|sparen tr. V. leave ⟨line etc.⟩ blank; (fig.) leave out; omit
Aussparung die; ~, ~en **(a)** (das Aussparen) leaving blank
(b) (Stelle) gap
aus|sperren 1 tr. V. lock out; shut ⟨animal⟩ out
2 itr. V. lock the workforce out
Aus·sperrung die lockout
aus|spielen tr. V. **(a)** auch itr. (Kartenspiel) lead
(b) jmdn./etw. gegen jmdn./etw. ~: play sb./ sth. off against sb./sth.
Aus·sprache die **(a)** pronunciation
(b) (Gespräch) discussion
aus|sprechen 1 unr. tr. V. **(a)** pronounce
(b) (ausdrücken) express; voice ⟨suspicion, request⟩
2 unr. refl. V. **(a)** sich lobend/missbilligend usw. über jmdn./etw. ~: speak highly/ disapprovingly of etc. sb./sth.
(b) (offen sprechen) say what's on one's mind; **sich bei jmdm. ~:** have a heart-to-heart talk with sb.
(c) (Strittiges klären) talk things out (mit with)
3 unr. itr. V. (zu Ende sprechen) finish [speaking]
Aus·spruch der remark
aus|spucken 1 itr. V. spit
2 tr. V. spit out
aus|spülen tr. V. rinse out
Aus·stand der strike
aus|statten /ˈausˌʃtatn̩/ tr. V. provide (mit with); (mit Gerät) equip; (mit Möbeln, Teppichen, Gardinen usw.) furnish

Ausstattung die; ~, ~en **(a)** ▶ AUSSTATTEN provision; equipping; furnishing
(b) (Ausrüstung) equipment; (Innenausstattung eines Autos) trim
(c) (Einrichtung) furnishings pl.
aus|stehen 1 unr. itr. V. **noch ~** ⟨debt⟩ be outstanding; ⟨decision⟩ be still to be taken; ⟨solution⟩ be still to be found
2 unr. tr. V. **ich kann ihn/das nicht ~:** I can't stand him/it
aus|steigen unr. itr. V.; **(a)** mit sein get out; (aus einem Zug, Bus) get off
(b) (ugs.: sich nicht mehr beteiligen) **~ aus** opt out of; give up ⟨show business, job⟩; leave ⟨project⟩
(c) (ugs.: der Gesellschaft den Rücken kehren) drop out
Aussteiger der; ~s, ~, **Aussteigerin** die; ~, ~nen (ugs.) dropout (coll.)
aus|stellen tr. V. **(a)** put on display; display; (im Museum, auf einer Messe) exhibit
(b) (ausfertigen) make out ⟨cheque, prescription, receipt, bill⟩; issue ⟨visa, passport, certificate⟩; **einen Scheck auf jmdn. ~:** make out a cheque to sb.
(c) (ugs.: ausschalten) switch off ⟨cooker, radio, heating, engine⟩
Aus·stellung die **(a)** exhibition
(b) ▶ AUSSTELLEN B: making out; issuing
Ausstellungs-: ~gelände das exhibition site; **~katalog** der exhibition catalogue
aus|sterben unr. itr. V.; mit sein die out; ⟨species⟩ become extinct; **vom Aussterben bedroht sein** be threatened with extinction
Aus·steuer die trousseau (consisting mainly of household linen)
Aus·stieg der; ~[e]s, ~e **(a)** exit
(b) (ugs.) opting out (aus of); **der ~ aus einem Projekt/aus der Atomenergie** leaving a project/abandoning nuclear energy
aus|stopfen tr. V. stuff
Aus·stoß der (Wirtsch.) output
aus|stoßen unr. tr. V. **(a)** expel; give off, emit ⟨gas, fumes, smoke⟩
(b) give ⟨cry, whistle, laugh, sigh, etc.⟩; let out ⟨cry, scream, yell⟩; utter ⟨curse, threat, etc.⟩
aus|strahlen 1 tr. V. **(a)** (auch fig.) radiate; ⟨lamp⟩ give out ⟨light⟩
(b) (Rundf., Ferns.) broadcast
2 itr. V. **(a)** (radiate; ⟨light⟩ be given out; (fig.) ⟨pain⟩ spread
(b) auf jmdn./etw. ~ (fig.) communicate itself to sb./influence sth.
Aus·strahlung die (fig.) charisma
aus|strecken 1 tr. V. stretch out; put out ⟨feelers⟩
2 refl. V. stretch out
aus|streichen unr. tr. V. cross out
aus|strömen itr. V.; mit sein pour out; ⟨gas, steam⟩ escape

aus|suchen *tr. V.* choose; pick

Aus-tausch *der* (a) exchange; **im ~ für** *od.* **gegen** in exchange for
(b) (das Ersetzen) replacement (**gegen** with)

aus|tauschen *tr. V.* (a) exchange (**gegen** for)
(b) (ersetzen) replace (**gegen** with)

Austausch-: **~motor** *der* replacement engine; **~schüler** *der*, **~schülerin** *die* exchange pupil *or* student

aus|teilen *tr. V.* distribute (**an** + *Akk.* to); (aushändigen) hand out ⟨*books, post, etc.*⟩ (**an** + *Akk.* to); give ⟨*orders*⟩; deal [out] ⟨*cards*⟩; give out ⟨*marks, grades*⟩; serve ⟨*food etc.*⟩

Auster *die;* **~,** **~n** oyster

aus|tragen *unr. tr. V.* (a) deliver ⟨*newspapers, post*⟩
(b) ⟨*pregnant woman*⟩ carry ⟨*child*⟩ to full term; (nicht abtreiben) have ⟨*child*⟩
(c) (ausfechten) settle ⟨*conflict, differences*⟩; fight out ⟨*battle*⟩

Australien /au:sˈtraːliən/ *(das);* **~s** Australia

Australier *der;* **~s,** **~,** **Australierin** *die;* **~,** **~nen** Australian

australisch *Adj.* Australian

aus|treiben *unr. tr. V.* (a) exorcize, cast out ⟨*evil spirit, demon*⟩
(b) jmdm. etw. **~:** cure sb. of sth.

aus|treten ① *unr. tr. V.* (a) tread out ⟨*spark, cigarette end*⟩; trample out ⟨*fire*⟩
(b) (bahnen) tread out ⟨*path*⟩
(c) wear out ⟨*shoes*⟩
② *unr. itr. V.; mit sein* (a) (ugs.: zur Toilette gehen) pay a call (coll.)
(b) aus etw. **~** (ausscheiden) leave sth.

aus|trinken *tr. V.* drink up ⟨*drink*⟩; finish ⟨*glass, cup, etc.*⟩

Aus-tritt *der* leaving

aus|trocknen ① *tr. V.* dry out; dry up ⟨*river bed, marsh*⟩
② *itr. V.; mit sein* dry out; ⟨*river bed, pond, etc.*⟩ dry up; ⟨*skin, hair*⟩ become dry

aus|üben *tr. V.* practise ⟨*art, craft*⟩; follow ⟨*profession*⟩; carry on ⟨*trade*⟩; do ⟨*job*⟩; hold ⟨*office*⟩; wield ⟨*power, right, control*⟩

Aus-verkauf *der* sale

ausverkauft *Adj.* sold out

Aus-wahl *die* (a) choice
(b) (Sortiment) range; **viel/wenig ~ haben** have a wide/limited selection (**an** + *Dat.*, **von** of)

aus|wählen *tr. V.* choose (**aus** from)

Aus-wanderer *der*, **Aus-wanderin** *die* emigrant

aus|wandern *itr. V.; mit sein* emigrate

Aus-wanderung *die* emigration

auswärtig *Adj.* (a) non-local
(b) (das Ausland betreffend) foreign

auswärts *Adv.* (a) (nach außen) outwards

(b) (nicht zu Hause) ⟨*sleep*⟩ away from home; **~ essen** eat out
(c) (nicht am Ort) in another town; (Sport) away

Auswärts-spiel *das* (Sport) away match

aus|waschen *unr. tr. V.* wash out

aus|wechseln *tr. V.* (a) change (**gegen** + *Akk.* for)
(b) (ersetzen) replace (**gegen** with); (Sport) substitute ⟨*player*⟩

Aus-weg *der* way out (**aus** of)

ausweg-los ① *Adj.* hopeless
② *adv.* hopelessly

Ausweglosigkeit *die;* **~:** hopelessness

aus|weichen *unr. itr. V.; mit sein* get out of the way (*Dat.* of); (Platz machen) make way (*Dat.* for); **einem Schlag/Angriff ~:** dodge a blow/evade an attack; **dem Feind ~:** avoid [contact with] the enemy; **einer Frage ~:** evade a question; **eine ~de Antwort** an evasive answer

Ausweich-manöver *das* evasive manœuvre

aus|weinen *refl. V.* have a good cry; **sie hat sich bei mir darüber ausgeweint** (ugs.) she had a good cry on my shoulder about it

Ausweis *der;* **~es,** **~e** card; (Personalausweis) identity card

aus|weisen ① *unr. tr. V.* (a) expel (**aus** from)
(b) jmdn. als etw. **~:** show that sb. is/was sth.
② *unr. refl. V.* prove *or* establish one's identity [by showing one's papers]; **können Sie sich ~?** do you have any means of identification?

Ausweis-papiere *Pl.* identity papers

Aus-weisung *die* expulsion (**aus** from)

aus|weiten *tr. V.* stretch

aus-wendig *Adv.* etw. **~ können/lernen** know/learn sth. [off] by heart

aus|werfen *unr. tr. V.* (a) cast ⟨*net, anchor, rope, line, etc.*⟩
(b) (herausschleudern) throw out ⟨*sparks*⟩; ⟨*volcano*⟩ eject, spew out ⟨*lava, ash, etc.*⟩; eject ⟨*cartridge case*⟩

aus|werten *tr. V.* analyse and evaluate

Aus-wertung *die* analysis and evaluation

aus|wirken *refl. V.* have an effect (**auf** + *Akk.* on); **sich günstig ~:** have a favourable effect

Aus-wirkung *die* effect (**auf** + *Akk.* on)

Aus-wuchs *der* (a) (Wucherung) growth; excrescence (Med., Bot.)
(b) (fig.) unhealthy product; (Exzess) excess

aus|wuchten *tr. V.* (Technik) **die Räder ~:** balance the wheels

aus|zahlen ① *tr. V.* (a) pay out ⟨*money*⟩
(b) pay off ⟨*employee, worker*⟩; buy out ⟨*business partner*⟩
② *refl. V.* pay

aus|zählen *tr. V.* (a) count [up] ⟨*votes etc.*⟩
(b) (Boxen) count out

---

*alte Schreibung - vgl. Hinweis auf S. xiv

aus|zeichnen *tr. V.* **(a)** (mit einem Preisschild) mark
(b) (ehren) honour

Aus·zeichnung *die* **(a)** (von Waren) marking
(b) (Ehrung) honouring; (Orden) decoration; (Preis) award

aus|ziehen 1 *unr. tr. V.* **(a)** pull out ‹couch›; extend ‹table, tripod, etc.›
(b) (ablegen) take off ‹clothes›
(c) (entkleiden) undress; **sich ~:** get undressed
2 *unr. itr. V.; mit sein* move out (**aus** of)

Auszubildende *der/die; adj. Dekl.* (bes. Amtsspr.) trainee; (im Handwerk) apprentice

Aus·zug *der* **(a)** (das Ausziehen) move
(b) (Bankw.) statement
(c) (Textpassage) extract

auszugs·weise *Adv.* in extracts *or* excerpts; etw. ~ lesen read extracts from sth.

authentisch *Adj.* authentic

Autist *der; ~en, ~en,* **Autistin** *die; ~, ~nen* autistic

autistisch *Adj.* (Med.) autistic

Auto *das; ~s, ~s* car; automobile (Amer.); ~ fahren drive; (mitfahren) go in the car

auto-, Auto-: ~**bahn** *die* motorway (Brit.); expressway (Amer.); ~**biografie** /-----'-/ *die* autobiography; ~**biografisch** /----'--/ *Adj.* autobiographical; ~**bombe** *die* car bomb; ~**bus** *der* ▶ BUS; ~**dieb** *der,* ~**diebin** *die* car thief; ~**fähre** *die* car ferry; ~**fahren** *das;* ~~*s* driving; motoring; ~**fahrer** *der,* ~**fahrerin** *die* [car] driver; ~**fahrt** *die* drive; ~**gramm** /-·-'-/ *das;* ~~*s,* ~~*e* autograph; ~**kino** *das* drive-in cinema

Automat *der; ~en, ~en* **(a)** (Verkaufs~) [vending] machine; (Spiel~) slot machine
(b) (in der Produktion) robot

Automatik *die; ~, ~en* automatic control mechanism; (Getriebeautomatik) automatic transmission

automatisch (auch fig.) 1 *Adj.* automatic
2 *adv.* automatically

automatisieren *tr. V.* automate

Automatisierung *die; ~, ~en* automation

auto-, Auto-: ~**mobil** /---'-/ *das;* ~~*s,* ~~*e* (geh.) motor car; automobile (Amer.); ~**nom** /--'-/ 1 *Adj.* autonomous; 2 *adv.* autonomously; ~**nomie** /---'-/ *die;* ~~, ~~*n* autonomy; ~**nummer** *die* [car] registration number; ~**pilot** *der* (Flugw.) autopilot

Autopsie /auto'psi:/ *die; ~, ~n* post mortem [examination]

Autor *der; ~s, ~en* author

Auto-: ~**radio** *das* car radio; ~**reifen** *der* car tyre; ~**reise-zug** *der* Motorail train (Brit.); auto train (Amer.); ~**reparatur** *die* car repair; repair to the/a car

Autorin *die; ~, ~nen* authoress; author

autoritär *Adj.* authoritarian

Autorität *die; ~, ~en* authority

Auto-: ~**schalter** *der* drive-in counter; ~**schlange** *die* queue of cars; ~**schlüssel** *der* car key; ~**skooter** /-sku:tɐ/ *der;* ~~*s,* ~~: dodgem; bumper car; ~**stopp** *der* hitch-hiking; per ~stopp fahren, ~stopp machen hitch-hike; ~**telefon** *das* car telephone; ~**tür** *die* car door; ~**unfall** *der* car accident; ~**vermietung** *die* car rental firm; ~**wäsche** *die* car wash; ~**werkstatt** *die* garage

Avocado /avo'ka:do/ *die; ~, ~s* avocado [pear]

Axt *die; ~,* Äxte axe

Azalee /ats:a'le:ə/ *die; ~, ~n* azalea

Azubi *der; ~s, ~s/die; ~, ~s* (ugs.)
▶ AUSZUBILDENDE

Bb

b, B /beː/ *das;* ~, ~ (a) (Buchstabe) b/B
(b) (Musik) [key of] B flat

B *Abk.* = **Bundesstraße** ≈ A (Brit.)

Baby /'beːbi/ *das;* ~s, ~s baby

Baby·sitter /'beːbisɪtɐ/ *der;* ~s, ~;
Baby·sitterin *die;* ~, ~: babysitter

Bach *der;* ~[e]s, Bäche (a) stream; brook
(b) (Rinnsal) stream [of water]

Back·blech *das* baking sheet

Back·bord *das* (Seew., Luftf.) port [side]

Backe *die;* ~, ~n cheek

backen ① *unr. itr. V.* bake
② *unr. tr. V.* (a) bake
(b) (bes. südd.) ▶ BRATEN

Backen·zahn *der* molar

Bäcker *der;* ~s, ~: baker; er ist ~: he is a
baker; zum/beim ~: to the/at the baker's

Bäckerei *die;* ~, ~en baker's [shop]

Bäckerin *die;* ~, ~nen baker

Back-: ~**fisch** *der* fried fish (*in
breadcrumbs*); ~**form** *die* baking tin (Brit.);
baking pan (Amer.); ~**hähnchen** *das,*
~**hen** *das* (österr.), ~**huhn** *das* fried
chicken (*in breadcrumbs*); ~**ofen** *der* oven;
~**pulver** *das* baking powder; ~**stein** *der*
brick; ~**waren** *Pl.* bread, cakes, and
pastries

Bad *das;* ~[e]s, Bäder (a) bath; (das
Schwimmen) swim; (im Meer usw.) bathe; ein ~
nehmen (geh.) take a bath; (schwimmen) go for
a swim; (im Meer usw.) bathe
(b) (Badezimmer) bathroom; ein Zimmer mit ~:
a room with [private] bath
(c) (Schwimm~) [swimming] pool
(d) (Heil~) spa; (See~) [seaside] resort

Bade-: ~**anzug** *der* bathing costume;
~**hose** *die* bathing trunks *pl;* ~**mantel**
der dressing gown; bathrobe; ~**meister**
der, ~**meisterin** *die* swimming-pool
attendant; ~**mütze** *die* bathing cap

baden ① *itr. V.* (a) have a bath
(b) (schwimmen) bathe; ~ gehen go for a
bathe
② *tr. V.* bath ‹*child, patient, etc.*›; bathe
‹*wound, eye, etc.*›

Baden-Württemberg (*das*); ~s Baden-
Württemberg

Bäder ▶ BAD

Bade-: ~**strand** *der* bathing beach;
~**tuch** *das; Pl.* ~**tücher** bath towel;
~**wanne** *die* bath[tub]; ~**wasser** *das*
bath water; ~**zimmer** *das* bathroom

Badminton *das;* ~s badminton

*old spelling - see note on page xiv

Bagatelle *die;* ~, ~n trifle

Bagger *der;* ~s, ~: excavator;
(Schwimmbagger) dredger

Bagger·see *der* flooded gravel pit

Bahn *die;* ~, ~en (a) (Weg) path
(b) (Route) path; (eines Geschosses) trajectory
(c) (Sport) track; (für Pferderennen) course (Brit.);
track (Amer.); (für einzelne Teilnehmer) lane;
(Kegel~) alley; (Bowling~) lane
(d) (Eisen~) railways *pl.;* railroad (Amer.);
(Zug) train; jmdn. zur ~ bringen take sb. to
the station; [mit der] ~ fahren go by train
(e) (Straßen~) tram; streetcar (Amer.)

bahn-, Bahn-: ~**beamte** *der,*
~**beamtin** *die* railway or (Amer.) railroad
official; ~**brechend** *Adj.* pioneering;
~**brecher** *der,* ~**brecherin** *die;* ~~,
~~nen pioneer; ~**bus** *der* railway bus;
~**damm** *der* railway embankment

bahnen *tr. V.* clear ‹*way, path*›; jmdm./einer
Sache einen Weg ~ (fig.) pave the way for
sb./sth.

Bahn-: ~**fahrt** *die* train journey; ~**hof**
der [railway or (Amer.) railroad] station;
~**reise** *die* train journey; ~**schranke**
die level crossing (Brit.) or (Amer.) grade
crossing barrier/gate; ~**steig** *der;* ~~[e]s,
~~e [station] platform; ~**übergang** *der*
level crossing (Brit.); grade crossing (Amer.);
~**verbindung** *die* train connection

Bahre *die;* ~, ~n (a) (Trage) stretcher
(b) (Totenbahre) bier

Baiser /bɛ'zeː/ *das;* ~s, ~s meringue

Bajonett *das;* ~[e]s, ~e bayonet

Bakterie /bak'teːriə/ *die;* ~, ~n bacterium

Balance /ba'laŋsə/ *die;* ~, ~n balance

balancieren *itr., tr. V.; itr. mit sein*
balance

bald *Adv.* (a) soon; (leicht, rasch) quickly;
easily; wirds ~? get a move on, will you; bis
~! see you soon
(b) (ugs.: fast) almost

Baldrian /'baldriaːn/ *der;* ~s, ~e valerian

Balkan /'balkaːn/ *der;* ~s: der ~: the
Balkans *pl.;* (Gebirge) the Balkan Mountains
pl. auf dem ~: in the Balkans

Balken *der;* ~s, ~: beam

Balkon /bal'koːn/ *der;* ~s, ~s
/bal'kɔns/ *od.* ~e /bal'koːnə/ (a) balcony
(b) (im Theater, Kino) circle

Ball *der;* ~[e]s, Bälle (a) ball; ~ spielen play
ball
(b) (Fest) ball

Ballade *die;* ~, ~n ballad

Ballast *der;* ~[e]s, ~e ballast

Ballast·stoffe *Pl.* (Med.) roughage *sing.*
ballen ⎡1⎤ *tr. V.* clench ⟨*fist*⟩
⎡2⎤ *refl. V.* ⟨*fist*⟩ clench
Ballen *der;* ~s, ~ (a) (Packen) bale
(b) (Hand-, Fußballen) ball
Ballerina *die;* ~, Ballerinen ballerina
Ballett *das;* ~[e]s, ~e ballet
Ballett-: ~**schuh** *der* ballet shoe;
~**schule** *die* ballet school; ~**tänzer** *der,*
~**tänzerin** *die* ballet dancer
Ball-: ~**junge** *der* ballboy; ~**kleid** *das*
ball gown
Ballon /baˈlɔŋ/ *der;* ~s, ~s balloon
Ball-: ~**saal** *der* ballroom; ~**spiel** *das*
ball game; ~**spielen** *das;* ~~s playing
ball *no art.*
Ballungs·gebiet *das* conurbation
Balsam *der;* ~s, ~e balsam; (fig.) balm
Balte *der;* ~n, ~n, **Baltin** *die;* ~, ~nen
Balt
Baltikum *das;* ~s Baltic States *pl.*
baltisch *Adj.* Baltic
Bambus *der;* ~ *od.* ~ses, ~se bamboo
banal *Adj.* (a) banal
(b) (gewöhnlich) commonplace
Banane *die;* ~, ~n banana
Banause *der;* ~n, ~n, **Banausin** *die;* ~,
~nen (abwertend) philistine
band *1. u. 3. Pers. Sg. Prät. v.* BINDEN
Band¹ *das;* ~[e]s, Bänder (a) ribbon;
(Haar~, Hut~) band; (Schürzen~) string
(b) (Klebe~, Isolier~, Ton~ usw.) tape; *etw. auf*
~ (*Akk.*) **aufnehmen** tape[-record] sth.
(c) ▸ FÖRDERBAND;
(d) ▸ FLIESSBAND;
(e) am laufenden ~ (ugs.) nonstop
(f) (Anat.) ligament
Band² *der;* ~[e]s, Bände /ˈbɛndə/ volume
Band³ /bɛnt/ *die;* ~, ~s band; (Beat~,
Rock~ usw.) group
Bande¹ *die;* ~, ~n (a) gang
(b) (ugs.: Gruppe) mob (coll.)
Bande² *die;* ~, ~n (Sport) [perimeter]
barrier; (mit Reklame) billboards *pl.;* (Billard)
cushion
Banden-: ~**krieg** *der* gang war;
~**werbung** *die:* advertising on hoardings
around the perimeter of a football pitch etc.
Bänder ▸ BAND¹
Bänder-: ~**riss,** ***~**riß** *der* (Med.) torn
ligament; ~**zerrung** *die* (Med.) pulled
ligament
bändigen *tr. V.* tame ⟨*animal*⟩; control
⟨*person, anger, urge*⟩
Bandit *der;* ~en, ~en bandit
Band·scheibe *die* [intervertebral] disc
bang, bange; banger, bangst... *od.*
bänger, bängst...: ⎡1⎤ *Adj.* afraid; scared;
(besorgt) anxious; **mir ist/wurde** ~ **[zumute]** I
am/became scared
⎡2⎤ *adv.* anxiously
bangen *itr. V.* be anxious

Bank¹ *die;* ~, Bänke bench; (mit Lehne)
bench seat; (Kirchen~) pew; *etw.* **auf die lange**
~ **schieben** (ugs.) put sth. off
Bank² *die;* ~, ~en bank
Bankett¹ *das;* ~[e]s, ~e banquet
Bankett² *das;* ~[e]s, ~e (an Straßen)
shoulder; (unbefestigt) verge
Bank·geheimnis *das* (Wirtsch.) bankers'
duty to maintain confidentiality
Bankier /banˈkie:/ *der;* ~s, ~s banker
Bank-: ~**kauffrau** *die,* ~**kaufmann**
der [qualified] bank/building society/stock
market clerk; ~**konto** *das* bank account;
~**leit·zahl** *die* [bank] sort code; ~**note**
die banknote; bill (Amer.); ~**raub** *der* bank
robbery; ~**räuber** *der,* ~**räuberin** *die*
bank robber
bankrott *Adj.* bankrupt; **Bankrott** *od.* ***~
gehen go bankrupt
Bankrott *der;* ~[e]s, ~e bankruptcy; ~
machen go bankrupt; *s. auch* BANKROTT
Bankrott·erklärung *die* declaration of
bankruptcy; (fig.) declaration of [one's own]
failure
Bank-: ~**überfall** *der* bank raid;
~**verbindung** *die* particulars of one's
bank account; ~**wesen** *das* banking
system
Bann *der;* ~[e]s (fig. geh.) spell
bar ⎡1⎤ *Adj.* cash
⎡2⎤ *adv.* in cash; *etw.* **[in]** ~ **bezahlen** pay for
sth. in cash; pay cash for sth.
Bar *die;* ~, ~s bar
Bär *der;* ~en, ~en bear
Baracke *die;* ~, ~n hut
Barbar *der;* ~en, ~en barbarian
Barbarei *die;* ~, ~en (a) (Rohheit)
barbarity
(b) (Kulturlosigkeit) barbarism *no indef. art.*
Barbarin *die;* ~, ~nen barbarian
barbarisch ⎡1⎤ *Adj.* (a) (roh) barbarous
(b) (unzivilisiert) barbaric
⎡2⎤ *adv.* (a) (roh) barbarously
(b) (unzivilisiert) barbarically
Bar·dame *die* barmaid
bären-, Bären-: ~**dienst** *der:* jmdm.
einen ~**dienst** erweisen do sb. a disservice;
~**hunger** *der* (ugs.) einen ~**hunger haben/**
kriegen be famished (coll.) *or* starving (coll.)/
get famished (coll.) *or* ravenous (coll.);
~**stark** *Adj.* as strong as an ox *postpos.*
Barett *das;* ~[e]s, ~e (eines Geistlichen)
biretta; (eines Richters, Professors) cap;
(Baskenmütze) beret
bar·fuß *indekl. Adj.; nicht attr.* barefooted;
~ **herumlaufen/gehen** run about/go barefoot
barg *1. u. 3. Pers. Sg. Prät. v.* BERGEN
bar-, Bar-: ~**geld** *das* cash; ~**geld·los**
Adj. cashless; ~**hocker** *der* bar stool
Bariton /ˈba(:)ritɔn/ *der;* ~s, ~e baritone
Barkasse *die;* ~, ~n launch
barmherzig (geh.) ⎡1⎤ *Adj.* merciful ····⊱

b

2 *adv.* mercifully

Barmherzigkeit *die;* ~ (geh.) mercy

Barock *das od. der;* ~[s] (a) baroque
(b) (Zeit) baroque age

Baro·meter *das* barometer

Baron *der;* ~s, ~e baron; (als Anrede) [Herr]
~: ≈ my lord

Baronin *die;* ~, ~nen baroness; (als Anrede)
[Frau] ~: ≈ my Lady

Barren *der;* ~s, ~ (a) (Gold~, Silber~ usw.)
bar
(b) (Turngerät) parallel bars *pl.*

Barriere /baˈriɛːrə/ *die;* ~, ~n (auch fig.)
barrier

Barrikade *die;* ~, ~n barricade

barsch **1** *Adj.* curt
2 *adv.* curtly

Barsch *der;* ~[e]s, ~e perch

barst 1. u. 3. Pers. Sg. Prät. v. BERSTEN

Bart *der;* ~[e]s, Bärte (a) beard; (Oberlippen~,
Schnurr~) moustache
(b) (von Katzen, Mäusen, Robben) whiskers *pl.;*
(c) (am Schlüssel) bit

Barten·wal *der* (Zool.) whalebone whale

bärtig *Adj.* bearded

Bart·wuchs *der* growth of beard

Bar-: ~zahlung *die* cash payment;
~zahlungs·rabatt *der* cash discount

Basalt *der;* ~[e]s, ~e basalt

Basar *der;* ~s, ~e bazaar

Basis *die;* ~, Basen (a) (Grundlage) basis
(b) (Math., Archit., Milit.) base

Baske *der;* ~n, ~n Basque

Basken-: ~land *das* Basque region;
~mütze *die* beret

Baskin *die;* ~, ~nen Basque

Basket·ball /ˈbaː(ː)skət-/ *der* basketball

Bass, *Baß *der;* Basses, Bässe (Musik) (a)
bass
(b) (Instrument) double bass

Bassin /baˈsɛː/ *das;* ~s, ~s (Schwimmbecken)
pool; (im Garten) pond

Bassist *der;* ~en, ~en (Musik) (a) (Sänger)
bass
(b) (Instrumentalist) double-bass player; bassist;
(in einer Rockband) bass guitarist

Bassistin *die;* ~, ~nen ▶ BASSIST B

Bast *der;* ~[e]s, ~e bast; (Raffia~) raffia

basta *Interj.* (ugs.) that's enough; und damit
~! and that's that!

Bastelei *die;* ~, ~en; (a) (Gegenstand) piece
of handicraft work
(b) (ugs.: das Basteln) handicraft work

basteln **1** *tr. V.* make
2 *itr. V.* make things [with one's hands]

Bastion *die;* ~, ~en bastion

bat 1. u. 3. Pers. Sg. Prät. v. BITTEN

Bataillon /batalˈjoːn/ *das;* ~s, ~e (Milit.)
battalion

Batik *der;* ~s, ~en od. die; ~, ~en batik ·

Batist *der;* ~[e]s, ~e batiste

Batterie *die;* ~, ~n battery

batterie-, Batterie-: ~betrieb *der*
battery operation; ~betrieben *Adj.*
battery-operated; ~huhn *das* battery
chicken; (Henne) battery hen

Batzen *der;* ~s, ~ (ugs.) (a) (Klumpen) lump
(b) (Menge) pile (coll.)

Bau¹ *der;* ~[e]s, ~ten (a) (Errichtung)
building; im ~ sein be under construction
(b) (Gebäude) building
(c) auf dem ~ arbeiten (Bauarbeiter sein) be in
the building trade
(d) (Struktur) structure

Bau² *der;* ~[e]s, ~e (Kaninchenbau) burrow;
hole; (Fuchsbau) earth

Bau·arbeiten *Pl.* building work *sing.*

Bauch *der;* ~[e]s, Bäuche (auch fig.: von
Schiffen, Flugzeugen) belly

bauchig *Adj.* bulbous

Bauch-: ~laden *der* vendor's tray;
~landung *die* belly landing; ~nabel *der*
(ugs.) belly button (coll.); ~redner *der,*
~rednerin *die* ventriloquist;
~schmerzen *Pl.* stomach ache *sing.;*
~speichel·drüse *die* pancreas; ~tanz
der belly dance; ~tänzerin *die* belly
dancer; ~weh *das* (ugs.) tummy ache (coll.);
stomach ache

Bau·denkmal *das* architectural
monument

bauen **1** *tr. V.* build
2 *itr. V.* (a) build; wir wollen ~: we want to
build a house; (bauen lassen) we want to have
a house built
(b) auf jmdn./etw. ~ (fig.) rely on sb./sth.

Bauer¹ *der;* ~n, ~n (a) farmer; (mit niedrigem
sozialem Status) peasant
(b) (Schachfigur) pawn
(c) (Kartenspiele) ▶ BUBE

Bauer² *das od. der;* ~s, ~: [bird]cage

Bäuerin *die;* ~, ~nen (a) ▶ BAUER¹ A:
[lady] farmer; peasant [woman]
(b) (Frau eines Bauern) farmer's wife

bäuerlich *Adj.* farming *attrib.;* (ländlich)
rural

Bauern-: ~haus *das* farmhouse; ~hof
der farm

bau-, Bau-: ~fällig *Adj.* ramshackle;
unsafe ⟨roof, ceiling⟩; ~fälligkeit *die* bad
state of dilapidation; badly dilapidated state;
~herr *der,* ~herrin *die* client (*for whom a
house etc. is being built*); ~jahr *das* year of
construction; (bei Autos) year of manufacture;
~kasten *der* construction set; (mit
Holzklötzen) box of bricks;
~kasten·system *das* unit construction
system; ~klotz *der* building brick; ~kran
der construction crane

baulich *Adj.* structural

Baum *der;* ~[e]s, Bäume tree

Bau-: ~markt *der* (Kaufhaus) DIY

hypermarket; ~**maschine** die piece of construction plant or machinery; ~maschinen construction plant sing. or machinery

Bäumchen das; ~s, ~ small tree

Bau·meister der (hist.) [architect and] master builder

baumeln itr. V. (ugs.) dangle (**an** + Dat. from)

Baum-: ~**schule** die tree nursery; ~**stamm** der tree trunk; ~**sterben** das; ~~s, ~~: dying-off of trees; ~**stumpf** der tree stump; ~**wolle** die cotton

Bau·platz der site for building

bäurisch (abwertend) ①Adj. boorish ②adv. boorishly

Bau·satz der kit

Bausch der; ~[e]s, ~e od. **Bäusche** (a) (Watte~) a wad (b) etw. in ~ und Bogen verwerfen/ verdammen reject/condemn sth. wholesale

bauschen ①tr. V. billow ⟨sail, curtains, etc.⟩ ②refl. V. ⟨dress, sleeve⟩ puff out; (ungewollt) bunch up; (im Wind) ⟨curtain, flag, etc.⟩ billow [out]

bauschig Adj. puffed ⟨dress⟩; baggy ⟨trousers⟩

bau-, Bau-: ~**sparen** itr. V.; nur Inf. gebr. save with a building society; ~**sparkasse** die building society; ~**stein** der (a) building stone; (b) (Bestandteil) element; (Elektronik, DV) module; (c) (~klotz) building brick; ~**stelle** die building site; (beim Straßenbau) roadworks pl.; ~**stoff** der building material; ~**teil** das component

Bauten Pl.: ▶ BAU

Bau-: ~**unternehmer** der, ~**unternehmerin** die building contractor; ~**weise** die method of construction; ~**werk** das building; (Brücke, Staudamm) structure; ~**wirtschaft** die building or construction industry

Bayer der; ~n, ~n **Bayerin** die; ~, ~nen Bavarian

bay[e]risch Adj. Bavarian

Bayern (das) ~s Bavaria

Bazille die; ~, ~n (ugs.) ▶ BAZILLUS A

Bazillus der; ~, Bazillen (a) bacillus (b) (fig.) cancer

Bd. Abk. = **Band** Vol.

beabsichtigen tr. V. intend

beachten tr. V. (a) follow ⟨rule, regulations, instruction⟩; heed, follow ⟨advice⟩; obey ⟨traffic signs⟩; observe ⟨formalities⟩ (b) (berücksichtigen) take account of; (achten auf) pay attention to

beachtlich ①Adj. considerable ②adv. considerably

Beachtung die; ~ (a) ▶ BEACHTEN A: following; heeding; obeying

(b) (Berücksichtigung) consideration (c) (Aufmerksamkeit) attention

Beamte der; adj. Dekl. official; (Staats~) [permanent] civil servant; (Kommunal~) [established] local government officer; (Polizei~) [police] officer

Beamtin die; ~, ~nen ▶ BEAMTE

beängstigend Adj. worrying

beanspruchen tr. V. (a) claim; etw. ~ können be entitled to expect sth. (b) (ausnutzen) make use of ⟨person, equipment⟩; take advantage of ⟨hospitality, services⟩ (c) (erfordern) demand ⟨energy, attention, stamina⟩; take up ⟨time, space, etc.⟩

Beanspruchung die; ~, ~en demands pl. (Gen. on); die ~ durch den Beruf the demands of his/her job

beanstanden tr. V. take exception to; (sich beklagen über) complain about

Beanstandung die; ~, ~en complaint

beantragen tr. V. apply for

beantworten tr. V. answer; reply to ⟨letter⟩; return ⟨greeting⟩

bearbeiten tr. V. (a) deal with; handle ⟨case⟩ (b) edit ⟨text, document⟩ (c) (adaptieren) adapt (**für** for)

Bearbeitung die; ~, ~en (a) die ~ eines Antrags/eines Falles usw. dealing with an application/handling a case etc.; (b) (Adaption) adaptation

beaufsichtigen tr. V. supervise; look after ⟨child⟩

beauftragen tr. V. entrust

bebauen tr. V. build on; develop

bebaut Adj. ein [dicht] ~es Gebiet a densely built-up area; ein ~es Gelände a developed site

Bebauung die; ~, ~en (a) development (b) (Gebäude) buildings pl.

beben itr. V. shake

Beben das; ~s, ~ ▶ ERDBEBEN

bebildern tr. V. illustrate

Bebilderung die; ~, ~en illustrations pl.

Becher der; ~s, ~ (Glas~, Porzellan~) glass; tumbler; (Plastik~) beaker; cup; (Eis~) (aus Glas, Metall) sundae dish; (aus Pappe) tub; (Joghurt~) carton

Becken das; ~s, ~ (a) (Wasch~) basin; (Abwasch~) sink; (Toiletten~) pan (b) (Anat.) pelvis (c) Pl. (Musik) cymbals

bedacht Adj. auf etw. (Akk.) ~ sein be intent on sth.

bedächtig ①Adj. (a) deliberate; measured ⟨steps, stride, speech⟩ (b) (besonnen) thoughtful; well-considered ⟨words⟩ ②adv. (a) deliberately (b) (besonnen) thoughtfully

bedanken *refl. V.* say thank you; **sich bei jmdm. [für etw.]** ∼: thank sb. [for sth.]

Bedarf *der;* ∼[e]s need (**an** + *Dat.* of); requirement (**an** + *Dat.* for); (Bedarfsmenge) needs *pl.;* requirements *pl.;* **bei** ∼: if required

bedauerlich *Adj.* regrettable

bedauerlicher·weise *Adv.* regrettably

bedauern *tr., itr. V.* (a) feel sorry for; **sie lässt sich gerne** ∼: she likes being pitied
(b) (schade finden) regret; **ich bedaure sehr, dass** ...: I am very sorry that ...

Bedauern *das;* ∼s regret; **zu meinem** ∼: to my regret

bedauerns·wert *Adj.* (geh.) unfortunate ⟨*person*⟩

bedecken *tr. V.* cover

bedeckt *Adj.* overcast ⟨*sky*⟩

bedenken *unr. tr. V.* (a) consider
(b) (beachten) take into consideration

Bedenken *das;* ∼s, ∼ reservation (**gegen** about); **ohne** ∼: without hesitation

bedenken·los [1] *Adj.* unhesitating; (skrupellos) unscrupulous
[2] *adv.* without hesitation; (skrupellos) unscrupulously

bedenklich [1] *Adj.* (a) dubious ⟨*methods, transactions, etc.*⟩
(b) (bedrohlich) alarming
[2] *adv.* alarmingly

Bedenk·zeit *die* time for reflection

bedeuten *tr. V.* (a) mean; **was soll das** ∼? what does that mean?
(b) (sein) represent; **das bedeutet ein Wagnis** that is being really daring

bedeutend [1] *Adj.* (a) significant; important
(b) (groß) substantial; considerable ⟨*success*⟩ [2] *adv.* considerably

Bedeutung *die;* ∼, ∼en (a) meaning
(b) (Wichtigkeit) importance

bedeutungs-: ∼**los** *Adj.* insignificant; ∼**voll** [1] *Adj.* (a) significant; (b) (viel sagend) meaningful; meaning ⟨*look*⟩; [2] *adv.* meaningfully

bedienen [1] *tr. V.* (a) serve; **werden Sie schon bedient?** are you being served?
(b) (handhaben) operate ⟨*machine*⟩
[2] *itr. V.* serve
[3] *refl. V.* help oneself; **sich selbst** ∼ (im Geschäft, Restaurant usw.) serve oneself

Bedienstete *der/die; adj. Dekl.* (Amtsspr.) employee

Bedienung *die;* ∼, ∼en (a) (das Bedienen) service; ∼ **inbegriffen** service included
(b) (das Handhaben) operation
(c) (Servierer[in]) waiter/waitress

Bedienungs·anleitung *die* operating instructions *pl.*

bedingen *tr. V.* cause

---

*old spelling - see note on page xiv

Bedingung *die;* ∼, ∼en condition; **unter der** ∼, **dass** ...: on condition that ...

bedingungs·los *Adj.* unconditional

bedrängen *tr. V.* (a) besiege ⟨*town, fortress, person*⟩; put ⟨*opposing player*⟩ under pressure
(b) (belästigen) pester

Bedrängnis *die;* ∼, ∼se (geh.) (innere Not) distress; (wirtschaftliche Not) [great] difficulties *pl.;* **in** ∼ **geraten/sein** get into/be in great difficulties *pl.*

bedrohen *tr. V.* threaten

bedrohlich [1] *Adj.* (Unheil verkündend) ominous; (gefährlich) dangerous
[2] *adv.* (Unheil verkündend) ominously; (gefährlich) dangerously

Bedrohlichkeit *die;* ∼: dangerousness; (einer Krankheit usw.) dangerous nature

Bedrohung *die* threat (*Gen.* to)

bedrucken *tr. V.* print

bedrücken *tr. V.* depress

Beduine *der;* ∼n, ∼n, **Beduinin** *die;* ∼, ∼nen Bed[o]uin

bedürfen *unr. itr. V.* **jmds./einer Sache** ∼ (geh.) require *or* need sb./sth.

Bedürfnis *das;* ∼ses, ∼se need (**nach** for); **das** ∼ **haben, etw. zu tun** feel a need to do sth.

bedürfnislos *Adj.* ⟨*person*⟩ with few [material] needs; modest, simple ⟨*life*⟩; ∼ **sein** have few [material] needs

Bedürfnislosigkeit *die;* ∼: lack of [material] needs

bedürftig *Adj.* needy

Beef·steak /ˈbiːf-/ *das* [beef]steak; **deutsches** ∼: ≈ beefburger

beehren *tr. V.* (geh.) honour

beeiden *tr. V.* ∼, **dass** ...: swear [on oath] that ...; **eine Aussage** ∼: swear to the truth of a statement

beeilen *refl. V.* hurry [up (coll.)]

beeindrucken *tr. V.* impress

beeindruckend *Adj.* impressive

beeinflussen *tr. V.* influence

Beeinflussung *die;* ∼, ∼en influencing

beeinträchtigen *tr. V.* restrict ⟨*sights, freedom*⟩; detract from ⟨*pleasure, enjoyment, value*⟩; spoil ⟨*appetite, good humour*⟩; impair ⟨*quality, reactions, efficiency, vision, hearing*⟩; damage, harm ⟨*sales, reputation*⟩

Beeinträchtigung *die;* ∼, ∼en
▶ BEEINTRÄCHTIGEN: restriction; detracting (+ *Gen.* from); spoiling; impairment; damage (*Gen.* to)

beenden, beendigen *tr. V.* (a) end; finish ⟨*piece of work etc.*⟩; complete ⟨*studies*⟩
(b) (DV) quit ⟨*program*⟩

beengen *tr. V.* hinder, restrict ⟨*movements*⟩; (fig.) restrict ⟨*freedom [of action]*⟩; **beengt wohnen** live in cramped surroundings or conditions; **sich beengt fühlen** feel cramped

beerben tr. V. jmdn. ~: inherit sb.'s estate

beerdigen tr. V. bury

Beerdigung die; ~, ~en burial; (Trauerfeier) funeral

Beerdigungs-institut das [firm sing. of] undertakers pl.

Beere die; ~, ~n berry

Beet das; ~[e]s, ~e (Blumenbeet) bed; (Gemüsebeet) plot

befahrbar Adj. passable

befahren unr. tr. V. (a) drive on ⟨road⟩; drive across ⟨bridge⟩; use ⟨railway line⟩; **die Straße ist stark/wenig ~**: the road is heavily/little used; **eine stark ~e Straße** a busy road
(b) sail ⟨sea⟩; navigate, sail up/down ⟨river, canal⟩

befallen unr. tr. V. (a) overcome; ⟨misfortune⟩ befall; **von Panik/Angst ~ werden** be seized with panic/fear
(b) ⟨pests⟩ attack

befangen 1 Adj. (a) self-conscious ⟨person⟩
(b) (voreingenommen) biased
2 adv. self-consciously

Befangenheit die; ~ (a) self-consciousness
(b) (Voreingenommenheit) bias

befassen refl. V. **sich mit etw. ~**: occupy oneself with sth.; ⟨article, book⟩ deal with sth.; (etw. studieren) study sth.

Befehl der; ~[e]s, ~e (a) order
(b) **den ~ über jmdn./etw. haben** be in command of sb./sth.

befehlen 1 unr. tr., itr. V. order; (Milit.) order; **man befahl ihm zu warten** he was told to wait
2 unr. itr. V. **über jmdn./etw. ~**: have command of or be in command of sb./sth.

Befehls-haber der; ~s, ~ (Milit.) commander

befestigen tr. V. (a) fix; **etw. an der Wand ~**: fix sth. to the wall
(b) (haltbar machen) stabilize ⟨bank, embankment⟩; make up ⟨road, path, etc.⟩
(c) (sichern) fortify ⟨town etc.⟩; strengthen ⟨border⟩

Befestigung die; ~, ~en (a) fixing
(b) (Milit.) fortification

befeuchten tr. V. moisten; damp ⟨hair, cloth⟩

befiehlst, befiehlt 2., 3. Pers. Sg. Präsens v. BEFEHLEN

befinden unr. refl. V. be

Befinden das; ~s health; (eines Patienten) condition

befindlich Adj.(a) to be found postpos.; **das in der Kasse ~e Geld** the money in the till
(b) (in einem Zustand) **die im Bau ~en Häuser** the houses [which are/were] under construction

Befindlichkeit die; ~, ~en (geh.) state

beflecken tr. V. stain

befohlen 2. Part. v. BEFEHLEN

befolgen tr. V. follow, obey ⟨instruction, grammatical rule⟩; obey, comply with ⟨law, regulation⟩; follow ⟨advice, suggestion⟩

Befolgung die; ~ ▶ BEFOLGEN: following; obedience (Gen. to); compliance (Gen. with)

befördern tr. V. (a) carry; transport
(b) (aufrücken lassen) promote

Beförderung die; ~, ~en (a) carriage; transport; (von Personen) transport
(b) (das Aufrückenlassen) promotion

befragen tr. V. (a) question (**über** + Akk. about)
(b) (konsultieren) ask

Befragung die; ~, ~en (a) questioning
(b) (Konsultation) consultation
(c) (Umfrage) opinion poll

befreien 1 tr. V. (a) free; liberate ⟨country, people⟩ (**von** from)
(b) (freistellen) exempt (**von** from)
(c) **jmdn. von Schmerzen ~**: free sb. of pain
2 refl. V. free oneself (**von** from)

Befreier der, **Befreierin** die; ~, ~nen liberator

Befreiung die; ~ (a) ▶ BEFREIEN 1A: freeing; liberation
(b) (Freistellung) exemption
(c) **die ~ von Schmerzen** release from pain

befremden tr. V. jmdn. ~: put sb. off

Befremden das; ~s surprise and displeasure

befremdlich (geh.) 1 Adj. strange; odd
2 adv. strangely

befreunden refl. V. ▶ ANFREUNDEN; [**gut od. eng**] **befreundet sein** be [good or close] friends (**mit** with)

befriedigen tr. V. (a) satisfy; gratify ⟨lust⟩
(b) (ausfüllen) ⟨job, occupation, etc.⟩ fulfil
(c) (sexuell) satisfy; **sich [selbst] ~**: masturbate

befriedigend 1 Adj. satisfactory
2 adv. satisfactorily

Befriedigung die; ~ (a) ▶ BEFRIEDIGEN A: satisfaction; gratification
(b) (Genugtuung) satisfaction

befristet Adj. temporary ⟨visa⟩; fixed-term ⟨ban, contract⟩

befruchten tr. V. fertilize ⟨egg⟩; pollinate ⟨flower⟩; impregnate ⟨female⟩; **ein Tier künstlich ~**: artificially inseminate an animal

Befruchtung die; ~, ~en ▶ BEFRUCHTEN: fertilization; pollination; impregnation; **künstliche ~**: artificial insemination

Befugnis die; ~, ~se authority

befühlen tr. V. feel

Befund der (bes. Med.) result[s pl.]

befürchten tr. V. fear; **ich befürchte, dass ...**: I am afraid that ...

befürworten tr. V. support

b

begabt *Adj.* talented; gifted; **hoch** ~: highly talented *or* gifted

Begabung *die;* ~, ~**en** talent; gift

begann *1. u. 3. Pers. Sg. Prät. v.* BEGINNEN

begatten *tr. V.* mate with; ⟨*man*⟩ copulate with; **sich** ~: mate; ⟨*persons*⟩ copulate

Begattung *die;* ~, ~**en** mating; (bei Menschen) copulation

begeben *unr. refl. V.* (geh.) proceed; make one's way; go; **sich zu Bett** ~: retire to bed; **sich an die Arbeit** ~: commence work

Begebenheit *die;* ~, ~**en** (geh.) event; occurrence

begegnen *itr. V.; mit sein* jmdm. ~: meet sb.; **sich** (*Dat.*) ~: meet [each other]

Begegnung *die;* ~, ~**en (a)** meeting **(b)** (Sport) match

begehen *unr. tr. V.* **(a)** commit ⟨*crime, adultery, indiscretion, sin, suicide, faux-pas, etc.*⟩; make ⟨*mistake*⟩; **eine [furchtbare] Dummheit** ~: do something [really] stupid **(b)** (geh.: feiern) celebrate

begehren *tr. V.* desire

begehrens-wert *Adj.* desirable

begehrlich ⟨1⟩ *Adj.* greedy ⟨2⟩ *adv.* greedily

begehrt *Adj.* much sought-after

begeistern ⟨1⟩ *tr. V.* jmdn. **[für etw.]** ~: fire sb. with enthusiasm [for sth.] ⟨2⟩ *refl. V.* get enthusiastic **(für** about**)**

begeisternd *Adj.* rousing

begeistert ⟨1⟩ *Adj.* enthusiastic **(von** about**)** ⟨2⟩ *adv.* enthusiastically

Begeisterung *die;* ~: enthusiasm

begeisterungs-, Begeisterungs-: ~**fähig** *Adj.* ⟨*children, people, etc.*⟩ who are able to get enthusiastic *or* are capable of enthusiasm; ~**fähigkeit** *die* capacity for enthusiasm; ~**sturm** *der* storm of enthusiastic applause

Begierde *die;* ~, ~**n** desire **(nach** for**)**

begierig ⟨1⟩ *Adj.* eager ⟨2⟩ *adv.* eagerly

begießen *unr. tr. V.* water ⟨*plants*⟩

Beginn *der;* ~**[e]s** beginning; **[gleich] zu** ~: [right] at the beginning

beginnen ⟨1⟩ *unr. itr. V.* start; begin; **mit dem Bau** ~: start *or* begin building; **dort beginnt der Wald** the forest starts there ⟨2⟩ *unr. tr. V.* start; begin; start ⟨*argument*⟩; ~, **etw. zu tun** start to do sth.

beglaubigen *tr. V.* certify

Beglaubigung *die;* ~, ~**en** certification

begleichen *unr. tr. V.* settle ⟨*bill, debt*⟩; pay ⟨*sum*⟩

Begleit-brief *der* covering *or* accompanying letter

begleiten *tr. V.* accompany; jmdn. **nach Hause** ~: see sb. home

Begleiter *der;* ~**s**, ~, **Begleiterin** *die;* ~, ~**nen** companion; (zum Schutz) escort; (Führer[in]) guide

Begleitung *die;* ~, ~**en (a)** er **bot uns seine** ~ **an** he offered to accompany us; **in** ~ **eines Erwachsenen** accompanied by an adult **(b)** (Musik) accompaniment

beglückwünschen *tr. V.* congratulate **(zu** on**)**

begnadet *Adj.* (geh.) divinely gifted

begnadigen *tr. V.* pardon; reprieve

Begnadigung *die;* ~, ~**en** reprieving; (Straferlass) pardon; reprieve

begnügen *refl. V.* content oneself

Begonie /be'goːni̯ə/ *die;* ~, ~**n** begonia

begonnen *2. Part. v.* BEGINNEN

begraben *unr. tr. V.* bury

Begräbnis *das;* ~**ses**, ~**se** burial; (~feier) funeral

begreifen ⟨1⟩ *unr. tr. V.* understand; **er konnte nicht** ~, **was geschehen war** he could not grasp what had happened ⟨2⟩ *itr. V.* understand; **schnell** *od.* **leicht/ langsam** *od.* **schwer** ~: be quick/slow on the uptake

begreiflich *Adj.* understandable

begrenzen *tr. V.* limit, restrict **(auf** + *Akk.* to**)**

Begriff *der* **(a)** concept; (Terminus) term **(b)** (Auffassung) idea; **sich** (*Dat.*) **keinen** ~ **von etw. machen können** not be able to imagine sth.; **ein/kein** ~ **sein** be/not be well known **(c)** **im** ~ **sein** *od.* **stehen, etw. zu tun** be about to do sth.

begriffs-stutzig *Adj.* (abwertend) obtuse

Begriffsstutzigkeit *die;* ~ (abwertend) obtuseness

begründen *tr. V.* **(a)** give reasons for **(b)** (gründen) found; establish ⟨*fame, reputation*⟩

Begründer *der;* ~**s**, ~, **Begründerin** *die;* ~, ~**nen** founder

begründet *Adj.* well-founded; reasonable ⟨*demand, objection, complaint*⟩

Begründung *die;* ~, ~**en** reason[s]; **mit der** ~, **dass** ...: on the grounds that ...

begrüßen *tr. V.* **(a)** greet; ⟨*hostess, host*⟩ welcome **(b)** (fig.) welcome

Begrüßung *die;* ~, ~**en** greeting; (von Gästen) welcoming; (Zeremonie) welcome (*Gen.* for)

begünstigen *tr. V.* favour

Begünstigung *die;* ~: favouring

begutachten *tr. V.* **(a)** examine and report on **(b)** (ugs.) have a look at

Begutachtung *die;* ~, ~**en** examination

begütert *Adj.* wealthy

begütigen *tr. V.* placate

behaart *Adj.* hairy; **stark** ~ **sein** be covered with hair; **stark** ~**e Beine** very hairy legs

---

behäbig ⟦1⟧ *Adj.* slow and ponderous
⟦2⟧ *adv.* slowly and ponderously
behagen *itr. V.* **etw. behagt jmdm.** sb. likes sth.
Behagen *das;* ∼s pleasure
behaglich ⟦1⟧ *Adj.* comfortable
⟦2⟧ *adv.* comfortably
Behaglichkeit *die;* ∼: comfortableness
behalten *unr. tr. V.* **(a)** keep; **etw. für sich** ∼: keep sth. to oneself
(b) (zurück∼) be left with ⟨*scar, defect, etc.*⟩
(c) (sich merken) remember
Behälter *der;* ∼s, ∼ container; (für Abfälle) receptacle
behämmert *Adj.* (salopp) ▶ BEKLOPPT
behänd, behände ⟦1⟧ *Adj.* (geschickt) deft; (flink) nimble
⟦2⟧ *adv. s. Adj.:* deftly; nimbly
behandeln *tr. V.* (auch Med.) treat; handle ⟨*matter, machine, device*⟩; deal with ⟨*subject, question etc.*⟩
Behandlung *die;* ∼, ∼en treatment
behängen *tr. V.* hang
beharren *itr. V.* **auf etw.** (*Dat.*) ∼ (etw. nicht aufgeben) persist in sth.; (auf etw. bestehen) insist on sth.
beharrlich ⟦1⟧ *Adj.* dogged
⟦2⟧ *adv.* doggedly
Beharrlichkeit *die;* ∼: doggedness
behauen *unr. tr. V.* hew
behaupten ⟦1⟧ *tr. V.* **(a)** maintain; assert; ∼, **jmd. zu sein/etw. zu wissen** claim to be sb./know sth.; **man behauptet** *od.* **es wird behauptet, dass …:** it is said *or* claimed that …
(b) (verteidigen) maintain ⟨*position*⟩; retain ⟨*record*⟩
⟦2⟧ *refl. V.* **(a)** assert oneself; (nicht untergehen) hold one's ground; (dableiben) survive
(b) (Sport) win through
Behauptung *die;* ∼, ∼en assertion
Behausung *die;* ∼, ∼en dwelling
beheben *unr. tr. V.* remove ⟨*danger, difficulty*⟩; repair ⟨*damage*⟩; remedy ⟨*abuse, defect*⟩
Behebung *die;* ∼, ∼en ▶ BEHEBEN: removal; repair; remedying
beheimatet *Adj.* **an einem Ort/in einem Land** *usw.* ∼ **sein** be native to a place/to a country *etc.*
beheizbar *Adj.* heatable; **eine** ∼e **Heckscheibe** a heated rear window
beheizen *tr. V.* heat
behelfen *unr. refl. V.* make do
behelfs·mäßig ⟦1⟧ *Adj.* makeshift
⟦2⟧ *adv.* in a makeshift way
behelligen *tr. V.* bother; (zudringlich werden gegen) pester
***behend**, ***behende** ▶ BEHÄND, BEHÄNDE
beherbergen *tr. V.* accommodate
beherrschen ⟦1⟧ *tr. V.* **(a)** control; rule ⟨*country, people*⟩

(b) (meistern) control ⟨*vehicle, animal*⟩; be in control of ⟨*situation*⟩
(c) (bestimmen, dominieren) dominate ⟨*townscape, landscape, discussions*⟩
(d) (zügeln) control ⟨*feelings*⟩; control, curb ⟨*impatience*⟩
(e) (gut können) have mastered ⟨*instrument, trade*⟩; have a good command of ⟨*language*⟩
⟦2⟧ *refl. V.* control oneself
beherrscht ⟦1⟧ *Adj.* self-controlled
⟦2⟧ *adv.* with self-control
Beherrschung *die;* ∼ **(a)** control; (eines Volks, Landes usw.) rule
(b) (das Meistern) control
(c) (Beherrschtheit) self-control
(d) (das Können) mastery
beherzigen *tr. V.* take ⟨*sth.*⟩ to heart
beherzt ⟦1⟧ *Adj.* spirited
⟦2⟧ *adv.* spiritedly
behilflich *Adj.* **[jmdm.]** ∼ **sein** help [sb.] (bei with)
behindern *tr. V.* **(a)** hinder; impede ⟨*movement*⟩; hold up ⟨*traffic*⟩
(b) (Sport, Verkehrsw.) obstruct
behindert *Adj.* handicapped
Behinderte *der/die; adj. Dekl.* handicapped person; **die** ∼n the handicapped; **WC für** ∼: toilet for disabled persons
Behinderung *die;* ∼, ∼en **(a)** hindrance
(b) (Sport, Verkehrsw.) obstruction
(c) (Gebrechen) handicap
Behörde *die;* ∼, ∼n authority; (Amt, Abteilung) department
behördlich ⟦1⟧ *Adj.* official
⟦2⟧ *adv.* officially
behüten *tr. V.* protect (**vor** + *Dat.* from); (bewachen) guard
behutsam ⟦1⟧ *Adj.* careful
⟦2⟧ *adv.* carefully
bei *Präp. mit Dat.* **(a)** (nahe) near; (dicht an, neben) by; **wer steht da** ∼ **ihm?** who is standing there with him?; **etw.** ∼ **sich haben** have sth. with *or* on one; **sich** ∼ **jmdm. entschuldigen** apologize to sb.
(b) (unter) among; **war heute ein Brief für mich** ∼ **der Post?** was there a letter for me in the post today?
(c) (an) by; **jmdn.** ∼ **der Hand nehmen** take sb. by the hand
(d) (im Wohn-/Lebens-/Arbeitsbereich von); ∼ **uns tut man das nicht** we don't do that; ∼ **mir [zu Hause]** at my house; ∼ **uns um die Ecke/gegenüber** round the corner from us/opposite us; ∼ **seinen Eltern leben** live with one's parents; **wir sind** ∼ **ihr eingeladen** we have been invited to her house; **wir treffen uns** ∼ **uns/Peter** we'll meet at our/Peter's place; ∼ **uns in der Firma** in our company; ∼ **Schmidt** (auf Briefen) c/o Schmidt; ∼ **einer Firma sein** be with a company; ∼ **jmdm./ einem Verlag arbeiten** work for sb./a publishing house
(e) (im Bereich eines Vorgangs) at; ∼ **einer** ···⫶

Hochzeit/einem Empfang *usw.* be at a wedding/reception *etc.;* ∼ einem Unfall in an accident
(f) (im Werk von) ∼ Goethe in Goethe
(g) (im Falle von) in the case of; wie ∼ den Römern as with the Romans; ∼ der Hauskatze in the domestic cat
(h) (modal) ∼ Tag/Nacht by day/night; ∼ Tageslicht by daylight; ∼ Nebel in fog
(i) (im Falle des Auftretens von) „∼ Nässe Schleudergefahr" ‘slippery when wet'
(j) (angesichts) with; ∼ dieser Hitze in this heat; ∼ deinen guten Augen/ihrem Talent with your good eyesight/her talent
(k) (trotz) ∼ all seinem Engagement/seinen Bemühungen in spite of *or* despite *or* for all his commitment/efforts

bei|behalten *unr. tr. V.* keep; retain; keep up ⟨*custom, habit*⟩; keep to ⟨*course, method*⟩; preserve, maintain ⟨*way of life; attitude*⟩

bei|bringen *unr. tr. V.* **(a)** jmdm. etw. ∼: teach sb. sth.
(b) (ugs.: mitteilen) jmdm. ∼, dass ...: break it to sb. that ...
(c) (zufügen) jmdm./sich etw. ∼: inflict sth. on sb./oneself

Beichte *die;* ∼, ∼n confession *no def. art.*

beichten **1** *itr. V.* confess
2 *tr. V.* (auch fig.) confess

Beicht-: ∼**stuhl** *der* confessional; ∼**vater** *der* father confessor

beid... *Indefinitpron. u. Zahlw.* **1** *Pl.* ∼e both; (der/die/das eine oder der/die/das andere) either *sing.;* die ∼en the two; die/seine ∼en Brüder the/his two brothers; die ∼en ersten Strophen the first two verses; kennst du die ∼en? do you know those two?; alle ∼e both of us/you/them; ihr/euch ∼e you two; ihr/euch ∼e nicht neither of you; wir/uns ∼e the two of us/both of us; er hat ∼e Eltern verloren he has lost both [his] parents; mit ∼en Händen with both hands; ich habe ∼e gekannt I knew both of them; einer/eins von ∼en one of the two; keiner/keins von ∼en neither [of them]
2 *Neutr. Sg.;* ∼es both *pl.;* (das eine oder das andere) either; ∼es ist möglich either is possible; ich glaube ∼es/∼es nicht I believe both things/neither thing; das ist ∼es nicht richtig neither of those is correct

beiderlei *indekl. Adj.* ∼ Geschlechts of both sexes

beider·seits **1** *Präp. mit Gen.* on both sides of
2 *Adv.* on both sides

bei·einander *Adv.* together; ∼ Trost suchen seek comfort from each other

Bei·fahrer *der,* **Bei·fahrerin** *die* **(a)** passenger
(b) (berufsmäßig) co-driver; (im LKW) driver's mate

Bei·fahrer·sitz *der* passenger seat; (eines Motorrads) pillion

Bei·fall *der* **(a)** applause
(b) (Zustimmung) approval

bei·fällig **1** *Adj.* approving
2 *adv.* approvingly

beige /be:ʃ/ *Adj.* beige

Beige /be:ʃ/ *das;* ∼, ∼e *od.* (ugs.) ∼s beige

Bei·geschmack *der:* einen bitteren *usw.* ∼ haben have a slightly bitter *etc.* taste [to it]

Bei·hilfe *die* **(a)** aid; (Zuschuss) allowance
(b) (Rechtsw.: Mithilfe) aiding and abetting

bei|kommen *unr. itr. V.; mit sein* **(a)** (gewachsen sein) jmdm. ∼: get the better of sb.
(b) (bewältigen) den Schwierigkeiten/der Unruhe/jmds. Sturheit ∼: overcome the difficulties/deal with the unrest/cope with sb.'s obstinacy

Beil *das;* ∼[e]s, ∼e axe; (kleiner) hatchet

Bei·lage *die* **(a)** (Zeitungs∼) supplement
(b) (zu Speisen) side dish; (Gemüse) vegetables *pl.*

bei·läufig **1** *Adj.* casual
2 *adv.* casually

bei|legen *tr. V.* **(a)** enclose
(b) (schlichten) settle ⟨*dispute etc.*⟩

Bei·leid *das* sympathy; [mein] herzliches *od.* aufrichtiges ∼! please accept my sincere condolences

bei|liegen *unr. itr. V.* einem Brief ∼: be enclosed with a letter

bei·liegend *Adj.* enclosed; ∼ senden wir ...: please find enclosed ...

beim *Präp. + Art.* **(a)** = bei dem;
(b) ∼ Film sein be in films
(c) er will ∼ Arbeiten nicht gestört werden he doesn't want to be disturbed when working; ∼ Duschen sein be taking a shower

bei|messen *unr. tr. V.* attach

Bein *das;* ∼[e]s, ∼e leg; jmdm. ein ∼ stellen trip sb.; (fig.) put *or* throw a spanner *or* (Amer.) a monkey wrench in sb.'s works; wieder auf den ∼en sein be back on one's feet again

bei·nah[e] *Adv.* almost

Bei·name *der* epithet

Bein·bruch *der:* das ist [doch] kein ∼ (ugs.) it's not the end of the world

beinhalten *tr. V.* (Papierdt.) involve

-beinig *adj.* -legged

bei|pflichten *itr. V.* agree (*Dat.* with)

be|irren *tr. V.* sich durch nichts/von niemandem ∼ lassen not be deterred by anything/anybody

beisammen *Adv.* together

beisammen|haben *unr. tr. V.* **(a)** have got together
(b) er hat [sie] nicht alle beisammen (ugs.) he's not all there (coll.)

Beisammen·sein *das* get-together

Bei·schlaf *der* sexual intercourse

Bei·sein das: in jmds. ~: in the presence of sb. or in sb.'s presence
bei·seite Adv. aside
Beis[e]l das; ~s, ~ od. ~n (österr.) pub (Brit.); bar (Amer.)
bei|setzen tr. V. lay to rest; inter ⟨ashes⟩
Bei·setzung die; ~, ~en funeral; burial
Bei·spiel das example (für of); zum ~: for example; mit gutem ~ vorangehen set a good example
beispielhaft Adj. exemplary
beispiel·los Adj. unparalleled
beispiels·weise Adv. for example
beißen ① unr. tr., itr. V. (auch fig.) bite ② unr. refl. V. (ugs.) ⟨colours, clothes⟩ clash
beißend Adj. biting ⟨cold⟩; acrid ⟨smoke, fumes⟩; sharp ⟨frost⟩
Beiß·zange die ▶ KNEIFZANGE
Bei·stand der (geh.: Hilfe) aid
bei|stehen unr. itr. V. jmdm. ~: aid sb.
bei|steuern tr. V. contribute
Beitrag der; ~[e]s, Beiträge contribution; (Versicherungsbeitrag) premium; (Mitgliedsbeitrag) subscription
bei|tragen unr. tr., itr. V. contribute (zu to)
bei|treten unr. itr. V.; mit sein join ⟨union, club, etc.⟩; einem Abkommen/Pakt accede to ⟨pact, agreement⟩
Bei·tritt der joining
Bei·wagen der sidecar
Bei·werk das accessories pl.
bei|wohnen itr. V. einer Sache (Dat.) ~ (geh.) be present at sth.
Beize die; ~, ~n (Holzbearb.) [wood]stain
beizeiten Adv. in good time
beizen tr. V. (Holzbearb.) stain
bejahen /bə'ja:ən/ tr. V. (a) auch itr. answer ⟨sth.⟩ in the affirmative (b) (gutheißen) approve of; das Leben ~: have a positive or an affirmative attitude to life
Bejahung die; ~, ~en (a) affirmative reply (b) (das Gutheißen) approval
bejammern tr. V. lament
bejubeln tr. V. cheer; acclaim
bekämpfen tr. V. (a) fight against (b) combat ⟨disease, epidemic, pest, unemployment, crime, etc.⟩
Bekämpfung die; ~ (a) fight (Gen. against) (b) ▶ BEKÄMPFEN B: combating
bekannt Adj. (a) well-known; etw. ~ geben announce sth.; etw. ~ machen announce sth.; (der Öffentlichkeit) make sth. public; ~ werden become known; es ist nichts davon ~: nothing is known concerning it (b) jmd./etw. ist jmdm. ~: sb. knows sb./sth.; Darf ich ~ machen? Meine Eltern may I introduce my parents?

Bekannte der/die; adj. Dekl. acquaintance
Bekạnnt·gabe die; ~: announcement
*bekạnnt|geben ▶ BEKANNT A
bekạnntlich Adv. as is well known; etw. ist ~ der Fall sth. is known to be the case
*bekạnnt|machen ▶ BEKANNT A
Bekạnnt·machung die; ~, ~en announcement
Bekạnntschaft die; ~, ~en acquaintance
*bekạnnt|werden ▶ BEKANNT A
bekehren ① tr. V. convert ② refl. V. become converted
Bekehrung die; ~, ~en (auch fig.) conversion (zu to)
bekennen ① unr. tr. V. (a) confess; ~, dass ... admit that ... (b) (Rel.) profess ② refl. V. sich zum Islam ~: profess Islam; sich zu Buddha ~: profess one's faith in Buddha; sich zu seiner Schuld ~: confess one's guilt; sich schuldig/nicht schuldig ~: confess/not confess one's guilt; (vor Gericht) plead guilty/not guilty
Bekenntnis das; ~ses, ~se (a) confession (b) (Eintreten) ein ~ zum Frieden a declaration for peace (c) (Konfession) denomination
bekiffen refl. V. (ugs.) get stoned (sl.)
bekifft Adj. (ugs.) stoned
beklagen ① tr. V. (geh.) (a) (betrauern) mourn (b) (bedauern) lament ② refl. V. complain
bekleckern tr. V. (ugs.) etw./sich [mit Soße usw.] ~: drop or spill sauce etc. down sth./ oneself
bekleiden tr. V. (a) clothe; mit etw. bekleidet sein be wearing sth. (b) (geh.: innehaben) occupy ⟨office, position⟩
Bekleidung die; ~, ~en clothing; clothes pl.
beklemmend Adj. oppressive
Beklemmung die; ~, ~en oppressive feeling
beklommen Adj. uneasy; (stärker) apprehensive
bekloppt Adj. (salopp) barmy (Brit. coll.); loony (coll.)
beknackt Adj. (salopp) lousy (coll.); ein ~er Typ a berk (Brit. coll.); a jerk (coll.)
beknien tr. V. (ugs.) beg
bekommen ① unr. tr. V. (a) get; get, receive ⟨money, letter, reply, news, orders⟩; (erreichen) catch ⟨train, bus, flight⟩; was ~ Sie? (im Geschäft) can I help you?; (im Lokal, Restaurant) what would you like?; was ~ Sie [dafür]? how much is that?; Hunger/Durst ~: get hungry/thirsty; Angst/Mut ~: become frightened/take heart; er bekommt einen Bart he's growing a beard; sie bekommt eine ⋯⋗

Brust her breasts are developing; **Zähne** ~: ⟨baby⟩ teethe; **sie bekommt ein Kind** she's expecting a baby

(b) etw. durch die Tür/ins Auto ~: get sth. through the door/into the car

2 *unr. V.; in der Funktion eines Hilfsverbs zur Umschreibung des Passivs* get; **etw. geschenkt** ~: get [given] sth. *or* be given sth. as a present

3 *unr. itr. V.; mit sein* **jmdm. gut** ~: do sb. good; **jmdm. [gut]** ~: ⟨food, medicine⟩ agree with sb.; **wohl bekomms!** your [very good] health!

bekömmlich *Adj.* easily digestible

beköstigen *tr. V.* cater for

bekräftigen *tr. V.* reinforce ⟨statement⟩; reaffirm ⟨promise⟩

bekreuzigen *refl. V.* (kath. Kirche) cross oneself

bekriegen *tr. V.* wage war on; (fig.) fight; **sich** ~: be at war; (fig.) fight

bekümmern *tr. V.* **jmdn.** ~: cause sb. worry

bekümmert *Adj.* worried; (stärker) distressed

bekunden *tr. V.* express

belächeln *tr. V.* smile [pityingly/tolerantly etc.] at

beladen *unr. tr. V.* load ⟨ship⟩; load [up] ⟨car, wagon⟩; load up ⟨horse, donkey⟩

Belag *der;* ~[e]s, Beläge **(a)** coating **(b)** (Fußbodenbelag) covering; (Straßenbelag) surface; (Bremsbelag) lining **(c)** (von Kuchen, Scheibe Brot usw.) topping; (von Sandwiches) filling

belagern *tr. V.* (auch fig.) besiege

Belagerung *die;* ~, ~en siege; (fig.) besieging

Belang *der;* ~[e]s, ~e **(a) von/ohne** ~ **sein** be of importance/of no importance **(b)** *Pl.* (Interessen) interests

belangen *tr. V.* (Rechtsw.) sue; (strafrechtlich) prosecute

belang-los *Adj.* (trivial) trivial; (unerheblich) of no importance (**für** for)

Belanglosigkeit *die;* ~, ~en unimportance; (Trivialität) triviality

belassen *unr. tr. V.* leave

belastbar *Adj.* tough, resilient ⟨person⟩; **seelisch/körperlich** ~ **sein** be emotionally/physically tough *or* resilient; be able to stand emotional/physical stress; **ein** ~**er Mitarbeiter** an employee who can work under pressure

Belastbarkeit *die;* ~, ~n toughness; resilience; (von Mitarbeitern) ability to work under pressure

belasten *tr. V.* **(a) etw.** ~: put sth. under strain; (durch Gewicht) put weight on sth. **(b)** (beeinträchtigen) pollute ⟨atmosphere⟩; put pressure on ⟨environment⟩

(c) (in Anspruch nehmen) burden (**mit** with)
(d) jmdn. ~ ⟨responsibility, guilt⟩ weigh upon sb.; ⟨thought⟩ weigh upon sb.'s mind
(e) (Rechtsw.) incriminate
(f) (Geldw.) **jmds. Konto mit 100 DM** ~: debit sb.'s account with 100 DM

belästigen *tr. V.* bother; (sehr aufdringlich) pester; (sexuell) molest

Belästigung *die* ▶ BELÄSTIGEN: bothering; pestering; molestation

Belastung *die;* ~, ~en **(a)** strain; (das Belasten) straining; (durch Gewicht) loading; (Last) load
(b) die ~ **der Atmosphäre/Umwelt durch Schadstoffe** the pollution of the atmosphere by harmful substances/the pressure on the environment caused by harmful substances
(c) (Bürde, Sorge) burden

Belastungs-: ~**EKG** *das* (Med.) electrocardiogram after effort; ~**zeuge** *der,* ~**zeugin** *die* (Rechtsw.) witness for the prosecution

belaufen *unr. refl. V.* **sich auf ...** ⟨Akk.⟩ ~: come to ...

belauschen *tr. V.* eavesdrop on

beleben 1 *tr. V.* enliven; stimulate ⟨economy⟩
2 *refl. V.* ⟨market, economic activity⟩ revive, pick up

belebend 1 *Adj.* invigorating
2 *adv.* ~ **wirken** have an invigorating effect

belebt *Adj.* busy ⟨street, crossing, town, etc.⟩

Beleg *der;* ~[e]s, ~e (Beweisstück) piece of [supporting] documentary evidence; (Quittung) receipt

belegen *tr. V.* **(a)** (Milit.: beschießen) bombard; (mit Bomben) attack
(b) (mit Belag versehen) cover ⟨floor⟩; fill ⟨flan base, sandwich⟩; top ⟨open sandwich⟩; **eine Scheibe Brot mit Käse** ~: put some cheese on a slice of bread
(c) (in Besitz nehmen) occupy ⟨seat, room, etc.⟩
(d) (Hochschulw.) enrol for ⟨seminar, lecture course⟩
(e) den ersten/letzten Platz ~ (Sport) take first place/come last
(f) (nachweisen) prove; give a reference for ⟨quotation⟩

Belegschaft *die;* ~, ~en staff

belegt *Adj.* **(a) ein** ~**es Brot** an open *or* (Amer.) openface sandwich; (zugeklappt) a sandwich; **ein** ~**es Brötchen** a roll with topping; an open-face roll (Amer.); (zugeklappt) a filled roll; a sandwich roll (Amer.)
(b) (mit Belag bedeckt) furred ⟨tongue, tonsils⟩
(c) (heiser) husky ⟨voice⟩
(d) (nicht mehr frei) ⟨room, flat⟩ occupied

belehren *tr. V.* teach; instruct; (aufklären) enlighten; (informieren) inform; **ich lasse mich gern** ~: I'm quite willing to believe otherwise

Belehrung *die;* ~, ~en instruction; (Zurechtweisung) lecture

beleibt *Adj.* (geh.) portly

beleidigen *tr. V.* insult

beleidigt *Adj.* insulted; (gekränkt) offended

Beleidigung *die;* ~, ~en **(a)** insult **(b)** (Rechtsw.) (schriftlich) libel; (mündlich) slander

belesen *Adj.* well-read

beleuchten *tr. V.* light up; light ⟨stairs, room, street, etc.⟩

Beleuchtung *die;* ~, ~en lighting; (Anstrahlung) illumination

beleumdet *Adj.* übel/gut ~ sein have a bad/good reputation

Belgien /ˈbɛlgi̯ən/ *(das);* ~s Belgium

Belgier *der;* ~s, ~, **Belgierin** *die;* ~, ~nen Belgian

belgisch *Adj.* Belgian

belichten *tr. V.* (Fot.) expose; *itr.* **richtig/falsch/kurz** ~: use the right/wrong exposure/a short exposure time

Belichtung *die* (Fot.) exposure

Belieben *das;* ~s: nach ~: just as you/they *etc.* like

beliebig ① *Adj.* any
② *adv.* as you like/he likes *etc.;* ~ **lange/viele** as long/many as you like/he likes *etc.*

beliebt *Adj.* popular; favourite *attrib.*

Beliebtheit *die;* ~: popularity

beliefern *tr. V.* supply

bellen *itr. V.* bark

Belletristik /bɛleˈtrɪstɪk/ *die;* ~: belles-lettres *pl.*

belohnen *tr. V.* reward ⟨person, thing⟩

Belohnung *die;* ~, ~en reward

belüften *tr. V.* ventilate

Belüftung *die* ventilation

belügen *unr. tr. V.* lie to

belustigen *tr. V.* amuse

Belustigung *die;* ~, ~en amusement

bemächtigen *refl. V.* sich jmds./einer Sache ~ (geh.) seize sb./sth.

bemalen *tr. V.* paint; (verzieren) decorate

bemängeln *tr. V.* find fault with

bemerkbar *Adj.* sich ~ machen attract attention [to oneself]; (erkennbar werden) become apparent; (spürbar werden) make itself felt

bemerken *tr. V.* **(a)** (wahrnehmen) notice; **ich wurde nicht bemerkt** I was unobserved **(b)** (äußern) remark

bemerkenswert ① *Adj.* remarkable
② *adv.* remarkably

Bemerkung *die;* ~, ~en **(a)** (Äußerung) remark; comment **(b)** (Notiz) note; (Anmerkung) comment

bemitleiden *tr. V.* pity; feel sorry for

bemitleidens-wert *Adj.* pitiable

bemogeln *tr. V.* (ugs.) cheat; diddle (Brit. coll.)

bemühen *refl. V.* make an effort; sich ~, etw. zu tun endeavour to do sth.; sich um

etw. ~: try to obtain sth.; sich um eine Stelle ~: try to get a job; sich um jmdn. ~ (kümmern) seek to help sb.

Bemühung *die;* ~, ~en effort

benachbart *Adj.* neighbouring *attrib.*

benachrichtigen *tr. V.* notify (von of)

Benachrichtigung *die;* ~, ~en notification

benachteiligen *tr. V.* put at a disadvantage; (diskriminieren) discriminate against; **die sozial benachteiligten Schichten** the underprivileged classes

Benachteiligte *der/die; adj. Dekl.* disadvantaged person; **die** ~n the disadvantaged; those at a disadvantage; **die sozial** ~n the underprivileged; the socially deprived

benehmen *unr. refl. V.* behave

Benehmen *das;* ~s behaviour; **kein** ~ **haben** have no manners *pl.*

beneiden *tr. V.* envy; **jmdn. um etw.** ~: envy sb. sth.

beneidens-wert *Adj.* enviable

Benelux-länder *Pl.* Benelux countries

benennen *unr. tr. V.* name

Bengel *der;* ~s, ~ od. (nordd.) ~s **(a)** (abwertend: junger Bursche) young rascal **(b)** (fam.: kleiner Junge) little lad

benommen *Adj.* dazed; (durch Fieber, Alkohol) muzzy

benoten *tr. V.* mark (Brit.); grade (Amer.); **einen Test mit „gut"** ~: mark a test 'good' (Brit.); assign a grade of 'good' to a test (Amer.)

benötigen *tr. V.* need; require

benutzen *tr. V.* use

Benutzer *der;* ~s, ~: user

benutzer-freundlich *Adj.* user-friendly

Benutzerin *die;* ~, ~nen user

Benutzung *die;* ~: use

Benzin *das;* ~s petrol (Brit.); gasoline (Amer.); gas (Amer. coll.); (Wasch~) benzine

Benzol *das;* ~s, ~e (Chemie) benzene

beobachten *tr. V.* observe; watch

Beobachter *der;* ~s, ~, **Beobachterin** *die;* ~, ~nen observer

Beobachtung *die;* ~, ~en observation

bepacken *tr. V.* load

bepflanzen *tr. V.* plant

bequem ① *Adj.* **(a)** comfortable **(b)** (abwertend: träge) idle
② *adv.* **(a)** comfortably **(b)** (leicht) easily

bequemen *refl. V.* sich dazu ~, etw. zu tun (geh.) condescend to do sth.

Bequemlichkeit *die;* ~ **(a)** comfort **(b)** (Trägheit) idleness

berappen *tr., itr. V.* (ugs.) ▶ BLECHEN

beraten ① *unr. tr. V.* **(a)** advise; jmdn. gut/schlecht ~: give sb. good/bad advice **(b)** (besprechen) discuss ⟨plan, matter⟩ ⋯⋯>

2 *unr. itr. V.* über etw. (*Akk.*) ∼: discuss sth.

3 *unr. refl. V.* sich mit jmdm. ∼, ob ...: discuss with sb. whether ...

Berater *der;* ∼s, ∼, **Beraterin** *die;* ∼, ∼nen adviser

beratschlagen **1** *tr. V.* discuss **2** *itr. V.* über etw. (*Akk.*) ∼: discuss sth.

Beratung *die;* ∼, ∼en **(a)** advice *no indef. art.;* (durch Arzt, Rechtsanwalt) consultation **(b)** (Besprechung) discussion

berauben *tr. V.* (auch fig.) rob (*Gen.* of)

berauschen (geh.) **1** *tr. V.* (auch fig.) intoxicate **2** *refl. V.* become intoxicated (an + *Dat.* with)

Berber *der;* ∼s, ∼(a) Berber **(b)** (Teppich) Berber carpet/rug **(c)** (Nichtsesshafter) tramp

Berberin *die;* ∼, ∼nen ▶ BERBER A, C

berechenbar *Adj.* calculable; predictable (behaviour)

Berechenbarkeit *die;* ∼: calculability; (des Verhaltens) predictability

berechnen *tr. V.* **(a)** (auch fig.) calculate; predict (behaviour, consequences) **(b)** (anrechnen) charge; **jmdm. 10 Mark für etw.** od.: **jmdm. etw. mit 10 Mark** ∼: charge sb. 10 marks for sth.; **jmdm. zu viel** ∼: overcharge sb.

Berechnung *die;* ∼, ∼en **(a)** calculation **(b)** (Eigennutz) [calculating] self-interest

berechtigen *tr. V.* entitle; *itr.* **die Karte berechtigt zum Eintritt** the ticket entitles the bearer to admission

berechtigt *Adj.* **(a)** (gerechtfertigt) justified **(b)** (befugt) authorized

Berechtigung *die;* ∼, ∼en **(a)** (Befugnis) entitlement; (Recht) right **(b)** (Rechtmäßigkeit) legitimacy

bereden *tr. V.* **(a)** (besprechen) discuss **(b)** jmdn. ∼, etw. zu tun talk sb. into doing sth.

beredsam *Adj.* eloquent

Beredsamkeit *die;* ∼: eloquence

beredt *Adj.* (auch fig.) eloquent

Bereich *der;* ∼[e]s, ∼e area; **im privaten/staatlichen** ∼: in the private/public sector

bereichern *refl. V.* get rich

Bereicherung *die;* ∼, ∼en **(a)** money-making **(b)** (Nutzen) valuable acquisition

bereifen *tr. V.* put tyres on (car); put a tyre on (wheel)

Bereifung *die;* ∼, ∼en [set *sing.* of] tyres *pl.*

bereinigen *tr. V.* clear up (misunderstanding); settle, resolve (dispute)

bereisen *tr. V.* travel around *or* about;

travel through (towns); (beruflich) (representative etc.) cover (area); **fremde Länder** ∼: travel in foreign countries

bereit *Adj.* ready; ∼ sein, etw. zu tun be ready *or* willing to do sth.

bereiten *tr. V.* **(a)** prepare; make (tea, coffee) **(b)** (verursachen) cause (trouble, sorrow, difficulty, etc.)

bereit-: ∼|halten *unr. tr. V.* have ready; ∼|legen *tr. V.* lay out ready; ∼|liegen *unr. itr. V.* be ready

bereits *Adv.* already

Bereitschaft *die;* ∼: readiness; willingness

Bereitschafts·dienst *der;* ∼ haben (doctor, nurse) be on call; (policeman, fireman) be on standby duty; (chemist's) be on rota duty (for dispensing outside normal hours)

bereit-: ∼|stehen *unr. itr. V.* be ready; ∼|stellen *tr. V.* place ready; get ready (food, drinks); ready, make (money, funds) available; ∼willig **1** *Adj.* willing. **2** *adv.* readily

Bereitwilligkeit *die;* ∼: willingness

bereuen **1** *tr. V.* regret **2** *itr. V.* be sorry; (Rel.) repent

Berg *der;* ∼[e]s, ∼e **(a)** hill; (im Hochgebirge) mountain **(b)** (Haufen) huge pile; (von Akten, Abfall auch) mountain

berg-, Berg-: ∼ab /-'-/ *Adv.* downhill; ∼auf /-'-/ *Adv.* uphill; ∼bahn *die* mountain railway; (Seilbahn) mountain cableway; ∼bau *der* mining

bergen *unr. tr. V.* **(a)** rescue, save (person); salvage (ship, cargo, belongings) **(b)** (geh.: enthalten) hold

Berg-: ∼führer *der,* ∼führerin *die;* ∼∼, ∼∼nen mountain guide; ∼hütte *die* mountain hut

bergig *Adj.* hilly; (mit hohen Bergen) mountainous

Berg-: ∼kette *die* range *or* chain of mountains; mountain range *or* chain; ∼kristall *der* rock crystal; ∼land *das* hilly country *no indef. art;* (mit hohen Bergen) mountainous country *no indef. art.;* ∼mann *der; Pl.* ∼leute miner; ∼station *die* top station; ∼steigen *das;* ∼∼s mountaineering *no art.;* ∼steiger *der,* ∼steigerin *die;* ∼∼, ∼∼nen mountaineer

Bergung *die;* ∼, ∼en **(a)** rescue **(b)** (von Schiffen, Gut) salvaging

Berg-: ∼wacht *die* mountain rescue service; ∼werk *das* mine

Bericht *der;* ∼[e]s, ∼e report

berichten *tr., itr. V.* report

Bericht-: ∼erstatter *der;* ∼∼s, ∼∼, ∼erstatterin *die;* ∼∼, ∼∼nen reporter; ∼erstattung *die* reporting *no indef. art.*

berichtigen *tr. V.* correct

Berichtigung *die;* ~, ~en correction
berieseln *tr. V.* (a) (bewässern) irrigate
(b) sich ständig mit Musik ~ lassen (ugs. abwertend) constantly have music on in the background
Berlin *(das);* ~s Berlin
Berliner ⊡ *indekl. Adj.* Berlin
⊡ *der;* ~s, ~: (a) Berliner
(b) (Gebäck) [jam (Brit.) *or* (Amer.) jelly] doughnut
Berlinerin *die;* ~, ~nen Berliner
berlinisch *Adj.* Berlin *attrib.*
Bern *(das);* ~s Bern[e]
Bernhardiner *der;* ~s, ~: St. Bernard [dog]
Bern·stein *der* amber
bersten *unr. itr. V.; mit sein* (geh.) ‹ice› break up; ‹glass› shatter [into pieces]; ‹wall› crack up
berüchtigt *Adj.* notorious (**wegen** for); (verrufen) disreputable
berücksichtigen *tr. V.* take into account; consider ‹applicant, application, suggestion›
Berücksichtigung *die;* ~: **bei** ~ **aller Umstände** taking all the circumstances into account
Beruf *der;* ~[e]s, ~e occupation; (akademischer) profession; (handwerklicher) trade; **was sind Sie von** ~? what do you do for a living?
berufen[1] ⊡ *unr. tr. V.* (a) (einsetzen) appoint
(b) **berufe es nicht!** (ugs.) don't speak too soon!
⊡ *unr. refl. V.* **sich auf etw.** *(Akk.)* ~: refer to sth.; **sich auf jmdn.** ~: quote *or* mention sb.'s name
berufen[2] *Adj.* (a) competent; **aus** ~**em Munde** from somebody qualified to speak
(b) **sich dazu** ~ **fühlen, etw. zu tun** feel called to do sth.
beruflich ⊡ *Adj.* vocational ‹training etc.›; (bei akademischen Berufen) professional ‹training etc.›
⊡ *adv.* ~ **erfolgreich sein** be successful in one's career; **sich** ~ **weiterbilden** undertake further job training
berufs-, Berufs-: ~**akademie** *die* university of co-operative education; ~**ausbildung** *die* vocational training; ~**aussichten** *Pl.* job prospects (*in a particular profession etc.*); ~**berater** *der,* ~**beraterin** *die* vocational adviser; ~**beratung** *die* vocational guidance; ~**bild** *das* outline of a/the profession/trade as a career; ~**erfahrung** *die* [professional] experience; ~**geheimnis** *das* professional secret; (Schweigepflicht) professional secrecy; ~**krankheit** *die* occupational disease; ~**leben** *das* working life; ~**schule** *die* vocational school; ~**soldat** *der,* ~**soldatin** *die* regular

soldier; ~**sportler** *der* professional sportsman; ~**sportlerin** *die* professional sportswoman; ~**tätig** *Adj.* working *attrib.;* ~**tätig** *der/die; adj. Dekl.* working person; ~**tätige** *Pl.* working people; ~**verkehr** *der* rush hour traffic
Berufung *die;* ~, ~en (a) (für ein Amt) offer of an appointment (**auf, in, an** + *Akk.* to)
(b) (innerer Auftrag) vocation
(c) (das Sichberufen) **unter** ~ *(Dat.)* **auf jmdn./ etw.** referring *or* with reference to sb./sth.
(d) (Rechtsw.: Einspruch) appeal; ~ **einlegen** lodge an appeal
beruhen *itr. V.* **auf etw.** *(Dat.)* ~: be based on sth.; **etw. auf sich** ~ **lassen** let sth. rest
beruhigen /bə'ru:ɪgn/ ⊡ *tr. V.* calm [down]; pacify ‹child, baby›; salve ‹conscience›; (trösten) soothe; (von einer Sorge befreien) reassure
⊡ *refl. V.* ‹person› calm down; ‹sea› become calm
Beruhigung *die;* ~ ▶ BERUHIGEN 1: calming [down]; pacifying; salving; soothing; reassurance
Beruhigungs·mittel *das* tranquillizer
berühmt *Adj.* famous
berühmt-berüchtigt *Adj.* notorious
Berühmtheit *die;* ~, ~en (a) (Ruhm) fame
(b) (Mensch) celebrity
berühren *tr. V.* (a) touch; (fig.) touch on ‹topic, issue. etc.›; **sich** ~: touch
(b) (beeindrucken) affect; **das berührt mich nicht** it's a matter of indifference to me
Berührung *die;* ~, ~en touch; **mit jmdm./ etw. in** ~ *(Akk.)* **kommen** (auch fig.) come into contact with sb./sth.
besagen *tr. V.* say; (bedeuten) mean
besänftigen *tr. V.* calm [down]; pacify; calm, soothe ‹temper›
Besatz *der;* ~es, Besätze (Borte) trimming *no indef. art.*
Besatzung *die;* ~, ~en (a) (Mannschaft) crew
(b) (Milit.: Verteidigungstruppe) garrison
(c) (Milit.: Okkupationstruppen) occupying forces *pl.*
Besatzungs-: ~**macht** *die* occupying power; ~**zone** *die* occupied zone
besaufen *unr. refl. V.* (salopp) get canned (Brit. sl.) *or* bombed (Amer. sl.)
Besäufnis *das;* ~ses, ~se (salopp) booze-up (Brit. coll.): blast (Amer. coll.)
beschädigen *tr. V.* damage
Beschädigung *die;* ~, ~en (a) damaging
(b) (Schaden) damage
beschaffen[1] *tr. V.* obtain, get *(Dat.* for)
beschaffen[2] *Adj.* **so** ~ **sein, dass ...:** be such that ...
Beschaffenheit *die;* ~: properties *pl.*
Beschaffung *die;* ~: ▶ BESCHAFFEN: obtaining; getting
beschäftigen ⊡ *refl. V.* occupy oneself; ┅┅╬

sich viel mit Musik/den Kindern ~: devote a great deal of one's time to music/the children; **sehr beschäftigt sein** be very busy
2 *tr. V.* **(a)** (geistig in Anspruch nehmen) **jmdn. ~:** preoccupy sb.
(b) (angestellt haben) employ ⟨*workers, staff*⟩
(c) (zu tun geben) occupy; **jmdn. mit etw. ~:** give sb. sth. to occupy him/her
Beschäftigte *der/die; adj. Dekl.* employee
Beschäftigung *die; ~, ~en* **(a)** (Tätigkeit) activity
(b) (Anstellung, Stelle) job
(c) (mit einer Frage, einem Problem) consideration (**mit of**); (Studium) study (**mit of**)
(d) (von Arbeitskräften) employment
beschämen *tr. V.* shame
beschämend 1 *Adj.* **(a)** (schändlich) shameful
(b) (demütigend) humiliating
2 *adv.* shamefully
beschämt *Adj.* ashamed
Beschämung *die; ~:* shame
beschatten *tr. V.* **(a)** (geh.) shade
(b) (überwachen) shadow
beschaulich 1 *Adj.* peaceful ⟨*life, manner, etc.*⟩
2 *adv.* peacefully
Beschaulichkeit *die; ~:* peacefulness
Bescheid *der; ~[e]s, ~e* **(a)** (Auskunft) information; (Antwort) answer; reply; **jmdm. ~ geben** *od.* **sagen[, ob ...]** let sb. know or tell sb. [whether ...]; **sage bitte im Hotel ~, dass ...:** please let the hotel know that ...; **[über etw. (*Akk.*)] ~ wissen** know [about sth.]
(b) (Entscheidung) decision
bescheiden¹ 1 *unr. tr. V.* **jmdn./etw. abschlägig ~:** turn sb./sth. down
2 *unr. refl. V.* (geh.) be content
bescheiden² 1 *Adj.* modest
2 *adv.* modestly
Bescheidenheit *die; ~:* modesty
bescheinigen *tr. V.* confirm ⟨*sth.*⟩ in writing
Bescheinigung *die; ~, ~en* written confirmation *no indef. art.*; (Schein, Attest) certificate
bescheißen *unr. tr. V.* (derb) **jmdn. ~:** rip sb. off (coll.); screw sb. (coarse)
beschenken *tr. V.* give ⟨*sb.*⟩ a present/presents
bescheren *tr. V.* **jmdn. [mit etw.] ~:** give sb. [sth. as] a Christmas present/Christmas presents
Bescherung *die; ~, ~en* **(a)** (zu Weihnachten) giving out of the Christmas presents
(b) das ist ja eine schöne ~ (ugs.) this is a pretty kettle of fish
bescheuert *Adj.* (salopp) **(a)** (verrückt) barmy (Brit. coll.); nuts (coll.)
(b) (unangenehm) stupid ⟨*task, party, etc.*⟩

beschichten *tr. V.* (Technik) coat
Beschichtung *die; ~, ~en* (Technik) coating
beschießen *unr. tr. V.* fire at; (mit Artillerie) bombard
beschimpfen *tr. V.* abuse; swear at
Beschimpfung *die; ~, ~en* insult; ~en abuse *sing.*; insults
beschissen *Adj.* (derb) lousy (coll.); shitty (coarse)
Beschlag *der; ~[e]s, Beschläge* **(a)** fitting
(b) jmdn./etw. mit ~ belegen *od.* in ~ nehmen monopolize sb./sth.
beschlagen¹ 1 *unr. tr. V.* shoe ⟨*horse*⟩
2 *unr. itr. V.; mit sein* ⟨*window*⟩ mist up (Brit.), fog up (Amer.); (durch Dampf) steam up
beschlagen² *Adj.* knowledgeable
Beschlagnahme *die; ~, ~n* confiscation
beschlagnahmen *tr. V.* confiscate
Beschlagnahmung *die; ~, ~en*
▶ BESCHLAGNAHME
beschleunigen 1 *tr. V.* accelerate; speed up ⟨*work, delivery*⟩; quicken ⟨*pace, step[s], pulse*⟩
2 *refl. V.* ⟨*heart rate*⟩ increase; ⟨*pulse*⟩ quicken
3 *itr. V.* ⟨*driver, car, etc.*⟩ accelerate
Beschleunigung *die; ~, ~en*
▶ BESCHLEUNIGEN 1: acceleration; speeding up; quickening
beschließen *unr. tr. V.* **(a)** decide; pass ⟨*law*⟩; **~, etw. zu tun** decide *or* resolve to do sth.
(b) (beenden) end
Beschluss, *Beschluß *der;* Beschlusses, Beschlüsse decision; (gemeinsam gefasst) resolution; **einen ~ fassen** come to a decision/pass a resolution
beschluss·fähig, *beschluß·fähig *Adj.* quorate
Beschluss·fähigkeit, *Beschluß·fähigkeit *die* presence of a quorum
beschmieren *tr. V.* **etw./sich ~:** get sth./oneself in a mess
beschmutzen *tr. V.* make ⟨*sth.*⟩ dirty
beschneiden *unr. tr. V.* **(a)** cut ⟨*hedge*⟩; prune ⟨*bush*⟩; cut back ⟨*tree*⟩; **einem Vogel die Flügel ~:** clip a bird's wings
(b) (Med., Rel.) circumcise
Beschneidung *die; ~, ~en* **(a)**
▶ BESCHNEIDEN A: cutting; pruning; cutting back
(b) (Med., Rel.) circumcision
beschnüffeln *tr. V.* sniff at
beschönigen *tr. V.* gloss over
beschränken 1 *tr. V.* restrict (**auf** + *Akk.* **to**)
2 *refl. V.* **sich auf etw. (*Akk.*) ~:** restrict oneself to sth.
beschränkt 1 *Adj.* **(a)** (dumm) dull-witted
(b) (engstirnig) narrow-minded

---

*alte Schreibung - vgl. Hinweis auf S. xiv

2 *adv.* narrow-mindedly
Beschränktheit *die;* ∼: (a) (Dummheit) lack of intelligence
(b) (Engstirnigkeit) narrow-mindedness
Beschränkung *die;* ∼, ∼en restriction
beschreiben *unr. tr. V.* (a) write on; (voll schreiben) write ⟨page, side, etc.⟩
(b) (darstellen) describe
Beschreibung *die;* ∼, ∼en description
beschriften *tr. V.* label; inscribe ⟨stone⟩; letter ⟨sign, label, etc.⟩; (mit Adresse) address
beschuldigen *tr. V.* accuse (*Gen.* of)
Beschuldigte *der/die; adj. Dekl.* accused
Beschuldigung *die;* ∼, ∼en accusation
beschummeln *tr. V.* (ugs.) cheat; diddle (Brit. coll.)
Beschuss, *Beschuß *der;* Beschusses fire; [heftig *od.* stark] unter ∼ geraten/stehen *od.* liegen (auch fig.) come/be under [heavy] fire
beschützen *tr. V.* protect (**vor** + *Dat.* from)
Beschützer *der;* ∼s, ∼, **Beschützerin** *die;* ∼, ∼nen protector
Beschwerde *die;* ∼, ∼n (a) complaint (**gegen, über** + *Akk.* about)
(b) *Pl.* (Schmerz) pain *sing.;* (Leiden) trouble *sing.*
beschweren 1 *refl. V.* complain (**über** + *Akk., wegen* about); **sich bei jmdm.** ∼: complain to sb.
2 *tr. V.* weight down
beschwerlich *Adj.* arduous; (ermüdend) exhausting
beschwichtigen *tr. V.* pacify; mollify ⟨anger etc.⟩
Beschwichtigung *die;* ∼, ∼en pacification; (des Zorns usw.) mollification
beschwingt *Adj.* lively
beschwipst *Adj.* (ugs.) tipsy
beschwören *unr. tr. V.* (a) swear to; ∼, **dass ...:** swear that ...; **eine Aussage** ∼: swear a statement on oath
(b) charm ⟨snake⟩
(c) (erscheinen lassen) invoke ⟨spirit⟩
(d) (bitten) implore
Beschwörung *die;* ∼, ∼en (a) (Zauberspruch) spell; incantation
(b) ▶ BESCHWÖREN C: invoking
(c) (Bitte) entreaty
beseitigen *tr. V.* remove; eliminate ⟨error, difficulty⟩; dispose of ⟨rubbish⟩
Beseitigung *die;* ∼: ▶ BESEITIGEN: removal; elimination; disposal
Besen *der;* ∼s, ∼ broom; **ich fress einen** ∼, **wenn das stimmt** (salopp) I'll eat my hat if that's right (coll.); **neue** ∼ **kehren gut** (Spr.) a new broom sweeps clean (prov.)
besessen *Adj.* (a) possessed
(b) (fig.) obsessive ⟨gambler⟩; **von einer Idee** ∼ **sein** be obsessed with an idea
Besessenheit *die;* ∼ (a) possession

(b) obsessiveness
besetzen *tr. V.* (a) (mit Pelz, Spitzen) edge; trim; **mit Perlen besetzt** set with pearls
(b) (belegen; auch Milit.: erobern) occupy
(c) (vergeben) fill ⟨post, position, role, etc.⟩
besetzt *Adj.* occupied; ⟨table, seat⟩ taken *pred.;* (gefüllt) full; (Fernspr.) engaged; busy (Amer.)
Besetzung *die;* ∼, ∼en (a) (einer Stellung) filling
(b) (Film, Theater usw.) cast
(c) (Eroberung) occupation
besichtigen *tr. V.* see ⟨sights⟩; see the sights of ⟨town⟩; view ⟨house etc. for sale⟩
Besichtigung *die;* ∼, ∼en: **zur** ∼ **der Stadt/des Schlosses/der Wohnung** to see the sights of the town/to see the castle/to view the flat
besiedeln *tr. V.* settle
besiedelt *Adj.* **dicht/dünn** ∼: densely/ thinly populated
besiegen *tr. V.* defeat
besinnen *unr. refl. V.* (a) think it over
(b) **sich [auf jmdn./etw.]** ∼: remember [sb./ sth.]
Besinnung *die;* ∼: consciousness; **die** ∼ **verlieren** faint; [wieder] **zur** ∼ **kommen** regain consciousness
besinnungs-los 1 *Adj.* unconscious
2 *adv.* mindlessly
Besinnungslosigkeit *die;* ∼: unconsciousness *no art.*
Besitz *der* (a) property
(b) (das Besitzen) possession; **im** ∼ **einer Sache** (*Gen.*) **sein** be in possession of sth.
Besitz·anspruch *der* claim to ownership
besitzen *unr. tr. V.* own; have ⟨quality, talent, etc.⟩; (nachdrücklicher) possess
Besitzer *der;* ∼s, ∼, **Besitzerin** *die;* ∼, ∼nen owner
besoffen *Adj.* (salopp) canned (Brit. sl.); bombed (Amer. sl.)
Besoffene *der/die; adj. Dekl.* (salopp) drunk
besohlen *tr. V.* sole; **neu** ∼: resole
besonder... *Adj.* special; **ein** ∼**es Ereignis** an unusual *or* a special event; **keine** ∼**e Leistung** no great achievement
Besonderheit *die;* ∼, ∼en special feature; (Eigenart) peculiarity
besonders 1 *Adv.* particularly
2 *Adj.; nicht attr.; nur verneint* (ugs.) **nicht** ∼ **sein** be nothing special
besonnen 1 *Adj.* prudent
2 *adv.* prudently
Besonnenheit *die;* ∼: prudence
besorgen *tr. V.* (a) get; (kaufen) buy
(b) (erledigen) take care of
Besorgnis *die;* ∼, ∼se concern
besorgt 1 *Adj.* concerned (**um** about)
2 *adv.* with concern
Besorgung *die;* ∼, ∼en purchase

bespitzeln *tr. V.* spy on

besprechen *unr. tr. V.* discuss; (rezensieren) review

Besprechung *die;* ~, ~en discussion; (Konferenz) meeting; (Rezension) review

bespritzen *tr. V.* (a) splash; (mit einem Wasserstrahl) spray
(b) (beschmutzen) bespatter

besprühen *tr. V.* spray

besser ① *Adj.* (a) better; **umso** ~: so much the better
(b) (sozial höher gestellt) superior
② *adv.* [immer] **alles** ~ **wissen** always know better; **es** ~ **haben** be better off; **es geht ihr** ~: she feels better; ~ **gesagt** to be [more] precise
③ *Adv.* (lieber) **das lässt du** ~ **sein** *od.* (ugs.) **bleiben** you'd better not do that

*****besser|gehen** ► BESSER 2

bessern ① *refl. V.* improve; ⟨person⟩ mend one's ways
② *tr. V.* improve; reform ⟨criminal⟩

Besserung *die;* ~, ~en recovery; **gute** ~! get well soon

best... ① *Adj.* (a) best; **bei** ~**er Gesundheit/ Laune sein** be in the best of health/spirits *pl.;* **im** ~**en Falle** at best; **in den** ~**en Jahren, im** ~**en Alter** in one's prime; ~**e Grüße an ...** (*Akk.*) best wishes to ...; **mit den** ~**en Grüßen** *od.* **Wünschen** with best wishes; (als Briefschluss) ≈ yours sincerely
(b) **es ist** *od.* **wäre das Beste, wenn ...**: it would be best if ...; **der/die/das nächste Beste ...**: the first ... one comes across; **einen Witz zum Besten geben** entertain [those present] with a joke; **das Beste vom Besten** the very best; **sein Bestes tun** do one's best; **zu deinem Besten** for your benefit
② *adv.* **am** ~**en** best
③ *Adv.* **am** ~**en fährst du mit dem Zug** it would be best for you to go by train

Bestand *der;* ~, **Bestände** (a) existence, (Fort~) continued existence
(b) (Vorrat) stock (**an** + *Dat.* of)

bestanden *Adj.* **von** *od.* **mit etw.** ~ **sein** have sth. growing on it; **mit Tannen** ~**e Hügel** fir-covered hills

beständig ① *Adj.* (a) constant
(b) (gleich bleibend) constant; steadfast ⟨person⟩; settled ⟨weather⟩
(c) (widerstandsfähig) resistant (**gegen** to)
② *adv.* constantly

Beständigkeit *die;* ~ (a) steadfastness
(b) (Widerstandsfähigkeit) resistance (**gegen** to)

Bestand·teil *der* component

bestärken *tr. V.* confirm

bestätigen ① *tr. V.* confirm; endorse ⟨document⟩; acknowledge ⟨receipt⟩
② *refl. V.* be confirmed; ⟨rumour⟩ prove to be true

Bestätigung *die;* ~, ~en confirmation; (des Empfangs) acknowledgement; (schriftlich) letter of confirmation

bestatten *tr. V.* (geh.) inter (formal); bury

Bestattung *die;* ~, ~en (geh.) interment (formal); burial; (Feierlichkeit) funeral

Bestattungs-: ~**institut** *das,* ~**unternehmen** *das* [firm of] undertakers *pl.* or funeral directors *pl.;* funeral parlor (Amer.)

bestäuben *tr. V.* (a) dust
(b) (Biol.) pollinate

bestaunen *tr. V.* marvel at

bestechen *unr. tr. V.* bribe

bestechlich *Adj.* corruptible; open to bribery *postpos.*

Bestechung *die;* ~, ~en bribery *no indef. art.*

Bestechungs-: ~**geld** *das* bribe; ~**versuch** *der* attempted bribery

Besteck *das;* ~[e]s, ~e cutlery setting; (ugs.: Gesamtheit der Bestecke) cutlery

bestehen ① *unr. itr. V.* (a) exist; **es besteht [die] Aussicht/Gefahr, dass ...**: there is a prospect/danger that ...; **noch besteht die Hoffnung, dass ...**: there is still hope that ...; ~ **bleiben** remain; ⟨regulation⟩ remain in force
(b) (fortdauern) survive; last
(c) **aus etw.** ~: consist of sth.; (hergestellt sein) be made of sth.
(d) **auf etw.** (*Dat.*) ~: insist on sth.
② *unr. tr. V.* pass ⟨test, examination⟩

Bestehen *das;* ~**s** existence; **die Firma feiert ihr 10-jähriges** ~: the firm is celebrating its tenth anniversary

*****bestehen|bleiben** ► BESTEHEN 1A

bestehend *Adj.* existing; current ⟨conditions⟩

bestehlen *unr. tr. V.* rob

besteigen *unr. tr. V.* (a) climb; mount ⟨horse, bicycle⟩; ascend ⟨throne⟩
(b) board ⟨ship, aircraft⟩; get on ⟨bus, train⟩

Besteigung *die;* ~, ~en an ascent

bestellen *tr. V.* (a) *auch itr.* order (**bei** from); **würden Sie mir bitte ein Taxi** ~? would you order me a taxi?
(b) (reservieren lassen) reserve ⟨tickets, table⟩
(c) **jmdn. [für 10 Uhr] zu sich** ~: ask sb. to go/come to see one [at 10 o'clock]
(d) (ausrichten) **jmdm. etw.** ~: tell sb. sth.; **bestell deinem Mann schöne Grüße von mir** give your husband my regards

Bestellung *die;* ~, ~en (a) order
(b) (Reservierung) reservation

besten·falls *Adv.* at best

bestens *Adv.* extremely well

besteuern *tr. V.* tax

bestialisch ① *Adj.* (a) bestial
(b) (ugs.: schrecklich) ghastly (coll.)
② *adv.* (a) in a bestial manner
(b) (ugs.: schrecklich) awfully (coll.)

Bestialität *die;* ~: bestiality

---

*old spelling - see note on page xiv

besticken *tr. V.* embroider

Bestie /'bɛstjə/ *die;* ~, ~n beast

bestimmen ① *tr. V.* **(a)** (festsetzen) decide on; fix ⟨*price, time, etc.*⟩

(b) (vorsehen) intend; **das ist für dich bestimmt** that is meant for you

(c) (identifizieren) identify; determine ⟨*age, position*⟩; define ⟨*meaning*⟩

(d) (prägen) determine the character of

② *itr. V.* **(a)** make the decisions

(b) über jmdn. ~: tell sb. what to do; **[frei] über etw.** *(Akk.)* ~: do as one wishes with sth.

bestimmend ① *Adj.* decisive

② *adv.* decisively

bestimmt ① *Adj.* **(a)** (speziell) particular; (gewiss) certain; (genau) definite

(b) (festgelegt) fixed; given ⟨*quantity*⟩

(c) (Sprachw.) definite ⟨*article etc.*⟩

(d) (entschieden) firm

② *adv.* **(a)** (deutlich) clearly; (genau) precisely

(b) (entschieden) firmly

③ *Adv.* for certain; **du weißt es doch [ganz]** ~ **noch** I'm sure you must remember it; **ich habe das** ~ **liegen gelassen** I must have left it behind

Bestimmtheit *die;* ~: firmness; (im Auftreten) decisiveness

Bestimmung *die;* ~, ~en **(a)** (das Festsetzen) fixing

(b) (Vorschrift) regulation

(c) (Zweck) purpose

(d) ▶ BESTIMMEN 1c: identification; determination; definition

(e) (Sprachw.) modifier; **adverbiale** ~: adverbial qualification

best·möglich *Adj.* best possible

bestrafen *tr. V.* punish (**für,** wegen for); **es wird mit Gefängnis bestraft** it is punishable by imprisonment

Bestrafung *die;* ~, ~en punishment

bestrahlen *tr. V.* **(a)** illuminate; floodlight ⟨*building*⟩

(b) (Med.) treat ⟨*tumour, part of body*⟩ using radiotherapy

Bestrahlung *die;* ~, ~en (Med.) radiation [treatment] *no indef. art.*

Bestreben *das;* ~s endeavour[s *pl.*]

bestrebt *Adj.:* ~ sein, etw. zu tun endeavour to do sth.

Bestrebung *die;* ~, ~en effort; (Versuch) attempt

bestreichen *unr. tr. V.* **A mit B** ~: spread B on A

bestreiten *unr. tr. V.* **(a)** dispute; (leugnen) deny

(b) (finanzieren) finance ⟨*studies*⟩; pay for ⟨*studies, sb.'s keep*⟩; meet ⟨*costs, expenses*⟩

(c) (gestalten) carry ⟨*programme, conversation, etc.*⟩

bestreuen *tr. V.* sprinkle

Bestseller /'bɛstzɛlɐ/ *der;* ~s, ~: best seller

bestürzend *Adj.* disturbing; (erschreckend) alarming

bestürzt ① *Adj.* dismayed

② *adv.* with dismay

Bestürzung *die;* ~: dismay

Besuch *der;* ~[e]s, ~e **(a)** visit (*Gen.,* bei to); **ein** ~ **bei jmdm.** a visit to sb.; (kurz) a call on sb.

(b) (Teilnahme) attendance (*Gen.* at)

(c) (Gast) visitor; (Gäste) visitors *pl.;* ~ **haben** have visitors/a visitor

besuchen *tr. V.* **(a)** visit; (weniger formell) go to see ⟨*person*⟩; go to ⟨*exhibition, theatre, museum, etc.*⟩; (zur Besichtigung) go to see ⟨*church, exhibition, etc.*⟩

(b) die Schule/Universität ~: go to school/ university

Besucher *der;* ~s, ~, **Besucherin** *die;* ~, ~nen visitor

Besuchs-: ~**erlaubnis** *die* visiting permit; ~**zeit** *die* visiting time *or* hours *pl.;* **es ist keine** ~**zeit** it is not visiting time

besucht *Adj.* gut/schlecht ~: well/poorly attended ⟨*lecture, performance, etc.*⟩; much/ little frequented ⟨*restaurant etc.*⟩

Beta-blocker /-blɔkɐ/ *der;* ~s, ~ (Med.) betablocker

betagt *Adj.* (geh.) elderly

betasten *tr. V.* feel [with one's fingers]

betätigen ① *refl. V.* occupy oneself; **sich politisch/körperlich** ~: engage in political/ physical activity

② *tr. V.* operate ⟨*lever, switch, flush, etc.*⟩; apply ⟨*brake*⟩

Betätigung *die;* ~, ~en: **(a)** activity

(b) ▶ BETÄTIGEN 2: operation; application

betäuben *tr. V.* **(a)** (Med.) anaesthetize; deaden ⟨*nerve*⟩; **jmdn. örtlich** ~: give sb. a local anaesthetic

(b) (unterdrücken) deaden ⟨*pain*⟩; still ⟨*unease, fear*⟩

(c) (benommen machen) daze; (mit einem Schlag) stun

Betäubung *die;* ~, ~en: **(a)** (Med.) anaesthetization; (Narkose) anaesthesia

(b) (Benommenheit) daze

Betäubungs·mittel *das* narcotic; (Med.) anaesthetic

beteiligen ① *refl. V.* take part (**an** + *Dat.* in)

② *tr. V.* jmdn. [mit 10 %] an etw. (*Dat.*) ~: give sb. a [10%] share of sth.

beteiligt *Adj.* **(a)** involved (**an** + *Dat.* in)

(b) (finanziell) **an einem Unternehmen/am Gewinn** ~ **sein** have a share in a business/ in the profit

Beteiligte *der/die; adj. Dekl.* person involved

Beteiligung *die;* ~, ~en **(a)** participation (**an** + *Dat.* in)

(b) (Anteil) share (**an** + *Dat.* in)

beten ① *itr. V.* pray (**für,** um for)

② *tr. V.* say ⟨*prayer*⟩

beteuern tr. V. affirm; protest ⟨one's innocence⟩

Beteuerung die; ∼, ∼en ▶ BETEUERN: affirmation; protestation

Beton /be'tɔŋ, bes. österr.: be'toːn/ der; ∼s, ∼s /-ɔŋs/ od. (bes. österr.:) ∼e /-oːnə/ concrete

betonen tr. V. (a) stress ⟨word, syllable⟩
(b) (hervorheben) emphasize

betonieren tr. V. concrete; surface ⟨road etc.⟩ with concrete

betont ① Adj. (a) stressed
(b) (bewusst) studied
② adv. studiedly

Betonung die; ∼, ∼en (a) stressing
(b) (Akzent) stress; (Intonation) intonation
(c) (Hervorhebung) emphasis

betören tr. V. (geh.) captivate

betr. Abk. = **betreffs, betrifft** re

Betr. Abk. = **Betreff** re

Betracht: jmdn./etw. in ∼ ziehen consider sb./sth.; jmdn./etw. außer ∼ lassen disregard sb./sth.

betrachten tr. V. (a) look at
(b) jmdn./etw. als etw. ∼: regard sb./sth. as sth.
(c) (beurteilen) consider

Betrachter der; ∼s, ∼, **Betrachterin** die; ∼, ∼nen observer

beträchtlich ① Adj. considerable
② adv. considerably

Betrachtung die; ∼, ∼en (a) contemplation; (Untersuchung) examination
(b) (Überlegung) reflection

Betrachtungs-weise die way of looking at things; (Standpunkt) point of view

Betrag der; ∼[e]s, Beträge amount; „∼ dankend erhalten" 'received with thanks'

betragen ① unr. itr. V. be; (bei Geldsummen) come to; amount to
② unr. refl. V. behave

Betragen das; ∼s behaviour

Betreff der; ∼[e]s, ∼e (im Brief) heading

betreffen unr. tr. V. concern; ⟨new rule, change, etc.⟩ affect

betreffend Adj. concerning; der ∼e Sachbearbeiter the person dealing with this matter; in dem ∼en Fall in the case in question

betreffs Präp. mit Gen. (Amtsspr., Kaufmannsspr.) concerning

betreiben unr. tr. V. (a) proceed with, (energisch) press ahead with ⟨task, case, etc.⟩; pursue ⟨policy, studies⟩; carry on ⟨trade⟩; go in for ⟨sport⟩
(b) run ⟨business, shop⟩
(c) (in Betrieb halten) operate

betreten¹ unr. tr. V. (hineintreten in) enter; (treten auf) step on to; (begehen) walk on ⟨carpet, grass, etc.⟩; „Betreten verboten" 'Keep off'; (kein Eintritt) 'Keep out'

betreten² ① Adj. embarrassed
② adv. with embarrassment

betreuen tr. V. look after; care for ⟨invalid⟩; supervise ⟨youth group⟩; see to the needs of ⟨tourists, sportsmen⟩

Betreuung die; ∼: care no indef. art.

Betrieb der; ∼[e]s, ∼e (a) business; (Firma) firm
(b) (das In-Funktion-Sein) operation; außer ∼ sein not operate; (wegen Störung) be out of order; in/außer ∼ setzen start up/stop ⟨machine etc.⟩
(c) (ugs.: Treiben) bustle; (Verkehr) traffic; es herrscht großer ∼, es ist viel ∼: it's very busy

betrieblich Adj. firm's; company

Betriebs-: ∼angehörige der/die employee; ∼anleitung die, ∼anweisung die operating instructions pl.; ∼ausflug der staff outing; ∼ferien Pl. firm's annual close-down sing.; „Wegen ∼ferien geschlossen" 'closed for annual holidays'; ∼klima das working atmosphere; ∼rat der (a) works committee; (b) (Person) member of a/the works committee; ∼rätin die ▶ BETRIEBSRAT B; ∼system das (DV) operating system; ∼versammlung die meeting of the workforce; ∼wirt der, ∼wirtin die graduate in business management; ∼wirtschaft die business management

betrinken unr. refl. V. get drunk

betroffen ① Adj. upset; (bestürzt) dismayed
② adv. in dismay

Betroffenheit die; ∼: dismay

betrüblich Adj. gloomy

betrübt ① Adj. sad; gloomy ⟨face etc.⟩
② sadly; (schwermütig) gloomily

Betrug der; ∼[e]s deception; (Delikt) fraud

betrügen ① unr. tr. V. deceive; be unfaithful to ⟨husband, wife⟩; (Rechtsw.) defraud; (beim Spielen) cheat; jmdn. um 100 DM ∼: cheat or (coll.) do sb. out of 100 marks; (arglistig) swindle sb. out of 100 marks
② unr. itr. V. cheat; (bei Geschäften) swindle people

Betrüger der; ∼s, ∼: swindler; (Hochstapler) conman (coll.); (beim Spielen) cheat

Betrügerei die; ∼, ∼en deception; (beim Spielen usw.) cheating; (bei Geschäften) swindling

Betrügerin die; ∼, ∼nen swindler; (beim Spielen) cheat

betrunken Adj. drunken attrib.; drunk pred.

Betrunkene der/die; adj. Dekl. drunk

Bett das; ∼[e]s, ∼en (a) bed; ins od. zu ∼ gehen go to bed; die Kinder ins ∼ bringen put the children to bed
(b) (Feder∼) duvet

Bett-: ∼bezug der duvet cover; ∼decke die blanket; (gesteppt) quilt

Bettelei die; ∼, ∼en begging no art.

---

betteln *itr. V.* beg (um for)

bett·lägerig *Adj.* bedridden

Bett·laken *das* sheet

Bett·lektüre *die* bedtime reading *no indef. art.*

Bettler *der;* ∼s, ∼, **Bettlerin** *die;* ∼, ∼nen beggar

bett-, Bett-: ∼**reif** *Adj.* (ugs.) ready for bed *pred.;* ∼**ruhe** *die* bed rest; ∼**schwere** *die:* die nötige *od.* notwendige ∼schwere haben (ugs.) be ready for one's bed; ∼**tuch** *das; Pl.* ∼tücher sheet; ∼**wäsche** *die* bedlinen; ∼**zeug** *das* (ugs.) bedclothes *pl.*

betucht *Adj.* (ugs.) well-heeled (coll.); well-off

betupfen *tr. V.* dab

Beuge *die;* ∼, ∼n (Turnen) bend

beugen ① *tr. V.* (a) bend; bow ⟨head⟩ (b) (Sprachw.: flektieren) inflect ⟨word⟩ ② *refl. V.* (a) bend over; **sich nach vorn/ hinten** ∼: bend forwards/bend over backwards; **sich aus dem Fenster** ∼: lean out of the window (b) (sich fügen) give way

Beugung *die;* ∼, ∼en (Sprachw.) inflexion

Beule *die;* ∼, ∼n bump; (Vertiefung) dent

beulen *itr. V.* bulge

beunruhigen *tr., refl. V.* worry

beurlauben *tr. V.* (a) jmdn. [für zwei Tage] ∼: give sb. [two days'] leave of absence (b) (suspendieren) suspend

beurteilen *tr. V.* judge; assess ⟨situation etc.⟩

Beurteilung *die;* ∼, ∼en (a) judgement; (einer Lage usw.) assessment (b) (Gutachten) assessment

Beute *die;* ∼, ∼n (a) (Gestohlenes) haul; loot *no indef. art.;* (b) (von Raubtieren) prey; (eines Jägers) bag

Beute·kunst *die* looted art

Beutel *der;* ∼s, ∼ bag; (kleiner, für Tabak usw.) pouch

bevölkern *tr. V.* populate

Bevölkerung *die;* ∼, ∼en population; (Volk) people

Bevölkerungs-: ∼**dichte** *die* population density; ∼**explosion** *die* population explosion; ∼**zunahme** *die*, ∼**zuwachs** *der* increase in population

bevollmächtigen *tr. V.* authorize

Bevollmächtigte *der/die; adj. Dekl.* authorized representative

bevor *Konj.* before; ∼ du nicht unterschrieben hast until you have signed

bevor·munden *tr. V.* jmdn. ∼: impose one's will on sb.; sie wollen sich nicht länger ∼ lassen they do not want to be dictated to any longer

bevor|stehen *unr. itr. V.* be near; unmittelbar ∼: be imminent; jmdm. steht etw. bevor sth. is in store for sb.

bevorstehend *Adj.* forthcoming; unmittelbar ∼: imminent

bevorzugen *tr. V.* (a) (vorziehen) prefer (vor + *Dat.* to) (b) (begünstigen) favour; give preference *or* preferenzial treatment to (vor + *Dat.* over)

bevorzugt ① *Adj.* favoured; (privilegiert) privileged; preferenzial ⟨treatment⟩ ② *adv.* jmdn. ∼ behandeln give sb. preferential treatment

Bevorzugung *die;* ∼, ∼en (Begünstigung) preferential treatment

bewachen *tr. V.* guard; bewachter Parkplatz car park with an attendant

Bewacher *der;* ∼s, ∼, **Bewacherin** *die;* ∼, ∼nen guard

Bewachung *die;* ∼, ∼en guarding

bewaffnen ① *tr. V.* arm ② *refl. V.* (auch fig.) arm oneself (mit with)

bewaffnet *Adj.* armed; bis an die Zähne ∼: armed to the teeth

Bewaffnung *die;* ∼, ∼en (a) arming (b) (Waffen) weapons *pl.*

bewahren *tr. V.* (a) protect (vor + *Dat.* from) (b) (erhalten) seine Fassung ∼: retain one's composure; Stillschweigen ∼: remain silent

bewähren *refl. V.* prove oneself/itself

bewährt *Adj.* proven ⟨method, design, etc.⟩; well-tried ⟨recipe, cure⟩; reliable ⟨worker⟩

Bewährung *die;* ∼, ∼en (Rechtsw.) probation

Bewährungs-: ∼**frist** *die* (Rechtsw.) period of probation; ∼**helfer** *der*, ∼**helferin** *die* probation officer; ∼**zeit** *die* (Rechtsw.) probation period

bewaldet *Adj.* wooded

bewältigen *tr. V.* cope with; overcome ⟨difficulty, problem⟩; cover ⟨distance⟩

Bewältigung *die;* ∼, ∼en ▶ BEWÄLTIGEN: coping with; overcoming; covering

bewandert *Adj.* well-versed

Bewandtnis *die;* ∼, ∼se: mit etw. hat es [s]eine eigene/besondere ∼: there's a [special] story behind sth.

bewässern *tr. V.* irrigate

Bewässerung *die;* ∼, ∼en irrigation

bewegen[1] ① *tr. V.* (a) move (b) (ergreifen) move (c) (innerlich beschäftigen) preoccupy ② *refl. V.* move

bewegen[2] *unr. tr. V.* jmdn. dazu ∼, etw. zu tun ⟨thing⟩ induce sb. to do sth.; ⟨person⟩ prevail upon sb. to do sth.

Beweg·grund *der* motive

beweglich *Adj.* (a) movable; moving ⟨target⟩ (b) (rege) agile ⟨mind⟩

bewegt *Adj.* eventful; (unruhig) turbulent

Bewegung *die;* ∼, ∼en (a) movement; (bes. Technik, Physik) motion (b) (körperliche ∼) exercise

⸱⸱⸱⸲

b

(c) (Ergriffenheit) emotion
(d) (Bestreben, Gruppe) movement
Bewegungs·freiheit *die* freedom of movement
bewegungslos *Adj.* motionless
Bewegungslosigkeit *die;* ~: motionlessness
Beweis *der;* ~es, ~e proof (*Gen.,* für of); belastende ~e incriminating evidence
beweisbar *Adj.* provable
beweisen *unr. tr. V.* prove
Beweis-: ~**material** *das* evidence; ~**mittel** *das* (Rechtsw.) form of evidence; ~**stück** *das* piece of evidence; ~**stücke** evidence *sing.*
bewenden *unr. V.* es bei *od.* mit etw. ~ lassen content oneself with sth.
bewerben *unr. refl. V.* apply (bei to, um for)
Bewerber *der;* ~s, ~, **Bewerberin** *die;* ~, ~nen applicant
Bewerbung *die* application
Bewerbungs-: ~**bogen** *der* application form; ~**schreiben** *das* letter of application; ~**unterlagen** *Pl.* documents in support of an/the application
bewerfen *unr. tr. V.* jmdn./etw. mit etw. ~: throw sth. at sb./sth.
bewerkstelligen *tr. V.* pull off, manage ⟨*deal, sale, etc.*⟩; es ~, etw. zu tun contrive *or* manage to do sth.
bewerten *tr. V.* assess; rate; (dem Geldwert nach) value (mit at)
Bewertung *die;* ~, ~en assessment; (dem Geldwert nach) valuation
bewilligen *tr. V.* grant
Bewilligung *die;* ~, ~en granting
bewirken *tr. V.* bring about; cause
bewirten *tr. V.* feed; jmdn. mit etw. ~: serve sb. sth.
bewirtschaften *tr. V.* (a) manage ⟨*estate, farm, restaurant, business, etc.*⟩
(b) farm ⟨*fields, land*⟩
Bewirtung *die;* ~, ~en provision of food and drink
bewog *1. u. 3. Pers. Sg. Prät. v.* BEWEGEN²
bewohnbar *Adj.* habitable
bewohnen *tr. V.* inhabit, live in ⟨*house, area*⟩; live in ⟨*room, flat*⟩
Bewohner *der;* ~s, ~, **Bewohnerin** *die;* ~, ~nen (eines Hauses, einer Wohnung) occupant; (einer Stadt, eines Gebietes) inhabitant
bewohnt *Adj.* occupied ⟨*house etc.*⟩; inhabited ⟨*area*⟩
bewölken *refl. V.* cloud over; become overcast
bewölkt *Adj.* cloudy; overcast
Bewölkung *die;* ~, ~en cloud [cover]
Bewunderer *der;* ~s, ~, **Bewunderin** *die;* ~, ~nen admirer

bewundern *tr. V.* admire (wegen, für for)
bewunderns·wert ① *Adj.* admirable
② *adv.* admirably
Bewunderung *die;* ~: admiration
bewusst, *bewußt ① *Adj.* conscious ⟨*reaction, behaviour, etc.*⟩; (absichtlich) deliberate ⟨*lie, deception, attack, etc.*⟩; etw. ist/wird jmdm. ~: sb. is/becomes aware of sth.; sb. realizes sth.; sich (*Dat.*) einer Sache (*Gen.*) ~ sein/werden be/become aware of something
② *adv.* consciously; (absichtlich) deliberately
bewusst·los, *bewußt·los *Adj.* unconscious
Bewusstlosigkeit, *Bewußtlosigkeit *die;* ~: unconsciousness
Bewusst·sein, *Bewußt·sein *das* (a) consciousness; das ~ verlieren/ wiedererlangen lose/regain consciousness; bei vollem ~ sein be fully conscious
(b) (deutliches Wissen) awareness
bewusstseins-, *bewußtseins-, Bewusstseins-, *Bewußtseins-: ~**erweiternd** *Adj.* mind-expanding; psychedelic; ~**erweiterung** *die* expansion of consciousness; ~**trübung** *die* clouding *or* dimming of consciousness; ~**veränderung** *die* change of awareness *or* outlook
bezahlbar *Adj.* affordable
bezahlen ① *tr. V.* pay ⟨*person, bill, taxes, rent, amount*⟩; pay for ⟨*goods etc.*⟩; das macht sich bezahlt it pays off
② *itr. V.* pay; Herr Ober, ich möchte ~ *od.* bitte ~: waiter, the bill *or* (Amer.) check please
Bezahl·fernsehen *das* pay television; pay TV
Bezahlung *die;* ~, ~en payment; (Lohn, Gehalt) pay
bezaubernd ① *Adj.* enchanting
② *adv.* enchantingly
bezeichnen *tr. V.* (a) jmdn./sich/etw. als etw. ~: call sb./oneself/sth. sth.
(b) (Name, Wort sein für) denote
bezeichnend *Adj.* characteristic (für of)
Bezeichnung *die;* ~, ~en (a) marking; (Angabe durch Zeichen) indication
(b) (Name) name
bezeugen *tr. V.* testify to
bezichtigen *tr. V.* accuse
beziehen ① *unr. tr. V.* (a) cover ⟨*seat, cushion, etc.*⟩; die Betten frisch ~: put clean sheets on the beds
(b) (einziehen in) move into ⟨*house, office*⟩
(c) (Milit.) take up ⟨*position, post*⟩
(d) (erhalten) obtain ⟨*goods*⟩; take ⟨*newspaper*⟩; draw ⟨*pension, salary*⟩
(e) (in Beziehung setzen) apply (auf + *Akk.* to)
② *unr. refl. V.* (a) es/der Himmel bezieht sich it/the sky is clouding over *or* becoming overcast

---

*old spelling - see note on page xiv

(b) sich auf jmdn./etw. ~ (sich berufen auf) ⟨*person, letter, etc.*⟩ refer to sb./sth.; (betreffen) ⟨*question, statement, etc.*⟩ relate to sb./sth.; **wir ~ uns auf Ihr Schreiben vom 28. 8.** with reference to your letter of 28 August

Beziehung *die;* ~, ~**en (a)** relation; (Zusammenhang) connection (**zu** with); **zwischen A und B besteht keine/eine** ~: there is no/a connection between A and B **(b)** (Freundschaft, Liebes~) relationship **(c)** (Hinsicht) respect; **in mancher** ~: in many respects

beziehungs·weise *Konj.* and ... respectively; (oder) or

beziffern *tr. V.* estimate (**auf** + *Akk.* at); **den Schaden auf 3 000 DM** ~: estimate the damage at 3,000 marks

Bezirk *der;* ~[e]s, ~e district

bezug ▶ BEZUG D

Bezug *der* **(a)** (für Kissen usw.) cover; (für Polstermöbel) loose cover; slip cover (Amer.); (für Betten) duvet cover; (für Kopfkissen) pillowcase **(b)** (Erwerb) obtaining; (Kauf) purchase; ~ **einer Zeitung** taking a newspaper **(c)** *Pl.* salary *sing.;* **(d)** (Papierdt.) **mit** *od.* **unter** ~ **auf etw.** (*Akk.*) with reference to sth.; **in** ~ **auf jmdn./etw.** regarding sb./sth.; ~ **nehmend auf unser Telex** with reference to our telex

bezüglich *Präp. mit Gen.* regarding

bezwecken *tr. V.* aim to achieve

bezweifeln *tr. V.* doubt

bezwingen *unr. tr. V.* conquer ⟨*enemy, mountain, pain, etc.*⟩; defeat ⟨*opponent*⟩; capture ⟨*fortress*⟩

BH /beː'haː/ *der;* ~[s], ~[s] *Abk.* = **Büstenhalter** bra

Bibel *die;* ~, ~**n** (auch fig.) Bible

Biber *der;* ~**s,** ~: beaver

Bibliographie *die;* ~, ~**n** bibliography

bibliographisch *Adj.* bibliographical

Bibliothek *die;* ~, ~**en** library

Bibliothekar *der;* ~**s,** ~**e, Bibliothekarin** *die;* ~, ~**nen** librarian

biblisch *Adj.* biblical

Bidet /bi'deː/ *das;* ~**s,** ~**s** bidet

bieder *Adj.* unsophisticated; (langweilig) stolid; (treuherzig) trusting

biegen ⓵ *unr. tr. V.* bend ⓶ *unr. refl. V.* bend; (nachgeben) give ⓷ *unr. itr. V.; mit sein* turn

biegsam *Adj.* flexible; pliable ⟨*material*⟩

Biegsamkeit *die;* ~ ▶ BIEGSAM: flexibility; pliability

Biegung *die;* ~, ~**en** bend

Biene *die;* ~, ~**n** bee

Bienen-: ~**honig** *der* bees' honey; ~**königin** *die* queen bee; ~**korb** *der* straw hive; ~**stock** *der* beehive

Bier *das;* ~[e]s, ~**e** beer

Bier-: ~**bauch** *der* (ugs. spött.) beer belly;

~**brauerei** *die* brewery; ~**deckel** *der* beer mat; ~**dose** *die* beer can; ~**fass,** *~***faß** *das* beer barrel; ~**flasche** *die* beer bottle; ~**garten** *der* beer garden; ~**glas** *das* beer glass; ~**kasten** *der* beer crate; ~**trinker** *der,* ~**trinkerin** *die* beer drinker; ~**zelt** *das* beer tent

Biest *das;* ~[e]s, ~**er** (ugs. abwertend) **(a)** (Tier, Gegenstand) wretched thing **(b)** (Mensch) wretch

bieten ⓵ *unr. tr. V.* **(a)** offer; put on ⟨*programme etc.*⟩; provide ⟨*shelter, guarantee, etc.*⟩ **(b) ein schreckliches Bild** ~: present a terrible picture; **einen prächtigen Anblick** ~: be a splendid sight ⓶ *unr. refl. V.* **sich jmdm.** ~: present itself to sb. ⓷ *unr. itr. V.* bid

Bigamie *die;* ~: bigamy *no def. art.*

Bigamist *der;* ~**en,** ~**en, Bigamistin** *die;* ~, ~**nen** bigamist

Bikini *der;* ~**s,** ~**s** bikini

Bilanz *die;* ~, ~**en (a)** balance sheet **(b)** (Ergebnis) outcome; ~ **ziehen** take stock

Bild *das;* ~[e]s, ~**er (a)** picture **(b)** (Anblick) sight **(c)** (Metapher) image

bilden ⓵ *tr. V.* **(a)** form (**aus** from); (modellieren) mould (**aus** from); **eine Gasse** ~: make a path; **sich** (*Dat.*) **ein Urteil** ~: form an opinion **(b)** (ansammeln) build up ⟨*fund, capital*⟩ **(c)** (darstellen) be ⟨*exception etc.*⟩ **(d)** (erziehen) educate ⓶ *refl. V.* **(a)** form **(b)** (lernen) educate oneself

bildend *Adj.* **(a) die** ~**e Kunst, die** ~**en Künste** the plastic arts *pl.* (*including painting and architecture*) **(b)** (belehrend) educational

Bilder-: ~**buch** *das* picture book (*for children*); ~**geschichte** *die* picture story; ~**rahmen** *der* picture frame; ~**rätsel** *das* picture puzzle; (Rebus) rebus

bild-, Bild: ~**hauer** *der* sculptor; ~**hauerin** *die;* ~~, ~~**nen** sculptress; ~**hübsch** *Adj.* really lovely; stunningly beautiful ⟨*girl*⟩

bildlich ⓵ *Adj.* pictorial; (übertragen) figurative ⓶ *adv.* pictorially; (übertragen) figuratively

Bildnis /'bɪltnɪs/ *das;* ~**ses,** ~**se** portrait

Bild-: ~**qualität** *die* picture quality; ~**röhre** *die* (Ferns.) picture tube

Bild·schirm *der* (Ferns., Informationst.) screen

Bildschirm-: ~**gerät** *das* VDU; visual display unit; ~**schoner** *der;* ~~**s,** ~~ (DV) screen saver

bild-, Bild-: ~**schön** *Adj.* really lovely; stunningly beautiful ⟨*girl, woman*⟩; ~**telefon** *das* video telephone

Bildung *die;* ~, ~en (a) (Erziehung)
education; (Kultur) culture
(b) (das Formen) formation

Bildungs-: ~**lücke** *die* gap in one's
education; ~**wesen** *das* education system;
das ~**wesen** education

Bild·unterschrift *die* caption

Billard /'bɪljart, *österr.:* bi'ja:ɐ̯/ *das;* ~s, ~e
billiards

Billard-: ~**kugel** *die* billiard ball;
~**stock** *der* billiard cue; ~**tisch** *der*
billiard table

Billett /bɪl'jɛt/ *das;* ~[e]s, ~e *od.* ~s
(schweiz., veralt.) ticket

Billiarde *die;* ~, ~n thousand million
million; quadrillion (Amer.)

billig ☐1 *Adj.* (a) cheap
(b) (abwertend: primitiv) cheap ⟨trick⟩; feeble
⟨excuse⟩
☐2 *adv.* cheaply

Billig·angebot *das* special *or* cut-price
offer

billigen *tr. V.* approve

Billig-: ~**flug** *der* cheap flight;
~**lohn·land** *das* low-wage country

Billigung *die;* ~: approval

Billion *die;* ~, ~en trillion; million million

bimmeln *itr. V.* (ugs.) ring

bin *1. Pers. Sg. Präsens v.* SEIN[1]

binär *Adj.* binary

Binde *die;* ~, ~n (a) (Verband) bandage;
(Augenbinde) blindfold
(b) (Armbinde) armband

Binde-: ~**gewebe** *das* (Anat.) connective
tissue; ~**haut** *die* (Anat.) conjunctiva

binden ☐1 *unr. tr. V.* (a) (auch fig.) tie; knot
⟨tie⟩; make up ⟨wreath, bouquet⟩; **jmdn. an**
sich (*Akk.*) ~ (fig.) make sb. dependent on
one
(b) (fesseln, festhalten, zusammenhalten, fig.:
verpflichten, Buchw.) bind
(c) (Kochk.: legieren) thicken ⟨sauce⟩
☐2 *unr. refl. V.* tie oneself down

Binder *der;* ~s, ~ tie

Binde·strich *der* hyphen

Bind·faden *der* string

Bindung *die;* ~, ~en (a) (Beziehung)
relationship (an + *Akk.* to)
(b) (Verbundenheit) attachment (an + *Akk.* to)
(c) (Skibindung) binding

binnen *Präp. mit Dat. od.* (geh.) *Gen.* within

Binnenmarkt *der* (Wirtsch.) domestic *or*
home market; **europäischer** ~: internal
European market

Binsen·weisheit *die* truism

Bio- (ugs.) organic ⟨farmer, garden,
vegetables, etc.⟩

bio-, Bio-: ~**abfall** *der* biowaste;
~**chemie** *die* biochemistry; ~**graf** *der;*
~~en, ~~en biographer; ~**grafie** *die;*

~, ~~n biography; ~**grafin** *die;* ~~,
~~nen biographer; ~**grafisch** *Adj.*
biographical; ~**loge** *der;* ~~n, ~~n
biologist; ~**logie** *die;* ~~: biology *no art.;*
~**login** *der;* ~~, ~~nen biologist;
~**logisch** *Adj.* (a) biological; (b) (natürlich)
natural ⟨medicine, cosmetic, etc.⟩; ~**masse**
die biomass; ~**müll** *der* biowaste; ~**top**
der od. das; ~~s, ~~e (Biol.) biotope

Birke *die;* ~, ~n birch [tree]; (Holz)
birch[wood]

Birma (*das*)*;* ~s Burma

Birn·baum *der* pear tree

Birne *die;* ~, ~n (a) pear
(b) (Glühlampe) [light]bulb
(c) (salopp: Kopf) nut (coll.)

bis ☐1 *Präp. mit Akk.* (a) (zeitlich) until; till;
(die ganze Zeit über und bis zu einem bestimmten
Zeitpunkt) up until; up till; (nicht später als) by
(b) (räumlich) to; **dieser Zug fährt nur** ~
Offenburg this train only goes as far as
Offenburg; ~ **5 000 Mark** up to 5,000 marks
(c) ~ **auf** (einschließlich) down to; (mit Ausnahme
von) except for
☐2 *Adv.* ~ **zu 6 Personen** up to six people
☐3 *Konj.* (a) (nebenordnend) to
(b) (unterordnend) until; till; (österr.: sobald)
when

Bisam·ratte *die* muskrat

Bischof *der;* ~s, Bischöfe, **Bischöfin** *die;*
~, ~nen bishop

bischöflich *Adj.* episcopal

bi·sexuell ☐1 *Adj.* bisexual
☐2 *adv.* bisexually

bis·her *Adv.* up to now; (aber jetzt nicht mehr)
until now; till now

bisherig *Adj.* (vorherig) previous; (momentan)
present

Biskaya /bɪs'ka:ja/ *die;* ~: the Bay of
Biscay

Biskuit /bɪs'kvi:t/ *das od. der;* ~[e]s, ~s *od.*
~e (a) sponge biscuit
(b) (~teig) sponge

bis·lang *Adv.:* ▶ BISHER

Bison *der;* ~s, ~s bison

Biss, *Biß *der;* Bisses, Bisse bite

bisschen, *bißchen *indekl.*
Indefinitpron. (a) *adj.* **ein** ~ **Geld/Wasser** a
bit of *or* a little money/a drop of *or* a little
water; **ein/kein** ~ **Angst haben** be a bit/not a
bit frightened
(b) *adv.* **ein/kein** ~: a bit *or* a little/not a *or*
one bit
(c) *subst.* **ein** ~: a bit; a little; (bei
Flüssigkeiten) a drop; a little; **das/kein** ~: the
little [bit]/not a *or* one bit

Bissen *der;* ~s, ~ mouthful

bissig ☐1 *Adj.* (a) ~ **sein** ⟨dog⟩ bite; **ein** ~**er**
Hund a dog that bites; „**Vorsicht,** ~**er Hund"**
'beware of the dog'
(b) cutting ⟨remark, tone, etc.⟩
☐2 *adv.* ⟨say⟩ cuttingly

Biss·wunde, *Biß·wunde *die* bite

---

*alte Schreibung - vgl. Hinweis auf S. xiv

bist 2. *Pers. Sg. Präsens v.* SEIN[1]

Bistum /'bɪstuːm/ *das;* ∼s, **Bistümer** bishopric; diocese

bis·weilen *Adv.* (geh.) from time to time

Bit /bɪt/ *das;* ∼s, ∼[s] (DV) bit

bitte 1 *Adv.* please
   2 *Interj.* (a) (Bitte, Aufforderung) please; **zwei Tassen Tee,** ∼: two cups of tea, please; ∼[, **nehmen Sie doch Platz]**! do take a seat; **Noch eine Tasse Tee? – [Ja]** ∼! Another cup of tea? – Yes, please
   (b) (Aufforderung, etw. entgegenzunehmen) ∼ [schön *od.* sehr]! there you are!
   (c) (Ausdruck des Einverständnisses) ∼ [gern]! certainly; of course; **Entschuldigung! – Bitte!** [I'm] sorry! – That's all right!
   (d) ∼ [schön *od.* sehr]! (im Laden, Lokal) yes, please?
   (e) [wie] ∼? (Nachfrage) sorry?
   (f) **Vielen Dank! – Bitte [schön** *od.* **sehr]** Many thanks! – Not at all *or* you're welcome

Bitte *die;* ∼, ∼n request; (inständig) plea

bitten *unr. tr. V.* (a) *auch itr.* ask (**um** for); **darf ich Sie um Feuer/ein Glas Wasser** ∼? could I ask you for a light/a glass of water, please?
   (b) (einladen) ask

bitter 1 *Adj.* (a) bitter; plain ⟨*chocolate*⟩
   (b) (fig.) (verbittert) bitter
   (c) (schmerzlich) bitter, painful, hard ⟨*loss*⟩; hard ⟨*time, fate, etc.*⟩; dire ⟨*need*⟩; desperate ⟨*poverty*⟩; grievous ⟨*injustice, harm*⟩
   2 *adv.* (sehr stark) desperately; ⟨*regret*⟩ bitterly

bitter-: ∼**böse** 1 *Adj.* furious; 2 *adv.* furiously; ∼**kalt** *Adj.* bitterly cold

bitterlich 1 *Adj.* slightly bitter ⟨*taste*⟩
   2 *adv.* (heftig) ⟨*cry, complain, etc.*⟩ bitterly

bitter-süß *Adj.* (auch fig.) bitter-sweet

Bitt·steller *der;* ∼s, ∼, **Bitt·stellerin** *die;* ∼, ∼nen petitioner

Biwak *das;* ∼s, ∼s (bes. Milit., Bergsteigen) bivouac

bizarr 1 *Adj.* bizarre
   2 *adv.* bizarrely

Bizeps *der;* ∼[es], ∼e biceps

Blähung *die;* ∼, ∼en flatulence *no art., no pl.*

Blamage /bla'maːʒə/ *die;* ∼, ∼n disgrace

blamieren 1 *tr. V.* disgrace
   2 *refl. V.* disgrace oneself; (sich lächerlich machen) make a fool of oneself

blank *Adj.* shiny

Blanko-: ∼**scheck** *der* (auch fig.) blank cheque; ∼**vollmacht** *die* (auch fig.) carte blanche

Bläschen /'blɛːsçən/ *das;* ∼s, ∼ (a) [small] bubble
   (b) (in der Haut) [small] blister

Blase *die;* ∼, ∼n (a) bubble
   (b) (in der Haut) blister
   (c) (Harn∼) bladder

Blase·balg *der;* ∼s, **Blasebälge** bellows *pl.*

blasen 1 *unr. itr. V.* blow
   2 *unr. tr. V.* (a) blow
   (b) (spielen) play ⟨*musical instrument, tune, melody, etc.*⟩

Bläser *der;* ∼s, ∼, **Bläserin** *die;* ∼, ∼nen (Musik) wind player

blasiert (abwertend) 1 *Adj.* blasé
   2 *adv.* in a blasé way

Blas-: ∼**instrument** *das* wind instrument; ∼**kapelle** *die* brass band; ∼**musik** *die* brass-band music

Blasphemie /blasfe'miː/ *die;* ∼, ∼n blasphemy

Blas·rohr *das* blowpipe

blass, *blaß 1 *Adj.* pale
   2 *adv.* palely

Blässe *die;* ∼: paleness

Blatt *das;* ∼[e]s, **Blätter** (a) (von Pflanzen) leaf
   (b) (Papier) sheet
   (c) (Buchseite usw.) page; **etw. vom** ∼ **spielen** sight-read sth.
   (d) (Zeitung) paper
   (e) (Spielkarten) hand
   (f) (am Werkzeug, Ruder) blade

Blättchen *das;* ∼s, ∼ (a) (von Pflanzen) [small] leaf
   (b) (Papier) [small] sheet

blättern *itr. V.* **in einem Buch** ∼: leaf through a book

Blätter·teig *der* puff pastry

Blatt-: ∼**gold** *das* gold leaf; ∼**grün** *das* chlorophyll; ∼**laus** *die* aphid

blau *Adj.* blue; **ein** ∼**er Fleck** a bruise; ∼ **sein** (fig. ugs.) be tight (coll.); **das Blaue vom Himmel herunterlügen** (ugs.) lie like anything

Blau *das;* ∼s, ∼ *od.* (ugs.:) ∼s blue

blau-, Blau-: ∼**äugig** *Adj.* (a) blue-eyed; (b) (naiv) naive; ∼**beere** *die* bilberry; ∼**grau** *Adj.* blue-grey; ∼**grün** *Adj.* blue-green

bläulich *Adj.* bluish

blau-, Blau-: ∼**licht** *das* flashing blue light; ∼**|machen** *itr. V.* (ugs.) skip work; ∼**mann** *der; Pl.* ∼**männer** (ugs.) boiler suit; ∼**säure** *die* (Chemie) prussic acid; ∼**stichig** *Adj.* (Fot.) with a blue cast *postpos., not pred.;* ∼**stichig sein** have a blue cast

Blazer /'bleːzɐ/ *der;* ∼s, ∼: blazer

Blech *das;* ∼[e]s, ∼e (a) sheet metal; (Stück Blech) metal sheet
   (b) (Back∼) [baking] tray

Blech-: ∼**bläser** *der,* ∼**bläserin** *die* brass player; **die** ∼**bläser** (im Orchester) the brass [section] *sing;* ∼**büchse** *die,* ∼**dose** *die* tin

blechen *tr., itr. V.* (ugs.) cough up (coll.)

blechern 1 *Adj.* (metallisch klingend) tinny ⟨*sound, voice*⟩
   2 *adv.* tinnily

Blech-: ∼**musik** *die* (abwertend) brass-band music; ∼**napf** *der* metal bowl

Blechner der; ~s, ~, **Blechnerin** die;
~, ~nen (südd.) ▶ KLEMPNER
Blech-: ~**schaden** der (Kfz-W.) damage no
indef. art. to the bodywork; ~**trommel** die
tin drum
blecken tr. V. die Zähne ~: bare one's/its
teeth
Blei das; ~[e]s, ~e lead
Bleibe die; ~, ~n place to stay
bleiben unr. itr. V.; mit sein (a) stay;
remain; ~ Sie bitte am Apparat hold the line
please; **wo bleibt er so lange?** where has he
got to?; **auf dem Weg** ~: keep to the path;
sitzen ~: stay or remain sitting down or
seated; **bei etw.** ~ (fig.: an etw. festhalten) keep
to sth.
(b) (übrig bleiben) be left; remain
(c) etw. ~ lassen give sth. a miss
bleibend Adj. lasting; permanent (damage)
*****bleiben|lassen** ▶ BLEIBEN C
bleich Adj. pale
bleichen[1] tr. V. bleach
bleichen[2] regelm., veralt. auch unr. itr. V.
become bleached
blei-, Blei-: ~**frei** Adj. unleaded (fuel);
~**kristall** das lead crystal; ~**kugel** die
lead ball; (Geschoss) lead bullet; ~**schwer**
Adj. heavy as lead postpos.; ~**stift** der
pencil; mit ~**stift** in pencil; ~**stift·spitzer**
der pencil sharpener
Blende die; ~, ~n (a) (Lichtschutz) shade; (am
Fenster) blind
(b) (Optik, Film, Fot.) diaphragm; (Blendenzahl)
aperture setting
blenden[1] tr. V. (a) (auch fig.) dazzle
(b) (blind machen) blind
[2] itr. V. (light) be dazzling
blendend[1] Adj. es geht mir ~: I feel
wonderfully well
[2] adv. wir haben uns ~ amüsiert we had a
marvellous time
blich 1. u. 3. Pers. Sg. Prät. v. BLEICHEN[2]
Blick der; ~[e]s, ~e (a) look; (flüchtig) glance
(b) (Ausdruck) look in one's eyes; **mit
misstrauischem** ~: with a suspicious look in
one's eye
(c) (Aussicht) view; **ein Zimmer mit** ~ **aufs
Meer** a room with a sea view
(d) (Urteil[skraft]) eye
blicken[1] itr. V. look; (flüchtig) glance
[2] tr. V. **sich** ~ **lassen** put in an appearance
Blick-: ~**fang** der eye-catcher; **als** ~**fang
dienen** serve to catch the eye; ~**feld** das
field of vision; ~**kontakt** der eye contact;
~**punkt** der view; ~**winkel** der (a) angle
of vision; (b) (fig.) point of view; viewpoint
blieb 1. u. 3. Pers. Sg. Prät. v. BLEIBEN
blies 1. u. 3. Pers. Sg. Prät. v. BLASEN
blind[1] Adj. (a) (auch fig.) blind; ~ **werden**
go blind
(b) (trübe) clouded (glass)

(c) **ein** ~**er Passagier** a stowaway
(d) ~**er Alarm** a false alarm
[2] adv. (a) (ohne hinzusehen) without looking;
(wahllos) blindly
(b) (unkritisch) (trust) implicitly; (obey) blindly
Blind-: ~**bewerbung** die unsolicited
application; ~**darm** der (a) caecum; (b)
(volkst.: Wurmfortsatz) appendix
Blinde der/die; adj. Dekl. blind person;
blind man/woman; **die** ~**n** the blind
Blinde-kuh: ~ **spielen** play blind man's
buff
Blinden-: ~**hund** der guide dog;
~**schrift** die Braille
Blindheit die; ~ (auch fig.) blindness
blindlings Adv. blindly; (trust) implicitly
blind-, Blind-: ~**schleiche** die; ~, ~n
slowworm; ~**wütig**[1] Adj. raging (anger,
hatred, fury, etc.); wild (rage); [2] adv. in a
blind rage
blinken[1] itr. V. (a) (light, glass, crystal)
flash; (star) twinkle; (metal, fish) gleam
(b) (Verkehrsw.) indicate
[2] tr. V. flash
Blinker der; ~s, ~: indicator [light]
Blink-: ~**licht** das (a) flashing light; (b)
▶ BLINKER; ~**zeichen** das flashlight signal
blinzeln itr. V. blink; (mit einem Auge, um ein
Zeichen zu geben) wink
Blitz der; ~es, ~e (a) lightning no indef.
art.; **ein** ~: a flash of lightning; [**schnell**] **wie
der** ~: like lightning
(b) (Blitzlicht) flash
blitz-, Blitz-: ~**ab·leiter** der lightning
conductor; ~**artig**[1] Adj. lightning;
[2] adv. like lightning; (disappear) in a flash;
~**blank** Adj. (ugs.) ~**blank** [geputzt]
sparkling clean; brightly polished (shoes)
blitzeblank ▶ BLITZBLANK
blitzen itr. V. unpers. **es blitzte** (einmal)
there was a flash of lightning; (mehrmals)
there was lightning
(b) (glänzen) (light, glass, crystal) flash;
(metal) gleam
blitz-, Blitz-: ~**gerät** das flash [unit];
~**licht** das flash[light]; ~**schnell**[1] Adj.
lightning attrib.; ~**schnell sein** be like
lightning; [2] adv. like lightning; (disappear)
in a flash; ~**start** der lightning start
Block der; ~[e]s, Blöcke od. ~s (a) Pl. nur
Blöcke (Brocken) block
(b) (Wohnblock) block
(c) Pl. nur Blöcke (Gruppierung von politischen
Kräften, Staaten) bloc
(d) (Schreibblock) pad
Blockade die; ~, ~n blockade
Block-: ~**flöte** die recorder; ~**haus** das,
~**hütte** die log cabin
blockieren tr. V. block; jam (telephone
line); halt (traffic); lock (wheel, machine, etc.)
Block·schrift die block capitals pl.
blöd[e] (ugs.)[1] Adj. (a) (dumm) stupid;
idiotic (coll.)

---

*old spelling - see note on page xiv

(b) (unangenehm) stupid
2 *adv.* stupidly; idiotically (coll.)
Blödel̲ei *die;* ∼, ∼**en** silly joke
blödeln *itr. V.* make silly jokes
Blödheit *die;* ∼, ∼**en** stupidity
blöd-, Blöd-: ∼**mann** *der; Pl.* ∼**männer**
(salopp) stupid idiot (coll.); ∼**sinn** *der* (ugs.)
nonsense; **mach doch keinen** ∼**sinn!** don't be
stupid; ∼**sinnig** (ugs.) 1 *Adj.* idiotic (coll.);
2 *adv.* idiotically (coll.)
blöken *itr. V.* ⟨sheep⟩ bleat; ⟨cattle⟩ low
blond *Adj.* fair-haired, blond ⟨man, race⟩;
blonde ⟨woman⟩; blond/blonde, fair ⟨hair⟩
Blondine *die;* ∼, ∼**n** blonde
bloß 1 *Adj.* **(a)** (nackt) naked
(b) (nichts als) mere ⟨words, promises,
triviality, suspicion, etc.⟩; **der** ∼**e Gedanke
daran** the mere thought of it
2 *Adv.* (ugs.: nur) only
3 *Partikel* **was hast du dir** ∼ **dabei
gedacht?** what on earth were you thinking
of?
Blöße *die;* ∼: **sich** (*Dat.*) **eine/keine** ∼
geben show a/not show any weakness
bloß|stellen *tr. V.* show up; expose
⟨swindler, criminal, etc.⟩
Blouson /bluˈzõ:/ *das od. der;* ∼**s**, ∼**s**
blouson
blubbern *itr. V.* (ugs.) bubble
Bluejeans /ˈbluːdʒiːns/ *Pl. od. die; die;* ∼, ∼:
[blue] jeans *pl.*
Blues /bluːs/ *der;* ∼, ∼: blues *pl.*
Bluff *der;* ∼**s**, ∼**s** bluff
bluffen *tr., itr. V.* bluff
blühen *itr. V.* **(a)** ⟨plant⟩ flower, be in
flower *or* bloom; ⟨flower⟩ be in bloom, be
out; ⟨tree⟩ be in blossom; ∼**de Gärten**
gardens full of flowers
(b) (florieren) thrive
(c) (ugs.: bevorstehen) **jmdm.** ∼: be in store for
sb.; **das kann dir auch noch** ∼: the same
could happen to you
blühend *Adj.* **(a)** (frisch, gesund) glowing
⟨colour, complexion, etc.⟩; radiant ⟨health⟩
(b) (übertrieben) vivid ⟨imagination⟩
Blümchen *das;* ∼**s**, ∼: [little] flower
Blume *die;* ∼, ∼**n (a)** flower
(b) (des Weines) bouquet
(c) (des Biers) head
blumen-, Blumen-: ∼**beet** *das* flower
bed; ∼**erde** *die* potting compost;
∼**geschäft** *das* florist's;
∼**geschmückt** *Adj.* flower-bedecked;
adorned with flowers *postpos.;* ∼**kasten**
der flower box; (vor einem Fenster) window
box; ∼**kohl** *der* cauliflower; ∼**strauß** *der;
Pl.* ∼**sträuße** bunch of flowers; (Bukett)
bouquet of flowers; ∼**topf** *der* flowerpot;
∼**vase** *die* [flower] vase; ∼**zwiebel** *die*
bulb
Bluse *die;* ∼, ∼**n** blouse
Blut *das;* ∼[e]s blood
blut-, Blut-: ∼**arm** *Adj.* (Med.) anaemic;

∼**armut** *die* (Med.) anaemia; ∼**bad** *das*
bloodbath; ∼**bahn** *die* bloodstream;
∼**bank** *die; Pl.* ∼∼**en** (Med.) blood bank;
∼**befleckt** *Adj.* bloodstained;
∼**beschmiert** *Adj.* smeared with blood
postpos.; ∼**buche** *die* copper beech;
∼**druck** *der; Pl.* ∼**drücke** blood pressure
Blüte *die;* ∼, ∼**n (a)** flower; bloom; (eines
Baums) blossom; ∼**n treiben** flower; ⟨tree⟩
blossom
(b) (das Blühen) flowering; (Baumblüte)
blossoming
Blut·egel *der;* ∼**s**, ∼: leech
bluten *itr. V.* bleed (aus from)
blüten-, Blüten-: ∼**blatt** *das* petal;
∼**honig** *der* blossom honey; ∼**staub** *der*
pollen; ∼**weiß** *Adj.* sparkling white
Bluter *der;* ∼**s**, ∼, **Bluterin** *die;* ∼, ∼**nen**
(Med.) haemophiliac
Blut·erguss, *Blut·erguß *der*
haematoma; (blauer Fleck) bruise
Bluter·krankheit *die* haemophilia *no art.*
Blut-: ∼**fleck[en]** *der* bloodstain;
∼**gefäß** *das* (Anat.) blood vessel;
∼**gerinnsel** *das;* ∼∼**s**, ∼∼ blood clot;
∼**gruppe** *die* blood group;
∼**hochdruck** *der* high blood pressure;
∼**hund** *der* bloodhound
blutig (a) bloody; **jmdn.** ∼ **schlagen** beat
sb. to a pulp
(b) (fig. ugs.: völlig) complete ⟨beginner,
layman, etc.⟩
blut-, Blut-: ∼**jung** *Adj.* very young;
∼**konserve** *die* container of stored blood;
∼**konserven** stored blood; ∼**körperchen**
das; ∼∼**s**, ∼∼: blood corpuscle; **rote/weiße**
∼**körperchen** red/white corpuscles;
∼**krebs** *der* leukaemia; ∼**kreislauf** *der*
blood circulation; ∼**lache** *die* pool of
blood; ∼**leer** *Adj.* bloodless; ∼**leere** *die*
restricted blood supply; ∼**orange** *die*
blood orange; ∼**plasma** *das* (Physiol.) blood
plasma; ∼**probe** *die* **(a)** (∼entnahme,
∼untersuchung) blood test; **(b)** (kleine ∼menge)
blood sample; ∼**rache** *die* blood revenge;
∼**rot** *Adj.* blood-red; ∼**rünstig** 1 *Adj.*
bloodthirsty; 2 *adv.* bloodthirstily;
∼**schande** *die* incest; ∼**spende** *die* (das
Spenden) giving *no indef. art.* of blood;
(∼menge) blood donation; ∼**spender** *der;*
∼**spenderin** *die* blood donor; ∼**spur** *die*
trail of blood; ∼**stillend** *Adj.* styptic
bluts-, Bluts-: ∼**tropfen** *der* drop of
blood; ∼**verwandt** *Adj.* related by blood
postpos.; ∼**verwandtschaft** *die* blood
relationship
Blut-: ∼**tat** *die* (geh.) bloody deed;
∼**transfusion** *die* blood transfusion;
∼**übertragung** *die* blood transfusion
Blutung *die;* ∼, ∼**en (a)** bleeding *no indef.
art., no pl.;*
(b) (Regelblutung) period
blut-, Blut-: ∼**unterlaufen** *Adj.*
suffused with blood *postpos.;* bloodshot ⋯⟩

⟨eyes⟩; ~**vergießen** das; ~~s bloodshed;
~**vergiftung** die blood poisoning no indef.
art., no pl.; ~**wurst** die black pudding;
~**zucker·spiegel** der (Physiol.) blood-
sugar level

Bö die; ~, ~en gust [of wind]

Bob der; ~, ~s bob[sleigh]

Bob-: ~**bahn** die bob[sleigh] run;
~**fahrer** der, ~**fahrerin** die bobber

Bock[1] der; ~[e]s, Böcke (a) (Reh~,
Kaninchen~) buck; (Ziegen~) billy goat; he-
goat; (Schafs~) ram; **einen/keinen ~ auf etw.**
(Akk.) **haben** (ugs.) fancy/not fancy sth.;
einen/keinen ~ haben, etw. zu tun (ugs.)
fancy/not fancy doing sth.
(b) (Gestell) trestle
(c) (Turngerät) buck

Bock[2] das; ~s (Bier) bock [beer]

Bock·bier das bock [beer]

bocken itr. V. refuse to go on; (vor einer
Hürde) refuse; (sich aufbäumen) buck

bockig [1] Adj. stubborn and awkward
[2] adv. stubbornly [and awkwardly]

Bocks·horn das: **sich ins ~ jagen lassen**
(ugs.) let oneself be browbeaten

Bock-: ~**springen** das; ~~s (Turnen)
vaulting [over the buck]; ~**wurst** die
bockwurst

Boden der; ~s, Böden (a) (Erd~) ground;
(Fuß~) floor; **am ~ zerstört [sein]** (ugs.) [be]
shattered (coll.); **bleiben wir doch auf dem ~
der Tatsachen** (fig.) let's stick to the facts
(b) (unterste Fläche) bottom; (Torten~) base
(c) (Dach~, Heu~) loft

boden-, Boden-: ~**belag** der floor-
covering; ~**ertrag** der crop yield;
~**fläche** die land area; ~**frost** der ground
frost; ~**kammer** die attic; ~**los** Adj. (a)
bottomless; (b) (ugs.: unerhört) incredible
⟨foolishness, meanness, etc.⟩; ~**nebel** der
ground fog/mist; ~**satz** der sediment;
~**schätze** Pl. mineral resources

Boden·see der; ~s Lake Constance

boden-, Boden-: ~**ständig** Adj.
indigenous ⟨culture, population, etc.⟩;
~**turnen** das floor exercises pl.; ~**welle**
die bump

Bodybuilding /ˈbɔdibɪldɪŋ/ das; ~s
bodybuilding no art.

Böe die; ~, ~n ▶ Bö

bog 1. u. 3. Pers. Sg. Prät. v. BIEGEN

Bogen der; ~s, ~, (südd., österr.:) Bögen (a)
curve; (Math.) arc
(b) (Archit.) arch
(c) (Waffe, Musik: Geigen~ usw.) bow
(d) (Papier~) sheet

bogen-, Bogen-: ~**fenster** das arched
window; ~**förmig** Adj. arched;
~**schießen** das; ~~s archery no art.

Boheme /boˈɛːm/ die; ~: bohemian society

Bohemien /boeˈmjɛ̃ː/ der; ~s, ~s
bohemian

Bohle die; ~, ~n [thick] plank

Böhnchen das; ~s, ~: [small] bean

Bohne die; ~, ~n bean; **nicht die ~** (ugs.)
not one little bit

Bohnen-: ~**eintopf** der bean stew;
~**kaffee** der real coffee; ~**kraut** das
savory; ~**stange** die (auch ugs.: Mensch)
beanpole; ~**stroh** das: **dumm wie ~stroh**
(ugs.) as thick as two short planks (coll.);
~**suppe** die bean soup

bohnern tr., itr. V. polish

Bohner·wachs das floor polish

bohren [1] tr. V. (a) bore; (mit Bohrer,
Bohrmaschine) drill, bore ⟨hole⟩; sink ⟨well,
shaft, pole, post etc.⟩ (in + Akk. into)
(b) (bearbeiten) drill ⟨wood, concrete, etc.⟩
(c) (drücken in) poke (in + Akk. in[to])
[2] itr. V. (a) drill; **in der Nase ~:** pick one's
nose; **nach Öl/Wasser usw. ~:** drill for oil/
water etc.;
(b) (ugs.: drängen, fragen) keep on
[3] refl. V. bore its way

bohrend Adj. (a) gnawing ⟨pain, hunger,
remorse⟩
(b) (hartnäckig) piercing ⟨look etc.⟩; probing
⟨question⟩

Bohrer der; ~s, ~ drill

Bohr-: ~**insel** die drilling rig;
~**maschine** die drill; ~**schrauber** der
power drill/screwdriver; ~**turm** der
derrick

Bohrung die; ~, ~en drill hole

böig Adj. gusty

Boiler /ˈbɔylɐ/ der; ~s, ~: water heater

Boje die; ~, ~n buoy

Bolivien /boˈliːvi̯ən/ (das); ~s Bolivia

Böller·schuss, *Böller·schuß der gun
salute

Boll·werk das bulwark; (fig.) bulwark;
bastion; stronghold

Bolschewik der; ~en, ~i, (abwertend:) ~en,
Bolschewikin die; ~, ~nen Bolshevik

Bolschewismus der; ~: Bolshevism no
art.

Bolschewist der; ~en, ~en,
Bolschewistin die; ~, ~nen Bolshevist

bolschewistisch Adj. Bolshevik

bolzen (ugs.) itr. V. kick the ball about

Bolzen der; ~s, ~: bolt

bombardieren tr. V. (a) bomb
(b) (fig. ugs.) bombard

Bombardierung die; ~, ~en (a) (Milit.)
bombing
(b) (fig. ugs.) bombardment

bombastisch [1] Adj. bombastic
[2] adv. bombastically

Bombe die; ~, ~n bomb

bomben-, Bomben-: ~**angriff** der
bomb attack; ~**anschlag** der bomb attack;
~**attentat** das bomb attack; ~**drohung**

---

die bomb threat; **~erfolg** *der* (ugs.) smash hit (coll.); **~fest** *Adj.* (ugs.: unveränderbar) dead certain; **~fest stehen** be dead certain; be a dead cert (Brit. coll.); **~form** *die* (ugs.) top form; **~sicher** *Adj.* (ugs.: gewiss) dead certain; **das ist eine ~sichere Sache** that's dead certain; that's a dead cert (Brit. coll.) *or* a sure thing (Amer.); **~stimmung** *die* (ugs.) tremendous *or* fantastic atmosphere (coll.); **~trichter** *der* bomb crater

Bomber *der;* **~s, ~:** bomber

Bon /bɔŋ/ *der;* **~s, ~s (a)** voucher; coupon **(b)** (Kassenzettel) receipt

Bonbon /bɔŋ'bɔŋ/ *der od.* (österr. nur) *das;* **~s, ~s** sweet (Brit.); candy (Amer.); (fig.) treat

bongen *tr. V.* (ugs.) ring up; **gebongt sein** (ugs.) be fine; **ist gebongt!** (ugs.) fine!

Bongo *das;* **~[s], ~s** *od. die;* **~, ~s** bongo [drum]

Bonmot /bõ'mo:/ *das;* **~s, ~s** bon mot

Bonze *der;* **~n, ~n** bigwig (coll.)

Boom /bu:m/ *der;* **~s, ~s** boom

Boot *das;* **~[e]s, ~e** boat

Boots-: ~fahrt *die* boat trip; **~haus** *das* boathouse; **~steg** *der* landing stage; **~verleih** *der* boat hire

Bord¹ *das;* **~[e]s, ~e** shelf

Bord² *der;* **~[e]s, ~e** (eines Schiffes) side; **an ~:** on board; **über ~:** overboard

Bordell *das;* **~s, ~e** brothel

Bord·stein *der* kerb

Bordüre *die;* **~, ~n** edging

borgen *tr. V.:* ▶ LEIHEN

Borke *die;* **~, ~n** bark

Borken·käfer *der* bark beetle

borniert 1 *Adj.* bigoted 2 *adv.* in a bigoted way

Börse *die;* **~, ~n** stock market; (Gebäude) stock exchange

Börsen-: ~krach *der* stock market crash; **~makler** *der* stockbroker

Borste *die;* **~, ~n** bristle

borstig *Adj.* bristly

Borte *die;* **~, ~n** braiding *no indef. art.;* edging *no indef. art.*

bös ▶ BÖSE

bös·artig 1 *Adj.* **(a)** (heimtückisch) malicious ⟨person, remark, etc.⟩; vicious ⟨animal⟩ **(b)** (Med.) malignant 2 *adv.* maliciously

Bös·artigkeit *die;* **~ (a)** maliciousness; (von Tieren) viciousness **(b)** (Med.) malignancy

Böschung *die;* **~, ~en** embankment

böse 1 *Adj.* **(a)** wicked; evil **(b)** (übel) bad ⟨times, illness, dream, etc.⟩; nasty ⟨experience, affair, situation, trick, surprise, etc.⟩ **(c)** (ugs.) (wütend) mad (coll.); (verärgert) cross (coll.) **(d)** (fam.: ungezogen) naughty

(e) (ugs.: arg) terrible (coll.) ⟨pain, fall, shock, disappointment, storm, etc.⟩ 2 *adv.* **(a)** (übel) ⟨end⟩ badly; **es war doch nicht ~ gemeint** I didn't mean it nastily **(b)** (wütend) angrily; (verärgert) crossly (coll.) **(c)** (ugs.: sehr) terribly (coll.)

boshaft 1 *Adj.* malicious 2 *adv.* maliciously

Boshaftigkeit *die;* **~, ~en (a)** maliciousness **(b)** (Bemerkung) malicious remark

Bosheit *die;* **~, ~en (a)** malice **(b)** (Bemerkung) malicious remark

Boss, *Boß *der;* **Bosses, Bosse** (ugs.) boss (coll.)

bös·willig 1 *Adj.* malicious; wilful ⟨desertion⟩ 2 *adv.* maliciously; wilfully ⟨desert⟩

Bös·willigkeit *die;* **~:** malice; maliciousness

bot *1. u. 3. Pers. Sg. Prät. v.* BIETEN

Botanik *die;* **~:** botany *no art.*

botanisch 1 *Adj.* botanical 2 *adv.* botanically

Bötchen *das;* **~s, ~:** little boat

Bote *der;* **~n, ~n (a)** messenger **(b)** (Laufbursche) errand boy

Botin *die;* **~, ~nen** ▶ BOTE: **(a)** messenger **(b)** errand girl

Botschaft *die;* **~, ~en (a)** message **(b)** (diplomatische Vertretung) embassy

Botschafter *der;* **~s, ~, Botschafterin** *die;* **~, ~nen** ambassador

Böttcher *der;* **~s, ~, Böttcherin** *die;* **~, ~nen** cooper

Bottich *der;* **~s, ~e** tub

Bouillon /bul'jɔŋ/ *die;* **~, ~s** bouillon

Boulevard /bulə'va:ɐ̯/ *der;* **~s, ~s** boulevard

Boulevard-: ~blatt *das* ▶ BOULEVARDZEITUNG; **~presse** *die* (abwertend) popular press; **~stück** *das* (Theater) boulevard drama; **~zeitung** *die* (abwertend) popular rag (derog.); tabloid

Bourgeoisie /bʊrʒoa'zi:/ *die;* **~, ~n** bourgeoisie

Boutique /bu'ti:k/ *die;* **~, ~s** *od.* **~n** boutique

Bowle /'bo:lə/ *die;* **~, ~n** punch (made of wine, champagne, sugar, and fruit or spices)

bowlen /'boʊlən/ *itr. V.* bowl

Bowling /'boʊlɪŋ/ *das;* **~s, ~s** [tenpin] bowling

Bowling·bahn *die* bowling alley

Box *die;* **~, ~en (a)** box **(b)** (Lautsprecher) speaker **(c)** (Pferdebox) [loose] box **(d)** (Motorsport) pit

boxen 1 *itr. V.* box; **gegen jmdn. ~:** fight sb.; box [against] sb. 2 *tr. V.* punch

Boxer *der;* ~s, ~ (Sportler, Hund) boxer
Boxerin *die;* ~, ~nen boxer
Box-: ~**handschuh** *der* boxing glove;
~**kampf** *der* boxing match; (im Streit) fist
fight; ~**ring** *der* boxing ring; ~**sport** *der*
boxing *no art.*
Boy /bɔy:/ *der;* ~s, ~s servant; (im Hotel)
pageboy
Boykott /bɔy:'kɔt/ *der;* ~[e]s, ~s boycott
boykottieren *tr. V.* boycott
brach¹ *1. u. 3. Pers. Sg. Prät. v.* BRECHEN
brach² *Adj.* fallow; (auf Dauer) uncultivated
Brachial-gewalt *die* brute force
Brach-land *das* fallow [land]; (auf Dauer)
uncultivated land
brach|liegen *unr. itr. V.* (auch fig.) lie
fallow; (auf Dauer) lie waste
brachte *1. u. 3. Pers. Sg. Prät. v.* BRINGEN
Branche /'brã:ʃə/ *die;* ~, ~n [branch of]
industry
Branchen-verzeichnis *das* classified
directory; (Telefonbuch) Yellow Pages ® *pl.*
Brand *der;* ~[e]s, Brände fire; beim ~ der
Scheune when the barn caught fire; etw. in
~ stecken set fire to sth.
Brand-anschlag *der* arson attack (auf +
Akk. on)
branden *itr. V.* (geh.) break
Branden-burg (*das*) ~s Brandenburg
brand-, Brand-: ~**marken** *tr. V.* brand
‹person›; denounce ‹thing›; ~**neu** *Adj.* (ugs.)
brand-new; ~**salbe** *die* ointment for burns;
~**schaden** *der* fire damage *no pl., no*
indef. art.; ~**stelle** *die* burn; ~**stifter**
der, ~**stifterin** *die* arsonist; ~**stiftung**
die arson
Brandung *die;* ~, ~en surf
Brand-wunde *die* burn
brannte *1. u. 3. Pers. Sg. Prät. v.* BRENNEN
Brannt-wein *der* spirits *pl.;* (Sorte) spirit
Brasilianer *der;* ~s, ~, **Brasilianerin**
die; ~, ~nen Brazilian
brasilianisch *Adj.* Brazilian
Brasilien /bra'zi:liən/ (*das*) ~s Brazil
brät *3. Pers. Sg. Präsens v.* BRATEN
Brat-apfel *der* baked apple
braten *unr. tr., itr. V.* fry; (im Backofen) roast
Braten *der;* ~s, ~ (a) joint
(b) roast [meat] *no indef. art.*
Braten-: ~**saft** *der* meat juice[s *pl.*];
~**soße** *die* gravy
Brat-: ~**fett** *das* [cooking] fat; ~**fisch** *der*
fried fish; ~**hähnchen** *das,* (südd., österr.)
~**hendl** *das* roast chicken; (gegrillt) broiled
chicken; ~**hering** *der* fried herring;
~**kartoffeln** *Pl.* fried potatoes; home fries
(Amer.); ~**pfanne** *die* frying pan; ~**spieß**
der spit; ~**wurst** *die* [fried/grilled] sausage
Brauch *der;* ~[e]s, Bräuche custom

brauchbar *Adj.* useful; (benutzbar) usable;
wearable ‹clothes›
brauchen ① *tr. V.* (a) (benötigen) need
(b) (aufwenden müssen) mit dem Auto braucht
er zehn Minuten; it takes him ten minutes by
car; wie lange brauchst du dafür? how long
will it take you?; (im Allgemeinen) how long
does it take you?
(c) (benutzen, gebrauchen) use; ich könnte es
gut ~: I could do with it
② *mod. V.;* 2. *Part* brauchen: need; du
brauchst nicht zu helfen there is no need [for
you] to help; du brauchst doch nicht gleich
zu weinen there's no need to start crying
Brauchtum /'brau:xtu:m/ *das;* ~s,
Brauchtümer custom
Braue *die;* ~, ~n [eye]brow
brauen *tr. V.* brew
Brauerei *die;* ~, ~en brewery
braun *Adj.* brown; ~ werden (sonnengebräunt)
get a tan; ~ gebrannt [sun]-tanned
Braun *das;* ~s, ~, (ugs.) ~s brown
Braun-bär *der* brown bear
Bräune *die;* ~: [sun]tan
bräunen *tr. V.* (a) tan; sich ~: get a tan
(b) (Kochk.) brown
braun-, Braun-: *∗*~**gebrannt** ▶ BRAUN;
~**kohle** *die* brown coal; lignite
bräunlich *Adj.* brownish
Bräunung *die;* ~, ~en browning
Braus ▶ SAUS
Brause *die;* ~, ~n (a) fizzy drink; (~pulver)
sherbet
(b) (veralt.: Dusche) shower
brausen ① *itr. V.* (a) ‹wind, water, etc.›
roar
(b) (sich schnell bewegen) race
(c) *auch refl.:* ▶ DUSCHEN 1;
② *tr. V.* ▶ DUSCHEN 2
Brause-: ~**pulver** *das* sherbet;
~**tablette** *die* effervescent tablet
Braut *die;* ~, Bräute bride
Bräutigam *der;* ~s, ~e [bride]groom
Braut-: ~**jungfer** *die* bridesmaid;
~**kleid** *das* wedding dress; ~**paar** *das*
bride and groom
brav ① *Adj.* (a) (artig) good
(b) (redlich) honest
② *adv.* nun iss schön ~ deine Suppe be a
good boy/girl and eat up your soup
bravo /'bra:vo/ *Interj.* bravo
Bravo *das;* ~s, ~s cheer
Bravo-ruf *der* cheer
BRD *Abk.* = **Bundesrepublik**
Deutschland FRG
Brech-: ~**bohne** *die* green bean; ~**eisen**
das crowbar
brechen ① *unr. tr. V.* (a) break; sich (*Dat.*)
den Arm/das Genick ~: break one's arm/
neck
(b) (ablenken) break ‹waves›; refract ‹light›

(c) (bezwingen) overcome ⟨*resistance*⟩; break ⟨*will, silence, record, blockade, etc.*⟩
(d) (nicht einhalten) break ⟨*agreement, contract, promise, the law, etc.*⟩
(e) (ugs.: erbrechen) bring up
2 *unr. itr. V.* **(a)** *mit sein* break; **brechend voll sein** be full to bursting
(b) *mit jmdm.* ∼: break with sb.
(c) *mit sein* **durch etw.** ∼: break through sth.
(d) (ugs.: sich erbrechen) throw up
3 *unr. refl. V.* ⟨*waves etc.*⟩ break; ⟨*rays etc.*⟩ be refracted

Brecher *der;* ∼s, ∼: breaker
Brech-: ∼**mittel** *das* emetic; ∼**reiz** *der* nausea; ∼**stange** *die* crowbar
Bredouille /breˈdʊljə/ *die;* ∼, ∼n (ugs.) **in der** ∼ **sein** *od.* **sitzen** be in real trouble; **in die** ∼ **kommen** get into real trouble
Brei *der;* ∼[e]s, ∼e (Hafer∼) porridge (Brit.), oatmeal (Amer.) *no indef. art.*; (Reis∼) rice pudding; (Grieß∼) semolina *no indef. art.*
breiig *Adj.* mushy
breit **1** *Adj.* **(a)** wide; broad, wide ⟨*hips, face, shoulders, forehead, etc.*⟩; **etw.** ∼**er machen** widen sth.; **die Beine** ∼ **machen** open one's legs; **ein 5 cm** ∼**er Saum** a hem 5 cm wide
(b) (groß) **die** ∼**e Masse** the general public
(c) **sich** ∼ **machen** take up room; (sich ausbreiten) be spreading
2 *adv.* ∼ **gebaut** sturdily built
breit·beinig **1** *Adj.* rolling ⟨*gait*⟩
2 *adv.* with one's legs apart
Breite *die;* ∼, ∼n **(a)** ▸ BREIT 1A: width; breadth
(b) (Geogr.) latitude
breiten (geh.) *tr., refl. V.* spread
Breiten-: ∼**grad** *der* degree of latitude; parallel (∼kreis); ∼**kreis** *der* parallel
breit-, Breit-: *∗∼|***machen** ▸ BREIT 1C; ∼**schult[e]rig** *Adj.* broad-shouldered; ∼**seite** *die* long side; (eines Schiffes) side; ∼**|treten** *unr. tr. V.* (ugs. abwertend) go on about; ∼**wand** *die* (Kino) big screen
Bremen (*das*); ∼s Bremen
Brems-: ∼**backe** *die* brake shoe; ∼**belag** *der* brake lining
Bremse¹ *die;* ∼, ∼n brake
Bremse² *die;* ∼, ∼n (Insekt) horsefly
bremsen *tr. V.* **(a)** *auch itr.* brake
(b) (fig.) slow down ⟨*rate, development, production, etc.*⟩; restrict ⟨*imports etc.*⟩
Brems-: ∼**klotz** *der* brake pad; ∼**licht** *das* brake light; ∼**pedal** *das* brake pedal; ∼**spur** *die* skid mark; ∼**weg** *der* braking distance; ∼**zug** *der* brake cable
brenn·bar *Adj.* combustible
brennen **1** *unr. itr. V.* **(a)** burn; ⟨*house etc.*⟩ be on fire; **schnell/leicht** ∼: catch fire quickly/easily; **es brennt!** fire!
(b) (glühen) be alight

(c) (leuchten) be on; **das Licht** ∼ **lassen** leave the light on
(d) **die Sonne brannte** the sun was burning down
(e) (schmerzen) ⟨*wound etc.*⟩ sting; ⟨*feet etc.*⟩ be sore
(f) **darauf** ∼, **etw. zu tun** be dying to do sth.
2 *unr. tr. V.* **(a)** burn ⟨*hole, pattern, etc.*⟩; **einem Tier ein Zeichen ins Fell** ∼: brand an animal
(b) (mit Hitze behandeln) fire ⟨*porcelain etc.*⟩; distil ⟨*spirits*⟩
(c) (rösten) roast ⟨*coffee beans, almonds, etc.*⟩
brennend **1** *Adj.* (auch fig.) burning; lighted ⟨*cigarette*⟩; urgent ⟨*topic*⟩
2 *adv.* **es interessiert mich** ∼, **ob** ...: I'm dying to know whether ...
Brenner *der;* ∼s, ∼: burner
Brennerei *die;* ∼, ∼en distillery
*∗***Brennessel** *die;* ∼, ∼n ▸ BRENNNESSEL
Brenn-: ∼**glas** *das* burning glass; ∼**holz** *das* firewood; ∼**material** *das* fuel; ∼**nessel** *die* stinging nettle; ∼**ofen** *der* kiln; ∼**punkt** *der* focus; ∼**spiritus** *der* methylated spirits *pl.*; ∼**stoff** *der* fuel; ∼**weite** *die* (Optik) focal length
brenzlig *Adj.* **(a)** ⟨*smell, taste, etc.*⟩ of burning *not pred.*;
(b) (ugs.: gefährlich) dicey (coll.)
Bresche *die;* ∼, ∼n gap; breach; **[für jmdn.] in die** ∼ **springen** stand in [for sb.]
Brett *das;* ∼[e]s, ∼er **(a)** board; (lang und dick) plank; (Diele) floorboard; **schwarzes** ∼: noticeboard; **ein** ∼ **vor dem Kopf haben** (fig. ugs.) be thick
(b) *Pl.* (Ski) skis
Bretter-: ∼**wand** *die* wooden partition; ∼**zaun** *der* wooden fence
Brett·spiel *das* board game
Brezel *die;* ∼, ∼n pretzel
Bridge /brɪtʃ/ *das;* ∼: bridge
Brief *der;* ∼[e]s, ∼e letter
Brief-: ∼**beschwerer** *der;* ∼∼s, ∼∼: paperweight; ∼**block** *der; Pl.* ∼∼s *od.* ∼**blöcke** writing pad; ∼**bogen** *der* sheet of writing paper; ∼**freund** *der*, ∼**freundin** *die* penfriend; pen pal (coll.); ∼**freundschaft** *die* penfriendship; ∼**geheimnis** *das* privacy of the post; ∼**karte** *die* correspondence card; ∼**kasten** *der* **(a)** postbox; **(b)** (privat) letter box; ∼**kopf** *der* **(a)** letter heading; **(b)** (aufgedruckt) letterhead; ∼**kuvert** *das* (veralt.) ▸ ∼UMSCHLAG
brieflich **1** *Adj.* written
2 *adv.* by letter
Brief·marke *die* [postage] stamp
Briefmarken-: ∼**album** *das* stamp album; ∼**sammler** *der*, ∼**sammlerin** *die* stamp collector; ∼**sammlung** *die* stamp collection
Brief-: ∼**öffner** *der* letter-opener; ∼**papier** *das* writing paper; ∼**partner** ⋯⋗

der, ~**partnerin** *die* penfriend;
~**schreiber** *der,* ~**schreiberin** *die*
[letter-]writer; ~**tasche** *die* wallet;
~**taube** *die* carrier pigeon; ~**träger** *der*
postman; letter-carrier (Amer.); ~**trägerin**
die postwoman; [female] letter-carrier (Amer.);
~**umschlag** *der* envelope; ~**waage** *die*
letter scales *pl.;* ~**wahl** *die* postal vote;
~**wechsel** *der* correspondence

Bries *das;* ~**es,** ~**e** (Kochk.) sweetbreads *pl.*

briet *1. u. 3. Pers. Sg. Prät. v.* BRATEN

Brigade *die;* ~**,** ~**n** (Milit.) brigade

Brikett *das;* ~**s,** ~**s** briquette

brillant /brɪl'jant/ 1 *Adj.* brilliant
2 *adv.* brilliantly

Brillant *der;* ~**en,** ~**en** brilliant

Brillant-: ~**ring** *der* (brilliant-cut) diamond
ring; ~**schmuck** *der* (brilliant-cut) diamond
jewellery

Brillanz /brɪl'jants:/ *die;* ~: brilliance

Brille *die;* ~**,** ~**n** (a) glasses *pl.;* ~ ~
pl.; **eine** ~: a pair of glasses *or* spectacles;
eine ~ **tragen** wear glasses *or* spectacles
(b) (ugs.: Klosettbrille) [lavatory] seat

Brillen-: ~**etui** *das,* ~**futteral** *das*
glasses case; spectacle case; ~**glas** *das*
[spectacle] lens; ~**schlange** *die* spectacled
cobra; ~**träger** *der,* ~**trägerin** *die*
person who wears glasses; ~**träger/-trägerin**
sein wear glasses

Brimborium *das;* ~**s** (ugs. abwertend) hoo-ha
(coll.)

bringen *unr. tr. V.* (a) (her~) bring; (hin~)
take; **jmdm. Glück/Unglück** ~: bring sb.
[good] luck/bad luck; **jmdm. eine Nachricht**
~: bring sb. news
(b) (begleiten) take; **jmdn. nach Hause/zum**
Bahnhof ~: take sb. home/to the station
(c) **es zu etwas/nichts** ~: get somewhere/get
nowhere
(d) **jmdn. ins Gefängnis** ~ ⟨crime, misdeed⟩
land sb. in gaol; **jmdn. wieder auf den**
rechten Weg ~ (fig.) get sb. back on the
straight and narrow; **jmdn. zum Lachen/zur**
Verzweiflung ~: make sb. laugh/drive sb. to
despair; **jmdn. dazu** ~, **etw. zu tun** get sb. to
do sth.; **etw. hinter sich** ~ (ugs.) get sth. over
and done with
(e) **jmdn. um seinen Besitz** ~: do sb. out of
his property
(f) (präsentieren) present; (veröffentlichen)
publish; (senden) broadcast
(g) **ein Opfer** ~: make a sacrifice
(h) **einen großen Gewinn/hohe Zinsen** ~:
make a large profit/earn high interest
(i) **das bringt es mit sich, dass** ...: that
means that ...
(j) (verursachen) cause

brisant *Adj.* explosive

Brisanz *die;* ~: explosiveness

Brise *die;* ~**,** ~**n** breeze

---

*alte Schreibung - vgl. Hinweis auf S. xiv

Britannien (*das*)*;* ~**s** Britain; (hist.)
Britannia

Brite *der;* ~**n,** ~**n** Briton; **die** ~**n** the
British; **er ist [kein]** ~: he is [not] British

Britin *die;* ~**,** ~**nen** Briton; British girl/
woman

britisch *Adj.* British; **die Britischen Inseln**
the British Isles

bröckelig *Adj.* crumbly

bröckeln 1 *itr. V.* (a) crumble
(b) *mit sein* **von der Wand** ~: crumble away
from the wall
2 *tr. V.* crumble

Brocken *der;* ~**s,** ~ (von Brot) hunk; (von
Fleisch) chunk; (von Lehm, Kohle, Erde) lump; **ein**
paar ~ **Englisch** (fig.) a smattering of English

brodeln *itr. V.* bubble

Broiler /'brɔyːlɐ/ *der;* ~**s,** ~ (regional)
▶ BRATHÄHNCHEN

Brokat *der;* ~[**e**]**s,** ~**e** brocade

Brokkoli *der;* ~**s,** ~[**s**] broccoli

Brom-beere *die* blackberry

Bronchie /'brɔnçiə/ *die;* ~**,** ~**n** bronchial
tube

Bronchitis *die;* ~**,** bronchitis

Bronze /'brõːsə/ *die;* ~: bronze

Bronze-: ~**medaille** *die* bronze medal;
~**zeit** *die* Bronze Age

Brosche *die;* ~**,** ~**n** brooch

Broschüre *die;* ~**,** ~**n** booklet

Brösel *der;* ~**s,** ~: breadcrumb

bröselig *Adj.* crumbly

bröseln *itr. V.* crumble

Brot *das;* ~[**e**]**s,** ~**e** bread *no pl., no indef.*
art.; (Laib) loaf [of bread]; (Scheibe) slice [of
bread]

Brot-: ~**aufstrich** *der* spread; ~**belag**
der topping; (im zusammengeklappten Brot) filling

Brötchen *das;* ~**s,** ~: roll

Brot-: ~**erwerb** *der* way to earn a living;
~**korb** *der* bread basket; ~**laib** *der* loaf [of
bread]; ~**messer** *das* bread knife;
~**rinde** *die* [bread] crust; ~**zeit** *die* (südd.)
(a) (Pause) [tea/coffee/lunch] break; (b)
(Vesper) snack; (Vesperbrot) sandwiches *pl.*

Browser /'braʊzɐ/ *der;* ~**s,** ~ (DV) browser

Bruch *der;* ~[**e**]**s,** **Brüche** (a) break; **in die**
Brüche gehen (zerbrechen) get broken; (fig.)
break up
(b) (Med.: Knochen~) fracture; break
(c) (Med.: Eingeweide~) hernia
(d) (fig.) (eines Versprechens) breaking; (eines
Abkommens, Gesetzes) violation
(e) (Math.) fraction

brüchig *Adj.* (a) brittle ⟨rock, brickwork⟩
(b) (fig.) crumbling ⟨relationship, marriage,
etc.⟩

Bruch-: ~**landung** *die* crash-landing;
~**rechnen** *das* fractions *pl.;* ~**strich** *der*
fraction line; ~**stück** *das* fragment; ~**teil**
der fraction; **im** ~**teil einer Sekunde** in a
split second

Brücke *die;* ~, ~n **(a)** (auch: Kommandobrücke, Zahnmed., Bodenturnen, Ringen) bridge
(b) (Landungsbrücke) gangway
(c) (Teppich) rug

Brücken-: ~**bogen** *der* arch [of a/the bridge]; ~**geländer** *das* parapet; ~**kopf** *der* (Milit., auch fig.) bridgehead

Bruder *der;* ~s, Brüder brother
Brüderchen *das;* ~s, ~: little brother
brüderlich [1] *Adj.* brotherly
[2] *adv.* in a brotherly way
Brüderlichkeit *die;* ~: brotherliness
Brüderschaft *die;* ~: [mit jmdm.] ~ trinken drink to close friendship [with sb.] (*agreeing to use the familiar 'du' form*)

Brühe *die;* ~, ~n **(a)** stock; (als Suppe) clear soup
(b) (ugs. abwertend) (Getränk) muck; (verschmutztes Wasser) filthy water

brühen *tr. V.* **(a)** blanch
(b) (auf~) brew, make ⟨tea⟩; make ⟨coffee⟩

brüh-, Brüh-: ~**warm** *Adj.* etw. ~warm weitererzählen (ugs.) pass sth. on straight away; ~**würfel** *der* stock cube

brüllen [1] *itr. V.* **(a)** ⟨bull, cow, etc.⟩ bellow; ⟨lion, tiger, etc.⟩ roar
(b) (ugs.) (schreien) roar; (weinen) howl
[2] *tr. V.* yell

brummen *tr., itr. V.* **(a)** ⟨insect⟩ buzz; ⟨bear⟩ growl; ⟨engine etc.⟩ drone
(b) (unmelodisch singen) drone
(c) (mürrisch sprechen) mumble

Brummer *der;* ~s, ~ (ugs.) **(a)** (Fliege) bluebottle
(b) (LKW) heavy lorry (Brit.) *or* truck

brummig *Adj.* (ugs.) grumpy

Brumm-: ~**kreisel** *der* humming top; ~**schädel** *der* (ugs.) thick head

brünett *Adj.* dark-haired ⟨person⟩; dark ⟨hair⟩

Brünette *die;* ~, ~n brunette

Brunnen *der;* ~s, ~ **(a)** well
(b) (Springbrunnen) fountain

Brunnen-kresse *die* watercress

Brunst *die;* ~, Brünste (von männlichen Tieren) rut; (von weiblichen Tieren) heat

Brunst-zeit *die* (bei männlichen Tieren) rutting season; (bei weiblichen Tieren) [season of] heat

brüsk [1] *Adj.* brusque
[2] *adv.* brusquely

brüskieren *tr. V.* offend; (stärker) insult; (schneiden) snub

Brüssel (*das*); ~s Brussels

Brust *die;* ~, Brüste **(a)** chest
(b) (der Frau) breast
(c) (Hähnchen~) breast; (Rinder~) brisket
(d) (Brustschwimmen) breaststroke

brüsten *refl. V.* sich mit etw. ~: boast about sth.

brust-, Brust-: ~**kasten** (ugs.) chest;

~**korb** *der* (Anat.) thorax (Anat.); ~**krebs** *der* breast cancer; ~**schwimmen** *unr. itr. V.; nur im Inf.* do [the] breaststroke; ~**schwimmen** *das* breaststroke; ~**tasche** *die* breast pocket

Brüstung *die;* ~, ~en parapet; (Balkon~) balustrade

Brust-warze *die* nipple

Brut *die;* ~, ~en **(a)** brooding
(b) (Jungtiere, auch fig. scherzh.: Kinder) brood

brutal [1] *Adj.* brutal; violent ⟨attack, programme, etc.⟩; brute ⟨force, strength⟩
[2] *adv.* brutally

Brutalität *die;* ~, ~en **(a)** brutality
(b) (Handlung) act of brutality

brüten *itr. V.* **(a)** brood
(b) (grübeln) ponder (**über** + *Dat.* over); **brütend** ~ **heiß:** (ugs.) boiling hot

Brüter *der;* ~s, ~ (Kernphysik) breeder

Brut-: ~**kasten** *der* incubator; ~**reaktor** *der* (Kernphysik) breeder reactor; ~**stätte** *die* (auch fig.) breeding ground

brutto *Adv.* gross

Brutto-: ~**einkommen** *das* gross income; ~**gehalt** *das* gross salary; ~**sozialprodukt** *das* (Wirtsch.) gross national product

brutzeln [1] *itr. V.* sizzle
[2] *tr. V.* (ugs.) fry [up]

BSE /beːsˈeː/ *die;* ~: BSE

Bub *der;* ~en, ~en (südd., österr., schweiz.) boy; lad

Bube *der;* ~n, ~n (Kartenspiele) jack; knave

Bubi *der;* ~s, ~s **(a)** [little] boy *or* lad
(b) (salopp: Schnösel) young lad

Buch *das;* ~[e]s, Bücher book; (Dreh~) script; **über etw.** (*Akk.*) ~ **führen** keep a record of sth.

Buch-: ~**besprechung** *die* book review; ~**binder** *der,* ~**binderin** *die;* ~~, ~~**nen** bookbinder; ~**druck** *der* letterpress printing

Buche *die;* ~, ~n **(a)** beech [tree]
(b) (Holz) beech[wood]

Buch-ecker *die;* ~, ~n beech nut

buchen *tr. V.* **(a)** enter
(b) (vorbestellen) book

Bücher-brett *das* bookshelf

Bücherei *die;* ~, ~en library

Bücher-: ~**regal** *das* bookshelves *pl.;* ~**schrank** *der* bookcase; ~**wurm** *der* (scherzh.) bookworm; ~**verbrennung** *die* burning of books

Buch-: ~**fink** *der* chaffinch; ~**führung** *die* bookkeeping; ~**halter** *der,* ~**halterin** *die* bookkeeper; ~**haltung** *die* **(a)** accountancy; **(b)** (Abteilung) accounts department; ~**händler** *der,* ~**händlerin** *die* bookseller; ~**handlung** *die* bookshop; ~**klub** *der* book club; ~**laden** *der; Pl.* ~**läden** ▶ ~HANDLUNG; ~**messe** *die* book fair; ~**rücken** *der* spine

Buchs·baum /'bʊks-/ *der* box [tree]
Buchse /'bʊksə/ *die;* ~, ~n **(a)** (Elektrot.)
socket
  (b) (Technik) bush
Büchse /'byksə/ *die;* ~, ~n **(a)** tin
  (b) (ugs.: Sammel~) [collecting] box
  (c) (Gewehr) rifle; (Schrot~) shotgun
Büchsen- ▶ DOSEN-
Buchstabe *der;* ~ns, ~n letter; (Druckw.)
character; **ein großer/kleiner** ~: a capital
[letter]/small letter
buchstabieren *tr. V.* spell
buchstäblich *Adv.* literally
Bucht *die;* ~, ~en bay
Buchung *die;* ~, ~en **(a)** entry
  (b) (Vorbestellung) booking
Buckel *der;* ~s, ~ **(a)** hump; **einen** ~
machen ⟨cat⟩ arch its back; ⟨person⟩ hunch
one's shoulders
  (b) (ugs.: Rücken) back; **rutsch mir den** ~
runter! (salopp) get lost! (coll.)
buckeln *itr. V.* (ugs.) bow and scrape; **vor**
jmdm. ~: kowtow to sb.
bücken *refl. V.* bend down
bucklig *Adj.* hunchbacked
Bucklige *der/die; adj. Dekl.* hunchback
Bückling[1] *der;* ~s, ~e (ugs. scherzh.:
Verbeugung) bow
Bückling[2] *der;* ~s, ~e (Hering) bloater
buddeln *itr., tr. V.* (ugs.) dig
Buddha /'bʊda/ *der;* ~s, ~s Buddha
Buddhismus *der;* ~: Buddhism *no art.*
Buddhist *der;* ~en, ~en, **Buddhistin**
die; ~, ~nen Buddhist
buddhistisch *Adj.* Buddhist *attrib.*
Bude *die;* ~, ~n **(a)** kiosk; (Markt~) stall;
(Jahrmarkts~) booth
  (b) (Bau~) hut
  (c) (ugs.) (Haus) dump (coll.); (Zimmer) room;
digs *pl.* (Brit. coll.)
Budget /by'dʒe:/ *das;* ~s, ~s budget
Büfett *das;* ~[e]s, ~s *od.* ~e **(a)** sideboard
  (b) (Schanktisch) bar
  (c) (Verkaufstisch) counter
  (d) kaltes ~: cold buffet
Büffel *der;* ~s, ~: buffalo
büffeln (ugs.) [1] *itr. V.* swot (Brit. coll.); cram
  [2] *tr. V.* swot up (Brit. coll.); cram
Buffet /by'fe:/ *das;* ~s, ~s ▶ BÜFETT
Bug *der;* ~[e]s, ~e *u.* Büge bow
Bügel *der;* ~s, ~ **(a)** (Kleider~) hanger
  (b) (Brillen~) earpiece
  (c) (an einer Tasche, Geldbörse) frame
bügel-, Bügel-: ~**brett** *das* ironing
board; ~**eisen** *die* iron; ~**falte** *die*
[trouser] crease; ~**frei** *Adj.* non-iron
bügeln *tr., itr. V.* iron
bugsieren /bʊ'ksi:rən/ *tr. V.* (ugs.) shift;
manœuvre; steer ⟨person⟩

buh *Interj.* boo
Buh *das;* ~s, ~s (ugs.) boo
buhen *itr. V.* (ugs.) boo
buhlen *itr. V.* (geh. abwertend) **um jmds.**
Gunst ~: court sb.'s favour
Buh·mann *der* whipping boy
Buhne /'bu:nə/ *die;* ~, ~n groyne
Bühne *die;* ~, ~n **(a)** stage; **ein Stück auf**
die ~ **bringen** put on *or* stage a play
  (b) (Theater) theatre
bühnen-, Bühnen-: ~**arbeiter** *der,*
~**arbeiterin** *die* stagehand;
~**ausstattung** *die* stage set; ~**bild** *das*
[stage] set; ~**bildner** *der;* ~~s, ~~,
~**bildnerin** *die;* ~~, ~~nen stage
designer; ~**reif** *Adj.* ⟨play etc.⟩ ready for the
stage; ⟨imitation etc.⟩ worthy of the stage;
dramatic ⟨entrance etc.⟩
Buh·ruf *der* boo
buk *1. u. 3. Pers. Sg. Prät. v.* BACKEN
Bukett *das;* ~s, ~s *od.* ~e (geh.) bouquet
Bulette *die;* ~, ~n (bes. berl.) rissole
Bulgare *der;* ~n, ~n Bulgarian
Bulgarien /bʊl'ga:rjən/ (*das*); ~s Bulgaria
Bulgarin *die;* ~, ~nen Bulgarian
bulgarisch *Adj.* Bulgarian
Bull-: ~**auge** *das* circular porthole;
~**dogge** *die* bulldog; ~**dozer** /-do:zɐ/ *der;*
~~s, ~~: bulldozer
Bulle *der;* ~n, ~n **(a)** bull
  (b) (salopp: Polizist) cop (coll.)
Bullen·hitze *die* (ugs.) sweltering *or* boiling
heat
Bulletin /byl'tɛ̃:/ *das;* ~s, ~s bulletin
bullig [1] *Adj.* **(a)** beefy ⟨person, appearance,
etc.⟩; chunky ⟨car⟩
  (b) (drückend) sweltering ⟨heat⟩
  [2] *adv.* ~ **heiß** boiling hot
Bull·terrier *der* bull terrier
bum *Interj.* bang
Bumerang *der;* ~s, ~e *od.* ~s boomerang
Bummel *der;* ~s, ~ **(a)** stroll (**durch**
around)
  (b) (durch Lokale) pub crawl (coll.)
Bummelei *die;* ~, ~en (ugs.) **(a)** dawdling
  (b) (Faulenzerei) loafing about
bummelig (ugs.) [1] *Adj.* **(a)** slow
  (b) (nachlässig) slipshod
  [2] *adv.* **(a)** slowly
  (b) (nachlässig) in a slipshod way
bummeln *itr. V.* **(a)** *mit sein* stroll (**durch**
around); **durch die Kneipen** ~: go on a pub
crawl (Brit. coll.)
  (b) (trödeln) dawdle
  (c) (faulenzen) laze about
bums *Interj.* bang
Bums *der;* ~es, ~e (ugs.) bang; (dumpfer)
thud
bumsen *itr. V.* (ugs.) **(a)** bang; (dumpfer)
thump; *unpers.* **es bumste ganz furchtbar**
there was a terrible bang/thud
  (b) *mit sein* (stoßen) bang

Bund[1] *der;* ~[e]s, **Bünde (a)** (Vereinigung) association; (Bündnis, Pakt) alliance
(b) (föderativer Staat) federation
(c) (an Röcken, Hosen) waistband

Bund[2] *das;* ~[e]s, ~e bunch

Bündchen *das;* ~s, ~ band

Bündel *das;* ~s, ~ bundle

bündeln *tr. V.* bundle up ⟨*newspapers, old clothes, rags, etc.*⟩; tie ⟨*banknotes etc.*⟩ into bundles/a bundle; tie ⟨*flowers, radishes, carrots, etc.*⟩ into bunches/a bunch; sheave ⟨*straw, hay, etc.*⟩

Bundes- federal; (in Namen, Titeln) Federal

bundes-, Bundes-: ~**bürger** *der,*
~**bürgerin** *die* (veralt.) West German citizen; ~**deutsch** *Adj.* (veralt.) West German; ~**ebene** *die:* auf ~**ebene** at federal *or* national level; ~**gerichtshof** *der* Federal Supreme Court; ~**kabinett** *das* Federal Cabinet; ~**kanzler** *der* **(a)** Federal Chancellor; **(b)** (schweiz.) Chancellor of the Confederation; ~**land** *das* [federal] state; (österr.) province; ~**liga** *die* national division; ~**minister** *der,* ~**ministerin** *die* Federal Minister; ~**ministerium** *das* Federal Ministry; ~**präsident** *der,* ~**präsidentin** *die* **(a)** [Federal] President; **(b)** (schweiz.) President of the Confederation; ~**rat** *der* Bundesrat; ~**regierung** *die* Federal Government; ~**republik** *die* federal republic; **die** ~**republik Deutschland** The Federal Republic of Germany; ~**straße** *die* federal highway; ≈ A road (Brit.); ~**tag** *der* Bundestag

Bundestags-: ~**abgeordnete** *der/die* member of parliament; member of the Bundestag; ~**präsident** *der,* ~**präsidentin** *die* President of the Bundestag; ~**wahl** *die* parliamentary *or* general election

bundes-, Bundes-: ~**trainer** *der,* ~**trainerin** *die* national team manager; ~**verfassungs-gericht** *das* Federal Constitutional Court; ~**verwaltungs-gericht** *das* Supreme Administrative Court; ~**wehr** *die* [Federal] Armed Forces *pl.;* ~**weit** *Adj., adv.* nationwide

Bund-: ~**falten** *Pl.* pleats; ~**falten·hose** *die* pleat[ed]-front trousers *pl.;* ~**hose** *die* knee breeches

bündig [1] *Adj.* **(a)** succinct
(b) (schlüssig) conclusive
[2] *adv.* **(a)** succinctly
(b) (schlüssig) conclusively

Bündnis *das;* ~ses, ~se alliance

Bungalow /'bʊŋgalo/ *der;* ~s, ~s bungalow

Bunker *der;* ~s, ~ **(a)** bunker
(b) (Luftschutzbunker) air-raid shelter

bunt [1] *Adj.* **(a)** colourful; (farbig) coloured; ~**e Farben/Kleidung** bright colours/brightly coloured clothes
(b) (fig.) varied ⟨*programme etc.*⟩

[2] *adv.* **(a)** colourfully; ~ **bemalt** brightly painted
(b) (fig.) **ein** ~ **gemischtes Programm** a varied programme

bunt-, Bunt-: *~**bemalt** ▶ BUNT 2A; ~**papier** *das* coloured paper; ~**specht** *der* spotted woodpecker; ~**stift** *der* coloured pencil/crayon

Bürde *die;* ~, ~n (geh.) weight; load

Burg *die;* ~, ~en **(a)** castle
(b) (Strand~) wall of sand

Bürge *der;* ~n, ~n guarantor

bürgen *itr. V.* **(a) für jmdn./etw.** ~: vouch for sb./sth.
(b) (fig.) guarantee

Bürger *der;* ~s, ~, **Bürgerin** *die;* ~, ~nen citizen

Bürger-: ~**initiative** *die* citizens' action group; ~**krieg** *der* civil war

bürgerlich *Adj.* **(a)** (staats~) civil ⟨*rights, marriage, etc.*⟩; civic ⟨*duties*⟩
(b) (dem Bürgertum zugehörig) middle-class; **die** ~**e Küche** good plain cooking
(c) (Polit.) non-socialist; (nicht marxistisch) non-Marxist

bürger-, Bürger-: ~**meister** *der,* ~**meisterin** *die* mayor; ~**nah** *Adj.* which/who reflects the general public's interests *postpos., not pred.;* ~**pflicht** *die* duty as a citizen; ~**steig** *der;* ~~s, ~~e pavement (Brit.); sidewalk (Amer.)

Bürgertum /'--tu:m/ *das;* ~s **(a)** middle class
(b) (Großbürgertum) bourgeoisie

Bürgin *die;* ~, ~nen ▶ BÜRGE

Bürgschaft *die;* ~, ~en **(a)** guarantee
(b) (Betrag) penalty

Büro *das;* ~s, ~s office

Büro-: ~**angestellte** *der/die* office worker; ~**artikel** *der* item of office equipment; ~**haus** *das* office block; ~**klammer** *die* paper clip; ~**kraft** *die* clerical worker

Bürokrat *der;* ~en, ~en bureaucrat

Bürokratie *die;* ~, ~n bureaucracy

Bürokratin *die;* ~, ~nen bureaucrat

bürokratisch [1] *Adj.* bureaucratic
[2] *adv.* bureaucratically

Büro·technik *die* office technology

Bürschchen /'bʏrʃçən/ *das;* ~, ~: little fellow

Bursche *der;* ~n, ~n **(a)** boy; lad
(b) (abwertend: Kerl) guy (coll.)

burschikos [1] *Adj.* **(a)** sporty ⟨*look, clothes*⟩; [tom]boyish ⟨*behaviour, girl, haircut*⟩
(b) (ungezwungen) casual ⟨*comment, behaviour, etc.*⟩
[2] *adv.* **(a)** [tom]boyishly
(b) (ungezwungen) in a colloquial way

Bürste *die;* ~, ~n brush

bürsten *tr. V.* brush

Bus *der;* ~ses, ~se bus
Bus-bahnhof *der* bus station
Busch *der;* ~[e]s, Büsche bush; **auf den ~ klopfen** (fig. ugs.) sound things out
Büschel *das;* ~s, ~: tuft; (von Heu, Stroh) handful
Busen *der;* ~s, ~ bust
Bus-: ~**fahrer** *der,* ~**fahrerin** *die* bus driver; ~**haltestelle** *die* bus stop; ~**linie** *die* bus route
Bussard *der;* ~s, ~e buzzard
Buße *die;* ~, ~n (Rel.) penance *no art.*
büßen 1 *tr. V.* **(a)** atone for **(b)** (fig.) pay for
2 *itr. V.* **(a) für etw.** ~: atone for sth. **(b)** (fig.) pay
Buß-geld *das* (Rechtsw.) fine
Buß- und Bettag *der* (ev. Kirche) Day of Prayer and Repentance (*Wednesday eleven days before the first Sunday in Advent*)

Büsten-halter *der* bra; brassière (formal)
Butan-gas *das* butane gas
Butt *der;* ~[e]s, ~e flounder; butt
Bütten-papier *das* handmade paper (*with deckle edge*)
Butter *die;* ~: butter; **es ist alles in** ~ (ugs.) everything's fine
butter-, Butter-: ~**berg** *der* (ugs.) butter mountain; ~**blume** *die* (Sumpfdotterblume) marsh marigold; (Hahnenfuß) buttercup; ~**brot** *das* slice of bread and butter; (zugeklappt) sandwich; ~**creme** *die* buttercream; ~**milch** *die* buttermilk; ~**weich** *Adj.* beautifully soft
b. w. *Abk.* = **bitte wenden** p.t.o.
Bypass /'baipɑs/ *der;* ~es, Bypässe (Med.) bypass
Byte /bait/ *das;* ~s, ~[s] (DV) byte
bzw. *Abk.* = **beziehungsweise**

Cc

c, C /ʦeː/ *das;* ~, ~: **(a)** (Buchstabe) c/C **(b)** (Musik) [key of] C
C *Abk.* = **Celsius** C
ca. *Abk.* = **cirka** c.
Café *das;* ~s, ~s café
Cafeteria *die;* ~, ~s cafeteria
cal *Abk.* = [**Gramm]kalorie** cal.
Callboy /'kɔːlbɔɪ/ *der;* ~s, ~s call-boy
Callgirl /'kɔːlgəːl/ *das;* ~s, ~s call girl
Camp /kɛmp/ *das;* ~s, ~s camp
campen *itr. V.* camp
Camping *das;* ~s camping
Camping-: ~**bus** *der* motor caravan; camper; ~**kocher** *der* camping stove; ~**platz** *der* campsite; campground (Amer.)
Canasta *das;* ~s canasta
Cannabis /'kanabɪs/ *der;* ~: cannabis
Cantilever-bremse /'kɛntiliːvɐ-/ *die* cantilever brake
Caravan /'ka(ː)ravan/ *der;* ~s, ~s (Wohnwagen) caravan; trailer (Amer.)
Cashflow /kɛʃ'floʊ/ *der;* ~s (Wirtsch.) [gross] cash flow
Castor-: ~**behälter** *der* Castor container; Castor cask; ~**transport** *der* Castor transport
Catcher /'kɛtʃɐ/ *der;* ~s, ~, **Catcherin** *die;* ~, ~nen all-in wrestler

Cayenne-pfeffer /ka'jɛn-/ *der* cayenne [pepper]
CD /ʦeː'deː/ *die;* ~, ~s CD
CD-ROM /ʦede'rɔm/ *die;* ~, ~[s] (DV) CD-ROM
CD-ROM-Laufwerk *das* (DV) CD-ROM drive
CD-Spieler /ʦeː'deː-/ *der* compact disc player
CDU *Abk.* = **Christlich-Demokratische Union [Deutschlands]** [German] Christian Democratic Party
C-Dur /'ʦeː-/ *das* C major
Cellist /tʃɛ'lɪst/ *der;* ~en, ~en, **Cellistin** *die;* ~, ~nen cellist
Cello /'tʃɛlo/ *das;* ~s, ~s od. **Celli** cello
Celsius: 20 Grad ~: 20 degrees Celsius or centigrade
Cembalo /'tʃɛmbalo/ *das;* ~s, ~s od. **Cembali** harpsichord
Ceylon /'ʦailɔn/ (*das*); ~s (hist.) Ceylon (Hist.)
Champagner /ʃam'panjɐ/ *der;* ~s, ~ champagne (from Champagne)
Champignon /'ʃampɪnjɔn/ *der;* ~s, ~s mushroom
Chance /'ʃãːsə/ *die;* ~, ~n **(a)** chance **(b)** *Pl.* (Aussichten) prospects; [**bei jmdm**] ~**n haben** stand a chance [with sb.]
Chancen-gleichheit *die* (Soziol.) equality *no art.* of opportunity

---

*alte Schreibung - vgl. Hinweis auf S. xiv

Chaos /'k.../ *das;* ~: chaos *no art.*

Chaot /ka'o:t/ *der;* ~en, ~en, **Chaotin** *die;* ~, ~nen(a) (Politik) anarchist (trying to undermine society)
(b) (salopp: unordentlicher Mensch) **ein [furchtbarer]** ~ **sein** be [terribly] disorganized

chaotisch ① *Adj.* chaotic
② *adv.* chaotically; **es geht** ~ **zu** there is chaos

Charakter /ka.../ *der;* ~s, ~e /...'te:rə/ character

charakterisieren *tr. V.* characterize

charakteristisch *Adj.* characteristic (für of)

charakterlich ① *Adj.* character *attrib.;*
② *adv.* in [respect of] character

charakter·los *Adj.* unprincipled; (niederträchtig) despicable; (labil) spineless

Charisma /'ça:rɪsma/ *das;* ~s, **Charismen** charisma

charismatisch /çarɪs'ma:tɪʃ/ *Adj.* charismatic

charmant /ʃar'mant/ ① *Adj.* charming
② *adv.* charmingly

Charme /ʃarm/ *der;* ~s charm

Charter- /'tʃartɐ-/: ~**flug** *der* charter flight; ~**maschine** *die* chartered aircraft

Charts /tʃarts/ *Pl.* charts

Chassis /ʃa'si:/ *das;* ~ /ʃa'si:(s),/ ~ /ʃa'si:s/ chassis

chatten /'tʃɛtn/ *itr. V.* (DV Jargon) chat

Chauffeur /ʃɔ'fø:ɐ/ *der;* ~s, ~e, **Chauffeurin** /ʃɔ'fø:rɪn/ *die;* ~, ~nen driver; (privat angestellt) chauffeur

checken /'tʃɛkn/ *tr. V.* (a) (bes. Technik: kontrollieren) check; examine
(b) (salopp: begreifen) twig (coll.); (bemerken) spot; **ich habe das noch nicht gecheckt** I haven't got it yet

Check·liste *die* checklist; (Passagierliste) passenger list

Chef /ʃɛf/ *der;* ~s, ~s, **Chefin** /'ʃɛfɪn/ *die;* ~, ~nen (Leiter[in]) head; (der Polizei, des Generalstabs) chief; (einer Partei, Bande) leader; (Vorgesetzte[r]) superior; boss (coll.)

Chef-: ~**koch** *der,* ~**köchin** *die* chef; head cook; ~**sekretärin** *die* director's secretary

Chemie *die;* ~ (a) chemistry *no art.;*
(b) (ugs.: Chemikalien) chemicals *pl.*

Chemikalie /çemi'ka:liə/ *die;* ~, ~n chemical

Chemiker *der;* ~s, ~, **Chemikerin** *die;* ~, ~nen (graduate) chemist

chemisch ① *Adj.* chemical
② *adv.* chemically

Chemo·therapie *die* (Med.) chemotherapy

Chicorée /'ʃikore/ *die;* ~s *od. die;* ~: chicory

Chiffon /'ʃɪfõ/ *der;* ~s, ~s chiffon

Chiffre /'ʃɪfrə/ *die;* ~, ~n (a) (Zeichen) symbol
(b) (Geheimzeichen) cipher
(c) (in Annoncen) box number

Chile /'tʃi:le, 'çi:lə/ *(das);* ~s Chile

Chilene /tʃi'le:nə, çi'le:nə/ *der;* ~n, ~n, **Chilenin** *die;* ~, ~nen Chilean

chilenisch *Adj.* Chilean

Chili /'tʃi:li/ *der;* ~s, ~es (a) *Pl.* (Schoten) chillies
(b) (Gewürz) chilli [powder]

China *(das);* ~s China

Chinese *der;* ~n, ~n, **Chinesin** *die;* ~, ~nen Chinese

chinesisch *Adj.* Chinese

Chip /tʃɪp/ *der;* ~s, ~s (a) (Spielmarke) chip
(b) (Kartoffel~) [potato] crisp (Brit.) *or* (Amer.) chip
(c) (Elektronik) [micro]chip

Chip·karte *die* smart card

Chirurg *der;* ~en, ~en surgeon

Chirurgie *die;* ~, ~n (a) surgery *no art.;*
(b) (Abteilung) surgical department; (Station) surgical ward

Chirurgin *die;* ~, ~nen surgeon

chirurgisch ① *Adj.* surgical
② *adv.* surgically; by surgery

Chlor /k.../ *das;* ~s chlorine

Chloroform /k.../ *das;* ~s chloroform

Chlorophyll /k.../ *das;* ~s chlorophyll

Cholera *die;* ~: cholera

cholerisch *Adj.* irascible; choleric ⟨temperament⟩

Cholesterin *das;* ~s cholesterol

Chor *der;* ~[e]s, **Chöre** /'kø:rə/ (auch Archit.) choir; (in Oper, Sinfonie, Theater; Komposition) chorus; **im** ~ **rufen** shout in chorus

Choral *der;* ~s, **Choräle** (Kirchenlied) chorale

Choreograph /koreo'gra:f/ *der;* ~en, ~en choreographer

Choreographie *die;* ~, ~n choreography

Choreographin *die;* ~, ~nen choreographer

choreographisch *Adj.* choreographic

Chose /'ʃo:zə/ *die;* ~, ~n (ugs.) stuff; **die ganze** ~: the whole lot (coll.) *or* (coll.) shoot

Chow-Chow /tʃau'tʃau/ *der;* ~s, ~s chow

Christ /k.../ *der;* ~en, ~en Christian

Christ-: ~**baum** *der* (bes. südd.) Christmas tree; ~**demokrat** *der,* ~**demokratin** *die* (Politik) Christian Democrat

Christenheit *die;* ~: Christendom *no art.*

Christentum *das;* ~s Christianity *no art.;*
(Glaube) Christian faith

Christin *die;* ~, ~nen Christian

Christ·kind *das* Christ-child *(as bringer of Christmas gifts)*

christlich ① *Adj.* Christian
② *adv.* in a [truly] Christian spirit

Christ-: ~**messe** *die* (kath. Rel.) Christmas ···⟩

Mass; ~**mette** die; ~~, ~~n (kath. Rel.) Christmas Mass; (ev. Rel.) midnight service [on Christmas Eve]; ~**rose** die Christmas rose; ~**stollen** der stollen; [German] Christmas loaf (with candied fruit, almonds, etc.)

Christus (der); ~ od. Christi Christ

Chrom /k.../ das; ~s chromium

Chromosom /k.../ das; ~s, ~en (Biol.) chromosome

Chromosomen·satz der (Biol.) chromosome set

Chronik /k.../ die; ~, ~en chronicle

chronisch Adj. chronic

Chrysantheme /k.../ die; ~, ~n chrysanthemum

City /'sɪti/ die; ~, ~s city centre

clean /kli:n/ Adj. (ugs.) clean (coll.); ~ werden come off drugs

clever /'klɛvɐ/ [1] Adj. (raffiniert) shrewd; (intelligent, geschickt) clever
[2] adv.: s. Adj.: shrewdly; cleverly

Clique /'klɪkə/ die; ~, ~n (a) (abwertend) clique
(b) (Freundeskreis) set; (größere Gruppe) crowd (coll.)

Clown /klaun/ der; ~s, ~s, **Clownin** /'klaunɪn/ die; ~, ~nen clown

Club ▶ KLUB

cm Abk. = **Zentimeter** cm.

Co. Abk. = **Compagnie** Co.

Coach /koutʃ/ der; ~s, ~s (Sport) coach; (bes. Fußball: Trainer) manager

coachen /'koutʃn/ tr., itr. V. (Sport) coach; (Trainer sein) manage

Cockpit das; ~s, ~s cockpit

Cocktail /'kɔkteil/ der; ~s, ~s cocktail

Cognac Ⓦ /'kɔnjak/ der; ~s, ~s Cognac

Cola /'ko:la/ das; ~s, ~s od. die; ~, ~s (ugs.) Coke ®

Color- (Fot.) colour ⟨film, slide, etc.⟩

Colt Ⓦ der; ~s, ~s Colt ® [revolver]

Comeback /kam'bɛk/ das; ~s, ~s comeback; ein ~ feiern stage a comeback

Comic·heft das comic

Computer /kɔm'pju:tɐ/ der; ~s, ~: computer

computer·gestützt Adj. computer-aided; computer-assisted

computerisieren tr. V. computerize ⟨data, system⟩; (aufbereiten) make ⟨data⟩ computer-compatible

computer-, Computer-: ~**raum** der computer rooom; ~**spiel** das computer game ~**unterstützt** Adj. computer-aided; computer-assisted

Container /kɔn'te:nɐ/ der; ~s, ~: container; (für Müll) [refuse] skip

cool /ku:l/ (ugs.) [1] Adj. cool; ~ bleiben keep one's cool (coll.)
[2] adv. coolly (coll.)

Cord der; ~[e]s, ~e od. ~s cord; (~samt) corduroy

Corned Beef /'kɔ:nd'bi:f/ das; ~s corned beef

Couch /kautʃ/ die, (schweiz. auch:) der; ~, ~es sofa

Coup /ku:/ der; ~s, ~s coup

Coupon /ku'pō:/ der; ~s, ~s coupon; voucher

Courage /ku'ra:ʒə/ die; ~ (ugs.) courage

Cousin /ku'zɛ̃:/ der; ~s, ~s, **Cousine** die; ~, ~n cousin

Cover /'kavɐ/ das; ~s, ~s (a) (von Illustrierten) cover
(b) (von Schallplatten) sleeve

covern /'kavɐn/ tr. V. cover ⟨song, record⟩

Cowboy /'kaubɔy:/ der; ~s, ~s cowboy

Credo ▶ KREDO

Creme /kre:m/ die; ~, ~s, (schweiz.:) ~n cream

CSU Abk. = **Christlich-Soziale Union** CSU

CT (Med.) Abk. = **Computertomographie** CT

Curry /'kœri/ das; ~s, ~s curry powder

Curry·wurst die: sliced fried sausage sprinkled with curry powder and served with ketchup

Cursor /'kə:sɐ/ der; ~s, ~s (DV) cursor

Cyberspace /'saɪ:bɐspeɪs/ der; ~ (DV) cyberspace

Dd

d, D /deː/ *das;* ~, ~ **(a)** (Buchstabe) d/D
(b) (Musik) [key of] D

D *Abk.* = **Damen**

da **1** *Adv.* **(a)** (dort) there; **da draußen/ drinnen/drüben/unten** out/in/over/down there; **da, wo** where
(b) (hier) here
(c) (zeitlich) then; (in dem Augenblick) at that moment
(d) (deshalb) **der Zug war schon weg, da habe ich den Bus genommen** the train had already gone, so I took the bus
(e) (ugs.: in diesem Fall) **da kann man nichts machen** there's nothing one can do about it
(f) **da sein** (existieren) exist; (übrig sein) be left; (anwesend sein) be about *or* around; (im Haus, zu Hause sein) be in; (zu sprechen sein) be available; (angekommen, eingetroffen sein) have arrived; (fig.) ⟨*case*⟩ have occurred; ⟨*moment*⟩ have arrived; ⟨*situation*⟩ have arisen; **ich bin gleich wieder da** I'll be right *or* straight back
2 *Konj.* (weil) as; since

da·bei *Adv.* **(a)** with it/him/her/them; **nahe ~:** close by; **~ sein** (anwesend sein) be there; be present (**bei** at); (teilnehmen) take part (**bei** in)
(b) (währenddessen) at the same time; (bei diesem Anlass) then; on that occasion; **die ~ entstehenden Kosten** the expense involved; [gerade] **~ sein, etw. zu tun** be just doing sth.
(c) (außerdem) **~ [auch]** what is more
(d) (hinsichtlich dessen) about it/them; **was hast du dir denn ~ gedacht?** what 'were you thinking of?

dabei-: ~**|bleiben** *unr. itr. V.; mit sein* stay there; be there; ~**|haben** *unr. tr. V.* have with one; ***~**|sein** ▶ DABEI A, B; ~**|stehen** *unr. itr. V.* stand there

da|bleiben *unr. itr. V.; mit sein* stay there; (hier bleiben) stay here

Dach *das;* ~[e]s, Dächer roof

Dach-: ~**antenne** *die* roof aerial; ~**boden** *der* loft; **auf dem** ~**boden** in the loft; ~**decker** /-dɛkɐ/ *der;* ~~s, ~~, ~**deckerin** *die;* ~~, ~~nen roofer; ~**fenster** *das* skylight; (~gaube) dormer window; ~**garten** *der* roof garden; ~**gaube** *die* dormer window; ~**gepäckträger** *der* (Kfz-W.) roof rack; ~**geschoss**, ***~**geschoß** *das* attic [storey]; ~**kammer** *die* attic [room]; ~**luke** *die* skylight; ~**pappe** *die* roofing felt; ~**rinne** *die* gutter

Dachs /daks/ *der;* ~es, ~e badger

Dach·stuhl *der* roof truss

dachte *1. u. 3. Pers. Sg. Prät. v.* DENKEN

Dach-: ~**terrasse** *die* roof terrace; ~**wohnung** *die* attic flat (Brit.) *or* (Amer.) apartment; ~**ziegel** *der* roof tile; ~**zimmer** *das* attic room

Dackel *der;* ~s, ~: dachshund

da·durch *Adv.* **(a)** through it/them
(b) (durch diesen Umstand) as a result; (durch dieses Mittel) by this [means]

da·für *Adv.* **(a)** for it/them; ~, **dass ...** (wenn man berücksichtigt, dass) considering that ...; (damit) so that ...; ~ **sorgen** [, **dass ...**] see to it [that ...]
(b) ~ **sein** be in favour [of it]; **ein Beispiel** ~ **ist ...:** an example of this is ...
(c) (als Gegenleistung) in return [for it]; (beim Tausch) in exchange; (stattdessen) instead
(d) **etwas/nichts** ~ **können** be/not be responsible

*****dafür|können** ▶ DAFÜR D

dagegen *Adv.* **(a)** against it/them; **etwas ~ haben** have sth. against it; **ich habe nichts ~:** I've no objection; ~ **sein** be against it
(b) (im Vergleich dazu) by *or* in comparison

da·heim *Adv.* (bes. südd., österr., schweiz.) **(a)** (zu Hause) at home; ⟨*nach Präp.*⟩ home
(b) (in der Heimat) [back] home

da·her *Adv.* **(a)** from there
(b) (durch diesen Umstand) hence
(c) (deshalb) therefore; so

daher|kommen *unr. itr. V.* come along

da·hin *Adv.* **(a)** there
(b) (fig.) ~ **musste es kommen** it had to come to that
(c) **bis ~:** to there; (zeitlich) until then
(d) ~ **sein** be *or* have gone
(e) (in diesem Sinne) ~ [**gehend**], **dass ...:** to the effect that ...

da·hinten *Adv.* over there

da·hinter *Adv.* behind it/them; (folgend) after it/them

Dahlie /ˈdaːlɪə/ *die;* ~, ~n dahlia

da-: ~**|lassen** *unr. tr. V.* (ugs.) leave [there]; (hier lassen) leave here; ~**|liegen** *unr. itr. V.* lie there

dalli *Adv.* (ugs.) [~] ~! get a move on!

damalig *Adj.* at that *or* the time *postpos.*

damals *Adv.* at that time

Damast *der;* ~[e]s, ~e damask

Dame *die;* ~, ~n **(a)** (Frau) lady
(b) (Schach, Kartenspiele) queen
(c) (Spiel) draughts (Brit.); checkers (Amer.)

Damen-: ~**binde** *die* sanitary towel (Brit.) *or* (Amer.) napkin; ~**friseur** *der,* ⋯⋗

∼**friseurin** *die* ladies' hairdresser; ∼**rad** *das* lady's bicycle; ∼**toilette** *die* ladies' toilet

da·mịt ① *Adv.* (a) with it/them (b) (gleichzeitig) with that (c) (daher) thus ② *Konj.* so that

dämlich (ugs. abwertend) ① *Adj.* stupid ② *adv.* stupidly

Dạmm *der;* ∼[e]s, Dämme embankment; levee (Amer.); (Deich) dike; (Stau∼) dam

dämmern *itr. V.* es dämmert (morgens) it is getting light; (abends) it is getting dark

Dämmerung *die;* ∼, ∼en (a) (Abend∼) twilight; dusk (b) (Morgen∼) dawn

Dämon *der;* ∼s, ∼en /dɛˈmoːnən/ demon

dämonisch *Adj.* demonic

dämonisieren *tr. V.* demonize; portray as a demon/demons

Dạmpf *der;* ∼[e]s, Dämpfe steam *no pl., no indef. art.*

Dạmpf·bügel·eisen *das* steam iron

dạmpfen *itr. V.* steam (vor + *Dat.* with)

dämpfen *tr. V.* (a) (garen) steam ⟨*fish, vegetables, potatoes*⟩ (b) (mildern) muffle ⟨*sound*⟩; cushion, absorb ⟨*blow, impact, shock*⟩

Dạmpfer *der;* ∼s, ∼: steamer

Dạmpf-: ∼**kochtopf** *der* pressure cooker; ∼**maschine** *die* steam engine; ∼**nudel** *die* (südd., Kochk.) steamed yeast dumpling; ∼**walze** *die* steamroller

da·nach *Adv.* (a) (zeitlich) after it/that; then (b) (räumlich) after it/them (c) (entsprechend) in accordance with it/them

Däne *der;* ∼n, ∼n Dane

da·neben *Adv.* (a) beside him/her/it/them *etc.;* (b) (im Vergleich dazu) in comparison

da·neben-: ∼|**benehmen** *unr. refl. V.* (ugs.) blot one's copybook (coll.); ∼|**gehen** *unr. itr. V.; mit sein* miss [the target]; ∼|**schießen** *unr. itr. V.* miss [the target]

Dänemark (*das*); ∼s Denmark

Dänin *die;* ∼, ∼nen Dane; Danish woman/girl

dänisch *Adj.* Danish

dạnk *Präp. mit Dat. u. Gen.* thanks to

Dạnk *der;* ∼[e]s thanks *pl.;* mit [vielem *od.* bestem] ∼ zurück thanks for the loan; (bes. geschrieben) returned with thanks!; vielen/besten/herzlichen ∼! thank you very much

dạnkbar ① *Adj.* grateful; (anerkennend) appreciative ⟨*child, audience, etc.*⟩; [jmdm.] für etw. ∼ sein be grateful [to sb.] for sth. ② *adv.* gratefully

Dạnkbarkeit *die;* ∼: gratitude

dạnke *Höflichkeitsformel* thank you; (ablehnend) no, thank you; ∼ schön/sehr/vielmals thank you very much

dạnken ① *itr. V.* (Dank aussprechen) thank; ich danke Ihnen vielmals thank you very much; na, ich danke! (ugs.) no, 'thank you! ② *tr. V.* [aber bitte,] nichts zu ∼: don't mention it

Dạnke·schön *das;* ∼s thank-you

dạnn *Adv.* (a) then; was ∼? what happens then?; noch drei Tage, ∼ ist Ostern another three days and it will be Easter; bis ∼: see you then; ∼ und wann now and then (b) (in diesem Falle) then; in that case; ∼ will ich nicht weiter stören in that case I won't disturb you any further; [na,] ∼ eben nicht! in that case, forget it!; nur ∼, wenn ...: only if ...

daran /daˈran/ *Adv.* (a) (an dieser/diese Stelle, an diesem/diesen Gegenstand) on it/them; dicht ∼: close to it/them; nahe ∼ sein, etw. zu tun be on the point of doing sth. (b) (hinsichtlich dieser Sache) about it/them; ∼ ist nichts zu machen there's nothing one can do about it; kein Wort ∼ ist wahr not a word of it is true; mir liegt viel ∼: it means a lot to me (c) ich wäre beinahe ∼ erstickt I almost choked on it; er ist ∼ gestorben he died of it

daran|setzen *tr. V.* devote ⟨*energy etc.*⟩ to it; summon up ⟨*ambition*⟩ for it; (aufs Spiel setzen) risk ⟨*one's life, one's honour*⟩ for it

darauf *Adv.* (a) on it/them; (oben ∼) on top of it/them (b) er hat ∼ geschossen he shot at it/them (c) (danach) after that; ein Jahr ∼/kurz ∼ starb er he died a year later/shortly afterwards; ∼ folgend following

darauf-: *∼**folgend** ▶ DARAUF c; ∼**hin** /-'-'-/ *Adv.* (a) thereupon; (b) (unter diesem Gesichtspunkt) with a view to this/that

daraus *Adv.* (a) from it/them; out of it/them (b) mach dir nichts ∼: don't worry about it; was ist ∼ geworden? what has become of it?

dạr|bieten (geh.) *unr. tr. V.* (aufführen, vortragen) perform; es wurden Gedichte und Lieder dargeboten a recital of poems and songs was presented

Dạrbietung *die;* ∼, ∼en (geh.) (a) presentation (b) (Aufführung) performance; (beim Varieté usw.) act

dạrf *1. u. 3. Pers. Sg. Präsens v.* DÜRFEN

dạrfst *2. Pers. Sg. Präsens v.* DÜRFEN

darịn *Adv.* (a) in it/them (b) (in dieser Hinsicht) in that respect

dạr|legen *tr. V.* explain; set forth ⟨*reasons, facts*⟩

Dạrlehen *das;* ∼s, ∼: loan; ein ∼ aufnehmen get *or* raise a loan; jmdm. ein ∼ gewähren give *or* grant sb. a loan

Dạrm *der;* ∼[e]s, Därme intestines *pl.;* bowels *pl.*

---

*alte Schreibung - vgl. Hinweis auf S. xiv

dar|stellen *tr. V.* (a) depict; portray; **etw. grafisch ∼:** present sth. graphically
(b) (verkörpern) play; act
(c) (schildern) describe ⟨*person, incident, etc.*⟩; present ⟨*matter, argument*⟩
(d) (sein, bedeuten) represent

Darsteller *der; ∼s, ∼:* actor

Darstellerin *die; ∼, ∼nen* actress

Darstellung *die* (a) representation; (Schilderung) portrayal; (Bild) picture; **grafische/schematische ∼:** diagram; (Graph) graph
(b) (Beschreibung, Bericht) description; account;
(c) (einer Theaterrolle) interpretation; **seine ∼ des Mephisto** his portrayal *or* interpretation of Mephisto

darüber *Adv.* (a) over it/them; **∼ stehen** (fig.) be above such things
(b) **∼ hinaus** in addition [to that]; (noch obendrein) what is more
(c) (über dieser/diese Angelegenheit) about it/them
(d) (über diese Grenze, dieses Maß hinaus) over [that]

*****darüber|stehen** ▶ DARÜBER A

darum *Adv.* (a) [a]round it/them
(b) (diesbezüglich) **ich sorge mich ∼:** I worry about it
(c) /'--/ (deswegen) for that reason

darunter *Adv.* (a) (unter dem Genannten/das Genannte) under it/them
(b) (unter dieser Grenze, diesem Maß) less; **Bewerber im Alter von 40 Jahren und ∼:** applicants aged 40 and under

das 1 *best. Art. Nom. u. Akk.* the
2 *Demonstrativpron.* (a) *attr.* **das Kind war es** it was 'that child
(b) *allein stehend* **das** [da] that one; **das** [hier] this one [here]
3 *Relativpron.* (Mensch) who; that; (Sache, Tier) which; that

*****da|sein** ▶ DA 1F

Da-sein *das* existence

Daseins-berechtigung *die* right to exist; **das findet darin** *od.* **dadurch seine ∼:** this justifies its existence

da|sitzen *unr. itr. V.* sit there

dasjenige ▶ DERJENIGE

dass, *daß *Konj.* (a) that; **entschuldigen Sie bitte, ∼ ich mich verspätet habe** please forgive me for being late; **ich verstehe nicht, ∼ sie ihn geheiratet hat** I don't understand why she married him
(b) (nach Pronominaladverbien o. Ä.) [the fact] that; **das liegt daran, ∼ du nicht aufgepasst hast** that comes from your not paying attention
(c) (im Konsekutivsatz) that; [so]**∼:** .so that
(d) (im Finalsatz) so that
(e) (im Ausruf) **∼ mir das passieren musste!** why did it have to [go and] happen to me!

dasselbe ▶ DERSELBE

da|stehen *unr. itr. V.* (a) stand there

(b) (fig.) **gut ∼:** be in a good position; [ganz] **allein ∼:** be [all] alone in the world

Datei /da'tai:/ *die; ∼, ∼en* data file

Daten 1 ▶ DATUM
2 *Pl.* data

Daten-: ∼autobahn *die* (DV) data highway; **∼bank** *die; Pl.* **∼∼en** data bank; **∼erfassung** *die* data collection *or* capture; **∼schutz** *der* data protection *no def. art.;* **∼träger** *der* data carrier; **∼verarbeitung** *die* data processing *no def. art.*

datieren *tr. V.* date

Dativ *der; ∼s, ∼e* (Sprachw.) dative [case]

Dativ-objekt *das* (Sprachw.) indirect object

Dattel *die; ∼, ∼n* date

Dattel-palme *die* date palm

Datum *das; ∼s,* **Daten** date

Dauer *die; ∼* (a) length; **für die ∼ eines Jahres** *od.* **von einem Jahr** for a period of one year
(b) (Fortbestehen) **von ∼ sein** last [long]; **auf die ∼:** in the long run; **auf ∼:** permanently

dauer-; Dauer-: ∼auftrag *der* (Bankw.) standing order; **∼haft** 1 *Adj.* (a) [long-]lasting ⟨*peace, friendship, etc.*⟩; (b) (haltbar) durable; 2 *adv.* lastingly; **∼karte** *die* season ticket; **∼lauf** *der* jogging *no art.;* **ein ∼lauf** a jog

dauern *itr. V.* last; ⟨*job etc.*⟩ take; **einen Moment, es dauert nicht lange** just a minute, it won't take long

dauernd 1 *Adj.* constant ⟨*noise, interruptions, etc.*⟩; permanent ⟨*institution*⟩
2 *adv.* constantly; **er kommt ∼ zu spät** he keeps on arriving late

Dauer-: ∼regen *der* continuous rain; **∼stellung** *die* permanent position; **∼welle** *die* perm; **∼wurst** *die* smoked sausage ⟨*with good keeping properties, esp. salami*⟩; **∼zustand** *der* permanent state [of affairs]; **zum ∼zustand werden** become permanent *or* a permanent state

Daumen *der; ∼s, ∼:* thumb

Daune *die; ∼, ∼n* down [feather]; **∼n** down *sing.*

davon *Adv.* (a) (von dieser Stelle entfernt, weg) from it/them; (von dort) from there; (mit Entfernungsangabe) away [from it/them]
(b) (hinsichtlich dieser Sache) about it/them
(c) (durch diese Angelegenheit verursacht) by it/them; **das kommt ∼!** (ugs.) [there you are,] that's what happens
(d) **ich hätte gern ein halbes Pfund ∼:** I would like half a pound of that/those
(e) **∼ kann man nicht leben** you can't live on that

davon-: ∼|fahren *unr. itr. V.; mit sein* leave; (mit dem Auto) drive off; (mit dem Fahrrad, Motorrad) ride off; **∼|kommen** *unr. itr. V.; mit sein* get away; **∼|laufen** *unr. itr. V.; mit sein* run away; **∼|tragen** *unr. tr. V.* (a) ⋯⟩

carry away; take away ⟨*rubbish*⟩; **(b)** (geh.:
erringen) gain ⟨*a victory, fame*⟩; **(c)** (geh.: sich
zuziehen) receive ⟨*injuries*⟩

da·vor *Adv.* **(a)** in front of it/them; ~
liegen/stehen *usw.* lie/stand *etc.* in front of
it/them
(b) (zeitlich) before [it/them]

*davor|liegen *usw.* ▶ DAVOR A

Dax *der;* ~: Dax [index]

da·zu *Adv.* **(a)** (zusätzlich zu dieser Sache) with
it/them; (gleichzeitig) at the same time;
(außerdem) what is more
(b) (diesbezüglich) about it/them
(c) (zu diesem Zweck) for it
(d) (zu diesem Ergebnis) to it; ~ **reicht unser
Geld nicht** we haven't enough money for that

dazu-: ~|**geben** *unr. tr. V.* add;
~|**gehören** *tr. V.* belong to it/them;
~|**kommen** *unr. itr. V.; mit sein* **(a)**
(hinkommen) arrive; **(b)** (hinzukommen) **kommt
noch etwas dazu?** is there anything else
[you would like]?; ~ **kommt, dass ...** (fig.)
what's more, ...; on top of that ...;
~|**rechnen** *tr. V.* add on; ~|**tun** *unr. tr. V.*
(ugs.) add

da·zwischen *Adv.* in between; between
them; (darunter) among them

dazwischen-: ~|**kommen** *unr. itr. V.;
mit sein* **(a)** mit dem Finger ~**kommen** get
one's finger caught [in it]; **(b)** (es verhindern)
prevent it; **es ist mir etwas** ~**gekommen** I
had problems; ~|**reden** *itr. V.* interrupt

DDR *Abk.* = **Deutsche
Demokratische Republik** GDR; East
Germany

Deal /di:l/ *der od. das;* ~s, ~s (salopp) deal

dealen /'di:lən/ *itr. V.* (ugs.) push drugs; mit
LSD ~: push LSD

Dealer *der;* ~s, ~, **Dealerin** *die;* ~,
~**nen** (ugs.) pusher

Debatte *die;* ~, ~n debate (über + *Akk.*
on); **zur** ~ **stehen** be under discussion

Debüt /de'by:/ *das;* ~s, ~s debut

Deck *das;* ~[e]s, ~s deck

Deck·bett *das* ▶ OBERBETT

Decke *die;* ~, ~n **(a)** (Tisch~) tablecloth
(b) (Woll~, Pferde~, fig.) blanket; (Reise~) rug
(c) (Zimmer~) ceiling

Deckel *der;* ~s, ~ **(a)** lid; (auf Flaschen,
Gläsern usw.) top; (Schacht~, Uhr~, Buch~ usw.)
cover
(b) (Bier~) beer mat

decken ① *tr. V.* **(a)** etw. über etw. (*Akk.*)
~: spread sth. over sth.
(b) roof ⟨*house*⟩; cover ⟨*roof*⟩
(c) den Tisch ~: lay the table
(d) (schützen; Finanzw., Versicherungsw.) cover
(e) (befriedigen) meet ⟨*need, demand*⟩
② *itr. V.* (den Tisch decken) lay the table

Deck·mantel *der* cover

Deckung *die;* ~, ~en (Schutz; auch fig.)
cover (esp. Mil.); (Boxen) guard; (bes. Fußball)
defence; **in** ~ **gehen** take cover
(b) (Befriedigung) meeting
(c) (Finanzw., Versicherungsw.) cover[ing]

deckungs·gleich *Adj.* (Geom.) congruent

defekt *Adj.* defective; faulty; ~ **sein** have a
defect; be faulty; (nicht funktionieren) not be
working

Defekt *der;* ~[e]s, ~e defect, fault (**an** +
Dat. in)

defensiv ① *Adj.* defensive
② *adv.* defensively

Defensive *die;* ~, ~n defensive; **in der** ~:
on the defensive; **die** ~ (Sport) defensive play

definieren *tr. V.* define

Definition *die;* ~, ~en definition

definitiv ① *Adj.* definitive
② *adv.* finally

Defizit *das;* ~s, ~e **(a)** deficit
(b) (Mangel) deficiency

deformieren *tr. V.* **(a)** (verformen) distort
(b) (entstellen) deform (also fig.)

deftig *Adj.* (ugs.) **(a)** [good] solid *attrib.*
⟨*meal etc.*⟩; [nice] big ⟨*sausage etc.*⟩
(b) (derb) crude, coarse ⟨*joke, speech, etc.*⟩

Degen *der;* ~s, ~ **(a)** (Waffe) [light] sword
(b) (Fechtsport) épée

degradieren *tr. V.* demote

Degradierung *die;* ~, ~en **(a)** (im Rang)
demotion
(b) (Herabwürdigung) degradation; reduction
(**zu** to the level of)

dehnbar *Adj.* **(a)** (elastisch) ⟨*material etc.*⟩
that stretches *not pred.*; elastic ⟨*waistband
etc.*⟩
(b) (fig.: vage) elastic; **das ist ein** ~**er Begriff**
it's a loose concept

Dehnbarkeit *die;* ~: elasticity

dehnen *tr., refl. V.* stretch

Deich *der;* ~[e]s, ~e dike

Deichsel /'daiksļ/ *die;* ~, ~n shaft

deichseln *tr. V.* (ugs.) fix

dein *Possessivpron.* your; **viele Grüße von**
~**em Emil** with best wishes, yours Emil; **das
Buch dort, ist das** ~[e]s? that book over
there, is it yours?; **du und die Deinen** (geh.)
you and yours

deiner *Gen. des Personalpronomens* **du** (geh.)
of you

deiner·seits *Adv.* (von deiner Seite) on your
part; (auf deiner Seite) for your part

deinet·wegen *Adv.* because of you; (für
dich) on your behalf; (dir zuliebe) for your sake

Dekade /de'ka:də/ *die;* ~, ~n decade

dekadent *Adj.* decadent

Dekadenz *die;* ~: decadence

deklamieren *tr., itr. V.* recite

Deklination *die;* ~, ~en (Sprachw.)
declension

deklinieren *tr. V.* (Sprachw.) decline

dekodieren *tr. V.* (fachspr.) decode

Dekolleté /dekɔl'te:/ *das;* ∼s, ∼s low[-cut] neckline; décolletage

Dekor *das;* ∼s, ∼s *od.* ∼e decoration; (Muster) pattern

Dekorateur /dekora'tø:ɐ̯/ *der;* ∼s, ∼e, **Dekorateurin** *die;* ∼, ∼nen (Schaufenster∼) window dresser; (von Innenräumen) interior designer

Dekoration *die;* ∼, ∼en decorations *pl.;* (Schaufenster∼) window display

dekorativ [1] *Adj.* decorative [2] *adv.* decoratively

dekorieren *tr. V.* decorate ⟨room etc.⟩; dress ⟨shop window⟩

Deko-stoff *der* furnishing fabric

Dekret *das;* ∼[e]s, ∼e decree

Delegation *die;* ∼, ∼en delegation

delegieren *tr. V.* (a) send as a delegate/as delegates
(b) delegate ⟨task etc.⟩ (**an** + *Akk.* to)

Delegierte *der/die; adj. Dekl.* delegate

Delfin ▶ DELPHIN

delikat *Adj.* (a) delicious; (fein) delicate ⟨bouquet, aroma⟩
(b) (heikel) delicate

Delikatesse *die;* ∼, ∼n delicacy

Delikt *das;* ∼[e]s, ∼e offence

Delinquent *der;* ∼en, ∼en, **Delinquentin** *die;* ∼, ∼nen offender

Delirium *das;* ∼s, Delirien delirium

Delle *die;* ∼n (ugs.) dent

Delphin *der;* ∼s, ∼e dolphin

dem [1] *best. Art., Dat. Sg. v.* DER¹ 1 *u.* DAS 1: to the; (nach Präp.) the
[2] *Demonstrativpron., Dat. Sg. v.* DER¹ 2 *u.* DAS 2: (a) *attr.* that; **gib es dem Mann** give it to 'that man
(b) *allein stehend* **gib es nicht dem, sondern dem da!** don't give it to him, give it to that man/child *etc.;*
[3] *Relativpron., Dat. Sg. v.* DER¹ 3 *u.* DAS 3 (Person) that/whom; (Sache) that/which; **der Mann/das Kind, dem ich das Geld gab** the man/the child to whom I gave the money to

Demagoge *der;* ∼n, ∼n, **Demagogin** *die;* ∼, ∼nen demagogue

demagogisch *Adj.* demagogic

Dementi *das;* ∼s, ∼s denial

dementieren [1] *tr. V.* deny [2] *itr. V.* deny it

dem-: ∼**entsprechend** [1] *Adj.* appropriate; [2] *adv.* accordingly; (vor Adjektiven) correspondingly; ∼**gemäß** *Adv.* (a) (infolgedessen) consequently; (b) (entsprechend) accordingly; ∼**jenigen** ▶ DERJENIGE; ∼**nach** *Adv.* therefore; ∼**nächst** *Adv.* shortly

Demo *die;* ∼, ∼s (ugs.) demo; **auf der** ∼: at the demo

Demokrat *der;* ∼en, ∼en democrat; (Parteimitglied) Democrat

Demokratie *die;* ∼, ∼n democracy

Demokratin *die;* ∼, ∼nen ▶ DEMOKRAT

demokratisch [1] *Adj.* democratic [2] *adv.* democratically

demokratisieren *tr. V.* democratize

demolieren *tr. V.* wreck; smash up ⟨furniture⟩

Demonstrant *der;* ∼en, ∼en, **Demonstrantin** *die;* ∼, ∼nen demonstrator

Demonstration *die;* ∼, ∼en demonstration (**für** in support of, **gegen** against)

demonstrativ [1] *Adj.* (a) pointed (b) (Sprachw.) demonstrative [2] *adv.* pointedly

Demonstrativ·pronomen *das* (Sprachw.) demonstrative pronoun

demonstrieren [1] *itr. V.* demonstrate (**für** in support of, **gegen** against) [2] *tr. V.* demonstrate

dem·selben ▶ DERSELBE

Demut *die;* ∼: humility

demütig [1] *Adj.* humble [2] *adv.* humbly

demütigen [1] *tr. V.* humiliate [2] *refl. V.* humble oneself

Demütigung *die;* ∼, ∼en humiliation

dem-zufolge *Adv.* consequently

den¹ [1] *best. Art., Akk. Sg. v.* DER¹ 1: the
[2] *Demonstrativpron., Akk. Sg. v.* DER¹ 2: (a) *attr.* that; **ich meine den Mann** I mean 'that man
(b) *allein stehend* **ich meine den [da]** I mean 'that one
[3] *Relativpron., Akk. Sg. v.* DER¹ 3 (Person) that/whom; (Sache) that/which; **der Mann, den ich gesehen habe** the man that I saw

den² [1] *best. Art., Dat. Pl. v.* DER¹ 1, DIE¹ 1, DAS 1: the
[2] *Demonstrativpron. Dat. Pl. v.* DER¹ 2A, DIE¹ 2A, DAS 2A: those

denen [1] *Demonstrativpron., Dat. Pl. v.* DER¹ 2B, DIE¹ 2B, DAS 2B them; **gib es** ∼, **nicht den anderen** give it to 'them, not to the others
[2] *Relativpron., Dat. Pl. v.* DER¹ 3, DIE¹ 3, DAS 3 (Personen) that/whom; (Sachen) that/which; **die Menschen,** ∼ **wir Geld gegeben haben** the people to whom we gave money; **die Tiere,** ∼ **er geholfen hat** the animals that he helped

denjenigen ▶ DERJENIGE

denkbar [1] *Adj.* conceivable [2] *adv.* (sehr, äußerst) extremely

denken [1] *unr. itr. V.* think (**an** + *Akk.* of, **über** + *Akk.* about); **wie denkst du darüber?** what do you think about it?; what's your opinion of it?; **schlecht von jmdm.** ∼: think badly of sb.; **denk daran, dass .../zu ...:** don't forget that .../to ...; **ich denke nicht daran!** ···⊱

no way!; not on your life!; **ich denke nicht daran, das zu tun** I've no intention of doing that

2 *unr. tr. V.* think; **wer hätte das gedacht?** who would have thought it?; **eine gedachte Linie** an imaginary line

3 *unr. refl. V.* (a) (sich vorstellen) imagine (b) sich (*Dat.*) **bei etw. etwas** ∼: mean something by sth.; **ich habe mir nichts [Böses] dabei gedacht** I didn't mean any harm [by it]

Denken *das;* ∼s thinking; (Denkweise) thought

Denker *der;* ∼s, ∼, **Denkerin** *die;* ∼, ∼nen thinker

denk·faul *Adj.* mentally lazy

Denk-: ∼**fehler** *der* flaw in one's reasoning; ∼**mal** *das; Pl.* ∼**mäler od.** ∼**e** monument; memorial; **jmdm. ein** ∼ **errichten od. setzen** erect or put up a memorial to sb.

Denkmal[s]·schutz *der* protection of historic monuments; **unter** ∼**stehen/stellen** be/put under a preservation order

denk-, Denk-: ∼**pause** *die* pause for thought; ∼**sport·aufgabe** *die* brain teaser; ∼**vermögen** *das* ability to think [creatively]; ∼**würdig** *Adj.* memorable; ∼**zettel** *der* lesson

denn 1 *Konj.* (a) (kausal) for; because (b) (geh.: als) than

2 *Adv.* **es sei** ∼, ...: unless ...

3 *Partikel* (in Fragesätzen) **wie geht es dir** ∼? tell me, how are you?; **wie heißt du** ∼? tell me your name; **warum** ∼ **nicht?** why ever not?

dennoch *Adv.* nevertheless

denselben ▶ DERSELBE

Denunziant *der;* ∼en, ∼en, **Denunziantin** *die;* ∼, ∼nen informer; grass (sl.)

denunzieren *tr. V.* denounce; (bei der Polizei) inform against; grass on (sl.) (**bei** to)

Deo *das;* ∼s, ∼s, **Deodorant** *das;* ∼s, ∼s (auch:) ∼e deodorant

Deo·spray *das* deodorant spray

Deponie *die;* ∼, ∼n tip (Brit.); dump

deponieren *tr. V.* put; (im Safe o. Ä.) deposit

Deportation *die;* ∼, ∼en transportation; (ins Ausland) deportation

deportieren *tr. V.* transport; (ins Ausland) deport

Deportierte *der/die; adj. Dekl.* transportee; (ins Ausland) deportee

Depot /de'po:/ *das;* ∼s, ∼s (a) depot; (Lagerhaus) warehouse; (für Möbel usw.) depository; (im Freien, für Munition o. Ä.) dump; (in einer Bank) strongroom; safe deposit (b) (hinterlegte Wertgegenstände) deposits *pl.*

Depp *der;* ∼en (auch:) ∼s, ∼en (auch:) ∼e (bes. südd., österr., schweiz. abwertend)
▶ DUMMKOPF

**alte Schreibung - vgl. Hinweis auf S. xiv

Depression *die;* ∼, ∼en depression

depressiv 1 *Adj.* depressive

2 *adv.* ∼ **veranlagt sein** have a tendency towards depression

deprimieren *tr. V.* depress

deprimierend *Adj.* depressing

deprimiert 1 *Adj.* depressed

2 *adv.* dejectedly

der¹ 1 *best. Art. Nom.* the; **der Tod** death; **der „Faust"** 'Faust'; **der Bodensee/Mount Everest** Lake Constance/Mount Everest; **der Iran/Sudan** Iran/the Sudan; **der Mensch/Mann ist ...:** man is .../men are ...

2 *Demonstrativpron.* (a) *attr.* that; **der Mann war es** it was 'that man (b) *allein stehend* he; **der war es** it was 'him; **der** [da] (Person) that man/boy; (Sache) that one; **der** [hier] (Person) this man/boy; (Sache) this one

3 *Relativpron.* (Person) who/that; (Sache) which/that; **der Mann, der da drüben entlanggeht** the man walking along over there

4 *Relativ- u. Demonstrativpron.* the one who

der² 1 *best. Art.* (a) *Gen. Sg. v.* DIE¹ 1: **der Hut der Frau** the woman's hat; **der Henkel der Tasse** the handle of the cup (b) *Dat. Sg. v.* DIE¹ 1 to the; (nach Präp.) the (c) *Gen. Pl. v.* DER¹ 1, DIE¹ 1, DAS 1: **das Haus der Freunde** our/their *etc.* friends' house; **das Bellen der Hunde** the barking of the dogs

2 *Demonstrativpron.* (a) *Gen. Sg. v.* DIE¹ 2: of the; of that (b) *Dat. Sg. v.* DIE¹ 2 *attr.* **der Frau** [da/hier] **gehört es** it belongs to that woman there/this woman here (c) *Gen. Pl. v.* DER¹ 2A, DIE¹ 2A, DAS 2A: of those

3 *Relativpron.; Dat. Sg. v.* DIE¹ 3: **die Frau, der ich es gegeben habe** the woman I gave it to; **die Katze, der er einen Tritt gab** the cat [that] he kicked

der·art *Adv.* so; **es hat lange nicht mehr** ∼ **geregnet** it hasn't rained as hard as that for a long time; **sie hat** ∼ **geschrien, dass ...:** she screamed so much that ...

der·artig 1 *Adj.* such

2 *adv.* ▶ DERART

derb 1 *Adj.* (a) (tough) (material); stout, (shoes) (b) (kraftvoll, deftig) earthy (scenes, humour) 2 *adv.* (a) strongly (made, woven, etc.) (b) (kraftvoll, deftig) earthily

deren 1 *Relativpron.* (a) *Gen. Sg. v.* DIE¹ 3 (Personen) whose; (Sachen) of which (b) *Gen. Pl. v.* DER¹ 3, DIE¹ 3, DAS 3 (Personen) whose; (Sachen) **Maßnahmen,** ∼ **Folgen wir noch nicht absehen können** measures, the consequences of which we cannot yet foresee

2 *Demonstrativpron.* (a) *Gen. Sg. v.* DIE¹ 2: **meine Tante, ihre Freundin und** ∼ **Hund** my aunt, her friend and her dog

(b) *Gen. Pl. v.* DER[1] 2, DIE[1] 2, DAS 2: meine Verwandten und ∼ Kinder my relatives and their children

derent-: ∼wegen *Adv.* [1] *relativ* (Personen) because of whom; (Sachen) because of which; [2] *demonstrativ* because of them; ∼willen *Adv.* um ∼willen (Personen) for whose sake; (Sachen) for the sake of which

derer *Demonstrativpron.; Gen. Pl. v.* DER[1] 2, DIE[1] 2, DAS 2 of those

der-gleichen *indekl. Demonstrativpron.* **(a)** *attr.* such; like that *postpos., not pred.;* **(b)** *allein stehend* that sort of thing

Derivat *das;* ∼[e]s, ∼e derivative

der-jenige, die-jenige, das-jenige *Demonstrativpron.* **(a)** *attr.* that; *Pl.* those **(b)** *allein stehend* that one; *Pl.* those

derlei *indekl. Demonstrativpron.:* ▶ DERGLEICHEN

der-maßen *Adv.* ∼ schön *usw.,* dass ...: so beautiful *etc.* that ...

derselbe, dieselbe, dasselbe *Demonstrativpron.* **(a)** *attr.* the same **(b)** *allein stehend* the same one; *Pl.* the same people; **er sagt immer dasselbe** he always says the same thing; **noch einmal dasselbe, bitte** (ugs.) [the] same again please

der-zeit *Adv.* at present

der-zeitig *Adj.* present; current

des [1] *best. Art.; Gen. Sg. v.* DER[1] 1, DAS 1: **die Mütze des Jungen** the boy's cap; **das Klingeln des Telefons** the ringing of the telephone
[2] *Demonstrativpron.; Gen. Sg. v.* DER[1] 2, DAS 2: **er ist der Sohn des Mannes, der ...:** he's the son of the man who ...

Deserteur /dezɛrˈtøːɐ̯/ *der;* ∼s, ∼e, **Deserteurin** /dezɛrˈtøːrɪn/ *die;* ∼, ∼nen deserter

desertieren *itr. V.; mit sein* desert

des-gleichen *Adv.* likewise; **er ist Arzt,** ∼ **sein Sohn** he is a doctor, as is his son

des-halb *Adv.* for that reason; ∼ **bin ich zu dir gekommen** that is why I came to you

Design /diˈzaɪn/ *das;* ∼s, ∼s design

Designer /diˈzaɪnɐ/ *der;* ∼s, ∼, **Designerin** *die;* ∼, ∼nen designer

Designer-droge /-'---/ *die;* ∼, ∼n designer drug

Desinfektion *die;* ∼, ∼nen disinfection

Desinfektions-mittel *das* disinfectant

desinfizieren *tr. V.* disinfect

Desinteresse *das;* ∼s lack of interest

Despot /dɛsˈpoːt/ *der;* ∼en, ∼en, **Despotin** *die;* ∼, ∼nen despot; (fig. abwertend) tyrant

despotisch [1] *Adj.* despotic
[2] *adv.* despotically

des-selben ▶ DERSELBE

dessen [1] *Relativpron.; Gen. Sg. v.* DER[1] 3, DAS 3 *attr.* (Person) whose; (Sache) of which

[2] *Demonstrativpron.; Gen. Sg. v.* DER[1] 2, DAS 2: mein Onkel, sein Sohn und ∼ Hund my uncle, his son, and 'his dog

Dessert /dɛˈseːɐ̯/ *das;* ∼s, ∼s dessert

Destille *die;* ∼, ∼n distillery

destillieren *tr. V.* (Chemie) distil

desto *Konj., vor Komp.* je eher, ∼ besser the sooner the better

des-wegen *Adv.* ▶ DESHALB

Detail /deˈtai̯/ *das;* ∼s, ∼s detail

detailliert [1] *Adj.* detailed
[2] *adv.* in detail; sehr ∼: in great detail

Detektiv *der;* ∼s, ∼e, **Detektivin** *die;* ∼, ∼nen [private] detective

Detonation *die;* ∼, ∼en detonation; explosion

detonieren *itr. V.; mit sein* detonate; explode

Deut keinen ∼: not one bit

deuten [1] *itr. V.* point; [mit dem Finger] auf jmdn./etw. ∼: point [one's finger] at sb./ sth.
[2] *tr. V.* interpret

deutlich [1] *Adj.* clear
[2] *adv.* clearly

Deutlichkeit *die;* ∼ **(a)** clarity **(b)** (Eindeutigkeit) clearness

deutsch [1] *Adj.* German; **Deutsche Mark** Deutschmark; German mark
[2] *adv.* Deutsch sprechen/schreiben speak/ write German

Deutsch *das;* ∼[s] German; gutes/fließend ∼ sprechen speak good/fluent German; auf *od.* in ∼: in German; auf [gut] ∼ (ugs.) in plain English

Deutsche¹ *der/die; adj. Dekl.* German; **er ist** ∼r he is German

Deutsche² *das; adj. Dekl.* das ∼: German; aus dem ∼n/ins ∼ übersetzen translate from/into German

Deutschland (*das*); ∼s Germany

deutsch-, Deutsch-: ∼lehrer *der,* ∼lehrerin *die* German teacher; ∼sprachig *Adj.* **(a)** German-speaking; **(b)** German-language *attrib.;* ∼unterricht *der* German teaching; (Unterrichtsstunde) German lesson

Deutung *die;* ∼, ∼en interpretation

Devise *die;* ∼, ∼n motto

Devisen *Pl.* foreign currency *sing.*

Devisen-: ∼börse *die* foreign exchange market; ∼kurs *der* exchange rate; rate of exchange

Dezember *der;* ∼s, ∼: December

dezent [1] *Adj.* quiet ⟨colour, pattern, suit⟩; subdued ⟨lighting, music⟩
[2] *adv.* discreetly; ⟨dress⟩ unostentatiously

dezimal *Adj.* decimal

Dezimal-: ∼system *das* decimal system; ∼zahl *die* decimal [number]

dezimieren *tr. V.* decimate

dgl. *Abk.* = **dergleichen, desgleichen**

d. h. *Abk.* = **das heißt** i.e.

Di. *Abk.* = **Dienstag** Tue[s].

Dia *das;* ~s, ~s slide

Diabetes *der;* ~: diabetes

Diabetiker *der;* ~s, ~, **Diabetikerin** *die;* ~, ~nen diabetic

Diagnose /dia'gno:zə/ *die;* ~, ~n diagnosis

diagonal 1 *Adj.* diagonal
2 *adv.* diagonally

Diagonale *die;* ~, ~n diagonal

Diagramm *das* graph; (von Gegenständen) diagram

Dialekt *der;* ~[e]s, ~e dialect

Dialog *der;* ~[e]s, ~e dialogue

Dialog·fenster *das* (DV) dialogue box

Dialyse /dia'ly:zə/ *die;* ~, ~n (Physik, Chemie, Med.) dialysis

Diamant *der;* ~en, ~en diamond

***diät** ▶ DIÄT

Diät *die;* ~, ~en diet; **eine** ~ **einhalten** keep to a diet; ~ **essen** be on a diet; ~ **kochen** cook according to a/one's diet

Diäten *Pl.* [parliamentary] allowance *sing.*

dich 1 *Akk. von* DU you
2 *Akk. des Reflexivpron. der 2. Pers. Sg.* yourself

dicht 1 *Adj.* (a) thick; dense ⟨*forest, hedge, crowd*⟩; heavy, dense ⟨*traffic*⟩
(b) (undurchlässig) (für Luft) airtight; (für Wasser) watertight
2 *adv.* (a) densely ⟨*populated, wooded*⟩; ~ **bebaut** heavily built up
(b) (undurchlässig) tightly
(c) *mit Präp.* (nahe) ~ **neben** right next to

***dicht·be:baut** ▶ DICHT 2A

Dichte *die;* ~ (Physik, fig.) density

dichten 1 *itr. V.* write poetry
2 *tr. V.* (verfassen) write; compose

Dichter *der;* ~s, ~: poet; (Schriftsteller) writer; author

Dichterin *die;* ~, ~nen poet[ess]; (Schriftstellerin) writer; author[ess]

dichterisch *Adj.* poetic; (schriftstellerisch) literary

dicht|machen *tr., itr. V.* (ugs.) shut; (endgültig) shut down

Dichtung¹ *die;* ~, ~en seal; (am Hahn usw.) washer; (am Vergaser, Zylinder usw.) gasket

Dichtung² *die;* ~, ~en (a) work of literature; (in Versform) poetic work; poem
(b) (Dichtkunst) literature; (in Versform) poetry

dick 1 *Adj.* (a) thick; stout ⟨*tree*⟩; fat ⟨*person, legs, etc.*⟩; swollen ⟨*cheek, ankle, tonsils, etc.*⟩; ~ **werden** get fat; **5 cm** ~ **sein** be 5 cm thick
(b) (ugs.) big ⟨*mistake*⟩; hefty ⟨*salary*⟩
2 *adv.* thickly; **etw.** ~ **unterstreichen** underline sth. heavily; **sich** ~ **anziehen** wrap

up warm[ly]; **etw. 5 cm** ~ **schneiden** cut sth. 5 cm. thick; ~ **geschwollen** (ugs.) badly swollen

Dicke¹ *die;* ~: thickness; (von Menschen, Körperteilen) fatness

Dicke² *der/die; adj. Dekl.* (ugs.) fatty (coll.)

dick·fellig (ugs.) *Adj.* thick-skinned

Dickfelligkeit *die;* ~ (ugs.) insensitivity

Dickicht /'dɪkɪçt/ *das;* ~[e]s, ~e thicket

dick-, Dick-: ~**kopf** *der* (ugs.) mule (coll.); **ein** ~**kopf sein** be stubborn as a mule; **einen** ~**kopf haben** be pigheaded; ~**köpfig** *Adj.* (ugs.) pigheaded; ~**macher** *der* (ugs.) fattening food; ~**milch** *die* sour milk

die¹ 1 *best. Art. Nom.* the; **die Helga** (ugs.) Helga; **die Frau/Menschheit** women *pl./* mankind
2 *Demonstrativpron.* (a) *attr.* **die Frau war es** it was 'that woman
(b) *allein stehend* she; **die war es** it was 'her; **die** [da] (Person) that woman/girl; (Sache) that one
3 *Relativpron. Nom.* (Person) who; that; (Sache, Tier) which; that
4 *Relativ- u. Demonstrativpron.* the one who

die² 1 *best. Art.* (a) *Akk. Sg. v.* DIE¹ 1 the; **ich sah die Frau** I saw the women
(b) *Nom. u. Akk. Pl. v.* DER¹ 1, DIE¹ 1, DAS 1: the
2 *Demonstrativpron. Nom. u. Akk. Pl. v.* DER¹ 1, DIE¹ 1, DAS 1: *attr.* **ich meine die Männer, die ...** I mean those men who ...; *allein stehend* **ich meine die** [da] I mean 'them
3 *Relativpron.* (a) *Akk. Sg. v.* DIE¹ 3 (Person) who; (Sache) that
(b) *Nom. u. Akk. Pl. v.* DER¹ 3, DIE¹ 3, DAS 3 (Personen) whom; (Sachen) which; **die Männer, die ich gesehen habe** the men I saw

Dieb *der;* ~[e]s, ~e thief

Diebin *die;* ~, ~nen [woman] thief

diebisch 1 *Adj.* (a) thieving
(b) (verstohlen) mischievous
2 *adv.* mischievously

Diebstahl *der;* ~[e]s, Diebstähle theft

die·jenige ▶ DERJENIGE

Diele *die;* ~, ~n hall[way]

dienen *itr. V.* serve; **womit kann ich** ~? what can I do for you?

Diener *der;* ~s, ~: servant; **einen** ~ **machen** (ugs.) bow; make a bow

Dienerin *die;* ~, ~nen maid; servant

dienlich *Adj.* helpful

Dienst *der;* ~[e]s, ~e (a) (Tätigkeit) work; (von Soldaten, Polizeibeamten, Krankenhauspersonal usw.) duty; **seinen** ~ **antreten** start work/go on duty; ~ **haben** be at work/on duty; ⟨*doctor*⟩ be on call; ⟨*chemist*⟩ be open
(b) (Arbeitsverhältnis) post; **Major außer** ~: retired major
(c) (Tätigkeitsbereich) service; *s. auch* ÖFFENTLICH;
(d) (Hilfe) service

---

*old spelling - see note on page xiv

Diens·tag *der* Tuesday; **am** ∼: on Tuesday; ∼**, der 1. Juni** Tuesday, 1 June; **er kommt** ∼: he is coming on Tuesday; **ab nächsten** ∼: from next Tuesday [onwards]; ∼ **in einer Woche** a week on Tuesday; ∼ **vor einer Woche** a week last Tuesday

diens·tags *Adv.* on Tuesday[s]

dienst-, Dienst-: ∼**bereit** *Adj.* ⟨chemist⟩ open *pred.*; ⟨doctor⟩ on call; ⟨dentist⟩ on duty; ∼**bote** *der,* ∼**botin** *die* servant; ∼**eifrig** *Adj.* zealous; ∼**frei** *Adj.* free ⟨time⟩; ∼**geheimnis** *das* (a) professional secret; (im Staatsdienst) official secret; (b) professional secrecy; (im Staatsdienst) official secrecy; ∼**grad** *der* (Milit.) rank; ∼**leister** *der;* ∼**s,** ∼**,** ∼**leisterin** *die;* ∼∼**,** ∼∼**nen** (Firma, auch DV) service provider; ∼**leistung** *die* (auch Wirtsch.) service

Dienstleistungs-: ∼**branche** *die* (Wirtsch.) (a) service industry; (b) ▶ ∼SEKTOR; ∼**sektor** *der* (Wirtsch.) service sector

dienstlich ① *Adj.* business ⟨call⟩; (im Staatsdienst) official ⟨letter, call, etc.⟩ ② *adv.* on business; (im Staatsdienst) on official business

Dienst-: ∼**reise** *die* business trip; ∼**stelle** *die* office; ∼**wagen** *der* official car; (Geschäftswagen) company car; ∼**weg** *der* official channels *pl.*; ∼**zeit** *die* (a) period of service; (b) (tägliche Arbeitszeit) working hours *pl.*

dies ▶ DIESER

dies·bezüglich *adv.* regarding this

diese ▶ DIESER

Diesel *der;* ∼**s,** ∼: diesel

die·selbe ▶ DERSELBE

Diesel·motor *der* diesel engine

dieser, diese, dieses, dies *Demonstrativpron.* (a) *attr.* this; *Pl.* these (b) *allein stehend* this one; *Pl.* these; **dies alles** all this; **dies und das,** (geh.) **dieses und jenes** this and that

diesig *Adj.* hazy

dies-: ∼**mal** *Adv.* this time; ∼**seits** ① *Präp. mit Gen.* on this side of; ② *Adv.* ∼**seits von** on this side of .

Dietrich *der;* ∼**s,** ∼**e** picklock

diffamieren *tr. V.* defame

Diffamierung *die;* ∼**,** ∼**en** defamation

Differential *usw.* ▶ DIFFERENZIAL *usw.*

Differenz *die;* ∼**,** ∼**en** difference; (Meinungsverschiedenheit) difference [of opinion]

Differenzial /dɪfərɛnʦiːaːl/ *das;* ∼**s,** ∼**e** (a) (Math.) differential (b) (Technik) differential [gear]

Differenzial·rechnung *die* (Math.) differential calculus

differenziert *Adj.* complex; subtly differentiated ⟨methods, colours⟩; sophisticated ⟨taste⟩

diffus ① *Adj.* (a) (Physik, Chemie) diffuse

(b) (geh.) vague; vague and confused ⟨idea, statement, etc.⟩ ② *adv.* in a vague and confused way

digital (DV) ① *Adj.* digital ② *adv.* digitally

Digital- digital ⟨clock, display, etc.⟩

digitalisieren *tr. V.* (DV) digitalize

Diktat *das;* ∼**[e]s,** ∼**e** dictation

Diktator *der;* ∼**s,** ∼**en, Diktatorin** *die;* ∼**,** ∼**nen** dictator

diktatorisch ① *Adj.* dictatorial ② *adv.* dictatorially

Diktatur *die;* ∼**,** ∼**en** dictatorship

diktieren *tr. V.* dictate

Diktier·gerät *das* dictating machine

Dilemma *das;* ∼**s,** ∼**s** dilemma

Dilettant /dileˈtant/ *der;* ∼**en,** ∼**en, Dilettantin** *die;* ∼**,** ∼**nen** dilettante

dilettantisch ① *Adj.* dilettante; amateurish ② *adv.* amateurishly

Dill *der;* ∼**[e]s,** ∼**e** dill

Dimension *die;* ∼**,** ∼**en** (Physik, fig.) dimension

DIN /diːn/ *Abk.* = **Deutsche Industrie-Norm[en]** *German Industrial Standard[s];* DIN; **DIN-A4-Format** A4

Ding¹ *das;* ∼**[e]s,** ∼**e** (a) thing (b) **nach Lage der** ∼**e** the way things are; **persönliche/private** ∼**e** personal/private matters; **ein** ∼ **der Unmöglichkeit sein** be quite impossible; **vor allen** ∼**en** above all (c) **guter** ∼**e sein** (geh.) be in good spirits

Ding² *das;* ∼**[e]s,** ∼**er** (ugs.) thing; **das ist ja ein** ∼**!** that's really something

Dinkel *der;* ∼**s,** ∼ (Landw.) spelt

Dino *der;* ∼**s,** ∼**s** (ugs.) dinosaur

Dino·saurier *der;* ∼**s,** ∼: dinosaur

Diode *die;* ∼**,** ∼**n** (Elektrot.) diode

Dioden·rücklicht *das* LED rear light

Dioxin *das;* ∼**s** (Chemie) dioxin

Diözese *die;* ∼**,** ∼**n** diocese

Dipl.-Ing. *Abk.* = **Diplomingenieur** *academically qualified engineer*

Diplom *das;* ∼**s,** ∼**e** ≈ [first] degree (*in a scientific or technical subject*); (für einen Handwerksberuf) diploma

Diplom- qualified

Diplomat *der;* ∼**en,** ∼**en, Diplomatin** *die;* ∼**,** ∼**nen** diplomat

diplomatisch ① *Adj.* diplomatic ② *adv.* diplomatically

dir ① *Dat. von* DU to you; (nach Präp.) you; **Freunde von** ∼: friends of yours ② *Dat. des Reflexivpron. der 2. Pers. Sg.* yourself

direkt ① *Adj.* direct ② *adv.* straight; directly; **etw.** ∼ **übertragen** broadcast sth. live

Direkt·flug *der* direct flight

Direktion *die;* ~, ~en management;
(Büroräume) managers' offices *pl.*

Direktor *der;* ~s, ~en, **Direktorin** *die;*
~, ~nen director; (einer Schule) headmaster/
headmistress; (einer Strafanstalt) governor; (einer
Abteilung) manager

Direkt·übertragung *die* live broadcast

Dirigent *der;* ~en, ~en, **Dirigentin** *die;*
~, ~nen conductor

dirigieren *tr. V.* (a) *auch itr.* conduct
(b) (führen) steer

Disc·jockey /'dıskdʒɔke/ *der* disc jockey

Disco /'dısko:/ *die;* ~, ~s disco

Diskette *die;* ~, ~n (DV) floppy disk

Disketten·laufwerk *das* (DV) [floppy-
]disk drive

Diskont·satz *der* (Finanzw.) discount rate

Diskothek *die;* ~, ~en discothèque

Diskrepanz *die;* ~, ~en discrepancy

diskret ⓵ *Adj.* (vertraulich) confidential;
(taktvoll) discreet; tactful
⓶ *adv.* (vertraulich) confidentially; (taktvoll)
discreetly; tactfully

Diskretion *die;* ~ (a) (Verschwiegenheit, Takt)
discretion
(b) (Unaufdringlichkeit) discreetness

diskriminieren *tr. V.* discriminate against

Diskriminierung *die;* ~, ~en
discrimination

Diskussion *die;* ~, ~en discussion; zur ~
stehen be under discussion

Diskussions-: ~**beitrag** *der*
contribution to a/the discussion; ~**leiter**
der chair[man] [of the discussion];
~**leiterin** *die* chair[woman] [of the
discussion]

diskutieren ⓵ *itr. V.* über etw. (*Akk.*) ~:
discuss sth.
⓶ *tr. V.* discuss

Disqualifikation *die;* ~, ~en (auch Sport)
disqualification

disqualifizieren *tr. V.* disqualify

Distanz *die;* ~, ~en (auch fig.) distance

distanzieren *refl. V.* sich von jmdm./etw.
~ (fig.) dissociate oneself from sb./sth.

distanziert *Adj.* reserved

Distel *die;* ~, ~n thistle

Distel·fink *der* goldfinch

Disziplin *die;* ~, ~en discipline;
(Selbstbeherrschung) [self-]discipline

disziplinieren ⓵ *tr. V.* discipline
⓶ *refl. V.* discipline oneself

diszipliniert ⓵ *Adj.* well-disciplined;
(beherrscht) disciplined
⓶ *adv.* in a well-disciplined way; (beherrscht)
in a disciplined way

divers... /di'vɛrs.../ *Adj.* various; (mehrer...)
several

Dividende /divi'dɛndə/ *die;* ~, ~n (Wirtsch.)
dividend

dividieren *tr. V.* divide

Division *die;* ~, ~en (auch Milit.) division

DM *Abk.* = **Deutsche Mark** DM

D-Mark /'de:-/ *die* Deutschmark

DNS *Abk.* (Chemie)
= **Desoxyribonukleinsäure** DNA

Do. *Abk.* = **Donnerstag** Thur[s].

doch ⓵ *Konj.* but
⓶ *Adv.* (a) (jedoch) but
(b) (dennoch) all the same; still
(c) (geh.: nämlich) **wusste er ~, dass ...**:
because he knew that ...
(d) (entgegen allen gegenteiligen Behauptungen,
Annahmen) **er war also ~ der Mörder!** so he
'was the murderer!
(e) (ohnehin) in any case
⓷ *Interj.* **Das stimmt nicht. – Doch!** That's
not right. – [Oh] yes it is!; **Hast du keinen
Hunger? – Doch!** Aren't you hungry? – Yes [I
am]!
⓸ *Partikel* (a) (Ungeduld ausdrückend) **pass ~
auf!** [oh] do be careful!; **das ist ~ nicht zu
glauben** that's just incredible
(b) (Zweifel ausdrückend) **du hast ~ meinen
Brief erhalten?** you did get my letter, didn't
you?
(c) (Überraschung ausdrückend) **das ist ~ Karl!**
there's Karl!
(d) (verstärkt Bejahung/Verneinung ausdrückend)
gewiss/sicher ~: [why] certainly; of course;
ja ~: [yes,] all right; **nicht ~!** (abwehrend)
[no,] don't!
(e) (Wunsch verstärkend) **wäre es ~ ...:** if only
it were ...

Docht *der;* ~[e]s, ~e wick

Dock *das;* ~s, ~s dock

Dogge *die;* ~, ~n: [deutsche] ~: Great
Dane

Dogma *das;* ~s, Dogmen (auch fig.) dogma

dogmatisch (Theol., auch fig.) *Adj.* dogmatic

Dohle *die;* ~, ~n jackdaw

Doktor *der;* ~s, ~en (auch ugs.: Arzt) doctor;
(Titel) Doctor

Doktor·arbeit *die* doctoral thesis

Doktor·grad *der* doctorate; doctor's degree

Doktorin *die;* ~, ~nen ▶ DOKTOR

Doktor·titel *der* title of doctor

Doktrin *die;* ~, ~en doctrine

Dokument *das;* ~[e]s, ~e document

Dokumentar-: ~**bericht** *der*
documentary report; ~**film** *der*
documentary [film]

Dokumentation *die;* ~, ~en (a)
documentation
(b) (Bericht) documentary report

dokumentieren *tr. V.* (a) document; (fig.)
demonstrate
(b) (festhalten) record

Dolch *der;* ~[e]s, ~e dagger

Dolde *die;* ~, ~n (Bot.) umbel

doll (bes. nordd., salopp) ⓵ *Adj.* (a)
(ungewöhnlich) incredible

---

*alte Schreibung - vgl. Hinweis auf S. xiv

(b) (großartig) great (coll.)
2 *adv.* **(a)** (großartig) fantastically [well] (coll.)
(b) (sehr) ⟨*hurt*⟩ dreadfully (coll.), like mad

Dollar *der;* ~s, ~s dollar; **zwei** ~: two dollars

dolmetschen *itr. V.* act as interpreter

Dolmetscher *der;* ~s, ~,
Dolmetscherin *die;* ~, ~nen interpreter

Dom *der;* ~[e]s, ~e cathedral

dominieren *itr. V.* dominate

dominikanisch *Adj.* Dominican; **die Dominikanische Republik** the Dominican Republic

Domino *das;* ~s, ~s (Spiel) dominoes *sing.*

Domizil *das;* ~s, ~e (geh.) domicile; residence

Dom-pfaff *der;* ~en *od.* ~s, ~en (Zool.) bullfinch

Dompteur /dɔmp'tøːɐ/ *der;* ~s, ~e,
Dompteurin /dɔmp'tøːrɪn/ *die;* ~, ~nen,
Dompteuse /dɔmp'tøːzə/ *die;* ~, ~n tamer

Donau *die;* ~: Danube

Donner *der;* ~s, ~: thunder

donnern *itr. V.* **(a)** (*unpers.*) thunder
(b) (fig.) thunder; ⟨*engine*⟩ roar

Donners-tag *der* Thursday; *s. auch*
DIENSTAG

donnerstags *Adv.* on Thursday[s]; *s. auch* DIENSTAGS

Donner-wetter *das* (ugs.) **(a)** (Krach) row
(b) /'--'--/ **zum** ~ [noch einmal]! damn it!; ~! my word

doof (ugs.) 1 *Adj.* stupid; dumb (coll.)
2 *adv.* stupidly

Doping /'doːpɪŋ/ *das;* ~s (Sport) taking drugs

Doping-kontrolle *die* (Sport) drug[s] test

Doppel *das,* ~s, ~ **(a)** (Kopie) duplicate; copy
(b) (Sport) doubles *sing. or pl.*

doppel-, Doppel-: ~**bett** *das* double bed; ~**bock** *das* extra-strong bock beer;
~**decker** *der;* ~~s, ~~: biplane;
~**deutig** /-ˌdɔy̆tɪç/ 1 *Adj.* **(a)** ambiguous;
(b) (anzüglich) suggestive; 2 *adv.* **(a)** ambiguously; **(b)** (anzüglich) suggestively;
~**fenster** *das* double-glazed window;
~**gänger** *der;* ~~s, ~~, ~**gängerin**
die; ~~, ~~nen double; ~**haus** *das* pair of semi-detached houses; ~**haus-hälfte**
die semi[-detached house]; ~**kinn** *das* double chin; ~**klick** *der;* ~~s, ~~s (DV) double click; ~**moral** *die* double standards
pl.; ~**pass,** *·*~**paß** *der* (ugs.) der ~pass dual nationality *no art.;* ~**punkt** *der* colon;
~**stunde** *die* double period

doppelt 1 *Adj.* double; **die** ~**e Menge** twice the quantity; **mit** ~**er Kraft arbeiten** work with twice as much energy

2 *adv.* ~ **so groß/alt wie** ...: twice as large/ old as ...; **sich** ~ **anstrengen** try twice as hard

Doppelte *das; adj. Dekl.* **das** ~ **bezahlen** pay twice as much; pay double

Doppel-: ~**tür** *die* double door;
~**zentner** *der* 100 kilograms; ~**zimmer**
das double room

Dorf *das;* ~[e]s, Dörfer village; **auf dem** ~: in the country

Dorf-: ~**bewohner** *der,*
~**bewohnerin** *die* villager; ~**depp** *der*
(bes. südd., österr.) village idiot; ~**trottel** *der* village idiot

Dorn *der;* ~[e]s, ~en thorn; **jmdm. ein** ~ **im Auge sein** annoy sb. intensely

dornig *Adj.* thorny

Dorn-röschen (*das*) the Sleeping Beauty

dörren *tr. V.* dry

Dörr-: ~**fleisch** *das* (südd.) lean bacon;
~**obst** *das* dried fruit

Dorsch *der;* ~[e]s, ~e cod

dort *Adv.* there; ~ **bleiben** stay there; *s. auch* DA 1A

dort-: ***~|**bleiben** ▶ DORT; ~**her** *Adv.*
[von] ~her from there; ~**hin** *Adv.* there

dortig *Adj.* there

Dose *die;* ~, ~n **(a)** (Blech~) tin; (Pillen~) box; (Zucker~) bowl
(b) (Konserven~) can; tin (Brit.); (Bier~) can

dösen *itr. V.* (ugs.) doze

Dosen-: ~**bier** *das* canned beer; ~**milch**
die canned *or* (Brit.) tinned milk; ~**öffner**
der can-opener; tin-opener (Brit.)

dosieren *tr. V. etw.* ~: measure out the required dose of sth.

Dosierung *die;* ~, ~en **(a)** measuring out; (das Zuführen) administering; (fig.) dispensing
(b) ▶ DOSIS

Dosis *die;* ~, Dosen dose

Dossier /dɔ'sjeː/ *das,* (veraltet:) *der;* ~s, ~s dossier

Dotter *der od. das;* ~s, ~: yolk

Dotter-blume *die* marsh marigold

doubeln /'duːbl̩n/ *tr. V.* stand in for ⟨*actor*⟩; use a stand-in for ⟨*scene*⟩; **sich** ~ **lassen** use *or* have a stand-in

Dozent *der;* ~en, ~en, **Dozentin** *die;* ~, ~nen lecturer (für in)

dpa *Abk.* = **Deutsche Presse-Agentur** German Press Agency

Dr. *Abk.* = **Doktor** Dr

Drache *der;* ~n, ~n (Myth.) dragon

Drachen *der;* ~s, ~ **(a)** kite
(b) (Fluggerät) hang-glider

Dragee, Dragée /dra'ʒeː/ *das;* ~s, ~s dragee

Draht *der;* ~[e]s, Drähte **(a)** wire
(b) (Leitung) wire; (Telefonleitung) line; wire
(c) (Telefonverbindung) line

draht-, Draht-: ~**los** (Nachrichtenw.)
1 *Adj.* wireless; 2 *adv. etw.* ~**los**   ····✦

telegrafieren/übermitteln radio sth.; ～**seil**
das [steel] cable; ～**seil·bahn** *die* cable
railway; ～**zieher** *der;* ～～s, ～～,
～**zieherin** *die;* ～～, ～～nen (fig.) wire
puller

drall *Adj.* strapping ⟨*girl*⟩; full, rounded
⟨*cheeks, face, bottom*⟩

Drama *das;* ～s, Dramen drama; (fig., ugs.)
disaster

Dramatiker *der;* ～s, ～, **Dramatikerin**
die; ～, ～nen dramatist

dramatisch ① *Adj.* dramatic
② *adv.* dramatically

dramatisieren *tr. V.* dramatize

dramaturgisch *adj.* dramaturgical

dran *Adv.* (ugs.) (a) häng das Schild ～! put
the sign up!
(b) arm ～ sein be in a bad way; gut/schlecht
～ sein be well off/badly off; früh/spät ～ sein
be early/late; ich bin ～: it's my turn

dran|bleiben *unr. itr. V.; mit sein* (ugs.) (am
Telefon) hang on (coll.)

drang 1. u. 3. Pers. Sg. Prät. v. DRINGEN

Drang *der;* ～[e]s, Dränge urge

dränge 1. u. 3. Pers. Sg. Konjunktiv II v.
DRINGEN

drängeln (ugs.) ① *itr. V.* (a) push [and
shove]
(b) (auf jmdn. einreden) go on (coll.)
② *tr. V.* (a) push; shove
(b) (einreden auf) go on at (coll.)
③ *refl. V.* sich nach vorn ～: push one's way
to the front

drängen ① *itr. V.* (a) push
(b) die Zeit drängt time is pressing
② *tr. V.* (a) push
(b) (antreiben) press; urge
③ *refl. V.* crowd

drangsalieren *tr. V.* (quälen) torment;
(plagen) plague

dran-: ～|**halten** *unr. refl. V.* (ugs.) get a
move on (coll.); ～|**kommen** *unr. itr. V.; mit
sein* (ugs.) have one's turn; ～|**nehmen** *unr.
tr. V.* (ugs.) (beim Friseur usw.) see to; (beim Arzt)
see

drastisch ① *Adj.* drastic ⟨*measure, means*⟩
② *adv.* drastically; ⟨*punish*⟩ severely

drauf *Adv.* (ugs.) on it

drauf-, Drauf-: ～**gänger** *der;* ～～s, ～～,
～**gängerin** *die;* ～～, ～～nen daredevil;
～**gängerisch** *Adj.* daring; ～|**gehen**
unr. itr. V.; mit sein (ugs.) (a) (umkommen) kick
the bucket (coll.); (b) (verbraucht werden) go (für
on); ～|**zahlen** (ugs.) ① *tr. V.* noch etwas/
1250 DM ～zahlen fork out (coll.) *or* pay a bit
more/an extra 1,250 marks; ② *itr. V.*
(Unkosten haben) ich zahle dabei noch ～: it's
costing me money

draußen *Adv.* outside; hier/da ～: out here/
there; von/nach ～: from outside/outside

Dreck *der;* ～[e]s (a) (ugs.) dirt; (sehr viel)
filth; (Schlamm) mud
(b) (salopp abwertend: Angelegenheit) mach
deinen ～ allein do it yourself; das geht dich
einen [feuchten] ～ an (salopp) none of your
damned business (coll.)
(c) (salopp abwertend: Zeug) junk *no indef. art.*

Dreck·arbeit *die* (auch fig.) dirty work *no
indef. art., no pl.*/dirty job

dreckig ① *Adj.* (a) (ugs., auch fig.) dirty;
(sehr schmutzig) filthy
(b) (salopp: unverschämt) cheeky
② *adv.* (a) es geht ihm ～ (ugs.) he's in a bad
way
(b) (salopp: unverschämt) cheekily

Dreck-: ～**sau** *die,* ～**schwein** *das* (derb)
filthy swine

Dreh *der;* ～s, ～s (ugs.) (a) den ～
heraushaben have [got] the knack
(b) [so] um den ～: about that

Dreh-: ～**arbeiten** *Pl.* (Film) shooting *sing.*
(zu of); ～**bank** *die; Pl.* ～bänke lathe;
～**buch** *das* screenplay; [film] script

drehen ① *tr. V.* (a) turn
(b) (formen) twist ⟨*rope, thread*⟩; roll
⟨*cigarette*⟩
(c) (Film) shoot ⟨*scene*⟩; film ⟨*report*⟩; make
⟨*film*⟩
② *itr. V.* (a) ⟨*car*⟩ turn; ⟨*wind*⟩ change
(b) an etw. (*Dat.*) ～: turn sth.
(c) (Film) shoot; film
③ *refl. V.* (a) turn
(b) (ugs.: zum Gegenstand haben) sich um etw.
～: be about sth.

Dreh-: ～**kreuz** *das* turnstile; ～**orgel** *die*
barrel organ; ～**ort** *der* (Film) location;
～**restaurant** *das* revolving restaurant;
～**stuhl** *der* swivel chair; ～**tür** *die*
revolving door

Drehung *die;* ～, ～en turn; (um einen
Mittelpunkt) revolution

Dreh-: ～**zahl** *die* revolutions *or* (coll.) revs
(*esp. per minute*); ～**zahl·messer** *der;*
～～s, ～～: revolution counter; rev counter
(coll.); tachometer

drei *Kardinalz.* three;

Drei *die;* ～, ～en three; eine ～ schreiben
(Schulw.) get a C

drei-, Drei-: ～**eck** *das* (Geom.) triangle;
～**eckig** *Adj.* triangular; ～**ein·halb**
Bruchz. three and a half

Dreier *der;* ～s, ～ (ugs.) three

dreierlei *indekl. Adj.* (a) *attr.* three kinds
or sorts of; three different
(b) *subst.* three [different] things

drei-, Drei-: ～**fach** *Vervielfältigungsz.*
triple; die ～fache Menge three times the
amount; ～**fache** *das; adj. Dekl.* das
～fache kosten cost three times as much; das
～fache von 3 ist 9 three times three is nine;
～**faltigkeit** *die;* ～～ (christl. Rel.) Trinity;
～**hundert** *Kardinalz.* three hundred;
～**jährig** *Adj.* (3 Jahre alt) three-year-old
attrib.; (3 Jahre dauernd) three-year *attrib.;*

~**kampf** *der* (Sport) triathlon; ~**klang** *der* triad; ~**köpfig** *Adj.* ⟨family, crew⟩ of three; ~**mal** *Adv.* three times; ~**malig** *Adj.* **eine** ~**malige Wiederholung** three repeats

drein (ugs.) ▶ DAREIN

drein-: ~|**blicken,** ~|**schauen** *itr. V.* look

drei-, Drei-: ~**rad** *das* tricycle; ~**satz** *der* rule of three; ~**seitig** *Adj.* three-sided ⟨figure⟩; three-page ⟨letter, leaflet, etc.⟩

dreißig *Kardinalz.* thirty; *s. auch* ACHTZIG

dreißigjährig *Adj.* (30 Jahre alt) thirty-year-old *attrib.;* (30 Jahre dauernd) thirty-year *attrib.*

dreißigst... *Ordinalz.* thirtieth

Dreißigstel *das;* ~**s,** ~: thirtieth

dreist ① *Adj.* brazen; barefaced ⟨lie⟩ ② *adv.* brazenly

drei-stellig *Adj.* three-figure *attrib.*

Dreistigkeit *die;* ~, ~**en (a)** brazenness **(b)** (Handlung) brazen act

drei-, Drei-: ~**tausend** *Kardinalz.* three thousand; ~**teilig** *Adj.* three-part *attrib.;* three-piece *attrib.* ⟨suit⟩; ***~**viertel** ▶ VIERTEL; ~**viertel-stunde** /---'--/ *die* three-quarters of an hour; ~**viertel-takt** /-'---/ *der* three-four time; ~**zehn** *Kardinalz.* thirteen; *s. auch* ACHTZEHN

Dresche *die;* ~ (salopp) walloping (coll.); thrashing

dreschen ① *unr. tr. V.* **(a)** thresh **(b)** (salopp: schlagen) wallop (coll.); thrash ② *unr. itr. V.* thresh

dressieren *tr. V.* train ⟨animal⟩

Dressur *die;* ~, ~**en** training

Drill *der;* ~[e]s drilling; (Milit.) drill

drillen *tr. V.* (auch Milit.) drill

Drilling *der;* ~**s,** ~**e** triplet

drin *Adv.* (ugs.) **(a)** in it **(b)** ▶ DRINNEN

dringen *unr. itr. V.* **(a)** *mit* sein **durch/in** etw. ~: penetrate sth. **(b)** *mit* sein **in jmdn.** ~ (geh.) press sb. **(c)** **auf etw.** (Akk.) ~: insist upon sth.

dringend ① *Adj.* urgent; strong ⟨suspicion, advice⟩ ② *adv.* urgently; ⟨advise, suspect⟩ strongly; ~ **erforderlich** essential

dringlich ① *Adj.* urgent ② *adv.* urgently

Dringlichkeit *die;* ~: urgency

drinnen *Adv.* inside; (im Haus) indoors; inside

dritt *in* **wir waren zu** ~: there were three of us

dritt... *Ordinalz.* third

Drittel *das,* (schweiz. meist *der*); ~**s,** ~: third

dritteln *tr. V.* split *or* divide three ways

drittens *Adv.* thirdly

DRK *Abk.* = **Deutsches Rotes Kreuz** German Red Cross

Dr. med. *Abk.* = **doctor medicinae** MD

droben *Adv.* (südd., österr., sonst geh.) up there

Droge *die;* ~, ~**n** drug

drogen-, Drogen-: ~**abhängig** *Adj.* addicted to drugs *postpos.;* ~**abhängige** *der/die; adj. Dekl.* drug addict; ~**abhängigkeit** *die* drug addiction; ~**beratungs-stelle** *die* drug advice centre; ~**gefährdet** *Adj.* at risk from drugs *postpos.;* ~**handel** *der* drug trafficking; ~**konsum** *der* drug-taking; ~**konsument** *der,* ~**konsumentin** *die* drug user; ~**missbrauch,** *~**mißbrauch** *der* drug abuse; ~**rausch** *der* [state of] drug intoxication; **etw. im** ~**rausch tun** do sth. while under the influence of drugs *or* while [high (coll.)] on drugs; ~**süchtig** *Adj.* ▶ ~ABHÄNGIG; ~**szene** *die* drug scene

Drogerie *die;* ~, ~**n** chemist's [shop] (Brit.); drugstore (Amer.)

Drogist *der;* ~**en,** ~**en, Drogistin** *die;* ~, ~**nen** chemist (Brit.); druggist (Amer.)

drohen *itr., mod. V.* threaten; (bevorstehen) be threatening; **jmdm. droht etw.** sb. is threatened with sth.

drohend *Adj.* threatening; (bevorstehend) impending

Drohne *die;* ~, ~**n** drone

dröhnen *itr. V.* boom; ⟨machine⟩ roar

Drohung *die;* ~, ~**en** threat

drollig ① *Adj.* funny; comical; (niedlich) sweet; cute (Amer.) ② *adv.: s. Adj.:* comically; sweetly; cutely (Amer.)

Dromedar *das;* ~**s,** ~**e** dromedary

Drops *der od. das;* ~, ~: fruit *or* (Brit.) acid drop

drosch *1. u. 3. Pers. Sg. Prät. v.* DRESCHEN

Drossel *die;* ~, ~**n** thrush

drosseln *tr. V.* **(a)** turn down ⟨heating, air conditioning⟩; throttle back ⟨engine⟩ **(b)** (herabsetzen) reduce

Dr. phil. *Abk.* = **doctor philosophiae** Dr

drüben *Adv.* **dort** *od.* **da** ~: over there; ~ **auf der anderen Seite** over on the other side

Druck¹ *der;* ~[e]s, Drücke **(a)** (auch fig.) pressure **(b)** **ein** ~ **auf den Knopf** a touch of the button

Druck² *der;* ~[e]s, ~**e (a)** printing; **in** ~ **gehen** go to press **(b)** (Produkt) print

Druck-buchstabe *der* printed letter

drucken *tr., itr. V.* print

drücken ① *tr. V.* **(a)** press; press, push ⟨button⟩; squeeze ⟨juice, pus⟩ (aus out of); **jmdm. die Hand** ~: squeeze sb.'s hand **(b)** (liebkosen) **jmdn.** ~: hug [and squeeze] sb. **(c)** ⟨shoe etc.⟩ pinch ····⟩

d

(d) (herabsetzen) push down ⟨*price, rate*⟩;
depress ⟨*sales*⟩; bring down ⟨*standard*⟩
2 *itr. V.* (a) press; **auf den Knopf** ~: press
or push the button; **„bitte** ~**":** 'push'
(b) (Druck verursachen) ⟨*shoe etc.*⟩ pinch
3 *refl. V.* (ugs.: sich entziehen) shirk; **sich vor
etw.** (*Dat.*) ~: get out of sth.

drückend *Adj.* (a) heavy ⟨*debt, taxes*⟩;
serious ⟨*worries*⟩; grinding ⟨*poverty*⟩
(b) (schwül) oppressive

Drucker *der;* ~**s,** ~: printer

Druckerei *die;* ~, ~**en** printing works;
(Firma) printing house; printer's

Druckerin *die;* ~, ~**nen** printer

druck-, Druck-: ~fehler *der* misprint;
printer's error; ~**knopf** *der* press stud
(Brit.); snap fastener; ~**luft** *die* compressed
air; ~**mittel** *das* means of bringing
pressure to bear (**gegenüber** on); ~**reif**
1 *Adj.* ready for publication; (~**fertig**) ready
for press; **2** *adv.* ⟨*speak*⟩ in a polished
manner; ~**sache** *die* (Postw.) printed
matter; ~**schrift** *die* (a) printed writing;
(b) (Schriftart) type[face]; (c) (Schriftwerk)
pamphlet

drum *Adv.* (ugs.) (a) ▶ DARUM;
(b) [a]round; **alles** *od.* **das [ganze] Drum und
Dran** (bei einer Mahlzeit) all the trimmings; (bei
einer Feierlichkeit) all the palaver that goes with
it (coll.)

Drum·herum *das;* ~**s** everything that
goes/went with it

drunter *Adv.* (ugs.) underneath; **es** *od.* **alles
geht** ~ **und drüber** everything is topsy-turvy

Drüse *die;* ~, ~**n** gland

Dschungel /'dʒʊŋl̩/ *der;* ~**s,** ~ (auch fig.)
jungle

dt. *Abk.* = **deutsch** G.

Dtzd. *Abk.* = **Dutzend** doz.

du *Personalpron.;* 2. *Pers. Sg. Nom.* you; **Du
zueinander sagen** use the familiar form in
addressing one another; *s. auch* ⟨*Gen.*⟩
DEINER, (*Dat.*) DIR, (*Akk.*) DICH

Dübel *der;* ~**s,** ~: plug

ducken **1** *refl. V.* duck
2 *itr. V.* (fig. abwertend) humble oneself (**vor** +
Dat. before)

Duckmäuser *der;* ~**s,** ~,
Duckmäuserin *die;* ~, ~**nen** (abwertend)
moral coward

Duckmäusertum *das;* ~**s** (abwertend)
moral cowardice

Dudel·sack *der* bagpipes *pl.*

Duell *das;* ~**s,** ~**e** duel

duellieren *refl. V.* fight a duel

Duett *das;* ~[**e**]**s,** ~**e** (Musik) duet; **im** ~
singen sing a duet

Duft *der;* ~[**e**]**s, Düfte** scent; (von Parfüm,
Blumen) scent; fragrance; (von Kaffee usw.)
aroma

duften *itr. V.* smell (**nach** of)

dulden *tr. V.* tolerate; put up with

duldsam **1** *Adj.* tolerant (**gegen** towards)
2 *adv.* tolerantly

Duma *die:* **die** ~: the Duma

dumm, dümmer, dümmst... **1** *Adj.*
(a) stupid
(b) (unvernünftig) foolish
(c) (ugs.: töricht, albern) idiotic; silly
(d) (ugs.: unangenehm) nasty ⟨*feeling*⟩;
annoying ⟨*habit*⟩; **das wird mir jetzt zu** ~
(ugs.) I've had enough of it
2 *adv.* (ugs.) idiotically

Dumme *der/die; adj. Dekl.* fool; **der/die** ~
sein (ugs.) be the loser

dummer·weise *Adv.* (a) unfortunately;
(ärgerlicherweise) annoyingly
(b) (törichterweise) foolishly

Dummheit *die;* ~, ~**en** (a) stupidity
(b) (unkluge Handlung) stupid thing

Dumm·kopf *der* (ugs.) nitwit (coll.)

dumpf **1** *Adj.* (a) dull ⟨*thud, rumble of
thunder*⟩; muffled ⟨*sound, thump*⟩
(b) (muffig) musty
(c) (stumpfsinnig) dull
2 *adv.* (a) ⟨*echo*⟩ hollowly
(b) (stumpfsinnig) apathetically

Dumping /'dampɪŋ/ *das;* ~**s** (Wirtsch.)
dumping

Dumping·preis *der* dumping price

Düne *die;* ~, ~**n** dune

düngen **1** *tr. V.* fertilize ⟨*soil, lawn*⟩;
spread fertilizer on ⟨*field*⟩; scatter fertilizer
around ⟨*plants*⟩
2 *itr. V.* **gut** ~ ⟨*substance*⟩ be a good
fertilizer

Dünger *der;* ~**s,** ~: fertilizer

dunkel **1** *Adj.* (auch fig.) dark; (tief) deep
⟨*voice, note*⟩; (undeutlich) vague
2 *adv.* (a) (tief) ⟨*speak*⟩ in a deep voice
(b) (undeutlich) vaguely

Dünkel *der;* ~**s** (geh.) arrogance; (Einbildung)
conceit[edness]

dunkel-: ~blond *Adj.* light brown ⟨*hair*⟩;
⟨*person*⟩ with light brown hair; ~**häutig**
Adj. dark-skinned

Dunkelheit *die;* ~: darkness

Dunkel·kammer *die* darkroom

dunkeln *itr. V.* (*unpers.*) **es dunkelt** (geh.) it
is growing dark

Dunkel·ziffer *die* number of unrecorded
cases

dünn **1** *Adj.* thin; slim ⟨*book*⟩; fine
⟨*stocking*⟩; watery ⟨*coffee, tea, beer*⟩
2 *adv.* thinly ⟨*sliced, populated*⟩; lightly
⟨*dressed*⟩

Dunst *der;* ~[**e**]**s, Dünste** (a) haze; (Nebel)
mist
(b) (Geruch) smell

dünsten *tr. V.* steam ⟨*fish, vegetables*⟩;
braise ⟨*meat*⟩; stew ⟨*fruit*⟩

dunstig *Adj.* hazy

Duo *das;* ~s, ~s (Musik) duet; (fig. scherzh.) duo; pair

Duplikat *das;* ~[e]s, ~e duplicate

duplizieren *tr. V.* duplicate

Dur *das;* ~ (Musik) major [key]

durch [1] *Präp. mit Akk.* **(a)** (räumlich) through

(b) (modal) by; ~ **Boten** by courier; **zehn [geteilt]** ~ **zwei** ten divided by two

[2] *Adv.* **(a)** (hin~) **das ganze Jahr** ~: throughout the whole year

(b) (ugs.: vorbei) **es war 3 Uhr** ~: it was gone 3 o'clock

(c) ~ **und** ~ **nass/überzeugt** wet through [and through]/completely *or* totally convinced

(d) [durch etw.] ~ **sein** be through [sth.]

(e) ~ **sein** (abgefahren sein) ⟨*train, bus, etc.*⟩ have gone

(f) ~ **sein** (fertig sein) have finished; **durch etw.** ~ **sein** have got through sth.

(g) ~ **sein** ⟨*cheese*⟩ be ripe; ⟨*meat*⟩ be well done

durch|arbeiten [1] *tr. V.* work through [2] *itr. V.* work through; **die Nacht** ~: work through the night

durch·aus *Adv.* absolutely; perfectly, quite ⟨*correct, possible, understandable*⟩; **das ist** ~ **richtig** that is entirely right; ~ **nicht** by no means

durch|beißen *unr. tr. V.* bite through

durch|blättern *tr. V.* leaf through

Durch·blick *der* (ugs.) **den [absoluten]** ~ **haben** know [exactly] what's going on

durch|blicken *itr. V.* **(a)** look through; **durch etw.** ~: look through sth.

(b) ~ **lassen, dass ...**/**wie ...**: hint that .../at how ...

Durch·blutung *die* flow of blood (+ *Gen.* to); [blood] circulation

Durchblutungs·störung *die* disturbance of the blood supply

durch|bohren¹ *tr. V.* drill through ⟨*wall, plank*⟩; drill ⟨*hole*⟩

durch·bohren² *tr. V.* pierce

durch|brechen¹ [1] *unr. tr. V.* **etw.** ~: break sth. in two

[2] *unr. itr. V.; mit sein* **(a)** break in two

(b) (hervorkommen) ⟨*sun*⟩ break through

(c) (einbrechen) fall through ⟨*ice, floor, etc.*⟩

durch·brechen² *unr. tr. V.* break through

durch|brennen *unr. itr. V.; mit sein* **(a)** ⟨*heating coil, lightbulb*⟩ burn out; ⟨*fuse*⟩ blow

(b) (ugs.: weglaufen) (von zu Hause) run away; (mit der Kasse, mit dem Geliebten/der Geliebten) run off

durch|bringen *unr. tr. V.* get through; (bei Wahlen) **jmdn.** ~: get sb. elected; **seine Familie/sich** ~: support one's family/oneself

Durch·bruch *der* (fig.) breakthrough

durch·dacht *Adj.* **ein wenig/gut** ~**er Plan**

a badly/well thought-out plan; **nicht [genügend]** ~ **sein** not be sufficiently well thought-out

durch|drehen [1] *tr. V.* put ⟨*meat*⟩ through the mincer *or* (Amer.) grinder

[2] *itr. V. auch mit sein* (ugs.) crack up (coll.)

durch|dringen¹ *unr. tr. V.; mit sein* ⟨*rain, sun*⟩ come through

durch·dringen² *unr. tr. V.* penetrate; **jmdn.** ~ ⟨*idea*⟩ take hold of sb. [completely]

durch·ein·ander *Adv.* ~ **bringen** (+ *Akk.*) (in Unordnung bringen) get ⟨*room, flat*⟩ into a mess; get ⟨*papers, file*⟩ into a muddle; muddle up ⟨*papers, file*⟩; (verwirren) confuse; (verwechseln) confuse ⟨*names, etc.*⟩; get ⟨*names etc.*⟩ mixed up; ~ **sein** ⟨*papers, desk, etc.*⟩ be in a muddle; (verwirrt sein) be confused; (aufgeregt sein) be flustered

Durcheinander *das;* ~s **(a)** muddle; mess

(b) (Wirrwarr) confusion

*durcheinander|bringen
▶ DURCHEINANDER

durch|exerzieren *tr. V.* (ugs.) go through, practise ⟨*rules, multiplication tables*⟩; rehearse ⟨*situation*⟩

durch|fahren *unr. itr. V.; mit sein* **(a)** [durch etw.] ~: drive through [sth.]

(b) (nicht anhalten) go straight through; (mit dem Auto) drive straight through; **der Zug fährt [in H.] durch** the train doesn't stop [at H.]

Durch·fahrt *die* **(a)** „~ **verboten"** 'no entry except for access'; **auf der** ~ **sein** be passing through

(b) (Weg) thoroughfare; „**bitte [die]** ~ **freihalten"** 'please do not obstruct'

Durch·fall *der* diarrhoea *no art.*

durch|fallen *unr. itr. V.; mit sein* **(a)** fall through

(b) (ugs.: nicht bestehen) fail

durch|finden *unr. refl. V.* find one's way through

durchführbar *Adj.* practicable

Durchführbarkeit *die;* ~: practicability;

durch|führen [1] *tr. V.* carry out; put into effect ⟨*decision, programme*⟩; perform ⟨*operation*⟩; hold ⟨*meeting, election, examination*⟩

[2] *itr. V.* **durch etw.**/**unter etw.** (*Dat.*) ~ ⟨*track, road*⟩ go through/under sth.

Durch·führung *die* carrying out; (einer Operation) performing; (einer Versammlung, Wahl, Prüfung) holding; (eines Wettbewerbs) staging

Durch·gang *der* **(a)** passage[way]; „**kein** ~", „~ **verboten"** 'no thoroughfare'

(b) (Phase) stage; (einer Versuchsreihe) run; (Sport, Wahlen) round

Durchgangs-: ~**straße** *die* through road; ~**verkehr** *der* through traffic

durch|geben *unr. tr. V.* announce ⟨*news*⟩; ···⟶

give ⟨*results, weather report*⟩; **eine Meldung
im Radio/Fernsehen** ∼: make an
announcement on the radio/on television

durch·gefroren *Adj.* frozen stiff; chilled
to the bone

durch|gehen [1] *unr. itr. V.; mit sein* **(a)**
[**durch etw.**] ∼: go *or* walk through [sth.]
(b) (hindurchdringen) [**durch etw.**] ∼: ⟨*rain,
water*⟩ come through [sth.]
(c) (direkt zum Ziel führen) ⟨*train etc.*⟩ go [right]
through ⟨*flight*⟩ go direct
(d) (andauern) go on (**bis zu** until)
(e) (hingenommen werden) ⟨*discrepancy*⟩ be
tolerated; ⟨*mistake, discourtesy*⟩ be allowed to
pass; **jmdm. etw.** ∼ **lassen** let sb. get away
with sth.
(f) ⟨*horse*⟩ bolt
[2] *unr. tr. V.; mit sein* go through
⟨*newspaper, text*⟩

durch·gehend [1] *Adj.* **(a)** continuous
⟨*line, pattern, etc.*⟩; constantly recurring
⟨*motif*⟩
(b) (direkt) through *attrib.* ⟨*train, carriage*⟩;
direct ⟨*flight, connection*⟩
[2] *adv.* ∼ **geöffnet haben/bleiben** be/stay
open all day

durchgeknallt *Adj.* (ugs.) crazy

durch·geschwitzt *Adj.* ⟨*person*⟩ soaked
or bathed in sweat; ⟨*clothes*⟩ soaked with
sweat; sweat-soaked *attrib.* ⟨*clothes*⟩

durch|greifen *unr. itr. V.* [hart] ∼: take
drastic measures *or* steps

durch|halten [1] *unr. itr. V.* hold out; (bei
einer schwierigen Aufgabe) see it through
[2] *unr. tr. V.* stand

durch|hängen *unr. itr. V.* sag

durch|kämmen *tr. V.* **(a)** comb ⟨*hair*⟩
through
(b) (durchsuchen) comb ⟨*area etc.*⟩

durch|kommen *unr. itr. V.; mit sein* **(a)**
come through; (mit Mühe) get through
(b) (ugs.: beim Telefonieren) get through
(c) (durchgehen, -fahren usw.) **durch etw.** ∼:
come through sth.
(d) (ugs.: überleben) pull through

durch·kreuzen[1] *tr. V.* cross out

durch·kreuzen[2] *tr. V.* (vereiteln) frustrate

durch|lassen *unr. tr. V.* **(a)** jmdn. [durch
etw.] ∼: let sb. through [sth.]
(b) (durchlässig sein) let ⟨*light, water, etc.*⟩
through

durchlässig *Adj.* permeable; (porös)
porous; (undicht) leaky; ⟨*raincoat, shoe*⟩ that
lets in water

Durch·lauf *der* (Sport, DV) run

durch|laufen[1] [1] *unr. itr. V.; mit sein* **(a)**
[**durch etw.**] ∼: run through [sth.];
(durchrinnen) trickle through [sth.]
(b) (passieren) ⟨*runners*⟩ run *or* pass through
(c) (ohne Pause laufen) run without stopping
[2] *unr. tr. V.* go through ⟨*soles*⟩

---

*old spelling - see note on page xiv

durch·laufen[2] *unr. tr. V.* go through
⟨*phase, stage*⟩

durchlaufend [1] *Adj.* continuous
[2] *adv.* ⟨*numbered, marked*⟩ in sequence

durch|lesen *unr. tr. V.* **etw.** [**ganz**] ∼: read
sth. [all the way] through

durch·leuchten *tr. V.* x-ray; (fig.)
investigate ⟨*case, matter, problem, etc.*⟩
thoroughly

durch·löchern *tr. V.* make holes in

durch|machen (ugs.) [1] *tr. V.* **(a)** undergo
⟨*change*⟩; complete ⟨*training course*⟩; go
through ⟨*stage, phase*⟩; serve
⟨*apprenticeship*⟩
(b) (erleiden) go through
(c) (durcharbeiten) work through ⟨*lunch break
etc.*⟩
[2] *itr. V.* (durcharbeiten) work [right] through;
(durchfeiern) celebrate all night/day etc.; keep
going all night/day etc.

Durchmesser *der;* ∼s, ∼: diameter

durch|nehmen *unr. tr. V.* (Schulw.:
behandeln) do

durch|pauken *tr. V.* (ugs.) force through
⟨*law, regulation, etc.*⟩

durch|peitschen *tr. V.* (ugs. abwertend)
railroad ⟨*law, application, etc.*⟩ through

durch|probieren *tr. V.* taste ⟨*wines, cakes,
etc.*⟩ one after another

durch·queren *tr. V.* cross; travel across
⟨*country*⟩; ⟨*train*⟩ go through ⟨*country*⟩

durch|rechnen *tr. V.* calculate ⟨*costs etc.*⟩
[down to the last penny]; check ⟨*bill*⟩
thoroughly

Durch·reise *die* journey through

durch|reisen *itr. V.; mit sein* travel
through

Durchreise·visum *das* transit visa

durch|reißen [1] *unr. tr. V.* **etw.** ∼: tear
sth. in two *or* in half
[2] *unr. itr. V.; mit sein* ⟨*fabric, garment*⟩ rip,
tear; ⟨*thread, rope*⟩ snap [in two]

durch|rosten *itr. V.; mit sein* rust through

durchs *Präp. + Art.* = **durch das**

Durch·sage *die* announcement; (an eine
bestimmte Person) message

durchschaubar *Adj.* transparent; **leicht**
∼: easy to see through

durch·schauen *tr. V.* see through ⟨*person,
plan, etc.*⟩; see ⟨*situation*⟩ clearly

durch|schlafen *unr. itr. V.* sleep [right]
through

Durch·schlag *der* **(a)** (Kopie) carbon [copy]
(b) (Küchengerät) strainer

durch|schlagen *unr. tr. V.* **etw.** ∼: chop
sth. in two

durchschlagend *Adj.* resounding
⟨*success*⟩; decisive ⟨*effect, measures*⟩;
conclusive ⟨*evidence*⟩

durch|schneiden *unr. tr. V.* cut through

⟨thread, cable⟩; cut ⟨ribbon, sheet of paper⟩ in two; cut ⟨throat, umbilical cord⟩; **etw. in der Mitte ~**: cut sth. in half

Durch·schnitt der average; **im ~**: on average; **über/unter dem ~ liegen** be above/below average

durchschnittlich [1] Adj. **(a)** nicht präd. average ⟨growth, performance, output⟩ **(b)** (ugs.: nicht außergewöhnlich) ordinary ⟨life, person, etc.⟩ **(c)** (mittelmäßig) modest; ordinary ⟨appearance⟩ [2] adv. ⟨earn etc.⟩ on [an] average; **~ groß** of average height

Durchschnitts-: **~alter** das average age; **~geschwindigkeit** die average speed; **~mensch** der average person; (Alltagsmensch) ordinary person; **~temperatur** die average temperature; **~wert** der average or mean value

Durch·schrift die carbon [copy]

durch|sehen [1] unr. itr. V. [durch etw.] **~**: look through [sth.] [2] unr. tr. V. look through

*durch|sein ▸ DURCH 2 D–G

durch|setzen [1] tr. V. carry through; achieve ⟨objective⟩; enforce ⟨demand, claim⟩ [2] refl. V. assert oneself; ⟨idea etc.⟩ find or gain acceptance

Durch·sicht die: nach **~** der Unterlagen after looking or checking through the documents

durchsichtig Adj. (auch fig.) transparent

durch|sprechen unr. tr. V. talk ⟨matter etc.⟩ over; discuss ⟨matter etc.⟩ thoroughly

durch|stehen unr. tr. V. stand ⟨pace, boring job⟩; come through ⟨difficult situation⟩; get over ⟨illness⟩

durch|stellen tr. V. put ⟨call⟩ through (**in** + Akk., **auf** + Akk. to)

durch|streichen unr. tr. V. cross out; (in Formularen) delete

durch·suchen tr. V. search (**nach** for); search, scour ⟨area⟩ (**nach** for)

Durchsuchung die; **~, ~en** search

durch|treten unr. tr. V. press ⟨clutch pedal, brake pedal⟩ right down

durchtrieben (abwertend) [1] Adj. crafty; sly [2] adv. craftily; slyly

durch·wachsen Adj. **~er Speck** streaky bacon

Durch·wahl die **(a)** direct dialling; **mein Apparat hat keine ~**: I don't have an outside line **(b)** ▸ DURCHWAHLNUMMER

durch|wählen itr. V. **(a)** dial direct **(b)** (bei Nebenstellenanlagen) dial straight through

Durchwahl·nummer die number of the/one's direct line

durch|zählen tr. V. count; count up

durch|ziehen [1] unr. tr. V. jmdn./etw. [durch etw.] **~**: pull sb./sth. through [sth.]; **ein Gummiband [durch etw.] ~**: draw an elastic through [sth.] [2] unr. itr. V.; mit sein pass through; ⟨soldiers⟩ march through

Durch·zug der draught

dürfen [1] unr. Modalverb; 2. Part. **dürfen**: **(a) etw. tun ~**: be allowed to do sth.; **darf ich rauchen?** may I smoke?; **was darf es sein?** can I help you? **(b)** Konjunktiv II + Inf. **das dürfte der Grund sein** that is probably the reason [2] unr. tr., itr. V. **er hat nicht gedurft** he was not allowed to

durfte 1. u. 3. Pers. Sg. Prät. v. DÜRFEN

dürfte 1. u. 3. Pers. Sg. Konjunktiv II v. DÜRFEN

dürr Adj. **(a)** withered; arid, barren ⟨ground, earth⟩ **(b)** (mager) scrawny

Dürre die; **~, ~n** drought

Durst der; **~[e]s** thirst; **~ haben** be thirsty; **ich habe ~ auf ein Bier** I could just drink a beer

durstig Adj. thirsty

durst-, Durst-: **~löscher** der thirst-quencher; **~stillend** Adj. thirst-quenching; **~strecke** die lean period or time

Dusche die; **~, ~n** shower

duschen itr., refl. V. have a shower

Düse die; **~, ~n** (Technik) nozzle; (eines Vergasers) jet

Düsen-: **~flugzeug** das jet aircraft; **~motor** der jet engine

düster [1] Adj. **(a)** dark; gloomy; dim ⟨light⟩ **(b)** (fig.) gloomy; sombre ⟨colour, music⟩ [2] adv. (fig.) gloomily

Dutzend das; **~s, ~e** dozen; **zwei ~**: two dozen

dutzend·weise Adv. in [their] dozens (coll.)

duzen tr. V. call ⟨sb.⟩ 'du' (the familiar form of address)

Duz·freund der, **Duz·freundin** die good friend (whom one addresses with 'du')

dynamisch [1] Adj. (auch fig.) dynamic [2] adv. dynamically

Dynamit das; **~s** dynamite

Dynamo der; **~s, ~s** dynamo

Dynastie die; **~, ~n** dynasty

D-Zug /ˈdeː-/ der express train

Ee

e, E /e:/ *das;* ~, ~ **(a)** (Buchstabe) e/E
(b) (Musik) [key of] E

Ebbe *die;* ~, ~n ebb tide; (Zustand) low tide;
es ist ~: the tide is out

eben ① *Adj.* **(a)** flat
(b) (glatt) level
② *adv.* **(a)** (gerade jetzt) just
(b) (kurz) [for] a moment

Ebene *die,* ~, ~n **(a)** plain; **in der** ~: on
the plain
(b) (Geom., Physik) plane
(c) (fig.) level

eben·falls *Adv.* likewise; as well; **danke,** ~:
thank you, [and] [the] same to you

Eben·holz *das* ebony

eben·so *Adv.* **(a)** *mit Adjektiven, Adverben*
just as; **ich mag Erdbeeren** ~ **gern [wie...]** I
like strawberries just as much [as ...]; ~
gern würde ich an den Strand gehen I would
just as soon go to the beach; ~ **gut** just as
well
(b) *mit Verben* in exactly the same way

***ebenso·gern** *usw.* ▶ EBENSO A

Eber *der;* ~s, ~: boar

Eber·esche *die* rowan; mountain ash

ebnen *tr. V.* level ⟨ground⟩

Echo *das;* ~s, ~s echo

echt ① *Adj.* **(a)** genuine; real ⟨love,
friendship⟩
(b) (typisch) real, typical
② *adv.* **(a)** (ugs. verstärkend) really
(b) (typisch) typically

Eck *das;* ~s, ~e (südd., österr.:) ~e corner

Eck-: ~**ball** *der* (Sport) corner [kick/hit/
throw]; **einen** ~**ball treten** take a corner;
~**bank** *die; Pl.* ~**bänke** corner seat

Ecke *die;* ~, ~n corner; **an der** ~: on *or* at
the corner; **um die** ~: round the corner

eckig *Adj.* square; angular

Eck·zahn *der* canine tooth

edel *Adj.* **(a)** thoroughbred ⟨horse⟩; species
⟨rose⟩
(b) (großmütig) noble[-minded], high-minded
⟨person⟩; noble ⟨thought, gesture, feelings,
deed⟩; honourable ⟨motive⟩

Edel-: ~**metall** *das* precious metal;
~**nutte** *die* (salopp) high-class tart (sl.);
~**pilz·käse** *der* blue[-veined] cheese;
~**stahl** *der* stainless steel; ~**stein** *der*
precious stone; gem[stone]

Edition *die;* ~, ~en edition

Edutainment /ɛdjuˈtɛmmənt/ *das;* ~s
edutainment

---

*alte Schreibung - vgl. Hinweis auf S. xiv

EDV *Abk.* = **elektronische
Datenverarbeitung** EDP

EEG *Abk.*
= **Elektroenzephalogramm** EEG; **ein
EEG machen lassen** have an EEG

Efeu *der;* ~s ivy

Effekt *der;* ~[e]s, ~e effect

effekt·voll *Adj.* effective; dramatic ⟨pause,
gesture, entrance⟩

EG *Abk.* **(a)** = **Europäische
Gemeinschaft** EC
(b) = **Erdgeschoss**

egal *Adj.* (ugs.: einerlei) **es ist jmdm.** ~: it's all
the same to sb.; **[ganz]** ~, **wie/wer** *usw.* ...:
no matter how/who *etc.* ...

Egge *die;* ~, ~n harrow

E-Gitarre *die* electric guitar

Egoist *der;* ~en, ~en, **Egoistin** *die;* ~,
~nen egoist

egoistisch ① *Adj.* egoistic[al]
② *adv.* egoistically

ehe *Konj.* before

Ehe *die;* ~, ~n marriage

Ehe-: ~**bett** *das* marriage bed; (Doppelbett)
double bed; ~**bruch** *der* adultery; ~**frau**
die wife; (verheiratete Frau) married woman;
~**krach** *der* (ugs.) row; ~**leute** *Pl.*
married couple

ehelich *Adj.* marital; matrimonial; conjugal
⟨rights, duties⟩; legitimate ⟨child⟩

ehemalig *Adj.* former

ehe-, Ehe-: ~**mann** *der; Pl.* ~**männer**
husband; (verheirateter Mann) married man;
~**mündig** *Adj.* (Rechtsspr.) of marriageable
age *postpos.;* ~**mündig sein** be of
marriageable age *or* of an age to marry;
~**mündigkeit** *die* (Rechtsspr.) being of
marriageable age; ~**paar** *das* married
couple

eher *Adv.* **(a)** (früher) earlier; sooner
(b) (lieber) rather; sooner

Ehe-: ~**ring** *der* wedding ring;
~**scheidung** *die* divorce; ~**vertrag** *der*
(Rechtsw.) marriage contract

Ehre *die;* ~, ~n honour; **jmdm.** ~ **antun** pay
tribute to sb.

ehren *tr. V.* **(a)** honour; **Sehr geehrter Herr
Müller!/Sehr geehrte Frau Müller!** Dear Herr
Müller/Dear Frau Müller
(b) (Ehre machen) **deine Hilfsbereitschaft ehrt
dich** your willingness to help does you credit

ehren-, Ehren-: ~**amt** *das* honorary
position *or* post; ~**amtlich** ① *Adj.*

honorary ⟨*position, membership*⟩; voluntary ⟨*help, worker*⟩; ② *adv.* in an honorary capacity; (freiwillig) on a voluntary basis

ehrenhaft *Adj.* honourable

ehren-, Ehren-: ∼**rührig** *Adj.* defamatory ⟨*allegations*⟩; ∼**sache** *die:* das ist ∼sache that is a point of honour; ∼sache! you can count on me!; ∼**voll** *Adj.* honourable; ∼**wert** *Adj.* (geh.) worthy; ∼**wort** *das; Pl.* ∼∼e: ∼wort [!/?] word of honour [!/?]

ehrerbietig *Adj.* (geh.) respectful

Ehr·furcht *die* reverence (vor + *Dat.* for)

ehrfürchtig *Adj.* reverent

ehr-, Ehr-: ∼**gefühl** *das* sense of honour; ∼**geiz** *der* ambition; ∼**geizig** *Adj.* ambitious

ehrlich *Adj.* honest; genuine ⟨*concern, desire, admiration*⟩; upright ⟨*character*⟩

Ehrlichkeit *die;* ∼ ▶ EHRLICH: honesty; genuineness; uprightness

ehr·los *Adj.* dishonourable

Ehrung *die;* ∼, ∼en: die ∼ der Preisträger the prize-giving (Brit.) *or* (Amer.) awards ceremony; bei der ∼ der Sieger when the winners were awarded their medals/trophies

ehr·würdig *Adj.* venerable

Ei *das;* ∼[e]s, ∼er egg

Eiche *die;* ∼, ∼n oak [tree]; (Holz) oak [wood]

Eichel *die;* ∼, ∼n acorn

eichen *tr. V.* calibrate ⟨*measuring instrument, thermometer*⟩; standardize ⟨*weights, measures, containers, products*⟩; adjust ⟨*weighing scales*⟩

Eich·hörnchen *das* squirrel

Eid *der;* ∼[e]s, ∼e oath

Eidechse /ˈaɪdɛksə/ *die;* ∼, ∼n lizard

eides·stattlich *Adj.* (Rechtsw.) eine ∼e Erklärung a statutory declaration

Ei·dotter *der od. das* egg yolk

Eier-: ∼**becher** *der* eggcup; ∼**kuchen** *der* pancake; (Omelett) omelette; ∼**likör** *der* egg flip; ∼**stock** *der* (Physiol., Zool.) ovary; ∼**uhr** *die* egg timer

Eifer *der;* ∼s eagerness

Eifer·sucht *die* jealousy (auf + *Akk.* of)

eifer·süchtig *Adj.* jealous (auf + *Akk.* of)

eifrig *Adj.* eager

Ei·gelb *das;* ∼[e]s, ∼e egg yolk

eigen *Adj.* own; (selbstständig) separate

eigen-, Eigen-: ∼**art** *die* (Wesensart) particular nature; (Zug) peculiarity; eine ∼art dieser Stadt one of the characteristic features of this city; ∼**artig** *Adj.* peculiar; strange; odd; ∼**artigerweise** *Adv.* strangely [enough]; oddly [enough]; ∼**artigkeit** *die* peculiarity; strangeness; oddness; ∼**brötelei** *die;* ∼∼, ∼∼en taking an [unduly] independent line; — ∼**brötler** *der;* ∼∼s, ∼∼, ∼**brötlerin**

die; ∼∼, ∼∼nen loner; lone wolf; ∼**dynamik** *die* inherent dynamism; ∼**händig** ① *Adj.* personal ⟨*signature*⟩; holographic ⟨*will, document*⟩; ② *adv.* ⟨*present, sign*⟩ personally; ∼**heim** *das* house of one's own

Eigenheit *die;* ∼, ∼en peculiarity

eigen-, Eigen-: ∼**initiative** *die* initiative of one's own; ∼**lob** *das* self-praise; ∼**mächtig** *Adj.* unauthorized; ∼**name** *der* proper name; ∼**nützig** *Adj.* self-seeking; selfish ⟨*motive*⟩

eigens *Adv.* specially

Eigenschaft *die;* ∼, ∼en quality; characteristic; (von Sachen, Stoffen) property

Eigenschafts·wort *das; Pl.* **Eigenschaftswörter** adjective

eigen-, Eigen-: ∼**sinn** *der* obstinacy; ∼**sinnig** *Adj.* obstinate; ∼**ständig** *Adj.* independent; ∼**ständigkeit** *die;* ∼∼: independence

eigentlich ① *Adj.* (wirklich) actual; real; (wahr) true; (ursprünglich) original ② *Adv.* actually ③ *Partikel* wie spät ist es ∼? tell me, what time is it?; was willst du ∼? what exactly do you want?

Eigen·tor *das* (Ballspiele, fig.) own goal

Eigentum *das;* ∼s property; (einschließlich Geld usw.) assets *pl.*

Eigentümer *der;* ∼s, ∼: owner; (Hotel∼, Geschäfts∼) proprietor

Eigentümerin *die;* ∼, ∼nen owner; (Hotel∼, Geschäfts∼) proprietress; proprietor

Eigentums·wohnung *die* owner-occupied flat (Brit.); condominium apartment (Amer.)

eigen-, Eigen-: ∼**vorsorge** private [pension] provision; ∼**willig** *Adj.* self-willed

eignen *refl. V.* be suitable

Eigner *der;* ∼s, ∼, **Eignerin** *die;* ∼, ∼nen owner

Eignung *die;* ∼: suitability; seine ∼ zum Fliegen his aptitude for flying

Eignungs-: ∼**prüfung** *die,* ∼**test** *der* aptitude test

Eil-: ∼**bote** *der,* ∼**botin** *die* special messenger; „durch *od.* per ∼boten" (veralt.) 'express'; ∼**brief** *der* express letter

Eile *die;* ∼: hurry; in ∼ sein be in a hurry

eilen *itr. V.* (a) *mit sein* hurry; (besonders schnell) rush (b) (dringend sein) be urgent; „eilt!" 'urgent'

eilig ① *Adj.* (a) hurried; es ∼ haben be in a hurry (b) (dringend) urgent ② *adv.* hurriedly

Eil·zug *der* semi-fast train

Eimer *der;* ∼s, ∼: bucket; (Milch∼) pail; (Abfall∼) bin; ein ∼ [voll] Wasser a bucket of water; im ∼ sein (salopp) be up the spout (coll.)

ein¹ [1] *Kardinalz.* one; ~ für alle Mal, *~
für allemal* once and for all
[2] *unbest. Art.* a/an
[3] *Indefinitpron.* ▶ IRGENDEIN A; *s. auch*
EINER

ein² (elliptisch) ~ – aus (an Schaltern) on – off

Einakter *der;* ~s, ~: one-act play

einander *reziprokes Pron.; Dat. u. Akk.*
(geh.) each other; one another

ein|arbeiten *tr. V.* train ⟨employee⟩

ein·armig *Adj.* one-armed

ein|äschern *tr. V.* cremate

ein|atmen *tr., itr. V.* breathe in

ein·äugig *Adj.* one-eyed

Ein·bahn·straße *die* one-way street

Ein·band *der; Pl.* Einbände binding

Ein·bau *der; Pl.* ~ten fitting; (eines Motors)
installation

ein|bauen *tr. V.* build in, fit; install
⟨engine, motor⟩

Einbau·küche *die* fitted kitchen

ein·beinig *Adj.* one-legged

ein|berufen *unr. tr. V.* summon; call

Ein·berufung *die* (a) (das Einberufen) calling
(b) (zur Wehrpflicht) call-up; conscription; draft
(Amer.)

Einbett·zimmer *das* single room

ein|beziehen *unr. tr. V.* include

ein|biegen *unr. itr. V.; mit sein* turn

ein|bilden *refl. V.* (a) sich ⟨Dat.⟩ etw. ~:
imagine sth.
(b) (ugs.) sich ⟨Dat.⟩ etwas ~: be conceited
(auf + Akk. about)

Ein·bildung *die* (a) imagination
(b) (falsche Vorstellung) fantasy
(c) (Hochmut) conceitedness

ein|binden *unr. tr. V.* bind ⟨book⟩; etw. neu
~: rebind sth.

ein|blenden *tr. V.* (Rundf., Ferns., Film) insert

Ein·blick *der* (a) view; ~ in etw. ⟨Akk.⟩
haben be able to see into sth.
(b) (Durchsicht) jmdm. ~ in etw. ⟨Akk.⟩
gewähren allow sb. to look at *or* examine
sth.
(c) (Kenntnis) insight

ein|brechen *unr. itr. V.* (a) *mit haben od.
sein* break in; in eine Bank ~: break into a
bank; bei jmdm. ~: burgle sb.
(b) *mit sein* (einstürzen) ⟨roof, ceiling⟩ cave in
(c) *mit sein* (durchbrechen) fall through

Ein·brecher *der;* ~s, ~, **Einbrecherin**
die; ~, ~nen burglar

ein|bringen *unr. tr. V.* (a) bring in
⟨harvest⟩
(b) (verschaffen) Gewinn/Zinsen ~: yield a
profit/bring in interest; jmdm. Ruhm ~:
bring sb. fame
(c) (Parl.: vorlegen) introduce ⟨bill⟩
(d) invest ⟨capital, money⟩

Ein·bruch *der* (a) burglary; ein ~ in eine
Bank a break-in at a bank
(b) (das Einstürzen) collapse

einbürgern [1] *tr. V.* naturalize
[2] *refl. V.* ⟨custom, practice⟩ become
established; ⟨person, plant, animal⟩ become
naturalized

Ein·bürgerung *die;* ~, ~en naturalization

Ein·buße *die* loss

ein|büßen *tr. V.* lose; (durch eigene Schuld)
forfeit

ein|checken *tr., itr. V.* (Flugw.) check in

ein|cremen *tr. V.* put cream on ⟨hands
etc.⟩; sich ~: put cream on

ein|dämmen *tr. V.* (fig.) check; stem

ein|decken [1] *refl. V.* stock up
[2] *tr. V.* (ugs.: überhäufen) jmdn. mit Arbeit ~:
swamp sb. with work

Eindecker *der;* ~s, ~ (Flugw.) monoplane

eindeutig *Adj.* clear

Eindeutigkeit *die;* ~, ~en clarity

ein|dringen *unr. itr. V.; mit sein* in etw.
⟨Akk.⟩ ~: penetrate into sth.; ⟨bullet⟩ pierce
sth.; (allmählich) ⟨water, sand, etc.⟩ seep into
sth.

ein·dringlich *Adj.* urgent; impressive
⟨voice⟩; forceful, powerful ⟨words⟩

Eindringling *der;* ~s, ~e intruder

Ein·druck *der; Pl.* Eindrücke impression

ein|drücken *tr. V.* smash in ⟨mudguard,
bumper⟩; stave in ⟨side of ship⟩; smash ⟨pier,
column, support⟩; break ⟨window⟩; crush
⟨ribs⟩; flatten ⟨nose⟩

eindrucks·voll [1] *Adj.* impressive
[2] *adv.* impressively

eine ▶ EIN¹

ein|ebnen *tr. V.* level

eineiig /ˈaɪnʲaɪ̯ɪç/ *Adj.* identical ⟨twins⟩

ein-ein·halb *Bruchz.* one and a half; ~
Stunden an hour and a half

ein|engen *tr. V.* (a) jmdn. ~: restrict sb.'s
movement[s]
(b) (fig.) restrict

einer, eine, eines, eins *Indefinitpron.*
(man) one; (jemand) someone; somebody;
(fragend, verneint) anyone; anybody; kaum einer
hardly anybody; ein[e]s ist sicher one thing
is for sure

Einer *der;* ~s, ~ (a) (Math.) unit
(b) (Sport) single sculler; im ~: in the single
sculls

einerlei *Adj.* ~, ob/wo/wer *usw.* no matter
whether/where/who *etc.*; es ist ~: it makes
no difference

Einerlei *das;* ~s monotony

einerseits *Adv.* on the one hand

ein·fach [1] *Adj.* (a) simple
(b) (nicht mehrfach) single ⟨knot, ticket,
journey⟩
[2] *Partikel* simply; just

Einfachheit *die;* ~: simplicity

ein|fädeln [1] *tr. V.* thread (in + Akk. into)

---

2 *refl. V.* (Verkehrsw.) filter in

ein|fahren **1** *unr. itr. V.; mit sein* come in; ⟨*train*⟩ pull in; **in den Bahnhof ∼:** pull into the station

2 *unr. tr. V.* **(a)** bring in ⟨*harvest*⟩
(b) (beschädigen) knock down ⟨*wall*⟩; smash in ⟨*mudguard*⟩

Ein-fahrt *die* **(a)** (das Hineinfahren) entry; **Vorsicht bei der ∼ des Zuges!** stand clear [of the edge of the platform], the train is approaching
(b) (Zufahrt) entrance; (Autobahn∼) slip road; „**keine ∼**" 'no entry'

Ein-fall *der* **(a)** (Idee) idea
(b) (Licht∼) incidence (Optics)

ein|fallen *unr. itr. V.; mit sein* **(a)** jmdm. ∼: occur to sb.; **was fällt dir denn ein!** what do you think you're doing?
(b) (in Erinnerung kommen) **ihr Name fällt mir nicht ein** I cannot think of her name; **plötzlich fiel ihr ein, dass ...:** suddenly she remembered that ...
(c) (von Licht) come in

einfalls-, Einfalls-: ∼**los** *Adj.* unimaginative; lacking in ideas; ∼**losigkeit** *die;* ∼∼: unimaginativeness; lack of ideas; ∼**reich** *Adj.* imaginative; full of ideas; ∼**reichtum** *der* imaginativeness; wealth of ideas; ∼**tor** *das* gateway

Einfalt *die;* ∼: simpleness; simple-mindedness

einfältig *Adj.* simple; naïve; naïve ⟨*remarks*⟩

Ein-familien-haus *das* house (as opposed to block of flats etc.)

ein|fangen *unr. tr. V.* catch

ein|fassen *tr. V.* border; edge; frame ⟨*picture*⟩; set ⟨*gem*⟩; edge ⟨*grave, lawn, etc.*⟩

Ein-fassung *die* ▸ EINFASSEN: border; edging; frame; setting

ein|fetten *tr. V.* grease; dubbin ⟨*leather*⟩; **sich** (*Dat.*) **die Haut/Hände ∼:** rub cream into one's skin/hands

ein|finden *unr. refl. V.* arrive; (sich treffen) meet; ⟨*crowd*⟩ gather

ein|fliegen *unr. tr. V.* fly in

ein|flößen *tr. V.* **(a)** jmdm. Tee ∼: pour tea into sb.'s mouth
(b) (fig.) jmdm. Angst ∼: put fear into sb.

Ein-fluss, *Ein-fluß *der* influence

einfluss-, *einfluß-, Einfluss-, *Einfluß-: ∼**bereich** *der* sphere of influence; ∼**nahme,** *die;* ∼∼: exertion of influence (**auf** + *Akk.* on); ∼**reich** *Adj.* influential

ein-förmig *Adj.* monotonous

ein|frieren **1** *unr. itr. V.; mit sein* freeze; ⟨*pipes*⟩ freeze up
2 *unr. tr. V.* **(a)** deep-freeze ⟨*food*⟩
(b) (fig.) freeze

ein|fügen *tr. V.* **(a)** fit in; **etw. in etw.** (*Akk.*) ∼: fit sth. into sth.
(b) (DV) insert; paste

ein|fühlen *refl. V.* **sich in jmdn. ∼:** empathize with sb.

einfühlsam *Adj.* understanding

Ein-fühlung *die;* ∼: empathy (**in** + *Akk.* with)

Ein-fuhr *die;* ∼, ∼**en** ▸ IMPORT

ein|führen *tr. V.* **(a)** (als Neuerung) introduce ⟨*fashion, method, technology*⟩
(b) (importieren) import

Einfuhr-: ∼**sperre** *die,* ∼**stopp** *der* embargo or ban on imports

Ein-führung *die* introduction

Einfuhr-verbot *das* ▸ ∼SPERRE

Ein-gabe *die* **(a)** (Gesuch) petition; (Beschwerde) complaint
(b) (DV) input

Eingabe-gerät *das* (DV) input device

Ein-gang *der* entrance; „**kein ∼**" 'no entry'

ein-gängig *Adj.* catchy

eingangs *Adv.* at the beginning; *or* start

Eingangs-: ∼**halle** *die* entrance hall; (eines Hotels, Theaters) foyer; ∼**tür** *die* (von Kaufhaus, Hotel usw.) [entrance] door; (von Wohnung, Haus usw.) front door

ein|geben *unr. tr. V.* (DV) feed in; **etw. in den Computer ∼:** feed sth. into the computer

ein-gebildet *Adj.* **(a)** imaginary ⟨*illness*⟩
(b) (arrogant) conceited

Eingeborene *der/die; adj. Dekl.* (veralt.) native

ein-gefahren *Adj.* long-established; deep-rooted ⟨*prejudice*⟩; **sich auf** *od.* **in ∼en Bahnen** *od.* **Gleisen bewegen** go on in the same old way

ein|gehen **1** *unr. itr. V.; mit sein* **(a)** arrive
(b) (fig.) **in die Geschichte ∼:** go down in history
(c) (schrumpfen) shrink
(d) **auf eine Frage ∼/nicht ∼:** go into *or* deal with/ignore a question; **auf jmdn. ∼:** be responsive to sb.; **auf jmdn. nicht ∼:** ignore sb.'s wishes
2 *unr. tr. V.* enter into ⟨*contract, matrimony*⟩; take ⟨*risk*⟩; accept ⟨*obligation*⟩

eingehend *Adj.* detailed

Ein-gemachte *das; adj. Dekl.* preserved fruit/vegetables

ein|gemeinden *tr. V.* incorporate ⟨*village*⟩ (**in** + *Akk.*, nach into)

ein-geschnappt *Adj.* (ugs.) huffy

Ein-geständnis *das* confession; admission

ein|gestehen *unr. tr. V.* admit

Eingeweide *das;* ∼s, ∼: entrails *pl.*; innards *pl.*

ein|gewöhnen *refl. V.* get used to one's new surroundings

ein|gießen *unr. tr., itr. V.* pour in

ein|gliedern tr. V. integrate (in + Akk. into); incorporate ⟨village, company⟩ (in + Akk. into); (einordnen) include (in + Akk. in)

Ein·gliederung die ▶ EINGLIEDERN: integration; incorporation; inclusion

ein|graben unr. tr. V. bury (in + Akk. in); sink ⟨pile, pipe⟩ (in + Akk. into)

ein|gravieren tr. V. engrave (in + Akk. on)

ein|greifen unr. itr. V. intervene (in + Akk. in)

Ein·griff der (a) intervention (in + Akk. in) (b) (Med.) operation

ein|haken ① tr. V. (a) (mit Haken befestigen) fasten
(b) sich ∼: link arms
② refl. V. sich bei jmdm. ∼: link arms with sb.

Ein·halt der: jmdm./einer Sache ∼ gebieten od. tun (geh.) halt sb./sth.

ein|halten ① unr. tr. V. keep ⟨appointment⟩; meet ⟨deadline, commitments⟩; keep to ⟨diet, speed limit, agreement⟩; observe ⟨regulation⟩
② unr. itr. V. (geh.) stop

ein·heimisch Adj. native; home attrib. ⟨team⟩

Einheimische der/die; adj. Dekl. local

Einheit die; ∼, ∼en unity

einheitlich ① Adj. unified; (unterschiedslos) uniform ⟨dress⟩; standard ⟨procedure, practice⟩
② adv. ∼ gekleidet sein be dressed the same

einhellig ① Adj. unanimous
② adv. unanimously

ein|holen ① tr. V. (a) catch up with ⟨person, vehicle⟩
(b) make up ⟨arrears, time⟩
② itr. V. (ugs.) ▶ EINKAUFEN 1

ein·hundert Kardinalz. ▶ HUNDERT

einig Adj. sich (Dat.) ∼ sein be agreed; sich (Dat.) ∼ werden reach agreement

einig... Indefinitpron. u. unbest. Zahlwort some; ∼e wenige a few; ∼e Hundert several hundred

einigen ① tr. V. unite
② refl. V. reach an agreement

einigermaßen Adv. somewhat

Einigkeit die; ∼ (a) unity
(b) (Übereinstimmung) agreement

ein·jährig Adj. (ein Jahr alt) one-year-old attrib.; one year old pred.; (ein Jahr dauernd) one-year attrib.

Ein·kauf der (a) Einkäufe machen do some shopping
(b) (eingekaufte Ware) purchase
(c) (Abteilung) purchasing department

ein|kaufen ① itr. V. shop; ∼ gehen go shopping
② tr. V. buy; purchase

---

*alte Schreibung - vgl. Hinweis auf S. xiv

Ein·käufer der, **Ein·käuferin** die buyer; purchaser

Einkaufs-: ∼**bummel** der [leisurely] shopping expedition; ∼**liste** die shopping list; ∼**preis** der (Kaufmannsspr.) wholesale price; ∼**tasche** die shopping bag; ∼**zentrum** das shopping centre; ∼**zettel** der shopping list

ein|kehren itr. V.; mit sein stop; in einem Wirtshaus ∼: stop at an inn

ein|klammern tr. V. etw. ∼: put sth. in brackets; bracket sth.

Ein·klang der harmony; in od. im ∼ stehen accord

ein|kleben tr. V. stick in

ein|kleiden tr. V. clothe

ein|klemmen tr. V. (a) (quetschen) catch
(b) (fest einfügen) clamp

ein|kochen tr. V. preserve ⟨fruit etc.⟩

Einkommen das; ∼s, ∼: income

Einkommen·steuer die income tax

ein|kreisen tr. V. (a) etw. ∼: put a circle round sth.
(b) (umzingeln) surround

Einkünfte Pl. income sing.; feste ∼: a regular income

ein|laden¹ unr. tr. V. load ⟨goods⟩

ein|laden² unr. tr. V. invite ⟨person⟩ (zu for)

einladend Adj. inviting

Ein·ladung die invitation

Ein·lage die (a) (in Brief) enclosure
(b) (Kochk.) vegetables, dumplings, etc. added to a clear soup;
(c) (Schuh∼) arch support
(d) (Programm∼) interlude

ein|lagern tr. V. store; lay in ⟨stores⟩

Einlass, *Einlaß der; Einlasses, Einlässe admission

ein|lassen unr. tr. V. (a) (hereinlassen) admit; let in
(b) (einfüllen) run ⟨water⟩

Ein·lauf der (Med.) enema

ein|laufen ① unr. itr. V.; mit sein (a) ⟨ship⟩ come in
(b) (kleiner werden) shrink
② unr. tr. V. wear in ⟨shoes⟩

ein|leben refl. V. settle down

ein|legen tr. V. (a) load ⟨film⟩; engage ⟨gear⟩
(b) (Kochk.) pickle

ein|leiten tr. V. (a) introduce
(b) induce ⟨birth⟩
(c) lead in; etw. in etw. (Akk.) ∼: lead sth. into sth.

Ein·leitung die (a) introduction
(b) (einer Geburt) induction

ein|leuchten itr. V. jmdm. ∼: be clear to sb.

einleuchtend Adj. plausible

ein|liefern tr. V. take ⟨letter, person⟩ (bei, in + Akk. to)

Einlieger·wohnung *die* ≈ granny flat

ein|lösen *tr. V.* cash ‹*cheque*›

ein|machen *tr. V.* preserve ‹*fruit etc.*›; (in Gläser) bottle

einmal ⟨1⟩ *Adv.* (a) once; **noch ~ so groß [wie]** twice as big [as]; **etw. noch ~ tun** do sth. again
(b) /'--/ (später) one day; (früher) once; **es war ~ ...:** once upon a time there was ...
⟨2⟩ *Partikel* **nicht ~:** not even; **wieder ~:** yet again

Einmal-eins *das;* **~:** [multiplication] tables *pl.*

einmalig ⟨1⟩ *Adj.* (a) unique; one-off ‹*payment, purchase*›
(b) (ugs.) fantastic (coll.)
⟨2⟩ *adv.* (ugs.) really fantastically (coll.)

Ein-marsch *der* (a) entry
(b) (Besetzung) invasion (in + *Akk.* of)

ein|marschieren *itr. V.; mit sein* march in

ein|massieren *tr. V.* massage *or* rub in

ein|mauern *tr. V.* (a) immure ‹*prisoner, traitor*›; wall in ‹*relic, treasure*›
(b) (ins Mauerwerk einfügen) **etw. in die Wand usw. ~:** set sth. into the wall *etc.*

ein|mischen *refl. V.* interfere (**in** + *Akk.* in)

ein|motten *tr. V.* **etw. ~:** put sth. into mothballs; (fig.) mothball

Ein-mündung *die* (von Straßen) junction

einmütig ⟨1⟩ *Adj.* unanimous
⟨2⟩ *adv.* unanimously

ein|nähen *tr. V.* sew in

Einnahme *die;* **~, ~n** (a) income; (Staats~) revenue; (Kassen~) takings *pl.;*
(b) (von Arzneimitteln) taking
(c) (einer Stadt, Burg) taking

Einnahme-quelle *die* source of income; (des Staates) source of revenue

ein|nehmen *unr. tr. V.* (a) take; (verdienen) earn
(b) (ausfüllen) take up ‹*amount of room*›
(c) (beeinflussen) **jmdn. für sich ~:** win sb. over

einnehmend *Adj.* winning ‹*manner*›; **ein ~es Wesen haben** (scherzh.) take everything one can get

Ein-öde *die* barren waste

ein|ölen *tr. V.* (a) (mit Öl einreiben) **sich/jmdn. ~:** put *or* rub oil on oneself/sb.
(b) (ölen) oil

ein|ordnen ⟨1⟩ *tr. V.* arrange; put in order
⟨2⟩ *refl. V.* (a) (Verkehrsw.) get into the correct lane; „~" 'get in lane'
(b) (sich einfügen) fit in

ein|packen ⟨1⟩ *tr. V.* pack (**in** + *Akk.* in); (einwickeln) wrap [up]
⟨2⟩ *itr. V.* (ugs.) **er kann ~:** he's had it (coll.)

ein|parken *tr., itr. V.* park

ein|pflanzen *tr. V.* (a) plant
(b) (Med., fig.) implant

ein|prägen *tr. V.* (a) stamp (**in** + *Akk.* into, on)
(b) (fig.) **sich** (*Dat.*) **etw. ~:** memorize sth.; **jmdm. etw. ~:** impress sth. on sb.

einprägsam *Adj.* easily remembered

ein|pudern *tr. V.* powder; **sich** (*Dat.*) **das Gesicht ~:** powder one's face

ein|rahmen *tr. V.* frame

ein|räumen *tr. V.* (a) put away
(b) (füllen) **seinen Schrank ~:** put one's things away in one's cupboard; **ein Zimmer ~:** put the furniture into a room
(c) (zugestehen) admit

ein|reden ⟨1⟩ *tr. V.* **jmdm. etw. ~:** talk sb. into believing sth.; **sich** (*Dat.*) **~, dass ...:** persuade oneself that ...
⟨2⟩ *itr. V.* **auf jmdn. ~:** talk insistently to sb.

ein|regnen *refl. V.; unpers.* **es hat sich eingeregnet** it's begun to rain steadily

ein|reiben *unr. tr. V.* rub ‹*substance*› in; **etw. mit Öl ~:** rub oil into sth.

ein|reichen *tr. V.* submit; lodge ‹*complaint*›; tender ‹*resignation*›

ein|reihen ⟨1⟩ *refl. V.* **sich in etw.** (*Akk.*) **~:** join sth.
⟨2⟩ *tr. V.* **jmdn. in eine Kategorie ~:** place sb. in a category

Einreiher *der;* **~s, ~:** single-breasted suit/ jacket

Ein-reise *die* entry

Einreise-erlaubnis *die* entry permit

ein|reisen *itr. V.; mit sein* enter; **nach Schweden ~:** enter Sweden

ein|reißen ⟨1⟩ *unr. tr. V.* (a) pull down ‹*building*›
(b) (einen Riss machen in) tear; rip
⟨2⟩ *unr. itr. V.; mit sein* tear; rip

ein|renken *tr. V.* (a) (Med.) set
(b) (ugs.: bereinigen) sort out

ein|richten ⟨1⟩ *refl. V.* **sich schön ~:** furnish one's home beautifully; **sich häuslich ~:** make oneself at home
⟨2⟩ *tr. V.* furnish ‹*flat, house*›; fit out ‹*shop*›; equip ‹*laboratory*›

Ein-richtung *die* (a) furnishing
(b) (Mobiliar) furnishings *pl.*

ein|rollen ⟨1⟩ *tr. V.* roll up ‹*carpet etc.*›; put ‹*hair*› in curlers
⟨2⟩ *itr. V.; mit sein* roll in

ein|rosten *itr. V.; mit sein* go rusty

ein|rücken ⟨1⟩ *itr. V.; mit sein* (einmarschieren) move in
⟨2⟩ *tr. V.* indent ‹*line, heading, etc.*›

eins ⟨1⟩ *Kardinalz.* one; **es ist ~:** it is one o'clock; **~ zu null** one-nil; **~ zu ~:** one all; **„~, zwei, drei"** 'ready, steady, go'
⟨2⟩ *Adj.* **mir ist alles ~:** it's all the same to me
⟨3⟩ *Indefinitpron.* ▶ IRGENDEIN A

Eins *die;* **~, ~en** (a) one
(b) (Schulnote) one; A

einsam *Adj.* (a) lonely ‹*person, decision*›
(b) (einzeln) solitary ‹*tree, wanderer*› ⋯⊱

(c) (abgelegen) isolated
(d) (menschenleer) deserted
Einsamkeit *die;* ~ **(a)** loneliness
(b) (Alleinsein) solitude
(c) (Abgeschiedenheit) isolation
ein|sammeln *tr. V.* **(a)** (auflesen) pick up; gather up
(b) (sich aushändigen lassen) collect in; collect ⟨tickets⟩
Ein·satz *der* **(a)** (aus Stoff) inset; (in Kochtopf, Nähkasten usw.) compartment
(b) (Betrag) stake
(c) (Gebrauch) use; (von Truppen) deployment
Einsatz-: ~**befehl** *der* order to go into action; **den** ~**befehl haben** have operational command; ~**leiter** *der,* ~**leiterin** *die* head of operations; ~**wagen** *der* (der Polizei) police car; (der Feuerwehr) fire engine; (Notarztwagen) ambulance
ein|saugen *unr.* (*auch regelm.*) *tr. V.* suck in; breathe [in] ⟨fresh air⟩
ein|schalten ① *tr. V.* **(a)** switch on ⟨radio, TV, electricity, etc.⟩
(b) (fig.) call in ⟨press, police, expert, etc.⟩ ② *refl. V.* **(a)** switch [itself] on
(b) (eingreifen) intervene (**in** + *Akk.* in)
Einschalt·quote *die* (Rundf.) listening figures *pl.;* (Fems.) viewing figures *pl.*
ein|schärfen *tr. V.* **jmdm. etw.** ~: impress sth. [up]on sb.
ein|schätzen *tr. V.* judge ⟨person⟩; assess ⟨situation, income, damages⟩; (schätzen) estimate
Ein·schätzung *die* ▶ EINSCHÄTZEN: judging; assessment; estimation
ein|schenken *tr., itr. V.* **(a)** (eingießen) pour [out]; **jmdm. etw.** ~: pour out sth. for sb.
(b) (füllen) fill [up] ⟨glass, cup⟩
ein|scheren *itr. V.; mit sein* **auf eine Fahrspur** ~: get *or* move into a lane
ein|schicken *tr. V.* send in
ein|schieben *unr. tr. V.* **(a)** push in
(b) (einfügen) insert; put on ⟨trains, buses⟩
ein|schiffen *tr., refl. V.* embark
einschl. *Abk.* = **einschließlich** incl.
ein|schlafen *unr. itr. V.; mit sein* **(a)** fall asleep
(b) (verhüll.: sterben) pass away
(c) (gefühllos werden) go to sleep
ein|schläfern *tr. V.* **(a)** **jmdn.** ~: send sb. to sleep, (betäuben) put sb. to sleep
(b) (schmerzlos töten) **ein Tier** ~: put an animal to sleep
einschläfernd ① *Adj.* soporific ② *adv.* ~ **wirken** have a soporific effect
ein|schlagen ① *unr. tr. V.* **(a)** knock in
(b) (zertrümmern) smash [in]
(c) (einwickeln) wrap up ⟨present⟩; cover ⟨book⟩

*old spelling - see note on page xiv

② *unr. itr. V.* **(a)** ⟨bomb⟩ land; ⟨lightning⟩ strike
(b) **auf jmdn./etw.** ~: rain blows on sb./sth.
einschlägig ① *Adj.* specialist ⟨journal, shop⟩; relevant ⟨literature, passage⟩ ② *adv.* **er ist** ~ **vorbestraft** he has previous convictions for a similar offence/similar offences
ein|schleichen *unr. refl. V.* steal in
ein|schließen *unr. tr. V.* **(a)** **etw. in etw.** (*Dat.*) ~: lock sth. up [in sth.]; **jmdn./sich** ~: lock sb./oneself in
(b) (umgeben) surround
einschließlich ① *Präp. mit Gen.* including; ~ **der Unkosten** including expenses ② *adv.* **bis** ~ **30. Juni** up to and including 30 June
ein|schmeicheln *refl. V.* **sich bei jmdm.** ~: ingratiate oneself with sb.
ein|schmuggeln *tr. V.* smuggle in
ein|schneiden *unr. tr. V.* **(a)** make a cut in
(b) (einritzen) carve
einschneidend *Adj.* drastic
ein|schneien *itr. V.; mit sein* get snowed in
Ein·schnitt *der* cut
ein|schränken ① *tr. V.* **(a)** reduce, curb ⟨expenditure, consumption⟩
(b) (einengen) limit; restrict; **jmdn. in seinen Rechten** ~: limit *or* restrict sb.'s rights ② *refl. V.* economize
Einschränkung *die;* ~, ~**en (a)** restriction; limitation
(b) (Vorbehalt) reservation
ein|schrauben *tr. V.* screw in
ein|schreiben *unr. tr. V.* **(a)** (Postw.) register ⟨letter⟩
(b) (eintragen) **sich/jmdn.** ~: enter one's/sb.'s name
Ein·schreiben *das* (Postw.) registered letter; **per** ~: by registered mail
ein|schreiten *unr. itr. V.* intervene
ein|schrumpfen *itr. V.; mit sein* shrivel up; (fig.) dwindle
ein|schüchtern *tr. V.* intimidate
ein|schulen *tr. V.* **eingeschult werden** start school
ein|sehen *unr. tr. V.* **(a)** (überblicken) see into
(b) (prüfend lesen) look at
(c) (erkennen) realize
(d) (begreifen) see
ein|seifen *tr. V.* lather
ein-seitig ① *Adj.* **(a)** on one side *postpos.;*
(b) (tendenziös) one-sided ② *adv.* **(a)** on one side
(b) (tendenziös) one-sidedly
ein|senden *unr.* (*auch regelm.*) *tr. V.* send [in]

Ein·sender der, **Ein·senderin** die; ~,
~nen sender; (bei einem Preisausschreiben)
entrant

Einsende·schluss,
*****Einsende·schluß** der closing date
ein|setzen 1 tr. V. (a) (hineinsetzen) put in
(b) put on ⟨special train etc.⟩
(c) (ernennen) appoint
(d) (in Aktion treten lassen) use
(e) (aufs Spiel setzen) stake ⟨money⟩
(f) (riskieren) risk
2 itr. V. begin; ⟨storm⟩ break
3 refl. V. (sich engagieren) **ich werde mich
dafür ~, dass ...:** I shall do what I can to
see that ...; **sich nicht genug ~:** ⟨pupil⟩ be
lacking application; ⟨minister⟩ be lacking in
commitment

Ein·sicht die (a) view (**in** + Akk. into)
(b) (Einblick) **~ in die Akten nehmen** take or
have a look at the files
(c) (Erkenntnis) insight

einsichtig Adj. (a) (verständnisvoll)
understanding
(b) (verständlich) comprehensible

Ein·siedler der, **Ein·siedlerin** die
hermit

ein·silbig Adj. (a) monosyllabic ⟨word⟩
(b) (fig.) taciturn ⟨person⟩

Einsilbigkeit die; ~ (fig.) taciturnity

ein|sinken unr. itr. V. sink in

ein|sitzen unr. itr. V. (Rechtsw.) serve a
prison sentence; **er sitzt für drei Jahre ein** he
is serving three years or a three-year
sentence

Einsitzer der; ~s, ~: single-seater

einsitzig Adj. single-seater attrib.

ein|spannen tr. V. harness ⟨horse⟩; put in
⟨paper⟩; fix ⟨fabric⟩; clamp ⟨work⟩

ein|sparen tr. V. save

Einsparung die; ~, ~en saving (**an** + Dat.
in); ~**en an Kosten/Energie/Material** savings
or economies in costs/energy/materials

ein|speichern tr. V. (DV) feed in; input

ein|speisen tr. V. (Technik, DV) feed in

ein|sperren tr. V. lock up

einsprachig Adj. monolingual

ein|springen unr. itr. V.; mit sein stand
in; (aushelfen) step in and help out

ein|spritzen tr. V. inject; **jmdm. etw. ~:**
inject sb. with sth.

Einspritz·motor der fuel-injection engine

Ein·spruch der objection (**gegen** to)

einspurig 1 Adj. single-track ⟨road⟩
2 adv. **die Autobahn ist nur ~ befahrbar**
only one lane of the motorway is open

einst Adv. (geh.) once

ein|stampfen tr. V. pulp ⟨books⟩

Ein·stand der: **seinen ~ geben** celebrate
starting a new job

ein|stecken tr. V. (a) put in
(b) (mitnehmen) put ⟨sth.⟩ in one's pocket/bag
etc.

ein|stehen unr. itr. V. **für jmdn. ~:** vouch
for sb.; **für etw. ~:** take responsibility for
sth.

ein|steigen unr. itr. V.; mit sein (a) (in ein
Fahrzeug) get in; **in ein Auto ~:** get into a car;
in den Bus ~: get on the bus
(b) (eindringen) climb in

einstellbar Adj. adjustable

ein|stellen 1 tr. V. (a) (einordnen) put
away ⟨books etc.⟩
(b) (unterstellen) put in ⟨car, bicycle⟩
(c) (beschäftigen) take on ⟨workers⟩
(d) (regulieren) adjust
(e) (beenden) stop; call off ⟨search, strike⟩
(f) (Sport) equal ⟨record⟩
2 refl. V. (a) arrive
(b) ⟨pain, worry⟩ begin; ⟨success⟩ come;
⟨symptoms, consequences⟩ appear
(c) **sich auf etw.** (Akk.) **~:** prepare oneself
for sth.; **sich schnell auf neue Situationen ~:**
adjust quickly to new situations

ein·stellig Adj. single-figure attrib.

Ein·stellung die (a) (von Arbeitskräften)
employment
(b) (Regulierung) adjustment
(c) (Beendigung) stopping
(d) (Sport) **die ~ eines Rekordes** the
equalling of a record
(e) (Ansicht) attitude; **ihre politische/religiöse
~:** her political/religious views pl.;
(f) (Film) take

Ein·stich der (a) insertion
(b) (~stelle) puncture; prick

Ein·stieg der; ~[e]s, ~e (Eingang) entrance;
(Tür) door/doors; „**kein ~**' 'exit only'

Einstiegs·droge die come-on drug

ein|stimmen 1 itr. V. join in
2 tr. V. **jmdn. auf etw.** (Akk.) **~:** get sb. in
the [right] mood for sth.

einstimmig 1 Adj. (a) (Musik) for one
voice
(b) (einmütig) unanimous ⟨decision, vote⟩
2 adv. (a) (Musik) in unison
(b) (einmütig) unanimously

ein·stöckig Adj. single-storey attrib.

ein|stöpseln tr. V. plug in ⟨telephone,
electrical device⟩

Ein·strahlung die irradiation; (Sonnen~)
insolation

ein|streichen unr. tr. V. (ugs.: für sich
behalten) pocket ⟨money, winnings, etc.⟩; (ugs.
abwertend) rake in (coll.) ⟨money, profits, etc.⟩

ein|studieren tr. V. rehearse

ein|stufen tr. V. classify; categorize

ein·stündig Adj. one-hour attrib.

ein|stürmen itr. V. **mit Fragen auf jmdn.
~:** besiege sb. with questions

Ein·sturz der collapse

ein|stürzen itr. V.; mit sein collapse

einst·weilen Adv. for the time being

eintägig Adj. one-day attrib.

Eintags·fliege die (Zool.) mayfly; (fig. ugs.)
seven-day wonder

ein|tauchen ① *tr. V.* dip; (untertauchen) immerse
② *itr. V.; mit sein* dive in; ⟨*submarine*⟩ dive

ein|tauschen *tr. V.* exchange (**gegen** for)

ein·tausend *Kardinalz.:* ▶ TAUSEND

ein|teilen *tr. V.* **(a)** divide up; classify ⟨*plants, species*⟩
(b) (disponieren, verplanen) organize

einteilig *Adj.* one-piece

ein|tippen *tr. V.* (in die Kasse) register; (in einen Rechner) key in

eintönig ① *Adj.* monotonous
② *adv.* monotonously

Eintönigkeit *die;* ∼: monotony

Ein·topf *der* stew

Ein·tracht *die* harmony

ein·trächtig *Adj.* harmonious

Eintrag *der;* ∼[e]s, **Einträge** entry

ein|tragen *unr. tr. V.* **(a)** enter
(b) (Amtsspr.) register

einträglich *Adj.* lucrative

ein|treffen *unr. itr. V.; mit sein* **(a)** arrive
(b) (verwirklicht werden) come true

ein|treiben *unr. tr. V.* collect ⟨*taxes, debts*⟩; (durch Gerichtsverfahren) recover ⟨*debts, money*⟩

Eintreibung *die;* ∼, ∼**en** (von Steuern, Schulden) collection; (durch Gerichtsverfahren) recovery

ein|treten ① *unr. itr. V.; mit sein* **(a)** enter; **bitte, treten Sie ein!** please come in
(b) (Mitglied werden) **in einen Verein/einen Orden** ∼: join a club/enter a religious order
(c) (Raumfahrt) enter
② *unr. tr. V.* kick in ⟨*door, window, etc.*⟩

ein|trichtern *tr. V.* (salopp) **jmdm. etw.** ∼: drum sth. into sb.

Ein·tritt *der* **(a)** entry; entrance; **vor dem** ∼ **in die Verhandlungen** (fig.) before entering into negotiations
(b) (Beitritt) **der** ∼ **in einen Verein/einen Orden** joining a club/entering a religious order
(c) (von Raketen) entry
(d) (Zugang, Eintrittsgeld) admission
(e) (Beginn) onset; ∼ **der Dunkelheit** nightfall

Eintritts-: ∼**geld** *das* admission fee; ∼**karte** *die* admission ticket; ∼**preis** *der* admission charge

ein|trocknen *itr. V.; mit sein* dry; ⟨*water, toothpaste*⟩ dry up; ⟨*leather*⟩ dry out; ⟨*berry, fruit*⟩ shrivel

ein|üben *tr. V.* practise

Ein·vernehmen *das;* ∼**s** harmony; (Übereinstimmung) agreement

ein·vernehmlich (Amtsspr.) ① *Adv.* conjointly
② *adj.* conjoint

einverstanden *Adj.* ∼ **sein** agree; **mit jmdm./etw.** ∼ **sein** approve of sb./sth.

Ein·verständnis *das* consent (**zu** to)

Ein·waage *die* (Kaufmannsspr.) contents *pl.*

ein|wachsen *unr. itr. V.; mit sein* grow into the flesh; **eingewachsen** ingrown ⟨*toenail*⟩

Einwand *der;* ∼[e]s, **Einwände** objection (**gegen** to)

Ein·wanderer *der,* **Ein·wanderin** *die* immigrant

ein|wandern *itr. V.; mit sein* immigrate (**in** + *Akk.* into)

Ein·wanderung *die* immigration

Einwanderungs-: ∼**behörde** *die* immigration authorities *pl.;* ∼**land** *das* country of immigration

einwand·frei ① *Adj.* flawless; impeccable ⟨*behaviour*⟩; indisputable ⟨*proof*⟩
② *adv.* flawlessly; ⟨*behave*⟩ impeccably; ⟨*prove*⟩ beyond question

ein|wechseln *tr. V.* **(a)** change ⟨*money*⟩
(b) (Sport) substitute ⟨*player*⟩

ein|wecken *tr. V.* preserve; bottle

Ein·weg-: ∼**flasche** *die* non-returnable bottle; ∼**spritze** *die* disposable [hypodermic] syringe

ein|weichen *tr. V.* soak

ein|weihen *tr. V.* open [officially] ⟨*bridge, road*⟩; dedicate ⟨*monument*⟩

Einweihung *die;* ∼, ∼**en** ▶ EINWEIHEN: [official] opening; dedication

ein|weisen *unr. tr. V.* **(a)** (in eine Tätigkeit) introduce
(b) (in ein Amt) install

ein|wenden *unr.* (*auch regelm.*) *tr. V.* **dagegen lässt sich vieles** ∼: there is a lot to be said against that

ein|werfen *unr. tr. V.* **(a)** mail ⟨*letter*⟩; insert ⟨*coin*⟩
(b) smash ⟨*window*⟩
(c) throw in ⟨*ball*⟩
(d) (bemerken, sagen) throw in ⟨*remark*⟩

ein|wickeln *tr. V.* wrap [up]

ein|willigen *itr. V.* agree (**in** + *Akk.* to)

Einwilligung *die;* ∼, ∼**en** agreement

ein|winken *tr. V.* (Verkehrsw.) guide in ⟨*aircraft, car*⟩

ein|wirken (a) (beeinflussen) **auf jmdn.** ∼: influence sb.
(b) (eine Wirkung ausüben) have an effect (**auf** + *Akk.* on)

Ein·wirkung *die* (Einfluss) influence; (Wirkung) effect

Einwohner *der;* ∼**s**, ∼, **Einwohnerin** *die;* ∼, ∼**nen** inhabitant

Einwohner·zahl *die* population

Ein·wurf *der* **(a)** insertion; (von Briefen) mailing
(b) (Ballspiele) throw-in
(c) (Bemerkung) interjection

Ein·zahl *die* singular

ein|zahlen *tr. V.* pay in; **Geld auf ein Konto** ∼: pay money into an account

Ein·zahlung *die* payment

ein|zäunen *tr. V.* fence in; enclose

---

*alte Schreibung - vgl. Hinweis auf S. xiv

Einzäunung die; ∼, ∼en fencing-in

ein|zeichnen tr. V. draw or mark in

einzeilig Adj. one-line attrib.

Einzel das; ∼s, ∼ (Sport) singles pl.

Einzel-: ∼**bett** das single bed; ∼**fall** der (a) particular case; (b) (Ausnahme) isolated case; ∼**gänger** der; ∼∼s, ∼∼, ∼**gängerin** die; ∼∼, ∼∼nen loner; ∼**haft** die solitary confinement;

Einzel·handel der retail trade

Einzelhandels·preis der retail price

Einzel·händler der, ∼**händlerin** die retailer

Einzelheit die; ∼, ∼en (a) detail (b) (einzelner Umstand) particular

Einzel·kind das only child

Einzeller der; ∼s, ∼ (Biol.) unicellular organism

einzeln Adj. (a) (für sich allein) individual (b) (allein stehend) solitary ⟨building, tree⟩; single ⟨lady, gentleman⟩ (c) ∼e (wenige) a few; (einige) some (d) substantivisch der/jeder Einzelne the/each individual; Einzelnes (manches) some things pl.; das Einzelne the particular

Einzel-: ∼**preis** der individual price; ∼**teil** das individual part; ∼**zelle** die single cell; ∼**zimmer** das single room

ein|ziehen ① unr. tr. V. (a) put in; thread in ⟨tape, elastic⟩ (b) (einholen) haul in ⟨net⟩ (c) (einatmen) breathe in ⟨scent, fresh air⟩; inhale ⟨smoke⟩ (d) (einberufen) call up ⟨recruits⟩ (e) (beitreiben) collect ② unr. itr. V.; mit sein (a) ⟨liquid⟩ soak in (b) (einkehren) enter (c) (in eine Wohnung) move in

einzig ① Adj. only; kein ∼es Wort not a single word ② adv. (a) intensivierend bei Adj. extraordinarily (b) (ausschließlich) only; das ∼ Wahre the only thing

einzig·artig ① Adj. unique ② adv. uniquely

Einzigartigkeit die, **Einzigkeit** die uniqueness

Ein·zug der (a) entry (in + Akk. into) (b) (in eine Wohnung) move

Einzugs·bereich der catchment area

Eis das; ∼es (a) ice; ∼ laufen ice-skate (b) (Speise∼) ice cream; ein ∼ am Stiel an ice lolly (Brit.) or (Amer.) ice pop

Eis-: ∼**bahn** die ice rink; ∼**bär** der polar bear; ∼**becher** der ice cream sundae; ∼**bein** das (Kochk.) knuckle of pork; ∼**berg** der iceberg; ∼**beutel** der ice bag; ∼**blume** die frost flower; ∼**bombe** die (Gastr.) bombe glacée; ∼**brecher** der icebreaker; ∼**café** das ice cream parlour

Ei·schnee der stiffly beaten egg white

Eis·diele die ice cream parlour

Eisen das; ∼s, ∼: iron

Eisen·bahn die (a) railway; railroad (Amer.); mit der ∼ fahren go by train (b) (Bahnstrecke) railway line; railroad track (Amer.)

Eisenbahn·abteil das railway or (Amer.) railroad compartment

Eisenbahner der; ∼s, ∼: railwayman; railway worker; railroader (Amer.)

Eisenbahnerin die; ∼, ∼nen railway worker

Eisenbahn·unglück das train crash

Eisen-: ∼**erz** das iron ore; ∼**kette** die iron chain; ∼**ring** der iron ring; ∼**stange** die iron bar; ∼**waren** Pl. ironmongery sing.; ∼**zeit** die Iron Age

eisern ① Adj. (auch fig.) iron ② adv. resolutely; ⟨save, train⟩ with iron determination; ∼ durchgreifen take drastic measures

eis-, Eis-: ∼**fach** das freezing compartment; ∼**frei** Adj. ice-free; ∼**gekühlt** Adj. iced; ∼**glatt** Adj. (a) icy ⟨road⟩; (b) /'··'/ (ugs.) ⟨floor, steps⟩ as slippery as ice; ∼**glätte** die black ice; ∼**hockey** das ice hockey

eisig ① Adj. (a) icy ⟨wind, cold⟩; icy [cold] ⟨water⟩ (b) (fig.) frosty ② adv. (a) ∼ kalt sein be icy cold (b) (fig.) ⟨smile⟩ frostily

*eisig·kalt Adj. ▶ EISKALT 1A

eis-, Eis-: ∼**kaffee** der iced coffee; ∼**kalt** ① Adj. (a) ice-cold ⟨drink⟩; freezing cold ⟨weather⟩; (b) (gefühllos) icy; ice-cold ⟨look⟩; ② adv. es lief mir ∼ am Rücken a cold shiver went down my spine; ∼**kunst·lauf** der figure skating; ∼**kunst·läufer** der, ∼**kunst·läuferin** die figure skater; ∼**lauf** der ice skating; *∼\|**laufen** ▶ EIS A; ∼**laufen** das; ∼∼s ice skating; ∼**läufer** der, ∼**läuferin** die ice skater

Ei·sprung der (Physiol.) ovulation

Eis-: ∼**regen** der sleet; ∼**schrank** der refrigerator; ∼**sport** der ice sports pl.; ∼**tanz** der (Sport) ice dancing; ∼**waffel** die [ice cream] wafer; ∼**wein** der: wine made from grapes frozen on the vine; ∼**würfel** der ice cube; ∼**zapfen** der icicle; ∼**zeit** die ice age

eitel Adj. vain

Eitelkeit die; ∼, ∼en vanity

Eiter der; ∼s pus

eitern itr. V. suppurate

eitrig Adj. suppurating

Ei·weiß das; ∼es, ∼e (a) egg white (b) (Protein) protein

eiweiß-: ∼**arm** Adj. low-protein attrib.; low in protein postpos.; ∼**reich** Adj. high-protein attrib.; rich in protein postpos.

Ejakulation die; ∼, ∼en (Physiol.) ejaculation

Ekel[1] *der;* ~s revulsion; [einen] ~ vor etw.
(*Dat.*) haben have a revulsion for sth.
Ekel[2] *das;* ~s, ~ (ugs. abwertend) horror; **er
ist ein [altes] ~:** he is quite obnoxious
ekelhaft *Adj.* revolting ⟨sight⟩; horrible
⟨weather, person⟩
ekeln [1] *refl. V.* be disgusted; **sich vor etw.**
(*Dat.*) ~: find sth. repulsive
[2] *tr., itr. V.* (*unpers.*) **es ekelt mich** *od.* **mir
ekelt davor** I find it revolting
eklig *Adj.* (a) ▶ EKELHAFT;
(b) (ugs.: gemein) nasty
Ekstase /ɛkˈstaːzə/ *die;* ~, ~n ecstasy
Ekzem *das;* ~s, ~e (Med.) eczema
Elan *der;* ~s zest; vigour
elastisch *Adj.* elasticated ⟨material⟩;
springy ⟨surface⟩; supple ⟨person, body⟩
Elastizität *die;* ~: elasticity; (Federkraft)
springiness; (Geschmeidigkeit) suppleness
Elch *der;* ~[e]s, ~e elk; (in Nordamerika)
moose
Elefant *der;* ~en, ~en elephant
elegant [1] *Adj.* elegant
[2] *adv.* elegantly
Eleganz *die;* ~: elegance
elektrifizieren *tr. V.* electrify
Elektrifizierung *die;* ~, ~en
electrification
Elektriker *der;* ~s, ~, **Elektrikerin** *die;*
~, ~nen electrician
elektrisch [1] *Adj.* electric; electrical
⟨resistance, wiring, system⟩
[2] *adv.* ~ **kochen** cook with electricity; ~
geladen sein be electrically charged
elektrisieren [1] *tr. V.* (Med.) treat using
electricity
[2] *refl. V.* get an electric shock
Elektrizität *die;* ~ electricity
Elektrizitäts·werk *das* power station
elektro-, Elektro-: ~**artikel** *der*
electrical appliance; ~**auto** *das* electric
car; ~**gerät** *das* electrical appliance;
~**geschäft** *das* electrical shop *or* (Amer.)
store; ~**herd** *der* electric cooker;
~**magnet** *der* electromagnet;
~**magnetisch** [1] *Adj.* electromagnetic;
[2] *adv.* electromagnetically; ~**mobil** *das;*
~~s, ~~e electric car; ~**motor** *der*
electric motor
Elektron *das;* ~s, ~en /-ˈtroːnən/ electron
Elektronen-: ~**[ge]hirn** *das* (ugs.)
electronic brain (coll.); ~**hülle** *die* electron
shell; ~**rechner** *der* electronic computer
Elektronik *die;* ~ (a) electronics *sing., no
art.;*
(b) (Teile) electronics *pl.*
Elektronik·schrott *der* scrapped
electrical appliances *pl.*
elektronisch [1] *Adj.* electronic
[2] *adv.* electronically

elektro-, Elektro-: ~**rasierer** *der*
electric shaver; ~**smog** *der* (Jargon)
electronic smog; ~**statisch** [1] *Adj.*
electrostatic; [2] *adv.* electrostatically;
~**technik** *die* electrical engineering *no
art.;* ~**techniker** *der,* ~**technikerin**
die (a) electronics engineer; (b) (Elektriker)
electrician
Element *das;* ~[e]s, ~e element
elementar *Adj.* (a) (grundlegend)
fundamental
(b) (einfach) elementary ⟨knowledge⟩
(c) (naturhaft) elemental ⟨force⟩
Elementar·teilchen *das* (Physik)
elementary particle
elend *Adj.* wretched; miserable
Elend *das;* ~s misery
Elends-: ~**quartier** *das* slum [dwelling];
~**viertel** *das* slum area
elf *Kardinalz.* eleven
Elf *die;* ~, ~en (a) eleven
(b) (Sport) team; side
Elfe *die;* ~, ~n fairy
Elfen·bein *das* ivory
Elfenbein-: ~**schnitzerei** *die* ivory
carving; ~**turm** *der* (fig.) ivory tower
Elf·meter *der* (Fußball) penalty; **einen** ~
schießen take a penalty
Elfmeter·schießen *das;* ~s (Fußball)
durch ~: by *or* on penalties
eliminieren *tr. V.* eliminate
elitär *adj.* élitist; **ein** ~**es Bewusstsein an**
élite-awareness
Elite *die;* ~, ~n élite
Elite·truppe *die* (Milit.) élite *or* crack force
Ell·bogen *der; Pl.* ~: elbow
Elle *die;* ~, ~n (a) (Anat.) ulna
(b) (frühere Längeneinheit) cubit
(c) (veralt.: Maßstock) ≈ yardstick
Ellen·bogen *der; Pl.* ~: ▶ ELLBOGEN
Ellipse *die;* ~, ~n ellipse
Elsass, *Elsaß *das;* ~ *od.* Elsasses
Alsace
Elster *die;* ~, ~n magpie
elterlich *Adj.* parental
Eltern *Pl.* parents *pl.*
eltern-, Eltern-: ~**abend** *der* (Schulw.)
parents' evening; ~**bei·rat** *der* (Schulw.)
parents' association; ~**haus** *das* home;
~**los** *Adj.* orphaned; ~**teil** *der* parent
Email /eˈmaiː/ *das;* ~s, ~s, **Emaille**
/eˈmaljə/ *die;* ~, ~n enamel
E-Mail /ˈiːmeɪl/ *die;* ~, ~s (DV) e-mail
Emanzipation *die;* ~, ~en emancipation
emanzipieren *refl. V.* emancipate
emanzipiert *Adj.* emancipated;
emancipated, liberated ⟨woman⟩
Embargo *das;* ~s, ~s embargo
Emblem *das;* ~s, ~e emblem
Embryo *der;* ~s, ~nen /-yˈoːnən/ *od.* ~s
embryo

Emigrant der; ~en, ~en, **Emigrantin** die; ~, ~nen emigrant; (Flüchtling) emigré

Emigration die; ~, ~en (das Emigrieren) emigration

emigrieren itr. V.; mit sein emigrate

Emission (a) (Physik, Ökologie) emission (b) (Ausgabe [von Briefmarken, Wertpapieren]) issue

Emotion die; ~, ~en emotion

emotional [1] Adj. emotional; emotive ⟨topic, question⟩ [2] adv. emotionally

Empfang der; ~[e]s, Empfänge reception; (Entgegennahme) receipt

empfangen unr. tr. V. receive

Empfänger der; ~s, ~ (a) recipient; (eines Briefs) addressee (b) (Empfangsgerät) receiver

Empfängerin die; ~, ~nen ▶ EMPFÄNGER A

empfänglich Adj. (a) receptive (für to) (b) (beeinflussbar) susceptible

Empfänglichkeit die; ~ (a) (Zugänglichkeit) receptivity, receptiveness (für to) (b) (Beeinflussbarkeit) susceptibility (für to)

Empfängnis die; ~: conception

Empfängnis·verhütung die contraception

empfangs-, Empfangs-: ~berechtigt Adj. authorized to receive payment/goods postpos.; ~chef der head receptionist; ~dame die receptionist; ~halle die reception lobby

empfehlen [1] unr. tr. V. recommend [2] unr. refl. V. (a) take one's leave (b) unpers. es empfiehlt sich, ... zu ...: it's advisable to ...

empfehlens·wert Adj. (a) to be recommended postpos.; recommendable (b) (ratsam) advisable

Empfehlung die; ~, ~en (a) recommendation (b) (Empfehlungsschreiben) letter of recommendation

empfiehl Imperativ Sg. v. EMPFEHLEN

empfiehlst 2. Pers. Sg. Präsens v. EMPFEHLEN

empfiehlt 3. Pers. Sg. Präsens v. EMPFEHLEN

empfinden unr. tr. V. (a) (wahrnehmen) feel (b) (auffassen) etw. als Beleidigung ~: feel sth. to be an insult

Empfinden das; ~s feeling; für mein od. nach meinem ~: to my mind

empfindlich [1] Adj. (a) sensitive; fast ⟨film⟩ (b) (leicht beleidigt) sensitive (c) (anfällig) zart und ~: delicate (d) (spürbar) severe ⟨punishment, shortage⟩ [2] adv. ~ auf etw. (Akk.) reagieren (sensibel) be susceptible to sth.; (beleidigt) react oversensitively to sth.

Empfindlichkeit die; ~, ~en ▶ EMPFINDLICH: sensitivity; severity; (eines Films) speed

empfindsam Adj. sensitive ⟨nature⟩

Empfindung die; ~, ~en (Gefühl) feeling

empfing 1. u. 3. Pers. Sg. Prät. v. EMPFANGEN

empfohlen [1] 2. Part. v. EMPFEHLEN; [2] Adj. recommended

empirisch [1] Adj. empirical [2] adv. empirically

empor Adv. (geh.) upwards

Empore die; ~, ~n gallery

empören [1] tr. V. fill with indignation; outrage [2] refl. V. become indignant or outraged

empörend Adj. outrageous

empört Adj. outraged

Empörung die; ~, ~en outrage

emsig [1] Adj. industrious ⟨person⟩; bustling ⟨activity⟩ [2] adv. industriously

Emu der; ~s, ~s (Zool.) emu

Ende das; ~s, ~n end; am ~ der Straße/ Stadt at the end of the road/town; am/bis/ gegen ~ des Monats at/by/towards the end of the month; ~ April at the end of April; zu ~ sein ⟨patience, war⟩ be at an end; ⟨school⟩ be over; ⟨film, game⟩ have finished; ~ gut, alles gut all's well that ends well (prov.)

End·effekt der im ~: in the end; in the final analysis

enden itr. V. (a) end; ⟨programme⟩ finish (b) in der Gosse ~: end up in the gutter; (dort sterben) die in the gutter

end-, End-: ~ergebnis das final result; ~gültig [1] Adj. final ⟨consent, decision⟩; conclusive ⟨evidence⟩; [2] adv. das ist ~gültig vorbei that's all over and done with; sich ~gültig trennen separate for good; ~haltestelle die terminus; ~kampf der (Sport) final; (Milit.) final battle; ~lauf der (Sport) final

endlich [1] Adv. (a) (nach langer Zeit) at last (b) (schließlich) in the end [2] Adj. finite

end-, End-: ~los [1] Adj. (a) (ohne Ende) infinite; (ringförmig) continuous; (b) (nicht enden wollend) endless; interminable ⟨speech⟩; [2] adv. ~los lange dauern be interminably long; ~lösung die (ns. verhüll.) Final Solution ⟨to the Jewish question⟩; ~resultat das final result; ~runde die (Sport) final; ~spiel das (Sport) final; ~spurt der (bes. Leichtathletik) final spurt; ~stadium das final stage; (Med.) terminal stage; ~station die terminus; ~summe die [sum] total

Endung die; ~, ~en (Sprachw.) ending

End-: ~verbraucher der, ~verbraucherin die (Wirtsch.) consumer; ····⫶

~**ziffer** *die* final number; **das Los mit der**
~**ziffer 4** the coupon with a number ending
in 4

Energie *die;* ~, ~**n** energy

energie-, Energie-: ~**bewusst,**
*∗~**bewußt** Adj.* energy-conscious; ~**mix**
der mix of energy sources; ~**politik** *die*
energy policy; ~**quelle** *die* energy source;
~**spar·lampe** *die* energy-saving lamp;
~**verbrauch** *der* energy consumption;
~**versorgung** *die* energy supply;
~**wirtschaft** *die* energy sector

energisch ⒈ *Adj.* (a) energetic ⟨*person*⟩;
firm ⟨*action*⟩
(b) forceful ⟨*voice, words*⟩
⒉ *adv.* (a) energetically; ~ **durchgreifen**
take drastic action
(b) ⟨*reject, say*⟩ forcefully; ⟨*stress*⟩
emphatically; ⟨*deny*⟩ strenuously

eng /ɛŋ/ ⒈ *Adj.* (a) (schmal) narrow
(b) (dicht) close ⟨*writing*⟩
(c) (fest anliegend) close-fitting
(d) (beschränkt) narrow
(e) (nahe) close ⟨*friend*⟩
⒉ *adv.* (a) (dicht) ~ [**zusammen**]**sitzen/stehen**
sit/stand close together
(b) (fest anliegend) ~ **anliegen/sitzen** fit closely
(c) (beschränkt) **etw. zu** ~ **auslegen** interpret
sth. too narrowly
(d) (nahe) closely

Engagement /ãgaʒə'mã:/ *das;* ~**s**, ~**s**
(a) (Einsatz) involvement; **sein** ~ **für etw.** his
commitment to sth.; **sein** ~ **gegen etw.** his
committed stand against sth.
(b) (eines Künstlers) engagement

engagiert *Adj.* committed ⟨*literature, film,
director*⟩; **politisch/sozial** ~ **sein** be
politically/socially committed *or* involved

Engagiertheit *die;* ~: commitment;
involvement

Enge *die;* ~, ~**n** confinement

Engel *der;* ~**s**, ~: angel

eng·herzig *Adj.* petty

England ⟨*das*⟩ ~**s** England

Engländer *der;* ~**s**, ~: Englishman/
English boy; **er ist** ~: he is English; **die** ~:
the English

Engländerin *die;* ~, ~**nen** Englishwoman/
English girl; **sie ist** ~: she is English

englisch ⒈ *Adj.* English; **die** ~**e Sprache/**
Literatur the English language/English
literature
⒉ *adv.* ~ **sprechen** speak English

Englisch *das;* ~[**s**] English

englisch-, Englisch-: ~**lehrer** *der,*
~**lehrerin** *die* English teacher;
~**sprachig** *Adj.* (a) (Englisch-language
⟨*book, magazine*⟩; (b) (Englisch sprechend)
English-speaking ⟨*population, country*⟩;
~**unterricht** *der* English teaching;
(Unterrichtsstunde) English lesson

∗alte Schreibung - vgl. Hinweis auf S. xiv

Eng·pass, ∗Eng·paß *der* (a) defile
(b) (fig.) bottleneck

eng·stirnig *Adj.* narrow-minded

Enkel *der;* ~**s**, ~: grandson

Enkelin *die;* ~, ~**nen** granddaughter

Enkel·kind *das* grandchild

enorm ⒈ *Adj.* enormous ⟨*sum, costs*⟩;
tremendous (coll.) ⟨*effort*⟩; immense ⟨*strain*⟩
⒉ *adv.* tremendously (coll.)

Ensemble /ã'sã:bl̩/ *das;* ~, ~**s** ensemble;
(Theater~) company

entarten *itr. V.; mit sein* degenerate

entbehren *tr. V.* (verzichten auf) do without

entbehrlich *Adj.* dispensable

Entbehrung *die;* ~, ~**en** privation

entbinden ⒈ *unr. tr. V.* (a) **jmdn. von**
einem Versprechen ~: release sb. from a
promise; **seines Amtes** *od.* **von seinem Amt**
entbunden werden be relieved of [one's]
office
(b) **jmdn.** ~ (Med.) deliver sb.'s baby
⒉ *unr. itr. V.* give birth

Entbindung *die* (Med.) delivery

Entbindungs·station *die* maternity
ward

entblößen ⒈ *refl. V.* take one's clothes off;
⟨*exhibitionist*⟩ expose oneself
⒉ *tr. V.* uncover ⟨*one's arm etc.*⟩

entdecken *tr. V.* (a) discover
(b) (ausfindig machen) **jmdn.** ~: find sb.; **etw.**
~: find *or* discover sth.

Entdecker *der;* ~**s**, ~, **Entdeckerin**
die; ~, ~**nen** discoverer

Entdeckung *die;* ~, ~**en** discovery

Ente *die;* ~, ~**n** duck

entehren *tr. V.* dishonour; ~**d** degrading

enteignen *tr. V.* expropriate

Enteignung *die;* ~, ~**en** expropriation

enterben *tr. V.* disinherit

entern *tr., itr. V.* board ⟨*ship*⟩

entfachen *tr. V.* (geh.) (a) kindle, light
⟨*fire*⟩
(b) (fig.) provoke ⟨*quarrel, argument*⟩; arouse
⟨*passion, enthusiasm*⟩

entfallen *unr. itr. V.; mit sein* (a) (aus dem
Gedächtnis) **es ist mir** ~: it escapes me
(b) (zugeteilt werden) **auf jmdn./etw.** ~: be
allotted to sb./sth.
(c) (wegfallen) lapse

entfalten ⒈ *tr. V.* (a) open [up]; unfold
⟨*map etc.*⟩
(b) (fig.) display ⟨*ability, talent*⟩
⒉ *refl. V.* (a) open [up]
(b) (fig.) ⟨*personality, talent, etc.*⟩ develop

Entfaltung *die;* ~, ~**en** (fig.) (a) (Entwicklung)
development
(b) ▶ ENTFALTEN 1B: display

entfernen ⒈ *tr. V.* remove; take out
⟨*tonsils etc.*⟩
⒉ *refl. V.* go away

entfernt ⒈ *Adj.* (a) (fern) remote; **das ist**

od. **liegt weit** ∼ **von der Stadt** it is a long way from the town; **10 km/zwei Stunden** ∼: 10 km/two hours away
(b) slight ⟨*acquaintance*⟩; distant ⟨*relation*⟩; slight ⟨*resemblance*⟩
2 *adv.* **(a)** (fern) remotely
(b) slightly ⟨*acquainted*⟩; distantly ⟨*related*⟩

Entfernung *die;* ∼, ∼**en (a)** (Abstand) distance
(b) (das Beseitigen) removal

entfesseln *tr. V.* unleash

entflammen 1 *tr. V.* arouse ⟨*enthusiasm etc*⟩
2 *itr. V.; mit sein* flare up

entfliehen *unr. itr. V.; mit sein* escape; **jmdm.** ∼: escape from sb.

entfremden 1 *tr. V.* **(a)** etw. seinem Zweck ∼: use sth. for a different purpose
(b) (Philos., Soziol.) entfremdet alienated
2 *refl. V.* **sich jmdm./einer Sache** ∼: become estranged from sb./unfamiliar with sth.

Entfremdung *die;* ∼, ∼**en** alienation; estrangement

entführen *tr. V.* kidnap ⟨*child etc.*⟩; hijack ⟨*plane, lorry, etc.*⟩

Entführer *der,* **Entführerin** *die*
▶ ENTFÜHREN: kidnapper; hijacker

Entführung *die* ▶ ENTFÜHREN: kidnapping; hijacking

entgegen 1 *Adv.* towards
2 *Präp. mit Dat.* ∼ **meinem Wunsch** against my wishes; ∼ **dem Befehl** contrary to orders

entgegen-, Entgegen-: ∼|**bringen** *unr. tr. V.* (fig.) show ⟨*love, understanding*⟩; ∼|**fahren** *unr. itr. V.; mit sein* jmdm. ∼**fahren** come/go to meet sb.; ∼|**gehen** *unr. itr. V.; mit sein* **(a)** jmdm. ∼**gehen** go to meet sb.; **(b)** (fig.) be heading for ⟨*catastrophe, hard times*⟩; ∼**gesetzt 1** *Adj.* **(a)** (umgekehrt) opposite ⟨*end, direction*⟩; **(b)** (gegensätzlich) opposing; **2** *adv.* genau ∼**gesetzt handeln/denken** do/think exactly the opposite; ∼|**kommen** *unr. itr. V.; mit sein* jmdm. ∼**kommen** come to meet sb.; (Zugeständnisse machen) be accommodating towards sb.; ∼|**kommen** *das;* ∼∼**s** cooperation; (Zugeständnis) concession; ∼**kommend** *Adj.* obliging; ∼|**nehmen** *unr. itr. V.* receive; ∼|**treten** *unr. itr. V.; mit sein* go/come up to; (fig.) stand up to ⟨*difficulties*⟩

entgegnen *tr. V.* retort; reply

entgehen *unr. itr. V.; mit sein* **(a)** (entkommen) escape
(b) jmdm. entgeht etw. sb. misses sth.

entgeistert *Adj.* dumbfounded

Entgelt *das;* ∼[e]s, ∼e payment; fee

entgiften *tr. V.* decontaminate ⟨*substance etc.*⟩; detoxicate ⟨*body etc.*⟩

entgleisen *itr. V.; mit sein* **(a)** be derailed
(b) (fig.) make a/some faux pas

entgräten *tr. V.* fillet

enthaaren *tr. V.* remove hair from

Enthaarungs·mittel *das* hair remover

enthalten¹ 1 *unr. tr. V.* contain
2 *unr. refl. V.* **sich einer Sache** (*Gen.*) ∼: abstain from sth.; **sich der Stimme** ∼: abstain

enthalten² *Adj.* **in etw.** (*Dat.*) ∼ **sein** be contained in sth.; **das ist im Preis** ∼: that is included in the price

enthaltsam 1 *Adj.* abstemious; (sexuell) abstinent
2 *adv.* ∼ **leben** live in abstinence

Enthaltsamkeit *die;* ∼: abstinence

Enthaltung *die;* ∼, ∼**en** abstention

enthaupten *tr. V.* (geh.) behead

enthäuten *tr. V.* skin

entheben *unr. tr. V.* (geh.) relieve

enthemmt *Adj.* uninhibited

enthüllen *tr. V.* unveil ⟨*monument etc.*⟩; reveal ⟨*face, truth, secret*⟩

Enthüllung *die;* ∼, ∼**en** ▶ ENTHÜLLEN: unveiling; revelation

Enthusiasmus /ɛntuˈzjasmʊs/ *der;* ∼: enthusiasm

Enthusiast *der;* ∼**en,** ∼**en,** **Enthusiastin** *die;* ∼, ∼**nen** enthusiast

enthusiastisch 1 *Adj.* enthusiastic
2 *adv.* enthusiastically

entkalken *tr. V.* decalcify

entkleiden *tr. V.* (geh.) **(a)** undress
(b) (berauben) strip

entkommen *unr. itr. V.; mit sein* escape

entkorken *tr. V.* uncork ⟨*bottle*⟩

entkräften *tr. V.* **(a)** weaken; **völlig** ∼: exhaust
(b) (fig.) refute ⟨*argument etc.*⟩

Entkräftung *die;* ∼, ∼**en (a)** debility; **völlige** ∼: exhaustion
(b) (fig.) refutation

entladen 1 *unr. tr. V.* unload
2 *unr. refl. V.* **(a)** ⟨*storm*⟩ break
(b) (fig.) ⟨*anger etc.*⟩ erupt; ⟨*aggression etc.*⟩ be released

entlang 1 *Präp. mit Akk. u. Dat.* along
2 *Adv.* along; **hier/dort** ∼, **bitte!** this/that way please!

entlang-: ∼|**fahren** *unr. itr. V.; mit sein* **(a)** drive along; **(b)** (streichen) go along; ∼|**gehen** *unr. itr. V.; mit sein* ⟨*person*⟩ go or walk along; ∼|**laufen** *unr. itr. V.; mit sein* **(a)** walk/run along; **(b)** (verlaufen) go or run along

entlarven *tr. V.* expose

entlassen *unr. tr. V.* **(a)** (aus dem Gefängnis) release; (aus dem Krankenhaus, der Armee) discharge
(b) (aus einem Arbeitsverhältnis) dismiss; (wegen Arbeitsmangels) make redundant (Brit.); lay off

Entlassung *die;* ∼, ∼**en** ▶ ENTLASSEN: release; discharge; dismissal; redundancy (Brit.); laying off

entlasten *tr. V.* **(a)** relieve

(b) (Rechtsw.) exonerate ⟨*defendant*⟩

Entlastung *die;* ~, ~en **(a)** relief
(b) (Rechtsw.) exoneration; defence

entlaufen *unr. itr. V.; mit sein* run away;
ein ~**er Sträfling/Sklave** an escaped convict/a
runaway slave

entlausen *tr. V.* delouse

entledigen *refl. V.* **sich jmds./einer Sache**
(*Gen.*) ~ (geh.) rid oneself of sb./sth.

entleeren *tr. V.* empty; evacuate ⟨*bowels,
bladder*⟩

entlegen *Adj.* remote

entleihen *unr. tr. V.* borrow

entlocken *tr. V.* (geh.) **jmdm. etw.** ~: elicit
sth. from sb.

entlohnen *tr. V.* pay

Entlohnung *die;* ~, ~en payment; (Lohn)
pay

entlüften *tr. V.* ventilate

Entlüfter *der;* ~s, ~: ventilator

entmachten *tr. V.* deprive of power

entmilitarisieren *tr. V.* demilitarize

entmündigen *tr. V.* incapacitate

Entmündigung *die;* ~, ~en
incapacitation

entmutigen *tr. V.* discourage

Entnahme *die;* ~, ~n (von Wasser) drawing;
(von Blut) extraction

Entnazifizierung *die;* ~, ~en
denazification

entnehmen *unr. tr. V.* **(a)** etw. [einer
Sache (*Dat.*)] ~: take sth. [from sth.]
(b) (ersehen aus) gather (*Dat.* from)

entnervend *Adj.* nerve-racking

entnervt *Adj.* ~ **sein** be worn down; have
reached *or* be at the end of one's tether; **er
gab** ~ **auf** he had reached the end of his
tether and gave up

entpuppen *refl. V.* **sich als etw./jmd.** ~:
turn out to be sth./sb.

entrahmen *tr. V.* skim ⟨*milk*⟩

entreißen *unr. tr. V.* **jmdm. etw.** ~: snatch
sth. from sb.

entrichten *tr. V.* (Amtsspr.) pay ⟨*fee*⟩

entrümpeln *tr. V.* clear out

Entrümpelung *die;* ~, ~en clear-out

entrüsten ① *refl. V.* **sich [über etw. (*Akk.*)]**
~: be indignant [at *or* about sth.]
② *tr. V.* (empören) **jmdn.** ~: make sb.
indignant

Entrüstung *die;* ~, ~en indignation (über
+ *Akk.* at, about)

Entsafter *der;* ~s, ~: juice extractor

entsagen *itr. V.* **einer Sache (*Dat.*)** ~ (geh.)
renounce sth.

Entsagung *die;* ~, ~en (geh.) renunciation

entschädigen *tr. V.* compensate (**für** for);
jmdn. für etw. ~ (fig.) make up for sth.

Entschädigung *die;* ~, ~en
compensation

entschärfen *tr. V.* defuse; tone down
⟨*discussion, criticism*⟩

entscheiden ① *unr. refl. V.* **(a)** decide
(b) (*unpers.*) **morgen entscheidet es sich,
ob** ...: I/we/you will know tomorrow
whether ...
② *unr. itr. V.* **über etw. (*Akk.*)** ~: settle sth.
③ *unr. tr. V.* decide on ⟨*dispute*⟩; decide
⟨*outcome, result*⟩

entscheidend ① *Adj.* crucial; decisive
⟨*action*⟩
② *adv.* **jmdn./etw.** ~ **beeinflussen** have a
decisive influence on sb./sth.

Entscheidung *die;* ~, ~en decision

entschieden ① *Adj.* **(a)** (entschlossen)
determined; resolute
(b) (eindeutig) definite
② *adv.* resolutely; **das geht** ~ **zu weit** that is
going much too far

Entschiedenheit *die;* ~: decisiveness;
etw. mit ~ **behaupten/verneinen** state/deny
sth. categorically; **etw. mit** ~ **fordern** demand
sth. emphatically

entschlafen *unr. itr. V.; mit sein* pass
away

entschließen *unr. refl. V.* decide

Entschließung *die;* ~, ~en resolution

entschlossen *Adj.* determined

Entschlossenheit *die;* ~: determination

Entschluss, *Entschluß *der;*
Entschlusses, Entschlüsse decision

entschlüsseln *tr. V.* decipher

entschuldigen ① *refl. V.* apologize
② *tr.* (*auch itr.*) **(a)** excuse ⟨*person*⟩; **sich** ~
lassen ask to be excused; ~ **Sie [bitte]!** (bei
Fragen, Bitten) excuse me; (bedauernd) I'm sorry

Entschuldigung *die;* ~, ~en **(a)** apology
(b) (Grund) excuse
(c) (Höflichkeitsformel) ~**!** (bei Fragen, Bitten)
excuse me; (bedauernd) [I'm] sorry

entschwinden *unr. itr. V.; mit sein* (geh.)
disappear; vanish

entsetzen ① *refl. V.* be horrified
② *tr. V.* horrify; **über etw. (*Akk.*) entsetzt
sein** be horrified by sth.

Entsetzen *das;* ~s horror

entsetzlich ① *Adj.* **(a)** horrible ⟨*accident,
crime, etc.*⟩
(b) (ugs.: stark) terrible ⟨*thirst, hunger*⟩
② *adv.* terribly (coll.)

entsinnen *unr. refl. V.* **sich jmds./einer
Sache** ~: remember sb./sth.

entsorgen *tr. V.* (Amtsspr., Wirtsch.) dispose
of ⟨*waste etc.*⟩

Entsorgung *die;* ~, ~en (Amtsspr., Wirtsch.)
waste disposal

entspannen ① *tr. V.* relax
② *refl. V.* **(a)** ⟨*person*⟩ relax
(b) (fig.) ⟨*situation, tension*⟩ ease

Entspannung *die;* ~ **(a)** relaxation
(b) (politisch) easing of tension; détente

---

*old spelling - see note on page xiv

Entspạnnungs-politik *die* policy of
détente

entsprẹchen *unr. itr. V.* (a) (übereinstimmen
mit) **einer Sache** (*Dat.*) **~:** correspond to sth.;
der Wahrheit/den Tatsachen ~: be in
accordance with the truth/the facts
(b) (nachkommen) **einem Wunsch ~:** comply
with a request; **den Anforderungen ~:** meet
the requirements

entsprẹchend [1] *Adj.* (a) corresponding;
(angemessen) appropriate
(b) (dem~) in accordance *postpos.;*
[2] *adv.* (a) (angemessen) appropriately
(b) (dem~) accordingly
[3] *Präp. mit Dat.* in accordance with

entsprịngen *unr. itr. V.; mit sein* (a)
⟨*river*⟩ rise
(b) (entstehen aus) **einer Sache** (*Dat.*) **~:**
spring from sth.

entstẹhen *unr. itr. V.; mit sein* (a)
originate; ⟨*quarrel, friendship, etc.*⟩ arise
(b) (gebildet werden) be formed (**aus** from,
durch by)
(c) (sich ergeben) occur; (als Folge) result

Entstẹhung *die; ~:* origin

entstẹinen *tr. V.* stone

entstẹllen *tr. V.* (a) disfigure
(b) (verfälschen) distort ⟨*text, facts*⟩

Entstẹllung *die; ~, ~en* (a)
disfigurement
(b) (Verfälschung) distortion

entstören *tr. V.* (Elektrot.) suppress ⟨*engine,
electrical appliance*⟩

Entstörungs-stelle *die* fault repair
service

enttạrnen *tr. V.* uncover

enttäuschen *tr. V.* disappoint

enttäuschend *Adj.* disappointing

enttäuscht *Adj.* disappointed; dashed
⟨*hopes*⟩

Enttäuschung *die; ~, ~en*
disappointment

entwạchsen *unr. itr. V.; mit sein* **einer
Sache** (*Dat.*) **~.** grow out of sth.

entwạffnen *tr. V.* (auch fig.) disarm

entwạffnend *Adj.* disarming

entwạrnen *itr. V.* sound the all-clear

Entwạrnung *die; ~, ~en* all-clear

entwässern *tr. V.* drain

Entwässerung *die; ~, ~en* drainage

ẹntweder *Konj.: ~ ... oder* either ... or

entwẹichen *unr. itr. V.; mit sein* escape

entwẹnden *tr. V.* (geh.) purloin

entwẹrfen *unr. tr. V.* design ⟨*furniture,
dress*⟩; draft ⟨*novel etc.*⟩; draw up ⟨*plans etc.*⟩

entwẹrten *tr. V.* (a) cancel ⟨*ticket, postage
stamp*⟩
(b) devalue ⟨*currency*⟩

Entwẹrter *der; ~s, ~:* ticket-cancelling
machine

entwịckeln [1] *refl. V.* develop

[2] *tr. V.* produce ⟨*vapour, smell*⟩; display
⟨*ability, characteristic*⟩; develop ⟨*equipment,
photograph, film*⟩; elaborate ⟨*theory, ideas*⟩

Entwịcklung *die; ~, ~en* (a)
development; (von Dämpfen usw.) production;
in der ~ sein ⟨*young person*⟩ be adolescent
(b) (Darlegung) elaboration
(c) (Fot.) developing

Entwịcklungs-: **~helfer** *der,*
~helferin *die* development aid worker;
~hilfe *die* [development] aid; **~land** *das*
developing country; **~politik** *die*
development aid policy

entwịrren *tr. V.* disentangle

entwịschen *itr. V.; mit sein* (ugs.) get
away

entwöhnen *tr. V.* wean

entwürdigend *Adj.* degrading

Entwụrf *der; ~, Entwürfe* (a) design
(b) (Konzept) draft

entwụrzeln *tr. V.* uproot

entziẹhen [1] *unr. tr. V.* (a) take away
(b) (nicht zugestehen) withdraw
[2] *unr. refl. V.* **sich seinen Pflichten** (*Dat.*)
~: evade one's duty; **das entzieht sich
meiner Kontrolle** that is beyond my control

Entziẹhung *die; ~, ~en* (a) withdrawal
(b) (Entziehungskur) withdrawal treatment *no
indef. art.*

entzịffern *tr. V.* decipher

entzückend *Adj.* delightful

entzückt *Adj.* delighted

Entzug *der; ~[e]s* withdrawal

Entzugs-erscheinung *die* withdrawal
symptom

entzündbar *Adj.* [in]flammable

entzünden [1] *tr. V.* light ⟨*fire*⟩; strike
⟨*match*⟩
[2] *refl. V.* (a) ignite
(b) (anschwellen) become inflamed

entzündlich *Adj.* (a) [in]flammable
⟨*substance*⟩
(b) (Med.) inflammatory

Entzündung *die; ~, ~en* inflammation

entzwei *Adj.* (geh.) in pieces

entzweien *refl. V.* fall out

entzwei|gehen *unr. itr. V.; mit sein* (geh.)
break

Ẹnzian *der; ~s, ~e* gentian

Enzyklika *die; ~, Enzykliken* encyclical

Enzyklopädie *die; ~, ~n* encyclopaedia

enzyklopädisch *Adj.* encyclopaedic

Epen ▸ EPOS

Epidemiẹ *die; ~, ~n* epidemic

epigonal *Adj.* (geh.) ▸ EPIGONENHAFT

Epigone *der; ~n, ~n* (geh.) imitator

epigonenhaft *Adj.* (geh.) imitative;
unoriginal

Epigonin *die; ~, ~nen* ▸ EPIGONE

Epik /'e:pɪk/ *die; ~* (Literaturw.) epic poetry

Epilepsie die; ~, ~n (Med.) epilepsy no art.
Epileptiker der; ~s, ~, **Epileptikerin**
die; ~, ~nen epileptic
epileptisch Adj. epileptic
episch Adj. epic
Episode die; ~, ~n episode
Epoche die; ~, ~n epoch
Epos /'e:pɔs/ das; ~, Epen epic [poem]; epos
er Personalpron. 3. Pers. Sg. Nom. Mask. he;
(betont) him; (bei Dingen/Tieren) it; s. auch IHM;
IHN; SEINER
erachten tr. V. (geh.) consider; etw. als od.
für seine Pflicht ~: consider sth. [to be] one's
duty
erarbeiten tr. V. work for
Erb-anlage die hereditary disposition
erbarmen refl. V. (geh.) take pity (Gen. on)
Erbarmen das; ~s pity
erbärmlich [1] Adj. (a) (elend) wretched
(b) (unzulänglich) pathetic
(c) (abwertend: gemein) mean; wretched
(d) (sehr groß) terrible ⟨hunger, fear, etc.⟩
[2] adv. terribly
erbauen [1] tr. V. (a) build
(b) (geh.: erheben) uplift
[2] refl. V. sich an etw. (Dat.) ~: be uplifted
by sth.
Erbauer der; ~s, ~, **Erbauerin** die; ~,
~nen architect
Erbe[1] das; ~s (a) inheritance
(b) (Vermächtnis) legacy
Erbe[2] der; ~n ~n heir
erben tr. (auch itr.) V. inherit
erbetteln tr. V. get by begging
erbeuten tr. V. carry off, get away with
⟨valuables, prey, etc.⟩; capture ⟨enemy plane,
tank, etc.⟩
Erb-: ~**faktor** der hereditary factor;
~**folge** die succession; ~**gut** das (Biol.)
genetic make-up
Erbin die; ~, ~nen heiress
erbitten unr. tr. V. (geh.) request
erbittern tr. V. enrage
erbittert [1] Adj. bitter
[2] adv. ~ kämpfen wage a bitter struggle
Erb-krankheit die hereditary disease
erblassen itr. V.; mit sein (geh.) turn pale;
blanch (literary)
erbleichen itr. V.; mit sein (geh.)
▶ ERBLASSEN
erblich Adj. hereditary ⟨title, disease⟩
erblicken tr. V. (geh.) catch sight of; (fig.)
see
erblinden itr. V.; mit sein lose one's sight
erblühen itr. V.; mit sein (geh.) bloom;
blossom
Erb-masse die (Biol.) genetic make-up
erbost Adj. furious
erbrechen [1] unr. tr. V. bring up ⟨food⟩

[2] unr. itr., refl. V. vomit
Erbrechen das; ~s vomiting
erbringen unr. tr. V. produce
Erbschaft die; ~, ~en inheritance
Erbschaft[s]-steuer die estate or death
duties pl.
Erb-: ~**schleicher** der; ~~s, ~~
(abwertend) legacy hunter; ~**schleicherei**
die; ~~, ~~en (abwertend) legacy hunting;
~**schleicherin** die; ~~, ~~nen
▶ ~SCHLEICHER
Erbse die; ~, ~n pea
Erb-: ~**stück** das heirloom; ~**sünde** die
original sin; ~**teil** das share of an/the
inheritance
Erd-: ~**achse** die earth's axis;
~**anziehung** die earth's gravitational
pull; ~**apfel** der (bes. österr.) ▶ KARTOFFEL;
~**atmosphäre** die earth's atmosphere;
~**beben** das earthquake; ~**beere** die
strawberry; ~**boden** der ground; earth;
etw. dem ~boden gleichmachen raze sth. to
the ground
Erde die; ~, ~n (a) (Erdreich) soil; earth
(b) (fester Boden) ground
(c) (Welt) earth; world
(d) (Planet) Earth
erdenklich Adj. conceivable
Erd-: ~**gas** das natural gas;
~**geschoss,** *~**geschoß** das ground
floor; first floor (Amer.); ~**kugel** die
terrestrial globe; earth; ~**kunde** die
geography; ~**magnetismus** der
terrestrial magnetism; ~**nuss,** *~**nuß** die
peanut; ~**oberfläche** die earth's surface;
~**öl** das oil; ~öl exportierende Länder oil-
exporting countries
erdöl-, Erdöl-: *~**exportierend**
▶ ERDÖL; ~**gewinnung** die oil production;
~**leitung** die oil pipeline
erdrosseln tr. V. strangle
erdrücken tr. V. (a) crush
(b) (fig.: belasten) overwhelm
erdrückend Adj. overwhelming;
oppressive ⟨heat, silence⟩
Erd-: ~**rutsch** der landslide;
~**rutsch-sieg** der (Politik) landslide
victory; ~**teil** der continent
erdulden tr. V. endure ⟨sorrow, misfortune⟩;
tolerate ⟨insults⟩; (über sich ergehen lassen)
undergo
Erd-: ~**umdrehung** die rotation of the
earth; ~**umlauf-bahn** die orbit [of the
earth]
ereifern refl. V. get excited
ereignen refl. V. happen; ⟨accident, mishap⟩
occur
Ereignis das; ~ses, ~se event; occurrence
ereignis-reich Adj. eventful
Eremit der; ~en, ~en, **Eremitin** die; ~,
~nen hermit
ererbt Adj. inherited

---

erfahren[1] *unr. tr. V.* (a) find out; learn; (hören) hear
(b) (geh.: erleben) experience; (erleiden) suffer

erfahren[2] *Adj.* experienced

Erfahrung *die;* ∼, ∼en experience; ∼en sammeln gain experience *sing.;* etw. in ∼ bringen discover sth.

erfahrungs·gemäß *Adv.* in our/my experience

erfassen *tr. V.* (a) (mitreißen) catch
(b) (begreifen) grasp ⟨situation, etc.⟩
(c) (registrieren) record

Erfassung *die;* ∼, ∼en registration

erfinden *unr. tr. V.* invent; **das ist alles erfunden** it is pure fabrication

Erfinder *der;* ∼s, ∼, **Erfinderin** *die;* ∼, ∼nen (a) inventor
(b) (Urheber) creator

erfinderisch *Adj.* inventive; (schlau) resourceful

Erfindung *die;* ∼, ∼en invention

erflehen *tr. V.* (geh.) beg

Erfolg *der;* ∼[e]s, ∼e success; **keinen** ∼ **haben** be unsuccessful

erfolgen *itr. V.; mit sein* take place; occur; **es erfolgte keine Reaktion** there was no reaction

erfolg-, Erfolg-: ∼los [1] *Adj.* unsuccessful; [2] *adv.* unsuccessfully; ∼**losigkeit** *die;* ∼∼: lack of success; ∼**reich** [1] *Adj.* successful; [2] *adv.* successfully

Erfolgs·erlebnis *das* feeling of achievement

erfolg·versprechend *Adj.* promising

erforderlich *Adj.* required; necessary

erfordern *tr. V.* require; demand

erforschen *tr. V.* discover ⟨facts, causes, etc.⟩; explore ⟨country⟩

Erforschung *die;* ∼ research (+ *Gen.* into); (eines Landes usw.) exploration

erfreuen [1] *tr. V.* please
[2] *refl. V.* **sich an etw.** (*Dat.*) ∼: take pleasure in sth.

erfreulich *Adj.* pleasant

erfreulicherweise *Adv.* happily

erfrieren [1] *unr. itr. V.; mit sein* freeze to death; ⟨plant, harvest, etc.⟩ be damaged by frost
[2] *unr. refl. V.* **sich** (*Dat.*) **die Finger** ∼: get frostbite in one's fingers

Erfrierung *die;* ∼, ∼en frostbite *no pl.;* ∼**en an den Händen/Füßen** frostbitten hands/feet

erfrischen [1] *tr.* (auch itr.) *V.* refresh
[2] *refl. V.* freshen oneself up

erfrischend (auch fig.) *Adj.* refreshing

Erfrischung *die;* ∼, ∼en (auch fig.) refreshment

Erfrischungs-: ∼**getränk** *das* soft

drink; ∼**raum** *der* refreshment room; ∼**tuch** *das; Pl.* ∼**tücher** tissue wipe; towelette

erfüllen [1] *tr. V.* grant ⟨wish, request⟩; fulfil ⟨contract⟩; carry out ⟨duty⟩; meet ⟨condition⟩
[2] *refl. V.* ⟨wish⟩ come true

Erfüllung *die:* in ∼ gehen come true

erfunden *Adj.* fictional ⟨story⟩

ergänzen *tr. V.* (a) (vervollständigen) complete; (erweitern) add to
(b) (hinzufügen) add ⟨remark⟩

Ergänzung *die;* ∼, ∼en (a) (Vervollständigung) completion; (Erweiterung) enlargement
(b) (Zusatz) addition; (zu einem Gesetz) amendment

ergattern *tr. V.* (ugs.) manage to grab

ergaunern *tr. V.* get by underhand means

ergeben[1] [1] *unr. refl. V.* (a) **sich in etw.** (*Akk.*) ∼: submit to sth.
(b) (kapitulieren) surrender (*Dat.* to)
(c) (folgen, entstehen) arise (**aus** from)
[2] *unr. tr. V.* result in

ergeben[2] *Adj.* (a) (zugeneigt) devoted
(b) (resignierend) **mit** ∼**er Miene** with an expression of resignation

Ergebnis *das;* ∼ses, ∼se result

ergebnis·los *Adj.* fruitless

ergehen *unr. refl. V.* **sich in etw.** (*Dat.*) ∼: indulge in sth.

ergiebig *Adj.* rich ⟨deposits, resources⟩; fertile ⟨topic⟩

Ergiebigkeit *die;* ∼ ▶ ERGIEBIG: richness; fertility

ergonomisch [1] *Adj.* ergonomic
[2] *adv.* ergonomically

ergötzen (geh.) [1] *tr. V.* enthrall
[2] *refl. V.* **sich an etw.** (*Dat.*) ∼: be delighted by sth.

ergrauen *itr. V.; mit sein* go grey

ergreifen *unr. tr. V.* (a) (greifen) grab
(b) (festnehmen) catch ⟨thief etc.⟩
(c) (fig.: erfassen) seize
(d) (fig.: aufnehmen) take up ⟨career⟩; take ⟨initiative, opportunity⟩
(e) (fig.: bewegen) move

ergreifend *Adj.* moving

ergriffen *Adj.* moved

Ergriffenheit *die;* ∼: **voller** ∼: deeply moved

ergründen *tr. V.* ascertain; discover ⟨cause⟩

Erguss, *Erguß *der* (geh. abwertend) outburst; **ein poetischer** ∼: a poetic outpouring

erhaben *Adj.* solemn ⟨moment⟩; awe-inspiring ⟨sight⟩; sublime ⟨beauty⟩; **über etw.** (*Akk.*) ∼ **sein** be above sth.

Erhalt *der;* ∼ (Amtsdt.) receipt

erhalten *unr. tr. V.* **(a)** receive ⟨*letter, news, gift*⟩; be given ⟨*order*⟩; get ⟨*good mark, impression*⟩
(b) (bewahren) preserve ⟨*town, building*⟩
erhältlich *Adj.* obtainable
Erhaltung *die;* ~: preservation; (des Friedens) maintenance
erhängen *tr. V.* hang
erhärten *tr. V.* strengthen ⟨*suspicion, assumption*⟩; substantiate ⟨*claim*⟩
erheben ① *unr. tr. V.* **(a)** raise
(b) (verlangen) levy ⟨*tax*⟩; charge ⟨*fee*⟩
② *unr. refl. V.* **(a)** rise
(b) (rebellieren) rise up **(gegen** against)
erhebend *Adj.* uplifting
erheblich ① *Adj.* considerable
② *adv.* considerably
Erhebung *die;* ~, ~en **(a)** (Anhöhe) elevation
(b) (Aufstand) uprising
(c) (Umfrage) survey
(d) (Einziehen) (von Steuern) levying; (von Gebühren) charging
erheitern *tr. V.* jmdn. ~: cheer sb. up
Erheiterung *die;* ~, ~en amusement
erhellen *tr. V.* light up
erhitzen ① *tr. V.* heat ⟨*liquid*⟩; jmdn. ~: make sb. hot
② *refl. V.* heat up; ⟨*person*⟩ become hot
erhoffen *tr. V.* sich ⟨*Dat.*⟩ viel/wenig von etw. ~: expect a lot/little from sth.
erhöhen ① *tr. V.* increase ⟨*prices, productivity, etc.*⟩
② *refl. V.* ⟨*rent, prices*⟩ rise
Erhöhung *die;* ~, ~en increase (*Gen.* in)
erholen *refl. V.* (auch fig.) recover **(von** from); (sich ausruhen) have a rest
erholsam *Adj.* restful
Erholung *die;* ~: ▶ ERHOLEN: recovery; rest; ~ **brauchen** need a rest
erholungs-bedürftig *Adj.* in need of a rest *postpos.*
Erholungs-urlaub *der* holiday for convalescence
erhören *tr. V.* (geh.) hear
Erika *die;* ~, ~s *od.* Eriken (Bot.) erica
erinnern ① *refl. V.* sich an jmdn./etw. ~: remember sb./sth.; sich [daran] ~, dass ...: remember *or* recall that ...
② *tr. V.* jmdn. an etw./jmdn. ~: remind sb. of sth./sb.
Erinnerung *die;* ~, ~en memory (an + *Akk.* of); etw. [noch gut] in ~ haben [still] remember sth. [well]; zur ~ an jmdn./etw. in memory of sb./sth.
Erinnerungs-lücke *die* gap in one's memory
erjagen *tr. V.* **(a)** catch
(b) (gewinnen) win ⟨*fame*⟩; make ⟨*money, fortune*⟩

erkalten *tr. V.; mit sein* cool
erkälten *refl. V.* catch cold
Erkältung *die;* ~, ~en cold
Erkältungs-krankheit *die* cold
erkämpfen *tr. V.* win; den Sieg ~: gain a victory
erkaufen *tr. V.* **(a)** (durch Opfer) win
(b) (durch Geld) buy
erkennbar *Adj.* recognizable; (sichtbar) visible
erkennen *unr. tr. V.* **(a)** recognize
(b) (deutlich sehen) make out
erkenntlich *Adj.* **(a)** sich [für etw.] ~ zeigen show one's appreciation for sth.
(b) ▶ ERKENNBAR
Erkenntnis *die;* ~, ~se discovery; zu der ~ **kommen, dass** ...: come to the realization that ...
Erkennungs-: ~**melodie** *die* (einer Sendung) theme music; (eines Senders) signature tune; ~**zeichen** *das* sign [to recognize sb. by]
Erker *der;* ~s, ~: bay window
Erker-fenster *das* bay window
erklärbar *Adj.* explicable
erklären ① *tr. V.* **(a)** explain
(b) (mitteilen) state; declare
(c) jmdn. für tot ~: pronounce someone dead; jmdn. zu etw. ~: name sb. as sth
② *refl. V.* sich einverstanden/bereit ~: declare oneself [to be] in agreement/willing
erklärlich *Adj.* understandable
erklärt *Adj.* declared
Erklärung *die;* ~, ~en **(a)** (Darlegung) explanation
(b) (Mitteilung) statement
erklimmen *unr. tr. V.* (geh.) climb
erklingen *unr. itr. V.; mit sein* ring out
erkranken *itr. V.; mit sein* become ill **(an** + *Dat.* with); **schwer erkrankt sein** be seriously ill
Erkrankung *die;* ~, ~en illness; (eines Körperteils) disease
erkunden *tr. V.* reconnoitre ⟨*terrain*⟩
erkundigen *refl. V.* sich nach jmdn./etw. ~: ask after sb./enquire about sth.
Erkundigung *die;* ~, ~en enquiry
Erkundung *die;* ~, ~en (meist Milit.) reconnaissance
Erkundungs-: ~**fahrt** *die* exploratory trip; ~**flug** *der* reconnaissance flight
erlahmen *itr. V.; mit sein* tire; ⟨*strength*⟩ flag
erlangen *tr. V.* gain; obtain ⟨*credit, visa*⟩; reach ⟨*age*⟩
Erlass, *Erlaß *der;* Erlasses, Erlasse decree
erlassen *unr. tr. V.* **(a)** enact ⟨*law*⟩; declare ⟨*amnesty*⟩; issue ⟨*warrant*⟩
(b) (verzichten auf) remit ⟨*sentence*⟩
erlauben ① *tr. V.* **(a)** allow
(b) (ermöglichen) permit

---

*old spelling - see note on page xiv

2 *refl. V.* sich (*Dat.*) etw. ~: permit oneself sth

Erlaubnis *die;* ~, ~se permission; (Schriftstück) permit

erläutern *tr. V.* explain; comment on ⟨*picture etc.*⟩; annotate ⟨*text*⟩

Erläuterung *die* explanation

Erle *die;* ~, ~n alder

erleben *tr. V.* experience; **etwas Schreckliches** ~: have a terrible experience; **er wird das nächste Jahr nicht mehr** ~: he won't see next year; **du kannst was** ~! (ugs.) you won't know what's hit you!

Erlebnis *das;* ~ses, ~se experience

erledigen **1** *tr. V.* deal with ⟨*task*⟩; settle ⟨*matter*⟩; **ich muss noch einige Dinge erledigen** I must see to a few things; **sie hat alles pünktlich erledigt** she got everything done on time

2 *refl. V.* ⟨*matter, problem*⟩ resolve itself; **vieles erledigt sich von selbst** a lot of things sort them'selves out

erledigt *Adj.* closed ⟨*case*⟩; (ugs.) worn out ⟨*person*⟩

erlegen *tr. V.* shoot ⟨*animal*⟩

erleichtern *tr. V.* (a) make easier
(b) (befreien) relieve

Erleichterung *die;* ~, ~en (a) zur ~ der Arbeit to make the work easier
(b) (Befreiung) relief
(c) (Verbesserung, Milderung) alleviation

erleiden *unr. tr. V.* suffer

erlernbar *Adj.* learnable

erlernen *tr. V.* learn

erlesen *Adj.* superior ⟨*wine*⟩; choice ⟨*dish*⟩

erleuchten *tr. V.* (a) light
(b) (geh.: mit Klarheit erfüllen) inspire

Erleuchtung *die;* ~, ~en inspiration

erliegen *unr. itr. V.; mit sein* succumb (*Dat.* to); **einem Irrtum** ~: be misled; **einer Krankheit** (*Dat.*) ~: die from an illness

erlogen *Adj.* made up

Erlös *der;* ~es, ~e proceeds *pl.*

erlöschen *unr. itr. V.; mit sein* ⟨*fire*⟩ go out; **ein erloschener Vulkan** an extinct volcano

erlösen *tr. V.* save, rescue (**von** from)

Erlöser *der;* ~s, ~ (a) saviour
(b) (christl. Rel.) redeemer

Erlöserin *die;* ~, ~nen ▶ ERLÖSER A

Erlösung *die;* ~, ~en release (**von** from)

ermächtigen *tr. V.* authorize

Ermächtigung *die;* ~, ~en authorization

ermahnen *tr. V.* admonish; tell (coll.); (warnen) warn

Ermahnung *die;* ~, ~en admonition; (Warnung) warning

Ermang[e]lung *die;* ~: in ~ (+ *Gen.*) (geh.) in the absence of

ermäßigen *tr. V.* reduce

Ermäßigung *die;* ~, ~en reduction

ermatten (geh.) **1** *itr. V.; mit sein* become exhausted
2 *tr. V.* exhaust, tire

ermessen *unr. tr. V.* estimate, gauge

Ermessen *das;* ~s estimation

ermitteln **1** *tr. V.* ascertain ⟨*facts*⟩; discover ⟨*culprit, address*⟩; establish ⟨*identity, origin*⟩; decide ⟨*winner*⟩; calculate ⟨*quota, rates, data*⟩
2 *itr. V.* (Rechtsw.) investigate

Ermittlung *die;* ~, ~en (a) (das Ermitteln)
▶ ERMITTELN A: ascertainment; discovery; establishment
(b) (Untersuchung) investigation

ermöglichen *tr. V.* enable

ermorden *tr. V.* murder

Ermordung *die;* ~, ~en murder

ermüden **1** *itr. V.; mit sein* tire
2 *tr. V.* tire; make tired

ermüdend *Adj.* tiring

Ermüdung *die;* ~, ~en tiredness

ermuntern *tr. V.* encourage

ermunternd *Adj.* encouraging

ermutigen *tr. V.* encourage

Ermutigung *die;* ~, ~en encouragement

ernähren **1** *tr. V.* (a) feed ⟨*young, child*⟩
(b) (unterhalten) keep ⟨*family, wife*⟩
2 *refl. V.* feed oneself

Ernährer *der;* ~s, ~, **Ernährerin** *die;* ~, ~nen breadwinner

Ernährung *die;* ~: feeding; (Nahrung) diet

Ernährungs·wissenschaft *die* dietetics *sing., no art.*

ernennen *unr. tr. V.* appoint

Ernennung *die* appointment (**zu** as)

erneuerbar *Adj.* renewable; ~e Energien renewable sources of energy

erneuern *tr. V.* (a) replace
(b) (wiederherstellen) renovate ⟨*roof, building*⟩; (fig.) thoroughly reform ⟨*system*⟩

Erneuerung *die;* ~, ~en (a) replacement
(b) (Wiederherstellung) renovation

erneut **1** *Adj.* renewed
2 *adv.* once again

erniedrigen *tr. V.* humiliate

Erniedrigung *die;* ~, ~en humiliation

ernst **1** *Adj.* (a) serious
(b) (aufrichtig) genuine ⟨*intention, offer*⟩
(c) (gefahrvoll) serious ⟨*injury*⟩; grave ⟨*situation*⟩
2 *adv.* seriously; **jmdn./etw.** ~ nehmen take sb./sth. seriously; ~ gemeint serious; sincere ⟨*wish*⟩

Ernst *der;* ~[e]s (a) seriousness; **das ist mein [voller]** ~: I mean that [quite] seriously; **etw. im** ~ meinen mean sth. seriously
(b) (Wirklichkeit) **daraus wurde [blutiger/ bitterer]** ~: it became [deadly] serious; **der** ~ **des Lebens** the serious side of life

ernst-, Ernst-: ~fall *der;* im ~fall when the real thing happens; **~gemeint* ····⊹

▶ ERNST 2; ~**haft** ① *Adj.* serious; ② *adv.* seriously; ~**haftigkeit** *die;* ~~: seriousness

ernstlich ① *Adj.* (a) serious (b) (aufrichtig) genuine ⟨*wish*⟩ ② *adv.* (a) seriously (b) (aufrichtig) genuinely ⟨*sorry, repentant*⟩

Ernte *die;* ~, ~n (a) harvest (b) (Ertrag) crop; **die ~ einbringen** bring in the harvest

Ernte-dank-fest *das* harvest festival

ernten *tr. V.* harvest

ernüchtern *tr. V.* sober up; (fig.) bring down to earth; ~**d** sobering

Ernüchterung *die;* ~, ~en (fig.) disillusionment

Eroberer *der;* ~s, ~, **Eroberin** *die;* ~, ~nen conqueror

erobern *tr. V.* (a) conquer; take ⟨*town, fortress*⟩ (b) seize ⟨*power*⟩

Eroberung *die;* ~, ~en conquest; (einer Stadt, Festung) taking

eröffnen *tr. V.* (a) open; start ⟨*business, practice*⟩ (b) (mitteilen) **jmdm. etw. ~:** reveal sth. to sb. (c) **ein Testament ~:** read a will

Eröffnung *die;* ~, ~en (a) opening; (einer Sitzung) start (b) (Mitteilung) revelation (c) (Testaments~) reading

erogen *Adj.* erogenous ⟨*zone*⟩

erörtern *tr. V.* discuss

Erörterung *die;* ~, ~en discussion

Eros-Center *das* [licensed] brothel; eros centre

Erosion *die;* ~, ~en erosion

Erotik *die;* ~: eroticism

erotisch *Adj.* erotic

Erpel *der;* ~s, ~: drake

erpicht *Adj.* **in auf etw.** (*Akk.*) ~ **sein** be keen on sth.

erpressbar, *erpreßbar *Adj.* blackmailable; susceptible to blackmail *postpos.*

Erpressbarkeit, *Erpreßbarkeit *die;* ~: susceptibility to blackmail

erpressen *tr. V.* (a) (nötigen) blackmail (b) (erlangen) extort ⟨*money etc.*⟩

Erpresser *der;* ~s, ~, **Erpresserin** *die;* ~, ~nen blackmailer

Erpressung *die;* ~, ~en blackmail *no indef. art.;* (von Geld, Geständnis) extortion

Erpressungs-versuch *der* blackmail attempt

erproben *tr. V.* test ⟨*medicine*⟩ (**an** + *Akk.* on)

Erprobung *die;* ~, ~en testing

erquickend *Adj.* (geh.) refreshing

erraten *unr. tr. V.* guess

errechnen *tr. V.* calculate

erregen ① *tr. V.* (a) annoy (b) (sexuell) arouse (c) (verursachen) arouse ② *refl. V.* get excited

erregend *Adj.* exciting; (sexuell) arousing

Erreger *der;* ~s, ~ (Med.) pathogen

erregt *Adj.* excited; (sexuell) aroused

Erregung *die;* ~, ~en excitement

erreichbar *Adj.* (a) within reach *postpos.;* (b) **der Ort ist mit dem Zug ~:** the place can be reached by train

erreichen *tr. V.* (a) reach; **den Zug ~:** catch the train; **er ist telefonisch zu ~:** he can be contacted by telephone (b) (durchsetzen) achieve ⟨*goal, aim*⟩

errichten *tr. V.* (a) build ⟨*house, bridge, etc.*⟩ (b) (aufstellen) erect

erringen *unr. tr. V.* gain ⟨*victory*⟩; reach ⟨*first etc. place*⟩

erröten *itr. V.; mit sein* blush

Errungenschaft *die;* ~, ~en achievement

Ersatz *der;* ~es (a) replacement (b) (Entschädigung) compensation

Ersatz-: ~**frau** *die* replacement; (Sport) substitute; ~**kasse** *die* private health insurance company; ~**mann** *der; Pl.* ~**männer** *od.* ~**leute** *die* replacement; (Sport) substitute; ~**rad** *das* spare wheel; ~**reifen** *der* spare tyre; ~**spieler** *der,* ~**spielerin** *die* (Sport) substitute [player]; ~**teil** *das* (bes. Technik) spare part; spare (Brit.)

ersaufen *unr. itr. V.; mit sein* (salopp) drown

ersäufen *tr. V.* drown

erschaffen *unr. tr. V.* create

Erschaffung *die* creation

erschaudern *itr. V.; mit sein* (geh.) shudder (**bei** at)

erscheinen *unr. itr. V.; mit sein* ⟨*book*⟩ be published

Erscheinung *die;* ~, ~en (a) (Vorgang) phenomenon (b) (äußere Gestalt) appearance (c) (Vision) apparition; **eine ~ haben** see a vision

Erscheinungs-: ~**bild** *das* appearance; ~**form** *die* manifestation; ~**weise** *die* ~**weise einer Zeitung** the frequency of publication of a newspaper; **wöchentliche/ monatliche ~weise** weekly/monthly publication

erschießen *unr. tr. V.* shoot dead

Erschießung *die;* ~, ~en shooting

erschlaffen *itr. V.; mit sein* ⟨*muscle, limb*⟩ become limp; ⟨*skin*⟩ grow slack

erschlagen¹ *unr. tr. V.* strike dead; kill

erschlagen² *Adj.* (ugs.) (a) (erschöpft) worn out

---

*alte Schreibung - vgl. Hinweis auf S. xiv

(b) (verblüfft) **wie** ~ **sein** be flabbergasted (coll.) or thunderstruck

erschließen unr. tr. V. develop ⟨area, building land⟩; tap ⟨resources⟩

erschöpfen tr. V. exhaust

erschöpfend Adj. exhaustive

erschöpft Adj. exhausted

Erschöpfung die; ~, ~en exhaustion

Erschöpfungs·zustand der state of exhaustion

erschrecken[1] unr. itr. V.; mit sein be startled; **vor etw.** (Dat.) od. **über etw.** (Akk.) ~: be startled by sth.

erschrecken[2] tr. V. frighten; scare

erschrecken[3] unr. od. regelm. refl. V. get a fright

erschreckend Adj. alarming

erschrocken [1] 2. Part. v. ERSCHRECKEN[1]; [2] Adj. frightened

erschüttern tr. V. (auch fig.) shake

erschütternd Adj. deeply distressing; deeply shocking ⟨conditions⟩

Erschütterung die; ~, ~en **(a)** vibration; (der Erde) tremor **(b)** (Ergriffenheit) shock; (Trauer) distress

erschweren tr. V. **etw.** ~: make sth. more difficult

erschwerend [1] Adj. complicating ⟨factor⟩ [2] adv. **es kommt** ~ **hinzu, dass er …:** to make matters worse he …

Erschwernis die; ~, ~se difficulty

erschwinglich Adj. reasonable

ersehen unr. tr. V. see; **aus etw. zu** ~ **sein** be evident from sth.

ersetzen tr. V. **(a)** replace (**durch** by) **(b)** (erstatten) reimburse ⟨expenses⟩; **jmdm. einen Schaden** ~: compensate sb. for damages

Ersetzung die; ~, ~en (von Kosten usw.) reimbursement; **die** ~ **von Schäden** compensation for damage

ersichtlich Adj. apparent

ersinnen unr. tr. V. (geh.) devise

erspähen tr. V. (geh.) espy (literary); catch sight of

ersparen tr. V. save

Ersparnis die; ~, ~se saving

ersprießlich Adj. (geh.) fruitful ⟨contacts, collaboration⟩

erst [1] Adv. **(a)** (zu~) first; ~ **einmal** first [of all] **(b)** (nicht eher als) **eben** ~: only just; ~ **nächste Woche** not until next week; **er war** ~ **zufrieden, als …:** he was not satisfied until … **(c)** (nicht mehr als) only [2] Partikel **so was lese ich gar nicht** ~: I don't even start reading that sort of stuff

erst… Ordinalz. **(a)** first; **etw. das** ~**e Mal**

tun do sth. for the first time; **am Ersten [des Monats]** on the first [of the month]; **als Erster/Erste etw. tun** be the first to do sth. **(b)** (best…) **das** ~**e Hotel** the best hotel; **der/ die Erste [der Klasse]** the top boy/girl [of the class]

erstarren itr. V.; mit sein ⟨jelly, plaster⟩ set; ⟨limbs, fingers⟩ grow stiff

erstatten tr. V. **(a)** reimburse ⟨expenses⟩ **(b) Anzeige gegen jmdn.** ~: report sb. [to the police]

Erstattung die; ~, ~en (von Kosten) reimbursement

Erst·aufführung die première

erstaunen tr. V. astonish

Erstaunen das; ~s astonishment

erstaunlich [1] Adj. astonishing [2] adv. astonishingly

erstaunlicher·weise Adv. astonishingly or amazingly [enough]

erstaunt Adj. astonished; amazed

Erst·ausgabe die first edition

erstechen unr. tr. V. stab [to death]

erstehen (geh.) [1] unr. tr. V. (kaufen) purchase [2] unr. itr. V.; mit sein ⟨difficulties, problems⟩ arise

ersteigen unr. tr. V. climb

ersteigern tr. V. buy [at an auction]

erstellen tr. V. (Papierdt.) **(a)** (bauen) build **(b)** (anfertigen) make ⟨assessment⟩; draw up ⟨plan, report, list⟩

erste·mal ▶ MAL[1]

ersten·mal ▶ MAL[1]

erstens Adv. firstly; in the first place

erster… Adj. the former

erst·geboren Adj. first-born

ersticken [1] itr. V.; mit sein suffocate; (sich verschlucken) choke [2] tr. V. **(a)** (töten) suffocate **(b)** smother ⟨flames⟩

erstklassig [1] Adj. first-class [2] adv. superbly

erstmals Adv. for the first time

erstrangig Adj. **(a)** first-class **(b)** (vordringlich) of top priority postpos.

erstreben tr. V. strive for

erstrebens·wert Adj. ⟨ideals etc.⟩ worth striving for; desirable ⟨situation⟩

erstrecken refl. V. **(a)** (sich ausdehnen) stretch **(b)** (dauern) **sich über 10 Jahre** ~: carry on for 10 years

Erst·stimme die first vote

erstürmen tr. V. take by storm

ersuchen tr. V. (geh.) ask; **jmdn.** ~, **etw. zu tun** request sb. to do sth.

ertappen tr. V. catch ⟨thief, burglar⟩

erteilen tr. V. give ⟨advice, information⟩; give, grant ⟨permission⟩

Erteilung die; ~, ~en giving; (einer Genehmigung) granting

ertönen itr. V.; mit sein sound

Ertrag der; ~[e]s, Erträge (a) yield
(b) (Gewinn) return

ertragen unr. tr. V. bear

erträglich Adj. tolerable; bearable ⟨pain⟩

ertrag·reich Adj. lucrative ⟨business⟩; productive ⟨land, soil⟩

ertränken tr. V. drown

ertrinken unr. itr. V.; mit sein be drowned; drown

erübrigen 1 tr. V. spare ⟨money, time⟩
2 refl. V. be unnecessary

erwachen itr. V.; mit sein (geh.) awake

Erwachen das; ~s (auch fig.) awakening

erwachsen¹ unr. itr. V.; mit sein (a) grow (aus out of); ⟨rumour⟩ spread
(b) (sich ergeben) ⟨difficulties, tasks⟩ arise

erwachsen² Adj. grown-up attrib.; ~ sein be grown up

Erwachsene der/die; adj. Dekl. adult; grown-up

erwägen unr. tr. V. consider

Erwägung die; ~, ~en consideration; etw. in ~ ziehen take sth. into consideration

erwählen tr. V. (geh.) choose

erwähnen tr. V. mention

erwähnens·wert Adj. worth mentioning postpos.

Erwähnung die; ~, ~en mention

erwärmen 1 tr. V. heat
2 refl. V. (warm werden) ⟨air, water⟩ warm up

Erwärmung die; ~: eine ~ der Luft/des Wassers an increase in air/water temperature; bei ~ der Flüssigkeit when the liquid is heated

erwarten tr. V. expect; jmdn. am Bahnhof ~: wait for sb. at the station

Erwartung die; ~, ~en expectation

erwartungs-: ~gemäß Adv. as expected; ~voll Adj. expectant

erwecken tr. V. (a) (auf~) wake
(b) (erregen) arouse ⟨longing, pity⟩

erweichen tr. V. soften

erweisen 1 unr. tr. V. (a) prove
(b) (bezeigen) jmdm. Achtung ~: show respect to sb.
2 unr. refl. V. sich als etw. ~: prove to be sth.

erweitern 1 tr. V. widen ⟨river, road⟩; expand ⟨library, business⟩; enlarge ⟨collection⟩; dilate ⟨pupil, blood vessel⟩
2 refl. V. ⟨road, river⟩ widen; ⟨pupil, blood vessel⟩ dilate

Erweiterung die; ~, ~en ▶ ERWEITERN: widening; expansion; enlargement; dilation

Erwerb der; ~[e]s (a) (Aneignung) acquisition
(b) (Kauf) purchase

---

*old spelling - see note on page xiv

erwerben unr. tr. V. (a) (verdienen) earn
(b) (sich aneignen) gain
(c) (kaufen) acquire

erwerbs-, Erwerbs-: ~fähig Adj. capable of gainful employment postpos.; able to work postpos.; ~fähigkeit die ability to work; ~los Adj.: ▶ ARBEITSLOS; ~lose der/die; adj. Dekl.: ▶ ARBEITSLOSE; ~tätig Adj. gainfully employed; ~unfähig Adj. incapable of gainful employment postpos.; unable to work postpos.

Erwerbung die acquisition; (Gekauftes) purchase

erwidern tr. V. (a) reply
(b) (reagieren auf) return ⟨greeting, visit⟩; reciprocate ⟨sb.'s feelings⟩

Erwiderung die; ~, ~en (a) reply (auf + Akk. to)
(b) ▶ ERWIDERN B: return; reciprocation

erwiesen Adj. proved; proven ⟨fact⟩

erwiesener·maßen Adv. as has been proved

erwirken tr. V. obtain

erwirtschaften tr. V. etw. ~: obtain sth. by careful management

erwischen tr. V. (ugs.) (a) catch ⟨culprit, train, bus⟩
(b) (greifen) grab
(c) (bekommen) manage to get
(d) (unpers.) es hat ihn erwischt (ugs.) (er ist tot) he's bought it (sl.); (er ist krank) he's got it; (er ist verletzt) he's been hurt; (scherzh.: er ist verliebt) he's got it bad (coll.)

erwünscht Adj. wanted

erwürgen tr. V. strangle

Erz /ɛrts: od. eːrts:/ das; ~es, ~e ore

erzählen tr. (auch itr.) V. tell ⟨joke, story⟩; jmdm. etw. ~: tell sb. sth.

Erzähler der, **Erzählerin** die storyteller; (Autor[in]) writer [of stories]; narrative writer

Erzählung die; ~, ~en narration; (Bericht) account; (Literaturw.) story

Erz-: ~bischof der archbishop; ~bistum das, ~diözese die archbishopric; archdiocese; ~engel der archangel

erzeugen tr. V. produce; generate ⟨electricity⟩

Erzeuger der; ~s, ~ (Vater) father

Erzeugnis das; ~ses, ~se product

Erzeugung die; ~, ~en (von Lebensmitteln usw.) production; (von Industriewaren) manufacture; (Strom~) generation

Erz·feind der, **Erz·feindin** die arch enemy

erziehen unr. tr. V. bring up; (in der Schule) educate; ein Kind zu Sauberkeit und Ordnung ~: bring a child up to be clean and tidy

Erzieher der; ~s, ~, **Erzieherin** die; ~, ~nen educator; (Pädagoge) educationalist; (Lehrer) teacher

Erziehung die; ~, ~en upbringing; (Schul~) education

Erziehungs-: ∼**berechtigte** der/die;
adj. Dekl. parent or [legal] guardian;
∼**urlaub** der child-rearing leave

erzielen tr. V. reach ⟨agreement,
compromise, speed⟩; achieve ⟨result, effect⟩;
make ⟨profit⟩; obtain ⟨price⟩

erzürnen (geh.) tr. V. anger; (stärker) incense

erzwingen unr. tr. V. force

es Personalpron.; 3. Pers. Sg. Nom. u. Akk.
Neutr. **(a)** (s. auch Gen. seiner; Dat. ihm)
(Sache) it; (weibliche Person) she/her; (männliche
Person) he/him
(b) ohne Bezug auf ein bestimmtes Subst.,
mit unpers. konstruierten Verben, als
formales Satzglied it; **ich bin es** it's me; **wir
sind traurig, ihr seid es auch** we are sad, and
so are you; **es sei denn, [dass]** ...: unless ...;
es ist genug! that's enough; **es hat geklopft**
there was a knock; **es klingelt** someone is
ringing; **es wird schöner** the weather is
improving; **es geht ihm gut/schlecht** he is
well/unwell; **es wird gelacht** there is
laughter; **es lässt sich aushalten** it is
bearable; **er hat es gut** he has it good; **er
meinte es gut** he meant well

Esche die; ∼, ∼n (Bot.) ash

Esel der; ∼s, ∼ **(a)** donkey; ass
(b) (ugs.: Dummkopf) ass (coll.)

Esels-: ∼**brücke** die (ugs.) mnemonic;
∼**ohr** das (ugs.: umgeknickte Stelle) dog-ear

Eskalation die; ∼, ∼en escalation

eskalieren tr., itr. V. escalate

Eskapade /ɛska'paːdə/ die; ∼, ∼n
escapade; (Seitensprung) amorous adventure

Eskimo der; ∼[s], ∼[s] Eskimo

Eskimofrau die Eskimo woman

Eskorte die; ∼, ∼n escort

eskortieren tr. V. escort

Espe die; ∼, ∼n aspen

Essay /'ɛse/ der od. das; ∼s, ∼s essay

essbar, *eßbar Adj. edible; **nicht** ∼:
inedible

essen unr. tr., itr. V. eat; **etw. gern** ∼: like
sth.; **sich satt** ∼: eat one's fill; **gut** ∼: have a
good meal; (immer) eat well; ∼ **gehen** go out
for a meal

Essen das; ∼s, ∼ (Mahlzeit) meal; (Speise)
food; [das] ∼ **machen/kochen** get/cook the
meal

Essen[s]-: ∼**marke** die meal ticket;
∼**zeit** die mealtime

Essenz die; ∼, ∼en essence

Esser der; ∼s, ∼, **Esserin** die; ∼, ∼nen:
er ist ein schlechter Esser he has a poor
appetite

Essig der; ∼s, ∼e vinegar

Essig-gurke die pickled gherkin

Ess-, *Eß-: ∼**kastanie** die sweet
chestnut; ∼**löffel** der (Suppenlöffel) soup
spoon; (für Nach-, Vorspeise) dessert spoon;
∼**stäbchen** das chopstick; ∼**teller** der

dinner plate; ∼**tisch** der dining table;
∼**waren** Pl. food sing.; ∼**zimmer** das
dining room

Establishment /ɪs'tɛblɪʃmənt/ das; ∼s,
∼s Establishment

Este der; ∼n, ∼n, **Estin** die; ∼, ∼nen
Estonian

Est·land (das); ∼s Estonia

Estragon /'ɛstragɔn/ der; ∼s tarragon

Estrich /'ɛstrɪç/ der; ∼s, ∼e composition
floor

Eszett /ɛs'tsːɛt/ das; ∼, ∼ [the letter] ß

etablieren tr. V. establish; set up

etabliert Adj. established

Etablissement /etablɪs(ə)'mãː/ das; ∼s,
∼s establishment

Etage /e'taːʒə/ die; ∼, ∼n floor; storey

Etappe die; ∼, ∼n stage

Etat /e'taː/ der; ∼s, ∼s budget

etepetete /eːtəpe'teːtə/ Adj. (ugs.) fussy;
finicky

Ethik die; ∼, ∼en **(a)** ethics sing.;
(b) (sittliche Normen) ethics pl.

ethisch Adj. ethical

ethnisch [1] Adj. ethnic; ∼**e Säuberung**
ethnic cleansing
[2] adv. ethnically

Etikett das; ∼[e]s, ∼en od. ∼e od. ∼s
label

Etikette die; ∼, ∼n etiquette

Etiketten·schwindel der (abwertend)
playing with names

etikettieren tr. V. label

etlich... Indefinitpron. u. unbest. Zahlwort:
Sg. quite a lot of; Pl. quite a few

Etüde die; ∼, ∼n (Musik) étude

Etui /ɛt'viː/ das; ∼s, ∼s case

etwa [1] Adv. **(a)** (ungefähr) about; ∼ **so groß
wie** ...: about as large as ...; ∼ **so** roughly
like this
(b) (beispielsweise) for example
[2] Partikel **störe ich** ∼? am I disturbing
you at all?

etwaig... /'ɛtva(ː)ɪg.../ Adj. possible

etwas Indefinitpron. **(a)** something; (fragend,
verneinend) anything; **irgend**∼: something
(b) (Bedeutsames) **aus ihm wird** ∼: he'll make
something of himself
(c) (ein Teil) some; (fragend, verneinend) any; ∼
von dem Geld some of the money
(d) (ein wenig) a little; ∼ **lauter/besser** a little
louder/better

Etymologie die; ∼, ∼n etymology

EU Abk. = **Europäische Union** EU

euch [1] Dat. u. Akk. Pl. des Personalpron.
ihr you
[2] Dat. u. Akk. Pl. des Reflexivpron. der 2.
Pers. Pl. yourselves

euer[1] Possessivpron. your; **Grüße von
eu[e]rer Helga/eu[e]rem Hans** Best wishes,
Yours, Helga/Hans

euer² *Gen. des Personalpron.* ihr (geh.) wir werden ~ gedenken we will remember you

Eule *die;* ~, ~n owl; ~n nach Athen tragen carry coals to Newcastle

Eunuch *der;* ~en, ~en eunuch

Euphorie *die;* ~, ~n (bes. Med., Psych.) euphoria

euphorisch (bes. Med., Psych.) ⓵ *Adj.* euphoric
⓶ *adv.* euphorically

eure ▶ EUER¹

eurer·seits ▶ DEINERSEITS

euret·wegen *Adv.* ▶ DEINETWEGEN

Euro *der;* ~[s], ~[s] Euro

Eurocheque /ˈɔyˌroʃɛk/ *der;* ~s, ~s Eurocheque

Europa (das); ~s Europe

Europäer *der;* ~s, ~, **Europäerin** *die;* ~, ~nen European

europäisch *Adj.* European; die Europäische Union the European Union

Europa-: ~meister *der,* ~meisterin *die* (Sport) European champion; ~meisterschaft *die* (Sport) (a) (Wettbewerb) European Championship; (b) (Sieg) European title; ~parlament *das* European Parliament; ~pokal *der* (Sport) European cup; ~rat *der* Council of Europe; ~straße *die* European long-distance road

Euro·scheck *der* ▶ EUROCHEQUE

Euter *das od. der;* ~s, ~: udder

ev. *Abk.* = **evangelisch** ev.

e.V., E.V. *Abk.* = **eingetragener Verein**

evakuieren /evakuˈiːrən/ *tr. V.* evacuate

Evakuierung *die;* ~, ~en evacuation

evangelisch /evaŋˈɡeːlɪʃ/ *Adj.* Protestant

Evangelium *das;* ~s, Evangelien (a) (auch fig.) gospel
(b) (christl. Rel.) Gospel

Event /iˈvɛnt/ *der od. das;* ~s, ~s event

Eventualität /eventualiˈtɛːt/ *die;* ~, ~en eventuality; contingency

eventuell ⓵ *Adj.* possible
⓶ *adv.* possibly; perhaps

Evolution /evoluˈtsi̯oːn/ *die;* ~, ~en evolution

evtl. *Abk.* = **eventuell**

EWG *Abk.* = **Europäische Wirtschaftsgemeinschaft** EEC

ewig ⓵ *Adj.* eternal; (abwertend) never-ending
⓶ *adv.* eternally; for ever

Ewig·gestrige *der/die; adj. Dekl.* (abwertend) ein ~r sein be an old reactionary

Ewigkeit *die;* ~, ~en (a) eternity
(b) (ugs.) es dauert eine ~: it takes ages (coll.)

ex *Adv.* (ugs.) etw. ex trinken drink sth. down in one (coll.)

Ex- (vor Personenbez.: vormalig) ex-

exakt *Adj.* exact; precise

Exaktheit *die;* ~: precision; exactness

Examen *das;* ~s, ~ od. Examina examination

exekutieren *tr. V.* (a) execute
(b) (österr.) ▶ PFÄNDEN

Exekution *die;* ~, ~en (a) execution
(b) (österr.) ▶ PFÄNDUNG

Exekutive *die;* ~, ~n (Rechtsw., Politik) executive

Exempel *das;* ~s, ~: example

Exemplar *das;* ~s, ~e specimen; (Buch, Zeitung usw.) copy

exemplarisch *Adj.* exemplary

exerzieren *tr., itr. V.* drill

Exhibitionist *der;* ~en, ~en, **Exhibitionistin** *die;* ~, ~nen (Psych., fig.) exhibitionist

exhibitionistisch (Psych.) ⓵ *Adj.* exhibitionist
⓶ *adv.* er ist ~ veranlagt he has exhibitionist tendencies

Exil *das;* ~s, ~e exile

exiliert *Adj.* exiled

Exil·regierung *die* government in exile

existentiell ▶ EXISTENZIELL

Existenz *die;* ~, ~en (a) existence
(b) (Lebensgrundlage) livelihood
(c) (Mensch) character

Existenz·grundlage *die* basis of one's livelihood

existenziell *Adj.* existential; in etw. (*Dat.*) eine ~e Bedrohung sehen see in sth. a threat to one's existence

Existenz-: ~kampf *der* struggle for existence; ~minimum *das* subsistence level

existieren *itr. V.* exist

Exitus *der;* ~ (Med.) death

exkl. *Abk.* = **exklusiv[e]** excl.

exklusiv ⓵ *Adj.* exclusive
⓶ *adv.* exclusively

exklusive *Präp.* + *Gen.* exclusive of

Exklusiv·vertrag *der* exclusive contract

Exkommunikation *die;* ~, ~en excommunication

Exkursion *die;* ~, ~en study trip

exotisch ⓵ *Adj.* exotic
⓶ *adv.* exotically

expandieren *tr., itr. V.* expand

Expansion *die;* ~, ~en expansion

Expedition *die;* ~, ~en expedition

Experiment *das;* ~[e]s, ~e experiment

experimentell ⓵ *Adj.* experimental
⓶ *adv.* experimentally

experimentieren *itr. V.* experiment

Experte *der;* ~n, ~n, **Expertin** *die;* ~, ~nen expert (für in)

Experten·system *das* (DV) expert system

explizit ⓵ *Adj.* explicit

---

*alte Schreibung - vgl. Hinweis auf S. xiv

2 *adv.* ⟨*describe, define*⟩ explicitly

explodieren *itr. V.; mit sein* (auch fig.) explode; ⟨*costs*⟩ rocket

Explosion *die;* ~, ~en explosion

explosiv 1 *Adj.* (auch fig.) explosive
2 *adv.* explosively

Exponent *der;* ~en, ~en (Math.) exponent

exponiert *Adj.* exposed

Export¹ *der;* ~[e]s, ~e export

Export² *das;* ~s, ~e (Bier) export; **zwei** ~: two export

Export-: ~**artikel** *der* export; ~**bier** *das* export beer

Exporteur /ɛkspɔrˈtøːɐ̯/ *der;* ~s, ~e, **Exporteurin** *die;* ~, ~nen (Wirtsch.) exporter

Export-: ~**firma** *die* exporter; ~**handel** *der* export trade

exportieren *tr., itr. V.* export

Express-gut, *Expreß-gut *das* express freight

Expressionismus *der;* ~: expressionism *no art.*

expressionistisch *Adj.* expressionist

exquisit 1 *Adj.* exquisite
2 *adv.* exquisitely

extern *Adj.* external

extra *Adv.* (a) (gesondert) ⟨*pay*⟩ separately
(b) (zusätzlich, besonders) extra
(c) (eigens) especially

Extra *das;* ~s, ~s extra

Extra-blatt *das* special edition

Extrakt *der;* ~[e]s, ~e extract

extra-terrestrisch *Adj.* (Astron.) extraterrestrial

extravagant /-vaˈgant/ *Adj.* flamboyant; flamboyantly furnished ⟨*flat*⟩

Extravaganz /-vaˈgants:/ *die;* ~, ~en
(a) flamboyance
(b) *Pl.* seine ~en his flamboyance *sing.*

extravertiert /-vɛrˈtiːɐ̯t/ *Adj.* (Psych.) extrovert[ed]

Extravertiertheit *die;* ~ (Psych.) extroversion

Extra-wurst *die* (fig. ugs.) eine ~ bekommen get special treatment *or* special favours

extrem *Adj.* extreme

Extrem *das;* ~s, ~e extreme

Extrem-fall *der* extreme case

Extremismus *der;* ~: extremism

Extremist *der;* ~en, ~en, **Extremistin** *die;* ~, ~nen extremist

extremistisch *Adj.* extremist

Extremität /ɛkstremiˈtɛːt/ *die;* ~, ~en
(a) extremity
(b) (das Extremsein) extremeness

Extrem-wert *der* (Math.) extremum

Exzellenz *die;* ~, ~en Excellency

Exzentriker *der;* ~s, ~, **Exzentrikerin** *die;* ~, ~nen eccentric

exzentrisch 1 *Adj.* eccentric
2 *adv.* eccentrically

Exzess, *Exzeß *der;* Exzesses, Exzesse excess

exzessiv /ɛksts:ɛˈsiːf/ 1 *Adj.* excessive
2 *adv.* excessively

Ff

f, F /ɛf/ *das;* ~, ~ (a) (Buchstabe) f/F
(b) (Musik) [key of] F

f. *Abk.* = **folgend** f.

Fa. *Abk.* = **Firma**

Fabel *die;* ~, ~n fable; (Kern einer Handlung) plot

fabelhaft 1 *Adj.* (ugs.: großartig) fantastic (coll.)
2 *adv.* (ugs.) fantastically (coll.)

Fabrik *die;* ~, ~en factory

Fabrikant *der;* ~en, ~en manufacturer

Fabrikat *das;* ~[e]s, ~e product; (Marke) make

Fabrikation *die;* ~: production

Fabrikations-fehler *der* manufacturing fault; factory fault

Fabrik-: ~**besitzer** *der,* ~**besitzerin** *die* factory owner; ~**direktor** *der,* ~**direktorin** *die* works manager

fabrizieren *tr. V.* (ugs. abwertend) knock together (coll.)

fabulieren *itr. V.* invent stories; spin yarns

Fach *das;* ~[e]s, Fächer (a) compartment; (für Post) pigeonhole
(b) (Studien~, Unterrichts~) subject; (Wissensgebiet) field; (Berufszweig) trade; **ein Mann vom** ~: an expert

Fach-: ~**arbeiter** *der,* ~**arbeiterin** *die* skilled worker; ~**arzt** *der,* ~**ärztin** *die* specialist (**für in**); ~**bereich** *der* (Hochschulw.) faculty; school; (in der Schule) department

fächer-übergreifend *Adj:*
▶ FACHÜBERGREIFEND

Fach-: ~**frau** *die* expert; ~**geschäft** *das* specialist shop; ~**hochschule** *die* college (*offering courses in a special subject*)

fachlich *Adj.* specialist ⟨*knowledge, work*⟩; technical ⟨*problem, explanation, experience*⟩

fach-, Fach-: ~**mann** *der; Pl.* ~**männer** *od.* ~**leute** expert; ~**terminus** *der* specialist/technical term; ~**übergreifend** [1] *Adj.* interdisciplinary ⟨*teaching*⟩; [2] *adv.* ⟨*think, argue*⟩ along interdisciplinary lines; ⟨*teach*⟩ using interdisciplinary methods; ~**werk** *das* (Bauweise) half-timbered construction; ~**werk·haus** *das* half-timbered house; ~**zeitschrift** *die* specialist/technical journal

Fackel *die:* ~, ~n torch

fade *Adj.* insipid; **ein** ~**r Beigeschmack** (fig.) a flat aftertaste

Faden *der;* ~**s, Fäden** thread; **ein** ~: a piece of thread

faden·scheinig *Adj.* threadbare; flimsy ⟨*excuse*⟩

Fagott *das;* ~[e]s, ~e bassoon

fähig *Adj.* (a) (begabt) able; capable (b) **zu etw.** ~ **sein** be capable of sth.

Fähigkeit *die;* ~, ~en (a) ability; capability; **geistige** ~**en** intellectual faculties (b) (Imstandesein) ability (zu to)

fahl *Adj.* pale; pallid; wan ⟨*light*⟩

fahnden *itr. V.* search (**nach** for)

Fahndung *die;* ~, ~en search

Fahne *die;* ~, ~n flag

Fahr·bahn *die* carriageway

Fähr·betrieb *der* ferry service; (von mehreren Fähren) ferry services *pl.*

Fähre *die;* ~, ~n ferry

fahren [1] *unr. itr. V.; mit sein* (a) (als Fahrzeuglenker) drive; (mit dem Fahrrad, Motorrad usw.) ride (b) (als Mitfahrer; mit öffentlichem Verkehrsmittel) go (**mit** by); (mit dem Aufzug/der Rolltreppe/der Seilbahn) take the lift (Brit.) *or* (Amer.) elevator/escalator/cable car; (per Anhalter) hitch-hike (c) (reisen) go; **in Urlaub** ~: go on holiday (d) (los~) go; leave (e) ⟨*motor vehicle, train, lift, cable car*⟩ go; ⟨*ship*⟩ sail; **mein Auto fährt nicht** my car won't go (f) (verkehren) ⟨*train etc.*⟩ run (g) **etw.** ~ **lassen** (loslassen) let sth. go; (fig.: aufgeben) abandon sth. [2] *unr. tr. V.* (a) (fortbewegen) drive ⟨*car, lorry, train, etc.*⟩; ride ⟨*bicycle, motor cycle*⟩ (b) **50/80 km/h** ~: do 50/80 k.p.h.; **hier muss man 50 km/h** ~: you've got to keep to 50 k.p.h. here; sail ⟨*boat*⟩; **Auto** ~: drive [a car]; **Kahn** *od.* **Boot/Kanu** ~: go boating/canoeing; **Ski** ~: ski; **U-Bahn** ~: ride on the underground (Brit.) *or* (Amer.) subway (c) (befördern) take

Fahrenheit: 70 Grad ~: 70 degrees Fahrenheit

Fahrer *der;* ~**s,** ~: driver

Fahrerflucht *die:* **wegen** ~: for failing to stop after [being involved in] an accident; ~ **begehen** fail to stop after [being involved in] an accident

Fahrerin *die;* ~, ~**nen** driver

Fahr-: ~**gast** *der* passenger; ~**geld** *das* fare

fahrig *Adj.* nervous

fahr-, Fahr-: ~**karte** *die* ticket; ~**karten·automat** *der* ticket machine; ~**karten·schalter** *der* ticket window; ~**lässig** [1] *Adj.* negligent ⟨*behaviour*⟩; ~**lässige Tötung/Körperverletzung** (Rechtsw.) causing death/injury through [culpable] negligence; [2] *adv.* negligently; ~**lehrer** *der,* ~**lehrerin** *die* driving instructor

Fähr·mann *der; Pl.* **Fährmänner** *od.* **Fährleute** ferryman

fahr-, Fahr-: ~**plan** *der* timetable; schedule (Amer.); ~**plan·mäßig** [1] *Adj.* scheduled ⟨*departure, arrival*⟩; [2] *adv.* ⟨*depart, arrive*⟩ according to schedule, on time; ~**preis** *der* fare; ~**prüfung** *die* driving test; ~**rad** *das* bicycle; cycle; **mit dem** ~**rad fahren** cycle; ride a bicycle; ~**rad·kurier** *der,* ~**rad·kurierin** *die* bicycle *or* bike messenger; bicycle *or* bike courier; ~**rad·ständer** *der* bicycle rack; ~**schein** *der* ticket; ~**schein·automat** *der* ticket machine; ~**schein·entwerter** *der* ticket cancelling machine; ~**schule** *die* driving school; ~**spur** *die* traffic lane

fährst *2. Pers. Sg. Präsens v.* FAHREN

Fahr-: ~**stuhl** *der* lift (Brit.); elevator (Amer.); (für Lasten) hoist; ~**stunde** *die* driving lesson

Fahrt *die;* ~, ~**en** (a) journey; **freie** ~ **haben** have a clear run; (Schiffsreise) voyage; (kurze Reise, Ausflug) trip (b) (Geschwindigkeit) **in voller** ~: at full speed

fährt *3. Pers. Sg. Präsens v.* FAHREN

Fährte *die* trail; **jmds.** ~ **verfolgen** track sb.

Fahrt·kosten *Pl.* (für öffentliche Verkehrsmittel) fare/fares; (für Autoreisen) travel costs

Fahr·treppe *die* escalator

Fahrt·richtung *die* direction; **in** ~ **parken** park in the direction of the traffic; **die** ~ **ändern** change direction

fahr·tüchtig *Adj.* ⟨*driver*⟩ fit to drive; ⟨*vehicle*⟩ roadworthy

Fahrt-: ~**wind** *der* airflow; ~**ziel** *das* destination

Fahr-: ~**wasser** *das* shipping channel; fairway; **in ein gefährliches** ~**wasser geraten** (fig.) get on to dangerous ground; ~**werk** *das* (Flugw.) undercarriage; ~**zeit** *die* travelling time; ~**zeug** (Luft~) aircraft; (Wasser~) vessel; ~**zeug·papiere** *Pl.* vehicle documents *pl.*

fair /fɛːɐ̯/ ① *Adj.* fair (**gegen** to)
② *adv.* fairly
Fäkalien /fɛːˈkaːli̯ən/ *Pl.* faeces *pl.*
Fakten ▸ FAKTUM
faktisch ① *Adj.* real; actual
② *adv.* **das bedeutet ~ ...**: it means in
effect ...
Faktor *der;* ~s, ~en (auch Math.) factor
Faktum *das;* ~s, **Fakten** fact
Fakultät *die;* ~, ~en (Hochschulw.) faculty
Falke *der;* ~n, ~n (auch Politik fig.) hawk
Fall *der;* ~[e]s, **Fälle (a)** (Sturz) fall; **zu ~
kommen** have a fall; **jmdn. zu ~ bringen** (fig.)
bring about sb.'s downfall
(b) (das Fallen) descent; **der freie ~:** free fall
(c) (Ereignis; Rechtsw., Med., Grammatik) case; (zu
erwartender Umstand) eventuality; **es ist [nicht]
der ~:** it is [not] the case; **gesetzt den ~:**
assuming; **auf jeden ~, in jedem ~, auf alle
Fälle** in any case; **auf keinen ~:** on no
account
Falle *die;* ~, ~n (auch fig.) trap
fallen *unr. itr. V.; mit sein* **(a)** fall; **jmdn./
etw. ~ lassen** drop sb./sth.
(b) (hin~, stürzen) fall [over]; **über einen Stein
~:** trip over a stone
(c) ⟨prices, light, glance, choice⟩ fall;
⟨temperature, water level⟩ fall, drop; ⟨fever⟩
subside; ⟨shot⟩ be fired
(d) (im Kampf sterben) die; fall (literary)
fällen *tr. V.* **(a)** fell ⟨tree, timber⟩
(b) **ein Urteil ~** ⟨judge⟩ pass sentence; ⟨jury⟩
return a verdict
*fallen|lassen ▸ FALLEN A
fällig *Adj.* due
Fall-obst *das* windfalls *pl.*
Fallout /fɔːlˈaʊt/ *der;* ~s, ~s (Kernphysik)
fallout
falls *Konj.* **(a)** (wenn) if
(b) (für den Fall, dass) in case
Fall-schirm *der* parachute; **mit dem ~
abspringen** (im Notfall) parachute out; (als
Sport) make a [parachute] jump
falsch ① *Adj.* **(a)** (unecht, imitiert) false ⟨teeth,
plait⟩; imitation ⟨jewellery⟩
(b) (gefälscht) forged; assumed ⟨name⟩
(c) (irrig, fehlerhaft) wrong
② *adv.* wrongly; **die Uhr geht ~:** the clock
is wrong
fälschen *tr. V.* forge
Fälscher *der;* ~s, ~, **Fälscherin** *die;* ~,
~nen forger
Falschgeld *das* counterfeit money
fälschlich ① *Adj.* false
② *adv.* falsely
Falsch-meldung *die* false report
Fälschung *die;* ~, ~en fake
Falt-blatt *das* leaflet; (in Zeitungen,
Zeitschriften, Büchern) insert
Falte *die;* ~, ~n **(a)** crease
(b) (im Stoff) fold; (mit scharfer Kante) pleat
(c) (Haut~) wrinkle

falten ① *tr. V.* fold; **die Hände ~:** fold one's
hands
② *refl. V.* (auch Geol.) fold; ⟨skin⟩ become
wrinkled
Falten-rock *der* pleated skirt
Falter *der;* ~s, ~ (Nacht~) moth; (Tag~)
butterfly
faltig (a) *Adj.* ⟨clothes⟩ gathered [in folds];
wrinkled ⟨skin, hands⟩
(b) (zerknittert) creased
-fältig *Adj., adv.* -fold
Falz *der;* ~es, ~e fold
falzen *tr. V.* fold; seam
familiär *Adj.* **(a)** family ⟨problems, worries⟩
(b) (zwanglos) familiar; informal
Familie /faˈmiːli̯ə/ *die;* ~, ~n family; ~
Meyer the Meyer family
Familien-: ~**angehörige** *der/die*
member of the family; ~**feier** *die* family
party; ~**grab** *das* family grave; ~**leben**
das family life; ~**name** *der* surname;
~**planung** *die* family planning *no art.;*
~**stand** *der* marital status; ~**vater** *der:*
~**vater sein** be the father of a family; **ein
guter ~vater** a good husband and father
Fan /fɛn/ *der;* ~s, ~s fan
Fanatiker *der;* ~s, ~, **Fanatikerin** *die;*
~, ~nen fanatic; (religiös) fanatic; zealot
fanatisch ① *Adj.* fanatical
② *adv.* fanatically
fanatisieren *tr. V.* rouse to fanaticism;
der fanatisierte Mob the fanatically excited
mob
fand *1. u. 3. Pers. Sg. Prät. v.* FINDEN
Fanfare *die;* ~, ~n (Signal) fanfare
Fang *der;* ~[e]s, **Fänge (a)** (Tier~) trapping;
(von Fischen) catching
(b) (Beute) bag; (von Fischen) catch
fangen ① *unr. tr. V.* catch; capture
⟨fugitive etc.⟩; **jmdn./ein Tier gefangen halten**
hold sb. prisoner/keep an animal in
captivity; **jmdn. gefangen nehmen** take sb.
prisoner
② *unr. refl. V.* **(a)** (in eine Falle geraten) be
caught
(b) (wieder in die normale Lage kommen) **sich
[gerade] noch ~:** [just] manage to steady
oneself
Fang-frage *die* catch question
Fantasie *die;* ~, ~n **(a)** imagination
(b) (Produkt der ~) fantasy
fantasie-los ① *Adj.* unimaginative
② *adv.* unimaginatively
Fantasielosigkeit *die;* ~: lack of
imagination; (Eintönigkeit) dullness
fantasieren *itr. V.* **(a)** indulge in
fantasies, fantasize (**von** about)
(b) (Med.: irrereden) talk deliriously.
fantasievoll ① *Adj.* imaginative
② *adv.* imaginatively
fantastisch ① *Adj.* **(a)** fantastic; ⟨idea⟩
divorced from reality
(b) (ugs.: großartig) fantastically (coll.)

Farb-: ~**bild** das (Foto) colour photo; ~**dia** das colour slide; ~**drucker** der (DV) colour printer

Farbe die; ~, ~n (a) colour
(b) (für Textilien) dye; (zum Malen, Anstreichen) paint; ~**n mischen/auftragen** mix/apply paint

farb-echt Adj. colour-fast

färben ① tr. V. dye
② refl. V. change colour; **sich schwarz/rot** usw. ~: turn black/red etc.
③ itr. V. (ugs.: ab~) ⟨material, blouse etc.⟩ run

-farben Adj. coloured

farben-, Farben-: ~**blind** Adj. colour-blind; ~**froh** Adj. colourful; ~**pracht** die colourful splendour; ~**prächtig** Adj. vibrant with colour postpos.

Farb-: ~**fernsehen** das colour television; ~**fernseher** der (ugs.) colour telly (coll.) or television; ~**film** der colour film; ~**foto** das colour photo

farbig ① Adj. (a) coloured
(b) (bunt, auch fig.) colourful
② adv. colourfully

-farbig Adj. -coloured

Farbige der/die; adj. Dekl. coloured man/woman; Pl. coloured people

farblich ① Adj. in colour postpos.; as regards colour postpos;
② adv. etw. ~ abstimmen match sth. in colour

farb-, Farb-: ~**los** Adj. (auch fig.) colourless; clear ⟨varnish⟩; neutral ⟨shoe polish⟩; ~**losigkeit** die; ~~ (auch fig.) colourlessness; ~**stift** der coloured pencil; ~**stoff** der (a) (Med., Biol.) pigment; (b) (für Textilien) dye; (c) (für Lebensmittel) colouring; ~**ton** der; Pl. ~**töne** shade; ~**tupfen,** ~**tupfer** der spot of colour

Färbung die; ~, ~en colouring

Farn der; ~[e]s, ~e, **Farn-kraut** das fern

Fasan der; ~[e]s, ~e[n] pheasant

Fasching der; ~s, ~e od. ~s [pre-Lent] carnival

Faschismus der; ~: fascism no art.

Faschist der; ~en, ~en, **Faschistin** die; ~, ~nen fascist

faschistisch Adj. fascist

faseln itr. V. (ugs. abwertend) drivel

Faser die; ~, ~n fibre

fasern itr. V. fray

Fass, *Faß das; Fasses, Fässer barrel; (Öl~) drum; (kleines Bier~) keg; (kleines Sherry~ usw.) cask; **Bier vom** ~: draught beer; **ein** ~ **ohne Boden** an endless drain on sb.'s resources

Fassade die; ~, ~n façade

fassbar, *faßbar Adj. (a) tangible ⟨results⟩

(b) (verständlich) comprehensible

Fass-bier, *Faß-bier das draught beer; beer on draught

fassen ① tr. V. (a) (greifen) grasp; take hold of
(b) (festnehmen) catch ⟨thief, culprit⟩
(c) (aufnehmen können) ⟨hall, tank⟩ hold
(d) (begreifen) **ich kann es nicht** ~: I cannot take it in
(e) **einen Entschluss** ~: make or take a decision
② itr. V. (greifen) **nach etw.** ~: reach for sth.; **in etw.** (Akk.) ~: put one's hand in sth.

fasslich, *faßlich Adj. comprehensible

Fasson /fa'sõ:/ die; ~, ~s style; shape

Fassung die; ~, ~en (a) (Form) version
(b) (Selbstbeherrschung) composure; **die** ~ **bewahren** keep one's composure; **die** ~ **verlieren** lose one's self-control; **jmdn. aus der** ~ **bringen** upset sb.
(c) (für Glühlampen) holder

fassungs-los Adj. stunned

fast Adv. almost; nearly; ~ **nie** hardly ever

fasten itr. V. fast

Fast-nacht die carnival; ~ **feiern** celebrate Shrovetide or the carnival

Fastnachts-: ~**brauch** der Shrovetide custom; ~**dienstag** der Shrove Tuesday; ~**zug** der carnival procession

faszinieren tr. V. fascinate

faszinierend ① Adj. fascinating
② adv. fascinatingly

fatal Adj. (a) (peinlich, misslich) awkward
(b) (verhängnisvoll) fatal

fauchen itr. V. ⟨cat⟩ hiss; ⟨tiger, person⟩ snarl

faul Adj. (a) (verdorben) rotten; bad ⟨food, tooth⟩; foul ⟨water, air⟩
(b) (träge) lazy

Fäule die; ~: foulness

faulen itr. V.; meist mit sein rot; ⟨water⟩ go foul; ⟨meat, fish⟩ go off

faulenzen itr. V. laze about; loaf about (derog.)

Faulenzer der; ~s, ~, **Faulenzerin** die; ~, ~nen idler; lazybones sing. (coll.)

Faulheit die; ~: laziness

faulig Adj. stagnating ⟨water⟩; ~ **schmecken/riechen** taste/smell off

Fäulnis die; ~: rottenness

Faul-: ~**pelz** der (fam.) lazybones sing. (coll.); ~**tier** das (a) (Zool.) sloth; (b) (ugs.: Faulenzer[in]) ▶ ~PELZ

Fauna die; ~, **Faunen** (Zool.) fauna

Faust die; ~, **Fäuste** fist; **eine** ~ **machen** clench one's fist; **das passt wie die** ~ **aufs Auge** (ugs.) (passt nicht) that clashes horribly; (passt) that matches perfectly; **auf eigene** ~: on one's own initiative

Fäustchen das; ~s, ~: **sich** (Dat.) **ins** ~ **lachen** laugh up one's sleeve

---

*alte Schreibung - vgl. Hinweis auf S. xiv

faust·dick *Adj.* as thick as a man's fist *postpos.;* (fig.) barefaced ⟨*lie*⟩

Fäustling *der;* ∼s, ∼e mitten

Faust·regel *die* rule of thumb

Favorit /favo'ri:t/ *der;* ∼en, ∼en, **Favoritin** *die;* ∼, ∼nen favourite

Fax *das;* ∼, ∼[e] fax

Fax·anschluss, *Fax·anschluß *der* fax line

faxen *tr. V.* fax

Faxen *Pl.* (ugs.) fooling around

Fax-: ∼**gerät** *das* fax machine; ∼**nachricht** *der* fax message; ∼**nummer** *die* fax number

Fazit *das;* ∼s, ∼s *od.* ∼e result

FCKW *Abk.* = **Fluorchlorkohlenwasserstoff** CFC

FCKW-frei *Adj* CFC-free

FDP, F.D.P. *Abk.* = **Freie Demokratische Partei**

Feature /'fi:tʃe/ *das;* ∼s, ∼s (Rundf., Ferns., Zeitungsw.) feature

Februar *der;* ∼[s], ∼e February

fechten *unr. itr., tr. V.* fence

Fechter *der;* ∼s, ∼, **Fechterin** *die;* ∼, ∼nen fencer

Feder *die;* ∼, ∼n (a) (Vogel∼) feather (b) (zum Schreiben) nib (c) (Technik) spring

feder-, Feder-: ∼**ball** *der* (a) (Spiel) badminton; (b) (Ball) shuttlecock; ∼**bett** *das* duvet (Brit.); stuffed quilt (Amer.); ∼**führend** *Adj.* in charge *postpos.;* ∼**halter** *der* fountain pen; ∼**leicht** *Adj.* ⟨*person*⟩ as light as a feather; featherweight ⟨*object*⟩; ∼**lesen** *das:* nicht viel ∼lesen[s] mit jmdm./etw. machen give sb./sth. short shrift

federn ① *itr. V.* ⟨*springboard, floor, etc.*⟩ be springy ② *tr. V.* (mit einer Federung versehen) spring; das Bett ist gut gefedert the bed is well-sprung

Federung *die;* ∼, ∼en (Kfz-W.) suspension

Fee *die;* ∼, ∼n fairy

Feedback /'fi:dbæk/ *das;* ∼s, ∼s feedback

Fege·feuer *das* purgatory

fegen ① *tr. V.* (a) (bes. nordd.: säubern) sweep (b) (schnell entfernen) brush ② *itr. V.* sweep up

Fehde *die;* ∼, ∼n feud

Fehde·hand·schuh *der* jmdm. den ∼ hinwerfen throw down the gauntlet to sb.

fehl *Adv.* ∼ am Platz[e] sein be out of place

Fehl·anzeige *die:* ∼! (ugs.) no chance! (coll.)

fehlen *itr. V.* (a) (nicht vorhanden sein) ihm fehlt das Geld he has no money (b) (ausbleiben) be absent

(d) (verschwunden sein) be missing; in der Kasse fehlt Geld money is missing from the till

(d) (vermisst werden) er/das wird mir ∼: I shall miss him/that

(e) (erforderlich sein) be needed; ihm ∼ noch zwei Punkte zum Sieg he needs only two points to win; es fehlte nicht viel, und ich wäre eingeschlafen I all but fell asleep

(f) *unpers.* (mangeln) es fehlt an Lehrern there is a lack of teachers

(g) (krank sein) was fehlt Ihnen? what seems to be the matter?; fehlt dir etwas? is there something wrong?

Fehl-: ∼**entscheidung** *die* wrong decision; ∼**entwicklung** *die* abortive development

Fehler *der;* ∼s, ∼ (a) (Irrtum) mistake; error; (Sport) fault (b) (schlechte Eigenschaft) fault

fehler·frei *Adj.* faultless

fehlerhaft *Adj.* faulty; defective; imperfect ⟨*pronunciation*⟩

Fehler·quelle *die* source of error

fehl-, Fehl-: ∼**geburt** *die* miscarriage; ∼**investition** *die* (bes. Wirtsch.) bad investment; ∼**planung** *die* [piece of] bad planning *no art.;* ∼**schlag** *der* failure; ∼|**schlagen** *unr. itr. V.; mit sein* fail; ∼**start** *der* (Leichtathletik) false start; ∼**tritt** *der* (fig. geh.) slip; ∼**urteil** *das* (a) (Rechtsw.) ein ∼urteil fällen ⟨*jury*⟩ return a wrong verdict; ⟨*judge*⟩ pass a wrong judgement (b) (falsche Beurteilung) error of judgement; ∼**verhalten** *das* (fehlerhaftes Verhalten) incorrect conduct; ∼**zündung** *die* (Technik) misfire

Feier *die;* ∼, ∼n (a) (Veranstaltung) party; (aus festlichem Anlass) celebration (b) (Zeremonie) ceremony

Feier·abend *der* (Arbeitsschluss) finishing time; nach ∼: after work; ∼ machen finish work

feierlich ① *Adj.* ceremonial ⟨*act etc.*⟩; solemn ⟨*silence*⟩ ② *adv.* solemnly; ceremoniously

Feierlichkeit *die;* ∼, ∼en (a) solemnity (b) (Veranstaltung) celebration

feiern ① *tr. V.* (a) celebrate ⟨*birthday, wedding, etc.*⟩ (b) acclaim ⟨*artist, sportsman, etc.*⟩ ② *itr. V.* celebrate

Feier·tag *der* holiday; ein gesetzlicher/kirchlicher ∼: a public holiday/religious festival

feig[e] ① *Adj.* cowardly ② *adv.* in a cowardly way

Feige *die;* ∼, ∼n fig

Feigheit *die;* ∼: cowardice

Feigling *der;* ∼s, ∼e coward

Feile *die;* ∼, ∼n file

feilen *tr., itr. V.* file

feilschen *itr. V.* haggle (um over)

fein ⓵ *Adj.* (a) fine; finely-ground ⟨*flour*⟩; finely-granulated ⟨*sugar*⟩
(b) (hochwertig) high-quality ⟨*fruit, soap, etc.*⟩; fine ⟨*silver, gold, etc.*⟩; fancy ⟨*cakes, pastries, etc.*⟩
(c) (ugs.: erfreulich) great (coll.)
(d) **sich ∼ machen** (ugs.) dress up
⓶ *adv.* **∼ [he]raus sein** (ugs.) be sitting pretty (coll.)

Feind *der;* ∼[e]s, ∼e, **Feindin** *die;* ∼, ∼nen enemy

feindlich ⓵ *Adj.* (a) hostile
(b) (Milit.) enemy ⟨*attack, activity*⟩
⓶ *adv.* in a hostile manner

Feindschaft *die;* ∼, ∼en enmity

feind·selig *Adj.* hostile

Feind·seligkeit *die;* ∼, ∼en hostility; ∼en (Milit.) hostilities

Feinheit *die;* ∼, ∼en (a) fineness; delicacy
(b) (Nuance) subtlety

fein-, Fein-: ∼**kost·geschäft** *das* delicatessen; **∼|**machen** ▶ FEIN 1D; ∼**schmecker** *der;* ∼∼s, ∼∼, ∼**schmeckerin** *die;* ∼∼, ∼∼nen gourmet; ∼**sinnig** *Adj.* sensitive and subtle; ∼**waschmittel** *das* mild detergent

feist *Adj.* (meist abwertend) fat

Feld *das;* ∼[e]s, ∼er (a) field
(b) (Sport: Spiel∼) pitch; field
(c) (auf Formularen) box; space; (auf Brettspielen) space; (auf dem Schachbrett) square
(d) (Tätigkeitsbereich) field; sphere

Feld-: ∼**herr** *der* (veralt.) commander; ∼**marschall** *der* Field Marshal; ∼**salat** *der* corn salad; ∼**stecher** *der;* ∼∼s, ∼∼ binoculars *pl.*; ∼**versuch** *der* (Wissensch.) field experiment; ∼**webel** *der;* ∼∼s, ∼∼ (Milit.) sergeant; ∼**weg** *der* path; track; ∼**zug** *der* (Milit., fig.) campaign

Felge *die;* ∼, ∼n [wheel] rim

Fell *das;* ∼[e]s, ∼e (a) (Haarkleid) fur; (Pferde∼, Hunde∼, Katzen∼) coat; (Schaf∼) fleece
(b) (Material) fur
(c) (abgezogen) hide; **ein dickes ∼ haben** (ugs.) be thick-skinned

Fels *der;* ∼en, ∼en rock

Felsen *der;* ∼s, ∼: rock; (an der Steilküste) cliff

felsen-, Felsen-: ∼**fest** *Adj.* firm; unshakeable ⟨*opinion, belief*⟩; ∼**küste** *die* rocky coast *or* coastline

felsig *Adj.* rocky

Fels-: ∼**spalte** *die* crevice [in the rock]; ∼**wand** *die* rock face

feminin *Adj.* feminine

Feminismus *der;* ∼: feminism *no art.*

Feminist *der;* ∼en, ∼en, **Feministin** *die;* ∼, ∼nen feminist

Fenchel *der;* ∼s fennel

Fenster *das;* ∼s, ∼: window

Fenster-: ∼**bank** *die Pl.* ∼bänke window sill; ∼**laden** *der* [window] shutter; ∼**leder** *das* wash leather; ∼**platz** *der* window seat; ∼**putzer** *der;* ∼∼s, ∼∼, ∼**putzerin** *die;* ∼∼, ∼∼nen window cleaner; ∼**rahmen** *der* window frame; ∼**scheibe** *die* window pane

Ferien /'feːriən/ *Pl.* holiday[s *pl.*] (Brit.); vacation (Amer.); **in die ∼ fahren** go on holiday/vacation; **∼ haben** have a *or* be on holiday/vacation

Ferien-: ∼**arbeit** *die* vacation work; **eine ∼arbeit** a vacation job; ∼**haus** *das* holiday house (Brit.); vacation house (Amer.); ∼**job** *der* vacation job; ∼**ort** *der* holiday resort (Brit.); vacation resort (Amer.); ∼**paradies** *das* holiday[maker's] paradise (Brit.); vacationer['s] paradise (Amer.); ∼**wohnung** *die* holiday flat *or* apartment (Brit.); vacation apartment (Amer.)

Ferkel *das;* ∼s, ∼: piglet

fern ⓵ *Adj.* distant; **jmdn./etw. ∼ halten** keep sb./sth. away
⓶ *adv.* **∼ von der Heimat** far from home
⓷ *Präp. mit Dat.* (geh.) far [away] from

fern-, Fern-: ∼**bedienung** *die* remote control; ∼|**bleiben** *unr. itr. V.; mit sein* (geh.) stay away

Ferne *die;* ∼, ∼n distance

ferner *Adv.* furthermore

fern-, Fern-: ∼**fahrer** *der*, ∼**fahrerin** *die* long-distance lorry driver (Brit.) *or* (Amer.) trucker; ∼**flug** *der* long-distance *or* long-haul flight; ∼**gelenkt** *Adj.* remote-controlled; ∼**gespräch** *das* long-distance call; ∼**gesteuert** *Adj.* ▶ ∼GELENKT; ∼**glas** *das* binoculars *pl.;* ∼|**halten** ▶ FERN 1; ∼**heizung** *die* district heating system; ∼**lenkung** *die* remote control; ∼**licht** *das* (Kfz-W.) full beam; ∼**melde-amt** *das* telephone exchange; ∼**ost:** **in/aus/nach ∼ost** in/from/to the Far East; ∼**rohr** *das* telescope; ∼**ruf** *der* telephone number; ∼**schreiben** *das* telex [message]; ∼**schreiber** *der* telex [machine]

Fernseh-: ∼**antenne** *die* television aerial (Brit.) *or* (Amer.) antenna; ∼**apparat** *der* television [set]

fern|sehen *unr. itr. V.* watch television

Fern·sehen *das;* ∼s television; **im ∼:** on television

Fern·seher *der;* ∼s, ∼ (ugs.) telly (Brit. coll.); TV

Fernseh-: ∼**gebühren** *Pl.* television licence fee; ∼**gerät** *das* television [set]; ∼**journalist** *der*, ∼**journalistin** *die* television reporter; ∼**kanal** *der* television channel; ∼**programm** *das* (a) (Sendungen) television programmes *pl.*; (b) (Kanal) television channel; (c) (Blatt, Programmheft) television [programme] guide; ∼**publikum** *das* viewing public; ∼**sender** *der*

**old spelling - see note on page xiv

television transmitter; **~sendung** *die* television programme; **~serie** *die* television series; **~spiel** *das* television play; **~zuschauer** *der*, **~zuschauerin** *die* television viewer

Fern·sicht *die* (Aussicht) view; (gute Sicht) visibility

Fern·sprecher *der* telephone

Fernsprech-: **~gebühren** *Pl.* telephone charges; **~teilnehmer** *der*, **~teilnehmerin** *die* telephone subscriber; telephone customer (Amer.)

Fern-: **~steuerung** *die* (Technik) remote control; **~straße** *die* major road; **~studium** *das* correspondence course; ≈ Open University course (Brit.); **~unterricht** *der* correspondence courses *pl.*; **~verkehr** *der* long-distance traffic; **~zug** *der* long-distance train

Ferse *die;* **~,** **~n** heel

fertig *Adj.* (a) finished ⟨*manuscript, picture, etc.*⟩; **das Essen ist ~:** lunch/dinner *etc.* is ready; [mit etw.] **~ sein/werden** have finished/finish [sth.]; **etw. ~ machen** finish sth. (b) (bereit, verfügbar) ready (**zu, für** for) (c) (ugs.: erschöpft) shattered (coll.); **jmdn. ~ machen** (erschöpfen) wear sb. out; (schikanieren) wear sb. down; (deprimieren) get sb. down (d) **etw. ~ bekommen** *od.* **bringen** *od.* (ugs.) **kriegen** manage sth; **etw. ~ stellen** complete sth.

fertig-, Fertig-: **~bau** *der; Pl.* **~~ten** prefabricated building; **~bauweise** *die* prefabricated construction; prefabrication; *****~|bringen** ▶ FERTIG D

fertigen *tr. V.* make

Fertig-: **~gericht** *das* ready-to-serve meal; **~haus** *das* prefabricated house; prefab (coll.)

Fertigkeit *die;* **~,** **~en** skill

fertig-, Fertig-: *****~|machen** ▶ FERTIG A, C; *****~|stellen** ▶ FERTIG D; **~stellung** *die* completion

Fertigung *die;* **~:** production; manufacture

Fessel *die;* **~,** **~n** fetter; shackle; (Kette) chain

fesseln *tr. V.* (a) tie up; **ans Bett/ans Haus/ an den Rollstuhl gefesselt sein** (fig.) be confined to [one's] bed/tied to the house/ confined to a wheelchair (b) (faszinieren) ⟨*book*⟩ grip; ⟨*work, person*⟩ fascinate

fesselnd ① *Adj.* compelling ② *adv.* compellingly

fest ① *Adj.* (a) (nicht flüssig *od.* gasförmig) solid (b) firm ⟨*bandage*⟩; sound ⟨*sleep*⟩; sturdy ⟨*shoes*⟩; strong ⟨*fabric*⟩; solid ⟨*house, shell*⟩; steady ⟨*voice*⟩; **der ~en Überzeugung sein, dass …:** be of the firm opinion that … (c) (dauernd) permanent ⟨*address*⟩; fixed ⟨*income*⟩ ② *adv.* (a) ⟨*tie, grip*⟩ tight[ly]

(b) (ugs. auch **~e**) ⟨*work*⟩ with a will; ⟨*eat*⟩ heartily; ⟨*sleep*⟩ soundly (c) ⟨*believe, be convinced*⟩ firmly; **sich auf jmdn./etw. ~ verlassen** rely one hundred per cent on sb./sth. (d) (endgültig) firmly; **etw. ~ vereinbaren** come to a firm arrangement about sth. (e) (auf Dauer) permanently; **~ befreundet sein** be close friends; (als Paar) be going steady

Fest *das;* **~[e]s,** **~e** (a) celebration; (Party) party (b) (Feiertag) festival; **frohes ~!** happy Christmas/Easter!

fest-, Fest-: **~akt** *der* ceremony; **~|binden** *unr. tr. V.* tie [up]; **~|bleiben** *unr. itr. V.; mit sein* stand firm; **~essen** *das* banquet; **~|fahren** *unr. itr., refl. V.* (itr. V. mit sein) get stuck; (fig.) get bogged down; **~|halten** ① *unr. tr. V.* (a) (halten, packen) hold on to; (b) (nicht weiterleiten) withhold ⟨*letter, parcel, etc.*⟩; (c) (verhaftet haben) hold, detain ⟨*suspect*⟩; ② *unr. refl. V.* **sich an jmdn./etw. ~halten** hold on to sb./sth.

festigen ① *tr. V.* strengthen; consolidate ⟨*position*⟩ ② *refl. V.* ⟨*friendship, ties*⟩ become stronger

Festival /'fɛstivl/ *das;* **~s,** **~s** festival

fest-, Fest-: **~|kleben** *tr., itr. V.; mit sein* stick (**an** + *Dat.* to); **~land** *das* (Kontinent) continent; (im Gegensatz zu den Inseln) mainland; **~|legen** *tr. V.* (a) fix ⟨*time, deadline, price*⟩; arrange ⟨*programme*⟩; (b) (verpflichten) **sich [auf etw. (***Akk.***)] ~legen** [lassen] commit oneself [to sth.]; **jmdn. [auf etw. (***Akk.***)] ~legen** tie sb. down [to sth.]

festlich ① *Adj.* festive ⟨*atmosphere*⟩; formal ⟨*dress*⟩ ② *adv.* festively; formally

fest-, Fest-: **~|machen** *tr. V.* (a) (befestigen) fix; (b) (fest vereinbaren) arrange ⟨*meeting etc.*⟩; **~|nageln** *tr. V.* (a) (befestigen) nail (**an** + *Dat.* to); (b) (ugs.: festlegen) **jmdn. [auf etw. (***Akk.***)] ~nageln** tie sb. down [to sth.]; **~nahme** *die;* **~~,** **~~n** arrest; **bei seiner ~nahme** when he was/is arrested; **~|nehmen** *unr. tr. V.* arrest; **~platte** *die* (DV) fixed disk; **~rede** *die* speech; **~|schnallen** *tr. V.* tie (**an** + *Dat.* to); **~|sitzen** *unr. itr. V.* be stuck; **~|stehen** *unr. itr. V.* ⟨*order, appointment, etc.*⟩ have been fixed; ⟨*decision*⟩ be definite; ⟨*fact*⟩ be certain; **~|stellen** *tr. V.* (a) establish ⟨*identity, age, facts*⟩; (b) (wahrnehmen) detect; diagnose ⟨*illness*⟩; **~stellung** *die* (a) establishment; (b) (Wahrnehmung) realization; **die ~stellung machen, dass …:** realize that …

Fest·tag *der* holiday; (Ehrentag) special day

Festung *die;* **~,** **~en** fortress

fest-, Fest-: **~zeit** *die* holiday (Brit.) *or* (Amer.) vacation [period]; **~zelt** *das* marquee; **~|ziehen** *unr. tr. V.* pull tight

Fete *die;* **~,** **~n** (ugs.) party

fẹtt 1 *Adj.* (a) fatty ‹*food*›; ~**er Speck** fat
bacon
(b) (sehr dick) fat
(c) (Druckw.) bold
2 *adv.* (a) ~ **essen** eat fatty foods
(b) ~ **gedruckt** bold

Fẹtt *das;* ~[e]s, ~e fat; ~ **ansetzen** ‹*animal*›
fatten up; ‹*person*› put on weight

fẹtt-, Fẹtt-: ~**arm** *Adj.* low-fat ‹*food*›; low
in fat *pred.;* ~**auge** *das* speck of fat;
~**creme** *die* enriched [skim] cream;
~**druck** *der* bold type; ~**fleck[en]** *der*
grease mark; *~**gedruckt** ▶ FETT 2B;
~**gehalt** *der* fat content

fẹttig *Adj.* greasy

fẹtt-, Fẹtt-: ~**leibig** *Adj.* obese;
~**leibigkeit** *die;* ~~: obesity;
~**näpfchen** *das:* ins ~**näpfchen treten**
(scherzh.) put one's foot in it; ~**polster** *das*
subcutaneous fat *no indef. art.;* fat pad;
~**reich** *Adj.* high-fat; ~**säure** *die* (Chemie)
fatty‿acid; ~**wanst** *der* (salopp abwertend)
fatso (coll.)

Fẹtus *der;* ~ *od.* ~**ses**, ~**se** *od.* **Fẹten** (Med.)
foetus

Fẹtzen *der;* ~**s**, ~: scrap

feucht *Adj.* damp; humid ‹*climate*›

feucht‑fröhlich *Adj.* (ugs. scherzh.) merry
‹*company*›; boozy (coll.) ‹*evening*›

Feuchtigkeit *die* moisture

Feuchtigkeits‑creme *die* (Kosmetik)
moisturizing cream; moisturizer

feucht-: ~**kalt** *Adj.* cold and damp;
~**warm** *Adj.* muggy

feudal *Adj.* (a) feudal ‹*system*›
(b) aristocratic ‹*regiment etc.*›
(c) (ugs.: vornehm) plush ‹*hotel etc.*›

Feuer *das;* ~**s**, ~ (a) fire; jmdm. ~ **geben**
give sb. a light
(b) (Brand) fire; blaze; ~**!** fire!
(c) (Milit.) das ~ **einstellen** cease fire

feuer-, Feuer-: ~**alarm** *der* fire alarm;
~**eifer** *der* enthusiasm; zest; ~**fest** *Adj.*
heat-resistant ‹*dish, plate*›; fireproof
‹*material*›; ~**gefährlich** *Adj.*
[in]flammable; ~**holz** *das* firewood;
~**leiter** *die* (bei Häusern) fire escape; (beim
~wehrauto) [fireman's] ladder; ~**löscher**
der; ~~**s**, ~~: fire extinguisher;
~**melder** *der;* ~~**s**, ~~: fire alarm

feuern 1 *tr. V.* (a) (ugs.: entlassen) fire (coll.);
sack (coll.)
(b) (ugs.: schleudern, werfen) fling
2 *itr. V.* (Milit.) fire (**auf** + *Akk.* at)

feuer-, Feuer-: ~**rot** *Adj.* fiery red;
~**schlucker** *der,* ~**schluckerin** *die;*
~~, ~~**nen** fire-eater; ~**sirene** *die* fire
siren; ~**stein** *der* flint; ~**versicherung**
die fire insurance; ~**waffe** *die* firearm;
~**wehr** *die;* ~~, ~~**en** fire service;
~**wehr‑auto** *das* fire engine;
~**wehr‑mann** *der; Pl.* ~**männer** *od.*

~**leute** fireman; ~**wehr‑wagen** *der* fire
engine; ~**werk** *das* firework display;
(~werkskörper) fireworks *pl.;*
~**werks‑körper** *der* firework; ~**zeug**
das lighter

Feuilleton /fœjə'tõ:/ *das;* ~**s**, ~**s** arts
section

feurig *Adj.* fiery

ff. *Abk.* = **folgende [Seiten]** ff.

Ffm. *Abk.* = **Frankfurt am Main**

Fiaker /'fi̯akɐ/ *der;* ~**s**, ~ (österr.) cab

Fiasko *das;* ~**s**, ~**s** fiasco

Fibel *die;* ~, ~**n** reader; primer

ficht /fɪçt/ *Imperativ Sg. u. 3. Pers. Sg.*
Präsens v. FECHTEN

Fichte *die;* ~, ~**n** spruce

ficken *tr., itr. V.* (vulg.) fuck (coarse)

fick[e]rig *Adj.* (landsch.: nervös) nervous

fidel *Adj.* (ugs.) jolly

Fieber *das;* ~**s** [high] temperature; (über
38°C) fever; ~ **haben** have a [high]
temperature/a fever; **bei jmdm.** ~ **messen**
take sb.'s temperature

fieber‑frei *Adj.* ‹*person*› free from fever

fieberhaft *Adj.* feverish

fieberig *Adj.* feverish

fiebern *itr. V.* have a temperature

Fieber‑thermometer *das* [clinical]
thermometer

fiebrig *Adj.* feverish

Fiedel *die;* ~, ~**n** (veralt., scherzh.) fiddle

fiel *1. u. 3. Pers. Sg. Prät. v.* FALLEN

fiepen *itr. V.* ‹*dog*› whimper; ‹*bird*› cheep

fies 1 *Adj.* (ugs.) nasty ‹*person, character*›
2 *adv.* in a nasty way

Figur *die;* ~, ~**en** (a) (einer Frau) figure; (eines
Mannes) physique
(b) (Bildwerk) figure
(c) (geometrisches Gebilde) shape
(d) (Spielstein) piece
(e) (Persönlichkeit) figure
(f) (literarische Gestalt) character

fiktiv *Adj.* fictitious

Filet /fi'le:/ *das;* ~**s**, ~**s** fillet

Filiale *die;* ~, ~**n** branch

Filigran *das;* ~**s**, ~**e** filigree

Film *der;* ~[e]s, ~**e** (a) (Fot.) film
(b) (Kino~) film; movie (Amer. coll.)

Filme‑macher *der,* **Filme‑macherin**
die film-maker

filmen *tr., itr. V.* film

Film-: ~**festival** *das* film festival;
~**festspiele** *Pl.* film festival *sing.;*
~**industrie** *die* film industry; ~**kamera**
die film camera; (Schmalfilmkamera) cine
camera; ~**kunst** *die* cinematic art;
~**musik** *die* film music; (eines einzelnen ~s)
theme music; ~**plakat** *das* film poster;
~**produzent** *der,* ~**produzentin** *die*
film producer; ~**regisseur** *der,*
~**regisseurin** *die* film director;

~**schauspieler** *der*,
~**schauspielerin** *die* film actor; ~**star**
der film star

Filter *der*, ~s, ~: filter

filtern *tr. V.* filter

Filter-: ~**papier** *das* filter paper;
~**zigarette** *die* [filter-]tipped cigarette

Filz *der*; ~es, ~e felt

filzen *tr. V.* (ugs.: durchsuchen) search ⟨room,
car, etc.⟩; frisk ⟨person⟩

Filz·stift *der* felt-tip pen

Fimmel *der*; ~s, ~: einen ~ für etw. haben
(ugs. abwertend) have a thing about sth. (coll.)

Finale *das*; ~s, ~[s] (a) (Sport) final
(b) finale

Finalist *der*; ~en, ~en, **Finalistin** *die*;
~, ~nen (Sport) finalist

Finanz *die*; ~: finance *no art.*

Finanz-: ~**amt** *das* (a) (Behörde) ≈ Inland
Revenue; (b) (Gebäude) tax office;
~**beamte** *der*, ~**beamtin** *die* tax officer

Finanzen *Pl.* finances

finanziell /finan'ts:iɛl/ *Adj.* financial

finanzieren *tr. V.* finance

Finanzierung *die*; ~, ~en financing

finanz-, Finanz-: ~**kraft** *die* financial
strength; ~**kräftig** *Adj.* financially
powerful; ~**lage** *die* financial situation;
~**minister** *der*, ~**ministerin** *die*
minister of finance; ~**politik** *die* (des
Staates, eines Unternehmens) financial policy;
(allgemeine) politics of finance

Findel·kind *das* foundling

finden *unr. tr. V.* (a) find
(b) Freunde ~: make friends
(c) (einschätzen, beurteilen) etw. gut/richtig ~:
think sth. is good/right; wie ~ Sie dieses
Bild? what do you think of this painting?

Finder *der*; ~s, ~: finder

Finder·lohn *der* reward [for finding sth.]

findig *Adj.* resourceful

Findling *der*; ~s, ~e (a) (Findelkind)
foundling
(b) (Geol.) erratic block

fing *1. u. 3. Pers. Sg. Prät. v.* FANGEN

Finger *der*; ~s, ~: finger; lange ~ machen
(ugs.) get itchy fingers

Finger-: ~**abdruck** *der* fingerprint;
~**fertigkeit** *die* dexterity;
~**handschuh** *der* glove [with fingers];
~**hut** *der* thimble; ~**kuppe** *die* fingertip

fingern *itr. V.* fiddle; an etw. (*Dat.*) ~:
fiddle with sth.; nach etw. ~: fumble
[around] for sth.

Finger-: ~**nagel** *der* fingernail; ~**spitze**
die fingertip; ~**spitzen·gefühl** *das*
feeling

fingieren *tr. V.* fake; ein fingierter Name a
false name

Fink *der*; ~en, ~en finch

Finne *der*; ~n, ~n, **Finnin** *die*; ~, ~nen
Finn

finnisch *Adj.* Finnish

Finnland *(das)*; ~s Finland

finster ① *Adj.* dark; dimly-lit ⟨pub,
district⟩
② *adv.* jmdn. ~ ansehen give sb. a black
look

Finsternis *die*; ~, ~se darkness; (auch bibl.,
fig.) dark

Finte *die*; ~, ~n trick; jmdn. durch eine ~
täuschen deceive sb. by trickery

Firlefanz *der*; ~es (ugs. abwertend) frippery;
trumpery

firm *Adj.* in etw. (*Dat.*) ~ sein be well up in
sth.

Firma *die*; ~, Firmen firm; company

Firmen-: ~**inhaber** *der*, ~**inhaberin**
die owner of the/a company; ~**schild** *das*
company's name plate; ~**zeichen** *das*
trademark

Firmung *die*; ~, ~en confirmation

First *der*; ~[e]s, ~e ridge

Fisch *der*; ~[e]s, ~e (a) fish; [fünf] ~e
fangen catch [five] fish; kleine ~e (fig.) small
fry
(b) (Astrol.) die ~e Pisces; er ist [ein] ~: he is
a Piscean

fischen ① *tr. V.* (a) fish for
(b) (ugs.) etw. aus etw. ~: fish sth. out of sth.
② *itr. V.* fish; nach etw. ~: fish for sth.

Fischer *der*; ~s, ~: fisherman

Fischer-: ~**boot** *das* fishing boat; ~**dorf**
das fishing village

Fischerei *die*; ~: fishing

Fischerin *die*; ~, ~nen fisherwoman

Fisch-: ~**fang** *der*: vom ~fang leben
make a/one's living by fishing; auf ~fang
gehen go fishing; ~**geschäft** *das*
fishmonger's [shop] (Brit.); fish store (Amer.);
~**grät[en]·muster** *das* (Textilw.)
herringbone pattern; ~**industrie** *die*
fishing industry; ~**konserve** *die* canned
fish; ~**kutter** *der* fishing trawler;
~**stäbchen** *das* (Kochk.) fish finger;
~**sterben** *das* death of the fish

Fiskus *der*; ~, Fisken *od.* ~se Government
(*as managing the State finances*)

Fitness-zentrum *das* fitness centre

Fittich *der*; ~[e]s, ~e (dichter.) wing

fix ① *Adj.* (ugs.) quick; ein ~er Bursche a
bright lad; ~ und fertig quite finished; (völlig
erschöpft) completely shattered (coll.)
② *adv.* (ugs.) quickly; mach ~! hurry up!

fixen *itr. V.* (Drogenjargon) fix (sl.)

Fixer *der*; ~s, ~, **Fixerin** *die*; ~, ~nen
(Drogenjargon) fixer

fixieren *tr. V.* (a) fix one's gaze on; jmdn.
scharf ~: gaze sharply at sb.
(b) (geh.: schriftlich niederlegen) take down

Fix·stern *der* (Astron.) fixed star

Fjord /fjɔrt/ *der*; ~[e]s, ~e fiord

FKK /ɛf ka: 'ka:/ *Abk.*
= **Freikörperkultur** nudism *no art.;*
naturism *no art.*

FKK-Strand *der* nudist beach

flach *Adj.* (a) flat
(b) (niedrig) low
(c) (nicht tief) shallow ⟨water, dish⟩

Fläche *die;* ~, ~n (a) area
(b) (Ober~) surface
(c) (Geom.) area; (einer dreidimensionalen Figur)
side

Flächen-: ~**inhalt** *der* area; ~**maß** *das*
unit of square measure; ~**staat** *der*
territorial state

flach, Flach-: ~|**fallen** *itr. V.; mit sein*
(ugs.) ⟨trip⟩ fall through; ⟨event⟩ be cancelled;
~**land** *das* lowland

Flachs *der;* ~es flax

flachsen *itr. V.* mit jmdm. ~ (ugs.) joke
with sb.

Flach·zange *die* flat tongs *pl.*

flackern *itr. V.* flicker

Fladen *der;* ~s, ~: *flat, round unleavened
cake made with oat or barley flour*

Flagge *die;* ~, ~n flag

flaggen *itr. V.* put out the flags

flambieren *tr. V.* (Kochk.) flambé

Flamme *die;* ~, ~n (a) flame
(b) (Brennstelle) burner

Flanell *der;* ~s, ~e flannel

flanieren *itr. V.; mit Richtungsangabe mit
sein* stroll

Flanke *die;* ~, ~n (a) (Weiche) flank
(b) (Ballspiele: Vorlage) centre
(c) (Teil des Spielfeldes) wing

Flasche *die;* ~, ~n bottle; eine ~ Wein a
bottle of wine; dem Kind die ~ geben feed
the baby

Flaschen-: ~**bier** *das* bottled beer;
~**öffner** *der* bottle-opener; ~**post** *die*
message in a/the bottle; ~**zug** *der* block and
tackle

flatterhaft *Adj.* fickle

flattern *itr. V.; mit Richtungsangabe mit
sein* flutter

flau *Adj.* (a) slack ⟨breeze⟩
(b) (leicht übel) queasy ⟨feeling⟩

Flaum *der;* ~[e]s fuzz

Flausch *der;* ~[e]s, ~e brushed wool

flauschig *Adj.* fluffy

Flause *die;* ~, ~n; *meist Pl.* (ugs.) er hat nur
~n im Kopf he can never think of anything
sensible

Flaute *die;* ~, ~n (a) (Seemannsspr.) calm
(b) (Kaufmannsspr.) fall[-off] in trade

Flechte *die;* ~, ~n (a) (Bot.) lichen
(b) (Med.) eczema

flechten *unr. tr. V.* plait ⟨hair⟩; weave
⟨basket, mat⟩

Fleck *der;* ~[e]s, ~e (a) stain

---
*old spelling - see note on page xiv

(b) (andersfarbige Stelle) patch

flecken *itr. V.* stain

flecken·los ① *Adj.* spotless
② *adv.* spotlessly

Fleck·entferner *der* stain or spot
remover

fleckig *Adj.* stained; blotchy ⟨face, skin⟩

Fleder·maus *die* bat

Flegel *der;* ~s, ~ (abwertend) lout

Flegelei *die;* ~, ~en (abwertend) loutish
behaviour

flegelhaft *Adj.* (abwertend) loutish

flegeln *refl. V.* (abwertend) sich auf ein Sofa/
in einen Sessel ~: flop on to a sofa/into an
armchair

flehen /'fle:ən/ *itr. V.* plead (um for)

Fleisch *das;* ~[e]s (a) flesh; ~ fressend
(Biol.) carnivorous
(b) (Nahrungsmittel) meat

Fleisch·brühe *die* bouillon; consommé

Fleischer *der;* ~s, ~: butcher

Fleischerei *die;* ~, ~en butcher's shop

fleisch·fressend *Adj.* carnivorous

Fleisch·fresser *der* (Biol.) carnivore

fleischig *Adj.* plump ⟨hands, face⟩; fleshy
⟨leaf, fruit⟩

Fleisch-: ~**käse** *der;* ~~s, ~~: meat
loaf; ~**klößchen** *das;* ~~s, ~~: small
meat ball; ~**pastete** *die* (Kochk.) pâté;
~**salat** *der* (Kochk.) meat salad;
~**vergiftung** *die* food poisoning [from
meat]; ~**waren** *Pl.* meat products; ~**wolf**
der mincer; ~**wunde** *die* flesh wound;
~**wurst** *die* pork sausage

Fleiß *der;* ~es hard work; (Eigenschaft)
diligence

fleißig ① *Adj.* hard-working
② *adv.* hard; ~ lernen learn as much as one
can

flennen *itr. V.* (ugs.) blubber

fletschen *tr., itr. V.* die Zähne od. mit den
Zähnen ~: bare one's teeth

Fleurop Ⓦ /'flɔy:rɔp/ *die* Interflora ®

flexibel ① *Adj.* flexible
② *adv.* flexibly

flicht *Imperativ Sg. u. 3. Pers. Sg. Präsens v.*
FLECHTEN

flicken *tr. V.* mend; repair ⟨engine, cable⟩

Flicken *der;* ~s, ~: patch

Flick-: ~**werk** *das* (abwertend) botched-up
job; ~**zeug** *das* repair kit

Flieder *der;* ~s, ~: lilac

Fliege *die;* ~, ~n (a) fly
(b) (Schleife) bow tie

fliegen ① *unr. itr. V.; mit sein* (a) fly
(b) (ugs.: fallen) vom Pferd/Fahrrad ~: fall off
a/the horse/bicycle
(c) (ugs.: entlassen werden) get the sack (coll.);
von der Schule ~: be chucked out [of the
school] (coll.)
② *unr. tr. V.* fly

Fliegen-: ~**draht** der fly screen;
~**fenster** das wire-mesh window;
~**gewicht** das (Schwerathletik) flyweight;
~**pilz** der fly agaric

Flieger der; ~s, ~: pilot

Flieger·alarm der air-raid warning

Fliegerin die; ~, ~nen pilot

fliegerisch Adj. aeronautical

fliehen /'fliːən/ unr. itr. V.; mit sein flee
(vor + Dat. from); (aus dem Gefängnis usw.)
escape (aus from); **ins Ausland/über die
Grenze** ~: flee the country/escape over the
border

Flieh·kraft die (Physik) centrifugal force

Fliese die; ~, ~n tile

Fließ·band das conveyor belt; **am** ~
arbeiten od. (ugs.) **stehen** work on the
assembly line

fließen unr. itr. V.; mit sein flow; ~**des
Wasser** running water; **eine Sprache** ~**d
sprechen** speak a language fluently

Flimmer·kasten der, **Flimmer·kiste**
die (ugs.) telly (coll.); box (coll.)

flimmern itr. V. shimmer

flink [1] Adj. nimble ⟨fingers⟩; sharp ⟨eyes⟩;
quick ⟨hands⟩
[2] adv. quickly

Flinkheit die; ~ ▶ FLINK 1: nimbleness;
sharpness; quickness

Flinte die; ~, ~n shotgun; **die** ~ **ins Korn
werfen** (fig.) throw in the towel

Flirt der; ~s, ~s flirtation

flirten itr. V. flirt

Flittchen das; ~s, ~ (ugs. abwertend)
floozie

Flitter der; ~s frippery; trumpery

Flitter·wochen Pl. honeymoon sing.

flitzen itr. V.; mit sein (ugs.) shoot; dart

Flitzer der; ~s, ~ (ugs.) sporty job (coll.)

floaten /'floʊtn/ tr., itr. V. (Wirtsch.) float

flocht 1. u. 3. Pers. Sg. Prät. v. FLECHTEN

Flocke die; ~, ~n (a) flake
(b) (Staub~) piece of fluff

flockig Adj. fluffy

flog 1. u. 3. Pers. Sg. Prät. v. FLIEGEN

floh 1. u. 3. Pers. Sg. Prät. v. FLIEHEN

Floh der; ~[e]s, Flöhe flea

Floh-: ~**markt** der flea market; ~**zirkus**
der flea circus

Flora die; ~, Floren flora

Florett das; ~[e]s, ~e foil

florieren itr. V. flourish

Florist der; ~en, ~en, **Floristin** die; ~,
~nen [qualified] flower arranger

Floskel die; ~, ~n cliché

floss 1. u. 3. Pers. Sg. Prät. v. FLIESSEN

Floß das; ~es, Flöße raft

Flosse die; ~, ~n (a) (Zool., Flugw.) fin
(b) (zum Tauchen) flipper

flößen tr., itr. V. float

Flößer der; ~s, ~: raftsman

Flößerin die; ~, ~nen raftswoman

Flöte die; ~, ~n flute; (Block~) recorder

flöten [1] itr. V. ⟨bird⟩ flute; ~ **gehen** (ugs.)
⟨money⟩ go down the drain; ⟨time⟩ be wasted
[2] tr. V. whistle

***flöten|gehen** ▶ FLÖTEN 1

flott [1] Adj. (a) (schwungvoll) lively
(b) (schick) smart
[2] adv. ⟨work⟩ quickly; ⟨dance, write⟩ in a
lively manner; ⟨be dressed⟩ smartly

Flotte die; ~, ~n fleet

flott|machen tr. V. refloat ⟨ship⟩; get
⟨car⟩ back on the road

Flöz das; ~es, ~e (Bergbau) seam

Fluch der; ~[e]s, Flüche curse; oath

fluchen itr. V. curse; swear

Flucht die; ~: flight

flucht·artig [1] Adj. hurried; hasty
[2] adv. hurriedly; hastily

flüchten [1] itr. V.; mit sein **vor jmdm./etw.**
~: flee from sb./sth.; **vor der Polizei** ~: run
away from the police
[2] refl. V. take refuge

Flucht-: ~**fahrzeug** das getaway vehicle;
~**helfer** der, ~**helferin** die person who
aids/aided an/the escape; ~**hilfe** die aiding
an escape

flüchtig [1] Adj. (a) fugitive
(b) cursory; superficial ⟨insight⟩
[2] adv. (a) (oberflächlich) cursorily
(b) (eilig) hurriedly

Flüchtigkeit die; ~, ~en cursoriness

Flüchtigkeits·fehler der slip

Flüchtling der; ~s, ~e refugee

Flüchtlings-: ~**elend** das hardship
among refugees; ~**hilfe** die refugee relief;
(Organisation) refugee relief agency; ~**lager**
das refugee camp; ~**treck** der long stream
of refugees

Flucht·weg der escape route

Flug der; ~[e]s, Flüge flight

Flug-: ~**bahn** die trajectory; ~**blatt** das
pamphlet; leaflet

Flügel der; ~s, ~ (a) wing
(b) (Klavier) grand piano

Flügel·mutter die; Pl. ~n wing nut

Flug·gast der [air] passenger

flügge Adj. fully-fledged

Flug-: ~**gesellschaft** die airline;
~**hafen** der airport; ~**hafen·steuer** die
airport tax; ~**linie** die (a) (Strecke) air
route; (b) (Gesellschaft) airline; ~**lotse** der,
~**lotsin** die air traffic controller; ~**platz**
der airfield; ~**schein** der air ticket;
~**schreiber** der flight recorder;
~**verbindung** die air connection;
~**verkehr** der air traffic

Flug·zeug das aeroplane (Brit.); airplane
(Amer.); aircraft

Flugzeug-: ~**absturz** der plane crash;
~**entführer** der, ~**entführerin** die   ···⊹

[aircraft] hijacker; ~**entführung** *die*
[aircraft] hijack[ing]; ~**katastrophe** *die*
air disaster; ~**träger** *der* aircraft carrier

Flunder *die;* ~, ~n flounder

flunkern *itr. V.* tell stories

Fluor *das;* ~s (Chemie) fluorine

Fluor·chlor·kohlen·wasserstoff *der*
(Chemie) chlorofluorocarbon

Flur¹ *der;* ~[e]s, ~e (Korridor) corridor; (Diele)
[entrance] hall; **im/auf dem** ~: in the
corridor/hall

Flur² *die;* ~, ~en farmland *no indef. art.*

Fluss, *Fluß *der;* Flusses, Flüsse river;
(fließende Bewegung) flow

fluss-, *fluß-, Fluss-, *Fluß-:
~**ab[wärts]** *Adv.* downstream;
~**auf[wärts]** *Adv.* upstream; ~**bett** *das*
river bed

Flüsschen, *Flüßchen *das;* ~s, ~:
small river

Fluss·diagramm *das* (DV, Arbeitswiss.) flow
chart

flüssig ☐ *Adj.* (a) liquid
(b) (fließend, geläufig) fluent
(c) **einen Betrag** ~ **machen** make a sum of
money available
☐ *adv.* ⟨write, speak⟩ fluently

Flüssig·gas *das* liquid gas

Flüssigkeit *die;* ~, ~en (a) liquid; (auch
Gas) fluid
(b) (Geläufigkeit) fluency

Flüssig·kristall·anzeige *die* (Technik)
liquid crystal display

*flüssig|machen ▶ FLÜSSIG 1c

Fluss·pferd, *Fluß·pferd *das*
hippopotamus

flüstern *itr., tr. V.* whisper

Flut *die;* ~, ~en (a) tide
(b) (geh.: Wassermasse) flood

fluten *itr. V.; mit sein* (geh.) flood

Flut·licht *das* floodlight

focht *1. u. 3. Pers. Sg. Prät. v.* FECHTEN

Föderalismus *der;* ~: federalism *no art.*

föderalistisch *Adj.* federalist

Fohlen *das;* ~s, ~: foal

Föhn *der;* ~[e]s, ~e (a) föhn
(b) (Haartrockner) hair-drier

föhnen *tr. V.* blow-dry

Folge *die;* ~, ~n (a) (Auswirkung)
consequence; (Ergebnis) consequence; result
(b) (Aufeinander~) succession;
(zusammengehörend) sequence
(c) (Fortsetzung) (einer Sendung) episode; (eines
Romans) instalment

Folge·erscheinung *die* consequence

folgen *itr. V.; mit sein* follow; **jmdm. im Amt/**
in der Regierung ~: succeed sb. in office/in
government; **auf etw.** (*Akk.*) ~: follow sth.;
aus etw. ~: follow from sth.

folgend *Adj.* following; **der/die/das**

Folgende the next in order; **im Folgenden** *od.*
in Folgendem in [the course of] the following
discussion/passage *etc.*

folgendermaßen *Adv.* as follows; (so) in
the following way

folge·richtig ☐ *Adj.* logical; consistent
⟨behaviour, action⟩
☐ *adv.* logically; ⟨act, behave⟩ consistently

Folge·richtigkeit *die* (einer Entscheidung,
Schlussfolgerung) logicality; (eines Verhaltens, einer
Handlung) consistency

folgern ☐ *tr. V.* etw. aus etw. ~: infer sth.
from sth.
☐ *itr. V.* **richtig** ~: draw a/the correct
conclusion

Folgerung *die;* ~, ~en conclusion

Folge·schaden *der* (a) damaging after-
effects
(b) (Versicherungsw.) consequential damage

folglich *Adv.* consequently

folgsam ☐ *Adj.* obedient
☐ *adv.* obediently

Folgsamkeit *die;* ~: obedience

Folie /'fo:liə/ *die;* ~, ~n (Metall~) foil;
(Plastik~) film

Folklore *die;* ~ (a) folklore
(b) (Musik) folk music

folkloristisch ☐ *Adj.* folkloric
☐ *adv.* in a folkloric way

Folter *die;* ~, ~n torture; **jmdn. auf die** ~
spannen (fig.) keep sb. in an agony of
suspense

Folterer *der;* ~s, ~, **Folterin** *die;* ~,
~nen torturer

foltern *tr. V.* torture; (fig.) torment

Folterung *die;* ~, ~en torture

Fön (Ⓦ) *der;* ~[e]s, ~e hairdrier

Fond /fõ:/ *der;* ~s, ~s (geh.) back

Fonds /fõ:/ *der;* ~ /fõ:(s),/ ~ /fõ:s/ fund

Fondue /fõ'dy:/ *die;* ~, ~s *od. das;* ~s, ~s
(Kochk.) fondue

*fönen ▶ FÖHNEN

Fontäne *die;* ~, ~n jet; (Springbrunnen)
fountain

forcieren /fɔr'si:rən/ *tr. V.* step up
⟨production⟩; intensify ⟨efforts⟩; push
forward ⟨developments⟩

Förderer *der;* ~s, ~: patron

Förderin *die;* ~, ~nen patroness

fordern *tr. V.* (a) demand
(b) (in Anspruch nehmen) make demands on

fördern *tr. V.* (a) promote; patronize,
support ⟨artist, art⟩; further ⟨investigation⟩;
foster ⟨talent, tendency⟩; improve ⟨appetite⟩;
aid ⟨digestion, sleep⟩
(b) (Bergbau, Technik) mine ⟨coal, ore⟩; extract
⟨oil⟩

Forderung *die;* ~, ~en (a) demand
(b) (Kaufmannsspr.) claim (an + *Akk.* against)

Förderung *die;* ~, ~en (a) ▶ FÖRDERN A:
promotion; patronage; support; furthering;
fostering; improvement; aiding

---

*alte Schreibung - vgl. Hinweis auf S. xiv

(b) (Bergbau, Technik) output; (das Fördern) mining; (von Erdöl) extraction

Forelle die; ∼, ∼n trout

Form die; ∼, ∼en **(a)** shape; **in ∼ von Tabletten** in the form of tablets
(b) (bes. Sport: Verfassung) form; **in ∼ sein** be on form
(c) (vorgeformtes Modell) mould; (Back∼) baking tin
(d) (Darstellungs∼, Umgangs∼) form

formal 1 Adj. formal
2 adv. formally

formalisieren tr. V. formalize

Formalität die; ∼, ∼en formality

Format das; ∼[e]s, ∼e **(a)** size; (Buch∼, Papier∼, Bild∼) format
(b) (Persönlichkeit) stature

formatieren tr. V. (DV) format

formbar Adj. malleable

Form-: ∼**blatt** das form; ∼**brief** der form letter

Formel die; ∼, ∼n formula

formell Adj. formal

formen tr. V. **(a)** (gestalten) form; shape
(b) (bilden, prägen) mould, form ⟨character, personality⟩

Form·fehler der irregularity

formieren tr., refl. V. form

förmlich 1 Adj. **(a)** formal
(b) (regelrecht) positive
2 adv. **(a)** formally
(b) (geradezu) **sich ∼ fürchten** be really afraid

form·los Adj. **(a)** informal
(b) (gestaltlos) shapeless

Form·sache die formality

Formular das; ∼s, ∼e form

formulieren tr. V. formulate

Formulierung die; ∼, ∼en **(a)** (das Formulieren) formulation; (eines Entwurfes, Gesetzes) drafting
(b) (formulierter Text) formulation

form·vollendet 1 Adj. perfectly executed ⟨pirouette, bow, etc.⟩; ⟨poem⟩ perfect in form
2 adv. faultlessly

forsch Adj. forceful

forschen itr. V. **(a)** nach jmdm./etw. ∼: search or look for sb./sth.
(b) (als Wissenschaftler) research

Forscher der; ∼s, **Forscherin** die; ∼, ∼nen researcher

Forschung die; ∼, ∼en research

Forschungs-: ∼**reaktor** der research reactor; ∼**reisende** der/die explorer

Forst der; ∼[e]s, ∼e[n] forest

Förster der; ∼s, ∼, **Försterin** die; ∼, ∼nen forest warden

Forst·wirtschaft die forestry

Forsythie /fɔrˈzyːtsɪə/ die; ∼, ∼n forsythia

fort Adv. **(a)** ▶ WEG;

(b) (weiter) **und so ∼:** and so on

fort-, Fort-: ∼**an** /-ˈ-/ Adv. from now/then on; ∼**bestand** der continuation; (eines Staates) continued existence; ∼|**bewegen** 1 tr. V. move; shift; 2 refl. V. move [along]; ∼|**bilden** tr. V. sich/jmdn. ∼bilden continue one's/sb.'s education; ∼**bildung** die further education; (beruflich) further training; ∼**bildungs·kurs** der further education course; (beruflich) training course; ∼|**bleiben** unr. itr. V.; mit sein fail to come; ∼|**bringen** unr. tr. V.:
▶ WEGBRINGEN; ∼**dauer** die continuation; ∼|**dauern** itr. V. continue; ∼|**fahren** 1 unr. itr. V. **(a)** mit sein leave; **(b)** auch mit sein (weitermachen) continue; go on; 2 unr. tr. V. drive away; ∼|**führen** tr. V. **(a)** lead away; **(b)** (fortsetzen) continue; ∼**gang** der **(a)** departure (**aus** from); **(b)** (Weiterentwicklung) progress; ∼|**gehen** unr. itr. V.; mit sein leave; **geh ∼!** go away!; ∼**geschritten** Adj. advanced; ∼**geschrittene** der/die; adj. Dekl. advanced student/player; ∼|**kommen** unr. itr. V.; mit sein ▶ WEGKOMMEN A, B; ∼|**laufen** unr. itr. V.; mit sein **(a)**
▶ WEGLAUFEN; **(b)** (sich ∼setzen) continue; ∼**laufend** 1 Adj. continuous; 2 adv. continuously; ∼|**pflanzen** refl. V. **(a)** reproduce [oneself/itself]; **(b)** (sich verbreiten) ⟨idea, mood⟩ spread; ⟨sound, light⟩ travel; ∼**pflanzung** die; ∼∼: reproduction; ∼|**schaffen** tr. V. take away; ∼|**schreiben** unr. tr. V. update; (in die Zukunft) project forward; ∼**schreibung** die updating; (in die Zukunft) forward projection; ∼|**schreiten** unr. itr. V.; mit sein ⟨process⟩ continue; ⟨time⟩ move on; ∼**schritt** der progress; ∼**schritte** progress sing.; **ein ∼schritt** a step forward; ∼**schrittlich** 1 Adj. progressive; 2 adv. progressively; ∼**schrittlichkeit** die; ∼∼: progressiveness; ∼|**setzen** 1 tr. V. continue; 2 refl. V. continue; ∼**setzung** die; ∼∼, ∼∼en **(a)** (das ∼setzen) continuation; **(b)** (anschließender Teil) instalment; ∼**setzungs·roman** der serial; serialized novel; ∼|**während** 1 Adj. continual; 2 adv. continually; ∼|**werfen** unr. tr. V.: ▶ WEGWERFEN

fossil Adj. fossilized; fossil attrib.

Foto das; ∼s, ∼s photo; ∼**s machen** take photos

Foto-: ∼**album** das photo album; ∼**apparat** der camera

fotogen Adj. photogenic

Foto·graf der; ∼en, ∼en photographer

Fotografie die; ∼, ∼n **(a)** photography no art.
(b) (Lichtbild) photograph

fotografieren tr. V. photograph; take a photograph/photographs of

Fotografin die; ∼, ∼nen photographer

foto-, Foto-: ~**kopie** *die* photocopy; ~**kopieren** *tr., itr. V.* photocopy; ~**kopierer** *der* photocopier

Foto-: ~**labor** *das* photographic laboratory; ~**modell** *das* photographic model

Foul /fauːl/ *das;* ~s, ~s (Sport) foul (**an** + *Dat.* **on**)

Foul·spiel /'fauːl-/ *das* foul

Foyer /foa'jeː/ *das;* ~s, ~s foyer

FPÖ *Abk.* = **Freiheitliche Partei Österreichs**

Fr. *Abk.* (**a**) = **Franken** SFr.
(**b**) = **Frau;**
(**c**) = **Freitag** Fri.

Fracht *die;* ~, ~en (Schiffs~, Luft~) cargo; freight; (Bahn~, LKW~) goods *pl.;* freight

Fracht·brief *der* consignment note; waybill

Frachter *der;* ~s, ~: freighter

Fracht-: ~**gut** *das* slow freight; slow goods *pl.;* ~**schiff** *das* cargo ship

Frack *der;* ~[e]s, Fräcke *pl.;* evening dress

Frage *die;* ~, ~n question; (Angelegenheit) issue; **in** ~: ▶ INFRAGE

Fragebogen *der* questionnaire; (Formular) form

fragen ① *tr., itr. V.* (**a**) ask
(**b**) (sich erkundigen) **nach etw.** ~: ask *or* inquire about sth.
(**c**) (nachfragen) ask for
② *refl. V.* **sich** ~, **ob** ...: wonder whether ...

Frage·zeichen *das* question mark

fraglich *Adj.* (**a**) doubtful
(**b**) (betreffend) in question *postpos.;* relevant

Fragment *das;* ~[e]s, ~e fragment

frag·würdig *Adj.* (**a**) questionable
(**b**) (zwielichtig) dubious

Fragwürdigkeit *die;* ~, ~en
(**a**) questionableness
(**b**) (Zwielichtigkeit) dubiousness

Fraktion *die;* ~, ~en parliamentary party; (mit zwei Parteien) parliamentary coalition

Fraktions- (Parl.)**:** ~**führer** *der,* ~**führerin** *die* leader of the parliamentary party/coalition; ~**zwang** *der* obligation to vote in accordance with party policy

frank *Adv.* ~ **und frei** frankly and openly; openly and honestly

Franken *der;* ~s ~: [Swiss] franc

Frankfurter *die;* ~, ~ (Wurst) frankfurter

frankieren *tr. V.* frank

Frank·reich (*das*)*;* ~s France

Franse *die;* ~, ~n strand [of a/the fringe]

Franzose *der;* ~n, ~n Frenchman; **er ist** ~: he is French; **die** ~**n** the French

Französin *die;* ~, ~nen Frenchwoman

französisch *Adj.* French

Französisch *das;* ~[s] French

Fräse *die;* ~, ~n (für Holz) moulding machine; (für Metall) milling machine

fraß *1. u. 3. Pers. Sg. Prät. v.* FRESSEN

Fraß *der;* ~es (derb) muck

Fratze *die;* ~, ~n (**a**) hideous face
(**b**) (ugs.: Grimasse) grimace

Frau *die;* ~, ~en (**a**) woman
(**b**) (Ehe~) wife
(**c**) (Titel, Anrede) ~ **Schulze** Mrs Schulze; (in Briefen) **Sehr geehrte** ~ **Schulze** Dear Madam; (bei persönlicher Bekanntschaft) Dear Mrs/Miss/ Ms Schulze

Frauen-: ~**arzt** *der,* ~**ärztin** *die* gynaecologist; ~**bewegung** *die* women's movement; ~**emanzipation** *die* female emancipation; women's emancipation; ~**gefängnis** *das* women's prison; ~**gruppe** *die* women's group; ~**haus** *das* battered wives' refuge; ~**klinik** *die* gynaecological hospital *or* clinic; ~**misshandlung,** ***~**mißhandlung** *die* abuse of women; ~**recht** *das* women's right; ~**rechtlerin** *die;* ~~, ~~nen feminist; Women's Libber (coll.); ~**zeitschrift** *die* women's magazine; ~**zimmer** *das* (abwertend) female

Fräulein *das;* ~s, ~ (*ugs.* ~s) (**a**) (junges ~) young lady; (ältliches ~) spinster
(**b**) (Titel, Anrede) ~ **Mayer/Schulte** Miss Mayer/Schulte

fraulich ① *Adj.* feminine
② *adv.* in a feminine way

frech ① *Adj.* (**a**) impertinent; cheeky; barefaced ⟨lie⟩
(**b**) (keck, kess) saucy
② *adv.* impertinently; cheekily

Frech·dachs *der* (ugs., meist scherzh.) cheeky little thing

Frechheit *die;* ~, ~en (**a**) impertinence; cheek
(**b**) (Äußerung) impertinent *or* cheeky remark

frei ① *Adj.* (**a**) (unabhängig) free
(**b**) (nicht angestellt) freelance
(**c**) (ungezwungen) free and easy
(**d**) (nicht mehr in Haft) free
(**e**) (offen) open; **im Freien sitzen/übernachten** sit out of doors/spend the night in the open; **ständig im Freien übernachten** sleep rough
(**f**) (unbesetzt) vacant; free
(**g**) (kostenlos) free ⟨food, admission⟩
(**h**) (verfügbar) spare; free ⟨time⟩
② *adv.* freely

frei-, Frei-: ~**bad** *das* open-air swimming pool; ~**|bekommen** ① *unr. itr. V.* (ugs.) get time off; ② *unr. tr. V.* **jmdn./etw.** ~**bekommen** get sb./sth. released; ~**beruflich** ① *Adj.* self-employed; freelance; ⟨doctor, lawyer⟩ in private practice; ② *adv.* ~**beruflich tätig sein/ arbeiten** work freelance/practise privately; ~**betrag** *der* (Steuerw.) [tax] allowance; ~**bier** *das* free beer

Freier *der;* ~s, ~ (veralt.) suitor

frei-, Frei-: ~**exemplar** *das* (Buch) free

copy; (Zeitung) free issue; **~frau** die
baroness; **~gabe** die release; **~|geben**
unr. tr. V. release; **~gebig** Adj. generous;
open-handed; **~gebigkeit** die; **~~**:
generosity; open-handedness; **~gehege**
das outdoor enclosure; **~gepäck** das
baggage allowance; **~hafen** der free port;
~|halten unr. tr. V. (a) treat; (b) (offen
halten) keep ⟨entrance, roadway⟩ clear;
Einfahrt **~halten!** no parking in front of
entrance; **~handels·zone** die free-trade
zone; **~händig** adv. ⟨cycle⟩ without
holding on

Freiheit die; **~**, **~en** (a) freedom; **~**,
Gleichheit, Brüderlichkeit Liberty, Equality,
Fraternity
(b) (Vorrecht) freedom; privilege

freiheitlich [1] Adj. liberal ⟨philosophy,
conscience⟩; **~** und demokratisch free and
democratic
[2] adv. liberally

Freiheits-: ~beraubung die (jur.)
wrongful detention; **~strafe** die (Rechtsw.)
term of imprisonment; prison sentence

frei-, Frei-: ~herr der baron; **~karte**
die complimentary ticket; **~|kaufen** tr. V.
ransom ⟨hostage⟩; buy the freedom of
⟨slave⟩; **~|kommen** unr. itr. V. aus dem
Gefängnis **~kommen** be released from
prison; **~körper·kultur** die nudism no
art.; naturism no art.; **~land** das open
ground; **~|lassen** unr. tr. V. set free;
release; **~|legen** tr. V. uncover

freilich Adv. of course

Frei·licht-: ~bühne die, **~theater** das
open-air theatre

frei-, Frei-: ~|machen [1] refl. V. (ugs.:
frei nehmen) take time off; [2] tr. V. (Postw.)
frank; etw. mit 0,50 DM **~machen** put a 50-
pfennig stamp on sth.; **~marke** die
postage stamp; **~mütig** [1] Adj. candid;
frank; [2] adv. candidly; frankly;
~mütigkeit die; **~~**: candidness;
frankness; **~schaffend** Adj. freelance;
~schärler der; **~~s, ~~,**
~schärlerin die; **~~, ~~nen** irregular
[soldier]; **~|schwimmen** unr. refl. V.
sich **~schwimmen** pass the 15-minute
swimming test; **~|sprechen** unr. tr. V.
(a) (Rechtsw.) acquit; (b) (für unschuldig erklären)
exonerate (von from); **~spruch** der
(Rechtsw.) acquittal; **~|stellen** tr. V. (a)
jmdm. etw. **~stellen** leave sth. up to sb.; (b)
(befreien) release ⟨person⟩; jmdn. vom
Wehrdienst **~stellen** exempt sb. from
military service; **~stoß** der (Fußball) free
kick

Frei·tag der Friday; s. auch DIENSTAG usw.

freitags Adv. on Friday[s]; s. auch
DIENSTAGS

frei-, Frei-: ~tod der (verhüll.) suicide no
art.; **~treppe** die [flight of] steps;
~übung die; meist Pl. (Sport) keep-fit
exercise; **~wild** das fair game; **~willig**

[1] Adj. voluntary ⟨decision⟩; optional
⟨subject⟩; [2] adv. voluntarily; sich **~willig**
melden volunteer; **~willige** der/die; adj.
Dekl. volunteer; **~zeichen** das ringing
tone;

Frei·zeit die spare time

Freizeit-: ~beschäftigung die hobby;
leisure pursuit; **~gestaltung** die (Soziol.,
Päd.) leisure activity; **~park** der
amusement park

frei-, Frei-: ~zügig Adj. (a) generous; (b)
(gewagt, unmoralisch) risqué ⟨remark, film,
dress⟩; **~zügigkeit** die; **~~** (a)
generosity; (b) (freie Wahl des Wohnsitzes)
freedom of domicile

fremd Adj. (a) foreign
(b) (nicht eigen) other people's; of others
postpos.;
(c) (unbekannt) strange

fremd-, Fremd-: ~arbeiter der,
~arbeiterin die (veralt., schweiz.) foreign
worker; **~artig** Adj. strange

Fremde¹ der/die; adj. Dekl. (a) stranger
(b) (Ausländer) foreigner

Fremde² die; **~** (geh.) die **~**: foreign parts
pl.

fremden-, Fremden-: ~feindlich
Adj. xenophobic; hostile to strangers/
foreigners postpos.; **~feindlichkeit** die
xenophobia; hostility towards foreigners;
~führer der, **~führerin** die tourist guide;
~hass, ****~haß** der xenophobia; hatred of
foreigners; **~verkehr** der tourism no art.;
~zimmer das room

fremd-, Fremd-: ~|gehen unr. itr. V.;
mit sein (ugs.) be unfaithful; **~herrschaft**
die foreign domination; **~ländisch** Adj.
foreign; (exotisch) exotic

Fremdling der; **~s, ~e** (veralt.) stranger

fremd-, Fremd-: ~sprache die foreign
language; **~sprachen·assistent** der,
~sprachen·assistentin die foreign-
language assistant; **~sprachig** Adj.
bilingual/multilingual ⟨staff, secretary⟩;
foreign ⟨literature⟩; foreign-language
⟨edition, teaching⟩; **~sprachlich** Adj.
foreign-language ⟨teaching⟩; foreign ⟨word⟩;
~wort das; Pl. **~wörter** foreign word

frenetisch [1] Adj. frenetic
[2] adv. frenetically

Frequenz die; **~**, **~en** (Physik) frequency;
(Med.: Puls**~**) rate

Fressalien /frɛˈsaljən/ Pl. (ugs. scherzh.)
grub (coll.)

Fresse die; **~**, **~n** (derb) (a) (Mund) gob (sl.)
(b) (Gesicht) mug (coll.)

fressen [1] unr. tr. V. (a) ⟨animal⟩ eat; (sich
ernähren von) feed on
(b) (ugs.: verschlingen) swallow up ⟨money,
time, distance⟩; drink ⟨petrol⟩
(c) (zerstören) eat away
(d) (derb: von Menschen) guzzle
[2] unr. itr. V. (von Tieren) feed; (derb: von
Menschen) stuff one's face (sl.)

Fressen das; ~s (a) (für Hunde, Katzen usw.)
food; (für Vieh) feed
(b) (derb: Essen) grub (coll.)

Fresserei die; ~, ~en (derb) guzzling

Freude die; ~, ~n joy; (Vergnügen) pleasure;
~ an etw. (Dat.) haben take pleasure in sth.

Freuden-: ~fest das celebration; ein
~fest feiern hold a celebration; ~haus das
house of pleasure; ~tag der happy day

freudestrahlend Adj. beaming with joy;

freudig Adj. joyful; joyous ⟨heart⟩;
delightful ⟨surprise⟩

freud·los Adj. joyless;

freuen 1 refl. V. be glad (über + Akk.
about); (froh sein) be happy; sich auf etw.
(Akk.) ~: look forward to sth.
2 tr. V. please; es freut mich, dass ... I am
pleased or glad that ...; das hat ihn sehr
gefreut he was very pleased about it

Freund der; ~es, ~e (a) friend
(b) (Verehrer, Geliebter) boyfriend

Freundes·kreis der circle of friends; im
engen ~: among close friends

Freundin die; ~, ~nen (a) friend
(b) (Geliebte) girlfriend; (älter) lady friend

freundlich 1 Adj. (a) kind ⟨face⟩; friendly
⟨reception⟩
(b) (angenehm) pleasant
(c) (freundschaftlich) friendly
2 adv. jmdm. ~ danken thank sb. kindly

Freundlichkeit die; ~: kindness

Freundschaft die; ~, ~en friendship; mit
jmdm. ~ schließen make friends with sb.

freundschaftlich 1 Adj. friendly
2 adv. in a friendly way

Frevel /'fre:fl/ der; ~s, ~ (geh., veralt.)
crime; outrage

frevelhaft (geh.) 1 Adj. wicked ⟨deed,
rebellion, person⟩; criminal ⟨stupidity⟩
2 adv. wickedly

Friede der; ~ns, ~n (älter, geh.) ▶ FRIEDEN

Frieden der; ~s, ~: peace

Friedens-: ~abkommen das peace
agreement; (Friedensvertrag) peace treaty;
~bewegung die peace movement;
~bruch der violation of the peace;
~forschung die peace studies pl., no art.;
~konferenz die peace conference;
~nobelpreis der Nobel Peace Prize;
~pfeife die pipe of peace; ~richter der,
~richterin die lay magistrate dealing
with minor offences; ≈ Justice of the Peace;
~taube die dove of peace;
~verhandlungen Pl. peace negotiations;
~vertrag der peace treaty; ~zeiten Pl.
peacetime sing.

fried·fertig Adj. peaceable ⟨person,
character⟩

Fried·fertigkeit die; ~: peaceableness

Fried·hof der cemetery; (Kirchhof) graveyard

friedlich 1 Adj. peaceful

2 adv. peacefully

Friedlichkeit die; ~: peacefulness

fried·liebend Adj. peace-loving

frieren unr. itr. V. (a) be or feel cold
(b) mit sein (gefrieren) freeze

Frikadelle die; ~, ~n rissole

frisch 1 Adj. fresh; new-laid ⟨egg⟩; clean
⟨linen, underwear⟩; wet ⟨paint⟩
2 adv. freshly

Frische die; ~ freshness; geistige ~:
mental alertness; körperliche ~: physical
fitness

Frisch-: ~fleisch das fresh meat;
~halte·beutel der airtight bag; ~luft
die fresh air; ~milch die fresh milk

Friseur /fri'zø:ɐ̯/ der; ~s, ~e, **Friseuse**
/fri'zø:zə/ die; ~, ~n hairdresser

frisieren tr. V. jmdn./sich ~: do sb.'s/one's
hair; sich ~ lassen have one's hair done

friss, *friß Imperativ Sg. v. FRESSEN

frisst, *frißt 2. u. 3. Pers. Sg. Präsens v.
FRESSEN

Frist die; ~, ~en (a) time; period; die ~
verlängern extend the deadline
(b) (begrenzter Aufschub) extension

frist-: ~gemäß, ~gerecht Adj., adv.
within the specified time postpos.; (bei
Anmeldung usw.) before the closing date
postpos.; ~los 1 Adj. instant; 2 adv.
without notice

Frisur die; ~, ~en hairstyle

fritieren tr. V. deep-fry

frivol /fri'vo:l/ Adj. (a) (schamlos) suggestive
⟨remark, picture, etc.⟩; risqué ⟨joke⟩; earthy
⟨man⟩; flighty ⟨woman⟩
(b) (leichtfertig) frivolous

froh Adj. (a) happy; cheerful ⟨person, mood⟩;
good ⟨news⟩
(b) (ugs.: erleichtert) pleased, glad (über + Akk.
about)

fröhlich Adj. cheerful; happy

Fröhlichkeit die; ~: cheerfulness; (eines
Festes, einer Feier) gaiety

Froh-: ~natur die cheerful person; ~sinn
der cheerfulness; gaiety

fromm; ~er od. frömmer, ~st... od.
frömmst... 1 Adj. pious, devout ⟨person⟩;
devout ⟨Christian⟩
2 adv. piously

Frömmigkeit die; ~: piety; devoutness

Fron·leichnam /fro:n-/ (das); ~s [the
feast of] Corpus Christi

Front die; ~, ~en (a) (Gebäude~) front;
façade
(b) (Kampfgebiet) front [line]

frontal 1 Adj. head-on ⟨collision⟩; frontal
⟨attack⟩
2 adv. ⟨collide⟩ head-on; ⟨attack⟩ from the
front

Front·antrieb der (Kfz-W.) front-wheel
drive

fror 1. u. 3. Pers. Sg. Prät. v. FRIEREN

---

*alte Schreibung - vgl. Hinweis auf S. xiv

Frosch *der;* ∼[e]s, Frösche frog
Frosch-: ∼**mann** *der; Pl.* ∼**männer**
frogman; ∼**perspektive** *die* worm's-eye
view; ∼**schenkel** *der* frog's leg
Frost *der;* ∼[e]s, Fröste frost
Frostbeule *die* chilblain
frösteln *itr. V.* feel chilly
Frost·grenze *die* (Met.) 0° C isotherm;
(Geol.) frost line
frostig ⓵ *Adj.* (auch fig.) frosty
⓶ *adv.* frostily
Frostigkeit *die;* ∼: frostiness
Frost-: ∼**schaden** *der* frost damage;
∼**schutz·mittel** *das* (a) frost protection
agent; (b) (Kfz-W.) antifreeze
Frottee *das* u. *der;* ∼s, ∼s terry towelling
Frottee·handtuch *das* terry towel
frottieren *tr. V.* rub; towel
frotzeln ⓵ *tr. V.* tease
⓶ *itr. V.* über jmdn./etw. ∼: make fun of
sb./sth.
Frucht *die;* ∼, Früchte fruit
frucht·bar *Adj.* fertile; fruitful ⟨*work, idea,
etc.*⟩
Fruchtbarkeit *die;* ∼: fertility;
fruitfulness
Frucht·becher *der* fruit sundae
fruchten *tr. V.* nichts ∼: be no use
fruchtig *Adj.* fruity
frucht·los *Adj.* fruitless, vain ⟨*efforts*⟩
Frucht·losigkeit *die;* ∼∼: fruitlessness
Frucht-: ∼**saft** *der* fruit juice;
∼**wasser** *das; Pl.* ∼**wässer** (Anat.)
amniotic fluid; waters *pl.* (coll.)
früh ⓵ *Adj.* (a) early
(b) (vorzeitig) premature
⓶ *adv.* early; heute ∼: this morning
früh·auf: von ∼ from early childhood
on[wards]
Frühaufsteher *der;* ∼s, ∼,
Frühaufsteherin *die;* ∼, ∼nen early
riser
Frühe *die;* ∼: in aller ∼: at the crack of
dawn
früher ⓵ *Adj., nicht präd.* (a) (vergangen)
earlier; former
(b) (ehemalig) former ⟨*owner, occupant,
friend*⟩
⓶ *adv.* formerly; ∼ war er ganz anders he
used to be quite different
Früh·erkennung *die* (Med.) early
recognition
frühestens *Adv.* at the earliest
Früh·geburt *die* (a) premature birth
(b) (Kind) premature baby
Früh·jahr *das* spring
Frühjahrsmüdigkeit *die* springtime
tiredness
Frühling *der;* ∼s, ∼e spring
Frühlings·anfang *der* first day of
spring

früh-, Früh-: ∼**reif** *Adj.* precocious
⟨*child*⟩; ∼**schoppen** *der* morning drink;
(um Mittag) lunchtime drink; ∼**sport** *der*
early-morning exercise
Früh·stück *das;* ∼s, ∼e breakfast
frühstücken *itr. V.* have breakfast
Frühstücks-: ∼**fernsehen** *das*
breakfast television; ∼**pause** *die* morning
break; coffee break
früh-, Früh-: ∼**warn·system** *das* early
warning system; ∼**zeitig** ⓵ *Adj.* early;
(vorzeitig) premature; ⓶ *adv.* early; (vorzeitig)
prematurely
Frustration *die;* ∼, ∼en (Psych.)
frustration
frustrieren *tr. V.* frustrate
Fuchs *der;* ∼es, Füchse fox
fuchsen *tr. V.* annoy; vex
fuchs·teufels·wild *Adj.* (ugs.) livid (coll.)
Fuchtel *die;* ∼: unter jmds. ∼ (ugs.) under
sb.'s thumb
fuchteln *itr. V.* (ugs.) mit etw. ∼: wave sth.
about
Fuder *das;* ∼s, ∼: cartload
Fuge¹ *die;* ∼, ∼n joint; (Zwischenraum) gap
Fuge² *die;* ∼, ∼n (Musik) fugue
fügen ⓵ *tr. V.* place; set; etw zu etw. ∼ (fig.)
add sth. to sth.
⓶ *refl. V.* (a) (sich ein∼) sich in etw. (*Akk.*)
∼: fit into sth.
(b) (gehorchen) sich ∼: fall into line
fügsam *Adj.* obedient
fühlbar *Adj.* noticeable
fühlen ⓵ *tr., itr. V.* feel
⓶ *refl. V.* sich krank ∼: feel sick
Fühler *der;* ∼s, ∼: feeler; antenna
Fühlungnahme *die;* ∼: initial contact
fuhr 1. u. 3. Pers. Sg. Prät. *v.* FAHREN
Fuhre *die;* ∼, ∼n load
führen ⓵ *tr. V.* (a) lead; jmdn. durch ein
Haus/eine Stadt ∼: show sb. around a
house/town; durch das Programm führt [Sie]
Klaus Frank Klaus Frank will present the
programme
(b) (verkaufen) stock, sell ⟨*goods*⟩
(c) (durch∼) Gespräche/Verhandlungen ∼:
hold conversations/negotiations; eine
glückliche Ehe ∼: be happily married
(d) (leiten) manage, run ⟨*company, business,
pub, etc.*⟩; lead ⟨*party, country*⟩; command
⟨*regiment*⟩
(e) (Amtsspr.) drive ⟨*train, motor, vehicle*⟩
(f) (als Kennzeichnung, Bezeichnung haben) bear;
einen Titel/Künstlernamen ∼: have a title/
use a stage name
(g) (angelegt haben) keep ⟨*diary, list, file*⟩
(h) (registrieren) jmdn. in einer Liste/Kartei ∼:
have sb. on a list/on file
(i) (tragen) etw. bei *od.* mit sich ∼: have sth.
on one; eine Waffe/einen Ausweis bei sich
∼: carry a weapon/a pass
⓶ *itr. V.* (a) lead
(b) (an der Spitze liegen) lead; be ahead

führend *Adj.* leading; high-ranking
⟨*official*⟩; prominent ⟨*position*⟩

Führer *der;* ~s, ~ (a) (Leiter) leader
(b) (Fremdenführer, Buch) guide

Führerin *die;* ~, ~nen ▶ FÜHRER

führer-, Führer-: ~**los** ⑴ *Adj.*
leaderless; (ohne Lenker) driverless ⟨*car*⟩
⑵ *adv.* ▶ 1: without a leader; without a
driver; ~**schein** *der* driving licence (Brit.);
driver's license (Amer.); ~**schein-entzug**
der disqualification from driving; driving
ban

Führung *die;* ~, ~en (a) ▶ FÜHREN 1D:
management; running; leadership; command
(b) (Fremden führung) guided tour
(c) (führende Position) lead

Führungs-: ~**kraft** *die* manager;
~**spitze** *die* (Politik) top leadership; (im
Betrieb) top management; ~**zeugnis** *das:*
document issued by police certifying that
holder has no criminal record

Fuhr-: ~**unternehmer** *der,*
~**unternehmerin** *die* haulage
contractor; ~**werk** *das* cart

Fülle *die;* ~ (a) wealth; abundance
(b) (Körper~) corpulence

füllen ⑴ *tr. V.* (a) fill; (Kochk.) stuff
(b) (fig.) fill in ⟨*gap, time*⟩
⑵ *refl. V.* (voll werden) fill [up]

Füller *der;* ~s, ~ (ugs.) [fountain] pen

Füll-federhalter *der* fountain pen

füllig *Adj.* corpulent, portly ⟨*person*⟩; ample
⟨*figure, bosom*⟩

Füllung *die;* ~, ~en stuffing; (Kochk.;
Zahnmed.) filling; (in Schokolade) centre

fummeln *itr. V.* (ugs.) (a) (fingern) fiddle
(b) (erotisch) pet

Fund *der;* ~[e]s, ~e (auch Archäol.) find

Fundament *das;* ~[e]s, ~e (a) (Bauw.)
foundations *pl.;*
(b) (Basis) base; basis

fundamental *Adj.* fundamental

Fundamentalismus *der;* ~:
fundamentalism

Fundamentalist *der;* ~en, ~en,
Fundamentalistin *die;* ~, ~nen
fundamentalist

Fund-: ~**büro** *das* lost property office
(Brit.); lost and found office (Amer.); ~**grube**
die treasure house

fundieren *tr. V.* underpin

fündig *Adj.* ~ sein yield something; ~
werden make a find; (bei Bohrungen) make a
strike

Fund-ort *der* place *or* site where sth. is/was
found

fünf *Kardinalz.* five

Fünf *die;* ~, ~en five; (Schulnote) E

fünf-, Fünf-: ~**eck** *das* pentagon; ~**fach**
Vervielfältigungsz. fivefold; ~**fache** *das;*

adj. Dekl. five times as much; ~**hundert**
Kardinalz. five hundred; ~**kampf** *der*
(Sport) pentathlon

Fünfling *der;* ~s, ~e quintuplet; quin (coll.)

fünf-: ~**mal** *Adv.* five times; ~**stellig**
Adj. five-figure

fünft... *Ordinalz.* fifth

Fünf-tagewoche *die* five-day [working]
week

fünf-tausend *Kardinalz.* five thousand

fünftel *Bruchz.* fifth

Fünftel *das* (schweiz. meist *der*); ~s, ~: fifth

fünftens *Adv.* fifthly

fünf-zehn *Kardinalz.* fifteen

fünfzig *Kardinalz.* fifty

Fünfzig *die;* ~: fifty

fünfziger *indekl. Adj.* die Fünfzigerjahre the
fifties

Fünfziger *der;* ~s, ~ (a) (ugs.) fifty-pfennig
piece
(b) (50-Jähriger) fifty-year-old

Fünfzig-: ~**mark-schein** *der* fifty-mark
note; ~**pfennig-stück** *das* fifty-pfennig
piece

fünfzigst... *Ordinalz.* fiftieth

fungieren *itr. V.* als etw. ~ ⟨*person*⟩ act as
sth.; ⟨*word etc.*⟩ function as sth.

Funk *der;* ~s radio

Funk-ausstellung *die* radio and
television exhibition

Funke *der;* ~ns, ~n (auch fig.) spark

funkeln *itr. V.* ⟨*light, star*⟩ twinkle; ⟨*gold,
diamonds*⟩ glitter; ⟨*eyes*⟩ blaze

funken *tr. V.* radio; ⟨*transmitter*⟩ broadcast

Funker *der;* ~s, ~, **Funkerin** *die;* ~,
~nen radio operator

Funk-: ~**gerät** *das* radio set; (tragbar)
walkie-talkie; ~**haus** *das* broadcasting
centre; ~**kolleg** *das* radio-based [adult
education] course; ~**sprech-gerät** *das*
radiophone; (tragbar) walkie-talkie;
~**spruch** *der* radio signal; (Nachricht) radio
message; ~**station** *die,* ~**stelle** *die* radio
station; ~**stille** *die* radio silence;
~**streife** *die* [police] radio patrol; ~**taxi**
das radio taxi; ~**telefon** *das* radiotelephone

Funktion *die;* ~, ~en function

Funktionär *der;* ~s, ~e official;
functionary

funktionieren *itr. V.* work; function

funktions-tüchtig *Adj.* working; sound
⟨*organ*⟩

Funk-: ~**turm** *der* radio tower;
~**verbindung** *die* radio contact

Funzel *die;* ~, ~n (ugs.) useless light

für *Präp. mit Akk.* for; etw. ~ ungültig
erklären declare sth. invalid; *s. auch* WAS 1

Furche *die;* ~, ~n (a) furrow
(b) (Wagenspur) rut

Furcht *die;* ~: fear; ~ **vor jmdm./etw. haben** fear sb./sth.

furchtbar [1] *Adj.* **(a)** dreadful **(b)** (ugs.: unangenehm) terrible (coll.) [2] *adv.* (ugs.) terribly (coll.)

fürchten [1] *refl. V.* **sich [vor jmdm./etw.]** ~: be afraid *or* frightened [of sb./sth.] [2] *tr. V.* be afraid of; **ich fürchte, [dass]** ...: I'm afraid [that] ...

fürchterlich *Adj., adv.* ▶ FURCHTBAR

furcht·los [1] *Adj.* fearless [2] *adv.* fearlessly

furchtsam [1] *Adj.* timid [2] *adv.* timidly

für·einander *Adv.* for one another; for each other

Furie /'fuːriə/ *die;* ~, ~n Fury

Furnier *das;* ~s, ~e veneer

Für·sorge *die;* ~ **(a)** care **(b)** (veralt.: Sozialhilfe) welfare **(c)** (veralt.: Sozialamt) social services *pl.*

für·sorglich [1] *Adj.* considerate [2] *adv.* considerately

Für·sprache *die* support

Für·sprecher *der,* **Für·sprecherin** *die* advocate

Fürst *der;* ~en, ~en prince

Fürstentum *das;* ~s, Fürstentümer principality

Fürstin *die;* ~, ~nen princess

fürstlich [1] *Adj.* **(a)** royal **(b)** (fig.: üppig) lavish [2] *adv.* lavishly

Furt *die;* ~, ~en ford

Furunkel *der od. das;* ~s, ~: boil; furuncle

Für·wort *das; Pl.* -wörter pronoun

Furz *der;* ~es, Fürze (derb) fart (coarse); **einen ~ lassen** let off a fart; **jeder ~** (fig.) the slightest thing

furzen *itr. V.* (derb) fart (coarse)

Fusion *die;* ~, ~en amalgamation; (von Konzernen) merger

fusionieren *itr. V.* merge

Fuß *der;* ~es, Füße foot; (einer Lampe, Säule) base; (von Möbeln) leg; **zu ~ gehen** go on foot;

walk; **bei** ~! heel!; (fig.) **auf freiem ~ sein** be at large; **auf großem ~ leben** live in great style

Fuß·ball *der* **(a)** (Ballspiel) [Association] football **(b)** (Ball) football

Fußballer *der;* ~s, ~, **Fußballerin** *die;* ~, ~nen footballer

Fußball-: ~**platz** *der* football ground; (Spielfeld) football pitch; ~**spiel** *das* **(a)** football match; **(b)** (Sportart) football *no art.;* ~**spieler** *der,* ~**spielerin** *die* football player

Fuß·boden *der* floor

Fußboden·heizung *die* underfloor heating

fußen *itr. V.* **auf etw.** (*Dat.*) ~: be based on sth.

Fuß·ende *das* foot

Fußgänger *der;* ~s, ~, **Fußgängerin** *die;* ~, ~nen pedestrian

Fußgänger-: ~**brücke** *die* footbridge; ~**übergang** *der,* ~**überweg** *der* pedestrian crossing; ~**unterführung** *die* pedestrian subway; ~**zone** *die* pedestrian precinct

Fuß-: ~**nagel** *der* toenail; ~**note** *die* footnote; ~**stapfen** *der;* ~~s, ~~: footprint; ~**tritt** *der* kick; ~**volk** *das* **(a)** (hist.) footmen *pl.;* **(b)** (abwertend: Untergeordnete) lower ranks *pl.;* ~**weg** *der* footpath

futsch *Adj.* (salopp) ~ **sein** have gone for a burton (Brit. coll.)

Futter[1] *das;* ~s (Tiernahrung) feed; (für Pferde, Kühe) fodder

Futter[2] *das;* ~s, ~ (von Kleidungsstücken usw.) lining

Futteral *das;* ~s, ~e case

Futter·mittel *das* animal food

füttern[1] *tr. V.* feed

füttern[2] *tr. V.* (mit Futter[2] ausstatten) line

Futter·pflanze *die* fodder plant; forage plant

Fütterung *die;* ~, ~en feeding

Futur *das;* ~s, ~e (Sprachw.) future [tense]

Fuzzi *der;* ~s, ~s (salopp) bozo (sl.)

Gg

g, G /ge:/ *das;* ~, ~ **(a)** (Buchstabe) g/G
  (b) (Musik) [key of] G
g *Abk.* **(a)** = **Gramm** g
  (b) = **Groschen**
gab *1. u. 3. Pers. Sg. Prät. v.* GEBEN
Gabe *die;* ~, ~n **(a)** (geh.: Geschenk, Talent)
  gift
  (b) (Almosen, Spende) alms *pl.*
Gabel *die;* ~, ~n fork; (Telefon~) cradle
gabeln *refl. V.* fork
Gabel-: ~**schlüssel** *der* flat spanner;
  ~**stapler** *der;* ~~s, ~~: forklift truck
Gabelung *die;* ~, ~en fork
Gaben·tisch *der* gift table
gackern *itr. V.* **(a)** cluck
  (b) (ugs.: lachen) cackle
gaffen *itr. V.* (abwertend) gape; gawp (coll.)
Gaffer *der;* ~s, ~, **Gafferin** *die;* ~, ~nen
  gaper; starer
Gag /gɛk/ *der;* ~s, ~s **(a)** (Theater, Film) gag
  (b) (Besonderheit) gimmick
Gage /'ga:ʒə/ *die;* ~, ~n salary; (für einzelnen
  Auftritt) fee
gähnen *itr. V.* (auch fig.) yawn
Gala /'ga:la, *auch* 'gala/ *die;* ~: formal dress
galant ⯐ *Adj.* gallant; (amourös) amorous
  ⯑ *adv.* gallantly
Gala·vorstellung *die* gala performance
Galeere *die;* ~, ~n galley
Galerie *die;* ~, ~n gallery
Galgen *der* gallows *sing.*
Galgen-: ~**frist** *die* reprieve; ~**humor**
  der gallows humour
Galle *die;* ~, ~n **(a)** (Gallenblase) gall
  [bladder]
  (b) (Sekret) (bei Tieren) gall; (bei Menschen) bile
Galopp *der;* ~s, ~s *od.* ~e gallop
galoppieren *itr. V.; meist mit sein* gallop
galt *1. u. 3. Pers. Sg. Prät. v.* GELTEN
galvanisch /gal'va:nɪʃ/ *Adj.* galvanic
Gamasche *die;* ~, ~n gaiter; (bis zum
  Knöchel reichend) spat
Gambe *die;* ~, ~n (Musik) viola da gamba
Gamma·strahlen *Pl.* (Physik, Med.) gamma
  rays
gammelig *Adj.* (ugs.) **(a)** bad; rotten
  (b) (unordentlich) scruffy
gammeln *itr. V.* **(a)** (ugs.) go off
  (b) (nichts tun) loaf around; bum around (Amer.
  coll.)
Gammler *der;* ~s, ~, **Gammlerin** *die;*
  ~, ~nen (ugs.) dropout (coll.)

---

*alte Schreibung - vgl. Hinweis auf S. xiv

Gämse *die;* ~, ~n chamois
gäng: ~ und gäbe sein be quite usual
Gang *der;* ~[e]s, Gänge **(a)** walk; gait
  (b) (Besorgung) errand
  (c) (Verlauf) course
  (d) (Technik) gear
  (e) (Flur) (in Zügen, Gebäuden usw.) corridor;
  (Verbindungs~) passage[way]; (im Theater, Kino,
  Flugzeug) aisle
  (f) (Kochk.) course
gangbar *Adj.* passable; (fig.) practicable
Gängel·band *das:* jmdn. am ~ führen keep
  sb. in leading reins
gängeln *tr. V.* (ugs.) jmdn. ~: boss sb.
  around
gang·genau *Adj.* accurate
Gang·genauigkeit *die* accuracy
gängig *Adj.* **(a)** (üblich) common; (aktuell)
  current
  (b) (leicht verkäuflich) popular
Gang·schaltung *die* (Technik) gear system;
  (Art) gear change
Gangway /'gænweɪ/ *die;* ~, ~s gangway
Ganove /ga'no:və/ *der;* ~n, ~n (ugs.
  abwertend) crook (coll.)
Gans *die;* ~, Gänse goose
Gänse-: ~**blümchen** *das* daisy;
  ~**braten** *der* roast goose; ~**füßchen** *das;*
  ~~s, ~~ (ugs.) ▸ ANFÜHRUNGSZEICHEN;
  ~**haut** *die* (fig.) gooseflesh; goose pimples
  pl.; ~**marsch** im ~marsch in single *or*
  Indian file
Gänserich *der;* ~s, ~e gander
ganz ⯐ *Adj.* **(a)** (gesamt) whole; entire; **den**
  ~en Tag/das ~e Jahr all day/year
  (b) (ugs.: alle) **die** ~en Kinder/Leute/Gläser
  usw. all the children/people/glasses *etc.;*
  (c) (vollständig) whole
  (d) (ugs.: ziemlich [groß]) **eine** ~e Menge/ein
  ~er Haufen quite a lot/quite a pile
  (e) (ugs.: unversehrt) intact; **etw. wieder** ~
  machen mend sth.
  ⯑ *adv.* quite
Ganze *das; adj. Dekl.* **(a)** whole
  (b) (alles) **das** ~: the whole thing
gänzlich *Adv.* entirely
ganz-: ~**tägig** ⯐ *Adj.* all-day; **eine**
  ~tägige Arbeit a full-time job; ⯑ *adv.* all
  day; ~**tags** *Adv.* arbeiten work full-time
Ganztags-: ~**schule** *die* all-day school;
  (System) all-day schooling *no art.;* ~**stelle**
  die full-time job
gar¹ *Adj.* cooked; done *pred.*
gar² *Partikel* **(a)** (überhaupt) ~ nicht [wahr]
  not [true] at all; ~ nichts nothing at all; ~

niemand *od.* keiner nobody at all; ~ keines
not a single one; ~ kein Geld no money at
all
(b) (südd., österr., schweiz.: verstärkend) ~ zu
only too
(c) (geh.: sogar) even
Garage /ga'raːʒə/ *die;* ~, ~n garage
Garagen-: ~firma *die* garage startup;
~wagen *der* garaged car
Garant *der;* ~en, ~en guarantor
Garantie *die;* ~, ~n guarantee
Garantie-frist *die* guarantee period
garantieren ①*tr. V.* guarantee
②*itr. V.* für etw. ~: guarantee sth.
garantiert *Adv.* (ugs.) wir kommen ~ zu
spät we're dead certain to arrive late (coll.)
Garantie-schein *der* guarantee
[certificate]
Garantin *die;* ~, ~nen guarantor
Garaus /'gaːʀlaʊːs/: jmdm. den ~ machen
do sb. in (coll.)
Garbe *die;* ~, ~n **(a)** sheaf
(b) (Geschoss~) burst of fire
Garde *die;* ~, ~n guard
Garderobe *die;* ~, ~n **(a)** wardrobe;
clothes *pl.;*
(b) (Flur~) coat rack
(c) (im Theater usw.) cloakroom; checkroom
(Amer.)
Garderoben-frau *die* cloakroom *or*
(Amer.) checkroom attendant
Gardine *die;* ~, ~n **(a)** net curtain
(b) (landsch., veralt.) curtain
Gardinen-: ~predigt *die* (ugs.) telling-off
(coll.); (einer Ehefrau zu ihrem Mann) curtain
lecture; ~stange *die* curtain rail
garen *tr., itr. V.* cook
gären *regelm.* (auch unr.) *itr. V.* ferment;
(fig.) seethe
Garn *das;* ~[e]s, ~e **(a)** thread; (Näh~)
cotton
(b) (Seew.) yarn
Garnele *die;* ~, ~n shrimp
garnieren *tr. V.* **(a)** decorate
(b) (Gastr.) garnish
Garnison *die;* ~, ~en garrison
Garnitur *die;* ~, ~en **(a)** set; (Wäsche) set of
[matching] underwear; (Möbel) suite
(b) (ugs.) die erste/zweite ~: the first/second-
rate people *pl.*
garstig *Adj.* nasty; bad ‹behaviour›
Garstigkeit *die;* ~, ~en **(a)** nastiness
(b) (Handlung) piece of nastiness
Gärtchen *das;* ~s, ~: little garden
Garten *der;* ~s, Gärten garden
Garten-: ~abfall *der* garden waste;
~abfälle garden waste; ~arbeit *die*
gardening; ~bau *der* horticulture; ~fest
das garden party; ~haus *das* summer
house; ~laube *die* summerhouse; garden
house; ~lokal *das* beer garden; (Restaurant)
open-air café; ~schau *die* horticultural

show; ~wirtschaft *die* ▶ ~LOKAL;
~zwerg *der* **(a)** garden gnome; **(b)** (salopp
abwertend) little runt
Gärtner *der;* ~s, ~: gardener
Gärtnerei *die;* ~, ~en nursery
Gärtnerin *die;* ~, ~nen gardener
Gärung *die;* ~, ~en fermentation
Gas *das;* ~es, ~e **(a)** gas
(b) (Treibstoff) petrol (Brit.); gasoline (Amer.);
gas (Amer. coll.); ~ wegnehmen take one's
foot off the accelerator; ~ geben accelerate;
put one's foot down (coll.)
gas-, Gas-: ~flasche *die* gas cylinder;
(für einen Herd, Ofen) gas bottle; ~förmig
Adj. gaseous; ~hahn *der* gas tap; ~herd
der gas cooker; ~kammer *die* gas
chamber; ~leitung *die* gas pipe; (Hauptrohr)
gas main; ~maske *die* gas mask;
~pedal *das* accelerator [pedal]; gas pedal
(Amer.); ~pistole *die* pistol that fires gas
cartridges
Gasse *die;* ~, ~n lane; (österr.) street
Gassen-junge *der* (abwertend) street
urchin
Gast *der;* ~[e]s, Gäste **(a)** guest
(b) (Besucher eines Lokals) patron
(c) (Besucher) visitor
Gast-: ~arbeiter, *der,* ~arbeiterin
die immigrant *or* guest worker; ~dozent
der, ~dozentin *die* (Hochschulw.) visiting
lecturer
Gäste-: ~buch *das* guest book; ~haus
das guest house; ~zimmer *das* (privat)
guest room; spare room; (im Hotel) room
gast-, Gast-: ~freundlich *Adj.*
hospitable; ~freundlichkeit *die,*
~freundschaft *die* hospitality;
~geber *der* host; ~geberin *die* hostess;
~haus *das,* ~hof *der* inn
gastieren *itr. V.* give a guest performance
gastlich *Adj.* hospitable
Gastlichkeit *die;* ~: hospitality
Gast-professor *der,*
Gast-professorin *die* visiting professor
Gastronom *der;* ~en, ~en restaurateur
Gastronomie *die;* ~: catering *no art.;*
(Gaststättengewerbe) restaurant trade
Gastronomin *die;* ~, ~nen restaurateur
Gast-: ~spiel *das* guest performance;
~stätte *die* public house; (Speiselokal)
restaurant; ~wirt *der* publican; landlord;
(eines Restaurants) [restaurant] proprietor;
(Pächter) restaurant manager; ~wirtin *die*
▶ ~WIRT: publican; landlady; [restaurant]
proprietress *or* owner; restaurant
manageress; ~wirtschaft *die* ▶ ~STÄTTE
Gas-: ~vergiftung *die* gas poisoning *no*
indef. art.; ~versorgung *die* gas supply;
~werk *das* gasworks *sing.;* ~zähler *der*
gas meter
Gatte *der;* ~n, ~n husband
Gatter *das;* ~s, ~ **(a)** (Zaun) fence;
(Lattenzaun) fence; paling ⋯❖

(b) (Tor) gate

Gattin *die;* ∼, ∼**nen** (geh.) wife

Gattung *die;* ∼, ∼**en (a)** kind; sort;
(Kunst∼) genre; form
(b) (Biol.) genus

GAU *der;* ∼s, ∼s *Abk.* = **größter
anzunehmender Unfall** MCA;
maximum credible accident

Gaudi *das;* ∼s (bayr., österr.) *die;* ∼ (ugs.) bit
of fun

Gaukler *der;* ∼s, ∼, **Gauklerin** *die;* ∼,
∼**nen (a)** (veralt.: Taschenspieler[in]) itinerant
entertainer
(b) (geh.: Betrüger[in]) charlatan

Gaul *der;* ∼[e]s, **Gäule** nag (derog.)

Gaumen *der;* ∼s, ∼: palate

Gauner *der;* ∼s, ∼ (abwertend) crook (coll.);
rogue

Gaunerei *die;* ∼, ∼**en** swindle

Gaunerin *die;* ∼, ∼**nen** ▶ GAUNER

Gauner·sprache *die* thieves' cant *or*
Latin

Gaze /'gaːzə/ *die;* ∼, ∼**n** gauze

geachtet *Adj.* respected

Geäst *das;* ∼[e]s branches *pl.*

geb. *Abk.* **(a)** = **geboren;**
(b) = **geborene**

Gebäck *das;* ∼[e]s, ∼**e** cakes and pastries
pl.; (Kekse) biscuits *pl.;* (Törtchen) tarts *pl.*

gebacken 2. *Part. v.* BACKEN

Gebälk *das;* ∼[e]s, ∼**e** beams *pl.;* (Dach∼)
rafters *pl.*

gebar 1. u. 3. *Pers. Sg. Prät. v.* GEBÄREN

Gebärde *die;* ∼, ∼**n** gesture

gebärden *refl. V.* behave

gebären *unr. tr. V.* bear; give birth to; *s.
auch* GEBOREN

gebär·fähig *Adj.* Frauen im ∼fähigen Alter
women of child-bearing age.

Gebär·mutter *die; Pl.* Gebärmütter womb

Gebäude *das;* ∼s, ∼ **(a)** building
(b) (Gefüge) structure

gebaut *Adj.* gut ∼ sein have a good figure

Gebein *das;* ∼[e]s, ∼**e** *Pl.* (geh.) bones *pl.;*
(sterbliche Reste) [mortal] remains

Gebell *das;* ∼[e]s barking; (der Jagdhunde)
baying

geben ① *unr. tr. V.* give; jmdm. die Hand
∼: shake sb.'s hand; ∼ Sie mir bitte Herrn N.
please put me through to Mr N.; Unterricht
∼: teach; **eins plus eins gibt zwei** one and
one is *or* makes two; **etw. von sich** ∼: utter
sth.
② *unr. tr. V.* (unpers.) **es gibt** there is/are;
heute gibts Fisch we're having fish today;
morgen gibt es Schnee it'll snow tomorrow
③ *unr. itr. V.* **(a)** (Karten austeilen) deal
(b) (Sport: aufschlagen) serve
④ *unr. refl. V.* **(a)** sich [natürlich/steif] ∼:
act *or* behave [naturally/stiffly]

(b) das gibt sich noch it will get better

Gebet *das;* ∼[e]s, ∼**e** prayer

gebeten 2. *Part. v.* BITTEN

Gebets-: ∼**mühle** *die* prayer wheel;
∼**teppich** *der* (islam. Rel.) prayer mat

gebiert 3. *Pers. Sg. Präsens v.* GEBÄREN

Gebiet *das;* ∼[e]s, ∼**e** region; area;
(Staats∼) territory; (Bereich, Fach) field

gebieten (geh.) **(a)** command; order
(b) (erfordern) demand

Gebieter *der;* ∼s, ∼ (veralt.) master

Gebieterin *die;* ∼, ∼**nen** (veralt.) mistress

gebieterisch (geh.) *Adj.* imperious;
(herrisch) domineering; peremptory ⟨tone⟩

Gebiets·anspruch *der* territorial claim

Gebilde *das;* ∼s, ∼: object; (Bauwerk)
structure

gebildet *Adj.* educated

Gebimmel *das;* ∼s (ugs.) ringing; (von
kleinen Glocken) tinkling

Gebirge *das;* ∼s, ∼: mountain range; im
∼: in the mountains

gebirgig *Adj.* mountainous

Gebiss, *Gebiß *das;* Gebisses, Gebisse
(a) set of teeth; teeth *pl.;*
(b) (Zahnersatz) denture; plate (coll.); (für beide
Kiefer) dentures *pl.*

gebissen 2. *Part. v.* BEISSEN

geblasen 2. *Part. v.* BLASEN

geblichen 2. *Part. v.* BLEICHEN

geblümt *Adj.* flowered

Geblüt *das;* ∼[e]s (geh.) blood

gebogen 2. *Part. v.* BIEGEN

geboren ① 2. *Part. v.* GEBÄREN;
② *Adj.* blind/taub ∼ sein be born blind/deaf;
Frau Anna Schmitz ∼**e** Meyer Mrs Anna
Schmitz née Meyer

geborgen ① 2. *Part. v.* BERGEN;
② *Adj.* safe; secure

Geborgenheit *die;* ∼: security

geborsten 2. *Part. v.* BERSTEN

gebot 1. u. 3. *Pers. Sg. Prät. v.* GEBIETEN

Gebot *das;* ∼[e]s, ∼**e (a)** (Grundsatz) precept;
die Zehn ∼**e** (Rel.) the Ten Commandments
(b) (Vorschrift) regulation

geboten ① 2. *Part. v.* BIETEN, GEBIETEN;
② *Adj.* (ratsam) advisable; (notwendig)
necessary

Gebr. *Abk.* = **Gebrüder** Bros.

gebracht 2. *Part. v.* BRINGEN

gebrannt 2. *Part. v.* BRENNEN

gebraten 2. *Part. v.* BRATEN

Gebrauch *der* **(a)** use
(b) (Brauch) custom

gebrauchen *tr. V.* use

gebräuchlich *Adj.* **(a)** normal;
customary
(b) (häufig) common

gebrauchs-, Gebrauchs-:
∼**anweisung** *die* instructions *pl.* [for

use]; ~**fertig** Adj. ready for use pred.;
~**gegenstand** der item of practical use;
~**wert** der utility value

gebraucht Adj. second-hand; used ⟨car⟩

Gebraucht·wagen der used car

Gebrechen das; ~s, ~ (geh.) affliction

gebrechlich Adj. infirm

Gebrechlichkeit die; ~: infirmity

gebrochen ⓵ 2. Part. v. BRECHEN;
⓶ Adj. ~es Englisch/Deutsch broken
English/German
⓷ adv. ~ Deutsch sprechen speak broken
German

Gebrüder Pl.: die ~ Meyer Meyer Brothers

Gebrüll das; ~[e]s roaring

Gebrumm das; ~[e]s (von Bären) growling;
(von Flugzeugen, Bienen) droning; (von Insekten)
buzz[ing]

gebückt Adj. in ~er Haltung bending
forward

Gebühr die; ~, ~en charge; (Maut) toll;
(Anwalts~) fee

gebühren (geh.) itr. V. jmdm. gebührt
Achtung usw. sb. deserves respect etc.

Gebühren·anzeiger der (Fernspr.)
telephone meter

gebührend ⓵ Adj. fitting
⓶ adv. fittingly

gebühren-, Gebühren-:
~**ermäßigung** die reduction of charges/
fees; ~**frei** ⓵ Adj. free of charge pred.;
⓶ adv. free of charge; ~**pflichtig** Adj.
eine ~pflichtige Verwarnung a fine and a
caution; ~**vignette** die [Swiss] motorway
fee sticker

gebunden ⓵ 2. Part. v. BINDEN;
⓶ Adj. (verpflichtet) bound

Geburt die; ~, ~en birth

Geburten-: ~**kontrolle** die birth
control; ~**rate** die birth rate; ~**ziffer** die
birth rate

gebürtig Adj. ein ~er Schwabe a Swabian
by birth

Geburts-: ~**anzeige** die birth
announcement; ~**datum** das date of birth;
~**haus** das: das ~haus Beethovens the
house where Beethoven was born;
Beethoven's birthplace; ~**helfer** der,
~**helferin** die (Arzt, Ärztin) obstetrician;
~**hilfe** die (Med.) obstetrics sing.; (von einer
Hebamme) midwifery; ~**ort** der place of birth; ~**tag**
der birthday; jmdm. zum ~tag gratulieren
wish sb. many happy returns of the day;
~**ur·kunde** die birth certificate

Gebüsch das; ~[e]s, ~e bushes pl.

gedacht 2. Part. v. DENKEN, GEDENKEN

Gedächtnis das; ~ses, ~se (a) memory
(b) (Andenken) memory

Gedächtnis-: ~**lücke** die gap in one's
memory; ~**schwund** der loss of memory

gedämpft Adj. subdued ⟨mood⟩; subdued,
soft ⟨light⟩; muffled ⟨sound⟩

Gedanke der; ~ns, ~n (a) thought; der ~
an etw. (Akk.) the thought of sth.
(b) Pl. (Meinung) ideas
(c) (Einfall) idea

gedanken-, Gedanken-: ~**gang** der
train of thought; ~**gut** das thought;
christliches ~gut Christian thought;
staatszersetzendes ~gut subversive ideas
pl.; ~**los** ⓵ Adj. unconsidered; (zerstreut)
absent-minded; ⓶ adv. without thinking;
(zerstreut) absent-mindedly; ~**losigkeit** die;
~~ (Zerstreutheit) absent-mindedness;
(Unüberlegtheit) lack of thought; ~**strich** der
dash; ~**verloren** Adv. lost in thought;
~**voll** ⓵ Adj. pensive; ⓶ adv. pensively

gedanklich ⓵ Adj. intellectual
⓶ adv. intellectually

Gedärm das; ~[e]s, ~e intestines pl.;
bowels pl., (eines Tieres) entrails pl.

Gedeck das; ~[e]s, ~e (a) place setting;
cover
(b) (Menü) set meal
(c) (Getränk) drink [with a cover charge]

gedeihen unr. itr. V.; mit sein (a) thrive;
(wirtschaftlich) flourish; prosper
(b) (fortschreiten) progress

gedenken unr. itr. V. (a) jmds./einer
Sache ~ (geh.) remember sb./sth.; (in einer
Feier) commemorate sb./sth.
(b) etw. zu tun ~: intend to do or doing sth.

Gedenk·stätte die memorial

Gedicht das; ~[e]s, ~e poem

gediegen ⓵ Adj. solid ⟨furniture⟩; sound
⟨piece of work⟩
⓶ adv. ~ gebaut/verarbeitet solidly built/
made

gedieh 1. u. 3. Pers. Sg. Prät. v. GEDEIHEN

gediehen 2. Part. v. GEDEIHEN

Gedränge das; ~s (a) pushing and
shoving; (Menge) crush; crowd
(b) ins ~ kommen od. geraten get into
difficulties

gedroschen 2. Part. v. DRESCHEN

gedrungen ⓵ 2. Part. v. DRINGEN;
⓶ Adj. stocky; thickset

Geduld die; ~: patience

gedulden refl. V. be patient; ~ Sie sich
bitte ein paar Minuten please be so good as
to wait a few minutes

geduldig ⓵ Adj. patient
⓶ adv. patiently

Gedulds-: ~**probe** die trial of one's
patience; ~**spiel** das puzzle

gedurft 2. Part. v. DÜRFEN

geeignet Adj. suitable; (richtig) right

Gefahr die; ~, ~en (a) danger; (Bedrohung)
danger; threat (für to); bei ~: in case of
emergency
(b) (Risiko) risk; auf eigene ~: at one's own
risk

gefährden *tr. V.* endanger; jeopardize ⟨*enterprise, success, position, etc.*⟩

gefährdet *Adj.* ⟨*people, adolescents, etc.*⟩ at risk *postpos.*

Gefährdung *die;* ~, ~en (a) endangering; (eines Unternehmens, einer Position usw.) jeopardizing

(b) (Gefahr) threat (+ *Gen.* to)

gefahren *2. Part. v.* FAHREN

gefährlich ① *Adj.* dangerous; (gewagt) risky

② *adv.* dangerously

gefahr·los ① *Adj.* safe

② *adv.* safely

Gefährt *das;* ~[e]s, ~e (geh.) vehicle

Gefährte *der;* ~n, ~n, **Gefährtin** *die;* ~, ~nen (geh.) companion; (Ehemann/Ehefrau) partner in life

Gefälle *das;* ~s, ~: slope; incline; (einer Straße) gradient

gefallen[1] *unr. itr. V.* (a) das gefällt mir [gut] I like it [a lot]

(b) sich (*Dat.*) etw. ~ lassen put up with sth.

gefallen[2] *2. Part. v.* FALLEN, GEFALLEN

Gefallen[1] *der;* ~s, ~: favour

Gefallen[2] *das;* ~s pleasure

Gefallene *der;* *adj. Dekl.* soldier killed in action; die ~n the fallen

Gefälle·strecke *die* incline

gefällig ① *Adj.* (a) obliging; helpful

(b) (anziehend) pleasing; agreeable ⟨*programme, behaviour*⟩

② *adv.* pleasingly; agreeably

Gefälligkeit *die;* ~, ~en favour

gefälligst *Adv.* (ugs.) kindly

gefangen *2. Part. v.* FANGEN

Gefangene *der/die; adj. Dekl.* prisoner

gefangen-: *~|halten, *~|nehmen ▶ FANGEN 1

Gefangenschaft *die;* ~, ~en captivity

Gefängnis *das;* ~ses, ~se (a) prison; gaol

(b) (Strafe) imprisonment

Gefängnis-: ~strafe *die* prison sentence; ~wärter *der,* ~wärterin *die* [prison] warder

Gefasel *das;* ~s (ugs. abwertend) twaddle (coll.); drivel (derog.)

Gefäß *das;* ~es, ~e (a) vessel; container

(b) (Anat.) vessel

gefasst, *gefaßt *Adj.* (a) calm; composed

(b) in auf etw. (*Akk.*) [nicht] ~ sein [not] be prepared for sth.

Gefecht *das;* ~[e]s, ~e battle

Gefieder *das;* ~s, ~: plumage; feathers *pl.*

gefiedert *Adj.* feathered

geflissentlich ① *Adj.* deliberate

② *adv.* deliberately

geflochten *2. Part. v.* FLECHTEN

geflogen *2. Part. v.* FLIEGEN

geflohen *2. Part. v.* FLIEHEN

geflossen *2. Part. v.* FLIESSEN

Geflügel *das;* ~s poultry

Geflügel·schere *die* poultry shears *pl.*

geflügelt *Adj.* winged ⟨*insect, seed*⟩; ein ~es Wort (fig.) a standard *or* familiar quotation

gefochten *2. Part. v.* FECHTEN

Gefolge *das;* ~s, ~: entourage

Gefolgschaft *die;* ~, ~en: jmdm. ~ leisten obey *or* follow sb.; give one's allegiance to sb.; jmdm. die ~ verweigern refuse to obey *or* follow sb.; refuse to give sb. one's allegiance

gefragt *Adj.* in great demand *postpos.;* sought-after

gefräßig *Adj.* (abwertend) greedy

Gefreite *der; adj. Dekl.* (Milit.) lance corporal (Brit.); private first class (Amer.); (Marine) able seaman; (Luftw.) aircraftman first class (Brit.); airman third class (Amer.)

gefressen *2. Part. v.* FRESSEN

gefrieren *unr. itr. V.; mit sein* freeze

gefrier-, Gefrier-: ~fach *das* freezing compartment; ~punkt *der* freezing point; ~schrank *der* freezer; ~|trocknen *tr. V.; meist im Inf. u. 2. Part.* freeze-dry; ~truhe *die* [chest] freezer

gefroren *2. Part. v.* FRIEREN, GEFRIEREN

gefrustet *Adj.* (ugs.) frustrated

Gefüge *das;* ~s, ~: structure

gefügig *Adj.* compliant; docile ⟨*animal*⟩

Gefühl *das;* ~s, ~e (a) sensation; feeling

(b) (Gemütsverfassung) feeling

gefühl·los *Adj.* (a) numb

(b) (herzlos, kalt) unfeeling

gefühls-, Gefühls-: ~betont *Adj.* emotional; ~duselei *die;* ~~ (ugs. abwertend) mawkishness; ~mäßig *Adj.* emotional ⟨*reaction*⟩; ⟨*action*⟩ based on emotion; ~regung *die* emotion

gefühl·voll ① *Adj.* sensitive; (ausdrucksvoll) expressive

② *adv.* sensitively; expressively

gefüllt *2. Part. v.* FÜLLEN

gefunden *2. Part. v.* FINDEN; *s. auch* FRESSEN B

Gegacker *das;* ~s (a) (dauerndes Gackern) cackling

(b) (ugs.: Kichern) giggling

gegangen *2. Part. v.* GEHEN

gegeben *2. Part. v.* GEBEN

gegebenen·falls *Adv.* should the occasion arise

gegen *Präp. mit Akk.* (a) against; ~ etw. stoßen knock into sth.; ein Mittel ~ Krebs a cure for cancer; ~ die Abmachung contrary to the agreement

(b) ~ Abend/Morgen towards evening/dawn; ~ vier Uhr around 4 o'clock

(c) (im Vergleich zu) compared with

(d) (im Ausgleich für) for; ~ **Quittung** against a receipt

Gegen-: ~**angriff** der counter-attack; ~**argument** das counter-argument; ~**besuch** der return visit

Gegend die; ~, ~**en (a)** area **(b)** (Körperregion) region

Gegen-: ~**darstellung** die: eine ~darstellung [der Sache] an account [of the matter] from an opposing point of view; ~**druck** der counter pressure

gegen-einander Adv. against each other or one another

gegen-, Gegen-: ~**gewicht** das counterweight; ein ~gewicht zu od. gegen etw. bilden (fig.) counterbalance sth.; ~**gift** das antidote; ~**kandidat** der, ~**kandidatin** die opposing candidate; rival candidate; ~**leistung** die service in return; ~**mittel** das (gegen Gift) antidote; (gegen Krankheit) remedy; ~**partei** die opposing side; other side; (Sport) opposing side or team; ~**probe** die cross-check; ~**satz** der **(a)** (Gegenteil) opposite; im ~satz zu in contrast to or with; unlike **(b)** (Widerspruch) conflict; ~**sätzlich** Adj. conflicting; ~**schlag** der counterstroke; zum ~schlag ausholen prepare to counter-attack or strike back; ~**seite** die **(a)** (einer Straße, eines Flusses usw.) other side; far side; **(b)** ▶ ~**PARTEI**; ~**seitig** ⟦1⟧ Adj. (wechselseitig) mutual; ⟦2⟧ adv. sich ~seitig helfen/überbieten help/outdo each other or one another; ~**seitigkeit** die; ~~: reciprocity; auf ~seitigkeit (Dat.) beruhen be mutual; ~**spieler** der, ~**spielerin** die opponent; (Sport) opposite number

Gegen-stand der object; (Thema) subject; topic

gegenständlich Adj. (Kunst) representational; (Philos.) objective

gegenstands-los Adj. **(a)** (hinfällig) invalid **(b)** (grundlos, unbegründet) unfounded ⟨accusation, complaint, jealousy⟩; baseless ⟨fear⟩

gegen-, Gegen-: ~**stimme** die vote against; ohne ~stimme unanimously; ~**stück** das companion piece; (fig.) counterpart; ~**teil** das opposite; im ~teil on the contrary; ~**teilig** Adj. opposite; contrary; ~**tor** das (Sport) goal for the other side

gegen-über Präp. mit Dat. **(a)** opposite **(b)** (in Bezug auf) ~ jmdm. od. jmdm. ~ freundlich sein be kind to sb. **(c)** (im Vergleich zu) compared with

gegenüber-, Gegenüber-: ~|**stehen** unr. itr. V. **(a)** jmdm./einer Sache ~stehen stand facing sb./sth.; (fig.) face sb./sth.; **(b)** jmdm./einer Sache feindlich/wohlwollend ~stehen be ill/well disposed towards sb./sth.; ~|**stellen** tr. V. confront; ~**stellung** die **(a)** confrontation; **(b)**

(Vergleich) comparison; **(c)** (zur Identifizierung) identification parade; ~|**treten** unr. itr. V.; mit sein jmdm./einer Sache ~treten (auch fig.) face sb./sth.

Gegen-verkehr der oncoming traffic

Gegenwart die; ~ **(a)** present **(b)** (Anwesenheit) presence **(c)** (Grammatik) present [tense]

gegenwärtig ⟦1⟧ Adj. present ⟦2⟧ adv. at present; at the moment

Gegen-: ~**wehr** die resistance; ~**wert** der equivalent; ~**wind** der head wind; ~**zug** der (Brettspiele, fig.) countermove

gegessen 2. Part. v. ESSEN

geglichen 2. Part. v. GLEICHEN

geglitten 2. Part. v. GLEITEN

Gegner der; ~s, ~, **Gegnerin** die; ~, ~**nen (a)** adversary; opponent **(b)** (Sport) opponent

gegnerisch Adj. opposing; opponents' ⟨goal⟩

Gegnerschaft die; ~ (Einstellung) hostility; antagonism

gegolten 2. Part. v. GELTEN

gegoren 2. Part. v. GÄREN

gegossen 2. Part. v. GIESSEN

gegriffen 2. Part. v. GREIFEN

Gehabe das; ~s (abwertend) affected behaviour; **ihr wichtigtuerisches** ~: her pompous behaviour

gehabt Adj. (ugs.: schon da gewesen) same old (coll.); usual; **wie** ~: as before

Gehalt¹ der; ~[e]s, ~e **(a)** meaning **(b)** (Anteil) content

Gehalt² das (österr. auch: der); ~[e]s, **Gehälter** salary

gehalten 2. Part. v. HALTEN

Gehalts-: ~**abrechnung** die salary statement; payslip; ~**empfänger** der, ~**empfängerin** die salary earner; ~**erhöhung** die salary increase; ~**zettel** der salary slip

gehalt-voll Adj. nutritious ⟨food⟩; ⟨novel, speech⟩ rich in substance

gehässig Adj. (abwertend) spiteful

Gehässigkeit die; ~, ~**en (a)** (Wesen) spitefulness **(b)** (Äußerung) spiteful remark

gehauen 2. Part. v. HAUEN

gehäuft Adj. ein ~er Teelöffel/Esslöffel a heaped teaspoon/tablespoon

Gehäuse das; ~s, ~ (einer Maschine) casing; housing; (einer Kamera, Uhr) case

geh-behindert Adj. able to walk only with difficulty postpos.; disabled

Gehege das; ~s, ~ **(a)** (Jägerspr.) preserve; jmdm. ins ~ kommen (fig.) poach on sb.'s preserve; sich (Dat.) [gegenseitig] ins ~ kommen (fig.) encroach on each other's territory **(b)** (im Zoo) enclosure

geheim [1] *Adj.* (a) secret; etw. ~ halten
keep sth. secret
(b) (mysteriös) mysterious
[2] *adv.* ~ abstimmen vote by secret ballot
geheim-, Geheim-: ~**agent** *der,*
~**agentin** *die* secret agent; ~**dienst** *der*
secret service; **~|**halten** ▸ GEHEIM 1A
Geheimnis *das;* ~**ses,** ~**se** secret
Geheimnis·tuerei *die;* ~ (ugs.)
secretiveness
geheimnis·voll *Adj.* mysterious
Geheim·nummer *die* (a) (Bankw.) personal
identification number; PIN
(b) (Telefonnummer) ex-directory number;
unlisted number (Amer.)
Geheim·zahl *die* ▸ GEHEIMNUMMER A
Geheiß *das:* auf jmds. ~ (geh.) at sb.'s
behest
gehen [1] *unr. itr. V.; mit sein* (a) walk; go;
über die Straße ~: cross the street
(b) (sich irgendwohin begeben) go
(c) (regelmäßig besuchen) attend
(d) (weg~) go; leave
(e) (in Funktion sein) work; meine Uhr geht
falsch my watch is wrong
(f) (möglich sein) ja, das geht yes, I/we can
manage that; das geht nicht that can't be
done
(g) (ugs.: gerade noch angehen) Hast du gut
geschlafen? – Es geht Did you sleep well? –
Not too bad
(h) (sich entwickeln) der Laden/das Geschäft
geht gut/gar nicht the shop/business is doing
well/not doing well at all; es ist gut
gegangen it turned out well
(i) (unpers.) wie geht es dir? How are you?;
jmdm. geht es gut/schlecht (gesundheitlich) sb.
is well/not well; (geschäftlich) sb. is doing well/
badly
(j) (unpers.) (sich um etw. handeln) worum geht
es hier? what is this all about?
(k) sich ~ lassen (sich nicht beherrschen) lose
control of oneself; (sich vernachlässigen) let
oneself go
(l) (ein Liebespaar sein) mit jmdm. ~: go out
with sb.
[2] *unr. tr. V.* (zurücklegen) 10 km ~: walk 10
km
****gehen|lassen** ▸ GEHEN 1K
geheuer *Adj.* (a) in diesem Gebäude ist es
nicht ~: this building is eerie
(b) ihr war doch nicht [ganz] ~: she felt [a
little] uneasy
(c) die Sache ist [mir] nicht ganz ~: [I feel]
there's something odd about this business
Gehilfe *der;* ~**n,** ~**n, Gehilfin** *die;* ~,
~**nen** assistant
Gehirn *das;* ~**[e]s,** ~**e** brain
Gehirn-: ~**erschütterung** *die*
concussion; ~**schlag** *der* stroke;
~**wäsche** *die* brainwashing *no indef. art.*
gehoben [1] 2. Part. v. HEBEN;

*old spelling - see note on page xiv

[2] *Adj.* (a) higher; senior (position)
(b) (gewählt) elevated, refined
geholfen 2. Part. v. HELFEN
Gehör *das;* ~**[e]s** [sense of] hearing; [etw.]
nach dem ~ singen/spielen sing/play [sth.]
by ear; das absolute ~ (Musik) absolute pitch
gehorchen *itr. V.* jmdm. ~: obey sb.
gehören [1] *itr. V.* (a) jmdm. ~: belong to
sb.
(b) (Teil eines Ganzen sein) zu jmds. Freunden/
Aufgaben ~: be one of sb.'s friends/part of
sb.'s duties
(c) (passend sein) dein Roller gehört nicht in
die Küche! your scooter does not belong in
the kitchen!
(d) (nötig sein) es hat viel Fleiß dazu gehört it
took a lot of hard work; dazu gehört sehr viel
that takes a lot
[2] *refl. V.* (sich schicken) be fitting; es gehört
sich [nicht], … zu …: it is [not] good
manners to …
gehörig [1] *Adj.* (a) proper
(b) (ugs.: beträchtlich) ein ~er Schrecken/eine
~e Portion Mut a good fright/a good deal of
courage
[2] *adv.* (ugs.: beträchtlich) ~ essen/trinken eat/
drink heartily
gehorsam *Adj.* obedient
Gehorsam *der;* ~**s** obedience
Geh·steig *der;* ~**[e]s,** ~**e** pavement (Brit.);
sidewalk (Amer.)
Geht·nicht·mehr *das:* bis zum ~ (salopp)
ad nauseam
Gehupe *das;* ~**s** honking; hooting
Geier *der;* ~**s,** ~: vulture
Geige *die;* ~, ~**n** violin
Geiger *der;* ~**s,** ~, **Geigerin** *die;* ~,
~**nen** violin player; violinist
Geiger·zähler *der* (Physik) Geiger counter
geil *Adj.* (a) (oft abwertend: sexuell erregt) randy;
horny (sl.); (lüstern) lecherous
(b) (Jugendspr.) great (coll.); fabulous (coll.)
Geilheit *die;* ~ ▸ GEIL A randiness;
horniness (sl.); lecherousness
Geisel *die;* ~, ~**n** hostage
Geisel-: ~**nahme** *die;* ~~, ~~**n** taking
of hostages; ~**nehmer** *der;* ~~**s,** ~~,
~**nehmerin** *die;* ~~, ~~**nen** terrorist/
guerrilla *etc.* holding the hostages
Geißel *die;* ~, ~**n** (hist., auch fig.) scourge
Geist *der;* ~**[e]s,** ~**er** (a) (Verstand) mind
(b) (Scharfsinn) wit
(c) (innere Einstellung) spirit
(d) (denkender Mensch) mind; intellect; ein
großer/kleiner ~: a great mind/a person of
limited intellect
(e) (überirdisches Wesen) spirit; der Heilige ~
(christl. Rel.) the Holy Ghost *or* Spirit
(f) (Gespenst) ghost
Geister-: ~**bahn** *die* ghost train;
~**fahrer** *der;* ~**fahrerin** *die: person*
driving on the wrong side of the road or the
wrong carriageway

geisterhaft *Adj.* ghostly; eerie ⟨*atmosphere*⟩

Geister·hand *die:* wie von *od.* durch ∼: as if by an invisible hand

geistes-, Geistes-: ∼**abwesend** ① *Adj.* absent-minded; ② *adv.* absent-mindedly; ∼**blitz** *der* (ugs.) brainwave; ∼**gegenwart** *die* presence of mind; ∼**gegenwärtig** ① *Adj.* quick-witted; ② *adv.* with great presence of mind; ∼**krank** *Adj.* mentally ill; ∼**krankheit** *die* mental illness; ∼**wissenschaften** *Pl.* arts; humanities; ∼**wissenschaftler** *der*, ∼**wissenschaftlerin** *die* arts scholar; scholar in the humanities; ∼**zustand** *der* mental state

geistig ① *Adj.* (a) intellectual; (Psych.) mental

(b) alcoholic ⟨*drinks*⟩

② *adv.* intellectually; (Psych.) mentally

geistlich *Adj.* sacred ⟨*song, music*⟩; religious ⟨*order, book, writings*⟩

Geistliche *der; adj. Dekl.* clergyman

geist-, Geist-: ∼**los** *Adj.* dim-witted; (trivial) trivial; ∼**losigkeit** *die;* ∼∼: dim-wittedness; (Trivialität) triviality; ∼**reich** ① *Adj.* witty; (klug) clever; ② *adv.:* wittily; cleverly; ∼**tötend** *Adj.* soul-destroying ⟨*work, job*⟩; stupefyingly boring ⟨*chatter, drivel*⟩

Geiz *der;* ∼es meanness; (Knauserigkeit) miserliness

geizen *itr. V.* be mean

Geiz·hals *der* (abwertend) skinflint

geizig *Adj.* mean; (knauserig) miserly

gekannt 2. *Part. v.* KENNEN

Gekicher *das;* ∼s giggling

geklungen 2. *Part. v.* KLINGEN

geknickt *Adj.* (ugs.) dejected

gekniffen 2. *Part. v.* KNEIFEN

gekommen 2. *Part. v.* KOMMEN

gekonnt ① 2. *Part. v.* KÖNNEN; ② *Adj.* accomplished; (hervorragend ausgeführt) masterly

gekrochen 2. *Part. v.* KRIECHEN

gekünstelt ① *Adj.* artificial ② *adv.* er lächelte ∼: he gave a forced smile

Gelächter *das;* ∼s, ∼: laughter

geladen 2. *Part. v.* LADEN

Gelände *das;* ∼s, ∼ (a) (Landschaft) ground; terrain

(b) (Grundstück) site; (von Schule, Krankenhaus usw.) grounds *pl.*

Geländer *das;* ∼s, ∼: banisters *pl.*; handrail; (am Balkon, an einer Brücke) railing[s *pl.*]; (aus Stein) parapet

gelang 3. *Pers. Sg. Prät. v.* GELINGEN

gelangen *itr. V.; mit sein* an etw. (*Akk.*)/zu etw. ∼: reach sth.; (fig.) zu Ansehen ∼: gain esteem

gelassen ① 2. *Part. v.* LASSEN; ② *Adj.* calm; (gefasst) composed

Gelassenheit *die;* ∼: calmness; (Gefasstheit) composure

Gelatine /ʒelaˈtiːnə/ *die;* ∼: gelatine

gelaufen 2. *Part. v.* LAUFEN

geläufig *Adj.* (vertraut) common ⟨*expression, concept*⟩

gelaunt *Adj.* gut ∼: cheerful; schlecht ∼: bad-tempered; gut/schlecht ∼ sein be in a good/bad mood

gelb *Adj.* yellow

Gelb *das;* ∼s, ∼ *od.* (ugs.) ∼s yellow

gelblich *Adj.* yellowish; yellowed ⟨*paper*⟩; sallow ⟨*skin*⟩

Gelb-sucht *die* (Med.) jaundice

Geld *das;* ∼es, ∼er money; großes ∼: large denominations *pl.;* kleines/bares ∼: change/cash

geld-, Geld-: ∼**automat** *der* cash dispenser; ∼**beutel** *der* (bes. südd.) purse; ∼**börse** *die* purse; ∼**buße** *die* fine; ∼**gier** *die* avarice; ∼**gierig** *Adj.* avaricious; ∼**institut** *das* financial institution; ∼**mangel** *der* lack of money; ∼**mittel** *Pl.* financial resources; ∼**preis** *der* cash prize; ∼**rück·gabe** *die* (a) ∼rückgabe verlangen ask for one's money back; Anspruch auf ∼rückgabe haben be entitled to one's money back; (b) (eines Automaten) coin return; ∼**schein** *der* banknote; bill (Amer.); ∼**schrank** *der* safe; ∼**schwierigkeiten** *Pl.* financial difficulties *or* straits; ∼**spende** *die* donation; contribution; ∼**strafe** *die* fine; ∼**stück** *das* coin; ∼**wechsel** *der* exchanging of money; „∼wechsel" 'bureau de change'

Gelee /ʒeˈleː/ *der od. das;* ∼s, ∼s jelly

gelegen ① 2. *Part. v.* LIEGEN; ② *Adj.* (passend) convenient

Gelegenheit *die;* ∼, ∼en opportunity; (Anlass) occasion

Gelegenheits-: ∼**arbeit** *die* casual work; ∼**kauf** *der* bargain

gelegentlich ① *Adj.* occasional ② *adv.* occasionally

gelehrig *Adj.* ⟨*child*⟩ who is quick to learn; ⟨*animal*⟩ that is quick to learn

gelehrt *Adj.* learned

Gelehrte *der/die; adj. Dekl.* scholar

Geleit *das;* ∼[e]s, ∼e (geh.) sie bot uns ihr ∼ an she offered to accompany us

geleiten *tr. V.* (geh.) escort

Geleit·schutz *der* (Milit.) escort

Gelenk *das;* ∼[e]s, ∼e joint

gelenkig ① *Adj.* agile ⟨*person*⟩; supple ⟨*limb*⟩ ② *adv.* agilely

Gelenkigkeit *die;* ∼: agility; (von Gliedmaßen) suppleness

gelernt *Adj.* qualified

gelesen 2. *Part. v.* LESEN

Geliebte *der/die; adj. Dekl.* lover/mistress

geliefert Adj.: ~ sein (salopp) have had it (coll.)

geliehen 2. Part. v. LEIHEN

gelind[e] ⊡ Adj. mild
⊡ adv. mildly; ~e gesagt to put it mildly

gelingen unr. itr. V.; mit sein succeed

Gelingen das; ~s success

gelitten 2. Part. v. LEIDEN

gellen itr. V. (a) (hell schallen) ring out
(b) (nachhallen) ring

geloben tr. V. (geh.) vow; das Gelobte Land the Promised Land

gelogen 2. Part. v. LÜGEN

gelöst Adj. relaxed

gelten ⊡ unr. itr. V. (a) (gültig sein) be valid; ⟨banknote, coin⟩ be legal tender; ⟨law etc.⟩ be in force
(b) (angesehen werden) als etw. ~: be regarded as sth.
(c) (+ Dat.) (bestimmt sein für) be directed at
⊡ unr. tr. V. (a) (wert sein) sein Wort gilt viel/wenig his word carries a lot of/little weight
(b) unpers. es gilt, etw. zu tun it is essential to do sth.

geltend: etw. ~ machen assert sth.

Geltung die; ~ (a) validity; für jmdn. ~ haben apply to sb.
(b) (Wirkung) recognition; zur ~ kommen show to [its best] advantage

Geltungs-bedürfnis das need for recognition

gelungen ⊡ 2. Part. v. GELINGEN;
⊡ Adj. (a) (ugs.: spaßig) priceless
(b) (ansprechend) inspired

gemächlich /gə'mɛ(:)çlɪç/ ⊡ Adj. leisurely
⊡ adv. in a leisurely manner

Gemächlichkeit die; ~: leisureliness

gemacht: ein ~er Mann sein (ugs.) be a made man

Gemahl der; ~s, ~e (geh.) consort; husband

Gemahlin die; ~, ~nen (geh.) consort; wife

Gemälde das; ~s, ~: painting

gemäß Präp. + Dat. in accordance with

gemäßigt Adj. moderate; qualified ⟨optimism⟩; temperate ⟨climate⟩

Gemecker[e] das; ~s (a) (von Schafen, Ziegen) bleating
(b) (ugs. abwertend: Nörgelei) griping (coll.); grousing (coll.); moaning

gemein ⊡ Adj. (a) vulgar ⟨joke, expression⟩; nasty ⟨person⟩
(b) (niederträchtig) mean; dirty ⟨lie⟩; mean ⟨trick⟩
⊡ adv. in a mean or nasty way

Gemeinde die; ~, ~n (a) municipality; (Bewohner) community
(b) (Pfarr~) parish
(c) (versammelte Gottesdienstteilnehmer) congregation

Gemeinde-: ~rat der (a) (Gremium) local council; (b) (Mitglied) local councillor;
~rätin die local councillor;
~schwester die district nurse;
~verwaltung die local administration

gemein·gefährlich Adj. dangerous to the public

Gemein·gut das (geh.) common property

Gemeinheit die; ~, ~en (a) meanness
(b) (Handlung) mean trick

gemein·nützig Adj. serving the public good postpos., not pred.; (wohltätig) charitable

gemeinsam ⊡ Adj. (a) common ⟨interests, characteristics⟩; mutual ⟨acquaintance, friend⟩; joint ⟨property, account⟩; shared ⟨experience⟩; ~e Interessen/Merkmale haben have interests/characteristics in common
(b) (miteinander unternommen) joint; viel Gemeinsames haben have a lot in common
⊡ adv. together

Gemeinsamkeit die; ~, ~en common feature

Gemeinschaft die; ~, ~en (a) community
(b) (Verbundenheit) coexistence

gemeinschaftlich ▶ GEMEINSAM

gemein·verständlich Adj. generally comprehensible

Gemein·wohl das public good

gemessen ⊡ 2. Part. v. MESSEN;
⊡ Adj. (würdevoll) measured ⟨steps, tones, language⟩; deliberate ⟨words, manner of speaking⟩

Gemetzel das; ~s, ~: massacre

gemieden 2. Part. v. MEIDEN

Gemisch das; ~[e]s, ~e mixture (aus, von of)

gemocht 2. Part. v. MÖGEN

gemolken 2. Part. v. MELKEN

*Gemse ▶ GÄMSE

Gemurmel das; ~s murmuring

Gemüse das; ~s, ~: vegetables pl.

gemusst, * gemußt 2. Part. v. MÜSSEN

Gemüt das; ~[e]s, ~er (a) nature
(b) (Empfindungsvermögen) heart
(c) (Mensch) soul

gemütlich ⊡ Adj. snug; cosy; (bequem) comfortable; (ungezwungen) informal
⊡ adv. cosily; (bequem) comfortably; ~ beisammensitzen sit pleasantly together

Gemütlichkeit die; ~: snugness; (Zwanglosigkeit) informality

gemüts-, Gemüts-: ~krank Adj. (Med., Psych.) emotionally disturbed; ~mensch der (ugs.) even-tempered person

gemüt·voll Adj. warm-hearted; (empfindsam) sentimental

Gen das; ~s, ~e (Biol.) gene

genannt 2. Part. v. NENNEN

genas 1. u. 3. Pers. Sg. Prät. v. GENESEN

genau ⊡ Adj. (a) (exakt) exact; precise

(b) (sorgfältig, gründlich) meticulous; ⟨person⟩; careful ⟨study⟩
[2] adv. **(a)** exactly; precisely; ∼ um 8⁰⁰ at 8 o'clock precisely
(b) (gerade, eben) just
(c) (als Verstärkung) just
(d) (als Zustimmung) exactly; precisely
(e) (sorgfältig) ∼ arbeiten/etw. ∼ durchdenken work/think sth. out meticulously; ∼ genommen strictly speaking
*****genau·genommen** ▶ GENAU 2E
Genauigkeit die; ∼ **(a)** (Exaktheit) exactness; precision; (einer Waage) accuracy
(b) (Sorgfalt) meticulousness
genau·so Adv. **(a)** mit Adjektiven just as
(b) mit Verben in exactly the same way; (in demselben Maße) just as much
genaustens Adv. etw. ∼ durchdenken/ beachten think sth. out/observe sth. most meticulously
Gendarm /ʒanˈdarm/ der; ∼en, ∼en (österr., sonst veralt.) village or local policeman or constable
Gendarmerie /ʒandarməˈriː/ die; ∼, ∼n (österr., sonst veralt.) village or local constabulary
genehm Adj. jmdm. ∼ sein (geh.) (jmdm. passen) be convenient to sb.; (jmdm. angenehm sein) be acceptable to sb.
genehmigen tr. V. approve ⟨plan, alterations, application⟩; authorize ⟨stay⟩; grant ⟨request⟩; give permission for ⟨demonstration⟩; sich (Dat.) etw. ∼ (ugs.) treat oneself to sth.
Genehmigung die; ∼, ∼en **(a)** ▶ GENEHMIGEN; approval; authorization; granting; permission (Gen. for)
(b) (Schriftstück) permit; (Lizenz) licence
geneigt Adj. in ∼ sein, etw. zu tun be inclined to do sth.
General der; ∼s, ∼e od. Generäle general
General-: ∼direktor der chairman; president (Amer.); ∼direktorin die chairwoman; president (Amer.)
generalisieren tr., itr. V. generalize
Generalisierung die; ∼, ∼en generalization
general-, General-: ∼probe die (auch fig.) dress rehearsal; ∼streik der general strike; ∼überholen tr. V.; nur im Inf. und 2. Part. gebr. (bes. Technik) etw. ∼überholen give sth. a general overhaul; ∼vertreter der, ∼vertreterin die general representative; ∼vollmacht die (Rechtsw.) full or unlimited power of attorney
Generation die; ∼, ∼en generation
Generations·konflikt der generation gap
Generator der; ∼s, ∼en generator
generell [1] Adj. general [2] adv. generally
genervt Adj. annoyed
genesen unr. itr. V.; mit sein (geh.) recover

Genesung die; ∼, ∼en (geh.) recovery
genetisch (Biol.) Adj. genetic
Genf (das); ∼s Geneva
Genfer [1] der; ∼s, ∼: Genevese [2] Adj. Genevese; der ∼ See Lake Geneva
Genferin die; ∼, ∼nen Genevese
Gen·forschung die (Biol.) genetic research
genial Adj. brilliant
Genialität die; ∼: genius
Genick das; ∼[e]s, ∼e back or nape of the neck
Genie /ʒeˈniː/ das; ∼s, ∼s genius
genieren /ʒeˈniːrən/ refl. V. be embarrassed
genießbar Adj. (essbar) edible; (trinkbar) drinkable; er ist heute nicht ∼ (fig. ugs.) he is unbearable today
genießen unr. tr. V. enjoy
Genießer der; ∼s, ∼, **Genießerin** die; ∼, ∼nen: er ist ein richtiger Genießer he is a regular 'bon viveur'; sie ist eine stille Genießerin she enjoys life [to the full] in her own quiet way
genießerisch [1] Adj. appreciative [2] adv. appreciatively; ⟨drink, eat⟩ with relish
Genitale das; ∼s, Genitalien /geniˈtaːliən/, **Genital·organ** das genital organ
Genitiv der; ∼s, ∼e (Sprachw.) genitive [case]
Gen·manipulation die genetic manipulation
gen·manipuliert Adj. genetically engineered; genetically manipulated
Genom /geˈnoːm/ das; ∼s, ∼e, (Biol.) genome
genommen 2. Part. v. NEHMEN
genoss, *genoß 1. u. 3. Pers. Sg. Prät. v. GENIESSEN
Genosse der; ∼n, ∼n comrade
genossen 2. Part. v. GENIESSEN
Genossenschaft die; ∼, ∼en cooperative
Genossin die; ∼, ∼nen comrade
gen-, Gen-: ∼technik die, ∼technisch [1] Adj. genetic engineering ⟨techniques, research etc.⟩; ⟨research, developments etc.⟩ in genetic engineering [2] adv. by genetic engineering; ∼technisch verändert genetically altered or modified; altered or modified by genetic engineering; ∼technologie die genetic engineering no art.
genug Adv. enough
genügen itr. V. **(a)** be enough
(b) einer Sache (Dat.) ∼: satisfy sth.
genügend [1] Adj. **(a)** enough
(b) (befriedigend) satisfactory [2] adv. enough
genügsam Adj. modest
Genugtuung /-tuːʊŋ/ die; ∼, ∼en satisfaction

Genus das; ∼, Genera (Sprachw.) gender
Genuss, *Genuß der; Genusses, Genüsse
(a) consumption
(b) (Wohlbehagen) etw. mit ∼ essen/lesen eat
sth. with relish/enjoy reading sth.
genüsslich, *genüßlich Adv. ⟨eat,
drink⟩ with relish
Geograph der; ∼en, ∼en geographer
Geographie die; ∼: geography no art.
Geographin die; ∼, ∼nen geographer
geographisch Adj. geographic[al]
Geologe der; ∼n, ∼n geologist
Geologie die; ∼: geology no art.
Geologin die; ∼, ∼nen geologist
geologisch Adj. geological
Geometrie die; ∼: geometry no art.
geometrisch Adj. geometric[al]
Gepäck das; ∼[e]s luggage (Brit.); baggage
(Amer.); (am Flughafen) baggage
Gepäck-: ∼annahme die (a) checking
in the luggage/baggage; (b) (Schalter) [in-
counter of the] luggage office (Brit.) or
baggage office (Amer.); (zur Aufbewahrung) [in-
counter of the] left-luggage office (Brit.) or
checkroom (Amer.); (am Flughafen) baggage
check-in; **∼aufbewahrung** die left-
luggage office (Brit.); checkroom (Amer.);
(Schließfächer) luggage lockers (Brit.); baggage
lockers (Amer.); **∼ausgabe** die [out-counter
of the] luggage office (Brit.) or (Amer.) baggage
office; (zur Aufbewahrung) [out-counter of the]
left-luggage office (Brit.) or (Amer.) checkroom;
(am Flughafen) baggage reclaim; **∼kontrolle**
die baggage check; **∼netz** das luggage rack
(Brit.); baggage rack (Amer.); **∼schalter** der
▶ ∼ANNAHME B; **∼schein** der luggage
ticket (Brit.); baggage check (Amer.); **∼träger**
der (a) porter; (b) (am Fahrrad) carrier; rack
Gepard der; ∼s, ∼e cheetah; hunting
leopard
gepfeffert Adj. (ugs.) steep (coll.) ⟨price,
rent, etc.⟩
Gepfeife das; ∼s (ugs. abwertend)
[continuous, tuneless] whistling
gepfiffen 2. Part. v. PFEIFEN
gepflegt Adj. (a) well-groomed; spruce
⟨appearance⟩; neat ⟨clothing⟩
(b) (hochwertig) choice ⟨food, drink⟩
Gepflogenheit die; ∼, ∼en (geh.) custom;
(Gewohnheit) habit
Geplapper das; ∼s (ugs., oft abwertend)
prattling
geplättet Adj. (salopp) flabbergasted
Gepolter das; ∼s clatter
gepriesen 2. Part. v. PREISEN
Gequake das; ∼s (ugs.) croaking; (von
Enten) quacking
Gequäke das; ∼s (ugs.) bawling
gequält Adj. forced ⟨smile, gaiety⟩; pained
⟨expression⟩

---

*old spelling - see note on page xiv

gequollen 2. Part. v. QUELLEN
gerade ① Adj. (a) straight; etw. ∼ biegen
bend sth. straight; straighten sth. [out]; ∼
stehen stand up straight
(b) (nicht schief) upright
(c) (aufrichtig) forthright; direct
(d) (Math.) even ⟨number⟩
② Adv. just; (direkt) right
Gerade die; ∼, ∼n; auch adj. Dekl. (Geom.)
straight line
gerade-: ∼aus Adv. straight ahead;
∼|biegen unr. tr. V. (ugs.: bereinigen)
straighten out; **∼heraus** /—'-/ (ugs.) Adv.
etw. ∼heraus sagen say sth. straight out;
∼so Adv. ∼so groß/lang wie ...: just as big/
long as ...; ∼|**stehen** unr. itr. V. (fig.:
einstehen) für etw. ∼stehen accept
responsibility for sth.; **∼zu** Adv. really;
(beinahe) almost
gerad-, Gerad-: ∼linig ① Adj. (a)
straight; direct, lineal ⟨descent, descendant⟩
(b) (aufrichtig) straightforward; ② adv.
(a) ∼linig verlaufen run in a straight line
(b) (aufrichtig) ∼linig handeln/denken be
straightforward; **∼linigkeit** die; ∼∼
(a) straightness; (b) (Aufrichtigkeit)
straightforwardness
gerammelt Adv. ∼ voll (ugs.) [jam-]packed
(coll.); packed out (coll.)
Geranie /ge'ra:niə/ die; ∼, ∼n geranium
gerann 3. Pers. Sg. Prät. v. GERINNEN
gerannt 2. Part. v. RENNEN
gerät 3. Pers. Sg. Präsens v. GERATEN[1]
Gerät das; ∼[e]s, ∼e (a) piece of
equipment; (Fernseher, Radio) set; (Garten∼)
tool
(b) (Turnen) piece of apparatus
geraten[1] unr. itr. V.; mit sein (a) (gelangen)
get
(b) (werden) turn out; (gut ∼) turn out well
geraten[2] ① 2. Part. v. RATEN, GERATEN[1]
② Adj. advisable
Geratewohl: aufs ∼ (ugs.) ⟨select⟩ at
random; wir fuhren aufs ∼ los (ugs.) we went
for a drive just to see where we ended up
geraum Adj. (geh.) considerable
geräumig Adj. spacious ⟨room⟩; roomy
⟨cupboard etc.⟩
Geräusch das; ∼[e]s, ∼e sound;
(unerwünscht) noise
geräusch-, Geräusch-: ∼arm ① Adj.
quiet; ② adv. quietly; **∼los** ① Adj. silent
② adv. (a) silently; (b) (fig. ugs.) without
[any] fuss; **∼pegel** der noise level; **∼voll**
Adj. noisy
gerben tr. V. tan ⟨hides, skins⟩
gerecht ① Adj. just; (unparteiisch) fair
② adv. justly
gerechtfertigt Adj. justified
Gerechtigkeit die; ∼: justice
Gerechtigkeits-sinn der sense of justice
Gerede das; ∼s (abwertend) (a) (ugs.) talk
(b) (Klatsch) gossip

geregelt *Adj.* regular, steady ⟨*job*⟩

gereizt *Adj.* irritable

Gericht¹ *das;* ~[e]s, ~e court; (Richter) bench; (Gebäude) court [house]; **das Jüngste** ~ (Rel.) the Last Judgement

Gericht² *das;* ~[e]s, ~e dish

gerichtlich ① *Adj.* judicial; legal ⟨*proceedings*⟩
② *adv.* jmdn. ~ **verfolgen** take sb. to court

Gerichts-: ~**hof** *der* Court of Justice; ~**kosten** *Pl.* legal costs; ~**saal** *der* courtroom; ~**verfahren** *das* legal proceedings *pl.;* **ein** ~**verfahren einleiten** institute legal *or* court proceedings; **ohne** ~**verfahren** without trial; ~**vollzieher** *der;* ~~s, ~~, ~**vollzieherin** *die;* ~~, ~~nen bailiff

gerieben 2. *Part. v.* REIBEN

geriffelt *Adj.* corrugated ⟨*surface, sheet metal*⟩; fluted ⟨*column*⟩; ribbed ⟨*glass*⟩

gering *Adj.* (a) low; little ⟨*value*⟩; small ⟨*quantity, amount*⟩; short ⟨*distance, time*⟩ (b) (unbedeutend) slight; minor ⟨*role*⟩; **nicht im Geringsten** not in the slightest *or* least; **jmdn./etw.** ~ **achten** *od.* **schätzen** have a low opinion of *or* think very little of sb./sth.; **den Erfolg/Reichtümer** ~ **achten** *od.* **schätzen** set little store by success/riches

geringfügig ① *Adj.* slight; minor ⟨*alteration, injury*⟩; trivial ⟨*amount, detail*⟩
② *adv.* slightly

Geringfügigkeit *die;* ~, ~en triviality

***gering|schätzen** ▶ GERING B

geringschätzig *Adj.* disdainful; disparaging ⟨*remark*⟩

gerinnen *unr. itr. V.; mit sein* ⟨*blood*⟩ clot; ⟨*milk*⟩ curdle

Gerippe *das;* ~s, ~: skeleton

gerippt *Adj.* ribbed; fluted ⟨*glass, column*⟩

gerissen ① 2. *Part. v.* REISSEN;
② *Adj.* (ugs.) crafty

geritten 2. *Part. v.* REITEN

geritzt *Adj.* (salopp) etw. **ist** ~: sth. is [all] settled; **ist** ~**!** will do! (coll.)

Germane *der;* ~n, ~n, **Germanin** *die;* ~, ~nen (hist.) ancient German; Teuton

germanisch *Adj.* (auch fig.) Germanic; Teutonic

Germanistik *die;* ~: German studies *pl.,* no art.

gern[e]; lieber, am liebsten *Adv.* (a) etw. ~ **tun** like *or* enjoy doing sth.; **er spielt lieber Tennis als Golf** he prefers playing tennis to golf; **etw.** ~**/am liebsten essen** like sth./like sth. best; **ja,** ~**/aber** ~: yes, of course; certainly!
(b) (durchaus) **das glaube ich** ~: I can well believe that

gerochen 2. *Part. v.* RIECHEN

Geröll *das;* ~s, ~e debris; (größer) boulders *pl.*

geronnen 2. *Part. v.* RINNEN, GERINNEN

Gerste *die;* ~: barley

Gersten-korn *das* (Med.) sty

Gerte *die;* ~, ~n switch

Geruch *der;* ~[e]s, Gerüche smell; (von Blumen) scent

Gerücht *das;* ~[e]s, ~e rumour

gerufen 2. *Part. v.* RUFEN

geruhsam ① *Adj.* peaceful; leisurely ⟨*stroll*⟩
② *adv.* leisurely; quietly

Geruhsamkeit *die;* ~: peacefulness; (eines Spaziergangs) leisureliness

Gerümpel *das;* ~s junk

gerungen 2. *Part. v.* RINGEN

Gerüst *das;* ~[e]s, ~e scaffolding *no pl., no indef. art.*

gesamt *Adj.* whole; entire

gesamt-, Gesamt-: ~**deutsch** *Adj.* all-German; ~**eindruck** *der* general impression

Gesamtheit *die:* **die** ~ **der Bevölkerung** the entire population

Gesamt-: ~**schule** *die* comprehensive [school]; ~**werk** *das* œuvre; (Bücher) complete works *pl.*

gesandt 2. *Part. v.* SENDEN

Gesandte *der/die; adj. Dekl.* envoy

Gesandtschaft *die;* ~, ~en legation

Gesang *der;* ~[e]s, Gesänge (a) singing (b) (Lied) song

Gesang-: ~**buch** *das* hymn book; ~**verein** *der* choral society

Gesäß *das;* ~es, ~e backside; buttocks *pl.*

geschaffen 2. *Part. v.* SCHAFFEN 1

Geschäft *das;* ~[e]s, ~e (a) business; (Transaktion) [business] deal; **mit jmdm.** ~**e/ein** ~ **machen** do business with sb./strike a bargain *or* do a deal with sb.; **ein gutes** ~ **machen** make a good profit (b) (Laden) shop; store (Amer.)

Geschäfte-macher *der,* **Geschäfte-macherin** *die* (abwertend) profit-seeker

geschäftig *Adj.* bustling

geschäftlich ① *Adj.* business *attrib.*
② *adv.* on business

geschäfts-, Geschäfts-: ~**bedingungen** *Pl.* terms [and conditions] of trade; ~**brief** *der* business letter; ~**frau** *die* businesswoman; ~**freund** *der,* ~**freundin** *die* business associate; ~**führer** *der* manager; (Vereinswesen) secretary; ~**führerin** *die* ▶~FÜHRER: manageress; secretary; ~**führung** *die* management; ~**gebaren** *das* business *no art.;* business practices *pl.;* ~**inhaber** *der,* ~**inhaberin** *die* owner of the/a business; ~**jahr** *das* financial year; ~**kosten** *Pl.* **auf** ~**kosten** on expenses; ~**lage** *die* [business] position; ~**leitung** *die* ▶~FÜHRUNG; ~**leute** ▶~MANN; ~**mann** *der; Pl.* ~**leute** businessman;

~**ordnung** die standing orders pl.; (im Parlament) [rules pl. of] procedure;
~**partner** der, ~**partnerin** die business partner; ~**reise** die business trip; ~**schluss** der closing time; ~**stelle** die branch; (einer Partei, eines Vereins) office; ~**straße** die shopping street; ~**tüchtig** Adj. able, ⟨businessman, landlord, etc.⟩; ~**viertel** das business quarter; (Einkaufszentrum) shopping district; ~**wagen** der company car; ~**zeit** die business hours pl.; (im Büro) office hours pl.

geschah 3. Pers. Sg. Prät. v. GESCHEHEN

geschehen unr. itr. V.; mit sein happen; occur; (ausgeführt werden) be done; **jmdm. geschieht etw.** sth. happens to sb.

gescheit Adj. (a) (intelligent) clever (b) (ugs.: vernünftig) sensible

Gescheitheit die; ~: cleverness

Geschenk das; ~[e]s, ~e present; gift

Geschenk-: ~**artikel** der gift; ~**packung** die gift pack

Geschichte die; ~, ~n (a) history (b) (Erzählung) story

geschichtlich Adj. (a) historical (b) (bedeutungsvoll) historic

Geschichts-: ~**atlas** der historical atlas; ~**buch** das history book

Geschick¹ das; ~[e]s, ~e (geh.) fate

Geschick² das; ~[e]s skill

Geschicklichkeit die; ~: skilfulness; skill

geschickt ① Adj. (a) skilful (b) (klug) clever; adroit ② adv. (a) (gewandt) skilfully (b) (klug) cleverly; adroitly

geschieden 2. Part. v. SCHEIDEN

geschienen 2. Part. v. SCHEINEN

Geschirr das; ~[e]s, ~e (a) crockery; (benutzt) dishes pl.; (b) (für Zugtier) harness

Geschirr-: ~**spül·maschine** die dishwasher; ~**tuch** das; Pl. ~**tücher** tea towel; dish towel (Amer.)

geschissen 2. Part. v. SCHEISSEN

geschlafen 2. Part. v. SCHLAFEN

geschlagen 2. Part. v. SCHLAGEN

Geschlecht das; ~[e]s, ~er (a) sex (b) (Generation) generation (c) (Sippe) family (d) (Sprachw.) gender

geschlechtlich Adj. sexual

geschlechts-, Geschlechts-: ~**akt** der sex[ual] act; ~**chromosom** das (Biol.) sex chromosome; ~**krank** Adj. ⟨person⟩ suffering from VD; ~**krankheit** die venereal disease; ~**organ** das sex[ual] organ; genital organ; ~**teil** das genitals pl.; ~**verkehr** der sexual intercourse; ~**wort** das ▶ ARTIKEL A

---

*alte Schreibung - vgl. Hinweis auf S. xiv

geschlichen 2. Part. v. SCHLEICHEN

geschliffen ① 2. Part. v. SCHLEIFEN; ② Adj. polished

geschlossen ① 2. Part. v. SCHLIESSEN; ② Adj. united ⟨action, front⟩; unified ⟨procedure⟩; **eine** ~**e Ortschaft** a built-up area

Geschlossenheit die; ~: unity

geschlungen 2. Part. v. SCHLINGEN

Geschmack der; ~[e]s, Geschmäcke taste

geschmacklos ① Adj. tasteless ② adv. tastelessly

Geschmacklosigkeit die; ~, ~en lack of [good] taste; bad taste; (Äußerung) tasteless remark

Geschmack[s]·sache die **das ist** ~: that is a question or matter of taste

geschmack·voll ① Adj. tasteful ② adv. tastefully

Geschmatze das; ~s (ugs. abwertend) smacking one's lips no art.; (beim Essen) noisy eating no art.

Geschmeide das; ~s, ~ (geh.) jewellery no pl.

geschmeidig ① Adj. (a) sleek ⟨hair, fur⟩; soft ⟨leather, boots, skin⟩ (b) (gelenkig) supple ⟨fingers⟩; lithe ⟨body, movement, person⟩ ② adv. (gelenkig) agilely

Geschmeidigkeit die; ~: ▶ GESCHMEIDIG 1: sleekness; suppleness; softness; litheness

geschmissen 2. Part. v. SCHMEISSEN

geschmolzen 2. Part. v. SCHMELZEN

Geschmuse das; ~s (ugs.) cuddling; (eines Pärchens) kissing and cuddling

Geschnetzelte das; adj. Dekl.: small, thin slices of meat [cooked in sauce]

geschnitten 2. Part. v. SCHNEIDEN

geschoben 2. Part. v. SCHIEBEN

geschollen 2. Part. v. SCHALLEN

gescholten 2. Part. v. SCHELTEN

Geschöpf das; ~[e]s, ~e creature

geschoren 2. Part. v. SCHEREN

Geschoss¹, *****Geschoß** das; Geschosses, Geschosse projectile; (Kugel) bullet; (Rakete) missile

Geschoss², *****Geschoß** das; Geschosses, Geschosse floor; storey

geschossen 2. Part. v. SCHIESSEN

geschraubt Adj. (ugs.) stilted

Geschrei das; ~s (a) shouting; (von Verletzten, Tieren) screaming; screams pl.; (b) (ugs. fig) fuss

geschrieben 2. Part. v. SCHREIBEN

geschrie[e]n 2. Part. v. SCHREIEN

geschritten 2. Part. v. SCHREITEN

geschunden 2. Part. v. SCHINDEN

Geschütz das; ~es, ~e [big] gun

Geschütz·feuer das artillery fire; shell fire

geschützt Adj. (a) sheltered

(b) (unter Naturschutz) protected
(c) ~er Geschlechtsverkehr sex with a condom
Geschwader *das;* ~s, ~ (Marine) squadron; (Luftwaffe) wing (Brit.); group (Amer.)
Geschwätz *das;* ~es (ugs. abwertend) prattling; (Klatsch) gossip
geschwätzig *Adj.* (abwertend) talkative
geschweige *Konj.* ~ [denn] let alone; never mind
geschwiegen *2. Part. v.* SCHWEIGEN
geschwind (bes. südd.) [1] *Adj.* swift; quick [2] *adv.* swiftly; quickly
Geschwindigkeit *die;* ~, ~en speed
Geschwindigkeits-: ~begrenzung *die,* ~beschränkung *die* speed limit
Geschwister *Pl.* brothers and sisters
geschwollen [1] *2. Part. v.* SCHWELLEN; [2] *Adj.* **(a)** swollen **(b)** (fig. abwertend) pompous [3] *adv.* pompously
geschwommen *2. Part. v.* SCHWIMMEN
geschworen *2. Part. v.* SCHWÖREN
Geschworene *der/die; adj. Dekl.* juror
Geschwulst *die;* ~, Geschwülste tumour
geschwunden *2. Part. v.* SCHWINDEN
geschwungen [1] *2. Part. v.* SCHWINGEN; [2] *Adj.* curved
Geschwür *das;* ~s, ~e ulcer; (Furunkel) boil
gesehen *2. Part v.* SEHEN
Geseire *das;* ~s (ugs.) drivel
Geselle *der;* ~n, ~n journeyman; (Kerl) fellow
gesellen *refl. V.* sich zu jmdm. ~: join sb.
gesellig *Adj.* sociable; ein ~er Abend/~es Beisammensein a convivial evening/a friendly get-together
Geselligkeit *die;* ~: die ~ lieben enjoy [good] company
Gesellin *die;* ~, ~nen journeyman; journeywoman (rare)
Gesellschaft *die;* ~, ~en **(a)** society **(b)** (Veranstaltung) party **(c)** (Kreis von Menschen) group of people **(d)** (Wirtschaft) company
Gesellschafter *der;* ~s, ~ **(a)** ein guter ~ sein be good company **(b)** (Wirtsch.) partner; (Teilhaber) shareholder
Gesellschafterin *die;* ~, ~nen **(a)** [lady] companion **(b)** (Wirtsch.) partner; (Teilhaberin) shareholder
gesellschaftlich *Adj.* social
gesellschafts-, Gesellschafts-: ~fähig *Adj.* (auch fig.) socially acceptable; ~ordnung *die* social order; ~reise *die* group tour; ~schicht *die* stratum of society; ~spiel *das* party game
gesessen *2. Part. v.* SITZEN
Gesetz *das;* ~es, ~e **(a)** law; (geschrieben) statute **(b)** (Regel) rule

gesetz-, Gesetz-: ~buch *das* statute book; ~gebend *Adj.* legislative; ~geber *der* legislator; (Organ) legislature; ~gebung *die;* ~: legislation
gesetzlich [1] *Adj.* legal; statutory ⟨holiday⟩; lawful ⟨heir, claim⟩ [2] *adv.* legally
gesetz-, Gesetz-: ~los *Adj.* lawless; ~losigkeit *die;* ~~: lawlessness; ~mäßig [1] *Adj.* **(a)** law-governed; ~mäßig sein be governed by *or* obey a [natural] law/[natural] laws; **(b)** (gesetzlich) legal; (rechtmäßig) lawful; [2] *adv.* in accordance with a [natural] law/[natural] laws; ~mäßigkeit *die* **(a)** conformity to a [natural] law/[natural] laws; **(b)** (Gesetzlichkeit) legality; (Rechtmäßigkeit) lawfulness
gesetzt *Adj.* staid
Gesetztheit *die;* ~: staidness
gesetz·widrig *Adj.* illegal; unlawful
Gesetz·widrigkeit *die* illegality; unlawfulness
Gesicht *das;* ~[e]s, ~er face; (fig.) das ~ einer Stadt the appearance of a town
Gesichts-: ~ausdruck *der* expression; look; ~creme *die* face cream; ~punkt *der* point of view; ~wasser *das* face lotion; ~züge *Pl.* features
Gesindel *das;* ~s (abwertend) rabble
gesinnt *Adj.* christlich/sozial ~ [sein] [be] Christian-minded/public-spirited; jmdm. freundlich ~ sein be well-disposed towards sb.
Gesinnung *die;* ~, ~en [basic] convictions *pl.;* [fundamental] beliefs *pl.*
gesinnungs-, Gesinnungs-: ~los (abwertend) *Adj.* unprincipled; ~wandel *der* change of attitude
gesittet *Adj.* well-behaved; well-mannered
gesogen *2. Part. v.* SAUGEN
gesondert [1] *Adj.* separate [2] *adv.* separately
gesonnen *Adj.* ~ sein, etw. zu tun feel disposed to do sth.
gesotten *2. Part. v.* SIEDEN
Gespann *das;* ~[e]s, ~e **(a)** (Zugtiere) team **(b)** (Wagen) horse and carriage **(c)** (Menschen) couple; pair
gespannt *Adj.* **(a)** eager; rapt ⟨attention⟩; ~ zuhören listen with rapt attention **(b)** tense ⟨situation, atmosphere⟩; strained ⟨relationships⟩
Gespenst *das;* ~[e]s, ~er **(a)** ghost **(b)** (geh.: Gefahr) spectre
gespenstig, gespenstisch *Adj.* ghostly; eerie ⟨building, atmosphere⟩
gespie[e]n *2. Part. v.* SPEIEN
gesponnen *2. Part. v.* SPINNEN
Gespött *das;* ~[e]s mockery; ridicule
Gespräch *das;* ~[e]s, ~e conversation; (Diskussion) discussion; (Telefon~) call (mit to)

g

gesprächig *Adj.* talkative

Gesprächs-: ~**partner** *der,*
~**partnerin** *die:* wer war dein ~partner/
deine ~partnerin? who were you talking to?;
~**stoff** *der* topics *pl.* of conversation;
~**thema** *das* topic of conversation

gesprochen 2. *Part. v.* SPRECHEN

gesprossen 2. *Part. v.* SPRIESSEN

gesprungen 2. *Part. v.* SPRINGEN

Gespür *das;* ~s feel

gest. *Abk.* = **gestorben** d.

Gestalt *die;* ~, ~en (a) build
(b) (Mensch, Persönlichkeit) figure
(c) (in der Dichtung) character
(d) (Form) form

gestalten *tr. V.* fashion; lay out ⟨*public gardens*⟩; shape ⟨*character, personality*⟩; arrange ⟨*party, conference, etc.*⟩

Gestaltung *die;* ~, ~en ▶ GESTALTEN: fashioning; laying out; arranging

gestand 1. u. 3. *Pers. Sg. Prät. v.* GESTEHEN

gestanden ① 2. *Part. v.* STEHEN, GESTEHEN;
② *Adj.* ein ~er Mann a grown man; ein ~er Parlamentarier an experienced *or* seasoned parliamentarian

geständig *Adj.:* ~ sein have confessed

Geständnis *das;* ~ses, ~se confession

Gestank *der;* ~[e]s (abwertend) stench; stink

Gestapo *die;* ~ (ns.) Gestapo

gestatten ① *tr., itr. V.* permit; allow; ~ Sie, dass ich ...: may I ...?
② *refl. V.* sich (*Dat.*) etw. ~: allow oneself sth.

Geste /'ɡɛstə, 'ɡeːstə/ *die;* ~, ~n (auch fig.) gesture

Gesteck *das;* ~[e]s, ~e flower arrangement

gestehen *tr., itr. V.* confess

Gestein *das;* ~[e]s, ~e rock

Gestell *das;* ~[e]s, ~e (a) (für Weinflaschen) rack; (zum Wäschetrocknen) horse
(b) (Unterbau) frame

gestern *Adv.* yesterday

gestiegen 2. *Part. v.* STEIGEN

gestikulieren *itr. V.* gesticulate

Gestirn *das;* ~[e]s, ~e star

gestochen ① 2. *Part. v.* STECHEN;
② *Adj.* extremely neat ⟨*handwriting*⟩

gestohlen 2. *Part. v.* STEHLEN

Gestöhne *das;* ~s groaning

gestorben 2. *Part. v.* STERBEN

gestoßen 2. *Part. v.* STOSSEN

Gestrampel *das;* ~s (ugs.) kicking about; (beim Radfahren) pedalling

Gesträuch *das;* ~[e]s, ~e shrubbery; bushes *pl.*

gestreift *Adj.* striped

gestrichen ① 2. *Part. v.* STREICHEN;
② *Adj.* level ⟨*measure*⟩

gestrig *Adj.* yesterday's

gestritten 2. *Part. v.* STREITEN

Gestrüpp *das;* ~[e]s, ~e undergrowth

gestunken 2. *Part. v.* STINKEN

Gestüt *das;* ~[e]s, ~e stud [farm]

Gesuch *das;* ~[e]s, ~e request (um for); (Antrag) application (um for)

gesucht *Adj.* (a) [much] sought-after
(b) (gekünstelt) laboured

gesund; gesünder, *seltener:* ~er,
gesündest..., *seltener:* ~est... *Adj.* healthy; wieder ~ werden get better; bleib ~! look after yourself!

gesunden *itr. V.; mit sein* ⟨*person*⟩ recover, get well, regain one's health

Gesundheit *die;* ~: health; ~! (ugs.) bless you!

gesundheitlich ① *Adj.; nicht präd.* ~e Betreuung health care; sein ~er Zustand [the state of] his health
② *adv.* wie geht es Ihnen ~? how are you?

gesundheits-, Gesundheits-: ~**amt** *das* [local] public health department;
~**gefährdend** *Adj.* ~gefährdend sein be a danger to health; ~gefährdende Bakterien/ Produkte bacteria that are a danger to health/products that are a health risk;
~**gefährdung** *die* risk to health;
~**schädlich** *Adj.* detrimental to [one's] health *postpos.;* ~**zeugnis** *das* certificate of health; ~**zustand** *der* state of health

gesungen 2. *Part. v.* SINGEN

gesunken 2. *Part. v.* SINKEN

getan 2. *Part. v.* TUN

Getier *das;* ~[e]s (geh.) animals *pl.*

Getöse *das;* ~s [thunderous] roar; (von vielen Menschen) din

getragen 2. *Part. v.* TRAGEN

Getränk *das;* ~[e]s, ~e drink; beverage (formal)

getrauen *refl. V.* dare

Getreide *das;* ~s grain

Getreide-: ~**anbau** *der* growing of cereals; ~**handel** *der* corn trade

getrennt ① *Adj.* separate
② *adv.* ⟨*pay*⟩ separately; ⟨*sleep*⟩ in separate rooms

getreten 2. *Part. v.* TRETEN

getreu ① *Adj.* (geh.) exact; faithful ⟨*image*⟩
② *adv.* (geh.) ⟨*report, describe*⟩ faithfully

Getriebe *das;* ~s, ~: gears *pl.;* (in einer Maschine) gear system

getrieben 2. *Part. v.* TREIBEN

getroffen 2. *Part. v.* TREFFEN, TRIEFEN

getrogen 2. *Part. v.* TRÜGEN

getrost ① *Adj.* confident
② *adv.* confidently; du kannst es mir ~ glauben you can take my word for it

getrunken 2. *Part. v.* TRINKEN

Getto *das;* ~s, ~s ghetto

---

*old spelling - see note on page xiv

Getue das; ~s (ugs. abwertend) fuss (**um** about)

Getümmel das; ~s tumult

geübt Adj. accomplished; practised ⟨eye, ear⟩

Gewächs das; ~es, ~e plant

gewachsen [1] 2. Part. v. WACHSEN; [2] jmdm./einer Sache ~ sein be a match for sb./be equal to sth.

gewagt Adj. daring; (gefährlich) risky; (fast anstößig) risqué ⟨joke etc.⟩

gewählt [1] Adj. refined [2] adv. in a refined manner

Gewähr die; ~: guarantee; keine ~ übernehmen be unable to guarantee sth.

gewähren tr. V. grant; give ⟨pleasure, joy⟩

gewähr·leisten tr. V. guarantee

Gewahrsam der; ~s (a) (Obhut) safe-keeping (b) (Haft) custody

Gewährs·mann der; Pl. ~männer od. ~leute, **Gewährs·person** die informant; source

Gewalt die; ~, ~en (a) power (b) (Willkür) force (c) (körperliche Kraft) force; violence

gewalt-, Gewalt-: ~akt der act of violence; ~anwendung die use of force or violence ~bereit Adj. ⟨person⟩ prone to violence; ⟨group, organization⟩ prepared to resort to or use violence; ~bereitschaft die: s. ~BEREIT: propensity to violence; willingness to resort to or use violence

Gewalten·teilung die separation of powers

gewaltig [1] Adj. (a) (immens) huge (b) (imponierend) mighty, huge, massive ⟨building etc⟩; monumental ⟨literary work etc.⟩ [2] adv. (ugs.) very much

gewalt·los [1] Adj. non-violent [2] adv. without violence

Gewalt·losigkeit die; ~: non-violence

gewaltsam [1] Adj. forcible ⟨expulsion⟩; enforced ⟨separation⟩; violent ⟨death⟩ [2] adv. forcibly

gewalt·tätig Adj. violent

Gewalt·tätigkeit die (a) (gewalttätige Art) violence (b) ▶ GEWALTAKT

Gewand das; ~[e]s, Gewänder (geh.) robe; gown

gewandt [1] 2. Part. v. WENDEN; [2] Adj. skilful; (körperlich) agile [3] adv. skilfully; (körperlich) agilely

Gewandtheit die; ~: ▶ GEWANDT 2: skill; skilfulness; agility

gewann 1. u. 3. Pers. Sg. Prät. v. GEWINNEN

gewaschen 2. Part. v. WASCHEN

Gewässer das; ~s, ~: stretch of water

Gewebe das; ~s, ~ (a) (Stoff) fabric (b) (Med., Biol.) tissue

Gewehr das; ~[e]s, ~e rifle; (Schrot~) shotgun

Geweih das; ~[e]s, ~e antlers pl.

Gewerbe das; ~s, ~: business; (Handel, Handwerk) trade

Gewerbe-: ~freiheit die right to carry on a business or trade; ~ordnung die laws pl. governing trade and industry; ~schein der licence to carry on a business or trade; ~treibende der/die; adj. Dekl. tradesman/tradeswoman; ~zweig der branch of trade

gewerblich [1] Adj. commercial; business attrib.; (industriell) industrial [2] adv. ~ tätig sein work

gewerbs·mäßig Adj. professional

Gewerkschaft die; ~, ~en trade union

Gewerkschaft[l]er der; ~s, ~, **Gewerkschaft[l]erin** die; ~, ~nen trade unionist

gewerkschaftlich [1] Adj. [trade] union attrib.; [2] adv. ~ organisiert sein belong to a [trade] union

Gewerkschafts·funktionär der, **Gewerkschafts·funktionärin** die [trade] union official

gewesen 2. Part. v. SEIN[1]

gewichen 2. Part. v. WEICHEN

Gewicht das; ~[e]s, ~e (auch fig.) weight; [nicht] ins ~ fallen be of [no] consequence

Gewicht·heben das; ~s weightlifting

gewichtig Adj. weighty

Gewichts·klasse die (Sport) weight [division or class]

gewieft Adj. (ugs.) cunning

gewiesen 2. Part. v. WEISEN

gewillt Adj. in [nicht] ~ sein, etw. zu tun be [un]willing to do sth.

Gewimmel das; ~s throng; (von Insekten) teeming mass

Gewinde das; ~s, ~ (Technik) thread

Gewinn der; ~[e]s, ~e (a) profit (b) (Preis einer Lotterie) prize; (beim Spiel) winnings pl.; (c) (Sieg) win

Gewinn·beteiligung die (Wirtsch.) profit sharing; (Betrag) profit-sharing bonus

gewinn·bringend Adj. lucrative

gewinnen [1] unr. tr. V. win; gain ⟨time, influence, validity, etc.⟩ [2] unr. itr. V. win (**bei** at)

gewinnend Adj. winning

Gewinner der; ~s, ~, **Gewinnerin** die; ~, ~nen winner

Gewinn-: ~quote die share of prize money; ~spanne die profit margin; ~sucht die greed for profit

Gewinnung die; ~ (a) (von Kohle, Erz usw.) mining; extraction; (von Öl) recovery; (von Metall aus Erz) extraction (b) (Erzeugung) production

Gewinn·zahl *die* winning number

Gewirr *das;* ~[e]s **(a)** tangle
(b) (Durcheinander) **ein** ~ **von Ästen** a maze of
branches

gewiss, *gewiß 1 *Adj.* certain
2 *adv.* certainly

Gewissen *das;* ~s, ~: conscience

gewissenhaft 1 *Adj.* conscientious
2 *adv.* conscientiously

gewissen·los *Adj.* unscrupulous

Gewissens·bisse *Pl.* pangs of conscience

gewissermaßen *Adv.* (sozusagen) as it
were; (in gewissem Sinne) to a certain extent

Gewissheit, *Gewißheit *die;* ~, ~en
certainty

Gewitter *das;* ~s, ~: thunderstorm

Gewitter·wolke *die* thundercloud

gewittrig *Adj.* thundery

gewitzt *Adj.* shrewd

gewoben 2. *Part. v.* WEBEN

gewogen 1 2. *Part. v.* WIEGEN
2 *Adj.* (geh.) well disposed (+ *Dat.* towards)

gewöhnen 1 *tr. V.* jmdn. an jmdn./etw. ~:
get sb. used to sb./sth.; accustom sb. to sb./
sth.
2 *refl. V.* sich an jmdn./etw. ~: get used *or*
get *or* become accustomed to sb./sth.;
accustom oneself to sb./sth.

Gewohnheit *die;* ~, ~en habit

gewohnheits-, Gewohnheits-:
~**mäßig** 1 *Adj.* habitual ⟨drinker etc.⟩;
automatic ⟨reaction etc.⟩; 2 *adv.* (regelmäßig)
habitually; ~**mensch** *der* creature of
habit; ~**tier** *das* (scherzh.) creature of habit;
~**trinker, ~trinkerin** *die* habitual
drinker; ~**verbrecher** *der,*
~**verbrecherin** *die* (Rechtsw.) habitual
criminal

gewöhnlich 1 *Adj.* **(a)** normal; ordinary
(b) (gewohnt, üblich) usual
(c) (abwertend: ordinär) common
2 *adv.* **(a)** [für] ~: usually; **wie** ~: as usual
(b) (abwertend: ordinär) in a common way

gewohnt *Adj.* **(a)** usual
(b) etw. (*Akk.*) ~ **sein** be used to sth.

Gewölbe *das;* ~s, ~: vault

gewonnen 2. *Part. v.* GEWINNEN

geworben 2. *Part. v.* WERBEN

geworfen 2. *Part. v.* WERFEN

gewrungen 2. *Part. v.* WRINGEN

Gewühl *das;* ~[e]s milling crowd

gewunden 2. *Part. v.* WINDEN

Gewürz *das;* ~es, ~e spice; (würzende Zutat)
seasoning

Gewürz-: ~**gurke** *die* pickled gherkin;
~**nelke** *die* clove

gewusst, *gewußt 2. *Part. v.* WISSEN

gez. *Abk.* = **gezeichnet** sgd.

Gezeit *die;* ~, ~en tide

Gezerre *das;* ~s wrangling

gezielt 1 *Adj.* specific ⟨questions,
measures, etc.⟩; deliberate ⟨insult,
indiscretion⟩; well-directed ⟨advertising
campaign⟩
2 *adv.* ⟨proceed, act⟩ purposefully

geziemen (geh. veralt.) 1 *itr. V.* jmdm.
[nicht] ~: [ill] befit sb
2 *refl. V.* be proper; **sich für jmdn.** ~: befit
sb.

geziert 1 *Adj.* (abwertend) affected
2 *adv.* (abwertend) affectedly

gezogen 2. *Part. v.* ZIEHEN

Gezwitscher *das;* ~s twittering

gezwungen 1 2. *Part. v.* ZWINGEN
2 *Adj.* forced

gezwungenermaßen *Adv.* of necessity

gib *Imperativ Sg. Präsens v.* GEBEN

gibst 2. *Pers. Sg. Präsens v.* GEBEN

gibt 3. *Pers. Sg. Präsens v.* GEBEN

Gicht *die;* ~: gout

Giebel *der;* ~s, ~: gable

Gier *die;* ~: greed (**nach** for)

gierig 1 *Adj.* greedy
2 *adv.* greedily

gießen 1 *unr. tr. V.* **(a)** pour (**in** + *Akk.*
into, **über** + *Akk.* over)
(b) (verschütten) spill (**über** + *Akk.* over)
(c) (begießen) water
2 *unpers.* (ugs.) pour [with rain]

Gießer *der;* ~s, ~: caster

Gießerei *die;* ~, ~en foundry

Gießerin *die;* ~, ~nen caster

Gift *das;* ~[e]s, ~e poison; (Schlangen~)
venom

gift·grün *Adj.* garish green

giftig *Adj.* poisonous; venomous ⟨snake⟩;
toxic, poisonous ⟨substance, gas, chemical⟩;
(fig.) venomous

Gift-: ~**mord** *der* [murder by] poisoning;
~**mörder** *der,* ~**mörderin** *die* poisoner;
~**müll** *der* toxic waste; ~**pilz** *der*
poisonous mushroom; [poisonous] toadstool;
~**schlange** *die* venomous snake;
~**schrank** *der* poison cabinet *or* cupboard;
~**stachel** *der* poisonous sting; ~**zahn**
der poison fang

Gigant *der;* ~en, ~en giant

gigantisch *Adj.* gigantic

Gilde *die;* ~, ~n (hist.) guild

gilt 3. *Pers. Sg. Präsens v.* GELTEN

Gimpel *der;* ~s, ~: bullfinch

Gin /dʒɪn/ *der;* ~s gin

ging 1. *u.* 3. *Pers. Sg. Prät. v.* GEHEN

Ginster *der;* ~s, ~: broom

Gipfel *der;* ~s, ~: peak; (höchster Punkt des
Berges) summit; (fig.) height

Gipfel·konferenz *die* summit conference

gipfeln *itr. V.* in etw. (*Dat.*) ~: culminate in
sth.

Gipfel·treffen *das* summit meeting

Gips *der;* ~es, ~e plaster; gypsum (Chem.)

Gips·abdruck *der* plaster cast

gipsen *tr. V.* plaster; put ⟨*leg, arm, etc.*⟩ in plaster

Gips·verband *der* plaster cast

Giraffe *die;* ~, ~n giraffe

Girlande *die;* ~, ~n festoon

Giro /'ʒiːro/ *das;* ~s, ~s, *österr. auch* **Giri** (Finanzw.) giro

Giro·konto *das* (Finanzw.) current account

gis, Gis *das;* ~, ~ (Musik) G sharp

Gischt *der;* ~[e]s, ~e *od.* **die;** ~, ~en spray

Gitarre *die;* ~, ~n guitar

Gitarrist *der;* ~en, ~en, **Gitarristin** *die;* ~, ~nen guitarist

Gitter *das;* ~s, ~: bars *pl.;* (vor Fenster-, Türöffnungen) grille; (in der Straßendecke, im Fußboden) grating; (Geländer) railing[s *pl.*]

Gitter·fenster *das* barred window

Glacé·hand·schuh /gla'seː.../ *der* kid glove

Gladiole *die;* ~, ~n gladiolus

Glanz *der;* ~es (a) (von Licht, Sternen, Augen) brightness; (von Haar, Metall, Perlen, Leder usw.) lustre; sheen

(b) (der Jugend, Schönheit) radiance; (des Adels usw.) splendour

glänzen *itr. V.* (a) (Glanz ausstrahlen) shine; ⟨*hair, metal, etc.*⟩ gleam; ⟨*elbows, trousers, etc.*⟩ be shiny

(b) (Bewunderung erregen) shine (**bei** at)

glänzend (ugs.) ⓵ *Adj.* (a) shining; gleaming ⟨*hair, metal, etc.*⟩; shiny ⟨*elbows, trousers, etc.*⟩

(b) (bewundernswert) brilliant; splendid ⟨*references, marks, results, etc.*⟩

⓶ *adv.* ~ mit jmdm. auskommen get on very well with sb.; **es geht mir/uns** ~: I am/we are very well

glanz-, Glanz-: ~**leistung** *die* (auch iron.) brilliant performance; ~**los** *Adj.* dull; lacklustre; ~**nummer** *die* star turn; ~**voll** ⓵ *Adj.* brilliant; sparkling ⟨*variety number*⟩; ⓶ *adv.* brilliantly

Glas *das;* ~es, Gläser (a) glass

(b) (Trinkgefäß) glass; **zwei** ~ *od.* Gläser Wein two glasses of wine

(c) (Behälter) jar

Glas: ~**bläser** *der,* **Glas·bläserin** *die* glass-blower; ~**bank** *die* bottle bank

Gläschen *das;* ~s, ~ (a) [little] glass

(b) (kleines Gefäß) [little] [glass] jar

Glaser *der;* ~s, ~, **Glaserin** *die;* ~, ~nen glazier

gläsern *Adj.* glass

Glas·faser *die* glass fibre

glasieren *tr. V.* (a) glaze

(b) (Kochk.) ice; glaze ⟨*meat*⟩

glasig *Adj.* (a) glassy

(b) (Kochk.) transparent

Glas·malerei *die* stained glass

Glasur *die;* ~, ~en (a) glaze

(b) (Kochk.) icing; (auf Fleisch) glaze

glatt ⓵ *Adj.* (a) smooth; (rutschig) slippery

(b) (ugs.: offensichtlich) downright ⟨*lie*⟩; outright ⟨*deception, fraud*⟩; flat ⟨*refusal*⟩

⓶ *adv.* (a) smoothly; ~ **gehen** (ugs.) go smoothly

(b) (ugs.: rückhaltlos) jmdm. etw. ~ ins Gesicht sagen tell sb. sth. straight to his/her face; ⟨*reject, deny*⟩ flatly

Glätte *die;* ~: smoothness; (Rutschigkeit) slipperiness

Glatt·eis *das* glaze; ice; (auf der Straße) black ice

glätten *tr. V.* smooth out ⟨*piece of paper, etc.*⟩; smooth [down] ⟨*feathers, fur, etc.*⟩; plane ⟨*wood etc.*⟩

glatt-: **~*|**gehen** ▶ GLATT 2A; ~**weg** *Adv.* (ugs.) etw. ~weg ablehnen/ignorieren turn sth. down flat/simply ignore sth.; **das ist** ~**weg erlogen/erfunden** that's a downright lie/that's pure invention

Glatze *die;* ~, ~n bald head; **eine** ~ **haben/bekommen** be/go bald

Glaube *der;* ~ns faith (an + *Akk.* in); (Überzeugung, Meinung) belief (an + *Akk.* in)

glauben ⓵ *tr. V.* (a) (meinen) think

(b) (für wahr halten) believe; **das glaube ich dir nicht** I don't believe you; **das glaubst du doch selbst nicht!** [surely] you can't be serious; **sie glaubt ihm jedes Wort** she believes every word he says; **ob du es glaubst oder nicht ...** believe it or not ...; **das ist doch kaum zu** ~ (ugs.) it's incredible

⓶ *itr. V.* believe (an + *Akk.* in)

Glaubens-: ~**bekenntnis** *das* creed; ~**freiheit** *die* religious freedom; ~**krieg** *der* religious war; ~**sache** *die* (ugs.) matter of faith or belief

glaubhaft ⓵ *Adj.* credible

⓶ *adv.* convincingly

gläubig ⓵ *Adj.* devout; (vertrauensvoll) trusting

⓶ *adv.* devoutly; (vertrauensvoll) trustingly

Gläubige *der/die; adj. Dekl.* believer

Gläubiger *der;* ~s, ~: creditor

glaub·würdig ⓵ *Adj.* credible

⓶ *adv.* convincingly

Glaubwürdigkeit *die;* ~: credibility

gleich ⓵ *Adj.* (a) (identisch, von derselben Art) same; ~ **bleiben** remain the same; ⟨*speed, temperature, etc.*⟩ remain constant; ~ **bleibend** constant, steady ⟨*temperature, speed, etc.*⟩; (~berechtigt, ~wertig, Math.) equal

(b) (ugs.: gleichgültig) **es ist mir völlig** *od.* **ganz** ~: I couldn't care less (coll.); **ganz** ~, **wer anruft, ...**: no matter who calls, ...

⓶ *adv.* (a) (übereinstimmend) ~ **groß/alt** *usw.* **sein** be the same height/age *etc.*; ~ **gut/schlecht** *usw.* equally good/bad *etc.*;

(b) (in derselben Weise) ~ **aufgebaut/gekleidet** having the same structure/wearing identical clothes ···⟶

(c) (sofort) at once; straight away; (bald) in a moment

(d) (räumlich) right; just; ~ **rechts/links** immediately to the right/left

gleich-, Gleich-: ~**alt[e]rig** /-alt(ə)rɪç/ *Adj.* of the same age (mit as); ~**artig** **1** *Adj.* of the same kind *postpos.* (+ *Dat.* as); (sehr ähnlich) very similar (+ *Dat.* to); **2** *adv.* in the same way; ~**berechtigt** *Adj.* having equal rights *postpos.;* ~**berechtigte Partner** equal partners; ~**berechtigung** *die* equal rights *pl.;* *~**bleiben**, ~**bleibend** ▶ GLEICH 1A

gleichen *unr. itr. V.* jmdm./einer Sache ~: be like *or* resemble sb./sth.;

gleichermaßen *Adv.* equally

gleich-, Gleich-: ~**falls** *Adv.* (auch) also; (ebenfalls) likewise; **danke** ~**falls!** thank you, [and] the same to you; ~**förmig** **1** *Adj.* **(a)** (einheitlich) uniform; **(b)** (monoton) monotonous; **2** *adv.* **(a)** (einheitlich) uniformly; **(b)** (monoton) monotonously; ~**geschlechtlich** *Adj.* homosexual; ~**gewicht** *das* balance; ~**gewichts-störung** *die* disturbance of one's sense of balance; ~**gültig** **1** *Adj.* indifferent (**gegenüber** towards); (belanglos) trivial; **das ist mir** ~**gültig** it's a matter of indifference to me; **2** *adv.* indifferently; ~**gültigkeit** *die* indifference (**gegenüber** towards)

Gleichheit *die;* ~, ~**en (a)** identity; (Ähnlichkeit) similarity

(b) (gleiche Rechte) equality

Gleichheits-zeichen *das* equals sign

gleich-, Gleich-: ~|**kommen** *unr. itr. V.; mit sein* **(a)** (entsprechen) be tantamount to; **(b)** (die gleiche Leistung erreichen) jmdm./einer Sache [an etw. (*Dat.*)] ~**kommen** equal sb./ sth. [in sth.]; ~|**machen** *tr. V.* make equal; ~**macherei** *die;* ~~, ~~**en** (abwertend) levelling down (derog.); egalitarianism; ~**mäßig** **1** *Adj.* regular ⟨*interval, rhythm*⟩; uniform ⟨*acceleration, distribution*⟩; even ⟨*heat*⟩; **2** *adv.* ⟨*breathe*⟩ regularly; **etw.** ~**mäßig verteilen/auftragen** distribute sth. equally/apply sth. evenly; ~**mut** *der* equanimity; ~**mütig** **1** *Adj.* calm; composed; **2** *adv.* with equanimity; calmly; ~**namig** *Adj.*(a) of the same name *postpos.;* **(b)** (Math.) ~**namige Brüche** fractions with a common denominator; **Brüche** ~**namig machen** reduce fractions to a common denominator

Gleichnis *das;* ~**ses,** ~**se** (Allegorie) allegory; (Parabel) parable

gleichsam *Adv.* (geh.) as it were

gleich-, Gleich-: ~|**schalten** *tr. V.* force into line; ~**schenk[e]lig** *Adj.* (Math.) isosceles; ~**schritt** *der* marching in step; ~**seitig** *Adj.* (Math.) equilateral; ~|**setzen** *tr. V.* equate; ~|**stellen** *tr. V.* equate; ~**strom** *der* (Elektrot.) direct current

---

*old spelling - see note on page xiv

Gleichung *die;* ~, ~**en** equation

gleich-: ~**wertig** *Adj.* of the same value *postpos.;* ~**wohl** /-'·- *od.* '--/ *Adv.* nevertheless; ~**zeitig** **1** *Adj.* simultaneous; **2** *adv.* at the same time

Gleis *das;* ~**es,** ~**e** track; (Bahnsteig) platform; (einzelne Schiene) rail

gleiten *unr. itr. V.; mit sein* glide; ⟨hand⟩ slide

Gleit-: ~**flug** *der* glide; ~**zeit** *die* flexitime; flexible working hours *Pl.*

Gletscher *der;* ~**s,** ~: glacier

Gletscher-spalte *die* crevasse

glich 1. u. 3. Pers. Sg. Prät. v. GLEICHEN

Glied *das;* ~**[e]s,** ~**er (a)** limb; (Finger~, Zehen~) joint

(b) (Ketten~, auch fig.) link

(c) (Teil eines Ganzen) section; (Mitglied) member

gliedern **1** *tr. V.* structure; organize ⟨thoughts⟩

2 *refl. V.* **sich in Gruppen/Abschnitte** *usw.* ~: be divided into groups/sections *etc.*

Gliederung *die;* ~, ~**en** structure

Glied-: ~**maße** /-ma:sə/ *die;* ~, ~**n** limb; ~**satz** *der* (Sprachw.) subordinate clause

glimmen *unr. od. regelm. itr. V.* glow

Glimm-stängel, ***Glimm-stengel** *der* (ugs. scherzh.) fag (coll.); ciggy (coll.)

glimpflich **1** *Adj.* **(a) der Unfall nahm ein** ~**es Ende** the accident turned out not to be too serious

(b) (mild) lenient ⟨*sentence, punishment*⟩ **2** *adv.* **(a)** (ohne Schaden) ~ **davonkommen** get off lightly

(b) (mild) leniently

glitschig *Adj.* (ugs.) slippery

glitt 1. u. 3. Pers. Sg. Prät. v. GLEITEN

glitzern *itr. V.* ⟨star⟩ twinkle; ⟨*diamond, decorations*⟩ sparkle; ⟨*snow, eyes, tears*⟩ glisten

global **1** *Adj.* **(a)** global; worldwide **(b)** (umfassend) all-round ⟨*education*⟩; overall ⟨*control, planning, etc.*⟩

(c) (allgemein) general **2** *adv.* **(a)** worldwide

(b) (umfassend) in overall terms

(c) (allgemein) in general terms

globalisieren *tr. V.* globalize

Globalisierung *die;* ~, ~**en** globalization

Globen ▶ GLOBUS

Globetrotter *der;* ~**s,** ~: globetrotter

Globus *der;* ~ *od.* ~**ses,** **Globen** globe

Glöckchen *das;* ~**s,** ~: [little] bell

Glocke *die;* ~, ~**n** bell

Glocken-: ~**blume** *die* (Bot.) campanula; ~**rock** *der* widely flared skirt; ~**spiel** *das* **(a)** carillon; (mit einer Uhr gekoppelt auch) chimes *pl.;* **(b)** (Instrument) glockenspiel

glomm 1. u. 3. Pers. Sg. Prät. v. GLIMMEN

Glorien-schein /ˈgloːriən-/ *der* glory; (um den Kopf, fig.) halo

glorifizieren *tr. V.* glorify

Glorifizierung *die;* ~, ~en glorification
glor·reich ① *Adj.* glorious
  ② *adv.* gloriously
Glossar *das;* ~s, ~e glossary
Glosse *die;* ~, ~n commentary; (spöttische Bemerkung) sneering comment
Glotze *die;* ~, ~n (salopp) box (coll.); goggle-box (Brit. coll.)
glotzen *itr. V.* (abwertend) goggle; gawp (coll.)
Glotz·kiste *die* (salopp) box (coll.); goggle-box (Brit. coll.)
Glück *das;* ~[e]s (a) luck; [es ist] ein ~, dass ...: it's lucky that ...; [kein] ~ haben be [un]lucky; viel ~! [the] best of luck!; zum ~ *od.* zu meinem/seinem *usw.* ~: luckily *or* fortunately [for me/him *etc.*]
  (b) happiness
Glucke *die;* ~, ~n brood hen
glücken *tr. V.; mit sein* succeed; etw. glückt jmdm. sb. is successful with sth.
gluckern *itr. V.* gurgle; glug
glücklich ① *Adj.* (a) happy (über + Akk. about)
  (b) (erfolgreich) lucky ⟨winner⟩; successful ⟨outcome⟩; safe ⟨journey⟩
  (c) (vorteilhaft) fortunate
  ② *adv.* (a) (erfolgreich) successfully
  (b) (vorteilhaft, zufrieden) happily ⟨chosen, married⟩
glücklicher·weise *Adv.* fortunately; luckily
glück·selig ① *Adj.* blissfully happy
  ② *adv.* blissfully
Glück·seligkeit *die;* ~: bliss
glucksen *itr. V.* (a) ▶ GLUCKERN;
  (b) (lachen) chuckle
Glücks-: ~klee *der* four-leaf clover; ~pfennig *der* lucky penny; ~pilz *der* (ugs.) lucky devil (coll.)
Glück[s]·sache *die:* das ist ~: it's a matter of luck
Glücks·spiel *das* game of chance
glück·strahlend *Adj.* radiantly happy
Glücks·zahl *die* lucky number
Glück·wunsch *der* congratulations *pl.;* herzlichen ~ zum Geburtstag! happy birthday!
Glüh·birne *die* lightbulb
glühen *itr. V.* glow
glühend ① *Adj.* red-hot ⟨metal etc.⟩; blazing ⟨heat⟩; ardent ⟨admirer etc.⟩; passionate ⟨words, letter, etc.⟩
  ② *adv.* ⟨love⟩ passionately; ⟨admire⟩ ardently; ~ heiß blazing hot
Glüh-: ~wein *der* mulled wine; ~würmchen *das;* ~~s, ~~ (ugs.) (weiblich) glow-worm; (männlich) firefly
Glut *die;* ~, ~en embers *pl.;*
  (b) (geh.: Leidenschaft) passion
glut·rot *Adj.* fiery red
Glyzerin *das;* ~s glycerine

GmbH *Abk.* = **Gesellschaft mit beschränkter Haftung** ≈ plc, PLC
Gnade *die;* ~, ~n (Gunst) favour; (Rel.) grace; (Milde) mercy
gnaden-, Gnaden-: ~brot *das:* jmdm./ einem Tier das ~brot geben keep sb./an animal in his/her/its old age; ~frist *die* reprieve; ~gesuch *das* plea for clemency; ~los (auch fig.) ① *Adj.* merciless; ② *adv.* mercilessly; ~losigkeit *die;* ~~: mercilessness; ~schuss, ***~schuß *der* coup de grâce ⟨by shooting⟩
gnädig *Adj.* gracious; (glimpflich) lenient ⟨sentence etc.⟩
Gnom *der;* ~en, ~en gnome
Gockel *der;* ~s, ~ (bes. südd., sonst ugs. scherzh.) cock
Gold *das;* ~[e]s gold
Gold·barren *der* gold bar
golden ① *Adj.* (aus Gold) gold; (herrlich) golden ⟨days, memories, etc.⟩
  ② *adv.* like gold
Gold-: ~fisch *der* goldfish; ~füllung *die* gold filling; ~grube *die* (auch fig.) gold mine; ~hamster *der* golden hamster
goldig *Adj.* sweet
gold-, Gold-: ~richtig (ugs.) *Adj.* absolutely right; ~schmied *der,* ~schmiedin *die* goldsmith; ~schnitt *der* gilt; ~währung *die* (Wirtsch.) currency tied to the gold standard
Golf¹ *der;* ~[e]s, ~e gulf
Golf² *das;* ~s (Sport) golf
Golf-: ~platz *der* golf course; ~schläger *der* golf club; ~spieler *der,* ~spielerin *die* golfer; ~strom *der* Gulf Stream
Gondel *die;* ~, ~n gondola
gondeln *itr. V.; mit sein* (ugs.) (a) (mit einem Boot) cruise
  (b) (reisen) travel around
  (c) (herumfahren) cruise around
Gong *der;* ~s, ~s gong
gongen *itr. V.* es hat gegongt the gong has sounded
gönnen *tr. V.* jmdm. etw. ~: not begrudge sb. sth.; sich/jmdm. etw. ~: allow oneself/sb. sth.
Gönner *der;* ~s, ~: patron
gönnerhaft (abwertend) *Adj.* patronizing
Gönnerin *die;* ~, ~nen patroness
gor *3. Pers. Sg. Prät. v.* GÄREN
Göre *die;* ~, ~n (nordd., oft abwertend) kid (coll.)
Gorilla *der;* ~s, ~s gorilla
goss, ***goß *1. u. 3. Pers. Sg. Prät. v.* GIESSEN
Gosse *die;* ~, ~n gutter
Gotik *die;* ~ (Stil) Gothic [style]; (Epoche) Gothic period
gotisch *Adj.* Gothic
Gott *der;* ~es, Götter (a) God; grüß [dich] ⋯▸

~! (landsch.) hello!; um ~es Willen (bei Erschrecken) for God's sake; (bei einer Bitte) for heaven's sake
(b) (übermenschliches Wesen) god

Gottes-: ~**dienst** der service; ~**haus** das (geh.) house of God; ~**lästerung** die blasphemy

Gottheit die; ~, ~en deity

Göttin die; ~, ~nen goddess

göttlich [1] Adj. (auch fig.) divine
[2] adv. divinely

gott-, Gott-: ~**lob** adv. thank goodness; ~**los** [1] Adj. (a) ungodly ⟨life etc.⟩; impious ⟨words, speech, etc.⟩; (b) (Gott leugnend) godless ⟨theory etc.⟩; [2] adv. (verwerflich) irreverently; ~**vater** der God the Father; ~**verlassen** Adj. (ugs.: abseits) godforsaken; ~**vertrauen** das trust in God

Götze der; ~n, ~n (auch fig.) idol

Götzen-: ~**bild** das idol; ~**diener** der idolater; ~**dienerin** die idolatress

Gouverneur /guvɛrˈnøːɐ̯/ der; ~s, ~e governor

Grab das; ~[e]s, Gräber grave; das Heilige ~: the Holy Sepulchre; das ~ des Unbekannten Soldaten the tomb of the Unknown Warrior

graben unr. tr., itr. V. dig

Graben der; ~s, Gräben ditch; (Schützen~) trench; (Festungs~) moat

Grab-: ~**hügel** der grave mound; ~**kammer** die burial chamber; ~**mal** das; Pl. ~mäler, geh. ~male monument; ~**schändung** die desecration of a/the grave/of [the] graves

grabschen [1] tr. V. grab; snatch
[2] itr. V. nach etw. ~: grab at sth.

gräbst 2. Pers. Sg. Präsens v. GRABEN

gräbt 3. Pers. Sg. Präsens v. GRABEN

Grab-stein der gravestone

Grabung die; ~, ~en (bes. Archäol.) excavation

Gracht die; ~, ~en canal

Grad der; ~[e]s, ~e degree; (Milit.) rank

grade (ugs.) ▶ GERADE

Grad-messer der gauge, yardstick (für of)

graduell [1] Adj. gradual; slight ⟨difference etc.⟩
[2] adv. gradually; ⟨different⟩ in degree

graduiert Adj. graduate; ein ~er Ingenieur an engineering graduate

Graf der; ~en, ~en count; (britischer ~) earl

Graffito der od. das; ~[s], Graffiti (a) (Kunst) graffito
(b) Pl. (Kritzelei) graffiti

Grafik die; ~, ~en graphic art[s pl.]; (Kunstwerk) graphic; (Druck) print

Grafiker der; ~s, ~, **Grafikerin** die; ~, ~nen [graphic] designer; (Künstler[in]) graphic artist

grafisch [1] Adj. graphic
[2] adv. graphically

Gräfin die; ~, ~nen countess

Grafschaft die; ~, ~en (a) count's land; (in Großbritannien) earldom
(b) (Verwaltungsbezirk) county

Gram der; ~[e]s (geh.) grief; sorrow

grämen [1] tr. V. grieve
[2] refl. V. grieve (über + Akk., um over)

Gramm das; ~s, ~e gram

Grammatik die; ~, ~en grammar

grammatisch [1] Adj. grammatical
[2] adv. grammatically

Grammophon ⓌⓏ das; ~s, ~e gramophone; phonograph (Amer.)

Granat der; ~[e]s, ~e (Schmuckstein) garnet

Granat-apfel der pomegranate

Granate die; ~, ~n shell; (Hand~) grenade

Granat-feuer das shellfire no pl., no indef. art.

grandios [1] Adj. magnificent
[2] adv. magnificently

Granit der; ~s, ~e granite

grantig (südd., österr. ugs.) [1] Adj. bad-tempered
[2] adv. bad-temperedly

Grapefruit /ˈgreːpfruːt/ die; ~, ~s grapefruit

Graph der; ~en, ~en (Math., Naturw.) graph

Graphik usw.: ▶ GRAFIK usw.

Graphit der; ~s, ~e graphite

Gras das; ~es, Gräser (a) grass; über etw. (Akk.) ~ wachsen lassen (ugs.) let the dust settle on sth.
(b) (Drogenjargon) grass (sl.)

grasen itr. V. graze

Gras-: ~**halm** der blade of grass; ~**land** das grassland; ~**narbe** die turf

grässlich, *gräßlich [1] Adj. (a) (abscheulich) horrible; terrible ⟨accident⟩
(b) (ugs.: unangenehm) dreadful (coll.)
(c) (ugs.: sehr stark) terrible (coll.)
[2] adv. (a) (abscheulich) horribly; terribly
(b) (ugs.: unangenehm) terribly (coll.)
(c) (ugs.: sehr) terribly (coll.)

Grässlichkeit, *Gräßlichkeit die; ~, ~enz (a) (Abscheulichkeit) horribleness; (eines Unfalls) terribleness
(b) (unangenehme Art) dreadfulness (coll.)

Grat der; ~[e]s, ~e ridge

Gräte die; ~, ~n [fish] bone

Gratifikation die; ~, ~en bonus

gratinieren tr. V. (Gastr.) brown [the top of]; gratinierter Blumenkohl cauliflower au gratin

gratis Adv. free [of charge]; gratis

Gratis-: ~**aktie** die (Börsenw.) bonus share; ~**muster** das, ~**probe** die free sample

Grätsche die; ~, ~n (Turnen) straddle; (Sprung) straddle vault

---

*alte Schreibung - vgl. Hinweis auf S. xiv

Gratulant *der;* ~en, ~en, **Gratulantin** *die;* ~, ~nen well-wisher

Gratulation *die;* ~, ~en congratulations *pl.*

gratulieren *itr. V.* jmdm. ~: congratulate sb.; jmdm. zum Geburtstag ~: wish sb. many happy returns [of the day]

Grat·wanderung *die* ridge walk; (fig.) balancing act

grau *Adj.* grey; (trostlos) dreary; drab; ~ meliert greying ⟨hair⟩

Gräuel *der;* ~s, ~ (a) etw./jmd. ist jmdm. ein ~: sb. loathes *or* detests sth./sb.
(b) (geh.) (~tat) atrocity

Gräuel·tat *die* atrocity

grauen[1] *itr. V.* (geh.) der Morgen/der Tag graut morning/day is breaking

grauen[2] *itr. V.* (unpers.) ihm graut [es] davor/vor ihr he dreads [the thought of] it/ he's terrified of her

Grauen *das;* ~s, ~: horror (vor + *Dat.* of)

grauen·haft [1] *Adj.* horrifying; (ugs.: sehr unangenehm) terrible (coll.)
[2] *adv.* horrifyingly; (ugs.: sehr unangenehm) terribly (coll.)

grauhaarig *Adj.* grey-haired

gräulich [1] *Adj.* (a) horrifying
(b) (unangenehm) awful
[2] *adv.* (a) horrifyingly
(b) (unangenehm) terribly

*grau·meliert ▶ GRAU

Graupe *die;* ~, ~n (a) grain of pearl barley
(b) *Pl.* (Gericht) pearl barley *sing.*

Graupel *die;* ~, ~n soft hail pellet; ~n soft hail; graupel

graupeln *itr. V.* (unpers.) es graupelt there's soft hail falling

grausam [1] *Adj.* (a) cruel
(b) (furchtbar) terrible; dreadful
[2] *adv.* (a) cruelly
(b) (furchtbar) terribly, dreadfully

Grausamkeit *die;* ~, ~en (a) cruelty
(b) (Handlung) act of cruelty

grausen [1] *tr., itr. V.* (unpers.) es grauste ihm *od.* ihn davor/vor ihr he dreaded it/he was terrified of her
[2] *refl. V.* sich vor etw./jmdm. ~: dread sth./ be terrified of sb.

Grausen *das;* ~s horror

grausig *Adj., adv.* ▶ GRAUENHAFT

gravieren *tr. V.* engrave

gravierend *Adj.* serious, grave

Gravierung *die;* ~, ~en engraving

Gravitation *die;* ~ (Physik, Astron.) gravitation

Gravur /gra'vuːɐ̯/ *die;* ~, ~en engraving

Grazie /'graːtsjə/ *die;* ~, ~n (a) (Anmut) gracefulness
(b) (Myth.) Grace

greif·bar [1] *Adj.* (a) in ~er Nähe (fig.)

within reach; der Urlaub ist in ~e Nähe gerückt (fig.) the holiday is just coming up [now]
(b) (deutlich) tangible; concrete
(c) (ugs.: verfügbar) available
[2] *adv.* ~ nahe (fig.) within reach

greifen [1] *unr. tr. V.* (a) (ergreifen) take hold of; grasp; (rasch ~) seize
(b) (fangen) catch
[2] *unr. itr. V.* (a) in/unter/hinter etw./sich (*Akk.*) ~: reach into/under/behind sth./one; nach etw. ~: reach for sth.; (hastig) make a grab for sth.
(b) (Technik) grip

Greis *der;* ~es, ~e old man

Greisin *die;* ~, ~nen old woman

grell [1] *Adj.* (a) (hell) glaring, ⟨light, sun, etc.⟩
(b) (auffallend) garish ⟨colour etc.⟩; loud ⟨dress, pattern, etc.⟩
(c) (schrill) shrill, ⟨cry, voice, etc.⟩
[2] *adv.* (a) (hell) with glaring brightness
(b) (auffallend) gegen *od.* von etw. ~ abstechen contrast sharply with sth.
(c) (schrill) shrilly

Gremium *das;* ~s, Gremien committee

Grenze *die;* ~, ~n (a) boundary; (Staats~) border; (gedachte Trennungslinie) borderline
(b) (fig.) limit

grenzen *itr. V.* an etw. (*Akk.*) ~: border [on] sth.

grenzen·los [1] *Adj.* boundless; (fig.) boundless, unbounded ⟨joy, wonder, jealousy, grief, etc.⟩; unlimited ⟨wealth, power⟩; limitless ⟨patience, ambition⟩; extreme ⟨tiredness, anger, foolishness⟩
[2] *adv.* endlessly; (fig.) beyond all measure

Grenzen·losigkeit *die;* ~: boundlessness

Grenz-: ~gänger *der;* ~s, ~, ~gängerin *die;* ~, ~nen [regular] commuter across the border *or* frontier; ~konflikt *der* border *or* frontier conflict; ~land *das* border *or* frontier area; ~posten *der* border *or* frontier guard; ~stein *der* boundary stone; ~übergang *der* border crossing-point; ~übertritt *der* crossing of the border; der ungesetzliche ~übertritt crossing the border illegally; ~verkehr *der* [cross-]border traffic

Gretchen·frage *die* crucial question; sixty-four-thousand-dollar question (coll.)

*Greuel ▶ GRÄUEL

*Greueltat ▶ GRÄUELTAT

*greulich ▶ GRÄULICH

Grieche *der;* ~n, ~n Greek

Griechen·land (*das*); ~s Greece

griechisch [1] *Adj.* Greek
[2] *adv.* ⟨speak, write⟩ in Greek

Griechisch *das;* ~[s] Greek *no art.*

Griechin *die;* ~, ~nen Greek

griesgrämig [1] *Adj.* grumpy
[2] *adv.* in a grumpy manner

Grieß *der;* ~es, ~e semolina

g

Grieß-brei der semolina

griff 1. u. 3. Pers. Sg. Prät. v. GREIFEN

Griff der; ∼[e]s, ∼e (a) grip; grasp
(b) (Knauf, Henkel) handle

griff·bereit Adj. ready to hand postpos.

Griffel der; ∼s, ∼: slate pencil

griffig Adj. (a) (handlich) handy
(b) (gut greifend) that grips well postpos., not pred.; non-slip ⟨surface, floor⟩

Grill der; ∼s, ∼s grill; (Rost) barbecue

Grille die; ∼, ∼n (a) cricket
(b) (sonderbarer Einfall) whim

grillen ⓵ tr. V. grill
⓶ itr. V. im Garten ∼: have a barbecue in the garden

Grill-platz der barbecue area

Grimasse die; ∼, ∼n grimace

grimmig ⓵ Adj. furious ⟨person⟩; grim ⟨expression⟩
⓶ adv. grimly

grinsen itr. V. grin; (höhnisch) smirk

Grippe die; ∼, ∼n (a) influenza; flu (coll.)
(b) (volkst.: Erkältung) cold

Grips der; ∼es brains pl.

grob ⓵ Adj. (a) coarse; thick ⟨wire⟩; rough ⟨work⟩
(b) (ungefähr) rough
(c) (schwerwiegend) gross; flagrant ⟨lie⟩
(d) (barsch) rude
⓶ adv. (a) coarsely
(b) (ungefähr) roughly
(c) (schwerwiegend) grossly
(d) (barsch) rudely

Grobheit die; ∼, ∼en (a) rudeness
(b) (Äußerung) rude remark

Grobian der; ∼[e]s, ∼e lout

Grog der; ∼s, ∼s grog

groggy Adj. (a) (Boxen) groggy
(b) (ugs.: erschöpft) whacked [out] (coll.); all in (coll.)

grölen ⓵ tr. V. (ugs. abwertend) bawl [out]; roar, howl ⟨approval⟩
⓶ itr. V. bawl

Groll der; ∼[e]s (geh.) rancour

grollen itr. V. (geh.) (a) [mit] jmdm. ∼: bear a grudge against sb.
(b) ⟨thunder⟩ rumble

Grönland (das); ∼s Greenland

Gros /groː/ das; ∼ /groːs/, ∼ /groːs/ bulk

Groschen der; ∼s, ∼ (a) (österreichische Münze) groschen
(b) (ugs.: Zehnpfennigstück) ten-pfennig piece; (fig.) penny; cent (Amer.)

groß; größer, größt... ⓵ Adj. (a) big, large; great ⟨length, width, height⟩; tall ⟨person⟩; wide ⟨selection⟩; 1m² ∼: 1m² in area; im Großen und Ganzen by and large
(b) (älter) big ⟨brother, sister⟩; (erwachsen) grown-up
(c) (lange dauernd) long, lengthy

*old spelling - see note on page xiv

(d) intense ⟨heat, cold⟩; high ⟨speed⟩; great, major ⟨event, artist, work⟩
⓶ adv. (ugs.: besonders) greatly; ∼ geschrieben werden (ugs.) be stressed; s. auch GROSSSCHREIBEN

groß-, Groß-: ∼**abnehmer** der, ∼**abnehmerin** die bulk buyer or purchaser; ∼**aktionär** der, ∼**aktionärin** die (Wirtsch.) principal or major shareholder; ∼**artig** ⓵ Adj. magnificent; splendid; ⓶ adv. magnificently; splendidly; ∼**auftrag** der (Wirtsch.) large order

Großbritannien (das); ∼s the United Kingdom; [Great] Britain

Groß-buchstabe der capital [letter]

Größe die; ∼, ∼n size; (Höhe, Körper∼) height; (fig.) greatness; die ∼ der Katastrophe the [full] extent of the catastrophe

Groß-eltern Pl. grandparents

Größen-ordnung die order [of magnitude]; in einer ∼ von einer Milliarde Mark in the order of a thousand million or a billion marks

großen-teils Adv. largely; for the most part

Größen-wahn der delusions pl. of grandeur

größer ▶ GROSS

Groß-: ∼**fahndung** die large-scale search; ∼**familie** die (Soziol.) extended family; (mehrere Kleinfamilien) composite family; ∼**handel** der wholesale trade; ∼**händler** der, ∼**händlerin** die wholesaler; ∼**industrielle** der/die; adj. Dekl. big industrialist

Grossist der; ∼en, ∼en, **Grossistin** die; ∼, ∼nen (Kaufmannsspr.) wholesaler

groß-, Groß-: ∼**macht** die great power; ∼**maul** das (ugs. abwertend) bigmouth (coll.); ∼**mut** die; ∼∼; generosity; ∼**mütig** Adj. generous; ∼**mutter** die; Pl. ∼mütter grandmother; ∼**rechner** der (DV) mainframe [computer]; ∼**reinemachen** das; ∼∼s (ugs.) thorough cleaning; ∼|**schreiben** unr. tr. V. write ⟨word⟩ with a capital; s. auch GROSS ⓶; ∼**spurig** (abwertend) ⓵ Adj. boastful; (hochtrabend) pretentious; ⓶ adv. boastfully; (hochtrabend) pretentiously; ∼**stadt** die city; large town; ∼**städter** der, ∼**städterin** die city-dweller

größt... ▶ GROSS

Groß-teil der (a) (Hauptteil) major part
(b) (nicht unerheblicher Teil) large part

größten-teils Adv. for the most part

größt-möglich Adj. greatest possible

groß-, Groß-: ∼|**tun** unr. itr. V. boast; ∼**unternehmen** das (Wirtsch.) large-scale enterprise; big concern; ∼**vater** der grandfather; ∼**verbraucher** der, ∼**verbraucherin** die bulk or large consumer; ∼|**ziehen** unr. tr. V. bring up;

raise; rear ⟨*animal*⟩; **~zügig** ① *Adj.*
generous; grand and spacious ⟨*building,
garden, etc.*⟩; ② *adv.* generously;
~zügigkeit *die;* **~:** generosity

grotesk ① *Adj.* grotesque
② *adv.* grotesquely

Grotte *die;* **~,** **~n** grotto

grub *1. u. 3. Pers. Sg. Prät. v.* GRABEN

Grübchen *das;* **~s,** **~:** dimple

Grube *die;* **~,** **~n** pit; (Bergbau) mine

grübeln *itr. V.* ponder (**über** + *Dat.* on,
over)

Gruben-arbeiter *der,*
  Gruben-arbeiterin *die* miner;
mineworker

grüezi *Interj.* (schweiz.) hallo

Gruft *die;* **~,** Grüfte vault; (in einer Kirche)
crypt

grün *Adj.* green

Grün *das;* **~s,** **~** *od.* (ugs.) **~s** (a) green
(b) (Pflanzen) greenery

Grün-anlage *die* green space; (Park) park

Grund *der;* **~[e]s,** Gründe (a) ground; (eines
Gewässers) bottom; **im ~e [genommen]**
basically
(b) (Ursache, Veranlassung) reason; **auf ~:**
▶ AUFGRUND

Grund-: **~besitz** *der* (a) (Eigentum an Land)
ownership of land; (b) (Land) land; **~buch**
das land register

gründen ① *tr. V.* (a) found; set up,
establish ⟨*business*⟩; start [up] ⟨*club*⟩
(b) (aufbauen) base ⟨*plan, theory, etc.*⟩ (**auf** +
Akk. on)
② *itr. V.* **auf** *od.* **in etw.** (*Dat.*) **~:** be based
on sth.
③ *refl. V.* **sich auf etw.** (*Akk.*) **~:** be based
on sth.

Gründer *der;* **~s,** **~,** **Gründerin** *die;* **~,**
~nen founder

Grund-erwerb[s]-steuer *die* (Steuerw.)
land transfer tax

Grund-gesetz *das* Basic Law

grundieren *tr. V.* prime

Grundierung *die;* **~,** **~en** (a) (das
Grundieren) priming
(b) (erster Anstrich) priming coat

grund-, Grund-: **~kenntnis** *die* basic
knowledge *no pl.* (**in** + *Dat.* of); **~lage** *die*
basis; foundation

Grundlagen-forschung *die* basic
research

grund-legend ① *Adj.* fundamental, basic
(für to); seminal ⟨*idea, work*⟩
② *adv.* fundamentally

gründlich ① *Adj.* thorough
② *adv.* thoroughly

Gründlichkeit *die;* **~:** thoroughness

grund-los ① *Adj.* groundless
② *adv.* **sich ~ aufregen/ängstigen** be
needlessly agitated/alarmed

Grund-nahrungsmittel *das* basic
food[stuff]

Grün-donnerstag *der* Maundy Thursday

Grund-: **~ordnung** *die* basic
fundamental [constitutional] order;
~prinzip *das* fundamental principle;
~recht *das* basic *or* constitutional right;
~riss, *****~riß** *der* (a) (Bauw.) [ground] plan;
(b) (Leitfaden) outline; **~satz** *der* principle

grund-sätzlich ① *Adj.* (a) fundamental
⟨*difference, question, etc.*⟩
(b) (aus Prinzip) ⟨*opponent etc.*⟩ on principle
(c) (allgemein) ⟨*agreement etc.*⟩ in principle
② *adv.* (a) fundamentally
(b) (aus Prinzip) on principle
(c) (allgemein) in principle

Grund-: **~schule** *die* primary school;
~stein *der* foundation stone;
~stein-legung *die;* **~~,** **~~en** laying of
the foundation stone; **~stück** *das* plot [of
land]

Gründung *die;* **~,** **~en** ▶ GRÜNDEN 1A:
foundation; setting up; establishing; starting
[up]

Grund-: **~wasser** *das* (Geol.) ground
water; **~wortschatz** *der* (Sprachw.) basic
vocabulary; **~zug** *der* essential feature

Grüne¹ *das; adj. Dekl.* green; **im ~n/ins ~:**
[out] in/into the country

Grüne² *der/die; adj. Dekl.* (Politik) member of
the Green Party; **die ~n** the Greens

Grün-: **~fläche** *die* green space; (im Park)
lawn; **~gürtel** *der* green belt; **~land** *das*
(Landw.) (Wiese) meadow land; (Weide)
pastureland; **~pflanze** *die* foliage plant;
~schnabel *der* (abwertend) [young]
whippersnapper; (Neuling) greenhorn;
~span *der* verdigris; **~streifen** *der*
central reservation (*grassed and often with
trees and bushes*)

grunzen *tr., itr. V.* grunt

Gruppe *die;* **~,** **~n** (a) group
(b) (Klassifizierung) class; category

Gruppen-: **~druck** *der* group pressure;
~dynamik *die* (Sozialpsych.) group
dynamics *sing., no art.;* **~leiter** *der,*
~leiterin *die* group leader; **~reise** *die*
(Touristik) group travel *no pl., no art.;* **eine
~reise nach London machen** travel to
London with a group; **~sieg** *der* (Sport) top
place in the group

gruppieren ① *tr. V.* arrange
② *refl. V.* form a group/groups

Gruppierung *die;* **~,** **~en** grouping

gruselig *Adj.* eerie; creepy

gruseln ① *tr., itr. V.* (*unpers.*) **es gruselt
jmdn.** *od.* **jmdm.** sb.'s flesh creeps
② *refl. V.* be frightened

Gruß *der;* **~es,** Grüße (a) greeting; (Milit.)
salute
(b) (im Brief) **mit herzlichen Grüßen** [with]
best wishes; **mit bestem ~/freundlichen
Grüßen** yours sincerely

grüßen 1 *tr. V.* (a) greet; (Milit.) salute
(b) (Grüße senden) grüße deine Eltern [ganz herzlich] von mir please give your parents my [kindest] regards; grüß dich! (ugs.) hello *or* (coll.) hi [there]!
2 *itr. V.* say hello; (Milit.) salute

Grütze *die;* ~, ~n groats *pl.;* rote ~: red fruit pudding (*made with fruit juice, fruit and cornflour, etc.*)

gucken *itr. V.* (ugs.) (a) look; (heimlich) peep
(b) (hervorsehen) stick out
(c) (dreinschauen) look

Guck·loch *das* spyhole

Guerilla /ɡeˈrɪlja/ *die;* ~, ~s guerrilla war; (Einheit) guerrilla unit

Gulasch /ˈɡʊlaʃ, ˈɡuːlaʃ/ *das od. der;* ~[e]s, ~e *od.* ~s goulash

Gulden *der;* ~s, ~: guilder

gültig *Adj.* valid; current ⟨note, coin⟩

Gültigkeit *die;* ~: validity; ~ haben/ erlangen be/become valid

Gummi *der od. das;* ~s, ~[s] rubber

Gummi-: ~band *das* rubber *or* elastic band; (in Kleidung) elastic *no indef. art.;* ~bärchen *das;* ~~s, ~~: jelly baby; ~baum *der* rubber plant

gummieren *tr. V.* gum

Gummi-: ~handschuh *der* rubber glove; ~knüppel *der* [rubber] truncheon; ~sohle *die* rubber sole; ~stiefel *der* rubber boot; (für Regenwetter) wellington [boot] (Brit.)

Gunst *die;* ~ (a) favour; goodwill
(b) zu ~en ▶ ZUGUNSTEN

günstig 1 *Adj.* favourable; propitious ⟨sign⟩; auspicious ⟨moment⟩; beneficial ⟨influence⟩; good
2 *adv.* favourably; etw. ~ beeinflussen have *or* exert a beneficial influence on sth.

günstig[st]en·falls *Adv.* at best

Gurgel *die;* ~, ~n throat; jmdm. die ~ zudrücken throttle sb.

gurgeln *itr. V.* gargle

Gurke *die;* ~, ~n cucumber; (eingelegt) gherkin

gurren *itr. V.* (auch fig.) coo

Gurt *der;* ~[e]s, ~e strap; (im Auto, Flugzeug) [seat] belt

Gürtel *der;* ~s, ~: belt

Gürtel-: ~linie *die* waist[line]; das war ein Schlag unter die ~linie (fig. ugs.) that was hitting below the belt (fig. coll.); ~reifen *der* radial[-ply] tyre

Gurt·straffer *der;* ~s, ~ (Kfz.-W.) [seat-]belt tensioner

Guru *der;* ~s, ~s guru

GUS *Abk.* = **Gemeinschaft Unabhängiger Staaten** CIS

Guss, *Guß *der;* Gusses, Güsse (a) (das Gießen) casting

(b) (ugs.: Regenschauer) downpour

Guss·eisen, *Guß·eisen, *das* cast iron
guss·eisern, *guß·eisern *Adj.* cast-iron

gut; besser, best... 1 *Adj.* good; fine ⟨wine⟩; ein ~es neues Jahr a happy new year; ~ tun do good; mir ist nicht ~: I'm not feeling well; ~ aussehend good-looking; ~en Appetit! enjoy your lunch/dinner *etc.*!; eine ~e Stunde [von hier] a good hour [from here]
2 *adv.* (a) well; ~ gemeint well-meant; so ~ wie nichts next to nothing
(b) (mühelos) easily; *s. auch* BESSER, BEST...

Gut *das;* ~[e]s, Güter (a) property; (Besitztum, auch fig.) possession
(b) (landwirtschaftlicher Grundbesitz) estate
(c) (Fracht~, Ware) item; Güter goods; (Fracht~) freight *sing.;* goods (Brit.)

gut-, Gut-: ~achten *das;* ~~s, ~~: [expert's] report; ~artig *Adj.* (a) good-natured; (b) (nicht gefährlich) benign; ~artigkeit *die* (a) good nature; goodnaturedness; (b) (Ungefährlichkeit) benignity; *~aussehend ▶ GUT 1; ~bürgerlich *Adj.* good middle-class; ~bürgerliche Küche good plain cooking; ~dünken *das;* ~~s discretion

Güte *die;* ~: goodness; kindness; (Qualität) quality

Gute·nacht·kuss, *Gute·nacht·kuß *der* goodnight kiss

Güter-: ~abfertigung *die* (a) (Abfertigung von Waren) dispatch of freight *or* (Brit.) goods; (b) (Annahmestelle) freight *or* (Brit.) goods office; ~bahnhof *der* freight depot; goods station (Brit.); ~wagen *der* goods wagon (Brit.); freight car (Amer.); ~zug *der* goods train (Brit.); freight train (Amer.)

gut-, Gut-: *~|gehen ▶ GEHEN H, I; *~gelaunt ▶ GELAUNT; *~gemeint ▶ GUT 2A; ~gläubig *Adj.* innocently trusting; *~haben ▶ GUT 3, ~~: credit balance; ~|heißen *unr. tr. V.* approve of; ~herzig *Adj.* kind-hearted

gütig 1 *Adj.* kindly
2 *adv.* ~ lächeln give a kindly smile

gütlich *Adj.* amicable

gut-, Gut-: ~|machen *tr. V.* make good ⟨damage⟩; put right ⟨omission, mistake, etc.⟩; ~mütig *Adj.* good-natured; ~mütigkeit *die;* ~~: good nature

Guts·besitzer *der,* **Guts·besitzerin** *die* owner of a/the estate; landowner

gut-, Gut-: ~schein *der* voucher, coupon (für, auf + Akk. for); ~|schreiben *unr. tr. V.* credit; ~schrift *die* credit

Guts·hof *der* estate; manor

gut-: *~|tun ▶ GUT 1; ~willig 1 *Adj.* willing; (entgegenkommend) obliging; 2 *adv.* etw. ~willig herausgeben/versprechen hand sth. over voluntarily/promise sth. willingly

Gymnasium *das;* ~s, Gymnasien ≈ grammar school

Gymnạstik *die;* ~: physical exercises *pl.;* (Turnen) gymnastics *sing.*

Gynäkologe *der;* ~n, ~n,
Gynäkologin *die;* ~, ~nen gynaecologist

H h

h, H /ha:/ *das;* ~, ~(a) (Buchstabe) h/H
(b) (Musik) [key of] B

h *Abk.* (a) = **Uhr** hrs
(b) = **Stunde** hr[s]

H *Abk.* (a) = **Herren;**
(b) = **Haltestelle**

ha¹ /ha(:)/ *Interj.* (a) (Überraschung) ah
(b) (Triumph) aha

ha² *Abk.* = **Hektar** ha

Haar *das;* ~[e]s, ~e hair; **blonde** ~e *od.*
blondes ~ **haben** have fair hair; (fig.) ~e **auf
den Zähnen haben** (ugs. scherzh.) be a tough
customer; **um ein** ~ (ugs.) very nearly

Haar-: ~**ausfall** *der* hair loss; ~**bürste**
die hairbrush; ~**büschel** *das* tuft of hair

haaren *itr. V.* moult

Haares·breite *die:* **um** ~: by a hair's
breadth

haar-, Haar-: ~**festiger** *der;* ~s, ~:
setting lotion; ~**genau** (ugs.) ⓵ *Adj.* exact;
⓶ *adv.* exactly

haarig *Adj.* hairy

haar-, Haar-: ~**klemme** *die* hairgrip;
~**nadel** *die* hairpin; ~**nadel·kurve** *die*
hairpin bend; ~**schnitt** *der* haircut;
(modisch) hairstyle; ~**spalterei** *die;* ~~,
~~en (abwertend) hair-splitting; **das ist doch**
~**spalterei** that's splitting hairs; ~**spange**
die hairslide; ~**sträubend** *Adj.* (a)
(grauenhaft) hair-raising; (b) (empörend)
outrageous; shocking; ~**teil** *das* hairpiece;
~**waschmittel** *das* shampoo;
~**wasser** *das* hair lotion

Habe *die;* ~ (geh.) possessions *pl.*

haben ⓵ *unr. tr. V.* have; have got; **heute**
~ **wir schönes Wetter** the weather is fine
today; **es gut/schlecht/schwer** ~: have it
good (coll.)/have a bad time [of it]/have a
difficult time; **du hast zu gehorchen** you
must obey; **das Jahr hat 12 Monate** there are
12 months in a year
⓶ *refl. V.* (ugs.: sich aufregen) make a fuss
⓷ *Hilfsverb* have; **ich habe/hatte ihn eben
gesehen** I've/I'd just seen him; **er hat es
gewusst** he knew it
⓸ *mod. V.* **du hast zu gehorchen** you must
obey; **er hat sich nicht einzumischen** he's not
to interfere

Haben *das;* ~s, ~ (Kaufmannsspr.) credit

Habe·nichts *der;* ~, ~e pauper

Haben-: ~**seite** *die* (Kaufmannsspr.) credit
side; ~**zinsen** *Pl.* interest *sing.* on
deposits

Hab·gier *die* (abwertend) greed

hab·gierig ⓵ *Adj.* (abwertend) greedy
⓶ *adv.* greedily

Habicht *der;* ~s, ~e hawk

Hab-: ~**seligkeiten** *Pl.* [meagre]
belongings; ~**sucht** *die;* (abwertend) greed;
avarice

Hachse *die;* ~, ~n (südd.) knuckle

Hack *das;* ~s (ugs., bes. nordd.) mince

Hack·braten *der* meat loaf

Hacke¹ *die;* ~, ~n hoe; (Pickel) pick[axe]

Hacke² *die;* ~, ~n (bes. nordd. u. md.) heel

hacken ⓵ *itr. V.* (a) hoe
(b) (picken) peck
⓶ *tr. V.* (a) hoe ⟨garden, flower bed, etc.⟩
(b) (zerkleinern) chop; chop [up] ⟨meat,
vegetables, etc.⟩

Hacker *der;* ~s, ~, **Hackerin** *die;* ~,
~nen (DV-Jargon) hacker

hacke·zu *Adj.* (salopp) paralytic [drunk]
(coll.)

Hack·fleisch *das* minced meat; mince

Häcksel *der od. das;* ~s (Landw.) chaff

hadern *itr. V.* (geh.) **mit etw.** ~: be at odds
with sth.

Hafen *der;* ~s, Häfen harbour; port

Hafen-: ~**arbeiter** *der,* ~**arbeiterin**
die dock worker; docker; ~**kneipe** *die*
dockland pub (Brit.) *or* (Amer.) bar;
~**rundfahrt** *die* trip round the harbour;
~**stadt** *die* port; ~**viertel** *das* dock area

Hafer *der;* ~s oats *pl.*

Hafer-: ~**brei** *der* porridge; ~**flocken**
Pl. porridge oats

Haff *das;* ~[e]s, ~s *od.* ~e lagoon

-haft *Adj., adv.* -like

Haft *die;* ~ (a) (Gewahrsam) custody; (aus
politischen Gründen) detention
(b) (Freiheitsstrafe) imprisonment

haftbar *Adj.* (bes. Rechtsspr.) **für etw.** ~ **sein**
be liable for sth.

Haft·befehl *der* (Rechtsw.) warrant [of
arrest]

haften¹ *itr. V.* stick (sich festsetzen) ⟨smell,
dirt, etc.⟩; cling (**an** + *Dat.* to); ~ **bleiben** ···⊹

stick; **(an/auf** + *Dat.* to); ⟨*smell, smoke*⟩ cling **(an/auf** + *Dat.* to); (ugs.: im Gedächtnis bleiben) stick

haften² *itr. V.* für jmdn./etw. ~: be responsible for sb./liable for sth.; (Rechtsw., Wirtsch.) be liable

***haften|bleiben** ▶ HAFTEN¹

Häftling *der;* ~s, ~e prisoner

Haft·pflicht *die* liability (für for)

Haftpflicht·versicherung *die* personal liability insurance; (für Autofahrer) third party insurance

Haft-: ~**prüfung** *die* (Rechtsw.) review of a/ the remand in custody; ~**schale** *die* contact lens; ~**strafe** *die* (Rechtsspr. veralt.) prison sentence

Haftung *die;* ~, ~en liability; Gesellschaft mit [un]beschränkter ~: [un]limited [liability] company

Hagebutte *die;* ~, ~n (a) (Frucht) rose hip **(b)** (ugs.: Heckenrose) dog rose

Hagel *der;* ~s, ~ (auch fig.) hail

hageln *itr., tr. V.* (unpers.) hail

Hagel-: ~**schaden** *der* damage *no pl.* caused by hail; ~**schauer** *der* [short] hailstorm; ~**schlag** *der* hail

hager *Adj.* gaunt

haha /ha'ha(:)/ *Interj.* ha ha

Häher *der;* ~s, ~: jay

Hahn¹ *der;* ~[e]s, Hähne cock; (Wetter~) weathercock

Hahn² *der;* ~[e]s, Hähne, *fachspr.:* ~en (a) tap; faucet (Amer.) **(b)** (bei Waffen) hammer

Hähnchen *das;* ~s, ~: chicken

Hahnen·fuß *der* buttercup

Hai *der;* ~s, ~e shark

Häkchen *das;* ~s, ~ (a) [small] hook **(b)** (Zeichen) mark; (beim Abhaken) tick

häkeln *tr., itr. V.* crochet

Häkel·nadel *die* crochet hook

haken ① *tr. V.* hook (an + *Akk.* on to) ② *itr. V.* (klemmen) be stuck

Haken *der;* ~s, ~ (a) hook **(b)** (Zeichen) tick **(c)** (ugs.: Schwierigkeit) catch **(d)** (Boxen) hook

haken-, Haken-: ~**förmig** ① *Adj.* hooked; hook-shaped; ② *adv.* ~förmig gebogen hooked; hook-shaped; ~**kreuz** *das* swastika; ~**nase** *die* hooked nose; hook nose

halb ① *Adj. u. Bruchz.* half; eine ~e Stunde/ein ~er Meter half an hour/a metre; zum ~en Preis [at] half price; ~ Europa/die ~e Welt half of Europe/the world; es ist ~ eins it's half past twelve; die ~e Wahrheit half [of] the truth; [noch] ein ~es Kind sein be hardly more than a child ② *adv.* ~ voll/leer half-full/-empty; ~ offen

*old spelling - see note on page xiv

half-open; ~ **angezogen** half dressed; ~ **links/rechts** (Fußball) ⟨*play*⟩ [at] inside left/ right

Halb·dunkel *das* semi-darkness

Halbe *der od. die od. das; adj. Dekl.* (ugs.) half litre (*of beer etc.*)

Halb·edelstein *der* (veralt.) semi-precious stone

halber *Präp. mit Gen.; nachgestellt* (wegen) on account of; (um ... willen) for the sake of

halb-, Halb-: ~**finale** *das* (Sport) semi-final; ~**gar** *Adj.* half-cooked; ~**gefror[e]ne** *das; adj. Dekl.* soft ice cream

Halbheit *die;* ~, ~en (abwertend) half measure

halbieren *tr. V.* cut/tear ⟨*object*⟩ in half; halve ⟨*amount, number*⟩

halb-, Halb-: ~**insel** *die* peninsula; ~**jahr** *das* six months *pl.;* half year; ~**jährlich** ① *Adj.* six-monthly; ② *adv.* every six months; ~**kreis** *der* semicircle; ~**kugel** *die* hemisphere; ~**lang** *Adj.* mid-length ⟨*hair*⟩; mid-calf length ⟨*coat, dress, etc.*⟩; ~**links** /-'-/ *Adv.* (Fußball) ⟨*play*⟩ [at] inside left; ~**mast** *Adv.* at half-mast; ~**mond** *der* (a) (Mond) half-moon; (b) (Figur) crescent; *~**offen** *Adj.:* ▶ HALB 2; ~**pension** *die* half-board; ~**rechts** /-'-/ *Adv.* (Fußball) ⟨*play*⟩ [at] inside right; ~**schlaf** *der* light sleep; im ~schlaf liegen be half asleep; doze; ~**schuh** *der* shoe; ~**starke** *der; adj. Dekl.* (ugs. abwertend) [young] hooligan

halb·tags *Adv.* ⟨*work*⟩ part-time; (morgens/ nachmittags) ⟨*work*⟩ [in the] mornings/ afternoons

Halbtags-: ~**arbeit** *die,* ~**beschäftigung** *die* part-time job; (morgens/nachmittags) morning/afternoon job; ~**schule** *die* half-day school; ~**stelle** *die* part-time job; (morgens/nachmittags) morning/ afternoon job

halb-, Halb-: *~**voll** *Adj.:* ▶ HALB 2; ~**wegs** *Adv.* to some extent; ~**wüchsig** /-vy:ksɪç/ *Adj.* adolescent; ~**wüchsige** *der/die; adj. Dekl.* adolescent; ~**zeit** *die* (bes. Fußball) (a) half; (b) (Pause) half-time; ~**zeit·pause** *die* (Sport) half-time

Halde *die;* ~, ~n (Bergbau) slag heap

half *1. u. 3. Pers. Sg. Prät. v.* HELFEN

Hälfte *die;* ~, ~n (a) half **(b)** (ugs.: Teil) part

Halfter¹ *der od. das;* ~s, ~: halter

Halfter² *die;* ~, ~n; *auch das;* ~s, ~: holster

Hall *der;* ~[e]s, ~e (a) (geh.) reverberation **(b)** (Echo) echo

Halle *die;* ~, ~n hall; (Fabrik~) shed; (Hotel~, Theater~) foyer

hallen *itr. V.* (a) reverberate; ⟨*shot, bell, cry*⟩ ring out **(b)** (widerhallen) echo

Hallen- indoor ⟨*swimming pool, handball*⟩

Hallig *die;* ~, ~**en** small low island (*particularly one of those off Schleswig-Holstein*)

hallo *Interj.* hello

Hallo *das;* ~s, ~s cheering

Halluzination *die;* ~, ~**en** hallucination

Halm *der;* ~[e]s, ~e stalk; stem

Hals *der;* ~es, **Hälse** neck; (Kehle) throat; ~ über Kopf (ugs.) in a rush

hals-, Hals-: ~**ab·schneider** *der,* ~**ab·schneiderin** *die* (ugs. abwertend) shark; ~**band** *das* (für Tiere) collar; ~**bruch** *der:* ▸ ~- UND BEINBRUCH; ~**entzündung** *die* inflammation of the throat; ~**kette** *die* necklace; ~-**Nasen-Ohren-Arzt** *der,* ~-**Nasen-Ohren-Ärztin** *die* ear, nose, and throat specialist; ~**schlagader** *die* carotid [artery]; ~**schmerzen** *Pl.* sore throat *sing.;* ~**starrig** *Adj.* (abwertend) stubborn; obstinate; ~**tuch** *das; Pl.* ~**tücher** cravat; (des Cowboys) neckerchief; ~ **und Beinbruch** *Interj.* (scherzh.) good luck; ~**weh** *das* (ugs.) ▸ ~SCHMERZEN

halt *Interj.* stop

Halt *der;* ~[e]s, ~e (a) hold
(b) (Stopp) stop; ~ **machen** stop

haltbar *Adj.* (a) ~ sein ⟨*food*⟩ keep [well]; ~ bis 5. 3. use by 5 March
(b) (nicht verschleißend) hard-wearing ⟨*material, clothes*⟩
(c) (aufrechtzuerhalten) tenable ⟨*hypothesis etc.*⟩

Haltbarkeit *die;* ~ (Strapazierfähigkeit) durability

Halte·bucht *die* (Verkehrsw.) lay-by (Brit.); turnout (Amer.)

halten ① *unr. tr. V.* (a) (auch Milit.) hold; **die Hand vor den Mund** ~: put one's hand in front of one's mouth
(b) (Ballspiele) save ⟨*shot, penalty, etc.*⟩
(c) (bewahren) keep; (beibehalten, aufrechterhalten) keep up ⟨*speed etc.*⟩; maintain ⟨*temperature, equilibrium*⟩
(d) (erfüllen) keep; **sein Wort/ein Versprechen** ~: keep one's word/a promise
(e) (besitzen, beschäftigen, beziehen) keep ⟨*chickens etc.*⟩; take ⟨*newspaper, magazine, etc.*⟩
(f) (einschätzen) **jmdn. für reich/ehrlich** ~: think sb. is rich/honest; **viel von jmdm.** ~: think a lot of sb.
(g) (ab~, veranstalten) give, ⟨*speech, lecture*⟩ ② *unr. itr. V.* (a) (stehen bleiben) stop
(b) (unverändert, an seinem Platz bleiben) last
(c) (Sport) save
(d) (beistehen) **zu jmdm.** ~: stand by sb. ③ *unr. refl. V.* (a) (sich durchsetzen, behaupten) **wir werden uns/die Stadt wird sich nicht länger** ~ **können** we/the town won't be able to hold out much longer
(b) (sich bewähren) **sich gut** ~: do well
(c) (unverändert bleiben) ⟨*weather, flowers, etc.*⟩ last; ⟨*milk, meat, etc.*⟩ keep

(d) (Körperhaltung haben) **sich schlecht/gerade** ~: hold oneself badly/straight
(e) (bleiben) **sich auf den Beinen/im Sattel** ~: stay on one's feet/in the saddle; **sich links/rechts** ~: keep [to the] left/right; **sich an etw.** (*Akk.*) ~: keep to sth.

Halte·punkt *der* stop

Halter *der;* ~s, ~ (a) (Fahrzeug~) keeper
(b) (Tier~) owner
(c) (Vorrichtung) holder

Halterin *die;* ~, ~**nen** (a) ▸ HALTER A: keeper
(b) ▸ HALTER B: owner

Halterung *die;* ~, ~**en** support

Halte-: ~**stelle** *die* stop; ~**verbot** *das* (a) „~verbot" 'no stopping'; **hier ist** ~**verbot** this is a no-stopping zone; (b) (Stelle) no-stopping zone; ~**verbots·schild** *das* no-stopping sign

-haltig, (österr.) **-hältig:** vitamin~/silber~ *usw.* containing vitamins/silver etc. postpos., not pred.; **vitamin**~ **sein** contain vitamins

halt-, Halt-: ~**los** *Adj.* (a) (labil) ~**los sein** be a weak character; **ein** ~**loser Mensch** a weak character; (b) (unbegründet) unfounded; ~**losigkeit** *die;* ~ ~ (a) (Labilität) weakness of character; (b) (mangelnde Begründung) unfoundedness; ***~|**machen** ▸ HALT B

Haltung *die;* ~, ~**en** (a) (Körper~) posture
(b) (Pose) manner
(c) (Einstellung) attitude
(d) (Fassung) composure

Halunke *der;* ~n, ~n scoundrel; villain

Hamburger *der;* ~s, ~ (Frikadelle) hamburger

hämisch ① *Adj.* malicious ② *adv.* maliciously

Hammel *der;* ~s, ~ (a) wether
(b) (Fleisch) mutton

Hammel·fleisch *das* mutton

Hammer *der;* ~s, **Hämmer** (a) hammer; (Holz~) mallet; ~ **und Sichel** hammer and sickle
(b) (Technik) ram

hämmern *itr., tr. V.* hammer

Hämorrhoiden /hɛmɔrɔˈiːdn̩/ *Pl.* (Med.) haemorrhoids; piles

Hampel·mann *der* (a) jumping jack
(b) (ugs. abwertend) puppet

hampeln *itr. V.* (ugs.) jump about

Hamster *der;* ~s, ~: hamster

hamstern *tr., itr. V.* (a) (horten) hoard
(b) (Lebensmittel tauschen) barter goods for [food]

Hand *die;* ~, **Hände** hand; **eine** ~ **voll** a handful; **jmdm. die** ~ **geben** shake sb.'s hand; ~ **und Fuß/weder** ~ **noch Fuß haben** (ugs.) make sense/no sense; **alle** *od.* **beide Hände damit voll haben,** etw. zu tun (ugs.) have one's hands full doing sth.; **die Hände in den Schoß legen** sit back and do nothing; **etw. aus der** ~ **geben** let sth. out of one's hands; ~ **in** ~ **arbeiten** work hand in hand; ⋯✧

etw. zur ~ haben have sth. handy; **zu Händen [von]** Herrn Müller attention Herr Müller; **unter der** ~ (fig.) on the quiet

Hand-: ~**arbeit** die **(a)** handicraft; **etw. in** ~**arbeit herstellen** make sth. by hand; **(b)** (Gegenstand) handmade article; **(c)** (Nadelarbeit) [piece of] needlework; ~**ball** der handball; ~**besen** der brush; ~**betrieb** der manual operation; ~**bewegung** die **(a)** movement of the hand; **(b)** (Geste) gesture; ~**bremse** die handbrake; ~**buch** das handbook; (technisches ~buch) manual

Händchen das; ~s, ~: [little] hand

Hände ▶ HAND

Hände-: ~**druck** der; Pl. ~drücke handshake; ~**klatschen** das; ~~s clapping

Handel der; ~s trade; ~ **treiben** trade; ~ **treibend** trading ⟨nation⟩

handeln [1] itr. V. **(a)** trade; deal **(b)** (feilschen) haggle **(c)** (agieren) act **(d)** (sich verhalten) behave **(e) von etw.** od. **über etw.** (Akk.) ~ ⟨book, film, etc.⟩ be about or deal with sth. [2] refl. V. (unpers.) **es handelt sich um ...:** it is a matter of ...; (es dreht sich um) it's about ...

handels-, Handels-: ~**abkommen** das trade agreement; ~**bank** die; Pl. ~~en merchant bank; ~**bilanz** die **(a)** (eines Betriebes) balance sheet; **(b)** (eines Staates) balance of trade; ~**einig**, ~**eins: mit** jmdm. ~einig od. ~eins werden/sein agree/ have agreed terms with sb.; ~**flotte** die merchant fleet; ~**gesellschaft** die company; ~**kammer** die: ▶ INDUSTRIE- UND HANDELSKAMMER; ~**klasse** die grade; ~**marine** die merchant navy; ~**partner** der, ~**partnerin** die trading partner; ~**register** das register of companies; ~**schiff** das merchant ship; ~**schule** die commercial college; ~**straße** die (hist.) trade route; ~**üblich** Adj. **übliche Praktiken/Größen** standard business practices/standard [commercial] sizes; ~**unternehmen** das trading concern; ~**vertreter** der, ~**vertreterin** die [sales] representative; travelling salesman/ saleswoman; ~**vertretung** die trade mission; ~**zentrum** das trading centre

hände-ringend Adv. (ugs.: dringend) ⟨need⟩ urgently; ⟨search for sb./sth.⟩ desperately

hand-, Hand-: ~**feger** der brush; ~**fest** Adj. **(a)** robust; sturdy; **(b)** substantial ⟨meal etc.⟩; **(c)** solid ⟨proof⟩; concrete ⟨suggestion⟩; complete ⟨lie⟩; well-founded ⟨argument⟩; ~**fläche** die palm [of one's/the hand]; flat of one's/the hand; ~**gas** das (Kfz-W.) hand throttle; ~**gearbeitet** Adj. handmade; ~**gelenk** das wrist; ~**gemenge** das fight; ~**gepäck** das hand baggage; ~**geschrieben** Adj. handwritten;

~**granate** die hand grenade; ~**greiflich** Adj. **(a)** (tätlich) ~**greiflich werden** start using one's fists; **(b)** tangible ⟨success, advantage, proof, etc.⟩; palpable ⟨contradiction, error⟩; obvious ⟨fact⟩; ~**griff** der **(a) mit einem** ~**griff/wenigen** ~**griffen** in one movement/ without much trouble; (schnell) in no time at all/next to no time; **(b)** (am Koffer, an einem Werkzeug) handle; ~**habe** die; ~~, ~~n: **eine [rechtliche]** ~**habe [gegen jmdn.]** a legal handle [against sb.]; ~**haben** tr. V. **(a)** handle; operate ⟨device, machine⟩; **(b)** (praktizieren) implement ⟨law etc.⟩; ~**habung** die; ~~, ~~en **(a)** handling; (eines Gerätes, einer Maschine) operation; **(b)** (Durchführung) implementation

Handikap /'hɛndikɛp/ das; ~s, ~s (auch Sport) handicap

handikapen /'hɛndikɛpn/ tr. V. handicap

Hand-: ~**käse** der (landsch.) small, hand-formed curd cheese; ~**koffer** der [small] suitcase; ~**kuss**, *~**kuß** der kiss on sb.'s hand; ~**langer** der; ~~s, ~~, ~**langerin** die; ~~, ~~nen (ungelernter Arbeiter) labourer; (abwertend) lackey; ~**lauf** der handrail

Händler der; ~s, ~, **Händlerin** die; ~, ~nen trader

handlich Adj. handy; easily carried ⟨parcel, suitcase⟩; easily portable ⟨television, camera⟩

Handlung die; ~, ~en **(a)** (Vorgehen) action; (Tat) act **(b)** (Fabel) plot

handlungs-, Handlungs-: ~**arm** Adj. short on action pred.; ~**fähig** Adj. able to act pred.; working attrib. ⟨majority⟩; ~**freiheit** die freedom of action; ~**reisende** der/die ▶ HANDELSVERTRETER; ~**weise** die conduct

hand-, Hand-: ~**puppe** die glove or hand puppet; ~**schelle** die handcuff; ~**schlag** der handshake; ~**schrift** die handwriting; ~**schriftlich** [1] Adj. handwritten; [2] adv. by hand; ~**schuh** der glove; ~**schuh-fach** das glove compartment; ~**signiert** Adj. signed; ~**spiegel** der hand mirror; ~**stand** der (Turnen) handstand; ~**tasche** die handbag; ~**tuch** das; Pl. -tücher towel; ~**umdrehen: im** ~**umdrehen** in no time at all; ~**verlesen** Adj. hand-picked; *~**voll** ▶ HAND; ~**wäsche** die washing by hand

Hand-werk das craft; (als Beruf) trade; **sein** ~ **kennen/beherrschen** know one's job

Handwerker der; ~s, ~: tradesman

Handwerkerin die; ~, ~nen tradeswoman;

handwerklich Adj. **ein** ~**er Beruf** a [skilled] trade

Handwerks-zeug das tools pl.

Handy /'hɛndi/ das; ~s, ~s mobile [phone]

Hand-zeichen das sign [with one's hand]; (eines Autofahrers) hand signal; (Abstimmung) show of hands

---

*alte Schreibung - vgl. Hinweis auf S. xiv

Hanf der; ~[e]s hemp

Hang der; ~[e]s, **Hänge** slope; (Neigung) tendency

Hänge-: ~**brücke** die suspension bridge; ~**lampe** die pendant light; ~**matte** die hammock

hängen[1] unr. itr. V.; südd., österr., schweiz. mit sein hang (**an** + Dat. from); (an einem Fahrzeug) be hitched (**an** + Dat. to); [mit der Ärmel usw. an/in etw. (Dat.) ~ bleiben get one's sleeve etc. caught on/in sth.; ~ bleiben (ugs.: haften) stick (**an/auf** + Dat.) to; (ugs.: verweilen) get stuck (coll.)

hängen[2] [1] tr. V. (a) hang (**in/über** + (Akk.)) in/over; **an/auf** + Akk. on) (b) (befestigen) hitch up (**an** + Akk. to); couple on ‹railway carriage, etc.› (**an** + Akk. to) [2] refl. V. (a) sich an etw. (Akk.) ~: hang on to sth. (b) (sich festsetzen) cling (**an** + Akk. to)

*****hängen|bleiben ▶** HÄNGEN[1]

hängend Adj. hanging

Hänge-schrank der wall cupboard

Hang·lage die hillside location

Hansaplast ⓦ das; ~[e]s sticking plaster; Elastoplast ®

hänseln tr. V. tease

Hanse-stadt die Hanseatic city

Hantel die; ~, ~n (Sport) (kurz) dumb-bell; (lang) barbell

hantieren itr. V. be busy

Häppchen das; ~s, ~ (a) [small] morsel (b) (Appetithappen) canapé

Happen der; ~s, ~: morsel

happig Adj. (ugs.) ~e Preise fancy prices (coll.)

Happyend, Happy-End /ˈhɛpiˈlɛnt/ das; ~[s], ~s happy ending

Hardware /ˈhaːdwɛə/ die; ~, ~s (DV) hardware

Harfe die; ~, ~n harp

Harke die; ~, ~n rake

harken tr. V. rake

harm·los [1] Adj. (a) (ungefährlich) harmless; slight ‹injury, cold, etc.›; mild ‹illness›; safe ‹medicine, bend, road, etc.› (b) (arglos) innocent; harmless ‹fun, pastime, etc.› [2] adv. (a) (ungefährlich) harmlessly (b) (arglos) innocently

Harmlosigkeit die; ~ (a) (Ungefährlichkeit) harmlessness; (einer Krankheit) mildness; (eines Medikamentes) safety (b) (Arglosigkeit, harmloses Verhalten) innocence

Harmonie die; ~, ~n (auch fig.) harmony

harmonieren itr. V. (a) harmonize (b) (miteinander auskommen) get on well

Harmonika die; ~, ~s od. **Harmoniken** harmonica

harmonisch [1] Adj. harmonious; (Musik) harmonic [2] adv. harmoniously; (Musik) harmonically

harmonisieren tr. V. coordinate; etw. mit etw. ~ (Wirtsch.) bring sth. into line with sth.

Harmonisierung die; ~, ~en (Wirtsch.) harmonization

Harmonium das; ~s, **Harmonien** harmonium

Harn der; ~[e]s, ~e (Med.) urine

Harn-blase die bladder

Harnisch der; ~s, ~e armour

Harpune die; ~, ~n harpoon

harpunieren tr. V. harpoon

harren itr. V. (geh.) jmds./einer Sache od. auf jmdn./etw. ~: await sb./sth.

harsch [1] Adj. (a) (vereist) crusted (b) (barsch) harsh [2] adv. harshly

Harsch der; ~[e]s crusted snow

hart; härter, härtest... [1] Adj. (a) hard; ~ gekocht hard-boiled ‹egg› (b) tough ‹situation, job›; harsh ‹reality, truth› (c) (streng) harsh ‹penalty, punishment, judgement›; tough ‹measure, law, course› (d) (rau) rough ‹game, opponent› [2] adv. hard chair; (a) (mühevoll) ‹work› hard (b) (streng) harshly (c) (nahe) close (**an** + Dat. to)

Härte die; ~, ~n (a) (auch Physik) hardness (b) (Widerstandsfähigkeit) toughness (c) (schwere Belastung) hardship (d) (Strenge) harshness (e) (Heftigkeit) (eines Aufpralls usw.) force; (eines Streits) violence (f) (Rauheit) roughness

Härte-fall der (a) case of hardship (b) (ugs.: Person) hardship case

härten tr., itr. V. harden

härter ▶ HART

härtest... ▶ HART

hart-, Hart-: *~**gekocht ▶** HART 1A; ~**geld** das coins pl.; ~**gummi** das hard rubber; ~**herzig** [1] Adj. hard-hearted [2] adv. hard-heartedly; ~**herzigkeit** die; ~~: hard-heartedness; ~**käse** der hard cheese; ~**näckig** [1] Adj. (a) (eigensinnig) obstinate; stubborn; (b) (ausdauernd) dogged [2] adv. (a) (eigensinnig) obstinately; stubbornly; (b) (ausdauernd) doggedly; ~**näckigkeit** die; ~~ (a) (Eigensinn) obstinacy; stubbornness; (b) (Ausdauer) doggedness

Härtung die; ~, ~en hardening; (von Stahl auch) tempering

Hart-wurst die dry sausage

Harz das; ~es, ~e resin

Harzer Käse der; ~ ~s, ~ ~: Harz [Mountain] cheese

Haschee (Kochk.) das; ~s, ~s hash

Haschen[1] tr. V. (veralt.) catch

haschen[2] itr. V. (ugs.) smoke [hash] (coll.)

Häschen /ˈhɛːsçən/ das; ~, ~s bunny

Haschisch das od. der; ~[s] hashish

Haschisch·rausch der [state of] hashish intoxication; etw. im od. bei einem ~rausch tun do sth. while under the effects of hashish or while [high (coll.)] on hashish

Hase der; ~n, ~n (a) hare
(b) (landsch.) ▶ KANINCHEN

Hasel·nuss, *Ha̱sel-nuß die hazelnut

Hasen-: ~fuß der (spöttisch abwertend) coward; chicken (coll.); ~scharte die (Med.) harelip

Haspel die; ~, ~n (Technik) (für Garn) reel; (für ein Seil, Kabel) drum

Hass, *Haß der; Hasses hatred (auf + Akk., gegen of, for)

hassen tr., itr. V. hate

hass·erfüllt, *haß·erfüllt Adj. filled with hatred postpos.

hässlich, *häßlich ① Adj. (a) ugly
(b) (gemein) nasty
(c) (unangenehm) awful ‹weather, cold, situation, etc.›
② adv. (a) ‹dress› unattractively
(b) (gemein) nastily

Hässlichkeit, *Häßlichkeit die; ~, ~en (a) (Aussehen) ugliness
(b) (Gesinnung) nastiness

hast 2. Pers. Sg. Präsens v. HABEN

Hast die; ~: haste

hasten itr. V.; mit sein hurry

hastig ① Adj. hasty; hurried
② adv. hastily; hurriedly

hat 3. Pers. Sg. Präsens v. HABEN

hätscheln tr. V. caress

hatschi Interj. atishoo

hatte 1. u. 3. Pers. Sg. Prät. v. HABEN

hätte 1. u. 3. Pers. Sg. Konjunktiv II v. HABEN

Haube die; ~, ~n (a) bonnet; (einer Krankenschwester) cap
(b) (Kfz-W.) bonnet (Brit.); hood (Amer.)

Hauch der; ~[e]s, ~e (geh.) (a) (Atem, auch fig.) breath
(b) (Luftzug) breath of wind
(c) (leichter Duft) delicate smell
(d) (dünne Schicht) [gossamer-]thin layer

hauch·dünn Adj. gossamer-thin ‹material, dress›; wafer-thin ‹layer, slice, majority›

hauchen itr. V. breathe (gegen, auf + Akk. on)

Haue die; ~, ~n (a) (südd., österr.: Hacke) hoe
(b) (ugs.: Prügel) a hiding (coll.)

hauen ① unr. tr. V. (a) (ugs.: schlagen) belt; clobber (coll.)
(b) (ugs.: auf einen Körperteil) belt (coll.); hit
(c) (herstellen) carve ‹figure, statue, etc.› (in + Akk. in)
② unr. itr. V. (a) (ugs.: prügeln) er haut immer gleich he's quick to hit out
(b) (auf einen Körperteil) belt (coll.); hit
(c) (ugs.: auf/gegen etw. schlagen) thump

*old spelling - see note on page xiv

③ unr. refl. V. (ugs.: sich prügeln) have a punch-up (coll.)

Hauer der; ~s, ~ (Jägerspr.) tusk; (fig.) fang

Haufen der; ~s, ~: heap; pile; (Gruppe) bunch (coll.)

häufen ① tr. V. heap, pile (auf + Akk. on to); (aufheben) hoard ‹money, supplies›
② refl. V. (sich mehren) pile up

häufig ① Adj. frequent
② adv. frequently; often

Häufigkeit die; ~, ~en frequency

Häufung die; ~, ~en increasing frequency

Haupt das; ~[e]s, Häupter (geh., auch fig.) head

haupt-, Haupt-: ~bahnhof der main station; ~beruflich ① Adj. seine ~berufliche Tätigkeit his main occupation; ② adv. er ist ~beruflich als Elektriker tätig his main occupation is that of electrician; ~darsteller der (Theater, Film) male lead; ~darstellerin die (Theater, Film) female lead; ~eingang der main entrance; ~einschalt·zeit die peak or prime viewing time; ~fach das major; ~figur die main character; ~film der main feature; ~gang der (a) main corridor;
(b) ▶ ~GERICHT; ~gebäude das main building; ~gericht das main course; ~gewinn der first prize

Häuptling der; ~s, ~e chief[tain]

haupt-, Haupt-: ~mahlzeit die main meal; ~mann der; Pl. ~leute (Milit.) captain; ~person die central figure; ~postamt das main post office; ~quartier das (Milit., auch fig.) headquarters sing. or pl.; ~reise-zeit die high season; peak [holiday] season; ~rolle die main role; lead; die ~rolle spielen (fig.) play the leading role; ~sache die main thing; ~sächlich ① Adv. mainly; principally; ② Adj.; nicht präd. main; principal; ~saison die high season; ~satz der main clause; (allein stehend) sentence; ~schalter der (Elektrot.) mains switch; ~schlagader die aorta; ~schul·abschluss, *~schul·abschluß der ≈ secondary school leaving certificate; ~schule die ≈ secondary modern school; ~schüler der, ~schülerin die ≈ secondary modern school pupil; ~sitz der head office; headquarters pl.; ~stadt die capital [city]; ~städtisch Adj. metropolitan; ~straße die main street; ~thema das main topic or theme; (Musik) main theme; ~verkehr der bulk of the traffic

Hauptverkehrs-: ~straße die main road; ~zeit die rush hour

Haupt-: ~versammlung die (Wirtsch.) shareholders' meeting; ~wache die main police station; ~wort das (Sprachw.) noun

hau ruck Interj. heave[-ho]

Haus das; ~es, Häuser (a) house; (Amts-,

Firmengebäude usw.) building; (Heim) home; nach ~e home; zu ~e at home; das erste ~ am Platze the best hotel in the town **(b)** ~ halten be economical

haus-, Haus-: ~**angestellte** der/die domestic servant; ~**apotheke** die medicine cabinet; ~**arbeit** die housework; (Schulw.) homework; ~**arrest** der house arrest; ~**arzt** der, ~**ärztin** die family doctor; ~**aufgabe** die homework; ~**backen** ⟦1⟧ Adj. plain; unadventurous ⟨clothes⟩; ⟦2⟧ adv. ⟨dress⟩ unadventurously; ~**besetzer** der; ~~s, ~~, ~**besetzerin** die; ~~, ~~nen squatter; ~**besitzer** der houseowner; (Vermieter) landlord; ~**besitzerin** die houseowner; (Vermieterin) landlady; ~**besuch** der house call; ~**boot** das houseboat

Häuschen /ˈhɔy:sçən/ das; ~s, ~: small house; aus dem ~ sein (ugs.) be over the moon (coll.)

hausen itr. V. **(a)** (ugs. abwertend) live **(b)** (Verwüstungen anrichten) [furchtbar] ~: wreak havoc

Häuser·block der block [of houses]

haus-, Haus-: ~**flur** der hall[way]; (im Obergeschoss) landing; ~**frau** die housewife; ~**freund** der **(a)** friend of the family; **(b)** (verhüll.: Liebhaber) man friend (euphem.); ~**freundin** die friend of the family; ~**friedens·bruch** der (Rechtsw.) trespass; ~**gebrauch** der domestic use; das reicht für den ~gebrauch (ugs.) it's good enough to get by (coll.); ~**gehilfin** die [home] help; ~**gemacht** Adj. home-made

Haus·halt der **(a)** household **(b)** (Arbeit im ~) housekeeping; jmdm. den ~ führen keep house for sb. **(c)** (Politik) budget

*****haus|halten** ► HAUS B

Haushälterin die; ~, ~nen housekeeper

Haushalts-: ~**artikel** der household article; ~**debatte** die (Politik) budget debate; ~**geld** das housekeeping money; ~**jahr** das financial year; ~**kasse** die housekeeping money; ~**plan** der budget; ~**waren** Pl. household goods

haus-, Haus-: ~**herr** der **(a)** (Familienoberhaupt) head of the household; **(b)** (als Gastgeber) host; **(c)** (Rechtsspr.) (Eigentümer) owner; (Mieter) occupier ~**herrin** die **(a)** ► ~HERR A; **(b)** ► ~HERR B; ~**hoch** ⟦1⟧ Adj. as high as a house; (fig.) overwhelming; ⟦2⟧ adv. (fig.) ~hoch gewinnen win hands down

hausieren itr. V. [mit etw.] ~: hawk [sth.]; peddle [sth.]; „Hausieren verboten" 'no hawkers'

Hausierer der; ~s, ~, **Hausiererin** die; ~, ~nen pedlar; hawker

häuslich Adj. **(a)** domestic **(b)** (das Zuhause liebend) home-loving

Hausmacher·art die: nach ~: home-made-style attrib.

Haus·mann der: man who stays at home and does the housework; (Ehemann) househusband

Hausmanns·kost die plain cooking

Haus-: ~**marke** die **(a)** house wine; **(b)** (ugs.: bevorzugtes Getränk) favourite tipple (coll.); ~**meister** der, ~**meisterin** die caretaker; ~**mittel** das household remedy; ~**musik** die music at home; ~**nummer** die house number; ~**ordnung** die house rules pl.; ~**putz** der spring-clean; (regelmäßig) clean-out

Haus·rat der household goods pl.

Hausrat·versicherung die [household or home] contents insurance

Haus-: ~**schlüssel** der front-door key; house key; ~**schuh** der slipper; ~**segen** der: bei ihnen hängt der ~segen schief (ugs. scherzh.) they've been having a row

Haussuchung die; ~, ~en house search

Haussuchungs·befehl der search warrant

Haus-: ~**telefon** das internal telephone; ~**tier** das **(a)** pet; **(b)** (Nutztier) domestic animal; ~**tür** die front door; ~**verbot** das ban on entering the house/pub/restaurant etc.; ~**verwalter** der, ~**verwalterin** die manager [of the block]; ~**wirt** der landlord; ~**wirtin** die landlady; ~**wirtschaft** die domestic science and home economics; ~**zelt** das ridge tent

Haut die; ~, Häute skin; aus der ~ fahren (ugs.) go up the wall (coll.)

Haut-: ~**arzt** der, ~**ärztin** die skin specialist; ~**ausschlag** der [skin] rash

häuten ⟦1⟧ tr. V. skin; flay ⟦2⟧ refl. V. shed its skin/their skins

haut-, Haut-: ~**eng** Adj. skintight; ~**farbe** [skin] colour; ~**krankheit** die skin disease; ~**krebs** der skin cancer

Häutung die; ~, ~en **(a)** ► HÄUTEN 1: skinning; flaying **(b)** (das Sichhäuten) eine Eidechse bei der ~: a lizard shedding its skin

Haxe die; ~, ~n ► HACHSE

he Interj. (ugs.) hey

Heb·amme die midwife

Hebel der; ~s, ~: lever

heben unr. tr. V. **(a)** lift; raise ⟨baton, camera, glass⟩ **(b)** (verbessern) raise ⟨standard, level⟩; increase ⟨turnover, self-confidence⟩; improve ⟨mood⟩; enhance ⟨standing⟩; boost ⟨morale⟩

hecheln¹ itr. V. (ugs. abwertend) gossip

hecheln² itr. V. pant [for breath]

Hecht der; ~[e]s, ~e pike

Hecht·sprung der **(a)** (Turnen) Hecht vault **(b)** (Schwimmen) racing dive; (vom Sprungturm) pike-dive

Heck das; ~[e]s, ~e od. ~s stern; (Flugzeug~) tail; (Auto~) rear

Heck·antrieb der (Kfz-W.) rear-wheel drive

Hẹcke *die;* ~, ~n (a) hedge
(b) (wild wachsend) thicket
Hẹcken-: ~**rose** *die* dogrose; ~**schütze**
der, ~**schützin** *die* sniper
Hẹck·scheibe *die* rear window
Heer *das;* ~[e]s, ~e armed forces *pl.;* (für
den Landkrieg, fig.) army
Hefe *die;* ~, ~n yeast
Hefe·teig *der* yeast dough
Hẹft¹ *das;* ~[e]s, ~e (geh.) haft; handle
Hẹft² *das;* ~[e]s, ~e (a) (bes. Schule)
exercise book
(b) (Nummer einer Zeitschrift) issue
Hẹftchen *das;* ~s, ~: book [of tickets/
stamps *etc.*]
hẹften ⟦1⟧ *tr. V.* (a) (mit einer Nadel) pin; (mit
einer Klammer) clip; (mit Klebstoff) stick
(b) (Schneiderei) tack
(c) (Buchbinderei) stitch; (mit Klammern) staple
⟦2⟧ *refl. V.* **sich an jmds. Fersen** (*Akk.*) ~:
stick hard on sb.'s heels
Hẹfter *der;* ~s, ~: [loose-leaf] file
hẹftig ⟦1⟧ *Adj.* violent; heavy ⟨rain, shower,
blow⟩; severe ⟨pain⟩; ⟨person⟩ with a violent
temper
⟦2⟧ *adv.* ⟨rain, snow, breathe⟩ heavily; ⟨hit⟩
hard; ⟨quarrel⟩ violently
Hẹftigkeit *die;* ~: ▸ HEFTIG 1: violence;
heaviness; severity
Hẹft-: ~**klammer** staple; ~**pflaster** *das*
sticking plaster; ~**zwecke** *die*
▸ REISSZWECKE
hegen *tr. V.* (a) (bes. Forstw., Jagdw.) look
after, tend
(b) (geh.: umsorgen) look after
(c) (fig.) feel ⟨contempt, hatred, mistrust⟩;
cherish ⟨hope, wish, desire⟩; harbour
⟨grudge, suspicion⟩
Hehl *der od. das:* **kein[en]** ~ **aus etw.
machen** make no secret of sth.
Hehler *der;* ~s, ~: receiver [of stolen
goods]
Hehlerei *die;* ~, ~en (Rechtsw.) receiving
[stolen goods] *no art.*
Hehlerin *die;* ~, ~nen ▸ HEHLER
Heide¹ *der;* ~n, ~n heathen
Heide² *die;* ~, ~n heath; (Landschaft)
heathland
Heide-: ~**kraut** *das* heather; ~**land** *das*
moorland; heathland
Heidel·beere *die* bilberry
Heidin *die;* ~, ~nen heathen
heidnisch *Adj.* heathen
heikel *Adj.* (a) (schwierig) delicate, ticklish
⟨matter, subject⟩; ticklish tricky ⟨problem,
question, situation⟩
(b) (wählerisch) fussy (**in Bezug auf** + *Akk.*
about)
heil *Adj.* (nicht entzwei) in one piece; **wieder** ~
sein ⟨injured part⟩ have healed [up]

Heil *das;* ~s (a) (Wohlergehen) benefit
(b) (Rel.) salvation
Heiland *der;* ~[e]s, ~e Saviour
Heil·anstalt *die* (Anstalt für Kranke od.
Süchtige) sanatorium; (psychiatrische Klinik)
mental hospital
heilbar *Adj.* curable
Heil·butt *der* halibut
heilen ⟦1⟧ *tr. V.* cure; heal ⟨wound⟩
⟦2⟧ *itr. V.; mit sein* ⟨wound⟩ heal [up];
⟨fracture⟩ mend
heil·froh *Adj.* very glad
heilig *Adj.* (a) holy; **die Heiligen Drei Könige**
the Three Kings *or* Wise Men; the Magi; **die
Heilige Schrift** the Holy Scriptures *pl.;* **der
Heilige Abend** Christmas Eve
(b) (geh.: unantastbar) sacred ⟨right, tradition,
cause, etc.⟩
Heilig·abend *der* Christmas Eve
Heilige *der/die; adj. Dekl.* saint
heiligen *tr. V.* keep ⟨tradition, Sabbath,
etc.⟩; **der Zweck heiligt die Mittel** the end
justifies the means
Heiligen·schein *der* gloriole; (um den
Kopf) halo
Heiligkeit *die;* ~: holiness
Heiligtum *das;* ~s, Heiligtümer shrine
Heil-: ~**kraut** *das* medicinal herb;
~**mittel** *das* (auch fig.) remedy (**gegen** for);
(Medikament) medicament; ~**praktiker** *der,*
~**praktikerin** *die* non-medical
practitioner
heilsam *Adj.* salutary
Heils·armee *die* Salvation Army
Heilung *die;* ~, ~en (einer Wunde) healing;
(von Krankheit, Kranken) curing
Heim *das;* ~[e]s, ~e (a) (Zuhause) home
(b) (Anstalt, Alters~) home; (für Obdachlose)
hostel
Heim·arbeit *die* outwork
Heimat *die;* ~, ~en (a) (Ort) home; home
town/village; (Land) home; homeland
(b) (Ursprungsland) natural habitat
Heimat-: ~**kunde** *die* local history,
geography, and natural history; ~**land** *das*
native land; (fig.) home
heimatlich *Adj.* native ⟨dialect⟩; nostalgic
⟨emotions⟩
heimat-, Heimat-: ~**los** *Adj.* homeless;
~**museum** *das* museum of local history;
~**ort** *der* home town/village; ~**stadt** *die*
home town; ~**vertriebene** *der/die; adj.
Dekl.* expellee [from his/her homeland]
heim-, Heim-: ~|**bringen** *unr. tr. V.* (a)
jmdn. ~: take *or.* see sb. home; (b) bring
home; ~**computer** *der* home computer;
~|**fahren** ⟦1⟧ *unr. itr. V.; mit sein* drive
home; ⟦2⟧ *unr. tr. V.* drive home; ~**fahrt** *die*
journey home; (mit dem Auto) drive home;
~|**gehen** *unr. itr. V.; mit sein* go home
heimisch *Adj.* (einheimisch) indigenous,

native ⟨*plants, animals, etc.*⟩ (in + *Dat.* to);
domestic ⟨*industry*⟩; **sich ~ fühlen** feel at
home; **~ werden [in** (+ *Dat.*)] settle in[to]

heim-, Heim-: ~kehr *die;* ~: return
home; homecoming; **~|kehren** *itr. V.; mit
sein* return home (aus from); **~|kommen**
unr. itr. V.; mit sein come home

heimlich 1 *Adj.* secret
2 *adv.* secretly

Heimlichkeit *die;* ~, **~en** secret

heim-, Heim-: ~reise *die* journey home;
~spiel *das* (Sport) home match *or* game;
~|suchen *tr. V.* ⟨*storm, earthquake,
epidemic*⟩ strike; ⟨*disease*⟩ afflict;
⟨*nightmares, doubts*⟩ plague; **~suchung**
die; ~~, **~~en** affliction; visitation;
~tückisch 1 *Adj.* (bösartig) malicious;
(fig.) insidious ⟨*disease*⟩; 2 *adv.* maliciously;
~wärts *Adv.* (nach Hause zu) home; (in
Richtung Heimat) homeward[s]; **~weg** *der*
way home; **~weh** *das* homesickness;
~weh haben be homesick (nach for);
~|zahlen *tr. V.* jmdm. etw. **~zahlen** pay
sb. back for sth.

Heinzel-männchen *das* brownie

Heirat *die;* ~, **~en** marriage

heiraten 1 *itr. V.* get married
2 *tr. V.* marry

Heirats-: ~antrag *der:* jmdm. einen
~antrag machen propose to sb.; **~anzeige**
die announcement of a/the forthcoming
marriage; **~schwindler** *der,*
~schwindlerin *die: person who makes a
spurious offer of marriage for purposes of
fraud*

heiser 1 *Adj.* hoarse
2 *adv.* in a hoarse voice

Heiserkeit *die;* ~: hoarseness

heiß 1 *Adj.* hot; jmdm. ist ~: sb. feels hot;
etw. ~ machen heat sth. up; heated ⟨*debate,
argument*⟩; fierce ⟨*fight, battle*⟩; ardent
⟨*wish, love*⟩; ein **~es Thema** a controversial
subject
2 *adv.* ⟨*fight*⟩ fiercely; ⟨*love*⟩ dearly; ⟨*long*⟩
fervently

heißen *unr. itr. V.* (den Namen tragen) be
called; (bedeuten) mean; (lauten) ⟨*saying*⟩ go;
(*unpers.*) **es heißt, dass ...:** they say that ...;
in dem Artikel heißt es ...: in the article it
says that ...

Heiß-luft *die* hot air

Heißluft-backofen *der* fan oven

heiter *Adj.* cheerful, happy ⟨*person,
nature*⟩; happy, merry ⟨*laughter*⟩; fine
⟨*weather, day*⟩

Heiterkeit *die;* ~ (a) (Frohsinn)
cheerfulness
(b) (Belustigung) merriment

heizbar *Adj.* heated

Heiz-decke *die* electric blanket

heizen 1 *itr. V.* have the heating on
2 *tr. V.* heat ⟨*room etc.*⟩

Heizer *der;* ~s, ~, **Heizerin** *die;* ~,
~nen stoker

Heiz-: ~kissen *das* heating pad;
~körper *der* radiator; **~ofen** *der* stove;
heater; **~platte** *die* hotplate

Heizung *die;* ~, **~en (a)** [central] heating
no pl., no indef. art.;
(b) (ugs.: Heizkörper) radiator

Hektar *das od. der;* ~s, **~e** hectare

Hektik *die;* ~: hectic rush; (des Lebens)
hectic pace

hektisch *Adj.* hectic

Held *der;* ~en, **~en** hero

heldenhaft 1 *Adj.* heroic
2 *adv.* heroically

Heldentum *das;* ~s heroism

Heldin *die;* ~, **~nen** heroine

helfen *unr. itr. V.* help; jmdm. [bei etw.] ~:
help sb. [with sth.]; (*unpers.*) **es hilft nichts**
it's no use *or* good

Helfer *der;* ~s, ~, **Helferin** *die;* ~, **~nen**
helper; (Mitarbeiter[in]) assistant; (eines
Verbrechens) accomplice

Helikopter *der;* ~s, ~: helicopter

hell 1 *Adj.* (a) (von Licht erfüllt) light; well-lit
⟨*stairs*⟩
(b) (klar) bright ⟨*day, sky, etc.*⟩
(c) (viel Licht spendend) bright ⟨*light, lamp,
star, etc.*⟩
(d) (blass) light ⟨*colour*⟩; fair ⟨*skin, hair*⟩;
light-coloured ⟨*clothes*⟩
(e) (akustisch) high, clear ⟨*sound, voice*⟩;
ringing ⟨*laugh*⟩
(f) (klug) bright
(g) (ugs.: absolut) sheer, utter ⟨*madness,
foolishness, despair*⟩
2 *adv.* brightly

hell-: ~blau *Adj.* light blue; **~blond** *Adj.*
very fair; light blonde

Helle *das; adj. Dekl.* ≈ lager

Heller *der;* ~s, ~: heller; **bis auf den
letzten ~/bis auf ~ und Pfennig** (ugs.) down
to the last penny *or* (Amer.) cent

hell-: ~grün *Adj.* light green; **~häutig**
Adj. fair-skinned

Helligkeit *die;* ~, **~en** (auch Physik)
brightness

hell-, Hell-: ~rot *Adj.* light red;
~sehen *unr. itr. V.; nur im Inf.* **~sehen
können** have second sight; **~seher** *der,*
~seherin *die* clairvoyant; **~wach** *Adj.*
wide awake

Helm *der;* ~[e]s, **~e** helmet

Hemd *das;* ~[e]s, **~en** shirt; (Unterhemd)
[under]vest; undershirt

Hemds-ärmel *der* shirtsleeve

hemmen *tr. V.* (a) (verlangsamen) slow
[down]
(b) (aufhalten) check; stem ⟨*flow*⟩
(c) (beeinträchtigen) hinder

Hemmung *die;* ~, **~en (a)** (Gehemmtheit)
inhibition
(b) (Bedenken) scruple

hemmungs·los ① *Adj.* unrestrained
② *adv.* unrestrainedly

Hendl *das;* ~s, ~[n] (bayr., österr.) chicken;
(Brathähnchen) [roast] chicken

Hengst *der;* ~[e]s, ~e (Pferd) stallion

Henkel *der;* ~s, ~: handle

Henker *der;* ~s, ~: hangman; (Scharfrichter,
auch fig.) executioner

Henne *die;* ~, ~n hen

her /heːɐ̯/ *Adv.* ~ damit give it to me; give it
here (coll.); **vom Fenster** ~: from the window;
wo ist er ~? where is he from?; **von ihrer**
Kindheit ~: since childhood; **von der**
Konzeption ~: as far as the basic design is
concerned; **hinter jmdm.** ~ **sein** be
after sb./sth.; **einen Monat/lange** ~ **sein** be a
month/a long time ago; **es ist lange** ~, **dass**
wir...: it is a long time since we...

herab *Adv.* down; **von oben** ~ (fig.)
condescendingly

herab-: ~|**hängen** *unr. itr. V.* hang
[down] (von from); ~**hängende Schultern**
drooping shoulders; ~|**lassen** ① *unr. tr.*
V. let down; lower; ② *unr. refl. V.* (iron.: bereit
sein) sich ~**lassen, etw. zu tun** condescend to
do sth.; ~**lassend** ① *Adj.* condescending;
patronizing (**zu** towards); ② *adv.*
condescendingly; patronizingly; ~|**sehen**
unr. itr. V. **auf jmdn.** ~**sehen** look down on
sb.; ~|**setzen** *tr. V.* (a) reduce; (b)
(abwerten) belittle

heran *Adv.* **an etw.** (*Akk.*) ~: right up to
sth.

heran-, Heran-: ~|**bilden** *tr. V.* train
[up]; (auf der Schule, Universität) educate;
~|**bringen** *unr. tr. V.* (a) bring [up] (**an** +
Akk., **zu** to); (b) (vertraut machen) **jmdn. an etw.**
(*Akk.*) ~**bringen** introduce sb. to sth.;
~|**fahren** *unr. itr. V.; mit sein* drive up (**an**
+ *Akk.* to); ~|**kommen** *unr. itr. V.; mit*
sein **an etw.** (*Akk.*) ~**kommen** come near to
sth.; (erreichen) reach sth.; (erwerben) obtain
sth.; ~|**reifen** *itr. V.; mit sein* ⟨fruit, crops⟩
ripen; **zur Frau** ~**reifen** mature into a
woman; ~|**treten** *unr. itr. V.; mit sein* (sich
wenden) **an jmdn.** ~**treten** approach sb.;
~|**wachsen** *unr. itr. V.; mit sein* grow up;
~**wachsende** der/die; adj. Dekl. young
person; ~|**ziehen** *unr. tr. V.* pull over; pull
up ⟨chair⟩; **etw. zu sich** ~**ziehen** pull sth.
towards one

herauf *Adv.* up

herauf-: ~|**beschwören** *tr. V.* (a)
(verursachen) cause ⟨disaster, war, crisis⟩; (b)
(erinnern) evoke ⟨memories etc.⟩; ~|**kommen**
unr. itr. V.; mit sein (nach oben kommen) come
up; ~|**setzen** *tr. V.* increase, put up
⟨prices, rents, interest rates, etc.⟩

heraus *Adv.* ~ **aus den Federn!/dem Bett!**
rise and shine!/out of bed!

heraus-, Heraus-: ~|**bekommen** *unr.*
tr. V. (a) (entfernen) get out (**aus** of); (b) (ugs.:

lösen) work out ⟨problem, answer, etc.⟩; solve
⟨puzzle⟩; (c) (ermitteln) find out; (d) (als
Wechselgeld bekommen) **5 DM** ~**bekommen** get
back 5 marks change; **ich bekomme noch 5**
DM ~: I still have 5 marks [change] to come;
~|**bringen** *unr. tr. V.* (a) (nach außen bringen)
bring out (**aus** of); (b) (nach draußen begleiten)
show out; (c) (veröffentlichen) bring out;
(aufführen) put on, stage ⟨play⟩; screen ⟨film⟩;
(d) (auf den Markt bringen) bring out; (e) (populär
machen) make widely known; ~|**fahren**
① *unr. itr. V.; mit sein* (a) (nach außen fahren)
aus etw. ~**fahren** drive/ride out of sth.; (b)
(fahrend herauskommen) come out; ② *unr. tr. V.*
den Wagen [aus dem Hof] ~**fahren** drive the
car out [of the yard]; **jmdn.** ~**fahren** drive sb.
out (**zu** to); ~|**finden** ① *unr. tr. V.* find out;
trace ⟨fault⟩; ② *unr. itr. V.* find one's way
out (**aus** of); ~|**fordern** ① *tr. V.* (a) (auch
Sport) challenge; (b) (heraufbeschwören) provoke
⟨person, resistance, etc.⟩; invite ⟨criticism⟩;
court ⟨danger⟩; ② *itr. V.* **zu etw.** ~**fordern**
provoke sth.; (Provokation) provocation;
~|**forderung** *die* (auch Sport)
challenge; (Provokation) provocation;
~|**geben** ① *unr. tr. V.* (a) (aushändigen)
hand over ⟨property, person, hostage, etc.⟩;
(zurückgeben) give back; (b) (als Wechselgeld
zurückgeben) **5 DM/zu viel** ~**geben** give 5
marks/too much change; (c) (veröffentlichen)
publish; (d) issue ⟨stamp, coin, etc.⟩; ② *unr.*
itr. V. give change; ~**geber** *der;* ~~s, ~~,
~**geberin** *die;* ~~, ~~**nen** publisher;
(Redakteur[in]) editor; ~|**gehen** *unr. itr. V.;*
mit sein (a) go out (**aus** of); (b) (sich entfernen
lassen) ⟨stain etc.⟩ come out; ~|**halten** *unr.*
refl. V. keep out; ~|**hängen** *tr. V.* hang out
(**aus** of); ~|**helfen** *unr. itr. V.* **jmdm.**
~**helfen** (auch fig.) help sb. out (**aus** of);
~|**holen** *tr. V.* (a) (nach außen holen) bring
out; (b) (ugs.: erwirken) win ⟨wage increase,
advantage, etc.⟩; ~|**kommen** *unr. itr. V.;*
mit sein (a) come out (**aus** of); (b) (erscheinen;
ugs.: auf den Markt kommen, bekannt werden) come
out; ~|**nehmen** *unr. tr. V.* (a) take out
(**aus** of); (b) (ugs.: entfernen) take out
⟨appendix, tonsils, tooth, etc.⟩; ~|**reden** *refl.*
V. (ugs.) talk one's way out (**aus** of);
~|**reißen** *unr. tr. V.* (a) tear out (**aus** of);
pull up ⟨plant⟩; (b) (aus der Umgebung, der
Arbeit) tear away (**aus** from); **die Krankheit hat**
ihn aus der Arbeit ~**gerissen** the illness has
interrupted his work; (c) (Mängel ausgleichen)
den zunächst etwas langweiligen Abend
~**reißen** rescue what had been rather a
boring evening; **die Eins im Aufsatz reißt die**
Drei im Diktat heraus the A for the essay
makes up for the C in the dictation;
~|**rutschen** *itr. V.; mit sein* (ugs.) ⟨remark
etc.⟩ slip out; ~|**stellen** *refl. V.* **es stellte**
sich ~, **dass ...**: it turned out that ...;
~|**suchen** *tr. V.* pick out; look out ⟨file⟩

herb *Adj.* [slightly] sharp ⟨taste⟩; dry ⟨wine⟩;
[slightly] sharp ⟨smell, perfume⟩; bitter
⟨disappointment⟩; severe ⟨face, features⟩;
austere ⟨beauty⟩; harsh ⟨words, criticism⟩

---

*old spelling - see note on page xiv

herbei-: ~**eilen** *itr. V.; mit sein* hurry over; ~**laufen** *unr. itr. V.; mit sein* come running up

Herberge *die;* ~**, ** ~**n** (veralt.: Gasthaus) inn

Herbergs-: ~**mutter** *die, Pl.* ~**mütter,** ~**vater** *der* warden [of the/a youth hostel]

her|bringen *unr. tr. V.* etw. ~: bring sth. [here]

Herbst *der;* ~[e]s, ~**e** autumn; fall (Amer.); *s. auch* FRÜHLING

Herbst·anfang *der* beginning of autumn

herbstlich *Adj.* autumn *attrib.;* autumnal

Herd *der;* ~[e]s, ~**e** cooker; (fig.) centre (*of disturbance/rebellion*)

Herde *die;* ~**, ** ~**n** herd

Herd·platte *die* hot-plate

herein-: ~**bitten** *unr. tr. V.* jmdn. ~ bitten ask *or* invite sb. in; ~**brechen** *unr. itr. V.; mit sein* (geh.) ⟨*night, evening, dusk*⟩ fall; (*winter*) set in; (*storm*) strike, break; ~**bringen** *unr. tr. V.* bring in; ~**fallen** *unr. itr. V.; mit sein* (ugs.) be taken for a ride (coll.); be done (coll.); ~**kommen** *unr. itr. V.; mit sein* come in; ~**lassen** *unr. tr. V.* let in; ~**legen** *tr. V.* (ugs.) jmdn. ~legen take sb. for a ride (coll.) (mit, bei with); ~**platzen** *itr. V.; mit sein* (ugs.) burst in; ~**schneien** *unr. itr. V.; mit sein* (ugs.) turn up out of the blue (coll.)

her-, Her-: ~**fahrt** *die* journey here; ~**fallen** *unr. itr. V.; mit sein* über jmdn. ~fallen attack sb.; (gierig zu essen beginnen) über etw. (*Akk.*) ~fallen fall upon sth.; ~**gang** *der:* der ~gang der Ereignisse the sequence of events; ~**geben** *unr. tr. V.* hand over; (weggeben) give away; ~**gehen** *unr. itr. V.; mit sein* neben/vor/hinter jmdm. ~gehen walk along beside/in front of/ behind sb.; ~**haben** *unr. tr. V.* (ugs.) wo hat er/sie das ~? where did he/she get that from?; ~**halten** *unr. itr. V.* ~halten müssen [für jmdn./etw.] be the one to suffer [for sb./sth.]; ~**hören** *itr. V.* listen

Hering *der;* ~**s,** ~**e** (a) herring (b) (Zeltpflock) peg

her-: ~**kommen** *unr. itr. V.; mit sein* come here; ~**kömmlich** *Adj.* conventional; traditional ⟨*custom*⟩

Herkunft *die;* ~**, ** Herkünfte origin

Herkunfts·land *das* country of origin

her-: ~**laufen** *unr. itr. V.; mit sein* vor/ hinter/neben jmdm. ~laufen run [along] in front of/behind/alongside sb.; (nachlaufen) hinter jmdm. ~laufen run after sb.; (fig.) chase sb. up; ~**leiten** *tr., refl. V.* derive (aus, von from); ~**machen** (ugs.) *refl. V.* sich über etw. (*Akk.*) ~machen get stuck into sth. (coll.)

Hermelin *der;* ~**s,** ~**e** (Pelz) ermine

hermetisch 1 *Adj.* hermetic 2 *adv.* hermetically

Heroin *das;* ~**s** heroin

Heroin-sucht *die* heroin addiction

heroin·süchtig *Adj.* addicted to heroin *postpos.*

Herr *der;* ~**n,** ~**en (a)** (Mann) gentleman **(b)** (Titel, Anrede) ~ Schulze Mr Schulze; Sehr geehrter ~ Schulze! Dear Sir; (bei persönlicher Bekanntschaft) Dear Mr Schulze; meine ~**en** gentlemen **(c)** (Gebieter) master

herren-, Herren-: ~**ausstatter** *der* [gentle]men's outfitter; ~**los** *Adj.* abandoned ⟨*car, luggage*⟩; stray ⟨*dog, cat*⟩; ~**salon** *der* men's hairdressing salon; ~**schuh** *der* man's shoe; ~schuhe men's shoes; ~**toilette** *die* [gentle]men's toilet

Herr·gott *der;* ~**s:** der [liebe]/unser ~: the Lord [God]; God

Herrgotts·frühe *die* in aller ~: at the crack of dawn

her|richten *tr. V.* (bereitmachen) get ⟨*room, refreshments, etc.*⟩ ready; arrange ⟨*table*⟩; (in Ordnung bringen) renovate

Herrin *die;* ~**, ** ~**en** mistress

herrisch 1 *Adj.* overbearing; imperious 2 *adv.* imperiously

herrlich 1 *Adj.* marvellous; magnificent ⟨*view, clothes*⟩ 2 *adv.* marvellously

Herrlichkeit *die;* ~**, ** ~**en (a)** (Schönheit) magnificence; splendour **(b)** (herrliche Sache) marvellous thing

Herrschaft *die;* ~**, ** ~**en (a)** rule; (Macht) power **(b)** *Pl.* (Damen u. Herren) ladies and gentlemen

herrschen *itr. V.* rule; ⟨*monarch*⟩ reign, rule; draußen ~ 30° Kälte it's 30° below outside

Herrscher *der;* ~**s,** ~**, Herrscherin** *die;* ~**, ** ~**en** ruler

herrsch-, Herrsch-: ~**sucht** *die* thirst for power; (herrisches Wesen) domineering nature; ~**süchtig** *Adj.* domineering

her-: ~**rühren** *itr. V.* von jmdm./etw. ~rühren come from sb./stem from sth.; ***~**sein** ▸ HER; ~**stellen** *tr. V.* produce; manufacture; make

Hersteller *der;* ~**s,** ~**, Herstellerin** *die;* ~**, ** ~**en** producer

Her·stellung *die* production; manufacture

herüber *Adv.* over

herum *Adv.* um … ~ (Richtung) round; (Anordnung) around; um Weihnachten ~: around Christmas; ~ sein (ugs.: vergangen sein, vorüber sein) have passed

herum-: ~**ärgern** *refl. V.* (ugs.) sich mit jmdm./etw. ~ärgern keep getting annoyed with sb./sth.; ~**drehen** 1 *tr. V.* (ugs.) turn ⟨*key*⟩; turn over ⟨*coin, mattress, hand, etc.*⟩ 2 *refl. V.* turn [a]round; ~**fahren** (ugs.) 1 *unr. itr. V.; mit sein* (sich plötzlich herumdrehen) spin round; 2 *unr. tr. V.* jmdn. [in der Stadt] ~fahren drive sb. around the town; ~**führen** 1 *tr. V.* jmdn. [in der Stadt] ~führen show sb. around the town; ····⟶

2 *itr. V.* um etw. ~führen ⟨road etc.⟩ go round sth.; ~|**gehen** *unr. itr. V.; mit sein* (vergehen) pass; um etw. ~gehen go round sth.; etw. ~gehen lassen circulate sth.; pass; ~|**kommandieren** (ugs.) 1 *tr. V.* jmdn. ~kommandieren boss (coll.) *or* order sb. around *or* about; 2 *itr. V.* boss (coll.) *or* order people around *or* about; ~|**kommen** *unr. itr. V.; mit sein* (ugs.) (a) (vermeiden können) um etw. [nicht] ~kommen [not] be able to get out of sth.; (b) (viel reisen) get around *or* about; in der Welt ~kommen see a lot of the world; ~|**laufen** *unr. itr. V.; mit sein* (a) walk/(schneller) run around *or* about; um etw. ~laufen go round sth.; (b) (gekleidet sein) wie ein Hippie ~laufen go about looking like a hippie; ~|**lungern** *itr. V.* (salopp) loaf around; ~|**schlagen** *unr. refl. V.* (ugs.) sich mit Problemen/Einwänden ~schlagen grapple with problems/battle against objections; *~|**sein** ▶ HERUM; ~|**sitzen** *unr. itr. V.* (ugs.) sit around *or* about; ~|**sprechen** *unr. refl. V.* get around *or* about; ~|**stöbern** *itr. V.* (ugs.) keep rummaging around *or* about (in + *Dat.* in); ~|**treiben** *unr. refl. V.* (ugs. abwertend) sich auf den Straßen/in Discos ~treiben hang around the streets/in discos; sich in der Welt ~treiben roam about the world

herunter *Adv.* (a) (nach unten) down; [körperlich] ~ sein be in poor health (b) (fort) off; ~ vom Sofa! [get] off the sofa!

herunter-: ~|**bringen** *unr. tr. V.* bring down; ~|**fallen** *unr. itr. V.; mit sein* fall down; vom Tisch/Stuhl ~fallen fall off the table/chair; ~|**gehen** *unr. itr. V.; mit sein* (a) come down; (b) (niedriger werden) ⟨temperature⟩ drop; ⟨prices⟩ come down, fall; ~**gekommen** 1 2. *Part. v.* ~KOMMEN; 2 *Adj.* poor ⟨health⟩; dilapidated ⟨building⟩; run-down ⟨area⟩; down and out ⟨person⟩; ~|**handeln** *tr. V.* (ugs.) einen Preis ~handeln beat down a price; ~|**hängen** *unr. itr. V.* hang down; ~|**hauen** *unr. tr. V.* (ugs.) jmdm. eine ~hauen give sb. a clout round the ear (coll.); ~|**kommen** *unr. itr. V.; mit sein* (a) come down; (b) (ugs.: verfallen) go to the dogs (coll.); ~|**lassen** *unr. tr. V.* lower; ~|**schlucken** *tr. V.* swallow; *~|**sein** ▶ HERUNTER A; ~|**spielen** *tr. V.* (ugs.) play down

hervor *Adv.* aus ... ~: out of

hervor-: ~|**heben** *unr. tr. V.* stress; ~**ragend** 1 *Adj.* outstanding[ly good]; 2 *adv.* ~ragend geschult outstandingly well trained; ~ragend spielen/arbeiten play/work outstandingly well; ~|**tun** *unr. refl. V.* distinguish oneself; (wichtig tun) show off

Herz *das;* ~ens, ~en heart; (Kartenspiel) hearts *pl.;* von ~en kommen come from the heart; ein ~ für die Armen haben feel for the poor; ein ~ für Kinder haben have a love of children; schweren ~ens with a heavy

heart; etw. auf dem ~en haben have sth. on one's mind; es nicht übers ~ bringen, etw. zu tun not have the heart to do sth.; sich (*Dat.*) etw. zu ~en nehmen take sth. to heart

Herz-: ~**an·fall** *der* heart attack; ~**beschwerden** *Pl.* heart trouble *sing.*

herzens-, Herzens-: ~**gut** /'--'/ *Adj.* kind-hearted; ~**lust** *die:* nach ~lust to one's heart's content

herzhaft 1 *Adj.* hearty; (nahrhaft) hearty ⟨meal⟩; (von kräftigem Geschmack) tasty 2 *adv.* heartily; (nahrhaft) er isst gern ~: he likes to have a hearty meal

her|ziehen *unr. itr. V.; mit sein od. haben* (ugs.) über jmdn./etw. ~: run sb./sth. down

herzig 1 *Adj.* sweet; delightful 2 *adv.* sweetly; delightfully

herz-, Herz-: ~**infarkt** *der* heart attack; ~**klappen·fehler** *der* (Med.) valvular defect *or* insufficiency; ~**klopfen** *das;* ~~s: jmd. hat ~klopfen sb.'s heart is pounding; ~**krank** *Adj.* ⟨person⟩ with a heart condition; ~**kranz·gefäß** *das* coronary vessel

herzlich 1 *Adj.* warm ⟨smile, reception⟩; kind ⟨words, regards⟩; (ehrlich gemeint) sincere; ~en Dank many thanks 2 *adv.* warmly; (ehrlich gemeint) sincerely; ⟨congratulate⟩ heartily; ~ wenig very *or* (coll.) precious little

Herzlichkeit *die;* ~: warmth; kindness; (Aufrichtigkeit) sincerity

herz·los 1 *Adj.* heartless 2 *adv.* heartlessly

Herzog *der;* ~s, Herzöge duke

Herzogin *die;* ~, ~nen duchess

Herz·rhythmus·störung *die* (Med.) disturbance of the heart *or* cardiac rhythm

herz-, Herz-: ~**schlag** *der* heartbeat; (Herzversagen) heart failure; ~**schmerz** *der* pain in the region of the heart; ~**schrittmacher** *der* (Anat., Med.) [cardiac] pacemaker; ~**transplantation** *die* (Med.) heart transplantation; ~**zerreißend** 1 *Adj.* heart-rending; 2 *adv.* heart-rendingly

Hessen (*das*); ~s Hesse

hetero·sexuell *Adj.* heterosexual

Hetze *die;* ~ (a) [mad] rush (b) (abwertend) smear campaign

hetzen 1 *tr. V.* (a) hunt (b) (antreiben) rush 2 *itr. V.* (a) (in großer Eile sein) rush (b) *mit sein* (hasten) rush; (rennen) dash; race

Hetz-: ~**kampagne** *die* (abwertend) smear campaign; (gegen eine Minderheit) hate campaign; ~**rede** *die* (abwertend) inflammatory speech

Heu *das;* ~[e]s hay

Heuchelei *die;* ~: hypocrisy

heucheln 1 *itr. V.* be a hypocrite 2 *tr. V.* feign

Heuchler *der;* ~s, ~, **Heuchlerin** *die;* ~, ~nen hypocrite

heuchlerisch [1] *Adj.* hypocritical [2] *adv.* hypocritically

heuer *Adv.* (südd., österr., schweiz.) this year

Heuer *die;* ~, ~n (Seemannsspr.) pay; wages *pl.*

Heu·ernte *die* (a) hay harvest (b) (Ertrag) hay crop

heulen *itr. V.* (a) howl; ‹siren etc.› wail (b) (ugs.: weinen) howl; bawl

Heurige *der; adj. Dekl.* (bes. österr.) (a) (Wein) new wine (b) (Weinlokal) inn with new wine on tap

Heu-: ~**schnupfen** *der* hay fever; ~**schrecke** *die* grasshopper

heute *Adv.* today; ~ früh early this morning; ~ Morgen/Abend this morning/ evening; ~ Mittag [at] midday today; ~ Nacht tonight; (letzte Nacht) last night; ~ in einer Woche a week [from] today; today week; ~ vor einer Woche a week ago today

heutig *Adj.* (a) (von diesem Tag) today's; der ~e Tag today (b) (gegenwärtig) today's; of today *postpos.;* in der ~en Zeit nowadays

heut·zu·tage *Adv.* nowadays

Hexe *die;* ~, ~n witch

hexen *itr. V.* work magic

Hexen·schuss, *Hexen-schuß *der* lumbago *no indef. art.*

Hexerei *die;* ~, ~en witchcraft; (von Kunststücken usw.) magic

Hickhack *das od. der;* ~s, ~s (ugs.) squabbling; bickering

hieb *1. u. 3. Pers. Sg. Prät. v.* HAUEN

Hieb *der;* ~[e]s, ~e (a) (Schlag) blow; (mit der Peitsche) lash (b) *Pl.* (ugs.: Prügel) hiding *sing.*

hieb·fest *Adj.:* hieb- und stichfest watertight; cast-iron

hielt *1. u. 3. Pers. Sg. Prät. v.* HALTEN

hier *Adv.* (a) here; [von] ~ oben/unten [from] up/down here (b) (jetzt) now; von ~ an from now on

hieran *Adv.* here; sich ~ festhalten hold on to this; (fig.) im Anschluss ~: immediately after this

Hierarchie /hierar'çi:/ *die;* ~, ~n hierarchy

hierauf *Adv.* (a) on here; (darauf) on this; wir werden ~ zurückkommen we'll come back to this (b) (danach) after that; then (c) (infolgedessen) whereupon

hieraus *Adv.* out of here; (aus dieser Tatsache, Quelle) from this

hier-: ~|**behalten** *unr. tr. V.* jmdn./etw. ~behalten keep sb./sth. here; ~**bei** *Adv.* (a) (bei dieser Gelegenheit) Diese Übung ist sehr schwierig. Man kann sich ~bei leicht verletzen. This exercise is very difficult. You

can easily injure yourself doing it; (b) (bei der erwähnten Sache) here; ~|**bleiben** *unr. itr. V.; mit sein* stay here; ~**durch** *Adv.* through here; (aufgrund dieser Sache) because of this; ~**für** *Adv.* for this

hier·her *Adv.* here; ich gehe bis ~ und nicht weiter I'm going this far and no further; ~**gehören** belong here; (hierfür wichtig sein) be relevant [here]; ~**kommen** *mit sein* come here

hier·hin *Adv.* here; bis ~: up to here

hier-: ~**in** *Adv.* (a) (räumlich) in here; (b) in this; ~**mit** *Adv.* with this/these; ~mit ist der Fall erledigt that puts an end to the matter; ~**nach** *Adv.* (anschließend) after that

Hieroglyphe /hiero.../ *die;* ~, ~n hieroglyph

hier-: *~**sein** ▶ HIER A; ~**über** *Adv.* (a) (über dem Erwähnten) above here; (über das Erwähnte) over here; (b) (das Erwähnte betreffend) about this/these; ~**von** *Adv.* of this/these; ~**zu** *Adv.* with this; (hinsichtlich dieser Sache) about this; ~zu gehört/gehören ...: this includes/these include; ~zu reicht mein Geld nicht I haven't got enough money for that; ~**zu·lande** *Adv.* [here] in this country

hiesig *Adj.* local

hieß *1. u. 3. Pers. Sg. Prät. v.* HEISSEN

Hi-Fi-Anlage /'hai:fi-/ *die* hi-fi system

high /hai/ *Adj.* (ugs.) high (coll.)

Hightech-, High-Tech- /'haitɛk-/ high-tech

Hilfe *die;* ~, ~n (a) help; (für Notleidende) aid; relief; zu ~! help! (b) (Hilfskraft) help; (im Geschäft) assistant

Hilfe-: ~**leistung** *die* help; ~**ruf** *der* cry for help; ~**stellung** *die* (Turnen) jmdm. ~stellung geben act as spotter for sb.

hilflos [1] *Adj.* helpless [2] *adv.* helplessly

Hilflosigkeit *die;* ~ helplessness

hilfs-, Hilfs-: ~**bedürftig** *Adj.* (a) (schwach) in need of help *postpos.;* (b) (notleidend) in need; needy; ~**bereit** *Adj.* helpful; ~**bereitschaft** *die* helpfulness; ~**gelder** *Pl.* aid money *sing.;* ~**kraft** *die* assistant; ~**mittel** *das* aid; ~**organisation** *die* aid or relief organization; ~**programm** *das* aid or relief programme; ~**verb** *das,* ~**zeitwort** *das* (Sprachw.) auxiliary [verb]

Himalaja *der;* ~[s]: der/im ~: the/in the Himalayas *pl.*

Him·beere *die* raspberry

Himmel *der;* ~s, ~ sky; (Rel.) heaven; ~ noch [ein]mal! for Heaven's sake!

himmel-, Himmel-: ~**bett** *das* four-poster bed; ~**blau** *Adj.* sky-blue; clear blue ‹eyes›; ~**fahrt** *die* (Rel.) (a) Christi/Mariä ~fahrt the Ascension of Christ/the Assumption of the Virgin Mary; (b) (Festtag) [Christi] ~: Ascension Day *no art.*

h

Himmels-: ∼**richtung** *die* point of the compass; ∼**schlüsselchen** *das;* ∼∼**s**, ∼∼**:** cowslip

himmel·weit *Adj.* enormous, vast ⟨*difference*⟩

himmlisch *Adj.* (auch fig.) heavenly

hin *Adv.* **(a)** (räumlich) **zur Straße** ∼ **liegen** face the road
(b) (zeitlich) **gegen Mittag** ∼: towards midday
(c) (in Verbindungen) **nach außen** ∼: outwardly; **auf meinen Rat** ∼: on my advice; **auf seine Bitte** ∼: at his request
(d) (in Wortpaaren) ∼ **und zurück** there and back; **einmal Köln** ∼ **und zurück** a return [ticket] to Cologne; ∼ **und her** to and fro; back and forth; ∼ **und wieder** [every] now and then
(e) ∼ **sein** (ugs.: verloren sein); be gone; (ugs.: nicht mehr brauchbar sein); have had it (coll.); ⟨*car*⟩ be a write-off; (salopp: tot sein) have snuffed it (sl.); **von jmdm./etw. ganz** ∼ **sein** (ugs.: hingerissen sein) be mad about sb./bowled over by sth.

hinab *Adv.* ⯈ HINUNTER

hinab|- ⯈ HINUNTER-

hinauf *Adv.* up; **bis** ∼ **zu** up to

hinauf-: ∼|**fahren** *unr. itr. V.; mit sein* go up; (im Auto) drive up; (mit einem Motorrad) ride up; ∼|**gehen** *unr. itr. V.; mit sein* **(a)** (nach oben gehen) go up; **(b)** (nach oben führen) lead up; **(c)** (ugs.: steigen) ⟨*prices, taxes, etc.*⟩ go up; rise; ∼|**klettern** *itr. V.; mit sein* climb up; ∼|**steigen** *unr. itr. V.; mit sein* climb up; ∼|**ziehen** ⌊1⌋ *unr. tr. V.* pull up; ⌊2⌋ *unr. itr. V.; mit sein* move up; ⌊3⌋ *unr. refl. V.* (sich erstrecken) stretch up

hinaus *Adv.* **(a)** (räumlich) out
(b) (zeitlich) **auf Jahre** ∼: for years to come
(c) (etw. überschreitend) **über etw.** (*Akk.*) ∼: in addition to sth.
(d) **über etw.** (*Akk.*) ∼ **sein** be past sth.

hinaus-: ∼|**bringen** *unr. tr. V.* jmdn./etw. ∼**bringen** see sb. out/take sth. out (aus of); ∼|**fahren** ⌊1⌋ *unr. itr. V.; mit sein* **aus etw.** ∼**fahren** (mit dem Auto) drive out of sth.; (mit dem Zweirad) ride out of sth.; ⟨*car, bus*⟩ go out of sth.; ⟨*train*⟩ pull out of sth.; **zum Flugplatz** ∼**fahren** drive out to the airport; ⌊2⌋ *unr. tr. V.* jmdn./etw. ∼**fahren** drive sb./take sth. out; ∼|**fallen** *unr. itr. V.; mit sein* fall out (aus of); ∼|**finden** *unr. itr. V.* find one's way out (aus of); ∼|**gehen** *unr. itr. V.; mit sein* **(a)** go out (aus of); **(b)** (gerichtet sein) **das Zimmer geht zum Garten/nach Westen** ∼: the room looks out on to the garden/faces west; ∼|**kommen** *unr. itr. V.; mit sein* come out (aus of); ∼|**laufen** *unr. itr. V.; mit sein* **(a)** run out (aus of); **(b)** (als Ergebnis haben) **auf etw.** (*Akk.*) ∼**laufen** lead to sth.; ∼|**sehen** *unr. itr. V.* look out; **zum Fenster** ∼**sehen** look out of the window; *∗*∼|**sein** ⯈ HINAUS D; ∼|**tragen** *unr. tr. V.* jmdn./etw. ∼**tragen** carry sb./sth. out; ∼|**werfen** *unr. tr. V.*

(auch ugs. fig.) throw out (aus of); ∼|**ziehen** ⌊1⌋ *unr. tr. V.* **(a)** (nach draußen ziehen) jmdn./ etw. ∼**ziehen** pull sb./sth. out (aus of); tow ⟨*ship*⟩ out; **(b)** (verzögern) put off; delay; ⌊2⌋ *unr. refl. V.* be delayed; ∼|**zögern** ⌊1⌋ *tr. V.* delay; ⌊2⌋ *refl. V.* be delayed

hin-, Hin-: ∼|**blick** *der:* **im** od. **in** ∼**blick auf etw.** (*Akk.*) (wegen) in view of; (hinsichtlich) with regard to; ∼|**bringen** *unr. tr. V.* jmdn./etw. ∼**bringen** take sb./sth. [there]; ∼|**denken** *unr. itr. V.* **wo denkst du hin?** (ugs.) whatever are you thinking of?

hinderlich *Adj.* ∼ **sein** get in the way

hindern *tr. V.* **(a)** (abhalten) jmdn. ∼: stop sb. (**an** + *Dat.* from)
(b) (behindern) hinder

Hindernis *das;* ∼**ses**, ∼**se** obstacle

hin|deuten *itr. V.* **(a)** auf jmdn./etw. od. zu jmdn./etw. ∼: point to sb./sth.
(b) **auf etw.** (*Akk.*) ∼ → (fig.) point to sth.

Hindu *der;* ∼[**s**], ∼[**s**] Hindu

Hinduismus *der;* ∼ Hinduism *no art.*

hin·durch *Adv.* **(a)** (räumlich) **durch den Wald** ∼: through the wood
(b) (zeitlich) **das ganze Jahr** ∼: throughout the year

hinein *Adv.* **(a)** (räumlich) in; **in etw.** (*Akk.*) ∼: into sth.
(b) (zeitlich) **bis in den Morgen/tief in die Nacht** ∼: till morning/far into the night

hinein-: ∼|**bringen** *unr. tr. V.* take in; ∼|**fahren** (mit dem Auto) drive in; (mit dem Zweirad) ride in; **in etw.** (*Akk.*) ∼**fahren** drive/ ride into sth.; ∼|**fallen** *unr. itr. V.; mit sein* fall in; **in etw.** (*Akk.*) ∼**fallen** fall into sth.; ∼|**gehen** *unr. itr. V.; mit sein* go in; **in etw.** (*Akk.*) ∼**gehen** go into sth.; ∼|**gucken** *itr. V.* (ugs.) look in; **in etw.** (*Akk.*) ∼**gucken** look in[to] sth.; ∼|**kommen** *unr. itr. V.; mit sein* **(a)** come in; **in etw.** (*Akk.*) ∼**kommen** come into sth.; **(b)** (gelangen, auch fig.) get in; **in etw.** (*Akk.*) ∼**kommen** get into sth.; ∼|**reden** *itr. V.* jmdm. **in seine Angelegenheiten/ Entscheidungen usw.** ∼**reden** interfere in sb.'s affairs/decisions *etc.*; ∼|**sehen** *unr. itr. V.* look in; **in etw.** (*Akk.*) ∼**sehen** look into sth.; ∼|**versetzen** *refl. V.* **sich in** jmdn. *od.* jmds. **Lage** ∼**versetzen** put oneself in sb.'s position; ∼|**ziehen** *unr. tr. V.* **(a)** pull *or* draw in; **etw./jmdn. in etw.** (*Akk.*) ∼**ziehen** pull *or* draw sth./sb. into sth.; **(b)** (verwickeln) jmdn. **in eine Angelegenheit/ einen Streit/Skandal** ∼**ziehen** drag sb. into an affair/a dispute/scandal

hin-, Hin-: ∼|**fahren** ⌊1⌋ *unr. itr. V.; mit sein* go there; ⌊2⌋ *unr. tr. V.* jmdn. ∼**fahren** drive sb. there; ∼**fahrt** *die* journey there; (Seereise) voyage out; ∼|**fallen** *unr. itr. V.; mit sein* **(a)** fall over; **(b)** jmdm. **fällt etw.** ∼: sb. drops sth.; **etw.** ∼**fallen lassen** drop sth.; ∼**fällig** *Adj.* **(a)** infirm; frail; **(b)** (ungültig) invalid; ∼|**fliegen** *unr. itr. V.; mit sein* fly there; ∼**flug** *der* outward flight

hing *1. u. 3. Pers. Sg. Prät. v.* HÄNGEN

Hin·gabe *die;* ~: devotion; (Eifer) dedication

Hingebung *die;* ~: devotion

hingebungs·voll [1] *Adj.* devoted [2] *adv.* devotedly; with devotion; ⟨listen⟩ with rapt attention; ⟨dance, play⟩ with abandon

hin·gegen *Konj., Adv.* (jedoch) however; (andererseits) on the other hand

hin-, Hin-: ~|**gehen** *unr. itr. V.; mit sein* **(a)** go [there]; **zu jmdm./etw.** ~**gehen** go to sb./sth.; **(b)** (verstreichen) ⟨time⟩ go by; ~|**halten** *unr. tr. V.* **(a)** hold out; **(b)** (warten lassen) jmdn. ~**halten** keep sb. waiting; ~**halte-taktik** *die* delaying tactics *pl.;* ~|**hören** *itr. V.* listen

hinken /ˈhɪŋkn̩/ *itr. V.* **(a)** walk with a limp **(b)** *mit sein* (hinkend gehen) limp

hin-, Hin-: ~|**kommen** *unr. itr. V.; mit sein* **(a)** get there; **(b)** (an einen Ort gehören) go; belong; **(c)** (ugs.: stimmen) be right; ~**länglich** [1] *Adj.* sufficient; (angemessen) adequate; [2] *adv.* sufficiently; (angemessen) adequately; ~|**legen** [1] *tr. V.* put; (weglegen) put down; [2] *refl. V.* lie down; ~**reichend** [1] *Adj.* sufficient; (angemessen) adequate; [2] *adv.* sufficiently; (angemessen) adequately; ~**reise** *die* journey there; (mit dem Schiff) voyage out; ~**reißend** *Adj.* enchanting ⟨person, picture, view⟩; captivating ⟨speaker, play⟩; ~|**richten** *tr. V.* execute; ~**richtung** *die* execution

Hinrichtungs·kommando *das* firing squad

hin-, Hin-: ~|**sehen** *unr. itr. V.* look; *~|**sein** ▶ HIN E; ~|**setzen** [1] *tr. V.* put; [2] *refl. V.* sit down; ~**sicht** *die* in gewisser ~**sicht** in a way/in some respects *or* ways; **in jeder** ~**sicht** in every respect; **in finanzieller** ~**sicht** financially; ~**sichtlich** *Präp. mit Gen.* (Amtsspr.) with regard to; (in Anbetracht) in view of; ~|**stellen** [1] *tr. V.* put; put up ⟨building⟩; (absetzen) put down; [2] *refl. V.* stand

hinten *Adv.* at the back; **sich ~ anstellen** join the back of the queue (Brit.) *or* (Amer.) line; **weiter** ~: further back; (in einem Buch) further on; **die Adresse steht ~ auf dem Brief** the address is on the back of the envelope; **nach ~ hinaus liegen/gehen** be at the back; **die anderen sind ganz weit** ~: the others are a long way back

hinter [1] *Präp. mit Dat.* behind; (nach) after; **3 km ~ der Grenze** 3 km beyond the frontier; **eine Prüfung ~ sich haben** (fig.) have got an examination over [and done] with; **viele Enttäuschungen/eine Krankheit ~ sich haben** have experienced many disappointments/have got over an illness [2] *Präp. mit Akk.* behind

hinter... *Adj.; nicht präd.* back

hinter-, Hinter-: ~**einander** *Adv.* **(a)** (räumlich) one behind the other; **(b)** (zeitlich) one after another *or* the other; ~**gedanke** *der* ulterior motive; ~**gehen** /-ˈ-ˈ-/ *unr. tr. V.* deceive; ~**grund** *der* background; ~**grund-bericht** *der* background report; ~**gründig** [1] *Adj.* enigmatic; [2] *adv.* enigmatically; ~**grund-information** *die* item *or* piece of background information; ~**grundinformationen** [items *or* pieces of] background information *sing.;* ~**halt** *der* ambush; ~**hältig** [1] *Adj.* underhand; [2] *adv.* in an underhand manner; ~**her** *Adv.* (räumlich) behind; (nachher) afterwards; ~**hof** *der* courtyard; ~**land** *das* hinterland; (Milit.) back area; ~**lassen** /-ˈ-ˈ-/ *unr. tr. V.* leave; ~**legen** /-ˈ-ˈ-/ *tr. V.* deposit (bei with); ~**list** *die* guile; deceit; ~**listig** *Adj.* deceitful; ~**mann** *der* **(a)** person behind; **(b)** (Gewährsmann) [secret] informant

Hintern *der;* ~s, ~ (ugs.) backside; bottom

hinter-, Hinter-: ~**rad** *das* rear wheel; ~**sinn** *der* deeper meaning; ~**sinnig** *Adj.* ⟨remark, story, etc.⟩ with a deeper meaning; ~**teil** *das* backside; behind; ~**treffen** *das* (ugs.): **ins** ~**treffen geraten** *od.* **kommen** fall behind; ~**treiben** /-ˈ-ˈ-/ *unr. tr. V.* foil ⟨plan⟩; prevent ⟨marriage, promotion⟩; block ⟨law, investigation, reform⟩; ~**treppe** *die* back stairs *pl.;* ~**tür** *die* back door; ~**wäldler** *der;* ~~s, ~~ (spött.) backwoodsman; ~**wäldlerin** *die;* ~~, ~~**nen** backwoodswoman; ~**wäldlerisch** *Adj.* (spött.) backwoods *attrib.* ⟨views, attitudes, manners, etc.⟩

hinüber *Adv.* over; across

Hin- und Rück·fahrt *die* journey there and back; round trip (Amer.)

hinunter *Adv.* down

hinunter-: ~|**fahren** [1] *unr. itr. V.; mit sein* go down; (mit dem Auto) drive down; (mit dem Fahrrad) ride down; [2] *unr. tr. V.* jmdn./ein Auto/eine Ladung ~**fahren** drive sb. down/drive a car down/take a load down; ~|**gehen** *unr. itr. V.; mit sein* go down; ⟨aircraft⟩ descend; ~|**klettern** *itr. V.; mit sein* climb down; ~|**reichen** [1] *tr. V.* hand down; [2] *itr. V.* (sich bis hinunter erstrecken) reach down (**bis auf** + *Akk.* to)

hin·weg *Adv.* **(a)** (geh.) ~ **mit dir!** away with you! **(b) über etw.** ~: over sth.

Hin·weg *der* way there

hinweg-: ~|**gehen** *unr. itr. V.; mit sein* **über etw.** (*Akk.*) ~**gehen** pass over sth.; ~|**kommen** *unr. itr. V.; mit sein* **über etw.** (*Akk.*) ~**kommen** get over sth.; ~|**setzen** *refl. V.* **sich über etw.** (*Akk.*) ~**setzen** ignore sth.

Hinweis /ˈhɪnvaɪs/ *der;* ~**es**, ~**e** hint; **unter ~ auf** (+ *Akk.*) with reference to

hin-: ~|**weisen** [1] *unr. itr. V.* **auf jmdn./ etw.** ~**weisen** point to sb./sth.; [2] *unr. tr. V.* **jmdn. auf etw.** (*Akk.*) ~**weisen** point sth. out to sb.; ~**weisend** *Adj.* (Grammatik) demonstrative; ~|**werfen** *unr. tr. V.* throw ⸱⸱⸱⸢

down; ~|**ziehen** ① *unr. tr. V.* pull, draw (**zu** to, towards); ② *unr. itr. V.; mit sein* (umziehen) move there; **wo ist sie ~gezogen?** where did she move to?; ③ *unr. refl. V.* **(a)** (sich erstrecken) drag on (**über** + *Akk.* for); **(b)** (sich verzögern) be delayed

hinzu-: ~|**fügen** *tr. V.* add; ~|**kommen** *unr. itr. V.; mit sein* **(a)** come along; **(b)** (hinzugefügt werden) **zu etw.** ~**kommen** be added to sth.; **es kommt noch** ~, **dass** ...: there is also the fact that ...; ~|**tun** *unr. tr. V.* (ugs.) add

Hiobs·botschaft *die* bad news

Hirn *das;* ~[e]s, ~e **(a)** brain **(b)** (Speise; ugs.: Verstand) brains *pl.*

Hirsch *der;* ~[e]s, ~e deer; (Rothirsch) red deer; (männlicher Rothirsch) stag; (Speise) venison

Hirse *die;* ~, ~n millet

Hirt *der;* ~en, ~en, **Hirte** *der;* ~n, ~n herdsman; (Schaf~) shepherd

Hirtin *die;* ~, ~nen shepherdess

hissen *tr. V.* hoist

historisch *Adj.* **(a)** historical **(b)** (geschichtlich bedeutungsvoll) historic

Hit *der;* ~[s], ~s (ugs.) hit

Hitler·jugend *die* Hitler Youth

Hit·parade *die* hit parade

Hitze *die;* ~: heat

hitze-, Hitze-: ~**beständig** *Adj.* heat-resistant; ~**frei** *Adj.* ~**frei haben** have the rest of the day off [school/work] because of excessively hot weather; ~**periode** *die* hot spell; spell *or* period of hot weather; ~**welle** *die* heat wave

hitzig *Adj.* **(a)** hot-tempered **(b)** (erregt) heated ⟨*discussion etc.*⟩

hitz-, Hitz-: ~**kopf** *der* hothead; ~**köpfig** *Adj.* hot-headed; ~**schlag** *der* heatstroke

HIV-: ~-**Anti·körper** *der* HIV antibody; ~-**Infektion** *die* HIV infection; ~-**infiziert** *Adj.* HIV-infected; ~-**kontaminiert** *Adj.* HIV-contaminated; ~-**positiv** *Adj.* HIV-positive; ~-**Test** *der* HIV test; ~-**verseucht** *Adj.* HIV-contaminated

hl *Abk.* = **Hektoliter** hl

H-Milch *die;* ~ long-life *or* UHT milk

HNO-Arzt *der,* **HNO-Ärztin** *die* ENT specialist

hob *1. u. 3. Pers. Sg. Prät. v.* HEBEN

Hobby *das;* ~s, ~s hobby

Hobel *der;* ~s, ~ **(a)** plane **(b)** (Küchengerät) [vegetable] slicer

Hobel·bank *die; Pl.* Hobel·bänke woodworker's bench

hobeln *tr., itr. V.* **(a)** plane **(b)** (schneiden) slice

hoch; höher, höchst... ① *Adj.* high; tall

⟨tree, mast⟩; long ⟨grass⟩; deep ⟨snow, water⟩; heavy ⟨fine⟩; large ⟨sum, amount⟩; severe, extensive ⟨damage⟩; senior ⟨official, officer, post⟩; high-level ⟨diplomacy, politics⟩; **höchste Gefahr** extreme danger; **es ist höchste Zeit, dass** ...: it is high time that ...; **das hohe C** top C; **vier ~ zwei** (Math.) four to the power [of] two; four squared ② *adv.* (in großer Höhe) high; (nach oben) up; (zahlenmäßig viel, sehr) highly; ~ **begabt** highly gifted; ~ **empfindlich** highly sensitive ⟨instrument, device, material, etc.⟩; fast ⟨film⟩; extremely delicate ⟨fabric⟩; ~ **gestellt** ⟨person⟩ in a high position; important ⟨person⟩; ~ **verschuldet/versichert** heavily in debt/insured for a large sum [of money]; **etw.** ~ **und heilig versprechen** promise sth. faithfully

Hoch *das;* ~s, ~s **(a)** (Hochruf) **ein [dreifaches]** ~ **auf jmdn. ausbringen** give three cheers for sb. **(b)** (Met.) high

Hoch·achtung *die* great respect

hochachtungs·voll *Adv.* (Briefschluss) yours faithfully

hoch-, Hoch-: ~**aktuell** *Adj.* highly topical; ~**amt** *das* (kath. Rel.) high mass; ~**arbeiten** *refl. V.* work one's way up; ~**begabt** *Adj.* highly gifted; ~**betagt** *Adj.* aged; ~**betrieb** *der* (ugs.) **es herrschte** ~**betrieb im Geschäft** the shop was at its busiest; ~**blüte** *die* golden age; ~**burg** *die* stronghold; ~**deutsch** *Adj.* High German; ~**deutsch** *das,* ~**deutsche** *das* High German; ~**druck** *der; Pl.* ~**drücke** (Physik, Met.) high pressure; ***~**empfindlich** ▶ HOCH 2; ~|**fahren** *unr. itr. V.; mit sein* **(a)** (ugs.) go up; (mit dem Auto) drive up; (mit dem Fahrrad, Motorrad) ride up; **(b)** (auffahren) start up; **aus dem Sessel** ~**fahren** start [up] from one's chair; **(c)** (aufbrausen) flare up; ~**finanz** *die;* ~~: high finance; ~**fliegend** *Adj.* ambitious; ~**form** *die* top form; ~**gebirge** *das* [high] mountains *pl.*; ~**gefühl** *das* [feeling of] elation; ~|**gehen** *unr. itr. V.; mit sein* (ugs.) go up; (zornig werden) blow one's top (coll.); explode; (explodieren) ⟨bomb, mine⟩ go off; ~**genuss**, ***~**genuß** *der:* **ein** ~**genuss sein** be a real delight; ~**geschlossen** *Adj.* high-necked ⟨dress⟩; ***~**gestellt** ▶ HOCH 2; ~**glanz** *der:* **etw. auf** ~**glanz bringen** give sth. a high polish; (fig.) make sth. spick and span; ~**gradig** ① *Adj.* extreme; ② *adv.* extremely; ~|**halten** *unr. tr. V.* hold up; ~**haus** *das* high-rise building; ~|**heben** *unr. tr. V.* lift up; raise ⟨arm, leg, hand⟩; ~**interessant** *Adj.* extremely interesting; ~**kant** *Adv.* (ugs.) **jmdn.** ~**kant hinauswerfen** chuck sb. out (coll.); throw sb. out on his/her ear (coll.); ~|**kommen** *unr. itr. V.; mit sein* (ugs.) come up; (vorwärts kommen) get on; ~**konjunktur** *die* (Wirtsch.) boom; **auf dem Automarkt herrscht** ~**konjunktur** the car market is booming;

**alte Schreibung - vgl. Hinweis auf S. xiv

~|**krempeln** *tr. V.* roll up; ~**land** *das* highlands *Pl.;* ~|**leben** *itr. V.* jmdn./etw. ~**leben lassen** cheer sb./sth.; **er lebe ~!** three cheers for him; ~**leistungs·sport** *der* top-level sport; ~**modern** *Adj.* ultra-modern; ~**mut** *der* arrogance; ~**mütig** *Adj.* arrogant; ~**näsig** *Adj.* (abwertend) stuck-up; ~|**nehmen** *unr. tr. V.* (ugs.: verspotten) jmdn. ~**nehmen** pull sb.'s leg; ~**ofen** *der* blast furnace; ~**prozentig** *Adj.* high-proof ‹spirits›; ~|**rechnen** project; ~**rechnung** *die* (Statistik) projection; ~**ruf** *der* cheer; ~**saison** *die* high season; ~|**schlagen** ① *unr. tr. V.* turn up ‹collar, brim›; ② *unr. itr. V.; mit sein* ‹water, waves› surge up; ‹flames› leap up; ~**schule** *die* college; (Universität) university

Hochsee·fischerei *die* deep-sea fishing no art.

hoch-, Hoch-: ~**sitz** *der* (Jägerspr.) raised hide; ~**sommer** *der* high summer; ~**spannung** *die* (Elektrot.) high voltage; ~|**spielen** *tr. V.* blow up

höchst *Adv.* extremely; most

höchst... ▸ HOCH

Hoch·stapler /ˈʃtaːplɐ/ *der;* ~s, ~: confidence trickster; conman (coll.); (Aufschneider) fraud

höchsten·falls *Adv.* at [the] most *or* the outside; at the very most

höchstens *Adv.* at most; (bestenfalls) at best

Höchst-: ~**fall** *der:* im ~**fall** at [the] most; ~**form** *die* (bes. Sport) peak form; ~**geschwindigkeit** *die* top speed; (Geschwindigkeitsbegrenzung) speed limit

Hoch·stimmung *die* high spirits *pl.*

höchst-, Höchst-: ~**leistung** *die* supreme performance; (Ergebnis) supreme achievement; ~**maß** *das:* ein ~**maß an etw.** (Dat.) a very high degree of sth.; ~**persönlich** ① *Adj.* personal; ② *adv.* in person; ~**temperatur** *die* maximum *or* highest temperature; ~**wahrscheinlich** *Adv.* very probably; ~**wert** *der* maximum value

hoch-, Hoch-: ~**tour** *die:* auf ~**touren laufen** run at full speed; (intensiv betrieben werden) be in full swing; ~**trabend** (abwertend) ① *Adj.* high-flown; ② *adv.* in a high-flown manner; ~|**treiben** *unr. tr. V.* force up ‹prices etc.›; ~**verrat** *der* high treason; ~**wasser** *das* (Flut) high tide; (Überschwemmung) flood; ~**wertig** *Adj.* high-quality ‹goods›; highly nutritious ‹food›; ~**würden** *der;* ~~[s] (veralt.) Reverend Father

Hoch·zeit *die;* ~, ~en wedding

Hochzeits-: ~**feier** *die* wedding; ~**nacht** *die* wedding night; ~**reise** *die* honeymoon [trip]

Hocke *die;* ~, ~n (a) (Körperhaltung) squat; crouch

(b) (Turnen) squat vault

hocken ① *itr. V.* (a) *mit haben od.* (südd.) *sein* squat; crouch

(b) *mit haben od.* (südd.) *sein* (ugs.: sich aufhalten) sit around

② *refl. V.* crouch down

Hocker *der;* ~s, ~: stool

Höcker *der;* ~s, ~: hump; (auf der Nase) bump; (auf dem Schnabel) knob

Hockey /ˈhɔki/ *das;* ~s hockey

Hoden *der;* ~s, ~: testicle

Hoden·bruch *der* (Med.) scrotal hernia

Hof *der;* ~[e]s, Höfe (a) courtyard; (Schul~) playground; (Bauern~) [prison] yard

(b) (Bauern~) farm

(c) (Herrscher, Hofstaat) court

Hof·dame *die* lady of the court; (Begleiterin der Königin) lady-in-waiting

hof·fähig *Adj.* presentable at court *pred.*

hoffen ① *tr. V.* hope

② *itr. V.* hope; **auf etw.** (Akk.) ~: hope for sth.; (Vertrauen setzen auf) **auf jmdn./etw.** ~: put one's faith in sb./sth.

hoffentlich *Adv.* hopefully; ~**!** let's hope so

Hoffnung *die;* ~, ~en hope

hoffnungs-, Hoffnungs-: ~**los** ① *Adj.* hopeless; despairing ‹person›; ② *adv.* hopelessly; ~**losigkeit** *die;* ~~: despair; (der Lage) hopelessness; ~**voll** ① *Adj.* (a) hopeful; full of hope *pred.;* (b) (erfolgversprechend) promising; ② *adv.* (a) full of hope; (b) (erfolgversprechend) promisingly

höflich ① *Adj.* polite

② *adv.* politely

Höflichkeit *die;* ~: politeness

hoh... ▸ HOCH

Höhe /ˈhøːə/ *die;* ~, ~n height; **etw. in die ~ heben** lift sth. up; **das ist ja die ~!** (fig. ugs.) that's the limit!

Hoheit *die;* ~, ~en sovereignty (über + Akk. over); **Seine/Ihre** ~: His/Your Highness

Hoheits-: ~**gebiet** *das* [sovereign] territory; ~**gewässer** *das* territorial waters

Höhen-: ~**angst** *die* fear of heights; ~**flug** *der* (fig.) flight; ~**lage** *die* altitude; ~**luft** *die* mountain air; ~**messer** *der* altimeter; ~**sonne** *die* (Med.) sun lamp; ~**unterschied** *der* difference in altitude; ~**zug** *der* (Geogr.) range of hills; (Bergkette) range of mountains; mountain range

Höhe·punkt *der* high point; (einer Veranstaltung) high spot; highlight; (einer Laufbahn, des Ruhms) peak; pinnacle; (Orgasmus; eines Stückes) climax

höher /ˈhøːɐ/ ▸ HOCH

hohl *Adj.* hollow

Höhle *die;* ~, ~n (a) cave; (größer) cavern

(b) (Tierbau) lair

Hohl-: ~**maß** das measure of capacity;
~**raum** der cavity; [hollow] space;
~**spiegel** der concave mirror

Hohn der; ~[e]s scorn; derision

höhnen (geh.) itr. V. jeer

höhnisch [1] Adj. scornful
[2] adv. scornfully

Hokuspokus der; ~: hocus-pocus;
(abwertend: Drum und Dran) fuss

hold Adj. (dichter. veralt.) fair; lovely; lovely
⟨sight, smile⟩

holen [1] tr. V. (a) fetch; get
(b) (ab~) fetch
(c) (ugs.: erlangen) get ⟨prize etc.⟩; carry off
⟨medal, trophy, etc.⟩
[2] refl. V. (ugs.: sich zuziehen) catch; sich (Dat.)
[beim Baden] einen Schnupfen ~: catch a
cold [swimming]

Holland (das); ~s Holland

Holländer der; ~s, ~: Dutchman

Holländerin die; ~, ~nen Dutchwoman

holländisch Adj. Dutch

Hölle die; ~, ~n hell no art.

Höllen-lärm der (ugs.) diabolical noise or
row (coll.)

höllisch [1] Adj. (a) infernal; ⟨spirits,
torments⟩ of hell
(b) (ugs.: sehr groß) tremendous (coll.)
[2] adv. (ugs.: sehr) hellishly (coll.)

Holm der; ~[e]s, ~e (Turnen) bar

Holocaust der; ~[s] Holocaust

holpern itr. V. mit sein (fahren) jolt; bump

holprig Adj. (a) bumpy; rough
(b) (stockend) halting ⟨speech⟩; clumsy ⟨verses,
style, language, etc.⟩

Holunder der; ~s, ~: elder

Holz das; ~es, Hölzer wood; (Bau~, Tischler~)
timber; wood

Holz-: ~**bein** das wooden leg; ~**bläser**
der, **Holz-bläserin** die woodwind player

hölzern Adj. (auch fig.) wooden

holz-, Holz-: ~**fäller** der; ~s, ~~:
woodcutter; lumberjack (Amer.); ~**frei** Adj.
wood-free ⟨paper⟩

holzig Adj. woody

Holz-: ~**klotz** der block of wood; (als
Spielzeug) wooden block; ~**kohle** die
charcoal; ~**kopf** der (salopp abwertend)
blockhead; ~**pantoffel** der clog;
~**scheit** das piece of wood; (Brenn~) piece
of firewood; ~**schnitt** der (a) (Technik)
woodcutting no art.; (b) (Blatt) woodcut;
~**schuh** der clog; ~**stoß** der pile of wood;
~**weg** der: auf dem ~weg sein be on the
wrong track (fig.); ~**wolle** die wood wool;
~**wurm** der woodworm

homogen Adj. homogeneous

homöopathisch Adj. homoeopathic

Homo-sexualität die; ~: homosexuality

homo-sexuell [1] Adj. homosexual

[2] adv. ~ veranlagt sein have homosexual
tendencies

Honig der; ~s, ~e honey

Honig-kuchen der honey cake

Honig-wabe die honeycomb

Honorar das; ~s, ~e fee; (Autoren~) royalty

Honoratioren /honora'tsːjoːrən/ Pl.
notabilities

honorieren tr. V. (a) jmdn. ~: pay sb. [a/
his/her fee]
(b) (würdigen) appreciate; (belohnen) reward

Hopfen der; ~s, ~: hop; bei ihm ist ~ und
Malz verloren (ugs.) he's a hopeless case

hopp Interj. quick; look sharp

hoppeln itr. V.; mit sein hop; (über + Akk.
across, over)

hoppla Interj. oops; whoops

hopsen itr. V.; mit sein (ugs.) (springen) jump;
(hüpfen) ⟨animal⟩ hop; ⟨child⟩ skip; ⟨ball⟩
bounce

Hopser der; ~s, ~ (ugs.) [little] jump

Hör-apparat der hearing aid

hörbar [1] Adj. audible
[2] adv. audibly; (geräuschvoll) noisily

Hör-buch das audiobook

horchen itr. V. listen (auf + Akk. to);
(heimlich zuhören) eavesdrop

Horde die; ~, ~n horde; (von Halbstarken)
mob

hören [1] tr. V. hear; (anhören) listen to
[2] itr. V. hear; (zuhören) listen; auf jmdn./
jmds. Rat ~: listen to sb./sb.'s advice

Hören-sagen das: vom ~: from hearsay

Hörer der; ~s, ~ (a) listener
(b) (Telefon~) receiver

Hörerin die; ~, ~nen listener

Hörerschaft die; ~, ~en audience

Hör-: ~**fehler** der (a) das war ein ~fehler
he/she etc. misheard; (b) (Schwerhörigkeit)
hearing defect; ~**funk** der radio; im ~funk
on the radio; ~**funk-sendung** die radio
programme; ~**gerät** das hearing aid

hörig Adj.: jmdm. ~ sein be submissively
dependent on sb.; (sexuell) be sexually
enslaved to sb.

Horizont der; ~[e]s, ~e (auch Geol., fig.)
horizon

horizontal [1] Adj. horizontal
[2] adv. horizontally

Horizontale die; ~, ~n (a) (Linie)
horizontal line
(b) (Lage) die ~: the horizontal

Hormon das; ~s, ~e hormone

Horn das; ~[e]s, Hörner horn

Hörnchen das; ~s, ~ (Gebäck) croissant

Horn-haut die (a) callus; hard skin no
indef. art.;
(b) (am Auge) cornea

Hornisse die; ~, ~n hornet

Horoskop das; ~s, ~e horoscope

---

*old spelling - see note on page xiv

horrend *Adj.* shocking (coll.), horrendous (coll.) ⟨*price*⟩; colossal (coll.) ⟨*sum, amount, rent*⟩

Hör·rohr *das* stethoscope

Horror *der;* ~s horror

Horror-: ~**film** *der* horror film; ~**roman** *der* horror novel

Hör-: ~**saal** *der* lecture theatre *or* hall; ~**spiel** *das* radio play

Horst *der;* ~[e]s, ~e eyrie

Hort *der;* ~[e]s, ~e ▸ KINDERHORT

horten *tr. V.* hoard; stockpile ⟨*raw materials*⟩

Hortensie /hɔr'tɛnzjə/ *die;* ~, ~n hydrangea

Hör·weite *die:* in/außer ~weite in/out of earshot

Höschen /'høːsçən/ *das;* ~s, ~: trousers *pl.;* pair of trousers; (kurzes ~) shorts *pl.;* pair of shorts

Hose *die;* ~, ~n **(a)** trousers *pl.;* pants *pl.* (Amer.); (Unter~) pants *pl.;* (Freizeit~) slacks *pl.;* (Bund~) breeches *pl.;* (Reit~) riding breeches *pl.;* **eine** ~: a pair of trousers/ pants/slacks *etc.;*
(b) (fig.) **die** ~**n anhaben** (ugs.) wear the trousers; **die** ~**n runterlassen** (salopp) come clean (coll.); **in die** ~[n] **gehen** (salopp) be a [complete] flop (coll.); **es ist tote** ~ (Jugendspr.) there's nothing doing (coll.)

Hosen-: ~**anzug** *der* trouser suit (Brit.); pant suit; ~**matz** *der;* ~~es, ~~e od. ~**mätze** (ugs. scherzh.) toddler; ~**rock** *der* culottes *pl.;* ~**tasche** *die* trouser pocket; pants pocket (Amer.); ~**träger** *Pl.* braces; suspenders (Amer.); pair of braces/ suspenders

Hospital *das;* ~s, ~e od. **Hospitäler** hospital

Hospiz *das;* ~es, ~e hospice

Hostie /'hɔstjə/ *die;* ~, ~n (christl. Rel.) host

Hotel *das;* ~s, ~s hotel

Hotel·bar *die* hotel bar

Hotel garni /- gar'niː/ *das;* ~ ~, ~s ~s /- gar'niː/ bed-and-breakfast hotel

Hotelier /hotɛ' lje/ *der;* ~s, ~s hotelier

Hotline /'hɔtlaɪn/ *die;* ~, ~s hotline

hüben *Adv.* over here

hübsch ① *Adj.* pretty; nice ⟨*area, flat, voice, tune, etc.*⟩; nice-looking ⟨*boy, person*⟩; **ein** ~**es Sümmchen** (ugs.) a tidy sum (coll.); **das ist eine** ~**e Geschichte** (ugs. iron.) this is a fine *or* pretty kettle of fish (coll.)
② *adv.* prettily; (ugs.: sehr) ~ **kalt** perishing cold

Hub·schrauber *der;* ~s, ~: helicopter

Hubschrauber·lande·platz *der* heliport; (kleiner) helicopter pad; landing pad

huckepack *Adv.* jmdn. ~ **tragen** (ugs.) give sb. a piggyback

hudeln *itr. V.* (bes. südd., österr.) be sloppy (**bei** in)

Huf *der;* ~[e]s, ~e hoof

huf-, Huf-: ~**eisen** *das* horseshoe; ~**eisen·förmig** ① *Adj.* horseshoe-shaped; ② *adv.* in [the shape of] a horseshoe; ~**schmied** *der* farrier

Hüfte *die;* ~, ~n hip

Hüft-: ~**gelenk** *das* (Anat.) hip joint; ~**gürtel** *der* girdle

Hügel *der;* ~s, ~ hill

hügelig *Adj.* hilly

Huhn *das;* ~[e]s, **Hühner** chicken; (Henne) chicken; hen

Hühnchen *das;* ~s, ~: small chicken; **mit jmdm. [noch] ein** ~ **zu rupfen haben** (ugs.) [still] have a bone to pick with sb.

Hühner-: ~**auge** *das* (am Fuß) corn; ~**brühe** *die* chicken broth

hui /hui/ *Interj.* whoosh

huldigen *itr. V.* jmdm. ~: pay tribute to sb.

Huldigung *die;* ~, ~en tribute

Hülle *die;* ~, ~n cover

hüllen *tr. V.* (geh.) wrap

Hülse *die;* ~, ~n **(a)** case
(b) (Bot.) pod

Hülsen·frucht *die* **(a)** (Frucht) fruit of a leguminous plant; **Hülsenfrüchte** pulse *sing.;*
(b) (Pflanze) legume; leguminous plant

human *Adj.* humane

Humanismus *der;* ~: humanism; (Epoche) Humanism *no art.*

humanitär *Adj.* humanitarian

Humbug *der;* ~s (ugs.) humbug

Hummel *die;* ~, ~n bumble-bee

Hummer *der;* ~s, ~: lobster

Humor *der;* ~s humour; (Sinn für ~) sense of humour; **den** ~ **nicht verlieren** remain good-humoured

Humorist *der;* ~en, ~en, **Humoristin** *die;* ~, ~nen **(a)** (Autor[in]) humorist
(b) (Vortragskünstler[in]) comedian

humoristisch *Adj.* humorous

humor-: ~**los** *Adj.* humourless; ~**losigkeit** *die;* ~~: humourlessness; lack of humour; ~**voll** *Adj.* humorous

humpeln *itr. V.* **(a)** auch mit sein walk with a limp
(b) mit sein (sich ~d fortbewegen) limp

Hund *der;* ~es, ~e **(a)** dog; **auf den** ~ **kommen** (ugs.) go to the dogs (coll.); **vor die** ~**e gehen** (ugs.) go to the dogs (coll.); (sterben) kick the bucket (coll.)
(b) (abwertend) bastard (sl.)

hunde-, Hunde-: ~**elend** *Adj.* (ugs.) [really] wretched *or* awful; ~**hütte** *die* [dog] kennel; ~**kuchen** *der* dog biscuit; ~**müde** *Adj.* (ugs.) dog-tired; ~**rasse** *die* breed of dog

hundert *Kardinalz.* **(a)** a *or* one hundred
(b) (ugs.: viele) hundreds of

Hundert[1] *das;* ~s, ~e hundred

Hundert² *die;* ~, ~en hundred
Hunderter *der;* ~s, ~ (ugs.) hundred-
mark/-dollar *etc.* note
hundert·mal *Adv.* a hundred times; **auch
wenn du dich** ~ **beschwerst** (ugs.) however
much you complain
Hundert-: ~**mark·schein** *der* hundred-
mark note; ~**meter·lauf** *der* (Leichtathletik)
hundred metres *sing.*
hundert·prozentig [1] *Adj.* **(a)** [one-
]hundred per cent *attrib.;*
(b) (ugs.: völlig) a hundred per cent
(c) (ugs.: ganz sicher) absolutely reliable
[2] *adv.* (ugs.) **ich bin nicht** ~ **sicher** I'm not a
hundred per cent sure
hundertst... /'hʊndɐts:t.../ *Ordinalz.*
hundredth
hundertstel /'hʊndɐts:tl̩/ *Bruchz.*
hundredth
Hundertstel *das* (schweiz. meist *der*); ~s, ~:
hundredth
hundert·tausend *Kardinalz.* a or one
hundred thousand
Hunde-: ~**scheiße** *die* (derb) dog shit
(coarse); ~**steuer** *die* dog licence fee;
~**zwinger** *der* dog run
Hündin *die;* ~, ~nen bitch
Hüne *der;* ~n, ~n giant
Hünen·grab *das* megalithic tomb;
(Hügelgrab) barrow
Hunger *der;* ~s **(a)** ~ **bekommen/haben**
get/be hungry
(b) (geh.: Verlangen) hunger; (nach Ruhm, Macht)
craving
Hunger·kur *die* starvation diet
hungern *itr. V.* go hungry; starve; **nach etw.**
~: (fig.) hunger for sth.
Hungers·not *die* famine
Hunger-: ~**streik** *der* hunger strike;
~**tuch** *das:* **am** ~**tuch nagen** (ugs. scherzh.)
be on the breadline
hungrig *Adj.* (auch geh. fig.) hungry (nach
for)
Hupe *die;* ~, ~n horn
hupen *itr. V.* sound one's horn; **dreimal** ~:
hoot three times
hüpfen *itr. V.; mit sein* hop; (ball) bounce
Hürde *die;* ~, ~n hurdle
Hürden·lauf *der* (Leichtathletik) hurdling;
(Wettbewerb) hurdles *pl.*
Hure *die;* ~, ~n (abwertend) whore
huren *itr. V.* (abwertend) whore
hurra *Interj.* hurray; hurrah; ~/**Hurra
schreien** cheer
Hurra *das;* ~s, ~s cheer
hurtig [1] *Adj.* rapid
[2] *adv.* quickly
huschen *itr. V.; mit sein* (lautlos u. leichtfüßig)

⟨*person*⟩ steal; (lautlos u. schnell) dart; ⟨*mouse,
lizard, etc.*⟩ dart; ⟨*smile*⟩ flit; ⟨*light*⟩ flash;
⟨*shadow*⟩ slide quickly
hüsteln *itr. V.* give a slight cough
husten [1] *itr. V.* cough; (Husten haben) have
a cough
[2] *tr. V.* cough up ⟨*blood, phlegm*⟩
Husten *der;* ~s, ~: cough
Husten-: ~**anfall** *der* coughing fit; fit of
coughing; ~**bonbon** *das* cough drop;
~**reiz** *der* tickling in the throat; ~**saft** *der*
cough mixture; ~**tropfen** *Pl.* cough drops
Hut¹ *der;* ~es, Hüte hat; (fig.) **da geht einem/
mir der** ~ **hoch** (ugs.) it makes you/me mad
(coll.); **das kann er sich** (*Dat.*) **an den** ~
stecken (ugs. abwertend) he can keep it (coll.)
Hut² *die;* ~ (geh.) keeping; care; **auf der** ~
sein be on one's guard
hüten [1] *tr. V.* look after; tend ⟨*sheep, cattle*⟩
[2] *refl. V.* be on one's guard
Hut·schnur *die:* **das geht mir über die** ~
(ugs.) that's going too far
Hütte *die;* ~, ~n **(a)** hut; (ärmliches Haus)
shack; hut
(b) (Eisen~) iron [and steel] works *sing.* or
pl.;
(c) (Jagd~) [hunting] lodge
Hütten-: ~**käse** *der* cottage cheese;
~**schuh** *der* slipper sock
Hyäne *die;* ~, ~n hyena
Hyazinthe *die;* ~, ~n hyacinth
Hydrant *der;* ~en, ~en hydrant
Hydrat *das;* ~[e]s, ~e (Chemie) hydrate
Hydraulik *die;* ~ (Technik) **(a)** (Theorie)
hydraulics *sing., no art.;*
(b) (Vorrichtungen) hydraulics *pl.*
hydraulisch (Technik) [1] *Adj.* hydraulic
[2] *adv.* hydraulically
Hydro·kultur *die* (Gartenbau) hydroponics
sing.
Hygiene *die;* ~ **(a)** (Gesundheitspflege) health
care
(b) (Sauberkeit) hygiene
hygienisch [1] *Adj.* hygienic
[2] *adv.* hygienically
Hymne /'hʏmnə/ *die;* ~, ~n hymn;
(National~) national anthem
Hypnose *die;* ~, ~n hypnosis
hypnotisieren *tr. V.* hypnotize
Hypochonder /hypo'xɔndɐ/ *der;* ~s, ~,
Hypochonderin *die;* ~, ~nen
hypochondriac
hypochondrisch *Adj.* hypochondriac
Hypotenuse *die;* ~, ~n (Math.) hypotenuse
Hypothek *die;* ~, ~en (Bankw.) mortgage;
(fig.) burden
Hypothese *die;* ~, ~n hypothesis
hypothetisch [1] *Adj.* hypothetical
[2] *adv.* hypothetically
Hysterie *die;* ~, ~n hysteria
hysterisch [1] *Adj.* hysterical
[2] *adv.* hysterically

*alte Schreibung - vgl. Hinweis auf S. xiv

Ii

i, I /i:/ *das;* ∼, ∼ i/I; **das Tüpfelchen** *od.* **der Punkt auf dem** ∼ (fig.) the final touch

i *Interj.* ugh; **i bewahre, i wo** (ugs.) [good] heavens, no!

i.A. *Abk.* = **im Auftrag[e]** p.p.

IC *Abk.* = **Intercity** IC

ICE *Abk.* = **Intercityexpress[zug]** ICE

ich *Personalpron.; 1. Pers. Sg. Nom.* I; **immer** ∼ (ugs.) [it's] always me; ∼ **nicht** not me; **Menschen wie du und** ∼: people like you and me; *s. auch* (*Gen.*) MEINER, (*Dat.*) MIR, (*Akk.*) MICH

Ich *das;* ∼[s], ∼[s] **(a)** self

(b) (Psych.) ego

Ichform *die* first person

Icon /ˈaɪkən/ *das;* ∼s, ∼s (DV) icon

ideal ① *Adj.* ideal

② *adv.* ideally

Ideal *das;* ∼s, ∼e ideal

Ideal-: ∼**bild** *das* ideal; ∼**fall** *der* ideal case; ∼**gewicht** *das* ideal weight

idealisieren *tr. V.* idealize

Idealismus *der;* ∼ (auch Philos.) idealism

Idealist *der;* ∼en, ∼en, **Idealistin** *die;* ∼, ∼nen idealist

idealistisch (auch Philos.) ① *Adj.* idealistic

② *adv.* idealistically

Idee *die;* ∼, ∼n **(a)** idea

(b) (ein bisschen) **eine** ∼: a shade; **eine** ∼ [Salz/Pfeffer] a touch [of salt/pepper]

ideell *Adj.* non-material; (geistig-seelisch) spiritual

ideen·los *Adj.* [completely] lacking in ideas *postpos.*

Identifikation /identifikaˈtsjoːn/ *die;* ∼, ∼en (auch Psych.) identification

identifizieren ① *tr. V.* identify

② *refl. V.* (auch Psych.) **sich mit jmdm./etw.** ∼: identify with sb./sth.

identisch *Adj.* identical

Identität *die;* ∼: identity

Ideologe *der;* ∼n, ∼n ideologue

Ideologie *die;* ∼, /-iːən/ ideology

Ideologin *die;* ∼, ∼nen ideologue

ideologisch ① *Adj.* ideological

② *adv.* ideologically

Idiot *der;* ∼en, ∼en (auch ugs. abwertend) idiot

Idioten-, Idioten-: ∼**hügel** *der* (ugs. scherzh.) nursery slope; ∼**sicher** *Adj.* (ugs. scherzh.) foolproof

Idiotie *die;* ∼, ∼n /-iːən/ **(a)** idiocy

(b) (ugs. abwertend: Dummheit) madness

Idiotin *die;* ∼, ∼nen (auch ugs. abwertend) idiot

idiotisch ① *Adj.* **(a)** (Psych.) severely subnormal

(b) (ugs. abwertend) idiotic

② *adv.* (auch ugs. abwertend) idiotically

Idol *das;* ∼s, ∼e (auch bild. Kunst) idol

Idyll *das;* ∼s, ∼e idyll

Idylle *die;* ∼, ∼n idyll

idyllisch *Adj.* idyllic

Igel *der;* ∼s, ∼: hedgehog

Iglu *der od. das;* ∼s, ∼s igloo

Ignoranz /ɪɡnoˈrants/ *die;* ∼: ignorance

ignorieren *tr. V.* ignore

ihm *Dat. von* ER, ES: (bei männlichen Personen) him; (bei weiblichen Personen) her; (bei Dingen, Tieren) it; **gib es** ∼: give it to him; give him it; **Freunde von** ∼: friends of his

ihn *Akk. von* ER (bei männlichen Personen) him; (bei Dingen, Tieren) it

ihnen *Dat. von* SIE, *Pl.* them; **gib es** ∼: give it to them; give them it; **Freunde von** ∼: friends of theirs

Ihnen *Dat. von* SIE you; **ich habe es** ∼ **gegeben** I gave it to you; **Freunde von** ∼: friends of yours

ihr[1] /iːɐ̯/ *Dat. von* SIE, *Sg.* (bei Personen) her; (bei Dingen, Tieren) it

ihr[2], *Personalpron.; 2. Pers. Pl. Nom.* you

ihr[3] *Possessivpron.* **(a)** *Sg.* (einer Person) her; (eines Tieres, einer Sache) its

(b) *Pl.* their

Ihr *Possessivpron.* (Anrede) your; ∼ **Hans Meier** (Briefschluss) yours, Hans Meier; **welcher Mantel ist** ∼**er?** which coat is yours?

ihrer (a) *Gen. von* SIE, *Sg.* (geh.) **wir gedachten** ∼: we remembered her

(b) *Gen. von* SIE, *Pl.* (geh.) **wir werden** ∼ **gedenken** we will remember them; **es waren** ∼ **zwölf** there were twelve of them

Ihrer *Gen. von* SIE (geh.) **wir werden** ∼ **gedenken** we will remember you

ihrerseits *Adv.* for her/their part; (von ihr/ ihnen) on her/their part

Ihrerseits *Adv.:* ▸ DEINERSEITS

ihres·gleichen *indekl. Pron.* people *pl.* like her/them; (abwertend) the likes of her/ them

Ihres·gleichen *indekl. Pron.* people *pl.* like you; (abwertend) the likes of you

ihret·wegen *Adv.:* ▸ MEINETWEGEN: because of her/them; for her/their sake; about her/them; as far as she is/they are concerned

Ihret·wegen *Adv.:* ▸ DEINETWEGEN

Ikone *die;* ∼, ∼n icon

illegal ① *Adj.* illegal
  ② *adv.* illegally
Illegalität *die;* ~, ~en illegality
illegitim *Adj.* (geh.) illegitimate
illuminieren *tr. V.* illuminate
Illusion *die;* ~, ~en illusion
illusorisch *Adj.* illusory; (zwecklos)
  pointless
Illustration *die;* ~, ~en illustration
illustrieren *tr. V.* illustrate
Illustrierte *die; adj. Dekl.* magazine
Iltis *der;* ~ses, ~se polecat; (Pelz) fitch
im *Präp. + Art.* (a) = in dem;
  (b) (räumlich) in the; **im Theater** at the theatre;
  im Fernsehen on television; **im Bett** in bed
  (c) (zeitlich) **im Mai** in May; **im letzten Jahr**
  last year; **im Alter von** ... at the age of ...
  (d) (Verlauf) etw. **im Sitzen tun** do sth. [while]
  sitting down; **im Gehen sein** be going
Image /'ɪmɪtʃ/ *das;* ~[s], ~s image
imaginär *Adj.* (geh., Math.) imaginary
Imbiss, *Imbiß *der; Imbisses, Imbisse* (a)
  (kleine Mahlzeit) snack
  (b) ▶ IMBISSSTUBE
Imbiss-stube, *Imbiß-stube *die* café
Imitation *die;* ~, ~en imitation
imitieren *tr. V.* imitate
Imker *der;* ~s, ~, **Imkerin** *die;* ~, ~nen
  bee-keeper
Immatrikulation *die;* ~, ~en (Hochschulw.)
  registration
immatrikulieren *tr., refl. V.* (Hochschulw.)
  register
immer *Adv.* (a) always; **schon** ~: always; ~
  wieder time and time again; ~, **wenn** every
  time that
  (b) **immer + Komp.:** ~ **dunkler** darker and
  darker; ~ **mehr** more and more
  (c) (ugs.: jeweils) ~ **drei Stufen auf einmal**
  three steps at a time
  (d) (auch) **wo/wer/wann/wie [auch]** ~:
  wherever/whoever/whenever/however
  (e) (verstärkend) ~ **noch, noch** ~: still
  (f) (ugs.: bei Aufforderung) ~ **geradeaus!** keep
  [going] straight on
immer-, Immer-: ~**fort** *Adv.* all the
  time; ~**grün** *Adj.* evergreen; ~**grün** *das*
  periwinkle; ~**hin** *Adv.* (a) (wenigstens) at any
  rate; (b) (trotz allem) all the same; (c)
  (schließlich) after all; ~**zu** *Adv.* (ugs.) the
  whole time
Immigrant *der;* ~en, ~en,
  Immigrantin *die;* ~, ~nen immigrant
Immigration *die;* ~, ~en immigration
immigrieren *itr. V.; mit sein* immigrate
Immobilien *Pl.* property *sing.;* real estate
  sing.
immun (a) (Med., fig.) immune (**gegen** to)
  (b) (Rechtsspr.) ~ **sein** have immunity

Immunität *die;* ~, ~en (a) (Med.)
  immunity (**gegen** to)
  (b) (Rechtsspr.) immunity (**gegen** from)
Immun-schwäche *die* (Med.)
  immunodeficiency; immune deficiency
Imperativ *der;* ~s, ~e (a) (Sprachw.)
  imperative
  (b) (Philos.) **[kategorischer]** ~: [categorical]
  imperative
Imperfekt *das;* ~s, ~e (Sprachw.) imperfect
  [tense]
Imperialismus *der;* ~: imperialism *no
  art.*
imperialistisch *Adj.* imperialistic
Imperium *das;* ~s, Imperien (hist., fig.)
  empire
impfen *tr. V.* vaccinate; inoculate
Impf-: ~**pass, *~paß** *der* vaccination
  certificate; ~**stoff** *der* vaccine
Impfung *die;* ~, ~en vaccination
implantieren *tr. V.* (Med.) implant
imponieren *itr. V.* impress
imponierend ① *Adj.* impressive
  ② *adv.* impressively
Imponier-gehabe *das* (Verhaltensf.)
  display; (fig.) showing off
Import *der;* ~[e]s, ~e import
Importeur /ɪmpɔr'tøːɐ̯/ *der;* ~s, ~e,
  Importeurin *die;* ~, ~nen importer
importieren *tr., itr. V.* import
imposant ① *Adj.* imposing; impressive
  ⟨achievement⟩
  ② *adv.* imposingly
impotent *Adj.* impotent
Impotenz *die;* ~: impotence
imprägnieren *tr. V.* impregnate;
  (wasserdicht machen) waterproof
Improvisation *die;* ~, ~en improvisation
improvisieren *tr., itr. V.* improvise
Impuls *der;* ~es, ~e stimulus; (innere
  Regung) impulse
impulsiv ① *Adj.* impulsive
  ② *adv.* impulsively
imstande *Adv.* ~ **sein, etw. zu tun** be able
  to do sth.
in[1] ① *Präp. mit Dat.* (auf die Frage: wo?/wann?/
  wie?) in; **er hat** ~ **Tübingen studiert** he
  studied at Tübingen; *s. auch* IM;
  ② *Präp. mit Akk.* (auf die Frage: wohin?) into; *s.
  auch* INS
in[2] *Adj.:* ~ **sein** (ugs.) be in
In-anspruchnahme *die;* ~, ~n (starke
  Belastung) demands *pl.*
In-begriff *der* quintessence
inbegriffen *Adj.* included
In-betrieb-nahme *die;* ~, ~n,
  In-betrieb-setzung *die;* ~, ~n bringing
  into service
In-brunst *die;* ~ (geh.) fervour; (der Liebe)
  ardour

in·brünstig (geh.) ⓵ *Adj.* fervent; ardent ⟨*love*⟩
⓶ *adv.* fervently; ⟨*love*⟩ ardently

in·dem *Konj.* (a) (während) while; (gerade als) as
(b) (dadurch, dass) ∼ man etw. tut by doing sth.

Inder *der;* ∼s, ∼, **Inderin** *die;* ∼, ∼nen Indian

in·dessen ⓵ *Konj.* (geh.) (a) (während) while
(b) (wohingegen) whereas
⓶ *Adv.* (a) (inzwischen) meanwhile; in the mean time
(b) (jedoch) however

Index *der;* ∼ *od.* ∼es, ∼e *od.* **Indizes** (a) *Pl.* ∼e *od.* **Indizes** (Register) index
(b) *Pl.* ∼e (kath. Kirche) Index

Indianer *der;* ∼s, ∼: [American] Indian

Indianer·häuptling *der* Indian chief

Indianerin *die;* ∼, ∼nen [American] Indian

indianisch *Adj.* Indian

Indien /'ɪndiən/ (*das*); ∼s India

in·different *Adj.* indifferent

Indikativ *der;* ∼s, ∼e /-iːvə/ (Sprachw.) indicative [mood]

Indikator *der;* ∼s, ∼en (auch Chemie, Technik) indicator

in·direkt ⓵ *Adj.* indirect
⓶ *adv.* indirectly

indisch *Adj.* Indian

in·diskret *Adj.* indiscreet

In·diskretion *die;* ∼, ∼en indiscretion

Individualist *der;* ∼en, ∼en, **Individualistin** *die;* ∼, ∼nen (geh.) individualist

Individualität *die;* ∼, ∼en (geh.) (a) individuality
(b) (Persönlichkeit) personality

individuell ⓵ *Adj.* individual; private ⟨*property, vehicle, etc.*⟩
⓶ *adv.* individually

Individuum *das;* ∼s, Individuen (auch Chemie, Biol.) individual

Indiz *das;* ∼es, ∼ien (a) (Rechtsw.) piece of circumstantial evidence; ∼ien circumstantial evidence *sing.;*
(b) (Anzeichen) sign (**für** of)

Indizes ▶ INDEX

Indizien·beweis *der* (Rechtsw.) piece of circumstantial evidence; ∼e circumstantial evidence *sing.*

indoktrinieren *tr. V.* indoctrinate

Indonesien /ɪndo'neːziən/ (*das*); ∼s Indonesia

Indonesier *der;* ∼s, ∼, **Indonesierin** *die;* ∼, ∼nen Indonesian

indonesisch *Adj.* Indonesian

industrialisieren *tr. V.* industrialize

Industrialisierung *die;* ∼: industrialization

Industrie *die;* ∼, ∼n industry

Industrie-: ∼**betrieb** *der* industrial firm; ∼**gebiet** *das* industrial area; ∼**kauffrau** *die,* ∼**kaufmann** *der: person with three years' business training employed on the business side of an industrial company*

industriell ⓵ *Adj.* industrial
⓶ *adv.* industrially

Industrielle *der/die; adj. Dekl.* industrialist

Industrie-: ∼**staat** *der* industrial nation; ∼**stadt** *die* industrial town

Industrie- und Handels·kammer *die* Chamber of Industry and Commerce

Industriezweig *der* branch of industry

in·einander *Adv.* ∼ **greifen** mesh together (lit. or fig); ∼ **verliebt sein** be in love with each other *or* one another; ∼ **verschlungene Ornamente** intertwined decorations

*ineinander|greifen ▶ INEINANDER

infam ⓵ *Adj.* disgraceful
⓶ *adv.* disgracefully

Infanterie *die;* ∼, ∼n (Milit.) infantry

infantil (Psych., Med., sonst abwertend) ⓵ *Adj.* infantile
⓶ *adv.* in an infantile way

Infarkt *der;* ∼[e]s, ∼e (Med.) infarction

Infekt *der;* ∼[e]s, ∼e (Med.) infection

Infektion *die;* ∼, ∼en (Med.) (a) (Ansteckung) infection
(b) (ugs.: Entzündung) inflammation

Infektions-: ∼**gefahr** *die* (Med.) risk of infection; ∼**herd** *der* (Med.) seat of the/an infection; ∼**krankheit** *die* (Med.) infectious disease

Inferno *das;* ∼s (geh.) inferno

Infinitiv *der;* ∼s, ∼e (Sprachw.) infinitive

infizieren ⓵ *tr. V.* infect
⓶ *refl. V.* become infected; **sich bei jmdm.** ∼: be infected by sb.

in flagranti *Adv.* (geh.) in flagrante [delicto]

Inflation *die;* ∼, ∼en (Wirtsch.) inflation; (Zeit der ∼) period of inflation

inflationär *Adj.* inflationary

Inflations·rate *die* inflation rate; rate of inflation

in·folge ⓵ *Präp.* + *Gen.* as a result of
⓶ *Adv.* ∼ **von etw.** (*Dat.*) as a result of sth.

infolge·dessen *Adv.* consequently

Informatik *die;* ∼: computer science *no art.*

Informatiker *der;* ∼s, ∼, **Informatikerin** *die;* ∼, ∼nen computer scientist

Information *die;* ∼, ∼en (a) information *no pl., no indef. art.* (**über** + *Akk.* about, on); **eine** ∼: [a piece of] information
(b) (Büro) information bureau; (Stand) information desk

Informations-: ∼**büro** *das* information ···⟩

bureau *or* office; ~**freiheit** *die* freedom of information; ~**material** *das* informational literature; ~**quelle** *die* source of information; ~**vielfalt** *die* variety of information

informativ *Adj.* informative

informieren 1 *tr. V.* inform (über + Akk. about)
2 *refl. V.* inform oneself, find out (über + Akk. about)

in-frage: ~ kommen be possible; das kommt nicht ~ (ugs.) that is out of the question

Infra-rot *das* (Physik) infra-red radiation

Infra-struktur *die* infrastructure

Infusion *die;* ~, ~en (Med.) infusion

Ing. *Abk.* = **Ingenieur**

In-gebrauch-nahme *die;* ~, ~n: vor ~ des Geräts before operating the appliance

Ingenieur /ɪnʒeˈni̯øːɐ̯/ *der;* ~s, ~e,
Ingenieurin *die;* ~, ~nen [qualified] engineer

Ingwer *der;* ~s, ~: ginger

Inhaber *der;* ~s, ~, **Inhaberin** *die;* ~, ~nen (a) holder
(b) (Besitzer) owner

inhaftieren *tr. V.* take into custody; detain

Inhaftierung *die;* ~, ~en detention

inhalieren *tr. V.* inhale

Inhalt *der;* ~[e]s, ~e (a) contents *pl.;*
(b) (einer Geschichte usw.) content
(c) (bes. Math.) (Flächen~) area; (Raum~) volume

inhaltlich 1 *Adj.* an ~en Gesichtspunkten gemessen from the point of view of content
2 *adv.* ~ ist der Aufsatz gut the essay is good as regards content; ~ übereinstimmen be the same in content

Inhalts-: ~**angabe** *die* summary [of contents]; synopsis; (eines Films, Dramas) synopsis; ~**verzeichnis** *das* table of contents; (auf einem Paket) list of contents

in-human *Adj.* (a) (unmenschlich) inhuman
(b) (rücksichtslos) inhumane

Initiale *die;* ~, ~n initial [letter]

Initiative *die;* ~, ~n initiative

Initiator *der;* ~s, ~en, **Initiatorin** *die;* ~, ~nen initiator; (einer Organisation) founder

Injektion *die;* ~, ~en (Med.) injection

injizieren *tr. V.* (Med.) inject

Inkarnation *die;* ~, ~en incarnation

inkl. *Abk.* = **inklusive** incl.

inklusive /ɪnkluˈziːvə/ 1 *Präp.* + Gen. (bes. Kaufmannsspr.) including
2 *Adv.* inclusive

inkognito *Adv.* (geh.) incognito

in-kompetent *Adj.* incompetent

In-kompetenz *die* incompetence

in-konsequent 1 *Adj.* inconsistent
2 *adv.* inconsistently

In-konsequenz *die* inconsistency

in-korrekt 1 *Adj.* incorrect
2 *adv.* incorrectly

In-korrektheit *die;* ~, ~en
(a) (Fehlerhaftigkeit) incorrectness
(b) (Fehler) mistake

In-kraft-treten *das;* ~s: mit [dem] ~ des Gesetzes when the law comes/came into force

Inkubations-zeit *die;* ~, ~en (Med.) incubation period

In-land *das* (a) im ~: at home
(b) (Binnenland) interior; inland; im/ins ~: inland

inländisch *Adj.* domestic; home-produced (goods)

Inlands-: ~**markt** *der* domestic market; ~**porto** *das* inland postage

in-mitten 1 *Präp.* + Gen. (geh.) in the midst of
2 *Adv.* ~ von in the midst of

inne|haben *unr. tr. V.* hold, occupy (position); hold (office)

innen *Adv.* inside; (auf/an der Innenseite) on the inside

innen-, Innen-: ~**architekt** *der,*
~**architektin** *die* interior designer;
~**aufnahme** *die* (Fot.) indoor photo[graph]; (Film) interior shot; ~**einrichtung** *die* furnishings *pl.;* ~**hof** *der* inner courtyard;
~**leben** *das* (a) [inner] thoughts and feelings *pl.;* (b) (oft scherzh.: Ausstattung) inside; ~**minister** *der,* ~**ministerin** *die* Minister of the Interior; ≈ Home Secretary (Brit.); ≈ Secretary of the Interior (Amer.);
~**ministerium** *das* Ministry of the Interior; ≈ Home Office (Brit.); ≈ Department of the Interior (Amer.); ~**politik** *die* (eines Staates) home affairs *pl.;* (einer Regierung) domestic policy/policies *pl.;* ~**politisch**
▶~POLITIK: 1 *Adj.* ~politische Fragen matters of domestic policy; 2 *adv.* as regards home affairs/domestic policy;
~**stadt** *die* town centre; downtown (Amer.); (einer Großstadt) city centre

inner... *Adj.* inner; (inländisch; Med.) internal; inside (pocket, lane)

Innere *das; adj. Dekl.* inside; (eines Gebäudes, Wagens, Schiffes) interior; inside; (eines Landes) interior

Innereien *Pl.* entrails; (Kochk.) offal *sing.*

inner-halb 1 *Präp.* + Gen. (a) within; ~ der Familie/Partei (fig.) within the family/party
(b) (binnen) within; ~ einer Woche within a week
2 *Adv.* (a) ~ von within
(b) (im Verlauf) ~ von zwei Jahren within two years

innerlich 1 *Adj.* inner
2 *adv.* inwardly

innerst... *Adj.* innermost

Innerste *das; adj. Dekl.* innermost being

inne|wohnen itr. V. (geh.) etw. wohnt jmdm./einer Sache ~: sb./sth. possesses sth.

innig ⟨1⟩ Adj. deep ⟨affection, sympathy⟩; fervent ⟨wish⟩; intimate ⟨friendship⟩; **mein ~ster Dank** my sincerest thanks
⟨2⟩ adv. ⟨love⟩ with all one's heart

Innigkeit die; ~: depth; (einer Beziehung) intimacy

innovativ Adj. innovative

Innung /'ɪnʊŋ/ die; ~, ~en [trade] guild

in·offiziell ⟨1⟩ Adj. unofficial
⟨2⟩ adv. unofficially

in puncto as regards

ins Präp. + Art. **(a)** = in das
(b) (räumlich) to the; **~ Bett gehen** go to bed
(c) **~ Schlendern geraten** go into a skid

Insasse der; ~n, ~n, **Insassin** die; ~, ~nen **(a)** (Fahrgast) passenger
(b) (Bewohner[in]) inmate

ins·besond[e]re Adv. particularly; in particular

In·schrift die inscription

Insekt /ɪn'zɛkt/ das; ~s, ~en insect

Insel die; ~, ~n island

Insel-: ~bewohner der, **~bewohnerin** die islander; **~gruppe** die group of islands; **~staat** die island state; **~welt** die islands pl.

Inserat das; ~[e]s, ~e advertisement (in a newspaper)

Inserent der; ~en, ~en, **Inserentin** die; ~, ~nen advertiser

inserieren itr. V. advertise

ins·geheim Adv. secretly

ins·gesamt Adv. in all; altogether; (alles in allem) all in all

insofern ⟨1⟩ Adv. /ɪn'zoːfɛrn/ (in dieser Hinsicht) to this extent; **~ als** in so far as
⟨2⟩ Konj. /ɪnzoˈfɛrn/ (falls) provided [that]

Insolvenz·verfahren das insolvency proceedings pl.

insoweit ⟨1⟩ adv. /ɪn'zoːvaiːt/ ▶ INSOFERN 1; ⟨2⟩ Konj. /ɪnzoˈvaiːt/ ▶ INSOFERN 2

in spe /ɪn 'speː/ future attrib.; **mein Schwiegersohn ~ ~**: my future son-in-law

Inspektion die; ~, ~en inspection; (Kfz-W.) service

Inspiration die; ~, ~en inspiration

inspirieren tr. V. inspire

inspizieren tr. V. inspect

Installateur /ɪnstalaˈtøːɐ̯/ der; ~s, ~e, **Installateurin** die; ~, ~nen plumber; (Gas~) [gas] fitter; (Heizungs~) heating engineer; (Elektro~) electrician

Installation die; ~, ~en installation; (Rohre) plumbing no pl.

installieren tr. V. install

in·stand Adv. etw. ist gut/schlecht ~: sth. is in good/poor condition; **etw. ~ halten** keep sth. in good condition; **etw. ~ setzen/ bringen** repair sth.

Instand·haltung die maintenance

in·ständig ⟨1⟩ Adj. urgent
⟨2⟩ adv. urgently

Instand·setzung die; ~, ~en repair; (Renovierung) renovation

Instanz /ɪn'stants:/ die; ~, ~en **(a)** authority
(b) (Rechtsw.) **[die] erste/zweite/dritte ~**: the court of original jurisdiction/the appeal court/the court of final appeal; **durch alle ~en gehen** go through all the courts

Instinkt /ɪn'stɪŋkt/ der; ~[e]s, ~e instinct

instinktiv ⟨1⟩ Adj. instinctive
⟨2⟩ adv. instinctively

Institut /ɪnstɪ'tuːt/ das; ~[e]s, ~e institute

Institution die; ~, ~en (auch fig.) institution

Instruktion /ɪnstrʊk'tsːoːn/ die; ~, ~en instruction

Instrument /ɪnstru'mɛnt/ das; ~[e]s, ~e instrument

instrumental (Musik) ⟨1⟩ Adj. instrumental
⟨2⟩ adv. instrumentally

Insulin das; ~s insulin

inszenieren tr. V. stage; put on; (Regie führen bei) direct; (fig.) (einfädeln) engineer; (organisieren) stage

Inszenierung die; ~, ~en staging; (Regie) direction; (Aufführung) production

intakt Adj. **(a)** (unbeschädigt) intact
(b) (funktionsfähig) in [proper] working order postpos.; healthy ⟨economy⟩

integer Adj. **eine integre Persönlichkeit** a person of integrity; **~ sein** be a person of integrity

Integral das; ~s, ~e (Math.) integral

Integration die; ~, ~en (auch Math.) integration

integrieren tr. V. integrate

Intellekt der; ~[e]s intellect

intellektuell Adj. intellectual

Intellektuelle der/die; adj. Dekl. intellectual

intelligent ⟨1⟩ Adj. intelligent
⟨2⟩ adv. intelligently

Intelligenz die; ~, ~en **(a)** intelligence
(b) (Gesamtheit der Intellektuellen) intelligentsia

Intelligenz·quotient der intelligence quotient

Intendant der; ~en, ~en, **Intendantin** die; ~, ~nen (Theater) manager and artistic director; (Fernseh~, Rundfunk~) director general

Intensität die; ~: intensity

intensiv ⟨1⟩ Adj. (gründlich) intensive (kräftig) intense
⟨2⟩ adv. intensively

intensivieren tr. V. intensify; increase ⟨exports⟩; strengthen ⟨connections⟩

Intensiv·station die intensive-care unit

interaktiv Adj. interactive

Intercityzug der inter-city train

interessant ⟨1⟩ Adj. interesting ⋯⟩

2 *adv.* ~ **schreiben** write in an interesting way

interessanterweise *Adv.* interestingly enough

Interesse *das;* ~s, ~n interest; ~ **an jmdm./etw. haben** be interested in sb./sth.

interesse-halber *Adv.* out of interest

Interessen-gebiet *das* field of interest

Interessent *der;* ~en, ~en, **Interessentin** *die;* ~, ~nen interested person; (möglicher Käufer/mögliche Käuferin) potential buyer

Interessen-verband *der* [organized] interest group

Interessen-vertretung *die* (a) representation
(b) (Vertreter von Interessen) representative body

interessieren **1** *refl. V.* **sich für jmdn./ etw. ~:** be interested in sb./sth.
2 *tr. V.* interest; **das interessiert mich nicht** I'm not interested [in it]

interessiert *Adj.* interested (**an** + *Dat.* in)

Interjektion *die;* ~, ~en interjection

Inter-: ~**kontinental-rakete** *die* (Milit.) intercontinental ballistic missile; ~**mezzo** *das;* ~~s, ~~s *od.* ~**mezzi** (Theat., Musik) intermezzo; (fig.) interlude; intermezzo

intern **1** *Adj.* internal
2 *adv.* internally

Internat *das;* ~[e]s, ~e boarding school

inter-, Inter-: ~**national** **1** *Adj.* international; **2** *adv.* internationally; ~**nationale** *die;* ~, ~n (a) International; Internationale; (b) (Lied) Internationale

Internats-: ~**schule** *die* boarding school; ~**schüler** *der,* ~**schülerin** *die* boarding school pupil; boarder

Internet /'ɪntɛnɛt/ *das;* ~s Internet; **im ~:** on the Internet

Internet-anschluss *der,*
***Internet-anschluß** *der* Internet connection; connection to the Internet; **einen ~ haben** be connected to the Internet

internieren *tr. V.* (Milit.) intern

Internierung *die;* ~, ~en internment

Internist *der;* ~en, ~en, **Internistin** *die;* ~, ~nen (Med.) internist

Interpol *die;* ~: Interpol *no art.*

Interpret *der;* ~en, ~en interpreter (*of music, text, events, etc.*)

Interpretation *die;* ~, ~en interpretation (*of music, text, events, etc.*)

interpretieren *tr. V.* interpret (*music, texts, events, etc.*)

Interpretin *die;* ~, ~nen ▶ INTERPRET

Interpunktion *die;* ~ (Sprachw.) punctuation

Intervall /ɪntɛ'val/ *das;* ~s, ~e (Musik, Math.) interval

intervenieren *itr. V.* (geh., Politik) intervene

Intervention *die;* ~, ~en (geh., Politik) intervention; (Protest) representations *pl.*

Interview /ɪntɐ'vjuː/ *das;* ~s, ~s interview

interviewen /ɪntɐ'vjuːən/ *tr. V.* interview

Interviewer *der;* ~s, ~, **Interviewerin** *die;* ~, ~nen interviewer

intialisieren *tr. V.* (DV) initialize

intim **1** *Adj.* intimate
2 *adv.* ~ **befreundet sein** be intimate friends

Intimität *die;* ~, ~en intimacy

Intim-: ~**partner** *der,* ~**partnerin** *die* intimate partner; sexual partner; ~**sphäre** *die* private life

in-tolerant *Adj.* intolerant

In-toleranz *die* intolerance (**gegenüber** of)

Intonation *die;* ~, ~en intonation

Intranet *das* ~s, ~s (DV) Intranet

in-transitiv **1** *Adj.* (Sprachw.) intransitive
2 *adv.* intransitively

intravenös (Med.) **1** *Adj.* intravenous
2 *adv.* intravenously

Intrige *die;* ~, ~n intrigue

Intuition *die;* ~, ~en intuition

intuitiv **1** *Adj.* intuitive
2 *adv.* intuitively

intus: **etw. ~ haben** (ugs.) (begriffen haben) have got sth. into one's head; (gegessen od. getrunken haben) have put sth. away (coll.)

invalide *der; adj. Dekl.* invalid

Invasion *die;* ~, ~en invasion

Inventar *das;* ~s, ~e (einer Firma) fittings and equipment *pl.;* (eines Hauses, Büros) furnishings and fittings *pl.*

inventarisieren *tr. V.* inventory; draw up *or* make an inventory of

Inventur *die;* ~, ~en stock-taking

investieren *tr., itr. V.* (auch fig.) invest (**in** + *Akk.* in)

Investition *die;* ~, ~en investment

Investitions-güter *Pl.* (Wirtsch.) capital goods

Investor *der;* ~s, ~en /-'toːrən/, **Investorin** *die;* ~, ~nen (Wirtsch.) investor

in-wie-fern *Adv.* in what way; (bis zu welchem Grade) to what extent

in-wie-weit *Adv.* to what extent·

In-zahlung-nahme *die;* ~, ~n part exchange; trade in (Amer.)

Inzest *der;* ~[e]s, ~e incest

In-zucht *die;* ~: inbreeding

in-zwischen *Adv.* (a) (seither) in the meantime; since [then]
(b) (bis zu einem Zeitpunkt) (in der Gegenwart) by now; (in der Vergangenheit/Zukunft) by then
(c) (währenddessen) meanwhile

IOK *Abk.* **Internationales Olympisches Komitee** IOC

Ion /iːn/ *das;* ~s, ~en (Physik, Chemie) ion

ionisieren *tr. V.* (Physik, Chemie) ionize

Iono·sphäre *die* ionosphere

Irak (*das*); ~s *od. der*; ~[s] Iraq

Iraker *der*; ~s, ~, **Irakerin** *die*; ~, ~nen Iraqi

irakisch Iraqi

Iran (*das*); ~s *od. der*; ~[s] Iran

Iraner *der*; ~s, ~, **Iranerin** *die*; ~, ~nen Iranian

iranisch *Adj.* Iranian

irden *Adj.* earthen[ware]

irdisch *Adj.* (a) earthly; worldly ‹goods, pleasures, possessions› (b) (zur Erde gehörig) terrestrial; **das** ~**e Leben** life on earth

Ire *der*; ~n, ~n Irishman

irgend *Adv.* (a) ~ **so ein Politiker** (ugs.) some politician [or other]; ~ **so etwas** something like that (b) (irgendwie) **wenn** ~ **möglich** if at all possible

irgend-: ~**ein** *Indefinitpron.* (a) *attr.* some; (fragend, verneinend) any; (b) *subst.* ~**einer**/~**eine** someone; somebody; (fragend, verneinend) anyone; anybody; ~**eines** *od.* (ugs.) ~**eins** any one; ~**einmal** *Adv.* sometime; ~**etwas** something; (fragend, verneinend) anything; ~**jemand** *Indefinitpron.* someone; somebody; (fragend, vereinend) anyone; anybody; ~**wann** *Adv.* [at] some time [or other]; (zu jeder beliebigen Zeit) [at] any time; ~**was** *Indefinitpron.* (ugs.) something [or other]; (fragend, verneinend) anything; ~**welch** *Indefinitpron.* some; (fragend, verneinend) any; ~**wer** *Indefinitpron.* (ugs.) somebody or other (coll.); (fragend, verneinend) anyone; anybody; ~**wie** *Adv.* somehow; ~**wo** *Adv.* somewhere; (fragend, verneinend) anywhere; ~**woher** *Adv.* from somewhere; (fragend, verneinend) from anywhere; ~**wohin** *Adv.* somewhere; (fragend, verneinend) anywhere

Irin *die*; ~, ~nen Irishwoman

Iris *die*; ~, ~ (Bot., Anat.) iris

irisch *Adj.* Irish

Irland (*das*); ~s Ireland

Ironie *die*; ~, ~n irony

ironisch ① *Adj.* ironic; ironical ② *adv.* ironically

ir·rational ① *Adj.* irrational ② *adv.* irrationally

irre ① *Adj.* (a) insane (b) (salopp: faszinierend) amazing (coll.) ② *adv.* (salopp) terribly (coll.)

Irre *der/die; adj. Dekl.* madman/madwoman; lunatic; (fig.) lunatic

irre-, Irre-: ~|**führen** *tr. V.* mislead; (täuschen) deceive; ~**führung** *die:* **eine bewusste** ~**führung** a deliberate attempt to mislead; ~**führung der Öffentlichkeit** misleading the public

ir·relevant *Adj.* irrelevant (für to)

irre|machen *tr. V.* disconcert; put off

irren ① *refl. V.* be mistaken; **Sie haben sich in der Nummer geirrt** you've got the wrong number ② *itr. V.* (a) **da** ~ **Sie** you are wrong there (b) *mit sein* (ziellos umherstreifen) wander

Irren-: ~**anstalt** *die* (veralt. abwertend) mental home; ~**haus** *das* (abwertend) [lunatic] asylum

ir·reparabel *Adj.* irreparable

Irr·fahrt *die* wandering

irriger·weise *Adv.* mistakenly

Irritation *die*; ~, ~en irritation

irritieren *tr., itr. V.* (a) (verwirren) put off (b) (stören) disturb

Irr-, Irr-: ~**licht** *das* will o' the wisp; ~**sinn** *der* (a) insanity; madness; (b) (ugs. abwertend) lunacy; ~**sinnig** ① *Adj.* (a) (geistig gestört) insane; mad; (absurd) idiotic; (b) (ugs.: extrem) terrible (coll.); terrific (coll.) ‹speed, heat, cold›; ② *adv.* (ugs.) terribly (coll.)

Irrtum *der*; ~s, Irrtümer mistake; ~**!** wrong!; **im** ~ **sein** be wrong *or* mistaken

irrtümlich ① *Adj.* incorrect ② *adv.* by mistake

Irr·weg *der* error; **diese Methode hat sich als** ~ **erwiesen** this method has proved to be wrong

Ischias *der od. das od.* (Med.) *die*; ~: sciatica

Islam /ɪsˈlaːm *od.* ˈɪslam/ *der*; ~[s] Islam

islamisch *Adj.* Islamic

Islamismus *der*; ~: Islamic fundamentalism; Islamism

Islamist *der*; ~en, ~en, **Islamistin** *die*; ~, ~nen Islamic fundamentalist; Islamist

islamistisch *Adj.* Islamic fundamentalist; Islamist

Island (*das*); ~s Iceland

Isländer *der*; ~s, ~, **Isländerin** *die*; ~, ~nen Icelander

isländisch *Adj.* Icelandic

Isolation *die*; ~, ~en ▸ ISOLIERUNG

Isolator *der*; ~s, ~en insulator

Isolier·band *das* insulating tape

isolieren *tr. V.* (a) isolate (b) (Technik) insulate ‹wiring, wall, etc.›; lag ‹boilers, pipes, etc.›

Isolier·station *die* (Med.) isolation ward

Isolierung *die*; ~, ~en (a) isolation (b) (Technik) ▸ ISOLIEREN B: insulation; lagging

Isotop *das*; ~s, ~e isotope

Israel /ˈɪsraeːl/ (*das*); ~s Israel

Israeli *der*; ~[s], ~[s]/*die*; ~, ~[s] Israeli

israelisch *Adj.* Israeli

Israelit *der*; ~en, ~en, **Israelitin** *die*; ~, ~nen Israelite

israelitisch *Adj.* Israelite

iss, *iß *Imperativ Sg. v.* ESSEN

isst, *ißt *2. u. 3. Pers. Sg. Präsens v.* ESSEN

ist 3. Pers. Sg. Präsens v. SEIN
Italien /i'taːli̯ən/ (das); ∼s Italy
Italiener der; ∼s, ∼, **Italienerin** die; ∼,
∼nen Italian

italienisch Adj. Italian
I-Tüpfel[chen] das; ∼s, ∼: final touch;
bis aufs [letzte] ∼: down to the last detail
i.V. Abk. = **in Vertretung**

Jj

j, **J** /jɔt, österr.: jeː/ das; ∼, ∼: j/J
ja ① Interj. yes; (nachgestellt: nicht wahr?) won't
you/doesn't it etc.?
② Partikel **Sie wissen ja, dass** ...: you know,
of course, that ...; **da seid ihr ja!** there you
are!
Ja das; ∼[s], ∼[s] yes; **mit ∼ stimmen** vote
yes
Jacht die; ∼, ∼en yacht
Jacke die; ∼, ∼n jacket; (gestrickt) cardigan
Jacken-kleid das dress and jacket
combination
Jacket-krone /'dʒɛkɪt-/ die (Zahnmed.)
jacket crown
Jackett /ʒa'kɛt/ das; ∼s, ∼s jacket
Jade die; ∼: jade
Jagd die; ∼, ∼en (a) die ∼: shooting;
hunting; **auf die ∼ gehen** go hunting/
shooting
(b) (Veranstaltung) shoot; (Hetzjagd) hunt
(c) (Verfolgung) hunt; (Verfolgungsjagd) chase; **auf
jmdn./etw. ∼ machen** hunt for sb./sth.
Jagd-: ∼**beute** die bag; kill; ∼**bomber**
der (Luftwaffe) fighter-bomber; ∼**flieger** der,
∼**fliegerin** die (Luftwaffe) fighter pilot;
∼**flugzeug** das (Luftwaffe) fighter aircraft;
∼**gewehr** das sporting gun; ∼**horn** das
hunting horn; ∼**hund** der gun dog;
∼**hütte** die shooting box; ∼**revier** das
preserve; shoot; ∼**schein** der game
licence; ∼**wurst** die chasseur sausage;
∼**zeit** die open season
jagen ① tr. V. (a) hunt ⟨game, fugitive,
criminal, etc.⟩; shoot ⟨game, game birds⟩;
(hetzen) chase ⟨fugitive, criminal, etc.⟩
(b) (treiben) drive; **jmdn. aus dem Haus ∼:**
throw sb. out of the house
② itr. V. (die Jagd ausüben) go shooting or
hunting
Jäger der; ∼s, ∼: (a) hunter
(b) (Milit.) rifleman
(c) (Soldatenspr.: Jagdflugzeug) fighter
Jäger-hut der huntsman's hat
Jägerin die; ∼, ∼nen huntress
Jäger-: ∼**latein** das (scherzh.) [hunter's]
tall story/stories; **das ist das reinste ∼latein**

that's all wild exaggeration; ∼**rock** der
hunting jacket; ∼**schnitzel** das (Kochk.)
escalope chasseur
Jaguar der; ∼s, ∼e jaguar
jäh ① Adj. (geh.) (a) sudden; abrupt ⟨change,
movement, stop⟩; sudden, sharp ⟨pain⟩
(b) (steil) steep; precipitous
② adv. (a) ⟨change⟩ abruptly
(b) (steil) ⟨fall, drop⟩ steeply
jählings Adv. (geh.) (a) (plötzlich) ⟨change,
end, stop⟩ suddenly, abruptly; ⟨die⟩ suddenly
(b) (steil) steeply
Jahr das; ∼[e]s, ∼e year; **ein halbes ∼:** six
months; **im ∼[e] 1908** in [the year] 1908; **er
ist zwanzig ∼e [alt]** he is twenty years old;
Kinder bis zu zwölf ∼en children up to the
age of twelve; **zwischen den ∼en** between
Christmas and the New Year
jahr-aus Adv. ∼, jahrein year in, year out
jahre-lang ① Adj. [many] years of; long-
standing ⟨feud, friendship⟩
② adv. for [many] years
jähren refl. V. **heute jährt sich zum zehnten
Mal, dass** ...: it is ten years ago today that ...
Jahres-: ∼**bilanz** die (Wirtsch.,
Kaufmannsspr.) annual balance [of accounts];
(Dokument) annual balance sheet;
∼**einkommen** das annual income;
∼**ende** das end of the year; ∼**frist:** **in** od.
innerhalb od. **binnen ∼frist** within [a period
of] a or one year; ∼**hälfte** die: **die erste/
zweite ∼hälfte** the first/secound half or six
months of the year; ∼**karte** die yearly
season ticket; ∼**tag** der anniversary;
∼**umsatz** der annual turnover; ∼**urlaub**
der annual holiday or (formal) leave or (Amer.)
vacation; ∼**wechsel** der turn of the year;
zum ∼wechsel die besten Wünsche best
wishes for the New Year; ∼**zahl** die date;
∼**zeit** die season
Jahr-gang der (a) (Altersklasse) year; **der ∼
1900** those born in 1900
(b) (eines Weines) vintage
(c) (einer Zeitschrift) set [of issues] for a/the
year
Jahr-hundert das century
Jahrhundert-wende die turn of the
century
-jährig (a) (... Jahre alt) **ein elfjähriges Kind**
an eleven-year-old child

---

*alte Schreibung - vgl. Hinweis auf S. xiv

(b) (... Jahre dauernd) ... year's/years'; **nach vierjähriger Vorbereitung** after four years' preparation; **mit dreijähriger Verspätung** three years late

jährlich ⒈ *Adj.;* annual; yearly ⒉ *adv.* annually; yearly; **zweimal ~**: twice a year

Jahr-: **~markt** *der* fair; funfair; **~tausend** *das* thousand years; millennium; **~tausend-wende** *die* turn of the millennium; **~zehnt** *das* decade

jahrzehnte-lang ⒈ *Adj.; nicht präd.* decades of ‹practice, experience, etc.› ⒉ *adv.* for decades

Jäh-zorn *der* violent anger

jäh-zornig ⒈ *Adj.* violent-tempered ⒉ *adv.* in a blind rage

ja-ja *Part.* (ugs.) **(a)** (seufzend) **~[, so ist das Leben]** oh well[, that's life] **(b)** (ungeduldig) **~[, ich komme schon]!** all right, all right[, I'm coming]!

Jalousie /ʒalu'ziː/ *die; ~, ~n* Venetian blind

Jamaika (das); -s Jamaica

Jamaikaner *der; ~s, ~,* **Jamaikanerin** *die; ~, ~nen* Jamaican

Jammer *der; ~s* [mournful] wailing; (Elend) misery

jämmerlich ⒈ *Adj.* **(a)** pitiful **(b)** wretched ‹appearance, existence, etc.›; paltry, meagre ‹quantity› ⒉ *adv.* pitifully

jammern *itr. V.* wail; (sich beklagen) moan

jammer-schade *Adj.* (ugs.) **es ist ~, dass ...:** it's a crying shame that ...; **es ist ~ um ihn** it's a great pity about him

Janker *der; ~s, ~* (südd., österr.) Alpine jacket

Januar *der; ~[s], ~e* January

Japan (das); ~s Japan

Japaner *der; ~s, ~,* **Japanerin** *die; ~, ~nen* Japanese

japanisch *Adj.* Japanese

japsen *itr. V.* (ugs.) pant

Jargon /ʒar'gõ:/ *der; ~s, ~s* jargon

Jasmin *der; ~s, ~e* jasmine

Ja-stimme *die* yes-vote

jäten *tr., itr. V.* weed; **Unkraut ~:** weed

Jauche *die; ~, ~n* liquid manure

Jauche-grube *die* liquid-manure reservoir

jauchzen *itr. V.* cheer; **vor Freude ~:** shout for joy

Jauchzer *der; ~s, ~:* cry of delight

jaulen *itr. V.* howl

Jause *die; ~, ~n* (österr.) **(a)** snack; **eine ~ machen** have a snack **(b)** (Nachmittagskaffee) [afternoon] tea

ja-wohl *Part.* certainly

Ja-wort *das* consent; **jmdm. das ~ geben** consent to marry sb.

Jazz /dʒæz od. dʒɛs od. jats:/ *der; ~:* jazz

jazzen /'dʒɛsn̩ od. 'jatsn̩/ *itr. V.* play jazz

Jazzer /'dʒɛsɐ od. 'jats:ɐ/ *der; ~s, ~,* **Jazzerin** *die; ~, ~nen* jazz musician

Jazz-: **~keller** *der* jazz cellar; **~tanz** *der* jazz dance

je¹ ⒈ *Adv.* **(a)** (jemals) ever; **mehr/besser denn je** more/better than ever **(b)** (jeweils) **je zehn Personen** ten people at a time; **sie kosten je 30 DM** they cost 30 DM each **(c)** (entsprechend) **je nach Gewicht** according to weight ⒉ *Präp. mit Akk.* per; for each ⒊ *Konj.* **je länger, je lieber** the longer the better; **je nachdem** it all depends

je² *Interj.* **ach je, wie schade!** oh dear, what a shame!

Jeans /dʒiːnz/ *Pl. od. die; ~, ~:* jeans *pl.;* denims *pl.*

jede ► JEDER

jeden-falls *Adv.* **(a)** in any case **(b)** (zumindest) at any rate

jeder, jede, jedes *Indefinitpron. u. unbest. Zahlwort* ⒈ *attr.* **(a)** (alle) every **(b)** (alle einzeln) each **(c)** (jeglicher) all ⒉ *allein stehend* **(a)** (alle) everyone; everybody **(b)** (alle einzeln) **jedes der Kinder** each of the children

jeder-: **~mann** *Indefinitpron.* everyone; everybody; **~zeit** *Adv.* [at] any time

jedes ► JEDER

*jedes-mal ► MAL¹

je-doch *Konj., Adv.* however

je-her /od. '-'-/ *Adv.* **seit od. von ~:** always; since time immemorial

jemals *Adv.* ever

jemand *Indefinitpron.* someone; somebody; (fragend, verneinend) anyone; anybody

Jemen (das); ~s od. der; ~[s] Yemen

jener, jene, jenes *Demonstrativpron.* (geh.) ⒈ *attr.* that; (im Pl.) those ⒉ *allein stehend* that one; (im Pl.) those

jenseits ⒈ *Präp. mit Gen.* on the other side of; (in größerer Entfernung) beyond ⒉ *Adv.* on the other side; **~ von** on the other side of

Jenseits *das; ~:* hereafter; beyond

Jersey¹ /'dʒøːɐ̯zi/ *der; ~[s], ~s* (Textilind.) jersey

Jersey² *das; ~s, ~s* (Sport: Trikot) jersey

Jesus (der); Jesu Jesus

Jet /dʒɛt/ *der; ~[s], ~s* jet; **mit einem ~ fliegen/reisen** fly/travel by jet

jetzig *Adj.* current

jetzt *Adv.* **(a)** just now; **bis ~:** up to now; **bis ~ noch nicht** not yet; **von ~ an od. ab** from now on[wards]; **erst ~ od. ~ erst** only just; **schon ~:** already **(b)** (heutzutage) now; nowadays

jeweilig *Adj.* (a) (in einem bestimmten Fall) particular
(b) (zu einer bestimmten Zeit) current; of the time *postpos., not pred.;*
(c) (zugehörig, zugewiesen) respective

jeweils *Adv.* (a) (jedesmal) ~ am ersten/letzten Mittwoch des Monats on the first/last Wednesday of each month
(b) (zur Zeit) at the time

Jg. *Abk.* = **Jahrgang**

Jh. *Abk.* = **Jahrhundert** c.

JH *Abk.* = **Jugendherberge**

jiddisch /'jɪdɪʃ/ *Adj.* Yiddish

Job /dʒɔp/ *der;* ~s, ~s (ugs.; auch DV) job

jobben /dʒɔbn̩/ *itr. V.* (ugs.) do a job/jobs

Job-: ~**killer** *der* destroyer of jobs; ~**sharing** /'-ʃɛərɪŋ/ *das;* ~~s jobsharing

Joch *das;* ~[e]s, ~e yoke

Jockei, Jockey /'dʒɔkə od. 'dʒɔki/ *der;* ~s, ~s jockey

Jod *das;* ~[e]s iodine

jodeln *itr., tr. V.* yodel

jod-haltig *Adj.* iodiferous

Joga *der od. das;* ~[s] yoga

joggen /'dʒɔgn̩/ *itr. V.; mit Richtungsangabe mit sein* jog

Jogging-anzug *der* jogging suit

Joghurt /'jo:gʊrt/ *der od. das;* ~[s], ~[s] yoghurt

Joghurt-becher *der* yoghurt pot (Brit.) or (Amer.) container

Johannis-beere *die* currant; rote/weiße/schwarze ~n redcurrants/white currants/blackcurrants

johlen *itr. V.* yell; (vor Wut) howl

Joint /dʒɔɪnt/ *der;* ~s, ~s (ugs.) joint (sl.)

Jolle *die;* ~, ~n keel-centreboard yawl

Jongleur /ʒɔŋ'lø:ɐ̯/ *der;* ~s, ~e, **Jongleurin** /~, ~nen juggler

jonglieren *tr., itr. V.* juggle

Joppe *die;* ~, ~n heavy jacket

Jordanien *(das);* ~s Jordan

Jordanier *der;* ~s, ~, **Jordanierin** *die;* ~, ~nen Jordanian

jordanisch *Adj.* Jordanian

Jot *das;* ~, ~: j, J

Journalismus *der;* /ʒʊr.../ ~: journalism no art.

Journalist *der;* ~en, ~en, **Journalistin** *die;* ~, ~nen journalist

journalistisch 1 *Adj.;* journalistic; eine ~e Ausbildung a training in journalism
2 *adv.* journalistically; ~ tätig sein be a journalist

Joystick /'dʒɔystik/ *der;* ~s, ~s (DV) joystick

jr. *Abk.* = **junior** Jr.

Jubel *der;* ~s rejoicing; jubilation; (laut) cheering

Jubel-jahr *das* jubilee; alle ~e [einmal] once in a blue moon

jubeln *itr. V.* cheer; über etw. (*Akk.*) ~: rejoice over sth.

Jubilar *der;* ~s, ~e man celebrating his anniversary/birthday

Jubilarin *die;* ~, ~nen woman celebrating her anniversary/birthday

Jubiläum *das;* ~s, Jubiläen anniversary; (eines Monarchen) jubilee

jubilieren *itr. V.* (geh.) jubilate (literary); rejoice

juchzen *itr. V.* (ugs.) shout with glee

jucken 1 *tr., itr. V.* (a) mir juckt die Haut I itch; es juckt mich hier I've got an itch here
(b) (Juckreiz verursachen) irritate
2 *tr. V.* (reizen, verlocken) es juckt mich, das zu tun I am itching to do it
3 *refl. V.* (ugs.: sich kratzen) scratch

Juck-reiz *der* itch

Jude *der;* ~n, ~n Jew

Juden-: ~**hass**, ***~**haß** *der* anti-Semitism; hatred of [the] Jews; ~**stern** *der* (ns.) Star of David

Judentum *das;* ~s (a) (Volk) Jewry; Jews *pl.;*
(b) (Kultur u. Religion) Judaism

Juden-verfolgung *die* persecution of [the] Jews

Jüdin *die;* ~, ~nen Jewess

jüdisch *Adj.* Jewish

Judo *das;* ~[s] judo no art.

Jugend *die;* ~ (a) youth
(b) (Jugendliche) young people

jugend-, Jugend-: ~**amt** *das* youth office (*agency responsible for education and welfare of young people*); ~**arbeitslosigkeit** *die* youth unemployment; ~**arrest** *der* detention in a community home; ~**bewegung** *die* (hist.) [German] youth Movement; ~**buch** *das* book for young people; ~**frei** *Adj.* ⟨film, book, etc.⟩ suitable for persons under 18; nicht ~frei ⟨film⟩ not U-certificate *pred.;* ~**gefährdend** *Adj.* liable to have an undesirable influence on the moral development of young people *postpos.;* ~**heim** *das* youth centre; ~**herberge** *die* youth hostel; ~**klub** *der* youth club; ~**kriminalität** *die* juvenile delinquency

jugendlich *Adj.* (a) young ⟨offender, customer, etc.⟩
(b) (für Jugendliche charakteristisch) youthful

Jugendliche *der/die; adj. Dekl.* young person; die ~n the young people

Jugend-: ~**liebe** *die* sweetheart of one's youth; ~**schutz** *der* protection of young people; ~**schutz-gesetz** *das* laws *pl.* protecting young people; ~**sprache** *die* young people's language no art.; ~**stil** *der* art nouveau; (in Deutschland) Jugendstil; ~**strafanstalt** *die* detention centre;

**old spelling - see note on page xiv

~**strafe** *die* youth custody sentence;
~**sünde** *die* youthful folly; ~**zeit** *die*
youth; ~**zentrum** *das* youth centre

Jugo·slawe *der* Yugoslav

Jugo·slawien (*das*) ~s Yugoslavia

Jugo·slawin *die* Yugoslav

jugo·slawisch *Adj.* Yugoslav[ian]

Julei *der;* ~[s], ~s ▶ JULI

Juli *der;* ~[s], ~s July; *s. auch* APRIL

jung *Adj.;* jünger, jüngst... (a) young; new
⟨*project, undertaking, sport, marriage, etc.*⟩
(b) (letzt...) recent; **in jüngster Zeit** recently

Junge¹ *der;* ~n, ~n *od.* (ugs.) Jung[en]s
boy

Junge² *das; adj. Dekl.* **ein** ~**s** one of the
young; ~ **kriegen** give birth to young

jungen *itr. V.* give birth; ⟨*cat*⟩ have kittens;
⟨*dog*⟩ have pups

jungenhaft *Adj.* boyish

jünger *Adj.* youngish; **sie ist noch** ~: she is
still quite young; *s. auch* JUNG

Jünger *der;* ~s, ~, **Jüngerin** *die;* ~,
~**nen** follower

Jungfer *die;* ~, ~n (abwertend: ältere ledige
Frau) spinster

Jungfern·fahrt *die* maiden voyage

Jungfern·häutchen *das;* ~s, ~: hymen

Jung·frau *die* (a) virgin
(b) (Astrol.) Virgo

jung·fräulich *Adj.* (geh., auch fig.) virgin

Jung·geselle *der* bachelor

Jung·gesellin *die* bachelor girl

Jüngling *der;* ~s, ~e (geh., spött.) youth;
boy

jüngst *Adv.* (geh.) recently

jüngst... ▶ JUNG

Jüngste *der/die; adj. Dekl.* youngest [one]

Jung-: ~**verheiratete** *der/die; adj.*

Dekl., young married man/woman; **die**
~**verheirateten** the newly-weds; ~**wähler**
der, ~**wählerin** *die* first-time voter

Juni *der;* ~[s], ~s June; *s. auch* APRIL

junior *indekl. Adj.; nach Personennamen*
junior

Junior *der;* ~s, ~en (a) (oft scherzh.) junior
(joc.)
(b) (Kaufmannsspr.) junior partner

Junior-: ~**chef** *der* owner's *or* (coll.) boss's
son; ~**chefin** *die* owner's *or* (coll.) boss's
daughter

Juno *der;* ~[s], ~s ▶ JUNI

Junta /'xʊnta/ *die;* ~, Junten junta

Jura law *sing.;* ~ **studieren** read Law

Jurist *der;* ~en, ~en, **Juristin** *die;* ~,
~**nen** lawyer; jurist

juristisch *Adj.* legal

Jury /ʒy'riː/ *die;* ~, ~s (a) (Preisrichter) panel
[of judges]; jury
(b) (Sachverständige) panel [of experts]

just *Adv.* (veralt., noch scherzh.) just; ~ **in
diesem Augenblick** just at that moment; at
that very moment

justieren *tr. V.* adjust

Justierung *die;* ~, ~en adjustment

Justiz *die;* ~: justice; (Behörden) judiciary

Justiz-: ~**irrtum** *der* miscarriage of
justice; ~**minister** *der,* ~**ministerin**
die Minister of Justice; ~**ministerium**
das Ministry of Justice; ~**mord** *der*
judicial murder; ~**vollzugs·anstalt** *die*
(Amtsspr.) penal institution (formal); prison

Jute *die;* ~: jute

Jütland (*das*); ~s Jutland

Juwel *das od. der;* ~s, ~en piece of
jewellery; (Edelstein) jewel

Juwelier /juvə'liːɐ̯/ *der;* ~s jeweller

Juwelier·geschäft *das* jeweller's shop

Jux *der;* ~es, ~e (ugs.) joke

Kk

k, K /ka:/ *das;* ~, ~: k/K

Kabarętt *das;* ~s, ~s *od.* ~e **(a)** satirical revue
(b) (Ensemble) cabaret act

Kabarettist *der;* ~en, ~en, **Kabarettistin** *die;* ~, ~nen revue performer

kabarettistisch *Adj.* [satirical] revue *attrib.;* ~e Szenen scenes in the style of a [satirical] revue

kabbeln *refl. V.* (ugs.) bicker (**mit** with)

Kabel *das;* ~s, ~: cable; (für kleineres Gerät) flex

Kabel·fernsehen *das* cable television

Kabeljau *der;* ~s, ~e *od.* ~s cod

kabeln *tr., itr. V.* (veralt.) cable

Kabine *die;* ~, ~n **(a)** cabin
(b) (Umkleideraum, abgeteilter Raum) cubicle
(c) (einer Seilbahn) [cable] car

Kabinętt *das;* ~s, ~e Cabinet

Kabrio *das;* ~s, ~s, **Kabriolętt** *das;* ~s, ~s convertible

Kąchel *die;* ~, ~n [glazed] tile

kącheln *tr. V.* tile

Kąchel·ofen *der* tiled stove

Kącke *die;* ~ (derb; auch fig.) shit (coarse); crap (coarse)

kącken *itr. V.* (derb) shit (coarse); crap (coarse)

Kadaver *der;* ~s, ~: carcass

Kader *der od.* (schweiz.) *das;* ~s, ~ **(a)** cadre
(b) (Sport) squad

Käfer *der;* ~s, ~: beetle

Kąff *das;* ~s, ~s *od.* **Käffer** (ugs. abwertend) dump (coll.)

Kaffee /'kafe *od.* (österr.) ka'fe:/ *der;* ~s, ~s **(a)** coffee
(b) (Nachmittags~) afternoon coffee; ~ **trinken** have afternoon coffee

Kaffee-: ~**kanne** *die* coffee pot; ~**kränzchen** *das* (veralt.) **(a)** (Zusammentreffen) coffee afternoon; **(b)** (Gruppe) coffee circle; ~**maschine** *die* coffee maker; ~**mühle** *die* coffee grinder; ~**satz** *der* coffee grounds *pl.;* ~**tante** *die* (ugs. scherzh.) coffee addict

Käfig *der;* ~s, ~e cage

kahl *Adj.* **(a)** (ohne Haare) bald; jmdn. ~ **scheren** shave sb.'s head
(b) (ohne Grün, schmucklos) bare; etw. ~ **fressen** strip sth. bare

kahl-, Kahl-: **~|***fressen** ▶ KAHL B;

~**köpfig** *Adj.* bald[-headed]; **~|***scheren** ▶ KAHL A; ~**schlag** *der* **(a)** clear-felling *no indef. art.;* **(b)** (Waldfläche) clear-felled area

Kahn *der;* ~[e]s, Kähne **(a)** (Ruder~) rowing boat; (Stech~) punt
(b) (Lastschiff) barge

Kai *der;* ~s, ~s quay

Kaiser *der;* ~s, ~: emperor

Kaiserin *die;* ~, ~nen empress

Kaiser-: ~**krone** *die* imperial crown; ~**reich** *das* empire; ~**schnitt** *der* Caesarean section; ~**wetter** *das* (scherzh.) glorious, sunny weather (*for an event*)

Kajüte *die;* ~, ~n (Seemannsspr.) cabin

Kakao /ka'kau:/ *der;* ~s, ~s cocoa; jmdn./ etw. durch den ~ ziehen (ugs.) make fun of sb./sth.

Kakerlak *der;* ~s *od.* ~en, ~en cockroach

Kąktus *der;* ~, Kakteen cactus

Kalauer *der;* ~s, ~: corny joke (coll.); (Wortspiel) atrocious *or* (coll.) corny pun

Kąlb *das;* ~[e]s, Kälber **(a)** calf
(b) (ugs.: ~fleisch) veal

kąlben *itr. V.* calve

Kąlb·fleisch *das* veal

Kąlbs-: ~**braten** *der* (Kochk.) roast veal *no indef. art.;* (Gericht) roast of veal; ~**leder** *das* calfskin; ~**schnitzel** *das* veal cutlet

Kalender *der;* ~s, ~: calendar; (Taschen~) diary

Kalender-: ~**jahr** *das* calendar year; ~**monat** *der* calendar month

Kalęsche *die;* ~, ~n (hist.) barouche

Kali *das;* ~s, ~s potash

Kaliber *das;* ~s, ~: **(a)** (Technik, Waffenkunde) calibre
(b) (ugs., oft abwertend) sort; kind

Kalifornien /kali'fɔrnjən/ *(das);* ~s California

Kalium (Chemie) *das;* ~s potassium

Kąlk *der;* ~[e]s, ~e calcium carbonate; (Baustoff) lime; quicklime

kąlken *tr. V.* whitewash

Kąlk-: ~**mangel** *der* calcium deficiency; ~**stein** *der* limestone

Kalkül *das od. der;* ~s, ~e (geh.) calculation

Kalkulation *die;* ~, ~en (auch Wirtsch.) calculation

kalkulieren *tr. V.* calculate ⟨cost, price⟩; cost ⟨product, article⟩

Kalorie *die;* ~, ~n calorie

kalorien-, Kalorien-: ~**arm** ① *Adj.*

low-calorie *attrib.;* ~**arm sein** be low in calories; ②*adv.* ~**arm kochen** cook low-calorie meals; ~**gehalt** *der* calorie content

kalt; **kälter, kältest...** ① *Adj.* cold; frosty ‹*atmosphere, smile*›; ~ **bleiben** (fig.) remain unmoved; **jmdn.** ~ **lassen** (ugs.) leave sb. unmoved; (nicht interessieren) leave sb. cold (coll.) ② *adv.* (a) ~ **duschen** have a cold shower **Getränke/Sekt** ~ **stellen** cool drinks/chill champagne (b) (nüchtern) coldly (c) (abweisend, unfreundlich) frostily

kalt-, Kalt-: *~|**bleiben** ▶ KALT 1; ~**blütig** ① *Adj.* (a) cool-headed; (b) (abwertend: skrupellos) cold-blooded; ② *adv.* (a) coolly; (abwertend: skrupellos) cold-bloodedly; ~**blütigkeit** *die;* ~~: ▶ ~BLÜTIG A, B: cool-headedness; cold-bloodedness

Kälte *die;* ~ cold; (fig.) coldness

Kälte-: ~**einbruch** *der* (Met.) sudden onset of cold weather; ~**grad** *der* degree of frost

kälter ▶ KALT

kältest... ▶ KALT

Kälte-welle *die* cold spell

kalt-, Kalt-: ~**gepresst,** *~**gepreßt** *Adj.* cold-pressed; ~**herzig** *Adj.* cold-hearted; *~**lächelnd** *Adv.* (ugs. abwertend) etw. ~**lächelnd tun** take callous pleasure in doing sth.; *~|**lassen** ▶ KALT 1; ~|**machen** *tr. V.* (salopp) jmdn. ~**machen** do sb. in (sl.); ~**miete** *die* rent exclusive of heating; ~**schale** *die: cold sweet soup made with fruit, beer, wine, or milk;* ~**schnäuzig** (ugs.) ① *Adj.* cold and insensitive; (frech) insolent; ② *adv.* coldly and insensitively; (frech) insolently; ~**stellen** *tr. V.* (ugs.) jmdn. ~**stellen** put sb. out of the way (coll. joc.)

kam *1. u. 3. Pers. Prät. v.* KOMMEN

Kambodscha *(das);* ~s Cambodia

käme *1. u. 3. Pers. Konjunktiv II v.* KOMMEN

Kamel *das;* ~s, ~e camel

Kamera *die;* ~, ~s camera

Kamerad *der;* ~en, ~en, **Kameradin** *die;* ~, ~nen companion; (Freund[in]) friend; (Mitschüler[in]) mate; (Soldat[in]) comrade; (Sport) teammate

Kameradschaft *die;* ~: comradeship

kameradschaftlich ① *Adj.* comradely ② *adv.* in a comradely way

Kamera-: ~**frau** *die* camerawoman; ~**mann** *der Pl.;* ~**männer** *od.* ~**leute** cameraman; ~**team** *das* camera crew

Kamerun /'kaməru:n/ *(das);* ~s Cameroon; the Cameroons *pl.*

Kamille *die;* ~, ~n camomile

Kamin *der, schweiz.: die;* ~s, ~e fireplace

Kamin-feger *der,* **Kamin-fegerin** *die* (bes. südd.) ▶ SCHORNSTEINFEGER

Kamm *der;* ~[e]s, **Kämme** (a) comb

(b) (bei Hühnern usw.) comb
(c) (Gebirgs~) ridge

kämmen *tr. V.* comb

Kammer *die;* ~, ~n (a) storeroom (b) (Biol., Med., Technik, Waffenkunde) chamber (c) (Parl.) chamber

Kammer-: ~**diener** *der* (veralt.) valet; ~**jäger** *der,* ~**jägerin** *die* pest controller; ~**musik** *die* chamber music; ~**sänger** *der,* ~**sängerin** *die: title awarded to singer of outstanding merit;* ~**zofe** *die* (veralt.) lady's maid

Kamm-garn *das* worsted

Kampagne /kam'panjə/ *die;* ~, ~n campaign

Kampf *der;* ~[e]s, **Kämpfe** (a) (militärisch) battle (**um** for) (b) (zwischen persönlichen Gegnern) fight; (fig.) struggle (c) (Wett~) contest; (Boxen) contest; bout (d) (Einsatz aller Mittel) fight (**um, für** for; **gegen** against)

kampf-, Kampf-: ~**abstimmung** *die* (Politik) crucial vote; ~**bereit** *Adj.* ready to fight *postpos.;* ‹*army, troops*› ready for battle

kämpfen *itr. V.* (a) fight (b) (Sport: sich messen) ‹*team*› play; ‹*wrestler, boxer*› fight

Kampfer *der;* ~s camphor

Kämpfer *der;* ~s, ~, **Kämpferin** *die;* ~, ~nen fighter

kampf-, Kampf-: ~**fähig** *Adj.* ‹*troops*› fit for action; ‹*boxer etc.*› fit to fight; ~**handlungen** *Pl.* fighting *sing.;* ~**preis** *der* (Wirtsch.) cut price; ~**richter** *der,* ~**richterin** *die* (Sport) judge; ~**unfähig** *Adj.* ‹*troops*› unfit for action; ‹*boxer etc.*› unfit to fight

kampieren *itr. V.* camp

Kanada *(das);* ~s Canada

Kanadier /ka'na:diɐ/ *der;* ~s, ~, **Kanadierin** *die;* ~, ~nen Canadian

kanadisch *Adj.* Canadian

Kanal *der;* ~s, **Kanäle** (a) canal (b) (Geogr.) **der** ~: the [English] Channel (c) (für Abwässer) sewer (d) (zur Entwässerung, Bewässerung) channel; (Graben) ditch (e) (Rundf., Ferns., Weg der Information) channel

Kanalisation *die;* ~, ~en sewerage system; sewers *pl.*

kanalisieren *tr. V.* (a) (lenken) channel ‹*energies, goods, etc.*› (b) (schiffbar machen) canalize

Kanal-tunnel *der* Channel Tunnel

Kanaren *Pl.* Canaries

Kanarien-vogel /ka'na:riən-/ *der* canary

Kanarische Inseln *Pl.* Canary Islands

Kandare *die;* ~, ~n curb bit; **jmdn. an die** ~ **nehmen** (fig.) take sb. in hand

Kandidat *der;* ~en, ~en, **Kandidatin** *die;* ~, ~nen (a) candidate (b) (beim Quiz usw.) contestant

Kandidatur die; ~, ~en candidature (auf + Akk. for)

kandidieren itr. V. stand [as a candidate] (für for)

kandieren tr. V. candy; kandiert crystallized ‹orange, petal›; glacé ‹cherry, pear›; candied ‹peel›

Kandis der; ~, **Kandis·zucker** der rock candy

Känguru, *Känguruh das; ~s, ~s kangaroo

Kaninchen das; ~s, ~: rabbit

Kanister der; ~s, ~: can; [metal/plastic] container

kann 1. u. 3. Pers. Sg. Präsens v. KÖNNEN

Kännchen das; ~s, ~: [small] pot; (für Milch) [small] jug

Kanne die; ~, ~n (a) pot; (für Milch, Wein, Wasser) jug
(b) (Henkel~) can; (für Milch) pail; (beim Melken) churn

kannst 2. Pers. Sg. Präsens v. KÖNNEN

kannte 1. u. 3. Pers. Sg. Prät. v. KENNEN

Kanon der; ~s, ~s canon

Kanone die; ~, ~n cannon; (fig. ugs.: Könner) ace

Kantate die; ~, ~n (Musik) cantata

Kante die; ~, ~n edge

kantig Adj. square-cut ‹timber, stone›; rough-edged ‹rock›; angular ‹face›; square ‹chin›

Kantine die; ~, ~n canteen

Kanton der; ~s, ~e canton

kantonal 1 Adj. cantonal
2 adv. on a cantonal basis

Kantor der; ~s, ~en choirmaster and organist

Kantorin die; ~, ~nen choirmistress and organist

Kanu das; ~s, ~s canoe

Kanüle die; ~, ~n (Med.) cannula

Kanzel die; ~, ~n (a) pulpit
(b) (Flugw.) cockpit

Kanzlei die; ~, ~en (a) (veralt.: Büro) office
(b) (Anwalts~) chambers pl. (of barrister); office (of lawyer)

Kanzler der; ~s, ~ chancellor

Kap das; ~s, ~s cape

Kapazität die; ~, ~en (a) capacity
(b) (Experte) expert

Kapelle die; ~, ~n (a) (Archit.) chapel
(b) (Musik~) band; [light] orchestra

Kapell·meister der,
Kapell·meisterin die bandmaster/ -mistress; (im Orchester) conductor; (im Theater usw.) musical director

Kaper die; ~, ~n caper usu. in pl.

kapern tr. V. (a) (hist.) capture

*old spelling - see note on page xiv

(b) (ugs.) jmdn. [für etw.] ~: rope sb. in[to sth.]

kapieren (ugs.) 1 tr. V. (ugs.) get (coll.)
2 itr. V. kapiert? got it? (coll.)

Kapital das; ~s, ~e od. ~ien (a) capital
(b) (fig.) asset

Kapital·anlage die (Wirtsch.) capital investment

Kapitalismus der; ~: capitalism no art.

Kapitalist der; ~en, ~en, **Kapitalistin** die; ~, ~nen capitalist

kapitalistisch Adj. capitalistic

Kapital·verbrechen das serious offence; (mit Todesstrafe bedroht) capital offence

Kapitän der; ~s, ~e, **Kapitänin** die; ~, ~nen captain

Kapitel das; ~s, ~: chapter

Kapitulation die; ~, ~en surrender; capitulation; **seine ~ erklären** admit defeat

kapitulieren itr. V. (a) surrender; capitulate
(b) (fig.: aufgeben) give up; **vor etw.** (Dat.) ~: give up in the face of sth.

Kaplan der; ~s, Kapläne (kath. Kirche) chaplain; (Hilfsgeistlicher) curate

Kappe die; ~, ~n cap

kappen tr. V. (a) (Seemannsspr.) cut
(b) (beschneiden) cut back ‹hedge etc.›; (abschneiden) cut off ‹branches etc.›

Käppi das; ~s, ~s garrison cap

Kapsel die; ~, ~n capsule

Kapstadt (das); ~s Cape Town

kaputt Adj. (a) broken; **das Telefon ist ~:** the phone is not working
(b) (ugs.: erschöpft) shattered (coll.)

kaputt-: ~|gehen unr. itr. V.; mit sein (ugs.) (entzweigehen) break; ‹machine› break down, (coll.) pack up; ‹lightbulb› go; (zerbrechen) be smashed; **~|lachen** refl. V. (ugs.) kill oneself [laughing] (coll.); **~|machen** (ugs.) 1 tr. V. break; spoil ‹sth. made with effort›; ruin ‹clothes, furniture, etc.›; finish ‹person› off; 2 refl. V. wear oneself out

Kapuze die; ~, ~n hood; (bei Mönchen) cowl; hood

Kapuziner der; ~s, ~: Capuchin [friar]

Karabiner der; ~s, ~: carbine

Karaffe die; ~, ~n carafe; (mit Glasstöpsel) decanter

Karambolage /karambo'la:ʒə/ die; ~, ~n (ugs.) crash; collision

***Karamel** usw. ▶ KARAMELL usw.

Karamell der (schweiz.: das); ~s caramel

Karamell·bonbon der od. das caramel [toffee]

Karat das; ~[e]s, ~e carat

Karate das; ~[s] karate

Karawane die; ~, ~n caravan

Kardinal der; ~s, Kardinäle (kath. Kirche) cardinal

Kardinal-: ~**fehler** der cardinal error;
~**tugend** die cardinal virtue; ~**zahl** die
cardinal [number]

Karenz die; ~, ~en, **Karenz·zeit** die
waiting period

Kar·freitag der Good Friday

karg ⓵ Adj. meagre ⟨wages etc.⟩; frugal
⟨meal etc.⟩; poor ⟨light, accommodation⟩;
(wenig fruchtbar) barren
⓶ adv. ~ **bemessen sein** ⟨helping⟩ be
mingy (Brit. coll.); ⟨supply⟩ be scanty; ~ **leben**
live frugally

kärglich ⓵ Adj. meagre, poor ⟨wages etc.⟩;
poor ⟨light⟩; frugal ⟨meal⟩; scanty ⟨supply⟩
⓶ adv. poorly ⟨lit, paid, rewarded⟩

karibisch Adj. Caribbean

kariert Adj. check, checked ⟨material,
pattern⟩; check ⟨jacket etc.⟩; squared ⟨paper⟩

Karies /'kaːri̯ɛs/ die; ~: caries

Karikatur die; ~, ~en cartoon; (Porträt)
caricature

Karikaturist der; ~en, ~en,
Karikaturistin die; ~, ~nen cartoonist;
(Porträtist) caricaturist

karikieren tr. V. caricature

kariös Adj. (Zahnmed.) carious

karitativ Adj. charitable

Karl /karl/ (der) Charles; ~ **der Große**
Charlemagne

Karneval /'karnəval/ der; ~s, ~e od. ~s
carnival; ~ **feiern** join in the carnival
festivities

karnevalistisch Adj. carnival attrib.

Karnevals-: ~**kostüm** das carnival
costume; ~**verein** der carnival society;
~**zug** der carnival procession

Karnickel das; ~s, ~ (landsch.) rabbit

Kärnten (das); ~s Carinthia

Karo das; ~s, ~s (a) square; (auf der Spitze
stehend) diamond
(b) (Karomuster) check
(c) (Kartenspiel: Farbe) diamonds pl.;
(d) (Kartenspiel: Karte) diamond

Karosse die; ~, ~n [state] coach

Karosserie die; ~, ~n bodywork

Karotte die; ~, ~n small carrot

Karpaten Pl. Carpathians; Carpathian
Mountains

Karpfen der; ~s, ~: carp

Karre die; ~, ~n (bes. nordd.) (a) ▶ KARREN;
(b) (abwertend: Fahrzeug) [old] heap (coll.)

Karree das; ~s, ~s: ums ~ **gehen/fahren**
walk/drive round the block

karren tr. V. (a) cart
(b) (salopp: mit einem Auto) run (coll.)

Karren der; ~s, ~ (bes. südd., österr.) cart;
(zweirädrig) barrow

Karriere /ka'ri̯eːrə/ die; ~, ~n career; ~
machen make a [successful] career for
oneself

Kärrner·arbeit die donkey work

Kar·samstag der Easter Saturday

Karte die; ~, ~n card; (Speise~) menu;
(Fahr~, Flug~, Eintritts~) ticket; (Land~) map;
alles auf eine ~ setzen stake everything on
one chance

Kartei die; ~, ~en card file

Kartei-: ~**karte** die file card; ~**kasten**
der file-card box

Kartell das; ~s, ~e (Wirtsch., Politik) cartel

Kartell-: ~**amt** das: government body
concerned with the control and supervision of
cartels; ≈ Monopolies and Mergers
Commission (Brit.); ~**gesetz** das law
relating to cartels; ≈ monopolies law
(Brit.)

Karten-: ~**haus** das house of cards;
~**spiel** das (a) (Spiel mit Karten) card game;
(b) (Satz Spielkarten) pack or (Amer.) deck [of
cards]; ~**telefon** das cardphone;
~**vorverkauf** der advance booking

Kartoffel die; ~, ~n potato

Kartoffel-: ~**brei** der mashed potatoes
pl.; mash (coll.); ~**chips** Pl. [potato] crisps
(Brit.) or (Amer.) chips; ~**käfer** der Colorado
beetle; ~**kloß** der potato dumpling;
~**puffer** der potato pancake (made from
grated raw potatoes); ~**püree** das: ▶ ~BREI

Karton /kar'tɔŋ/ der; ~s, ~s (a) (Pappe)
card[board]
(b) (Schachtel) cardboard box

Karussell das; ~s, ~s od. ~e merry-go-
round; carousel (Amer.); (kleineres) roundabout

Kar·woche die Holy Week

karzinogen Adj. (Med.) carcinogenic

Karzinom das; ~s, ~e (Med.) carcinoma

kaschieren tr. V. conceal; hide; disguise
⟨fault⟩

Kaschmir[1] (das); ~s Kashmir

Kaschmir[2] der; ~s, ~e (Textilw.) cashmere

Käse der; ~s, ~: cheese; (ugs. abwertend:
Unsinn) rubbish

Käse-: ~**blatt** das (salopp abwertend) rag;
~**glocke** die cheese dome

Kaserne die; ~, ~n barracks sing. or pl.

käse·weiß Adj. (ugs.) [as] white as a sheet

käsig Adj. (ugs.) pasty; pale

Kasino das; ~s, ~s (a) (Spiel~) casino
(b) (Offiziers~) [officers'] mess
(c) (Speiseraum) canteen

Kasko·versicherung die (Voll~)
comprehensive insurance; (Teil~) insurance
against theft, fire, or act of God

Kasper der; ~s, ~: ≈ Punch; (fig. ugs.)
clown

Kasperl das; ~s, ~[n] (österr.), **Kasperle**
das od. der; ~s, ~: ▶ KASPER

Kasper-: ~**puppe** die ≈ Punch and Judy
puppet; ~**theater** das ≈ Punch and Judy
show; (Puppenbühne) ≈ Punch and Judy
theatre

Kasse die; ~, ~n (a) cash box; (Registrier~)
till ⋯⃗

(b) (Ort zum Bezahlen) cash desk; (im Supermarkt) checkout; (in einer Bank) counter
(c) (Kassenraum) cashier's office
(d) (Theater~, Kino~) box office

Kạsseler das; ~s smoked loin of pork

Kạssen-: ~**arzt** der, ~**ärztin** die: doctor who treats members of health insurance schemes; ~**bon** der sales slip; receipt; ~**lage** die financial situation; **die** ~**lage der Firma** the state of the company's finances; **nach** ~**lage** as finances allow/allowed; **eine Rentenpolitik nach** ~**lage** a pensions policy dependent on what finances will allow; ~**patient** der, ~**patientin** die: patient who is a member of a health insurance scheme; ~**wart** der; ~~s, ~~e, ~**wartin** die; ~~, ~~nen treasurer; ~**zettel** der:
▶ ~BON

Kassẹtte die; ~, ~n **(a)** box; case
(b) (mit Büchern, Schallplatten) boxed set; (Tonband~, Film~) cassette

Kassẹtten-: ~**deck** das cassette deck; ~**recorder**, ~**rekorder** der; ~~s, ~~: cassette recorder

kassieren ① tr. V. **(a)** collect
(b) (ugs.: wegnehmen) confiscate; take away ⟨driving licence⟩
② itr. V. **bei jmdm.** ~: give sb. his/her bill or (Amer.) check; (ohne Rechnung) settle up with sb.; **darf ich bei Ihnen** ~? would you like your bill?/can I settle up with you?

Kassierer der; ~s, ~, **Kassiererin** die; ~, ~nen cashier; (bei einem Verein) treasurer

Kastanie /kas'ta:niə/ die; ~, ~n chestnut

kastanien·braun Adj. chestnut

Kästchen das; ~s, ~ **(a)** small box
(b) (vorgedrucktes Quadrat) square; (auf Fragebögen) box

Kạste die; ~, ~n caste

kasteien refl. V. **(a)** (als Bußübung) chastise oneself
(b) (sich Entbehrungen auferlegen) deny oneself

Kasteiung die; ~, ~en **(a)** (als Bußübung) self-chastisement
(b) (Auferlegung von Entbehrungen) self-denial

Kastẹll das; ~s, ~e **(a)** (hist.: röm. Lager) fort
(b) (Burg) castle

Kạsten der; ~s, Kästen **(a)** box; (für Flaschen) crate
(b) (ugs.: Briefkasten) postbox
(c) (ugs. abwertend) (Gebäude) barracks sing. or pl.; (Auto) heap (coll.); (fig. ugs.) **etw. auf dem** ~ **haben** have got it up top (coll.)

Kạsten·brot das tin [loaf]

Kastration /kastra'tsi̯o:n/ die; ~, ~en castration

kastrieren tr. V. castrate

Kat der; ~s, ~s (ugs.) ▶ KATALYSATOR B

Katalọg der; ~[e]s, ~e (auch fig.) catalogue

katalogisieren tr. V. catalogue

Katalysator der; ~s, ~en **(a)** (Chemie, fig.) catalyst
(b) (Kfz-W.) catalytic converter

Katamaran der od. das; ~s, ~e catamaran

katapultieren tr. V. (auch fig.) catapult; eject ⟨pilot⟩

Katạrrh /ka'tar/ der; ~s, ~e (Med.) catarrh

katastrophal /katastro'fa:l/ ① Adj. disastrous; (stärker) catastrophic
② adv. disastrously; (stärker) catastrophically

Katastrophe /katas'tro:fə/ die; ~, ~n (Unglück) disaster; (stärker, auch Literaturw.) catastrophe

Katastrophen-: ~**alarm** der disaster alert; ~**gebiet** das disaster area; ~**schutz** der (Organisation) emergency services pl.; (Maßnahmen) disaster procedures pl.

Kategorie die; ~, ~n category

kategorisch ① Adj. categorical
② adv. categorically

Kater der; ~s, ~ **(a)** tomcat
(b) (ugs.) hangover

Kathedrale die; ~, ~n cathedral

Katholik der; ~en, ~en, **Katholikin** die; ~, ~nen [Roman] Catholic

katholisch Adj. [Roman] Catholic

Katholizismus der; ~: [Roman] Catholicism no art.

Katz die ~ **und Maus [mit jmdm.] spielen** (ugs.) play cat and mouse [with sb.]; **für die** ~ **sein** (salopp) be a waste of time

Kätzchen das; ~s, ~ **(a)** little cat; pussy; (junge Katze) kitten
(b) meist Pl. catkin

Kạtze die; ~, ~n cat

katzen-, Kạtzen-: ~**auge** das reflector; Cat's-eye ®; ~**jammer** der **(a)** (Kater) hangover; **(b)** (fig.) mood of depression; ~**musik** die (ugs. abwertend) terrible row (coll.); ~**sprung** der stone's throw; ~**wäsche** die (ugs.) ~**wäsche machen** have a lick and a promise (coll.)

Kauderwelsch das; ~[s] gibberish no indef. art.

kauen tr., itr. V. chew; **[die] Nägel** ~: bite one's nails

kauern itr., refl. V. crouch [down]; (ängstlich) cower

Kauf der; ~[e]s, Käufe **(a)** (das Kaufen) buying; purchasing (formal)
(b) (das Gekaufte) purchase

kaufen ① tr. V. buy; purchase
② itr. V. (einkaufen) shop

Käufer der; ~s, ~, **Käuferin** die; ~, ~nen buyer; purchaser (formal)

Kauf-: ~**frau** die (Geschäftsfrau) businesswoman; (Händlerin) trader; ~**haus** das department store; ~**kraft** die (Wirtsch.) **(a)** (Wert des Geldes) purchasing power; **(b)** (Zahlungsfähigkeit) spending power

---

*alte Schreibung - vgl. Hinweis auf S. xiv

käuflich ☐1 *Adj.* (a) for sale *postpos.;*
(b) (bestechlich) venal; ~ **sein** be easily
bought
☐2 *adv.* etw. ~ **erwerben/erstehen** purchase
sth.

Kauf·mann *der; Pl.* **Kaufleute** (a)
(Geschäftsmann) businessman; (Händler) trader
(b) (Besitzer) shopkeeper; (eines
Lebensmittelladens) grocer

kaufmännisch *Adj.* commercial;
business *attrib.*

Kauf-: ~**preis** *der* purchase price;
~**vertrag** *der* contract of sale; (beim
Hauskauf) title deed

Kau·gummi *der od. das;* ~**s,** ~**s** chewing
gum

Kaukasus *der;* ~: the Caucasus

Kaulquappe *die;* ~, ~**n** tadpole

kaum *Adv.* hardly; scarcely; ~ **hatte er
Platz genommen, als ...:** no sooner had he
sat down than ...

kausal *Adj.* (geh., Sprachw.) causal

Kau·tabak *der* chewing tobacco

Kaution *die;* ~, ~**en** (a) (bei Freilassung eines
Gefangenen) bail
(b) (beim Mieten einer Wohnung) deposit

Kautschuk *der;* ~**s,** ~**e** rubber

Kauz *der;* ~**es,** **Käuze** (a) (Wald~) tawny
owl; (Stein~) little owl
(b) (Sonderling) strange fellow; oddball (coll.)

Kavalier /kava'liːɐ̯/ *der;* ~**s,** ~**e** gentleman

Kavaliers·delikt *das* trifling offence

Kavallerie /kavalə'riː/ *die;* ~, ~**n** (Milit.
hist.) cavalry

Kavallerist *der;* ~**en,** ~**en** cavalryman

Kaviar /'kaːvi̯ar/ *der;* ~**s,** ~**e** caviare

kcal *Abk.* = **Kilo[gramm]kalorie** kcal

keck ☐1 *Adj.* (a) cheeky; saucy (Brit.)
(b) (veralt.: verwegen) bold
(c) (flott) jaunty, pert ⟨hat etc.⟩
☐2 *adv.* (a) cheekily; saucily (Brit.)
(b) (veralt.: verwegen) boldly
(c) (flott) jauntily

Keckheit *die;* ~, ~**en** (a) cheek; sauce
(Brit.)
(b) (veralt.: Kühnheit) boldness

Kegel *der;* ~**s,** ~ (a) cone
(b) (Spielfigur) skittle; (beim Bowling) pin

Kegel-: ~**bahn** *die* skittle alley;
~**förmig** *Adj.* conical

kegeln ☐1 *itr. V.* play skittles *or* ninepins
☐2 *tr. V.* **eine Partie** ~: play a game of
skittles *or* ninepins; **eine Neun** ~: score a
nine

Kehle *die;* ~, ~**n** throat

Kehl·kopf *der* (Anat.) larynx

Kehlkopf·krebs *der* (Med.) cancer of the
larynx

Kehre *die;* ~, ~**n** sharp bend

kehren¹ ☐1 *tr. V.* turn
☐2 *refl. V.* turn

kehren² ☐1 *itr. V.* (bes. südd.) sweep; do the
sweeping
☐2 *tr. V.* sweep; (mit einem Handfeger) brush

Kehricht *der od. das;* ~**s** (schweiz.: Müll)
refuse; garbage (Amer.)

Kehr·seite *die* (a) back; (einer Münze,
Medaille) reverse; (scherzh.) (Gesäß) backside
(b) (nachteiliger Aspekt) drawback;
disadvantage

kehrt|machen *itr. V.* (ugs.) turn [round
and go] back

keifen *itr. V.* (abwertend) nag

Keil *der;* ~**[e]s,** ~**e** (a) (zum Spalten) wedge
(b) (zum Festklemmen) chock; (unter einer Tür)
wedge

keilen *refl. V.* (ugs.: sich prügeln) fight; scrap

Keiler *der;* ~**s,** ~ (Jägerspr.) wild boar

Keilerei *die;* ~, ~**en** (ugs.) punch-up (coll.);
fight

Keil-: ~**riemen** *der* (Technik) V-belt;
~**schrift** *die* cuneiform script

Keim *der;* ~**[e]s,** ~**e** (Bot.) shoot; (Biol.)
embryo

Keim-: ~**bahn** *die* (Biol.) germ line;
~**drüse** *die* (Zool., Med.) gonad

keimen *itr. V.* germinate; (fig.) ⟨hope⟩ stir

keim-, Keim-: ~**frei** *Adj.* germ-free;
sterile; ~**zelle** *die* nucleus

kein *Indefinitpron.* (a) no
(b) (ugs.: nicht ganz, nicht einmal) less than

kein... *Indefinitpron.* ~**er/**~**e** nobody; no
one; ~**s von beiden** neither [of them]

keinerlei *indekl. Adj.* no ... what[so]ever

keines-: ~**falls** *Adv.* on no account;
~**wegs** *Adv.* by no means

kein·mal *Adv.* not [even] once

Keks *der;* ~ *od.* ~**es,** ~ *od.* ~**e** biscuit
(Brit.); cookie (Amer.)

Kelch *der;* ~**[e]s,** ~**e** goblet; (Rel.) chalice

Kelle *die;* ~, ~**n** (a) ladle
(b) (Signalstab) signalling disc
(c) (Maurer~) trowel

Keller *der;* ~**s,** ~: cellar; (~geschoss)
basement

Keller·assel *die;* ~, ~**n** woodlouse

Kellerei *die;* ~, ~**en** winery; (Kellerräume)
[wine] cellars *pl.*

Keller-: ~**geschoss,** *** ~**geschoß** *das*
basement; ~**wohnung** *die* basement flat
(Brit.) *or* (Amer.) apartment

Kellner *der;* ~**s,** ~: waiter

Kellnerin *die;* ~, ~**nen** waitress

kellnern *itr. V.* (ugs.) work as a waiter/
waitress

Kelte *der;* ~**n,** ~**n** Celt

Kelter *die;* ~, ~**n** winepress

keltern *tr. V.* press ⟨grapes etc.⟩

Keltin *die;* ~, ~**nen** Celt

keltisch *Adj.* Celtic

Kenia (*das*)*;* ~**s** Kenya

Kenianer der; ~s, ~, **Kenianerin** die;
~, ~nen Kenyan

kennen unr. tr. V. know; jmdn./etw. ~
lernen get to know sb./sth.; jmdn. **lernen**
(jmdm. erstmals begegnen) meet sb.; jmdn. **als**
etw. ~ **lernen** come to know sb. as sth.

Kenner der; ~s, ~: expert (+ Gen. on); (von
Wein, Speisen) connoisseur

Kenner·blick der expert eye; mit ~: with
an expert eye

Kennerin die; ~, ~nen ▶ KENNER

Kenn·marke die [police] identification
badge; ≈ [police] warrant card or (Amer.) ID
card

kenntlich Adj.: ~ **sein** be recognizable (**an**
by); etw./jmdn. ~ **machen** mark sth./make
sb. [easily] identifiable

Kenntnis die; ~, ~se knowledge

kennen|lernen ▶ KENNEN

Kenntnisnahme die; ~ (Papierdt.) **nach ~**
der Akten after giving the documents my/his
etc. attention

kenntnis·reich Adj. well-informed;
knowledgeable

kenn-, Kenn-: ~**wort** das; Pl. ~wörter
code word; (Parole) password; code word;
~**zahl** die index; ~**zeichen** das (a) sign;
(b) (Erkennungszeichen) badge; (auf einem
Behälter, einer Ware usw.) label; (am Fahrzeug)
registration number; ~**zeichnen** tr. V. (a)
mark; label; mark (way); (b) (charakterisieren)
characterize; ~**zeichnend** Adj. typical,
characteristic (für of)

kentern itr. V. mit sein capsize

Keramik die; ~, ~en ceramics pl.; pottery;
(Gegenstand) piece of pottery

Kerbe die; ~, ~n notch

Kerbel der; ~s chervil

Kerb·holz das: etwas auf dem ~ **haben**
(ugs.) have done a job (sl.)

Kerker der; ~s, ~ (hist.) dungeons pl.;
(einzelne Zelle) dungeon

Kerl der; ~s, ~e (nordd., md. auch: ~s)
(ugs.) fellow (coll.); bloke (Brit. coll.)

Kern der; ~[e]s, ~e pip; (von Steinobst) stone;
(von Nüssen usw.) kernel; (Atom~) nucleus; (fig.)
der ~ einer Sache the heart of a matter; **der**
harte ~: the hard core

kern-, Kern-: ~**energie** die nuclear
energy no art.; ~**gehäuse** das core;
~**geschäft** das core business; ~**gesund**
Adj. fit as a fiddle pred.

kernig Adj. earthy (language); forceful
(speech); pithy (saying)

kern-, Kern-: ~**kraft** die nuclear power;
~**kraftwerk** das nuclear power station or
plant; ~**los** Adj. seedless; ~**obst** das
pomaceous fruit; ~**physik** die nuclear
physics sing., no art.; ~**reaktor** der
nuclear reactor; ~**seife** die washing soap;
~**spaltung** die (Physik) nuclear fission no

art.; ~**spin·tomographie**
/ˈkɛrnspɪntomoɡrafiː/ die; ~~ (Med.)
[nuclear] magnetic resonance imaging;
~**waffe** die nuclear weapon; ~**zeit** die
core time

Kerze die; ~, ~n candle

kerzen-, Kerzen-: ~**gerade,** (ugs.)
~**grade** ① Adj. dead straight; ② adv. bolt
upright; ~**halter** der candle holder;
~**leuchter** der candlestick; ~**licht** das
the light of a candle/of candles; **bei ~licht** by
candlelight

kess, *keß ① Adj. (a) pert; jaunty (hat,
dress, etc.)
(b) (frech) cheeky
② adv. (a) (flott) jauntily
(b) (frech) cheekily

Kessel der; ~s, ~ (a) kettle; (zum Kochen)
pot; (Wasch~) copper
(b) (Berg~) basin-shaped valley
(c) (Milit.) encircled area

Kessel-: ~**stein** der scale; ~**treiben**
das (Hetzkampagne) witch-hunt

Kette die; ~, ~n chain; (Hals~) necklace;
(von Ereignissen) string

ketten tr. V. chain (**an** + Akk. to)

Ketten-: ~**hund** der guard dog (kept on a
chain); ~**rauchen** das; ~~s chain-
smoking no art.; ~**raucher** der,
~**raucherin** die chain-smoker; ~**säge**
die chain saw; ~**schaltung** die derailleur
gears pl.

Ketzer der; ~s, ~ (auch fig.) heretic

Ketzerei die; ~, ~en (auch fig.) heresy

Ketzerin die; ~, ~nen ▶ KETZER

keuchen itr. V. gasp for breath

Keuch·husten der whooping cough no
art.

Keule die; ~, ~n (a) club
(b) (Kochk.) leg

keusch ① Adj. chaste
② adv. ~ **leben** lead a chaste life

Keuschheit die; ~: chastity

Kfz Abk. = **Kraftfahrzeug**

kg Abk. = **Kilogramm** kg

KG Abk. = **Kommanditgesellschaft**

kichern itr. V. giggle

kicken (ugs.) ① itr. V. play football
② tr. V. kick

kidnappen /ˈkɪtnɛpn̩/ tr. V. kidnap

Kidnapper der; ~s, ~, **Kidnapperin**
die; ~, ~nen kidnapper

Kiebitz der; ~es, ~e lapwing; peewit

Kiefer[1] der; ~s, ~: jaw; (~knochen) jawbone

Kiefer[2] die; ~, ~n pine[tree]

Kiefer·höhle die (Anat.) maxillary sinus

Kiefern·holz das pine [wood]

Kiel der; ~[e]s, ~e keel

kiel·holen tr. V. (Seemannsspr.) keelhaul
(person)

Kiel·wasser das wake

Kieme *die;* ~, ~n gill

Kien *der;* ~[e]s resinous wood

Kies *der;* ~es, ~e gravel; (auf dem Strand) shingle

Kiesel *der;* ~s, ~: pebble

Kiesel·stein *der* pebble

Kies-: ~**grube** *die* gravel pit; ~**weg** *der* gravel path

kiffen *itr. V.* (ugs.) smoke pot (sl.) *or* grass (sl.)

Kiffer *der;* ~s, ~, **Kifferin** *die;* ~, ~nen (ugs.) pothead (sl.)

kikeriki /kikəriˈkiː/ *Interj.* (Kinderspr.) cock-a-doodle-doo

Killer *der;* ~s, ~, **Killerin** *die;* ~, ~nen (salopp) killer; (gegen Bezahlung) hit man

Kilo *das;* ~s, ~[s] kilo

Kilo·gramm *das* kilogram

Kilometer *der;* ~s, ~: kilometre

kilometer-, Kilometer-: ~**lang** [1] *Adj.* miles long *pred.;* [2] *adv.* for miles [and miles]; ~**stand** *der* mileage reading

Kilowatt·stunde *die* (Physik; bes. Elektrot.) kilowatt-hour

Kimme *die;* ~, ~n sighting notch

Kimono *der;* ~s, ~s kimono

Kind *das;* ~[e]s, ~er (a) child; ein ~ erwarten be expecting
(b) [~er,] ~er! my goodness!

Kinder-: ~**arzt** *der,* ~**ärztin** *die* paediatrician; ~**betreuung** *die* child care; ~**bett** *das* cot; (für größeres Kind) child's bed; ~**dorf** *das* children's village

Kinderei *die;* ~, ~en childishness *no indef. art., no pl.*

kinder-, Kinder-: ~**erziehung** *die* bringing up of children; ~**feindlich** *Adj.* hostile to children *pred.;* ~**freundlich** *Adj.* fond of children *pred.;* ⟨town, resort⟩ which caters for children; ⟨planning, policy⟩ which caters for the needs of children; ~**garten** *der* nursery school; ~**gärtnerin** *die* nusery-school teacher; ~**geld** *das* child benefit; ~**heilkunde** *die* paediatrics *sing., no art.;* ~**hort** *der* day home for schoolchildren; ~**krankheit** *die* (a) (Infektionskrankheit) children's disease *or* illness; **(b)** *Pl.* (fig.) ⟨town⟩ teething troubles; ~**krippe** *die* crèche; day nursey; ~**lähmung** *die* poliomyelitis; ~**leicht** (ugs.) Adj. childishly simple; dead easy; **das ist** ~**leicht** it's kid's stuff (coll.); it's child's play; ~**lieb** *Adj.* fond of children *pred.;* ~**los** *Adj.* childless; ~**reich** *Adj.* with many children *postpos., not pred.;* ~**sterblichkeit** *die* child mortality; ~**stube** *die* eine gute/schlechte ~stube gehabt haben have been well/badly brought up; ~**tages·heim** *das,* ~**tages·stätte** *die* day nursery; crèche ~**teller** *der* (auf der Speisekarte) children's menu; ~**wagen** *die* pram (Brit.); baby carriage (Amer.); (Sportwagen) pushchair (Brit.); stroller (Amer.)

Kindes-: ~**alter** *das* childhood; ~**misshandlung,** ***~**mißhandlung** *die* (Rechtsw.) child abuse

Kindheit *die;* ~: childhood

kindisch [1] *Adj.* childish, infantile; naïve ⟨ideas⟩
[2] *adv.* childishly

kindlich [1] *Adj.* childlike
[2] *adv.* ⟨behave⟩ in a childlike way

Kinkerlitzchen *Pl.* (ugs.) trifles

Kinn *das;* ~[e]s, ~e chin

Kinn-: ~**haken** *der* hook to the chin; ~**lade** *die* jaw

Kino *das;* ~s, ~s cinema (Brit.); movie theater (Amer.)

Kino-: ~**gänger** *der;* ~~s, ~~, ~**gängerin** *die;* ~~, ~~nen cinema-goer (Brit.); movie-goer (Amer.); ~**karte** *die* cinema ticket (Brit.); movie ticket (Amer.)

Kiosk *der;* ~[e]s, ~e kiosk

Kippe¹ *die;* ~, ~n (ugs.) cigarette end; dog-end (coll.)

Kippe² *die;* ~, ~n (a) (Bergmannsspr.) slag heap
(b) etw. steht auf der ~ (fig.) it's touch and go with sth.; (etw. ist noch nicht entschieden) sth. hangs in the balance

kippen [1] *tr. V.* (a) tip [up]
(b) (ausschütten) tip [out]
(c) (ugs.: trinken) knock back (coll.); einen ~: have a quick one (coll.) *or* a drink
[2] *itr. V.; mit sein* tip over; ⟨person⟩ topple; ⟨boat⟩ overturn; ⟨car⟩ roll over

Kipp-: ~**fenster** *das* horizontally pivoted window; ~**schalter** *der* tumbler switch

Kirche *die;* ~, ~n church; in die ~ gehen go to church

Kirchen-: ~**fest** *das* church festival; ~**lied** *das* hymn; ~**musik** *die* church music; ~**steuer** *die* church tax

Kirch-: ~**gänger** *der;* ~~s, ~~, ~**gängerin** *die;* ~~, ~~nen churchgoer; ~**hof** *der* (veralt.) churchyard

kirchlich [1] *Adj.* ecclesiastical; church *attrib.* ⟨wedding, funeral⟩
[2] *adv.* ~ getraut/begraben werden have a church wedding/funeral

Kirch-: ~**turm** *der* [church] steeple; (ohne Turmspitze) church tower; ~**weih** *die;* ~~, ~~en fair (held on the anniversary of the consecration of a church)

Kirmes *die;* ~, **Kirmessen** (bes. md., niederd.)
▶ KIRCHWEIH

Kirsch·baum *der* cherry [tree]

Kirsche *die;* ~, ~n cherry

Kirsch-: ~**torte** *die* cherry gateau; (mit Tortenboden) cherry flan; ~**wasser** *das; Pl.* ~**wässer** kirsch

Kissen *das;* ~s, ~: cushion; (Kopf~) pillow

k

Kiste die; ~, ~n box; (Truhe) chest; (Latten~) crate

Kita die; ~, ~s day nursery; crèche

Kitsch der; ~[e]s kitsch

kitschig Adj. kitschy

Kitt der; ~[e]s, ~e putty; (für Porzellan, Kacheln usw.) cement

Kittchen das; ~s, ~ (ugs.) clink (sl.)

Kittel der; ~s, ~ (a) overall; (eines Arztes usw.) white coat
(b) (hemdartige Bluse) smock

kitten tr. V. cement [together]

Kitz das; ~es, ~e (Reh~) fawn; (Ziegen~, Gämsen~) kid

kitzeln tr., itr. V. tickle

kitzlig Adj. (auch fig.) ticklish

KKW Abk. = **Kernkraftwerk**

Klacks der; ~es, ~e (ugs.) dollop (coll.); (~ Senf) dab; **etw. ist nur ein ~ [für jmdn.]** (fig.) sth. is no trouble at all [for sb.]

Kladde die; ~, ~n rough book

Kladderadatsch der; ~[e]s, ~e (ugs.) unholy mess (coll.)

klaffen itr. V. yawn; ⟨hole, wound⟩ gape

kläffen itr. V. (abwertend) yap

Kläffer der; ~s, ~ (ugs. abwertend) yapping dog; yapper

Klafter der od. das; ~s, ~ (Raummaß für Holz) cord

Klage die; ~, ~n (a) (Äußerung der Trauer) lament
(b) (Beschwerde) complaint
(c) (Rechtsw.) action; (im Strafrecht) charge

klagen ⓵ itr. V. (a) (geh.: jammern) wail; (stöhnend) moan
(b) (sich beschweren) complain (**über** + Akk. about)
(c) (bei Gericht) take legal action
⓶ tr. V. **jmdm. sein Leid/seine Not ~:** pour out one's sorrows pl./troubles pl.

Kläger der; ~s, ~, **Klägerin** die; ~, ~nen (im Zivilrecht) plaintiff; (im Strafrecht) prosecuting party; (bei einer Scheidung) petitioner

kläglich Adj. (a) (Mitleid erregend) pitiful
(b) (minderwertig) pathetic
(c) (erbärmlich) despicable ⟨behaviour, role, compromise⟩; pathetic ⟨result, defeat⟩

Klamauk der; ~s (ugs. abwertend) fuss; (Lärm, Krach) row (coll.)

klamm Adj. (a) (feucht) cold and damp
(b) (steif) numb

Klammer die; ~, ~n (Wäsche~) peg; (Haar~) [hair]grip; (Zahn~) brace; (Büro~) paper clip; (Heft~) staple; (Schriftzeichen) bracket

klammern ⓵ refl. V. **sich an jmdn./etw. ~** (auch fig.) cling to sb./sth.
⓶ tr. V. (a) **eine Wunde ~:** close a wound with a clip/clips

(b) (mit einer Büroklammer) clip; (mit einer Heftmaschine) staple; (mit Wäscheklammern) peg

Klamotten Pl. (salopp) (Kleidung) gear sing. (coll.); (Kram) stuff sing.

Klampfe die; ~, ~n (volkst.: Gitarre) guitar

klang 1. u. 3. Pers. Sg. Prät. v. KLINGEN

Klang der; ~[e]s, **Klänge (a)** (Ton) sound
(b) (~farbe) tone

Klapp-bett das folding bed

Klappe die; ~, ~n (a) [hinged] lid; (am LKW) tailgate; (seitlich) side gate; (am Kombiwagen) back; (am Ofen) [drop-]door
(b) (an Musikinstrumenten) key; (an einer Trompete) valve
(c) (Filmjargon) clapperboard
(d) (salopp: Mund) trap (sl.)

klappen ⓵ tr. V. **nach oben/unten ~:** turn up/down ⟨collar, hat brim⟩; lift up/put down ⟨lid⟩; **nach vorne/hinten ~:** tilt forward/back ⟨seat⟩
⓶ itr. V. (a) ⟨door, shutter⟩ bang
(b) (stoßen) bang
(c) (ugs.: gelingen) work out all right

klapperig Adj. rickety

klappern itr. V. (a) rattle
(b) (ein Klappern erzeugen) make a clatter

Klapper·schlange die rattlesnake

Klapp·fahrrad das folding bicycle

klapprig Adj. rickety

Klapp-: ~**sitz** der tip-up seat; ~**stuhl** der folding chair

Klaps der; ~es, ~e (ugs.) smack; slap

Klaps-mühle die (salopp) loony bin (sl.)

klar ⓵ Adj. (a) clear; straight ⟨question, answer⟩; clear ⟨Dat.⟩ **über etw.** ⟨Dat.⟩ **werden** realize sth.; **jmdm. ~ werden** become clear to sb.; **sich** ⟨Dat.⟩ **über etw.** ⟨Akk.⟩ **im Klaren sein** realize sth.; **etw. ~ machen** (ugs.) make sth. clear
(b) (fertig) ready
⓶ adv. clearly; ~ **sehen** understand the matter

Klär·anlage die sewage treatment plant

Klare der; ~n, ~n schnapps

klären ⓵ tr. V. (a) settle ⟨question, issue, matter⟩; clarify ⟨situation⟩; clear up ⟨case, affair, misunderstanding⟩
(b) (reinigen) purify; treat ⟨effluent, sewage⟩
⓶ refl. V. (a) ⟨situation⟩ become clear; ⟨question, issue, matter⟩ be settled
(b) (rein werden) ⟨liquid, sky⟩ clear; ⟨weather⟩ clear [up]

klar|gehen unr. itr. V.; mit sein (ugs.) go OK (coll.)

Klarheit die; ~: clarity; **sich** ⟨Dat.⟩ **über etw.** ⟨Akk.⟩ ~ **verschaffen** clarify sth.

Klarinette die; ~, ~n clarinet

klar-: ~|**machen** tr. V. (Seemannsspr.) get ready; *~|**sehen** ▶ KLAR 2

klaro Adj., Interj. (ugs.) of course; it goes without saying; ~, **dass** ...: it goes without saying that ...

Klarsicht·folie *die* transparent film

klar|stellen *tr. V.* clear up; clarify

Klar·text *der* (auch DV) clear text; **im** ~**text** (fig.) in plain language

Klärung *die;* ~, ~**en** (a) clarification (b) (Reinigung) purification; (von Abwässern) treatment

*****klar|werden** ▶ KLAR 1A

Klär·werk *das* sewage works *sing. or pl.*

klasse (ugs.) ☐1 *indekl. Adj.* great (coll.) ☐2 *adv.* marvellously

Klasse *die;* ~, ~**n** (a) (Schul~) class; (Raum) classroom; (Stufe) year; grade (Amer.) (b) (Sport) league; (Boxen) division (c) (Fahrzeug~, Boots~, Qualitätsstufe) class; **das ist einsame** *od.* **ganz große** ~! (ugs.) that's [just] great (coll.) *or* marvellous!

klassen-, Klassen-: ~**arbeit** *die* (Schulw.) [written] class test; ~**buch** *das* (Schulw.) *book recording details of pupils' attendance, behaviour, and of topics covered in each lesson;* ≈ [class] register; ~**fahrt** *die* (Schulw.) class outing; ~**gesellschaft** *die* (Soziol.) class society; ~**kampf** *der* (marx.) class struggle; ~**lehrer** *der,* ~**lehrerin** *die* (Schulw.) class teacher; ~**los** *Adj.* (Soziol.) classless; ~**sprecher** *der,* ~**sprecherin** *die* (Schulw.) class spokesman; ~**treffen** *das* (Schulw.) class reunion; ~**ziel** *das* (Schulw.) required standard *(for pupils in a particular class);* ~**zimmer** *das* (Schulw.) classroom

klassifizieren *tr. V.* classify (**als** as)

Klassifizierung *die;* ~, ~**en** classification

Klassik *die;* ~ (a) (Antike) classical antiquity *no art.;* (b) (Zeit kultureller Höchstleistung) classical period

Klassiker *der;* ~**s**, ~, **Klassikerin** *die;* ~, ~**nen** classical writer/composer

klassisch *Adj.* classical; (vollendet, zeitlos; auch iron.) classic

Klassizismus *der;* ~: classicism

Klatsch *der;* ~[e]**s**, ~**e** (a) (ugs. abwertend) gossip (b) (Geräusch) smack

Klatsch·base *die* (ugs. abwertend) gossip

klatschen *itr. V.* (a) *auch mit sein (waves, wet sails)* slap (b) (mit den Händen; applaudieren) clap (c) (schlagen) slap (d) (ugs. abwertend: reden) gossip (**über** + *Akk.* about)

klatschhaft *Adj.* gossipy; fond of gossip *pred.*

klatsch-, Klatsch-: ~**mohn** *der* corn poppy; ~**nass**, *****~**naß** *Adj.* (ugs.) sopping wet; dripping wet *(hair);* ~**spalte** *die* (ugs. abwertend) gossip column

Klaue *die;* ~, ~**n** (a) claw; (von Raubvögeln) talon; (salopp: Hand) mitt (coll.) (b) (salopp abwertend: Schrift) scrawl

klauen (ugs.) ☐1 *tr. V.* pinch (coll.); **jmdm. etw.** ~: pinch sth. from sb. ☐2 *itr. V.* pinch (coll.) things

Klause *die;* ~, ~**n** hermitage; (Klosterzelle) cell

Klausel *die;* ~, ~**n** clause; (Bedingung) condition; (Vorbehalt) proviso

Klausur *die;* ~, ~**en** [examination] paper; (Examen) examination; **eine** ~ **schreiben** take a[n examination] paper/an examination

Klausur-: ~**arbeit** *die* [examination] paper; ~**tagung** *die* private meeting

Klavier /kla'viːɐ̯/ *das;* ~**s**, ~**e** piano

Klebe·folie *die* adhesive film

kleben ☐1 *itr. V.* (a) stick (**an** + *Dat.* to) (b) (ugs.: klebrig sein) be sticky (**von, vor** + *Dat.* with) ☐2 *tr. V.* (a) (befestigen) stick; (mit Klebstoff) glue; **jmdm. eine** ~ (salopp) belt sb. one (coll.) (b) (reparieren) stick *or* glue *(vase etc.)* back together

Kleber *der;* ~**s**, ~: adhesive; glue

klebrig *Adj.* sticky

Kleb-: ~**stoff** *der* adhesive; glue; ~**streifen** *der* adhesive *or* sticky tape

kleckern (ugs.) *itr. V.* make a mess

Klecks *der;* ~**es**, ~**e** (a) stain; (nicht aufgesogen) blob; (Tintenfleck) [ink] blot (b) (ugs.: kleine Menge) spot; (von Senf, Mayonnaise) dab

klecksen *itr. V.* (a) make a stain/stains; (mit Tinte) make a blot/blots; *(pen)* blot (b) (ugs. abwertend: schlecht malen) daub

Klee *der;* ~**s** clover

Klee·blatt *das* cloverleaf

Kleid *das;* ~**es**, ~**er** (a) dress (b) *Pl.* (Kleidung) clothes

kleiden ☐1 *refl. V.* dress ☐2 *tr. V.* (a) dress (b) *(jmdm. stehen)* suit

Kleider-: ~**bügel** *der* clothes hanger; coat hanger; ~**bürste** *die* clothes brush; ~**haken** *der* coat hook; ~**schrank** *der* wardrobe; ~**spende** *die* donation of [second-hand] clothes *or* clothing; ~**ständer** *der* coat stand

kleidsam *Adj.* becoming

Kleidung *die;* ~: clothes *pl.*

Kleidungs·stück *das* garment

klein ☐1 *Adj.* (a) little; small; **er ist** ~**er als ich** he is shorter than me; **etw.** ~ **schneiden** cut sth. into small pieces; **Zwiebeln** ~ **schneiden/hacken** chop up onions [small] (b) (jung) little; **von** ~ **auf** from an early age (c) (von kurzer Dauer) little, short *(while);* short *(walk, break, holiday);* brief *(moment)* (d) (von geringer Menge) small; low *(price);* ~**es Geld haben** have some [small] change (e) (von geringem Ausmaß) small *(party, gift);* scant *(attention);* slight *(cold, indisposition, mistake, irregularity);* minor *(event, error)* ⋯⋗

(f) (unbedeutend) lowly ⟨*employee*⟩; minor ⟨*official*⟩; ~ **anfangen** (ugs.) start off in a small way

[2] *adv.* **die Heizung ~/~er einstellen** turn the heating down low/lower; **ein Wort ~ schreiben** write a word with a small initial letter

klein-, Klein-: ~**aktionär** *der*, ~**aktionärin** *die* (Wirtsch.) small shareholder; ~**anzeige** *die* (Zeitungsw.) small *or* classified advertisement; ~**asien** (*das*) Asia Minor; ~**buchstabe** *der* small letter; ~**bürger** *der*, ~**bürgerin** *die* lower middle-class person; (abwertend: Spießbürger) petit bourgeois; ~**bürgerlich** *Adj.* **(a)** (das Kleinbürgertum betreffend) lower middle-class; **(b)** (abwertend: spießbürgerlich) petit bourgeois

Kleine¹ *der; adj. Dekl.* **(a)** (kleiner Junge) little boy

(b) (ugs. Anrede) little man

Kleine² *die; adj. Dekl.* **(a)** (kleines Mädchen) little girl

(b) (ugs. Anrede) love; (abwertend) little madam

klein-, Klein-: ~**familie** *die* (Soziol.) nuclear family; ~**geld** *das* [small] change; ~**gläubig** *Adj.* sceptical

Kleinigkeit *die;* ~, ~**en** small thing; (Einzelheit) [small] detail; **ich habe noch eine ~ zu erledigen** I still have a small matter to attend to; **eine ~ essen** have a [small] bite to eat; **eine ~ für jmdn. sein** be no trouble for sb.

klein-, Klein-: ~**kind** *das* small child; ~**kram** *der* (ugs.) odds and ends *pl.;* (unbedeutende Dinge) trivial matters *pl.;* ~**kredit** *der* (Bankw.) personal loan (*repayable within two years*); ~|**kriegen** *tr. V.* (ugs.) **(a)** (zerkleinern) crush [to pieces]; **(b)** (zerstören) smash; break; **(c)** (aufbrauchen) get through; **(d)** jmdn. ~**kriegen** get sb. down (coll.); (durch Drohungen) intimidate sb.; (gefügig machen) bring sb. into line; ~**kunst** *die* cabaret; ~**laut** [1] *Adj.* subdued; (verlegen) sheepish; [2] *adv.* in a subdued fashion; (verlegen) sheepishly

kleinlich (abwertend) [1] *Adj.* pernickety; (ohne Großzügigkeit) mean; (engstirnig) small-minded; petty

[2] *adv.* meticulously

Kleinod *das;* ~[e]s, ~e *od.* ~ien (geh.) **(a)** (Schmuckstück) piece of jewellery; (Edelstein) jewel

(b) (Kostbarkeit) gem

klein-, Klein-: ~|**rechnen** *tr. V.* undercalculate; ***~|**schneiden** ▸ KLEIN 1A; ~**stadt** *die* small town; ~**städter** *der,* ~**städterin** *die* small-town dweller

Kleinste *der/die/das; adj. Dekl.* youngest boy/girl/child

klein|stellen *tr. V.* turn down [low]

Klein·wagen *der* small car

**old spelling - see note on page xiv

Kleister *der;* ~**s**, ~: paste

Klementine *die;* ~, ~**n** clementine

Klemme *die;* ~, ~**n** clip; **in der ~ sein** *od.* **sitzen** (ugs.) be in a fix (coll.)

klemmen [1] *tr. V.* **(a)** (befestigen) tuck; stick (coll.)

(b) (quetschen) **sich** (*Dat.*) **den Fuß/die Hand ~:** get one's foot/hand caught *or* trapped

[2] *refl. V.* **sich hinter etw.** (*Akk.*) ~ (fig. ugs.) put some hard work into sth.

[3] *itr. V.* ⟨*door, drawer, etc.*⟩ stick

Klempner *der;* ~**s**, ~, **Klempnerin** *die;* ~, ~**nen** tinsmith; (Installateur[in]) plumber

Kleptomanie *die;* ~ (Psych.) kleptomania *no art.*

klerikal *Adj.* (auch abwertend) clerical; church ⟨*property*⟩

Klerus *der;* ~: clergy

Klette *die;* ~, ~**n** bur; (Pflanze) burdock

klettern *itr. V.; mit sein* (auch fig.) climb; **auf einen Baum ~:** climb a tree

Kletter·pflanze *die* creeper; (Bot.) climbing plant; climber

Klett·verschluss, *Klett·verschluß *der* Velcro ® fastening

klicken *itr. V.* click

Klient *der;* ~**en**, ~**en, Klientin** *die;* ~, ~**nen** client

Klima *das;* ~**s**, ~**s** *od.* **Klimate** climate

Klima-anlage *die* air conditioning *no indef. art.*

klimatisch *Adj.* climatic

klimatisieren *tr. V.* air-condition

Klima-wechsel *der* change of climate

Klimm·zug *der* (Turnen) pull-up

klimpern [1] *itr. V.* jingle

[2] *tr. V.* (ugs. abwertend) plunk out ⟨*tune etc.*⟩

Klinge *die;* ~, ~**n** blade

Klingel *die;* ~, ~**n** bell

Klingel-: ~**beutel** *der* offertory bag; collection bag; ~**knopf** *der* bell push

klingeln *itr. V.* ring; ⟨*alarm clock*⟩ go off; **es klingelt** (an der Tür) there is a ring at the door; (Telefon) the telephone is ringing

klingen *unr. itr. V.* sound; **die Glocken klangen** the bells were ringing

Klinik *die;* ~, ~**en** hospital; (spezialisiert) clinic

Klinke *die;* ~, ~**n** door handle

Klinker *der;* ~**s**, ~: [Dutch] clinker

klipp *Adv.* ~ **und klar** (ugs.) quite plainly

Klippe *die;* ~, ~**n** rock

klirren *itr. V.* clink; ⟨*weapons in fight*⟩ clash; ⟨*window pane*⟩ rattle; ⟨*chains, spurs*⟩ rattle; ⟨*harness*⟩ jingle

Klischee *das;* ~**s**, ~**s** cliché

klitsch-nass, *klitsch-naß *Adj.* (ugs.) sopping wet; (tropfnass) dripping wet

klitze-klein *Adj.* (ugs.) teeny[-weeny] (coll.)

Klo *das;* ~s, ~s (ugs.) loo (Brit. coll.); john (Amer. coll.)

Kloake *die;* ~, ~n cesspit; (Kanal) sewer

klobig *Adj.* heavy and clumsy[-looking] ⟨*shoes, furniture*⟩; bulky ⟨*figure*⟩; (plump) clumsy

Klon *der;* ~s, ~e (Biol.) clone

klonen *tr. V.* clone

Klo-papier *das* (ugs.) loo paper (Brit. coll.); toilet paper

klopfen ⓵ *itr. V.* (a) (schlagen) knock
(b) (pulsieren) ⟨*heart*⟩ beat; ⟨*pulse*⟩ throb
⓶ *tr. V.* beat ⟨*carpet*⟩

Klöppel *der;* ~s, ~ (Glocken~) clapper

klöppeln *tr., itr. V.* [etw.] ~: make [sth. in] pillow lace

Klops *der;* ~es, ~e (nordostd.) meat ball

Klosett *das;* ~s, ~s od. ~e lavatory

Kloß *der;* ~es, **Klöße** dumpling; (Fleisch~) meat ball

Kloster *das;* ~s, **Klöster** (Mönchs~) monastery; (Nonnen~) convent

Klotz *der;* ~es, **Klötze** block [of wood]; (Stück eines Baumstamms) log

Klub *der;* ~s, ~s club

Klub·sessel *der* club chair

Kluft¹ *die;* ~, ~en (ugs.) gear (coll.); (Uniform) garb

Kluft² *die;* ~, **Klüfte** (veralt.) (Spalte) cleft; (im Gletscher) crevasse; (Abgrund) chasm; (fig.) gulf

klug; **klüger, klügst…** *Adj.* clever; bright ⟨*child, pupil*⟩; intelligent ⟨*eyes*⟩; (vernünftig) wise; sound ⟨*advice*⟩; (geschickt) shrewd ⟨*politician, negotiator, question*⟩; astute ⟨*businessman*⟩

Klugheit *die;* ~ ▶ KLUG: cleverness; brightness; intelligence; wisdom; soundness; shrewdness; astuteness

klumpen *itr. V.* go lumpy

Klumpen *der;* ~s, ~: lump; **ein** ~ **Gold** a gold nugget

km *Abk.* = **Kilometer** km.

knabbern ⓵ *tr. V.* nibble
⓶ *itr. V.* **an etw.** (*Dat.*) ~: nibble [at] sth.

Knabe *der;* ~n, ~n (geh. veralt./südd., österr., schweiz.) boy; (ugs.: Bursche) chap (coll.)

knabenhaft ⓵ *Adj.* boyish
⓶ *adv.* boyishly

Knäcke·brot *das* crispbread; (Scheibe) slice of crispbread

knacken ⓵ *itr. V.* (a) ⟨*bed, floor, etc.*⟩ creak
(b) *mit sein* (ugs.: zerbrechen) snap; ⟨*window*⟩ crack
⓶ *tr. V.* (a) crack ⟨*nut, shell*⟩
(b) (salopp: aufbrechen) crack ⟨*safe*⟩ [open]; break into ⟨*car, bank, etc.*⟩

knackig *Adj.* (a) crisp
(b) (ugs.: attraktiv) delectable

Knacks *der;* ~es, ~e (ugs.) crack; (fig.: Defekt) **einen** ~ **bekommen** ⟨*person*⟩ have a breakdown; ⟨*health*⟩ suffer

Knall *der;* ~[e]s, ~e bang

knallen ⓵ *itr. V.* (a) ⟨*shot*⟩ ring out; ⟨*firework*⟩ go bang; ⟨*cork*⟩ pop; ⟨*door*⟩ slam; ⟨*whip, rifle*⟩ crack; **mit der Tür** ~: slam the door
(b) (ugs.: schießen) shoot, fire (**auf** + *Akk.* at)
(c) (Ballspiele ugs.) **aufs Tor** ~: belt the ball/ puck at the goal (coll.)
⓶ *tr. V.* (a) (ugs.) slam down; (werfen) sling (coll.)
(b) (ugs.: schlagen) **jmdm. eine** ~ (salopp) belt sb. one (coll.)

knall-: ~**hart** (ugs.) ⓵ *Adj.* very tough ⟨*demands, measures, etc.*⟩; ⟨*person*⟩ as hard as nails; ⓶ *adv.* brutally; **gegen etw.** ~**hart vorgehen** take very tough action against sth.; ~**rot** *Adj.* bright *or* vivid red; **sie wurde** ~**rot** she turned as red as a beetroot

knapp ⓵ *Adj.* (a) meagre; narrow ⟨*victory, lead*⟩; narrow, bare ⟨*majority*⟩; **die Vorräte wurden** ~: supplies ran short; **vor einer** ~**en Stunde** just under an hour ago
(b) (eng) tight-fitting ⟨*garment*⟩; (zu eng) tight ⟨*garment*⟩
(c) (kurz) terse ⟨*reply, greeting*⟩; succinct ⟨*description, account, report*⟩
⓶ *adv.* (a) ~ **bemessen sein** be meagre, ⟨*time*⟩ be limited; ~ **gewinnen/verlieren** win/ lose narrowly; **er ist** ~ **fünfzig** he is just this side of fifty
(b) (eng) ~ **sitzen** fit tightly; (zu eng) be a tight fit
(c) (kurz) ⟨*reply*⟩ tersely; ⟨*describe, summarize*⟩ succinctly

Knappheit *die;* ~ (a) (Mangel) shortage (**an** + *Dat.* of)
(b) (Kürze) (einer Antwort, eines Grußes) terseness; (einer Beschreibung, eines Berichts) succinctness

Knarre *die;* ~, ~n (salopp: Gewehr) shooting iron (coll.)

knarren *itr. V.* creak

Knast *der;* ~[e]s, **Knäste** od. ~e (ugs.) (a) (Strafe) bird (sl.); time
(b) (Gefängnis) clink (sl.); prison

Knatsch *der;* ~[e]s (ugs.: Ärger) trouble

knattern *itr. V.* clatter; ⟨*sail*⟩ flap; ⟨*radio*⟩ crackle

Knäuel *der od. das;* ~s, ~ ball; (wirres ~) tangle

Knauf *der;* ~[e]s, **Knäufe** knob; (eines Schwertes, Dolches) pommel

knauserig *Adj.* (ugs. abwertend) stingy; tight-fisted

knausern *itr. V.* (ugs. abwertend) be stingy; skimp

knautschen (ugs.) ⓵ *tr. V.* crumple; crease ⟨*dress*⟩
⓶ *itr. V.* ⟨*dress, material*⟩ crease

Knebel *der;* ~s, ~ (a) gag
(b) (Griff) toggle

knebeln *tr. V.* gag

Knecht *der;* ~[e]s, ~e farm labourer

knechten *tr. V.* (geh.) reduce to slavery; enslave; (unterdrücken) oppress

Knechtschaft *die;* ~, ~en (geh.) bondage; slavery

kneifen [1] *unr. tr., itr. V.* pinch
[2] *unr. itr. V.* (a) ‹clothes› be too tight
(b) (ugs.: sich drücken) chicken (coll.) out (**vor** + *Dat.* of)

Kneif·zange *die* pincers *pl.*

Kneipe *die;* ~, ~n (ugs.) pub (Brit. coll.); bar (Amer.)

Kneipen·tour *die* (ugs.) pub crawl

kneippen *itr. V.* (ugs.) take a Kneipp cure

Kneipp·kur *die* Kneipp cure

kneten *tr. V.* (a) (bearbeiten) knead ‹dough, muscles›; work ‹clay›
(b) (formen) model ‹figure›

Knet·masse *die* Plasticine ®

Knick *der;* ~[e]s, ~e sharp bend; (Falz) crease

knicken [1] *tr. V.* (a) (brechen) snap
(b) (falten) crease ‹page, paper, etc.›
[2] *itr. V.; mit sein* snap

knick[e]rig *Adj.* (ugs. abwertend) stingy

Knick[e]rigkeit *die;* ~ (ugs. abwertend) stinginess

Knicks *der;* ~es, ~e curtsy

knicksen *itr. V.* curtsy (**vor** + *Dat.* to)

Knie *das;* ~s, ~ /ˈkniː(ə)/ (a) knee
(b) (Biegung) sharp bend

knie-, Knie-: ~**beuge** *die* knee bend; ~**bund·hose** *die* knee breeches *pl.;* ~**fall** *der:* einen ~**fall tun** *od.* **machen** (auch fig.) go down on one's knees (**vor** + *Dat.* before); ~**kehle** *die* hollow of the knee

knien /ˈkniː(ə)n/ [1] *itr. V.* kneel
[2] *refl. V.* kneel [down]

Knie-: ~**scheibe** *die* kneecap; ~**strumpf** *der* knee-length sock

Kniff *der;* ~[e]s, ~e (a) pinch
(b) (Falte) crease
(c) (Kunstgriff) trick

knipsen *tr. V.* (a) (entwerten) clip; punch
(b) (fotografieren) take a snap[shot] of

Knirps *der;* ~es, ~e ((Ⓦ) *Taschenschirm*) telescopic umbrella
(b) (ugs.: Junge) nipper (coll.)

knirschen *itr. V.* crunch; **mit den Zähnen** ~: grind one's teeth

knistern *itr. V.* rustle; ‹wood, fire› crackle

knittern *tr., itr. V.* crease; crumple

knobeln *itr. V.* (mit Würfeln) play dice

Knob·lauch *der* garlic

Knoblauch·zehe *die* clove of garlic

Knöchel *der;* ~s, ~: ankle; (am Finger) knuckle

Knochen *der;* ~s, ~: bone

knochen-, Knochen-: ~**bau** *der* bone structure; ~**bruch** *der* fracture; ~**hart** *Adj.* (ugs.) rock-hard; ~**mark** *das* bone marrow

knochig *Adj.* bony

Knödel *der;* ~s, ~ (bes. südd., österr.) dumpling

Knöllchen *das;* ~s, ~ (ugs.: Strafzettel) [parking] ticket

Knolle *die;* ~, ~n tuber

Knopf *der;* ~[e]s, Knöpfe button; (Knauf) knob

knöpfen *tr. V.* button [up]

Knopf·loch *das* buttonhole

Knorpel *der;* ~s, ~ (Anat.) cartilage; (im Steak o. Ä.) gristle

knorrig *Adj.* gnarled

Knospe *die;* ~, ~n bud

knospen *itr. V.* bud

knoten *tr. V.* knot

Knoten *der;* ~s, ~: knot; (Haartracht) bun; knot; (Med.) lump

Knoten·punkt *der* junction; intersection

Know-how /noʊˈhaʊ:/ *das;* ~[s] know-how

knuffen *tr. V.* poke

Knüller *der;* ~s, ~ (ugs.) sensation; (Angebot, Verkaufsartikel) sensational offer

knüpfen *tr. V.* (a) tie (**an** + *Akk.* to); **Bedingungen an etw.** (*Akk.*) ~: attach conditions to sth.
(b) (durch Knoten herstellen) knot; make ‹net›

Knüppel *der;* ~s, ~ cudgel; (Polizei~) truncheon

knüppel-, Knüppel-: ~**dick** *Adv.* (ugs.) **es kam** ~**dick** it was one disaster after the other; ~**schaltung** *die* (Kfz-W.) floor[-type] gear change

knurren *itr. V.* (a) ‹animal› growl; (wütend) snarl; (fig.) ‹stomach› rumble
(b) (murren) grumble (**über** + *Akk.* about)

knusprig *Adj.* crisp; crusty ‹bread, roll›

knutschen (ugs.) [1] *tr. V.* smooch with (coll.); (sexuell berühren) pet; **sich** ~: smooch (coll.)/pet
[2] *itr. V.* smooch (coll.); (sich sexuell berühren) pet

k. o. /kaːˈoː/ *Adj.* (a) (Boxen) **jmdn. k. o. schlagen** knock sb. out
(b) (ugs.: übermüdet) all in (coll.)

koalieren *itr. V.* (Politik) form a coalition (**mit** with)

Koalition *die;* ~, ~en coalition

Koax·kabel *das* (Technik Jargon) coax [cable]; coaxial cable

Kobalt *das;* ~s (Chemie) cobalt

Kobold *der;* ~[e]s, ~e goblin

Kobra *die;* ~, ~s cobra

Koch *der;* ~[e]s, Köche cook; (Küchenchef) chef

Koch·buch *das* cookery book (Brit.); cookbook (Amer.)

---

*alte Schreibung - vgl. Hinweis auf S. xiv

kochen [1] *tr. V.* (a) boil; (zubereiten) cook 〈*meal*〉; make 〈*purée, jam*〉; **Tee** ∼: make some tea
(b) (waschen) boil
[2] *itr. V.* (a) (Speisen zubereiten) cook
(b) (sieden) 〈*water, milk, etc.*〉 boil

Kocher *der;* ∼s, ∼ [small] stove; (Kochplatte) hotplate

Köcher *der;* ∼s, ∼ (für Pfeile) quiver

Koch·feld *das* ceramic hob

Köchin *die;* ∼, ∼nen cook

Koch-: ∼**löffel** *der* wooden spoon; ∼**nische** *die* kitchenette; ∼**salz** *das* common salt; ∼**topf** *der* [cooking] pot; ∼**wäsche** *die* washing that is to be boiled

Köder *der;* ∼s, ∼: bait

ködern *tr. V.* lure

Koffein *das;* ∼s caffeine

koffein·frei *Adj.* decaffeinated

Koffer *der;* ∼s, ∼: [suit]case

Koffer-: ∼**kuli** *der* luggage trolley; ∼**radio** *das* portable radio; ∼**raum** *der* boot (Brit.); trunk (Amer.)

Kognak /ˈkɔnjak/ *der;* ∼s, ∼s brandy; *s. auch* COGNAC

Kohl *der;* ∼[e]s (a) cabbage
(b) (ugs. abwertend: Unsinn) rubbish; rot (coll.)

Kohl·dampf *der* (salopp) ∼ **haben** be ravenously hungry

Kohle *die;* ∼, ∼n (a) coal
(b) (salopp: Geld) dough (coll.)

Kohle·hydrat ▶ KOHLENHYDRAT

kohlen[1] *itr. V.* smoulder; 〈*wick*〉 smoke

kohlen[2] *itr. V.* (fam.) (lügen) tell fibs; (übertreiben) exaggerate

Kohlen-: ∼**dioxid**, ∼**dioxyd** /--ʹ---/ *das* (Chemie) carbon dioxide; ∼**grube** *die* coal mine; ∼**händler** *der*, ∼**händlerin** *die* coal merchant; ∼**hydrat** *das* (Chemie) carbohydrate; ∼**monoxid**, ∼**monoxyd** /--ʹ---/ *das* (Chemie) carbon monoxide; ∼**säure** *die* carbonic acid; ∼**stoff** *der* carbon

Kohle·papier *das* carbon paper

Köhler *der;* ∼s, ∼: charcoal burner

Kohle·zeichnung *die* charcoal drawing

Kohl-: ∼**kopf** *der* [head of] cabbage; ∼**rübe** *die* swede

Koitus *der;* ∼, Koitus (geh.) sexual intercourse; coitus (formal)

Koje *die;* ∼, ∼n (a) (Seemannsspr.) bunk; berth
(b) (Ausstellungsstand) stand
(c) (ugs. scherzh.: Bett) bed

Kokain *das;* ∼s cocaine

kokett [1] *Adj.* coquettish
[2] *adv.* coquettishly

kokettieren *itr. V.* mit etw. ∼: make much play with sth.

Kokos·nuss, ***Kokos·nuß *die* coconut

Koks *der;* ∼es coke

Kolben *der;* ∼s, ∼ (a) (Technik) piston

(b) (Chemie: Glas∼) flask
(c) (Teil des Gewehrs) butt

Kolchose /kɔlˈço:zə/ *die;* ∼, ∼n kolkhoz; Soviet collective farm

Kolibri *der;* ∼s, ∼s hummingbird

Kolik *die;* ∼, ∼en colic

Kollaborateur /kɔlaboraˈtø:ɐ̯/ *der;* ∼s, ∼e, **Kollaborateurin** *die;* ∼, ∼nen collaborator

Kollaps *der;* ∼es, ∼e collapse

Kolleg *das;* ∼s, ∼s lecture

Kollege *der;* ∼n, ∼n colleague

kollegial [1] *Adj.* helpful and considerate
[2] *adv.* 〈*act etc.*〉 like a good colleague/good colleagues

Kollegin *die;* ∼, ∼nen colleague

Kollegium *das;* ∼s, Kollegien (a) (Gruppe) group; (unmittelbar zusammenarbeitend) team
(b) (Lehrkörper) [teaching] staff

Kollekte *die;* ∼, ∼n collection

Kollektion *die;* ∼, ∼en collection; (Sortiment) range

kollektiv [1] *Adj.* collective
[2] *adv.* collectively

kollidieren *itr. V.* (a) mit sein collide
(b) (fig.) conflict

Kollier /kɔˈlie:/ *das;* ∼s, ∼s necklace

Kollision *die;* ∼, ∼en collision

Köln (*das*); ∼s Cologne

Kölner [1] *indekl. Adj.* Cologne *attrib.;* (in Köln) in Cologne *postpos., not pred;* 〈*suburb, archbishop, mayor, speciality*〉 of Cologne
[2] *der;* ∼s, ∼: inhabitant of Cologne; (von Geburt) native of Cologne

Kölnerin *die;* ∼, ∼nen ▶ KÖLNER 2

Kolonialisierung *die;* ∼, ∼en colonialization

Kolonialismus *der;* ∼: colonialism *no art.*

Kolonie *die;* ∼, ∼n colony

kolonisieren *tr. V.* colonize

Kolonisierung *die;* ∼, ∼en colonization

Kolonne *die;* ∼, ∼n column

Koloss, ***Koloß *der;* Kolosses, Kolosse (auch fig. ugs.) giant

kolossal [1] *Adj.* (a) colossal; gigantic
(b) (ugs.: sehr groß) tremendous (coll.); incredible (coll.) 〈*rubbish, nonsense*〉
[2] *adv.* (ugs.) tremendously (coll.)

Kolumbianer *der;* ∼s, ∼,
Kolumbianerin *die;* ∼, ∼nen Colombian

Kolumbien /koˈlʊmbiən/ (*das*); ∼s Colombia

Kombination *die;* ∼, ∼en (a) combination
(b) (gedankliche Verknüpfung) deduction; piece of reasoning
(c) (Kleidungsstücke) ensemble; suit; (Herren∼) suit

kombinieren [1] *tr. V.* combine
[2] *itr. V.* deduce; reason

Kombi-: ~**wagen** der estate [car]; station wagon (Amer.); ~**zange** die combination pliers pl.

Komet der; ~en, ~en comet

Komfort /kɔm'foːɐ̯/ der; ~s comfort

komfortabel ① Adj. comfortable ② adv. comfortably

Komik die; ~: comic effect; (komisches Element) comic element

Komiker der; ~s, ~, **Komikerin** die ~, ~en (a) (Vortragskünstler[in]) comedian
(b) (Darsteller[in]) comic actor

komisch Adj. (a) comical; funny
(b) (seltsam) funny

Komitee das; ~s, ~s committee

Komma das; ~s, ~s od. ~ta comma; (Math.) decimal point; **zwei** ~ **acht** two point eight

Kommandant der; ~en, ~en (Milit.) commanding officer

Kommandeur /kɔman'døːɐ̯/ der; ~s, ~e (Milit.) ▶ KOMMANDANT

kommandieren ① tr. V. (a) command; be in command of; order ⟨retreat, advance⟩
(b) (ugs.) jmdn. ~: boss sb. about (coll.) ② itr. V. (ugs.) boss people about (coll.)

Kommandit-gesellschaft die (Wirtsch.) limited partnership

Kommando das; ~s, ~s command

kommen unr. itr. V.; mit sein (a) come; **angelaufen** ~: come running along; (auf jmdn. zu) come running up
(b) (gelangen, geraten) get; **unter ein Auto** ~: be knocked down by a car; **wie kommst du darauf?** what gives you that idea?
(c) ~ **lassen** (bestellen) order ⟨taxi⟩; **den Arzt/ die Polizei** ~ **lassen** send for a doctor/the police
(d) (aufgenommen werden) **zur Schule/aufs Gymnasium** ~: start school/grammar school
(e) (auftauchen) ⟨seeds, plants⟩ come up; ⟨buds, flowers⟩ come out; ⟨teeth⟩ come through
(f) (seinen festen Platz haben) go; belong; **in die Schublade** ~: go or belong in the drawer; (seinen Platz erhalten) **in die Mannschaft** ~: get into the team; **auf den ersten Platz** ~: go into first place
(g) (Gelegenheit haben) **dazu** ~, **etw. zu tun** get round to doing sth.
(h) (sich ereignen) come about; **wie kommt es, dass ...**: how is it that ...; how come that ... (coll.)
(i) (etw. erlangen) **zu Geld** ~: become wealthy; **zu Erfolg/Ruhm** usw. ~: gain success/fame etc.

kommend Adj. (a) (folgend) next; **in den** ~**en Jahren** in years to come
(b) (mit großer Zukunft) **der** ~**e Mann/Meister** the coming man/future champion

Kommentar der; ~s, ~e commentary; (Stellungnahme) comment; **kein** ~! no comment!

Kommentator der; ~s, ~en, **Kommentatorin** die; ~, ~nen commentator

kommentieren tr. V. (a) (erläutern) furnish with a commentary ⟨text, work⟩
(b) (Stellung nehmen zu) comment on

kommerziell ① Adj. commercial ② adv. commercially

Kommiss, *Kommiß der; Kommisses (Soldatenspr.) army

Kommissar der; ~s, ~e, **Kommissarin** die; ~, ~nen (a) (Beamter/ Beamtin der Polizei) detective superintendent
(b) (staatlicher Beauftragter/staatliche Beauftragte) commissioner

Kommission die; ~, ~en (a) (Gremium) committee; (Prüfungs~) commission
(b) etw. **in** ~ **nehmen/haben/geben** (Wirtsch.) take/have sth. on commission/give sth. to a dealer for sale on commission

Kommode die; ~, ~n chest of drawers

kommunal Adj. local; (bei einer städtischen Gemeinde) municipal; local

Kommunal-wahl die local [government] elections pl.

Kommunikation die; ~, ~en (Sprachw., Soziol.) communication

Kommunion die; ~, ~en (kath. Kirche) [Holy] Communion

Kommuniqué /kɔmyni'keː/ das; ~s, ~s communiqué

Kommunismus der; ~: communism

Kommunist der; ~en, ~en, **Kommunistin** die; ~, ~nen communist

kommunistisch ① Adj. communist ② adv. Communist-⟨influenced, led, ruled, etc.⟩

kommunizieren itr. V. (a) (geh.) communicate
(b) (kath. Kirche) receive [Holy] Communion

Komödiant der; ~en, ~en, **Komödiantin** die; ~, ~nen (veralt.) actor/ actress; player; (abwertend: Heuchler[in]) play-actor

Komödie /ko'møːdiə/ die; ~, ~n comedy; (Theater) comedy theatre

Kompagnon /kɔmpan'jõ:/ der; ~s, ~s (Wirtsch.) partner; associate

kompakt Adj. solid

Kompanie die; ~, ~n company

Komparativ der; ~s, ~e (Sprachw.) comparative

Kompass, *Kompaß der; Kompasses, Kompasse compass

kompatibel Adj. (Nachrichtenw., Sprachw.) compatible

Kompatibilität die; ~, ~en compatibility

Kompensation die; ~, ~en (Wirtsch., Physik, geh.) compensation

kompensieren tr. V. etw. mit etw. od. durch etw. ~: compensate for sth. by sth.

kompetent Adj. competent

Kompetenz *die;* ~, ~en competence; (bes. Rechtsw.) authority

komplett ⟨1⟩ *Adj.* complete
⟨2⟩ *adv.* fully ⟨*furnished, equipped*⟩; (ugs.: ganz und gar) completely

komplettieren *tr. V.* complete

Komplett-preis *der* all-inclusive price

komplex *Adj.* complex

Komplex *der;* ~es, ~e (auch Psych.) complex

Komplexität *die;* ~: complexity

Komplikation *die;* ~, ~en (auch Med.) complication

Kompliment *das;* ~[e]s, ~e compliment

Komplize *der;* ~n, ~n (abwertend) accomplice

komplizieren *tr. V.* complicate

kompliziert ⟨1⟩ *Adj.* complicated
⟨2⟩ *adv.* ~ aufgebaut sein have a complicated or complex structure

Kompliziertheit *die;* ~: complexity; complicatedness

Komplizin *die;* ~, ~nen ▶ KOMPLIZE

Komplott *das;* ~[e]s, ~e plot; conspiracy

komponieren *tr., itr. V.* compose

Komponist *der;* ~en, ~en,
  Komponistin *die;* ~, ~nen composer

Komposition *die;* ~, ~en composition

Kompost *der;* ~[e]s, ~e, compost

Kompost-haufen *der* compost heap

kompostierbar *Adj.* compostable

kompostieren *tr. V.* compost

Kompott *das;* ~[e]s, ~e stewed fruit; compote

Kompresse *die;* ~, ~n (Med.) **(a)** (Umschlag) [wet] compress
(b) (Mull) [gauze] pad

Kompression *die;* ~, ~en (Physik, Technik, Med., DV) compression

Kompressor *der;* ~s, ~en (Technik) compressor

komprimieren *tr. V.* (auch Physik, Technik, DV) compress

Kompromiss, *Kompromiß *der;* Kompromisses, Kompromisse compromise

**kompromiss-, *kompromiß-,
  Kompromiss-, *Kompromiß-:**
  ~bereit *Adj.* willing to compromise *pred.;*
  ~los ⟨1⟩ *Adj.* uncompromising; ⟨2⟩ *adv.*
  uncompromisingly; ~vorschlag *der*
  compromise proposal

kompromittieren *tr. V.* compromise

Kondensation *die;* ~, ~en (Physik, Chemie) condensation

Kondensator *der;* ~s, ~en (Elektrot.) capacitor

kondensieren *tr., itr. V.* (*itr. auch mit sein*) (Physik, Chemie) condense

Kondens-: ~milch *die* condensed milk;
  ~streifen *der* condensation trail;
  ~wasser *das* condensation

Kondition *die;* ~, ~en condition; **eine gute/schlechte** ~ **haben** be/not be in good condition *or* shape; **keine** ~ **haben** be out of condition; (fig.) have no stamina

Konditional-satz *der* (Sprachw.) conditional clause

Konditions-training *das* fitness training

Konditor *der;* ~s, ~en pastry cook

Konditorei *die;* ~, ~en cake shop; (Lokal) café

kondolieren *itr. V.* offer one's condolences; **jmdm. [zu jmds. Tod]** ~: offer one's condolences to sb. [on sb.'s death]

Kondom *das od. der;* ~s, ~e condom

Konfekt *das;* ~[e]s **(a)** confectionery; sweets *pl.* (Brit.); candies *pl.* (Amer.)
(b) (bes. südd., österr., schweiz.: Teegebäck) [small] fancy biscuits *pl.* (Brit.) *or* (Amer.) cookies *pl.*

Konfektion *die;* ~, ~en ready-made garments *pl.*

Konferenz *die;* ~, ~en conference; (Besprechung) meeting

konferieren *itr. V.* confer (über + Akk. on, about)

Konfession *die;* ~, ~en denomination

konfessionell ⟨1⟩ *Adj.* denominational
⟨2⟩ *adv.* as regards denomination; ~
[un]gebunden sein have [no] denominational ties

Konfetti *das;* ~[s] confetti

Konfirmand *der;* ~en, ~en,
  Konfirmandin *die;* ~, ~nen (ev. Rel.) confirmand

Konfirmation *die;* ~, ~en (ev. Rel.) confirmation

konfirmieren *tr. V.* (ev. Rel.) confirm

konfiszieren *tr. V.* (bes. Rechtsw.) confiscate

Konfitüre *die;* ~, ~n jam

Konflikt *der;* ~[e]s, ~e conflict

Konföderation *die;* ~, ~en confederation

konform *Adj.* concurring *attrib.;* ~ gehen be in agreement

Konformismus *der;* ~: conformism

Konformist *der;* ~en, ~en,
  Konformistin *die;* ~, ~: conformist

konformistisch ⟨1⟩ *Adj.* conformist
⟨2⟩ *adv.* in a conformist way

Konfrontation *die;* ~, ~en confrontation

konfrontieren *tr. V.* confront

konfus ⟨1⟩ *Adj.* confused
⟨2⟩ *adv.* in a confused fashion

Kongo[1] *der;* ~[s] (Fluss) Congo

Kongo[2] *(das);* ~s *od. der;* ~[s] (Staat) the Congo

Kongress, *Kongreß *der;* Kongresses, Kongresse congress; conference; **der** ~ (USA) Congress

Kongress-halle, *Kongreß-halle *die* conference hall

k

König *der;* ~s, ~e king
Königin *die;* ~, ~nen queen
königlich [1] *Adj.* **(a)** royal
(b) (vornehm) regal
(c) (reichlich) princely ⟨*gift, salary, wage*⟩
[2] *adv.* ⟨*pay*⟩ handsomely; (ugs.:
außerordentlich) ⟨*enjoy oneself*⟩ immensely (coll.)
König-reich *das* kingdom
Königs-haus *das* royal house
Königtum *das;* ~s, Königtümer **(a)**
(Monarchie) monarchy
(b) (veralt.: Reich) kingdom
Konjugation *die;* ~, ~en (Sprachw.)
conjugation
konjugieren *tr. V.* (Sprachw.) conjugate
Konjunktion *die;* ~, ~en (Sprachw.)
conjunction
Konjunktiv *der;* ~s, ~e (Sprachw.)
subjunctive
Konjunktur *die;* ~, ~en (Wirtsch.) **(a)**
(wirtschaftliche Lage) [level of] economic
activity; economy; (Tendenz) economic trend
(b) (Hoch~) boom; (Aufschwung) upturn [in the
economy]
konjunkturell *Adj.* economic
Konjunktur-politik *die* (Wirtsch.) measures
pl. aimed at avoiding violent fluctuations in
the economy
konkav (Optik) [1] *Adj.* concave
[2] *adv.* concavely
konkret [1] *Adj.* concrete
[2] *adv.* in concrete terms
konkretisieren *tr. V.* etw. ~: put sth. in
concrete terms
Konkurrent *der;* ~en, ~en,
Konkurrentin *die;* ~, ~nen (Sport,
Wirtsch.) competitor
Konkurrenz *die;* ~, ~en (Sport, Wirtsch.)
competition
konkurrenz-, Konkurrenz-: ~**fähig**
Adj. competitive; ~**kampf** *der* competition;
(zwischen zwei Menschen) rivalry
konkurrieren *itr. V.* compete
Konkurs *der;* ~es, ~e **(a)** (Bankrott)
bankruptcy; ~ machen *od.* in ~ gehen go
bankrupt
(b) (gerichtliches Verfahren) bankruptcy
proceedings *pl.*
können [1] *unr. Modalverb; 2. Part.* können:
(a) be able to; **er kann gut reden/tanzen** he is
a good talker/dancer; **ich kann nicht schlafen**
I cannot *or* (coll.) can't sleep; **kann das
explodieren?** could it explode?; **man kann nie
wissen** you never know; **es kann sein, dass
...**: it could be that ...; **kann ich Ihnen helfen?**
can I help you?
(b) (Grund haben) **du kannst ganz ruhig sein**
you don't have to worry; **das kann man wohl
sagen!** you could well say that
(c) (dürfen) **kann ich gehen?** can I go?; ~ **wir
mit[kommen]?** can we come too?

[2] *unr. tr. V.* (beherrschen) know ⟨*language*⟩;
be able to play ⟨*game*⟩; **sie kann das [gut]**
she can do that [well]; **etw./nichts für etw.** ~:
be/not be responsible for sth.
[3] *unr. itr. V.* **(a)** (fähig sein) **er kann nicht
anders** there's nothing else he can do; (es ist
seine Art) he can't help it (coll.)
(b) (Zeit haben) **ich kann heute nicht** I can't
today (coll.)
(c) (ugs.: Kraft haben) **kannst du noch [weiter]?**
can you go on?
(d) (ugs.: umgehen ~) **[gut] mit jmdm.** ~: get
on [well] with sb.
Können *das;* ~s ability
Könner *der;* ~s, ~, **Könnerin** *die;* ~,
~nen expert
konnte *1. u. 3. Pers. Sg. Prät. v.* KÖNNEN
könnte *1. u. 3. Pers. Sg. Konjunktiv II v.*
KÖNNEN
Konsens-gespräch *das* (Politik)
discussion aimed at reaching a consensus
konsequent [1] *Adj.* consistent; (folgerichtig)
logical
[2] *adv.* consistently; (folgerichtig) logically
Konsequenz *die;* ~, ~en **(a)** (Folge)
consequence
(b) (Unbeirrbarkeit) determination
konservativ [1] *Adj.* conservative
[2] *adv.* conservatively
Konservative *der/die; adj. Dekl.*
conservative
Konservatorium *das;* ~s, Konservatorien
conservatoire; conservatory (Amer.)
Konserve *die;* ~, ~n **(a)** (Büchse) can; tin
(Brit.)
(b) (konservierte Lebensmittel) preserved food; (in
Dosen) canned *or* (Brit.) tinned food
Konserven-: ~**büchse** *die,* ~**dose** *die*
can; tin (Brit.)
konservieren *tr. V.* preserve; conserve
⟨*work of art*⟩
Konservierung *die;* ~, ~en preservation
Konservierungs-mittel *das*
preservative
konsolidieren *tr. V.* consolidate
Konsolidierung *die;* ~, ~en (Festigung)
consolidation
Konsonant *der;* ~en, ~en consonant
Konsortium *das;* ~s, Konsortien (Wirtsch.)
consortium
konspirativ /kɔnspiraˈtiːf/ *Adj.*
conspiratorial
konstant /kɔnˈstant/ [1] *Adj.* **(a)** constant
(b) (beharrlich) persistent
[2] *adv.* **(a)** constantly
(b) (beharrlich) persistently
Konstellation /kɔnstɛlaˈtsi̯oːn/ *die;* ~,
~en **(a)** (von Parteien usw.) grouping; (von
Umständen) combination
(b) (Astron., Astrol.) constellation
konstituieren /kɔnstituˈiːrən/ [1] *tr. V.*
(gründen) constitute; set up
[2] *refl. V.* be constituted

---

*alte Schreibung - vgl. Hinweis auf S. xiv

Konstitution /kɔnstitu'tsːjoːn/ *die;* ∼,
∼en constitution
konstruieren /kɔnstru'iːrən/ *tr. V.* (a)
(entwerfen) design
(b) (aufbauen, Geom. Sprachw.) construct
(c) (abwertend) fabricate
Konstrukteur /kɔnstrʊk'tøːɐ̯/ *der;* ∼s,
∼e, **Konstrukteurin** *die;* ∼, ∼nen
designer; design engineer
Konstruktion /kɔnstrʊk'tsjoːn/ *die;* ∼,
∼en (a) (Aufbau, Geom., Sprachw.)
construction; (das Entwerfen) designing
(b) (Entwurf) design; (Bau) construction
konstruktiv [1] *Adj.* constructive
[2] *adv.* constructively
Konsul *der;* ∼s, ∼n (Dipl., hist.) consul
Konsulat *das;* ∼[e]s, ∼e (Dipl., hist.)
consulate
Konsulin *die;* ∼, ∼nen ▶ KONSUL
konsultieren *tr. V.* (auch fig.) consult
Konsum *der;* ∼s consumption
Konsument *der;* ∼en, ∼en,
Konsumentin *die;* ∼, ∼nen consumer
Konsum·gesellschaft *die* consumer
society
konsumieren *tr. V.* consume
Kontakt *der;* ∼[e]s, ∼e contact; **mit** *od.*
jmdm. ∼ **haben/halten** be/remain in contact
with sb.
kontakt-, Kontakt-: ∼**freudig** *Adj.*
sociable; ∼**linse** *die* contact lens; ∼**mann**
der; Pl.: ∼**männer** *od.* ∼**leute** (Agent) contact;
∼**person** *die* (Med.) contact
Kontamination *die;* ∼, ∼en
contamination
kontaminieren *tr. V.* contaminate
Konten ▶ KONTO
kontern *tr., itr. V.* (Boxen, auch fig.) counter;
(Ballspiele) counter-attack
Konter·revolution *die* counter-
revolution
Kontinent *der;* ∼[e]s, ∼e continent
kontinental *Adj.* continental
Kontingent *das;* ∼[e]s, ∼e quota
kontinuierlich [1] *Adj.* steady
[2] *adv.* steadily
Kontinuität *die;* ∼: continuity
Konto *das;* ∼s, Konten *od.* Konti account;
ein laufendes ∼: a current account
Konto-: ∼**auszug** *der* (Bankw.) [bank]
statement; ∼**bewegung** *die* transaction;
∼**nummer** *die* account number
Kontor *das;* ∼s, ∼e branch; (einer Reederei)
office
Konto·stand *der* (Bankw.) balance; state of
an/one's account
kontra [1] *Präp. mit Akk.* (Rechtsspr., auch
fig.) versus
[2] *Adv.* against
Kontra *das;* ∼s, ∼s (Kartenspiele) double;
jmdm. ∼ **geben** (fig. ugs.) flatly contradict sb.

Kontrahent *der;* ∼en, ∼en,
Kontrahentin *die;* ∼, ∼nen adversary;
opponent
konträr *Adj.* contrary; opposite
Kontrast *der;* ∼[e]s, ∼e contrast
Kontroll·abschnitt *der* stub
Kontrolle *die;* ∼, ∼n (a) (Überwachung)
surveillance
(b) (Überprüfung) check; (bei Waren, bei
Lebensmitteln) inspection
(c) (Herrschaft) control; **die** ∼ **über etw.** (Akk.)
verlieren lose control of sth.
Kontrolleur /kɔntrɔ'løːɐ̯/ *der;* ∼s, ∼e,
Kontrolleurin *die;* ∼, ∼nen inspector
Kontroll·gang *der* tour of inspection;
(eines Nachtwächters) round; (eines Polizisten)
patrol
kontrollieren *tr. V.* (a) (überwachen) check;
monitor
(b) (überprüfen) check; inspect ⟨goods, food⟩
(c) (beherrschen) control
Kontrollturm *der* control tower
kontrovers [1] *Adj.* conflicting; (strittig)
controversial
[2] *adv.* **sich** ∼ **zu etw. äußern** express
conflicting opinions on sth.
Kontroverse /kɔntro'vɛrzə/ *die;* ∼, ∼n
controversy (um, über + Akk. about)
Kontur *die;* ∼, ∼en contour; outline
Konvention /kɔnvɛn'tsjoːn/ *die;* ∼, ∼en
convention
konventionell [1] *Adj.* (a) conventional
(b) (förmlich) formal
[2] *adv.* (a) conventionally
(b) (förmlich) formally
Konversation /kɔnvɛrza'tsjoːn/ *die;* ∼,
∼en conversation
Konversations·lexikon *das*
encyclopaedia
konvertieren [1] *itr. V.; auch mit sein*
(Rel.) be converted
[2] *tr. V.* (Wirtsch., DV) convert
konvex /kɔn'vɛks/ (Optik) [1] *Adj.* convex
[2] *adv.* convexly
Konvoi /kɔn'vɔy/ *der;* ∼s, ∼s (bes. Milit.)
convoy
Konzentration *die;* ∼, ∼en
concentration
Konzentrations-: ∼**fähigkeit** *die*
ability to concentrate; ∼**lager** *das* (bes. ns.)
concentration camp
konzentrieren *refl., tr. V.* concentrate;
sich auf etw. (Akk.) ∼: concentrate on sth.
konzentriert [1] *Adj.* concentrated
[2] *adv.* with concentration
Konzept *das;* ∼[e]s, ∼e (a) [rough] draft
(b) (Programm) programme; (Plan) plan
Konzern *der;* ∼[e]s, ∼e (Wirtsch.) group [of
companies]
Konzert *das;* ∼[e]s, ∼e (a) (Komposition)
concerto
(b) (Veranstaltung) concert

k

Konzert·saal der concert hall

Konzession die; ~, ~en (a) (Amtsspr.) licence

(b) (Zugeständnis) concession

Konzil das; ~s, ~e od. ~ien (kath. Kirche) council

konzipieren tr. V. draft; design ⟨device, car, etc.⟩

Kooperation die; ~, ~en cooperation no indef. art.

kooperativ [1] Adj. cooperative
[2] adv. cooperatively

kooperieren tr. V. cooperate

Koordinate die; ~, ~n coordinate

Koordinaten·system das (Math.) system of coordinates

koordinieren tr. V. coordinate

Kopenhagen (das); ~s Copenhagen

Kopf der; ~[e]s, Köpfe (a) head; ein ~ Salat a lettuce; ~ an ~: shoulder to shoulder; (im Wettlauf) neck and neck; (fig.) ~ stehen (ugs.: überrascht sein) be bowled over; nicht wissen, wo einem der ~ steht not know whether one is coming or going; ~ hoch! chin up!; den ~ hängen lassen become disheartened
(b) (Person) person; ein kluger/fähiger ~ sein be a clever/able man/woman; pro ~: per head; die führenden Köpfe der Wirtschaft the leading minds in the field of economics
(c) (Wille) seinen ~ durchsetzen make sb. do what one wants
(d) (Verstand) mind; head; sich (Dat.) den ~ zerbrechen (ugs.) rack one's brains (über + Akk. over)

Kopf-: ~bahnhof der terminal station; ~bedeckung die headgear; ohne ~bedeckung without anything on one's head

Köpfchen das; ~s, ~: brains pl.; ~ muss man haben you've got to have it up here (coll.)

köpfen tr. V. (a) decapitate; (hinrichten) behead
(b) (Fußball) head

kopf-, Kopf-: ~ende das head end; ~haut die [skin of the] scalp; ~hörer der headphones pl.; ~kissen das pillow; ~lastig Adj. down by the head pred.; ~los [1] Adj. rash; (in Panik) panic-stricken; [2] adv. rashly; ~los davonrennen flee in panic; ~rechnen itr. V.; nur im Inf. gebr. do mental arithmetic; ~rechnen das mental arithmetic; ~salat der head lettuce; ~schmerz der headache; ~schmerzen haben have a headache sing.; ~sprung der header; ~stand der headstand; *~|stehen ▶ KOPF A; ~stein·pflaster das cobblestones pl.; ~tuch das; Pl. ~tücher headscarf; ~weh das (ugs.) headache; ~weh haben have a headache; ~zerbrechen das; ~s: etw. bereitet od.

macht jmdm. ~zerbrechen sb. has to rack his/her brains about sth.; (etw. macht jmdm. Sorgen) sth. is a worry to sb.

Kopie die; ~, ~n copy; (Durchschrift) carbon copy; (Fotokopie) photocopy; (Fot., Film) print

kopieren tr. V. copy; (fotokopieren) photocopy; (Fot., Film) print

Kopierer der; ~s, ~: [photo]copier

Kopier·gerät das photocopier

Kopilot der; ~en, ~en, **Kopilotin** die; ~, ~nen (Flugw.) co-pilot

Koppel¹ das; ~s, ~, österr.: die; ~, ~n (Gürtel) [leather] belt (as part of a uniform)

Koppel² die; ~, ~n paddock

koppeln tr. V. couple (an + Akk. to); dock ⟨spacecraft⟩

Koppelung ▶ KOPPLUNG

Kopplung die; ~, ~en coupling; (Raumf.) docking

kopulieren itr. V. copulate

Koralle die; ~, ~n coral

Koran der; ~s, ~e Koran

Korb der; ~es, Körbe (a) basket
(b) jmdm. einen ~ geben turn sb. down

Korb·ball der netball

Kord der; ~[e]s (a) corduroy; cord
(b) ▶ KORDSAMT

Kordel die; ~, ~n cord

Kord·samt der cord velvet

Korea (das); ~s Korea

Koreaner der; ~s, ~, **Koreanerin** die; ~, ~nen Korean

koreanisch Adj. Korean

Korinthe die; ~, ~n currant

Kork der; ~s, ~e cork

Korken der; ~s, ~: cork

Korken·zieher der; ~s, ~: corkscrew

Korn¹ das; ~[e]s, Körner (a) (Frucht) grain; (Getreide~) grain [of corn]; (Pfeffer~) corn
(b) o. Pl. (Getreide) corn; grain
(c) (Salz~, Sand~) grain; (Hagel~) stone

Korn² der; ~[e]s, ~ (ugs.) corn schnapps; corn liquor (Amer.)

Korn·blume die cornflower

Körnchen das; ~s, ~: tiny grain; (von Sand usw.) [tiny] grain; granule

Körner ▶ KORN

Korn·feld das cornfield

körnig Adj. granular

Korona die; ~, Koronen crowd (coll.)

Körper der; ~s, ~: body

körper-, Körper-: ~bau der physique; ~behindert Adj. physically handicapped; ~behinderte der/die physically handicapped person; ~behinderte Pl. physically handicapped people; ~geruch der body odour; BO (coll.); ~größe die height

körperlich [1] Adj. physical
[2] adv. physically

Körper·pflege die body care no art.

---

*old spelling - see note on page xiv

Körperschaft[s]·steuer *die* (Steuerw.) corporation tax

Körper-: ~spray *der od. das* deodorant spray; **~teil** *der* part of the/one's body; **~verletzung** *die* (Rechtsw.) bodily harm *no indef. art.*

Korps /koːɐ̯/ *das;* ~ /koːɐ̯(s),/ ~ /koːɐ̯s/ **(a)** (Milit.) corps
(b) (Studentenverbindung) student duelling society

korpulent *Adj.* corpulent

korrekt [1] *Adj.* correct
[2] *adv.* correctly

korrekter·weise *Adv.* to be [strictly] correct

Korrektheit *die;* ~: correctness

Korrektor *der;* ~s, ~en /-'toːrən/, **Korrektorin** *die;* ~, ~nen proof-reader

Korrektur *die;* ~, ~en correction

Korrespondent *der;* ~en, ~en, **Korrespondentin** *die;* ~, ~nen correspondent

Korrespondenz *die;* ~, ~en correspondence

korrespondieren *itr. V.* correspond (mit with)

Korridor *der;* ~s, ~e corridor

korrigieren *tr. V.* correct; revise ⟨opinion, view⟩

korrodieren *tr., itr. V.* (itr. mit sein) (bes. Chemie, Geol.) corrode

Korrosion *die;* ~, ~en (auch Geol., Med.) corrosion

korrosions-, Korrosions-: ~beständig *Adj.,* ~fest *Adj.* corrosion-resistant; **~schutz** *der* protection against corrosion

korrupt *Adj.* corrupt

Korruption *die;* ~, ~en corruption

Korsett *das;* ~s, ~s od. ~e corset

Korsika (*das*) ~s Corsica

Kortison *das;* ~s (Med.) cortisone

koscher *Adj.* kosher

Kose-: ~form *die* familiar form; **~name** *der* pet name

Kosinus *der;* ~, ~ od. ~se (Math.) cosine

Kosmetik *die;* ~ **(a)** beauty culture *no art.;*
(b) (fig.) cosmetic procedures *pl.*

Kosmetikerin *die;* ~, ~nen cosmetician; beautician

Kosmetikum *das;* ~s, Kosmetika cosmetic

kosmetisch [1] *Adj.* (auch fig.) cosmetic
[2] *adv.* jmdn. ~ beraten give sb. advice on beauty care; **sich ~ behandeln lassen** have beauty treatment

kosmisch *Adj.* cosmic ⟨ray, dust, etc.⟩; space ⟨age, station, research, etc.⟩; meteoric ⟨iron⟩

Kosmos *der;* ~: cosmos

Kost *die;* ~: food; ~ **und Logis** board and lodging

kostbar [1] *Adj.* valuable; precious ⟨time⟩
[2] *adv.* expensively ⟨dressed⟩; luxuriously ⟨decorated⟩

Kostbarkeit *die;* ~, ~en **(a)** (Sache) treasure
(b) (Eigenschaft) value

kosten¹ [1] *tr. V.* taste; try
[2] *itr. V.* (probieren) have a taste

kosten² *tr. V.* **(a)** cost
(b) (erfordern) take; cost ⟨lives⟩

Kosten *Pl.* cost *sing.;* costs; (Auslagen) expenses; (Rechtsw.) costs; **auf jmds. ~:** at sb.'s expense

kosten-, Kosten-: ~deckend *Adj.* that covers/cover [one's] costs *postpos., not pred.;* **~erstattung** *die* reimbursement of costs; **~los** [1] *Adj.* free; [2] *adv.* free of charge; **~pflichtig** (Rechtsw.) [1] *Adj.* eine ~pflichtige Verwarnung a fine and a caution; [2] *adv.* eine Klage ~pflichtig abweisen dismiss a case with costs; **ein Auto ~pflichtig abschleppen** tow a car away at the owner's expense; **~punkt** *der* (ugs.) **~punkt?** how much is it/are they?; **~punkt 25 DM** it costs/they cost 25 marks; **~stelle** *die* (Wirtsch.) cost centre; **~vor·anschlag** *der* estimate

Kost·gänger *der;* ~s, ~, **Kost·gängerin** *die;* ~, ~nen (veralt.) boarder

köstlich [1] *Adj.* delicious; (unterhaltsam) delightful
[2] *adv.* ⟨taste⟩ delicious; **sich ~ amüsieren/unterhalten** enjoy oneself enormously (coll.)

Köstlichkeit *die;* ~, ~en (Sache) delicacy

Kost·probe *die;* ~, ~n taste

kost·spielig *Adj.* costly

Kostüm *das;* ~s, ~e **(a)** suit
(b) (Theater~, Verkleidung) costume

kostümieren *tr. V.* dress up

Kot *der;* ~[e]s, ~e excrement

Kotangens *der;* ~, ~ (Math.) cotangent

Kotelett /kɔt'lɛt/ *das;* ~s, ~s chop; (vom Nacken) cutlet

Koteletten *Pl.* side whiskers

Köter *der;* ~s, ~ (abwertend) cur

Kot·flügel *der* (Kfz-W.) wing

kotzen *itr. V.* (derb) puke (coarse)

KP *Abk.* = **Kommunistische Partei** CP

Krabbe *die;* ~, ~n (a) (Zool.) crab
(b) (ugs.: Garnele) shrimp; (größer) prawn

krabbeln [1] *itr. V.; mit sein* crawl
[2] *tr. V.* (ugs.: kraulen) tickle

Krach *der;* ~[e]s, Kräche **(a)** (Lärm) noise; row
(b) (lautes Geräusch) crash
(c) (ugs.: Streit) row

krachen [1] *itr. V.* **(a)** (Krach auslösen) ⟨thunder⟩ crash; ⟨shot⟩ ring out ⋯⟩

(b) *mit sein* (ugs.: bersten) ⟨*ice*⟩ crack; ⟨*bed*⟩ collapse
(c) *mit sein* (ugs.: mit Krach auftreffen) crash
2 *refl. V.* (ugs.) row (coll.)

krächzen *itr. V.* ⟨*raven, crow*⟩ caw; ⟨*parrot*⟩ squawk; ⟨*person*⟩ croak

kraft *Präp. + Gen.* (Amtsspr.) ~ **[meines]** Amtes by virtue of my office; ~ **Gesetzes** by law

Kraft *die;* ~, Kräfte strength; (Wirksamkeit) power; (Physik) force; (Arbeits~) employee; **mit letzter** ~: with one's last ounce of strength; **aus eigener** ~: by one's own efforts; **mit vereinten Kräften werden wir …**: if we join forces *or* combine our efforts we will …; **außer** ~ **setzen** repeal ⟨*law*⟩; countermand ⟨*order*⟩; **außer** ~ **sein/treten** no longer be/cease to be in force; **in** ~ **treten/sein/bleiben** come into/be in/remain in force

Kraft-: ~**aufwand** *der* effort; ~**brühe** *die* strong meat broth; ~**fahrer** *der,* ~**fahrerin** *die* driver; motorist;

Kraft·fahrzeug *das* motor vehicle

Kraftfahrzeug-: ~**brief** *der* vehicle registration document; logbook (Brit.); ~**schein** *der* vehicle registration document; ~**steuer** *die* vehicle tax

kräftig **1** *Adj.* strong; vigorous ⟨*plant, shoot*⟩; powerful, hefty ⟨*blow, kick, etc.*⟩; nourishing ⟨*soup, bread, meal, etc.*⟩ **2** *adv.* powerfully ⟨*built*⟩; ⟨*rain, snow*⟩ heavily; ⟨*eat*⟩ heartily

kräftigen *tr. V.* ⟨*holiday, air, etc.*⟩ invigorate; ⟨*food etc.*⟩ fortify

kraft-, Kraft-: ~**meier** *der;* ~~s, ~~ (ugs.: abwertend) muscleman; ~**probe** *die* trial of strength; ~**rad** *das* (Amtsspr.) motorcycle; ~**stoff** *der* (Kfz-W.) fuel; ~**stoff-verbrauch** *der* fuel consumption; ~**voll** **1** *Adj.* powerful; **2** *adv.* powerfully; ~**wagen** *der* motor vehicle; ~**werk** *das* power station

Kragen *der;* ~s, ~, (südd., österr. u. schweiz. auch:) Krägen collar

Kragen-weite *die* collar size

Krähe /ˈkrɛːə/ *die;* ~, ~n crow

krähen *itr. V.* (auch fig.) crow

Krähen·füße *Pl.* (ugs.) crow's feet

krakeelen *itr. V.* (ugs.) kick up a row (coll.)

krakeln *tr., itr. V.* (ugs.) scrawl

kraklig *Adj.* (ugs. abwertend) scrawly

Kralle *die;* ~, ~n claw

krallen **1** *refl. V.* sich an etw. (Akk.) ~ ⟨*cat*⟩ dig its claws into sth.; ⟨*person*⟩ clutch sth. [tightly]
2 *tr. V.* (fest greifen) **die Finger in/um etw.** (Akk.) ~: dig one's fingers into sth./clutch sth. [tightly] with one's fingers

Kram *der;* ~[e]s (ugs.) **(a)** stuff; (Gerümpel) junk
(b) (Angelegenheit) affair

kramen **1** *itr. V.* in etw. (Dat.) ~: rummage about in sth.
2 *tr. V.* (ugs.) etw. aus etw. ~: fish (coll.) sth. out of sth.

Krämer *der;* ~s, ~, **Krämerin** *die;* ~, ~nen grocer

Kram·laden *der* (ugs. abwertend) junk shop

Krampf *der;* ~[e]s, Krämpfe **(a)** cramp; (Zuckung) spasm
(b) painful strain; (sinnloses Tun) senseless waste of effort

Krampf·ader *die* varicose vein

krampfhaft **1** *Adj.* convulsive; (verbissen) desperate
2 *adv.* convulsively; (verbissen) desperately

Kran *der;* ~[e]s, Kräne **(a)** crane
(b) (südwestd.: Wasserhahn) tap; faucet (Amer.)

Kranich *der;* ~s, ~e crane

krank; kränker, kränkst… *Adj.* ill *usu. pred.;* sick; bad ⟨*leg, tooth*⟩; diseased ⟨*plant, organ*⟩; (fig.) ailing ⟨*economy, business*⟩; ~ **werden** be taken ill

Kranke *der/die; adj. Dekl.* sick man/woman; (Patient) patient

kränkeln *itr. V.* be in poor health

kränken *tr. V.* jmdn. ~: hurt sb. *or* sb.'s feelings

Kranken-: ~**geld** *das* sickness benefit; ~**gymnastik** *die* remedial *or* medical gymnastics *sing.;* physiotherapy; ~**gymnastin** *die;* ~~, ~~nen remedial gymnast; medical gymnast; physiotherapist; ~**haus** *das* hospital; ~**kasse** *die* health insurance scheme; (Körperschaft) health insurance institution; (privat) health insurance company; ~**pfleger** *der* male nurse; ~**schein** *der* health insurance certificate; ~**schwester** *die* nurse; ~**versicherung** *die* **(a)** (Versicherung) health insurance; **(b)** (Unternehmen) health insurance company; ~**wagen** *der* ambulance

kränker ▶ KRANK

krank|feiern *itr. V.* (ugs.) skive off work (coll.) [pretending to be ill]

krankhaft **1** *Adj.* pathological; morbid ⟨*growth, state, swelling, etc.*⟩
2 *adv.* pathologically; morbidly ⟨*swollen, sensitive*⟩

Krankheit *die;* ~, ~en **(a)** illness; (bestimmte Art, von Pflanzen, Organen) disease
(b) (Zeit des Krankseins) illness

Krankheits-erreger *der* pathogen

kränklich *Adj.* ailing

krank|schreiben *tr. V.* give ⟨*person*⟩ a medical certificate

kränkst… ▶ KRANK

Kränkung *die;* ~, ~en: eine ~: an injury to one's/sb.'s feelings

Kranz *der;* ~es, Kränze wreath; garland; (auf einem Grab usw.) wreath

Kränzchen *das;* ~s, ~: coffee circle; coffee klatch (Amer.)

Krapfen *der;* ~s, ~: doughnut

krass, *kraß [1] *Adj.* blatant ‹case›; flagrant ‹injustice›; stark ‹contrast›; complete ‹contradiction›; sharp ‹difference›; out-and-out ‹egoist›
[2] *adv.* sich ~ ausdrücken put sth. bluntly; sich von etw. ~ unterscheiden be in stark contrast to sth

Krater *der;* ~s, ~: crater

Kratz·bürste *die* (ugs. scherzh.) prickly so-and-so

kratzen [1] *tr. V.* scratch; (entfernen) scrape
[2] *itr. V.* (a) scratch
(b) (jucken) itch

Kratzer *der;* ~s, ~ (ugs.) scratch

kratzig *Adj.* itchy ‹material›

Kraul *das;* ~s (Sport) crawl

kraulen¹ [1] *itr. V.* do the crawl
[2] *tr. V.; auch mit sein* eine Strecke ~: cover a distance using the crawl

kraulen² *tr. V.* jmdm. das Kinn ~: tickle sb. under the chin; jmdn. in den Haaren ~: run one's fingers through sb.'s hair

kraus *Adj.* creased ‹skirt etc.›; frizzy ‹hair›

Krause *die;* ~, ~n (Kragen) ruff; (am Ärmel) ruffle

kräuseln [1] *tr. V.* ruffle ‹water, surface›; gather ‹material etc.›; frizz ‹hair›
[2] *refl. V.* ‹hair› go frizzy; ‹water› ripple; ‹smoke› curl up

Kraut *das;* ~[e]s, Kräuter (a) herb
(b) (bes. südd., österr.: Kohl) cabbage

Kraut·salat *der* coleslaw

Krawall *der;* ~s, ~e (a) riot
(b) (ugs.: Lärm) row (coll.)

Krawatte *die;* ~, ~n tie

kraxeln *itr. V.; mit sein* (bes. südd., österr. ugs.) climb; (mit Mühe) clamber

kreativ [1] *Adj.* creative
[2] *adv.* ~ veranlagt sein have a creative bent

Kreativität *die;* ~: creativity

Kreatur *die;* ~, ~en creature

Krebs *der;* ~es, ~e (a) crustacean; (Fluss~) crayfish; (Krabbe) crab
(b) (Krankheit) cancer
(c) (Astrol.) Cancer; the Crab

krebs-, Krebs-: ~ erregend, ~erzeugend *Adj.* carcinogenic; ~forschung *die* cancer research; ~geschwulst *die* cancerous growth or tumour; ~geschwür *das* (volkst.) cancerous ulcer; (fig. geh.) cancer; ~krank *Adj.* ~krank sein have cancer; ~rot *Adj.* as red as a lobster *postpos.*

Kredit *der;* ~[e]s, ~e credit; (Darlehen) loan

kredit-, Kredit-: ~institut *das* credit institution; ~karte *die* credit card; mit ~karte bezahlen pay by credit card; ~nehmer *der;* ~~s, ~~, ~nehmerin *die;* ~~, ~~nen borrower; ~würdig *Adj.* (Finanzw.) creditworthy

Kreide *die;* ~, ~n chalk

kreide-bleich *Adj.* as white as a sheet *postpos.*

Kreide-felsen *der* chalk cliff

kreieren /kreˈiːrən/ *tr. V.* create

Kreis *der;* ~es, ~e circle; (Verwaltungsbezirk) district; (Wahl~) ward

Kreis-bahn *die* orbit

kreischen *itr. V.* screech; ‹door› creak

Kreisel *der;* ~s, ~ (Kinderspielzeug) top; (ugs.: Kreisverkehr) roundabout

kreisen *itr. V.; auch mit sein* ‹planet› revolve (um around); ‹satellite etc.› orbit; ‹aircraft, bird› circle

kreis-, Kreis-: ~förmig *Adj.* circular; ~lauf *der* (Physiol.) circulation; (der Natur, des Lebens usw.) cycle; ~lauf-störungen *Pl.* (Med.) circulatory trouble *sing.;* ~rund *Adj.* [perfectly] round; ~säge *die* circular saw

Kreiß-saal *der* (Med.) delivery room

Kreis-: ~stadt *die* chief town of a/the district; ~verkehr *der* roundabout

Krem *die;* ~, ~s ▶ CREME

Krematorium *das;* ~s, Krematorien crematorium

Krempe *die;* ~, ~n brim

Krempel *der;* ~s (ugs. abwertend) stuff; (Gerümpel) junk

krepieren *itr. V.; mit sein* (salopp) ‹person› snuff it (sl.)

Krepp *der;* ~s, ~s od. ~e crêpe

*Kreppapier *das,* **Krepp-papier** *das* crêpe paper

Kresse *die;* ~, ~n (Bot.) cress

Kreta (*das*); ~s Crete

Kreuz *das;* ~es, ~e (a) cross; (Kreuzzeichen) sign of the cross
(b) (Teil des Rückens) small of the back; jmdn. aufs ~ legen (salopp) take sb. for a ride (coll.)
(c) (Kartenspiel) (Farbe) clubs *pl.;* (Karte) club
(d) (Autobahn) interchange
(e) (Musik) sharp

kreuzen [1] *tr. V.* (auch Biol.) cross
[2] *refl. V.* (a) (überschneiden) cross
(b) (zuwiderlaufen) clash (mit with)
[3] *itr. V.; mit haben od. sein* (fahren) cruise

Kreuz-: ~fahrer *der* (hist.) crusader; ~fahrt *die* cruise; ~feuer *das* (Milit., auch fig.) crossfire; ~gang *der* cloister

kreuzigen *tr. V.* crucify

Kreuzigung *die;* ~, ~en crucifixion

Kreuz-: ~otter *die* adder; [common] viper; ~ritter *der* (hist.) crusader; ~schlitz-schraube *die* Phillips screw ®; ~schmerzen *Pl.* pain *sing.* in the small of the back; ~spinne *die* cross spider; garden spider

Kreuzung *die;* ~, ~en (a) crossroads *sing.*
(b) (Biol.) crossing; cross-breeding; (Ergebnis) cross

kreuz-, Kreuz-: ~ **verhör** *das* cross- ⋯⋰

examination; ∼**weise** *Adv.* crosswise;
∼**wort·rätsel** *das* crossword [puzzle];
∼**zug** *der* (hist., fig.) crusade

kribbelig *Adj.* (ugs.) (vor Ungeduld) fidgety;
(nervös) edgy

kribbeln *itr. V.* (jucken) tickle; (prickeln)
tingle

kriechen *unr. itr. V.* (a) *mit sein* ‹insect,
baby› crawl; ‹plant› creep; ‹person, animal›
creep, crawl
(b) *auch mit sein* (fig. abwertend) crawl (**vor** +
Dat. to)

Kriecher *der;* ∼s, ∼, **Kriecherin** *die;* ∼,
∼nen (abwertend) crawler

Kriech·spur *die* (Verkehrsw.) crawler lane

Krieg *der;* ∼[e]s, ∼e war; ∼ **führend**
warring; belligerent

kriegen *tr. V.* (ugs.) get; (erreichen) catch
‹train, bus, etc.›

Krieger *der;* ∼s, ∼, **Kriegerin** *die;* ∼,
∼nen warrior

kriegerisch *Adj.* (a) (kampflustig) warlike
(b) (militärisch) military; **eine** ∼**e**
Auseinandersetzung an armed conflict

*****krieg·führend** ▶ KRIEG

kriegs-, Kriegs-: ∼**beil** *das* tomahawk;
das ∼**beil begraben** (scherzh.) bury the
hatchet; ∼**bemalung** *die* (Völkerk.)
warpaint; ∼**beschädigt** *Adj.* war-
disabled; ∼**beschädigte** *der/die/adj.*
Dekl. war invalid; ∼**dienst** *der* (a) (im
Krieg) active service; (b) (Wehrdienst) military
service; **den** ∼**dienst verweigern** be a
conscientious objector;
∼**dienst·verweigerer** *der* conscientious
objector; ∼**ende** *das* end of the war; **bei/**
vor ∼**ende** at/before the end of the war;
∼**erklärung** *die* declaration of war;
∼**gefangene** *der* prisoner of war; POW;
∼**gefangenschaft** *die* captivity;
∼**opfer** *das* war victim; ∼**schiff** *das*
warship; ∼**verbrechen** *das* (Rechtsw.) war
crime; ∼**verbrecher** *der*,
∼**verbrecherin** *die* war criminal;
∼**waise** *die* war orphan

Krimi *der;* ∼[s], ∼[s] (ugs.) crime thriller

Kriminal·beamte *der*,
Kriminal·beamtin *die* [plain-clothes]
detective

kriminalisieren *tr. V.* jmdn. ∼: make sb.
turn to crime

kriminalistisch ①*Adj.* ‹methods,
practice› of criminalistics; ‹abilities› in the
field of criminalistics
②*adv.* ‹proceed etc.› using the methods of
criminalistics

Kriminalität *die;* ∼: crime no art.

Kriminal-: ∼**polizei** *die* criminal
investigation department; ∼**roman** *der*
crime novel; (mit Detektiv als Held) detective
novel

*old spelling - see note on page xiv

kriminell ①*Adj.* criminal
②*adv.* ∼ **veranlagt sein** have criminal
tendencies; ∼ **handeln** act illegally

Kriminelle *der/die; adj. Dekl.* criminal

Krimskrams *der;* ∼[es] (ugs.) stuff

Kringel *der;* ∼s, ∼ (Kreis) [small] ring;
(Kritzelei) round squiggle; (Gebäck) [ring-
shaped] biscuit

kringeln *refl. V.* curl [up]; ‹hair› go curly;
sich ∼ **[vor Lachen]** (ugs.) kill oneself
[laughing] (coll.)

Kripo *die;* ∼ (ugs.) die ∼: ≈ the CID

Krippe *die;* ∼, ∼n (a) (Futtertrog) manger;
crib
(b) (Weihnachts∼) model of a nativity scene
(c) (Kinder∼) crèche

Krise *die;* ∼, ∼n (auch Med.) crisis

kriseln *itr. V.* (unpers.) **es kriselt in ihrer**
Ehe/in der Partei their marriage is in
trouble/the party is in a state of crisis

Krisen-: ∼**gebiet** *das* crisis area; ∼**herd**
der trouble spot

Kristall[1] /krɪsˈtal/ *der;* ∼s, ∼e crystal

Kristall[2] *das;* ∼s crystal no indef. art.

Kristallisation *die;* ∼, ∼en (bes. Chemie)
crystallization

kristallisieren *itr. V.* (bes. Chemie)
crystallize

Kriterium *das;* ∼s, Kriterien criterion

Kritik *die;* ∼, ∼en (a) criticism no indef.
art. (an + *Dat.* of); **an jmdm./etw.** ∼ **üben**
criticize sb./sth.
(b) (Besprechung) review

Kritiker *der;* ∼s, ∼, **Kritikerin** *die;* ∼,
∼nen critic

kritik·los ①*Adj.* uncritical
②*adv.* uncritically

kritisch ①*Adj.* critical
②*adv.* critically

kritisieren *tr. V.* criticize; review ‹book,
play, etc.›

kritzeln ①*itr. V.* (schreiben) scribble;
(zeichnen) doodle
②*tr. V.* scribble

Kroatien /kroˈaːtsi̯ən/ ‹das›; ∼s Croatia

kroatisch *Adj.* Croatian

kroch 1. u. 3. Pers. Sg. Prät. v. KRIECHEN

Krokant *der;* ∼s praline

Krokette *die;* ∼, ∼n (Kochk.) croquette

Krokodil *das;* ∼s, ∼e crocodile

Krokodils·tränen *Pl.* (ugs.) crocodile
tears

Krokus *der;* ∼, ∼ od. ∼se crocus

Krone *die;* ∼, ∼n crown; (eines Baumes) top;
crown; (einer Welle) crest; **die** ∼ **der**
Schöpfung the pride of creation

krönen *tr. V.* (auch fig.) crown

Kronen·korken *der* crown cork

Kron-: ∼**juwelen** *Pl.* the crown jewels;

∼**leuchter** *der* chandelier; ∼**prinz** *der* crown prince; ∼**prinzessin** *die* crown princess

Krönung *die;* ∼, ∼en coronation; (fig.) culmination

Kron-zeuge *der*, **Kron-zeugin** *die* (Rechtsw.) person who turns Queen's/King's evidence; **als** ∼ **auftreten** turn Queen's/King's evidence

Kropf *der;* ∼[e]s, Kröpfe (Med.) goitre

Kröte *die;* ∼, ∼n (a) toad
(b) *Pl.* (salopp: Geld) **ein paar/eine ganze Menge** ∼n **verdienen** earn a few bob (Brit. coll.)/a fair old whack (coll.)

Krücke *die;* ∼, ∼n crutch

Krück-stock *der* walking stick

Krug *der;* ∼[e]s, Krüge jug; (größer) pitcher; (Bier∼) mug

Krume *die;* ∼, ∼n crumb

Krümel *der;* ∼s, ∼: crumb

krümeln *itr. V.* (a) crumble
(b) (Krümel machen) make crumbs

krumm ① *Adj.* (a) bent ⟨nail, back⟩; crooked ⟨stick, branch, etc.⟩; bandy ⟨legs⟩; **sich über etw.** (Akk.) ∼ **lachen** (ugs.) fall about laughing over sth.
(b) (ugs.: unrechtmäßig) crooked
(c) etw. ∼ **nehmen** (ugs.) take sth. the wrong way
② *adv.* crookedly

krümmen ① *tr. V.* bend
② *refl. V.* (a) (sich winden) writhe
(b) (krumm verlaufen) ⟨road, path, river⟩ bend

krumm-: *∼|**lachen** ▶ KRUMM 1A; *∼|**nehmen** ▶ KRUMM 1C

Krümmung *die;* ∼, ∼en bend

Krüppel *der;* ∼s, ∼: cripple

Kruste *die;* ∼, ∼n crust; (vom Braten) crisp

Kruzifix *das;* ∼es, ∼e crucifix

Krypta *die;* ∼, Krypten (Archit.) crypt

Kuba (das) ∼s Cuba

Kubaner *der;* ∼s, ∼, **Kubanerin** *die;* ∼, ∼nen Cuban

Kübel *der;* ∼s, ∼: pail

Kubik- cubic ⟨metre, foot, etc.⟩

Küche *die;* ∼, ∼n kitchen; (Einrichtung) kitchen furniture *no indef. art.;* (Kochk.) cooking; cuisine; **kalte/warme** ∼: cold/hot food

Kuchen *der;* ∼s, ∼: cake; (Obst∼) flan; (Torte) gateau

Küchen-: ∼**abfälle** *Pl.* kitchen scraps; ∼**chef** *der*, ∼**chefin** *die* chef

Kuchen-: ∼**form** *die* cake tin; ∼**gabel** *die* pastry fork

Küchen-: ∼**gerät** *das* kitchen utensil; (als Kollektivum) kitchen utensils *pl.;* ∼**maschine** *die* food processor; ∼**meister** *der*, ∼**meisterin** *die* chef; ∼**messer** *das* kitchen knife; ∼**schabe** *die* cockroach; ∼**schrank** *der* kitchen cupboard; ∼**tisch** *der* kitchen table

Kuckuck *der;* ∼s, ∼e (a) cuckoo; **zum** ∼ [**noch mal**]**!** (salopp) for crying out loud! (coll.)
(b) (scherzh.: Pfandsiegel) bailiff's seal (*placed on distrained goods*)

Kuckucks-uhr *die* cuckoo clock

Kufe *die;* ∼, ∼n runner; (von Flugzeugen, Hubschraubern) skid

Kugel *die;* ∼, ∼n (a) ball; (Geom.) sphere; (Kegeln) bowl; (beim Kugelstoßen) shot
(b) (ugs.: Geschoss) bullet

Kugel-lager *das* (Technik) ball bearing

kugeln ① *tr. V.* roll
② *refl. V.* **sich** [**vor Lachen**] ∼ (ugs.) double *or* roll up [laughing]

kugel-, Kugel-: ∼**rund** /-'-'-/ *Adj.* round as a ball *postpos.;* (scherzh.: dick) rotund; tubby; ∼**schreiber** *der* ball pen; Biro ®; ∼**sicher** *Adj.* bulletproof; ∼**stoßen** *das;* ∼∼s shot[-put]; (Disziplin) putting the shot *no art.*

Kuh *die;* ∼, Kühe cow

Kuh-: ∼**fladen** *der* cowpat; ∼**handel** *der* (ugs. abwertend) shady horse-trading *no indef. art.;* **ein** ∼**handel** a bit of shady horse-trading; ∼**haut** *die:* **das geht auf keine** ∼**haut** (fig. salopp) it's absolutely staggering

kühl ① *Adj.* cool; **etw.** ∼ **lagern** keep sth. in a cool place
② *adv.* coolly

Kuhle *die;* ∼, ∼n (ugs.) hollow

Kühle *die;* ∼: coolness

kühlen ① *tr. V.* cool; chill ⟨wine⟩; refrigerate ⟨food⟩
② *itr. V.* ⟨cold compress, ointment, breeze, etc.⟩ have a cooling effect

Kühler *der;* ∼s, ∼ (a) (am Auto) radiator; (Kühlerhaube) bonnet (Brit.); hood (Amer.)
(b) (Sekt∼) ice bucket

Kühler-haube *die* bonnet (Brit.); hood (Amer.)

Kühl-: ∼**fach** *das* frozen food compartment; ∼**haus** *das* cold store; ∼**raum** *der* cold store; cold-storage room; ∼**schrank** *der* refrigerator; fridge (Brit. coll.); icebox (Amer.); ∼**truhe** *die* [chest] freezer; (im Lebensmittelgeschäft) freezer [cabinet]

Kühlung *die;* ∼, ∼en cooling; (Vorrichtung) cooling system; (für Lebensmittel) refrigeration system

Kühl-wasser *das* cooling water

kühn ① *Adj.* bold; (dreist) audacious
② *adv.* boldly; (gewagt) daringly; (dreist) audaciously

Kühnheit *die;* ∼: boldness; (Gewagtheit) daringness; (Dreistigkeit) audacity

Kuh-stall *der* cowshed

Küken *das;* ∼s, ∼: chick

kulant *Adj.* obliging; fair ⟨terms⟩

Kulanz *die;* ∼: willingness to oblige

Kuli *der;* ∼s, ∼s (a) coolie
(b) (ugs.) ballpoint; Biro ®

k

kulinarisch *Adj.* culinary

Kulisse *die;* ~, ~n piece of scenery; flat; (Hintergrund) backdrop; **die** ~**n** the scenery *sing.;* **hinter den** ~**n** (fig.) behind the scenes

kullern (ugs.) *itr. V. mit sein* roll

Kult *der;* ~[e]s, ~e (auch fig.) cult

Kult·film *der* cult film

kultivieren *tr. V.* (auch fig.) cultivate

kultiviert ① *Adj.* cultured; (vornehm) refined

② *adv.* in a cultured manner; (vornehm) in a refined manner

Kultur *die;* ~, ~en (a) culture; (kultivierte Lebensart) refinement; **ein Mensch von** ~: a cultured person

(b) (Zivilisation, Lebensform) civilization

Kultur-: ~**abkommen** *das* cultural agreement; ~**austausch** *der* cultural exchange; ~**beutel** *der* sponge bag (Brit.); toilet bag

kulturell ① *Adj.* cultural

② *adv.* culturally

Kultur-: ~**film** *der* documentary film; ~**geschichte** *die* history of civilization; (einer bestimmten Kultur) cultural history; ~**politik** *die* cultural and educational policy

Kultus·minister *der,* **Kultus·ministerin** *die* minister for education and cultural affairs

Kümmel *der;* ~s, ~: caraway [seed]; (Branntwein) kümmel

Kummer *der;* ~s sorrow; grief; (Ärger, Sorgen) trouble; ~ **um** *od.* **über jmdn.** grief for sb.; **jmdm.** ~ **machen** give sb. trouble

kümmerlich *Adj.* (a) (schwächlich) puny; stunted ⟨*vegetation, plants*⟩

(b) (ärmlich) wretched; miserable

(c) (abwertend: gering) miserable; meagre ⟨*knowledge, leftovers*⟩

kümmern ① *refl. V.* (a) sich um jmdn./etw. ~: take care of sb./sth.

(b) (sich befassen mit) **sich nicht um Politik** ~: not be interested in politics

② *tr. V.* concern

Kumpan *der;* ~s, ~e, **Kumpanin** *die;* ~, ~nen (ugs.) (a) pal (coll.); buddy (coll.)

(b) (abwertend: Mittäter[in]) accomplice

Kumpel *der;* ~s, ~ (a) (Bergmannsspr.) miner

(b) (salopp: Kamerad) pal (coll.); buddy (coll.)

Kumulus·wolke *die* (Met.) cumulus cloud

kündbar *Adj.* terminable ⟨*contract*⟩; redeemable ⟨*loan, mortgage*⟩

Kunde¹ *der;* ~n, ~n customer; (eines Architekten-, Anwaltsbüros, einer Versicherung usw.) client

Kunde² *die;* ~ (geh.) tidings *pl.* (literary)

Kunden·dienst *der* service to customers; (Wartung) after-sales service

Kundgebung *die;* ~, ~en rally

---

kundig *Adj.* (kenntnisreich) knowledgeable; (sachverständig) expert

kündigen ① *tr. V.* cancel ⟨*subscription, membership*⟩; terminate ⟨*contract, agreement*⟩; **seine Stellung** ~: hand in one's notice (**bei** to)

② *unr. itr. V.* (a) (ein Mietverhältnis beenden) ⟨*tenant*⟩ give notice; **jmdm.** ~ ⟨*landlord*⟩ give sb. notice to quit; **zum 1. Juli** ~: give notice for 1 July

(b) (ein Arbeitsverhältnis beenden) ⟨*employee*⟩ hand in one's notice (**bei** to); **jmdm.** ~ ⟨*employer*⟩ give sb. his/her notice

Kündigung *die;* ~, ~en (a) (der Mitgliedschaft, eines Abonnements) cancellation; (eines Vertrags) termination

(b) (eines Arbeitsverhältnisses) **jmdm. die** ~ **aussprechen** give sb. his/her notice

Kündigungs-: ~**frist** *die* period of notice; ~**schutz** *der* protection against wrongful dismissal

Kundin *die;* ~, ~nen customer/client

Kundschaft *die;* ~, ~en ▶ KUNDE¹: customers *pl.;* clientele

Kundschafter *der;* ~s, ~, **Kundschafterin** *die;* ~, ~nen scout

kund|tun (geh.) *unr. tr. V.* announce

künftig ① *Adj.* future

② *adv.* in future

Kunst *die;* ~, Künste (a) art; **die bildende** ~, **die bildenden Künste** the plastic arts *pl.;* **die schönen Künste** [the] fine arts

(b) (das Können) skill; **die ärztliche** ~: medical skill; **das ist keine** ~! (ugs.) there's nothing 'to it

kunst-, Kunst-: ~**ausstellung** *die* art exhibition; ~**buch** *das* art book; ~**druck** *der; Pl.* ~~e (a) [fine] art print;(b) (Druckw.) fine-art printing; ~**erzieher** *der,* ~**erzieherin** *die* art teacher; ~**faser** *die* synthetic fibre; ~**führer** *der* guide to cultural and artistic monuments [of an/the area]; ~**genuss,** ***~**genuß** *der* enjoyment of art; (Ereignis) artistic treat; ~**gerecht** ① *Adj.* expert; ② *adv.* expertly; ~**geschichte** *die* art history; ~**geschichtlich** ① *Adj.* art historical ⟨*studies, evidence, expertise*⟩; ⟨*work*⟩ on art history; ② *adv.* ~ **geschichtlich interessiert/versiert** interested/well versed in art history; ~**gewerbe** *das* arts and crafts *pl.;* ~**griff** *der* trick; dodge; ~**halle** *die* art gallery; ~**händler** *der,* ~**händlerin** *die* [fine-]art dealer; ~**handwerk** *das* craftwork; ~**kritiker** *der,* ~**kritikerin** *die* art critic; ~**leder** imitation leather

Künstler *der;* ~s, ~, **Künstlerin** *die;* ~, ~nen (a) artist; (Zirkus~, Varietee~) artiste

(b) (Könner) genius (**in** + *Dat.* at)

künstlerisch ① *Adj.* artistic

② *adv.* artistically

Künstler·name *der* stage name

künstlich ① *Adj.* (a) artificial

(b) (gezwungen) forced ⟨*laugh, cheerfulness, etc.*⟩

[2] *adv.* artificially

kunst-, Kunst-: ∼**licht** *das* artificial light; ∼**los** *Adj.* plain; ∼**postkarte** *die* art postcard; ∼**saal** *der* art room; ∼**sammler** *der*, ∼**sammlerin** *die* art collector; ∼**sammlung** *die* art collection; ∼**schatz** *der* art treasure; ∼**stoff** *der* synthetic material; plastic; ∼**stück** *das* trick; **das ist kein** ∼**stück** (ugs.) it's no great feat; ∼**turnen** *das* gymnastics *sing.*; ∼**voll** [1] *Adj.* ornate and artistic; (kompliziert) elaborate; [2] *adv.* **(a)** ornately *or* elaborately and artistically; **(b)** (geschickt) skilfully; ∼**werk** *das* work of art

kunter·bunt [1] *Adj.* multi-coloured; (abwechslungsreich) varied; (ungeordnet) jumbled ⟨*confusion, muddle, etc.*⟩

[2] *adv.* ⟨*painted, printed*⟩ in many colours; ∼ **durcheinander sein** be higgledy-piggledy

Kupfer *das;* ∼s **(a)** copper

(b) (∼geschirr) copperware; (∼geld) coppers *pl.*

Kupfer-: ∼**geld** *das* coppers *pl.;* ∼**stich** *der* **(a)** copperplate engraving *no art.;* **(b)** (Blatt) copperplate print *or* engraving

Kuppe *die;* ∼, ∼n **(a)** [rounded] hilltop **(b)** (Finger∼) tip; end

Kuppel *die;* ∼, ∼n dome; (kleiner) cupola

Kuppelei *die;* ∼: procuring

kuppeln *itr. V.* operate the clutch

Kuppelung ▶ KUPPLUNG

Kuppler *der;* ∼s, ∼: procurer

Kupplerin *die;* ∼, ∼nen procuress

Kupplung *die;* ∼, ∼en **(a)** (Kfz-W.) clutch **(b)** (Technik: Vorrichtung zum Verbinden) coupling

Kur *die;* ∼, ∼en [health] cure; (ohne Aufenthalt im Badeort) course of treatment

Kür *die;* ∼, ∼en (Eiskunstlauf) free programme; (Turnen) optional exercises *pl.*

Kurbel *die;* ∼, ∼n crank [handle]; (an Spieldosen, Grammophonen) winder; (an einem Brunnen) [winding] handle

kurbeln *tr. V.* etw. nach oben/unten ∼: wind sth. up/down

Kurbel·welle *die* (Technik) crankshaft

Kürbis *der;* ∼ses, ∼se pumpkin

Kurde *der;* ∼n, ∼n, **Kurdin** *die;* ∼, ∼nen Kurd

kurdisch *Adj.* Kurdish

Kur-: ∼**fürst** *der* (hist.) Elector; ∼**gast** *der* visitor to a/the spa; (Patient) patient at a/the spa

Kurier *der;* ∼s, ∼e courier

kurieren *tr. V.* (auch fig.) cure (**von** of)

Kurierin *die;* ∼, ∼nen ▶ KURIER

kurios [1] *Adj.* curious [2] *adv.* curiously; strangely; oddly

Kuriosität *die;* ∼, ∼en **(a)** strangeness **(b)** (Gegenstand) curiosity; curio

Kur-: ∼**konzert** *das* concert [at a spa]; ∼**ort** *der* spa; ∼**pfuscher** *der*, ∼**pfuscherin** *die* (ugs. abwertend) quack

Kurs *der;* ∼es, ∼e **(a)** (Richtung) course; **ein harter/weicher** ∼ (fig.) a hard/soft line **(b)** (von Wertpapieren) price; (von Devisen) exchange rate; **der** ∼ **des Dollars** the dollar rate

(c) (Lehrgang) course; (Teilnehmer) class

Kürschner *der;* ∼s, ∼, **Kürschnerin** *die;* ∼, ∼nen furrier

kursieren *itr. V.; auch mit sein* circulate

Kurs·teilnehmer *der*, **Kurs·teilnehmerin** *die* course participant

Kursus *der;* ∼, Kurse ▶ KURS

Kurs·wagen *der* (Eisenb.) through carriage

Kur·taxe *die;* visitors' tax (*at a spa*)

Kurve *die;* ∼, ∼n **(a)** (einer Straße) bend **(b)** (Geom.) curve **(c)** (in der Statistik, Temperatur∼ usw.) graph

kurven *itr. V.; mit sein* **(a)** ⟨*aircraft*⟩ circle; ⟨*tanks etc.*⟩ circle [round] **(b)** (ugs.: fahren) drive around

kurven·reich *Adj.* winding; twisting

kurz; kürzer, kürzest... [1] *Adj.* short; (zeitlich; knapp) short, brief; quick ⟨*look*⟩ [2] *adv.* **(a)** (zeitlich) briefly; (knapp) ∼ **gesagt** in a word

(b) (wenig) just; ∼ **vor/hinter der Kreuzung** just before/past the crossroads; ∼ **vor/nach Pfingsten** just before/after Whitsun

kurz-, Kurz-: ∼**arbeit** *die* short-time working; ∼**ärm[e]lig** *Adj.* short-sleeved

Kürze *die;* ∼ **(a)** shortness **(b)** (geringe Dauer) shortness; brevity; **in** ∼: shortly

(c) (Knappheit) brevity

Kürzel *das;* ∼s, ∼: shorthand symbol

kürzen *tr. V.* shorten; abridge ⟨*article, book*⟩; cut ⟨*pension, budget*⟩

kürzer ▶ KURZ

kurzer·hand *Adv.* without more ado

kürzest... ▶ KURZ

kurz-, Kurz-: ∼**fristig** [1] *Adj.* **(a)** ⟨*refusal, resignation, etc.*⟩ at short notice; **(b)** (für kurze Zeit) short-term; [2] *adv.* **(a)** at short notice; **(b)** (für kurze Zeit) for a short time; (auf kurze Sicht) in the short term; (in kurzer Zeit) without delay; ∼**geschichte** *die* short story; ∼**haar-frisur** *die* bob; bobbed hairstyle; ∼**lebig** *Adj.* (auch fig.) short-lived; ∼**lebigkeit** *die;* ∼∼: short-livedness

kürzlich *Adv.* recently; not long ago

kurz-, Kurz-: ∼**meldung** *die* brief report; (während einer anderen Sendung) news flash; ∼**parker** *der;* ∼∼s, ∼∼, ∼**parkerin** *die;* ∼∼, ∼∼nen short-stay (Brit.) *or* short-term parker; ∼**schluss, ***∼**schluß** *der* (Elektrot.) short circuit; ∼**sichtig** (auch fig.) [1] *Adj.* short-sighted; [2] *adv.* short-sightedly; ∼**sichtigkeit** *die;* ∼∼ (auch fig.) short-sightedness

Kurzstrecken·rakete *die* short-range
missile
Kürzung *die;* ~, ~en cut
kurz-, Brit.-: ~**waren** *Pl.* haberdashery
sing. (Brit.); notions (Amer.); ~**welle** *die*
(Physik, Rundf.) short wave; ~**weilig** *Adj.*
entertaining; ~**zeitig** ⊡ *Adj.* brief; ⊡ *adv.*
briefly
kuschelig *Adj.* cosy
kuscheln *refl. V.* sich an jmdn. ~: snuggle
up to sb.
Kuschel·tier *das* cuddly toy
kuschen *itr. V.* knuckle under (**vor** + *Dat.*
to)
Kusine *die;* ~, ~n ▶ COUSINE
Kuss, *Kuß *der;* Kusses, Küsse kiss
kuss·echt, *kuß·echt *Adj.* kissproof
küssen *tr., itr. V.* kiss
Kuss·hand, *Kuß·hand *die:* jmdm. eine
~ zuwerfen blow sb. a kiss; **mit** ~ (ugs.)
gladly
Küste *die;* ~, ~n coast
Küsten-: ~**linie** *die* coastline; ~**wache**
die coastguard [service]

Küster *der;* ~s, ~, **Küsterin** *die;* ~,
~nen sexton
Kutsche *die;* ~, ~n coach
Kutscher *der;* ~s, ~, **Kutscherin** *die;*
~, ~nen coach driver
kutschieren ⊡ *itr. V.; mit sein* drive, ride
[in a coach]
⊡ *tr. V.* jmdn. ~: drive sb. [in a coach]
Kutte *die;* ~, ~n [monk's/nun's] habit
Kutter *der;* ~s, ~: cutter
Kuvert /ku've:ɐ̯/ *das;* ~s, ~s envelope;
(geh.: Gedeck) cover
Kuwait /ku'vai:t/ (*das);* ~s Kuwait
Kybernetik *die;* ~: cybernetics *sing.*
Kybernetiker *der;* ~s, ~,
Kybernetikerin *die;* ~, ~nen
cybernetician; cyberneticist
kybernetisch *Adj.* cybernetic
KZ *Abk.* = **Konzentrationslager**
KZ-Häftling *der,* **KZler** *der;* ~s, ~,
KZlerin *die;* ~, ~nen concentration-camp
prisoner

Ll

l, L /ɛl/ *das;* ~, ~: l/L
l *Abk.* = **Liter** l.
Lab *das;* ~[e]s, ~e rennet
labberig *Adj.* (ugs. abwertend) (a) (fade)
wishy-washy; ~ **schmecken** taste of nothing
(b) (weich) floppy, limp ⟨material⟩; floppy
⟨trousers, dress, etc.⟩
laben (geh.) ⊡ *tr. V.* jmdn. ~: give sb.
refreshment
⊡ *refl. V.* refresh oneself (**an** + *Dat.*, **mit**
with)
labern *itr. V.* (ugs. abwertend) rabbit (Brit. coll.)
or babble on
labil *Adj.* (a) (Med.) delicate ⟨constitution,
health⟩; poor ⟨circulation⟩
(b) (auch Psych.) unstable ⟨person, character,
situation, etc.⟩
Labor *das;* ~s, ~s, *auch:* ~e laboratory
Laboratorium *das;* ~s, Laboratorien
laboratory
Labyrinth *das;* ~[e]s, ~e maze; labyrinth
Lache¹ *die;* ~, ~n (ugs.) laugh
Lache² /'la(:)xə/ *die;* ~, ~n puddle; (von Blut,
Öl) pool
lächeln *itr. V.* smile (**über** + *Akk.* at)
Lächeln *das;* ~s smile

lachen ⊡ *itr. V.* laugh (**über** + *Akk.* at)
⊡ *tr. V.* was gibt es denn zu ~? what's so
funny?
Lachen *das;* ~s laughter; **ein lautes** ~: a
loud laugh
lächerlich ⊡ *Adj.* ridiculous; ludicrous
⟨argument, statement⟩
⊡ *adv.* ridiculously
Lächerlichkeit *die;* ~: ridiculousness;
(von Argumenten, Behauptungen usw.)
ludicrousness
lachhaft *Adj.* ridiculous
Lachs *der;* ~es, ~e salmon
Lack *der;* ~[e]s, ~e varnish; (für Metall,
Lackarbeiten) lacquer
lackieren *tr. V.* varnish; spray ⟨car⟩
Lack·leder *das* patent leather
Lade *die;* ~, ~n (landsch.) drawer
Lade·hemmung *die* jam
laden¹ ⊡ *unr. tr. V.* load; (Physik) charge
⊡ *unr. itr. V.* load [up]
laden² *unr. tr. V.* (a) (Rechtsspr.) summon
(b) (geh.: einladen) invite
Laden *der;* ~s, Läden (a) shop; store
(Amer.); **der** ~ **läuft** (ugs.) business is good
(b) (Fensterladen) shutter
Laden-: ~**dieb** *der,* ~**diebin** *die*
shoplifter; ~**diebstahl** *der* shoplifting;

---
*old spelling - see note on page xiv

∼schluss, **∼***schluß** *der* shop *or* (Amer.) store closing time; **∼tisch** *der* [shop] counter

Lade-: **∼rampe** *die* loading ramp; **∼raum** *der* (beim Auto) luggage space; (beim Flugzeug, Schiff) hold; (bei LKWs) payload space

lädieren *tr. V.* damage

lädst *2. Pers. Sg. Präsens v.* LADEN

lädt *3. Pers. Sg. Präsens v.* LADEN

Ladung *die;* ∼, ∼en **(a)** (Schiffs∼, Flugzeug∼) cargo; (eines LKW) load **(b)** (beim Sprengen, Schießen; Physik) charge **(c)** (Rechtsspr.: Vor∼) summons *sing.*

lag *1. u. 3. Pers. Sg. Prät. v.* LIEGEN

Lage *die;* ∼, ∼n **(a)** situation; **eine gute ∼ haben** be well situated **(b)** (Art des Liegens) position **(c)** (Situation) situation

Lage-plan *der* map of the area

Lager *das;* ∼s, ∼ **(a)** camp **(b)** storeroom; (in Geschäften, Betrieben) stockroom **(c)** (Warenbestand) stock

Lager-: **∼bestand** *der* (Wirtsch.) stock; **den ∼bestand aufnehmen** do a stocktake; **∼feuer** *das* campfire; **∼halle** *die* warehouse

lagern ⟨1⟩ *tr. V.* **(a)** store **(b)** (hinlegen) lay down ⟨2⟩ *itr. V.* **(a)** camp **(b)** (liegen) lie; ⟨*foodstuffs, medicines, etc.*⟩ be kept

Lager-: **∼platz** *der* campsite; **∼raum** storeroom; (im Geschäft, Betrieb) stockroom

Lagerung *die;* ∼, ∼en storage

Lagune *die;* ∼, ∼n lagoon

lahm *Adj.* **(a)** (gelähmt) lame; (ugs.: unbeweglich) stiff **(b)** (ugs.: unzureichend) lame ⟨*excuse, explanation, etc.*⟩ **(c)** (ugs. abwertend: matt) dreary

lahmen *itr. V.* be lame

lähmen *tr. V.* paralyse; (fig.) paralyse ⟨*economy, industry*⟩; bring ⟨*traffic*⟩ to a standstill

Lähmung *die;* ∼, ∼en paralysis; (fig.) (der Wirtschaft, Industrie) paralysis; **zu einer ∼ des Verkehrs führen** bring traffic to a standstill

Laib *der;* ∼[e]s, ∼e loaf; **ein [halber] ∼ Brot** [half] a loaf of bread

Laich *der;* ∼[e]s, ∼e spawn

laichen *itr. V.* spawn

Laie *der;* ∼n, ∼n (Mann) layman; (Frau) laywoman

Lakai *der;* ∼en, ∼en lackey; liveried footman

Lake *die;* ∼, ∼n brine

Laken *das;* ∼s, ∼ (bes. nordd.) sheet

Lakritze *die;* ∼, ∼n liquorice

lallen *tr., itr. V.* ⟨*baby*⟩ babble; ⟨*drunk/ drowsy person*⟩ mumble

Lamelle *die;* ∼, ∼n (einer Jalousie) slat; (eines Heizkörpers) rib

lamentieren *itr. V.* (ugs.) moan (**über** + *Akk.* about)

Lametta *das;* ∼s lametta

Lamm *das;* ∼[e]s, Lämmer lamb

lamm-, Lamm-: **∼fell** *das* lambskin; **∼fleisch** *das* lamb; **∼fromm** ⟨1⟩ *Adj.* ⟨*person*⟩ as meek as a [little] lamb; ⟨2⟩ *adv.* ⟨*answer*⟩ like a lamb

Lämpchen *das;* ∼s, ∼: small *or* little light; **ein rotes ∼:** a little red light

Lampe *die;* ∼, ∼n light; (Tisch∼, Öl∼, Signal∼) lamp

Lampen-: **∼fieber** *das* stage fright; **∼schirm** *der* [lamp]shade

Lampion /lamˈpi̯ɔŋ/ *der;* ∼s, ∼s Chinese lantern

Land *das;* ∼es, Länder *od.* (veralt.) ∼e **(a)** land *no indef. art.;* (dörfliche Gegend) country *no indef. art.;* **an ∼:** ashore; **auf dem ∼ wohnen** live in the country **(b)** (Staat) country; **hier zu ∼e** [here] in this country **(c)** (Bundesland) Land; state; (österr.) province

Land-: **∼arbeiter** *der,* **∼arbeiterin** *die* agricultural worker; farm worker; **∼bevölkerung** *die* rural population

Lande-: **∼anflug** *der* (Flugw.) [landing] approach; **∼bahn** *die* (Flugw.) [landing] runway; **∼erlaubnis** *die* (Flugw.) permission to land *no art.*

landen ⟨1⟩ *itr. V.; mit sein* **(a)** land; (ankommen) arrive **(b)** (ugs.: gelangen) land up ⟨2⟩ *tr. V.* **(a)** land ⟨*aircraft, troops, passengers, fish, etc.*⟩ **(b)** (ugs.: zustande bringen) pull off ⟨*victory, coup*⟩; have ⟨*smash hit*⟩

Ländereien *Pl.* estates

Länder-: **∼kampf** *der* (Sport) international match; **∼spiel** *das* (Sport) international [match]

Landes-: **∼innere** *das* interior [of the country]; **∼kunde** *die* regional studies *pl., no art.;* **∼regierung** *die* government of a/ the Land/province; **∼sprache** *die* language of the country

Lande-steg *der* landing stage; jetty

Landes-: **∼tracht** *die* national costume *or* dress; **∼verrat** *der* (Rechtsw.) treason; **∼währung** *die* currency of a/the country

land-, Land-: **∼flucht** *die* migration from the land *or* countryside [to the towns]; **∼friedens-bruch** *der* (Rechtsw.) breach of the peace; **∼gewinnung** *die* reclamation of land; **∼haus** *das* country house; **∼karte** *die* map; **∼kreis** *der* district; **∼läufig** *Adj.* widely accepted

ländlich *Adj.* rural; country *attrib.* ⟨*life*⟩

Land-: **∼luft** *die* country air; **∼plage** *die* (fig.) pest; nuisance; **∼ratte** *die* (ugs.) landlubber

Landschaft die; ~, ~en landscape;
(ländliche Gegend) countryside
landschaftlich ① Adj. regional
② adv. ~ herrlich gelegen sein be in a
glorious natural setting; **die Umgebung der
Stadt ist ~ sehr schön** the town is in or has
a beautiful natural setting
Land·schul·heim das ▶ SCHULLANDHEIM
Lands-: ~**mann** der; Pl. ~leute fellow
countryman; compatriot; ~**männin** die;
~~, ~~nen fellow countrywoman;
compatriot
Land-: ~**straße** die country road; (im
Gegensatz zur Autobahn) ordinary road;
~**streicher** der; ~~s, ~~,
~**streicherin** die; ~~, ~~nen tramp;
~**strich** der area; ~**tag** der Landtag; state
parliament; (österr.) provincial parliament
Landung die; ~, ~en landing
Landungs·brücke die [floating] landing
stage
land-, Land-: ~**weg** der overland route;
auf dem ~weg overland; ~**wirt** der,
~**wirtin** die farmer; ~**wirtschaft** die
agriculture no art.; farming no art.;
~**wirtschaftlich** ① Adj. agricultural;
② adv. ~wirtschaftlich genutzt werden be
used for agricultural purposes; ~**zunge** die
(Geogr.) tongue of land
lang; länger, längst... ① Adj. long; (ugs.:
groß) tall
② adv. [for] a long time; **eine Sekunde/
mehrere Stunden** ~: for a second/several
hours
lang-: ~**ärm[e]lig** Adj. long-sleeved;
~**atmig** ① Adj. long-winded; ② adv. long-
windedly; ⟨relate⟩ at great length
lange; länger, am längsten Adv. (a) a long
time; **bist du schon ~ hier?** have you been
here long?
(b) (bei weitem) **ich bin noch ~ nicht fertig** I'm
nowhere near finished; **hier is es ~ nicht so
schön** it isn't nearly as nice here
Länge die; ~, ~n length; (Geogr.) longitude
langen (ugs.) ① itr. V. (a) be enough
(b) (greifen) reach (**in** + Akk. into; **auf** + Akk.
on to; **nach** for)
② tr. V. **jmdm. eine** ~ (ugs.) give sb. a clout
[around the ear] (coll.)
Längen·grad der (Geogr.) degree of
longitude
länger ① ▶ LANG, LANGE;
② Adj. **seit** ~**er Zeit** for quite some time
Lange·weile die; ~ od. **Langenweile**
boredom; ~ **haben** be bored
lang-, Lang-: ~**fristig** ① Adj. long-term;
long-dated ⟨loan⟩; ② adv. on a long-term
basis; ~**jährig** Adj. ⟨customer, friend⟩ of
many years' standing; long-standing
⟨friendship⟩; ~**jährige Erfahrung** many years

of experience; ~**lauf** der (Skisport) cross-
country; ~**lebig** Adj. long-lived ⟨animals,
organisms⟩; durable ⟨goods, materials⟩
länglich Adj. oblong
lang-, Lang-: ~**mut** die; ~~:
forbearance; ~**mütig** Adj. forbearing;
~**mütigkeit** die; ~~: forbearance
längs ① Präp. + Gen. od. (selten) Dat. along
② Adv.lengthways
Längs·achse die longitudinal axis
langsam ① Adj. slow
② adv. (a) slowly; ~, **aber sicher** (ugs.)
slowly but surely
(b) (allmählich) gradually
Lang-: ~**schläfer** der, ~**schläferin** die
late riser; ~**spiel·platte** die long-playing
record; LP
Längs·schnitt der longitudinal section
längst Adv. (a) (schon lange) a long time ago
(b) (bei weitem) **hier ist es ~ nicht so schön** it
isn't nearly as nice here
längst... ▶ LANG
längstens Adv. (ugs.) (höchstens) at [the]
most; (spätestens) at the latest
Languste die; ~, ~n spiny lobster
lang-, Lang-: ~**weilen** ① tr. V. bore;
② refl. V. be bored; ~**weilig** ① Adj.
boring; dull ⟨place⟩; ② adv. boringly;
~**welle** die (Physik, Rundf.) long wave;
~**wierig** Adj. lengthy; prolonged ⟨search⟩
Lanze die; ~, ~n lance; (zum Werfen) spear
Laos (das); Laos' Laos
Laote der; ~n, ~n, **Laotin** die; ~, ~nen
Laotian
lapidar ① Adj. (kurz, aber wirkungsvoll)
succinct; (knapp) terse
② adv. succinctly/tersely
Lappalie /laˈpaːli̯ə/ die; ~, ~n trifle
Lappe der; ~n, ~n Lapp
Lappen der; ~s, ~: cloth; (Fetzen) rag;
(Wasch~) flannel
Lappin die; ~, ~nen Lapp
läppisch Adj. silly
Lapp·land (das); ~s Lapland
Laptop der; ~s, ~s (DV) laptop
Lärche die; ~, ~n larch
Lärm der; ~[e]s noise; (Krach) din; row (coll.)
Lärm·belästigung die disturbance
caused by noise
lärmen itr. V. make a noise or (coll.) row
Lärm-: ~**pegel** der noise level; ~**schutz**
der (a) protection against noise;
(b) (Vorrichtung) noise barrier; noise or sound
insulation no indef. art.; ~**schutz·wand**
die sound-insulating wall
Larve die; ~, ~n grub; larva
las 1. u. 3. Pers. Sg. Prät. v. LESEN
lasch ① Adj. limp ⟨handshake⟩; feeble
⟨action, measure⟩; lax ⟨upbringing⟩
② adv. s. Adj.: limply; feebly; laxly

---

*alte Schreibung - vgl. Hinweis auf S. xiv

Lạsche *die;* ~, ~n (Gürtel~) loop; (eines Briefumschlags) flap; (Schuh~) tongue

Laser /'leɪzɐ/ *der;* ~s, ~ (Physik) laser

Lạser-: ~**drucker** *der* (DV) laser printer; ~**pointer** *der* (DV) laser pointer

lạss, ***laß** *Imperativ Sg. v.* LASSEN

lạssen 1 *unr. tr. V.* (a) *mit Inf. + Akk.* (2. *Part.* lassen) (veranlassen) **etw. tun/machen/ bauen/waschen** ~: have *or* get sth. done/ made/built/washed; **jmdn. warten** ~: keep sb. waiting; **jmdn. grüßen** ~: send one's regards to sb.; **jmdn. kommen/rufen** ~: send for sb.

(b) *mit Inf. + Akk.* (2.Part. lassen) (erlauben) **jmdn. etw. tun** ~: let sb. do sth.; allow sb. to do sth.

(c) (belassen) **jmdn. in Frieden** ~: leave sb. in peace

(d) (hinein~/heraus~) let *or* allow (**in** + *Akk.* into, **aus** out of)

(e) (unterlassen) stop

(f) (zurück~; bleiben ~) leave

(g) (überlassen) **jmdn. etw.** ~: let sb. have sth.

(h) (als Aufforderung) **lass/lasst uns gehen/ fahren!** let's go!

(i) (verlieren) lose; (ausgeben) spend

2 *unr. refl. V.* **die Tür lässt sich leicht öffnen** the door opens easily; **das lässt sich nicht beweisen** it can't be proved

3 *unr. itr. V.* (a) (ugs.) **Lass mal. Ich mache das schon** Leave it. I'll do it

(b) (veranlassen) **ich lasse bitten** would you ask him/her/them to come in

lạssig 1 *Adj.* casual

2 *adv.* casually

lạsst, ***läßt** *3. Pers. Sg. Präsens v.* LASSEN

Lạst *die;* ~, ~en load; (Gewicht) weight; (Bürde) burden

lạsten *itr. V.* be a burden; **auf jmdm./etw.** ~: weigh heavily [up]on sb./sth.

Lạster[1] *der;* ~s, ~ (ugs.: Lkw) truck; lorry (Brit.)

Lạster[2] *das;* ~s, ~: vice

lạsterhaft *Adj.* (abwertend) depraved

lạstern 1 *itr. V.* (abwertend) **über jmdn./etw.** ~: make malicious remarks about sb./sth.

2 *tr. V.* (veralt.) blaspheme against

lạstig *Adj.* tiresome; troublesome ⟨illness, cough, etc.⟩

Lạst-: ~**schrift** *die* debit; ~**wagen** *der* truck; lorry (Brit.)

Lasụr *die;* ~, ~en varnish; (farbig) glaze

Latein *das;* ~s Latin

Latein-amerika (*das*) Latin America

lateinisch *Adj.* Latin

latẹnt *Adj.* latent

Latẹrne *die;* ~, ~n (a) (Leuchte) lamp; lantern (Naut.)

(b) (Straßen~) street light

Latẹrnen-pfahl *der* lamp post

Latrịne *die;* ~, ~n latrine

lạtschen *itr. V.; mit sein* (salopp) trudge; (schlurfend) slouch

Lạtschen *der;* ~s, ~ (ugs.) old worn-out shoe/slipper

Lạtte *die;* ~, ~n (a) lath; (Zaun~) pale

(b) (Sport: Quer~ des Tores) [cross]bar

(c) (Leichtathletik) bar

Lạtten-: ~**rost** *der* (auf dem Boden) duckboards *pl.;* (eines Bettes) slatted frame ~**zaun** *der* paling fence

Lạtz *der;* ~es, **Lätze** bib

Lätzchen *das;* ~s, ~: bib

lau *Adj.* tepid, lukewarm ⟨water etc.⟩; mild ⟨wind, air, evening, etc.⟩

Laub *das;* ~[e]s leaves *pl.;* **dichtes** ~: thick foliage

Laub-baum *der* broad-leaved tree

Laube *die;* ~, ~n summer house; (überdeckter Sitzplatz) bower; arbour

Laub-: ~**frosch** *der* tree frog; ~**säge** *die* fretsaw; ~**wald** *der* deciduous wood/forest

Lauch *der;* ~[e]s (Porree) leek

Lauer *die;* **auf der** ~ **liegen** *od.* **sein** (ugs.) (jmdm. auflauern) lie in wait

lauern *itr. V.* (auch fig.) lurk

Lauf *der;* ~[e]s, **Läufe** (a) running

(b) (Sport: Wettrennen) heat

(c) (Ver~) course; **im** ~[e] **der Zeit** in the course of time; **im** ~[e] **der Jahre/des Tages** over the years/during the day

(d) (von Schusswaffen) barrel

Lauf-bahn *die* (a) (Werdegang) career

(b) (Leichtathletik) running track

laufen 1 *unr. itr. V.; mit sein* (a) run; (beim Eislauf) skate; (beim Ski~) ski; (gehen) go; (zu Fuß gehen) walk; **in** (*Akk.*)/**gegen etw.** ~: walk into sth./gegen etw. ~: keep running to the doctor

(b) (im Gang sein) ⟨machine⟩ be running; ⟨radio, television, etc.⟩ be on; (funktionieren) ⟨machine⟩ run; ⟨radio, television, etc.⟩ work

(c) (gelten) ⟨contract, agreement, engagement, etc.⟩ run

(d) (gespielt werden) ⟨programme, play, etc.⟩ be on

2 *unr. tr. u. itr. V.* (a) *mit sein* (zurücklegen) (zu Fuß) walk; (rennen) run

(b) *mit sein* (erzielen) **einen Rekord** ~: set up a record

(c) *mit haben od. sein* **Ski/Schlittschuh/ Rollschuh** ~: ski/skate/roller-skate

laufend 1 *Adj.* (a) (ständig) regular ⟨interest, income⟩; recurring ⟨costs⟩

(b) (gegenwärtig) current ⟨issue, year, month, etc.⟩

2 *adv.* constantly; ⟨increase⟩ steadily

Läufer *der;* ~s, ~ (a) (Sport) runner; (Handball; Fußball veralt.) halfback

(b) (Teppich) (long narrow) carpet

Läuferin *die;* ~, ~nen ▶ LÄUFER A

Lauf-feuer *das* brush fire; **wie ein** ~: like wildfire

Lauf-: ~**masche** *die* ladder; ~**pass,** ⋯⊹

*∼**paß** der: er hat seiner Freundin den ∼**pass** gegeben (ugs.) he finished with his girlfriend (coll.); ∼**schritt** der: im ∼schritt, marsch, marsch! at the double, quick march!

läufst 2. Pers. Sg. Präsens v. LAUFEN

Lauf·stall der playpen

läuft 3. Pers. Sg. Präsens v. LAUFEN

Laufwerk das (Technik) mechanism; (DV) drive

Lauge die; ∼, ∼n (a) soapy water (b) (Chemie) alkaline solution

Laugen·brezel die (südd.) pretzel

Laune die; ∼, ∼n mood

launenhaft Adj. temperamental; (unberechenbar) capricious

launig witty

launisch Adj.: ▶ LAUNENHAFT

Laus die; ∼, Läuse louse

Laus·bub der little rascal

Lausch·aktion die, **Lausch·angriff** der bugging operation (coll.)

lauschen itr. V. (a) (horchen) listen (b) (zuhören) listen [attentively]

Lauscher der; ∼s, ∼, **Lauscherin** die; ∼, ∼nen eavesdropper

lauschig Adj. cosy, snug ⟨corner⟩

lausig 1 Adj. (ugs.) (a) (abwertend: unangenehm, schäbig) lousy (coll.); rotten (coll.) (b) (sehr groß) perishing (Brit. coll.), freezing ⟨cold⟩; terrible (coll.) ⟨heat⟩ 2 adv. terribly (coll.)

laut[1] 1 Adj. loud; (geräuschvoll) noisy 2 adv. loudly; (geräuschvoll) noisily

laut[2] Präp. + Gen. od. Dat. (Amtsspr.) according to

Laut der; ∼[e]s, ∼e sound

Laute die; ∼, ∼n lute

lauten itr. V. ⟨answer, instruction, slogan⟩ be, run; ⟨letter, passage, etc.⟩ read, go; ⟨law⟩ state

läuten 1 tr., itr. V. ring; ⟨alarm clock⟩ go off 2 itr. V. (bes. südd.: klingeln) ring; es läutete the bell rang or went (zu for)

lauter[1] Adj. (geh.) honourable ⟨person, intentions, etc.⟩; honest ⟨truth⟩

lauter[2] indekl. Adj. nothing but; sheer ⟨nonsense, joy, etc.⟩

läutern tr. V. (geh.) reform ⟨character⟩; purify ⟨soul⟩

Läuterung die; ∼, ∼en (geh.) reformation; (der Seele) purification

laut·hals Adv. at the top of one's voice; ∼ lachen roar with laughter

lautlich 1 Adj. phonetic 2 adv. phonetically

laut-, Laut-: ∼los 1 Adj. silent; soundless; (wortlos) silent; 2 adv. silently; soundlessly; ∼**schrift** die (Phon.) phonetic alphabet; (Umschrift) phonetic transcription;

---

*old spelling - see note on page xiv

∼**sprecher** der loudspeaker; (einer Stereoanlage usw.) speaker; ∼**stark** 1 Adj. loud; vociferous, loud ⟨protest⟩; 2 adv. loudly; ⟨protest⟩ vociferously; ∼**stärke** die volume

lau·warm Adj. lukewarm

Lava die; ∼, **Laven** (Geol.) lava

Lavendel der; ∼s, ∼: lavender

Lawine die; ∼, ∼n (auch fig.) avalanche; eine ∼ von Protesten (fig.) a storm of protest

Lawinen·gefahr die danger of avalanches

lax 1 Adj. lax 2 adv. laxly

Laxheit die; ∼: laxness; laxity

Layout /lɛɪˈaʊt/ das; ∼s, ∼s (Druckw., Elektronik) layout

Lazarett das; ∼[e]s, ∼e military hospital

Lead·sänger /ˈliːt-/ der, **Lead·sängerin** die lead singer

leasen /ˈliːzn̩/ tr. V. rent; (für längere Zeit mieten) lease ⟨car etc.⟩

leben itr. V. live; (lebendig sein) be alive; leb[e] wohl! farewell!; von seiner Rente/seinem Gehalt ∼: live on one's pension/salary

Leben das; ∼s, ∼ (a) life; das ∼: life; sich (Dat.) das ∼ nehmen take one's [own] life; am ∼ sein/bleiben be/stay alive; ums ∼ kommen lose one's life (b) (Betriebsamkeit) auf dem Markt herrschte ein reges ∼: the market was bustling with activity; das ∼ auf der Straße the comings and goings in the street

lebend Adj. living; live ⟨animal⟩

lebendig 1 Adj. living; (lebhaft) lively 2 adv. (lebhaft) in a lively way

Lebendigkeit die; ∼: liveliness

lebens-, Lebens-: ∼abend der (geh.) evening of one's life (literary); ∼**art** die (a) way of life; (b) (Umgangsformen) manners pl.; ∼**aufgabe** die life's work; ∼**bejahend** Adj. ⟨person⟩ with a positive attitude to life; ∼**bereich** der area of life; ∼**dauer** die lifespan; ∼**ende** das end [of one's life]; ∼**erinnerungen** Pl. memories of one's life; (aufgezeichnet) memoirs; ∼**erwartung** die life expectancy; ∼**fähig** Adj. (auch fig.) viable; ∼**freude** die zest for life; ∼**froh** Adj. full of zest for life postpos.; ∼**gefahr** die mortal danger; „Achtung, ∼gefahr!" 'danger'; ∼**gefährlich** 1 Adj. highly dangerous; critical ⟨injury⟩; 2 adv. critically ⟨injured, ill⟩; ∼**gefährte** der, ∼**gefährtin** die (geh.) companion through life (literary); ∼**geister** Pl. jmds. ∼geister [wieder] wecken put new life into sb.; ∼**groß** Adj. life-size; ∼**größe** die: eine Statue in ∼größe a life-size statue

Lebens·haltung die cost of living

Lebenshaltungs-: ∼index der (Wirtsch.) cost-of-living index; ∼**kosten** Pl. cost of living sing.

lebens-, Lebens-: ∼jahr das year of [one's] life; ∼**kraft** die vitality;

~**künstler** der, ~**künstlerin** die: ein [echter/wahrer] ~künstler a person who always knows how to make the best of things; ~**lage** die situation [in life]; ~**lang** [1] Adj. lifelong; [2] adv. all one's life; ~**länglich** [1] Adj. ~länglicher Freiheitsentzug life imprisonment; [2] adv. jmdn. ~länglich gefangen halten keep sb. imprisoned for life; ~**lauf** der curriculum vitae; c.v.; ~**licht** das (geh.) flame of life (literary); jmdm. das ~licht ausblasen od. auspusten (ugs.) send sb. to kingdom come (coll.); ~**lustig** Adj. ⟨person⟩ full of the joys of life

Lebens·mittel das food[stuff]; ~ Pl. food sing.

Lebensmittel-: ~**abteilung** die food department; ~**geschäft** das food shop; ~**vergiftung** die food poisoning

lebens-, Lebens-: ~**müde** Adj. weary of life pred.; ~**notwendig** Adj. essential; ~**raum** der (a) (Umkreis) lebensraum; (b) (Biol.) ▶ BIOTOP; ~**retter** der, ~**retterin** die rescuer; ~**standard** der standard of living; ~**unterhalt** der: seinen ~unterhalt verdienen/bestreiten earn one's living/support oneself; ~**versicherung** die life insurance; ~**wandel** der way of life; ~**weg** der [journey through] life; ~**weise** die way of life; ~**zeichen** das sign of life; ~**zeit** die life[span]; auf ~zeit for life

Leber die; ~, ~n liver

Leber-: ~**fleck** der liver spot; ~**käse** der: meat loaf made with mincemeat, [minced liver,] eggs, and spices; ~**tran** der fish-liver oil; (des Kabeljaus) cod-liver oil; ~**wurst** die liver sausage; ~**zirrhose** die (Med.) cirrhosis of the liver

Lebe-: ~**wesen** das living being; ~**wohl** /-'--/ das; ~~[e]s, ~~ od. ~~e (geh.) farewell

lebhaft [1] Adj. (a) lively; busy ⟨traffic⟩; brisk ⟨business⟩
(b) (deutlich) vivid ⟨idea, picture, etc.⟩
(c) (kräftig) bright ⟨colour⟩; vigorous ⟨applause, opposition⟩
[2] adv. (a) in a lively way
(b) (deutlich) vividly
(c) (kräftig) brightly ⟨coloured⟩

leb-, Leb-: ~**kuchen** der ≈ gingerbread; ~**los** Adj. lifeless; ~**zeiten** Pl. bei od. zu jmds. ~zeiten during sb.'s lifetime

lechzen itr. V. (geh.) nach einem Trunk ~: long for a drink; nach Rache usw. ~: thirst for revenge etc.

leck Adj. leaky; ~ sein leak

Leck das; ~[e]s, ~s leak

lecken¹ [1] tr. V. lick
[2] itr. V. an etw. (Dat.) ~: lick sth.

lecken² itr. V. (leck sein) leak

lecker Adj. tasty ⟨meal⟩; delicious ⟨cake etc.⟩; good ⟨smell, taste⟩

Lecker·bissen der delicacy; ein musikalischer ~ (fig.) a musical treat

Leckerei die; ~, ~en (ugs.) dainty; (Süßigkeit) sweet [meat]

led. Abk. = **ledig**

Leder das; ~s, ~: leather

Leder-: ~**handschuh** der leather glove; ~**hose** die leather shorts pl.; lederhosen pl.; (lang) leather trousers; ~**jacke** die leather jacket; ~**riemen** der [leather] strap; ~**waren** Pl. leather goods

ledig Adj. single; eine ~e Mutter an unmarried mother

Ledige der/die; adj. Dekl. single person

lediglich Adj. merely

leer Adj. empty; clean ⟨sheet of paper⟩; ~ stehend empty, unoccupied

Leere die; ~ (auch fig.) emptiness

leeren tr., refl. V. empty

leer-, Leer-: ~**gefegt** Adj. deserted ⟨street, town⟩; wie ~gefegt deserted; ~**lauf** der im ~lauf den Berg hinunterfahren ⟨driver⟩ coast down the hill in neutral; ⟨cyclist⟩ freewheel down the hill; *~**stehend** ▶ LEER; ~**taste** die space bar

Leerung die; ~, ~en emptying; (von Briefkästen) collection

Lefze die; ~, ~n lip

legal [1] Adj. legal
[2] adv. legally

legalisieren tr. V. legalize

Legalisierung die; ~, ~en legalization

Legalität die; ~: legality

legen [1] tr. V. (a) lay [down]
(b) (verlegen) lay ⟨pipe, cable, carpet, tiles, etc.⟩
[2] tr., itr. V. ⟨hen⟩ lay
[3] refl. V. (a) lie down
(b) (nachlassen) die down; abate; ⟨enthusiasm⟩ wear off, subside

legendär Adj. legendary

Legende die; ~, ~n legend

leger /le'ʒeːɐ̯/ [1] Adj. casual
[2] adv. casually

legieren tr. V. alloy

Legierung die; ~, ~en alloy

Legislative die; ~, ~n (Politik) legislature

Legislatur·periode die legislative period

legitim Adj. legitimate

Legitimation die; ~, ~en (a) legitimation
(b) (Ausweis) proof of identity

legitimieren [1] tr. V. (a) (rechtfertigen) justify
(b) (bevollmächtigen) authorize
(c) (für legitim erklären) legitimize ⟨child, relationship⟩
[2] refl. V. show proof of one's identity

Legitimität die; ~: legitimacy

Lehm der; ~s loam; (Ton) clay

Lehne *die;* ~, ~n (Rücken~) back; (Arm~) arm

lehnen ① *tr., refl. V.* lean (**an** + *Akk.,* **gegen** against)
② *itr. V.* be leaning (**an** + *Dat.* against)

Lehn-: ~**stuhl** *der* armchair; ~**wort** *das; Pl.* ~**wörter** loanword

Lehr-: ~**auftrag** *der* lectureship; ~**buch** *das* textbook

Lehre *die;* ~, ~n (a) apprenticeship
(b) (Weltanschauung) doctrine
(c) (Theorie, Wissenschaft) theory
(d) (Erfahrung) lesson

lehren *tr., itr. V.* teach

Lehrer *der;* ~s, ~ (auch fig.) teacher; (Ausbilder) instructor

Lehrer-: ~**ausbildung** *die* teacher training *no art.;* ~**ausflug** *die* staff outing

Lehrerin *die;* ~, ~nen teacher

Lehrer-: ~**kollegium** *das* teaching staff; faculty (Amer.); ~**konferenz** *das* staff meeting; ~**zimmer** *das* staffroom

Lehr-: ~**gang** *der* course (**für, in** + *Dat.* in); ~**jahr** *das* year as an apprentice; ~**körper** *der* (Amtsspr.) teaching staff; faculty (Amer.)

Lehrling *der;* ~s, ~e apprentice; (in kaufmännischen Berufen) trainee

lehr-, Lehr-: ~**plan** *der* (Schulw.) syllabus; (Gesamtlehrgang) curriculum; ~**reich** *Adj.* informative; ~**stelle** *die* apprenticeship; (in kaufmännischen Berufen) trainee post; ~**stoff** *der* (Schulw.) syllabus

Leib *der;* ~[e]s, ~er (geh.) body; **mit** ~ **und Seele** Arzt/Krankenschwester *usw.* sein be a dedicated doctor/nurse *etc.;* **mit** ~ **und Seele dabei sein** put one's whole heart into it

Leibes-: ~**übungen** *Pl.* (Schulw.) physical education *sing.;* PE; ~**visitation** *die;* ~~, ~~en body search

Leib-gericht *das* favourite dish

leibhaftig *Adj.* in person *postpos.;* (echt) real

leiblich *Adj.* physical ‹*well-being*›; (blutsverwandt) real

Leib-: ~**schmerzen** *Pl.* abdominal pain *sing.;* ~**wächter** *der,* ~**wächterin** *die* bodyguard

Leiche *die;* ~, ~n [dead] body; corpse

Leichen *der* hearse

leichen-, Leichen-: ~**blass**, ***~**blaß** *Adj.* deathly pale; ~**schau-haus** *das* morgue; ~**wagen** *der* hearse

Leichnam *der;* ~s, ~e (geh.) body

leicht ① *Adj.* light; lightweight ‹*suit, material*›; easy ‹*task, question, job, etc.*›; slight ‹*accent, illness, wound, doubt, etc.*›; mild ‹*cigar, cigarette*›; ~ **fallen** be easy; **das fällt mir** ~: it's easy for me; **jmdm./sich etw.** ~ **machen** make sth. easy for sb./oneself; **etw.** ~ **nehmen** make light of sth.

─────────
*alte Schreibung - vgl. Hinweis auf S. xiv

② *adv.* lightly ‹*built*›; (einfach, schnell, spielend) easily; (geringfügig) slightly; ~ **verletzt** slightly injured

leicht-, Leicht-: ~**athletik** *die* [track and field] athletics *sing.;* ***~**fallen** ► LEICHT 1; ~**fertig** ① *Adj.* careless ‹*behaviour, person*›; rash ‹*promise*›; ill-considered, slapdash ‹*plan*›; ② *adv.* carelessly; ~**gläubig** *Adj.* gullible

Leichtigkeit *die;* ~ (geringes Gewicht) lightness; (Mühelosigkeit) ease

leicht-, Leicht-: ***~|**machen** ► LEICHT 1; ***~|**nehmen** ► LEICHT 1; ~**sinn** *der* carelessness *no indef. art.;* (mit Gefahr verbunden) recklessness *no indef. art.;* ~**sinnig** ① *Adj.* careless; (sich, andere gefährdend) reckless; (fahrlässig) negligent; ② *adv.* carelessly; (gefährlich) recklessly; ‹*promise*› rashly; ~**sinniger-weise** *Adv.* carelessly; (gefährlicherweise) recklessly; ‹*promise*› rashly; ***~**verletzt** ► LEICHT 2

leid *Adj.* **etw./jmdn.** ~ **sein/werden** (ugs.) be/get fed up with sth./sb. (coll.); *s. auch* LEID²

Leid¹ *das;* ~[e]s (a) (Schmerz) suffering; (Kummer) grief; sorrow
(b) (Unrecht) wrong; (Böses) harm

Leid²: **es tut mir** ~, [**dass**]...: I'm sorry [that]...; **er tut mir** ~: I feel sorry for him

leiden ① *unr. itr. V.* suffer (**an, unter** + *Dat.* from)
② *unr. tr. V.* (a) **jmdn.** [**gut**] ~ **können** *od.* **mögen** like sb.
(b) (geh.: ertragen müssen) suffer ‹*hunger, thirst, etc.*›

Leiden *das;* ~s, ~ (a) (Krankheit) illness; (Gebrechen) complaint
(b) (Qual) suffering

leidend *Adj.* (a) (krank) ailing
(b) (schmerzvoll) strained ‹*voice*›; martyred ‹*expression*›

Leidenschaft *die;* ~, ~en passion (**zu, für** for)

leidenschaftlich ① *Adj.* passionate; vehement ‹*protest*›
② *adv.* passionately; (eifrig) dedicatedly; **etw.** ~ **gern tun** adore doing sth.

Leidens-genosse *der,* **Leidens-genossin** *die* fellow sufferer

leider *Adv.* unfortunately

leidig *Adj.* tiresome

leidlich *Adj.* reasonable

Leid-tragende *der/die; adj. Dekl.* victim

Leier *die;* ~, ~n lyre

leihen *unr. tr. V.* (a) **jmdm. etw.** ~: lend sb. sth.
(b) (entleihen) borrow

Leih-: ~**gabe** *die* loan (*Gen.* from); ~**gebühr** *die* hire *or* (Amer.) rental charge; (bei Büchern) borrowing fee; ~**haus** *das* pawnbroker's; pawnshop; ~**mutter** *die; Pl.* ~**mütter** surrogate mother; ~**wagen** *der* hire *or* (Amer.) rental car

Leim *der;* ~[e]s glue

leimen *tr. V.* glue (**an** + *Akk.* to)

Leine *die;* ~, ~n rope; (Wäsche~, Angel~) line; (Hunde~) lead (esp. Brit.); leash; ~ **ziehen** (ugs.) clear off

leinen *Adj.* linen ‹*tablecloth, sheet, etc.*›

Leinen *das;* ~s (a) (Gewebe) linen
(b) (Buchw.) cloth

Leinen·band *der* cloth-bound volume

Lein·wand *die* (a) linen; (grob) canvas
(b) (des Malers) canvas
(c) (für Filme und Dias) screen

leise [1] *Adj.* (a) quiet; soft ‹*steps, music, etc.*›
(b) (leicht) faint; slight; slight, gentle ‹*touch*›
[2] *adv.* (a) quietly
(b) (leicht; kaum merklich) slightly; ‹*touch, rain*› gently

Leiste *die;* ~, ~n strip; (Holz~) batten; (profiliert) moulding

leisten [1] *tr. V.* do ‹*work*›; (schaffen) achieve ‹*a lot, nothing*›; **jmdm. Hilfe** ~: help sb.
[2] *refl. V.* (ugs.) **sich** (*Dat.*) **etw.** ~: treat oneself to sth.; **sich** (*Dat.*) **etw.** [**nicht**] ~ **können** [not] be able to afford sth.

Leisten·bruch *der* rupture

Leistung *die;* ~, ~en (a) (Qualität bzw. Quantität der Arbeit) performance
(b) (Errungenschaft) achievement; (im Sport) performance
(c) (Leistungsvermögen, Physik: Arbeits~) power
(d) (Zahlung, Zuwendung) payment; (Versicherungsw.) benefit
(e) (Dienst~) service

leistungs-, Leistungs-: ~**druck** *der* (bei Arbeitnehmern) pressure to work harder; (bei Sportlern, Schülern) pressure to achieve *or* to do well; ~**fähig** *Adj.* capable ‹*person*›; (körperlich) able-bodied; ~**gesellschaft** *die* competitive society; ~**prinzip** *das* competitive principle; ~**sport** *der* competitive sport *no art.*

Leit·artikel *der* (Zeitungsw.) leading article; leader

leiten *tr. V.* (a) (anführen) lead; head; be head of ‹*school*›; (verantwortlich sein für) be in charge of ‹*project, expedition, etc.*›; manage ‹*factory, enterprise*›; (den Vorsitz führen bei) chair; conduct ‹*orchestra, choir*›; ~**der Angestellter** manager
(b) (begleiten, führen) lead
(c) (lenken) direct; route ‹*traffic*›; (um~) divert

Leiter[1] *der;* ~s, ~: leader; (einer Abteilung) head; (eines Instituts) director; (einer Schule) head teacher; headmaster (Brit.); principal (esp. Amer.); (Vorsitzender) chair[man]

Leiter[2] *die;* ~, ~n ladder

Leiterin *die;* ~, ~nen ▶ LEITER[1]; (einer Schule) head teacher; headmistress (Brit.); principal (esp. Amer.)

Leit-: ~**motiv** *das* (Musik, Literaturw., fig.)
(a) leitmotiv; (b) (Leitgedanke) dominant *or*

central theme; ~**planke** *die* crash barrier; guardrail (Amer.)

Leitung *die;* ~, ~en (a) ▶ LEITEN A: leading; heading; being in charge; management; chairing
(b) (einer Expedition usw.) leadership; (Verantwortung) responsibility (*Gen.* for); (eines Betriebes, Unternehmens) management; (einer Sitzung, Diskussion) chairmanship
(c) (leitende Personen) management; (einer Schule) head and senior staff
(d) (Rohr~) pipe; (Haupt~) main
(e) (Draht, Kabel) cable; (für ein Gerät) lead
(f) (Telefon~) line

Leitungs·wasser *das* tap water

Leit·zins[satz] *der* (Finanzw.) discount rate; ≈ base rate

Lektion /lɛkˈtsi̯oːn/ *die;* ~, ~en lesson

Lektor *der;* ~s, ~en (a) (Hochschulw.) *junior university teacher in charge of practical or supplementary classes etc.;*
(b) (im Verlag) [publisher's] editor

Lektüre *die;* ~, ~n (a) reading
(b) (Lesestoff) reading [matter]

Lende *die;* ~, ~n loin

Lenden-: ~**gegend** *die* loins *pl.;* lumbar region (Anat.); ~**schurz** *der* loincloth; ~**wirbel** *der* (Anat.) lumbar vertebra

lenken *tr. V.* (a) *auch itr.* steer; be at the controls of ‹*aircraft*›; guide ‹*missile*›; (fahren) drive ‹*car etc.*›
(b) direct ‹*thoughts etc.*› (**auf** + *Akk.* to); turn ‹*attention*› (**auf** + *Akk.* to)
(c) (kontrollieren) control ‹*person, press, economy*›; govern ‹*state*›

Lenker *der;* ~s, ~ (a) handlebars *pl.;*
(b) (Fahrer) driver

Lenkerin *die;* ~, ~nen ▶ LENKER B

Lenk-: ~**rad** *das* steering wheel; ~**rad·schloss,** ***~**rad·schloß** *das* (Kfz-W.) steering [wheel] lock; ~**stange** *die* handlebars *pl.*

Lenz *der;* ~es, ~e (dichter. veralt.) spring

Leopard *der;* ~en, ~en leopard

Lepra *die;* ~: leprosy *no art.*

Lerche *die;* ~, ~n lark

lernen [1] *itr. V.* study; (als Lehrling) train
[2] *tr. V.* learn (**aus** from)

lesbar *Adj.* legible; (klar) lucid ‹*style*›; (verständlich) comprehensible

Lesbe *die;* ~, ~n (ugs.) lesbian

Lesbierin /ˈlɛsbi̯ərɪn/ *die;* ~, ~nen lesbian

lesbisch *Adj.* Lesbian

Lese-: ~**brille** *die* reading glasses *pl.;* ~**buch** *das* reader

lesen[1] *unr. tr., itr. V.* read

lesen[2] *unr. tr. V.* (a) pick ‹*grapes, berries, fruit*›; gather ‹*firewood*›; **Ähren** ~: glean [ears of corn]
(b) (aussondern) pick over

Leser *der;* ~s, ~: reader

Leserbrief der reader's letter; ~e readers' letters; „~e" (Zeitungsrubrik) 'Letters to the editor' **Leserin** die; ~, ~nen reader
Leserkreis der readership
leserlich [1] Adj. legible
[2] adv. legibly
Lese-zeichen das bookmark
Lesung die; ~, ~en reading
Lette der; ~n, ~n, **Lettin** die; ~, ~nen Latvian
lettisch Adj. Latvian; Lettish ⟨language⟩
Lett-land (das); ~s Latvia
Letzt: zu guter ~: in the end
letzt... Adj. last; ~en Endes in the end; (äußerst...) ultimate; (neuest...) latest ⟨news⟩
*letzte-mal: ▶ MAL[1]
*letzen-mal: ▶ MAL[1]
letzter... Adj. latter
letztlich Adv. ultimately; in the end
Leucht·diode die light-emitting diode; LED
Leuchte die; ~, ~n light
leuchten itr. V. (a) ⟨moon, sun, star, etc.⟩ be shining; ⟨fire, face⟩ glow
(b) shine a/the light; jmdm. ~: light the way for sb.
leuchtend Adj. (a) shining ⟨eyes⟩; brilliant ⟨colours⟩; bright ⟨blue, red, etc.⟩
(b) (großartig) shining ⟨example⟩
Leuchter der; ~s, ~: candelabrum; (für eine Kerze) candlestick
Leucht-: ~**farbe** die luminous paint; ~**kugel** die flare; ~**reklame** die neon sign; ~**stoff·lampe** die fluorescent light or lamp; ~**turm** der lighthouse; ~**ziffer·blatt** das luminous dial
leugnen [1] tr. V. deny
[2] itr. V. deny it
Leukämie die; ~, ~n (Med.) leukaemia
Leumund der; ~[e]s (geh.) reputation
Leute Pl. people; die reichen/alten ~: the rich/the old
Leutnant der; ~s, ~s second lieutenant (Milit.)
leut·selig [1] Adj. affable
[2] adv. affably
Lexikon das; ~s, Lexika od. Lexiken encyclopaedia ⟨Gen., für of⟩
Libanese der; ~n, ~n, **Libanesin** die; ~, ~nen Lebanese
Libanon (das) od. der; ~s Lebanon
Libelle die; ~, ~n dragonfly
liberal [1] Adj. liberal
[2] adv. liberally
Liberale der/die; adj. Dekl. liberal
liberalisieren tr. V. liberalize; relax ⟨import controls⟩
Libero der; ~s, ~s (Fußball) sweeper

Libyen (das); ~s Libya
libysch Adj. Libyan
licht Adj. (a) light
(b) (dünn bewachsen) sparse; thin
Licht das; ~[e]s, ~er (a) light
(b) (elektrisches) light
(c) Pl. auch ~e (Kerze) candle
licht-, Licht-: ~**bild** das [small] photograph ⟨for passport etc.⟩; ~**empfindlich** Adj. sensitive to light
lichten[1] [1] tr. V. thin out ⟨trees etc.⟩
[2] refl. V. ⟨trees⟩ thin out; ⟨hair⟩ grow thin; ⟨fog, mist⟩ lift
lichten[2] tr. V. (Seemannsspr.) den/die Anker ~: weigh anchor
lichterloh [1] Adj. blazing ⟨fire⟩; leaping ⟨flames⟩
[2] adv. ~ brennen be blazing fiercely
Lichter·meer das sea of lights
Licht-: ~**hupe** die headlight flasher; ~**jahr** das (Astron.) light year; ~**kegel** der beam; ~**maschine** die (Kfz-W.) (mit Gleichstrom) dynamo; (mit Wechselstrom) alternator; generator (esp. Amer.); ~**reklame** die neon sign; ~**schalter** der light switch; ~**schranke** die photoelectric beam; ~**schutz·faktor** der protection factor ⟨against sunburn⟩
Lichtung die; ~, ~en clearing
Lid das; ~[e]s, ~er eyelid
lieb [1] Adj. (a) (liebevoll) kind ⟨words, gesture⟩
(b) (liebenswert) likeable; nice; (stärker) lovable ⟨child, girl, pet⟩; ~ aussehen look sweet or (Amer.) cute
(c) (artig) good ⟨child, dog⟩
(d) (geschätzt) dear; sein liebstes Spielzeug his favourite toy; ~er Hans/~e Else! (am Briefanfang) dear Hans/Else
(e) (angenehm) welcome; es wäre mir ~/~er, wenn ...: I should be glad/should prefer it if ...
(f) jmdn. ~ haben love sb.; (gern haben) be fond of sb.
[2] adv. (a) (liebenswert) kindly
(b) (artig) nicely
Liebe die; ~, ~n (a) love; ~ zu jmdm./zu etw. love for sb./of sth.; aus ~ [zu jmdm.] for love [of sb.]; tu mir die ~ und ...: do me a favour and ...; mit ~: lovingly; with loving care
(b) (ugs.: geliebter Mensch) love
Liebelei die; ~, ~en flirtation
lieben [1] tr. V. (a) jmdn. ~: love sb.; (sexuell) make love to sb.; sich ~: be in love; (sexuell) make love
(b) etw. ~: be fond of sth.; (stärker) love sth.
[2] itr. V. be in love
liebend Adv. etw. ~ gern tun [simply] love doing sth.
liebens·würdig Adj. kind; charming ⟨smile⟩
lieber Adv. (a) ▶ GERN;

(b) better; **lass das ∼:** better not do that

Liebes-: ∼**brief** *der* love letter; ∼**paar** *das* courting couple; ∼**roman** *der* romantic novel

liebe·voll ⟦1⟧ *Adj.* loving *attrib.* ⟨*care*⟩; affectionate ⟨*embrace, gesture, person*⟩ ⟦2⟧ *adv.* lovingly; affectionately; (mit Sorgfalt) lovingly

***lieb|haben** ▶ LIEB 1F

Liebhaber *der;* ∼**s,** ∼ **(a)** lover **(b)** (Interessierter, Anhänger) enthusiast ⟨*Gen.* for⟩; (Sammler) collector

Liebhaberei *die;* ∼, ∼: hobby

Liebhaberin *die;* ∼, ∼**nen** ▶ LIEBHABER

lieblich ⟦1⟧ *Adj.* charming; (angenehm) sweet ⟨*scent, sound*⟩ ⟦2⟧ *adv.* sweetly; (angenehm) pleasingly

Liebling *der;* ∼**s,** ∼**e** (bes. als Anrede) darling; (bevorzugte Person) favourite

Lieblings- favourite

lieb·los ⟦1⟧ *Adj.* loveless ⟦2⟧ *adv.* **(a)** without affection **(b)** (ohne Sorgfalt) without proper care

liebsten: am ∼: ▶ GERN

Liechtenstein *(das);* ∼**s** Liechtenstein

Lied *das;* ∼[e]s, ∼**er** song

liederlich *Adj.* slovenly; messy ⟨*hairstyle, person*⟩

Lieder-: ∼**macher** *der;* ∼∼**s,** ∼∼; ∼**macherin** *die;* ∼∼, ∼∼**nen** singer-songwriter

lief *1. u. 3. Pers. Sg. Prät. v.* LAUFEN

Lieferant *der;* ∼**en,** ∼**en, Lieferantin** *die;* ∼, ∼**nen** supplier

lieferbar *Adj.* available; (vorrätig) in stock

Liefer·bedingungen *Pl.* terms of delivery

liefern *tr. V.* **(a)** (bringen) deliver (**an** + *Akk.* to); (zur Verfügung stellen) supply **(b)** (hervorbringen) produce; provide ⟨*eggs, honey, examples, raw material, etc.*⟩

Liefer-: ∼**schein** *der* delivery note; ∼**termin** *der* delivery date

Lieferung *die;* ∼, ∼**en** delivery

Liefer-: ∼**wagen** *der* [delivery] van; ∼**zeit** *die* delivery time

Liege *die;* ∼, ∼**n** daybed; (zum Ausklappen) bed settee; (als Gartenmöbel) sunlounger

liegen *unr. itr. V.* lie; ⟨*person*⟩ be lying down; (sich befinden) be; ⟨*object*⟩ be [lying]; ⟨*town, house, etc.*⟩ be [situated]; **im Bett ∼:** lie in bed; ∼ **bleiben** (liegen gelassen werden) stay; be left; (vergessen werden) be left behind; (unerledigt bleiben) be left undone; (nicht aufstehen) stay [lying]; **[im Bett] ∼ bleiben** stay in bed; **etw. ∼ lassen** leave sth.; (vergessen) leave sth. [behind]; (unerledigt lassen) leave sth. undone; **einen Brief ∼ lassen** (nicht abschicken) leave a letter unposted; (nicht öffnen) leave a letter unopened; **das liegt an ihm** *od.* **bei ihm** it is up to him; (ist seine Schuld) it is his fault; **es**

liegt mir nicht it doesn't suit me; (es spricht mich nicht an) it doesn't appeal to me; (ich mag es nicht) I don't like it; **daran liegt ihm viel/wenig/nichts** he sets great/little/no store by that

liegen-: *∼**|bleiben** ▶ LIEGEN; *∼**|lassen** ▶ LIEGEN

Liege-: ∼**stuhl** *der* deckchair; ∼**stütz** *der;* ∼∼**es,** ∼∼**e** press-up; ∼**wagen** *der* couchette car; ∼**wiese** *die* sunbathing lawn

lieh *1. u. 3. Pers. Sg. Prät. v.* LEIHEN

lies *Imperativ Sg. v.* LESEN

ließ *1. u. 3. Pers. Sg. Prät. v.* LASSEN

liest *3. Pers. Sg. Präsens v.* LESEN

Lift *der;* ∼[e]s, ∼**e** *od.* ∼**s (a)** lift (Brit.); elevator (Amer.) **(b)** *Pl.:* ∼**e** (Ski∼, Sessel∼) lift

Liga *die;* ∼, **Ligen** league; (Sport) division

Likör *der;* ∼**s,** ∼**e** liqueur

lila *indekl. Adj.* mauve; (dunkel∼) purple

Lila *das;* ∼**s** *od.* (ugs.) ∼**s** mauve; (Dunkel∼) purple

Lilie /'liːli̯ə/ *die;* ∼, ∼**n** lily

Liliputaner *der;* ∼**s,** ∼, **Liliputanerin** *die;* ∼, ∼**nen** dwarf

Limit *das;* ∼**s,** ∼**s** limit

Limo *die, auch: das;* ∼, ∼[s] (ugs.) fizzy drink

Limonade *die;* ∼, ∼**n** fizzy drink; (Zitronen∼) lemonade

Limousine *die;* ∼, ∼**n** [large] saloon (Brit.) *or* (Amer.) sedan

Linde *die;* ∼, ∼**n** lime [tree]

lindern *tr. V.* relieve ⟨*suffering, pain*⟩; slake ⟨*thirst*⟩

Lineal *das;* ∼**s,** ∼**e** ruler

Linie /'liːni̯ə/ *die;* ∼, ∼**n** line; (Verkehrsstrecke) route; **die ∼ 12** (Verkehrsw.) the number 12; **auf die [schlanke] ∼ achten** (ugs. scherzh.) watch one's figure; **auf der ganzen ∼** (fig.) all along the line

linien-, Linien-: ∼**bus** *der* regular bus; ∼**flug** *der* scheduled flight; ∼**richter** *der,* ∼**richterin** *die* (Fußball usw.) linesman; (Tennis) line judge; (Rugby) touch judge; ∼**treu** ⟦1⟧ *Adj.* loyal to the party line *postpos.;* ⟦2⟧ *adv.* ⟨*act*⟩ in accordance with the party line

linieren, liniieren *tr. V.* rule

link... *Adj.* **(a)** left **(b)** (innen, nicht sichtbar) wrong, reverse ⟨*side*⟩ **(c)** (in der Politik) left-wing

linkisch ⟦1⟧ *Adj.* awkward ⟦2⟧ *adv.* awkwardly

links *Adv.* on the left; (Politik) on the left wing

links-, Links-: ∼**abbieger** *der,* ∼**abbiegerin** *die* (Verkehrsw.) motorist/cyclist/car *etc.* turning left; ∼**außen** *der;* ∼∼, ∼∼ (Ballspiele) left wing; outside left; ∼**extremist** *der,* ∼**extremistin** *die* ┄╍╍┄

(Politik) left-wing extremist; ~**händer** der;
~~s, ~~, ~**händerin** die; ~~, ~~nen
left-hander; ~**kurve** die left-hand bend;
~**radikal** (Politik)⒈ Adj. radical left-
wing;⒉ adv. eine ~radikal orientierte Gruppe
a group with a radical left-wing orientation;
~**radikale** der/die left-wing radical;
~**radikalismus** der left-wing radicalism;
~**verkehr** der driving no art. on the left

Linoleum das; ~s linoleum; lino

Linse die; ~, ~n (a) (Bot., Kochk.) lentil
(b) (Med., Optik) lens

Lippe die; ~, ~n lip

Lippen-stift der lipstick

liquid Adj. (Wirtsch.) liquid ⟨funds, resources⟩;
solvent ⟨business⟩

liquidieren (verhüll.: töten; Wirtsch.) liquidate

lispeln itr. V. lisp

Lissabon (das); ~s Lisbon

List die; ~, ~en (a) [cunning] trick
(b) (listige Art) cunning

Liste die; ~, ~n list; **schwarze** ~: blacklist

listig ⒈ Adj. cunning; crafty
⒉ adv. cunningly; craftily

Litauen (das); ~s Lithuania

Litauer der; ~s, ~, **Litauerin** die; ~,
~nen Lithuanian

litauisch Adj. Lithuanian

Liter der, auch: das; ~s, ~: litre

literarisch Adj. literary

Literatur die; ~, ~en literature

Literatur-: ~**geschichte** die literary
history; history of literature;
~**verzeichnis** das list of references

liter-weise Adv. by the litre; in litres

Litfaß-säule die advertising column

Lithografie, Lithographie die; ~, ~n
(Druck) lithograph

litt 1. u. 3. Pers. Sg. Prät. v. LEIDEN

Litze die; ~, ~n braid

live /lai:f/ (Rundf., Ferns.); ⒈ Adj. live
⒉ adv. live; **in dieser Sendung wird nur** ~
gesungen in this programme all the singing
is live

Live-: ~**sendung**, *~**Sendung** die
(Rundf., Ferns.) live programme;
~**übertragung** die (Rundf., Ferns.) live
broadcast

Lizenz die; ~, ~en licence

Lizenz-gebühr die licence fee; (Verlagsw.)
royalty

Lkw, LKW /ɛlka:'ve:/ der; ~[s], ~[s] Abk.
= **Lastkraftwagen** truck; lorry (Brit.)

Lob das; ~[e]s, ~e praise no indef. art.

Lobby /'lɔbi/ die; ~, ~s od. **Lobbies** lobby

loben tr. V. praise

lobens-wert ⒈ Adj. praiseworthy;
laudable; commendable
⒉ adv. laudably; commendably

---

*alte Schreibung - vgl. Hinweis auf S. xiv

löblich Adj. commendable

Lob-lied das song of praise

Loch das; ~[e]s, **Löcher** hole

lochen tr. V. punch holes/a hole in; punch
⟨ticket⟩

Locher der; ~s, ~: punch

löcherig Adj. full of holes pred.

Locke die; ~, ~n curl

locken tr. V. (a) lure
(b) (reizen) tempt

Locken-wickler der [hair] curler

locker ⒈ Adj. loose; (entspannt) relaxed
⟨position, muscles⟩; slack ⟨rope, rein⟩; (fig.)
relax ⟨regulation, law, etc.⟩
⒉ adv. ~ **sitzen** ⟨tooth, screw, nail⟩ be loose;
(entspannt, ungezwungen) loosely

locker|lassen unr. itr. V. (ugs.) **nicht** ~:
not give up

lockern ⒈ tr. V. loosen; slacken [off] ⟨rope
etc.⟩; relax ⟨muscles, limbs⟩
⒉ refl. V. ⟨brick, tooth, etc.⟩ work itself loose;
⟨person⟩ loosen up

Lockerung die; ~, ~en (a) loosening; (fig.:
von Bestimmung, Gesetz usw.) relaxation
(b) (Entspannung) loosening up; relaxation

lockig Adj. curly

Lock-vogel der decoy

Loden-mantel der loden coat

Löffel der; ~s, ~: spoon; (als Maßangabe)
spoonful; (Jägerspr.) ear

löffeln tr. V. spoon [up]

log 1. u. 3. Pers. Sg. Prät. v. LÜGEN

Logarithmus der; ~, **Logarithmen** (Math.)
logarithm; log

Loge /'lo:ʒə/ die; ~, ~n box

logieren itr. V. (veralt.) stay

Logik die; ~: logic

logisch ⒈ Adj. logical
⒉ adv. logically

logischer-weise Adv. logically;
(selbstverständlich) naturally

logo Adj. (salopp) [**ist doch**] ~! you bet! (coll.);
of course!

Lohn der; ~[e]s, **Löhne** (a) wage[s pl.]; pay
no indef. art., no pl.
(b) (Belohnung) reward

Lohn-büro das payroll office

lohnen ⒈ refl., itr. V. be worth it
⒉ tr. V. be worth

lohnend Adj. rewarding

Lohn-steuer die income tax

Lohn-: ~**steuer-karte** die income-tax
card; ~**streifen** der payslip; ~**tüte** die
pay packet (Brit.); wage packet

lokal Adj. local

Lokal das; ~s, ~e pub (Brit. coll.); bar (Amer.);
(Speise~) restaurant

Lokalität die; ~, ~en locality

Lokal-: ~**blatt** das local paper;
~**patriotismus** der local patriotism;

∼teil der (Zeitungsw.) local section;
∼termin der (Rechtsspr.) visit to the scene
[of the crime]

Lok·führer der, **Lok·führerin** die:
▶ LOKOMOTIVFÜHRER

Lokomotive /lokomo'ti:və/ die; ∼, ∼n
locomotive

Lokomotiv·führer der,
Lokomotiv·führerin die engine driver
(Brit.); engineer (Amer.)

Lokus der; ∼ od. ∼ses, ∼ od. ∼se (salopp)
loo (Brit. coll.); john (Amer. coll.)

London (das) ∼s London

Londoner ① indekl. Adj. London
② der; ∼s, ∼: Londoner

Londonerin die; ∼, ∼nen Londoner

Lorbeer der; ∼s, ∼en (a) laurel
(b) (Gewürz) bayleaf

Lore die; ∼, ∼n car; (kleiner) tub

los ① Adj. (a) (gelöst, ab) off
(b) es ist etwas ∼: there is something going
on
(c) jmdn./etw. ∼ sein be rid of sb./sth.
② Adv. (als Aufforderung) come on!

Los das; ∼es, ∼e (a) lot
(b) (Lotterie∼) ticket

Lösch·blatt das piece of blotting paper

löschen tr. V. (a) put out; extinguish;
seinen Durst ∼ (fig.) quench one's thirst
(b) (tilgen) delete ⟨entry⟩; erase ⟨recording,
memory, etc.⟩

Lösch-: ∼fahrzeug das fire engine;
∼papier das blotting paper

lose ① Adj. loose
② adv. loosely

Löse·geld das ransom

losen itr. V. draw lots (um for)

lösen ① tr. V. (a) remove ⟨stamp,
wallpaper⟩; etw. von etw. ∼: remove sth.
from sth.
(b) (lockern) undo ⟨screw, belt, tie⟩
(c) (klären) solve; resolve ⟨contradiction,
conflict⟩
(d) (annullieren) break off ⟨engagement⟩;
cancel ⟨contract⟩; sever ⟨relationship⟩
(e) (kaufen) buy, obtain ⟨ticket⟩
② refl. V. (a) (lose werden) come off; (sich
lockern) ⟨wallpaper, plaster⟩ come off;
⟨packing, screw⟩ come loose
(b) (sich klären) ⟨puzzle, problem⟩ be solved
(c) (sich auflösen) dissolve

los-: ∼fahren unr. itr. V.; mit sein set off;
(wegfahren) move off; ∼gehen unr. itr. V.;
mit sein (a) (aufbrechen) set off; (b) (ugs.:
beginnen) start; (c) (ugs.: abgehen) ⟨button,
handle, etc.⟩ come off; ∼kommen unr.
itr. V.; mit sein (ugs.) (a) (wegkommen) get
away; (b) (freikommen) get free; ∼lassen unr. tr. V.
(a) (nicht festhalten) let go of; (b) (freilassen) let
⟨person, animal⟩ go; ∼legen itr. V. (ugs.)
get going

löslich Adj. soluble

Löslichkeit die; ∼: solubility

los|machen tr. V. (ugs.) let ⟨animal⟩ loose;
untie ⟨string, line, rope⟩; unhitch ⟨trailer⟩

Los·nummer die [lottery-]ticket number

los-: ∼reißen unr. refl. V. break free or
loose; ∼sagen refl. V. sich von jmdm./etw.
∼sagen break with sb./sth.; ∼schlagen
unr. itr. V. (bes. Milit.) attack; launch one's
attack

Löss, *Löß der; Lösses, Lösse (Geol.) loess

Losung die; ∼, ∼en slogan; (Milit.: Kennwort)
password

Lösung die; ∼, ∼en (a) solution (Gen., für
to)
(b) ▶ LÖSEN 1D: breaking off; cancellation;
severing

los|werden unr. tr. V.; mit sein get rid of

Lot das; ∼[e]s, ∼e plumb [bob]; [nicht] im ∼
sein be [out of] plumb

löten tr. V. solder

Lotion die; ∼, ∼en lotion

Löt·kolben der soldering iron

lot·recht ① Adj. perpendicular; vertical
② adv. perpendicularly; vertically

Lotse der; ∼n, ∼n (Seew.) pilot

lotsen tr. V. guide

Lotsin die ▶ LOTSE

Lotterie die; ∼, ∼n lottery

Lotto das; ∼s, ∼s national lottery

Lotto-: ∼schein der national-lottery
coupon; ∼zahlen Pl. winning national-
lottery numbers

Löt·zinn das [tin-lead] solder

Löwe der; ∼n, ∼n (a) lion
(b) (Astrol.) Leo; the Lion

Löwen-: ∼anteil der lion's share;
∼mäulchen das; ∼∼s, ∼∼: snapdragon;
∼zahn der dandelion

Löwin die; ∼, ∼nen lioness

loyal /loa'ja:l/ ① Adj. loyal
② adv. loyally

Loyalität die; ∼: loyalty

LP /el'pe:/ die; ∼, ∼[s] Abk.
= **Langspielplatte** LP

LSD /ɛles'de:/ das; ∼[s] LSD

Luchs der; ∼es, ∼e lynx

Lücke die; ∼, ∼n gap

lücken-, Lücken-: ∼büßer der, ∼∼s,
∼∼, ∼büßerin die; ∼∼, ∼∼nen (ugs.)
stopgap; ∼haft Adj. sketchy; ∼los Adj.
complete

lud 1. u. 3. Pers. Sg. Prät. v. LADEN

Luder das; ∼s, ∼ (salopp) so-and-so (coll.)

Luft die; ∼, Lüfte air; an die frische ∼
gehen get out in[to] the fresh air; die ∼
anhalten hold one's breath; tief ∼ holen take
a deep breath; in die ∼ gehen (fig. ugs.) blow
one's top (coll.)

luft-, Luft-: ∼angriff der (Milit.) air raid;
∼ballon der balloon; ∼brücke die
airlift; ∼dicht Adj. airtight; ∼druck der
(a) (Physik) air pressure; (b) (Druckwelle) blast

lüften ① *tr. V.* **(a)** air ⟨*room, clothes, etc.*⟩
(b) raise ⟨*hat*⟩
(c) disclose ⟨*secret*⟩
② *itr. V.* air the room/house *etc*

luft-, Luft-: ~**fahrt** *die* aviation *no art.;*
~**feuchtigkeit** *die* [atmospheric]
humidity; ~**gekühlt** *Adj.* air-cooled;
~**getrocknet** *Adj.* air-dried; ~**gewehr**
das air rifle; airgun

luftig *Adj.* airy ⟨*room, building, etc.*⟩; light
⟨*clothes*⟩

Luft·kissen·boot *das* hovercraft

luft-, Luft-: ~**leer** *Adj.* **ein** ~**leerer Raum**
a vacuum; ~**linie** *die* **1000 km** ~**linie** 1,000
km. as the crow flies; ~**loch** *das* air hole;
~**matratze** *die* airbed; air mattress; Lilo
®; ~**pirat** *der*, ~**piratin** *die* [aircraft]
hijacker; ~**post** *die* airmail; **etw. per** *od.*
mit ~**post schicken** send sth. [by] airmail;
~**pumpe** *die* air pump; **(für Fahrrad)** [bicycle]
pump; ~**röhre** *die* (Anat.) windpipe;
~**schiff** *das* airship; ~**schloss,**
*∗~**schloß** *das* castle in the air; ~**schutz**
der air-raid protection *no art.;*
~**schutz-bunker,** ~**schutz-keller,**
~**schutz-raum** *der* air-raid shelter;
~**verschmutzung** *die* air pollution;
~**waffe** *die* air force; ~**zug** *der* [gentle]
breeze; (in Zimmern, Gebäuden) draught

Lüge *die;* ~, ~n lie

lügen *itr., tr. V.* lie; **das ist gelogen!** that's a
lie!

Lügner *der;* ~s, ~, **Lügnerin** *die;* ~,
~**nen** liar

Luke *die;* ~, ~n (Dach~) skylight; (bei
Schiffen) hatch; (Keller~) trapdoor

lukrativ ① *Adj.* lucrative
② *adv.* lucratively

Lümmel *der;* ~s, ~: lout; (ugs., fam.: Bengel)
rascal

Lump *der;* ~en, ~en scoundrel

lumpen (ugs.) *tr. V.* **sich nicht** ~ **lassen**
splash out (coll.)

Lumpen *der;* ~s, ~ rag

Lumpen-: ~**sammler** *die* rag-and-bone
man; ~**sammlerin** *die* rag-and-bone
woman

Lunge *die;* ~, ~n lungs *pl.*

Lungen-: ~**entzündung** *die* pneumonia
no indef. art.; ~**krebs** *der* lung cancer;
~**zug** *der* inhalation

Lunte *die;* ~, ~n fuse; match

Lupe *die;* ~, ~n magnifying glass

Lurch *der;* ~[e]s, ~e amphibian

Lust *die;* ~ **(a)** ~ **haben, etw. zu tun** feel
like doing sth.
(b) (Vergnügen) pleasure; joy

lustig ① *Adj.* **(a)** merry; jolly; enjoyable
⟨*time*⟩
(b) (komisch) funny
② *adv.* **(a)** merrily
(b) (komisch) funnily

lust-, Lust-: ~**los** ① *Adj.* listless; ② *adv.*
listlessly; ~**spiel** *das* comedy

lutherisch *Adj.* Lutheran

lutschen ① *tr. V.* suck
② *itr. V.* suck; **an etw.** (Dat.) ~: suck sth.

Luxemburg (*das*)*;* ~s Luxembourg

luxuriös ① *Adj.* luxurious
② *adv.* luxuriously

Luxus *der;* ~: luxury

Lymphe *die;* ~, ~n lymph

Lymph·knoten *der* lymph node

lynchen *tr. V.* lynch

Lyrik *die;* ~: lyric poetry

Lyriker *der;* ~s, ~, **Lyrikerin** *die;* ~,
~**nen** lyric poet; lyricist

lyrisch *Adj.* lyrical; lyric ⟨*poetry*⟩

Lyzeum *das;* ~s, Lyzeen girls' high school

M m

m, M /ɛm/ *das;* ~, ~ m/M

m *Abk.* = **Meter** m

Mach·art *die* style; (Schnitt) cut

machbar *Adj.* feasible

machen ① *tr. V.* **(a)** make; **aus Plastik/Holz**
usw. **gemacht** made of plastic/wood *etc.;* **sich**
(Dat.) **etw.** ~ **lassen** have sth. made; **etw. aus**
jmdm. ~: make sb. into sth.; **jmdn. zum**
Präsidenten *usw.* ~: make sb. president *etc.;*

jmdm./sich [einen] Kaffee ~: make [some]
coffee for sb./oneself
(b) (verursachen) **jmdm. Arbeit** ~: make [extra]
work for sb.; **das macht das Wetter** that's
[because of] the weather
(c) (ausführen) do ⟨*job, repair, etc.*⟩; **einen**
Spaziergang ~: go for a walk; **eine Reise** ~:
go on a journey; **einen Besuch [bei jmdm.]**
~: pay [sb.] a visit
(d) (tun) do; **was machst du da?** what are you
doing?; **so etwas macht man nicht** that [just]
isn't done
(e) **was macht ...?** (wie ist es um ... bestellt?)

---

*∗old spelling - see note on page xiv

how is ...?; **was macht die Gesundheit/ Arbeit?** how are you keeping/how is the job [getting on]?
(f) (ergeben) (beim Rechnen) be; (bei Geldbeträgen) come to; **zwei mal zwei macht vier** two times two is four; **das macht 12 DM** that is 12 marks; (Endsumme) that comes to 12 marks
(g) (schaden) **was macht das schon?** what does it matter?; **macht nichts!** (ugs.) it doesn't matter
(h) (teilnehmen an) **einen Kursus** od. **Lehrgang** ~: take a course
(i) mach's gut! (ugs.) look after yourself!; (auf Wiedersehen) so long!
②*refl. V.* **(a) sich an etw.** (*Akk.*) ~: get down to sth.
(b) (ugs.: sich entwickeln) do well
(c) mach dir nichts daraus! (ugs.) don't let it bother you
③*itr. V.* **(a) mach schon!** (ugs.) get a move on! (coll.)
(b) das macht hungrig/durstig it makes you hungry/thirsty; **das macht dick** it's fattening
Machenschaften *Pl.* (abwertend) wheeling and dealing *sing.*
Macher *der;* ~s, ~, **Macherin** *die;* ~, ~nen (ugs.) doer; **der Typ des Machers** the dynamic type who just gets on with things
Macho /'matʃːo/ *der;* ~s, ~s (abwertend) macho
Macht *die;* ~, **Mächte** power; **an die** ~ **kommen** come to power
Macht-: ~**bereich** *der* sphere of influence; ~**haber** *der;* ~~s, ~~, ~**haberin** *die;* ~~, ~~nen ruler
mächtig ① *Adj.* **(a)** powerful
(b) (beeindruckend groß) mighty
② *adv.* (ugs.) terribly (coll.)
macht-, Macht-: ~**kampf** *der* power struggle; ~**los** *Adj.* powerless; **gegen etw.** ~**los sein** be powerless in the face of sth.; ~**probe** *die* trial of strength
Mach·werk *das* (abwertend) shoddy effort
Macke *die;* ~, ~n **(a)** (salopp: Tick) fad
(b) (ugs.: Defekt) defect
Mädchen *das;* ~s, ~ **(a)** girl
(b) (Haus~) maid
mädchenhaft *Adj.* girlish
Mädchen·name *der* **(a)** girl's name
(b) (Name vor der Ehe) maiden name
Made *die;* ~, ~n maggot
madig *Adj.* maggoty; **jmdn./etw.** ~ **machen** (ugs.) run sb./sth. down
Madonna *die;* ~, **Madonnen** madonna
mag 1. u. 3. Pers. Sg. Präsens v. MÖGEN
Magazin *das;* ~s, ~e **(a)** (Lager) store; (für Waren) stockroom
(b) (für Patronen, Dias, Film usw.; Zeitschrift) magazine
Magazin·sendung *die* magazine programme
Magen *der;* ~s, **Mägen** od. ~: stomach

magen-, Magen-: ~**bitter** *der;* ~~s, ~~: bitters *pl.;* ~**geschwür** *das* stomach ulcer; ~**krebs** *der* cancer of the stomach; ~**schmerzen** *Pl.* stomach ache *sing.*
mager *Adj.* **(a)** thin
(b) (fettarm) low-fat; low in fat *pred.;* lean ⟨*meat*⟩
(c) (fig.) poor ⟨*soil, harvest*⟩; meagre ⟨*profit, increase, success, report, etc.*⟩; thin ⟨*programme*⟩
Mager-: ~**milch** *die* skim[med] milk; ~**quark** *der* low-fat curd cheese; ~**sucht** *die* (Med.) wasting disease; (Anorexie) anorexia
Magie *die;* ~: magic
Magier /'maːgiɐ/ *der;* ~s, ~, **Magierin** *die;* ~, ~nen (auch fig.) magician
magisch *Adj.* magic ⟨*powers*⟩; (geheimnisvoll) magical
Magistrat *der;* ~[e]s, ~e City Council
Magnat *der;* ~en, ~en magnate
Magnet *der;* ~en od. ~[e]s, ~e magnet
Magnet·band *das; Pl.* **Magnet·bänder** magnetic tape
magnetisch ① *Adj.* magnetic
② *adv.* magnetically
magnetisieren *tr. V.* magnetize
Magnetismus *der;* ~: magnetism
Magnet·nadel *die* [compass] needle
Mahagoni *das;* ~s mahogany
Mäh·drescher *der* combine harvester
mähen ① *tr. V.* mow; cut ⟨*corn*⟩
② *itr. V.* mow; (Getreide ~) reap
Mahl *das;* ~[e]s, **Mähler** (geh.) meal; repast (formal)
mahlen *unr. tr., itr. V.* grind
Mahl·zeit meal
Mähne *die;* ~, ~n mane
mahnen *tr. V.* urge; remind ⟨*debtor*⟩
Mahn-: ~**mal** *das; Pl.* ~~e od. ~**mäler** memorial (erected as a warning to future generations); ~**schreiben** *das* reminder
Mahnung *die;* ~, ~en **(a)** exhortation; (Warnung) admonition
(b) ▶ MAHNSCHREIBEN
Mai *der;* ~[e]s od. ~: May
Mai-: ~**baum** *der* maypole; ~**feiertag** *der* May Day no def. art.; ~**glöckchen** *das* lily of the valley; ~**käfer** *der* May bug
Mais *der;* ~es maize; corn (esp. Amer.); (als Gericht) sweet corn
Mais·kolben *der* corn cob; (als Gericht) corn on the cob
Majestät *die;* ~, ~en **(a)** (Titel) Majesty; **Eure** ~: Your Majesty
(b) (geh.) majesty
majestätisch ① *Adj.* majestic
② *adv.* majestically
Majonäse *die;* ~, ~n mayonnaise
Major *der;* ~s, ~e (Milit.) major
Majoran *der;* ~s, ~e marjoram
makaber *Adj.* macabre

Makedonien /make'do:njən/ (das); ~s Macedonia

Makel der; ~s, ~ (geh.) (a) (Schmach) stigma (b) (Fehler) blemish

makel·los [1] Adj. flawless; spotless ⟨white, cleanness⟩
[2] adv. immaculately; spotlessly ⟨clean⟩

Make-up /me:k'|ap/ das; ~s, ~s make-up

Makkaroni Pl. macaroni sing.

Makler der; ~s, ~, **Maklerin** die; ~, ~nen (a) (Häusermakler) estate agent (Brit.); realtor (Amer.)
(b) (Börsenmakler) broker

Makrele die; ~, ~n mackerel

Makro der od. das; ~s, ~s (DV) macro

Makrone die; ~, ~n macaroon

mal [1] Adv. times; (bei Flächen) by
[2] Partikel komm ~ her! come here!

Mal¹ das; ~[e]s, ~e time; das erste/zweite ~, zum ersten/zweiten ~: for the first/second time; beim ersten/zweiten ~: the first/second time; das letzte, zum letzten ~: for the last time; letztes, beim letzten ~: last time; jedes ~: every time; mit einem ~[e] all at once

Mal² das; ~[e]s, ~e od. Mäler mark; (Muttermal) birthmark; (braun) mole

Malaie der; ~n, ~n, **Malaiin** die; ~, ~nen Malay

Malaria die; ~: malaria

Malaysia (das); ~s Malaysia

Mal-buch das colouring book

malen tr., itr. V. paint; decorate ⟨flat, room, walls⟩

Maler der; ~s, ~: painter

Malerei die; ~, ~en painting

Malerin der; ~, ~nen painter

malerisch [1] Adj. picturesque
[2] adv. picturesquely

mal|nehmen unr. tr., itr. V. multiply (mit by)

malträtieren tr. V. maltreat; ill-treat

Malz-bier das malt beer

Mama die; ~, ~s (fam.) mamma

Mami die; ~, ~s (fam.) mummy (Brit. coll.); mommy (Amer. coll.)

Mammut das; ~s, ~e od. ~s mammoth

mampfen tr., itr. V. (salopp) munch; nosh (coll.)

man Indefinitpron. im Nom. one; you 2nd person; (irgendjemand) somebody; (die Behörden, die Leute dort) they pl.; (die Menschen im Allgemeinen) people pl; ~ hat mir gesagt ...: I was told ...

Management /'mɛnɪdʒ:mənt/ das; ~s, ~s management

managen /'mɛnɪdʒ:n/ tr. V. (a) (ugs.) fix; organize
(b) (betreuen) manage ⟨singer, artist, player⟩

Manager /'mɛnɪdʒ:ɐ/ der; ~s, ~, **Managerin** die; ~, ~nen manager; (eines Fußballvereins) club secretary

manch Indefinitpron. (a) attr. many a; in [so] ~er Beziehung in many respects
(b) allein stehend ~er many a person/man; ~e Pl. some; (viele) many; [so] ~es a number of things; (allerhand Verschiedenes) all kinds of things

mancherlei indekl. Adj. (a) attr. various; a number of
(b) allein stehend various things

manch·mal Adv. sometimes

Mandant der; ~en, ~en, **Mandantin** die; ~, ~nen client

Mandarine die; ~, ~n mandarin [orange]

Mandel die; ~, ~n (a) almond
(b) (Anat.) tonsil

Mandel-entzündung die tonsillitis no indef. art.

Manege /ma'ne:ʒə/ die; ~, ~n (im Zirkus) ring; (in der Reitschule) arena

Mangel¹ der; ~s, Mängel (a) (Fehlen) lack (an + Dat. of); (Knappheit) shortage, lack (an + Dat. of)
(b) (Fehler) defect

Mangel² die; ~, ~n [large] mangle

mangelhaft [1] Adj. faulty ⟨goods, German, English, etc.⟩; (unzulänglich) inadequate ⟨knowledge, lighting⟩; (Schulw.) die Note „~" the mark 'unsatisfactory'; (bei Prüfungen) the fail mark
[2] adv. faultily; (unzulänglich) inadequately

mangeln¹ itr. V.; unpers. es mangelt an etw. (Dat.) (etw. fehlt) there is a lack of sth.; (etw. ist unzureichend vorhanden) there is a shortage of sth.; jmdm./einer Sache mangelt es an etw. (Dat.) sb./sth. lacks sth.

mangeln² tr. V. mangle

mangels Präp. mit Gen. in the absence of

Mango die; ~, ~s mango

Mangold der; ~[e]s [Swiss] chard

Manie die; ~, ~n mania

Manier die; ~, ~en (a) manner
(b) Pl. (Umgangsformen) manners

manierlich [1] Adj. (a) (fam.) well-mannered; well-behaved ⟨child⟩
(b) (ugs.: einigermaßen gut) decent
[2] adv. (a) (fam.) nicely
(b) (ugs.: einigermaßen gut) ganz/recht ~: quite/really nicely

Manifest das; ~[e]s, ~e manifesto

Maniküre die; ~: manicure

maniküren tr. V. manicure

Manipulation die; ~, ~en (geh.) manipulation

manipulieren tr. V. manipulate; rig ⟨election result etc.⟩

Manko das; ~s, ~s shortcoming; deficiency

Mann der; ~[e]s, Männer (a) man
(b) (Ehemann) husband

Männchen das; ~s, ~ (a) little man

(b) (Tier∼) male; ∼ **machen** ⟨*animal*⟩ sit up and beg

Mannequin /'manəkɛ̃/ *das;* ∼s, ∼s mannequin; [fashion] model

männer-, Männer-: ∼**beruf** *der* all-male profession; (überwiegend von Männern ausgeübt) male-dominated profession; ∼**mordend** *Adj.* (ugs. scherzh.) man-eating (fig.); ∼**sache** *die:* das ist ∼sache that's men's business; ∼**überschuss**, *∗*∼**überschuß** *der* surplus of men

mannig·fach *Adj.* multifarious

männlich ① *Adj.* **(a)** male **(b)** ▶ MASKULIN 1; ② *adv.* in a masculine way

Mannschaft *die;* ∼, ∼en (Sport, auch fig.) team; (Schiffs-, Flugzeugbesatzung) crew; (Milit.) unit

Mannschafts-: ∼**führer** *der*, ∼**führerin** *die* (Sport) team captain; ∼**kapitän** *der*, ∼**kapitänin** *die* (Sport) team captain; ∼**spiel** *das* (Sport) team game

Manöver *das;* ∼s, ∼ **(a)** (Milit.) exercise; ∼ *Pl.* manœuvres **(b)** (Bewegung; fig. abwertend: Trick) manœuvre

manövrieren *itr., tr. V.* manœuvre

Mansarde *die;* ∼, ∼n attic; (Zimmer) attic room

Manschette *die;* ∼, ∼n cuff

Manschetten·knopf *der* cuff link

Mantel *der;* ∼s, Mäntel coat

Manteltarif·vertrag *der* (Wirtsch.) framework collective agreement [on working conditions]

Manuskript *das;* ∼[e]s, ∼e **(a)** manuscript; (Typoskript) typescript **(b)** (Notizen) notes *pl.*

Mappe *die;* ∼, ∼n **(a)** folder **(b)** (Aktentasche) briefcase; (Schul∼) schoolbag

Marathon·lauf /...tɔn.../ *der* marathon

Märchen *das;* ∼s, ∼: fairy story; fairy tale; (ugs.: Lüge) [tall] story (coll.)

Märchen·buch *das* book of fairy stories

märchenhaft ① *Adj.* magical ② *adv.* magically; (ugs.) fantastically (coll.)

Margarine *die;* ∼: margarine

Margerite *die;* ∼, ∼n ox-eye daisy

Maria (*die*)*;* ∼s *od.* (Rel.) Mariä Mary

Marien·käfer *der* ladybird

Marihuana *das;* ∼s marijuana

Marinade *die;* ∼, ∼n (Kochk.) marinade; (Salatsoße) [marinade] dressing

Marine *die;* ∼, ∼n fleet; (Kriegs∼) navy

marinieren *tr. V.* marinade; **marinierte Heringe** soused herrings

Marionette *die;* ∼, ∼n puppet; marionette

Marionetten·theater *das* puppet theatre

Mark¹ *die;* ∼, ∼: mark; **Deutsche ∼:** Deutschmark

Mark² *das;* ∼[e]s **(a)** (Knochen∼) marrow **(b)** (Frucht∼) pulp

markant *Adj.* striking; prominent ⟨*figure, nose, chin*⟩; clear-cut ⟨*features, profile*⟩

Marke *die;* ∼, ∼n **(a)** (Waren∼) brand; (Fabrikat) make **(b)** (Brief∼, Rabatt∼, Beitrags∼) stamp **(c)** (Essen∼) meal ticket **(d)** (Erkennungs∼) [identification] disc; (Dienst∼) [police] identification badge; ≈ warrant card (Brit.) *or* (Amer.) ID card

Marken-: ∼**artikel** *der* proprietary *or* (Brit.) branded article; ∼**zeichen** *das* trade mark

Marketing *das;* ∼s (Wirtsch.) marketing

markieren ① *tr. V.* **(a)** mark **(b)** (ugs.: vortäuschen) sham ⟨*illness, breakdown, etc.*⟩ ② *itr. V.* (ugs.: simulieren) put it on (coll.)

Markierung *die;* ∼, ∼en marking

Markt *der;* ∼[e]s, Märkte market; (∼platz) market place *or* square; **freitags ist ∼:** Friday is market day

markt-, Markt-: ∼**anteil** *der* share of the market; ∼**beherrschend** *Adj.* market-dominating *attrib.;* ∼**einführung** *die* launch; ∼**forschung** *die* market research *no def. art.;* ∼**frau** *die* market woman; ∼**führer** *der*, ∼**führerin** *die* market leader; ∼**halle** *die* covered market; ∼**lücke** *die* gap in the market; ∼**platz** *der* market place; ∼**stand** *der* market stall; ∼**wirtschaft** *die* market economy

Marmelade *die;* ∼, ∼n jam; (Orangen∼) marmalade

Marmor *der;* ∼s marble

Marokkaner *der;* ∼s, ∼, **Marokkanerin** *die;* ∼, ∼nen Moroccan

marokkanisch *Adj.* Moroccan

Marokko (*das*) *;* ∼s Morocco

Marone *die;* ∼, ∼n [sweet] chestnut

Mars *der;* ∼: Mars *no def. art.*

Marsch¹ *der;* ∼[e]s, Märsche march; (Wanderung) [long] walk

Marsch² *die;* ∼, ∼en fertile marshland

Marsch·flug·körper *der* cruise missile

marschieren *itr. V.; mit sein* march; (wandern) walk

Marsch-: ∼**musik** *die* march music; ∼**verpflegung** *die* (Milit.) marching rations *pl.;*

Mars-: ∼**mensch** *der* Martian; ∼**sonde** *die* (Raumfahrt) Mars probe

Marter *die;* ∼, ∼n (geh.) torture; (seelisch) torment

martern *tr. V.* (geh.) torture

Märtyrer *der;* ∼s, ∼, **Märtyrerin** *die;* ∼, ∼nen martyr

Martyrium *das;* ∼s, Martyrien martyrdom

Marxismus *der;* ∼: Marxism *no art.*

Marxist *der;* ∼en, ∼en, **Marxistin** *die;* ∼, ∼nen Marxist

marxistisch *Adj.* Marxist

März *der;* ∼[es] March

Marzipan *das;* ~s marzipan

Masche *die;* ~, ~n stitch; (Lauf~) run; ladder (Brit.); (beim Netz) mesh

Maschen-draht *der* wire netting

Maschine *die;* ~, ~n (a) (auch ugs.: Motorrad) machine

(b) (ugs.: Automotor) engine

(c) (Flugzeug) [aero]plane

(d) (Schreib~) typewriter; ~ **schreiben** type

maschine-geschrieben *Adj.* typewritten

maschinell ⟦1⟧ *Adj.* machine *attrib.;* by machine *postpos.;* ⟦2⟧ *adv.* by machine; ~ **hergestellt** machine-made

Maschinen-: ~**gewehr** *das* machine gun; ~**pistole** *die* sub-machine gun; ~**schlosser** *der,* ~**schlosserin** *die* fitter

*****maschine|schreiben** ▶ MASCHINE D

Masern *Pl.* measles *sing.* or *pl.*

Maserung *die;* ~, ~en [wavy] grain

Maske *die;* ~, ~n mask

Masken-: ~**ball** *der* masked ball; ~**bildner** *der,* ~~s, ~~, ~**bildnerin** *die;* ~~, ~~nen make-up artist

Maskerade *die;* ~, ~n [fancy-dress] costume

maskieren ⟦1⟧ *tr. V.* mask ⟦2⟧ *refl. V.* put on a mask/masks

Maskottchen *das;* ~s, ~: [lucky] mascot

maskulin /*auch:* '---/ ⟦1⟧ *Adj.* (auch Sprachw.) masculine ⟦2⟧ *adv.* in a masculine way

Masochismus *der;* ~ (Psych.) masochism *no art.*

Masochist *der;* ~en, ~en, **Masochistin** *die;* ~, ~nen (Psych.) masochist

masochistisch (Psych.) ⟦1⟧ *Adj.* masochistic ⟦2⟧ *adv.* masochistically; ~ **veranlagt sein** have masochistic tendencies

maß *1. u. 3. Pers. Sg. Prät. v.* MESSEN

Maß[1] *das;* ~es, ~e (a) measure (für of); (fig.) **das** ~ **ist voll** enough is enough

(b) (Größe) measurement

(c) (Grad) degree (**an** + *Dat.* of); **in großem/ gewissem** ~**e** to a great/certain extent

(d) ~ **halten** exercise moderation

Maß[2] *die;* ~, ~[e] (bayr., österr.) litre [of beer]

Massage /ma'saːʒə/ *die;* ~, ~n massage

Massaker *das;* ~s, ~: massacre

Maß-: ~**anzug** *der* made-to-measure suit; ~**arbeit** *die* (a) custom-made item; (Kleidungsstück) made-to-measure item; **(b)** (genaue Arbeit) neat work

Masse *die;* ~, ~n (a) mass

(b) (Gemisch) mixture

Maß-einheit *die* unit of measurement

Massen-: ~**arbeitslosigkeit** *die* mass unemployment; ~**entlassungen** *Pl.* mass redundancies *pl.;* ~**grab** *das* mass grave

massenhaft ⟦1⟧ *Adj.* in huge numbers *postpos.;* ⟦2⟧ *adv.* on a huge scale

massen-, Massen-: ~**karambolage** *die* multiple crash; ~**kommunikations-mittel** *das* medium of mass communication; mass medium; ~**medium** *das* mass medium; ~**mörder** *der,* ~**mörderin** *die* mass murderer; ~**produktion** *die* mass production; ~**vernichtung** *die* mass extermination; ~**vernichtungs-waffen** *Pl.* weapons of mass destruction; ~**weise** *Adv.* in huge numbers

Masseur /maˈsøːɐ̯/ *der;* ~s, ~e masseur

Masseurin *die;* ~, ~nen, **Masseuse** /maˈsøːzə/ *die;* ~, ~n masseuse

maß-gebend, maß-geblich ⟦1⟧ *Adj.* authoritative ⟨book, expert, opinion⟩; definitive ⟨text⟩; influential ⟨person, circles, etc.⟩; decisive ⟨factor, influence, etc.⟩ ⟦2⟧ *adv.* ⟨influence⟩ to a considerable extent; (entscheidend) decisively

*****maß|halten** ▶ MAß[1] D

massieren *tr. V.* massage

mäßig ⟦1⟧ *Adj.* moderate; (mittel~) mediocre ⟦2⟧ *adv.* in moderation; moderately ⟨gifted, talented⟩; (mittel~) indifferently

mäßigen *refl. V.* (geh.) **(a)** practise *or* exercise moderation

(b) (sich beherrschen) control *or* restrain oneself

Mäßigkeit *die;* ~: moderation

Mäßigung *die;* ~: moderation

massiv ⟦1⟧ *Adj.* **(a)** solid

(b) (heftig) massive ⟨demand⟩; crude ⟨accusation, threat⟩; strong ⟨attack, criticism, pressure⟩ ⟦2⟧ *adv.* ⟨attack⟩ strongly; ⟨accuse, threaten⟩ crudely

maß-, Maß-: ~**krug** *der* (südd., österr.) litre beer mug; (aus Steingut) stein; ~**los** ⟦1⟧ *Adj.* extreme; gross ⟨exaggeration, insult⟩; excessive ⟨demand, claim⟩; boundless ⟨ambition, greed, sorrow, joy⟩; ⟦2⟧ *adv.* extremely; ⟨exaggerate⟩ grossly; ~**nahme** *die;* ~~, ~~n measure; ~**regel** *die* regulation; (Maßnahme) measure; ~**regeln** *tr. V.* (zurechtweisen) reprimand; (bestrafen) discipline; ~**stab** *der* **(a)** standard; **(b)** (einer Karte, eines Modells usw.) scale; ~**voll** ⟦1⟧ *Adj.* moderate; ⟦2⟧ *adv.* in moderation

Mast *der;* ~[e]s, ~en, *auch:* ~e (Schiffs~, Antennen~) mast; (Stange, Fahnen~) pole; (Hochspannungs~) pylon

mästen *tr. V.* fatten

Masturbation *die;* ~, ~en masturbation

masturbieren *itr., tr. V.* masturbate

Match /mɛtʃ/ *das od.* der; ~[e]s, ~s *od.* ~e match

Material *das;* ~s, ~ien material; (Bau~; Hilfsmittel) materials *pl.*

Materialismus *der;* ~: materialism

Materialist *der;* ~en, ~en, **Materialistin** *die;* ~, ~nen materialist

materialistisch 1 *Adj.* materialistic 2 *adv.* materialistically

Materie *die;* ~, ~n (a) matter (b) (geh.: Thema, Gegenstand) subject matter

materiell 1 *Adj.* (finanziell) financial 2 *adv.* materially; (finanziell) financially

Mathe *die;* ~ (ugs.) maths *sing.* (Brit. coll.); math (Amer. coll.)

Mathematik *die;* ~: mathematics *sing.*, no art.

mathematisch 1 *Adj.* mathematical 2 *adv.* mathematically

Matjes *der;* ~, ~: matie [herring]

Matratze *die;* ~, ~n mattress

Matrose *der;* ~n, ~n sailor; seaman

Matsch *der;* ~[e]s (ugs.) mud; (breiiger Schmutz) sludge; (Schnee~) slush

matschig *Adj.* (ugs.) (a) muddy; slushy ⟨snow⟩ (b) (weich) mushy; squashy ⟨fruit⟩

matt 1 *Adj.* (a) weak; feeble ⟨applause, reaction⟩ (b) (glanzlos) matt; dull ⟨metal, mirror, etc.⟩ (c) (undurchsichtig) frosted ⟨glass⟩; pearl ⟨lightbulb⟩ (d) subdued; (Schach) checkmated; ~! checkmate! 2 *adv.* (a) (kraftlos) weakly (b) (mäßig) ⟨protest, contradict⟩ feebly

Matte *die;* ~, ~n mat

Matt-scheibe *die* (ugs.) telly (Brit. coll.); box (coll.)

Matur *die;* ~ (schweiz.), **Matura** *die;* ~a (österr., schweiz.) ▶ ABITUR

Mätzchen *das;* ~s, ~: ~ machen (ugs.) fool about or around

Mauer *die;* ~, ~n wall

mauern 1 *tr. V.* build 2 *itr. V.* lay bricks

Mauer-: ~segler *der* swift; ~werk *das* (a) masonry; (aus Ziegeln) brickwork; (b) (Mauern) walls *pl.*

Maul *das;* ~[e]s, Mäuler (von Tieren) mouth; (derb: Mund) gob (sl.)

Maul-: ~esel *der* mule; ~korb *der* (auch fig.) muzzle; ~tier *das* mule

Maul-wurf *der* mole

Maulwurfs-: ~haufen *der*, ~hügel *der* molehill

Maurer *der;* ~s, ~, **Maurerin** *die;* ~, ~nen bricklayer

Maus *die;* ~, Mäuse mouse

Mauschelei *die;* ~, ~en (ugs. abwertend) shady wheeling and dealing no indef. art.

mauscheln *itr. V.* (ugs. abwertend) engage in shady wheeling and dealing

Mäuschen *das;* ~s, ~: little mouse

mäuschen-still *Adj.* ~ sein be as quiet as a mouse

Mause-falle *die* mousetrap

mausern *refl. V.* moult

Maus: ~klick *der;* ~~s, ~~s (DV) mouse click; ~taste *die* (DV) mouse button; ~zeiger *der* (DV) mouse pointer

Maut *die;* ~, ~en toll

maximal 1 *Adj.* maximum 2 *adv.* ~ zulässige Geschwindigkeit maximum permitted speed

Maxime *die;* ~, ~n maxim

maximieren *tr. V.* maximize

Maximum *das;* ~s, Maxima maximum (an + *Dat.* of)

Maxi-single *die* maxi-single

Mayonnaise /majɔ'nɛːzə/ *die;* ~, ~n mayonnaise

Mäzen *der;* ~s, ~e (geh.) patron

Mäzenin *die;* ~, ~nen patroness

MdB, M.d.B. *Abk.* = **Mitglied des Bundestages** Member of the Bundestag

m. E. *Abk.* = **meines Erachtens** in my opinion or view

Mechanik *die;* ~: mechanics *sing.*, no art.

Mechaniker *der;* ~s, ~, **Mechanikerin** *die;* ~, ~nen mechanic

mechanisch 1 *Adj.* mechanical; power attrib. ⟨loom, press⟩ 2 *adv.* mechanically

Mechanismus *der;* ~, Mechanismen mechanism

meckern *itr. V.* (a) (auch fig.) bleat (b) (ugs.: nörgeln) grumble; moan

Mecklenburg-Vorpommern *(das);* ~s Mecklenburg-Western Pomerania

Medaille /me'daljə/ *die;* ~, ~n medal

Medaillen-gewinner *der*, **Medaillen-gewinnerin** *die* medallist; medal winner

Medaillon /medal'jõː/ *das;* ~s, ~s (a) locket (b) (Kochk., bild. Kunst) medallion

medial *Adj.* (in den Medien) in the media *postpos.*; (von den Medien) by the media *postpos.*; eine ~e Präsenz a media presence; ein ~es Spektakel a media spectacle

Medien-: ~angebot *das* range of media; ~konzern *der* media concern; ~landschaft *die* media scene; ~politik *die* media policy; ~präsenz *die* media presence

Medikament *das;* ~[e]s, ~e medicine; (Droge) drug

Meditation *die;* ~, ~en meditation

meditieren *itr. V.* meditate (**über** + *Akk.* [up]on)

Medium *das;* ~s, Medien medium

Medizin die; ∼, ∼en medicine

Mediziner der; ∼s, ∼, **Medizinerin** die; ∼, ∼nen doctor; (Student[in]) medical student

medizinisch 1 Adj. medical; medicinal ⟨bath etc.⟩; medicated ⟨toothpaste, soap, etc.⟩ 2 adv. medically

Meer das; ∼[e]s, ∼e (auch fig.) sea; am ∼: by the sea

Meer-enge die straits pl.; strait

Meeres-: ∼**boden** der sea bed or bottom or floor; ∼**bucht** die bay; ∼**früchte** Pl. (Kochk.) seafood sing.; ∼**kunde** die oceanography no art.; ∼**spiegel** der sea level

Meer-: ∼**jungfrau** die mermaid; ∼**katze** die guenon; ∼**rettich** der horseradish; ∼**schweinchen** das; ∼∼s, ∼∼: guinea pig; ∼**wasser** das sea water

Meeting /ˈmiːtɪŋ/ das; ∼s, ∼s meeting

mega-, Mega- mega-

Mega-byte das (DV) megabyte

Megaphon das; ∼s, ∼e megaphone; loud hailer

Mehl das; ∼[e]s flour

mehlig Adj. (a) floury (b) mealy ⟨potato, apple, etc.⟩

Mehl-: ∼**sack** der flour sack; (Sack voll Mehl) sack of flour; ∼**tau** der mildew; ∼**wurm** der mealworm

mehr 1 Indefinitpron. more 2 Adv. (a) more (b) nicht ∼: not … any more; no longer; es war niemand ∼ da there was no one left; das wird nie ∼ vorkommen it will never happen again; da ist nichts ∼ zu machen there is nothing more to be done

mehr-, Mehr-: ∼**bändig** Adj. in several volumes postpos.; ∼**bereichs-öl** das (Technik) multi-purpose oil; ∼**deutig** 1 Adj. ambiguous; 2 adv. ambiguously

mehren (geh.) refl. V. increase

mehrer- Indefinitpron. u. unbest. Zahlwort (a) attr. several (b) allein stehend ∼e several people; ∼es several things pl.

mehr-fach 1 Adj. multiple; (wiederholt) repeated 2 adv. several times; (wiederholt) repeatedly

Mehrheit die; ∼, ∼en majority

Mehrheits-: ∼**beschluss**, *∼**beschluß** der, ∼**entscheidung** die majority decision

mehr-, Mehr-: ∼**jährig** Adj. lasting several years postpos.; ∼**malig** Adj.; nicht präd. repeated; ∼**mals** Adv. several times; (wiederholt) repeatedly; ∼**parteien-system** das multi-party system; ∼**sprachig** Adj. multilingual; ∼**stimmig** (Musik) 1 Adj. for several voices postpos.; ein ∼stimmiges Lied a part-

song; 2 adv. ∼stimmig singen sing in harmony; ∼**teilig** Adj. in several parts postpos.

Mehrweg-: ∼**flasche** die returnable or reusable bottle; ∼**verpackung** die reusable packaging

Mehr-: ∼**wert** der (Wirtsch.) surplus value; ∼**wert-steuer** die (Wirtsch.) value added tax (Brit.); VAT (Brit.); sales tax (Amer.); ∼**zahl** die (a) (Sprachw.) plural; (b) (Mehrheit) majority

meiden unr. tr. V. (geh.) avoid

Meile die; ∼, ∼n mile

mein Possessivpron. my; ∼e Damen und Herren ladies and gentlemen; das Buch dort, ist das ∼[e]s? that book over there, is it mine?

Mein-eid der perjury no indef. art.; einen ∼ schwören commit perjury

meinen 1 itr. V. think 2 tr. V. (a) think (b) (sagen wollen, im Sinn haben) mean (c) (beabsichtigen) mean; intend; es gut mit jmdm. ∼: mean well by sb. (d) (sagen) say

meiner Gen. von ICH (geh.) gedenkt ∼: remember me; erbarme dich ∼: have mercy upon me

meinerseits Adv. for my part; ganz ∼: the pleasure is [all] mine

meinetwegen Adv. (a) because of me; (mir zuliebe) for my sake; (um mich) about me (b) /auch: -ˈ-/ (von mir aus) as far as I'm concerned; ∼! if you like

Meinung die; ∼, ∼en opinion (zu on, über + Akk. about); er ist der ∼, dass … he is of the opinion or takes the view that …; meiner ∼ nach in my opinion; ganz meine ∼: I agree entirely; einer ∼ sein be of the same opinion

Meinungs-: ∼**forschung** die opinion research; ∼**freiheit** die freedom to form and express one's own opinions; (Redefreiheit) freedom of speech; ∼**umfrage** die [public] opinion poll; ∼**verschiedenheit** die difference of opinion

Meise die; ∼, ∼n tit[mouse]

Meißel der; ∼s, ∼: chisel

meißeln tr. V. chisel; carve ⟨statue, sculpture⟩ with a chisel

meist Adv. mostly

meist... Indefinitpron. u. unbest. Zahlw. most; die ∼en Leute …: most people …; am ∼en most

meistens Adv. ▶ MEIST

Meister der; ∼s, ∼ (a) master (b) (Werk∼, Polier) foreman (c) (Sport) champion

Meister-brief der master craftsman's diploma or certificate

meisterhaft 1 Adj. masterly 2 adv. in a masterly manner

Meisterin die; ∼, ∼nen ▶ MEISTER A,C

meistern *tr. V.* master

Meister·prüfung *die* examination for the/one's master craftsman's diploma *or* certificate

Meisterschaft *die;* ∼, ∼en **(a)** mastery **(b)** (Sport) championship

Meister-: ∼**stück** *das* masterpiece (**an** + *Dat.* of); ∼**titel** *der* (Sport) championship [title]; ∼**werk** *das* masterpiece (**an** + *Dat.* of)

Melancholie /melaŋko:'li:/ *die;* ∼ (Gemütszustand) melancholy; (Psych.) melancholia

melancholisch ⟨1⟩ *Adj.* melancholy; melancholy, melancholic ⟨*person, temperament*⟩ ⟨2⟩ *adv.* melancholically

melden ⟨1⟩ *tr. V.* report; (registrieren lassen) register ⟨*birth, death, etc.*⟩ (*Dat.* with) ⟨2⟩ *refl. V.* **(a)** report **(b)** (am Telefon) answer **(c)** (ums Wort bitten) put one's hand up **(d)** (von sich hören lassen) get in touch (**bei** with)

Meldung *die;* ∼, ∼en **(a)** report; (Nachricht) piece of news **(b)** (Wort∼) request to speak

meliert *Adj.* mottled; [grau] ∼es Haar hair streaked with grey

melken *regelm.* (*auch unr.*) *tr. V.* milk

Melodie *die;* ∼, ∼n melody; (Weise) tune

melodisch ⟨1⟩ *Adj.* melodic ⟨2⟩ *adv.* melodically

Melone *die;* ∼, ∼n **(a)** melon **(b)** (ugs.: Hut) bowler [hat]

Membran *die;* ∼, ∼en **(a)** (Technik) diaphragm **(b)** (Biol., Chemie) membrane

Memoiren /me'mo̯a:rən/ *Pl.* memoirs

Menge *die;* ∼, ∼n **(a)** quantity; amount **(b)** (große) lot (coll.); **eine** ∼ (ugs.) lots [of it/ them] (coll.) **(c)** (Menschen∼) crowd **(d)** (Math.) set

Mengen-: ∼**lehre** *die* set theory *no art.;* ∼**rabatt** *der* bulk discount

Meniskus *der;* ∼, Menisken (Anat., Optik) meniscus

Menopause *die;* ∼, ∼n (Physiol.) menopause

Mensa *die;* ∼, ∼s *od.* Mensen refectory, canteen (*of university, college*)

Mensch *der;* ∼en, ∼en **(a)** (Gattung) der ∼: man; **die** ∼en man *sing.;* human beings; mankind *sing.;* **(b)** (Person) person; man/woman; ∼en people

menschen-, Menschen-: ∼**affe** *der* anthropoid [ape]; ∼**auflauf** *der* crowd [of people]; ∼**feind** *der,* ∼**feindin** *die* misanthropist; ∼**fresser** *der* (ugs.) cannibal; ∼**freund** *der,* ∼**freundin** *die* philanthropist; ∼**handel** *der* trade *or* traffic in human beings; ∼**kenner** *der,*

∼**kennerin** *die* judge of human nature; ∼**kenntnis** *die;* ability to judge human nature; ∼**leben** *das* life; ∼**leer** *Adj.* deserted; ∼**menge** *die* crowd [of people]; ∼**recht** *das* human right; ∼**schlag** *der* breed [of people]; ∼**seele** *die:* keine ∼seele not a [living] soul

Menschens-kind: ∼! (salopp) (erstaunt) good heavens; good grief; (vorwurfsvoll) for heaven's sake

menschen-, Menschen-: ∼**unwürdig** ⟨1⟩ *Adj.* ⟨*accommodation*⟩ unfit for human habitation; ⟨*conditions*⟩ unfit for human beings; ⟨*behaviour*⟩ unworthy of a human being; ⟨2⟩ *adv.* ⟨*treat*⟩ in a degrading and inhumane way; ⟨*live, be housed*⟩ in conditions unfit for human beings; ∼**verstand** *der* human intellect; ∼**würde** *die* human dignity *no art.*

Menschheit *die;* ∼: mankind *no art.;* humanity *no art.;* human race

menschlich ⟨1⟩ *Adj.* **(a)** human **(b)** (annehmbar) civilized **(c)** (human) humane ⟨*person, treatment, etc.*⟩ ⟨2⟩ *adv.* **(a)** er ist mir ∼ sympathisch I like him as a person **(b)** (human) humanely

Menschlichkeit *die;* ∼: humanity *no art.*

Mensen ▶ MENSA

Menstruation *die;* ∼, ∼en (Physiol.) menstruation; (Periode) [menstrual] period

Mentalität *die;* ∼, ∼en mentality

Menü *das;* ∼s, ∼s (auch DV) menu

Menü-leiste *die* (DV) menu bar

merkbar ⟨1⟩ *Adj.* noticeable ⟨2⟩ *adv.* noticeably

Merk·blatt leaflet

merken ⟨1⟩ *tr. V.* notice ⟨2⟩ *refl. V.* sich (*Dat.*) etw. ∼: remember sth.

merklich ▶ MERKBAR

Merkmal *das;* ∼s, ∼e feature

Merkur *der;* ∼s Mercury

merkwürdig ⟨1⟩ *Adj.* strange; odd ⟨2⟩ *adv.* strangely; oddly

messbar, *meßbar *Adj.* measurable

Messe¹ *die;* ∼, ∼n (Gottesdienst, Musik) mass

Messe² *die;* ∼, ∼n (Ausstellung) [trade] fair

messen ⟨1⟩ *unr. tr. V.* **(a)** *auch itr.* measure **(b)** (beurteilen) judge (**nach** by) ⟨2⟩ *unr. refl. V.* (geh.) compete (**mit** with)

Messer *das;* ∼s, ∼: knife

messer-, Messer-: ∼**scharf** ⟨1⟩ *Adj.* razor-sharp; (fig.) incisive ⟨*logic*⟩; razor-sharp ⟨*wit, intellect*⟩; ⟨2⟩ *adv.* (fig. ugs.) ⟨*argue*⟩ incisively; ∼**stecherei** *die;* ∼, ∼∼en knife fight; fight with knives; ∼**stich** *der* knife thrust; (Wunde) knife wound

Mess-gerät, *Meß-gerät *das* measuring device; (Zähler) meter

Messias *der;* ∼, ∼se Messiah

Messing *das;* ~s brass
Mess·instrument, *Meß·instrument
das measuring instrument
Messung *die;* ~, ~en measurement
Metall *das;* ~s, ~e metal
metallic *indekl. Adj.* metallic [grey/blue/
etc.]
Metall·industrie *die* metal-processing and
metal-working industries *pl.*
metallisch *Adj.* metallic; metal *attrib.*,
metallic ⟨conductor⟩
Metapher *die;* ~, ~n metaphor
metaphorisch (Stilk.) [1] *Adj.* metaphorical
[2] *adv.* metaphorically
Meta·physik *die;* ~: metaphysics *sing., no
art.*
Metastase *die;* ~, ~n (Med.) metastasis
Meteor *der;* ~s, ~e meteor
Meteorit *der;* ~en *od.* ~s, ~e[n] meteorite
Meteorologe *der;* ~n, ~n meteorologist
Meteorologie *die;* ~: meteorology *no art.*
Meteorologin *die;* ~, ~nen meteorologist
meteorologisch [1] *Adj.* meteorological
[2] *adv.* meteorologically
Meter *der od. das;* ~s, ~: metre
meter-, Meter-: ~**dick** *Adj.* (sehr dick)
metres thick *postpos.;* ~**hoch** *Adj.* metres
high *postpos.;* ⟨snow⟩ metres deep; ~**maß**
das tape measure; (Stab) [metre] rule
Methan *das;* ~s methane
Methode *die;* ~, ~n method
methodisch [1] *Adj.* methodological; (nach
einer Methode vorgehend) methodical
[2] *adv.* methodologically; (nach einer Methode)
methodically
Metier /me'tje:/ *das;* ~s, ~s profession
Metrik *die;* ~, ~en metrics
metrisch [1] *Adj.*(a) (Verslehre, Musik)
metrical
(b) (auf den Meter bezogen) metric
[2] *adv.* metrically
Metropole *die;* ~, ~n metropolis
Mett·wurst *die:* soft smoked sausage made
of minced pork and beef
Metzger *der;* ~s, ~ (bes. westmd., südd.,
schweiz.) butcher
Metzgerei *die;* ~, ~en (bes. westmd., südd.,
schweiz.) butcher's [shop]
Meute *die;* ~, ~n (a) (Jägerspr.) pack
(b) (ugs. abwertend) mob
Meuterei *die;* ~, ~en mutiny
meutern *itr. V.* (a) mutiny; ⟨prisoners⟩ riot
(b) (ugs.: Unwillen äußern) moan
Mexikaner *der;* ~s, ~, **Mexikanerin**
die; ~, ~ Mexican
mexikanisch *Adj.* Mexican
Mexiko (*das*) ~s Mexico
MEZ *Abk.* = **mitteleuropäische Zeit**
CET

mg *Abk.* = **Milligramm** mg
MG /ɛm'geː/ *das;* ~s, ~s *Abk.*
= **Maschinengewehr**
Mi. *Abk.* = **Mittwoch** Wed.
miau *Interj.* miaow
miauen *itr. V.* miaow
mich [1] *Akk. von* ICH me
[2] *Akk. des Reflexivpron. der 1.Pers. Sg.*
myself
mick[e]rig *Adj.* (ugs.) miserable; measly
(coll.); puny ⟨person⟩
mied *1. u. 3. Pers. Sg. Prät. v.* MEIDEN
Mieder·waren *Pl.* corsetry *sing.*
Miene *die;* ~, ~n expression
mies (ugs.) [1] *Adj.* lousy (coll.)
[2] *adv.* lousily (coll.)
Mies-: ~**macher** *der,* ~**macherin** *die*
(ugs. abwertend) carping critic; (Spielverderber)
killjoy; ~**muschel** *die* [common] mussel
Miete *die;* ~, ~n rent; (für ein Auto, Boot) hire
charge; **zur** ~ **wohnen** live in rented
accommodation
mieten *tr. V.* rent; (für kürzere Zeit) hire
Mieter *der;* ~s, ~, **Mieterin** *die;* ~, ~nen
tenant
Miets·haus *das* block of rented flats (Brit.)
or (Amer.) apartments
Miet-: ~**erhöhung** *die* rent increase;
~**vertrag** *der* tenancy agreement;
~**wagen** *der* hire car
Migräne *die;* ~, ~n migraine
Migrant *der;* ~en, ~en, **Migrantin** *die;*
~, ~nen migrant
mikro-, Mikro- micro-
Mikrobe *die;* ~, ~n microbe
mikro-, Mikro-: ~**film** *der* microfilm;
~**phon** /-'-'-/ *das;* ~~s, ~~e microphone;
~**skop** /-'-'-/ *das;* ~~s, ~~e microscope;
~**skopisch** /-'-'-/ [1] *Adj.* microscopic;
[2] *adv.* microscopically; ~**welle** *die* (ugs.)
microwave [oven]
Milbe *die;* ~, ~n mite
Milch *die;* ~: milk
Milch·flasche *die* milk bottle
milchig [1] *Adj.* milky
[2] *adv.* **weiß** milky-white
Milch-: ~**kaffee** *der* coffee with plenty of
milk; ~**kännchen** *das;* ~~s, ~~: milk
jug; ~**reis** *der* rice pudding; ~**straße** *die*
Milky Way; Galaxy; ~**zahn** *der* milk tooth
mild, milde [1] *Adj.* mild; lenient ⟨judge,
judgement⟩; soft ⟨light⟩; smooth ⟨brandy⟩
[2] *adv.* (gütig) leniently; (gelinde) mildly
Milde *die;* ~: mildness; (Güte) leniency
mildern *tr. V.* moderate; mitigate
⟨punishment⟩
Milderung *die;* ~: ▶ MILDERN: moderation;
mitigation
Milieu /mi'ljøː/ *das;* ~s, ~s environment
militant *Adj.* militant

Militär¹ *das;* ~s armed forces *pl.;* military; (Soldaten) soldiers *pl.*

Militär² *der;* ~s, ~s [high-ranking military] officer

Militär-: ~**dienst** *der* military service; ~**diktatur** *die* military dictatorship

militärisch *Adj.* military

militarisieren *tr. V.* militarize

Militarismus *der;* ~ (abwertend) militarism

Militarist *der;* ~en, ~en (abwertend) militarist

Militär-: ~**macht** *die* military power; ~**putsch** *der* military putsch

Military /'mɪlɪtərɪ/ *die;* ~, ~s (Reiten) three-day event

Miliz *die;* ~, ~en militia; (Polizei) police

Mill. *Abk.* = **Million** m.

milli-, Milli- milli-

Milliarde *die;* ~, ~n billion

Milli-: ~**gramm** *das* milligram; ~**meter** *der od. das* millimetre; ~**meter·papier** *das* [graph] paper ruled in millimetre squares

Million *die;* ~, ~en million

Millionär *der;* ~s, ~e millionaire

Millionen-: ~**schaden** *der* damage no *pl.,* no indef. art. running into millions; ~**stadt** *die* town with over a million inhabitants

millionst... *Ordinalz.* millionth

Milz *die;* ~: spleen

Mimik *die;* ~: gestures and facial expressions *pl.*

Mimose *die;* ~, ~n (a) mimosa (b) (fig.) oversensitive person

mimosenhaft [1] *Adj.* oversensitive [2] *adv.* oversensitively

minder *Adv.* (geh.) less

minder... *Adj.* inferior ⟨goods, brand⟩

minder·bemittelt *Adj.* without much money *postpos., not pred.;* ~**sein** not have much money; **geistig** ~ (fig. salopp abwertend) not all that bright (coll.)

Minderheit *die;* ~, ~en minority

minder·jährig *Adj.* ⟨child etc.⟩ who is/was a minor

Minder·jährige *der/die; adj. Dekl.* minor

mindern *tr. V.* (geh.) reduce

Minderung *die;* ~, ~en reduction (Gen. in)

minder·wertig *Adj.* inferior

mindest... *Adj.* least; (geringst...) slightest; **das ist das Mindeste** *od.* ~**e, was du tun kannst** it is the least you can do

mindestens *Adv.* at least

Mindest·haltbarkeits·datum *das* best-before date

Mine *die;* ~, ~n (a) (Bergwerk, Sprengkörper) mine (b) (Bleistift~) lead; (Kugelschreiber~, Filzschreiber~) refill

Mineral *das;* ~s, ~e *od.* Mineralien mineral

Mineralogie *die;* ~: mineralogy *no art.*

Mineral-: ~**öl** *das* mineral oil; ~**wasser** *das* mineral water

Mini *das;* ~s, ~s (Mode) mini

Mini- mini-

Miniatur *die;* ~, ~en miniature

minimal [1] *Adj.* minimal; marginal ⟨advantage, lead⟩; very slight ⟨benefit, profit⟩ [2] *adv.* minimally

Minimum *das;* ~s, Minima minimum (an + Dat. of)

minimieren *tr. V.* (bes. Math.) minimize

Minister *der;* ~s, ~, **Ministerin** *die;* ~, ~nen minister (für for); (eines britischen Hauptministeriums) Secretary of State (für for); (eines amerikanischen Hauptministeriums) Secretary (für of)

Ministerium *das;* ~s, Ministerien Ministry; Department (Amer.)

Minister·präsident *der,* **Minister·präsidentin** *die* (a) (eines deutschen Bundeslandes) minister-president (b) (Premierminister[in]) Prime Minister

Minister·rat *der* Council of Ministers

Ministrant *der;* ~en, ~en, **Ministrantin** *die;* ~, ~nen (kath. Kirche) server

Minorität *die;* ~, ~en ▶ MINDERHEIT

minus *Konj., Adv.* (bes. Math.) minus

Minus *das;* ~: deficit

Minus·zeichen *das* minus sign

Minute *die;* ~, ~n minute

minuten·lang [1] *Adj.* lasting [for] several minutes *postpos.;* [2] *adv.* for several minutes

Minuten·zeiger *der* minute hand

Mio. *Abk.* = **Million[en]** m.

mir [1] *Dat. von* ICH to me; (nach Präpositionen) me; **Freunde von** ~: friends of mine; **gehen wir zu** ~: let's go to my place; **von** ~ **aus** as far as I'm concerned [2] *Dat. des Reflexivpron. der 1. Pers. Sg.* myself

Mirabelle *die;* ~, ~n mirabelle

Misch-: ~**brot** *das* bread made from wheat and rye flour; ~**ehe** *die* mixed marriage

mischen [1] *tr. V.* mix [2] *refl. V.* (a) (sich ver~) mix (mit with); ⟨smell, scent⟩ blend (mit with) (b) (sich ein~) **sich in etw.** (Akk.) ~: interfere in sth.

Misch·farbe *die* non-primary colour

Mischling *der;* ~s, ~e half-caste

Mischmasch *der;* ~[e]s, ~e (ugs., meist abwertend) hotchpotch; mishmash

Misch·pult *das* (Film, Rundf., Ferns.) mixing desk *or* console

Mischung *die;* ~, ~en mixture; (Tee~, Kaffee~, Tabak~) blend; (Pralinen~) assortment

Misch·wald *der* mixed [deciduous and coniferous] forest

miserabel (ugs.) ① *Adj.* dreadful (coll.) ② *adv.* dreadfully (coll.); **ihm geht es gesundheitlich ~:** he's in a bad way

Misere *die;* ~, ~n (geh.) wretched *or* dreadful state; (Elend) misery; (Not) distress

miss, *miß *Imperativ Sg. v.* MESSEN

miss·achten, *miß·achten *tr. V.* **(a)** (ignorieren) disregard; ignore **(b)** (geringschätzen) be contemptuous of

miss·billigen, *miß·billigen *tr. V.* disapprove of

Miss·billigung, *Miß·billigung *die* disapproval

Miss·brauch, *Miß·brauch *der:* ▶ MISSBRAUCHEN: abuse; misuse

miss·brauchen, *miß·brauchen *tr. V.* abuse; misuse; abuse ⟨*trust*⟩

missen *tr. V.* (geh.) jmdn./etw. nicht ~ mögen not want to be without sb./sth.

Miss·erfolg, *Miß·erfolg *der* failure

Misse·tat *die* (geh. veralt.) misdeed

miss·fallen, *miß·fallen *unr. itr. V.* etw. missfällt jmdm. sb. dislikes sth.

Missfallen, *Mißfallen *das;* ~s displeasure; (Missbilligung) disapproval

Miss·geschick, *Miß·geschick *das* mishap

miss·glücken, *miß·glücken *itr. V.;* mit sein fail

miss·gönnen, *miß·gönnen *tr. V.* jmdm. etw. ~: begrudge sb. sth.

Miss·griff, *Miß·griff *der* error of judgement

miss·handeln, *miß·handeln *tr. V.* maltreat

Miss·handlung, *Miß·handlung *die* maltreatment

Mission *die;* ~, ~en mission

Missionar *der;* ~s, ~e, **Missionarin** *die;* ~, ~nen missionary

Miss·kredit, *Miß·kredit *der:* jmdn./etw. in ~ bringen bring sb./sth. into discredit

misslang, *mißlang *1. u. 3. Pers. Sg. Prät. v.* MISSLINGEN

missliebig, *mißliebig *Adj.* unpopular

misslingen, *mißlingen *unr. itr. V.; mit sein* fail

Misslingen, *Mißlingen *das;* ~s failure

misslungen, *mißlungen *2. Part. v.* MISSLINGEN

Miss·mut, *Miß·mut *der* ill humour no indef. art.

miß·mutig, *miß·mutig ① *Adj.* bad-tempered; sullen ⟨*face*⟩ ② *adv.* bad-temperedly

Miss·stand, *Miß·stand *der* deplorable state of affairs no pl.

---

*alte Schreibung - vgl. Hinweis auf S. xiv

misst, *mißt *2. u. 3. Pers. Sg. Präsens v.* MESSEN

miss·trauen, *miß·trauen *itr. V.* jmdm./einer Sache ~: mistrust or distrust sb./sth.

Misstrauen, *Miß·trauen *das;* ~s mistrust, distrust (**gegen** of)

misstrauisch, *miß·trauisch ① *Adj.* mistrustful; distrustful ② *adv.* mistrustfully; distrustfully

miss·verständlich, *miß·verständlich ① *Adj.* unclear; ⟨formulation, concept, etc.⟩ that could be misunderstood ② *adv.* ⟨express oneself, describe⟩ in a way that could be misunderstood

Miss·verständnis, *Miß·verständnis *das* misunderstanding

miss·verstehen, *miß·verstehen *unr. tr. V.* ich missverstehe, missverstanden, misszuverstehen misunderstand

Miss·wirtschaft, *Miß·wirtschaft *die* mismanagement

Mist *der;* ~[e]s **(a)** dung; (Dünger) manure; (mit Stroh usw. gemischt) muck **(b)** (Misthaufen) dung/manure/muck heap **(c)** (ugs. abwertend) (Unsinn) rubbish no indef. art.; (Minderwertiges) junk no indef. art.

Mistel *die;* ~, ~n mistletoe

Mist·haufen *der* dung/manure/muck heap

mit ① *Präp. mit Dat.* with; **ein Zimmer ~ Frühstück** a room with breakfast included; **~ 50 [km/h] fahren** drive at 50 [k.p.h]; **~ der Bahn/dem Auto fahren** go by train/car; **~ 20 [Jahren] (a)** at [the age of] twenty ② *adv.* too; as well **(b) seine Arbeit war ~ am besten** (ugs.) his work was among the best

Mit·arbeit *die* collaboration (**bei/an** + *Dat.* on); (Mithilfe) assistance (**bei, in** + *Dat.* in); (Beteiligung) participation (**in** + *Dat.* in)

mit|arbeiten *itr. V.* collaborate (**bei/an** + *Dat.* on) (sich beteiligen) participate (**in** + *Dat.* in)

Mit·arbeiter *der,* **Mit·arbeiterin** *die* **(a)** collaborator; **freier ~:** freelance worker **(b)** (Angestellter) employee

mit|bekommen *unr. tr. V.* **(a)** etw. ~: be given sth. to take with one **(b)** (wahrnehmen) be aware of; (durch Hören, Sehen) hear/see

mit|bestimmen ① *itr. V.* have a say ② *tr. V.* have an influence on

Mit·bestimmung *die* participation (**bei** in); (der Arbeitnehmer) co-determination

mit|bringen *unr. tr. V.* **(a)** etw. ~: bring sth. with one; jmdm./sich etw. ~: bring sth. with one for sb./bring sth. back for oneself **(b)** (haben) have ⟨ability, gift, etc.⟩

Mitbringsel *das;* ~s, ~: [small] present; (Andenken) [small] souvenir

Mit·bürger der, **Mit·bürgerin** die fellow
citizen; **ältere Mitbürger** (Amtsspr.) senior
citizens

mit-einander Adv. (a) with each other or
one another; ~ **sprechen** talk to each other
or one another
(b) (gemeinsam) together

mit|erleben tr. V. (a) witness ⟨events etc.⟩
(b) (mitmachen) be alive during

mit|fahren unr. itr. V.; mit sein **bei jmdm.**
[im Auto] ~: go/travel with sb. [in his/her
car]; (mitgenommen werden) get a lift with sb.
[in his/her car]

mit·fühlend ① Adj. sympathetic
② adv. sympathetically

mit|führen tr. V. (a) (Amtsspr.: bei sich tragen)
etw. ~: carry sth. [with one]
(b) (transportieren) ⟨river, stream⟩ carry along

mit|geben unr. tr. V. **jmdm. etw.** ~: give
sb. sth. to take with him/her; (fig.) provide
sb. with sth.

Mit·gefühl das sympathy

mit|gehen unr. itr. V.; mit sein (a) go too;
mit jmdm. ~: go with sb.
(b) (sich mitreißen lassen) **begeistert** ~:
respond enthusiastically

Mit·gift die; ~, ~en (veralt.) dowry

Mit·glied das member (Gen., **in** + Dat. of)

Mitglieder·versammlung die general
meeting

Mitglieds-: ~**ausweis** der membership
card; ~**beitrag** der membership
subscription

Mitgliedschaft die; ~: membership (+
Gen., **in** + Dat.) of

Mitglied[s]·staat der member state or
country

mit|halten unr. itr. V. keep up (**bei** in, **mit**
with)

mit|helfen unr. itr. V. help (**bei, in** + Dat.
with)

mit·hilfe ① Präp. mit Gen. with the help
or aid of
② Adv. ~ **von** with the help or aid of

Mit·hilfe die help; assistance

mit|hören ① tr. V. listen to; (zufällig)
overhear ⟨conversation, argument, etc.⟩;
(abhören) listen in on
② itr. V. listen; (zufällig) overhear

mit|kommen unr. itr. V.; mit sein (a)
come too; **kommst du mit?** are you coming
[with me/us]?
(b) (Schritt halten) keep up

Mit·läufer der, **Mit·läuferin** die
(abwertend) [mere] supporter

Mit·laut der consonant

Mit·leid das pity, compassion (**mit** for);
(Mitgefühl) sympathy (**mit** for)

Mit·leidenschaft die: **jmdn./etw. in** ~
ziehen affect sb./sth.

mit·leidig ① Adj. compassionate;
(mitfühlend) sympathetic

② adv. compassionately; (mitfühlend)
sympathetically

mit|machen ① tr. V. (a) (teilnehmen an) go
on ⟨trip⟩; join in ⟨joke⟩; follow ⟨fashion⟩;
fight in ⟨war⟩; do ⟨course, seminar⟩; **das
mache ich nicht mit** (ugs.) I can't go along
with it
(b) (ugs.: erleiden) **zwei Weltkriege/viele
Bombenangriffe mitgemacht haben** have
been through two world wars/many bomb
attacks
② itr. V. (a) (sich beteiligen) join in
(b) (ugs.: funktionieren) **mein Herz/Kreislauf
macht nicht mit** my heart/circulation can't
take it

Mit·mensch der fellow human being

mit|nehmen unr. tr. V. (a) **jmdn.** ~: take
sb. with one; **etw.** ~: take sth. with one;
(verhüll.: stehlen) walk off with sth. (coll.);
(kaufen) take sth.; **Essen/Getränke zum
Mitnehmen** food/drinks to take away or
(Amer.) to go
(b) (in Mitleidenschaft ziehen) **jmdn.** ~: take it
out of sb.

mit|reden itr. V. (a) join in the
conversation
(b) (mitbestimmen) have a say

Mit·reisende der/die fellow passenger

mit|reißen unr. tr. V. **die Begeisterung/
seine Rede hat alle Zuhörer mitgerissen** the
audience was carried away with
enthusiasm/by his speech

mit-samt Präp. mit Dat. together with

mit|schneiden unr. tr. V. (Rundf., Fems.)
record [live]

Mit·schuld die share of the blame or
responsibility (**an** + Dat. for)

Mit·schüler der, **Mit·schülerin** die
schoolfellow

mit|spielen itr. V. (a) join in the game
(b) in einem Film ~: be in a film; in einem
Orchester/in od. bei einem Fußballverein ~:
play in an orchestra/for a football club

Mit·spieler der, **Mit·spielerin** die
player; (in derselben Mannschaft) teammate

*****mittag** ▶ MITTAG

Mittag der; ~s, ~e (a) midday no art.;
gegen ~: around midday; **zu** ~ **essen** have
lunch; **heute/Montag** ~: at midday today/on
Monday
(b) (ugs.: Mittagspause) lunch hour

Mittag-essen das lunch

mittags Adv. at midday; **12 Uhr** ~: 12 noon

Mittags-: ~**pause** die lunch hour;
~**ruhe** die period of quiet after lunch;
~**zeit** die (a) (Zeit gegen 12 Uhr) lunchtime
no art.; (b) (Mittagspause) lunch hour

Mitte die; ~, ~n middle; (eines Kreises, einer
Kugel, Stadt) centre; ~ **des Monats/Jahres** in
the middle of the month/year

mit|teilen tr. V. **jmdm. etw.** ~: tell sb. sth.;
(informieren) inform sb. of sth.

mitteilsam *Adj.* communicative;
(gesprächig) talkative

Mit·teilung *die* communication;
(Bekanntgabe) announcement

Mittel *das;* ~s, ~ **(a)** means; (Methode) way;
method; (Werbe~, Propaganda~ usw.) device
(*Gen.* for); **mit allen** ~**n versuchen, etw. zu
tun** try by every means to do sth.
(b) (Arznei) **ein** ~ **gegen Husten** *usw.* a cure
for coughs *etc.;*
(c) *Pl.* (Geldmittel) funds; [financial] resources;
(Privatmittel) means

Mittel·alter *das* Middle Ages *pl.*

mittel·alterlich *Adj.* medieval

mittelbar ⬚1 *Adj.* indirect
⬚2 *adv.* indirectly

mittel-, Mittel-: ~**ding** *das* **ein** ~**ding
sein** be something in between; ~**europa**
(*das*) Central Europe; ~**finger** *der* middle
finger; ~**gebirge** *das* low mountains *pl.;*
~**groß** *Adj.* medium-sized; ⟨*person*⟩ of
medium height; ~**klasse·wagen** *der*
medium-sized car; ~**linie** *die* centre line;
(Fußball) half-way line; ~**los** *Adj.* without
means *postpos.;* ~**mäßig** *Adj.* mediocre;
~**meer** *das* Mediterranean [Sea]; ~**punkt**
der **(a)** (Geom.) centre; (einer Strecke) midpoint;
(b) (Mensch/Sache im Zentrum) centre of
attention; ~**scheitel** *der* centre parting;
~**schule** *die* ▶ REALSCHULE; ~**stand** *der*
middle class; ~**strecken·rakete** *die*
medium-range missile; ~**streifen** *der*
central reservation; median strip (Amer.);
~**weg** *der* middle course; ~**welle** *die*
(Physik, Rundf.) medium wave

mitten *Adv.* ~ **an/auf etw.** (*Akk./Dat.*) in
the middle of sth.; ~ **durch die Stadt** right
through the town

mitten-: ~**drin** *Adv.* [right] in the middle;
~**durch** *Adv.* [right] through the middle

Mitter·nacht *die* midnight *no art.*

Mitternachts·sonne *die* midnight sun

Mittler *der;* ~s, ~ mediator

mittler... *Adj.* middle; moderate ⟨*speed*⟩;
medium-sized ⟨*company, town*⟩; medium
⟨*quality, size*⟩; (durchschnittlich) average; **die** ~**e
Reife** (Schulw.) *standard of achievement for
school-leaving certificate at a Realschule or
for entry to the sixth form in a Gymnasium*

Mittlerin *die;* ~, ~**nen** mediator

Mittler·rolle *die* mediating role

mittler·weile *Adv.* since then; (bis jetzt) by
now; (unterdessen) in the meantime

Mittwoch *der;* ~[e]s, ~e Wednesday; *s.
auch* DIENSTAG

mittwochs *Adv.* on Wednesday[s]

mit·unter *Adv.* from time to time

mit·wirken *itr. V.* **an etw.** (*Dat.*)/**bei etw.** ~:
collaborate on/be involved in sth.; **in einem
Orchester/Theaterstück** ~: play in an
orchestra/act *or* appear in a play

Mitwirkende *der/die adj. Dekl.* (an einer
Sendung) participant; (in einer Show) performer;
(in einem Theaterstück) actor

Mit·wisser *der;* ~s ~, **Mit·wisserin** *die;*
~, ~**nen:** ~ **einer Sache** (*Gen.*) **sein** be an
accessory to sth.

mixen *tr. V.* mix; **sich** (*Dat.*) **einen Drink** ~:
fix oneself a drink

Mixer *der;* ~s, ~, **(a)** (Bar~) barman;
bartender (Amer.)
(b) (Gerät) blender and liquidizer

Mixerin *die;* ~, ~**nen** barmaid

mm *Abk.* = **Millimeter** mm.

Mo. *Abk.* = **Montag** Mon.

Mob *der;* ~s (abwertend) mob

Möbel *das;* ~s, ~ **(a)** *Pl.* furniture *sing., no
indef. art.;*
(b) piece of furniture

Möbel·wagen *der* furniture van; removal
van

mobil *Adj.* **(a)** mobile; *s. auch* MOBILMACHEN;
(b) (ugs.) (lebendig) lively

Mobiliar *das;* ~s furnishings *pl.*

mobilisieren *tr. V.* **(a)** (Milit., fig.) mobilize
(b) (aktivieren) activate

mobil|machen *itr. V.* mobilize

Mobilmachung *die;* ~, ~**en** mobilization

Mobil·telefon *das* cellular phone

möblieren *tr. V.* furnish

mochte *1. u. 3. Pers. Sg. Prät. v.* MÖGEN

möchte *1. u. 3. Pers. Sg. Konjunktiv II v.*
MÖGEN

Mode *die;* ~, ~**n** fashion

Mode·farbe *die* fashionable colour

Modell *das;* ~s, ~e (auch fig.) model; **jmdm.**
~ **sitzen** *od.* **stehen** sit for sb.

modellieren *tr. V.* model, mould ⟨*figures,
objects*⟩; mould ⟨*clay, wax*⟩

Modell·kleid *das* model dress

Modem *der od. das;* ~s, ~s (DV) modem

Moden·schau *die* fashion show

Moder *der;* ~s mould; (~geruch) mustiness

Moderation *die;* ~, ~**en** (Rundf., Ferns.)
presentation

Moderator *der;* ~s, ~**en**, **Moderatorin**
die; ~, ~**nen** (Rundf., Ferns.) presenter

moderieren *tr. V.* (Rundf., Ferns.) present
⟨*programme*⟩

modern¹ *itr. V.; auch mit sein* go mouldy

modern² ⬚1 *Adj.* modern; (modisch)
fashionable
⬚2 *adv.* in a modern manner; (modisch)
fashionably

modernisieren *tr. V.* modernize

Mode-: ~**schöpfer** *der* couturier;
~**schöpferin** *die* couturière; ~**wort** *das;*
Pl. ~wörter vogue word; ~**zeitschrift** *die*
fashion magazine

modifizieren *tr. V.* (geh.) modify

modisch ⬚1 *Adj.* fashionable
⬚2 *adv.* fashionably

---

*old spelling - see note on page xiv

Mofa *das;* ∼s, ∼s [low-powered] moped
Mogelei *die;* ∼, ∼en (ugs.) cheating *no pl.*
mogeln *itr. V.* cheat
Mogel·packung *die* (abwertend) deceptive packaging
mögen [1] *unr. Modalverb; 2.Part.* mögen: **(a)** (wollen) want to; **das hätte ich sehen** ∼: I would have liked to see that **(b)** (geh.: sollen) **das mag genügen** that should be enough **(c)** (Vermutung, Möglichkeit) **sie mag/mochte vierzig sein** she must be/must have been [about] forty; [das] **mag sein** maybe **(d)** *Konjunktiv II* (den Wunsch haben) **ich/sie möchte gern wissen …**: I would/she would like to know … [2] *unr. tr. V.* like; **sie mag keine Rosen** she does not like roses; **sie** ∼ **sich** they're fond of one another; **möchten Sie ein Glas Wein?** would you like a glass of wine?; **ich möchte lieber Tee** I would prefer tea [3] *unr. itr. V.* **(a)** (es wollen) like to **(b) ich möchte nach Hause** I want to go home; **er möchte zu Herrn A** he would like to see Mr A
möglich *Adj.* possible; **es war ihm nicht** ∼ [zu kommen] he was unable [to come]; **alles Mögliche** (ugs.) all sorts of things; [das ist doch] **nicht** ∼! impossible!; **sein Möglichstes tun** do one's utmost
möglicher·weise *Adv.* possibly
Möglichkeit *die;* ∼, ∼en **(a)** possibility; (Methode) way; **es besteht die** ∼, **dass …:** there is a possibility that … **(b)** (Gelegenheit) opportunity; chance
möglichst *Adv.* **(a)** if [at all] possible **(b)** ∼ **schnell** as fast as possible
Mohammed *(der)* Muhammad
Mohammedaner *der;* ∼s, ∼, **Mohammedanerin** *die;* ∼, ∼nen Muslim; Muhammadan
mohammedanisch *Adj.* Muslim; Muhammadan
Mohn *der;* ∼s poppy; (Samen) poppy seed; (auf Brot, Kuchen) poppy seeds *pl.*
Mohn-: ∼**blume** *die* poppy; ∼**brötchen** *das* poppy-seed roll; ∼**kuchen** *der* poppy-seed cake
Möhre *die;* ∼, ∼n carrot
Mohren-kopf *der* chocolate marshmallow
Mohr·rübe *die* carrot
mokieren *refl. V.* (geh.) **sich über etw.** *(Akk.)* ∼: scoff at sth.; **sich über jmdn.** ∼: mock sb.
Mokka *der;* ∼s strong black coffee
Molch *der;* ∼[e]s, ∼e newt
Mole *die;* ∼, ∼n [harbour] mole
Molekül *das;* ∼s, ∼e molecule
molekular *Adj.* molecular
molk *1. u. 3. Pers. Sg. Prät. v.* MELKEN
Molkerei *die;* ∼, ∼en dairy
Moll *das;* ∼ (Musik) minor [key]

mollig [1] *Adj.* **(a)** (rundlich) plump **(b)** (warm) snug [2] *adv.* snugly; ∼ **warm** warm and snug
Moment[1] *der;* ∼[e]s, ∼e moment; **jeden** ∼ (ugs.) [at] any moment; **im** ∼: at the moment
Moment[2] *das;* ∼[e]s, ∼e factor, element (für in)
momentan [1] *Adj.* **(a)** present **(b)** (vorübergehend) temporary; (flüchtig) momentary [2] *adv.* **(a)** at present **(b)** (vorübergehend) temporarily
Monaco *(das);* ∼s Monaco
Monarch *der;* ∼en, ∼en monarch
Monarchie *die;* ∼, ∼n monarchy
Monarchin *die;* ∼, ∼nen monarch
Monat *der;* ∼s, ∼e month; **im** ∼ **April** in the month of April
monatelang [1] *Adj.* lasting for months *postpos., not pred.;* [2] *adv.* for months [on end]
monatlich [1] *Adj.* monthly [2] *adv.* every month; (pro Monat) per month
Monats-: ∼**ende** *das* end of the month; ∼**erste** *der; adj. Dekl.* first [day] of the month; ∼**hälfte** *die* half of the month; ∼**karte** *die* monthly season ticket; ∼**letzte** *der; adj. Dekl.* last day of the month
Mönch *der;* ∼[e]s, ∼e monk
Mond *der;* ∼[e]s, ∼e moon; **auf** od. **hinter dem** ∼ **leben** (fig. ugs.) be a bit behind the times; **nach dem** ∼ **gehen** (ugs.) ‹clock, watch› be hopelessly wrong
Mond-: ∼**fähre** *die* (Raumf.) lunar module; ∼**finsternis** *die* eclipse of the moon; ∼**landung** *die* moon landing; ∼**licht** *das* moonlight; ∼**phase** *die* moon's phase
Mongole *der;* ∼n, ∼n **(a)** Mongol **(b)** (Bewohner der Mongolei) Mongolian
Mongolei *die;* ∼: Mongolia
Mongolin *die;* ∼, ∼nen ▶ MONGOLE
Monitor *der;* ∼s, ∼en monitor
mono-, Mono-: mono-
Mono·gramm *das;* ∼s, ∼e monogram
Monographie *die;* ∼, ∼n monograph
Monolog *der;* ∼s, ∼e monologue
Monopol *das;* ∼s, ∼e monopoly (auf + *Akk.,* für in, of)
monoton [1] *Adj.* monotonous [2] *adv.* monotonously
Monotonie *die;* ∼, ∼n monotony
Monster *das;* ∼s, ∼: monster; (hässlich) [hideous] brute
Monstren ▶ MONSTRUM
monströs *Adj.* monstrous
Monstrum *das;* ∼s, **Monstren (a)** monster **(b)** (Sache) hulking great thing (coll.)
Monsun *der;* ∼s, ∼e (Geogr.) monsoon
Mon·tag *der* Monday; *s. auch* DIENSTAG
Montage /mɔn'taːʒə/ *die;* ∼, ∼n **(a)** ···⟶

(Zusammenbau) assembly; (Einbau) installation; (Aufstellen) erection; (Anbringen) fitting (**an** + *Akk. od. Dat.* to); mounting (**auf** + *Akk. od. Dat.* on)
(b) (Film, bild. Kunst, Literaturw.) montage

montags *Adv.* on Monday[s]

montieren *tr. V.* (a) (zusammenbauen) assemble (**aus** from); erect ⟨*building*⟩
(b) (anbringen) fit (**an** + *Akk. od. Dat.* to; **auf** + *Akk. od. Dat.* on); (einbauen) install (**in** + *Akk.* in); (befestigen) fix (**an** + *Akk. od. Dat.* to)

Monument *das;* ~[e]s, ~e monument

monumental *Adj.* monumental

Moor *das;* ~[e]s, ~e bog; (Bruch) marsh

Moos *das;* ~es, ~e moss

Moped /'moːpɛt/ *das;* ~s, ~s moped

Mops *der;* ~es, Möpse pug [dog]; (salopp: dicke Person) podge (coll.)

Moral *die;* ~ (a) (Norm) morality
(b) (Sittlichkeit) morals *pl.;*
(c) (Selbstvertrauen) morale
(d) (Lehre) moral

moralisch ⟨1⟩ *Adj.* (a) moral
(b) (tugendhaft) virtuous
⟨2⟩ *adv.* (a) morally
(b) (tugendhaft) virtuously

moralisieren *itr. V.* (geh.) moralize

Moralist *der;* ~en, ~en, **Moralistin** *die;* ~, ~nen moralist

Moral·predigt *die* (abwertend) [moralizing] lecture; homily

Morast *der;* ~[e]s, ~e *od.* Moräste (a) bog; swamp
(b) (Schlamm) mud

Mord *der;* ~[e]s, ~e murder (**an** + *Dat.* of); (durch ein Attentat) assassination; **einen** ~ **begehen** commit murder

Mord-: ~**anschlag** *der* attempted murder (**auf** + *Akk.* of); (Attentat) assassination attempt (**auf** + *Akk.* on); ~**drohung** *die* murder threat

morden *tr., itr. V.* murder

Mörder *der;* ~s, ~: murderer (esp. Law); killer; (politischer) assassin

Mörderin *die;* ~, ~nen murderer; murderess; (politische) assassin

mörderisch ⟨1⟩ *Adj.* murderous
⟨2⟩ *adv.* (ugs.) dreadfully (coll.)

Mord·fall *der* murder case

mords-, Mords- (ugs.) terrific (coll.)

mords·mäßig *Adj.* terrific (coll.); tremendous (coll.); (entsetzlich) terrible (coll.)

Mord-: ~**verdacht** *der* suspicion of murder; ~**versuch** *der* attempted murder; (Attentat) assassination attempt; ~**waffe** *die* murder weapon

morgen *Adv.* tomorrow; ~ **in einer Woche** tomorrow week; a week tomorrow; ~ **um diese Zeit** this time tomorrow; **bis** ~**!** until tomorrow!; see you tomorrow!

Morgen *der;* ~s, ~: morning; **am** ~: in the morning; **am folgenden** *od.* **nächsten** ~: next morning; **früh am** ~, **am frühen** ~: early in the morning; **heute** ~: this morning; **guten** ~**!** good morning!

morgendlich *Adj.* morning

Morgen-: ~**grauen** *das* daybreak; ~**mantel** *der* dressing gown; ~**rot** *das* (geh.) rosy dawn

morgens *Adv.* in the morning; (jeden Morgen) every morning; **Dienstag** *od.* **dienstags** ~: on Tuesday morning[s]; **von** ~ **bis abends** from morning to evening

morgig *Adj.* tomorrow's

Morphium *das;* ~s morphine

morphium·süchtig *Adj.* addicted to morphine *pred.*

morsch *Adj.* (auch fig.) rotten

Mörser *der;* ~s, ~ (Gefäß, Geschütz) mortar

Mörtel *der;* ~s mortar

Mosaik *das;* ~s, ~en *od.* ~e mosaic

Mosambik (*das*); ~s Mozambique

Moschee *die;* ~, ~n mosque

Moschus *der;* ~: musk

Mosel *die;* ~: Moselle

Mosel·wein *der* Moselle [wine]

mosern *itr. V.* (ugs.) gripe (coll.) (**über** + *Akk.*)

Moskau (*das*); ~s Moscow

Moskauer ⟨1⟩ *indekl. Adj.* Moscow *attrib.;*
⟨2⟩ *der;* ~s, ~: Muscovite

Moskauerin *die;* ~, ~nen Muscovite

Moskito *der;* ~s, ~s mosquito

Moslem *der;* ~s, ~s ▶ MUSLIM

Moslemin *die;* ~, ~nen ▶ MUSLIMIN

moslemisch ▶ MUSLIMISCH

Most *der;* ~[e]s, ~e (a) [cloudy fermented] fruit juice
(b) (landsch.: neuer Wein) new wine

Mostrich *der;* ~s (nordostd.) mustard

Motel *das;* ~s, ~s motel

Motiv *das;* ~s, ~e (a) motive
(b) (fachspr.: Thema) motif; theme; (Kunst) subject

Motor *der;* ~s, ~en engine; (Elektro~) motor

Motor·haube *die* (Kfz-W.) bonnet (Brit.); hood (Amer.)

motorisieren *tr. V.* motorize

Motor-: ~**rad** *das* motor cycle; ~**rad·fahrer** *der,* ~**rad·fahrerin** *die* motorcyclist; ~**roller** *der* motor scooter; ~**schaden** *der* engine trouble *no indef. art.*

Motte *die;* ~, ~n moth

Motten·kugel *die* mothball

Motto *das;* ~s, ~s motto; (Schlagwort) slogan

Möwe *die;* ~, ~n gull

Mrd. *Abk.* = **Milliarde** bn.

Mücke *die;* ~, ~n midge; (größer) mosquito

Mücken·stich *der* midge/mosquito bite

Mucks *der;* ~**es,** ~**e** (ugs.) murmur [of protest]; **keinen** ~ **sagen** not utter a [single] word

müde ⟦1⟧ *Adj.* tired; (ermattet) weary; (schläfrig) sleepy; **jmdn./etw.** *od.* **jmds./einer Sache** ~ **sein** (geh.) be tired of sb./sth. ⟦2⟧ *adv.* wearily; (schläfrig) sleepily

Müdigkeit *die;* ~: tiredness

muffelig (ugs.) ⟦1⟧ *Adj.* grumpy ⟦2⟧ *adv.* grumpily

muffig *Adj.* musty

Mühe *die;* ~, ~**n** trouble; **sich** (*Dat.*) **mit jmdm./etw.** ~ **geben** take [great] pains over sb./sth.; **mit Müh und Not** with great difficulty

mühelos ⟦1⟧ *Adj.* effortless ⟦2⟧ *adv.* effortlessly

mühe·voll *Adj.* laborious; painstaking ⟨*work*⟩

Mühle *die;* ~, ~**n** (a) mill; (Kaffee~) [coffee] grinder (b) (Spiel) nine men's morris

Mühsal *die;* ~, ~**e** (geh.) tribulation; (Strapaze) hardship

mühsam ⟦1⟧ *Adj.* laborious ⟦2⟧ *adv.* laboriously

müh·selig (geh.) ⟦1⟧ *Adj.* laborious; arduous ⟨*journey, life*⟩ ⟦2⟧ *adv.* with [great] difficulty

Mulde *die;* ~, ~**n** hollow

Mull *der;* ~**[e]s** (Stoff) mull; (Verband~) gauze

Müll *der;* ~**s** refuse; rubbish; garbage (Amer.); trash (Amer.); (Industrie~) [industrial] waste

Müll-: ~**abfuhr** *die* refuse *or* (Amer.) garbage collection; ~**ablade·platz** *der* [refuse] dump *or* (Brit.) tip

Müll·binde *die* gauze bandage

Müll·deponie *die* (Amtsspr.) refuse disposal site

Müller *der;* ~**s,** ~: miller

Müll-: ~**halde** *die* refuse dump; ~**kippe** *die* ▶ MÜLLABLADEPLATZ; ~**mann** *der;* (ugs.) dustman (Brit.); garbage man (Amer.); ~**sack** *der* refuse bag; ~**schlucker** *der* rubbish *or* (Amer.) garbage chute; ~**tonne** *die* dustbin (Brit.); garbage *or* trash can (Amer.); ~**tüte** *die* bin bag; ~**wagen** *der* dustcart (Brit.); garbage truck (Amer.)

mulmig *Adj.* (ugs.) uneasy

Multimedia·technik *die* (DV) multimedia technology

Multiplex *das;* ~**es,** ~**e** multiplex

Multiplikation *die;* ~, ~**en** (Math.) multiplication

multiplizieren *tr. V.* multiply (**mit** by)

Mumie /'muːmiə/ *die;* ~, ~**n** mummy

Mumm *der;* ~**s** (ugs.) (Mut) guts *pl.* (coll.); (Tatkraft) drive; zap (coll.); (Kraft) muscle power

Mumps *der od. die;* ~: mumps *sing.*

München (*das*); ~**s** Munich

Münch[e]ner ⟦1⟧ *indekl. Adj.* Munich *attrib* ⟦2⟧ *der;* ~**s,** ~: inhabitant/native of Munich

Münch[e]nerin *die;* ~, ~**nen** ▶ MÜNCH[E]NER 2

Mund *der;* ~**[e]s, Münder** mouth; **er küsste sie auf den** ~: he kissed her on the lips; **mit vollem** ~ **sprechen** speak with one's mouth full; **den** ~ **nicht aufmachen** (fig. ugs.) not say anything; **den** *od.* **seinen** ~ **halten** (ugs.) (zu sprechen aufhören) shut up (coll.); (nichts sagen) not say anything; (nichts verraten) keep quiet (**über** + *Akk.* about); **sie ist nicht auf den** ~ **gefallen** (fig. ugs.) she's never at a loss for words

Mund·art *die* dialect

münden *itr. V.; mit sein* **in etw.** (*Akk.*) ~: ⟨*river*⟩ flow into sth.; ⟨*corridor, street*⟩ lead into sth.

mund-, Mund-: ~**faul** *Adj.* (ugs.) uncommunicative; ~**gerecht** *Adj.* bite-sized; ~**geruch** *der* bad breath *no indef. art.*; ~**harmonika** *die* mouth organ

mündig *Adj.* of age *pred.;* ~ **werden** come of age

mündlich ⟦1⟧ *Adj.* oral ⟦2⟧ *adv.* orally

Mund·stück *das* mouthpiece; (bei Zigaretten) tip

mund·tot *Adj.* **jmdn.** ~ **machen** silence sb.

Mündung *die;* ~, ~**en** (a) mouth; (größere Trichter~) estuary (b) (bei Feuerwaffen) muzzle

Mund·wasser *das; Pl.* ~**wässer** mouthwash

Mund-zu-Mund-Beatmung *die* mouth-to-mouth resuscitation

Munition *die;* ~: ammunition

munkeln *tr., itr. V.* (ugs.) **man munkelt, dass** ...: there is a rumour that ...

Münster *das;* ~**s,** ~: minster; (Dom) cathedral

munter ⟦1⟧ *Adj.* (a) cheerful; (lebhaft) lively ⟨*eyes, game*⟩ (b) (wach) awake ⟦2⟧ *adv.* cheerfully

Munterkeit *die;* ~: cheerfulness

Münz·automat *der* slot machine

Münze *die;* ~, ~**n** coin

Münz-: ~**fernsprecher** *der* payphone; pay station (Amer.); ~**tankstelle** *die* coin-in-the-slot petrol (Brit.) *or* (Amer.) gas station; ~**wechsler** *der* change machine

mürbe *Adj.* crumbly ⟨*biscuit, cake, etc.*⟩; tender ⟨*meat*⟩; soft ⟨*fruit*⟩; **jmdn.** ~ **machen** (fig.) wear sb. down

Murmel *die;* ~, ~**n** marble

murmeln *tr., itr. V.* mumble; mutter; (sehr leise) murmur

Murmel·tier *das* marmot

murren *itr. V.* grumble

mürrisch ⟦1⟧ *Adj.* grumpy ⋯⋗

2 *adv.* grumpily

Mus *das od. der;* ~es, ~e purée

Muschel *die;* ~, ~n (a) mussel; (Schale) [mussel] shell

(b) (am Telefon) (Hör~) earpiece; (Sprech~) mouthpiece

Muse *die;* ~, ~n muse

Museum *das;* ~s, Museen museum

Musik *die;* ~, ~en music

musikalisch 1 *Adj.* musical

2 *adv.* musically

Musikant *der;* ~en, ~en, **Musikantin** *die;* ~, ~nen musician

Musik·box *die* jukebox

Musiker *der;* ~s, ~, **Musikerin** *die;* ~, ~nen musician

Musik-: ~**hochschule** *die* college of music; ~**instrument** *das* musical instrument; ~**saal** *der* (in der Schule) music room; ~**sender** *der* music station; ~**stück** *das* piece of music; ein ~stück Chopins/von Chopin a piece by Chopin; ~**stunde** *die* music lesson; ~**szene** *die* music scene

musisch 1 *Adj.* artistic; ⟨education⟩ in the arts

2 *adv.* artistically

musizieren *itr. V.* play music; (bes. unter Laien) make music

Muskat *der;* ~[e]s, ~e nutmeg

Muskat·nuss, *Muskat·nuß *die* nutmeg

Muskel *der;* ~s, ~n muscle

Muskel-: ~**kater** *der* stiff muscles *pl.;* ~**kraft** *die* muscle power; ~**krampf** *der* cramp; ~**pille** *die* (scherzh.) muscle-building pill; muscle builder ~**protz** *der* (ugs.) muscleman; ~**zerrung** *die* (Med.) pulled muscle; sich (*Dat.*) eine ~zerrung zuziehen pull a muscle

Muskulatur *die;* ~, ~en musculature; muscular system

muskulös *Adj.* muscular

Müsli *das;* ~s, ~s muesli

Muslim *der;* ~s, ~e od. ~s Muslim

Muslimin *die;* ~, ~nen Muslim [woman]

muslimisch 1 *Adj.* Muslim

2 *adv.* on Muslim principles; ~ erzogen werden be brought up in the Muslim faith

muss, *muß *1. u. 3.Pers. Sg. Präsens v.* MÜSSEN

Muss, *Muß *das;* ~: necessity; must (coll.)

Muße *die;* ~: leisure

müssen 1 *unr. Modalverb; 2.Part.* **müssen:** (a) have to; er muss es tun he must do it; he has to *or* (coll.) has got to do it; das muss 1968 gewesen sein it must have been in 1968; er muss gleich hier sein he will be here at any moment

*old spelling - see note on page xiv

(b) *Konjunktiv II* es müsste doch möglich sein it ought to be possible; reich müsste man sein! how nice it would be to be rich!

2 *unr. itr. V.* ich muss nach Hause I have to *or* must go home; ich muss mal (fam.) I need to spend a penny (Brit. coll.) *or* (Amer. coll.) go to the john

müßig 1 *Adj.* idle ⟨person⟩; ⟨hours, weeks, life⟩ of leisure

2 *adv.* idly

Müßig-: ~**gang** *der* leisure; (Untätigkeit) idleness ~**gänger** *der;* ~~s, ~~, ~**gängerin** *die;* ~~, ~~nen idler; ~gänger *Pl.* people with time on their hands

musste, *mußte *1. u. 3. Pers. Sg. Prät. v.* MÜSSEN

Muster *das;* ~s, ~ (a) (Vorlage) pattern

(b) (Vorbild) model (an + *Dat.* of)

(c) (Verzierung) pattern

(d) (Warenprobe) sample

muster-, Muster-: ~**beispiel** *das* perfect example; ~**gültig** 1 *Adj.* exemplary; impeccable ⟨order⟩; 2 *adv.* in an exemplary fashion; ~**prozess,** *~prozeß** *der* test case

mustern *tr. V.* (a) eye

(b) (Milit.: ärztlich untersuchen) jmdn. ~: give sb. his medical

Musterung *die;* ~, ~en (a) scrutiny

(b) (Milit.: von Wehrpflichtigen) medical examination; medical

Mut *der;* ~[e]s courage

mutig 1 *Adj.* brave

2 *adv.* bravely

mut·los *Adj.* dejected; (entmutigt) disheartened

Mut·losigkeit *die;* ~: dejection

mutmaßen *tr., itr. V.* conjecture

mutmaßlich *Adj.* supposed; suspected ⟨murderer etc.⟩

Mutmaßung *die;* ~, ~en conjecture

Mut·probe *die* test of courage

Mutter¹ *die;* ~, Mütter mother

Mutter² *die;* ~, ~n nut

mütterlich 1 *Adj.* (a) maternal ⟨line, love, instincts, etc.⟩

(b) (fürsorglich) motherly ⟨woman, care⟩

2 *adv.* in a motherly way

mütterlicher·seits *Adv.* on the/his/her *etc.* mother's side

Mütterlichkeit *die;* ~: motherliness; (mütterliche Gefühle) motherly feeling

Mutter-: ~**liebe** *die* motherly love *no art.;* ~**mal** *das;* ~~e birthmark

Mutterschaft *die;* ~: motherhood

Mutterschafts·urlaub *der* maternity leave

mutter-, Mutter-: ~**seelen·allein** *Adj.* all alone; ~**söhnchen** *das* mummy's *or* (Amer.) mama's boy; ~**sprache** *die* mother tongue; ~**tag** *der* Mother's Day *no def. art.*

Mutti *die;* ∼, ∼s mummy (Brit. coll.); mum (Brit. coll.); mommy (Amer. coll.); mom (Amer. coll.)

mut·willig [1] *Adj.* wilful; wanton ⟨destruction⟩
[2] *adv.* wilfully

Mütze *die;* ∼, ∼n cap

MW *Abk.* (Rundf.) = **Mittelwelle** MW

Mw.-St., MwSt. *Abk.* **Mehrwertsteuer** VAT

mysteriös [1] *Adj.* mysterious
[2] *adv.* mysteriously

Mystik *die;* ∼: mysticism

Mystery- /ˈmɪstəri/ mystery *attrib.*

Mythologie *die;* ∼, ∼n mythology

mythologisch *Adj.* mythology

Mythos *der;* ∼, Mythen myth

Nn

n, N /ɛn/ *das;* ∼, ∼: n/N

N *Abk.* = **Nord[en]** N

na *Interj.* (ugs.) well; **na so [et]was!** well I never!; **na und?** (wennschon) so what?; (beschwichtigend) **na, na, na!** now, now, come along; (triumphierend) **na also!** there you are!; (unsicher) **na, ich weiß nicht** hmm, I'm not sure; (ärgerlich) **na, was soll das denn?** now what's all this about?; (drohend) **na warte!** just [you] wait!

Nabe *die;* ∼, ∼n hub

Nabel *der;* ∼s, ∼: navel

Nabel-: ∼**bruch** *der* (Med.) umbilical hernia; ∼**schnur** *die* umbilical cord

Naben·schaltung *die* hub gear

nach [1] *Präp. mit Dat.* (a) (räumlich) to; **der Zug** ∼ **München** the train for Munich *or* the Munich train; ∼ **Hause gehen** go home; ∼ **Osten [zu]** eastwards; [towards the] east (b) (zeitlich) after; **zehn [Minuten]** ∼ **zwei** ten [minutes] past two (c) (mit bestimmten Verben, bezeichnet das Ziel der Handlung) for (d) (bezeichnet [räumliche und zeitliche] Reihenfolge) after; ∼ **Ihnen/dir!** after you (e) (gemäß) according to; ∼ **meiner Ansicht** *od.* **Meinung, meiner Ansicht** *od.* **Meinung** ∼: in my view *or* opinion; ∼ **der neusten Mode gekleidet** dressed in [accordance with] the latest fashion; **dem Gesetz** ∼: in accordance with the law; by law; ∼ **etw. schmecken/ riechen** taste/smell of sth. [2] *Adv.* (a) (räumlich) **[alle] mir** ∼**!** [everybody] follow me! (b) (zeitlich) ∼ **und** ∼: little by little; gradually; ∼ **wie vor** still

nach|ahmen *tr. V.* imitate

Nachahmung *die;* ∼, ∼en imitation

Nachbar *der;* ∼n, ∼n neighbour

Nachbar·haus *das* house next door

Nachbarin *die;* ∼, ∼nen neighbour

Nachbar·land *das* neighbouring country

Nachbarschaft *die;* ∼, ∼en (a) the whole neighbourhood (b) (Beziehungen) **gute** ∼: good neighbourliness (c) (Gegend) neighbourhood; (Nähe) vicinity

Nach·beben *das* aftershock

nach|bestellen *tr. V.* [noch] etw. ∼: order more of sth.; ⟨shop⟩ reorder sth.

Nach·bildung *die* (a) copying (b) (Gegenstand) copy

nach|blicken *tr. V.* (geh.) jmdm./einer Sache ∼: gaze after sb./sth.

nach|datieren *tr. V.* backdate

nach·dem *Konj.* (a) after (b) ▶ JE[1] 3

nach|denken *unr. itr. V.* think; **denk mal [gut** *od.* **scharf] nach** have a [good] think

Nach·denken *das* thought

nachdenklich [1] *Adj.* thoughtful
[2] *adv.* thoughtfully

Nach·druck *der; Pl.* ∼e (a) **mit** ∼: emphatically (b) (Druckw.) reprint

nachdrücklich [1] *Adj.* emphatic
[2] *adv.* emphatically

Nachdrücklichkeit *die;* ∼: emphatic nature

nach|dunkeln *itr. V.;* mit sein get darker

Nach·durst *der* morning-after thirst

nach|eifern *itr. V.* jmdm. ∼: emulate sb.

nach·einander *Adv.* one after the other

nach|empfinden *unr. tr. V.* empathize with ⟨feeling⟩; share ⟨delight, sorrow⟩

Nach·erzählung *die* retelling [of a story]; (Schulw.) reproduction

Nachfahr *der;* ∼en, ∼en, **Nachfahrin** *die;* ∼, ∼nen (geh.) descendant

nach|fahren *unr. itr. V.;* mit sein follow [on]; jmdm. ∼: follow sb.

Nach·folge *die* succession

Nachfolger *der;* ∼s, ∼, **Nachfolgerin** *die;* ∼, ∼nen successor

Nach·forschung *die* investigation

Nach·frage *die* demand (**nach** for)

nach|fragen *itr. V.* ask; inquire; **bei jmdm.
~:** ask sb.; **ob ich mal ~ soll?** should I ask
about it *or* make inquiries?

nach|fühlen *tr. V.* empathize with; **das
kann ich dir ~!** I know how you feel!

nach|füllen *tr. V.* top up; **Salz/Wein ~:** put
[some] more salt/wine in

nach|geben *unr. itr. V.* give way

Nach·gebühr *die* excess postage

nach|gehen *unr. itr. V.; mit sein* **(a)**
jmdm./einer Sache ~: follow sb./sth.; **einer
Sache ~** (fig.) look into a matter; **einem Beruf
~:** practise a profession
(b) (nicht aus dem Kopf gehen) **jmdm. ~:** remain
on sb.'s mind
(c) ⟨clock, watch⟩ be slow; **[um] eine Stunde
~:** be an hour slow

Nach·geschmack *der* aftertaste

nach·giebig *Adj.* indulgent

Nachgiebigkeit *die; ~:* indulgence

nach·haltig ① *Adj.* **(a)** lasting
(b) (Ökologie) sustainable
② *adv.* **(a)** (auf längere Zeit) for a long time
(b) (Ökologie) sustainably

Nach·hause·weg *der* way home

nach|helfen *unr. itr. V.* help

nach·her /*auch: '--*/ *Adv.* afterwards; (später)
later [on]; **bis ~!** see you later!

Nach·hilfe *die* coaching

Nachhilfe·unterricht *der* coaching

***nach·hinein, Nachhinein:* im ~**
(nachträglich) afterwards; later; (zurückblickend)
with hindsight

nach|holen *tr. V.* (nachträglich erledigen) catch
up on ⟨work, sleep⟩; make up for ⟨working
hours missed⟩

nach|jagen *itr. V.; mit sein* **jmdm./einer
Sache ~:** chase after sb./sth.

Nachkomme *der; ~n, ~n* descendant

nach|kommen *unr. itr. V.; mit sein* follow
[later]; come [on] later

Nachkommenschaft *die; ~:*
descendants *pl.*

Nachkömmling *der; ~s, ~e* much
younger child (than the rest)

Nach·kriegs- post-war ⟨generation, period,
etc.⟩

Nach·lass, *Nach·laß *der;* Nachlasses,
Nachlasse *od.* Nachlässe **(a)** estate
(b) (Kaufmannsspr.: Rabatt) discount

nach|lassen ① *unr. itr. V.* let up; ⟨pain,
stress, pressure⟩ ease; ⟨effect⟩ wear off;
⟨interest, enthusiasm, strength, courage⟩
wane; ⟨health, hearing, memory⟩ deteriorate;
⟨business⟩ drop off
② *unr. tr. V.* (Kaufmannsspr.) give a discount
of

nach·lässig ① *Adj.* careless

② *adv.* carelessly

Nach·lässigkeit *die; ~, ~en* carelessness

Nachlass·verwalter *der,*
Nachlass·verwalterin, *die* (Rechtsw.)
executor

nach|laufen *unr. itr. V.; mit sein* **jmdm./
einer Sache ~:** run after sb./sth.

nach|lesen *unr. tr. V.* look up

nach|lösen ① *tr. V.* **eine Fahrkarte ~:** buy
a ticket [on the train, bus, etc.]
② *itr. V.* pay the excess [fare]

nach|machen *tr. V.* (auch tun) copy;
(imitieren) imitate; (genauso herstellen) reproduce
⟨period furniture etc.⟩; forge ⟨signature⟩

***nach·mittag** ▶ NACHMITTAG

Nach·mittag *der* afternoon; **am ~:** in the
afternoon; **am späten ~:** late in the
afternoon; **heute ~:** this afternoon

nach·mittags *Adv.* in the afternoon;
dienstags *od.* **Dienstag ~:** on Tuesday
afternoons; **um vier Uhr ~:** at four in the
afternoon; at 4 p.m.

Nachnahme *die; ~, ~n:* **per ~:** cash on
delivery; COD

Nach·name *der* surname

Nach·porto *das* excess postage

nachprüfbar *Adj.* verifiable

nach|prüfen *tr., itr. V.* check

nach|rechnen *tr. V.* check ⟨figures⟩

Nach·rede *die:* **üble ~:** malicious gossip;
(Rechtsw.) defamation [of character]

nach|rennen *unr. itr. V.:* ▶ NACHLAUFEN

Nachricht *die; ~, ~en* **(a)** news *no pl.;* **das
ist eine gute ~:** that is [a piece of] good
news; **eine ~ hinterlassen** leave a message
(b) *Pl.* (Ferns., Rundf.) news *sing.;* **~en hören**
listen to the news

Nachrichten-: **~sprecher** *der,*
~sprecherin *die* newsreader

nach|rücken *itr. V.; mit sein* move up

Nach·ruf *der* obituary (**auf** + *Akk.* of)

nach|rufen *unr. tr., itr. V.* **jmdm.** [**etw.**] **~:**
call [sth.] after sb.

nach|rüsten ① *itr. V.* counter-arm
② *tr. V.* (Technik: zusätzlich ausstatten) **mit etw. ~**
(+ *Akk.*) equip additionally with sth.;
upgrade ⟨television, hi-fi, etc.⟩ with sth.

nach|sagen *tr. V.* **(a)** (wiederholen) repeat
(b) **man sagt ihm nach, er sei ...:** he is said
to be ...; **jmdm. Schlechtes ~:** speak ill of sb.

Nach·saison *die* late season

nach|schicken *tr. V.* **(a)** (durch die Post
o. Ä.) forward
(b) **jmdm. jmdn. ~:** send sb. after sb.

Nach·schlag *der* (ugs.: zusätzliche Portion)
second helping; seconds *pl.*

nach|schlagen ① *unr. tr. V.* look up
② *unr. itr. V.* **im Lexikon/Wörterbuch ~:**
consult the encyclopaedia/dictionary

Nachschlage·werk *das* work of
reference

Nach·schlüssel *der* duplicate key

---

nach|schmeißen *unr. tr. V.* (ugs.) **man kriegt sie nachgeschmissen** you get them for next to nothing

Nach·schub *der* (Milit.) **(a)** supply **(an +** *Dat.* of) **(b)** (~material) supplies *pl.* **(an +** *Dat.* of)

nach|sehen ① *unr. itr. V.* **(a)** jmdm./einer Sache ~: gaze after sb./sth. **(b)** (kontrollieren) check **(c)** (nachschlagen) have a look ② *unr. tr. V.* **(a)** (nachlesen) look up **(b)** (überprüfen) check [over]

Nach·sehen *das:* **das** ~ **haben** not get a look-in; (nichts abbekommen) be left with nothing

nach|senden *unr. od. regelm. tr. V.* forward

Nach·sicht *die* leniency

nachsichtig ① *Adj.* lenient **(gegen, mit** towards) ② *adv.* leniently

Nachsichtigkeit *die;* ~: leniency

Nach·silbe *die* (Sprachw.) suffix

nach|sitzen *unr. itr. V.* be in detention; **[eine Stunde]** ~ **müssen** have [an hour's] detention

Nach·spann *der;* ~[e]s, ~e (Film, Ferns.) [final] credits *pl.*

Nach·speise *die* dessert; sweet

Nach·spiel *das:* **die Sache wird noch ein** ~ **haben** this affair will have repercussions; **ein gerichtliches** ~ **haben** result in court proceedings

nach|spionieren *itr. V.* jmdm. ~: spy on sb.

nach|sprechen *unr. tr. V.* [jmdm.] etw. ~: repeat sth. [after sb.]

nächst... *Sup. zu* NAH: *Adj.* next; (kürzest) shortest ⟨way⟩; **am** ~**en Tag** the next day; **beim** ~**en Mal, das** ~**e Mal** the next time; **der** ~**e bitte!** next [one], please; **wer kommt als** ~**er dran?** whose turn is it next?

Nächste *der; adj. Dekl.* (geh.) neighbour

nach|stehen *unr. itr. V.* jmdm. an etw. (*Dat.*) nicht ~: be sb.'s match in sth.; jmdm./ einer Sache in nichts ~: be in no way inferior to sb./sth.

nach·stehend ① *Adj.* following ② *adv.* below

Nächsten·liebe *die* charity [to one's neighbour]

nächstens *Adv.* **(a)** shortly **(b)** (ugs.: wenn es so weitergeht) if it goes on like this

nächst-: ~**liegend** *Adj.* first, immediate ⟨problem⟩; [most] obvious ⟨explanation etc.⟩; ~**möglich** *Adj.* earliest possible

nach|suchen *itr. V.* (geh.) **um etw.** ~: request sth.; (bes. schriftlich) apply for sth.

*nacht ▸ NACHT

Nacht *die;* ~, **Nächte** night; **gestern/ morgen/Dienstag** ~: last night/tomorrow

night/on Tuesday night; **heute** ~: tonight; **bei** ~, **in der** ~: at night[-time]; **über** ~ **bleiben** stay overnight; **gute** ~! good night!

nacht-, Nacht-: ~**arbeit** *die* night work *no art.;* ~**blind** *Adj.* night-blind; ~**blindheit** *die* night blindness; ~**creme** *die* night cream; ~**dienst** *der* night duty; ~**dienst haben** be on night duty; ⟨chemist's shop⟩ be open late

Nach·teil *der* disadvantage

nachteilig ① *Adj.* detrimental; harmful ② *adv.* detrimentally; harmfully

Nacht-: ~**essen** *das* (bes. südd., schweiz.) ▸ ABENDESSEN; ~**hemd** *das* nightshirt

Nachtigall *die;* ~, ~**en** nightingale

nächtigen *itr. V.* (österr., sonst geh.) spend the night

Nach·tisch *der* dessert; sweet

nächtlich *Adj.* nocturnal; night ⟨sky⟩; ⟨darkness, stillness⟩ of the night

Nacht·lokal *das* night spot (coll.)

nach|tragen *unr. tr. V.* (schriftlich ergänzen) insert; add

nach·tragend *Adj.* unforgiving; (rachsüchtig) vindictive

nachträglich ① *Adj.* later; subsequent ⟨apology⟩; (verspätet) belated ⟨greetings, apology⟩ ② *adv.* afterwards; subsequently; (verspätet) belatedly

nach|trauern *itr. V.* jmdm./einer Sache ~: bemoan the passing of sb./sth.

Nacht·ruhe *die* night's sleep

nachts *Adv.* at night; **Montag** *od.* **montags** ~: on Monday nights; **um 3 Uhr** ~: at 3 o'clock in the morning

Nacht-: ~**schicht** *die* night shift; ~**schwester** *die* night nurse; ~**tisch** *der* bedside table; ~**tisch·lampe** *die* bedside light; ~**topf** *der* chamber pot; ~**wächter** *der,* ~**wächterin** *die* nightwatchman

Nach·untersuchung *die* follow-up examination; check-up

nach|vollziehen *unr. tr. V.* reconstruct; (begreifen) comprehend

nach|wachsen *unr. itr. V.; mit sein* [wieder] ~: grow again

Nach·wehen *Pl.* (Med.) afterpains; (fig. geh.) unpleasant after-effects

Nachweis *der;* ~**es**, ~**e** proof *no indef. art.* (*Gen.,* **über +** *Akk.* of); (Zeugnis) certificate (**über +** *Akk.* of)

nachweisbar ① *Adj.* demonstrable ⟨fact, truth, error, defect, guilt⟩; detectable ⟨substance, chemical⟩ ② *adv.* demonstrably

nach|weisen *unr. tr. V.* prove

nachweislich *Adv.* as can be proved

Nach·welt *die* posterity *no art.;* future generations *pl., no art.*

n

nach|winken itr. V. jmdm./einer Sache ~:
wave after sb./sth.

Nach·wirkung die after-effect

Nach·wort das; Pl. ~e afterword

Nach·wuchs der (a) (fam.: Kind[er])
offspring

  (b) (junge Kräfte) new blood; (für eine Branche
usw.) new recruits pl.; (in der Ausbildung)
trainees pl.

nach|zahlen tr., itr. V. **(a)** pay later

  (b) (zusätzlich zahlen) **25 DM** ~: pay another 25
marks

nach|zählen tr., itr. V. [re]count

Nach·zahlung die additional payment

nach|ziehen unr. itr. V.**(a)** (ugs.: ebenso
handeln) do likewise; follow suit

  (b) mit sein (nachträglich übersiedeln) **jmdm.** ~:
[go to] join sb.

Nachzügler der; ~s, ~, **Nachzüglerin**
die; ~, ~nen straggler; (spät Ankommende[r])
latecomer

Nackedei der; ~s, ~s (fam. scherzh.)
[kleiner] ~: naked little thing

Nacken der; ~s, ~: back or nape of the
neck; (Hals) neck

nackt Adj. naked; bare ⟨feet, legs, arms,
skin, fists⟩; (fig.) plain ⟨truth, fact⟩; bare
⟨existence⟩

Nackt·bade·strand der nudist beach

Nackte der/die; adj. Dekl. naked man/
woman

Nackt·foto das nude photo

Nadel die; ~, ~n needle; (Steck~, Hut~,
Haar~) pin; **an der** ~ **hängen** (fig. ugs.) be on
the needle (sl.)

Nadel·baum der conifer

Nadeldrucker der (DV) dot-matrix printer

nadeln itr. V. ⟨tree⟩ shed its needles

Nadel·wald der coniferous forest

Nagel der; ~s, Nägel nail; **den** ~ **auf den
Kopf treffen** (fig. ugs.) hit the nail on the head

Nagel-: ~**bürste** die nailbrush; ~**feile**
die nail file; ~**lack** der nail varnish (Brit.);
nail polish

nageln tr. V. nail (**an** + Akk. to, **auf** + Akk.
on); (Med.) pin

nagel·neu Adj. (ugs.) brand-new

Nagel·schere die nail scissors pl.

nagen ⓵ itr. V. gnaw; **an etw.** (Dat.) ~:
gnaw [at] sth.

  ⓶ tr. V. gnaw off; **ein Loch ins Holz** ~: gnaw
a hole in the wood

Nage·tier das rodent

nah ▸ NAHE

Nah·aufnahme die (Fot.) close-up
[photograph]

nahe /'naːə,/ näher /'nɛːə,/ nächst... ⓵ Adj.
(a) (räumlich) near pred.; close pred.; nearby
attrib.;

  (b) (zeitlich) imminent; near pred.

(c) (eng) close ⟨relationship etc.⟩

  ⓶ adv. **(a)** (räumlich) ~ **an** (+ Dat./Akk.), ~
bei close to; ~ **gelegen** nearby; **von** ~**m** from
close up; **jmdm.** ~ **gehen** affect sb. deeply;
eine Sache (Dat.) ~ **kommen** come close to
sth.; ⟨amount⟩ approximate to sth.; **jmdm./
sich** [menschlich] ~ **kommen** get to know
sb./one another well; **jmdm/sich** [menschlich]
näher kommen get on closer terms with sb.;
jmdm. ~ **stehen** be on intimate terms with
sb.; **jmdm. etw.** ~ **legen** (fig.) suggest sth. to
sb.; **einen Verdacht/einen Gedanken** usw. ~
legen give rise to a suspicion/thought etc.;
~ **liegen** (fig.) ⟨thought⟩ suggest itself;
⟨suspicion, question⟩ arise

  (b) (zeitlich) ~ **an die achtzig** (ugs.) pushing
eighty (coll.)

  (c) (eng) closely

  ⓷ Präp. mit Dat. (geh.) near; close to

Nähe die; ~: closeness

nahe-: ~**bei** Adv. nearby; close by;
~|**gehen** usw. ▸ NAHE 2A; ~**liegend** Adj.
obvious ⟨reason, solution⟩

nahen itr. V.; mit sein (geh.) draw near; **sein/
ihr** usw. **Ende nahte** the end was near

nähen ⓵ itr. V. sew; (Kleider machen) make
clothes

  ⓶ tr. V. **(a)** sew ⟨seam, hem⟩; make ⟨dress
etc.⟩

  (b) (Med.) stitch

näher ⓵ Komp. zu nahe;

  ⓶ Adj. **(a)** (kürzer) shorter ⟨way, road⟩

  (b) (genauer) more precise ⟨information⟩;
closer ⟨investigation, inspection⟩

  ⓷ adv. **(a)** bitte treten Sie ~! please come
in/nearer/this way

  (b) (genauer) more closely; (im Einzelnen) in
[more] detail

***näher|kommen** ▸ NAHE 2A

nähern refl. V. approach; **sich jmdm./einer
Sache** ~: approach sb./sth.

nahe-: *~|**stehen** ▸ NAHE 2A; ~**zu** Adv.
almost; nearly; (mit Zahlenangabe) close on

Näh-: ~**garn** das [sewing] cotton;
~**kasten** der sewing box

nahm 1. u. 3. Pers. Sg. Prät. v. NEHMEN

Näh-: ~**maschine** die sewing machine;
~**nadel** die sewing needle

nah·östlich Adj. Middle Eastern

Nähr·boden der culture medium; (fig.)
breeding ground

nähren ⓵ tr. V. feed (mit on)

  ⓶ refl. V. (geh.) **sich von etw.** ~: live on sth.;
⟨animal⟩ feed on sth.

nahrhaft Adj. nourishing

Nahrung die; ~: food

Nahrungs·mittel das food [item]; ~ Pl.
foodstuffs

Nähr·wert der nutritional value

Näh·seide die sewing silk

Naht die; ~, Nähte seam

naht·los ⓵ Adj. seamless; (fig.) perfectly
smooth ⟨transition⟩

---

*old spelling - see note on page xiv

2 *adv.* Studium und Beruf gehen nicht ∼ ineinander über there is not a perfectly smooth transition from study to work

Nah-: ∼**verkehr** *der* local traffic; ∼**verkehrs·zug** *der* local train

Näh·zeug *das* sewing things *pl.*

naiv 1 *Adj.* naïve
2 *adv.* naïvely

Naivität *die;* ∼: naïvety

Name *der;* ∼ns, ∼n name

namens *Adv.* by the name of

Namens-: ∼**schild** *das* (a) (an Türen usw.) nameplate; (b) (zum Anstecken) name badge; ∼**tag** *der* name day

namentlich 1 *Adj.* by name *postpos.;*
2 *adv.* by name
3 *Adv.* (besonders) particularly

namhaft *Adj.* (a) (berühmt) noted (b) (ansehnlich) noteworthy ⟨sum, difference⟩; notable ⟨contribution, opportunity⟩

nämlich *Adv.* (a) er kann nicht kommen, er ist ∼ krank he cannot come, as he is ill (b) (und zwar) namely

nannte *1. u. 3. Pers. Sg. Prät. v.* NENNEN

nanu *Interj.* ∼, was machst du denn hier? hello, what are you doing here?; ∼, Sie gehen schon? what, you're going already?

Napf *der;* ∼[e]s, Näpfe bowl (esp. for animal's food)

Narbe *die;* ∼, ∼n scar

narbig *Adj.* scarred

Narkose *die;* ∼, ∼n (Med.) narcosis

narkotisieren *tr. V.* (Med.) anaesthetize ⟨patient⟩; put ⟨patient⟩ under a general anaesthetic

Narr *der;* ∼en, ∼en fool

Narren·freiheit *die* freedom to do as one pleases

Närrin *die;* ∼, ∼nen fool

närrisch 1 *Adj.* crazy; carnival-crazy ⟨season⟩
2 *adv.* crazily

Narzisse *die;* ∼, ∼n narcissus

naschen 1 *itr. V.* (Süßes essen) eat sweet things; (heimlich essen) have a nibble
2 *tr. V.* eat ⟨sweets, chocolate, etc.⟩; er hat Milch genascht he has been at the milk

Nascherei *die;* ∼, ∼en (a) [continually] eating sweet things; hör auf mit der ∼! don't keep eating sweet things all the time! (b) (Süßigkeit) ∼en sweets

naschhaft *Adj.* sweet-toothed; ∼ sein have a sweet tooth

Nase *die;* ∼, ∼n nose; die ∼ voll haben (ugs.) have had enough

Nasen-: ∼**bluten** *das;* ∼∼s bleeding from the nose; ∼**loch** *das* nostril; ∼**spitze** *die* tip of the/one's nose; jmdm. etw. an der ∼spitze ansehen (fig. ugs.) tell sth. by sb.'s face; ∼**tropfen** *Pl.* nose drops; ∼**wurzel** *die* root of the nose

nase-: ∼**rümpfend** 1 *Adj.* disapproving

2 *adv.* disdainfully; ∼**weis** 1 *Adj.* precocious; pert ⟨remark, reply⟩; 2 *adv.* precociously

Nas·horn *das* rhinoceros

**nass, *naß; nasser od.* nässer, nassest... *od.* nässest...: *Adj.* wet; sich/das Bett ∼ machen wet oneself/one's bed

Nässe *die;* ∼: wetness

nass·kalt, *naß·kalt *Adj.* cold and wet

Nass·rasur, *Naß·rasur *die* wet shaving *no art.*

Nation *die;* ∼, ∼en nation

national 1 *Adj.* national
2 *adv.* nationally

National-: ∼**elf** *die* (Fußball) national side; ∼**hymne** *die* national anthem

Nationalisierung *die;* ∼, ∼en nationalization

Nationalismus *der;* ∼: nationalism *usu. no art.*

nationalistisch 1 *Adj.* nationalist; nationalistic
2 *adv.* nationalistically

Nationalität *die;* ∼, ∼en nationality

national,- National-: ∼**mannschaft** *die* national team; ∼**sozialismus** *der* National Socialism; ∼**sozialist** *der*, ∼**sozialistin** *die* National Socialist; ∼**sozialistisch** *Adj.* National Socialist; ∼**spieler** *der*, ∼**spielerin** *die* (Sport) national player; international; ∼**staat** *der* nation state; ∼**stolz** *der* national pride; ∼**versammlung** *die* National Assembly

NATO, Nato *die;* ∼: NATO, Nato *no art.*

Natron *das;* ∼∼s [doppeltkohlensaures] ∼: sodium bicarbonate; [kohlensaures] ∼: sodium carbonate

Natter *die;* ∼, ∼n colubrid

Natur *die;* ∼, ∼en nature; die freie ∼: [the] open countryside

Naturalien /natu'ra:ljən/ *Pl.* natural produce *sing.* (used as payment); in ∼ (Dat.) bezahlen pay in kind

Naturalismus *der;* ∼: naturalism

naturalistisch 1 *Adj.* naturalistic
2 *adv.* naturalistically

Naturell *das;* ∼s, ∼e temperament

natur-, Natur-: ∼**erscheinung** *die* natural phenomenon; ∼**farben** *Adj.* natural-coloured; ∼**freund** *der*, ∼**freundin** *die* nature lover; ∼**gemäß** *Adv.* naturally; ∼**geschichte** *die* natural history; ∼**gesetz** *das* law of nature; ∼**getreu** 1 *Adj.* lifelike ⟨portrait, imitation⟩; faithful ⟨reproduction⟩; 2 *adv.* ⟨draw⟩ true to life; ⟨reproduce⟩ faithfully; ∼**heilkunde** *die* naturopathy *no art.;* ∼**katastrophe** *die* natural disaster

natürlich 1 *Adj.* natural
2 *adv.* ⟨laugh, behave⟩ naturally
3 *Adv.* (a) (selbstverständlich, wie erwartet) naturally; of course (b) (zwar) of course

Natürlichkeit *die;* ~: naturalness
natur-, Natur-: ~**park** *der* ≈ national park; ~**produkt** *das* natural product; ~**schutz** *der* [nature] conservation; **unter** ~**schutz** (*Dat.*) **stehen** be protected by law; be a protected species/variety/area *etc.*; ~**schutz-gebiet** *das* nature reserve; ~**talent** *das* [great] natural talent *or* gift; (begabter Mensch) naturally talented *or* gifted person; ~**verbunden** *Adj.* ⟨*person*⟩ in tune with nature; ~**volk** *das* primitive people; ~**wissenschaft** *die* natural science *no art.;* ~**wissenschaftler** *der,* ~**wissenschaftlerin** *die* [natural] scientist; ~**wissenschaftlich** ⓵ *Adj.* scientific; ⓶ *adv.* scientifically; ~**wunder** *das* miracle *or* wonder of nature
Navigation *die;* ~: navigation *no art.*
navigieren *tr., itr. V.* navigate
n. Chr. *Abk.* = **nach Christus** AD
Neandertaler *der;* ~s, ~: Neanderthal man
Nebel *der;* ~s, ~: fog; (weniger dicht) mist
nebelig ▶ NEBLIG
Nebel-: ~**scheinwerfer** *der* fog lamp; ~**schluss-leuchte,** ***~**schluß-leuchte** *die* rear fog lamp; ~**schwaden** *Pl.* swathes of mist; ~**wand** *die* wall of fog
neben ⓵ *Präp. mit Dat.* **(a)** (Lage) next to; beside **(b)** (außer) apart from; aside from (Amer.) **(c)** (verglichen mit) beside ⓶ *Präp. mit Akk.* (Richtung) next to; beside
neben-, Neben-: ~**an** *Adv.* next door; ~**bei** *Adv.* **(a)** ⟨*work*⟩ on the side; (zusätzlich) as well; **(b)** (beiläufig) ⟨*remark, ask*⟩ by the way; ⟨*mention*⟩ in passing; ~**beruf** *der* second job; sideline; ~**beruflich** ⓵ *Adj.* **eine** ~**berufliche Tätigkeit** a second job; ⓶ *adv.* on the side; **er arbeitet** ~**beruflich als Übersetzer** he translates as a sideline; ~**beschäftigung** *die* second job; sideline; ~**buhler** *der,* ~**buhlerin** *die* rival
neben-einander *Adv.* **(a)** next to each other; ⟨*be sitting, standing*⟩ next to one another, side by side; (fig.: zusammen) ⟨*live, exist*⟩ side by side; ~ **wohnen** live next door to each other; ~ **legen** (+ *Akk.*) lay *or* place ⟨*objects*⟩ next to each other *or* side by side **(b)** (gleichzeitig) together
***nebeneinander|legen *usw.* ▶ NEBENEINANDER A
Neben-: ~**erwerb** *der* secondary occupation; ~**fach** *das* subsidiary subject; minor (Amer.); ~**fluss,** ***~**fluß** *der* tributary; ~**gebäude** *das* **(a)** annexe; outbuilding **(b)** (Nachbargebäude) neighbouring building; ~**geräusch** *das* background noise; ~**haus** *das* house next door
neben-her *Adv.* ▶ NEBENBEI

nebenher-: ~|**fahren** *unr. itr. V.; mit sein* drive/ride alongside; ~|**gehen** *unr. itr. V.; mit sein* walk alongside
neben-, Neben-: ~**höhle** *die* (Anat.) paranasal sinus; ~**kläger** *der,* ~**klägerin** *die* (Rechtsw.) accessory prosecutor; ~**kosten** *Pl.* **(a)** additional costs; **(b)** (bei Mieten) heating, lighting, and services; ~**produkt** *das* by-product; ~**rolle** *die* supporting role; ~**sache** *die* minor matter; ~**sachen** inessentials; ~**sächlich** *Adj.* of minor importance *postpos.;* unimportant; minor ⟨*detail*⟩; ~**sächlichkeit** *die;* ~~, ~~**en** (Unwichtiges) matter of minor importance; unimportant matter; ~**satz** *der* (Sprachw.) subordinate clause; ~**stelle** *die* extension; ~**straße** *die* side street; ~**tätigkeit** *die* second job; sideline; ~**tisch** *der* next table; ~**verdienst** *der* additional income; ~**wirkung** *die* side effect; ~**zimmer** *das* next room
neblig *Adj.* foggy; (weniger dicht) misty
Necessaire /nesɛˈsɛːɐ̯/ *das;* ~s, ~s sponge bag (Brit.); toilet bag (Amer.)
necken *tr. V.* tease
Neckerei *die;* ~: teasing
nee (ugs.) no; nope (Amer. coll.)
Neffe *der;* ~n, ~n nephew
negativ ⓵ *Adj.* negative ⓶ *adv.* ⟨*answer*⟩ in the negative
Negativ *das;* ~s, ~e (Fot.) negative
Neger *der;* ~s, ~: Negro
Negerin *die;* ~, ~**nen** Negress
nehmen *unr. tr. V.* take; **sich** (*Dat.*) **etw.** ~: take sth.; (sich bedienen) help oneself to sth.; **auf sich** (*Akk.*) ~: take on ⟨*responsibility, burden*⟩; **jmdm./einer Sache etw.** ~: deprive sb./sth. of sth.; **was nehmen Sie dafür?** how much do you charge for it?
Neid *der;* ~[e]s envy; jealousy
neiden *tr. V.* (geh.) **jmdm. etw.** ~: envy sb. [for] sth.
Neid-hammel *der* (salopp abwertend) envious sod (sl.)
neidisch ⓵ *Adj.* envious ⓶ *adv.* enviously
neigen ⓵ *tr. V.* tip; tilt; incline ⟨*head, upper part of body*⟩ ⓶ *refl. V.:* ⟨*person*⟩ lean; ⟨*ship*⟩ heel over, list; ⟨*scales*⟩ tip ⓷ *itr. V.* **(a)** zu Erkältungen/Krankheiten ~: be prone to colds/illnesses **(b)** (tendieren) tend
Neigung *die;* ~, ~**en (a)** (Vorliebe) inclination **(b)** (Tendenz) tendency
nein *Interj.* no
Nein *das;* ~[s], ~[s] no
Nein-stimme *die* no-vote
Nektar *der;* ~s, ~e (Bot.) nectar
Nektarine *die;* ~, ~**n** nectarine

***alte Schreibung - vgl. Hinweis auf S. xiv

Nelke *die;* ~, ~n (a) pink; (Dianthus
caryophyllus) carnation
(b) (Gewürz) clove

nennen [1] *unr. tr. V.* (a) call
(b) (angeben) give ⟨*name, date of birth,
address, reason, price, etc.*⟩
(c) (anführen) give ⟨*example*⟩; (erwähnen)
mention ⟨*person, name*⟩
[2] *unr. refl. V.* ⟨*person, thing*⟩ be called

nennens·wert *Adj.* considerable
⟨*influence, changes, delays, damage*⟩; **kaum**
~e **Veränderungen** changes scarcely worth
mentioning

Nenner *der;* ~s, ~ (Math.) denominator

neo-, Neo- neo-

Neon *das;* ~s neon

Neon-: ~**licht** *das* neon light; ~**röhre**
die neon tube

Nepal (*das*)*;* ~s Nepal

Nepp *der;* ~s (ugs. abwertend) daylight
robbery *no art.;* rip-off (coll.)

neppen *tr. V.* (ugs. abwertend) rook; rip
⟨*tourist, customer, etc.*⟩ off (sl.)

Nepper *der;* ~s, ~, **Nepperin** *die;* ~,
~nen (ugs. abwertend) shark; rip-off merchant
(coll.)

Nepp·lokal *das* (ugs. abwertend) clip joint
(coll.)

Nerv *der;* ~s, ~en nerve; **die ~en verlieren**
lose control [of oneself]; **jmdm. auf die ~en
gehen** *od.* **fallen** get on sb.'s nerves

nerven (salopp) [1] *tr. V.* **jmdn.** ~: get on
sb.'s nerves
[2] *itr. V.* be wearing on the nerves

nerven-, Nerven-: ~**aufreibend** *Adj.*
nerve-racking; ~**bündel** *das* (ugs.) bundle
of nerves (coll.); ~**gift** *das* neurotoxin;
~**heil·anstalt** *die* (veralt.) psychiatric
hospital; ~**krank** *Adj.* ⟨*person*⟩ suffering
from a nervous disease; ~**probe** *die*
mental trial; ~**säge** *die* (salopp) pain in the
neck (coll.); ~**zusammen·bruch** *der*
nervous breakdown

nervig *Adj.* (auch fig.) sinewy

nervlich *Adj.* nervous ⟨*strain*⟩

nervös [1] *Adj.* (auch Med.) nervous; jittery
⟨*person*⟩
[2] *adv.* nervously

Nervosität *die;* ~ nervousness

nerv·tötend *Adj.* nerve-racking ⟨*wait*⟩;
soul-destroying ⟨*activity, work*⟩

Nerz *der;* ~es, ~e mink

Nerz·mantel *der* mink coat

Nessel *die;* ~, ~n nettle

Nest *das;* ~[e]s, ~er (a) nest
(b) (fam.: Bett) bed
(c) (ugs. abwertend: kleiner Ort) little place

nett [1] *Adj.* nice; (freundlich) kind
[2] *adv.* nicely; (freundlich) nicely; kindly

netter·weise *Adv.* kindly

netto *Adv.* ⟨*weigh, earn, etc.*⟩ net

Netto-: ~**einkommen** *das* net income;
~**gehalt** *das* net salary; ~**preis** *der* net
price

Netz *das;* ~es, ~e (a) net; (Einkaufs~) string
bag; (Gepäck~) [luggage] rack
(b) (Spinnen~) web
(c) (Netzwerk) network; (für Strom, Wasser, Gas)
mains *pl.*

Netz-: ~**haut** *die* (Anat.) retina; ~**werk**
das (auch Elektrot.) network

neu [1] *Adj.* new; **die ~este Mode** the latest
fashion; **das ist mir ~:** that is news to me;
der/die Neue the new man/woman/boy/girl
[2] *adv.* (a) ~ **tapeziert/gestrichen**
repapered/repainted; **sich ~ einrichten**
refurnish one's home
(b) (gerade erst) **diese Ware ist ~ eingetroffen**
this item has just come in; ~ **eröffnet**
newly-opened; (wieder eröffnet) reopened

neu·artig *Adj.* new; ~e **Lebensmittel** novel
foods

Neu·artigkeit *die;* ~~: novelty

neu-, Neu-: ~**bau** *der; Pl.* ~~ten new
house/building; ~**bau·wohnung** *die* flat
(Brit.) *or* (Amer.) apartment in a new block/
house; ~**beginn** *der* new beginning

neuerdings *Adv.* **er trägt ~ eine Brille** he
has recently started wearing glasses

*****neu·eröffnet** ▶ NEU 2B

Neu·eröffnung *die* (a) opening
(b) (Wiedereröffnung) reopening

Neuerung *die;* ~, ~en innovation

neu·geboren *Adj.* newborn

Neu·gier, Neugierde *die;* ~: curiosity;
(Wissbegierde) inquisitiveness

neu·gierig [1] *Adj.* curious; inquisitive;
inquisitive ⟨*person*⟩; **ich bin ~, was er dazu
sagt** I'm curious to know what he'll say
about it
[2] *adv.* ⟨*ask*⟩ inquisitively; ⟨*peer*⟩ nosily (coll.
derog.)

Neuheit *die;* ~, ~en (a) novelty
(b) (Neues) new product/gadget/article *etc.*

Neuigkeit *die;* ~, ~en piece of news; ~en
news *sing.*

Neu-: ~**jahr** *das* New Year's Day; ~**land**
das (fig.) new ground

neulich *Adv.* recently; ~ **morgens** the
other morning

Neuling *der;* ~s, ~e newcomer; (auf einem
Gebiet) novice

Neu·mond *der* new moon

neun *Kardinalz.* nine

Neun *die;* ~, ~en nine

neun-: ~**hundert** *Kardinalz.* nine
hundred; ~**jährig** *Adj.* (9 Jahre alt) nine-
year-old *attrib.;* (9 Jahre dauernd) nine-year
attrib.; ~**mal** *Adv.* nine times

neunt... *Ordinalz.* ninth

neun·tausend *Kardinalz.* nine thousand

Neuntel *das* (schweiz. meist *der*)*;* ~s, ~:
ninth

neuntens *Adv.* ninthly

neun-zehn *Kardinalz.* nineteen

neunzig *Kardinalz.* ninety

neunziger *indekl. Adj.* **die ~ Jahre** the nineties

neunzigst... *Ordinalz.* ninetieth

neuralgisch *Adj.* **(a)** (Med.) neuralgic **(b)** (empfindlich) **das ist mein ~er Punkt** it's a sore *or* touchy point with me.

neu-reich *Adj.* nouveau riche

Neurodermitis *die;* **~, Neurodermitiden** (Med.) neurodermatitis

Neurologe *der;* **~n, ~n** neurologist

Neurologie *die;* **~:** neurology

Neurologin *die;* **~, ~nen** neurologist

neurologisch *Adj.* neurological

Neurose *die;* **~, ~n** (Med., Psych.) neurosis

Neurotiker *der;* **~s, ~, Neurotikerin** *die;* **~, ~nen** (Med., Psych., auch ugs.) neurotic

neurotisch *Adj.* (Med., Psych., auch ugs.) neurotic

Neu-see-land *(das);* **~s** New Zealand

Neuseeländer *der;* **~s, ~, Neuseeländerin** *die;* **~, ~nen** New Zealander

neutral ⟦1⟧ *Adj.* neutral ⟦2⟧ *adv.* **sich ~ verhalten** remain neutral

Neutralität *die;* **~, ~en** neutrality

Neutron *das;* **~s, ~en** neutron

Neutrum *das;* **~s, Neutra** (österr. nur so) *od.* **Neutren** (Sprachw.) neuter

neu-, Neu-: **~wert** *der* value when new; **~wertig** *Adj.* as new; **~zeit** *die* modern age; **~zeitlich** *Adj.* modern

nicht *Adv.* not; **~!** [no,] don't!; **~ rostend** non-rusting ⟨blade⟩; stainless ⟨steel⟩; **~ [wahr]?** isn't it/he/she *etc.;* don't you/we/they *etc.;* **du magst das, ~ [wahr]?** you like that, don't you?; **was du ~ sagst!** you don't say!

nicht-, Nicht- non-

Nicht-angriffs-pakt *der* nonaggression pact

Nichte *die;* **~, ~n** niece

nichtig *Adj.* **(a)** (geh.) vain ⟨things, pleasures, etc.⟩; trivial ⟨reason⟩ **(b)** (Rechtsspr.) void

Nicht-raucher *der* non-smoker; **„~raucher"** 'no smoking'

*nicht-rostend ▶ NICHT

nichts *Indefinitpron.* nothing; **ich möchte ~:** I don't want anything; **~ sagend** (fig.) empty; (ausdruckslos) expressionless ⟨face⟩

nichts-desto-weniger *Adv.* nevertheless; none the less

nichts-, Nichts-: **~nutz** *der;* **~~es, ~~e** (veralt.) good-for-nothing; **~nutzig** *Adj.* (veralt.) good-for-nothing *attrib.;* worthless ⟨existence⟩; ***~sagend** ▶ NICHTS; **~tun** *das* idleness *no art.*

Nickel *das;* **~s** nickel

nicken *itr. V.* nod

nie *Adv.* never

nieder ⟦1⟧ *Adj.; nicht präd.* lower ⟨class, intelligence⟩; minor ⟨official⟩; lowly ⟨family, origins, birth⟩; menial ⟨task⟩ ⟦2⟧ *Adv.* down

nieder-, Nieder-: **~gang** *der* fall; decline; **~gehen** *unr. itr. V.; mit sein* ⟨plane etc., rain, avalanche⟩ come down; **~geschlagen** *Adj.* dejected; **~geschlagenheit** *die;* **~:** dejection; **~lage** *die* defeat

Nieder-lande *Pl.:* **die ~:** the Netherlands

Niederländer *der;* **~s, ~:** Dutchman

Niederländerin *die;* **~, ~nen** Dutchwoman

niederländisch *Adj.* Dutch; Netherlands *attrib.* ⟨government, embassy, etc.⟩

nieder-, Nieder-: **~lassen** *unr. refl. V.* **(a)** set up in business; ⟨doctor, lawyer⟩ set up in practice; **(b)** (seinen Wohnsitz nehmen) settle; **~lassung** *die;* **~~, ~~en** (Wirtsch.) branch; **~legen** *tr. V.* **(a)** (geh.: hinlegen) lay *or* put down; lay ⟨wreath⟩; **(b)** (fig.) resign [from] ⟨office⟩; relinquish ⟨command⟩

Nieder-sachsen *(das)* Lower Saxony

nieder-, Nieder-: **~schlag** *der* precipitation; **~schlagen** *unr. tr. V.* **(a)** **jmdn. ~schlagen** knock sb. down; **(b)** (beenden) suppress, put down ⟨revolt, uprising, etc.⟩; **(c)** (senken) lower ⟨eyes, eyelids⟩; **~schmetternd** *Adj.* shattering ⟨experience, news⟩; devastating ⟨result, review⟩; **~trächtig** ⟦1⟧ *Adj.* malicious ⟨person, slander, lie, etc.⟩; (verachtenswert) despicable ⟨person⟩; base ⟨misrepresentation, slander, lie⟩; ⟦2⟧ *adv.* ⟨betray, lie, treat⟩ in a despicable way; **~trächtigkeit** *die;* **~~, ~~en (a)** ▶ ~TRÄCHTIG 1: maliciousness; despicableness; baseness; **(b)** (gemeine Handlung) despicable act

Niederung *die;* **~, ~en** low-lying area; (an Flussläufen, Küsten) flats *pl.;* (Tal) valley

niedlich ⟦1⟧ *Adj.* sweet; cute (Amer. coll.) ⟦2⟧ *adv.* sweetly

niedrig ⟦1⟧ *Adj.* low; lowly ⟨origins, birth⟩; base ⟨instinct, desire, emotion⟩; vile ⟨motive⟩ ⟦2⟧ *adv.* ⟨hang, fly⟩ low

Niedrig-: **~lohn-land** *das* country with a low-wage country; **~wasser** *das* **(a)** (von Seen/Flüssen) **bei ~wasser** when the [level of the] lake/river is low; **(b)** (bei Ebbe) low tide; low water; **bei ~wasser** at low tide *or* low water

niemals *Adv.* never

niemand *Indefinitpron.* nobody; no one

Niemands-land *das* (auch fig.) no man's land

Niere *die;* **~, ~n** kidney

Nieren-: **~entzündung** *die* nephritis; **~stein** *der* kidney stone

nieseln *unpers. itr. V.* drizzle

Niesel·regen *der* drizzle
niesen *itr. V.* sneeze
Niete¹ *die;* ~, ~n (a) (Los) blank
  (b) (ugs.: Mensch) dead loss (coll.) (in + *Dat.* at)
Niete² *die;* ~, ~n rivet
nieten *tr. V.* rivet
niet- und nagelfest: [alles] was nicht ~
  ist (ugs.) [everything] that's not nailed *or*
  screwed down
Nikolaus /'nɪkolays/ *der;* ~, ~e (ugs.)
  Nikoläuse (a) St Nicholas
  (b) (Tag) St Nicholas' Day
Nikotin *das;* ~s nicotine
nikotin·arm *Adj.* low-nicotine *attrib.;* low
  in nicotine *pred.*
Nikotin·sucht *die* nicotine addiction
Nil *der;* ~[s] Nile
Nil·pferd *das* hippopotamus
nimm *Imperativ Sg. v.* NEHMEN
nippen *itr. V.* sip
nirgends, nirgend·wo *Adv.* nowhere
Nische *die;* ~, ~n niche; (Erweiterung eines
  Raumes) recess
nisten *itr. V.* nest
Nitrat *das;* ~[e]s, ~e nitrate
Niveau /ni'vo:/ *das;* ~s, ~s level;
  (Qualitäts~) standard
Nixe *die;* ~, ~n nixie; (mit Fischschwanz)
  mermaid
nobel *Adj.* (a) (geh.) noble; noble[-minded]
  ⟨person⟩
  (b) (oft spött.: luxuriös) elegant; posh (coll.)
Nobel·preis *der* Nobel prize
noch ⓵ *Adv.* (a) ([wie] bisher) still; ~ nicht
  not yet; sie sind immer ~ nicht da they're
  still not here; ich habe Großvater ~ gekannt
  I'm old enough to have known grandfather;
  er hat ~ Glück gehabt he was lucky; das
  geht ~: that's [still] all right
  (b) (als Rest einer Menge) ich habe [nur] ~
  zehn Mark I've [only] ten marks left; es sind
  ~ 10 km bis zur Grenze it's another 10 km.
  to the border
  (c) (bevor etw. anderes geschieht) just; ich will ~
  [schnell] duschen I just want to have a
  [quick] shower
  (d) (irgendwann einmal) some time; one day; er
  wird ~ anrufen/kommen he will still call/
  come
  (e) (womöglich) if you're/he's *etc.* not careful;
  du kommst ~ zu spät! you'll be late if
  you're not careful
  (f) (drückt eine geringe zeitliche Distanz aus) only;
  gestern habe ich ihn ~ gesehen I saw him
  only yesterday
  (g) (nicht später als) ~ am selben Abend the
  [very] same evening
  (h) (außerdem, zusätzlich) wer war ~ da? who
  else was there?; ~ etwas Kaffee? [would you
  like] some more coffee?; Geld/Kleider *usw.* ~
  und ~ heaps and heaps of money/clothes
  etc. (coll.)
  (i) er ist ~ größer [als Karl] he is even taller

[than Karl]; er will ~ mehr haben he wants
even more; jeder ~ so dumme Mensch
versteht das anyone, however stupid, can
understand that
  (j) wie heißt sie [doch] ~? [now] what's her
  name again?
  ⓶ *Partikel* das ist ~ Qualität! that's what I
  call quality; der wird sich ~ wundern (ugs.)
  he's in for a surprise; er kann ~ nicht
  einmal lesen he can't even read
  ⓷ *Konj.* (und auch nicht) nor; weder ... noch
  neither ... nor
noch·mals *Adv.* again
Nominativ *der;* ~s, ~e (Sprachw.)
  nominative [case]
nominieren *tr. V.* nominate
Nominierung *die;* ~, ~en nomination
Nonne *die;* ~, ~n nun
Nord (bes. Seemannsspr., Met.) ▶ NORDEN
nord-, Nord-: ~afrika (das) North
  Africa; ~amerika (das) North America;
  ~deutsch *Adj.* North German
Norden *der;* ~s north; der ~: the North;
  nach ~: northwards
Nord·irland (das) Northern Ireland
nordisch *Adj.* Nordic
Nord·kap *das* North Cape
nördlich ⓵ *Adj.* (a) (im Norden gelegen)
  northern
  (b) (nach, aus dem Norden) northerly
  (c) (aus dem Norden kommend, für den Norden
  typisch) Northern
  ⓶ *adv.* northwards; ~ von ...: [to the] north
  of ...
  ⓷ *Präp. mit Gen.* [to the] north of
Nord-: ~licht *das* northern lights *pl.;*
  aurora borealis; ein ~licht/~lichter the
  northern lights; ~pol *der* North Pole
Nordrhein-Westfalen (das)*;* ~s North
  Rhine-Westphalia
Nord·see *die;* ~: North Sea
nord·wärts *Adv.* northwards
Nord·wind *der* northerly wind
Nörgelei *die;* ~, ~en (abwertend) grumbling
nörgeln *itr. V.* (abwertend) moan, grumble
  (an + *Dat.* about)
Norm *die;* ~, ~en (a) norm
  (b) (geforderte Arbeitsleistung) quota
  (c) (Sport) qualifying standard
  (d) (technische, industrielle ~) standard
normal ⓵ *Adj.* normal
  ⓶ *adv.* normally
Normal·benzin *das* ≈ two-star petrol
  (Brit.); regular (Amer.)
normalerweise *Adv.* normally
normalisieren ⓵ *tr. V.* normalize
  ⓶ *refl. V.* return to normal
Normalität *die;* ~: normality *no def. art.*
Normal·zustand *der* normal state
Normandie *die;* ~: Normandy
normen *tr. V.,* **normieren** *tr. V.*
  standardize

Norwegen (das); ~s Norway
Norweger der; ~s, ~, **Norwegerin** die;
~, ~nen Norwegian
norwegisch Adj. Norwegian
Nostalgie die; ~: nostalgia
Not die; ~, **Nöte** (a) (Gefahr) **in** ~ **sein** be in
desperate straits
(b) (Mangel, Armut) need; poverty [and
hardship]; ~ **leiden** suffer poverty [and
hardship]; **in** ~ **geraten/sein** encounter hard
times/be suffering want [and deprivation]
(c) (Verzweiflung) distress
(d) (Sorge, Mühe) trouble; **mit knapper** ~: by
the skin of one's teeth
(e) (veralt.: Notwendigkeit) necessity; **zur** ~: if
need be
Notar der; ~s, ~e notary
Notariat das; ~[e]s, ~e (a) (Amt)
notaryship
(b) (Kanzlei) notary's office
not-, Not-: ~**arzt** der doctor on
[emergency] call; ~**aufnahme** die
casualty department; casualty no art.;
~**ausgang** der emergency exit;
~**bremse** die emergency brake; ~**dienst**
der ▶ BEREITSCHAFTSDIENST; ~**durft** die; ~
(geh.) **seine [große/kleine]** ~**durft verrichten**
relieve oneself; ~**dürftig** [1] Adj. makeshift
⟨shelter, repair⟩; scanty ⟨cover, clothing⟩;
[2] adv. scantily ⟨clothed⟩
Note die; ~, ~n (a) (Zeichen) note
(b) Pl. (Text) music sing.;
(c) (Schul~) mark
(d) (Eislauf, Turnen) score
Notebook /'noutbʊk/ das; ~s, ~s (DV)
notebook [computer]
not-, Not-: ~**fall** der (a) emergency; (b) **im**
~**fall** (nötigenfalls) if need be; ~**falls** Adv. if
need be; ~**gedrungen** Adv. of necessity
notieren [1] tr. V. [sich (Dat.)] etw. ~:
make a note of sth.
[2] itr. V. (Börsenw., Wirtsch.) be quoted (**mit** at)
Notierung die; ~, ~en (Börsenw., Wirtsch.)
quotation; (Preis) quoted [price] (**für** of); (von
Devisen) rate (**für** for)
nötig [1] Adj. necessary; **etw./jmdn.** ~ **haben**
need sth./sb.
[2] adv. **er braucht** ~ **Hilfe** he is in urgent
need of help
nötigen tr. V. compel; force; (Rechtsspr.)
coerce
Nötigung die; ~, ~en (bes. Rechtsspr.)
intimidation; coercion
Notiz die; ~, ~en note; (Zeitungs~) brief
report; **von jmdm./etw. [keine]** ~ **nehmen**
take [no] notice of sb./sth.
Notiz-: ~**block** der; Pl. ~blocks, schweiz.:
~blöcke notepad; ~**buch** das notebook
not-, Not-: ~**lage** die serious difficulties
pl.; ~**landen** itr. V.; mit sein; **ich notlande,
notgelandet, notzulanden** do an emergency

landing; ~**landung** die emergency landing;
~**leidend** Adj. needy; ~**lösung** die
stopgap; ~**lüge** die evasive lie; (aus
Rücksichtnahme) white lie
notorisch [1] Adj. notorious
[2] adv. notoriously
Not-: ~**ruf** der (a) (Hilferuf) emergency call;
(eines Schiffes) Mayday call; (b) (Nummer)
emergency number; ~**ruf·nummer** die
emergency number; ~**ruf·säule** die
emergency telephone (mounted in a pillar);
~**stand** der crisis; (Staatsrecht) state of
emergency; ~**unterkunft** die emergency
accommodation no pl., no indef. art.;
~**wehr** die self-defence
not·wendig Adj. necessary
Notwendigkeit die; ~, ~en necessity
Not·zucht die (Rechtsw. veralt.) rape; ~ **[an
jmdm.] begehen** od. **verüben** commit rape [on
sb.]
Novelle die; ~, ~n (Literaturw.) novella
November der; ~[s], ~: November
Novität die; ~, ~en novelty; (neue Erfindung)
innovation; (neue Schallplatte) new release;
(neues Buch) new publication
Nr. Abk. = **Nummer** No
Nu der: **im Nu** in no time
Nuance /'nÿä:sə/ die; ~, ~n nuance; (Grad)
shade
nüchtern [1] Adj. (nicht betrunken; realistisch)
sober; (ungeschminkt) bare, plain ⟨fact⟩; **der
Patient muss** ~ **sein** the patient's stomach
must be empty
[2] adv. soberly
Nüchternheit die; ~: sobriety
nuckeln (ugs.) itr. V. suck (**an** + Dat. at)
Nudel die; ~, ~n piece of spaghetti/
vermicelli/tortellini etc.; (als Suppeneinlage)
noodle; ~**n** (Teigwaren) pasta sing.; (als
Suppeneinlage) noodles
Nugat /'nu:gat/ der; auch das; ~s nougat
nuklear [1] Adj. nuclear
[2] adv. ~ **angetrieben** nuclear-powered
Nuklear-: ~**medizin** die nuclear
medicine no art.; ~**waffe** die nuclear
weapon
null Kardinalz. nought; ~ **Komma sechs**
[nought] point six; **gegen** ~ **Uhr** around
twelve midnight
Null die; ~, ~en (a) nought; zero; **in** ~
Komma nichts (ugs.) in less than no time;
gleich ~ **sein** (fig.) be practically zero; **auf** ~
stehen ⟨indicator, needle, etc.⟩ be at zero
(b) (ugs.: Versager) failure; dead loss (coll.)
Null-: ~**punkt** der zero;
~**summen·spiel** das zero-sum game
*****numerieren** tr. V. number
*****Numerierung** die; ~, ~en numbering
Numerus clausus der; ~: fixed number
of students admissible to a university to study
a particular subject; numerus clausus
Nummer die; ~, ~n (a) number; **ein Wagen**

n

mit [einer] Münchner ~: a car with a Munich registration; **ich bin unter der ~ 242679 zu erreichen** I can be reached on 242679
(b) (Ausgabe) issue
(c) (Größe) size
Nummern·schild das number plate; license plate (Amer.)
nummerieren tr.V. number
Nummerierung die; ~, ~en numbering
nun [1] adv. now
[2] Partikel now; **das hast du ~ davon!** it serves you right!; **kommst du ~ mit oder nicht?** now are you coming or not?; **~ gut** [well,] all right; **~, ~!** now, come on; **~ ja** ...: well, yes ...
nur [1] adv. **(a)** (nicht mehr als) only; just
(b) (ausschließlich) only; **nicht ~ ..., sondern auch ...:** not only ..., but also ...; **~ so zum Spaß** just for fun
[2] Konj. but; **ich kann dir das Buch leihen, ~ nicht heute** I can lend you the book, only not today
[3] Partikel **wenn er ~ hier wäre** if only he were here; **~ zu!** go ahead; **lass dich ~ nicht erwischen** just don't let me/them etc. catch you; **was sollen wir ~ tun?** what on earth are we going to do?; **so schnell er ~ konnte** just as fast as he could
Nürnberg (das); ~s Nuremberg
nuscheln tr., itr. V. (ugs.) mumble
Nuss, *Nuß die; ~, Nüsse nut
Nuss-, *Nuß-: ~**baum**, der walnut tree; ~**knacker** der nutcrackers pl.; ~**schale** die nutshell
Nüster die; ~, ~n nostril
Nut die; ~, ~en (Technik) groove

Nutte die; ~, ~n (derb) tart (sl.); hooker (Amer. sl.)
nutz-: ~**bar** Adj. usable; exploitable, utilizable ⟨mineral resources, invention⟩; cultivatable ⟨land, soil⟩; ~**bringend**
[1] Adj. useful; (gewinnbringend) profitable
[2] adv. profitably
nutzen [1] tr. V. **(a)** use; exploit, utilize ⟨natural resources⟩; cultivate ⟨land, soil⟩; harness ⟨energy source⟩; exploit ⟨advantage⟩
(b) (be-, ausnutzen) use; make use of
[2] itr. V. ▶ NÜTZEN 1
Nutzen der; ~s **(a)** benefit; [jmdm.] **von ~ sein** be of use [to sb.]
(b) (Profit) profit
nützen [1] itr. V. be of use (Dat. to); **nichts ~:** be no use
[2] tr. V. ▶ NUTZEN 1
nützlich Adj. useful
Nützlichkeit die; ~: usefulness
nutzlos [1] Adj. useless; (vergeblich) vain attrib.; in vain pred.;
[2] adv. uselessly; (vergeblich) in vain
Nutz·losigkeit die; ~: uselessness; (Vergeblichkeit) futility
Nutznießer der; ~s, ~, **Nutznießerin** die; ~, ~nen beneficiary
Nutzung die; ~, ~en use; (des Landes, des Bodens) cultivation; (von Bodenschätzen) exploitation; utilization; (einer Energiequelle) harnessing
Nylon Ⓦ /'naɪlɔn/ das; ~s nylon
Nymphe die; ~, ~n (Myth., Zool.) nymph
Nymphomanin die; ~, ~nen (Psych.) nymphomaniac

Oo

o, O das; ~, ~: o/O
ö, Ö das; ~, ~: o/O umlaut
O Abk. = **Ost[en]** E
Oase die; ~, ~n (auch fig.) oasis
ob Konj. **(a)** whether
(b) und ob! of course!
OB Abk. = **Oberbürgermeister[in]**
Obacht die; ~ (bes. südd.) caution; **~ auf jmdn./etw. geben** take care of sb./sth.; (aufmerksam sein) pay attention to sb./sth.
Obdach das; ~[e]s (geh.) shelter
obdach·los Adj. homeless
Obdachlose der/die; adj. Dekl. homeless person/man/woman; **die ~n** the homeless
Obdachlosen-: ~**heim** das hostel for the homeless; ~**siedlung** die estate of houses for the homeless

Obdachlosigkeit die; ~: homelessness
Obduktion die; ~, ~en (Med., Rechtsw.) post mortem [examination]; autopsy
obduzieren tr. V. carry out or perform a/ the postmortem [examination] or autopsy on
O-Beine Pl. bandy legs; bow legs
oben Adv. **(a)** hier/dort ~: up here/there; **weiter ~:** further up; **nach ~:** upwards; **von ~:** from above; **von ~ herab** (fig.) condescendingly
(b) (im Gebäude) upstairs; **nach ~:** upstairs
(c) (am oberen Ende, zum oberen Ende hin) at the top; **nach ~ [hin]** towards the top; **von ~:** from the top; **~ ohne** topless
(d) (an der Oberseite) on top
(e) (in einer Hierarchie, Rangfolge) at the top
(f) ([weiter] vorn im Text) above; **~ genannt** above-mentioned

*oben·genannt ▶ OBEN F

Ober *der;* ~s, ~: waiter; **Herr** ~**!** waiter!

ober... *Adj.* upper *attrib.;* top *attrib.*

Ober-: ~**arm** *der* upper arm;
~**bekleidung** *die* outer clothing;
~**bürgermeister** *der* mayor; ~**fläche**
die surface; (Flächeninhalt) surface area

oberflächlich ⒈ *Adj.* superficial
⒉ *adv.* superficially

Ober·geschoss, *Ober·geschoß *das*
upper storey; **im fünften** ~: on the fifth floor
(Brit.) *or* (Amer.) the sixth floor

ober·halb ⒈ *Adv.* above; ~ **von** above
⒉ *Präp. mit Gen.* above

Ober-: ~**hand** *die* die ~hand [über jmdn./
etw.] haben have the upper hand [over sb./
sth.]; die ~hand [über jmdn./etw.] gewinnen/
bekommen gain *or* get the upper hand [over
sb./sth.]; ~**haupt** *das* head; (einer
Verschwörung) leader; ~**hemd** *das* shirt;
~**kiefer** *der* upper jaw; ~**körper** *der*
upper part of the body; ~**lippen·bart** *der*
moustache; ~**schenkel** *der* thigh;
~**schicht** *die* (Soziol.) upper class;
~**schule** *die* secondary school; ~**seite**
die top

oberst... ▶ OBER...

Ober-: ~**stufe** *die* (Schulw.) upper school;
~**teil** *das od. der* top [part]; (eines Bikinis,
Anzugs, Kleids usw.) top [half]; ~**wasser** *das*
headwater; (fig.) ~**wasser haben** feel in a
strong position; ~**wasser bekommen/kriegen**
have one's hand strengthened

ob·gleich *Konj.* ▶ OBWOHL

obig *Adj.* above

Objekt *das;* ~s, ~e object; (Kaufmannsspr.:
Immobilie) property

objektiv ⒈ *Adj.* objective
⒉ *adv.* objectively

Objektiv *das;* ~s, ~e lens

Objektivität *die;* ~: objectivity

Obrigkeit *die;* ~, ~en authorities *pl.*

ob·schon *Konj.* (geh.) although

Obst *das;* ~[e]s fruit

Obst-: ~**baum** *der* fruit tree; ~**garten**
der orchard; ~**kuchen** *der* fruit flan

Obstler *der;* ~s, ~ (bes. südd.) fruit brandy

Obst-: ~**saft** *der* fruit juice; ~**salat** *der*
fruit salad; ~**wein** *der* fruit wine

obszön ⒈ *Adj.* obscene
⒉ *adv.* obscenely

Obszönität *die;* ~, ~en obscenity

ob·wohl *Konj.* although; though

Ochse /ˈɔksə/ *der;* ~n, ~n (a) ox; bullock
(b) (salopp) numskull (coll.)

Ochsen·schwanz·suppe *die* oxtail
soup

od. *Abk.* = **oder**

öde *Adj.* (a) deserted; desolate ⟨*area,
landscape*⟩

(b) (unfruchtbar) barren
(c) (langweilig) tedious; dreary ⟨*life, time,
existence*⟩

Öde *die;* ~ ▶ ÖDE A–C: desertedness;
desolateness; barrenness; tediousness;
dreariness

oder *Konj.* or; (in Fragen) **er ist doch hier,** ~**?**
he is here, isn't he? (zweifelnd) he is here – or
isn't he?

Öd·land *das* uncultivated land

Oeuvre /ˈøːvrə/ *das;* ~, ~s (geh.) œuvre

OEZ *Abk.* = **osteuropäische Zeit** EET

Ofen *der;* ~s, **Öfen** heater; (Kohle~) stove;
(Back~) oven; (Brenn~, Trocken~) kiln

Ofen·rohr *das* [stove] flue

offen ⒈ *Adj.* (a) open; ~ **bleiben** stay open;
etw. ~ **lassen** leave sth. open; ~ **stehen** be
open; **ein** ~**es Hemd** a shirt with the collar
unfastened; ~ **haben** *od.* **sein** be open; ~**es**
Licht a naked light

(b) (frei) vacant ⟨*job, post*⟩
(c) (ungewiss, ungeklärt) open ⟨*question*⟩;
uncertain ⟨*result*⟩; ~ **bleiben** remain open;
⟨*decision*⟩ be left open
(d) (noch nicht bezahlt) outstanding ⟨*bill*⟩
(e) (freimütig, aufrichtig) frank [and open]
⟨*person*⟩; frank, candid ⟨*look, opinion, reply*⟩
⒉ *adv.* openly; ~ **gesagt** frankly; to be
frank

offen·bar ⒈ *Adj.* obvious
⒉ *adv.* obviously

Offenbarung *die;* ~, ~en revelation

*offen|bleiben ▶ OFFEN 1A, C

Offen·heit *die;* ~ ▶ OFFEN E: frankness
[and openness]; candour

offen-: ~**kundig** ⒈ *Adj.* obvious; ⒉ *adv.*
obviously; ***~|lassen** ▶ OFFEN 1A;
~**sichtlich** ⒈ *Adj.* obvious; ⒉ *adv.*
obviously

offensiv ⒈ *Adj.* (a) offensive
(b) (Sport) attacking
⒉ *adv.* (a) offensively
(b) (Sport) ~ **spielen** play an attacking game

Offensive *die;* ~, ~n (auch Sport) offensive

*offen|stehen ▶ OFFEN 1A

öffentlich ⒈ *Adj.* public; state *attrib.*,
[state-]maintained ⟨*school*⟩; **der** ~**e Dienst**
the civil service
⒉ *adv.* publicly; ⟨*perform, appear*⟩ in public

Öffentlichkeit *die;* ~: public

offiziell ⒈ *Adj.* official
⒉ *adv.* officially

Offizier *der;* ~s, ~e, **Offizierin** *die;* ~,
~nen officer

öffnen ⒈ *tr. V.* open; turn on ⟨*tap*⟩; undo
⟨*coat, blouse, button, zip*⟩
⒉ *itr. V.* (a) [jmdm.] ~: open the door [to
sb.]
(b) (geöffnet werden) ⟨*shop, bank, etc.*⟩ open
⒊ *refl. V.* open

Öffner *der;* ~s, ~: opener

Öffnung *die;* ~, ~en opening

Öffnungs·zeiten *Pl.* opening times

Offroader /ɔfˈrəʊdɐ/ *der;* ~**s**, ~: offroader

oft *Adv.* **öfter, am öftesten** often; **wie oft soll ich dir noch sagen, dass …?** how many [more] times do I have to tell you that …?

öfter *Adv.* now and then

oftmals *Adv.* often; frequently

OG *Abk.* = **Obergeschoss**

ohne [1] *Präp. mit Akk.* without; ~ **mich!** [you can] count me out!; ~ **weiteres** (leicht, einfach) easily; (ohne Einwand) readily
[2] *Konj.* ~ **zu zögern** without hesitation

ohne·hin *Adv.* anyway

Ohnmacht *die;* ~, ~**en** (a) faint; **in** ~ **fallen** faint
(b) (Machtlosigkeit) powerlessness; impotence

ohnmächtig [1] *Adj.* (a) unconscious; ~ **werden** faint; ~ **sein** have fainted
(b) (machtlos) powerless; impotent
[2] *adv.* impotently; ~ **zusehen** watch helplessly

Ohr *das;* ~[e]s, ~**en** ear; **gute/schlechte** ~**en haben** have good/poor hearing *sing.*; **jmdn. übers** ~ **hauen** (fig. ugs.) put one over on sb. (coll.)

Öhr *das,* ~[e]s, ~**e** eye

ohren-, Ohren-: ~**arzt,** *der,* ~**ärztin,** *die* otologist; ear specialist; ~**betäubend** [1] *Adj.* ear-splitting; deafening; deafening ⟨applause⟩; [2] *adv.* deafeningly; ~**sausen** *das;* ~**s** ringing in the *or* one's ears; tinnitus (Med.); ~**schmerz** *der* earache; ~**schmerzen haben** have [an] earache *sing.*

ohr-, Ohr-: ~**feige** *die* box on the ears; ~**feigen** *tr. V.* jmdn. ~**feigen** box sb.'s ears; **ich könnte mich** ~**feigen!** (ugs.) I could kick myself!; ~**läppchen** *das* ear lobe; ~**ring** *der* earring; ~**wurm** *der* (a) earwig; (b) (ugs.: Melodie) catchy tune; **ein** ~**wurm sein** be really catchy

okay /oˈkeɪ/ (ugs.) *Interj., Adj., adv.* OK (coll.); okay (coll.)

öko-, Öko- eco-

Ökologie *die;* ~: ecology

ökologisch [1] *Adj.* ecological
[2] *adv.* ecologically

ökonomisch [1] *Adj.* (a) economic
(b) (sparsam) economical
[2] *adv.* economically

Öko-: ~**produkt** *das* ecoproduct; environmentally friendly *or* safe product; ~**steuer** *die* eco-tax; ~**system** *das* ecosystem

Oktober *der;* ~[s], ~: October

ökumenisch *Adj.* (christl. Rel.) ecumenical

Öl *das;* ~[e]s, ~**e** oil; **in Öl malen** paint in oils

ölen *tr. V.* oil

Öl-: ~**embargo** *das* oil embargo; ~**farbe** *die* (a) oil-based paint; (b) (zum Malen) oil paint; ~**gemälde** *das* oil painting

ölig *Adj.* oily

Olive *die;* ~, ~**n** olive

Oliven-: ~**baum** *der* olive tree; ~**öl** *das* olive oil

Öl-: ~**ofen** *der* oil heater; ~**pest** *die* oil pollution *no indef. art.*; ~**quelle** *die* oil well; ~**sardine** *die* sardine in oil; **eine Dose** ~**sardinen** a tin of sardines; ~**teppich** *der* oil slick; ~**wechsel** *der* (bes. Kfz-W.) oil change

Olympiade *die;* ~, ~**n** Olympic Games *pl.*; Olympics *pl.*

Olympia-: ~**sieger** *der,* ~**siegerin** *die* Olympic champion; ~**stadion** *das* Olympic stadium

olympisch *Adj.* Olympic; **die Olympischen Spiele** the Olympic Games; the Olympics

Oma *die;* ~, ~**s** (fam.) granny (coll./child lang.)

Omelett /ɔm(ə)ˈlɛt/ *das;* ~[e]s, ~**e** *od.* ~**s** omelette

Omi *die;* ~, ~**s** ▶ OMA

Omnibus *der;* ~**ses**, ~**se** omnibus (formal); (Privat- und Reisebus auch) coach

Onanie *die;* ~: onanism *no art.*; masturbation *no art.*

onanieren *itr. V.* masturbate

Onkel *der;* ~**s**, ~ *od.* (ugs.) ~**s** uncle

online /ˈɔnlaɪn/ [1] *Adj.* online; ~ **gehen** go online
[2] *Adv.* online

Online·shopping *das* online shopping

OP /oːˈpeː/ *der;* ~[s], ~[s] *Abk.* = **Operationssaal**

Opa *der;* ~**s**, ~**s** (fam.) grandad (coll./child lang.)

Opal *der;* ~**s**, ~**e** opal

OPEC /ˈoːpɛk/ *die;* ~: *Abk.* OPEC

Oper *die;* ~, ~**n** opera; (Opernhaus) Opera; opera house

Operation *die;* ~, ~**en** operation

Operations·saal *der* operating theatre (Brit.) *or* room

operativ [1] *Adj.*(Med.) operative
[2] *adv.* (Med.) by operation/surgery; **etw.** ~ **entfernen** operate to remove sth.

Operette *die;* ~, ~**n** operetta

operieren [1] *tr. V.* operate on ⟨patient⟩
[2] *itr. V.* operate

Opern·glas *das* opera glass[es *pl.*]

Opfer *das;* ~**s**, ~ (a) sacrifice
(b) (Geschädigter) victim

opfern *tr. V.* (auch fig.) sacrifice; offer up ⟨fruit, produce, etc.⟩

Opi *der* ~**s**, ~**s** ▶ OPA

Opium *das;* ~**s** opium

opponieren *itr. V.* gegen jmdn./etw. ~: oppose sb./sth.

Opposition *die;* ~, ~**en** opposition

oppositionell *Adj.* opposition *attrib.* ⟨group, movement, etc.⟩; ⟨newspaper, writer, artist, etc.⟩ opposed to the government

Optik *die;* ~: optics *sing., no art.*

Optiker *der;* ~s, ~, **Optikerin** *die;* ~,
~nen optician

optimal ①*Adj.* optimal; optimum *attrib.;*
②*adv.* jmdn. ~ beraten give sb. the best
possible advice

optimieren *tr. V.* optimize

Optimierung *die;* ~, ~en optimization

Optimismus *der;* ~: optimism

Optimist *der;* ~en, ~en, **Optimistin** *die;*
~, ~nen optimist

optimistisch ①*Adj.* optimistic
②*adv.* optimistically

optisch ①*Adj.* optical; visual ⟨*impression*⟩;
eine ~e Täuschung an optical illusion
②*adv.* optically; visually ⟨*impressive,*
effective⟩

orange /o'rãː(ə)/ *indekl. Adj.* orange

Orange *die;* ~, ~n orange

Orangen-: ~**marmelade** *die* orange
marmalade; ~**saft** *der* orange juice

Orchester /ɔr'kɛstɐ/ *das;* ~s, ~: orchestra

Orden *der;* ~s, ~ (a) order
(b) (Ehrenzeichen) decoration

ordentlich ①*Adj.* (a) [neat and] tidy; neat
⟨*handwriting, clothes*⟩
(b) (anständig) respectable; proper ⟨*manners*⟩
(c) (planmäßig) ordinary ⟨*meeting*⟩; ~es
Mitglied full member
(d) (ugs.: richtig) proper; real; ein ~es Stück
Kuchen a nice big piece of cake
(e) (ugs.: recht gut) decent ⟨*wine, flat, marks,*
etc.⟩; ganz ~: pretty good
②*adv.* (a) tidily; neatly; ⟨*write*⟩ neatly
(b) (anständig) properly
(c) (ugs.: gehörig) ~ feiern have a real good
celebration (coll.)
(d) (ugs.: recht gut) ⟨*ski, speak, etc.*⟩ really well

ordern *tr., itr. V.* (Kaufmannsspr.) order

Ordinal-zahl *die* ordinal [number]

ordinär ①*Adj.* vulgar
②*adv.* vulgarly

Ordinate *die;* ~, ~n (Math.) ordinate

ordnen *tr. V.* arrange; sein Leben/seine
Finanzen ~: straighten out one's life/put
one's finances in order

Ordner *der;* ~s, ~ (Hefter) file

Ordnung *die;* ~, ~en order; (geregelter
Ablauf) routine; ~ halten keep things tidy; in
~ sein (ugs.) be OK (coll.) or all right; hier ist
etw. nicht in ~: there's something wrong
here; sie ist in ~ (ugs.) she's OK (coll.); in ~!
(ugs.) OK!(coll.); all right!

ordnungs-, Ordnungs-: ~**gemäß**
①*Adj.* ⟨*conduct etc.*⟩ in accordance with the
regulations; ②*adv.* in accordance with the
regulations; ~**halber** *Adv.* as a matter of
form; ~**widrig** (Rechtsw.) ①*Adj.* ⟨*actions,*
behaviour, etc.⟩ contravening the regulations;
illegal ⟨*parking*⟩; ②*adv.* ~widrig parken

park illegally; ~**widrigkeit** *die* (Rechtsw.)
infringement of the regulations; ~**zahl** *die*
ordinal [number]

Organ *das;* ~s, ~e organ; (ugs.: Stimme)
voice

Organisation *die;* ~, ~en organization

Organisator *der;* ~s, ~en,
Organisatorin *die;* ~, ~nen organizer

organisatorisch *Adj.* organizational

organisch ①*Adj.* organic
②*adv.* organically

organisieren ①*tr. V.* organize
②*itr. V.* gut ~ können be a good organizer
③*refl. V.* organize

Organismus *der;* ~, Organismen organism

Organist *der;* ~en, ~en, **Organistin** *die;*
~, ~nen organist

Organ-spender *der,*
Organ-spenderin *die* organ donor

Orgasmus *der;* ~, Orgasmen orgasm

Orgel *die;* ~, ~n organ

Orgie /'ɔrgiə/ *die;* ~, ~n (auch fig.) orgy

Orient /'oːri̯ɛnt/ *der;* ~s Middle East and
south-western Asia (including Afghanistan
and Nepal); der Vordere ~: the Middle East

orientalisch *Adj.* oriental

orientieren ①*refl. V.* (a) get one's
bearings
(b) sich über etw. (Akk.) ~ (fig.) inform
oneself about sth.
(c) sich an etw. (Dat.) ~ (fig.) be oriented
towards sth.; ⟨*policy, advertising*⟩ be geared
towards sth.
②*tr. V.* (unterrichten) inform (über + Akk.
about)

Orientierung *die;* ~ (a) die ~ verlieren
lose one's bearings
(b) (Unterrichtung) zu Ihrer ~: for your
information

Orientierungs-sinn *der* sense of
direction

original ①*Adj.* original
②*adv.* ~ italienischer Espresso genuine
Italian espresso coffee; etw. ~ übertragen
broadcast sth. live

Original *das;* ~s, ~e original

Original-: ~**fassung** *die* original version;
~**gemälde** *das* original painting

Originalität *die;* ~: originality

Original-ton *der; Pl.* Original-töne (Film,
Ferns.) direct sound; original sound

originell ①*Adj.* original
②*adv.* with originality

Orkan *der;* ~[e]s, ~e hurricane

Ornament *das;* ~[e]s, ~e ornament

Ort¹ /ɔrt/ *der;* ~[e]s, ~e place; (Dorf) village;
(Stadt) town; an ~ und Stelle there and then

Ort²: vor ~ (fig.) on the spot

orthodox *Adj.* orthodox

Orthographie *die;* ~, ~n orthography

orthographisch ①*Adj.* orthographic; ~e
Fehler spelling mistakes

---

*alte Schreibung - vgl. Hinweis auf S. xiv

2 *adv.* orthographically
Orthopäde *der;* ~n, ~n orthopaedic specialist
orthopädisch 1 *Adj.* orthopaedic
2 *adv.* orthopaedically
örtlich 1 *Adj.* (auch Med.) local
2 *adv.* (auch Med.) locally; ~ **betäubt werden** be given a local anaesthetic
Ortschaft *die;* ~, ~en (Dorf) village; (Stadt) town
Orts-: ~**gespräch** *das* (Fernspr.) local call; ~**name** *der* place name; ~**netz·kennzahl** *die* (Fernspr.) dialling code; area code (Amer.)
Öse *die;* ~, ~n eye
Ossi *der;* ~s, ~s (salopp) East German
Ost (bes. Seemannsspr., Met.) ▶ OSTEN
ost-, Ost-: ~**block** *der* Eastern bloc; ~**deutsch** *Adj.* Eastern German; (hist.: auf die DDR bezogen) East German; ~**deutschland** (*das*) Eastern Germany; (hist.: DDR) East Germany
Osten *der;* ~s east; **der** ~: the East; **der Ferne** ~: the Far East; **der Nahe** ~: the Middle East
Oster-: ~**ei** *das* Easter egg; ~**glocke** *die* daffodil; ~**hase** *der* Easter hare (*said to bring children their Easter Eggs*); ~**montag** *der* Easter Monday *no def. art.*
Ostern *das;* ~, ~: Easter; **Frohe** *od.* **Fröhliche** ~! Happy Easter!; **zu** ~: at Easter
Österreich (*das*)*;* ~s Austria
Österreicher *der;* ~s, **Österreicherin** *die* ~, ~nen Austrian
österreichisch *Adj.* Austrian

Oster·sonntag *der* Easter Sunday *no def. art.*
Ost·europa (*das*) Eastern Europe
Ostler *der;* ~s, ~, **Ostlerin** *die;* ~, ~nen (ugs.) East German
östlich 1 *Adj.* (a) (im Osten gelegen) eastern (b) (nach, aus dem Osten) easterly (c) (aus dem Osten kommend, für den Osten typisch; Politik) Eastern; ⟨*influence, policies*⟩ of the East
2 *adv.* eastwards; ~ **von** ...: [to the] east of ...
3 *Präp. mit Gen.* [to the] east of
Ost·see *die;* ~: Baltic [Sea]
ost·wärts *Adv.* eastwards
Ost·wind *der* easterly wind
Otter[1] *der;* ~s, ~ (Fisch~) otter
Otter[2] *die;* ~, ~n (Viper) adder; viper
Otto·motor *der* Otto engine
out /aʊt/ *Adj.* ~ **sein** (ugs.) be out
Outfit /ˈaʊtfɪt/ *das;* ~[s], ~s outfit
Ouvertüre /uverˈtyːrə/ *die;* ~, ~n (auch fig.) overture (*Gen.* to)
oval *Adj.* oval
Ovation *die;* ~, ~en ovation; **jmdm.** ~**en darbringen** give sb. an ovation
Ozean *der;* ~s, ~e ocean
Ozean·dampfer *der* ocean liner
Ozon *der od. das;* ~s ozone
Ozon-: ~**alarm** *der* ozone alert; ~**loch** *das* hole in the ozone layer; ~**schicht** *die* ozone layer; ~**zerstörung** *die* ozone destruction

Pp

p, P /peː/ *das;* ~, ~: p/P
paar *indekl. Indefinitpron.* **ein** ~ ...: a few ...; (zwei od. drei) a couple of ...
Paar *das;* ~[e]s, ~e pair; (Mann und Frau) couple; **ein** ~ **Würstchen** two sausages
paaren *refl. V.* ⟨*animals*⟩ mate; ⟨*people*⟩ copulate
Paar·lauf *der* pairs *pl.*
paar·mal *Adv.* **ein** ~ a few times; (zwei- oder dreimal) a couple of times
Paarung *die;* ~, ~en (Zool.) mating
paar·weise *Adv.* in pairs
Pacht *die;* ~, ~en lease; **etw. in** ~ **nehmen** lease sth.; **etw. in** ~ **haben** have sth. on lease; **etw. in** ~ **geben** lease sth.
pachten *tr. V.* lease

Pächter *der;* ~s, ~, **Pächterin** *die;* ~, ~nen leaseholder; (eines Hofes) tenant
Pacht-: ~**vertrag** *der* lease; ~**zins** *der; Pl.* ~~e rent
Pack[1] *der;* ~[e]s, ~e *od.* **Päcke** (a) pack (b) ▶ PACKEN
Pack[2] *das;* ~[e]s (ugs. abwertend) rabble
Päckchen *das;* ~s, ~ (a) package; (auch Postw.) small parcel; (Bündel) packet (b) ▶ PACKUNG A
packen 1 *tr. V.* (a) pack (b) (fassen) grab [hold of]; (fig.) **Furcht packte ihn/er wurde von Furcht gepackt** he was seized with fear
2 *itr. V.* (Koffer usw. ~) pack
Packen *der;* ~s, ~: pile; (zusammengeschnürt) bundle; (von Geldscheinen) wad

packend 1 *Adj.* gripping
2 *adv.* grippingly
Pack·papier *das* [stout] wrapping paper
Packung *die; ~, ~en* (a) packet; pack (esp. Amer.)
(b) (Med., Kosmetik) pack
Pädagoge *der; ~n, ~n* (Erzieher, Lehrer) teacher; (Wissenschaftler) educationalist
Pädagogik *die; ~:* [theory and methodology of] education
Pädagogin *die; ~, ~nen* ▶ PÄDAGOGE
pädagogisch 1 *Adj.* educational; **seine ~en** Fähigkeiten his teaching ability *sing.;* 2 *adv.* educationally ⟨*sound, wrong*⟩
Paddel *das; ~s, ~:* paddle
Paddel·boot *das* canoe
paddeln *itr. V.; mit sein* paddle; (als Sport) canoe
Päderast *der; ~en, ~en* pederast
pädophil *Adj.* paedophile
Pädophile *der; adj. Dekl.* paedophile
paffen 1 *tr. V.* puff at ⟨*pipe etc.*⟩ 2 *itr. V.* puff away
Page /'paːʒə/ *der; ~n, ~n* bellboy
Paket *das; ~[e]s, ~e* pile; (zusammengeschnürt) bundle; (Eingepacktes, Post~) parcel; (Packung) packet; pack (esp. Amer.)
Paket-: ~**karte** *die* parcel dispatch form; ~**schalter** *der* parcels counter
Pakistan *(das)* ~s Pakistan
Pakistaner *der; ~s, ~*, **Pakistanerin** *die; ~, ~nen*, **Pakistani** *der; ~[s], ~[s]* Pakistani
pakistanisch *Adj.* Pakistani
Pakt *der; ~[e]s, ~e* pact
paktieren *itr. V.* make *or* do a deal/deals
Palast *der; ~[e]s, Paläste* palace
Palästina *(das)* ~s Palestine
Palästinenser *der; ~s, ~*, **Palästinenserin** *die; ~, ~nen* Palestinian
palästinensisch *Adj.* Palestinian
Palaver /pa'laːve/ *das; ~s, ~* (ugs. abwertend) palaver
palavern *itr. V.* (ugs. abwertend) palaver
Palette *die; ~, ~n* (a) palette
(b) (bes. Werbespr.: Vielfalt) diverse range; **die ganze ~:** the whole range
(c) (Technik, Wirtsch.: Untersatz) pallet
paletti *Adj.* **alles ~** (ugs.) everything's OK (coll.) *or* all right
Palme *die; ~, ~n* palm [tree]
Pampelmuse *die; ~, ~n* grapefruit
Panade *die; ~, ~n* (Kochk.) breadcrumb coating
Panama *(das)* ~s Panama
Panama·kanal *der; ~s* Panama Canal
Panel /'pɛnl/ *das; ~s, ~s* panel

Pan·flöte *die* pan pipes *pl.*
panieren *tr. V.* bread; coat ⟨*sth.*⟩ with breadcrumbs
Panier·mehl *das* breadcrumbs *pl.*
Panik *die; ~, ~en* panic
Panik-: ~**mache** *die; ~~* (abwertend) panicmongering; ~**macher** *der*, ~**macherin** *die* (abwertend) panicmonger
Panne *die; ~, ~n* (a) breakdown; (Reifen~) puncture; flat [tyre]
(b) (Missgeschick) mishap
Pannen·dienst *der* breakdown service
Panorama *das; ~s, Panoramen* panorama
Panter, *Panther *der; ~s, ~:* panther
Pantoffel *der; ~s, ~n* backless slipper
Pantomime *die; ~, ~n* mime
Panzer *der; ~s, ~* (a) (Milit.) tank
(b) (Zool.) armour *no indef. art.;* (von Schildkröten, Krebsen) shell
Panzer·glas *das* bulletproof glass
panzern *tr. V.* armour[-plate]
Panzer·schrank *der* safe
Papa *der; ~s, ~s* (ugs.) daddy (coll.)
Papagei *der; ~en od. ~s, ~e[n]* parrot
Paparazzo *der; ~s, Paparazzi* paparazzo
Paperback /'peɪpəbæk/ *das; ~s, ~s* paperback
Papi *der; ~s, ~s* (ugs.) daddy (coll.)
Papier *das; ~s, ~e* (a) paper
(b) *Pl.* (Ausweis[e]) [identity] papers
(c) (Finanzw.: Wert~) security
Papier-: ~**geld** *das* paper money; ~**korb** *der* waste-paper basket
Pappe *die; ~, ~n* cardboard
Pappel *die; ~, ~n* poplar
päppeln *tr. V.* feed up
Papp·karton *der* cardboard box
Paprika *der; ~s, ~[s]* (a) pepper
(b) (Gewürz) paprika
Papst *der; ~[e]s, Päpste*, **Päpstin** *die; ~, ~nen* pope
päpstlich *Adj.* papal
Para *der; ~s, ~s* para (coll.)
Parabel *die; ~, ~n* (a) (bes. Literaturw.) parable
(b) (Math.) parabola
Parade *die; ~, ~n* parade
Parade·beispiel *das* perfect example
Paradeiser *der; ~s, ~* (österr.) tomato
Paradies *das; ~es, ~e* paradise
paradiesisch *Adj.* paradisical; (herrlich) heavenly
Paradigma *das; ~s, Paradigmen* paradigm
paradox *Adj.* paradoxical
Para·gleiten *das; ~s*, **Para·gliding** /'paraglaːdɪŋ/ *das; ~s* paragliding
Paragraph *der; ~en, ~en* section; (in Vertrag) clause
parallel 1 *Adj.* parallel
2 *adv.* ~ **verlaufen** run parallel (mit, zu to)

Parallele *die;* ~, ~n parallel
Parallelogramm *das;* ~s, ~e parallelogram
Parallel-straße *die* street running parallel (*Gen.* to)
Para-nuss, *Para-nuß *die* Brazil nut
Parasit *der;* ~en, ~en (auch fig.) parasite
parat *Adj.* ready
Pardon /par'dõ/ *der od. das;* ~s pardon; ~! I beg your pardon
Parfum /par'fœː/, **Parfüm** *das;* ~s, ~s perfume
Parfümerie *die;* ~, ~en perfumery
parfümieren *tr. V.* perfume
Pariser 1 *indekl. Adj.* Parisian; Paris *attrib.;*
  2 *der;* ~s, ~ (a) (Einwohner) Parisian
  (b) (ugs.: Kondom) French letter (coll.)
Pariserin *die;* ~, ~nen Parisian
Parität *die;* ~, ~en parity
Park /park/ *der;* ~s, ~s park; (Schloss~ usw.) grounds *pl.*
Parka *der;* ~s, ~s parka
parken *tr., itr. V.* park; „Parken verboten!" 'No Parking'
Parkett *das;* ~[e]s, ~e (a) parquet floor
  (b) (Theater) [front] stalls *pl.;* parquet (Amer.)
Parkett-: ~[fuß]boden *der* parquet floor; ~handel *der* (Börsenw.) floor trading
Park-: ~gebühr *die* parking fee; ~haus *das* multi-storey car park
parkieren *tr., itr. V.* (schweiz.) ▶ PARKEN
Park-: ~lücke *die* parking space; ~platz *der* car park; parking lot (Amer.); (für ein einzelnes Fahrzeug) parking space;
  ~scheibe *die* parking disc; ~schein *der* car park ticket; ~uhr *die* parking meter; ~verbot *das* ban on parking; im ~verbot stehen be parked illegally; ~verbots-schild *das* no-parking sign
Parlament *das;* ~[e]s, ~e parliament
Parlamentarier *der;* ~s, ~, **Parlamentarierin** *die;* ~, ~nen member of parliament
parlamentarisch *Adj.* parliamentary
Parodie *die;* ~, ~n parody (auf + *Akk.* of)
Parole *die;* ~, ~n (a) (Wahlspruch) motto; (Schlagwort) slogan
  (b) (bes. Milit.: Kennwort) password
Partei *die;* ~, ~en (a) (Politik, Rechtsw.) party
  (b) (Gruppe, Mannschaft) side; für jmdn. ~ ergreifen *od.* nehmen side with sb.
Partei-gänger *der;* ~s, ~, **Partei-gängerin** *die;* ~, ~nen (oft abwertend) [loyal] party supporter·
parteiisch 1 *Adj.* biased
  2 *adv.* in a biased manner
parteilich 1 *Adj.* (parteiisch) biased
  2 *adv.* in a biased manner
Parteilichkeit *die;* ~ (einseitige Parteinahme) bias; partiality
partei-, Partei-: ~los *Adj.* (Politik)

independent (*MP*); ~lose *der/die; adj. Dekl.* (Politik) independent; person not attached to a party; ~nahme *die;* ~~, ~~n partisanship; taking sides *no art.;*
~politik *die* party politics *sing.;*
~politisch 1 *Adj.* party political;
  2 *adv.* from a party political point of view;
~tag *der* party conference *or* (Amer.) convention
Parterre *das;* ~s, ~s ground floor; first floor (Amer.)
Partie *die;* ~, ~n (a) part
  (b) (Spiel, Sport: Runde) game; (Golf) round
  (c) eine gute ~ [für jmdn.] sein be a good match [for sb.]
Partisan *der;* ~s *od.* ~en, ~en, **Partisanin** *die,* ~, ~nen guerrilla; (gegen Besatzungstruppen im Krieg) partisan
Partitur *die;* ~, ~en (Musik) score
Partizip *das;* ~s, ~ien /-'tsːiːpiən/ (Sprachw.) participle
Partner *der;* ~s, ~, **Partnerin** *die;* ~, ~nen partner
Partnerschaft *die;* ~, ~en partnership
partnerschaftlich 1 *Adj.* (cooperation etc.) on a partnership basis
  2 *adv.* in a spirit of partnership
Partner-: ~schule *die* partner school; ~stadt *die* twin town (Brit.); sister city *or* town (Amer.); ~vermittlung *die* (a) matchmaking; (b) (Agentur) [introduction and] matchmaking agency;
  ~vermittlungs-büro *das:* ▶ PARTNER ~VERMITTLUNG B
Party /'paːɐ̯ti/ *die;* ~, ~s party
Parzelle *die;* ~, ~n [small] plot [of land]
Pass, *Paß *der;* Passes, Pässe (a) (Reisepass) passport
  (b) (Gebirgspass; Ballspiele) pass
passabel 1 *Adj.* reasonable; presentable (appearance)
  2 *adv.* reasonably well
Passage /pa'saːʒə/ *die;* ~, ~n (a) [shopping] arcade
  (b) (Abschnitt) passage
Passagier /pasa'ʒiːɐ̯/ *der;* ~s, ~e passenger; blinder ~: stowaway
Passagier-: ~dampfer *der* passenger steamer; ~flugzeug *das* passenger aircraft
Passagierin *die;* ~, ~nen passenger
Passagier-liste *die* passenger list
Pass-amt, *Paß-amt *das* passport office
Passant *der;* ~en, ~en, **Passantin** *die;* ~, ~nen passer-by
Pass-bild, *Paß-bild *das* passport photograph
Pässe ▶ PASS
passen *itr. V.* (a) (die richtige Größe/Form haben) fit
  (b) (geeignet sein) be suitable (auf + *Akk.*, zu for); (harmonieren) (colour etc.) match; zu etw./ ⋯⋗

jmdm. ∼: go well with sth./be well suited to sb.; **zueinander** ∼ ⟨*things*⟩ go well together; ⟨*two people*⟩ be suited to each other
(c) (genehm sein) jmdm. ∼ ⟨*time*⟩ suit sb.
(d) (Kartenspiel) pass

passend *Adj.* **(a)** (geeignet) suitable ⟨*dress, present, etc.*⟩; right ⟨*words, expression, moment*⟩
(b) (harmonierend) matching ⟨*shoes etc.*⟩

Pass·foto, *Paß·foto *das* ▶ PASSBILD

passierbar *Adj.* passable ⟨*road*⟩; navigable ⟨*river*⟩; negotiable ⟨*path*⟩

passieren ① *tr. V.* pass; **die Grenze** ∼: cross the border
② *itr. V.; mit sein* happen

Passion *die;* ∼, ∼en **(a)** passion
(b) (christl. Rel.) Passion

passioniert *Adj.* passionate ⟨*collector, card player, huntsman*⟩

passiv ① *Adj.* passive
② *adv.* passively

Passiv *das;* ∼s, ∼e (Sprachw.) passive

Passivität *die;* ∼: passivity

Pass-, *Paß-: ∼kontrolle *die* passport check; **∼straße** *die* [mountain] pass road; **∼wort** *das; Pl.* ∼wörter (DV) password; **∼zwang** *der* obligation to carry a passport

Paste *die;* ∼, ∼n paste

Pastell *das;* ∼[e]s, ∼e **(a)** (Farbton) pastel shade
(b) (Maltechnik) pastel *no art.*

Pastell-: ∼farbe *die* pastel colour; **∼ton** *der* pastel shade

Pastete *die;* ∼, ∼n **(a)** (gefüllte) vol-au-vent
(b) (in einer Schüssel o. Ä. gegart) pâté; (in einer Hülle aus Teig gebacken) pie

pasteurisieren *tr. V.* pasteurize

Pastille *die;* ∼, ∼n pastille

Pastor *der;* ∼s, ∼en, **Pastorin** *die;* ∼, ∼nen pastor

Pate *der;* ∼n, ∼n godfather; (männlich od. weiblich) godparent

Paten-: ∼kind *das* godchild; **∼onkel** *der* godfather; **∼stadt** *die* ▶ PARTNERSTADT

patent (ugs.) ① *Adj.* **(a)** (tüchtig) capable
(b) (zweckmäßig) ingenious
② *adv.* ingeniously; neatly ⟨*solved*⟩

Patent *das;* ∼[e]s, ∼e **(a)** (Schutz) patent; **etw. zum** *od.* **als** ∼ **anmelden** apply for a patent for sth.
(b) (Erfindung) [patented] invention

Patent·amt *das* Patent Office

Paten·tante *die* godmother

patentieren *tr. V.* patent

Patent-: ∼lösung *die* patent remedy (**für,** zu for); **∼rezept** *das* patent remedy (gegen, für for)

Pater *der;* ∼s, ∼ *od.* Patres (kath. Kirche) Father

Paternoster *der;* ∼s, ∼ (Aufzug) paternoster [lift]

pathetisch ① *Adj.* emotional ⟨*speech, manner*⟩; melodramatic ⟨*gesture*⟩; pompous ⟨*voice*⟩
② *adv.* emotionally; (dramatisch) [melo]dramatically

Pathos *das;* ∼: emotionalism

Patience /pa'sïā:s/ *die;* ∼, ∼n [game of] patience; **∼n/eine** ∼ **legen** play patience/a game of patience

Patient /pa'tsi̯ɛnt/ *der;* ∼en, ∼en, **Patientin** *die;* ∼, ∼nen patient

Patin *die;* ∼, ∼nen godmother

Patres ▶ PATER

Patriot *der;* ∼en, ∼en, **Patriotin** *die;* ∼, ∼nen patriot

patriotisch ① *Adj.* patriotic
② *adv.* patriotically

Patriotismus *der;* ∼: patriotism

Patrone *die;* ∼, ∼n cartridge

Patrouille /pa'trʊljə/ *die;* ∼, ∼n patrol

patrouillieren /patrʊl'ji:rən/ *itr. V.; auch mit sein* be on patrol

Patsche *die;* ∼, ∼n (ugs.) ▶ KLEMME

patschen *itr. V., mit sein* (ugs.) splash

patsch·nass, *patsch·naß *Adj.* (ugs.) sopping wet

patt *Adj.* (Schach) stalemated

Patt *das;* ∼s, ∼s (Schach; auch fig.) stalemate

Patt·situation *die* [position of] stalemate

Patzer *der;* ∼s, ∼ (ugs.) slip (coll.); boob (coll.)

patzig (ugs.) ① *Adj.* snotty (coll.); (frech) cheeky
② *adv.* snottily (coll.); (frech) cheekily

Pauke *die;* ∼, ∼n kettledrum; **auf die** ∼ **hauen** (ugs.) (feiern) paint the town red (coll.); (sich lautstark äußern) come right out with it

pauken (ugs.) ① *tr. V.* swot up (Brit. sl.), bone up on (Amer. coll.) ⟨*facts, figures, etc.*⟩; **Latein/Mathe** ∼: swot up one's Latin/maths
② *itr. V.* swot (Brit. sl.); (fürs Examen) cram (coll.)

pausbäckig *Adj.* chubby-faced; chubby ⟨*face*⟩

pauschal ① *Adj.* **(a)** all-inclusive ⟨*price, settlement*⟩
(b) (verallgemeinernd) sweeping ⟨*judgement, criticism, statement*⟩; indiscriminate ⟨*prejudice*⟩; wholesale ⟨*discrimination*⟩
② *adv.* **(a)** ⟨*cost*⟩ all in all; ⟨*pay*⟩ in a lump sum
(b) (ohne zu differenzieren) wholesale

Pauschale *die;* ∼, ∼n flat-rate payment

Pauschal-: ∼preis *der* flat rate; (Inklusivpreis) all-in price; **∼reise** *die* package holiday; (mit mehreren Reisezielen) package tour

Pause *die;* ∼, ∼n break; (Ruhe∼) rest; (Theater) interval (Brit.); intermission (Amer.)

pausen *tr. V.* trace; (eine Lichtpause machen) Photostat (*Brit.* ®)

---

*alte Schreibung - vgl. Hinweis auf S. xiv

pausen-, Pausen-: ~**brot** *das*
sandwich *(eaten during break)*; ~**hof** *der*
school yard; ~**los** [1] *Adj.* incessant *(noise,
moaning, questioning)*; continous *(work,
operation)*
[2] *adv.* incessantly; *(work)* non-stop

Pavian /'pa:vi̯a:n/ *der;* ~**s,** ~**e** baboon

Pavillon /'pavɪljɔn/ *der;* ~**s,** ~**s** pavilion

Pazifik *der;* ~**s** Pacific

pazifisch *Adj.* Pacific *(area)*; **der Pazifische
Ozean** the Pacific Ocean

Pazifismus *der;* ~: pacifism *no art.*

Pazifist *der;* ~**en,** ~**en, Pazifistin** *die;*
~, ~**nen** pacifist

pazifistisch [1] *Adj.* pacifist
[2] *adv.* in a pacifist way

PC *der;* ~[s], ~[s] (DV) PC

PDS *Abk.* = **Partei des
Demokratischen Sozialismus**
Party of Democratic Socialism

Peanuts /'pi:nʌts/ *Pl.* peanuts (coll.)

Pech *das;* ~[e]s, ~e (a) pitch
(b) (Missgeschick) bad luck

pech·schwarz *Adj.* (ugs.) jet-black

Pedal *das;* ~**s,** ~**e** pedal

Pedant *der;* ~**en,** ~**en, Pedantin** *die;* ~,
~**nen** pedant

pedantisch [1] *Adj.* pedantic
[2] *adv.* pedantically

Pediküre *die;* ~, ~**n** pedicure

pediküren *tr. V.* pedicure

Pegel *der;* ~**s,** ~ (a) water level indicator;
(Tide~) tide gauge
(b) (Wasserstand) water level

peilen *tr. V.* take a bearing on *(transmitter,
fixed point)*

Pein *die;* ~ (geh.) torment

peinigen *tr. V.* (geh.) torment; (foltern)
torture

peinlich [1] *Adj.* (a) embarrassing;
awkward *(question, position, pause)*; **es ist
mir sehr ~:** I feel very bad (coll.) *or*
embarrassed about it
(b) (äußerst genau) meticulous
[2] *adv.* (a) unpleasantly *(surprised)*
(b) (überaus [genau]) meticulously

Peinlichkeit *die;* ~, ~**en** (a)
embarrassment; **die ~ der Situation** the
awkwardness of the situation
(b) (Genauigkeit) meticulousness
(c) (peinliche Situation) embarrassing situation

Peitsche *die;* ~, ~**n** whip

peitschen *tr. V.* whip; (fig.) *(storm, waves,
rain)* lash

Pelikan *der;* ~**s,** ~**e** pelican

Pelle *die;* ~, ~**n** (bes. nordd.) skin; (abgeschält)
peel

pellen (bes. nordd.) *tr., refl. V.* peel

Pell·kartoffel *die* potato boiled in its skin

Pelz *der;* ~**es,** ~**e** (a) fur; coat; (des toten
Tieres) skin; pelt
(b) (Material) fur; (~mantel) fur coat

Pelz·mantel *der* fur coat

Pendel *das;* ~**s,** ~: pendulum

pendeln *itr. V.* (a) swing [to and fro]; (mit
weniger Bewegung) dangle
(b) *mit sein (bus, ferry, etc.)* operate a
shuttle service; *(person)* commute

Pendler *der;* ~**s,** ~, **Pendlerin** *die;* ~,
~**nen** commuter

penetrant [1] *Adj.* (a) penetrating *(smell,
taste)*; overpowering *(stink, perfume)*
(b) (aufdringlich) pushing, (coll.) pushy
(person); overbearing *(tone, manner)*;
aggressive *(question)*
[2] *adv.* (a) overpoweringly
(b) (aufdringlich) overbearingly

penibel [1] *Adj.* over-meticulous *(person)*;
(pedantisch) pedantic
[2] *adv.* painstakingly; over-meticulously
(dressed)

Penis *der;* ~, ~**se** penis

pennen *itr. V.* (salopp) (a) (schlafen) kip (coll.)
(b) (fig.: nicht aufpassen) be half asleep
(c) (koitieren) **mit jmdm.** ~: sleep with sb.

Penner *der;* ~**s,** ~, **Pennerin** *die;* ~,
~**nen** (salopp) tramp (Brit.); hobo (Amer.)

Pensen ▶ PENSUM

Pension /pāˈzi̯o:n/ *die;* ~, ~**en** (a)
(Ruhestand) **in ~ gehen** retire; **in ~ sein** be
retired
(b) (Ruhegehalt) [retirement] pension
(c) (Haus für [Ferien]gäste) guest house
(d) (Unterkunft u. Verpflegung) board

Pensionär /pāzi̯oˈnɛːɐ̯/ *der;* ~**s,** ~**e,**
Pensionärin *die;* ~, ~**nen** retired civil
servant

pensionieren *tr. V.* pension off; retire;
sich [vorzeitig] ~ lassen take [early]
retirement; **ein pensionierter Schulmeister/
Politiker** a retired schoolmaster/politician

Pensionierung *die;* ~, ~**en** retirement

Pensions-: ~**alter** *das* retirement age;
~**anspruch** *der* pension entitlement

Pensum *das;* ~**s, Pensen** work quota

per *Präp. mit Akk.* (a) (mittels) by; ~ **Adresse
X** care of X; c/o X
(b) (Kaufmannsspr.: [bis] zum) by; (am) on
(c) (Kaufmannsspr.: pro) per

perfekt [1] *Adj.* (a) perfect *(crime, host)*;
faultless *(English, French, etc.)*
(b) ~ **sein** (ugs.: abgeschlossen, fertig sein) be
finalized
[2] *adv.* perfectly

Perfekt *das;* ~**s** (Sprachw.) perfect

Perfektion *die;* ~: perfection

perfektionieren *tr. V.* perfect

Perfektionismus *der;* ~: perfectionism

Perfektionist *der;* ~**en,** ~**en,**
Perfektionistin *die;* ~, ~**nen**
perfectionist

perfektionistisch [1] *Adj.* perfectionist
(standards etc.)
[2] *adv.* in a perfectionist manner

p

Pergamẹnt·papier *das* greaseproof paper

Periọde *die;* ~, ~n period

Pẹrle *die;* ~, ~n (a) (auch fig.) pearl
(b) (aus Holz, Glas o. Ä.) bead

Pẹrlmutt *das;* ~s mother-of-pearl

Perlon ⓌⓏ *das;* ~s ≈ nylon

Pẹrser *der;* ~s, ~ (a) Persian
(b) ▸ PERSERTEPPICH

Pẹrserin *die;* ~, ~nen Persian

Pẹrser·teppich *der* Persian carpet

Persiạner *der;* ~s, ~ (Mantel) Persian lamb
coat

Pẹrsien (*das);* ~s Persia

pẹrsisch *Adj.* Persian

Persọn *die;* ~, ~en person; (in der Dichtung,
im Film) character

Personạl *das;* ~s (in einem Betrieb o. Ä.) staff;
(im Haushalt) domestic staff *pl.*

Personạl-: ~**abbau** *der* reduction in
staff; (in mehreren Abteilungen/Betrieben) staff cuts
pl.; ~**abteilung** *die* personnel department;
~**ausweis** *der* identity card; ~**büro** *das*
personnel office; ~**chef** *der,* ~**chefin** *die*
personnel manager

Personạlien *Pl.* personal particulars

Personạl-: ~**kosten** *Pl.* (Wirtsch.,
Verwaltung) staff costs; ~**mangel** *der* staff
shortage; ~**pronomen** *das* (Sprachw.)
personal pronoun; ~**rat** *der* (a) (Ausschuss)
staff council (*for civil servants*); (b) (Mitglied)
staff council representative; ~**rätin** *die;*
▸ ~RAT B

Personẹn-: ~**kraftwagen** *der* (bes.
Amtsspr.) private car *or* (Amer.) automobile;
~**name** *der* personal name; ~**wagen** *der*
(Auto) [private] car; automobile (Amer.); (im
Unterschied zum Lastwagen) passenger car *or*
(Amer.) automobile; ~**zug** *der* stopping train

Personifikatiọn *die;* ~, ~en
personification

personifiziẹren *tr. V.* personify

Personifiziẹrung *die;* ~, ~en
personification

persọ̈nlich ① *Adj.* personal; ~ werden get
personal
② *adv.* personally; (auf Briefen) 'private [and
confidential]'

Persọ̈nlichkeit *die;* ~, ~en (a)
personality
(b) (Mensch) person of character; **eine** ~ **sein**
have a strong personality; ~**en des**
öffentlichen Lebens public figures

Perspektịve *die;* ~, ~n perspective;
(Blickwinkel) angle; (Zukunftsaussicht) prospect

Peru (*das);* ~s Peru

Peruạner *der;* ~s, ~, **Peruạnerin** *die;*
~, ~nen Peruvian

peruạnisch *Adj.* Peruvian

Perụ̈cke *die;* ~, ~n wig

pervẹrs *Adj.* perverted

---

*old spelling - see note on page xiv

Perversiọn *die;* ~, ~en perversion

Pessimịsmus *der;* ~: pessimism

Pessimịst *der;* ~en, ~en, **Pessimịstin**
die; ~, ~nen pessimist

pessimịstisch ① *Adj.* pessimistic
② *adv.* pessimistically

Pẹst *die;* ~: plague

Pestizịd *das;* ~s, ~e pesticide

Petersịlie /petɐˈziːliə/ *die;* ~: parsley

Petitiọn *die;* ~, ~en (Amtsspr.) petition

Petrọleum /peˈtroːleʊm/ *das;* ~s paraffin
(Brit.); kerosene (Amer.)

Pẹtrus (*der);* **Pẹtri** (christl. Rel.: Apostel) St
Peter

pẹtzen (Schülerspr.) ① *itr. V.* tell tales; sneak
(Brit. school coll.)
② *tr. V.* ~, **dass** ...: tell teacher/sb.'s parents
that ...

Pf *Abk.* = **Pfennig**

Pfad *der;* ~[e]s, ~e path

Pfad-: ~**finder** *der* Scout; ~**finderin** *die;*
~, ~nen Guide (Brit.); girl scout (Amer.)

Pfạffe *der;* ~n, ~n (abwertend) cleric; Holy
Joe (derog.)

Pfahl *der;* ~[e]s, Pfähle post; stake

Pfạnd *das;* ~[e]s, Pfänder (a) security;
pledge (esp. fig.)
(b) (für Flaschen usw.) deposit (**auf** + *Dat.* on)

pfạ̈nden *tr. V.* seize [under distress] (Law)
(*goods, chattels*); attach (*wages etc.*) (Law)

Pfạnd·flasche *die* returnable bottle (*on*
which a deposit is payable)

Pfạ̈ndung *die;* ~, ~en seizure; distraint
(Law); (von Geldsummen, Vermögensrechten)
attachment (Law)

Pfạnne *die;* ~, ~n [frying] pan

Pfạnn·kuchen *der* (a) pancake
(b) (Berliner) doughnut

Pfarrẹi *die;* ~, ~en (a) (Bezirk) parish
(b) (Dienststelle) parish office
(c) ▸ PFARRHAUS

Pfạrrer *der;* ~s, ~ pastor; (anglikanisch)
vicar; (von Freikirchen) minister

Pfạrrerin *die;* ~, ~nen [woman] pastor; (in
Freikirchen) [woman] minister

Pfạrr·haus *das* vicarage; (katholisch)
presbytery; (in Schottland) manse

Pfạu *der;* ~[e]s, ~en peacock

Pfauen·auge *das* peacock butterfly

Pfd. *Abk.* = **Pfund** lb.

Pfẹffer *der;* ~s, ~: pepper

Pfẹffer-: ~**kuchen** *der* ≈ gingerbread;
~**minze** *die* peppermint [plant];
~**minz·tee** *der* peppermint tea; ~**mühle**
die pepper mill

pfẹffern *tr. V.* season with pepper

Pfẹffer·streuer *der;* ~s, ~: pepper pot

Pfeife *die;* ~, ~n pipe; (Triller~) whistle

pfeifen ① *unr. itr. V.* whistle; ⟨*bird*⟩ sing;

(auf einer Trillerpfeife o. Ä.) ⟨*policeman, referee, etc.*⟩ blow one's whistle; **auf jmdn./etw. ~** (ugs.) not give a damn about sb./sth.

2 *unr. tr. V.* whistle ⟨*tune etc.*⟩; ⟨*bird*⟩ sing ⟨*song*⟩; (auf einer Pfeife) pipe, play ⟨*tune etc.*⟩

Pfeil *der;* ~[e]s, ~e arrow

Pfeiler *der;* ~s, ~: pillar; (Brücken~) pier

Pfennig *der;* ~s, ~e pfennig; **es kostet 20 ~:** it costs 20 pfennig[s]

pferchen *tr. V.* cram; pack

Pferd *das;* ~[e]s, ~e horse; (Schachfigur) knight; **mit ihr kann man ~e stehlen** (ugs.) she's game for anything

Pferde-: ~**rennen** *das* horse race; (Sportart) horseracing; ~**schwanz** *der* (Frisur) ponytail; ~**stall** *der* stable

pfiff *1. u. 3. Pers. Sg. Prät. v.* PFEIFEN

Pfiff *der;* ~[e]s, ~e (a) whistle
(b) (ugs.: besonderer Reiz) style

Pfifferling *der;* ~s, ~e chanterelle; **keinen** *od.* **nicht einen ~ wert sein** (ugs.) be not worth a bean (coll.)

pfiffig 1 *Adj.* smart; bright ⟨*idea*⟩; artful ⟨*smile, expression*⟩
2 *adv.* artfully

Pfingsten *das;* ~, ~: Whitsun

Pfingst-: ~**montag** *der* Whit Monday *no def. art.;* ~**sonntag** *der* Whit Sunday *no def. art.*

Pfirsich *der;* ~s, ~e peach

Pflanze *die;* ~, ~n plant

pflanzen *tr. V.* plant

Pflanzen-öl *das* vegetable oil

pflanzlich *Adj.* plant *attrib.* ⟨*life, motif*⟩; vegetable ⟨*dye, fat*⟩

Pflaster *das;* ~s, ~ (a) (Straßen~) road surface; (auf dem Gehsteig) pavement; **ein teures/gefährliches ~** (ugs.) an expensive/dangerous place *or* spot to be
(b) (Wund~) sticking plaster

pflastern *tr. V. (auch itr.) V.* surface; (mit Kopfsteinpflaster, Steinplatten) pave

Pflaster-stein *der* paving stone; (Kopfstein) cobblestone

Pflaume *die;* ~, ~n plum; **getrocknete ~n** [dried] prunes

Pflege *die;* ~: care; (Maschinen~, Fahrzeug~) maintenance; (fig.: von Beziehungen, Kunst, Sprache) cultivation; **jmdn./etw. in ~ (Akk.) nehmen** look after sb./sth.

pflege-, Pflege-: ~**bedürftig** *Adj.* needing care *or* attention *postpos.;* ⟨*person*⟩ in need of care; ~**bedürftig sein** need looking after; need attention; ~**eltern** *Pl.* foster-parents; ~**fall** *der:* **ein ~fall sein** be in [permanent] need of nursing; ~**heim** *das* nursing home (esp. Brit.); ~**kind** *das* foster-child; ~**leicht** *Adj.* easy-care *attrib.* ⟨*textiles, flooring*⟩

pflegen 1 *tr. V.* look after; care for; take care of ⟨*skin, teeth, floor*⟩; look after ⟨*bicycle,*

car, machine⟩; look after, tend ⟨*garden, plants*⟩; cultivate ⟨*relations, arts, interests*⟩; foster ⟨*contacts, cooperation*⟩; pursue ⟨*hobby*⟩
2 *mod. V.* **etw. zu tun ~:** usually do sth.

Pflege-personal *das* nursing staff

Pfleger *der;* ~s, ~ (a) (Krankenpfleger) [male] nurse
(b) (Tierpfleger) keeper

Pflegerin *die;* ~, ~nen (a) (Krankenpflegerin) nurse
(b) (Tierpflegerin) keeper

Pflege-versicherung *die* (*long-term*) [nursing-]care insurance

Pflicht *die;* ~, ~en duty

pflicht-, Pflicht-: ~**bewusst,** ***~**bewußt** 1 *Adj.* conscientious; 2 *adv.* with a sense of duty; ~**bewusstsein,** ***~**bewußtsein** *das,* sense of duty; ~**fach** *das* compulsory subject; ~**gefühl** *das* sense of duty; ~**übung** *die* (fig.) ritual exercise; ~**verteidiger** *der,* ~**verteidigerin** *die* (Rechtsw.) defense counsel appointed by the court; assigned counsel

Pflock *der;* ~[e]s, Pflöcke peg

pflücken *tr. V.* pick

Pflug *der;* ~[e]s, Pflüge plough

pflügen *tr., itr. V.* plough

Pforte *die;* ~, ~n (Tor) gate; (Tür) door; (Eingang) entrance

Pförtner *der;* ~s, ~, **Pförtnerin** *die;* ~, ~nen porter; (eines Wohnblocks, Büros) doorkeeper; (am Tor) gatekeeper

Pförtner-loge *die* porter's lodge

Pfosten *der;* ~s, ~: post

Pfote *die;* ~, ~n paw

Pfropf *der;* ~[e]s, ~e blockage

pfropfen *tr. V.* (ugs.) cram; stuff; **gepfropft voll** crammed [full]; packed

Pfropfen *der;* ~s, ~: stopper; (Korken) cork; (für Fässer) bung

pfui *Interj.* ugh; **~ rufen** boo

Pfund *das;* ~[e]s, ~e pound

Pfusch *der;* ~[e]s (a) (ugs. abwertend) **das ist ~:** it's a botch-up
(b) (österr.: Schwarzarbeit) work done on the side (*and not declared for tax*); (nach Feierabend) moonlighting (coll.)

pfuschen *itr. V.* (a) (ugs. abwertend) botch it; do a botched-up job
(b) (österr.: schwarzarbeiten) do work on the side (*not declared for tax*); (nach Feierabend) moonlight (coll.)

Pfütze *die;* ~, ~n puddle

Phänomen *das;* ~s, ~e phenomenon

Phantasie *usw.:* ▶ FANTASIE *usw.*

Pharma-: ~**berater** *der,* ~**beraterin** *die:* ▶ ~REFERENT; ~**industrie** *die* pharmaceutical industry

Pharmakologie *die;* ~: pharmacology *no art.*

Pharma·referent *der,*
Pharma·referentin *die* pharmaceutical representative

pharmazeutisch *Adj.* pharmaceutical

Phase *die;* ∼, ∼n phase

Philosoph *der;* ∼en, ∼en philosopher

Philosophie *die;* ∼, ∼n philosophy

philosophieren *itr. (auch tr.) V.* philosophize

Philosophin *die;* ∼, ∼nen philosopher

philosophisch ① *Adj.* philosophical; ⟨*dictionary, principles*⟩ of philosophy
② *adv.* philosophically

Phosphat *das;* ∼[e]s, ∼e (Chemie) phosphate

Photo *das;* ∼s, ∼s ▶ FOTO

Phrase *die;* ∼, ∼n (abwertend) [empty] phrase; cliché

Physik *die;* ∼: physics *sing., no art.*

physikalisch *Adj.* physics *attrib.* ⟨*experiment, formula, research, institute*⟩; physical ⟨*map, process*⟩

Physiker *der;* ∼s, ∼, **Physikerin** *die;* ∼, ∼nen physicist

physisch ① *Adj.* physical
② *adv.* physically

Pianist *der;* ∼en, ∼en, **Pianistin** *die;* ∼, ∼nen pianist

Pickel *der;* ∼s, ∼: pimple

picken ① *itr. V.* peck (**nach** at; **an** + *Akk.,* **gegen** on, against)
② *tr. V.* ⟨*bird*⟩ peck; (ugs.) ⟨*person*⟩ pick

Picknick *das;* ∼s, ∼e *od.* ∼s picnic

piek·fein (ugs.) ① *Adj.* posh (coll.)
② *adv.* poshly (coll.)

piepe, piep·egal *Adj.* [jmdm.] ∼ **sein** (ugs.) not matter at all [to sb.]; **es ist mir** ∼ (ugs.) I don't give a damn

Piepen *Pl.* (salopp: Geld) dough *sing.* (coll.)

piep[s]en *itr. V.* (ugs.) squeak; ⟨*small bird*⟩ cheep; **bei dir piept's wohl!** (salopp) you must be off your rocker (coll.); **zum Piepen sein** (ugs.) be a hoot *or* a scream (coll.)

Pietät /piˈtɛːt/ *die;* ∼: respect; (Ehrfurcht) reverence

Pik *das;* ∼[s], ∼[s] (Kartenspiel) (a) (Farbe) spades *pl.;*
(b) (Karte) spade

pikant ① *Adj.* (a) piquant
(b) (fig.: witzig) ironical
(c) (verhüll.: schlüpfrig) racy ⟨*joke, story*⟩
② *adv.* piquantly ⟨*seasoned*⟩

pikiert ① *Adj.* piqued
② *adv.* ⟨*reply, say*⟩ in an aggrieved tone

Pilger *der;* ∼s, ∼, **Pilgerin** *die;* ∼, ∼nen pilgrim

pilgern *itr. V.* go on a pilgrimage

Pille *die;* ∼, ∼n pill

Pilot *der;* ∼en, ∼en, **Pilotin** *die;* ∼, ∼nen pilot

Pils *das;* ∼, ∼: Pils

Pilz *der;* ∼es, ∼e fungus; (Speise∼, auch fig.) mushroom

Pinguin *der;* ∼s, ∼e penguin

Pinie /ˈpiːni̯ə/ *die;* ∼, ∼n [stone *or* umbrella] pine

pinkeln *itr. V.* (salopp) pee (coll.)

Pinsel *der;* ∼s, ∼: brush; (Mal∼) paintbrush

Pinzette *die;* ∼, ∼n tweezers *pl.*

Pionier *der;* ∼s, ∼e (Milit.) sapper; (fig.: Wegbereiter) pioneer

Pionierin *die;* ∼, ∼nen pioneer

Pionier·arbeit *die* pioneering work

Pipi *das;* ∼s (Kinderspr.) ∼ **machen** do wee-wees (sl.); ∼ **müssen** have to do wee-wees *or* have a wee (sl.)

Pirat *der;* ∼en, ∼en, **Piratin** *die;* ∼, ∼nen pirate

pissen *itr. V.* (derb) piss (coarse)

Pistazie /pɪsˈtaːtsi̯ə/ *die;* ∼, ∼n pistachio

Piste *die;* ∼, ∼n (Ski∼) piste; (Renn∼) course; (Flugw.) runway

Pistole *die;* ∼, ∼n pistol

Pizza *die;* ∼, ∼s *od.* Pizzen pizza

Pkw, PKW /ˈpeːkaːveː/ *der;* ∼[s], ∼[s] [private] car; automobile (Amer.)

plädieren *itr. V.* (Rechtsw.) plead (**auf** + *Akk.* for); (fig.) argue

Plädoyer /plɛdo̯aˈjeː/ *das;* ∼s, ∼s (Rechtsw.) summing up (*for the defence/prosecution*); (fig.) plea

Plage *die;* ∼, ∼n (a) nuisance
(b) (ugs.: Mühe) bother; trouble

plagen ① *tr. V.* (a) torment
(b) (ugs.: bedrängen) harass; (mit Bitten, Fragen) pester
② *refl. V.* (a) (sich abmühen) slave away
(b) (leiden) **sich mit etw.** ∼: be bothered by sth.

Plagiat *das;* ∼[e]s, ∼e plagiarism *no art.*

Plakat *das;* ∼[e]s, ∼e poster

Plakette *die;* ∼, ∼n badge

Plan *der;* ∼[e]s, **Pläne** (a) plan
(b) (Karte) map; plan

Plane *die;* ∼, ∼n tarpaulin

planen *tr., itr. V.* plan

Planet *der;* ∼en, ∼en planet

planieren *tr. V.* level; grade

Planier·raupe *die* bulldozer

Planke *die;* ∼, ∼n plank

plan-: ∼**los** ① *Adj.* aimless; (ohne System) unsystematic; ② *adv.* ▶ 1: aimlessly; unsystematically; ∼**mäßig** ① *Adj.* (a) scheduled ⟨*service, steamer*⟩; ∼**mäßige Ankunft/Abfahrt** scheduled time of arrival/departure; (b) (systematisch) systematic
② *adv.* (a) (wie geplant) according to plan; (pünktlich) on schedule; (b) (systematisch) systematically

Plansch·becken *das* paddling pool

planschen *itr. V.* splash [about]

---

*alte Schreibung - vgl. Hinweis auf S. xiv

Plantage /plan'ta:ʒə/ *die;* ~, ~n plantation

Planung *die;* ~, ~en planning

Plan-wirtschaft *die* planned economy

Plastik¹ *die;* ~, ~en sculpture

Plastik² *das;* ~s (ugs.) plastic

Plastik-beutel *der*, **Plastik-tüte** *die* plastic bag

Platane *die;* ~, ~n plane tree

Platin *das;* ~s platinum

platschen *itr. V.* (a) splash
(b) *mit sein* (~d auftreffen) splash (**an** + *Akk.,* **gegen** against)

plätschern *itr. V.* (a) splash; ⟨*rain*⟩ patter; ⟨*stream*⟩ burble
(b) *mit sein* ⟨*stream*⟩ burble along

platt *Adj.* flat; **ein Platter** (ugs.) a flat (coll.); etw. ~ **machen** (salopp abwertend) close sth. down

Platt *das;* ~[s] [local] Low German dialect

Plättchen *das;* ~s, ~: small plate *or* disc

platt-deutsch *Adj.* Low German

Platte *die;* ~, ~n (a) (Stein~) slab; (Metall~) plate; sheet; (Span~, Hartfaser~ usw.) board; (Tisch~) [table] top; (Grab~) [memorial] slab
(b) (Koch~) hotplate
(c) (Schall~) [gramophone] record
(d) (Teller) plate; (zum Servieren, aus Metall) dish; **kalte** ~: selection of cold meats [and cheese]

Platten-spieler *der* record player

Platt-fuß *der* (a) flat foot
(b) (ugs.: Reifenpanne) flat (coll.)

Platz *der;* ~es, **Plätze** (a) square
(b) (Sport~) ground; (Spielfeld) field; (Tennis~, Volleyball~ usw.) court; (Golf~) course
(c) (Stelle, wo jmd., etw. hingehört) place; **nicht** *od.* **fehl am** ~[e] **sein** (fig.) be out of place
(d) (Sitz~) seat; (am Tisch, Steh~ usw.) place; ~ **nehmen** sit down
(e) (bes. Sport: Platzierung) place
(f) (Ort) place; **am** ~: in the town/village
(g) (Raum) space; room; ~ **machen** make room (*Dat.* for)

Platz-angst *die* (volkst.: Klaustrophobie) claustrophobia

Plätzchen *das;* ~s, ~ (a) little place
(b) (Keks) biscuit (Brit.); cookie (Amer.)

platzen *itr. V.; mit sein* (a) burst; (explodieren) explode
(b) (ugs.: scheitern) fall through; **der Wechsel/ das Treffen ist geplatzt** the bill has bounced (coll.)/the meeting is off
(c) **in eine Versammlung** ~ (ugs.) burst into a meeting

Platz-: ~**karte** *die* reserved-seat ticket; ~**konzert** *das* open-air concert (*by a military or brass band*); ~**mangel** *der* lack of space; ~**not** *die* [acute] lack of space; ~**regen** *der* cloudburst; ~**wunde** *die* lacerated wound

Plauderei *die;* ~, ~en chat

plaudern *itr. V.* chat

plausibel *Adj.* plausible

Play-boy /'pleɪbɔɪ/ *der* playboy

Player /'pleɪɐ/ *der;* ~, ~: player

pleite (ugs.) ~ **sein** ⟨*person*⟩ be broke (coll.); ⟨*company*⟩ have gone bust (coll.); *s. auch* PLEITE A

Pleite *die;* ~, ~n (ugs.) (a) (Bankrott) bankruptcy *no def. art.;* ~ **gehen/machen** go bust (coll.)
(b) (Misserfolg) washout (coll.)

Pleite-: ~**geier** *der* (ugs.) spectre of bankruptcy; ~**wirtschaft** *die* (ugs.) bankrupt economy

Plissee *das;* ~s, ~s accordion pleats *pl.*

Plombe *die;* ~, ~n (a) (Siegel) [lead] seal
(b) (veralt.: Zahnfüllung) filling

plombieren *tr. V.* (a) (versiegeln) seal
(b) (veralt.) fill ⟨*tooth*⟩

plötzlich ① *Adj.* sudden
② *adv.* suddenly

Plötzlichkeit *die;* ~: suddenness

plump ① *Adj.* (a) (dick) plump; (unförmig) ungainly ⟨*shape*⟩; (rundlich) bulbous
(b) (schwerfällig) clumsy ⟨*movements, style*⟩
(c) (fig.) (dreist) crude ⟨*lie, deception, trick*⟩; (leicht durchschaubar) blatantly obvious; (unbeholfen) clumsy ⟨*excuse, advances*⟩; crude ⟨*joke, forgery*⟩
② *adv.* (a) (schwerfällig) clumsily
(b) (fig.) in a blatantly obvious manner

Plumpheit *die;* ~ (a) (Dicke) plumpness; (Unförmigkeit) ungainliness; (Rundlichkeit) bulbousness
(b) (Schwerfälligkeit) clumsiness
(c) (abwertend: Dreistigkeit) blatant nature

plumps *Interj.* bump; thud; (ins Wasser) splash; ~ **machen** go bump

Plumps *der;* ~es, ~e (ugs.) bump; thud; (ins Wasser) splash

plumpsen *itr. V.* fall with a bump; thud; (ins Wasser) splash

Plünderer *der;* ~s, ~, **Plünderin** *die;* ~, ~nen looter

plündern *itr., tr. V.* (a) loot; plunder ⟨*town*⟩
(b) (scherzh.) raid ⟨*larder, fridge, account*⟩

Plünderung *die;* ~, ~en looting; (einer Stadt) plundering; ~en cases of looting/ plundering

Plural *der;* ~s, ~e plural

Pluralismus *der;* ~: pluralism

pluralistisch ① *Adj.* pluralistic
② *adv.* pluralistically; along pluralistic lines

plus *Konj., Adv.* plus

Plus *das;* ~: surplus; (Vorteil) advantage

Plüsch *der;* ~[e]s, ~e plush

Plusquam-perfekt *das* pluperfect [tense]

PLZ *Abk.* = Postleitzahl

Po *der;* ~s, ~s (ugs.) bottom

Pöbel *der;* ~s rabble

pöbeln *itr. V.* make rude *or* coarse remarks

pochen *itr. V.* (klopfen) knock (**gegen/an** + *Akk.* at, on); (geh.: pulsieren) ⟨*heart*⟩ pound

Pocken *Pl.* smallpox *sing.*

Podest *das od. der;* ∼[e]s, ∼e rostrum

Podium *das;* ∼s, **Podien** (Plattform) platform; (Bühne) stage; (trittartige Erhöhung) rostrum

Poesie *die;* ∼: poetry

Poet *der;* ∼en, ∼en (veralt.) poet; bard (literary)

poetisch ① *Adj.* poetic[al]
② *adv.* poetically

Pogrom *das od. der;* ∼s, ∼e pogrom

Pointe /'pŏɛ̃:tə/ *die;* ∼, ∼n (eines Witzes) punch line; (einer Geschichte) point; (eines Sketches) curtain line

pointiert /pŏɛ̃'ti:ɐ̯t/ ① *Adj.* pointed ⟨*remark*⟩
② *adv.* pointedly

Pokal *der;* ∼s, ∼e (a) (Trinkgefäß) goblet (b) (Siegestrophäe, ∼wettbewerb) cup

Pökel·fleisch *das* salt meat

pökeln *tr. V.* salt

Poker *das od. der;* ∼s poker

Poker·gesicht *das* poker face

pokern *itr. V.* play poker

Pol *der;* ∼s, ∼e pole

Polar·licht *das* aurora; polar lights *pl.*

Polaroid·kamera ⓦ *die* Polaroid camera ®

Pole *der;* ∼n, ∼n Pole

polemisch ① *Adj.* polemic[al]
② *adv.* polemically

Polen *das;* ∼s Poland

Polente *die;* ∼ (salopp) cops *pl.* (coll.)

Police /po'li:sə/ *die;* ∼, ∼n (Versicherungsw.) policy

polieren *tr. V.* polish

Poli·klinik *die* outpatients' clinic

Polin *die;* ∼n, ∼nen Pole

Polit·büro *das* politburo

Politik *die;* ∼, ∼en (a) politics *sing.*, no art. (b) (eine spezielle ∼) policy

Politiker *der;* ∼s, ∼, **Politikerin** *die;* ∼, ∼nen politician

politisch ① *Adj.* political
② *adv.* politically

politisieren ① *itr. V.* talk politics
② *tr. V.* make politically active

Politur *die;* ∼, ∼en polish

Polizei *die;* ∼, ∼en police *pl.*

Polizei-: ∼**auto** *das* police car; ∼**beamte** *der* police officer; ∼**kontrolle** *die* police check

polizeilich ① *Adj.* police; ∼e Meldepflicht obligation to register with the police
② *adv.* by the police

Polizei-: ∼**präsidium** *das* police headquarters *sing. or pl.;* ∼**revier** *das*

police station; ∼**streife** *die* police patrol; ∼**stunde** *die* closing time; ∼**wache** *die* police station

Polizist *der;* ∼en, ∼en policeman

Polizistin *die;* ∼, ∼nen policewoman

Pollen *der;* ∼s, ∼ (Bot.) pollen

Poller *der;* ∼s, ∼: bollard

polnisch *Adj.* Polish

Polster *das;* ∼s, ∼: upholstery no pl., no indef. art.

Polster·möbel *Pl.* upholstered furniture *sing.*

polstern *tr. V.* upholster ⟨*furniture*⟩

poltern *itr. V.* (a) crash about (b) *mit sein* der Karren polterte über das Pflaster the cart clattered over the cobblestones

Polyp *der;* ∼en, ∼en (Zool., Med.) polyp

Pommern (*das*)*;* ∼s Pomerania

Pommes frites /pɔm'frit/ *Pl.* chips (Brit.); French fries (Amer.)

pompös ① *Adj.* grandiose
② *adv.* grandiosely

Pony¹ /'pɔni/ *das;* ∼s, ∼s pony

Pony² *der;* ∼s, ∼s (Frisur) fringe

Popel *der;* ∼s, ∼ (ugs.) bogy (sl.)

popelig (ugs. abwertend) ① *Adj.* crummy (coll.); lousy (coll.); (durchschnittlich) second-rate
② *adv.* crummily (sl.)

Popeline·mantel *der* poplin coat

popeln *itr. V.* (ugs.) [in der Nase] ∼: pick one's nose

Pop-: ∼**musik** *die* pop music; ∼**star** *der* pop star

populär ① *Adj.* popular (**bei** with)
② *adv.* popularly

popularisieren *tr. V.* popularize

Popularität *die;* ∼: popularity

Pore *die;* ∼s, ∼n pore

Porno *der;* ∼s, ∼s (ugs.) porn[o] film/ magazine *etc.*

Pornographie *die;* ∼: pornography

pornographisch ① *Adj.* pornographic
② *adv.* pornographically

Porree *der;* ∼s leek

Portal *das;* ∼s, ∼e portal

Portemonnaie /pɔrtmɔ'ne:/ *das;* ∼s, ∼s purse

Porti *Pl.* ▶ PORTO

Portier /pɔr'tje:/ *der;* ∼s, ∼s, österr.: /pɔr'ti:ɐ̯/ *der;* ∼s, ∼e porter

Portion /pɔr'ts:jo:n/ *die;* ∼, ∼en (a) (beim Essen) portion; helping (b) (ugs.: Anteil) amount

Porto *das;* ∼s, ∼s od. **Porti** postage (**für** on, for)

Portugal (*das*)*;* ∼s Portugal

Portugiese *der;* ∼n, ∼n, **Portugiesin** *die;* ∼, ∼nen Portuguese

portugiesisch *Adj.* Portuguese

Portwein *der* port

Porzellan *das;* ~s porcelain; china
Posaune *die;* ~, ~n trombone
Position /pozi'tsi̯oːn/ *die;* ~, ~en position
positiv [1] *Adj.* positive
  [2] *adv.* positively
Positiv *das;* ~s, ~e (Fot.) positive
Possessiv-pronomen *das* (Sprachw.)
  possessive pronoun
Post *die;* ~, ~en (a) post (Brit.); mail; **etw.**
  mit der *od.* **per** ~ **schicken** send sth. by post
  or mail; **die** ~ **geht ab** (fig. ugs.) it's all
  happening; **ab 20 Uhr geht die** ~ **ab** (fig. ugs.)
  it'll all be happening from 8 o'clock; **auch**
  beim Publikum geht die ~ **ab** (fig. ugs.) the
  audience is having a ball too (coll.)
  (b) (Postamt) post office
Post-: ~**amt** *das* post office;
  ~**anweisung** *die* postal remittance form;
  ~**auto** *das* mail van; ~**bote** *der* (ugs.)
  postman (Brit.); mailman (Amer.); ~**botin** *die*
  (ugs.) postwoman (Brit.); mailwoman (Amer.)
Posten *der;* ~s, ~ (a) post
  (b) (bes. Milit.: Wachmann) sentry
post-, Post-: ~**fach** *das* post office *or* PO
  box; (im Büro, Hotel usw.) pigeonhole; ~**karte**
  die postcard; ~**lagernd** *Adj., adv.* poste
  restante; general delivery (Amer.);
  ~**leit·zahl** *die* postcode; Zip code (Amer.);
  ~**stempel** *der* (Abdruck) postmark;
  ~**wendend** *Adv.* by return [of post]
potent *Adj.* potent
Potenz *die;* ~, ~en (a) potency
  (b) (Math.) power
potenzieren *tr. V.* (Math.) **mit 5** ~: raise to
  the power [of] 5
Pracht *die;* ~: splendour
prächtig, pracht·voll [1] *Adj.* splendid
  [2] *adv.* splendidly
prädestiniert *Adj.* predestined
Prädikat *das;* ~[e]s, ~e (a) (Auszeichnung)
  rating
  (b) (Sprachw.) predicate
Prag (*das*) ~s Prague
prägen *tr. V.* (a) emboss
  (b) mint (coin)
  (c) (fig.: beeinflussen) shape
prägnant [1] *Adj.* concise; succinct
  [2] *adv.* concisely; succinctly
Prägung *die;* ~, ~en embossing; (von
  Münzen) minting
prahlen *itr. V.* boast, brag (mit about)
Prahler *der;* ~s, ~: boaster; braggart
Prahlerei *die;* ~, ~en (abwertend) boasting;
  bragging; ~en boasts
Prahlerin *die;* ~, ~nen boaster; braggart
Praktik *die;* ~, ~en practice
Praktika ▶ PRAKTIKUM
praktikabel *Adj.* practicable; practical
Praktikant *der;* ~en, ~en,
  Praktikantin *die;* ~, ~nen (a) (in einem
  Betrieb) student trainee

  (b) (an der Hochschule) physics/chemistry
  student (doing a period of practical training)
Praktikum *das;* ~s, Praktika period of
  practical training
praktisch [1] *Adj.* practical; ~**er Arzt**
  general practitioner
  [2] *adv.* practically; (auf die Praxis bezogen;
  wirklich) in practice
praktizieren *tr. V.* practise
Praline *die;* ~, ~n [filled] chocolate
prall *Adj.* (a) hard ⟨ball⟩; bulging ⟨sack,
  wallet, bag⟩; big strong ⟨attrib. ⟨thighs,
  muscles, calves⟩; well-rounded ⟨breasts⟩
  (b) (intensiv) blazing ⟨sun⟩
prallen *itr. V.; mit sein* crash (**gegen/auf/an**
  + *Akk.* into); collide (**gegen/auf/an** + *Akk.*
  with)
Prämie /'prɛːmi̯ə/ *die;* ~, ~n (a)
  (Leistungs~; Wirtschaft) bonus; (Belohnung)
  reward; (Spar~, Versicherungs~) premium
  (b) (einer Lotterie) [extra] prize
prämieren *tr. V.* award a prize to ⟨person,
  film⟩; give an award for ⟨best essay etc.⟩
Pranger *der;* ~s, ~ (hist.) pillory
Pranke *die;* ~, ~n paw
Präparat *das;* ~[e]s, ~e preparation
präparieren [1] *tr. V.* prepare
  [2] *refl. V.* (geh.: sich vorbereiten) prepare
  oneself
Präposition *die;* ~, ~en (Sprachw.)
  preposition
Prärie *die;* ~, ~n prairie
Präsens /'prɛːzɛns/ *das;* ~ (Sprachw.)
  present [tense]
präsentieren *tr. V.* present
Präservativ *das;* ~s, ~e condom
Präsident *der;* ~en, ~en, **Präsidentin**
  die; ~, ~nen president
Präsidium *das;* ~s, Präsidien (a)
  committee
  (b) (Vorsitz) chairmanship
  (c) (Polizei~) police headquarters *sing. or pl.*
prasseln *itr. V.* pelt down; ⟨shots⟩ clatter;
  ⟨fire⟩ crackle
prassen *itr. V.* live extravagantly;
  (schlemmen) feast
Präteritum *das;* ~s (Sprachw.) preterite
  [tense]
Prävention *die;* ~, ~en prevention
Praxis *die;* ~, Praxen (a) (im Unterschied zur
  Theorie) practice *no art.;* (Erfahrung) [practical]
  experience
  (b) (eines Arztes, Anwalts usw.) practice; (Räume)
  (eines Arztes) surgery (Brit.); office (Amer.);
  (eines Anwalts usw.) office
präzise [1] *Adj.* precise
  [2] *adv.* precisely
Präzision *die;* ~: precision
predigen [1] *itr. V.* deliver a/the sermon
  [2] *tr. V.* preach
Prediger *der;* ~s, ~, **Predigerin** *die;* ~,
  ~nen preacher

p

Predigt die; ~, ~en sermon
Preis der; ~es, ~e: (a) (Kaufpreis) price (**für** of)
(b) (Belohnung) prize
Preis-: ~**anstieg** der rise or increase in prices; ~**aus·schreiben** das [prize] competition; ~**bindung** die (Wirtsch.) price-fixing
Preisel·beere die cranberry
preisen unr. tr. V. (geh.) praise
preis-, Preis-: ~**erhöhung** die price increase or rise; ~**geld** das prize money; ~**günstig** ⒈ Adj. ⟨goods⟩ available at unusually low prices; ⟨purchases⟩ at favourable prices; inexpensive ⟨holiday⟩; **das** ~**günstigste Angebot** the best bargain or value; **das ist [sehr]** ~**günstig** that is [very] good value; ⒉ adv. at a low price; ~**günstig herstellen/verkaufen/bekommen** produce/sell/get sth. at a low price; ~**kampf** der price war; ~**liste** die price list; ~**nachlass, *~nachlaß** der price reduction; ~**richter** der, ~**richterin** die judge; ~**schild** das price tag; ~**senkung** die price reduction or cut; ~**steigerung** die rise or increase in prices; ~**tafel** die price list; ~**träger** der, ~**trägerin** die prizewinner; ~**verleihung** die presentation [of prizes/awards]; ~**wert** ⒈ Adj. good value pred.; ⒉ adv. ⟨eat⟩ at a reasonable price; **dort kann man** ~**wert einkaufen** you get good value for money there
prellen tr. V. (a) (betrügen) cheat (**um** out of); **die Zeche** ~: avoid paying the bill
(b) (verletzen) bash; bruise
Prellung die; ~, ~en bruise
Premiere /prə'mie:rə/ die; ~, ~n opening night
Presse die; ~, ~n (a) press; (Zitronen~) squeezer
(b) (Zeitungen) press
Presse-: ~**erklärung** die press statement; ~**freiheit** die freedom of the press; ~**information** die press release; ~**konferenz** die press conference; ~**meldung** die press report
pressen tr. V. press
Presse·sprecher der, ~**sprecherin** die spokesman; press officer
Press·luft-, *Preß·luft-: ~**bohrer** der pneumatic drill; ~**hammer** der pneumatic hammer
Prestige /prɛs'ti:ʒə/ das; ~s prestige
prickeln itr. V. tingle
pries 1. u. 3. Pers. Sg. Prät. v. PREISEN
Priester der; ~s, ~: priest
Priesterin die; ~, ~nen priestess
prima (ugs.) ⒈ indekl. Adj. great (coll.)
⒉ adv. ⟨taste⟩ great (coll.); ⟨sleep⟩ fantastically well (coll.)

primär ⒈ Adj. primary
⒉ adv. primarily
Primel die; ~, ~n primula; (Schlüsselblume) cowslip
primitiv ⒈ Adj. primitive; (einfach, schlicht) simple
⒉ adv. primitively; (einfach, schlicht) in a simple manner
Prim·zahl die (Math.) prime [number]
Prinz der; ~en, ~en prince
Prinzessin die; ~, ~nen princess
Prinzip das; ~s, ~ien /-'tsi:piən/ principle; **aus** ~: on principle; **im** ~: in principle
prinzipiell ⒈ Adj. in principle postpos., not pred.; ⟨rejection⟩ on principle
⒉ adv. (im Prinzip) in principle; (aus Prinzip) on principle
Prion das; ~, ~en (Biol.) prion
Prise die; ~, ~n pinch
privat ⒈ Adj. private; (persönlich) personal
⒉ adv. privately
Privat-: ~**adresse** die private or home address; ~**angelegenheit** die private matter; ~**besitz** der private property; ~**eigentum** das private property
privatisieren tr. V. (Wirtsch.) privatize; transfer into private ownership
Privatisierung die; ~, ~en (Wirtsch.) privatization; transfer into private ownership
Privat-: ~**leben** das private life; ~**lehrer** der, ~**lehrerin** die private tutor; ~**patient** der, ~**patientin** die private patient; ~**schule** die private school; (Eliteschule in Großbritannien) public school; ~**unterricht** der private tuition; ~**vermögen** das private fortune; ~**versicherung** die private insurance; ~**weg** der private way; ~**wirtschaftlich** Adj. private-sector attrib.
privilegiert Adj. privileged
pro Präp. mit Akk. per; ~ **Stück** each; a piece
pro- pro-; ~**westlich**/~**kommunistisch** pro-western/pro-communist
Probe die; ~, ~n (a) test
(b) (Muster, Teststück) sample
(c) (Theater~, Orchester~) rehearsal
Probe-: ~**fahrt** die trial run; (vor dem Kauf, nach einer Reparatur) test drive; ~**jahr** das probationary year
proben tr., itr. V. rehearse
probe·weise Adv. ⟨employ⟩ on a trial basis
Probe·zeit die probationary period
probieren ⒈ tr. V. (a) try; have a go at
(b) (kosten) taste; try
(c) (aus~) try out; (an~) try on ⟨clothes, shoes⟩
⒉ itr. V. (a) (versuchen) try
(b) (kosten) have a taste
Problem das; ~s, ~e problem

---

*alte Schreibung - vgl. Hinweis auf S. xiv

problematisch *Adj.* problematic[al]
problematisieren *tr. V.* etw. ~: expound
the problems of sth.
problem·los [1] *Adj.* problem-free
[2] *adv.* without any problems
Product-placement
/'prɔdaktpleɪsmənt/ *das;* ~s, ~ product
placement
Produkt *das;* ~[e]s, ~e (auch Math., fig.)
product
Produktion *die;* ~, ~en production
produktiv [1] productive; prolific ⟨*writer,
artist, etc.*⟩
[2] *adv.* ⟨*work, cooperate*⟩ productively
Produktivität *die;* ~: productivity
Produzent *der;* ~en, ~en,
Produzentin *die;* ~, ~nen producer
produzieren *tr. V.* produce
Prof. *Abk.* = **Professor** Prof.
professionell [1] *Adj.* professional
[2] *adv.* professionally
Professor *der;* ~s, ~en, **Professorin**
die; ~, ~nen professor
Professur *die;* ~, ~en professorship,
chair (**für** in)
Profi *der;* ~s, ~s (ugs.) pro (coll.)
Profil *das;* ~s, ~e (a) (Seitenansicht) profile;
im ~: in profile
(b) (von Reifen, Schuhsohlen) tread
Profit *der;* ~[e]s, ~e profit
profitieren *itr. V.* profit (**von, bei** by)
profund *Adj.* (geh.) profound; deep
Prognose *die;* ~, ~n prognosis; (Wetter~,
Wirtschafts~) forecast
prognostizieren *tr. V.* (geh.) forecast;
predict
Programm *das;* ~s, ~e programme;
program (Amer., Computing); (Ferns.: Sender)
channel
Programm-: ~**fehler** *der* (DV) program
error; error in the/a program; ~**heft** *das*
programme; ~**hinweis** *der* programme
announcement
programmieren *tr. V.* (a) (DV) program
(b) (auf etw. festlegen) programme
Programmierer *der;* ~s, ~,
Programmiererin *die;* ~, ~nen (DV)
programmer
Programm-: ~**vorschau** *die* (im
Fernsehen) preview [of the week's/evening's
etc. viewing]; (im Kino) trailers *pl.;*
~**zeitschrift** *die* radio and television
magazine
progressiv [1] *Adj.* progressive
[2] *adv.* progressively
Projekt *das;* ~[e]s, ~e project
Projekt-management *das* project
management
Projektor /proˈjɛktɔr/ *der;* ~s, ~en
/-ˈtoːrən/ projector
Projekt·tage *Pl.* (Schulw.) project[-work]
days

projizieren /projiˈtsiːrən/ *tr. V.* (Optik)
project
proklamieren *tr. V.* proclaim
Prolet *der;* ~en, ~en (abwertend) peasant
Proletariat *das;* ~[e]s proletariat
Proletarier /proleˈtaːriɐ/ *der;* ~s, ~:
proletarian
proletarisch *Adj.* proletarian
prollig *Adj.* (salopp) boorish
Promenade *die;* ~, ~n promenade
Promille *das;* ~s, ~: [part] per thousand;
er fährt nur ohne ~ (ugs.) he never drinks
and drives; **er hatte 1,8** ~: he had a blood
alcohol level of 1.8 per thousand
Promille-grenze *die* (ugs.) legal [alcohol]
limit
prominent *Adj.* prominent
Prominente *der/die; adj. Dekl.* prominent
figure
Prominenz *die;* ~: prominent figures *pl.*
Promotion /promoˈtsi̯oːn/ *die;* ~ (Wirtsch.)
promotion; **für etw.** ~ **machen** promote sth.
promovieren [1] *itr. V.* (a) (die Doktorwürde
erlangen) gain *or* obtain a/one's doctorate
(b) (eine Dissertation schreiben) do a doctorate
(**über** + *Akk.* on)
[2] *tr. V.* confer a doctorate *or* the degree of
doctor on
prompt [1] *Adj.* prompt
[2] *adv.* (a) promptly
(b) (ugs., meist iron.: wie erwartet) [and] sure
enough
Promptheit *die;* ~: promptness
Pronomen *das;* ~s, ~ *od.* Pronomina
(Sprachw.) pronoun
Propaganda *die;* ~: propaganda
propagieren *tr. V.* propagate
Propan·gas *das* propane
Propeller *der;* ~s, ~ propeller
Prophet *der;* ~en, ~en, **Prophetin** *die;*
~, ~nen prophet
prophezeien *tr. V.* prophesy (*Dat.* for);
predict ⟨*result, weather*⟩
Proportion *die;* ~, ~en proportion
Prosa *die;* ~: prose
Prosa·literatur *die* prose writing
prosit *Interj.* your [very good] health; ~
Neujahr! happy New Year!
Prospekt *der od.* (bes. österr.) *das;* ~[e]s,
~e (Werbeschrift) brochure; (Werbezettel) leaflet
prost *Interj.* (ugs.) cheers (Brit. coll.)
Prostituierte *die/der; adj. Dekl.* prostitute
Prostitution *die;* ~: prostitution *no art.*
Protagonist *der;* ~en, ~en,
Protagonistin *die;* ~, ~nen (geh.)
protagonist
Protest *der;* ~[e]s, ~e protest
Protestant *der;* ~en, ~en,
Protestantin *die;* ~, ~nen Protestant
protestantisch *Adj.* Protestant

p

Protestantismus *der;* ~: Protestantism *no art.*

protestieren *itr. V.* protest, make a protest (**gegen** against, about)

Protest·kundgebung *die* protest rally

Prothese *die;* ~, ~n artificial limb; prosthesis (Med.); (Zahn~) set of dentures; dentures *pl.*

Protokoll *das;* ~s, ~e (a) (wörtlich mitgeschrieben) transcript; (Ergebnis~) minutes *pl.;* (bei Gericht) record; **etw. zu** ~ **geben** make a statement about sth.
(b) (diplomatisches Zeremoniell) protocol

protokollieren ① *tr. V.* take down; take the minutes of ⟨meeting⟩; minute ⟨remark⟩ ② *itr. V.* take the minutes; (bei Gericht) keep the record

protzen *itr. V.* (ugs.) swank (coll.); show off; **mit etw.** ~: show sth. off

protzig (ugs. abwertend) ① *Adj.* swanky (coll.); showy ② *adv.* swankily (coll.)

Proviant *der;* ~s, ~e provisions *pl.*

Provinz *die;* ~, ~en province

provinziell ① *Adj.* provincial ② *adv.* provincially

Provision *die;* ~, ~en (Kaufmannsspr.) commission

provisorisch ① *Adj.* provisional; temporary ② *adv.* temporarily

Pro·vitamin *das* provitamin

Provokation *die;* ~, ~en provocation

provozieren *tr. V.* provoke

Prozedur *die;* ~, ~en procedure

Prozent *das;* ~[e]s, ~e (a) *nach Zahlenangaben Pl. ungebeugt* per cent *sing.;* **fünf** ~: five per cent
(b) *Pl.* (ugs.) (Gewinnanteil) share *sing.* of the profits; (Rabatt) discount *sing.;* **auf etw.** (Akk.) ~e **bekommen** get a discount on sth.

-prozentig *adj.* -per-cent

Prozent-: ~**punkt** *der* percentage point; ~**rechnung** *die* percentage calculation; ~**satz** *der* percentage

prozentual ① *Adj.* percentage ② *adv.* ~ **am Gewinn beteiligt sein** have a percentage share in the profits

Prozess, *Prozeß *der; Prozesses, Prozesse* (a) trial; (Fall) [court] case; **einen** ~ **gewinnen/verlieren** win/lose a case
(b) (Vorgang) process

prozessieren *itr. V.* go to court; **gegen jmdn.** ~: bring an action against sb.

Prozess·kosten, *Prozeß·kosten *Pl.* legal costs

Prozessor *der;* ~s, ~en (DV) [central] processor

prüde (abwertend) ① *Adj.* prudish ② prudishly

---
*old spelling - see note on page xiv

Prüderie *die;* ~ (abwertend) prudery; prudishness

prüfen *tr. V.* (a) *auch itr.* examine ⟨pupil, student, etc.⟩; **mündlich/schriftlich geprüft werden** have an oral/a written examination
(b) (untersuchen) examine (**auf** + *Akk.* for); check ⟨device, machine, calculation⟩ (**auf** + *Akk.* for); investigate ⟨complaint⟩; (testen) test (**auf** + *Akk.* for)
(c) (kontrollieren) check; examine ⟨accounts, books⟩
(d) (vor einer Entscheidung) check ⟨price⟩; examine ⟨offer⟩; consider ⟨application⟩

Prüfer *der;* ~s, ~, **Prüferin** *die;* ~, ~nen
(a) inspector; (Buch~) auditor
(b) (im Examen) examiner

Prüfling *der;* ~s, ~e examinee; [examination] candidate

Prüfung *die;* ~, ~en (a) examination; exam (coll.); **eine** ~ **machen** *od.* **ablegen** take an examination
(b) ▶ PRÜFEN B–D: examination; check; investigation; test; consideration

Prügel *Pl.* (Schläge) beating *sing.;* (als Strafe für Kinder) hiding (coll.)

Prügelei *die;* ~, ~en (ugs.) punch-up (coll.); fight

Prügel·knabe *der* whipping boy

prügeln ① *tr. V.* (*auch itr.*) *V.* beat ② *refl. V.* **sich** ~: fight; **sich mit jmdm.** [**um etw.**] ~: fight sb. [over *or* for sth.]

Prunk *der;* ~[e]s splendour; magnificence

Prunk-: ~**bau** *der; Pl.* ~~ten magnificent building; ~**stück** *das* showpiece

PS /peː'|ɛs/ *das;* ~, ~: *Abk.* = **Pferdestärke** h.p.

Psalm *der;* ~s, ~en psalm

Psychiater *der;* ~s, ~, **Psychiaterin** *die;* ~, ~nen psychiatrist

Psychiatrie *die;* ~: psychiatry *no art.*

psychisch ① *Adj.* psychological; mental ⟨process, illness⟩ ② *adv.* psychologically; ~ **gesund/krank sein** be mentally fit/ill

psycho-: Psycho- /psyːço-/: ~**loge** *der;* ~~n, ~~n psychologist; ~**logie** *die;* ~~: psychology; ~**login** *die;* ~~, ~~nen psychologist; ~**logisch** ① *Adj.* psychological; ② *adv.* psychologically; ~**path** *der;* ~~en, ~~en, ~**pathin** *die;* ~~, ~~nen psychopath

Psychose *die;* ~, ~n psychosis

psychotisch *Adj.* psychotic

pubertär *Adj.* pubertal

Pubertät *die;* ~: puberty

pubertieren *itr. V.* reach puberty; ~d pubescent

publik *Adj.* ~ **sein/werden** be/become public knowledge

Publikum *das;* ~s (a) (Zuschauer, Zuhörer) audience; (bei Sportveranstaltungen) crowd
(b) (Kreis von Interessierten) public; (eines Schriftstellers) readership

(c) (Besucher) clientele

Publikums-: ~**erfolg** der success with the public; ~**liebling** der idol of the public; ~**sport** der spectator sport

publizieren tr. (auch itr.) V. publish

Publizität die; ~: publicity

Pudding der; ~s, ~e od. ~s thick, usually flavoured, milk-based dessert; ≈ blancmange

Pudel der; ~s, ~: poodle

Puder der; ~s, ~: powder

Puder·dose die powder compact

pudern tr. V. powder

Puder·zucker der icing sugar (Brit.); confectioners' sugar (Amer.)

Puff¹ der; ~[e]s, **Püffe** (ugs.) **(a)** (Stoß) thump; (leichter/kräftiger Stoß mit dem Ellenbogen) nudge/dig
(b) (Knall) bang

Puff² der od. das; ~s, ~s (salopp: Bordell) knocking shop (Brit. sl.); brothel

puffen (ugs.) tr. V.: ▶ PUFF¹ A: thump; nudge/dig

Puff·reis der puffed rice

Pulli der; ~s, ~s (ugs.), **Pullover** der; ~s, ~: pullover; sweater

Pullunder der; ~s, ~: slipover

Puls der; ~es, ~e pulse

Puls·ader die artery

Pult das; ~[e]s, ~e desk; (Lese~) lectern

Pulver das; ~s, ~: powder

pulverisieren tr. V. pulverize; powder

Pulver·kaffee der instant coffee

pumm[e]lig Adj. (ugs.) chubby

Pumpe die; ~, ~n pump

pumpen tr., itr. V. **(a)** (auch fig.) pump
(b) (salopp) ▶ LEIHEN A, B

Pump-: ~**spray** das pump spray; ~**zerstäuber** der pump-action atomizer

Punkt der; ~[e]s, ~e **(a)** (Tupfen) dot; (größer) spot
(b) (Satzzeichen) full stop
(c) (I-Punkt) dot
(d) (Stelle) point; **ein schwacher/wunder** ~ (fig.) a weak/sore point
(e) (Gegenstand, Thema, Abschnitt) point; (einer Tagesordnung) item
(f) (Bewertungs~) point; (bei einer Prüfung) mark
(g) ~ **12 Uhr** at 12 o'clock on the dot

pünktlich 1 Adj. punctual
2 adv. punctually; on time

Pünktlichkeit die; ~: punctuality

Punsch der; ~[e]s, ~e od. **Pünsche** punch

Pupille die; ~, ~n pupil

Puppe die; ~, ~n **(a)** doll[y]
(b) (Marionette) puppet; marionette

Puppen-: ~**stube** die doll's house; dollhouse (Amer.); ~**wagen** der doll's pram

pur Adj. **(a)** (rein) pure
(b) (unvermischt) neat ⟨whisky etc.⟩; straight

Püree das; ~s, ~s **(a)** purée
(b) ▶ KARTOFFELBREI

pürieren tr. V. (Kochk.) purée ⟨potatoes, apples, etc.⟩; (zerstampfen) mash

Purpur der; ~s crimson

purzeln itr. V.; mit sein (fam.) tumble

pushen tr. V. **(a)** (Drogenjargon) push
(b) (Journalistenjargon) push

Puste die; ~ (salopp) puff; breath

Pustel die; ~, ~n pimple; pustule (Med.)

pusten (ugs.) tr., itr. V. blow

Pute die; ~, ~n turkey hen; (als Braten) turkey

Puter der; ~s, ~: turkeycock; (als Braten) turkey

Putsch der; ~[e]s, ~e putsch; coup [d'état]

putschen itr. V. organize a putsch or coup

Putsch·versuch der attempted putsch or coup

Putz der; ~es plaster; (für Außenmauern) rendering

putzen tr. V. **(a)** (blank reiben) polish
(b) (säubern) clean; groom ⟨horse⟩; [sich (Dat.)] **die Zähne/die Nase** ~: clean or brush one's teeth/blow one's nose
(c) auch itr. (sauber machen) clean ⟨room, shop, etc.⟩; ~ **gehen** work as a cleaner
(d) (vorbereiten) wash and prepare ⟨vegetables⟩

Putz-: ~**fimmel** der (ugs. abwertend) mania for cleaning; ~**frau** die cleaner

putzig Adj. (ugs.) (entzückend) sweet; cute (Amer.); (possierlich) funny; comical

Putz-: ~**lappen** der [cleaning] rag; cloth; ~**leute** Pl. cleaners; ~**mann** der cleaner; ~**mittel** das cleaning agent; ~**tuch** das; Pl. ~**tücher** cloth; (Lappen) [cleaning] rag

puzzeln /ˈpʊzln̩/ itr. V. do jigsaw puzzles/a jigsaw [puzzle]

Puzzle /ˈpʊzl/ das; ~s, ~s, **Puzzlespiel** das jigsaw [puzzle]

Pyjama /pyˈdʒaːma/ der (österr., schweiz. auch: das); ~s, ~s pyjamas pl.

Pyramide die; ~, ~n pyramid

pyramiden·förmig Adj. pyramidal; pyramid-shaped

Python der; ~s, ~s od. ~en, **Python·schlange** die python

p

Qq

q, Q /ku:/ *das;* ~, ~: q/Q
Quacksalber *der;* ~s, ~,
  Quacksalberin *die;* ~, ~nen (abwertend)
  quack [doctor]
Quader *der;* ~s, ~ *od.* (österr.:) ~n (a)
  (Steinblock) ashlar block; [rectangular] block
  of stone
  (b) (Geom.) rectangular parallelepiped;
  cuboid
Quadrat *das;* ~[e]s, ~e square
quadratisch *Adj.* square
Quadrat-: ~**meter** *der od. das* square
  metre; ~**wurzel** *die* (Math.) square root (aus
  of); ~**zahl** *die* square number
quaken *itr. V.* ‹duck› quack; ‹frog› croak
Qual *die;* ~, ~en (a) torment
  (b) (Schmerzen) agony; ~en pain *sing.;* agony
  sing.; (seelisch) torment *sing.*
quälen *tr. V.* (a) torment ‹person, animal›;
  be cruel to ‹animal›; (foltern) torture
  (b) (plagen) ‹cough etc.› plague; (belästigen)
  pester
Quälerei *die;* ~, ~en (a) torment; (Folter)
  torture; (Grausamkeit) cruelty
  (b) (das Belästigen) pestering
Qualifikation *die;* ~, ~en (a) (Ausbildung)
  qualifications *pl.*
  (b) (Sport) qualification
qualifizieren *refl. V.* (a) gain
  qualifications
  (b) (Sport) qualify
qualifiziert *Adj.* (a) ‹work, post› requiring
  particular qualifications
  (b) (sachkundig) competent; skilled ‹work›
Qualität *die;* ~, ~en quality
qualitativ ① *Adj.* qualitative; ‹difference,
  change› in quality
  ② *adv.* with regard to quality
Qualitäts-erzeugnis *das* quality product
Qualle *die;* ~, ~n jellyfish
Qualm *der;* ~[e]s [thick] smoke
qualmen *itr. V.* (a) give off clouds of [thick]
  smoke
  (b) (ugs.: rauchen) puff away
qualmig *Adj.* (ugs.) thick with smoke
  postpos.; smoke-filled
qual·voll ① *Adj.* agonizing
  ② *adv.* agonizingly
Quantität *die;* ~, ~en quantity
quantitativ ① *Adj.* quantitative
  ② *adv.* quantitatively
Quantum *das;* ~s, Quanten quota (an +
  Dat. of); (Dosis) dose

Quarantäne /karan'tɛ:nə/ *die;* ~, ~n
  quarantine
Quark *der;* ~s quark
Quark-speise *die* quark dish
Quartal *das;* ~s, ~e quarter [of the year]
Quartett *das;* ~[e]s, ~e (a) quartet
  (b) (Spiel) ≈ Happy Families; (Satz von vier
  Karten) set [of four]
Quartier *das;* ~s, ~e accommodation *no
  indef. art.;* accommodations *pl.* (Amer.); place
  to stay; (Mil.) quarters *pl.*
Quarz *der;* ~es, ~e quartz
Quarz·uhr *die* quartz clock; (Armbanduhr)
  quartz watch
quasi *Adv.* [so] ~: more or less; (so gut wie)
  as good as
quasseln (ugs.) ① *itr. V.* chatter; rabbit on
  (Brit. sl.) (von about)
  ② *tr. V.* spout, babble ‹nonsense›
Quaste *die;* ~, ~n tassel
Quatsch *der;* ~[e]s (ugs.) (a) (Äußerung)
  rubbish
  (b) (Handlung) nonsense; (Unfug) messing
  about; **lass den** ~: stop that nonsense
quatschen (ugs.) ① *itr. V.* (a) (dumm reden)
  rabbit on (Brit. coll.)
  (b) (klatschen) gossip; **es wird so viel
  gequatscht** there is so much gossip
  (c) (sich unterhalten) [have a] chat *or* (coll.)
  natter
  ② *tr. V.* (äußern) spout ‹nonsense, rubbish›
Quatsch-kopf *der* (salopp) stupid
  chatterbox; (Schwätzer, Schwafler) windbag
Queck·silber *das* mercury
Quell-bewölkung *die* (Met.) cumulus
  clouds *pl.*
Quelle *die;* ~, ~n spring; (eines Flusses; fig.)
  source
quellen *unr. itr. V.; mit sein* (a) ‹liquid›
  gush, stream; (aus der Erde) well up; ‹smoke›
  billow
  (b) (sich ausdehnen) swell [up]
Quell-wasser *das; Pl.* ~ *od.* Quell-wässer
  spring water
quengeln *itr. V.* (auch tr.) *V.* (ugs.) (a) (weinen)
  ‹baby› whimper, (coll.) grizzle
  (b) (drängen) nag
  (c) (nörgeln) carp
quer *Adv.* sideways; (schräg) diagonally;
  (rechtwinklig) at right angles; ~ **durch/über**
  (+ *Akk.*) straight through/across
Quer-: ~**achse** *die* transverse axis;
  ~**denker** *der,* ~**denkerin** *die* lateral
  thinker

Quere *die* jmdm. in die ∼ kommen bump into sb. (coll.); (fig.: jmdn. behindern) get in sb.'s way (coll.)

quer-, Quer-: ∼**flöte** *die* transverse flute; ∼**format** *das* landscape format; ∼**kopf** *der* (ugs.) awkward cuss (coll.); (komischer Kauz) oddball (coll.); ∼**köpfig** *Adj.* awkward; perverse; ∼**schläger** *der* deflected shot; ricochet; ∼**schnitt** *der* (*auch fig.*) cross section; ∼**schnitt[s]-gelähmt** *Adj.* (Med.) paraplegic; ∼**straße** *die* intersecting road; ∼**treiber** *der;* ∼∼s, ∼∼, ∼**treiberin** *die;* ∼∼, ∼∼nen (ugs. abwertend) troublemaker

Querulant *der;* ∼en, ∼en, **Querulantin** *die;* ∼, ∼nen (abwertend) malcontent

quetschen *tr. V.* crush; sich (*Dat.*) die Hand ∼: get one's hand caught

Quetschung *die;* ∼, ∼en bruise; contusion (Med.)

quietschen *itr. V.* squeak; ⟨brakes, tyres⟩ squeal, screech; (ugs.) ⟨person⟩ squeal, shriek

Quirl *der;* ∼[e]s, ∼e long-handled blender *with a star-shaped head*

quirlig *Adj.* lively; (flink) nimble

quitt *Adj.* (ugs.) quits

Quitte *die;* ∼, ∼n quince

quittieren *tr. V.* (a) *auch itr.* acknowledge, confirm ⟨receipt, condition⟩; give a receipt for ⟨sum, invoice⟩
(b) etw. mit etw. ∼: react *or* respond to sth. with sth.

Quittung *die;* ∼, ∼en (a) receipt
(b) (fig.) come-uppance (coll.)

Quiz /kvɪs/ *das;* ∼, ∼: quiz

quoll *1. u. 3. Pers. Sg. Prät. v.* QUELLEN

Quote *die;* ∼, ∼n proportion

Quoten-regelung *die: requirement that women should be adequately represented*

Quotient *der;* ∼en, ∼en (Math.) quotient (aus of)

Rr

r, R /ɛr/ *das;* ∼, ∼: r/R

Rabatt *der;* ∼[e]s, ∼e discount

Rabatte *die;* ∼, ∼n border

Rabbi *der;* ∼[s], ∼nen *od.* ∼s (a) (Titel) Rabbi
(b) (Person) rabbi

Rabbiner *der;* ∼s, ∼: rabbi

Rabe *der;* ∼n, ∼n raven

Rabenmutter *die; Pl.* Rabenmütter (abwertend) uncaring [brute of a] mother

rabiat ① *Adj.* violent; brutal; ruthless ⟨methods⟩
② *adv.* (gewalttätig) violently; brutally

Rache *die;* ∼: revenge; [an jmdm.] ∼ nehmen take revenge [on sb.]

Rache-akt *der* (geh.) act of revenge, reprisal (*Gen.* by, on the part of)

Rachen *der;* ∼s, ∼ (a) (Schlund) pharynx (Anat.)
(b) (Maul) mouth; maw (literary); (fig.) jaws *pl.*

rächen ① *tr. V.* avenge ⟨person, crime⟩; take revenge for ⟨insult, crime⟩
② *refl. V.* (a) take one's revenge
(b) ⟨mistake etc.⟩ take its/their toll

Rachitis *die;* ∼ (Med.) rickets *sing.*

Rach-sucht *die* (geh.) lust for revenge

rach-süchtig (geh.) ① *Adj.* vengeful
② *adv.* vengefully

Rad *das;* ∼es, Räder (a) wheel; das fünfte ∼ am Wagen sein (fig. ugs.) be superfluous; ein ∼ abhaben (fig. ugs.) have a screw loose (coll.)

(b) (Fahrrad) bicycle; bike (coll.); ∼ fahren cycle; ride a bicycle *or* (coll.) bike

Radar *der od. das;* ∼s radar

Radar-: ∼**falle** *die* (ugs.) [radar] speed trap; ∼**kontrolle** *die* [radar] speed check; ∼**schirm** *der* radar screen

Rad-dampfer *der* paddle steamer

radeln *itr. V.; mit sein* (ugs., bes. südd.) cycle

Rädels-führer *der,* **Rädels-führerin** *die* (abwertend) ringleader

rad-, Rad-: *∼fahren* ▶ RAD B; ∼**fahrer** *der,* ∼**fahrerin** *die* cyclist

Radien ▶ RADIUS

radieren *tr. (auch itr.) V.* erase

Radier-gummi *der* rubber [eraser]

Radierung *die;* ∼, ∼en (Grafik) etching

Radieschen *das;* ∼s, ∼: radish

radikal ① *Adj.* radical; drastic ⟨measure, method, cure⟩
② *adv.* radically; (vollständig) totally

Radikalismus *der;* ∼: radicalism

Radikalität *die;* ∼: radicalness; radical nature

Radio *das* (südd., schweiz. auch: *der*); ∼s, ∼s radio; ∼ hören listen to the radio

radio-, Radio-: ∼**aktiv** /⎯⎯'-/ ① *Adj.* radioactive; ② *adv.* radioactively; ∼**aktivität** /⎯⎯'-/ *die* radioactivity; ∼**sender** *der* radio station; ∼**wecker** *der* radio alarm clock

Radius *der;* ∼, Radien radius

Rad-: ~**kappe** die hubcap; ~**lager** das
wheel bearing

Radler der; ~s, ~: (a) cyclist
  (b) (bes. südd.: Getränk) shandy

Radlerin die; ~, ~**nen** cyclist

Rad-: ~**rennbahn** die cycle racing track;
~**rennen** das cycle race; (Sport) cycle
racing; ~**sport** der cycling no def. art.;
~**tour** die cycling tour; ~**weg** der cycle
path or track

raffen tr. V. (a) snatch; rake in (coll.)
  ⟨money⟩; etw. [an sich] ~: seize sth.; (eilig)
  snatch sth.
  (b) gather ⟨material, curtain⟩

Raffinerie die; ~, ~**n** refinery

Raffinesse die; ~, ~**n** (a) (Schlauheit) guile;
  ingenuity
  (b) (Finesse) refinement

raffiniert ⊞ Adj. (a) ingenious ⟨plan,
  design⟩; (verfeinert) refined, subtle ⟨colour,
  scheme, effect⟩; sophisticated ⟨dish, cut (of
  clothes)⟩
  (b) (gerissen) cunning ⟨person, trick⟩
  ⊡ adv. (a) ingeniously; (verfeinert) with great
  refinement/sophistication
  (b) (gerissen) cunningly

Raffiniertheit die; ~ (a) (Klugheit)
  ingenuity; (Verfeinerung) refinement;
  sophistication
  (b) (Gerissenheit) cunning

Raft das; ~s, ~s raft

raften itr. V. raft

Rafting das; ~s rafting

Rage /'ra:ʒə/ die; ~ (ugs.) fury

ragen itr. V. (a) (vertikal) rise [up];
  ⟨mountains⟩ tower up
  (b) (horizontal) project, stick out (in + Akk.
  into; über + Akk. over)

Ragout /ra'gu:/ das; ~s, ~s ragout

Rahm der; ~[e]s cream

rahmen tr. V. frame

Rahmen der; ~s, ~ (a) frame; (Fahrgestell)
  chassis
  (b) (fig.) framework

Rakete die; ~, ~**n** rocket; (Lenkflugkörper)
  missile

rammen tr. V. ram

Rampe die; ~, ~**n** (a) (Lade~) [loading]
  platform
  (b) (schiefe Fläche) ramp

Rampen-licht das: im ~ [der
  Öffentlichkeit] stehen be in the limelight

Ramsch der; ~[e]s, ~e (ugs.) (a) (Ware)
  trashy goods pl.;
  (b) (Kram) junk

ran Adv. (ugs.) (a) ▶ HERAN;
  (b) (fang[t] an) off you go; (fangen wir an) let's
  go
  (c) (greif[t] an) go at him/them!

Rand der; ~[e]s, **Ränder** (a) edge; (Einfassung)

border; (Hut~) brim; (Brillen~, Gefäß~,
Krater~) rim; (eines Abgrunds) brink; (auf einem
Schriftstück) margin; (Weg~) verge; (Stadt~)
outskirts pl.;
  (b) (Schmutz~) mark; (rund) ring

randalieren itr. V. riot

Randalierer der; ~s, ~,
  Randaliererin die; ~, ~**nen** hooligan

rand-, Rand-: ~**bemerkung** die
  marginal note or comment; ~**gruppe** die
  (Soziol.) fringe or marginal group; ~**stein**
  der kerb; ~**voll** Adj. ⟨glass etc.⟩ full to the
  brim

rang 1. u. 3. Pers. Sg. Prät. v. RINGEN

Rang der; ~[e]s, **Ränge** (a) rank; (in der
  Gesellschaft) status
  (b) (im Theater) circle; erster ~: dress circle;
  zweiter ~: upper circle; dritter ~: gallery

rangieren /raŋ'ʒi:rən/ tr. V. shunt ⟨trucks
  etc.⟩; switch ⟨cars⟩ (Amer.)

Rang-: ~**liste** die ranking list; **Nummer
  eins der internationalen** ~**liste** number one
  in the world rankings; ~**ordnung** die
  order of precedence; (Verhaltensf.) pecking
  order

Ranke die; ~, ~**n** (Bot.) tendril

ranken refl. V. climb, grow (an + Dat. up,
  über + Akk. over)

Ranking /'ræŋkɪŋ/ das; ~s ranking

rann 1. u. 3. Pers. Sg. Prät. v. RINNEN

rannte 1. u. 3. Pers. Sg. Prät. v. RENNEN

Ranzen der; ~s, ~: satchel

ranzig Adj. rancid

Rap /ræp/ der; ~[s], ~s rap

Rappe der; ~n, ~n black horse

rappen /'ræpn̩/ itr. V. rap

Rappen der; ~s, ~: [Swiss] centime

Rapper /'ræpɐ/ der; ~s, ~, **Rapperin** die;
  ~, ~**nen** rapper

Raps der; ~es (Bot.) rape

rar Adj. scarce; (selten) rare

Rarität die; ~, ~**en** rarity

rasant (ugs.) ⊞ Adj. tremendously fast (coll.)
  ⟨car, horse, etc.⟩
  ⊡ adv. at terrific speed (coll.)

rasch ⊞ Adj. quick; speedy, swift ⟨end,
  action, decision, progress⟩
  ⊡ adv. quickly; ⟨decide, end, proceed⟩
  swiftly, rapidly

rascheln itr. V. rustle; ⟨mouse etc.⟩ make a
  rustling noise

rasen itr. V. (a) mit sein (ugs.: eilen) dash or
  rush [along]; (fahren) tear or race along; (fig.)
  ⟨pulse⟩ race
  (b) (toben) ⟨person⟩ rage

Rasen der; ~s, ~: grass no indef. art.;
  (gepflegte Rasenfläche) lawn

rasend ⊞ Adj. (a) (sehr schnell) breakneck
  attrib. ⟨speed⟩
  (b) (tobend) raging
  (c) (heftig) violent
  ⊡ adv. (ugs.) incredibly (coll.)

---
*old spelling - see note on page xiv

Rasen·mäher *der;* ~s, ~: lawn-mower

Raser *der;* ~s, ~ (ugs. abwertend) speed
merchant (coll.); (rücksichtslos) road hog

Raserei *die;* ~, ~en (ugs.) tearing along *no
art.*

Raserin *die;* ~, ~nen ▶ RASER

Rasier·apparat *der* [safety] razor;
(elektrisch) electric shaver

rasieren *tr. V.* shave; **sich** ~: shave; **sich
nass/trocken/elektrisch** ~: have a wet
shave/have a dry shave/use an electric
shaver

Rasierer *der;* ~s, ~ (ugs.) [electric] shaver

Rasier-: ~**klinge** *die* razor blade;
~**messer** *das* cutthroat razor; ~**pinsel**
der shaving brush; ~**schaum** *der* shaving
foam; ~**seife** *die* shaving soap;
~**wasser** *das* aftershave; (vor der Rasur)
pre-shave lotion

Räson /rɛ'zɔŋ/ *die* zur ~ kommen come to
one's senses; jmdn. zur ~ bringen make sb.
see reason

Rasse *die;* ~, ~n (a) breed
(b) (Menschen~) race

Rassel *die;* ~, ~n rattle

rasseln *itr. V.* rattle

Rassen-: ~**hass,** ***~**haß** *der* racial
hatred *no art.;* ~**krawall** *der* race riot;
~**trennung** *die* racial segregation *no art.*

Rassismus *der;* ~: racism; racialism

Rassist *der;* ~en, ~en, **Rassistin** *die;*
~, ~nen racist; racialist

rassistisch *Adj.* racist; racialist

Rast *die;* ~, ~en rest; ~ machen stop for a
break

rasten *itr. V.* rest; take a rest *or* break

Raster *der;* ~s, ~ (a) (Druckw.) screen
(b) (fig.) [conceptual] framework; set pattern

Rast-: ~**haus** *das* roadside café; (an der
Autobahn) motorway restaurant; ~**hof** *der*
[motorway] motel [and service area];
~**platz** *der* (a) place to rest; (b) (an
Autobahnen) parking place (*with benches and
WCs*); picnic area; ~**stätte** *die* service
area

Rasur *die;* ~, ~en shave

Rat *der;* ~[e]s, Räte (a) advice; ein ~: a
word of advice
(b) (Gremium) council

rät *3. Pers. Sg. Präsens v.* RATEN

Rate *die,* ~, ~n (a) (Teilbetrag) instalment;
etw. auf ~n kaufen buy sth. by instalments
or (Brit.) on hire purchase *or* (Amer.) on the
installment plan
(b) (Statistik) rate

raten [1] *unr. itr. V.* (a) jmdm. ~: advise sb.
(b) (schätzen) guess
[2] *tr. V.* (a) jmdm. ~, etw. zu tun advise sb.
to do sth.
(b) (erraten) guess

Raten·zahlung *die* payment by
instalments

Rat·haus *das* town hall

Ratifizierung *die;* ~, ~en ratification

Rätin *die;* ~, ~nen councillor

Ration *die;* ~, ~en ration

rational *Adj.* rational

rationalisieren *tr., itr. V.* rationalize

rationell [1] *Adj.* efficient; (wirtschaftlich)
economic
[2] *adv.* efficiently; (wirtschaftlich) economically

rationieren *tr. V.* ration

rat·los [1] *Adj.* baffled; helpless ⟨look⟩
[2] *adv.* helplessly

Rat·losigkeit *die;* ~: helplessness

ratsam *Adj.* advisable

Ratschlag *der* [piece of] advice

Rätsel *das;* ~s, ~ (a) riddle; (Bilder~,
Kreuzwort~ usw.) puzzle
(b) (Geheimnis) mystery

rätselhaft [1] *Adj.* mysterious;
(unergründlich) enigmatic
[2] *adv.* mysteriously; (unergründlich)
enigmatically

rätseln *itr. V.* puzzle, rack one's brains
(über + *Akk.* over); ~, wer .../ob ...: try to
work out who .../whether ...

Ratte *die;* ~, ~n (auch fig.) rat

rau [1] *Adj.* (a) (nicht glatt) rough
(b) (nicht mild) harsh, raw ⟨climate, winter⟩;
raw ⟨wind⟩
(c) (kratzig) husky, hoarse ⟨voice⟩
(d) (entzündet) sore ⟨throat⟩
(e) (grob, nicht feinfühlig) rough; harsh ⟨words,
tone⟩
[2] *adv.* (a) (kratzig) ⟨speak etc.⟩ huskily,
hoarsely
(b) (grob, nicht feinfühlig) roughly

Raub *der;* ~[e]s (a) robbery
(b) (Beute) stolen goods *pl.*

Raub·bau *der* overexploitation (an + *Dat.*
of); ~ an etw. (*Dat.*) treiben over-exploit sth.

rauben *tr. V.* steal; kidnap ⟨person⟩; jmdm.
etw. ~: rob sb. of sth.; (geh.: wegnehmen)
deprive sb. of sth.

Räuber *der;* ~s, ~, **Räuberin** *die;* ~,
~nen robber

Raub-: ~**fisch** *der* predatory fish;
~**kopie** *die* pirated copy; ~**mord** *der*
(Rechtsw.) murder (an + *Dat.* of) in the
course of a robbery *or* with robbery as
motive; ~**tier** *das* predator; ~**überfall**
der robbery (auf + *Akk.* of); ~**vogel** *der*
bird of prey

Rauch *der;* ~[e]s smoke

rauchen [1] *itr. V.* smoke
[2] *tr. V.* (auch itr.) *V.* smoke ⟨cigarette, pipe,
etc.⟩; „Rauchen verboten" 'No smoking'

Raucher *der;* ~s, ~: smoker

Raucher-: ~**abteil** *das* smoking
compartment; smoker; ~**husten** *der*
smoker's cough

Raucherin *die;* ~, ~nen smoker

räuchern *tr. V.* smoke ⟨meat, fish⟩

rauchig *Adj.* smoky; husky ‹*voice*›

Rauch-: ∼**melder** *der* smoke detector;
∼**schwaden** *der* cloud of smoke;
∼**verbot** *das* ban on smoking; ∼**wolke**
die cloud of smoke

räudig *Adj.* mangy

rauf *Adv.* (ugs.) up; ∼ **mit euch!** up you go!;
s. auch HERAUF; HINAUF

Rau·faser·tapete *die* woodchip wallpaper

raufen ① *itr., refl. V.* fight
② *tr. V.* **sich** (*Dat.*) **die Haare/den Bart** ∼:
tear one's hair/at one's beard

Rauferei *die;* ∼, ∼**en** fight

*∗**rauh** *usw.* ▶ RAU *usw.*

Raum *der;* ∼[e]s, **Räume** (a) (Wohn∼, Nutz∼)
room
(b) (Gebiet) area; region
(c) (Platz) room; space

räumen *tr. V.* (a) clear [away]; clear ‹*snow*›
(b) (an einen Ort) clear; move
(c) (freimachen) clear ‹*street, building,
warehouse, stocks, etc.*›
(d) (verlassen) vacate

Raum·fahrt *die;* ∼: space travel

räumlich ① *Adj.* (a) spatial; **aus** ∼**en
Gründen** for reasons of space
(b) (dreidimensional) three-dimensional;
stereoscopic ‹*vision*›
② *adv.* (a) spatially
(b) (dreidimensional) three-dimensionally

Räumlichkeit *die;* ∼, ∼**en** (a) *Pl.* rooms
(b) (räumliche Wirkung) three-dimensionality

Raum-: ∼**schiff** *das* spaceship; ∼**sonde**
die space probe

Räumung *die;* ∼, ∼**en** (a) clearing
(b) (das Verlassen) vacation; vacating
(c) (wegen Gefahr) evacuation
(d) (eines Lagers) clearance

Räumungs·verkauf *der* (Kaufmannsspr.)
clearance sale

raunen *tr., itr. V.* (geh.) whisper

Raupe *die;* ∼, ∼**n** caterpillar

Rau·reif *der* hoar frost

raus *Adv.* (ugs.) out; ∼ **mit euch!** out you go!;
s. auch HERAUS; HINAUS

Rausch *der;* ∼[e]s, **Räusche** (a) state of
drunkenness
(b) (starkes Gefühl) transport; **der** ∼ **der
Geschwindigkeit** the exhilaration *or* thrill of
speed

rauschen *itr. V.* ‹*water, wind, torrent*›
rush; ‹*trees, leaves*› rustle; ‹*skirt, curtains,
silk*› swish; ‹*waterfall, strong wind*› roar;
‹*rain*› pour down

Rausch·gift *das* drug; narcotic; ∼ **nehmen**
take drugs; be on drugs

Rauschgift-: ∼**händler** *der,*
∼**händlerin** *die* drug trafficker; ∼**sucht**
die drug addiction

raus∣fliegen *unr. itr. V.; mit sein* (ugs.) be
fired (coll.)

räuspern *refl. V.* clear one's throat

raus∣schmeißen *unr. tr. V.* (ugs.) chuck
(coll.) ‹*objects*› out *or* away; give ‹*employee*›
the push (coll.) *or* sack (coll.); chuck (coll.) *or*
throw ‹*customer, drunk, tenant*› out (**aus** of)

Raute *die;* ∼, ∼**n** (Geom.) rhombus

Rave /reɪv/ *der;* ∼s, ∼s rave

Raver /ˈreɪvɐ/ *der;* ∼s, ∼, **Raverin** *die;* ∼,
∼**nen** raver

Razzia *die;* ∼, **Razzien** raid

reagieren *itr. V.* react (**auf** + *Akk.* to)

Reaktion *die;* ∼, ∼**en** reaction (**auf** + *Akk.*
to)

reaktionär *Adj.* reactionary

Reaktionär *der;* ∼**s**, ∼**e** reactionary

Reaktor *der;* ∼**s**, ∼**en** /-ˈtoːrən/ reactor

real ① *Adj.* real
② *adv.* actually

realisieren *tr. V.* (geh.) realize

Realismus *der;* ∼: realism

Realist *der;* ∼**en**, ∼**en**, **Realistin** *die;* ∼,
∼**nen** realist

realistisch ① *Adj.* realistic
② *adv.* realistically

Realität *die;* ∼, ∼**en** reality

Real·schule *die* ≈ secondary modern
school (Brit. Hist.)

Rebe *die;* ∼, ∼**n** (a) vine shoot
(b) (Weinstock) [grape] vine

Rebell *der;* ∼**en**, ∼**en**, **Rebellin** *die;* ∼,
∼**nen** rebel

rebellieren *itr. V.* rebel (**gegen** against)

Rebellion *die;* ∼, ∼**en** rebellion

rebellisch *Adj.* rebellious

Reb-: ∼**huhn** *das* partridge; ∼**stock** *der*
vine

rechen *tr. V.* (bes. südd.) rake

Rechen *der;* ∼**s**, ∼ (bes. südd.) rake

Rechen-: ∼**fehler** *der* arithmetical error;
∼**maschine** *die* calculator

Rechenschaft *die;* ∼: account; **jmdn. für
etw. zur** ∼ **ziehen** call *or* bring sb. to account
for sth.

Rechenschafts·bericht *der* report

Recherche /reˈʃɛrʃə/ *die;* ∼, ∼**n** (a) (geh.)
investigation; enquiry
(b) (DV) search

recherchieren *itr., tr. V.* (geh.) investigate

rechnen ① *tr. V.* (a) **eine Aufgabe** ∼: work
out a problem
(b) (veranschlagen) reckon; estimate; **gut/rund
gerechnet** at a generous/rough estimate
(c) (berücksichtigen) take into account
(d) (einbeziehen) count
② *itr. V.* (a) do *or* make a calculation/
calculations; **gut/schlecht** ∼ **können** be good/
bad at figures
(b) (zählen) reckon
(c) (ugs.: berechnen) calculate; estimate

(d) (wirtschaften) budget carefully
(e) auf jmdn./etw. od. mit jmdn./etw. ∼: count on sb./sth.
(f) mit etw. ∼ (etw. einkalkulieren) reckon with sth.; (etw. erwarten) expect sth.

Rechnen *das;* ∼s arithmetic

Rechner *der;* ∼s, ∼: calculator; (Computer) computer

rechnerisch *Adj.* arithmetical

Rechnung *die;* ∼, ∼en **(a)** calculation
(b) (schriftliche Kosten∼) bill; invoice
(Commerc.); [jmdm.] etw. in ∼ stellen charge [sb.] for sth.

recht ⒈ *Adj.* **(a)** (geeignet, richtig) right
(b) (gesetzmäßig, anständig) right; proper; ∼ **und billig** right and proper
(c) (wunschgemäß) jmdm. ∼ **sein** be all right with sb.
(d) (wirklich, echt) real
⒉ *adv.* **(a)** (geeignet) du kommst gerade ∼: you are just in time
(b) (richtig) correctly
(c) (gesetzmäßig, anständig) properly
(d) (wunschgemäß) es jmdm. ∼ machen please sb.
(e) (wirklich, echt) really
(f) (ziemlich) quite; rather; *s. auch* RECHT D

Recht *das;* ∼[e]s, ∼e **(a)** (Rechtsordnung) law
(b) (Rechtsanspruch) right; **sein** ∼ **fordern** *od.* **verlangen** demand one's rights
(c) (Berechtigung) right (**auf** + *Akk.* to); **gleiches** ∼ **für alle!** equal rights for all!; **im** ∼ **sein** be in the right; **zu** ∼: rightly
(d) ∼ **haben** be right; **jmdm.** ∼ **geben** admit that sb. is right

recht... *Adj.* **(a)** right; right[-hand] 〈edge〉
(b) (außen, sichtbar) right 〈side〉
(c) (in der Politik) right-wing

recht·fertigen *tr. V.* justify (**vor** + *Dat.* to)

Recht·fertigung *die* justification

rechtlich ⒈ *Adj.* legal
⒉ *adv.* legally

Rechtlichkeit *die;* ∼ *s.:* RECHTMÄSSIGKEIT

recht·los *Adj.* without rights *postpos.*

Rechtlosigkeit *die;* ∼: lack of rights

rechtmäßig ⒈ *Adj.* lawful; rightful; legitimate 〈claim〉
⒉ *adv.* lawfully; rightfully

Rechtmäßigkeit *die;* ∼: legality; (eines Anspruchs) legitimacy

rechts *Adv.* **(a)** on the right; **von** ∼: from the right
(b) (Politik) on the right wing

Rechts-: ∼**abbieger** *der,*
∼**abbiegerin** *die* (Verkehrsw.) motorist/ cyclist/car *etc.* turning right; ∼**anwalt** *der,* ∼**anwältin** *die* lawyer; solicitor (Brit.); attorney (Amer.); (vor Gericht) barrister (Brit.); attorney[-at-law] (Amer.); advocate (Scot.);
∼**außen** /·'-·/ *der;* ∼, ∼ (Ballspiele) right wing; outside right

recht-, Recht-: ∼**schaffen** ⒈ *Adj.*

honest; ⒉ *adv.* honestly;
∼**schreib·fehler** *der* spelling mistake;
∼**schreibung** *die* orthography

rechts-, Rechts-: ∼**empfinden** *das* sense of [what is] right and wrong;
∼**extremist** *der,* ∼**extremistin** *die* (Politik) right-wing extremist; ∼**händer** *der;* ∼∼s, ∼∼, ∼**händerin** *die;* ∼∼, ∼∼nen right-hander; ∼**kräftig** (Rechtsw.) ⒈ *Adj.* final [and absolute] 〈decision, verdict, etc.〉;
⒉ *adv.* jmdn. ∼**kräftig verurteilen** pass a final sentence on sb.; ∼**kurve** *die* right-hand bend

Recht·sprechung *die;* ∼, ∼en administration of justice; (eines Gerichts) jurisdiction

rechts-, Rechts-: ∼**radikal** (Politik) ⒈ *Adj.* radical right-wing; ⒉ *adv.* **eine** ∼**radikal orientierte Gruppe** a group with a radical right-wing orientation; ∼**radikale** *der/die* right-wing radical;
∼**radikalismus** *der* right-wing radicalism; ∼**staat** *der* [constitutional] state founded on the rule of law;
∼**staatlich** *Adj.* founded on the rule of law *postpos.;* ∼**verkehr** *der* driving *no art.* on the right; ∼**verletzung** *die* (Rechtsw.) infringement *or* violation of the law;
∼**widrig** ⒈ *Adj.* unlawful; ⒉ *adv.* unlawfully; ∼**widrigkeit** *die* (a) unlawfulness; **(b)** (Handlung) unlawful act

recht-: ∼**wink[e]lig** *Adj.* right-angled;
∼**zeitig** ⒈ *Adj.* timely; (pünktlich) punctual; ⒉ *adv.* in time; (pünktlich) on time

Reck *das;* ∼[e]s, ∼e *od.* ∼s horizontal bar

recken ⒈ *tr. V.* stretch
⒉ *refl. V.* stretch oneself

recyceln /ri'saɪ:kln̩/ *tr. V.; 2. Part.* **recycelt** recycle

Recycling /ri'saɪ:klɪŋ/ *das;* ∼s recycling

Recycling·papier /ri'saɪ:klɪŋ-/ *das* recycled paper

Redakteur /redak'tøːɐ̯/ *der;* ∼s, ∼e,
Redakteurin *die;* ∼, ∼nen editor

Redaktion *die;* ∼, ∼en **(a)** (Redakteure) editorial staff
(b) (Büro) editorial department *or* office/ offices *pl.*

redaktionell ⒈ *Adj.* editorial
⒉ *adv.* editorially

Rede *die;* ∼, ∼n **(a)** (Ansprache) address; speech; **eine** ∼ **halten** give *or* make a speech
(b) (Vortrag) rhetoric
(c) (Äußerung, Ansicht) **nicht der** ∼ **wert sein** be not worth mentioning; **jmdn. zur** ∼ **stellen** make someone explain himself/ herself; **von jmdm./etw. ist die** ∼: there is some talk about sb./sth.; **es ist die** ∼ **davon, dass** ...: it is being said *or* people are saying that ...; **davon kann keine** ∼ **sein** it's out of the question

reden ⒈ *tr. V.* talk; **Unsinn** ∼: talk nonsense; **kein Wort** ∼: not say *or* speak a word   ⋯⋄

2 *itr. V.* (a) (sprechen) talk; speak; **viel/wenig**
~: talk a lot (coll.)/not talk much
(b) (sich äußern, eine Rede halten) speak; **gut ~**
können be a good speaker
(c) (sich unterhalten) talk; **mit jmdm./über jmdn.**
~: talk to/about sb.

Redens·art *die* (a) expression; (Sprichwort)
saying
(b) *Pl.* (Phrase) empty *or* meaningless words

Rede·wendung *die* (Sprachw.) idiom

redlich 1 *Adj.* honest
2 *adv.* honestly

Redlichkeit *die;* ~: honesty

Redner *der;* ~s, ~, **Rednerin** *die* ~,
~nen (a) speaker
(b) (Rhetoriker) orator

red·selig *Adj.* talkative

reduzieren 1 *tr. V.* reduce (**auf** + *Akk.* to)
2 *refl. V.* decrease; diminish

Reeder *der;* ~s, ~: shipowner

Reederei *die;* ~, ~en shipping firm

Reederin *die;* ~, ~nen shipowner

reell 1 *Adj.* honest, straight ⟨person, deal,
etc.⟩; sound, solid ⟨business, firm, etc.⟩;
straight ⟨offer⟩
2 *adv.* honestly

Reet *das;* ~s (nordd.) reeds *pl.*

Referat *das;* ~[e]s, ~e (a) paper
(b) (kurzer schriftlicher Bericht) report

Referendar *der;* ~s, ~e, **Referendarin**
die; ~, ~nen *candidate for a higher civil-
service post who has passed the first state
examination and is undergoing in-service
training*

Referenz *die;* ~, ~en (Person, Stelle) referee;
jmdn. als ~ angeben give sb.'s name *or* give
sb. as a reference

referieren *itr. V.* über etw. (*Akk.*) ~:
present a paper on sth.; (zusammenfassend)
give a report on sth.

reflektieren *tr. V.* reflect

Reflex *der;* ~es, ~e reflex

Reflexion *die;* ~, ~en reflection

Reflexiv·pronomen *das* (Sprachw.)
reflexive pronoun

Reform *die;* ~, ~en reform

Reformation *die;* ~ (hist.) Reformation

Reformations·fest *das* Reformation Day

Reform·haus *das* health food shop

reformieren *tr. V.* reform

Refrain /rə'frɛ̃:/ *der;* ~s, ~s chorus

Regal *das;* ~s, ~e [set *sing.* of] shelves *pl.*

rege 1 *Adj.* (a) (betriebsam) busy ⟨traffic⟩;
brisk ⟨demand, trade, business, etc.⟩
(b) (lebhaft) lively; keen ⟨interest⟩
2 *adv.* (a) (betriebsam) actively
(b) (lebhaft) actively

Regel *die;* ~, ~n (a) rule; **nach allen ~n**
der Kunst (fig.) well and truly

(b) rule; custom; **die ~ sein** be the rule; **in**
der *od.* **aller ~:** as a rule
(c) (Menstruation) period

regel·mäßig 1 *Adj.* regular
2 *adv.* regularly

Regel·mäßigkeit *die* regularity

regeln 1 *tr. V.* (a) settle ⟨matter, question,
etc.⟩; put ⟨finances, affairs, etc.⟩ in order
(b) (einstellen, regulieren) regulate; (steuern)
control
2 *refl. V.* take care of itself

regelrecht 1 *Adj.* (ugs.: richtiggehend)
proper (coll.); real; real ⟨shock⟩; real, absolute
⟨scandal⟩; complete, utter ⟨flop, disaster⟩; **ich**
hatte ~e Angst I was really afraid
2 *adv.* (ugs.: richtiggehend) really

Regelung *die;* ~, ~en (a) ▶ REGELN 1A, B:
settlement; putting in order; regulation;
control
(b) (Vorschrift) regulation

regen 1 *tr. V.* (geh.) move
2 *refl. V.* (a) (sich bewegen) move
(b) (geh.) ⟨hope, doubt, desire, conscience⟩ stir

Regen *der;* ~s, ~ (a) rain; **vom** *od.* **aus**
dem ~ in die Traufe kommen (fig.) jump out
of the frying pan into the fire
(b) (fig.) shower

Regen-: ~**bogen** *der* rainbow; ~**mantel**
der raincoat; mackintosh; ~**schirm** *der*
umbrella; ~**tag** *der* rainy day; ~**wald** *der*
(Geogr.) rainforest; ~**wasser** *das*
rainwater; ~**wetter** *das* wet weather;
~**wolke** *die* rain cloud; ~**wurm** *der*
earthworm; ~**zeit** *die* rainy season

Regie /re'ʒi:/ *die;* ~ (a) (Theater, Film, Ferns.,
Rundf.) direction; **die ~ bei etw. haben** *od.*
führen direct sth.
(b) (Leitung, Verwaltung) management

regieren 1 *itr. V.* rule (**über** + *Akk.* over);
⟨party, administration⟩ govern
2 *tr. V.* rule; govern; ⟨monarch⟩ reign over

Regierung *die;* ~, ~en (a) (Herrschaft) rule;
(eines Monarchen) reign
(b) (Kabinett) government

Regierungs·sitz *der* seat of government

Regiment *das;* ~[e]s, ~e *od.* ~er (a) *Pl.*
~e (Herrschaft) rule
(b) *Pl.* ~er (Milit.) regiment

Region *die;* ~, ~en region

regional 1 *Adj.* regional
2 *adv.* regionally

Regisseur /reʒɪ'sø:ɐ̯/ *der;* ~s, ~e,
Regisseurin *die;* ~, ~nen director

Register *das;* ~s, ~ (a) index
(b) (amtliche Liste) register
(c) (Musik) (bei Instrumenten) register; (Orgel~)
stop

registrieren *tr. V.* (a) register
(b) (bewusst wahrnehmen) note; register

Regler *der;* ~s, ~ (Technik) regulator;
(Kybernetik) control

reg·los *Adj.* motionless

---

*old spelling - see note on page xiv

(r)

regnen 1 *itr., tr. V.* (*unpers.*) rain; **es regnet** it is raining
2 *itr. V.; mit sein* (fig.) rain down

regnerisch *Adj.* rainy

regulär *Adj.* (a) proper; normal ⟨*working hours*⟩
(b) (normal, üblich) normal

regulieren *tr. V.* regulate

Regulierung *die;* ~, ~**en** regulation

Regung *die;* ~, ~**en** (geh.: Gefühl) stirring

regungs·los *Adj.* motionless

Reh *das;* ~**[e]s,** ~**e** roe deer

Rehabilitation *die;* ~, ~**en** rehabilitation

rehabilitieren *tr. V.* rehabilitate

Reh-: ~**bock** *der* roebuck; ~**kitz** *das* fawn [of a/the roe deer]

Reibach *der;* ~**s** (ugs.) profits *pl.;* **einen [kräftigen]** ~ **machen** make a killing (coll.)

Reibe *die;* ~, ~**n, Reib·eisen** *das* grater

reiben 1 *unr. tr. V.* (a) rub
(b) (zerkleinern) grate
2 *unr. itr. V.* rub (**an** + *Dat.* on)

Reib·fläche *die* striking surface (*of matchbox*)

Reibung *die;* ~, ~**en** (Physik, fig.) friction

reibungs·los 1 *Adj.* smooth
2 *adv.* smoothly

reich 1 *Adj.* (a) (vermögend) rich
(b) (prächtig) costly ⟨*goods, gifts*⟩; rich ⟨*décor, finery*⟩
(c) (üppig) rich; abundant ⟨*harvest*⟩; abundant ⟨*mineral resources*⟩; ~ **an etw.** (*Dat.*) **sein** be rich in sth.
(d) (vielfältig) rich ⟨*collection, possibilities*⟩; wide, large ⟨*selection, choice*⟩; wide ⟨*knowledge, experience*⟩
2 *adv.* richly

Reich *das;* ~**[e]s,** ~**e** (a) empire; (König~) kingdom; realm; **das [Deutsche]** ~ (hist.) the German Reich *or* Empire; **das Dritte** ~ (hist.) the Third Reich
(b) (fig.) realm

reichen 1 *itr. V.* (a) (ausreichen) be enough; **das Geld reicht nicht** I/we *etc.* haven't got enough money; **jetzt reichts mir aber!** now I've had enough!; **danke, es reicht** that's enough, thank you
(b) (sich erstrecken) reach; ⟨*forest, fields, etc.*⟩ extend
2 *tr. V.* (a) pass; hand; **jmdm. die Hand** ~: hold out one's hand to sb.; **sich** (*Dat.*) **die Hand** ~: shake hands
(b) (servieren) serve ⟨*food, drink*⟩

reich·haltig *Adj.* extensive; varied ⟨*programme*⟩; substantial ⟨*meal*⟩

Reich·haltigkeit *die;* ~~: extensiveness; (eines Programms) varied content; (einer Mahlzeit) substantialness

reichlich 1 *Adj.* large; ample ⟨*space, time*⟩; good ⟨*hour, year*⟩
2 *adv.* (a) amply
(b) (mehr als) over; more than

(c) (ugs.: ziemlich, sehr) a bit too ⟨*cheeky, dear, late*⟩

Reichtum *der;* ~**s, Reichtümer** (a) wealth (**an** + *Dat.* of)
(b) *Pl.* (Vermögenswerte) riches

Reich·weite *die* reach; (eines Geschützes, Senders, Flugzeugs) range

reif *Adj.* (a) ripe ⟨*fruit, grain, cheese*⟩; mature ⟨*brandy, cheese*⟩; ~ **für etw. sein** (ugs.) be ready for sth.
(b) (erwachsen, ausgewogen) mature

Reif[1] *der;* ~**[e]s** hoar frost

Reif[2] *der;* ~**[e]s,** ~**e** (geh.) ring; (Arm~) bracelet; (Diadem) circlet

Reife *die;* ~ (a) ripeness; (von Menschen, Gedanken, Produkten) maturity
(b) (Reifung) ripening
(c) **mittlere** ~ (Schulw.) *school-leaving certificate usually taken after the fifth year of secondary school*

reifen 1 *itr. V.; mit sein* (a) ⟨*fruit, cereal, cheese*⟩ ripen
(b) (geh.: älter, reifer werden) mature (**zu** into)
(c) ⟨*idea, plan, decision*⟩ mature
2 *tr. V.* ripen ⟨*fruit, cereal*⟩

Reifen *der;* ~**s,** ~ (a) hoop
(b) (Gummi~) tyre
(c) ▶ REIF[2]

Reifen-: ~**druck** *der; Pl.* ~**drücke** tyre pressure; ~**panne** *die* puncture; ~**wechsel** *der* tyre change

Reif·glätte *die* ice on the roads

reiflich 1 *Adj.* [very] careful
2 *adv.* [very] carefully

Reifung *die;* ~: ▶ REIFEN 1: ripening; maturing; maturation

Reigen *der;* ~**s,** ~ (a) round dance
(b) (fig.) **den** ~ **eröffnen** start off

Reihe *die;* ~, ~**n** (a) row; **in Reih und Glied** (Milit.) in rank and file; **aus der** ~ **tanzen** (fig. ugs.) be different
(b) (Reihenfolge) series; **er/sie** *usw.* **ist an der** ~: it's his/her *etc.* turn; **der** ~ **nach, nach der** ~: in turn
(c) (größere Anzahl) number

reihen (geh.) *tr. V.* string; thread

Reihen-: ~**folge** *die* order; ~**haus** *das* terraced house

Reiher *der;* ~**s,** ~: heron

Reim *der;* ~**[e]s,** ~**e** rhyme

reimen 1 *itr. V.* make up rhymes
2 *tr., refl. V.* rhyme (**auf** + *Akk.* with)

rein[1] *Adv.* (ugs.) ~ **mit dir!** in you go/come!

rein[2] 1 *Adj.* (a) (unvermischt) pure
(b) (nichts anderes als) pure; sheer; plain, unvarnished ⟨*truth*⟩
(c) (frisch, sauber) clean; fresh ⟨*clothes, sheet of paper, etc.*⟩; pure, clean ⟨*water, air*⟩; clear ⟨*complexion*⟩; **etw. ins Reine schreiben** make a fair copy of sth.; **etw. ins Reine bringen** clear sth. up
2 *Adv.* purely; ~ **gar nichts** (ugs.) absolutely nothing

Rein·fall *der* (ugs.) let-down
rein|fallen *unr. itr. V.; mit sein* (ugs.)
▶ HEREINFALLEN
Rein·gewinn *der* net profit
Reinheit *die;* ~ (a) purity
  (b) (Sauberkeit) cleanness; (des Wassers, der Luft)
  purity; (der Haut) clearness
reinigen *tr. V.* clean; purify ⟨effluents, air,
  water, etc.⟩; **Kleider** [chemisch] ~ **lassen**
  have clothes [dry-]cleaned
Reinigung *die;* ~, ~**en** (a) ▶ REINIGEN:
  cleaning; purification; dry-cleaning
  (b) (Betrieb) [dry-]cleaner's
reinlich *Adj.* cleanly
Reinlichkeit *die;* ~: cleanliness
rein, Rein-: ~**rassig** *Adj.* thoroughbred
  ⟨animal⟩; ~|**reiten** *tr. V.* (ugs.) jmdn.
  ~**reiten** drag sb. in (fig.); ~**schrift** *die* fair
  copy
rein|ziehen *unr. tr. V.* (a) ▶ HINEINZIEHEN;
  (b) sich (Dat.) etw. ~**ziehen** (salopp) take
  ⟨drug⟩; watch ⟨film, show, video⟩
Reis *der;* ~**es** rice
Reis·brei *der* rice pudding
Reise *die;* ~, ~**n** journey; (kürzere Fahrt,
  Geschäfts~) trip; (Ausflug) outing; trip;
  (Schiffs~) voyage; **eine** ~ **machen** go on a
  trip/an outing; **auf** ~**n sein** travel; (nicht zu
  Hause sein) be away; **glückliche** od. **gute** ~!
  have a good journey
reise-, Reise-: ~**andenken** *das*
  souvenir; ~**boom** *das* tourist boom;
  ~**büro** *das* travel agent's; travel agency;
  ~**bus** *der* coach; ~**freiheit** the freedom of
  travel; ~**führer** *der* (a) (Reiseleiter) courier;
  (b) (Buch) guidebook; ~**führerin** *die*
  courier; ~**gepäck** *das* luggage (Brit.);
  baggage (Amer.); (am Flughafen) baggage;
  ~**gesellschaft** *die* (a) (Reisegruppe) party
  of tourists; (b) (ugs.: Reiseveranstalter) tour
  operator; ~**kosten** *Pl.* travel expenses;
  ~**krank** *Adj.* travel-sick; ~**krankheit** *die*
  travel sickness no pl.; ~**leiter** *der*,
  ~**leiterin** *die* courier
reisen *itr. V.; mit sein* (a) travel
  (b) (abreisen) leave; set off
Reisende *der/die; adj. Dekl.* traveller;
  (Fahrgast) passenger
Reise-: ~**pass, *~paß** *der* passport;
  ~**planung** *die* travel planning; **die**
  ~**planung umstellen** change one's travel
  plans; ~**prospekt** *der* travel brochure;
  ~**route** *die* route; ~**scheck** *der*
  traveller's cheque; ~**tasche** *die* holdall;
  ~**verkehr** *der* holiday traffic;
  ~**wetterbericht** *der* holiday weather
  forecast; ~**ziel** *das* destination
Reisig *das;* ~**s** brushwood
Reiß·brett *das* drawing board
reißen ①*unr. tr. V.* (a) tear; (in Stücke) tear
  up

  (b) (ziehen an) pull; (heftig) yank (coll.)
  (c) (werfen, ziehen) jmdn. **zu Boden/in die Tiefe**
  ~: knock sb. to the ground/drag sb. down
  into the depths
  (d) (töten) ⟨wolf, lion, etc.⟩ kill ⟨prey⟩
  (e) etw. an sich ~ (fig.) seize sth.
  ②*unr. itr. V.* (a) *mit sein* ⟨paper, fabric⟩
  tear, rip; ⟨rope, thread⟩ break, snap; ⟨film⟩
  break; ⟨muscle⟩ tear
  (b) (zerren) an etw. (Dat.) ~: pull at sth.
  ③*unr. refl. V.* (ugs.: sich bemühen um) **sie** ~
  sich um die Eintrittskarten they are fighting
  each other to get tickets
reißend *Adj.* rapacious ⟨animal⟩; raging
  ⟨torrent⟩; ~**en Absatz finden** sell like hot
  cakes
reißerisch (abwertend) ① *Adj.* sensational;
  lurid ⟨headline⟩; garish, lurid ⟨colour⟩
  ② *adv.* sensationally
Reiß-: ~**leine** *die* (Flugw.) ripcord;
  ~**nagel** *der:* ▶ ~ZWECKE; ~**verschluss,**
  *~verschluß** *der* zip [fastener];
  ~**zwecke** *die* drawing pin (Brit.);
  thumbtack (Amer.)
reiten ① *unr. itr. V.; meist mit sein* ride
  ② *unr. tr. V.; auch mit sein* ride; **Schritt/**
  Trab/Galopp ~: ride at a walk/trot/gallop
Reiten *das;* ~**s** riding no art.
Reiter *der;* ~**s**, ~, **Reiterin** *die;* ~, ~**nen**
  rider
Reit-: ~**hose** *die* riding breeches pl.;
  ~**pferd** *das* saddle horse; ~**stiefel** *der*
  riding boot
Reiz *der;* ~**es**, ~**e** (a) (Physiol.) stimulus
  (b) (Anziehungskraft) attraction; appeal no pl.;
  (des Verbotenen, der Ferne usw.) lure
  (c) (Zauber) charm
reizbar *Adj.* irritable
Reizbarkeit *die;* ~: irritability
reizen ① *tr. V.* (a) annoy; tease ⟨animal⟩;
  (herausfordern, provozieren) provoke; *s. auch*
  GEREIZT
  (b) (Physiol.) irritate
  (c) (Interesse erregen bei) jmdn. ~: attract sb.;
  appeal to sb.
  (d) (Kartenspiele) bid
  ② *itr. V.* (Kartenspiele) bid
reizend ① *Adj.* charming; delightful, lovely
  ⟨child⟩
  ② *adv.* charmingly
reizlos *Adj.* unattractive; ⟨landscape,
  scenery⟩ lacking in charm
reizvoll *Adj.* (a) (hübsch) charming
  (b) (interessant) attractive
rekeln *refl. V.* (ugs.) stretch
Reklamation /reklamaˈtsɪ̯oːn/ *die;* ~,
  ~**en** complaint (**wegen** about)
Reklame *die;* ~, ~**n** (a) advertising no
  indef. art.; ~ **für jmdn./etw. machen** promote
  sb./advertise or promote sth.
  (b) (ugs.: Werbemittel) advert (Brit. coll.); ad (coll.);
  (im Fernsehen, Radio auch) commercial

---
*alte Schreibung - vgl. Hinweis auf S. xiv

Reklame-: ~**schild** *das* advertising sign; ~**tafel** *die* advertising hoarding; (klein) advertising board

reklamieren ⟨1⟩ *itr. V.* complain ⟨2⟩ *tr. V.* **(a)** complain about (**bei** to, **wegen** on account of) **(b)** (beanspruchen) claim

rekonstruieren *tr. V.* reconstruct

Rekord *der;* ~[e]s, ~e record

Rekord·halter *der,* **Rekord·halterin** *die,* **Rekord·inhaber** *der,* **Rekord·inhaberin** *die* record holder

Rekrut *der;* ~en, ~en (Milit.) recruit

Rektor *der;* ~s, ~en **(a)** (einer Schule) head[master] **(b)** (Universitäts~) Rector; ≈ Vice-Chancellor (Brit.); (einer Fachhochschule) principal

Rektorin *die;* ~, ~nen **(a)** (einer Schule) head[mistress] **(b)** ▶ REKTOR B

Relation *die;* ~, ~en relation

relativ ⟨1⟩ *Adj.* relative ⟨2⟩ *adv.* relatively

relativieren *tr. V.* relativize

Relativierung *die;* ~, ~en relativization

Relativ-: ~**pronomen** *das* (Sprachw.) relative pronoun; ~**satz** *der* (Sprachw.) relative clause

relaxed /ri'lɛkst/ *Adj.* (salopp) laid-back (coll.)

relevant /rele'vant/ *Adj.* relevant (**für** to)

Relevanz *die;* ~: relevance (**für** to)

Relief *das;* ~s, ~s *od.* ~e relief

Religion *die;* ~, ~en religion

religiös ⟨1⟩ *Adj.* religious ⟨2⟩ *adv.* in a religious manner

Religiosität *die;* ~: religiousness

Relikt *das;* ~[e], ~e relic

Reling *die;* ~, ~s *od.* ~e [deck] rail

Reliquie /re'li:kvjə/ *die;* ~, ~n relic

Remis *das;* ~ /rə'mi:(s)/, ~ /rə'mi:s/ (bes. Schach) draw

Ren *das;* ~s, ~s *od.* ~e reindeer

Renaissance /rənɛ'sã:s/ *die;* ~, ~n **(a)** Renaissance **(b)** (Wiederaufleben) revival

Rendezvous /rãde'vu:/ *das;* ~ /...'vu:(s)/, ~ /'rãde'vu:s/ rendezvous

Renn·bahn *die* (Sport) racetrack; (für Pferde) racecourse

rennen *unr. itr. V.; mit sein* run; **an/gegen jmdn./etw.** ~: run *or* bang into sb./sth.

Rennen *das;* ~s, ~: running; (Pferde~, Auto~) racing; (Wettbewerb) race

Renner *der;* ~s, ~ (ugs.: Verkaufserfolg) big seller

Renn-: ~**fahrer** *der,* ~**fahrerin** *die* racing driver; ~**pferd** *das* racehorse; ~**rad** *das* racing cycle; ~**wagen** *der* racing car

renommiert *Adj.* renowned

renovieren *tr. V.* renovate; redecorate ⟨room, flat⟩

Renovierung *die;* ~, ~en renovation; (eines Zimmers, einer Wohnung) redecoration

rentabel ⟨1⟩ *Adj.* profitable ⟨2⟩ *adv.* profitably

Rentabilität *die;* ~ (bes. Wirtsch.) profitability

Rente *die;* ~, ~n **(a)** pension **(b)** (Kapitalertrag) annuity

Renten-: ~**alter** *das* pensionable age *no art.;* ~**empfänger** *der,* ~**empfängerin** *die* pensioner; ~**versicherung** *die* pension scheme

Ren·tier *das* reindeer

rentieren *refl. V.* be profitable; ⟨equipment, machinery⟩ pay its way

Rentner *der;* ~s, ~, **Rentnerin** *die;* ~, ~nen pensioner

Reparatur *die;* ~, ~en repair (**an** + *Dat.* to)

Reparatur-werkstatt *die* repair [work]shop; (für Autos) garage

reparieren *tr. V.* repair; mend

Repertoire /repɛ'tǒa:ɐ̯/ *das;* ~s, ~s repertoire

Report *der;* ~[e]s, ~e, **Reportage** /repɔr'ta:ʒə/ *die;* ~, ~n report

Reporter *der;* ~s, ~, **Reporterin** *die;* ~, ~nen reporter

Repräsentant *der;* ~en, ~en, **Repräsentantin** *die;* ~, ~nen representative

repräsentativ *Adj.* representative

repräsentieren *tr. V.* represent

Repressalie /reprɛ'sa:lǐə/ *die;* ~, ~n repressive measure

Reproduktion *die* reproduction

reproduzieren *tr. V.* reproduce

Reptil *das;* ~s, ~ien reptile

Republik *die;* ~, ~en republic

republikanisch *Adj.* republican

Reservat *das;* ~[e]s, ~e **(a)** reservation **(b)** (Naturschutzgebiet) reserve

Reserve *die;* ~, ~n reserve

Reserve-: ~**rad** *das* spare wheel; ~**reifen** *der* spare tyre

reservieren *tr. V.* reserve

reserviert ⟨1⟩ *Adj.* reserved ⟨2⟩ *adv.* in a reserved way

Reserviertheit *die;* ~: reserve

Reservierung *die;* ~, ~en reservation

Reservoir /rezɛr'vǒa:ɐ̯/ *das;* ~s, ~e (auch fig.) reservoir (**an** + *Dat.* of)

Residenz *die;* ~, ~en **(a)** residence **(b)** (Hauptstadt) [royal] capital

Resignation *die;* ~, ~en resignation

resignieren *itr. V.* give up

resigniert ⟨1⟩ *Adj.* resigned ⟨2⟩ *adv.* resignedly

resolut ⟨1⟩ *Adj.* resolute ⋯⟩

2 *adv.* resolutely

Resolution *die;* ~, ~en resolution

Resonanz *die;* ~, ~en resonance

resozialisieren *tr. V.* (bes. Rechtsspr.) reintegrate into society

Resozialisierung *die;* ~, ~en (bes. Rechtsspr.) reintegration into society

Respekt *der;* ~[e]s (a) (Achtung) respect (**vor** + *Dat.* for)
(b) (Furcht) **jmdm.** ~ **einflößen** intimidate sb.

respektabel 1 *Adj.* respectable
2 *adv.* respectably

respektieren *tr. V.* respect

respekt·los 1 *Adj.* disrespectful
2 *adv.* disrespectfully

Respekt·losigkeit *die;* ~: disrespectfulness

respekt·voll 1 *Adj.* respectful
2 *adv.* respectfully

Ressort /rɛˈsoːɐ̯/ *das;* ~s, ~s area of responsibility; (Abteilung) department

Ressource /rɛˈsʊrsə/ *die;* ~, ~n resource

Rest *der;* ~[e]s, ~e (a) rest; **ein** ~ **von** a little bit of
(b) (Endstück) remnant
(c) (Math.) remainder

Rest·alkohol *der* residual alcohol

Restaurant /rɛstoˈrãː/ *das;* ~s, ~s restaurant

restaurieren *tr. V.* restore

restlich *Adj.* remaining

rest·los 1 *Adj.* complete
2 *adv.* completely

Rest·müll *der* general waste; non-recyclable waste

Resultat *das;* ~[e]s, ~e result

resultieren *itr. V.* result

Retorte *die;* ~, ~n retort

Retorten-baby *das* (ugs.) test tube baby

Retrospektive *die;* ~, ~n (a) (Rückblick) retrospective view; **in der** ~: in retrospect
(b) (Ausstellung) retrospective

retten 1 *tr. V.* save; (vor Gefahr) save; rescue; (befreien) rescue; **jmdm. das Leben** ~: save sb.'s life
2 *refl. V.* (fliehen) escape (**aus** from)

Retter *der;* ~s, ~, **Retterin** *die;* ~, ~nen rescuer

Rettich *der;* ~s, ~e radish

Rettung *die* rescue; (vor Zerstörung) saving

rettungs-, Rettungs-: ~**aktion** *die* rescue operation; ~**boot** *das* lifeboat; ~**hubschrauber** *der* rescue helicopter; ~**los** 1 *Adj.* hopeless; inevitable ‹*disaster*›; 2 *adv.* hopelessly; ~**ring** *der* lifebelt

Reue *die;* ~: remorse (**über** + *Akk.* for); (Rel.) repentance

reuen *tr. V.* **etw. reut jmdn.** sb. regrets sth.

---

reu·mütig *Adj.* remorseful; repentant ‹*sinner*›

Reuse *die;* ~, ~n fish trap

Revanche /reˈvãːʃ(ə)/ *die;* ~, ~n revenge; (Sport) return match/fight/game

revanchieren *refl. V.* (a) get one's revenge, (coll.) get one's own back (**bei** on)
(b) **sich bei jmdm. für eine Einladung** ~ (ugs.) return sb.'s invitation

Revers /rəˈveːɐ̯/ *das od.* (österr.) *der;* ~ /rəˈvɛːɐ̯s/, ~ /rəˈvɛːɐ̯s/ lapel

reversibel /revɛrˈziːbl̩/ *Adj.* (Technik, Med.) reversible

revidieren /reviˈdiːrən/ *tr. V.* (abändern) revise; amend ‹*law, contract*›

Revier /reˈviːɐ̯/ *das;* ~s, ~e (a) (Aufgabenbereich) province
(b) (Zool.) territory
(c) (Polizei~) (Dienststelle) [police] station; (Bereich) district; (des einzelnen Polizisten) beat

Revision /reviˈzi̯oːn/ *die;* ~, ~en (a) revision; (Änderung) amendment
(b) (Rechtsw.) appeal [on a point/points of law]; ~ **einlegen, in die** ~ **gehen** lodge an appeal [on a point/points of law]

Revolte /reˈvɔltə/ *die;* ~, ~n revolt

revoltieren /revɔlˈtiːrən/ *itr. V.* revolt, rebel (**gegen** against); (fig.) ‹*stomach*› rebel

Revolution /revoluˈtsi̯oːn/ *die;* ~, ~en (auch fig.) revolution

revolutionär 1 *Adj.* revolutionary
2 *adv.* in a revolutionary way

Revolutionär *der;* ~s, ~e, **Revolutionärin** *die;* ~, ~nen revolutionary

Revolver /reˈvɔlvɐ/ *der;* ~s, ~: revolver

Rezept *das;* ~[e]s, ~e (a) (Med.) prescription
(b) (Anleitung) recipe

rezept·frei 1 *Adj.* ~**e Mittel** medicines obtainable without a prescription
2 *adv.* **etw.** ~ **verkaufen/erhalten** sell/obtain sth. without a prescription *or* over the counter

Rezeption *die;* ~, ~en reception *no art.*

rezept·pflichtig *Adj.* ‹*drug etc.*› obtainable only on prescription

Rezession *die;* ~, ~en (Wirtsch.) recession

R-Gespräch /ˈɛr-/ *das* (Fernspr.) reverse-charge call (Brit.); collect call (Amer.)

Rhabarber *der;* ~s rhubarb

Rhein *der;* ~[e]s Rhine

rheinisch *Adj.* Rhenish; ‹*speciality etc.*› of the Rhine region

Rhein·land *das;* ~[e]s Rhineland

Rheinland-Pfalz (*das*); ~: the Rhineland-Palatinate

Rhetorik *die;* ~, ~en rhetoric

Rheuma *das;* ~s (ugs.) rheumatism

rheumatisch (Med.) 1 *Adj.* rheumatic
2 *adv.* rheumatically

---

*old spelling - see note on page xiv

Rheumatismus *der;* ~, **Rheumatismen**
(Med.) rheumatism

Rhinozeros *das;* ~[ses], ~se rhinoceros;
rhino (coll.)

Rhododendron *der od. das;* ~s,
Rhododendren rhododendron

rhythmisch [1] *Adj.* rhythmical; rhythmic
[2] *adv.* rhythmically

Rhythmus *der;* ~, **Rhythmen** (auch fig.)
rhythm

richten [1] *tr. V.* (a) direct ⟨*gaze*⟩ (auf +
Akk. at, towards); turn ⟨*eyes, gaze*⟩ (auf +
Akk. towards); point ⟨*torch, telescope, gun*⟩
(auf + *Akk.* at); aim ⟨*gun, missile, telescope,
searchlight*⟩ (auf + *Akk.* on); (fig.) direct
⟨*activity, attention*⟩ (auf + *Akk.* towards);
address ⟨*letter, remarks, words*⟩ (an + *Akk.*
to); level ⟨*criticism*⟩ (an + *Akk.* at)
(b) (geraderichten) straighten
(c) (aburteilen) judge; (verurteilen) condemn; *s.
auch* ZUGRUNDE A;
[2] *refl. V.* (a) (sich hinwenden) **sich auf jmdn./
etw. ~** (auch fig.) be directed towards sb./sth.
(b) **sich an jmdn./etw. ~** ⟨*person*⟩ turn on
sb./sth.; ⟨*appeal, explanation*⟩ be directed at
sb./sth.; **sich gegen jmdn./etw. ~** ⟨*person*⟩
criticize sb./sth.; ⟨*criticism, accusations, etc.*⟩
be aimed *or* levelled at sb./sth.
(c) (sich orientieren) **sich nach jmdn./jmds.
Wünschen ~**: fit in with sb./sb.'s wishes
(d) (abhängen) **sich nach jmdn./etw. ~**:
depend on sb./sth.
[3] *itr. V.* (urteilen) judge

Richter *der;* ~s, ~, **Richterin** *die;* ~,
~nen judge

Richt·geschwindigkeit *die*
recommended maximum speed

richtig [1] *Adj.* (a) right; (zutreffend) right;
correct; accurate ⟨*prophecy, premonition*⟩;
etw. ~ stellen correct sth.
(b) (ordentlich) proper
(c) (wirklich, echt) real
[2] *adv.* (a) right; correctly
(b) (ordentlich) properly
(c) (richtiggehend) really

richtig·gehend [1] *Adj.* real; proper (coll.)
[2] *adv.* really

Richtigkeit *die;* ~: correctness; **etw. hat
seine ~, mit etw. hat es seine ~**: sth. is
right; **das wird schon seine ~ haben** I'm
sure it's all right *or* (coll.) OK

***richtig|stellen** ▸ RICHTIG 1A

Richt-: ~linie *die* guideline; **~schnur**
die; Pl. **~~en** (fig.) guiding principle

Richtung *die;* ~, ~en (a) direction; **in ~**
Ulm in the direction of Ulm
(b) (fig.: Tendenz) movement; trend

richtung·weisend *Adj.* ⟨*idea, resolution,
paper, speech*⟩ that points the way ahead

rieb *1. u. 3. Pers. Sg. Prät. v.* REIBEN

riechen [1] *unr. tr. V.* (a) smell
(b) (wittern) ⟨*dog etc.*⟩ pick up the scent of
[2] *unr. itr. V.* (a) smell; **an jmdm./etw. ~**:
smell sb./sth.

(b) (einen Geruch haben) smell (**nach** of)

rief *1. u. 3. Pers. Sg. Prät. v.* RUFEN

Riegel *der;* ~s, ~ (a) bolt
(b) **ein ~ Schokolade** a bar of chocolate

Riemen *der;* ~s, ~ (a) strap; (Treib~, Gürtel)
belt; **sich am ~ reißen** (ugs.) pull oneself
together; get a grip on oneself
(b) (Ruder) [long] oar

Riese *der;* ~n, ~n giant

rieseln *itr. V.; mit Richtungsangabe mit
sein* trickle [down]; ⟨*snow*⟩ fall gently

Riesen- giant; enormous ⟨*selection, profit,
portion*⟩; tremendous (coll.) ⟨*effort, rejoicing,
success*⟩; terrific (coll.), terrible (coll.)
⟨*stupidity, scandal, fuss*⟩

riesen-, Riesen-: ~groß *Adj.*
enormous; huge; terrific (coll.) ⟨*surprise*⟩;
~schritt *der* giant stride

riesig [1] *Adj.* enormous; huge; vast
⟨*country*⟩; tremendous ⟨*effort, progress*⟩
[2] *adv.* (ugs.) tremendously (coll.); terribly
(coll.)

Riesin *die;* ~, ~nen giantess

Riesling *der;* ~s, ~e Riesling

riet *1. u. 3. Pers. Sg. Prät. v.* RATEN

Riff *das;* ~[e]s, ~e reef

rigoros [1] *Adj.* rigorous
[2] *adv.* rigorously

Rille *die;* ~, ~n groove

Rind *das;* ~[e]s, ~er (a) cow; (Stier) bull;
~er cattle *pl.;*
(b) (~fleisch) beef

Rinde *die;* ~, ~n (a) (Baum~) bark
(b) (Brot~) crust; (Käse~) rind

Rinder·braten *der* roast beef *no indef.
art.;* (roh) roasting beef *no indef. art.*

Rinder·wahnsinn *der* mad cow disease

Rind-: ~fleisch *das* beef; **~vieh** *das* (a)
cattle *pl.;* (b) (ugs. abwertend) ass; [stupid] fool

Ring *der;* ~[e]s, ~e ring

Ringel·natter *die* ring snake

ringen [1] *unr. tr. V.* (Sport, fig.) wrestle; (fig.:
kämpfen) struggle, fight (**um** for; **gegen, mit**
with); **nach Luft ~**: struggle for breath
[2] *unr. tr. V.* **die Hände ~**: wring one's
hands

Ringen *das;* ~s (Sport) wrestling *no art.*

Ring-: ~finger *der* ring finger; **~kampf**
der (a) [stand-up] fight; (b) (Sport) wrestling
bout

rings *Adv.* all around

rings·herum *Adv.* all around [it/them *etc.*]

Ring·straße *die* ring road

rings-: ~um, ~umher *Adv.* all around

Rinne *die;* ~, ~n channel; (Dach~, Rinnstein)
gutter; (Abfluss) drainpipe

rinnen *unr. itr. V.; mit sein* run

Rinn·stein *der* gutter

Rippchen *das;* ~s, ~ (Kochk. südd.) rib [of
pork]

Rippe *die;* ~, ~n rib

Rippen·bruch der (Med.) rib fracture

Risiko das; ∼s, Risiken risk

Risiko-: ∼**faktor** der risk factor;
∼**gruppe** die risk group

riskant ① Adj. risky
② adv. riskily

riskieren tr. V. risk

riss, **riß 1. u. 3. Pers. Sg. Prät. v. REISSEN*

Riss, **Riß der; Risses, Risse tear; (Spalt, Sprung) crack*

rissig Adj. cracked; chapped ⟨lips⟩

ritt 1. u. 3. Pers. Sg. Prät. v. REITEN

Ritt der; ∼[e]s, ∼e ride

Ritter der; ∼s, ∼: knight

Ritter·sporn der delphinium

rittlings Adv. astride

Ritze die; ∼, ∼n crack; [narrow] gap

ritzen tr. V. scratch

Rivale der; ∼n, ∼n, **Rivalin** die; ∼, ∼nen rival

Rivalität die; ∼, ∼en rivalry no indef. art.

Roastbeef /'roːstbiːf/ das; ∼s, ∼s roast [sirloin (Brit.) of] beef

Robbe die; ∼, ∼n seal

Robe die; ∼, ∼n robe; (schwarz) gown

Roboter der; ∼s, ∼: robot

robust Adj. robust

roch 1. u. 3. Pers. Sg. Prät. v. RIECHEN

Rochade die; ∼, ∼n (Schach) castling

röcheln itr. V. give the death rattle

Rock[1] der; ∼[e]s, Röcke skirt

Rock[2] der; ∼[s] (Musik) rock [music]

Rock and Roll /'rɔk ɛnt 'rɔl/ der; ∼[s], ∼[s] rock and roll no pl.

Rock·band die rock band

rocken itr. V. rock

Rocker der; ∼s, ∼: rocker

rockig Adj. rock ⟨music⟩; rock-like ⟨jazz etc.⟩

Rock·musik die rock music

Rodel·bahn die toboggan run; (Sport) luge run

rodeln itr. V.; mit sein sledge; toboggan

roden tr. V. clear ⟨wood, land⟩; (ausgraben) grub up ⟨tree⟩

Rogen der; ∼s, ∼: roe

Roggen der; ∼s rye

Roggen-: ∼**brot** das rye bread; ein ∼brot a loaf of rye bread; ∼**brötchen** das rye-bread roll

roh ① Adj. (a) raw ⟨food⟩; unboiled ⟨milk⟩; unfinished ⟨wood⟩
(b) (ungenau) rough
(c) (brutal) brutish; brute attrib. ⟨force⟩
② adv. (a) (ungenau) roughly
(b) (brutal) brutishly; (grausam) callously; (grob) coarsely

Roh-: ∼**bau** der shell [of a/the building];

∼**kost** die raw fruit and vegetables pl.;
∼**material** das raw material; ∼**öl** das crude oil

Rohr das; ∼[e]s, ∼e (a) (Leitungs∼) pipe; (als Bauteil) tube
(b) o. Pl. (Röhricht) reeds pl.;
(c) o. Pl. (Werkstoff) reed

Röhre die; ∼, ∼n tube; (Elektronen∼) valve (Brit.); tube (Amer.)

Roh·stoff der raw material

Rokoko das; ∼[s] rococo

*Rolladen ▶ ROLLLADEN

Roll·bahn die (Flugw.) taxiway

Rolle die; ∼, ∼n (a) (Spule) reel
(b) (zylindrischer [Hohl]körper; Zusammengerolltes) roll
(c) (Walze) roller
(d) (Rad) [small] wheel; (an Möbeln usw.) castor; (für Gardine, Schiebetür usw.) runner
(e) (Turnen, Kunstflug) roll
(f) (Theater, Film usw., fig.) role; part; (Soziol.) role; **es spielt keine ∼**: it is of no importance; (es macht nichts aus) it doesn't matter

rollen ① tr. V. roll
② itr. V. mit sein ⟨ball, wheel, etc.⟩ roll; ⟨vehicle⟩ move; ⟨aircraft⟩ taxi

Roller der; ∼s, ∼: scooter

Roll-: ∼**feld** das runway[s] and taxiway[s]; ∼**kragen** der polo neck; ∼**laden** der [roller] shutter; ∼**mops** der rollmops; ∼**schuh** der roller skate; ∼**schuh laufen** roller-skate; ∼**splitt** der loose chippings pl.; ∼**stuhl** der wheelchair; ∼**treppe** die escalator

Rom (das) ∼s Rome

Roman der; ∼s, ∼e novel

Romantik die; ∼: romanticism; die ∼: Romanticism

romantisch ① Adj. romantic
② adv. romantically

Romanze die; ∼, ∼n romance

Römer der; ∼s, ∼, **Römerin** die; ∼, ∼nen Roman

römisch-katholisch Adj. Roman Catholic

röntgen tr. V. X-ray

Röntgen-: ∼**aufnahme** die, ∼**bild** das X-ray [image/photograph or picture]; ∼**strahlen** Pl. X-rays

rosa ① indekl. Adj. pink
② adv. pink

Rosa das; ∼s, ∼ od. ∼s pink

Rose die; ∼, ∼n rose

rosé indekl. Adj. pale pink

Rosé der; ∼s, ∼s rosé [wine]

Rosen-: ∼**kohl** der [Brussels] sprouts pl.; ∼**kranz** der (kath. Kirche) rosary; **einen ∼kranz beten** say a rosary; ∼**montag** der the day before Shrove Tuesday

rosig Adj. (a) rosy; pink ⟨piglet etc.⟩
(b) (fig.) rosy; optimistic ⟨mood⟩

Rosine *die;* ~, ~n raisin
Rosmarin *der;* ~s rosemary
Ross, *Roß *das;* Rosses, Rosse *od.* Rösser
horse; steed (poet./joc.); **hoch zu** ~: on
horseback; **auf dem** *od.* **seinem hohen** ~
sitzen (fig.) be on one's high horse
Ross-, *Roß-: ~**haar** *das* horsehair;
~**kastanie** *die* horse chestnut
Rost[1] *der;* ~[e]s, ~e (a) (Gitter) grating;
(eines Ofens, einer Feuerstelle) grate; (Brat~) grill
(b) (Bett~) base
Rost[2] *der;* ~[e]s rust
Rost-: ~**braten** *der* grilled steak;
~**bratwurst** *die* grilled sausage
rosten *itr. V.; auch mit sein* rust
rösten /'rœstn̩, 'rø:stn̩/ *tr. V.* roast; toast
⟨bread⟩
rost·frei *Adj.* stainless ⟨steel⟩
Rösti *die;* ~ (schweiz. Kochk.) thinly sliced
fried potatoes *pl.*
rostig *Adj.* rusty
rot [1] *Adj.* red; ~ **werden** turn red; ⟨person⟩
blush; ⟨traffic light⟩ change to red
[2] *adv.* red
Rot *das;* ~s, ~ *od.* ~s red
Rot·barsch *der* rosefish
Röte *die;* ~: red[ness]
röten [1] *tr. V.* redden
[2] *refl. V.* go *or* turn red
rot·haarig *Adj.* red-haired
Rot·hirsch *der* red deer
rotieren *itr. V.* (a) rotate
(b) (ugs.: hektisch sein) get into a flap (coll.)
Rot-: ~**käppchen** *das;* ~s Little Red
Riding Hood; ~**kehlchen** *das;* ~s, ~~:
robin [redbreast]; ~**kohl** *der,* (bes. südd.,
österr.) ~**kraut** *das* red cabbage
rötlich *Adj.* reddish
Rot-: ~**licht** *das* red light; **bei** ~**licht**
under a red light; ~**stift** *der* red pencil
Rötung *die;* ~, ~en reddening
Rot·wein *der* red wine
Rotz *der;* ~es (salopp) snot (sl.)
rotzen (derb) [1] *itr. V.* (a) blow one's nose
loudly
(b) (Schleim in den Mund ziehen) sniff back
one's snot (sl.)
(c) (ausspucken) gob (sl.)
[2] *tr. V.* spit
rotz·frech (salopp) [1] *Adj.* insolent; snotty
(sl.)
[2] *adv.* insolently; snottily (sl.)
Rouge /ru:ʒ/ *das;* ~s, ~s rouge
Roulade /ru:la:də/ *die;* ~, ~n (Kochk.)
[beef/veal/pork] olive
Route /'ru:tə/ *die;* ~, ~n route
Routine /ru'ti:nə/ *die;* ~ (a) (Erfahrung)
experience; (Übung) practice
(b) (Gewohnheit) routine *no def. art.*
routiniert /ruti'ni:ɐ̯t/[1] *Adj.* (gewandt)
expert; skilled; (erfahren) experienced

[2] *adv.* expertly; skilfully
Rowdy /'rau:di/ *der;* ~s, ~s (abwertend)
hooligan
Rübe *die;* ~, ~n turnip; **Rote** ~: beetroot;
Gelbe ~ (südd.) carrot
rüber *Adv.* (ugs.) over
Rubin *der;* ~s, ~e ruby
Rubrik *die;* ~, ~en column; (fig.: Kategorie)
category
Ruck *der;* ~[e]s, ~e jerk
Rück·blick *der* look back (**auf** + *Akk.* at);
retrospective view (**auf** + *Akk.* of)
rücken *itr., tr. V.* move
Rücken *der;* ~s, ~: back; (Buch~) spine
Rücken-: ~**deckung** *die* (a) (bes. Milit.)
rear cover; (b) (fig.) backing; ~**lehne** *die*
[chair/seat] back; ~**mark** *das* (Anat.) spinal
cord; ~**schmerzen** *Pl.* backache *sing.;*
~**schwimmen** *das* backstroke; ~**wind**
der tail wind
rück-, Rück-: ~|**erstatten** *tr. V.; nur*
im Inf. u. 2. Part. repay; ~**erstattung** *die*
repayment; ~**fahr·karte** *die,*
~**fahr·schein** *der* return [ticket];
~**fahrt** *die* return journey; ~**fall** *der* (Med.,
auch fig.) relapse; ~**fällig** *Adj.* (Med., auch fig.)
relapsed ⟨patient, alcoholic, etc.⟩; ~**fällig**
werden have a relapse; ⟨alcoholic etc.⟩ go
back to one's old ways; ⟨criminal⟩ commit a
second offence; ~**flug** *der* return flight;
~**frage** *die* query; ~**gabe** *die* return;
~**gang** *der* drop, fall (*Gen.* in); ~**gängig**
Adj. ~**gängig machen** cancel ⟨agreement,
decision, etc.⟩; ~**grat** *das;* ~~[e]s, ~~e
spine; (bes. fig.) backbone; ~**halt** *der*
support; backing; ~**halt·los** [1] *Adj.*
unreserved, unqualified ⟨support⟩; [2] *adv.*
unreservedly; ~**kehr** *die;* ~~: return;
~**kopp[e]lung** *die* (Elektrot.) feedback;
~**lage** *die* savings *pl.;* ~**läufig** *Adj.*
decreasing ⟨number⟩; declining ⟨economic
growth etc.⟩; falling ⟨rate, production, etc.⟩;
~**licht** *das* rear *or* tail light
rücklings *Adv.* on one's back
Rück-: ~**nahme** *die;* ~~: taking back;
~**reise** *die* return journey; ~**ruf** *der*
(Fernspr.) return call
Ruck·sack *der* rucksack; (Touren~)
backpack
Rucksack·urlaub *der* backpacking
holiday
rück-, Rück-: ~**schlag** *der* setback;
~**schritt** *der* retrograde step; ~**seite** *die*
back; (einer Münze usw.) reverse; far side;
~**sicht** *die* consideration; ~**sicht auf jmdn.**
nehmen show consideration for *or* towards
sb.; ~**sicht·nahme** *die;* ~~:
consideration; ~**sichts·los** [1] *Adj.*
inconsiderate; thoughtless; (verantwortungslos)
reckless ⟨driver⟩; (schonungslos) ruthless;
[2] *adv. s. Adj:* inconsiderately; recklessly;
ruthlessly; ~**sichtslosigkeit** *die;* ~~,
~~en ▸ RÜCKSICHTSLOS: lack of
consideration; recklessness; ruthlessness; ⋯⟶

~**sichts·voll** ① *Adj.* considerate; ② *adv.*
considerately; ~**sitz** *der* back seat;
~**spiegel** *der* rear-view mirror;
~**sprache** *die* consultation; ~**stand** *der*
(a) (Rest) residue; (b) (ausstehende Zahlung)
arrears *pl.;* (c) (Zurückbleiben hinter dem gesetzten
Ziel) Sport: hinter dem Gegner)
deficit; [mit etw.] im ~**stand** sein/in ~**stand**
(*Akk.*) geraten be/get behind [with sth.];
~**ständig** *Adj.* (a) backward; (b) (schon
länger fällig) outstanding *(payment, amount)*;
(wages) still owing; ~**strahler** *der*
reflector; ~**tritt** *der* resignation (**von** from);
(von einer Kandidatur, einem Vertrag usw.)
withdrawal (**von** from)

rückwärts *Adv.* backwards

Rückwärts·gang *der* reverse [gear]

rück-, Rück-: ~**weg** *der* return journey;
~**wirkend** ① *Adj.* retrospective;
backdated *(pay increase)*; ② retrospectively;
~**zahlung** *die* repayment; ~**zug** *der*
retreat

Rüde *der;* ~**n,** ~**n** [male] dog

Rudel *das;* ~**s,** ~: herd; (von Wölfen, Hunden)
pack

Ruder *das;* ~**s,** ~ (a) (Riemen) oar
(b) (Steuer~) rudder

Ruder·boot *das* rowboat; rowing boat (Brit.)

Rudergänger *der;* ~~**s,** ~~, ~**gast** *der*
(Seemannsspr.) helmsman

rudern ① *itr. V.; mit sein* row
② *tr. V.* row

Ruder·regatta *die* rowing regatta

Ruf *der;* ~**[e]s,** ~**e** (a) call; (Schrei) shout;
cry; (Tierlaut) call
(b) (fig.: Forderung) call (**nach** for)
(c) (Telefonnummer) telephone [number]
(d) (Leumund) reputation

rufen ① *unr. itr. V.* call (**nach** for); (schreien)
shout (**nach** for); *(animal)* call
② *unr. tr. V.* (a) (ausrufen) call; (schreien)
shout
(b) (herbeirufen, anrufen) **jmdn.** ~: call sb.;
jmdn. zu Hilfe ~: call to sb. to help

Ruf-: ~**mord** *der* character assassination;
~**mord·kampagne** *die* smear campaign;
~**name** *der* first name (*by which one is
generally known*); ~**nummer** *die* telephone
number

Rüge *die;* ~, ~**n** reprimand

rügen *tr. V.* reprimand *(person)* (**wegen** for);
censure *(carelessness etc.)*

Ruhe *die;* ~ (a) (Stille) silence; ~ [**bitte**]!
quiet *or* silence [please]!
(b) (Ungestörtheit) peace; **jmdn. mit etw. in** ~
lassen stop bothering sb. with sth.
(c) (Unbewegtheit) rest
(d) (Erholung) rest *no def. art.;*
(e) (Gelassenheit) calm[ness]; composure; [**die**]
~ **bewahren/die** ~ **verlieren** keep calm/lose
one's composure; **in** [**aller**] ~: [really] calmly

*old spelling - see note on page xiv

ruhe·los ① *Adj.* restless
② *adv.* restlessly

ruhen *itr. V.* (a) (ausruhen) rest
(b) (geh.: schlafen) sleep
(c) (stillstehen) *(work, business)* have stopped;
(production, firm) be at a standstill

Ruhe-: ~**pause** *die* break; ~**stand** *der*
retirement; **in den** ~**stand gehen/versetzt
werden** go into retirement/be retired;
~**störung** *die* disturbance; (Rechtsw.)
disturbance of the peace; ~**tag** *der* closing
day; „**Dienstag** ~**tag**" 'closed on Tuesdays'

ruhig ① *Adj.* (a) (still, leise) quiet
(b) (friedlich, ungestört) peaceful *(times, life,
valley, etc.)*; quiet *(talk, reflection, life)*
(c) (unbewegt) calm *(sea, weather)*; still *(air)*;
(fig.) peaceful *(melody)*; (gleichmäßig) steady
(breathing, hand, steps); smooth *(flight,
crossing)*
(d) (gelassen) calm *(voice etc.)*; quiet, calm
(person)
② *adv.* (a) (still, leise) quietly; **sich** ~
verhalten keep quiet
(b) (friedlich, ohne Störungen) peacefully; (ohne
Zwischenfälle) uneventfully; *(work, think)* in
peace
(c) (unbewegt) *(sit, lie, stand)* still; (gleichmäßig)
(burn, breathe) steadily; *(run, fly)* smoothly
(d) (gelassen) *(speak, watch, sit)* calmly
③ *Adv.* by all means

Ruhm *der;* ~**[e]s** fame

rühmen ① *tr. V.* praise
② *refl. V.* boast (+ *Gen.* about)

ruhm·reich *Adj.* glorious *(victory, history)*;
celebrated *(general, army, victory)*

Ruhr *die;* ~, ~**en** dysentery *no art.*

Rühr·ei *das* scrambled egg[s *pl.*]

rühren ① *tr. V.* (a) (umrühren) stir; (einrühren)
stir *(egg, powder, etc.)* (**an, in** + *Akk.* into)
(b) (bewegen) move *(limb, fingers, etc.)*
(c) (fig.) move; touch
② *itr. V.* (a) (umrühren) stir
(b) (geh.: herrühren) **das rührt daher, dass ...:**
that stems from the fact that ...
③ *refl. V.* (a) (sich bewegen) move
(b) (Milit.) **rührt euch!** at ease!

rührend ① *Adj.* touching
② *adv.* touchingly

rühr·selig ① *Adj.* (a) emotional *(person)*
(b) (allzu gefühlvoll) over-sentimental; *(manner,
mood, etc.)*; maudlin, (coll.) tear-jerking *(play,
song, etc.)*
② *adv.* (allzu gefühlvoll) in an over-sentimental
manner

Rühr·seligkeit *die* sentimentality

Rührung *die;* ~: emotion

Ruine *die;* ~, ~**n** ruin

ruinieren *tr. V.* ruin

rülpsen *itr. V.* (ugs.) burp

rum *Adv.* (ugs.) ▶ HERUM

Rum *der;* ~**s,** ~**s** rum

Rumäne *der;* ~**n,** ~**n** Romanian

Rumänien *(das);* ~**s** Romania

Rumänin *die;* ∼, ∼**nen** Romanian
rumänisch *Adj.* Romanian
Rummel *der;* ∼**s** (ugs.) **(a)** commotion;
　(Aufhebens) fuss (**um** about)
　(b) (Jahrmarkt) fair
Rummel·platz *der* (bes. nordd.) fairground
Rumpel·kammer *die* (ugs.) boxroom
　(Brit.); junk room
rumpeln *itr. V.* (ugs.) bump and bang about
Rumpf *der;* ∼**[e]s, Rümpfe** **(a)** trunk [of the
　body]
　(b) (beim Schiff) hull
　(c) (beim Flugzeug) fuselage
rümpfen *tr. V.* **die Nase [bei etw.]** ∼:
　wrinkle one's nose [at sth.]; **über jmdn./etw.**
　die Nase rümpfen (fig.) look down one's nose
　at sb./turn up one's nose at sth.
Rumpsteak /'rumpste:k/ *das;* ∼**s,** ∼**s**
　rump steak
rum|treiben *unr. refl. V.* (ugs.)
　▶ HERUMTREIBEN
rund ⟨1⟩ *Adj.* **(a)** round
　(b) (dicklich) plump ⟨*arms etc.*⟩; chubby
　⟨*cheeks*⟩; fat ⟨*stomach*⟩
　(c) (ugs.: ganz) round ⟨*dozen, number, etc.*⟩
　⟨2⟩ *Adv.* **(a)** (ugs.: etwa) about
　(b) ∼ **um jmdn./etw.** [all] around sb./sth.
Rund-: ∼**blick** *der* panorama; view in all
　directions; ∼**brief** *der* circular [letter]
Runde *die;* ∼, ∼**n** **(a)** (Sport: Strecke) lap
　(b) (Sport: Durchgang usw.) round; **über die** ∼**n**
　kommen (fig. ugs.) get by; manage
　(c) (Personenkreis) circle; (Gesellschaft)
　company
　(d) (Rundgang) round
　(e) (Lage) round
rund-, Rund-: ∼**erneuern** *tr. V.;* ich
　runderneuere, runderneuert, rundzuerneuern
　(Kfz-W.) remould; ∼**fahrt** *die* tour (durch
　of); ∼**funk** *der* **(a)** radio; **(b)** (Einrichtung,
　Gebäude) radio station
Rundfunk-: ∼**anstalt** *die* broadcasting
　corporation; ∼**gebühren** *Pl.* radio licence
　fees; ∼**gerät** *das* radio set; ∼**sendung**
　die radio programme; ∼**sprecher** *der,*
　∼**sprecherin** *die* radio announcer
rund-, Rund-: ∼**gang** *der* round (durch
　of); ∼**herum** *Adv.* **(a)** (ringsum) all around;
　(b) (völlig) completely
rundlich *Adj.* **(a)** roundish
　(b) (mollig) plump

Rund-: ∼**reise** *die* [circular] tour (durch
　of); ∼**schreiben** *das:* ▶ ∼BRIEF; ∼**weg**
　der circular path *or* walk
runter *Adv.* (ugs.) ∼ [da]! get off [there]; *s.*
　auch HERUNTER; HINUNTER
Runzel *die;* ∼, ∼**n** wrinkle
runz[e]lig *Adj.* wrinkled
runzeln *tr. V.* **die Stirn/die Brauen** ∼:
　wrinkle one's brow/knit one's brows;
　(ärgerlich) frown
rupfen *tr. V.* **(a)** pluck ⟨*goose, hen, etc.*⟩
　(b) (abreißen) pull up ⟨*weeds, grass*⟩; pull off
　⟨*leaves etc.*⟩
ruppig *Adj.* (abwertend) gruff ⟨*person,*
　behaviour⟩; sharp ⟨*tone*⟩; **er war** ∼ **zu ihr** he
　was short with her; he snapped at her
Rüsche *die;* ∼, ∼**n** ruche; frill
Ruß *der;* ∼**es** soot
Russe *der;* ∼**n,** ∼**n** Russian
Rüssel *der;* ∼**s,** ∼ (des Elefanten) trunk; (des
　Schweins) snout; (bei Insekten u. Ä.) proboscis
rußen *itr. V.* give off sooty smoke .
Russin *die;* ∼, ∼**nen** Russian
russisch ⟨1⟩ *Adj.* Russian
　⟨2⟩ *adv.* (auf ∼) in Russian
Russisch *das;* ∼**[s]** Russian
Russ·land, *Ruß·land ⟨*das*⟩; ∼**s** Russia
rüsten *itr. V.* arm
rüstig *Adj.* sprightly; active
rustikal ⟨1⟩ *Adj.* country-style ⟨*food, inn,*
　clothes, etc.⟩; rustic ⟨*furniture*⟩
　⟨2⟩ *adv.* in [a] country style
Rüstung *die;* ∼, ∼**en** **(a)** armament *no*
　art.; (Waffen) arms *pl.;* weapons *pl.*
　(b) (hist.) suit of armour
Rüstungs-: ∼**industrie** *die* armaments
　or arms industry; ∼**kontrolle** *die* arms
　control; ∼**stopp** *der* arms freeze;
　∼**wettlauf** *der* arms race
Rute *die;* ∼, ∼**n** switch; (Birken∼, Angel∼,
　Wünschel∼) rod
Rutsch *der* guten ∼ [ins neue Jahr]! (ugs.)
　happy New Year!
Rutsch·bahn *die* slide
Rutsche *die;* ∼, ∼**n** chute
rutschen *itr. V.; mit sein* slide; ⟨*clutch,*
　carpet⟩ slip
rutschig *Adj.* slippery
rütteln *tr., itr. V.* shake

Ss

s, S /ɛs/ *das;* ~, ~ s/S

s *Abk.* = **Sekunde** sec.; s.

s. *Abk.* = **siehe**

S *Abk.* **(a)** = **Süden** S.
 (b) (österr.) = **Schilling** Sch.

S. *Abk.* = **Seite** p.

Sa. *Abk.* = **Samstag** Sat.

Saal *der;* ~[e]s, **Säle (a)** hall; (Ballsaal) ballroom
 (b) (Publikum) audience

Saar·land *das;* ~[e]s Saarland; Saar (esp. Hist.)

Saat *die;* ~, ~en **(a)** (das Gesäte) [young] crops *pl.*
 (b) (das Säen) sowing
 (c) (Samenkörner) seed[s *pl.*]

Säbel *der;* ~s, ~: sabre

Sabotage /zabo'ta:ʒə/ *die;* ~, ~n sabotage *no art.*

Sabotage-akt *der* act of sabotage

sabotieren *tr.* V. sabotage

Sach-: ~**bearbeiter** *der,* ~**bearbeiterin** *die* person responsible (**für** for); (Experte) specialist, expert (**für** on); ~**beschädigung** *die* (Rechtsw.) wilful damage to property; ~**buch** *das* [popular] non-fiction book; ~**bücher lesen** read non-fiction *sing.*

sach·dienlich *Adj.* useful

Sache *die;* ~, ~n **(a)** things
 (b) (Angelegenheit) matter; business (esp. derog.); **zur ~ kommen** come to the point
 (c) (Rechtssache) case
 (d) (Anliegen) cause

sach-, Sach-: ~**gebiet** *das* subject [area]; field; ~**gemäß**, ~**gerecht** 1 *Adj.* proper; correct; 2 *adv.* properly; correctly; ~**kenntnis** *die* expertise; knowledge of the subject; ~**kundig** 1 *Adj.* with a knowledge of the subject *postpos.*, *not pred.;* 2 *adv.* expertly

sachlich 1 *Adj.* **(a)** (objektiv) objective; (nüchtern) functional ‹building, style, etc.›; matter-of-fact ‹letter etc.›
 (b) (sachbezogen) factual ‹error›
 2 *adv.* **(a)** (objektiv) objectively; ‹state› as a matter of fact; (nüchtern) ‹furnished› in a functional style; ‹written› in a matter-of-fact way
 (b) (sachbezogen) factually ‹wrong›

sächlich *Adj.* (Sprachw.) neuter

Sachlichkeit *die;* ~: objectivity; (Nüchternheit) functionalism

Sach-: ~**register** *das* [subject] index; ~**schaden** *der* damage [to property] *no indef. art.*

Sachse *der;* ~n, ~n Saxon

Sachsen (*das*); ~s Saxony

Sachsen-Anhalt (*das*); ~s Saxony-Anhalt

Sächsin *die;* ~, ~nen Saxon

sacht, sachte 1 *Adj.* **(a)** (behutsam) gentle
 (b) (leise) quiet
 2 *adv.* **(a)** gently
 (b) (leise) quietly

Sach-: ~**verhalt** *der;* ~~[e]s, ~~e facts *pl.* [of the matter]; ~**verstand** *der* expertise; grasp of the subject; ~**verständige** *der/die; adj. Dekl.* expert

Sack *der;* ~[e]s, **Säcke** sack; (aus Papier, Kunststoff) bag

Sack-: ~**gasse** *die* cul-de-sac; ~**hüpfen** *das;* ~~s sack race

Sadismus *der;* ~: sadism *no art.*

Sadist *der;* ~en, ~en, **Sadistin** *die;* ~, ~nen sadist

sadistisch 1 *Adj.* sadistic
 2 *adv.* sadistically

säen *tr.* (*auch itr.*) V. sow

Saft *der;* ~[e]s, **Säfte (a)** juice
 (b) (in Pflanzen) sap

saftig *Adj.* **(a)** juicy; sappy ‹stem›; lush ‹meadow, green›
 (b) (ugs.) hefty ‹slap, blow›; steep (coll.) ‹prices, bill›; crude ‹joke, song, etc.›; strongly-worded ‹letter etc.›

saft-, Saft-: ~**laden** *der* (salopp abwertend) lousy outfit (coll.); ~**los** *Adj.* **(a)** juiceless
 (b) (fig.) feeble, anodyne ‹language›; ~**- und kraftlos** feeble; wishy-washy; (*adv.*) without any zest; ~**sack** *der* (derb abwertend) bastard (coll.)

Sage *die;* ~, ~n legend; (bes. nordische) saga

Säge *die;* ~, ~n saw

Säge-: ~**blatt** *das* saw blade; ~**mehl** sawdust

sagen 1 *tr.* V. **(a)** say; **was ich noch ~ wollte** [oh] by the way; **unter uns gesagt** between you and me
 (b) (mitteilen) **jmdm. etw. ~:** say sth. to sb.; (zur Information) tell sb. sth.
 (c) (nennen) **zu jmdm./etw. X ~:** call sb./sth. X
 (d) (anordnen, befehlen) tell
 2 *refl.* V. **sich** (*Dat.*) **etw. ~:** say sth. to oneself

sägen *tr., itr.* V. saw

Säge-: ~späne *Pl.* wood shavings;
~**werk** *das* sawmill

sah *1. u. 3. Pers. Sg. Prät. v.* SEHEN

Sahne *die;* ~: cream

Saison /zɛ'zõː/ *die;* ~, ~s season

saisonal /zɛzo'naːl/ [1] *Adj.* seasonal
[2] *adv.* ⟨fluctuate⟩ according to the season

Saite *die;* ~, ~n string

Saiten·instrument *das* stringed
instrument

Sakko *der od. das;* ~s, ~s jacket

Sakrament *das;* ~[e]s, ~e sacrament

Sakristei *die;* ~, ~en sacristy

säkularisieren *tr. V.* secularize ⟨property,
art, etc.⟩; deconsecrate ⟨church⟩

Salami *die;* ~, ~[s] salami

Salami-taktik *die* step-by-step policy

Salat *der;* ~[e]s, ~e (a) salad
(b) [grüner] ~: lettuce; **ein Kopf** ~: a [head
of] lettuce

Salat-: ~**besteck** *das* salad servers *pl.;*
~**soße** *die* salad dressing

Salbe *die;* ~, ~n ointment

Salbei *der od. die. die;* ~: sage

Saldo *der;* ~s, ~s *od.* Saldi (Buchf., Finanzw.)
balance

Säle ▶ SAAL

Salmiak *der od. das;* ~: sal ammoniac

Salmonelle *die;* ~, ~n salmonella

Salon /za'lõː/ *der;* ~s, ~s (a) (Raum)
drawing room
(b) (Geschäft) [hair *etc.*] salon

salopp [1] *Adj.* casual ⟨clothes⟩; informal
⟨behaviour⟩
[2] *adv.* ⟨dress⟩ casually

Salto *der;* ~s, ~s *od.* Salti somersault; (beim
Turnen auch) salto

Salut *der;* ~[e]s, ~e (Milit.) salute; ~
schießen fire a salute

salutieren *itr. V.* (bes. Milit.) salute

Salut·schuss, *Salut·schuß *der* (Milit.)
gun salute

Salve *die;* ~, ~n (Milit.) salvo; (aus Gewehren)
volley

Salz *das;* ~es, ~e salt

salzen *tr. V.* salt

salzig *Adj.* salty

Salz-: ~**kartoffel** *die* boiled potato;
~**säure** *die* (Chemie) hydrochloric acid;
~**stange** *die* salt stick; ~**streuer** *der;*
~~s, ~~: salt sprinkler; salt shaker
(Amer.); ~**wasser** *das* (a) (zum Kochen)
salted water; (b) (Meerwasser) salt water

Sambia (*das*) ~s Zambia

Samen *der;* ~s, ~ (a) (Samenkorn) seed
(b) (Samenkörner) seed[s *pl.*]
(c) (Sperma) sperm; semen

Samen-: ~**bank** *die; Pl.* ~~en (Med.,
Tiermed.) sperm bank; ~**erguss**,
*~**erguß** *der* ejaculation; ~**korn** *das* seed

Sammel-: ~**büchse** *die* collecting box;
~**mappe** *die* folder; file

sammeln [1] *tr. (auch itr.) V.* (a) collect;
gather ⟨honey, firewood, fig.: experiences,
impressions, etc.⟩; gather, pick ⟨berries etc.⟩
(b) (zusammenkommen lassen) gather ⟨people⟩
[together]; assemble ⟨people⟩; cause ⟨light
rays⟩ to converge
[2] *refl. V.* gather [together]

Sammler *der;* ~s, ~: collector

Sammlung *die;* ~, ~en (a) collection
(b) [innere] ~: composure

Samstag *der;* ~[e]s, ~e Saturday; *s. auch*
DIENSTAG

samstags *Adv.* on Saturdays

samt [1] *Präp. mit Dat.* together with
[2] *Adv.* ~ **und sonders** one and all

Samt *der;* ~[e]s, ~e velvet

samten *Adj.* velvet

Samt·handschuh *der* velvet glove; **jmdn.
mit** ~**en anfassen** (fig.) handle sb. with kid
gloves

samtig *Adj.* velvety

sämtlich *Indefinitpron. u. unbest. Zahlwort*
all the

Sand *der;* ~[e]s sand

Sandale *die;* ~, ~n sandal

Sand-: ~**bank** *die; Pl.* ~bänke sandbank;
~**dorn** *der; Pl.* ~~e (Bot.) hippopha;
[Echter] ~**dorn** sea buckthorn ~**düne** *die*
sand dune

sandig *Adj.* sandy

sand-, Sand-: ~**kasten** *der* [child's]
sandpit; sandbox (Amer.); ~**kuchen** *der*
Madeira cake; ~**mann** *der,*
~**männchen** *das* sandman; ~**stein** *der*
sandstone; ~**strahlen** *tr. V.* (Technik)
sandblast; ~**strand** *der* sandy beach

sandte *1. u. 3. Pers. Sg. Prät. v.* SENDEN

sanft [1] *Adj.* gentle; (leise) soft; (friedlich)
peaceful
[2] *adv.* gently; (leise) softly; (friedlich)
peacefully

Sänfte *die;* ~, ~n litter; (geschlossen) sedan
chair

Sanftheit *die;* ~: gentleness; (von Klängen,
Licht, Farben) softness

Sanftmut *die;* ~: gentleness; **mit** ~:
gently; (nachsichtig) leniently

sanftmütig [1] *Adj.* gentle; docile ⟨horse⟩
[2] *adv.* gently

Sanftmütigkeit *die;* ~: gentleness;
(Fügsamkeit) docility

sang *1. u. 3. Pers. Sg. Prät. v.* SINGEN

Sänger *der;* ~s, ~, **Sängerin** *die;* ~,
~nen singer

sanieren [1] *tr. V.* (a) redevelop ⟨area⟩;
rehabilitate ⟨building⟩; (renovieren) renovate
[and improve] ⟨flat etc.⟩
(b) (Wirtsch.) restore ⟨firm⟩ to profitability · · · ⟩

S

2 *refl. V.* ⟨*company etc.*⟩ restore itself to profitability; ⟨*person*⟩ get oneself out of the red

Sanierung *die;* ~, ~**en (a)** ▶ SANIEREN A: redevelopment; rehabilitation; renovation
(b) ▶ SANIEREN B: restoration to profitability

sanitär *Adj.* sanitary

Sanitäter *der;* ~**s,** ~, **Sanitäterin** *die;* ~, ~**nen** first-aid worker; (im Krankenwagen) ambulance worker

sank *1. u. 3. Pers. Sg. Prät. v.* SINKEN

Sanktion *die;* ~, ~**en** sanction

sanktionieren *tr. V.* sanction

Sanktionierung *die;* ~, ~**en** sanctioning *no indef. art.*

sann *1. u. 3. Pers. Sg. Prät. v.* SINNEN

Saphir *der;* ~**s,** ~**e** sapphire

Sardelle *die;* ~, ~**n** anchovy

Sardine *die;* ~, ~**n** sardine

Sarg *der;* ~**[e]s, Särge** coffin

Sarkasmus *der;* ~: sarcasm

sarkastisch 1 *Adj.* sarcastic
2 *adv.* sarcastically

saß *1. u. 3. Pers. Sg. Prät. v.* SITZEN

Satan *der* (bibl.) Satan *no def. art.*

Satellit *der;* ~**en,** ~**en** satellite

Satelliten-: ~**fernsehen** *das* satellite television; ~**schüssel** *die* (ugs.) satellite dish; ~**technologie** *die* satellite technology

Satire *die;* ~, ~**n** satire

satirisch 1 *Adj.* satirical
2 *adv.* satirically; with a satirical touch

satt *Adj.* **(a)** full [up] *pred.*; well-fed; **sich** ~ **essen/trinken** eat/drink as much as one wants; eat/drink one's fill
(b) jmdn./etw. ~ **haben** (ugs.) be fed up with sb./sth. (coll.)

Sattel *der;* ~**s, Sättel** saddle

satteln 1 *tr. V.* saddle
2 *itr. V.* saddle the/one's horse

sättigen *itr. V.* be filling

Sattler *der;* ~**s,** ~, **Sattlerin** *die;* ~, ~**nen** saddler; (allgemein) leather worker

Satz *der;* ~**es, Sätze (a)** (sprachliche Einheit) sentence
(b) (Musik) movement
(c) (Tennis, Volleyball) set; (Tischtennis, Badminton) game
(d) (Sprung) leap; jump
(e) (Amtsspr.: Tarif) rate
(f) (Set) set
(g) (Bodensatz) sediment; (von Kaffee) grounds *pl.*

Satz-glied *das,* **Satz-teil** *der* (Sprachw.) component part [of a/the sentence]

Satzung *die;* ~, ~**en** articles of association *pl.*; statutes *pl.*

Satz-zeichen *das* punctuation mark

Sau *die;* ~, **Säue (a)** (weibliches Schwein) sow

(b) (bes. südd.: Schwein) pig
(c) die ~ **rauslassen** (fig. ugs.) let one's hair down

sau-, Sau- (salopp) bloody ... (Brit. sl.); damn ... (coll.)

sauber 1 *Adj.* **(a)** clean; **etw.** ~ **machen** clean sth.; ~ **machen** (putzen) clean; do the cleaning
(b) (sorgfältig) neat
2 *adv.* **(a)** (sorgfältig) neatly
(b) (fehlerlos) [**sehr**] ~: [quite] perfectly

Sauberkeit *die;* ~: cleanness

säuberlich 1 *Adj.* neat
2 *adv.* neatly; **fein** ~ **geordnet/verpackt** *usw.* neatly arranged/packed *etc.*

*sauber|machen ▶ SAUBER 1A

säubern *tr. V.* **(a)** clean
(b) (befreien) clear, rid (**von** of); purge ⟨*party, government, etc.*⟩ (**von** of)

Säuberung *die;* ~, ~**en (a)** cleaning
(b) (Entfernung) purging
(c) (Politik) purge; **ethnische** ~ (verhüll.) ethnic cleansing

Säuberungs-aktion *die* (Politik) purge; clean-up operation

Sauce ▶ SOSSE

Saudi *der;* ~**s,** ~**s** Saudi

Saudi-Arabien (*das*) Saudi Arabia

sauer 1 *Adj.* **(a)** sour; pickled ⟨*herring, gherkin, etc.*⟩; acid[ic] ⟨*wine, vinegar*⟩; **saurer Regen** acid rain
(b) (ugs.: verärgert) cross, annoyed (**auf** + *Akk.* with)
2 *adv.* in vinegar

Sauer-braten *der:* braised beef marinated in vinegar and herbs; sauerbraten (Amer.)

Sauerei *die;* ~, ~**en** (salopp abwertend) **(a)** (Unflätigkeit) obscenity
(b) (Gemeinheit) bloody scandal (coll.)

Sauer-: ~**kirsche** *die* sour cherry; ~**kraut** *das* sauerkraut

säuerlich *Adj.* [leicht] ~: slightly sour; slightly sharp ⟨*sauce*⟩

Sauer-: ~**stoff** *der* oxygen; ~**stoff-gerät** *das* oxygen apparatus; ~**stoff-mangel** *der* lack of oxygen; ~**teig** *der* leaven

saufen 1 *unr. itr. V.* (salopp: trinken) drink; swig (coll.); (Alkohol trinken) drink; booze (coll.)
2 *unr. tr. V.* (salopp: trinken) drink

Säufer *der;* ~**s,** ~ (salopp) boozer (coll.)

säuft *3. Pers. Sg. Präsens v.* SAUFEN

saugen 1 *tr. V.* (a) *auch unr.* suck
(b) *auch itr.* (staubsaugen) vacuum; hoover (coll.)
2 *regelm.* (*auch unr.*) *itr. V.* **an etw.** (*Dat.*) ~: suck [at] sth.
3 *unr.* (*auch regelm.*) *refl. V.* **sich voll etw.** ~: become soaked with sth.

säugen *tr. V.* suckle

Säuge-tier *das* (Zool.) mammal

Säugling *der;* ~**s,** ~**e** baby

Säuglings-: ~**alter** das infancy; babyhood; ~**pflege** die baby care

Säule die; ~, ~**n** column; (nur als Stütze, auch fig.) pillar

Saum der; ~[e]s, Säume hem

säumen tr. V. hem; (fig. geh.) line

säumig (geh.) Adj. tardy

Sauna die; ~, ~s od. Saunen sauna

Säure die; ~, ~n (a) (von Früchten) sourness; (von Wein, Essig) acidity; (von Soßen) sharpness (b) (Chemie) acid

säure-: ~**beständig** Adj. acid-resistant; ~**frei** Adj. acid-free

Saure-gurken-zeit, Saure-Gurken-Zeit die (ugs.) silly season (Brit.)

Saurier /ˈzauˌriɐ̯/ der; ~s, ~: large prehistoric reptile

Saus: in ~ und Braus leben live the high life

säuseln ① itr. V. ⟨leaves, branches, etc.⟩ rustle; ⟨wind⟩ murmur ② tr. V. (iron.: sagen) whisper

sausen itr. V. (a) ⟨wind⟩ whistle; ⟨storm⟩ roar; ⟨head, ears⟩ buzz (b) mit sein ⟨person⟩ rush; ⟨vehicle⟩ roar (c) mit sein ⟨whip, bullet, etc.⟩ whistle

sau-, Sau-: ~**stall** der (fig. salopp abwertend) hole (coll.); dump (coll.); ~**stark** Adj. (salopp) bloody brilliant (sl.); ~**wetter** das (salopp abwertend) lousy weather (coll.); ~**wohl** Adj. sich ~wohl fühlen (salopp) feel bloody (Brit. sl.) or (coll.) damn good or great

Savanne /zaˈvanə/ die; ~, ~n savannah

Saxophon das; ~s, ~e saxophone

SB- /ɛsˈbeː-/ self-service attrib.

S-Bahn /ˈɛs-/ die city and suburban railway

Scanner /ˈskænɐ/ der; ~s, ~ (DV, Med., graf. Technik) scanner

Schabe die; ~, ~n cockroach

schaben tr., itr. V. scrape

Schaber der; ~s, ~: scraper

schäbig ① Adj. (a) (abgenutzt) shabby (b) (jämmerlich, gering) pathetic (c) (gemein) shabby ② adv. (a) (abgenutzt) shabbily (b) (jämmerlich) miserably (c) (gemein) meanly

Schablone die; ~, ~n pattern

Schach das; ~s, ~s (a) (Spiel) chess (b) (Stellung) check; jmdn./etw. in ~ halten (ugs. fig.) keep sb./sth. in check

Schach-: ~**brett** das chessboard; ~**figur** die chess piece; ~**spiel** das (a) (Spiel) chess; (das Spielen) chess-playing; (b) (Brett und Figuren) chess set

Schacht der; ~[e]s, Schächte shaft

Schachtel die; ~, ~n (a) box; eine ~ Zigaretten a packet or (Amer.) pack of cigarettes (b) alte ~ (salopp abwertend) old bag (sl.)

schade Adj. [ach, wie] ~! [what a] pity or

shame; [es ist] ~ um jmdn./etw. it's a pity or shame about sb./sth.; für jmdn./für od. zu etw. zu ~ sein be too good for sb./sth.

Schädel der; ~s, ~: skull; (Kopf) head

Schädel-basis-bruch der (Med.) basal skull fracture

Schädel-bruch der (Med.) skull fracture

schaden itr. V. jmdm./einer Sache ~: damage or harm sb./sth.

Schaden der; ~s, Schäden (a) damage no pl., no indef. art.; ein kleiner/großer ~: little/ major damage (b) (Nachteil) disadvantage

schaden-, Schaden-: ~**ersatz** der (Rechtsw.) damages pl.; ~**freude** die malicious pleasure; ~**froh** ① Adj. gloating; ~froh sein gloat; ② adv. with malicious pleasure

schadhaft Adj. defective

Schadhaftigkeit die; ~: defectiveness

schädigen tr. V. damage ⟨health, reputation, interests⟩; harm, hurt ⟨person⟩; cause losses to ⟨firm, industry, etc.⟩

Schädigung die; ~, ~en damage no pl., no indef. art. ⟨Gen. to⟩

schädlich Adj. harmful

Schädling der; ~s, ~e pest

Schad-stoff der harmful chemical

schadstoff-arm Adj. (bes. Kfz-W.) low in harmful substances postpos.; clean-exhaust attrib. ⟨vehicle⟩

Schaf das; ~[e]s, ~e (a) sheep (b) (ugs.: Dummkopf) twit (Brit. coll.)

Schaf-bock der ram

Schäfchen das; ~s, ~: [little] sheep; (Lamm) lamb

Schäfchen-wolke die fleecy cloud

Schäfer der; ~s, ~: shepherd

Schäfer-hund der sheepdog; [deutscher] ~: Alsatian

Schäferin die; ~, ~nen shepherdess

Schaf-fell das sheepskin

schaffen ① unr. tr. V. (a) create (b) auch regelm. (herstellen) create ⟨conditions, jobs, situation, etc.⟩; make ⟨room, space, fortune⟩ ② tr. V. (a) (bewältigen) manage; es ~, etw. zu tun manage to do sth. (b) (ugs.: erschöpfen) wear out (c) etw. aus etw./in etw. (Akk.) ~: get sth. out of/into sth. ③ itr. V. (a) (südd.: arbeiten) work (b) sich (Dat.) zu ~ machen busy oneself; jmdm. zu ~ machen cause sb. trouble

Schaffner der; ~s ~ (im Bus) conductor; (im Zug) guard (Brit.); conductor (Amer.)

Schaffnerin die; ~, ~nen (im Bus) conductress (Brit.); (im Zug) guard (Brit.); conductress (Amer.)

Schaffung die; ~: creation

Schafott das; ~[e]s, ~e scaffold

Schafs-käse der sheep's milk cheese

S

Schaf·wolle *die* sheep's wool

Schakal *der;* ~s, ~e jackal

schal *Adj.* stale ⟨*drink, taste, smell, joke*⟩; empty ⟨*words, feeling*⟩

Schal *der;* ~s, ~s *od.* ~e scarf

Schale *die;* ~, ~n (a) (Obstschale) skin; (abgeschälte ~) peel *no pl.;*
(b) (Nussschale, Eierschale) shell
(c) (Schüssel) bowl; (flacher) dish
(d) sich in ~ werfen *od.* schmeißen (ugs.) get dressed [up] to the nines

schälen ① *tr. V.* peel ⟨*fruit, vegetable*⟩; shell ⟨*egg, nut, pea*⟩
② *refl. V.* peel

Schall *der;* ~[e]s, ~e *od.* Schälle sound

Schall·dämpfer *der* (a) silencer
(b) (Musik) mute

schall·dicht *Adj.* soundproof

schallen *regelm.* (*auch unr.*) *itr. V.* ring out; ~des Gelächter ringing laughter

Schall-: ~**geschwindigkeit** *die* speed *or* velocity of sound; ~**mauer** *die* sound *or* sonic barrier; ~**platte** *die* record

Schalotte *die;* ~, ~n shallot

schalt *1. u. 3. Pers. Sg. Prät. v.* SCHELTEN

schalten ① *tr. V.* switch
② *itr. V.* (a) (Schalter betätigen) switch, turn (auf + *Akk.* to)
(b) ⟨*machine*⟩ switch (auf + *Akk.* to)
(c) (im Auto) change [gear]
(d) ~ und walten manage one's affairs
(e) (ugs.: begreifen) twig (coll.); catch on (coll.)

Schalter *der;* ~s, ~ (a) switch
(b) (Post-, Bankschalter usw.) counter

Schalter-: ~**beamte** *der*, ~**beamtin** *die* counter clerk; (im Bahnhof) ticket clerk; ~**halle** *die* hall; (im Bahnhof) booking hall (Brit.); ticket office

Schalt·jahr *das* leap year

Schaltung *die;* ~, ~en (Elektrot.) circuit; wiring system

Scham *die;* ~: shame

schämen *refl. V.* be ashamed (*Gen.,* für, wegen *of*)

Scham·gefühl *das* sense of shame

schamhaft ① *Adj.* bashful
② *adv.* bashfully

scham·los ① *Adj.* (a) (skrupellos, dreist) shameless
(b) (unanständig) indecent; shameless ⟨*person*⟩
② *adv.* (a) (skrupellos, dreist) shamelessly
(b) (unanständig) indecently

Schampon *das;* ~s, ~s ▶ SHAMPOO

schamponieren *tr. V.* shampoo

Schande *die;* ~: disgrace

schändlich ① *Adj.* disgraceful
② *adv.* disgracefully

Schändlichkeit *die;* ~: disgracefulness

Schar *die;* ~, ~en crowd; horde

scharen·weise *Adv.* in swarms *or* hordes

scharf; schärfer, schärfst... ① *Adj.* (a) sharp
(b) (stark gewürzt, brennend, stechend) hot; strong ⟨*drink, vinegar, etc.*⟩; caustic ⟨*chemical*⟩; pungent ⟨*smell*⟩
(c) (durchdringend) shrill; (hell) harsh; (kalt) biting ⟨*cold, wind, etc.*⟩; sharp ⟨*frost*⟩
(d) (deutlich wahrnehmend) keen
(e) (schnell) fast; hard ⟨*ride, gallop, etc.*⟩
(f) (explosiv) live; (Ballspiele) powerful ⟨*shot*⟩
(g) das ~e S (bes. österr.) the letter 'ß'
(h) ~ auf jmdn./etw. sein (ugs.) really fancy sb. (coll.)/be really keen on sth.
② *adv.* (a) ~ würzen/abschmecken season/flavour highly; ~ riechen smell pungent
(b) (durchdringend) shrilly; (hell) harshly; (kalt) bitingly
(c) (deutlich wahrnehmend) ⟨*listen, watch, etc.*⟩ closely, intently; ⟨*think, consider, etc.*⟩ hard
(d) (deutlich hervortretend) sharply
(e) (schonungslos) ⟨*attack, criticize, etc.*⟩ sharply, strongly; ⟨*watch, observe, etc.*⟩ closely
(f) (schnell) fast; ~ bremsen brake hard *or* sharply

Schärfe *die;* ~ (a) sharpness
(b) (von Geschmack) hotness; (von Chemikalien) causticity; (von Geruch) pungency
(c) (Intensität) shrillness; (des Frostes) sharpness

schärfen ① *tr. V.* (auch fig.) sharpen
② *refl. V.* become sharper *or* keener

scharf-, Scharf-: ~**kantig** *Adj.* sharp-edged; ~**macher** *der* (ugs.) rabble-rouser; ~**macherei** *die;* ~~, ~~en (ugs.) rabble-rousing; ~**macherin** *die:* ▶ ~MACHER; ~**sichtig** *Adj.* sharp-sighted; perspicacious; ~**sinn** *der* astuteness; ~**sinnig** ① *Adj.* astute; ② *adv.* astutely

Scharlach *der;* ~s (Med.) scarlet fever

Scharlatan *der;* ~s, ~e (abwertend) charlatan

Scharnier *das;* ~s, ~e hinge

scharren ① *itr. V.* (a) scrape
(b) (wühlen) scratch
② *tr. V.* scrape, scratch out ⟨*hole, hollow, etc.*⟩

Schaschlik *der od. das;* ~s, ~s (Kochk.) shashlik

Schatten *der;* ~s, ~ (a) shadow
(b) (schattiger Bereich) shade

Schatten-: ~**kabinett** *das* (Politik) shadow cabinet; ~**riss**, *~**riß** *der* silhouette; ~**seite** *die* shady side; die ~seiten des Lebens kennen lernen (fig.) get to know the dark side of life

schattig *Adj.* shady

Schatz *der;* ~es, Schätze treasure *no indef. art.*

schätzen ① *tr. V.* (a) estimate; sich glücklich ~: deem oneself lucky
(b) (ugs.: annehmen) reckon
(c) (würdigen, hoch achten) jmdn. ~: hold sb. in high esteem

S

2 *itr. V.* guess

Schätzung *die;* ~, ~en estimate

Schätz·wert *der* estimated value

Schau *die;* ~, ~en (a) (Ausstellung) exhibition

(b) (Vorführung) show

(c) zur ~ stellen (ausstellen) exhibit; display; (offen zeigen) display

Schauder *der;* ~s, ~: shiver

schauderhaft 1 *Adj.* terrible

2 *adv.* terribly

schaudern *itr. V.* (a) (vor Kälte) shiver (b) (vor Angst) shudder

schauen (bes. südd., österr., schweiz.)

1 *itr. V.* (a) look

(b) (sich kümmern um) **nach jmdm./etw.** ~: take *or* have a look at sb./sth.

(c) (achten) **auf etw.** (*Akk.*) ~: set store by sth.

(d) (ugs.: sich bemühen) **schau, dass du ...**: see *or* mind that you ...

(e) (nachsehen) have a look

2 *tr. V.* Fernsehen ~: watch television

Schauer *der;* ~s, ~: shower

Schauer·geschichte *die* horror story

schauerlich 1 *Adj.* (a) horrifying (b) (ugs.: fürchterlich) terrible (coll.)

2 (ugs.: fürchterlich) terribly (coll.)

Schaufel *die;* ~, ~n shovel; (Kehr~) dustpan

schaufeln *tr. V.* shovel; (graben) dig

Schau·fenster *das* shop window

Schaufenster-: ~**bummel** *der:* einen ~**bummel machen** go window shopping; ~**einbruch** *der* raid on a shop window

Schaukel *die;* ~, ~n (a) swing (b) (Wippe) see-saw

schaukeln 1 *itr. V.* (a) swing; (im Schaukelstuhl) rock

(b) (sich hin und her bewegen) sway [to and fro]; (sich auf und ab bewegen) ⟨ship, boat⟩ pitch and toss; ⟨vehicle⟩ bump [up and down]

2 *tr. V.* rock

Schaukel-: ~**pferd** *das* rocking horse; ~**stuhl** *der* rocking chair

Schau·lustige *der/die; adj. Dekl.* curious onlooker

Schaum *der;* ~s, Schäume (a) foam; (von Seife usw.) lather; (von Getränken, Suppen usw.) froth

(b) (Geifer) foam; froth

schäumen *itr. V.* foam; froth; ⟨soap etc.⟩ lather; ⟨beer, fizzy drink, etc.⟩ froth [up]

Schaum·gummi *der* foam rubber

schaumig *Adj.* frothy; **Butter und Zucker** ~ **rühren** beat butter and sugar until fluffy

Schaum-: ~**schläger** *der* (abwertend) boaster; ~**schlägerei** *die* (abwertend) boasting; ~**schlägerin** *die:* ▶ ~SCHLÄGER; ~**stoff** *der* [plastic] foam; ~**wein** *der* sparkling wine

Schau·platz *der* scene

schaurig *Adj.* (furchtbar) dreadful; frightful; (unheimlich) eerie

Schau-: ~**spiel** *das* (a) (Drama) drama *no art.;* (b) (ernstes Stück) play; (c) (geh.: Anblick) spectacle; ~**spieler** *der* actor; ~**spielerin** *die* actress; ~**steller** *der;* ~~s, ~~: showman; ~**stellerin** *die;* ~~, ~~nen showwoman

Scheck *der;* ~s, ~s cheque

Scheck-: ~**heft** *das* chequebook; ~**karte** *die* cheque card

scheel (ugs.) 1 *Adj.* disapproving; (neidisch) envious; jealous

2 *adv.* disapprovingly; (neidisch) enviously; jealously

scheffeln *tr. V.* (ugs.) rake in (coll.)

Scheibe *die;* ~, ~n (a) disc

(b) (abgeschnittene) slice

(c) (Glasscheibe) pane [of glass]; (Fensterscheibe) [window] pane

Scheiben-: ~**bremse** *die* disc brake; ~**wasch·anlage** *die* (Kfz-W.) windscreen washer system *or* unit; ~**wischer** *der* windscreen wiper

Scheide *die;* ~, ~n (a) sheath

(b) (Anat.) vagina

scheiden *unr. tr. V.* dissolve ⟨marriage⟩; divorce ⟨married couple⟩; **sich** ~ **lassen** get divorced *or* get a divorce

Scheidung *die;* ~, ~en divorce

Schein *der;* ~[e]s, ~e (a) (Lichtschein) light (b) (Anschein) appearances *pl., no art.;* (Täuschung) pretence; **etw. nur zum** ~ **tun** [only] pretend to do sth.; make a show of doing sth.

(c) (Geldschein) note

scheinbar 1 *Adj.* apparent; seeming

2 *adv.* seemingly

scheinen *unr. itr. V.* (a) shine

(b) (den Eindruck erwecken) seem; appear; **mir scheint, [dass] ...**: it seems *or* appears to me that ...

schein-, Schein-: ~**heilig** 1 *Adj.* hypocritical; 2 *adv.* hypocritically; ~**heiligkeit** *die* hypocrisy; ~**tot** *Adj.* (a) (Med.) apparently *or* seemingly dead; (b) (salopp: sehr alt) with one foot in the grave *postpos.;* ~**werfer** *der* floodlight; (am Auto) headlight; ~**werfer·licht** *das* floodlight; (des Autos) headlights *pl.;* (im Theater, Museum usw.) spotlight [beam]

Scheiße *die;* ~ (derb) shit (coarse); crap (coarse)

scheiß·egal *Adj.* (derb) ~ **sein** not matter a damn (sl.); **das ist mir** ~: I don't give a damn (sl.) *or* (coarse) shit

scheißen *unr. itr. V.* (derb) [have *or* (Amer.) take a] shit (coarse); crap (coarse); have a crap (coarse)

Scheiß·kerl *der* (derb) bastard (coll.)

Scheitel *der;* ~s, ~: parting

scheiteln *tr. V.* part ⟨hair⟩

scheitern *itr. V.; mit sein* fail; ⟨talks, marriage⟩ break down; ⟨plan, project⟩ fail, fall through

Schelle *die;* ~, ~n bell

schellen *itr. V.* (westd.) ▶ KLINGELN

Schell·fisch *der* haddock

Schelm *der;* ~[e]s, ~e rascal; rogue

schelmisch ①*Adj.* roguish
②*adv.* roguishly

Schelte *die;* ~, ~n (geh.) scolding

schelten (südd., geh.) ①*unr. itr. V.* **auf** *od.* **über jmdn./etw.** ~: moan about sb./sth.
②*unr. tr. V.* scold

Schema *das;* ~s, ~s *od.* ~ta *od.* **Schemen** pattern

schematisch ①*Adj.* (a) diagrammatic
(b) (mechanisch) mechanical
②*adv.* (a) in diagram form
(b) (mechanisch) mechanically

Schemel *der;* ~s, ~ (a) stool
(b) (südd.: Fußbank) footstool

Schenkel *der;* ~s, ~: thigh

schenken *tr. V.* (a) give; **jmdm. etw.** [**zum Geburtstag**] ~: give sb. sth. *or* sth. to sb. [as a birthday present *or* for his/her birthday]
(b) (ugs.: erlassen) **jmdm./sich etw.** ~: spare sb./oneself sth.

scheppern *itr. V.* (ugs.) clank

Scherbe *die;* ~, ~n fragment

Schere *die;* ~, ~n (a) scissors *pl.;* **eine** ~: a pair of scissors
(b) (Zool.) claw

scheren¹ *unr. tr. V.* crop; (von Haar befreien) shear, clip ⟨sheep⟩

scheren² *tr., refl. V.* **sich um jmdn./etw. nicht** ~: not care about sb./sth.

Schererei *Pl.* (ugs.) trouble *no pl.*

Scherz *der;* ~es, ~e joke

scherzen *itr. V.* joke

scherzhaft ①*Adj.* jocular
②*adv.* jocularly

scheu ①*Adj.* shy; timid ⟨animal⟩; (ehrfürchtig) awed
②*adv.* shyly; (von Tieren) timidly

Scheu *die;* ~ (a) shyness; (Ehrfurcht) awe
(b) (von Tieren) timidity

scheuchen *tr. V.* shoo; drive

scheuen ①*tr. V.* shrink from; shun ⟨people, light, company, etc.⟩
②*refl. V.* **sich vor etw.** (*Dat.*) ~: be afraid of *or* shrink from sth.
③*itr. V.* ⟨horse⟩ shy (**vor** + *Dat.* at)

scheuern ①*tr., itr. V.* (a) (reinigen) scour; scrub
(b) (reiben) rub; chafe
②*tr. V.* (reiben an) rub

Scheuer-: ~**pulver** *das* scouring powder; ~**tuch** *das; Pl.* ~**tücher** scouring cloth

Scheune *die;* ~, ~n barn

Scheusal *das;* ~s, ~e monster

---

scheußlich ①*Adj.* (a) dreadful
(b) (ugs.: äußerst unangenehm) dreadful (coll.); ghastly (coll.) ⟨weather, taste, smell⟩
②*adv.* (a) dreadfully
(b) (ugs.: sehr) dreadfully (coll.)

Scheußlichkeit *die;* ~, ~en (a) dreadfulness
(b) (etw. Scheußliches) dreadful thing

Schi *usw.* ▶ SKI *usw.*

Schicht *die;* ~, ~en (a) (Lage) layer; (Geol.) stratum; (von Farbe) coat; (sehr dünn) film
(b) (Gesellschaftsschicht) stratum
(c) (Arbeitsschicht) shift; ~ **arbeiten** work shifts; be on shift work

Schicht·arbeit *die* shift work

schichten *tr. V.* stack

schick ①*Adj.* (a) stylish; chic ⟨clothes, fashions⟩; smart ⟨woman, girl, man⟩
(b) (ugs.: großartig, toll) great (coll.); fantastic (coll.)
②*adv.* stylishly; smartly ⟨furnished, decorated⟩

schicken ①*tr. V.* send; **jmdm. etw.** ~, **etw. an jmdn.** ~: send sth. to sb.; send sb. sth.
②*itr. V.* **nach jmdm.** ~: send for sb.
③*refl. V.* (veralt.: sich ziemen) be proper *or* fitting

Schickeria *die;* ~ (ugs.) smart set

Schicksal *das;* ~s, ~e: [das] ~: fate; destiny; (schweres Los) fate

Schicksals·schlag *der* stroke of fate

Schiebe·dach *das* sunroof

schieben ①*unr. tr. V.* (a) push
(b) (stecken) put
(c) **etw. auf jmdn./etw.** ~: blame sb./sth. for sth.
②*unr. refl. V.* **sich durch die Menge** ~: push one's way through the crowd
③*unr. itr. V.* push; (heftig) shove

Schiebe·tür *die* sliding door

Schiebung *die;* ~, ~en (ugs.) (a) shady deal
(b) (Begünstigung) pulling strings

schied *1. u. 3. Pers. Sg. Prät. v.* SCHEIDEN

Schieds·richter *der,*
Schieds·richterin *die* referee; (Tennis, Hockey, Kricket) umpire

schief ①*Adj.* (a) (schräg) leaning ⟨wall, fence, post⟩; (nicht parallel) crooked; sloping ⟨surface⟩; worn[-down] ⟨heels⟩
(b) (fig.: verzerrt) distorted ⟨picture, presentation, view, impression⟩; false ⟨comparison⟩
②*adv.* (a) (schräg) **das Bild hängt/der Teppich liegt** ~: the picture/carpet is crooked; **der Tisch steht** ~: the table isn't level
(b) (fig.: verzerrt) **etw.** ~ **darstellen** give a distorted account of sth.
(c) ~ **gehen** *od.* **laufen** (ugs.) go wrong

Schiefer *der;* ~s (Gestein) slate

***schief-:** ~|**gehen,** ~|**laufen** ▶ SCHIEF 2c

---

schielen itr. V. (a) squint; **auf dem rechten
Auge** ∼: have a squint in one's right eye
(b) (ugs.: blicken) look out of the corner of
one's eye
schien 1. u. 3. Pers. Sg. Prät. v. SCHEINEN
Schien·bein das shinbone
Schiene die; ∼, ∼n (a) rail
(b) (Gleitschiene) runner
(c) (Med.: Stütze) splint
schienen tr. V. jmds. Arm/Bein ∼: put
sb.'s arm/leg in a splint/splints
schießen die; ∼, ∼en (a) shoot; **auf
jmdn./etw.** ∼: shoot/fire at sb./sth.
(b) mit sein (strömen) gush; (spritzen) spurt
(c) mit sein (schnell wachsen) shoot up
[2] unr. tr. V. (a) shoot; fire ⟨bullet, missile,
rocket⟩
(b) (Fußball) score ⟨goal⟩
(c) (ugs.: fotografieren) **einige Aufnahmen** ∼:
take a few snaps
Schießerei die; ∼, ∼en (a) shooting no
indef. art., no pl.;
(b) (Schusswechsel) gun battle
Schiff das; ∼[e]s, ∼e (a) ship; **mit dem** ∼:
by ship or sea
(b) (Archit.) (Mittelschiff) nave; (Querschiff)
transept; (Seitenschiff) aisle
***Schiffahrt** ▶ SCHIFFFAHRT
schiffbar Adj. navigable
Schiff-: ∼**bau** der shipbuilding no art.;
∼**bruch** der (veralt.) shipwreck; [mit etw.]
∼bruch erleiden (fig.) fail [in sth.];
∼**brüchige** der/die; adj. Dekl.
shipwrecked man/woman
Schiffer der; ∼s, ∼, **Schifferin** die; ∼,
∼nen boatman/boatwoman; (eines Lastkahns)
bargee; (Kapitän[in]) skipper
Schiff·fahrt die shipping no indef. art.;
(Schifffahrtskunde) navigation
Schiffs-: ∼**arzt** der ship's doctor;
∼**brücke** die pontoon bridge; ∼**junge**
der ship's boy; ∼**reise** die voyage;
(Vergnügungsreise) cruise; ∼**verkehr** der
shipping traffic
Schikane die; ∼, ∼n (a) harassment no
indef. art.
(b) mit allen ∼n (ugs.) ⟨kitchen, house⟩ with
all mod cons (Brit. coll.); ⟨car, bicycle, stereo⟩
with all the extras
schikanieren tr. V. harass
Schild[1] der; ∼[e]s, ∼e shield
Schild[2] das; ∼[e]s, ∼er sign; (Nummernschild)
number plate; (Namensschild) nameplate; (auf
Denkmälern, Gebäuden usw.) plaque; (Etikett)
label
Schild·drüse die (Med.) thyroid [gland]
schildern tr. V. describe
Schild·kröte die tortoise; (Meeresschildkröte)
turtle
Schilf das; ∼[e]s (a) reed
(b) (Röhricht) reeds pl.
schillern itr. V. shimmer
Schilling der; ∼s, ∼e schilling

schilt 3. Pers. Sg. Präsens v. SCHELTEN
Schimmel der; ∼s, ∼ (a) mould; (auf Leder,
Papier) mildew
(b) (Pferd) white horse
schimmelig Adj. mouldy; mildewy
⟨paper, leather⟩
schimmeln itr. V.; auch mit sein go
mouldy; ⟨leather, paper⟩ get covered with
mildew
Schimmel·pilz der mould
Schimmer der; ∼s (Schein) gleam; (von
Seide) shimmer; sheen; **keinen** ∼ **[von etw.]
haben** (ugs.) not have the faintest idea [about
sth.] (coll.)
schimmern itr. V. gleam; ⟨water, sea⟩
glisten, shimmer; ⟨metal⟩ glint, gleam; ⟨silk
etc.⟩ shimmer
schimmlig ▶ SCHIMMELIG
Schimpanse der; ∼n, ∼n chimpanzee
schimpfen[1] itr. V. (a) carry on (coll.)
(auf, über + Akk. about); (meckern) grumble,
moan (auf, über + Akk. at)
(b) mit jmdm. ∼: tell sb. off; scold sb.
[2] tr. V. jmdn. ∼: tell sb. off
Schimpf·wort das; Pl. **Schimpf·wörter**
(Beleidigung) insult; (derbes Wort) swear word
schinden unr. tr. V. maltreat; ill-treat; **Zeit**
∼ (ugs.) play for time
Schinderei die; ∼, ∼en (Strapaze, Qual)
struggle; (Arbeit) toil
Schinken der; ∼s, ∼: ham
Schinken·speck der bacon
Schippe die; ∼, ∼n (Schaufel) shovel
Schirm der; ∼[e]s, ∼e umbrella; brolly
(Brit. coll.); (Sonnenschirm) sunshade
Schirm-: ∼**herr** der patron; ∼**herrin** die
patroness; ∼**herrschaft** die patronage;
∼**ständer** der umbrella stand
schiss, *schiß 1. u. 3. Pers. Sg. Prät. v.
SCHEISSEN
Schlacht die; ∼, ∼en battle
schlachten tr. (auch itr.) V. slaughter; kill
⟨rabbit, chicken, etc.⟩
Schlachter der; ∼s, ∼ (nordd.) butcher
Schlachterei die; ∼, ∼en (nordd.)
butcher's [shop]
Schlacht-: ∼**feld** das battlefield; ∼**hof**
der abattoir; ∼**tier** das animal kept for
meat; (kurz vor der Schlachtung) animal for
slaughter
Schlachtung die; ∼, ∼en slaughter[ing]
Schlacht·vieh das animals pl. kept for
meat; (kurz vor der Schlachtung) animals pl. for
slaughter
Schlacke die; ∼, ∼n cinders pl.;
(Hochofen∼) slag
Schlaf der; ∼[e]s sleep; **einen leichten/
festen/gesunden** ∼ **haben** be a light/heavy/
good sleeper
Schlaf·anzug der pyjamas pl.
Schläfchen das; ∼s, ∼: nap; snooze (coll.)
Schläfe die; ∼, ∼n temple

S

schlafen *unr. itr. V.* **(a)** (auch fig.) sleep; **tief** *od.* **fest** ∼: be sound asleep; **lange** ∼: sleep for a long time; (am Morgen) sleep in; ∼ **gehen** go to bed
(b) (ugs.: nicht aufpassen) be asleep

Schläfer *der;* ∼**s,** ∼**, Schläferin** *die;* ∼, ∼**nen** sleeper

schlaff ⒈ *Adj.* **(a)** slack; flabby ⟨*stomach, muscles*⟩
(b) (schlapp, matt) limp ⟨*body, hand, handshake*⟩; shaky ⟨*knees*⟩
⒉ *adv.* **(a)** slackly
(b) (schlapp, matt) limply

Schlaf-: ∼**gelegenheit** *die* place to sleep; ∼**mittel** *das* sleep-inducing drug

schläfrig ⒈ *Adj.* sleepy
⒉ *adv.* sleepily

Schläfrigkeit *die;* ∼: sleepiness

Schlaf-: ∼**saal** *der* dormitory; ∼**sack** sleeping bag

schläft *3. Pers. Sg. Präsens v.* SCHLAFEN

Schlaf-: ∼**tablette** *die* sleeping pill; ∼**wagen** *der* sleeping car; sleeper; ∼**zimmer** *das* bedroom

Schlag *der;* ∼**[e]s, Schläge (a)** blow; (Faust∼) punch; (Klaps) slap; (Tennis, Golf) stroke; shot; ∼ **auf** ∼ (fig.) in quick succession
(b) (Aufprall) bang; (dumpf) thud; (Klopfen) knock
(c) (des Herzens, Pulses) beating; (eines Pendels) swinging
(d) (einzelne rhythmische Bewegung) beat; (eines Pendels) swing
(e) (Töne) (einer Uhr) striking; (einer Glocke) ringing
(f) (einzelner Ton) (Stundenschlag) stroke; (Glockenschlag) ring; ∼ **acht Uhr** on the stroke of eight

schlag-, Schlag-: ∼**ader** *die* artery; ∼**anfall** *der* stroke; ∼**artig** ⒈ *Adj.* very sudden; ⒉ *adv.* quite suddenly; ∼**baum** *der* barrier; ∼**bohrer** *der,* ∼**bohr·maschine** *die* percussion drill; hammer drill

schlagen ⒈ *unr. tr. V.* **(a)** hit; beat; strike; (mit der Faust) punch; hit; (mit der flachen Hand) slap
(b) (mit Richtungsangabe) hit ⟨*ball*⟩; **einen Nagel in etw.** (*Akk.*) ∼: knock a nail into sth.
(c) (rühren) beat ⟨*mixture*⟩; whip ⟨*cream*⟩; (mit einem Schneebesen) whisk
(d) (läuten) ⟨*clock*⟩ strike; ⟨*bell*⟩ ring
(e) (legen) throw
(f) (einwickeln) wrap (**in** + *Akk.* in)
(g) (besiegen, übertreffen) beat
⒉ *unr. itr. V.* **(a)** **er schlug mit der Faust auf den Tisch** he beat the table with his fist
(b) **mit den Flügeln** ∼ ⟨*bird*⟩ beat or flap its wings

(c) *mit sein* (prallen) bang; **mit dem Kopf auf etw.** (*Akk.*)/**gegen etw.** ∼: bang one's head on/against sth.
(d) *mit sein* jmdm. **auf den Magen** ∼: affect sb.'s stomach
(e) (pulsieren) ⟨*heart, pulse*⟩ beat; (heftig) ⟨*heart*⟩ pound; ⟨*pulse*⟩ throb
(f) (läuten) ⟨*clock*⟩ strike; ⟨*bell*⟩ ring
⒊ *unr. refl. V.* fight; **sich mit jmdm.** ∼: fight with sb.

Schlager *der;* ∼**s,** ∼ **(a)** pop song
(b) (Erfolg) (Buch) best seller; (Ware) best-selling line; (Film, Stück, Lied) hit

Schläger *der;* ∼**s,** ∼ **(a)** (Raufbold) tough; thug
(b) (Tennis, Federball, Squash) racket; (Tischtennis, Kricket) bat; ([Eis]hockey, Polo) stick; (Golf) club

Schlägerei *die;* ∼, ∼**en** brawl; fight

Schlägerin *die;* ∼, ∼**nen** ▶ SCHLÄGER A

Schlager·sänger *der,* **Schlager·sängerin** *die* pop singer

schlag-, Schlag-: ∼**fertig** *Adj.* quick-witted ⟨*reply*⟩; ⟨*person*⟩ who is quick at repartee; ∼**fertigkeit** *die* quickness at repartee; ∼**licht** *das* (Kunst, Fot.) shaft of light; **ein** ∼**licht auf etw. werfen** highlight sth.; ∼**loch** *das* pothole; ∼**obers** *das;* ∼∼ (österr.), ∼**rahm** *der* (bes. südd., österr., schweiz.), ∼**sahne** *die* whipping cream; (geschlagen) whipped cream; ∼**seite** *die* list; [**starke** *od.* **schwere**] ∼**seite haben/bekommen** be listing [heavily] *or* have a [heavy] list/ develop a [heavy] list; ∼**stock** *der* cudgel; (für Polizei) truncheon; ∼**wort** *das* **(a)** *Pl. meist* ∼∼**e** (Parole) slogan; catchphrase; **(b)** *Pl.* ∼**wörter** (Buchw.: Stichwort) headword; ∼**zeile** *die* headline; ∼**zeug** *das* drums *pl.*

schlaksig (ugs.) *Adj.* gangling; lanky

Schlamassel *der od. das;* ∼**s** (ugs.) mess

Schlamm *der;* ∼**[e]s,** ∼**e** *od.* **Schlämme (a)** mud
(b) (Schlick) sludge

schlammig *Adj.* **(a)** muddy
(b) (schlickig) sludgy; muddy

Schlamperei *die;* ∼, ∼**en** (ugs. abwertend) sloppiness

schlampig (ugs. abwertend) ⒈ *Adj.* **(a)** (liederlich) slovenly
(b) (nachlässig) sloppy, slipshod ⟨*work*⟩
⒉ *adv.* **(a)** (liederlich) in a slovenly way
(b) (nachlässig) sloppily

schlang *1. u. 3. Pers. Sg. Prät. v.* SCHLINGEN

Schlange *die;* ∼, ∼**n (a)** snake
(b) (Warteschlange) queue; line (Amer.); ∼ **stehen** queue; stand in line (Amer.)
(c) (Autoschlange) tailback (Brit.); backup (Amer.)

schlängeln *refl. V.* ⟨*snake*⟩ wind [its way]; ⟨*road*⟩ wind, snake [its way]

Schlangen·linie *die* wavy line

schlank *Adj.* slim ⟨*person*⟩; slim, slender ⟨*build, figure*⟩

Schlankheit *die;* ~ ▶ SCHLANK: slimness; slenderness

Schlankheits·kur *die* slimming diet

schlapp *Adj.* (a) worn out; tired out; (wegen Schwüle) listless; (wegen Krankheit) run-down

(b) (ugs.: ohne Schwung) wet (coll.); feeble

(c) slack ⟨*rope, cable*⟩; loose ⟨*skin*⟩; flabby ⟨*stomach, muscles*⟩

Schlappe *die;* ~, ~n setback

schlapp|machen *itr. V.* (ugs.) flag; (zusammenbrechen) flake out (coll.); (aufgeben) give up

Schlaraffen·land *das;* ~[e]s Cockaigne

schlau ① *Adj.* (a) shrewd; astute; (gerissen) wily; crafty; cunning

(b) (ugs.: gescheit) clever; bright; smart; **aus jmdm. nicht ~ werden** (ugs.) not be able to make sb. out

② *adv.* shrewdly; astutely; (gerissen) craftily; cunningly

Schlauch *der;* ~[e]s, Schläuche (a) hose

(b) (im Reifen) tube

Schlauch·boot *das* rubber dinghy; inflatable [dinghy]

schlauchen (ugs.) *tr., auch itr. V.* jmdn. ~: take it out of sb.

schlauch·los *Adj.* tubeless ⟨*tyre*⟩

Schläue *die;* ~: shrewdness; astuteness; (Gerissenheit) wiliness; craftiness; cunning

Schlaufe *die;* ~, ~n loop

schlecht ① *Adj.* (a) bad; poor, bad ⟨*food, quality, style, harvest, health, circulation*⟩; poor ⟨*salary, eater, appetite*⟩; poor-quality ⟨*goods*⟩; bad, weak ⟨*eyes*⟩; **um jmdn./mit etw. steht es ~:** sb./sth. is in a bad way; **jmdn. ~ machen** run sb. down; disparage sb.

(b) (böse) bad; wicked

(c) (ungenießbar) off; **das Fleisch ist ~ geworden** the meat has gone off

② *adv.* (a) badly; **er sieht/hört ~:** his sight is poor/he has poor hearing; **über jmdn.** *od.* **von jmdm. ~ sprechen** speak ill of sb.; ~ **bezahlt** badly *or* poorly paid

(b) (schwer) **heute geht es ~:** today is difficult

(c) ~ **und recht, mehr ~ als recht** after a fashion

schlecht-: *~**bezahlt** ▶ SCHLECHT 2A; *~|**gehen** ▶ GEHEN I; *~**gelaunt** ▶ GELAUNT

Schlechtigkeit *die;* ~: badness; wickedness

***schlecht|machen** ▶ SCHLECHT 1A

schlecken (bes. südd., österr.) *tr. V.* lap up

schleichen ① *unr. itr. V.; mit sein* creep; (heimlich) creep; sneak; ⟨*cat*⟩ slink, creep; (langsam fahren) crawl along

② *unr. refl. V.* creep; sneak; ⟨*cat*⟩ slink, creep

schleichend *Adj.* insidious ⟨*disease*⟩; slow[-acting] ⟨*poison*⟩; creeping ⟨*inflation*⟩; gradual ⟨*crisis*⟩

Schleich·werbung *die* surreptitious advertising

Schleier *der;* ~s, ~: veil

schleier·haft *Adj.* jmdm. ~ **sein/bleiben** be/remain a mystery to sb.

Schleife *die;* ~, ~n (a) bow; (Fliege) bow tie

(b) (starke Biegung) loop

schleifen[1] *unr. tr. V.* grind; cut ⟨*diamond, glass*⟩; (mit Schleifpapier usw.) sand; (schärfen) sharpen

schleifen[2] ① *tr. V.* (a) (auch fig.) drag

(b) (niederreißen) raze ⟨*sth.*⟩ [to the ground]

② *itr. V.; auch mit sein* drag; **die Kupplung ~ lassen** (Kfz-W.) slip the clutch

Schleim *der;* ~[e]s, ~e mucus; (im Hals) phlegm; (von Schnecken) slime

schleimig *Adj.* (auch fig.) slimy; (Physiol., Zool.) mucous

schlemmen *itr. V.* have a feast

Schlemmer *der;* ~s, ~: gourmet

schlendern *itr. V.; mit sein* stroll

Schlenker *der;* ~s, ~ (ugs.) swerve; **einen ~ machen** swerve

schlenkern *tr., itr. V.* swing; **mit den Armen ~:** swing one's arms

Schleppe *die;* ~, ~n train

schleppen ① *tr. V.* (a) (ziehen) tow ⟨*vehicle, ship*⟩

(b) (tragen) carry; lug

(c) (ugs.: mitnehmen) drag

② *refl. V.* drag *or* haul oneself

schleppend *Adj.* (nicht zügig) slow

Schlepper *der;* ~s, ~ (a) (Schiff) tug

(b) (Traktor) tractor

Schlepper·organisation *die: organization smuggling illegal immigrants and emigrants*

Schlepp-: ~**lift** *der* T-bar [lift]; ~**tau** *das* towline; **in jmds. ~tau** (fig.) in sb.'s wake

Schleswig-Holstein (*das*); ~s Schleswig-Holstein

Schleuder *die;* ~, ~n sling; (mit Gummiband) catapult (Brit.); slingshot (Amer.)

schleudern ① *tr. V.* hurl

② *itr. V.; mit sein* ⟨*vehicle*⟩ skid

schleunigst *Adv.* (a) (auf der Stelle) at once; immediately; straight away

(b) (eilends) hastily; with all haste

Schleuse *die;* ~, ~n lock

schlich *1. u. 3. Pers. Sg. Prät. v.* SCHLEICHEN

schlicht ① *Adj.* (a) simple; plain ⟨*pattern, furniture*⟩

(b) (unkompliziert) simple, unsophisticated ⟨*person, view, etc.*⟩

② *adv.* simply; simply, plainly ⟨*dressed, furnished*⟩

schlichten ① *tr. V.* settle ⟨*argument etc.*⟩; settle ⟨*industrial dispute etc.*⟩ by mediation

② *itr. V.* mediate

S

Schlichtheit die; ~ ▶ SCHLICHT A, B:
simplicity; plainness; unsophisticatedness

Schlick der; ~[e]s, ~e silt

schlief 1. u. 3. Pers. Sg. Prät. v. SCHLAFEN

Schließe die; ~, ~n clasp; (Schnalle) buckle

schließen [1] unr. tr. V. (a) close; shut;
turn off ⟨tap⟩; fasten ⟨belt, bracelet⟩; do up
⟨button, zip⟩; close ⟨street, route, border,
electrical circuit⟩; fill, close ⟨gap⟩
(b) (außer Betrieb setzen) close [down] ⟨shop,
school⟩
(c) etw./jmdn./sich in etw. (Akk.) ~: lock
sth./sb./oneself in sth.
(d) (beenden) close ⟨meeting, proceedings,
debate⟩; end, conclude ⟨letter, speech, lecture⟩
(e) (eingehen, vereinbaren) conclude ⟨treaty,
pact, ceasefire, agreement⟩; reach ⟨settlement,
compromise⟩; enter into ⟨contract⟩
(f) (folgern) infer (**aus** from)
[2] unr. itr. V. (a) close, shut
(b) (enden) end; conclude
(c) [aus etw.] auf etw. (Akk.) ~: infer sth.
[from sth.]
[3] unr. refl. V. ⟨door, window⟩ close, shut;
⟨wound, circle⟩ close

Schließ·fach das locker; (bei der Post) PO
box; (bei der Bank) safe-deposit box

schließlich Adv. (a) finally; in the end
(b) (immerhin, doch) after all

schliff 1. u. 3. Pers. Sg. Prät. v. SCHLEIFEN

Schliff der; ~[e]s, ~e (a) cutting; (von
Messern, Sensen usw.) sharpening
(b) (Art, wie etw. geschliffen wird) cut; (von
Messern, Scheren usw.) edge
(c) einem Brief/Text usw. den letzten ~
geben put the finishing touches pl. to a
letter/text etc.

schlimm [1] Adj. (a) grave, serious ⟨error,
mistake, accusation, offence⟩; bad, serious
⟨error, mistake⟩
(b) (übel) bad; nasty, bad ⟨experience⟩; [das ist
alles] halb so ~: it's not as bad as all that;
ist nicht ~! [it] doesn't matter
[2] adv. ~ dran sein be in a bad way; (in einer
Notlage) be in dire straits

schlimmsten·falls Adv. if the worst
comes to the worst

Schlinge die; ~, ~n (a) loop; (für den Arm)
sling; (zum Erhängen) noose
(b) (Fanggerät) snare

Schlingel der; ~s, ~: rascal; rogue

schlingen [1] unr. tr. V. etw. um etw. ~:
loop sth. round sth.
[2] unr. refl. V. sich um etw. ~: wind itself
round sth.
[3] unr. itr. V. bolt one's food

schlingern itr. V.; mit sein ⟨ship, boat⟩ roll;
⟨train, vehicle⟩ lurch from side to side

Schlips der; ~es, ~e tie

Schlitten der; ~s, ~: sledge; sled;
(Pferdeschlitten) sleigh; (Rodelschlitten) toboggan;
~ fahren go tobogganing

schlittern itr. V. slide

Schlitt-: ~schuh der [ice] skate; ~schuh
laufen od. fahren [ice-]skate;
~schuh-laufen das [ice] skating no art.;
~schuh-läufer der, ~schuh-läuferin
die [ice] skater

Schlitz der; ~es, ~e (a) slit; (am Briefkasten,
Automaten) slot
(b) (Hosenschlitz) flies pl.; fly

schlitz-, Schlitz-: ~auge das slit eye;
~äugig Adj. slit-eyed; ~ohr das (ugs.)
wily or crafty devil; ~ohrig (ugs.) [1] Adj.
wily; crafty; [2] adv. craftily

schloss, *schloß 1. u. 3. Pers. Sg. Prät. v.
SCHLIESSEN

Schloss, *Schloß das; Schlosses,
Schlösser (a) lock; (Vorhänge~) padlock;
hinter ~ und Riegel (ugs.) behind bars
(b) (Verschluss) clasp
(c) (Wohngebäude) castle; (Palast) palace;
(Herrschaftshaus) mansion·

Schlosser der; ~s, ~, **Schlosserin** die;
~, ~nen metalworker; (Maschinenschlosser)
fitter; (für Schlösser) locksmith

Schlot der; ~[e]s, ~e od. **Schlöte** chimney
[stack]; (eines Schiffes) funnel

schlottern itr. V. (a) shake
(b) ⟨clothes⟩ hang loose

Schlucht die; ~, ~en ravine

schluchzen itr. V. sob

Schluck der; ~[e]s, ~e od. **Schlücke**
swallow; mouthful; (großer ~) gulp; (kleiner ~)
sip

Schluck·auf der; ~s hiccups pl.

Schlückchen das; ~s, ~: sip

schlucken [1] tr. V. swallow; etw. hastig
~: gulp sth. down
[2] itr. V. swallow

Schlucker der; ~s, ~: armer ~ (ugs.) poor
devil or (Brit. coll.) blighter

schluderig ▶ SCHLUDRIG

schludern itr. V. (ugs.) work sloppily

schludrig (ugs.) [1] Adj. (a) slipshod ⟨work,
examination⟩; botched ⟨job⟩; slapdash
⟨person, work⟩
(b) (schlampig [aussehend]) scruffy
[2] adv. (a) in a slipshod or slapdash way
(b) (schlampig) scruffily

schlug 1. u. 3. Pers. Sg. Prät. v. SCHLAGEN

Schlummer der; ~s (geh.) slumber (poet./
rhet.)

schlummern itr. V. (geh.) slumber (poet./
rhet.)

Schlund der; ~[e]s, Schlünde [back of the]
throat; pharynx (Anat.)

schlüpfen itr. V.; mit sein slip; [aus dem
Ei] ~ ⟨chick⟩ hatch out

Schlüpfer der; ~s, ~ (für Damen) knickers
pl. (Brit.); panties pl.; (für Herren) [under]pants
pl. or trunks pl.

schlüpfrig Adj. (a) slippery
(b) (anstößig) lewd

*old spelling - see note on page xiv

Schlüpfrigkeit *die;* ∼, ∼en (a) (feuchte Glätte) slipperiness
(b) (Anstößigkeit) lewdness

schlurfen *itr. V.; mit sein* shuffle

schlürfen [1] *tr. V.* slurp [up] (coll.)
[2] *itr. V.* slurp (coll.)

Schluss, *Schluß *der;* Schlusses, Schlüsse (a) (eines Vortrags o. Ä.) conclusion; (eines Buchs, Schauspiels usw.) ending; **am** *od.* **zum** ∼: at the end; (schließlich) in the end
(b) (Folgerung) conclusion

Schlüssel *der;* ∼s, ∼: key

Schlüssel-: ∼**bein** *das* collarbone; clavicle (Anat.); ∼**blume** *die* cowslip; (Primel) primula; ∼**bund** *der od. das* bunch of keys; ∼**figur** *die* key figure; ∼**loch** *das* keyhole; ∼**stellung** *die* key position

schluss·folgern, *schlußfolgern *tr. V.* conclude (aus from)

Schluss·folgerung, *Schluß·folgerung *die* conclusion, inference (aus from); ∼en ziehen draw conclusions

schlüssig [1] *Adj.* (a) conclusive ⟨proof, evidence⟩; convincing, logical ⟨argument, conclusion⟩
(b) sich (*Dat.*) ∼ werden make up one's mind
[2] *adv.* conclusively

Schlüssigkeit *die;* ∼: conclusiveness

Schluss-, *Schluß-: ∼**licht** *das* tail or rear light; ∼**strich** *der* [bottom] line; ∼**verkauf** *der* [end-of-season] sale[s *pl.*]

schmächtig *Adj.* slight

schmackhaft *Adj.* tasty

Schmähung *die;* ∼, ∼en diatribe; ∼en abuse *sing.;* invective *sing.*

schmal; ∼er *od.* schmäler, ∼st... *od.* schmälst... *Adj.* narrow; slim, slender ⟨hips, hands, figure, etc.⟩; thin ⟨lips, face, nose, etc.⟩

schmälern *tr. V.* diminish; restrict ⟨rights⟩

Schmalz¹ *das;* ∼es dripping; (Schweineschmalz) lard

Schmalz² *der;* ∼es (abwertend) schmaltz (coll.)

Schmalz·brot *das* slice of bread and dripping

schmalzig (abwertend) [1] *Adj.* schmaltzy (coll.)
[2] *adv.* with slushy sentimentality

schmarotzen *itr. V.* (fig.) sponge; freeload (coll.)

Schmarren *der;* ∼s, ∼ (österr., auch südd.) *pancake broken up with a fork after frying*

schmatzen *itr. V.* smack one's lips; (geräuschvoll essen) eat noisily

Schmaus *der;* ∼es, Schmäuse (veralt., scherzh.) [good] spread (coll.)

schmecken [1] *itr. V.* taste (nach of); [gut] ∼: taste good; **schmeckt es [dir]?** are you enjoying it *or* your meal?

[2] *tr. V.* taste; (kosten) sample

schmeicheln *itr. V.* jmdm. ∼: flatter sb.

Schmeichler *der;* ∼s, ∼,
Schmeichlerin *die;* ∼, ∼nen flatterer

schmeißen (ugs.) [1] *unr. tr. V.* chuck (coll.); sling (coll.); (schleudern) fling; hurl
[2] *unr. refl. V.* throw oneself; (mit Wucht) hurl oneself
[3] *unr. itr. V.* mit etw. [nach jmdm.] ∼: chuck sth. [at sb.] (coll.)

Schmeiß·fliege *die* blowfly; (blaue) bluebottle

schmelzen [1] *unr. itr. V.; mit sein* melt; (fig.) ⟨doubts, apprehension, etc.⟩ dissolve, fade away
[2] *unr. tr. V.* melt; smelt ⟨ore⟩; render ⟨fat⟩

Schmelz-: ∼**käse** *der* processed cheese; ∼**wasser** *das* melted snow and ice; meltwater (Geol.)

Schmerz *der;* ∼es, ∼en (a) (physisch) pain; (dumpf u. anhaltend) ache; **wo haben Sie** ∼**en?** where does it hurt?; ∼**en haben** be in pain
(b) (psychisch) pain; (Kummer) grief

schmerz·empfindlich *Adj.* sensitive to pain *pred.*

Schmerz·empfindlichkeit *die;* ∼: sensitivity to pain

schmerzen [1] *tr. V.* jmdn. ∼: hurt sb.; (jmdm. Kummer bereiten) grieve sb.; cause sb. sorrow
[2] *itr. V.* hurt

schmerz·frei *Adj.* free of pain *pred.;* painless ⟨operation⟩

Schmerz·grenze *die* (fig.) jetzt/dann ist die ∼ erreicht this/that is the absolute limit

schmerzhaft *Adj.* painful

schmerzlich [1] *Adj.* painful; distressing
[2] *adv.* painfully

schmerz-, Schmerz-: ∼**lindernd** *Adj.* pain-relieving; ∼**los** [1] *Adj.* painless; [2] *adv.* painlessly; ∼**stillend** *Adj.* pain-killing; ∼**tablette** *die* pain-killing tablet

Schmetterling *der;* ∼s, ∼e butterfly

schmettern [1] *tr. V.* (a) hurl (an + *Akk.* at, gegen against)
(b) (laut spielen, singen usw.) blare out ⟨march, music⟩; ⟨person⟩ sing lustily ⟨song⟩
(c) (Tennis usw.) smash ⟨ball⟩
[2] *itr. V.* ⟨trumpet, music, etc.⟩ blare out

Schmied *der;* ∼[e]s, ∼e blacksmith

Schmiede *die;* ∼, ∼n smithy; forge

schmieden *tr. V.* (auch fig.) forge

Schmiedin *die;* ∼, ∼nen ▸ SCHMIED

schmiegen [1] *refl. V.* snuggle, nestle (in + *Akk.* in); sich an jmdm. ∼: snuggle [close] up to sb.
[2] *tr. V.* press (an + *Akk.* against)

schmieren [1] *tr. V.* (a) lubricate
(b) (streichen) spread ⟨butter, jam, etc.⟩ (auf + *Akk.* on); Brote ∼: spread slices of bread
[2] *tr. V.* (a) ⟨oil, grease⟩ lubricate
(b) (ugs: unsauber schreiben) ⟨person⟩ scrawl, scribble; ⟨pen, ink⟩ smudge, make smudges

schmierig *Adj.* greasy

Schmier-: ~**mittel** *das* lubricant; ~**seife** *die* soft soap

schmilzt *2. u. 3. Pers. Sg. Präsens v.* SCHMELZEN

Schminke *die;* ~, ~n make-up

schminken [1] *tr. V.* make up ⟨*face, eyes*⟩ [2] *refl. V.* make oneself up

schmirgeln *tr. V.* rub down; (bes. mit Sandpapier) sand

Schmirgel·papier *das* emery paper; (Sandpapier) sandpaper

schmiss, *schmiß *1. u. 3. Pers. Sg. Prät. v.* SCHMEISSEN

Schmöker *der;* ~s, ~ (ugs.) lightweight adventure story/romance

schmökern (ugs.) [1] *itr. V.* bury oneself in a book [2] *tr. V.* bury oneself in ⟨*book*⟩

schmollen *itr. V.* sulk

Schmoll·mund *der* pouting mouth

schmolz *1. u. 3. Pers. Sg. Prät. v.* SCHMELZEN

Schmor·braten *der* braised beef

schmoren [1] *tr. V.* braise [2] *itr. V.* (a) braise (b) (ugs.: schwitzen) swelter

schmuck *Adj.* attractive

Schmuck *der;* ~[e]s (a) jewelry; jewellery (esp. Brit.) (b) ▶ SCHMUCKSTÜCK (c) (Zierde) decoration

schmücken *tr. V.* decorate; embellish ⟨*writings, speech*⟩

schmuck-, Schmuck-: ~**kästchen** *das,* ~**kasten** *der* jewelry *or* (esp. Brit.) jewellery box; ~**los** *Adj.* plain; bare ⟨*room*⟩; ~**losigkeit** *die;* ~~: plainness; (eines Zimmers) bareness; ~**stück** *das* piece of jewelry *or* (esp. Brit.) jewellery

schmuddelig *Adj.* (ugs.) grubby; mucky (coll.); (schmutzig u. unordentlich) messy; grotty (Brit. coll.)

Schmuggel *der;* ~s smuggling *no art.*

schmuggeln *tr., itr. V.* smuggle (in + *Akk.* into; aus out of)

Schmuggler *der;* ~s, ~, **Schmugglerin** *die;* ~, ~nen smuggler

schmunzeln *itr. V.* smile to oneself

schmusen *itr. V.* (ugs.) cuddle; ⟨*couple*⟩ kiss and cuddle

Schmutz *der;* ~es dirt; (Schlamm) mud

schmutzen *itr. V.* get dirty

schmutzig *Adj.* dirty

Schmutz·wasser *das* dirty water; (Abwasser) sewage

Schnabel *der;* ~s, Schnäbel (a) beak (b) (ugs.: Mund) gob (sl.)

Schnake *die;* ~, ~n (a) daddy-long-legs (b) (bes. südd.: Stechmücke) mosquito

Schnalle *die;* ~, ~n buckle

schnallen *tr. V.* (a) (mit einer Schnalle festziehen) buckle ⟨*shoe, belt*⟩; fasten ⟨*strap*⟩ (b) (mit Riemen/Gurten befestigen) strap (auf + *Akk.* on to)

schnalzen *itr. V.* [mit der Zunge/den Fingern] ~: click one's tongue/snap one's fingers

Schnäppchen *das;* ~s, ~ (ugs.) snip (Brit. coll.); [real] bargain; ein ~ machen get a [real] bargain

schnappen [1] *itr. V.* nach jmdm./etw. ~ ⟨*animal*⟩ snap at sb./sth.; nach Luft ~: gasp for breath [2] *tr. V.* ⟨*dog, bird, etc.*⟩ snatch; [sich ⟨*Dat.*⟩] jmdn./etw. ~ (ugs.) ⟨*person*⟩ grab sb./sth.; (mit raschem Zugriff) snatch sb./sth

Schnapp·schuss, *Schnapp·schuß *der* snapshot

Schnaps *der;* ~es, Schnäpse (a) spirit; (Klarer) schnapps (b) (Spirituosen) spirits *pl.*

schnarchen *itr. V.* snore

schnattern *itr. V.* (a) ⟨*goose etc.*⟩ cackle, gaggle (b) (ugs.: eifrig schwatzen) jabber [away]; chatter

schnauben *itr. V.* snort (vor with)

schnaufen *itr. V.* puff (vor with)

Schnauze *die;* ~, ~n (a) (von Tieren) muzzle; (der Maus usw.) snout; (Maul) mouth (b) (derb: Mund) gob (sl.); [halt die] ~! shut your trap! (sl.)

schnauzen *tr., itr. V.* (ugs.) bark; (ärgerlich) snap; snarl

Schnecke *die* snail; (Nacktschnecke) slug

Schnecken·haus *das* snail shell

Schnee *der;* ~s snow

schnee-, Schnee-: ~**ball** *der* snowball; ~**besen** *der* whisk; ~**flocke** *die* snowflake; ~**gestöber** *das* snow flurry; ~**glöckchen** *das* snowdrop; ~**kette** *die* snow chain; ~**matsch** *der* slush; ~**pflug** *der* snowplough; ~**schmelze** *die;* ~~, ~~n melting of the snow; thaw; ~**sturm** *der* snowstorm; ~**treiben** *das* driving snow; ~**wehe** *die* snowdrift; ~**weiß** *Adj.* snow-white; as white as snow *postpos.*

Schneewittchen *das;* ~s Snow White

Schneid·brenner *der* (Technik) cutting torch; oxyacetylene cutter

Schneide *die;* ~, ~n [cutting] edge

schneiden [1] *unr. itr. V.* cut (in + *Akk.* into) [2] *unr. tr. V.* (a) cut; (in Scheiben) slice ⟨*bread, sausage, etc.*⟩; (klein ~) cut up, chop ⟨*wood, vegetables*⟩; (stutzen) prune ⟨*tree, bush*⟩; trim ⟨*beard*⟩; cut, mow ⟨*grass*⟩; sich ⟨*Dat.*⟩ die Haare ~ lassen have one's hair cut (b) eine Kurve ~: cut a corner

Schneider *der;* ~s, ~: tailor; (Damenschneider) dressmaker

---

*alte Schreibung - vgl. Hinweis auf S. xiv

Schneiderei *die;* ~, ~en tailor's shop; (Damenschneider) dressmaker's shop

Schneiderin *die;* ~, ~nen ▶ SCHNEIDER

schneidern *tr. V.* make; make, tailor ⟨suit⟩

Schneide·zahn *der* incisor

schneien [1] *itr., tr. V.* (unpers.) snow; **es schneit** it is snowing
[2] *itr. V.; mit sein* (fig.) rain down; fall like snow

Schneise *die;* ~, ~n (Wald~) aisle; (als Feuerschutz) firebreak

schnell [1] *Adj.* quick ⟨journey, decision, service, etc.⟩; fast ⟨car, skis, road, track, etc.⟩; quick, swift ⟨progress, movement, blow, action⟩
[2] *adv.* quickly; ⟨drive, move, etc.⟩ fast, quickly; ⟨spread⟩ quickly, rapidly; (bald) soon ⟨sold, past, etc.⟩; **mach** ~**!** (ugs.) move it! (coll.)

schnellen *itr. V.; mit sein* shoot (aus + *Dat.* out of; in + *Akk.* into)

Schnelligkeit *die;* ~, ~en speed

Schnell-: ~**imbiss**, **~**imbiß** *der* snackbar; ~**koch·topf** *der* pressure cooker

schnellstens *Adv.* as quickly as possible

Schnell-: ~**straße** *die* expressway; ~**zug** *der* express [train]

Schnepfe *die;* ~, ~n snipe

schneuzen [1] *tr. V.* **sich/einem Kind die Nase** ~: blow one's/a child's nose
[2] *refl. V.* blow one's nose

schnippeln (ugs.) [1] *itr. V.* snip [away] (**an** + *Dat.* at)
[2] *tr. V.* shred ⟨vegetables⟩; chop ⟨beans etc.⟩ [finely]

schnippen [1] *itr. V.* snap one's fingers (**nach** at)
[2] *tr. V.* flick (**von** off, from)

schnippisch [1] *Adj.* pert ⟨reply, tone, etc.⟩
[2] *adv.* pertly

Schnipsel *der od. das;* ~s, ~: scrap; (aus Papier, Stoff) snippet; shred

schnipseln ▶ SCHNIPPELN

schnitt *1. u. 3. Pers. Sg. Prät. v.* SCHNEIDEN

Schnitt *der;* ~[e]s, ~e (a) cut
(b) (das Mähen) (von Gras) mowing; (von Getreide) harvest

Schnitt-: ~**blume** *die* cut flower; ~**bohne** *die* French bean

Schnittchen *das;* ~s, ~: canapé; [small] open sandwich

Schnitte *die;* ~, ~n slice; **eine** ~ [Brot] a slice of bread

Schnitt·fläche *die* cut surface

schnittig [1] *Adj.* stylish, smart ⟨suit, appearance, etc.⟩; (sportlich) racy ⟨car, yacht, etc.⟩
[2] *adv.* stylishly; (sportlich) racily

Schnitt-: ~**lauch** *der* chives *pl.*; ~**menge** *die* (Math.) intersection; ~**punkt**

der intersection; (Geom.) point of intersection; ~**stelle** *die* (DV) interface; ~**wunde** *die* cut; (lang u. tief) gash

Schnitzel *das;* ~s, ~ (a) (Fleisch) [veal/pork] escalope
(b) (von Papier) scrap; (von Holz) shaving

schnitzeln *tr. V.* chop up ⟨vegetables⟩ [into small pieces]; shred ⟨cabbage⟩

schnitzen *tr., itr. V.* carve

schnodderig (ugs.) [1] *Adj.* brash
[2] *adv.* brashly

schnöde (geh.) [1] *Adj.* (a) (verachtenswert) contemptible
(b) (gemein) contemptuous, scornful ⟨glance, reply, etc.⟩
[2] *adv.* (gemein) contemptuously; ⟨exploit, misuse⟩ flagrantly

Schnorchel *der;* ~s, ~: snorkel

Schnörkel *der;* ~s, ~: scroll; (der Handschrift, in der Rede) flourish

schnorren *tr., itr. V.* (ugs.) scrounge (coll.) (**bei, von** + *Dat.* off)

Schnorrer *der;* ~s, ~, **Schnorrerin** *die;* ~, ~nen (ugs.) scrounger (coll.)

Schnösel *der;* ~s, ~ (ugs. abwertend) young whippersnapper

schnüffeln *itr. V.* (a) sniff
(b) (ugs.: spionieren) snoop [about] (coll.)
(c) (Drogenjargon: Dämpfe ~) sniff [glue/paint etc.]

Schnüffler *der;* ~s, ~, **Schnüfflerin** *die;* ~, ~nen (a) (ugs.) Nosey Parker; (Spion) snooper (coll.)
(b) (Drogenjargon) [glue-, paint-, etc.]sniffer

Schnulze *die;* ~, ~n (ugs. abwertend) (Lied/Melodie) slushy song/tune; (Theaterstück, Film, Fernsehspiel) tear jerker (coll.); slushy play

schnupfen [1] *tr. V.* sniff; **Tabak** ~: take snuff
[2] *itr. V.* take snuff

Schnupfen *der;* ~s, ~: [head] cold; [den od. einen] ~ **haben** have a [head] cold

Schnupf·tabak *der* snuff

schnuppe: **das/er ist mir** ~/**mir völlig** ~ (ugs.) I don't care/I couldn't care less about it/him (coll.)

schnuppern *itr. V.* sniff; **an etw.** (*Dat.*) ~: sniff sth.

Schnur *die;* ~, **Schnüre** (a) (Bindfaden) piece of string; (Kordel) piece of cord
(b) (ugs.: Kabel) flex (Brit.); lead; cord (Amer.)

schnüren *tr. V.* tie ⟨bundle, string, etc.⟩; tie, lace up ⟨shoe, corset, etc.⟩

schnur·los *Adj.* cordless

Schnurr·bart *der* moustache

schnurren *itr. V.* ⟨cat⟩ purr; ⟨machine⟩ hum

Schnür-: ~**schuh** *der* lace-up shoe; ~**senkel** *der;* ~s, ~ (bes. nordd.) [shoe]lace; (für Stiefel) bootlace

schnur·stracks *Adv.* (ugs.) straight

schob *1. u. 3. Pers. Prät. v.* SCHIESSEN

S

Schock der; ~[e]s, ~s shock

schockieren tr. V. shock; **über etw.** (Akk.) **schockiert sein** be shocked at sth.

Schöffe der; ~n, ~n lay judge (acting together with another lay judge and a professional judge)

Schöffen-gericht das: court presided over by a professional judge and two lay judges

Schöffin die; ~, ~nen ▶ SCHÖFFE

Schokolade die; ~, ~n (a) chocolate
(b) (Getränk) [drinking] chocolate

Schokolade[n]-: ~**eis** das chocolate ice cream; ~**guss**, *~**guß** der chocolate icing; ~**pudding** der chocolate blancmange; ~**torte** die chocolate cake or gateau

scholl 1. u. 3. Pers. Sg. Prät. v. SCHALLEN

Scholle die; ~, ~n (a) (Erdscholle) clod [of earth]
(b) (Eisscholle) [ice] floe
(c) (Fisch) plaice

schon ① Adv. (a) (bereits) (oft nicht übersetzt) already; (in Fragen) yet; **wie lange bist du ~ hier?** how long have you been here?
(b) (fast gleichzeitig) there and then
(c) (jetzt) ~ **[mal]** now; (inzwischen) meanwhile
(d) (selbst, sogar) even; (nur) only
(e) (ohne Ergänzung, ohne weiteren Zusatz) on its own; **[allein]** ~ **der Gedanke daran** the mere thought of it; ~ **deshalb** for this reason alone
(f) (wohl) really; **Lust hätte ich ~, aber ...:** I'd certainly like to, but ...
② Partikel (a) (ugs. ungeduldig: endlich) **nun komm ~!** come on!; hurry up!
(b) (beruhigend: bestimmt) all right
(c) (durchaus) **das ist ~ möglich** that is quite possible

schön ① Adj. (a) beautiful; handsome ⟨youth, man⟩
(b) (angenehm) pleasant, nice ⟨day, holiday, dream, relaxation, etc.⟩; fine ⟨weather⟩; (nett) nice; **das war eine ~e Zeit** those were wonderful days
(c) (gut) good
(d) (in Höflichkeitsformeln) ~**e Grüße** best wishes; **recht ~en Dank für ...:** thank you very much for ...
(e) ~**!** (ugs.: einverstanden) OK (coll.); all right
(f) (iron.: leer) ~**e Worte** fine[-sounding] words; (schmeichlerisch) honeyed words
(g) (ugs.: beträchtlich) handsome, (coll.) tidy ⟨sum, fortune, profit⟩; considerable ⟨quantity, distance⟩; pretty good ⟨pension⟩
(h) (iron.: unerfreulich) nice (coll. iron.); **das sind ja ~e Aussichten!** this is a fine lookout sing. (iron.)
(i) **sich ~ machen** smarten oneself up
② adv. (a) beautifully
(b) (angenehm, erfreulich) nicely; ~ **warm/weich/langsam** nice and warm/soft/slow
(c) (gut) well

(d) (in Höflichkeitsformeln) **bitte ~, können Sie mir sagen, ...:** excuse me, could you tell me ...
(e) (iron.) **wie es so ~ heißt, wie man so ~ sagt** as they say
(f) (ugs.: beträchtlich) really; (vor einem Adjektiv) pretty; **ganz ~ arbeiten müssen** have to work jolly hard (Brit. coll.)
③ Partikel (ugs.) **bleib ~ liegen!** lie there and be good

schonen ① tr. V. treat ⟨clothes, books, furniture, etc.⟩ with care; (schützen) protect ⟨hands, furniture⟩; (nicht strapazieren) spare ⟨voice, eyes, etc.⟩; conserve ⟨strength⟩
② refl. V. take things easy

Schönheit die; ~, ~en beauty

Schönheits-: ~**chirurgie** die cosmetic surgery no art.; ~**pflege** die beauty care no art.

Schon-kost die light food

*****schön|machen** (ugs.) ▶ SCHÖN 1I

Schonung die; ~, ~en (a) (Nachsicht) consideration; (nachsichtige Behandlung) considerate treatment; (nach Krankheit/Operation) [period of] rest; (von Gegenständen) careful treatment
(b) (Jungwald) [young] plantation

schonungs·los ① Adj. unsparing, ruthless ⟨criticism etc.⟩; blunt ⟨frankness⟩
② adv. unsparingly; ⟨say⟩ without mincing one's words

Schonungslosigkeit die; ~: ruthlessness; (Strenge) rigour

Schopf der; ~[e]s, Schöpfe shock of hair

schöpfen tr. V. (a) scoop [up] ⟨water, liquid⟩; (mit einer Kelle) ladle ⟨soup⟩
(b) (geh.: einatmen) draw, take ⟨breath⟩

Schöpfer der; ~s, ~: creator; (Gott) Creator

Schöpferin die; ~, ~nen creator

schöpferisch ① Adj. creative
② adv. creatively

Schöpf-: ~**kelle** die, ~**löffel** der ladle

Schöpfung die; ~, ~en (geh.) creation; die ~ (die Welt) Creation

Schoppen der; ~s, ~: [quarter-litre/half-litre] glass of wine/beer

schor 1. u. 3. Pers. Sg. Prät. v. SCHEREN

Schorf der; ~[e]s, ~e scab

Schorle die; ~, ~n wine with mineral water; ≈ spritzer

Schorn-stein der chimney; (Lokomotive, Schiff usw.) funnel

Schornstein·feger der; ~s, ~, **Schornstein·fegerin** die; ~, ~nen chimney sweep

schoss, *****schoß** 1. u. 3. Pers. Sg. Prät. v. SCHIESSEN

Schoß der; ~es, Schöße lap

Schote die; ~, ~n pod

Schotte der; ~n, ~n Scot; Scotsman; die ~n the Scots; the Scottish

---

*old spelling - see note on page xiv

Schotten-rock *der* tartan skirt; (Kilt) kilt

Schottin *die;* ~, ~**nen** Scot; Scotswoman

schottisch *Adj.* Scottish; ~**er Whisky** Scotch whisky

Schottland *(das);* ~**s** Scotland

schräg ① *Adj.* diagonal ⟨*line, beam, cut, etc.*⟩; sloping ⟨*surface, roof, wall, side, etc.*⟩; slanting, slanted ⟨*writing, eyes, etc.*⟩; tilted ⟨*position of the head etc., axis*⟩
② *adv.* at an angle; (diagonal) diagonally

Schräge *die;* ~, ~**n (a)** (schräge Fläche) sloping surface
(b) (Neigung) slope

Schräg-strich *der* oblique stroke

schrak *1. u. 3. Pers. Sg. Prät. v.* SCHRECKEN

Schramme *die;* ~, ~**n** scratch

schrammen *tr. V.* scratch

Schrank *der;* ~**[e]s, Schränke** cupboard; closet (Amer.); (Glas~; kleiner Wand~) cabinet; (Kleiderschrank) wardrobe; (Bücher~) bookcase

Schränkchen *das;* ~**s,** ~: cabinet

Schranke *die;* ~, ~**n (a)** (auch fig.) barrier
(b) (fig.: Grenze) limit

Schraube *die;* ~, ~**n** bolt; (Holz-, Blechschraube) screw

schrauben *tr. V.* **(a)** ▶ SCHRAUBE: bolt/ screw (an, auf + *Akk.* on to)
(b) (drehen) screw ⟨*nut, hook, lightbulb, etc.*⟩ (auf + *Akk.* into; in + *Akk.* into)

Schrauben-: ~**schlüssel** *der* spanner; ~**zieher** *der;* ~**s,** ~: screwdriver

Schraub-verschluss, **Schraub-verschluß* *der* screw top

Schreber-garten *der* ≈ allotment (*cultivated primarily as a garden*)

Schreck *der;* ~**[e]s,** ~**e** fright; scare; (Schock) shock; **jmdm. einen** ~ **einjagen** give sb. a fright

schrecken *regelm. (auch unr.) itr. V.* start [up]; **aus dem Schlaf** ~: awake with a start; start from one's sleep

Schrecken *der;* ~**s,** ~: fright; scare; (Entsetzen) horror; (große Angst) terror; **jmdm. einen** ~ **einjagen** give sb. a fright

schreckhaft *Adj.* easily scared

Schreckhaftigkeit *die;* ~: easily scared nature; tendency to take fright

schrecklich ① *Adj.* terrible
② *adv.* terribly

Schredder *der;* ~**s,** ~: shredder

schreddern *tr. V.* shred

Schrei *der;* ~**[e]s,** ~**e** cry; (lauter Ruf) shout; (durchdringend) yell; (gellend) scream; (kreischend) shriek

Schreib-block *der; Pl.* ~**s od.** Schreib-blöcke writing pad

schreiben ① *unr. itr. V.* write; (mit der Schreibmaschine) type; **an einem Roman usw.** ~: be writing a novel *etc.;* **jmdm. od. an jmdn.** ~: write to sb.

② *unr. tr. V.* write; (mit der Schreibmaschine) type; **wie schreibt man dieses Wort?** how is this word spelt?
③ *unr. refl. V.* be spelt

Schreiben *das;* ~**s,** ~ **(a)** writing *no def. art.;*
(b) (Brief) letter

Schreiber *der;* ~**s,** ~: writer; (Verfasser) author

Schreiberin *die;* ~, ~**en** writer; (Verfasserin) authoress

Schreib-: ~**marke** *die* (DV) cursor; ~**maschine** *die* typewriter; ~**maschinen-papier** *das* typing paper; ~**papier** *das* writing paper; ~**schutz** *der* (DV) write protection; ~**tisch** *der* desk

Schreibung *die;* ~, ~**en** spelling

Schreib-: ~**waren** *Pl.* stationery *sing.;* ~**waren-geschäft** *das* stationer's

schreien *unr. itr. V.* ⟨*person*⟩ cry [out]; (laut rufen/sprechen) shout; (durchdringend) yell; (gellend) scream; ⟨*baby*⟩ yell, bawl; **zum Schreien sein** (ugs.) be a scream (coll.)

Schrei-hals *der* (ugs.) **(a)** (Kind) bawler
(b) (abwertend: Randalierer) rowdy

Schreiner *der;* ~**s,** ~, (bes. südd.)
▶ TISCHLER

Schreinerei *die;* ~, ~**en** (bes. südd.)
▶ TISCHLEREI

Schreinerin *die;* ~, ~**nen** (bes. südd.)
▶ TISCHLERIN

schreiten *unr. itr. V.; mit sein* (geh.) walk; (mit großen Schritten) stride

schrickst *2. Pers. Sg. Präsens v.* SCHRECKEN

schrickt *3. Pers. Sg. Präsens v.* SCHRECKEN

schrie *1. u. 3. Pers. Sg. Prät. v.* SCHREIEN

schrieb *1. u. 3. Pers. Sg. Prät. v.* SCHREIBEN

Schrieb *der;* ~**[e]s,** ~**e** (ugs.) missive (coll.)

Schrift *die;* ~, ~**en (a)** (System) script; (Alphabet) alphabet
(b) (Handschrift) [hand]writing
(c) (Werk) work

Schrift-art *die* (Druckw.) [type]face

schriftlich ① *Adj.* written
② *adv.* in writing

Schrift-: ~**steller** *der;* ~~**s,** ~~, ~**stellerin** *die;* ~~, ~~**nen** writer; ~**stück** *das* [official] document; ~**wechsel** *der* correspondence; ~**zeichen** *das* character; ~**zug** *der* (Namenszug) lettering; (als Firmenzeichen) logo

schrill ① *Adj.* shrill
② *adv.* shrilly

schrillen *itr. V.* shrill; sound shrilly

schritt *1. u. 3. Pers. Sg. Prät. v.* SCHREITEN

Schritt *der;* ~**[e]s,** ~**e (a)** step; **einen** ~ **machen od. tun** take a step
(b) *Pl.* (Geräusch) footsteps
(c) (Entfernung) pace
(d) (Gleich~) **aus dem** ~ **kommen** get out of step ⋯⋗

(e) (Gangart) walk; seinen ~ verlangsamen/
beschleunigen slow/quicken one's pace; [mit
jmdm./etw.] ~ halten (auch fig.) keep up or
keep pace [with sb./sth.]
(f) (Schrittgeschwindigkeit) walking pace; „~
fahren" 'dead slow'
(g) (fig.: Maßnahme) step; measure

Schritt-: ~geschwindigkeit die
walking pace; ~macher der,
~macherin die pacemaker

schroff 1 Adj. **(a)** precipitous ‹rock etc.›
(b) (plötzlich) sudden ‹transition, change›;
(krass) stark ‹contrast›
(c) (barsch) curt ‹refusal, manner›; brusque
‹manner, behaviour, tone›
2 adv. **(a)** ‹rise, drop› sheer; ‹fall away›
precipitously
(b) (plötzlich, unvermittelt) suddenly
(c) (barsch) curtly; ‹interrupt› abruptly;
‹treat› brusquely

schröpfen tr. V. (ugs.) fleece

Schrot der od. das; ~[e]s, ~e **(a)** (coarse
meal; (aus Getreide) whole meal (Brit.); whole
grain
(b) (Munition) shot

schroten tr. V. grind ‹grain etc.› [coarsely];
crush ‹malt› [coarsely]

Schrot-: ~flinte die shotgun; ~kugel
die pellet

Schrott der; ~[e]s, ~e **(a)** scrap [metal];
ein Auto zu ~ fahren (ugs.) write a car off
(b) (salopp fig.) rubbish

schrott-reif Adj. ready for the scrap heap
postpos.

schrubben tr. (auch itr.) V. scrub

Schrubber der; ~s, ~: [long-handled]
scrubbing brush

Schrulle die; ~, ~n cranky idea; (Marotte)
quirk

schrumpelig Adj. (ugs.) wrinkly

schrumpeln itr. V.; mit sein (ugs.) ‹skin› go
wrinkled; ‹apple etc.› shrivel

schrumpfen itr. V.; mit sein shrink;
‹metal, rock› contract; ‹apple etc.› shrivel;
‹skin› go wrinkled; (abnehmen) decrease;
‹supplies, capital, hopes› dwindle

Schrumpf-: ~leber die cirrhotic liver;
~niere die cirrhotic kidney

Schub der; ~[e]s, Schübe **(a)** (Physik) thrust
(b) (Med.: Phase) phase; stage
(c) (Gruppe, Anzahl) batch

Schuber der; ~s, ~: slip case

Schub-: ~fach das drawer; ~karre die,
~karren der wheelbarrow; ~lade die
drawer

Schubs der; ~es, ~e (ugs.) shove

schubsen tr. (auch itr.) V. (ugs.) push;
shove

schub-weise Adv. (Med.) in phases or
stages

schüchtern 1 Adj. **(a)** shy ‹person, smile,
etc.›; shy, timid ‹voice, knock, etc.›
(b) (fig.: zaghaft) tentative, cautious ‹attempt,
beginnings, etc.›
2 adv. shyly; ‹knock, ask, etc.› timidly

Schüchternheit die; ~: shyness

Schuft der; ~[e]s, ~e scoundrel

schuften (ugs.) itr. V. slave away

Schufterei die; ~ (ugs.) slaving away no
indef. art.; slog

Schuh der; ~[e]s, ~e shoe; (hoher ~, Stiefel)
boot; jmdm. etw. in die ~e schieben (fig. ugs.)
pin the blame for sth. on sb.

Schuh-: ~anzieher der; ~s, ~:
shoehorn; ~band das; Pl. ~bänder (bes.
südd.) shoelace; ~creme die shoe polish;
~größe die shoe size; welche ~größe hast
du? what size shoe[s] do you take?; ~löffel
der shoehorn; ~macher der,
~macherin die shoemaker; ~sohle die
sole [of a/one's shoe]

Schul-: ~abschluss, *~abschluß der
school-leaving qualification; ~arbeit die
(a) ▶ ~AUFGABE; **(b)** (österr.: Klassenarbeit)
[written] class test; ~aufgabe die item of
homework; ~aufgaben homework sing.;
~beirat der school advisory board;
~buch das school book; ~bus der school
bus

schuld ▶ SCHULD B

Schuld die; ~, ~en **(a)** guilt; er ist sich
(Dat.) keiner ~ bewusst he is not conscious
of having done any wrong
(b) (Verantwortlichkeit) blame; es ist [nicht]
seine ~: it is [not] his fault; [an etw. (Dat.)]
~ haben od. schuld sein be to blame [for
sth.]
(c) (Verpflichtung zur Rückzahlung) debt; 5000
Mark ~en haben have debts of 5,000 marks;
owe 5,000 marks

schuld-bewusst, *schuld-bewußt
1 Adj. guilty ‹look, face, etc.›
2 adv. guiltily

schulden tr. V. owe; was schulde ich
Ihnen? how much do I owe you?

Schuld-gefühl das feeling of guilt

schuldig Adj. **(a)** guilty; der [an dem
Unfall] ~e Autofahrer the driver to blame
[for the accident]
(b) jmdm. etw. ~ sein/bleiben owe sb. sth.
(c) (gebührend) due; proper

Schuldige der/die; adj. Dekl. guilty person;
(im Strafprozess) guilty party

Schuldigkeit die; ~, ~en duty; meine
[verdammte] Pflicht und ~: my bounden
duty; seine ~ getan haben (fig.) have served
its/his purpose

Schul-direktor der, **Schul-direktorin**
die head teacher; headmaster/headmistress

schuld-, Schuld-: ~los Adj. innocent
(an + Dat. of); ~spruch der verdict of
guilty

---
*alte Schreibung - vgl. Hinweis auf S. xiv

Schule *die;* ~, ~n school; **zur** *od.* **in die** ~ **gehen, die** ~ **besuchen** go to school; **auf** *od.* **in der** ~: at school

schulen *tr. V.* train

Schüler *der;* ~s, ~: pupil; (Schuljunge) schoolboy

Schüler-austausch *der* school exchange

Schülerin *die;* ~, ~nen pupil; (Schulmädchen) schoolgirl

Schüler-mit-verwaltung *die* pupil participation *no art.* in school administration

schul-, Schul-: ~**ferien** *Pl.* school holidays *or* (Amer.) vacation *sing.;* ~**fernsehen** *das* educational television; television for schools; ~**fest** *das* school open day; ~**frei** *Adj.* ⟨*day*⟩ off school; **morgen ist/haben wir** ~**frei** there is/we have no school tomorrow; ~**frei bekommen** be let off school; ~**hof** *der* school yard; ~**jahr** *das* (a) school year; (b) (Klasse) year; ~**junge** *der* schoolboy; ~**kind** *das* schoolchild; ~**klasse** *die* [school] class; ~**land·heim** *das* [school's] country hostel (*visited by school classes*); ~**mädchen** *das* schoolgirl; ~**ordnung** *die* school rules *pl.;* ~**pflicht** *die* obligation to attend school; **die Einführung der [allgemeinen]** ~**pflicht** the introduction of compulsory school attendance [for all children]; ~**pflichtig** *Adj.* required to attend school *postpos.;* ~**pflichtig sein** have to attend school; **im** ~**pflichtigen Alter** of school age; ~**ranzen** *der* [school] satchel; ~**sportfest** *das* inter-school sports day; ~**sprecher** *der* pupils' representative; ≈ head boy; ~**sprecherin** *die* pupils' representative; ≈ head girl; ~**tag** *der* school day; ~**tasche** *die* schoolbag; (Ranzen) [school] satchel; ~**uniform** *die* school uniform

Schulter *die;* ~, ~n shoulder; **jmdm. auf die** ~ **klopfen** pat sb. on the shoulder *or* (fig.) back

Schulter·blatt *das* (Anat.) shoulder blade

schultern *tr. V.* shoulder; **das Gewehr** ~: shoulder arms

Schul-: ~**weg** *der* way to school; ~**zeit** *die* schooldays *pl.*

Schummelei *die;* ~, ~en (ugs.) ▶ MOGELEI

schummeln *itr., tr., refl. V.* (ugs.) ▶ MOGELN

schummerig *Adj.* dim ⟨*light etc.*⟩; dimly lit ⟨*room etc.*⟩

Schummler *der;* ~s, ~, **Schummlerin** *die;* ~, ~nen (ugs.) cheat

Schund *der;* ~[e]s trash

Schuppe *die;* ~, ~n (a) scale (b) *Pl.* (auf dem Kopf) dandruff *sing.;* (auf der Haut) flaking skin *sing.*

schuppen 1 *tr. V.* scale ⟨*fish*⟩ 2 *refl. V.* ⟨*skin*⟩ flake; ⟨*person*⟩ have flaking skin

Schuppen *der;* ~s, ~ (a) shed

(b) (ugs.: Lokal) joint (coll.)

schüren *tr. V.* (a) poke ⟨*fire*⟩ (b) (fig.) stir up ⟨*hatred, envy, etc.*⟩

schürfen 1 *itr. V.* scrape 2 *tr. V.* (a) **sich** (*Dat.*) **das Knie** *usw.* ~: graze one's knee *etc.;* (b) (Bergbau) mine ⟨*ore etc.*⟩ open-cast *or* (Amer.) opencut

Schürf·wunde *die* graze; abrasion

Schurke *der;* ~n, ~n, **Schurkin** *die;* ~, ~nen rogue

Schur·wolle *die* new wool

Schürze *die;* ~, ~n apron; (Latzschürze) pinafore

Schuss, *Schuß *der;* **Schusses, Schüsse** (a) shot (**auf** + *Akk.* at); **weit** *od.* **weitab vom** ~ (fig. ugs.) well away from the action (b) (Menge Munition/Schießpulver) round; **drei** ~ **Munition** three rounds of ammunition (c) (Schusswunde) gunshot wound (d) (kleine Menge) dash (e) (Drogenjargon) shot; fix (sl.) (f) (Skisport) schuss; ~ **fahren** schuss (g) (ugs.) **etw. in** ~ **bringen/halten** get sth. into/keep sth. in [good] shape

Schüssel *die;* ~, ~n bowl; (flacher) dish

schusselig (ugs.) 1 *Adj.* scatterbrained 2 *adv.* in a scatterbrained way

Schusseligkeit *die;* ~ (ugs.) scatterbrained way

Schuss-, *Schuß-: ~**linie** *die* line of fire; **in die/jmds.** ~**linie geraten** *od.* **kommen** (auch fig.) come under fire/come under fire from sb.; ~**verletzung** *die* gunshot wound; ~**waffe** *die* weapon (*firing a projectile*); (Gewehr usw.) firearm; ~**wechsel** *der* exchange of shots

Schuster *der;* ~s, ~, **Schusterin** *die;* ~, ~nen (ugs.) shoemaker; (jmd., der Schuhe repariert) shoe repairer

Schutt *der;* ~[e]s rubble; „~ **abladen verboten"** 'no tipping'; 'no dumping'

Schüttel·frost *der* [violent] shivering fit

schütteln 1 *tr. V.* (a) shake; **den Kopf [über etw.** (*Akk.*)] ~: shake one's head [over sth.]; **jmdm. die Hand** ~: shake sb.'s hand; shake sb. by the hand (b) (*unpers.*) **es schüttelte ihn [vor Kälte]** he was shaking [with *or* from cold] 2 *refl. V.* shake oneself/itself 3 *itr. V.* **mit dem Kopf** ~: shake one's head

schütten 1 *tr. V.* pour ⟨*liquid, flour, etc.*⟩; (unabsichtlich) spill ⟨*liquid, flour, etc.*⟩; tip ⟨*rubbish, coal, etc.*⟩ 2 *itr. V.* (*unpers.*) (ugs.: regnen) pour [down]

schütter *Adj.* sparse; thin

Schutt-: ~**halde** *die* pile *or* heap of rubble; ~**haufen** *der* pile of rubble; (Abfallhaufen) rubbish heap

Schutz *der;* ~es protection (**vor** + *Dat.*, **gegen** against); (Zuflucht) refuge; ~ **suchend** seeking protection *postpos.*

schutz-, Schutz-: ~**bedürftig** *Adj.* in ⋯⟩

need of protection *postpos.;*
~**behauptung** *die* (bes. Rechtsw.) attempt
to justify one's behaviour; ~**blech** *das*
mudguard; ~**brief** *der* (Kfz-W.) travel
insurance; (Dokument) travel insurance
certificate

Schütze *der;* ~**n,** ~**n** (a) marksman
(b) (Fußball usw.) scorer
(c) (Milit.: einfacher Soldat) private
(d) (Astrol.) Sagittarius

schützen ⟦1⟧ *tr. V.* protect **(vor** + *Dat.* from,
gegen against); safeguard *⟨interest, property,
etc.⟩* **(vor** + *Dat.* from); **gesetzlich geschützt**
registered [as a trade mark]
⟦2⟧ *itr. V.* provide *or* give protection **(vor** +
Dat. from, **gegen** against); (vor Wind, Regen)
give shelter **(vor** + *Dat.* from)

Schützen·fest *das: shooting competition
with fair*

Schutz·engel *der* guardian angel

Schützen-: ~**graben** *der* trench;
~**panzer** *der* armoured personnel carrier;
~**verein** *der* rifle club

Schutz-: ~**helm** *der* helmet; (bei
Motorradfahrern usw.) crash helmet; (bei
Bauarbeitern usw.) safety helmet; ~**hütte** *die*
(a) (Unterstand) shelter; (b) (Berghütte)
mountain hut; ~**impfung** *die* vaccination

Schützin *die;* ~**,** ~**nen** (a) markswoman
(b) (Fußball usw.) scorer

Schützling *der;* ~**s,** ~**e** protégé;
(Anvertrauter) charge

schutz-, Schutz-: ~**los** *Adj.* defenceless;
~**mann** *der; Pl.* ~**männer** *od.* ~**leute** (ugs.
veralt.) [police] constable; copper (Brit. coll.);
~**patron** *der,* ~**patronin** *die* patron
saint; ~**schicht** *die* protective layer **(aus**
of); (flüssig aufgetragen) protective coating;
*~**suchend** ▶ SCHUTZ; ~**umschlag** *der*
dust jacket

schwabbelig *Adj.* flabby *⟨stomach,
person, etc.⟩*; wobbly *⟨jelly etc.⟩*

schwabbeln *itr. V.* (ugs.) wobble

Schwabe *der;* ~**n,** ~**n** Swabian

Schwaben *(das);* ~**s** Swabia

Schwäbin *die;* ~**,** ~**nen** Swabian

schwäbisch *Adj.* Swabian

schwach; schwächer, schwächst… ⟦1⟧ *Adj.*
(a) weak; weak, delicate *⟨child, woman⟩*;
frail *⟨invalid, old person⟩*; low-powered
⟨engine, bulb, amplifier, etc.⟩; weak, poor
⟨eyesight, memory, etc.⟩; poor *⟨hearing⟩*;
delicate *⟨health, constitution⟩*; ~ **werden**
grow weak; (fig.: schwanken) weaken; (fig.:
nachgeben) give in
(b) (nicht gut) poor *⟨pupil, player,
performance, result, etc.⟩*; weak *⟨argument,
opponent, play, film, etc.⟩*
(c) (gering, niedrig) poor, low *⟨attendance etc.⟩*;
slight *⟨effect, resistance, gradient, etc.⟩*; light

*old spelling - see note on page xiv

⟨wind, rain, current⟩; faint *⟨voice, pressure,
hope, smile, smell⟩*; weak, faint *⟨pulse⟩*; faint,
dim *⟨light⟩*; pale *⟨colour⟩*
(d) (wenig konzentriert) weak *⟨solution, coffee,
poison, etc.⟩*
(e) (Sprachw.) weak
⟦2⟧ *adv.* (a) weakly
(b) (nicht gut) poorly
(c) (in geringem Maße) poorly *⟨attended,
developed⟩*; slightly *⟨poisonous, sweetened,
inclined⟩*; *⟨rain⟩* slightly; *⟨remember, glow,
smile⟩* faintly
(d) (Sprachw.) ~ **gebeugt** weak

Schwäche *die;* ~**,** ~**n** weakness; **eine** ~
für jmdn./etw. haben have a soft spot for sb./
a weakness for sth.

Schwäche·anfall *der* sudden feeling of
faintness

schwächen *tr. V.* weaken

schwächlich *Adj.* weakly *⟨person⟩*; frail
⟨old person, constitution⟩

Schwächling *der;* ~**s,** ~**e** weakling

schwach-, Schwach-: ~**punkt** *der*
weak point; ~**sinn** *der* (a) (Med.) mental
deficiency; (b) (ugs.) [idiotic (coll.)] rubbish;
~**sinnig** ⟦1⟧ *Adj.* (a) (Med.) mentally
deficient; (b) (ugs.) idiotic (coll.), nonsensical
⟨measure, policy, etc.⟩; rubbishy *⟨film etc.⟩*;
⟦2⟧ *adv.* (ugs.) idiotically (coll.); stupidly

Schwächung *die;* ~**,** ~**en** weakening

Schwaden *der;* ~**s,** ~**:** [thick] cloud

schwafeln (ugs.) ⟦1⟧ *itr. V.* rabbit on (Brit.
coll.), waffle (**von** about)
⟦2⟧ *tr. V.* blether *⟨nonsense⟩*

Schwager *der;* ~**s, Schwäger** brother-in-
law

Schwägerin *die;* ~**,** ~**nen** sister-in-law

Schwalbe *die;* ~**,** ~**n** swallow

Schwall *der;* ~**[e]s,** ~**e** torrent

schwamm *1. u. 3. Pers. Sg. Prät. v.*
SCHWIMMEN

Schwamm *der;* ~**[e]s, Schwämme** (a)
sponge; ~ **drüber!** (ugs.) [let's] forget it
(b) (südd., österr.: Pilz) mushroom

Schwammerl *das;* ~**s,** ~**[n]** (bayr., österr.)
mushroom

schwammig ⟦1⟧ *Adj.* (a) spongy
(b) (aufgedunsen) flabby, bloated *⟨face, body,
etc.⟩*
(c) (abwertend: unpräzise) woolly *⟨concept,
manner of expression, etc.⟩*
⟦2⟧ *adv.* (unpräzise) vaguely

Schwammigkeit *die;* ~ (a) sponginess
(b) (abwertend: Aufgedunsenheit) flabbiness;
bloated appearance
(c) (abwertend: Vagheit) woolliness

Schwan *der;* ~**[e]s, Schwäne** swan

schwand *1. u. 3. Pers. Sg. Prät. v.*
SCHWINDEN

schwang *1. u. 3. Pers. Sg. Prät. v.*
SCHWINGEN

schwanger *Adj.* pregnant (**von** by)

Schwangere *die; adj. Dekl.* expectant
mother; pregnant woman

schwängern *tr. V.* make ⟨*woman*⟩
pregnant

Schwangerschaft *die;* ~, ~**en**
pregnancy

Schwangerschafts-: ~**abbruch** *der*
termination of pregnancy; abortion;
~**verhütung** *die* contraception;
~**vertretung** *die* **(a)** maternity[-leave]
cover; **die** ~**vertretung für jmdn. machen**
cover for sb. while she is on maternity
leave; **(b)** (Person) person covering [a period
of] maternity leave

Schwank *der;* ~[e]s, Schwänke comic tale;
(auf der Bühne) farce

schwanken *itr. V.; mit Richtungsangabe
mit sein* **(a)** sway; ⟨*boat*⟩ rock; (heftiger) roll;
⟨*ground, floor*⟩ shake
(b) (fig.: unbeständig sein) ⟨*prices, temperature,
etc.*⟩ fluctuate; ⟨*number, usage, etc.*⟩ vary
(c) (fig.: unentschieden sein) waver; (zögern)
hesitate

Schwankung *die;* ~, ~**en** variation; (der
Kurse usw.) fluctuation

Schwanz *der;* ~**es**, Schwänze **(a)** tail
(b) (salopp: Penis) prick (coarse); cock (coarse)

Schwänzchen *das;* ~**s**, ~**(a)** [little] tail
(b) (fam.: Penis) willy (coll.)

schwänzeln *itr. V.* wag its tail/their tails

schwänzen *tr., itr. V.* (ugs.) skip, cut
⟨*lesson etc.*⟩; **[die Schule]** ~: play truant *or*
(Amer.) hookey

schwappen *itr. V.* slosh

Schwarm *der;* ~[e]s, Schwärme **(a)** swarm
(b) (fam.: Angebetete[r]) idol; heart-throb

schwärmen *itr. V.* **(a)** *mit
Richtungsangabe mit sein* swarm
(b) (begeistert sein) **für jmdn./etw.** ~: be mad
about *or* really keen on sb./sth.; **von etw.** ~:
go into raptures about sth.

schwärmerisch [1] *Adj.* rapturous
[2] *adv.* rapturously

Schwarte *die;* ~, ~**n (a)** rind
(b) (ugs.: dickes Buch) tome

schwarz; schwärzer, schwärzest… [1] *Adj.*
(a) black; Black ⟨*person*⟩; filthy[-black]
⟨*hands, fingernails, etc.*⟩; **mir wurde Schwarz
vor den Augen** everything went black **der**
~**e Erdteil** *od.* **Kontinent** the Dark Continent;
das Schwarze Meer the Black Sea; **ins
Schwarze treffen** (fig.) hit the nail on the
head
(b) (illegal) illicit ⟨*deal, exchange, etc.*⟩; **der**
~**e Markt** the black market
(c) ~ **sehen** look on the black side; be
pessimistic (**für** about)
[2] *adv.* (illegal) illegally

Schwarz *das;* ~[**es**], ~: black

Schwarz·brot *das* black bread

Schwarze *der/die; adj. Dekl.* Black

schwärzen *tr. V.* blacken

schwarz-, Schwarz-: ~|**fahren** *unr.*

itr. V.; mit sein dodge paying the fare;
~**fahrer** *der,* ~**fahrerin** *die* fare dodger;
~**haarig** *Adj.* black-haired; ~**handel** *der*
black market (**mit** in); (Tätigkeit) black
marketeering (**mit** in); ~**markt** *der* black
market; ~|**sehen** *unr. itr. V.* watch
television without a licence; *s. auch*
SCHWARZ 1C; ~**seher** *der,* ~**seherin** *die*
(a) (ugs.) pessimist; **(b)** (jmd, der schwarz
fernsieht) [television] licence dodger

Schwärzung *die;* ~, ~**en** blackening

schwarz-, Schwarz-: ~**wald** *der;*
~[e]s Black Forest; ~**weiß** *Adj.* black and
white; ~**weiß·film** *der* black and white
film; ~**weiß·foto** *das* black and white
photo; ~**wurzel** *die* black salsify

schwatzen, (bes. südd.) **schwätzen**
[1] *itr. V.* chat; (über belanglose Dinge) chatter;
natter (coll.)
[2] *tr. V.* say; talk ⟨*nonsense, rubbish*⟩

Schwätzer *der;* ~**s**, ~, **Schwätzerin**
die; ~, ~**nen** chatterbox; (klatschhafter Mensch)
gossip

schwatzhaft *Adj.* talkative; (klatschhaft)
gossipy

Schwatzhaftigkeit *die;* ~:
talkativeness; (Klatschsucht) gossipiness

Schwebe *die:* **in der** ~ **sein/bleiben** (fig.)
be/remain in the balance

Schwebe-: ~**bahn** *die* cableway;
~**balken** *der* (Turnen) [balance] beam

schweben *itr. V.* **(a)** ⟨*bird, balloon, etc.*⟩
hover; ⟨*cloud, balloon, mist*⟩ hang; **in Gefahr**
~ (fig.) be in danger
(b) *mit sein* (durch die Luft) float

Schwede *der;* ~**n**, ~**n** Swede

Schweden (*das*) ~**s** Sweden

Schwedin *die;* ~, ~**nen** Swede

schwedisch *Adj.* Swedish

Schwefel *der;* ~**s** sulphur

Schwefel-: ~**dioxid**, ~**dioxyd** *das*
(Chemie) sulphur dioxide; ~**säure** *die*
(Chemie) sulphuric acid; ~**wasserstoff**
der (Chemie) hydrogen sulphide

Schweif *der;* ~[e]s, ~**e** tail

schweifen *itr. V.; mit sein* (geh.; auch fig.)
wander

Schweige·geld *das* hush money

schweigen *unr. itr. V.* remain *or* stay
silent; say nothing; **ganz zu** ~ **von** …: not to
mention …

Schweigen *das;* ~**s** silence

schweigsam *Adj.* silent; quiet

Schweigsamkeit *die;* ~: silence;
quietness

Schwein *das;* ~[e]s, ~**e (a)** pig
(b) (Fleisch) pork
(c) (salopp: gemeiner Mensch) swine;
(Schmutzfink) mucky devil (coll.); mucky pig
(coll.)
(d) (salopp: Mensch) **ein armes** ~: a poor
devil; **kein** ~ **war da** there wasn't a bloody
(Brit. sl.) *or* (coll.) damn soul there ⋯⟫

(e) (ugs.: Glück) [**großes**] ~ **haben** have a [big] stroke of luck; (davonkommen) get away with it (coll.)

Schweine-: ~**braten** der roast pork no indef. art.; ~**fleisch** das pork; ~**kotelett** das (Kochk.) pork chop

Schweinerei die; ~, ~en (ugs.) **(a)** (Schmutz) mess

(b) (Gemeinheit) mean or dirty trick

Schweine-: ~**schnitzel** das escalope of pork; ~**stall** der (auch fig.) pigsty; pigpen (Amer.); ~**steak** das pork steak;

schweinisch (ugs.) Adj. **(a)** (schmutzig) filthy

(b) (unanständig) dirty; smutty

Schweins·leder das pigskin

Schweiß der; ~es sweat; **mir brach der** ~ **aus** I broke out in a sweat

Schweiß-: ~**ausbruch** der sweat; ~**brenner** der welding torch; ~**drüse** die (Anat.) sweat gland

schweißen tr., itr. V. weld

Schweißer der; ~s, ~, **Schweißerin** die; ~, ~nen welder

schweiß-, Schweiß-: ~**fuß** sweaty foot; ~**gebadet** Adj. bathed in sweat postpos.; ~**nass**, *~**naß** Adj. sweaty; damp with sweat pred.; ~**perle** die bead of sweat

Schweiz die; ~: Switzerland no art.

Schweizer der; ~s, ~: Swiss

schweizer·deutsch Adj. Swiss German

Schweizerin die; ~, ~nen Swiss

schweizerisch Adj. Swiss

schwelen (auch fig.) smoulder

schwelgen itr. V. feast

Schwelle die; ~, ~n **(a)** threshold

(b) (Eisenbahnschwelle) sleeper (Brit.); [cross] tie (Amer.)

schwellen unr. itr. V.; mit sein swell; ⟨limb, face, cheek, etc.⟩ swell [up]

Schwellen·land das: country at the stage of economic take-off

Schwellung die; ~, ~en (Med.) swelling

Schwemme die; ~, ~n glut (an + Dat. of)

Schwemm·land das alluvial land

Schwengel der; ~s, ~ **(a)** (der Glocke) clapper

(b) (der Pumpe) handle

Schwenk der; ~s, ~s **(a)** (Drehung) swing

(b) (Film, Ferns.) pan

schwenken ① tr. V. **(a)** swing; wave ⟨flag, handkerchief⟩

(b) (spülen) rinse

② itr. V.; mit sein ⟨marching column⟩ swing, wheel; ⟨camera⟩ pan; ⟨path, road, car⟩ swing

schwer ① Adj. **(a)** heavy; **2 Kilo** ~ **sein** weigh two kilos

(b) (mühevoll) heavy ⟨work⟩; hard, tough ⟨job⟩; hard ⟨day⟩; difficult ⟨birth⟩; **es** ~/**nicht** ~

---

haben have it hard/easy; **sich mit** od. **bei etw.** ~ **tun** (ugs.) have trouble with sth.; **jmdm. fällt etw.** ~: sb. finds sth. difficult; **jmdm./ sich etw.** ~ **machen** make sth. difficult for sb./oneself

(c) (schlimm) severe ⟨shock, disappointment, strain, storm⟩; serious, grave ⟨wrong, injustice, error, illness, blow, reservation⟩; serious ⟨accident, injury⟩; heavy ⟨punishment, strain, loss, blow⟩; **etw.** ~ **nehmen** take sth. seriously

② adv. **(a)** heavily ⟨built, laden, armed⟩; ~ **tragen** be carrying sth. heavy [with difficulty]

(b) ⟨work⟩ hard; ⟨breathe⟩ heavily; ~ **hören** be hard of hearing

(c) (schwierig) with difficulty; ~ **verdaulich** (auch fig.) hard to digest pred.

(d) (sehr) seriously ⟨injured, ill⟩; greatly, deeply ⟨disappointed⟩; ⟨punish⟩ severely, heavily; ~ **verunglücken** have a serious accident

Schwer-: ~**arbeiter** der worker engaged in heavy physical work; ~**behinderte** der/die severely handicapped person; (körperlich auch) severely disabled person; **die** ~**behinderten** the severely handicapped/ disabled; ~**beschädigte** der/die; adj. Dekl. severely disabled person

Schwere die; ~ **(a)** weight

(b) (Schwerkraft) gravity

(c) ▶ SCHWER 1C; severity; seriousness; gravity; heaviness

schwere·los Adj. weightless

Schwerelosigkeit die; ~: weightlessness

schwer-, Schwer-: *~|**fallen** ▶ SCHWER 1B; ~**fällig** ① Adj. (auch fig.) ponderous; cumbersome ⟨bureaucracy, procedure⟩; ② adv. ponderously; ~**fälligkeit** die: ▶ ~FÄLLIG: ponderousness; cumbersomeness; ~**gewicht** das **(a)** (Sport) heavyweight; **(b)** (Schwerpunkt) main focus; ~**hörig** Adj. hard of hearing pred.; ~**hörigkeit** die; ~~: hardness of hearing; ~**industrie** die heavy industry; ~**kraft** die gravity; *~**krank** ▶ SCHWER 2D

schwerlich Adv. hardly

schwer-, Schwer-: *~|**machen** ▶ SCHWER 1B; ~**metall** das heavy metal; ~**mütig** ① Adj. melancholic; ② adv. melancholically; *~|**nehmen** ▶ SCHWER 1C; ~**punkt** der centre of gravity; (fig.) main focus; (Hauptgewicht) main stress

Schwert das; ~[e]s, ~er sword

Schwert-: ~**fisch** der swordfish; ~**lilie** die iris

schwer|tun ▶ SCHWER 1B

Schwert·wal der (Orka) killer whale

schwer-, Schwer-: ~**verbrecher** der, ~**verbrecherin** die serious offender; *~**verdaulich** ▶ SCHWER 2C; *~**verletzt** ▶ SCHWER 2D; ~**wiegend** Adj. serious; momentous ⟨decision⟩

Schwester die; ~, ~n **(a)** sister

---

*alte Schreibung - vgl. Hinweis auf S. xiv

(b) (Krankenschwester) nurse

schwesterlich ⟦1⟧ *Adj.* sisterly
  ⟦2⟧ *adv.* ~ **handeln** act in a sisterly way

schwieg *1. u. 3. Pers. Prät. v.* SCHWEIGEN

Schwieger-: ~**eltern** *Pl.* parents-in-law;
~**mutter** *die; Pl.* ~mütter mother-in-law;
~**sohn** *der* son-in-law; ~**tochter** *die*
daughter-in-law; ~**vater** *der* father-in-law

Schwiele *die;* ~, ~n callus; ~n **an den**
Händen horny hands

schwielig *Adj.* callused; ~e **Hände** horny
hands

schwierig *Adj.* difficult

Schwierigkeit *die;* ~, ~en difficulty

Schwierigkeits-grad *der* degree of
difficulty; (von Lehrmaterial usw.) level of
difficulty

Schwimm-: ~**bad** *das* swimming baths
pl. (Brit.); swimming pool; ~**becken** *das*
swimming pool

schwimmen ⟦1⟧ *unr. itr. V.* **(a)** *meist mit*
sein swim
  (b) *meist mit sein* (treiben, nicht untergehen)
float
  (c) (ugs.: unsicher sein) be all at sea; **ins**
Schwimmen geraten start to flounder
  ⟦2⟧ *unr. tr. V.; auch mit sein* swim

Schwimmen *das;* ~s: swimming *no art.*

Schwimmer *der;* ~s, ~ **(a)** swimmer
  (b) (Technik) float

Schwimmerin *die;* ~, ~nen swimmer

Schwimm-: ~**flosse** *die* flipper;
~**lehrer** *der,* ~**lehrerin** *die* swimming
instructor; ~**weste** *die* life jacket

Schwindel *der;* ~s **(a)** dizziness;
giddiness
  (b) (Betrug) swindle; (Lüge) lie

schwindel-frei *Adj.* ~ **sein** have a head
for heights

schwindelig ▶ SCHWINDLIG

schwindeln *itr. V.* **(a)** (unpers.) **mich** *od.*
mir schwindelt I feel dizzy *or* giddy
  (b) (lügen) tell fibs

schwinden *unr. itr. V.; mit sein* fade;
⟨supplies, money⟩ run out; ⟨effect⟩ wear off;
⟨fear, mistrust⟩ lessen; ⟨powers, influence⟩
wane

Schwindler *der;* ~s, ~, **Schwindlerin**
die; ~, ~nen (Lügner[in]) liar; (Betrüger[in])
swindler; (Hochstapler[in]) confidence trickster

schwindlig *Adj.* dizzy; giddy; **jmdm. wird**
es ~: sb. gets dizzy *or* giddy

schwingen ⟦1⟧ *unr. itr. V.* **(a)** *mit sein*
swing
  (b) (vibrieren) vibrate
  ⟦2⟧ *unr. tr. V.* swing; wave ⟨flag, wand⟩;
brandish ⟨sword, axe, etc.⟩
  ⟦3⟧ *unr. refl. V.* **sich aufs Pferd/Fahrrad** ~:
leap on to one's horse/bicycle

Schwingung *die;* ~, ~en **(a)** swinging;
(Vibration) vibration
  (b) (Physik) oscillation

Schwips *der;* ~es, ~e (ugs.) **einen** ~
haben be tipsy

schwirren *itr. V. mit sein* ⟨arrow, bullet,
etc.⟩ whiz; ⟨bird⟩ whirr; ⟨insect⟩ buzz

schwitzen *itr. V.* (auch fig.) sweat

schwor *1. u. 3. Pers. Sg. Prät. v.* SCHWÖREN

schwören ⟦1⟧ *unr. tr., itr. V.* swear
⟨fidelity, friendship⟩; swear, take ⟨oath⟩
  ⟦2⟧ *unr. itr. V.* swear an/the oath

Schwuchtel *die;* ~, ~n (salopp) queen (sl.)

schwul *Adj.* (ugs.) gay (coll.)

schwül *Adj.* sultry; close

Schwule *der; adj. Dekl.* (ugs.) gay (coll.);
(abwertend) queer (sl.)

Schwüle *die;* ~: sultriness

schwülstig ⟦1⟧ *Adj.* bombastic; pompous;
over-ornate ⟨art, architecture⟩
  ⟦2⟧ *adv.* bombastically; pompously

Schwund *der;* ~[e]s decrease, drop ⟨Gen.
in⟩; (an Interesse) waning; falling off

Schwung *der;* ~[e]s, Schwünge **(a)**
(Bewegung) swing
  (b) (Linie) sweep
  (c) (Geschwindigkeit) momentum; ~ **holen**
build *or* get up momentum
  (d) (Antrieb) drive; energy
  (e) (mitreißende Wirkung) sparkle

schwung-haft *Adj.* thriving; brisk,
flourishing ⟨trade, business⟩

schwung-voll ⟦1⟧ *Adj.* **(a)** lively
  (b) (kraftvoll) vigorous; sweeping ⟨movement,
gesture⟩; bold ⟨handwriting, line, stroke⟩
  ⟦2⟧ *adv.* spiritedly; (kraftvoll) with great vigour

Schwur *der;* ~[e]s, Schwüre **(a)** (Gelöbnis)
vow
  (b) (Eid) oath

Schwur-gericht *das:* court with a jury

sechs *Kardinalz.* six

Sechs *die;* ~, ~en six

sechs-, Sechs-: ~**eck** *das* hexagon;
~**eckig** *Adj.* hexagonal; ~**fach**
Vervielfältigungsz. sixfold; ~**hundert**
Kardinalz. six hundred; ~**mal** *Adv.* six
times

sechst... *Ordinalz.* sixth

sechs-tausend *Kardinalz.* six thousand

sechstel *Bruchz.* sixth

Sechstel *das,* (schweiz. meist *der*); ~s, ~:
sixth

sechstens *Adv.* sixthly

sechzehn *Kardinalz.* sixteen

sechzig *Kardinalz.* sixty

sechzigst... *Ordinalz.* sixtieth

SED *Abk.* (DDR) = **Sozialistische**
Einheitspartei Deutschlands
Socialist Unity Party of Germany ⟨state
party of the former DDR⟩

See¹ *der;* ~s, ~n lake

See² *die;* ~: **die** ~: the sea; **an die** ~ **fahren**
go to the seaside; **auf hoher** ~: on the high
seas

see-, See-: ~**bad** *das* seaside health   ⋯⟶

resort; ~**fahrt** die seafaring no art.; sea travel no art.; ~**gang** der leichter/starker od. hoher od. schwerer ~gang light/heavy or rough sea; ~**hund** der [common] seal; (Pelz)seal[skin]; ~**igel** der sea urchin; ~**krank** Adj. seasick; ~**krankheit** die seasickness; ~**lachs** der pollack

Seele die; ~, ~n soul; (Psyche) mind

Seelen·leben das (geh.) inner life

seelen·ruhig 1 Adj. calm; unruffled 2 adv. calmly

seelisch 1 Adj. psychological ⟨cause, damage, tension⟩; mental ⟨equilibrium, breakdown, illness, health⟩ 2 adv. ~ bedingt sein have psychological causes; ~ krank mentally ill

Seel·sorge die pastoral care

Seelsorger der; ~s, ~, **Seelsorgerin** die; ~, ~nen pastoral worker; (Geistliche[r]) pastor

see-, See-: ~**macht** die sea power; ~**mann** der; Pl. ~leute seaman; sailor; ~**meile** die nautical mile; ~**not** die distress [at sea]; in ~not geraten get into difficulties pl.; ~**pferd[chen]** das sea horse; ~**räuber** der, ~**räuberin** die pirate; ~**reise** die voyage; (Kreuzfahrt) cruise; ~**rose** die waterlily; ~**stern** der starfish; ~**tüchtig** Adj. seaworthy; ~**zunge** die sole

Segel das; ~s, ~: sail

Segel-: ~**boot** das sailing boat; ~**flieger** der, ~**fliegerin** die glider pilot; ~**flugzeug** das glider

segeln itr. V.; mit sein sail

Segel-: ~**schiff** das sailing ship; ~**tuch** das; Pl. ~~e sailcloth

Segen der; ~s, ~: blessing; (Gebet in der Messe) benediction

Segler der; ~s, ~: yachtsman

Seglerin die; ~, ~nen yachtswoman

segnen tr. V. bless

seh·behindert Adj. partially sighted; visually handicapped

sehen 1 unr. itr. V. (a) see; schlecht/gut ~: have bad/good eyesight; mal ~, wir wollen od. werden ~ (ugs.) we'll see; siehste! (ugs.) there, you see! (b) (hinsehen) look (auf + Akk. at); sieh mal od. doch! look!; siehe da! lo and behold! 2 unr. tr. V. (a) (auch fig.) see; jmdn./etw. [nicht] zu ~ bekommen [not] get to see sb./ sth.; ich habe ihn kommen [ge]~: I saw him coming (b) (ansehen) watch ⟨television programme⟩

sehens·wert Adj. worth seeing postpos.

Sehens·würdigkeit die; ~, ~en sight

Seher der; ~s, ~, **Seherin** die; ~, ~nen seer; prophet/prophetess

Seh-: ~**fehler** der sight defect; defect of vision; ~**kraft** die sight

Sehne die; ~, ~n (a) tendon (b) (Bogen~) string

sehnen refl. V. sich nach jmdm./etw. ~: long or yearn for sb./sth.

sehnig Adj. (a) stringy ⟨meat⟩ (b) (kräftig) sinewy ⟨figure, legs, etc.⟩

sehnlichst 1 Adj. das ist mein ~es Verlangen/mein ~er Wunsch that's what I long for most/that's my dearest wish 2 adv. etw. ~ herbeiwünschen look forward longingly to sth.

Sehn·sucht die longing; ~ nach jmdm. haben long to see sb.

sehn·süchtig Adj. longing attrib., yearning attrib. ⟨desire, look, gaze, etc.⟩

sehr Adv. (a) mit Adj. u. Adv. very; ~ viel a great deal; jmdn. ~ gern haben like sb. a lot (coll.) or a great deal (b) mit Verben very much; greatly; danke ~! thank you or thanks [very much]; bitte ~, Ihr Steak! here's your steak, sir/madam

Seh-: ~**schärfe** die visual acuity; ~**test** der eye test; ~**vermögen** das sight

sei 1. u. 3. Pers. Sg. Präsens Konjunktiv u. Imperativ Sg. v. SEIN

seicht 1 Adj. (auch fig.) shallow 2 adv. (fig.) shallowly

Seichtheit die; ~ (auch fig.) shallowness

seid 2. Pers. Pl. Präsens u. Imperativ Pl. v. SEIN

Seide die; ~, ~n silk

Seidel das; ~s, ~: beer mug

seiden Adj. silk

Seiden·papier das tissue paper

seidig 1 Adj. silky 2 adv. silkily

Seife die; ~, ~n soap

Seifen-: ~**blase** die soap bubble; ~**oper** die (ugs.) soap opera; ~**schale** die soap dish; ~**schaum** der lather

Seil das; ~s, ~e rope; (Drahtseil) cable

Seil·bahn die cableway

seil|hüpfen itr. V.; nur im Inf. u. 2. Part.; mit sein ▶ SEILSPRINGEN

Seilschaft die; ~, ~en (Bergsteigen) rope; (fig.) followers pl.

seil-, Seil-: ~|**springen** unr. itr. V.; nur im Inf. u. 2. Part.; mit sein skip; ~**tänzer** der, ~**tänzerin** die tightrope walker; ~**winde** die cable winch

sein[1] 1 unr. itr. V. be; (existieren) be; exist; (sich ereignen) be; happen; wie dem auch sei be that as it may; er ist Schwede/Lehrer he is Swedish or a Swede/a teacher; bist du es? is that you?; mir ist kalt/besser I am or feel cold/better; mir ist schlecht I feel sick; drei und vier ist od. (ugs.) sind sieben three and four is or makes seven; es ist drei Uhr/Mai/Winter it is three o'clock/May/winter; er ist aus Berlin he is or comes from Berlin; was darf es ~? (im Geschäft) what can I get you?; es war einmal ein Prinz once upon a time there was a prince

2 *mod. V.* (in der Funktion von können/müssen + Passiv) **es ist niemand zu sehen** there's no one to be seen; **das war zu erwarten** that was to be expected; **die Schmerzen sind kaum zu ertragen** the pain is hardly bearable; **die Richtlinien sind strengstens zu beachten** the guidelines are to be strictly followed

3 *Hilfsverb* **(a)** (zur Perfektumschreibung) have; **er ist gestorben** he has died

(b) (zur Bildung des Zustandspassivs) be; **wir sind gerettet worden/wir waren gerettet** we were saved

sein² *Possessivpron.* (einer männlichen Person) his; (einer weiblichen Person) her; (einer Sache, eines Tiers) its; (nach man) one's; his (Amer.)

Sein *das;* ~s (Philos.) being; (Dasein) existence; ~ **und Schein** appearance and reality

seiner (geh.) *Gen. von* ER: **sich ~ erbarmen** have pity on him; ~ **gedenken** remember him

seiner-: ~**seits** *Adv.* for his part; (von ihm) on his part; ~**zeit** *Adv.* at that time

seines-gleichen *indekl. Pron.* his own kind

seinet·wegen *Adv.* ▶ MEINETWEGEN: because of him; for his sake; about him; as far as he is concerned

seismo-, Seismo-: ~**graph** *der;* ~~en, ~~en seismograph; ~**loge** *der;* ~~n, ~~n seismologist; ~**logie** *die;* ~~: seismology *no art.;* ~**login** *die;* ~~, ~~nen seismologist; ~**logisch** 1 *Adj.* seismological; 2 *adv.* seismologically

seit 1 *Präp. mit Dat.* (Zeitpunkt) since; (Zeitspanne) for; **ich bin ~ zwei Wochen hier** I've been here [for] two weeks

2 *Konj.* since; ~ **du hier wohnst** since you have been living here

seit·dem 1 *Adv.* since then

2 *Konj.* ▶ SEIT 2

Seite *die;* ~, ~n **(a)** side; **zur** *od.* **auf die ~ gehen** move aside *or* to one side; ~ **an ~:** side by side; **jmdm. zur ~ stehen** stand by sb.; **von allen ~n** (auch fig.) from all sides; **nach allen ~n** in all directions; (fig.) on all sides

(b) (Buch-, Zeitungsseite) page

Seiten-: ~**ansicht** *die* side view; ~**aufprall·schutz** *der* side impact protection; ~**hieb** *der* (fig.) sideswipe (**auf** + *Akk.* at); ~**ruder** *das* (Flugw.) rudder

seitens *Präp. mit Gen.* (Papierdt.) on the part of

Seiten-: ~**sprung** *der* infidelity; ~**straße** *die* side street; ~**wind** *der* side wind; crosswind; ~**zahl** *die* **(a)** page number; **(b)** (Anzahl der Seiten) number of pages

seit·her *Adv.* since then

seitlich 1 *Adj.* at the side (postpos.)

2 *adv.* (an der Seite) at the side; (von der Seite) from the side; (nach der Seite) to the side

seit·wärts *Adv.* sideways

Sekretär *der;* ~s, ~e **(a)** secretary **(b)** (Schreibschrank) bureau (Brit.)

Sekretariat *das;* ~[e]s, ~e [secretary's/ secretaries'] office

Sekretärin *die;* ~, ~nen secretary

Sekt *der;* ~[e]s, ~e high-quality sparkling wine; ≈ champagne

Sekte *die;* ~, ~n sect

Sektor *der;* ~s, ~en **(a)** (Fachgebiet) field; sphere; **industrieller/wirtschaftlicher ~:** industrial/economic sector **(b)** (Geom.; Besatzungszone) sector

sekundär 1 *Adj.* secondary

2 *adv.* secondarily

Sekundar-: ~**schule** *die* (schweiz.) secondary school; ~**stufe** *die* secondary stage (*of education*)

Sekunde *die;* ~, ~n **(a)** (auch Math., Musik) second **(b)** (ugs.: Augenblick) second; moment

Sekunden·zeiger *der* second hand

selb... *Demonstrativpron.* same;

selber *indekl. Demonstrativpron.* ▶ SELBST 1

selbst 1 *indekl. Demonstrativpron.* myself/ yourself/himself/herself/itself/ourselves/ yourselves/themselves; **von ~:** automatically; ~ **gemacht** home-made

2 *Adv.* even

Selbst·achtung *die* self-respect; self-esteem

selb·ständig 1 *Adj.* independent; self-employed ⟨*business man, tradesman, etc.*⟩; **sich ~ machen** set up on one's own

2 *adv.* independently; ~ **denken** think for oneself

Selbständigkeit *die;* ~: independence

selbst-, Selbst-: ~**auslöser** *der* (Fot.) delayed-action shutter release; ~**bedienung** *die* self-service *no art.;* ~**befriedigung** *die* masturbation *no art.;* ~**beherrschung** *die* self-control *no art.;* ~**bestätigung** *die* (Psych.) self-affirmation *no art.;* ~**bewusst**, ***~**bewußt** 1 *Adj.* self-confident; 2 *adv.* self-confidently; ~**bewusstsein**, ***~**bewußtsein** *das* self-confidence *no art.;* ~**erkenntnis** *die* self-knowledge *no art.;* ~**gefällig** 1 *Adj.* self-satisfied; smug; 2 *adv.* smugly; ~**gefälligkeit** *die* self-satisfaction; smugness; ***~**gemacht** ▶ SELBST 1; ~**gespräch** *das* conversation with oneself; ~**hilfe** *die* self-help *no art.;* **Hilfe zur ~hilfe leisten** help people to help themselves; ~**hilfe-gruppe** *die* self-help group; ~**los** 1 *Adj.* selfless; 2 *adv.* selflessly; unselfishly; ~**mord** *der* suicide *no art.;* ~**mörder** *der,* ~**mörderin** *die* suicide; ~**sicher** 1 *Adj.* self-confident; 2 *adv.* in a self-confident manner; ~**ständig** *usw.;* ▶ SELBSTÄNDIG *usw.;* ~**süchtig** 1 *Adj.* selfish; 2 *adv.* selfishly; ~**tätig** 1 *Adj.* automatic; ⋯⋅∴

S

2 *adv.* automatically; **~verständlich** 1 *Adj.* natural; **etw. für ~verständlich halten** regard sth. as a matter of course; (für gegeben hinnehmen) take sth. for granted; 2 *adv.* naturally; of course; **~verständlichkeit** *die* matter of course; **etw. mit der größten ~verständlichkeit tun** do sth. as if it were the most natural thing in the world; **~vertrauen** *das* self-confidence; **~verwaltung** *die* self-government *no art.;* **~zweck** *der* end in itself

selektieren *tr. V.* select; pick out

Selektion *die;* ~, ~en selection

selektiv 1 *Adj.* selective
2 *adv.* selectively

selig 1 *Adj.* (a) (Rel.) blessed
(b) (tot) late [lamented]
(c) (glücklich) blissful ⟨*idleness, slumber, etc.*⟩; blissfully happy ⟨*person*⟩
2 *adv.* blissfully

Seligkeit *die;* ~, ~en bliss *no pl.;* [blissful] happiness *no pl.*

Sellerie *der;* ~s, ~[s] *od.* die; ~, ~: celeriac; (Stangen~) celery

selten 1 *Adj.* rare; infrequent ⟨*visit, visitor*⟩
2 *adv.* (a) rarely
(b) (sehr) exceptionally; uncommonly

Seltenheit *die;* ~, ~en rarity

Seltenheits·wert *der;* ~[es] rarity value

Selters·wasser *das* seltzer [water]

seltsam 1 *Adj.* strange; odd
2 *adv.* strangely

Semester *das;* ~s, ~: semester

Semester·ferien *Pl.* [university] vacation *sing.*

Semi·finale *das* (Sport) semi-final

Semi·kolon *das;* ~s, ~s semicolon

Seminar *das;* ~s, ~e (a) seminar (über + *Akk.* on)
(b) (Institut) department

Semit *der;* ~en, ~en, **Semitin** *die;* ~, ~nen Semite

semitisch *Adj.* Semitic

Semmel *die;* ~, ~n (bes. österr., bayr., ostmd.) [bread] roll

Semmel·knödel *der* (bayr., österr.) bread dumpling

Senat *der;* ~[e]s, ~e senate

Senator *der;* ~s, ~en, **Senatorin** *die;* ~, ~nen senator

senden[1] *unr.* (auch regelm.) *tr. V.* (geh.) send

senden[2] *regelm.* (schweiz. unr.) *tr., itr. V.* broadcast ⟨*programme, play, etc.*⟩; transmit ⟨*signals, Morse, etc.*⟩

Sender *der;* ~s, ~: [broadcasting] station; (Anlage) transmitter

Sende·reihe *die* series [of programmes]

Sender·such·lauf *der* (Rundf., Ferns.) [automatic] station search

Sende·schluss, *Sende·schluß *der* close down

Sende·zeit *die* (Rundf., Ferns.) broadcasting time; **die ~ um zehn Minuten überschreiten** overrun by ten minutes

Sendung *die;* ~, ~en (a) consignment
(b) (Rundf., Ferns.) programme

Senf *der;* ~[e]s, ~e mustard

senil 1 *Adj.* (Med., auch abwertend) senile
2 *adv.* in a senile manner

senior *nach Personennamen* senior

Senior *der;* ~s, ~en (a) (Kaufmannsspr.) senior partner
(b) (Sport) senior [player]
(c) (Rentner) senior citizen

Senioren·heim *das* home for the elderly

Seniorin *die;* ~, ~nen ▶ SENIOR

Senke *die;* ~, ~n hollow

senken 1 *tr. V.* lower
2 *refl. V.* ⟨*curtain, barrier, etc.*⟩ fall, come down; ⟨*ground, building, road*⟩ subside, sink; ⟨*water level*⟩ fall, sink

senk-, Senk-: ~fuß *der* flat foot; **~recht** 1 *Adj.* vertical; **~recht zu etw.** perpendicular to sth.; 2 *adv.* vertically; **~rechte** *die;* ~~, ~n; *auch adj. Dekl.* vertical; (Geom.: Gerade) perpendicular

Sensation *die;* ~, ~en sensation

sensationell 1 *Adj.* sensational
2 *adv.* sensationally

Sense *die;* ~, ~n scythe

sensibel 1 *Adj.* sensitive
2 *adv.* sensitively

sensibilisieren *tr. V.* (geh.) make ⟨*person*⟩ more sensitive (für to)

Sensibilität *die;* ~: sensitivity

sentimental 1 *Adj.* sentimental
2 *adv.* sentimentally

Sentimentalität *die;* ~, ~en sentimentality

separat 1 *Adj.* separate; self-contained ⟨*flat etc.*⟩
2 *adv.* separately

September *der;* ~[s], ~: September

Serbe *der;* ~n, ~n Serb; Serbian

Serbien *(das);* ~s Serbia

Serbin *die;* ~, ~nen ▶ SERBE

serbisch *Adj.* Serbian

Serenade *die;* ~, ~n serenade

Serie /'ze:rɪə/ *die;* ~, ~n series

serien·mäßig 1 *Adj.* standard ⟨*product, model, etc.*⟩
2 *adv.* (a) ~ **gefertigt** *od.* **gebaut** produced in series
(b) (nicht als Sonderausstattung) ⟨*fitted, supplied, etc.*⟩ as standard

seriös *Adj.* respectable ⟨*person, hotel, etc.*⟩; trustworthy ⟨*firm, partner, etc.*⟩; serious ⟨*offer, applicant, artist, etc.*⟩

S

Seriosität *die;* ~ (geh.) **(a)** (Solidität) respectability; (Vertrauenswürdigkeit) trustworthiness
(b) (Ernsthaftigkeit) seriousness
Serpentine *die;* ~, ~n hairpin bend
Serum *das;* ~s, Seren serum
Service¹ /zɛrˈviːs/ *das;* ~, ~: [dinner *etc.*] service
Service² /ˈzøːɐ̯vɪs/ *der;* ~, ~s /ˈzøːɐ̯vɪsɪs/ (Bedienung, Kundendienst) service
servieren *tr. V.* serve
Serviererin *die;* ~, ~nen waitress
Serviette /zɛrˈvi̯ɛtə/ *die;* ~, ~n napkin; serviette (Brit.)
Servo-: ~bremse *die* servo[-assisted] brake; **~lenkung** *die* power[-assisted] steering *no indef. art.*
Servus /ˈzɛrvʊs/ *Interj.* (bes. südd., österr.) (beim Abschied) goodbye; so long (coll.); (zur Begrüßung) hello
Sesam *der;* ~s sesame seeds *pl.*
Sessel *der;* ~s, ~ **(a)** armchair
(b) (österr.: Stuhl) chair
Sessel-lift *der* chairlift
sesshaft, *seßhaft *Adj.* settled; ~ werden settle down
Sesshaftigkeit, *Seßhaftigkeit *die;* ~: settled way of life
Set *das od. der;* ~[s], ~s **(a)** set, combination (aus of)
(b) (Deckchen) table- *or* place mat
setzen ⓵ *refl. V.* **(a)** sit [down]; **setzen Sie sich** sit down; take a seat; **sich aufs Sofa** *usw.* ~: sit on the sofa *etc.;*
(b) ⟨coffee, froth, *etc.*⟩ settle; ⟨sediment⟩ sink to the bottom
⟨2⟩ *tr. V.* **(a)** put
(b) (einpflanzen) plant ⟨tomatoes, potatoes, *etc.*⟩
(c) (aufziehen) hoist ⟨flag *etc.*⟩; set ⟨sails, navigation lights⟩
(d) (Druckw.) set ⟨manuscript *etc.*⟩
⟨3⟩ *itr. V.* **(a)** meist mit sein (springen) leap; jump
(b) über einen Fluss ~ (mit einer Fähre o. Ä.) cross a river
(c) (beim Wetten) bet; **auf ein Pferd/auf Rot** ~: back a horse/put one's money on red
Setzer *der;* ~s, ~, **Setzerin** *die;* ~, ~nen (Druckw.) [type]setter
Setzling *der;* ~s, ~e seedling
Seuche *die;* ~, ~n epidemic
Seuchen-gefahr *die* danger of an epidemic
seufzen *itr., tr. V.* sigh
Seufzer *der;* ~s, ~: sigh
Sex *der;* ~[es] sex *no art.*
Sexismus *der;* ~: sexism *no art.*
sexistisch ⓵ *Adj.* sexist
⟨2⟩ *adv.* ⟨behave, think, *etc.*⟩ in a sexist manner
Sexualität *die;* ~: sexuality *no art.*
Sexual-: ~kunde *die* (Schulw.) sex

education *no art.;* **~leben** *das* sex life;
~partner *der,* **~partnerin** *die* sexual partner; **~trieb** *der* sex[ual] drive *or* urge;
~verbrechen *das* sex crime;
~verbrecher *der* sex offender
sexuell ⓵ *Adj.* sexual
⟨2⟩ *adv.* sexually
sezieren *tr. V.* dissect ⟨corpse⟩
sfr., sFr. *Abk.* **Schweizer Franken**
Shampoo /ˈʃamˈpuː/, **Shampoon** /ʃamˈpoːn/ *das;* ~s, ~s shampoo
Shareholdervalue /ˈʃɛəhoʊldəvælju:/ *der;* ~s, ~s shareholder value
Sherry /ˈʃɛrɪ/ *der;* ~s, ~s sherry
Show /ʃoʊ/ *die;* ~, ~s show
siamesisch *Adj.* Siamese
Siam-katze *die* Siamese cat
Sibirien (*das*); ~s Siberia
sich *Reflexivpron. der 3. Pers. Sg. und Pl. Akk. und Dat.* **(a)** himself/herself/itself/themselves; (auf man bezogen) oneself; (auf das Anredepronomen Sie bezogen) yourself/yourselves; ~ **freuen/wundern/schämen/täuschen** be pleased/surprised/ashamed/mistaken; ~ **sorgen** worry
(b) (reziprok) one another, each other
Sichel *die;* ~, ~n sickle
sicher ⓵ *Adj.* **(a)** safe ⟨road, procedure, *etc.*⟩; secure ⟨job, investment, *etc.*⟩
(b) reliable ⟨evidence, source⟩; certain ⟨proof⟩; reliable, sure ⟨judgment, taste, *etc.*⟩
(c) (selbstbewusst) [self-]assured ⟨person, manner⟩
(d) (gewiss) certain; sure
⟨2⟩ *adv.* **(a)** safely
(b) (zuverlässig) reliably; ~ **[Auto] fahren** be a safe driver
(c) (selbstbewusst) [self-]confidently
⟨3⟩ *Adv.* certainly
sicher|gehen *unr. itr. V.; mit sein* play safe
Sicherheit *die;* ~, ~en **(a)** safety; (der Öffentlichkeit) security; jmdn./etw. in ~ [vor etw. (*Dat.*)] bringen save *or* rescue sb./sth. [from sth.]
(b) (Gewissheit) certainty
(c) (Wirtsch.: Bürgschaft) security
sicherheits-, Sicherheits-:
~abstand *der* (Verkehrsw.) safe distance between vehicles; **~gurt** *der* seat belt;
~halber *Adv.* to be on the safe side;
~nadel *die* safety pin; **~schloss, *~schloß** *das* safety lock
sicherlich *Adv.* certainly
sichern *tr. V.* **(a)** make ⟨door *etc.*⟩ secure; (garantieren) safeguard ⟨rights, peace⟩; (schützen) protect ⟨rights *etc.*⟩; **sich (*Dat.*) etw.** ~: secure sth.
(b) (DV) back up
sicher|stellen *tr. V.* **(a)** impound ⟨goods, vehicle⟩
(b) guarantee ⟨supply, freedom, *etc.*⟩

Sicher·stellung *die* (a) ▶ SICHERSTELLEN
A: impounding
(b) (Gewährleistung) guarantee

Sicherung *die;* ~, ~en (a) safeguarding;
(das Schützen) protection
(b) (Elektrot.) fuse
(c) (techn. Vorrichtung) safety catch

Sicherungs·kopie *die* (DV) back-up
[copy]

Sicht *die;* ~: view (auf + *Akk.*, in + *Akk.* of);
gute *od.* klare/schlechte ~: good/poor
visibility; in ~ kommen come into sight;
außer ~ sein be out of sight

sichtbar ① *Adj.* visible; (fig.) apparent
⟨*reason*⟩
② *adv.* visibly

sichten *tr. V.* sight

sichtlich ① *Adj.* obvious; evident
② *adv.* obviously; evidently; visibly
⟨*impressed*⟩

Sichtung *die;* ~, ~en sighting

Sicht-: ~**verhältnisse** *Pl.* visibility
sing.; ~**vermerk** *der* visa; ~**weite** *die*
visibility *no art.;* außer/in ~weite sein be out
of/in sight

sickern *itr. V.; mit sein* seep; (spärlich fließen)
trickle

sie ① *Personalpron.;* 3. *Pers. Sg. Nom. Fem.*
she; (betont) her; (bei Dingen, Tieren) it; *s. auch*
IHR¹, IHRER A
② *Personalpron.;* 3. *Pers. Pl. Nom.* they;
(betont) them; *s. auch* IHNEN, IHRER B;
③ *Akk. von* SIE 1: her; (bei Dingen, Tieren) it
④ *Akk. von* SIE 2A: them

Sie *Personalpron.;* 3. *Pers. Pl. Nom. u. Akk;*
Anrede an eine od. mehrere Personen you; *s.*
auch IHNEN; IHRER

Sieb *das;* ~[e]s, ~e sieve; (für Tee) strainer

sieben¹ *tr. V.* (a) sieve ⟨*flour etc.*⟩; riddle
⟨*sand, gravel, etc.*⟩
(b) (auswählen) screen ⟨*candidates*⟩

sieben² *Kardinalz.* seven

Sieben *die;* ~, ~en seven

sieben-, Sieben-: ~**fach**
Vervielfältigungsz. sevenfold; ~**mal** *Adj.*
seven times; ~**sachen** *Pl.* (ugs.) **meine/**
deine *usw.* ~sachen my/your *etc.* belongings
or (coll.) bits and pieces

siebt... *Ordinalz.* seventh

siebtel *Bruchz.* seventh

Siebtel *das,* (schweiz. meist *der*); ~s, ~:
seventh

siebtens *Adv.* seventhly

sieb·zehn *Kardinalz.* seventeen

siebzig *Kardinalz.* seventy

siebzigst... *Ordinalz.* seventieth

siedeln *itr. V.* settle

sieden *unr. od. regelm. itr. V.* boil

Siede·punkt *der* (auch fig.) boiling point

Siedler *der;* ~s, ~: settler

Siedlung *die;* ~, ~en (a) (Wohngebiet)
[housing] estate
(b) (Niederlassung) settlement

Sieg *der;* ~e victory, (bes. Sport) win
(über + *Akk.* over)

Siegel *das;* ~s, ~: seal; (von Behörden) stamp

siegen *itr. V.* win; **über jmdn.** ~: gain *or*
win a victory over sb.; (bes. Sport) win
against sb.; beat sb.

Sieger *der;* ~s, ~: winner; (Mannschaft)
winners *pl.;* (einer Schlacht) victor

Sieger·ehrung *die* presentation ceremony;
awards ceremony

Siegerin *die;* ~, ~nen winner

sieges·sicher ① *Adj.* confident of victory
pred.;
② *adv.* confident of victory

sieg·gewohnt *Adj.* ⟨*army*⟩ accustomed to
victory; ⟨*team*⟩ used to winning

sieh, siehe *Imperativ Sg. v.* SEHEN

siehst 2. *Pers. Sg. Präsens v.* SEHEN

sieht 3. *Pers. Sg. Präsens v.* SEHEN

siezen *tr. V.* call ⟨*sb.*⟩ 'Sie' (*the polite form*
of address)

Signal *das;* ~s, ~e signal

signalisieren *tr. V.* indicate ⟨*danger,*
change, etc.⟩

Signatur *die;* ~, ~en (a) initials *pl.;* (Kürzel)
abbreviated signature; (des Künstlers)
autograph
(b) (Unterschrift) signature
(c) (in einer Bibliothek) shelf mark

signieren *tr. V.* sign; autograph ⟨*one's own*
work⟩

Silbe *die;* ~, ~n syllable

Silber *das;* ~s (a) silver
(b) (silbernes Gerät) silver[ware]

Silber·medaille *die* silver medal

silbern ① *Adj.* silver; silvery ⟨*moonlight,*
shade, gleam, etc.⟩
② *adv.* ⟨*shine, shimmer, etc.*⟩ with a silvery
lustre

Silber·papier *das* silver paper

Silhouette /zi'luɛtə/ *die;* ~, ~n silhouette

Silicium *das;* ~s silicon

Silikon *das;* ~s, ~e (Chemie) silicone

Silo *der od. das;* ~s, ~s silo

Silvester *der od. das;* ~s, ~: New Year's
Eve

Silvester·nacht *die* night of New Year's
Eve

Simbabwe (*das*) ~s Zimbabwe

simpel ① *Adj.* (a) simple ⟨*question, task*⟩
(b) (beschränkt) simple-minded ⟨*person*⟩;
simple ⟨*mind*⟩
② *adv.* (a) simply
(b) (beschränkt) in a simple-minded manner

Simpel *der;* ~s, ~ (bes. südd. ugs.)
simpleton; fool

Sims *der od. das;* ~es, ~e ledge; sill;
(Kamin~) mantelpiece

Simulant *der;* ~en, ~en **Simulantin**
die; ~, ~nen malingerer
Simulation *die;* ~, ~en simulation
simulieren 1 *tr. V.* feign, sham ⟨*illness, emotion, etc.*⟩; simulate ⟨*situation, condition, etc.*⟩
2 *itr. V.* feign illness
simultan 1 *Adj.* simultaneous
2 *adv.* simultaneously
sind *1. u. 3. Pers. Pl. Präsens v.* SEIN[1]
Sinfonie *die;* ~, ~n symphony
Sinfonie-orchester *das* symphony orchestra
singen *unr. tr., itr. V.* sing
Single[1] /'zɪŋ/ *die;* ~, ~s (Schallplatte) single
Single[2] *der;* ~s, ~s single person; ~s single people *no art.*
Single[3] *das;* ~s, ~s (Badminton, Tennis) singles *sing. or pl.*
Singular *der;* ~s singular
Sing-vogel *der* songbird
sinken *unr. itr. V.; mit sein* (a) ⟨*ship, sun*⟩ sink, go down; ⟨*plane, balloon*⟩ descend, go down
(b) (niedersinken) fall
(c) (niedriger werden) ⟨*temperature, level*⟩ fall, drop
(d) (an Wert verlieren; nachlassen; abnehmen) fall, go down
Sinn *der;* ~[e]s, ~e (a) sense
(b) *Pl.* (geh.: Bewusstsein) senses; mind *sing.;* **nicht bei** ~**en sein** be out of one's senses *or* mind
(c) (Gefühl, Verständnis) feeling
(d) (Bedeutung) meaning
(e) (Ziel u. Zweck) point
Sinn-bild *das* symbol
Sinnes-: ~**organ** *das* sense organ; sensory organ; ~**täuschung** *die* trick of the senses
sinn-gemäß 1 *Adj.* **eine** ~**e Übersetzung** a translation which conveys the general sense
2 *adv.* **etw.** ~ **übersetzen/wiedergeben** translate the general sense of sth./give the gist of sth.
sinnlich *Adj.* sensory ⟨*impression, perception, stimulus*⟩; sensual ⟨*love, mouth*⟩; sensuous ⟨*pleasure, passion*⟩
Sinnlichkeit *die;* ~: sensuality
sinn-los 1 *Adj.* (a) senseless
(b) (zwecklos) pointless
2 *adv.* (a) senselessly
(b) (zwecklos) pointlessly
Sinnlosigkeit *die;* ~ (a) senselessness
(b) (Zwecklosigkeit) pointlessness
sinn-voll 1 *Adj.* (a) (vernünftig) sensible
(b) (einen Sinn ergebend) meaningful
2 *adv.* (a) (vernünftig) sensibly
(b) (einen Sinn ergebend) meaningfully
Sint-flut *die* Flood; Deluge
sintflut-artig 1 *Adj.* torrential
2 *adv.* in torrents

Sinto *der;* ~, Sinti Sinte
Sippe *die;* ~, ~n (a) (Völkerk.) sib
(b) (ugs.: Verwandtschaft) clan
Sippschaft *die;* ~, ~en (ugs.) ▶ SIPPE B
Sirene *die;* ~, ~n siren
Sirup *der;* ~s, ~e syrup
Sitte *die;* ~, ~n (a) (Brauch) custom; tradition
(b) (moralische Norm) common decency
(c) *Pl.* (Benehmen) manners
sitten-widrig *Adj.* (a) (Rechtsw.) illegal ⟨*methods, advertising, etc.*⟩
(b) (unmoralisch) immoral ⟨*behaviour*⟩
sittlich 1 *Adj.* moral
2 *adv.* morally
Sittlichkeit *die;* ~: morality
Sittlichkeits-: ~**verbrechen** *das* sexual crime; ~**verbrecher** *der,* ~**verbrecherin** *die* sex offender
Situation *die;* ~, ~en situation
situiert *Adj.* **gut/schlechter** (usw.) ~ well off/worse off *etc.*
Sitz *der;* ~es, ~e (a) seat
(b) (Verwaltungssitz) headquarters *sing. or pl.;*
(c) (von Kleidungsstücken) fit
Sitz-bank *die; Pl.* Sitzbänke bench
sitzen *unr. itr. V.; mit sein; südd., österr., schweiz. mit sein* (a) sit
(b) (sein) be
(c) ([gut] passen) fit
(d) ~ **bleiben** (nicht versetzt werden) stay down [a year]; (unverheiratet bleiben) be left on the shelf; **auf etw.** (*Dat.*) ~ **bleiben** (für etw. keinen Käufer finden) be left *or* (coll.) stuck with sth.; **jmdn.** ~ **lassen** (ugs.) (nicht heiraten) jilt sb.; (im Stich lassen) leave sb. in the lurch; **etw. nicht auf sich** (*Dat.*) ~**lassen** not take sth.
sitzen-: *~|**bleiben** ▶ SITZEN D; *~|**lassen** ▶ SITZEN D
Sitz-platz *der* seat
Sitzplatz-stadion *das* all-seater stadium
Sitzung *die;* ~, ~en meeting; (eines Parlaments) sitting; session
Sitzungs-saal *der* conference hall
Skala *die;* ~, Skalen scale
Skalp *der;* ~s, ~e scalp
Skalpell *das;* ~s, ~e scalpel
skalpieren *tr. V.* scalp
Skandal *der;* ~s, ~e scandal
skandalös *Adj.* scandalous
Skandinavien (*das*) ~s Scandinavia
Skandinavier *der;* ~s, ~: Scandinavian
skandinavisch *Adj.* Scandinavian
Skat *der;* ~[e]s, ~e *od.* ~s skat
Skateboard /'skeɪtbɔːd/ *das;* ~s, ~s skateboard
Skateboarder /'skeɪtbɔːdɐ/ *der;* ~s, ~, **Skateboarderin** *die;* ~, ~nen skateboarder
Skelett *das;* ~[e]s, ~e skeleton
Skepsis *die;* ~: scepticism

S

skeptisch [1] *Adj.* sceptical
  [2] *adv.* sceptically
Ski /ʃiː/ *der;* ~s, ~er *od.* ~: ski; ~ **laufen**
  od. **fahren** ski
Ski-: ~**läufer** *der,* ~**läuferin** *die* skier;
  ~**lehrer** *der,* ~**lehrerin** *die* ski
  instructor; ~**lift** *der* ski lift; ~**springen**
  das; ~~s ski jumping *no art.*
Skinhead /'skɪnhɛd/ *der;* ~s, ~s skinhead
Skizze *die;* ~, ~n sketch
Skizzen·block *der* sketch pad
skizzieren *tr. V.* sketch
Sklave *der;* ~n, ~n slave
Sklaven·händler *der,*
  Sklaven·händlerin *die* slave trader
Sklaverei *die;* ~: slavery *no art.*
Sklavin *die;* ~, ~nen slave
sklavisch [1] *Adj.* slavish
  [2] *adv.* slavishly
Skonto *der od. das;* ~s, ~s (Kaufmannsspr.)
  [cash] discount
Skorbut *der;* ~[e]s scurvy *no art.*
Skorpion *der;* ~s, ~e scorpion; (Astrol.)
  Scorpio
Skrupel *der;* ~s, ~: scruple
skrupel·los [1] *Adj.* unscrupulous
  [2] *adv.* unscrupulously
Skrupellosigkeit *die;* ~:
  unscrupulousness
Skulptur *die;* ~, ~en sculpture
skurril [1] *Adj.* absurd; droll ⟨*person*⟩
  [2] *adv.* absurdly
Skurrilität *die;* ~, ~en absurdity
Slalom *der;* ~s, ~s slalom
Slawe *der;* ~n, ~n, **Slawin** *die;* ~, ~nen
  Slav
slawisch *Adj.* Slav[ic]; Slavonic
Slip *der;* ~s, ~s briefs *pl.*
Slogan /'sloːgn̩/ *der;* ~s, ~s slogan
Slowake *der;* ~n, ~n Slovak
Slowakei *die;* ~: Slovakia *no art.*
Slowakin *die;* ~, ~nen Slovak
Slowene *der;* ~n, ~n Slovene; Slovenian
Slowenien /sloˈveːni̯ən/ *(das);* ~s Slovenia
Slowenin *die;* ~, ~nen Slovene; Slovenian
Slum /slam/ *der;* ~s, ~s slum
Smaragd *der;* ~[e]s, ~e emerald
Smog *der;* ~[s], ~s smog
Smoking *der;* ~s, ~s dinner jacket *or*
  (Amer.) tuxedo and dark trousers
Snowboard /'snoʊbɔːd/ *das;* ~s, ~s
  snowboard
Snowboarder /'snoʊbɔːdɐ/ *der;* ~s, ~,
  Snowboarderin *die;* ~, ~nen
  snowboarder
so [1] *Adv.* (a) (auf diese Weise; in, von dieser Art)
  like this/that; this/that way; **weiter so!** carry
  on in the same way!; **so gennant** so-called
  (b) (dermaßen, überaus) so

(c) (genauso) as; **so wenig/viel wie** *od.* **als** as
  little/much as; **halb/doppelt so viel** half/
  twice as much; **so weit wie möglich** as far as
  possible; **so weit** (im großen Ganzen) by and
  large; (bis jetzt) up to now; **so weit sein** (ugs.)
  be ready; **so gut ich konnte** as best I could
  (d) (ugs.: solch) such; **so ein Idiot!** what an
  idiot!; **so einer/eine/eins** one like that
  (e) *betont* (eine Zäsur ausdrückend) right; OK
  (coll.)
  (f) (ugs.: schätzungsweise) about
  [2] *Partikel* (a) just; **ach, das hab' ich nur so**
  gesagt oh, I didn't mean anything by that
  (b) (in Aufforderungssätzen verstärkend) **so komm**
  doch come on now
s. o. *Abk.* = **siehe oben**
So. *Abk.* = **Sonntag** Sun.
Soap /soʊp/ *die;* ~, ~s soap [opera]
sobald *Konj.* as soon as
Socke *die;* ~, ~n sock
Sockel *der;* ~s, ~ (a) (einer Säule, Statue)
  plinth
  (b) (unterer Teil eines Hauses, Schrankes) base
so·dass, ****sodaß** *Konj.* (a) (damit) so that
  (b) (und deshalb) and so
Soda·wasser *das* soda; soda water
Sod·brennen *das;* ~s heartburn
so·eben *Adv.* just
Sofa *das;* ~s, ~s sofa; settee
so·fern *Konj.* provided [that]
soff *1. u. 3. Pers. Sg. Prät. v.* SAUFEN
so·fort *Adv.* immediately; at once
sofortig *Adj.* (unmittelbar) immediate
Sofort·maßnahme *die* immediate
  measure
Software /'sɔftvɛːɐ̯/ *die;* ~, ~s (DV)
  software
sog *1. u. 3. Pers. Sg. Prät. v.* SAUGEN
Sog *der;* ~[e]s, ~e suction; (bei Schiffen)
  wake; (bei Fahr-, Flugzeugen) slipstream; (von
  Wasser, auch fig.) current
so·gar *Adv.* even
*****so·genannt** ▶ so 1A
so·gleich *Adv.* immediately; at once
Sohle *die;* ~, ~n (a) (Schuh~) sole;
  (Einlege~) insole
  (b) (Fuß~) sole [of the foot]
Sohn *der;* ~es, Söhne son
Soja-: ~**bohne** *die* soy[a] bean; ~**soße**
  die soy[a] sauce
so·lang[e] *Konj.* so *or* as long as
solar *Adj.* solar
Solar·energie *die* (Physik.) solar energy
Solarium *das;* ~s, Solarien solarium
Solar-: ~**kraftwerk** *das:*
  ▶ SONNENKRAFTWERK; ~**technik** *die*
  (Energietechnik) solar technology *no art.;*
  ~**zelle** *die* (Physik, Elektrot.) solar cell
solch *Demonstrativpron.* (a) *attr.* such; **das**
  macht ~**en Spaß!** it's so much fun!
  (b) *allein stehend* ~**e wie die** people like that

---

*alte Schreibung - vgl. Hinweis auf S. xiv

Sọld *der;* ~[e]s, ~e [military] pay

Soldạt *der;* ~en, ~en soldier

Soldạten·friedhof *der* military *or* war cemetery

Soldạtin *die;* ~, ~nen [female *or* woman] soldier

soldạtisch ⟨1⟩ *Adj.* military ⟨*discipline, expression, etc.*⟩; soldierly ⟨*figure, virtue*⟩ ⟨2⟩ *adv.* in a military manner

Sọ̈ldner *der;* ~s, ~, **Sọ̈ldnerin** *die;* ~, ~nen mercenary

solidạrisch ⟨1⟩ *Adj.* ~es Verhalten zeigen show one's solidarity ⟨2⟩ *adv.* ~ handeln/sich ~ verhalten act in/show solidarity

solidarisieren *refl. V.* show [one's] solidarity

Solidaritạ̈t *die;* ~: solidarity

solịde ⟨1⟩ *Adj.* **(a)** solid; sturdy ⟨*shoes, material*⟩; [good-]quality ⟨*goods*⟩ **(b)** (gut fundiert) sound ⟨*work, education, knowledge*⟩; solid ⟨*firm*⟩ **(c)** (anständig) respectable ⟨*person, life, profession*⟩ ⟨2⟩ *adv.* **(a)** solidly ⟨*built*⟩; sturdily ⟨*made*⟩ **(b)** (gut fundiert) soundly ⟨*educated, constructed*⟩ **(c)** (anständig) ⟨*live*⟩ respectably, steadily

Solidịtạ̈t *die;* ~: ▶ SOLIDE 1 A-C: solidness; sturdiness; soundness; respectability

Solịst *der;* ~en, ~en, **Solịstin** *die;* ~, ~nen soloist

Sọll *das;* ~[s], ~[s] **(a)** (Bankw.) debit **(b)** (Arbeits~) quota; **sein ~ erfüllen** *od.* erreichen achieve one's target

sọllen ⟨1⟩ *unr. Modalverb; 2. Part.* sollen: **(a)** (bei Aufforderung, Anweisung, Auftrag) **was soll ich als Nächstes tun?** what should I do next?; [sagen Sie ihm,] **er soll hereinkommen** tell him to come in **(b)** (bei Wunsch, Absicht, Vorhaben) **das sollte ein Witz sein** that was meant to be a joke; **was soll denn das heißen?** what is that supposed to mean? **(c)** (bei Ratlosigkeit) **was soll ich nur machen?** what am I to do? **(d)** (Notwendigkeit ausdrückend) **man soll so etwas nicht unterschätzen** it shouldn't be taken so lightly **(e)** *häufig im Konjunktiv II* (Erwartung, Wünschenswertes ausdrückend) **du solltest dich schämen** you ought to be ashamed of yourself; **das hättest du besser nicht tun ~:** it would have been better if you hadn't done that **(f)** (jmdm. beschieden sein) **er sollte seine Heimat nicht wieder sehen** he was never to see his homeland again **(g)** *im Konjunktiv II* (eine Möglichkeit ausdrückend) **wenn du ihn sehen solltest, sage ihm bitte ...:** if you should see him, please tell him ... **(h)** *im Präsens* (sich für die Wahrheit nicht

verbürgend) **das Restaurant soll sehr teuer sein** the restaurant is supposed *or* said to be very expensive **(i)** *im Konjunktiv II* (Zweifel ausdrückend) **sollte das sein Ernst sein?** is he really being serious? **(j)** (können) **mir soll es gleich sein** it's all the same to me ⟨2⟩ *tr., itr. V.* **was soll das?** what's the idea?; **was soll ich dort?** what would I do there?

Sọlo *das;* ~s, ~s *od.* Sọli solo

so·mịt /*auch:* '--/ *Adv.* consequently; therefore

Sọmmer *der;* ~s, ~: summer

Sọmmer·ferien *Pl.* summer holidays

sọmmerlich ⟨1⟩ *Adj.* summer; summery ⟨*warmth, weather*⟩; summer's *attrib.* ⟨*day, evening*⟩ ⟨2⟩ *adv.* **es war ~ warm** it was as warm as summer

sọmmer-, Sọmmer-: ~**reifen** *der* standard tyre; ~**schluss·verkauf,** ***~**schluß·verkauf** *der* summer sale/sales; ~**sprosse** *die* freckle; ~**sprossig** *Adj.* freckled; ~**zeit** *die* (Uhrzeit) summer time

Sonạte *die;* ~, ~n (Musik) sonata

Sọnde *die;* ~, ~n probe; (zur Ernährung) tube

Sọnder-: ~**angebot** *das* special offer; ~**ausgabe** *die* **(a)** special edition; **(b)** (Steuern.: private Aufwendungen) tax-deductible expenditure; **(c)** (Extraausgabe) extra expense

sọnderbar ⟨1⟩ *Adj.* strange; odd ⟨2⟩ *adv.* strangely; oddly

sọnderbarer·weise *Adv.* strangely *or* oddly enough

Sọnder-: ~**fall** *der* special case; ~**genehmigung** *die* special permit

sọnder·gleichen *Adv., nachgestellt* **eine Frechheit/Unverschämtheit ~:** the height of cheek/impudence

sọnderlich *Adv.* particularly

Sọnderling *der;* ~s, ~e strange *or* odd person

Sọnder-: ~**marke** *die* special issue [stamp]; ~**müll** *der* hazardous waste

sọndern¹ *tr. V.* (geh.) separate (von from)

sọndern² *Konj.* but; **nicht nur ..., ~ [auch] ...:** not only ... but also ...

Sọnder-: ~**nummer** *die* special edition *or* issue; ~**preis** *der* special *or* reduced price; ~**schule** *die* special school; ~**schul·lehrer** *der,* ~**schul·lehrerin** *die* teacher at a special school; ~**wunsch** *der* special request *or* wish; ~**zug** *der* special train

sondieren *tr. V.* sound out

Sonẹtt *das;* ~[e]s, ~e sonnet

Sọnn·abend *der* (bes. nordd.) Saturday; *s. auch* DIENSTAG

sọnn·abends *Adv.* on Saturday[s]

Sọnne *die;* ~, ~n sun; (Licht der ~) sun[light]

S

sonnen *refl. V.* sun oneself

sonnen-, Sonnen-: ∼**aufgang** *der* sunrise; ∼**baden** *itr. V.* sunbathe; ∼**blume** *die* sunflower; ∼**brand** *der* sunburn *no indef. art.;* ∼**brille** *die* sunglasses *pl.;* ∼**energie** *die* solar energy; ∼**finsternis** *die* solar eclipse; ∼**hut** *der* sun hat; ∼**kollektor** *der* (Energietechnik) solar collector; ∼**kraftwerk** *das* solar power station; ∼**licht** *das* sunlight; ∼**milch** *die* suntan lotion; ∼**öl** *das* sun oil; ∼**schein** *der* sunshine; ∼**schirm** *der* sunshade; ∼**schutz-creme** *die* suntan lotion; ∼**stich** *der* sunstroke *no indef. art.;* ∼**strahl** *der* ray of sun[shine]; ∼**uhr** *die* sundial; ∼**untergang** *der* sunset

sonnig *Adj.* sunny

Sonn-tag *der* Sunday; *s. auch* DIENSTAG

sonn-täglich ☐ *Adj.* Sunday *attrib.;* ☐ *adv.* ∼ **gekleidet** dressed in one's Sunday best

sonntags *Adv.* on Sunday[s]

sonst *Adv.* (a) der ∼ so freundliche Mann ...: the man, who is/was usually so friendly, ...; **alles war wie** ∼: everything was [the same] as usual; ∼ **was** (ugs.) something else; (fragend, verneint) anything else; ∼ **wer** (ugs.) somebody else; (fragend, verneint) anybody else; ∼ **wo** (ugs.) somewhere else; (fragend, verneint) anywhere else; ∼ **noch was?** (ugs., auch iron.) anything else?; **wer/was/wie/wo [denn]** ∼? who/what/how/where else? (b) (andernfalls) otherwise; or

sonstig... *Adj.* other; further

*∗**sonst·was** *usw.* ▶ SONST A

so-oft *Konj.* whenever

sophistisch ☐ *Adj.* sophistic[al] ☐ *adv.* sophistically

Sopran *der;* ∼**s,** ∼**e** (Musik) soprano; (im Chor) sopranos *pl.*

Sopranistin *die;* ∼, ∼**nen** soprano

Sorge *die;* ∼, ∼**n** worry; **keine** ∼**!** I don't [you] worry!

sorgen ☐ *refl. V.* worry (**um** about) ☐ *itr. V.* **für jmdn./etw.** ∼: take care of sb./sth.

sorgen-, Sorgen-: ∼**frei** ☐ *Adj.* carefree; ☐ *adv.* ∼**frei leben** live in a carefree manner; ∼**kind** *das* (auch fig.) problem child; ∼**voll** ☐ *Adj.* worried; ☐ *adv.* worriedly

Sorg-falt *die;* ∼: care

sorg-fältig ☐ *Adj.* careful ☐ *adv.* carefully

sorg-los ☐ *Adj.* (a) (ohne Sorgfalt) careless (b) (unbekümmert) carefree ☐ *adv.* ∼ **mit etw. umgehen** treat sth. carelessly

Sorglosigkeit *die;* ∼ (a) (Mangel an Sorgfalt) carelessness (b) (Unbekümmertheit) carefreeness

sorgsam ☐ *Adj.* careful ☐ *adv.* carefully

Sorte *die;* ∼, ∼**n** (a) sort; type; kind (b) *Pl.* (Devisen) foreign currency *sing.*

Sorten-kurs *der* (Bankw.) exchange rate

sortieren *tr. V.* sort [out] ⟨*pictures, letters, washing, etc.*⟩; grade ⟨*goods etc.*⟩

Sortiment *das;* ∼**[e]s,** ∼**e** range (**an** + *Dat.* of)

so-sehr *Konj.* however much

Soße *die;* ∼, ∼**n** sauce; (Bratensoße) gravy; sauce; (Salatsoße) dressing

sott *1. u. 3. Pers. Sg. Prät. v.* SIEDEN

Souffleur /zuˈfløːɐ̯/ *der;* ∼**s,** ∼**e,** **Souffleuse** /zuˈfløːzə/ *die;* ∼, ∼**n** prompter

soufflieren /zuˈfliːrən/ *tr. V.* prompt

Sound-: ∼**check** /ˈsaʊndtʃɛk/ *der;* ∼∼**s,** ∼∼**s** sound check; ∼**karte** *die* (DV) sound card

Souvenir /suvəˈniːɐ̯/ *das;* ∼**s,** ∼**s** souvenir

souverän /zuvəˈrɛːn/ *Adj.* sovereign

Souveränität *die;* ∼: sovereignty

so-viel *Konj.* as *or* so far as; *s. auch* so 1B

so-weit *Konj.* (a) as *or* so far as; *s. auch* SO 1B; (b) (in dem Maße, wie) [in] so far as; *s. auch* SO 1B

*∗**so-wenig** ▶ SO 1B

so-wie *Konj.* (a) (und) as well as (b) (sobald) as soon as

so-wie-so *Adv.* anyway

sowjetisch *Adj.* Soviet

Sowjet-union *die* (1922–1991) Soviet Union

so-wohl *Konj.* ∼ ... **als** *od.* **wie [auch]** ...: both ... and ...; ... as well as ...

sozial ☐ *Adj.* social ☐ *adv.* socially

sozial-, Sozial-: ∼**abgaben** *Pl.* social welfare contributions; ∼**arbeiter** *der,* ∼**arbeiterin** *die* social worker; ∼**demokrat** *der,* ∼**demokratin** *die* Social Democrat; ∼**demokratisch** *Adj.* social democratic; ∼**dienst** *der* community services department; ∼**hilfe** *die* social welfare; ∼**hilfe-empfänger** *der,* ∼**hilfe-empfängerin** *die* welfare recipient

Sozialismus *der;* ∼: socialism *no art.;*

Sozialist *der;* ∼**en,** ∼**en, Sozialistin** *die;* ∼, ∼**nen** socialist

sozialistisch ☐ *Adj.* socialist ☐ ∼ **regierte Länder** countries with socialist governments

Sozial-: ∼**kunde** *die* social studies *sing., no art.;* ∼**politik** *die* social policy; ∼**produkt** *das* (Wirtsch.) national product; ∼**staat** *der* welfare state

Soziologe *der;* ∼**n,** ∼**n** sociologist

Soziologie *die;* ∼: sociology

Soziologin *die;* ∼, ∼**nen** sociologist

soziologisch ☐ *Adj.* sociological

2 *adv.* sociologically

Sozius *der;* ∼, ∼se **(a)** *Pl. auch:* **Sozii** (Wirtsch.: Teilhaber) partner

(b) (beim Motorrad) pillion

so-zu-sagen *Adv.* as it were

Spachtel *der;* ∼s, *od. die;* ∼, ∼n putty knife; (zum Malen) palette knife

Spachtel·masse *die* filler

spachteln *tr. V.* **(a)** stop, fill ⟨*hole, crack, etc.*⟩; smooth over ⟨*wall, panel, surface, etc.*⟩

(b) (ugs.: essen) put away (coll.) ⟨*food, meal*⟩

Spagat *der od. das;* ∼[e]s, ∼e splits *pl.;* [einen] ∼ **machen** do the splits

Spaghetti *Pl.* spaghetti *sing.*

spähen *itr. V.* peer; (durch ein Loch, eine Ritze usw.) peep

Späher *der;* ∼s, ∼, **Späherin** *die;* ∼, ∼nen (Milit.) scout; (Posten) lookout; (Spitzel) informer

Spalier *das;* ∼s, ∼e **(a)** trellis

(b) (Ehren∼) guard of honour; ∼ **stehen** line the route; ⟨*soldiers*⟩ form a guard of honour

Spalt *der;* ∼[e]s, ∼e opening; (im Fels) fissure; crevice; (zwischen Vorhängen) chink; gap; (langer Riss) crack

Spalte *die;* ∼, ∼n **(a)** crack; (Felsspalte) crevice

(b) (Druckw.) column

spalten *unr.* (*auch regelm.*) *tr., refl. V.* split

Spaltung *die;* ∼, ∼en (auch fig.) splitting; (fig.: das Gespaltensein) split

Span *der;* ∼[e]s, Späne (Hobelspan) shaving

Span·ferkel *das* suckling pig

Spange *die;* ∼, ∼n clasp; (Haarspange) hairslide (Brit.); barrette (Amer.); (Armspange) bracelet; bangle

Spaniel /'ʃpaːnjəl/ *der;* ∼s, ∼s spaniel

Spanien /'ʃpaːnjən/ (*das*) ∼s Spain

Spanier /'ʃpaːniɐ/ *der;* ∼s, ∼, **Spanierin** *die;* ∼, ∼nen Spaniard

spanisch *Adj.* Spanish

Span·korb *der* chip basket; chip

spann 1. u. 3. P. Sing. Prät. v. SPINNEN

spannen 1 *tr. V.* **(a)** tighten ⟨*violin string, violin bow, etc.*⟩; draw ⟨*bow*⟩; tension ⟨*spring, tennis net, drumhead, saw blade*⟩; stretch ⟨*fabric, shoe, etc.*⟩; draw *or* pull ⟨*line*⟩ tight *or* taut; flex ⟨*muscle*⟩; cock ⟨*gun, camera shutter*⟩

(b) (befestigen) put up ⟨*washing line*⟩; stretch ⟨*net, wire, tarpaulin, etc.*⟩ (**über** + *Akk.* over)

(c) (schirren) harness (**vor, an** + *Akk.* to)

2 *refl. V.* **(a)** become *or* go taut; ⟨*muscles*⟩ tense

(b) (geh.: sich wölben) **sich über etw.** (*Akk.*) ∼: span sth.

3 *itr. V.* ⟨*clothing*⟩ be [too] tight; ⟨*skin*⟩ be taut

spannend 1 *Adj.* exciting; (stärker) thrilling

2 *adv.* excitingly; (stärker) thrillingly

Spannung *die;* ∼, ∼en **(a)** excitement; (Neugier) suspense

(b) (eines Romans, Films usw.) suspense

(c) (Zwistigkeit, Nervosität) tension

(d) (Elektrot.) voltage

Spannungs·gebiet *das* (Politik.) area of tension

Spann·weite *die* [wing]span

Span·platte *die* chipboard

Spar-: ∼**buch** *das* savings book; ∼**büchse** *die* money box

sparen 1 *tr. V.* save

2 *itr. V.* **(a)** save; **für od. auf etw.** (*Akk.*) ∼: save up for sth.

(b) (sparsam wirtschaften) economize (**mit** on); **an etw.** (*Dat.*) ∼: be sparing with sth.; (beim Einkauf) economize on sth.

Sparer *der;* ∼s, ∼, **Sparerin** *die;* ∼, ∼nen saver

Spargel *der;* ∼s, ∼, (schweiz. auch) *die;* ∼, ∼n asparagus *no pl., no indef. art.*

Spar-: ∼**groschen** *der* (ugs.) nest egg; savings *pl.;* ∼**kasse** *die* savings bank; ∼**konto** *das* savings *or* deposit account

spärlich 1 *Adj.* sparse ⟨*vegetation, beard, growth*⟩; thin ⟨*hair, applause*⟩; scanty ⟨*leftovers, knowledge, news, evidence, clothing*⟩; poor ⟨*lighting*⟩

2 *adv.* sparsely, thinly ⟨*populated, covered*⟩; poorly ⟨*lit, attended*⟩; scantily ⟨*dressed*⟩

sparsam 1 *Adj.* thrifty ⟨*person*⟩; (wirtschaftlich) economical; **mit etw.** ∼ **sein** be economical with sth.

2 *adv.* ∼ **mit der Butter/dem Papier umgehen** use butter/paper sparingly; economize on butter/paper

Sparsamkeit *die;* ∼: thrift[iness]; (Wirtschaftlichkeit) economicalness

Sparte *die;* ∼, ∼n **(a)** (Teilbereich) area; (eines Geschäfts) line [of business]

(b) (Rubrik) section

Sparten·kanal *der* special-interest channel

Spar-: ∼**vertrag** *der* savings agreement; ∼**zins** *der; Pl.* ∼∼en interest *no pl.* on a savings account

Spaß *der;* ∼es, Späße **(a)** (Vergnügen) fun; ∼ **an etw.** (*Dat.*) **haben** enjoy sth.; [jmdm.] ∼ **machen** be fun [for sb.]; **viel** ∼! have a good time!

(b) (Scherz) joke; (Streich) prank; **er macht nur** ∼: he's only joking; ∼ **beiseite!** joking aside; ∼ **muss sein!** there's no harm in a joke; ∼ **verstehen** be able to take a joke; **im** *od.* **zum** *od.* **aus** ∼: as a joke; for fun

spaßen *itr. V.* **(a)** (Spaß machen) joke

(b) **er lässt nicht mit sich** ∼: he won't stand for any nonsense; **mit ihm/damit ist nicht zu** ∼: he/it is not to be trifled with

spaßes·halber *Adv.* for the fun of it; for fun

spaßig *Adj.* funny; comical; amusing

Spaß·macher *der,* **Spaß·macherin** *die* joker

S

spät ⓵ *Adj.* late; **wie ~ ist es?** what time is
it?
  ⓶ *adv.* late; **~ am Abend** late in the evening
Spaten *der; ~s, ~:* spade
später ⓵ *Adj.* (a) later ⟨*years, generations,
etc.*⟩
  (b) (zukünftig) future ⟨*owner, wife, etc.*⟩
  ⓶ *Adv.* later; **bis ~!** I see you later!
spätestens *Adv.* at the latest
Spatz *der; ~en, ~en* (a) sparrow
  (b) (fam.: Liebling) pet
Spätzle *Pl.* spaetzle; *kind of noodles*
spazieren *itr. V.; mit sein* stroll; **~ gehen**
go for a walk; **~ fahren** go for a ride; **ein
Kind [im Kinderwagen] ~ fahren** take a baby
for a walk [in a pram]
*spazieren|fahren usw. ▶ SPAZIEREN
Spazier-: **~gang** *der* walk; **~gänger**
der; ~~s, ~~, **~gängerin** *die; ~~,*
~~nen person out for a walk
SPD ~ *Abk.* = **Sozialdemokratische
Partei Deutschlands** SPD
Specht *der; ~[e]s, ~e* woodpecker
Speck *der; ~[e]s, ~e* (a) bacon fat;
(Schinkenspeck) bacon
  (b) (ugs. scherzh.: Fettpolster) fat; flab (coll.)
speckig *Adj.* greasy
Spediteur /ʃpediˈtøːɐ̯/ *der; ~s, ~e,*
Spediteurin *die; ~, ~nen* carrier;
haulage contractor; (Möbelspediteur) furniture
remover
Spedition *die; ~, ~en* ▶ SPEDITIONSFIRMA
Speditions-firma *die* forwarding agency;
(per Schiff) shipping agency;
(Transportunternehmen) haulage firm; firm of
hauliers; (per Schiff) firm of carriers;
(Möbelspedition) removal firm
Speer *der; ~[e]s, ~e* (a) spear
  (b) (Sportgerät) javelin
Speichel *der; ~s* saliva
Speicher *der; ~s, ~* (a) storehouse;
(Lagerhaus) warehouse
  (b) (südd.: Dachboden) loft
  (c) (Elektronik) memory
Speicher-kapazität *die* storage capacity;
(DV) memory *or* storage capacity
speichern *tr. V.* store
speien (geh.) *unr. tr., itr. V.* spit
Speise *die; ~, ~n* (a) (Gericht) dish
  (b) (geh.: Nahrung) food
Speise-: **~eis** *das* ice cream; **~fisch** *der*
food fish; **~gaststätte** *die* restaurant;
~kammer *die* larder; **~karte** *die* menu;
~lokal *das* restaurant
speisen (geh.) ⓵ *itr. V.* eat; (dinieren) dine
  ⓶ *tr. V.* eat; (dinieren) dine on
Speise-: **~saal** *der* dining hall; (im Hotel, in
einer Villa usw.) dining room; **~wagen** *der*
restaurant car (Brit.); **~zettel** *der* menu

**alte Schreibung - vgl. Hinweis auf S. xiv

Spektakel *der; ~s, ~* (ugs.) (Lärm) row
(coll.); rumpus (coll.)
spektakulär ⓵ *Adj.* spectacular
  ⓶ *adv.* spectacularly
Spekulation *die; ~, ~en* speculation
spekulieren *itr. V.* (a) (ugs.) **darauf ~, etw.
tun zu können** count on being able to do sth.
  (b) (Wirtsch.) speculate (**mit** in)
Spelunke *die; ~, ~n* (ugs. abwertend) dive
(coll.)
Spelze *die; ~, ~n* husk
Spende *die; ~, ~n* donation; contribution
spenden *tr., itr. V.* (a) donate; give
  (b) (fig. geh.) give ⟨*light*⟩; afford, give ⟨*shade*⟩;
give off ⟨*heat*⟩
Spenden-aktion *die* campaign for
donations
Spender *der; ~s, ~,* **Spenderin** *die; ~,*
~nen donor; donator; (Organspender,
Blutspender) donor
Spender-organ *das* donor organ
spendieren *tr. V.* (ugs.) get, buy ⟨*drink,
meal, etc.*⟩; stand ⟨*round*⟩
Spengler *der; ~s, ~,* **Spenglerin** *die;
~, ~nen* (südd., österr., schweiz.) ▶ KLEMPNER
Sperling *der; ~s, ~e* sparrow
Sperma *das; ~s,* **Spermen** sperm; semen
Sperma-bank *die; Pl. ~en* sperm bank
sperr-, Sperr-: **~angel·weit** *Adv.* (ugs.)
~angel·weit offen *od.* **geöffnet** wide open;
~bezirk *der* (a) restricted *or* prohibited
area; (b) (für Prostituierte) *area in which
prostitution is prohibited;* (c)
(Gesundheitswesen) infected area
Sperre *die; ~, ~n* (a) barrier; (Straßensperre)
roadblock; (Milit.) obstacle
  (b) (fig.) ban; (Handelssperre) embargo; (Import-,
Exportsperre) blockade; (Nachrichten~) [news]
blackout
sperren ⓵ *tr. V.* (a) close; close off ⟨*area*⟩;
block ⟨*entrance, access, etc.*⟩; lock
⟨*mechanism etc.*⟩
  (b) cut off ⟨*water, gas, electricity, etc.*⟩
  (c) (Bankw.) stop ⟨*cheque, overdraft facility*⟩;
freeze ⟨*bank account*⟩
  (d) (einsperren) **ein Tier/jmdn. in etw. (Akk.) ~:**
shut an animal/sb. in sth.
  (e) (Sport: von der Teilnahme ausschließen) ban
  (f) (Druckw.: spationieren) print ⟨*word, text*⟩
with the letters spaced
  ⓶ *refl. V.* **sich [gegen etw.] ~:** balk [at sth.]
Sperr·holz *das* plywood
sperrig *Adj.* unwieldy
Sperr-: **~müll** *der* bulky refuse (*for which
there is a separate collection service*); **~sitz**
der (im Kino) seat in the back stalls; (im Zirkus)
front seat; (im Theater) seat in the front stalls;
~stunde *die* closing time
Sperrung *die; ~, ~en* ▶ SPERREN A-C, E:
closing; closing off; cutting off; stopping;
freezing; banning
Spesen *Pl.* expenses; **auf ~:** on expenses

Spezi *der;* ~s, ~[s] (südd., österr., schweiz. ugs.) [bosom] pal (coll.); chum (coll.)

spezialisieren *refl. V.* specialize (**auf** + *Akk.* in)

Spezialist *der;* ~en, ~en, **Spezialistin** *die;* ~, ~nen specialist

Spezialität *die;* ~, ~en speciality

speziell ① *Adj.* special; specific ⟨*question, problem, etc.*⟩
② *Adv.* especially; (eigens) specially

spezifisch ① *Adj.* specific; characteristic ⟨*smell, style*⟩
② *adv.* specifically

Sphäre *die;* ~, ~n (auch fig.) sphere

spicken *tr. V.* lard

spie *1. u. 3. Pers. Sg. Prät. v.* SPEIEN

Spiegel *der;* ~s, ~ (a) mirror
(b) (Wasserspiegel, fig.: Konzentration) level

spiegel-, Spiegel-: ~**bild** *das* reflection; ~**blank** *Adj.* shining; ~**ei** *das* fried egg; ~**glatt** *Adj.* like glass *postpos.;* as smooth as glass *postpos.*

spiegeln ① *itr. V.* (a) (glänzen) shine; gleam
(b) (als Spiegel wirken) reflect the light
② *tr. V.* reflect; mirror
③ *refl. V.* be mirrored *or* reflected

Spiegel·reflex·kamera *die* reflex camera

Spiegelung *die;* ~, ~en (a) (auch fig., Math.) reflection
(b) (Med.) speculum examination

spiegel·verkehrt ① *Adj.* back-to-front ⟨*lettering*⟩; **eine** ~**e Abbildung** a mirror image
② *adv.* **etw.** ~ **abbilden** reproduce sth. as a *or* in mirror image

Spiel *das;* ~[e]s, ~e (a) play
(b) (Glücks, Gesellschaftsspiel) game; (Wettspiel) game; match; **auf dem** ~ **stehen** be at stake; **etw. aufs** ~ **setzen** put sth. at stake; risk sth.

Spiel·bank *die;* *Pl.* ~en casino

spielen ① *itr. V.* (a) play; **auf der Gitarre** ~: play the guitar; **um Geld** ~: play for money
(b) (als Schauspieler) act; perform
(c) **der Roman/Film spielt im 17. Jahrhundert/in Berlin** the novel/film is set in the 17th century/in Berlin
(d) (fig.) **das Blau spielt ins Violette** the blue is tinged with purple
② *tr. V.* (a) play; **Cowboy** ~: play at being a cowboy; **Geige** *usw.* ~: play the violin *etc.;*
(b) (aufführen, vorführen) put on ⟨*play*⟩; show ⟨*film*⟩; perform ⟨*piece of music*⟩; play ⟨*record*⟩; **den Beleidigten/Unschuldigen** ~ (fig.) act offended/play the innocent

spielend *Adv.* easily

Spieler *der;* ~s, ~: player; (Glücksspieler) gambler

Spielerei *die;* ~, ~en (a) playing *no art.;* (im Glücksspiel) gambling *no art.;*

(b) **eine** ~ **mit Worten/Zahlen** playing [around] with words/numbers

Spiel·ergebnis *das* match result

Spielerin *die;* ~, ~nen ▶ SPIELER

spielerisch *Adj.* playful

Spiel-: ~**feld** *das* field; pitch (Brit.); (Tennis, Squash, Volleyball usw.) court; ~**film** *der* feature film; ~**kamerad** *der* playmate; ~**karte** *die* playing card; ~**leitung** *die* (a) (Sport) control of the match; (b) ▶ REGIE; ~**plan** *der* programme; ~**platz** *der* playground; ~**raum** *der* room to move (fig.); scope; latitude; ~**regel** *die* (auch fig.) rule of the game; **gegen die** ~**regeln verstoßen** (auch fig.) break the rules; ~**sachen** *Pl.* toys; ~**verderber** *der;* ~s, ~, ~**verderberin** *die;* ~, ~nen spoilsport; ~**waren** *Pl.* toys; ~**zeit** *die* (a) (Theater: Saison) season; (b) (Sport) playing time; **die normale** ~**zeit** normal time; ~**zeug** *das* (a) toy; (fig.) toy; plaything; (b) (Gesamtheit) toys *pl.*

Spieß *der;* ~es, ~e (a) (Waffe) spear; **den** ~ **umdrehen** *od.* **umkehren** (ugs.) turn the tables
(b) (Bratspieß) spit
(c) (Fleischspieß) kebab
(d) (Soldatenspr.) [company] sergeant major

Spieß·bürger *der,* **Spießbürgerin** *die* (abwertend) [petit] bourgeois

Spießer *der;* ~s, ~, **Spießerin** *die;* ~, ~nen (abwertend) [petit] bourgeois

spießig (abwertend) ① *Adj.* [petit] bourgeois
② *adv.* ⟨*think, behave, etc.*⟩ in a [petit] bourgeois way

Spinat *der;* ~[e]s, ~e spinach

Spind *der od. das;* ~[e]s, ~e locker

Spindel *die;* ~, ~n spindle

Spinne *die;* ~, ~n spider

spinnen ① *unr. tr. V.* spin (fig.); plot ⟨*intrigue*⟩; think up ⟨*idea*⟩; hatch ⟨*plot*⟩
② *unr. itr. V.* (a) spin
(b) (ugs.: verrückt sein) be crazy *or* (coll.) nuts

Spinnen·netz *das* spider's web

Spinner *der;* ~s, ~ (a) (Beruf) spinner
(b) (ugs. abwertend) nutcase (coll.); idiot

Spinnerei *die;* ~, ~en spinning mill

Spinnerin *die;* ~, ~nen ▶ SPINNER

Spinn-: ~**rad** *das* spinning wheel; ~**webe** *die;* ~, ~n cobweb

Spion *der;* ~s, ~e (a) spy
(b) (Guckloch) spyhole

Spionage /ʃpio'na:ʒə/ *die;* ~: spying; espionage

spionieren *itr. V.* spy

Spionin *die;* ~, ~nen spy

Spirale *die;* ~, ~n spiral

Spiral·feder *die* coil spring

Spirituose *die;* ~, ~n spirit *usu. in pl.*

Spiritus *der;* ~, ~se spirit; ethyl alcohol

Spiritus·kocher *der* spirit stove

S

Spital *das;* ∼s, **Spitäler** (bes. österr., schweiz.) hospital

spitz ① *Adj.* (a) pointed; sharp ⟨*pencil, needle, stone, etc.*⟩; fine ⟨*pen nib*⟩; (Geom.) acute ⟨*angle*⟩
(b) (schrill) shrill ⟨*cry etc.*⟩
(c) (boshaft) cutting ⟨*remark etc.*⟩
② *adv.* **(a)** ∼ **zulaufen** taper to a point; ∼ **zulaufend** pointed
(b) (boshaft) cuttingly

Spitz *der;* ∼**es,** ∼**e** spitz

spitz-, Spitz-: ∼**bart** *der* goatee; ∼**bube** *der* (scherzh.: Schlingel) rascal; ∼**bübisch** ① *Adj.* mischievous; ② *adv.* mischievously

spitze *indekl. Adj.* (ugs.) ▶ KLASSE

Spitze *die;* ∼, ∼**n** **(a)** point; (Pfeil∼, Horn∼ usw.) tip
(b) (oberes Ende) top; (eines Berges) summit
(c) (Zigarren-, Haar-, Zweigspitze) end; (Schuhspitze) toe; (Finger-, Nasenspitze) tip
(d) (vorderes Ende) front; **an der** ∼ **liegen** (Sport) be in the lead *or* in front
(e) (führende Position) top
(f) (einer Firma, Organisation usw.) head; (einer Hierarchie) top; (leitende Gruppe) management
(g) (Höchstwert) maximum; peak
(h) [**absolute/einsame**] ∼ **sein** (ugs.) be [absolutely] great (coll.)
(i) (fig.: Angriff) dig (**gegen** at)
(j) (Textilwesen) lace

Spitzel *der;* ∼s, ∼: informer

spitzen *tr. V.* sharpen ⟨*pencil*⟩; purse ⟨*lips, mouth*⟩; prick up ⟨*ears*⟩

Spitzen-: ∼**erzeugnis** *das* top-quality product; ∼**kandidat** *der,* ∼**kandidatin** *die* leading *or* top candidate; ∼**klasse** *die* top class; ∼**qualität** *die* top quality; ∼**reiter** *der* **(a)** top rider; (fig.) leader; **(b)** (Mannschaft) top team; **(c)** (Ware) top *or* best seller; ∼**reiterin** *die:* ▶ ∼REITER A; ∼**sportler** *der* top sportsman; ∼**sportlerin** *die* top sportswoman

Spitzer *der;* ∼s, ∼: [pencil] sharpener

spitz-, Spitz-: ∼**findig** *Adj.* hair-splitting; ∼**findigkeit** *die;* ∼∼, ∼∼**en** **(a)** hair-splitting; **(b)** (etwas Spitzfindiges) nicety; ∼**hacke** *die* pick; ∼|**kriegen** *tr. V.* (ugs.) tumble to (coll.); ∼**maus** *die* shrew; ∼**name** *der* nickname

Spleen /ʃpliːn/ *der;* ∼s, ∼e *od.* ∼s strange habit; eccentricity

Splitt *der;* ∼[e]s, ∼e [stone] chippings *pl.;* (zum Streuen) grit

Splitter *der;* ∼s, ∼: splinter; (Granat-, Bombensplitter) splinter

splitter·faser·nackt *Adj.* (ugs.) absolutely stark naked; completely starkers *pred.* (Brit. coll.)

splittern *itr. V.* **(a)** (Splitter bilden) splinter
(b) *mit sein* (in Splitter zerbrechen) ⟨*glass, windscreen, etc.*⟩ shatter

---

*old spelling - see note on page xiv

splitter·nackt *Adj.* (ugs.) stark naked; starkers *pred.* (Brit. coll.)

Splitter·partei *die* splinter party

SPÖ *Abk.* = **Sozialistische Partei Österreichs** Austrian Socialist Party

sponsern *tr. V.* sponsor

Sponsor *der;* ∼s, ∼en sponsor

spontan ① *Adj.* spontaneous
② *adv.* spontaneously

Spontaneität /ʃpɔntaneiˈtɛːt/ *die;* ∼: spontaneity

sporadisch ① *Adj.* sporadic
② *adv.* sporadically

Spore *die;* ∼, ∼n spore

Sporn *der;* ∼[e]s, **Sporen** (des Reiters) spur; **einem Pferd die Sporen geben** spur a horse

Sport *der;* ∼[e]s **(a)** sport; (als Unterrichtsfach) sport; PE; ∼ **treiben** do sport
(b) (Hobby, Zeitvertreib) hobby; pastime

Sport-: ∼**art** *die* [form of] sport; ∼**fest** *das* sports festival; (einer Schule) sports day; ∼**flugzeug** *das* sports plane; ∼**geist** *der* sportsmanship; ∼**halle** *die* sports hall; ∼**journalist** *der,* ∼**journalistin** *die* sports journalist; ∼**kleidung** *die* sportswear

Sportler *der;* ∼s, ∼: sportsman

Sportlerin *die;* ∼, ∼nen sportswoman

sportlich ① *Adj.* **(a)** sporting *attrib.;*
(b) (fair) sportsmanlike; sporting
(c) (fig.: flott, rasant) sporty ⟨*car, driving, etc.*⟩
(d) (zu sportlicher Leistung fähig) sporty, athletic ⟨*person*⟩
(e) (jugendlich wirkend) sporty, smart but casual ⟨*clothes*⟩; smart but practical ⟨*hairstyle*⟩
② *adv.* **(a)** as far as sport is concerned
(b) (fair) sportingly
(c) (fig.: flott, rasant) in a sporty manner

Sport-: ∼**platz** *der* sports field; (einer Schule) playing field/fields *pl.;* ∼**schuh** *der* sports shoe; ∼**stadion** *das* [sports] stadium; ∼**teil** *der* sport[s] section; ∼**verein** *der* sports club; ∼**wagen** *der* **(a)** (Auto) sports car; **(b)** (Kinderwagen) pushchair (Brit.); stroller (Amer.); ∼**zentrum** *das* sports centre

Spot /spɔt/ *der;* ∼s, ∼s **(a)** (Werbespot) commercial; advertisement; ad (coll.)
(b) (Leuchte) spotlight; spotlamp

Spott *der;* ∼[e]s mockery; (höhnischer) ridicule; derision

spott·billig *Adj., adv.* (ugs.) dirt cheap

spötteln *itr. V.* mock [gently]; poke *or* make [gentle] fun

spotten *itr. V.* **(a)** mock; poke *or* make fun; (höhnischer) ridicule; be derisive
(b) einer Sache ⟨*Gen.*⟩ ∼: be contemptuous of *or* scorn sth.

Spötter *der;* ∼s, ∼, **Spötterin** *die;* ∼, ∼nen mocker

spöttisch ① *Adj.* mocking; (höhnischer) derisive
② *adv.* mockingly

Spọtt·preis *der* (ugs.) ridiculously low price

sprach *1. u. 3. Pers. Sg. Prät. v.* SPRECHEN

Sprạche *die;* ~, ~n (a) language; **in englischer** ~: in English
(b) (Sprechweise) way of speaking; speech; (Stil) style
(c) etw. **zur** ~ **bringen** bring sth. up; raise sth.; **heraus mit der** ~! come on, out with it!

Sprạchen·schule *die* language school

Sprạch-: ~**fehler** *der* speech impediment or defect; ~**führer** *der* phrase book; ~**grenze** *die* language boundary; ~**kenntnisse** *Pl.* knowledge *sing.* of a language/languages; ~**kurs** *der* language course; ~**labor** *das* language laboratory or (coll.) lab

sprạchlich ①*Adj.* linguistic
②*adv.* linguistically

sprạch-, Sprạch-: ~**los** *Adj.* (überrascht) speechless; ~**problem** *das* language problem; ~**rohr** *das* (Repräsentant) spokesman; (Propagandist) mouthpiece; ~**schule** *die* language school; ~**unterricht** *der* language teaching

sprạng *1. u. 3. Pers. Sg. Prät. v.* SPRINGEN

Spray /ʃpreː/ *das od. der;* ~s, ~s spray

Sprạy·dose *die* aerosol [can]

sprạyen *tr., itr. V.* spray

Sprẹch-: ~**anlage** *die* intercom (coll.); ~**chor** *der* chorus

sprẹchen ①*unr. itr. V.* speak (**über** + *Akk.* about; **von** about, of); (sich unterhalten, sich besprechen auch) talk (**über** + *Akk.*, **von** about); ⟨parrot etc.⟩ talk; **deutsch/flüsternd** ~: speak German/in a whisper; **für/gegen** etw. ~: speak in favour of/against sth.; **mit jmdm.** ~: speak or talk with or to sb.; **mit wem spreche ich?** who is speaking please?
②*unr. tr. V.* (a) speak ⟨language, dialect⟩; say ⟨word, sentence⟩; „**Hier spricht man Deutsch**" 'German spoken'
(b) (rezitieren) say, recite ⟨poem, text⟩; say ⟨prayer⟩
(c) **jmdn.** ~: speak to sb.
(d) (aussprechen) pronounce ⟨name, word, etc.⟩

Sprẹcher *der;* ~s, ~, **Sprẹcherin** *die;* ~, ~nen (a) spokesman/spokeswoman
(b) (Ansager[in]) announcer; (Nachrichtensprecher[in]) newscaster; newsreader
(c) (Kommentator[in], Erzähler[in]) narrator

Sprẹch-: ~**funk·gerät** *das* radiotelephone; (Walkie-talkie) walkie-talkie; ~**stunde** *die* consultation hours *pl.;* (eines Arztes) surgery; ~**stunden·hilfe** *die* (eines Arztes) receptionist; (eines Zahnarztes) assistant; ~**zimmer** *das* consulting room

sprẹizen *tr. V.* spread ⟨fingers, toes, etc.⟩; **die Beine** ~: spread one's legs apart; open one's legs

Sprẹiz·fuß *der* (Med.) spread foot

sprẹngen *tr. V.* (a) blow up; blast ⟨rock⟩; **etw. in die Luft** ~: blow sth. up
(b) (gewaltsam öffnen, aufbrechen) force [open] ⟨door⟩; force ⟨lock⟩; burst, break ⟨bonds, chains⟩; (fig.) break up ⟨meeting, demonstration⟩
(c) (besprengen) water ⟨flower bed, lawn⟩; sprinkle ⟨street, washing⟩ with water; (verspritzen) sprinkle; (mit dem Schlauch) spray

Sprẹng-: ~**stoff** *der* explosive; ~**stoff·anschlag** *der* bomb attack

Sprẹnkel *der;* ~s, ~: spot; dot; speckle

sprẹnkeln *tr. V.* sprinkle spots of ⟨colour⟩; sprinkle ⟨water⟩

Spreu *die;* ~: chaff

sprich *Imperativ Sg. v.* SPRECHEN

sprichst *2. Pers. Sg. Präsens v.* SPRECHEN

spricht *3. Pers. Sg. Präsens v.* SPRECHEN

Sprich·wort *das; Pl.* Sprichwörter proverb

sprießen *unr. itr. V.; mit sein* ⟨leaf, bud⟩ shoot, sprout; ⟨seedlings⟩ come or spring up; ⟨beard⟩ sprout

Spring·brunnen *der* fountain

springen ①*unr. itr. V.* (a) *mit sein* (auch Sport) jump; (mit Schwung) leap; spring; jump; ⟨frog, flea⟩ hop, jump; (sich in Sprüngen fortbewegen) bound
(b) *mit sein* (fig.) ⟨pointer, milometer, etc.⟩ jump (**auf** + *Akk.* to); ⟨traffic lights⟩ change (**auf** + *Akk.* to); ⟨spark⟩ leap; ⟨ball⟩ bounce
(c) *mit sein* ⟨string, glass, porcelain, etc.⟩ break; (Risse, Sprünge bekommen) crack
②*unr. tr. V.; auch mit sein* (Sport) perform ⟨somersault, twist dive, etc.⟩

Springer *der;* ~s, ~ (a) (Sport) jumper
(b) (Schachfigur) knight

Springerin *die;* ~, ~nen (Sport) jumper

spring·lebẹndig *Adj.* extremely lively; full of beans *pred.* (coll.)

Spring·reiten *das* showjumping *no art.*

Sprinkler *der;* ~s, ~: sprinkler

sprinten *itr. V.* (*auch tr.*) *V.; mit sein* sprint

Sprinter *der;* ~s, ~, **Sprinterin** *die;* ~, ~nen (Sport) sprinter

Sprit *der;* ~[e]s, ~e (a) (ugs.: Treibstoff) gas (Amer. coll.); juice (sl.); petrol (Brit.)
(b) (ugs.: Schnaps) shorts *pl.*

Spritze *die;* ~, ~n (a) syringe
(b) (Injektion) injection
(c) (der Feuerwehr) hose; (Löschfahrzeug) fire engine

spritzen ①*tr. V.* (a) (versprühen) spray; (verspritzen) splash; (in Form eines Strahls) spray, squirt ⟨water, foam, etc.⟩; pipe ⟨cream etc.⟩
(b) (bespritzen, besprühen) water ⟨lawn, tennis court⟩; water, spray ⟨street, yard⟩; spray ⟨plants, crops, etc.⟩; (mit Lack) spray ⟨car etc.⟩; **jmdn. nass** ~: splash sb.; (mit Wasserpistole, Schlauch) spray sb.
(c) (injizieren) inject ⟨drug etc.⟩; (ugs.: einer Injektion unterziehen) **jmdn./sich** ~: give sb. an injection/inject oneself ⋯⋯∴

2 *itr. V.; mit Richtungsangabe mit sein* ⟨*hot fat*⟩ spit; ⟨*mud etc.*⟩ spatter, splash; ⟨*blood, water*⟩ spurt

Spritzer *der;* ~s, ~ (kleiner Tropfen) splash; (von Farbe) splash; spot

spritzig 1 *Adj.* (a) sparkling ⟨*wine*⟩; tangy ⟨*fragrance, perfume*⟩
(b) lively ⟨*show, music, article*⟩; sparkling ⟨*performance*⟩; racy ⟨*style*⟩; nippy (coll.); zippy ⟨*car, engine*⟩; agile ⟨*person*⟩
2 *adv.* sparklingly ⟨*produced, performed, etc.*⟩; racily ⟨*written*⟩

Spritz·tour *die* (ugs.) spin

spröd, spröde *Adj.* (a) brittle ⟨*glass, plastic, etc.*⟩; dry ⟨*hair, lips, etc.*⟩; (rissig) chapped ⟨*lips, skin*⟩; (rauh) rough ⟨*skin*⟩
(b) (fig.: abweisend) aloof ⟨*person, manner, nature*⟩

Sprödheit, Sprödigkeit *die;* ~ (a)
▶ SPRÖDE A: brittleness; dryness; roughness
(b) (fig.: abweisendes Wesen) aloofness

spross, *sproß *1. u. 3. Pers. Sg. Prät. v.* SPRIESSEN

Spross, *Sproß *der;* Sprosses, Sprosse (Bot.) shoot

Sprosse *die;* ~, ~n (a) (auch fig.) rung
(b) (eines Fensters) glazing bar

Sprössling, *Sprößling *der;* ~s, ~e (ugs. scherzh.) offspring; **seine** ~e his offspring *pl.*

Sprotte *die;* ~, ~n sprat

Spruch *der;* ~[e]s, Sprüche (Wahlspruch) motto; (Sinnspruch) maxim; (Ausspruch) saying; aphorism; (Zitat) quotation

spruch·reif *Adj.* **das ist noch nicht** ~: that's not definite, so people mustn't start talking about it yet

Sprudel *der;* ~s, ~ (a) sparkling mineral water
(b) (österr.) fizzy drink

sprudeln *itr. V.; mit sein* bubble; ⟨*lemonade, champagne, etc.*⟩ fizz, effervesce

Sprudel·wasser *das* sparkling mineral water

Sprüh·dose *die* aerosol [can]

sprühen 1 *tr. V.* spray
2 *itr. V.; mit Richtungsangabe mit sein* ⟨*sparks, spray*⟩ fly; (fig.) ⟨*eyes*⟩ sparkle (**vor** + *Dat.* with); ⟨*intellect, wit*⟩ sparkle

Sprüh·regen *der* drizzle; fine rain

Sprung *der;* ~[e]s, Sprünge (a) (auch Sport) jump; (schwungvoll) leap; (Satz) bound; (fig.) leap; **keine großen Sprünge machen können** (fig. ugs.) not be able to afford many luxuries; **auf dem** ~[e] **sein** (fig. ugs.) be in a rush
(b) (ugs.: kurze Entfernung) stone's throw
(c) (Riss) crack

Sprung·brett *das* (auch fig.) springboard

sprunghaft 1 *Adj.* (a) erratic ⟨*person, character, manner*⟩; disjointed ⟨*conversation, thoughts*⟩

(b) (unvermittelt) sudden
(c) (ruckartig) rapid ⟨*change*⟩; sharp ⟨*increase*⟩
2 *adv.* ▶ 1B–C: disjointedly; suddenly; rapidly; sharply

Sprunghaftigkeit *die;* ~: ▶ SPRUNGHAFT 1A: erraticness; disjointedness

Sprung·tuch *das; Pl.* Sprungtücher safety blanket

Spucke *die;* ~: spit

spucken 1 *itr. V.* spit; **in die Hände** ~ (fig.: an die Arbeit gehen) go to work with a will
2 *tr. V.* spit; cough up ⟨*blood, phlegm*⟩

Spuk *der;* ~[e]s, ~e [ghostly *or* supernatural] manifestation

spuken *itr. V.; unpers.* **hier/in dem Haus spukt es** this place/the house is haunted

Spül·bürste *die* washing-up brush

Spule *die;* ~, ~n spool; (für Tonband, Film) spool; reel

Spüle *die;* ~, ~n sink unit; (Becken) sink

spulen *tr., itr. V.* spool; (am Tonbandgerät) wind

spülen 1 *tr. V.* (a) rinse; bathe ⟨*wound*⟩
(b) (landsch.: abwaschen) wash up ⟨*dishes, glasses, etc.*⟩; **Geschirr** ~: wash up
2 *itr. V.* (a) (beim WC) flush [the toilet]
(b) (den Mund ausspülen) rinse out [one's mouth]
(c) (landsch.) ▶ ABWASCHEN 2

Spül-: ~**maschine** *die* dishwasher; ~**mittel** *das* washing-up liquid; ~**tuch** *das; Pl.* ~tücher dish cloth; ~**wasser** *das* (a) rinse water; (b) (Abwaschwasser) dishwater

Spund *der;* ~[e]s, ~e/Spünde (a) *Pl.* Spünde (Zapfen) bung
(b) *Pl.* ~e (ugs.) [**junger** *od.* **grüner**] ~ young greenhorn *or* tiro

Spur *die;* ~, ~en (a) (Abdruck im Boden) track; (Folge von Abdrücken) tracks *pl.*; (fig.) a hot trail; **jmdm./einer Sache auf der** ~ **sein** be on to the track *or* trail of sb./sth.
(b) (Anzeichen) trace; (eines Verbrechens) clue (*Gen.* to)
(c) (sehr kleine Menge; auch fig.) trace
(d) (Verkehrsw.: Fahrspur) lane; **die** ~ **wechseln** change lanes

spürbar 1 *Adj.* noticeable; distinct, perceptible ⟨*improvement*⟩; evident ⟨*relief, embarrassment*⟩
2 *adv.* noticeably, perceptibly; (sichtlich) clearly ⟨*relieved, on edge*⟩

spüren *tr. V.* feel; (instinktiv) sense

spur·los 1 *Adj.* total, complete ⟨*disappearance*⟩
2 *adv.* ⟨*disappear*⟩ completely *or* without trace

Spür·sinn *der* (feiner Instinkt) intuition

Spurt *der;* ~[e]s, ~s *od.* ~e spurt

spurten *itr. V.* (a) mit Richtungsangabe mit sein spurt
(b) mit sein (ugs.: schnell laufen) sprint

sputen *refl. V.* (veralt.) make haste

---

*alte Schreibung - vgl. Hinweis auf S. xiv

St. *Abk.* **(a)** = **Sankt** St.
 (b) = **Stück**

Staat *der;* ∼[e]s, ∼en state

staatlich ⚊ *Adj.* state *attrib.; ⟨power, unity, etc.⟩* of the state; state-owned *⟨factory etc.⟩*
 ② *adv.* by the state; ∼ anerkannt/geprüft state-approved/-certified

staats-, Staats-: ∼**angehörige** *der/ die* national; ∼**angehörigkeit** *die* nationality; ∼**anwalt** *der,* ∼**anwältin** *die* public prosecutor; ∼**bürger** *der,* ∼**bürgerin** *die* citizen; er ist deutscher ∼bürger he is a German citizen *or* national; ∼**bürgerlich** *Adj.* civil *⟨rights⟩;* civic *⟨duties, loyalty⟩;* ⟨education, attitude⟩ as a citizen; ∼**bürgerschaft** *die*
 ▶∼ANGEHÖRIGKEIT; ∼**gewalt** *die* authority of the state; (Exekutive) executive power; ∼**grenze** *die* state frontier *or* border; ∼**mann** *der; Pl.* -männer statesman; ∼**oberhaupt** *das* head of state; ∼**präsident** *der,* ∼**präsidentin** *die* [state] president; ∼**sicherheit** *die* **(a)** state security; **(b)** (DDR ugs.)
 ▶∼SICHERHEITSDIENST;
 ∼**sicherheits·dienst** *der* (DDR) State Security Service

Stab *der;* ∼[e]s, **Stäbe (a)** rod; (länger) pole; (eines Käfigs, Gitters, Geländers) bar
 (b) (Milit.) staff
 (c) (Team) team

Stäbchen *das;* ∼s, ∼**(a)** (kleiner Stab) little rod; [small] stick
 (b) (Essstäbchen) chopstick

stabil ⚊ *Adj.* sturdy *⟨chair, cupboard⟩;* robust, sound *⟨health⟩;* stable *⟨prices, government, economy, etc.⟩*
 ② *adv.* ∼ gebaut solidly built

stabilisieren ⚊ *tr. V.* stabilize
 ② *refl. V.* **(a)** stabilize
 (b) *⟨health, circulation, etc.⟩* become stronger

Stabilität *die;* ∼ **(a)** (einer Konstruktion) sturdiness; (von Gesundheit, Konstitution usw.) robustness; soundness
 (b) (das Beständigsein) stability

Stab·lampe *die* torch (Brit.); flashlight (Amer.)

Stabs·arzt *der,* **Stabs·ärztin** *die* (Milit.) medical officer, MO *(with the rank of captain)*

stach *1. u. 3. Pers. Sg. Prät. v.* STECHEN

Stachel *der;* ∼s, ∼n **(a)** spine; (Dorn) thorn
 (b) (Giftstachel) sting
 (c) (Spitze) spike; (an Stacheldraht) barb

Stachel-: ∼**beere** *die* gooseberry;
 ∼**draht** *der* barbed wire

stachelig *Adj.* prickly

Stadion *das;* ∼s, Stadien stadium

Stadium *das;* ∼s, Stadien stage

Stadt *die;* ∼, Städte **(a)** town; (Großstadt) city; die ∼ Basel the city of Basel; in die ∼ gehen go into town; go downtown (Amer.)
 (b) (Verwaltung) town council; (in der Großstadt) city council; city hall *no art.* (Amer.)

Stadt-: ∼**bahn** *die* urban railway;
 ∼**bummel** *der* (ugs.) einen ∼bummel machen take a stroll through the town/city centre

Städter *der;* ∼s, ∼, **Städterin** *die;* ∼, ∼nen **(a)** town-dweller; (Großstädter, -städterin) city-dweller
 (b) (Stadtmensch) townie (coll.)

Städte·tour *die* city tour

Stadt-: ∼**führer** *der* town/city guidebook;
 ∼**führung** *die* guided tour of the town/ city; ∼**gespräch** *das:* ∼gespräch sein be the talk of the town

städtisch ⚊ *Adj.* **(a)** (kommunal) municipal
 (b) (urban) urban *⟨life, way of life, etc.⟩*
 ② *adv.* (kommunal) municipally

Stadt-: ∼**mauer** *die* town/city wall;
 ∼**mitte** *die* town centre; (einer Großstadt) city centre; downtown area (Amer.); ∼**park** *der* municipal park; ∼**plan** *der* [town/city] street plan *or* map; ∼**rand** *der* outskirts *pl.* of the town/city; am ∼rand on the outskirts of the town/city; ∼**rundfahrt** *die* sightseeing tour round a/the town/city; ∼**teil** *der* district; part [of a/the town]; ∼**tor** *das* town/city gate; ∼**viertel** *das* district

Staffel *die;* ∼, ∼n **(a)** (Sport: Mannschaft) relay team
 (b) (Sport: Staffellauf) relay race
 (c) (Luftwaffe: Einheit) flight
 (d) (Eskorte) escort formation

Staffelei *die;* ∼, ∼en easel

staffeln *tr. V.* **(a)** (aufstellen, formieren) arrange in a stagger *or* in an echelon
 (b) (einteilen, abstufen) grade *⟨salaries, fees, prices⟩;* stagger *⟨times, arrivals, starting places⟩*

stahl *1. u. 3. Pers. Sg. Prät. v.* STEHLEN

Stahl *der;* ∼[e]s, Stähle *od.* ∼e steel

Stahl-: ∼**beton** *der* reinforced concrete;
 ∼**blech** *das* sheet steel

stählern *Adj.* steel

stak *1. u. 3. Pers. Sg. Prät. v.* STECKEN

Stall *der;* ∼[e]s, Ställe (Pferde-, Rennstall) stable; (Kuhstall) cowshed; (Hühnerstall) [chicken] coop; (Schweinestall) [pig]sty; (für Kaninchen, Kleintiere) hutch; (für Schafe) pen

Stallung *die;* ∼, ∼en (Pferdestall) stable; (Kuhstall) cowshed; (Schweinestall) [pig]sty

Stamm *der;* ∼[e]s, Stämme **(a)** (Baumstamm) trunk
 (b) (Volksstamm) tribe

Stamm-: ∼**aktie** *die* (Wirtsch.) ordinary share; ∼**baum** *der* family tree; (eines Tieres) pedigree

stammeln *tr., itr. V.* stammer

stammen *itr. V.* come (**aus, von** from); (datieren) date (**aus, von** from)

Stamm-: ∼**gast** *der* (im Lokal/Hotel) regular customer/visitor; regular (coll.); ∼**tisch** *der* (a) (Tisch) regulars' table (coll.); (b) (Runde) group of regulars (coll.); (c) (Treffen) get-together with the regulars (coll.)

stampfen 1 *itr. V.* (a) (laut auftreten) stamp (b) *mit sein* (sich fortbewegen) tramp; (mit schweren Schritten) trudge
2 *tr. V.* (a) **mit den Füßen den Rhythmus** ∼: tap the rhythm with one's feet (b) (feststampfen) compress (c) (zerkleinern) mash ⟨*potatoes*⟩

stand *1. u. 3. Pers. Sg. Prät. v.* STEHEN

Stand *der;* ∼[e]s, Stände (a) (das Stehen) standing position; [**bei jmdm.** *od.* **gegen jmdn.**] **einen schweren** ∼ **haben** (fig.) have a tough time [of it] [with sb.]
(b) (Standort) position
(c) (Verkaufsstand; Box für ein Pferd) stall; (Messestand, Informationsstand) stand; (Zeitungsstand) [newspaper] kiosk
(d) (erreichte Stufe; Zustand) state; **etw. auf den neu[e]sten** ∼ **bringen** bring sth. up to date; **außer** ∼[e] ▶ AUSSERSTANDE; **im** ∼[e] ▶ IMSTANDE;
(e) (des Wassers, Flusses) level; (des Thermometers, Zählers, Barometers) reading; (der Kasse, Finanzen) state; (eines Himmelskörpers) position
(f) (Familienstand) status
(g) (Gesellschaftsschicht) class; (Berufsstand) trade; (Ärzte, Rechtsanwälte) [professional] group

Standard *der;* ∼s, ∼s standard

standardisieren *tr. V.* standardize

Standardisierung *die;* ∼, ∼en standardization

Ständchen *das;* ∼s, ∼: serenade; **jmdm. ein** ∼ **bringen** serenade sb.

Ständer *der;* ∼s, ∼: stand; (Kleider∼) coat stand; (Wäsche∼) clothes horse

standes-, Standes-: ∼**amt** *das* registry office; ∼**amtlich** 1 *Adj.* registry office ⟨*wedding, document*⟩; 2 *adv.* ∼**amtlich heiraten** get married in a registry office; ∼**beamte** *der,* ∼**beamtin** *die* registrar

stand-, Stand-: ∼**fest** *Adj.* steady; stable; strong ⟨*stalk, stem*⟩; ∼**haft** 1 *Adj.* steadfast; 2 *adv.* steadfastly; ∼**haftigkeit** *die;* ∼∼: steadfastness; ∼**halten** *unr. itr. V.* stand firm; **einer Sache** (*Dat.*) ∼**halten** withstand sth.

ständig 1 *Adj.* constant ⟨*noise, worry, pressure, etc.*⟩; permanent ⟨*residence, correspondent, staff, member, etc.*⟩; standing ⟨*committee*⟩; regular ⟨*income*⟩
2 *adv.* constantly

Stand-: ∼**licht** *das* (Kfz-W.) sidelights *pl.;* ∼**ort** *der* (a) position; (eines Betriebes usw.) location; site; (b) (Milit.: Garnison) garrison;

base; ∼**punkt** *der* (fig.) point of view; viewpoint; **auf dem** ∼**punkt stehen, dass** ...: take the view that ...; ∼**spur** *die* (Verkehrsw.) hard shoulder; ∼**uhr** *die* grandfather clock

Stange *die;* ∼, ∼n pole; (aus Metall) bar; (dünner) rod; (Kleiderstange) rail; (Vogelstange) perch; **ein Anzug von der** ∼ (ugs.) an off-the-peg-suit

Stängel *der;* ∼s, ∼: stem; stalk

Stangen-: ∼**brot** *das* French bread; ∼**spargel** *der* asparagus spears *pl.*

stank *1. u. 3. Pers. Sg. Prät. v.* STINKEN

Stapel *der;* ∼s, ∼: pile; **ein** ∼ **Holz** a pile or stack of wood

stapeln 1 *tr. V.* pile up; stack
2 *refl. V.* pile up

stapfen *itr. V.; mit sein* tramp

Star[1] *der;* ∼[e]s, ∼e *od.* (schweiz.) ∼en (Vogel) starling

Star[2] *der;* ∼s, ∼s (berühmte Persönlichkeit) star

Star[3] *der;* ∼[e]s (Med.) **grauer** ∼: cataract; **grüner** ∼: glaucoma

starb *1. u. 3. Pers. Sg. Prät. v.* STERBEN

stark; stärker, stärkst... 1 *Adj.* (a) strong; potent ⟨*drink, medicine, etc.*⟩; powerful ⟨*engine, lens, voice, etc.*⟩; (ausgezeichnet) excellent; *s. auch* STÜCK C;
(b) (dick) thick; stout ⟨*rope, string*⟩; (verhüll.: korpulent) well-built (euphem.)
(c) (zahlenmäßig groß, umfangreich) sizeable, large; big ⟨*demand*⟩; **eine 100 Mann** ∼**e Truppe** a 100-strong unit
(d) (heftig, intensiv) heavy; severe ⟨*frost, pain*⟩; strong ⟨*impression, current, resistance, dislike*⟩; grave ⟨*doubt, reservations*⟩; great ⟨*exaggeration, interest*⟩; loud ⟨*applause*⟩
(e) (Jugendspr.: großartig) great (coll.); fantastic (coll.)
2 *adv.* (a) (sehr, überaus, intensiv) (mit Adj.) very; heavily ⟨*indebted, stressed*⟩; greatly ⟨*increased, reduced, enlarged*⟩; strongly ⟨*emphasized, characterized*⟩; badly ⟨*damaged, worn, affected*⟩; (mit Verb) heavily ⟨*exaggerate, impress*⟩ greatly; ⟨*enlarge, reduce, increase*⟩ considerably; ⟨*support, oppose, suspect*⟩ strongly; ⟨*remind*⟩ very much; ∼ **erkältet sein** have a heavy or bad cold
(b) (Jugendspr.: großartig) fantastically (coll.)

Stark-bier *das* strong beer

Stärke *die;* ∼, ∼n (a) strength; (eines Motors) power; (einer Glühbirne) wattage
(b) (Dicke) thickness; (Technik) gauge
(c) (zahlenmäßige Größe) strength
(d) (besondere Fähigkeit, Vorteil) strength; **jmds.** ∼/**nicht jmds.** ∼ **sein** be sb.'s forte/not be sb.'s strong point
(e) (Intensität) strength; (von Sturm, Schmerzen, Abneigung) intensity; (von Frost) severity; (von Lärm, Verkehr) volume
(f) (organischer Stoff) starch

stärken 1 *tr. V.* (a) strengthen; boost ⟨*power, prestige*⟩; ⟨*drink, food, etc.*⟩ fortify ⟨*person*⟩
(b) (steif machen) starch ⟨*washing etc.*⟩

---

*old spelling - see note on page xiv

⟨2⟩ *refl. V.* refresh oneself
Stärkung *die;* ~, ~en (a) strengthening
(b) (Erfrischung) refreshment
starr ⟨1⟩ *Adj.* (a) rigid; (steif) stiff (vor +
Dat. with); fixed ⟨*expression, smile, stare*⟩
(b) (nicht abwandelbar) inflexible, rigid ⟨*law,
rule, principle*⟩
(c) (unnachgiebig) inflexible ⟨*person, attitude,
etc.*⟩
⟨2⟩ *adv.* rigidly; (steif) stiffly
starren *itr. V.* (a) stare (in + *Akk.* into, **auf,
an, gegen** + *Akk.* at); **jmdm. ins Gesicht** ~:
stare sb. in the face
(b) vor/von Schmutz ~: be filthy
starr-, Starr-: ~**sinn** *der* pigheadedness;
~**sinnig** *Adj.* pigheaded; ~**sinnigkeit**
die pigheadedness
Start *der;* ~[e]s, ~s start; (eines Flugzeugs)
take-off; (einer Rakete) launch
Start·bahn *die* [take-off] runway
start·bereit *Adj.* ready to start *postpos.;*
⟨*aircraft*⟩ ready for take-off
starten ⟨1⟩ *itr. V.; mit sein* (a) start;
⟨*aircraft*⟩ take off; ⟨*rocket*⟩ blast off, be
launched
(b) (den Motor anlassen) start the engine
⟨2⟩ *tr. V.* start; launch ⟨*rocket, satellite,
attack*⟩; start [up] ⟨*engine, machine, car*⟩
Stasi *die;* ~: *Abk.* (DDR ugs.)
Staatssicherheit
Stasi·akte *die* Stasi file
Station *die;* ~, ~en (a) station
(b) (Haltestelle) stop
(c) (Zwischenhalt, Aufenthalt) stopover; ~
machen stop over or off
(d) (im Krankenhaus) ward
stationär ⟨1⟩ *Adj.* (Med.) ⟨*treatment*⟩ in
hospital, as an inpatient
⟨2⟩ *adv.* (Med.) in hospital; **jmdn.** ~
behandeln treat sb. as an inpatient
stationieren *tr. V.* station ⟨*troops*⟩; deploy
⟨*weapons, bombers, etc.*⟩
Stationierung *die;* ~, ~en stationing;
(von Waffen, Raketen usw.) deployment
Stations-: ~**arzt** *der,* ~**ärztin** *die* ward
doctor; ~**schwester** *die* ward sister;
~**taste** *die* (Rundf.) preset [tuning] button;
preset
statisch *Adj.* static
Statistik *die;* ~: statistics *sing., no art.*
statistisch ⟨1⟩ *Adj.* statistical
⟨2⟩ *adv.* statistically
statt ⟨1⟩ *Präp. mit Gen.* instead of; *s. auch*
STATTDESSEN
⟨2⟩ *Konj.* ▶ ANSTATT
statt·dessen *Adv.* instead [of this]
statt|finden *unr. itr. V.* take place;
⟨*process, development*⟩ occur
statthaft *Adj.* permissible
stattlich ⟨1⟩ *Adj.* (a) well-built; imposing
⟨*figure, stature, building, etc.*⟩; fine ⟨*farm,
estate*⟩; impressive ⟨*trousseau, collection*⟩
(b) (beträchtlich) considerable

⟨2⟩ *adv.* impressively
Statue *die;* ~, ~n statue
Statur *die;* ~, ~en build
Status *der;* ~, ~ /'ʃtaːtuːs/ status
Status quo *der;* ~ (geh.) status quo
Statut *das;* ~[e]s, ~en statute
Stau *der;* ~[e]s, ~s *od.* ~e (a) build-up
(b) (von Fahrzeugen) tailback (Brit.); backup
(Amer.)
Staub *der;* ~[e]s dust; ~ **wischen** dust; ~
saugen vacuum; *or* (Brit. coll.) hoover; **sich
aus dem** ~[e] **machen** (fig. ugs.) make oneself
scarce (coll.)
stauben *itr. V.* cause dust
staubig *Adj.* dusty
staub-, Staub-: ~**saugen** *itr., tr. V.* ich
staubsauge, staubgesaugt, staubzusaugen
vacuum; (Brit. coll.) hoover; ~**sauger** *der*
vacuum cleaner; Hoover (*Brit.* ®); ~**tuch**
das; Pl. ~tücher duster
Stau·damm *der* dam
Staude *die;* ~, ~n (Bot.) herbaceous
perennial
stauen ⟨1⟩ *tr. V.* dam [up] ⟨*stream, river*⟩;
staunch ⟨*blood*⟩
⟨2⟩ *refl. V.* ⟨*water, blood, etc.*⟩ accumulate,
build up; ⟨*people*⟩ form a crowd; ⟨*traffic*⟩
form a tailback/tailbacks (Brit.) *or* (Amer.)
backup/backups
staunen *itr. V.* be amazed *or* astonished
(über + *Akk.* at); (beeindruckt sein) marvel
(über + *Akk.* at); ~**d** with *or* in amazement
Staunen *das;* ~s amazement (über + *Akk.*
at); (Bewunderung) wonderment
Stau-: ~**see** *der* reservoir; ~**stufe** *die*
barrage
Stauung *die;* ~, ~en (a) (eines Bachs,
Flusses) damming; (des Blutes, Wassers)
stemming the flow; (das Sichstauen) build-up
(b) (Verkehrsstau) tailback (Brit.); backup
(Amer.); jam
Std. *Abk.* = **Stunde** hr.
Steak /steːk/ *das;* ~s, ~s steak
stechen ⟨1⟩ *unr. itr. V.* (a) prick; ⟨*wasp,
bee*⟩ sting; ⟨*mosquito*⟩ bite
(b) (hineinstechen) **mit etw. in etw.** (*Akk.*) ~:
stick *or* jab sth. into sth.
⟨2⟩ *unr. tr. V.* (mit dem Messer, Schwert) stab;
(mit der Nadel, mit einem Dorn usw.) prick; ⟨*bee,
wasp*⟩ sting; ⟨*mosquito*⟩ bite; **sich in den
Finger** ~: prick one's finger
stechend *Adj.* penetrating, pungent
⟨*smell*⟩; penetrating ⟨*glance, eyes*⟩
Stech-: ~**mücke** *die* mosquito; gnat;
~**uhr** *die* time clock
Steck-: ~**brief** *der* description [of a/the
wanted person]; (Plakat) 'wanted' poster;
~**dose** *die* socket; power point
stecken ⟨1⟩ *tr. V.* (a) put
(b) (mit Nadeln) pin ⟨*hem, lining, etc.*⟩; pin
[on] ⟨*badge*⟩; pin up ⟨*hair*⟩
⟨2⟩ *itr. V.* be; ~ **bleiben** get stuck; **den
Schlüssel [im Schloss]** ~ **lassen** leave the ···⟩

S

key in the lock; **wo steckt meine Brille?** (ugs.) where have my glasses got to or gone?; **hinter etw.** (Dat.) ~ (fig. ugs.) be behind sth.

stecken-, Stecken-: *~|**bleiben**
▶ STECKEN 2; *~|**lassen** ▶ STECKEN 2;
~**pferd** das (a) (Spielzeug) hobby horse; **(b)** (Liebhaberei) hobby

Stecker der; ~s, ~: plug

Steck·nadel die pin

Steg der; ~[e]s, ~e (Brücke) [narrow] bridge; (Laufbrett) gangplank; (Boots~) landing stage

Steg·reif der: aus dem ~: impromptu

Steh·auf·männchen das tumbling figure; tumbler

stehen unr. itr. V.; südd., österr., schweiz. mit sein **(a)** stand
(b) (sich befinden) be; ⟨upright object, building⟩ stand
(c) (einen bestimmten Stand haben) **auf etw.** (Dat.) ~ ⟨needle, hand⟩ point to sth.; **das Barometer steht tief/auf Regen** the barometer is reading low/indicating rain; **das Spiel/es steht 1:1** (Sport) the score is one all; **die Sache steht gut/schlecht** things are going well/badly
(d) (einen bestimmten Kurs, Wert haben) ⟨currency⟩ stand (**bei** at); **wie steht das Pfund?** what is the rate for the pound?
(e) (nicht in Bewegung sein) be stationary; ⟨machine etc.⟩ be at a standstill; **meine Uhr steht** my watch has stopped; ~ **bleiben** (anhalten) stop; ⟨traffic⟩ come to a standstill; (stehen gelassen werden) stay; be left; (zurückgelassen werden) be left behind; (der Zerstörung entgehen) ⟨building⟩ be left standing; **etw.** ~ **lassen** (nicht entfernen) leave sth.; (vergessen) leave sth. [behind]
(f) (geschrieben, gedruckt sein) be; **in der Zeitung steht, dass ...:** it says in the paper that ...
(g) (Sprachw.: gebraucht werden) ⟨subjunctive etc.⟩ occur; be found
(h) jmdm. [gut] ~ ⟨dress etc.⟩ suit sb. [well]
(i) auf etw. (Akk.) ~ (ugs., bes. Jugendspr.: mögen) be into sth. (coll.); **sie steht total auf ihn** she's nuts about him

*steh|en|bleiben, *steh|en|lassen
▶ STEHEN E

Steh·lampe die standard lamp (Brit.); floor lamp (Amer.)

stehlen unr. tr., itr. V. steal; s. auch
GESTOHLEN 2

Steh·platz der (im Theater usw.) standing place; (im Bus) space to stand

Steiermark die; ~: Styria no art.

steif ① Adj. **(a)** stiff; (ugs.: erigiert) erect ⟨penis⟩
(b) (Seemannsspr.: stark) stiff ⟨wind, breeze⟩
(c) (förmlich) stiff; formal
② adv. stiffly

Steifheit die; **(a)** ~ stiffness
(b) (Förmlichkeit) formality; stiffness

steigen ① unr. itr. V.; mit sein **(a)** climb; ⟨mist, smoke, sun⟩ rise; ⟨balloon⟩ climb, rise;

auf die Leiter ~: get on to the ladder; **in den/ aus dem Bus/Zug** ~: board or get on/get off or out of the bus/train
(b) (ansteigen, zunehmen) rise; ⟨price, cost, salary, output⟩ increase; rise; ⟨debts, tension⟩ increase, mount; ⟨chances⟩ improve
② unr. tr. V.; mit sein climb ⟨stairs, steps⟩

Steiger der; ~s, ~ (Bergbau) overman

steigern ① tr. V. **(a)** increase ⟨speed, value, sales, consumption, etc.⟩ (**auf** + Akk. to); step up ⟨demands, production, etc.⟩; raise ⟨standards, requirements⟩; (verstärken) intensify ⟨fear, tension⟩; heighten ⟨effect⟩
(b) (Sprachw.) compare ⟨adjective⟩
② refl. V. ⟨confusion, speed, profit, etc.⟩ increase; ⟨pain, excitement, tension, etc.⟩ become more intense; ⟨costs⟩ escalate; ⟨effect⟩ be heightened

Steigerung die; ~, ~en **(a)** increase (Gen. in); (Verstärkung) intensification; (einer Wirkung) heightening; (Verbesserung) improvement (Gen. in); (bes. Sport: Leistungssteigerung) improvement [in performance]
(b) (Sprachw.) comparison

Steigung die; ~, ~en gradient

steil ① Adj. steep; meteoric ⟨career⟩; rapid ⟨rise⟩
② adv. steeply

Steil-: ~**hang** der steep escarpment; ~**küste** die (Geogr.) cliffs pl.

Stein der; ~[e]s, ~e stone; (Fels) rock; (Baustein) [stone]block; **mir fällt ein** ~ **vom Herzen** that's a weight off my mind

Stein-: ~**bock** der **(a)** ibex; **(b)** (Astrol.) Capricorn; the Goat; ~**bruch** der quarry

steinern Adj. stone

Stein·gut das earthenware

stein·hart Adj. rock-hard

steinig Adj. stony

steinigen tr. V. stone ⟨person⟩

Stein-: ~**kohle** die [hard] coal; ~**metz** der; ~~en, ~~en, ~**metzin** die; ~~, ~~nen stonemason; ~**obst** das stone fruit; ~**pilz** der cep; ~**schlag** der rock fall; „**Achtung** ~**schlag**" 'beware falling rocks'; ~**zeit** die Stone Age; (fig.) stone age

Steiß·bein das (Anat.) coccyx

Stelle die; ~, ~n **(a)** place; an jmds. ~ **treten** take sb.'s place; **ich an deiner** ~ ...: ... if I were you; **an achter** ~ **liegen** be in eighth place; **die erste** ~ **hinter** od. **nach dem Komma** (Math.) the first decimal place; **an** ~ (+ Gen.) instead of; **auf der** ~: immediately
(b) (begrenzter Bereich) patch; (am Körper) spot
(c) (Passage) passage; (Punkt im Ablauf einer Rede usw.) point
(d) (Arbeitsstelle) job; post; **eine freie** ~**: a** vacancy
(e) (Dienststelle) office; (Behörde) authority

stellen ① tr. V. **(a)** put; (mit Sorgfalt) place; (aufrecht hin~) stand
(b) (ein~) set ⟨points, clock, scales⟩; **den**

Wecker auf 6 Uhr ∼: set the alarm for 6 o'clock; **die Heizung höher/niedriger** ∼: turn the heating up/down **(c)** (bereitstellen) provide **(d) jmdn. besser** ∼: ⟨firm⟩ improve sb.'s pay; **gut/schlecht/besser gestellt** comfortably/badly/better off **(e)** verblasst put ⟨question⟩; set ⟨task, topic, condition⟩; make ⟨application, demand, request⟩; **jmdm. eine Frage** ∼: ask sb. a question ② refl. V. **(a)** place oneself; **sich auf die Zehenspitzen** ∼: stand on tiptoe **(b) sich schlafend/taub/tot** usw. ∼: feign sleep/deafness/death etc.; pretend to be asleep/deaf/dead etc.

stellen-, Stellen-: ∼**angebot** das offer of a job; (Inserat) job advertisement; „∼**angebote"** 'situations vacant'; ∼**anzeige** die job advertisement; ∼**gesuch** das 'situation wanted' advertisement; ∼**markt** der job market; ∼**profil** das job profile; ∼**suche** die job-hunting no art.; search for a job; ∼**weise** Adv. in places; ∼**wert** der **(a)** (Math.) place value; **(b)** (fig.: Bedeutung) standing; status

Stellung die; ∼, ∼en position; **zu etw.** ∼ **nehmen** express one's opinion on sth.

Stellungnahme die; ∼, ∼n opinion; (kurze Äußerung) statement

stell-, Stell-: ∼**vertretend** ① Adj. acting; (von Amts wegen) deputy ⟨minister, director, etc.⟩; ② adv. as a deputy; ∼**vertreter** der, ∼**vertreterin** die deputy

Stelze die; ∼, ∼n stilt

stelzen itr. V.; mit sein strut; stalk

stemmen ① tr. V. **(a)** (hochstemmen) lift [above one's head] **(b)** (drücken) brace ⟨feet, knees⟩ **(gegen** against) ② refl. V. **sich gegen etw.** ∼: brace oneself against sth.

Stempel der; ∼s, ∼: stamp; (Poststempel) postmark

stempeln tr. V. stamp ⟨passport, form⟩; postmark ⟨letter⟩; cancel ⟨postage stamp⟩

*****Stengel** ▶ STÄNGEL

steno-, Steno-: ∼**gramm** das shorthand text; ∼**graph** der; ∼∼en, ∼∼en stenographer; ∼**graphie** die; ∼∼, ∼∼n stenography no art.; shorthand no art.; ∼**graphieren** itr. V. do shorthand; ∼**graphin** die; ∼∼, ∼∼nen stenographer; ∼**typistin** die; ∼∼, ∼∼nen shorthand typist

Stepp-decke die quilt

Steppe die; ∼, ∼n steppe

steppen¹ tr. (auch itr.) V. backstitch

steppen² itr. V. (tanzen) tap dance

Steppke der; ∼s, ∼s (ugs., bes. berlin.) lad; nipper (coll.)

sterben unr. itr. V.; mit sein die; **im Sterben liegen** lie dying

sterbens-krank Adj. mortally ill

sterblich Adj. mortal

Sterbliche der/die; adj. Dekl. mortal; **ein gewöhnlicher** ∼**r** an ordinary mortal or person

Sterblichkeit die; ∼: mortality

stereo Adv. in stereo

Stereo das; ∼s stereo

Stereo-: ∼**anlage** die stereo [system]; ∼**aufnahme** die stereo recording

steril Adj. sterile

Sterling /'stɛːlɪŋ/: **Pfund** ∼: pound/pounds sterling

Stern der; ∼[e]s, ∼e star

Sternchen das; ∼s, ∼ (Druckw.) asterisk

Stern-schnuppe die; ∼, ∼n shooting star

Stethoskop das; ∼s, ∼e (Med.) stethoscope

Steuer¹ das; ∼s, ∼: [steering] wheel; (von Schiffen) helm

Steuer² die; ∼, ∼n tax

steuer-, Steuer-: ∼**belastung** die tax burden; ∼**berater** der, ∼**beraterin** die tax consultant or adviser; ∼**bord** das od. (österr.) der (Seew., Flugw.) starboard; ∼**erhöhung** die tax increase; ∼**erklärung** die tax return; ∼**ermäßigung** die tax relief; ∼**frau** die (Rudersport) cox; ∼**frei** Adj. tax-free

steuerlich ① Adj. tax ⟨advantages, benefits, etc.⟩ ② adv. ∼ **absetzbar** tax-deductible

Steuer·mann der; Pl. ∼**leute** od. ∼**männer** (Rudersport) cox

steuern ① tr. V. (fahren) steer; (fliegen) pilot, fly ⟨aircraft⟩; fly ⟨course⟩ ② itr. V. **(a)** be at the wheel; (auf dem Schiff) be at the helm **(b)** mit sein (Kurs nehmen, ugs.: sich hinbewegen; auch fig.) head

Steuer-: ∼**oase** die (ugs.) tax haven; ∼**senkung** die (Steuerw.) tax cut; reduction in taxation

Steuerung die; ∼, ∼en **(a)** (System) controls pl.; **(b)** ▶ STEUERN 1: steering; piloting; flying

Steward /'stjuːɐt/ der; ∼s, ∼s steward

Stewardess, *Stewardeß /'stjuːɐdɛs/ die; ∼, Stewardessen stewardess

stich Imper. Sg. v. STECHEN

Stich der; ∼[e]s, ∼e **(a)** (mit einer Waffe) stab **(b)** (mit einem Dorn, einer Nadel) prick; (von Wespe, Biene usw.) sting; (Mückenstich usw.) bite **(c)** (Stichwunde) stab wound **(d)** (beim Nähen) stitch **(e)** (Schmerz) stabbing or shooting pain **(f)** (Kartenspiel) trick ⋯⋗

(g) jmdn./etw. im ~ lassen leave sb. in the lurch/abandon sth.

Stichelei die; ~, ~en (ugs. abwertend) **(a)** (Bemerkung) dig; gibe
(b) hör auf mit deiner ~: stop getting at me/ him etc. (coll.)

sticheln itr. V. make snide remarks (coll.) (gegen about)

stich-, Stich-: ~**flamme** die tongue of flame; ~**haltig** Adj. sound ⟨argument, reason⟩; valid ⟨assertion, reply⟩; conclusive ⟨evidence⟩; ~~:
▶ ~HALTIG: soundness; validity; conclusiveness

Stichling der; ~s, ~e stickleback

Stich-probe die [random] sample; (bei Kontrollen) spot check

stichst 2. Pers. Sg. Präsens v. STECHEN

sticht 3. Pers. Sg. Präsens v. STECHEN

Stich-: ~**tag** der set date; deadline; ~**wunde** die stab wound

sticken ① itr. V. do embroidery
② tr. V. embroider

Stickerei die; ~, ~en embroidery no pl.; (gestickte Arbeit) piece of embroidery

Stick-garn das embroidery thread

stickig Adj. stuffy; stale ⟨air⟩

Stick-: ~**oxid,** ~**oxyd** das nitrogen oxide; ~**oxid-emission,** ~**oxyd-emission** die nitrogen oxide emission; ~**stoff** der nitrogen; ~**stoff-oxid,** ~**stoff-oxyd** das nitrogen oxide

Stief- step ⟨brother, child, mother, etc.⟩

Stiefel der; ~s, ~ boot

stief-, Stief-: ~**mutter** die; Pl. ~mütter stepmother; ~**mütterchen** das; ~~s, ~~ (Bot.) pansy; ~**mütterlich** ① Adj. poor, shabby ⟨treatment⟩; ② adv. ~mütterlich behandeln treat ⟨person⟩ poorly or shabbily; neglect ⟨pet, flowers, doll, problem⟩; ~**vater** der stepfather

stieg 1. u. 3. Pers. Sg. Prät. v. STEIGEN

Stieglitz der; ~es, ~e goldfinch

stiehl Imp. Sg. v. STEHLEN

stiehlst 2. Pers. Sg. Präsens v. STEHLEN

stiehlt 3. Pers. Sg. Präsens v. STEHLEN

Stiel der; ~[e]s, ~e (Griff) handle; (Besenstiel) [broom]stick; (für Süßigkeiten) stick; (bei Gläsern) stem; (bei Blumen) stem; (an Obst usw.) stalk

Stier der; ~[e]s, ~e bull; (Astrol.) Taurus; the Bull

stieren itr. V. stare [vacantly] (auf + Akk. at)

Stier-kampf der bullfight

stieß 1. u. 3. Pers. Sg. Prät. v. STOSSEN

Stift der; ~[e]s, ~e **(a)** (aus Metall) pin; (aus Holz) peg
(b) (Bleistift) pencil; (Malstift) crayon; (Schreibstift) pen

stiften tr. V. **(a)** found, establish ⟨monastery, hospital, etc.⟩; endow ⟨prize, scholarship⟩; (als Spende) donate, give **(für** to)
(b) (herbeiführen) cause, create ⟨unrest, confusion, strife, etc.⟩; bring about ⟨peace, order, etc.⟩; arrange ⟨marriage⟩

Stifter der; ~s, ~, **Stifterin** die; ~, ~nen founder; (Spender) donor

Stiftung die; ~, ~en (Rechtsspr.) foundation; endowment

Stift-zahn der (Zahnmed.) post crown

stigmatisieren tr. V. stigmatize

Stil der; ~[e]s, ~e style

Stil-bruch der inconsistency of style

stilistisch ① Adj. stylistic
② adv. stylistically

still ① Adj. quiet; (ohne Geräusche) silent; still; (reglos) still; (wortlos) silent; (heimlich) secret; **der Stille Ozean** the Pacific [Ocean]
② adv. quietly; (geräuschlos) silently; (wortlos) in silence

Stille die; ~: quiet; (Geräuschlosigkeit) silence; stillness

***stillegen** ▶ STILLLEGEN

stillen ① tr. V. **(a)** ein Kind ~: breastfeed a baby
(b) (befriedigen) satisfy; quench ⟨thirst⟩
(c) (eindämmen) stop ⟨bleeding, tears, pain⟩
② itr. V. breastfeed

still-, Still-: ~**halten** unr. itr. V. keep or stay still; ~**legen** tr. V. close or shut down; close ⟨railway line⟩; ~**schweigen** das silence; ~schweigen bewahren maintain silence; keep silent; ~**schweigend** ① Adj. silent; (ohne Abmachung) tacit ⟨assumption, agreement⟩; ② adv. in silence; (ohne Abmachung) tacitly; ~**sitzen** unr. itr. V. sit still; ~**stand** der standstill; ~**stehen** unr. itr. V. **(a)** ⟨factory, machine⟩ stand idle; ⟨traffic⟩ be at a standstill; ⟨heart etc.⟩ stop; **(b)** (Milit.) stand to attention

Stimm-bruch der: er ist im ~: his voice is breaking

Stimme die; ~, ~n **(a)** voice
(b) (bei Wahlen) vote

stimmen ① itr. V. **(a)** be right or correct; stimmt es, dass …? is it true that …?
(b) (seine Stimme geben) vote; mit Ja ~: vote yes or in favour
② tr. V. **(a)** (in eine Stimmung versetzen) make
(b) (Musik) tune ⟨instrument⟩

Stimm-: ~**enthaltung** die abstention; ~**gabel** die (Musik) tuning fork

stimmig Adj. harmonious; **die Argumentation ist [in sich (Dat.)] ~:** the argument is consistent

Stimm-: ~**lage** die **(a)** voice; **(b)** (Musik) voice; register; ~**recht** das right to vote

Stimmung die; ~, ~en **(a)** mood
(b) (Atmosphäre) atmosphere

stimmungs-voll ① Adj. atmospheric
② adv. ⟨describe, light⟩ atmospherically; ⟨sing, recite⟩ with great feeling

---

*old spelling - see note on page xiv

Stimm·zettel *der* ballot paper
stimulieren *tr. V.* stimulate
Stink·bombe *die* stink bomb
stinken *unr. itr. V.* stink (**nach** of)
stink·faul *Adj.* (salopp abwertend) bone idle (coll.)
stinkig *Adj.* (salopp abwertend) stinking; smelly
stink-: ~**normal** (salopp) ① *Adj.* dead (coll.) *or* boringly ordinary; ② *adv.* in a dead ordinary way (coll.); ~**reich** *Adj.* (salopp) stinking rich (coll.)
Stipendium *das;* ~s, Stipendien (als Auszeichnung) scholarship; (als finanzielle Unterstützung) grant
stirb *Imp. Sg. v.* STERBEN
stirbst *2. Pers. Sg. Präsens v.* STERBEN
stirbt *3. Pers. Sg. Präsens v.* STERBEN
Stirn *die;* ~, ~en forehead; brow
Stirn-: ~**höhle** *die* (Anat.) frontal sinus; ~**runzeln** *das;* ~~s frown; ~**seite** *die* front [side]
stöbern *itr. V.* (ugs.) rummage
stochern *itr. V.* poke
Stock¹ *der;* ~[e]s, Stöcke (a) stick; (Zeigestock) pointer; stick; (Taktstock) baton; (Skistock) pole; stick
(b) (Pflanze) (Rosenstock) [rose] bush; (Rebstock) vine
Stock² *der;* ~[e]s, ~ (Etage) floor; storey; **in welchem** ~? on which floor?
stock·dunkel *Adj.* (ugs.) pitch-dark
stocken *itr. V.* (a) ⟨*traffic*⟩ be held up; ⟨*conversation, production*⟩ stop; ⟨*business*⟩ slacken; ⟨*journey*⟩ be interrupted
(b) (innehalten) falter
stock·finster *Adj.* (ugs.) pitch-dark
Stöckel·schuhe *Pl.* high heels
-stöckig -storey *attr.;* -storeyed
stock·nüchtern *Adj.* (ugs.) stone-cold sober
Stockung *die;* ~, ~en hold-up (*Gen.* in)
Stockwerk *das* floor; storey
Stoff *der;* ~[e]s, ~e (a) material; fabric
(b) (Materie) substance
(c) (Philos.) matter
(d) (Thema) subject [matter]; (Gesprächsthema) topic
(e) (salopp: Rauschgift) stuff (sl.); dope (sl.)
stofflich *Adj.* material
Stofflichkeit *die;* ~: materiality
Stoff·wechsel *der* metabolism
stöhnen *itr. V.* moan; (vor Schmerz) groan
Stola *die;* ~, Stolen shawl; (Pelzstola) stole
Stollen *der;* ~s, ~ (a) (Kuchen) Stollen
(b) (Bergbau) gallery
(c) (bei Sportschuhen) stud
stolpern *itr. V.; mit sein* stumble; trip
stolz ① *Adj.* proud (**auf** + *Akk.* of); **eine** ~**e Summe** (ugs.) a tidy sum
② *adv.* proudly
Stolz *der;* ~es pride (**auf** + *Akk.* in)

stolzieren *itr. V.; mit sein* strut
stop /stɔp/ *Interj.* stop; (Verkehrsw.) halt
stopfen *tr. V.* (a) darn
(b) (hineintun) stuff
(c) (füllen) stuff ⟨*cushion, quilt, etc.*⟩; fill ⟨*pipe*⟩; plug, stop [up] ⟨*hole, leak*⟩
Stopf-: ~**garn** *das* darning cotton; ~**nadel** *die* darning needle
Stopp *der;* ~s, ~s stop; (Einstellung) freeze (*Gen.* on)
Stoppel *die;* ~, ~n stubble *no pl.*
stoppelig *Adj.* stubbly
stoppen *tr., itr. V.* stop
Stopp-: ~**licht** *das* stop light; ~**schild** *das* stop sign; ~**uhr** *die* stopwatch
Stöpsel *der;* ~s, ~: plug
Stör *der;* ~s, ~e sturgeon
Storch *der;* ~[e]s, Störche stork
stören ① *tr. V.* (a) disturb; disrupt ⟨*court proceedings, lecture, church service, etc.*⟩; interfere with ⟨*transmitter, reception*⟩
(b) (missfallen) bother
② *itr. V.* (a) disturb
(b) (Unruhe stiften) make *or* cause trouble
③ *refl. V.* **sich an jmdm./etw.** ~: take exception to sb./sth.
Störenfried *der;* ~[e]s, ~e troublemaker
Stör·fall *der* (Technik) fault
störrisch ① *Adj.* stubborn
② *adv.* stubbornly
Störung *die;* ~, ~en (a) disturbance; (einer Gerichtsverhandlung, Vorlesung, eines Gottesdienstes usw.) disruption; **bitte entschuldigen Sie die** ~**, aber …:** I'm sorry to bother you, but …
(b) **eine technische** ~: a technical fault
Stoß *der;* ~es, Stöße (a) (mit der Faust) punch; (mit dem Fuß) kick; (mit dem Kopf, den Hörnern) butt; (mit dem Ellbogen) dig
(b) (mit einer Waffe) (Stich) thrust; (Schlag) blow
(c) (beim Schwimmen, Rudern) stroke
(d) (Stapel) pile; stack
stoßen ① *unr. tr. V.* (a) *auch itr.* (mit der Faust) punch; (mit dem Fuß) kick; (mit dem Kopf, den Hörnern) butt; (mit dem Ellbogen) dig
(b) (hineintreiben) plunge, thrust ⟨*dagger, knife*⟩; push ⟨*stick, pole*⟩
(c) (schleudern) push; **die Kugel** ~: put the shot
② *unr. itr. V.* (a) *mit sein* (auftreffen) bump (**gegen** into); **mit dem Kopf gegen etw.** ~: bump one's head on sth.
(b) *mit sein* (fig.) **auf etw.** (*Akk.*) ~ ⟨*etw. entdecken*⟩ come upon sth.; **auf Ablehnung** ~ ⟨*abgelehnt werden*⟩ meet with disapproval
(c) (grenzen) **an etw.** (*Akk.*) ~ ⟨*room, property, etc.*⟩ be [right] next to sth.
③ *unr. refl. V.* bump *or* knock oneself; **sich an etw.** (*Dat.*) ~ (fig.) object to sth.
Stoß-: ~**seufzer** *der* heartfelt groan; ~**stange** *die* bumper
stößt *3. Pers. Sg. Präsens v.* STOSSEN
stoß-, Stoß-: ~**weise** *Adv.* (a) ⋯⇨

spasmodically; **(b)** (in Stapeln) by the pile; in piles; ~**zahn** der tusk; ~**zeit** die peak time; (Hauptverkehrszeit) rush hour

Stotterer der; ~s, ~, **Stotterin** die; ~, ~**nen** stutterer

stottern 1 itr. V. stutter
2 tr. V. stutter [out]

Str. Abk. **Straße** St./Rd.

stracks Adv. **(a)** (direkt) straight
(b) (sofort) straight away

straf·bar Adj. punishable

Strafe die; ~, ~**n** punishment; (Rechtsspr.) penalty; (Freiheitsstrafe) sentence; (Geldstrafe) fine

strafen tr. V. punish

straff 1 Adj. **(a)** tight, taut ⟨rope, lines, etc.⟩; firm ⟨breasts, skin⟩
(b) (energisch) tight ⟨organization, planning, etc.⟩; strict ⟨discipline, leadership, etc.⟩
2 adv. **(a)** [zu] ~ sitzen ⟨clothes⟩ be [too] tight
(b) (energisch) tightly, strictly

straf·fällig Adj. ~ werden commit a criminal offence

straffen tr. V. **(a)** tighten; firm ⟨skin⟩
(b) (fig.) tighten up ⟨text, procedure, organization, etc.⟩

straf-, Straf-: ~**frei** Adj. ~frei ausgehen go unpunished; ~**freiheit** die exemption from punishment; ~**gefangene** der/die prisoner; ~**gericht** das (fig.) judgement; ein ~gericht des Himmels divine judgement; ~**gesetz·buch** das penal code

sträflich 1 Adj. criminal
2 adv. criminally

Sträfling der; ~s, ~e prisoner

straf-, Straf-: ~**los** Adj. unpunished; ~**rechtlich** 1 Adj. criminal attrib. ⟨case, investigation, responsibility⟩; 2 adv. under criminal law; etw. ~rechtlich verfolgen prosecute sth.; ~**tat** die criminal offence; ~**täter** der, ~**täterin** die offender; ~**verfahren** das criminal proceedings pl.; ~**vollzug** der (System) penal system; ~**zettel** der (ugs.) [parking, speeding, etc.] ticket

Strahl der; ~[e]s, ~**en** (auch Phys., Math., fig.) ray; (von Scheinwerfern, Taschenlampen) beam; (von Flüssigkeit) jet

Strahle·mann der (ugs.) man/boy with the smiling face

strahlen itr. V. **(a)** shine; bei ~dem Wetter/ Sonnenschein in glorious sunny weather/in glorious sunshine; ~d weiß sparkling white
(b) (glänzen) sparkle
(c) (lächeln) beam (**vor** + Dat. with)

Strahler der; ~s, ~ **(a)** radiator
(b) (Heizstrahler) radiant heater

Strahlung die; ~, ~**en** radiation

Strähne die; ~, ~**n** strand; eine graue ~: a grey streak

strähnig 1 Adj. straggly ⟨hair⟩
2 adv. in strands

stramm 1 Adj. **(a)** (straff) tight, taut ⟨rope, line, etc.⟩; tight ⟨clothes⟩
(b) (kräftig) strapping ⟨girl, boy⟩; sturdy ⟨legs, body⟩
(c) (gerade) upright, erect ⟨posture, etc.⟩
2 adv. **(a)** (straff) tightly
(b) (kräftig) sturdily ⟨built⟩

strampeln itr. V. ⟨baby⟩ kick [his/her feet]

Strand der; ~[e]s, Strände beach; **am** ~: on the beach

Strand-: ~**bad** das bathing beach (on river, lake); ~**burg** die sand den (built as a windbreak)

stranden itr. V.; mit sein ⟨ship⟩ run aground

Strand-: ~**korb** der basket chair; ~**urlaub** der beach holiday; beach vacation (Amer.)

Strang der; ~[e]s, Stränge rope

Strapaze die; ~, ~**n** strain no pl.

strapazieren tr. V. be a strain on ⟨person, nerves⟩

strapazier·fähig Adj. hard-wearing ⟨clothes, shoes⟩; durable ⟨material⟩

Straße die; ~, ~**n** (in Ortschaften) street; road; (außerhalb) road

Straßen-: ~**bahn** die tram (Brit.); streetcar (Amer.); ~**bahn·haltestelle** die tram stop (Brit.); ~**bau·arbeiten** Pl. roadworks; ~**café** das pavement café; street café; ~**ecke** die street corner; ~**feger** der, ~**fegerin** die; ~~, ~~**nen** (bes. nordd.) road sweeper; ~**graben** der ditch [at the side of the road]; ~**karte** die road map; ~**kehrer** der; ~~s, ~~, ~~**kehrerin** die; ~~, ~~**nen** (bes. südd.) road sweeper; ~**kriminalität** die street crime; ~**musikant** der, ~**musikantin** die street musician; busker; ~**raub** der street robbery; (gewalttätig) mugging; ~**räuber** der, ~**räuberin** die street robber; (gewalttätig) mugger; ~**schild** das street name sign; ~**sperre** die roadblock; ~**verkehr** der traffic

Strategie die; ~, ~**n** strategy

strategisch 1 Adj. strategic
2 adv. strategically

Strato·sphäre die stratosphere

sträuben 1 tr. V. ruffle [up] ⟨feathers⟩; bristle ⟨fur, hair⟩
2 refl. V. **(a)** ⟨hair, fur⟩ bristle, stand on end; ⟨feathers⟩ become ruffled
(b) (sich widersetzen) resist

Strauch der; ~[e]s, Sträucher shrub

straucheln itr. V.; mit sein (geh.) stumble

Strauß¹ der; ~es, Sträuße bunch of flowers; bouquet [of flowers]

Strauß² der; ~es, ~e (Vogel) ostrich

Sträußchen das; ~s, ~: posy

streben itr. V. **(a)** mit sein make one's way briskly

(b) (trachten) strive (**nach** for)

Stre̲ber *der;* ~**s;** ~ (abwertend) pushy person (coll.); (in der Schule) swot (Brit. coll.); grind (Amer. coll.)

stre̲bsam *Adj.* ambitious and industrious

Stre̲cke *die;* ~, ~**n** distance; (Abschnitt, Route) route; (Eisenbahn~) line

stre̲cken [1] *tr. V.* (gerade machen) stretch ‹*arms, legs*›; (dehnen) stretch [out] ‹*arms, legs, etc.*›; **den Kopf aus dem Fenster** ~: stick one's head out of the window (coll.)
[2] *refl. V.* stretch out

stre̲cken·weise *Adv.* in places; (fig.: zeitweise) at times

Stre̲ich *der;* ~[e]**s,** ~**e** trick; prank; **jmdm. einen** ~ **spielen** play a trick on sb.

stre̲icheln *tr. V.* stroke

stre̲ichen [1] *unr. tr. V.* **(a)** stroke
(b) (anstreichen) paint; „**frisch gestrichen**" 'wet paint'
(c) (auftragen) spread ‹*butter, jam, ointment, etc.*›; (bestreichen) **ein Brötchen mit Butter/mit Honig** ~: butter a roll/spread honey on a roll
(d) (tilgen) delete; cancel ‹*train, flight*›
[2] *unr. itr. V.* **(a)** stroke; **jmdm. über den Kopf** ~: stroke sb.'s head
(b) (anstreichen) paint

Stre̲icher *der;* ~**s,** ~, **Stre̲icherin** *die;* ~, ~**nen** (Musik) string player; **die Streicher:** the strings

Stre̲ich-: ~**holz** *das* match; ~**instrument** *das* string[ed] instrument; ~**käse** *der* cheese spread; ~**wurst** *die* [soft] sausage for spreading; ≈ meat spread

Stre̲ife *die;* ~, ~**n (a)** (Personen) patrol
(b) (Streifengang) patrol

stre̲ifen [1] *tr. V.* **(a)** (leicht berühren) touch; ‹*shot*› graze
(b) (kurz behandeln) touch [up]on ‹*problem, subject, etc.*›
(c) den Ring vom Finger ~: slip the ring off one's finger; **die Ärmel nach oben** ~: pull/push up one's sleeves
[2] *itr. V. mit sein* roam

Stre̲ifen *der;* ~**s,** ~ **(a)** stripe
(b) (Stück, Abschnitt) strip

Stre̲ifen·wagen *der* patrol car

stre̲ifig *Adj.* streaky

Stre̲if·licht *das* streak of light; **ein** ~**licht auf etw.** (*Akk.*) **werfen** (fig.) highlight sth.

Stre̲ik *der;* ~[e]**s,** ~**s** strike; **in den** ~ **treten** come out *or* go on strike

Stre̲ik·brecher *der,* **Stre̲ik·brecherin** *die;* ~, ~**nen** strike-breaker; blackleg (derog.)

stre̲iken *itr. V.* **(a)** strike; be on strike; (in den Streik treten) come out *or* go on strike; strike
(b) (ugs.: nicht mitmachen) go on strike
(c) (ugs.: nicht funktionieren) pack up (coll.)

Stre̲ikende *der/die; adj. Dekl.* striker

Stre̲ik·posten *der* picket

Stre̲it *der;* ~[e]**s,** ~**e** (Zank) quarrel; (Auseinandersetzung) dispute; argument

stre̲iten *unr. itr., refl. V.* quarrel; argue; (sich zanken) quarrel

Streiter̲ei *die;* ~, ~**en** arguing *no pl., no indef. art.;* (Gezänk) quarrelling *no pl.*

Stre̲itigkeit *die;* ~, ~**en** *meist Pl.* **(a)** quarrel; argument
(b) (Streitfall) dispute

Stre̲it·kräfte *Pl.* armed forces

stre̲ng [1] *Adj.* **(a)** strict; severe ‹*punishment*›; stringent, strict ‹*rule, regulation, etc.*›; stringent ‹*measure*›; rigorous ‹*examination, check, test, etc.*›; stern ‹*reprimand, look*›; absolute ‹*discretion*›; complete ‹*rest*›
(b) (schmucklos, herb) austere, severe ‹*cut, collar, style, etc.*›; severe ‹*face, features, hairstyle, etc.*›
(c) (durchdringend) pungent, sharp ‹*taste, smell*›
(d) (rau) severe ‹*winter*›; sharp, severe ‹*frost*›
[2] *adv.* ‹*mark, judge, etc.*› strictly, severely; ‹*punish*› severely; ‹*look, reprimand*› sternly; ‹*smell*› strongly

Stre̲nge *die;* ~ **(a)** ▸ STRENG A: strictness; severity; stringency; rigour; sternness
(b) (von [Gesichts]zügen) severity
(c) (von Geruch, Geschmack) pungency; sharpness
(d) ▸ STRENG D: severity; sharpness

stre̲ngstens *Adv.* [most] strictly

Stre̲ss, *Stre̲ß *der;* Stresses stress

stre̲ssen (ugs.) [1] *tr. V.* **jmdn.** ~: put sb. under stress; **vollkommen gestresst sein** be under an enormous amount of stress; **die gestressten Großstädter** the stressed city-dwellers
[2] *itr. V.* be stressful

Stre̲u *die;* ~, ~**en** straw

stre̲uen *tr. V.* **(a)** spread ‹*manure, sand, grit*›; sprinkle ‹*salt, herbs, etc.*›; strew, scatter ‹*flowers*›
(b) *auch itr.* **die Straßen [mit Sand/Salz]** ~: grit/salt the roads

stre̲unen *itr. V.; meist mit sein* wander *or* roam about *or* around; ~**de Katzen/Hunde** stray cats/dogs

Stre̲usel·kuchen *der* streusel cake

strich *1. u. 3. Pers. Sg. Prät. v.* STREICHEN

Stri̲ch *der;* ~[e]**s,** ~**e** (Linie) line; (Gedankenstrich) dash; (Schrägstrich) diagonal; (Binde-, Trennungsstrich) hyphen; **auf den** ~ **gehen** (salopp) walk the streets

stri̲cheln *tr. V.* **(a)** sketch in [with short lines]
(b) (schraffieren) hatch

Stri̲ch-: ~**junge** *der* (salopp) [young] male prostitute; ~**mädchen** *das* (salopp) streetwalker; hooker (Amer. sl.); ~**punkt** *der* semicolon

Stri̲ck *der;* ~[e]**s,** ~**e** cord; (Seil) rope; **jmdm. aus etw. einen** ~ **drehen** (fig.) use sth. against sb.

S

stricken *tr., itr. V.* knit

Strick-: ∼**jacke** *die* cardigan; ∼**nadel** *die* knitting needle; ∼**zeug** *das* knitting

striegeln *tr. V.* groom ⟨*horse*⟩

strikt ⊡ *Adj.* strict
⊡ *adv.* strictly

Strip *der;* ∼s, ∼s strip[tease]

Strippe *die;* ∼, ∼n (ugs.) string; **an der** ∼ **hängen** (fig.) be on the phone (coll.); (dauernd) hog the phone (coll.)

Stripper *der;* ∼s, ∼, **Stripperin** *die;* ∼, ∼**nen** (ugs.) stripper

Striptease /'ſtrɪptiːs/ *der od. das;* ∼: striptease

stritt *1. u. 3. Pers. Sg. Prät. v.* STREITEN

strittig *Adj.* contentious ⟨*point, problem*⟩; disputed ⟨*territory*⟩; ⟨*question*⟩ in dispute, at issue

Stroh *das;* ∼[e]s straw

Stroh-: ∼**blume** *die* (a) (Immortelle) immortelle; (b) (Korbblütler) strawflower; ∼**halm** *der* straw; ∼**witwe** *die* (ugs. scherzh.) grass widow; ∼**witwer** *der* (ugs. scherzh.) grass widower

Strolch *der;* ∼[e]s, ∼e (fam. scherzh.: Junge) rascal

Strom *der;* ∼[e]s, Ströme river; (fig.) stream; (Strömung; Elektrizität) current; (∼versorgung) electricity; **unter** ∼ **stehen** be live

strom-: ∼**abwärts** *Adv.* downstream; ∼**auf**[**wärts**] *Adv.* upstream

strömen *itr. V.; mit sein* stream

Strömung *die;* ∼, ∼en current; (Met.) airstream; (fig.) trend

Strophe *die;* ∼, ∼n verse; (einer Ode) strophe

strotzen *itr. V.* von *od.* vor etw. (*Dat.*) ∼: be full of sth.; von *od.* vor Gesundheit ∼: be bursting with health

strubbelig *Adj.* tousled

Strudel *der;* ∼s, ∼ (a) whirlpool
(b) (bes. südd., österr.: Gebäck) strudel

Struktur *die;* ∼, ∼en structure

strukturieren *tr. V.* structure; neu ∼: restructure

Strumpf *der;* ∼[e]s, Strümpfe stocking; (Socke, Knie∼) sock

Strumpf-: ∼**band** *das* garter; (Straps) suspender (Brit.); garter (Amer.); ∼**hose** *die* tights *pl.* (Brit.); pantyhose (esp. Amer.)

Strunk *der;* ∼[e]s, Strünke stem; stalk; (Baumstrunk) stump

struppig *Adj.* shaggy; tangled, tousled ⟨*hair*⟩

Stube *die;* ∼, ∼n (a) (veralt.: Wohnraum) [living] room; parlour (dated)
(b) (Milit.) [barrack] room

Stuben·fliege *die* [common] housefly

Stück *das;* ∼[e]s, ∼e (a) piece; (kleines) bit; (Teil, Abschnitt) part; **ein** ∼ **Kuchen** a piece *or*

---

*old spelling - see note on page xiv

slice of cake; **ein** ∼ **Zucker/Seife** a lump of sugar/a piece *or* bar of soap; **im** *od.* **am** ∼: unsliced ⟨*sausage, cheese, etc.*⟩
(b) (Einzelstück) item; (Exemplar) specimen; **ich nehme 5** ∼: I'll take five [of them]; **30 Pfennig das** ∼: thirty pfennigs each; ∼ **für** ∼: piece by piece; (eins nach dem andern) one by one; **das ist** [**ja**] **ein starkes** ∼ (ugs.) that's a bit much; **ein faules/freches** ∼ (salopp) a lazy/cheeky thing *or* devil
(c) (Bühnenstück) play; (Musikstück) piece

Stückchen *das;* ∼s, ∼: [little] piece; bit

stückeln *tr. V.* put together ⟨*sleeve, curtain*⟩ with patches

Student *der;* ∼en, ∼en (a) student
(b) (österr.: Schüler) [secondary-school] pupil

Studenten·wohnheim *das* student hostel; hall of residence

Studentin *die;* ∼, ∼nen ▶ STUDENT

Studie /'ſtuːdjə/ *die;* ∼, ∼n study

Studien-: ∼**aufenthalt** *der* study visit (in + *Dat.* to); ∼**dauer** *die* length of study; **eine neunsemestrige** ∼**dauer** nine semesters of study; ∼**freund** *der,* ∼**freundin** *die* university/college friend; ∼**gebühr** *die* tuition fee; ∼**platz** *der* university/college place; ∼**reise** *die* study trip

studieren *tr., itr. V.* study

Studierende *der/die; adj. Dekl.* student

Studio *das;* ∼s, ∼s studio

Studium *das;* ∼s, Studien study; (Studiengang) course of study

Stufe *die;* ∼, ∼n (a) step; (einer Treppe) stair; „**Vorsicht,** ∼**!**' 'mind the step'
(b) (Raketenstufe, Geol., fig.: Stadium) stage; (Niveau) level; (Grad) degree; (Rang) grade

Stuhl *der;* ∼[e]s, Stühle chair

Stuhl-: ∼**gang** *der* bowel movement[s]; (Kot) stool; ∼**lehne** *die* (Rückenlehne) chair back; (Armlehne) chair arm

stülpen *tr. V.* etw. auf *od.* über etw. (*Akk.*) ∼: pull/put sth. on to *or* over sth.

stumm *Adj.* dumb ⟨*person*⟩; (schweigsam) silent; (wortlos) wordless; mute ⟨*glance, gesture*⟩

Stumme *der/die; adj. Dekl.* mute; **die** ∼n the dumb

Stummel *der;* ∼s, ∼: stump; (Bleistiftstummel) stub; (Zigaretten-/Zigarrenstummel) [cigarette/cigar] butt

Stumm·film *der* silent film

Stümper *der;* ∼s, ∼: botcher; bungler

stümperhaft ⊡ *Adj.* incompetent; botched ⟨*job*⟩; (laienhaft) amateurish ⟨*attempt, drawing*⟩
⊡ *adv.* incompetently; (laienhaft) amateurishly

Stümperin *die;* ∼, ∼nen botcher, bungler

stümpern *itr. V.* work incompetently; (pfuschen) bungle

stumpf *Adj.* (a) blunt ⟨*pin, needle, knife, etc.*⟩

(b) (glanzlos, matt) dull ⟨*paint, hair, metal, colour, etc.*⟩

Stumpf *der;* ∼[e]s, **Stümpfe** stump

Stumpf·sinn *der* **(a)** apathy
(b) (Monotonie) monotony; tedium

stumpf·sinnig ① *Adj.* **(a)** apathetic; vacant ⟨*look*⟩
(b) (monoton) tedious; soul-destroying ⟨*job, work*⟩
② *adv.* **(a)** apathetically; ⟨*stare*⟩ vacantly
(b) (monoton) tediously

Stunde *die;* ∼, ∼n hour; (Unterrichts∼) lesson; **eine** ∼ **Aufenthalt/Pause** an hour's stop/break; a stop/break of an hour

stünde *1. u. 3. Pers. Sg. Konjunktiv II v.* STEHEN

stunden *tr. V.* **jmdm. einen Betrag** *usw.* ∼: allow sb. to defer payment of a sum *etc.*

stunden-, Stunden-: ∼**kilometer** *der* kilometre per hour; k.p.h.; ∼**lang** ① *Adj.* lasting hours *postpos.;* ② *adv.* for hours; ∼**lohn** *der* hourly wage; ∼**plan** *der* timetable; ∼**zeiger** *der* hour hand

-stündig *adj.* -hour

stündlich *Adj., adv.* hourly

-stündlich *adj.* -hourly; **zwei**∼/**halb**∼: two-hourly/half-hourly; *adv.* every two hours/half an hour

Stundung *die;* ∼, ∼en deferment of payment

Stups *der;* ∼es, ∼e (ugs.) push; shove; (leicht) nudge

stupsen *tr. V.* (ugs.) push; shove; (leicht) nudge

Stups-nase *die* snub nose

stur (ugs.) ① *Adj.* **(a)** obstinate; dogged ⟨*insistence*⟩; (phlegmatisch) dour
(b) (unbeirrbar) dogged; persistent
(c) (stumpfsinnig) tedious
② *adv.* **(a)** obstinately
(b) (unbeirrbar) doggedly
(c) (stumpfsinnig) tediously; ⟨*learn, copy*⟩ mechanically

stürbe *1. u. 3. Pers. Sg. Konjunktiv II v.* STERBEN

Sturheit *die;* ∼ (ugs.) **(a)** obstinacy; pigheadedness; (phlegmatisches Wesen) dourness
(b) (Stumpfsinnigkeit) deadly monotony

Sturm *der;* ∼[e]s, **Stürme** **(a)** storm; (heftiger Wind) gale
(b) (Milit.) assault (**auf** + *Akk.* on); ∼ **klingeln** ring the [door]bell like mad

stürmen ① *itr. V.* **(a)** *unpers.* **es stürmt** [**heftig**] it's blowing a gale
(b) *mit sein* (rennen) rush; (verärgert) storm
② *tr. V.* (Milit.) storm ⟨*town, position, etc.*⟩; (fig.) besiege ⟨*booking office, shop, etc.*⟩

Stürmer *der;* ∼s, ∼ (Sport) striker; forward

stürmisch ① *Adj.* **(a)** stormy; (fig.) tempestuous, turbulent
(b) (ungestüm) tumultuous ⟨*applause,*

welcome, reception⟩; wild ⟨*enthusiasm*⟩; passionate ⟨*lover, embrace, temperament*⟩; vehement ⟨*protest*⟩
② *adv.* ⟨*protest*⟩ vehemently; ⟨*embrace*⟩ impetuously, passionately; ⟨*demand*⟩ clamorously; ⟨*applaud*⟩ wildly

Sturz *der;* -es, **Stürze** **(a)** fall; (Unfall) accident
(b) (fig.: von Preis, Temperatur usw.) [sharp] fall, drop (*Gen.* in)
(c) (Verlust des Amtes, der Macht) fall; (Absetzung) overthrow; (Amtsenthebung) removal from office

Sturz-bach *der* [mountain] torrent; (fig.: von Fragen usw.) torrent

sturz-besoffen *Adj* (ugs.) paralytic [drunk] (coll.)

stürzen ① *itr. V.; mit sein* **(a)** fall; (fig.) ⟨*temperature, exchange rate, etc.*⟩ drop [sharply]; ⟨*prices*⟩ tumble; ⟨*government*⟩ fall, collapse
(b) (laufen) rush; dash
(c) (fließen) stream; pour
② *refl. V.* **sich auf jmdn./etw.** ∼ (auch fig.) pounce on sb./sth.; **sich in etw.** (*Akk.*) ∼: throw oneself into sth.
③ *tr. V.* **(a)** throw; (mit Wucht) hurl
(b) (umdrehen) upturn ⟨*mould*⟩; turn out ⟨*pudding, cake, etc.*⟩
(c) (des Amtes entheben) oust ⟨*person*⟩ [from office]; (gewaltsam) overthrow ⟨*leader, government*⟩

Sturz-: ∼**flug** *der* (Flugw.) [nose]dive; **im** ∼**flug** in a [nose]dive; ∼**helm** *der* crash helmet

Stuss, *Stuß *der;* **Stusses** (ugs. abwertend) rubbish; twaddle (coll.)

Stute *die;* ∼, ∼n mare

Stütze *die;* ∼, ∼n (auch fig.) support

stutzen¹ *itr. V.* stop short

stutzen² *tr. V.* trim; dock ⟨*tail*⟩; clip ⟨*ear, hedge, wing*⟩; prune ⟨*tree, bush*⟩

stützen ① *tr. V.* support; (mit Pfosten o. Ä.) prop up; (aufstützen) rest ⟨*head, hands, arms, etc.*⟩
② *refl. V.* **sich auf jmdn./etw.** ∼: lean *or* support oneself on sb./sth.

stutzig *Adj.* ∼ **werden** begin to wonder; **jmdn.** ∼ **machen** make sb. wonder

Styropor Ⓦ *das;* ∼s polystyrene [foam]

s. u. *Abk. =* **siehe unten** see below

Subjekt *das;* ∼[e]s, ∼e **(a)** subject
(b) (abwertend: Mensch) creature

subjektiv ① *Adj.* subjective
② *adv.* subjectively

Subjektivität *die;* ∼: subjectivity

***substantiell ▶** SUBSTANZIELL

Substantiv *das;* ∼s, ∼e (Sprachw.) noun

Substanz *die;* ∼, ∼en **(a)** (auch fig.) substance
(b) (Grundbestand) **die** ∼: the reserves *pl.*

substanziell ① *Adj.* substantial
② *adv.* substantially

S

subtil ①Adj. subtle
②adv. subtly
Subtilität die; ~, ~en subtlety
sub·tropisch Adj. subtropical
Subvention die; ~, ~en (Wirtsch.) subsidy
Suche die; ~, ~n search (nach for); **auf der**
~ **[nach jmdm./etw.] sein** be looking/
(intensiver) searching [for sb./sth.]
suchen ①tr. V. (a) look for; (intensiver)
search for; „Leerzimmer gesucht"
'unfurnished room wanted'
(b) (bedacht sein auf, sich wünschen) seek
⟨protection, advice, company, warmth, etc.⟩;
look for ⟨adventure⟩
②itr. V. search; **nach jmdm./etw.** ~: look/
search for sb./sth.
Sucherei die; ~, ~en (ugs., oft abwertend)
[endless] searching no pl.
Sucht die; ~, Süchte od. ~en (a) addiction
(nach to); **[bei jmdm.] zur** ~ **werden** (auch fig.)
become addictive [in sb.'s case]
(b) Pl. **Süchte** (übermäßiges Verlangen) craving
(nach for)
süchtig Adj. (a) addicted
(b) (fig.) **nach etw.** ~ **sein** be obsessed with
sth.
Sucht·kranke die/der addict
Süd (bes. Seemannsspr., Met.) ▶ SÜDEN
Süd-: ~**afrika** (das) South Africa;
~**amerika** (das) South America
Sudan (das); ~s od. der; ~s Sudan
Süden der; ~s south; **der** ~: the South;
Süd·frucht die tropical [or sub-tropical]
fruit
Südländer der; ~s, ~, **Südländerin**
die; ~, ~nen Southern European
südländisch Adj. Southern [European];
Latin ⟨temperament⟩; ~ **aussehen** have Latin
looks
südlich ①Adj. (a) southern
(b) (nach, von Süden) southerly
(c) (aus dem Süden) Southern
②adv. southwards
③Präp. mit Gen. [to the] south of
süd-, Süd-: ~**licht** das southern lights pl.;
(einzelne Erscheinung) display of the southern
lights; ~**pol** der South Pole; ~**see** die;
~~: **die** ~**see:** the South Seas pl.;
~**see·insel** die South Sea island; ~**tirol**
(das) South Tyrol; ~**wärts** Adv.
southwards; ~**wind** der south or southerly
wind
Sues·kanal der; ~s Suez Canal
Sühne die; ~, ~n (geh.) atonement;
expiation
sühnen tr., itr. V. [für] etw. ~: atone for or
pay the penalty for sth.
Sultanine die; ~, ~n sultana
Sülze die; ~, ~n (a) diced meat/fish in
aspic; (vom Schweinskopf) brawn
(b) (Aspik) aspic

sülzen tr., itr. V. (salopp) ▶ QUATSCHEN 1A, 2
Summe die; ~, ~n sum
summen ①itr. V. hum; (lauter, heller) buzz
②tr. V. hum ⟨tune, song, etc.⟩
summieren refl. V. add up (auf + Akk. to)
Sumpf der; ~[e]s, Sümpfe marsh; (bes. in den
Tropen) swamp
sumpfig Adj. marshy
Sund der; ~[e]s, ~e (Geogr.) sound
Sünde die; ~, ~n sin; (fig.) misdeed;
transgression
Sünden·bock der (ugs.) scapegoat
Sünder der; ~s, ~, **Sünderin** die; ~,
~nen sinner
sündigen itr. V. sin
Super das; ~s, ~: four star (Brit.); premium
(Amer.)
super- ultra- ⟨long, high, fast, modern,
masculine, etc.⟩
Super- super⟨hero, car, group, etc.⟩; terrific
(coll.), tremendous (coll.) ⟨success, offer,
chance, idea, etc.⟩
Super·benzin das four-star petrol (Brit.);
premium (Amer.)
Superlativ der; ~s, ~e (Sprachw.)
superlative
Super-: ~**macht** die super power;
~**markt** der supermarket
Suppe die; ~; ~n soup
Suppen·löffel der soup spoon
Surf·brett /'sə:f-/ das surfboard
surfen /'sə:fn̩/ itr. V. surf
Surfer /'sə:fɐ/ der; ~s, ~, **Surferin** die;
~, ~nen surfer
surren itr. V. (a) (summen) hum; ⟨camera,
fan⟩ whirr
(b) mit sein (schwirren) whirr
suspekt ①Adj. suspicious; **jmdm.** ~ **sein**
arouse sb.'s suspicions
②adv. suspiciously
süß ①Adj. sweet
②adv. sweetly
süßen tr. V. sweeten
Süßigkeit die; ~, ~en sweet (Brit.); candy
(Amer.); ~**en** sweets (Brit.); candy sing. (Amer.);
(als Ware) confectionery sing.
süßlich ①Adj. (a) [slightly] sweet; on the
sweet side pred.;
(b) (sentimental) mawkish
②adv. ⟨write, paint⟩ mawkishly
süß-, Süß-: ~**most** der unfermented fruit
juice; ~**sauer** ①Adj. sweet-and-sour; (fig.)
wry ⟨smile, face⟩; ②adv. (a) etw. ~**sauer**
zubereiten give sth. a sweet-and-sour flavour;
(b) (fig.) ⟨smile⟩ wryly; ~**speise** die sweet;
dessert; ~**stoff** der sweetener; ~**wasser**
das fresh water
Symbol das; ~s, ~e symbol
symbolisch ①Adj. symbolic
②adv. symbolically
Sympathie die; ~, ~n sympathy (**für** with)

sympathisch ①*Adj.* congenial, likeable ⟨*person, manner*⟩; appealing ⟨*voice, appearance, material*⟩ ②*adv.* in an appealing way; (angenehm) agreeably

Symphonie *usw.* ▶ SINFONIE *usw.*

Symptom *das;* ~s, ~e (Med., geh.) symptom (*Gen.*, **für**, von of)

symptomatisch (Med., geh.) *Adj.* symptomatic (**für** of)

Synagoge *die;* ~, ~n synagogue

synchron ①*Adj.* (a) synchronous (b) (Sprachw.) synchronic ②*adv.* (a) synchronously (b) (Sprachw.) synchronically

Synchronisation *die;* ~, ~en ▶ SYNCHRONISIERUNG

synchronisieren *tr. V.* (a) (Film) dub ⟨*film*⟩ (b) (Technik, fig.) synchronize ⟨*watches, operations, etc.*⟩; **synchronisiertes Getriebe** synchromesh [gearbox]

Synchronisierung *die;* ~, ~en (a) (Film) dubbing (b) (Technik, fig.) synchronization

Synthese *die;* ~, ~n synthesis (*Gen.*, **von**, **aus** of)

Synthesizer /'sɪntəsaɪzɐ/ *der;* ~s, ~ (Musik) synthesizer

synthetisch ①*Adj.* synthetic ②*adv.* synthetically

Syrer *der;* ~s, ~, **Syrerin** *die;* ~, ~nen Syrian

Syrien /'zy:riən/ *(das);* ~s Syria

syrisch *Adj.* Syrian

System *das;* ~, ~e system

systematisch ①*Adj.* systematic ②*adv.* systematically

System-fehler *der* fault in the system

Szenario *das;* ~s, ~s scenario

Szene /'sts:e:nə/ *die;* ~, ~n (auch fig.) scene

Szenen-wechsel *der* (Theater) scene change

Tt

t, T /te:/ *das;* ~, ~: t/T

t *Abk.* = **Tonne** t

Tab. *Abk.* = **Tabelle**

Tabak *der;* ~s, ~e tobacco

Tabaks-pfeife *die* [tobacco] pipe

tabellarisch *Adj.* tabular; **ein** ~**er Lebenslauf** a curriculum vitae in tabular form

Tabelle *die;* ~, ~n table

Tabellen-kalkulation *die* (DV) performing calculations using a spreadsheet; (Program) spreadsheet program

Tabernakel *das od. der;* ~s, ~: tabernacle

Tablett *das;* ~[e]s, ~s *od.* ~e tray

Tablette *die;* ~, ~n tablet

tabletten-süchtig *Adj.* addicted to pills *postpos.*

tabu *Adj.* taboo

Tabu *das;* ~s, ~s taboo

tabuisieren *tr. V.* etw. ~: taboo sth.; make sth. taboo

Ta-cheles [mit jmdm.] ~ **reden** (ugs.) do some straight talking [to sb.]

Tacho *der;* ~s, ~s (ugs.) speedo (coll.)

Tacho-: ~**meter** *der od. das* speedometer; ~**stand** *der* (ugs.: Kilometerstand) mileometer *or* odometer reading

Tadel *der;* ~s, ~ (a) censure (b) (im Klassenbuch) black mark

tadel-los ①*Adj.* impeccable; immaculate ⟨*hair, clothing, suit, etc.*⟩; perfect ⟨*condition, teeth, pronunciation, German, etc.*⟩ ②*adv.* ⟨*dress*⟩ impeccably; ⟨*fit, speak, etc.*⟩ perfectly; ⟨*live, behave, etc.*⟩ irreproachably

tadeln *tr. V.* jmdn. [für *od.* wegen etw.] ~: rebuke sb. [for sth.]

Tafel *die;* ~, ~n (a) (Schiefertafel) slate; (Wandtafel) blackboard (b) (plattenförmiges Stück) slab; **eine** ~ **Schokolade** a bar of chocolate (c) (Gedenktafel) plaque (d) (geh.: festlicher Tisch) table

Täfelchen *das;* ~s, ~: ▶ TAFEL B: [small] slab; [small] bar

tafeln *itr. V.* (geh.) feast

täfeln *tr. V.* panel

Tafel-: ~**spitz** *der* (österr.) boiled fillet of beef; ~**wasser** *das* [bottled] mineral water; ~**wein** *der* table wine

taff *Adj.* (ugs.) tough

Taft *der;* ~[e]s, ~e taffeta

Tag *der;* ~[e]s, ~e day; **am** ~[e] during the day[time]; **guten** ~! hello; (bei Vorstellung) how do you do?; **an diesem** ~: on this day; **dreimal am** ~: three times a day; **am folgenden** ~: the next day; **eines** ~**es** one day; some day

tag-aus *Adv.* ~, **tagein** day in, day out; day after day

Tage-buch *das* diary

tag·ein *Adv.* ▶ TAGAUS

tage·lang ⒈ *Adj.* lasting for days *postpos.;* **nach ~em Regen** after days of rain ⒉ *adv.* for days [on end]

tagen *itr. V.* meet; **das Gericht/Parlament tagt** the court/parliament is in session

tages-, Tages-: **~aktuell** *Adj.* **die ~aktuellen Nachrichten** the [current] news of the day; **die ~aktuellen Kurse** the rates of exchange current on the day; **~anbruch** *der* daybreak; dawn; **~ausflug** *der* day's outing; **~karte** *die* (a) (Gastron.) menu of the day; (b) (Fahr-, Eintrittskarte) day ticket; **~kasse** *die* (a) box office (*open during the day*); (b) (Tageseinnahme) day's takings *pl.;* **~licht** *das* daylight; **~licht·projektor** *der* overhead projector; **~zeit** *die* time of day; **~zeitung** *die* daily newspaper; daily

-tägig (a) (... Tage alt) **ein sechstägiges Küken** a six-day-old chick (b) (... Tage dauernd) **nach dreitägiger Vorbereitung** after three days' preparation

täglich ⒈ *Adj.* daily ⒉ *adv.* every day; **zweimal ~:** twice a day; **~ drei Tabletten einnehmen** take three tablets daily

tags *Adv.* (a) by day; in the daytime (b) **~ zuvor/davor** the day before; **~ darauf** the next *or* following day; the day after

tags·über *Adv.* during the day

tag·täglich (intensivierend) ⒈ *Adj.* day-to-day; daily ⒉ *adv.* every single day

Tagung *die;* **~, ~en** conference

Taifun *der;* **~s, ~e** typhoon

Taille /ˈtaljə/ *die;* **~, ~n** waist

Taiwan (*das*) **~s** Taiwan

Takt *der;* **~[e]s, ~e** (a) (Musik) time; (Einheit) bar; measure (Amer.); **aus dem ~ kommen** lose the beat (b) (rhythmischer Bewegungsablauf) rhythm (c) (Feingefühl) tact

Takt·gefühl *das* sense of tact

taktieren *itr. V.* proceed tactically; **vorsichtig/klug ~:** use caution/clever tactics

Taktik *die;* **~, ~en: [eine] ~:** tactics *pl.*

taktisch ⒈ *Adj.* tactical ⒉ *adv.* tactically

taktlos ⒈ *Adj.* tactless ⒉ *adv.* tactlessly

Taktlosigkeit *die;* **~, ~en** (a) (taktlose Art) tactlessness (b) (taktlose Handlung) piece of tactlessness

taktvoll ⒈ *Adj.* tactful ⒉ *adv.* tactfully

Tal *das;* **~[e]s, Täler** valley

Talent *das;* **~[e]s, ~e** talent (**zu, für** for); (Mensch) talented person

talentiert *Adj.* talented

---

*old spelling - see note on page xiv

Talg *der;* **~[e]s, ~e** suet; (zur Herstellung von Seife, Kerzen usw.) tallow

Talisman *der;* **~s, ~e** talisman

Tampon *der;* **~s, ~s** tampon

Tamtam *das;* **~s** (ugs. abwertend) [**großes**] **~:** [a big] fuss

Tang *der;* **~[e]s, ~e** seaweed

Tangente *die;* **~, ~n** (Math.) tangent

Tank *der;* **~s, ~s** tank

tanken *tr., itr. V.* fill up; **Öl ~:** fill up with oil

Tanker *der;* **~s, ~:** tanker

Tank-: **~säule** *die* petrol pump (Brit.); gasoline pump (Amer.); **~stelle** *die* petrol station (Brit.); gas station (Amer.); **~wagen** *der* tanker; **~wart** *der;* **~s, ~e, ~wartin** *die;* **~, ~nen** petrol pump attendant (Brit.); gas station attendant (Amer.)

Tanne *die;* **~, ~n** fir [tree]

Tannen-: **~baum** *der* (ugs.) fir tree; (Weihnachtsbaum) Christmas tree; **~grün** *das* fir sprigs *pl.;* **~zapfen** *der* fir cone; **~zweig** *der* fir branch

Tansania (*das*); **~s** Tanzania

Tante *die;* **~, ~n** (a) aunt (b) (Kinderspr.: Frau) lady (c) (ugs.: Frau) woman

Tanz *der;* **~es, Tänze** dance

Tanz-: **~abend** *der* evening dance; **~bar** *die* night spot (coll.) with dancing; **~café** *das* coffee house with dancing

tanzen *itr., tr. V.* dance

Tänzer *der;* **~s, ~, Tänzerin** *die;* **~, ~nen** dancer; (Ballett tänzer[in]) ballet dancer

Tanz-: **~fläche** *die* dance floor; **~lokal** *das* café/restaurant with dancing; **~orchester** *das* dance band; **~stunde** *die* (a) (~kurs) dancing class; (b) (einzelne Stunde) dancing lesson

Tapete *die;* **~, ~n** wallpaper

Tapeten·wechsel *der* (ugs.) change of scene

tapezieren *tr. V.* [wall]paper

tapfer ⒈ *Adj.* brave ⒉ *adv.* bravely

Tapferkeit *die;* **~:** courage; bravery

tappen *itr. V.* (a) *mit sein* patter (b) (tastend greifen) grope (**nach** for)

Taps *der;* **~es, ~e** (ugs. abwertend) clumsy oaf

Tarif *der;* **~s, ~e** charge; (Post-, Wassertarif) rate; (Verkehrstarif) fares *pl.;* (Zolltarif) tariff; (Lohntarif) [wage] rate; (Gehaltstarif) [salary] scale

tarnen ⒈ *tr., itr. V.* camouflage ⒉ *refl. V.* camouflage oneself

Tasche *die;* **~, ~n** bag; (in Kleidung, Rucksack usw.) pocket; **jmdm. auf der ~ liegen** (fig. ugs.) live off sb.

Taschen-: **~buch** *das* paperback; **~dieb** *der,* **~diebin** *die* pickpocket; **~geld** *das* pocket money; **~lampe** *die* [pocket] torch (Brit.) *or* (Amer.) flashlight;

∼**messer** *das* penknife; ∼**rechner** *der* pocket calculator; ∼**tuch** *das; Pl.* ∼**tücher** handkerchief; ∼**uhr** *die* pocket watch

Tasse *die;* ∼, ∼**n** cup

Tastatur *die;* ∼, ∼**en** keyboard

Taste *die;* ∼, ∼**n** **(a)** (eines Musikinstruments, einer Schreibmaschine) key
(b) (Pedal) pedal [key]
(c) (am Telefon, Radio, Fernsehgerät, Taschenrechner usw.) button

tasten 1 *itr. V.* (fühlend suchen) grope, feel (nach for)
2 *refl. V.* (sich tastend bewegen) grope *or* feel one's way

Tasten-telefon *das* push-button telephone

tat *1. u. 3. Pers. Sg. Prät. v.* TUN

Tat *die;* ∼, ∼**en** act; (das Tun) action; **eine gute** ∼: a good deed; **in der** ∼ (verstärkend) actually; (zustimmend) indeed

Tatar *das;* ∼[s] steak tartare

Tat-bestand *der* **(a)** facts *pl.* [of the matter *or* case]
(b) (Rechtsw.) elements *pl.* of an offence

Täter *der;* ∼s, ∼, **Täterin** *die;* ∼, ∼**nen** culprit

tätig *Adj.* **(a)** ∼ **sein** work
(b) (rührig, aktiv) active

tätigen *tr. V.* (Kaufmannsspr., Papierdt.) transact ⟨*business, deal, etc.*⟩

Tätigkeit *die;* ∼, ∼**en** activity; (Arbeit) job

tat-, Tat-: ∼**kraft** *die* energy; drive; ∼**kräftig** 1 *Adj.* energetic ⟨*person*⟩; 2 *adv.* energetically

tätlich 1 *Adj.* physical ⟨*clash, attack, resistance, etc.*⟩; **gegen jmdn.** ∼ **werden** become violent towards sb.
2 *adv.* physically; **jmdn.** ∼ **angreifen** attack sb. physically; assault sb.

Tat-ort *der* scene of a/the crime

tätowieren *tr. V.* tattoo

Tätowierung *die;* ∼, ∼**en** tattoo

Tat-sache *die* fact

tatsächlich 1 *Adj.* actual; real
2 *adv.* actually; really

tätscheln *tr. V.* pat

Tattoo /tɛˈtuː/ *das;* ∼s, ∼s tattoo

tat-verdächtig *Adj.* suspected

Tat-waffe *die* weapon [used in the crime]

Tatze *die;* ∼, ∼**n** paw

Tat-zeit *die* time of the crime

Tau¹ *der;* ∼[e]s dew

Tau² *das;* ∼[e]s, ∼e (Seil) rope

taub *Adj.* **(a)** deaf
(b) (wie abgestorben) numb
(c) empty ⟨*nut*⟩

Taube¹ *die;* ∼, ∼**n** pigeon; (Turteltaube; auch Politik fig.) dove

Taube² *der/die; adj. Dekl.* deaf person; deaf man/woman; **die** ∼**n** the deaf

Taubheit *die;* ∼: deafness

taub-stumm *Adj.* deaf and dumb

Taub-stumme *der/die; adj. Dekl.* deaf mute

tauchen 1 *itr. V.* **(a)** *auch mit* sein dive (nach for)
(b) *mit* sein (eintauchen) dive; (auftauchen) rise; emerge
2 *tr. V.* **(a)** (eintauchen) dip
(b) (untertauchen) duck

Taucher *der;* ∼s, ∼: diver; (mit Flossen und Atemgerät) skin diver

Taucher-: ∼**anzug** *der* diving suit; ∼**brille** *die* diving goggles *pl.*

Taucherin *die;* ∼, ∼**nen** ▶ TAUCHER

Tauch-sieder *der;* ∼s, ∼: portable immersion heater

tauen 1 *itr. V.* **(a)** *unpers.* **es taut** it's thawing
(b) *mit* sein (schmelzen) melt
2 *tr. V.* melt; thaw

Taufe *die;* ∼, ∼**n** (christl. Rel.) **(a)** (Sakrament) baptism
(b) (Zeremonie) christening; baptism

taufen *tr. V.* **(a)** baptize
(b) (einen Namen geben) christen

taugen *itr. V.* nichts/nicht viel/etwas ∼: be no/not much/some good *or* use

tauglich *Adj.* [nicht] ∼: [un]suitable; (für Militärdienst) fit [for service]

Taumel *der;* ∼s **(a)** [feeling of] dizziness
(b) (Rausch) frenzy; fever

taumelig *Adj.* dizzy; giddy

taumeln *itr. V.* **(a)** *auch mit* sein (wanken) reel, sway (**vor** + *Dat.* with)
(b) *mit* sein (taumelnd gehen) stagger

Tausch *der;* ∼[e]s, ∼e exchange; **ein guter/ schlechter** ∼: a good/bad deal

tauschen 1 *tr. V.* exchange (**gegen** for); **sie tauschten die Plätze** they changed places
2 *itr. V.* **mit jmdm.** ∼ (fig.) change places with sb.

täuschen 1 *tr. V.* deceive; **wenn mich nicht alles täuscht** unless I'm completely mistaken
2 *itr. V.* be deceptive
3 *refl. V.* be wrong *or* mistaken (**in** + *Dat.* about)

täuschend 1 *Adj.* remarkable, striking ⟨*similarity, imitation*⟩
2 *adv.* remarkably

Täuschung *die;* ∼, ∼**en** deception; (Selbst∼) delusion

tausend *Kardinalz.* **(a)** a *or* one thousand
(b) (ugs.: sehr viele) thousands of; ∼ **Dank/ Küsse** a thousand thanks/kisses

Tausend *das;* ∼s, ∼e thousand

tausend-ein[s] *Kardinalz.* a *or* one thousand and one

Tausender *der;* ∼s, ∼ (ugs.) (Tausendmarkschein usw.) thousand-mark/-dollar *etc.* note; (Betrag) thousand marks/dollars *etc.*

tausenderlei *indekl. Adj.* (ugs.) a thousand and one different ⟨*answers, kinds, etc.*⟩

tausend·mal *Adv.* a thousand times

Tausend·mark·schein *der* thousand-mark note

tausendst... *Ordinalz.* thousandth; *s. auch* ACHT...

tausendstel *Bruchz.* thousandth

Tausendstel *das* (schweiz. meist *der*); ~s, ~: thousandth

Tau-: ~**wasser** *das* meltwater; ~**wetter** *das* thaw; ~**ziehen** *das*; ~~s (auch fig.) tug-of-war

Taxe *die*; ~, ~n (a) (Taxi) taxi
(b) (Gebühr) charge

Taxi *das*; ~s, ~s taxi

taxieren *tr. V.* estimate

Taxi-: ~**fahrer** *der*, ~**fahrerin** *die* taxi driver; ~**stand** *der* taxi rank (Brit.); taxi stand

Tb /teː'beː/, **Tbc** /teːbeː'tseː/ *die*; ~: *Abk.* = **Tuberkulose** TB

Team /tiːm/ *das*; ~s, ~s team

Team·arbeit *die* teamwork

Technik *die*; ~, ~en (a) technology; (Studienfach) engineering *no art.*;
(b) (technische Ausrüstung) equipment
(c) (Arbeitsweise, Verfahren) technique

Techniker *der*; ~s, ~, **Technikerin** *die*; ~, ~nen technical expert

technisch ① *Adj.* technical; technological ⟨*progress, age*⟩
② *adv.* technically; technologically ⟨*advanced*⟩

Techno /'tɛkno/ *das od. der*; ~s techno

Technologie *die*; ~, ~n technology

technologisch ① *Adj.* technological
② *adv.* technologically

Techno-party *die* techno party

Tee *der*; ~s, ~s tea

TEE /teː|eː'|eː/ *der*; ~[s], ~[s] *Abk.* = **Trans-Europ-Express** TEE

Tee-: ~**beutel** *der* tea bag; ~**kanne** *die* teapot; ~**löffel** *der* teaspoon

Teenie /'tiːni/ *der*; ~s, ~s (ugs.) young teenager

Tee-: sieb *das* tea strainer; ~**tasse** *die* teacup

Teich *der*; ~[e]s, ~e pond

Teig *der*; ~[e]s, ~e dough; (Kuchen-, Biskuitteig) pastry; (Pfannkuchen-, Waffelteig) batter

Teig·waren *Pl.* pasta *sing.*

Teil (a) *der*; ~[e]s, ~e part; **fünfter** ~: fifth
(b) *der od. das*; ~[e]s, ~e (Anteil; Beitrag) share
(c) *der*; ~[e]s, ~e (beteiligte Person[en]; Rechtsw.: Partei) party
(d) *das*; ~[e]s, ~e (Einzelteil) part

teil·bar *Adj.* divisible (**durch** by)

Teilbarkeit *die*; ~: divisibility

Teilchen *das*; ~s, ~ (a) (kleines Stück) [small] part
(b) (Partikel) particle

teilen ① *tr. V.* (a) divide (**durch** by)
(b) (aufteilen) share (**unter** + *Dat.* among)
② *refl. V.* sich (*Dat.*) etw. [mit jmdm.] ~: share sth. [with sb.]

Teiler *der*; ~s, ~ (Math.) factor

teil|haben *unr. itr. V.* share (**an** + *Dat.* in)

Teilhaber *der*; ~s, ~, **Teilhaberin** *die*; ~, ~nen partner

Teil·kasko·versicherung *die: insurance giving limited cover*

Teilnahme *die*; ~, ~n (a) participation (**an** + *Dat.* in); ~ **an einem Kurs** attendance at a course
(b) (Interesse) interest (**an** + *Dat.* in)
(c) (geh.: Mitgefühl) sympathy

teilnahms·los *Adj.* indifferent

Teilnahmslosigkeit *die*; ~: indifference

teilnahms·voll ① *Adj.* compassionate
② *adv.* compassionately

teil|nehmen *unr. itr. V.* [an etw. (*Dat.*)] ~: take part [in sth.]; [an einem Lehrgang] ~: attend [a course]

Teilnehmer *der*; ~s, ~, **Teilnehmerin** *die*; ~, ~nen (a) participant (*Gen.*, **an** + *Dat.* in); (bei Wettbewerb auch) competitor, contestant (**an** + *Dat.* in)
(b) (Fernspr.) subscriber

teils *Adv.* partly

Teilung *die*; ~, ~en division

teil·weise ① *Adv.* partly
② *adj.* partial

Teilzeit-: ~**arbeit** *die* part-time work *no indef. art.*; ~**job** *der* part-time job

Teint /tɛ̃ː/ *der*; ~s, ~s complexion

Telefon /'teːlefoːn, *auch* teleˈfoːn/ *das*; ~s, ~e telephone; phone; **ans** ~ **gehen** answer the [tele]phone

Telefon-: ~**anruf** *der* [tele]phone call; ~**anschluss**, *~anschluß der* telephone; line; ~**apparat** *der* telephone

Telefonat *das*; ~[e]s, ~e telephone call

Telefon-: ~**buch** *das* [tele]phone book *or* directory; ~**gespräch** *das* telephone conversation

telefonieren *itr. V.* make a [tele]phone call; **mit jmdm.** ~: talk to sb. [on the telephone]

telefonisch ① *Adj.* telephone *attrib.*
② *adv.* by telephone

Telefonist *der*; ~en, ~en, **Telefonistin** *die*; ~, ~nen telephonist; (in einer Firma) switchboard operator

Telefon-: ~**karte** *die* phonecard; ~**nummer** *die* [tele]phone number; ~**rechnung** *die* [tele]phone bill; ~**verzeichnis** *das* [tele]phone list; ~**zelle** *die* [tele]phone booth *or* (Brit.) box; call box (Brit.); ~**zentrale** *die* telephone exchange

---

Telegraf *der;* ~en, ~en telegraph
Telegrafie *die;* ~: telegraphy *no art.*
telegrafieren *itr., tr. V.* telegraph
telegrafisch [1] *Adj.* telegraphic
[2] *adv.* by telegraph *or* telegram
Telegramm *das* telegram
Tele·objektiv *das* (Fot.) telephoto lens
Tele·text *der* teletext *no art.*
Teller *der;* ~s, ~: plate
Tempel *der;* ~s, ~: temple
Temperament *das;* ~[e]s, ~e (a)
(Wesensart) temperament
(b) (Schwung) **eine Frau mit** ~: a woman with
spirit; **das** ~ **geht oft mit mir durch** I often
lose my temper
temperament·voll *Adj.* spirited ⟨person,
speech, dance, etc.⟩
Temperatur *die;* ~, ~en temperature
Temperatur-: ~**anstieg** *der* rise in
temperature; ~**rückgang** *der* drop *or* fall
in temperature
Tempo *das;* ~s, ~s *od.* Tempi (a) *Pl.* ~s
speed
(b) (Musik) tempo; time
Tempo·limit *das* (Verkehrsw.) speed limit
Tempus *das;* ~, Tempora (Sprachw.) tense
Tendenz *die;* ~, ~en trend
tendieren *itr. V.* tend (**zu** towards)
Teneriffa (*das*); ~s Tenerife
Tennis *das;* ~: tennis *no art.*
Tennis-: ~**ball** *der* tennis ball; ~**platz**
der tennis court; ~**schläger** *der* tennis
racket; ~**schuh** *der* tennis shoe;
~**schule** *die* tennis school; ~**spieler**
der, ~**spielerin** *die* tennis player
Tenor *der;* ~s, Tenöre, (österr. auch:) ~e
(Musik) tenor; (im Chor) tenors *pl.;* tenor
voices *pl.*
Teppich *der;* ~s, ~e carpet; (kleiner) rug
Teppich·boden *der* fitted carpet
Termin *der;* ~s, ~e date; (Anmeldung)
appointment; (Verabredung) engagement;
(Rechtsw.) hearing
Terminal /'tø:ɐ̯mɪnəl/ *das;* ~s, ~s
terminal
Termin-: ~**geschäft** *das* (Börsenw.)
forward transaction *or* operation;
~**kalender** *der* appointments book
Terminus *der;* ~, Termini term
Terpentin *das,* (österr. meist:) *der;* ~s (a)
(Harz) turpentine
(b) (ugs.: Terpentinöl) turps *sing.* (coll.)
Terpentin·öl *das* oil of turpentine
Terrain /tɛ'rɛ̃:/ *das;* ~s, ~s terrain
Terrasse *die;* ~, ~n terrace
Terrier /'tɛrɪɐ̯/ *der;* ~s, ~: terrier
Terrine *die;* ~, ~n tureen
Territorium *das;* ~s, Territorien territory
Terror *der;* ~s terrorism *no art.*
Terror·anschlag *der* terrorist attack
terrorisieren *tr. V.* (a) terrorize

(b) (ugs.: belästigen) pester
Terrorismus *der;* ~: terrorism *no art.*
Terrorist *der;* ~en, ~en, **Terroristin**
die; ~, ~nen terrorist
Terz *die;* ~, ~en (Musik) third
Test *der;* ~[e]s, ~s *od.* ~e test
Testament *das;* ~[e]s, ~e (a) will
(b) (christl. Rel.) Testament
Test·bogen *der* test paper
testen *tr. V.* test (**auf** + *Akk.* for)
teuer [1] *Adj.* expensive; dear *usu. pred.;*
wie ~ **war das?** how much did that cost?
[2] *adv.* expensively; dearly; **etw.** ~ **kaufen/**
verkaufen pay a great deal for sth./sell sth.
at a high price
Teuerung *die;* ~, ~en rise in prices
Teuerungs·rate *die* rate of price
increases
Teufel *der;* ~s, ~: devil
Teufels·zeug *das* (ugs.) terrible stuff (coll.)
teuflisch [1] *Adj.* (a) devilish, fiendish
⟨plan, trick, etc.⟩; diabolical ⟨laughter,
pleasure, etc.⟩
(b) (ugs.: groß, intensiv) terrible (coll.); dreadful
(coll.)
[2] *adv.* (a) diabolically
(b) (ugs.) terribly (coll.)
Text *der;* ~[e]s, ~e text; (Wortlaut) wording;
(eines Theaterstücks) script; (einer Oper) libretto;
(eines Liedes, Chansons usw.) words *pl.;* (eines
Schlagers) words *pl.;* lyrics *pl.;* (zu einer
Abbildung) caption
texten *tr. V.* write ⟨song, advertisement,
etc.⟩
Textilien *Pl.* (a) textiles
(b) (Fertigwaren) textile goods
Textil·industrie *die* textile industry
Text·verarbeitung *die* text processing;
word processing
Thailand (*das*); ~s Thailand
Theater *das;* ~s, ~ (a) theatre; **ins** ~
gehen go to the theatre; **im** ~: at the
theatre; ~ **spielen** act; (fig.) play-act; pretend
(b) (fig. ugs.) fuss
Theater-: ~**abonnement** *das* theatre
subscription [ticket]; ~**stück** *das* [stage]
play
Theke *die;* ~, ~n (a) (Schanktisch) bar
(b) (Ladentisch) counter
Thema *das;* ~s, Themen subject; topic;
(einer Abhandlung) subject; theme; (Leitgedanke)
theme
Themse *die;* ~: Thames
Theologe *der;* ~n, ~n theologian
Theologie *die;* ~, ~n theology *no art.*
Theologin *die;* ~, ~: theologian
theologisch [1] *Adj.* theological
[2] *adv.* theologically
theoretisch [1] *Adj.* theoretical
[2] *adv.* theoretically
Theorie *die;* ~, ~n theory

Therapeut der; ~en, ~en,
 Therapeutin die; ~, ~nen therapist;
 therapeutist
therapeutisch [1] Adj. therapeutic
 [2] adv. therapeutically
Therapie die; ~, ~n therapy (gegen for)
therapieren tr. V. treat
Thermo·meter das (österr. u. schweiz. der
 od. das) thermometer
Thermos·flasche Ⓦ die Thermos flask
 ®; vacuum flask
Thermostat der; ~[e]s od. ~en, ~e od.
 ~en thermostat
These die; ~, ~n thesis
Thron der; ~[e]s, ~e throne
Thun·fisch der tuna
Thüringen (das); ~s Thuringia
Thüringer Wald der; ~ ~[e]s Thuringian
 Forest
Thymian der; ~s, ~e thyme
Tick der; ~[e]s, ~s (a) (ugs.: Schrulle) quirk;
 thing (coll.)
 (b) (ugs.: Nuance) tiny bit; shade
ticken itr. V. tick; **du tickst wohl nicht
 richtig** (salopp) you must be off your rocker
 (coll.)
Ticket das; ~s, ~s ticket
tief [1] Adj. (auch fig.) deep; (niedrig) low; low
 ‹neckline, bow›; deep; intense ‹pain,
 suffering›
 [2] adv. deep; (niedrig) low; (intensiv) deeply;
 ‹stoop, bow› low; ‹breathe, inhale› deeply
Tief das; ~s, ~s (Met.) low
tief·blau Adj. deep blue
Tief·druck der (Met.) low pressure
Tiefe die; ~, ~n depth; **in die ~ stürzen**
 plunge into the depths
tief-, Tief-: ~**garage** die underground
 car park; ~**greifend** [1] Adj. profound;
 profound, deep ‹crisis›; far-reaching
 ‹improvement›; [2] adv. profoundly;
 ~**gründig** Adj. profound; ~|**kühlen** tr. V.
 [deep-]freeze
Tief·kühl-: ~**fach** das freezer
 [compartment]; ~**kost** die frozen food
tief-, Tief-: ~**punkt** der low [point];
 ~**schlag** der (Boxen) low punch; punch
 below the belt (lit. or fig.); ~**see** die (Geogr.)
 deep sea; ~**sinnig** [1] Adj. profound;
 [2] adv. profoundly
Tiefst·temperatur die minimum or
 lowest temperature
Tiegel der; ~s, ~ (zum Kochen) pan;
 (Schmelztiegel) crucible; (Behälter) pot
Tier das; ~[e]s, ~e animal
Tier-: ~**arzt** der, ~**ärztin** die veterinary
 surgeon; vet; ~**garten** der zoo; zoological
 garden; ~**heim** das animal home
tierisch [1] Adj. (a) animal attrib.; savage
 ‹cruelty, crime›

(b) (ugs.: unerträglich groß) terrible (coll.); ~**er
Ernst** deadly seriousness
 [2] adv. (a) ‹roar› like an animal; savagely
 ‹cruel›
 (b) (ugs.: unerträglich) terribly (coll.)
tier-, Tier-: ~**kreis** der (Astron., Astrol.)
 zodiac; ~**kreis·zeichen** das (Astron.,
 Astrol.) sign of the zodiac; ~**lieb** Adj. animal-
 loving attrib.; fond of animals postpos.;
 ~**park** der zoo; ~**pfleger** der,
 ~**pflegerin** die animal keeper;
 ~**quälerei** /---'-/ die cruelty to animals;
 ~**reich** das animal kingdom
Tiger der; ~s, ~: tiger
tilgen tr. V. (a) (geh.) delete ‹word, letter,
 error›; erase ‹record, endorsement›; (fig.) wipe
 out ‹shame, guilt, traces›
 (b) (Wirtsch., Bankw.) repay; pay off
Tilgung die; ~, ~en (a) (geh.) ▶ TILGEN A:
 deletion; erasure; wiping out
 (b) (Wirtsch., Bankw.) repayment
Tilsiter der; ~s, ~: Tilsit [cheese]
Tinte die; ~, ~n ink; **in der ~ sitzen** (ugs.)
 be in the soup (coll.)
Tinten-: ~**fisch** der cuttlefish; (Krake)
 octopus; ~**strahl·drucker** der (DV) ink-jet
 printer
*Tip, Tipp der; ~s, ~s (a) (ugs.) tip
 (b) (bei Toto, Lotto usw.) [row of] numbers
tippen [1] itr. V. (a) **an/gegen etw.** (Akk.) ~:
 tap sth.
 (b) (ugs.: Maschine schreiben) type
 (c) (wetten) do the pools/lottery etc.; **im Lotto
 ~:** do the lottery
 [2] tr. V. (a) tap
 (b) (ugs.: mit der Maschine schreiben) type
 (c) (setzen auf) choose; **sechs Richtige ~:**
 make six correct selections
Tipp-: ~**fehler** der typing error or
 mistake; ~**gemeinschaft** die pools/
 lottery etc. syndicate
tipp·topp (ugs.) [1] Adj. (tadellos)
 immaculate; (erstklassig) tip-top
 [2] adv. immaculately
Tirol (das); ~s [the] Tyrol
Tiroler der; ~s, ~, **Tirolerin** die; ~,
 ~nen Tyrolese; Tyrolean
Tisch der; ~[e]s, ~e table; **reinen ~
 machen** (ugs.) sort things out
Tisch-: ~**dame** die dinner partner;
 ~**decke** die tablecloth; ~**gebet** das grace
 no pl.; ~**herr** der dinner partner; ~**lampe**
 die table lamp
Tischler der; ~s, ~: joiner; (bes. Kunst~)
 cabinetmaker
Tischlerei die; ~, ~en ▶ TISCHLER: (a)
 (Werkstatt) joiner's/cabinetmaker's [workshop]
 (b) (Handwerk) joinery/cabinetmaking
Tischlerin die; ~, ~nen ▶ TISCHLER
Tisch-: ~**nachbar** der person next to one
 [at table]; ~**platte** die table top; ~**tennis**
 das table tennis; ~**tuch** das; Pl. ~**tücher**

tablecloth; **~wäsche** *die* table linen;
~wein *der* table wine; **~zeit** *die*
lunchtime

Titel *der;* ~s, ~ (a) title
(b) (ugs.: Musikstück, Song usw.) number

Titel-: **~bild** *das* cover picture; **~blatt**
das title page; **~rolle** *die* title role;
~seite (a) (einer Zeitung, Zeitschrift) [front]
cover; (b) (eines Buchs) title page

Titte *die;* ~, ~n (derb) tit (coarse)

titulieren *tr. V.* call

tja /tja(:)/ *Interj.* [yes] well; (Resignation
ausdrückend) oh, well

Toast /to:st/ *der;* ~[e]s, ~e *od.* ~s toast

Toast·brot *das* [sliced white] bread for
toasting

toasten *tr. V.* toast

Toaster *der;* ~s, ~: toaster

toben *itr. V.* (a) go wild (vor + *Dat.* with);
(fig.) ⟨storm, sea, battle⟩ rage
(b) (tollen) romp *or* charge about
(c) mit sein (laufen) charge

Tochter *die;* ~, Töchter (a) daughter
(b) (Wirtsch.) subsidiary

Tochter·gesellschaft *die* (Wirtsch.)
subsidiary [company]

Tod *der;* ~[e]s, ~e death; eines natürlichen/
gewaltsamen ~es sterben die a natural/
violent death; jmdn. zum ~e verurteilen
sentence sb. to death

tod·ernst [1] *Adj.* deadly serious
[2] *adv.* deadly seriously

Todes-: **~anzeige** *die* (a) (in einer Zeitung)
death notice; (b) (Karte) card announcing a
person's death; **~fall** *der* death; (in der
Familie) bereavement; **~nachricht** *die*
news of his/her/their *etc.* death; **~opfer**
das death; fatality; **~strafe** *die* death
penalty; **~ursache** *die* cause of death;
~urteil *das* death sentence;
~verachtung *die* [utter] fearlessness in
the face of death; etw. mit ~verachtung
essen/trinken (ugs.) force sth. down [without
showing one's distaste]

Tod·feind *der,* Tod-feindin *die* deadly
enemy

tod·krank *Adj.* critically ill

tödlich [1] *Adj.* (a) fatal ⟨accident, illness,
outcome, etc.⟩; lethal, deadly ⟨poison, bite,
shot, trap, etc.⟩; lethal ⟨dose⟩
(b) (sehr groß, ausgeprägt) deadly ⟨hatred,
seriousness, certainty, boredom⟩
[2] *adv.* (a) fatally
(b) (sehr) terribly (coll.)

tod-, Tod-: **~müde** *Adj.* dead tired;
~schick (ugs.) [1] *Adj.* dead smart (coll.);
[2] *adv.* dead smartly (coll.); **~sicher** (ugs.)
[1] *Adj.* sure-fire (coll.); [2] *adv.* for certain *or*
sure; **~sünde** *die* (auch fig.) deadly *or*
mortal sin; **~unglücklich** *Adj.* (ugs.)
extremely *or* desperately unhappy

Toilette /toa'lɛtə/ *die;* ~, ~n toilet

Toiletten·papier *das* toilet paper

toi, toi, toi /'tɔy: 'tɔy: 'tɔy:/ *Interj.* good
luck!; (unberufen!) touch wood!

Tokio (*das*); ~s Tokyo

tolerant [1] *Adj.* tolerant (gegen of)
[2] *adv.* tolerantly

Toleranz *die;* ~: tolerance

tolerierbar *Adj.* tolerable

tolerieren *tr. V.* tolerate

toll [1] *Adj.* (a) (ugs.) (großartig) great (coll.);
fantastic (coll.); (erstaunlich) amazing; (heftig,
groß) enormous ⟨respect⟩; terrific (coll.) ⟨noise,
storm⟩
(b) (wild) wild
[2] *adv.* (a) (ugs.: großartig) terrifically well
(coll.)
(b) (ugs.: heftig) ⟨rain, snow⟩ like billy-o (coll.)
(c) (wild) bei dem Fest ging es ~ zu it was a
wild party

Tolle *die;* ~, ~n quiff

tollen *itr. V.* (a) romp about
(b) mit sein romp

toll-, Toll-: **~kühn** [1] *Adj.* daredevil
attrib.; daring; [2] *adv.* daringly; **~wut** *die*
rabies *sing.;* **~wütig** *Adj.* rabid

Tollpatsch *der;* ~[e]s, ~e (ugs.) clumsy *or*
awkward creature

tollpatschig (ugs.) [1] *Adj.* clumsy;
awkward
[2] *adv.* clumsily; awkwardly

*Tollpatsch usw. ▶ TOLLPATSCH *usw.*

Tölpel *der;* ~s, ~: fool

tölpelhaft [1] *Adj.* foolish
[2] *adv.* foolishly

Tomate *die;* ~, ~n tomato

Tomaten·mark *das* tomato purée

Tombola *die;* ~, ~s raffle

Ton¹ *der;* ~[e]s, ~e clay

Ton² *der;* ~[e]s, Töne (a) (auch Physik, Musik;
beim Telefon) tone; (Klang) note
(b) (Film, Ferns. usw., Tonwiedergabe) sound
(c) (ugs.: Äußerung) word
(d) (Farb~) shade
(e) (Akzent) stress

ton-, Ton-: **~angebend** *Adj.*
predominant; **~art** *die* (a) (Musik) key; (b)
(fig.) tone; **~band** *das; Pl.* **~bänder** tape;
~band·gerät *das* tape recorder;
~effekt *der* sound effect

tönen [1] *itr. V.* (geh.) sound; ⟨bell⟩ sound,
ring; (schallen, widerhallen) resound
[2] *tr. V.* (färben) tint

Ton-: **~fall** *der* tone; (Intonation) intonation;
~höhe *die* pitch; **~leiter** *die* (Musik) scale

Tonne *die;* ~, ~n (a) (Behälter) drum;
(Mülltonne) bin; (Regentonne) water butt
(b) (Gewicht) tonne

tonnen·weise *Adv., adj.* by the ton

Ton·qualität *die* sound quality

Tönung *die;* ~, ~en tint; shade

Tool /tu:l/ *das;* ~s, ~s (DV) tool

Topf *der;* ~es, Töpfe (a) pot; (Braten~,
Schmor~) casserole; (Stielkasserolle) saucepan ⋯⊱

(b) (zur Aufbewahrung) pot
(c) (Krug) jug
(d) (Nachttopf) chamber pot; (für Kinder) potty (Brit. coll.)
(e) (Blumentopf) [flower]pot

Topf·blume die [flowering] pot plant

Töpfchen das; ~s, ~: potty (Brit. coll.)

Töpfer der; ~s, ~ potter

Töpferei die; ~, ~en **(a)** (Handwerk) pottery no art.;
(b) (Werkstatt) pottery; potter's workshop
(c) (Erzeugnis) piece of pottery; ~en pottery sing.

Töpferin die; ~, ~nen ▶ TÖPFER

Topf-: ~lappen der oven cloth; ~pflanze die pot plant

Tor¹ das; ~[e]s, ~e **(a)** gate; (einer Garage, Scheune) door; (fig.) gateway
(b) (Ballspiele) goal
(c) (Ski) gate

Tor² der; ~en, ~en (geh.: Narr) fool

Torf der; ~[e]s, ~e peat

Torheit die; ~, ~en (geh.) **(a)** foolishness
(b) (Handlung) foolish act

Tor·hüter der, **Tor·hüterin** die (Ballspiele) goalkeeper

töricht (geh.) ⊡ Adj. foolish
⊡ adv. foolishly

torkeln itr. V.; mit sein stagger

Tor·mann der; Pl. **Tormänner** od. **Torleute** (Ballspiele) goalkeeper

Tornister /tɔrˈnɪstɐ/ der; ~s, ~: knapsack; (Schulranzen) satchel

torpedieren tr. V. (Milit., fig.) torpedo

Torpedo der; ~s, ~s torpedo

Törtchen das; ~s, ~: tartlet

Torte die; ~, ~n (Creme-, Sahnetorte) gateau; (Obsttorte) [fruit] flan

Torten-: ~boden der flan case; (ohne Rand) flan base; ~guss, *~guß der glaze; ~heber der; ~s, ~: cake slice

Tortur die; ~, ~en **(a)** ordeal
(b) (veralt.: Folter) torture

Tor-: ~wart der; ~~[e]s, ~~e, ~wartin die; ~~, ~~nen (Ballspiele) goalkeeper; ~weg der gateway

tosen itr. V. roar; ⟨storm⟩ rage

tot Adj. dead; ~ umfallen drop dead; sich ~ stellen pretend to be dead; play dead; ~ geboren stillborn

total ⊡ Adj. total
⊡ adv. totally

Total·ausverkauf der clearance sale

totalitär (Politik) ⊡ Adj. totalitarian
⊡ adv. in a totalitarian way; ⟨organized, run⟩ along totalitarian lines

Total·schaden der (Versicherungsw.) **an beiden Fahrzeugen entstand ~:** both vehicles were a write-off

tot|ärgern refl. V. (ugs.) get livid (coll.)

Tote der/die; adj. Dekl. dead person; **die ~n** the dead

töten tr., itr. V. kill; deaden ⟨nerve etc.⟩

toten-, Toten-: ~blass, *~blaß, ~bleich Adj. deathly pale; ~gräber der; ~~s, ~~, ~gräberin die; ~~, ~~nen gravedigger; ~kopf der **(a)** skull; **(b)** (als Symbol) death's head; (mit gekreuzten Knochen) skull and crossbones; ~schädel der skull; ~sonntag der (ev. Kirche) Sunday before Advent on which the dead are commemorated; ~still Adj. deathly quiet; ~stille die deathly silence; ~wache die vigil by the body

tot-, Tot-: ~|fahren unr. tr. V. [run over and] kill; *~geboren ▶ TOT; ~geburt die still birth; ~|lachen refl. V. (ugs.) kill oneself laughing; **zum Totlachen sein** be killing (coll.)

Toto das od. der; ~s, ~s **(a)** (Pferdetoto) tote (coll.); **im ~:** on the tote
(b) (Fußballtoto) [football] pools pl.; **[im] ~ spielen** do the pools

Toto·schein der; ▶ TOTO: pools coupon/ (coll.) tote ticket

tot-, Tot-: ~|schießen unr. tr. V. (ugs.) jmdn. ~schießen shoot sb. dead; ~schlag der (Rechtsw.) manslaughter no indef. art.; ~|schlagen unr. tr. V. beat to death; *~|stellen ▶ TOT; ~|treten unr. tr. V. trample ⟨person⟩ to death; step on and kill ⟨insect⟩

Tötung die; ~, ~en killing; **fahrlässige ~** (Rechtsspr.) manslaughter by culpable negligence

Touch /tatʃ/ der; ~s, ~s (ugs.) touch

tough /taf/ Adj. (ugs.) tough

Toupet /tuˈpeː/ das; ~s, ~s toupee

toupieren /tuˈpiːrən/ tr. V. backcomb

Tour /tuːɐ̯/ die; ~, ~en tour **(durch** of); (kürzere Fahrt, Ausflug) trip; (mit dem Auto) drive; (mit dem Fahrrad) ride; (feste Strecke) route; **in einer ~** (ugs.) the whole time

touren /ˈtuːrən/ itr. V.; mit sein tour

Tourismus /tuˈrɪsmʊs/ der; ~: tourism no art.

Tourismus·branche die tourism industry; tourist industry;

Tourist der; ~en, ~en tourist

Touristen-: ~klasse die tourist class; ~zentrum das tourist centre

Touristin die; ~, ~nen tourist

Tournee /tʊrˈneː/ die; ~, ~s od. ~n tour; **auf ~ sein/gehen** be/go on tour

Trab der; ~[e]s trot; **im ~:** at a trot; **im ~ reiten** trot

traben itr. V.; mit sein (auch ugs.: laufen) trot

Tracht die; ~, ~en **(a)** (Volkstracht) national costume; (Berufstracht) uniform
(b) **eine ~ Prügel** a thrashing; (als Strafe) a hiding

trachten itr. V. (geh.) strive **(nach** for, after)

Tradition die; ~, ~en tradition

traditionell ①*Adj.* traditional
②*adv.* traditionally

traf *1. u. 3. Pers. Sg. Prät. v.* TREFFEN

träfe *1. u. 3. Pers. Sg. Konjunktiv II v.*
TREFFEN

Trafik *die;* ～, ～en (österr.) tobacconist's
[shop]

Trag·bahre *die* stretcher

tragbar *Adj.* (a) portable
(b) wearable ⟨*clothes*⟩
(c) (finanziell) supportable ⟨*cost, debt, etc.*⟩
(d) (erträglich) bearable; tolerable

träge ①*Adj.* sluggish
②*adv.* sluggishly

Trage *die;* ～, ～n (a) (Bahre) stretcher
(b) (Traggestell) pannier

tragen ①*unr. tr. V.* (a) carry
(b) (bringen) take
(c) (ertragen) bear ⟨*fate, destiny*⟩; bear, endure
⟨*suffering*⟩
(d) (halten) hold; **einen/den linken Arm in der
Schlinge** ～: have one's arm/one's left arm
in a sling
(e) (von unten stützen) support
(f) (belastbar sein durch) be able to carry *or*
take ⟨*weight*⟩
(g) (übernehmen, aufkommen für) bear, carry
⟨*costs etc.*⟩; take ⟨*blame, responsibility,
consequences*⟩
(h) (am Körper) wear ⟨*clothes, wig, glasses,
jewellery, etc.*⟩
(i) have ⟨*false teeth, beard, etc.*⟩
(j) (hervorbringen) ⟨*tree*⟩ bear ⟨*fruit*⟩; ⟨*field*⟩
produce ⟨*crops*⟩
②*unr. itr. V.* (a) carry
(b) (am Körper) **man trägt [wieder] kurz/lang**
short/long skirts are in fashion [again]
(c) **der Baum trägt gut** the tree produces a
good crop

tragend *Adj.* (Stabilität gebend) load-bearing;
supporting ⟨*wall, column, function, etc.*⟩

Träger *der;* ～s, ～ (a) porter
(b) (Austräger) paper boy/girl; delivery boy/
girl
(c) (Bauw.) girder; [supporting] beam
(d) (an Kleidung) strap; (Hosenträger) braces *pl.;*
(e) (Inhaber) ⟨*eines Amts*⟩ holder; ⟨*eines Namens,
Titels*⟩ bearer; ⟨*eines Preises*⟩ winner

Trägerin *die;* ～, ～nen ▶ TRÄGER A, B, E

Trage·tasche *die* carrier bag

Trag-: ～**fähigkeit** *die* load-bearing
capacity; ～**fläche** *die* wing;
～**flügel·boot** *das* hydrofoil

Trägheit *die;* ～, ～en sluggishness

Tragik *die;* ～: tragedy

tragi·komisch ①*Adj.* tragicomic
②*adv.* tragicomically

tragisch ①*Adj.* tragic; **das ist nicht [so]**
～ (ugs.) it's not the end of the world (coll.)
②*adv.* tragically

Tragödie /tra'gø:dȷə/ *die;* ～, ～n tragedy

Trag·weite *die* consequences *pl.*

Trainer /'trɛːnɐ/ *der;* ～s, ～, **Trainerin**
die; ～, ～nen coach; trainer; (einer
Fußballmannschaft) manager

trainieren ①*tr. V.* (a) train; coach
⟨*swimmer, tennis player*⟩; manage ⟨*football
team*⟩; exercise ⟨*muscles etc.*⟩
(b) (üben, einüben) practise ⟨*exercise, jump,
etc.*⟩; **Fußball** ～: do football training
②*itr. V.* train

Training /'trɛːnɪŋ/ *das;* ～s, ～s training *no
indef. art.*

Trainings-: ～**anzug** *der* track suit;
～**hose** *die* track-suit bottoms *pl.* ～**lager**
das training camp

Trakt *der;* ～[e]s, ～e section; (Flügel) wing

Traktor *der;* ～s, ～en tractor

trällern *itr., tr. V.* warble

trampeln ①*itr. V.* (a) [mit den Füßen] ～:
stamp one's feet
(b) *mit sein* (treten) trample (**auf** + *Akk.* on)
②*tr. V.* trample

Trampel·pfad *der* [beaten] path

trampen /'trɛmpn̩/ *itr. V. mit sein* hitch-
hike

Tramper *der;* ～s, ～, **Tramperin** *die;* ～,
～nen hitch-hiker

Trampolin *das;* ～s, ～e trampoline

Tramway /'tramve/ *die;* ～, ～s (österr.)
tram (Brit.); streetcar (Amer.)

Tran *der;* ～[e]s train-oil

Trance /'trã:s(ə)/ *die;* ～, ～n trance; **in** ～:
in a trance

tranchieren /trã'ʃiːrən/ *tr. V.* carve

Träne *die;* ～, ～n tear; ～**n lachen** laugh till
one cries

tränen *itr. V.* ⟨*eyes*⟩ water

tranig *Adj.* (ugs. abwertend: langsam) sluggish;
slow

trank *1. u. 3. Pers. Sg. Prät. v.* TRINKEN

Tränke *die;* ～, ～n watering place

tränken *tr. V.* (a) water
(b) (sich voll saugen lassen) soak

Transfer *der;* ～s, ～s (bes. Wirtsch., Sport)
transfer

Transfer·summe *die* transfer fee

Trans·formator *der;* ～s, ～en
transformer

Transistor *der;* ～s, ～en transistor

Transit /tran'ziːt, *auch:* 'tranzɪt/ *das;* ～s,
～s transit visa

transitiv (Sprachw.) ①*Adj.* transitive
②*adv.* transitively

Transit·verkehr *der* transit traffic

transparent *Adj.* transparent; (Licht
durchlassend) translucent

Transparent *das;* ～[e]s, ～e (Spruchband)
banner; (Bild) transparency

Transparenz *die;* ～ transparency

Transport *der;* ～[e]s, ～e (a)
transportation ⋯⟩

(b) (beförderte Lebewesen od. Sachen) (mit dem Zug) trainload; (mit mehreren Fahrzeugen) convoy; (Fracht) consignment

transportabel *Adj.* transportable; (tragbar) portable

Transporteur /...'tø:ɐ̯/ *der;* ~s, ~e, **Transporteurin** *die;* ~, ~nen carrier

transport·fähig *Adj.* moveable

transportieren *tr. V.* transport ⟨goods, people⟩; move ⟨patient⟩

Transport·kosten *Pl.* carriage *sing.;* transport costs

Transvestit *der;* ~en, ~en transvestite

Trapez *das;* ~es, ~e **(a)** (Geom.) trapezium (Brit.); trapezoid (Amer.)
(b) (im Zirkus) trapeze

trappeln *itr. V.; mit sein* patter [along]; ⟨feet⟩ patter; ⟨hoofs⟩ go clip-clop

Trara *das;* ~s (ugs.) razzmatazz (coll.)

Trasse *die;* ~, ~n (Verkehrsweg) [marked-out] route *or* line

trat *1. u. 3. Pers. Sg. Prät. v.* TRETEN

Tratsch *der;* ~[e]s (ugs.) gossip; tittle-tattle

tratschen *itr. V.* (ugs.) gossip; (schwatzen) chatter

Traube *die;* ~, ~n **(a)** bunch; (von Johannisbeeren usw.) cluster
(b) (Weinbeere~) grape
(c) (Menschenmenge) bunch; cluster

trauen [1] *itr. V.* jmdm./einer Sache ~: trust sb./sth.
[2] *refl. V.* dare
[3] *tr. V.* (verheiraten) ⟨vicar, registrar, etc.⟩ marry

Trauer *die;* ~ **(a)** grief (über + *Akk.* over); (um einen Toten) mourning (um + *Akk.* for)
(b) (Trauerzeit) [period of] mourning
(c) ~ tragen be in mourning

Trauer-: ~**fall** *der* bereavement; ~**feier** *die* memorial ceremony; (beim Begräbnis) funeral ceremony; ~**karte** *die* [pre-printed] card of condolence; ~**kleidung** *die* mourning clothes *pl.*

trauern *itr. V.* mourn; um jmdn. ~: mourn for sb.

Trauer-: ~**spiel** *das* tragedy; (fig. ugs.) deplorable business; ~**weide** *die* weeping willow

träufeln *tr. V.* [let] trickle (in + *Akk.* into); drip ⟨ear drops etc.⟩

Traum *der;* ~[e]s, Träume /'trɔʏmə/ dream

Trauma *das;* ~s, Traumen *od.* ~ta (Psych., Med.) trauma

traumatisch (Psych., Med.) [1] *Adj.* traumatic
[2] *adv.* traumatically

träumen [1] *itr. V.* dream (von of, about); (unaufmerksam sein) [day]dream
[2] *tr. V.* dream

Träumer *der;* ~s, ~, **Träumerin** *die;* ~, ~nen dreamer

träumerisch [1] *Adj.* dreamy
[2] *adv.* dreamily

traumhaft (ugs.) [1] *Adj.* marvellous; fabulous (coll.)
[2] *adv.* fabulously (coll.)

Traum·urlaub *der* dream holiday

traurig [1] *Adj.* **(a)** sad; unhappy ⟨childhood, youth⟩; painful ⟨duty⟩
(b) (kümmerlich) sorry ⟨state etc.⟩; miserable ⟨result⟩
[2] *adv.* sadly

Traurigkeit *die;* ~: sadness; sorrow

Trau-: ~**ring** *der* wedding ring; ~**schein** *der* marriage certificate

Trauung *die;* ~, ~en wedding [ceremony]

Trau·zeuge *der,* **Trau·zeugin** *die* witness ⟨at wedding ceremony⟩

Trecker *der;* ~s, ~: tractor

Treff *der;* ~s, ~s (ugs.) rendezvous; (Ort) meeting place

treffen [1] *unr. tr. V.* **(a)** hit; ⟨punch, blow, object⟩ strike; **ihn trifft keine Schuld** he is in no way to blame
(b) (erschüttern) affect [deeply]; (verletzen) hurt
(c) (begegnen) meet
(d) (vorfinden) come upon, find ⟨anomalies etc.⟩; **es gut/schlecht ~:** be *or* strike lucky/be unlucky
(e) (als Funktionsverb) make ⟨arrangements, choice, preparations, decision, etc.⟩
[2] *unr. itr. V.* **(a)** ⟨person, shot, etc.⟩ hit the target; **nicht ~:** miss [the target]
(b) *mit sein* auf etw. (*Akk.*) ~: come upon sth.; **auf Widerstand/Ablehnung/Schwierigkeiten ~:** meet with resistance/rejection/difficulties
[3] *unr. refl. V.* **(a)** sich mit jmdm. ~: meet sb.
(b) *unpers.* es trifft sich gut/schlecht it is convenient/inconvenient

Treffen *das;* ~s, ~: meeting

treffend [1] *Adj.* apt
[2] *adv.* aptly

Treffer *der;* ~s, ~ **(a)** (Milit., Boxen, Fechten usw.) hit; (Schlag) blow; (Ballspiele) goal
(b) (Gewinn) win; (Los) winner

trefflich (geh.) [1] *Adj.* excellent; splendid ⟨person⟩
[2] *adv.* excellently; splendidly

treff-, Treff-: ~**punkt** *der* meeting place; ~**sicher** [1] *Adj.* accurate ⟨language, mode of expression⟩; unerring ⟨judgement⟩; [2] *adv.* accurately; ~**sicherheit** *die* accuracy

Treib·eis *das* drift-ice

treiben [1] *unr. tr. V.* **(a)** drive
(b) (sich beschäftigen mit) go in for ⟨farming, cattle breeding, etc.⟩; study ⟨French etc.⟩; carry on, pursue ⟨studies, trade, craft⟩; **viel Sport ~:** do a lot of sport; **es wüst/übel/toll ~** (ugs.) lead a dissolute/bad life/live it up

② *unr. itr. V. meist, mit Richtungsangabe nur, mit sein* drift

Treiben *das;* ~s (a) (Durcheinander) bustle (b) (Tun) activities *pl.;* doings *pl.*

Treib-: ~**gas** *das* propellant; ~**haus** *das* hothouse; ~**haus-effekt** *der* greenhouse effect; ~**haus-gas** *das* greenhouse gas; ~**stoff** *der* fuel

Trekking *das;* ~s trekking

Trenchcoat /'trɛntʃkoʊt/ *der;* ~s, ~s trench coat

Trend *der;* ~s, ~s trend (**zu** + *Dat.* towards); (Mode) vogue

trendig *Adj.* (ugs.) modern and fashionable

trennen ① *tr. V.* (a) separate (**von** from); sever ⟨*head, arm*⟩
(b) (auftrennen) unpick ⟨*dress, seam*⟩
(c) (teilen) divide ⟨*word, parts of a room etc., fig.: people*⟩
② *refl. V.* (a) (voneinander weggehen) part [company]
(b) (eine Partnerschaft auflösen) ⟨*couple, partners*⟩ split up
(c) **sich von etw.** ~: part with sth.

Trennung *die;* ~, ~en (von Menschen) separation (**von** from); (von Gegenständen) parting; (von Wörtern) division

trepp-: ~**ab** *Adv.* down the stairs; ~**auf** *Adv.* up the stairs

Treppe *die;* ~, ~n staircase; [flight *sing.* of] stairs *pl.;* (im Freien, auf der Bühne) [flight *sing.* of] steps *pl.*

Treppen-: ~**absatz** *der* half-landing; ~**geländer** *das* banisters *pl.;* ~**haus** *das* stairwell; ~**stufe** *die* stair; (im Freien) step

Tresen *der;* ~s, ~ (bes. nordd.) bar; (Ladentisch) counter

Tresor *der;* ~s, ~e safe

Tret-boot *das* pedalo

treten ① *unr. itr. V.* (a) *mit sein* step (**in** + *Akk.* into, **auf** + *Akk.* on to)
(b) (seinen Fuß setzen) **auf etw.** (*Akk.*) ~ tread on sth.
(c) (ausschlagen) kick
② *unr. tr. V.* (a) (Tritt versetzen) kick ⟨*person, ball, etc.*⟩
(b) (trampeln) trample ⟨*path*⟩
(c) (mit dem Fuß niederdrücken) step on ⟨*brake, pedal*⟩; operate ⟨*bellows, clutch*⟩

treu ① *Adj.* faithful; loyal; faithful ⟨*husband, wife*⟩; loyal ⟨*ally, subject*⟩; **jmdm.** ~ **sein** be true to sb.; **sich selbst** (*Dat.*)/ **seinem Glauben** ~ **bleiben** be true to oneself/one's faith
② *adv.* faithfully; loyally

Treue *die;* ~ (a) loyalty; (von [Ehe]partnern) fidelity
(b) (Genauigkeit) accuracy

treu-, Treu-: ~**hand[anstalt]** *die* (Wirtschaft) German privatization agency; ~**herzig** ① *Adj.* ingenuous; (naiv) naïve; (unschuldig) innocent; ② *adv.* ingenuously; (naiv) naïvely; (unschuldig) innocently;

~**herzigkeit** *die;* ~~: ingenuousness; (Naivität) naivety; (Unschuld) innocence; ~**los** ① *Adj.* disloyal, faithless ⟨*friend, person*⟩; unfaithful ⟨*husband, wife, lover*⟩; ② *adv.* faithlessly

Tribunal *das;* ~s, ~e tribunal

Tribüne *die;* ~, ~n [grand]stand

Tribut *der;* ~[e]s, ~e due; **einer Sache** (*Dat.*) ~ **zollen** pay the price for sth.

Trichter *der;* ~s, ~ funnel

Trick *der;* ~s, ~s trick; (fig.: List) ploy

Trick-film *der* animated cartoon [film]

trieb 1. u. 3. *Pers. Sg. Prät. v.* TREIBEN

Trieb *der;* ~[e]s, ~e (a) (innerer Antrieb) impulse; (Drang) urge; (Verlangen) [compulsive] desire
(b) (Spross) shoot

trieb-, Trieb-: ~**feder** *die* mainspring; (fig.) driving *or* motivating force; ~**haft** ① *Adj.* compulsive; carnal ⟨*sensuality*⟩; ② *adv.* compulsively; ~**täter** *der,* ~**täterin** *die,* ~**verbrecher** *der,* ~**verbrecherin** *die: offender committing a crime in gratifying a compulsive desire;* (Sexualtäter) sexual offender; ~**wagen** *der* (Eisenb.) railcar; ~**werk** *das* engine

triefen *unr. od. regelm. itr. V.* (a) *mit sein* (fließen) (in Tropfen) drip; (in kleinen Rinnsalen) trickle
(b) (nass sein) be dripping wet; ⟨*nose*⟩ run

triff *Imperativ Sg. v.* TREFFEN

trifft 3. *Pers. Sg. Präsens v.* TREFFEN

triftig *Adj.* good ⟨*reason, excuse*⟩; valid, convincing ⟨*motive, argument*⟩

Trikot¹ /tri'ko:/ *der od. das;* ~s, ~s (Stoff) cotton jersey

Trikot² /tri'ko:/ *das;* ~s, ~ (ärmellos) singlet; (eines Tänzers) leotard; (eines Fußballspielers) shirt

Triller *der;* ~s, ~: trill

trillern ① *itr. V.* trill
② *tr. V.* warble ⟨*song*⟩

Triller-pfeife *die* police/referee's whistle

Trillion *die;* ~, ~en quintillion

Trimm-dich-Pfad *der* keep-fit trail

trimmen *tr. V.* (durch Sport) get ⟨*person*⟩ into shape

trinken ① *unr. itr. V.* drink; **auf jmdn./etw.** ~: drink to sb./sth.
② *unr. tr. V.* drink; **einen Kaffee/ein Bier** ~: have a coffee/beer

Trinker *der;* ~s, ~: alcoholic

Trinkerei *die;* ~, ~en drinking *no art.*

Trinkerin *die;* ~, ~nen alcoholic

Trink-: ~**geld** *das* tip; ~**halle** *die* (a) (in einem Heilbad) pump room; (b) (Kiosk) refreshment kiosk; (größer) refreshment stall; ~**wasser** *das* drinking water; „kein ~wasser" 'not for drinking'

Trio *das;* ~s, ~s (Musik, fig.) trio

Trip *der;* ~s, ~s (a) (ugs.: Ausflug) trip; jaunt
(b) (Drogenjargon: Rausch) trip (coll.) ⋯❖

(c) (Drogenjargon: Dosis) fix (sl.)

trippeln itr. V.; mit sein trip; ⟨child⟩ patter

trist Adj. dreary; dismal

tritt Imperativ Sg. u. 3. Pers. Sg. Präsens v.
TRETEN

Tritt der; ~[e]s, ~e (Schritt; Trittbrett) step;
(Fußtritt) kick

Tritt-: ~**brett** das step; ~**brett·fahrer**
der, ~**brett·fahrerin** die (fig. abwertend) ≈
free rider (Amer.); person who profits from
another's work

Triumph der; ~[e]s, ~e triumph

triumphieren itr. V. **(a)** exult
(b) (siegen) be triumphant; triumph (lit. or fig.)
(über + Akk. over)

trivial ① Adj. **(a)** (platt) banal; trite;
(unbedeutend) trivial
(b) (alltäglich) humdrum ⟨life, career⟩
② adv. (platt) banally; ⟨say etc.⟩ tritely

trocken ① Adj. (auch fig.) dry
② adv. drily

Trocken·haube die [hood-type] hairdrier

Trockenheit die; ~, ~en **(a)** dryness
(b) (Dürreperiode) drought

trocken-, Trocken-: ~|**legen** tr. V. **(a)**
ein Baby ~legen change a baby's nappies
(Brit.) or (Amer.) diapers; **(b)** (entwässern) drain
⟨marsh, pond, etc.⟩; ~**milch** die dried milk;
~|**reiben** unr. tr. V. rub ⟨hair, child, etc.⟩
dry; wipe ⟨crockery, window, etc.⟩ dry

trocknen ① itr. V.; meist mit sein dry
② tr. V. dry

Troddel die; ~, ~n tassel

Trödel der; ~s (ugs.) junk; (für den Flohmarkt)
jumble

trödeln itr. V. **(a)** (ugs.) dawdle (mit over)
(b) mit sein (ugs.: schlendern) saunter

Trödler der; ~s, ~, **Trödlerin** die; ~,
~nen (ugs.) junk dealer

troff 1. u. 3. Pers. Sg. Prät. v. TRIEFEN

trog 1. u. 3. Pers. Sg. Prät. v. TRÜGEN

Trog der; ~[e]s, Tröge trough

trollen (ugs.) refl. V. push off (coll.)

Trommel die; ~, ~n drum

Trommel·bremse die drum brake

trommeln itr. V. **(a)** beat the drum; (als
Beruf, Hobby usw.) play the drums
(b) ([auf etw.] schlagen, auftreffen) drum (auf +
Akk. on, an + Akk. against)

Trommel·wirbel der drum roll

Trommler der; ~s, ~ drummer

Trompete die; ~, ~n trumpet

trompeten ① itr. V. play the trumpet; (fig.)
⟨elephant⟩ trumpet
② tr. V. play ⟨piece⟩ on the trumpet

Trompeter der; ~s, ~, **Trompeterin**
die; ~, ~nen trumpeter

Tropen Pl. tropics

Tropen- tropical

Tropen·helm der sun helmet

Tropf der; ~[e]s, ~e (Med.) drip

Tröpfchen das; ~s, ~: droplet; (kleine
Menge) drop

tröpfeln ① itr. V. **(a)** mit sein drip (auf +
Akk. on to, aus, von from)
(b) unpers. (ugs.: leicht regnen) es tröpfelt it's
spitting [with rain]
② tr. V. let ⟨sth.⟩ drip (in + Akk. into, auf +
Akk. on to)

tropfen ① itr. V.; mit Richtungsangabe mit
sein drop; ⟨tears⟩ fall; unpers. es tropft [vom
Dach usw.] water is dripping from the roof
etc.;
② tr. V. let ⟨sth.⟩ drip (in + Akk. into, auf +
Akk. on to)

Tropfen der; ~s, ~ drop; ein guter/edler ~:
a good/fine vintage

Tropf·stein·höhle die limestone cave
with stalactites and/or stalagmites

Trophäe die; ~, ~n (hist., Jagd, Sport) trophy

tropisch Adj. tropical

Tross, *Troß der; Trosses, Trosse
(a) (Milit.) baggage train
(b) (Gefolge) retinue; (fig.: Zug) procession [of
hangers-on]

Trost der; ~[e]s consolation; (bes. geistlich)
comfort; nicht [ganz od. recht] bei ~ sein
(ugs.) be out of one's mind

trösten ① tr. V. comfort, console (mit with)
② refl. V. console oneself

tröstlich Adj. comforting

trost·los Adj. **(a)** hopeless; (verzweifelt) in
despair postpos.;
(b) (deprimierend, öde) miserable; dreary;
hopeless ⟨situation⟩

Trostlosigkeit die; ~ **(a)** (einer Person, der
Lage usw.) hopelessness; (Verzweiflung)
despair
(b) (Öde) dreariness

Trost·preis der consolation prize

Tröstung die; ~, ~en comfort no indef. art.

Trott der; ~[e]s, ~e trot; (fig.) routine

Trottel der; ~s, ~ (ugs.) fool

trottelig (ugs.) ① Adj. doddery
② adv. in a feeble-minded way

trotten itr. V.; mit sein trot [along]

trotz Präp. mit Gen., seltener mit Dat. in
spite of; despite

Trotz der; ~es defiance

trotz·dem /auch: ′-′-/ Adv. nevertheless

trotzen itr. V. **(a)** (geh.: widerstehen) jmdm./
einer Sache ~ (auch fig.) defy sb./sth.
(b) (trotzig sein) be contrary

trotzig ① Adj. defiant; (widerspenstig)
contrary; difficult ⟨child⟩
② adv. defiantly

trüb[e] ① Adj. **(a)** (nicht klar) murky ⟨stream,
water⟩; cloudy ⟨liquid, wine, juice⟩;
(schlammig) muddy ⟨puddle⟩; (schmutzig) dirty
⟨glass, window pane⟩; dull ⟨eyes⟩

---

*alte Schreibung - vgl. Hinweis auf S. xiv

(b) (nicht hell) dim ⟨*light*⟩; dull, dismal ⟨*day, weather*⟩; grey, overcast ⟨*sky*⟩
2 *adv.* ⟨*shine, light*⟩ dimly

Trubel *der;* ~s [hustle and] bustle; **sie stürzten sich in den dicksten ~:** they plunged into the thick of the hurly-burly

trüben 1 *tr. V.* **(a)** make ⟨*liquid*⟩ cloudy; cloud ⟨*liquid*⟩
(b) (beeinträchtigen) dampen ⟨*mood*⟩; mar ⟨*relationship*⟩; cloud ⟨*judgement*⟩
2 *refl. V.* ⟨*liquid*⟩ become cloudy; ⟨*eyes*⟩ become dull; ⟨*sky*⟩ darken

Trübsal *die;* ~, ~e (geh.) **(a)** (Leiden) affliction
(b) (Kummer) grief; ~ **blasen** (ugs.) mope (**wegen** over, about)

trüb-, Trüb-: ~**selig** 1 *Adj.* **(a)** (öde) dreary, depressing ⟨*place, area, colour*⟩; **(b)** (traurig) gloomy; 2 *adv.* (traurig) gloomily; ~**seligkeit** *die:* **(a)** (Ödheit) dreariness; **(b)** (Traurigkeit) gloom; ~**sinn** *der* melancholy; ~**sinnig** 1 *Adj.* melancholy; 2 *adv.* gloomily

Trübung *die;* ~, ~en **(a)** clouding; (des Auges) dimming
(b) (Beeinträchtigung) deterioration; (der Stimmung) dampening

trudeln *itr. V. mit sein* roll

Trüffel *die;* ~, ~n truffle

trug *1. u. 3. Pers. Prät. v.* TRAGEN

trüge *1. u. 3. Pers. Sg. Konjunktiv II v.* TRAGEN

trügen 1 *unr. tr. V.* deceive
2 *unr. itr. V.* be deceptive; ⟨*feeling, deception*⟩ be a delusion

trügerisch 1 *Adj.* deceptive; false ⟨*hope, sign, etc.*⟩; treacherous ⟨*ice*⟩
2 *adv.* deceptively

Truhe *die;* ~, ~n chest

Trümmer *Pl.* (eines Gebäudes) rubble *sing.;* (Ruinen) ruins; (eines Flugzeugs usw.) wreckage *sing.;* (kleinere Teile) debris *sing.*

Trümmer·haufen *der* pile *or* heap of rubble

Trumpf *der;* ~[e]s, Trümpfe (auch fig.) trump [card]; (Farbe) trumps *pl.;* ~ **sein** (fig.: Mode sein) be the in thing

trumpfen *itr. V.* play a trump

Trunk *der;* ~[e]s, Trünke (geh.) (Getränk) drink; beverage (formal)

Trunkenheit *die;* ~: drunkenness; ~ **am Steuer** drink-driving

Trunk·sucht *die* alcoholism *no art.*

trunk·süchtig *Adj.* alcoholic; ~ **sein** be an alcoholic

Trupp *der;* ~s, ~s troop; (von Arbeitern, Gefangenen) gang; (von Soldaten, Polizisten) squad

Truppe *die;* ~, ~n (a) (Einheit der Streitkräfte) unit
(b) *Pl.* (Soldaten) troops
(c) (Streitkräfte) [armed] forces *pl.;* (Heer) army
(d) (Gruppe von Schauspielern, Artisten) troupe; (von Sportlern) squad

Trut·hahn *der* turkey [cock]

tschau *Interj.* (ugs.) ciao (coll.)

Tscheche *der;* ~n, ~n Czech

Tschechien (*das*) ~s Czech Republic

Tschechin *die;* ~, ~nen Czech

tschechisch *Adj.* Czech

Tschechoslowakei *die;* ~ (hist.) Czechoslovakia *no art.*

tschechoslowakisch *Adj.* (hist.) Czechoslovak[ian]

tschüs *Interj.* (ugs.) bye (coll.)

Tsd. *Abk.* = **Tausend**

T-Shirt /'tiːʃəːt/ *das;* ~s, ~s T-shirt

Tube *die;* ~, ~n tube

Tuberkulose *die;* ~, ~n (Med.) tuberculosis *no art.*

Tuch *das;* ~[e]s, Tücher *od.* ~e (a) *Pl.* Tücher cloth; (Kopf-, Halstuch) scarf
(b) *Pl.* ~e (Gewebe) cloth

Tuch·fühlung *die* (scherzh.) physical contact

tüchtig 1 *Adj.* **(a)** efficient; (fähig) capable, competent (**in** + *Dat.* at)
(b) (ugs.: beträchtlich) sizeable ⟨*piece, portion*⟩; big ⟨*gulp*⟩; hearty ⟨*eater, appetite*⟩
2 *adv.* **(a)** efficiently; (fähig) competently
(b) (ugs.: sehr) really ⟨*cold, warm*⟩; ⟨*snow, rain*⟩ good and proper (coll.); ⟨*eat*⟩ heartily

Tüchtigkeit *die;* ~: efficiency; (Fähigkeit) ability; competence; (Fleiß) industry

Tücke *die;* ~, ~n (a) (Hinterhältigkeit) deceit[fulness]; (List) guile
(b) ([verborgene] Gefahr/Schwierigkeit) [hidden] danger/difficulty

tuckern *itr. V.; mit Richtungsangabe mit sein* chug

tückisch 1 *Adj.* **(a)** (hinterhältig) wily; (betrügerisch) deceitful
(b) (gefährlich) treacherous ⟨*bend, slope, spot, etc.*⟩
2 *adv.* craftily

tüfteln *itr. V.* (ugs.) fiddle (**an** + *Dat.* with); do finicky work (**an** + *Dat.* on); (geistig) rack one's brains (**an** + *Dat.* over)

Tugend *die;* ~, ~en virtue

tugendhaft 1 *Adj.* virtuous
2 *adv.* virtuously

Tüll *der;* ~s, ~e tulle

Tülle *die;* ~, ~n (bes. nordd.) spout

Tulpe *die;* ~, ~n tulip

tummeln *refl. V.* romp [about]

Tummel·platz *der* (auch fig.) playground

Tumor *der;* ~s, ~en (Med.) tumour

Tümpel *der;* ~s, ~ pond

Tumult *der;* ~[e]s, ~e tumult; commotion; (Protest) uproar

tun 1 *unr. tr. V.* (a) do; **so etwas tut man nicht** that is just not done; [**etwas**] **mit etw./ jmdm. zu ~ haben** be concerned with sth./ have dealings with sb.
(b) *als Funktionsverb* make ⟨*remark, catch, etc.*⟩; take ⟨*step, jump*⟩; do ⟨*deed*⟩ ⋯⟶

(c) (bewirken) work, perform ⟨miracle⟩
(d) (antun) jmdm. etw. ~: do sth. to sb.
(e) es ~ (ugs.: genügen) be good enough
(f) (ugs.: irgendwohin bringen) put
2 *unr. itr. V.* (a) (ugs.: funktionieren) work
(b) freundlich/geheimnisvoll ~: pretend to be or (coll.) act friendly/act mysteriously
3 *unr. refl. V.; unpers.* **es hat sich einiges getan** quite a bit has happened

Tünche *die;* ~, ~n distemper; wash; [weiße] ~: whitewash

tünchen *tr.* (*auch itr.*) *V.* distemper; weiß ~: whitewash

Tunell *das;* ~s, ~s (südd., österr., schweiz.)
▶ TUNNEL

tunen /'tjuːnən/ *tr. V.* (Kfz-W.) tune

Tuner /'tjuːnɐ/ *der;* ~s, ~(a) (Elektronik) tuner
(b) (Kfz-W.) tuner; tuning expert

Tunesien /tuˈneːzi̯ən/ (*das*) ~s Tunisia

tunesisch *Adj.* Tunisian

Tunke *die;* ~, ~n (bes. ostmd.) sauce; (Bratensoße) gravy

tunken *tr. V.* (bes. ostmd.) dip

tunlichst *Adv.* (geh.) (a) (möglichst) as far as possible
(b) (unbedingt) at all costs

Tunnel *der;* ~s, ~ od. ~s tunnel

tupfen *tr. V.* (a) dab
(b) (mit Tupfen versehen) dot

Tupfen *der;* ~s, ~: dot; (größer) spot

Tupfer *der;* ~s, ~ (Med.) swab

Tür *die;* ~, ~en door; (Garten~) gate; **an die** ~ **gehen** (öffnen) [go and] answer the door; **vor die** ~ **gehen** go outside

Turban *der;* ~s, ~e turban

Turbine *die;* ~, ~n turbine

turbulent 1 *Adj.* (auch fachspr.) turbulent
2 *adv.* (auch fachspr.) turbulently

Turbulenz *die;* ~, ~en (auch Physik, Astron., Met.) turbulence *no pl.*

Tür-griff *der* door handle

Türke *der;* ~n, ~n Turk

Türkei *die;* ~: Turkey *no art.*

türken *tr. V.* (ugs.) fake ⟨scene, letter, document, etc.⟩; make up ⟨story, report⟩

Türkin *die;* ~, ~nen Turk

türkis *indekl. Adj.* turquoise

Türkis *der;* ~es, ~e turquoise

türkisch *Adj.* Turkish

Tür-klinke *die* door handle

Turm *der;* ~[e]s, Türme (a) tower; (spitzer Kirchturm) spire; steeple
(b) (Schach) rook
(c) (Sprungturm) diving platform

Türmchen *das;* ~s, ~: turret

türmen[1] 1 *tr. V.* (stapeln) stack up; (häufen) pile up
2 *refl. V.* be piled up; ⟨clouds⟩ gather

türmen[2] *itr. V.; mit sein* (salopp) scarper (Brit. coll.)

Turm-falke *der* kestrel

turnen 1 *itr. V.* do gymnastics; (Schulw.) do gym
2 *tr. V.* do, perform ⟨exercise, routine⟩

Turnen *das;* ~s gymnastics *sing., no art.;* (Schulw.) gym *no art.;* PE *no art.*

Turner *der;* ~s, ~, **Turnerin** *die;* ~, ~nen gymnast

Turn-: ~halle *die* gymnasium; ~hemd *das* [gym] singlet; ~hose *die* gym shorts *pl.*

Turnier *das;* ~s, ~e (auch hist.) tournament; (Reitturnier) show; (Tanzturnier) competition

Turn-schuh *der* gym shoe

Turnus *der;* ~, ~se regular cycle

Turn-verein *der* gymnastics club

Tür-: ~öffner *der* door-opener; ~rahmen *der* doorframe

turteln *itr. V.* (scherzh.: zärtlich sein) bill and coo

Tusch *der;* ~[e]s, ~e fanfare

Tusche *die;* ~, ~n Indian (Brit.) or (Amer.) India ink

Tuschelei *die;* ~, ~en (a) (das Tuscheln) whispering
(b) (Äußerung) whisper

tuscheln *itr., tr. V.* whisper

Tussi *die;* ~, ~s (salopp) female (derog.)

Tüte *die;* ~, ~n bag

tuten *itr. V.* hoot; ⟨siren, [fog]horn⟩ sound

Tutor *der;* ~s, ~en, **Tutorin** *die;* ~, ~nen (Päd.) tutor

Tycoon /tai̯ˈkuːn/ *der;* ~s, ~s tycoon

Typ *der;* ~s, ~en (a) type
(b) *Gen. auch* ~en (ugs.: Mann) bloke (Brit. coll.)

Type *die;* ~, ~n (Druck-, Schreibmaschinentype) type

Typhus *der;* ~: typhoid [fever]

typisch 1 *Adj.* typical (für of)
2 *adv.* typically

Typographie *die;* ~, ~n (Druckw.) typography

typographisch (Druckw.) 1 *Adj.* typographical
2 *adv.* typographically

Tyrann *der;* ~en, ~en (auch fig.) tyrant

Tyrannei *die;* ~, ~en (auch fig.) tyranny

Tyrannin *die;* ~, ~nen ▶ TYRANN

tyrannisch 1 *Adj.* tyrannical
2 *adv.* tyrannically

tyrannisieren *tr. V.* tyrannize

U u

u, U /u:/ *das;* ~, ~: u/U

u. *Abk.* = **und**

ü, Ü /y:/ *das;* ~, ~: u umlaut

U-Bahn *die* underground (Brit.); subway (Amer.); (bes. in London) tube

U-Bahnhof *der;* **U-Bahn-Station** *die* underground station (Brit.); subway station (Amer.); (bes. in London) tube station

übel *Adj.* **(a)** foul, nasty ⟨*smell, weather*⟩; bad, nasty ⟨*headache, cold, taste*⟩; nasty ⟨*consequences, situation*⟩; sorry ⟨*state, affair*⟩; foul, (coll.) filthy ⟨*mood*⟩; **nicht ~** (ugs.) not bad at all

(b) (unwohl) **jmdm. ist/wird ~:** sb. feels sick

(c) (verwerflich) bad; wicked; nasty, dirty ⟨*trick*⟩

(d) jmdm. etw. ~ nehmen hold sth. against sb.; **etw. ~ nehmen** take offence at sth.

Übel *das;* ~s, ~: evil

Übelkeit *die;* ~, ~en nausea

***übel|nehmen** ▶ ÜBEL D

Übel·täter *der,* **Übel·täterin** *die* wrongdoer

üben *tr. V.* **(a)** (auch itr.) practise; rehearse ⟨*scene, play*⟩; practise on ⟨*musical instrument*⟩

(b) (trainieren, schulen) exercise ⟨*fingers*⟩; train ⟨*memory*⟩

über 1 *Präp. mit Dat.* **(a)** (Lage, Standort) over; above; (in einer Rangfolge) above; **~ jmdm. wohnen** live above sb.; **zehn Grad ~ Null** ten degrees above zero; **sie trug eine Jacke ~ dem Kleid** she wore a jacket over her dress

(b) (während) during; **~ dem Lesen/der Arbeit einschlafen** fall asleep over one's book/magazine *etc.*/over one's work

2 *Präp. mit Akk.* **(a)** (Richtung) over; (quer hinüber) across; **~ Ulm nach Stuttgart** via Ulm to Stuttgart

(b) (während) over; (für die Dauer von) for

(c) (betreffend) about; **~ etw. reden/schreiben** talk/write about sth.; **ein Scheck/eine Rechnung ~ 1000 Mark** a cheque/bill for 1,000 marks

(d) Kinder ~ 10 Jahre children over ten [years of age]

3 *Adv.* **(a)** (mehr als) over

(b) ~ und ~: all over

über·all /*od.* --'-/ *Adv.* **(a)** everywhere

(b) (bei jeder Gelegenheit) always

überall-: ~her *Adv.* from all over the place; **~hin** *Adv.* everywhere

Über·angebot *das* surplus (an + *Dat.* of); (Schwemme) glut (an + *Dat.* of)

über·anstrengen *tr. V.; ich*
überanstrenge, überanstrengt, zu überanstrengen overtax ⟨*person, energy*⟩; strain ⟨*eyes, nerves, heart*⟩; **sich ~:** overexert oneself

über·arbeiten 1 *tr. V.* rework; revise ⟨*text, edition*⟩

2 *refl. V.* overwork

über·aus *Adv.* (geh.) extremely

über·backen *unr. tr. V.* **etw. mit Käse** *usw.* **~:** top sth. with cheese *etc.* and brown it lightly [under the grill/in a hot oven]

Über·bein *das* (Med.) ganglion

über·belichten *tr. V.;* ich überbelichte, überbelichtet, überzubelichten (Fot.) overexpose

über·bieten *unr. tr. V.* **(a)** outbid (um by)

(b) (übertreffen) surpass; outdo ⟨*rival*⟩; break ⟨*record*⟩ (um by); exceed ⟨*target*⟩ (um by)

Über·blick *der* **(a)** view; **einen guten ~ über etw.** (Akk.) **haben** have a good view over sth.

(b) (Abriss) survey

(c) (Einblick) overall view

über·blicken *tr. V.* ▶ ÜBERSEHEN A, B

über·bringen *unr. tr. V.* deliver; convey ⟨*greetings, congratulations*⟩

über·brücken *tr. V.* bridge ⟨*gap, gulf*⟩; reconcile ⟨*difference*⟩

Überbrückung *die;* ~, ~en (fig.) bridging; (von Gegensätzen) reconciliation

über·buchen *tr. V.* overbook

überdacht *Adj.* covered ⟨*terrace, station platform, etc.*⟩

über·dauern *tr. V.* survive ⟨*war, separation, hardship*⟩

über·dehnen *tr. V.* overstretch; strain ⟨*muscle*⟩

über·dies *Adv.* moreover

Über·dosis *die* overdose

Über·druck *der; Pl.* Überdrücke excess pressure

Überdruss, ***Überdruß** *der;* Überdrusses surfeit (an + *Dat.* of)

überdrüssig *Adj.* **jmds./einer Sache ~ sein/werden** be/grow tired of sb./sth.

über·eignen *tr. V.* **jmdm. etw. ~:** transfer sth. *or* make sth. over to sb.

Über·eignung *die* transfer (an + *Akk.* to)

über·eilen *tr. V.* rush; **übereilt** overhasty

über·einander *Adv.* **(a)** one on top of the other; **Holzscheite** *usw.:* **~ legen** lay pieces of wood *etc.* one on top of the other; **Arme/ Beine ~ schlagen** fold one's arms/cross one's legs

(b) ⟨*talk etc.*⟩ about each other

*übereinander|legen *usw.*
▶ ÜBEREINANDER A

überein|kommen *unr. itr. V.; mit sein*
agree; come to an agreement

Überein-kommen *das;* ~s, ~,
Übereinkunft *die;* ~, Übereinkünfte
agreement

überein|stimmen *itr. V.* **(a)** (einer Meinung
sein) agree (**in** + *Dat.* on)
(b) (sich gleichen) ⟨*colours, styles*⟩ match;
⟨*figures, statements, reports, results*⟩ tally,
agree; ⟨*views, opinions*⟩ coincide

Überein-stimmung *die* agreement (**in** +
Dat. on; *Gen.* between)

über-empfindlich ①*Adj.* oversensitive
(**gegen** to); (Med.) hypersensitive (**gegen** to)
② *adv.* oversensitively; (Med.)
hypersensitively

Über-empfindlichkeit *die*
oversensitivity (**gegen** to); (Med.)
hypersensitivity (**gegen** to)

über|fahren¹ ① *unr. tr. V.* jmdn. ~: ferry
or take sb. over
② *unr. itr. V.; mit sein* cross over

über-fahren² *unr. tr. V.* **(a)** run over
(b) (hinwegfahren über) cross; go over
⟨*crossroads*⟩

Über-fahrt *die* crossing (**über** + *Akk.* of)

Über-fall *der* attack (**auf** + *Akk.* on); (aus
dem Hinterhalt) ambush (**auf** + *Akk.* on); (mit
vorgehaltener Waffe) hold-up; (auf eine Bank o. Ä.)
raid (**auf** + *Akk.* on)

über-fallen *unr. tr. V.* **(a)** attack; raid
⟨*bank, enemy position, village, etc.*⟩;
(hinterrücks) ambush; (mit vorgehaltener Waffe)
hold up
(b) (überkommen) ⟨*tiredness, homesickness,
fear*⟩ come over

über-fällig *Adj.* overdue

über-fliegen *unr. tr. V.* **(a)** fly over; overfly
(formal)
(b) (flüchtig lesen) skim [through]

über-flügeln *tr. V.* outshine; outstrip

Über-fluss, *Über-fluß *der* abundance
(**an** + *Dat.* of); (Wohlstand) affluence

über-flüssig *Adj.* superfluous; unnecessary
⟨*purchase, words, work*⟩

über-fluten *tr. V.* (auch fig.) flood

Über|flutung *die;* ~, ~en (auch fig.)
flooding

über-fordern *tr. V.* jmdn. [mit etw.] ~:
overtax sb. [with sth.]; ask *or* demand too
much of sb. [with sth.]

über-fragen *tr. V.* da bin ich überfragt
I don't know the answer to that

über-fremden *tr. V.* überfremdet werden/
sein ⟨*country*⟩ be dominated [by foreign
influences]

Über-fremdung *die;* ~, ~en domination
[by foreign influences]

über-frieren *unr. itr. V.; mit sein* freeze
over; ~de Nässe black ice

über|führen¹ *tr. V.* transfer

über-führen² *tr. V.* **(a)** ▶ ÜBERFÜHREN¹;
(b) jmdn. [eines Verbrechens] ~: find sb.
guilty [of a crime]; convict sb. [of a
crime]

Über-führung *die* **(a)** transfer
(b) (eines Verdächtigen) conviction
(c) (Brücke) bridge; (Hochstraße) overpass; (für
Fußgänger) [foot]bridge

über-füllt *Adj.* crammed full (**von** with); (mit
Menschen) overcrowded (**von** with);
oversubscribed ⟨*course*⟩

Über-gabe *die* **(a)** handing over (**an** + *Akk.*
to); (von Macht) handing over
(b) (Auslieferung an den Gegner) surrender (**an** +
Akk. to)

Über-gang *der* **(a)** crossing
(b) (Stelle zum Überqueren) crossing;
(Bahnübergang) level crossing (Brit.); grade
crossing (Amer.); (Grenzübergang) crossing point
(c) (Wechsel, Überleitung) transition (**zu, auf** +
Akk. to)

über-geben ① *unr. tr. V.* **(a)** hand over;
pass ⟨*baton*⟩
(b) (übereignen) transfer, make over (*Dat.* to)
(c) (ausliefern) surrender (*Dat.*, **an** + *Akk.* to)
(d) eine Straße dem Verkehr ~: open a road
to traffic
② *unr. refl. V.* (sich erbrechen) vomit

über|gehen¹ *unr. itr. V.; mit sein* **(a)** pass
(b) zu etw. ~: go over to sth.
(c) in etw. (*Akk.*) ~ (zu etw. werden) turn into
sth.

über-gehen² *unr. tr. V.* **(a)** (nicht beachten)
ignore
(b) (auslassen, überspringen) skip [over]
(c) (nicht berücksichtigen) pass over

über-geordnet *Adj.* higher ⟨*court,
authority, position*⟩; greater ⟨*significance*⟩;
superordinate ⟨*concept*⟩

Über-gewicht *das* **(a)** excess weight
(b) (fig.) predominance

über-gewichtig *Adj.* overweight

über-glücklich *Adj.* blissfully happy;
(hocherfreut) overjoyed

über|greifen *unr. itr. V.* auf etw. (*Akk.*) ~:
spread to sth.

Über-griff *der* (unrechtmäßiger Eingriff)
encroachment (**auf** + *Akk.* on); infringement
(**auf** + *Akk.* of); (Angriff) attack (**auf** + *Akk.*
on)

Über-größe *die* outsize

überhand: ~ nehmen get out of hand;
⟨*attacks, muggings, etc.*⟩ increase alarmingly;
⟨*weeds*⟩ run riot

über|hängen *tr. V.* sich (*Dat.*) eine Jacke
~: put a jacket round one's shoulders; sich
(*Dat.*) das Gewehr/die Tasche ~: hang the
rifle/bag over one's shoulder

über-häufen *tr. V.* jmdn. mit etw. ~: heap
or shower sth. on sb.

---

*alte Schreibung - vgl. Hinweis auf S. xiv

überhaupt Adv. (a) in general
(b) ∼ **nicht** not at all; ∼ **keine Zeit haben** have no time at all; ∼ **nichts** nothing at all

überheblich 1 Adj. arrogant; supercilious ⟨grin⟩
2 adv. arrogantly; ⟨grin⟩ superciliously

Überheblichkeit die; ∼: arrogance

über·holen 1 tr. V. (a) overtake (esp. Brit.); pass (esp. Amer.)
(b) (übertreffen) outstrip
(c) (wieder instand setzen) overhaul
2 itr. V. overtake (esp. Brit.); pass (esp. Amer.)

Überholspur die overtaking lane (esp. Brit.); pass lane (esp. Amer.)

überholt Adj. (veraltet) outdated

Überholung die; ∼, ∼en overhaul

Überhol·verbot das ban on overtaking

über·hören tr. V. not hear

über·irdisch 1 Adj. celestial; heavenly; (übernatürlich) supernatural
2 adv. celestially; (übernatürlich) supernaturally

über|kochen itr. V.; mit sein (auch fig. ugs.) boil over

über·kommen unr. tr. V. Mitleid/Ekel/Furcht überkam mich I was overcome by pity/revulsion/fear

über·laden unr. tr. V. (auch fig.) overload

über·lassen unr. tr. V. (a) jmdm. etw. ∼: let sb. have sth.
(b) sich (Dat.) selbst ∼ sein be left to one's own devices
(c) etw. jmdm. ∼ (etw. jmdn. entscheiden/tun lassen) leave sth. to sb.

über·lasten tr. V. overload; overtax ⟨person⟩; (mit Arbeit) overwork ⟨person⟩

Über·lauf der overflow

über|laufen[1] unr. itr. V.; mit sein (a) overflow
(b) (auf die gegnerische Seite überwechseln) defect; ⟨partisan⟩ go over to the other side

über·laufen[2] unr. tr. V. seize; ein Frösteln/Schauer überlief mich, es überlief mich [eis]kalt a cold shiver ran down my spine

überlaufen[3] Adj. overcrowded

Über·läufer der, **Über·läuferin** die (auch fig.) defector

über·leben tr. V. survive

Über·lebende der/die; adj. Dekl. survivor

über|legen[1] tr. V. jmdm. etw. ∼: put sth. over sb.

über·legen[2] 1 tr. V. consider; think about; es sich anders ∼: change one's mind
2 itr. V. think

überlegen[3] 1 Adj. (a) superior; clear, convincing ⟨win, victory⟩; jmdm. ∼ sein be superior to sb. (an + Dat. in)
(b) (herablassend) supercilious
2 adv. (a) in a superior manner; ⟨play⟩ much the better; ⟨win, argue⟩ convincingly
(b) (herablassend) superciliously

Überlegenheit die; ∼: superiority

überlegt 1 Adj. carefully considered
2 adv. in a carefully considered way

Überlegung die; ∼, ∼en (a) thought
(b) (Gedanke) idea; ∼en (Gedankengang) thoughts

über·liefern tr. V. hand down

Über·lieferung die tradition

überlisten tr. V. outwit

überm Präp. + Art. = über dem

Über·macht die superior strength; (zahlenmäßig) superior numbers pl.

über·mannen tr. V. overcome

Über·maß das excessive amount, excess (an + Dat. of)

über·mäßig 1 Adj. excessive
2 adv. excessively

über·menschlich Adj. superhuman

über·mitteln tr. V. send; (als Mittler weitergeben) pass on, convey ⟨greetings, regards, etc.⟩

über·morgen Adv. the day after tomorrow

über·müden tr. V. overtire; **übermüdet** overtired; exhausted

Übermüdung die; ∼: overtiredness; exhaustion

Über·mut der high spirits pl.

übermütig 1 Adj. high-spirited
2 adv. high-spiritedly

über·nächst... Adj. im ∼en Jahr, ∼es Jahr the year after next; am ∼en Tag two days later

über·nachten itr. V. stay overnight

übernächtigt Adj. ⟨person⟩ tired or worn out [through lack of sleep]; tired ⟨face, look, etc.⟩

Übernachtung die; ∼, ∼en overnight stay; ∼ und Frühstück bed and breakfast

Übernahme die; ∼ (von Waren, einer Sendung) taking delivery no art.; (einer Idee usw.) adoption, taking over no indef. art.; (der Macht, einer Praxis usw.) take over

über·natürlich Adj. supernatural

über·nehmen 1 unr. tr. V. (a) take delivery of ⟨goods, consignment⟩; take over ⟨power, practice, business, etc.⟩; take on ⟨job, position, etc.⟩; undertake to pay ⟨costs⟩
(b) (sich zu Eigen machen) adopt ⟨ideas, methods, subject, etc.⟩ (von from); borrow ⟨word, phrase⟩ (von from)
2 unr. refl. V. overdo things or it; sich mit etw. ∼: take on too much with sth.

Über·produktion die (Wirtsch., Med.) overproduction

über·prüfen tr. V. check (auf + Akk. for); review ⟨issue, situation, results⟩

Über·prüfung die (a) checking no indef. art. (auf + Akk. for)
(b) (Kontrolle) check; (einer Lage, Frage usw.) review

über·queren tr. V. cross

u

über·ragen *tr. V.* **(a)** jmdn./etw. ~: tower above sb./sth.
(b) (übertreffen) jmdn. an etw. (*Dat.*) ~: be head and shoulders above sb. in sth.

überragend ①*Adj.* outstanding ②*adv.* outstandingly

über·raschen *tr. V.* surprise

Überraschung *die;* ~, ~en surprise

über·reden *tr. V.* persuade

Überredung *die;* ~: persuasion

über·regional ①*Adj.* national ⟨*newspaper, radio station*⟩ ②*adv.* nationally

über·reichen *tr. V.* [jmdm.] etw. ~: present sth. [to sb.]

Überreichung *die;* ~: presentation

über·reif *Adj.* over-ripe

über·rumpeln *tr. V.* jmdn. ~: take sb. by surprise

über·runden *tr. V.* **(a)** (Sport) lap **(b)** (übertreffen) outstrip

übers *Präp. + Art.* = über das

über·sättigen *tr. V.* supersaturate ⟨*solution*⟩; glut ⟨*market*⟩; satiate ⟨*public*⟩

Überschall-: ~**flugzeug** *das* supersonic aircraft; ~**geschwindigkeit** *die* supersonic speed

über·schatten *tr. V.* overshadow; cast its/their shadow over; (fig.) cast a shadow over

über·schätzen *tr. V.* overestimate; overrate ⟨*artist, talent, etc.*⟩

Über·schätzung *die* ▶ ÜBERSCHÄTZEN: overestimation; overrating

überschaubar *Adj.* eine ~e Menge/Zahl a manageable quantity/number

über·schauen *tr. V.* ▶ ÜBERSEHEN A, B

Über·schlag *der* **(a)** rough calculation *or* estimate **(b)** (Turnen) handspring **(c)** ▶ LOOPING

über|schlagen[1] ①*unr. tr. V.* die Beine ~: cross one's legs ②*unr. itr. V.; mit sein* ⟨*wave*⟩ break

über·schlagen[2] ①*unr. tr. V.* **(a)** skip ⟨*chapter, page, etc.*⟩ **(b)** (ungefähr berechnen) calculate *or* estimate roughly ②*unr. refl. V.* go head over heels; ⟨*car*⟩ turn over

über|schnappen *itr. V.; mit sein* (ugs.) go crazy

über·schneiden *unr. refl. V.* cross, intersect; (fig.) overlap

über·schreiben *unr. tr. V.* **(a)** entitle; head ⟨*chapter, section*⟩ **(b)** etw. jmdm. od. auf jmdn. ~: transfer sth. to sb.

über·schreiten *unr. itr. V.* cross; (fig.) exceed

Über·schrift *die* heading; (in einer Zeitung) headline; (Titel) title

Über·schuss, *****Über·schuß** *der* surplus (an + *Dat.* of)

überschüssig *Adj.* surplus

über·schütten *tr. V.* cover

Überschwang *der;* ~[e]s exuberance

über·schwänglich ①*Adj.* effusive ⟨*words etc.*⟩; wild ⟨*joy, enthusiasm*⟩ ②*adv.* effusively

über·schwemmen *tr. V.* (auch fig.) flood

Überschwemmung *die;* ~, ~en flood; (das Überschwemmen) flooding *no pl.*

***über·schwenglich** ▶ ÜBERSCHWÄNGLICH

Über·see: aus od. von ~: from overseas; in/nach ~: overseas

über·sehen *unr. tr. V.* **(a)** look out over **(b)** (abschätzen) assess ⟨*damage, situation, consequences, etc.*⟩ **(c)** (nicht sehen) overlook; miss; miss ⟨*turning, signpost*⟩ **(d)** (ignorieren) ignore

über·senden *unr.* (auch regelm.) *tr. V.* send

über|setzen[1] ①*tr. V.* ferry over ②*itr. V.; auch mit sein* cross [over]

über·setzen[2] *tr., itr. V.* (auch fig.) translate

Über·setzer *der,* **Übersetzerin** *die;* ~, ~nen translator

Übersetzung *die;* ~, ~en translation

Über·sicht *die* **(a)** overall view, overview (über + *Akk.* of) **(b)** (Darstellung) survey; (Tabelle) summary

über·sichtlich ①*Adj.* clear; ⟨*crossroads*⟩ which allows a clear view ②*adv.* clearly

Übersichtlichkeit *die;* ~: clarity; (einer Kreuzung) clear layout

über|siedeln[1], **über·siedeln**[2] *itr. V.; mit sein* move (nach to)

Über·siedler *der,* **Über·siedlerin** *die* migrant

überspannt *Adj.* exaggerated ⟨*ideas, behaviour, gestures*⟩; extreme ⟨*views*⟩; inflated ⟨*demands, expectations*⟩

über·spielen *tr. V.* **(a)** (hinweggehen über) cover up; smooth over ⟨*difficult situation*⟩ **(b)** (aufnehmen) [auf ein Tonband] ~: transfer ⟨*record*⟩ to tape; put ⟨*record*⟩ on tape

über·spitzen *tr. V.* etw. ~: push *or* carry sth. too far

über·springen *unr. tr. V.* **(a)** jump ⟨*obstacle*⟩ **(b)** (auslassen) miss out

über|stehen[1] *unr. itr. V.; südd., österr., schweiz. mit sein* jut out

über·stehen[2] *unr. tr. V.* come through ⟨*danger, war, operation*⟩; get over ⟨*illness*⟩

über·steigen *unr. tr. V.* **(a)** climb over **(b)** (fig.) exceed

über·stimmen *tr. V.* outvote

---

*old spelling - see note on page xiv

über|streifen *tr. V.* [sich (*Dat.*)] etw. ∼: slip sth. on

über|stülpen *tr. V.* pull on ⟨*hat etc.*⟩

Über·stunde *die:* ∼n machen do overtime

über·stürzen [1] *tr. V.* rush
[2] *refl. V.* rush; (rasch aufeinander folgen) ⟨*events, news, etc.*⟩ come thick and fast

überstürzt [1] *Adj.* hurried ⟨*escape, departure*⟩; overhasty ⟨*decision*⟩
[2] *adv.* ⟨*decide, act*⟩ overhastily; ⟨*depart*⟩ hurriedly

über·tölpeln *tr. V.* dupe; con (coll.)

über·tönen *tr. V.* drown out

Übertrag *der;* ∼[e]s, Überträge (bes. Buchf.) carry-over

über·tragbar *Adj.* transferable (auf + *Akk.* to); (auf etw. anderes anwendbar) applicable (auf + *Akk.* to); (übersetzbar) translatable; (ansteckend) infectious ⟨*disease*⟩

über·tragen *unr. tr. V.* (a) transfer (auf + *Akk.* to); transmit ⟨*power, torque, etc.*⟩ (auf + *Akk.* to); communicate ⟨*disease, illness*⟩ (auf + *Akk.* to); carry over ⟨*subtotal*⟩; (auf etw. anderes anwenden) apply (auf + *Akk.* to); (übersetzen) translate
(b) (senden) broadcast ⟨*concert, event, match, etc.*⟩; (im Fernsehen) televise
(c) (geben) jmdm. Aufgaben/Pflichten *usw.* ∼: hand over tasks/duties *etc.* to sb.; (anvertrauen) entrust sb. with tasks/duties *etc.*

Übertragung *die;* ∼, ∼en (a)
▶ ÜBERTRAGEN A: transference; transmission; communication; carrying over; application; translation
(b) (das Senden) broadcasting; (Sendung) broadcast; (im Fernsehen) televising/television broadcast

über·treffen *unr. tr. V.* (a) surpass, outdo (an + *Dat.* in); break ⟨*record*⟩
(b) (übersteigen) exceed

über·treiben *unr. tr. V.* (a) auch itr. exaggerate
(b) (zu weit treiben) overdo

Übertreibung *die;* ∼, ∼en exaggeration

über|treten¹ *unr. itr. V.; mit sein* change sides; **zum Katholizismus/Islam** ∼: convert to Catholicism/Islam

über·treten² *unr. tr. V.* contravene ⟨*law*⟩; violate ⟨*regulation, prohibition*⟩

Übertretung *die;* ∼, ∼en (a)
▶ ÜBERTRETEN²: contravention; violation
(b) (Vergehen) misdemeanour

übertrieben *Adj.* [1] exaggerated; (übermäßig) excessive ⟨*care, thrift, etc.*⟩
[2] *adv.* excessively

Über·tritt *der* change of allegiance, switch (zu to); (Rel.) conversion (zu to)

über·trumpfen *tr. V.* outdo

über·tünchen *tr. V.* cover with whitewash; (fig.) cover up

über·vorteilen *tr. V.* cheat

über·wachen *tr. V.* keep under surveillance ⟨*suspect, agent, area, etc.*⟩;

supervise ⟨*factory, workers, process*⟩; control ⟨*traffic*⟩; monitor ⟨*progress, production process, experiment, patient*⟩

Überwachung *die;* ∼, ∼en
▶ ÜBERWACHEN: surveillance; supervision; controlling; monitoring

über·wältigen *tr. V.* (a) overpower
(b) (fig.) ⟨*sleep, emotion, fear, etc.*⟩ overcome; ⟨*sight, impressions, beauty, etc.*⟩ overwhelm

überwältigend [1] *Adj.* overwhelming ⟨*sight, impression, victory, majority, etc.*⟩; overpowering ⟨*smell*⟩; stunning ⟨*beauty*⟩
[2] *adv.* stunningly ⟨*beautiful*⟩

über·weisen *unr. tr. V.* (a) transfer ⟨*money*⟩ (an, auf + *Akk.* to)
(b) refer ⟨*patient*⟩ (an + *Akk.* to)

Über·weisung *die* (a) transfer (an, auf + *Akk.* to)
(b) (Summe) remittance
(c) (eines Patienten) referral (an + *Akk.* to)

überwiegend [1] /auch --'--/ *Adj.* overwhelming
[2] *adv.* mainly

über·winden [1] *unr. tr. V.* overcome; get past ⟨*stage*⟩
[2] *unr. refl. V.* overcome one's reluctance; sich [dazu] ∼, etw. zu tun bring oneself to do sth.

Über·windung *die* (a) ▶ ÜBERWINDEN 1: overcoming; getting past
(b) (das Sichüberwinden) es war eine große ∼ für ihn it cost him a great effort

über·wuchern *tr. V.* overgrow

Über·zahl *die* majority

überzählig *Adj.* surplus

über·zeugen [1] *tr. V.* convince
[2] *itr. V.* be convincing

überzeugend [1] *Adj.* convincing
[2] *adv.* convincingly

überzeugt *Adj.* convinced

Über·zeugung *die* (feste Meinung) conviction

über|ziehen¹ *unr. tr. V.* pull on

über·ziehen² *unr. tr. V.* (a) etw. mit etw. ∼: cover sth. with sth.
(b) overdraw ⟨*account*⟩ (um by)

Überziehungs·kredit *der* (Finanzw.) overdraft facility

überzüchtet *Adj.* overbred; over-sophisticated ⟨*engines, systems*⟩

Überzug *der* (a) (Beschichtung) coating
(b) (Bezug) cover

üblich *Adj.* usual; (normal) normal; (gebräuchlich) customary

üblicher·weise *Adv.* usually

U-Boot *das* submarine; sub (coll.)

übrig *Adj.* remaining *attrib.;* (ander...) other; alle ∼en Gäste ...: all the other guests ...; im Übrigen besides; es ist etwas ∼: there is some left; ∼ bleiben be left; ⟨*food, drink*⟩ be left over; ∼ lassen (+ *Akk.*) leave; leave ⟨*food, drink*⟩ over

u

***übrig|bleiben** ▶ ÜBRIG
übrigens *Adv.* by the way
***übrig|lassen** ▶ ÜBRIG
Übung *die;* ~, ~en (a) exercise
(b) (das Üben, Geübtsein) practice
UdSSR *Abk. die;* ~ (1922–1991) = **Union der Sozialistischen Sowjetrepubliken** USSR
Ufer *das;* ~s, ~: bank; (des Meers) shore
UG *Abk.* = **Untergeschoss**
Uganda (*das*); ~s Uganda
Uhr *die;* ~, ~en (a) clock; (Armband-, Taschenuhr) watch; (Wasser-, Gasuhr) meter; (an Messinstrumenten) dial; gauge; **auf die** *od.* **nach der** ~ **sehen** look at the time; **rund um die** ~ (ugs.) round the clock
(b) **acht** ~: eight o'clock; **wie viel** ~ **ist es?** what's the time?; what time is it?
Uhr-: ~**armband** *das* watch strap; ~**kette** *die* watch chain; ~**macher** *der*, ~**macherin** *die* watchmaker/clockmaker; ~**werk** *das* clock/watch mechanism; ~**zeiger** *der* clock/watch hand; ~**zeiger·sinn** *der:* im/entgegen dem ~zeigersinn clockwise/anticlockwise; ~**zeit** *die* time; jmdn. nach der ~zeit fragen ask sb. the time
Uhu *der;* ~s, ~s eagle owl
Ukraine *die;* ~: Ukraine
Ukrainer *der;* ~s, ~, **Ukrainerin** *die;* ~, ~nen Ukrainian
UKW *Abk.* = **Ultrakurzwelle** VHF
UKW-Sender *der* VHF station; ≈ FM station
Ulk *der;* ~s, ~e lark (coll.); (Streich) trick; [practical] joke
ulkig (ugs.) ① *Adj.* funny ② *adv.* in a funny way
Ulme *die;* ~, ~n elm
Ultimatum *das;* ~s, Ultimaten ultimatum
Ultra·kurz·welle *die* ultra-short wave; (Rundf.: Wellenbereich) very high frequency; VHF
Ultra·schall *der* (Physik, Med.) ultrasound
Ultraschall·untersuchung *die* (Med.) ultrasound examination
ultra·violett *Adj.* ultraviolet
um ① *Präp. mit Akk.* (a) (räumlich) [a]round; **um die Ecke** round the corner
(b) (zeitlich) (genau) at; (etwa) around [about]
(c) **Tag um Tag/Stunde um Stunde** day after day/hour after hour
(d) (bei Maß- u. Mengenangaben) by
② *Adv.* around; about; **um [die] 10 Mark/50 Personen [herum]** around *or* about ten marks/50 people
③ *Konj.* (a) (final) **um ... zu** [in order] to
(b) (konsekutiv) **er ist groß genug/ist noch zu klein, um ... zu ...:** he is big enough/is still too young to ...

um|ändern *tr. V.* change; revise ⟨*text, novel*⟩; alter ⟨*garment*⟩
um·armen *tr. V.* embrace; (an sich drücken) hug
Umarmung *die;* ~, ~en embrace; hug
Um·bau *der;* ~[e]s, ~ten ▶ UMBAUEN: rebuilding; alteration; conversion; (fig.) reorganization
um|bauen *tr.,* *auch itr. V.* rebuild; (leicht ändern) alter; (zu etw. anderem) convert (**zu** into); (fig.) reorganize ⟨*system, administration, etc.*⟩
um|benennen *unr. tr. V.* change the name of; rename
um|biegen ① *unr. tr. V.* bend ② *unr. itr. V.; mit sein* turn
um|binden *unr. tr. V.* put on
um|blättern ① *tr. V.* turn [over] ② *itr. V.* turn the page/pages
um|blicken *refl. V.* (a) look around
(b) (zurückblicken) [turn to] look back (**nach** at)
um|bringen *unr. tr. V.* kill
Um·bruch *der* (a) radical change; (Umwälzung) upheaval
(b) (Druckw.) make-up; (Ergebnis) page proofs *pl.*
um|buchen ① *tr. V.* change (**auf** + *Akk.* to) ② *itr. V.* change one's booking (**auf** + *Akk.* to)
Um·buchung *die* change of booking
um|datieren *tr. V.* change the date of; redate ⟨*contract, letter, etc.*⟩
um|denken *unr. itr. V.* revise one's thinking; rethink; **ein Prozess des Umdenkens** a process of rethinking
um|drehen ① *tr. V.* turn round; turn over ⟨*coin, hand, etc.*⟩; turn ⟨*key*⟩ ② *refl. V.* turn round; (den Kopf wenden) turn one's head ③ *itr. V.; auch mit sein* (ugs.: umkehren) turn back; (ugs.: wenden) turn round
Um·drehung *die* turn; (eines Motors usw.) revolution; rev (coll.)
um·einander *Adv.* **sich** ~ **kümmern/sorgen** take care of/worry about each other *or* one another
um|fahren[1] *unr. tr. V.* knock down
um|fahren[2] *unr. tr. V.* go round; make a detour round ⟨*obstruction etc.*⟩; (im Auto) drive round; (im Schiff) sail round; (auf einer Umgehungsstraße) bypass ⟨*town, village, etc.*⟩
um|fallen *unr. itr. V.; mit sein* (a) fall over
(b) (zusammenbrechen) collapse; **tot** ~: fall down dead
Um·fang *der* (a) circumference; (eines Quadrats usw.) perimeter; (eines Baums, Menschen usw.) girth
(b) (Größe) size
(c) (Ausmaß) extent
umfang·reich *Adj.* extensive; substantial ⟨*book*⟩
um·fassen *tr. V.* (a) grasp; (umarmen) embrace

---
*alte Schreibung - vgl. Hinweis auf S. xiv

(b) (enthalten) contain; (einschließen) include; span, cover ⟨*period*⟩

umfassend ① *Adj.* full ⟨*reply, information, survey, confession*⟩; extensive, wide ⟨*knowledge, powers*⟩ ② *adv.* ⟨*inform*⟩ fully

Um·feld *das* (Psych., Soziol.) milieu

um|formen *tr. V.* reshape; revise ⟨*poem, novel*⟩; transform ⟨*person*⟩

Um·frage *die* survey; (Politik) opinion poll

um|füllen *tr. V.* etw. in etw. (*Akk.*) ∼: transfer sth. into sth.

um|funktionieren *tr. V.* change the function of; etw. zu etw. ∼: turn sth. into sth.

Um·gang *der* **(a)** (gesellschaftlicher Verkehr) contact
(b) (das Umgehen) den ∼ mit Pferden lernen learn how to handle horses

umgänglich *Adj.* affable; (gesellig) sociable

Umgangs-: ∼**form** *die* gute/schlechte/ keine ∼formen haben have good/bad/no manners; ∼**sprache** *die* colloquial language

um·garnen *tr. V.* beguile

um·geben *unr. V.* **(a)** surround; ⟨*hedge, fence, wall, etc.*⟩ enclose
(b) etw. mit etw. ∼: surround sth. with sth.; (einfrieden) enclose sth. with sth.

Umgebung *die;* ∼, ∼en surroundings *pl.;* (Nachbarschaft) neighbourhood; (eines Ortes) surrounding area

um|gehen[1] *unr. itr. V.; mit sein* **(a)** (im Umlauf sein) ⟨*list, rumour, etc.*⟩ go round, circulate; ⟨*illness, infection*⟩ go round
(b) (spuken) hier geht ein Gespenst um this place is haunted
(c) (behandeln) mit jmdm. freundlich/liebevoll usw. ∼: treat sb. kindly/lovingly *etc.;* er kann mit Geld nicht ∼: he can't handle money

um·gehen[2] *unr. tr. V.* **(a)** go round; make a detour round; (auf einer Umgehungsstraße) bypass ⟨*town etc.*⟩
(b) (vermeiden) avoid; evade ⟨*question, issue*⟩
(c) (nicht befolgen) circumvent ⟨*law, restriction, etc.*⟩; evade ⟨*obligation, duty*⟩

umgehend ① *Adj.* immediate ② *adv.* immediately

Umgehung *die;* ∼, ∼en **(a)** durch ∼ der Innenstadt by bypassing *or* avoiding the town centre
(b) ▶ UMGEHEN[2] C: circumvention; evasion

Umgehungs·straße *die* bypass

umgekehrt ① *Adj.* inverse ⟨*ratio, proportion*⟩; reverse ⟨*order*⟩; opposite ⟨*sign*⟩ ② *adv.* inversely ⟨*proportional*⟩; vom Englischen ins Deutsche und ∼ übersetzen translate from English into German and vice versa

um|gestalten *tr. V.* reshape; remodel; redesign ⟨*square, park, room, etc.*⟩

um|graben *unr. tr. V.* dig over

Um·hang *der* cape

um|hängen *tr. V.* **(a)** etw. ∼: hang sth. somewhere else
(b) jmdm./sich einen Mantel/eine Decke ∼: drape a coat/blanket round sb.'s/one's shoulders

um|hauen *unr. tr. V.* fell; (fig.) knock down

um·her *Adv.* around

umher- ▶ HERUM-

um|hören *refl. V.* keep one's ears open; (direkt fragen) ask around

um·jubeln *tr. V.* cheer

um|kehren ① *itr. V.; mit sein* turn back ② *tr. V.* turn upside down; turn over ⟨*sheet of paper*⟩; (nach links drehen) turn ⟨*garment etc.*⟩ inside out; (nach rechts drehen) turn ⟨*garment etc.*⟩ right side out

um|kippen ① *itr. V.; mit sein* **(a)** fall over; ⟨*boat*⟩ capsize, turn over; ⟨*vehicle*⟩ overturn
(b) (ugs.: ohnmächtig werden) keel over
(c) (Ökologie) ⟨*river, lake*⟩ reach the stage of biological collapse ② *tr. V.* tip over; knock over ⟨*lamp, vase, glass, cup*⟩; capsize ⟨*boat*⟩; turn ⟨*boat*⟩ over; overturn ⟨*vehicle*⟩

um|klappen *tr. V.* fold down

Umkleide·kabine *die* changing cubicle

um|knicken *itr. V.; mit sein* **(a)** [mit dem Fuß] ∼: go over on one's ankle
(b) ⟨*branch*⟩ bend and snap

um|kommen *unr. itr. V.; mit sein* die; (bei einem Unglück, durch Gewalt) get killed; die; ⟨*food*⟩ go off

Um·kreis *der* surrounding area; im ∼ von 5 km within a radius of 5 km.

um·kreisen *tr. V.* circle; ⟨*spacecraft, satellite*⟩ orbit; ⟨*planet*⟩ revolve [a]round

Um·lauf *der* **(a)** (von Planeten) revolution
(b) (Zirkulation) circulation; in *od.* im ∼ sein be circulating; ⟨*coin, banknote*⟩ be in circulation; in ∼ bringen circulate; bring ⟨*coin, banknote*⟩ into circulation

Umlauf·bahn *die* (Astron., Raumf.) orbit

Um·laut *der* (Sprachw.) umlaut

um|legen *tr. V.* **(a)** (um einen Körperteil) put on
(b) (verlegen) transfer ⟨*patient, telephone call*⟩
(c) (salopp: ermorden) jmdn. ∼: bump sb. off (coll.)

um|leiten divert

Um·leitung *die* diversion

umliegend *Adj.* surrounding ⟨*area*⟩; (nahe) nearby ⟨*building*⟩

um|modeln *tr. V.* (ugs.) change ⟨*house, flat*⟩ round; refashion, alter ⟨*jacket etc.*⟩

um·nachtet *Adj.* (geh.) deranged

Umnachtung *die;* ∼, ∼en (geh.) derangement

um|pflanzen *tr. V.* transplant

um|pflügen *tr. V.* plough up

um|räumen ① *tr. V.* rearrange ② *itr. V.* rearrange things

um|rechnen tr. V. convert (**in** + Akk. into)

Um-rechnung die conversion (**in** + Akk. into)

Umrechnungs·kurs der exchange rate

um|reißen[1] unr. tr. V. pull ⟨mast, tree⟩ down; knock ⟨person⟩ down; ⟨wind⟩ tear ⟨tent etc.⟩ down

um-reißen[2] unr. tr. V. outline; summarize ⟨subject, problem, situation⟩

um|rennen unr. tr. V. [run into and] knock down

um-ringen tr. V. surround

Um-riss, *Um-riß der (auch fig.) outline

um|rühren tr. V. (auch itr.) V. stir

um|rüsten tr. V. (Technik) convert (**auf** + Akk. to, **zu** into)

ums /ʊms/ Präp. + Art. (a) = um das; (b) ∼ Leben kommen lose one's life

um|satteln itr. V. (ugs.) change jobs; ⟨student⟩ change courses

Um-satz der turnover; (Verkauf) sales pl. (**an** + Dat. of); ∼ machen (ugs.) make money

um|säumen tr. V. hem

um|schalten [1] tr. V. (auch fig.) switch [over] (**auf** + Akk. to); move ⟨lever⟩ [2] itr. V. switch or change over (**auf** + Akk. to)

Um-schlag der (a) cover (b) (Briefumschlag) envelope (c) (Schutzumschlag) jacket; (einer Broschüre, eines Heftes) cover (d) (Med.: Wickel) compress; (warm) poultice

um|schlagen [1] unr. tr. V. (a) turn up ⟨sleeve, collar, trousers⟩; turn over ⟨page⟩ (b) (umladen, verladen) turn round, trans-ship ⟨goods⟩ [2] unr. itr. V.; mit sein change (**in** + Akk. into); ⟨wind⟩ veer [round]

um|schreiben[1] unr. tr. V. rewrite

um-schreiben[2] unr. tr. V. (a) (in Worte fassen) describe; (definieren) define ⟨meaning, sb.'s task, etc.⟩; (paraphrasieren) paraphrase ⟨word, expression⟩ (b) (Sprachw.) construct (**mit** with)

Um-schreibung die description; (Definition) definition; (Verhüllung) circumlocution (Gen. for)

Um-schrift die (Sprachw.) transcription

um|schulen [1] tr. V. (beruflich) retrain [2] itr. V. retrain (**auf** + Akk. as)

Umschulung die; ∼: retraining (**auf** + Akk. as)

um|schütten tr. V. (a) pour [into another container]; decant ⟨liquid⟩ (b) (verschütten) spill

Um-schweif der circumlocution; ohne ∼e without beating about the bush

Um-schwung der complete change; (in der Politik usw.) U-turn

um|sehen unr. refl. V. (a) look; sich im Zimmer ∼: look [a]round the room (b) (zurücksehen) look round or back

umseitig Adj., adv. overleaf

um|setzen tr. V. (a) move; (auf anderen Posten usw.) move, transfer (**in** + Akk. to); (umpflanzen) transplant; (in anderen Topf) repot (b) (verwirklichen) implement ⟨plan⟩; translate ⟨plan, intention, etc.⟩ into action or reality; realize ⟨ideas⟩ (c) (Wirtsch.) turn over, have a turnover of ⟨x marks etc.⟩; sell ⟨shares, goods⟩

Um-sicht die circumspection

um-sichtig [1] Adj. circumspect [2] adv. circumspectly

um|siedeln [1] tr. V. resettle [2] itr. V.; mit sein move (**in** + Akk., **nach** to)

um-so Konj. je ... ∼: the ..., the; ∼ besser/ schlimmer! all the better/worse!

um-sonst Adv. (a) (unentgeltlich) free; for nothing (b) (vergebens) in vain

Um-stand der (a) (Gegebenheit) circumstance; (Tatsache) fact; unter Umständen possibly (b) (Aufwand) business; macht keine [großen] Umstände please don't go to any bother

umstände·halber Adv. owing to circumstances; „∼ zu verkaufen" 'forced to sell'

umständlich [1] Adj. involved, elaborate ⟨procedure, method, description, explanation, etc.⟩; elaborate, laborious ⟨preparation, check, etc.⟩; awkward, difficult ⟨journey, job⟩; (weitschweifig) long-winded; (Umstände machend) awkward ⟨person⟩ [2] adv. in an involved or roundabout way; (weitschweifig) at great length

Umstands·kleid das maternity dress

umstehend Adj. standing round postpos.

um|steigen unr. itr. V. change (**in** + Akk. [on] to)

um|stellen[1] [1] tr. V. (a) rearrange, change round ⟨furniture, books, etc.⟩; reorder ⟨words etc.⟩; transpose ⟨two words⟩ (b) (anders einstellen) reset ⟨lever, switch, points, clock⟩ (c) (ändern) change or switch over (**auf** + Akk. to) [2] refl. V. adjust (**auf** + Akk. to)

um-stellen[2] tr. V. surround

um|stimmen tr. V. win ⟨person⟩ round

um|stoßen unr. tr. V. (a) knock over (b) (rückgängig machen) change ⟨plan, decision⟩; (zunichte machen) upset, wreck ⟨plan, theory⟩

umstritten Adj. disputed; controversial ⟨book, author, policy, etc.⟩

Um-sturz der coup

um|stürzen [1] tr. V. overturn; (fig.) topple, overthrow ⟨political system, government⟩ [2] itr. V. overturn; ⟨wall, building, chimney⟩ fall down

umstürzlerisch Adj. subversive

---

*old spelling - see note on page xiv

Umsturz·versuch der attempted coup

Um-tausch der exchange

um|tauschen tr. V. exchange ⟨goods, article⟩ (gegen for); change ⟨dollars, pounds, etc.⟩ (in + Akk. into)

um|topfen tr. V. repot ⟨plant⟩

Um-trunk der communal drink

um|tun unr. refl. V. (ugs.) look [a]round; sich nach etw. ∼: be on the lookout for sth.

Umwälzung die; ∼, ∼en (fig.) revolution

um|wandeln tr. V. convert ⟨substance, building, etc.⟩ (in + Akk. into); (ändern) change; alter

Um-weg der detour

Um-welt die (a) environment
(b) (Menschen) people pl. around sb.

umwelt-, Umwelt-: ∼bedingt Adj. caused by the or one's environment postpos.; ∼belastung die environmental pollution no indef. art.; ∼bewusst, *∼bewußt Adj. environmentally conscious or aware; ∼feindlich [1] Adj. inimical to the environment postpos.; ecologically undesirable; [2] adv. in an ecologically undesirable way; ⟨drive, behave⟩ without regard for the environment; ∼freundlich [1] Adj. environmentally friendly; [2] adv. in an environmentally friendly way; ∼katastrophe die environmental disaster; ∼schädlich [1] Adj. harmful to the environment postpos.; ecologically harmful; [2] adv. in an ecologically harmful way; ∼schutz der environmental protection no art.; ∼schützer der; ∼∼s, ∼∼, ∼schützerin die; ∼∼, ∼, ∼nen environmentalist; conservationist; ∼verschmutzung die pollution [of the environment]

um|wenden regelm. (auch unr.) tr. V. (a) turn over ⟨page, joint, etc.⟩
(b) turn round ⟨vehicle, horse⟩

um·werben unr. tr. V. court; woo; **viel umworben** much-courted

um|werfen unr. tr. V. (a) knock over; knock ⟨person⟩ down or over; (fig. ugs.: aus der Fassung bringen) bowl ⟨person⟩ over; stun ⟨person⟩
(b) (fig. ugs.: umstoßen) knock ⟨plan⟩ on the head (coll.)

umwerfend (ugs.) [1] Adj. fantastic (coll.); stunning (coll.)
[2] adv. fantastically [well] (coll.); brilliantly

um·wickeln tr. V. wrap; bind; (mit einem Verband) bandage

Umzäunung die; ∼, ∼en fence, fencing (Gen. round)

um|ziehen [1] unr. itr. V.; mit sein move (an + Akk., in + Akk., nach to)
[2] unr. tr. V. jmdn. ∼: change sb. or get sb. changed; **sich** ∼: change or get changed

um·zingeln tr. V. surround; encircle

Umzingelung die; ∼: encirclement

Um-zug der (a) move; (von Möbeln) removal
(b) (Festzug) procession

UN Pl. UN sing.

unabänderlich [1] Adj. unalterable; irrevocable ⟨decision⟩
[2] adv. irrevocably

unabhängig [1] Adj. independent (von of); (unbeeinflusst) unaffected (von by)
[2] adv. independently (von of); ∼ **davon, ob** .../was .../wo ... usw. irrespective or regardless of whether .../what .../where ... etc

Unabhängigkeit die; ∼: independence

unabkömmlich Adj. indispensable; **sie ist im Moment** ∼: she is otherwise engaged

unablässig [1] Adj. incessant
[2] adv. incessantly

unabsichtlich [1] Adj. unintentional
[2] adv. unintentionally

unabwendbar Adj. inevitable

unachtsam [1] Adj. (a) inattentive
(b) (nicht sorgfältig) careless
[2] adv. (ohne Sorgfalt) carelessly

Unachtsamkeit die; ∼ (a) inattentiveness
(b) (mangelnde Sorgfalt) carelessness

unangebracht Adj. inappropriate

unangefochten Adj. unchallenged; (Rechtsw.) uncontested ⟨verdict, will, etc.⟩

unangenehm [1] Adj. unpleasant (Dat. for); (peinlich) embarrassing ⟨question, situation⟩
[2] adv. unpleasantly

unannehmbar Adj. unacceptable

Unannehmlichkeit die; ∼, ∼en trouble

unansehnlich Adj. unprepossessing; plain ⟨girl⟩

unanständig [1] Adj. improper; (anstößig) indecent; dirty ⟨joke⟩; rude ⟨word, song⟩
[2] adv. improperly

Unanständigkeit die; ∼, ∼en impropriety; indecency; (Obszönität) obscenity

unappetitlich [1] Adj. unappetizing; (fig.) unsavoury ⟨joke⟩; disgusting ⟨washbasin, nails, etc.⟩
[2] adv. unappetizingly

Unart die; ∼, ∼en bad habit

unartig Adj. naughty

unästhetisch Adj. unpleasant ⟨sight etc.⟩; ugly ⟨building etc.⟩

unauffällig [1] Adj. inconspicuous; unobtrusive ⟨scar, defect, skill, behaviour, surveillance, etc.⟩; discreet ⟨signal, elegance⟩
[2] adv. inconspicuously; unobtrusively

unauffindbar Adj. untraceable; ∼ **sein od. bleiben** be nowhere to be found

unaufgefordert Adv. without being asked

unaufhaltsam [1] Adj. inexorable
[2] adv. inexorably

unaufmerksam Adj. inattentive (gegenüber to); careless ⟨driver⟩

unaufrichtig Adj. insincere

Unaufrichtigkeit *die;* ~, ~en insincerity
unausbleiblich *Adj.* inevitable
unausgegoren *Adj.* (abwertend) immature
unausstehlich *Adj.* unbearable ⟨*person, noise, smell, etc.*⟩; insufferable ⟨*person*⟩; intolerable ⟨*noise, smell*⟩.
unausweichlich *Adj.* unavoidable; inevitable
unbändig ① *Adj.* (a) boisterous
(b) (überaus groß/stark) unbridled
② *adv.* (a) wildly
(b) (sehr, äußerst) unrestrainedly; tremendously (coll.)
unbarmherzig *Adj.* merciless
unbeabsichtigt ① *Adj.* unintentional
② *adv.* unintentionally
unbeachtet *Adj.* unnoticed
unbedacht ① *Adj.* rash; thoughtless
② *adv.* rashly; thoughtlessly
unbedenklich *adv.* without second thoughts
unbedeutend ① *Adj.* insignificant; minor ⟨*artist, poet*⟩; slight, minor ⟨*improvement, change, error*⟩
② *adv.* slightly
unbedingt ① *Adj.* absolute
② *adv.* absolutely
③ *Adv.* (auf jeden Fall) whatever happens
unbefangen *Adj.* (a) (ungehemmt) uninhibited
(b) (unvoreingenommen) impartial
Unbefangenheit *die;* ▶ UNBEFANGEN A, B: uninhibitedness; impartiality
unbefriedigend *Adj.* unsatisfactory
unbefristet ① *Adj.* for an indefinite period *postpos.;* indefinite ⟨*strike*⟩; unlimited ⟨*visa*⟩
② *adv.* for an indefinite period
unbefugt ① *Adj.* unauthorized
② *adv.* without authorization
unbegreiflich *Adj.* incomprehensible (*Dat.,* für to); incredible ⟨*love, goodness, stupidity, carelessness, etc.*⟩
unbegrenzt ① *Adj.* unlimited
② *adv.* ⟨*stay, keep, etc.*⟩ indefinitely
Unbehagen *das;* ~s uneasiness, disquiet; (Sorge) concern (an + *Dat.* about)
unbehaglich ① *Adj.* uneasy ⟨*feeling, atmosphere*⟩; uncomfortable ⟨*thought, room*⟩
② *adv.* uneasily
unbeherrscht *Adj.* uncontrolled; er ist ~: he has no self-control
Unbeherrschtheit *die;* ~: lack of self-control
unbeholfen ① *Adj.* clumsy
② *adv.* clumsily
unbekannt *Adj.* (a) unknown; (nicht vertraut) unfamiliar; unidentified ⟨*caller, donor*⟩; „Empfänger ~" 'not known at this address'

(b) (nicht vielen bekannt) little known; obscure ⟨*poet, painter, etc.*⟩
Unbekannte[1] *der/die; adj. Dekl.* unknown or unidentified man/woman; (Fremde[r]) stranger
Unbekannte[2] *die; adj. Dekl.* (Math.; auch fig.) unknown
unbekleidet *Adj.* without any clothes on *postpos.;* bare ⟨*torso etc.*⟩; naked ⟨*corpse*⟩
unbekümmert ① *Adj.* carefree; (ohne Bedenken, lässig) casual
② *adv.* (a) in a carefree way
(b) (ohne Bedenken) without caring or worrying
unbeleuchtet *Adj.* unlit ⟨*street, corridor, etc.*⟩; ⟨*vehicle*⟩ without [any] lights
unbeliebt *Adj.* unpopular (bei with)
unbemannt *Adj.* unmanned
unbemerkt *Adj., adv.* unnoticed
unbenutzt *Adj.* unused
unbequem ① *Adj.* (a) uncomfortable
(b) (lästig) awkward, embarrassing ⟨*question, opinion*⟩; troublesome ⟨*politician etc.*⟩; unpleasant ⟨*criticism, truth, etc.*⟩
② *adv.* uncomfortably
unberechenbar ① *Adj.* unpredictable
② *adv.* unpredictably
unberechtigt *Adj.* (a) (ungerechtfertigt) unjustified
(b) (unbefugt) unauthorized
unberührt *Adj.* untouched; sie ist noch ~: she is still a virgin
unbescheiden *Adj.* presumptuous
unbeschrankt *Adj.* ⟨*crossing*⟩ without gates, with no gates
unbeschreiblich ① *Adj.* indescribable; unimaginable ⟨*fear, beauty*⟩; ⟨*fear, beauty*⟩ beyond description
② *adv.* indescribably ⟨*beautiful*⟩; unbelievably ⟨*busy*⟩
unbesorgt *Adj.* unconcerned; seien Sie ~: don't [you] worry
unbeständig *Adj.* changeable ⟨*weather*⟩; fickle ⟨*lover etc.*⟩
unbestimmt ① *Adj.* (a) indefinite; indeterminate ⟨*age, number*⟩; (ungewiss) uncertain
(b) (ungenau) vague
(c) (Sprachw.) indefinite ⟨*article, pronoun*⟩
② *adv.* (ungenau) vaguely
unbestreitbar *Adj.* indisputable; unquestionable
unbestritten ① *Adj.* undisputed; ~ ist, dass … it is undisputed that …; there is no disputing that …
② *adv.* indisputably
unbewacht *Adj.* unsupervised; unattended ⟨*car park*⟩
unbewaffnet *Adj.* unarmed
unbeweglich *Adj.* motionless; still ⟨*air, water*⟩; fixed ⟨*gaze, expression*⟩

---

*alte Schreibung - vgl. Hinweis auf S. xiv

unbewegt *Adj.* motionless; fixed
⟨*expression*⟩

unbewohnbar *Adj.* uninhabitable

unbewohnt *Adj.* uninhabited ⟨*area*⟩;
unoccupied ⟨*house, flat*⟩

unbewusst, *unbewußt *Adj.*
unconscious

unbrauchbar *Adj.* unusable; (untauglich)
useless ⟨*method, person*⟩

und *Konj.* and; (folglich) [and] so; **ich ~**
tanzen? what, me dance?; **sei so gut ~ mach**
das Fenster zu be so good as to shut the
window

Undank *der;* ~[e]s: ingratitude

undankbar *Adj.* ungrateful ⟨*person,*
behaviour⟩

undenkbar *Adj.* unthinkable;
inconceivable

undeutlich ① *Adj.* unclear; indistinct;
(ungenau) vague ⟨*idea, memory, etc.*⟩
② *adv.* indistinctly; (ungenau) vaguely

undicht *Adj.* leaky; leaking; ~e **Fenster**
windows which do not fit tightly

Unding *das* **ein ~ sein** be preposterous *or*
ridiculous

undurchführbar *Adj.* impracticable

undurchlässig *Adj.* impermeable;
(wasserdicht) watertight; waterproof; (luftdicht)
airtight

uneben *Adj.* uneven

Unebenheit *die;* ~, ~en **(a)** unevenness
(b) (unebene Stelle) lumpy *or* uneven patch

unehelich *Adj.* illegitimate ⟨*child*⟩;
unmarried ⟨*mother*⟩

unehrlich ① *Adj.* dishonest
② *adv.* dishonestly; by dishonest means

uneigennützig *Adj.* unselfish

Uneigennützigkeit *die;* ~:
unselfishness

uneinig *Adj.* ⟨*party*⟩ divided by
disagreement; [sich (*Dat.*)] ~ **sein** disagree

Uneinigkeit *die;* ~: disagreement (in +
Dat. on)

uneins *Adj.* ~ **sein** be divided (in + *Dat.*
on); ⟨*persons*⟩ be at variance *or* at cross
purposes (in + *Dat.* over)

unempfindlich *Adj.* **(a)** insensitive
(**gegen** to)
(b) (immun) immune (**gegen** to, against)
(c) (strapazierfähig) hard-wearing

unendlich ① *Adj.* infinite; boundless;
(zeitlich) endless; (Math.) infinite
② *adv.* infinitely ⟨*lovable, sad*⟩;
immeasurably ⟨*happy*⟩; ⟨*happy*⟩ beyond
measure

unentbehrlich *Adj.* indispensable (*Dat.,*
für to)

unentgeltlich */od.* '—'/ ① *Adj.* free
② *adv.* free of charge; ⟨*work*⟩ for nothing,
without pay

unentschieden ① *Adj.* unsettled;
undecided ⟨*question*⟩; (Sport, Schach) drawn

② *adv.* ~ **spielen** draw

Unentschieden *das;* ~s, ~ (Sport, Schach)
draw

unentwegt */od.* --'-/ ① *Adj.* **(a)** (beharrlich)
persistent ⟨*fighter, champion, efforts*⟩
(b) (unaufhörlich) constant; incessant
② *adv.* **(a)** (beharrlich) persistently
(b) (unaufhörlich) constantly; incessantly

unerbittlich ① *Adj.* (auch fig.) inexorable;
unsparing ⟨*critic*⟩; relentless ⟨*battle,*
struggle⟩; implacable ⟨*hate, enemy*⟩
② *adv.* (auch fig.) inexorably

unerfahren *Adj.* inexperienced

unerfreulich ① *Adj.* unpleasant; bad
⟨*news*⟩
② *adv.* unpleasantly

unerheblich *Adj.* insignificant

unerhört ① *Adj.* (empörend) outrageous
② *adv.* outrageously

unerlaubt ① *Adj.* unauthorized
② *adv.* without authorization

unerledigt *Adj.* not dealt with *postpos.*

unermüdlich ① *Adj.* tireless, untiring
(**bei, in** + *Dat.* in)
② *adv.* tirelessly

unerreichbar *Adj.* inaccessible; (fig.)
unattainable

unerreicht *Adj.* unequalled

unersättlich *Adj.* insatiable

unerschöpflich *Adj.* inexhaustible

unersetzlich *Adj.* irreplaceable

unerträglich */od.* '—-/ *Adj.* unbearable;
intolerable ⟨*situation, conditions, etc.*⟩

unerwartet ① *Adj.* unexpected; **es kam**
für alle ~: it came as a surprise to
everybody
② *adv.* unexpectedly

unerwünscht *Adj.* unwanted; unwelcome
⟨*interruption, visit, visitor*⟩; undesirable ⟨*side*
effects⟩

unfähig *Adj.* **(a)** ~ **sein, etw. zu tun** (ständig)
be incapable of doing sth.; (momentan) be
unable to do sth.
(b) (inkompetent) incompetent

Unfähigkeit *die* **(a)** inability
(b) (Inkompetenz) incompetence

unfair ① *Adj.* unfair (**gegen** to)
② *adv.* unfairly

Un·fall *der;* ~[e]s, Unfälle accident

Unfall-: ~**arzt** *der,* ~**ärztin** *die* casualty
doctor; ~**flucht** *die* (Rechtsspr.) ~**flucht**
begehen fail to stop after [being involved in]
an accident; ~**opfer** *das* accident victim;
~**stelle** *die* scene of an/the accident;
~**versicherung** *die* accident insurance

unfehlbar *Adj.* infallible

Unfehlbarkeit *die;* ~: infallibility

unförmig *Adj.* shapeless; huge ⟨*legs,*
hands, body⟩; bulky, ungainly ⟨*shape, shoes,*
etc.⟩

unfrei *Adj.* not free *pred.;* subject,
dependent ⟨*people*⟩; ⟨*life*⟩ of bondage

u

unfreiwillig [1] *Adj.* involuntary;
(erzwungen) enforced ⟨*stay*⟩; (nicht beabsichtigt)
unintended ⟨*publicity, joke, humour*⟩
[2] *adv.* involuntarily; without wanting to;
(unbeabsichtigt) unintentionally

unfreundlich [1] *Adj.* unfriendly (**zu**,
gegen to); unkind ⟨*words, remark*⟩
[2] *adv.* in an unfriendly way

Unfreundlichkeit *die;* ~: unfriendliness

unfrisiert *Adj.* ungroomed ⟨*hair*⟩

unfruchtbar *Adj.* infertile; (fig.)
unproductive

Unfruchtbarkeit *die;* ~: infertility; (fig.)
unproductiveness

Unfug *der;* ~[e]s (a) [piece of] mischief;
grober ~: public nuisance
(b) (Unsinn) nonsense

Ungar *der;* ~n, ~n, **Ungarin** *die;* ~,
~nen Hungarian

ungarisch *Adj.* Hungarian

Ungarn (*das*); ~s Hungary

ungeachtet *Präp. mit Gen.* (geh.)
notwithstanding; despite

ungebildet *Adj.* uneducated

ungeboren *Adj.* unborn

ungebräuchlich *Adj.* uncommon; rare;
rarely used ⟨*method, process*⟩

ungebrochen *Adj.* (fig.) unbroken ⟨*will,
person*⟩; undiminished ⟨*strength, courage*⟩

ungedeckt *Adj.* uncovered ⟨*cheque*⟩

Ungeduld *die;* ~: impatience

ungeduldig [1] *Adj.* impatient
[2] *adv.* impatiently

ungeeignet *Adj.* unsuitable; (für eine
Aufgabe) unsuited (**für, zu** to, for)

ungefähr [1] *Adj.* approximate; rough
⟨*idea, outline*⟩
[2] *adv.* approximately; roughly

ungefährlich *Adj.* safe; harmless ⟨*animal,
person, illness, etc.*⟩

ungeheizt *Adj.* unheated

ungeheuer [1] *Adj.* enormous; tremendous
⟨*strength, energy, effort, enthusiasm, fear,
success, pressure, etc.*⟩; vast, immense
⟨*fortune, knowledge*⟩; (schrecklich) terrible
(coll.), terrific (coll.) ⟨*pain, rage*⟩
[2] *adv.* tremendously; terribly (coll.)
⟨*difficult, clever*⟩

Ungeheuer *das;* ~s, ~ (auch fig.) monster

ungeheuerlich *Adj.* monstrous;
outrageous

Ungeheuerlichkeit *die;* ~, ~en (a)
monstrous nature; outrageousness
(b) (Vorgang) monstrous *or* outrageous thing

ungehindert *Adj.* unimpeded

ungehörig [1] *Adj.* improper; (frech)
impertinent
[2] *adv.* improperly; (frech) impertinently

ungehorsam *Adj.* disobedient (**gegenüber**
to)

Ungehorsam *der;* ~s disobedience
(**gegenüber** to)

ungekürzt *Adj.* unabridged ⟨*edition, book*⟩;
uncut ⟨*film, speech*⟩

ungelegen [1] *Adj.* das kommt mir sehr ~/
nicht ~: that is very inconvenient *or*
awkward/quite convenient for me
[2] *adv.* inconveniently

ungelernt *Adj.* unskilled

ungemütlich [1] *Adj.* uninviting, cheerless
⟨*room, flat*⟩; uncomfortable, unfriendly
⟨*atmosphere*⟩
[2] *adv.* uncomfortably ⟨*furnished*⟩

ungenau [1] *Adj.* inaccurate; imprecise,
inexact ⟨*definition, formulation, etc.*⟩;
(undeutlich) vague ⟨*memory, idea, impression*⟩
[2] *adv.* inaccurately; ⟨*define*⟩ imprecisely,
inexactly; ⟨*remember*⟩ vaguely

ungeniert /ˈʊnʒeniːɐ̯t/ [1] *Adj.* free and
easy; uninhibited
[2] *adv.* openly; ⟨*yawn*⟩ unconcernedly;
⟨*undress etc.*⟩ without any embarrassment

ungenießbar *Adj.* (nicht essbar) inedible;
(nicht trinkbar) undrinkable; (fig. ugs.)
unbearable

ungenügend [1] *Adj.* inadequate; die Note
„~"/ein Ungenügend (Schulw.) the/an
'unsatisfactory' [mark]
[2] *adv.* inadequately

ungepflegt *Adj.* neglected ⟨*garden, park,
car, etc.*⟩; unkempt ⟨*person, appearance,
hair*⟩; uncared-for ⟨*hands*⟩

ungerade *Adj.* odd ⟨*number*⟩

ungerecht [1] *Adj.* unjust, unfair (**gegen**,
zu, gegenüber to)
[2] *adv.* unjustly; unfairly

Ungerechtigkeit *die;* ~, ~en injustice

ungern *Adv.* reluctantly; etw. ~ tun not like
or dislike doing sth.

ungerührt *Adj.* unmoved

ungeschält *Adj.* unpeeled ⟨*fruit*⟩

ungeschehen *Adj.* etw. ~ machen undo
sth.

Ungeschicklichkeit *die;* ~, ~en
(a) clumsiness
(b) (etwas Ungeschicktes) piece of clumsiness

ungeschickt [1] *Adj.* clumsy; awkward
[2] *adv.* clumsily; awkwardly

ungesetzlich [1] *Adj.* unlawful; illegal
[2] *adv.* unlawfully; illegally

ungestempelt *Adj.* uncancelled ⟨*stamp*⟩

ungestört *Adj.* undisturbed; uninterrupted
⟨*development*⟩

ungesund *Adj.* (auch fig.) unhealthy

Ungetüm *das;* ~s, ~e monster

ungewiss, *ungewiß *Adj.* uncertain;
über etw. (*Akk.*) im Ungewissen sein be
uncertain *or* unsure about sth.

Ungewissheit, *Ungewißheit *die;* ~,
~en uncertainty

ungewöhnlich [1] *Adj.* (a) unusual

(b) (sehr groß) exceptional ⟨*strength, beauty, ability, etc.*⟩; outstanding ⟨*achievement, success*⟩
② *adv.* **(a)** ⟨*behave*⟩ abnormally, strangely
(b) (enorm) exceptionally

ungewohnt ① *Adj.* unaccustomed; (nicht vertraut) unfamiliar ⟨*method, work, surroundings, etc.*⟩
② *adv.* unusually

ungewollt ① *Adj.* unwanted; (unbeabsichtigt) unintentional; inadvertent
② *adv.* unintenionally; inadvertently

Ungeziefer *das;* ~s vermin *pl.*

ungezogen ① *Adj.* naughty; badly behaved; bad ⟨*behaviour*⟩; (frech) cheeky
② *adv.* naughtily; ⟨*behave*⟩ badly

ungezwungen *Adj.* natural, unaffected ⟨*person, behaviour, cheerfulness*⟩; (nicht förmlich) informal, free and easy ⟨*tone, conversation, etc.*⟩

ungläubig ① *Adj.* **(a)** disbelieving
(b) (Rel.) unbelieving
② *adv.* in disbelief

unglaublich ① *Adj.* incredible
② *adv.* (ugs.: äußerst) incredibly (coll.)

unglaubwürdig *Adj.* implausible; untrustworthy, unreliable ⟨*witness etc.*⟩

ungleich ① *Adj.* unequal; odd, unmatching ⟨*socks, gloves, etc.*⟩; (unähnlich) dissimilar
② *adv.* **(a)** unequally
(b) (ungleichmäßig) unevenly

ungleichmäßig ① *Adj.* uneven
② *adv.* unevenly

Unglück *das;* ~[e]s, ~e **(a)** (Unfall) accident; (Flugzeugunglück, Zugunglück) crash; accident
(b) (Not) misfortune; (Leid) suffering
(c) (Pech) bad luck; ~ haben be unlucky; **das bringt** ~: that's unlucky
(d) (Schicksalsschlag) misfortune

unglücklich ① *Adj.* **(a)** unhappy
(b) (nicht vom Glück begünstigt) unfortunate ⟨*person*⟩; (bedauernswert, arm) hapless ⟨*person, animal*⟩
(c) (ungünstig, ungeschickt) unfortunate ⟨*moment, combination, meeting, etc.*⟩; unhappy ⟨*end, choice, solution*⟩
② *adv.* **(a)** unhappily
(b) (ungünstig) unfortunately; (ungeschickt) unhappily, clumsily ⟨*translated, expressed*⟩

unglücklicher·weise *Adv.* unfortunately

Unglücks·fall *der* accident

Ungnade *die* [bei jmdm.] in ~ (*Akk.*) **fallen/in** ~ (*Dat.*) **sein** fall/be out of favour [with sb.]

ungnädig *Adj.* bad-tempered; grumpy

ungültig *Adj.* invalid; void (esp. Law); spoilt ⟨*vote, ballot paper*⟩; disallowed ⟨*goal*⟩

Ungunst *die* zu jmds. ~en to sb.'s disadvantage

ungünstig ① *Adj.* **(a)** unfavourable; unfortunate, bad ⟨*shape, layout*⟩
(b) (unpassend) inconvenient ⟨*time*⟩; (ungeeignet) inappropriate, inconvenient ⟨*time, place*⟩
② *adv.* **(a)** unfavourably; badly ⟨*designed, laid out*⟩
(b) (unpassend) inconveniently

ungut *Adj.* nichts für ~! no offence [meant]! (coll.)

unhandlich *Adj.* unwieldy

Unheil *das;* ~s disaster

unheilbar ① *Adj.* incurable
② *adv.* incurably

unheil·voll *Adj.* disastrous; (verhängnisvoll) fateful

unheimlich ① *Adj.* **(a)** eerie
(b) (ugs.) (schrecklich) terrible (coll.) ⟨*hunger, headache, etc.*⟩ terrific (coll.) ⟨*fun etc.*⟩
② *adv.* **(a)** eerily
(b) (ugs.: äußerst) terribly (coll.); incredibly (coll.) ⟨*quick, long*⟩

unhöflich ① *Adj.* impolite
② *adv.* impolitely

Unhöflichkeit *die;* ~, ~en impoliteness

unhygienisch ① *Adj.* unhygienic
② *adv.* unhygienically

Uni *die;* ~, ~s (ugs.) university

Uniform *die;* ~, ~en uniform

uninteressant *Adj.* uninteresting; (nicht von Belang) of no interest *postpos.;* unimportant

Union *die;* ~, ~en union

Universität *die;* ~, ~en university

Universum *das;* ~s universe

unkenntlich *Adj.* unrecognizable ⟨*person, face*⟩; indecipherable ⟨*writing, stamp*⟩

Unkenntnis *die;* ~: ignorance

unklar *Adj.* unclear; sich (*Dat.*) über etw. (*Akk.*) im Unklaren sein be unclear *or* unsure about sth.

unkonventionell ① *Adj.* unconventional
② *adv.* unconventionally

Unkosten *Pl.* **(a)** [extra] expense *sing.;* expenses
(b) (ugs.: Ausgaben) costs; expenditure *sing.*

Unkosten·beitrag *der* contribution towards expenses

Unkraut *das;* ~[e]s, Unkräuter weeds *pl.*

unkultiviert *Adj.* uncultivated

unlauter *Adj.* (geh.) dishonest; ~er **Wettbewerb** (Rechtsspr.) unfair competition

unleserlich ① *Adj.* illegible
② *adv.* illegibly

unmäßig ① *Adj.* immoderate; excessive
② *adv.* excessively; ⟨*eat, drink*⟩ to excess

Unmenge *die* mass; enormous number/amount

Unmensch *der;* ~en, ~en brute

unmenschlich ① *Adj.* **(a)** inhuman; brutal; appalling ⟨*conditions*⟩
(b) (entsetzlich) appalling

 ⋯⋮⟩

u

2 *adv.* **(a)** in an inhuman way **(b)** (entsetzlich) appallingly (coll.)

unmissverständlich, *unmißverständlich* 1 *Adj.* **(a)** (eindeutig) unambiguous **(b)** (offen, direkt) blunt ‹*answer, refusal*›; unequivocal ‹*language*›
2 *adv.* **(a)** (eindeutig) unambiguously **(b)** (offen, direkt) bluntly; unequivocally

unmittelbar 1 *Adj.* immediate; direct ‹*contact, connection, influence, etc.*›
2 *adv.* immediately; directly

unmöbliert *Adj.* unfurnished

unmodern 1 *Adj.* old-fashioned; (nicht modisch) unfashionable
2 *adv.* in an old-fashioned way; (nicht modisch) unfashionably

unmöglich 1 *Adj.* impossible; (ugs.: seltsam) incredible
2 *adv.* (ugs.) ‹*behave*› impossibly; ‹*dress*› ridiculously
3 *Adv.* (ugs.) **ich/es** *usw.* **kann ~ ...**: I/it *etc.* can't possibly ...

unmoralisch 1 *Adj.* immoral
2 *adv.* immorally

unmündig *Adj.* under-age

Unmut *der;* ~[e]s (geh.) displeasure; annoyance

unnachsichtig 1 *Adj.* merciless; unmerciful
2 *adv.* mercilessly; ‹*punish*› unmercifully

unnahbar *Adj.* unapproachable

unnatürlich 1 *Adj.* unnatural; forced ‹*laugh*›
2 *adv.* unnaturally; ‹*laugh*› in a forced way; ‹*speak*› affectedly

unnötig 1 *Adj.* unnecessary
2 *adv.* unnecessarily

unnütz *Adj.* useless

UNO *die;* ~: UN

unordentlich 1 *Adj.* **(a)** untidy **(b)** (ungeregelt) disorderly ‹*life*›
2 *adv.* untidily; ‹*tie, treat, etc.*› carelessly

Unordnung *die;* ~: disorder; mess

unparteiisch 1 *Adj.* impartial
2 *adv.* impartially

unpassend 1 *Adj.* inappropriate; unsuitable ‹*dress etc.*›
2 *adv.* inappropriately; unsuitably ‹*dressed etc.*›

unpersönlich 1 *Adj.* impersonal; distant, aloof ‹*person*›
2 *adv.* impersonally; ‹*answer, write*› in impersonal terms

unpraktisch 1 *Adj.* unpractical
2 *adv.* in an unpractical way

unproblematisch *Adj.* unproblematic

unproduktiv *Adj.* unproductive

unpünktlich 1 *Adj.* unpunctual ‹*person*›; late, unpunctual ‹*payment*›
2 *adv.* late

Unpünktlichkeit *die;* ~: lack of punctuality

Unrecht *das;* ~[e]s wrong; **zu ~**: wrongly; **~ haben** be wrong; **jmdm. ~ tun** do sb. an injustice

unrechtmäßig 1 *Adj.* unlawful
2 *adv.* unlawfully

unredlich (geh.) **1** *Adj.* dishonest
2 *adv.* dishonestly

Unredlichkeit *die;* ~, ~en **(a)** dishonesty **(b)** (Handlung) dishonest act

unregelmäßig 1 *Adj.* irregular
2 *adv.* irregularly

Unregelmäßigkeit *die;* ~, ~en irregularity

unreif *Adj.* **(a)** unripe **(b)** (nicht erwachsen) immature

unrentabel *Adj.* unprofitable

Unruhe *die;* ~, ~n (auch fig.) unrest; (Lärm) noise; (Unrast) restlessness; (Besorgnis) anxiety

unruhig 1 *Adj.* **(a)** restless; (besorgt) anxious; unsettled, troubled ‹*time*› **(b)** (laut) noisy **(c)** (ungleichmäßig) uneven ‹*breathing, pulse, etc.*›; fitful ‹*sleep*›; disturbed ‹*night*›
2 *adv.* **(a)** restlessly; (besorgt) anxiously **(b)** (ungleichmäßig) unevenly; ‹*sleep*› fitfully

uns 1 (a) *Akk. von* WIR us **(b)** *Dat. von* WIR; **gib es ~**: give it to us; **bei ~**: at our home or (coll.) place
2 *Reflexivpron. der 1. Pers. Pl.* **(a)** *refl.* ourselves **(b)** *reziprok* one another

unsachlich 1 *Adj.* unobjective
2 *adv.* without objectivity

unsauber 1 *Adj.* **(a)** dirty **(b)** (nachlässig) untidy; sloppy
2 *adv.* (nachlässig) untidily

unschädlich *Adj.* harmless

unscharf *Adj.* blurred ‹*photo, picture*›

unscheinbar *Adj.* inconspicuous

unschlagbar *Adj.* unbeatable

Unschuld *die;* ~: innocence; (Jungfräulichkeit) virginity

unschuldig 1 *Adj.* innocent
2 *adv.* innocently

unselbständig, unselbstständig *Adj.* dependent [on other people]

unser¹ *Possessivpron. der 1. Pers. Pl.* our; **das ist ~s** that is ours

unser² *Gen. von* WIR (geh.) of us; **in ~ aller/ beider Interesse** in the interest of all/both of us

unser-einer, unsereins *Indefinitpron.* (ugs.) the likes of us *pl.;* our sort (coll.)

unserer-seits *Adv.* for our part; (von uns) on our part

unser[e]s-gleichen *indekl. Indefinitpron.* people *pl.* like us

unsert-wegen *Adv.:* ▶ MEINETWEGEN: because of us; for our sake; about us; as far as we are concerned

unsicher 1 *Adj.* uncertain; (nicht selbstsicher) insecure
2 *adv.* ⟨walk, stand, etc.⟩ unsteadily; (nicht selbstsicher) ⟨smile, look⟩ diffidently

Unsicherheit *die;* ~: uncertainty; (fehlende Selbstsicherheit) insecurity

unsichtbar *Adj.* invisible (**für** to)

Unsinn *der;* ~[e]s nonsense; ~ **machen** mess *or* fool about

unsinnig *Adj.* nonsensical ⟨statement, talk, etc.⟩; absurd, ridiculous ⟨demand etc.⟩

Unsitte *die;* ~, ~n bad habit

unsittlich 1 *Adj.* indecent
2 *adv.* indecently

unsr... ▶ UNSER¹

unsterblich *Adj.* immortal

Unsterblichkeit *die;* ~: immortality

unstreitig 1 *Adj.* indisputable
2 *adv.* indisputably

unsympathisch *Adj.* uncongenial, disagreeable ⟨person⟩; unpleasant ⟨characteristic, nature, voice⟩

Untat *die;* ~, ~en misdeed; evil deed

untätig *Adj.* idle; ~ **herumsitzen/zusehen** sit around doing nothing/stand idly by

untauglich *Adj.* unsuitable; (für Militärdienst) unfit [for service] *postpos.*

unten *Adv.* (a) down; **hier/da** ~: down here/there; **von** ~: from below
(b) (in Gebäuden) downstairs; **nach** ~: downstairs
(c) (am unteren Ende, zum unteren Ende hin) at the bottom; ~ [**links**] **auf der Seite/im Schrank** at the bottom [left] of the page/cupboard
(d) (an der Unterseite) underneath
(e) (im Text) below; ~ **genannt** undermentioned (Brit.); mentioned below *postpos.*

*unten·genannt ▶ UNTEN E

unter 1 *Präp. mit Dat.* (Lage, Standort) under; (zwischen) among[st]; **Mengen** ~ **100 Stück** quantities of less than 100; ~ **Angst/ Tränen** in *or* out of fear/in tears
2 *Präp. mit Akk.* under; (zwischen) among[st]; ~ **Null sinken** drop below zero
3 *Adv.* less than; ~ **30** [**Jahre alt**] **sein** be under 30 [years of age]

unter... *Adj.* lower; bottom; (ganz unten) bottom; (in der Rangfolge o. Ä.) lower

Unter·arm *der* forearm

unterbelichten *tr. V.;* **ich unterbelichte, unterbelichtet, unterzubelichten** (Fot.) underexpose

Unter·bewusstsein,
*Unter·bewußtsein *das* subconscious

unter·bleiben *unr. itr. V.; mit sein* **etw. unterbleibt** sth. does not occur *or* happen

unter·brechen *unr. tr. V.* interrupt; break ⟨journey, silence⟩

Unter·brechung *die* ▶ UNTERBRECHEN: interruption; break (*Gen.* in)

unter|bringen *unr. tr. V.* (a) put
(b) (beherbergen) put up

Unterbringung *die;* ~, ~en accommodation *no indef. art.*

unter|buttern *tr. V.* (ugs.) push aside (fig.)

*unter·der·hand ▶ HAND

unter·dessen ▶ INZWISCHEN

unter·drücken *tr. V.* suppress; hold back ⟨comment, question, answer, criticism, etc.⟩; oppress ⟨minority etc.⟩

Unterdrückung *die;* ~, ~en (a) (das Unterdrücken) suppression
(b) (das Unterdrücktwerden, -sein) oppression

unter·einander *Adv.* (a) (räumlich) one below the other
(b) (miteinander) among[st] ourselves/ themselves *etc.*

unter·ernährt *Adj.* undernourished

Unter·ernährung *die* malnutrition

Unter·führung *die* underpass; (für Fußgänger) subway (Brit.); [pedestrian] underpass (Amer.)

unter-, Unter-: ~**gang** *der* (a) (Sonnenuntergang, Monduntergang usw.) setting; (b) (von Schiffen) sinking; (c) (das Zugrundegehen) decline; ~|**gehen** *unr. itr. V.; mit sein* (a) ⟨sun, star, etc.⟩ set; ⟨ship⟩ sink, go down; ⟨person⟩ drown, go under; (b) (zugrunde gehen) come to an end; ~**geordnet** *Adj.* secondary ⟨role, importance, etc.⟩; subordinate ⟨position, post, etc.⟩; ~**geschoss, *~geschoß** *das* basement; ~**gewicht** *das* underweight; ~**grund** *der* (bes. Politik) underground; ~**grund·bahn** *die* underground [railway] (Brit.); subway (Amer.); ~|**haken** *tr. V.* (ugs.) jmdn. ~**haken** take sb.'s arm; ~**halb** 1 *Adv.* below; ~**halb von** below; 2 *Präp. mit Gen.* below; ~**halt** *der* (a) living; (b) (Zahlung) maintenance; (c) (Instandhaltung[skosten]) upkeep

unter-, Unter-: ~**halten** 1 *unr. tr. V.* (a) support; (b) (instand halten) maintain ⟨building⟩; (c) (betreiben) run, keep ⟨car, hotel⟩; (d) (pflegen) maintain, keep up ⟨contact, correspondence⟩; (e) entertain ⟨guest, audience⟩; 2 *unr. refl. V.* (a) talk; converse; (b) (sich vergnügen) enjoy oneself; ~**haltsam** *Adj.* entertaining; ~**haltung** *die* (a) (Versorgung) support; (b) (Instandhaltung) maintenance; (c) (Gespräch) conversation; (d) (Zeitvertreib) entertainment

unter-, Unter-: ~**händler** *der,* ~**händlerin** *die* (bes. Politik) negotiator; ~**hemd** *das* vest (Brit.); undershirt (Amer.); ~**holz** *das* underwood; undergrowth; ~**hose** *die* (für Männer) briefs *pl.;* [under]pants *pl.;* (für Frauen) panties *pl.;* knickers *pl.* (Brit.); ~**irdisch** 1 *Adj.* underground; 2 *adv.* underground; ~|**jubeln** *tr. V.* (ugs.) jmdm. etw. ~**jubeln** palm sth. off on sb.; ~**kiefer** *der* lower ⋯⟩

jaw; ∼|**kommen** *unr. itr. V.; mit sein* find
accommodation; ∼**kühlt** *Adj.* ∼**kühlt sein**
be suffering from hypothermia *or* exposure

Unterkunft *die;* ∼, **Unterkünfte**
accommodation *no indef. art.;* lodging *no
indef. art.;* ∼ **und Frühstück** bed and
breakfast; ∼ **und Verpflegung** board and
lodging

Unter·lage *die* **(a)** (Schreibunterlage) pad; (für
eine Schreibmaschine usw.) mat
(b) *Pl.* documents; papers

unter-, Unter-: ∼**lassen** *unr. tr. V.*
refrain from [doing]; ∼**lassung** *die;* ∼∼,
∼∼**en** omission; failure;
∼**lassungs·sünde** *die* (ugs.) sin of
omission; ∼**laufen** *unr. itr. V.; mit sein*
occur; jmdm. **ist ein Fehler/Irrtum** ∼**laufen** sb.
made a mistake; ∼**legen** *Adj.* inferior;
jmdm. ∼**legen sein** be inferior to sb. **(an +**
Dat. in); ∼**leib** *der* lower abdomen

unter·liegen *unr. itr. V.* **(a)** *mit sein* (besiegt
werden) lose; be beaten *or* defeated
(b) (unterworfen sein) be subject to

Unter·lippe *die* lower lip

unterm *Präp. + Art.* = **unter dem**

unter·malen *tr. V.* accompany

Unter·malung *die;* ∼, ∼**en**
accompaniment (*Gen.* to)

unter·mauern *tr. V.* (mit Argumenten, Fakten
absichern) back up

Unter-: ∼**miete** *die* subtenancy; sublease;
∼**mieter** *der,* ∼**mieterin** *die* subtenant;
lodger

untern (ugs.) *Präp. + Art.* = **unter den**

unter-, Unter-: ∼**nehmen** *unr. tr. V.* **(a)**
(durchführen) undertake; make; take ⟨*steps*⟩; **(b)**
etwas ∼**nehmen** do something; ∼**nehmen**
das; ∼∼**s**, ∼∼ **(a)** (Vorhaben) enterprise; **(b)**
(Firma) concern; ∼**nehmer** *der;* ∼∼**s**, ∼∼,
∼**nehmerin** *die;* ∼∼, ∼∼**nen** employer

unternehmerisch [1] *Adj.*
entrepreneurial
[2] *adv.* ⟨*think*⟩ in an entrepreneurial *or*
businesslike way

unter·nehmungs·lustig *Adj.* active; **sie
ist sehr** ∼ she is always out doing things

Unter·offizier *der* **(a)** non-commissioned
officer
(b) (Dienstgrad) corporal

unter|ordnen [1] *tr. V.* subordinate
[2] *refl. V.* accept a subordinate role

Unter·redung *die;* ∼, ∼**en** discussion

Unter·richt *der;* ∼**[e]s**, ∼**e** instruction;
(Schulunterricht) teaching; (Schulstunden) classes
pl.

unter·richten [1] *tr. V.* **(a)** teach
(b) (informieren) inform **(über +** *Akk.* of, about)
[2] *itr. V.* (Unterricht geben) teach
[3] *refl. V.* (sich informieren) inform oneself
(über + *Akk.* about)

Unterrichts·stunde *die* lesson; period

───────────

*old spelling - see note on page xiv

Unter·rock *der* [half] slip

unter|rühren *tr. V.* stir in

unters *Präp. + Art.* = **unter das**

unter·sagen *tr. V.* forbid; prohibit

Unter·satz *der* ▶ **UNTERSETZER**

unter-, Unter-: ∼**schätzen** *tr. V.*
underestimate ⟨*amount, effect, etc.*⟩;
underrate ⟨*talent, ability, etc.*⟩; ∼**scheiden**
[1] *unr. tr. V.* distinguish; [2] *unr. refl. V.*
differ **(durch** in, **von** from); ∼**scheidung**
die (Vorgang) differentiation; (Resultat)
distinction

Unter-: ∼**schenkel** *der* shank; lower leg;
∼**schicht** *die* (Soziol.) lower class

Unter·schied *der;* ∼**[e]s**, ∼**e** difference

unterschiedlich [1] *Adj.* different;
(uneinheitlich) variable; varying
[2] *adv.* **[sehr/ganz]** ∼: in [very/quite]
different ways

unterschieds·los [1] *Adj.* uniform; equal
⟨*treatment*⟩
[2] *adv.* ⟨*treat*⟩ equally; (ohne Benachteiligung)
without discrimination

unter·schlagen *unr. tr. V.* embezzle
⟨*money, funds, etc.*⟩; (unterdrücken) intercept
⟨*letter*⟩; withhold ⟨*fact, news, information,
etc.*⟩

Unter·schlupf *der;* ∼**[e]s**, ∼**e** shelter;
(Versteck) hiding place; hideout

unter|schlüpfen *itr. V.; mit sein* (ugs.)
hide out

unter·schreiben *unr. itr., tr. V.* sign

Unter-: ∼**schrift** *die* signature; (Bild∼)
caption; ∼**see-boot** *das* submarine;
∼**setzer** *der* mat; (für Gläser) coaster

untersetzt *Adj.* stocky

Unter·stand *der* (Schutzbunker) dugout;
(Unterschlupf) shelter

unter·stehen [1] *unr. itr. V.* jmdm. ∼: be
subordinate *or* answerable to sb.
[2] *unr. refl. V.* dare

unter|stellen¹ [1] *tr. V.* (zur Aufbewahrung)
keep; store ⟨*furniture*⟩
[2] *refl. V.* take shelter

unter·stellen² *tr. V.* **(a)** jmdm. **eine
Abteilung** ∼: put sb. in charge of a
department; **die Behörde ist dem Ministerium
unterstellt** the office is under the ministry
(b) (unterschieben) jmdm. **böse Absichten** *usw.*
∼: insinuate that sb.'s intentions *etc.* are bad

Unter·stellung *die* (falsche Behauptung)
insinuation

unter·streichen *unr. tr. V.* **(a)** underline
(b) (hervorheben) emphasize

Unter·streichung *die;* ∼, ∼**en**
(a) underlining
(b) (das Betonen) emphasizing

unter·stützen *tr. V.* support

Unter·stützung *die;* ∼, ∼**en (a)** support
(b) (finanzielle Hilfe) allowance; (für Arbeitslose)
[unemployment] benefit *no art.*

unter·suchen *tr. V.* examine; (überprüfen)

test (auf + *Akk.* for); (aufzuklären suchen) investigate; (durchsuchen) search (auf + *Akk.*, nach for)

Untersuchung *die;* ~, ~en **(a)**
▸ UNTERSUCHEN: examination; test; investigation; search **(b)** (wissenschaftliche Arbeit) study

Untersuchungs·haft *die* imprisonment *or* detention while awaiting trial

Unter·tasse *die* saucer

unter|tauchen ① *itr. V.; mit sein* **(a)** (im Wasser) dive [under] **(b)** (verschwinden) disappear ② *tr. V.* duck

Unter·tell *das od. der* bottom part

unter·teilen *tr. V.* divide; (gliedern) subdivide

Unter·titel *der* subtitle

unter·treiben *unr. itr. V.* play things down

Untertreibung *die;* ~, ~en understatement

unter·vermieten *tr., itr. V.* sublet

unter·wandern *tr. V.* infiltrate

Unter·wanderung *die* infiltration *no indef. art.*

Unter·wäsche *die* underwear

unterwegs *Adv.* on the way; (nicht zu Hause) out [and about]

unter·weisen *unr. tr. V.* (geh.) instruct

Unter·welt *die;* ~: underworld

unter·werfen ① *unr. tr. V.* **(a)** subjugate ⟨people, country⟩ **(b)** (unterziehen) subject (*Dat.* to) ② *unr. refl. V.* sich [jmdm./einer Sache] ~: submit [to sb./sth.]

Unterwerfung *die;* ~, ~en **(a)** (das Unterwerfen) subjugation (unter + *Akk.* to) **(b)** (das Sichunterwerfen) submission (unter + *Akk.* to)

unterwürfig ① *Adj.* obsequious ② *adv.* obsequiously

unter·zeichnen *tr. V.* sign

unter·ziehen ① *unr. tr. V.* etw. einer Untersuchung/Überprüfung (*Dat.*) ~: examine/check sth. ② *unr. refl. V.* sich einer Operation (*Dat.*) ~: undergo *or* have an operation

untragbar *Adj.* unbearable

untreu *Adj.* disloyal; (in der Ehe, Liebe) unfaithful

Untreue *die;* ~: disloyalty; (in der Ehe, Liebe) unfaithfulness

untröstlich *Adj.* inconsolable

Untugend *die;* ~, ~en bad habit

unüberlegt ① *Adj.* rash ② *adv.* rashly

unübersehbar ① *Adj.* **(a)** (offenkundig) conspicuous **(b)** (sehr groß) enormous ② *adv.* (sehr) extremely

unübersichtlich ① *Adj.* unclear; confusing ⟨arrangement⟩; blind ⟨bend⟩; broken ⟨country etc.⟩ ② *adv.* unclearly; confusingly ⟨arranged⟩

unübertrefflich ① *Adj.* superb ② *adv.* superbly

unübertroffen *Adj.* unsurpassed

unumgänglich *Adj.* [absolutely] necessary

Unumgänglichkeit *die;* ~: absolute necessity

unumwunden ① *Adj.* frank ② *adv.* frankly; openly

ununterbrochen ① *Adj.* incessant ② *adv.* incessantly

unveränderlich *Adj.* unchangeable

unverantwortlich ① *Adj.* irresponsible ② *adv.* irresponsibly

unverbesserlich *Adj.* incorrigible

unverbindlich ① *Adj.* **(a)** not binding *pred.;* without obligation *postpos;* **(b)** (reserviert) non-committal ⟨answer, words⟩; impersonal ⟨attitude⟩ ② *adv.* ⟨send, reserve⟩ without obligation

unverbleit *Adj.* unleaded

unverblümt ① *Adj.* blunt ② *adv.* bluntly

unverbraucht *Adj.* untouched; unspent ⟨energy⟩; fresh ⟨air⟩

unverdaut *Adj.* undigested

unverdorben *Adj.* unspoilt

unverdrossen *Adj.* undeterred; (unverzagt) undaunted

unvereinbar *Adj.* incompatible (mit with)

Unvereinbarkeit *die;* ~: incompatibility (mit with)

unverfänglich *Adj.* harmless

unverfroren *Adj.* insolent; impudent

unvergänglich *Adj.* immortal ⟨fame⟩; unchanging ⟨beauty⟩; abiding ⟨recollection⟩

unvergesslich, *unvergeßlich *Adj.* unforgettable

unvergleichlich ① *Adj.* incomparable ② *adv.* incomparably

unverheiratet *Adj.* unmarried

unverhofft ① *Adj.* unexpected ② *adv.* unexpectedly

unverhohlen ① *Adj.* unconcealed ② *adv.* openly

unverkäuflich *Adj.* diese Vase ist ~: this vase is not for sale/(nicht absetzbar) unsaleable

unvermeidlich *Adj.* unavoidable; (sich als Folge ergebend) inevitable

Unvermögen *das;* ~s lack of ability

unvermutet ① *Adj.* unexpected ② *adv.* unexpectedly

unvernünftig *Adj.* stupid; foolish

unverrichtet *Adj.* ~er Dinge without having achieved anything

u

unverschämt 1 *Adj.* **(a)** impertinent ⟨*person, manner, words, etc.*⟩; barefaced ⟨*lie*⟩ **(b)** (ugs.: sehr groß) outrageous ⟨*price, luck, etc.*⟩ 2 *adv.* impertinently; ⟨*lie*⟩ barefacedly; blatantly

Unverschämtheit *die;* ~, ~en impertinence

unversehens *Adv.* suddenly

unversehrt *Adj.* unscathed; (unbeschädigt) undamaged

unverständlich *Adj.* incomprehensible

Unverständnis *das;* ~ses lack of understanding

unverträglich *Adj.* **(a)** quarrelsome **(b)** incompatible ⟨*blood groups, medicines, transplant tissue*⟩

unverwechselbar *Adj.* unmistakable; distinctive

unverwüstlich *Adj.* indestructible

unverzeihlich *Adj.* unforgivable

unverzüglich 1 *Adj.* prompt 2 *adv.* promptly

unvollkommen 1 *Adj.* **(a)** imperfect **(b)** (unvollständig) incomplete 2 *adv.* **(a)** imperfectly **(b)** (unvollständig) incompletely

Unvollkommenheit *die;* ~: **(a)** imperfectness **(b)** (Unvollständigkeit) incompleteness

unvollständig *Adj.* incomplete

Unvollständigkeit *die;* ~: incompleteness

unvorhergesehen *Adj.* unforeseen; unexpected ⟨*visit*⟩

unvorhersehbar *Adj.* unforeseeable

unvorsichtig 1 *Adj.* careless; (unüberlegt) rash 2 *adv.* carelessly; (unüberlegt) rashly

Unvorsichtigkeit *die;* ~ ▶ UNVORSICHTIG 1: carelessness; rashness

unvorstellbar 1 *Adj.* inconceivable 2 *adv.* unimaginably

unvorteilhaft *Adj.* **(a)** unattractive ⟨*figure, appearance*⟩ **(b)** (ohne Vorteil) unfavourable, poor ⟨*purchase, exchange*⟩; unprofitable ⟨*business*⟩

unwahr *Adj.* untrue

Unwahrheit *die;* ~, ~en **(a)** untruthfulness **(b)** (Äußerung) untruth

unwahrscheinlich 1 *Adj.* **(a)** improbable; unlikely **(b)** (ugs.: sehr viel) incredible (coll.) 2 *adv.* (ugs.: sehr) incredibly (coll.)

Unwahrscheinlichkeit *die;* ~: improbability

unwegsam *Adj.* [almost] impassable

unweiblich *Adj.* unfeminine

unweigerlich 1 *Adj.* inevitable

2 *adv.* inevitably

Unwesen *das:* sein ~ treiben (abwertend) be up to one's mischief *or* one's tricks

Unwetter *das;* ~s, ~: [thunder]storm

unwichtig *Adj.* unimportant

Unwichtigkeit *die;* ~, ~en **(a)** unimportance **(b)** (etw. Unwichtiges) unimportant thing

unwiderruflich 1 *Adj.* irrevocable 2 *adv.* irrevocably

unwiderstehlich *Adj.* irresistible

unwiederbringlich (geh.) 1 *Adj.* irretrievable 2 *adv.* irretrievably

Unwille[n] *der;* Unwillens displeasure

unwillig 1 *Adj.* indignant; (widerwillig) unwilling 2 *adv.* indignantly; (widerwillig) unwillingly

unwillkürlich 1 *Adj.* **(a)** spontaneous ⟨*cry, sigh*⟩; instinctive ⟨*reaction, movement, etc.*⟩ **(b)** (Physiol.) involuntary ⟨*movement etc.*⟩ 2 *adv.* **(a)** ⟨*shout etc.*⟩ spontaneously; ⟨*react, move, etc.*⟩ instinctively **(b)** (Physiol.) ⟨*move etc.*⟩ involuntarily

unwirklich (geh.) *Adj.* unreal

Unwirklichkeit *die;* ~, ~en unreality

unwirksam *Adj.* ineffective

Unwirksamkeit *die;* ~: ineffectiveness

unwirsch 1 *Adj.* surly; ill-natured 2 *adv.* ill-naturedly

unwirtschaftlich 1 *Adj.* uneconomic ⟨*procedure etc.*⟩; (nicht sparsam) uneconomical ⟨*driving etc.*⟩ 2 *adv.* ⟨*work, drive, etc.*⟩ uneconomically

Unwissenheit *die;* ~: ignorance

unwissentlich 1 *Adj.* unconscious 2 *adv.* unknowingly; unwittingly

unwohl *Adv.* unwell; mir ist ~: I don't feel well

Unwohlsein *das;* ~s indisposition

unwürdig *Adj.* **(a)** undignified ⟨*person, behaviour*⟩; degrading ⟨*treatment*⟩ **(b)** (unangemessen) unworthy

unzählig *Adj.* innumerable; countless

Unze *die;* ~, ~n ounce

unzeitgemäß *Adj.* anachronistic

unzerbrechlich *Adj.* unbreakable

unzertrennlich *Adj.* inseparable

Unzucht *die:* ~ treiben fornicate; gewerbsmäßige ~: prostitution

unzüchtig 1 *Adj.* obscene ⟨*letter, gesture*⟩ 2 *adv.* ⟨*touch, approach, etc.*⟩ indecently; ⟨*speak*⟩ obscenely

unzufrieden *Adj.* dissatisfied; (stärker) unhappy

Unzufriedenheit *die;* ~: dissatisfaction; (stärker) unhappiness

unzugänglich *Adj.* inaccessible ⟨*area, building, etc.*⟩; unapproachable ⟨*character, person, etc.*⟩

---

unzulänglich (geh.) 1 *Adj.* insufficient
2 *adv.* insufficiently

unzumutbar *Adj.* unreasonable

unzurechnungsfähig *Adj.* not
responsible for one's actions *pred.;*
(geistesgestört) of unsound mind *postpos.*

unzustellbar *Adj.* (Postw.) „∼": 'not
known [at this address]'

unzutreffend *Adj.* inappropriate; (falsch)
incorrect

unzuverlässig *Adj.* unreliable

Unzuverlässigkeit *die;* ∼: unreliability

unzweckmäßig 1 *Adj.* unsuitable;
(unpraktisch) impractical
2 *adv.* unsuitably; (unpraktisch) impractically

Update /'apdeit/ *das;* ∼s, ∼s (DV) update

üppig 1 *Adj.* lush ⟨*vegetation*⟩; thick ⟨*hair,
beard*⟩; full ⟨*bosom, lips*⟩; voluptuous ⟨*figure,
woman*⟩; (fig.) sumptuous, opulent ⟨*meal*⟩
2 *adv.* luxuriantly; (fig.) sumptuously

Ur·abstimmung *die* [*esp.* strike] ballot

Ural *der;* ∼[s] Urals *pl.;* Ural Mountains *pl.*

ur·alt *Adj.* very old; ancient

Uran *das;* ∼s uranium

Ur·aufführung *die* première; first night *or*
performance; (eines Films) première; first
showing

urbar *Adj.* ein Stück Land ∼ machen
cultivate a piece of land

Ur·einwohner *der,* **Ur·einwohnerin**
die native inhabitant

Ur·enkel *der* great-grandson

Urgroß-: ∼**eltern** *Pl.* great-grandparents;
∼**mutter** *die; Pl.* ∼**mütter** great-
grandmother; ∼**vater** *der* great-
grandfather

Ur·heber *der;* ∼s, ∼: originator; initiator;
(bes. Rechtsspr.: Verfasser, Autor) author

Urheber·recht *das* copyright

urig *Adj.* natural ⟨*person*⟩; real ⟨*beer*⟩; cosy
⟨*pub*⟩

Urin *der;* ∼s, ∼e (Med.) urine

urinieren *itr. V.* urinate

Ur·knall *der* big bang

Ur·kunde *die;* ∼, ∼n document;
(Bescheinigung, Siegerurkunde, Diplom usw.)
certificate

Urlaub *der;* ∼[e]s, ∼e holiday[s] (Brit.);
vacation (esp. Amer.); (bes. Milit.) leave

urlaubs-, Urlaubs-: ∼**geld** *das* holiday
pay *or* money; (gespartes Geld) holiday
money; ∼**ort** *der* holiday resort; ∼**reif**
Adj. ∼reif sein (ugs.) be ready for a holiday;
∼**reise** *die* holiday [trip]; ∼**zeit** *die*
holiday period *or* season

Urne *die;* ∼, ∼n urn; (Wahlurne) [ballot] box

Ur·oma *die* (fam.) great-granny (coll./child
lang.)

Ur·opa *der* (fam.) great-grandpa (coll./child
lang.)

Ur·sache *die* cause

Ur·sprung *der* origin

ur·sprünglich 1 *Adj.* (a) original ⟨*plan,
price, form, material, etc.*⟩
(b) (natürlich) natural
2 *adv.* (a) originally
(b) (natürlich) naturally

Urteil *das;* ∼s, ∼e judgement; (Strafe)
sentence; (Gerichtsurteil) verdict

urteilen *itr. V.* form an opinion; judge;
über etw./jmdn. ∼: judge sth./sb.

urteils-, Urteils-: ∼**fähig** *Adj.*
competent *or* able to judge *postpos.;*
∼**fähigkeit** *die* competence *or* ability to
judge; ∼**vermögen** *das* competence to
judge

Ur·wald *der* primeval forest; (tropisch)
jungle

ur·wüchsig *Adj.* natural ⟨*landscape,
power*⟩; earthy ⟨*language, humour*⟩

Urwüchsigkeit *die;* ∼ ▶ URWÜCHSIG:
naturalness; earthiness

USA *Pl.* USA

User /'ju:zɐ/ *der;* ∼s, ∼, **Userin** *die;* ∼,
∼nen (bes. DV, Drogenjargon) user

usw. *Abk.* = **und so weiter** etc.

Utensil *das;* ∼s, ∼ien /...jən/ piece of
equipment; ∼ien equipment *sing.*

Utopie *die;* ∼, ∼n utopian dream

utopisch *Adj.* utopian

UV *Abk.* = **Ultraviolett** UV

Vv

v, V /vau:/ *das;* ~, ~: v/V
v. *Abk.* = **von**
vage /'va:gə/ [1] *Adj.* vague
[2] *adv.* vaguely
Vagina /va'gi:na/ *die;* ~, Vaginen (Anat.)
vagina
vaginal *Adj.* (Anat.) vaginal
vakant /va'kant/ *Adj.* vacant
Vakuum *das;* ~s, Vakuen vacuum
vakuum-verpackt *Adj.* vacuum-packed
Valentins-tag /'va:lɛnti:ns-/ *der* [St]
Valentine's Day
Van /væn/ *der;* ~s, ~s (Kfz.-W.) multi-
purpose vehicle; MPV
Vandale /van'da:la/ *usw.* ▶ WANDALE
Vanille /va'nɪljə/ *die;* ~: vanilla
Vanille-: ~eis *das* vanilla ice cream;
~pudding *der* vanilla pudding; ~zucker
der vanilla sugar
variabel /va'rịa:bḷ/ [1] *Adj.* variable
[2] *adv.* variably
Variante /va'rịantə/ *die;* ~, ~n (geh.)
variant; variation
variieren *tr., itr.* V. vary
Vase /'va:zə/ *die;* ~, ~n vase
Vaseline /vaze'li:nə/ *die;* ~: Vaseline ®
Vater *der;* ~s, Väter father; **Gott** ~: God the
Father
Vater-land *das* fatherland
väterlich [1] *Adj.* (a) paternal ⟨*line, love,
instincts, etc.*⟩
(b) (fürsorglich) fatherly
[2] *adv.* in a fatherly way
väterlicherseits *Adv.* on the/his/her *etc.*
father's side
Vaterschaft *die;* ~, ~en fatherhood
Vater-: ~tag *der* Father's Day *no def. art.;*
~unser *das;* ~~s, ~~: Lord's Prayer
Vati *der;* ~s, ~s (fam.) dad[dy] (coll.)
Vatikan /vati'ka:n/ *der;* ~s Vatican
v. Chr. *Abk.* = **vor Christus** BC
Vegetarier /vege'ta:rịɐ/ *der;* ~s, ~,
Vegetarierin *die;* ~, ~nen vegetarian
vegetarisch [1] *Adj.* vegetarian
[2] *adv.* er isst *od.* lebt ~: he is a vegetarian
Vegetation *die;* ~, ~en vegetation *no
indef. art.*
vegetieren *itr.* V. vegetate
Veilchen *das;* ~s, ~: violet
Vene /'ve:nə/ *die;* ~, ~n vein
Venedig /ve'ne:dɪç/ (*das*) ~s Venice

Venezolaner /venɛts:o'la:nɐ/ *der;* ~s, ~,
Venezolanerin *die;* ~, ~nen Venezuelan
venezolanisch *Adj.* Venezuelan
Venezuela (*das*); ~s Venezuela
Ventil /vɛn'ti:l/ *das;* ~s, ~e valve
Ventilator /vɛnti'la:tɔr/ *der;* ~s, ~en
ventilator
Venus /'ve:nʊs/ *die;* ~: Venus *no def. art.*
verabreden [1] *tr.* V. arrange
[2] *refl.* V. sich im Park/zum Tennis/für den
folgenden Abend ~: arrange to meet in the
park/for tennis/next evening
Verabredung *die;* ~, ~en (a)
arrangement
(b) (verabredete Zusammenkunft) appointment;
eine ~ absagen call off a meeting
verabscheuen *tr.* V. detest; loathe
verabschieden [1] *tr.* V. (a) say goodbye
to
(b) (aus dem Dienst) retire ⟨*general, civil
servant, etc.*⟩
[2] *refl.* V. sich [von jmdm.] ~: say goodbye
[to sb.]
Verabschiedung *die;* ~, ~en (a) leave-
taking
(b) (aus dem Dienst) retirement
verachten *tr.* V. despise
verächtlich [1] *Adj.* (a) contemptuous
(b) (verachtenswürdig) contemptible
[2] *adv.* contemptuously
Verächtlichkeit *die;* ~: contempt;
contemptuousness
Verachtung *die;* ~: contempt
verallgemeinern *tr., itr.* V. generalize
Verallgemeinerung *die;* ~, ~en
generalization
veralten *itr.* V.; *mit sein* become obsolete
Veranda /ve'randa/ *die;* ~, Veranden
veranda; porch
veränderlich *Adj.* changeable
verändern *tr., refl.* V. change
Veränderung *die;* ~, ~en change (Gen.
in)
verängstigen *tr.* V. frighten; scare
verankern *tr.* V. fix ⟨*tent, mast, pole, etc.*⟩;
(mit einem Anker) anchor
veranlagen *tr.* V. (Steuerw.) assess (mit at)
veranlagt *Adj.* künstlerisch/praktisch ~
sein have an artistic bent/be practically
minded
Veranlagung *die;* ~, ~en [pre]disposition
veranlassen *tr.* V. cause; induce; ~, dass
... see to it that ...

---

*old spelling - see note on page xiv

Veranlassung *die;* ~, ~en reason

veranschaulichen *tr. V.* illustrate

veranschlagen *tr. V.* estimate (**mit** at)

veranstalten *tr. V.* organize; hold, give ⟨*party*⟩; hold ⟨*auction*⟩; do ⟨*survey*⟩

Veranstalter *der;* ~s, ~, **Veranstalterin** *die;* ~, ~nen organizer

Veranstaltung *die;* ~, ~en (a) (das Veranstalten) organizing; organization
(b) (etw., was veranstaltet wird) event

verantworten ⓵ *tr. V.* etw. ~: take responsibility for sth.
⓶ *refl. V.* sich für etw. ~: answer for sth.; sich vor jmdm. ~: answer to sb

verantwortlich *Adj.* responsible

Verantwortung *die;* ~, ~en responsibility (**für** for)

verantwortungs-: ~**bewusst,** ***~**bewußt** *Adj.* responsible; ~**los** *Adj.* irresponsible; ~**voll** *Adj.* responsible

verarbeiten *tr. V.* use; etw. zu etw. ~: make sth. into sth.; (geistig bewältigen) assimilate ⟨*film, experience, impressions*⟩

Verarbeitung *die;* ~, ~en (a) (das Verarbeiten) use
(b) (Art der Fertigung) finish; **Schuhe in erstklassiger** ~: shoes with a first-class finish

verärgern *tr. V.* annoy

verarzten *tr. V.* (ugs.) patch up (coll.) ⟨*person*⟩; fix (coll.) ⟨*wound etc.*⟩

verausgaben *refl. V.* wear oneself out; **sie hat sich total verausgabt** (finanziell) she has completely spent out

veräußern *tr. V.* dispose of ⟨*property*⟩

Verb /vɛrp/ *das;* ~s, ~en verb

verbal /vɛr'baːl/ *Adj.* ⓵ (auch Sprachw.) verbal
⓶ *adv.* verbally

Verband *der* (a) (Binde) bandage; dressing
(b) (Vereinigung) association

verbandeln *tr. V.* link closely

Verband[s]-: ~**kasten** *der* first-aid box; ~**material** *das* dressing materials *pl.*

Verband-zeug *das* first-aid things *pl.*

Verbannung *die;* ~, ~en banishment

verbeamten *tr. V.* make ⟨*person*⟩ a civil servant

verbergen *unr. tr. V.* hide; conceal

verbessern ⓵ *tr. V.* (a) improve
(b) (korrigieren) correct
⓶ *refl. V.* (a) improve
(b) ([beruflich] aufsteigen) better oneself

Verbesserung *die* (a) improvement
(b) (Korrektur) correction

Verbesserungs-vorschlag *der* suggestion for improvement

verbeugen *refl. V.* bow (**vor** + *Dat.* to)

Verbeugung *die;* ~, ~en bow

verbeulen *tr. V.* dent

verbieten *unr. tr. V.* (a) forbid; jmdm. etw.

~: forbid sb. sth.; „**Betreten des Rasens/ Rauchen verboten**" 'keep off the grass'/'no smoking'
(b) (für unzulässig erklären) ban

verbinden ⓵ *unr. tr. V.* (a) (bandagieren) bandage; dress
(b) (zubinden) bind; jmdm. die Augen ~: blindfold sb.
(c) (zusammenfügen) join
(d) (in Beziehung bringen) connect (**durch** by); link ⟨*towns, lakes, etc.*⟩ (**durch** by)
(e) (verknüpfen) combine ⟨*abilities, qualities, etc.*⟩
(f) auch *intr.* (telefonisch) jmdn. [mit jmdm.] ~: put sb. through [to sb.]
⓶ *unr. refl. V.* (a) (auch Chemie) combine (**mit** with)
(b) (sich zusammentun) join [together]; join forces

verbindlich ⓵ *Adj.* (a) friendly
(b) (bindend) obligatory; compulsory; binding ⟨*agreement, decision, etc.*⟩
⓶ *adv.* (a) (freundlich) in a friendly manner
(b) ~ zusagen definitely agree; jmdm. etw. ~ zusagen make sb. a firm offer of sth

Verbindung *die;* ~, ~en (a) (das Verknüpfen) linking
(b) (Zusammenhalt) join; connection
(c) (verknüpfende Strecke) link
(d) (durch Telefon, Funk, Verkehrsmittel) connection (**nach** to)
(e) (Kombination) combination; in ~ mit etw. in conjunction with sth.
(f) (Kontakt) contact; sich mit jmdm. in ~ setzen get in touch *or* contact with sb.
(g) (Zusammenhang) connection

verbissen ⓵ *Adj.* dogged; doggedly determined
⓶ *adv.* doggedly

verbitten *unr. refl. V.* sich (*Dat.*) etw. ~: refuse to tolerate sth.

verbittern *tr. V.* embitter

Verbitterung *die;* ~, ~en bitterness; embitterment

verblassen *itr. V.; mit sein* (auch fig. geh.) fade

Verbleib *der;* ~[e]s (geh.) whereabouts *pl.*

verbleiben *unr. itr. V.; mit sein* remain; **wie seid ihr verblieben?** what did you arrange?

verbleien *tr. V.* (Technik) lead ⟨*petrol*⟩

Verblendung *die;* ~, ~en blindness

verblüffen *tr.* (auch *itr.*) *V.* amaze

verblüffend ⓵ *Adj.* amazing
⓶ *adv.* amazingly

Verblüffung *die;* ~, ~en amazement

verblühen *itr. V.; mit sein* (auch fig.) fade

verbluten *itr.* (auch *refl.*) *V.; mit sein* bleed to death

verbohrt *Adj.* pigheaded

verborgen *Adj.* (abgelegen) secluded; (nicht sichtbar) hidden

Verbot *das;* ~[e]s, ~e ban (*Gen.*, **von** on)

Verbots-schild *das; Pl.* ~er sign (prohibiting sth.); (Verkehrsw.) prohibitive sign

Verbrauch *der;* ~[e]s consumption (von, an + *Dat.* of)

verbrauchen *tr. V.* use; consume ⟨*food, drink*⟩; use up ⟨*provisions*⟩; spend ⟨*money*⟩; consume, use ⟨*fuel*⟩; (fig.) use up ⟨*strength, energy*⟩

Verbraucher *der;* ~s, ~, **Verbraucherin** *die;* ~, ~nen consumer

Verbraucher-schutz *der* consumer protection

Verbrechen *das;* ~s, ~: crime (an + *Dat.*, gegen against)

Verbrechens-: ~rate *die* crime rate; ~verhütung *die* crime prevention

Verbrecher *der;* ~s, ~, **Verbrecherin** *die;* ~, ~nen criminal

verbrecherisch *Adj.* criminal

verbreiten [1] *tr. V.* spread; radiate ⟨*optimism, calm, etc.*⟩
[2] *refl. V.* spread

Verbreitung *die;* ~, ~en (a) ▶ VERBREITEN 1: spreading; radiation
(b) (Ausbreitung) spread

verbrennen [1] *unr. itr. V.; mit sein* burn
[2] *tr. V.* burn; cremate ⟨*dead person*⟩; sich (*Dat.*) den Mund ~ (fig.) say too much

Verbrennung *die;* ~, ~en (a) ▶ VERBRENNEN 2: burning; cremation
(b) (Wunde) burn

verbringen *unr. tr. V.* spend

verbummeln *tr. V.* (ugs.) (a) waste ⟨*time*⟩
(b) (vergessen) forget [all] about; clean forget; (verlieren) lose

verbünden *refl. V.* form an alliance

Verbündete *der/die; adj. Dekl.* ally

verbüßen *tr. V.* serve ⟨*sentence*⟩

Verdacht *der;* ~[e]s, ~e *od.* Verdächte suspicion; wen hast du in ~? who do you suspect?

verdächtig [1] *Adj.* suspicious
[2] *adv.* suspiciously

Verdächtige *der/die; adj. Dekl.* suspect

verdächtigen *tr. V.* suspect

Verdächtigung *die;* ~, ~en suspicion

verdammen *tr. V.* condemn; (Rel.) damn ⟨*sinner*⟩

verdampfen [1] *itr. V.; mit sein* evaporate
[2] *tr. V.* evaporate

verdanken *tr. V.* jmdm./einer Sache etw. ~: owe sth. to sb./sth.

verdarb *1. u. 3. Pers. Sg. Prät. v.* VERDERBEN

verdattert (ugs.) *Adj.* flabbergasted; (verwirrt) dazed; stunned

verdauen [1] *tr. V.* (auch fig.) digest
[2] *itr. V.* digest [one's food]

verdaulich *Adj.* digestible

Verdauung *die;* ~: digestion

Verdeck *das;* ~[e]s, ~e top; hood (Brit.); (bei Kinderwagen) hood

verdecken *tr. V.* hide; cover

verderben [1] *unr. itr. V.; mit sein* go bad or off; spoil
[2] *unr. tr. V.* spoil; (stärker) ruin; spoil ⟨*appetite, enjoyment, fun, etc.*⟩
[3] *unr. refl. V.* sich (*Dat.*) den Magen/die Augen ~: give oneself an upset stomach/ ruin one's eyesight

Verderben *das;* ~s ruin

verderblich *Adj.* perishable ⟨*food*⟩; pernicious ⟨*influence, effect, etc.*⟩

verdeutlichen *tr. V.* etw. ~: make sth. clear; (erklären) explain sth.

verdichten *refl. V.* ⟨*fog, smoke*⟩ thicken, become thicker; (fig.) ⟨*suspicion, rumour*⟩ grow; ⟨*feeling*⟩ intensify

verdienen [1] *tr. V.* (a) earn
(b) (wert sein) deserve
[2] *itr. V.* beide Eheleute ~: husband and wife are both earning

Verdiener *der;* ~s, ~, **Verdienerin** *die;* ~, ~nen wage earner

Verdienst¹ *der;* ~[e]s, ~e income; earnings *pl.*

Verdienst² *das;* ~[e]s, ~e merit

verdienst-voll [1] *Adj.* commendable; ⟨*person*⟩ of outstanding merit
[2] *adv.* commendably

verdient [1] *Adj.* (a) ⟨*person*⟩ of outstanding merit; sich um etw. ~ machen render outstanding services to sth.
(b) (gerecht, zustehend) well-deserved
[2] *adv.* deservedly

verdientermaßen *Adv.* deservedly

verdoppeln [1] *tr. V.* double; (fig.) double, redouble ⟨*efforts etc.*⟩
[2] *refl. V.* double

verdorben *2. Part. v.* VERDERBEN

verdorren *itr. V.; mit sein* wither [and die]; ⟨*meadow*⟩ scorch

verdrängen *tr. V.* (a) drive out ⟨*inhabitants*⟩; (fig.: ersetzen) displace
(b) (Psych.) repress; (bewusst) suppress

verdrehen *tr. V.* (a) twist ⟨*joint*⟩; roll ⟨*eyes*⟩
(b) (ugs. abwertend: entstellen) twist ⟨*words, facts, etc.*⟩

verdrießen *unr. tr. V.* (geh.) irritate; annoy

verdrießlich [1] *Adj.* morose
[2] *adv.* morosely

verdross, *verdroß *1. u. 3. Pers. Sg. Prät. v.* VERDRIESSEN

verdrossen [1] *Adj.* (missmutig) morose; (missmutig und lustlos) sullen
[2] *adv.* (missmutig) morosely; (missmutig und lustlos) sullenly

Verdruss, *Verdruß *der;* Verdrusses, Verdrusse annoyance

verdunkeln *tr. V.* darken; (vollständig) black out ⟨*room, house, etc.*⟩

Verdunk[e]lung *die;* ∼, ∼en darkening; (vollständig) blackout

verdünnen *tr. V.* dilute

verdunsten *itr. V.; mit sein* evaporate

verdünnen *tr. V.* dilute

verdunsten *itr. V.; mit sein* evaporate

Verdunstung *die;* ∼: evaporation

verdursten *itr. V.; mit sein* die of thirst

verdutzt *Adj.* taken aback *pred.;* nonplussed; (verwirrt) baffled

Verdutztheit *die;* ∼: bafflement

verehren *tr. V.* (a) venerate **(b)** (geh.: bewundern) admire; (ehrerbietig lieben) worship

Verehrer *der;* ∼s, ∼, **Verehrerin** *die;* ∼, ∼en admirer

Verehrung *die;* ∼ (a) veneration **(b)** (Bewunderung) admiration

vereidigen *tr. V.* swear in

Vereidigung *die;* ∼, ∼en swearing in

Verein *der;* ∼s, ∼e organization; (der Kunstfreunde usw.) association; society; (Sportverein) club

vereinbar *Adj.* compatible

vereinbaren *tr. V.* agree; arrange ⟨*meeting etc.*⟩

Vereinbarung *die;* ∼, ∼en (a) agreeing; (eines Termins usw.) arranging **(b)** (Abmachung) agreement

vereinfachen *tr. V.* simplify

Vereinfachung *die;* ∼, ∼en simplification

vereinheitlichen *tr. V.* standardize

Vereinheitlichung *die;* ∼, ∼en standardization

vereinigen *tr., refl. V.* unite; (in der Wirtschaft) merge

vereinigt *Adj.* united

Vereinigung *die;* ∼, ∼en (a) organization **(b)** (das Vereinigen) uniting; (von Unternehmen) merging

vereinsamen *itr. V.; mit sein* become [increasingly] lonely *or* isolated

Vereinsamung *die;* ∼: loneliness; isolation

vereinzelt ① *Adj.* occasional ② *adv.* (zeitlich) occasionally; (örtlich) here and there

Vereinzelung *die;* ∼, ∼en isolation

vereisen *itr. V.; mit sein* freeze *or* ice over; ⟨*wing*⟩ ice up; ⟨*lock*⟩ freeze up

vereiteln *tr. V.* thwart

Vereitelung *die;* ∼: thwarting

vereitern *itr. V.; mit sein* go septic

verenden *itr. V.; mit sein* perish; die

verengen *refl. V.* narrow; ⟨*pupils*⟩ contract

vererben *tr. V.* leave, bequeath ⟨*property*⟩ (*Dat.,* an + *Akk.* to)

Vererbung *die;* ∼, ∼en heredity *no art.*

verewigen ① *tr. V.* immortalize

② *refl. V.* (ugs.: Spuren hinterlassen) leave one's mark

verfahren ① *unr. refl. V.* lose one's way ② *unr. itr. V.; mit sein* proceed

Verfahren *das;* ∼s, ∼ (a) procedure; (Technik) process; (Methode) method **(b)** (Rechtsw.) proceedings *pl.*

Verfall *der;* ∼[e]s (a) decay; (fig.: der Preise, einer Währung) collapse **(b)** (Auflösung) decline

verfallen *unr. itr. V.; mit sein* (a) (baufällig werden) fall into disrepair **(b)** (körperlich) ⟨*strength*⟩ decline **(c)** (untergehen) ⟨*empire*⟩ decline; ⟨*morals, morale*⟩ deteriorate **(d)** (ungültig werden) expire

Verfalls-datum *das* use-by date; (ugs.: Mindesthaltbarkeitsdatum) best-before date

verfälschen *tr. V.* distort, misrepresent ⟨*statement, message*⟩; falsify, misrepresent ⟨*facts, history, truth*⟩; falsify ⟨*painting, banknote*⟩; adulterate ⟨*wine, milk, etc.*⟩

Verfälschung *die* ▶ VERFÄLSCHEN: distortion; misrepresentation; falsification; adulteration

verfassen *tr. V.* write; draw up ⟨*resolution*⟩

Verfasser *der;* ∼s, ∼, **Verfasserin** *die;* ∼, ∼nen writer; (eines Buchs, Artikels usw.) author; writer

Verfassung *die;* ∼, ∼en (a) (Politik) constitution **(b)** (Zustand) state [of health/mind]; in guter/ schlechter ∼ sein be in good/poor shape

verfassungs-gemäß ① *Adj.* constitutional; in accordance with the constitution *postpos.;* ② *adv.* constitutionally; in accordance with the constitution

verfaulen *itr. V.; mit sein* rot

verfehlen *tr. V.* miss

Verfehlung *die;* ∼, ∼en misdemeanour; (Rel.: Sünde) transgression

verfeinden *refl. V.* sich ∼ mit make an enemy of

verfeinern *tr. V.* improve; refine ⟨*method, procedure*⟩

Verfeinerung *die;* ∼, ∼en ▶ VERFEINERN: improvement; refinement

verfertigen *tr. V.* produce

verfilmen *tr. V.* film; make a film of

Verfilmung *die;* ∼, ∼en (a) (das Verfilmen) filming **(b)** (Film) film [version]

verfinstern ① *tr. V.* obscure ⟨*sun etc.*⟩ ② *refl. V.* (auch fig.) darken

Verfinsterung *die;* ∼, ∼en darkening

verflixt (ugs.) ① *Adj.* (a) (ärgerlich) awkward, unpleasant ⟨*situation, business, etc.*⟩ **(b)** (verdammt) blasted (Brit.); blessed; confounded; ∼ [noch mal]! [damn and] blast! (Brit. coll.)

⋯⟶

(c) (sehr groß) **er hat ~es Glück gehabt** he was damned lucky (coll.)
2 *adv.* (sehr) damned (coll.)
verflọssen *Adj.* (ugs.) former
verfluchen *tr. V.* curse
verflụcht **1** *Adj.* (salopp) damned (coll.); bloody (Brit. sl); **~ [noch mal]!** damn [it]! (coll.)
2 *adv.* (sehr) damned (coll.)
verfọlgen *tr. V.* pursue; hunt, track ⟨*animal*⟩; **etw. [strafrechtlich] ~:** prosecute sth.
Verfọlgte *der/die; adj. Dekl.* victim of persecution
Verfọlgung *die;* **~, ~en (a)** pursuit; (eines Ziels, Plans usw.) pursuance
(b) [strafrechtliche] **~:** prosecution
Verfọlgungs-: ~jagd *die* pursuit; chase; **~wahn** *der* (Psych.) persecution mania
verfrẹssen *Adj.* (salopp) greedy
verfügen **1** *tr. V.* (anordnen) order; (dekretieren) decree
2 *itr. V.* **über etw.** (*Akk.*) **[frei] ~ können** be free to decide what to do with sth.; **über etw.** (*Akk.*) **~** (etw. haben) have sth. at one's disposal
Verfügung *die;* **~, ~en (a)** (Anordnung) order; (Dekret) decree
(b) (Disposition) **etw. zur ~ haben** have sth. at one's disposal; **jmdm. etw. zur ~ stellen** put sth. at sb.'s disposal
verführen *tr. V.* **(a)** (verleiten) tempt
(b) (sexuell) seduce
Verführer *der;* **~s, ~:** seducer
Verführerin *der;* **~, ~nen** seductress
verführerisch **1** *Adj.* **(a)** (verlockend) tempting
(b) (aufreizend) seductive
2 *adv.* **(a)** (verlockend) temptingly
(b) (aufreizend) seductively
Verführung *die;* **~, ~en (a)** temptation
(b) (sexuell) seduction
vergạngen *Adj.* **(a)** (vorüber, vorbei) bygone, former ⟨*times, years, etc.*⟩
(b) (letzt...) last ⟨*year, week, etc.*⟩
Vergạngenheit *die;* **~ (a)** past
(b) (Grammatik: Präteritum) past tense
vergạ̈nglich *Adj.* transient; transitory; ephemeral
Vergạ̈nglichkeit *die;* **~:** transience
Vergaser *der;* **~s, ~:** carburettor
vergạß *1. u. 3. Pers. Sg. Prät. v.* VERGESSEN
Vergasung *die;* **~, ~en (a)** (von Kohle) gasification
(b) (Tötung) gassing
(c) **bis zur ~** (ugs.) ad nauseam
vergeben *unr. tr. V.* **(a)** *auch itr.* (geh.: verzeihen) forgive; **jmdm. etw. ~:** forgive sb. [for] sth.
(b) throw away ⟨*chance, goal, etc.*⟩

(c) (geben) place ⟨*order*⟩ (**an** + *Akk.* with); award ⟨*grant, prize*⟩ (**an** + *Akk.* to)
vergebens **1** *Adv.* in vain; vainly
2 *adj.* **es war ~:** it was of *or* to no avail
vergeblich **1** *Adj.* futile; vain, futile ⟨*attempt, efforts*⟩
2 *adv.* in vain
Vergebung *die;* **~:** (geh.) forgiveness
vergegenwạ̈rtigen /od. ---'---/ *refl. V.* **sich** (*Dat.*) **etw. ~:** imagine sth.; (erinnern) recall sth.
vergehen *unr. itr. V.; mit sein* ⟨*time*⟩ pass [by], go by; ⟨*pain*⟩ wear off, pass; ⟨*pleasure*⟩ fade
Vergehen *das;* **~s, ~:** crime; (Rechtsspr.) offence
vergeigen *tr. V.* (ugs.) botch up ⟨*test, performance, etc.*⟩; lose ⟨*game, match*⟩
vergẹlten *unr. tr. V.* repay
vergẹssen *unr. tr.* (*auch itr.*) *V.* forget
Vergẹssenheit *die;* **~:** oblivion
vergẹsslich, *vergẹßlich *Adj.* forgetful
vergeuden *tr. V.* waste
Vergeudung *die;* **~, ~en** waste
vergewạltigen *tr. V.* rape
Vergewạltigung *die;* **~, ~en** rape
vergewịssern *refl. V.* make sure (*Gen.* of)
vergießen *unr. tr. V.* spill; **Tränen ~:** shed tears
vergịften *tr. V.* (auch fig.) poison
Vergịftung *die;* **~, ~en** poisoning
vergịss, *vergịß *Imper. Sg. v.* VERGESSEN
Vergịss-mein-nicht, *Vergịß-mein-nicht *das;* **~[e]s, ~[e]** forget-me-not
vergịsst, *vergịßt *2. u. 3. Pers. Sg. Präs. v.* VERGESSEN
Vergleich *der;* **~[e]s, ~e (a)** comparison; **im ~ zu** *od.* **mit etw.** in comparison with sth.; compared with *or* to sth.
(b) (Rechtsw.) settlement
vergleichbar *Adj.* comparable
vergleichen *tr. V.* compare
Vergleichs-form *die* (Sprachw.) comparative/superlative form
verglühen *itr. V.; mit sein* ⟨*log, wick, fire, etc.*⟩ smoulder and go out; ⟨*satellite, rocket, wire, etc.*⟩ burn out
vergnügen *refl. V.* enjoy oneself; have a good time
Vergnügen *das;* **~s, ~:** pleasure; (Spaß) fun; **viel ~!** (auch iron.) have fun!
vergnüglich *Adj.* amusing; entertaining
vergnügt **1** *Adj.* cheerful
2 *adv.* cheerfully
Vergnügungs-viertel *das* pleasure district
vergọlden *tr. V.* gold-plate ⟨*jewellery etc.*⟩; (mit Blattgold) gild
vergraben *unr. tr. V.* bury
vergrạ̈mt *Adj.* careworn

---

*old spelling - see note on page xiv

vergraulen tr. V. (ugs.) put off
vergreifen unr. refl. V. **sich an jmdm. ~:** assault sb.
vergriffen Adj. out of print pred.
vergrößern [1] tr. V. **(a)** (erweitern) extend ⟨room, area, building, etc.⟩ **(b)** (vermehren) increase **(c)** (größer reproduzieren) enlarge ⟨photograph etc.⟩ [2] refl. V. **(a)** (größer werden) ⟨firm, business, etc.⟩ expand **(b)** (zunehmen) increase [3] itr. V. ⟨lens etc.⟩ magnify
Vergrößerung die; ~, ~en **(a)** ▶ VERGRÖSSERN 1, 2: extension; increase; enlargement; expansion **(b)** (Foto) enlargement
Vergrößerungs-glas das magnifying glass
Vergünstigung die; ~, ~en privilege
vergüten tr. V. **(a)** (erstatten) jmdm. etw. ~: reimburse sb. for sth. **(b)** (bes. Papierdt.: bezahlen) remunerate, pay for ⟨work, services⟩
Vergütung die; ~, ~en **(a)** (Rückerstattung) reimbursement **(b)** (Geldsumme) remuneration
verhaften tr. V. arrest; **Sie sind verhaftet** you are under arrest
Verhaftung die; ~, ~en arrest
verhalten unr. refl. V. **(a)** behave; (reagieren) react **(b)** (beschaffen sein) be
Verhalten das; ~s behaviour
Verhaltens·weise die behaviour
Verhältnis das; ~ses, ~se **(a)** ein ~ von drei zu eins a ratio of three to one **(b)** (persönliche Beziehung) relationship (**zu** with); **mit jmdm. ein ~ haben** (ugs.) have an affair with sb. **(c)** Pl. (Umstände) conditions
verhältnis·mäßig Adv. relatively; comparatively
Verhältnis·wort das; Pl. ~wörter (Sprachw.) preposition
verhandeln [1] itr. V. **(a)** negotiate (**über** + Akk. about) **(b)** (strafrechtlich) try a case; (zivilrechtlich) hear a case [2] tr. V. **(a)** etw. ~: negotiate over sth. **(b)** (strafrechtlich) try ⟨case⟩; (zivilrechtlich) hear ⟨case⟩
Verhandlung die; ~, ~en **(a)** ~en negotiations **(b)** (strafrechtlich) trial; (zivilrechtlich) hearing; **die ~ gegen X** the trial of X
verhängen tr. V. impose ⟨fine, punishment⟩ (**über** + Akk. on); declare ⟨state of emergency, state of siege⟩; (Sport) award, give ⟨penalty etc.⟩
Verhängnis das; ~ses, ~se undoing
verhängnis·voll Adj. disastrous
verharmlosen tr. V. play down

Verharmlosung die; ~, ~en playing down
verhärmt Adj. careworn
verharren itr. V. (geh.) remain
verhärten [1] tr. V. harden; make ⟨person⟩ hard [2] refl. V. ⟨tissue⟩ become hardened
verhasst, *verhaßt Adj. hated; detested
verhätscheln tr. V. (ugs.) pamper
verhauen (ugs.) unr. tr. V. beat up; (als Strafe) beat
verheben unr. refl. V. do oneself an injury [while lifting sth.]
verheeren tr. V. devastate; lay waste [to]
verheerend Adj. **(a)** devastating **(b)** (ugs.: scheußlich) ghastly (coll.)
verhehlen tr. V. (geh.) conceal (Dat. from)
verheilen itr. V.; mit sein ⟨wound⟩ heal [up]
verheimlichen tr. V. [jmdm.] etw. ~: keep sth. secret [from sb.]
Verheimlichung die; ~, ~en concealment
verheiraten refl. V. get married; **sich mit jmdm. ~:** marry sb.; get married to sb.
Verheiratete der/die; adj. Dekl. married person; married man/woman
Verheiratung die; ~, ~en marriage
verheizen tr. V. **(a)** burn; use as fuel **(b)** (abwertend: rücksichtslos einsetzen) burn out ⟨athlete, skier, etc.⟩; use ⟨troops⟩ as cannon fodder
verhelfen unr. itr. V. jmdm./einer Sache zu etw. ~: help sb./sth. to get/achieve sth.
verherrlichen tr. V. glorify
Verherrlichung die; ~, ~en glorification
verheult Adj. (ugs.) ⟨eyes⟩ red from crying; ⟨face⟩ puffy or swollen from crying
verhexen tr. V. (auch fig.) bewitch
verhindern tr. V. prevent
Verhinderung die; ~, ~en prevention
verhöhnen tr. V. mock
Verhöhnung die; ~, ~en mockery
Verhör das; ~[e]s, ~e interrogation; questioning; (bei Gericht) examination
verhören [1] tr. V. interrogate; question; (bei Gericht) examine [2] refl. V. mishear
verhüllen tr. V. cover; (fig.) disguise
verhüllend Adj. (Literaturw.) euphemistic
Verhüllung die; ~, ~en covering; (fig.) disguising
verhungern itr. V.; mit sein die of starvation; starve [to death]
verhunzen tr. V. (ugs. abwertend) ruin; mess up; ruin ⟨landscape, townscape, etc.⟩
verhüten tr. V. prevent
Verhütung die; ~, ~en prevention; (Empfängnisverhütung) contraception
Verhütungs·mittel das contraceptive

verirren refl. V. (a) get lost; lose one's way; ⟨animal⟩ stray
(b) (irgendwohin gelangen) stray (in, an + Akk. into)

verjagen tr. V. chase away

verjüngen [1] tr. V. rejuvenate
[2] refl. V. (schmaler werden) taper; become narrower; narrow

verkalken itr. V.; mit sein (a) ⟨tissue⟩ calcify; ⟨arteries⟩ become hardened
(b) (ugs.: senil werden) become senile

Verkauf der; ~[e]s, Verkäufe sale

verkaufen tr. V. (auch fig.) sell ⟨Dat., an + Akk. to); „zu ~" 'for sale'

Verkäufer der; ~s, ~ **Verkäuferin** die; ~, ~nen (a) seller; vendor (formal)
(b) (Berufsbez.) sales or shop assistant; (im Außendienst) salesman/saleswoman

verkäuflich Adj. (zum Verkauf geeignet) saleable; (zum Verkauf bestimmt) for sale postpos.

verkaufs-offen Adj. der ~e Samstag Saturday on which the shops are open all day

Verkaufs-preis der retail price

Verkehr der; ~s (a) traffic
(b) (Kontakt) contact; communication
(c) (Geschlechtsverkehr) intercourse

verkehren itr. V. (a) auch mit sein (fahren) run; ⟨aircraft⟩ fly
(b) (in Kontakt stehen) mit jmdm. ~: associate with sb.
(c) (zu Gast sein) bei jmdm. ~: visit sb. regularly

verkehrs-, Verkehrs-: ~ampel die traffic lights pl.; ~amt das tourist information office; ~aufkommen das volume of traffic; ~hindernis das obstruction to traffic; ~knotenpunkt der [traffic] junction; ~kontrolle die traffic check; ~meldung die traffic announcement or flash; ~mittel das means of transport; die öffentlichen ~mittel public transport sing.; ~polizist der traffic policeman; ~polizistin die traffic policewoman; ~schild das; Pl. ~~er traffic sign; road sign; ~sicher Adj. roadworthy; ~teilnehmer der, ~teilnehmerin die road user; ~unfall der road accident; ~weg der traffic route; ~zeichen das traffic sign; road sign

verkehrt [1] Adj. wrong
[2] adv. wrongly; alles ~ machen do everything wrong

verkennen unr. tr. V. fail to recognize; misjudge ⟨situation⟩

verklagen tr. V. sue; take to court; eine Firma auf Schadenersatz ~: sue a company for damages

verkleben [1] itr. V.; mit sein stick together
[2] tr. V. (zukleben) seal up ⟨hole⟩; (festkleben) stick [down] ⟨floor covering etc.⟩

verkleiden tr. V. disguise; (kostümieren) dress up; sich ~: disguise oneself/dress [oneself] up

Verkleidung die; ~, ~en (a) disguising; (das Kostümieren) dressing up
(b) (Kleidung) disguise; (bei einer Party) fancy dress

verkleinern [1] tr. V. (a) make smaller
(b) (verringern) reduce ⟨size, number, etc.⟩
(c) (kleiner reproduzieren) reduce ⟨photograph etc.⟩
[2] refl. V. become smaller; ⟨number⟩ decrease

Verkleinerungs-form die (Sprachw.) diminutive form

verknallen refl. V. (ugs.: sich verlieben) fall head over heels in love (in + Akk. with); in jmdn. verknallt sein be crazy about sb. (coll.)

verknittern tr. V. crumple

verknoten tr. V. tie; knot

verknüpfen tr. V. (a) (knoten) tie; knot
(b) (in Beziehung setzen) link

verkochen itr. V.; mit sein (a) boil away
(b) (breiig werden, zerfallen) boil down to a pulp

verkohlen itr. V. char

verkommen¹ unr. itr. V.; mit sein go to the dogs; (moralisch, sittlich) go to the bad

verkommen² Adj. depraved

verköstigen tr. V. feed; provide with meals

verkraften tr. V. cope with

verkrampfen refl. V. ⟨muscle⟩ become cramped; ⟨person⟩ tense up

Verkrampfung die; ~, ~en tenseness; tension

verkriechen unr. refl. V. ⟨animal⟩ creep [away]; ⟨person⟩ hide [oneself away]

verkrümeln refl. V. (ugs.: sich entfernen) slip off or away

verkrümmt Adj. bent ⟨person⟩; crooked ⟨finger⟩; curved ⟨spine⟩

Verkrümmung die; ~, ~en crookedness

verkrüppeln tr. V. cripple

verkümmern itr. V.; mit sein ⟨person, animal⟩ go into a decline; ⟨plant etc.⟩ become stunted; ⟨talent, emotional life, etc.⟩ wither away

verkünden tr. V. announce; pronounce ⟨judgement⟩; promulgate ⟨law, decree⟩

verkündigen tr. V. (geh.) announce; proclaim

Verkündigung die; ~, ~en announcement; proclamation

Verkündung die; ~, ~en announcement; (von Urteilen) pronouncement; (von Gesetzen, Verordnungen) promulgation

verkürzen tr. V. (a) (verringern) reduce; (abkürzen) shorten
(b) (abbrechen) cut short ⟨stay, life⟩; put an end to, end ⟨suffering⟩

verladen unr. tr. V. load

---

*alte Schreibung - vgl. Hinweis auf S. xiv

Verlag *der;* ∼[e]s, ∼e publishing house *or* firm; publisher's

verlagern *tr. V.* shift; (an einen anderen Ort) move; (fig.) transfer; shift ⟨*emphasis*⟩

Verlagerung *die* moving; **eine ∼ des Schwergewichts** (fig.) a shift in emphasis

verlanden *itr. V.; mit sein* silt up

Verlandung *die;* ∼, ∼en silting up

verlangen *tr. V.* demand; (nötig haben) ⟨*task etc.*⟩ require, call for ⟨*patience, knowledge, experience, skill, etc.*⟩; (berechnen) charge; (sehen/sprechen wollen) ask for; **du wirst am Telefon verlangt** you're wanted on the phone (coll.)

Verlangen *das;* ∼s, ∼ (a) desire (**nach** for)
(b) **auf ∼:** on request

verlängern *tr. V.* extend; lengthen, make longer ⟨*skirt, sleeve, etc.*⟩; renew ⟨*passport, driving licence, etc.*⟩

Verlängerung *die;* ∼, ∼en ▶ VERLÄNGERN: extension; lengthening; renewal

Verlängerungs·schnur *die* extension lead *or* (Amer.) cord

verlangsamen *tr. V.* **das Tempo/seine Schritte ∼:** reduce speed/slacken one's pace; slow down

verlassen¹ 1 *unr. refl. V.* rely, depend (**auf** + *Akk.* on)
2 *unr. tr. V.* (a) leave
(b) (sich trennen von) desert; abandon; forsake; leave, desert ⟨*wife, family, etc.*⟩

verlassen² *Adj.* deserted ⟨*street etc.*⟩; empty ⟨*house*⟩; (öd) desolate ⟨*region etc.*⟩

verlässlich, *verläßlich 1 *Adj.* reliable
2 *adv.* reliably

Verlauf *der;* ∼[e]s, Verläufe course

verlaufen 1 *unr. itr. V.; mit sein* (a) (sich erstrecken) run
(b) (ablaufen) ⟨*test, rehearsal, etc.*⟩ go; ⟨*party etc.*⟩ go off
2 *unr. refl. V.* get lost; lose one's way

Verlaufs·form *die* (Sprachw.) progressive *or* continuous form

verlautbaren *tr. V.* announce [officially]

Verlautbarung *die;* ∼, ∼en announcement

verlauten *itr. V.; mit sein* be reported; **wie verlautet** according to reports

verleben *tr. V.* spend

verlebt *Adj.* dissipated

verlegen¹ *tr. V.* (a) mislay
(b) (verschieben) postpone (**auf** + *Akk.* until); (vor∼) bring forward (**auf** + *Akk.* to); **einen Termin ∼:** alter an appointment
(c) (verlagern) move; transfer ⟨*patient*⟩
(d) (legen) lay ⟨*cable, pipe, carpet, etc.*⟩

verlegen² 1 *Adj.* embarrassed
2 *adv.* in embarrassment

Verlegenheit *die;* ∼, ∼en (a) (Befangenheit) embarrassment; **jmdn. in ∼ bringen** embarrass sb.
(b) (Unannehmlichkeit) embarrassing situation

Verleger *der;* ∼s, ∼, **Verlegerin** *die;* ∼, ∼nen publisher

Verleih *der;* ∼[e]s, ∼e (a) hiring out; (von Autos) renting *or* hiring out
(b) (Unternehmen) hire firm; (Filmverleih) distribution company; (Videoverleih) video library; (Autoverleih) rental *or* hire firm

verleihen *unr. tr. V.* (a) hire out; rent *or* hire out ⟨*car*⟩; (umsonst) lend [out]
(b) (überreichen) award; confer ⟨*award, honour*⟩

Verleihung *die;* ∼, ∼en (a) ▶ VERLEIHEN A: hiring out; renting out; lending [out]
(b) ▶ VERLEIHEN B: awarding; conferring; (Zeremonie) award; conferment

verleiten *tr. V.* **jmdn. dazu ∼, etw. zu tun** lead *or* induce sb. to do sth.

verlernen *tr. V.* forget

verlesen 1 *unr. tr. V.* read out
2 *unr. refl. V.* (falsch lesen) make a mistake/mistakes in reading

verletzen *tr. V.* (a) injure; (durch Schuss, Stich) wound
(b) (kränken) hurt ⟨*person, feelings*⟩
(c) (verstoßen gegen) violate; infringe ⟨*regulation*⟩; break ⟨*agreement, law*⟩

verletzlich *Adj.* vulnerable

Verletzlichkeit *die;* ∼: vulnerability

Verletzte *der/die; adj. Dekl.* casualty; (durch Schuss, Stich) wounded person

Verletzung *die;* ∼, ∼en (a) (Wunde) injury
(b) (Kränkung) hurting
(c) ▶ VERLETZEN C: violation; infringement; breaking

verleugnen *tr. V.* deny; disown ⟨*friend, relation*⟩

Verleugnung *die;* ∼, ∼en denial; (eines Freundes, Verwandten) disownment

verleumden *tr. V.* slander; (schriftlich) libel

verleumderisch *Adj.* slanderous; (in Schriftform) libellous

Verleumdung *die;* ∼, ∼en slander; (in Schriftform) libel

verlieben *refl. V.* fall in love (**in** + *Akk.* with)

Verliebte *der/die; adj. Dekl.* lover

verlieren *unr. tr., itr. V.* lose

Verlierer *der;* ∼s, ∼, **Verliererin** *die;* ∼, ∼nen loser

verloben *refl. V.* get engaged; **verlobt sein** be engaged

Verlobte *der/die; adj. Dekl.* fiancé/fiancée

verlockend *Adj.* tempting

Verlockung *die;* ∼, ∼en temptation

verlogen *Adj.* lying, mendacious ⟨*person*⟩; false ⟨*morality etc.*⟩

verlor *1. u. 3. Pers. Sg. Prät. v.* VERLIEREN

verloren 1 *2. Part. v.* VERLIEREN ⋯⋮

2 *Adj.* lost; wasted ⟨*effort*⟩; ~ **gehen** get lost
*verloren|gehen ▶ VERLOREN 2
verlosen *tr. V.* raffle
Verlosung *die;* ~, ~en raffle; draw
verlottern *itr. V.; mit sein* ⟨*person*⟩ go to seed
Verlust *der;* ~[e]s, ~e loss (an + *Dat.* of)
vermachen *tr. V.* jmdm. etw. ~: leave *or* bequeath to sb.; (fig.: schenken, überlassen) give sth. to sb.
vermählen *refl. V.* (geh.) sich [jmdm. *od.* mit jmdm.] ~: marry *or* wed [sb.]
Vermählung *die;* ~, ~en (geh.) **(a)** marriage
(b) (Fest) wedding ceremony
vermarkten *tr. V.* market ⟨*goods etc.*⟩
Vermarktung *die;* ~, ~en marketing
vermehren **1** *tr. V.* increase (um by)
2 *refl. V.* **(a)** increase
(b) (sich fortpflanzen) reproduce
Vermehrung *die;* ~, ~en **(a)** increase (*Gen.* in)
(b) (Fortpflanzung) reproduction
vermeiden *unr. tr. V.* avoid
Vermeidung *die;* ~, ~en avoidance
vermeintlich *Adj.* supposed
vermengen *tr. V.* mix **(miteinander together)**
Vermerk *der;* ~[e]s, ~e note; (amtlich) remark
vermerken *tr. V.* make a note of; note [down]; (in Akten, Wachbuch usw.) record
vermessen¹ *unr. tr. V.* measure; survey ⟨*land, site*⟩
vermessen² *Adj.* (geh.) presumptuous
vermieten *tr. (auch itr.) V.* rent [out], let [out] (an + *Akk.* to); hire [out] ⟨*boat, car, etc.*⟩; „Zimmer zu ~" 'room to let'
Vermieter *der;* ~s, ~: landlord
Vermieterin *die;* ~, ~nen landlady
Vermietung *die;* ~, ~en ▶ VERMIETEN: renting [out]; letting [out]; hiring [out]
vermindern **1** *tr. V.* reduce; decrease; reduce, lessen ⟨*danger, stress*⟩; lower ⟨*resistance*⟩; reduce ⟨*debt*⟩
2 *refl. V.* decrease; ⟨*resistance*⟩ diminish
Verminderung *die* ▶ VERMINDERN 1: reduction; decreasing; lessening; lowering; **eine ~ der Einnahmen** a decrease in revenues
verminen *tr. V.* mine
vermischen **1** *tr. V.* mix **(miteinander together)**; blend ⟨*teas, tobaccos, etc.*⟩
2 *refl. V.* mix; (fig.) mingle; ⟨*races, animals*⟩ interbreed
Vermischung *die;* ~ ▶ VERMISCHEN: mixing; blending; (fig.) mingling
vermissen *tr. V.* **(a)** miss
(b) (nicht haben) **ich vermisse meinen Ausweis** my identity card is missing

Vermisste, *Vermißte *der/die; adj. Dekl.* missing person
vermitteln **1** *itr. V.* mediate, act as [a] mediator (in + *Dat.* in)
2 *tr. V.* **(a)** (herbeiführen) arrange; negotiate ⟨*transaction, ceasefire, compromise*⟩
(b) (besorgen) jmdm. eine Stelle ~: find sb. a job
(c) (weitergeben) impart ⟨*knowledge, insight, values, etc.*⟩; communicate ⟨*message, information, etc.*⟩; convey ⟨*feeling*⟩; pass on ⟨*experience*⟩
Vermittler *der;* ~s, ~, **Vermittlerin** *die;* ~, ~nen **(a)** (Mittler) mediator
(b) ▶ VERMITTELN 2c: imparter; communicator; conveyer
(c) (von Berufs wegen) agent
Vermittlung *die;* ~, ~en **(a)** (Schlichtung) mediation
(b) ▶ VERMITTELN 2A: arrangement; negotiation
(c) ▶ VERMITTELN 2c: imparting; communicating; conveying
(d) (Telefonzentrale) exchange; (in einer Firma) switchboard
vermöbeln *tr. V.* (ugs.) beat up; (als Strafe) thrash
vermögen (geh.) *unr. tr. V.* etw. zu tun ~: be able to do sth.; be capable of doing sth.
Vermögen *das;* ~s, ~ **(a)** (geh.: Fähigkeit) ability
(b) (Besitz) fortune; **er hat ~:** he has money
vermögend *Adj.* wealthy; well-off
Vermögen[s]·steuer *die* wealth tax
vermummen *tr. V.* wrap up [warmly]; (verbergen) disguise
vermurksen *tr. V.* (ugs.) mess up; muck up (Brit. sl.)
vermuten *tr. V.* suspect; **das ist zu ~:** that is what one would suppose *or* expect; we may assume that;
vermutlich **1** *Adj.* probable
2 *Adv.* presumably; (wahrscheinlich) probably
Vermutung *die;* ~, ~en supposition
vernachlässigen *tr. V.* neglect; (unberücksichtigt lassen) ignore; disregard
Vernachlässigung *die;* ~, ~en neglect
vernarben *itr. V.; mit sein* [form a] scar; heal (lit. or fig.)
vernehmbar *Adj.* (geh.) audible
vernehmen *unr. tr. V.* **(a)** (geh.: hören, erfahren) hear
(b) (verhören) question
vernehmlich **1** *Adj.* [clearly] audible
2 *adv.* audibly
Vernehmung *die;* ~, ~en questioning
verneigen *refl. V.* (geh.) bow (vor + *Dat.* to, (literary) before)
verneinen *tr. (auch itr.) V.* **(a)** say 'no' to ⟨*question*⟩; answer ⟨*question*⟩ in the negative
(b) (Sprachw.) negate
Verneinung *die;* ~, ~en (Sprachw.) negation

vernetzen tr. V. (Chemie, Technik) interlink

vernichten tr. V. destroy; exterminate ⟨pests, vermin⟩

vernichtend [1] Adj. crushing ⟨defeat⟩; shattering ⟨blow⟩; (fig.) devastating ⟨criticism⟩; devastating, withering ⟨glance⟩ [2] adv. **den Feind** ∼ **schlagen** inflict a crushing defeat on the enemy

Vernichtung die; ∼, ∼en destruction; (von Schädlingen) extermination

Vernichtungs-: ∼**lager** das extermination camp; ∼**waffe** die weapon of annihilation

Vernunft die; ∼: reason

vernünftig [1] Adj. (a) sensible (b) (ugs.: ordentlich, richtig) decent [2] adv. (a) sensibly (b) (ugs.: ordentlich, richtig) ⟨talk, eat⟩ properly; ⟨dress⟩ sensibly

veröffentlichen tr. V. publish

Veröffentlichung die; ∼, ∼en publication

verordnen tr. V. [jmdm. etw.] ∼: prescribe [sth. for sb.]

Verordnung die; ∼, ∼en prescribing

verpachten tr. V. lease

verpacken tr. V. pack; wrap up ⟨present, parcel⟩

Verpackung die (a) packing (b) (Umhüllung) packaging no pl.; wrapping

verpassen tr. V. miss

verpennen (salopp) [1] itr. V. oversleep [2] tr. V. (a) (vergessen) forget (b) (verschlafen) sleep through ⟨morning etc.⟩

verpesten tr. V. (abwertend) pollute

Verpestung (abwertend) die; ∼, ∼en pollution

verpflanzen tr. V. (auch Med.) transplant; graft ⟨skin⟩

Verpflanzung die; ∼, ∼en (Med.) transplant[ing]; (von Haut) graft

verpflegen tr. V. cater for; feed

Verpflegung die; ∼, ∼en (a) catering no indef. art. (Gen. for) (b) (Nahrung) food; **Unterkunft und** ∼: board and lodging

verpflichten [1] tr. V. (a) oblige; commit; (festlegen, binden) bind (b) (einstellen, engagieren) engage ⟨manager, actor, etc.⟩ [2] refl. V. undertake; promise; **sich vertraglich** ∼: sign a contract

Verpflichtung die; ∼, ∼en (a) obligation; commitment (b) (Engagement) engaging; engagement

verpfuschen tr. V. (ugs.) make a mess of; muck up (Brit. sl.)

verpissen refl. V. (salopp) piss off (Brit. sl.); beat it (coll.)

verpönt Adj. scorned; (tabu) taboo

verprügeln tr. V. beat up; (zur Strafe) thrash

Verputz der; ∼es plaster; (auf Außenwänden) rendering

verputzen tr. V. plaster; render ⟨outside wall⟩

verquer Adj. (absonderlich) weird, outlandish ⟨idea⟩

verquirlen tr. V. mix [with a whisk]; whisk

verquollen Adj. swollen

verrammeln tr. V. barricade

Verrat der; ∼[e]s betrayal (an + Dat. of)

verraten unr. tr. V. (a) betray (an + Akk. to) (b) (ugs.: mitteilen) jmdm. den Grund usw. ∼: tell sb. the reason etc.; (c) (erkennen lassen) show, betray ⟨feelings, surprise, fear, etc.⟩; show ⟨influence, talent⟩

Verräter der; ∼s, ∼: traitor

Verräterin die; ∼, ∼nen traitress

verräterisch Adj. treacherous ⟨plan, purpose, act, etc.⟩

verraucht Adj. smoke-filled; smoky

verrechnen [1] tr. V. include ⟨amount etc.⟩; (gutschreiben) credit ⟨cheque etc.⟩ to another account [2] refl. V. miscalculate

Verrechnungs-scheck der crossed cheque

verregnen itr. V.; mit sein be spoilt or ruined by rain

verreiben unr. tr. V. rub in

verreisen itr. V.; mit sein go away

verrenken tr. V. dislocate

Verrenkung die; ∼, ∼en dislocation

verrichten tr. V. perform

verriegeln tr. V. bolt

verringern [1] tr. V. reduce [2] refl. V. decrease

Verringerung die; ∼: reduction; decrease (Gen., von in)

Verriss, *Verriß der (ugs.) damning review or criticism (über + Akk. of)

verrosten itr. V.; mit sein rust; **verrostet** rusty

verrückt (ugs.) [1] Adj. (a) mad; ∼ **werden** go mad or insane (b) (überspannt, ausgefallen) crazy ⟨idea, fashion, prank, day, etc.⟩ [2] adv. crazily; ⟨behave⟩ crazily or like a madman; ⟨dress etc.⟩ in a mad or crazy way

Verrückte der/die; adj. Dekl. (ugs.) madman/madwoman; lunatic

verrufen Adj. disreputable

verrühren tr. V. stir together; mix

verrutschen itr. V. slip

Vers der; ∼es, ∼e verse

versagen itr. V. fail; ⟨machine, engine⟩ stop [working]; **menschliches Versagen** human error

Versager der; ∼s, ∼, **Versagerin** die; ∼, ∼nen failure

V

versalzen unr. tr. V. put too much salt in/
on; (fig. ugs.) spoil

versammeln tr., refl. V. assemble

Versammlung die; ~, ~en (a) meeting
(b) (Gremium) assembly

Versand der; ~[e]s (a) dispatch
(b) (ugs.: Versandhaus) mail order firm

Versand-: ~**handel** der mail order
business; ~**haus** das mail order firm

versauen tr. V. (salopp) (a) (verschmutzen)
mess up; make mucky (coll.)
(b) (verderben) foul up (coll.)

versäumen tr. V. (a) (verpassen) miss; lose
⟨time, sleep⟩
(b) (vernachlässigen, unterlassen) neglect ⟨duty,
task⟩

verschaffen tr. V. jmdm. etw. ~: provide
sb. with sth.; get sb. sth.; sich (Dat.) etw. ~:
get hold of sth.; obtain sth.

verschämt ① Adj. bashful
② adv. bashfully

verschandeln tr. V. (ugs.) spoil; ruin

verschenken tr. V. give away

verscheuchen tr. V. chase away

verscheuern tr. V. (ugs.) flog (Brit. sl.) ⟨Dat.,
an + Akk. to⟩

verschicken tr. V. ▶ VERSENDEN

verschieben ① unr. tr. V. (a) shift; move
(b) (aufschieben) put off, postpone (auf + Akk.
till)
② unr. refl. V. be postponed (um for); ⟨start⟩
be put back or delayed (um by)

Verschiebung die; ~, ~en postponement

verschieden ① Adj. (a) different (von
from)
(b) (vielfältig) various; die ~sten ...: all sorts
of ...; die ~en ...: the various ...
(c) **Verschiedenes** various things pl.;
② adv. differently

verschieden·artig ① Adj. different in
kind pred.; (mehr als zwei) diverse
② adv. diversely

Verschiedenheit die; ~, ~en difference;
(unter mehreren) diversity

verschiedentlich Adv. on various
occasions

verschimmeln itr. V.; mit sein go mouldy;
verschimmelt mouldy

verschlafen¹ ① unr. itr. (auch refl.) V.
oversleep
② unr. tr. V. (a) (schlafend verbringen) sleep
through ⟨morning, journey, etc.⟩
(b) (versäumen) not wake up in time for
⟨appointment⟩; not wake up in time to catch
⟨train, bus⟩
(c) (ugs.: vergessen) forget about ⟨appointment
etc.⟩

verschlafen² Adj. half asleep; (fig.) sleepy
⟨town⟩

Verschlag der; ~[e]s, **Verschläge** shed

verschlagen¹ unr. tr. V. die Seite ~: lose
one's place or page; jmdm. die Sprache ~:
leave sb. speechless

verschlagen² ① Adj. sly; shifty
② adv. slyly; shiftily

verschlechtern ① tr. V. make worse
② refl. V. get worse; deteriorate

Verschlechterung die; ~, ~en
worsening, deterioration (Gen. in)

Verschleiß der; ~es, ~e (a) wear no
indef. art.;
(b) (Verbrauch) consumption (an + Dat. of)

verschleißen ① unr. itr. V.; mit sein wear
out
② unr. tr. V. wear out; (fig.) run down, ruin
⟨one's nerves, one's health⟩; use up ⟨energy,
ability, etc.⟩

verschleppen tr. V. (a) carry off; take
away ⟨person⟩
(b) (weiterverbreiten) carry, spread ⟨disease,
bacteria, mud, etc.⟩
(c) (verzögern) delay; (in die Länge ziehen) draw
out; let ⟨illness⟩ drag on [and get worse]

verschleudern tr. V. (a) sell dirt cheap
(coll.); (mit Verlust) sell at a loss
(b) (verschwenden) squander

verschließbar Adj. closable; lockable
⟨suitcase, drawer, etc.⟩; [luftdicht] ~: sealable
⟨container etc.⟩

verschließen unr. tr. V. (a) close; stop,
(mit einem Korken) cork ⟨bottle⟩
(b) (abschließen) lock; lock up ⟨house etc.⟩
(c) (wegschließen) lock away (in + Dat. od.
Akk. in)

verschlimmern ① tr. V. make worse
② refl. V. get worse; ⟨position, conditions⟩
deteriorate, worsen

Verschlimmerung die; ~, ~en
worsening

verschlingen unr. tr. V. (a) [inter]twine
⟨threads etc.⟩ (zu into)
(b) (essen, fressen) devour ⟨food⟩; (fig.) devour
⟨novel, money, etc.⟩

verschlissen 2. Part. v. VERSCHLEISSEN 2

verschlossen Adj. (wortkarg) taciturn;
(zurückhaltend) reserved

Verschlossenheit die; ~: taciturnity;
(Zurückhaltung) reserve

verschlucken ① tr. V. swallow
② refl. V. choke

Verschluss, *Verschluß der (am BH, an
Schmuck usw.) fastener; fastening; (an Taschen,
Schmuck) clasp; (an Schuhen, Gürteln) buckle; (am
Schrank, Fenster, Koffer usw.) catch; (an Flaschen)
top; (Stöpsel) stopper

verschmähen tr. V. (geh.) spurn

verschmerzen tr. V. get over

verschmieren tr. V. smear ⟨window etc.⟩;
(beim Schreiben) mess up ⟨paper⟩; scrawl all
over ⟨page⟩; smudge ⟨ink⟩

verschmitzt ① Adj. mischievous
② adv. mischievously

---

*alte Schreibung - vgl. Hinweis auf S. xiv

verschmutzen ① *itr. V.; mit sein* get dirty; ⟨*river etc.*⟩ become polluted
② *tr. V.* dirty; soil; pollute ⟨*air, water, etc.*⟩
Verschmutzung *die; ∼, ∼en* (der Umwelt) pollution; (von Stoffen, Teppichen usw.) soiling
verschnaufen *itr.* (*auch refl.*) *V.* have *or* take a breather
verschneit *Adj.* snow-covered *attrib.;* covered with snow *postpos.*
verschnörkelt *Adj.* ornate
verschnüren *tr. V.* tie up
verschollen *Adj.* missing
verschonen *tr. V.* spare; **jmdn. mit etw. ∼:** spare sb. sth.
verschönern *tr. V.* brighten up
verschränken *tr. V.* fold ⟨*arms*⟩; cross ⟨*legs*⟩; clasp ⟨*hands*⟩
verschrecken *tr. V.* frighten *or* scare [off *or* away]
verschreiben ① *unr. tr. V.* (Med.: verordnen) prescribe
② *unr. refl. V.* **(a)** make a slip of the pen **(b) sich einer Sache** (*Dat.*) ∼: devote oneself to sth.
verschreibungs-pflichtig *Adj.* available only on prescription *postpos.*
verschrie[e]n *Adj.* notorious (**wegen** for)
verschroben *Adj.* eccentric, cranky ⟨*person*⟩; cranky, weird ⟨*ideas*⟩
verschrotten *tr. V.* scrap
Verschrottung *die; ∼, ∼en* scrapping
verschulden ① *tr. V.* be to blame for ⟨*accident, death, etc.*⟩
② *refl. V.* get into debt
Verschulden *das; ∼s* guilt; **durch eigenes ∼:** through one's own fault
verschuldet *Adj.* in debt *postpos.* **(bei** to); **hoch ∼:** deeply in debt
verschütt: **∼ gehen** (ugs.) do a vanishing trick *or* disappearing act (coll.)
verschütten *tr. V.* **(a)** spill **(b)** (begraben) bury ⟨*person*⟩ [alive].
∗verschütt|gehen ▶ VERSCHÜTT
verschwägert *Adj.* related by marriage *postpos.*
verschweigen *unr. tr. V.* conceal (*Dat.* from)
verschwenden *tr. V.* waste (**an** + *Akk.* on)
Verschwender *der; ∼s, ∼,* **Verschwenderin** *die; ∼, ∼nen* (von Geld) spendthrift; (von Dingen) wasteful person
verschwenderisch ① *Adj.* wasteful ⟨*person*⟩; ⟨*life*⟩ of extravagance
② *adv.* wastefully
Verschwendung *die; ∼, ∼en* wastefulness; extravagance
verschwiegen *Adj.* discreet; (still, einsam) secluded
Verschwiegenheit *die; ∼:* secrecy; (Diskretion) discretion
verschwimmen *unr. itr. V.; mit sein* blur

verschwinden *unr. itr. V.; mit sein* disappear; vanish; **verschwinde [hier]!** off with you!; go away!; hop it! (coll.); **ich muss mal ∼** (ugs. verhüll.) I have to pay a visit (coll.) *or* (Brit. coll.) spend a penny
verschwindend ① *Adj.* tiny
② *adv.* ∼ **klein** tiny; minute; ∼ **wenig** a tiny amount
verschwommen ① *Adj.* blurred ⟨*photograph, vision*⟩; blurred, hazy ⟨*outline*⟩; vague, woolly ⟨*idea, concept, formulation, etc.*⟩
② *adv.* vaguely; ⟨*remember*⟩ hazily
versehen ① *unr. tr. V.* **(a)** (ausstatten) provide; equip ⟨*car, factory, machine, etc.*⟩ **(b)** (ausüben, besorgen) perform ⟨*duty etc.*⟩
② *unr. refl. V.* make a slip; slip up
Versehen *das; ∼s, ∼:* oversight; slip; **aus ∼:** by mistake; inadvertently
versehentlich ① *Adv.* by mistake; inadvertently
② *adj.* inadvertent
Versehrte *der/die; adj. Dekl.* disabled person; **die ∼n** the disabled
versenden *unr.* (*auch regelm.*) *tr. V.* send ⟨*letter, parcel*⟩; send out ⟨*invitations*⟩; dispatch ⟨*goods*⟩
versetzen ① *tr. V.* **(a)** move; transfer, move ⟨*employee*⟩; (in die nächsthöhere Klasse) move ⟨*pupil*⟩ up, (Amer.) promote ⟨*pupil*⟩ (**in** + *Akk.* to); (umpflanzen) transplant, move ⟨*plant*⟩; (fig.) transport (**in** + *Akk.* to) **(b)** (nicht geradlinig anordnen) stagger **(c)** (verpfänden) pawn **(d)** (verkaufen) sell **(e)** (ugs.: vergeblich warten lassen) stand ⟨*person*⟩ up (coll.) **(f)** (vermischen) mix **(g)** (erwidern) retort **(h) etw. in Bewegung/Tätigkeit ∼:** set sth. in motion/operation; **jmdn. in die Lage ∼, etw. zu tun** put sb. in a position to do sth.; **jmdm. einen Stoß/Fußtritt/Schlag** *usw.* ∼: give sb. a push/kick/deal sb. a blow *etc.;*
② *refl. V.* **sich in jmds. Lage** (*Akk.*) ∼: put oneself in sb.'s position *or* place
Versetzung *die; ∼, ∼en* (eines Schülers) moving up, (Amer.) promotion (**in** + *Akk.* to); (eines Angestellten) transfer
verseuchen *tr. V.* (auch fig.) contaminate; **radioaktiv ∼:** contaminate with radioactivity
Verseuchung (auch fig.) *die; ∼, ∼en* contamination
Versicherer *der; ∼s, ∼,* **Versicherin** *die; ∼, ∼nen* insurer
versichern *tr. V.* **(a)** assert ⟨*sth.*⟩ **(b)** (vertraglich schützen) insure (**bei** with)
Versicherte *der/die; adj. Dekl.* insured |person|
Versicherung *die* **(a)** (Beteuerung) assurance **(b)** (Schutz durch Vertrag) insurance; (Vertrag) insurance |policy| (**über** + *Akk.* for); (Gesellschaft) insurance |company|

Versicherungs-: ~**beitrag** *der*
insurance premium; ~**betrug** *der*
insurance fraud; ~**gesellschaft** *die*
insurance company; ~**nehmer** *der*; ~~s,
~~, ~**nehmerin** *die*; ~~, ~~nen policy
holder; ~**police** *die* insurance policy
versickern *itr. V.; mit sein* ‹*river etc.*›
drain *or* seep away
versiegeln *tr. V.* seal
versiegen *itr. V.; mit sein* (geh.) dry up;
run dry
versinken *unr. itr. V.; mit sein* sink; **im
Schlamm** ~: sink into the mud
verslumen /...'slamən/ *itr. V.; mit sein* turn
into a slum; **ein verslumter Stadtteil** a slum
district
versoffen *Adj.* (salopp abwertend) boozy (coll.)
versöhnen ① *refl. V.* **sich** [**miteinander**] ~:
become reconciled; **sich mit jmdm.** ~: make
it up with sb.
② *tr. V.* reconcile
Versöhnung *die;* ~, ~en reconciliation
versonnen ① *Adj.* dreamy
② *adv.* dreamily
versorgen *tr. V.* (a) supply
(b) (unterhalten, ernähren) provide for ‹*children,
family*›
(c) (sorgen für) look after; **jmdn. ärztlich** ~:
give sb. medical care; (kurzzeitig) give sb.
medical attention
Versorger *der;* ~s, ~, **Versorgerin** *die;*
~, ~nen breadwinner
Versorgung *die;* ~, ~en (a) supply[ing]
(b) (Unterhaltung, Ernährung) support[ing]
(c) (Bedienung, Pflege) care; **ärztliche** ~:
medical care *or* treatment; (kurzzeitig) medical
attention
Verspannung *die* (Med.: der Muskulatur)
tension
verspäten *refl. V.* be late
verspätet *Adj.* late ‹*arrival etc.*›; belated
‹*greetings, thanks*›; ~ **eintreffen** arrive late
Verspätung *die;* ~, ~en lateness;
(verspätetes Eintreffen) late arrival; [**fünf
Minuten**] ~ **haben** be [five minutes] late
versperren *tr. V.* block; obstruct ‹*view*›
verspielen *tr. V.* gamble away; (fig.)
squander, throw away ‹*opportunity, chance*›;
forfeit ‹*right, credibility, etc*›
verspielt ① *Adj.* (auch fig.) playful; fanciful;
fantastic ‹*form, design, etc.*›
② *adv.* playfully (lit. or fig.); ‹*dress, designed*›
fancifully, fantastically
verspotten *tr. V.* mock; ridicule
Verspottung *die;* ~, ~en mocking;
ridiculing
versprechen ① *unr. tr. V.* promise; **sich**
(*Dat.*) **etw. von etw./jmdm.** ~: hope for sth. *or*
to get sth. from sth./sb.
② *unr. refl. V.* make a slip/slips of the
tongue

Versprechen *das;* ~s, ~,
Versprechung *die;* ~, ~en promise
versprühen *tr. V.* spray
verspüren *tr. V.* feel
verstaatlichen *tr. V.* nationalize
Verstaatlichung *die;* ~, ~en
nationalization
Verstand *der;* ~[e]s (Fähigkeit zu denken)
reason *no art.;* (Fähigkeit, Begriffe zu bilden)
mind; (Vernunft) [common] sense *no art.;* **hast
du denn den** ~ **verloren?** (ugs.) have you
taken leave of your senses?
verständig ① *Adj.* sensible
② *adv.* sensibly
verständigen ① *tr. V.* notify, inform
(**von, über** + *Akk.* of)
② *refl. V.* (a) make oneself understood; **sich
mit jmdm.** ~: communicate with sb.
(b) (sich einigen) **sich** [**mit jmdm.**] **über/auf etw.**
(*Akk.*) ~: come to an understanding [with
sb.] about *or.* on sth
Verständigkeit *die;* ~: understanding;
intelligence
Verständigung *die;* ~, ~en (a)
notification
(b) (das Sichverständlichmachen) communication
no art.;
(c) (Einigung) understanding
Verständigungs-schwierigkeit *die*
difficulty of communication
verständlich ① *Adj.* (a) comprehensible;
(deutlich) clear ‹*pronunciation, presentation,
etc.*›; **sich** ~ **machen** make oneself
understood; **jmdm. etw.** ~ **machen** make sth.
clear to sb.
(b) (begreiflich, verzeihlich) understandable
② *adv.* comprehensibly; (deutlich) ‹*speak,
express oneself, present*› clearly
verständlicher·weise *Adv.*
understandably
Verständlichkeit *die;* ~:
comprehensibility; clarity
Verständnis *das;* ~ses, ~se
understanding; **ich habe volles** ~ **dafür, dass
...:** I fully understand that ...; **für die
Unannehmlichkeiten bitten wir um** [**Ihr**] ~: we
apologize for the inconvenience caused
verständnis-: ~**los** ① *Adj.*
uncomprehending; ② *adv.*
uncomprehendingly; ~**voll** ① *Adj.*
understanding; ② *adv.* understandingly
verstärken ① *tr. V.* (a) strengthen
(b) (zahlenmäßig) reinforce ‹*troops etc.*› (**um
by**); enlarge ‹*orchestra, choir*› (**um by**)
(c) (intensiver machen) intensify, increase
‹*effort, contrast*›; strengthen, increase
‹*impression, suspicion*›; (größer machen)
increase ‹*pressure, voltage, effect, etc.*›; (lauter
machen) amplify ‹*signal, sound, guitar, etc.*›
② *refl. V.* increase
Verstärker *der;* ~s, ~: amplifier
Verstärkung *die;* ~, ~en (a)
strengthening

---

*old spelling - see note on page xiv

(b) (zahlenmäßig) reinforcement (esp. Mil.)
(c) (Zunahme) increase (*Gen.* in); (der Lautstärke) amplification
(d) (zusätzliche Person[en]) reinforcements *pl.*

verstauben *itr. V.; mit sein* get dusty; gather dust (lit. or fig.)

verstaubt *Adj.* (fig. abwertend) old-fashioned; outmoded

verstauchen *tr. V.* sprain; **sich** (*Dat.*) **den Fuß/die Hand** ∼: sprain one's ankle/wrist

Verstauchung *die;* ∼, ∼**en** sprain

verstauen *tr. V.* pack (**in** + *Dat. od. Akk.* in[to]); (bes. im Boot/Auto) stow (**in** + *Dat. od. Akk.* in)

Versteck *das;* ∼**[e]s,** ∼**e** hiding place: ∼ **spielen** play hide-and-seek

verstecken [1] *tr. V.* hide (**vor** + *Dat.* from)
[2] *refl. V.* **sich** [**vor jmdm./etw.**] ∼: hide [from sb./sth.]

versteckt *Adj.* hidden; (heimlich) secret ⟨*malice, activity, etc.*⟩; disguised ⟨*foul*⟩

verstehen [1] *unr. tr. V.* understand; **wie soll ich das** ∼? how am I to interpret that?; **jmdn./etw. falsch** ∼: misunderstand sb./sth.
[2] *unr. refl. V.* **sich mit jmdm.** ∼: get on with sb.; **das versteht sich** [**von selbst**] that goes without saying

versteigern *tr. V.* auction; **etw.** ∼ **lassen** put sth. up for auction

Versteigerung *die;* ∼, ∼**en** auction

versteinern *itr. V.; mit sein* ⟨*plant, animal*⟩ fossilize, become fossilized; ⟨*wood etc.*⟩ petrify, become petrified

Versteinerung *die;* ∼, ∼**en (a)** (das Versteinern) fossilization; (von Holz) petrification
(b) (Fossil) fossil

verstellbar *Adj.* adjustable

verstellen [1] *tr. V.* **(a)** (falsch platzieren) misplace
(b) (anders einstellen) adjust ⟨*seat etc.*⟩; alter [the adjustment of] ⟨*mirror etc.*⟩; reset ⟨*alarm clock, points, etc.*⟩
(c) (versperren) block, obstruct
(d) (zur Täuschung verändern) disguise ⟨*voice, handwriting*⟩
[2] *refl. V.* pretend

Verstellung *die;* ∼, ∼**en** pretence; (der Stimme, Schrift) disguising

versteuern *tr. V.* pay tax on

verstimmen *tr. V.* put ⟨*person*⟩ in a bad mood; (verärgern) annoy

verstimmt *Adj.* **(a)** (Musik) out of tune *pred.;*
(b) (verärgert) put out, peeved, disgruntled (**über** + *Akk.* by, about); **ein** ∼**er Magen** an upset stomach

Verstimmung *die;* ∼, ∼**en** bad mood

verstockt *Adj.* obdurate; stubborn

Verstocktheit *die;* ∼: obduracy; stubbornness

verstohlen [1] *Adj.* furtive

[2] *adv.* furtively

verstopfen [1] *tr. V.* block; **verstopft sein** ⟨*pipe, drain, jet, nose, etc.*⟩ be blocked [up] (**durch, von** with)
[2] *itr. V.; mit sein* become blocked

Verstopfung *die;* ∼, ∼**en** (Med.) constipation

verstorben *Adj.* late (deceased)

Verstorbene *der/die; adj. Dekl.* (geh.) deceased

verstören *tr. V.* distress

verstört *Adj.* distraught

Verstoß *der;* ∼**es, Verstöße** violation (**gegen** of)

verstoßen [1] *unr. tr. V.* disown
[2] *unr. itr. V.* **gegen etw.** ∼: infringe sth

verstreichen [1] *unr. tr. V.* apply, put on ⟨*paint*⟩; spread ⟨*butter etc.*⟩
[2] *unr. itr. V.; mit sein* (geh.) ⟨*time*⟩ pass [by]

verstreuen *tr. V.* scatter; put down ⟨*bird food, salt*⟩; (versehentlich) spill

verstricken [1] *tr. V.* **jmdn. in etw.** (*Akk.*) ∼: involve sb. in sth.; draw sb. into sth.
[2] *refl. V.* **sich in etw.** (*Akk.*) ∼: become entangled *or* caught up in sth

verstümmeln *tr. V.* mutilate; (fig.) garble ⟨*report*⟩; chop, mutilate ⟨*text*⟩

verstummen *itr. V.; mit sein* (geh.) fall silent; ⟨*music, noise, conversation*⟩ cease

Versuch *der;* ∼**[e]s,** ∼**e** attempt; (Experiment) experiment (**an** + *Dat.* on); (Probe) test

versuchen *tr. V.* **(a)** try; attempt
(b) (probieren) try ⟨*cake etc.*⟩

versündigen *refl. V.* **sich an jmdm./etw.** ∼: sin against sb./sth.

versüßen *tr. V.* **jmdm./sich etw.** ∼ (fig.) make sth. more pleasant for sb./oneself

vertauschen *tr. V.* exchange; switch; reverse ⟨*roles, poles*⟩; **etw. mit** *od.* **gegen etw.** ∼: exchange sth. for sth.

verteidigen *tr. V.* defend

Verteidiger *der;* ∼**s,** ∼, **Verteidigerin** *die;* ∼, ∼**nen** (auch Sport) defender; (Rechtsw.) defence counsel

Verteidigung *die,* ∼, ∼**en** defence

Verteidigungs-minister *der,* **Verteidigungs-ministerin** *die* minister of defence

verteilen *tr. V.* distribute, hand out ⟨*leaflets, prizes, etc.*⟩ (**an** + *Akk.* to, **unter** + *Akk.* among); share [out], distribute ⟨*money, food*⟩ (**an** + *Akk.* to, **unter** + *Akk.* among); allocate ⟨*work*⟩; distribute ⟨*weight etc.*⟩ (**auf** + *Akk.* over); spread ⟨*cost*⟩ (**auf** + *Akk.* among); distribute, spread ⟨*butter, seed, dirt, etc.*⟩

Verteilung *die;* ∼, ∼**en** distribution; (der Rollen, der Arbeit) allocation

verteuern [1] *tr. V.* make ⟨*goods*⟩ more expensive
[2] *refl. V.* become more expensive

V

verteufeln *tr. V.* condemn; denigrate

Verteufelung *die;* ~, ~en condemnation; denigration

vertiefen [1] *tr. V.* (auch fig.) deepen (um by) [2] *refl. V.* **sich** ~ **in** (+ *Akk.*); **in etw.** (*Akk.*) **vertieft sein** be engrossed in sth ⟨*book, work, etc.*⟩: bury oneself in

Vertiefung *die;* ~, ~en (Mulde) depression; hollow

vertikal [1] *Adj.* vertical [2] *adv.* vertically

Vertikale *die;* ~, ~n ▶ SENKRECHTE

vertilgen *tr. V.* (a) (vernichten) exterminate ⟨*vermin*⟩; kill off ⟨*weeds*⟩ (b) (ugs.: verzehren) devour, (joc.) demolish ⟨*food*⟩

vertonen *tr. V.* set ⟨*text, poem*⟩ to music

Vertonung *die;* ~, ~en setting

Vertrag *der;* ~[e]s, Verträge contract; (zwischen Staaten) treaty

vertragen [1] *unr. tr. V.* endure; tolerate (esp. Med.); (aushalten, leiden können) stand; bear; **ich vertrage keinen Kaffee** coffee disagrees with me [2] *unr. refl. V.* **sich mit jmdm.** ~: get on *or* along with sb.; (passen) **sich mit etw.** ~: go with sth

vertraglich [1] *Adj.* contractual [2] *adv.* contractually; by contract

verträglich *Adj.* (a) digestible ⟨*food*⟩ (b) (umgänglich) goodnatured; easy to get on with *pred.*

vertrauen *itr. V.* **jmdm./einer Sache** ~: trust sb./sth.; **auf etw.** (*Akk.*) ~: [put one's] trust in sth.

Vertrauen *das;* ~s trust; confidence; **jmdn. ins** ~ **ziehen** take sb. into one's confidence

vertrauen-erweckend *Adj.* inspiring

vertrauens-, Vertrauens-: ~**bruch** *der* breach of trust; ~**lehrer** *der,* ~**lehrerin** *die* (Schulw.) liaison teacher (liaising between staff and pupils); ~**person** *die* person in a position of trust; ~**sache** *die* matter *or* question of trust; ~**selig** *Adj.* all too trusting; ~**voll** [1] *Adj.* trusting ⟨*relationship*⟩; ⟨*collaboration, cooperation*⟩ based on trust; (zuversichtlich) confident; [2] *adv.* trustingly; (zuversichtlich) confidently; ~**würdig** *Adj.* trustworthy

vertraulich [1] *Adj.* (a) confidential (b) (freundschaftlich, intim) familiar ⟨*manner, tone, etc.*⟩; intimate ⟨*conversation*⟩ [2] *adv.* (a) confidentially (b) (freundschaftlich, intim) in a familiar way

Vertraulichkeit *die;* ~, ~en (a) confidentiality (b) (vertrauliche Information) confidence (c) (distanzloses Verhalten) familiarity; (Intimität) intimacy

vertraut *Adj.* (a) close ⟨*friend etc.*⟩; intimate ⟨*circle, conversation, etc.*⟩

(b) (bekannt) familiar; **jmdn./sich mit etw.** ~ **machen** familiarize sb./oneself with sth.

Vertraute *der/die; adj. Dekl.* close friend

vertreiben *unr. tr. V.* (a) drive out (aus of); drive away ⟨*animal, smoke, clouds*⟩ (aus from); fight off ⟨*tiredness, troubles*⟩ (b) (verkaufen) sell

vertreten [1] *unr. tr. V.* (a) stand in *or* deputize for ⟨*colleague etc.*⟩; ⟨*teacher*⟩ cover for ⟨*colleague*⟩ (b) (eintreten für, repräsentieren) represent ⟨*person, firm, interests, constituency, country, etc.*⟩; (Rechtsw.) act for ⟨*person, prosecution, etc.*⟩; ~ **sein** be represented (c) (einstehen für, verfechten) support ⟨*point of view, principle*⟩; hold ⟨*opinion*⟩; advocate ⟨*thesis etc.*⟩ [2] *unr. refl. V.* **sich** (*Dat.*) **die Füße** *od.* **Beine** ~ (ugs.) stretch one's legs

Vertreter *der;* ~s, ~, **Vertreterin** *die;* ~, ~nen (a) (Stellvertreter[in]) deputy; stand-in (b) (Repräsentant[in]) representative; (Handelsvertreter[in]) sales representative; commercial traveller (c) (Verfechter[in], Anhänger[in]) supporter; advocate

Vertretung *die;* ~, ~en deputy; (Delegierte[r]) representative; (Delegation) delegation (Handelsvertretung) [sales] agency; **eine diplomatische** ~: a diplomatic mission

Vertriebene *der/die; adj. Dekl.* expellee [from his/her homeland]

vertrocknen *itr. V.; mit sein* dry up

vertrödeln *tr. V.* (ugs. abwertend) dawdle away, waste ⟨*time*⟩

vertrösten *tr. V.* put ⟨*person*⟩ off (auf + *Akk.* until)

vertun [1] *unr. tr. V.* waste [2] *unr. refl. V.* (ugs.) make a slip

vertuschen *tr. V.* hush up ⟨*scandal etc.*⟩; keep ⟨*truth etc.*⟩ secret

Vertuschung *die;* ~, ~en hushing up; **eine** ~: a hush-up *or* cover-up

verübeln *tr. V.* **jmdm. eine Äußerung** *usw.* ~: take sb.'s remark *etc.* amiss

verüben *tr. V.* commit ⟨*crime etc.*⟩

verunglücken *itr. V.; mit sein* have an accident; ⟨*car etc.*⟩ be involved in an accident; **mit dem Auto/Flugzeug** ~: be in a car/an air accident *or* crash

Verunglückte *der/die; adj. Dekl.* accident victim; casualty

verunreinigen *tr. V.* pollute; contaminate ⟨*water, milk, flour, oil*⟩

verunsichern *tr. V.* **jmdn.** ~: make sb. feel unsure *or* uncertain

verunstalten *tr. V.* disfigure

Verunstaltung *die;* ~, ~en disfigurement

veruntreuen *tr. V.* embezzle

Veruntreuung *die;* ~, ~en embezzlement

verunzieren *tr. V.* spoil the look of

verursachen *tr. V.* cause

---

*alte Schreibung - vgl. Hinweis auf S. xiv

verurteilen *tr. V.* pass sentence on; sentence; (fig.) condemn ⟨*behaviour, action*⟩; **jmdn. zum Tode ∼:** sentence *or* condemn sb. to death

Verurteilte *der/die; adj. Dekl.* convicted man/woman

Verurteilung *die; ∼, ∼en* sentencing; (fig.) condemnation

vervollkommnen *tr. V.* perfect

vervollständigen *tr. V.* complete

verwachsen *Adj.* deformed

verwählen *refl. V.* misdial

verwahren ⓵ *tr. V.* keep [safe] ⓶ *refl. V.* protest

verwahrlosen *itr. V.; mit sein* get in a bad state; ⟨*house, building*⟩ fall into disrepair; ⟨*garden, hedge*⟩ become overgrown; ⟨*person*⟩ let oneself go; **verwahrlost** neglected; overgrown ⟨*hedge, garden*⟩; dilapidated ⟨*house, building*⟩; unkempt ⟨*person, appearance, etc.*⟩; (in der Kleidung) ragged ⟨*person*⟩

Verwahrlosung *die; ∼:* (eines Gebäudes) dilapidation; (einer Person) advancing decrepitude

verwaisen *itr. V.* be orphaned

verwalten *tr. V.* (a) administer ⟨*estate, property*⟩; run ⟨*house*⟩; hold ⟨*money*⟩ in trust (b) (leiten) run, manage ⟨*hostel, kindergarten, etc.*⟩; (regieren) administer ⟨*area, colony, etc.*⟩; govern ⟨*country*⟩

Verwalter *der; ∼s, ∼,* **Verwalterin** *die; ∼, ∼nen* administrator; (eines Amts usw.) manager; (eines Nachlasses) trustee

Verwaltung *die; ∼, ∼en* (a) administration; (eines Landes) government; (eines Amtes) tenure; (einer Aufgabe) performance (b) (Organ) administration

verwandeln ⓵ *tr. V.* convert (in + *Akk.,* zu into); (völlig verändern) transform (in + *Akk.,* zu into) ⓶ *refl. V.* **sich in etw.** (*Akk.*) *od.* **zu etw. ∼:** turn *or* change into sth.; (bei chemischen Vorgängen usw.) be converted into sth

Verwandlung *die; ∼, ∼en* conversion (in + *Akk.,* zu into); (völlige Veränderung, das Sichverwandeln) transformation (in + *Akk.,* zu into)

verwandt[1] 2. *Part. v.* VERWENDEN

verwandt[2] *Adj.* related (mit to); (fig.) similar ⟨*views, ideas, forms*⟩

Verwandte *der/die; adj. Dekl.* relative; relation

Verwandtschaft *die; ∼, ∼en* (a) relationship (mit to); (fig.) affinity (b) (Verwandte) relatives *pl.;* relations *pl.;* **die ganze ∼:** all one's relatives

verwandtschaftlich *Adj.* family ⟨*ties, relationships, etc.*⟩

verwarnen *tr. V.* warn, caution (wegen for)

Verwarnung *die; ∼, ∼en* warning; caution

verwechseln *tr. V.* (a) [miteinander] ∼: confuse ⟨*two things/people*⟩; **etw. mit etw./ jmdn. mit jmdm. ∼:** mistake sth. for sth./sb. for sb.; confuse sth. with sth./sb. with sb. (b) (vertauschen) mix up

Verwechslung *die; ∼, ∼en* (a) [case of] confusion (b) (Vertauschung) mixing up; **eine ∼:** a mix-up

verwegen ⓵ *Adj.* daring; (auch fig.) audacious ⓶ *adv.* (auch fig.) audaciously

Verwegenheit *die; ∼:* daring; (auch fig.) audacity

verwehren *tr. V.* **jmdm. etw. ∼:** refuse *or* deny sb. sth.

Verwehung *die; ∼, ∼en* [snow]drift

verweigern *tr. V.* refuse

Verweigerung *die; ∼, ∼en* refusal

Verweis *der; ∼es, ∼e* (a) reference (auf + *Akk.* to); (Querverweis) cross reference (b) (Tadel) reprimand

verweisen *unr. tr. V.* (a) **jmdn./einen Fall** *usw.* **an jmdn./etw. ∼** (auch Rechtsspr.) refer sb./a case *etc.* to sb./sth. (b) (wegschicken) **jmdn. von der Schule/aus dem Saal ∼:** expel sb. from the school/send sb. out of the room; **einen Spieler vom Platz ∼:** send a player off [the field] (c) *auch itr.* (hinweisen) **[jmdn.] auf etw.** (*Akk.*) ∼: refer [sb.] to sth.

verwelken *itr. V.; mit sein* wilt

verwendbar *Adj.* usable

Verwendbarkeit *die; ∼:* usability

verwenden *unr. od. regelm. tr. V.* (a) use (zu, für for) (b) (aufwenden) spend ⟨*time*⟩ (auf + *Akk.* on)

Verwendung *die; ∼, ∼en* use

verwerfen *unr. tr. V.* reject; dismiss ⟨*thought*⟩

verwerflich (geh.) ⓵ *Adj.* reprehensible ⓶ *adv.* reprehensibly

verwertbar *Adj.* utilizable; usable

verwerten *tr. V.* utilize, use (zu for); make use of ⟨*suggestion, experience, knowledge, etc.*⟩

verwesen *itr. V.; mit sein* decompose

Verwesung *die; ∼:* decomposition

verwickeln ⓵ *refl. V.* get tangled up *or* entangled; **sich in etw.** (*Akk. od. Dat.*) ∼: get caught [up] in sth. ⓶ *tr. V.* involve

Verwicklung *die; ∼, ∼en* complication

verwildern *itr. V.* ⟨*garden*⟩ become overgrown; ⟨*domestic animal*⟩ return to the wild

verwirklichen ⓵ *tr. V.* realize ⟨*dream*⟩; realize, put into practice ⟨*plan, proposal, idea, etc.*⟩; carry out ⟨*project, intention*⟩ ⓶ (a) *refl. V.* ⟨*hope, dream*⟩ be realized

····⫶

V

(b) (sich voll entfalten) **sich [selbst]** ∼: realize one's [full] potential; fulfil oneself

Verwirklichung *die;* ∼, ∼en realization; (eines Wunsches, einer Hoffnung) fulfilment

verwirren *tr. (auch itr.) V.* confuse; **verwirrt** confused; ∼d bewildering

Verwirrung *die;* ∼, ∼en confusion

verwischen *tr. V.* smudge ⟨signature, writing, etc.⟩; smear ⟨paint⟩; (fig.) cover up ⟨tracks⟩

verwittern *itr. V.; mit sein* weather

Verwitterung *die;* ∼, ∼en weathering

verwitwet *Adj.* widowed

verwöhnen *tr. V.* spoil

verwöhnt *Adj.* spoilt; (anspruchsvoll) discriminating; ⟨taste, palate⟩ of a gourmet

verworren *Adj.* confused, muddled ⟨ideas, situation, etc.⟩

verwunden *tr. V.* wound; injure

Verwundete *der/die; adj. Dekl.* casualty; **die** ∼**n** the wounded

Verwundung *die;* ∼, ∼en wound

verwünschen *tr. V.* curse

verwüsten *tr. V.* devastate

Verwüstung *die;* ∼, ∼en devastation

verzagen *itr. V.; mit sein od. haben* despair; lose heart; **verzagt sein** be despondent

Verzagtheit *die;* ∼: despondency; despair

verzählen *refl. V.* miscount

verzanken *refl. V.* (ugs.) **sich [mit jmdm. wegen etw.]** ∼: fall out [with sb. over sth.]

verzaubern *tr. V.* cast a spell on; bewitch; (fig.) enchant; **jmdn. in etw. (Akk.)** ∼: transform sb. into sth.

Verzehr *der;* ∼[e]s consumption

verzehren *tr. V.* consume

Verzeichnis *das;* ∼ses, ∼se list; (Register) index

verzeihen *unr. tr., itr. V.* forgive; (entschuldigen) excuse ⟨behaviour, remark, etc.⟩; ∼ **Sie [bitte], können Sie mir sagen ...?** excuse me, could you tell me ...?

Verzeihung *die;* ∼: forgiveness; ∼! sorry!; **jmdn. um** ∼ **bitten** apologize to sb.

verzerren *tr. V.* (a) contort ⟨face etc.⟩ (**zu** into)
(b) (akustisch, optisch) distort ⟨sound, image⟩; **etw. verzerrt darstellen** (fig.) present a distorted account *or* picture of sth.

Verzicht *der;* ∼[e]s, ∼e (a) renunciation (**auf** + *Akk.* of)
(b) (auf Reichtum, ein Amt usw.) relinquishment (**auf** + *Akk.* of)

verzichten *itr. V.* do without; ∼ **auf** (+ *Akk.*) do without; (sich enthalten) refrain from; (aufgeben) give up ⟨share, smoking, job, etc.⟩; renounce ⟨inheritance⟩; relinquish ⟨right, privilege⟩; (opfern) sacrifice ⟨holiday, salary⟩

verziehen¹ *2. Part. v.* VERZEIHEN

verziehen² ⓵ *unr. tr. V.* (a) screw up ⟨face, mouth, etc.⟩
(b) (schlecht erziehen) spoil
⓶ *unr. refl. V.* (a) (aus der Form geraten) go out of shape; ⟨wood⟩ warp
(b) (wegziehen) ⟨clouds, storm⟩ move away, pass over: ⟨fog, mist⟩ disperse
(c) (ugs.: weggehen) take oneself off
⓷ *unr. itr. V.; mit sein* move [away]; „**Empfänger [unbekannt] verzogen**" 'no longer at this address'

verzieren *tr. V.* decorate

Verzierung *die;* ∼, ∼en decoration

verzögern ⓵ *tr. V.* (a) delay (**um** by)
(b) (verlangsamen) slow down
⓶ *refl. V.* be delayed (**um** by)

Verzögerung *die;* ∼, ∼en delay (*Gen.* in); (Verlangsamung) slowing down

verzollen *tr. V.* pay duty on

Verzug *der;* ∼[e]s delay; **im** ∼ **sein/in** ∼ **kommen** be/fall behind

verzweifeln *itr. V.; mit sein* despair; **über etw./jmdn.** ∼: despair at sth./of sb.

verzweifelt ⓵ *Adj.* despairing ⟨person⟩; desperate ⟨situation, attempt, effort, struggle, etc⟩; ∼ **sein** be in despair
⓶ *adv.* desperately

Verzweiflung *die;* ∼: despair

verzweigen *refl. V.* branch [out]

Veteran /vete'ra:n/ *der;* ∼en, ∼en,
Veteranin *die;* ∼, ∼nen (auch fig.) veteran

Vetter *der;* ∼s, ∼n cousin

vgl. *Abk.* = **vergleiche** cf.

v. H. *Abk.* = **vom Hundert** per cent

via /'vi:a/ *Präp.* via

Viadukt /via'dʊkt/ *das od. der;* ∼[e]s, ∼e viaduct

Viagra ⓌⓏ/'viagra/ *das;* ∼s Viagra ®

vibrieren /vi'bri:rən/ *itr. V.* vibrate

Video *das;* ∼s, ∼s (ugs.) video

video-, Video- /'vi:deo-/: video

Video-: ∼**clip** *der;* ∼∼s, ∼∼s video; ∼**gerät** *das* video machine; ∼**kassette** *die* video cassette; ∼**recorder**, ∼**rekorder** *der* video recorder; ∼**text** *der* videotex[t]

Videothek *die;* ∼, ∼en video library

Vieh *das;* ∼[e]s (a) (Nutztiere) livestock *sing. or pl.;*
(b) (Rinder) cattle *pl.*

Vieh·zucht *die* [live]stock/cattle breeding *no art.*

viel ⓵ *Indefinitpron. u. unbest. Zahlw.* (a) *Sg.* a great deal of; a lot of (coll.); **wie/nicht/zu** ∼: how/not/too much; ∼**[es]** (vielerlei) much; **der** ∼**e Regen** all the rain; **um** ∼**es jünger** a great deal younger
(b) *Pl.* many; **gleich** ∼**[e]** the same number of; **die** ∼**en Menschen** all the people
⓶ *Adv.* (a) (oft, lange) a great deal; a lot (coll.)
(b) (wesentlich) much; a great deal; a lot (coll.); ∼ **zu klein** much too small

---
*old spelling - see note on page xiv

vielerlei *indekl. Adj.* **(a)** *attr.* many different; all kinds *or* sorts of **(b)** *allein stehend* all kinds of things

viel-, Viel-: ~**fach** [1] *Adj.* **(a)** multiple;. **die** ~**fache Menge** many times the amount; **(b)** (vielfältig) many kinds of; [2] *adv.* many times; ~**falt** *die;* ~~: diversity; ~**fältig** [1] *Adj.* many and diverse; [2] *adv.* in many different ways

vielleicht *Adv.* perhaps; maybe

viel-: ~**mals** *Adv.* ich bitte ~mals um Entschuldigung I'm very sorry; **danke** ~mals thank you very much; ~**mehr** /*od.* -'-/ *Konj. u. Adv.* rather; ~**sagend** [1] *Adj.* meaningful; [2] *adv.* meaningfully; ~**seitig** *Adj.* versatile ⟨person⟩; ~**versprechend** [1] *Adj.* [very] promising; [2] *adv.* [very] promisingly

vier *Kardinalz.* four

Vier *die;* ~, ~**en** four; **eine** ~ **schreiben/ bekommen** (Schulw.) ≈ get a D

vier-, Vier-: (*s. auch* ACHT-, ACHT-); ~**beiner** *der;* ~~s, ~~ (ugs.) four-legged friend; ~**beinig** *Adj.* four-legged; ~**eck** *das* quadrilateral; (Rechteck) rectangle; (Quadrat) square; ~**eckig** *Adj.* quadrilateral; (rechteckig) rectangular; ~**fach** *Vervielfältigungsz.* fourfold; quadruple; ~**fache** *das; adj. Dekl.* um das ~**fache:** fourfold; by four times the amount; ~**hundert** *Kardinalz.* four hundred

Vierling *der;* ~s, ~e quadruplet

vier-, Vier-: ~**mal** *Adv.* four times; ~**spurig** *Adj.* four-lane ⟨road, motorway⟩; ~**spurig sein** have four lanes; ~**stellig** *Adj.* four-figure *attrib.;* ~**sterne-hotel** /-'----/ *das* four-star hotel

viert... *Ordinalz.* fourth

vier·tausend *Kardinalz.* four thousand;

viertel /'fɪrtl̩/ *Bruchz.* quarter; **ein** ~ **Pfund** a quarter of a pound; **drei** ~ **Liter** three quarters of a litre

Viertel /'fɪrtl̩/ *das* (schweiz. meist *der*); ~s, ~ **(a)** quarter; ~ **vor/nach eins** [a] quarter to/past one; **drei** ~: three-quarters **(b)** (Stadtteil) quarter; district

viertel-, Viertel-: ~**finale** *das* (Sport) quarter-final; ~**jahr** *das* three months *pl.;* ~**jährlich** [1] *Adj.* quarterly; [2] *adv.* quarterly; ~**liter** *der* quarter of a litre; ~**note** *die* (Musik) crotchet (Brit.); quarter note (Amer.); ~**pfund** *das* quarter [of a] pound; ~**stunde** *die* quarter of an hour; ~**stündig** *Adj.* quarter-of-an-hour; ~**stündlich** [1] *Adj.* every quarter of an hour *postpos.;* [2] *adv.* every quarter of an hour

viertens *Adv.* fourthly

viertürig *Adj.* four-door *attrib.;* ~ **sein** have four doors

Vierwaldstätter See, (schweiz.:) **Vierwaldstättersee** *der* Lake Lucerne

vier- /'fɪr-:/ ~**zehn** *Kardinalz.* fourteen; **für**

vierzehn Tage for a fortnight; ~**zehn·tägig** *Adj.* two-week; ~**zehn·täglich** [1] *Adj.* fortnightly; [2] *adv.* fortnightly

vierzig /'fɪrtsɪç/ *Kardinalz.* forty; *s. auch* ACHTZIG

vierzigst... *Ordinalz.* fortieth; *s. auch* ACHT...

Vikar /vi'kaːɐ̯/ *der;* ~s, ~e, **Vikarin** *die;* ~, ~**nen (a)** (kath. Kirche) locum tenens **(b)** (ev. Kirche) ≈ [trainee] curate

Villa /'vɪla/ *die;* ~, **Villen** villa

Villen-viertel *das* exclusive residential district

violett /vio'lɛt/ purple; violet

Violett *das;* ~s, ~e *od. ugs.* ~s purple; violet; (im Spektrum) violet

Violine /vio'liːnə/ *die;* ~, ~**n** (Musik) violin

Viper /'viːpɐ/ *die;* ~, ~**n** viper; adder

Viren ▶ VIRUS

virtuell /vɪr'tu̯ɛl/ [1] *Adj.* **(a)** potential **(b)** (DV, Optik) virtual ⟨memory, image;⟩ ~**e Wirklichkeit** virtual reality [2] *adv.* virtually

virtuos /vɪr'tu̯oːs/ [1] *Adj.* virtuoso ⟨performance etc.⟩ [2] *adv.* in a virtuoso manner

Virtuose *der;* ~n, ~n, **Virtuosin** *die;* ~, ~**nen** virtuoso

Virtuosität *die;* ~: virtuosity

Virus /'viːrʊs/ *das;* ~, **Viren** virus

Visa ▶ VISUM

Visage /vi'zaːʒə/ *die;* ~, ~**n** (salopp abwertend) mug (coll.); (Miene) expression

Visen ▶ VISUM

Visier /vi'ziːɐ̯/ *das;* ~s, ~e (am Helm) visor; (an der Waffe) backsight

Vision /vi'zi̯oːn/ *die;* ~, ~**en** vision

Visite /vi'ziːtə/ *die;* ~, ~**n** round; ~ **machen** do one's round

Visiten-karte *die* visiting card

Visum /'viːzʊm/ *das;* ~s, **Visa** *od.* **Visen** visa

vital *Adj.* vital

Vitalität *die;* ~: vitality

Vitamin /vita'miːn/ *das;* ~s, ~e vitamin

vitamin-, Vitamin-: ~**arm** *Adj.* low in vitamins *postpos.;* ~**mangel** *der* vitamin deficiency; ~**reich** *Adj.* rich in vitamins *postpos.*

Vitrine /vi'triːnə/ *die;* ~, ~**n** display case; (Möbel) display cabinet

Vize- vice-

Vogel *der;* ~s, **Vögel** bird; **einen** ~ **haben** (salopp) be off one's rocker (coll.)

Vogel-: ~**käfig** *der* birdcage; ~**nest** *das* bird's nest; ~**perspektive** *die* bird's-eye view; ~**scheuche** *die;* ~~, ~~**n** scarecrow

Vokabel /vo'kaːbl̩/ *die;* ~, ~**n** word; ~**n** vocabulary *sing.*

Vokal /vo'ka:l/ *der;* ~s, ~e (Sprachw.) vowel

volks-, Volks-: ~**abstimmung** *die* plebiscite; ~**eigen** *Adj.* (DDR) publicly *or* nationally owned; ~**entscheid** *der* (Politik) referendum; ~**fest** *das* public festival; (Jahrmarkt) fair; ~**hochschule** *die* adult education centre; ~**kammer** *die* (DDR) Volkskammer; People's Chamber; ~**kunde** *die* folklore; ~**lied** *das* folk song; ~**musik** *die* folk music; ~**polizei** *die* (DDR) People's Police; ~**republik** *die* People's Republic; ~**stamm** *der* tribe; ~**tanz** *der* folk dance; ~**tracht** *die* traditional costume; (eines Landes) national costume; ~**trauer·tag** *der* (Bundesrepublik Deutschland) national remembrance day

volkstümlich ① *Adj.* popular ② *adv.* ~ schreiben write in terms readily comprehensible to the layman

volks-, Volks-: ~**verhetzung** *die;* ~~: incitement of the people; ~**vertreter** *der,* ~**vertreterin** *die* representative of the people; ~**wirt** *der,* ~**wirtin** *die* economist; ~**wirtschaft** *die* national economy; (Fach) economics *sing., no art.;* ~**wirtschaftlich** ① *Adj.* economic; ② *adv.* economically; ~**zählung** *die* [national] census; ~**zorn** *der* public anger

voll ① *Adj.* full; ample ⟨bosom⟩; (salopp: betrunken) plastered (sl.); ~ von od. mit etw. sein be full of sth.; ~ laufen fill up; etw. ~ laufen lassen fill sth. [up]; etw. ~ füllen fill sth. up; etw. ~ gießen fill sth. [up]; etw. ~ tanken fill sth. up; bitte ~ tanken fill it up, please; etw. ~ machen fill sth. up; [sich] (*Dat.*)] die Hosen/Windeln ~ machen (ugs.) mess one's pants/nappy; jmdn. nicht für ~ nehmen not take sb. seriously ② *adv.* fully; ~ und ganz completely

**voll·abern▸ VOLLLABERN

voll·auf /*od.* '-'--/ *Adv.* completely

**voll·laufen ▸ VOLL 1

voll-, Voll-: ~**automatisch** ① *Adj.* fully automatic; ② *adv.* fully automatically; ~**bad** *das* bath; ~**bart** *der* full beard; ~**bringen** /-'--/ *unr. tr. V.* (geh.) accomplish; achieve

Völle·gefühl *das* feeling of fullness

voll·enden *tr. V.* complete

vollendet ① *Adj.* accomplished ⟨performance⟩; perfect ⟨gentleman, host, manners, reproduction⟩ ② *adv.* ⟨play⟩ in an accomplished manner

vollends *Adv.* completely

Voll·endung *die* completion

voller *indekl. Adj.* full of; ~ Flecken covered with stains

Volley·ball /'vɔlibal/ *der* volleyball

voll-, Voll-: ~**führen** /-'--/ *tr. V.* perform;

**~|füllen ▸ VOLL 1; ~gas *das* ~gas geben put one's foot down; mit ~gas at full throttle; **~|gießen ▸ VOLL 1

völlig ① *Adj.* complete; total ② *adv.* completely; totally; du hast ~ Recht you are absolutely right

voll-, Voll-: ~**jährig** *Adj.* of age pred.; ~jährig werden come of age; ~**jährigkeit** *die;* ~: majority *no art.;* ~**kasko·versicherung** *die* fully comprehensive insurance

voll·kommen ① *Adj.* (a) /-'-- od. '---/ (vollendet) perfect (b) /'---/ (vollständig) complete; total ② /'---/ *adv.* completely; totally

voll-, Voll-: ~**korn·brot** *das* wholemeal (Brit.) *or* (Amer.) wholewheat bread; ~|**labern** *tr. V.* (ugs.) jmdn. ~labern rabbit on at sb. (coll.); **~|laufen ▸ VOLL 1; **~|machen ▸ VOLL 1; ~**macht** *die;* ~~, ~~en (a) authority; (b) (Urkunde) power of attorney; ~**milch** *die* full-cream milk; ~**milch·schokolade** *die* full-cream milk chocolate; ~**mond** *der* full moon; ~**pension** *die* full board *no art.;* ~**ständig** ① *Adj.* complete; full ⟨text, address, etc.⟩; ② *adv.* completely; ⟨list⟩ in full; ~**ständigkeit** *die;* ~: completeness; ~**strecken** /-'--/ *tr. V.* enforce ⟨penalty, fine, law⟩; carry out ⟨sentence⟩ (an + *Dat.* on); **~|tanken ▸ VOLL 1; ~**treffer** *der* direct hit; ein ~treffer sein (fig.) hit the bull's eye; ~**versammlung** *die* general meeting; (der UNO) General Assembly; ~**zählig** *Adj.* complete

voll·ziehen *unr. tr. V.* carry out (an + *Dat.* on); execute, carry out ⟨order⟩; perform ⟨sacrifice, ceremony, sexual intercourse⟩

Voll·zug *der:* ▸ VOLLZIEHEN: carrying out; execution; performance

Volt /vɔlt/ *das;* ~ *od.* ~[e]s, ~: (Physik, Elektrot.) volt

Volumen /vo'lu:mən/ *das;* ~s, ~: volume

vom *Präp. + Art.* (a) = von dem; (b) (räumlich) from the; links/rechts ~ Eingang to the left/right of the entrance; ~ Stuhl aufspringen jump up out of one's chair (c) (zeitlich) ~ Morgen bis zum Abend from morning till night; ~ ersten Januar an [as] from the first of January (d) (zur Angabe der Ursache) das kommt ~ Rauchen/Alkohol that comes from smoking/drinking alcohol; jmdn. ~ Sehen kennen know sb. by sight

von *Präp. mit Dat.* (a) (räumlich) from; nördlich/südlich ~ Mannheim to the north/south of Mannheim; rechts/links ~ mir on my right/left; ~ hier an *od.* (ugs.) ab from here on[ward]; ~ Mannheim aus from Mannheim (b) (zeitlich) from; ~ jetzt an *od.* (ugs.) ab from now on; ~ heute/morgen an [as] from today/tomorrow; starting today/tomorrow; in der

---

**alte Schreibung - vgl. Hinweis auf S. xiv

Nacht ~ Freitag auf *od.* zu Samstag during Friday night; **das Brot ist** ~ **gestern** it's yesterday's bread
(c) (anstelle eines Genitivs) of; **acht** ~ **hundert/ zehn** eight out of a hundred/ten
(d) (zur Angabe des Urhebers, der Ursache, beim Passiv) by; **der Roman ist** ~ **Fontane** the novel is by Fontane; **müde** ~ **der Arbeit sein** be tired from work[ing]; **sie hat ein Kind** ~ **ihm** she has a child by him
(e) (zur Angabe von Eigenschaften) of; **eine Fahrt** ~ **drei Stunden** a three-hour drive
von·ei·nạn·der *Adv.* from each other *or* one another
vonstạtten *Adv.* ~ **gehen** proceed
vor ⓵ *Präp. mit Dat.* **(a)** (räumlich) in front of; (weiter vorn) ahead of; in front of; (nicht ganz so weit wie) before; (außerhalb) outside; **kurz** ~ **der Abzweigung** just before the turn-off; ~ **der Stadt** outside the town; **etw.** ~ **sich haben** (fig.) have sth. before one; **das liegt noch** ~ **mir** (fig.) I still have that to come *or* have that ahead of me
(b) (zeitlich) before; **es ist fünf [Minuten]** ~ **sieben** it is five [minutes] to seven
(c) (bei Reihenfolge, Rangordnung) before; **knapp** ~ **jmdm. siegen** win just ahead *or* in front of sb.
(d) (aufgrund von) with; ~ **Freude strahlen** beam with joy; ~ **Hunger/Durst umkommen** (ugs.) die of hunger/thirst
(e) ~ **fünf Minuten/10 Jahren/Wochen** *usw.* five minutes/ten years/weeks ago; **heute** ~ **einer Woche** a week ago today
⓶ *Präp. mit Akk.* in front of; ~ **sich hin** to oneself
Vor·abend *der* evening before; (fig.) eve
Vor·ahnung *die* premonition; presentiment; **dunkle/schlimme** ~**en** dark forebodings
vor·ạn *Adv.* forward[s] ahead; first
vorạn-: ~|**gehen** *unr. itr. V.; mit sein* **(a)** go first; **(b)** (Fortschritte machen) make progress; ~|**kommen** *unr. itr. V.; mit sein* **(a)** make headway; **(b)** (Fortschritte machen) make progress; ~|**treiben** *unr. tr. V.* push ahead
Vor·arbeiter *der* foreman
Vor·arbeiterin *die* forewoman
vor·aus ⓵ /ˈ--/ *Präp. mit Dat., nachgestellt* in front; **jmdm./seiner Zeit** ~ **sein** (fig.) be ahead of sb./one's time
⓶ *Adv.* **im Voraus** /-ˈ--/ in advance
voraus-, Voraus-: ~|**gehen** *unr. itr. V.; mit sein* **(a)** go [on] ahead; **(b)** (zeitlich) **einem Ereignis** ~**gehen** precede an event; ~**sage** *die* ▶ VORHERSAGE; ~|**sagen** *tr. V.* predict; ~|**sehen** *unr. tr. V.* foresee; ~|**setzen** *tr. V.* **(a)** (als gegeben ansehen) assume; ~**gesetzt, [dass]** ...: provided [that] ...; **(b)** (erfordern) require ⟨skill, experience, etc.⟩; presuppose ⟨good organization, planning, etc.⟩; ~**setzung** *die;* ~~, ~~**en (a)** (Annahme) assumption; (Prämisse) premiss;

(b) (Vorbedingung) prerequisite; **unter der** ~**setzung, dass** ...: on condition *or* on the precondition that ...; ~**sichtlich** ⓵ *Adj.* anticipated; ⓶ *adv.* probably
Vor·bau *der; Pl.* ~**ten** porch
Vor·behalt *der;* ~[e]s, ~e reservation; **unter dem** ~, **dass** ...: with the reservation that ...
vor|behalten *unr. tr. V.* **sich** *(Dat.)* **etw.** ~: reserve oneself sth.; „**Änderungen** ~" 'subject to alterations'
vor·behalt·los ⓵ *Adj.* unreserved; unconditional
⓶ *adv.* unreservedly; without reservation[s]
vor·bei *Adv.* **(a)** (räumlich) past; by; **an etw.** *(Dat.)* ~: past sth.
(b) (zeitlich) past; over; (beendet) finished; over; **es ist acht Uhr** ~ (ugs.) it is past *or* gone eight o'clock
vorbei-: ~|**fahren** *unr. itr. V.; mit sein* **(a)** drive/ride past; pass; **an jmdm.** ~**fahren** drive/ride past *or* pass sb.; **(b)** (ugs.: einen kurzen Besuch machen) [**bei jmdm./der Post**] ~**fahren** drop in (coll.) [at sb.'s/at the post office]; ~|**gehen** *unr. itr. V.; mit sein* **(a)** pass; go past; **an jmdm./etw.** ~**gehen** pass *or* go past sb./sth.; **der Schuss ist** ~**gegangen** the shot missed; **(b)** (ugs.: einen kurzen Besuch machen) [**bei jmdm./der Post**] ~**gehen** drop in (coll.) [at sb.'s/at the post office]; **(c)** (vergehen) pass; ~|**kommen** *unr. itr. V.; mit sein* pass; **an etw.** *(Dat.)* ~**kommen** pass sth.; ~|**reden** *itr. V.* **an etw.** *(Dat.)* ~**reden** talk round sth. without getting to the point; **aneinander** ~**reden** talk at cross purposes; ~|**schießen** *unr. itr. V.* miss
vor·belastet *Adj.* handicapped (**durch** by); **erblich** ~ **sein** have an inherited defect
vor|bereiten *tr. V.* prepare; **jmdn./sich auf** *od.* **für etw.** ~: prepare sb./oneself for sth.
Vor·bereitung *die;* ~, ~**en** preparation; ~**en [für etw.] treffen** make preparations for sth.
vor|bestellen *tr. V.* order in advance
Vor·bestellung *die* advance order
vor·bestraft *Adj.* with a previous conviction/previous convictions *postpos., not pred.*
vor|beugen ⓵ *tr. V.* bend ⟨head, upper body⟩ forward; **sich** ~: lean forward ⓶ *itr. V.* **einer Sache** *(Dat.)* *od.* **gegen etw.** ~: prevent sth.
Vor·beugung *die* prevention (**gegen** of); **zur** ~: as a preventive
Vor·bild *das* model; **jmdm. ein gutes** ~ **sein** be a good example to sb.
vor·bildlich ⓵ *Adj.* exemplary ⓶ *adv.* in an exemplary way
vor|bringen *unr. tr. V.* say; **eine Forderung/ein Anliegen** ~: make a demand/ express a desire; **Argumente** ~: present arguments
vor·christlich *Adj.* pre-Christian

vor|datieren tr. V. postdate

vorder... Adj. front; **der Vordere Orient** the Middle East

Vorder-: ~**grund** der foreground; **im** ~**grund stehen** (fig.) be prominent or to the fore; ~**mann** der; Pl. ~**männer** person in front; **jmdn. auf** ~**mann bringen** (ugs.) lick sb. into shape

vor|drängen refl. V. push [one's way] forward or to the front; (fig.) push oneself forward

vor|dringen unr. itr. V.; mit sein push forward; advance

vor-dringlich ① Adj. (a) priority attrib. ⟨treatment⟩
(b) (dringlich) urgent
② adv. (a) as a matter of priority
(b) (dringlich) as a matter of urgency

Vor-druck der; Pl. ~**e** form

vor-eilig ① Adj. rash
② adv. rashly

vor-einander Adv. (a) one in front of the other
(b) (einer dem anderen gegenüber) opposite each other; face to face
(c) **Angst** ~ **haben** be afraid of each other

vor-eingenommen Adj. prejudiced; biased; **für/gegen jmdn.** ~ **sein** be prejudiced in sb.'s favour/against sb.

Vor-eingenommenheit die; ~, ~**en** prejudice; bias

vor|enthalten unr. tr. V.; **ich enthalte vor** (od. seltener: **vorenthalte**), **vorenthalten**, **vorzuenthalten: jmdm. etw.** ~: withhold sth. from sb.

vor-erst /od. -'-/ Adv. for the present

Vorfahr der; ~**en**, ~**en** forefather

vor|fahren unr. itr. V.; mit sein (a) (ankommen) drive/ride up
(b) (weiter nach vorn fahren) ⟨person⟩ drive or move forward; ⟨car⟩ move forward
(c) (vorausfahren) drive or go on ahead

Vor-fahrt die right of way; „~ **beachten/ gewähren**" 'give way'

Vorfahrt[s]-: ~**schild** das; Pl. ~~**er** right-of-way sign; ~**straße** die main road

Vor-fall der incident; occurrence

vor|fallen unr. itr. V.; mit sein (a) (sich ereignen) happen; occur
(b) (nach vorn fallen) fall forward

Vor-film der supporting film

vor|finden unr. tr. V. find

Vor-freude die anticipation

vor|führen tr. V. show ⟨film, slides, etc.⟩; present ⟨circus act, programme⟩; perform ⟨play, trick, routine⟩; (demonstrieren) demonstrate; **jmdn. dem Richter** ~: bring sb. before the judge

Vor-führung die show; (eines Theaterstücks) performance

Vor-gang der occurrence; (Amtsspr.) file

Vorgänger der; ~**s**, ~, **Vorgängerin** die; ~, ~**nen** predecessor

Vor-garten der front garden

vor|geben unr. tr. V. pretend

Vor-gebirge das promontory

vor-gefasst, *vor-gefaßt Adj. preconceived

vor|gehen unr. itr. V.; mit sein (a) (ugs.: nach vorn gehen) go forward
(b) (vorausgehen) go on ahead; **jmdn.** ~ **lassen** let sb. go first
(c) ⟨clock⟩ be fast
(d) (einschreiten) **gegen jmdn./etw.** ~: take action against sb./sth.
(e) (verfahren) proceed
(f) (sich abspielen) happen; go on
(g) (Vorrang haben) have priority; come first

Vor-geschmack der foretaste

Vor-gesetzte der/die; adj. Dekl. superior

vor-gestern Adv. the day before yesterday

vor|greifen unr. itr. V. **jmdm.** ~: anticipate sb.; jump in ahead of sb.

vor|haben unr. tr. V. intend; (geplant haben) plan

Vor-haben das; ~**s**, ~: plan; (Projekt) project

Vor-halle die entrance hall; (eines Theaters, Hotels) foyer

vor|halten unr. tr. V. (a) hold up; **mit vorgehaltener Schusswaffe** at gunpoint
(b) (zum Vorwurf machen) **jmdm. etw.** ~: reproach sb. for sth.

Vor-haltungen Pl. **jmdm. [wegen etw.]** ~ **machen** reproach sb. [for sth.]

vorhanden Adj. existing; (verfügbar) available; ~ **sein** exist or be in existence/be available

Vor-hang der (auch Theater) curtain

Vorhänge-schloss, *Vorhänge-schloß das padlock

Vor-haut die foreskin

vor-her /od. -'-/ beforehand; (davor) before

vorher|gehen unr. itr. V.; mit sein **in den** ~**den Wochen** in the preceding weeks

Vor-herrschaft die supremacy

vor|herrschen itr. V. predominate

vorher-, Vorher-: ~**sage** die prediction; (des Wetters) forecast; ~|**sagen** tr. V. predict; forecast ⟨weather⟩; ~|**sehen** unr. tr. V. ▶ VORAUSSEHEN

vor-hin /od. -'-/ Adv. a short time or while ago

vorig... Adj. last

Vor-jahr das previous year

vor-jährig Adj. of the previous year

Vor-kämpfer der, **Vor-kämpferin** die pioneer

Vorkehrungen Pl. precautions

Vor-kenntnis die background knowledge

vor|kommen *unr. itr. V.; mit sein* **(a)** (sich ereignen) happen **(b)** (vorhanden sein) occur **(c)** (erscheinen) seem; **das Lied kommt mir bekannt vor** I seem to know the song

Vorkommnis *das;* ~ses, ~se incident; occurrence

vor|laden *unr. tr. V.* summon

Vor·ladung *die* summons

Vor·lage *die* **(a)** ▶ VORLEGEN: presentation; showing; production; submission; tabling **(b)** (Entwurf) draft **(c)** (Muster) pattern; (Modell) model

Vor·lauf *der* (eines Bandgeräts) fast forward

Vor·läufer *der,* **Vor·läuferin** *die* precursor; forerunner

vor·läufig ⟦1⟧ *Adj.* temporary; provisional; interim ⟨order, agreement⟩ ⟦2⟧ *adv.* for the time being

vor·laut ⟦1⟧ *Adj.* forward ⟦2⟧ *adv.* forwardly

vor|legen *tr. V.* present; show, produce ⟨certificate, identity card, etc.⟩; show ⟨sample⟩; submit ⟨evidence⟩; table ⟨parliamentary bill⟩

vor|lesen *unr. tr., itr. V.* read aloud or out; read ⟨story, poem, etc.⟩ aloud; **jmdm. [etw.]** ~: read [sth.] to sb.

Vor·lesung *die* lecture; (Vorlesungsreihe) series or course of lectures

vor·letzt... *Adj.* last but one; penultimate ⟨page, episode, etc.⟩

vorlieb: **mit jmdm./etw.** ~ **nehmen** put up with sb./sth.; (sich begnügen) make do with sb./sth.

Vor·liebe *die* preference

*vorlieb|nehmen ▶ VORLIEB

vor|liegen *unr. itr. V.* be with sb.; **die Ergebnisse liegen uns noch nicht vor** we do not have the results yet; **im** ~**den Fall** in the present case

vor|lügen *unr. tr. V.* (ugs.) **jmdm. etwas** ~: lie to sb.

vorm *Präp. + Art.* **(a)** = vor dem; **(b)** (räumlich) in front of the **(c)** (zeitlich, bei Reihenfolge) before the

vor|machen *tr. V.* (ugs.) **jmdm. etw.** ~: show sb. sth.; (vortäuschen) kid (coll.) or fool sb.

vormalig *Adj.* former

vormals *Adv.* formerly

Vor·marsch *der* (auch fig.) advance

vor|merken *tr. V.* make a note of; **ich habe Sie für den Kurs vorgemerkt** I've put you down for the course

*vor·mittag ▶ VORMITTAG

Vor·mittag *der* morning; **heute/morgen/ gestern** ~: this/tomorrow/yesterday morning

vor·mittags *Adv.* in the morning

Vor·mund *der; Pl.* ~e od. Vormünder guardian

Vor·name *der* first or Christian name

vorn[e] *Adv.* at the front; **nach** ~: to the front; **von** ~: from the front; **noch einmal von** ~ **anfangen** start afresh; **von** ~ **bis hinten** (ugs.) from beginning to end

vornehm ⟦1⟧ *Adj.* (nobel; adelig) noble; (kultiviert) distinguished; (elegant) exclusive ⟨district, hotel, restaurant, resort⟩; elegant ⟨villa, clothes⟩ ⟦2⟧ *adv.* nobly; (elegant) elegantly

vor|nehmen *unr. refl. V.* **sich** (*Dat.*) **etw.** ~: plan sth.; **sich** (*Dat.*) ~**, mit dem Rauchen aufzuhören** resolve to give up smoking

vorn-: ~**herein:** **von** ~**herein** from the outset; ~**über** *Adv.* forwards

Vor·ort *der* suburb

vor|programmieren *tr. V.* (auch fig.) pre-programme

Vor·rang *der* **(a)** priority (**vor** + *Dat.* over) **(b)** (bes. österr.: Vorfahrt) right of way

Vor·rat *der* supply, stock (**an** + *Dat.* of)

vorrätig *Adj.* in stock *postpos.*

Vor·raum *der* anteroom

vor|rechnen *tr. V.* **jmdm. etw.** ~: work sth. out or calculate sth. for sb.; **jmdm. seine Fehler** ~ (fig.) enumerate sb.'s mistakes

Vor·recht *das* privilege

Vor·redner *der,* **Vor·rednerin** *die* previous speaker; **mein Vorredner:** the previous speaker

Vor·richtung *die* device

vor|rücken ⟦1⟧ *tr. V.* move forward; advance ⟨chess piece⟩ ⟦2⟧ *itr. V.; mit sein* move forward; **auf den 5. Platz** ~: move up to fifth place

Vor·ruhestand *der* early retirement

vors *Präp. + Art.* = vor das

vor|sagen *tr. V.* **(a)** *auch itr.* **jmdm. [die Antwort]** ~: tell sb. the answer; (flüsternd) whisper the answer to sb. **(b)** (aufsagen) recite

Vor·saison *die* start of the season; early [part of the] season

Vor·satz *der* intention

vorsätzlich ⟦1⟧ *Adj.* intentional; wilful ⟨murder, arson, etc.⟩ ⟦2⟧ *adv.* intentionally

Vor·schau *die* preview

Vor·schein *der:* **zum** ~ **kommen** appear; (entdeckt werden) come to light

vor|schieben *unr. tr. V.* **(a)** push ⟨bolt⟩ across **(b)** (nach vorn schieben) push forward

vor|schießen *unr. tr. V.* **jmdm. Geld** ~: advance sb. money

Vorschlag *der* suggestion; proposal

vor|schlagen *unr. tr. V.* [jmdm.] **etw.** ~: suggest or propose sth. [to sb.]

vor·schreiben *unr. tr. V.* stipulate, set ⟨conditions⟩; lay down ⟨rules⟩; prescribe ⟨dose⟩

Vor·schrift *die* instruction; order; (gesetzliche od. amtliche Bestimmung) regulation

vorschrifts·mäßig ① *Adj.* correct; proper
② *adv.* correctly; properly

Vor·schub *der* jmdm./einer Sache ∼ leisten encourage sb./encourage *or* promote *or* foster sth.

Vorschul·alter *das* preschool age

Vor·schuss, *Vor·schuß *der* advance

vor|schwärmen *itr. V.* jmdm. von jmdm./ etw. ∼: rave about sb./sth. to sb. (coll.)

vor|schweben *itr. V.* jmdm. schwebt etw. vor sb. has sth. in mind

vor|sehen ① *unr. tr. V.* (a) plan; etw. für/ als etw. ∼: intend sth. for/as sth.
(b) ⟨law, plan, contract, etc.⟩ provide for
② *unr. refl. V.* sich [vor jmdm./etw.] ∼: be careful [of sb./sth.]

vor|setzen *tr. V.* jmdm. etw. ∼: serve sb. sth.; (fig.) serve *or* dish sb. up sth.

Vor·sicht *die* care; (bei Risiko, Gefahr) caution; care; **zur** ∼: as a precaution; ∼! be careful!; „∼, Stufe!" 'mind the step!'

vorsichtig ① *Adj.* careful; (bei Risiko, Gefahr) cautious; **sei** ∼! be careful!; take care!
② *adv.* carefully; with care

vorsichts·halber *Adv.* as a precaution; to be on the safe side

Vorsichts·maßnahme *die* precautionary measure; precaution

Vor·silbe *die* [monosyllabic] prefix

vor|singen *unr. tr. V.* [jmdm.] etw. ∼: sing sth. [to sb.]

Vor·sitz *der* chairmanship

Vorsitzende *der/die; adj. Dekl.* chair[person]; (bes. Mann) chairman; (Frau auch) chairwoman

Vor·sorge *die* precautions *pl.;* (für den Todesfall, Krankheit, Alter) provisions *pl.*

vor|sorgen *itr. V.* für etw. ∼: make provisions for sth.; provide for sth.

Vorsorge-untersuchung *die* (Med.) medical check-up

vorsorglich *adv.* as a precaution

Vor·spann *der* (Film, Ferns.) opening credits *pl.*

Vor·speise *die* starter; hors d'œuvre

Vor·spiel *das* (Theater) prologue; (Musik) prelude

vor|spielen *tr. V.* (a) play ⟨piece of music⟩ (*Dat.* to, for); act out, perform ⟨scene⟩ (*Dat.* for, in front of)
(b) (vorspiegeln) jmdm. etw. ∼: feign sth. to sb.

vor|sprechen ① *unr. tr. V.* (a) (zum Nachsprechen) jmdm. etw. ∼: pronounce *or* say sth. first for sb.
(b) (zur Prüfung) recite
② *unr. itr. V.* audition

Vor·sprung *der* lead (vor + *Dat.* over)

---

*alte Schreibung - vgl. Hinweis auf S. xiv

Vor·stadt *die* suburb

Vor·stand *der* (einer Firma) board [of directors]; (eines Vereins, einer Gesellschaft) executive committee; (einer Partei) executive

vor|stehen *unr. itr. V.* (a) project; jut out; ⟨teeth, chin⟩ stick out; ∼de Zähne buck teeth; projecting teeth
(b) (geh.: leiten) einer Institution ∼: be the head of an institution

vor|stellen ① *tr. V.* jmdm./sich jmdm. ∼: introduce sb./oneself to sb.; (bei Bewerbung) sich ∼: come/go for [an] interview; die Uhr [um eine Stunde] ∼: put the clock forward [one hour]
② *refl. V.* sich (*Dat.*) etw. ∼: imagine sth.

Vor·stellung *die* (a) (Begriff) idea
(b) (Fantasie) imagination
(c) (Aufführung) performance; (im Kino) showing

Vorstellungs-gespräch *das* interview

Vor·stoß *der* advance

vor|stoßen *unr. itr. V.; mit sein* advance; push forward

Vor·strafe *die* previous conviction

vor|strecken *tr. V.* stretch ⟨arm, hand⟩ out; advance ⟨money, sum⟩

Vor·tag *der* day before

vor|täuschen *tr. V.* feign; simulate ⟨reality etc.⟩; fake ⟨crime⟩

Vor·teil *[od. 'fortail] der* advantage

vorteilhaft ① *Adj.* advantageous
② *adv.* advantageously

Vortrag *der;* ∼[e]s, Vorträge talk; (wissenschaftlich) lecture; einen ∼ halten give a talk/lecture

vor|tragen *unr. tr. V.* (a) sing ⟨song⟩; perform, play ⟨piece of music⟩; recite ⟨poem⟩
(b) (darlegen) present ⟨case, matter, request, demands⟩; lodge, make ⟨complaint⟩; express ⟨wish, desire⟩

vor·trefflich ① *Adj.* excellent
② *adv.* excellently

Vortrefflichkeit *die;* ∼: excellence

vorüber *Adv.* over; (räumlich) past

vorüber|gehen *unr. itr. V.; mit sein* (a) go *or* walk past; pass by; an jmdm./etw. ∼: go past sb./sth.; pass sb./sth.; (achtlos) pass sb./ sth. by
(b) (vergehen) pass; ⟨pain⟩ go

vorübergehend ① *Adj.* temporary; passing ⟨interest, infatuation⟩; brief ⟨illness, stay⟩
② *adv.* temporarily; (für kurze Zeit) for a short time; briefly

Vor·urteil *das* bias; (voreilige Schlussfolgerung) prejudice

Vor·vergangenheit *die* (Sprachw.) pluperfect

Vor·verkauf *der* advance sale of tickets

vor|verlegen tr. V. (zeitlich) bring forward (auf + Akk. to; um by)

Vor·wahl die, **Vorwähl·nummer** die (Fernspr.) dialling code

Vorwand der; ~[e]s, Vorwände pretext; (Ausrede) excuse

vor|warnen tr. V. jmdn. ~: give sb. advance warning; warn sb. [in advance]; **vorgewarnt sein** be forewarned

Vor·warnung die [advance] warning

vor·wärts Adv. forwards; (weiter) onwards; ~ **kommen** make progress; (im Beruf, Leben) get on; get ahead

***vorwärts|kommen** ▶ VORWÄRTS

vor·weg Adv. beforehand

vorweg|nehmen unr. tr. V. anticipate

vor|weisen unr. tr. V. produce

vor|werfen unr. tr. V. jmdm. etw. ~: reproach sb. with sth.; (beschuldigen) accuse sb. of sth.

vor·wiegend Adv. mainly

vor·witzig Adj. bumptious; pert ⟨child⟩

Vor·wort das; Pl. ~e foreword

Vor·wurf der reproach; (Beschuldigung) accusation

vorwurfs·voll ① Adj. reproachful
② adv. reproachfully

Vor·zeichen das (a) (Omen) omen
(b) (Math.) [algebraic] sign

vor|zeigen tr. V. produce; show

Vor·zeit die prehistory

vorzeitig ① Adj. premature; early ⟨retirement⟩
② adv. prematurely

vor|ziehen unr. tr. V. prefer

Vor·zimmer das outer office

Vor·zug der (a) preference (**gegenüber** over)
(b) (gute Eigenschaft) good quality; merit

vorzüglich ① Adj. excellent; first-rate
② adv. excellently

vulgär /vʊlˈɡɛːɐ̯/ ① Adj. vulgar
② adv. in a vulgar way

Vulgarität /vʊlɡariˈtɛːt/ die; ~, ~en vulgarity

Vulkan /vʊlˈkaːn/ der; ~s, ~e volcano

vulkanisch Adj. volcanic

vulkanisieren tr. V. vulcanize

v. u. Z. Abk. = **vor unserer Zeit[rechnung]** BC

W w

w, W /veː/ das; ~s, ~: w/W

W Abk. (a) = **West, Westen** W.
(b) = **Watt** W.

Waage die; ~, ~n (a) [pair sing. of] scales pl.
(b) (Astrol.) [die] ~: Libra; **er ist [eine]** ~: he is a Libra or Libran

waage·recht ① Adj. horizontal
② adv. horizontally

Waage·rechte die; ~, ~n; also adj. Dekl. horizontal

Waag·schale die scale pan

Wabe die; ~, ~n honeycomb

wach ① Adj. awake
② adv. alertly; attentively

Wache die; ~, ~n (a) (Milit.) guard or sentry duty; (Seew.) watch [duty]
(b) (Wächter, Milit.) guard; (Seew.) watch
(c) (Polizei~) police station

wachen itr. V. (geh.) be awake; **bei jmdm.** ~: stay up at sb.'s bedside; sit up with sb.

Wachheit die; ~: alertness

Wach·hund der guard dog

Wacholder der; ~s, ~: juniper

Wach·posten der (Milit.) guard

Wachs das; ~es, ~e wax

wachsam Adj. watchful; vigilant

Wachsamkeit die; ~: vigilance

wachsen¹ unr. itr. V.; mit sein grow

wachsen² tr. V. wax

Wachs-: ~**figur** die waxwork; ~**figuren·kabinett** das waxworks sing. or pl.; waxworks museum

wächst 2. u. 3. Pers. Sg. Präsens v. WACHSEN

Wachs·tuch das Pl. Wachstücher (Tischtuch) oilcloth tablecloth

Wachstum das; ~s growth

Wachtel die; ~, ~n quail

Wächter der; ~s, ~: guard; (Nacht-, Turmwächter) watchman; (Parkwächter) [park-]keeper

Wächterin die; ~, ~nen ▶ WÄCHTER

Wach[t]·turm der watchtower

wackelig Adj. (a) wobbly ⟨chair, table, etc.⟩; loose ⟨tooth⟩
(b) (ugs.: kraftlos, schwach) frail

Wackel·kontakt der (Elektrot.) loose connection

wackeln itr. V. wobble; ⟨tooth etc.⟩ be loose; ⟨house, window, etc.⟩ shake; **mit dem Kopf/den Ohren** ~: waggle one's head/ears

wacker (veralt.) ① Adj. upright   ···⦙·

2 *adv.* valiantly; **sich** ~ **halten** put up a good show

Wade *die;* ~, ~**n** (Anat.) calf

Waden-krampf *der* cramp in one's calf

Waffe *die;* ~, ~**n** weapon

Waffel *die;* ~, ~**n** waffle; (dünne Waffel, Eiswaffel) wafer; (Eistüte) cone

Waffen-: ~**gewalt** *die* mit ~**gewalt** by force of arms; ~**handel** *der* arms trade; ~**händler** *der,* ~**händlerin** *die* arms dealer; ~**schein** *der* firearms licence; ~**stillstand** *der* armistice

Wage-mut *der* daring

wage-mutig *Adj.* daring

wagen 1 *tr. V.* risk; [es] ~, etw. zu tun dare to do sth.
    2 *refl. V.* sich irgendwohin/nicht irgendwohin ~: venture somewhere/not dare to go somewhere

Wagen *der;* ~**s**, ~: (PKW) car; (Pferdewagen) cart; (Eisenb.: Personenwagen) coach; (Eisenb.: Güterwagen) truck; (Straßenbahnwagen) car; (Kinder-, Puppenwagen) pram (Brit.); baby carriage (Amer.); (Sportwagen) pushchair (Brit.); stroller (Amer.)

Wagen-heber *der* jack

Waggon /va'gɔŋ, *südd., österr.:* va'goːn/ *der;* ~**s**, ~**s**, *südd., österr.:* ~**s**, ~**e** wagon; truck (Brit.); car (Amer.)

waghalsig 1 *Adj.* daring; (leichtsinnig) reckless
    2 *adv.* daringly; ⟨speculate⟩ riskily; (leichtsinnig) recklessly

Wagnis *das;* ~**ses**, ~**se** daring exploit *or* feat; (Risiko) risk

Wahl *die;* ~, ~**en** (a) choice; **eine/seine** ~ **treffen** make a/one's choice
    (b) (in ein Gremium, Amt usw.) election; **geheime** ~: secret ballot

wahl-berechtigt *Adj.* eligible *or* entitled to vote *postpos.*

Wahl-beteiligung *die* turn-out

wählen 1 *tr. V.* (a) choose; (aus~) select
    (b) (Fernspr.) dial ⟨number⟩
    (c) (durch Stimmabgabe) elect
    (d) (stimmen für) vote for ⟨party, candidate⟩
    2 *itr. V.* (a) choose
    (b) (Fernspr.) dial
    (c) (stimmen) vote

Wähler *der;* ~**s**, ~: voter

Wahl-ergebnis *das* election result

Wählerin *die;* ~, ~**nen** voter

wählerisch *Adj.* choosy; particular (**in** + *Dat.* about)

Wählerschaft *die;* ~, ~**en** electorate; **die** ~ **der SPD** the SPD's voters *pl.;* those who vote for the SPD

wahl-, Wahl-: ~**fach** *das* (Schulw.) optional subject; ~**gang** *der* ballot; ~**geheimnis** *das* secrecy of the ballot; ~**geschenk** *das* pre-election bonus;

~**kabine** *die* polling booth; ~**kampf** *der* election campaign; ~**kreis** *der* constituency; ~**lokal** *das* polling station; ~**los** 1 *Adj.* indiscriminate; 2 *adv.* indiscriminately; ~**niederlage** *die* election defeat; ~**recht** *das* right to vote

Wähl-scheibe *die* (Fernspr.) dial

Wahl-: ~**sieg** *der* election victory; ~**spruch** *der* motto; ~**system** *das* electoral system; ~**urne** *die* ballot box

Wahn *der;* ~[**e**]**s** mania; delusion

Wahn-sinn *der* (a) insanity; madness
    (b) (ugs.: Unvernunft) madness; lunacy

wahnsinnig 1 *Adj.* (a) (geistesgestört) insane; mad
    (b) (ugs.: ganz unvernünftig) mad; crazy
    (c) (ugs.: groß, heftig, intensiv) terrific (coll.) ⟨effort, speed, etc.⟩; terrible (coll.) ⟨fright, job, pain⟩
    2 *adv.* (ugs.) incredibly (coll.); terribly (coll.)

wahr *Adj.* (a) true; nicht ~? *translation depends on preceding verb form:* **du hast Hunger, nicht** ~? you're hungry, aren't you?; **nicht** ~, **er weiß es doch?** he does know, doesn't he?
    (b) (wirklich) real ⟨reason, motive, feelings, joy, etc.⟩; actual ⟨culprit⟩; (echt) true, real ⟨friend, friendship, love, art⟩

wahren *tr. V.* (geh.) preserve ⟨balance, equality, neutrality, etc.⟩; maintain ⟨authority, right⟩; (verteidigen) defend

während *itr. V.* (geh.) last

während 1 *Konj.* (a) (zeitlich) while
    (b) (adversativ) whereas
    2 *Präp. mit Gen.* during; (über einen Zeitraum von) for

wahr|haben *unr. tr. V.* etw. nicht ~ **wollen** not want to admit sth.

wahrhaft (geh.) 1 *Adj.* true
    2 *adv.* truly

wahrhaftig 1 *Adj.* (geh.) truthful ⟨person⟩
    2 *adv.* really; genuinely

Wahrheit *die;* ~, ~**en** truth

wahrheits-getreu 1 *Adj.* truthful; faithful ⟨account⟩
    2 *adv.* truthfully; ⟨portray⟩ faithfully

wahr|nehmen *unr. tr. V.* (a) (mit den Sinnen erfassen) perceive; (spüren) feel; detect ⟨sound, smell⟩; (bemerken) notice; (erkennen, ausmachen) make out
    (b) (nutzen) take advantage of ⟨opportunity⟩; exploit ⟨advantage⟩; exercise ⟨right⟩
    (c) (vertreten) look after ⟨sb.'s interests, affairs⟩
    (d) (erfüllen, ausführen) carry out, perform ⟨function, task, duty⟩; fulfil ⟨responsibility⟩

Wahrnehmung *die;* ~, ~**en** (a) perception; (eines Sachverhalts) awareness; (eines Geruchs, eines Tons) detection
    (b) (Nutzung) (eines Rechts) exercise; (einer Gelegenheit, eines Vorteils) exploitation
    (c) (Vertretung) representation
    (d) (einer Funktion, Aufgabe, Pflicht) performance; execution; (einer Verantwortung) fulfilment

---

*old spelling - see note on page xiv

wahr·sagen 2. *Part.* gewahrsagt ⟨1⟩ *itr. V.* tell fortunes

⟨2⟩ *tr. V.* predict, foretell ⟨*future*⟩

Wahrsager *der;* ~s, ~, **Wahrsagerin** *die;* ~, ~nen fortune-teller

wahrscheinlich ⟨1⟩ *Adj.* probable; likely

⟨2⟩ *adv.* probably

Wahrscheinlichkeit *die;* ~, ~en probability; likelihood

Währung *die;* ~, ~en currency

Währungs-: ~**reform** *die* currency reform; ~**union** *die* currency union; ~-, Wirtschafts- und Sozialunion social, economic, and currency union

Wahr·zeichen *das* symbol; (einer Stadt, einer Landschaft) [most famous] landmark

Waise *die;* ~, ~n orphan

Waisen·haus *das* orphanage

Wal *der;* ~[e]s, ~e whale

Wald *der;* ~[e]s, Wälder wood; (größer) forest

Wald·brand *der* forest fire

Wäldchen *das;* ~s, ~: copse

Wald-: ~**meister** *der* (Bot.) woodruff; ~**sterben** *das;* ~~s death of the forest [as a result of pollution]

Wal·fang *der* whaling *no def. art.;* auf ~ gehen/sein go/be whaling

Waliser *der;* ~s, ~: Welshman

Waliserin *die;* ~, ~nen Welshwoman

walisisch *Adj.* Welsh

Walkman ⓦ /'wɔkmən/ *der;* ~s, Walkmen /'wɔkmən/ Walkman ®; personal stereo

Wall *der;* ~[e]s, Wälle earthwork; embankment; rampart (esp. Mil.)

Wall-: ~**fahrer** *der* pilgrim; ~**fahrt** *die* pilgrimage; ~**fahrts·ort** *der* place of pilgrimage

Wal·nuss, *Wal·nuß *die* walnut

Wal·ross, *Wal·roß *das; Pl.* -rosse walrus

walten *itr. V.* (geh.) ⟨good sense, good spirit⟩ prevail; ⟨peace, silence, harmony, etc.⟩ reign

Walze *die;* ~, ~n roller; (Straßen~) [road] roller; (Schreib~) platen

walzen *tr. V.* roll ⟨field, road, steel, etc.⟩

wälzen ⟨1⟩ *tr. V.* roll; heave ⟨heavy object⟩; (fig.) shove ⟨blame, responsibility⟩ (auf + Akk. on); etw. in Mehl *usw.* ~ (Kochk.) toss sth. in flour *etc.;* Probleme ~ (fig. ugs.) mull over problems

⟨2⟩ *refl. V.* roll; (auf der Stelle) roll about *or* around; (im Krampf, vor Schmerzen) writhe around

Walzer *der;* ~s, ~: waltz

wand *1. u. 3. Pers. Sg. Prät. v.* WINDEN

Wand *die;* ~, Wände wall; (Trennwand) partition; (bewegliche Trennwand) screen; (eines Behälters, Schiffs) side

Wandale *der;* ~n, ~n, **Wandalin** *die;* ~, ~nen vandal

Wandalismus *der;* ~: vandalism

Wandel *der;* ~s change

wandeln *refl., tr. V.* change (in + Akk. into)

Wanderer *der;* ~s, ~, **Wanderin** *die;* ~, ~nen rambler; hiker

Wander·karte *die* rambler's [path] map

wandern *itr. V.;* *mit sein* (a) hike; ramble

(b) (ugs.: gehen; fig.) wander (lit. or fig.)

(c) (ziehen, reisen) travel; (ziellos) roam; ⟨exhibition, circus, theatre⟩ tour, travel; ⟨animal, people, tribe⟩ migrate

Wander·tag *der* day's hike (*for a class or school*)

Wanderung *die;* ~, ~en (a) hike; walking tour; eine ~ machen go on a hike *or* a walking tour

(b) (Zool., Soziol.) migration

Wander-: ~**urlaub** *der* walking holiday; ~**weg** *der* footpath (*constructed for ramblers*)

Wand-: ~**gemälde** *das* mural; ~**lampe** *die* wall light

Wandlung *die;* ~, ~en change; (grundlegend) transformation

Wand-: ~**malerei** *die* (Bild) mural; ~**schrank** *der* wall cupboard *or* (Amer.) closet

wandte *1. u. 3. Pers. Prät. v.* WENDEN

Wange *die;* ~, ~n (geh.) cheek

Wankelmut *der* (geh.) vacillation

wankel·mütig *Adj.* (geh.) vacillating

wanken *itr. V.* (a) sway; ⟨person⟩ totter; (unter einer Last) stagger

(b) *mit sein* (unsicher gehen) stagger; totter

wann *Adv.* when; seit ~ wohnst du dort? how long have you been living there?

Wanne *die;* ~, ~n bath[tub]

Wanze *die;* ~, ~n bug (coll.)

Wappen *das;* ~s, ~: coat of arms

wappnen *refl. V.* (geh.) forearm oneself

war *1. u. 3. Pers. Sg. Prät. v.* SEIN

warb *1. u. 3. Pers. Sg. Prät. v.* WERBEN

ward (geh.) *1. u. 3. Pers. Sg. Prät. v.* WERDEN

Ware *die;* ~, ~n (a) goods ~[n] *pl.;*

(b) (Artikel) article; commodity (Econ., fig.); (Erzeugnis) product

Waren-: ~**angebot** *das* supply [of goods]; (Sortiment) range of goods; ~**haus** *das* department store; ~**korb** *der* (Statistik) basket of goods; ~**lager** *das* (einer Fabrik o. Ä.) stores *pl.;* (eines Geschäftes) stockroom; (größer) warehouse; ~**muster** *das,* ~**probe** *die* sample; ~**zeichen** *das* trade mark

warf *1. u. 3. Pers. Sg. Prät. v.* WERFEN

warm; wärmer, wärmst ... ⟨1⟩ *Adj.* (auch fig.) warm; hot ⟨meal, food, bath, spring⟩; keen, lively ⟨interest⟩ das Essen ~ machen heat up the food; „~" (auf Wasserhahn) 'hot'

⟨2⟩ *adv.* warmly; ~ essen/duschen have a hot meal/shower

Wärme *die;* ~: warmth; (Hitze; auch Physik) heat

W

wärmen ① *tr. V.* warm; (aufwärmen) warm up ⟨food, drink⟩
② *itr. V.* be warm; (warm halten) keep one warm

Wärme-pumpe *die* (Technik) heat pump

Warm-front *die* (Met.) warm front

warm|halten *unr. tr. V.* (ugs.) **sich** (*Dat.*) **jmdn.** ~: keep on the right side of sb.

Warm-wasser-: ~**bereiter** *der;* ~s, ~: water heater; ~**heizung** *die* hot-water heating

Warn-: ~**blinkanlage** *die* (Kfz-W.) hazard warning lights *pl.;* ~**dreieck** *das* (Kfz-W.) hazard warning triangle

warnen *tr.* (auch itr.) *V.* warn (vor + *Dat.* of, about); **jmdn.** [davor] ~, etw. zu tun warn sb. against doing sth.

Warn-: ~**schild** *das; Pl.* ~~er warning sign; ~**schuss,** ***~**schuß** *der* warning shot; ~**signal** *das* warning signal; ~**streik** *der* token strike

Warnung *die;* ~, ~en warning (vor + *Dat.* of, about)

Warschau (*das*); ~s Warsaw

Warte-: ~**halle** *die* waiting room; (Flugw.) departure lounge; ~**liste** *die* waiting list

warten ① *itr. V.* wait (auf + *Akk.* for)
② *tr. V.* service ⟨car etc.⟩

Wärter *der;* ~s, ~, **Wärterin** *die;* ~, ~nen attendant; (Tier-, Zoo-, Leuchtturmwärter[in]) keeper; (Krankenwärter[in]) orderly; (Gefängniswärter[in]) warder

Warte-: ~**saal** *der* waiting room; ~**zimmer** *das* waiting room

Wartung *die;* ~, ~en service; (das Warten) servicing; (Instandhaltung) maintenance

warum *Adv.* why

Warze *die;* ~, ~n wart; (Brust~) nipple

was ① *Interrogativpron. Nom. u. Akk. u.* (*nach Präp.*) *Dat. Neutr.;* ~ kostet das? what or how much does that cost?; **ach** ~! (ugs.) oh, come on!; ~ für ein .../~ für ...: what sort or kind of ...
② *Relativpron. Nom. u. Akk. u.* (*nach Präp.*) *Dat. Neutr.;* [das,] ~: what; **alles,** ~ ...: everything or all that ...; **vieles/nichts/etwas,** ~ ...: much/nothing/something that ...; ~ **mich betrifft,** [so] ...: as far as I'm concerned, ...
③ *Indefinitpron. Nom. u. Akk. u.* (*nach Präp.*) *Dat. Neutr.* (ugs.) ▶ ETWAS;
④ *Adv.* (ugs.) (warum, wozu) why; what ... for

Wasch-: ~**anlage** *die* car wash; ~**automat** *der* washing machine; ~**becken** *das* washbasin

Wäsche *die;* ~, ~n **(a)** (zu waschende Textilien) washing; (für die Wäscherei) laundry
(b) (Unterwäsche) underwear
(c) (das Waschen) washing *no pl.;* (einmalig) wash; **in der** ~ **sein** be in the wash

wasch-echt *Adj.* **(a)** colour-fast ⟨textile, clothes⟩; fast ⟨colour⟩
(b) (fig.) genuine

Wäsche-: ~**klammer** *die* clothes peg (Brit.); clothespin (Amer.); ~**korb** *der* laundry basket; ~**leine** *die* clothes line

waschen ① *unr. tr. V.* wash; **sich** ~: wash [oneself]; have a wash; **Wäsche** ~: do the/ some washing
② *unr. itr. V.* do the washing

Wäscherei *die;* ~, ~en laundry

Wäsche-: ~**schleuder** *die* spin drier; ~**trockner** *der* (a) (Maschine) tumble drier; **(b)** (Gestell) clothes airer

wasch-, Wasch-: ~**gelegenheit** *die* washing facilities *pl.;* ~**küche** *die* laundry room; ~**lappen** *der* [face] flannel; washcloth (Amer.); ~**maschine** *die* washing machine; ~**maschinen-fest** *Adj.* machine washable; ~**mittel** *das* detergent; ~**pulver** *das* washing powder; ~**raum** *der* washing room; ~**schüssel** *die* washing bowl; ~**straße** *die* [automatic] car wash

wäscht 3. *Pers. Sg. Präsens v.* WASCHEN

Wasch-wasser *das* washing water

Wasser *das;* ~s, ~/**Wässer** **(a)** water
(b) *Pl.* **Wässer** (Mineral-, Tafelwasser) mineral water; (Heilwasser) water
(c) (Gewässer) **ein fließendes/stehendes** ~: a moving/stagnant stretch of water
(d) ~ **lassen** pass water

wasser-, Wasser-: ~**bad** *das* (Kochk.) bain-marie; ~**ball** *der* **(a)** beachball; **(b)** (Spiel) water polo; ~**dampf** *der* steam; ~**dicht** *Adj.* waterproof ⟨clothing, watch, etc.⟩; watertight ⟨container, seal, etc.⟩; ~**fall** *der* waterfall; ~**farbe** *die* watercolour; ~**hahn** *der* water tap; faucet (Amer.)

wässerig ▶ WÄSSRIG

Wasser-: ~**kessel** *der* kettle; ~**leitung** *die* water pipe; (Hauptleitung) water main; ~**mann** *der* (Astrol.) [der] ~mann Aquarius; **er/sie ist [ein]** ~~: he/she is an Aquarian

wassern *itr. V.; mit sein* land [on the water]

wässern *tr. V.* soak; (Fot.) wash ⟨negative, print⟩

wasser-, Wasser-: ~**pflanze** *die* aquatic plant; ~**qualität** *die* water quality; ~**rohr** *das* water pipe; ~**scheu** *Adj.* scared of water; ~**schlauch** *der* [water] hose; ~**schutz-polizei** *die* river/lake police; ~**ski**[1] *der* waterski; ~**ski fahren** waterski; ~**ski**[2] *das;* ~~s waterskiing *no art.;* ~**spiegel** *der* **(a)** (Oberfläche) surface [of the water]; **(b)** (Niveau) water level; ~**sport** *der* water sport *no art.;* ~**spülung** *die* flush

Wasser-stoff *der* hydrogen

Wasser-stoff-: ~**bombe** *die* hydrogen

bomb; ~**per·oxid,** ~**per·oxyd,**
~**super·oxid,** ~**super·oxyd** *das*
(Chemie) hydrogen peroxide
Wasser-: ~**strahl** *der* jet of water;
~**straße** *die* waterway; ~**temperatur**
die water temperature; ~**tiefe** *die* depth of
the water; ~**tropfen** *der* drop of water;
~**turm** *der* water tower; ~**werfer** *der*
water cannon; ~**werk** *das* waterworks
sing.; ~**zeichen** *das* watermark
wässrig, ***wäßrig** *Adj.* watery
waten *itr. V.; mit sein* wade
Waterloo *das;* ~s, ~s Waterloo *no art.;*
sein ~ erleben meet one's Waterloo
watscheln *itr. V.; mit sein* waddle
Watt[1] *das;* ~[e]s, ~en mudflats *pl.*
Watt[2] *das;* ~s, ~ (Technik, Physik) watt
Watte *die;* ~, ~n cotton wool
Watte·bausch *der* wad of cotton wool
Watten·meer *das* tidal shallows *pl.*
wattiert *Adj.* quilted; padded ⟨*shoulder
etc., envelope*⟩
WC *das;* ~[s], ~[s] toilet; WC
weben *tr., itr. V.* weave
Weber *der;* ~s, ~, **Weberin** *die;* ~, ~nen
weaver
Website /web'saɪt/ *die;* ~, ~s (DV) Web
site
Web·stuhl *der* loom
Wechsel *der;* ~s, ~ **(a)** (das Auswechseln)
change; (Geldwechsel) exchange
(b) (Aufeinanderfolge) alternation; **im** ~:
alternately; (bei mehr als zwei) in rotation
(c) (das Überwechseln) move; (Sport) transfer
(d) (Bankw.) bill of exchange ⟨**über** + *Akk.*
for⟩
wechsel-, Wechsel-: ~**geld** *das*
change; ~**haft** *Adj.* changeable; ~**jahre**
Pl. change of life *sing.;* menopause *sing.;*
~**kurs** *der* exchange rate
wechseln [1] *tr. V.* **(a)** change; das Hemd
~: change one's shirt; die Wohnung ~:
move home
(b) ([aus]tauschen) exchange ⟨*letters, glances,
etc.*⟩
(c) (umwechseln) change ⟨*money, note, etc.*⟩ (**in**
+ *Akk.* into)
[2] *itr. V.* change
wechsel-, Wechsel-: ~**seitig** [1] *Adj.*
mutual; [2] *adv.* mutually; ~**strom** *der*
(Elektrot.) alternating current; ~**stube** *die*
bureau de change; ~**wähler** *der,*
~**wählerin** *die* (Politik) floating voter;
~**wirkung** *die* interaction
wecken *tr. V.* jmdn. [aus dem Schlaf] ~:
wake sb. [up]; (fig.: hervorrufen) arouse
⟨*interest, curiosity, anger*⟩
Wecker *der;* ~s, ~: alarm clock
wedeln *itr. V.* ⟨*tail*⟩ wag; [mit dem
Schwanz] ~ ⟨*dog*⟩ wag its tail
weder *Konj.* ~ A noch B neither A nor B
weg *Adv.* away; (verschwunden, weggegangen)

gone; **er ist schon seit einer Stunde** ~: he
left an hour ago; **weit** ~: far away; a long
way away
Weg *der;* ~[e]s, ~e **(a)** (Fußweg) path;
(Feldweg) track
(b) (Zugang) way; (Passage, Durchgang) passage;
sich (*Dat.*) **einen** ~ **durch etw. bahnen** clear
a path *or* way through sth.
(c) (Route, Verbindung) way; route
(d) (Strecke, Entfernung) distance; (Gang) walk;
(Reise) journey; **auf dem kürzesten** ~: by the
shortest route; (auch fig.)
half-way; **sich auf den** ~ **machen** set off;
etw. in die ~**e leiten** get sth. under way
(e) (ugs.: Besorgung) errand
(f) (Methode) way; (Mittel) means
weg-: ~|**bleiben** *unr. itr. V.; mit sein*
(nicht kommen) stay away; (nicht nach Hause
kommen) stay out; ~|**bringen** *unr. tr. V.*
take away; (zur Reparatur, Wartung usw.) take in
Wegelagerei *die;* ~: highway robbery
Wegelagerer *der;* ~s, ~: highwayman
Wegelagerin *die;* ~, ~nen
highwaywoman
wegen *Präp. mit Gen.* **(a)** because of; ~
Umbau[s] geschlossen closed for alterations
(b) (um ... willen) for the sake of; ~ **der
Kinder**/(ugs.) ~ **dir** for the children's/your sake
(c) (bezüglich) about; regarding
weg-: ~|**fahren** [1] *unr. itr. V.; mit sein*
(a) leave; (im Auto) drive off; (losfahren) set off;
(b) (irgendwohin fahren) go away; [2] *unr. tr. V.*
drive away; (mit dem Handwagen usw.) take
away; ~|**fallen** *unr. itr. V.; mit sein* be
discontinued; (nicht mehr zutreffen) no longer
apply; ~|**fliegen** *unr. itr. V.; mit sein* fly
away; (weggeblasen werden) fly off; ~|**gehen**
unr. itr. V. **(a)** leave; (ugs.: ausgehen) go out;
(ugs.: wegziehen) move away; **(b)** (verschwinden)
⟨*spot, fog, etc.*⟩ go away; **(c)** (sich entfernen
lassen) ⟨*stain*⟩ come out; ~|**jagen** *tr. V.*
chase away; ~|**kommen** *unr. itr. V.; mit
sein* **(a)** get away; **(b)** (abhanden kommen) go
missing; **(c)** gut/schlecht usw. ~kommen [bei etw.]
~kommen (ugs.) come off well/badly etc. [in
sth.]; ~|**kriegen** *tr. V.* get rid of ⟨*cold,
pain, etc.*⟩; get out, get rid of ⟨*stain*⟩;
~|**lassen** *unr. itr. V.* **(a)** jmdn. ~lassen let
sb. go; (ausgehen lassen) let sb. out; **(b)**
(auslassen) leave out; omit; ~|**laufen** *unr.
itr. V.; mit sein* run away (**von, vor** + *Dat.*
from); ~|**legen** *tr. V.* put aside; (an seinen
Platz legen) put away; ~|**nehmen** *unr. tr. V.*
(a) take away; move ⟨*head, arm*⟩; **(b)** jmdm.
etw. ~nehmen take sth. away from sb.;
~|**schicken** *tr. V.* **(a)** send off ⟨*letter,
parcel*⟩; **(b)** send ⟨*person*⟩ away;
~|**schmeißen** *unr. tr. V.* (ugs.) chuck
away (coll.); ~|**schnappen** *tr. V.* (ugs.)
jmdm. etw. ~schnappen/vor der Nase
~schnappen snatch sth. away from sb./from
under sb.'s nose; ~|**schütten** *tr. V.* pour
away; ~|**sehen** *unr. itr. V.* look away;
~|**stellen** *tr. V.* put away; (beiseite stellen) ⋯⫶

put aside; ∼|**stoßen** *unr. tr. V.* push *or* shove away; ∼|**tragen** *unr. tr. V.* carry away

Weg·weiser *der;* ∼s, ∼: signpost

weg-: ∼|**werfen** *unr. tr. V.* (auch fig.) throw away; ∼**werfend** *Adj.* dismissive ⟨*gesture, remark*⟩; ∼|**wischen** *tr. V.* wipe away; ∼**zappen** (ugs.) **1** *tr. V.* etw. ∼**zappen** switch sth. off [by changing channels]; **2** *itr. V.* switch to another channel; ∼**ziehen 1** *unr. tr. V.* pull away; draw back curtain; pull off blanket; **2** *unr. itr. V.; mit sein* (a) (umziehen) move away; (b) (wandern) ⟨*animals, nomads, etc.*⟩ leave [on their migration]

weh (ugs.) *Adj.* sore; *s. auch* WEHTUN

Wehe *die;* ∼, ∼n: ∼n haben have contractions; **in den** ∼**n liegen** be in labour

wehen *itr. V.* (a) (blasen) blow (b) (flattern) flutter

weh-, Weh-: ∼**leidig** (abwertend) **1** *Adj.* (überempfindlich) soft; (weinerlich) whining *attrib.;* **2** *adv.* self-pityingly; (weinerlich) whiningly; ∼**mut** *die;* ∼ (geh.) wistful nostalgia; ∼**mütig** *Adj.* wistfully nostalgic

Wehr¹ *die;* ∼, ∼en: sich [gegen jmdn./etw.] **zur** ∼ **setzen** make a stand [against sb./sth.]; resist [sb./sth.]

Wehr² *das;* ∼[e]s, ∼e weir

Wehrdienst *der* military service *no art.;* **seinen** ∼ **ableisten** do one's military service

Wehr·dienst-: ∼**verweigerer** *der;* ∼s, ∼: conscientious objector; ∼**verweigerung** *die* conscientious objection

wehren *refl. V.* defend oneself

wehr-, Wehr-: ∼**los** *Adj.* defenceless; ∼**losigkeit** *die;* ∼: defencelessness; ∼**pflicht** *die* military service; **die allgemeine** ∼**pflicht** compulsory military service; ∼**pflichtig** *Adj.* liable for military service *postpos.;* ∼**sold** *der* military pay; ∼**übung** *die* reserve duty [re]training exercise

weh|tun *unr. itr. V.* (ugs.) hurt; **mir tut der Magen/Kopf/Rücken weh** my stomach/head/back is aching *or* hurts; **jmdm./sich** ∼: hurt sb./oneself

Weib *das;* ∼[e]s, ∼er (veralt., ugs.) woman; female (derog.)

Weibchen *das;* ∼s, ∼: female

Weiber·held *der* (ugs.) ladykiller

weiblich 1 *Adj.* (a) female (b) (für die Frau typisch; Sprachw.) feminine **2** *adv.* femininely

Weiblichkeit *die;* ∼: femininity

Weibs·bild *das* (a) (ugs.) woman (b) (salopp abwertend) female

weich 1 *Adj.* (auch fig.) soft; **ein** ∼**es** *od.* ∼ **gekochtes Ei** a soft-boiled egg **2** *adv.* softly

Weiche¹ *die;* ∼, ∼n (Flanke) flank

Weiche² *die;* ∼, ∼n points *pl.* (Brit.); switch (Amer.)

weichen *unr. itr. V.; mit sein* move; **vor jmdm./einer Sache** ∼: give way to sb./sth.

***weich·gekocht* ►** WEICH 1

weichlich 1 *Adj.* soft; (ohne innere Festigkeit) weak **2** *adv.* softly

Weich·macher *der* (Chemie, Technik) plasticizer

Weide¹ *die;* ∼, ∼n willow

Weide² *die;* ∼, ∼n pasture

weiden *itr., tr. V.* graze

Weiden·kätzchen *das* willow catkin

weigern *refl. V.* refuse

Weigerung *die;* ∼, ∼en refusal

Weih·bischof *der* (kath. Kirche) suffragan bishop

Weihe *die;* ∼, ∼n (Rel.) consecration; (kath. Kirche: Priester-, Bischofsweihe) ordination

weihen *tr. V.* (a) (Rel.) consecrate; (zueignen) dedicate (*Dat.* to) (b) (kath. Kirche: ordinieren) ordain

Weiher *der;* ∼s, ∼: [small] pond

Weihnachten *das;* ∼, ∼: Christmas; **frohe** *od.* **fröhliche** *od.* **gesegnete** ∼! Merry *or* Happy Christmas!

weihnachtlich *Adj.* Christmassy

Weihnachts-: ∼**baum** *der* Christmas tree; ∼**feiertag** *der:* **der erste/zweite** ∼**feiertag** Christmas Day/Boxing Day; ∼**fest** *das* Christmas; ∼**geld** *das* Christmas bonus; ∼**geschenk** *das* Christmas present *or* gift; ∼**lied** *das* Christmas carol; ∼**mann** *der; Pl.* ∼**männer** Father Christmas; Santa Claus; ∼**markt** *der* Christmas fair; ∼**tag** *der:* **►** ∼FEIERTAG; ∼**zeit** *die* Christmas time

Weih-: ∼**rauch** *der* incense; ∼**wasser** *das* (kath. Kirche) holy water

weil *Konj.* because

Weile *die;* ∼: while

weilen *itr. V.* (geh.) stay; (sein) be

Wein *der;* ∼[e]s, ∼e wine

Wein-: ∼**berg** *der* vineyard; ∼**berg·schnecke** *die* [edible] snail; ∼**brand** *der* brandy

weinen *itr. V.* cry (über + *Akk.* over, about); (aus Trauer, Kummer) cry, weep (**um** for)

weinerlich 1 *Adj.* tearful; weepy **2** *adv.* tearfully

wein-, Wein-: ∼**essig** *der* wine vinegar; ∼**flasche** wine bottle; ∼**glas** *das* wineglass; ∼**handlung** *die* wine merchant's; ∼**karte** *die* wine list; ∼**krampf** *der* crying fit; fit of crying; ∼**lokal** *das* wine bar; ∼**probe** *die* wine-tasting [session]; ∼**rebe** *die* grapevine; ∼**rot** *Adj.* wine-red; ∼**schaum·creme**

---

*old spelling - see note on page xiv

die (Kochk.) zabaglione; ~**stock** *der; Pl.*
~**stöcke** [grape]vine; ~**stube** *die* wine
bar; ~**traube** *die* grape

weise 1 *Adj.* wise
2 *adv.* wisely

Weise *die;* ~, ~n (a) (Art, Verfahren) way
(b) (Melodie) tune; melody

weisen 1 *unr. tr. V.* (geh.: zeigen) show;
jmdn. aus dem Zimmer ~: send sb. out of
the room
2 *unr. itr. V.* (irgendwohin zeigen) point

Weisheit *die;* ~, ~en (a) wisdom
(b) (Erkenntnis) wise insight; (Spruch) wise
saying

Weisheits·zahn *der* wisdom tooth

weis|machen *tr. V.* (ugs.) das kannst du
mir nicht ~! you can't expect me to swallow
that!

weiß[1] *1. u. 3. Pers. Sg. Präsens v.* WISSEN

weiß[2] *Adj.* white

Weiß *das;* ~[e]s, ~: white

weis·sagen *tr. V.* prophesy

Weissagung *die;* ~, ~en prophecy

Weiß-: ~**bier** *das* wheat beer; white beer;
~**brot** *das* white bread; ~**dorn** *der;* ~~s,
~~e hawthorn

Weiße *der/die; adj. Dekl.* white; white man/
woman

weißen *tr. V.* paint white; (tünchen)
whitewash

weiß-, Weiß-: ~**gold** *das* white gold;
~**haarig** *Adj.* white-haired; ~**haarig sein**
have white hair; ~**herbst** *der* ≈ rosé
wine; ~**kohl** *der,* (bes. südd., österr.)
~**kraut** *das* white cabbage

weißlich *Adj.* whitish

Weiß·macher *der* whitener

weißt *2. Pers. Sg. Präsens v.* WISSEN

Weiß-: ~**wein** *der* white wine; ~**wurst**
die veal sausage

Weisung *die;* ~, ~en (geh., sonst Amtsspr.)
instruction; (Direktive) directive

Weisungs·befugnis *die* authority to
issue instructions/directives

weit 1 *Adj.* wide; long ⟨way⟩; jmdm. zu ~
sein ⟨clothes⟩ be too loose on sb.
2 *adv.* (a) (räumlich ausgedehnt) ~ geöffnet
wide open; ~ und breit war niemand zu
sehen there was no one to be seen
anywhere; ~ verbreitet widespread;
common; common ⟨plant, animal⟩; ~ gereist
widely travelled
(b) (lang) far; ~er further; farther; am
~esten [the] furthest or farthest; ~ [entfernt
od. weg] wohnen live a long way away or
off; live far away; ~ reichend long-range;
(fig.) far-reaching ⟨importance, consequences⟩;
sweeping ⟨changes, powers⟩; extensive
⟨relations, influence⟩; von ~em from a
distance; das geht zu ~ (fig.) that is going
too far
(c) (zeitlich entfernt) ~ nach Mitternacht well
past midnight

(d) (in der Entwicklung) far

Weit·blick *der* far-sightedness

Weite *die;* ~, ~n (a) (räumliche Ausdehnung)
expanse
(b) (bes. Sport: Entfernung) distance
(c) (eines Kleidungsstückes) width

weiten 1 *tr. V.* widen
2 *refl. V.* widen; ⟨pupil⟩ dilate

weiter *Adv.* (a) ▸ WEITER 2;
(b) und so ~: and so on
(c) (weithin, anschließend) then
(d) (außerdem, sonst) ~ nichts nothing more
or else

weiter... *Adj.* further; bis auf ~es for the
time being; *s. auch* OHNE

weiter-, Weiter-: ~|**bilden** *tr. V.:*
▸ FORTBILDEN; ~**bildung** *die:*
▸ FORTBILDUNG; ~|**bringen** *unr. tr. V.* die
Diskussion brachte uns nicht ~: the
discussion did not get us any further
[forward]; ~|**erzählen** *tr. V.* (a) continue
telling; *itr.* erzähl weiter! do carry or go on;
(b) (~sagen) pass on; ~|**fahren** *unr. itr. V.;*
mit sein continue [on one's way]; (weiterreisen)
travel on; ~|**führen** *tr.., itr. V.* continue;
~|**geben** *unr. tr. V.* pass on; ~|**gehen**
unr. itr. V.; mit sein go on; bitte ~**gehen!**
please move along or keep moving!; ~**hin**
Adv. (a) (immer noch) still; (b) (künftig) in
future; (c) (außerdem) in addition;
~|**kommen** *unr. itr. V.; mit sein* (a) get
further; (b) (Fortschritte machen) make
progress; im Beruf ~**kommen** get on in one's
career; ~|**machen** (ugs.) *itr. V.* carry on;
go on; ~|**reichen** *tr. V.* pass on;
~|**sagen** *tr. V.* pass on; ~|**sehen** *unr.
itr. V.* see

Weiterungen *Pl.* complications;
difficulties

weiter-, Weiter-:
~**verarbeiten** *tr. V.* process;
~**verarbeitung** *die* processing

weit-, Weit-: ~**gehend** 1 *Adj.*
extensive, wide, sweeping ⟨powers⟩; far-
reaching ⟨support, concessions, etc.⟩; wide
⟨support, agreement, etc.⟩; general
⟨renunciation⟩; 2 *adv.* to a large or great
extent; *~**gereist** ▸ WEIT 2A; ~**hin** *Adv.*
for miles around; ~**läufig** 1 *Adj.* (a)
(ausgedehnt) extensive; (geräumig) spacious; (b)
(entfernt) distant; 2 *adv.* (a) (ausgedehnt)
spaciously; (b) (entfernt) distantly;
~**räumig** 1 *Adj.* spacious ⟨room, area,
etc.⟩; wide ⟨gap, space⟩; 2 *adv.* spaciously;
*~**reichend** ▸ WEIT 2B; ~**sichtig** *Adj.*
long-sighted; ~**sichtigkeit** *die;* ~~: long-
sightedness; ~**sprung** *der* (Sport) long
jump (Brit.); broad jump (Amer.);
*~**verbreitet** ▸ WEIT 2A;
~**winkel·objektiv** *das* wide-angle lens

Weizen *der;* ~s wheat

Weizen·bier *das:* ▸ WEISSBIER

welch 1 *Interrogativpron.* (bei Wahl aus einer ⋯⋅⦂

unbegrenzten Menge) what; (bei Wahl aus einer begrenzten Menge) (*adj.*) which; (*subst.*) which one
[2] *Relativpron.* (bei Menschen) who; (bei Sachen) which
[3] *Indefinitpron.* some; (in Fragen) any

welk *Adj.* withered ⟨*skin, hands, etc.*⟩; wilted ⟨*leaves, flower*⟩; limp ⟨*lettuce*⟩

welken *itr. V.; mit sein* ⟨*plant, flower*⟩ wilt

Well-blech *das* corrugated iron

Welle *die;* ~, ~n **(a)** (auch fig.) wave; (Rundf.: Wellenlänge) wavelength
(b) (Technik) shaft

wellen-, Wellen-: ~**bad** *das* artificial wave pool; ~**bereich** *der* (Rundf.) waveband; ~**brecher** *der* breakwater; ~**gang** *der* swell; bei starkem ~gang in heavy seas; ~**länge** *die* wavelength; ~**sittich** *der* budgerigar

Well-fleisch *das* boiled belly pork

wellig *Adj.* wavy ⟨*hair*⟩; undulating ⟨*scenery, hills, etc.*⟩; uneven ⟨*surface, track, etc.*⟩

Well-pappe *die* corrugated cardboard

Wels *der;* ~es, ~e catfish

Welt *die;* ~, ~en **(a)** world; auf der ~: in the world; die Alte/Neue ~: the Old/New World; die Dritte/Vierte ~ the Third/Fourth World; auf die od. zur ~ kommen be born; alle ~ (fig. ugs.) the whole world; everybody **(b)** (Weltall) universe

welt-, Welt-: ~**all** *das* universe; ~**anschauung** *die* world view; ~**ausstellung** *die* world fair; ~**berühmt** *Adj.* world-famous; ~**bevölkerung** *die* world population; population of the world

Welten-bummler *der;* ~s, ~, **Welten-bummlerin** *die;* ~, ~nen globetrotter

welt-, Welt-: ~**erfolg** *der* worldwide success; ~**fremd** [1] *Adj.* unworldly; [2] *adv.* unrealistically; ~**frieden** *der* world peace; ~**karte** *die* map of the world; ~**klima** *das* world climate; ~**krieg** *der* world war; der Erste/Zweite ~krieg the First/Second World War

weltlich *Adj.* **(a)** worldly **(b)** (nicht geistlich) secular

welt-, Welt-: ~**literatur** *die* world literature *no art.;* ~**macht** *die* world power; ~**markt** *der* (Wirtsch.) world market; ~**meister** *der,* ~**meisterin** *der* world champion; ~**meisterschaft** *die* world championship; ~**politik** *die* world politics *pl.;* ~**rangliste** *die* world ranking list; world rankings *pl.;* ~**raum** *der* space *no art.;* ~**reise** *die* world tour; ~**rekord** *der* world record; ~**religion** *die* world religion; ~**sicherheits-rat** *der* (Pol.) [United Nations] Security Council; ~**sprache** *die* world language; ~**stadt**

die cosmopolitan city; ~**weit** [1] *Adj.* worldwide; [2] *adv.* throughout the world; ~**wirtschaft** *die* world economy; ~**wunder** *das:* die sieben ~wunder the Seven Wonders of the World

wem *Dat. von* WER [1] *Interrogativpron.* to whom; who ... to; mit/von/zu ~: with/from/ to whom; who ... with/from/to
[2] *Relativpron.* the person to whom ...; the person who ... to
[3] *Indefinitpron.* (ugs.: jemandem) to somebody *or* someone; (fragend od. verneint) to anybody *or* anyone

wen *Akk. von* WER [1] *Interrogativpron.* whom; who (coll.); an/für ~: to/for whom ...; who ... to/for
[2] *Relativpron.* the person whom
[3] *Indefinitpron.* (ugs.: jemanden) somebody; someone; (fragend od. verneint) anybody; anyone

Wende *die;* ~, ~n change (zu for)

Wende-kreis *der* **(a)** (Geogr.) tropic **(b)** (Kfz-W.) turning circle

Wendel-treppe *die* spiral staircase

wenden¹ [1] *tr., auch itr. V.* (auf die andere Seite) turn [over]; (in die entgegengesetzte Richtung) turn [round]; bitte ~! please turn over
[2] *itr. V.* turn [round]
[3] *refl. V.* sich zum Besseren/Schlechteren ~: take a turn for the better/worse

wenden² [1] *unr.* (auch regelm.) *tr. V.* turn
[2] *unr.* (auch regelm.) *refl. V.* **(a)** ⟨*person*⟩ turn
(b) (sich richten) sich an jmdn. [um Rat] ~: turn to sb. [for advice]

Wende-: ~**platz** *der* turning area; ~**punkt** *der* turning point

wendig [1] *Adj.* **(a)** agile; manœuvrable ⟨*vehicle, boat, etc.*⟩
(b) (gewandt) astute
[2] *adv.* **(a)** (beweglich) agilely
(b) (gewandt) astutely

Wendigkeit *die;* ~ **(a)** agility; (eines Flugzeugs) manœuvrability
(b) (Gewandtheit) astuteness

Wendung *die;* ~, ~en **(a)** (Änderung der Richtung) turn
(b) (Veränderung) change

wenig [1] *Indefinitpron. u. unbest. Zahlw.*
(a) *Sing.* little; das ist ~: that isn't much; zu ~ Zeit/Geld haben not have enough time/ money; ein Exemplar/50 Mark zu ~: one copy too few/50 marks too little
(b) *Pl.* a few; mit ~en Worten in a few words
[2] *Adv.* little; ~ mehr not much more

weniger [1] *Komp. von* WENIG; *Indefinitpron. u. unbest. Zahlw.* (+ *Sg.*) less; (+ *Pl.*) fewer; immer ~: less and less
[2] *Komp. von* WENIG; *Adv.* less; das ist ~ angenehm/erfreulich/schön that is not very pleasant/pleasing/nice; *s. auch* MEHR 1;
[3] *Konj.* less; fünf ~ drei five, take away three

---

*alte Schreibung - vgl. Hinweis auf S. xiv

wenigst... 1 *Sup. von* WENIG 1; least; **am ~en** least

2 *Sup. von* WENIG 2: **am ~en** the least

wenigstens *Adv.* at least

wenn *Konj.* **(a)** (konditional) if; **außer ~:** unless; **~ es nicht anders geht** if there's no other way
(b) (temporal) when; **jedes Mal** *od.* **immer, ~:** whenever
(c) (konzessiv) **wenn ... auch** even though
(d) (in Wunschsätzen) if only

wenn·gleich *Konj.* (geh.) even though; although

wer *Nom. Mask. u. Fem.; s. auch* (*Gen.*) WESSEN; (*Dat.*) WEM; (*Akk.*) WEN
1 *Interrogativpron.* who; **~ von ...:** which of...
2 *Relativpron.* the person who; (jeder, der) anyone *or* anybody who
3 *Indefinitpron.* (ugs.: jemand) someone; (in Fragen, Konditionalsätzen) anyone; anybody

Werbe-: ~abteilung *die* advertising *or* publicity department; **~agentur** *die* advertising agency; **~aktion** *die* advertising campaign; **~block** *der; pl.* **~blöcke** commercial break; **~fernsehen** *das* television commercials *pl.*; **~funk** *der* radio commercials *pl.*; **~geschenk** *das* [promotional] free gift

werben 1 *unr. itr. V.* advertise; **für etw. ~:** advertise sth.
2 *unr. tr. V.* attract ⟨readers, customers, etc.⟩; recruit ⟨soldiers, members, etc.⟩

Werbe-: ~pause *die* commercial break; **~spot** *der* commercial; advertisement; ad (coll.); **~spruch** *der* advertising slogan

Werbung *die; ~:* advertising; **für etw. ~ machen** advertise sth.

Werde·gang *der* career

werden 1 *unr. itr. V.; mit sein* become; get; **älter ~:** get *or* grow old[er]; **wahnsinnig** *od.* **verrückt ~:** go mad; **das muss anders ~:** things have to change; **wach ~:** wake up; **rot ~:** go *or* turn red; **Arzt/Professor ~:** become a doctor/professor; **zu etw. ~:** become sth.; **es wird [höchste] Zeit** it is [high] time; **es wird 10 Uhr** it is nearly 10 o'clock; **es wird Herbst** autumn is coming; **sind die Fotos [etwas] geworden?** (ugs.) have the photos turned out [well]?
2 *Hilfsverb; 2. Part.* **worden (a)** (zur Bildung des Futurs) **wir ~ uns um ihn kümmern** we will take care of him; **es wird gleich regnen** it is going to rain any minute; **es wird um die 80 Mark kosten** (ich vermute, es kostet um die 80 Mark) it will cost around 80 marks
(b) (zur Bildung des Passivs) **du wirst gerufen** you are being called; **er wurde gebeten** he was asked

werfen 1 *unr. tr. V.* throw; drop ⟨bombs⟩
2 *unr. itr. V.* **(a)** throw; **mit etw. ~:** throw sth.
(b) (Junge kriegen) give birth; ⟨dog, cat⟩ litter

3 *unr. refl. V.* throw oneself; **sich vor einen Zug ~:** throw oneself under a train

Werft *die; ~, ~en* shipyard

Werk *das; ~[e]s, ~e* **(a)** work
(b) (Betrieb, Fabrik) factory; works *sing. or pl.;* **ab ~:** ex works

Werk·bank *die; Pl.* **Werkbänke** workbench

werken *itr. V.* work

Werken *das; ~s* (Schulw.) handicraft

Werk[s]-: ~angehörige *der/die* factory *or* works employee; **~arzt** *der*, **~ärztin** *die* factory *or* works doctor

werk-, Werk-: ~statt *die;* **~statt, ~stätten** workshop; (Kfz-W.) garage; **~stoff** *der* material; **~tag** *der* working day; workday; **~tags** *Adv.* on weekdays; **~tätig** *Adj.* working; **~tätige** *der/die; adj. Dekl.* worker; **~zeug** *das* (auch fig.) tool; (Gesamtheit von Werkzeugen) tools *pl.*

Werkzeug-: ~kasten *der* toolbox; **~macher** *der*, **~macherin** *die* tool maker

Wermut *der; ~[e]s, ~s* **(a)** (Pflanze) wormwood
(b) (Wein) vermouth

wert *Adj.* (geh.) esteemed; (als Anrede) my dear ...; **etw./nichts ~ sein** be worth sth./be worthless

Wert *der; ~[e]s, ~e* value; **im ~[e] von ...:** worth ...; **~ auf etw.** (*Akk.*) **legen** set great store by *or* on sth.

wert·beständig *Adj.* of lasting value *postpos.*

werten *tr., itr. V.* judge; assess

wert-, Wert-: ~gegenstand *der* valuable object; **~gegenstände** valuables; **~los** *Adj.* worthless; valueless; **~papier** *das* (Wirtsch.) security; **~sache** *die* valuable item; **~sachen** valuables; **~sendung** *die* (Postw.) registered item; **~stoff** *der* recyclable material

Wertung *die; ~, ~en* judgement

Wert·urteil *das* value judgement

wert·voll *Adj.* valuable; (moralisch) estimable

Wesen *das; ~s* nature

wesentlich 1 *Adj.* fundamental (für to); **im W~en** essentially
2 *adv.* (erheblich) considerably; much

wes·halb *Adv.* ▶ WARUM

Wespe *die; ~, ~n* wasp

Wespen·nest *das* wasp's nest; **in ein ~stechen** (fig. ugs.) stir up a hornets' nest

wessen *Interrogativpron.* **(a)** *Gen. von* WER whose
(b) *Gen. von* WAS: **~ wird er beschuldigt?** what is he accused of?

Wessi *der; ~s, ~s* (salopp) West German

West (bes. Seemannsspr., Met.) ▶ WESTEN

west·deutsch *Adj.* Western German; (hist.: auf die alte BRD bezogen) West German

W

West·deutschland (das) Western
Germany; (hist.: alte BRD) West Germany
Weste die; ~, ~n waistcoat (Brit.); vest
(Amer.)
Westen der; ~s west; der ~: the West
Western der; ~[s], ~: western
West·europa (das) Western Europe
Westfalen (das); ~s Westphalia
westfälisch Adj. Westphalian
West·indien (das) the West Indies pl.
westlich 1 Adj. (a) western
(b) (nach Westen) westerly
(c) (aus dem Westen) Western
2 adv. westwards
3 Präp. mit Gen. [to the] west of
west·wärts Adv. [to the] west
West·wind der west[erly] wind
wes·wegen Adv. ▶ WARUM
Wett·bewerb der; ~[e]s, ~e (a)
competition
(b) (Wirtsch.) competition no indef. art.
Wette die; ~, ~n bet; eine ~ [mit jmdm.]
abschließen make a bet [with sb.]; mit jmdm.
um die ~ laufen race sb.
wett·eifern itr. V.; 2. Part. gewetteifert: mit
jmdm. [um etw.] ~: compete with sb. [for
sth.]
wetten itr. V. bet; mit jmdm. ~: have a bet
with sb.; mit jmdm. um etw. ~: bet sb. sth.
Wetter das; ~s weather
wetter-, Wetter-: ~aussichten Pl.
weather outlook sing.; ~bericht der
weather report; (Vorhersage) weather forecast;
~dienst der weather or meteorological
service; ~fühlig Adj. sensitive to [changes
in] the weather postpos.; ~fühligkeit die;
~~: sensitivity to [changes in] the weather;
~karte die weather chart; weather map;
~lage die weather situation; ~satellit
der weather satellite; ~vorhersage die
weather forecast; ~warte die weather
station
wett-, Wett-: ~kampf der competition;
~lauf der race; ~|machen tr. V. make up
for (durch with); ~rennen das race;
~rüsten das; ~~s arms race; ~streit
der contest
wetzen tr. V. sharpen; whet
WEZ Abk. = **Westeuropäische Zeit**
GMT
Whirlpool /'wɔːlpuːl/ der; ~s, ~s whirlpool
[bath]
Whiskey /'vɪskɪ/ der; ~s ~s whiskey
Whisky /'vɪskɪ/ der; ~s, ~s whisky
wich 1. u. 3. Pers. Sg. Prät. v. WEICHEN
wichtig Adj. important
Wichtigkeit die; ~: importance
Wicke die; ~, ~n vetch; (im Garten) sweet
pea
Wickel der; ~s, ~: compress

wickeln tr. V. wind; (einwickeln) wrap (in +
Akk. in); (auswickeln) unwrap (aus + Dat.
from); (abwickeln) unwind (von from); ein Kind
~: change a baby's nappy
Widder der; ~s, ~: (a) ram
(b) (Astrol.) Aries
wider Präp. mit Akk. (geh.) against
wider-: ~fahren unr. itr. V.; mit sein (geh.)
etw. ~fährt jmdm. sth. happens to sb.;
~legen tr. V. etw. ~legen refute sth.; jmdn.
~legen prove sb. wrong
widerlich 1 Adj. revolting; repulsive
⟨person, behaviour, etc.⟩; awful ⟨headache
etc.⟩
2 adv. revoltingly; ⟨behave⟩ in a repugnant
or repulsive manner; awfully ⟨cold, sweet,
etc.⟩
Widerlichkeit die; ~, ~en (abwertend)
(a) repulsiveness
(b) (Äußerung/Handlung) revolting remark/
action
wider-, Wider-: ~rede die: keine ~rede!
don't argue!; ~ruf der retraction; [bis] auf
~ruf until revoked; ~rufen /-'--/ unr. tr.,
auch itr. V. retract ⟨statement, claim,
confession, etc.⟩; ~setzen /-'--/ refl. V. sich
jmdm./einer Sache ~setzen oppose sb./sth.;
~spenstig 1 Adj. unruly; stubborn
⟨horse, mule, etc.⟩; 2 adv. wilfully;
~|spiegeln, ~spiegeln /-'--/ 1 tr. V.
mirror; (fig.) reflect; 2 refl. V. be mirrored;
(fig.) be reflected; ~sprechen /-'--/ unr.
itr. V. contradict; ~spruch der (a)
(Widerrede, Protest) opposition; protest; (b) (etw.
Unvereinbares) contradiction; im ~spruch zu
od. mit etw. stehen contradict sth.; be
contradictory to sth.; ~sprüchlich Adj.
contradictory ⟨news, statements, etc.⟩;
inconsistent ⟨behaviour, attitude, etc.⟩
Wider·stand der (a) resistance (gegen to)
(b) (Hindernis) opposition
widerstands-, Widerstands-:
~fähig Adj. robust; resistant ⟨material
etc.⟩; hardy ⟨animal, plant⟩; ~fähigkeit
die robustness; (von Material usw.) resistance;
(von Tier, Pflanze) hardiness; ~los Adj., adv.
without resistance postpos.
wider-, Wider-: ~stehen /-'--/ unr. itr.
V. (a) (nicht nachgeben) [jmdm./einer Sache]
~stehen resist [sb./sth.]; (b) (standhalten)
jmdm./einer Sache ~stehen withstand sb./
sth.; ~streben /-'--/ itr. V. etw. ~strebt
jmdm. sb. dislikes or detests sth.; ~wärtig
1 Adj. revolting, repugnant ⟨smell, taste,
etc.⟩; offensive ⟨person, behaviour, etc.⟩;
2 adv. ⟨behave etc.⟩ in an offensive manner;
~wille der aversion (gegen to); ~willig
1 Adj. reluctant; unwilling; 2 adv.
reluctantly; unwillingly
widmen 1 tr. V. (a) dedicate
(b) (verwenden für/auf) devote
2 refl. V. sich jmdm./einer Sache ~: attend
to sb./sth.; (ausschließlich) devote oneself to
sb./sth.

Wjdmung *die;* ∼, ∼**en** dedication (**an** + *Akk.* to)

widrig *Adj.* unfavourable; adverse

Widrigkeit *die;* ∼, ∼**en** adversity

wie ⟦1⟧ *Interrogativadv.* how; ∼ **viel/viele** how much/many; ∼ **[bitte]**? [I beg your] pardon?; ∼ **spät ist es?** what time is it? ⟦2⟧ *Relativadv.* ∼ **er es tut** the way *or* manner in which he does it ⟦3⟧ *Konj.* **(a)** *Vergleichspartikel* as; **[so]** ... ∼ ...: as ... as ...; **ich fühlte mich** ∼ ...: I felt as if I were ...; „**N**" ∼ „**Nordpol**" N for November **(b)** (zum Beispiel) like; such as **(c)** (und, sowie) as well as; both

wieder *Adv.* again; **alles ist** ∼ **beim Alten** everything is back as it was before; **ich bin gleich** ∼ **da** I'll be right back (coll.); **etw.** ∼ **finden** find sth. again; **etw.** ∼ **gutmachen** make sth. good; put sth. right; **den Schaden** ∼ **gutmachen** pay for the damage; **jmdn.** ∼ **wählen** re-elect sb.; **jmdn.** ∼ **beleben** revive *or* resuscitate sb.; **jmdn./etw.** ∼ **erkennen** recognize sb./sth.

wieder-, Wieder-: ∼**|aufbau** /-'-'-/ *der* reconstruction; rebuilding; **der wirtschaftliche** ∼**aufbau** economic recovery; ∼**|bekommen** *unr. tr. V.* get back; *∗*∼**|beleben** ▶ WIEDER; ∼**belebungs·versuch** *der* attempt at resuscitation; ∼**eingliederung** *die* reintegration (**in** + *Akk.* in); *∗*∼**|erkennen** ▶ WIEDER; *∗*∼**|finden** ▶ WIEDER; ∼**gabe** *die* (Bericht) report; (Übersetzung) rendering; (Reproduktion) reproduction; ∼**geben** *unr. tr. V.* **(a)** (zurückgeben) give back; **(b)** (berichten) report; (wiederholen) repeat; ∼**geburt** *die* (christl. Rel., fig. geh.) rebirth

*∗***wieder·gut|machen** ▶ WIEDER

wieder|haben *unr. tr. V.* (auch fig.) have back

wieder-: ∼**her|stellen** *tr. V.* **(a)** re-establish ⟨contact, peace⟩; **(b)** (reparieren) restore ⟨building⟩; ∼**holen** ⟦1⟧ *tr. V.* repeat; (repetieren) revise ⟨lesson, vocabulary, etc.⟩; ⟦2⟧ *refl. V.* **(a)** (wieder dasselbe sagen) repeat oneself; **(b)** (erneut geschehen) happen again; **(c)** (wiederkehren) be repeated; recur

wieder|holen *tr. V.* fetch *or* get back

wiederholt ⟦1⟧ *Adj.* repeated ⟦2⟧ *adv.* repeatedly

Wiederholung *die;* ∼, ∼**en** repetition; (eines Fußballspiels usw.) replay; (einer Sendung) repeat; (einer Aufführung) repeat performance; (von Lernstoff) revision

Wiederholungs·täter *der,* **Wiederholungs·täterin** *die* habitual offender

Wieder·hören *das:* [auf od. Auf] ∼! goodbye! (at end of telephone call)

wieder-, Wieder-: ∼**kehren** *itr. V.; mit sein* (geh.) return; ∼**kommen** *unr. itr. V.; mit sein* **(a)** (zurückkommen) return; come back; **(b)**

(noch einmal kommen) come back *or* again; **(c)** (sich noch einmal ereignen) ⟨opportunity, past⟩ come again; ∼**|kriegen** *tr. V.* (ugs.) get back; ∼**schauen** *das:* [auf] ∼**schauen!** (südd., österr.) goodbye!; ∼**|sehen** *unr. tr. V.* see again; ∼**sehen** *das;* ∼**s,** ∼: reunion; **[auf]** ∼**sehen!** goodbye!; ∼**um** *Adv.* **(a)** (erneut) again; **(b)** (andererseits) on the other hand; ∼**verwendung** *die* reuse; ∼**verwertung** *die* recycling; ∼**wahl** *die* re-election; *∗*∼**|wählen** *tr. V.* WIEDER

Wiege *die;* ∼, ∼**n** (auch fig.) cradle

wiegen¹ *unr. itr., tr. V.* weigh

wiegen² *tr. V.* rock; shake ⟨head⟩

Wiegen·lied *das* lullaby; cradle song

wiehern *itr. V.* whinny; (lauter) neigh

Wien *(das);* ∼**s** Vienna

Wiener¹ *der;* ∼**s,** ∼: Viennese

Wiener² *Adj.* Viennese; *s. auch* WÜRSTCHEN

Wienerin *die;* ∼, ∼**nen** Viennese

wienerisch *Adj.* Viennese

wies *1. u. 3. Pers. Sg. Prät. v.* WEISEN

Wiese *die;* ∼, ∼**n** meadow; (Rasen) lawn

wie·so *Interrogativadv.* why

*∗***wie·viel** /od. '--/ ▶ VIEL, WIE, UHR B

wie·viel·mal /od. -'--/ *Interrogativadv.* how many times

wievielt... /od. '--/ *Interrogativadj.* **der** ∼**e Band?** which number volume?; **der Wievielte ist heute?** what is the date today?

wie·weit *Interrogativadv.* to what extent; how far

wild ⟦1⟧ *Adj.* (auch fig.) wild; (wütend) furious ⟨cursing, shouting, etc.⟩; ∼**es Parken** illegal parking; ∼**er Streik** wildcat strike; ∼ **auf etw./jmdn. sein** (ugs.) be mad *or* crazy about sth./sb. (coll.); ∼ **werden** get furious; **jmdn.** ∼ **machen** infuriate sb. ⟦2⟧ *adv.* **(a)** wildly; **wie** ∼ (ugs.) like mad (coll.) **(b)** (ordnungswidrig) illegally

Wild *das;* ∼**[e]s (a)** (Tiere, Fleisch) game **(b)** (einzelnes Tier) [wild] animal

Wild·bret /-brɛt/ *das;* ∼**s** (geh.) game

Wilde *der/die; adj. Dekl.* savage

Wilderei *die;* ∼, ∼**en** poaching *no pl., no art.*

Wilderer *der;* ∼**s,** ∼, **Wilderin** *die;* ∼, ∼**nen** poacher

wild·fremd *Adj.* completely strange

Wild·gans *die* wild goose

Wildheit *die;* ∼: wildness

Wild-: ∼**katze** *die* wild cat; ∼**leder** *das* suede

Wildnis *die;* ∼, ∼**se** wilderness

Wild-: ∼**pferd** *das* wild horse; ∼**schwein** *das* wild boar; ∼**wasser** *das Pl.* ∼∼: mountain torrent; ∼**wechsel** *der* game crossing; ∼**west·film** *der* western

will *1. u. 3. Pers. Sg. Präsens v.* WOLLEN

Wille *der;* ∼**ns** will; (Wunsch) wish

W

willen *Präp. mit Gen.* um jmds./einer Sache ~: for sb.'s/sth.'s sake

Willen *der;* ~s ▶ WILLE

willen-los 1 *Adj.* will-less
2 *adv.* will-lessly

willens *Adj.* ~ sein, etw. zu tun (geh.) be willing to do sth.

willens-, Willens-: ~**schwach** *Adj.* weak-willed; ~**schwäche** *die* weakness of will; ~**stark** *Adj.* strong-willed; ~**stärke** *die* strength of will

willentlich 1 *Adj.* deliberate
2 *adv.* deliberately; on purpose

willig 1 *Adj.* willing
2 *adv.* willingly

will·kommen *Adj.* welcome; jmdn. ~ heißen welcome sb.

Will·kür *die;* ~: arbitrary use of power; (Handlung o. Ä.) arbitrariness

willkürlich 1 *Adj.* arbitrary; (vom Willen gesteuert) voluntary ⟨*muscle, movement, etc.*⟩
2 *adv.* arbitrarily; (vom Willen gesteuert) voluntarily

wimmeln *itr. V.* von Fischen/Fehlern ~: be teeming with fish/mistakes

wimmern *itr. V.* whimper

Wimpel *der;* ~s, ~: pennant

Wimper *die;* ~, ~n [eye]lash

Wimpern·tusche *die* mascara

Wind *der;* ~[e]s, ~e wind

Wind·beutel *der* cream puff

Winde *die;* ~, ~n winch

Windel *die;* ~, ~n nappy (Brit.); diaper (Amer.)

Windel·höschen *das* nappy pants *pl.*

winden 1 *unr. tr. V.* (geh.) make ⟨*wreath, garland*⟩; etw. um etw. ~: wind sth. around sth.
2 *unr. refl. V.* ⟨*plant, tendrils*⟩ wind (um around); ⟨*snake*⟩ coil [itself], wind itself (um around); sich vor Schmerzen ~: writhe in pain

Windes·eile *die:* in ~: in next to no time

Wind-: ~**hose** *die* (Met.) whirlwind; ~**hund** *der* greyhound

windig *Adj.* windy

Wind-: ~**kanal** *der* (Technik) wind tunnel; ~**mühle** *die* windmill; ~**pocken** *Pl.* chickenpox *sing.;* ~**schatten** *der* lee; ~**schutz·scheibe** *die* windscreen (Brit.); windshield (Amer.); ~**stärke** *die:* ~stärke 7/9 *usw.* wind force 7/9 *etc.;* ~**still** *Adj.* windless; still; ~**stoß** *der* gust of wind; ~**surfer** *der,* ~**surferin** *die* windsurfer; ~**surfing** *das;* ~~s windsurfing *no art.*

Windung *die;* ~, ~en (a) bend
(b) (spiralförmiger Verlauf) spiral; (einer Spule usw.) winding

Wink *der;* ~[e]s, ~e sign; (Hinweis) hint; (Ratschlag) tip; hint

Winkel *der;* ~s, ~ (a) (Math.) angle; **toter** ~: blind spot
(b) (Ecke; auch fig.) corner

winkelig *Adj.* twisty ⟨*streets*⟩

winken 1 *itr. V.* (a) wave; mit etw. ~: wave sth.
(b) (auffordern heranzukommen) jmdm. ~: beckon sb. over; einem Taxi ~: hail a taxi
2 *tr. V.* beckon; jmdn. zu sich ~: beckon sb. over [to one]

winklig *Adj.* ▶ WINKELIG

winseln *itr. V.* ⟨*dog*⟩ whimper

Winter *der;* ~s, ~: winter

Winter-: ~**anfang** *der* beginning of winter; ~**garten** *der* conservatory

winterlich 1 *Adj.* wintry; winter *attrib.* ⟨*clothing, break*⟩
2 *adv.* ~ kalt cold and wintry

Winter-: ~**reifen** *der* winter tyre; ~**schlussverkauf,** *~**schlußverkauf** *der* winter sale[s *pl.*]; ~**sport** *der* winter sports *pl.;* ~**urlaub** *der* winter holiday; ~**zeit** *die* wintertime

Winzer *der;* ~s, ~, **Winzerin** *die;* ~, ~nen winegrower

winzig 1 *Adj.* tiny
2 *adv.* ~ klein tiny; minute

Winzigkeit *die;* ~, ~en (a) tininess; minuteness
(b) (Kleinigkeit) tiny thing; triviality

Wipfel *der;* ~s, ~: treetop

Wippe *die;* ~, ~n see-saw

wippen *itr. V.* bob up and down; (hin und her) bob about; (auf einer Wippe) see-saw

wir *Personalpron.; 1. Pers. Pl. Nom.* we; *s. auch (Gen.)* UNSER *(Dat.)* UNS; *(Akk.)* UNS

wirb *Imperativ Sg. v.* WERBEN

Wirbel *der;* ~s, ~ (a) (kreisende Bewegung) (im Wasser) whirlpool; (in der Luft) whirlwind; (kleiner) eddy; (von Rauch, beim Tanz) whirl
(b) (Trubel) hurly-burly
(c) (Aufsehen) fuss
(d) (Anat.) vertebra

wirbeln 1 *itr. V. mit sein* whirl; ⟨*water, snowflakes*⟩ swirl
2 *tr. V.* swirl ⟨*leaves, dust*⟩; whirl ⟨*dancer*⟩

Wirbel-: ~**säule** *die* spinal column; ~**sturm** *der* cyclone

wirbt *3. Pers. Sg. Präsens v.* WERBEN

wird *3. Pers. Sg. Präsens v.* WERDEN

wirf *Imperativ Sg. v.* WERFEN

wirft *3. Pers. Sg. Präsens v.* WERFEN

wirken *itr. V.* (a) (eine Wirkung haben) have an effect; gegen etw. ~: be effective against sth.
(b) (erscheinen) seem; appear

wirklich 1 *Adj.* real
2 *Adv.* really

Wirklichkeit *die;* ~, ~en reality; in ~: in reality

wirksam 1 *Adj.* effective
2 *adv.* effectively

Wirksamkeit *die;* ~: effectiveness

---

*alte Schreibung - vgl. Hinweis auf S. xiv

Wirk·stoff *der* active agent

Wirkung *die;* ~, ~en effect (**auf** + *Akk.* on); **mit** ~ **vom 1. Juli** (Amtsspr.) with effect from 1 July

wirkungs-, Wirkungs-: ~**grad** *der* (Technik) efficiency; ~**los** [1] *Adj.* ineffective; [2] *adv.* ineffectively; ~**losigkeit** *die;* ~~: ineffectiveness; ~**voll** [1] *Adj.* effective; [2] *adv.* effectively

wirr *Adj.* (unordentlich) tousled ⟨hair, beard⟩; tangled ⟨ropes, roots⟩; (unklar, verwirrt) confused

Wirren *Pl.* turmoil *sing.*

Wirrwarr *der;* ~s chaos; (von Stimmen) clamour

Wirsing *der;* ~s, **Wirsing·kohl** *der* savoy [cabbage]

Wirt *der;* ~[e]s, ~e landlord

Wirtin *die;* ~, ~nen landlady

Wirtschaft *die;* ~, ~en (a) economy; (Geschäftsleben) commerce and industry (b) (Gaststätte) public house; pub (Brit. coll.); bar (Amer.) (c) (Haushalt) household (d) (ugs. abwertend: Unordnung) mess; shambles *sing.*

wirtschaften *itr. V.* **mit dem Geld gut** ~: manage one's money well; **mit Verlust/ Gewinn** ~: run at a loss/profit

wirtschaftlich [1] *Adj.* (a) economic (b) (finanziell) financial (c) (sparsam, rentabel) economical [2] *adv.; s. Adj.:* economically; financially

Wirtschaftlichkeit *die;* ~: economic viability

Wirtschafts-: ~**hilfe** *die* economic aid *no indef. art.;* ~**krieg** *der* economic war; (Kriegsführung) economic warfare; ~**kriminalität** *die* economic crime *no art.;* ~**krise** *die* economic crisis; ~**lehre** *die* economics *sing.;* ~**minister** *der,* ~**ministerin** *die* minister for economic affairs; ~**politik** *die* economic policy; ~**union** *die* economic union; *s. auch* WÄHRUNGSUNION; ~**wunder** *das* (ugs.) economic miracle

Wirts-: ~**haus** *das* pub (Brit. coll.); ~**leute** *Pl.* landlord and landlady

Wisch *der;* ~[e]s, ~e (salopp) piece *or* bit of paper

wischen *itr., tr. V.* wipe; **Staub** ~: do the dusting; dust

wispern *itr., tr. V.* whisper

wiss-, *wiß-, Wiss, *Wiß-: ~**begier,** ~**begierde** *die* thirst for knowledge; ~**begierig** *Adj.* eager for knowledge; ⟨child⟩ eager to learn

wissen [1] *unr. tr. V.* know; **von jmdm./etw. nichts [mehr]** ~ **wollen** want to have nothing [more] to do with sb./sth. [2] *unr. itr. V.* **von etw./um etw.** ~: know about sth.

Wissen *das;* ~s knowledge; **meines/ unseres** ~s to my/our knowledge

Wissenschaft *die;* ~, ~en science

Wissenschaftler *der;* ~s ~, **Wissenschaftlerin** *die;* ~, ~nen academic; (Naturwissenschaft) scientist

wissenschaftlich [1] *Adj.* scholarly; (naturwissenschaftlich) scientific [2] *adv.* in a scholarly manner; (naturwissenschaftlich) scientifically

wissens-wert *Adj.* ~ **sein** be worth knowing

wissentlich [1] *Adj.* deliberate [2] *adv.* knowingly; deliberately

wittern [1] *itr. V.* sniff the air [2] *tr. V.* get wind of; (fig.: ahnen) sense

Witterung *die;* ~, ~en (a) (Wetter) weather *no indef. art;* (b) (Jägerspr.) (Geruchssinn) sense of smell; (Geruch) scent

Witwe *die;* ~, ~n widow; ~ **werden** be widowed

Witwen-rente *die* widow's pension

Witwer *der;* ~s, ~: widower; ~ **werden** be widowed

Witz *der;* ~es, ~e joke

Witz-: ~**blatt** *das* humorous magazine; ~**bold** *der;* ~~es, ~~e joker

Witzelei *die;* ~, ~en (a) teasing (b) (witzelnde Bemerkung) joke

witzeln *itr. V.* joke (**über** + *Akk.* about)

Witz·figur *die* (a) (in Witzen) joke character (b) (ugs. abwertend) figure of fun

witzig [1] *Adj.* funny [2] *adv.* amusingly

witz-los *Adj.* (a) dull (b) (ugs.: sinnlos) pointless

wo [1] *Adv.* where [2] *Konj.* (a) (da, weil) seeing that (b) (obwohl) although; when

wo·anders *Adv.* somewhere else

wo·bei *Adv.* (a) (interrogativ) ~ **hast du sie ertappt?** what did you catch her doing? (b) (relativisch) **er gab sechs Schüsse ab,** ~ **einer der Täter getötet wurde** he fired six shots – one of the criminals was killed

Woche *die;* ~, ~n week; **in dieser/der nächsten/der letzten** ~: this/next/last week; **heute in/vor einer** ~: a week today/a week ago today

wochen-, Wochen-: ~**bett** *das:* **im** ~**bett liegen** be lying in; ~**ende** *das* weekend; ~**lang** [1] *Adj.* lasting weeks *postpos;* [2] *adv.* for weeks [on end]; ~**stunde** *die* (Schulw.) period per week; ~**tag** *der* weekday (*including Saturday*); ~**tags** *Adv.* on weekdays [and Saturdays]

wöchentlich *Adj., adv.* weekly

Wochen-zeitung *die* weekly newspaper

-wöchig (a) (... Wochen alt) ... -week-old (b) (... Wochen dauernd) ... week's/weeks'; ...-week

Wöchnerin die; ~, ~nen woman who has just given birth

Wodka der; ~s, ~s vodka

wo·durch Adv. (a) (interrogativ) how (b) (relativisch) as a result of which

wo·für Adv. (a) (interrogativ) for what (b) (relativisch) for which

wog 1. u. 3. Pers. Sg. Prät. v. WIEGEN

Woge die; ~, ~n wave

wo·gegen ⓵ Adv. (a) (interrogativ) against what; what ... against (b) (relativisch) against which; which ... against ⓶ Konj. whereas

wogen itr. V. (geh.) ⟨sea⟩ surge; (fig.) ⟨corn⟩ wave

wo·her Adv. (a) (interrogativ) where ... from; ~ weißt du das? how do you know that? (b) (relativisch) where ... from

wo·hin Adv. (a) (interrogativ) where [... to] (b) (relativisch) where

wo·hingegen Konj. whereas

wohl ⓵ Adv. (a) well; jmdm. ist nicht ~, jmd. fühlt sich nicht ~: sb. does not feel well (b) (behaglich) at ease; happy; leb ~!/leben Sie ~! farewell! (c) (durchaus) well (d) (ungefähr) about (e) etw. tut jmdm. ~: sth. does sb. good ⓶ Partikel probably; ~ kaum hardly

Wohl das; ~[e]s welfare; auf jmds. ~ trinken drink sb.'s health; zum ~! cheers!

wohl-, Wohl-: ~auf /·'·/ Adj. (geh.) ~auf sein be well; ~befinden das well-being; ~behagen das sense of well-being; ~behalten Adj. safe and well ⟨person⟩; undamaged ⟨thing⟩; ~fahrts·staat der welfare state; ~gefallen das; ~~s pleasure; ~gemerkt Adv. please note; ~habend Adj. prosperous; ~habenheit die; ~~: prosperity

wohlig ⓵ Adj. pleasant; agreeable ⓶ adv. ⟨sigh, purr, etc.⟩ with pleasure

wohl-, Wohl-: ~klang der (geh.) melodious sound; ~schmeckend Adj. (geh.) delicious; ~stand der prosperity; ~stands·gesellschaft die affluent society; ~tat die (a) (gute Tat) good deed; (Gefallen) favour; (b) (Genuss) blissful relief; ~tätig Adj. charitable; ~tuend Adj. agreeable; *~tun ▸ WOHL 1 E; ~verdient Adj. well-earned; ~weislich Adv. deliberately; ~wollen das; ~~s goodwill; ~wollend ⓵ Adj. benevolent; favourable ⟨judgement, opinion⟩; ⓶ adv. benevolently; ⟨judge, consider⟩ favourably

Wohn-: ~anhänger der caravan; trailer (Amer.); ~block der; Pl. ~~s, od. ~blöcke residential block

wohnen itr. V. live; (kurzfristig) stay

wohn-, Wohn-: ~gemeinschaft die

---

*old spelling - see note on page xiv

group sharing a flat (Brit.) or (Amer.) apartment/house; ~haft Adj. resident (in + Dat. in); ~heim das (für Alte, Behinderte) home; (für Obdachlose, Lehrlinge) hostel; (für Studenten) hall of residence

wohnlich Adj. homely

Wohn-: ~mobil das; ~~s, ~~e motor home; ~ort der place of residence; ~siedlung die residential estate; (mit gleichartigen Häusern) housing estate; ~sitz der place of residence; ohne festen ~sitz of no fixed abode

Wohnung die; ~, ~en (a) flat (Brit.); apartment (Amer.) (b) (Unterkunft) lodging

Wohnungs-: ~not die housing crisis; serious housing shortage; ~schlüssel der key to the flat (Brit.) or (Amer.) apartment; ~suche die search for a flat (Brit.) or (Amer.) apartment; auf ~suche sein be flat-hunting; ~tür die door of the flat (Brit.) or (Amer.) apartment; ~verlust der loss of one's home

Wohn-: ~verhältnisse Pl. living conditions; ~wagen der caravan; trailer (Amer.); ~zimmer das living room

wölben ⓵ tr. V. curve; vault, arch ⟨roof, ceiling⟩ ⓶ refl. V. curve; ⟨bridge, ceiling⟩ arch

Wölbung die; ~, ~en curve; (einer Decke) arch; vault

Wolf der; ~[e]s, Wölfe wolf

Wolke die; ~, ~n cloud

wolken-, Wolken-: ~bruch der cloudburst; ~bruch·artig Adj. torrential; ~decke die [unbroken] cloud no indef. art.; die ~decke riss auf the clouds broke; ~kratzer der skyscraper; ~los Adj. cloudless

wolkig Adj. cloudy

Wolle die; ~, ~n wool

wollen¹ Adj. woollen

wollen² ⓵ unr. Modalverb; 2. Part. wollen: etw. tun ~ (den Wunsch haben, etw. zu tun) want to do sth.; (die Absicht haben, etw. zu tun) be going to do sth.; die Wunde will nicht heilen the wound [just] won't heal ⓶ unr. itr. V. du musst nur ~, dann ... you only have to want to want, then ... ganz wie du willst just as you like; ich will nach Hause (ugs.) I want to go home; zu wem ~ Sie? whom do you want to see? ⓷ unr. tr. V. want; das habe ich nicht gewollt I never meant that to happen

wo·mit Adv. (a) (interrogativ) ~ schreibst du? what do you write with? (b) (relativisch) ~ du schreibst which or that you write with; (more formal) with which you write

wo·möglich Adv. possibly

wo·nach Adv. (a) (interrogativ) after what; what ... after; ~ suchst du? what are you looking for?

(b) (relativisch) after which; which ... after

Wonne *die;* ∼, ∼n (geh.) bliss *no pl.;* ecstasy; (etw., was Freude macht) joy

wonnig *Adj.* sweet

woran *Adv.* **(a)** (interrogativ) ∼ **denkst du?** what are you thinking of?
(b) (relativisch) **nichts,** ∼ **man sich anlehnen könnte** nothing one could lean against

worauf (a) (interrogativ) ∼ **wartest du?** what are you waiting for?
(b) (relativisch) **etwas,** ∼ **man sich verlassen kann** something one can rely on
(c) (relativisch: woraufhin) whereupon

woraus *Adv.* **(a)** (interrogativ) ∼ **schließt du das?** what do you infer that from?
(b) (relativisch) **es gab nichts,** ∼ **wir den Wein hätten trinken können** there was nothing for us to drink the wine out of

worden *2. Part. v.* WERDEN 2

worin *Adv.* **(a)** (interrogativ) in what; what ... in
(b) (relativisch) in which; which ... in

Workaholic /wɔːkəˈhɔlɪk/ *der;* ∼s, ∼s: workaholic

Wort *das;* ∼[e]s, Wörter/∼e **(a)** *Pl.* Wörter, (auch:) ∼e word; ∼ **für** ∼: word for word; **DM 1000** (in ∼en: **tausend)** DM 1,000 (in words: one thousand)
(b) *Pl.* ∼e (Äußerung) word; **mir fehlen die** ∼e I'm lost for words; **Dr. Meyer hat das** ∼: it's Dr Meyer's turn to speak
(c) *Pl.* ∼e (Spruch) saying; (Zitat) quotation
(d) *Pl.* ∼e (geh.: Text) words *pl.;* **in** ∼ **und Bild** in words and pictures
(e) *Pl.* ∼e (Versprechen) word; **[sein]** ∼ **halten** keep one's word

Wort-bruch *der* breaking one's word *no art.*

wort-brüchig *Adj.* ∼ **werden** break one's word

Wörter-buch *das* dictionary

wort-, Wort-: ∼**getreu** *Adj.* word-for-word; ∼**karg** ⓵ *Adj.* taciturn ⟨person⟩; ⓶ *adv.* taciturnly; ∼**kargheit** *die* taciturnity; ∼**laut** *der* wording; **im [vollen]** ∼**laut** verbatim

wörtlich ⓵ *Adj.* **(a)** word-for-word
(b) (der eigentlichen Bedeutung entsprechend) literal
⓶ *adv.: s. Adj.:* word for word; literally

wort-, Wort-: ∼**los** ⓵ *Adj.* silent; wordless; ⓶ *adv.* without saying a word; ∼**meldung** *die:* **gibt es noch** ∼**meldungen?** does anyone else wish to speak?; ∼**spiel** *das* play on words; pun; ∼**wechsel** *der* exchange of words; ∼**wörtlich** *Adj.* word-for-word

worüber *Adv.* **(a)** (interrogativ) over what ...; what ... over
(b) (relativisch) over which; which ... over

worum *Adv.* **(a)** (interrogativ) around what; what ... around

(b) (relativisch) around which; which ... around

worunter *Adv.* **(a)** (interrogativ) under what; what ... under
(b) (relativisch) under which; which ... under

wo-von *Adv.* **(a)** (interrogativ) from where; where ... from
(b) (relativisch) from which; which ... from

wo-vor *Adv.* **(a)** (interrogativ) in front of what; what ... in front of
(b) (relativisch) in front of which; which ... in front of

wo-zu *Adv.* **(a)** (interrogativ) to what; what ... to; (wofür) what ... for
(b) (relativisch) ∼ **du dich auch entschließt** whatever you decide on

Wrack *das;* ∼[e]s, ∼s *od.* ∼e wreck

wrang *1. und 3. Pers. Sg. Prät. v.* WRINGEN

wringen *unr. tr. V.* (bes. nordd.) wring

Wucher *der;* ∼s profiteering; (beim Verleihen von Geld) usury

wuchern *itr. V.* **(a)** *auch mit sein ⟨plants, weeds, etc.⟩* proliferate, run wild
(b) (Wucher treiben) **[mit etw.]** ∼: profiteer [on sth.]; (beim Verleihen von Geld) lend [sth.] at extortionate interest rates

Wucherung *die;* ∼, ∼en growth

wuchs *1. u. 3. Pers. Sg. Prät. v.* WACHSEN

Wuchs *der;* ∼es (Gestalt) stature

Wucht *die;* ∼: force; (von Schlägen) power; weight

wuchtig ⓵ *Adj.* **(a)** (voller Wucht) powerful; mighty
(b) (schwer, massig) massive
⓶ *adv.* powerfully

wühlen ⓵ *itr. V.* **(a)** dig; (mit der Schnauze, dem Schnabel) root (nach for); ⟨mole⟩ tunnel, burrow
(b) (ugs.: suchen) rummage [around] (nach for)
⓶ *tr. V.* burrow; tunnel out ⟨burrow⟩

wulstig *Adj.* bulging

wund *Adj.* sore; **sich** ∼ **liegen** get bed sores

Wunde *die;* ∼, ∼n wound

wunder, Wunder[1] (ugs.): **er denkt, er sei** ∼ **wer** he thinks he's really something; **sie bildet sich** ∼ **was darauf ein** she's terribly pleased with herself about it (coll.)

Wunder[2] *das;* ∼s, ∼ **(a)** miracle; ∼ **wirken** (fig. ugs.) work wonders; **ein/kein** ∼ **sein** (ugs.) be a/no wonder
(b) (etw. Erstaunliches) wonder

wunderbar ⓵ *Adj.* **(a)** miraculous
(b) (sehr schön, herrlich) wonderful; marvellous
⓶ *adv.* **(a)** (sehr schön, herrlich) wonderfully; marvellously
(b) (ugs.: sehr) wonderfully

Wunder-: ∼**kerze** *die* sparkler; ∼**kind** *das* child prodigy

wunderlich ⓵ *Adj.* strange; odd
⓶ *adv.* strangely; oddly

W

wundern ① *tr. V.* surprise; **mich wundert** *od.* **es wundert mich, dass ...**: I'm surprised that ...
② *refl. V.* **sich über jmdn./etw. ~**: be surprised at sb./sth

wunder-: ~schön ① *Adj.* simply beautiful; (herrlich) simply wonderful; ② *adv.* quite beautifully; **~voll** ① *Adj.* wonderful; ② *adv.* wonderfully

*****wund|liegen** ▶ WUND

Wund·starr·krampf *der* (Med.) tetanus

Wunsch *der;* **~[e]s, Wünsche** wish **(nach to** have); (Sehnen) desire **(nach** for); **haben Sie [sonst] noch einen ~?** will there be anything else?; **auf jmds. ~**: at sb.'s wish; **mit den besten/herzlichsten Wünschen** with best/warmest wishes

wünschbar *Adj.* (bes. schweiz.) desirable

Wünschel-: ~rute *die* divining rod; **~ruten·gänger** *der;* **~~s, ~~,** **~ruten·gängerin** *die;* **~~, ~~nen** diviner

wünschen *tr. V.* **(a)** sich *(Dat.)* etw. **~**: want sth.; (im Stillen) wish for sth.
(b) (in formelhaften Wünschen) wish; **jmdm. alles Gute/frohe Ostern ~**: wish sb. all the best/a happy Easter
(c) *auch itr. V.* (begehren) want; **was ~ Sie?, Sie ~?** (im Lokal) what may I do you like?; (in einem Geschäft) can I help you?

Wunsch-: ~kind *das* wanted child; **~konzert** *das* request concert; (im Rundfunk) request programme; **~zettel** *der* (zum Geburtstag *usw.*) list of presents one would like

wurde *1. u. 3. Pers. Sg. Prät. v.* WERDEN

würde *1. u. 3. Pers. Sg. Konjunktiv II v.* WERDEN

Würde *die;* **~**: dignity

würde·los ① *Adj.* undignified; (schimpflich) disgraceful
② *adv.* in an undignified way; (schimpflich) disgracefully

Würdelosigkeit *die;* **~** ▶ WÜRDELOS: lack of dignity; disgracefulness

Würden·träger *der,* **Würden·trägerin** *die* dignitary

würde·voll ① *Adj.* dignified
② *adv.* with dignity

würdig ① *Adj.* **(a)** dignified
(b) (wert) worthy
② *adv.* **(a)** with dignity
(b) (angemessen) worthily

würdigen *tr. V.* **(a)** (anerkennen, beachten) recognize; (schätzen) appreciate; (lobend hervorheben) acknowledge
(b) (für wert halten) **jmdn. keines Blickes/keiner Antwort ~**: not deign to look at/answer sb.

Wurf *der;* **~[e]s, Würfe (a)** throw; (beim Kegeln) bowl

*alte Schreibung - vgl. Hinweis auf S. xiv

(b) *o. Pl.* (das Werfen) throwing/pitching/bowling
(c) (Zool.) litter

Würfel *der;* **~s, ~**: cube; (Spielwürfel) dice; *die* (formal)

Würfel·becher *der* dice cup

würfeln ① *itr. V.* throw the dice; **um etw. ~**: play dice for sth.
② *tr. V.* **(a)** throw
(b) (in Würfel schneiden) dice

Würfel-: ~spiel *das* dice; (Brettspiel) dice game; **~zucker** *der* cube sugar

Wurf·geschoss, *Wurf·geschoß *das* missile

würgen ① *tr. V.* strangle; throttle
② *itr. V.* (Brechreiz haben) retch

Wurm *der;* **~[e]s, Würmer** worm; (Made) maggot

wurmig *Adj.,* **wurm·stichig** *Adj.* worm-eaten; (madig) maggoty

Wurst *die;* **~, Würste** sausage; **es geht um die ~** (fig. ugs.) the crunch has come; **jmdm. ist jmd./etw. ~** (ugs.) sb. doesn't care about sb./sth.

Wurst·bude *die* ▶ WÜRSTCHENBUDE

Würstchen *das;* **~s, ~ (a)** [small] sausage; **Frankfurter/Wiener ~**: frankfurter/wienerwurst
(b) (fig. ugs.) nobody; (hilfloser Mensch) poor soul

Würstchen·bude *die* sausage stand

Wurstelei *die;* **~, ~en** (ugs. abwertend) pottering about *no pl.*

wursteln *itr. V.* (ugs.) potter

Wurst·salat *der: piquant salad with pieces of sausage, onion rings, boiled eggs and/or cheese*

Würze *die;* **~, ~n** spice; seasoning

Wurzel *die;* **~, ~n** (auch fig.) root

wurzeln *itr. V.* take root

würzen *tr. V.* season

würzig *Adj.* tasty; full-flavoured ⟨beer, wine⟩; aromatic ⟨fragrance⟩; tangy ⟨air⟩

Würzigkeit *die;* **~** ▶ WÜRZIG 1: tastiness; full flavour; aromatic fragrance; tanginess

wusch *1. u. 3. Pers. Sg. Prät. v.* WASCHEN

wusste, *wußte *1. und 3. Pers. Sg. Prät. v.* WISSEN

wüsste, *wüßte *1. und 3. Pers. Sg. Konjunktiv II v.* WISSEN

wüst ① *Adj.* **(a)** (öde) desolate
(b) (unordentlich) chaotic
(c) (ungezügelt) wild; (unanständig) rude
② *adv.* **(a)** (unordentlich) chaotically
(b) (ungezügelt) wildly

Wust *der;* **~[e]s** (abwertend) jumble; (fig.) welter; **ein ~ von Daten/Vorschriften** a mass of data/regulations

Wüste *die;* **~, ~n** desert

Wut *die;* **~**: rage; fury

wüten *itr. V.* (auch fig.) rage; (zerstören) wreak havoc

wütend [1] *Adj.* furious; angry ⟨*voice, mob*⟩
[2] *adv.* furiously; in a fury

Xx

x¹, X /ɪks/ *das;* ∼, ∼: x/X
x² *unbest. Zahlwort* (ugs.) umpteen (coll.)
x-Achse *die* (Math.) x-axis
X-Beine *Pl.* knock knees
x-beinig *Adj.* knock-kneed
x-beliebig *Adj.* (ugs.) [irgend]ein ∼er/ [irgend]eine ∼e/[irgend]ein ∼es any old (coll. attrib.); **jeder** ∼**e Ort** any old place (coll.)

X-Chromosom *das* (Biol.) X-chromosome
x-fach [1] *Vervielfältigungsz.* **die** ∼**e Menge** (Math.) x times the amount; (ugs.) umpteen times the amount (coll.)
[2] *adv.* (ugs.) ∼ **erprobt sein** ⟨*tested etc.*⟩ umpteen times (coll.)
x-mal *Adv.* (ugs.) umpteen times (coll.)
x-t... *Ordinalz.* (ugs.) umpteenth (coll.)
Xylophon *das;* ∼s, ∼e xylophone

Yy

y, Y /ˈʏpsilɔn/ *das;* ∼, ∼: y/Y
y-Achse *die* (Math.) y-axis
Yacht ▶ JACHT
Y-Chromosom *das* (Biol.) Y-chromosome

Yoga ▶ JOGA
Ypsilon *das;* ∼[s], ∼s y, Y; (im griechischen Alphabet) upsilon

Zz

z, Z /tsɛt/ *das;* ∼, ∼: z/Z
Zack: **auf** ∼ **sein** (ugs.: tüchtig sein) be on the ball (coll.) *or* one's toes; **jmdn. auf** ∼ **bringen** (ugs.) knock sb. into shape (coll.)
Zacke *die;* ∼, ∼n point; peak; (einer Säge, eines Kamms) tooth; (einer Gabel, Harke) prong
Zacken *der;* ∼s: ▶ ZACKE
zackig [1] *Adj.* (a) (gezackt) jagged; (mit kleinen, regelmäßigen Zacken) serrated
(b) (schneidig) dashing; smart; rousing ⟨*music*⟩; brisk ⟨*orders, tempo*⟩; lively ⟨*organization*⟩
[2] *adv.* (a) (gezackt) jaggedly
(b) (schneidig) smartly; ⟨*play music*⟩ rousingly
zaghaft [1] *Adj.* timid; (zögernd) hesitant
[2] *adv.* timidly; (zögernd) hesitantly
Zaghaftigkeit *die;* ∼: timidity; (Zögern) hesitancy
zäh [1] *Adj.* (a) tough; heavy ⟨*dough, soil*⟩; (dickflüssig) glutinous; viscous ⟨*oil*⟩

(b) (widerstandsfähig) tough ⟨*person*⟩
(c) (beharrlich) tenacious; tough ⟨*negotiations*⟩; dogged ⟨*resistance*⟩
[2] *adv.* (beharrlich) tenaciously; ⟨*resist*⟩ doggedly
Zähheit *die;* ∼: (a) (Festigkeit) toughness; (des Teigs, Bodens) heaviness; (Dickflüssigkeit) glutinousness; (von Öl) viscosity
(b) (Widerstandsfähigkeit) toughness
(c) (Beharrlichkeit) tenacity; (des Widerstands) doggedness
Zähigkeit *die;* ∼ (a) (Widerstandsfähigkeit) toughness
(b) (Beharrlichkeit) tenacity; **mit** ∼: tenaciously
Zahl *die;* ∼, ∼en number; (Ziffer) numeral; (Zahlenangabe, Geldmenge) figure; **in den roten/ schwarzen** ∼**en** in the red/black
zahlbar *Adj.* (Kaufmannsspr.) payable
zahlen [1] *tr. V.* pay (**an** + *Akk.* to) ⋯⟩

2 *itr. V.* pay; [ich möchte] bitte ~ (im Lokal) [can I have] the bill, please!

zählen 1 *itr. V.* (a) count; zu einer Gruppe usw. ~: be one of *or* belong to a group *etc.*; (b) auf jmdn./etw. ~: count on sb./sth 2 *tr. V.* count; jmdn. zu seinen Freunden ~: count sb. among one's friends

zahl-, Zahl-: ~**karte** *die* (Postw.) paying-in slip; ~**los** *Adj.* countless; ~**reich** *Adj.* numerous

Zahlung *die;* ~, ~en payment

Zählung *die;* ~, ~en counting; eine ~: a count

zahlungs-, Zahlungs-: ~**bilanz** *die* (Wirtsch.) balance of payments; ~**fähig** *Adj.* solvent; ~**fähigkeit** *die* solvency; ~**mittel** *das* means of payment; ~**unfähig** *Adj.* insolvent; ~**unfähigkeit** *die* insolvency

Zahl·wort *das; Pl.* Zahl·wörter (Sprachw.) numeral

zahm 1 *Adj.* tame 2 *adv.* tamely

zähmen *tr. V.* (auch fig.) tame

Zahn *der;* ~[e]s, Zähne tooth; (Reißzahn) fang; (an einer Briefmarke usw.) serration

Zahn-: ~**arzt** *der,* ~**ärztin** *die* dentist; (mit chirurgischer Ausbildung) dental surgeon; ~**bürste** *die* toothbrush

zahnen *itr. V.* ⟨baby⟩ be teething

zahn-, Zahn-: ~**ersatz** *der* denture; ~**fleisch** *das* gum; (als Ganzes) gums *pl.;* ~**fleisch-bluten** *das;* ~~s bleeding gums *pl.;* ~**los** *Adj.* toothless; ~**lücke** *die* gap in one's teeth; ~**pasta** *die,* ~~, ~**pasten** toothpaste; ~**pflege** *die* dental care; ~**prothese** *die* dentures *pl.;* [set *sing.* of] false teeth *pl.;* ~**rad** *das* gearwheel; (für Ketten) sprocket; ~**schmerzen** *der* toothache *sing.;* ~**seide** *die* dental floss; ~**spange** *die* [tooth] brace; ~**stein** *der* tartar; ~**stocher** *der;* ~~s, ~~: toothpick; ~**weh** *das* (ugs.) toothache

Zange *die;* ~, ~n (a) (Werkzeug) pliers *pl.;* (Eiswürfel-, Zuckerzange) tongs *pl.;* (Geburtszange) forceps *pl.;* (Kneifzange) pincers *pl.;* eine ~: a pair of pliers/tongs/forceps/pincers (b) (bei Tieren) pincer

Zank *der;* ~[e]s squabble; row

zanken *refl.* (auch itr.) V. squabble, bicker (um *od.* über + *Akk.* over)

zänkisch *Adj.* quarrelsome

Zäpfchen *das;* ~s, ~: suppository

zapfen *tr. V.* tap, draw ⟨beer, wine⟩

Zapfen *der;* ~s, ~ (a) (Bot.) cone (b) (Stöpsel) bung

Zapf·säule *die* petrol pump (Brit.); gasoline pump (Amer.)

zappeln *itr. V.* wriggle; ⟨child⟩ fidget

zappen /ˈzɛpn̩/ *itr. V.* (ugs.) zap (coll.)

Zar *der;* ~en, ~en (hist.) Tsar

Zarin *die;* ~, ~nen (hist.) Tsarina

zart 1 *Adj.* (auch fig.) delicate; soft ⟨skin⟩; tender ⟨bud, shoot; meat, vegetables⟩; fine ⟨biscuits⟩; gentle ⟨kiss, touch⟩; soft ⟨pastel colours⟩ 2 *adv.* (empfindlich) delicately; ⟨kiss, touch⟩ gently

Zartheit *die;* ~: delicacy; (der Haut) softness; (von Fleisch, Gemüse) tenderness; (eines Kusses, einer Berührung) gentleness

zärtlich 1 *Adj.* tender 2 *adv.* tenderly

Zärtlichkeit *die;* ~, ~en (a) (Zuneigung) tenderness; affection (b) (Liebkosung) caress

Zauber *der;* ~s, ~ (a) (auch fig.) magic; (Bann) [magic] spell (b) (ugs. abwertend: Aufheben) fuss

Zauberei *die;* ~, ~en (a) (das Zaubern) magic (b) (Zaubertrick) magic trick

Zauberer *der;* ~s, ~: magician

zauber·haft 1 *Adj.* enchanting 2 *adv.* enchantingly

Zauberin *die;* ~, ~nen (a) sorceress (b) (Zauberkünstlerin) conjurer

Zauber·künstler *der,* **Zauberkünstlerin** *die* conjurer; magician

zaubern 1 *itr. V.* (a) do magic (b) (Zaubertricks ausführen) do conjuring tricks 2 *tr. V.* (auch fig.) conjure

zaudern *itr. V.* (geh.) delay

Zaum *der;* ~[e]s, Zäume bridle

zäumen *tr. V.* bridle

Zaum·zeug *das* bridle

Zaun *der;* ~[e]s, Zäune fence

Zaun·könig *der* wren

z. B. *Abk.* = zum Beispiel e.g.

ZDF *das;* ~: *Abk.* = Zweites Deutsches Fernsehen Second German Television Channel

Zebra *das;* ~s, ~s zebra

Zebra-streifen *der* zebra crossing (Brit.); pedestrian crossing

Zeche *die;* ~, ~n (a) (Rechnung) bill (Brit.); check (Amer.) (b) (Bergwerk) pit; mine

zechen *itr. V.* (veralt., scherzh.) tipple

Zecke *die;* ~, ~n (Zool.) tick

Zeder *die;* ~, ~n cedar

Zedern·holz *das* cedarwood

Zeh *der;* ~s, ~en, **Zehe** *die;* ~, ~n (a) toe (b) (Knoblauchzehe) clove

Zehen-spitze *die:* auf ~n on tiptoe

zehn *Kardinalz.* ten

Zehn *die;* ~, ~en ten

Zehner *der;* ~s, ~ (a) (ugs.: Geldschein, Münze) ten (b) (ugs.: Autobus) number ten (c) (Math.) ten

---

zehn-fach *Vervielfältigungsz.* tenfold

Zehnfache *das; adj. Dekl.* das ~: ten times as much

zehn-, Zehn-: ~**kampf** *der* (Sport) decathlon; ~**mal** *Adv.* ten times; ~**mark·schein** *der* ten-mark note; ~**pfennig·[brief]marke** *die* ten-pfennig stamp; ~**pfennig·stück** *das* ten-pfennig piece

zehnt... *Ordinalz.* tenth;

zehn-tausend *Kardinalz.* ten thousand

Zehntel *Bruchz.* tenth

Zehntel *das* (schweiz. meist *der*); ~s, ~: tenth

zehntens *Adv.* tenthly

zehren *itr. V.* von etw. ~: live on *or* off sth.

Zeichen *das;* ~s, ~: sign; (Markierung) mark; (Chemie, Math., auf Landkarten usw.) symbol; (Schrift~) character; jmdm. ein ~ geben signal to sb.

Zeichen-: ~**setzung** *die;* ~~: punctuation; ~**sprache** *die* sign language

zeichnen [1] *tr. V.* draw; (fig.) portray ⟨character⟩
[2] *itr. V.* draw

Zeichner *der;* ~s, ~, **Zeichnerin** *die;* ~, ~nen graphic artist; (Technik) draughtsman/-woman

Zeichnung *die;* ~, ~en drawing

zeichnungs-berechtigt *Adj.* with signatory powers *postpos.;* ~ sein have signatory powers

Zeige-finger *der* index finger; forefinger

zeigen [1] *itr. V.* point
[2] *tr. V.* show
[3] *refl. V.* (a) (sich sehen lassen) appear
(b) (sich erweisen) prove to be; es wird sich ~, ...: time will tell ...

Zeiger *der;* ~s, ~: pointer; (Uhrzeiger) hand

Zeile *die;* ~, ~n line; (Reihe) row

zeit *Präp. mit Gen.* ~ meines usw./unseres usw. Lebens all my etc. life/our etc. lives

Zeit *die;* ~, ~en (a) time *no art.;* mit der ~: with *or* in time; (allmählich) gradually; eine ~ lang for a while
(b) (Zeitpunkt) time; alles zu seiner ~: all in good time; *zur ~: at the moment
(c) (Zeit-, Lebensabschnitt) time; period; (Geschichtsabschnitt) age; period
(d) (Sprachw.) tense

zeit-, Zeit-: ~**alter** *das* age; era; ~**arbeit** *die* (Wirtsch.) temporary work; work as a temp (coll.); ~**druck** *der* pressure of time; unter ~druck under pressure; unter ~druck stehen be pressed for time; ~**geist** *der* spirit of the age; ~**gemäß** *Adj.* (modern) up-to-date; (aktuell) topical ⟨theme⟩; contemporary ⟨views⟩; ~**genosse** *der,* ~**genossin** *die* contemporary; ~**genössisch** *Adj.* contemporary; ~**geschehen** *das:* das

[aktuelle] ~geschehen current events *pl.;* ~**geschichte** *die* contemporary history *no art.*

zeitig *Adj., adv.* early

zeit-, Zeit-: ~**karte** *die* (Verkehrsw.) season ticket; *~**lang** ▶ ZEIT A; ~**lebens** *Adv.* all my/his/her etc. life

zeitlich [1] *Adj.* ⟨length, interval⟩ in time; chronological ⟨order, sequence⟩
[2] *adv.* with regard to time

zeit-, Zeit-: ~**los** [1] *Adj.* timeless; classic ⟨fashion, shape⟩; [2] *adv.* timelessly; ~**lupe** *die* slow motion; ~**mangel** *der* lack of time; ~**punkt** *der* moment; ~**raubend** *Adj.* time-consuming; ~**raum** *der* period; ~**schrift** *die* magazine; (bes. wissenschaftlich) journal; periodical; ~**spanne** *die* period

Zeitung *die;* ~, ~en [news]paper

Zeitungs-: ~**ausschnitt** *der* newspaper cutting; ~**notiz** *die* newspaper item

zeit-, Zeit-: ~**unterschied** *der* time difference; ~**verschwendung** *die* waste of time; ~**vertreib** *der;* ~~[e]s, ~~e pastime; zum ~vertreib to pass the time; ~**weilig** [1] *Adj.* temporary; [2] *adv.* temporarily; ~**weise** *Adv.* (gelegentlich) occasionally; (von Zeit zu Zeit) from time to time; ~**wort** *das;* Pl. ~wörter (Sprachw.) verb; ~**zünder** *der* time fuse

Zelle *die;* ~, ~n cell

Zelluloid /tsɛluˈlɔyt/ *das;* ~[e]s celluloid

Zelt *das;* ~[e]s, ~e tent; (Festzelt) marquee; (Zirkuszelt) big top

zelten *itr. V.* camp

Zelt-: ~**lager** *das* camp; ~**plane** *die* tarpaulin

Zement *der;* ~[e]s, ~e cement

Zensur *die;* ~, ~en (a) (Schulw.: Note) mark; grade (Amer.)
(b) (Kontrolle) censorship
(c) (Behörde) censors *pl.*

Zenti-: ~**meter** *der, auch: das* centimetre; ~**meter·maß** *das* [centimetre] measuring tape

Zentner *der;* ~s, ~ (a) metric hundredweight
(b) (österr., schweiz.) ▶ DOPPELZENTNER

zentral [1] *Adj.* central
[2] *adv.* centrally

Zentral-bank *die; Pl.* ~en (Finanzw.) central bank

Zentrale *die;* ~, ~n (a) (zentrale Stelle) head *or* central office; (der Polizei, einer Partei) headquarters *sing. or pl.;* (Funkzentrale) control centre
(b) (Telefonzentrale) [telephone] exchange; (eines Hotels, einer Firma o. Ä.) switchboard

Zentral-: ~**figur** *die* central figure; ~**heizung** *die* central heating; ~**speicher** *der* (DV) main memory

Zentren ▶ ZENTRUM

Zentrifugal-kraft *die* (Physik) centrifugal force

Z

Zentrifuge *die;* ~, ~n centrifuge

Zentrum *das;* ~s, Zentren centre; **im** ~: at the centre; (im Stadtzentrum) in the town/city centre

Zeppelin *der;* ~s, ~e Zeppelin

Zepter *das, auch: der;* ~s, ~: sceptre

zerbeißen *unr. tr. V.* bite in two

zerbersten *unr. itr. V.; mit sein* burst apart

zerbrechen ①*unr. itr. V.; mit sein* break [into pieces]; smash [to pieces]; ⟨*glass*⟩ shatter; (fig.) ⟨*marriage, relationship*⟩ break up
② *unr. tr. V.* break; smash, shatter ⟨*dishes, glass*⟩

zerbrechlich *Adj.* fragile; (fig.) frail

Zerbrechlichkeit *die;* ~: fragility; (fig.) frailty

zerbröckeln ① *itr. V.; mit sein* crumble away
② *tr. V.* break into small pieces

zerdrücken *tr. V.* mash

Zeremonie *die;* ~, ~n ceremony; (fig.) ritual

Zeremoniell *das;* ~s, ~e ceremonial

zerfallen *unr. itr. V.; mit sein* (auch fig.) disintegrate (in + *Akk.,* zu into); ⟨*building*⟩ fall into ruin, decay; ⟨*corpse*⟩ decompose, decay

zerfetzen *tr. V.* rip or tear to pieces; (fig.) tear apart ⟨*body, limb*⟩

zerfleischen *tr. V.* tear ⟨*person, animal*⟩ limb from limb

zerfressen *unr. tr. V.* (a) eat away; ⟨*moth etc.*⟩ eat holes in
(b) (zersetzen) corrode ⟨*metal*⟩; eat away ⟨*bone*⟩

zergehen *unr. itr. V.; mit sein* melt; (in Wasser, im Mund) ⟨*tablet etc.*⟩ dissolve

zerhacken *tr. V.* chop up (zu into)

zerhauen *unr. tr. V.* chop up

zerkleinern *tr. V.* chop up; (zermahlen) crush ⟨*rock etc.*⟩

zerknautschen *tr. V.* (ugs.) crumple

zerknirscht ① *Adj.* remorseful
② *adv.* remorsefully

zerknittern *tr. V.* crease; crumple

zerknüllen *tr. V.* crumple up [into a ball]

zerkratzen *tr. V.* scratch

zerkrümeln *tr. V.* crumble up

zerlegen *tr. V.* (a) dismantle; take to pieces
(b) (zerschneiden) cut up ⟨*animal, meat*⟩; carve ⟨*joint*⟩

zerlumpt *Adj.* ragged ⟨*clothes, person*⟩

zerplatzen *itr. V.; mit sein* burst

Zerr·bild *das* distorted image

zerreiben *unr. tr. V.* crush

zerreißen ① *unr. tr. V.* (a) tear up; (in kleine Stücke) tear to pieces; break ⟨*thread*⟩

(b) (beschädigen) tear ⟨*stocking, trousers, etc.*⟩ (an + *Dat.* on)
② *unr. itr. V.; mit sein* ⟨*thread, string, rope*⟩ break; ⟨*paper, cloth, etc.*⟩ tear

Zerreiß·probe *die* acid test

zerren ① *tr. V.* (a) drag
(b) sich (*Dat.*) einen Muskel/eine Sehne ~: pull a muscle/tendon
② *itr. V.* an etw. (*Dat.*) ~: tug or pull at sth

Zerrung *die;* ~, ~en pulled muscle/tendon

zerrütten *tr. V.* ruin; shatter ⟨*nerves*⟩

zerschellen *itr. V.; mit sein* be dashed or smashed to pieces

zerschlagen ① *unr. tr. V.* smash ⟨*plate, windscreen, etc.*⟩; smash up ⟨*furniture*⟩; (fig.) smash ⟨*spy ring etc.*⟩
② *unr. refl. V.* ⟨*plan, deal*⟩ fall through

zerschmettern *tr. V.* smash; shatter ⟨*glass, leg, bone*⟩

zerschneiden *unr. tr. V.* cut; (in Stücke) cut up; (in zwei Teile) cut in two

zersetzen *tr. V.* corrode ⟨*metal*⟩; decompose ⟨*organism*⟩

zersplittern *itr. V.; mit sein* ⟨*wood, bone*⟩ splinter; ⟨*glass*⟩ shatter

zerspringen *unr. itr. V.; mit sein* shatter; (Sprünge bekommen) crack

zerstäuben *tr. V.* spray

zerstören *tr. V.* destroy; ⟨*hooligan*⟩ smash up, vandalize; (fig.) ruin ⟨*health, life*⟩

Zerstörung *die;* ~, ~en ▶ ZERSTÖREN: destruction; smashing up; vandalization; (fig.) ruin[ation]

Zerstörungs·wut *die* destructive frenzy

zerstreuen ① *tr. V.* scatter; disperse ⟨*crowd*⟩; jmdn./sich ~ (ablenken) take sb.'s/ one's mind off things
② *refl. V.* disperse; (schneller) scatter

zerstreut ① *Adj.* distracted; (vergesslich) absent-minded
② *adv.* absentmindedly

Zerstreuung *die;* ~, ~en (Ablenkung) diversion

zerstückeln *tr. V.* break ⟨*sth.*⟩ up into small pieces; (zerschneiden) cut or chop ⟨*sth.*⟩ up into small pieces; dismember ⟨*corpse*⟩

zerteilen *tr. V.* divide into pieces; (zerschneiden) cut into pieces; cut up

Zertifikat *das;* ~[e]s, ~e certificate

zertrampeln *tr. V.* trample all over ⟨*flower bed etc.*⟩; trample ⟨*child etc.*⟩ underfoot

zertreten *unr. tr. V.* stamp on; stamp out ⟨*cigarette, match*⟩

zertrümmern *tr. V.* smash; smash, shatter ⟨*glass*⟩; smash up ⟨*furniture*⟩; wreck ⟨*car, boat*⟩; reduce ⟨*building*⟩ to ruins

Zerwürfnis *das;* ~ses, ~se (geh.) quarrel; dispute; (Bruch) rift

zerzausen *tr. V.* ruffle; zerzaust aussehen look dishevelled

zetern *itr. V.* scold [shrilly]; (sich beklagen) moan (über + *Akk.* about)

Zettel *der;* ~s, ~: slip *or* piece of paper; (mit einigen Zeilen) note; (Bekanntmachung) notice; (Formular) form; (Kassenzettel) receipt; (Handzettel) leaflet

Zeug *das;* ~[e]s, ~e (a) (ugs.) stuff; **dummes** ~: nonsense; rubbish **(b)** (Kleidung) things *pl.*

Zeuge *der;* ~n, ~n witness

zeugen *tr. V.* procreate; ⟨*man*⟩ father ⟨*child*⟩

Zeugen-aussage *die* testimony

Zeugin *die;* ~, ~nen witness

Zeugnis *das;* ~ses, ~se (a) (Schulw.) report **(b)** (Arbeitszeugnis) reference; testimonial **(c)** (Gutachten) certificate

Zeugung *die;* ~, ~en procreation; (eines Kindes) fathering

zeugungs-fähig *Adj.* fertile

z. Hd. *Abk.* = **zu Händen** attn.

Zicke *die;* ~, ~n (a) ▶ ZIEGE; **(b)** *Pl.* (ugs.: Dummheiten) stupid tricks; monkey business *sing.* (coll.); ~n **machen** mess about; (Schwierigkeiten machen) make trouble

Zickzack *der;* ~[e]s, ~e zigzag

Ziege *die;* ~, ~n goat; (Schimpfwort: Frau) cow (sl. derog.)

Ziegel *der;* ~s, ~ brick; (Dachziegel) tile

Ziegelei *die;* ~, ~en brickworks *sing.*

Ziegel-stein *der* brick

Ziegen-: ~**bock** *der* he- *or* billy goat; ~**käse** *der* goat's cheese

ziehen 1 *unr. tr. V.* (a) pull; (sanfter) draw; (zerren) tug; (schleppen) drag; **etw. nach sich** ~ (fig.) result in sth.; entail sth.
(b) (herausziehen) extract ⟨*tooth*⟩; take out, remove ⟨*stitches*⟩; draw ⟨*cord, sword, pistol*⟩; **den Hut** ~: raise one's hat; **die [Quadrat]wurzel** ~ (Math.) extract the square root
(c) (dehnen) stretch ⟨*elastic etc.*⟩; stretch out ⟨*sheets etc.*⟩
(d) (Gesichtspartien bewegen) make ⟨*face, grimace*⟩
(e) (bei Brettspielen) move ⟨*chessman etc.*⟩
(f) (zeichnen) draw ⟨*line etc.*⟩
(g) (anlegen) dig ⟨*trench*⟩; build ⟨*wall*⟩; erect ⟨*fence*⟩; put up ⟨*washing line*⟩; run, lay ⟨*cable, wires*⟩; draw ⟨*frontier*⟩
(h) (aufziehen) grow ⟨*plants, flowers*⟩; breed ⟨*animals*⟩
2 *unr. itr. V.* (a) (reißen) pull; **an etw.** (*Dat.*) ~: pull on sth.
(b) (funktionieren) ⟨*stove, pipe, chimney*⟩ draw
(c) *mit sein* (umziehen) move (**nach, in** + *Akk.* to)
(d) *mit sein* (gehen) go; (marschieren) march; (umherstreifen) roam; (weggehen) go away; leave; ⟨*fog, clouds*⟩ drift
(e) (saugen) draw; **an einer Zigarette/Pfeife** ~: draw on a cigarette/pipe
(f) ⟨*tea, coffee*⟩ draw
(g) (Kochk.) simmer
(h) *unpers.* **es zieht** there's a draught

3 *unr. refl. V.* ⟨*road*⟩ run, stretch; ⟨*frontier*⟩ run

Zieh-harmonika *die* piano accordion

Ziehung *die;* ~, ~en draw

Ziel *das;* ~[e]s, ~e (a) destination **(b)** (Sport) finish; (Ziellinie) finishing line; (Pferderennen) finishing post **(c)** (Zielscheibe; auch Milit.) target **(d)** (Zweck) aim; goal; **sein** ~ **erreichen** achieve one's objective *or* aim

ziel-bewusst, **ziel-bewußt* 1 *Adj.* determined 2 *adv.* determinedly

zielen *itr. V.* aim (**auf** + *Akk.*, at); (fig.) **auf jmdn./etw.** ~ ⟨*reproach, efforts, etc.*⟩ be aimed at sb./sth.

ziel-, Ziel-: ~**gruppe** *die* target group; ~**los** 1 *Adj.* aimless; 2 *adv.* aimlessly; ~**losigkeit** *die;* ~~: aimlessness; ~**scheibe** *die* (auch fig.) target (*Gen.* for); ~**strebig** 1 *Adj.* (a) purposeful; (b) (energisch) single-minded ⟨*person*⟩; 2 *adv.* (a) purposefully; (b) (energisch) single-mindedly; ~**strebigkeit** *die;* ~~ ▶ ~STREBIG: (a) purposefulness; (b) single-mindedness; ~**wahl** *die* (Fernspr.) one-touch dialling

ziemlich 1 *Adj.* (ugs.) fair, sizeable ⟨*quantity, number*⟩ 2 *adv.* (a) quite; fairly **(b)** (ugs.: fast) pretty well

Zierde *die;* ~, ~n (auch fig.) ornament

zieren *refl. V.* be coy

zierlich 1 *Adj.* dainty; petite, dainty ⟨*woman, figure*⟩ 2 *adv.* daintily

Zierlichkeit *die;* ~: daintiness; (einer Frau, Gestalt) petiteness; daintiness

Zier-pflanze *die* ornamental plant

Ziffer *die;* ~, ~n numeral; (in einer mehrstelligen Zahl) digit; figure

Ziffer-blatt *das* dial; face

zig *unbest. Zahlwort* (ugs.) umpteen (coll.)

Zigarette *die;* ~, ~n cigarette

Zigaretten-werbung *die* cigarette advertising

Zigarillo *der od. das;* ~s, ~s cigarillo; small cigar

Zigarre *die;* ~, ~n cigar

Zigeuner *der;* ~s, ~, **Zigeunerin** *die;* ~, ~nen gypsy

zig-mal *Adv.* (ugs.) umpteen times (coll.)

zig-tausend *unbest. Zahlwort* (ugs.) umpteen thousand (coll.)

Zimmer *das;* ~s, ~: room

Zimmer-mädchen *das* chambermaid

zimmern *tr. V.* make ⟨*shelves etc.*⟩

Zimmer-: ~**suche** *die* room-hunt; ~**vermittlung** *die* accommodation office

zimperlich 1 *Adj.* timid; (leicht angeekelt) squeamish; (prüde) prissy 2 *adv.: s. Adj.:* timidly; squeamishly; prissily

Zimperlichkeit die; ~, ~en (abwertend) timidity; (Neigung zum Ekel) squeamishness; (Prüderie) prissiness

Zimt der; ~[e]s, ~e cinnamon

Zink das; ~[e]s zinc

Zinke die; ~, ~n prong; (eines Kamms) tooth

Zinn das; ~[e]s tin; (Gegenstände) pewter[ware]

Zins der; ~es, ~en interest

Zinses·zins der compound interest

zins·los [1] Adj. interest-free [2] adv. free of interest

Zins·satz der interest rate

Zipfel der; ~s, ~ (einer Decke, eines Tisch-, Handtuchs usw.) corner; (Wurstzipfel, eines Halstuchs) [tail] end

Zipfel·mütze die [long-]pointed cap

zirka Adv. about; approximately

Zirkulation die, ~, ~en circulation

zirkulieren itr. V.; auch mit sein circulate

Zirkus der; ~, ~se (a) circus (b) (ugs.) (Trubel) hustle and bustle; (Krach) to-do

zirpen itr. V. chirp

zischeln tr. V. whisper angrily

zischen itr. V. (a) hiss; ‹hot fat› sizzle (b) mit sein hiss

Zitat das; ~[e]s, ~e quotation (aus from)

zitieren tr., itr. V. (a) quote; (Rechtsspr.) cite (b) (rufen) summon

Zitronat das; ~[e]s candied lemon peel

Zitrone die; ~, ~n lemon

Zitronen-: ~**limonade** die lemonade; ~**presse** die lemon squeezer; ~**saft** der lemon juice

Zitrus·frucht die citrus fruit

zittern itr. V. tremble (vor + Dat. with); (vor Kälte) shiver; (beben) ‹walls, windows› shake; vor jmdm./etw. ~: be terrified of sb./sth.

Zitter·partie die nail-biting affair

zittrig Adj. shaky; doddery ‹old man›

Zitze die; ~, ~n teat

zivil [1] Adj. (a) civilian; non-military ‹purposes›; civil ‹aviation, marriage, law, defence› (b) (annehmbar) decent [2] adv. (annehmbar) decently

Zivil das; ~s civilian clothes pl.

Zivil·bevölkerung die civilian population

Zivilisation /tsiːviliza'tsjoːn/ die; ~, ~en civilization

zivilisieren tr. V. civilize

zivilisiert [1] Adj. civilized [2] adv. in a civilized way

Zivilist der; ~en, ~en, **Zivilistin** die; ~, ~nen civilian

Zivil·kleidung die civilian clothes pl.

Zofe die; ~, ~n (hist.) lady's maid

zoffen refl. V. (ugs.) quarrel (mit with)

zog 1. u. 3. Pers. Sg. Prät. v. ZIEHEN

zögerlich [1] Adj. hesitant; tentative [2] adv. hesitantly; tentatively

zögern itr. V. hesitate; ohne zu ~: without hesitation

Zoll der; ~[e]s, Zölle (a) [customs] duty (b) (Behörde) customs pl.

zoll-, Zoll-: ~**amt** das customs house or office; ~**beamte** der, ~**beamtin** die customs officer; ~**erklärung** die customs declaration; ~**frei** [1] Adj. duty-free; free of duty pred.; [2] adv. free of duty; ~**kontrolle** die customs examination or check; ~**stock** der folding rule

Zone die; ~, ~n zone

Zoo der; ~s, ~s zoo

Zoologe der; ~n, ~n zoologist

Zoologie die; ~: zoology no art.

Zoologin die; ~, ~nen zoologist

zoologisch Adj. zoological; ~er Garten zoological gardens pl.

Zoom das; ~s, ~s (Film, Fot.) zoom

Zoom·objektiv das (Film, Fot.) zoom lens

Zopf der; ~[e]s, Zöpfe plait; (am Hinterkopf) pigtail

Zorn der; ~[e]s anger; (stärker) wrath; fury

zornig [1] Adj. furious [2] adv. furiously

Zote die; ~, ~n dirty joke

zotig [1] Adj. smutty; dirty ‹joke› [2] adv. smuttily

zottig Adj. shaggy

zu [1] Präp. mit Dat. (a) (Richtung) to; zu ... hin towards ...
(b) (zusammen mit) with; zu dem Käse gab es Wein there was wine with the cheese
(c) (Lage) at; zu beiden Seiten on both sides
(d) (zeitlich) at; zu Weihnachten at Christmas
(e) (Art u. Weise) zu meiner Zufriedenheit/ Überraschung to my satisfaction/surprise; (bei Mengenangaben) zu Dutzenden/zweien by the dozen/in twos
(f) (ein Zahlenverhältnis ausdrückend) ein Verhältnis von 3 zu 1 a ratio of 3 to 1
(g) (einen Preis zuordnend) at; for
(h) (Zweck) for
(i) (Ziel, Ergebnis) into; zu etw. werden turn into sth.
(j) (über) about; on; sich zu etw. äußern comment on sth.
(k) (gegenüber) freundlich/hässlich zu jmdm. sein be friendly/nasty to sb.; s. auch ZUM; ZUR;
[2] Adv. (a) (allzu) too; zu sehr/viel too much; zu wenig too little
(b) nachgestellt (Richtung) towards
[3] Konj. (a) mit Infinitiv to; was gibts da zu lachen? what is there to laugh about?
(b) mit 1. Part. die zu erledigende Post the letters pl. to be dealt with

Zubehör das; ~[e]s, ~e od. schweiz. ~den accessories pl.; (eines Staubsaugers, Mixers usw.) attachments pl.; (Ausstattung) equipment

Z

zu|bereiten tr. V. prepare ⟨meal etc.⟩; make up ⟨medicine, ointment⟩; (kochen) cook ⟨fish, meat, etc.⟩

zu|billigen tr. V. jmdm. etw. ~: grant or allow sb. sth.

zu|binden unr. tr. V. tie [up]

zu|blinzeln itr. V. jmdm. ~: wink at sb.

zu|bringen unr. tr. V. spend

Zu·bringer der; ~s, ~ (a) (Straße) access road
  (b) (Verkehrsmittel) shuttle

Zucht die; ~, ~en **(a)** breeding; (von Pflanzen) cultivation; **ein Pferd aus deutscher ~:** a German-bred horse
  (b) (geh.: Disziplin) discipline

züchten tr. V. (auch fig.) breed; cultivate ⟨plants⟩; culture ⟨bacteria, pearls⟩

Züchter der; ~s, ~, **Züchterin** die; ~, ~nen breeder; (von Pflanzen) grower [of new varieties]

züchtigen tr. V. (geh.) beat; thrash; (fig.: bestrafen) castigate

Züchtigung die; ~, ~en (geh.) beating; thrashing; (fig.: Bestrafung) castigation

Züchtung die; ~, ~en **(a)** breeding; (von Pflanzen) cultivation
  (b) (Zuchtergebnis) strain

zucken itr. V.; mit Richtungsangabe mit sein twitch; ⟨body, arm, leg, etc.⟩ jerk; (vor Schreck) start; ⟨flames⟩ flicker; **mit den Achseln/Schultern ~:** shrug one's shoulders

zücken tr. V. draw ⟨sword, dagger, knife⟩

Zucker der; ~s, ~ **(a)** sugar
  (b) (ugs.: Diabetes) diabetes; **~ haben** be a diabetic

zucker-, Zucker-: **~dose** die sugar bowl; **~hut** der sugar loaf; **~krank** Adj. diabetic

zuckern tr. V. sugar

Zucker·wasser das sugar water

Zuckung die; ~, ~en twitch

zu|decken tr. V. cover up; cover [over] ⟨well, ditch⟩; jmdn./sich ~: tuck sb./oneself up

zu|drehen tr. V. **(a)** (abdrehen) turn off
  (b) (zuwenden) jmdm. den Rücken ~: turn one's back on sb.

zu·dringlich ① Adj. pushy (coll.), pushing ⟨person, manner⟩; (sexuell) importunate ⟨person, manner⟩; prying ⟨glance⟩
  ② adv. importunately

Zu·dringlichkeit die; ~, ~en **(a)** pushiness (coll.); (in sexueller Hinsicht) importunate manner
  (b) (Handlung) ~en insistent advances or attentions

zu|drücken tr. V. press shut; push ⟨door⟩ shut; jmdm. die Kehle ~: choke or throttle sb.

zu-einander Adv. to one another

zu-erst Adv. **(a)** first
  (b) (anfangs) at first; to start with

(c) (erstmals) first

Zu·fahrt die **(a)** access [for vehicles]
  (b) (Straße, Weg) access road; (zum Haus) driveway

Zufahrts·straße die access road

Zu·fall der chance; (zufälliges Zusammentreffen von Ereignissen) coincidence; **durch ~:** by chance

zu|fallen unr. itr. V.; mit sein **(a)** ⟨door etc.⟩ slam shut; ⟨eyes⟩ close
  (b) (zukommen) jmdm. ~ ⟨task⟩ fall to sb.; ⟨prize, inheritance⟩ go to sb.

zu·fällig ① Adj. accidental; chance attrib. ⟨meeting, acquaintance⟩; random ⟨selection⟩
  ② adv. by chance; **wissen Sie ~, wie spät es ist?** (ugs.) do you by any chance know the time?

Zufalls·treffer der fluke

zu|fassen itr. V. make a snatch or grab

zu|faxen tr. V. jmdm. etw. ~: fax sth. to sb.; fax sb. sth.

zu|fliegen unr. itr. V.; mit sein (ugs.) ⟨door, window, etc.⟩ slam shut

Zu·flucht die refuge (vor + Dat. from); (vor Unwetter o. Ä.) shelter (vor + Dat. from)

Zufluchts·ort der place of refuge; sanctuary

Zu·fluss, *Zu·fluß der **(a)** (das Zufließen) inflow; supply; (fig.) influx
  (b) (Gewässer) feeder stream/river

zu|flüstern tr. V. jmdm. etw. ~: whisper sth. to sb.

zu·folge Präp. mit Dat.; nachgestellt according to

zu·frieden ① Adj. contented; (befriedigt) satisfied; **mit etw. ~ sein** be satisfied with sth.; **sich ~ geben** be satisfied; **jmdn. ~ stellen** satisfy sb.
  ② adv. contentedly

***zufrieden|geben** ▶ ZUFRIEDEN 1

Zufriedenheit die; ~: contentment; (Befriedigung) satisfaction

***zufrieden|stellen** ▶ ZUFRIEDEN 1

zufriedenstellend ① Adj. satisfactory
  ② adv. satisfactorily

zu|frieren unr. itr. V.; mit sein freeze over

zu|fügen tr. V. jmdm. etw. ~: inflict sth. on sb.; jmdm. Schaden/[ein] Unrecht ~: do sb. harm/an injustice

Zufuhr die; ~: supply; (Material) supplies pl.

zu|führen ① itr. V. auf etw. (Akk.) ~: lead towards sth.
  ② tr. V. **(a)** (zuleiten) einer Sache (Dat.) etw. ~: supply sth. to sth.
  (b) (bringen) einer Partei Mitglieder ~: bring new members to a party

Zug der; ~[e]s, Züge **(a)** (Bahn) train
  (b) (Kolonne) column; (Umzug) procession; (Demonstrationszug) march
  (c) (das Ziehen) pull; traction (Phys.)
  (d) (Vorrichtung) pull
  (e) (Wanderung) migration
  (f) (beim Brettspiel) move ⋯⟩

Z

(g) (Schluck) swig (coll.); mouthful; (großer Schluck) gulp; **das Glas auf einen** *od.* **in einem ~ leeren** empty the glass at one go
(h) (beim Rauchen) pull; drag (coll.)
(i) (Atemzug) breath
(j) (Zugluft; beim Ofen) draught
(k) (Gesichtszug) feature; (Wesenszug) characteristic; trait
Zu·gabe *die* **(a)** (Geschenk) [free] gift
(b) (im Konzert, Theater) encore
Zu·gang *der* **(a)** (Weg, auch fig.) access; (Eingang) entrance
(b) (das Hinzukommen) (von Personen) intake; (von Patienten) admission
(c) (Zuwachs) increase (**von** in)
zu·gange: ~ sein (ugs.) be busy *or* occupied
zugänglich *Adj.* **(a)** accessible; (geöffnet) open
(b) (zur Verfügung stehend) available (*Dat.*, **für** to); (verständlich) accessible (*Dat.*, **für** to)
(c) (aufgeschlossen) approachable ⟨*person*⟩
zu|geben *unr. tr. V.* admit; admit to ⟨*deed, crime*⟩
zu·gegen *Adj.* **~ sein** be present
zu|gehen *unr. itr. V.; mit sein* **(a) auf** jmdn./etw. **~:** approach sb./sth.
(b) jmdm. **~** (zugeschickt werden) be sent to sb.
(c) (ugs.: sich schließen) close; shut; **die Tür geht nicht zu** the door will not shut
zu·gehörig *Adj.* belonging to it/them *postpos., not pred.*
Zugehörigkeit *die;* **~:** belonging (**zu** to)
Zügel *der;* **~s, ~:** rein
zügel·los (fig.) **1** *Adj.* unrestrained; unbridled ⟨*rage, passion*⟩
2 *adv.* without restraint
Zügellosigkeit *die;* **~, ~en** lack of restraint; (Unzüchtigkeit) licentiousness
zügeln *tr. V.* rein [in] ⟨*horse*⟩; (fig.) curb, restrain ⟨*desire etc.*⟩
zu|gesellen *refl. V.* **sich** jmdm./einer Sache **~:** join sb./sth.
Zu·geständnis *das* concession
zu|gestehen *unr. tr. V.* admit; concede
zu·getan *Adj.* jmdm. [herzlich] **~ sein** (geh.) be [very] attached to sb.
zugig *Adj.* draughty, (im Freien) windy ⟨*corner etc.*⟩
zügig **1** *Adj.* speedy; rapid
2 *adv.* speedily; rapidly
Zügigkeit *die;* **~:** speediness; rapidity
zu·gleich *Adv.* at the same time
Zug-: ~luft *die* draught; **~maschine** *die* tractor; (von Sattelzug) tractor [unit]
zu|greifen *unr. itr. V.* **(a)** take hold
(b) (sich bedienen) help oneself
(c) (fleißig arbeiten) [hart *od.* kräftig] **~:** [really] knuckle down to it
Zu·griff *der* (Zugang) access (**auf** + *Akk.* to)
zu·grunde *Adv.* **(a) ~ gehen** (sterben) die

(an + *Dat.* of); (zerstört werden) be destroyed **(an** + *Dat.* by); **~ richten** destroy; (finanziell) ruin ⟨*company, person*⟩
(b) etw. einer Sache (*Dat.*) **~ legen** base sth. on sth.; **etw. liegt einer Sache ~:** sth. is based on sth.
zu|gucken *itr. V.* (ugs.) ▸ ZUSEHEN
zu·gunsten **1** *Präp. mit Gen.* in favour of
2 *Adv.* **~ von** in favour of
zu·gute *Adv.* jmdm. **seine Unerfahrenheit** *usw.* **~ halten** (geh.) make allowances for sb.'s inexperience *etc.;* **sich** (*Dat.*) **etwas/viel auf etw.** (*Akk.*) **~ tun** *od.* **halten** (geh.) be proud/very proud of sth.; **jmdm./einer Sache ~ kommen** stand sb./sth. in good stead
zu|haben *unr. itr. V.* (ugs.) ⟨*shop, office*⟩ be shut *or* closed
zu|halten *unr. tr. V.* hold closed; (nicht öffnen) keep closed
zu|hängen *tr. V.* cover ⟨*window, cage*⟩
zu|hauen (ugs.) **1** *unr. itr. V.* bang *or* slam ⟨*door, window*⟩ shut
2 *unr. itr. V.* hit *or* strike out
Zu·hause *das;* **~s** home
Zuhilfenahme *die;* **~:** utilization; **ohne/ unter ~ einer Sache** (*Gen.*)/**von etw.** without/ with the aid of sth.
zu|hören *itr. V.* jmdm./einer Sache **~:** listen to sb./sth.
Zu·hörer *der*, **Zu·hörerin** *die* listener
zu|kleben *tr. V.* seal ⟨*letter, envelope*⟩
zu|knallen (ugs.) **1** *tr. V.* slam
2 *itr. V.; mit sein* slam
zu|knöpfen *tr. V.* button up
zu|kommen *itr. V.; mit sein* **auf** jmdn. **~:** approach sb.
Zukunft *die;* **~:** future
Zu·lage *die* extra pay *no indef. art.;* additional allowance *no indef. art.*
zu|lassen *unr. tr. V.* **(a)** allow; permit
(b) (teilnehmen lassen) admit
(c) (mit einer Lizenz usw. versehen) **jmdn. als Arzt ~:** register sb. as a doctor
(d) (Kfz-W.) register ⟨*vehicle*⟩
(e) (geschlossen lassen) leave closed *or* shut ⟨*door, window, etc.*⟩
zu·lässig *Adj.* permissible; admissible ⟨*appeal*⟩
Zulassung *die;* **~, ~en** registration
Zu·lauf *der* **[viel] ~ haben** ⟨*shop, restaurant, etc.*⟩ enjoy a large clientele; ⟨*doctor, lawyer*⟩ have a large practice
zu|laufen *unr. itr. V.; mit sein* **(a) auf** jmdn./etw. **~** (auch fig.) run towards sb./sth.
(b) jmdm. **~** ⟨*cat, dog, etc.*⟩ adopt sb. as a new owner
zu|legen *refl. V.* **sich** (*Dat.*) **etw. ~:** get oneself sth.
zu·letzt *Adv.* **(a)** last [of all]
(b) (als Letzter/Letzte/Letztes) last
(c) (fig.: am wenigsten) least of all
(d) (schließlich, am Ende) in the end; **bis ~:** [right up] to *or* until the end

---

*alte Schreibung - vgl. Hinweis auf S. xiv

zu·liebe *Adv.* jmdm./einer Sache ∼: for sb.'s sake/for the sake of sth.

zum *Präp.* + *Art.* (a) = zu dem; (b) (räumlich: Richtung) to the (c) (räumlich: Lage) etw. ∼ **Fenster hinauswerfen** throw sth. out of the window (d) (Hinzufügung) **Milch** ∼ **Tee nehmen** take milk with [one's] tea (e) (zeitlich) at the; **spätestens** ∼ **15. April** by 15 April at the latest (f) (Zweck) ∼ **Spaß/Vergnügen** for fun/pleasure (g) (Folge) ∼ **Ärger seines Vaters** to the annoyance of his father

zu|machen *tr. V.* close; fasten, do up ⟨*dress*⟩; seal ⟨*envelope, letter*⟩; turn off ⟨*tap*⟩; put the top on ⟨*bottle*⟩; (stilllegen) close *or* shut down ⟨*factory, mine, etc.*⟩

zu·mal ① *Adv.* especially; particularly ② *Konj.* especially *or* particularly since

zumindest *Adv.* at least

zu|müllen *tr. V.* (ugs.) etw. ∼: bury sth. under rubbish; **mit etw. zugemüllt werden** be buried under sth.; **von etw. zugemüllt werden** (fig.) be buried under sth.

zu·mute *Adj.* jmdm. ist unbehaglich *usw.* ∼: sb. feels uncomfortable *etc.; mir war nicht danach* ∼: I didn't feel like it *or* in the mood

zu|muten *tr. V.* jmdm. etw. ∼ (abverlangen) expect *or* ask sth. of sb.; (antun) expect sb. to put up with sth.

Zumutung *die;* ∼, ∼en unreasonable demand; **eine** ∼ **sein** be unreasonable

zu·nächst *Adv.* (a) (als erstes) first; (anfangs) at first (b) (im Moment, vorläufig) for the moment

Zunahme *die;* ∼, ∼n increase (*Gen.,* an + *Dat.* in)

Zu·name *der* surname; last name

zünden ① *tr. V.* ignite ⟨*gas, fuel, etc.*⟩; detonate ⟨*bomb, explosive device, etc.*⟩; let off ⟨*fireworks*⟩; fire ⟨*rocket*⟩ ② *itr. V.* ⟨*rocket, engine*⟩ fire; ⟨*lighter, match*⟩ light; ⟨*gas, fuel, explosive*⟩ ignite

Zünd-: ∼holz *das* (bes. südd., österr.) match; ∼schlüssel *der* (Kfz-W.) ignition key

Zündung *die;* ∼, ∼en (a) ▶ ZÜNDEN 1: ignition; detonation; letting off; firing (b) (Kfz-W.: Anlage) ignition

zu|nehmen *unr. itr. V.* (a) increase (an + *Dat.* in); ⟨*moon*⟩ wax (b) (schwerer werden) put on *or* gain weight

Zu·neigung *die* affection

Zunge *die;* ∼, ∼n tongue; [jmdm.] **die** ∼ **herausstrecken** put one's tongue out [at sb.]

zu·nichte *Adj.* etw. ∼ **machen** ruin sth.

zu·oberst *Adv.* [right] on [the] top

zu·pass, *zu·paß: jmdm. ∼ **kommen** come [to sb.] at just the right time *or* moment

zupfen ① *itr. V.* an etw. (*Dat.*) ∼: pluck *or* pull at sth.

② *tr. V.* (a) etw. aus/von *usw.* etw. ∼: pull sth. out of/from *etc.* sth. (b) (auszupfen) pull out; pluck ⟨*eyebrows*⟩ (c) pluck ⟨*string, guitar, tune*⟩ (d) jmdn. am Ärmel ∼: pull *or* tug [at] sb.'s sleeve

zur *Präp.* + *Art.* (a) = zu der; (b) (räumlich, fig.: Richtung) to the; ∼ **Schule/Arbeit gehen** go to school/work (c) (räumlich: Lage) ∼ **Tür hereinkommen** come [in] through the door (d) (Zusammengehörigkeit, Hinzufügung) with the (e) (zeitlich) at the; ∼ **Stunde** at the moment; at present ∼ **Zeit** ▶ ZURZEIT (f) (Zweck) ∼ **Entschuldigung** by way of [an] excuse (g) (Folge) ∼ **vollen Zufriedenheit ihres Chefs** to the complete satisfaction of her boss

zurechnungs·fähig *Adj.* sound of mind *pred.*

zurecht-: ∼|**finden** *unr. refl. V.* find one's way [around]; ∼|**kommen** *unr. itr. V.; mit sein* get on (mit with); ∼|**legen** *tr. V.* lay out [ready]; jmdm. etw. ∼**legen** lay sth. out ready for sb.; ∼|**machen** *tr. V.* (ugs.) (a) (vorbereiten) get ready; (b) (herrichten) do up; (c) jmdn./sich ∼**machen** get sb. ready/get [oneself] ready; (schminken) make sb. up/put on one's make-up; ∼|**weisen** *unr. tr. V.* rebuke; reprimand ⟨*pupil, subordinate, etc.*⟩

zu|reden *itr. V.* jmdm. ∼: persuade sb.; (ermutigen) encourage sb.

Zürich (*das*); ∼s Zurich

zu·rück *Adv.* back; (weiter hinten) behind; **einen Schritt** ∼: a step backwards; ∼! get *or* go back!

zurück-, Zurück-: ∼|**behalten** *unr. tr. V.* (a) keep [back]; retain; (b) be left with ⟨*scar, heart defect, etc.*⟩; ∼|**bekommen** *unr. tr. V.* get back; **Sie bekommen 10 Mark** ∼: you get 10 marks change; ∼|**bleiben** *unr. itr. V.; mit sein* (a) remain; (b) (nicht mithalten) lag behind; (fig.) fall behind; (c) (bleiben) remain; ∼|**blicken** *unr. V.* look back; ∼|**erstatten** *tr. V.* refund; jmdm. etw. ∼**erstatten** refund sth. to sb.; ∼|**fahren** *unr. tr. V.; mit sein* (a) go back; return; (b) (nach hinten fahren) go back[wards]; ∼|**fallen** *unr. itr. V.; mit sein* (a) (in Rückstand geraten) fall behind; (b) (auf einen niedrigeren Rang) drop (auf + *Akk.* to); (c) an jmdn. ∼**fallen** ⟨*property*⟩ revert to sb.; (d) auf jmdn. ∼**fallen** ⟨*actions, behaviour*⟩ reflect [up]on sb.; ∼|**fliegen** *unr. itr. V.; mit sein* fly back; ∼|**führen** *tr. V.* etw. auf etw. (*Akk.*) ∼**führen** attribute sth. to sth.; ∼|**geben** *unr. tr. V.* give back; return; take back ⟨*defective goods*⟩; ∼|**gehen** *unr. itr. V.; mit sein* (a) go back; return; (b) (nach hinten) go back; (c) (verschwinden) disappear; ⟨*swelling, inflammation*⟩ go down; ⟨*pain*⟩ subside; (d) (sich verringern) decrease; ⟨*fever*⟩ abate; ⟨*flood*⟩ subside; ⟨*business*⟩ fall off; (e) (zurückgeschickt werden) be returned *or* sent back; ∼|**greifen** *unr. itr. V.* auf jmdn./etw. ⋯⟩

~**zurückgreifen** fall back on sb./sth.;
~**halten** 1 *unr. tr. V.* (a) jmdn. ~halten
hold sb. back; (von etw. abhalten) stop sb.; (b)
(am Vordringen hindern) keep back ‹*crowd, mob,
etc.*›; (c) (behalten) withhold ‹*news, letter, etc.*›;
(d) (nicht austreten lassen) hold back ‹*tears etc.*›;
2 *unr. refl. V.* restrain *or* control oneself;
sich in einer Diskussion ~halten keep in the
background in a discussion; ~**haltend**
1 *Adj.* (a) reserved; (b) (kühl, reserviert) cool,
restrained ‹*reception, response*›; (c) (Wirtsch.:
schwach) slack ‹*demand*›; 2 *adv.* ‹*behave*›
with reserve *or* restraint; (kühl, reserviert)
coolly; ~**haltung** *die* reserve; (Kühle,
Reserviertheit) coolness; (Wirtsch.) caution;
~**kehren** *itr. V.; mit sein* return; come
back; ~**kommen** *unr. itr. V.; mit sein*
come back; return; (zurückgelangen) get back;
~**kommen auf** (+ *Akk.*) come back to
‹*subject, question, point, etc.*›; ~**kriegen**
tr. V. (ugs.) ▶ ~BEKOMMEN; ~**lassen** *unr.*
tr. V. leave; ~**legen** *tr. V.* (a) put back; (b)
(reservieren) put aside, keep (*Dat.*, **für** for); (c)
(sparen) put away; (d) (hinter sich bringen) cover
‹*distance*›; ~**lehnen** *refl. V.* lean back;
~**nehmen** *unr. tr. V.* (auch fig. widerrufen)
take back; ~**rufen** *unr. tr. V.* (a) call back;
recall ‹*ambassador*›; (b) *auch itr.* (telefonisch)
call *or* (Brit.) ring back; ~**schauen** *itr. V.*
(bes. südd., österr., schweiz.) ▶ ~BLICKEN;
~**schicken** *tr. V.* send back;
~**schlagen** 1 *unr. tr. V.* (a) (nach hinten
schlagen) fold back ‹*cover, hood, etc.*›; turn
down ‹*collar*›; (b) (durch einen Schlag
zurückbefördern) hit back; (mit dem Fuß) kick
back; (c) (zum Rückzug zwingen, abwehren) beat
off, repulse ‹*enemy, attack*›; 2 *unr. itr. V.* (a)
hit back; ‹*enemy*› strike back, retaliate; (b)
mit sein ‹*pendulum*› swing back;
~**schrecken** *regelm.*, (veralt.) *unr., itr. V.,*
mit sein **vor etw.** (*Dat.*) ~schrecken (fig.)
shrink from sth.; **er schreckt vor nichts ~:**
he will stop at nothing; ~**senden** *unr. od.*
regelm. tr. V. (geh.) ▶ ~SCHICKEN; ~**treten**
unr. itr. V.; mit sein step back; (von einem Amt)
resign; step down; ‹*government*› resign; (von
einem Vertrag usw.) withdraw (**von** from); back
out (**von** of); (fig.: in den Hintergrund treten)
become less important; ~**weisen** *unr.*
tr. V. reject ‹*proposal, question, demand,
application, etc.*›; turn down, refuse ‹*offer,
request, help, etc.*›; turn away ‹*petitioner,
unwelcome guest*›; repudiate ‹*accusation,
claim, etc.*›; ~**werfen** *unr. tr. V.* throw
back; reflect ‹*light, sound*›; repulse ‹*enemy*›;
(fig.: in einer Entwicklung) set back; ~**zahlen**
tr. V. pay back; ~**ziehen** 1 *unr. tr. V.* (a)
pull back; draw back ‹*bolt, curtains, one's
hand, etc.*›; (b) (abziehen, zurückbeordern)
withdraw ‹*troops*›; recall ‹*ambassador*›; (c)
(rückgängig machen) withdraw; cancel ‹*order,
instruction*›; 2 *unr. refl. V.* withdraw
Zu·ruf *der* shout

zu|rufen *unr. tr. V.* jmdm. etw. ~: shout sth.
to sb.

zur·zeit *Adv.* at the moment

Zu·sage *die* (a) (auf eine Einladung hin)
acceptance; (auf eine Stellenbewerbung hin) offer
(b) (Versprechen) promise; undertaking

zu|sagen 1 *itr. V.* (a) accept
(b) jmdm. ~ (gefallen) appeal to sb.
2 *tr. V.* promise

zusammen *Adv.* together; ~ **sein**
(zusammenleben) be *or* live together

zusammen-, Zusammen-: ~**arbeit**
die cooperation *no indef. art.;* ~|**arbeiten**
itr. V. cooperate; ~|**binden** *unr. tr. V.* tie
together; ~|**brechen** *unr. itr. V.; mit sein*
collapse; (fig.) ‹*order, communications, system,
telephone network*› break down; ‹*traffic*›
come to a standstill; ~**bruch** *der* collapse;
(fig., auch psychisch, nervlich) breakdown;
~|**drücken** *tr. V.* press together;
~|**fahren** *unr. itr. V.; mit sein*
(zusammenzucken) start; jump; ~|**fallen** *unr.*
itr. V.; mit sein (a) collapse; (b) [zeitlich]
~fallen coincide; ~|**fassen** *tr. V.*
summarize; ~**fassung** *die* summary;
~|**fegen** *tr. V.* (bes. nordd.) sweep together;
~|**fließen** *unr. itr. V.; mit sein* ‹*rivers,
streams*› flow into each other; ~**fluss,**
*~fluß der confluence; ~|**fügen** *tr. V.* fit
together; ~|**führen** *tr. V.* bring together;
~|**gehören** *itr. V.* belong together;
~**gehörig** *Adj.* [closely] related *or*
connected ‹*subjects, problems, etc.*›; matching
attrib. ‹*pieces of tea service, cutlery, etc.*›;
~**gehörigkeit** *die;* ~~~: **ein starkes
Gefühl der ~gehörigkeit** a strong sense of
belonging together;
~**gehörigkeits·gefühl** *das* sense *or*
feeling of belonging together; ~**hang** *der*
connection; (einer Geschichte, Rede) coherence;
(Kontext) context; ~|**hängen** *unr. itr. V.* (a)
be joined [together]; (b) **mit etw.** ~hängen
(fig.) be related to sth.; (durch etw. [mit]
verursacht sein) be the result of sth.;
~|**kehren** *tr. V.* (bes. südd.) sweep together;
~**klappbar** *Adj.* folding; ~|**klappen** *tr.*
V. fold up; ~|**kommen** *unr. itr. V.; mit sein*
(a) meet; **mit jmdm.** ~**kommen** meet sb.; (b)
(zueinanderkommen; auch fig.) get together;
(gleichzeitig auftreten) occur *or* happen together;
~**kunft** *die;* ~~, ~**künfte** meeting;
~|**laufen** *unr. itr. V.; mit sein* (a) ‹*people,
crowd*› gather, congregate; (b) ‹*rivers,
streams*› flow into each other, join up;
~|**leben** *itr. V.* live together; ~**leben** *das*
living together *no art.;* ~|**legen** 1 *tr. V.*
(a) put *or* gather together; (b) (zusammenfalten)
fold [up]; (c) (miteinander verbinden)
amalgamate, merge ‹*classes, departments,
etc.*›; combine ‹*events*›; (d) put ‹*patients,
guests, etc.*› together [in the same room];
2 *itr. V.* club together; ~|**nehmen** 1 *unr.*
tr. V. summon up ‹*courage, strength,
understanding*›; 2 *unr. refl. V.* get *or* take a
grip on oneself; **nimm dich ~!** pull yourself

together!; ∼|**passen** itr. V. go together; ⟨persons⟩ be suited to each other; ∼**prall** der; ∼∼[e]s, ∼∼e collision; ∼|**prallen** itr. V.; mit sein collide (mit with); ∼|**schlagen** unr. tr. V. (verprügeln) beat up; *∼|**sein** ▸ ZUSAMMEN; ∼|**setzen** 1 tr. V. put together; 2 refl. V. (a) sich aus etw. ∼setzen be made up or composed of sth.; (b) (sich zueinander setzen) sit together; (zu einem Gespräch) get together; ∼**setzung** die; ∼∼, ∼∼en (a) putting together; (b) (Aufbau) composition; „∼setzung: ...“ (als Aufschrift auf Medikamentenpackung) 'ingredients: ...'; (c) (Sprachw.) compound; ∼**spiel** das (a) (von Musikern) ensemble playing; (von Darstellern) ensemble acting; (einer Mannschaft) teamwork; (b) (fig.) interplay; ∼|**stehen** unr. itr. V. stand together; ∼|**stellen** tr. V. put together; draw up ⟨list⟩; ∼**stoß** der collision; (fig.) clash (mit with); ∼|**stoßen** unr. itr. V.; mit sein collide (mit with); ∼|**treffen** unr. itr. V.; mit sein (a) meet; mit jmdm. ∼treffen meet sb.; (b) (zeitlich) coincide; ∼|**wachsen** unr. itr. V.; mit sein grow together; join [up]; ⟨bones⟩ knit together; (fig.) ⟨towns⟩ merge into one; ∼|**zählen** tr. V. add up; ∼|**ziehen** unr. itr. V.; mit sein move in together; mit jmdm. ∼ziehen move in with sb.; ∼|**zucken** itr. V.; mit sein start; jump

Zu·satz der addition; (Zugesetztes, Additiv) additive

zusätzlich 1 Adj. additional 2 adv. in addition

zu|schauen itr. V. (südd., österr., schweiz.) ▸ ZUSEHEN

Zu·schauer der, **Zu·schauerin** die; ∼, ∼nen spectator; (im Theater, Kino) member of the audience; (an einer Unfallstelle) onlooker; (Fernsehzuschauer) viewer; **die Zuschauer** (im Theater, Kino) the audience sing.

zu|schicken tr. V. send; jmdm. etw. ∼: send sth. to sb.

zu|schieben unr. tr. V. (a) push ⟨drawer, door⟩ shut (b) (fig.) jmdm. die Schuld ∼: lay the blame on sb.

Zu·schlag der (a) additional or extra charge; (für Nacht-, Feiertagsarbeit usw.) additional or extra payment (b) (Eisenb.) supplement

zu|schlagen 1 unr. tr. V. bang or slam ⟨door, window, etc.⟩ shut; close ⟨book⟩; (heftig) slam ⟨book⟩ shut 2 unr. itr. V. (a) mit sein ⟨door, trap⟩ slam or bang shut (b) (einen Schlag/Schläge führen) throw a blow/blows; (losschlagen) hit or strike out; (fig.) ⟨army, police, murderer⟩ strike

zu|schließen 1 unr. tr. V. lock 2 unr. itr. V. lock up

zu|schnüren tr. V. tie up

zu|schrauben tr. V. screw the lid or top on ⟨jar, flask⟩; screw ⟨lid, top⟩ on

Zu·schrift die letter; (auf eine Anzeige) reply

Zu·schuss, *Zu·schuß der contribution (zu towards)

zu|sehen unr. itr. V. (a) watch; jmdm. [beim Arbeiten usw.] ∼: watch sb. [working etc.] (b) (dafür sorgen) make sure; see to it

zu|senden unr. od. regelm. tr. V. ▸ ZUSCHICKEN

Zu·sendung die sending

zu|spitzen refl. V. become aggravated

zu|sprechen 1 unr. tr. V. (a) er sprach ihr Trost/Mut zu his words gave her comfort/ courage (b) jmdm. ein Erbe usw. ∼: award sb. an inheritance etc.; 2 unr. itr. V. jmdm. ermutigend/tröstend usw. ∼: speak encouragingly/comfortingly to sb.

Zu·stand der (a) condition; (bes. abwertend) state (b) (Stand der Dinge) state of affairs

zu·stande Adv. etw. ∼ bringen [manage to] bring about sth.; ∼ kommen come into being; (geschehen) take place

zu·ständig Adj. appropriate relevant ⟨authority, office, etc.⟩; [für etw.] ∼ sein (verantwortlich) be responsible [for sth.]

Zuständigkeit die; ∼, ∼en (Verantwortlichkeit) responsibility; (Kompetenz) competence

zu|stehen unr. itr. V. etw. steht jmdm. zu sb. is entitled to sth.

zu|steigen unr. itr. V.; mit sein get on; ist noch jemand zugestiegen? (im Bus) ≈ any more fares, please?; (im Zug) ≈ tickets, please!

zu|stellen tr. V. deliver ⟨letter, parcel, etc.⟩

zu|stimmen itr. V. agree; jmdm. [in einem Punkt] ∼: agree with sb. [on a point]; einer Sache (Dat.) ∼: agree to sth.

Zu·stimmung die (Billigung) approval (zu of); (Einverständnis) agreement (zu to, with)

zu|stoßen unr. itr. V.; mit sein jmdm. ∼: happen to sb.•

Zu·tat die ingredient

zu·teil Adv. jmdm./einer Sache ∼ werden (geh.) be granted to sb./sth.

zu|teilen tr. V. jmdm. jmdn./etw. ∼: allot or assign sb./sth. to sb.; jmdm. seine Portion ∼: mete out his/her share to sb.

zu|tragen unr. refl. V. (geh.) occur

zuträglich Adj. healthy ⟨climate⟩; jmdm./ einer Sache ∼ sein be good for sb./sth.; be beneficial to sb.

zu|trauen tr. V. jmdm. etw. ∼: believe sb. [is] capable of [doing] sth.; sich (Dat.) etw. ∼: think one can do or is capable of doing sth.

Zutrauen das; ∼s confidence, trust (zu in)

zutraulich 1 Adj. trusting 2 adv. trustingly

Zutraulichkeit *die;* ~: trust[fulness]

zu|treffen *unr. itr. V.* (a) be correct
(b) **auf** *od.* **für jmdn./etw.** ~: apply to sb./sth.

zutreffend ⟨1⟩ *Adj.* (a) correct; (treffend) accurate
(b) (geltend) applicable; relevant
⟨2⟩ *adv.* correctly

zu|trinken *unr. itr. V.* **jmdm.** ~: raise one's glass and drink to sb.

Zu·tritt *der* entry; admittance; „kein ~", „~ verboten" 'no entry'; 'no admittance'; ~ [zu etw.] haben have access [to sth.]

Zu·tun *das;* ~s: ohne jmds. ~: without sb.'s being involved

zu·unterst *Adv.* right at the bottom

zuverlässig ⟨1⟩ *Adj.* reliable; (verlässlich) dependable ⟨person⟩
⟨2⟩ *adv.* reliably

Zuverlässigkeit *die;* ~: reliability; (Verlässlichkeit) dependability

Zuversicht *die;* ~: confidence

zuversichtlich ⟨1⟩ *Adj.* confident
⟨2⟩ *adv.* confidently

***zuviel** ▸ ZU 2A

zu·vor *Adv.* before

zuvor|kommen *unr. itr. V.; mit sein* (a) **jmdm.** ~: beat sb. to it
(b) **einer Sache** (*Dat.*) ~: anticipate sth.

zuvorkommend ⟨1⟩ *Adj.* obliging; (höflich) courteous
⟨2⟩ *adv.* obligingly; (höflich) courteously

Zuvorkommenheit *die;* ~: courteousness; courtesy

Zuwachs *der;* ~es, Zuwächse increase (*Gen.,* an + *Dat.* in)

Zuwachs·rate *die* (bes. Wirtsch.) growth rate

Zu·wanderer *der,* **Zu·wanderin** *die* immigrant

Zu·wanderung *die* immigration

zu·weilen *Adv.* (geh.) now and again

zu|weisen *unr. tr. V.* **jmdm. etw.** ~: allocate *or* allot sb. sth.

zu|wenden *unr. od. regelm. refl. V.* **sich jmdm./einer Sache** ~ (auch fig.) turn to sb./ sth.

***zu·wenig** ▸ ZU 2A

zuwider *Adj.* **jmdm.** ~ **sein** be repugnant to sb.

zu|winken *itr. V.* **jmdm./einander** ~: wave to sb./one another

zu|zahlen *tr. V.* pay ⟨five marks etc.⟩ extra

zu|ziehen ⟨1⟩ *unr. tr. V.* pull ⟨door⟩ shut; draw ⟨curtain⟩; do up ⟨zip⟩
⟨2⟩ *unr. refl. V.* **sich** (*Dat.*) **eine Krankheit** ~: catch an illness
⟨3⟩ *unr. itr. V.; mit sein* move into the area

Zu·zug *der* influx

zuzüglich *Präp. mit Gen.* plus

zwang *1. u. 3. Pers. Sg. Prät. v.* ZWINGEN

---

*alte Schreibung - vgl. Hinweis auf S. xiv

Zwang *der;* ~[e]s, Zwänge (a) compulsion
(b) (unwiderstehlicher Drang) irresistible urge

zwängen ⟨1⟩ *tr. V.* squeeze
⟨2⟩ *refl. V.* squeeze [oneself]

zwanghaft *Adj.* obsessive

zwanglos ⟨1⟩ *Adj.* (a) informal; casual ⟨behaviour⟩
(b) (unregelmäßig) haphazard ⟨arrangement⟩
⟨2⟩ *adv.* (a) informally
(b) (unregelmäßig) haphazardly ⟨arranged⟩

Zwanglosigkeit *die;* ~: (a) informality
(b) (Unregelmäßigkeit) haphazard *or* casual manner

Zwangs·lage *die* predicament

zwangs·läufig ⟨1⟩ *Adj.* inevitable
⟨2⟩ *adv.* inevitably

zwanzig *Kardinalz.* twenty; *s. auch* ACHTZIG

zwanziger *indekl. Adj.* **die** ~ **Jahre** the twenties

Zwanzig·mark·schein *der* twenty-mark note

zwanzigst... *Ordinalz.* twentieth

zwar *Adv.* (a) admittedly
(b) **und** ~: to be precise

Zweck *der;* ~[e]s, ~e purpose; (Sinn) point; **es hat keinen** ~: it's pointless; **es hat keinen** ~, **das zu tun** there is no point in doing that

zweck-, Zweck-: ~**entfremden** *tr. V.* use for another purpose; ~**los** *Adj.* pointless; ~**losigkeit** *die;* ~~: pointlessness; ~**mäßig** ⟨1⟩ *Adj.* appropriate; expedient ⟨behaviour, action⟩; functional ⟨building, fittings, furniture⟩; ⟨2⟩ *adv.* appropriately ⟨arranged, clothed⟩; ⟨act⟩ expediently; ⟨equip, furnish⟩ functionally; ~**mäßigkeit** *die* appropriateness; (einer Handlung) expediency; (eines Gebäudes) functionalism

zwecks *Präp. mit Gen.* (Papierdt.) for the purpose of

zwei *Kardinalz.* two; *s. auch* ACHT[1]

Zwei *die;* ~, ~en (a) (Zahl) two
(b) (Schulnote) B

zwei-, Zwei-: ~**bettzimmer** *das* twin-bedded room; ~**deutig** ⟨1⟩ *Adj.* ambiguous; (fig.: schlüpfrig) suggestive ⟨remark, joke⟩; ⟨2⟩ *adv.* ambiguously; (fig.) suggestively; ~**deutigkeit** *die;* ~~, ~~en ambiguity; (fig.) suggestiveness; ~**dimensional** ⟨1⟩ *Adj.* two-dimensional; ⟨2⟩ *adv.* two-dimensionally; ~**ein·halb** *Bruchz.* two and a half

zweierlei *indekl. Adj.* (a) *attr.* two sorts *or* kinds of; two different ⟨sizes, kinds, etc.⟩; odd ⟨socks, gloves⟩
(b) *allein stehend* two [different] things

zwei·fach *Vervielfältigungsz.* double; (zweimal) twice

Zwei·fache *das; adj. Dekl.* **das** ~: twice as much

Zweifel *der;* ~s, ~: doubt (**an** + *Dat.* about); **etw. in** ~ **ziehen** question sth.

zweifelhaft *Adj.* (a) doubtful

(b) (fragwürdig) dubious; (suspekt) suspicious
zweifel·los *Adv.* undoubtedly
zweifeln *itr. V.* doubt; **an** jmdm./etw. ~: doubt sb./sth.; have doubts about sb./sth.
zweifels-, Zweifels-: ~**fall** *der* case of doubt; doubtful *or* problematic case; **im** ~**fall[e]** in case of doubt; if in doubt; ~**ohne** *Adv.* undoubtedly; without doubt
Zweig *der;* ~[e]s, ~e [small] branch; (meist ohne Blätter) twig
zwei-, Zwei-: ~**hundert** *Kardinalz.* two hundred; ~**mal** *Adv.* twice; ~**mark·stück** *das* two-mark piece; ~**pfennig·stück** *das* two-pfennig piece; ~**reiher** *der* double-breasted suit/coat/ jacket; ~**schneidig** *Adj.* double-edged; ~**sprachig** ① *Adj.* bilingual; ⟨sign⟩ in two languages; ② *adv.* bilingually; ⟨written⟩ in two languages; ⟨published⟩ in a bilingual edition; ~**spurig** *Adj.* **(a)** two-lane ⟨road⟩; **(b)** two-track ⟨vehicle⟩; **(c)** two- *or* twin-track ⟨recording⟩; ~**stellig** *Adj.* two-figure *attrib.* ⟨number, sum⟩; ~**stöckig** *Adj.* two-storey *attrib.;* ~stöckig sein have two storeys
zweit... *Ordinalz.* second; jeder Zweite every other one; s. *auch* ERST...
zwei·tägig *Adj.* (2 Tage alt) two-day-old *attrib.;* (2 Tage dauernd) two-day stint.
zweit·ältest... *Adj.* second oldest
zwei·tausend *Kardinalz.* two thousand
zweit·best... *Adj.* second best
*zweite·mal ▶ MAL[1]
*zweiten·mal ▶ MAL[1]
zweitens *Adv.* secondly; in the second place
Zweite[r]-Klasse-Abteil *das* second-class compartment
zweit·rangig *Adj.* of secondary importance *postpos.;* (zweitklassig) second-rate
Zweit·stimme *die* second vote
zwei·türig *Adj.* two-door ⟨car⟩
Zweit-: ~**wagen** *der* second car; ~**wohnung** *die* second home
Zwei·zimmer·wohnung *die* two-room flat (Brit.) *or* (Amer.) apartment
Zwerch·fell *das* (Anat.) diaphragm
Zwerg *der;* ~[e]s, ~e dwarf; (Gartenzwerg) gnome
Zwetsche *die;* ~, ~n damson plum
Zwieback *der;* ~[e]s, ~e *od.* Zwiebäcke rusk; (unzählbar) rusks *pl.*
Zwiebel *die;* ~, ~n onion; (Blumenzwiebel) bulb
zwie-, Zwie-: ~**gespräch** *das* (geh.) dialogue; ~**spalt** *der;* ~~[e]s, ~~e *od.* ~spälte [inner] conflict; ~**spältig** *Adj.* conflicting ⟨mood, feelings⟩; discordant ⟨impression⟩; (widersprüchlich) contradictory ⟨nature, attitude, person, etc.⟩
Zwilling *der;* ~s, ~e **(a)** twin **(b)** *Pl.* (Astrol.) Gemini; the Twins; er/sie ist [ein] ~: he/she is a Gemini

Zwillings-: ~**bruder** *der* twin brother; ~**paar** *das* pair of twins; ~**schwester** *die* twin sister
zwingen *unr. tr. V.* force; jmdn. [dazu] ~, etw. zu tun force *or* compel sb. to do sth.
zwingend *Adj.* compelling ⟨reason, logic⟩; conclusive ⟨proof, argument⟩; imperative ⟨necessity⟩
zwinkern *itr. V.* [mit den Augen] ~: blink; (als Zeichen) wink
Zwirn *der;* ~[e]s, ~e [strong] thread *or* yarn
zwischen *Präp. mit Dat./Akk.* between; (mitten unter) among[st]
zwischen-, Zwischen-: ~**durch** /-'-/ *Adv.* (zeitlich) between times; (zwischen zwei Zeitpunkten) in between; (von Zeit zu Zeit) from time to time; ~**fall** *der* incident; ~**landen** *itr. V.; mit sein* in X ~landen land in X on the way; ~**mahlzeit** *die* snack [between meals]; ~**menschlich** ① *Adj.* interpersonal ⟨relations⟩; ⟨contacts⟩ between people; ② *adv.* on a personal level; ~**raum** *der* space; gap; (Lücke) gap; ~**ruf** *der* interruption; viele ~rufe a great deal of heckling *sing.;* ~**wand** *die* dividing wall; partition; ~**zeit** *die* interim
Zwist *der;* ~[e]s, ~e (geh.) strife *no indef. art.;* (Fehde) feud; dispute
Zwistigkeit *die;* ~, ~en (geh.) dispute
zwitschern *itr.* (*auch tr.*) *V.* chirp
Zwitter *der;* ~s, ~ (Biol.) hermaphrodite
zwo *Kardinalz.* (ugs.; bes. zur Verdeutlichung) two
zwölf *Kardinalz.* twelve; ~ Uhr mittags/ nachts [twelve o'clock] midday/midnight; s. *auch* ACHT[1]
zwölft... *Ordinalz.* twelfth; s. *auch* ACHT...
zwölftel *Bruchz.* twelfth; s. *auch* ACHTEL
Zwölftel *das* (schweiz. meist *der*); ~s, ~: twelfth
zwot... *Ordinalz.* (ugs.; bes. zur Verdeutlichung) second
zwotens *Adv.* (ugs.; bes. zur Verdeutlichung) secondly
Zylinder /ts:i'lmdɐ/ *der;* ~s, ~ **(a)** cylinder; **(b)** (Hut) top hat
zylindrisch ① *Adj.* cylindrical ② *adv.* cylindrically
Zyniker *der;* ~s, ~, **Zynikerin** *die;* ~, ~nen cynic
zynisch ① *Adj.* cynical ② *adv.* cynically
Zynismus *der;* ~: cynicism
Zypern (*das*) ~s Cyprus
Zyprer *der;* ~s, ~, **Zyprerin** *die;* ~, ~nen Cypriot
Zypresse *die;* ~, ~n cypress
Zypriot *der;* ~en, ~en, **Zypriotin** *die;* ~, ~nen Cypriot
zypriotisch, zyprisch *Adj.* Cypriot
Zyste *die;* ~, ~n (Med.) cyst

→ Meine Familie und ich haben am Samstagmorgen beschlossen nach Inverness zufahren. Wir wollten in das Kino gehen. Das Kino liegt im Retail Park in Inverness in der Nähe von Culloden. Wir sind mit dem Auto gefahren. Wir sind um viertel nach neun abgefahren. Die Reise hat eine halb Stunde gedauert. Unterwegs hat man gesprochen und Radio gehört. Ich habe Seelöwen auf dem Cromarty gesehen.

→ Wir haben "Signs" in Kino in Inverness gesehen. Der Star heisst "Mel Gibson". Der Film hat um zehn Uhr angefangen. Die Karten haben alles zusammen zwanzig Pfund gekostet. Wir haben Püffnais und Bonbons und Cola gekauft.

→ Das Kino war voll. Wir haben Plätze hinten gefunden.

→ Der Film handelte sich um eine Fremdeninvasion der Welt. Es war ein Sciencefictionfilm. Es hat Spass gemacht. Es war der beste Film den ich je gesehen habe.

→ Der Film hat um halb eins geendet. Kurz vor dem Ende des Filmes, um fünfundzwanzig Minuten nach zwölf, haben wir beschlossen, den Kinosaal zu

• •

verlassen, damit wir die Menge Leute
vermeiden konnten, die direkt zum Ausgang
sich auf den Weg machen würde. Wir
haben das Auto schnell erreicht und
sind eine halbe Stunde später zu Hause
angekommen.

Festtags-, Feiertags- und Brauchtumskalender / Calendar of traditions, festivals, and holidays

January

1	8	15	22	29
2	9	16	23	30
3	10	17	24	31
4	11	18	25	
5	12	19	26	
6	13	20	27	
7	14	21	28	

February

1	8	15	22
2	9	16	23
3	10	17	24
4	11	18	25
5	12	19	26
6	13	20	27
7	14	21	28

March

1	8	15	22	29
2	9	16	23	30
3	10	17	24	31
4	11	18	25	
5	12	19	26	
6	13	20	27	
7	14	21	28	

Festtags-, Feiertags- und Brauchtumskalender

1 Januar New Year's Day Neujahr ist Feiertag und normalerweise ein ruhiger Tag, an dem man sich von den Silvesterfeierlichkeiten erholt.

2 Januar Feiertag in Schottland.

6 Januar Epiphany/Twelfth Night (Heilige Drei Könige) Mit diesem Tag sind keine bestimmten Bräuche verbunden, aber traditionellerweise werden Weihnachtsbaum und Weihnachtsschmuck dann weggeräumt.

25 Januar Burns Night Der Geburtstag des schottischen Dichters Robert Burns, der im 18. Jh. lebte. Schotten in aller Welt treffen sich an diesem Tag zu *Burns Suppers* (Burns-Essen). Dabei wird das Hauptgericht, der *haggis* (eine dem Saumagen ähnliche schottische Spezialität, die mit Innereien, Haferflocken, Zwiebeln und Gewürzen gefüllt ist), unter Dudelsackbegleitung zu Tisch getragen.

2 Februar Groundhog Day An diesem Tag soll einer Wetterregel in den USA zufolge das Murmeltier aus seinem Winterschlaf erwachen. Wenn es dann seinen Schatten sieht (d.h. wenn die Sonne scheint), bedeutet das noch weitere sechs Wochen Winterwetter.

14 Februar St Valentine's day (Valentinstag) Der Tag, an dem Liebespaare sich mit Blumen und Geschenken überraschen. Es ist auch üblich, eine anonyme Valentinskarte an jemanden zu schicken, den man mag.

1 März St David's Day (Davidstag) Der heilige David ist der Schutzheilige von Wales. Viele Waliser tragen an diesem Tag zu seinen Ehren eine Narzisse am Aufschlag.

17 März St. Patrick's Day (Patrickstag) Der heilige Patrick ist der Schutzheilige Irlands. Dieser Tag ist ein Feiertag in Irland und Nordirland und wird auch in den USA begangen. In New York finden Umzüge statt, und Iren in aller Welt treffen sich zu feuchtfröhlichen Feiern mit Musik und Tanz.

1 April April Fool's Day (Erster April) An diesem Tag schickt man sich gegenseitig in den April. Wer einem Aprilscherz zum Opfer fällt, gilt als *April Fool*.

23 April St George's Day (Georgstag) Der heilige Georg ist der Schutzheilige Englands.

4 Juli Independence Day (Unabhängigkeitstag) Ein Feiertag in den USA zum Gedenken an die Unabhängigkeit der Nation. Der Tag wird mit Umzügen, Feuerwerk und Flaggen gefeiert, und man trifft sich zum Essen im Freien oder zu Grillfesten.

12 Oktober Columbus Day (Kolumbustag) Feiertag in den USA zum Gedenken an die Entdeckung der Neuen Welt im Jahre 1492 durch Christoph Kolumbus.

31 Oktober Halloween Am Abend vor Allerheiligen vermischen sich Bräuche christlichen und heidnischen Ursprungs. Kinder verkleiden sich als Gespenster oder Hexen und spielen *Trick or Treat*, d.h. sie klingeln an den Haustüren in der Nachbarschaft und erwarten Süßigkeiten oder Geld. Wer ihnen nichts gibt, dem spielen sie einen Streich. In den USA feiern viele Familien Kostümfeste.

5 November Bonfire Night/Guy Fawkes. Dies ist der Jahrestag des *Gunpowder Plot*, ein von Guy Fawkes und anderen Verschwörern geplanter, aber fehlgeschlagener Sprengstoffanschlag auf die *Houses of Parliament* im Jahre 1605. Es werden Feuerwerke abgebrannt und Freudenfeuer entzündet, in denen eine Puppe, *the Guy*, verbrannt wird.

April

1	8	15	22	29
2	9	16	(23)	30
3	10	17	24	
4	11	18	25	
5	12	19	26	
6	13	20	27	
7	14	21	28	

May

(1)	8	15	22	29
2	9	16	23	30
3	10	17	24	31
4	11	18	25	
5	12	19	26	
6	13	20	27	
7	14	21	28	

June

1	8	15	22	29
2	9	16	23	30
3	10	17	24	
4	11	18	25	
5	12	19	26	
6	13	20	27	
7	14	21	28	

11 November Veterans' Day
Feiertag in den USA, der am Jahrestag des Endes des Ersten Weltkriegs zu Ehren der amerikanischen Veteranen und der Opfer aller Kriege begangen wird.

11 November Remembrance Sunday fällt in Großbritannien auf den Sonntag, der dem 11. November am nächsten liegt. Es ist ein Gedenktag für die Toten beider Weltkriege und späterer Konflikte. Traditionellerweise trägt man eine rote Mohnblume am Aufschlag, und Kränze aus Mohnblumen werden an den Kriegerdenkmälern niedergelegt.

30 November St Andrew's Day (Andreastag) Der heilige Andreas ist der Schutzheilige Schottlands.

24 Dezember Christmas Eve (Heiligabend, Heiliger Abend) Mit Heiligabend sind keine bestimmten Bräuche verbunden, allerdings gehen manche Leute zur Mitternachtsmesse.

25 Dezember Christmas Day (Weihnachten, erster Weihnachtstag) Der erste Weihnachtstag ist Feiertag. Die Bescherung findet morgens unter dem Weihnachtsbaum statt. In vielen Familien in Großbritannien finden die Kinder morgens einen Strumpf mit Süßigkeiten und kleinen Geschenken an ihrem Bett, den der Tradition zufolge *Father Christmas*, auch *Santa Claus* genannt, gebracht hat.

26 Dezember Boxing Day (Zweiter Weihnachtstag) Feiertag in Großbritannien.

26 Dezember St Stephen's Day (Stephanstag) Feiertag in der Republik Irland.

31 Dezember New Year's Eve (Silvester) In Schottland heißt Silvester Hogmanay. Dort ist es üblich, Freunde und Nachbarn um Mitternacht zu besuchen, um bis in die Morgenstunden zu essen und zu trinken. Es gibt den Brauch, ein Stück Kohle als Glücksbringer mitzunehmen.

Bewegliche Feste

Presidents' Day Der dritte Montag im Februar, Feiertag in den USA zu Ehren der Präsidenten George Washington und Abraham Lincoln.

Shrove Tuesday/Pancake Day (Faschingsdienstag) Traditionelles Fest vor dem Beginn der Fastenzeit, an dem man Pfannkuchen mit Zitronensaft und Zucker isst.

Mothers' Day/Mothering Sunday (Muttertag) In Großbritannien und Irland der vierte Sonntag in der Fastenzeit. Mütter bekommen an diesem Tag von ihren Kindern Karten und kleine Geschenke. In den USA (**Mothers' Day**) der zweite Sonntag im Mai.

Good Friday (Karfreitag) Feiertag in Großbritannien und Irland.

Easter Sunday (Ostern, Ostersonntag) Ostern wird von der Kirche gefeiert, und die Kinder bekommen Ostereier aus Schokolade.

Easter Monday (Ostermontag) Feiertag in Großbritannien und Irland.

Early May Bank Holiday Der dem 1 Mai am nächsten gelegene Montag ist in Großbritannien und Irland Feiertag.

Whitsun/Pentecost (Pfingsten) Pfingsten wird von der Kirche gefeiert, aber sonst nicht. Pfingstmontag war früher ein Feiertag in Großbritannien, wurde aber durch den **Spring Bank Holiday / Late May Bank Holiday** (Frühlingsfeiertag) am letzten Montag im Mai ersetzt.

Fathers' Day (Vatertag) Der dritte Sonntag im Juni. Väter bekommen an diesem Tag von ihren Kindern Karten und kleine Geschenke.

Late Summer Bank Holiday/August Bank Holiday Feiertag im Vereinigten Königreich am letzten Montag im August.

Labor Day (Tag der Arbeit) Wird in den USA am ersten Montag im September volksfestartig (u.a. mit Umzügen und Picknicks) begangen.

Thanksgiving In den USA der vierte Donnerstag im November. Ein Tag für Familien- und kirchliche Feiern, dessen Höhepunkt ein großes Essen bildet, bei dem es Truthahn mit Süßkartoffeln und Preiselbeersoße und danach Kürbiskuchen gibt.

Advent (Advent) In Großbritannien haben viele Kinder Advent Calendars (Adventskalender) mit einem Fenster für jeden Tag vom 1. bis zum 25. Dezember. Jedes Fenster, das geöffnet wird, zeigt ein weihnachtliches Bild.

Kalender / Calendar

Calendar of traditions, festivals, and holidays

July

1	8	15	22	29
2	9	16	23	30
3	10	17	24	31
(4)	11	18	25	
5	12	19	26	
6	13	20	27	
7	14	21	28	

August

1	8	15	22	29
2	9	16	23	30
3	10	17	24	31
4	11	18	25	
5	12	19	26	
6	13	20	27	
7	14	21	28	

September

1	8	15	22	29
2	9	16	23	30
3	10	17	24	
4	11	18	25	
5	12	19	26	
6	13	20	27	
7	14	21	28	

Feast days and festivals in German-speaking countries

1 January Neujahr New Year's Day is always a public holiday and tends to be a quiet day when people are recovering from the *Silvester* celebrations.

6 January Heilige Drei Könige Epiphany or Twelfth Night is a public holiday in Austria and some parts of southern Germany. In some areas, children dressed up as the Three Kings go from house to house to bless the homes for the coming year and collect money for charity. This is also traditionally the day when the Christmas tree is taken down.

2 February Mariä Lichtmess Candlemas is celebrated in the Catholic church but is not a public holiday.

1 April Erster April April Fool's Day is the time to make an April fool of your family and friends (*jdn. in den April schicken*) or to play an April fool trick (*Aprilscherz*).

1 May Erster Mai May Day is a public holiday in Germany, Austria and Switzerland. It is celebrated by trade unions as *Labour Day*, often with rallies and demonstrations. Many people simply use the day for a family outing or picnic, and in rural areas maypoles are put up in the villages.

3 October Tag der deutschen Einheit Germany's national holiday, the *Day of German Unity* commemorates German reunification on 3 October 1990.

26 October Nationalfeiertag Austria's national holiday.

31 October Reformationstag Reformation Day is a public holiday in some mainly Protestant parts of Germany and commemorates the Reformation.

1 November Allerheiligen All Saints' Day is a public holiday in Catholic parts of Germany and Austria.

2 November Allerseelen All Souls' Day is the day when Catholics remember their dead by visiting the cemeteries to pray and place wreaths, flowers and lighted candles on the graves. This is often done on 1 November as *Allerseelen* is not a public holiday.

11 November Martinstag St Martin's day is not a public holiday, but in Catholic areas the charitable Saint is commemorated with processions where children carry lanterns and sing songs. Traditional food includes the *Martinsgans* (roast goose) and *Martinsbrezel* (a kind of soft pretzel).

6 December Nikolaustag On the eve of St. Nicholas' Day, children put out their boots in the hope of finding presents and fruit, nuts and sweets in the morning. The Saint may also turn up in person, looking much like Santa Claus or Father Christmas.

24 December Heiligabend Christmas Eve is not a public holiday, but many firms and shops close early for the Christmas period. This is the day when traditionally the Christmas tree is put up and decorated. Christmas presents are given in the evening, and many people attend midnight mass.

25 December Erster Weihnachtstag Christmas Day is a public holiday in Germany, Austria and Switzerland. It tends to be a quiet day for family get-togethers, often with a traditional lunch of goose or carp.

26 December Zweiter Weihnachtstag Boxing Day is a public holiday in Germany, Austria and Switzerland. In Austria and Switzerland it is called *Stephanstag* (St Stephen's day).

31 December Silvester New Year's Eve is not a bank holiday, but firms and shops tend to close early. A party, or at least a meal with friends, is a must for *Silvester* evening. At midnight, the new year is toasted in Sekt (German sparkling wine), and everybody goes outside to admire the fireworks.

Calendar of traditions, festivals, and holidays

• •

October

1	8	15	22	29
2	9	16	23	30
◇3	10	17	24	□31
4	11	18	25	
5	○12	19	◇26	
6	13	20	27	
7	14	21	28	

November

◇1	8	15	22	29
◇2	9	16	23	○30
3	10	17	24	
4	□11	18	25	
○5	12	19	26	
6	13	20	27	
7	14	21	28	

December

1	8	15	22	29
2	9	16	23	30
3	10	17	□24	□31
4	11	18	□25	
5	12	19	□26	
◇6	13	20	27	
7	14	21	28	

Kalender / Calendar

Movable Feasts and festivals

Rosenmontag The day before Shrove Tuesday is not an official public holiday but many people, especially in the Rhineland, get the day off work or school to take part in the *Karneval* celebrations, which involve masked balls, fancy-dress parties and parades. The street parades in Düsseldorf, Cologne, Mainz and other cities are attended by thousands of revellers and shown live on television.

Faschingsdienstag Shrove Tuesday is the final day of *Fasching* (Carnival) in Southern Germany, with processions and fancy dress parties similar to Rosenmontag in the Northwest. In the far south, ancient customs to drive out the winter with bells and drums survive. The pre-Lent carnival in and around the Rhineland is called Karneval. Almost every town has its own carnival prince and princess, and organizes a street parade with decorated floats, which is watched by thousands of revellers in fancy dress.

Aschermittwoch Ash Wednesday marks the end of the carnival season and the beginning of Lent. This day is celebrated in the Catholic church but is not a public holiday.

Karfreitag Good Friday is a public holiday and generally a very quiet day. Catholics traditionally eat fish on this day.

Ostern Easter traditions include hiding Easter eggs (often dyed hardboiled eggs, or the chocolate variety) in the garden for the children. The *Osterhase* (Easter bunny) is supposed to have brought them. Ostermontag (Easter Monday) is also a public holiday.

Weißer Sonntag (Sunday after Easter) In the Catholic Church, first communion is traditionally taken on this Sunday.

Muttertag (second Sunday in May) On Mothers' day, children of all ages give their mothers small gifts, cards or flowers.

Christi Himmelfahrt (40 days after Easter) Ascension day is a public holiday in Germany, Austria and Switzerland. This day is also Fathers' day when fathers traditionally go out on daytrips or pub crawls.

Pfingsten (seventh Sunday after Easter) As *Pfingstmontag* (Whit Monday) is also a public holiday in Germany, Austria and Switzerland, Whitsun is a popular time to have a long weekend away.

Fronleichnam (second Thursday after Whitsun) Corpus Christi is a public holiday in Austria and in parts of Germany and Switzerland. In Catholic areas, processions and open-air masses are held.

Buß- und Bettag (third Wednesday in November, 11 days before the first Advent Sunday) This 'day of repentance and prayer' is a public holiday only in some parts of Germany.

Volkstrauertag (second Sunday before the beginning of Advent) In Germany, this is a national day of mourning to commemorate the dead of both world wars, and the victims of the Nazis.

Totensonntag (last Sunday before the beginning of Advent) Protestants remember their dead on this day.

Advent The four weeks leading up to Christmas, beginning with the 1. Adventssonntag (first Sunday in Advent) in late November or early December, still have a special significance in Germany, even for non-religious people. An Advent wreath with four candles is present in almost every German household during this time, and on each Sunday of Advent one more candle is lit.

□ Celebrated in German and English-speaking countries / In deutsch- und englischsprachigen Ländern begangene Tage

◇ Celebrated in German-speaking countries / In deutschsprachigen Ländern begangene Tage

○ Celebrated in English-speaking countries / In englischsprachigen Ländern begangene Tage

Abc der britischen und amerikanischen Kultur

ABC - American Broadcasting Company
Eine der größten amerikanischen Fernsehanstalten, gehört jetzt zur
Walt Disney Company.

ACT - American College Test
Ein Test, den Studierende in fast allen Staaten der USA bestehen müssen, um an
einem **College** zugelassen zu werden. Der Test wird normalerweise am Ende der
HIGH SCHOOL abgelegt und deckt eine Reihe von Kernfächern einschließlich
Englisch und Mathematik ab.

African American
Dies ist in den USA z.Z. der gebräuchlichste Begriff für Amerikaner afrikanischer
Abstammung.

Afro-Caribbean
Dies ist in Großbritannien und den USA zur Zeit der gebräuchlichste Begriff
für Menschen afrikanischer Herkunft, die in der Karibik leben oder aus der
Karibik kommen.

A level - Advanced level
Ein Examen, das von vielen Schülern in England und Wales, üblicherweise
im letzten Jahr der weiterführenden Schule, abgelegt wird. Die Abschlussnoten
(**grades**) werden in jedem Fach einzeln vergeben. Schüler, die ein Hochschulstudium
(**higher education**) anstreben, absolvieren in der Regel 3 bis 4 *A levels* und werden
von den Universitäten und anderen Institutionen entsprechend ihren
Abschlussnoten, besonders in den für ihr Studienfach relevanten Fächern,
ausgewählt.

Alliance Party (Northern Ireland)
Eine politische Partei in Nordirland, deren Ziel es ist, ein Ende des Konflikts
zwischen extremen religiösen Gruppen zu bewirken, indem sie Menschen mit
gemäßigten Ansichten beider Seiten zusammenführt.

American Indian ▶ NATIVE AMERICAN.

AS level - Advanced Supplementary level
Ein Abschlussexamen in einem bestimmten Fach, das in der Regel im letzten Jahr
der **Secondary School** von vielen Schülern in England und Wales abgelegt wird.
Ein *AS level* liegt zwischen einem **GCSE** und einem **A LEVEL** und zählt für den
Zugang zur Universität halb so viele Punkte wie ein *A level*. Viele Studierende legen
eine Mischung aus *A levels* und *AS levels* ab.

Asian American
Dies ist z.Z. der gebräuchlichste Begriff für einen Amerikaner asiatischer, besonders
fernöstlicher Abstammung.

BBC - British Broadcasting Corporation
Eine der wichtigsten britischen Fernseh- und Rundfunkanstalten. Sie erhielt 1927 die
Royal Charter, das königliche Privileg, finanziert sich über Fernsehgebühren, nicht
über Werbeeinnahmen, und ist zur unparteilichen Berichterstattung verpflichtet.

bed and breakfast
Überall in Großbritannien sieht man Schilder mit der Aufschrift *Bed & Breakfast* oder **B&B**. Sie weisen auf Privathäuser hin, die Unterkunft zu meist recht niedrigen Preisen anbieten, wobei im Zimmerpreis das Frühstück mit eingeschlossen ist. Die Gäste erhalten normalerweise ein üppiges traditionelles Frühstück mit Fruchtsaft, Müsli, warmem Essen - dazu gehört vor allem Spiegelei mit Speck - und Toast und Marmelade.

Big Issue
Eine Zeitung, die von Obdachlosen in vielen größeren und kleineren Städten in Großbritannien verkauft wird. Die Artikel haben oft ein sehr gutes Niveau, sie behandeln hauptsächlich soziale Themen oder Aspekte der Stadtkultur. Die Verkäufer kaufen die Zeitungen von einer zentralen Stelle und verkaufen sie zu einem festgelegten Preis. Den Gewinn dürfen sie behalten in der Hoffnung, dass sie dann leben können, ohne betteln zu müssen.

broadsheet
Ein Zeitung in Großbritannien, die auf großen Zeitungsbögen gedruckt wird, im Gegensatz zu den **TABLOIDS** , der Boulevardpresse, die auf halb so großen Bögen hergestellt wird. Das *broadsheet*-Format wird normalerweise mit der *quality press* (seriösen Presse) assoziiert, mit Zeitungen wie z.B. **THE GUARDIAN** und **THE TIMES**, während die meisten Zeitungen der *popular press* (Boulevardpresse), wie z.B. **The Mirror** und **The Sun** das *tabloid*-Format benutzen.

busking
Dies ist der informelle britische Ausdruck für das Musizieren an öffentlichen Plätzen, mit dem Zweck Geld einzunehmen. In den großen britischen Städten gibt es viele *buskers* (Straßenmusikanten), oft auf hohem Niveau. An einigen Plätzen ist es verboten, Straßenmusik zu machen, z.B. in der Londoner U-Bahn.

Cabinet
Das britische Kabinett ist ein Komitee von etwa 20 *Ministers* (Ministern), die vom Prime Minister (**Premierminister**) berufen werden. Jedes Mitglied ist für ein bestimmtes politisches Ressort verantwortlich und das Kabinett als Ganzes entscheidet über die Regierungspolitik. Das **shadow cabinet** (Schattenkabinett) wird vom Oppositionsführer berufen, so dass es im Fall eines Regierungswechsels, wie z.B. nach einer **general election** (Wahl), die Regierungsgeschäfte übernehmen kann.

Cambridge Certificate
Ein Sprachzertifikat über das Leistungsniveau von Lernenden, die Englisch als Fremdsprache studieren. Die Examen werden von der Universität Cambridge auf drei verschiedenen Niveaus abgenommen. Auf dem niedrigeren Niveau führt das Examen zum *First Certificate in English*, auf dem mittleren Niveau zum *Advanced Certificate in English*, und auf dem fortgeschrittenen Niveau führt es zum *Certificate of Proficiency in English*. Viele Sprachschulen innerhalb und außerhalb Großbritanniens bereiten Studierende auf diese Examen vor.

Capitol
Der Sitz des amerikanischen **CONGRESS** auf dem Capitol Hill in Washington.

CBS - Columbia Broadcasting System
Neben **ABC** und **NBC** eine der drei ersten amerikanischen nationalen Rundfunkgesellschaften.

Kultur

Ceefax

Ein Informationsservice, der in Großbritannien von der **BBC** angeboten wird und eine große Bandbreite abdeckt, von Wetterberichten bis zu Aktienkursen. Die Informationen können über den Fernseher abgerufen werden und erscheinen auf dem Bildschirm.

Channel Five

Ein britischer privater Fernsehsender, der populäre leichte Unterhaltung ausstrahlt.

Channel Four

Ein britischer privater Fernsehsender mit einem umfangreichen sozialen und kulturellen Programm. Er hat ein Renommee für exzellente Dokumentationen und für die Berichterstattung über kulturelle und künstlerische Ereignisse.

City

The City of London ist das Gebiet innerhalb der alten Stadtgrenzen von London. Heute ist es das Geschäfts- und Finanzzentrum Londons und viele Banken und andere Geldinstitute haben dort ihre Hauptstellen. Wenn Leute über die *City* sprechen, beziehen sie sich oft auf diese Institutionen und nicht auf den Ort.

City Technology College (CTC)

Eine Form der *secondary school* in Großbritannien, die gemeinsam von der Regierung und privaten Unternehmen eingerichtet wurde. Diese Colleges liegen in den Stadtzentren und legen besonderen Wert auf die Vermittlung von Mathematik, Naturwissenschaften und Technologie.

CNN - Cable News Network

Eine amerikanische Fernsehgesellschaft, die Nachrichten und Informationsprogramme 24 Stunden am Tag über Satellit überträgt.

college of further education (CFE)

Ein Collegetyp in Großbritannien, der Personen über 16 Jahren Voll- und Teilzeitkurse anbietet. Dazu gehören Vorbereitungskurse für **GCSE** und **A LEVELS** sowie Tages- und Abendkurse in diversen Fächern wie Fremdsprachen, Informatik, bis hin zu Töpferei und Autowartung.

community college

Ein Collegetyp in den Vereinigten Staaten, der eine Vielzahl von praktischen Kursen für die Allgemeinheit anbietet.

community service

In Großbritannien gibt es auf kommunaler Ebene ehrenamtliche Helfer, die z.B. Alte oder Behinderte pflegen oder Reparaturen an Gemeindezentren und anderen Einrichtungen ausführen. Diese Art von Sozialdienst wird manchmal auch Straftätern auferlegt, als Alternative zu einer Haftstrafe.

comprehensive school

Einer Gesamtschule entsprechende große staatliche weiterführende Schule in Großbritannien für Kinder aller Leistungsstufen im Alter von 11 bis 18 Jahren, die in einer bestimmten Gegend leben.

Congress

Die nationale gesetzgebende Versammlung in den Vereinigten Staaten. Der Kongress tritt im **CAPITOL** zusammen und besteht aus zwei Kammern, **SENATE** (Senat) und **HOUSE OF REPRESENTATIVES** (Repräsentantenhaus). Die Funktion des Kongresses ist es, Gesetze zu erlassen. Jedes Gesetz muss von beiden Kammern angenommen und anschließend vom **PRESIDENT** (Präsident) verabschiedet werden.

Conservative Party

Eine der Volksparteien Großbritanniens. Es ist eine Partei der politischen Rechten, die für Kapitalismus, freie Marktwirtschaft und private Industrie und Dienstleistung steht. Sie entwickelte sich etwa 1830 aus der alten *Tory Party* und wird auch heute noch häufig so genannt. Die Farbe der Partei ist Blau.

council

Gewählte Versammlung, die für die Verwaltung eines bestimmten Gebietes in Großbritannien zuständig ist. Dieses Gebiet kann eine **COUNTY** (Grafschaft) sein, Teil eines Landkreises, eine Stadt oder Teil einer größeren Stadt. Der *council* ist dafür verantwortlich, die Straßen und Gemeinschaftseinrichtungen instand zu halten, und stellt eine breite Palette öffentlicher Dienstleistungen bereit.

council house

Ein Haus in Großbritannien, das vom lokalen **COUNCIL** zu einem vergleichsweise niedrigen Preis vermietet wird. Diese Häuser und **council flats** (Sozialwohnungen) sind oft im Besitz des *councils*. Allerdings wurden ab 1980 viele dieser Wohnungen an ihre Bewohner verkauft.

council tax

Eine Steuer, die jeder Haushalt in Großbritannien an die lokale oder kommunale Verwaltung entrichten muss. Die Höhe der *council tax* berechnet sich aus dem Schätzwert des Hauses bzw. der Wohnung sowie aus der Anzahl der Personen im Haushalt.

county

Ein Verwaltungsbezirk in vielen Teilen Großbritanniens. Die *counties* bilden die Hauptverwaltungseinheiten und viele haben noch die alten Grenzen. Allerdings wurden in den letzten Jahrzehnten viele Grenzen und Namen geändert und die Bezeichnung *county* wird nicht mehr immer verwendet. In Schottland werden die Hauptverwaltungsbezirke jetzt **REGIONS** genannt.

Daily Telegraph - The Daily Telegraph

Eine britische überregionale Tageszeitung. Der *Sunday Telegraph* wird von demselben Verlagshaus publiziert. Die Zeitung zählt zu den **BROADSHEET**-Zeitungen und damit zur seriösen Presse. Sie vertritt Ansichten der politischen Rechten und wurde in der Vergangenheit durch die Äußerung von sehr rechten Positionen bekannt. Traditionell vertritt sie die Interessen der **CONSERVATIVE PARTY**, äußert jedoch auch oft Kritik an der konservativen Politik.

Democratic Party

Neben der **REPUBLICAN PARTY** eine der zwei großen politischen Parteien in den USA. Die demokratische Partei gilt als die liberalere, besonders in Fragen der Gesellschaftspolitik. Aus diesem Grund erhält sie viel Unterstützung aus den Reihen der Minderheitengruppierungen und Gewerkschaften.

Kultur

Downing Street

Der Name einer Straße in Westminster im Zentrum von London. Das Haus mit der Nummer 10 in der Downing Street ist der offizielle Sitz des Premierministers und Nummer 11 der des Finanzministers. Unter Journalisten ist der Ausdruck *Downing Street* oder *Number 10* gebräuchlich, wenn vom Amtssitz des Premierministers die Rede ist.

elementary school

Die Grundschule in den Vereinigten Staaten. Sie unterrichtet Kinder im Alter von sechs bis zwölf oder dreizehn Jahren. Diese Schulstufe wird auch als *grade school* oder *primary school* bezeichnet.

first school ▶ PRIMARY SCHOOL.

football pools

Eine dem Fußballtoto ähnliche beliebte Wettform in Großbritannien. Wer mitspielen will, lässt sich einmal wöchentlich *pools coupons* von einer der Toto-Gesellschaften zusenden. Man füllt die Wettscheine aus, indem man die Fußballergebnisse der nächsten Woche in Großbritannien vorhersagt. Für jedes Ergebnis wird gezahlt. Der Gewinn, der sich aus diesen Einzahlungen zusammensetzt, wird an diejenigen ausgezahlt, die dem Resultat am nächsten lagen. Dies kann bedeuten, dass unter Umständen eine sehr hohe Summe an eine einzelne Person ausgezahlt wird.

further education

In Großbritannien bedeutet *further education* in der Regel jede Form der Fortbildung für Personen über 16 Jahren, mit Ausnahme der Hochschulausbildung, die als **higher education** bezeichnet wird. In den Vereinigten Staaten schließt jedoch der Ausdruck *further education* auch ein Hochschulstudium mit ein.

Gaelic

Die alte Sprache der Kelten, wie sie noch von einigen Schotten und Iren gesprochen wird. Obgleich es beträchtliche Unterschiede zwischen dem schottischen und dem irischen Gälisch gibt, können die Sprecher einander verstehen. Das schottische Gälisch wird nur von etwa 40.000 Menschen im schottischen Hochland und auf den westschottischen Inseln gesprochen. Irisches Gälisch, das auch **Erse** oder einfach **Irish** genannt wird, erlebte in den letzten 50 Jahren eine bemerkenswerte Wiederbelebung. Es wird nun von vielen gesprochen und an Schulen als offizielle Sprache neben Englisch unterrichtet.

GCSE

Ein Examen in einem bestimmten Fach, das gewöhnlich im 5. Schuljahr von den meisten Schülern in England und Wales abgelegt wird. Die Abschlussnoten (**grades**) werden in jedem Fach einzeln vergeben. Das *GCSE* können Schüler aller Befähigungen ablegen, die meisten tun dies in einer Reihe von Fächern. Schüler, die danach **A LEVELS** machen wollen, brauchen eine bestimmte Anzahl von *GCSEs*, um dafür zugelassen zu werden. Es ist möglich, *GCSEs* mit den eher beruflich orientierten **GNVQ**s zu kombinieren.

GNVQ - General National Vocational Qualification

Ein Examen in einem bestimmten Fach, das gewöhnlich im 5. Schuljahr von den meisten Schülern in England und Wales abgelegt wird. *GNVQs* wurden 1992 als Alternative zu den **GCSEs** in einer Reihe von berufs- oder praxisorientierten Fächern eingeführt. Ihr Ziel ist es, Schüler auf das Berufsleben vorzubereiten. Viele Schüler legen ihre Examen mit einer Mischung aus *GNVQs* und **GCSEs** ab.

. . . .

GP - general practitioner

Ein *GP*, oft auch **family doctor** (Hausarzt) genannt, ist ein Arzt für
Allgemeinmedizin in Großbritannien. In einer Gemeinschaftspraxis arbeiten meist
mehrere *GPs*. Die Patienten der Praxis können den behandelnden Arzt frei wählen.
Durch den **NATIONAL HEALTH SERVICE** müssen Patienten ihren Arzt nicht
bezahlen, die Praxis wird direkt oder indirekt aus staatlichen Geldern finanziert.
Wenn nötig, kann ein *GP* einen Patienten zu einem Spezialisten überweisen oder ins
Krankenhaus einweisen. Die Praxis wird **surgery** genannt.

graduate school

Das Seminar einer Universität in den USA, das Kurse und Betreuung für graduierte
Studierende organisiert, die ihr Studium und/oder ihre Forschung nach dem 1.
Examen (nach ungefähr 3-4 Jahren Universitätsstudium) fortsetzen wollen.

grammar school

Eine dem Gymnasium vergleichbare Form der weiterführenden Schule in einigen
Gebieten Englands und Wales' für Schüler zwischen 11 und 18 Jahren. Schüler im
Alter von 11 oder 12 Jahren werden nach bestandener Aufnahmeprüfung zugelassen.
Grammar schools wurden seit 1965 größtenteils von **COMPREHENSIVE SCHOOLS**
ersetzt. In den USA ist *grammar school* ein anderer Name für **ELEMENTARY
SCHOOL**.

grant-maintained school

Eine Form der weiterführenden Schule in England und Wales, die von der Regierung
in London und nicht von der lokalen Regierung finanziert wird.

green card

Ein offizielles Dokument, das nichtamerikanische Bürger zur Erwerbstätigkeit in
den USA berechtigt. Die *green card* braucht jeder, der beabsichtigt, eine feste Stelle
in den USA anzutreten.

Green Party

Eine politische Partei in Großbritannien, die sich dem Umweltschutz verpflichtet
und Kritik an Industrien, Transportmitteln und Energiequellen übt, die sie für
umweltschädlich hält. Die Grünen sprechen sich gegen die Nutzung von
Atomenergie aus.

Greyhound bus

Ein Bus der *Greyhound Lines Company*, der größten Busgesellschaft in den
Vereinigten Staaten. *Greyhound*-Busse verkehren zwischen größeren und kleineren
Städten in den gesamten Vereinigten Staaten und sind vor allem bei jungen Leuten
und Touristen beliebt, die oft lange Strecken mit ihnen zurücklegen.

Guardian - The Guardian

Eine britische überregionale Tageszeitung. Der *Guardian* ist eine **BROADSHEET**-
Zeitung und zählt zur seriösen Presse. Politisch steht der Guardian links von der
Mitte, er berichtet ausführlich über soziale und kulturelle Themen.

Guardian Angels

Eine Jugendorganisation in den USA, die gegründet wurde, um Menschen vor
Verbrechen zu schützen. Ihre Mitglieder tragen rote Kappen und T-Shirts mit dem
Motto '*Dare to Care*' ('Trau dich zu helfen'). Sie arbeiten mit der Polizei zusammen
und sind unbewaffnet.

Kultur

• •

heritage centre

Ein Museumstyp in Großbritannien, der einem bestimmten Thema wie z.B. der Geschichte der lokalen Architektur oder einer bestimmten traditionellen Industrie oder Aktivität gewidmet ist. *Heritage centres* werden manchmal um alte Gebäude herum entwickelt.

high school

Eine weiterführende Schule in den USA, normalerweise für Schüler von vierzehn bis achtzehn Jahren. Auch in Großbritannien werden einige weiterführende Schulen als *high schools* bezeichnet.

House of Commons

Eines der zwei Häuser der britischen **HOUSES OF PARLIAMENT**, das Unterhaus des britischen Parlaments. Die gewählten **MEMBERS OF PARLIAMENT** treten hier zusammen, um innen- und außenpolitische Themen zu debattieren und über Gesetzesvorschläge abzustimmen.

House of Lords

Eines der zwei Häuser der britischen **HOUSES OF PARLIAMENT**, das Oberhaus des britischen Parlaments. Seine Mitglieder werden nicht gewählt und seine Aufgabe ist es, Gesetze, die vom **HOUSE OF COMMONS** verabschiedet wurden, zu diskutieren und sie entweder anzunehmen oder Änderungen vorzuschlagen. Das **HOUSE OF LORDS** fungiert auch als oberstes Gericht in Großbritannien.

House of Representatives

Das Unterhaus des amerikanischen **CONGRESS**. Es gibt 435 **REPRESENTATIVES** (Abgeordnete), die alle zwei Jahre gewählt werden. Proportional zu seiner Bevölkerung hat jeder Staat eine bestimmte Anzahl von Repräsentanten. Das *House of Representatives* bringt Gesetzesvorlagen ein und verabschiedet alle neuen Gesetze.

Houses of Parliament

Die zwei Häuser des britischen Parlaments: **HOUSE OF COMMONS** und **HOUSE OF LORDS**. Der Westminsterpalast, der Gebäudekomplex im Zentrum von London, wo beide Häuser untergebracht sind, ist auch als *Houses of Parliament* bekannt.

Independent - The Independent

Eine britische überregionale Tageszeitung. Ihr Pendant am Sonntag heißt *The Independent on Sunday*. Obgleich der *Independent* politisch eher links als rechts steht, strebt er, wie der Name schon andeutet, eine unabhängige überparteiliche Berichterstattung an. Der *Independent* ist eine BROADSHEET-Zeitung und zählt zur seriösen Presse.

independent school

Eine Privatschule in Großbritannien, die sich selbst finanziert, und zwar durch Elternbeiträge. Sie erhält keine staatliche Unterstützung. **PUBLIC SCHOOLS** und **PREPARATORY SCHOOLS** fallen in diese Kategorie.

infant school

Eine Grundschule in Großbritannien, die für die ersten drei Jahre Schulausbildung sorgt. Schulpflichtiges Alter in Großbritannien ist fünf. Oft ist die *infant school* Teil einer **PRIMARY SCHOOL**, zusammen mit einer **JUNIOR SCHOOL**, die Kinder bis zu ihrem 11. Lebensjahr betreut.

Kultur

. . . .

International Herald Tribune - The International Herald Tribune

Eine internationale amerikanische Zeitung. Sie hat ihren Sitz in Paris, wird täglich in 180 Ländern veröffentlicht und hat eine exzellente Reputation für seriöse und gründliche Berichterstattung. Es ist eine **BROADSHEET**-Zeitung.

Internet

Das Internet bietet eine Fülle von nützlichen Informationen über britische und amerikanische Kultur, Gesellschaft und Tagespolitik. Alle wichtigen Zeitungen und Zeitschriften haben Webseiten (z.B. http://www.the-times.co.uk und http://www.nytimes.com), ebenso die BBC (http://www.bbc.co.uk) und CNN (http://www.cnn.com).

interstate (highway)

Durch mehr als einen Bundesstaat führende Autobahn in den USA, *Interstates* haben ein rotblaues Zeichen, auf dem 'I' steht. Nord-Süd-*interstates* haben ungerade Nummern und Ost-West-*interstates* haben gerade. Sie sind in jeder Richtung vierspurig.

ITV - Independent Television

Die Gruppe von Fernsehgesellschaften, die in Großbritannien auf Channel 3 senden. Es gibt fünfzehn Regionen, von denen jede ihre eigenen Programme und Nachrichten empfangen kann. Daneben werden auf Channel 3 aber auch viele Gemeinschaftssendungen ausgestrahlt.

Jobcentre

In den meisten britischen Städten gibt es Beratungszentren, die verschiedene Dienste für Arbeitssuchende anbieten, z.B. werden freie Stellen ausgehängt und Bewerbungsgespräche mit Arbeitgebern vermittelt. Jobcentres werden vom *Employment Service* betrieben.

jobseeker's allowance

Eine staatliche Beihilfe, die Arbeitssuchenden in Großbritannien gewährt wird, wenn sie nachweisen können, dass sie sich um eine Anstellung bemühen.

junior high school

Eine Schule in den USA, die für die Ausbildung zwischen der **ELEMENTARY SCHOOL** und der **HIGH SCHOOL** sorgt und normalerweise an eine *high school* angeschlossen ist.

junior school

Eine staatliche Schule in Großbritannien für Kinder von sieben bis elf Jahren.

Labour Party

Eine der drei großen politischen Parteien in Großbritannien. 1924 übernahm die *Labour Party* zum ersten Mal die Regierung. Ihr Ziel war, die Interessen der Arbeiter und Gewerkschaften zu vertreten. In den letzten 20 Jahren ist die Partei generell von ihren linken Positionen abgerückt. Sie wird daher heute oft als **New Labour** bezeichnet. 1997 wurde die Partei unter der Führung von Tony Blair in die Regierungsverantwortung gewählt.

L-driver - learner driver

Eine Person in Großbritannien, die Auto- oder Motorradfahren lernt, indem sie schon vor dem Erwerb eines entsprechenden Führerscheins als Lenker oder Lenkerin eines Kraftfahrzeugs am öffentlichen Straßenverkehr teilnimmt. *L-drivers* müssen von einer Person begleitet werden, die eine gültige *driving licence* (Führerschein) besitzt und müssen so lange *L-plates* vorne und hinten am Auto haben, bis sie ihren driving test (Führerscheinprüfung) erfolgreich abgeschlossen haben. *L-plates* sind viereckige weiße Schilder mit einem roten 'L' darauf.

Liberal Democratic Party

Inoffiziell oft auch als *Lib Dems* bezeichnet. Die drittgrößte politische Partei Großbritanniens. Sie ging 1988 aus einem Zusammenschluss der *Liberal Party* und Mitgliedern der *Social Democratic Party* hervor.

Los Angeles Times - The Los Angeles Times

Eine in Los Angeles verlegte Tageszeitung, die zu den besten Zeitungen in den USA gezählt wird. Sie verkauft Artikel an Zeitungen in aller Welt .

Medicaid

Staatliche Krankenversicherung in den USA für Versicherungsnehmer unter 65 Jahren mit kleinem Einkommen.

Medicare

Staatliche Gesundheitsversorgung und Krankenversicherung in den USA für Versicherungsnehmer über 65 Jahren.

Member of Parliament (MP)

Ein Abgeordneter des **HOUSE OF COMMONS**, der eine der 659 *constituencies* (Wahlkreise) in England, Schottland, Wales und Nordirland repräsentiert.

middle school

Eine staatliche Schule in einigen Teilen von England and Wales, die Kinder im Alter von 8 bis 14 Jahren unterrichtet.

Mirror - The Mirror

Eine überregionale Tageszeitung. Am Sonntag erscheint ihr Pendant *The Sunday Mirror*. Der Mirror ist gemäßigt links und eine **TABLOID**-Zeitung, also ein Blatt, das zur Boulevardpresse gezählt wird.

motorway

Eine britische Autobahn. In Großbritannien gibt es ein gut ausgebautes Autobahnnetz, die meisten Autobahnen sind dreispurig. Sie sind mit dem Buchstaben 'M' und einer nachfolgenden Nummer gekennzeichnet und haben eine Geschwindigkeitsbegrenzung von 70 mph (112 kmh). Die britischen Autobahnen sind gebührenfrei.

National Health Service (NHS)

Das staatliche Gesundheitssystem in Großbritannien, das die ärztliche Versorgung gewährleistet. Es wird größtenteils aus öffentlichen Geldern finanziert. Ein Großteil der medizinischen Versorgung ist kostenlos. Kostenpflichtig sind jedoch Zahnarztbehandlungen und verschriebene Medikamente. Von der Zahlung ausgenommen sind Kinder, Jugendliche unter 18 Jahren und Rentner.

• •

National Insurance (NI)
Obligatorische Sozialabgaben von Arbeitgebern und Arbeitnehmern in
Großbritannien werden **National Insurance Contributions** genannt.
Jeder Erwachsene muss eine **National Insurance Number** haben. Mithilfe dieses
Systems werden verschiedene staatliche Zuwendungen finanziert wie z.B. die
JOBSEEKERS' ALLOWANCE, die Altersrenten sowie der **NATIONAL HEALTH
SERVICE**.

National Lottery
Eine Lotterie in Großbritannien, die ihre Einnahmen einer Vielzahl von Projekten
in der Kunst, dem Sport, nationalen historischen Stätten und wohltätigen Zwecken
zuführt.

National Trust
Eine Stiftung zur Erhaltung und Pflege von Stätten von historischem Interesse
oder besonderer Naturschönheiten. Der *National Trust* finanziert sich aus
Stiftungsgeldern und privaten Spenden und ist der größte Privateigner von
Land in Großbritannien. Er hat riesige Landflächen, Dörfer und Häuser gekauft
oder erhalten, von denen viele zu bestimmten Zeiten öffentlich zugänglich sind.

Native American
Dies ist die heute akzeptierte Bezeichnung für die Ureinwohner Nord- und
Südamerikas sowie der Karibik. Sie wird besonders im offiziellen Kontext dem
Ausdruck *American Indian* vorgezogen, da sie akkurater und positiver ist, denn
Indian rührt daher, dass Kolumbus bei seiner Ankunft in Amerika annahm, in
Indien zu sein. *American Indian* hat weiterhin weite Verbreitung und wird von
den betreffenden Völkern nicht als diskriminierend empfunden.

NBC - National Broadcasting Company
Die erste Rundfunkgesellschaft in den USA. Sie wurde 1926 gegründet.
Das erste NBC-Nachrichtenprogramm wurde 1940 ausgestrahlt.

News of the World - The News of the World
Eine britische Sonntagszeitung. Schwerpunkte der Berichterstattung sind die
Themen Verbrechen und Sport. Das Blatt ist besonders für seine
Sensationsberichterstattung über Prominente und die königliche Familie bekannt.
Es ist eine **TABLOID**-Zeitung, Teil der Boulevardpresse und ist in Großbritannien
die auflagenstärkste Zeitung.

NVQ - National Vocational Qualification
Eine Qualifikation in Großbritannien, die man durch Ausbildung und Trainee-
Umläufe am Arbeitsplatz oder in bestimmten Colleges und Schulen erhält.
Die Fächer sind konkret berufsbezogen und auf verschiedenen Niveaus angesiedelt.

Observer - The Observer
Eine britische Sonntagszeitung, die für die Qualität ihres investigativen
Journalismus bekannt ist. Ihre politische Position ist links von der Mitte, besonders
in sozialen Fragen. Der *Observer* ist eine **BROADSHEET**-Zeitung, zählt zur seriösen
Presse und gehört nun der **GUARDIAN**-Gruppe an.

Kultur

● ●

pantomime

Eine Form der Theateraufführung, die traditionell in den Wochen vor und nach Weihnachten auf Bühnen in ganz Großbritannien hauptsächlich für Kinder gezeigt wird. Die Handlung ist oft die komische Adaption eines Märchens oder einer Volkssage und sie bezieht die Zuschauer stark ein. Gemäß der Tradition wird die Rolle des *principal boy* oder Helden von einer Frau gespielt und die Rolle der *dame*, einer grotesken Frauenfigur, von einem Mann.

Parliament

Das britische Parlament ist die höchste gesetzgebende Gewalt in Großbritannien und besteht aus dem Souverän (dem König oder der Königin), dem **HOUSE OF LORDS** und dem **HOUSE OF COMMONS**.

PBS - Public Broadcasting Service

Ein staatlich geförderter Rundfunkdienst in den USA, bekannt für seine hohe Programmqualität. Er übermittelt sein Programm an eine Gruppe von lokalen Sendern, die keinen Gewinn anstreben und keine Werbung ausstrahlen.

Pentagon – The Pentagon

Das Gebäude in Arlington, Virginia, in dem die Verwaltungen des Verteidigungsministeriums untergebracht sind. Mit "das Pentagon" bezeichnen Journalisten oft die militärische Führung in den USA.

Plaid Cymru

Die nationalistische politische Partei in Wales. Ihr wesentliches Ziel ist die völlige Unabhängigkeit vom Vereinigten Königreich. Im Rahmen dieses Ziels sind Anstrengungen unternommen worden, **WELSH** (das Walisische) wieder zu beleben und die walisische Kultur zu pflegen.

preparatory school

Eine Privatschule in Großbritannien, auch **prep school** genannt, für Schüler im Alter von sieben bis dreizehn Jahren. Einige sind Tagesschulen, einige Internate und viele eine Mischung aus beidem. Eine *preparatory school* ist normalerweise entweder für Jungen oder für Mädchen, hat also keine gemischten Klassen. Die Eltern zahlen für die Ausbildung ihrer Kinder und andere Angebote innerhalb der Schule Schulgeld. Die meisten Schüler gehen anschließend auf eine **PUBLIC SCHOOL** (Privatschule). *Preparatory schools* und *public schools* nennen sich heute oft **INDEPENDENT SCHOOLS**.

President

Der Präsident der Vereinigten Staaten ist das Staatsoberhaupt, trägt außenpolitische Verantwortung und hat den Oberbefehl über die Streitkräfte. Er kann Bundesrichter und leitende Minister ernennen und wird vom **CONGRESS** gebeten, neue Gesetze zu bewilligen. Ein Präsident kann maximal für zwei *terms* (Legislaturperioden), also für 8 Jahre regieren.

primary school

Eine Grundschule in Großbritannien, die Kinder von fünf bis elf betreut.

public school

Eine Privatschule in England und Wales für Schüler im Alter von dreizehn bis achtzehn Jahren, die vorher meist eine **PREPARATORY SCHOOL** besucht haben. Die meisten *public schools* sind Internate, normalerweise entweder für Jungen oder Mädchen. Die Eltern zahlen für die Ausbildung ihrer Kinder und andere Angebote innerhalb der Schule Schulgeld. In Schottland und den USA ist eine *public school* eine staatliche Schule.

• •

Queen's Speech
Eine von den Mitgliedern des britischen Parlaments vorbereitete Rede, die von der Königin jährlich zur Parlamentseröffnung im Herbst im **HOUSE OF LORDS** verlesen wird. Dies ist ein wichtiger Anlass, denn in der Rede werden die Pläne der Regierung für das kommende Jahr vorgestellt.

region
Die größte Verwaltungseinheit in Schottland. Es gibt davon neun, jede mit einem eigenen **COUNCIL**.

Representative
Ein Mitglied des amerikanischen **HOUSE OF REPRESENTATIVES**.

Republican Party
Neben der **DEMOCRATIC PARTY** eine der zwei großen politischen Parteien in den USA. Sie wird als die konservativere der beiden Parteien eingestuft.

SAT
1 - **Scholastic Aptitude Test** Eine standardisierte Eignungsprüfung in den USA, die normalerweise im letzten Schuljahr der **HIGH SCHOOL** abgelegt wird und die für die meisten Colleges und Universitäten als Zulassungsvoraussetzung gilt.
2 - **Standard Assessment Test** Ein Test für Schüler im Alter von 7, 11 und 14 Jahren in allen Schulen in England und Wales zur Kontrolle ihres Wissensstandes.

Scottish Certificate of Education
Das am weitesten verbreitete Schulabschlusszeugnis in Schottland, das sein eigenes Ausbildungssystem hat. Die erste Prüfung wird mit 16 abgelegt und ist das Äquivalent zu den GCSE-Prüfungen in England, während die zweite Prüfung mit 17 abgelegt wird und das Äquivalent zu den **A-LEVELs** darstellt.

Scottish National Party (SNP)
Eine schottische Partei, deren Ziel es ist, eine vollkommen unabhängige schottische Regierung zu erwirken.

Scottish Parliament
Das schottische Parlament, dessen Mitglieder im *Palace of Holyroodhouse* in der Hauptstadt Edinburgh zusammentreten. Es wurde 1999 nach den schottischen Wahlen eröffnet und verleiht Schottland eine größere Autonomie gegenüber dem britischen Parlament in London.

SDLP - Social Democrat and Labour Party
Eine politische Partei in Nordirland, deren Ziel die rechtliche Gleichstellung von Katholiken und die Vereinigung Nordirlands mit der Republik Irland ist. Sie lehnt Gewalt als Mittel der Politik ab.

Senate - the United States Senate
Das Oberhaus des amerikanischen **CONGRESS**. Es gibt 100 gewählte **SENATORS** (Senatoren). Neue Gesetze müssen sowohl vom **HOUSE OF REPRESENTATIVES** als auch vom Senat verabschiedet werden.

Senator
Ein Mitglied des amerikanischen **SENATE**.

Kultur

- -

Shadow Cabinet ▶ CABINET

Silicon Valley
Ein scherzhafter Name für ein Gebiet im kalifornischen Santa Clara Valley, wo es eine besonders hohe Dichte an Computerfirmen und Elektronikunternehmen gibt. Der Name rührt daher, dass in der Elektronik mit Silicium gearbeitet wird.

Sinn Fein
Name einer 1905 in Irland gegründeten politischen Bewegung und Partei, deren ursprüngliche Ziele die Unabhängigkeit Irlands und eine Wiederbelebung der irischen Kultur waren und die heute, im Verein mit der IRA, ein vereinigtes republikanisches Irland anstrebt.

Stars and Stripes
Die amerikanische Nationalflagge.

Star-Spangled Banner
Die amerikanische Nationalhymne.

state school
Eine direkt oder indirekt vom Staat finanzierte Schule in Großbritannien, die keine Schulgebühren verlangt. Die meisten Kinder in Großbritannien besuchen solche staatlichen Schulen.

Sun - The Sun
Eine britische Tageszeitung, die für ihre Sensationsschlagzeilen und -berichterstattung sowie für ihre rechten Meinungen bekannt ist. Sie ist eine **TABLOID**-Zeitung, gehört zur Boulevardpresse und ist die auflagenstärkste Tageszeitung in Großbritannien.

tabloid
Eine Zeitung in Großbritannien, die auf kleinen Zeitungsbögen gedruckt wird, im Gegensatz zu den **BROADSHEETS**, die auf doppelt so großen Zeitungsbögen gedruckt werden. Das *tabloid*-Format wird normalerweise mit der popular press (Boulevardpresse) assoziiert, wie sie z.B. von **THE SUN** und **THE MIRROR** repräsentiert wird, während das *broadsheet-Format* von den meisten Zeitungen der *quality press* (seriösen Presse), wie z.B. **THE GUARDIAN** und **THE TIMES**, benutzt wird.

The Times, The White House *etc.* ▶ TIMES, WHITE HOUSE *etc.*

Times - The Times
Eine britische überregionale Tageszeitung, deren Pendant am Sonntag *The Sunday Times* ist. Sie ist eine **BROADSHEET**-Zeitung und zählt zur seriösen Presse. Sie ist politisch unabhängig, wird jedoch gemeinhin als konservativ angesehen. Sie ist die älteste Zeitung in England und wurde erstmals 1785 veröffentlicht.

TOEFL - Test of English as a Foreign Language
Ein Test zur Feststellung der englischen Sprachkenntnisse für Studierende, die an einer amerikanischen Universität studieren wollen und deren Muttersprache nicht Englisch ist.

Tory ▶ CONSERVATIVE PARTY.

Kultur

• •

Turner Prize

Ein jährlich ausgeschriebener Preis, der von der *Tate Gallery* in London für ein Werk eines britischen Künstlers unter 50 Jahren vergeben wird. Die Preisverleihung erhält ein breites Echo in der Presse und der öffentlichen Diskussion, da viele der Werke avantgardistisch und umstritten sind.

Ulster Democratic Unionist Party

Eine politische Partei in Nordirland, die stark von den Protestanten unterstützt wird und den Standpunkt vertritt, dass Nordirland Teil des Vereinigten Königreichs bleiben sollte.

Ulster Unionist Party

Von den politischen Parteien in Nordirland, die die Ansicht vertreten, dass Nordirland Teil des Vereinigten Königreichs bleiben sollte, ist dies die bedeutendste.

Union Jack

Die Nationalflagge des Vereinigten Königreichs. Sie setzt sich aus dem englischen *St George's Cross*, dem schottischen *St Andrew's Cross* und dem nordirischen *St Patrick's Cross* zusammen.

Washington Post - The Washington Post

Eine amerikanische überregionale Tageszeitung, die in Washington erscheint. Sie ist bekannt für ihre politische Berichterstattung, ihren investigativen Journalismus auf hohem Niveau und ihre Liberalität.

Welsh

Die alte keltische Sprache, wie sie in Wales gesprochen wird. Für mehr als 20% der Bevölkerung ist Walisisch noch die erste Sprache und hat, wie viele Minderheitensprachen, in den letzten 40 Jahren eine Wiederbelebung erfahren. Es ist zur Zeit die erste Sprache in vielen walisischen Schulen und offizielle Schilder sind normalerweise sowohl in *Welsh* als auch in Englisch beschriftet.

Welsh Assembly

Das walisische Parlament, dessen Mitglieder in der Hauptstadt Cardiff zusammentreten. Es wurde 1999 nach den walisischen Wahlen eröffnet und verleiht Wales eine größere Autonomie gegenüber dem britischen Parlament in London.

Westminster

Ein Stadtteil im Zentrum von London, in dem ein Großteil der Regierungsgebäude liegt. Das wichtigste unter ihnen ist der *Palace of Westminster*, auch **HOUSES OF PARLIAMENT** genannt, in dem beide Häuser des britischen Parlaments tagen. Ebenfalls im Stadtteil liegt die *Westminster Abbey*, wo alle englischen Königen und Königinnen seit William dem Eroberer gekrönt wurden.

Whitehall

Eine Straße im Zentrum von London, in der sich ein Großteil der Ministerien befindet. Journalisten bezeichnen mit *Whitehall* oft die Regierung und die Verwaltung Großbritanniens.

White House – The White House

Der offizielle (Arbeits-)Sitz des amerikanischen Präsidenten in Washington. Journalisten bezeichnen mit *the White House* häufig den Präsidenten und seine Berater.

A–Z of German life and culture

Abendbrot, Abendessen

For most Germans, **MITTAGESSEN** is still the main meal of the day. *Abendbrot* or *Abendessen* normally consists of bread, cheese, meats, perhaps a salad, and a hot drink. It is eaten by the whole family at about 6 or 7 p.m. *Abendessen* can also refer to a cooked meal, especially for people who are out at work all day.

Abitur

This is the final exam taken by pupils at a **GYMNASIUM**, usually when they are about 19. The result is based on continuous assessment during the last two years before the *Abitur*, plus examinations in four subjects. The *Abitur* is the obligatory qualification for university entrance.

ADAC - Allgemeiner Deutscher Automobil-Club

Europe's largest motoring organization, based in Munich, the *ADAC* acts as a powerful lobby for the German motorist. The *ADAC-Straßenwacht* provides free breakdown assistance for *ADAC* members.

Ampel-Koalition

A term describing any coalition between the **SPD** (the party colour is red), the **FDP** (yellow) and the Green Party. This type of coalition has become increasingly common in local government over the last ten years, with some **LÄNDER** ruled in this way.

AOK - Allgemeine Ortskrankenkasse

The largest health insurance organization in Germany. Foreign visitors to Germany who need medical assistance can get the necessary forms at the local *AOK* office.

Arbeitsamt

The local employment office to be found in every German town. It provides career guidance, helps the unemployed find new jobs, and processes all claims for **ARBEITSLOSENGELD** and related benefits. Unemployed people have to report to the *Arbeitsamt* once every three months to prove they are still looking for work.

Arbeitslosengeld

This is the benefit paid to all unemployed people who are looking for a new job and have already made a minimum contribution to the **ARBEITSLOSENVERSICHERUNG**. The benefit is a proportion of the person's previous pay, and is higher for people supporting children. After one year, it is reduced and called *Arbeitslosenhilfe*.

Arbeitslosenversicherung

This is the compulsory state-run insurance against unemployment. All *Arbeiter* and *Angestellte* have to pay into this scheme and in return are entitled to **ARBEITSLOSENGELD** and related benefits. This area has been subject to wide-ranging reforms in recent years.

ARD

An umbrella organization for the regional broadcasting stations of the various German **LÄNDER**, financed by licence fees plus a certain amount of advertising. The *ARD* broadcasts **DAS ERSTE**.

• •

Autobahn

Germany's motorway network is very extensive and not subject to a general speed limit, other than a recommended limit of about 80 mph. Many motorways have only two lanes. To ease congestion, lorries are not allowed to use the *Autobahn* on Sundays. German motorways are free, but on Austrian and Swiss motorways all vehicles must display a **VIGNETTE**.

BAföG - Bundesausbildungsförderungsgesetz

The grant which about a quarter of German students receive from the state. Whether they are entitled to *BAföG*, and how much they get, depends on the students' and their parents' financial circumstances. Half of the money is given in the form of a loan which has to be repaid later.

Bayern

Bayern (Bavaria), Germany's largest and southernmost **LAND**, is known for its beautiful scenery (the Alps and their foothills, as well as forests, rivers, and lakes, picturesque towns and villages), its excellent beer and food, and its lively cosmopolitan capital München (Munich). The Bavarians are said to be warm and hospitable, but also fiercely independent and very conservative.

Bausparen

German building societies expect people to have saved up a sizeable sum towards the purchase of a house before they will give them a mortgage. For this reason, many Germans have a *Bausparvertrag* (a tax-efficient savings contract for an agreed sum) with a building society, even if they are not planning to buy their **EIGENHEIM** for some time.

Beamte

This term covers civil servants and other officials, but also occupations like teachers and lecturers. *Beamte* are legally obliged to support the democratic system in Germany and are not allowed to go on strike. In return, they enjoy many privileges, such as total job security, private health insurance, and exemption from social security contributions.

Berlin

After **WIEDERVEREINIGUNG**, Berlin took over from Bonn as the capital of Germany, but the German government did not start moving there until 1998. This vibrant city in the heart of Europe lies on the river Spree. It has about 3.5 million inhabitants and is a major cultural and industrial centre.

Berufsausbildung ▶ LEHRE.

Berufsschule

A college for young people who are doing a **LEHRE**. They attend *Berufsschule* 2 days a week (or sometimes in blocks of several weeks) to continue their general education and receive formal training in their chosen type of job.

Betriebsrat

The staff in any German company with at least five employees are entitled to have a *Betriebsrat*. This is a committee elected by the workers to represent their interests as opposed to those of management. It allows workers to participate in decisions on pay and other benefits, redundancies, and even some business matters.

. . . .

Biergarten

A rustic open-air pub which is traditional in Bavaria but can now be found throughout Germany. It is usually set up for the summer in the yard of a pub or restaurant. A *Biergarten* is the best place to enjoy a beer and a simple meal on a summer's day.

Bild Zeitung

Germany's largest-selling daily newspaper, *Bild* is a typical tabloid with huge headlines, lots of photos, scandal stories, gossip and nude models. It is known for its right-wing views. *Bild* sells about 4.5 million copies every day, almost eight times more than any other newspaper in Germany. Its Sunday edition is called *Bild am Sonntag*.

Bodensee

This is the German name for Lake Constance, Germany's biggest lake, bordered by Germany, Switzerland, and Austria. The river Rhine flows through it. This popular recreation area enjoys a particularly mild climate, especially on the three islands Lindau, Mainau, and Reichenau.

Bonn

Bonn was the capital of the Federal Republic of Germany from 1949 until **BERLIN** was made the capital of a reunified Germany and remains home to a number of government institutions. This relatively small, quiet city of about 300,000 inhabitants enjoys a picturesque location on the river Rhine.

Bund

This term refers to the federal state as the top level of government, as opposed to the individual **LÄNDER** which make up the Federal Republic. *Bund* and *Länder* have different responsibilities, with the *Bund* in charge of foreign policy, defence, transport, health, employment, etc.

Bundesbank

Properly called the *Deutsche Bundesbank*, Germany's central bank is located in Frankfurt/Main. With the introduction of the Euro in 1999, some of its functions have passed to the European Central Bank (also in Frankfurt).

Bundeskanzler

The Chancellor is the head of government in Germany and Austria. The German chancellor is normally elected for 4 years by the MPs in the **BUNDESTAG** after being proposed by the **BUNDESPRÄSIDENT**. He chooses the ministers and decides on government policies.

Bundesland ▶ LAND.

Bundespräsident

The President is the head of state in Germany and Austria. The German president is elected for 5 years by the MPs and delegates from the **LÄNDER**. He (so far there have not been any women) acts mainly as a figurehead, representing Germany abroad, and does not get involved in party politics, although he often takes a moral lead in major issues like the reform of the education system.

• •

Bundesrat

This is the upper house of the German parliamentary system, where the **LÄNDER** are represented. The *Bundesrat* members are appointed by the Länder governments. It has to approve laws affecting the *Länder*, and also any changes to the **GRUNDGESETZ**. Sometimes the opposition parties actually hold a majority in the *Bundesrat*, which allows them to influence German legislation.

Bundestag

The lower house of the German parliament, which is elected every four years by the German people. The *Bundestag* is responsible for federal legislation, the federal budget, and electing the **BUNDESKANZLER**. Half of the MPs are elected directly and half by proportional representation, in a complicated voting system where each voter has two votes.

Bundeswehr

This is the name for the German armed forces, which come under the control of the defence minister. The *Bundeswehr* consists of professional soldiers and conscripts serving their **WEHRDIENST**. Until 1994, the **GRUNDGESETZ** did not allow German forces to be deployed abroad, but they now take part in certain operations, notably UN peacekeeping missions.

Bündnis 90/Die Grünen

This party came into being in 1993 as the result of a merger of the West German Green party and civil rights movements of the former GDR. It is the third largest force in the German parliament, committed to environmental and social issues.

CDU - Christlich-Demokratische Union

One of the main German political parties. It was founded in 1945 and is committed to Christian and conservative values. The *CDU* is not active in Bavaria. ▶ **CSU**.

Christkind

Traditionally, it is *Das Christkind* (the Christ Child) who brings Christmas presents to children on Christmas Eve. The concept of *der Weihnachtsmann* (Father Christmas) is relatively new in Germany.

CSU - Christlich-Soziale Union

The Bavarian sister party of the **CDU**. It was founded in 1946 and has enjoyed an absolute majority in Bavaria for over 30 years. Politically, it stands to the right of the *CDU*.

Das Erste

Also called **Erstes Programm**, this is the first German public TV channel, broadcast by **ARD**. Programming includes news, information, films, and entertainment. There is a limited amount of advertising, which is concentrated in 'blocks' at certain times of day and not after 8 p.m.

Der Spiegel

One of Germany's best-selling weekly news and current affairs magazines, *Der Spiegel* was founded in 1947 and is published in Hamburg. It has a liberal to left-wing outlook and has become synonymous with investigative journalism in Germany, as it has brought to light a number of major scandals in German business and politics over the years.

Culture

Deutsche Post

The previously state-run German postal system has undergone wide-ranging reforms in recent years which will effectively remove the *Deutsche Post* monopoly by 2002. The number of post offices has been reduced, but small post office agencies can now be found in shops, newsagents, and petrol stations. German letter boxes are yellow. Postal charges are relatively high, but the service is very reliable.

Deutsche Telekom

The previously state-run German telecommunications service has undergone extensive reforms and gradual privatization and is now a public limited company. Since 1998 when the market was opened up to competition, *Deutsche Telekom* has ceased to have a monopoly.

Deutsche Welle

The German equivalent of the BBC World Service, this radio station is financed and controlled by the German government and broadcasts programmes on German politics, business, arts, and culture, aimed at listeners abroad.

DGB - Deutscher Gewerkschaftsbund

The biggest trade-union umbrella organization in Germany, with about 8 million members in 13 individual unions. In recent years, the *DGB* has pursued a policy of moderation in its pay demands.

Die Republikaner

This ultra right-wing party was founded in 1983 and quickly became notorious for its xenophobic and nationalistic aims. After some success in the early 90s it now has very little support and is not represented in the **BUNDESTAG**.

Die Welt

A national daily newspaper which was founded in 1946 and is published in Hamburg. It has a large business section and is considered to be right-wing in its views.

Die Zeit

Germany's 'heaviest' weekly newspaper is published in Hamburg and is considered essential reading for academics and intellectuals. Former **BUNDESKANZLER** Helmut Schmidt is a joint editor. The paper offers in-depth analysis of current issues in politics, society, culture, and the arts.

documenta

This international contemporary art exhibition takes place in Kassel every 4 to 5 years. The 1997 *documenta* covered drama, music, film, talks and the Internet as well as art. It cost over 20 million DM and was subsidized heavily by the taxpayer and private sponsors.

Drittes Programm

One of the eight regional television channels run by the **ARD** and focussing on regional affairs and educational programmes.

Duales System

This is a waste disposal and recycling system which was introduced in Germany in 1993 and is operated by the private company *DSD*. All packaging materials marked with the **GRÜNER PUNKT** symbol are collected separately, and sorted into plastics, glass, paper and metal for recycling. Non-recyclable and compostable waste is still collected by the local refuse collection service.

Eigenheim

The level of home ownership in Germany is rising but still far lower than in Britain. Many people happily live in rented flats or houses, but most dream of buying or building their *Eigenheim* (own home) one day and save up towards it through the system of **BAUSPAREN**. German houses tend to be large and solidly built, usually with cellars, and are therefore relatively expensive. First-time buyers are usually middle-aged and expect to stay in their home for the rest of their lives.

Einwohnermeldeamt

Anybody who moves to Germany or relocates within Germany is legally obliged to register their address with the *Einwohnermeldeamt* within a week.

Entwerter

When travelling on buses and trams in Germany it is important to remember that you have to cancel (*entwerten*) your ticket in one of the *Entwerter* machines located inside the bus or tram. Your ticket, even if you have just bought it from the driver, is not valid without the stamp from the *Entwerter*.

Erste, Das ▶ DAS ERSTE.

Erziehungsgeld

A state benefit paid for up to two years to any mother or father who stays at home after the birth of a child to look after it. In 98% of cases, it is still the mother who claims *Erziehungsgeld*. Although this benefit is means-tested, almost all families receive some money for the first 6 months of the baby's life. In addition to this, parents receive **Kindergeld** (child benefit) for each child.

Erziehungsurlaub

A German mother or father who looks after a child at home is entitled to up to three years' extended maternity or paternity leave. At the end of this *Erziehungsurlaub* they are entitled to return to their old job. 95% of German mothers take time out of work for at least one year after the birth.

Eurocheque

The Eurocheque is the standard cheque issued by banks in Germany. It is backed up by the *Eurochequekarte* which can also be used at cash machines and for payments in shops. Although plastic cards have become more popular in Germany, many people (and shops and restaurants) still prefer cash.

Fachhochschule

This type of university provides shorter, more vocational and practically-based courses than those available at a **HOCHSCHULE**.

Fahrschule

Learner drivers in Germany have to take lessons from a qualified driving instructor at a *Fahrschule* (driving school) in a specially adapted car with dual controls. It is quite common to have 20 or 30 driving lessons before sitting the driving test, as there is no other way of getting driving practice on the road.

FDP - Freie Demokratische Partei

The German Liberal party, which was founded in 1948. This relatively small party tends to gain only 5 to 10% of the vote at general elections, but it has held the balance of power in various coalition governments both with the SPD and the CDU/CSU. It supports a free-market economy and the freedom of the individual.

Culture

Focus

A relatively new weekly news and current affairs magazine published in Munich.
It was set up in 1993 and is aimed at a centre-right readership, especially
businesspeople and professionals. *Focus* has become a serious competitor of **DER
SPIEGEL**, with shorter, easier-to-read articles and a more modern presentation.

Frankfurter Allgemeine Zeitung (FAZ)

One of Germany's most serious and widely respected daily newspapers.
It was founded in 1945 and is published in Frankfurt/Main. It tends to have
a centre-left to liberal outlook.

Frühstück

Breakfast in Germany typically consists of strong coffee, slices of bread or
fresh rolls with butter, jam, honey, sliced cheese and meat, and maybe a boiled egg.
For working people and schoolchildren, who have little time for breakfast first thing
in the morning, a *zweites Frühstück* is common at around 10 a.m.

Gastarbeiter

The term used for foreign workers from southern European countries, mainly
Turkey, former Yugoslavia, and Italy, many of whom came to Germany in the 60s and
70s. Despite the time that they have lived in Germany and the fact that their children
have grown up there, integration is still a widely discussed issue.

Gemeinde

The lowest level of local government, run by a local council chaired by the
Bürgermeister (mayor). *Gemeinden* have their own budget, with income from
local taxes. They pass local legislation and administer local affairs.

Gesamthochschule

A type of university established in some **LÄNDER** following reforms in the 60s
and combining **HOCHSCHULE** and **FACHHOCHSCHULE** under one roof, thereby
offering greater flexibility and a wider choice of subjects to the student.

Gesamtschule

A comprehensive secondary school introduced in the 70s and designed to replace
the traditional division into **GYMNASIUM, REALSCHULE,** and **HAUPTSCHULE**.
Pupils are taught different subjects at their own level and may take any of the
school-leaving exams, including the **ABITUR**.

Goethe-Institut

An organization for promoting German language and culture abroad. It is based in
Munich and runs about 140 institutes in over 70 countries, offering German language
classes, cultural events such as exhibitions, films and seminars, and a library of
German books and magazines and other documentation, which is open to the public.

Grundgesetz

The written German constitution which came into force in May 1949. It lays down
the basic rights of German citizens, the relationship between **BUND** and **LÄNDER**,
and the legal framework of the German state.

Grundschule

The primary school which all German children attend for four years from the age
of 6 (some children do not start until they are 7). Lessons are intense but pupils only
attend school for about 4 hours a day. At the end of the *Grundschule*, teachers and
parents decide together which type of secondary school the child should attend.

. . . .

Grüner Punkt

A symbol used to mark packaging materials which can be recycled. Any packaging carrying this logo is collected separately under the **DUALES SYSTEM** recycling scheme. Manufacturers have to buy a licence from the recycling company *DSD* to entitle them to use this symbol.

Gymnasium

The secondary school which prepares pupils for the **ABITUR**. The *Gymnasium* is attended after the **GRUNDSCHULE** by the most academically-inclined pupils. They spend nine years at this school, and during the last three years, they have some choice as to which subjects they study. ▶ **SCHULE**.

Hauptschule

The secondary school which prepares pupils for the **Hauptschulabschluss** (school-leaving certificate). The *Hauptschule* aims to give the least academically-inclined children a sound educational grounding. Pupils stay at the *Hauptschule* for 5 or 6 years after the **GRUNDSCHULE**. ▶ **SCHULE, LEHRE**.

Hochschule

German *Hochschulen* (universities) do not charge fees, and anybody who has passed the **ABITUR** is entitled to go to university (except for some subjects which have a **NUMERUS CLAUSUS**). They tend to be very large and impersonal institutions. Students may receive a **BAföG** grant and often take more than the minimum 8 semesters (4 years) to complete their course.

ICE - Intercityexpresszug

This high-speed train runs at two-hour intervals on a number of main routes in Germany, offering shorter journey times and better facilities than ordinary trains. A futuristic new *ICE* station has been built at Frankfurt airport.

IM - inoffizieller Mitarbeiter

This term refers to 'unofficial collaborators' of the **STASI**. These informers were often ordinary people in the former GDR who had been recruited or pressurized by the Stasi to spy on neighbours, family, and friends. However, some were prominent figures in the West.

Internet

A wealth of useful information on German politics, culture and so on can be obtained on the Internet, which is very popular in Germany. All the main German newspapers have web sites (e.g. http://www.focus.de), as do the television channels (e.g. http://www.ard.de) and organizations like the *Goethe-Institut* (http://goethe.de). In addition, many German towns and cities have web sites (e.g. http://www.berlin.de).

Kaffee

This refers not only to coffee as a drink but also to the small meal taken at about 4 in the afternoon, consisting of coffee and cakes or biscuits. It is often a social occasion as it is common to invite family or friends for *Kaffee und Kuchen* (rather than for lunch or dinner), especially on birthdays and other family occasions.

Kanton

The name for the individual autonomous states that make up Switzerland. There are 26 *Kantone*, with the largest having just over 1 million inhabitants. Each *Kanton* has its own government and its own constitution.

Kindergarten

Every German pre-school child has the right to attend *Kindergarten* (nursery or play school) between the ages of 3 and 6. Kindergarten concentrates on play, crafts, singing etc., and aims to foster the child's social and emotional development. There is no formal teaching at all, this being reserved for the **GRUNDSCHULE**.

Kindertagesstätte

Often called *Kita* for short, this is a day nursery intended for the children of working parents. The age range is usually from babies to 6, although some *Kitas* also offer after-school care for older children.

Kirchensteuer

Any taxpayer who is a member of one of the established churches in Germany (mainly Catholic and Protestant) has to pay *Kirchensteuer* (church tax). It is calculated as a proportion of income tax and is collected at source by the tax office, which then passes on the money to the relevant church.

Krankenkasse

There are many different health insurance organizations in Germany with the **AOK** being the largest. Contributions are high, due to the high standard (and cost) of health care in Germany. The *Krankenkassen* issue their members with plastic cards which entitle them to treatment by the doctor of their choice.

Kur

A health cure in a spa town lasting about 3 to 6 weeks and usually involving a special diet, exercise programmes, physiotherapy, massage etc. These are intended for people with minor complaints or recovering from illness and play an important role in preventative medicine in Germany. *Kuren* are paid for by the **KRANKENKASSEN**, with the patient making a contribution. A number of cutbacks have been made in this area in recent years.

Ladenschlusszeit

The strict regulations governing shop closing times in Germany were relaxed in 1996. Shops are allowed to stay open until 8 p.m. on weekdays and 4 p.m. on Saturdays, and bakeries may open for 3 hours on Sundays. However, the actual opening times vary, depending on the location and size of the shop.

Land

Germany is a federal republic consisting of 16 member states called *Länder* or *Bundesländer*. Five so-called neue *Bundesländer* were added after reunification in 1990. The Land has a degree of autonomy and is responsible for all educational and cultural affairs, the police, the environment, and local government. Austria is a federal state consisting of 9 *Länder*, and the Swiss equivalent is a **KANTON**.

Landtag

The parliament of a **LAND**, which is elected every 4 to 5 years using a similar mixed system of voting as for the **BUNDESTAG** elections.

Lehre

This type of apprenticeship is still the normal way to learn a trade or train for a practical career in Germany. A *Hauptschulabschluss* is the minimum requirement, although many young people with a *Realschulabschluss* or even *Lehre* opt to train in this way. A Lehre takes about 2 to 3 years and involves practial training by a **MEISTER(IN)** backed up by lessons at a **BERUFSSCHULE**, with an exam at the end.

● ●

Love Parade
A Techno music and dance festival which takes place in Berlin every summer, with about 1 million mainly young people attending. Originally a celebration of youth culture, it has become a major tourist attraction.

Markt
Weekly markets are still held in most German cities and towns, usually laid out very attractively in the picturesque market squares. Fresh fruit and vegetables, flowers, eggs, cheese and other dairy products, bread, meat and fish are available directly from the producer. Many Germans still buy most of their provisions *auf dem Markt*.

Meister(in)
A master craftsman or craftswoman who has completed rigorous training in his/her trade or vocation and has passed a final exam after several years' experience in a job. A *Meister(in)* is allowed to set up in business and train young people who are doing their **LEHRE**.

Mittagessen
This is a cooked meal eaten in the middle of the day and is the main meal of the day for most Germans. Schoolchildren come home from school in time for *Mittagessen* and most large companies have canteens where hot meals are served at lunchtime. On a Sunday, *Mittagessen* might consist of a starter like a clear broth, followed by a roast with gravy, boiled potatoes and vegetables, and a dessert.

Namenstag
This day is celebrated by many Germans, especially Catholics, in the same way as a birthday. It is the day dedicated to the saint whose name the person carries so, for example, someone called Martin would celebrate their *Namenstag* on *Martinstag* (November 11).

Numerus clausus
The *Numerus clausus* system is used to limit the number of students studying certain oversubscribed subjects such as medicine at German universities.
It means that only those students who have achieved a minimum average mark in their **ABITUR** are admitted.

Orientierungsstufe
The name given to the first two years at a **HAUPTSCHULE**, a **REALSCHULE**, or a **GYMNASIUM**. During this time pupils can find out if they are suited to the type of school they are attending, and at the end of the two years they may transfer to a different school.

Ossi
A colloquial and sometimes derogatory term for someone from East Germany, as opposed to a **WESSI** (someone from West Germany).

Parkscheibe
When parking your car in Germany in an area where the parking time is limited, you have to display a *Parkscheibe* (parking disc) in the windscreen, with the hands of the clock set to your arrival time. These blue cardboard or plastic discs are available at newsagents and department stores.

Culture

PDS - Partei des Demokratischen Sozialismus
A party formed in 1990 from the old East German SED. The ultra left-wing *PDS*
is against a free-market economy and demands the redistribution of wealth.
It has virtually no support in the former West Germany.

Pflegeversicherung
Compulsory nursing-care insurance which all employees have to pay into as part
of their **SOZIALABGABEN**. It was introduced in Germany in 1995 and pays for
the long-term nursing care of the elderly and the severely disabled. Employers and
employees make equal contributions to the scheme.

Polterabend
This is Germany's answer to stag and hen nights. The *Polterabend* usually takes
place a few days before the wedding and takes the form of a large party for the family
and friends of both bride and groom. Traditionally, the guests smash some crockery,
as this is supposed to bring luck to the couple.

Post ▶ DEUTSCHE POST.

Premiere
Germany's main Pay-TV channel was introduced in 1991 and can be received
via satellite or cable. *Premiere* subscribers can watch the latest feature films, sports
events, cutural programmes and documentaries uninterrupted by advertising.

Pro 7
Germany's third largest private television channel, *Pro 7* is financed entirely
by advertising and offers films, documentaries, and news programmes.

Realschule
The secondary school which prepares pupils for the *Realschulabschluss*
(school-leaving certificate).This type of school is in between **HAUPTSCHULE**
and **GYMNASIUM**, catering for less academic children who will probably train for
a practical career. Pupils stay at the *Realschule* for 6 years after the **GRUNDSCHULE**.
▶ SCHULE, LEHRE.

Rechtschreibreform
After much controversy, a reform aiming to simplify the strict rules governing
German spelling and punctuation was finally implemented in 1998. The old spelling
is still acceptable for a transitional period until 2005, but most newspapers and some
new books already use the new spelling.

Reichstag
This historic building in the centre of Berlin became the seat of the **BUNDESTAG**
in 1999. The refurbishment of the *Reichstag* included the addition of a glass cupola,
with a walkway open to visitors, which provides a spectacular viewing platform and
addition to the Berlin skyline.

Rentenversicherung
This is the compulsory state pension insurance in Germany. All employees have to
pay into it as part of their **SOZIALABGABEN**, with employers and the state also
making a contribution. The amount of the German state pension depends on the
contributions made by the individual, with allowances for years spent as a student
or carer.

Republikaner ▶ DIE REPUBLIKANER.

● ●

RTL
Germany's largest privately-owned television channel is the market leader in commercial television. It broadcasts films, sport, news, and entertainment and regularly achieves the highest viewing figures.

SAT 1
Germany's second largest privately-owned television channel broadcasts films, news, sport, and entertainment. It was the first commercial channel in the country.

3SAT
This satellite TV channel is run jointly by **ARD, ZDF**, and Swiss and Austrian TV.

Schule
German children do not start school until they are 6, and they are not allowed to leave school until they are at least 15. All children attend the **GRUNDSCHULE** for four years (six in Berlin) and either a **HAUPTSCHULE, REALSCHULE, GYMNASIUM**, or **GESAMTSCHULE**, depending on their ability. Some students stay at school until they are over 20 due to the system of **"SITZEN BLEIBEN"**.

Schultag - 1. Schultag
The first day at school is a big event for a German child, involving a ceremony at school and sometimes at church. The child is given a *Schultüte*, a large cardboard cone containing pens, small gifts, and sweets, to mark this special occasion.

Schützenfest
An annual festival celebrated in most towns, involving a shooting competition, parade and fair. The winners of the shooting competition are crowned *Schützenkönig* and *Schützenkönigin* for the year.

Schwarzwald
This is the German name for the Black Forest, a mountainous area in south-western Germany and a popular holiday destination for Germans and foreign tourists alike. The name refers to the large coniferous forests in the area.

sitzen bleiben
If German pupils fail more than one subject in their end-of-year school report, they have to repeat the year. This is colloquially referred to as *sitzen bleiben*, and it means that some pupils do not manage to sit their **ABITUR** until they are 20.

Skat
A popular card game for three players playing with 32 German cards. Keen players meet regularly for a game or even join a *Skat* club.

Solidaritätszuschlag
A tax surcharge introduced to help pay for the enormous cost of German reunification and rebuilding the economy in the East. It is payable by every German taxpayer or firm (in 1999 it was 5.5% of income tax and corporation tax).

Sozialabgaben
This term refers to the contributions every German taxpayer has to make towards the four main state insurance schemes: pension, health, nursing care, and unemployment. Altogether this amounts to over 40% of gross income, with employee and employer paying half each.

Culture

. . . .

SPD - Sozialdemokratische Partei Deutschlands

One of the main German political parties and the party with the biggest membership. Re-formed after the war in 1945, it is a workers' party supporting social democratic values.

Spiegel ▶ DER SPIEGEL.

Stammtisch

A large table reserved for regulars in most German pubs. The word is also used to refer to the group of people who meet around this table for a drink and lively discussion.

Stasi - Staatssicherheitsdienst

The secret service in the former GDR. With the help of an extensive network of informers, the *Stasi* built up personal files on over 6 million people, that is one third of the population. It was disbanded a year before re-unification. ▶ IM.

Süddeutsche Zeitung

This respected daily national newspaper was founded in 1945 and is published in Munich. It has a liberal outlook and is read mainly in southern Germany.

Trabant

A make of car produced in the former GDR. A *Trabant* or *Trabi* with its two-stroke engine and plastic body was a prized possession, and people had to wait for years to get one. After reunification, the *Trabant* came to symbolize the GDR era and has achieved cult status in Germany.

TÜV - Technischer Überwachungs-Verein

An independent organization responsible for testing the technical safety of vehicles and all types of machinery. Cars over three years old have to pass a *TÜV* safety and exhaust emission test every two years.

Vignette

In order to be able to use Austrian and Swiss motorways, all vehicles must display a sticker on the windscreen called a *Vignette*. These stickers are usually valid for one year, but foreign tourists in Austria can buy stickers for a period of 10 days or two months.

Volkshochschule (VHS)

A local adult education centre that can be found in every German town. The *VHS* offers low-cost daytime and evening classes in a wide range of subjects, including crafts, languages, music, and exercise.

Waldorfschule

An increasingly popular type of private school originally founded by the Austrian anthroposophist Rudolf Steiner in the 1920s. The main aim of these schools is to develop pupils' creative and cognitive abilities through music, art, and crafts.

Wehrdienst

Compulsory military service for young men in Germany (10 months), Switzerland (3 months) and Austria (6 months). Young Germans are generally called up when they are 19, although there are certain exemptions. Conscientious objectors may apply to do **ZIVILDIENST** instead.

● ●

Weihnachtsmarkt
During the weeks of Advent, these Christmas markets take place in most German towns, selling Christmas decorations, handmade toys and crib figures, traditional Christmas biscuits, and mulled wine to sustain the shoppers.

Weinstube
A cosy wine bar which offers a wide choice of wines and usually also serves a few dishes which are considered to go well with wine. A *Weinstube* tends be more upmarket than an ordinary pub, or else fairly rustic, especially in wine-growing areas.

Welt ▶ DIE WELT.

Wende
This word can refer to any major political or social change or turning point, but it is used especially to refer to the collapse of Communism in 1989, which was symbolized by the fall of the Berlin wall and eventually led to the WIEDERVEREINIGUNG in 1990.

Wessi
A colloquial and sometimes derogatory term for someone from West Germany, as opposed to an OSSI. The expression *Besserwessi*, a pun on *Besserwisser* ('know-all') is used by East Germans to describe a *Wessi* who thinks he knows it all.

Westdeutsche Allgemeine Zeitung (WAZ)
Germany's highest-circulation serious national paper. It was founded in 1948 and is published in Essen, catering mainly for the densely populated Ruhr area.

Wiedervereinigung
This is the German word for the reunification of Germany which officially took place on 3 October 1990, when the former GDR was incorporated into the Federal Republic. The huge financial and social costs of reunification are still being felt throughout Germany.

ZDF - Zweites Deutsches Fernsehen
The second German public TV channel which was founded in 1961 and broadcasts the *Zweites Programm* with entertainment, news, information and a limited amount of advertising.

Zeit ▶ DIE ZEIT.

Zivildienst
Community service which recognized conscientious objectors in Germany and Austria can choose to carry out instead of WEHRDIENST. It lasts 3 months longer than *Wehrdienst* (2 months longer in Austria) and usually involves caring for children, the elderly, the disabled, or the sick.

Culture

Letter-writing / Briefeschreiben

Holiday postcard

Letters / Briefe

■ Beginnings (informal): 'Lieber' here because it's a man; if it's a woman, use e.g. Liebe Elke.

To two people, repeat 'Liebe(r)': Lieber Hans, liebe Elke.

To a family: Liebe Schmidts, Liebe Familie Schmidt, or just Liebe Leute.

■ Address: Note that the title (Herrn, Frau, Fräulein) stands on the line above the name. Herr always has an n on the end in addresses.

The house number comes after the street name.

The postcode comes before the place, and if you're writing from outside the country put a D- for Germany, A- for Austria or CH- for Switzerland in front of it.

Heidelberg, den 6.8. 2000

Lieber Hans!

Einen schönen Gruß aus Alt-Heidelberg! Wir sind erst zwei Tage hier, aber schon sehr angetan von der Stadt und Umgebung, trotz der vielen Touristen. Allerdings ist es ziemlich schwül. Wir waren gestern abend in einem Konzert im Schlosshof, eine wunderbare Stimmung! Und dann die herrliche Aussicht auf Altstadt und Neckar von der Terrasse. Morgen machen wir eine Bootsfahrt, dann geht's am Donnerstag wieder nach Hause. Hoffentlich ist deine Mutter inzwischen wieder gesund.

Bis bald

Max und Sophie

Herrn

Hans Matthäus

Brucknerstr. 26

91052 Erlangen

■ Endings (informal): Herzlich or Herzlichst, Herzliche Grüße; more affectionately: Alles Liebe; Bis bald = See you soon .

Letters / Briefe

Postkarte aus dem Urlaub

- *Anrede: sehr einfach auf Postkarten, immer 'Dear' und der Vorname, der im englischen Sprachraum viel häufiger verwendet wird. Die Anrede kann auch entfallen.*

- *Meist keine Ortsangabe, wenn der Ort aus dem Inhalt oder dem Bild auf der Postkarte klar hervorgeht.*
  Datum – in den USA verwendet man die Reihenfolge Monat, Tag, Jahr, wenn ein Datum mit Ziffern angegeben ist – 8.6.2000

- *Adresse: Der Titel (Mr, Mrs, Miss, Ms) steht direkt vor dem Namen auf der gleichen Zeile.*

  Das Haus hat oft einen Namen anstelle einer (oder zusätzlich zur) Hausnummer, die übrigens vor dem Straßennamen steht.

  Es folgen (in GB) Ortschaft, meist auch Grafschaft, dann Postleitzahl (postcode), alles jeweils auf einer eigenen Zeile; in den USA Ortschaft und Postleitzahl (zipcode), mit dem auf zwei Buchstaben abgekürzten Namen des Staates davor:

  John Splaine Jr.
  1067 Blackwall Avenue
  Studio City
  CA 91604
  USA

6.8.2000

Dear John,

Greetings from old Heidelberg! Got here ① a couple of days ago, but already in love with the place (in spite of all the tourists). It's pretty sultry though. Last night we went to a concert in the castle courtyard, very atmospheric. And a terrific view of the river and the old town from the terrace. Tomorrow we're taking a boat trip, and then on Thursday we head for home. Hope ① your mother's fully recovered by now.

See you soon,

Mark and Juliet

Mr J. Roberts
The Willows
49 North Terrace
Kings Barton
Nottinghamshire
NG8 4LQ
England

- *Schlussformal:*
  All the best, Best wishes, *oder einfach* Yours; *auch* Love (from), *wenn man den Addressaten näher steht.*

- ① *Telegrammstil: die Angabe der Person entfällt auf Postkarten oft.*

. . . .

Christmas and New Year wishes

On a card:

Frohe Weihnachten und viel Glück im neuen Jahr

A bit more formal: Ein gesegnetes Weihnachtsfest und die besten Wünsche zum neuen Jahr

A bit less formal: Fröhliche Weihnachten und einen guten Rutsch ins neue Jahr

In a letter:

- *On most personal letters German speakers don't put their address at the top, but just the name of the place and the date*

Würzburg, den 20.12.2000

Liebe Karin, lieber Ferdinand,

euch und euren Kindern wünschen wir von Herzen frohe Weihnachten und ein glückliches neues Jahr. Wir hoffen, es geht euch allen gut, und dass wir uns bald mal wieder sehen werden. Es kommt uns so vor, als hätten wir uns eine Ewigkeit nicht gesehen.

Das vergangene Jahr war für uns sehr ereignisreich. Thomas hatte im Sommer einen Unfall mit dem Fahrrad, und brach sich den Arm und das Schlüsselbein. Sabine hat das Abitur gerade noch bestanden und ist jetzt an der Uni in Erlangen, studiert Sport. Der arme Michael ist im Oktober arbeitslos geworden und sucht immer noch nach einer Stelle.

Ihr müsst unbedingt vorbeikommen, wenn ihr das nächste Mal in der Gegend seid. Ruft doch einfach ein paar Tage vorher an, damit wir etwas ausmachen können.

Mit herzlichen Grüßen

Eure Gabi und Michael

. . . .

Weihnachts- und Neujahrsgrüße

Auf einer Karte:

> *[Best wishes for a] Happy* ① *Christmas and a Prosperous New Year*
>
> *All best wishes for Christmas and the New Year*
>
> *Wishing you every happiness this Christmas[tide] and in the New Year*

① *Oder etwas altmodisch:* Merry

In einem Brief:

> *44 Louis Gardens*
> *London NW6 4GM*
>
> *December 20th 2000*
>
> *Dear Peter and Claire,*
>
> *First of all, a very happy Christmas and all the best for the New Year to you and the children.① We hope you're all well② and that we'll see you again soon. It seems ages since we last met up.*
>
> *We've had a very eventful year. Last summer Gavin came off his bike and broke his arm and collarbone. Kathy scraped through her A levels and is now at Sussex doing European Studies. Poor Tony was made redundant in October and is still looking for a job.*
>
> *Do come and see us next time you are over this way. Just give us a ring a couple of days before so we can fix something.*
>
> *All best wishes*
>
> *Tony and Ann*

① *Oder (vor allem, wenn die Kinder älter sind):* to you and the family.
② *Informeller:* flourishing.

Letters / Briefe

Invitation (informal)

Hamm, den 22.4.2000

Liebe Jennie,

wäre es möglich, dass du ① in den Sommerferien zu uns kommst? Katrin und
Gottfried würden sich riesig freuen (ich und mein Mann natürlich auch). Wir
planen eine Reise zum Bodensee Ende Juli/Anfang August, du ① könntest gerne
mitfahren. Es ist wirklich sehr schön dort unten. Wir werden wahrscheinlich
zelten – hoffentlich hast du ① nichts dagegen!

Schreib bald, ob das für dich ① in Frage kommt.

Herzliche Grüße

Monika Pfortner

■ Beginning: if you put a comma after the name on the first line (which is usual), the letter proper
should start with a small letter.

① du, dich, dein etc.: although many people still write these with a capital in letters, this is not
necessary. But the formal Sie, Ihnen, Ihr must always have a capital.

Invitation (formal)

Invitations to parties are usually by word of mouth, while for weddings, announcements rather than
invitations are usually sent out:

Irene Brinkmann   Stefan Hoff

Wir heiraten am Samstag, den 20. April 2000,
um 14 Uhr in der Pfarrkirche Landsberg.

Goethestraße 12   Ulrichsweg 4

Landsberg   Altötting

Einladung (informell)

- *Die Absenderadresse befindet sich oben auf dem Brief selbst, entweder rechts oder in der Mitte, darunter das Datum.*

- *Das Datum im Englischen hat viele Formen:* May 10, 10 May, May 10th, 10th May *sind alle möglich und gleichermaßen richtig. In den USA verwendet man die Reihenfolge Monat, Tag, Jahr, wenn das Datum in Ziffern angegeben wird:* 05/10/2000

35 Winchester Drive
Stoke Gifford
Bristol
BS34 8PD

April 22nd 2000

Dear Klaus,

Is there any chance of your coming to stay with us in the summer holidays? Roy and Debbie would be delighted if you could (as well as David and me, of course). We hope to go to North Wales at the end of July/beginning of August, and you'd be very welcome to come too. It's really beautiful up there. We'll probably take tents – I hope that's OK by you.

Let me know as soon as possible if you can manage it.

All best wishes

Rachel Hemmings

Einladung (förmlich)

Zu einer Hochzeit mit anschließendem Empfang

Mr and Mrs Peter Thompson

request the pleasure of your company
at the marriage of their daughter

Hannah Louise
to
Steven David Warner

at St. Mary's Church, Little Bourton
on Saturday 25th July 2000 at 2 p.m.
and afterwards at the
Golden Cross Hotel, Billing

R.S.V.P.   *23 Santers Lane*
Little Bourton
Northampton
NN6 1AZ

Accepting an invitation

Edinburgh, den 2.5.2000

Liebe Frau Pfortner,

recht herzlichen Dank für Ihre liebe Einladung. Da ich noch keine festen Pläne für die Sommerferien habe, möchte ich sie sehr gerne annehmen. Allerdings darf ich nicht mehr als vier bis fünf Tage weg sein, da es meiner Mutter nicht sehr gut geht. Sie ① müssen mir sagen, was ich mitbringen soll (außer Edinburgh Rock!). Ist es sehr warm am Bodensee? Kann man im See schwimmen?

Natürlich habe ich nichts gegen Zelten. Auch hier in Schottland bei Wind und Regen macht es mir Spaß!

Ich freue mich auf ein baldiges Wiedersehen.

Herzliche Grüße

Jennie Stewart

---

① *Since this is a letter from a younger person writing to the mother of a friend, she uses the formal Sie form and possessive Ihr (always with capitals), and writes to her as "Frau Pfortner". On the other hand it was quite natural for Frau Pfortner to use the du form to her.*

Antwort auf eine Einladung (informell)

> Mozartstraße 5
> 32756 Detmold
> Germany
>
> 2 May 2000

Dear Mrs Hemmings,

Many thanks for your letter and kind invitation. Since I don't have anything fixed yet for the summer holidays, I'd be delighted to come. However I mustn't be away for more than four or five days since my mother hasn't been very well.

You must let me know what I should bring. How warm is it in North Wales? Can one swim in the sea? Camping is fine as far as I'm concerned, we take our tent everywhere.

Looking forward to seeing you again soon,

Yours

Klaus

Letters / Briefe

Antwort auf eine Einladung (förmlich)

> Greenacres
> Westway
> Balsall Common
> West Midlands
> CV7 8RR

■ Man wiederholt die Details von der Einladung, etwas vereinfacht.

Annahme:
Richard Willis has great pleasure in accepting Mr and Mrs Peter Thompson's kind invitation to the marriage of their daughter Hannah Louise to Steven Warner at St. Mary's Church, Little Bourton, on Saturday 25th July.

■ Im Falle einer Absage ist es oft höflicher, einen Brief zu schreiben, vor allem wenn man die Brauteltern gut kennt.

Absage:
Richard Willis regrets that he is unable to accept Mr and Mrs Peter Thompson's kind invitation ... , due to a prior engagement.

Replying to a job advertisement

David Baker
67 Whiteley Avenue
St George
Bristol
BS5 6TW

Softwarehaus WSO GmbH
Personalabteilung
Kanalstr. 75
D-75757 Pforzheim   Bristol, den 26.2.2000

Ihre Stellenanzeige im Tagblatt vom 23.2.2000

Sehr geehrte Damen und Herren, (1)

ich interessiere mich für die von Ihnen im Tagblatt vom 23. September ausgeschriebene Stelle eines Computergrafikers und würde mich freuen, wenn Sie mir nähere Informationen zuschicken könnten. (2)

Derzeit bin ich bei der Firma Wondersoft Ltd in Bristol tätig, aber mein Vertrag läuft schon Ende des Monats aus, (3) und ich möchte gerne in Deutschland arbeiten. Wie Sie meinem Lebenslauf entnehmen können, verfüge ich über ausgezeichnete Sprachkenntnisse sowie die geforderten Qualifikationen und einschlägige Berufserfahrung.

Zu einem Vorstellungsgespräch stehe ich jederzeit ab dem 6. Oktober zur Verfügung. Sie können mich ab diesem Datum unter der folgenden Adresse in Deutschland erreichen:

bei Gerber
Rudolfstr. 22
81925 München
Tel. (089) 460 99 507

Ich freue mich darauf, von Ihnen zu hören. (4)

Mit freundlichen Grüßen

David Baker

Anlage: Lebenslauf

(1) *Correct if the letter is addressed to the personnel department, but if it is addressed to the personnel manager (An den Personalleiter, ...) the letter begins:* Sehr geehrter Herr XY *or* Sehr geehrte Frau XY.

(2) *Or if you have enough details and want to apply for the job right away:* und möchte mich um diese Stellung bewerben.

(3) *Or if you are unemployed:* Derzeit bin ich arbeitslos, ...

(4) *Or:* Ihre Antwort erwarte ich mit Interesse.

Bewerbung auf eine Stellenanzeige hin

Humboldtweg 16
60247 Frankfurt a. M.
Germany
Tel. (069) 724 689

13th February 2000

The Personnel Manager ①
Patterson Software plc
Milton Estate
Bath BA6 8YZ

Dear Sir or Madam, ②

I am interested in the post of programmer advertised in the Guardian of 12th February and would be grateful if you could send me further particulars. ③

I am currently working for the Sempo Corporation in Frankfurt, but my contract finishes at the end of the month, and I would like ④ to come and work in the UK. As you can see from my CV (enclosed), I have an excellent command of English and also the required qualifications and experience.

I will be available for interview any time after 6th October, from which date I can be contacted at the following address in the UK:

c/o Lewis
51 Dexter Road
London N7 6BW
Tel. 0207 607 5512

I look forward to hearing from you. ⑤

Yours sincerely

Rita Steinmüller

Encl.

Letters / Briefe

① *Den Brief so addressieren, wenn in der Anzeige kein Name vorkommt; aber wenn es z.B. heißt* "Reply to Angela Summers", *dann* "Ms Angela Summers, ..."

② *Wenn der Name bekannt ist, dann* "Dear Ms Summers", "Dear Mr Wright" *etc.*

③ *Oder falls Sie schon genügend Informationen haben und sich bewerben wollen:* "and would like to apply for this position".

④ *Oder falls Sie arbeitslos sind:* "I am currently unemployed and would like ..."

⑤ *Oder:* "Thanking you in anticipation".

Letters / Briefe

Curriculum Vitae (CV) or (*Amer.*) Résumé

Lebenslauf

David Baker
67 Whiteley Avenue
St George
Bristol
BS5 6TW
Großbritannien

Tel. +43 (0)117 945 3421

geboren am 30.06.1970 in London, ledig①

Ausbildung

1986 O Levels in 7 Fächern (ungefähr = mittlere Reife), John Radcliffe School, Croydon

1988 A Levels in Mathematik, Höherer Mathematik, Informatik, Deutsch (ungefähr = Abitur), Croydon Sixth Form College

1989 Teilzeitarbeit in München, Abendkurse an der VHS

1990-94 University of Aston, Birmingham, B.Sc in Informatik

Berufstätigkeit

08/94 - 08/97 Traineeausbildung, anschließend Sotwareentwickler bei IBM

seit 09/97 Programmierer bei Wondersoft plc, Bristol

Entwicklung von Programmen für die Industrie; Schwerpunkt: Grafiksoftware

Besondere Kenntnisse

Fremdsprachen: Deutsch (fließend), Französisch (gut)

---

① *Or:* Verheiratet (mit einem Kind/zwei Kindern etc.); Geschieden (mit einem Kind/zwei Kindern etc.)

Lebenslauf

CURRICULUM VITAE ①

Name:	Rita Steinmüller
Address:	Humboldtweg 16 60247 Frankfurt a. M. Germany
Telephone:	+44 (0)69 724 689
Nationality:	German
Date of Birth:	11/3/1973
Marital status:	Single ②

Education:

1991-1995	Degree Course in Information Technology at Stuttgart University
1984-1991	Theodor-Heuss-Gymnasium, Eichborn Abitur examination (approx. A Level) in Mathematics, Physics, Economics and English

Employment:

1996-present	Program development engineer with Sempo-Informatik, Frankfurt, specializing in computer graphics
1995-1996	Trainee programmer with Oregon Germany, Rüsselsheim

Further skills:

Languages:	German (mother tongue), English (fluent spoken and written), French (good)
Interests:	Travel (many trips to the UK), chess, tennis

---

① *Oder (Amer.):* RÉSUMÉ
② *Oder:* Married (with one/two/three etc. children), Divorced (with one/two/three etc. children)

Enquiry to a tourist office

■ *A simple business-style letter. The recipient's address is on the left and the sender's on the right, with the date below.*

Verkehrsverein Heidelberg e.V. Silvia Sommer
Friedrich-Ebert-Anlage 2 Tannenweg 23
69117 Heidelberg 48149 Münster

24. April 2000

■ *The subject of the letter is centred.*

Hotels und Pensionen in Heidelberg

Sehr geehrte Damen und Herren,

■ *This is the standard formula for starting a business letter addressed to a firm or organization, and not to a particular person.*

würden Sie mir bitte freundlicherweise eine Liste der Hotels und Pensionen (der mittleren Kategorie) am Ort zusenden?

Ich möchte bitte auch Informationen über Busfahrten zu den Sehenswürdigkeiten der Umgebung in der zweiten Augusthälfte haben.

Mit freundlichen Grüßen

Silvia Sommer

■ *"Mit freundlichen Grüßen" is the standard ending for a formal or business letter; another possibility is "Mit besten Grüßen".*

Anfrage an ein Fremdenverkehrsbüro

■ *Diese Anrede verwendet man, wenn der Name des Adressaten nicht bekannt ist. Es wäre hier auch möglich, "The Manager" wegzulassen und das Tourist Office anzuschreiben; in diesem Fall könnte der Brief auch mit "Dear Sirs" anfangen.*

Am Grün 28
A-9026 Klagenfurt
Austria

4th May 2000

The Manager
Regional Tourist Office
3 Virgin Road
Canterbury
CT1 3AA

Dear Sir or Madam,

Please send me a list of hotels and guest houses in Canterbury in the medium price range.

I would also like details of coach trips to local sights in the second half of August.

Yours sincerely

Bruno Angermeyer

Letters / Briefe

■ *"Yours sincerely" ist der übliche Briefschluss für Geschäftsbriefe sowie für persönliche Briefe an Leute, die man nicht sehr gut kennt. "Yours faithfully" ist etwas altmodisch und wird nur noch für sehr formelle Geschäftsbriefe verwendet, vor allem in Rechtssachen.*

Letter-writing / Briefeschreiben

• •

Booking a hotel room

Hotel Goldener Pflug　　　　　　　　Tobias Schwarz
Ortsstraße 7　　　　　　　　　　　　Gartenstr. 19
69235 Steinbach　　　　　　　　　　76530 Baden-Baden

16. Juli 2000

Sehr geehrte Damen und Herren,

Ich wurde durch die Broschüre "Hotels und Pensionen im Naturpark Odenwald (Ausgabe 2000)" auf ihr Hotel aufmerksam.

Ich möchte für mich und meine Frau für die Zeit vom 2. bis 11. August (neun Nächte) ein ruhiges Doppelzimmer mit Dusche reservieren, sowie ein Einzelzimmer für unseren Sohn.

Falls Sie für diese Zeit etwas Passendes haben, informieren Sie mich doch bitte über den Preis und darüber, ob Sie eine Anzahlung wünschen.

Mit freundlichen Grüßen

Tobias Schwarz

Booking a campsite

Camilla Stumpf
Saalgasse 10
60311 Frankfurt

Camping am See
Frau Bettina Sattler
Auweg 6-10
87654 Waldenkirchen

■ For a business letter to a particular person, use "Sehr geehrte(r)" and the name. (If this letter were to a man, it would start "Sehr geehrter Herr Sattler").

Frankfurt, den 16.04.2000

Sehr geehrte Frau Sattler,

Ihr Campingplatz wurde mir von Herrn Stephan Seidel empfohlen, der schon mehrmals bei Ihnen war. ① Ich würde nun gerne vom 18. bis 25. Juli mit zwei Freunden eine Woche bei Ihnen verbringen. Könnten Sie uns bitte einen Zeltplatz ② möglichst in unmittelbarer Nähe des Sees ③ reservieren?

Würden Sie mir freundlicherweise mitteilen, ob Sie meine Reservierung annehemen können und ob Sie eine Anzahlung wünschen?

Außerdem wäre ich Ihnen dankbar für eine kurze Wegbeschreibung von der Autobahn.

Mit vielem Dank im Voraus und freundlichen Grüßen

Camilla Stumpf

① Or if you have found the campsite in a guide, say e.g.: "Ich habe Ihre Anschrift dem ACDA-Campingführer 2000 entnommen".

② Or if you have a caravan: "einen Stellplatz für einen Wohnwagen".

③ Alternatives: "in schattiger/geschützter Lage".

Hotelzimmerreservierung

The Manager   35 Prince Edward Road
Torbay Hotel   Oxford OX7 3AA
Dawlish
Devon   Tel. 01865 322435
EX37 2LR   23rd April 2000

Dear Sir or Madam,

I saw your hotel listed in the Inns of Devon guide for last year, and wish to reserve a double (or twin-bedded) room with shower ① in a quiet position from August 2nd - 11th (nine nights), also a single room for our son.

If you have anything suitable for this period please let me know the price and whether you require a deposit.

Yours sincerely

Charles Fairhurst

① *Alternativen:* "with bath", "with ensuite".

Campingplatzreservierung

22 Daniel Avenue
Caldwood
Leeds LS8 7RR
Tel. 01132 998767

25th April 2000

Mr Joseph Vale
Lakeside Park
Rydal
Cumbria
LA22 9RZ

Dear Mr Vale

Your campsite was recommended to me by James Dallas, who knows it from several visits.① I and two friends would like to come for a week from July 18th to 25th Could you please reserve us a site for one tent, ② preferably close to the shore.③

Please confirm the booking and let me know if you require a deposit. Would you also be good enough to send me instructions on how to reach you from the motorway.

Yours sincerely

Frances Good

① *Oder falls Sie den Campingplatz einem Führer entnommen haben, etwa:* "I found your site in the Tourist Board's list/ the Good Camper's Guide" *etc.*
② *Oder falls Sie einen Wohnwagen haben:* "a caravan site".
③ *Andere Möglichkeiten:* "in a shady/sheltered spot".

Letters / Briefe

. . . .

Cancelling a reservation

Herrn
Hans Knauer
Gasthaus Sonnenblick
Hauptstr. 6
D-94066 Bad Füssing
Germany   Aberdeen, den 2.6.2000

Sehr geehrter Herr Knauer,

leider muss ich meine/unsere Reservierung für die Woche vom 7. bis 13. August
① rückgängig machen. Wegen unvorhergesehener Umstände ② muss
ich/müssen wir auf meinen/unseren Urlaub verzichten.

Es tut mir aufrichtig Leid, dass ich so spät abbestellen muss, und hoffe, dass Sie
deswegen keine Unannehmlichkeiten haben.

Mit freundlichen Grüßen

Robert McDonald

---

① Or: "für die Zeit vom 7. bis 20. August" etc.
② Or more precisely: "Durch den überraschenden Tod meines Vaters/die Krankheit meines
   Mannes" etc.

Stornierung einer Reservierung

Mrs J. Warrington   Wernerstr. 17
Downlands   49835 Wietmarschen
Steyning   Germany
West Sussex
BN44 6LZ

                                     July 20th 2000

Dear Mrs Warrington,

Unfortunately I have to cancel my/our reservation for the week
of August 7th. ① Due to unforeseen circumstances ② I/we have
had to abandon my/our holiday plans.

I very much regret having to cancel [at such a late stage] and
hope it does not cause you undue inconvenience.

Yours sincerely

Elke Nordrup

---

① Oder: "for the period from August 7th to 14th".
② Oder genauer: "Owing to my father's sudden death/my husband's illness" etc

Sending an e-mail

The illustration shows a typical interface for sending e-mail.

Lieber Klaus

Vielen Dank fuer deine Nachricht von heute Morgen.
Der Termin, den du vorschlaegst, wuerde auch mir sehr gut passen.

Beste Gruesse,

Thomas

Das Verschicken von E-Mails

Die Abbildung zeigt eine typische Oberfläche zum Verschicken von E-Mails.

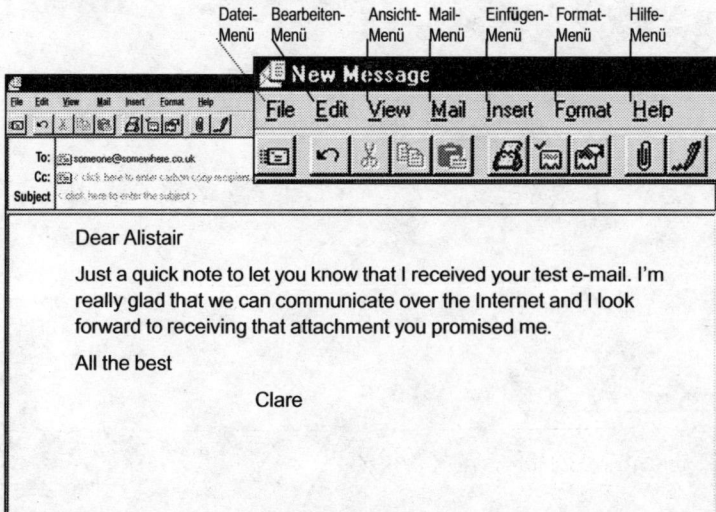

Dear Alistair

Just a quick note to let you know that I received your test e-mail. I'm really glad that we can communicate over the Internet and I look forward to receiving that attachment you promised me.

All the best

Clare

A, a¹ /eɪ/ *n.* A, a, *das;* **A road** Straße 1. Ordnung; ≈ Bundesstraße, *die*

a² /ə, *stressed* eɪ/ *indef. art.* ein/eine/ein; **he is a gardener/a Frenchman** er ist Gärtner/Franzose; **she did not say a word** sie sagte kein Wort

AA *abbr.* (Brit.) = **Automobile Association** britischer Automobilklub

aback /ə'bæk/ *adv.* **be taken ~:** erstaunt sein

abacus /'æbəkəs/ *n., pl.* **~es** *or* **abaci** /'æbəsaɪ/ Abakus, *der*

abandon /ə'bændən/ *v.t.* verlassen ⟨*Ort, Person*⟩; aufgeben ⟨*Prinzip*⟩; **~ed** verlassen, ausgesetzt ⟨*Kind, Tier*⟩

abase /ə'beɪs/ *v.t.* erniedrigen

abashed /ə'bæʃt/ *adj.* beschämt

abate /ə'beɪt/ *v.i.* nachlassen

abattoir /'æbətwɑː(r)/ *n.* Schlachthof, *der*

abbey /'æbɪ/ *n.* Abtei, *die*

abbot /'æbət/ *n.* Abt, *der*

abbreviate /ə'briːvɪeɪt/ *v.t.* abkürzen

ab'breviated dialling *n.* (Teleph.) Kurzwahl, *die*

abbreviation /əbriːvɪ'eɪʃn/ *n.* Abkürzung, *die*

abdicate /'æbdɪkeɪt/ *v.t.* abdanken

abdication /æbdɪ'keɪʃn/ *n.* Abdankung, *die*

abdomen /'æbdəmən/ *n.* Bauch, *der*

abdominal /æb'dɒmɪnl/ *adj.* Bauch-

abduct /əb'dʌkt/ *v.t.* entführen

abduction /əb'dʌkʃn/ *n.* Entführung, *die*

aberration /æbə'reɪʃn/ *n.* Abweichung, *die*

abet /ə'bet/ *v.t.,* -tt- helfen (+ *Dat.*); **aid and ~:** Beihilfe leisten (+ *Dat.*)

abhor /əb'hɔː(r)/ *v.t.,* -rr- verabscheuen

abhorrent /əb'hɒrənt/ *adj.* abscheulich

abide /ə'baɪd/ ① *v.i.* **~ by** befolgen ⟨*Gesetz, Vorschrift*⟩; [ein]halten ⟨*Versprechen*⟩ ② *v.t.* ertragen; **I can't ~ dogs** ich kann Hunde nicht ausstehen

ability /ə'bɪlɪtɪ/ *n.* (a) (capacity) Fähigkeit, *die;* **have the ~ to do sth.** etw. können (b) (cleverness) Intelligenz, *die* (c) (talent) Begabung, *die*

abject /'æbdʒekt/ *adj.* elend; bitter ⟨*Armut*⟩; demütig ⟨*Entschuldigung*⟩

ablaze /ə'bleɪz/ *adj.* **be ~:** in Flammen stehen

able /'eɪbl/ *adj.* (a) **be ~ to do sth.** etw. tun können (b) (competent) fähig

able-bodied /'eɪblbɒdɪd/ *adj.* kräftig; tauglich ⟨*Soldat, Matrose*⟩

ably /'eɪblɪ/ *adv.* geschickt; gekonnt

abnormal /æb'nɔːml/ *adj.* abnorm; a[b]normal ⟨*Interesse, Verhalten*⟩

abnormality /æbnɔː'mælɪtɪ/ *n.* Abnormität, *die*

aboard /ə'bɔːd/ ① *adv.* an Bord ② *prep.* an Bord (+ *Gen.*); **~ the bus** im Bus; **~ ship** an Bord

abode /ə'bəʊd/ *n.* **of no fixed ~:** ohne festen Wohnsitz

abolish /ə'bɒlɪʃ/ *v.t.* abschaffen

abolition /æbə'lɪʃn/ *n.* Abschaffung, *die*

abominable /ə'bɒmɪnəbl/ *adj.* abscheulich; scheußlich

aborigine /æbə'rɪdʒɪnɪ/ *n.* Ureinwohner, *der*

abort /ə'bɔːt/ *v.t.* abtreiben ⟨*Baby*⟩

abortion /ə'bɔːʃn/ *n.* Abtreibung, *die;* **backstreet ~:** illegale Abtreibung (durch Engelmacherin)

a'bortion pill *n.* Abtreibungspille, *die*

abortive /ə'bɔːtɪv/ *adj.* misslungen ⟨*Plan*⟩; fehlgeschlagen ⟨*Versuch*⟩

abound /ə'baʊnd/ *v.i.* **~ in sth.** an etw. (*Dat.*) reich sein

about /ə'baʊt/ ① *adv.* (a) (all around) rings[her]um; (here and there) überall; **all ~:** ringsumher (b) (near) **be ~:** da sein; hier sein (c) **be ~ to do sth.** gerade etw. tun wollen (d) **be out and ~:** aktiv sein (e) (approximately) ungefähr ② *prep.* (a) (all round) um [... herum] (b) (concerning) über (+ *Akk.*); **know ~ sth.** von etw. wissen; **a question ~ sth.** eine Frage zu etw.; **what was it ~?** worum ging es?

above /ə'bʌv/ ① *adv.* (a) (position) oben; (higher up) darüber (b) (direction) nach oben ② *prep.* (position) über (+ *Dat.*); (direction, more than) über (+ *Akk.*); **~ all** vor allem

above 'board *pred. adj.* einwandfrei; korrekt

a'bove-mentioned *adj.* oben erwähnt *od.* genannt

abrasion /ə'breɪʒn/ *n.* (graze) Hautabschürfung, *die*

abrasive /ə'breɪsɪv/ ① *adj.* (a) scheuernd; Scheuer- (b) (fig.: harsh) aggressiv ② *n.* Scheuermittel, *das*

abreast /ə'brest/ *adv.* (a) nebeneinander ⋯▶

(b) (fig.) **keep** ∼ **of** sth. sich über etw. (*Akk.*) auf dem Laufenden halten

abroad /ə'brɔːd/ *adv.* im Ausland; (direction) ins Ausland

abrupt /ə'brʌpt/ *adj.*, **a'bruptly** *adv.* **(a)** (sudden[ly]) abrupt; plötzlich
(b) (brusque[ly]) schroff

ABS *abbr.* = **anti-lock brake** *or* **braking system** ABS

abscess /'æbsɪs/ *n.* Abszess, *der*

abscond /əb'skɒnd/ *v.t.* sich entfernen

absence /'æbsəns/ *n.* Abwesenheit, *die;* the ∼ **of** sth. der Mangel an etw. (*Dat.*)

absent /'æbsənt/ *adj.* abwesend; **be** ∼ **from school/work** in der Schule/am Arbeitsplatz fehlen

absentee /æbsən'tiː/ *n.* Fehlende, *der/die;* Abwesende, *der/die;* ∼ **landlord** nicht auf seinem Gut lebender Gutsherr

absenteeism /æbsən'tiːɪzm/ *n.* [häufiges] Fernbleiben; (without good reason) Krankfeiern, *das* (ugs.)

absent-minded /æbsənt'maɪndɪd/ *adj.* geistesabwesend; (habitually) zerstreut

absolute /'æbsəluːt/ *adj.* absolut; ausgemacht ⟨*Lüge, Skandal*⟩; ∼ **majority** absolute Mehrheit

abso'lutely *adv.* absolut; völlig ⟨*verrückt*⟩; **you're** ∼ **right!** du hast völlig Recht; ∼ **not!** auf keinen Fall!

absolve /əb'zɒlv/ *v.t.* ∼ **from** entbinden von ⟨*Pflichten*⟩; lossprechen von ⟨*Schuld*⟩

absorb /əb'sɔːb/ *v.t.* **(a)** aufsaugen ⟨*Flüssigkeit*⟩
(b) abfangen ⟨*Schlag, Stoß*⟩
(c) (fig.: engross) ausfüllen

absorbency /əb'sɔːbənsɪ/ *n.* Saugfähigkeit, *die*

absorbent /əb'sɔːbənt/ *adj.* saugfähig

ab'sorbing *adj.* faszinierend

abstain /əb'steɪn/ *v.i.* ∼ **from** sth. sich einer Sache (*Gen.*) enthalten; ∼ **[from voting]** sich der Stimme enthalten

abstemious /əb'stiːmɪəs/ *adj.* enthaltsam

abstention /əb'stenʃn/ *n.* (from voting) Stimmenthaltung, *die*

abstinence /'æbstɪnəns/ *n.* Abstinenz, *die*

abstinent /'æbstɪnənt/ *adj.* abstinent

abstract /'æbstrækt/ ① *adj.* abstrakt ② *n.* Zusammenfassung, *die*

absurd /əb'sɜːd/ *adj.* absurd; (ridiculous) lächerlich

absurdity /əb'sɜːdɪtɪ/ *n.* Absurdität, *die*

ab'surdly *adv.* lächerlich

abundance /ə'bʌndəns/ *n.* [**an**] ∼ **of** sth. eine Fülle von etw.

abundant /ə'bʌndənt/ *adj.* reich (**in** an + *Dat.*)

abuse ① /ə'bjuːz/ *v.t.* beschimpfen ② /ə'bjuːs/ *n.* Beschimpfungen *Pl.*

abusive /ə'bjuːsɪv/ *adj.* beleidigend; **become** ∼: ausfallend werden

abysmal /ə'bɪzml/ *adj.* (coll.: bad) katastrophal (ugs.)

abyss /ə'bɪs/ *n.* Abgrund, *der*

AC *abbr.* = **alternating current** Ws

academic /ækə'demɪk/ *adj.* akademisch

academy /ə'kædəmɪ/ *n.* Akademie, *die*

accede /æk'siːd/ *v.i.* **(a)** zustimmen (**to** *Dat.*)
(b) ∼ **[to the throne]** den Thron besteigen

accelerate /ək'seləreɪt/ ① *v.t.* beschleunigen
② *v.i.* sich beschleunigen; ⟨*Auto, Fahrer:*⟩ beschleunigen

acceleration /əkselə'reɪʃn/ *n.* Beschleunigung, *die*

accelerator /ək'seləreɪtə(r)/ *n.* ∼ **[pedal]** Gas[pedal], *das*

accent /'æksənt/ *n.* Akzent, *der*

accentuate /ək'sentjʊeɪt/ *v.t.* betonen

accept /ək'sept/ *v.t.* **(a)** annehmen; entgegennehmen ⟨*Dank, Spende*⟩; übernehmen ⟨*Verantwortung*⟩
(b) (acknowledge) akzeptieren

acceptable /ək'septəbl/ *adj.* akzeptabel; annehmbar ⟨*Preis, Gehalt*⟩

acceptance /ək'septəns/ *n.* **(a)** Annahme, *die*
(b) (acknowledgement) Anerkennung, *die*

access /'ækses/ *n.* **(a)** (admission) **gain** ∼: Einlass finden
(b) (opportunity to use or approach) Zugang, *der* (**to** zu)

accessible /ək'sesɪbl/ *adj.* **(a)** (reachable) erreichbar
(b) (available, understandable) zugänglich (**to** für)

accession /ək'seʃn/ *n.* Amtsantritt, *der;* ∼ **[to the throne]** Thronbesteigung, *die*

accessory /ək'sesərɪ/ *n.* **(a)** accessories *pl.* Zubehör, *das*
(b) (dress article) Accessoire, *das*

'access road *n.* Zufahrtsstraße, *die*

accident /'æksɪdənt/ *n.* **(a)** Unfall, *der*
(b) (chance) Zufall, *der;* **by** ∼: zufällig
(c) (mistake) Versehen, *das;* **by** ∼: versehentlich

accidental /æksɪ'dentl/ *adj.* (chance) zufällig; (unintended) unbeabsichtigt

acci'dentally *adv.* (by chance) zufällig; (by mistake) versehentlich

'accident-prone *adj.* ∼ **person** Unfäller, *der* (Psych.); **he's such an** ∼ **boy** mit dem Jungen ist aber auch immer irgendwas (ugs.)

acclaim /ə'kleɪm/ *v.t.* feiern

acclimatisation, acclimatise
▶ ACCLIMATIZ-

acclimatization /əklaɪmətaɪ'zeɪʃn/ *n.* (lit. or fig.) Akklimatisation, *die*

acclimatize /ə'klaɪmətaɪz/ *v.t.* **get** *or* **become** ∼**d** sich akklimatisieren

accolade /'ækəleɪd/ *n.* ∼**[s]** (praise) Lob, *das*

accommodate /ə'kɒmədeɪt/ v.t. **(a)** unterbringen; (hold) Platz bieten (+ Dat.) **(b)** (oblige) gefällig sein (+ Dat.)

accommodating /ə'kɒmədeɪtɪŋ/ adj. zuvorkommend

accommodation /əkɒmə'deɪʃn/ n. Unterkunft, die

accommo'dation address n. Gefälligkeitsadresse, die

accompaniment /ə'kʌmpənɪmənt/ n. Begleitung, die

accompanist /ə'kʌmpənɪst/ n. Begleiter, der/Begleiterin, die

accompany /ə'kʌmpənɪ/ v.t. begleiten

accomplice /ə'kʌmplɪs/ n. Komplize, der/Komplizin, die

accomplish /ə'kʌmplɪʃ/ v.t. vollbringen ⟨Tat⟩; erfüllen ⟨Aufgabe⟩

accomplished /ə'kʌmplɪʃt/ adj. fähig; **he is an ~ speaker/dancer** er ist ein erfahrener Redner/vollendeter Tänzer

ac'complishment n. **(a)** (completion) Vollendung, die **(b)** (achievement) Leistung, die; (skill) Fähigkeit, die

accord /ə'kɔːd/ **1** n. Übereinstimmung, die; **of one's own ~:** aus eigenem Antrieb; **with one ~:** geschlossen **2** v.t. **~ sb. sth.** jmdm. etw. gewähren

accordance /ə'kɔːdəns/ n. **in ~ with** in Übereinstimmung mit

ac'cording adv. **~ to** nach; **~ to him** nach seiner Aussage

ac'cordingly adv. (as appropriate) entsprechend; (therefore) folglich

accordion /ə'kɔːdɪən/ n. Akkordeon, das

accost /ə'kɒst/ v.t. ansprechen

account /ə'kaʊnt/ n. **(a)** (Finance) Rechnung, die; (at bank, shop) Konto, das **(b)** (consideration) **take ~ of sth., take sth. into ~:** etw. berücksichtigen; **take no ~ of sth./sb.** etw./jmdn. unberücksichtigt lassen; **don't change your plans on my ~:** ändert nicht meinetwegen eure Pläne; **on ~ of** wegen; **on no ~:** auf [gar] keinen Fall **(c)** (report) Bericht, der **(d) call sb. to ~:** jmdn. zur Rechenschaft ziehen

■ **ac'count for** v.t. Rechenschaft ablegen über; (explain) erklären

accountable /ə'kaʊntəbl/ adj. verantwortlich

accountancy /ə'kaʊntənsɪ/ n. Buchhaltung, die

accountant /ə'kaʊntənt/ n. [Bilanz]buchhalter, der/-halterin, die

account: ~ holder n. Kontoinhaber, der/-inhaberin, die; **~ number** n. Kontonummer, die

accredited /ə'kredɪtɪd/ adj. anerkannt ⟨Schule, Anstalt, Buch, Regierung⟩; akkreditiert ⟨Botschafter, Diplomat⟩; zugelassen ⟨Journalist⟩

accrue /ə'kruː/ v.i. ⟨Zinsen:⟩ auflaufen; **~ to sb.** ⟨Reichtümer, Einnahmen:⟩ jmdm. zufließen

accumulate /ə'kjuːmjʊleɪt/ **1** v.t. sammeln **2** v.i. ⟨Menge, Staub:⟩ sich ansammeln; ⟨Geld:⟩ sich anhäufen

accumulation /əkjuːmjʊ'leɪʃn/ n. [An]sammeln, das; (being accumulated) Anhäufung, die

accuracy /'ækjʊrəsɪ/ n. Genauigkeit, die

accurate /'ækjʊrət/ adj., **'accurately** adv. genau; (correct[ly]) richtig

accusation /ækjuː'zeɪʃn/ n. Anschuldigung, die; (Law) Anklage, die

accusative /ə'kjuːzətɪv/ adj. & n. **~ [case]** Akkusativ, der

accuse /ə'kjuːz/ v.t. beschuldigen; (Law) anklagen (of wegen + Gen.)

accustom /ə'kʌstəm/ v.t. gewöhnen (to an + Akk.); **grow/be ~ed to sth.** sich an etw. (Akk.) gewöhnen/an etw. (Akk.) gewöhnt sein

accustomed /ə'kʌstəmd/ attrib. adj. gewohnt; üblich

ace /eɪs/ **1** n. As, das **2** adj. (coll.) klasse (ugs.); spitze (ugs.)

ache /eɪk/ **1** v.i. schmerzen; wehtun **2** n. Schmerz, der

achieve /ə'tʃiːv/ v.t. zustande bringen; erreichen ⟨Ziel, Standard⟩

a'chievement n, **(a)** ▶ ACHIEVE: Zustandebringen, das; Erreichen, das **(b)** (thing accomplished) Leistung, die

acid /'æsɪd/ **1** adj. sauer **2** n. Säure, die

'acid house n Acidhouse, das; **~ music/party** Acidhousemusik, die/Acidhouseparty, die

'acid: ~'rain n. saurer Regen; **~ test** n. (fig.) Feuerprobe, die

acidic /ə'sɪdɪk/ adj. säuerlich

acidity /ə'sɪdɪtɪ/ n. Säure, die

acknowledge /ək'nɒlɪdʒ/ v.t. **(a)** zugeben ⟨Tatsache, Fehler, Schuld⟩ **(b)** sich erkenntlich zeigen für ⟨Dienste, Bemühungen⟩; erwidern ⟨Gruß⟩ **(c)** bestätigen ⟨Empfang, Bewerbung⟩; **~ a letter** den Empfang eines Briefes bestätigen

acknowledg[e]ment /ək'nɒlɪdʒmənt/ n. **(a)** (admission) Eingeständnis, das **(b)** (thanks) Dank, der (of für) **(c)** (of letter) Bestätigung [des Empfangs]

acne /'æknɪ/ n. Akne, die

acorn /'eɪkɔːn/ n. Eichel, die

acoustic /ə'kuːstɪk/ adj. akustisch

a'coustics n. pl. Akustik, die

acquaint /ə'kweɪnt/ v.t. **be ~ed with sb.** mit jmdm. bekannt sein

acquaintance /ə'kweɪntəns/ n. **(a)** **~ with sb.** Bekanntschaft mit jmdm.; **make sb.'s ~:** jmds. Bekanntschaft machen ⸬

(b) (person) Bekannte, der/die

acquiesce /ækwɪ'es/ v.i. einwilligen (in in + Akk.)

acquire /ə'kwaɪə(r)/ v.t. sich (Dat.) anschaffen ⟨Gegenstände⟩; erwerben ⟨Besitz, Kenntnisse⟩

acquisition /ækwɪ'zɪʃn/ n. Erwerb, der; (thing) Anschaffung, die

acquisitive /ə'kwɪzɪtɪv/ adj. raffsüchtig

acquit /ə'kwɪt/ v.t., **-tt-** freisprechen

acquittal /ə'kwɪtl/ n. Freispruch, der

acre /'eɪkə(r)/ n. Acre, der

acrid /'ækrɪd/ adj. beißend ⟨Geruch, Rauch⟩; bitter ⟨Geschmack⟩

acrimonious /ækrɪ'məʊnɪəs/ adj. bitter; erbittert ⟨Streit⟩

acrobat /'ækrəbæt/ n. Akrobat, der/ Akrobatin, die

acrobatic /ækrə'bætɪk/ adj. akrobatisch

acrobatics /ækrə'bætɪks/ n. Akrobatik, die

acronym /'ækrənɪm/ n. Akronym, das

across /ə'krɒs/ **1** adv. (from one side to the other) darüber; (from here to there) hinüber; **be 9 miles ~:** 9 Meilen breit sein **2** prep. über (+ Akk.); (on the other side of) auf der anderen Seite (+ Gen.)

a'cross-the-board adj. pauschal; **an ~ pay rise** eine pauschale od. generelle Lohnerhöhung

acrylic /ə'krɪlɪk/ **1** adj. aus Acryl nachgestellt; Acryl-; **~ paint/fibre** Acrylfarbe, die/-faser, die **2** n. Acryl, das

act /ækt/ **1** n. **(a)** (deed) Tat, die **(b)** (Theatre) Akt, der **(c)** (pretence) Theater, das; **put on an ~:** Theater spielen **(d)** (Law) Gesetz, das **2** v.t. spielen ⟨Stück⟩ **3** v.i. **(a)** (perform actions) handeln; **(b)** (behave) sich verhalten; **~ as** fungieren als **(c)** (perform play) spielen **(d)** (have effect) **~ on sth.** auf etw. (Akk.) wirken

'acting **1** n. (Theatre etc.) die Schauspielerei **2** adj. (temporary) stellvertretend

action /'ækʃn/ n. **(a)** (doing sth.) Handeln, das; **take ~:** Schritte od. etwas unternehmen; **put a plan into ~:** einen Plan in die Tat umsetzen; **put sth. out of ~:** etw. außer Betrieb setzen **(b)** (act) Tat, die **(c)** (legal process) [Gerichts]verfahren, das **(d)** **die in ~:** im Kampf fallen

action: ~ committee, ~ group ns. [Inter-/Bürger- usw.]initiative, die; **~-packed** adj. spannend ⟨Buch, Roman⟩; **an ~-packed film** ein Film mit viel Aktion; **~'replay** n. Wiederholung [in Zeitlupe]

activate /'æktɪveɪt/ v.t. **(a)** in Gang setzen **(b)** (Chem., Phys.) aktivieren

active /'æktɪv/ adj., **'actively** adv. aktiv

activist /'æktɪvɪst/ n. Aktivist, der/ Aktivistin, die

activity /æk'tɪvɪtɪ/ n. Aktivität, die; **outdoor activities** Betätigung an der frischen Luft; **~ holiday** Aktivurlaub, der

actor /'æktə(r)/ n. Schauspieler, der

actress /'æktrɪs/ n. Schauspielerin, die

actual /'æktʃʊəl/ adj. eigentlich; wirklich ⟨Name⟩

'actually adv. (in fact) eigentlich; (by the way) übrigens; (believe it or not) sogar

acumen /'ækjʊmen/ Scharfsinn, der; **business ~:** Geschäftssinn, der

acupressure /'ækjuːpreʃə(r)/ n. (Med.) Akupressur, die

acupuncture /'ækjʊpʌnktʃə(r)/ n. Akupunktur, die

acute /ə'kjuːt/ adj. **(a)** spitz ⟨Winkel⟩ **(b)** (critical; Med.) akut

ad /æd/ n. (coll.) Annonce, die

AD abbr. = **Anno Domini** n.Chr.

adamant /'ædəmənt/ adj. unnachgiebig; **be ~ that …:** darauf bestehen, dass …

adapt /ə'dæpt/ v.t. **(a)** anpassen (to Dat.); **~ oneself to sth.** sich an etw. (Akk.) gewöhnen **(b)** bearbeiten ⟨Text, Theaterstück⟩

adaptable /ə'dæptəbl/ adj. anpassungsfähig

adaptation /ædəp'teɪʃn/ n. **(a)** Anpassung, die **(b)** (version) Adap[ta]tion, die; (of story, text) Bearbeitung, die

adapter, adaptor /ə'dæptə(r)/ n. Adapter, der

add /æd/ **1** v.t. hinzufügen (to Dat.); **~ two and two** zwei und zwei zusammenzählen **2** v.i. **~ to** vergrößern ⟨Schwierigkeiten, Einkommen⟩ ◾ **add 'up** **1** v.i. **~ up to sth.** (fig.) auf etw. (Akk.) hinauslaufen **2** v.t. zusammenzählen

adder /'ædə(r)/ n. Viper, die

addict **1** /ə'dɪkt/ v.t. **be ~ed** süchtig sein (to nach); **be ~ed to alcohol/smoking/drugs** alkohol-/nikotin-/drogensüchtig sein **2** /'ædɪkt/ n. Süchtige, der/die

addiction /ə'dɪkʃn/ n. Sucht, die (to nach)

addictive /ə'dɪktɪv/ adj. **be ~:** süchtig machen

addition /ə'dɪʃn/ n. **(a)** Hinzufügen, das; (adding up) Addieren, das; (process) Addition, die; **in ~:** außerdem; **in ~ to** zusätzlich zu **(b)** (thing added) Ergänzung, die (to zu)

additional /ə'dɪʃənl/ adj. zusätzlich

additionally /ə'dɪʃənəlɪ/ adv. außerdem

additive /'ædɪtɪv/ n. Zusatz, der

'add-on **1** n. (accessory) Zubehörteil, das; (for electrical appliance) Zusatzgerät, das; (addition) Zusatz, der

2 *adj.* ~ **accessory** Zubehörteil, *das*; (for electrical appliance) Zusatzgerät, *das*

address /əˈdres/ **1** *v.t.* (a) (mark with ~) adressieren (**to** an + *Akk.*)
(b) (speak to) anreden; sprechen zu ⟨*Zuhörern*⟩
2 *n.* (a) (on letter) Adresse, *die*
(b) (speech) Ansprache, *die*

ad'dress book *n.* Adressenbüchlein, *das*

addressee /ædreˈsiː/ *n.* Adressat, *der*/ Adressatin, *die*

ad'dress label *n.* Adressenaufkleber, *der*

adept /ˈædept, əˈdept/ *adj.* geschickt (**in, at** in + *Dat.*)

adequate /ˈædɪkwət/ *adj.* (a) angemessen (**to** *Dat.*); (suitable) passend
(b) (sufficient) ausreichend

'adequately *adv.* (a) (sufficiently) ausreichend
(b) (suitably) angemessen ⟨*gekleidet, qualifiziert usw.*⟩

adhere /ədˈhɪə(r)/ *v.i.* haften, (by glue) kleben (**to** an + *Dat.*)

adhesion /ədˈhiːʒn/ *n.* Haften, *das*

adhesive /ədˈhiːsɪv/ **1** *adj.* gummiert ⟨*Briefmarke*⟩; Klebe⟨*band*⟩; ~ **plaster** Heftpflaster, *das*
2 *n.* Klebstoff, *der*

adjacent /əˈdʒeɪsənt/ *adj.* angrenzend; ~ **to** neben (*position:* + *Dat.; direction:* + *Akk.*)

adjective /ˈædʒɪktɪv/ *n.* Adjektiv, *das*

adjoin /əˈdʒɔɪn/ *v.t.* grenzen an (+ *Akk.*)

adjourn /əˈdʒɜːn/ **1** *v.t.* (break off) unterbrechen; (put off) aufschieben
2 *v.i.* sich vertagen; ~ **for lunch/half an hour** [an etw. (*Akk.*)] einlegen die Mittagspause/halbstündige Pause einlegen

a'djournment *n.* (of court) Vertagung, *die;* (of meeting) Unterbrechung, *die*

adjudicate /əˈdʒuːdɪkeɪt/ *v.i.* (in court, tribunal) das Urteil fällen; (in contest) entscheiden

adjust /əˈdʒʌst/ **1** *v.t.* einstellen; ~ **sth.** [**to sth.**] etw. [an etw. (*Akk.*)] anpassen
2 *v.i.* ⟨*Person:*⟩ sich anpassen (**to** an + *Akk.*)

adjustable /əˈdʒʌstəbl/ *adj.* einstellbar; verstellbar ⟨*Gerät*⟩

a'djustment *n.* Einstellung, *die;* (to situation etc.) Anpassung, *die*

ad-lib /ædˈlɪb/ **1** *adj.* improvisiert
2 *v.i.*, **-bb-** improvisieren

adman /ˈædmæn/*n.* Werbe-, Reklamefachmann, *der*

admin /ˈædmɪn/ *n.* (coll.) Verwaltung, *die;* **an** ~ **problem** ein Verwaltungsproblem

'aedmzen administer /ædˈmɪnɪstə(r)/
(a) (manage) verwalten
(b) leisten ⟨*Hilfe*⟩; verabreichen ⟨*Medikamente*⟩

administration /ədmɪnɪˈstreɪʃn/ *n.* Verwaltung, *die*

administrative /ədˈmɪnɪstrətɪv/ *adj.* Verwaltungs-; **an** ~ **job** ein Verwaltungsposten

administrator /ədˈmɪnɪstreɪtə(r)/ *n.* Administrator, *der;* Verwalter, *der*

admirable /ˈædmərəbl/ *adj.* bewundernswert

admiral /ˈædmərəl/ *n.* Admiral, *der*

admiration /ædməˈreɪʃn/ *n.* Bewunderung, *die* (**of, for** für)

admire /ədˈmaɪə(r)/ *v.t.* bewundern

admirer /ədˈmaɪərə(r)/ *n.* Bewunderer, *der*/ Bewunderin, *die*

admiring /ədˈmaɪərɪŋ/ *adj.* bewundernd

admission /ədˈmɪʃn/ *n.* (a) (entry) Zutritt, *der*
(b) (charge) Eintritt, *der*
(c) (confession) Eingeständnis, *das*

admission: ~ **charge,** ~ **fee** *ns.* Eintrittspreis, *der;* ~ **money** *n.* Eintrittsgeld, *das;* ~**price** *n.* Eintrittspreis, *der;* ~ **ticket** *n.* Eintrittskarte, *die*

admit /ədˈmɪt/ *v.t.*, **-tt-:** (a) (let in) hinein-/ hereinlassen
(b) (acknowledge) zugeben

admittance /ədˈmɪtəns/ *n.* Zutritt, *der*

admittedly /ədˈmɪtɪdlɪ/ *adv.* zugegeben[ermaßen]

admonish /ədˈmɒnɪʃ/ *v.t.* ermahnen

ado /əˈduː/ *n.* **without more** ~: ohne weiteres Aufheben

adolescence /ædəˈlesns/ *n.* die Zeit des Erwachsenenwerdens

adolescent /ædəˈlesnt/ **1** *n.* Heranwachsende, *der/die*
2 *adj.* heranwachsend

adopt /əˈdɒpt/ *v.t.* (a) adoptieren
(b) (take over) annehmen ⟨*Glaube, Kultur*⟩
(c) (take up) übernehmen ⟨*Methode*⟩; einnehmen ⟨*Standpunkt, Haltung*⟩

adoption /əˈdɒpʃn/ *n.* (a) Adoption, *die*
(b) (taking over) Annahme, *die*
(c) (taking up) Übernahme, *die;* (of point of view) Einnahme, *die*

adorable /əˈdɔːrəbl/ *adj.* bezaubernd

adoration /ædəˈreɪʃn/ *n.* Verehrung, *die*

adore /əˈdɔː(r)/ *v.t.* verehren

adorn /əˈdɔːn/ *v.t.* schmücken

a'dornment *n.* Verzierung, *die;* ~**s** Schmuck, *der*

adrenalin /əˈdrenəlɪn/ *n.* Adrenalin, *das*

Adriatic /eɪdrɪˈætɪk/ *pr. n.* ~ **[Sea]** Adriatisches Meer

adrift /əˈdrɪft/ *adj.* **be** ~: treiben

adroit /əˈdrɔɪt/ *adj.* geschickt

adulation /ædjʊˈleɪʃn/ *n.* Vergötterung, *die*

adult /ˈædʌlt, əˈdʌlt/ **1** *adj.* erwachsen; **an** ~ **film/book** *etc.* ein Film/Buch *usw.* [nur] für Erwachsene
2 *n.* Erwachsene, *der/die;* ~ **education** Erwachsenenbildung, *die*

adulterate /ə'dʌltəreɪt/ v.t. verunreinigen
adultery /ə'dʌltərɪ/ n. Ehebruch, der
advance /əd'vɑːns/ ⓵ v.t. (a) (also Mil.)
vorrücken lassen
(b) (put forward) vorbringen ⟨Plan, Meinung⟩
(c) (further) fördern
(d) (pay before due date) vorschießen; ⟨Bank:⟩
leihen
⓶ v.i. (a) (also Mil.) vorrücken; ⟨Prozession:⟩
sich vorwärts bewegen
(b) (fig.: make progress) vorankommen
⓷ n. (a) Vorrücken, das; (fig.: progress)
Fortschritt, der
(b) usu. in pl. (personal approach)
Annäherungsversuch, der
(c) (on salary) Vorschuss, der
(d) in ~: im Voraus

ad'vance booking n. (for a film, play)
[vorherige] Kartenreservierung; (of a table in a
restaurant) [vorherige] Tischreservierung

advanced /əd'vɑːnst/ adj. fortgeschritten

advance: ~ **'notice** n. a week's ~ notice
Benachrichtigung eine Woche [im] Voraus;
give sb. ~ **notice of sth.** jmdn. im Voraus
von etw. in Kenntnis setzen; ~ **'payment**
n. Vorauszahlung, die

advantage /əd'vɑːntɪdʒ/ n. Vorteil, der;
take ~ **of sb.** jmdn. ausnutzen; **be to one's**
~: für jmdn. von Vorteil sein; **turn sth. to**
[one's] ~: etw. ausnutzen

advantageous /ædvən'teɪdʒəs/ adj.
vorteilhaft

advent /'ædvent/ n. Beginn, der; **A~:**
Advent, der

adventure /əd'ventʃə(r)/ n. Abenteuer, das

adventure: ~ **holiday** n
Abenteuerurlaub, der; ~ **playground** n.
(Brit.) Abenteuerspielplatz, der

adventurous /əd'ventʃərəs/ adj.
abenteuerlustig

adverb /'ædvɜːb/ n. Adverb, das

adversary /'ædvəsərɪ/ n. (enemy)
Widersacher, der/Widersacherin, die;
(opponent) Kontrahent, der/Kontrahentin, die

adverse /'ædvɜːs/ adj. (a) (unfavourable)
ungünstig
(b) (contrary) widrig ⟨Wind, Umstände⟩

adversity /əd'vɜːsɪtɪ/ n. (a) no pl. Not, die
(b) usu. in pl. Widrigkeit, die

advert /'ædvɜːt/ (Brit. coll.) ▶ ADVERTISEMENT

advertise /'ædvətaɪz/ ⓵ v.t. werben für;
(by small ad) inserieren; ausschreiben ⟨Stelle⟩
⓶ v.i. werben; (in newspaper) inserieren;
annoncieren

advertisement /əd'vɜːtɪsmənt/ n.
Anzeige, die; **TV** ~: Fernsehspot, der;
classified ~: Kleinanzeige, die

advertiser /'ædvətaɪzə(r)/ n. (in newspaper)
Inserent, der/Inserentin, die; (on radio, TV)
Auftraggeber/Auftraggeberin [der
Werbesendung]

advertising /'ædvətaɪzɪŋ/ n. Werbung, die;

attrib. Werbe-; ~ **agency/campaign/industry**
Werbeagentur, die/-kampagne, die/
-branche, die

advice /əd'vaɪs/ n. Rat, der; **take sb.'s** ~:
jmds. Rat (Dat.) folgen

advisable /əd'vaɪzəbl/ adj. ratsam

advise /əd'vaɪz/ v.t. beraten; ~ **sth.** zu etw.
raten; (inform) unterrichten (**of** über + Akk.);
~ **sb. to do sth.** jmdm. raten, etw. zu tun

adviser, advisor /əd'vaɪzə(r)/ n. Berater,
der/Beraterin, die

advisory /əd'vaɪzərɪ/ adj. beratend

advocate ⓵ /'ædvəkət/ n. (of a cause)
Befürworter, der/Befürworterin, die; (Law)
[Rechts]anwalt, der/-anwältin, die
⓶ /'ædvəkeɪt/ v.t. befürworten

advt. abbr. = **advertisement**

aerial /'eərɪəl/ ⓵ adj. Luft-;
~ **bombardment** Bombardierung [aus der
Luft]; ~ **photograph/photography**
Luftaufnahme, die/Luftaufnahmen Pl.
⓶ n. Antenne, die

aero- /eərəʊ/ in comb. Aero-

aerobic /eə'rəʊbɪk/ adj. (Biol.) aerob

ae'robics n. Aerobic, das

aerodynamic adj. aerodynamisch

aeronautics /eərə'nɔːtɪks/ n. Aeronautik,
die

aeroplane /'eərəpleɪn/ n. (Brit.) Flugzeug,
das

aerosol /'eərəsɒl/ n. (spray) Spray, der od.
das; (container) ~ **[spray]** Spraydose, die

'aerospace n., no art. Erdatmosphäre und
Weltraum; (technology) Luft- und Raumfahrt,
die

aesthetic /iːs'θetɪk/ adj. ästhetisch

afar /ə'fɑː/ adv. **from** ~: aus der Ferne

affable /'æfəbl/ adj. freundlich

affair /ə'feə(r)/ n. (a) (concern)
Angelegenheit, die
(b) in pl. (business) Geschäfte Pl.
(c) (love ~) Affäre, die; **have an** ~ **with sb.**
eine Affäre od. ein Verhältnis mit jmdm.
haben

affect /ə'fekt/ v.t. (a) sich auswirken auf (+
Akk.)
(b) (emotionally) betroffen machen

affectation /æfek'teɪʃn/ n. (studied display)
Verstellung, die; (artificiality) Affektiertheit, die

affected /ə'fektɪd/ adj. affektiert;
gekünstelt ⟨Sprache, Stil⟩

affection /ə'fekʃn/ n. Zuneigung, die

affectionate /ə'fekʃənət/ adj. anhänglich;
liebevoll ⟨Umarmung⟩

af'fectionately adv. liebevoll

affiliate /ə'fɪlɪeɪt/ v.t. **be** ~**d to sth.** an etw.
(Akk.) angegliedert sein

affinity /ə'fɪnɪtɪ/ n. (a) (relationship)
Verwandtschaft, die (**to** mit)
(b) (liking) Neigung, die (**for** zu); **feel an** ~ **to**
or for sb./sth. sich zu jmdm./etw. hingezogen
fühlen

affirm /ə'fɜːm/ *v.t.* (assert) bekräftigen ⟨*Absicht*⟩; beteuern ⟨*Unschuld*⟩; (state as a fact) bestätigen

affirmation /æfə'meɪʃn/ *n.* (of intention) Bekräftigung, *die;* (of fact) Bestätigung, *die*

affirmative /ə'fɜːmətɪv/ ⊡ *adj.* affirmativ; bejahend ⟨*Antwort*⟩
⊡ *n.* answer in the ∼: bejahend antworten

affirmative 'action *n.* (Amer.) positive Diskriminierung (fachspr.); Bevorzugung, *die*

afflict /ə'flɪkt/ *v.t.* (physically) plagen; (mentally) quälen; peinigen; **be ∼ed with sth.** von etw. befallen sein

affliction /ə'flɪkʃn/ *n.* Leiden, *das*

affluence /'æfluəns/ *n.* Reichtum, *der*

affluent /'æfluənt/ *adj.* reich; **the ∼ society** die Überflussgesellschaft

afford /ə'fɔːd/ *v.t.* **(a)** sich (*Dat.*) leisten **(b)** (provide) bieten; gewähren ⟨*Schutz*⟩

affordable /ə'fɔːdəbl/ *adj.* erschwinglich

affray /ə'freɪ/ *n.* Schlägerei, *die*

affront /ə'frʌnt/ ⊡ *v.t.* beleidigen
⊡ *n.* Beleidigung, *die*

afield /ə'fiːld/ *adv.* **far ∼** (direction) weit hinaus; (place) weit draußen

afloat /ə'fləʊt/ *pred. adj.* **(a)** (floating) über Wasser; flott ⟨*Schiff*⟩ **(b)** (at sea) auf See; **be ∼:** auf dem Meer treiben

afoot /ə'fʊt/ *pred. adj.* im Gange

aforementioned /ə'fɔːmenʃnd/, **aforesaid** /ə'fɔːsed/ *adjs.* oben erwähnt *od.* genannt

afraid /ə'freɪd/ *adj.* **be ∼** [of sb./sth.] [vor jmdm./etw.] Angst haben; **be ∼ to do sth.** Angst davor haben, etw. zu tun; **I'm ∼ so/ not** ich fürchte ja/nein

afresh /ə'freʃ/ *adv.* von neuem

Africa /'æfrɪkə/ *pr. n.* Afrika (*das*)

African /'æfrɪkən/ ⊡ *adj.* afrikanisch; **sb. is ∼:** jmd. ist Afrikaner/Afrikanerin
⊡ *n.* Afrikaner, *der*/Afrikanerin, *die*

Afro-Carib'bean ⊡ *adj.* afrokaribisch
⊡ *n.* Mensch afrokaribischer Herkunft *od.* Abstammung

after /'ɑːftə(r)/ ⊡ *adv.* **(a)** (later) danach **(b)** (behind) hinterher
⊡ *prep.* **(a)** (in time) nach; **two days ∼:** zwei Tage danach **(b)** (behind) hinter (+ *Dat.*) **(c)** ask ∼ sb./sth. nach jmdm./etw. fragen **(d)** ∼ all schließlich
⊡ *conj.* nachdem

after: ∼care *n.* (Med.) Nachbehandlung, *die* **∼-effect** *n.* Nachwirkung, *die*

aftermath /'ɑːftəmæθ, 'ɑːftəmɑːθ/ *n.* Nachwirkungen *Pl.*

after: ∼'noon *n.* Nachmittag, *der;* **this/ tomorrow ∼noon** heute/morgen Nachmittag; **in the ∼noon** am Nachmittag; (regularly) nachmittags; **∼-sales service** *n.*

Kundendienst, *der;* **∼shave** *n.* Aftershave, *das;* **∼taste** *n.* Nachgeschmack, *der;* **∼thought** *n.* nachträglicher Einfall

afterwards /'ɑːftəwədz/ *adv.* danach

again /ə'gen, ə'geɪn/ *adv.* wieder; (one more time) noch einmal; **∼ and ∼, time and [time] ∼:** immer wieder; **back ∼:** wieder zurück

against /ə'genst, ə'geɪnst/ *prep.* gegen

age /eɪdʒ/ ⊡ *n.* **(a)** Alter, *das;* **what ∼ are you?** wie alt bist du?; **at the ∼ of** im Alter von; **come of ∼:** volljährig werden; **be under ∼:** zu jung sein **(b)** (great period) Zeitalter, *das;* **∼s** (coll.: a long time) eine Ewigkeit
⊡ *v.t.* altern lassen
⊡ *v.i.* altern

'age bracket *n.* Altersstufe, *die*

aged *adj.* **(a)** /eɪdʒd/ **be ∼ five** fünf Jahre alt sein; **a boy ∼ five** ein fünfjähriger Junge **(b)** /'eɪdʒɪd/ (elderly) bejahrt

'age group *n.* Altersgruppe, *die*

ageism /'eɪdʒɪzm/ *n.* Diskriminierung aufgrund des Alters

ageist /'eɪdʒɪst/ *adj.* das Alter diskriminierend

ageless /'eɪdʒlɪs/ *adj.* nicht alternd ⟨*Person*⟩; (eternal) zeitlos

'age limit *n.* Altersgrenze, *die*

agency /'eɪdʒənsɪ/ *n.* (business establishment) Geschäftsstelle, *die;* (news/advertising ∼) Agentur, *die*

agenda /ə'dʒendə/ *n.* Tagesordnung, *die*

agent /'eɪdʒənt/ *n.* Vertreter, *der*/ Vertreterin, *die;* (spy) Agent, *der*/Agentin, *die*

age: ∼-old *adj.* uralt; **∼ range** *n.* Altersstufe, *die*

aggravate /'ægrəveɪt/ *v.t.* **(a)** (make worse) verschlimmern **(b)** (annoy) aufregen; ärgern

aggravating /'ægrəveɪtɪŋ/ *adj.* ärgerlich

aggravation /ægrə'veɪʃn/ *n.* **(a)** Verschlimmerung, *die* **(b)** (annoyance) Ärger, *der*

aggregate /'ægrɪgət/ ⊡ *n.* Gesamtmenge, *die*
⊡ *adj.* gesamt

aggression /ə'greʃn/ *n.* Aggression, *die*

aggressive /ə'gresɪv/ *adj.*, **ag'gressively** *adv.* aggressiv

ag'gressiveness *n.* Aggressivität, *die*

aggressor /ə'gresə(r)/ *n.* Aggressor, *der*

aggrieved /ə'griːvd/ *v.t.* (resentful) verärgert; (offended) gekränkt

aggro /'ægrəʊ/ *n.* (Brit. sl.) Zoff, *der* (ugs.); Krawall, *der;* **they are looking for ∼:** sie suchen Streit

aghast /ə'gɑːst/ *pred. adj.* bestürzt (über + *Akk.*)

agile /'ædʒaɪl/ *adj.* beweglich; flink ⟨*Bewegung*⟩

agility /ə'dʒɪlɪtɪ/ *n.* Beweglichkeit, *die;* (of movement) Flinkheit, *die*

agitate /'ædʒɪteɪt/ ① *v.t.* (a) (shake) schütteln
(b) (disturb) erregen
② *v.i.* agitieren

agitation /ædʒɪ'teɪʃn/ *n.* (a) (shaking) Schütteln, *das*
(b) (emotional) Erregung, *die*

agitator /'ædʒɪteɪtə(r)/ *n.* Agitator, *der*

AGM *abbr.* = **Annual General Meeting** JHV

agnostic /æg'nɒstɪk/ *n.* Agnostiker, *der*/ Agnostikerin, *die*

ago /ə'gəʊ/ *adv.* **ten years ~:** vor zehn Jahren; **[not] long ~:** vor [nicht] langer Zeit

agog /ə'gɒg/ *pred. adj.* gespannt

agonize /'ægənaɪz/ *v.i.* **~ over sth.** sich (*Dat.*) den Kopf über etw. (*Akk.*) zermartern

agony /'ægənɪ/ *n.* Todesqualen *Pl.*

'agony aunt *n.* (coll.) Briefkastentante, *die* (ugs. scherzh.)

agoraphobia /ægərə'fəʊbɪə/ *n.* (Psych.) Agoraphobie, *die*; Platzangst, *die*

agoraphobic /ægərə'fəʊbɪk/ *adj.* (Psych.) an Agoraphobie *od.* Platzangst leidend; **be ~:** an Agoraphobie *od.* Platzangst leiden

agree /ə'griː/ ① *v.i.* (a) (consent) einverstanden sein (**to, with** mit)
(b) (hold similar opinion) einer Meinung sein; **they ~d [with me]** sie waren derselben Meinung [wie ich]
(c) (reach similar opinion) **~ on sth.** sich über etw. (*Akk.*) einigen
(d) (harmonize) übereinstimmen
(e) **~ with sb.** (suit) jmdm. bekommen
② *v.t.* vereinbaren

agreeable /ə'griːəbl/ *adj.* (a) (pleasing) angenehm
(b) **be ~ [to sth.]** [mit etw.] einverstanden sein

agreeably /ə'griːəblɪ/ *adv.* angenehm

agreed /ə'griːd/ *adj.* einig; vereinbart ⟨*Summe, Zeit*⟩

a'greement *n.* Übereinstimmung, *die*; **be in ~ [about sth.]** sich (*Dat.*) [über etw. (*Akk.*)] einig sein

agricultural /ægrɪ'kʌltʃərl/ *adj.* landwirtschaftlich

agriculture /'ægrɪkʌltʃə(r)/ *n.* Landwirtschaft, *die*

aground /ə'graʊnd/ *adj.* **go** *or* **run ~:** auf Grund laufen

aha /ɑː'hɑː/ *int.* aha

ahead /ə'hed/ *adv.* voraus; **~ of** vor (+ *Dat.*); **be ~ of the others** (fig.) den anderen voraus sein

AI *abbr.* = **artificial intelligence** KI

aid /eɪd/ ① *v.t.* (a) **~ sb. [to do sth.]** jmdm. helfen[, etw. zu tun]; **~ed by** unterstützt von
(b) (promote) fördern
② *n.* (a) (help) Hilfe, *die*; **with the ~ of sth./ sb.** mit Hilfe einer Sache (*Gen.*)/mit jmds. Hilfe; **in ~ of sb./sth.** zugunsten von jmdm./ etw.

(b) (source of help) Hilfsmittel, *das* (**to** für)

'aid agency *n.* Hilfsorganisation, *die*; Hilfswerk, *das*

aide /eɪd/ *n.* Berater, *der*/Beraterin, *die*

Aids /eɪdz/ *n.* Aids (*das*); **~ test** Aidstest, *der*

'Aids-related *adj.* **~ disease/illness** durch Aids hervorgerufene Krankheit

'aid worker *n.* Helfer, *der*/Helferin, *die*; **~s** Hilfskräfte *Pl.*; Hilfspersonal, *das*

ailment /'eɪlmənt/ *n.* Gebrechen, *das*

aim /eɪm/ ① *v.t.* ausrichten ⟨*Schusswaffe, Rakete*⟩; **~ sth. at sb./sth.** etw. auf jmdn./etw. richten
② *v.i.* (a) zielen (**at** auf + *Akk.*)
(b) **~ to do sth.** beabsichtigen, etw. zu tun; **~ at** *or* **for sth.** (fig.) etwas anstreben
③ *n.* Ziel, *das*; **take ~ [at sth./sb.]** [auf etw./ jmdn.] zielen

'aimless *adj.*, **'aimlessly** *adv.* ziellos

air /eə(r)/ ① *n.* (a) Luft, *die*; **be/go on the ~:** senden; ⟨*Programm:*⟩ gesendet werden; **by ~:** mit dem Flugzeug; (by ~ mail) mit Luftpost
(b) (facial expression) Miene, *die*
(c) **put on ~s** sich aufspielen
② *v.t.* (ventilate) lüften; (make public) [öffentlich] darlegen

air: ~ bag *n.* (Motor Veh.) Airbag *der*; **side ~ bag** Seitenairbag, *der*; **~base** *n.* Luftwaffenstützpunkt, *der*; **~bed** *n.* Luftmatratze, *die*; **~borne** *adj.* **be ~borne** sich in der Luft befinden; **~ brake** *n.* Druckluftbremse, *die*; (flap) Luftbremse, *die*; **~brush** *n.* Spritzpistole, *die*; **~ bubble** *n.* Luftblase, *die*; **~ bus** *n.* Airbus, *der*; **~-conditioned** *adj.* klimatisiert; **~ conditioner** *n.* Klimaanlage, *die*; **~ conditioning** *n.* Klimaanlage, *die*; **~-cooled** *adj.* luftgekühlt; **~craft** *n., pl.* same Flugzeug, *das*; **~craft carrier** *n.* Flugzeugträger, *der*; **~ crew** *n.* Besatzung, *die*; Flugpersonal, *das*; **~ cushion** *n.* Luftkissen, *das*; **~ fare** *n.* Flugpreis, *der*; **~field** *n.* Flugplatz, *der*; **~ force** *n.* Luftwaffe, *die*; **~ freshener** *n.* Lufterfrischer, *der*; Luftverbesserer, *der*; **~gun** *n.* Luftgewehr, *das*; **~ hostess** *n.* Stewardess, *die*

airing /'eərɪŋ/ *n.* Auslüften, *das*; **these clothes need a good ~:** diese Kleider müssen gründlich gelüftet werden

airless /'eəlɪs/ *adj.* stickig ⟨*Zimmer, Büro*⟩; windstill ⟨*Nacht*⟩

air: ~ letter *n.* Aerogramm, *das*; **~lift** *n.* Luftbrücke, *die* (of für); **~line** *n.* Fluggesellschaft, *die*; Fluglinie, *die*; **~line pilot** [für eine Fluggesellschaft fliegender] Pilot; **~ liner** *n.* Verkehrsflugzeug, *das*; **~ mail** *n.* Luftpost, *die*; **by ~ mail** mit Luftpost; **~man** /'eəmən/ *n., pl.* **~men** / -mən/ Flieger, *der*; **~ mile** *n.* Flugmeile, *die*; **~plane** *n.* (Amer.) Flugzeug, *das*; **~ play** *n.* (Radio) das Spielen einer Platte im Radio;

the record receives *or* gets no/a great deal of
~**play** die Platte wird [überhaupt] nicht/
wird sehr häufig im Radio gespielt;
~ **pocket** n. (Aeronaut.) Luftloch, *das;*
~ **pollution** n. Luftverschmutzung, *die;*
~**port** n. Flughafen, *der;* ~**port tax**
Flughafengebühr, *die;* ~ **pressure** n.
Luftdruck, *der;* ~ **raid** n. Luftangriff, *der;*
~**raid shelter** n. Luftschutzraum, *der;*
~ **rifle** n. Luftgewehr, *das;* ~**sea
'rescue** n. Seenotrettungseinsatz aus der
Luft; ~**ship** n. Luftschiff, *das;* ~ **show** n.
Flugschau, *die;* ~**sick** adj. luftkrank;
~**stream** n. (Meteorol.) Luftströmung, *die;*
~**strike** n. Luftschlag, *der;*
~ **terminal** n. [Air-]Terminal, *der od. das;*
~**tight** adj. luftdicht; ~**time** n. Sendezeit,
die; ~ **traffic** n. Flugverkehr, *der;*
~**traffic control** n. Flugsicherung, *die;*
~**traffic controller** n. Fluglotse, *der;*
~ **travel** n. Fliegen, *das;* ~**waves** n. pl.
Äther, *der*

'**airy** adj. luftig ⟨*Büro, Zimmer*⟩

aisle /aɪl/ n. Gang, *der;* (of church)
Seitenschiff, *das*

ajar /ə'dʒɑː(r)/ adj. be ~: einen Spaltbreit
offen stehen

a.k.a. abbr. = **also known as** al.

akin /ə'kɪn/ adj. be ~ to sth. einer Sache
(*Dat.*) ähnlich sein

alarm /ə'lɑːm/ [1] n. (a) Alarm, *der;* give *or*
raise the ~: Alarm schlagen
(b) (fear) Angst, *die*
[2] v.t. aufschrecken

alarm: ~ **call** n. Weck[an]ruf, *der;*
~ '**clock** n. Wecker, *der*

alas /ə'læs/ int. ach

Albania /æl'beɪnɪə/ pr. n. Albanien (*das*)

Albanian /æl'beɪnɪən/ [1] adj. albanisch;
sb. is ~: jmd. ist Albaner/Albanerin
[2] n. (a) (person) Albaner, *der*/Albanerin, *die*
(b) (language) Albanisch, *das; see also*
ENGLISH 2 A

albatross /'ælbətrɒs/ n. Albatros, *der*

album /'ælbəm/ n. Album, *das*

alcohol /'ælkəhɒl/ n. Alkohol, *der*

'**alcohol-free** adj. alkoholfrei

alcoholic /ælkə'hɒlɪk/ [1] adj. alkoholisch
[2] n. Alkoholiker, *der*/Alkoholikerin, *die*

Alcoholics A'nonymous n. die
Anonymen Alkoholiker

alcoholism /'ælkəhɒlɪzm/ n.
Alkoholismus, *der*

alcopop /'ælkəʊpɒp/ n.: *alkoholhaltiges
Erfrischungsgetränk*

alcove /'ælkəʊv/ n. Alkoven, *der*

ale /eɪl/ n. Ale, *das*

alert /ə'lɜːt/ [1] adj. wachsam
[2] n. Alarmbereitschaft, *die;* on the ~: auf
der Hut
[3] v.t. alarmieren; ~ sb. [to sth.] jmdn. [vor
etw. (*Dat.*)] warnen

'**A level** n. (Brit. Sch.) ≈ Abitur, *das*

algebra /'ældʒɪbrə/ n. Algebra, *die*

Algeria /æl'dʒɪərɪə/ pr. n. Algerien (*das*)

Algerian /æl'dʒɪərɪən/ [1] adj. algerisch;
sb. is ~: jmd. ist Algerier/Algerierin
[2] n. Algerier, *der*/Algerierin, *die*

alias /'eɪlɪəs/ [1] adv. alias
[2] n. angenommener Name

alibi /'ælɪbaɪ/ n. Alibi, *das*

alien /'eɪlɪən/ [1] adj. (a) (strange) fremd
(b) (foreign) ausländisch
[2] n. (a) (from another world) Außerirdische,
der/die
(b) (Admin.: foreigner) Ausländer, *der*/
Ausländerin, *die*

alienate /'eɪlɪəneɪt/ v.t. befremden

alienation /eɪlɪə'neɪʃn/ n. Entfremdung,
die

alight¹ /ə'laɪt/ v.i. (a) aussteigen (from aus)
(b) ⟨*Vogel:*⟩ sich niedersetzen

alight² adj. be/catch ~: brennen; set sth.
~: etw. in Brand setzen

align /ə'laɪn/ v.t. (a) (place in a line)
ausrichten
(b) (bring into line) in eine Linie bringen

a'lignment n. Ausrichtung, *die;* out of ~:
nicht richtig ausgerichtet

alike /ə'laɪk/ pred. adj. ähnlich;
(indistinguishable) gleich

alimony /'ælɪmənɪ/ n. Unterhaltszahlung,
die

alive /ə'laɪv/ pred. adj. (a) lebendig
(b) (aware) be ~ to sth. sich (*Dat.*) einer
Sache (*Gen.*) bewusst sein
(c) (swarming) be ~ with wimmeln von

alkali /'ælkəlaɪ/ n., pl. ~s *or* ~es Alkali,
das

alkaline /'ælkəlaɪn/ adj. alkalisch

all /ɔːl/ [1] attrib. adj. (a) (entire extent or
quantity of) ganz; ~ **day** den ganzen Tag;
~ **my money** all mein Geld; mein ganzes
Geld
(b) (entire number of) alle; ~ **the books** alle
Bücher; ~ **my books** all[e] meine Bücher;
~ **the others** alle anderen
(c) (any whatever) jeglicher/jegliche/jegliches
(d) (greatest possible) in ~ **innocence** in aller
Unschuld
[2] n. (a) (~ persons) alle; ~ **of us** wir alle;
the happiest of ~: der/die Glücklichste
unter *od.* von allen
(b) (every bit) ~ **of it** alles; ~ **of the money**
das ganze Geld
(c) ~ **of** (coll.: as much as) be ~ **seven feet
tall** gut sieben Fuß groß sein
(d) (~ things) alles; ~ **I need is the money**
ich brauche nur das Geld; **that is** ~: das ist
alles; **the most beautiful of** ~: der/die/das
Schönste von allen; **most of** ~: am meisten;
it was ~ **but impossible** es war fast
unmöglich; **it's** ~ **the same to me** es ist mir
ganz egal; **can I help you at** ~? kann ich
Ihnen irgendwie behilflich sein?; **she has no
talent at** ~: sie hat überhaupt kein Talent; ⋯⊹

nothing at ∼: gar nichts; not at ∼ happy/well überhaupt nicht glücklich/gesund; not at ∼! überhaupt nicht!; (acknowledging thanks) gern geschehen!; if at ∼: wenn überhaupt; in ∼: insgesamt; ∼ in ∼: alles in allem (e) (Sport) two [goals] ∼: zwei zu zwei; (Tennis) thirty ∼: dreißig beide

3 adv. ganz; ∼ but fast; ∼ the better/worse [for that] um so besser/schlimmer; ∼ at once (suddenly) plötzlich; be ∼ 'in (exhausted) total erledigt sein (ugs.); sth. is ∼ right etw. ist in Ordnung; (tolerable) etw. ist ganz gut; I'm ∼ right mir geht es ganz gut; yes, ∼ right ja, gut; it's ∼ right by me das ist mir recht

allay /əˈleɪ/ v.t. zerstreuen ⟨Besorgnis, Befürchtungen⟩

all: ∼-'clear n. Entwarnung, die; **∼-day** adj. ganztägig ⟨Ausflug, Versammlung⟩

allegation /ælɪˈɡeɪʃn/ n. Behauptung, die; make ∼s against sb. Beschuldigungen gegen jmdn. erheben

allege /əˈledʒ/ v.t. behaupten

alleged /əˈledʒd/ adj., **allegedly** /əˈledʒɪdlɪ/ adv. angeblich

allegiance /əˈliːdʒəns/ n. Loyalität, die (to gegenüber)

allegorical /ælɪˈɡɒrɪkl/ adj. allegorisch

allegory /ˈælɪɡərɪ/ n. Allegorie, die

allergic /əˈlɜːdʒɪk/ adj. allergisch (to gegen)

allergy /ˈælədʒɪ/ n. Allergie, die

alleviate /əˈliːvɪeɪt/ v.t. abschwächen

alley /ˈælɪ/ n. [schmale] Gasse

alliance /əˈlaɪəns/ n. Bündnis, das; (league) Allianz, die

allied /ˈælaɪd/ adj. be ∼ to or with sb./sth. mit jmdm./etw. verbündet sein

alligator /ˈælɪɡeɪtə(r)/ n. Alligator, der

all: ∼-in adj. Pauschal-; **∼-night** adj. die ganze Nacht dauernd ⟨Sitzung⟩; durchgehend geöffnet ⟨Gaststätte⟩

allocate /ˈæləkeɪt/ v.t. zuweisen, zuteilen (to Dat.)

allocation /æləˈkeɪʃn/ n. Zuweisung, die; (ration) Zuteilung, die

allot /əˈlɒt/ v.t., -tt-: ∼ sth. to sb. jmdm. etw. zuteilen

al'lotment n. (Brit.: plot of land) ≈ Schrebergarten, der

all: ∼-out attrib. adj. mit allen [verfügbaren] Mitteln nachgestellt; **∼-over** attrib. adj. ∼-over tan nahtlose Bräune

allow /əˈlaʊ/ **1** v.t. erlauben; zulassen; ∼ sb. to do sth. jmdm. erlauben, etw. zu tun; be ∼ed to do sth. etw. tun dürfen
2 v.i. ∼ for sth. etw. berücksichtigen

allowance /əˈlaʊəns/ n. (a) Zuteilung, die; (for special expenses) Zuschuss, der (b) make ∼s for sth./sb. etw./jmdn. berücksichtigen

alloy /ˈælɔɪ/ n. Legierung, die

all: ∼-purpose adj. Universal-; Allzweck-; **∼-risks** attrib. adj. an ∼-risks insurance

eine alle gängigen Risiken abdeckende Versicherung; **∼-round** adj. Allround-; **∼-'rounder** n. Allroundtalent, das; **∼-seater** adj. voll bestuhlt ⟨Stadion⟩; **∼-time** adj. ∼-time record absoluter Rekord

allude /əˈluːd/ v.i. ∼ to sth beziehen auf (+ Akk.); (indirectly) anspielen auf (+ Akk.)

allusion /əˈluːʒn/ n. Hinweis, der; (indirect) Anspielung, die

ally /ˈælaɪ/ n. Verbündete, der/die; the Allies die Alliierten

almighty /ɔːlˈmaɪtɪ/ adj. allmächtig; the A∼: der Allmächtige

almond /ˈɑːmənd/ n. Mandel, die

almost /ˈɔːlməʊst/ adv. fast; beinahe

alms /ɑːmz/ n. Almosen, das

alone /əˈləʊn/ **1** pred. adj. allein; alleine (ugs.)
2 adv. allein

along /əˈlɒŋ/ **1** prep. entlang (position: + Dat.; direction: + Akk.)
2 adv. weiter; I'll be ∼ shortly ich komme gleich; all ∼: die ganze Zeit [über]

along'side **1** adv. daneben
2 prep. neben (position: + Dat.; direction: + Akk.)

aloof /əˈluːf/ **1** adv. abseits; hold ∼ from sb. sich von jmdm. fern halten
2 adj. distanziert

aloud /əˈlaʊd/ adv. laut; read [sth.] ∼: [etw.] vorlesen

alphabet /ˈælfəbet/ n. Alphabet, das

alphabetical /ælfəˈbetɪkl/ adj., **alpha'betically** adv. alphabetisch

alpine /ˈælpaɪn/ adj. alpin

Alps /ælps/ pr. n. pl. the ∼: die Alpen

already /ɔːlˈredɪ/ adv. schon

Alsation /ælˈseɪʃn/ n. [deutscher] Schäferhund

also /ˈɔːlsəʊ/ adv. auch; (moreover) außerdem

altar /ˈɔːltə(r), ˈɒltə(r)/ n. Altar, der

alter /ˈɔːltə(r), ˈɒltə(r)/ **1** v.t. ändern
2 v.i. sich verändern

alteration /ɔːltəˈreɪʃn, ɒltəˈreɪʃn/ n. Änderung, die

alternate **1** /ɔːlˈtɜːnət/ adj. sich abwechselnd
2 /ˈɔːltəneɪt/ v.t. abwechseln lassen
3 /ˈɔːltəneɪt/ v.i. sich abwechseln

al'ternately adv. abwechselnd

'alternating current n. (Electr.) Wechselstrom, der

alternative /ɔːlˈtɜːnətɪv/ **1** adj. alternativ; Alternativ-
2 n. (a) (choice) Alternative, die; ∼ fuel Alternativkraftstoff, der ⟨für Verbrennungsmotoren⟩; ∼ medicine Alternativmedizin, die
(b) (possibility) Möglichkeit, die

al'ternatively adv. oder aber; or ∼: oder aber auch

although /ɔːlˈðəʊ/ *conj.* obwohl

altimeter /ˈæltɪmiːtə(r)/ *n.* Höhenmesser, *der*

altitude /ˈæltɪtjuːd/ *n.* Höhe, *die*

altogether /ɔːltəˈgeðə(r)/ *adv.* völlig; (on the whole) im Großen und Ganzen; (in total) insgesamt; **not** ~ **[true/convincing]** nicht ganz [wahr/überzeugend]

altruist /ˈæltrʊɪst/ *n.* Altruist, *der*/ Altruistin, *die* (geh.)

altruistic /æltrʊˈɪstɪk/ *adj.* altruistisch

aluminium /æljʊˈmɪnɪəm/ (Brit.), **aluminum** /əˈluːmɪnəm/ (Amer.) *ns.* Aluminium, *das*

always /ˈɔːlweɪz/ *adv.* immer; (repeatedly) ständig

Alzheimer's disease /ˈæltshaɪmez dɪzɪːz/ *n.* Alzheimerkrankheit, *die*

am ▶ BE

AM *abbr.* = **amplitude modulation** AM

a.m. /ˈeɪˈem/ *adv.* vormittags; [at] **one/four** ~: [um] ein/vier Uhr früh

amalgamate /əˈmælgəmeɪt/ ① *v.t.* vereinigen
② *v.i.* sich vereinigen; ⟨*Firmen:*⟩ fusionieren

amalgamation /əmælgəˈmeɪʃn/ *n.* Vereinigung, *die;* (of firms) Fusion, *die*

amass /əˈmæs/ *v.t.* anhäufen

amateur /ˈæmətə(r)/ *n.* Amateur, *der; attrib.* Amateur-; Laien-

'amateurish *adj.* laienhaft; amateurhaft

amaze /əˈmeɪz/ *v.t.* verblüffen; verwundern

a'mazement *n.* Verblüffung, *die;* Verwunderung, *die*

amazing /əˈmeɪzɪŋ/ *adj.* (remarkable) erstaunlich; (astonishing) verblüffend

Amazon /ˈæməzən/ *pr. n.* **the** ~: der Amazonas

ambassador /æmˈbæsədə(r)/ *n.* Botschafter, *der*/Botschafterin, *die*

amber /ˈæmbə(r)/ ① *n.* **(a)** Bernstein, *der* **(b)** (traffic light) Gelb, *das*
② *adj.* Bernstein-; (colour) bernsteinfarben; gelb ⟨*Verkehrslicht*⟩

ambiguity /æmbɪˈgjuːɪtɪ/ *n.* Zweideutigkeit, *die*

ambiguous /æmˈbɪgjʊəs/ *adj.* zweideutig

ambition /æmˈbɪʃn/ *n.* Ehrgeiz, *der;* (aspiration) Ambition, *die*

ambitious /æmˈbɪʃəs/ *adj.* ehrgeizig

ambivalent /æmˈbɪvələnt/ *adj.* ambivalent

amble /ˈæmbl/ *v.i.* schlendern

ambulance /ˈæmbjʊləns/ *n.* Krankenwagen, *der;* Ambulanz, *die*

ambulance: ~ **chaser** *n.* (Amer.) *Anwalt oder sein Agent, der Unfallopfer dazu überredet, auf Schadenersatz zu klagen;*

~ **driver** *n.* Fahrer/Fahrerin eines/des Krankenwagens; ~ **man** *n.* Sanitäter, *der;* ~ **service** *n.* Rettungsdienst, *der*

ambush /ˈæmbʊʃ/ ① *n.* Hinterhalt, *der;* **lie in** ~: im Hinterhalt liegen
② *v.t.* [aus dem Hinterhalt] überfallen

amen /ɑːˈmen, eɪˈmen/ ① *int.* amen
② *n.* Amen, *das*

amenable /əˈmiːnəbl/ *adj.* zugänglich, aufgeschlossen (**to** *Dat.*)

amend /əˈmend/ *v.t.* berichtigen; abändern ⟨*Gesetzentwurf, Antrag*⟩

a'mendment *n.* (to motion) Abänderungsantrag, *der;* (to bill) Änderungsantrag, *der*

amends /əˈmendz/ *n. pl.* **make** ~ **[to sb.]** es [bei jmdm.] wieder gutmachen; **make** ~ **for** sth. etw. wieder gutmachen

amenity /əˈmiːnɪtɪ/ *n., usu. in pl.* **amenities** (of town) kulturelle und Freizeiteinrichtungen

America /əˈmerɪkə/ *pr. n.* Amerika (*das*)

American /əˈmerɪkən/ ① *adj.* amerikanisch; **sb. is** ~: jmd. ist Amerikaner/Amerikanerin; ~ **English** amerikanisches Englisch
② *n.* (person) Amerikaner, *der*/ Amerikanerin, *die*

American: ~ **'football** *n.* Football, *der;* ~ **'Indian** *n.* Indianer, *der*/Indianerin, *die*

Americanism /əˈmerɪkənɪzm/ *n.* (Ling.) Amerikanismus, *der*

Americanization /əmerɪkənaɪˈzeɪʃn/ *n.* Amerikanisierung, *die*

Americanize /əˈmerɪkənaɪz/ *v.t.* amerikanisieren

amiable /ˈeɪmɪəbl/ *adj.* umgänglich

amicable /ˈæmɪkəbl/ *adj.* freundschaftlich; gütlich ⟨*Einigung*⟩

amicably /ˈæmɪkəblɪ/ *adv.* in [aller] Freundschaft

amid[st] /əˈmɪd(st)/ *prep.* inmitten; (fig.: during) bei

amiss /əˈmɪs/ ① *pred. adj.* verkehrt; **is anything** ~? stimmt irgendetwas nicht?
② *adv.* **take** sth. ~: etw. übel nehmen

ammonia /əˈməʊnɪə/ *n.* Ammoniak, *das*

ammunition /æmjʊˈnɪʃn/ *n.* Munition, *die*

amnesia /æmˈniːzɪə/ *n.* Amnesie, *die*

amnesty /ˈæmnɪstɪ/ *n.* Amnestie, *die*

amniocentesis /æmnɪəʊsenˈtiːsɪs/ *n.* (Med.) Fruchtwasserentnahme, *die*

amok /əˈmɒk/ *adv.* **run** ~: Amok laufen

among[st] /əˈmʌŋ(st)/ *prep.* unter (+ *Dat.*); ~ **other things** unter anderem; **they often quarrel** ~ **themselves** sie streiten oft miteinander

amoral /eɪˈmɒrl/ *adj.* amoralisch

amorous /ˈæmərəs/ *adj.* verliebt; amourös ⟨*Abenteuer, Beziehung*⟩

amorphous /əˈmɔːfəs/ *adj.* formlos; amorph ⟨*Masse*⟩

a

amount /ə'maʊnt/ ① *v.i.* ~ **to sth.** sich auf etw. (*Akk.*) belaufen; (fig.) etw. bedeuten ② *n.* (a) (total) Betrag, *der;* Summe, *die* (b) (quantity) Menge, *die*

amp /æmp/ *n.* Ampere, *das*

amphetamine /æm'fetəmɪn/ *n.* (Med.) Amphetamin, *das*

amphibian /æm'fɪbɪən/ ① *adj.* amphibisch ② *n.* Amphibie, *die*

amphibious /æm'fɪbɪəs/ *adj.* amphibisch

amphitheatre /'æmfɪθɪətə(r)/ *n.* Amphitheater, *das*

ample /'æmpl/ *adj.* (a) (spacious) weitläufig ⟨*Garten, Räume*⟩; reichhaltig ⟨*Mahl*⟩ (b) (enough) ~ **room/food** reichlich Platz/zu essen

amplifier /'æmplɪfaɪə(r)/ *n.* Verstärker, *der*

amplify /'æmplɪfaɪ/ *v.t.* verstärken; (enlarge on) weiter ausführen

amputate /'æmpjoteɪt/ *v.t.* amputieren

amputation /æmpjʊ'teɪʃn/ *n.* Amputation, *die*

amuse /ə'mju:z/ *v.t.* (a) (interest) unterhalten; ~ **oneself by doing sth.** sich (*Dat.*) die Zeit damit vertreiben, etw. zu tun (b) (make laugh or smile) amüsieren

a'musement *n.* Belustigung, *die;* ~ **arcade** Spielhalle, *die*

amusing /ə'mju:zɪŋ/ *adj.* amüsant

an /ən, *stressed* æn/ *indef. art. see also* A²: ein/eine/ein

anaemia /ə'ni:mɪə/ *n.* Blutarmut, *die;* Anämie, *die*

anaemic /ə'ni:mɪk/ *adj.* blutarm; anämisch

anaesthetic /ænɪs'θetɪk/ *n.* Anästhetikum, *das;* general ~: Narkosemittel, *das;* local ~: Lokalanästhetikum, *das*

anaesthetist /ə'ni:sθətɪst/ *n.* Anästhesist, *der*/Anästhesistin, *die;* Narkose[fach]arzt, *der*/-ärztin, *die*

anagram /'ænəgræm/ *n.* Anagramm, *das*

analgesia /ænæl'dʒi:zɪə/ *n.* (Med.) Analgesie, *die*

analgesic /ænæl'dʒi:sɪk/ (Med.) ① *adj.* analgetisch ② *n.* Analgetikum, *das*

analog (Amer.) ▶ ANALOGUE

analogue /'ænəlɒg/ *n.* Entsprechung, *die;* Analogon, *das* (geh.); ~ **computer** Analogrechner, *der;* ~ **watch** Analoguhr, *die*

analogy /ə'nælədʒɪ/ *n.* Analogie, *die*

analyse /'ænəlaɪz/ *v.t.* analysieren

analysis /ə'nælɪsɪs/ *n.,* *pl.* **analyses** /ə'nælɪsi:z/ Analyse, *die*

analyst /'ænəlɪst/ *n.* (a) (Psych.) Analytiker, *der*/Analytikerin, *die* (b) (Econ., Polit., etc.) Experte, *der*/Expertin, *die*

analytic /ænə'lɪtɪk/, **analytical** /ænə'lɪtɪkl/ *adj.* analytisch

analyze (Amer.) ▶ ANALYSE

anarchic /ə'nɑ:kɪk/, **anarchical** /ə'nɑ:kɪkl/ *adj.* anarchisch; (anarchistic) anarchistisch

anarchist /'ænəkɪst/ *n.* Anarchist, *der*/ Anarchistin, *die*

anarchy /'ænəkɪ/ *n.* Anarchie, *die*

anatomical /ænə'tɒmɪkl/ *adj.* anatomisch

anatomy /ə'nætəmɪ/ *n.* Anatomie, *die*

ANC *abbr.* = **African National Congress** ANK

ancestor /'ænsestə(r)/ *n.* Vorfahr, *der*

ancestry /'ænsestrɪ/ *n.* Abstammung, *die*

anchor /'æŋkə(r)/ ① *n.* Anker, *der* ② *v.t.* verankern ③ *v.i.* ankern

anchorage /'æŋkərɪdʒ/ *n.* Ankerplatz, *der*

anchorman /'æŋkəmæn/ *n.* (Telev., Radio) Moderator, *der*

anchovy /'æntʃəvɪ/ *n.* Sardelle, *die*

ancient /'eɪnʃənt/ *adj.* alt; historisch ⟨*Gebäude usw.*⟩; (of antiquity) antik

and /ənd, *stressed* ænd/ *conj.* und; **for weeks** ~ **weeks** wochenlang; **better** ~ **better** immer besser

androgynous /æn'drɒdʒɪnəs/ *adj.* (Biol.) zwittrig

anecdote /'ænɪkdəʊt/ *n.* Anekdote, *die*

anemia, anemic (Amer.) ▶ ANAEM-

anesthetic *etc.* (Amer.) ▶ ANAESTHETIC *etc.*

angel /'eɪndʒl/ *n.* Engel, *der*

angelic /æn'dʒelɪk/ *adj.* engelhaft

anger /'æŋgə(r)/ ① *n.* Zorn, *der* (at über + Akk.); (fury) Wut, *die* (at über + *Akk.*) ② *v.t.* verärgern; (infuriate) wütend machen

angina [pectoris] /æn'dʒaɪnə ('pektərɪs)/ *n.* (Med.) Angina pectoris, *die*

angle¹ /'æŋgl/ *n.* (a) (Geom.) Winkel, *der;* **at an** ~ **of 60°** im Winkel von 60°; **at an** ~: schief (b) (fig.) Gesichtspunkt, *der*

angle² *v.i.* angeln; (fig.) ~ **for sth.** sich um etw. bemühen

angle: ~ **brackets** *n. pl.* spitze Klammern; ~ **grinder** *n.* Winkelschleifer, *der;* (with cutting disc) Flex, *die;* ~**parking** *n.* Schrägparken, *das*

angler /'æŋglə(r)/ *n.* Angler, *der*/Anglerin, *die*

Anglican /'æŋglɪkən/ ① *adj.* anglikanisch ② *n.* Anglikaner, *der*/Anglikanerin, *die*

Anglo- /æŋgləʊ/ *in comb.* anglo-/Anglo-

Anglo-Saxon /-'sæksn/ ① *n.* Angelsachse, *der*/Angelsächsin, *die;* (language) Angelsächsisch, *das* ② *adj.* angelsächsisch

angora [wool] /æŋ'gɔːrə/ *n.* Angorawolle, *die;* Mohair, *der*

angrily /'æŋgrɪlɪ/ *adv.* verärgert; (stronger) zornig

angry /'æŋgrɪ/ *adj.* böse; verärgert ⟨*Person, Stimme, Geste*⟩; (stronger) zornig; wütend; **be**

~ **at** *or* **about sth.** wegen etw. böse sein; **be**
~ **with** *or* **at sb.** mit jmdm. *od.* auf jmdn.
böse sein; **get** ~: böse werden

anguish /'æŋgwɪʃ/ *n.* Qualen *Pl.*

angular /'æŋgjʊlə(r)/ *adj.* eckig ‹*Gebäude,
Struktur*›; kantig ‹*Gesicht*›

animal /'ænɪməl/ 1 *n.* Tier, *das*
2 *adj.* tierisch

animal: A~ **Libe'ration Front** *n.*
Tierbefreiungsfront, *die;* ~ **lover** *n.*
Tierfreund, *der*/-freundin, *die;*
~ **pro'tectionist** *n.* Tierschützer, *der*/
-schützerin, *die;* ~ **'rights** *n. pl.* Tierrechte
Pl.; ~ **rights supporter** Tierrechtler, *der*/
Tierrechtlerin, *die*

animate 1 /'ænɪmeɪt/ *v.t.* beleben
2 /'ænɪmət/ *adj.* beseelt ‹*Leben, Körper*›;
belebt ‹*Objekt, Welt*›

animated /'ænɪmeɪtɪd/ *adj.* lebhaft
‹*Diskussion, Gebärde*›; ~ **cartoon**
Zeichentrickfilm, *der*

animation /ænɪ'meɪʃn/ *n.* **(a)**
Lebhaftigkeit, *die*
(b) (Cinemat.) Animation, *die*

animosity /ænɪ'mɒsɪtɪ/ *n.* Feindseligkeit,
die

aniseed /'ænɪsiːd/ *n.* Anis[samen], *der*

ankle /'æŋkl/ *n.* Fußgelenk, *das*

ankle: ~**-deep** *adj.* knöcheltief; ~ **sock**
n. Socke, *die;* (esp. for children) Söckchen, *das*

annex 1 /ə'neks/ *v.t.* annektieren ‹*Land,
Territorium*›
2 /'æneks/ *n.* Anbau, *der*

annexation /ænɪk'seɪʃn/ *n.* Annexion, *die;*
Annektierung, *die*

annexe ▶ ANNEX 2

annihilate /ə'naɪɪleɪt/ *v.t.* vernichten

annihilation /ənaɪɪ'leɪʃn/ *n.* Vernichtung,
die

anniversary /ænɪ'vɜːsərɪ/ *n.* Jahrestag,
der; **wedding** ~: Hochzeitstag, *der*

annotate /'ænəteɪt/ *v.t.* kommentieren

announce /ə'naʊns/ *v.t.* bekannt geben;
ansagen ‹*Programm*›; (over Tannoy etc.)
durchsagen; (in newspaper) anzeigen ‹*Heirat
usw.*›

an'nouncement *n.* Bekanntgabe, *die;*
(over Tannoy etc.) Durchsage, *die;* (in newspaper)
Anzeige, *die*

an'nouncer *n.* Ansager, *der*/Ansagerin,
die

annoy /ə'nɔɪ/ *v.t.* **(a)** ärgern
(b) (harass) schikanieren

annoyance /ə'nɔɪəns/ *n.* Verärgerung, *die;*
(nuisance) Plage, *die*

annoyed /ə'nɔɪd/ *adj.* **be** ~ **[at** *or* **with sb.**/
sth.] ärgerlich [auf *od.* über jmdn./über etw.]
sein; **he got very** ~: er hat sich darüber
sehr geärgert

an'noying *adj.* ärgerlich; lästig
‹*Gewohnheit, Person*›

annual /'ænjʊəl/ 1 *adj.* **(a)** (reckoned by the

year) Jahres-; ~ **income/subscription/rent/**
turnover/production/leave/salary
Jahreseinkommen, *das*/-abonnement, *das*/
-miete, *die*/-umsatz, *der*/-produktion, *die*/
-urlaub, *der*/-gehalt, *das;* ~ **rainfall** jährliche
Regenmenge
(b) (recurring yearly) [all]jährlich ‹*Ereignis,
Feier*›; Jahres‹*bericht, -hauptversammlung*›
2 *n.* **(a)** Jahrbuch, *das;* (of comic etc.)
Jahresalbum, *das*
(b) (plant) einjährige Pflanze

'annually *adv.* jährlich

annul /ə'nʌl/ *v.t.,* **-ll-** annullieren; auflösen
‹*Vertrag*›

anodyne /'ænədaɪn/ *adj.* (fig.) wohltuend;
(soothing) einlullend

anon. /ə'nɒn/ *abbr.* = **anonymous**
[author] anon.

anonymity /ænə'nɪmɪtɪ/ *n.* Anonymität,
die

anonymous /ə'nɒnɪməs/ *adj.* anonym

anorak /'ænəræk/ *n.* Anorak, *der*

anorexia /ænə'reksɪə/ *n.* Anorexie, *die*
(Med.); Magersucht, *die*

anorexic /ænə'reksɪk/ *adj.* anorektisch
(fachspr.); magersüchtig; **be** ~: an Anorexie
(Med.) *od.* Magersucht leiden

another /ə'nʌðə(r)/ 1 *pron.* **(a)** (an
additional one) noch einer/eine/eins; ein
weiterer/eine weitere/ein weiteres
(b) (counterpart) wieder einer/eine/eins
(c) (a different one) ein anderer/eine andere/
ein anderes
2 *adj.* **(a)** (additional) noch ein/eine; ein
weiterer/eine weitere/ein weiteres; **after**
~ **six weeks** nach weiteren sechs Wochen
(b) (different) ein anderer/eine andere/ein
anderes

answer /'ɑːnsə(r)/ 1 *n.* **(a)** (reply) Antwort,
die (to auf + *Akk.*)
(b) (to problem) Lösung, *die* (to *Gen.*); (to
calculation) Ergebnis, *das*
2 *v.t.* **(a)** beantworten ‹*Brief, Frage*›;
antworten auf (+ *Akk.*) ‹*Frage, Hilferuf,
Einladung, Inserat*›; eingehen auf (+ *Akk.*)
‹*Angebot, Vorschlag*›; sich stellen zu
‹*Beschuldigung*›; erhören ‹*Gebet*›; erfüllen
‹*Bitte, Wunsch*›; ~ **sb.** jmdm. antworten
(b) ~ **the door/bell** an die Tür gehen
3 *v.i.* **(a)** (reply) antworten; ~ **to sth.** sich zu
etw. äußern
(b) (be responsible) ~ **for sth.** für etw. die
Verantwortung übernehmen
(c) ~ **to a description** einer Beschreibung
(*Dat.*) entsprechen

answerable /'ɑːnsərəbl/ *adj.*
verantwortlich (**for** für; **to** *Dat.*)

answering: ~**machine** *n.*
Anrufbeantworter, *der;* ~ **service** *n.*
Fernsprechauftragsdienst, *der*

'answerphone (Brit.) ▶ ANSWERING
MACHINE

ant /ænt/ *n.* Ameise, *die*

antagonism /æn'tægənɪzm/ n. Feindseligkeit, die (towards, against gegenüber)

antagonist /æn'tægənɪst/ n. Gegner, der/ Gegnerin, die

antagonistic /æntægə'nɪstɪk/ adj. feindlich

antagonize /æn'tægənaɪz/ v.t. ~ sb. sich (Dat.) jmdn. zum Feind machen

antarctic /ænt'ɑːktɪk/ [1] adj. antarktisch [2] n. the A~: die Antarktis

antelope /'æntɪləʊp/ n. Antilope, die

antenatal /æntɪ'neɪtl/ adj. (concerning pregnancy) Schwangerschafts-; Schwangeren-; ~ care Schwangerenfürsorge, die; ~ clinic Klinik für werdende Mütter

antenna /æn'tenə/ n. (a) pl. ~e /æn'teniː/ (Zool.) Fühler, der (b) pl. ~s (tech., Amer.: aerial) Antenne, die

anthem /'ænθəm/ n. Chorgesang, der

anthology /æn'θɒlədʒɪ/ n. Anthologie, die

anthropologist /ænθrə'pɒlədʒɪst/ n. Anthropologe, der/Anthropologin, die

anthropology /ænθrə'pɒlədʒɪ/ n. Anthropologie, die

anti /'æntɪ/ [1] prep. gegen [2] adj. ablehnend

anti- /'æntɪ/ pref. anti-/Anti-

anti: ~**a'bortion** attrib. adj. ~-abortion protester Abtreibungsgegner, der/-gegnerin, die; ~-abortion protest/law Protest/Gesetz gegen Abtreibung; ~-abortion demonstration/movement Antiabtreibungsdemonstration, die/ -bewegung, die; ~-**abortionist** /æntɪə'bɔːʃənɪst/ n. Abtreibungsgegner, der/ -gegnerin, die; ~-**'aircraft** adj. (Mil.) Flugabwehr-; ~-aircraft gun Flak, die

antibiotic /æntɪbaɪ'ɒtɪk/ n. Antibiotikum, das

'antibody n. Antikörper, der

antic /'æntɪk/ n. (trick) Mätzchen, das (ugs.); (of clown) Possen, der

anticipate /æn'tɪsɪpeɪt/ v.t. (a) (expect) erwarten; (foresee) voraussehen; ~ trouble mit Ärger rechnen (b) (consider before due time) vorwegnehmen

anticipation /æntɪsɪ'peɪʃn/ n. Erwartung, die

anti'climax n. Abstieg, der

anti'clockwise adv., adj. gegen den Uhrzeigersinn

anti'cyclone n. Hochdruckgebiet, das

antidepressant /æntɪdɪ'presənt/ n. Antidepressivum, das

antidote /'æntɪdəʊt/ n. Gegenmittel, das (for, against, to gegen)

'antifreeze n. Frostschutzmittel, das

'anti-hero n. Antiheld, der

antihistamine /æntɪ'hɪstəmɪn/ n. (Med.) Antihistamin[ikum], das

'anti-lock adj. Antiblockier-; ~ brake or braking system Antiblockiersystem, das

anti'nuclear adj. Anti-Atom[kraft]-

antipathy /æn'tɪpəθɪ/ n. Antipathie, die; Abneigung, die

anti-person'nel adj. gegen Menschen gerichtet; ~ mine Schützenmine, die

antiperspirant /æntɪ'pɜːspɪrənt/ [1] adj. schweißhemmend; ~ spray Deodorantspray, der od. das [2] n. Antitranspirant, das

antiquated /'æntɪkweɪtɪd/ adj. antiquiert; veraltet

antique /æn'tiːk/ [1] adj. antik (Möbel, Schmuck usw.) [2] n. Antiquität, die; ~ shop Antiquitätenladen, der

antiquity /æn'tɪkwɪtɪ/ n. Altertum, das; Antike, die

anti-Semitic /æntɪsɪ'mɪtɪk/ adj. antisemitisch; judenfeindlich

anti-Semitism /æntɪ'semɪtɪzm/ n. Antisemitismus, der; Judenhass, der

anti'septic [1] adj. antiseptisch [2] n. Antiseptikum, das

anti'social adj. asozial

anti-'theft attrib. adj. Antidiebstahl-

antithesis /æn'tɪθəsɪs/ n., pl. antitheses /æn'tɪθəsiːz/ Gegenstück, das (of, to zu)

anti: ~'**toxin** n. (Med.) Antitoxin, das; ~'**virus** attrib. adj. (Comp.) Antivirus-; ~virus software Antivirensoftware, die

antivivisectionist /æntɪvɪvɪ'sekʃənɪst/ n. Vivisektionsgegner, der/-gegnerin, die

antler /'æntlə(r)/ n. Geweihsprosse, die; [pair of] ~s Geweih, das

anvil /'ænvɪl/ n. Amboss, der

anxiety /æŋ'zaɪətɪ/ n. Angst, die; (concern about future) Sorge, die (about wegen)

anxious /'æŋkʃəs/ adj. (a) (troubled) besorgt (about um) (b) (eager) sehnlich; be ~ for sth. sich nach etw. sehnen

'anxiously adv. (a) besorgt (b) (eagerly) sehnsüchtig

any /'enɪ/ [1] adj. (a) (some) [irgend]ein/ [irgend]eine; not ~: kein/keine; have you ~ wool/wine? haben Sie Wolle/Wein? (b) (one) ein/eine (c) (all, every) jeder/jede/jedes; [at] ~ time jederzeit (d) (whichever) jeder/jede/jedes [beliebige]; choose ~ [one] book/~ books you like suchen Sie sich (Dat.) irgendein Buch/ irgendwelche Bücher aus [2] pron. (a) (some) in condit., interrog., or neg. sentence (replacing sing. n.) einer/eine/ ein[e]s; (replacing collect. n.) welcher/welche/ welches; (replacing pl. n.) welche; not ~: keiner/keine/kein[e]s/Pl. keine; without ~: ohne (b) (no matter which) irgendeiner/irgendeine/ irgendein[e]s/irgendwelche Pl.

⟦3⟧ *adv.* do you feel ∼ **better today?** fühlen Sie sich heute [etwas] besser?; **if it gets** ∼ **colder** wenn es noch kälter wird; **I can't wait** ∼ **longer** ich kann nicht [mehr] länger warten

'anybody *n. & pron.* (a) (whoever) jeder (b) (somebody) [irgend]jemand; *after neg.* niemand

'anyhow *adv.* (a) ▶ ANYWAY
(b) (haphazardly) irgendwie

'anyone ▶ ANYONE

'anything ⟦1⟧ *n. & pron.* (a) (whatever thing) was [immer]; alles, was
(b) (something) irgendetwas; *after neg.* nichts
(c) (a thing of any kind) alles
⟦2⟧ *adv.* **not** ∼ **like as … as** keineswegs so … wie

'anyway *adv.* (a) (in any case, besides) sowieso
(b) (at any rate) jedenfalls

'anywhere *adv.* (a) (in any place) (wherever) überall, wo; wo [immer]; (somewhere) irgendwo; **not** ∼ **near as … as** (coll.) nicht annähernd so … wie
(b) (to any place) (wherever) wohin [auch immer]; (somewhere) irgendwohin

aorta /eɪ'ɔːtə/ *n.* (Anat.) Aorta, *die*

apart /ə'pɑːt/ *adv.* (a) (separately) getrennt; ∼ **from …:** außer …
(b) (into pieces) auseinander

apartheid /ə'pɑːteɪt/ *n.* Apartheid, *die*

apartment /ə'pɑːtmənt/ *n.* (a) (room) Apartment, *das*
(b) (Amer.: flat) Wohnung, *die*

apathetic /æpə'θetɪk/ *adj.* apathisch (**about** gegenüber)

apathy /'æpəθɪ/ *n.* Apathie, *die* (**about** gegenüber)

ape /eɪp/ ⟦1⟧ *n.* [Menschen]affe, *der*
⟦2⟧ *v.t.* nachahmen

aperitif /əperɪ'tiːf/ *n.* Aperitif, *der*

aperture /'æpətʃə(r)/ *n.* Öffnung, *die*

apex /'eɪpeks/ *n.* Spitze, *die*

aphid /'eɪfɪd/ *n.* Blattlaus, *die*

aphrodisiac /æfrə'dɪzɪæk/ *n.* Aphrodisiakum, *das*

apiece /ə'piːs/ *adv.* je; **they cost a penny** ∼: sie kosten einen Penny das Stück

apolitical /eɪpə'lɪtɪkl/ *adj.* apolitisch; unpolitisch

apologetic /əpɒlə'dʒetɪk/ *adj.* entschuldigend; **be** ∼: sich entschuldigen

apologize /ə'pɒlədʒaɪz/ *v.i.* sich entschuldigen (**to** bei)

apology /ə'pɒlədʒɪ/ *n.* Entschuldigung, *die;* **make an** ∼: sich entschuldigen (**to** bei)

apoplectic /æpə'plektɪk/ *adj.* apoplektisch; ∼ **fit** Schlaganfall, *der*

apoplexy /'æpəpleksɪ/ *n.* Apoplexie, *die* (fachspr.); Schlaganfall, *der*

apostle /ə'pɒsl/ *n.* Apostel, *der*

apostrophe /ə'pɒstrəfɪ/ *n.* Apostroph, *der;* Auslassungszeichen, *das*

appal (*Amer.*: **appall**) /ə'pɔːl/ *v.t.,* **-ll-** entsetzen

ap'palling *adj.* entsetzlich

apparatus /æpə'reɪtəs/ *n.* (equipment) Gerät, *das;* (gymnastic ∼) Geräte *Pl.;* (machinery, lit. or fig.) Apparat, *der;* **a piece of** ∼: ein Gerät

apparel /ə'pærəl/ *n.* Kleidung, *die;* Gewänder *Pl.* (geh.)

apparent /ə'pærənt/ *adj.* (a) (clear) offensichtlich; offenbar ⟨Bedeutung, Wahrheit⟩
(b) (seeming) scheinbar

ap'parently *adv.* (a) (clearly) offensichtlich
(b) (seemingly) scheinbar

apparition /æpə'rɪʃn/ *n.* [Geister]erscheinung, *die*

appeal /ə'piːl/ ⟦1⟧ *v.i.* (a) (Law etc.) Einspruch einlegen
(b) (make earnest request) ∼ **to sb. for sth./to do sth.** jmdn. etw. ersuchen/jmdn. ersuchen, etw. zu tun
(c) (address oneself) ∼ **to sb./sth.** an jmdn./ etw. appellieren
(d) (be attractive) ∼ **to sb.** jmdm. zusagen
⟦2⟧ *n.* (a) (Law etc.) Einspruch, *der* (**to** bei); (to higher court) Berufung, *die* (**to** bei)
(b) (request) Appell, *der;* **an** ∼ **to sb. for sth.** eine Bitte an jmdn. um etw.
(c) (attraction) Reiz, *der*

ap'pealing *adj.* (a) (imploring) flehend
(b) (attractive) ansprechend; verlockend ⟨Idee⟩

appear /ə'pɪə(r)/ *v.i.* (a) (become visible, arrive) erscheinen; ⟨Licht, Mond:⟩ auftauchen; (present oneself) auftreten
(b) (occur) vorkommen
(c) (seem) ∼ **[to be] …:** scheinen … [zu sein]

appearance /ə'pɪərəns/ *n.* (a) (becoming visible) Auftauchen, *das;* (arrival) Erscheinen, *das;* (of performer etc.) Auftritt, *der*
(b) (look) Äußere, *das;* **to all** ∼s allem Anschein nach
(c) (semblance) Anschein, *der*
(d) (occurrence) Vorkommen, *das*

appease /ə'piːz/ *v.t.* besänftigen; (Polit.) beschwichtigen

append /ə'pend/ *v.t.* anhängen (**to an** + *Akk.*); (add) anfügen (+ *Dat.*)

appendage /ə'pendɪdʒ/ *n.* Anhängsel, *das;* (addition) Anhang, *der*

appendicitis /əpendɪ'saɪtɪs/ *n.* Blinddarmentzündung, *die*

appendix /ə'pendɪks/ *n., pl.* **appendices** /ə'pendɪsiːz/ *or* ∼**es** (a) Anhang, *der* (**to** zu)
(b) (Anat.) Blinddarm, *der*

appetite /'æpɪtaɪt/ *n.* (a) Appetit, *der* (**for** auf + *Akk.*)
(b) (fig.) Verlangen, *das* (**for** nach)

appetizer /'æpɪtaɪzə(r)/ *n.* Appetitanreger, *der*

appetizing /'æpɪtaɪzɪŋ/ *adj.* appetitlich

applaud /ə'plɔːd/ ① v.i. applaudieren; [Beifall] klatschen
② v.t. applaudieren (+ Dat.)

applause /ə'plɔːz/ n. Beifall, der; Applaus, der

apple /'æpl/ n. Apfel, der

apple: ~ '**pie** gedeckte Apfeltorte; ~ '**sauce** n. Apfelmus, das

applet /'æplɪt/ n. (Comp.) Applet, das

'**apple tree** n. Apfelbaum, der

appliance /ə'plaɪəns/ n. Gerät, das

applicable /ə'plɪkəbl/ adj. (a) anwendbar (to auf + Akk.)
(b) (appropriate) geeignet; zutreffend ⟨Fragebogenteil⟩

applicant /'æplɪkənt/ n. Bewerber, der/ Bewerberin, die (for um); (claimant) Antragsteller, der/-stellerin, die

application /æplɪ'keɪʃn/ n. (a) (request) Bewerbung, die (for um); (for passport, licence, etc.) Antrag, der (for auf + Akk.); ~ form Antragsformular, das
(b) (putting) Auftragen, das (to auf + Akk.)
(c) (use) Anwendung, die
(d) (Comp.) Applikation, die

applicator /'æplɪkeɪtə(r)/ n. Applikator, der

apply /ə'plaɪ/ ① v.t. (a) auftragen ⟨Creme, Farbe⟩ (to auf + Akk.)
(b) (make use of) anwenden
② v.i. (a) (have relevance) zutreffen (to auf + Akk.)
(b) ~ [to sb.] for sth. [jmdn.] um etw. bitten; (for passport etc.) [bei jmdm.] etw. beantragen; (for job) sich [bei jmdm.] um etw. bewerben

appoint /ə'pɔɪnt/ v.t. (a) (fix) bestimmen; festlegen ⟨Zeitpunkt, Ort⟩
(b) (to job) einstellen; (to office) ernennen

appointee /əpɔɪn'tiː/ n. Ernannte, der/die; Berufene, der/die

ap'pointment n. (a) (to job) Einstellung, die; (to office) Ernennung, die (as zum/zur)
(b) (job) Stelle, die
(c) (arrangement) Termin, der; make an ~ with sb. sich (Dat.) von jmdm. einen Termin geben lassen; by ~: nach Anmeldung

appraisal /ə'preɪzl/ n. (evaluation) Bewertung, die

appraise /ə'preɪz/ v.t. (evaluate) bewerten

appreciable /ə'priːʃəbl/ adj. (a) (perceptible) nennenswert ⟨Unterschied, Einfluss⟩; spürbar ⟨Veränderung, Wirkung⟩; merklich ⟨Verringerung, Anstieg⟩
(b) (considerable) beträchtlich

appreciably /ə'priːʃəblɪ/ adv. (a) (perceptibly) spürbar ⟨verändern⟩; merklich ⟨sich unterscheiden⟩
(b) (considerably) beträchtlich

appreciate /ə'priːʃɪeɪt/ ① v.t. (a) ([correctly] estimate) [richtig] einschätzen; (understand) verstehen; (be aware of) sich (Dat.) bewusst sein (+ Gen.)
(b) (be grateful for) schätzen; (enjoy) genießen

② v.i. im Wert steigen

appreciation /əpriːʃɪ'eɪʃn/ n. (a) ([correct] estimation) [richtige] Einschätzung; (understanding) Verständnis, das (of für); (awareness) Bewusstsein, das
(b) (gratefulness) Dankbarkeit, die; (enjoyment) Gefallen, das (of an + Dat.)

appreciative /ə'priːʃətɪv/ adj. (grateful) dankbar (of für); (approving) anerkennend

apprehend /æprɪ'hend/ v.t. (a) (arrest) festnehmen
(b) (understand) erfassen

apprehension /æprɪ'henʃn/ n. Besorgnis, die

apprehensive /æprɪ'hensɪv/ adj. besorgt

apprentice /ə'prentɪs/ n. Lehrling, der (to bei)

ap'prenticeship n. (training) Lehre, die; (learning period) Lehrzeit, die

approach /ə'prəʊtʃ/ ① v.i. sich nähern; (in time) nahen
② v.t. (a) (come near to) sich nähern (+ Dat.)
(b) (approximate to) nahe kommen (+ Dat.)
(c) (appeal to) sich wenden an (+ Akk.)
③ n. (a) [Heran]nahen, das
(b) (approximation) Annäherung, die (to an + Akk.)
(c) (appeal) Herantreten, das (to an + Akk.)
(d) (access) Zugang, der; (road) Zufahrtsstraße, die

approachable /ə'prəʊtʃəbl/ adj. (a) (friendly) umgänglich
(b) (accessible) zugänglich

ap'proach road n. Zufahrtsstraße, die

appropriate ① /ə'prəʊprɪət/ adj. geeignet (to, for für)
② /ə'prəʊprɪeɪt/ v.t. sich (Dat.) aneignen

appropriately /ə'prəʊprɪətlɪ/ adv. gebührend; passend ⟨gekleidet, genannt⟩

approval /ə'pruːvl/ n. (a) (sanctioning) Genehmigung, die; (of proposal) Billigung, die; (agreement) Zustimmung, die
(b) on ~ (Commerc.) zur Probe

approve /ə'pruːv/ ① v.t. (a) (sanction) genehmigen ⟨Plan, Projekt⟩; billigen ⟨Vorschlag⟩
(b) (find good) gutheißen
② v.i. ~ of billigen; zustimmen (+ Dat.) ⟨Plan⟩

approving /ə'pruːvɪŋ/ adj. zustimmend ⟨Worte⟩; anerkennend ⟨Blicke⟩

approx. /ə'prɒks/ abbr. = **approximately** ca.

approximate /ə'prɒksɪmət/ adj. ungefähr attr.

ap'proximately adv. ungefähr

approximation /əprɒksɪ'meɪʃn/ n. (a) Annäherung, die (to an + Dat.)
(b) (estimate) Annäherungswert, der

APR abbr. = **annualized percentage rate** Jahreszinssatz, der

Apr. abbr. = **April** Apr.

après-ski /ˈæpreɪˈskiː/ n. Après-Ski, der; attrib. Après-Ski-

apricot /ˈeɪprɪkɒt/ n. Aprikose, die

April /ˈeɪprəl/ n. April, der; ~ **fool** April[s]narr, der; see also AUGUST

apron /ˈeɪprən/ n. Schürze, die

apt /æpt/ adj. (a) (suitable) passend; treffend ⟨Bemerkung⟩
(b) be ~ **to do sth.** dazu neigen, etw. zu tun

aptitude /ˈæptɪtjuːd/ n. Begabung, die

'aptly adv. passend

aqualung /ˈækwəlʌŋ/ n. Tauchgerät, das

aquaplane /ˈækwəpleɪn/ v.i. ⟨Reifen:⟩ aufschwimmen; ⟨Fahrzeug:⟩ [durch Aquaplaning] ins Rutschen geraten

aquarium /əˈkweərɪəm/ n., pl. ~s or aquaria /əˈkweərɪə/ Aquarium, das

Aquarius /əˈkweərɪəs/ n. (Astrol., Astron.) der Wassermann

aquatic /əˈkwætɪk/ adj. aquatisch; Wasser-; ~ **plant** Wasserpflanze, die

aqueduct /ˈækwɪdʌkt/ n. Aquädukt, der od. das

aqueous /ˈeɪkwɪəs, ˈækwɪəs/ adj. wässerig; wässrig

Arab /ˈærəb/ ① adj. arabisch
② n. Araber, der/Araberin, die

Arabian /əˈreɪbɪən/ ① adj. arabisch
② n. Araber, der/Araberin, die

Arabic /ˈærəbɪk/ ① adj. arabisch
② n. Arabisch, das; see also ENGLISH 2A

arable /ˈærəbl/ adj. bebaubar, landwirtschaftlich nutzbar ⟨Land⟩; ~ **land** (cultivated) Ackerland, das

arbitrary /ˈɑːbɪtrərɪ/ adj. willkürlich

arbitrate /ˈɑːbɪtreɪt/ ① v.t. schlichten ⟨Streit⟩
② v.i. ~ [upon sth.] [in einer Sache] vermitteln

arbitration /ɑːbɪˈtreɪʃn/ n. Vermittlung, die; (in industry) Schlichtung, die

arbitrator /ˈɑːbɪtreɪtə(r)/ n. Vermittler, der; (in industry) Schlichter, der

arboretum /ɑːbəˈriːtəm/ n., pl. arboreta /ɑːbəˈriːtə/ or (Amer.) ~s Arboretum, das; Baumgarten, der

arbour /ˈɑːbə(r)/ n. (Brit.) Laube, die

arc /ɑːk/ n. [Kreis]bogen, der; ~ **lamp**, ~ **light** Lichtbogenlampe, die; ~ **welding** Lichtbogen-, Elektroschweißung, die

arcade /ɑːˈkeɪd/ n. Arkade, die

arch /ɑːtʃ/ ① n. Bogen, der; (of foot) Wölbung, die
② v.t. beugen ⟨Rücken⟩; ~ **its back** ⟨Katze:⟩ einen Buckel machen

arch- pref. Erz-

archaeological /ɑːkɪəˈlɒdʒɪkl/ adj. archäologisch

archaeologist /ɑːkɪˈɒlədʒɪst/ n. Archäologe, der/Archäologin, die

archaeology /ɑːkɪˈɒlədʒɪ/ n. Archäologie, die

archaic /ɑːˈkeɪɪk/ adj. veraltet

arch'bishop n. Erzbischof, der

arch-'enemy n. Erzfeind, der/Erzfeindin, die

archeology etc. (Amer.) ▶ ARCHAEOLOGY etc.

archer /ˈɑːtʃə(r)/ n. Bogenschütze, der

archery /ˈɑːtʃərɪ/ n. Bogenschießen, das

archetype /ˈɑːkɪtaɪp/ n. (original) Urfassung, die; (typical specimen) Prototyp, der

architect /ˈɑːkɪtekt/ n. Architekt, der/ Architektin, die

architectural /ɑːkɪˈtektʃərl/ adj. architektonisch

architecture /ˈɑːkɪtektʃə(r)/ n. Architektur, die

archive /ˈɑːkaɪv/ ① n. Archiv, das; ~ **s** Archiv, das
② v.t. archivieren

arctic /ˈɑːktɪk/ ① adj. arktisch; A~ **Circle** nördlicher Polarkreis; A~ **Ocean** Nordpolarmeer, das
② n. the A~: die Arktis

ardent /ˈɑːdənt/ adj. leidenschaftlich; brennend ⟨Wunsch⟩; (eager) begeistert

ardor (Amer.), **ardour** (Brit.) /ˈɑːdə(r)/ n. Leidenschaft, die

arduous /ˈɑːdjʊəs/ adj. anstrengend

are ▶ BE

area /ˈeərɪə/ n. (a) (surface measure) Fläche, die; Flächeninhalt, der
(b) (region) Gelände, das; (of wood, marsh, desert) Gebiet, das; (of city, country) Gegend, die; **parking/picnic** ~: Park-/Picknickplatz, der
(c) (subject field) Gebiet, das

'area code n. (Amer. Teleph.) Gebietsvorwahl[nummer], die

arena /əˈriːnə/ n. Arena, die; **the political** ~: die politische Arena

aren't /ɑːnt/ (coll.) = are not; ▶ BE

Argentina /ɑːdʒənˈtiːnə/ pr. n. Argentinien (das)

Argentinian /ɑːdʒənˈtɪnɪən/ ① adj. argentinisch; **sb. is** ~: jmd. ist Argentinier/ Argentinierin
② n. Argentinier, der/Argentinierin, die

arguable /ˈɑːgjʊəbl/ adj. (questionable) fragwürdig

arguably /ˈɑːgjʊəblɪ/ adv. möglicherweise

argue /ˈɑːgjuː/ ① v.t. (a) (maintain) ~ **that** ...: die Ansicht vertreten, dass ...
(b) (with reasoning) darlegen ⟨Grund, Standpunkt⟩
② v.i. ~ **with sb.** sich mit jmdm. streiten; ~ **for/against sth.** für/gegen etw. eintreten; ~ **about sth.** sich über/um etw. (Akk.) streiten

argument /ˈɑːgjʊmənt/ n. (a) (reason) Begründung, die; ~**s for/against sth.** Argumente für/gegen etw.
(b) (reasoning process) Argumentieren, das ⋯⋗

(c) (disagreement, quarrel) Auseinandersetzung, *die*

argumentative /ɑːgjʊ'mentətɪv/ *adj.* widerspruchsfreudig

arid /'ærɪd/ *adj.* trocken

Aries /'eəriːz/ *n.* (Astrol; Astron.) der Widder

arise /ə'raɪz/ *v.i.*, **arose** /ə'rəʊz/, **arisen** /ə'rɪzn/ **(a)** (originate) entstehen
(b) (present itself) auftreten; ⟨*Gelegenheit:*⟩ sich bieten
(c) (result) ~ **from** *or* **out of** sth. von etw. herrühren

aristocracy /ærɪ'stɒkrəsɪ/ *n.* Aristokratie, *die*

aristocrat /'ærɪstəkræt/ *n.* Aristokrat, *der*/ Aristokratin, *die*

aristocratic /ærɪstə'krætɪk/ *adj.* aristokratisch

arithmetic /ə'rɪθmətɪk/ *n.* Arithmetik, *die*

arm¹ /ɑːm/ *n.* Arm, *der*

arm² ☐1 *n.* **(a)** *usu. in pl.* (weapon) Waffe, *die;* **up in** ~s (fig.) in Harnisch (**about** wegen)
(b) *in pl.* (heraldic device) Wappen, *das*
☐2 *v.t.* bewaffnen

armada /ɑː'mɑːdə/ *n.* Armada, *die*

arm: ~**band** *n.* Armbinde, *die;* ~**chair** *n.* Sessel, *der;* ~**chair politician/strategist** politischer Amateur/Amateurstratege, *der;* ~**chair critic** Hobby- *od.* Amateurkritiker, *der;* ~**chair travel** Reisen *Pl.* in der Fantasie

armed /ɑːmd/ *adj.* bewaffnet; ~ **forces** Streitkräfte *Pl.*

armistice /'ɑːmɪstɪs/ *n.* Waffenstillstand, *der*

armor (Amer.), **armour** (Brit.) /'ɑːmə(r)/ *n.* **(a)** (Hist.) Rüstung, *die*
(b) (steel plates) Panzerung, *die*

arm: ~**pit** *n.* Achselhöhle, *die;* ~**rest** *n.* Armlehne, *die*

arms: ~ **control** *n.* Rüstungskontrolle, *die; attrib.* Rüstungskontroll-; ~ **race** *n.* Rüstungswettlauf, *der;* ~ **trade** *n.* Waffenhandel, *der*

army /'ɑːmɪ/ *n.* Heer, *das;* **join the** ~: zum Militär gehen

aroma /ə'rəʊmə/ *n.* Duft, *der*

aromatherapy /ərəʊmə'θerəpɪ/ *n.* Aromatherapie, *die*

aromatic /ærə'mætɪk/ *adj.* aromatisch

arose ▶ ARISE

around /ə'raʊnd/ ☐1 *adv.* **(a)** (on every side) [all] ~: überall
(b) (round) herum
(c) (in various places) **ask/look** ~: herumfragen/sich umsehen
☐2 *prep.* **(a)** um [... herum]
(b) (approximately) ~ **3 o'clock** gegen 3 Uhr; sth. [costing] ~ **£2** etw. für ungefähr 2 Pfund

arouse /ə'raʊz/ *v.t.* **(a)** (awake) [auf]wecken
(b) (excite) erregen; erwecken ⟨*Interesse, Begeisterung*⟩; ~ **suspicion** Verdacht erregen

arrange /ə'reɪndʒ/ ☐1 *v.t.* **(a)** (order) anordnen
(b) (settle, agree) ausmachen, vereinbaren ⟨*Termin*⟩; planen ⟨*Urlaub*⟩; **they** ~**d to meet the following day** sie verabredeten sich für den nächsten Tag
☐2 *v.i.* (plan) sorgen (**for** für)

ar'rangement *n.* **(a)** (ordering, order) Anordnung, *die*
(b) (settling, agreement) Vereinbarung, *die*
(c) *in pl.* (plans) Vorkehrungen *Pl.;* **make** ~s Vorkehrungen treffen

arrears /ə'rɪəz/ *n. pl.* Schulden *Pl.;* **be in** ~ **with** sth. mit etw. im Rückstand sein; **be paid in** ~: rückwirkend bezahlt werden

arrest /ə'rest/ ☐1 *v.t.* **(a)** verhaften, (temporarily) festnehmen ⟨*Person*⟩
(b) (stop) aufhalten
☐2 *n.* Verhaftung, *die;* **under** ~: festgenommen

arrival /ə'raɪvl/ *n.* Ankunft, *die;* **new** ~s Neuankömmlinge

arrive /ə'raɪv/ *v.i.* **(a)** ankommen; ~ **at a conclusion/an agreement** zu einem Schluss/ einer Einigung kommen
(b) ⟨*Stunde, Tag, Augenblick:*⟩ kommen

arrogance /'ærəgəns/ *n.* Arroganz, *die*

arrogant /'ærəgənt/ *adj.* arrogant

arrow /'ærəʊ/ *n.* Pfeil, *der*

arse /ɑːs/ *n.* (coarse) Arsch, *der* (derb)

■ **arse a'bout, arse a'round** *v. i.* (Brit. coarse) herumalbern (ugs.); herumblödeln (ugs.)

'**arsehole** *n.* (coarse) Arschloch, *das* (derb)

arsenal /'ɑːsənl/ *n.* Waffenlager, *das*

arsenic /'ɑːsənɪk/ *n.* **(a)** Arsenik, *das*
(b) (element) Arsen, *das*

arson /'ɑːsn/ *n.* Brandstiftung, *die;* ~ **attack** Brandanschlag, *der*

arsonist /'ɑːsənɪst/ *n.* Brandstifter, *der*/ Brandstifterin, *die*

art /ɑːt/ *n.* **(a)** Kunst, *die;* **works of** ~: Kunstwerke *Pl.;* ~ **college** *or* **school** Kunsthochschule, *die;* ~**s and crafts** Kunsthandwerk, *das*
(b) *in pl.* (branch of study) Geisteswissenschaften *Pl.*

artery /'ɑːtərɪ/ *n.* (Anat.) Schlagader, *die;* Arterie, *die* (bes. fachspr.)

artful /'ɑːtfl/ *adj.* schlau

'**art gallery** *n.* Kunstgalerie, *die*

arthritic /ɑː'θrɪtɪk/ *adj.* arthritisch

arthritis /ɑː'θraɪtɪs/ *n.* Arthritis, *die* (fachspr.); Gelenkentzündung, *die*

artichoke /'ɑːtɪtʃəʊk/ *n.* [globe] ~: Artischocke, *die*

article /'ɑːtɪkl/ *n.* **(a)** (in magazine, newspaper; Ling.) Artikel, *der*
(b) **an** ~ **of furniture/clothing** ein Möbel-/ Kleidungsstück; **an** ~ **of value** ein Wertgegenstand

articulate /ɑːˈtɪkjʊlət/ *adj.* redegewandt; **be ∼/not very ∼:** sich gut/nicht sehr gut ausdrücken [können]

articulated /ɑːˈtɪkjʊleɪtɪd/ *adj.* ∼ **'lorry** Sattelzug, *der*

artificial /ɑːtɪˈfɪʃl/ *adj.* **(a)** künstlich; Kunst-; (not real) unecht; ∼ **limb** Prothese, *die* **(b)** (affected) gekünstelt

artificial: ∼ **insemi'nation** *n.* künstliche Befruchtung; (of animal) künstliche Besamung; ∼ **in'telligence** *n.* künstliche Intelligenz; ∼ **'language** *n.* Kunstsprache, *die;* ∼ **respi'ration** *n.* künstliche Beatmung

artillery /ɑːˈtɪlərɪ/ *n.* Artillerie, *die*

artisan /ˈɑːtɪzn, ɑːtɪˈzæn/ *n.* [Kunst]handwerker, *der*

artist /ˈɑːtɪst/ *n.* Künstler, *der*/Künstlerin, *die*

artiste /ɑːˈtiːst/ *n.* Artist, *der*/Artistin, *die*

artistic /ɑːˈtɪstɪk/ *adj.* **(a)** (of art) Kunst-; künstlerisch **(b)** (naturally skilled in art) künstlerisch veranlagt

'artless *adj.* arglos

art nouveau /ɑː nuːˈvəʊ/ *n.* Jugendstil, *der*

'art room *n.* Zeichensaal, *der*

'arts centre *n.* Kunstzentrum, *das*

'art work *n.* Bildmaterial, *das*

as /əz, stressed æz/ **1** *adv., conj.* **(a)** he is as tall as I am er ist so groß wie ich; **as quickly as you can/as possible** so schnell du kannst/wie möglich **(b)** (though) **small as he was** obwohl er klein war **(c)** (however much) **try as he might/would, he could not concentrate** sosehr er sich auch bemühte, er konnte sich nicht konzentrieren **(d)** *expr. manner* wie; **as you may already have heard, ...:** wie Sie vielleicht schon gehört haben, ...; **as it were** sozusagen **(e)** *expr. time* als; während; **as we climbed the stairs** als wir die Treppe hinaufgingen; **as we were talking** während wir uns unterhielten **(f)** *expr. reason* da **2** *prep.* **(a)** (in the function of) als; **as an artist** als Künstler; **speaking as a mother** ...: als Mutter ... **(b)** (like) wie **(c)** **the same as** ...: der-/die-/dasselbe wie ...; **such as** wie zum Beispiel **3** **as for** ...: was ... angeht *od.* betrifft; **as [it] is** wie die Dinge liegen; **the place is untidy enough as it is** es ist hier [so] schon unordentlich genug; **as of ...** (Amer.) von ... an; **as to** hinsichtlich (+ *Gen.*); **as yet** bis jetzt; noch

a.s.a.p. *abbr.* = **as soon as possible**

asbestos /æzˈbestɒs/ *n.* Asbest, *der*

asbestosis /æzbesˈtəʊsɪs/ *n.* (Med.) Asbestose, *die*

ascend /əˈsend/ **1** *v.i.* **(a)** (go up) hinaufsteigen; (climb up) hinaufklettern; (by vehicle) hinauffahren **(b)** (rise) aufsteigen; ⟨Hubschrauber:⟩ höhersteigen **(c)** (slope upwards) ⟨Hügel, Straße:⟩ ansteigen **2** *v.t.* **(a)** (go up) hinaufsteigen ⟨Treppe, Leiter, Berg⟩ **(b)** ∼ **the throne** den Thron besteigen

Ascension Day /əˈsenʃn/ *n.* Himmelfahrtstag, *der*

ascent /əˈsent/ *n.* Aufstieg, *der*

ascertain /æsəˈteɪn/ *v.t.* feststellen; ermitteln ⟨Fakten, Daten⟩

ascribe /əˈskraɪb/ *v.t.* zuschreiben (**to** *Dat.*)

asexual /eɪˈsekʃʊəl/ *adj.* (without sexuality) asexuell

ash¹ /æʃ/ *n.* (tree) Esche, *die*

ash² *n.* (from fire etc.) Asche, *die*

ashamed /əˈʃeɪmd/ *adj.* beschämt; **be ∼:** sich schämen (**of** wegen)

ash: ∼ **bin** *n.* Mülleimer, *der;* ∼ **blonde** **1** *adj.* aschblond; **2** *n.* Aschblonde, *der/die;* ∼**can** (Amer.) ▶ ∼ BIN

ashen /ˈæʃn/ *adj.* aschfahl ⟨Gesicht⟩

ashore /əˈʃɔː(r)/ *adv.* an Land

'ashtray *n.* Aschenbecher, *der*

Ash 'Wednesday *n.* Aschermittwoch, *der*

Asia /ˈeɪʃə/ *pr. n.* Asien (*das*)

Asian /ˈeɪʃən/ **1** *adj.* asiatisch **2** *n.* Asiat, *der*/Asiatin, *die*

aside /əˈsaɪd/ *adv.* beiseite; zur Seite

ask /ɑːsk/ **1** *v.t.* **(a)** fragen; ∼ **sb.** [**sth.**] jmdn. [nach etw.] fragen **(b)** (seek to obtain) ∼ **sth.** um etw. bitten; **how much are you** ∼**ing for that car?** wie viel verlangen Sie für das Auto?; ∼ **sb. to do sth.** jmdn. [darum] bitten, etw. zu tun **(c)** (invite) einladen **2** *v.i.* ∼ **after sb./sth.** nach jmdm./etw. fragen; ∼ **for sth./sb.** etw./jmdn. verlangen

askance /əˈskæns, əˈskɑːns/ *adv.* **look** ∼ **at sb.** jmdn. befremdet ansehen

askew /əˈskjuː/ *adv., pred. adj.* schief

asleep /əˈsliːp/ *pred. adj.* schlafend; **be/lie** ∼: schlafen; **fall** ∼: einschlafen

asparagus /əˈspærəgəs/ *n.* Spargel, *der*

aspect /ˈæspekt/ *n.* Aspekt, *der*

aspersion /əˈspɜːʃn/ *n.* **cast** ∼**s on sb./sth.** jmdn./etw in den Schmutz ziehen

asphalt /ˈæsfælt/ *n.* Asphalt, *der*

asphyxiate /æsˈfɪksɪeɪt/ *v.t. & i.* ersticken

aspiration /æspəˈreɪʃn/ *n.* Streben, *das*

aspire /əˈspaɪə(r)/ *v.i.* ∼ **to** *or* **after sth.** nach etw. streben

aspirin /ˈæspərɪn/ *n.* Aspirin Ⓦ, *das;* Kopfschmerztablette, *die*

ass¹ /æs/ *n.* Esel, *der*

ass² (Amer.) ▶ ARSE

assailant /əˈseɪlənt/ n. Angreifer, der/
Angreiferin, die

assassin /əˈsæsɪn/ n. Mörder, der/
Mörderin, die

assassinate /əˈsæsɪneɪt/ v.t. ermorden; **be**
~d einem Attentat zum Opfer fallen

assassination /əsæsɪˈneɪʃn/ n. Mord, der
(**of** an + Dat.); **~ attempt** Attentat, das (**on**
auf + Akk.)

assault /əˈsɔːlt/ ① n. Angriff, der; (fig.)
Anschlag, der
② v.t. angreifen

assemble /əˈsembl/ ① v.t. (a)
zusammentragen; zusammenrufen
‹Menschen›
(b) (fit together) zusammenbauen
② v.i. sich versammeln

assembly /əˈsemblɪ/ n. (a) (meeting)
Versammlung, die; (in school) Morgenandacht,
die
(b) (fitting together) Zusammenbau, der

as'sembly line n. Fließband, das

assent /əˈsent/ ① v.i. zustimmen (**to** Dat.)
② n. Zustimmung, die

assert /əˈsɜːt/ v.t. (a) geltend machen;
~ **oneself** sich durchsetzen
(b) (declare) behaupten; beteuern ‹Unschuld›

assertion /əˈsɜːʃn/ n. (a) Geltendmachen,
das
(b) (declaration) Behauptung, die

assertive /əˈsɜːtɪv/ adj. energisch ‹Person›;
bestimmt ‹Ton, Verhalten›

assertiveness /əˈsɜːtɪvnɪs/ n.
Bestimmtheit, die

assess /əˈses/ v.t. einschätzen; festsetzen
‹Steuer› (**at** auf + Akk.)

as'sessment n. (a) Einschätzung, die
(b) (tax to be paid) Steuerbescheid, der

asset /ˈæset/ n. (a) Vermögenswert, der
(b) (useful quality) Vorzug, der (**to** für); (person)
Stütze, die; (thing) Hilfe, die

'asset-stripping n.: Ankauf unrentabler
Unternehmen, von denen einzelne Teile
Gewinn bringend weiterverkauft werden

assiduous /əˈsɪdjʊəs/ adj. (a) (diligent) eifrig
(b) (conscientious) gewissenhaft

assign /əˈsaɪn/ v.t. (a) (allot) zuweisen (**to**
Dat.)
(b) (appoint) zuteilen; ~ **sb. to do sth.** jmdn.
damit betrauen, etw. zu tun

as'signment n. (a) (allotment) Zuweisung,
die; (appointment) Zuteilung, die
(b) (task) Aufgabe, die

assimilate /əˈsɪmɪleɪt/ v.t. angleichen (**to**,
with an + Akk.)

assimilation /əsɪmɪˈleɪʃn/ n. Angleichung,
die (**to**, **with** an + Akk.)

assist /əˈsɪst/ ① v.t. helfen (+ Dat.)
② v.i. helfen; ~ **with sth./in doing sth.** bei
etw. helfen/helfen, etw. zu tun

assistance /əˈsɪstəns/ n. Hilfe, die

assistant /əˈsɪstənt/ n. (helper) Helfer, der/
Helferin, die; (subordinate) Mitarbeiter, der/

Mitarbeiterin, die; (of professor, artist)
Assistent, der/Assistentin, die; (in shop)
Verkäufer, der/Verkäuferin, die; ~ **manager**
stellvertretender Geschäftsführer

associate ① /əˈsəʊʃɪət, əˈsəʊsɪət/ n.
(partner) Partner, der/Partnerin, die; (colleague)
Kollege, der/Kollegin, die
② /əˈsəʊʃɪeɪt, əˈsəʊsɪeɪt/ v.t. in Verbindung
bringen; **be ~d** in Verbindung stehen
③ /əˈsəʊʃɪeɪt, əˈsəʊsɪeɪt/ v.i. ~ **with sb.** mit
jmdm. Umgang haben

association /əsəʊsɪˈeɪʃn/ n. (a)
(organization) Vereinigung, die
(b) (mental connection) Assoziation, die
(c) (connection) Verbindung, die

assorted /əˈsɔːtɪd/ adj. gemischt

assortment /əˈsɔːtmənt/ n. Sortiment, das;
a good ~ of hats [to choose from] eine gute
Auswahl an Hüten

Asst. abbr. = **Assistant** Ass.

assume /əˈsjuːm/ v.t. (a) voraussetzen;
assuming that ...: vorausgesetzt, dass ...
(b) (undertake) übernehmen ‹Amt, Pflichten›
(c) (take on) annehmen ‹Namen, Rolle›

assumption /əˈsʌmpʃn/ n. Annahme, die;
going on the ~ that ...: vorausgesetzt, dass
...; **the A~** (Relig.) Mariä Himmelfahrt

assurance /əˈʃʊərəns/ n. (a) Zusicherung,
die
(b) (self-confidence) Selbstsicherheit, die

assure /əˈʃʊə(r)/ v.t. (a) versichern (+ Dat.)
(b) (convince) ~ **sb./oneself** jmdn./sich
überzeugen
(c) (make certain or safe) gewährleisten

assured /əˈʃʊəd/ adj. gewährleistet
‹Erfolg›; **be ~ of sth.** sich (Dat.) einer Sache
(Gen.) sicher sein

asterisk /ˈæstərɪsk/ n. Sternchen, das

astern /əˈstɜːn/ adv. (Naut., Aeronaut.)
achtern; (towards the rear) achteraus

asteroid /ˈæstərɔɪd/ n. Asteroid, der

asthma /ˈæsmə/ n. Asthma, das

asthmatic /æsˈmætɪk/ ① adj. asthmatisch
② n. Asthmatiker, der/Asthmatikerin, die

astonish /əˈstɒnɪʃ/ v.t. erstaunen

a'stonishing adj. erstaunlich

a'stonishment n. Erstaunen, das

astound /əˈstaʊnd/ v.t. verblüffen

a'stounding adj. erstaunlich

astray /əˈstreɪ/ adv. **sth. goes ~** (is mislaid)
etw. wird verlegt; (is lost) etw. geht verloren;
go/lead ~ (fig.) in die Irre gehen/führen

astride /əˈstraɪd/ ① adv. rittlings ‹sitzen›
② prep. rittlings auf (+ Dat.)

astringent /əˈstrɪndʒənt/ ① adj. scharf
② n. Adstringens, das

astrologer /əˈstrɒlədʒə(r)/ n. Astrologe,
der/Astrologin, die

astrological /æstrəˈlɒdʒɪkl/ adj.
astrologisch

astrology /əˈstrɒlədʒɪ/ n. Astrologie, die

astronaut /'æstrənɔ:t/ *n.* Astronaut, *der*/
Astronautin, *die*

astronautics /æstrə'nɔ:tɪks/ *n.*
Astronautik, *die;* Raumfahrt, *die*

astronomer /ə'strɒnəmə(r)/ *n.* Astronom,
der/Astronomin, *die*

astronomical /æstrə'nɒmɪkl/ *adj.*
astronomisch

astronomy /ə'strɒnəmɪ/ *n.* Astronomie,
die

astrophysics /æstrəʊ'fɪzɪks/ *n.*
Astrophysik, *die*

astute /ə'stju:t/ *adj.* scharfsinnig

asylum /ə'saɪləm/ *n.* (a) (Polit.) Asyl, *das;*
grant sb. ∼: jmdm. Asyl gewähren;
∼ seeker Asylsuchende, *der*/*die*
(b) ▶ LUNATIC ASYLUM

asymmetric /æsɪ'metrɪk, eɪsɪ'metrɪk/ *adj.*
asymmetrisch; unsymmetrisch

at /ət, *stressed* æt/ *prep.* (a) *expr. place* an
(+ *Dat.*); **at the station** am Bahnhof; **at the
baker's/butcher's/grocer's** beim Bäcker/
Fleischer/Kaufmann; **at the chemist's** in der
Apotheke/Drogerie; **at the supermarket** im
Supermarkt; **at the party** auf der Party; **at
the office/hotel** im Büro/Hotel; **at Dover** in
Dover
(b) *expr. time* **at Christmas** [zu *od.* an]
Weihnachten; **at six o'clock** um sechs Uhr;
at midnight um Mitternacht; **at midday** am
Mittag; **at [the age of] 40** mit 40; im Alter
von 40; **at this/the moment** in diesem/im
Augenblick *od.* Moment
(c) *expr. price* **at £2.50 [each]** zu *od.* für [je]
2,50 Pfund
(d) *expr. speed* **at 30 m.p.h.** *etc.* mit dreißig
Meilen pro Stunde *usw.*
(e) **at that** (at that point) dabei; (at that
provocation) daraufhin; (moreover) noch dazu

ate ▶ EAT

atheism /'eɪθɪɪzm/ *n.* Atheismus, *der*

atheist /'eɪθɪɪst/ *n.* Atheist, *der*/Atheistin,
die

Athens /'æθɪnz/ *pr. n.* Athen (*das*)

athlete /'æθli:t/ *n.* Athlet, *der*/Athletin, *die;*
(runner, jumper) Leichtathlet, *der*/-athletin, *die*

athletic /æθ'letɪk/ *adj.* sportlich

ath'letics *n.* Leichtathletik, *die*

Atlantic /ət'læntɪk/ ⨯1⨯ *adj.* atlantisch;
∼ **Ocean** Atlantischer Ozean
⨯2⨯ *pr. n.* Atlantik, *der*

atlas /'ætləs/ *n.* Atlas, *der*

ATM *abbr.* = **automated teller
machine**

atmosphere /'ætməsfɪə(r)/ *n.*
Atmosphäre, *die*

atmospheric /ætməs'ferɪk/ *adj.* (a)
atmosphärisch
(b) (fig.: evocative) stimmungsvoll

atom /'ætəm/ *n.* Atom, *das*

'atom bomb *n.* Atombombe, *die*

atomic /ə'tɒmɪk/ *adj.* Atom-

atomizer /'ætəmaɪzə(r)/ *n.* Zerstäuber, *der*

atone /ə'təʊn/ *v.i.* es wieder gutmachen;
∼ **for sth.** etw. wieder gutmachen

a'tonement *n.* Buße, *die*

atrocious /ə'trəʊʃəs/ *adj.* grauenhaft;
scheußlich ⟨*Wetter, Benehmen*⟩

a'trociously *adv.* grauenhaft; scheußlich
⟨*sich benehmen*⟩

atrocity /ə'trɒsɪtɪ/ *n.* (a) (wickedness)
Grauenhaftigkeit, *die*
(b) (deed) Gräueltat, *die*

attach /ə'tætʃ/ *v.t.* (a) (fasten) befestigen (**to**
an + *Dat.*); **please note ∼ed a copy of the
letter** beigeheftet ist eine Kopie des Briefes
(b) (fig.) ∼ **importance to sth.** einer Sache
(*Dat.*) Gewicht beimessen

attaché /ə'tæʃeɪ/ *n.* Attaché, *der*

at'taché case *n.* Diplomatenkoffer, *der*

attached /ə'tætʃt/ *adj.* (emotionally) **be ∼ to
sb./sth.** an jmdm./etw. hängen

at'tachment *n.* (a) (act or means of fastening)
Befestigung, *die*
(b) (affection) Anhänglichkeit, *die* (**to** an +
Akk.)
(c) (accessory) Zusatzgerät, *das*
(d) (Comp.) Attachment, *das;* Anlage, *die*

attack /ə'tæk/ ⨯1⨯ *v.t.* (a) angreifen;
(ambush, raid) überfallen; (fig.: criticize)
attackieren
(b) (affect) ⟨*Krankheit:*⟩ befallen
⨯2⨯ *v.i.* angreifen
⨯3⨯ *n.* Angriff, *der;* (ambush) Überfall, *der;* (fig.:
criticism) Attacke, *die;* (of illness) Anfall, *der*

at'tacker *n.* Angreifer, *der*/Angreiferin,
die

attacking /ə'tækɪŋ/ *adj.* offensiv
⟨*Spielweise, Spieler*⟩; angreifend ⟨*Truppen*⟩

attain /ə'teɪn/ *v.t.* erreichen

attainable /ə'teɪnəbl/ *adj.* erreichbar
⟨*Ziel*⟩; realisierbar ⟨*Hoffnung, Ziel*⟩

at'tainment *n.* Verwirklichung, *die*

attempt /ə'tempt/ ⨯1⨯ *v.t.* versuchen
⨯2⨯ *n.* Versuch, *der*

attend /ə'tend/ ⨯1⨯ *v.i.* (a) (give care and
thought) aufpassen; (apply oneself) ∼ **to sth.**
(deal with sth.) sich um etw. kümmern
(b) (be present) anwesend sein (**at** bei)
⨯2⨯ *v.t.* (a) (be present at) teilnehmen an
(+ *Dat.*); (go regularly to) besuchen
(b) (wait on) bedienen (+ *Dat.*)
(c) ⟨*Arzt:*⟩ behandeln

attendance /ə'tendəns/ *n.* Anwesenheit,
die; (number of people) Teilnehmerzahl, *die*

attendant /ə'tendənt/ *n.* (a) [lavatory] ∼:
Toilettenmann, *der*/-frau, *die;* [cloakroom]
∼: Garderobenmann, *der*/-frau, *die;* **museum**
∼: Museumswärter, *der*/-wärterin, *die*
(b) (member of entourage) Begleiter, *der*/
Begleiterin, *die*

attention /ə'tenʃn/ ⨯1⨯ *n.* (a)
Aufmerksamkeit, *die;* **attract [sb.'s]** ∼:
[jmdn.] auf sich (*Akk.*) aufmerksam machen;
pay ∼ to sb./sth. jmdn./etw. beachten; **pay** ···⊹

∼! gib Acht!; pass auf!; hold sb.'s ∼: jmds.
Interesse wach halten; ∼ **Miss Jones** (on
letter) zu Händen [von] Miss Jones
(b) (Mil.) **stand to** ∼: stillstehen
[2] *int.* (a) Achtung
(b) (Mil.) stillgestanden

attentive /ə'tentɪv/ *adj.* aufmerksam

attic /'ætɪk/ *n.* (room) Dachboden, *der;*
(habitable) Dachkammer, *die*

attire /ə'taɪə(r)/ *n.* Kleidung, *die*

attitude /'ætɪtjuːd/ *n.* (a) Haltung, *die*
(b) (mental ∼) Einstellung, *die*

attn. *abbr.* = **for the attention of**
z. H[d].

attorney /ə'tɜːnɪ/ *n.* (a) Bevollmächtigte,
der/die; **power of** ∼: Vollmacht, *die*
(b) (Amer.: lawyer) [Rechts]anwalt, *der/*
-anwältin, *die*

attract /ə'trækt/ *v.t.* (a) (draw) anziehen; auf
sich (*Akk.*) ziehen ⟨*Interesse, Blick, Kritik*⟩
(b) (arouse pleasure in) anziehend wirken auf
(+ *Akk.*)
(c) (arouse interest in) reizen (**about** an + *Dat.*)

attraction /ə'trækʃn/ *n.* (a) Anziehung,
die; (force, lit. or fig.) Anziehung[skraft], *die*
(b) (fig.: thing that attracts) Attraktion, *die;*
(charm) Verlockung, *die;* Reiz, *der*

attractive /ə'træktɪv/ *adj.* (a) anziehend
(b) (fig.) attraktiv; reizvoll ⟨*Vorschlag,
Möglichkeit, Idee*⟩

attribute [1] /'ætrɪbjuːt/ *n.* Eigenschaft, *die*
[2] /ə'trɪbjuːt/ *v.t.* zuschreiben (**to** *Dat.*)

attributive /ə'trɪbjʊtɪv/ *adj.* (Ling.)
attributiv

atypical /eɪ'tɪpɪkl/ *adj.* atypisch; untypisch

aubergine /'əʊbəʒiːn/ *n.* Aubergine, *die*

auburn /'ɔːbən/ *adj.* rötlich braun

auction /'ɔːkʃn/ [1] *n.* Versteigerung, *die*
[2] *v.t.* versteigern

auctioneer /ɔːkʃə'nɪə(r)/ *n.* Auktionator,
*der/*Auktionatorin, *die*

audacious /ɔː'deɪʃəs/ *adj.* (a) (daring) kühn;
verwegen
(b) (impudent) dreist

audacity /ɔː'dæsɪtɪ/ *n.* (a) (daringness)
Kühnheit, *die;* Verwegenheit, *die*
(b) (impudence) Dreistigkeit, *die*

audible /'ɔːdɪbl/ *adj.* hörbar

audience /'ɔːdɪəns/ *n.* (a) Publikum, *das*
(b) (formal interview) Audienz, *die* (**with** bei)

audio /'ɔːdɪəʊ/ *adj.* Ton-; ∼ **frequency**
Tonfrequenz, *die;* ∼ **equipment** Audioanlage,
die

audio: ∼**book** *n.* Hörbuch, *das;*
∼ **cassette** *n.* Audiokassette, *die;*
Tonkassette, *die;* ∼ **typist** *n.* Phonotypist,
der/-typistin, *die;* ∼**visual** *adj.* audiovisuell

audit /'ɔːdɪt/ [1] *n.* ∼ [**of the accounts**]
Rechnungsprüfung, *die*
[2] *v.t.* prüfen

audition /ɔː'dɪʃn/ [1] *n.* (singing) Vorsingen,
das; (dancing) Vortanzen, *das;* (acting)
Vorsprechen, *das*

[2] *v.i.* (sing) vorsingen; (dance) vortanzen;
(act) vorsprechen
[3] *v.t.* vorsingen/vortanzen/vorsprechen
lassen

auditor /'ɔːdɪtə(r)/ *n.* Buchprüfer, *der/*
-prüferin, *die*

auditorium /ɔːdɪ'tɔːrɪəm/ *n.*
Zuschauerraum, *der*

Aug. *abbr.* = **August** Aug.

augment /ɔːg'ment/ *v.t.* verbessern
⟨*Einkommen*⟩; aufstocken ⟨*Fonds*⟩

augur /'ɔːgə(r)/ [1] *v.t.* bedeuten;
versprechen ⟨*Erfolg*⟩
[2] *v.i.* ∼ **well/ill for sth./sb.** ein gutes/
schlechtes Zeichen für etw./jmdn. sein

August /'ɔːgəst/ *n.* August, *der;* **in** ∼: im
August; **last/next** ∼: letzten/nächsten
August; **the first of/on the first of** ∼: der
erste/am ersten August

aunt /ɑːnt/ *n.* Tante, *die*

auntie, aunty /'ɑːntɪ/ *n.* (coll.) Täntchen,
das; (with name) Tante, *die*

au pair /əʊ 'peə(r)/ *n.* Aupairmädchen, *das*

aura /'ɔːrə/ *n.* Aura, *die*

auspices /'ɔːspɪsɪs/ *n. pl.* **under the** ∼ **of**
sb./sth. unter jmds./einer Sache
Schirmherrschaft

auspicious /ɔː'spɪʃəs/ *adj.* günstig;
viel versprechend ⟨*Anfang*⟩

Aussie /'ɒzɪ/ (coll.) [1] *adj.* australisch
[2] *n.* Australier, *der/*Australierin, *die*

austere /ɒ'stɪə(r)/ *adj.* (a) (strict, stern)
streng
(b) (severely simple) karg

austerity /ɒ'sterɪtɪ/ *n.* (a) (strictness)
Strenge, *die*
(b) (severe simplicity) Kargheit, *die*
(c) (lack of luxuries) wirtschaftliche
Einschränkung

Australia /ɒ'streɪlɪə/ *pr. n.* Australien (*das*)

Australian /ɒ'streɪlɪən/ [1] *adj.* australisch;
sb. is ∼: jmd. ist Australier/Australierin
[2] *n.* Australier, *der/*Australierin, *die;*

Austria /'ɒstrɪə/ *pr. n.* Österreich (*das*)

Austrian /'ɒstrɪən/ [1] *adj.* österreichisch;
sb. is ∼ jmd. ist Österreicher/Österreicherin
[2] *n.* Österreicher, *der/*Österreicherin, *die*

authentic /ɔː'θentɪk/ *adj.* authentisch

authenticate /ɔː'θentɪkeɪt/ *v.t.*
authentifizieren; ∼ **sth.** die Echtheit einer
Sache (*Gen.*) bestätigen

authentication /ɔːθentɪ'keɪʃn/ *n.*
Bestätigung der Echtheit; (of information, report)
Bestätigung, *die*

authenticity /ɔːθen'tɪsɪtɪ/ *n.* Authentizität,
die

author /'ɔːθə(r)/ *n.* Autor, *der/*Autorin, *die;*
(profession) Schriftsteller, *der/*Schriftstellerin,
die

authoritarian /ɔːθɒrɪ'teərɪən/ [1] *adj.*
autoritär
[2] *n.* autoritäre Person

authoritative /ɔ:ˈθɒrɪtətɪv/ adj. maßgebend; zuverlässig ⟨Bericht, Information⟩

authority /ɔ:ˈθɒrɪtɪ/ n. (a) Autorität, die; in ∼: verantwortlich
(b) the authorities die Behörde[n]

authorization /ɔ:θəraɪˈzeɪʃn/ n. Genehmigung, die

authorize /ˈɔ:θəraɪz/ v.t. (a) ermächtigen; bevollmächtigen
(b) (sanction) genehmigen

auto /ˈɔ:təʊ/ n., pl. ∼s (Amer. coll.) Auto, das

auto- /ɔ:təʊ/ in comb. auto-/Auto-

autobio'graphical adj. autobiographisch

autobi'ography n. Autobiographie, die

autocrat /ˈɔ:təkræt/ n. Autokrat, der/ Autokratin, die

autocratic /ɔ:təˈkrætɪk/ adj. autokratisch

'autocross n. Autocross, das

Autocue ® /ˈɔ:təʊkju:/ n. Teleprompter ⓌⓏ, der

'autofocus n. (Photog.) Autofokus, der

autograph /ˈɔ:təgrɑ:f/ ① n. Autogramm, das
② v.t. signieren

auto-im'mune adj. (Med.) autoimmun; ∼ response Autoimmunantwort, die

automat /ˈɔ:təmæt/ n. (Amer.) (a) (slot machine) [Münz]automat, der
(b) (cafeteria) Automatenrestaurant, das

automate /ˈɔ:təmeɪt/ v.t. automatisieren

automated 'teller machine n. Geldautomat, der

automatic /ɔ:təˈmætɪk/ ① adj. automatisch; ∼ gear system, ∼ transmission Automatikgetriebe, das
② n. (weapon) automatische Waffe; (vehicle) Fahrzeug mit Automatikgetriebe

automatically /ɔ:təˈmætɪkəlɪ/ adv. automatisch

automation /ɔ:təˈmeɪʃn/ n. Automation, die

automaton /ɔ:ˈtɒmətən/ n., pl. ∼s or automata /ɔ:ˈtɒmətə/ Automat, der

automobile /ˈɔ:təməbi:l/ n. (Amer.) Auto, das

autonomous /ɔ:ˈtɒnəməs/ adj. autonom

autonomy /ɔ:ˈtɒnəmɪ/ n. Autonomie, die

'autopilot n. Autopilot, der; [fly] on ∼: mit Autopilot [fliegen]

autopsy /ˈɔ:tɒpsɪ/ n. Autopsie, die

auto: ∼save (Comp.) ① n. automatisches Speichern; ② v.t. automatisch speichern; ∼suggestion n. Autosuggestion, die; ∼timer n. [automatische] Schaltuhr

autumn /ˈɔ:təm/ n. Herbst, der; in [the] ∼: im Herbst

autumnal /ɔ:ˈtʌmnl/ adj. herbstlich

auxiliary /ɔ:gˈzɪljərɪ/ ① adj. Hilfs-
② n. (a) Hilfskraft, die
(b) (Ling.) Hilfsverb, das

avail /əˈveɪl/ ① n. be of no ∼: nichts nützen; to no ∼: vergebens
② v. refl. ∼ oneself of sth. von etw. Gebrauch machen

available /əˈveɪləbl/ adj. (a) (at one's disposal) verfügbar
(b) (obtainable) erhältlich; lieferbar ⟨Waren⟩

avalanche /ˈævəlɑ:nʃ/ n. Lawine, die

avarice /ˈævərɪs/ n. Geldgier, die; Habsucht, die

avaricious /ævəˈrɪʃəs/ adj. geldgierig; habsüchtig

avenge /əˈvendʒ/ v.t. rächen

avenue /ˈævənju:/ n. Allee, die; (fig.) Weg, der (to zu)

average /ˈævərɪdʒ/ ① n. Durchschnitt, der; on ∼: im Durchschnitt; durchschnittlich
② adj. durchschnittlich
③ v.t. (a) (find the ∼ of) den Durchschnitt ermitteln von
(b) (amount on ∼ to) durchschnittlich betragen
④ v.i. ∼ out at im Durchschnitt betragen

averse /əˈvɜ:s/ adj. be ∼ to sth. einer Sache ⟨Dat.⟩ abgeneigt sein

aversion /əˈvɜ:ʃn/ n. Abneigung, die (to gegen)

avert /əˈvɜ:t/ v.t. abwenden; verhüten ⟨Unfall⟩

aviary /ˈeɪvɪərɪ/ n. Vogelhaus, das

aviation /eɪvɪˈeɪʃn/ n. Luftfahrt, die

avid /ˈævɪd/ adj. (enthusiastic) begeistert; be ∼ for sth. (eager, greedy) begierig auf etw. (Akk.) sein

avocado /ævəˈkɑ:dəʊ/ n., pl. ∼s: ∼ [pear] Avocado[birne], die

avoid /əˈvɔɪd/ v.t. (a) meiden ⟨Ort⟩; ∼ a cyclist einem Radfahrer ausweichen; ∼ the boss when he's in a temper geh dem Chef aus dem Weg, wenn er schlechte Laune hat
(b) (refrain from, escape) vermeiden

avoidable /əˈvɔɪdəbl/ adj. vermeidbar

avoidance /əˈvɔɪdəns/ n. Vermeidung, die

await /əˈweɪt/ v.t. erwarten

awake /əˈweɪk/ ① v.i., awoke /əˈwəʊk/, awoken /əˈwəʊkn/ erwachen
② v.t., awoke, awoken wecken
③ pred. adj. wach; wide ∼: hellwach

awaken /əˈweɪkn/ v.t. & i. (esp. fig.)
▶ AWAKE 1, 2

award /əˈwɔ:d/ ① v.t. verleihen ⟨Preis, Auszeichnung⟩; zusprechen ⟨Sorgerecht, Entschädigung⟩; gewähren ⟨Zahlung, Gehaltserhöhung⟩
② n. (prize) Auszeichnung, die

a'ward-winning adj. preisgekrönt

aware /əˈweə(r)/ adj. be ∼ of sth. sich (Dat.) einer Sache (Gen.) bewusst sein; be ∼ that ...: sich (Dat.) [dessen] bewusst sein, dass ...

a'wareness n. Bewusstsein, das

awash /ə'wɒʃ/ *adj.* be ~ (flooded) unter Wasser stehen

away /ə'weɪ/ ① *adv.* **(a)** (at a distance) entfernt; **play** ~ (Sport) auswärts spielen **(b)** (to a distance) weg; fort **(c)** (absent) nicht da ② *adj.* (Sport) auswärts *präd.;* Auswärts-; ~ **match** Auswärtsspiel, *das;* ~ **team** Gastmannschaft, *die*

awe /ɔː/ *n.* Ehrfurcht, *die* (**of** vor + *Dat.*)

'**awe-inspiring** *adj.* Ehrfurcht gebietend; beeindruckend

awesome /'ɔːsəm/ *adj.* überwältigend; eindrucksvoll ‹*Schweigen*›; übergroß ‹*Verantwortung*›

awe: ~**stricken,** ~**struck** *adj.* [von Ehrfurcht] ergriffen; ehrfurchtsvoll ‹*Ausdruck, Staunen*›

awful /'ɔːfl/ *adj.,* '**awfully** *adv.* furchtbar

awkward /'ɔːkwəd/ *adj.* **(a)** (difficult to use) ungünstig; be ~ **to use** unhandlich sein **(b)** (clumsy) unbeholfen **(c)** (embarrassing) peinlich **(d)** (difficult) schwierig; ungünstig ‹*Zeitpunkt*›

awning /'ɔːnɪŋ/ *n.* (on house) Markise, *die;* (of tent) Vordach, *das*

awoke, awoken ▶ AWAKE

awry /ə'raɪ/ *adv.* schief; **go** ~ (fig.) schief gehen (ugs.); ‹*Plan.*› fehlschlagen

axe (*Amer.:* **ax**) /æks/ *n.* Axt, *die;* Beil, *das*

axis /'æksɪs/ *n., pl.* **axes** /'æksiːz/ Achse, *die*

axle /'æksl/ *n.* Achse, *die*

Bb

B, b /biː/ *n.* B, b, *das;* **B road** Straße 2. Ordnung; ≈ Landstraße, *die*

BA *abbr.* = **Bachelor of Arts**

babble /'bæbl/ *v.i.* **(a)** (talk incoherently) stammeln **(b)** (talk foolishly) [dumm] schwatzen **(c)** ‹*Bach:*› plätschern

baboon /bə'buːn/ *n.* Pavian, *der*

baby /'beɪbɪ/ *n.* **(a)** Baby, *das;* **have a** ~/**be going to have a** ~: ein Kind bekommen; **throw out** *or* **away the** ~ **with the bathwater** (fig.) das Kind mit dem Bade ausschütten **(b)** (childish person) **be a** ~: sich wie ein kleines Kind benehmen

baby: ~ **boom** *n.* Babyboom, *der;* ~**bouncer** *n.: federnd aufgehängter Sitz für Kleinkinder, in dem sie durch Wippen ihre Beine kräftigen sollen;* ~ **buggy,** ~ **carriage** *ns.* (Amer.) Kinderwagen, *der;* ~ **clothes** *n. pl.* Babykleidung, *die;* ~ **food** *n.* Babynahrung, *die*

'**babyish** *adj.* kindlich ‹*Aussehen*›; kindisch ‹*Benehmen, Person*›

baby: ~**minder** *n.* Tagesmutter, *die;* ~**sit** *v.i., forms as* SIT 1: babysitten (ugs.); auf das Kind/die Kinder aufpassen; ~**sitter** *n.* Babysitter, *der*/Babysitterin, *die;* ~**sitting** *n.* Babysitting, *das;* ~**snatcher** *n.* Kindesentführer, *der* /-entführerin, *die;* ~**talk** *n.* Babysprache, *die;* ~**walker** *n.* Laufstuhl, *der;* ~ **wipe** *n.* feuchtes Baby[pflege]tuch

bachelor /'bætʃələ(r)/ *n.* **(a)** Junggeselle, *der*

(b) (Univ.) **B**~ **of Arts/Science** Bakkalaureus der philosophischen Fakultät/der Naturwissenschaften

back /bæk/ ① *n.* **(a)** (of person, animal) Rücken, *der;* (of house, chair) Rückseite, *die;* (of vehicle) Heck, *das;* (inside car) Rücksitz, *der;* **stand** ~ **to** ~: Rücken an Rücken stehen; ~ **to front** verkehrt rum; **turn one's** ~ **on sb.** jmdm. den Rücken zuwenden; (fig.) jmdn. im Stich lassen; **turn one's** ~ **on sth.** (fig.) sich um etw. nicht kümmern; **get** *or* **put sb.'s** ~ **up** (fig.) jmdn. wütend machen; **be glad to see the** ~ **of sb./sth.** (fig.) froh sein, jmdn./ etw. nicht mehr sehen zu müssen; **have one's** ~ **to the wall** (fig.) mit dem Rücken zur Wand stehen; **put one's** ~ **into sth.** (fig.) sich für etw. mit allen Kräften einsetzen; **with the** ~ **of one's hand** mit dem Handrücken; **at the** ~ [**of the book**] hinten [im Buch] **(b)** (Sport: player) Verteidiger, *der* ② *adj.* hinter... ③ *adv.* zurück; **two miles** ~: vor zwei Meilen; ~ **and forth** hin und her; **there and** ~: hin und zurück; **a week/month** ~: vor einer Woche/vor einem Monat ④ *v.t.* **(a)** (assist) unterstützen **(b)** (bet on) wetten *od.* setzen auf (+ *Akk.*) **(c)** zurücksetzen [mit] ‹*Fahrzeug*› ⑤ *v.i.* zurücksetzen; ~ **into/out of sth.** rückwärts in etw. (*Akk.*)/aus etw. fahren; ~ **on to sth.** hinten an etw. (*Akk.*) grenzen

■ **back 'down** *v.i.* nachgeben

■ **back 'out** *v.i.* rückwärts herausfahren; ~ **out of sth.** (fig.) von etw. zurücktreten

■ **back 'up** *v.t.* **(a)** unterstützen; untermauern ‹*Anspruch, These*›

(b) (Comp.) sichern ⟨*Daten, Dokumente*⟩; ~ **up a file on to a floppy disk** von einer Datei eine Sicherungskopie auf Diskette machen

back: ~**ache** *n.* Rückenschmerzen *Pl.;* ~**-bencher** /bæk'bentʃə(r)/ *n.* (Brit. Parl.) [einfacher] Abgeordneter/[einfache] Abgeordnete; ~**bone** *n.* Rückgrat, *das;* ~**chat** *n.* (coll.) [freche] Widerrede; ~**date** *v.t.* zurückdatieren (**to** auf + *Akk.*); ~ '**door** *n.* Hintertür, *die*

'**backer** *n.* Geldgeber, *der*

back: ~'**fire** *v.i.* knallen; (fig.) fehlschlagen; **it** ~**fired on me/him** *etc.* der Schuss ging nach hinten los (ugs.); ~**gammon** /'bækgæmən/ *n.* (game) Backgammon, *das;* ≈ Tricktrack, *das;* ≈ Puff, *das;* ~**ground** *n.* Hintergrund, *der;* (social status) Herkunft, *die;* ~**hand** (Tennis etc.) ⟦1⟧ *adj.* Rückhand-; ⟦2⟧ *n.* Rückhand, *die;* ~'**handed** *adj.* **(a)** (Tennis etc.) Rückhand-; **(b)** (fig.) indirekt; zweifelhaft ⟨*Kompliment*⟩; ~'**hander** *n.* (coll.: bribe) Schmiergeld, *das*

'**backing** *n.* (support) Unterstützung, *die*

back: ~ **issue** ▶ ~ NUMBER; ~**lash** *n.* (fig.) Gegenreaktion, *die;* ~**log** *n.* Rückstand, *der;* ~ **number** *n.* (of periodical, magazine) alte Nummer; ~**pack** ⟦1⟧ *n.* Rucksack, *der;* ⟦2⟧ *v.i.* mit dem Rucksack [ver]reisen; ~**packer** *n.* Rucksackreisende, *der/die;* Rucksacktourist, *der/*-touristin, *die;* (hiker) Wanderer, *der/* Wanderin, *die* mit Rucksack; ~**packing** *n.* das [Ver]reisen mit dem Rucksack; (hiking) das Wandern mit dem Rucksack; *attrib.* ⟨*Reise usw.*⟩ mit dem Rucksack; ~ **pay** *n.* ausstehender Lohn/ausstehendes Gehalt; **he was reinstated with** ~ **pay** er wurde wieder eingestellt und erhielt eine Lohn-/ Gehaltsnachzahlung; **she was awarded £7,850 in** ~ **pay** sie erhielt eine Nachzahlung von 7 850 Pfund; ~'**pedal** *v.i.* **(a)** die Pedale rückwärts treten; **(b)** (fig.) einen Rückzieher machen (ugs.); ~**scratching** *n.* (fig. coll.) [mutual] ~**scratching** Klüngelei, *die* (abwertend); ~ '**seat** *n.* Rücksitz, *der;* ~**side** *n.* Hinterteil, *das* (ugs.); ~**space** *v.i.* die Rücktaste betätigen; ~'**stage** *adv.* go ~**stage** hinter die Bühne gehen; ~ **street** *n.* kleine Seitenstraße; ~**stroke** *n.* Rückenschwimmen, *das;* ~**track** *v.i.* wieder zurückgehen; (fig.) eine Kehrtwendung machen; ~**-up** *n.* (support) Unterstützung, *die;* ~**-up** [copy] (Comp.) Sicherungskopie, *die*

backward /'bækwəd/ ⟦1⟧ *adj.* **(a)** rückwärts gerichtet; Rückwärts- **(b)** (reluctant, shy) zurückhaltend **(c)** (underdeveloped) rückständig ⟨*Land, Region*⟩ ⟦2⟧ *adv.* ▶ BACKWARDS

backwards /'bækwədz/ *adv.* **(a)** nach hinten; **the child fell** [over] ~ **into the water** das Kind fiel rückwärts ins Wasser; **bend** *or* **lean over** ~ **to do sth.** (fig. coll.) sich zerreißen, um etw. zu tun (ugs.) **(b)** (oppositely to normal direction) rückwärts; ~ **and forwards** hin und her

back: ~**water** *n.* (fig.) Kaff, *das* (ugs.); ~ '**yard** *n.* Hinterhof, *der*

bacon /'beɪkn/ *n.* [Frühstücks]speck, *der*

bacterial /bæk'tɪərɪəl/ *adj.* bakteriell

bacterium /bæk'tɪərɪəm/ *n., pl.* **bacteria** /bæk'tɪərɪə/ Bakterie, *die*

bad /bæd/ *adj., worse* /wɜːs/, *worst* /wɜːst/ **(a)** schlecht; (rotten) schlecht, verdorben ⟨*Fleisch, Fisch, Essen*⟩; faul ⟨*Ei, Apfel*⟩; **not** ~ (coll.) nicht schlecht; nicht übel **(b)** (naughty) ungezogen, böse ⟨*Kind, Hund*⟩ **(c)** (offensive) [**use**] ~ **language** Kraftausdrücke [benutzen] **(d)** (regretful) **feel** ~ **about sth.** etw. bedauern; **I feel** ~ **about him** ich habe seinetwegen ein schlechtes Gewissen **(e)** (serious) schlimm ⟨*Sturz, Krise*⟩; schwer ⟨*Fehler, Krankheit, Unfall*⟩ **(f)** (Commerc.) **a** ~ **debt** eine uneinbringliche Schuld

bade ▶ BID 1B

badge /bædʒ/ *n.* Abzeichen, *das*

badger /'bædʒə(r)/ *n.* Dachs, *der*

'**badly** *adv., worse* /wɜːs/, *worst* /wɜːst/ **(a)** schlecht **(b)** schwer ⟨*verletzt, beschädigt*⟩ **(c)** (urgently) dringend

bad-mannered /bæd'mænəd/ *adj.* **be** ~: schlechte Manieren haben

badminton /'bædmɪntən/ *n.* Federball, *der;* (als Sport) Badminton, *das*

bad-tempered /bæd'tempəd/ *adj.* griesgrämig

baffle /'bæfl/ *v.t.* ~ **sb.** jmdm. unverständlich sein

baffling /'bæflɪŋ/ *adj.* rätselhaft

bag /bæg/ ⟦1⟧ *n.* Tasche, *die;* (sack) Sack, *der;* (hand~) Handtasche, *die;* (plastic ~) Beutel, *der;* (small paper ~) Tüte, *die;* ~**s of** (coll.: large amount) jede Menge ⟦2⟧ *v.t.,* -**gg**-: **(a)** in Säcke/Beutel/Tüten füllen **(b)** (claim possession of) sich (*Dat.*) schnappen (ugs.)

baggage /'bægɪdʒ/ *n.* Gepäck, *das*

baggage: ~ **allowance** *n.* Freigepäck, *das;* **be over/within one's** ~ **allowance** Übergepäck/kein Übergepäck haben; ~ **handler** *n.* Gepäckverlader, *der/* -verladerin, *die;* ~ **handling** *n.* Gepäckverladung, *die;* ~ **reclaim** *n.* Gepäckausgabe, *die*

baggy /'bægɪ/ *adj.* weit [geschnitten] ⟨*Kleid, Hose*⟩; (through long use) ausgebeult ⟨*Hose*⟩

'**bagpipe[s]** *n.* [*pl.*] Dudelsack, *der*

baguette /bæ'get/ *n.* Baguette, *die;* [französisches] Stangenweißbrot

Bahamas /bə'hɑːməz/ *pr. n. pl.* the ~: die Bahamas *Pl.*

bail¹ /beɪl/ ⊞ *n.* Kaution, *die;* be [out] on ~: gegen Kaution auf freiem Fuß sein ⊡ *v.t.* ~ sb. out jmdn. gegen Kaution freibekommen; (fig.) jmdm. aus der Klemme helfen (ugs.)

bail² *v.t.* (scoop) ~ [out] ausschöpfen

▪ **'bail out** *v.i.* ⟨Pilot:⟩ abspringen

bailiff /'beɪlɪf/ *n.* ≈ Gerichtsvollzieher, *der*

bait /beɪt/ ⊞ *v.t.* mit einem Köder versehen ⊡ *n.* Köder, *der*

bake /beɪk/ *v.t. & i.* backen; ~d beans gebackene Bohnen [in Tomatensoße]; ~d potato [in der Schale] gebackene Kartoffel

'baker *n.* Bäcker, *der*

bakery /'beɪkərɪ/ *n.* Bäckerei, *die*

baking: ~ **powder** *n.* Backpulver, *das;* ~ **sheet** *n.* Backblech, *das;* ~ **soda** *n.* Natron, *das;* ~ **tin** *n.* Backform, *die;* ~ **tray** *n.* Kuchenblech, *das*

balance /'bæləns/ ⊞ *n.* (a) (instrument) Waage, *die*
(b) (fig.) be *or* hang in the ~: in der Schwebe sein
(c) (steady position) Gleichgewicht, *das;* keep/ lose one's ~: das Gleichgewicht halten/ verlieren; (fig.) sein Gleichgewicht bewahren/ verlieren; strike a ~ between (fig.) den Mittelweg finden zwischen (+ *Dat.*)
(d) (Bookk.: difference) Bilanz, *die;* (state of bank account) Kontostand, *der;* on ~ (fig.) alles in allem; ~ sheet Bilanz, *die*
(e) (Econ.) ~ of payments Zahlungsbilanz, *die;* ~ of trade Handelsbilanz, *die*
(f) (remainder) Rest, *der*
⊡ *v.t.* (a) (weigh up) abwägen
(b) (bring into or keep in ~) balancieren; auswuchten ⟨Rad⟩
(c) (equal, neutralize) ausgleichen; ~ each other, be ~d sich ⟨*Dat.*⟩ die Waage halten

'balanced *adj.* ausgewogen; ausgeglichen ⟨Person, Team, Gemüt⟩

balcony /'bælkənɪ/ *n.* Balkon, *der*

bald /bɔːld/ *adj.* kahl ⟨Kopf⟩; kahlköpfig, glatzköpfig ⟨Person⟩; be/go ~: eine Glatze haben/bekommen

bald: ~**head** *n.* kahlköpfiger *od.* glatzköpfiger Mensch; Kahlkopf, *der* (ugs.); Glatzkopf, *der* (ugs.); ~-**'headed** *adj.* glatzköpfig; kahlköpfig

'balding *adj.* mit beginnender Glatze *nachgestellt;* be ~: kahl werden

'baldness *n.* Kahlheit, *die*

bale /beɪl/ *n.* Ballen, *der*

balk /bɔːk/ ⊞ *n.* they were ~ed in their plan ihr Plan wurde blockiert ⊡ *v.i.* sich sträuben (at gegen)

Balkan /'bɔːlkən/ ⊞ *adj.* Balkan- ⊡ *n. pl.* the ~s der Balkan

ball¹ /bɔːl/ *n.* (a) Ball, *der;* (Billiards etc., Croquet) Kugel, *die;* be on the ~ (coll.: be alert) auf Zack sein (ugs.)

(b) (of wool, string, fluff, etc.) Knäuel, *das*

ball² *n.* (dance) Ball, *der*

ballad /'bæləd/ *n.* Ballade, *die*

ballast /'bæləst/ *n.* Ballast, *der*

ball: ~ **'bearing** *n.* Kugellager, *das;* ~**boy** *n.* Balljunge, *der;* ~**cock** *n.* Schwimmer[regel]ventil, *das*

ballerina /bælə'riːnə/ *n.* Ballerina, *die*

ballet /'bæleɪ/ *n.* Ballett, *das;* ~ **dancer** Balletttänzer, *der*/-tänzerin, *die*

'ball game *n.* (a) Ballspiel, *das*
(b) (Amer.) Baseballspiel, *das;* a whole new ~ (fig. coll.) eine ganz neue Geschichte (ugs.); a different ~ (fig. coll.) eine andere Sache

ballistic /bə'lɪstɪk/ *adj.* ballistisch; go ~ (fig. coll.) ausrasten (salopp)

balloon /bə'luːn/ *n.* (a) Ballon, *der;* hot-air ~: Heißluftballon, *der*
(b) (toy) Luftballon, *der*

ballot /'bælət/ *n.* Abstimmung, *die;* [secret] ~: geheime Wahl

ballot: ~ **box** *n.* Wahlurne, *die;* ~ **paper** *n.* Stimmzettel, *der*

ball: ~**park** *n.* (Amer.) Baseballfeld, *das;* your estimate is not in the right ~park (fig.) mit deiner Schätzung liegst du völlig falsch (ugs.); ~ **pen,** ~**point** **'pen** *ns.* Kugelschreiber, *der;* ~**room** *n.* Tanzsaal, *der*

balls-up /'bɔːlzʌp/ *n.* (coarse) Scheiß, *der* (salopp abwertend); make a ~ of sth. bei etw. Scheiße bauen (derb)

balm /bɑːm/ *n.* Balsam, *der*

balmy /'bɑːmɪ/ *adj.* (mild) mild

balsa /'bɔːlsə, 'bɒlsə/ *n.* ~ [wood] Balsaholz, *das*

Baltic /'bɔːltɪk/ ⊞ *pr. n.* Ostsee, *die* ⊡ *adj.* ~ Sea Ostsee, *die*

balustrade /bælə'streɪd/ *n.* Balustrade, *die*

bamboo /bæm'buː/ *n.* Bambus, *der*

ban /bæn/ ⊞ *v.t.,* -nn- verbieten; ~ sb. from doing sth. jmdm. verbieten, etw. zu tun ⊡ *n.* Verbot, *das*

banal /bə'nɑːl/ *adj.* banal

banality /bə'nælɪtɪ/ *n.* Banalität, *die*

banana /bə'nɑːnə/ *n.* Banane, *die*

ba'nana skin *n.* Bananenschale, *die*

band /bænd/ ⊞ *n.* (a) Band, *das;* a ~ of light/colour ein Streifen Licht/Farbe
(b) (range of values) Bandbreite, *die*
(c) (organized group) Gruppe, *die;* (of robbers, outlaws, etc.) Bande, *die*
(d) (Mus.) [Musik]kapelle, *die;* (pop group, jazz ~) Band, *die*
⊡ *v.i.* ~ together [with sb.] sich [mit jmdm.] zusammenschließen

bandage /'bændɪdʒ/ ⊞ *n.* Verband, *der;* (as support) Bandage, *die*
⊡ *v.t.* verbinden; bandagieren ⟨[verstauchtes] Gelenk usw.⟩

b. & b. /biː ən 'biː/ *abbr.* = **bed & breakfast**

bandit /'bændɪt/ n. Bandit, der

band: ~**stand** n. Musiktribüne, die; ~**wagon** n. climb or jump on [to] the ~**wagon** (fig.) auf den fahrenden Zug aufspringen (fig.)

bandy[1] /'bændɪ/ v.t. they were ~ing words/ insults sie stritten sich/beschimpften sich gegenseitig

bandy[2] adj. krumm; he is ~-legged er hat O-Beine (ugs.)

bang /bæŋ/ [1] v.t. knallen (ugs.); schlagen; zuknallen (ugs.) ⟨Tür, Fenster, Deckel⟩; ~ one's head on sth. mit dem Kopf an etw. (Akk.) knallen (ugs.). [2] v.i. (strike) ~ [against sth.] [gegen etw.] knallen (ugs.); ~ shut ⟨Tür:⟩ zuknallen (ugs.). [3] n. (a) (blow) Schlag, der (b) (noise) Knall, der [4] adv. go ~ ⟨Gewehr, Feuerwerkskörper:⟩ krachen

'banger n. (coll.) (a) (sausage) Würstchen, das (b) (firework) Kracher, der (ugs.) (c) (car) Klapperkiste, die (ugs.)

bangle /'bæŋgl/ n. Armreif, der

banish /'bænɪʃ/ v.t. verbannen (from aus)

banister /'bænɪstə(r)/ n. [Treppen]geländer, das

banjo /'bændʒəʊ/ n., pl. ~s or ~es Banjo, das

bank[1] /bæŋk/ n. (a) (slope) Böschung, die (b) (of river) Ufer, das

bank[2] [1] n. (Finance) Bank, die [2] v.i. ~ at/with ...: ein Konto haben bei ...; ~ on sth. (fig.) auf etw. (Akk.) zählen [3] v.t. zur Bank bringen

bank: ~ **account** n. Bankkonto, das; ~ **balance** n. Kontostand, der; ~ **book** n. Sparbuch, das; ~ **card** n. Scheckkarte, die; ~ **charges** n. pl. Kontoführungskosten Pl.; ~ **clerk** n. Bankangestellte, der/die; ~ **draft** n. Bankakzept, die

'banker n. Bankier, der

banker's: ~ **card** ▸ BANK CARD; ~ **draft** ▸ BANK DRAFT; ~ **'order** n. Bankanweisung, die

bank 'holiday n. (Brit.) Feiertag, der

'banking n. Bankwesen, das

bank: ~ **loan** n. Bankdarlehen, das; take out a ~ loan bei einer Bank einen Kredit od. ein Darlehen aufnehmen; ~ **manager** n. Zweigstellenleiter/-leiterin [einer/der Bank]; ~**note** n. Banknote, die

bankrupt /'bæŋkrʌpt/ [1] n. Bankrotteur, der [2] adj. go ~: Bankrott machen [3] v.t. Bankrott machen

bankruptcy /'bæŋkrʌptsɪ/ n. Konkurs, der; Bankrott, der

'bank statement n. Kontoauszug, der

banner /'bænə(r)/ n. Banner, das; (on two poles) Spruchband, das

banns /bænz/ n. pl. Aufgebot, das

banquet /'bæŋkwɪt/ n. Bankett, das

bap /bæp/ n. ≈ Brötchen, das

baptism /'bæptɪzm/ n. Taufe, die

Baptist /'bæptɪst/ n. Baptist, der/Baptistin, die

baptize /bæp'taɪz/ v.t. taufen

bar /bɑː(r)/ [1] n. (a) Stange, die; (shorter, thinner also) Stab, der; (of cage, prison) Gitterstab, der; a ~ of soap ein Stück Seife; a ~ of chocolate eine Tafel Schokolade (b) (for refreshment) Bar, die; (counter) Theke, die [2] v.t., -rr-: (a) (fasten) verriegeln (b) ~ sb.'s way jmdm. den Weg versperren (c) (prohibit, hinder) verbieten; ~ sb. from doing sth. jmdn. daran hindern, etw. zu tun [3] prep. abgesehen von; ~ none ohne Einschränkung

barb /bɑːb/ n. Widerhaken, der

barbarian /bɑː'beərɪən/ n. Barbar, der

barbaric /bɑː'bærɪk/ adj. barbarisch

barbarity /bɑː'bærɪtɪ/ n. Grausamkeit, die

barbecue /'bɑːbɪkjuː/ [1] n. (a) (party) Grillparty, die (b) (food) Grillgericht, das; ~ sauce Grillsoße, die; Barbecuesoße, die [2] v.t. grillen

barbed wire /bɑːbd 'waɪə(r)/ n. Stacheldraht, der

barber /'bɑːbə(r)/ n. [Herren]friseur, der; ~'s shop (Brit.) Friseursalon, der

barbiturate /bɑː'bɪtjʊrət/ n. (Chem.) Barbiturat, das

bar: ~ **chart** n. Stabdiagramm, das; ~ **code** n. Strichcode, der

bare /beə(r)/ [1] adj. nackt; (leafless, unfurnished) kahl; (empty) leer; äußerst ⟨Notwendige⟩; do sth. with one's ~ hands etw. mit den bloßen Händen tun [2] v.t. entblößen ⟨Kopf, Arm, Bein⟩; blecken ⟨Zähne⟩

bare: ~**faced** /'beəfeɪst/ adj. (fig.) unverhüllt; ~**foot** [1] adj. barfüßig; [2] adv. barfuß

barely /'beəlɪ/ adv. kaum; knapp ⟨vermeiden, entkommen⟩

bargain /'bɑːgɪn/ [1] n. (a) (agreement) Abmachung, die; into the ~: darüber hinaus (b) (thing offered cheap) günstiges Angebot; (thing acquired cheaply) guter Kauf [2] v.i. (a) (discuss) handeln (b) ~ for or on sth. (expect sth.) mit etw. rechnen

bargain: ~ **'basement** n. Untergeschoss mit Sonderangeboten; ~ **hunter** n. Schnäppchenjäger, der/-jägerin, die; ~ **price** n. Sonderpreis, der

barge /bɑːdʒ/ [1] n. Kahn, der [2] v.i. ~ into sb. jmdn. anrempeln; ~ in (intrude) hineinplatzen/hereinplatzen (ugs.)

baritone /'bærɪtəʊn/ [1] n. Bariton, der [2] adj. Bariton-

bark[1] /bɑːk/ *n.* (of tree) Rinde, *die*

bark[2] ⓵ *n.* (of dog) Bellen, *das*
⓶ *v.i.* bellen; **be ~ing up the wrong tree** auf dem Holzweg sein

barley /'bɑːlɪ/ *n.* Gerste, *die*

bar: ~maid *n.* (Brit.) Bardame, *die;* **~man** /'bɑːmən/ *n., pl.* **~men** /'bɑːmən/ Barmann, *der*

barmy /'bɑːmɪ/ *adj.* (coll.: crazy) bescheuert (salopp)

barn /bɑːn/ *n.* (Brit.: for grain etc.) Scheune, *die;* (Amer.: for animals) Stall, *der*

barnacle /'bɑːnəkl/ *n.* Rankenfüßer, *der*

barn: ~ dance *n.* ≈ Schottische, *der;* **~storming** /'bɑːnstɔːmɪŋ/ *adj.* mitreißend

barometer /bə'rɒmɪtə(r)/ *n.* Barometer, *das*

baron /'bærn/ *n.* Baron, *der;* Freiherr, *der*

baroness /'bærənɪs/ *n.* Baronin, *die;* Freifrau, *die*

baroque /bə'rɒk/ ⓵ *n.* Barock, *das*
⓶ *adj.* barock

barracks /'bærəks/ *n. pl.* Kaserne, *die*

barrage /'bærɑːʒ/ *n.* (Mil.) Sperrfeuer, *das;* **a ~ of questions** ein Bombardement von Fragen

barrel /'bærl/ *n.* **(a)** Fass, *das*
(b) (of gun) Lauf, *der*

barren /'bærn/ *adj.* unfruchtbar

barricade /bærɪ'keɪd/ ⓵ *n.* Barrikade, *die*
⓶ *v.t.* verbarrikadieren

barrier /'bærɪə(r)/ *n.* Barriere, *die;* (at level crossing etc.) Schranke, *die*

barring /'bɑːrɪŋ/ *prep.* außer im Falle (+ *Gen.*)

barrister /'bærɪstə(r)/ *n.* (Brit.) **~-at-law**] Barrister, *der;* ≈ [Rechts]anwalt/-anwältin vor höheren Gerichten

barrow /'bærəʊ/ *n.* **(a)** Karre, *die;* Karren, *der*
(b) ▶ WHEELBARROW

barter /'bɑːtə(r)/ ⓵ *v.t.* [ein]tauschen; **~ sth. for sth. [else]** etw. für *od.* gegen etw. [anderes] [ein]tauschen
⓶ *v.i.* Tauschhandel treiben
⓷ *n.* Tauschhandel, *der*

base /beɪs/ ⓵ *n.* **(a)** (of lamp, mountain) Fuß, *der;* (of cupboard, statue) Sockel, *der;* (fig.: support) Basis, *die*
(b) (Mil.) Basis, *die;* Stützpunkt, *der*
⓶ *v.t.* **(a)** **be ~d on sth.** sich auf etw. (*Akk.*) gründen; **~ sth. on sth.** etw. auf etw. (*Dat.*) aufbauen
(b) *in pass.* **be ~d in Paris** (permanently) in Paris sitzen; (temporarily) in Paris sein

base: ~ball *n.* Baseball, *der;* **~line** *n.* Grundlinie, *die*

basement /'beɪsmənt/ *n.* Untergeschoss, *das;* **a ~ flat** eine Kellerwohnung

'base rate *n.* (Finance) Eckzins, *der*

bash /bæʃ/ *v.t.* (heftig) schlagen

bashful /'bæʃfl/ *adj.* schüchtern

basic /'beɪsɪk/ *adj.* grundlegend; Grund⟨prinzip, -bestandteil, -lohn, -gehalt *usw.*⟩; Haupt⟨problem, -grund, -sache⟩; **be ~ to sth.** wesentlich für etw. sein

basically /'beɪsɪkəlɪ/ *adv.* im Grunde; grundsätzlich ⟨*übereinstimmen*⟩; (mainly) hauptsächlich

basil /'bæzɪl/ *n.* Basilikum, *das*

basin /'beɪsn/ *n.* **(a)** Becken, *das;* (wash~) Waschbecken, *das;* (bowl) Schüssel, *die*
(b) (of river) Becken, *das*

basis /'beɪsɪs/ *n., pl.* **bases** /'beɪsiːz/ Basis, *die;* Grundlage, *die*

bask /bɑːsk/ *v.i.* sich [wohlig] wärmen

basket /'bɑːskɪt/ *n.* Korb, *der*

'basketball *n.* Basketball, *der*

Basle /bɑːl/ *pr. n.* Basel (*das*)

bass /beɪs/ ⓵ *n.* **(a)** Bass, *der*
(b) (coll.) (double ~) [Kontra]bass, *der;* (~ guitar) Bass, *der*
⓶ *adj.* Bass-

bass gui'tar *n.* Bassgitarre, *die*

bassoon /bə'suːn/ *n.* Fagott, *das*

'bass player *n.* Bassist, *der*/Bassistin, *die*

bastard /'bɑːstəd/ ⓵ *adj.* unehelich
⓶ *n.* **(a)** uneheliches Kind
(b) (sl.: disliked person) Schweinehund, *der* (derb)

baste /beɪst/ *v.t.* [mit Fett] begießen

bastion /'bæstɪən/ *n.* Bastei, *die*

bat[1] /bæt/ *n.* (Zool.) Fledermaus, *die*

bat[2] ⓵ *n.* (Sport) Schlagholz, *das;* (for table tennis) Schläger, *der;* **do sth. off one's own ~** (fig.) etw. auf eigene Faust tun
⓶ *v.t.*, **-tt-** schlagen

bat[3] *v.t.* **not ~ an eyelid** nicht mit der Wimper zucken

batch /bætʃ/ *n.* **(a)** (of loaves) Schub, *der*
(b) (of people) Gruppe, *die;* (of books, papers) Stapel, *der*

batch: ~ file *n.* (Comp.) Stapeldatei, *die;* **~ 'processing** *n.* (Comp.) Schub-, Stapelverarbeitung, *die*

bated /'beɪtɪd/ *v.t.* **with ~ breath** mit angehaltenem Atem

bath /bɑːθ/ ⓵ *n., pl.* **~s** /bɑːðz/ **(a)** Bad, *das;* **have** *or* **take a ~:** ein Bad nehmen
(b) (tub) Badewanne, *die;* **room with ~:** Zimmer mit Bad
(c) *usu. in pl.* (building) Bad, *das*
⓶ *v.t. & i.* baden

'bath cubes *n. pl.* Badesalz, *das*

bathe /beɪð/ *v.t. & i.* baden

bather /'beɪðə(r)/ *n.* Badende, *der/die*

bathing /'beɪðɪŋ/ *n.* Baden, *das*

bathing: ~ beach *n.* Badestrand, *der;* **~ costume** *n.* Badeanzug, *der;* **~ suit** *ns.* Badeanzug, *der;* **~ trunks** *n. pl.* Badehose, *die*

bath: ~ mat *n.* Badematte, *die;* **~robe** *n.* Bademantel, *der;* **~room** *n.* Badezimmer,

das; ~ **salts** *n. pl.* Badesalz, *das;*
~ **towel** *n.* Badetuch, *das;* ~**tub** ▶ BATH
1B; ~**water** *n.* Badewasser, *das*

baton /'bætn/ *n.* **(a)** (truncheon) Schlagstock, *der*
(b) (Mus.) Taktstock, *der*

batsman /'bætsmən/ *n., pl.* **batsmen**
/'bætsmən/ Schlagmann, *der*

battalion /bə'tæljən/ *n.* Bataillon, *das*

batter¹ /'bætə(r)/ *v.t.* (strike) einschlagen
auf (+ *Akk.*)

batter² *n.* (Cookery) [Back]teig, *der*

battery /'bætərɪ/ *n.* Batterie, *die*

battery: ~ **charger** *n.* Batterieladegerät,
das; ~ **'chicken** *n.* Batteriehuhn, *das;*
~ **'farming** *n.* Batteriehaltung, *die;*
~ **'hen** *n.* Batteriehuhn, *das;*
~**-operated** *adj.* batteriebetrieben

battle /'bætl/ **1** *n.* Schlacht, *die;* (fig.)
Kampf, *der*
2 *v.i.* kämpfen

battle: ~**axe** *n.* (coll.: woman)
Schreckschraube, *die* (ugs.); ~**field,**
~**ground** *ns.* Schlachtfeld, *das*

battlements /'bætlmənts/ *n. pl.* Zinnen
Pl.

'battleship *n.* Schlachtschiff, *das*

batty /'bætɪ/ *adj.* (coll.) bekloppt (salopp)

bauble /'bɔːbl/ *n.* Flitter, *der*

baulk ▶ BALK

Bavaria /bə'veərɪə/ *pr. n.* Bayern (*das*)

Bavarian /bə'veərɪən/ **1** *adj.* bay[e]risch;
sb. is ~: jmd. ist Bayer/Bayerin
2 *n.* Bayer, *der*/Bayerin, *die*

bawdy /'bɔːdɪ/ *adj.* zweideutig; (stronger)
obszön

bay¹ /beɪ/ *n.* (of sea) Bucht, *die*

bay² *n.* **(a)** (space in room) Erker, *der*
(b) [parking] ~: Stellplatz, *der*

bay³ *n.* hold *or* keep sb./sth. at ~: sich
(*Dat.*) jmdn./etw. vom Leib halten

'bayleaf *n.* Lorbeerblatt, *das*

bayonet /'beɪənɪt/ *n.* Bajonett, *das*

bayonet: ~ **fitting** *n.* Bajonettfassung,
die; ~ **plug** *n.* Stecker mit
Bajonettverschluss *od.* -fassung; ~ **socket**
n. Steckdose mit Bajonettfassung

bay 'window *n.* Erkerfenster, *das*

bazaar /bə'zɑː(r)/ *n.* Basar, *der*

BBC *abbr.* = **British Broadcasting
Corporation** BBC, *die*

BC *abbr.* = **before Christ** v.Chr.

be /biː/ *v., pres. t.* **I am** /əm, *stressed* æm/, **he
is** /ɪz/, **we are** /ə(r), *stressed* ɑː(r)/; *p.t.* **I was**
/wəz, *stressed* wɒz/, **we were** /wə(r), *stressed*
wɜː(r)/; *pres.p.* **being** /'biːɪŋ/; *p.p.* **been** /bɪn,
stressed biːn/ **1** *copula* **(a)** sein; **she is a
mother/an Italian/a teacher** sie ist Mutter/
Italienerin/Lehrerin; **be sensible!** sei
vernünftig!; **be ill/unwell** krank sein/sich
nicht wohl fühlen; **I am well** es geht mir gut;
I am hot mir ist heiß; **I am freezing** mich

friert es; **how are you/is she?** wie gehts
(ugs.)/geht es ihr?; **it is the 5th today** heute
haben wir den Fünften; **who's that?** wer ist
das?; **if I were you** an deiner Stelle; **it's hers**
es ist ihrs
(b) (cost) kosten; **how much are the eggs?**
was kosten die Eier?; **two times three is six,
two threes are six** zweimal drei ist *od.* sind
sechs
(c) (constitute) bilden
2 *v.i.* **(a)** (exist) [vorhanden] sein; **there is/
are** ...: es gibt ...; **for the time being**
vorläufig; **be that as it may** wie dem auch
sei
(b) (remain) bleiben; **I shan't be a moment** ich
komme sofort; **let it be** lass es sein; **let him/
her be** lass ihn/sie in Ruhe
(c) (happen) stattfinden; sein
(d) (go, come) **be off with you!** geh/geht!; **I'm
off home** ich gehe jetzt nach Hause; **she's
from Australia** sie stammt *od.* ist aus
Australien
(e) (go or come on visit) sein; **have you [ever]
been to London?** bist du schon einmal in
London gewesen?; **has anyone been?** ist
jemand da gewesen?
3 *v. aux.* **(a)** *forming passive* werden; **the
child was found** das Kind wurde gefunden;
German is spoken here hier wird Deutsch
gesprochen
(b) *forming continuous tenses, active* **he is
reading** er liest [gerade]; **I am leaving
tomorrow** ich reise morgen [ab]; **the train
was departing when I got there** der Zug fuhr
gerade ab, als ich ankam
(c) *forming continuous tenses, passive* **the
house is/was being built** das Haus wird/
wurde [gerade] gebaut
(d) *expr. arrangement, obligation* **be to**
sollen; **I am to go/to inform you** ich soll
gehen/Sie unterrichten
(e) *expr. destiny* **they were never to meet
again** sie sollten sich nie wieder treffen
(f) *expr. condition* **if I were to tell you that
...**: wenn ich dir sagen würde, dass ...
4 **bride-/husband-to-be** zukünftige Braut/
zukünftiger Ehemann

beach /biːtʃ/ *n.* Strand, *der;* **on the** ~: am
Strand; ~ **hat/holiday/shoe** Strandhut/
-urlaub/-schuh, *der*

beach: ~**ball** *n.* Wasserball, *der;* ~**wear**
n. Strandkleidung, *die*

beacon /'biːkn/ *n.* Leuchtfeuer, *das;* (Naut.)
Leuchtbake, *die*

bead /biːd/ *n.* Perle, *die;* ~**s** Perlen *Pl.;*
Perlenkette, *die;* ~**s of dew/sweat** Tau-/
Schweißtropfen

beady /'biːdɪ/ *adj.* ~ **eyes** Knopfaugen *Pl.*

beak /biːk/ *n.* Schnabel, *der*

beaker /'biːkə(r)/ *n.* Becher, *der*

beam /biːm/ **1** *n.* **(a)** (timber etc.) Balken,
der
(b) (ray etc.) [Licht]strahl, *der*
2 *v.i.* **(a)** (shine) strahlen; glänzen ···❖

(b) (smile) strahlen; ~ **at sb.** jmdn. anstrahlen

bean /biːn/ n. Bohne, die; **full of** ~s (fig. coll.) putzmunter (ugs.)

bean: ~**bag** n. **(a)** mit Bohnen gefülltes Säckchen zum Spielen; **(b)** (cushion) Knautschsessel, der; ~**curd** n. Soja[bohnen]quark, der; ~**pole** n. (lit. or fig.) Bohnenstange, die; ~**sprout** n. Sojabohnenkeim, der

bear¹ /beə(r)/ n. Bär, der

bear² ① v.t., bore /bɔː(r)/, borne /bɔːn/ **(a)** tragen; aufweisen ⟨Spuren, Ähnlichkeit⟩; tragen, führen ⟨Namen, Titel⟩; ~ **some/little relation to sth.** einen gewissen/wenig Bezug zu etw. haben
(b) (endure, tolerate) ertragen ⟨Schmerz, Kummer⟩; with neg. ertragen, aushalten ⟨Schmerz⟩; ausstehen ⟨Geruch, Lärm⟩
(c) (be fit for) vertragen; **it will not** ~ **scrutiny** es hält einer Überprüfung nicht stand; **it does not** ~ **thinking about** daran darf man gar nicht denken
(d) (give birth to) gebären ⟨Kind, Junges⟩
② v.i., bore, borne: ~ **left** ⟨Person:⟩ sich links halten; **the path** ~**s to the left** der Weg führt nach links
∎ **bear 'out** v.t. (fig.) bestätigen ⟨Bericht, Erklärung⟩; ~ **sb. out** jmdm. Recht geben
∎ **'bear with** v.t. Nachsicht haben mit

bearable /'beərəbl/ adj. erträglich

beard /bɪəd/ n. Bart, der

'bearded adj. bärtig. **be** ~: einen Bart haben

'bearer n. (carrier) Träger, der/Trägerin, die; (of message, cheque) Überbringer, der/Überbringerin, die

'bear hug n. kräftige Umarmung

'bearing n. **(a)** (behaviour) Verhalten, das
(b) (relation) Bezug, der; **have some/no** ~ **on sth.** relevant/irrelevant für etw. sein
(c) (Mech. Engin.) Lager, das
(d) (compass ~) Position, die; **take a compass** ~: den Kompasskurs feststellen; **get one's** ~**s** sich orientieren; (fig.) sich zurechtfinden

beast /biːst/ n. Tier, das; (fig.: brutal person) Bestie, die

'beastly adj., adv. (coll.) scheußlich

beat /biːt/ ① v.t., beat, beaten /'biːtn/ schlagen; klopfen ⟨Teppich⟩; (surpass) brechen ⟨Rekord⟩; **hard to** ~: schwer zu schlagen; **it** ~**s me how/why** ...: es ist mir ein Rätsel wie/warum ...; ~ **time** den Takt schlagen; ~ **it!** (coll.) hau ab! (ugs.); see also BEATEN 2
② v.i., beat, beaten schlagen (on auf + Akk.); ⟨Regen, Hagel:⟩ prasseln (against gegen)
③ n. **(a)** (stroke, throbbing) Schlagen, das; (Mus.) (rhythm) Takt, der; (single ~) Schlag, der
(b) (of policeman) Runde, die
∎ **beat 'off** v.t. abwehren ⟨Angriff⟩
∎ **beat 'up** v.t. zusammenschlagen ⟨Person⟩

beaten /'biːtn/ ① ▶ BEAT 1, 2
② adj. **(a)** off the ~ **track** weit abgelegen

'beating n. **(a)** (punishment) **a** ~: Schläge Pl.; Prügel Pl.
(b) (defeat) Niederlage, die
(c) take some/a lot of ~: nicht leicht zu übertreffen sein

'beat-up adj. (coll.) ramponiert (ugs.)

beautician /bju:'tɪʃn/ n. Kosmetiker, der/Kosmetikerin, die

beautiful /'bju:tɪfl/ adj. schön; wunderschön ⟨Augen, Aussicht, Morgen⟩

beautify /'bju:tɪfaɪ/ v.t. verschönern

beauty /'bju:tɪ/ n. Schönheit, die; (beautiful feature) Schöne, das; **the** ~ **of it** das Schöne daran

beauty: ~ **competition,** ~ **contest** ns. Schönheitswettbewerb, der; ~ **parlour** ▶ SALON; ~ **queen** n. Schönheitskönigin, die; ~ **salon** n. Kosmetiksalon, der; ~ **spot** n. Schönheitsfleck, der; (place) schönes Fleckchen [Erde]; ~ **treatment** n. Schönheitsbehandlung, die

beaver /'bi:və(r)/ n. Biber, der

became ▶ BECOME

because /bɪ'kɒz/ ① conj. weil
② adv. ~ **of** wegen (+ Gen.)

beckon /'bekn/ v.t. & i. winken (**to sb.** jmdm.); (fig.) locken

become /bɪ'kʌm/ ① copula, became /bɪ'keɪm/, become werden; ~ **a politician** Politiker werden; ~ **a nuisance/rule** zu einer Plage/zur Regel werden
② v.i., became, become werden; **what has** ~ **of him?** was ist aus ihm geworden?
③ v.t., became, become (suit) ~ **sb.** jmdm. stehen

becoming /bɪ'kʌmɪŋ/ adj. **(a)** (fitting) schicklich (geh.)
(b) (flattering) vorteilhaft ⟨Hut, Kleid, Frisur⟩

bed /bed/ n. **(a)** Bett, das; (without bedstead) Lager, das; **in** ~: im Bett; ~ **and breakfast** Zimmer mit Frühstück; **get out of/into** ~: aufstehen/ins Bett gehen; **go to** ~: ins Bett gehen; **put sb. to** ~: jmdn. ins Bett bringen; **make the** ~: das Bett machen
(b) (flat base) Unterlage, die; (of machine) Bett, das
(c) (in garden) Beet, das
(d) (of sea, lake) Grund, der; (of river) Bett, das

'bedclothes n. pl. Bettzeug, das

bedding /'bedɪŋ/ n. Matratze und Bettzeug

'bedding plant n. Freilandpflanze, die

bedlam /'bedləm/ n., no indef. art. Tumult, der

bed: ~**linen** n. Bettwäsche, die; ~**pan** n. Bettpfanne, die

bedraggled /bɪ'drægld/ adj. (soaked) durchnässt; (with mud) verdreckt

bed: ~**ridden** adj. bettlägerig; ~**room** n. Schlafzimmer, das; ~ **set'tee** n. Bettcouch, die; ~**side** n. Seite des Bettes, die; ~**side table/lamp** Nachttisch, der/Nachttischlampe, die; ~**sit,** ~'**sitter** ns. (coll.)

Wohnschlafzimmer, *das;* ∼**spread** *n.*
Tagesdecke, *die;* ∼**stead** *n.* Bettgestell,
das; ∼**time** *n.* Schlafenszeit, *die;* at ∼**time**
vor dem Zubettgehen; a ∼**time** story eine
Gutenachtgeschichte; ∼**-wetting** *n.*
Bettnässen, *das*

bee /biː/ *n.* Biene, *die*

beech /biːtʃ/ *n.* Buche, *die*

beef /biːf/ |1| *n.* **(a)** Rindfleisch, *das*
(b) (coll.: muscles) Muskeln *Pl.*
|2| *v.t.* ∼ **up** stärken

beef: ∼**burger** *n.* Beefburger, *der;*
∼**cake** *n.* (Amer. coll.) Muskeln *Pl.;* Bizeps,
der (ugs.)

bee: ∼**hive** *n.* Bienenstock, *der;*
∼**keeper** *n.* Imker, *der*/Imkerin, *die;*
∼**keeping** *n.* Imkerei, *die;* ∼**line** *n.*
make a ∼**line** for sth./sb. schnurstracks auf
etw./jmdn. zustürzen

been ▶ BE

beep /biːp/ |1| *n.* Piepton, *der;* (of car horn)
Tuten, *das*
|2| *v.i.* piepen; ⟨Signalhorn:⟩ hupen
|3| *v.t.* (esp. Amer.) ▶ BLEEP 3

beeper /ˈbiːpə(r)/ *n.* Piepser, *der*

beer /bɪə(r)/ *n.* Bier, *das*

beer: ∼ **barrel** *n.* Bierfass, *das;* ∼ **belly**
n. (coll.) Bierbauch, *der* (ugs.); ∼ **bottle** *n.*
Bierflasche, *die;* ∼ **can** *n.* Bierdose, *die;*
∼ **cellar** *n.* Bierkeller, *der;* ∼ **drinker** *n.*
Biertrinker, *der;* ∼ **garden** *n.* Biergarten,
der; ∼ **glass** *n.* Bierglas, *das;* ∼ **mat** *n.*
Bierdeckel, *der;* Bieruntersetzer, *der;*
∼ **mug** *n.* Bierkrug, *der*

beet /biːt/ *n.* Rübe, *die*

beetle /ˈbiːtl/ *n.* Käfer, *der*

'beetroot *n.* rote Beete *od.* Rübe

before /bɪˈfɔː(r)/ |1| *adv.* **(a)** (of time) vorher;
(already) schon; the day ∼: am Tag zuvor;
never ∼: noch nie
(b) (ahead in position) vor[aus]
|2| *prep.* (of time; position) vor (+ *Dat.*);
(direction) vor (+ *Akk.*); the day ∼ yesterday
vorgestern; ∼ now/then früher/vorher;
∼ Christ vor Christus; ∼ leaving, he phoned
bevor er wegging, rief er an
|3| *conj.* bevor

be'forehand *adv.* vorher; (in anticipation) im
Voraus

befriend /bɪˈfrend/ *v.t.* **(a)** (act as a friend to)
sich anfreunden mit
(b) (help) sich annehmen (+ *Gen.*)

beg /beg/ |1| *v.t.,* -gg-: **(a)** betteln um
(b) (ask earnestly for) ∼ sth. um etw. bitten
|2| *v.i.,* -gg- betteln (for um)

began ▶ BEGIN

beggar /ˈbegə(r)/ *n.* **(a)** Bettler, *der*/
Bettlerin, *die*
(b) (coll.) poor ∼: armer Teufel

begin /bɪˈgɪn/ |1| *v.t.,* -nn-, began /bɪˈgæn/,
begun /bɪˈgʌn/ ∼ sth. [mit] etw. beginnen;
∼ doing *or* to do sth. anfangen *od.*
beginnen, etw. zu tun

|2| *v.i.,* -nn-, began, begun anfangen;
∼ [up]on sth. etw. anfangen

be'ginner *n.* Anfänger, *der*/Anfängerin, *die*

be'ginning *n.* Anfang, *der;* at *or* in the ∼:
am Anfang; at the ∼ of February/the month
Anfang Februar/des Monats; from the ∼:
von Anfang an

begrudge /bɪˈgrʌdʒ/ *v.t.* ∼ sb. sth. jmdm.
etw. missgönnen; ∼ doing sth. etw. ungern
tun

begun ▶ BEGIN

behalf /bɪˈhɑːf/ *n.* on *or* (Amer.) in ∼ of sb./
sth. für jmdn./etw.; (more formally) im Namen
von jmdm./etw.

behave /bɪˈheɪv/ |1| *v.i.* sich verhalten;
sich benehmen; well-/ill- *or* badly ∼d brav/
ungezogen
|2| *v. refl.* ∼ oneself sich benehmen

behaviour /bɪˈheɪvjə(r)/ *n.* Verhalten, *das*

behead /bɪˈhed/ *v.t.* enthaupten

behind /bɪˈhaɪnd/ |1| *adv.* hinten; (further
back) be miles ∼: kilometerweit
zurückliegen; stay ∼: dableiben; leave sb./
sth. ∼: jmdn./etw. zurücklassen; fall ∼:
zurückbleiben; (fig.) in Rückstand geraten;
be/get ∼ with one's payments/rent mit
seinen Zahlungen/der Miete im Rückstand
sein/in Rückstand geraten
|2| *prep.* **(a)** hinter (+ *Dat.*); one ∼ the other
hintereinander
(b) (towards rear of) hinter (+ *Akk.*)

beige /beɪʒ/ |1| *n.* Beige, *das*
|2| *adj.* beige

being /ˈbiːɪŋ/ *n.* **(a)** (existence) Dasein, *das;*
in ∼: bestehend; come into ∼: entstehen
(b) (person etc.) Wesen, *das*

belated /bɪˈleɪtɪd/ *adj.,* **be'latedly** *adv.*
verspätet

belch /beltʃ/ |1| *v.i.* heftig aufstoßen;
rülpsen (ugs.)
|2| *n.* Rülpser, *der* (ugs.)

beleaguer /bɪˈliːgə(r)/ *v.t.* (lit. or fig.)
belagern

belfry /ˈbelfrɪ/ *n.* Glockenturm, *der*

Belgian /ˈbeldʒən/ |1| *adj.* belgisch; sb. is
∼: jmd. ist Belgier/Belgierin
|2| *n.* Belgier, *der*/Belgierin, *die*

Belgium /ˈbeldʒəm/ *pr. n.* Belgien (*das*)

belie /bɪˈlaɪ/ *v.t.,* belying /bɪˈlaɪɪŋ/
hinwegtäuschen über ⟨Tatsachen, wahren
Zustand⟩; nicht erfüllen ⟨Versprechen⟩; nicht
entsprechen ⟨Vorstellung (Dat.)⟩

belief /bɪˈliːf/ *n.* **(a)** Glaube, *der* (in an
+ *Akk.*); in the ∼ that …: in der
Überzeugung, dass …
(b) (Relig.) Glaube[n], *der*

believable /bɪˈliːvəbl/ *adj.* glaubhaft

believe /bɪˈliːv/ |1| *v.i.* glauben (in an
+ *Dat.*); (have faith) glauben (in an + *Akk.*)
⟨Gott, Himmel usw.⟩; I ∼ so/not ich glaube
schon/nicht

···‖

2 *v.t.* glauben; ∼ **sb.** jmdm. glauben; **I don't** ∼ **you** das glaube ich dir nicht; **make** ∼ **that** ...: so tun, als ob ...

believer /bɪˈliːvə(r)/ *n.* **(a)** Gläubige, *der/die* **(b) be a great** *or* **firm** ∼ **in sth.** viel von etw. halten

Belisha beacon /bəliˈʃə ˈbiːkn/ *n.* (Brit.) *gelbes Blinklicht an Zebrastreifen*

belittle /bɪˈlɪtl/ *v.t.* herabsetzen

bell /bel/ *n.* Glocke, *die;* (door∼) Klingel, *die*

belligerent /bɪˈlɪdʒərənt/ *adj.* Krieg führend ⟨Nation⟩; streitlustig ⟨Person⟩

bellow /ˈbeləʊ/ 1 *v.i.* brüllen 2 *v.t.* ∼ [out] brüllen ⟨Befehl⟩

bellows /ˈbeləʊz/ *n. pl.* Blasebalg, *der*

bell: ∼-**ringer** *n.* Glöckner, *der;* ∼-**ringing** *n.* Glockenläuten, *das*

belly /ˈbelɪ/ *n.* Bauch, *der*

belly: ∼**ache** *n.* Bauchschmerzen *Pl.;* ∼ **button** *n.* (coll.) Bauchnabel, *der;* ∼ **dance** *n.* Bauchtanz, *der*

belong /bɪˈlɒŋ/ *v.i.* ∼ **to sb./sth.** jmdm./zu etw. gehören; ∼ **to a club** einem Verein angehören; **where does this** ∼? wo gehört das hin?

be'longings *n. pl.* Habe, *die;* Sachen *Pl.;* **personal** ∼: persönlicher Besitz; persönliches Eigentum

beloved /bɪˈlʌvɪd/ 1 *adj.* geliebt 2 *n.* Geliebte, *der/die*

below /bɪˈləʊ/ 1 *adv.* **(a)** (position) unten; (lower down) darunter; **from** ∼: von unten [herauf] **(b)** (direction) nach unten; hinunter 2 *prep.* unter (position: + *Dat.;* direction: + *Akk.*)

belt /belt/ *n.* Gürtel, *der;* (for tools, weapons, ammunition) Gurt, *der;* (of trees) Streifen, *der* ∎ **belt along** *v.i.* (coll.) rasen (ugs.) ∎ **belt 'up** *v.i.* (Brit. coll.) die Klappe halten (salopp)

bemused /bɪˈmjuːzd/ *adj.* verwirrt

bench /bentʃ/ *n.* Bank, *die;* (work table) Werkbank, *die*

bench: ∼**mark** *n.* Höhenmarke, *die;* (fig.) Maßstab, *der;* Fixpunkt, *der;* ∼**marking** *n.* Benchmarking, *das* (fachspr.); Leistungsvergleich, *der;*

bend /bend/ 1 *n.* Beuge, *die;* (in road) Kurve, *die* 2 *v.t.,* **bent** /bent/ biegen; beugen ⟨Arm, Knie⟩; anwinkeln ⟨Bein⟩ 3 *v.i.* sich biegen; (bow) sich bücken ∎ **bend 'down** *v.i.* sich bücken ∎ **bend 'over** *v.i.* sich nach vorn beugen

beneath /bɪˈniːθ/ *prep.* **(a)** (unworthy of) ∼ **sb.,** ∼ **sb.'s dignity** unter jmds. Würde (*Dat.*) **(b)** (arch./literary: under) unter (+ *Dat.*)

benefactor /ˈbenɪfæktə(r)/ *n.* Wohltäter, *der;* (patron) Gönner, *der*

beneficial /benɪˈfɪʃl/ *adj.* nützlich; vorteilhaft ⟨Einfluss⟩

benefit /ˈbenɪfɪt/ 1 *n.* **(a)** Vorteil, *der;* **be of** ∼ **to sb./sth.** jmdm./einer Sache von Nutzen sein; **have the** ∼ **of** den Vorteil (+ *Gen.*); **for sb.'s** ∼: in jmds. Interesse (*Dat.*) **(b)** (allowance) Beihilfe, *die;* **unemployment** ∼: Arbeitslosenunterstützung, *die* 2 *v.t.* nützen (+ *Dat.*) 3 *v.i.* ∼ **by/from sth.** von etw. profitieren

benevolent /bɪˈnevələnt/ *adj.* **(a)** gütig **(b)** wohltätig ⟨Institution, Verein⟩

benign /bɪˈnaɪn/ *adj.* gütig; (Med.) gutartig

bent /bent/ 1 ▶ BEND 2, 3 2 *n.* (liking) Neigung, *die* **(for** zu) 3 **(a)** *adj.* krumm **(b)** (Brit. sl.: corrupt) link (salopp)

bequeath /bɪˈkwiːð/ *v.t.* ∼ **sth. to sb.** jmdm. etw. hinterlassen

bequest /bɪˈkwest/ *n.* Legat, *das* **(to** an + *Akk.*)

bereaved /bɪˈriːvd/ *n.* **the** ∼: der/die Hinterbliebene/die Hinterbliebenen

bereavement /bɪˈriːvmənt/ *n.* Trauerfall, *der*

beret /ˈbereɪ/ *n.* Baskenmütze, *die*

Berlin /bɜːˈlɪn/ *pr. n.* Berlin (*das*)

Berne /bɜːn/ *pr. n.* Bern (*das*)

berry /ˈberɪ/ *n.* Beere, *die*

berserk /bəˈsɜːk/ *adj.* rasend; **go** ∼: durchdrehen (ugs.)

berth /bɜːθ/ *n.* (for ship) Liegeplatz, *der;* (sleeping place) (in ship) Koje, *die;* (in train) Schlafwagenbett, *das*

beside /bɪˈsaɪd/ *prep.* **(a)** neben (+ *Dat.*); ∼ **the sea/lake** am Meer/See **(b) be** ∼ **the point** nichts damit zu tun haben **(c)** ∼ **oneself** außer sich

besides /bɪˈsaɪdz/ 1 *adv.* außerdem 2 *prep.* außer

besiege /bɪˈsiːdʒ/ *v.t.* belagern

besotted /bɪˈsɒtɪd/ *adj.* **be** ∼ **by** *or* **with sb.** in jmdn. vernarrt sein

bespectacled /bɪˈspektəkld/ *adj.* bebrillt

best /best/ 1 *adj.* best...; **the** ∼ **part of an hour** fast eine ganze Stunde 2 *adv.* am besten 3 *n.* **the** ∼: der/die/das Beste; **do one's** ∼: sein Bestes tun; **make the** ∼ **of it** das Beste daraus machen; **at** ∼: bestenfalls

best: ∼-**before date** *n.* Mindesthaltbarkeitsdatum, *das;* ∼ **'friend** *n.* bester Freund/beste Freundin; **be** ∼ **friends with sb.** sehr gut mit jmdm. befreundet sein; ∼ **'man** *n.* Trauzeuge, *der* (des Bräutigams); ∼ **'seller** *n.* Bestseller, *der;* (author) Bestsellerautor, *der;* ∼-**selling** *attrib. adj.* meistverkauft ⟨Schallplatte⟩; ∼-**selling book/novel** Bestseller, *der;* **a** ∼-**selling author/novelist** ein Bestsellerautor

bet /bet/ 1 *v.t. & i.,* -**tt**-, ∼ *or* ∼**ted** wetten; **I** ∼ **him £10** ich habe mit ihm um 10 Pfund gewettet; ∼ **on sth.** auf etw. (*Akk.*) setzen

[2] *n.* Wette, *die;* (fig. coll.) Tipp, *der*

beta-blocker /'biːtəblɒkə(r)/ *n.* (Med.)
Beta[rezeptoren]blocker, *der*

betray /bɪ'treɪ/ *v.t.* verraten (**to** an + *Akk.*)

betrayal /bɪ'treɪəl/ *n.* Verrat, *der*

better /'betə(r)/ [1] *adj.* besser; ∼ **and** ∼:
immer besser; **be much** ∼ (recovered) sich
viel besser fühlen; **get** ∼ (recover) besser
werden; **the** ∼ **part of sth.** der größte 'Teil
einer Sache (*Gen.*)
[2] *adv.* besser; ∼ 'off (financially) [finanziell]
besser gestellt; **be** ∼ **off than sb.** besser als
jmd. dran sein (ugs.); **be** ∼ **off without sb./**
sth. ohne jmdn./etw. besser dran sein; **I'd**
∼ **be off now** ich gehe jetzt besser
[3] *n.* **get the** ∼ **of sb./sth.** jmdn./etw.
unterkriegen (ugs.); **a change for the** ∼: eine
vorteilhafte Veränderung
[4] *v.t.* übertreffen

better-'quality *attrib. adj.* qualitativ
besser

'betting shop *n.* Wettbüro, *das*

between /bɪ'twiːn/ [1] *prep.* (a) [in] ∼:
zwischen (*position:* + *Dat.; direction:* + *Akk.*)
(b) (amongst) unter (+ *Dat.*); ∼ **ourselves,**
∼ **you and me** unter uns (*Dat.*) gesagt
(c) ∼ **them/us** (by joint action of) gemeinsam;
∼ **us we had 40p** wir hatten zusammen 40
Pence
[2] *adv.* [in] ∼: dazwischen; (in time)
zwischendurch

beverage /'bevərɪdʒ/ *n.* Getränk, *das*

beware /bɪ'weə(r)/ *v.t. & i.; only in imper.*
and inf. ∼ **[of]** sb./sth. sich vor jmdm./etw.
in Acht nehmen; ∼ **of doing sth.** sich davor
hüten, etw. zu tun; '∼ **of the dog**" „Vorsicht,
bissiger Hund!"

bewilder /bɪ'wɪldə(r)/ *v.t.* verwirren
be'wildering *adj.* verwirrend
be'wilderment *n.* Verwirrung, *die*

bewitch /bɪ'wɪtʃ/ *v.t.* verzaubern; (fig.)
bezaubern

beyond /bɪ'jɒnd/ [1] *adv.* (a) (in space)
jenseits; (on other side of wall, mountain range,
etc.) dahinter
(b) (in time) darüber hinaus
(c) (in addition) außerdem
[2] *prep.* (a) (at far side of) jenseits (+ *Gen.*)
(b) (later than) nach
(c) (out of reach or comprehension or range) über
… (+ *Akk.*) hinaus

bias /'baɪəs/ [1] *n.* Voreingenommenheit, *die*
[2] *v.t.,* **-s-** *or* **-ss-** beeinflussen; **be** ∼**ed in**
favour of/against sth./sb. für etw./jmdn.
eingestellt sein/gegen etw./jmdn.
voreingenommen sein

bib /bɪb/ *n.* Lätzchen, *das*

Bible /'baɪbl/ *n.* Bibel, *die*

biblical /'bɪblɪkl/ *adj.* biblisch

bibliography /bɪblɪ'ɒgrəfɪ/ *n.*
Bibliographie, *die*

biceps /'baɪseps/ *n.* Bizeps, *der*

bicker /'bɪkə(r)/ *v.i.* sich zanken

bicycle /'baɪsɪkl/ [1] *n.* Fahrrad, *das;*
attrib. Fahrrad-
[2] *v.i.* Rad fahren

bicycle: ∼ **clip** *n.* Hosenklammer, *die;*
∼ **courier** *n.* Fahrradkurier, *der/*
-kurierin, *die;* ∼ **lane** *n.* (reserved for cyclists)
Radfahrstreifen, *der;* (with priority for cyclists)
Schutzstreifen, *der* [für Radfahrer]; ∼ **path**
n. [Fahr]radweg, *der*

bid /bɪd/ [1] *v.t.* (a) -dd-, bid (at auction)
bieten
(b) -dd-, bade /bæd, beɪd/ *or* bid, bidden
/'bɪdn/ *or* bid: ∼ **sb. welcome/goodbye**
jmdn. willkommen heißen/sich von jmdm.
verabschieden
[2] *v.i.,* -dd-, bid (a) werben (**for** um)
(b) (at auction) bieten
[3] *n.* (a) (at auction) Gebot, *das*
(b) (attempt) Versuch, *der*

bidden ▶ BID 1B

'bidder *n.* Bieter, *der/*Bieterin, *die*

bide /baɪd/ *v.t.* ∼ **one's time** den richtigen
Augenblick abwarten

biennial /baɪ'enɪəl/ *n.* (Bot.) zweijährige
Pflanze; Bienne, *die* (fachspr.)

bifocal /baɪ'fəʊkl/ [1] *adj.* Bifokal-
[2] *n. in pl.* Bifokalgläser *Pl.*

big /bɪg/ *adj.* groß

bigamist /'bɪgəmɪst/ *n.* Bigamist, *der/*
Bigamistin, *die*

bigamy /'bɪgəmɪ/ *n.* Bigamie, *die*

big: ∼**head** *n.* (coll.) Fatzke, *der* (ugs.
abwertend); ∼-'**headed** *adj.* (coll.)
eingebildet

bigot /'bɪgət/ *n.* borniertter Mensch; (Relig.)
bigotter Mensch

bigoted /'bɪgətɪd/ *adj.* borniert

big: ∼ '**toe** *n.* große Zehe; ∼ '**top** *n.*
Zirkuszelt, *das;* ∼ '**wheel** *n.* (at fair)
Riesenrad, *das*

bike /baɪk/ (coll.) [1] *n.* (bicycle) Rad, *das;*
(motor cycle) Maschine, *die*
[2] *v.i.* Rad fahren/[mit dem] Motorrad
fahren

bike: ∼ **courier,** ∼ **messenger** *ns.* (on
motorbike) Motorradkurier, *der/*-kurierin, *die;*
(on bicycle) Fahrradkurier, *der/*-kurierin, *die;*
∼ **path** (esp. Amer.) ▶ BICYCLE PATH

bikini /bɪ'kiːnɪ/ *n.* Bikini, *der*

bilingual /baɪ'lɪŋgwəl/ *adj.* zweisprachig

bilious /'bɪljəs/ *adj.* (Med.) Gallen-; ∼ **attack**
Gallenanfall, *der*

bill¹ /bɪl/ *n.* (of bird) Schnabel, *der*

bill² *n.* (a) (Parl.) Gesetzentwurf, *der*
(b) (note of charges) Rechnung, *die;* **could we**
have the ∼ **please?** wir möchten zahlen
(c) (poster) '[stick] no ∼s' „[Plakate]
ankleben verboten"

'billboard *n.* Reklametafel, *die*

billet /'bɪlɪt/ [1] *n.* Quartier, *das*
[2] *v.t.* einquartieren (**with, on** bei)

'billfold *n.* (Amer.) Brieftasche, *die*

'billiard ball n. Billardkugel, *die*

billiards /'bɪljədz/ n. Billard[spiel], *das*

billion /'bɪljən/ n. **(a)** (thousand million) Milliarde, *die* **(b)** (esp. Brit. dated: million million) Billion, *die*

billionaire /bɪljə'neə(r)/ n. (Amer.) Milliardär, *der*

billy goat /'bɪlɪgəʊt/ n. Ziegenbock, *der*

bimbo /'bɪmbəʊ/ n. (coll. derog.) Puppe, *die* (salopp)

bin /bɪn/ n. Behälter, *der;* (for bread) Brotkasten, *der;* (for rubbish) Mülleimer, *der*

binary /'baɪnərɪ/ adj. binär

'bin bag n. Müllbeutel, *der*

bind /baɪnd/ v.t., **bound** /baʊnd/ **(a)** fesseln ‹*Person, Tier*›; (bandage) wickeln ‹*Glied, Baum*›; verbinden ‹*Wunde*› **(with** mit) **(b)** (fasten together) zusammenbinden **(c)** binden ‹*Buch*› **(d) be bound up with sth.** (fig.) eng mit etw. verbunden sein **(e) be bound to do sth.** (required) verpflichtet sein, etw. zu tun; (certain) etw. ganz bestimmt tun; **it is bound to rain** es wird bestimmt regnen

'binder n. (for papers) Hefter, *der;* (for magazines) Mappe, *die*

'binding ⬛1⬛ adj. bindend ‹*Vertrag, Abkommen*› **(on** für) ⬛2⬛ n. (of book) Einband, *der*

bingo /'bɪŋgəʊ/ n. Bingo, *das*

'bin liner n. Müllbeutel, *der*

binoculars /bɪ'nɒkjʊləz/ n. pl. **[pair of]** ~: Fernglas, *das*

bio'chemistry n. Biochemie, *die*

biodegradable /baɪəʊdɪ'greɪdəbl/ adj. biologisch abbaubar

biode'grade v.i. sich biologisch abbauen

biographer /baɪ'ɒgrəfə(r)/ n. Biograph, *der*/Biographin, *die*

biographical /baɪə'græfɪkl/ adj. biographisch

biography /baɪ'ɒgrəfɪ/ n. Biographie, *die*

biological /baɪə'lɒdʒɪkl/ adj. biologisch

biological: ~ **'clock** n. biologische Uhr; ~ **'warfare** n. biologische Kriegführung; Bakterienkrieg, *der;* ~ **'waste** n. Bio-Abfall, *der;* Biomüll, *der*

biologist /baɪ'ɒlədʒɪst/ n. Biologe, *der*/Biologin, *die*

biology /baɪ'ɒlədʒɪ/ n. Biologie, *die*

biopsy /'baɪɒpsɪ/ n. Biopsie, *die*

'biorhythm n. Biorhythmus, *der*

'biosphere n. Biosphäre, *die*

biotech'nology n. Biotechnologie, *die*

birch /bɜːtʃ/ n. Birke, *die*

bird /bɜːd/ n. Vogel, *der*

bird: ~ **bath** n. Vogelbad, *das;* ~ **cage** n. Vogelkäfig, *der;* ~**'s-eye 'view** n. Vogelperspektive, *die;* ~**'s nest** n. Vogelnest, *das;* ~ **table** n. Futterstelle für

Vögel; ~**watcher** n. Vogelbeobachter, *der*/-beobachterin, *die;* ~**watching** n. das Beobachten von Vögeln

Biro ® /'baɪrəʊ/ n., pl. ~**s** Kugelschreiber, *der;* Kuli, *der* (ugs.)

birth /bɜːθ/ n. **(a)** Geburt, *die;* **give** ~ ‹*Frau:*› entbinden; ‹*Tier:*› jungen; werfen; **give** ~ **to a child** ein Kind zur Welt bringen **(b)** (of movement, fashion, etc.) Aufkommen, *das*

birth: ~ **certificate** n. Geburtsurkunde, *die;* ~ **control** n. Geburtenkontrolle, *die;* ~**day** n. Geburtstag, *der;* attrib. Geburtstags-

'birthing pool n. Gebärwanne, *die*

birth: ~**mark** n. Muttermal, *das;* ~**place** n. Geburtsort, *der;* ~ **rate** n. Geburtenrate, *die*

biscuit /'bɪskɪt/ n. (Brit.) Keks, *der*

bisect /baɪ'sekt/ v.t. halbieren

bisexual /baɪ'seksjʊəl/ ⬛1⬛ adj. bisexuell ⬛2⬛ n. Bisexuelle, *der*/*die*

bishop /'bɪʃəp/ n. **(a)** (Eccl.) Bischof, *der* **(b)** (Chess) Läufer, *der*

bit¹ /bɪt/ n. **(a)** (for horse) Gebiss, *das* **(b)** (of drill) [Bohr]einsatz, *der*

bit² /bɪt/ n. **(a)** (piece) Stück, *das;* **not a** or **one** ~ (not at all) überhaupt nicht; **a** ~ **tired/too early** ein bisschen müde/zu früh; **be a** ~ **of a coward/ bully** ein ziemlicher Feigling sein/den starken Mann markieren (ugs.)

bit³ n. (Comp.) Bit, *das*

bit⁴ n. ▶ BITE 1, 2

bitch /bɪtʃ/ n. **(a)** (dog) Hündin, *die* **(b)** (sl. derog.: woman) Miststück, *das* (derb)

bitchy /'bɪtʃɪ/ adj. (coll.) gemein; gehässig

bite /baɪt/ ⬛1⬛ v.t., **bit** /bɪt/, **bitten** /'bɪtn/ beißen; ‹*Moskito usw.:*› stechen ⬛2⬛ v.i., **bit**, **bitten** beißen/stechen; (take bait) anbeißen ⬛3⬛ n. Biss, *der;* (piece) Bissen, *der;* (wound) Bisswunde, *die;* (by mosquito etc.) Stich, *der* ▪ **bite 'off** v.t. abbeißen

'bite-size adj. mundgerecht

biting /'baɪtɪŋ/ adj. beißend

bitten ▶ BITE 1, 2

bitter /'bɪtə(r)/ adj. bitter

'bitterly adv. bitterlich ‹*weinen, sich beschweren*›; ~ **cold** bitterkalt

'bitterness n. Bitterkeit, *die*

bizarre /bɪ'zɑː(r)/ adj. bizarr

black /blæk/ ⬛1⬛ adj. **(a)** schwarz; ~ **and blue** (fig.) grün und blau; **in** ~ **and white** (fig.) schwarz auf weiß; ~ **and white film** Schwarzweißfilm, *der;* **in the** ~ (in credit) in den schwarzen Zahlen **(b)** (dark-skinned) schwarz **(c)** B~ (person) Schwarze, *der*/*die* ⬛2⬛ n. **(a)** Schwarz, *das* **(b)** B~ (person) Schwarze, *der*/*die* ⬛3⬛ v.t. bestreiken ‹*Betrieb*›; boykottieren ‹*Arbeit*› ▪ **black 'out** ⬛1⬛ v.t. verdunkeln ⬛2⬛ v.i. das Bewusstsein verlieren

black: ∼**berry** /'blækbərɪ/ n. Brombeere, die; ∼**bird** n. Amsel, die; ∼**board** n. [Wand]tafel, die; ∼ **'box** n. (flight recorder) Flugschreiber, der; ∼**currant** n. schwarze Johannisbeere

blacken /'blækn/ v.t. schwärzen; verfinstern ⟨Himmel⟩

black: ∼ **'eye** n. blaues Auge; **B**∼ **'Forest** pr. n. Schwarzwald, der; ∼ **'hole** n. (Astron.) schwarzes Loch; ∼ **'ice** n. Glatteis, das; ∼**leg** n. (Brit.) Streikbrecher, der/-brecherin, die; ∼ **list** n. schwarze Liste; ∼**list** v.t. auf die schwarze Liste setzen; ∼**mail** [1] v.t. erpressen; [2] n. Erpressung, die; ∼ **market** n. schwarzer Markt

'blackness n. Schwärze, die; (darkness) Finsternis, die

black: ∼**out** n. (a) Verdunkelung, die; (Theatre, Radio) Blackout, der; (b) (Med.) have a ∼out das Bewusstsein verlieren; ∼ **'pudding** n. Blutwurst, die; **B**∼ **'Sea** pr. n. Schwarze Meer, das; ∼**smith** n. Schmied, der; ∼ **spot** n. Gefahrenstelle, die

bladder /'blædə(r)/ n. Blase, die

blade /bleɪd/ n. (a) (of sword, knife, razor, etc.) Klinge, die; (of saw, oar, propeller) Blatt, das (b) (of grass) Spreite, die

Blairite /'bleərɑɪt/ [1] adj. blairsch; Blairsch [2] n. Blair-Anhänger, der/-Anhängerin, die

blame /bleɪm/ [1] v.t. ∼ **sb. [for sth.]** jmdm. die Schuld [an etw. (Dat.)] geben; **be to** ∼ **[for sth.]** an etw. (Dat.) schuld sein; ∼ **sth. [for sth.]** etw. [für etw.] verantwortlich machen [2] n. Schuld, die

'blameless adj. untadelig

blancmange /blə'mɒnʒ/ n. Flammeri, der

bland /blænd/ adj. mild; (suave) verbindlich

blank /blæŋk/ [1] adj. (a) leer; kahl ⟨Wand, Fläche⟩ (b) (empty) frei [2] n. (a) (space) Lücke, die (b) (cartridge) Platzpatrone, die (c) draw a ∼: kein Glück haben

blank 'cheque n. Blankoscheck, der; (fig.) Blankovollmacht, die

blanket /'blæŋkɪt/ n. Decke, die; **wet '**∼ (fig.) Trauerkloß, der (ugs.)

blare /'bleə(r)/ [1] v.i. ⟨Lautsprecher:⟩ plärren; ⟨Trompete:⟩ schmettern [2] v.t. ∼ **[out]** [hinaus]plärren ⟨Worte⟩; [hinaus]schmettern ⟨Melodie⟩

blasé /'blɑːzeɪ/ adj. blasiert

blasphemous /'blæsfəməs/ adj. lästerlich

blasphemy /'blæsfəmɪ/ n. Blasphemie, die

blast /blɑːst/ [1] n. (a) **a** ∼ **[of wind]** ein Windstoß (b) (of horn) Tuten, das [2] v.t. (blow up) sprengen [3] int. verdammt
■ **blast 'off** v.i. abheben

blasted /'blɑːstɪd/ adj. (damned) verdammt (salopp)

'blast-off n. Abheben, das

blatant /'bleɪtənt/ adj. (a) (flagrant) eklatant (b) (unashamed) unverhohlen; unverfroren ⟨Lüge⟩

'blatantly adv. ▶ BLATANT: eklatant; unverhohlen

blaze /bleɪz/ [1] n. Feuer, das [2] v.i. brennen; lodern (geh.)

blazer /'bleɪzə(r)/ n. Blazer, der

bleach /bliːtʃ/ [1] v.t. bleichen [2] n. Bleichmittel, das

bleak /'bliːk/ adj. (a) öde ⟨Landschaft usw.⟩ (b) (unpromising) düster

bleat /bliːt/ v.i. ⟨Schaf:⟩ blöken; ⟨Ziege:⟩ meckern

bled ▶ BLEED

bleed /bliːd/ v.i., bled /bled/ bluten

bleep /bliːp/ [1] n. Piepen, das [2] v.i. ⟨Geigerzähler, Funksignal:⟩ piepen [3] v.t. ∼ **sb.** jmdn. über seinen Kleinempfänger od. (ugs.) Piepser rufen

bleeper /'bliːpə(r)/ n. Kleinempfänger, der; Piepser, der (ugs.)

blemish /'blemɪʃ/ n. Fleck, der

blend /blend/ [1] v.t. mischen [2] v.i. sich mischen lassen [3] n. Mischung, die

'blender n. Mixer, der

bless /bles/ v.t. segnen; ∼ **you!** (after sb. sneezes) Gesundheit!

blessed /'blesɪd/ adj. (a) (revered) heilig (b) (cursed) verdammt (salopp)

'blessing n. Segen, der

blew ▶ BLOW[1]

blight /blɑɪt/ n. (fig.) Fluch, der

blind /blɑɪnd/ [1] adj. blind; ∼ **in one eye** auf einem Auge blind [2] adv. blindlings [3] n. (a) Jalousie, die; (made of cloth) Rouleau, das; (of shop) Markise, die (b) pl. the n∼: die Blinden Pl. [4] v.t. blenden

blind: ∼ **'alley** n. (lit. or fig.) Sackgasse, die; ∼ **'corner** n. unübersichtliche Ecke; ∼ **'date** n. Verabredung mit einem/einer Unbekannten; ∼**fold** [1] v.t. die Augen verbinden (+ Dat.); [2] adj. mit verbundenen Augen nachgestellt

'blinding adj. blendend; **a** ∼ **headache** rasende Kopfschmerzen Pl.

'blindly adv. [wie] blind; (fig.) blindlings

'blindness n. Blindheit, die

'blind spot n. (Motor Veh.) toter Winkel; (fig.: weak spot) schwacher Punkt

blink /blɪŋk/ v.i. (a) blinzeln (b) (shine intermittently) blinken

'blinkers n. pl. Scheuklappen Pl.

bliss /blɪs/ n. [Glück]seligkeit, die

blissful /'blɪsfl/ adj. [glück]selig

blister /'blɪstə(r)/ [1] n. Blase, die ⋯⟩

② v.i. ⟨Haut:⟩ Blasen bekommen; ⟨Anstrich:⟩ Blasen werfen

'blister pack n. Klarsichtpackung, die

blizzard /ˈblɪzəd/ n. Schneesturm, der

bloated /ˈbləʊtɪd/ adj. (having overeaten) aufgedunsen; **I feel ~:** ich bin voll (ugs.)

blob /blɒb/ n. (drop) Tropfen, der; (small mass) Klacks, der (ugs.)

block /blɒk/ ① n. (a) Klotz, der; (for chopping on) Hackklotz, der; (of concrete or stone, building stone) Block, der
(b) (building) [Häuser]block, der; **~ of flats/ offices** Wohnblock, der/Bürohaus, das
② v.t. versperren ⟨Tür, Straße, Durchgang, Sicht⟩; verstopfen ⟨Pfeife, Abfluss⟩; verhindern ⟨Fortschritt⟩
■ **block 'out** v.t. ausschließen ⟨Licht, Lärm⟩
■ **block 'up** v.t. verstopfen; versperren ⟨Eingang⟩

blockade /blɒˈkeɪd/ ① n. Blockade, die
② v.t. blockieren

blockage /ˈblɒkɪdʒ/ n. Block, der; (of pipe, gutter) Verstopfung, die

block: ~ 'booking n. Gruppenbuchung, die; **~buster** n. **(a)** (bomb) [große] Fliegerbombe; **(b)** (fig.) Knüller, der (ugs.); **~ 'capital** n. Blockbuchstabe, der; **~head** n. Dummkopf, der; **~ 'letters** n. pl. Blockschrift, die

bloke /bləʊk/ n. (Brit. coll.) Typ, der (ugs.)

blonde /blɒnd/ ① adj. blond
② n. Blondine, die

blood /blʌd/ n. Blut, das

blood: ~ bank n. Blutbank, die; **~bath** n. Blutbad, das; **~ cell** n. Blutkörperchen, das; **~ clot** n. Blutgerinnsel, das; **~ donor** n. Blutspender, der/-spenderin, die; **~ group** n. Blutgruppe, die; **~hound** n. Bluthund, der; **~ plasma** n. Blutplasma, das; **~ poisoning** n. Blutvergiftung, die; **~ pressure** n. Blutdruck, der; **~ sample** n. Blutprobe, die; **~shed** n. Blutvergießen, das; **~shot** adj. blutunterlaufen; **~ sports** n. pl. Hetzjagd, die; **~stain** n. Blutfleck, der; **~stained** adj. blutbefleckt; **~stream** n. Blutstrom, der; **~ sugar** n. Blutzucker, der; **~ test** n. Blutprobe, die; **~thirsty** adj. blutrünstig; **~ transfusion** n. Bluttransfusion, die; **~ vessel** n. Blutgefäß, das

'bloody ① adj. **(a)** blutig; (running with blood) blutend
(b) (sl.: damned) verdammt (salopp)
② adv. (sl.: damned) verdammt (salopp)

bloom /bluːm/ ① n. Blüte, die; **be in ~:** in Blüte stehen
② v.i. blühen

blossom /ˈblɒsəm/ ① n. (flower) Blüte, die; (mass) Blütenmeer, das (geh.)
② v.i. blühen; ⟨Mensch:⟩ aufblühen

blot /blɒt/ ① n. (of ink) Tintenklecks, der; (stain) Fleck, der
② v.t., -tt- ablöschen ⟨Tinte, Papier⟩

■ **blot 'out** v.t. (fig.) auslöschen

blotchy /ˈblɒtʃɪ/ adj. fleckig

'blotting paper n. Löschpapier, das

blouse /blaʊz/ n. Bluse, die

blow¹ /bləʊ/ ① v.i., **blew** /bluː/, **blown** /bləʊn/ ⟨Wind:⟩ wehen; ⟨Sturm:⟩ blasen
② v.t., **blew, blown: (a)** blasen; ⟨Wind:⟩ wehen; machen ⟨Seifenblase⟩; **~ sb. a kiss** jmdm. eine Kusshand zuwerfen
(b) **~ one's nose** sich ⟨Dat.⟩ die Nase putzen
(c) **~ sth. to pieces** etw. in die Luft sprengen
■ **blow 'out** ① v.t. ausblasen
② v.i. ausgeblasen werden
■ **blow 'over** ① v.i. umgeblasen werden; ⟨Streit, Sturm:⟩ sich legen
② v.t. umblasen
■ **blow 'up** ① v.t. **(a)** (shatter) [in die Luft] sprengen
(b) aufblasen ⟨Ballon⟩; aufpumpen ⟨Reifen⟩
(c) (coll.: exaggerate) hochspielen
② v.i. (explode) explodieren

blow² n. **(a)** Schlag, der; (with axe) Hieb, der; **come to ~s** handgreiflich werden
(b) (disaster) [schwerer] Schlag

blow: ~-dry v.t. fönen; **~lamp** n. Lötlampe, die

blown ▶ BLOW¹

blow: ~torch (Amer.) ▶ ~LAMP; **~-up** n. (coll.: enlargement) Vergrößerung, die

blubber /ˈblʌbə(r)/ n. Walspeck, der

blue /bluː/ ① adj. blau
② n. **(a)** Blau, das
(b) **have the ~s** deprimiert sein
(c) (Mus.) **the ~s** der Blues
(d) **out of the ~:** aus heiterem Himmel

blue: ~bell n. Glockenblume, die; **~ 'blood** n. blaues Blut; **~bottle** n. Schmeißfliege, die; **~ 'cheese** n. Blauschimmelkäse, der; Edelpilzkäse, der; **~-collar** adj. **~-collar worker** Arbeiter, der/Arbeiterin, die; **~-eyed** adj. blauäugig; **be ~-eyed** blaue Augen haben; **~ 'jeans** n. pl. Blue jeans Pl.; **~ 'moon** n. **once in a ~ moon** alle Jubeljahre (ugs.); **~print** n. (fig.) Entwurf, der; **~ tit** n. (Ornith.) Blaumeise, die; **~ 'whale** n. Blauwal, der

bluff /blʌf/ ① n. Bluff, der (ugs.); **call sb.'s ~:** es darauf ankommen lassen (ugs.)
② v.i. & t. bluffen (ugs.)

blunder /ˈblʌndə(r)/ ① n. [schwerer] Fehler
② v.i. **(a)** (make mistake) einen [schweren] Fehler machen
(b) (move blindly) tappen

blunt /blʌnt/ ① adj. **(a)** stumpf
(b) (outspoken) direkt; glatt (ugs.) ⟨Ablehnung⟩
② v.t. ~ [the edge of] stumpf machen

'bluntly adv. direkt; glatt ⟨ablehnen⟩

blur /blɜː(r)/ ① v.t., **-rr-: (a)** verwischen
(b) (become indistinct) verschwimmen; **his vision was ~red** er sah alles verschwommen
② n. (smear) Fleck, der; (dim image) verschwommener Fleck

blurt /blɜːt/ v.t. ~ **out** herausplatzen mit (ugs.)

blush /blʌʃ/ 1 v.i. rot werden 2 n. Rotwerden, das

bluster /'blʌstə(r)/ v.i. sich aufplustern (ugs.)

blustery /'blʌstərɪ/ adj. stürmisch

BO abbr. (coll.) = **body odour** Körpergeruch, der

boar /bɔː(r)/ n. [wild] ~: Keiler, der

board /bɔːd/ 1 n. (a) Brett, das; (black~) Tafel, die; (notice~) schwarzes Brett; **above** ~ (fig.) einwandfrei; korrekt (b) (Commerc.) [of directors] Vorstand, der; (supervisory ~) Aufsichtsrat, der (c) (Naut., Aeronaut.) **on** ~: an Bord (d) ~ **and lodging** Unterkunft und Verpflegung; **full** ~: Vollpension, die 2 v.t. ~ **the ship/plane** an Bord des Schiffes/Flugzeuges gehen; ~ **the train/bus** in den Zug/Bus einsteigen
■ **board 'up** v.t. mit Brettern vernageln

'boarder n. (Sch.) Internatsschüler, der/ -schülerin, die

'board game n. Brettspiel, das

boarding: ~ **house** n. Pension, die; ~ **pass** n. Bordkarte, die; ~ **school** n. Internat, das

board: ~ **meeting** n. Vorstandssitzung, die; ~**room** n. Sitzungssaal, der

boast /bəʊst/ v.i. prahlen

boastful /'bəʊstfl/ adj. prahlerisch

boat /bəʊt/ n. Boot, das

boat: ~**house** n. Bootshaus, das; ~ **trip** n. Bootsfahrt, die

bob¹ /bɒb/ v.i., -bb-: ~ [up and down] sich auf und nieder bewegen

bob² n. (~sled) Bob, der

bobbin /'bɒbɪn/ n. Spule, die

bob: ~**sled**, ~**sleigh** ns. Bobschlitten, der

bodice /'bɒdɪs/ n. Mieder, das; (part of dress) Oberteil, das

bodily /'bɒdɪlɪ/ adj. körperlich; ~ **needs** leibliche Bedürfnisse

body /'bɒdɪ/ n. (a) Körper, der (b) (corpse) Leiche, die (c) (group) Gruppe, die; (with particular function) Organ, das

body: ~ **bag** n. Leichensack, der; ~**building** 1 n. Bodybuilding, das; 2 adj. ~**building food** Aufbaukost, die; ~ **clock** ▶ BIOLOGICAL CLOCK; ~**guard** n. (single) Leibwächter, der; (group) Leibwache, die; ~ **language** n. Körpersprache, die; ~ **odour** n. Körpergeruch, der; ~ **piercing** n. Piercing, das; ~ **weight** n. Körpergewicht, das; ~**work** n. Karosserie, die

bog /bɒg/ 1 n. Moor, das; (marsh, swamp) Sumpf, der 2 v.t., -gg-: **be/get** ~**ged down** (fig.) sich verzettelt haben/sich verzetteln

boggle /'bɒgl/ v.i. (coll.) **the mind** ~**s** da kann man nur [noch] staunen

bogus /'bəʊgəs/ adj. falsch

boil¹ /bɔɪl/ 1 v.i. & t. kochen 2 n. **come to/go off the** ~: zu kochen anfangen/aufhören; **bring to the** ~: zum Kochen bringen
■ **boil 'down** v.i. ~ **down to sth.** (fig.) auf etw. hinauslaufen
■ **boil 'over** v.i. überkochen

boil² n. (Med.) Furunkel, der

'boiler n. Kessel, der

boiler: ~**room** n. Kesselraum, der; ~ **suit** n. Overall, der

'boiling point n. Siedepunkt, der

boisterous /'bɔɪstərəs/ adj. ausgelassen

bold /bəʊld/ adj. (a) (courageous) mutig; (daring) kühn (b) auffallend ⟨Farbe, Muster⟩

'boldly adv. (courageously) mutig; (daringly) kühn

Bolivia /bə'lɪvɪə/ pr. n. Bolivien (das)

bollard /'bɒlɑːd/ n. (Brit.) Poller, der

bollocks /'bɒləks/ (coarse) 1 n. pl. Eier (derb) 2 int. Scheiße

bolster /'bəʊlstə(r)/ 1 n. (pillow) Nackenrolle, die 2 v.t. (fig.) stärken

bolt /bəʊlt/ 1 n. (a) (on door or window) Riegel, der; (on gun) Kammerverschluss, der (b) (metal pin) Schraube, die; (without thread) Bolzen, der 2 v.i. davonlaufen; ⟨Pferd:⟩ durchgehen; ⟨Fuchs, Kaninchen:⟩ flüchten 3 v.t. (a) verriegeln ⟨Tür, Fenster⟩ (b) (fasten with ~s) verschrauben/mit Bolzen verbinden (c) ~ [down] hinunterschlingen ⟨Essen⟩ 4 adv. ~ **upright** kerzengerade

bomb /bɒm/ 1 n. Bombe, die; ~ **attack** Bombenanschlag, der 2 v.t. bombardieren

bombard /bɒm'bɑːd/ v.t. beschießen

bom'bardment n. Beschuss, der

bombastic /bɒm'bæstɪk/ adj. bombastisch

bomb: ~ **blast** n. (blast wave) Druckwelle, die; (explosion) Bombenexplosion, die; ~ **disposal** n. Räumung von Bomben; ~ **disposal squad** Bombenräumkommando, das

bomber /'bɒmə(r)/ n. (Air Force) Bomber, der (ugs.)

bombing /'bɒmɪŋ/ n. Bombardierung, die

bomb: ~ **scare** n. Bombendrohung, die; ~**shell** n. Bombe, die; (fig.) Sensation, die

bond /bɒnd/ n. (a) Band, das; in pl. (shackles) Fesseln Pl. (b) (adhesion) Verbindung, die (c) (Commerc.) Anleihe, die

bone /bəʊn/ 1 n. Knochen, der; (of fish) Gräte, die ┄┄╬

2 *v.t.* den/die Knochen herauslösen aus; entgräten ⟨*Fisch*⟩

bone: ~ **'china** *n.* Knochenporzellan, *das;* ~ **'dry** *adj.* knochentrocken (ugs.); ~ **'idle** *adj.* stinkfaul (salopp); ~ **marrow** *n.* (Anat.) Knochenmark, *das;* ~**meal** *n.* Knochenmehl, *das*

bonfire /'bɒnfaɪə(r)/ *n.* Freudenfeuer, *das;* (for rubbish) Feuer, *das;* B~ **Night** (Brit.) [Abend des] Guy Fawkes Day (*mit Feuerwerk*)

bonnet /'bɒnɪt/ *n.* (a) (woman's) Haube, *die;* (child's) Häubchen, *das*
(b) (Brit. Motor Veh.) Motorhaube, *die*

bonus /'bəʊnəs/ *n.* zusätzliche Leistung; (to shareholders) Bonus, *der;* **Christmas** ~: Weihnachtsgratifikation, *die*

bony /'bəʊnɪ/ *adj.* (a) Knochen-; (like bone) knochenartig
(b) (skinny) knochendürr (ugs.); spindeldürr

boo /buː/ **1** *int.* (to surprise sb.) huh; (expr. disapproval, contempt) buh
2 *n.* Buh, *das* (ugs.)
3 *v.t.* ausbuhen (ugs.)
4 *v.i.* buhen (ugs.)

boob /buːb/ (Brit. coll.) *n.* (a) (mistake) Fehler, *der;* Schnitzer, *der* (ugs.)
(b) (breast) Titte, *die* (derb)

booby /'buːbɪ/ *n.* Trottel, *der* (ugs.)

booby: ~ **prize** *n:* Preis für den schlechtesten Teilnehmer an einem Wettbewerb; ~ **trap** *n.* (a) Falle, mit der man jmdm. einen Streich spielen will; (b) (Mil.) versteckte Sprengladung

book /bʊk/ **1** *n.* Buch, *das;* (for accounts) Rechnungsbuch, *das;* (for exercises) [Schreib]heft, *das*
2 *v.t.* buchen ⟨*Reise, Flug, Platz [im Flugzeug]*⟩; [vor]bestellen ⟨*Eintrittskarte, Tisch, Zimmer, Platz [im Theater]*⟩
3 *v.i.* buchen
▪ **book 'in** **1** *v.i.* sich eintragen
2 *v.t.* eintragen
▪ **book 'up** *v.i. & t.* buchen; **be** ~**ed up** ⟨*Hotel usw.*⟩ ausgebucht sein

book: ~**case** *n.* Bücherschrank, *der;* ~ **club** *n.* Buchklub, *der;* Buchgemeinschaft, *die;* ~**ends** *n. pl.* Buchstützen *Pl.*

bookie /'bʊkɪ/ *n.* (coll.) Buchmacher, *der*

'booking office *n.* [Fahrkarten]schalter, *der*

book: ~**keeper** *n.* Buchhalter, *der/* -halterin, *die;* ~**keeping** *n.* Buchführung, *die;* Buchhaltung, *die*

booklet /'bʊklɪt/ *n.* Broschüre, *die*

book: ~**maker** *n.* (in betting) Buchmacher, *der;* ~**mark** *n.* **1** (also Comp.) Lesezeichen, *das;* **2** *v.t.* (Comp.) mit einem Lesezeichen versehen; ~**seller** *n.* Buchhändler, *der/* -händlerin, *die;* ~**shelf** *n.* Bücherbord, *das;* ~**shop** *n.* Buchhandlung, *die;* ~**stall** *n.* Bücherstand, *der;* ~**store** *n.* (Amer.)

Buchhandlung, *die;* ~ **token** *n.* Büchergutschein, *der;* ~**worm** *n.* Bücherwurm, *der*

boom¹ /buːm/ *n.* (a) (for camera or microphone) Ausleger, *der*
(b) (Naut.) Baum, *der*

boom² **1** *v.i.* (a) dröhnen
(b) ⟨*Geschäft, Verkauf, Gebiet:*⟩ sich sprunghaft entwickeln
2 *n.* (a) Dröhnen, *das*
(b) (in business or economy) Boom, *der*

boomerang /'buːməræŋ/ *n.* Bumerang, *der*

boon /buːn/ *n.* Segen, *der* (**to** für)

boor /bʊə(r)/ *n.* Rüpel, *der*

boorish /'bʊərɪʃ/ *adj.* rüpelhaft

boost /buːst/ **1** *v.t.* ankurbeln ⟨*Wirtschaft*⟩; in die Höhe treiben ⟨*Preis, Wert*⟩; stärken ⟨*Selbstvertrauen, Moral*⟩
2 *n.* Auftrieb, *der*

boot /buːt/ **1** *n.* (a) Stiefel, *der;* **give sb. the** ~ (fig. coll.) jmdn. rausschmeißen (ugs.)
(b) (Brit.: of car) Kofferraum, *der*
2 *v.t.* (a) (coll.: kick) kicken (ugs.)
(b) (Comp.) ~ [**up**] booten

bootable /'buːtəbl/ *adj.* (Comp.) bootbar ⟨*System*⟩; ~ **disk** Bootdiskette, *die*

'boot disk *n.* (Comp.) Bootdiskette, *die*

booth /buːð/ *n.* (a) Bude, *die*
(b) (telephone ~) Zelle, *die*

'bootleg *adj.* (illegally sold/distilled) schwarz verkauft/gebrannt

booze /buːz/ (coll.) **1** *v.i.* saufen (derb)
2 *n.* Alkohol, *der*

'booze-up *n.* (coll.) Besäufnis, *das* (salopp); **have a** ~: saufen gehen (salopp) (ugs.)

border /'bɔːdə(r)/ **1** *n.* (a) Rand, *der;* (of tablecloth, handkerchief) Bordüre, *die*
(b) (of country) Grenze, *die*
(c) (flower bed) Rabatte, *die*
2 *attrib. adj.* Grenz⟨*stadt, -streit*⟩
3 *v.t.* (a) (adjoin) [an]grenzen an (+ *Akk.*)
(b) (put a ~ to, act as ~ to) umranden; einfassen
4 *v.i.* ~ **on** (a) ▸ 3A
(b) (resemble) grenzen an (+ *Akk.*)

border: ~ **crossing** *n.* Grenzübergang, *der;* ~**line** **1** *n.* Grenzlinie, *die;* **2** *adj.* **be** ~**line** auf der Grenze liegen; **a** ~**line case/** **candidate** ein Grenzfall

bore¹ /bɔː(r)/ **1** *v.t.* bohren
2 *n.* (of firearm) Kaliber, *das*

bore² **1** *n.* (a) **it's a real** ~: es ist wirklich ärgerlich; **what a** ~! wie ärgerlich!
(b) (person) Langweiler, *der* (ugs.)
2 *v.t.* langweilen; **be** ~**d** sich langweilen

bore³ ▸ BEAR²

boredom /'bɔːdəm/ *n.* Langeweile, *die*

'borehole *n.* Bohrloch, *das*

boring /'bɔːrɪŋ/ *adj.* langweilig

born /bɔːn/ **1** *v.t.* **be** ~: geboren werden
2 *adj.* geboren; **be a** ~ **orator** der geborene Redner sein

borne ▸ BEAR²

borough /ˈbʌrə/ n. (town) Stadt, die; (village) Gemeinde, die

borrow /ˈbɒrəʊ/ v.t. leihen (**from** von, bei); (from library) entleihen

'**borrower** n. (from bank) Kreditnehmer, der; (from library) Entleiher, der

Bosnia /ˈbɒznɪə/ n. Bosnien (das)

Bosnian /ˈbɒznɪən/ ⟨1⟩ adj. bosnisch; **sb. is ~**: jmd. ist Bosnier/Bosnierin ⟨2⟩ n. Bosnier, der/Bosnierin, die

bosom /ˈbʊzəm/ n. Brust, die

boss /bɒs/ (coll.) ⟨1⟩ n. Boss, der (ugs.); Chef, der ⟨2⟩ v.t. **~ [about** or **around]** herumkommandieren (ugs.)

'**bossy** adj. (coll.) herrisch

botanical /bəˈtænɪkl/ adj. botanisch

botanist /ˈbɒtənɪst/ n. Botaniker, der/ Botanikerin, die

botany /ˈbɒtənɪ/ n. Botanik, die

botch /bɒtʃ/ ⟨1⟩ v.t. pfuschen bei (ugs.) ⟨2⟩ v.i. pfuschen (ugs.)
■ **botch 'up** v.t. (bungle) verpfuschen (ugs.)

both /bəʊθ/ ⟨1⟩ adj. beide; **~ [the] brothers** beide Brüder ⟨2⟩ pron. beide; **~ [of them] are dead** beide sind tot; **~ of you/them are ...**: ihr seid/sie sind beide ... ⟨3⟩ adv. **~ A and B** sowohl A als [auch] B; **he and I were ~ there** er und ich waren beide da

bother /ˈbɒðə(r)/ ⟨1⟩ v.t. (a) **I can't be ~ed** ich habe keine Lust (b) (annoy) lästig sein (+ Dat.); ⟨Lärm, Licht:⟩ stören; ⟨Schmerz, Zahn:⟩ zu schaffen machen (+ Dat.); **I'm sorry to ~ you, but ...**: es tut mir Leid, wenn ich Sie störe, aber ... (c) (worry) Sorgen machen (+ Dat.); ⟨Problem, Frage:⟩ beschäftigen ⟨2⟩ v.i. **don't ~ to do it** Sie brauchen es nicht zu tun; **you needn't/shouldn't have ~ed** das wäre nicht nötig gewesen; **don't ~!** nicht nötig! ⟨3⟩ n. (a) (trouble) Ärger, der (b) (effort) Mühe, die ⟨4⟩ int. (coll.) wie ärgerlich!

bottle /ˈbɒtl/ ⟨1⟩ n. Flasche, die; **a ~ of beer** eine Flasche Bier ⟨2⟩ v.t. (a) (put into ~s) in Flaschen [ab]füllen (b) **~d beer** Flaschenbier, das (c) (preserve in jars) einmachen
■ **bottle 'up** v.t. (a) (conceal) in sich (Dat.) aufstauen (b) (trap) einschließen

bottle: ~ bank n. Altglasbehälter, der; **~neck** n. (fig.) Flaschenhals, der (ugs.); **~-opener** n. Flaschenöffner, der; **~ top** n. Flaschenverschluss, der

bottom /ˈbɒtəm/ ⟨1⟩ n. (a) unteres Ende; (of cup, glass, box) Boden, der; (of valley, well, shaft) Sohle, die; (of hill, cliff, stairs) Fuß, der (b) (buttocks) Hinterteil, das (ugs.) (c) (of sea, lake) Grund, der

(e) (farthest point) **at the ~ of the garden/street** hinten im Garten/am Ende der Straße (e) (underside) Unterseite, die (f) (fig.) **start at the ~**: ganz unten anfangen; **be ~ of the class** der/die Letzte in der Klasse sein ⟨2⟩ adj. (a) (lowest) unterst...; (lower) unter... (b) (fig.: last) letzt...

'**bottomless** adj. bodenlos; unendlich tief ⟨Meer, Ozean⟩

'**botulism** /ˈbɒtjuːlɪzm/ n. (Med.) Botulismus, der

bough /baʊ/ n. Ast, der

bought ▶ BUY 1

boulder /ˈbəʊldə(r)/ n. Felsbrocken, der

boulevard /ˈbuːləvɑːd/ n. Boulevard, der

bounce /baʊns/ ⟨1⟩ v.i. (a) springen (b) (coll.) ⟨Scheck:⟩ platzen (ugs.) ⟨2⟩ v.t. aufspringen lassen ⟨Ball⟩ ⟨3⟩ n. Aufprall, der

'**bouncer** n. (coll.) Rausschmeißer, der (ugs.)

bouncing /ˈbaʊnsɪŋ/ adj. stramm ⟨Baby⟩

bouncy /ˈbaʊnsɪ/ adj. gut springend ⟨Ball⟩; (fig.: lively) munter

bound¹ /baʊnd/ ⟨1⟩ n., usu. in pl. (limit) Grenze, die; **within the ~s of possibility** im Bereich des Möglichen; **sth. is out of ~s [to sb.]** der Zutritt zu etw. ist [für jmdn.] verboten ⟨2⟩ v.t. **be ~ed by sth.** durch etw. begrenzt werden

bound² /baʊnd/ ⟨1⟩ v.i. hüpfen ⟨2⟩ n. Satz, der

bound³ pred. adj. **be ~ for home/Frankfurt** auf dem Heimweg/nach Frankfurt unterwegs sein; **homeward ~**: auf dem Weg nach Hause

bound⁴ ▶ BIND

boundary /ˈbaʊndərɪ/ n. Grenze, die

'**boundless** adj. grenzenlos

bounty /ˈbaʊntɪ/ n. Kopfgeld, das

bouquet /buˈkeɪ/ n. [Blumen]strauß, der

bourgeois /ˈbʊəʒwɑː/ ⟨1⟩ n., pl. same Bürger, der/Bürgerin, die ⟨2⟩ adj. bürgerlich

bout /baʊt/ n. (a) (contest) Wettkampf, der (b) (fit) Anfall, der

boutique /buːˈtiːk/ n. Boutique, die

bow¹ /bəʊ/ n. (a) (curve, weapon, Mus.) Bogen, der (b) (knot, ribbon) Schleife, die

bow² /baʊ/ ⟨1⟩ v.i. (a) **~ [to sb.]** sich [vor jmdm.] verbeugen (b) (submit) sich beugen (**to** Dat.) ⟨2⟩ n. Verbeugung, die

bow³ /baʊ/ n. (Naut.) Bug, der

bowel /ˈbaʊəl/ n. (Anat.) **~s** pl., (Med.) **~:** Darm, der

bowl¹ /bəʊl/ n. (basin) Schüssel, die; (shallower) Schale, die; (of spoon) Schöpfteil, der; (of pipe) Kopf, der

bowl² ⟨1⟩ n. (a) (ball) Kugel, die   ⋯⋯⟩

(b) *in pl.* (game) Bowls, *das*
2 *v.i.* **(a)** (play ~s) Bowls spielen
(b) (Cricket) werfen
bow-legged /'bəʊlegɪd/ o-beinig (ugs.)
bowler¹ /'bəʊlə(r)/ *n.* (Cricket) Werfer, *der*
bowler² *n.* ~ [hat] Bowler, *der*
'bowling *n.* [tenpin] ~: Bowling, *das;* go ~:
bowlen gehen
bowling: ~ alley *n.* Bowlingbahn, *die;*
~ green *n.:* Rasenfläche für Bowls
bow /bəʊ/: **~string** *n.* Bogensehne, *die;*
~ 'tie *n.* Fliege, *die;* **~ window** *n.*
Erkerfenster, *das*
box¹ /bɒks/ *n.* **(a)** Kasten, *der;* (bigger) Kiste,
die; (of cardboard) Schachtel, *die*
(b) the ~ (coll.: television) der Kasten (ugs.
abwertend); die Flimmerkiste (scherzh.)
box² **1** *n.* he gave him a ~ on the ear[s] er
gab ihm eine Ohrfeige
2 *v.t.* **(a)** he ~ed his ears *or* ~ed him round
the ears er ohrfeigte ihn
(b) (Sport) ~ sb. gegen jmdn. boxen
3 *v.i.* (Sport) boxen
■ **box 'in** *v.t.* (enclose tightly) einklemmen
'boxer *n.* Boxer, *der*
'boxer shorts *n. pl.* Boxershorts *Pl.*
'boxing *n.* Boxen, *das*
boxing: B~ Day *n.* zweiter
Weihnachtsfeiertag; **~ glove** *n.*
Boxhandschuh, *der;* **~ match** *n.*
Boxkampf, *der;* **~ ring** *n.* Boxring, *der*
box: ~ junction *n.* (Brit.) gelb markierter
Kreuzungsbereich, in den man bei Stau nicht
einfahren darf; **~ number** *n.* (at newspaper
office) Chiffre, *die;* (at post office) Postfach, *das;*
~ office *n.* Kasse, *die;* be a ~ office
success ein Kassenerfolg sein; **~room** *n.*
(Brit.) Abstellraum, *der*
boy /bɔɪ/ *n.* Junge, *der*
'boy band *n.* Boyband, *die*
boycott /'bɔɪkɒt/ **1** *v.t.* boykottieren
2 *n.* Boykott, *der*
'boyfriend *n.* Freund, *der*
'boyish *adj.* jungenhaft
boy 'scout ▶ SCOUT 1A
bra /brɑː/ *n.* BH, *der* (ugs.)
brace /breɪs/ **1** *n.* **(a)** (connecting piece)
Klammer, *die;* (strut) Strebe, *die;* (Dent.)
[Zahn]spange, *die*
(b) *in pl.* (trouser straps) Hosenträger *Pl.*
2 *v. refl.* ~ oneself for sth. sich auf etw.
(*Akk.*) vorbereiten
bracelet /'breɪslɪt/ *n.* Armband, *das*
bracing /'breɪsɪŋ/ *adj.* belebend
bracken /'brækn/ *n.* [Adler]farn, *der*
bracket /'brækɪt/ **1** *n.* **(a)** (support)
Konsole, *die*
(b) (mark) Klammer, *die*
2 *v.t.* einklammern
brag /bræg/ *v.i. & t.,* -gg- prahlen (**about**
mit)

braid /breɪd/ **1** *n.* **(a)** (plait) Flechte, *die*
(geh.); Zopf, *der*
(b) (woven band) Borte, *die;* (on uniform) Litze,
die
2 *v.t.* flechten
Braille /breɪl/ *n.* Blindenschrift, *die*
brain /breɪn/ *n.* Gehirn, *das*
brain: ~child *n.* (coll.) Geistesprodukt, *das;*
~-dead *adj.* **(a)** (Med.) hirntot; **(b)** (coll.
derog.) hirnlos ‹Person›; **~less** *adj.* hirnlos;
~storm *n.* **(a)** Anfall geistiger
Umnachtung; **(b)** (Amer. coll.) ▶ ~WAVE;
~storming *n.* Brainstorming, *das;*
~ tumour *n.* Gehirntumor, *der;* **~wash**
v.t. einer Gehirnwäsche unterziehen;
~wave *n.* (coll.: inspiration) genialer Einfall
'brainy *adj.* intelligent
brake /breɪk/ **1** *n.* Bremse, *die*
2 *v.t. & i.* bremsen
brake: ~ block *n.* Bremsklotz, *der;*
~ cable *n.* Bremszug, *der;* Bremsseil, *das;*
~ fluid *n.* Bremsflüssigkeit, *die;* **~ light**
n. Bremslicht, *das;* **~ pad** *n.* Bremsbelag,
der; **~ shoe** *n.* Bremsbacke, *die*
'braking distance *n.* Bremsweg, *der*
bramble /'bræmbl/ *n.* Dornenstrauch, *der*
bran /bræn/ *n.* Kleie, *die*
branch /brɑːntʃ/ **1** *n.* **(a)** (bough) Ast, *der;*
(twig) Zweig, *der*
(b) (of artery, antlers) Ast, *der*
(c) (office) Zweigstelle, *die;* (shop) Filiale, *die*
2 *v.i.* sich verzweigen
■ **branch 'off** *v.i.* abzweigen
■ **branch 'out** *v.i.* (fig.) ~ out into sth. sich
auch mit etw. befassen
branch: ~ line *n.* (Railw.) Nebenstrecke,
die; **~ manager** *n.* Filialleiter, *der*/
-leiterin, *die;* **~ office** *n.* Zweigstelle, *die*
brand /brænd/ *n.* **(a)** (trade mark)
Markenzeichen, *das;* (goods of particular make)
Marke, *die*
(b) (mark) Brandmal, *das*
'brand image *n.* Markenimage, *das*
brandish /'brændɪʃ/ *v.t.* schwenken;
schwingen ‹Waffe›
brand: ~ leader *n.* (product)
marktführendes Produkt; (brand) führende
Marke, *die;* **~ name** *n.* Markenname, *der;*
~-'new *adj.* nagelneu (ugs.)
brandy /'brændɪ/ *n.* Weinbrand, *der;*
Kognak, *der*
brash /bræʃ/ *adj.* dreist
brass /brɑːs/ *n.* Messing, *das; attrib.*
Messing-; the ~ (Mus.) das Blech; **~ player**
(Mus.) Blechbläser, *der;* get down to ~ tacks
zur Sache kommen
brass 'band *n.* Blaskapelle, *die*
brassière /'bræzjə(r)/ *n.* Büstenhalter, *der*
brat /bræt/ *n.* Balg, *das od. der* (ugs.)
bravado /brə'vɑːdəʊ/ *n.* do sth. out of ~:
so waghalsig sein, etw. zu tun
brave /breɪv/ **1** *adj.* tapfer
2 *n.* [indianischer] Krieger

3 *v.t.* trotzen (+ *Dat.*)

'**bravely** *adv.* tapfer

bravery /'breɪvərɪ/ *n.* Tapferkeit, *die*

bravo /brɑː'vəʊ/ *int.* bravo

brawl /brɔːl/ 1 *v.i.* sich schlagen
2 *n.* Schlägerei, *die*

brawny /'brɔːnɪ/ *adj.* muskulös

bray /breɪ/ 1 Iah, *das*
2 *v.i.* ⟨*Esel:*⟩ iahen

brazen /'breɪzn/ 1 *adj.* dreist; (shameless)
schamlos
2 *v.t.* ~ [out] trotzen (+ *Dat.*); ~ it out (deny
guilt) es abstreiten; (not admit guilt) es nicht
zugeben

brazier /'breɪzɪə(r)/ *n.* Kohlenbecken, *das*

Brazil /brə'zɪl/ *pr. n.* Brasilien (*das*)

Bra'zil nut *n.* Paranuss, *die*

breach /briːtʃ/ 1 *n.* (a) (violation) Verstoß,
der; (of gegen); ~ of faith/duty
Vertrauensbruch, *der*/Pflichtverletzung, *die*
(b) (of relations) Bruch, *der*
(c) (gap) Bresche, *die;* (fig.) Riss, *der*
2 *v.t.* durchbrechen

bread /bred/ *n.* Brot, *das;* a piece of ~ and
butter ein Butterbrot

bread: ~ bin *n.* Brotkasten, *der;* ~board
n. [Brot]brett, *das;* ~crumb *n.* Brotkrume,
die; ~crumbs (coating) Paniermehl, *das;*
~ knife *n.* Brotmesser, *das;* ~line *n.* be
or live on/below the ~line gerade noch/nicht
einmal das Notwendigste zum Leben
haben; ~ 'roll *n.* Brötchen, *das*

breadth /bredθ/ *n.* Breite, *die*

'**breadwinner** *n.* Ernährer, *der*/
Ernährerin, *die*

break /breɪk/ 1 *v.t.*, broke /brəʊk/, broken
/'brəʊkn/ (a) brechen; (so as to damage)
zerbrechen; kaputtmachen (ugs.); zerreißen
⟨*Seil*⟩; (fig.: interrupt) unterbrechen; brechen
⟨*Bann, Zauber, Schweigen*⟩; the TV/my watch
is broken der Fernseher/meine Uhr ist
kaputt (ugs.); ~ the habit es sich (*Dat.*)
abgewöhnen
(b) (fracture) sich (*Dat.*) brechen ⟨*Arm, Bein
usw.*⟩
(c) brechen ⟨*Vertrag, Versprechen*⟩;
verstoßen gegen ⟨*Regel, Gesetz*⟩
(d) (surpass) brechen ⟨*Rekord*⟩
(e) (cushion) auffangen ⟨*Schlag, jmds. Fall*⟩
2 *v.i.*, broke, broken (a) kaputtgehen (ugs.);
⟨*Faden, Seil:*⟩ [zer]reißen; ⟨*Glas, Tasse,
Teller:*⟩ brechen; ⟨*Eis:*⟩ brechen; ~ in two/
in pieces durchbrechen/zerbrechen
(b) ~ into einbrechen in (+ *Akk.*) ⟨*Haus*⟩;
aufbrechen ⟨*Auto, Safe*⟩; ~ into laughter/
tears in Gelächter/Tränen ausbrechen;
~ into a trot/run zu traben/laufen anfangen
(c) (escape) ~ out of prison aus dem
Gefängnis ausbrechen; ~ free *or* loose sich
losreißen
(d) ⟨*Welle:*⟩ sich brechen (on/against an
+ *Dat.*)
(e) ⟨*Tag:*⟩ anbrechen; ⟨*Sturm:*⟩ losbrechen

(f) sb's voice is ~ing jmd. kommt in den
Stimmbruch
3 *n.* (a) Bruch, *der;* (of rope) Reißen, *das;* a
~ with sb./sth. ein Bruch mit jmdm./etw.
(b) (gap) Lücke, *die;* (broken place) Sprung, *der*
(c) (dash) they made a sudden ~: sie
stürmten plötzlich davon
(d) (interruption) Unterbrechung, *die;* (pause,
holiday) Pause, *die;* take *or* have a ~: Pause
machen
(e) (coll.: chance) Chance, *die*

▪ **break 'down** 1 *v.i.* zusammenbrechen;
⟨*Verhandlungen:*⟩ scheitern; ⟨*Auto:*⟩ eine
Panne haben
2 *v.t.* (a) aufbrechen ⟨*Tür*⟩; brechen
⟨*Widerstand*⟩; niederreißen ⟨*Barriere,
Schranke*⟩
(b) (analyse) aufgliedern

▪ **break 'in** 1 *v.i.* (into building etc.)
einbrechen
2 *v.t.* (a) zureiten ⟨*Pferd*⟩
(b) einlaufen ⟨*Schuhe*⟩
(c) ~ the door in die Tür aufbrechen

▪ '**break into** ▶ ~ 2B

▪ **break 'off** 1 *v.t.* abbrechen; abreißen
⟨*Faden*⟩; auflösen ⟨*Verlobung*⟩
2 *v.i.* (a) abbrechen
(b) (cease) aufhören

▪ **break 'out** *v.i.* ausbrechen; ~ out in
spots/a rash Pickel/einen Ausschlag
bekommen

▪ **break 'up** 1 *v.t.* (a) (~ into pieces)
zerkleinern; ausschlachten ⟨*Auto*⟩;
aufbrechen ⟨*Erde*⟩
(b) (disband) auflösen
2 *v.i.* (a) (~ into pieces, lit. or fig.) zerbrechen
(b) (disband) sich auflösen; ⟨*Schule:*⟩
schließen; ⟨*Schüler, Lehrer:*⟩ in die Ferien
gehen
(c) ~ up [with sb.] sich [von jmdm.] trennen

breakable /'breɪkəbl/ 1 *adj.* zerbrechlich
2 *n.* ~s zerbrechliche Dinge

breakage /'breɪkɪdʒ/ *n.* Zerbrechen, *das;*
~s must be paid for zerbrochene Ware muss
bezahlt werden

'**breakdown** *n.* (a) (of vehicle) Panne, *die;* (in
machine) Störung, *die;* ~ truck/van
Abschleppwagen, *der*
(b) (Med.) Zusammenbruch, *der*
(c) (analysis) Aufschlüsselung, *die*

'**breaker** *n.* (a) (wave) Brecher, *der*
(b) ~'s [yard] Autoverwertung, *die*

breakfast /'brekfəst/ 1 *n.* Frühstück, *das;*
for ~: zum Frühstück
2 *v.i.* frühstücken

breakfast: ~ cereal *n.* ≈
Frühstücksflocken *Pl.;* ~ 'television *n.*
Frühstücksfernsehen, *das*

'**break-in** *n.* Einbruch, *der*

'**breaking** ~ and entering (Law)
Einbruch, *der;* be at ~ point (mentally) die
Grenze der Belastbarkeit erreicht haben

break: ~neck *adj.* halsbrecherisch;   ⋯⟡

∼through n. Durchbruch, der; **∼up** n. Auflösung, die; (of relationship) Bruch, der; **∼water** n. Wellenbrecher, der

breast /brest/ n. Brust, die

breast: ∼bone n. Brustbein, das; **∼ cancer** n. Brustkrebs, der; **∼feed** v.t. & i. stillen; **∼stroke** n. Brustschwimmen, das

breath /breθ/ n. (a) Atem, der; **get one's ∼ back** wieder zu Atem kommen; **hold one's ∼:** den Atem anhalten; **be out of ∼:** außer Atem sein; **say sth. under one's ∼:** etw. vor sich (Akk.) hin murmeln (b) (one respiration) Atemzug, der

Breathalyser (Brit.), **Breathalyzer** ® /'breθəlaɪzə(r)/ n. Alcotest-Röhrchen ⓌⓏ, das; **∼ test** Alcotest ⓌⓏ, der

breathe /briːð/ ⓵ v.i. atmen; **∼ in** einatmen; **∼ out** ausatmen ⓶ v.t. (a) **∼ [in/out]** ein-/ausatmen (b) (utter) hauchen

'breather /'briːðə(r)/ n. Verschnaufpause, die

'breathing space n. Zeit zum Luftholen; (Fig.) Atempause, die

'breathless adj. atemlos (with vor + Dat.)

breath: ∼taking adj. atemberaubend; **∼ test** n. Alcotest ⓌⓏ, der

bred ▶ BREED 1, 2

breeches /'brɪtʃɪz/ n. pl. [pair of] ∼: [Knie]bundhose, die; [riding]∼: Reithose, die

breed /briːd/ ⓵ v.t., bred /bred/ (a) (cause) erzeugen (b) züchten ⟨Tiere, Pflanzen⟩ ⓶ v.i., bred sich vermehren ⓷ n. (of animals) Rasse, die

'breeding n. [good] ∼: gute Erziehung

'breeding ground n. (lit. or fig.) Brutstätte, die

breeze /briːz/ n. Brise, die

'breeze block n. (Building) ≈ Leichtstein, der

breezy /'briːzɪ/ adj. windig

brevity /'brevɪtɪ/ n. Kürze, die

brew /bruː/ ⓵ v.t. brauen ⟨Bier⟩; **∼ [up]** kochen ⟨Kaffee, Tee usw.⟩ ⓶ v.i. (a) ⟨Bier:⟩ gären; ⟨Kaffee, Tee:⟩ ziehen (b) ⟨Unwetter:⟩ sich zusammenbrauen ⓷ n. (brewed beer/tea) Bier, das/Tee, der

'brewer n. Brauer, der; (firm) Brauerei, die

brewery /'bruːərɪ/ n. Brauerei, die

bribe /braɪb/ ⓵ n. Bestechung, die ⓶ v.t. bestechen; **∼ sb. to do/into doing sth.** jmdn. bestechen, damit er etw. tut

bribery /'braɪbərɪ/ n. Bestechung, die

brick /brɪk/ ⓵ n. Ziegelstein, der; (toy) Bauklötzchen, das ⓶ adj. Ziegelstein-

brick: ∼layer n. Maurer, der; **∼laying** n. Mauern, das; **∼ 'wall** n. Backsteinmauer, die; **bang one's head against a ∼ wall** (fig.) mit dem Kopf gegen die Wand rennen (fig.)

bridal /'braɪdl/ adj. Braut-

bride /braɪd/ n. Braut, die

'bridegroom n. Bräutigam, der

bridesmaid /'braɪdzmeɪd/ n. Brautjungfer, die

bridge¹ /brɪdʒ/ ⓵ n. (a) Brücke, die (b) (Naut.) [Kommando]brücke, die (c) (of nose) Nasenbein, das (d) (of spectacles) Steg, der ⓶ v.t. eine Brücke bauen über (+ Akk.)

bridge² n. (Cards) Bridge, das

'bridging loan n. (Commerc.) Überbrückungskredit, der

bridle /'braɪdl/ n. Zaum, der

'bridle path n. Reitweg, der

brief¹ /briːf/ adj. (a) kurz; gering ⟨Verspätung⟩ (b) (concise) knapp; **in ∼, to be ∼:** kurz gesagt

brief² ⓵ n. (instructions) Instruktionen Pl.; (Law: case) Mandat, das ⓶ v.t. Instruktionen geben (+ Dat.); (inform) unterrichten

'briefcase n. Aktentasche, die

'briefing n. Briefing, das; (of reporters) Unterrichtung, die

'briefly adv. (a) kurz (b) (concisely) knapp; kurz

briefs /briːfs/ n. pl. [pair of] ∼: Slip, der

brigade /brɪ'geɪd/ n. (Mil.) Brigade, die

brigadier /brɪgə'dɪə(r)/ n. Brigadegeneral, der

bright /braɪt/ adj. (a) hell; grell ⟨Scheinwerfer[licht], Sonnenlicht⟩; strahlend ⟨Sonnenschein, Augen, Tag⟩; leuchtend ⟨Farbe, Blume⟩; **∼ intervals/periods** Aufheiterungen Pl. (b) (cheerful) fröhlich (c) (clever) intelligent

brighten /'braɪtn/ ⓵ v.t. **∼ [up]** aufhellen ⓶ v.i. **the weather** or **it is ∼ing [up]** es klärt sich auf

'brightly adv. (a) hell (b) (cheerfully) fröhlich

'brightness n. ▶ BRIGHT: (a) Helligkeit, die; Grelle, die; Strahlen, das; Leuchtkraft, die (b) Fröhlichkeit, die (c) Intelligenz, die

brilliance /'brɪlɪəns/ n. ▶ BRILLIANT: (a) Helligkeit, die; Leuchten, das (b) Genialität, die; Glanz, der

brilliant /'brɪljənt/ adj. (a) hell ⟨Licht⟩; leuchtend ⟨Farbe⟩ (b) genial ⟨Mensch, Gedanke, Leistung⟩; glänzend ⟨Verstand, Aufführung, Idee⟩

brim /brɪm/ ⓵ n. Rand, der; (of hat) [Hut]krempe, die ⓶ v.i., -mm-: **be ∼ming with sth.** randvoll mit etw. sein

brim-'full pred. adj. randvoll (**with** mit)

brine /braɪn/ n. Salzwasser, das

bring /brɪŋ/ *v.t.*, **brought** /brɔ:t/ (a) bringen; (as a present or favour) mitbringen; ~ sth. with one etw. mitbringen
(b) ~ sb. to do sth. jmdn. dazu bringen, etw. zu tun; **I could not ~ myself to do it** ich konnte es nicht über mich bringen, es zu tun
■ **bring a'bout** *v.t.* verursachen
■ **bring 'back** *v.t.* (a) (return) zurückbringen; (from a journey) mitbringen
(b) (recall) in Erinnerung bringen
(c) (restore, reintroduce) wieder einführen
■ **bring 'down** *v.t.* (a) herunterbringen
(b) (kill, wound) zur Strecke bringen
(c) senken ⟨Preise, Inflationsrate, Fieber⟩
■ **bring 'forward** *v.t.* (a) nach vorne bringen
(b) vorbringen ⟨Argument⟩; zur Sprache bringen ⟨Fall, Angelegenheit⟩
(c) vorverlegen ⟨Termin⟩ (to auf + Akk.)
■ **bring 'in** *v.t.* hereinbringen; einbringen ⟨Gesetzesvorlage, Verdienst, Summe⟩
■ **bring 'off** *v.t.* (conduct successfully) zustande bringen
■ **bring 'on** *v.t.* (a) (cause) verursachen
(b) (Sport) einsetzen
■ **bring 'out** *v.t.* (a) herausbringen
(b) hervorheben ⟨Unterschied⟩
(c) einführen ⟨Produkt⟩; herausbringen ⟨Buch, Zeitschrift⟩
■ **bring 'up** *v.t.* (a) heraufbringen
(b) (educate) erziehen; (rear) aufziehen
(c) zur Sprache bringen ⟨Angelegenheit, Thema, Problem⟩

brink /brɪŋk/ *n.* Rand, *der;* **be on the ~ of doing sth.** nahe daran sein, etw. zu tun
brisk /brɪsk/ *adj.* flott ⟨Gang⟩; forsch ⟨Person, Art⟩; frisch ⟨Wind⟩; (fig.) rege ⟨Handel, Nachfrage⟩; lebhaft ⟨Geschäft⟩
'briskly *adv.* flott
bristle /'brɪsl/ ① *n.* Borste, *die*
② *v.i.* (a) ~ [up] ⟨Haare:⟩ sich sträuben
(b) ~ with (fig.) starren vor (+ Dat.)
bristly /'brɪslɪ/ *adj.* borstig
Brit /brɪt/ *n.* (coll.) Brite, *der*/Britin, *die;* Engländer, *der*/Engländerin, *die* (ugs.)
Britain /'brɪtn/ *pr. n.* Großbritannien (*das*)
British /'brɪtɪʃ/ ① *adj.* britisch; **he/she is ~:** er ist Brite/sie ist Britin
② *n. pl.* **the ~:** die Briten
British 'Isles *pr. n. pl.* Britische Inseln
Briton /'brɪtn/ *n.* Brite, *der*/Britin, *die*
Brittany /'brɪtənɪ/ *pr. n.* Bretagne, *die*
brittle /'brɪtl/ *adj.* spröde ⟨Material⟩
broach /brəʊtʃ/ *v.t.* anschneiden ⟨Thema⟩
broad /brɔ:d/ *adj.* (a) breit; (extensive) weit ⟨Ebene, Land⟩; ausgedehnt ⟨Fläche⟩
(b) (explicit) klar ⟨Hinweis⟩; breit ⟨Lächeln⟩
(c) (main) grob; (generalized) allgemein
(d) stark ⟨Akzent⟩
broad 'bean *n.* Saubohne, *die*
broadcast /'brɔ:dkɑ:st/ ① *n.* Sendung, *die;* (live) Übertragung, *die*

② *v.t.*, **broadcast** senden; übertragen ⟨Livesendung⟩
③ *v.i.*, **broadcast** senden
'broadcaster *n.* (Radio, Telev.) jmd., *der durch häufige Auftritte im Rundfunk und Fernsehen, besonders als Interviewpartner, Diskussionsteilnehmer od. Kommentator, bekannt ist*
'broadcasting *n.* Senden, *das;* (live) Übertragen, *das;* **work in ~:** beim Funk arbeiten
broaden /'brɔ:dn/ ① *v.t.* (a) verbreitern
(b) ausweiten ⟨Diskussion⟩
② *v.i.* sich verbreitern; (fig.) sich erweitern
'broadly *adv.* (a) deutlich ⟨hinweisen⟩; breit ⟨grinsen, lächeln⟩
(b) (in general) allgemein ⟨beschreiben⟩; **~ speaking** allgemein gesagt
broad: ~'minded *adj.* tolerant;
~sheet *n.* (a) (Printing) Einblattdruck, *der;*
(b) (pamphlet) Flugblatt, *das;*
~'shouldered *adj.* breitschultrig;
~side *n.* Breitseite, *die*
brocade /brə'keɪd/ *n.* Brokat, *der*
broccoli /'brɒkəlɪ/ *n.* Brokkoli, *der*
brochure /'brəʊʃə(r)/ *n.* Broschüre, *die;* Prospekt, *der*
broil /'brɔɪl/ *v.t.* (esp. Amer.) grillen
broke /brəʊk/ ① ▶ BREAK 1, 2
② *pred. adj.* (coll.) pleite (ugs.)
broken /'brəʊkn/ ① ▶ BREAK 1, 2
② *adj.* (a) zerbrochen; gebrochen ⟨Bein, Hals⟩; verletzt ⟨Haut⟩; abgebrochen ⟨Zahn⟩; gerissen ⟨Seil⟩; kaputt (ugs.) ⟨Uhr, Fernsehen, Fenster⟩; **~ glass** Glasscherben *Pl.*
(b) (imperfect) gebrochen; **in ~ English** in gebrochenem Englisch
(c) (fig.) ruiniert ⟨Ehe⟩; gebrochen ⟨Mensch, Herz⟩
broken: ~-down *adj.* baufällig ⟨Gebäude⟩; kaputt (ugs.) ⟨Wagen⟩;
~'hearted *adj.* untröstlich
broker /'brəʊkə(r)/ *n.* Makler, *der*
brolly /'brɒlɪ/ *n.* (Brit. coll.) [Regen]schirm, *der*
bronchitis /brɒŋ'kaɪtɪs/ *n.* Bronchitis, *die*
bronze /brɒnz/ ① *n.* Bronze, *die*
② *attrib. adj.* Bronze-; (coloured like ~) bronzefarben
brooch /brəʊtʃ/ *n.* Brosche, *die*
brood /bru:d/ ① *n.* Brut, *die*
② *v.i.* [vor sich ⟨Akk.⟩ hin] brüten
brook /brʊk/ *n.* Bach, *der*
broom /bru:m/ *n.* (a) Besen, *der*
(b) (Bot.) Ginster, *der*
broom: ~ cupboard *n.* Besenschrank, *der;* **~stick** *n.* Besenstiel, *der*
broth /brɒθ/ *n.* Brühe, *die*
brothel /'brɒθl/ *n.* Bordell, *das*
brother /'brʌðə(r)/ *n.* Bruder, *der;* **my ~s and sisters** meine Geschwister ···⟩

'brotherhood n. (organization) Bruderschaft, die

'brother-in-law n., pl. brothers-in-law Schwager, der

brought ▶ BRING

brow /braʊ/ n. (a) (eye~) Braue, die
(b) (forehead) Stirn, die
(c) (of hill) Kuppe, die

'browbeat v.t., forms as BEAT 1 einschüchtern

brown /braʊn/ [1] adj. braun
[2] n. Braun, das

brown: ~ **'bread** n. ≈ Mischbrot, das;
~-**eyed** adj. braunäugig; be ~-eyed braune Augen haben

Brownie /'braʊnɪ/ n. Wichtel, die

brown: ~ **'paper** n. Packpapier, das;
~ **'rice** n. Naturreis, der

browse /braʊz/ v.i. [1] (a) weiden
(b) (in shop) sich umsehen; (read) blättern (through in + Dat.)
(c) (Comp.) suchen; ~ **through sth.** etw. durchsuchen
[2] (a) abgrasen ⟨Weide⟩; abfressen ⟨Blätter⟩
(b) (Comp.) ~ **sth** in etw. ⟨Dat.⟩ suchen

browser /'braʊzə(r)/ n. (Comp.) Browser, der

bruise /bruːz/ [1] n. (a) (Med.) blauer Fleck
(b) (on fruit) Druckstelle, die
[2] v.t. quetschen ⟨Obst, Pflanzen⟩;
~ **oneself/one's leg** sich stoßen/sich am Bein stoßen

brunch /brʌntʃ/ n. (coll.) Brunch, der;
ausgedehntes, spätes Frühstück

brunette /bruː'net/ [1] n. Brünette, die
[2] adj. brünett

brunt /brʌnt/ n. **bear the** ~ **of the attack/ financial cuts** von dem Angriff/von den Einsparungen am meisten betroffen sein

brush /brʌʃ/ [1] n. (a) Bürste, die; (for sweeping) Besen, der; (with short handle) Handfeger, der; (for painting or writing) Pinsel, der
(b) (skirmish) Zusammenstoß, der
(c) (light touch) flüchtige Berührung
[2] v.t. (a) kehren; fegen; abbürsten ⟨Kleidung⟩; ~ **one's teeth/hair** sich ⟨Dat.⟩ die Zähne putzen/die Haare bürsten
(b) (touch in passing) streifen
[3] v.i. ~ **past sb./sth.** jmdn./etw. streifen
■ **brush 'up** v.t. & i. ~ **up [on]** auffrischen ⟨Kenntnisse usw.⟩

brusque /brʊsk/ adj., **'brusquely** adv. schroff

Brussels /'brʌslz/ pr. n. Brüssel (das)

Brussels 'sprouts n. pl. Rosenkohl, der

brutal /'bruːtl/ adj. brutal

brutality /bruː'tælɪtɪ/ n. Brutalität, die

brutally /'bruːtəlɪ/ adv. brutal

brute /bruːt/ [1] n. (a) (animal) Bestie, die
(b) (person) Rohling, der
[2] attrib. adj. **by** ~ **force** mit roher Gewalt

B.Sc. abbr. = **Bachelor of Science**

BSE abbr. = **bovine spongiform encephalopathy** BSE

BST abbr. = **British Summer Time** Britische Sommerzeit

bubble /'bʌbl/ [1] n. Blase, die; (small) Perle, die
[2] v.i. ⟨Wasser, Schlamm, Lava⟩ Blasen bilden

bubble: ~ **bath** n. Schaumbad, das;
~ **pack** n. Klarsichtpackung, die;
~-**wrapped** adj. in Luftpolsterfolie verpackt

buck[1] /bʌk/ n. (deer, chamois) Bock, der; (rabbit, hare) Rammler, der

buck[2] n. **pass the** ~ **to sb.** jmdm. die Verantwortung aufhalsen

buck[3] (coll.) [1] v.i. ~ **'up** (a) (make haste) sich ranhalten (ugs.)
(b) (cheer up) ~ **up!** Kopf hoch!
[2] v.t. ~ **one's ideas up** (coll.) sich zusammenreißen

buck[4] n. (Amer. coll.) Dollar, der

bucket /'bʌkɪt/ n. Eimer, der

bucketful /'bʌkɪtfʊl/ n. Eimer [voll]

bucket: ~ **seat** n. Schalensitz, der;
~ **shop** n. [nicht ganz seriöses] Maklerbüro; (for air tickets) Reisebüro (das vor allem Billigflüge vermittelt)

buckle /'bʌkl/ [1] n. Schnalle, die
[2] v.t. (a) zuschnallen; ~ **sth. on/up** etw. anschnallen/festschnallen
(b) verbiegen ⟨Stoßstange, Rad⟩
[3] v.i. ⟨Rad, Metallplatte:⟩ [sich] verbiegen

bud /bʌd/ [1] n. Knospe, die; **come into** ~/**be in** ~: Knospen treiben
[2] v.i. -**dd**- Knospen treiben

Buddha /'bʊdə/ n. Buddha, der

Buddhism /'bʊdɪzm/ n. Buddhismus, der

Buddhist /'bʊdɪst/ [1] n. Buddhist, der/ Buddhistin, die
[2] adj. buddhistisch

budge /bʌdʒ/ [1] v.i. sich rühren;
⟨Gegenstand:⟩ sich bewegen
[2] v.t. bewegen

budgerigar /'bʌdʒərɪgɑː(r)/ n. Wellensittich, der

budget /'bʌdʒɪt/ [1] n. Etat, der; Haushalt[splan], der
[2] v.i. ~ **for sth.** etw. [im Etat] einplanen

'budget account n. Konto für laufende Zahlungen

budgie /'bʌdʒɪ/ n. (coll.) Wellensittich, der

buff /bʌf/ [1] adj. gelbbraun
[2] n. (coll.: enthusiast) Fan, der (ugs.)

buffalo /'bʌfələʊ/ n., pl. ~**es or same** Büffel, der

buffer /'bʌfə(r)/ n. Prellbock, der; (on vehicle; also fig.) Puffer, der

buffet /'bʊfeɪ/ n. Büfett, das

'buffet car n. Büfettwagen, der

bug /bʌg/ n. (also coll.: microphone) Wanze, die

bugger /'bʌɡə(r)/ (coarse) ①1 *n.* (as insult) Scheißkerl, *der* (derb)

②2 *v.t.* (damn) ~ you/him du kannst/der kann mich mal (derb); ~ it! ach du Scheiße! (derb)

■ ~ 'off *v.i.* abhauen (ugs.)

buggy /'bʌɡɪ/ *n.* (pushchair) Sportwagen, *der*

bugle /'bju:ɡl/ *n.* Bügelhorn, *das*

build /bɪld/ ①1 *v.t., built* /bɪlt/ bauen; (fig.) aufbauen ⟨System, Gesellschaft, Zukunft⟩

②2 *v.i.,* built bauen

③3 *n.* Körperbau, *der*

■ **build 'in** *v.t.* einbauen

■ **build 'on** *v.t.* aufbauen auf (+ *Dat.*); bebauen ⟨Gebiet⟩

■ **build 'up** ①1 *v.t.* aufhäufen ⟨Reserven, Mittel⟩; kräftigen ⟨Personen, Körper⟩; steigern ⟨Produktion, Kapazität⟩; stärken ⟨[Selbst]vertrauen⟩; aufbauen ⟨Firma, Geschäft⟩

②2 *v.i.* ⟨Spannung, Druck:⟩ zunehmen; ⟨Schlange, Rückstau:⟩ sich bilden; ⟨Verkehr:⟩ sich verdichten

'builder *n.* Bauunternehmer, *der*

'building *n.* (a) Bau, *der* (b) (structure) Gebäude, *das*

building: ~ **site** *n.* Baustelle, *die;* ~ **society** *n.* (Brit.) Bausparkasse, *die*

built ▶ BUILD 1, 2

built: ~**-in** *adj.* (a) eingebaut; Einbau⟨schrank, küche usw.⟩; (b) (fig.: instinctive) angeboren; ~**-up** *adj.* bebaut; ~**-up area** Wohngebiet, *das;* (Motor Veh.) geschlossene Ortschaft

bulb /bʌlb/ *n.* (a) (Bot., Hort.) Zwiebel, *die* (b) (of lamp) [Glüh]birne, *die*

Bulgaria /bʌl'ɡeərɪə/ *pr. n.* Bulgarien (*das*)

Bulgarian /bʌl'ɡeərɪən/ ①1 *adj.* bulgarisch; sb. is ~ *n.:* jmd. ist Bulgare/Bulgarin

②2 *n.* (a) (person) Bulgare, *der*/Bulgarin, *die* (b) (language) Bulgarisch, *das; see also* ENGLISH 2A

bulge /bʌldʒ/ ①1 *n.* Ausbeulung, *die;* ausgebeulte Stelle

②2 *v.i.* sich wölben

bulimia (nervosa) /bʊ'li:mɪə (nɜː'vəʊsə)/ *n.* Bulimie, *die;* Bulimia nervosa, *die* (fachspr.)

bulimic /bʊ'lɪmɪk/ ①1 *n.* Bulimiker, *der*/Bulimikerin, *die*

②2 *adj.* bulimisch

bulk /bʌlk/ *n.* (a) (large quantity) **in** ~: in großen Mengen

(b) (large shape) massige Gestalt

(c) (size) Größe, *die*

(d) (greater part) der größte Teil; (of population, votes) Mehrheit, *die*

bulk 'buying *n.* Großeinkauf, *der*

'bulky *adj.* sperrig ⟨Gegenstand⟩; massig ⟨Gestalt, Körper⟩

bull /bʊl/ *n.* Bulle, *der;* (esp. for bullfight) Stier, *der*

bull: ~ **bar** *n.* Rammschutz, *der;* Rammbügel, *der;* ~**dog** *n.* Bulldogge, *die*

bulldozer /'bʊldəʊzə(r)/ *n.* Planierraupe, *die*

bullet /'bʊlɪt/ *n.* Kugel, *die*

'bullet hole *n.* Einschuss, *der;* Einschussloch, *das*

bulletin /'bʊlɪtɪn/ *n.* Bulletin, *das*

'bulletin board *n.* (Comp.) schwarzes Brett

'bulletproof *adj.* kugelsicher

bull: ~**fight** *n.* Stierkampf, *der;* ~**fighter** *n.* Stierkämpfer, *der;* ~**fighting** *n.* Stierkämpfe *Pl.*

bullion /'bʊljən/ *n.* **gold** ~: Goldbarren *Pl.*

'bull neck *n.* Stiernacken, *der*

bullock /'bʊlək/ *n.* Ochse, *der*

bull: ~**ring** *n.* Stierkampfarena, *die;* ~**seye** *n.* (of target) Schwarze, *das;* ~**shit** (coarse) *n.* Scheiße, *die* (salopp abwertend)

bully /'bʊlɪ/ ①1 *n.* (schoolboy etc.) ≈ Rabauke, *der;* (boss) Tyrann, *der*

②2 *v.t.* schikanieren; (frighten) einschüchtern

bullying /'bʊlɪɪŋ/ *n.* Schikanieren, *das*

bum¹ /bʌm/ *n.* (Brit. coll.) Hintern, *der* (ugs.)

bum² *n.* (Amer. coll.: tramp) Penner, *der* (salopp)

bumble-bee /'bʌmblbi:/ *n.* Hummel, *die*

bumf /bʌmf/ *n.* (Brit. coll. derog.: papers) Papierkram, *der* (ugs.)

bump /bʌmp/ ①1 *n.* (a) (sound) Bums, *der;* (impact) Stoß, *der*

(b) (swelling) Beule, *die*

(c) (hump) Buckel, *der* (ugs.)

②2 *adv.* bums

③3 *v.t.* anstoßen

■ **'bump into** *v.t.* (a) stoßen an (+ *Akk.*)

(b) (meet by chance) zufällig [wieder]treffen

'bumper ①1 *n.* Stoßstange, *die;* ~**-to-**~ Stoßstange an Stoßstange

②2 *attrib. adj.* Rekord⟨ernte, -jahr⟩

'bumpy *adj.* holp[e]rig ⟨Straße, Fahrt, Fahrzeug⟩; uneben ⟨Fläche⟩; unruhig ⟨Flug⟩

bun /bʌn/ *n.* süßes Brötchen; (currant ~) Korinthenbrötchen, *das*

bunch /bʌntʃ/ *n.* (a) (of flowers) Strauß, *der;* (of grapes, bananas) Traube, *die;* (of parsley, radishes) Bund, *das;* ~ **of flowers/grapes** Blumenstrauß, *der*/Traube, *der;* **a** ~ **of keys** ein Schlüsselbund

(b) (lot) Anzahl, *die;* **the best or pick of the** ~: der/die/das Beste [von allen]

(c) (of people) Haufen, *der* (ugs.)

bundle /'bʌndl/ *n.* Bündel, *das;* (of papers) Packen, *der*

bung /bʌŋ/ ①1 *n.* Spund, *der*

②2 *v.t.* (coll.) schmeißen (ugs.)

■ **bung 'up** *v.i.* be/get ~**ed up** verstopft sein/verstopfen

bungalow /'bʌŋɡələʊ/ *n.* Bungalow, *der*

'bungee jumping /'bʌndʒɪ/ *n.* Bungeespringen, *das*

bungle /'bʌŋɡl/ *v.t.* stümpern bei

bunk /bʌŋk/ *n.* (in ship, lorry) Koje, *die;* (in sleeping car) Bett, *das;* (~ bed) Etagenbett, *das*

b

bunker /'bʌŋkə(r)/ n. Bunker, der

bunny /'bʌnɪ/ n. Häschen, das

buoy /bɔɪ/ n. Boje, die

buoyancy /'bɔɪənsɪ/ n. Auftrieb, der

buoyant /'bɔɪənt/ adj. (a) schwimmend; be ~: schwimmen

(b) (fig.) rege, lebhaft ⟨Markt⟩; heiter, munter ⟨Person⟩; **in ~ spirits** in Hochstimmung

burden /'bɜːdn/ 1 n. Last, die; **become a ~** (fig.) zur Last werden

2 v.t. belasten (with mit)

bureau /'bjʊərəʊ, bjʊə'rəʊ/ n. (a) (Brit.: writing desk) Sekretär, der

(b) (office) Büro, das

bureaucracy /bjʊə'rɒkrəsɪ/ n. Bürokratie, die

bureaucrat /'bjʊərəkræt/ n. Bürokrat, der/Bürokratin, die

bureaucratic /bjʊərə'krætɪk/ adj. bürokratisch

burger /'bɜːgə(r)/ n. (coll.) Hamburger, der

'burger bar n. (coll.) Hamburgerlokal, das

burglar /'bɜːglə(r)/ n. Einbrecher, der

burglar: ~ alarm n. Alarmanlage, die; **~-proof** adj. einbruch[s]sicher

burglary /'bɜːglərɪ/ n. Einbruch, der

burgle /'bɜːgl/ v.t. einbrechen in (+ Akk.); **the shop/he was ~d** in dem Laden/bei ihm wurde eingebrochen

burial /'berɪəl/ n. Begräbnis, das

burly /'bɜːlɪ/ adj. stämmig

Burma /'bɜːmə/ pr. n. Birma ⟨das⟩

Burmese /bɜː'miːz/ 1 adj. birmanisch; sb. **is ~:** jmd. ist Birmane/Birmanin

2 n., pl. same (a) (person) Birmane, der/ Birmanin, die

(b) (language) Birmanisch, das; see also ENGLISH 2A

burn /bɜːn/ 1 n. (on the skin) Verbrennung, die; (on material) Brandfleck, der

2 v.t., ~t /bɜːnt/ or ~ed (a) verbrennen; **~ oneself/one's hand** sich verbrennen/sich (Dat.) die Hand verbrennen; **~ a hole in sth.** ein Loch in etw. (Akk.) brennen

(b) als Brennstoff verwenden ⟨Gas, Öl usw.⟩; heizen mit ⟨Kohle, Holz, Torf⟩

(c) (spoil) anbrennen lassen ⟨Fleisch, Kuchen⟩; **be ~t** angebrannt sein

3 v.i., ~t or ~ed brennen; **~ to death** verbrennen; **she ~s easily** sie bekommt leicht einen Sonnenbrand

■ **burn 'down** v.t. & i. niederbrennen

'burned-out adj. (lit. or fig.) ausgebrannt

'burner n. Brenner, der

'burning adj. glühend ⟨Leidenschaft, Hass, Wunsch⟩; brennend ⟨Wunsch, Frage, Problem⟩

'burn-out n. Burn-out, das (Med.); totale Erschöpfung od. Entkräftung; **risk ~:** Gefahr laufen, sich zu übernehmen

burnt ▶ BURN 2, 3

'burnt-out ▶ BURNED-OUT

burp /bɜːp/ (coll.) 1 n. Rülpser, der (ugs.)

2 v.i. rülpsen (ugs.)

burrow /'bʌrəʊ/ 1 n. Bau, der

2 v.i. [sich (Dat.)] einen Gang graben

burst /bɜːst/ 1 n. (a) (split) Bruch, der

(b) (of firing) Salve, die

(c) (fig.) **a ~ of applause/cheering** ein Beifallsausbruch/Beifallsrufe Pl.

2 v.t., burst zum Platzen bringen; platzen lassen ⟨Luftballon⟩; **~ pipe** Rohrbruch, der

3 v.i., burst (a) platzen; ⟨Bombe:⟩ explodieren; ⟨Damm:⟩ brechen; ⟨Flussufer:⟩ überschwemmt werden; ⟨Furunkel, Geschwür:⟩ aufgehen

(b) **be ~ing with sth.** zum Bersten voll sein mit etw.; **be ~ing with pride/impatience/ excitement** vor Stolz/Ungeduld platzen/vor Aufregung außer sich sein

■ **'burst into** v.t. (a) eindringen in

(b) **~ into tears/laughter** in Tränen/ Gelächter ausbrechen; **~ into flames** in Brand geraten

■ **burst 'out** v.i. (a) herausstürzen

(b) (exclaim) losplatzen

(c) **~ out laughing/crying** in Lachen/Tränen ausbrechen

bury /'berɪ/ v.t. (a) begraben

(b) (hide) vergraben; **~ one's face in one's hands** das Gesicht in den Händen vergraben

(c) **~ one's teeth in sth.** seine Zähne in etw. (Akk.) graben

bus /bʌs/ n. Bus, der

bus: ~ company n. ≈ Verkehrsbetrieb, der; **~ conductor** n. Busschaffner, der/ -schaffnerin, die; **~ depot** ▶ ~ GARAGE; **~ driver** n. Busfahrer, der/-fahrerin, die; **~ fare** n. [Bus]fahrpreis, der; **~ garage** n. Busdepot, das

bush /bʊʃ/ n. (a) Busch, der

(b) (shrubs) Gebüsch, das

'bushy adj. buschig

busily /'bɪzɪlɪ/ adj. eifrig

business /'bɪznɪs/ n. (a) (trading operation) Geschäft, das; (company, firm) Betrieb, der; (large) Unternehmen, das; **how's ~ with you?** (lit. or fig.) was machen die Geschäfte [bei Ihnen]?; **~ is ~** (fig.) Geschäft ist Geschäft; **go out of ~:** Pleite gehen (ugs.); **go into ~:** Geschäftsmann-/frau werden

(b) (buying and selling) Geschäfte Pl.

(c) (task, province) Aufgabe, die; **mind your own ~!** kümmere dich um deine [eigenen] Angelegenheiten!

(d) (difficult matter) Problem, das

business: ~ address n. Geschäftsadresse, die; **~ card** n. Geschäftskarte, die; **~ class** 1 n., no pl. Businessklasse, die; attrib. Businessklasse-; 2 adv. **fly/travel ~ class** in der Businessklasse fliegen/reisen; **~ correspondence** n. Geschäftskorrespondenz, die; **~ hours** n. pl. Geschäftszeit, die; (in office) Dienstzeit, die; **~ letter** n. Geschäftsbrief, der; **~-like**

adj. geschäftsmäßig ⟨*Art*⟩; geschäftstüchtig
⟨*Person*⟩; ~ **lunch** *n.* Arbeitsessen, *das;*
~**man** *n.* Geschäftsmann, *der;* ~ **park** *n.*
Gewerbepark, *der;* ~ **plan** *n.*
Geschäftsplan, *der;* ~ **premises** *n. pl.*
Geschäftsräume *Pl.;* ~ **school** *n.*
kaufmännische Fachschule; ~ **studies** *n.*
pl. Wirtschaftslehre, *die;* ~ **trip** *n.*
Geschäftsreise, *die;* on a ~ trip auf
Geschäftsreise; ~**woman** *n.*
Geschäftsfrau, *die*

busker /'bʌskə(r)/ *n.* Straßenmusikant, *der*

bus: ~ **lane** *n.* (Brit.) Busspur, *die;* ~ **ride**
n. Busfahrt, *die;* B. is only an hour's ~ ride
away B. ist nur eine Busstunde entfernt;
~ **route** *n.* Buslinie, *die;* ~ **service** *n.*
Omnibusverkehr, *der;* (specific service)
Busverbindung, *die;* ~ **shelter** *n.*
Wartehäuschen, *das;* ~ **station** *n.*
Omnibusbahnhof, *der;* ~ **stop** *n.*
Bushaltestelle, *die*

bust[1] /bʌst/ *n.* (a) (sculpture) Büste, *die*
(b) ~ [**measurement**] Oberweite, *die*

bust[2] (coll.) [1] *adj.* kaputt (ugs.)
[2] *v.t.,* ~ed *or* bust (break) kaputtmachen
(ugs.); ~ **sth. open** etw. aufbrechen
[3] *v.i.,* ~ed *or* bust kaputtgehen (ugs.)

bus: ~ **terminal** *n.* Busbahnhof, *der;*
~ **ticket** *n.* Busfahrkarte, *die;*
Busfahrschein, *der*

bustle /'bʌsl/ [1] *v.i.* ~ about geschäftig hin
und her eilen
[2] *n.* Betrieb, *der*

bustling /'bʌslɪŋ/ *adj.* belebt ⟨*Straße,
Stadt, Markt usw.*⟩; rege ⟨*Tätigkeit*⟩

busy /'bɪzɪ/ [1] *adj.* (a) beschäftigt (at, with
mit); arbeitsreich ⟨*Leben*⟩; ziemlich hektisch
⟨*Zeit*⟩; I'm ~ now ich habe jetzt zu tun; he
was ~ packing er war mit Packen
beschäftigt
(b) (Amer. Teleph.) besetzt
[2] *v. refl.* ~ oneself sich beschäftigen (with
mit)

'busybody *n.* G[e]schaftlhuber, *der*

but [1] /bət, stressed bʌt/ *conj.* aber;
correcting after a negative sondern; not that
book ~ this one nicht das Buch, sondern
dieses
[2] /bət/ *prep.* außer (+ *Dat.*); the next/last
~ one der/die/das übernächste/vorletzte

butcher /'bʊtʃə(r)/ [1] *n.* Fleischer, *der/*
Fleischerin, *die*
[2] *v.t.* (murder) niedermetzeln

butler /'bʌtlə(r)/ *n.* Butler, *der*

butt[1] /bʌt/ *n.* (a) (of rifle) Kolben, *der*
(b) (of cigarette, cigar) Stummel, *der*

butt[2] *n.* (object of teasing or ridicule)
Zielscheibe, *die*

butt[3] [1] *n.* (push) (by person) [Kopf]stoß, *der;*
(by animal) Stoß [mit den Hörnern]
[2] *v.t. & i.* mit dem Kopf/den Hörnern
stoßen

■ **butt 'in** *v.i.* dazwischenreden

butter /'bʌtə(r)/ [1] *n.* Butter, *die*

[2] *v.t.* buttern

butter: ~ **bean** *n.* Mondbohne, *die;*
~**cup** *n.* Butterblume, *die;* ~ **dish** *n.*
Butterdose, *die;* ~**fingers** *n. sing.*
Tollpatsch, *der (beim Fangen usw.);* ~**fly**
(a) Schmetterling, *der;* (b) ~**fly** [**stroke**]
Delphinstil, *der;* ~ **mountain** *n.*
Butterberg, *der*

buttock /'bʌtək/ *n.* Hinterbacke, *die;*
Gesäßhälfte, *die;* ~s Gesäß, *das*

button /'bʌtn/ [1] *n.* Knopf, *der*
[2] *v.t.* ~ [up] zuknöpfen

'buttonhole [1] *n.* (a) Knopfloch, *das*
(b) (flower) Knopflochblume, *die*
[2] *v.t.* zu fassen kriegen (ugs.)

buttress /'bʌtrɪs/ *n.* (Archit.) Mauerstütze,
die

buxom /'bʌksəm/ *adj.* drall

buy /baɪ/ [1] *v.t.,* **bought** /bɔːt/ kaufen;
~ **sb./oneself sth.** jmdm./sich etw. kaufen
[2] *n.* [Ein]kauf, *der;* be a good ~: preiswert
sein

■ **buy 'up** *v.t.* aufkaufen

'buyer *n.* (a) Käufer, *der/*Käuferin, *die*
(b) (Commerc.) Einkäufer, *der/*Einkäuferin,
die

'buying power /'baɪɪŋ/ *n.* Kaufkraft, *die*

'buyout *n.* Aufkauf, *der;* Management-Buy-
Out, *das* (Wirtsch.)

buzz /bʌz/ [1] *n.* Summen, *das*
[2] *v.i.* summen

■ **buzz 'off** *v.i.* (coll.) abhauen (salopp)

'buzzer *n.* Summer, *der*

by /baɪ/ [1] *prep.* (a) (near, beside) an (+ *Dat.*);
bei; (next to) neben; ~ the window/river am
Fenster/Fluss
(b) (to position beside) zu
(c) (about, in the possession of) bei
(d) [all] by herself/himself etc. [ganz]
allein[e]
(e) (along) entlang; (via) über (+ *Akk.*)
(f) (passing) vorbei an (+ *Dat.*)
(g) (during) bei; by day/night bei Tag/Nacht
(h) (through the agency of) von; written by ...:
geschrieben von ...
(i) (through the means of) durch; by bus/ship
etc. mit dem Bus/Schiff *usw.;* by air/sea mit
dem Flugzeug/Schiff
(j) (not later than) bis; by now/this time
inzwischen
(k) (indicating unit) pro; by the minute/hour pro
Minute/Stunde; day by day/month by month
Tag für Tag/Monat für Monat; 10 ft. by 20 ft.
10 [Fuß] mal 20 Fuß
(l) (indicating amount) one by one einzeln; two
by two/three by three zu zweit/dritt
(m) (indicating factor) durch; 8 divided by 2 is 4
8 geteilt durch 2 ist 4
(n) (indicating extent) um; wider by a foot um
einen Fuß breiter
(o) (according to) nach
[2] *adv.* (a) (past) vorbei
(b) (near) close/near by in der Nähe
(c) by and large im Großen und Ganzen

bye[-bye] /'baɪ(baɪ)/ *int.* (coll.) tschüs (ugs.)

bye-law ▶ BY-LAW

'by-election *n.* Nachwahl, *die*

bygone /'baɪɡɒn/ *adj.* vergangen

'by-law *n.* (esp. Brit.) Verordnung, *die*

'bypass **1** *n.* **(a)** Umgehungsstraße, *die*
(b) (Med.) Bypass, *der;* ∼ **surgery** (Med.) eine
Bypassoperation/Bypassoperationen *Pl.*
2 *v.t.* **(a) the road** ∼**es the town** die Straße
führt um die Stadt herum

(b) (fig.) übergehen

'by-product *n.* Nebenprodukt, *das*

'byroad *n.* Nebenstraße, *die*

bystander /'baɪstændə(r)/ *n.* Zuschauer,
der/Zuschauerin, *die*

byte /'baɪt/ *n.* (Comp.) Byte, *das*

'byway *n.* Seitenweg, *der*

'byword *n.* Inbegriff, *der* (**for** Gen.)

Cc

C, c /siː/ *n.* C, c, *das*

C. *abbr.* **(a)** = **Celsius** C
(b) = **Centigrade** C

cab /kæb/ *n.* **(a)** (taxi) Taxi, *das*
(b) (of lorry, truck) Fahrerhaus, *das;* (of train)
Führerstand, *der*

cabaret /'kæbəreɪ/ *n.* Varietee, *das;*
(satirical) Kabarett, *das*

cabbage /'kæbɪdʒ/ *n.* Kohl, *der;* red/white
∼: Rot-/Weißkohl, *der*

'cab driver *n.* Taxifahrer, *der*/-fahrerin, *die*

cabin /'kæbɪn/ *n.* (in ship) (for passengers)
Kabine, *die;* (for crew) Kajüte, *die;* (in aircraft)
Kabine, *die*

cabinet /'kæbɪnɪt/ *n.* **(a)** Schrank, *der;* (in
bathroom, for medicines) Schränkchen, *das;*
[display] ∼: Vitrine, *die*
(b) the C∼ (Polit.) das Kabinett; **C**∼ **Minister**
Minister, *der*

cable /'keɪbl/ **1** *n.* **(a)** (rope) Kabel, *das;* (of
∼ car etc.) Seil, *das*
(b) (Electr., Teleph.) Kabel, *das*
(c) (message) Kabel, *das*
2 *v.t.* kabeln ⟨Mitteilung, Nachricht⟩

cable: ∼ **car** *n.* Drahtseilbahn, *die;*
∼ **'television,** ∼ **T'V** *ns.* Kabelfernsehen,
das

'cab rank *n.* (Brit.) Taxistand, *der;*
Droschken[halte]platz, *der* (Amtsspr.)

cache /kæʃ/ *n.* geheimes [Waffen-/Proviant-]
lager

cackle /'kækl/ **1** *n.* **(a)** (of hen) Gackern,
das
(b) (laughter) [meckerndes] Gelächter
2 *v.i.* **(a)** ⟨Henne:⟩ gackern
(b) (laugh) meckernd lachen

cactus /'kæktəs/ *n., pl.* **cacti** /'kæktaɪ/ *or*
∼**es** Kaktus, *der*

CAD *abbr.* = **computer-aided design**
CAD

caddie /'kædɪ/ *n.* (Golf) Caddie, *der*

caddy /'kædɪ/ *n.* Dose, *die*

cadet /kə'det/ *n.* Offiziersschüler, *der;*
naval/police ∼: Marinekadett/Anwärter für
den Polizeidienst

cadge /kædʒ/ *v.t.* [sich ⟨Dat.⟩] erbetteln

café, cafe /'kæfeɪ/ *n.* Lokal, *das;* (tea room)
Café, *das*

cafeteria /kæfɪ'tɪərɪə/ *n.* Cafeteria, *die*

cafetière /kæfə'tjeə/ *n.* Kaffeebereiter, *der*

caffeinated /'kæfɪneɪtɪd/ *adj.* koffeinhaltig

caffeine /'kæfiːn/ *n.* Koffein, *das*

cage /keɪdʒ/ **1** *n.* **(a)** Käfig, *der*
(b) (of lift) Fahrkabine, *die*
2 *v.t.* einsperren

cagey /'keɪdʒɪ/ *adj.* (coll.) zugeknöpft (ugs.);
be ∼ about sth. mit etw. hinterm Berg
halten (ugs.)

Cairo /'kaɪərəʊ/ *pr. n.* Kairo ⟨das⟩

cajole /kə'dʒəʊl/ *v.t.* ∼ sb. into sth./doing
sth. jmdm. etw. einreden/jmdm. einreden,
etw. zu tun

cake /keɪk/ **1** *n.* Kuchen, *der;* a ∼ of soap
ein Riegel *od.* Stück Seife
2 *v.t.* verkrusten; ∼d with dirt/blood
schmutz-/blutverkrustet

cal. *abbr.* = **calorie[s]** cal.

calamity /kə'læmɪtɪ/ *n.* Unheil, *das*

calcium /'kælsɪəm/ *n.* Kalzium, *das*

calculate /'kælkjʊleɪt/ **1** *v.t.* **(a)**
berechnen; (by estimating) ausrechnen
(b) be ∼d to do sth. darauf abzielen, etw. zu
tun
2 *v.i.* ∼ on doing sth. damit rechnen, etw.
zu tun

'calculated *adj.* kalkuliert ⟨Risiko⟩;
vorsätzlich ⟨Handlung⟩

calculation /kælkjʊ'leɪʃn/ *n.* **(a)** (result)
Rechnung, *die;* he is out in his ∼s er hat
sich verrechnet
(b) (calculating) Berechnung, *die*

calculator /'kælkjʊleɪtə(r)/ *n.* Rechner, *der*

calculus /'kælkjuːləs/ *n.* differential/integral ∼: Differenzial-/Integralrechnung, *die*

calendar /'kælɪndə(r)/ *n.* Kalender, *der; attrib.* Kalender-

calf¹ /kɑːf/ *n., pl.* **calves** Kalb, *das*

calf² *n., pl.* **calves** (Anat.) Wade, *die*

calibre (*Brit.; Amer.:* **caliber**) /'kælɪbə(r)/ *n.* Kaliber, *das*

calico /'kælɪkəʊ/ *n.* Kattun, *der*

California /kælɪ'fɔːnɪə/ *pr. n.* Kalifornien (*das*)

caliper ▶ CALLIPER

call /kɔːl/ **1** *v.i.* (a) rufen; ∼ to sb. jmdm. etwas zurufen; ∼ [out] for help um Hilfe rufen
(b) (*pay brief visit*) [kurz] besuchen (at *Akk.*); ∼ on sb. jmdn. besuchen; ∼ round vorbeikommen (ugs.); ∼ at a port/station einen Hafen anlaufen/an einem Bahnhof halten
(c) (Teleph.) who is ∼ing, please? wer spricht da, bitte?; thank you for ∼ing vielen Dank für Ihren Anruf!
2 *v.t.* (a) rufen; aufrufen (*Namen, Nummer*)
(b) (*cry to, summon*) rufen; (to a duty, to do sth.) aufrufen
(c) (by radio/telephone) rufen/anrufen; (initially) Kontakt aufnehmen mit
(d) (rouse) wecken
(e) einberufen (*Konferenz*); ausrufen (*Streik*)
(f) (name) nennen; he is ∼ed Bob er heißt Bob; what is it ∼ed in English? wie heißt das auf Englisch?
3 *n.* (a) Ruf, *der;* a ∼ for help ein Hilferuf; be on ∼: Bereitschaftsdienst haben
(b) (visit) Besuch, *der;* make *or* pay a ∼ on sb., make *or* pay sb. a ∼: jmdn. besuchen
(c) (telephone ∼) Anruf, *der;* give sb. a ∼: jmdn. anrufen; make a ∼: telefonieren
(d) (invitation, summons) Aufruf, *der*
(e) (need, occasion) Anlass, *der*
■ **call 'back 1** *v.t.* zurückrufen
2 *v.i.* zurückrufen; (come back) zurückkommen
■ **'call for** *v.t.* (a) (send for, order) bestellen
(b) (collect) abholen
(c) (require, demand) erfordern; this ∼s for a celebration das muss gefeiert werden
■ **'call 'in 1** *v.i.* vorbeikommen (ugs.) (on bei)
2 *v.t.* zu Rate ziehen (*Fachmann usw.*)
■ **call 'off** *v.t.* absagen (*Treffen, Verabredung*); rückgängig machen (*Geschäft*); lösen (*Verlobung*); (end) abbrechen (*Streik*)
■ **'call on** *v.t.* (a) ▶ ∼ 1B
(b) ▶ ∼ [UP]ON
■ **call 'out 1** *v.t.* alarmieren (*Truppen*); zum Streik aufrufen (*Arbeitnehmer*)
2 *v.i.* ▶ ∼ 1A
■ **call 'up** *v.t.* (a) (by telephone) anrufen
(b) (Mil.) einberufen
■ **'call [up]on** *v.t.* ∼ upon sb.'s generosity

an jmds. Großzügigkeit (*Akk.*) appellieren; ∼ [up]on sb. to do sth. jmdn. auffordern, etw. zu tun

'call box *n.* Telefonzelle, *die*

'caller *n.* (visitor) Besucher, *der*/Besucherin, *die;* (on telephone) Anrufer, *der*/Anruferin, *die*

'call girl *n.* Callgirl, *das*

'calling *n.* Beruf, *der*

calliper /'kælɪpə(r)/ *n.* (a) [a pair of] ∼s Tasterzirkel, *der*
(b) (Med.) Beinschiene, *die*

callous /'kæləs/ *adj.* gefühllos; herzlos (*Handlung, Verhalten*)

'call-up *n.* (Mil.) Einberufung, *die*

calm /kɑːm/ **1** *n.* (stillness) Stille, *die;* (serenity) Ruhe, *die*
2 *adj.* ruhig
3 *v.t.* ∼ sb. [down] jmdn. beruhigen
4 *v.i.* ∼ [down] sich beruhigen

'calmly *adv.* ruhig; gelassen

'calmness *n.* Ruhe, *die;* (of water) Stille, *die*

Calor gas ® /'kælə gæs/ *n.* Butangas, *das*

calorie /'kælərɪ/ *n.* Kalorie, *die*

calorific /kælə'rɪfɪk/ *adj.* ∼ value Heizwert, *der*

calves *pl. of* CALF¹, ²

CAM *abbr.* = **computer-aided manufacturing** CAM

camber /'kæmbə(r)/ *n.* Wölbung, *die*

camcorder /'kæmkɔːdə(r)/ *n.* Camcorder, *der;* Kamerarecorder, *der*

came ▶ COME

camel /'kæml/ *n.* Kamel, *das*

camera /'kæmərə/ *n.* Kamera, *die*

camera: ∼ **case** *n.* Kameratasche, *die;* ∼ **crew** *n.* Kamerateam, *das;* ∼**man** *n.* Kameramann, *der;* ∼**work** *n., no indef. art.* Kameraführung, *die*

camomile /'kæməmaɪl/ *n.* Kamille, *die;* ∼ **tea** Kamillentee, *der*

camouflage /'kæməflɑːʒ/ **1** *n.* Tarnung, *die*
2 *v.t.* tarnen

camp /kæmp/ **1** *n.* Lager, *das*
2 *v.i.* ∼ [out] campen; (in tent) zelten; go ∼ing Campen/Zelten fahren/gehen

campaign /kæm'peɪn/ **1** *n.* (a) (Mil.) Feldzug, *der*
(b) (organized action) Kampagne, *die;* publicity ∼: Werbekampagne, *die*
2 *v.i.* ∼ for/against sth. sich für etw. einsetzen/gegen etw. etwas unternehmen; be ∼ing (*Politiker:*) im Wahlkampf stehen

'camp bed *n.* Campingliege, *die*

'camper *n.* (person) Camper, *der*/Camperin, *die*

'campfire *n.* Lagerfeuer, *das*

'camping *n.* Camping, *das;* (in tent) Zelten, *das*

camping: ∼ **ground** ▶ ∼ SITE; ⋯⟡

~ **holiday** n. Campingurlaub, der; ~ **site** n. Campingplatz, der; ~ **stove** n. Campingkocher, der

'**campsite** n. Campingplatz, der

campus /'kæmpəs/ n. Campus, der

can¹ /kæn/ ⊡ n. (a) (milk ~, watering ~) Kanne, die; (for oil, petrol) Kanister, der; (Amer.: for refuse) Eimer, der
(b) (for preserving) [Konserven]dose, die; a ~ of tomatoes/beer eine Dose Tomaten/Bier
⊡ v.t., -nn- konservieren

can² /kən, stressed kæn/ v. aux., only in pres. can, neg. cannot /'kænət/, (coll.) can't /kɑːnt/, past could /kʊd/, neg. (coll.) couldn't /'kʊdnt/ können; (have right, be permitted) dürfen; können; I can't do that das kann ich nicht; (it would be wrong) das kann ich nicht tun; you can't smoke here hier dürfen Sie nicht rauchen; could you ring me tomorrow? könnten Sie mich morgen anrufen?; I could have killed him ich hätte ihn umbringen können; [that] could be [so] das könnte od. kann sein

Canada /'kænədə/ pr. n. Kanada (das)

Canadian /kə'neɪdɪən/ ⊡ adj. kanadisch; sb. is ~: jmd. ist Kanadier/Kanadierin
⊡ n. Kanadier, der/Kanadierin, die

canal /kə'næl/ n. Kanal, der

canary /kə'neərɪ/ n. Kanarienvogel, der

Ca'nary Islands pr. n. pl. Kanarische Inseln Pl.

cancel /'kænsl/ ⊡ v.t., (Brit.) -ll- (a) absagen ⟨Besuch, Urlaub, Reise, Sportveranstaltung⟩; ausfallen lassen ⟨Veranstaltung, Vorlesung, Zug, Bus⟩; fallen lassen ⟨Pläne⟩; rückgängig machen ⟨Einladung, Vertrag⟩; zurücknehmen ⟨Befehl⟩; stornieren ⟨Bestellung, Auftrag⟩; kündigen ⟨Abonnement⟩; abbestellen ⟨Zeitung⟩
(b) (Comp.) abbrechen
⊡ v.i., (Brit.) -ll-: (a) ~ [out] sich [gegenseitig] aufheben
(b) (Comp.) abbrechen

cancellation /kænsə'leɪʃn/ n. ▶ CANCEL 1A: Absage, die; Ausfall, der; Fallenlassen, das; Rückgängigmachen, das; Zurücknahme, die; Stornierung, die; Kündigung, die; Abbestellung, die

cancer /'kænsə(r)/ n. (a) (Med.) Krebs, der; ~ of the liver Leberkrebs, der
(b) C~ (Astrol., Astron.) der Krebs

candelabra /kændɪ'lɑːbrə/ n. Leuchter, der

candid /'kændɪd/ adj. offen; ehrlich ⟨Ansicht, Bericht⟩

candidate /'kændɪdət, 'kændɪdeɪt/ n. Kandidat, der/Kandidatin, die

candle /'kændl/ n. Kerze, die

candle: ~**light** n. Kerzenlicht, das; ~**stick** n. Kerzenhalter, der; (elaborate) Leuchter, der; ~**wick** n. (material) Frottierplüsch, der

candour (Brit., Amer.: **candor**) /'kændə(r)/ n. ▶ CANDID: Offenheit, die; Ehrlichkeit, die

candy /'kændɪ/ n. (Amer.) (sweets) Süßigkeiten Pl.; (sweet) Bonbon, das od. der

'**candyfloss** /'kændɪflɒs/ n. Zuckerwatte, die

cane /keɪn/ ⊡ n. (a) (stem) Rohr, das; (of raspberry, blackberry) Spross, der
(b) (material) Rohr, das
(c) (stick) [Rohr]stock, der
⊡ v.t. [mit dem Stock] schlagen

'**cane sugar** n. Rohrzucker, der

canine /'keɪnaɪn/ adj. (a) (of dog[s]) Hunde-
(b) ~ tooth Eckzahn, der

canister /'kænɪstə(r)/ n. Büchse, die; (for petrol, oil, etc.) Kanister, der

cannabis /'kænəbɪs/ n. (hashish) Haschisch, das; (marijuana) Marihuana, das

canned /kænd/ adj. Dosen-; in Dosen nachgestellt; ~ meat/fruit Fleisch-/Obstkonserven Pl.; ~ beer Dosenbier; ~ food [Lebensmittel]konserven Pl.; ~ music Musikkonserve, die

cannibal /'kænɪbl/ n. Kannibale, der/Kannibalin, die

cannibalism /'kænɪbəlɪzm/ n. Kannibalismus, der

cannon /'kænən/ ⊡ n. Kanone, die
⊡ v.i. (Brit.) ~ into sb./sth. mit etw./jmdm. zusammenprallen

'**cannon ball** n. Kanonenkugel, die

cannot ▶ CAN²

canny /'kænɪ/ adj. (shrewd) schlau

canoe /kə'nuː/ n. Paddelboot, das; (Indian ~, Sport) Kanu, das

canoeing /kə'nuːɪŋ/ n. Paddeln, das; (Sport) Kanufahren, das; Kanusport, der

canoeist /kə'nuːɪst/ n. Paddelbootfahrer, der/-fahrerin, die

canon /'kænən/ n. (a) (general law, criterion) Grundregel, die
(b) (Eccl.: person) Kanoniker, der

canonize /'kænənaɪz/ v.t. kanonisieren ⟨Heiligen⟩; heilig sprechen ⟨Märtyrer⟩

'**can-opener** n. Dosenöffner, der

canopy /'kænəpɪ/ n. Baldachin, der; (over entrance) Vordach, das

can't /kɑːnt/ (coll.) = CANNOT; ▶ CAN²

cantankerous /kæn'tæŋkərəs/ adj. streitsüchtig

canteen /kæn'tiːn/ n. Kantine, die

canter /'kæntə(r)/ ⊡ n. Handgalopp, der
⊡ v.i. leicht galoppieren

canvas /'kænvəs/ n. Leinwand, die

canvass /'kænvəs/ ⊡ v.t. Wahlwerbung treiben in ⟨einem Wahlkreis, Gebiet⟩; Wahlwerbung treiben bei ⟨Wählern, Bürgern⟩
⊡ v.i. werben (on behalf of für); ~ for votes um Stimmen werben

'**canvasser** n. (for votes) Wahlhelfer, der/

-helferin, *die*

canyon /'kænjən/ *n.* Cañon, *der*

cap /kæp/ ① *n.* (a) Mütze, *die;* (nurse's, servant's) Haube, *die;* (with peak) Schirmmütze, *die;* (skull⁓) Kappe, *die*
(b) (of bottle, jar) [Verschluss]kappe, *die;* (petrol ⁓, radiator ⁓) Deckel, *der*
② *v.t., -pp-:* (a) verschließen ⟨*Flasche*⟩; zudecken ⟨*Bohrloch*⟩; mit einer Schutzkappe versehen ⟨*Zahn*⟩
(b) (fig.) überbieten; **to ⁓ it all** obendrein

CAP *abbr.* = **Common Agricultural Policy** gemeinsame Agrarpolitik

capability /keɪpə'bɪlɪtɪ/ *n.* Fähigkeit, *die*

capable /'keɪpəbl/ *adj.* (a) **be ⁓ of sth.** ⟨*Person:*⟩ zu etw. imstande sein
(b) (gifted, able) fähig

capacity /kə'pæsɪtɪ/ *n.* (a) Fassungsvermögen, *das;* **the machine is working to ⁓:** die Maschine ist voll ausgelastet; **a seating ⁓ of 300** 300 Sitzplätze
(b) (measure) Rauminhalt, *der;* Volumen, *das;* **measure of ⁓:** Hohlmaß, *das*
(c) (position) Eigenschaft, *die;* **in his ⁓ as …:** in seiner Eigenschaft als …

cape¹ /keɪp/ *n.* (garment) Umhang, *der;* Cape, *das*

cape² *n.* (Geog.) Kap, *das;* **the C⁓** [**of Good Hope**] das Kap der Guten Hoffnung; **C⁓ Town** Kapstadt (*das*)

caper /'keɪpə(r)/ *v.i.* ⁓ [**about**] [herum]tollen

capful /'kæpfʊl/ *n.* **one ⁓:** der Inhalt einer Verschlusskappe

capillary /kə'pɪlərɪ/ *n.* Kapillare, *die* (fachspr.)

capital /'kæpɪtl/ ① *attrib. adj.* (a) Todes⟨*strafe, -urteil*⟩; Kapital⟨*verbrechen*⟩
(b) groß, Groß⟨*buchstabe*⟩
(c) (principal) Haupt⟨*stadt*⟩
② *n.* (a) (letter) Großbuchstabe, *der*
(b) (city, town) Hauptstadt, *die*
(c) (stock, wealth) Kapital, *das*

capitalism /'kæpɪtəlɪzm/ *n.* Kapitalismus, *der*

capitalist /'kæpɪtəlɪst/ ① *n.* Kapitalist, *der*/Kapitalistin, *die*
② *adj.* kapitalistisch

capitalize /'kæpɪtəlaɪz/ ① *v.t.* großschreiben ⟨*Buchstaben, Wort*⟩
② *v.i.* ⁓ **on sth.** aus etw. Kapital schlagen (ugs.)

capital 'punishment *n.* Todesstrafe, *die*

capitulate /kə'pɪtjʊleɪt/ *v.i.* kapitulieren

capitulation /kəpɪtjʊ'leɪʃn/ *n.* Kapitulation, *die*

cappuccino /kæpʊ'tʃiːnəʊ/ *n., pl.* ⁓s Cappuccino, *der*

capricious /kə'prɪʃəs/ *adj.* launisch

Capricorn /'kæprɪkɔːn/ *n.* (Astrol., Astron.) der Steinbock

capsize /kæp'saɪz/ ① *v.t.* zum Kentern bringen

② *v.i.* kentern

capsule /'kæpsjuːl/ *n.* Kapsel, *die*

Capt. *abbr.* = **Captain** Kapt.; Hptm.

captain /'kæptɪn/ ① *n.* Kapitän, *der;* (Army) Hauptmann, *der*
② *v.t.* ⁓ **a team** Kapitän einer Mannschaft sein

caption /'kæpʃn/ *n.* (heading) Überschrift, *die;* (under photograph, drawing) Bildunterschrift, *die;* (Cinemat., Telev.) Untertitel, *der*

captivate /'kæptɪveɪt/ *v.t.* fesseln

captivating /'kæptɪveɪtɪŋ/ *adj.* bezaubernd; einnehmend ⟨*Lächeln*⟩

captive /'kæptɪv/ ① *adj.* gefangen; **be taken ⁓:** gefangen genommen werden; **⁓ audience** unfreiwilliges Publikum
② *n.* Gefangener, *der*/Gefangene, *die*

captivity /kæp'tɪvɪtɪ/ *n.* Gefangenschaft, *die;* **be held in ⁓:** gefangen gehalten werden

captor /'kæptə(r)/ *n.* **his ⁓:** der, der/die, die ihn gefangen nahm

capture /'kæptʃə(r)/ ① *n.* (a) (of thief etc.) Festnahme, *die;* (of town) Einnahme, *die*
(b) (thing, person) Fang, *der*
② *v.t.* festnehmen ⟨*Person*⟩; [ein]fangen ⟨*Tier*⟩; einnehmen ⟨*Stadt*⟩; gefangen nehmen ⟨*Fantasie*⟩

car /kɑː(r)/ *n.* Auto, *das;* Wagen, *der;* **by ⁓:** mit dem Auto

carafe /kə'ræf/ *n.* Karaffe, *die*

caramel /'kærəmel/ *n.* Karamell, *der;* (toffee) Karamellbonbon, *das*

carat /'kærət/ *n.* Karat, *das;* **a 22-⁓ gold ring** in 22-karätiger Goldring

caravan /'kærəvæn/ *n.* (Brit.) Wohnwagen, *der*

'caravan site *n.* Campingplatz für Wohnwagen

carbohydrate /kɑːbəʊ'haɪdreɪt/ *n.* Kohlenhydrat, *das*

'car bomb *n.* Autobombe, *die*

carbon /'kɑːbən/ *n.* Kohlenstoff, *der*

carbon: ⁓ 'copy *n.* Durchschlag, *der;* **⁓ dioxide** /- daɪ'ɒksaɪd/ *n.* Kohlendyoxid, *das;* **⁓ mo'noxide** /-mə'nɒksaɪd/ *n.* (Chem.) Kohlenmonoxyd, *das;* **⁓ paper** *n.* Kohlepapier, *das*

car 'boot sale *n.:* Trödelmarkt, bei dem die Händler ihre Waren aus dem Kofferraum ihrer Autos heraus verkaufen

carburettor (Amer.: **carburetor**) /kɑːbə'retə(r)/ *n.* Vergaser, *der*

carcass (Brit. also: **carcase**) /'kɑːkəs/ *n.* Kadaver, *der*

'car crash *n.* Autounfall, *der*

card /kɑːd/ *n.* Karte, *die;* **play ⁓s** Karten spielen

card: ⁓board *n.* Pappe, *die;* **⁓board 'box** *n.* [Papp]karton, *der;* (smaller) [Papp]schachtel, *die;* **⁓ game** *n.* Kartenspiel, *das;* **⁓holder** *n.* Karteninhaber, *der*/-inhaberin, *die*

cardiac /'kɑːdɪæk/ adj. (of heart) Herz-
cardiac ar'rest n. Herzstillstand, der
cardigan /'kɑːdɪgən/ n. Strickjacke, die
cardinal /'kɑːdɪnl/ [1] adj. grundlegend
⟨Frage, Doktrin, Pflicht⟩; Kardinal⟨fehler,
-problem⟩; Haupt⟨punkt, -merkmal⟩
[2] n. (Eccl.) Kardinal, der
cardinal: ∼ 'number n. Kardinalzahl,
die; ∼ **'sin** n. Todsünde, die
'cardphone n. Kartentelefon, das
care /keə(r)/ [1] n. **(a)** (anxiety) Sorge, die
(b) (pains) Sorgfalt, die
(c) (caution) Vorsicht, die; **take** ∼: aufpassen
(d) medical ∼: ärztliche Betreuung
(e) (charge) Obhut, die (geh.); **put sb. in** ∼/
take sb. into ∼: jmdn. in Pflege geben/
nehmen; ∼ **of** (on letter) bei; **take** ∼ **of sb./sth.**
(ensure safety of) auf jmdn./etw. aufpassen;
(attend to) sich um jmdn./etw. kümmern
[2] v.i. ∼ **for sb./sth.** (look after) sich um
jmdn./etw. kümmern; (like) jmdn./etw. mögen;
∼ **to do sth.** etw. tun mögen; **I don't**
∼ [whether/how/what etc.] es ist mir
gleich[, ob/wie/was usw.]
career /kə'rɪə(r)/ [1] n. Beruf, der
[2] v.i. rasen; ⟨Pferd, Reiter:⟩ galoppieren
career: ∼ break n. Karriereknick, der;
∼**s adviser** n. Berufsberater, der/
-beraterin, die; ∼**s [advisory] service**
n. Berufsberatung, die; ∼ **woman** n.
Karrierefrau, die
'carefree adj. sorgenfrei
careful /'keəfl/ adj. (thorough) sorgfältig;
(cautious) vorsichtig; [be] ∼! Vorsicht!; **be**
∼ **of sb./sth.** (be cautious of) sich vor jmdm./
etw. in Acht nehmen; **be** ∼ **with sb./sth.**
vorsichtig mit jmdm./etw. umgehen
'carefully adv. (thoroughly) sorgfältig;
(attentively) aufmerksam; (cautiously) vorsichtig
careless /'keəlɪs/ adj. **(a)** (inattentive)
unaufmerksam; (thoughtless) gedankenlos;
leichtsinnig ⟨Fahrer⟩; nachlässig ⟨Arbeiter,
Arbeit⟩; gedankenlos ⟨Bemerkung,
Handlung⟩; unachtsam ⟨Fahren⟩
(b) (nonchalant) ungezwungen
'carelessly adv. (without care) nachlässig;
(thoughtlessly) gedankenlos
'carelessness n. (lack of care)
Nachlässigkeit, die; (thoughtlessness)
Gedankenlosigkeit, die
carer /'keərə(r)/ n. (for sick person) Pfleger,
der/Pflegerin, die
caress /kə'res/ [1] n. Liebkosung, die
[2] v.t. liebkosen
'caretaker n. Hausmeister, der/-meisterin,
die
'car ferry n. Autofähre, die
cargo /'kɑːgəʊ/ n. Fracht, die
'cargo boat, 'cargo ship ns. Frachter,
der
'car hire n. Autovermietung, die
Caribbean /kærɪ'biːən/ [1] n. **the** ∼: die
Karibik

[2] adj. karibisch
caricature /'kærɪkətjʊə(r)/ [1] n.
Karikatur, die
[2] v.t. karikieren
caring /'keərɪŋ/ adj. sozial ⟨Gesellschaft⟩;
fürsorglich ⟨Person⟩
carnage /'kɑːnɪdʒ/ n. Gemetzel, das
carnal /'kɑːnl/ adj. sinnlich
carnation /kɑː'neɪʃn/ n. [Garten]nelke, die
carnet /'kɑːneɪ/ n. (of motorist) Triptyk, das;
[camping] ∼: Ausweis für Camper
carnival /'kɑːnɪvl/ n. Volksfest, das
carnivorous /kɑː'nɪvərəs/ adj. Fleisch
fressend
carol /'kærl/ n. [Christmas] ∼:
Weihnachtslied, das
'car owner n. Autobesitzer, der/-besitzerin,
die
carp /kɑːp/ n., pl. same Karpfen, der
car: ∼ park n. Parkplatz, der; (building)
Parkhaus, das; ∼ **parking** n. Parken, das;
∼ **parking facilities are available** Parkplätze
[sind] vorhanden
carpenter /'kɑːpɪntə(r)/ n. Zimmermann,
der; (for furniture) Tischler, der/Tischlerin, die
carpentry /'kɑːpɪntrɪ/ n.
Zimmerhandwerk, das; (in furniture)
Tischlerhandwerk, das
carpet /'kɑːpɪt/ n. Teppich, der
carpet: ∼ slipper n. Hausschuh, der;
∼ **sweeper** n. Teppichkehrer, der
car: ∼ phone n. Autotelefon, das; ∼**port**
n. Einstellplatz, der; ∼ **radio** n. Autoradio,
das; ∼ **rental** ▶ CAR HIRE
carriage /'kærɪdʒ/ n. **(a)** (horse-drawn)
Kutsche, die
(b) (Railw.) Wagen, der
'carriageway n. Fahrbahn, die
'car ride n. Autofahrt, die
carrier /'kærɪə(r)/ n. **(a)** (bearer) Träger, der
(b) (firm) Transportunternehmen, das
carrier: ∼ bag n. Tragetasche, die;
∼ **pigeon** n. Brieftaube, die
carrot /'kærət/ n. Möhre, die
carry /'kærɪ/ v.t. **(a)** tragen; (emphasizing
destination) bringen
(b) (possess) besitzen ⟨Autorität, Gewicht⟩
■ **carry a'way** v.t. forttragen; **be** or **get**
carried away sich hinreißen lassen
■ **carry 'on** [1] v.t. fortführen; ∼ **on** [doing
sth.] weiterhin etw. tun
[2] v.i. weitermachen
■ **carry 'out** v.t. durchführen; ausführen
⟨Anweisung, Auftrag⟩; vornehmen
⟨Verbesserungen⟩
carry: ∼cot n. Babytragetasche, die;
∼**out** n. ∼**out** [meal] Essen od. Mahlzeit
zum Mitnehmen; **get a** ∼**out** sich (Dat.) in
einem Restaurant etw. zu essen holen
'carsick adj. **children are often** ∼: Kindern
wird beim Autofahren oft schlecht
cart /kɑːt/ [1] n. Wagen, der

2 *v.t.* (coll.) schleppen

'**car thief** *n.* Autodieb, *der/*-diebin, *die*

cartilage /'kɑ:tɪlɪdʒ/ *n.* Knorpel, *der*

carton /'kɑ:tn/ *n.* [Papp]karton, *der;* (of drink) Tüte, *die;* (of cream, yoghurt) Becher, *der*

cartoon /kɑ:'tu:n/ *n.* humoristische Zeichnung; (satirical) Karikatur, *die;* (film) Zeichentrickfilm, *der*

cartridge /'kɑ:trɪdʒ/ *n.* (a) (for gun) Patrone, *die*
(b) (of film; cassette) Kassette, *die*

'**cartwheel** *n.* (Gymnastics) Rad, *das;* turn *or* do ∼s Rad schlagen

carve /kɑ:v/ **1** *v.t.* (a) tranchieren ⟨*Fleisch, Braten, Hähnchen*⟩
(b) (from wood) schnitzen; (from stone) meißeln
2 *v.i.* ∼ **in wood/stone** in Holz schnitzen/in Stein meißeln

carving /'kɑ:vɪŋ/ *n.* (in or from wood) Schnitzerei, *die;* (in or from stone) Skulptur, *die*

'**carving knife** *n.* Tranchiermesser, *das*

'**car wash** *n.* Waschanlage, *die*

cascade /kæs'keɪd/ *n.* Kaskade, *die*

case¹ /keɪs/ *n.* (a) (instance, matter, set of arguments) Fall, *der;* it is [not] the ∼ that ...: es trifft [nicht] zu, dass ...; in ∼ ...: falls ...; [just] in ∼: für alle Fälle; in ∼ **of emergency** im Notfall; in any ∼: jedenfalls; in that ∼: in diesem Fall; in any ∼ (regardless of anything else) jedenfalls; I don't need it in any ∼: ich brauche es sowieso nicht
(b) (Med., Police, Soc. Serv., etc.) Fall, *der*
(c) (Law) Fall, *der;* (action) Verfahren, *das*
(d) (Ling.) Fall, *der;* Kasus, *der* (fachspr.)

case² *n.* (a) Koffer, *der;* (brief∼) [Akten]tasche, *die*
(b) (for spectacles, cigarettes) Etui, *das*
(c) (crate) Kiste, *die*
(d) [display] ∼: Schaukasten, *der*

cash /kæʃ/ **1** *n.* Bargeld, *das;* pay [in] ∼, pay ∼ down bar zahlen
2 *v.t.* einlösen ⟨*Scheck*⟩

cash: ∼ **account** *n.* Kassekonto, *das;* ∼ **and** '**carry** *n.* cash and carry; (store) Cash-and-carry-Laden, *der;* ∼**back** *n., no art.:* Barauszahlung eines Differenzbetrages bei Kauf mit Geldkarte; ∼**card** *n.* Geldautomatenkarte, *die;* ∼ **desk** *n.* (Brit.) Kasse, *die;* ∼ **discount** *n.* Skonto, *der od. das;* Barzahlungsrabatt, *der;* ∼ **dispenser** *n.* Geldautomat, *der*

cashew nut /'kæʃu:/ *n.* Cashewnuss, *die*

'**cash flow** *n.* Cashflow, *der*

cashier /kæ'ʃɪə(r)/ *n.* Kassierer, *der/* Kassiererin, *die*

'**cashless** *adj.* bargeldlos; the ∼ **society** die bargeldlose Gesellschaft

cashmere /'kæʃmɪə(r)/ *n.* Kaschmir, *der;* ∼ **wool/sweater** Kaschmirwolle, *die/* Kaschmirpullover, *der*

cash: ∼ **payment** *n.* Barzahlung, *die;*

make ∼ **payment** bar bezahlen; ∼**point** *n.* Geldautomat, *der;* ∼ **register** *n.* [Registrier]kasse, *die*

casino /kə'si:nəʊ/ *n.* Kasino, *das*

cask /kɑ:sk/ *n.* Fass, *das*

casket /'kɑ:skɪt/ *n.* (a) Kästchen, *das*
(b) (Amer.: coffin) Sarg, *der*

casserole /'kæsərəʊl/ *n.* Schmortopf, *der*

cassette /kə'set, kæ'set/ *n.* Kassette, *die*

cassette: ∼ **deck** *n.* Kassettendeck, *das;* ∼ **player** *n.* Kassettengerät, *das;* ∼ **recorder** *n.* Kassettenrekorder, *der*

cast /kɑ:st/ **1** *v.t.*, **cast** (a) werfen
(b) (shape, form) gießen
(c) abgeben ⟨*Stimme*⟩
2 *n.* (a) (Med.) Gipsverband, *der*
(b) (actors) Besetzung, *die*
■ **cast a'side** *v.t.* beiseite schieben ⟨*Vorschlag*⟩; vergessen ⟨*Sorgen*⟩; fallen lassen ⟨*Hemmungen*⟩
■ **cast 'off** *v.i. & t.* (Naut.) losmachen

castanets /kæstə'nets/ *n. pl.* Kastagnetten *Pl.*

'**castaway** *n.* Schiffbrüchige, *der/die*

caste /kɑ:st/ *n.* Kaste, *die*

cast 'iron *n.* Gusseisen, *das*

castle /'kɑ:sl/ *n.* Burg, *die;* (mansion) Schloss, *das*

'**cast-offs** *n. pl.* abgelegte Sachen *Pl.*

castor /'kɑ:stə(r)/ *n.* (wheel) Rolle, *die*

castor: ∼ '**oil** *n.* Rizinusöl, *das;* ∼ **sugar** *n.* Raffinade, *die*

castrate /kæ'streɪt/ *v.t.* kastrieren

castration /kæ'streɪʃn/ *n.* Kastration, *die*

casual /'kæʒʊəl/ *adj.* ungezwungen; leger ⟨*Kleidung*⟩; beiläufig ⟨*Bemerkung*⟩; flüchtig ⟨*Bekannter, Bekanntschaft, Blick*⟩; unbekümmert ⟨*Haltung, Einstellung*⟩

casual 'labour *n.* Gelegenheitsarbeit, *die*

'**casually** *adv.* ungezwungen; beiläufig ⟨*bemerken*⟩; flüchtig ⟨*anschauen*⟩; leger ⟨*sich kleiden*⟩

casualty /'kæʒʊəltɪ/ *n.* (a) (injured person) Verletzte, *der/die;* (in battle) Verwundete, *der/ die;* (dead person) Tote, *der/die*
(b) (hospital department) Unfallstation, *die*

'**casualty ward** *n.* Unfallstation, *die*

cat /kæt/ *n.* Katze, *die*

catalogue (Amer.: **catalog**) /'kætəlɒg/
1 *n.* Katalog, *der*
2 *v.t.* katalogisieren

catalyst /'kætəlɪst/ *n.* Katalysator, *der*

catalytic /kætə'lɪtɪk/ *adj.* ∼ **converter** Katalysator, *der*

catamaran /kætəmə'ræn/ *n.* Katamaran, *der*

catapult /'kætəpʌlt/ **1** *n.* Katapult, *das*
2 *v.t.* katapultieren

cataract /'kætərækt/ *n.* (a) Katarakt, *der*
(b) (Med.) grauer Star

catarrh /kə'tɑ:(r)/ *n.* Katarrh, *der*

catastrophe /kə'tæstrəfɪ/ n. Katastrophe, die

catastrophic /kætə'strɒfɪk/ adj. katastrophal

catch /kætʃ/ ① v.t., caught /kɔːt/ (a) fangen; ~ hold of sb./sth. jmdn./etw. festhalten; (to stop oneself falling) sich an jmdm./etw. festhalten; get sth. caught or ~ sth. on/in sth. mit etw. an/in etw. (Dat.) hängen bleiben; ~ one's finger in the door sich (Dat.) den Finger in der Tür einklemmen
(b) (travel by) nehmen; (be in time for) [noch] erreichen
(c) (surprise) ~ sb. doing sth. jmdn. [dabei] erwischen, wie er etw. tut (ugs.)
(d) (become infected with) sich (Dat.) zuziehen; ~ sth. from sb. sich bei jmdm. mit etw. anstecken; ~ a cold sich erkälten; ~ it (fig. coll.) etwas kriegen (ugs.)
(e) ~ sb.'s attention/interest jmds. Aufmerksamkeit erregen/jmds. Interesse wecken
② v.i., caught (a) (begin to burn) [anfangen zu] brennen
(b) (become hooked up) hängenbleiben; ⟨Haar, Faden:⟩ sich verfangen
③ n. (a) (of ball) make a ~: fangen
(b) (amount caught, lit. or fig.) Fang, der
(c) (difficulty) Haken, der (in an + Dat.)
(d) (of door) Schnapper, der
■ **catch 'on** v.i. (coll.) (a) (become popular) [gut] ankommen (ugs.)
(b) (understand) kapieren (ugs.)
■ **catch 'up** ① v.t. ~ sb. up, ~ up with s.b. jmdn. einholen
② v.i. ~ up gleichziehen; ~ up on sth. etw. nachholen

'catching adj. ansteckend

'catchphrase n. Slogan, der

'catchy adj. eingängig

'cat door n. Katzentür, die

categorical /kætɪ'gɒrɪkl/ adj. kategorisch

categorize (**categorise**) /'kætɪgəraɪz/ v.t. kategorisieren

category /'kætɪgərɪ/ n. Kategorie, die

cater /'keɪtə(r)/ v.i. ~ for sb./sth. für jmdn./ etw. [die] Speisen und Getränke liefern; (fig.) auf jmdn./etw. eingestellt sein

'caterer n. Lieferant von Speisen und Getränken

'catering n. (a) (trade) Gastronomie, die
(b) (service) Lieferung von Speisen und Getränken

caterpillar /'kætəpɪlə(r)/ n. Raupe, die

'cat flap ▶ CAT DOOR

cathedral /kə'θiːdrl/ n. Dom, der

Catherine wheel /'kæθrɪn wiːl/ n. Feuerrad, das

Catholic /'kæθəlɪk/ ① adj. katholisch
② n. Katholik, der/Katholikin, die

Catholicism /kə'θɒlɪsɪzm/ n. Katholizismus, der

catkin /'kætkɪn/ n. (Bot.) Kätzchen, das

'Cat's-eye ® n. (Brit.: on road) Bodenrückstrahler, der

cattle /'kætl/ n. pl. Rinder Pl.

'cattle market n. Viehmarkt, der; (fig.) Fleischbeschau, die (ugs. scherzh.)

'catwalk n. Laufsteg, der

caught ▶ CATCH 1, 2

cauldron /'kɔːldrən/ n. Kessel, der

cauliflower /'kɒlɪflaʊə(r)/ n. Blumenkohl, der

cause /kɔːz/ ① n. (a) Ursache, die (of für od. Gen.); (person) Verursacher, der/ Verursacherin, die; be the ~ of sth. etw. verursachen
(b) (reason) Grund, der; ~ for sth. Grund zu etw.
(c) (object of support) Sache, die; [in] a good ~: [für] eine gute Sache
② v.t. verursachen; erregen ⟨Aufsehen, Ärgernis⟩; hervorrufen ⟨Unruhe, Verwirrung⟩; ~ sb. worry/pain jmdm. Sorge/ Schmerzen bereiten; ~ sb. to do sth. jmdn. veranlassen, etw. zu tun

causeway /'kɔːzweɪ/ n. Damm, der

caustic /'kɔːstɪk/ adj. ätzend; (fig.) bissig; beißend ⟨Spott⟩

caution /'kɔːʃn/ ① n. (a) (warning) Vorsicht, die
(b) (warning) Warnung, die
② v.t. (warn) warnen; (warn and reprove) verwarnen (for wegen)

cautious /'kɔːʃəs/ adj., **'cautiously** adv. vorsichtig

cavalry /'kævəlrɪ/ n. Kavallerie, die

cave /keɪv/ n. Höhle, die
■ **cave 'in** v.i. einbrechen

'caveman n. Höhlenbewohner, der

cavern /'kævən/ n. Höhle, die

cavernous /'kævənəs/ adj. höhlenartig

caviar[e] /'kævɪɑː(r)/ n. Kaviar, der

cavity /'kævɪtɪ/ n. Hohlraum, der; (in tooth) Loch, das

'cavity wall n. Hohlmauer, die

CB abbr. = **citizen's band** CB

cc /siː'siː/ abbr. = **cubic centimetre(s)** cm³

CCTV abbr. = **closed-circuit television** CCTV

CD abbr. = **compact disc** CD, die; CD player CD-Spieler, der

CD-ROM /siːdiː'rɒm/ n. CD-ROM, die; ~ drive CD-ROM-Laufwerk, das

cease /siːs/ ① v.i. aufhören
② v.t. (a) (stop) aufhören
(b) (end) aufhören mit; einstellen ⟨Bemühungen⟩

'ceasefire n. Waffenruhe, die

cedar /'siːdə(r)/ n. Zeder, die

Ceefax ® /'siːfæks/ n. (Brit.) Bildschirmtextdienst der BBC

ceiling /'siːlɪŋ/ n. (a) Decke, die
(b) (upper limit) Maximum, das

celebrate /'selɪbreɪt/ *v.t. & i.* feiern

'celebrated *adj.* berühmt

celebration /selɪ'breɪʃn/ *n.* Feier, *die*

celebrity /sɪ'lebrɪtɪ/ *n.* Berühmtheit, *die*

celery /'selərɪ/ *n.* Sellerie, *der od. die*

celibate /'selɪbət/ *adj.* zölibatär (Rel.); ehelos

cell /sel/ *n.* Zelle, *die*

cellar /'selə(r)/ *n.* Keller, *der*

cellist /'tʃelɪst/ *n.* Cellist, *der*/Cellistin, *die*

cello /'tʃeləʊ/ *n., pl.* **~s** Cello, *das*

Cellophane ® /'seləfeɪn/ *n.* Cellophan ⒲, *das*

cellular 'phone /'seljʊlə(r)/ *n.* Mobiltelefon, *das*

cellulite /'seljʊlaɪt/ *n., no indef. art.:* überschüssige Fettdepots an Oberschenkeln und Hüften

Celsius /'selsɪəs/ *adj.* Celsius

cement /sɪ'ment/ ① *n.* Zement, *der* ② *v.t.* zementieren; (stick together) zusammenkleben

ce'ment mixer *n.* Betonmischmaschine, *die*

cemetery /'semɪtərɪ/ *n.* Friedhof, *der*

censor /'sensə(r)/ ① *n.* Zensor, *der* ② *v.t.* zensieren

'censorship *n.* Zensur, *die*

censure /'senʃə(r)/ *v.t.* tadeln

census /'sensəs/ *n.* Volkszählung, *die*

cent /sent/ *n.* Cent, *der*

centenary /sen'tiːnərɪ/ *adj. & n.* **~ [celebrations]** Hundertjahrfeier, *die*

center (Amer.) ▶ CENTRE

centigrade /'sentɪgreɪd/ ▶ CELSIUS

centimetre (*Brit.; Amer.:* **centimeter**) /'sentɪmiːtə(r)/ *n.* Zentimeter, *der*

centipede /'sentɪpiːd/ *n.* Tausendfüßler, *der*

central /'sentrl/ *adj.* zentral

Central: **~ A'merica** *pr. n.* Mittelamerika (*das*); **~ 'Europe** *pr. n.* Mitteleuropa (*das*); **~ Euro'pean** *adj.* mitteleuropäisch; **c~ 'heating** *n.* Zentralheizung, *die*

centralize /'sentrəlaɪz/ *v.t.* zentralisieren

central: **~ 'locking** *n.* (Motor Veh.) Zentralverriegelung, *die;* **~ 'nervous system** *n.* Zentralnervensystem, *das;* **~ 'processing unit** *n.* (Comp.) Zentraleinheit, *die;* **~ reservation** *n.* (Brit.) Mittelstreifen, *der*

centre /'sentə(r)/ (Brit.) ① *n.* (a) Mitte, *die;* (of circle) Mittelpunkt, *der* (b) (of area, city) Zentrum, *das* ② *adj.* mittler... ③ *v.i.* **~ on sth.** sich auf etw. (*Akk.*) konzentrieren; **~ [a]round sth.** sich um etw. drehen ④ *v.t.* (a) in der Mitte anbringen

(b) (concentrate) be **~d [a]round sth.** etw. zum Mittelpunkt haben; **~ sth. on sth.** etw. auf etw. (*Akk.*) konzentrieren

centre 'forward *n.* Mittelstürmer, *der*

centrifugal /sentrɪ'fjuːgl/ *adj.* **~ force** Zentrifugalkraft, *die;* Fliehkraft, *die*

century /'sentʃərɪ/ *n.* (hundred-year period from a year ..00) Jahrhundert, *das;* (hundred years) hundert Jahre

ceramic /sɪ'ræmɪk/ *adj.* keramisch

cereal /'sɪərɪəl/ *n.* Getreide, *das;* (breakfast dish) Getreideflocken *Pl.*

cerebral /'serɪbrl/ *adj.* (intellectual) intellektuell

ceremonial /serɪ'məʊnɪəl/ ① *adj.* feierlich; (prescribed for ceremony) zeremoniell ② *n.* Zeremoniell, *das*

ceremony /'serɪmənɪ/ *n.* Feier, *die;* (formal act) Zeremonie, *die*

certain /'sɜːtn, 'sɜːtɪn/ *adj.* (a) (settled, definite) bestimmt (b) **be ~ to do sth.** etw. bestimmt tun (c) (confident, sure to happen) sicher (d) (indisputable) unbestreitbar (e) **a ~ Mr Smith** ein gewisser Herr Smith; **to a ~ extent** in gewisser Weise

'certainly *adv.* (a) (admittedly) sicher[lich]; (definitely) bestimmt (b) (in answer) [aber] sicher; [most] **~ 'not!** auf [gar] keinen Fall!

certainty /'sɜːtntɪ, 'sɜːtɪntɪ/ *n.* (a) **be a ~:** sicher sein (b) (absolute conviction) Gewissheit, *die*

certificate /sə'tɪfɪkət/ *n.* Urkunde, *die;* (of action performed) Schein, *der*

certify /'sɜːtɪfaɪ/ *v.t.* bescheinigen; bestätigen; **this is to ~ that ...:** hiermit wird bescheinigt *od.* bestätigt, dass ...

cf. *abbr.* = **compare** vgl.

CFC *abbr.* = **chlorofluorocarbon** FCKW, *das;* **~-free** FCKW-frei

chafe /tʃeɪf/ *v.t.* wund scheuern

chaff /tʃɑːf/ *n.* Spreu, *die*

chaffinch /'tʃæfɪntʃ/ *n.* Buchfink, *der*

chagrin /'ʃægrɪn/ *n.* Kummer, *der*

chain /tʃeɪn/ ① *n.* Kette, *die;* **~ of shops/ hotels** Laden-/Hotelkette, *die* ② *v.t.* [an]ketten (**to** an + *Akk.*)

chain: **~ re'action** *n.* Kettenreaktion, *die;* **~saw** *n.* Kettensäge, *die;* **~-smoke** *v.t. & i.* Kette rauchen (ugs.); **~-smoker** *n.* Kettenraucher, *der*/-raucherin, *die;* **~ store** *n.* Kettenladen, *der*

chair /tʃeə(r)/ ① *n.* (a) Stuhl, *der;* (arm**~**, easy **~**) Sessel, *der* (b) (professorship) Lehrstuhl, *der* (c) (at meeting) Vorsitz, *der;* (**~**person) Vorsitzende, *der*/*die* ② *v.t.* den Vorsitz haben bei

chair: **~ back** *n.* Rückenlehne, *die;* **~lift** *n.* Sessellift, *der;* **~man** /'tʃeəmən/ *n., pl.* ⸱⸱⸹

~**men** /'tʃeəmən/ Vorsitzende, *der/die;*
~**person** *n.* Vorsitzende, *der/die;*
~**woman** *n.* Vorsitzende, *die*
chalet /'ʃæleɪ/ *n.* Chalet, *das*
chalk /tʃɔːk/ 〔**1**〕 *n.* Kreide, *die*
〔**2**〕 *v.t.* mit Kreide schreiben/malen *usw*
challenge /'tʃælɪndʒ/ 〔**1**〕 *n.*
Herausforderung, *die*
〔**2**〕 *v.t.* (a) (to contest etc.) herausfordern
(b) (fig.) auffordern; (question) infrage stellen
challenged /'tʃælɪndʒd/ *adj.* (euphem. or
joc.) behindert; **mentally ~:** geistig behindert
'**challenger** *n.* Herausforderer, *der/*
Herausforderin, *die*
challenging /'tʃælɪndʒɪŋ/ *adj.*
herausfordernd; fesselnd 〈*Problem*〉;
anspruchsvoll 〈*Arbeit*〉
chamber /'tʃeɪmbə(r)/ *n.* Kammer, *die*
chamber- ~**maid** *n.* Zimmermädchen,
das; ~ **music** *n.* Kammermusik, *die;*
C~ of 'Commerce *n.* Industrie- und
Handelskammer, *die;* ~ **pot** *n.* Nachttopf,
der
chameleon /kə'miːljən/ *n.* Chamäleon, *das*
chamois /'ʃæmwɑː/ *n.* (a) Gämse, *die*
(b) /'ʃæmɪ/ ~ **[leather]** Chamois[leder], *das*
champagne /ʃæm'peɪn/ *n.* Sekt, *der;* (from
Champagne) Champagner, *der*
cham'pagne glass *n.* Sektglas, *das*
champion /'tʃæmpɪən/ 〔**1**〕 *n.* (a) (defender)
Verfechter, *der/*Verfechterin, *die*
(b) (Sport) Meister, *der/*Meisterin, *die*
〔**2**〕 *v.t.* verfechten 〈*Sache*〉; sich einsetzen für
〈*Person*〉
'**championship** *n.* Meisterschaft, *die*
chance /tʃɑːns/ 〔**1**〕 *n.* (a) (fortune, trick of fate)
Zufall, *der; attrib.* zufällig; ~ **encounter**
Zufallsbegegnung, *die;* **game of ~:**
Glücksspiel, *das;* **by ~:** zufällig; **take a ~:** es
riskieren; **the ~s are that …:** es ist
wahrscheinlich, dass …; **by [any] ~, by some**
~ **or other** zufällig
(b) (opportunity, possibility) Chance, *die;* **get a/the**
~ **to do sth.** eine/die Gelegenheit haben,
etw. zu tun
〔**2**〕 *v.t.* riskieren
chancellor /'tʃɑːnsələ(r)/ *n.* Kanzler, *der;*
C~ of the Exchequer (Brit.) Schatzkanzler, *der*
chandelier /ʃændə'lɪə(r)/ *n.* Kronleuchter,
der
change /tʃeɪndʒ/ 〔**1**〕 *n.* (a) Veränderung,
die; Änderung, *die;* (of job, surroundings,
government, etc.) Wechsel, *der*
(b) (for the sake of variety) Abwechslung, *die;*
for a ~: zur Abwechslung
(c) (money) Wechselgeld, *das;* [loose or small]
~: Kleingeld, *das;* [here is] **15 marks ~:**
15 Mark zurück; **keep the ~:** [es] stimmt so
〔**2**〕 *v.t.* (a) (switch) wechseln; auswechseln
〈*Glühbirne, Batterie*〉; ~ **one's clothes** sich
umziehen; ~ **one's address/name** seine
Anschrift/seinen Namen ändern; ~ **trains/**
buses umsteigen

(b) (transform) verwandeln (**into** in + *Akk.*);
(alter) ändern
(c) (exchange) eintauschen (**for** für); wechseln
〈*Geld*〉
〔**3**〕 *v.i.* (a) (alter) sich ändern; 〈*Person, Land:*〉
sich verändern
(b) (into something else) sich verwandeln
(c) (put on other clothes) sich umziehen
(d) (~trains, buses, etc.) umsteigen
■ **change 'over** *v.i.* ~ **over from sth. to**
sth. von etw. zu etw. übergehen
changeable /'tʃeɪndʒəbl/ *adj.*
veränderlich
'**change[-giving] machine** *n.*
Geldwechsler, *der*
'**changeover** *n.* Wechsel, *der;* ~ **from sth.**
to sth. Umstellung von etw. auf etw. (*Akk.*)
'**changing room** *n.* (Brit.) Umkleideraum,
der
channel /'tʃænl/ 〔**1**〕 *n.* (also Telev., Radio)
Kanal, *der;* **the C~** (Brit.) der [Ärmel]kanal
〔**2**〕 *v.t.* (fig.) lenken
Channel: c~-hop *v.i.* (coll.) (a) (Telev.)
zappen (ugs.); (b) (cross the English Channel)
kurz mal über den Kanal fahren;
~ **Islands** *pr. n. pl.* Kanalinseln *Pl.;*
~ '**Tunnel** *n.* [Ärmel]kanaltunnel, *der*
chant /tʃɑːnt/ 〔**1**〕 *v.t.* skandieren; (Eccl.)
singen
〔**2**〕 *v.i.* Sprechchöre anstimmen; (Eccl.) singen
〔**3**〕 *n.* Sprechchor, *der;* (Eccl.) Gesang, *der*
chaos /'keɪɒs/ *n.* Chaos, *das*
chaotic /keɪ'ɒtɪk/ *adj.* chaotisch
chap¹ /tʃæp/ *n.* (Brit. coll.) Bursche, *der;* Kerl,
der
chap² *v.t.,* **-pp-** aufplatzen lassen
chapel /'tʃæpl/ *n.* Kapelle, *die*
chaperon /'ʃæpərəʊn/ 〔**1**〕 *n.*
Anstandsdame, *die*
〔**2**〕 *v.t.* beaufsichtigen
chaplain /'tʃæplɪn/ *n.* Kaplan, *der*
chapter /'tʃæptə(r)/ *n.* Kapitel, *das*
char /tʃɑː(r)/ *v.t. & i.,* **-rr-** verkohlen
character /'kærɪktə(r)/ *n.* (a) Charakter,
der
(b) (in novel etc.) Figur, *die*
(c) (coll.: extraordinary person) Original, *das*
(d) (symbol) Zeichen, *das*
characteristic /kærɪktə'rɪstɪk/ 〔**1**〕 *adj.*
charakteristisch (**of** für)
〔**2**〕 *n.* charakteristisches Merkmal
characterize /'kærɪktəraɪz/ *v.t.*
charakterisieren
'**characterless** *adj.* nichts sagend
charade /ʃə'rɑːd/ *n.* Scharade, *die;* (fig.)
Farce, *die*
charcoal /'tʃɑːkəʊl/ *n.* Holzkohle, *die*
charge /tʃɑːdʒ/ 〔**1**〕 *n.* (a) (price) Preis, *der;*
(for services) Gebühr, *die*
(b) **be in ~ of sth.** für etw. die
Verantwortung haben; **take ~:** die
Verantwortung übernehmen
(c) (Law: accusation) Anklage, *die*

(d) (attack) Angriff, *der*
(e) (of explosives, electricity) Ladung, *die*
2 *v.t.* **(a)** ~ sb. sth., ~ sth. to sb. jmdm. etw. berechnen
(b) (Law: accuse) anklagen **(with wegen)**
(c) (Electr.) [auf]laden ⟨*Batterie*⟩
(d) (rush at) angreifen
3 *v.i.* **(a)** (attack) angreifen
(b) (coll.: hurry) sausen

charge: ~ **account** *n.* (Amer.) Kreditkonto, *das;* ~ **card** *n.* Kreditkarte, *die*

charisma /kə'rızmə/ *n.* Charisma, *das*

charitable /'tʃærɪtəbl/ *adj.* **(a)** wohltätig
(b) (lenient) großzügig

charity /'tʃærɪtɪ/ *n.* **(a)** Wohltätigkeit, *die*
(b) (organization) wohltätige Organisation

charity: ~ **concert** *n.* Benefizkonzert, *das;* ~ **match** *n.* Benefizspiel, *das;* ~ **performance** *n.* Benefizvorstellung, *die;* Wohltätigkeitsvorstellung, *die;* ~ **shop** *n.:* Secondhandladen, dessen Erlöse einem wohltätigen Zweck dienen

charlady /'tʃɑːleɪdɪ/ *n.* (Brit.) Putzfrau, *die*

charlatan /'ʃɑːlətən/ *n.* Scharlatan, *der*

charm /tʃɑːm/ 1 *n.* **(a)** (act) Zauber, *der*
(b) (talisman) Talisman, *der*
(c) (attractiveness) Reiz, *der;* (of person) Charme, *der*
2 *v.t.* bezaubern

'charming *adj.* bezaubernd

chart /tʃɑːt/ 1 *n.* **(a)** (map) Karte, *die*
(b) (graph etc.) Schaubild, *das*
(c) the ~s die Hitliste
2 *v.t.* (fig.: describe) schildern

charter /'tʃɑːtə(r)/ 1 *n.* **(a)** Charta, *die*
(b) on ~ gechartert
2 *v.t.* chartern ⟨*Schiff, Flugzeug*⟩

chartered: ~ **ac'countant** *n.* (Brit.) Wirtschaftsprüfer, *der/*-prüferin, *die;* ~ **'aircraft** *n.* Charterflugzeug, *das;* Chartermaschine, *die*

charter: ~ **flight** *n.* Charterflug, *der;* ~ **plane** ▶ CHARTERED AIRCRAFT

charwoman /'tʃɑːwʊmən/ *n.* Putzfrau, *die*

chase /tʃeɪs/ 1 *n.* Verfolgungsjagd, *die*
2 *v.t.* (pursue) jagen; ~ sth. (fig.) einer Sache (*Dat.*) nachjagen
3 *v.i.* ~ after sb./sth. hinter jmdm./etw. herjagen
■ **chase 'up** *v.t.* (coll.) ausfindig machen

chasm /'kæzm/ *n.* Kluft, *die*

chassis /'ʃæsɪ/ *n., pl. same* /'ʃæsɪz/ Chassis, *das;* Fahrgestell, *das*

chaste /tʃeɪst/ *adj.* keusch

chastening /'tʃeɪsənɪŋ/ *adj.* ernüchternd

chastise /tʃæ'staɪz/ *v.t.* züchtigen

chastity /'tʃæstɪtɪ/ *n.* Keuschheit, *die*

chat /tʃæt/ 1 *n.* Schwätzchen, *das*
2 *v.i.,* -tt-: **(a)** plaudern; ~ with *or* to sb. about sth. mit jmdm. von etw. plaudern
(b) (Comp.) chatten
■ **chat 'up** *v.t.* (Brit. coll.) anmachen (ugs.)

chat: ~ **line** *n.* Chatline, *die;* ~ **room** *n.* (Comp.) Chat-Room, *der;* ~ **show** *n.* Talkshow, *die*

chattels /'tʃætəlz/ *n. pl.* bewegliche Habe (geh.)

chatter /'tʃætə(r)/ 1 *v.i.* **(a)** schwatzen
(b) ⟨*Zähne:*⟩ klappern
2 *n.* Schwatzen, *das*

'chatterbox *n.* Quasselstrippe, *die* (ugs.)

chatty /'tʃætɪ/ *adj.* gesprächig

chauffeur /'ʃəʊfə(r)/ 1 *n.* Fahrer, *der;* Chauffeur, *der*
2 *v.t.* fahren

chauvinist /'ʃəʊvɪnɪst/ *n.* Chauvinist, *der/* Chauvinistin, *die*

chauvinistic /ʃəʊvɪ'nɪstɪk/ *adj.* chauvinistisch

cheap /tʃiːp/ *adj., adv.* billig

cheapen /'tʃiːpn/ *v.t.* (fig.) herabsetzen

'cheaply *adv.* billig

cheat /tʃiːt/ 1 *n.* Schwindler, *der/* Schwindlerin, *die*
2 *v.t. & i.* betrügen

check¹ /tʃek/ 1 *n.* **(a)** Kontrolle, *die;* make/keep a ~ on kontrollieren
(b) (Amer.: bill) Rechnung, *die*
2 *v.t.* **(a)** (restrain) unter Kontrolle halten
(b) (examine) nachprüfen; kontrollieren ⟨*Fahrkarte*⟩
(c) (stop) aufhalten
3 *v.i.* ~ on sth. etw. überprüfen; ~ with sb. bei jmdm. nachfragen
■ **check 'in** *v.t. & i.* (at airport) einchecken
■ **check 'out** 1 *v.t.* überprüfen
2 *v.i.* abreisen
■ **check 'up** *v.i.* ~ up [on] überprüfen

check² *n.* (pattern) Karo, *das*

checkers /'tʃekəz/ (Amer.) ▶ DRAUGHTS

check: ~**in** *n.* Abfertigung, *die;* ~**list** *n.* Checkliste, *die;* ~**mate** 1 *n.* [Schach]matt, *das;* 2 *int.* [schach]matt; ~**out** [**desk**] *n.* Kasse, *die;* ~**point** *n.* Kontrollpunkt, *der;* ~**-up** *n.* (Med.) Untersuchung, *die*

cheek /tʃiːk/ *n.* **(a)** Backe, *die;* Wange, *die* (geh.)
(b) (impertinence) Frechheit, *die*

'cheekbone *n.* Backenknochen, *der*

'cheekily *adv.,* **'cheeky** *adj.* frech

cheep /tʃiːp/ 1 *v.i.* piep[s]en
2 *n.* Piep[s]en, *das*

cheer /tʃɪə(r)/ 1 *n.* **(a)** (applause) Beifallsruf, *der*
(b) in *pl.* (Brit. coll.: as a toast) prost!
(c) (Brit. coll.: thank you) danke
2 *v.t.* **(a)** (applaud) ~ sth./sb. etw. bejubeln/ jmdm. zujubeln
(b) (gladden) aufmuntern
3 *v.i.* jubeln
■ **cheer 'on** *v.t.* anfeuern ⟨*Sportler*⟩
■ **cheer 'up** 1 *v.t.* aufheitern
2 *v.i.* bessere Laune bekommen; ~ up! Kopf hoch!

c

cheerful /'tʃɪəfl/ adj. (in good spirits) fröhlich; (bright, pleasant) heiter

'**cheerfully** adv. vergnügt

'**cheering** [1] adj. fröhlich stimmend [2] n. Jubeln, das

cheerio /tʃɪərɪ'əʊ/ int. (Brit. coll.) tschüs (ugs.)

'**cheery** adj. fröhlich

cheese /tʃiːz/ n. Käse, der

cheese: ~**board** n. Käseplatte, die; ~**cake** n. Käsetorte, die

cheetah /'tʃiːtə/ n. Gepard, der

chef /ʃef/ n. Küchenchef, der; (as profession) Koch, der

chemical /'kemɪkl/ [1] adj. chemisch [2] n. Chemikalie, die

chemical 'warfare n. chemische Krieg[s]führung

chemist /'kemɪst/ n. (a) (scientist) Chemiker, der/Chemikerin, die (b) (Brit.: pharmacist) Drogist, der/Drogistin, die; ~s [shop] Drogerie, die

chemistry /'kemɪstrɪ/ n. Chemie, die

chemotherapy /kiːmə'θerəpɪ/ n. Chemotherapie, die

cheque /tʃek/ n. Scheck, der; pay by ~: mit [einem] Scheck bezahlen

cheque: ~**book** n. Scheckbuch, das; ~**book 'journalism** n. Scheckbuchjournalismus, der; ~ **card** n. Scheckkarte, die

cherish /'tʃerɪʃ/ v.t. hegen ‹Hoffnung, Gefühl›; in Ehren halten ‹[Erinnerungs]gegenstand›

cherry /'tʃerɪ/ n. Kirsche, die

chess /tʃes/ n., no art. das Schach[spiel]

chess: ~**board** n. Schachbrett, das; ~**man** n. Schachfigur, die; ~ **player** n. Schachspieler, der/-spielerin, die

chest /tʃest/ n. (a) Kiste, die (b) (Anat.) Brust, die; get sth. off one's ~ (fig. coll.) sich (Dat.) etw. von der Seele reden (c) ~ [measurement] Brustumfang, der

chestnut /'tʃesnʌt/ [1] n. (a) Kastanie, die (b) (colour) Kastanienbraun, das [2] adj. (colour) ~[-brown] kastanienbraun

'**chestnut tree** n. Kastanie, die

chest of 'drawers n. Kommode, die

chew /tʃuː/ v.t. & i. kauen

'**chewing gum** n. Kaugummi, der od. das

chic /ʃiːk/ adj. schick; elegant

chick /tʃɪk/ n. (a) Küken, das (b) (sl.: young woman) Biene, die (ugs.)

chicken /'tʃɪkɪn/ [1] n. (a) Huhn, das; (grilled, roasted) Hähnchen, das (b) (coll.: coward) Angsthase, der [2] adj. (coll.) feig[e] [3] v.i. ~ **out** (coll.) kneifen

chicken: ~**pox** /-pɒks/ n. Windpocken Pl.; ~ '**soup** n. Hühnersuppe, die; ~ **wire** n. Maschendraht, der

'**chickpea** n. Kichererbse, die

chicory /'tʃɪkərɪ/ n. (plant) Chicorée, der od. die; (for coffee) Zichorie, die

chief /tʃiːf/ [1] n. (a) Oberhaupt, das; (of tribe) Häuptling, der (b) (of department) Leiter, der; ~ of police Polizeipräsident, der [2] adj., usu. attrib. (a) Haupt- (b) (leading) führend

'**chiefly** adv. hauptsächlich

chieftain /'tʃiːftən/ n. Stammesführer, der

chilblain /'tʃɪlbleɪn/ n. Frostbeule, die

child /tʃaɪld/ n., pl. ~**ren** /'tʃɪldrən/ Kind, das

child: ~ **abuse** n. Kindesmisshandlung, die; ~**bearing** [1] n. Schwangerschaften Pl.; [2] adj. ~**bearing age** Gebäralter, das; of ~**bearing age** im gebärfähigen Alter; ~**birth** n. Geburt, die; ~**care** n. Kinderbetreuung die

'**childhood** n. Kindheit, die

childish /'tʃaɪldɪʃ/ adj., '**childishly** adv. kindisch

'**childishness** n. (behaviour) kindisches Benehmen

child: ~**less** adj. kinderlos; ~**like** adj. kindlich; ~**minder** /-maɪndə(r)/ n. Tagesmutter, die; ~**proof** adj. kindersicher; ~**proof door lock** (in car) Kindersicherung, die

children pl. of CHILD

'**child's play** n. (fig.) ein Kinderspiel

Chile /'tʃɪlɪ/ pr. n. Chile (das)

chill /tʃɪl/ [1] n. Kühle, die; (illness) Erkältung, die [2] v.t. kühlen

■ **chill out** v.i. (Amer. coll.) (relax) sich entspannen; (calm down) sich abregen (ugs.)

chilli /'tʃɪlɪ/ n., pl. ~**es** Chili, der

chilling /'tʃɪlɪŋ/ adj. (fig.) ernüchternd

'**chilly** adj. kühl; I am rather ~: mir ist ziemlich kühl

chime /tʃaɪm/ [1] n. Geläute, das [2] v.i. läuten; ‹Turmuhr:› schlagen

chimney /'tʃɪmnɪ/ n. Schornstein, der

chimney: ~ **breast** n. Kaminmantel, der; ~ **pot** n. ≈ Schornsteinkopf, der; ~ **sweep** n. Schornsteinfeger, der

chimpanzee /tʃɪmpən'ziː/ n. Schimpanse, der

chin /tʃɪn/ n. Kinn, das

china n. Porzellan, das; (crockery) Geschirr, das

China /'tʃaɪnə/ pr. n. China (das)

Chinese /tʃaɪ'niːz/ [1] adj. chinesisch; sb. is ~: jmd. ist Chinese/Chinesin [2] n. (a) pl. same (person) Chinese, der/Chinesin, die (b) (language) Chinesisch, das; see also ENGLISH 2A

chink n. (gap) Spalt, der

chip /tʃɪp/ [1] n. (a) Splitter, der (b) in pl. (Brit.: potato ~s) Pommes frites Pl.

545

(c) (Gambling, Comp.) Chip, *der*
2 *v.t.,* **-pp-** anschlagen
■ **chip 'in** (coll.) 1 *v.i.* **(a)** (interrupt) sich einmischen
(b) (contribute money) etwas beisteuern
2 *v.t.* (contribute) beisteuern
'**chipboard** *n.* Spanplatte, *die*
chipmunk /'tʃɪpmʌŋk/ *n.* Chipmunk, *das*
chippy /'tʃɪpɪ/ *n.* (Brit. coll.) Pommes-frites-Bude, *die;* Frittenbude, *die* (ugs.)
'**chip shop** (Brit.) ▶ CHIPPY
chiropodist /kɪ'rɒpədɪst/ *n.* Fußpfleger, *der*/-pflegerin, *die*
chiropody /kɪ'rɒpədɪ/ *n.* Fußpflege, *die*
chirp /tʃɜːp/ 1 *v.i.* zwitschern; ⟨Grille:⟩ zirpen
2 *n.* Zwitschern, *das;* Zirpen, *das*
chisel /'tʃɪzl/ 1 *n.* Meißel, *der;* (for wood) Stemmeisen, *das*
2 *v.t.,* (Brit.) **-ll-** meißeln; (in wood) hauen
chit /tʃɪt/ *n.* Notiz, *die*
chit-chat /'tʃɪttʃæt/ *n.* Plauderei, *die*
chivalrous /'ʃɪvlrəs/ *adj.* ritterlich
chivalry /'ʃɪvlrɪ/ *n.* Ritterlichkeit, *die*
chives /tʃaɪvz/ *n.* Schnittlauch, *der*
chloride /'klɔːraɪd/ *n.* Chlorid, *das*
chlorine /'klɔːriːn/ *n.* Chlor, *das*
chlorofluorocarbon /klɔːrəʊfluərəʊ'kɑːbən/ *n.* Chlorfluorkohlenstoff, *der*
chock /tʃɒk/ *n.* Bremsklotz, *der*
'**chock-a-block** *pred adj.* voll gepfropft
chocolate /'tʃɒklət/ *n.* Schokolade, *die*
chocolate 'biscuit *n.* Schokoladenkeks, *der*
choice /tʃɔɪs/ 1 *n.* **(a)** Wahl, *die;* **from ∼:** freiwillig
(b) (variety) Auswahl, *die*
2 *adj.* ausgewählt
choir /kwaɪə(r)/ *n.* Chor, *der*
'**choirboy** *n.* Chorknabe, *der*
choke /tʃəʊk/ 1 *v.t.* **(a)** ersticken
(b) (block up) verstopfen
2 *v.i.* (temporarily) keine Luft [mehr] bekommen; (permanently) ersticken (**on** an + *Dat.*)
3 *n.* (Motor Veh.) Choke, *der*
cholera /'kɒlərə/ *n.* Cholera, *die*
cholesterol /kə'lestərɒl/ *n.* Cholesterin, *das*
choose /tʃuːz/ 1 *v.t.,* chose /tʃəʊz/, chosen /'tʃəʊzn/ **(a)** wählen
(b) (decide) ∼/∼ **not to do sth.** sich dafür/ dagegen entscheiden, etw. zu tun
2 *v.i.,* chose, chosen wählen (**between** zwischen); ∼ **from** sth. aus etw./(from several) unter etw. (*Dat.*) [aus]wählen
choos[e]y /'tʃuːzɪ/ *adj.* wählerisch
chop /tʃɒp/ 1 *n.* **(a)** Hieb, *der*
(b) (of meat) Kotelett, *das*
(c) get the ∼ (coll.: be dismissed) rausgeworfen werden (ugs.)

2 *v.t.,* **-pp-** hacken ⟨Holz⟩; klein schneiden ⟨Fleisch, Gemüse⟩
'**chopper** *n.* (axe) Beil, *das;* (cleaver) Hackbeil, *das*
'**chopping board** *n.* Hackbrett, *das*
'**choppy** *adj.* bewegt
'**chopstick** *n.* [Ess]stäbchen, *das*
choral /'kɔːrl/ *adj.* Chor-
chord /kɔːd/ *n.* (Mus.) Akkord, *der*
chore /tʃɔː(r)/ *n.* [lästige] Routinearbeit
choreographer /kɒrɪ'ɒɡrəfə(r)/ *n.* Choreograph, *der*/Choreographin, *die*
choreography /kɒrɪ'ɒɡrəfɪ/ *n.* Choreographie, *die*
chortle /'tʃɔːtl/ 1 *v.i.* vor Lachen glucksen
2 *n.* Glucksen, *das*
chorus /'kɔːrəs/ *n.* **(a)** Chor, *der*
(b) (of song) Refrain, *der;* (in jazz) Chorus, *der*
chose, chosen ▶ CHOOSE
chow /tʃaʊ/ *n.* (Amer. sl.: food) Futter, *das* (salopp)
Christ /kraɪst/ *n.* Christus (*der*)
christen /'krɪsn/ *v.t.* taufen
'**christening** *n.* Taufe, *die*
Christian /'krɪstjən/ 1 *adj.* christlich
2 *n.* Christ, *der*/Christin, *die*
Christianity /krɪstɪ'ænɪtɪ/ *n.* das Christentum
'**Christian name** *n.* Vorname, *der*
Christmas /'krɪsməs/ *n.* Weihnachten, *das od. Pl.;* **merry** *or* **happy** ∼: frohe *od.* fröhliche Weihnachten; **at** ∼: [zu] Weihnachten
Christmas: ∼ **cake** *n.* Weihnachtskuchen, *der;* ∼ **card** *n.* Weihnachtskarte, *die;* ∼ **'carol** *n.* Weihnachtslied, *das;* ∼ **'Day** *n.* erster Weihnachtsfeiertag; ∼ **'Eve** *n.* Heiligabend, *der;* ∼ **present** *n.* Weihnachtsgeschenk, *das;* ∼ **tree** *n.* Weihnachtsbaum, *der*
chrome /krəʊm/**, chromium** /'krəʊmɪəm/ *ns.* Chrom, *das*
'**chromium-plated** *adj.* verchromt
chromosome /'krəʊməsəʊm/ *n.* Chromosom, *das*
chronic /'krɒnɪk/ *adj.* chronisch; ∼ **fatigue syndrome** chronisches Müdigkeitssyndrom
chronically /'krɒnɪkəlɪ/ *adv.* chronisch
chronicle /'krɒnɪkl/ *n.* Chronik, *die*
chronological /krɒnə'lɒdʒɪkl/ *adj.* chronologisch
chrysalis /'krɪsəlɪs/ *n., pl.* ∼**es** Puppe, *die*
chrysanthemum /krɪ'sænθɪməm/ *n.* Chrysantheme, *die*
chubby /'tʃʌbɪ/ *adj.* pummelig
chuck /tʃʌk/ *v.t.* (coll.) schmeißen (ugs.)
■ **chuck 'away, chuck 'out** *v.t.* (coll.) wegschmeißen (ugs.)
chuckle /'tʃʌkl/ 1 *v.i.* leise [vor sich hin] lachen (**at** über + *Akk.*)
2 *n.* leises, glucksendes Lachen

chug /tʃʌg/ v.i., -gg- tuckern

chum /tʃʌm/ n. (coll.) Kumpel, der (salopp)

chunk /tʃʌŋk/ n. dickes Stück

'chunky adj. (a) (small and sturdy) stämmig
(b) dick ⟨Pullover⟩

Chunnel /'tʃʌnl/ n. (Brit. coll.)
[Ärmel]kanaltunnel, der

church /tʃɜːtʃ/ n. Kirche, die; go to ~: in
die Kirche gehen; the C~ of England die
Kirche von England

'churchyard n. Friedhof, der (bei einer
Kirche); Kirchhof, der (veralt.)

churlish /'tʃɜːlɪʃ/ adj. (ill-bred) ungehobelt;
(surly) griesgrämig

churn /tʃɜːn/ n. (Brit.) Butterfass, das

churn 'out v.t. massenweise produzieren
(ugs.)

chute /ʃuːt/ n. Schütte, die; (for persons)
Rutsche, die

chutney /'tʃʌtnɪ/ n. Chutney, das

CIA abbr. (Amer.) = **Central
Intelligence Agency** CIA, der od. die

cicada /sɪ'kɑːdə/ n. Zikade, die

CID abbr. (Brit.) = **Criminal
Investigation Department** C.I.D.; the
~: die Kripo

cider /'saɪdə(r)/ n. ≈ Apfelwein, der

cigar /sɪ'gɑː(r)/ n. Zigarre, die

cigarette /sɪgə'ret/ n. Zigarette, die

cigarette: ~ **end** n. Zigarettenstummel,
der; ~ **lighter** n. Feuerzeug, das;
~ **packet** n. Zigarettenschachtel, die;
~ **paper** n. Zigarettenpapier, das

cinders /'sɪndəz/ n. pl. Asche, die

cine /'sɪnɪ/: ~ **camera** n. Filmkamera,
die; ~ **film** n. Schmalfilm, der

cinema /'sɪnɪmə/ n. Kino, das; go to the ~:
ins Kino gehen

cinema: ~ **complex** n. Kinocenter, das;
~-**goer** n. (Brit.) Kinogänger, der/-gängerin,
die

cinematography /sɪnɪmə'tɒgrəfɪ/ n.
Kinematographie, die

cinnamon /'sɪnəmən/ n. Zimt, der

cipher /'saɪfə(r)/ n. Geheimschrift, die; in
~: chiffriert

circle /'sɜːkl/ ① n. Kreis, der
② v.i. kreisen
③ v.t. umkreisen

circuit /'sɜːkɪt/ n. (a) (Electr.) Schaltung, die
(b) (Motor racing) Rundkurs, der

circular /'sɜːkjʊlə(r)/ ① adj. (round)
kreisförmig
② n. (letter, notice) Rundbrief, der;
Rundschreiben, das; (advertisement)
Werbeprospekt, der

circular: ~ **'letter** ▶ CIRCULAR 2; ~ **'saw**
n. Kreissäge, die

circulate /'sɜːkjʊleɪt/ ① v.i. zirkulieren;
⟨Personen, Wein usw.:⟩ herumgehen (ugs.)
② v.t. in Umlauf setzen; herumgehen lassen
⟨Buch, Bericht⟩ (around in + Dat.)

circulation /sɜːkjʊ'leɪʃn/ n. (a) (Physiol.)
Kreislauf, der; poor ~: Kreislaufstörungen
Pl.
(b) (copies sold) verkaufte Auflage

circulatory /sɜːkjʊ'leɪtərɪ, 'sɜːkjʊleɪtərɪ/
adj. (Physiol., Bot.) Kreislauf-; ~ **system**
Kreislauf, der

circumcise /'sɜːkəmsaɪz/ v.t. beschneiden

circumcision /sɜːkəm'sɪʒn/ n.
Beschneidung, die

circumference /sə'kʌmfərəns/ n.
Umfang, der

circumstances /'sɜːkəmstənsɪz/ n. pl.
Umstände Pl.; in or under the ~: unter
diesen Umständen; under no ~: unter
keinen Umständen

circus /'sɜːkəs/ n. Zirkus, der

CIS abbr. = **Commonwealth of
Independent States** GUS

cissy /'sɪsɪ/ ▶ SISSY

cistern /'sɪstən/ n. Wasserkasten, der; (in
roof) Wasserbehälter, der

citation /saɪ'teɪʃn/ n. Zitat, das

cite /saɪt/ v.t. (quote) zitieren; anführen
⟨Beispiel⟩

citizen /'sɪtɪzən/ n. (a) (of town, city) Bürger,
der/Bürgerin, die
(b) (of state) [Staats]bürger, der/-bürgerin, die

'citizenship n. Staatsbürgerschaft, die

citrus /'sɪtrəs/ n. ~ **[fruit]** Zitrusfrucht, die

city /'sɪtɪ/ n. [Groß]stadt, die

city 'centre n. Stadtzentrum, das

civic /'sɪvɪk/ adj. [staats]bürgerlich;
~ **centre** Verwaltungszentrum der Stadt

civil /'sɪvl/ adj. (a) (not military) zivil
(b) (polite, obliging) höflich
(c) (Law) Zivil-

civil: ~ **engi'neer** n. Bauingenieur, der/
-ingenieurin, die; ~ **engi'neering** n.
Hoch- und Tiefbau, der

civilian /sɪ'vɪljən/ ① n. Zivilist, der
② adj. Zivil-

civility /sɪ'vɪlɪtɪ/ n. Höflichkeit, die

civilization /sɪvɪlaɪ'zeɪʃn/ n. Zivilisation,
die

civilized /'sɪvɪlaɪzd/ adj. zivilisiert

civil: ~ **'law** n. Zivilrecht, das; ~ **'rights**
n. pl. Bürgerrechte Pl.; ~ **'servant** n. ≈
Staatsbeamte, der/-beamtin, die;
C~ **'Service** n. öffentlicher Dienst;
~ **'war** n. Bürgerkrieg, der

CJD abbr. = **Creutzfeldt-Jakob
disease**

clad /klæd/ adj. (arch./literary) gekleidet (in
in + Akk.)

claim /kleɪm/ ① v.t. (a) beanspruchen
⟨Thron, Gebiete⟩; fordern ⟨Lohnerhöhung,
Schadensersatz⟩; beantragen ⟨Sozialhilfe
usw.⟩
(b) (assert) behaupten
② v.i. (Insurance) Ansprüche geltend machen

3 *n.* Anspruch, *der* (**to** auf + *Akk.*); **lay** ∼ **to sth.** auf etw. (*Akk.*) Anspruch erheben

claimant /'kleɪmənt/ *n.* Antragsteller, *der*/ -stellerin, *die*

'**claim form** *n.* (**a**) (Insurance) Antragsformular, *das* (**b**) (for expenses) Spesenabrechnungsformular, *das*

clairvoyant /kleə'vɔɪənt/ 1 *n.* Hellseher, *der*/Hellseherin, *die* 2 *adj.* hellseherisch

clam /klæm/ 1 *n.* Klaffmuschel, *die* 2 *v.i.,* -mm-: ∼ **up** (coll.) den Mund nicht [mehr] aufmachen

clamber /'klæmbə(r)/ *v.i.* klettern

clammy /'klæmɪ/ *adj.* feucht; kalt und schweißig ⟨*Haut*⟩; klamm ⟨*Kleidung*⟩

clamour (*Brit.; Amer.*: **clamor**) /'klæmə(r)/ 1 *n.* (noise, shouting) Lärm, *der;* lautes Geschrei 2 *v.i.* ∼ **for sth.** nach etw. schreien

clamp /klæmp/ 1 *n.* Klammer, *die;* (for holding) Schraubzwinge, *die* 2 *v.t.* klemmen; einspannen ⟨*Werkstück*⟩ 3 *v.i.* (fig.) ∼ **down on sb./sth.** gegen jmdn./ etw. rigoros vorgehen

clan /klæn/ *n.* Sippe, *die;* (of Scottish Highlanders) Clan, *der*

clandestine /klæn'destɪn/ *adj.* heimlich

clang /klæŋ/ 1 *n.* (of bell) Läuten, *das;* (of hammer) Klingen, *das* 2 *v.i.* ⟨*Glocke:*⟩ läuten; ⟨*Hammer:*⟩ klingen

clap /klæp/ 1 *n.* (**a**) Klatschen, *das* (**b**) ∼ **of thunder** Donnerschlag, *der* 2 *v.i.,* -pp- klatschen 3 *v.t.,* -pp-: ∼ **one's hands** in die Hände klatschen; ∼ **sth.** etw. beklatschen; ∼ **sb.** jmdm. Beifall klatschen

'**clapping** *n.* Applaus, *der*

claret /'klærət/ 1 *n.* roter Bordeauxwein 2 *adj.* weinrot

clarification /klærɪfɪ'keɪʃn/ *n.* Klarstellung, *die*

clarify /'klærɪfaɪ/ *v.t.* klären ⟨*Situation usw.*⟩; (by explanation) klarstellen; erläutern ⟨*Bedeutung, Aussage*⟩

clarinet /klærɪ'net/ *n.* Klarinette, *die*

clarity /'klærɪtɪ/ *n.* Klarheit, *die*

clash /klæʃ/ 1 *v.i.* (**a**) scheppern (ugs.) (**b**) (meet in conflict) zusammenstoßen (**c**) (disagree) sich streiten (**d**) ⟨*Interesse, Ereignis:*⟩ kollidieren; ⟨*Farbe:*⟩ sich beißen (ugs.) (**with** mit) 2 *v.t.* gegeneinander schlagen 3 *n.* (**a**) (of cymbals) Dröhnen, *das* (**b**) (meeting in conflict) Zusammenstoß, *der* (**c**) (disagreement) Auseinandersetzung, *die* (**d**) (of personalities, colours) Unverträglichkeit, *die;* (of events) Überschneiden, *die*

clasp /klɑːsp/ 1 *n.* Verschluss, *der* 2 *v.t.* umklammern

class /klɑːs/ 1 *n.* Klasse, *die;* (in society) Gesellschaftsschicht, *die;* (Sch.: lesson) Stunde, *die* 2 *v.t.* einstufen (**as** als)

'**class-conscious** *adj.* klassenbewusst

classic /'klæsɪk/ 1 *adj.* klassisch 2 *n.* Klassiker, *der;* ∼**s** Altphilologie, *die*

classical /'klæsɪkl/ *adj.* klassisch

classifiable /'klæsɪfaɪəbl/ *adj.* klassifizierbar

classification /klæsɪfɪ'keɪʃn/ *n.* Klassifikation, *die*

classified /'klæsɪfaɪd/ *adj.* (**a**) (secret) geheim (**b**) ∼ **advertisement** Kleinanzeige, *die*

classify /'klæsɪfaɪ/ *v.t.* klassifizieren

'**classless** *adj.* klassenlos ⟨*Gesellschaft*⟩

class: ∼**mate** *n.* Klassenkamerad, *der*/ -kameradin, *die;* ∼**room** *n.* Klassenzimmer, *das;* ∼ **trip** *n.* Klassenfahrt, *die;* Klassenausflug, *der*

'**classy** *adj.* (coll.) klasse

clatter /'klætə(r)/ 1 *n.* Klappern, *das* 2 *v.i.* (**a**) klappern (**b**) (move or fall with a ∼) poltern

clause /klɔːz/ *n.* (**a**) Klausel, *die* (**b**) (Ling.) Teilsatz, *der;* [**subordinate**] ∼: Nebensatz, *der*

claustrophobia /klɒstrə'fəʊbɪə/ *n.* Klaustrophobie, *die*

claustrophobic /klɒstrə'fəʊbɪk/ *adj.* beengend ⟨*Ort*⟩

claw /klɔː/ 1 *n.* Kralle, *die;* (of crab etc.) Schere, *die* 2 *v.t.* kratzen

clay /kleɪ/ *n.* Lehm, *der;* (for pottery) Ton, *der*

clean /kliːn/ 1 *adj.* sauber; frisch ⟨*Wäsche, Hemd*⟩ 2 *adv.* glatt 3 *v.t.* sauber machen; putzen ⟨*Zimmer, Schuh*⟩; reinigen ⟨*Teppich, Kleidung, Wunde*⟩; ∼ **one's teeth** sich (*Dat.*) die Zähne putzen 4 *n.* **give sth. a** ∼: etw. putzen ■ **clean 'out** *v.t.* (**a**) sauber machen (**b**) (coll.) ∼ **sb. out** (take all sb.'s money) jmdn. [total] schröpfen (ugs.) ■ **clean 'up** 1 *v.t.* (**a**) aufräumen (**b**) (fig.) säubern 2 *v.i.* aufräumen

'**clean-cut** *adj.* klar [umrissen]; **his** ∼ **features** seine klar geschnittenen Gesichtszüge

'**cleaner** *n.* (**a**) Raumpfleger, *der*/-pflegerin, *die;* (woman also) Putzfrau, *die* (**b**) *usu. in pl.* (dry-∼) Reinigung, *die;* **take sth. to the** ∼'s etw. in die Reinigung bringen

cleanliness /'klenlɪnɪs/ *n.* Reinlichkeit, *die*

'**clean-living** *adj.* von untadeligem Lebenswandel *nachgestellt*

cleanly /'kliːnlɪ/ *adv.* sauber

cleanse /klenz/ v.t. [gründlich] reinigen

'**cleanser** n. Reinigungsmittel, das

'**clean-shaven** adj. glatt rasiert

'**cleansing cream** n. Reinigungscreme, die

clear /klɪə(r)/ ① adj. (a) klar; scharf ‹Bild›; make oneself ~: sich deutlich [genug] ausdrücken; make it ~ [to sb.] that …: [jmdm.] klar und deutlich sagen, dass … (b) (complete) three ~ days volle drei Tage (c) (unobstructed) frei; keep sth. ~ (not block) etw. freihalten ② adv. keep ~ of sth./sb. etw./jmdn. meiden; please stand or keep ~ of the door bitte von der Tür zurücktreten ③ v.t. (a) räumen ‹Straße›; abräumen ‹Schreibtisch›; freimachen ‹Abfluss, Kanal›; ~ a space for sb./sth. für jmdn./etw. Platz machen (b) (empty) räumen; leeren ‹Briefkasten› (c) (remove) wegräumen; beheben ‹Verstopfung› (d) (show to be innocent) freisprechen (e) (get permission for) ~ sth. with sb. etw. von jmdm. genehmigen lassen ④ v.i. (a) ‹Wetter, Himmel:› sich aufheitern (b) (disperse) sich verziehen ⑤ n. we're in the ~ (free of suspicion) auf uns fällt kein Verdacht; (free of trouble) wir haben es geschafft

■ **clear 'off** v.i. abhauen (salopp)

■ **clear 'out** ① v.t. ausräumen ② v.i. (coll.) verschwinden

■ **clear 'up** ① v.t. (a) wegräumen ‹Abfall›; aufräumen ‹Platz, Sachen› (b) (explain) klären ② v.i. (a) aufräumen (b) ‹Wetter:› sich aufhellen

clearance /'klɪərəns/ n. (a) (of obstruction) Beseitigung, die (b) (clear space) Spielraum, der

'**clearance sale** n. Räumungsverkauf, der

'**clear cut** adj. klar umrissen; klar ‹Abgrenzung, Ergebnis›

'**clearing** n. Lichtung, die

'**clearing bank** n. Clearingbank, die

'**clearly** adv. (a) (distinctly) klar; deutlich ‹sprechen› (b) (manifestly, unambiguously) eindeutig; klar ‹denken›

'**clearway** n. (Brit.) Straße mit Halteverbot

cleavage /'kli:vɪdʒ/ n. (between breasts) Dekolleté, das

cleaver /'kli:və(r)/ n. Hackbeil, das

clef /klef/ n. Notenschlüssel, der

cleft /kleft/ n. Spalte, die

clematis /'klemətɪs, klə'meɪtɪs/ n. Klematis, die

clementine /'klemənti:n, 'kleməntaɪn/ n. Klementine, die

clench /klentʃ/ v.t. zusammenpressen; ~ one's fist or fingers die Faust ballen; ~ one's teeth die Zähne zusammenbeißen

clergy /'klɜːdʒɪ/ n. pl. Geistlichkeit, die; Klerus, der

clergyman /'klɜːdʒɪmən/ n., pl. ~men /'klɜːdʒɪmən/ Geistliche, der

clerical /'klerɪkl/ adj. Büro‹arbeit, -personal›; ~ error Schreibfehler, der

clerk /klɑːk/ n. (in bank) Bankangestellte, der/die; (in office) Büroangestellte, der/die

clever /'klevə(r)/ adj. (a) klug (b) (skilful) geschickt (c) (ingenious) geistreich ‹Idee, Argument› (d) (smart, cunning) clever

'**cleverly** adv. (a) klug (b) (skilfully) geschickt

cliché /'kli:ʃeɪ/ n. Klischee, das

click /klɪk/ ① n. Klicken, das ② v.i. klicken ③ v.t. (Comp.) drücken ‹Maustaste›

■ **click on** v.i. (Comp.) anklicken

client /'klaɪənt/ n. (a) Klient, der/Klientin, die (b) (customer) Kunde, der/Kundin, die

clientele /kli:ɒn'tel/ n. (of shop) Kundschaft, die

cliff /klɪf/ n. Kliff, das

'**cliffhanger** n. Thriller, der

climate /'klaɪmət/ n. Klima, das

climatic /klaɪ'mætɪk/ adj. klimatisch

climax /'klaɪmæks/ n. Höhepunkt, der

climb /klaɪm/ ① v.t. hinaufsteigen; klettern auf ‹Baum›; ‹Auto:› hinaufkommen ‹Hügel› ② v.i. (a) klettern (up auf + Akk.) (b) ‹Flugzeug, Sonne:› aufsteigen ③ n. Aufstieg, der

■ **climb 'down** v.i. (a) hinunterklettern (b) (fig.) nachgeben

'**climbdown** n. Rückzieher, der (ugs.)

climber /'klaɪmə(r)/ n. Bergsteiger, der

'**climbing frame** n. Klettergerüst, das

clinch /klɪntʃ/ ① v.t. zum Abschluss bringen; perfekt machen (ugs.) ‹Geschäft› ② n. (Boxing) Clinch, der

cling /klɪŋ/ v.i., clung /klʌŋ/ sich klammern (to an + Akk.)

'**cling film** n. Klarsichtfolie, die

clinic /'klɪnɪk/ n. Klinik, die

clinical /'klɪnɪkl/ adj. (a) (Med.) klinisch (b) (dispassionate) nüchtern

clink /klɪŋk/ ① n. (of glasses) Klirren, das; (of coins) Klimpern, das ② v.i. ‹Flaschen:› klirren; ‹Münzen:› klimpern ③ v.t. klirren mit ‹Glas›; klimpern mit ‹Kleingeld›

clip¹ /klɪp/ ① n. Klammer, die; (for paper) Büroklammer, die ② v.t., -pp- klammern ([on] to an + Akk.)

clip² v.t., -pp- (cut) schneiden ‹Fingernägel, Haar, Hecke›; stutzen ‹Flügel›

clip: ~**board** n. (a) Klemmbrett, das; (b) (Comp.) Zwischenablage, die; ~ **frame** n. [rahmenloser] Bilderhalter

clipping /ˈklɪpɪŋ/ n. (a) (piece clipped off)
Schnipsel, der od. das
(b) (newspaper cutting) Ausschnitt, der

clique /kliːk/ n. Clique, die

clitoris /ˈklɪtərɪs/ n. Kitzler, der; Klitoris,
die (fachspr.)

cloak /kləʊk/ ⓵ n. Umhang, der
⓶ v.t. [ein]hüllen

'cloakroom n. Garderobe, die; (Brit.
euphem.: lavatory) Toilette, die

clock /klɒk/ ⓵ n. (a) Uhr, die; [work]
against the ∼: gegen die Zeit [arbeiten];
round the ∼: rund um die Uhr
(b) (coll.) (speedometer) Tacho, der (ugs.);
(milometer) ≈ Kilometerzähler, der
⓶ v.t. [up] zu verzeichnen haben
⟨Erfolg⟩; erreichen ⟨Geschwindigkeit⟩
▪ **clock 'in, clock 'on** v.i. [bei
Arbeitsantritt] stechen
▪ **clock 'off, clock 'out** v.i. [bei
Arbeitsschluss] stechen

clock 'radio n. Radiowecker, das

'clockwise adv., adj. im Uhrzeigersinn

'clockwork n. Uhrwerk, das; a ∼ car ein
Aufziehauto; **as regular as** ∼ (fig.) absolut
regelmäßig

clod /klɒd/ n. (of earth) Scholle, die

clog /klɒg/ ⓵ n. Clog, der; (traditional)
Holzschuh, der
⓶ v.t., **-gg-:** ∼ [up] verstopfen

cloister /ˈklɔɪstə(r)/ n. Kreuzgang, der

clone /kləʊn/ ⓵ n. Klon, der
⓶ v.t. klonen

close ⓵ /kləʊs/ adj. (a) (in space) dicht;
nahe; **be** ∼ **to sth.** nahe bei od. an etw.
(Dat.) sein; **at** ∼ **quarters** aus der Nähe
betrachtet
(b) (in time) nahe (**to** an + Dat.)
(c) eng ⟨Freund, Zusammenarbeit⟩; nahe
⟨Verwandte, Bekanntschaft⟩
(d) eingehend ⟨Untersuchung, Prüfung usw.⟩
(e) hart ⟨Wett[kampf], Spiel⟩; knapp
⟨Ergebnis⟩; **that was a** ∼ **call** or **shave!** (coll.)
das war knapp!
⓶ /kləʊs/ adv. nah[e]; ∼ **by** in der Nähe;
∼ **to sb./sth.** nahe bei jmdm./etw.
⓷ /kləʊz/ v.t. (a) (shut) schließen; zuziehen
⟨Vorhang⟩; schließen ⟨Laden, Fabrik⟩;
sperren ⟨Straße⟩
(b) (conclude) schließen ⟨Diskussion,
Versammlung⟩
⓸ /kləʊz/ v.i. (a) (shut) sich schließen
(b) ⟨Laden, Fabrik:⟩ schließen, (ugs.)
zumachen
⓹ /kləʊz/ n. Ende, das; Schluss, der; **come**
or **draw to a** ∼: zu Ende gehen; **bring** or
draw sth. to a ∼: etw. zu Ende bringen
▪ **close 'down** /kləʊz/ ⓵ v.t. schließen;
stilllegen ⟨Werk⟩
⓶ v.i. geschlossen werden; ⟨Werk:⟩
stillgelegt werden
▪ **close 'in** v.i. ⟨Nacht, Dunkelheit:⟩
hereinbrechen; ⟨Tage:⟩ kürzer werden; ∼ **in**
on umzingeln

▪ **close 'off** v.t. [ab]sperren

close-cropped /ˈkləʊskrɒpt/ adj. kurz
geschoren

closed /kləʊzd/ adj. geschlossen; **we're** ∼:
wir haben geschlossen

'closed-circuit adj. ∼ **television** interne
Fernsehanlage; (for supervision)
Videoüberwachungsanlage, die

close-down /ˈkləʊzdaʊn/ n. (Radio, Telev.)
Sendeschluss, der

closed 'shop n. Closed Shop, der

'close-knit /kləʊsˈnɪt/ adj. fest
zusammengewachsen

closely /ˈkləʊslɪ/ adv. (a) dicht
(b) (intimately) eng
(c) genau ⟨befragen, prüfen⟩; streng
⟨bewachen⟩

'close-range /ˈkləʊsreɪndʒ/ adj. ⟨Sicht,
Betrachtung⟩ aus nächster Nähe

closet /ˈklɒzɪt/ n. (Amer.: cupboard) Schrank,
der

close-up /ˈkləʊsʌp/ n. ∼ [picture/shot]
Nahaufnahme, die

closing /ˈkləʊzɪŋ/: ∼ **date** n. (for
competition) Einsendeschluss, der; (to take part)
Meldefrist, die; ∼ **time** n. (of pub)
Polizeistunde, die

closure /ˈkləʊʒə(r)/ n. Schließung, die; (of
road) Sperrung, die

clot /klɒt/ ⓵ n. (a) (blood) Gerinnsel, das
(b) (Brit. coll.: stupid person) Trottel, der
⓶ v.i., **-tt-** ⟨Blut:⟩ gerinnen

cloth /klɒθ/ n., pl. ∼**s** /klɒθs/ (a) Stoff, der;
Tuch, das
(b) (dish∼) Spültuch, das; (table∼)
[Tisch]decke, die

clothe /kləʊð/ v.t. kleiden

clothes /kləʊðz/ n. pl. Kleider Pl.; **put**
one's ∼ **on** sich anziehen; **take one's** ∼ **off**
sich ausziehen

clothes: ∼ **brush** n. Kleiderbürste, die;
∼ **hanger** n. Kleiderbügel, der; ∼ **horse**
n. Wäscheständer, der; ∼ **line** n.
Wäscheleine, die; ∼ **peg** (Brit.), ∼**pin**
(Amer.) ns. Wäscheklammer, die

clothing /ˈkləʊðɪŋ/ n. Kleidung, die

clotted cream /klɒtɪd ˈkriːm/ n. sehr
fetter Rahm

cloud /klaʊd/ n. (a) Wolke, die; **every** ∼ **has**
a silver lining (prov.) es hat alles sein Gutes
(b) ∼ **of dust/smoke** Staub-/Rauchwolke, die
▪ **cloud 'over** v.i. sich bewölken

'cloudburst n. Wolkenbruch, der

'cloudless adj. wolkenlos

'cloudy adj. bewölkt ⟨Himmel⟩; trübe
⟨Wetter, Flüssigkeit, Glas⟩

clout /klaʊt/ (coll.) ⓵ n. Schlag, der
⓶ v.t. hauen (ugs.)

clove[1] /kləʊv/ n. ∼ [of garlic]
[Knoblauch]zehe, die

clove[2] n. (spice) [Gewürz]nelke, die

clover /ˈkləʊvə(r)/ n. Klee, der   ···⟫

'cloverleaf n. Kleeblatt, das
clown /klaʊn/ [1] n. Clown, der
　[2] v.i. ~ [about or around] den Clown spielen
cloying /'klɔɪɪŋ/ adj. süßlich
club /klʌb/ [1] n. (a) (weapon) Keule, die; (golf ~) Schläger, der
　(b) (association) Klub, der; Verein, der
　(c) (Cards) Kreuz, das; ~s are trumps Kreuz ist Trumpf; **the ace/seven of** ~s das Kreuzas/die Kreuzsieben
　[2] v.t., -bb- (beat) prügeln; (with ~) knüppeln
　[3] v.i., -bb-: ~ **together** (to buy something) zusammenlegen
club 'sandwich n. (Amer.) Club-Sandwich, das; Doppeldecker, der (ugs.)
cluck /klʌk/ [1] n. Gackern, das
　[2] v.i. gackern
clue /klu:/ n. Anhaltspunkt, der; (in criminal investigation) Spur, die; **not have a** ~: keine Ahnung haben
'clueless adj. (coll.) unbedarft (ugs.)
clump /klʌmp/ n. Gruppe, die; (of grass) Büschel, das
clumsily /'klʌmzɪlɪ/ adv. ▸ CLUMSY: schwerfällig; unbeholfen; plump
clumsiness /'klʌmzɪnɪs/ n. ▸ CLUMSY: Schwerfälligkeit, die; Plumpheit, die
clumsy /'klʌmzɪ/ adj. schwerfällig, unbeholfen ⟨Person, Bewegung⟩; plump ⟨Form, Figur, Nachahmung⟩
clung ▸ CLING
cluster /'klʌstə(r)/ [1] n. (of grapes, berries) Traube, die; (of fruit, flowers) Büschel, das; (of stars, huts) Haufen, der
　[2] v.i. ~ **[a]round** sb./sth. sich um jmdn./etw. scharen od. drängen
clutch /klʌtʃ/ [1] v.t. umklammern
　[2] v.i. ~ **at sth.** nach etw. greifen; (fig.) sich an etw. ⟨Akk.⟩ klammern
　[3] n. (a) in pl. (fig.: control) Klauen Pl.
　(b) (Motor Veh.) Kupplung, die
clutter /'klʌtə(r)/ [1] n. Durcheinander, das
　[2] v.t. ~ **[up] the table/room** überall auf dem Tisch/im Zimmer herumliegen
cm. abbr. = **centimetre[s]** cm
c/o abbr. = **care of** bei; c/o
Co. abbr. (a) = **company** Co.
　(b) = **county**
coach /kəʊtʃ/ [1] n. (a) (horse-drawn) Kutsche, die
　(b) (Railw.) Wagen, der
　(c) (bus) [Reise]bus, der; **by** ~: mit dem Bus
　(d) (Sport) Trainer, der/Trainerin, die
　[2] v.t. trainieren
coaching /'kəʊtʃɪŋ/ n. (a) (teaching) Privatunterricht, der
　(b) (Sport) Training, das
coach: ~ **party** n. Reisegesellschaft, die; ~ **station** n. Busbahnhof, der; ~ **tour** n. Rundreise [im Omnibus]
coagulate /kəʊ'ægjʊleɪt/ [1] v.t. gerinnen lassen

coal /kəʊl/ n. Kohle, die
coal: ~**field** n. Kohlenrevier, das; ~ **fire** n. Kohlenfeuer, das; ~**-fired** adj. mit Kohle beheizt; kohlebeheizt
coalition /kəʊə'lɪʃn/ n. (Polit.) Koalition, die
coal: ~ **mine** n. [Kohlen]bergwerk, das; ~ **miner** n. [im Kohlenbergbau tätiger] Grubenarbeiter; ~ **mining** n. Kohlenbergbau, der
coarse /kɔːs/ adj. (a) (in texture) grob
　(b) (unrefined, obscene) derb
coast /kəʊst/ [1] n. Küste, die
　[2] v.i. im Freilauf fahren
coastal /'kəʊstl/ adj. Küsten-
'coaster n. (a) (mat) Untersetzer, der
　(b) (ship) Küstenmotorschiff, das
coast: ~**guard** n. Küstenwache, -wacht, die; ~**line** n. Küste, die
coat /kəʊt/ [1] n. (a) Mantel, der
　(b) (layer) Schicht, die; (of paint) Anstrich, der
　(c) (animal's hair, fur, etc.) Fell, das
　[2] v.t. überziehen; (with paint) streichen
'coat hanger n. Kleiderbügel, der
'coating n. Schicht, die
coat of 'arms n. Wappen, das
coax /kəʊks/ v.t. überreden
cobble /'kɒbl/ n. Kopfstein, der
cobbler /'kɒblə(r)/ n. Schuster, der
'cobblestone ▸ COBBLE
cobra /'kɒbrə/ n. Kobra, die
cobweb /'kɒbweb/ n. Spinnengewebe, das; Spinnennetz, das
cocaine /kə'keɪn/ n. Kokain, das
cock /kɒk/ [1] n. Hahn, der
　[2] v.t. spitzen ⟨Ohren⟩; ~ **a/the gun** den Hahn spannen
cock-a-hoop /kɒkə'hu:p/ adj. überschwänglich
cockatoo /kɒkə'tu:/ n. Kakadu, der
'cockcrow n. **at** ~: beim ersten Hahnenschrei
cockerel /'kɒkərəl/ n. junger Hahn
cock-eyed /'kɒkaɪd/ adj. (a) (crooked) schief
　(b) (absurd) verrückt
cockle /'kɒkl/ n. Herzmuschel, die
cockney /'kɒknɪ/ [1] adj. Cockney-
　[2] n. Cockney, der
'cockpit n. Cockpit, das
cockroach /'kɒkrəʊtʃ/ n. [Küchen-, Haus-] schabe, die
cocktail /'kɒkteɪl/ n. Cocktail, der
cocktail: ~ **cabinet** n. Hausbar, die; ~ **party** n. Cocktailparty, die
cocoa /'kəʊkəʊ/ n. Kakao, der
coconut /'kəʊkənʌt/ n. Kokosnuss, die
cocoon /kə'ku:n/ n. (Zool.) Kokon, der
cod /kɒd/ n., pl. same Kabeljau, der
COD abbr. = **cash on delivery,** (Amer.) = **collect on delivery** p. Nachn.

code /kəʊd/ ① n. (a) (statutes etc.)
Gesetzbuch, das; ~s of behaviour
Verhaltensnormen
(b) (system of signals) Code, der; be in ~:
verschlüsselt sein
② v.t. chiffrieren; verschlüsseln

code: ~ **name** n. Deckname, der;
~ **word** n. Kennwort, das

cod-liver 'oil n. Lebertran, der

co-driver /'kəʊdraɪvə(r)/ n. Beifahrer, der/
-fahrerin, die

coed /'kəʊed/ (esp. Amer. coll.) ① n.
Studentin, die
② adj. ~ **school** gemischte Schule

coeducational /kəʊedjʊ'keɪʃənl/ adj.
koedukativ; Koedukations-

coerce /kəʊ'ɜːs/ v.t. zwingen; ~ **sb. into
sth.** jmdn. zu etw. zwingen

coercion /kəʊ'ɜːʃn/ n. Zwang, der

coexist /kəʊɪg'zɪst/ v.i. koexistieren

coexistence /kəʊɪg'zɪstəns/ n.
Koexistenz, die

C. of E. /siːəv'iː/ abbr. = **Church of
England**

coffee /'kɒfɪ/ n. Kaffee, der; **three black/
white** ~s drei [Tassen] Kaffee ohne/mit
Milch

coffee: ~ **bar** n. Café, das; ~ **bean** n.
Kaffeebohne, die; ~ **break** n. Kaffeepause,
die; ~ **cup** n. Kaffeetasse, die;
~ **machine,** ~ **maker** ns.
Kaffeeautomat, der; ~ **pot** n. Kaffeekanne,
die; ~ **shop** n. Kaffeestube, die; ~ **table**
n. Couchtisch, der

coffin /'kɒfɪn/ n. Sarg, der

cog /kɒg/ n. (Mech.) Zahn, der

cogent /'kəʊdʒənt/ adj. überzeugend
⟨Argument⟩; zwingend ⟨Grund⟩

cognac /'kɒnjæk/ n. Cognac, der Ⓦ

cog: ~ **railway** n. Zahnradbahn, die;
~**wheel** n. Zahnrad, das

cohabit /kəʊ'hæbɪt/ v.i. zusammenleben;
in eheähnlicher Gemeinschaft leben
(Rechtsspr.)

cohere /kəʊ'hɪə(r)/ v.i. zusammenhalten

coherent /kəʊ'hɪərənt/ adj.
zusammenhängend

coherently /kəʊ'hɪərəntlɪ/ adv.
zusammenhängend; im Zusammenhang

coil /kɔɪl/ ① v.t. aufwickeln; (twist)
aufdrehen
② v.i. ~ **round sth.** etw. umschlingen
③ n. (a) ~s **of rope/wire** aufgerollte Seile
Pl./aufgerollter Draht
(b) (single turn) Windung, die
(c) (Electr.) Spule, die

'coil spring n. Spiralfeder, die

coin /kɔɪn/ ① n. Münze, die
② v.t. prägen ⟨Wort, Redewendung⟩

coincide /kəʊɪn'saɪd/ v.i. (a) (in time)
zusammenfallen
(b) (agree) übereinstimmen (**with** mit)

coincidence /kəʊ'ɪnsɪdəns/ n. Zufall, der

coincidental /kəʊɪnsɪ'dentl/ adj. zufällig

coincidentally /kəʊɪnsɪ'dentəlɪ/ adv.
gleichzeitig; (by coincidence) zufälligerweise

'coin-operated adj. Münz-

coke /kəʊk/ n. Koks, der

Col. abbr. = **Colonel** Obst.

colander /'kʌləndə(r)/ n. Sieb, das

cold /kəʊld/ ① adj. (a) kalt; **I am/feel** ~:
mir ist kalt
(b) (fig.) [betont] kühl ⟨Person, Aufnahme,
Begrüßung⟩
② adv. kalt
③ n. (a) Kälte, die
(b) (illness) Erkältung, die; ~ **[in the head]**
Schnupfen, der; **have a** ~: eine Erkältung/
[einen] Schnupfen haben

cold-blooded /'kəʊldblʌdɪd/ adj. (a)
wechselwarm ⟨Tier⟩
(b) kaltblütig ⟨Person, Mord⟩

'coldly adv. [betont] kühl

cold: ~-'**shoulder** v.t. schneiden (fig.);
~ '**storage** n. Kühllagerung, die; ~ '**war**
n. kalter Krieg

coleslaw /'kəʊlslɔː/ n. Krautsalat, der

collaborate /kə'læbəreɪt/ v.i. (a)
zusammenarbeiten; ~ [**with sb.**] **on sth.**
zusammen [mit jmdm.] an etw. (Dat.)
arbeiten
(b) (with enemy) kollaborieren

collaboration /kəlæbə'reɪʃn/ n.
Zusammenarbeit, die; (with enemy)
Kollaboration, die

collaborator /kə'læbəreɪtə(r)/ n.
Mitarbeiter, der/-arbeiterin, die; (with enemy)
Kollaborateur, der/Kollaborateurin, die

collage /'kɒlɑːʒ/ n. Collage, die

collapse /kə'læps/ ① n. (a) (of person)
Zusammenbruch, der
(b) (of structure) Einsturz, der
(c) (of negotiations) Scheitern, das; (of company)
Zusammenbruch, der
② v.i. (a) ⟨Person:⟩ zusammenbrechen
(b) ⟨Stuhl:⟩ zusammenbrechen; ⟨Gebäude:⟩
einstürzen
(c) ⟨Verhandlungen:⟩ scheitern;
⟨Unternehmen:⟩ zusammenbrechen
(d) (fold down) ⟨Regenschirm, Fahrrad, Tisch:⟩
sich zusammenklappen lassen

collapsible /kə'læpsɪbl/ adj. Klapp⟨stuhl,
-tisch, -fahrrad⟩

collar /'kɒlə(r)/ ① n. (a) Kragen, der
(b) (for dog) [Hunde]halsband, das
② v.t. schnappen (ugs.)

'collarbone n. Schlüsselbein, das

colleague /'kɒliːg/ n. Kollege, der/
Kollegin, die

collect /kə'lekt/ ① v.i. sich versammeln;
⟨Staub, Müll usw.:⟩ sich ansammeln
② v.t. sammeln; aufsammeln ⟨Müll, leere
Flaschen usw.⟩; (fetch) abholen ⟨Menschen,
Dinge⟩; ~ **one's wits/thoughts** seine
Gedanken sammeln   ⋯⋗

col'lected adj. (a) (gathered) gesammelt
(b) (calm) gesammelt; gelassen

collection /kə'lekʃn/ n. (a) (collecting)
Sammeln, das; (of goods, persons) Abholen, das
(b) (amount of money collected) Sammlung, die;
(in church) Kollekte, die
(c) (from postbox) Leerung, die
(d) (of stamps etc.) Sammlung, die

collective /kə'lektıv/ adj. kollektiv nicht
präd

collective 'bargaining n.
Tarifverhandlungen Pl.

collector /kə'lektə(r)/ n. (a) (of stamps etc.)
Sammler, der/Sammlerin, die
(b) (of taxes) Einnehmer, der/Einnehmerin,
die

col'lector's item, col'lector's piece
ns. Sammlerstück, das

college /'kɒlıdʒ/ n. (a) (esp. Brit. Univ.)
College, das
(b) (place of further education) Fach[hoch]schule,
die; go to ~ (esp. Amer.) studieren

collide /kə'laıd/ v.i. zusammenstoßen (with
mit)

collie /'kɒlı/ n. Collie, der

colliery /'kɒljərı/ n. Kohlengrube, die

collision /kə'lıʒn/ n. Zusammenstoß, der;
on a ~ course (lit. or fig.) auf Kollisionskurs

colloquial /kə'ləʊkwıəl/ adj.
umgangssprachlich

collusion /kə'luːʒn/ n. geheime Absprache

cologne ▶ EAU-DE-COLOGNE

Cologne /kə'ləʊn/ ①pr. n. Köln (das)
②attrib. adj. Kölner

Colombia /kə'lɒmbıə/ pr. n. Kolumbien
(das)

colon¹ /'kəʊlən/ n. Doppelpunkt, der

colon² /'kəʊlən, 'kəʊlɒn/ n. (Anat.)
Grimmdarm, der

colonel /kɜːnl/ n. Oberst, der

colonial /kə'ləʊnıəl/ adj. Kolonial-; kolonial

colonize /'kɒlənaız/ v.t. kolonisieren

colony /'kɒlənı/ n. Kolonie, die

color etc. (Amer.) ▶ COLOUR etc.

colossal /kə'lɒsl/ adj. ungeheuer; gewaltig
⟨Bauwerk⟩

colour /'kʌlə(r)/ (Brit.) ①n. Farbe, die; what
~ is it? welche Farbe hat es?; change ~: die
Farbe ändern; he is off ~: ihm ist nicht gut
②v.t. (a) (give ~ to) Farbe geben (+ Dat.)
(b) (paint) malen
(c) (stain, dye) färben
③v.i. ~ [up] erröten

'colour-blind adj. farbenblind

coloured /'kʌləd/ (Brit.) ①adj. (a) farbig
(b) (of non-white descent) farbig; ~ people
Farbige Pl.
②n. Farbige, der/die

colour: ~fast adj. farbecht; ~ film n.
Farbfilm, der

colourful /'kʌləfl/ adj. (Brit.) bunt;
anschaulich ⟨Sprache, Stil, Bericht⟩

'colouring n. (Brit.) (a) (colours) Farben Pl.
(b) ~ [matter] (in food etc.) Farbstoff, der

'colourless adj. (Brit.) farblos

colour: ~ **photograph** n.
Farbaufnahme, die; ~ **printer** n.
Farbdrucker, der; ~ **scheme** n.
Farb[en]zusammenstellung, die;
~ **supplement** n. Farbbeilage, die;
~ **television** n. Farbfernsehen, das; (set)
Farbfernsehgerät, das; ~ **transparency**
n. Farbdia, das

colt /kəʊlt/ n. [Hengst]fohlen, das

column /'kɒləm/ n. (a) Säule, die
(b) (of page) Spalte, die; sports ~: Sportteil,
der

columnist /'kɒləmıst/ n. Kolumnist, der/
Kolumnistin, die

coma /'kəʊmə/ n. Koma, das; in a ~: im
Koma

comb /kəʊm/ ①n. Kamm, der
②v.t. (a) kämmen; ~ sb.'s/one's hair
jmdm./sich die Haare kämmen
(b) (search) durchkämmen

combat /'kɒmbæt/ ①n. Kampf, der
②v.t. bekämpfen

combatant /'kɒmbətənt/ n. Kombattant,
der

combination /kɒmbı'neıʃn/ n.
Kombination, die; in ~: zusammen

combi'nation lock n.
Kombinationsschloss, das

combine ①/kəm'baın/ v.t.
zusammenfügen (into zu); verbinden
⟨Substanzen⟩
②v.i. (join together) ⟨Stoffe:⟩ sich verbinden
③/'kɒmbaın/ n. ~ [harvester] Mähdrescher,
der

combustible /kəm'bʌstıbl/ adj. brennbar

combustion /kəm'bʌstʃn/ n.
Verbrennung, die

come /kʌm/ v.i., came /keım/, come /kʌm/
kommen; ~ here! komm [mal] her!; [I'm]
coming! [ich] komme schon!; the train came
into the station der Zug fuhr in den Bahnhof
ein; Christmas is coming bald ist
Weihnachten; the handle has ~ loose der
Griff ist lose; nothing came of it es ist nichts
daraus geworden

■ **come a'bout** v.i. passieren

■ **come across** ①/-'-/ v.i. (be understood)
verstanden werden
②/'—/ v.t. begegnen (+ Dat.)

■ **come a'long** v.i. (coll.) (a) (hurry up)
~ along! komm/kommt!
(b) (make progress) ~ along nicely gute
Fortschritte machen
(c) (to place) mitkommen (with mit)

■ **come 'back** v.i. zurückkommen

■ **come by** ①/-'-/ v.t. (obtain) bekommen
②/'-'-/ v.i. vorbeikommen

■ **come 'down** v.i. (a) (fall) ⟨Schnee, Regen,
Preis:⟩ fallen
(b) (~ lower) herunterkommen
(c) (land) [not]landen; (crash) abstürzen

■ **come 'in** *v.i.* (enter) hereinkommen; ∼ **in!** herein!

■ **'come into** *v.t.* **(a)** (enter) hereinkommen in (+ *Akk.*)
(b) (inherit) erben

■ **come off** ⟨1⟩ /-'-/ *v.i.* **(a)** ⟨*Griff, Knopf:*⟩ abgehen; (be removable) sich abnehmen lassen
(b) (succeed) ⟨*Pläne, Versuche:*⟩ Erfolg haben
(c) (take place) stattfinden
⟨2⟩ /'--/ *v.t.* ▸ ∼ **off a horse/bike** vom Pferd/Fahrrad fallen; ∼ **'off it!** (coll.) nun mach mal halblang! (ugs.)

■ **come on** ⟨1⟩ /-'-/ *v.i.* **(a)** (continue coming, follow) kommen; ∼ **on!** komm, komm/kommt, kommt!; (encouraging) na, komm!
(b) (make progress) ∼ **on very well** gute Fortschritte machen
⟨2⟩ /'--/ *v.t.* ▸ ∼ UPON

■ **come 'out** *v.i.* **(a)** herauskommen
(b) (fig.) ⟨*Sonne, Wahrheit, Buch:*⟩ herauskommen
(c) ∼ **out with** herausrücken mit (ugs.)

■ **come 'over** ⟨1⟩ *v.i.* herüberkommen
⟨2⟩ *v.t.* kommen über (+ *Akk.*)

■ **come 'round** *v.i.* **(a)** (visit) vorbeischauen
(b) (recover) wieder zu sich kommen

■ **come 'through** ⟨1⟩ *v.i.* durchkommen
⟨2⟩ *v.t.* (survive) überleben

■ **come to** ⟨1⟩ /'--/ *v.t.* (amount to) ⟨*Rechnung, Kosten:*⟩ sich belaufen auf (+ *Akk.*), machen
⟨2⟩ /-'-/ *v.i.* wieder zu sich kommen

■ **'come under** *v.t.* **(a)** (be classed as or among) kommen unter (+ *Akk.*)
(b) (be subject to) kommen unter (+ *Akk.*)

■ **come 'up** *v.i.* **(a)** (∼ higher) hochkommen
(b) ∼ **up to sb.** (approach for talk) auf jmdn. zukommen
(c) (present itself) sich ergeben
(d) ∼ **up to** (reach) reichen bis an (+ *Akk.*); entsprechen (+ *Dat.*) ⟨*Erwartungen*⟩
(e) ∼ **up against sth.** (fig.) auf etw. (*Akk.*) stoßen
(f) ∼ **up with** vorbringen ⟨*Vorschlag*⟩; wissen ⟨*Lösung, Antwort*⟩

■ **'come upon** *v.t.* (meet by chance) begegnen (+ *Dat.*)

'comeback *n.* (to profession etc.) Come-back, *das*

comedian /kə'mi:dɪən/ *n.* Komiker, *der*

comedienne /kəmi:dɪ'en/ *n.* Komikerin, *die*

'comedown *n.* Abstieg, *der*

comedy /'kɒmɪdɪ/ **(a)** *n.* Lustspiel, *das;* Komödie, *die*
(b) (humour) Witz, *der;* Witzigkeit, *die*

comer /'kʌmə(r)/ *n.* **the competition is open to all** ∼s an dem Wettbewerb kann sich jeder beteiligen; **the first** ∼: derjenige, der zuerst kommt

comet /'kɒmɪt/ *n.* Komet, *der*

comeuppance /kʌm'ʌpəns/ *n.* **get one's** ∼: die Quittung kriegen (fig.)

comfort /'kʌmfət/ ⟨1⟩ *n.* **(a)** (consolation) Trost, *der*

(b) (physical well-being) Behaglichkeit, *die*
(c) *in pl.* Komfort, *der*
⟨2⟩ *v.t.* trösten

comfortable /'kʌmfətəbl/ *adj.* **(a)** bequem ⟨*Bett, Schuhe*⟩; komfortabel ⟨*Haus, Zimmer*⟩; **a** ∼ **victory** ein leichter Sieg
(b) (at ease) **be/feel** ∼: sich wohl fühlen

comfortably /'kʌmfətəblɪ/ *adv.* bequem; leicht ⟨*gewinnen*⟩

comforting /'kʌmfətɪŋ/ *adj.* beruhigend ⟨*Gedanke*⟩; tröstend ⟨*Worte*⟩; wohlig ⟨*Wärme*⟩

'comfort station *n.* (Amer.) öffentliche Toilette

comfy /'kʌmfɪ/ *adj.* (coll.) bequem; gemütlich ⟨*Haus, Zimmer*⟩

comic /'kɒmɪk/ ⟨1⟩ *adj.* komisch
⟨2⟩ *n.* **(a)** (comedian) Komiker, *der*/Komikerin, *die*
(b) (periodical) Comicheft, *das*

comical /'kɒmɪkl/ *adj.* komisch

coming /'kʌmɪŋ/ ⟨1⟩ *adj.* **in the** ∼ **week** kommende Woche
⟨2⟩ *n.* ∼**s and goings** das Kommen und Gehen

comma /'kɒmə/ *n.* Komma, *das*

command /kə'mɑ:nd/ ⟨1⟩ *v.t.* **(a)** (order) befehlen (**sb.** jmdm.)
(b) (be in ∼ of) befehligen ⟨*Schiff, Armee*⟩
(c) verfügen über (+ *Akk.*) ⟨*Gelder, Wortschatz*⟩
⟨2⟩ *n.* **(a)** Kommando, *das;* (in writing) Befehl, *der;* **have/take** ∼ **of** das Kommando über (+ *Akk.*) … haben/übernehmen
(b) (mastery, possession) Beherrschung, *die*

commandeer /kɒmən'dɪə(r)/ *v.t.* requirieren

com'mander *n.* Führer, *der*

com'manding *adj.* **(a)** gebieterisch ⟨*Erscheinung, Stimme*⟩; imposant ⟨*Gestalt*⟩
(b) beherrschend ⟨*Ausblick, Lage*⟩

commanding 'officer *n.* Befehlshaber, *der*/Befehlshaberin, *die*

com'mandment *n.* Gebot, *das*

commemorate /kə'meməreɪt/ *v.t.* gedenken (+ *Gen.*)

commemoration /kəmemə'reɪʃn/ *n.* Gedenken, *das;* **in** ∼ **of** zum Gedenken an (+ *Akk.*)

commemorative /kə'memərətɪv/ *adj.* Gedenk-; ∼ **of** zum Gedenken an (+ *Akk.*)

commence /kə'mens/ *v.t. & i.* beginnen

com'mencement *n.* Beginn, *der*

commend /kə'mend/ *v.t.* (praise) loben

commendable /kə'mendəbl/ *adj.* lobenswert; löblich

commendation /kɒmen'deɪʃn/ *n.* (praise) Lob, *das;* (official) Belobigung, *die;* (award) Auszeichnung, *die*

comment /'kɒment/ ⟨1⟩ *n.* Bemerkung, *die* (on über + *Akk.*); (note) Anmerkung, *die* (on über + *Akk.*); **no** ∼! (coll.) kein Kommentar! ···⟋

② *v.i.* ~ **on sth.** über etw. (*Akk.*)
Bemerkungen machen; **he** ~**ed that** ...: er
bemerkte, dass ...
commentary /'kɒməntəri/ *n.* **(a)**
Kommentar, *der* (**on** zu)
(b) (Radio, Telev.) [**live** *or* **running**] ~:
Livereportage, *die*
commentate /'kɒmənteɪt/ *v.i.* ~ **on sth.**
etw. kommentieren
commentator /'kɒmənteɪtə(r)/ *n.*
Kommentator, *der*/Kommentatorin, *die;*
(Sport) Reporter, *der*/Reporterin, *die*
commerce /'kɒmɜːs/ *n.* Handel, *der*
commercial /kə'mɜːʃl/ ① *adj.* Handels-;
kaufmännisch ⟨*Ausbildung*⟩
② *n.* Werbespot, *der*
commercial: ~ '**bank** *n.* private
Geschäftsbank; ~ '**break** *n.* Werbepause,
die
commercialism /kə'mɜːʃəlɪzm/ *n.*
Kommerzialismus, *der*
commercialize /kə'mɜːʃəlaɪz/ *v.t.*
kommerzialisieren
commercial: ~ '**radio** *n.* Werbefunk,
der; ~ '**television** *n.* Werbefernsehen,
das; ~ '**traveller** *n.* Handelsvertreter, *der*/
-vertreterin, *die;* ~ '**vehicle** *n.*
Nutzfahrzeug, *das*
commiserate /kə'mɪzəreɪt/ *v.i.* ~ **with sb.**
jmdm. sein Mitgefühl aussprechen (**on** zu)
commission /kə'mɪʃn/ ① *n.* **(a)** (official
body) Kommission, *die*
(b) (instruction, piece of work) Auftrag, *der*
(c) (Mil.) Ernennungsurkunde, *die*
(d) (pay of agent) Provision, *die*
(e) in/out of ~ ⟨*Auto, Maschine*⟩ in/außer
Betrieb
② *v.t.* beauftragen ⟨*Künstler*⟩; in Auftrag
geben ⟨*Gemälde usw.*⟩
commissionaire /kəmɪʃə'neə(r)/ *n.* (esp.
Brit.) Portier, *der*
commissioner /kə'mɪʃənə(r)/ *n.* (of police)
Präsident, *der*
commit /kə'mɪt/ *v.t.,* **-tt-:** **(a)** begehen
⟨*Verbrechen, Fehler, Ehebruch*⟩
(b) (pledge, bind) ~ **oneself/sb. to doing sth.**
sich/jmdn. verpflichten, etw. zu tun
(c) (entrust) anvertrauen (**to** *Dat.*)
(d) ~ **sb. for trial** jmdm. dem Gericht
überstellen
com'mitment *n.* Verpflichtung (**to**
gegenüber)
com'mitted *adj.* engagiert
committee /kə'mɪtɪ/ *n.* Ausschuss, *der*
commodity /kə'mɒdɪtɪ/ *n.* **(a)** household
~: Haushaltsartikel, *der*
(b) (St. Exch.) [vertretbare] Ware; (raw material)
Rohstoff, *der*
common /'kɒmən/ ① *adj.* **(a)** (belonging to
all) gemeinsam
(b) (public) öffentlich
(c) (usual) gewöhnlich; (frequent) häufig;
allgemein verbreitet ⟨*Sitte, Redensart*⟩

(d) (vulgar) ordinär
② *n.* **(a)** (land) Gemeindeland, *das*
(b) have sth./nothing/a lot in ~ [**with sb.**]
etw./nichts/viel [mit jmdm.] gemein[sam]
haben
common 'cold *n.* Erkältung, *die*
'**commoner** *n.* Bürgerliche *der*/*die*
common: ~ '**ground** *n.* gemeinsame
Basis; ~ '**knowledge** *n.* **it's [a matter of]**
~ **knowledge that** ... es ist allgemein
bekannt, dass ...; ~**law** *adj.* **she's his**
~**-law wife** sie lebt mit ihm in eheähnlicher
Gemeinschaft
'**commonly** *adv.* im Allgemeinen
common: **C**~ '**Market** *n.* gemeinsamer
Markt; ~**place** ① *n.* Gemeinplatz, *der;*
② *adj.* alltäglich; ~ **room** *n.* (Brit.)
Gemeinschaftsraum, *der;* (for lecturers)
Dozentenzimmer, *das*
Commons /'kɒmənz/ *n. pl.* **the [House of]**
~: das Unterhaus
common: ~ '**sense** *n.* gesunder
Menschenverstand; ~**sense** *adj.*
vernünftig; gesund ⟨*Ansicht, Standpunkt*⟩;
~**wealth** *n.* **the [British] C**~**wealth** das
Commonwealth
commotion /kə'məʊʃn/ *n.* Tumult, *der*
communal /'kɒmjʊnl/ *adj.* **(a)** (of or for the
community) gemeindlich
(b) (for common use) gemeinsam
commune /'kɒmjuːn/ *n.* Kommune, *die*
communicate /kə'mjuːnɪkeɪt/ ① *v.t.*
übertragen ⟨*Krankheit*⟩; übermitteln
⟨*Informationen*⟩; vermitteln ⟨*Gefühle, Ideen*⟩
② *v.i.* ~ **with sb.** mit jmdm. kommunizieren
communication /kəmjuːnɪ'keɪʃn/ *n.* **(a)**
(of information) Übermittlung, *die*
(b) (message) Mitteilung, *die* (**to** an + *Akk.*)
communication: ~ **cord** *n.* Notbremse,
die; ~**s satellite** *n.* Nachrichtensatellit,
der
communicative /kə'mjuːnɪkətɪv/ *adj.*
gesprächig
Communion /kə'mjuːnɪən/ *n.* **[Holy]** ~
(Protestant Ch.) das [heilige] Abendmahl; (RC
Ch.) die [heilige] Kommunion
communiqué /kə'mjuːnɪkeɪ/ *n.*
Kommuniqué, *das*
communism /'kɒmjʊnɪzm/ *n.*
Kommunismus, *der;* **C**~: der Kommunismus
Communist, communist /'kɒmjʊnɪst/
① *n.* Kommunist, *der*/Kommunistin, *die*
② *adj.* kommunistisch
community /kə'mjuːnɪtɪ/ *n.* **(a)** (organized
body) Gemeinwesen, *das;* **the Jewish** ~: die
jüdische Gemeinde
(b) *no pl.* (public) Öffentlichkeit, *die*
community: ~ '**care** *n.* ≈ ambulante
Betreuung; ~ **centre** *n.*
Gemeindezentrum, *das;* ~ '**charge** *n.* (Brit.)
Gemeindesteuer, *die;* ~ '**service** *n.*:

[*freiwilliger od. als Strafe auferlegter*]
sozialer Dienst; ~ **spirit** *n.*
Gemeinschaftsgeist, *der*
commute /kə'mju:t/ [1] *v.t.* umwandeln
⟨*Strafe*⟩ (**to** in + *Akk.*)
[2] *v.i.* pendeln
commuter /kə'mju:tə(r)/ *n.* Pendler, *der*/
Pendlerin, *die*
com'muter: ~ **belt** *n.* großstädtischer
Einzugsbereich; ~ **train** *n.* Pendlerzug, *der*
compact¹ /kəm'pækt/ *adj.* kompakt
compact² /'kɒmpækt/ *n.* Puderdose [mit
Puder(stein)]
compact 'disc *n.* Compactdisc, *die;*
~ **player** CD-Spieler, *der*
companion /kəm'pænjən/ *n.* Begleiter,
der/Begleiterin, *die*
com'panionship *n.* Gesellschaft, *die*
company /'kʌmpənɪ/ *n.* (a) (persons
assembled, companionship) Gesellschaft, *die;*
expect ~: Besuch *od.* Gäste erwarten; **keep
sb.** ~: jmdm. Gesellschaft leisten
(b) (firm) Gesellschaft, *die;* ~ **car**
Firmenwagen, *der;* ~ **policy**
Unternehmenspolitik, *die;* Firmenpolitik, *die*
(c) (of actors) Truppe, *die;* Ensemble, *das*
(d) (Mil.) Kompanie, *die*
comparable /'kɒmpərəbl/ *adj.*
vergleichbar (**to, with** mit)
comparably /'kɒmpərəblɪ/ *adv.* in
vergleichbarer Weise; vergleichbar
comparative /kəm'pærətɪv/ [1] *adj.* (a)
(relative) relativ; **in** ~ **comfort** relativ
komfortabel
(b) (Ling.) komparativ (fachspr.); **a**
~ **adjective/adverb** ein Adjektiv/Adverb im
Komparativ
[2] *n.* (Ling.) Komparativ, *der*
com'paratively *adv.* verhältnismäßig
compare /kəm'peə(r)/ [1] *v.t.* vergleichen
(**to, with** mit); ~**d with** *or* **to sb./sth.**
verglichen mit *od.* im Vergleich zu jmdm./
etw.
[2] *v.i.* sich vergleichen lassen
comparison /kəm'pærɪsn/ *n.* Vergleich,
der; **in** *or* **by** ~ [**with sb./sth.**] im Vergleich
[zu jmdm./etw.]
compartment /kəm'pɑ:tmənt/ *n.* (in
drawer, desk, etc.) Fach, *das;* (of railway carriage)
Abteil, *das*
compass /'kʌmpəs/ *n.* (a) *in pl.* [**a pair of**]
~**es** ein Zirkel
(b) (for navigating) Kompass, *der*
compassion /kəm'pæʃn/ *n.* Mitgefühl,
das (**for** mit)
compassionate /kəm'pæʃənət/ *adj.*
mitfühlend; **on** ~ **grounds** aus persönlichen
Gründen; (for family reasons) aus familiären
Gründen
compatibility /kəmpætɪ'bɪlɪtɪ/ *n.*
Vereinbarkeit, *die;* (of people)
Zueinanderpassen, *das;* (Comp.)
Kompatibilität, *die*

compatible /kəm'pætɪbl/ *adj.* vereinbar;
zueinander passend ⟨*Personen*⟩; (Comp.)
kompatibel
compel /kəm'pel/ *v.t.,* **-ll-** zwingen
compelling /kəm'pelɪŋ/ *adj.* bezwingend
compendium /kəm'pendɪəm/ *n.*
Kompendium, *das*
compensate /'kɒmpenseɪt/ [1] *v.i.* ~ **for**
sth. etw. ersetzen
[2] *v.t.* ~ **sb. for sth.** jmdn. für etw.
entschädigen
compensation /kɒmpen'seɪʃn/ *n.* Ersatz,
der; (for damages, injuries, etc.)
Schaden[s]ersatz, *der*
compère /'kɒmpeə(r)/ *n.* (Brit.)
Conférencier, *der*
compete /kəm'pi:t/ *v.i.* konkurrieren (**for**
um); (Sport) kämpfen
competence /'kɒmpɪtəns/ *n.* Fähigkeiten
Pl.
competent /'kɒmpɪtənt/ *adj.* fähig; **not**
~ **to do sth.** nicht kompetent, etw. zu tun
'competently *adv.* kompetent
competition /kɒmpɪ'tɪʃn/ *n.* (a) (contest)
Wettbewerb, *der;* (in magazine etc.)
Preisausschreiben, *das*
(b) (those competing) Konkurrenz, *die*
competitive /kəm'petɪtɪv/ *adj.*
wettbewerbsfähig ⟨*Preis, Unternehmen*⟩;
~ **sports** Leistungssport, *der*
competitor /kəm'petɪtə(r)/ *n.* Konkurrent,
der/Konkurrentin, *die;* (in contest, race)
Teilnehmer, *der*/-nehmerin, *die*
compile /kəm'paɪl/ *v.t.* zusammenstellen
complacency /kəm'pleɪsənsɪ/ *n.*
Selbstzufriedenheit, *die*
complacent /kəm'pleɪsənt/ *adj.*
selbstzufrieden
complain /kəm'pleɪn/ *v.i.* sich beklagen
(**about, at** über + *Akk.;* **to** bei); ~ **of sth.**
über etw. ⟨*Akk.*⟩ klagen
complaint /kəm'pleɪnt/ *n.* (a) Beschwerde,
die
(b) (ailment) Leiden, *das*
complement [1] /'kɒmplɪmənt/ *n.* (a)
(what completes) Vervollständigung, *die*
(b) (full number) **a** [**full**] ~: die volle Zahl; (of
people) die volle Stärke
[2] /'kɒmplɪment/ *v.t.* ergänzen
complementary /kɒmplɪ'mentərɪ/ *adj.*
(a) (completing) ergänzend
(b) (completing each other) einander ergänzend
complementary 'medicine *n.*
Komplementärmedizin, *die*
complete /kəm'pli:t/ [1] *adj.* (a)
vollständig; (in number) vollzählig
(b) (finished) fertig
(c) (absolute) völlig ⟨*Idiot*⟩; absolut
⟨*Katastrophe*⟩; total, (ugs.) blutig ⟨*Anfänger*⟩
[2] *v.t.* (a) (finish) beenden; fertig stellen
⟨*Gebäude, Arbeit*⟩
(b) ausfüllen ⟨*Formular*⟩
⋯⟩

com'pletely *adv.* völlig; absolut
⟨*erfolgreich*⟩
completion /kəm'pli:ʃn/ *n.* Beendigung,
die; (of building, work) Fertigstellung, *die*
complex /'kɒmpleks/ ⓵ *adj.* kompliziert
⓶ *n.* Komplex, *der*
complexion /kəm'plekʃn/ *n.*
Gesichtsfarbe, *die;* (fig.) Gesicht, *das*
-complexioned /kəm'plekʃnd/ *adj.* in
comb. **sallow-/fair-~**: mit gelblichem Teint/
mit hellem Teint
complexity /kəm'pleksɪtɪ/ *n.*
Kompliziertheit, *die*
complicate /'kɒmplɪkeɪt/ *v.t.*
komplizieren.
'complicated *adj.* kompliziert
complication /kɒmplɪ'keɪʃn/ *n.*
Komplikation, *die*
complicity /kəm'plɪsɪtɪ/ *n.* Mittäterschaft,
die (in bei)
compliment ⓵ /'kɒmplɪmənt/ *n.*
Kompliment, *das; in pl.* (formal greetings)
Grüße *Pl.;* **pay sb. a ~**: jmdn. ein
Kompliment machen
⓶ /'kɒmplɪment/ *v.t.* **~ sb. on sth.** jmdm.
Komplimente wegen etw. machen
complimentary /kɒmplɪ'mentərɪ/ *adj.* **(a)**
schmeichelhaft
(b) (free) Frei-
comply /kəm'plaɪ/ *v.i.* **~ with sth.** sich
nach etw. richten; **he refused to ~:** er wollte
sich nicht danach richten
component /kəm'pəʊnənt/ ⓵ *n.*
Bestandteil, *der*
⓶ *adj.* **a ~ part** ein Bestandteil
compose /kəm'pəʊz/ *v.t.* **(a)** bilden; **be ~d
of** sich zusammensetzen aus
(b) verfassen ⟨*Rede, Gedicht*⟩; abfassen
⟨*Brief*⟩
(c) (Mus.) komponieren
com'posed *adj.* (calm) gefasst
com'poser *n.* Komponist, *der*/
Komponistin, *die*
composition /kɒmpə'zɪʃn/ *n.* **(a)**
(constitution) (of soil etc.) Zusammensetzung, *die;*
(of picture) Aufbau, *der*
(b) (essay) Aufsatz, *der;* (Mus.) Komposition,
die
compost /'kɒmpɒst/ *n.* Kompost, *der*
compostable /'kɒmpɒstəbl/ *adj.*
kompostierbar
'compost heap *n.* Komposthaufen, *der*
composure /kəm'pəʊʒə(r)/ *n.* Gleichmut,
der
compound¹ ⓵ /'kɒmpaʊnd/ *adj.* **(a)**
zusammengesetzt
(b) (Med.) **~ fracture** komplizierter Bruch
⓶ /'kɒmpaʊnd/ *n.* **(a)** (mixture) Mischung, *die*
(b) (Ling.) Kompositum, *das*
(c) (Chem.) Verbindung, *die*
⓷ /kəm'paʊnd/ *v.t.* verschlimmern
⟨*Schwierigkeiten, Verletzung usw.*⟩

compound² /'kɒmpaʊnd/ *n.* umzäuntes
Gelände
compound 'interest *n.* Zinseszinsen *Pl.*
comprehend /kɒmprɪ'hend/ *v.t.* verstehen
comprehensible /kɒmprɪ'hensɪbl/ *adj.*
verständlich
comprehension /kɒmprɪ'henʃn/ *n.*
Verständnis, *das*
comprehensive /kɒmprɪ'hensɪv/ ⓵ *adj.*
(a) umfassend
(b) ~ school Gesamtschule, *die*
(c) (insurance) Vollkasko-
⓶ *n.* Gesamtschule, *die*
compress ⓵ /kəm'pres/ *v.t.* **(a)** (squeeze)
zusammenpressen (**into** zu)
(b) komprimieren ⟨*Luft, Gas, Bericht*⟩
(c) (Comp.) komprimieren
⓶ /'kɒmpres/ *n.* Kompresse, *die*
compression /kəm'preʃn/ *n.*
Kompression, *die*
compressor /kəm'presə(r)/ *n.*
Kompressor, *der*
comprise /kəm'praɪz/ *v.t.* (include)
umfassen; (consist of) bestehen aus
compromise /'kɒmprəmaɪz/ ⓵ *n.*
Kompromiss, *der*
⓶ *v.i.* Kompromisse/einen Kompromiss
schließen
⓷ *v.t.* kompromittieren
compromising /'kɒmprəmaɪzɪŋ/ *adj.*
kompromittierend
compulsion /kəm'pʌlʃn/ *n.* Zwang, *der;* **be
under no ~ to do sth.** keineswegs etw. tun
müssen
compulsive /kəm'pʌlsɪv/ *adj.* **(a)**
zwanghaft; **he is a ~ gambler** er ist dem
Spiel verfallen
(b) this book is ~ reading von diesem Buch
kann man sich nicht losreißen
compulsory /kəm'pʌlsərɪ/ *adj.*
obligatorisch
compunction /kəm'pʌŋkʃn/ *n.*
Schuldgefühle
computer /kəm'pju:tə(r)/ *n.* Computer, *der*
computer: ~-aided *adj.*
computergestützt; **~ ani'mation** *n.*
Computeranimation, *die;* **~-assisted** *adj.*
computergestützt; **~ 'dating** *n.*
Partnervermittlung per Computer; **~ dating
agency/service** Computer-
Partnervermittlung[sagentur], *die;* **~ game**
n. Computerspiel, *das;* **~ 'graphics** *n. pl.*
Computergraphik, *die*
computerisation, computerise
▸ COMPUTERIZ-
computerization /kəmpju:təraɪ'zeɪʃn/ *n.*
Computerisierung, *die*
computerize /kəm'pju:təraɪz/ *v.t.*
computerisieren
computer: ~-'literate *adj.* mit
Computern vertraut; **~-'operated** *adj.*
computergesteuert; rechnergesteuert;
~ program *n.* Programm, *das;*

~ **programmer** n. Programmierer, der/
Programmiererin, die; ~ **programming**
n. Programmieren, das; ~ **room** n.
Computerraum, der; ~ '**science** n.
Computerwissenschaft, die; ~ **terminal** n.
Terminal, das; ~ '**typesetting** n.
Computersatz, der; ~ **virus** n.
[Computer]virus, das od. der

computing /kəm'pju:tɪŋ/ n. EDV, die;
elektronische Datenverarbeitung; ~ **skills**
Computerkenntnisse Pl.

comrade /'kɒmreɪd, 'kɒmrɪd/ n. Kamerad,
der/Kameradin, die

'**comradeship** n. Kameradschaft, die

con /kɒn/ (coll.) 1 n. Schwindel, der
2 v.t., **-nn-** reinlegen (ugs.); ~ **sb. into sth.**
jmdm. etw. aufschwatzen (ugs.)

concave /'kɒnkeɪv/ adj. konkav

conceal /kən'si:l/ v.t. verbergen (**from** vor
+ Dat.)

con'cealment n. Verbergen, das

concede /kən'si:d/ v.t. zugeben

conceit /kən'si:t/ n. Einbildung, die

con'ceited adj. eingebildet

conceivable /kən'si:vəbl/ adj.
vorstellbar; **it is scarcely ~ that ...**: man
kann sich (Dat.) kaum vorstellen, dass ...

conceivably /kən'si:vəblɪ/ adj.
möglicherweise; **he cannot ~ have done it**
er kann es unmöglich getan haben

conceive /kən'si:v/ 1 v.t. (a) empfangen
⟨Kind⟩
(b) (form in mind) sich (Dat.) vorstellen; haben
⟨Idee, Plan⟩
2 v.i. (a) (become pregnant) empfangen
(b) ~ **of sth.** sich (Dat.) etw. vorstellen

concentrate /'kɒnsəntreɪt/ 1 v.t.
konzentrieren
2 v.i. sich konzentrieren (**on** auf + Akk.)

'**concentrated** adj. konzentriert

concentration /kɒnsən'treɪʃn/ n.
Konzentration, die

concen'tration camp n.
Konzentrationslager, das; KZ, das

concentric /kən'sentrɪk/ adj.
konzentrisch

concept /'kɒnsept/ n. Begriff, der; (idea)
Vorstellung, die

conception /kən'sepʃn/ (a) Vorstellung,
die (**of** von)
(b) (of child) Empfängnis, die

conceptual /kən'septjʊəl/ adj. begrifflich

conceptualize /kən'septjʊəlaɪz/ v.t.
begrifflich fassen

concern /kən'sɜːn/ 1 v.t. (a) (affect)
betreffen; **so far as ... is ~ed** was ... betrifft;
'**to whom it may ~**' ≈ „Bestätigung"; (on
certificate, testimonial) ≈ „Zeugnis"
(b) (interest) ~ **oneself with** or **about sth.** sich
mit etw. befassen
(c) (trouble) beunruhigen
2 n. (a) (anxiety) Besorgnis, die; (interest)
Interesse, das

(b) (matter) Angelegenheit, die
(c) (firm) Unternehmen, das

con'cerned /kən'sɜːnd/ adj. (a) (involved)
betroffen; (interested) interessiert; **as** or **so far
as I'm ~**: was mich betrifft
(b) (troubled) besorgt

con'cerning prep. bezüglich

concert /'kɒnsət/ n. Konzert, das

concerted /kən'sɜːtɪd/ adj. vereint

concert: ~**goer** n. Konzertbesucher,
der/-besucherin, die; ~ **hall** n. Konzertsaal,
der

concertina /kɒnsə'ti:nə/ n. Konzertina,
die

concerto /kən'tʃeətəʊ/ n. Konzert, das

concession /kən'seʃn/ n. Konzession, die

concessionary /kən'seʃənərɪ/ adj.
Konzessions-; ~ **rate/fare** ermäßigter Tarif

conciliatory /kən'sɪljətərɪ/ adj.
versöhnlich

concise /kən'saɪs/ adj. kurz und prägnant;
knapp, konzis ⟨Stil⟩

conclude /kən'klu:d/ 1 v.t. (a) (end)
beschließen
(b) (infer) schließen (**from** aus)
(c) (reach decision) beschließen
2 v.i. (end) schließen

concluding /kən'klu:dɪŋ/ adj.
abschließend

conclusion /kən'klu:ʒn/ n. (a) (end)
Abschluss, der; **in ~**: zum Abschluss
(b) (result) Ausgang, der
(c) (inference) Schluss, der; **draw** or **reach a
~**: zu einem Schluss kommen

conclusive /kən'klu:sɪv/ adj.,
con'clusively adv. schlüssig

concoct /kən'kɒkt/ v.t. zubereiten;
zusammenbrauen ⟨Trank⟩

concoction /kən'kɒkʃn/ n. Gebräu, das

concourse /'kɒnkɔːs/ n. Halle, die; **station
~**: Bahnhofshalle, die

concrete /'kɒnkri:t/ 1 adj. konkret
2 n. Beton, der; attrib. Beton-; **aus Beton**
präd

concrete/'kɒnkri:t/: ~ **mixer** n.
Betonmischer, der; Betonmischmaschine,
die; ~ '**poetry** n. konkrete Poesie

concur /kən'kɜː(r)/ v.i., **-rr-:** ~ [**with sb.**] [**in
sth.**] [jmdm.] [in etw. (Dat.)] zustimmen

concurrent /kən'kʌrənt/ adj.,
con'currently adv. gleichzeitig

concussion /kən'kʌʃn/ n.
Gehirnerschütterung, die

condemn /kən'dem/ v.t. (a) (censure)
verdammen
(b) (Law: sentence) verurteilen (**to** zu)
(c) für unbewohnbar erklären ⟨Gebäude⟩

condemnation /kɒndem'neɪʃn/ n.
Verdammung, die

condensation /kɒnden'seɪʃn/ n. (a)
(condensing) Kondensation, die
(b) (water) Kondenswasser, das

condense /kən'dens/ ① *v.t.* (a)
komprimieren; ∼d milk Kondensmilch, *die*
(b) (Phys., Chem.) kondensieren
② *v.i.* kondensieren

condescend /kɒndɪ'send/ *v.i.* ∼ to do sth.
sich dazu herablassen, etw. zu tun

conde'scending *adj.* herablassend

condescension /kɒndɪ'senʃn/ *n.* (derog.:
patronizing manner) Herablassung, *die*

condiment /'kɒndɪmənt/ *n.* Gewürz, *das*

condition /kən'dɪʃn/ *n.* (a) (stipulation)
[Vor]bedingung, *die;* on [the] ∼ that ...: unter
der Voraussetzung, dass ...
(b) in pl. (circumstances) Umstände *Pl.;*
weather/living ∼s Witterungs-/
Wohnverhältnisse; working ∼s
Arbeitsbedingungen
(c) (of athlete etc.) Form, *die;* (of thing) Zustand,
der; (of patient) Verfassung, *die*
(d) (Med.) Leiden, *das*

conditional /kən'dɪʃənl/ *adj.* (a) bedingt;
be ∼ [up]on sth. von etw. abhängen
(b) (Ling.) Konditional-

con'ditioner *n.* Frisiermittel, *das*

condolence /kən'dəʊləns/ *n.*
Anteilnahme, die; letter of ∼: Beileidsbrief,
der

condom /'kɒndɒm/ *n.* Kondom, *das od. der*

condominium /'kɒndə'mɪnɪəm/ *n.* (Amer.)
Appartementhaus [mit
Eigentumswohnungen]

condone /kən'dəʊn/ *v.t.* hinwegsehen über
(+ *Akk.*); (approve) billigen

conducive /kən'dju:sɪv/ *adj.* be ∼ to sth.
einer Sache (*Dat.*) förderlich sein

conduct ① /'kɒndʌkt/ *n.* (a) (behaviour)
Verhalten, *das*
(b) (way of ∼ing) Führung, *die*
② /kən'dʌkt/ *v.t.* (a) führen
(b) (Mus.) dirigieren
(c) (Phys.) leiten
(d) ∼ed tour Führung, *die*

conduction /kən'dʌkʃn/ *n.* (Phys.) Leitung,
die

conductor /kən'dʌktə(r)/ *n.* (a) (Mus.)
Dirigent, *der*/Dirigentin, *die*
(b) (of bus, tram) Schaffner, *der*

conductress /kən'dʌktrɪs/ *n.* Schaffnerin,
die

conduit /'kɒndjʊɪt/ *n.* (a) Leitung, *die;*
Kanal, *der* (auch fig.)
(b) (Electr.) Isolierrohr, *das*

cone /kəʊn/ *n.* (a) Kegel, *der;* (traffic ∼)
Leitkegel, *der*
(b) (Bot.) Zapfen, *der*
(c) ice-cream ∼: Eistüte, *die*

confectioner /kən'fekʃənə(r)/ *n.* ∼'s
[shop] Süßwarengeschäft, *das*

con'fectionery *n.* Süßwaren *Pl.*

confederate /kən'fedərət/ *adj.* verbündet

confederation /kən'fedə'reɪʃn/ *n.*
[Staaten]bund, *der*

confer /kən'fɜ:(r)/ ① *v.t.,* -rr-: ∼ sth. [up]on
sb. jmdm. etw. verleihen
② *v.i.,* -rr-: ∼ with sb. sich mit jmdm.
beraten

conference /'kɒnfərəns/ *n.* (a) Konferenz,
die
(b) be in ∼: in einer Besprechung sein

conference: ∼ **room** *n.* Konferenzraum,
der; ∼ **table** *n.* Konferenztisch, *der*

confess /kən'fes/ ① *v.t.* (a) gestehen
(b) (Eccl.) beichten
② *v.i.* (a) ∼ to sth. etw. gestehen
(b) (Eccl.) beichten (to sb. jmdm.)

confession /kən'feʃn/ *n.* (a) Geständnis,
das
(b) (Eccl.: of sins etc.) Beichte, *die*

confetti /kən'fetɪ/ *n.* Konfetti, *das*

confidant /'kɒnfɪdænt, kɒnfɪ'dænt/ *n.*
Vertraute, *der*

confidante /'kɒnfɪdænt, kɒnfɪ'dænt/ *n.*
Vertraute, *die*

confide /kən'faɪd/ ① *v.i.* ∼ in sb. sich
jmdm. anvertrauen
② *v.t.* ∼ sth. to sb. jmdm. etw. anvertrauen

confidence /'kɒnfɪdəns/ *n.* (a) (firm trust)
Vertrauen, *das;* have ∼ in sb./sth. Vertrauen
zu jmdm./etw. haben; have [absolute] ∼ that
...: [absolut] sicher sein, dass ...
(b) (assured expectation) Gewissheit, *die*
(c) (self-reliance) Selbstvertrauen, *das*
(d) in ∼: im Vertrauen; this is in [strict] ∼:
das ist [streng] vertraulich

'confidence trick *n.* (Brit.) Trickbetrug,
der

confident /'kɒnfɪdənt/ *adj.* zuversichtlich
(about in Bezug auf + *Akk.*)

confidential /kɒnfɪ'denʃl/ *adj.* vertraulich

confidentiality /kɒnfɪdenʃɪ'ælɪtɪ/ *n.*
Vertraulichkeit, *die*

confi'dentially *adv.* vertraulich

'confidently *adv.* zuversichtlich

confiding /kən'faɪdɪŋ/ *adj.,* **con'fidingly**
adv. vertrauensvoll

confine /kən'faɪn/ *v.t.* (a) einsperren; be
∼d to bed/the house ans Bett/Haus gefesselt
sein
(b) (fig.) ∼ oneself to doing sth. sich darauf
beschränken, etw. zu tun

con'fined *adj.* begrenzt

con'finement *n.* (imprisonment)
Einsperrung, *die*

confines /'kɒnfaɪnz/ *n. pl.* Grenzen *Pl.*

confirm /kən'fɜ:m/ *v.t.* bestätigen

confirmation /kɒnfə'meɪʃn/ *n.* (a)
Bestätigung, *die*
(b) (Protestant Ch.) Konfirmation, *die;* (RC Ch.)
Firmung, *die*

con'firmed *adj.* eingefleischt ‹*Junggeselle*›;
überzeugt ‹*Vegetarier*›

confiscate /'kɒnfɪskeɪt/ *v.t.*
beschlagnahmen

confiscation /kɒnfɪs'keɪʃn/ n.
Beschlagnahme, *die*

conflict [1] /'kɒnflɪkt/ n. (a) (fight) Kampf,
der
(b) (clashing) Konflikt, *der*
[2] /kən'flɪkt/ v.i. (be incompatible) sich (*Dat.*)
widersprechen; ~ **with sth.** einer Sache
(*Dat.*) widersprechen

con'flicting adj. widersprüchlich

conform /kən'fɔːm/ v.i. (a) entsprechen (to
Dat.)
(b) (comply) sich einfügen; ~ **to** or **with sth./**
with sb. sich nach etw./jmdm. richten

conformist /kən'fɔːmɪst/ n. Konformist,
der/Konformistin, *die*

conformity /kən'fɔːmɪtɪ/ n.
Übereinstimmung, *die* (with, to mit)

confound /kən'faʊnd/ v.t. (a) (defeat)
vereiteln
(b) (confuse) verwirren

con'founded adj. (coll. derog.) verdammt

confront /kən'frʌnt/ v.t. (a)
gegenüberstellen; ~ **sb. with sth./sb.** jmdn.
mit etw./[mit] jmdm. konfrontieren
(b) (stand facing) gegenüberstehen (+ *Dat.*)

confrontation /kɒnfrən'teɪʃn/ n.
Konfrontation, *die*

confuse /kən'fjuːz/ v.t. (a) (disorder)
durcheinander bringen
(b) (mix up mentally) verwechseln
(c) (perplex) verwirren

con'fused adj. konfus; wirr ‹Gedanken,
Gerüchte›; verworren ‹Lage, Situation›

confusing /kən'fjuːzɪŋ/ adj. verwirrend

confusion /kən'fjuːʒn/ n. (a) Verwirrung,
die; (mixing up) Verwechslung, *die*
(b) (embarrassment) Verlegenheit, *die*

congeal /kən'dʒiːl/ v.i. gerinnen

congenial /kən'dʒiːnɪəl/ adj. (agreeable)
angenehm

congenital /kən'dʒenɪtl/ adj. angeboren;
kongenital (fachspr.)

conger /'kɒŋgə(r)/ n. ~ [eel] Seeaal, *der*

congested /kən'dʒestɪd/ adj. verstopft
‹Straße, Nase›

congestion /kən'dʒestʃn/ n. (of traffic)
Stauung, *die;* **nasal** ~: verstopfte Nase

conglomerate /kən'glɒmərət/ n.
(Commerc.) Großkonzern, *der*

conglomeration /kənglɒmə'reɪʃn/ n.
Anhäufung, *die*

congratulate /kən'grætjʊleɪt/ v.t.
gratulieren (+ *Dat.*); ~ **sb./oneself on sth.**
jmdm./sich zu etw. gratulieren

congratulations /kəngrætjʊ'leɪʃnz/
[1] int. ~! herzlichen Glückwunsch! (on zu);
(on passing exam etc.) ich gratuliere!
[2] n. pl. Glückwünsche *Pl.*

congregate /'kɒŋgrɪgeɪt/ v.i. sich
versammeln

congregation /kɒŋgrɪ'geɪʃn/ n. (Eccl.)
Gemeinde, *die*

congress /'kɒŋgres/ n. Kongress, *der;* **C~**
(Amer.) der Kongress

congressional /kən'greʃənl/ adj.
Kongress-

conical /'kɒnɪkl/ adj. kegelförmig

conifer /'kɒnɪfə(r)/ n. Nadelbaum, *der*

coniferous /kə'nɪfərəs/ adj. Nadel-; ~ **tree**
Nadelbaum, *der;* Konifere, *die*

conjecture /kən'dʒektʃə(r)/ [1] n.
Vermutung, *die*
[2] v.t. vermuten
[3] v.i. Vermutungen anstellen

conjugate /'kɒndʒʊgeɪt/ v.t. (Ling.)
konjugieren

conjugation /kɒndʒʊ'geɪʃn/ n. (Ling.)
Konjugation, *die*

conjunction /kən'dʒʌŋkʃn/ n. (a)
Verbindung, *die;* **in** ~ **with** in Verbindung
mit
(b) (Ling.) Konjunktion, *die*

conjure /'kʌndʒə(r)/ v.i. zaubern; **conjuring**
trick Zaubertrick, *der*
■ **conjure 'up** v.t. heraufbeschwören

conjurer, conjuror /'kʌndʒərə(r)/ n.
Zauberkünstler, *der*/-künstlerin, *die*

connect /kə'nekt/ [1] v.t. verbinden (to,
with mit)
[2] v.i. ~ **with sth.** mit etw.
zusammenhängen

con'nected adj. zusammenhängend

connection, (Brit. also) **connexion**
/kə'nekʃn/ n. (a) (act, state) Verbindung, *die*
(b) (fig.: of ideas) Zusammenhang, *der;* **in**
~ **with** im Zusammenhang mit
(c) (train, bus, etc.) Anschluss, *der*

connoisseur /kɒnə'sɜː(r)/ n. Kenner, *der*

connotation /kɒnə'teɪʃn/ n. Assoziation,
die

conquer /'kɒŋkə(r)/ v.t. besiegen; erobern
‹Land›

conqueror /'kɒŋkərə(r)/ n. (of a country)
Eroberer, *der*

conquest /'kɒŋkwest/ n. Eroberung, *die*

conscience /'kɒnʃəns/ n. Gewissen, *das;*
have a clear/guilty ~: ein gutes/schlechtes
Gewissen haben

'conscience-stricken,
'conscience-struck adjs.
schuldbewusst

conscientious /kɒnʃɪ'enʃəs/ adj.
pflichtbewusst; (meticulous) gewissenhaft;
~ **objector** Wehrdienstverweigerer [aus
Gewissensgründen]

consci'entiously adv. pflichtbewusst;
(meticulously) gewissenhaft

conscious /'kɒnʃəs/ adj. (a) **he is not**
~ **of it** es ist ihm nicht bewusst
(b) pred. (awake) bei Bewusstsein präd.
(c) (realized by doer) bewusst ‹Versuch,
Bemühung›

'consciously adv. bewusst

'consciousness n. Bewusstsein, *das*

conscript ① /kən'skrɪpt/ v.t. einberufen
② /'kɒnskrɪpt/ n. Einberufene, der/die
conscription /kən'skrɪpʃn/ n.
Wehrpflicht, die
consecrate /'kɒnsɪkreɪt/ v.t. weihen
consecutive /kən'sekjʊtɪv/ adj.
aufeinander folgend ‹Monate, Jahre›;
fortlaufend ‹Zahlen›
con'secutively adj. hintereinander
consensus /kən'sensəs/ n. Einigkeit, die
consent /kən'sent/ ① v.i. zustimmen
② n. (agreement) Zustimmung, die (to zu); by
common or general ~: nach allgemeiner
Auffassung; age of ~: Ehemündigkeitsalter,
das
consequence /'kɒnsɪkwəns/ n. (a) (result)
Folge, die; in ~: folglich; as a ~:
infolgedessen
(b) (importance) Bedeutung, die
consequent /'kɒnsɪkwənt/ adj. daraus
folgend
'consequently adv. infolgedessen
conservation /kɒnsə'veɪʃn/ n. Erhaltung,
die; wildlife ~: Schutz wild lebender
Tierarten
conser'vation area n. (Brit.) (rural)
Landschaftsschutzgebiet, das; (urban) unter
Denkmalschutz stehendes Gebiet
conservationist /kɒnsə'veɪʃənɪst/ n.
Naturschützer, der/-schützerin, die
conservative /kən'sɜ:vətɪv/ ① adj. (a)
konservativ
(b) vorsichtig ‹Schätzung›
(c) C~ (Brit. Polit.) konservativ; the C~ Party
die Konservative Partei
② n. C~ (Brit. Polit.) Konservative, der/die
con'servatively adv. vorsichtig
‹geschätzt›
conservatory /kən'sɜ:vətərɪ/ n.
Wintergarten, der
conserve /kən'sɜ:v/ v.t. erhalten; schonen
‹Kräfte›
consider /kən'sɪdə(r)/ v.t. (a) (think about)
~ sth. an etw. (Akk.) denken; he's ~ing
emigrating er denkt daran, auszuwandern
(b) (reflect on) sich (Dat.) überlegen
(c) (regard as) halten für; all things ~ed alles
in allem
considerable /kən'sɪdərəbl/ adj.,
con'siderably adv. erheblich
considerate /kən'sɪdərət/ adj.
rücksichtsvoll; (thoughtfully kind)
entgegenkommend
considerately /kən'sɪdərətlɪ/ adv.
rücksichtsvoll; (obligingly) entgegenkommend
consideration /kənsɪdə'reɪʃn/ n. (a)
Überlegung, die; take sth. into ~: etw.
berücksichtigen; the matter is under ~: die
Angelegenheit wird geprüft
(b) (thoughtfulness) Rücksichtnahme, die
considered /kən'sɪdəd/ adj. (a) ~ opinion
feste od. ernsthafte Überzeugung

(b) be highly ~ [by others] [bei anderen] in
hohem Ansehen stehen
con'sidering prep. ~ sth. wenn man etw.
bedenkt; ~ [that] ...: wenn man bedenkt,
dass ...
consign /kən'saɪn/ v.t. anvertrauen (to
Dat.)
con'signment n. (Commerc.) Sendung, die;
(large) Ladung, die
consist /kən'sɪst/ v.i. ~ of bestehen aus
consistency /kən'sɪstənsɪ/ n. (a) (density)
Konsistenz, die
(b) (being consistent) Konsequenz, die
consistent /kən'sɪstənt/ adj. (a) (compatible)
[miteinander] vereinbar
(b) (uniform) gleich bleibend ‹Qualität›
(c) (unchanging) konsequent
consolation /kɒnsə'leɪʃn/ n. Trost, der
conso'lation prize n. Trostpreis, der
console /kən'səʊl/ v.t. trösten
consolidate /kən'sɒlɪdeɪt/ v.t. festigen
consolidation /kənsɒlɪ'deɪʃn/ n.
Festigung, die
consoling /kən'səʊlɪŋ/ adj. tröstlich
consonant /'kɒnsənənt/ n. Konsonant, der
consort /kən'sɔ:t/ v.i. verkehren (with mit)
consortium /kən'sɔ:tɪəm/ n., pl. consortia
/kən'sɔ:tɪə/ Konsortium, das
conspicuous /kən'spɪkjʊəs/ adj. (a)
(visible) unübersehbar
(b) (obvious) auffallend
con'spicuously adv. (a) (visibly)
unübersehbar
(b) (obviously) auffallend
conspiracy /kən'spɪrəsɪ/ n. (conspiring)
Verschwörung, die; (plot) Komplott, das
conspire /kən'spaɪə(r)/ v.i. sich
verschwören
constable /'kʌnstəbl, 'kɒnstəbl/ n. (Brit.)
Polizist, der/Polizistin, die
constabulary /kən'stæbjʊlərɪ/ n. Polizei,
die
constant /'kɒnstənt/ adj. (a) (unceasing)
ständig
(b) (unchanging) gleich bleibend
'constantly adv. (a) (unceasingly) ständig
(b) (unchangingly) konstant
constellation /kɒnstə'leɪʃn/ n. Sternbild,
das
consternation /kɒnstə'neɪʃn/ n.
Bestürzung, die
constipated /'kɒnstɪpeɪtɪd/ adj. be ~: an
Verstopfung leiden
constipation /kɒnstɪ'peɪʃn/ n.
Verstopfung, die
constituency /kən'stɪtjʊənsɪ/ n.
Wahlkreis, der
constituent /kən'stɪtjʊənt/ n. (a) (part)
Bestandteil, der
(b) (Polit.) Wähler, der/Wählerin, die
constitute /'kɒnstɪtjuːt/ v.t. (a) (form, be)
sein; ~ a threat to eine Gefahr sein für

(b) (make up) bilden

constitution /ˌkɒnstɪˈtjuːʃn/ n. **(a)** (of person) Konstitution, *die*
(b) (of state) Verfassung, *die*

constitutional /ˌkɒnstɪˈtjuːʃənl/ adj. (of constitution) der Verfassung *nachgestellt*; (in harmony with constitution) verfassungsmäßig

constrain /kənˈstreɪn/ v.t. zwingen

constraint /kənˈstreɪnt/ n. (limitation) Einschränkung, *die*

constrict /kənˈstrɪkt/ v.t. verengen

constriction /kənˈstrɪkʃn/ n. Verengung, *die*

construct /kənˈstrʌkt/ v.t. bauen; (fig.) erstellen ⟨*Plan*⟩

construction /kənˈstrʌkʃn/ n. **(a)** (constructing) Bau, *der;* **be under** ∼: im Bau sein
(b) (thing constructed) Bauwerk, *das*

constructive /kənˈstrʌktɪv/ adj. konstruktiv

consul /ˈkɒnsl/ n. Konsul, *der*

consulate /ˈkɒnsjʊlət/ n. Konsulat, *das*

consult /kənˈsʌlt/ v.t. konsultieren ⟨*Arzt, Fachmann*⟩; ∼ **a book** in einem Buch nachsehen

consultant /kənˈsʌltənt/ n. Berater, *der*/ Beraterin, *die;* (Med.) Chefarzt, *der*/-ärztin, *die*

consultation /ˌkɒnsəlˈteɪʃn/ n. Beratung, *die*

con'sulting room n. Sprechzimmer, *das*

consume /kənˈsjuːm/ v.t. verbrauchen; (eat, drink) konsumieren

con'sumer n. Verbraucher, *der*/ Verbraucherin, *die*

con'sumer goods n. pl. Konsumgüter Pl.

consumerism /kənˈsjuːmərɪzm/ n., no art. Konsumerismus, *der*

consumer: ∼ **pro'tection** n. Verbraucherschutz, *der;* ∼ **research** n. Verbrauchsforschung, *die;* Konsumforschung, *die*

consumption /kənˈsʌmpʃn/ n. Verbrauch, *der* (of an + *Dat.*); (eating or drinking) Verzehr, *der* (of von)

cont. abbr. = **continued** Forts.

contact 1 /ˈkɒntækt/ n. Berührung, *die;* (fig.) Kontakt, *der;* **be in** ∼ **with sth.** etw. berühren; **be in** ∼ **with sb.** (fig.) mit jmdm. Kontakt haben
2 /ˈkɒntækt, kənˈtækt/ v.t. sich in Verbindung setzen mit

'contact lens n. Kontaktlinse, *die*

contagious /kənˈteɪdʒəs/ adj. ansteckend

contain /kənˈteɪn/ v.t. **(a)** (hold, include) enthalten
(b) (prevent from spreading) aufhalten

con'tainer n. Behälter, *der;* (cargo ∼) Container, *der;* **cardboard/wooden** ∼: Pappkarton, *der*/Holzkiste, *die*

contaminate /kənˈtæmɪneɪt/ v.t. verunreinigen; (with radioactivity) verseuchen

contamination /kənˌtæmɪˈneɪʃn/ n. Verunreinigung, *die;* (with radioactivity) Verseuchung, *die*

contemplate /ˈkɒntəmpleɪt/ v.t. **(a)** betrachten; (mentally) nachdenken über (+ *Akk.*)
(b) (expect) rechnen mit; (consider) ∼ **sth./ doing sth.** an etw. (*Akk.*) denken/daran denken, etw. zu tun

contemplation /ˌkɒntəmˈpleɪʃn/ n. Betrachtung, *die;* (mental) Nachdenken, *das* (of über + *Akk.*)

contemporary /kənˈtempərərɪ/ 1 adj. zeitgenössisch
2 n. Zeitgenosse, *der*/-genossin, *die*

contempt /kənˈtempt/ n. Verachtung, *die* (of, for für)

contemptible /kənˈtemptɪbl/ adj. verachtenswert

contemptuous /kənˈtemptjʊəs/ adj. verächtlich

contend /kənˈtend/ v.i. **be able/have to** ∼ **with** fertig werden können/müssen mit

con'tender n. Bewerber, *der*/Bewerberin, *die*

content[1] /ˈkɒntent/ n. **(a)** in pl. Inhalt, *der;* [table of] ∼s Inhaltsverzeichnis, *das*
(b) (amount contained) Gehalt, *der* (of an + *Dat.*)

content[2] /kənˈtent/ 1 pred. adj. zufrieden
2 v.t. zufrieden stellen; ∼ **oneself with sth./ sb.** sich mit etw./jmdm. zufrieden geben

con'tented adj., **con'tentedly** adv. zufrieden

contention /kənˈtenʃn/ n. **(a)** Streit, *der*
(b) (point asserted) Behauptung, *die*

contentious /kənˈtenʃəs/ adj. strittig ⟨*Punkt, Thema*⟩

con'tentment n. Zufriedenheit, *die*

contest 1 /ˈkɒntest/ n. Wettbewerb, *der*
2 /kənˈtest/ v.t. **(a)** bestreiten; infrage stellen ⟨*Behauptung*⟩
(b) (Brit.: compete for) kandidieren für

contestant /kənˈtestənt/ n. (competitor) Teilnehmer, *der*/Teilnehmerin, *die*

context /ˈkɒntekst/ n. Kontext, *der;* **in/out of** ∼: im/ohne Kontext; **in this** ∼: in diesem Zusammenhang

contextual /kənˈtekstjʊəl/ adj. kontextuell

contextualize /kənˈtekstjʊəlaɪz/ v.t. (place in context) in einen Kontext einordnen

continent /ˈkɒntɪnənt/ n. Kontinent, *der;* **the C**∼: das europäische Festland

continental /ˌkɒntɪˈnentl/ adj. **(a)** kontinental
(b) **C**∼ (mainland European) kontinental[europäisch]

continental: ∼ **'breakfast** n. kontinentales Frühstück; ∼ **'quilt** n. (Brit.) [Stepp]federbett, *das*

con'tingency plan /kən'tɪndʒənsɪ/ n.
Alternativplan, der
contingent /kən'tɪndʒənt/ n. Kontingent,
das
continual /kən'tɪnjʊəl/ adj.,
con'tinually adv. (frequent[ly]) ständig;
(without stopping) unaufhörlich
continuation /kəntɪnjʊ'eɪʃn/ n.
Fortsetzung, die
continue /kən'tɪnjuː/ **1** v.t. fortsetzen; '~d
on page 2' „Fortsetzung auf Seite 2";
~ doing or to do sth. etw. weiter tun; it ~d
to rain es regnete weiter
2 v.i. (persist) ⟨Wetter, Zustand, Krise usw.:⟩
andauern; (persist in doing sth.) nicht aufhören;
~ with sth. mit etw. fortfahren
continuity /kɒntɪ'njuːɪtɪ/ n. Kontinuität,
die
continuous /kən'tɪnjʊəs/ adj. (a)
ununterbrochen; anhaltend ⟨Regen,
Sonnenschein⟩; ständig ⟨Kritik, Streit⟩;
durchgezogen ⟨Linie⟩
(b) (Ling.) ~ [form] Verlaufsform, die
con'tinuously adv. ununterbrochen;
ständig ⟨sich ändern⟩
contort /kən'tɔːt/ v.t. verdrehen
contortion /kən'tɔːʃn/ n. Verdrehung, die
contour /'kɒntʊə(r)/ n. Kontur, die; ~ map
Höhenlinienkarte, die
contraband /'kɒntrəbænd/ n.
Schmuggelware, die
contraception /kɒntrə'sepʃn/ n.
Empfängnisverhütung, die
contraceptive /kɒntrə'septɪv/ **1** adj.
empfängnisverhütend
2 n. Verhütungsmittel, das
contract **1** /'kɒntrækt/ n. Vertrag, der;
~ of employment Arbeitsvertrag, der; be
under ~ to do sth. vertraglich verpflichtet
sein, etw. zu tun
2 /kən'trækt/ v.t. (Med.) sich (Dat.) zuziehen
3 /kən'trækt/ v.i. (a) ~ to do sth. sich
vertraglich verpflichten, etw. zu tun
(b) (become smaller, be drawn together) sich
zusammenziehen
contraction /kən'trækʃn/ n. Kontraktion,
die
'contract killer n. Auftragskiller, der/
-killerin, die
contractor /kən'træktə(r)/ n.
Auftragnehmer, der/-nehmerin, die
contradict /kɒntrə'dɪkt/ v.t.
widersprechen (+ Dat.)
contradiction /kɒntrə'dɪkʃn/ n.
Widerspruch, der; in ~ to sb./sth. im
Widerspruch zu jmdm./etw.
contradictory /kɒntrə'dɪktərɪ/ adj.
widersprüchlich
contraflow /'kɒntrəfləʊ/ n. ~ system
Gegenverkehr auf einem Fahrstreifen
contralto /kən'træltəʊ/ n., pl. ~s Alt, der
contraption /kən'træpʃn/ n. (coll.)
[komisches] Gerät

contrary /'kɒntrərɪ/ **1** adj. (a)
entgegengesetzt; be ~ to sth. im Gegensatz
zu etw. stehen
(b) /kən'treərɪ/ (perverse) widerspenstig
2 n. the ~: das Gegenteil; on the ~: im
Gegenteil
3 adv. ~ to sth. entgegen einer Sache
contrast **1** /kən'trɑːst/ v.t.
gegenüberstellen
2 /'kɒntrɑːst/ n. Kontrast, der (with zu); in
~, ...: im Gegensatz dazu, ...; [be] in ~ with
sth. im Gegensatz zu etw. [stehen]
con'trasting adj. gegensätzlich
contravene /kɒntrə'viːn/ v.t. verstoßen
gegen
contravention /kɒntrə'venʃn/ n. Verstoß,
der (of gegen)
contribute /kən'trɪbjuːt/ **1** v.t. ~ sth. [to
or towards sth.] etw. [zu etw.] beitragen
2 v.i. ~ to charity für karitative Zwecke
spenden; ~ to the success of sth. zum Erfolg
einer Sache (Gen.) beitragen
contribution /kɒntrɪ'bjuːʃn/ n. Beitrag,
der; (for charity) Spende, die (to für); make a
~: einen Beitrag leisten; (to charity) etwas
spenden
contributor /kən'trɪbjʊtə(r)/ n. (to
encyclopaedia etc.) Mitarbeiter, der/
Mitarbeiterin, die
'con trick (Brit. coll.) ▶ CONFIDENCE TRICK
contrite /'kɒntraɪt/ adj. zerknirscht
contrive /kən'traɪv/ v.t. ~ to do sth. es
fertig bringen, etw. zu tun
contrived /kən'traɪvd/ adj. künstlich
control /kən'trəʊl/ **1** n. (a) Kontrolle, die
(of über + Akk.); keep ~ of sth. etw. unter
Kontrolle halten; be in ~ [of sth.] die
Kontrolle [über etw. (Akk.)] haben; [go or
get] out of ~: außer Kontrolle [geraten]; [get
sth.] under ~: [etw.] unter Kontrolle
[bringen]
(b) (device) Regler, der; ~s Schalttafel, die
2 v.t., -ll- kontrollieren; lenken ⟨Auto⟩;
zügeln ⟨Zorn⟩; regeln ⟨Verkehr⟩
control: ~ **centre** n. Kontrollzentrum,
das; ~ **con'trol desk** n. Schaltpult, das
con'troller n. (director) Leiter, der/Leiterin,
die
control: ~ **panel** n. Schalttafel, die;
~ **room** n. Kontrollraum, der; ~ **tower**
n. Kontrollturm, der
controversial /kɒntrə'vɜːʃl/ adj.
umstritten
controversy /'kɒntrəvɜːsɪ, kən'trɒvəsɪ/ n.
Auseinandersetzung, die
conurbation /kɒnɜː'beɪʃn/ n. Konurbation,
die (Soziol.); ≈ Stadtregion, die
convalesce /kɒnvə'les/ v.i. genesen
convalescence /kɒnvə'lesəns/ n.
Genesung, die
convection /kən'vekʃn/ n. (Phys., Meteorol.)
Konvektion, die
convector /kən'vektə(r)/ n. Konvektor, der

convene /kən'viːn/ [1] *v.t.* einberufen
[2] *v.i.* zusammenkommen

convenience /kən'viːnɪəns/ *n.* (a) for
sb.'s ~ zu jmds. Bequemlichkeit; **at your** ~:
wann es Ihnen passt
(b) (toilet) [**public**] ~: [öffentliche] Toilette

con'venience food *n.* Fertignahrung,
die

convenient /kən'viːnɪənt/ *adj.* günstig;
(useful) praktisch; **would it be** ~ **to** *or* **for
you?** würde es Ihnen passen?

con'veniently *adv.* (a) günstig ⟨gelegen,
angebracht⟩
(b) (opportunely) angenehmerweise

convent /'kɒnvənt/ *n.* Kloster, *das*

convention /kən'venʃn/ *n.* (a) Brauch,
der
(b) (assembly) Konferenz, *die*
(c) (agreement) Konvention, *die*

conventional /kən'venʃənl/ *adj.*
konventionell

converge /kən'vɜːdʒ/ *v.i.* ~ [**on each
other**] aufeinander zulaufen

conversant /kən'vɜːsənt/ *pred. adj.*
vertraut (**with** mit)

conversation /kɒnvə'seɪʃn/ *n.*
Unterhaltung, *die;* **have a** ~: ein Gespräch
führen

conversational /kɒnvə'seɪʃənl/ *adj.*
~ **English** gesprochenes Englisch

converse¹ /kən'vɜːs/ *v.i.* (formal) ~ [**with
sb.**] [**about** *or* **on sth.**] sich [mit jmdm.]
[über etw. (*Akk.*)] unterhalten

converse² /'kɒnvɜːs/ [1] *adj.*
entgegengesetzt; umgekehrt ⟨Fall, Situation⟩
[2] *n.* Gegenteil, *das*

conversely /kən'vɜːslɪ/ *adj.* umgekehrt

conversion /kən'vɜːʃn/ *n.* (a)
Umwandlung, *die* (**into** in + *Akk.*)
(b) (adaptation) Umbau, *der*
(c) (of person) Bekehrung, *die* (**to** zu)

con'version table *n.*
Umrechnungstabelle, *die*

convert [1] /kən'vɜːt/ *v.t.* umwandeln (**into**
in + *Akk.*); (Comp.) konvertieren ⟨Daten⟩;
~ **sb.** [**to sth.**] jmdn. [zu etw.] bekehren
[2] /kən'vɜːt/ *v.i.* ~ **into sth.** sich in etw.
(*Akk.*) umwandeln lassen
[3] /'kɒnvɜːt/ *n.* Konvertit, *der*/Konvertitin,
die

convertible /kən'vɜːtɪbl/ [1] *adj.* **be** ~ **into**
sth. sich in etw. (*Akk.*) umwandeln lassen
[2] *n.* Kabrio[lett], *das*

convex /'kɒnveks/ *adj.* konvex

convey /kən'veɪ/ *v.t.* (a) befördern
(b) (impart) vermitteln

conveyance /kən'veɪəns/ *n.* (a)
(transportation) Beförderung, *die*
(b) (formal: vehicle) Beförderungsmittel, *das*

con'veyancing *n.* (Law) ~ [**of property**]
[Eigentums]übertragung, *die*

conveyor /kən'veɪə(r)/ *n.* ~ [**belt**]
Förderband, *das*

convict [1] /'kɒnvɪkt/ *n.* Strafgefangene,
der/*die*
[2] /kən'vɪkt/ *v.t.* verurteilen

conviction /kən'vɪkʃn/ *n.* (a) (Law)
Verurteilung, *die* (**for** wegen)
(b) (belief) Überzeugung, *die*

convince /kən'vɪns/ *v.t.* überzeugen; ~ **sb.
that …:** jmdn. davon überzeugen, dass …; **be
~d that …:** davon überzeugt sein, dass …

convincing /kən'vɪnsɪŋ/ *adj.*,
con'vincingly *adv.* überzeugend

convivial /kən'vɪvɪəl/ *adj.* fröhlich

convoluted /'kɒnvəluːtɪd/ *adj.* (complex)
kompliziert

convoy /'kɒnvɔɪ/ *n.* Konvoi, *der;* **in** ~: im
Konvoi

convulse /kən'vʌls/ *v.t.* **be** ~**d with** sich
krümmen vor (+ *Dat.*)

convulsions /kən'vʌlʃnz/ *n. pl.* Krämpfe
Pl.

convulsive /kən'vʌlsɪv/ *adj.*,
con'vulsively *adv.* konvulsivisch

coo /kuː/ *v.i.* gurren

cook /kʊk/ [1] *n.* Koch, *der*/Köchin, *die*
[2] *v.t.* kochen ⟨Mahlzeit⟩; (fry, roast) braten;
(boil) kochen
[3] *v.i.* kochen
■ **cook 'up** *v.t.* erfinden ⟨Geschichte⟩

'cookbook *n.* (Amer.) Kochbuch, *das*

'cooker *n.* (Brit.) Herd, *der*

cookery /'kʊkərɪ/ *n.* Kochen, *das*

'cookery book *n.* (Brit.) Kochbuch, *das*

cookie /'kʊkɪ/ *n.* (a) (Amer.) Keks, *der*
(b) (Comp.) Cookie, *der*

'cooking *n.* Kochen, *das*

cooking: ~ **apple** *n.* Kochapfel, *der;*
~ **utensil** *n.* Küchengerät, *das*

cool /kuːl/ [1] *adj.* (a) kühl; **store in a**
~ **place** kühl aufbewahren
(b) (unemotional, unfriendly) kühl; (calm) ruhig
[2] *n.* Kühle, *die*
[3] *v.i.* abkühlen
[4] *v.t.* kühlen; (from high temperature) abkühlen
■ **cool 'down, cool 'off** *v.i.* & *t.*
abkühlen

cool: ~ **box** *n.* Kühlbox, *die;* ~-**headed**
adj. kühl; nüchtern

coolly /'kuːllɪ/ *adv.* (calmly) ruhig;
(unemotionally) kühl

coop /kuːp/ [1] *n.* (for poultry) Hühnerstall,
der
[2] *v.t.* ~ **up** einpferchen

cooperate /kəʊ'ɒpəreɪt/ *v.i.* mitarbeiten
(**in** bei); (with each other) zusammenarbeiten
(**in** bei)

cooperation /kəʊɒpə'reɪʃn/ *n.*
Zusammenarbeit, *die*

cooperative /kəʊ'ɒpərətɪv/ [1] *adj.*
kooperativ; (helpful) hilfsbereit
[2] *n.* Genossenschaft, *die*

coordinate /kəʊ'ɔːdɪneɪt/ *v.t.* koordinieren ····⊹

coordination /kəʊɔːdɪˈneɪʃn/ n. Koordination, *die*

co-owner /kəʊˈəʊnə(r)/ n. Miteigentümer, *der*/-eigentümerin, *die;* (of business) Mitinhaber, *der*/-inhaberin, *die*

cop /kɒp/ n. (coll.: police officer) Bulle, *der* (salopp)

cope /kəʊp/ v.i. ~ with sb./sth. mit jmdm./ etw. fertig werden

Copenhagen /kəʊpnˈheɪɡn/ pr. n. Kopenhagen (*das*)

copier /ˈkɒpɪə(r)/ n. (machine) Kopiergerät, *das*

co-pilot /ˈkəʊpaɪlət/ n. Kopilot, *der*/ Kopilotin, *die*

copious /ˈkəʊpɪəs/ adj. reichhaltig

'cop-out n. (coll.) Drückebergerei, *die* (ugs. abwertend); **that's a ~:** das ist Drückebergerei (ugs. abwertend)

copper¹ /ˈkɒpə(r)/ n. Kupfer, *das*

copper² (Brit. coll.) ▶ COP

coppice /ˈkɒpɪs/, **copse** /kɒps/ ns. Wäldchen, *das*

'cop shop n. (Brit. coll.) Wache, *die;* Revier, *das*

copula /ˈkɒpjʊlə/ n. (Ling.) Kopula, *die*

copulate /ˈkɒpjʊleɪt/ v.i. kopulieren

copy /ˈkɒpɪ/ ① n. (a) (reproduction) Kopie, *die* (b) (specimen) Exemplar, *das* ② v.t. & i. kopieren; (transcribe) abschreiben

copy: ~**cat** n. (coll.) you're such a ~cat! du musst immer alles nachmachen!; ~ **editor** n. Redakteur, *der*/Redakteurin, *die* (der/die nur nach schriftlichen Vorlagen arbeitet); ~ **protection** n. (Comp.) Kopierschutz, *der;* ~**right** n. Urheberrecht, *das* ~**writer** n. [Werbe]texter, *der*/-texterin, *die*

coral /ˈkɒrl/ n. Koralle, *die*

cord /kɔːd/ n. (a) Kordel, *die;* (strong string) Schnur, *die* (b) (cloth) Cord, *der* (c) in pl. (trousers) [pair of] ~s Cordhose, *die*

cordial /ˈkɔːdɪəl/ ① adj. herzlich ② n. (drink) Sirup, *der*

cordiality /kɔːdɪˈælɪtɪ/ n. Herzlichkeit, *die*

'cordially adv. herzlich

'cordless phone /ˈkɔːdlɪs/ n. Schnurlostelefon, *das*

cordon /ˈkɔːdn/ ① n. Kordon, *der* ② v.t. ~ [off] absperren

corduroy /ˈkɔːdərɔɪ, ˈkɔːdjʊrɔɪ/ n. Cordsamt, *der*

core /kɔː(r)/ ① n. (of fruit) Kerngehäuse, *das* ② v.t. entkernen

co-respondent /kəʊrɪˈspɒndənt/ n. Mitbeklagte, *der*/*die* (im Scheidungsprozess)

cork /kɔːk/ ① n. (a) (bark) Kork, *der* (b) (bottle stopper) Korken, *der* ② v.t. zukorken

cork: ~**screw** n. Korkenzieher, *der;* ~ **'tile** n. Korkplatte, *die*

cormorant /ˈkɔːmərənt/ n. Kormoran, *der*

corn¹ /kɔːn/ n. Getreide, *das*

corn² n. (on foot) Hühnerauge, *das*

cornea /ˈkɔːnɪə/ n. (Anat.) Hornhaut, *die;* Cornea, *die* (fachspr.)

corned beef /kɔːnd ˈbiːf/ n. Cornedbeef, *das*

corner /ˈkɔːnə(r)/ ① n. (a) Ecke, *die;* (curve) Kurve, *die;* **on the ~:** an der Ecke/in der Kurve (b) (of mouth, eye) Winkel, *der* ② v.t. (fig.) in die Enge treiben ③ v.i. die Kurve nehmen

corner: ~ **kick** n. (Footb.) Eckball, *der;* ~ **shop** n. Tante-Emma-Laden, *der* (ugs.); ~**stone** n. (fig.) Eckpfeiler, *der*

cornet /ˈkɔːnɪt/ n. (a) (Brit.: for ice cream) [Eis]tüte, *die* (b) (Mus.) Kornett, *das*

corn: ~**flakes** n. pl. Cornflakes Pl.; ~**flour** (Brit.) n. Maismehl, *das;* ~**flower** n. Kornblume, *die;* ~ **starch** (Amer.) n. Maismehl, *das*

'corny adj. (coll.: trite) abgedroschen

coronary /ˈkɒrənərɪ/ ① adj. (Anat.) koronar ② n. (Med.) ▶ CORONARY THROMBOSIS

coronary: ~ **'artery** n. Herzkranzarterie, *die;* Koronararterie, *die* (fachspr.); ~ **throm'bosis** n. Koronarthrombose, *die*

coronation /kɒrəˈneɪʃn/ n. Krönung, *die*

coroner /ˈkɒrənə(r)/ n. Coroner, *der;* Beamter, *der* gewaltsame od. unnatürliche Todesfälle untersucht

coronet /ˈkɒrənet/ n. Krone, *die*

corporal¹ /ˈkɔːpərl/ adj. körperlich

corporal² n. ≈ Hauptgefreite, *der*

corporate /ˈkɔːpərət/ adj. körperschaftlich

corporation /kɔːpəˈreɪʃn/ n. Stadtverwaltung, *die*

corpo'ration tax n. Körperschaftssteuer, *die*

corps /kɔː(r)/ n., pl. same /kɔːz/ Korps, *das*

corpse /kɔːps/ n. Leiche, *die*

corpulent /ˈkɔːpjʊlənt/ adj. korpulent

Corpus Christi /kɔːpəs ˈkrɪstɪ/ n. (Eccl.) Fronleichnam (*der*)

corpuscle /ˈkɔːpəsl/ n. [blood] ~ Blutkörperchen, *das*

corral /kəˈrɑːl/ (Amer.) ① n. Pferch, *der* ② v.t., -ll- einpferchen

correct /kəˈrekt/ ① v.t. korrigieren ② adj. korrekt; **that is ~:** das stimmt

correction /kəˈrekʃn/ n. Korrektur, *die*

cor'rectly adv. korrekt

correspond /kɒrɪˈspɒnd/ v.i. (a) ~ [to each other] einander entsprechen; ~ to sth. einer Sache (*Dat.*) entsprechen (b) (communicate) ~ with sb. mit jmdm. korrespondieren

correspondence /kɒrɪˈspɒndəns/ n. (a) Übereinstimmung, *die* (with, to mit) (b) (communication) Briefwechsel, *der*

corre'spondence course n. Fernkurs, der

correspondent /kɒrɪ'spɒndənt/ n. (reporter) Korrespondent, der/ Korrespondentin, die

corre'sponding adj. entsprechend (**to** Dat.)

corre'spondingly adv. entsprechend

corridor /'kɒrɪdɔ:(r)/ n. (a) Flur, der (b) (Railw.) [Seiten]gang, der

corroborate /kə'rɒbəreɪt/ v.t. bestätigen

corroboration /kərɒbə'reɪʃn/ n. Bestätigung, die

corrode /kə'rəʊd/ [1] v.t. zerfressen [2] v.i. zerfressen werden

corrosion /kə'rəʊʒn/ n. Korrosion, die

corrugated /'kɒrəgeɪtɪd/ adj. ~ **cardboard** Wellpappe, die; ~ **iron** Wellblech, das

corrupt /kə'rʌpt/ [1] adj. (depraved) verdorben (geh.); (influenced by bribery) korrupt [2] v.t. (deprave) korrumpieren; (bribe) bestechen

corruption /kə'rʌpʃn/ n. (moral deterioration) Verdorbenheit, die (geh.); (corrupt practices) Korruption, die

corset /'kɔ:sɪt/ n. Korsett, das

Corsica /'kɔ:sɪkə/ pr. n. Korsika (das)

cortège /kɔ:'teɪʒ/ n. Trauerzug, der

cortisone /'kɔ:tɪzəʊn/ n. Kortison, das; Cortison, das (fachspr.)

cosh /kɒʃ/ (Brit. coll.) [1] n. Totschläger, der [2] v.t. niederknüppeln

cosmetic /kɒz'metɪk/ [1] adj. kosmetisch [2] n. Kosmetikum, das

cosmic /'kɒzmɪk/ adj. kosmisch

cosmonaut /'kɒzmənɔ:t/ n. Kosmonaut, der/Kosmonautin, die

cosmopolitan /kɒzmə'pɒlɪtən/ adj. kosmopolitisch

cosmos /'kɒzmɒs/ n. Kosmos, der

cosset /'kɒsɪt/ v.t. [ver]hätscheln

cost /kɒst/ [1] n. (a) Kosten Pl. (b) (fig.) Preis, der; **at all** ~**s, at any** ~: um jeden Preis [2] v.t. (a) p.t., p.p. **cost** (lit. or fig.) kosten; **how much does it** ~? was kostet es? (b) p.t., p.p. **costed** (Commerc.: fix price of) ~ **sth.** den Preis für etw. kalkulieren

co-star /'kəʊstɑ:(r)/ (Cinemat., Theatre) [1] n. **be a/the** ~: eine der Hauptrollen/die zweite Hauptrolle spielen [2] v.i., -rr- eine der Hauptrollen spielen [3] v.t., -rr-: **the film** ~**red Robert Redford** der Film zeigte Robert Redford in einer der Hauptrollen

cost: ~ **cutting** n. Kostensenkung, die; ~**-cutting** adj. Spar-; ~**-effective** adj. rentabel

'costly adj. teuer

cost: ~ **of 'living** n.

Lebenshaltungskosten Pl.; ~**-of-living index** Lebenshaltungsindex, der; ~ **price** n. Selbstkostenpreis, der

costume /'kɒstju:m/ n. Kleidermode, die; (theatrical ~) Kostüm, das

costume 'jewellery n. Modeschmuck, der

cosy /'kəʊzɪ/ adj. gemütlich

cot /kɒt/ n. Kinderbett, das

'cot death n. (Brit.) plötzlicher Kindstod; Cot-death, der (Med.)

cottage /'kɒtɪdʒ/ n. Cottage, das

cottage: ~ **'cheese** n. Hüttenkäse, der; ~ **'hospital** n.: kleines [Land]krankenhaus ohne ständige ärztliche Betreuung; ~ **industry** n. Heimarbeit, die; ~ **'pie** n.: mit Kartoffelbrei überbackenes Hackfleisch

cotton /'kɒtən/ [1] n. Baumwolle, die; (thread) Baumwollgarn, das [2] attrib. adj. Baumwoll- [3] v.i. ~ **'on** (coll.) kapieren (ugs.)

cotton: ~ **reel** n. [Näh]garnrolle, die; ~ **'wool** n. Watte, die

couch /kaʊtʃ/ n. Couch, die

couchette /ku:'ʃet/ n. (Railw.) Liegewagenplatz, der

couch po'tato n. (coll.) Couchpotato[e], der

cough /kɒf/ [1] n. Husten, der [2] v.i. husten

cough: ~ **medicine** n. Hustenmittel, das; ~ **mixture** n. Hustensaft, der

could ▶ CAN²

couldn't /'kʊdnt/ (coll.) = could not; ▶ CAN²

council /'kaʊnsl/ n. Rat, der; **local** ~: Gemeinderat, der; **city/town** ~: Stadtrat, der; **C**~ **of Ministers** Ministerrat, der

council: ~ **estate** n. Wohnviertel mit Sozialwohnungen; ~ **flat** n. Sozialwohnung, die; ~ **house** n. Haus des sozialen Wohnungsbaus; ~ **housing** n. sozialer Wohnungsbau

councillor /'kaʊnsələ(r)/ n. Ratsmitglied, das

'council tax n. (Brit.) Gemeindesteuer, die

counsel /'kaʊnsl/ [1] n. (a) Rat[schlag], der (b) pl. same (Law) Rechtsanwalt, der/ -anwältin, die [2] v.t., (Brit.) -ll- beraten

counselling (Amer.: **counseling**) /'kaʊnsəlɪŋ/ n. Beratung, die; **marriage** ~: Eheberatung, die

counsellor, (Amer. **counselor**) /'kaʊnsələ(r)/ n. Berater, der/Beraterin, die

count¹ /kaʊnt/ [1] n. Zählen, das; **keep** ~ [**of sth.**] [etw.] zählen; **lose** ~: sich verzählen [2] v.t. (a) zählen (b) (include) mitzählen; **not** ~**ing** abgesehen von (c) (consider) halten für; ~ **oneself lucky** sich glücklich schätzen können ⋯⟩

3 v.i. (a) zählen; ~ [up] to ten bis zehn zählen
(b) (be included) zählen
■ **'count on** v.t. ~ on sb./sth. sich auf jmdn./etw. verlassen
■ **count 'up** v.t. zusammenzählen

count² n. (nobleman) Graf, der

'countdown n. Count-down, der od. das

countenance /'kaʊntɪnəns/ **1** n. (literary: face) Antlitz, das
2 v.t. (formal: approve) gutheißen

counter¹ /'kaʊntə(r)/ n. (a) (in shop) Ladentisch, der; (in cafeteria) Büfett, das; (in bank) Schalter, der
(b) (for games) Spielmarke, die

counter² **1** adj. Gegen-
2 v.t. (a) (oppose) begegnen (+ Dat.)
(b) (act against) kontern
3 adv. go ~ to zuwiderlaufen (+ Dat.)

counter: ~'act v.t. entgegenwirken (+ Dat.); ~attack n. Gegenangriff, der; ~balance v.t. (fig.) ausgleichen; ~-'espionage n. Spionageabwehr, die

counterfeit /'kaʊntəfɪt/ **1** adj. gefälscht; ~ money Falschgeld, das
2 v.t. fälschen

'counterfeiter n. Fälscher, der/Fälscherin, die

counterfoil /'kaʊntəfɔɪl/ n. Kontrollabschnitt, der

counter: ~part n. Gegenstück, das (of zu); ~pro'ductive adj. sth. is ~productive etw. bewirkt das Gegenteil des Gewünschten; ~sign v.t. gegenzeichnen; ~weight n. Gegengewicht, das

countess /'kaʊntɪs/ n. Gräfin, die

'countless adj. zahllos

countrified /'kʌntrɪfaɪd/ adj. ländlich

country /'kʌntrɪ/ n. (a) Land, das; sb's [home] ~: jmds. Heimat
(b) (~side) Landschaft, die; in the ~: auf dem Land; ~ road/air Landstraße, die/Landluft, die

country 'dancing n. Kontertanz, der

countryfied ▶ COUNTRIFIED

country: ~man /'kʌntrɪmən/, n. pl. ~men /'kʌntrɪmən/ Landsmann, der; ~side n. (a) (rural areas) Land, das; (b) (rural scenery) Landschaft, die

county /'kaʊntɪ/ n. (Brit.) Grafschaft, die

coup /kuː/ n. (a) Coup, der
(b) ▶ COUP D'ÉTAT

coup d'état /ku deɪ'ta:/ n. Staatsstreich, der

coupé /'ku:peɪ/ n. Coupé, das

couple /kʌpl/ **1** n. (a) (pair) Paar, das; (married) [Ehe]paar, das
(b) a ~ [of] (a few) ein paar; (two) zwei
2 v.t. koppeln

coupon /'ku:pɒn/ n. (a) (for rations) Marke, die
(b) (in advertisement) Coupon, der

courage /'kʌrɪdʒ/ n. Mut, der

courageous /kə'reɪdʒəs/ adj., **cou'rageously** adv. mutig

courgette /kʊə'ʒet/ n. (Brit.) Zucchino, der

courier /'kʊrɪə(r)/ n. (a) (Tourism) Reiseleiter, der/-leiterin, die
(b) (messenger) Kurier, der

'courier company n. Kurierdienst, der

course /kɔːs/ n. (a) (of ship, plane) Kurs, der; ~ [of action] Vorgehensweise, die
(b) of ~: natürlich
(c) in due ~: zu gegebener Zeit; in the ~ of the day/his life im Lauf[e] des Tages/seines Lebens
(d) (of meal) Gang, der
(e) (Sport) Kurs, der; [golf]~: [Golf]platz, der
(f) (Educ.) Kurs[us], der; go to or attend/do a ~ in sth. einen Kurs in etw. (Dat.) besuchen/machen
(g) (Med.) a ~ of treatment eine Kur

court /kɔːt/ **1** n. (a) Hof, der
(b) (Tennis, Squash) Platz, der
(c) (Law) Gericht, das
2 v.t. ~ sb. jmdn. umwerben

courteous /'kɜːtɪəs/ adj. höflich

courtesy /'kɜːtəsɪ/ n. Höflichkeit, die

'courtesy light n. (Motor Veh.) Innenbeleuchtung, die

court: ~ house n. (Law) Gerichtsgebäude, das; ~ martial n., pl. ~s martial (Mil.) Kriegsgericht, das; ~room n. (Law) Gerichtssaal, der

courtship /'kɔːtʃɪp/ n. Werben, das

court: ~ shoe n. Pumps, der; ~yard n. Hof, der

cousin /'kʌzn/ n. [first] ~: Cousin, der/Cousine, die

couturier /ku:'tjʊərjeɪ/ n. Couturier, der; Modeschöpfer, der

cove /kəʊv/ n. (Geog.) [kleine] Bucht

covenant /'kʌvənənt/ n. formelle Übereinkunft

cover /'kʌvə(r)/ **1** n. (a) (piece of cloth) Decke, die; (of cushion, bed) Bezug, der; (lid) Deckel, der; (of hole, engine, typewriter, etc.) Abdeckung, die
(b) (of book) Einband, der; (of magazine) Umschlag, der
(c) [send sth.] under separate ~: [etw.] mit getrennter Post [schicken]
(d) take ~ [from sth.] Schutz [vor etw. (Dat.)] suchen; under ~ (from rain) überdacht
2 v.t. (a) bedecken; beziehen ⟨Sessel, Kissen⟩; zudecken ⟨Pfanne⟩; the roses are ~ed with greenfly die Rosen sind voller Blattläuse
(b) (include) abdecken
(c) (Journ.) berichten über (+ Akk.)
(d) decken ⟨Kosten⟩
■ **cover 'up** **1** v.t. zudecken; (fig.) vertuschen
2 v.i. ~ up for sb. jmdn. decken

coverage /'kʌvərɪdʒ/ n. (Journ.) Berichterstattung, die

'cover charge n. [Preis für das] Gedeck

'covering n. Decke, die; (of chair, bed) Bezug, der

'covering letter n. Begleitbrief, der

'cover story n. (Journ.) Titelgeschichte, die

covert /'kʌvət/ adj. versteckt

cover: ∼-up n. Verschleierung, die; **∼ version** n. Coverversion, die

covet /'kʌvɪt/ v.t. begehren (geh.)

covetous /'kʌvɪtəs/ adj. begehrlich (geh.)

cow /kaʊ/ n. Kuh, die

coward /'kaʊəd/ n. Feigling, der

cowardice /'kaʊədɪs/ n. Feigheit, die

'cowardly adj. feig[e]

'cowboy n. Cowboy, der

cower /'kaʊə(r)/ v.i. sich ducken

cowherd n. Kuhhirte, der

'co-worker n. Kollege, der/Kollegin, die

cow: ∼ parsley n. (Bot.) Wiesenkerbel, der; **∼pat** n. Kuhfladen, der; **∼shed** n. Kuhstall, der; **∼slip** n. Schlüsselblume, die

coy /kɔɪ/ adj. gespielt schüchtern

cozy (Amer.) ▶ cosy

CPU abbr. (Comp.) = **central processing unit** ZE

crab /kræb/ n. Krabbe, die

'crab apple n. Holzapfel, der

crack /kræk/ ① n. (a) (noise) Krachen, das (b) (in china etc.) Sprung, der; (in rock) Spalte, die; (chink) Spalt, der (c) (coll.: try) **have a ∼ at** sth./doing sth. versuchen, etw. zu tun (d) (sl.: drug) ∼ [**cocaine**] Crack, das ② attrib. adj. (coll.) erstklassig ③ v.t. (a) knacken ⟨Nuss, Problem, Kode⟩ (b) (make a ∼ in) anschlagen ⟨Porzellan usw.⟩ (c) ∼ **a joke** einen Witz machen (d) ∼ **a whip** mit einer Peitsche knallen ④ v.i. ⟨Porzellan usw.:⟩ einen Sprung/ Sprünge bekommen ■ **crack 'down** v.i. (coll.) ∼ **down** [**on** sb./ sth.] [gegen jmdn./etw.] [hart] vorgehen ■ **crack 'up** v.i. (coll.) ⟨Person:⟩ zusammenbrechen

'crack-down n. (coll.) **there will be a ∼:** man wird hart durchgreifen; **have/order a ∼ on** sb./sth. drastische Maßnahmen gegen jmdn./etw. ergreifen/anordnen

cracked /krækt/ adj. gesprungen ⟨Porzellan usw.⟩; rissig ⟨Verputz⟩

cracker /'krækə(r)/ n. (a) [Christmas] ∼ ≈ Knallbonbon, der od. das (b) (biscuit) Cracker, der

'crackers pred. adj. (Brit. coll.) übergeschnappt (ugs.)

crackle /'krækl/ ① v.i. knistern; ⟨Feuer:⟩ prasseln ② n. Knistern, das

cradle /'kreɪdl/ ① n. Wiege, die ② v.t. wiegen

cradle:∼ -snatch v.i. (coll.) Your boyfriend/girlfriend is much younger than you. You're ∼-snatching Dein Freund/deine Freundin ist viel jünger als du. Du vergreifst dich ja an kleinen Kindern (ugs. scherzh.); ∼ **-snatcher** n. (fig. coll.) jmd., der mit einer sehr viel jüngeren Person eine Liebesbeziehung eingeht

craft /krɑːft/ n. (a) (trade) Handwerk, das; (art) Kunsthandwerk, das (b) pl. same (boat) Boot, das

craftily /'krɑːftɪlɪ/ adv. listig

craftsman /'krɑːftsmən/ n., pl. **craftsmen** /'krɑːftsmən/ Handwerker, der

craftsmanship /'krɑːftsmənʃɪp/ n. (skilled workmanship) handwerkliches Können

crafty /'krɑːftɪ/ adj. listig

crag /kræg/ n. Felsspitze, die

'craggy adj. (a) felsig (b) zerfurcht ⟨Gesicht⟩

cram /kræm/ ① v.t., -mm- (overfill) voll stopfen (ugs.); (force) stopfen ② v.i., -mm- (for exam) büffeln (ugs.)

cramp /kræmp/ ① n. (Med.) Krampf, der ② v.t. einengen

cramped /kræmpt/ adj. eng ⟨Raum⟩; gedrängt ⟨Handschrift⟩

cranberry /'krænbərɪ/ n. Preiselbeere, die

crane /kreɪn/ ① n. Kran, der ② v.t. ∼ **one's neck** den Hals recken

crane: ∼ driver n. Kranführer, der/ -führerin, die; **∼ fly** n. Schnake, die

crank¹ /kræŋk/ n. (Mech. Engin.) [Hand]kurbel, die

crank² n. Irre, der/die (salopp)

crank: ∼ arm n. (of bicycle) Tretkurbel, die; **∼shaft** n. (Mech. Engin.) Kurbelwelle, die

'cranky adj. (eccentric) schrullig

cranny /'krænɪ/ n. Ritze, die

crap /kræp/ n. (coarse) (a) (faeces) Scheiße, die (derb); **have a ∼:** scheißen (derb) (b) (nonsense) Scheiß, der (salopp)

crash /kræʃ/ ① n. (a) (noise) Krachen, das (b) (collision) Zusammenstoß, der; **have a ∼:** einen Unfall haben ② v.i. (a) (make a noise, go noisily) krachen (b) (have a collision) einen Unfall haben; ⟨Flugzeug, Flieger:⟩ abstürzen; ∼ **into** sth. gegen etw. krachen (c) (Finance etc., Computing) zusammenbrechen ③ v.t. (a) (smash) schmettern (b) (cause to have collision) einen Unfall haben mit

crash: ∼ barrier n. Leitplanke, die; **∼ course** n. Intensivkurs, der; **∼ diet** n. radikale Diät; ≈ Nulldiät, die; **∼ helmet** n. Sturzhelm, der; **∼land** ① v.t. **∼land a** plane mit einem Flugzeug bruchlanden; ② v.i. bruchlanden; **∼landing** n. Bruchlandung, die

crass /kræs/ adj. haarsträubend ⟨Dummheit, Unwissenheit⟩; (grossly stupid) strohdumm

crate /kreɪt/ n. Kiste, die

crater /'kreɪtə(r)/ n. Krater, der

cravat /krə'væt/ *n.* Krawatte, *die*

crave /kreɪv/ *v.t.* (a) (beg) erbitten
(b) (long for) sich sehnen nach

'craving *n.* Verlangen, *das* (**for** nach)

crawl /krɔːl/ ① *v.i.* (a) kriechen; ⟨*Baby, Insekt:*⟩ krabbeln
(b) (coll.) ~ **to sb.** vor jmdm. kriechen
② *n.* (a) **go at a** ~: im Schneckentempo fahren
(b) (swimming stroke) Kraulen, *das*

'crawler lane *n.* Kriechspur, *die*

crayfish /'kreɪfɪʃ/ *n., pl. same* Flusskrebs, *der*

crayon /'kreɪən/ *n.* [coloured] ~: Buntstift, *der;* (wax) Wachsmalstift, *der*

craze /kreɪz/ *n.* Begeisterung, *die*

crazy /'kreɪzɪ/ *adj.* verrückt; **be** ~ **about sb./sth.** (coll.) nach jmdm./etw. verrückt sein (ugs.)

creak /kriːk/ ① *n.* Knarren, *das*
② *v.i.* knarren

cream /kriːm/ ① *n.* (a) Sahne, *die*
(b) (dessert, cosmetic) Creme, *die*
② *adj.* ~[-coloured] creme[farben]

cream: ~ **cake** *n.* Cremetorte, *die;* (small) Cremetörtchen, *das;* (with whipped ~) Sahnetorte, *die*/Sahnetörtchen, *das;*
~ **'cheese** *n.* ≈ Frischkäse, *der;*
~ **'cracker** *n.* ≈ Cracker, *der;* ~ **'tea** *n.* Tee mit Marmeladetörtchen und Sahne

'creamy *adj.* (with cream) sahnig; (like cream) cremig

crease /kriːs/ ① *n.* (pressed) Bügelfalte, *die;* (accidental) Falte, *die*
② *v.t.* (press) eine Falte bügeln in (+ *Akk.*); (accidentally) zerknittern
③ *v.i.* Falten bekommen; knittern

'crease-resistant *adj.* knitterfrei

create /kriː'eɪt/ *v.t.* schaffen; verursachen ⟨*Verwirrung*⟩; machen ⟨*Eindruck*⟩

creation /kriː'eɪʃn/ *n.* Schaffung, *die;* (of the world) Schöpfung, *die* (geh.)

creative /kriː'eɪtɪv/ *adj.* kreativ

creator /kriː'eɪtə(r)/ *n.* Schöpfer, *der*/Schöpferin, *die*

creature /'kriːtʃə(r)/ *n.* Geschöpf, *das*

crèche /kreʃ/ *n.* [Kinder]krippe, *die*

credentials /krɪ'denʃlz/ *n. pl.* Zeugnis, *das*

credibility /kredɪ'bɪlɪtɪ/ *n.* Glaubwürdigkeit, *die*

credible /'kredɪbl/ *adj.* glaubwürdig

credit /'kredɪt/ ① *n.* (a) (honour) Ehre, *die;* **take the** ~ **for sth.** die Anerkennung für etw. einstecken
(b) (Commerc.) Kredit, *der*
(c) ~**s,** ~ **titles** (at beginning of film) Vorspann, *der;* (at end) Nachspann, *der*
② *v.t.* (a) glauben
(b) (Finance) gutschreiben

creditable /'kredɪtəbl/ *adj.* anerkennenswert

creditably /'kredɪtəblɪ/ *adv.* achtbar

credit: ~ **account** *n.* Kreditkonto, *das;*
~ **card** *n.* Kreditkarte, *die;* ~ **facilities** *n. pl.* [Kredit]fazilität, *die* (fachspr.); ~ **limit** *n.* Kreditlinie, *die*

creditor /'kredɪtə(r)/ *n.* Gläubiger, *der*/Gläubigerin, *die*

credit: ~ **rating** *n.* [Einschätzung der] Kreditwürdigkeit; **have a good/bad** ~ **rating** als kreditwürdig/kreditunwürdig eingeschätzt werden; ~**worthy** *adj.* kreditwürdig

creed /kriːd/ *n.* Glaubensbekenntnis, *das*

creek /kriːk/ *n.* (a) (Brit.: of coast) [kleine] Bucht
(b) (of river) [kurzer] Flussarm

creep /kriːp/ ① *v.i.,* crept [krept] kriechen; (move timidly, slowly, stealthily) schleichen
② *n.* (a) (coll.: person) Fiesling, *der* (salopp)
(b) (coll.) **give sb. the** ~**s** jmdn. nicht [ganz] geheuer sein

'creeper *n.* Kletterpflanze, *die*

'creepy *adj.* unheimlich

cremate /krɪ'meɪt/ *v.t.* einäschern

cremation /krɪ'meɪʃn/ *n.* Einäscherung, *die*

crematorium /kremə'tɔːrɪəm/ *n.* Krematorium, *das*

creosote /'kriːəsəʊt/ *n.* Kreosot, *das*

crept ▶ CREEP 1

crescendo /krɪ'ʃendəʊ/ *n., pl.* ~**s** (Mus.) Crescendo, *das;* (fig.) Zunahme, *die*

crescent /'kresənt/ *n.* Mondsichel, *die*

cress /kres/ *n.* Kresse, *die*

crest /krest/ *n.* Kamm, *der*

'crestfallen *adj.* niedergeschlagen

Crete /kriːt/ *pr. n.* Kreta (*das*)

cretin /'kretɪn/ *n.* (coll.) Trottel, *der*

Creutzfeldt-Jakob disease /'krɔɪtsfelt'jækɒb/ *n.* Creutzfeldt-Jakob-Krankheit, *die*

crevasse /krɪ'væs/ *n.* Gletscherspalte, *die*

crevice /'krevɪs/ *n.* Spalt, *der*

crew /kruː/ *n.* Besatzung, *die*

crew: ~**cut** *n.* Bürstenschnitt, *der;*
~ **neck** *n.* enger, runder Halsausschnitt; **a** ~-**neck pullover** ein Pullover mit engem, rundem Halsausschnitt

crib /krɪb/ ① *n.* Krippe, *die*
② *v.t.,* -**bb-** (coll.) abkupfern (salopp)

crick /krɪk/ *n.* **a** ~ [in one's neck/back] ein steifer Hals/Rücken

cricket¹ /'krɪkɪt/ *n.* Kricket, *das*

cricket² *n.* (Zool.) Grille, *die*

cricket: ~ **ball** *n.* Kricketball, *der;* ~ **bat** *n.* Schlagholz, *das*

'cricketer *n.* Kricketspieler, *der*/-spielerin, *die*

'cricket match *n.* Kricketspiel, *das*

cried ▶ CRY

crime /kraɪm/ *n.* (a) Verbrechen, *das*

(b) *collect.* **a wave of** ∼: eine Welle von Straftaten; ∼ **doesn't pay** Verbrechen lohnen sich nicht

crime: ∼ **prevention** *n.* Verbrechensverhütung, *die;* C∼ **Prevention Officer** *Polizeibeamter, dessen/-beamtin, deren Aufgabe aktive, vorbeugende Verbrechensbekämpfung ist;* ∼ **rate** *n.* Kriminalitätsrate, *die;* ∼ **wave** *n.* Welle von Straftaten; ∼ **writer** *n.* Kriminalschriftsteller, *der/-schriftstellerin, die*

criminal /'krɪmɪnl/ **1** *adj.* kriminell; strafbar; ∼ **act** *or* **deed/offence** Straftat, *die* **2** *n.* Kriminelle, *der/die*

criminal: ∼ **charge** *n.* Anklage, *die;* **face** ∼ **charges [for sth.]** sich [wegen etw.] vor Gericht zu verantworten haben; **there are** ∼ **charges against him** er steht unter Anklage; ∼ **'court** *n.* Strafgericht, *das;* ∼ **'law** *n.* Strafrecht, *das;* ∼ **'lawyer** *n.* Anwalt/Anwältin für Strafsachen; ∼ **'record** *n.* Strafregister, *das;* **have a** ∼ **record** vorbestraft sein

crimson /'krɪmzn/ **1** *adj.* purpurrot **2** *n.* Purpurrot, *das*

cringe /krɪndʒ/ *v.i.* zusammenzucken

crinkle /'krɪŋkl/ **1** *n.* Knitterfalte, *die* **2** *v.t.* zerknittern **3** *v.i.* knittern

cripple /'krɪpl/ **1** *n.* Krüppel, *der* **2** *v.t.* zum Krüppel machen; (fig.) lähmen

crippled /'krɪpld/ *adj.* verkrüppelt

crippling /'krɪplɪŋ/ *adj.* zur Verkrüppelung führend ⟨*Krankheit, Verletzung*⟩; (fig.) erdrückend ⟨*Preise, Inflationsrate, Steuern, Mieten*⟩; lähmend ⟨*Streik, Schmerzen*⟩

crisis /'kraɪsɪs/ *n., pl.* **crises** /'kraɪsi:z/ Krise, *die*

crisis: ∼ **area** *n.* Krisengebiet, *das;* ∼ **'management** *n.* Krisenmanagement, *das*

crisp /krɪsp/ **1** *adj.* knusprig **2** *n.* **(a)** *usu. in pl.* (Brit.: potato ∼) [Kartoffel]chip, *der* **(b) be burned to a** ∼: verbrannt sein

'crispbread *n.* Knäckebrot, *das*

'crispy *adj.* knusprig

criss-cross /'krɪskrɒs/ **1** *adj.* ∼ **pattern** Muster aus gekreuzten Linien **2** *adv.* kreuz und quer **3** *v.t.* wiederholt schneiden

criterion /kraɪ'tɪərɪən/ *n., pl.* **criteria** /kraɪ'tɪərɪə/ Kriterium, *das*

critic /'krɪtɪk/ *n.* Kritiker, *der/Kritikerin, die*

critical /'krɪtɪkl/ *adj.* kritisch; **be** ∼ **of sb./ sth.** jmdn./etw. kritisieren

critically /'krɪtɪkəlɪ/ *adv.* kritisch; ∼ **ill** ernstlich krank

critical 'mass *n.* (Phys.) kritische Masse

criticism /'krɪtɪsɪzm/ *n.* Kritik, *die* (of an + *Dat.*)

criticize /'krɪtɪsaɪz/ *v.t.* kritisieren (**for** wegen)

critique /krɪ'ti:k/ *n.* Kritik, *die*

croak /krəʊk/ **1** *n.* (of frog) Quaken, *das;* (of person) Krächzen, *das* **2** *v.i.* ⟨*Frosch:*⟩ quaken; ⟨*Person:*⟩ krächzen **3** *v.t.* krächzen

Croat /'krəʊæt/ *n.* **(a)** (person) Kroate, *der/* Kroatin, *die* **(b)** (language) Kroatisch, *das*

Croatia /krəʊ'eɪʃə/ *pr. n.* Kroatien (*das*)

Croatian /krəʊ'eɪʃn/ **1** *adj.* kroatisch; **sb. is** ∼: jmd. ist Kroate/Kroatin **2** *n.* ▶ CROAT

crochet /'krəʊʃeɪ/ **1** *n.* Häkelarbeit, *die;* ∼ **hook** Häkelhaken, *der* **2** *v.t.* häkeln

crock /krɒk/ *n.* (coll.) **[old]** ∼ (person) altes Wrack, *das* (fig.); (vehicle) [alte] Klapperkiste (ugs.)

crockery /'krɒkərɪ/ *n.* Geschirr, *das*

crocodile /'krɒkədaɪl/ *n.* Krokodil, *das*

crocus /'krəʊkəs/ *n.* Krokus, *der*

croft /krɒft/ *n.* **(a)** [kleines] Stück Acker-/ Weideland **(b)** (smallholding) [kleines] Pachtgut

'crofter *n.* (Brit.) Pächter, *der/Pächterin, die*

croissant /'krwɑ:sɑ̃/ *n.* Hörnchen, *das*

crony /'krəʊnɪ/ *n.* Kumpel, *der* (ugs.)

crook /krʊk/ *n.* **(a)** (coll.: rogue) Gauner, *der* **(b)** (shepherd's) Hirtenstab, *der*

crooked /'krʊkɪd/ *adj.* krumm; (fig.: dishonest) betrügerisch

crop /krɒp/ **1** *n.* [Feld]frucht, *die;* (season's yield) Ernte, *die* **2** *v.t.* stutzen ⟨*Haare usw.*⟩ ∎ **crop 'up** *v.i.* auftauchen

'crop dusting *n.* Schädlingsbekämpfung aus der Luft

'cropper *n.* (coll.) **come a** ∼: einen Sturz bauen (ugs.)

crop: ∼**-spraying** *n.* Schädlingsbekämpfung (mit Sprühmitteln); ∼ **top** *n.* bauch- *od.* nabelfreies Top

croquet /'krəʊkeɪ/ *n.* Krocket[spiel], *das*

croquette /krə'ket/ *n.* Krokette, *die*

cross /krɒs/ *n.* **(a)** Kreuz, *das* **(b)** (mixture) Mischung, *die* (**between** aus) **2** *v.t.* **(a)** [über]kreuzen; ∼ **one's arms/legs** die Arme verschränken/die Beine übereinander schlagen; **keep one's fingers** ∼**ed [for sb.]** (fig.) [jmdm.] die *od.* den Daumen drücken **(b)** (go across) kreuzen; überqueren ⟨*Straße, Gebirge*⟩; durchqueren ⟨*Land, Zimmer*⟩; ∼ **sb.'s mind** (fig.) jmdm. einfallen; **'**∼ **now'** „Gehen" **(c)** (Brit.) **a** ∼**ed cheque** ein Verrechnungsscheck **(d)** ∼ **oneself** sich bekreuzigen **3** *v.i.* aneinander vorbeigehen; ∼ **[in the post]** ⟨*Briefe:*⟩ sich kreuzen ···⟩

4 *adj.* verärgert; **sb. will be ~:** jmd. wird ärgerlich *od.* böse werden; **be ~ with sb.** böse auf jmdn. sein
■ **cross 'out** *v.t.* ausstreichen
■ **cross 'over** *v.t.* überqueren; *abs.* hinübergehen
cross: ~bar *n.* (a) [Fahrrad]stange, *die;* (b) (Sport) Querlatte, *die;* **~bones** *n. pl.* gekreuzte Knochen *Pl.* (*unter Totenkopf*); **~bow** /'krɒsbəʊ/ *n.* Armbrust, *die;* **~breed** **1** *n.* Hybride, *die;* (animal) Bastard, *der;* **2** *v.t.* kreuzen; **~Channel** *adj.* **~-Channel traffic/ferry** Verkehr/Fähre über den Kanal; **~check** **1** *n.* Gegenprobe, *die;* **2** *v.t.* [nochmals] nachprüfen; nachkontrollieren; **~country** **1** *adj.* Querfeldein-; **2** *adv.* querfeldein; **~cultural** *adj.* interkulturell; **~dressing** *n.* Crossdressing, *das;* **~examination** *n.* Kreuzverhör, *das;* **~examine** *v.t.* ins Kreuzverhör nehmen; **~eyed** /'krɒsaɪd/ *adj.* [nach innen] schielend; **be ~-eyed** schielen; **~'fertilize** *v.t.* fremdbestäuben; kreuzbefruchten; (fig.) sich gegenseitig befruchten; **~fire** *n.* Kreuzfeuer, *das;* **get caught in the ~fire** (fig.) ins Kreuzfeuer geraten
'crossing *n.* (a) (act) Überquerung, *die* (b) (pedestrian ~) Überweg, *der*
cross-legged /'krɒslegd/ *adv.* mit gekreuzten Beinen; (with feet across thighs) im Schneidersitz
'crossly *adv.* verärgert
cross: ~ 'purposes *n. pl.* **talk at ~ purposes** aneinander vorbeireden; **~'question** *v.t.* ins Kreuzverhör nehmen; **~refer** *v.i.* einen Querverweis machen (**to** auf + *Akk.*); **~ reference** *n.* Querverweis, *der;* **~roads** *n. sing.* Kreuzung, *die;* (fig.) Wendepunkt, *der;* **~ section** *n.* Querschnitt, *der;* **~word** *n.* **~word [puzzle]** Kreuzworträtsel, *das*
crotch /krɒtʃ/ *n.* (of trousers, body) Schritt, *der*
crotchet /'krɒtʃɪt/ *n.* (Brit. Mus.) Viertelnote, *die*
crouch /kraʊtʃ/ *v.i.* [sich zusammen]kauern
croupier /'kruːpɪə(r), 'kruːpɪeɪ/ *n.* Croupier, *der*
crow /krəʊ/ *n.* Krähe, *die;* **as the ~ flies** Luftlinie
'crowbar *n.* Brechstange, *die*
crowd /kraʊd/ **1** *n.* [Menschen]menge, *die* **2** *v.t.* füllen **3** *v.i.* sich sammeln
'crowded *adj.* überfüllt
'crowd-puller *n.* (coll.) Publikumsmagnet, *der*
crown /kraʊn/ **1** *n.* Krone, *die* **2** *v.t.* (a) krönen (b) überkronen 〈*Zahn*〉
crown 'jewels *n. pl.* Kronjuwelen *Pl.*

'crow's-foot *n., usu. in pl.* Krähenfuß, *der*
crucial /'kruːʃl/ *adj.* entscheidend (**to** für)
crucially /'kruːʃəlɪ/ *adv.* entscheidend; **be ~ important** von entscheidender Wichtigkeit sein
crucifix /'kruːsɪfɪks/ *n.* Kruzifix, *das*
crucifixion /kruːsɪ'fɪkʃn/ *n.* Kreuzigung, *die*
crucify /'kruːsɪfaɪ/ *v.t.* kreuzigen
crude /kruːd/ *adj.* (a) roh; **~ oil** Rohöl, *das* (b) (fig.) grob 〈*Entwurf, Worte*〉
cruel /'kruːəl/ *adj.* grausam
cruelty /'kruːəltɪ/ *n.* Grausamkeit, *die*
cruet /'kruːɪt/ *n.* (a) Essig-/Ölfläschchen, *das*
(b) ▶ CRUET STAND
'cruet stand *n.* Menage, *die*
cruise /kruːz/ **1** *v.i.* (at random) 〈*Fahrzeug, Fahrer:*〉 herumfahren **2** *n.* Kreuzfahrt, *die*
'cruise missile *n.* Marschflugkörper, *der*
'cruiser *n.* Kreuzer, *der*
crumb /krʌm/ *n.* Krümel, *der*
crumble /'krʌmbl/ **1** *v.t.* zerkrümeln 〈*Keks, Kuchen*〉 **2** *v.i.* 〈*Mauer:*〉 zusammenfallen
crumbly /'krʌmblɪ/ *adj.* krümelig 〈*Keks, Kuchen*〉; bröckelig 〈*Gestein*〉
crumpet /'krʌmpɪt/ *n.* weiches Hefeküchlein zum Toasten
crumple /'krʌmpl/ **1** *v.t.* (a) (crush) zerdrücken (b) (wrinkle) zerknittern **2** *v.i.* knittern
'crumple zone *n.* (Motor Veh.) Knautschzone, *die*
crunch /krʌntʃ/ **1** *v.t.* [geräuschvoll] knabbern 〈*Keks*〉 **2** *v.i.* 〈*Schnee, Kies:*〉 knirschen **3** *n.* Knirschen, *das;* **when it comes to the ~:** wenn es hart auf hart geht
'crunchy *adj.* knusprig
crusade /kruː'seɪd/ **1** *n.* (Hist.; also fig.) Kreuzzug, *der* **2** *v.i.* (fig.) zu Felde gehen
cru'sader *n.* (Hist.) Kreuzfahrer, *der*
crush /krʌʃ/ **1** *v.t.* (a) quetschen (b) (powder) zerstampfen (c) (fig.) niederschlagen **2** *n.* (a) (crowd) Gedränge, *das* (b) (coll.) **have/get a ~ on sb.** in jmdn. verknallt sein/sich in jmdn. verknallen (ugs.)
crush: ~ bar *n.* Bar, *die* (im *Foyer eines Theaters*); **~barrier** *n.* Absperrgitter, *das*
crushing /'krʌʃɪŋ/ *adj.* niederschmetternd 〈*Antwort*〉; vernichtend 〈*Niederlage, Schlag*〉
crust /krʌst/ *n.* Kruste, *die*
'crusty *adj.* knusprig
crutch /krʌtʃ/ *n.* Krücke, *die;* **go about on ~es** an Krücken gehen
crux /krʌks/ *n.* **the ~ of the matter** der springende Punkt bei der Sache

cry /kraɪ/ ⓵ n. (of grief) Schrei, der; (of words) Schreien, das; **a far ~ from** ... (fig.) etwas ganz anderes als ...
⓶ v.i. **(a)** rufen; (loudly) schreien
(b) (weep) weinen (**over** wegen)
▪ **cry 'off** v.i. absagen
▪ **cry 'out** v.i. aufschreien

'crying adj. **it's a ~ shame** es ist eine wahre Schande

crypt /krɪpt/ n. Krypta, die

cryptic /'krɪptɪk/ adj. geheimnisvoll

crystal /'krɪstl/ ⓵ n. **(a)** Kristall, der
(b) (glass) Bleikristall, das
⓶ adj. (made of ~ glass) kristallen; Kristalle⟨schale, -vase⟩

crystal: ~ clear adj. kristallklar; ; (fig.) glasklar; **~ 'glass** n. Bleikristall, das; Kristallglas, das

crystallize /'krɪstəlaɪz/ v.i. kristallisieren; (fig.) feste Form annehmen

cub /kʌb/ n. **(a)** Junge, das; (of wolf, fox, dog) Welpe, der
(b) Cub ▶ CUB SCOUT

Cuba /'kjuːbə/ pr. n. Kuba ⟨das⟩

cubby[hole] /'kʌbɪ(həʊl)/ n. Kämmerchen, das

cube /kjuːb/ n. Würfel, der

'cube sugar n. Würfelzucker, der

cubic /'kjuːbɪk/ adj. **(a)** würfelförmig
(b) Kubik⟨meter usw.⟩

cubicle /'kjuːbɪkl/ n. Kabine, die

cubism /'kjuːbɪzm/ n. (Art) Kubismus, der

cubist /'kjuːbɪst/ n. (Art) Kubist, der/ Kubistin, die

'Cub Scout n. Wölfling, der

cuckoo /'kʊkuː/ n. Kuckuck, der

'cuckoo clock n. Kuckucksuhr, die

cucumber /'kjuːkʌmbə(r)/ n. [Salat]gurke, die

cuddle /'kʌdl/ ⓵ n. enge Umarmung
⓶ v.t. schmusen mit; hätscheln ⟨kleines Kind⟩
⓷ v.i. schmusen

cuddly /'kʌdlɪ/ adj. zum Schmusen nachgestellt

cuddly 'toy n. Plüschtier, das

cudgel /'kʌdʒl/ n. Knüppel, der

cue¹ /kjuː/ n. (Billiards etc.) Queue, das

cue² n. (Theatre) Stichwort, das

cuff¹ /kʌf/ n. **(a)** Manschette, die; **off the ~** (fig.) aus dem Stegreif
(b) (Amer.: trouser turn-up) [Hosen]aufschlag, der

cuff² ⓵ v.t. **~ sb.** jmdm. einen Klaps geben
⓶ n. Klaps, der

'cuff link n. Manschettenknopf, der

cuisine /kwɪ'ziːn/ n. Küche, die

cul-de-sac /'kʌldəsæk/ n. Sackgasse, die

culinary /'kʌlɪnərɪ/ adj. kulinarisch

culminate /'kʌlmɪneɪt/ v.i. gipfeln; **~ in sth.** in etw. (Dat.) seinen Höchststand erreichen

culmination /kʌlmɪ'neɪʃn/ n. Höhepunkt, der

culottes /kjuː'lɒts/ n. pl. Hosenrock, der

culpable /'kʌlpəbl/ adj. schuldig ⟨Person⟩; strafbar ⟨Handlung⟩

culprit /'kʌlprɪt/ n. Täter, der/Täterin, die

cult /kʌlt/ n. Kult, der

cultivate /'kʌltɪveɪt/ v.t. kultivieren (auch fig.); bestellen ⟨Acker, Land⟩; anbauen ⟨Pflanzen⟩

cultivated /'kʌltɪveɪtɪd/ adj. kultiviert ⟨Manieren, Sprache, Geschmack⟩; kultiviert, gebildet ⟨Person⟩

cultivation /kʌltɪ'veɪʃn/ n. ▶ CULTIVATE: Kultivierung, die; Bestellen das; Anbau, der

culture /'kʌltʃə(r)/ n. Kultur, die

'cultured adj. kultiviert

'culture shock n. Kulturschock, der

cumbersome /'kʌmbəsəm/ adj. hinderlich ⟨Kleider⟩; sperrig ⟨Pakete⟩; schwerfällig ⟨Arbeitsweise⟩

cunning /'kʌnɪŋ/ ⓵ n. Schläue, die
⓶ adj. schlau

cup /kʌp/ n. **(a)** Tasse, die
(b) (prize, competition) Pokal, der
(c) (~ful) Tasse, die; **a ~ of coffee/tea** eine Tasse Kaffee/Tee

cupboard /'kʌbəd/ n. Schrank, der

'Cup Final n. Pokalendspiel, das

cupful /'kʌpfl/ n. Tasse, die; **a ~ of water** eine Tasse Wasser

'cup tie n. Pokalspiel, das

curable /'kjʊərəbl/ adj. heilbar

curate /'kjʊərət/ n. Kurat, der

curator /kjʊə'reɪtə(r)/ n. (of museum) Direktor, der/Direktorin, die

curb /kɜːb/ v.t. zügeln

'curd cheese n. ≈ Quark, der

curdle /'kɜːdl/ v.i. gerinnen

cure /kjʊə(r)/ ⓵ n. [Heil]mittel, das (**for** gegen); (fig.) Mittel, das
⓶ v.t. **(a)** heilen
(b) [ein]pökeln ⟨Fleisch⟩

'cure-all n. Allheilmittel, das

curfew /'kɜːfjuː/ n. Ausgangssperre, die

curiosity /kjʊərɪ'ɒsɪtɪ/ n. **(a)** Neugier[de], die
(b) (object) Wunderding, das

curious /'kjʊərɪəs/ adj. **(a)** (inquisitive) neugierig
(b) (strange, odd) seltsam

curl /kɜːl/ ⓵ n. Locke, die
⓶ v.t. locken
⓷ v.i. **(a)** sich locken
(b) ⟨Straße, Fluss:⟩ sich winden

'curler n. Lockenwickler, der

'curly adj. lockig   ···❖

'curly-haired adj. lockenköpfig; mit lockigem Haar

currant /'kʌrənt/ n. Korinthe, die

currency /'kʌrənsɪ/ n. (money) Währung, die; foreign currencies Devisen Pl.

current /'kʌrənt/ ① adj. (a) verbreitet ⟨Meinung⟩; gebräuchlich ⟨Wort⟩
(b) laufend ⟨Jahr, Monat⟩
(c) (the present) aktuell ⟨Ereignis, Mode⟩; Tages⟨politik, -preis⟩; ~ affairs Tagespolitik, die
② n. (a) (of water, air) Strömung, die
(b) (Electr.) Strom, der

'current account n. Girokonto, das

'currently adv. zur Zeit

curriculum /kə'rɪkjʊləm/ n. Lehrplan, der

curriculum vitae /- 'viːtaɪ/ n. Lebenslauf, der

curry¹ /'kʌrɪ/ n. Curry[gericht], das

curry² v.t. ~ favour [with sb.] sich [bei jmdm.] einschmeicheln

curse /kɜːs/ ① n. Fluch, der
② v.t. verfluchen
③ v.i. fluchen

cursor /'kɜːsə(r)/ n. Läufer, der; (on screen) Cursor, der; Schreibmarke, die

cursory /'kɜːsərɪ/ adj. flüchtig

curt /kɜːt/ adj. kurz angebunden; kurz und schroff ⟨Brief⟩

curtail /kɜː'teɪl/ v.t. kürzen; abkürzen ⟨Urlaub⟩; beschneiden ⟨Macht⟩

curtain /'kɜːtən/ n. Vorhang, der; draw or pull the ~s (open) die Vorhänge aufziehen; (close) die Vorhänge zuziehen

curtain: ~ **call** n. Vorhang, der; ~ **hook** n. Gardinenhaken, der; ~ **rod** n. Gardinenstange, die

curtsy /'kɜːtsɪ/ ① n. Knicks, der
② v.i. einen Knicks machen (to vor + Dat.)

curvaceous /kɜː'veɪʃəs/ adj. kurvenreich (ugs.); a ~ figure eine üppige Figur

curve /kɜːv/ ① v.t. krümmen
② v.i. ⟨Straße, Fluss:⟩ eine Biegung machen
③ n. Kurve, die

cushion /'kʊʃn/ ① n. Kissen, das
② v.t. dämpfen ⟨Aufprall, Stoß⟩

cushy /'kʊʃɪ/ adj. (coll.) bequem

custard /'kʌstəd/ n. ≈ Vanillesoße, die

'custard powder n. Vanillesoßenpulver, das

custodian /kʌs'təʊdɪən/ n. (of museum) Wächter, der/Wächterin, die; (of valuables) Hüter, der/Hüterin, die

custody /'kʌstədɪ/ n. (a) (care) Obhut, die
(b) (imprisonment) [be] in ~: in Haft [sein]; take sb. into ~: jmdn. verhaften od. festnehmen

custom /'kʌstəm/ n. (a) Brauch, der
(b) in pl. (duty on imports) Zoll, der

customary /'kʌstəmərɪ/ adj. üblich

'custom-built adj. spezial[an]gefertigt

customer /'kʌstəmə(r)/ n. Kunde, der/ Kundin, die

customize (customise) /'kʌstəmaɪz/ v.t. speziell anfertigen; (alter) umbauen

'custom-made adj. spezial[an]gefertigt; maßgeschneidert ⟨Kleidung⟩

customs: ~ **duty** n. Zoll, der; ~ **inspection** n. Zollkontrolle, die; ~ **officer** n. Zollbeamter, der/-beamtin, die

cut /kʌt/ ① v.t., -tt-, cut (a) schneiden; durchschneiden ⟨Seil⟩; ~ one's leg sich (Dat. od. Akk.) ins Bein schneiden
(b) abschneiden ⟨Scheibe⟩; schneiden ⟨Hecke⟩; mähen ⟨Getreide, Gras⟩; ~ one's nails sich (Dat.) die Nägel schneiden
(c) (reduce) senken ⟨Preise⟩; kürzen ⟨Lohn⟩; abbauen ⟨Arbeitsplätze⟩
(d) ~ sth. short (interrupt) etw. abbrechen
(e) (Comp.) ~ and paste ausschneiden und einfügen
② v.i., -tt-, cut (a) ⟨Messer:⟩ schneiden
(b) ~ through or across the field/park [quer] über das Feld/durch den Park gehen
③ n. (a) (act of cutting) Schnitt, der
(b) (stroke, blow) (with knife) Schnitt, der; (with sword, whip) Hieb, der
(c) (reduction) Kürzung, die; (in prices) Senkung, die; (in services) Verringerung, die
(d) (of meat) Stück, die

■ **cut a'way** v.t. abschneiden

■ **cut 'back** v.t. (a) (reduce) einschränken
(b) (prune) stutzen

■ **cut 'down** ① v.t. (a) fällen ⟨Baum⟩
(b) (reduce) einschränken
② v.i. ~ down on sth. etw. einschränken

■ **cut 'off** v.t. abschneiden; unterbrechen ⟨Telefongespräch, Sprecher⟩

■ **cut 'out** ① v.t. (a) ausschneiden (of aus)
(b) be ~ out for geeignet sein zu
② v.i. ⟨Motor:⟩ aussetzen

■ **cut 'up** v.t. zerschneiden

cut: ~**back** n. (reduction) Kürzung, die; ~ **'glass** n. Kristall[glas], das; ~**glass** adj. Kristall-

cutlery /'kʌtlərɪ/ n. Besteck, das

cutlet /'kʌtlɪt/ n. Kotelett, das

cut: ~**off** n. ~**off point** Trennungslinie, die; ~**out** n. (figure) Ausschneidefigur, die; ~**price** adj. herabgesetzt; ~**price offer** Billigangebot, das

'cutting ① adj. beißend ⟨Bemerkung, Antwort⟩
② n. (from newspaper) Ausschnitt, der

'cutting edge n. be at the ~ of technology auf dem Gebiet der Technologie führend sein; die Speerspitze der Technologie sein; be at the ~ of fashion auf dem Gebiet der Mode führend sein

c. v. abbr. = **curriculum vitae**

cyber: ~**cafe** /'saɪbəkæfeɪ/ n. Internet-Café das; ~**sex** /'saɪbəseks/ n., no art. Cybersex, der; ~**space** /'saɪbəspeɪs/ n., no art. Cyberspace, der

cycle /'saɪkl/ [1] *n.* **(a)** (recurrent period)
Zyklus, *der*
(b) (bicycle) Rad, *das*
[2] *v.i.* Rad fahren
cycle: ~ lane *n.* Fahrradspur, *die;*
~ race *n.* Radrennen, *das;* **~ track** *n.*
Rad[fahr]weg, *der;* (for racing) Radrennbahn,
die
cycling /'saɪklɪŋ/ *n.* (activity) Radfahren,
das; (sport) Radsport, *der;* **~ shorts**
Radlerhose, *die*
cyclist /'saɪklɪst/ *n.* Radfahrer, *der/*
-fahrerin, *die*
cyclone /'saɪkləʊn/ *n.* (violent hurricane)
Zyklon, *der*
cylinder /'sɪlɪndə(r)/ *n.* Zylinder, *der*
cylindrical /sɪ'lɪndrɪkl/ *adj.* zylindrisch
cymbal /'sɪmbl/ *n.* Beckenteller, *der;* **~s**
Becken *Pl.*

cynic /'sɪnɪk/ *n.* Zyniker, *der*
cynical /'sɪnɪkl/ *adj.* zynisch; bissig
⟨Bemerkung, Worte⟩
cynicism /'sɪnɪsɪzm/ *n.* Zynismus, *der*
Cyprus /'saɪprəs/ *pr. n.* Zypern (*das*)
czar ▶ TSAR
Czech /tʃek/ [1] *adj.* tschechisch; **sb. is ~:**
jmd. ist Tscheche/Tschechin
[2] *n.* **(a)** (language) Tschechisch, *das*
(b) (person) Tscheche, *der/*Tschechin, *die*
Czechoslovakia /tʃekəʊslə'vækɪə/ *pr. n.*
(Hist.) die Tschechoslowakei
Czechoslovakian /tʃekəʊslə'vækɪən/
(Hist.) [1] *adj.* tschechoslowakisch
[2] *n.* Tschechoslowake, *der/*
Tschechoslowakin, *die*
Czech Re'public *pr. n.* Tschechische
Republik; Tschechien (*das*)

Dd

D, d /diː/ *n.* D, d, *das*
dab /dæb/ [1] *n.* Tupfer, *der*
[2] *v.t.,* **-bb-** abtupfen; **~ sth. on** *or* **against**
sth. etw. auf etw. (*Akk.*) tupfen
dabble /'dæbl/ *v.i.* **~ in sth.** sich in etw.
(*Dat.*) versuchen
dachshund /'dækshʊnd/ *n.* Dackel, *der*
dad /dæd/ *n.* (coll.) Vater, *der*
daddy /'dædɪ/ *n.* (coll.) Vati, *der* (fam.)
daddy-'long-legs *n.* Schnake, *die*
daffodil /'dæfədɪl/ *n.* Osterglocke, *die*
daft /dɑːft/ *adj.* doof (ugs.)
dagger /'dægə(r)/ *n.* Dolch, *der*
daily /'deɪlɪ/ [1] *adj.* täglich; **~ [news]paper**
Tageszeitung, *die*
[2] *adv.* täglich
[3] *n.* Tageszeitung, *die*
dainty /'deɪntɪ/ *adj.* zierlich; anmutig
⟨Bewegung, Person⟩; zart ⟨Gesichtszüge⟩
dairy /'deərɪ/ *n.* **(a)** Molkerei, *die*
(b) (shop) Milchladen, *der*
dairy: ~ cattle *n.* Milchvieh, *das;*
~ farm *n.* Milchbetrieb, *der;* **~ farmer**
n. Milchbauer, *der;* **~ produce** *n.,*
~ products *n. pl.* Molkereiprodukte
dais /'deɪɪs/ *n.* Podium, *das*
daisy /'deɪzɪ/ *n.* Gänseblümchen, *das*
'daisy chain *n.* Kranz aus
Gänseblümchen
dam /dæm/ [1] *n.* [Stau]damm, *der*
[2] *v.t.,* **-mm-:** **(a)** **~ [up] sth.** etw. abblocken
(b) aufstauen ⟨Fluss⟩
damage /'dæmɪdʒ/ [1] *n.* Schaden, *der*

[2] *v.t.* beschädigen
damaging /'dæmɪdʒɪŋ/ *adj.* schädlich (**to**
für)
damn /dæm/ [1] *v.t.* verdammen
[2] *adj., adv., int.* (coll.) verdammt (ugs.)
[3] *n.* **he doesn't give** *or* **care a ~:** ihm ist es
völlig wurscht (ugs.)
damp /dæmp/ [1] *adj.* feucht
[2] *v.t.* ▶ DAMPEN
[3] *n.* Feuchtigkeit, *die*
dampen /'dæmpn/ *v.t.* befeuchten; (fig.)
dämpfen ⟨Begeisterung, Eifer⟩
'dampness *n.* Feuchtigkeit, *die*
'damp-proof *adj.* feuchtigkeitsbeständig;
~ course Sperrschicht, *die* (gegen
aufsteigende Bodenfeuchtigkeit)
dance /dɑːns/ [1] *v.i. & t.* tanzen
[2] *n.* **(a)** Tanz, *der*
(b) (party) Tanzveranstaltung, *die;* (private)
Tanzparty, *die*
dance: ~ floor *n.* Tanzfläche, *die;* **~ hall**
n. Tanzsaal, *der*
'dancer *n.* Tänzer, *der/*Tänzerin, *die*
'dance step *n.* Tanzschritt, *der*
dandelion /'dændɪlaɪən/ *n.* Löwenzahn,
der
dandruff /'dændrʌf/ *n.* [Kopf]schuppen *Pl.*
Dane /deɪn/ *n.* Däne, *der/*Dänin, *die*
danger /'deɪndʒə(r)/ *n.* Gefahr, *die;* **in/out**
of ~: in/außer Gefahr; **be in ~ of doing sth.**
⟨Person:⟩ Gefahr laufen, etw. zu tun

danger: ∼ **area** n. Gefahrenzone, die; ∼ **list** n. be on/off the ∼ list in/außer Lebensgefahr sein
dangerous /'deɪndʒərəs/ adj., **'dangerously** adv. gefährlich
danger: ∼ **signal** n. Warnzeichen, das; ∼ **zone** n. Gefahrenzone, die
dangle /'dæŋgl/ ⟨1⟩ v.i. baumeln (**from** an + Dat.)
⟨2⟩ v.t. baumeln lassen
Danish /'deɪnɪʃ/ ⟨1⟩ adj. dänisch; **sb. is** ∼: jmd. ist Däne/Dänin
⟨2⟩ n. Dänisch, das; see also ENGLISH 2A
dank /dæŋk/ adj. feucht
Danube /'dænjuːb/ pr. n. Donau, die
dare /deə(r)/ ⟨1⟩ v.t. **(a)** [es] wagen; ∼ **to do** sth. [es] wagen, etw. zu tun
(b) (challenge) ∼ **sb. to do** sth. jmdn. aufstacheln, etw. zu tun; **I** ∼ **you!** trau dich!
⟨2⟩ n. Mutprobe, die
daring /'deərɪŋ/ adj. (bold) kühn; waghalsig ⟨Kunststück, Tat⟩; (fearless) wagemutig
dark /dɑːk/ ⟨1⟩ adj. dunkel; (dark-haired) dunkelhaarig; ∼**-blue/-brown** dunkelblau/ -braun; ∼ **glasses** dunkle Brille
⟨2⟩ n. **(a)** Dunkel, das; **in the** ∼: im Dunkeln; **keep sb. in the** ∼ (fig.) jmdn. im Dunkeln lassen
(b) no art. (nightfall) Einbruch der Dunkelheit
darken /'dɑːkn/ v.t. verdunkeln
dark: ∼**-haired** adj. dunkelhaarig; ∼ **'horse** n. be a ∼ horse ein stilles Wasser sein
'darkness n. Dunkelheit, die
'darkroom n. Dunkelkammer, die
darling /'dɑːlɪŋ/ n. Liebling, der
darn /dɑːn/ v.t. stopfen
dart /dɑːt/ ⟨1⟩ n. **(a)** (missile) Pfeil, der
(b) (Sport) Wurfpfeil, der; ∼**s** sing. (game) Darts, das
⟨2⟩ v.i. sausen
'dartboard n. Dartsscheibe, die
dash /dæʃ/ ⟨1⟩ v.i. sausen
⟨2⟩ v.t. (fling) schleudern
⟨3⟩ n. **(a)** make a ∼: rasen (ugs.) (**for** zu)
(b) (horizontal stroke) Gedankenstrich, der
(c) (small amount) Schuss, der
'dashboard n. Armaturenbrett, das
data /'deɪtə, 'dɑːtə/ n. Daten Pl.
data: ∼**base** n. Datenbank, die; ∼ **capture** n. (Comp.) Datenerfassung, die; ∼ **file** n. (Comp.) Datei, die; ∼ **highway** n. (Comp.) Datenautobahn, die; ∼ **pro'tection** n. (Comp.) Datenschutz, der; ∼ **retrieval** n. (Comp.) Retrieval, das; Datenabruf, der; ∼ **security** n. (Comp.) Datensicherung, die; ∼ **storage** n. (Comp.) Datenspeicherung, die; (capacity) Speicherkapazität, die
date¹ /deɪt/ n. (Bot.) Dattel, die
date² ⟨1⟩ n. **(a)** Datum, das; (on coin etc.) Jahreszahl, die; ∼ **of birth** Geburtsdatum, das; **be out of** ∼: altmodisch sein; **to** ∼: bis heute

(b) (coll.: appointment) Verabredung, die; **have/ make a** ∼ **with** sb. mit jmdm. verabredet sein/sich mit jmdm. verabreden
⟨2⟩ v.t. **(a)** datieren
(b) (coll.: make seem old) alt machen
⟨3⟩ v.i. ∼ **back to/**∼ **from** stammen aus
dated /'deɪtɪd/ adj. altmodisch
date: ∼ **line** n. Datumsgrenze, die; ∼ **rape** n.: Vergewaltigung der eigenen Freundin oder Vergewaltigung einer Frau während einer Verabredung mit ihr; ∼ **stamp** n. Datumsstempel, der; ∼**-stamp** v.t. abstempeln; mit einem Datumsstempel versehen
'dating agency /'deɪtɪŋ/ n. Partnervermittlung, die
dative /'deɪtɪv/ adj. & n. ∼ [**case**] Dativ, der
daub /dɔːb/ v.t. (smear) beschmieren; (put crudely) schmieren
daughter /'dɔːtə(r)/ n. Tochter, die
'daughter-in-law n., pl. **daughters-in-law** Schwiegertochter, die
daunt /dɔːnt/ v.t. entmutigen
dawdle /'dɔːdl/ v.i. bummeln (ugs.)
dawn /dɔːn/ ⟨1⟩ v.i. dämmern; sth. ∼**s** [**up**]**on** sb. etw. dämmert jmdm
⟨2⟩ n. [Morgen]dämmerung, die; **at** ∼: im Morgengrauen
dawn 'chorus n. morgendlicher Gesang der Vögel
day /deɪ/ n. Tag, der; **all** ∼ [**long**] den ganzen Tag [lang]; **for two** ∼**s** zwei Tage [lang]; **the** ∼ **before yesterday/after tomorrow** vorgestern/übermorgen; ∼ **after** ∼: Tag für Tag; ∼ **in** ∼ **out** tagaus, tagein; **in the** ∼**s when** ...: zu der Zeit, als ...; **these** ∼**s** heutzutage; **in those** ∼**s** damals
day: ∼**bed** n. Liegesofa, das; ∼**break** n. Tagesanbruch, der; ∼ **care** n. Ganztagsbetreuung, die; ∼**dream** ⟨1⟩ n. Tagtraum, der; ⟨2⟩ v.i. träumen; ∼**dreamer** n. Tagträumer, der/-träumerin, die; ∼**light** n. Tageslicht, das; **in broad** ∼**light** am helllichten Tag[e]; ∼ **release** n. (Brit.) [tageweise] Freistellung zur Fortbildung; ∼ **re'turn** n. Tagesrückfahrkarte, die; ∼**time** n. Tag, der; ∼**-to-**∼ adj. [tag]täglich; ∼ **trip** n. Tagesausflug, der; ∼ **tripper** n. Tagesausflügler, der/ -ausflüglerin, die
daze /deɪz/ v.t. benommen machen
dazed /deɪzd/ adj. benommen
dazzle /'dæzl/ v.t. blenden
DC abbr. = **direct current** GS
dead /ded/ ⟨1⟩ adj. **(a)** tot
(b) plötzlich ⟨Halt⟩; genau ⟨Mitte⟩
(c) (numb) taub
⟨2⟩ adv. völlig; ∼ **straight** schnurgerade; ∼ **easy/slow** kinderleicht/ganz langsam; ∼ **on time** auf die Minute; ∼ **tired** todmüde
⟨3⟩ n. pl. **the** ∼: die Toten Pl.
deaden /'dedn/ v.t. dämpfen; betäuben ⟨Schmerz⟩

dead: ~ **'end** n. Sackgasse, die; ~ **'heat** n. totes Rennen; ~**line** n. [letzter] Termin; ~**lock** n. völliger Stillstand; ~ **'loss** n. (coll.) (worthless thing) totaler Reinfall (ugs.); (person) hoffnungsloser Fall (ugs.)

deadly /'dedlɪ/ adj. tödlich; (fig. coll.: boring) todlangweilig

dead: ~**pan** adj. unbewegt; **he looked** ~**pan** or **had a** ~**pan expression** er verzog keine Miene; **D**~ **'Sea** pr. n. Totes Meer; ~ **'wood** n. (fig.) **be just** ~ **wood** völlig überflüssig sein

deaf /def/ adj. ⊡ taub; ~ **and dumb** taubstumm
⊡ n. pl. **the** ~: die Gehörlosen Pl.

'deaf aid n. Hörgerät, das

deafen /'defn/ v.t. ~ **sb.** bei jmdm. zur Taubheit führen; **I was** ~**ed by the noise** (fig.) ich war von dem Lärm wie betäubt

'deafening adj. ohrenbetäubend

'deafness n. Taubheit, die

deal¹ /diːl/ ⊡ v.t., **dealt** /delt/ **(a)** (Cards) austeilen
(b) ~ **sb. a blow** jmdm. einen Schlag versetzen
⊡ v.i., **dealt (a)** (do business) ~ **in sth.** mit etw. handeln
(b) ~ **with sth.** (occupy oneself) sich mit etw. befassen; (manage) mit etw. fertig werden; (be about) von etw. handeln; ~ **with sb.** mit jmdm. fertig werden
⊡ n. (coll.: arrangement) Geschäft, das; **it's a** ~**!** abgemacht!; **big** ~**!** (iron.) na, und?
■ **deal 'out** v.t. verteilen

deal² n. **a great** or **good** ~: viel; (often) ziemlich viel; **a great** or **good** ~ **of** viel

'dealer n. **(a)** Händler, der
(b) (Cards) Geber, der; **he's the** ~: er gibt

'dealings n. pl. **have** ~ **with sb.** mit jmdm. zu tun haben

dealt ▶ DEAL¹ 1, 2

dean /diːn/ n. (Eccl.) Dechant, der

dear /dɪə(r)/ ⊡ adj. **(a)** lieb; **sb./sth. is** ~ **to sb.['s heart]** jmd. liebt jmdn./etw.; (beginning letter) **D**~ **Sir/Madam** Sehr geehrter Herr/ Sehr geehrte Dame; **D**~ **Mr Jones/Mrs Jones** Sehr geehrter Herr Jones/Sehr geehrte Frau Jones; **D**~ **Malcolm/Emily** Lieber Malcolm/ Liebe Emily
(b) (expensive) teuer
⊡ int. ~, ~**!, oh** ~ **me!, oh** ~**!** [ach] du liebe od. meine Güte!

'dearly adv. **(a)** von ganzem Herzen
(b) (at high price) teuer

dearth /dɜːθ/ n. Mangel, der (**of** an + Dat.)

death /deθ/ n. **(a)** Tod, der; **... to** ~: zu Tode ...; **bleed to** ~: verbluten
(b) (instance) Todesfall, der

death: ~**bed** n. Totenbett, das; **on one's** ~**bed** auf dem Sterbebett; ~ **certificate** n. (from doctor) Totenschein, der

deathly /'deθlɪ/ ⊡ adj. tödlich
⊡ adv. tödlich; ~ **still/quiet** totenstill

death: ~ **penalty** n. Todesstrafe, die; ~ **sentence** n. Todesurteil, das; ~ **trap** n. lebensgefährliche Sache; ~ **threat** n. Morddrohung, die

debatable /dɪ'beɪtəbl/ adj. (questionable) fraglich

debate /dɪ'beɪt/ n. Debatte, die

debilitating /dɪ'bɪlɪteɪtɪŋ/ adj. anstrengend ‹Klima›; schwächend ‹Krankheit›

debit /'debɪt/ ⊡ n. Soll, das
⊡ v.t. belasten ‹Konto›

debris /'debriː/ n. Trümmer Pl.

debt /det/ n. Schuld, die; **be in** ~: Schulden haben; **get into** ~: in Schulden geraten

debtor /'detə(r)/ n. Schuldner, der/ Schuldnerin, die

debug /diː'bʌg/ v.t., **-gg-** (coll.: remove defects from) von Fehlern befreien

début (Amer.: **debut**) /'deɪbuː, 'deɪbjuː/ n. Debüt, das

Dec. abbr. = **December** Dez.

decade /'dekeɪd/ n. Jahrzehnt, das

decadent /'dekədənt/ adj. dekadent

decaf, decaff /'diːkæf/ n. (coll.) or ® koffeinfreier Kaffee

decaffeinated /diː'kæfmeɪtɪd/ adj. entkoffeiniert

decanter /dɪ'kæntə(r)/ n. Karaffe, die

decay /dɪ'keɪ/ ⊡ v.i. verrotten; ‹Gebäude:› zerfallen; ‹Zahn:› faul werden
⊡ n. Verrotten, das; (of building) Zerfall, der; (of tooth) Fäule, die

deceased /dɪ'siːst/ ⊡ adj. verstorben
⊡ n. Verstorbene, der/die

deceit /dɪ'siːt/ n. Täuschung, die

deceitful /dɪ'siːtfl/ adj. falsch ‹Person, Art›; hinterlistig ‹Trick›

deceive /dɪ'siːv/ v.t. täuschen; (be unfaithful to) betrügen

December /dɪ'sembə(r)/ n. Dezember, der; see also AUGUST

decency /'diːsənsɪ/ n. Anstand, der

decent /'diːsənt/ adj. anständig

decentralization /diːsentrəlaɪ'zeɪʃn/ n. Dezentralisierung, die

decentralize /diː'sentrəlaɪz/ v.t. dezentralisieren

deception /dɪ'sepʃn/ n. Betrug, der; (being deceived) Täuschung, die

deceptive /dɪ'septɪv/ adj. trügerisch

decibel /'desɪbel/ n. Dezibel, das

decide /dɪ'saɪd/ ⊡ v.t. **(a)** (settle, judge) entscheiden über (+ Akk.)
(b) (resolve) ~ **that** ...: beschließen, dass ...; ~ **to do sth.** sich entschließen, etw. zu tun
⊡ v.i. sich entscheiden (**in favour of** zugunsten von, **against** gegen)

de'cided adj., **de'cidedly** adv. entschieden

deciduous /dɪ'sɪdjʊəs/ adj. ~ **tree** ≈ Laubbaum, der

decimal /'desɪml/ ① n. Dezimalbruch, der
② adj. Dezimal-

decimal: ~ **'currency** n.
Dezimalwährung, die; ~ **'fraction** n.
Dezimalbruch, der; ~ **'point** n. Komma,
das

decimate /'desɪmeɪt/ v.t. dezimieren

decipher /dɪ'saɪfə(r)/ v.t. entziffern

decision /dɪ'sɪʒn/ n. Entscheidung, die

decisive /dɪ'saɪsɪv/ adj. entscheidend

deck /dek/ n. (a) Deck, das; on ~: an Deck;
below ~[s] unter Deck
(b) (Amer.: pack) a ~ of cards ein Spiel
Karten

'deckchair n. Liegestuhl, der

declaration /deklə'reɪʃn/ n. Erklärung,
die

declare /dɪ'kleə(r)/ v.t. erklären; kundtun
(geh.) ⟨Wunsch, Absicht⟩; ~ sth./sb. [to be]
sth. etw./jmdn. für etw. erklären

declension /dɪ'klenʃn/ n. Deklination, die

decline /dɪ'klaɪn/ ① v.i. nachlassen;
⟨Anzahl:⟩ sinken
② v.t. (a) ablehnen
(b) (Ling.) deklinieren
③ n. ▶ 1: Nachlassen, das/Sinken, das (in
Gen.); be on the ~: nachlassen/sinken

decode /diː'kəʊd/ v.t. entziffern

decommission /diːkə'mɪʃən/ v.t.
stilllegen; außer Dienst stellen ⟨Schiff⟩

decompose /diːkəm'pəʊz/ v.i. sich
zersetzen

décor /'deɪkɔː(r)/ n. Ausstattung, die

decorate /'dekəreɪt/ v.t. (a) schmücken
⟨Raum, Straße, Baum⟩; verzieren ⟨Kuchen,
Kleid⟩; (paint) streichen; (wallpaper) tapezieren
(b) (award medal etc. to) auszeichnen

decoration /dekə'reɪʃn/ n. (a) Schmücken,
das; (with paint) Streichen, das; (with wallpaper)
Tapezieren, das; (of cake, dress) Verzieren, das
(b) (adornment) Schmuck, der
(c) (medal etc.) Auszeichnung, die

decorative /'dekərətɪv/ adj. dekorativ

decorator /'dekəreɪtə(r)/ n. Maler, der;
(paperhanger) Tapezierer, der

decorous /'dekərəs/ adj., **'decorously**
adv. schicklich (geh.)

decorum /dɪ'kɔːrəm/ n. Schicklichkeit, die
(geh.)

decoy /'diːkɔɪ/ n. Lockvogel, der

decrease ① /dɪ'kriːs/ v.i. abnehmen;
⟨Stärke:⟩ nachlassen
② /dɪ'kriːs/ v.t. [ver]mindern ⟨Wert, Lärm⟩;
schmälern ⟨Popularität, Macht⟩
③ /'diːkriːs/ n. Rückgang, der; (in weight)
Abnahme, die; (in strength) Nachlassen, das; (in
value, noise) Minderung, die

decree /dɪ'kriː/ ① n. Dekret, das; Erlass,
der
② v.t. verfügen

decrepit /dɪ'krepɪt/ adj. altersschwach;
(dilapidated) heruntergekommen

decriminalize /diː'krɪmɪnəlaɪz/ v.t.
entkriminalisieren

dedicate /'dedɪkeɪt/ v.t. ~ sth. to sb.
jmdm. etw. widmen

'dedicated adj. (a) (devoted) be ~ to sth./
sb. nur für etw./jmdn. leben
(b) (to vocation) hingebungsvoll; a ~ teacher
ein Lehrer mit Leib und Seele

dedication /dedɪ'keɪʃn/ n. (a) Widmung,
die (to Dat.)
(b) (devotion) Hingabe, die

deduce /dɪ'djuːs/ v.t. ~ sth. [from sth.] etw.
[aus etw.] schließen

deduct /dɪ'dʌkt/ v.t. ~ sth. [from sth.] etw.
[von etw.] abziehen

deduction /dɪ'dʌkʃn/ n. (a) (deducting)
Abzug, der
(b) (deducing, thing deduced) Ableitung, die
(c) (amount) Abzüge Pl.

deed /diːd/ n. (a) Tat, die
(b) (Law) Urkunde, die

deejay /'diːdʒeɪ/ n. (coll.) Diskjockey, der

deem /diːm/ v.t. erachten für

deep /diːp/ ① adj. (lit. or fig.) tief; tiefgründig
⟨Bemerkung⟩; water ten feet ~: drei Meter
tiefes Wasser; take a ~ breath tief Atem
holen; be ~ in thought in Gedanken
versunken sein
② adv. tief

'deepen ① v.t. vertiefen
② v.i. sich vertiefen

deep: ~**-'freeze** v.t. tiefgefrieren;
~**-fried** adj. frittiert

'deeply adv. (lit. or fig.) tief; äußerst
⟨interessiert, dankbar⟩

deep-'rooted adj. tief ⟨Abneigung⟩; tief
verwurzelt ⟨Tradition⟩

deer /dɪə(r)/ n., pl. same Hirsch, der; (roe ~)
Reh, das

de-escalate /diː'eskəleɪt/ v.t. deeskalieren

deface /dɪ'feɪs/ v.t. verunstalten

defamation /defə'meɪʃn/ n. Diffamierung,
die

defamatory /dɪ'fæmətərɪ/ adj.
diffamierend

default /dɪ'fɔːlt, dɪ'fɒlt/ ① n. (a) lose/go by
~: durch Abwesenheit verlieren/nicht zur
Geltung kommen; win by ~: durch
Nichterscheinen des Gegners gewinnen
(b) (Comp.) Voreinstellung, die
② v.i. ~ on one's payments/debts seinen
Zahlungsverpflichtungen nicht nachkommen

defeat /dɪ'fiːt/ ① v.t. besiegen
② n. (being ~ed) Niederlage, die; (~ing) Sieg,
der (of über + Akk.)

de'featist adj. defätistisch

defect ① /'diːfekt/ n. (a) (lack) Mangel, der
(b) (shortcoming) Fehler, der
② /dɪ'fekt/ v.i. überlaufen (to zu)

defection /dɪ'fekʃn/ n. Flucht, die

defective /dɪˈfektɪv/ adj. defekt ⟨Maschine⟩; fehlerhaft ⟨Material, Arbeiten, Methode⟩

defector /dɪˈfektə(r)/ n. Überläufer, der/ -läuferin, die

defence /dɪˈfens/ n. (Brit.) Verteidigung, die; (means of ∿) Schutz, der

de'fenceless adj. wehrlos

de'fence mechanism n. (Physiol., Psych.) Abwehrmechanismus, der

defend /dɪˈfend/ v.t. verteidigen

defendant /dɪˈfendənt/ n. (Law) (accused) Angeklagte, der/die; (sued) Beklagte, der/die

de'fender n. Verteidiger, der

defense etc. (Amer.) ▶ DEFENCE etc.

defensive /dɪˈfensɪv/ **1** adj. defensiv **2** n. be on the ∿: in der Defensive sein

defer¹ /dɪˈfɜː(r)/ v.t., -rr- aufschieben

defer² v.i., -rr-: ∿ [to sb.] sich [jmdm.] beugen

deference /ˈdefərəns/ n. Respekt, der; in ∿ to sb./sth. aus Achtung vor jmdm./etw.

deferential /defəˈrenʃl/ adj. respektvoll

defiance /dɪˈfaɪəns/ n. Trotz, der; in ∿ of sb./sth. jmdm./einer Sache zum Trotz

defiant /dɪˈfaɪənt/ adj., **de'fiantly** adv. trotzig

deficiency /dɪˈfɪʃənsɪ/ n. Mangel, der

deficient /dɪˈfɪʃnt/ adj. unzulänglich; sb./ sth. is ∿ in sth. jmdm./einer Sache mangelt es an etw. (Dat.)

deficit /ˈdefɪsɪt/ n. Defizit, das (of an + Dat.)

defile /dɪˈfaɪl/ v.t. verpesten ⟨Luft⟩; beflecken ⟨Reinheit, Unschuld⟩

define /dɪˈfaɪn/ v.t. definieren

definite /ˈdefɪnɪt/ adj. bestimmt; eindeutig ⟨Antwort, Entscheidung, Beschluss, Verbesserung⟩; klar umrissen ⟨Ziel, Plan⟩; klar ⟨Vorstellung⟩; genau ⟨Zeitpunkt⟩

'definitely **1** adv. bestimmt; eindeutig ⟨festlegen, größer sein, verbessert⟩; endgültig ⟨entscheiden⟩ **2** int. (coll.) na, klar (ugs.)

definition /defɪˈnɪʃn/ n. Definition, die; (Telev., Phot.) Schärfe, die

definitive /dɪˈfɪnɪtɪv/ adj. endgültig ⟨Beschluss, Antwort, Urteil⟩; (authoritative) maßgeblich

deflate /dɪˈfleɪt/ v.t. die Luft ablassen aus; (fig.) ernüchtern

deflation /dɪˈfleɪʃn/ n. (Econ.) Deflation, die

deflect /dɪˈflekt/ v.t. brechen ⟨Licht⟩; ∿ sb./sth. [from sb./sth.] jmdn./etw. [von jmdm./einer Sache] ablenken

deforestation /diːfɒrɪˈsteɪʃn/ n. Entwaldung, die; Abholzung, die

deform /dɪˈfɔːm/ v.t. deformieren

deformed /dɪˈfɔːmd/ adj. entstellt ⟨Gesicht⟩; verunstaltet ⟨Person, Körperteil⟩

deformity /dɪˈfɔːmɪtɪ/ n. (malformation) Verunstaltung, die

defraud /dɪˈfrɔːd/ v.t. ∿ sb. [of sth.] jmdn. [um etw.] betrügen

defray /dɪˈfreɪ/ v.t. bestreiten

defrost /diːˈfrɒst/ v.t. auftauen ⟨Speisen⟩; abtauen ⟨Kühlschrank⟩

deft /deft/ adj., **'deftly** adv. sicher und geschickt

defunct /dɪˈfʌŋkt/ adj. defekt ⟨Maschine⟩; veraltet ⟨Gesetz⟩

defuse /diːˈfjuːz/ v.t. entschärfen

defy /dɪˈfaɪ/ v.t. **(a)** (resist openly) ∿ sb. jmdm. trotzen **(b)** (refuse to obey) ∿ sb./sth. sich jmdm./ einer Sache widersetzen

degenerate /dɪˈdʒenəreɪt/ v.i. ∿ [into sth.] [zu etw.] verkommen

degradation /degrəˈdeɪʃn/ n. Erniedrigung, die

degrade /dɪˈgreɪd/ v.t. erniedrigen

degrading /dɪˈgreɪdɪŋ/ adj. entwürdigend; erniedrigend

degree /dɪˈgriː/ n. **(a)** Grad, der; 20 ∿s 20 Grad **(b)** (academic rank) [akademischer] Grad

de'gree course n. Studium, das

dehydrate /diːˈhaɪdreɪt/ v.t. austrocknen ⟨Körper⟩; ∿d dehydratisiert (fachspr.)

dehydration /diːhaɪˈdreɪʃn/ n. Dehydration, die (fachspr.); Austrocknung, die

de-ice /diːˈaɪs/ v.t. enteisen

deign /deɪn/ v.t. ∿ to do sth. sich [dazu] herablassen, etw. zu tun

deity /ˈdiːɪtɪ/ n. Gottheit, die

dejected /dɪˈdʒektɪd/ adj. niedergeschlagen

dejection /dɪˈdʒekʃn/ n. Niedergeschlagenheit, die

delay /dɪˈleɪ/ **1** v.t. (make late) aufhalten; verzögern ⟨Ankunft, Abfahrt⟩; the train has been ∿ed der Zug hat Verspätung **2** v.i. warten **3** n. **(a)** Verzögerung, die (to bei) **(b)** (Transport) Verspätung, die

delectable /dɪˈlektəbl/ adj. köstlich

delegate **1** /ˈdelɪgət/ n. Delegierte, der/ die **2** /ˈdelɪgeɪt/ v.t. delegieren (to an + Akk.)

delegation /delɪˈgeɪʃn/ n. Delegation, die

delete /dɪˈliːt/ v.t. streichen (from in + Dat.); (Comp.) löschen

de'lete key n. (Comp.) Löschtaste, die

deletion /dɪˈliːʃn/ n. Streichung, die; (Comp.) Löschung, die

deli /ˈdelɪ/ (coll.) ▶ DELICATESSEN

deliberate /dɪˈlɪbərət/ adj. **(a)** (intentional) absichtlich; bewusst ⟨Lüge, Irreführung⟩ **(b)** (fully considered) wohl überlegt

de'liberately adv. absichtlich

deliberation /dɪlɪbəˈreɪʃn/ n. Überlegung, die; (discussion) Beratung, die

delicacy /ˈdelɪkəsɪ/ n. **(a)** (tactfulness and care) Feingefühl, das ⋯⟡

(b) (food) Delikatesse, *die*

delicate /'delɪkət/ *adj.* zart; (requiring careful handling) empfindlich; delikat ⟨*Frage, Angelegenheit*⟩

delicatessen /delɪkə'tesən/ *n.* Feinkostgeschäft, *das*

delicious /dɪ'lɪʃəs/ *adj.* köstlich

delight /dɪ'laɪt/ **1** *v.t.* erfreuen
2 *v.i.* sb. ∼s in doing sth. es macht jmdm. Freude, etw. zu tun
3 *n.* Freude, *die* (at über + *Akk.;* in an + *Dat.*)

de'lighted *adj.* be ∼ ⟨*Person:*⟩ hocherfreut sein; be ∼ by *or* with sth. sich über etw. (*Akk.*) freuen

delightful /dɪ'laɪtfl/ *adj.* wunderbar; köstlich ⟨*Geschmack*⟩; reizend ⟨*Person, Landschaft*⟩

de'lightfully *adv.* wunderbar

delinquent /dɪ'lɪŋkwənt/ **1** *n.* Randalierer, *der*
2 *adj.* kriminell

delirious /dɪ'lɪrɪəs/ *adj.* be ∼: im Delirium sein; be ∼ [with sth.] (fig.) außer sich [vor etw. (*Dat.*)] sein

delirium /dɪ'lɪrɪəm/ *n.* Delirium, *das*

deliver /dɪ'lɪvə(r)/ *v.t.* **(a)** bringen; liefern ⟨*Ware*⟩; zustellen ⟨*Post, Telegramm*⟩; überbringen ⟨*Botschaft*⟩
(b) halten ⟨*Rede*⟩

delivery /dɪ'lɪvərɪ/ *n.* Lieferung, *die;* (of letters, parcels) Zustellung, *die*

delivery: ∼ **date** *n.* Liefertermin, *der;* ∼ **note** *n.* Lieferschein, *der;* ∼ **service** *n.* Zustelldienst, *der;* ∼ **van** *n.* Lieferwagen, *der*

delta /'deltə/ *n.* Delta, *das*

delude /dɪ'lju:d/ *v.t.* täuschen

deluge /'delju:dʒ/ **1** *n.* sintflutartiger Regen
2 *v.t.* überschwemmen

delusion /dɪ'lju:ʒn/ *n.* Illusion, *die*

de luxe /də'lʌks/ *adj.* Luxus-

demand /dɪ'mɑ:nd/ **1** *n.* Forderung, *die* (for nach); (for commodity) Nachfrage, *die;* sth./ sb. is in ∼: etw. ist gefragt/jmd. ist begehrt
2 *v.t.* verlangen (of, from von); fordern ⟨*Recht*⟩

de'manding *adj.* anspruchsvoll

demean /dɪ'mi:n/ *v. refl.* (lower one's dignity) ∼ oneself [to do sth.] sich [dazu] erniedrigen[, etw. zu tun]; ∼ oneself by sth./ doing sth. sich durch etw. erniedrigen/sich dadurch erniedrigen, dass man etw. tut

demeaning /dɪ'mi:nɪŋ/ *adj.* erniedrigend

demeanour (*Brit.; Amer.:* **demeanor**) /dɪ'mi:nə(r)/ *n.* Benehmen, *das*

demented /dɪ'mentɪd/ *adj.* wahnsinnig

dementia /dɪ'menʃə/ *n.* (Med.) Demenz, *die*

demerara /demə'reərə/ *n.* ∼ [sugar] brauner Zucker; Farin, *der*

demise /dɪ'maɪz/ *n.* (death) Ableben, *das* (geh.); (of firm, party, etc.) Untergang, *der*

demo /'deməʊ/ *n., pl.* ∼s (coll.) Demo, *die* (ugs.)

de'mobilize *v.t.* demobilisieren ⟨*Armee, Kriegsschiff*⟩; aus dem Kriegsdienst entlassen ⟨*Soldat*⟩

democracy /dɪ'mɒkrəsɪ/ *n.* Demokratie, *die*

Democrat /'deməkræt/ *n.* (Amer. Polit.) Demokrat, *der*/Demokratin, *die*

democratic /demə'krætɪk/ *adj.,* **democratically** /demə'krætɪkəlɪ/ *adv.* demokratisch

demolish /dɪ'mɒlɪʃ/ *v.t.* abreißen

demolition /demə'lɪʃn/ *n.* Abriss, *der;* ∼ **work** Abbrucharbeit, *die*

demon /'di:mən/ *n.* Dämon, *der*

demonstrably /'demənstrəblɪ, dɪ'mɒnstrəblɪ/ *adv.* nachweislich

demonstrate /'demənstreɪt/ **1** *v.t.* zeigen; (be proof of) zeigen; beweisen
2 *v.i.* demonstrieren

demonstration /demən'streɪʃn/ *n.* (also Pol. etc.) Demonstration, *die;* (proof) Beweis, *der*

demonstrative /də'mɒnstrətɪv/ *adj.* **(a)** offen ⟨*Person*⟩
(b) (Ling.) Demonstrativ-

demonstrator /'demənstreɪtə(r)/ *n.* (Pol. etc.) Demonstrant, *der*/Demonstrantin, *die*

demoralize /dɪ'mɒrəlaɪz/ *v.t.* demoralisieren

demote /di:'məʊt/ *v.t.* degradieren (to zu)

demotion /di:'məʊʃn/ *n.* Degradierung, *die* (to zu)

demur /dɪ'mɜ:(r)/ *v.i.,* -rr- Einwände erheben

demure /dɪ'mjʊə(r)/ *adj.* betont zurückhaltend

den /den/ *n.* Höhle, *die*

denial /dɪ'naɪəl/ *n.* (refusal) Verweigerung, *die;* (of request) Ablehnung, *die*

denier /'denjə(r)/ *n.* Denier, *das;* **20 ∼ stockings** 20-den-Strümpfe

denim /'denɪm/ *n.* Denim ⓌⓏ, *der;* Jeansstoff, *der;* ∼ **jacket** Jeansjacke, *die;* ∼s Bluejeans *Pl.*

Denmark /'denmɑ:k/ *pr. n.* Dänemark (*das*)

denomination /dɪnɒmɪ'neɪʃn/ *n.* (Relig.) Konfession, *die*

denote /dɪ'nəʊt/ *v.t.* bezeichnen

dénouement, denouement /deɪ'nu:mɑ̃/ *n.* Ausgang, *der*

denounce /dɪ'naʊns/ *v.t.* denunzieren; (accuse publicly) beschuldigen

dense /dens/ *adj.* **(a)** dicht; massiv ⟨*Körper*⟩
(b) (stupid) dumm

'densely *adv.* dicht; ∼ **packed** dicht gedrängt

density /'densɪtɪ/ *n.* Dichte, *die*

dent /dent/ **1** *n.* Beule, *die*

2 *v.t.* einbeulen

dental /'dentl/ *adj.* Zahn-; ~ **care** Zahnpflege, *die;* ~ **treatment** zahnärztliche Behandlung

dental: ~ **floss** /'dentl flɒs/ *n.* Zahnseide, *die;* ~ **surgeon** *n.* Zahnarzt, *der/*-ärztin, *die*

dentist /'dentɪst/ *n.* Zahnarzt, *der/*-ärztin, *die*

dentistry /'dentɪstrɪ/ *n.* Zahnheilkunde, *die*

denture /'dentʃə(r)/ *n.* ~**[s]** Zahnprothese, *die*

denunciation /dɪnʌnsɪ'eɪʃn/ *n.* Denunziation, *die;* (public accusation) Beschuldigung, *die*

deny /dɪ'naɪ/ *v.t.* (declare untrue) bestreiten; (refuse) ~ sb. sth. jmdm. etw. verweigern; ~ **sb.'s request** jmdm. seine Bitte abschlagen

deodorant /diːˈəʊdərənt/ 1 *adj.* deodorierend
2 *n.* Deodorant, *das*

depart /dɪ'pɑːt/ *v.i.* (a) (go away) weggehen (b) (set out, leave) abfahren; (on one's journey) abreisen (c) (fig.: deviate) abweichen (**from** von)

department /dɪ'pɑːtmənt/ *n.* Abteilung, *die;* (government ~) Ministerium, *das;* (of university) Seminar, *das*

de'partment store *n.* Kaufhaus, *das*

departure /dɪ'pɑːtʃə(r)/ *n.* (a) Abreise, *die;* (of train, bus, ship) Abfahrt, *die;* (of aircraft) Abflug, *der* (b) (deviation) ~ **from sth.** Abweichen von etw.

departure: ~ **gate** *n.* Flugsteig, *der;* ~ **lounge** *n.* Abflughalle, *die;* ~ **time** *n.* (of train, bus) Abfahrtzeit, *die;* (of aircraft) Abflugzeit, *die*

depend /dɪ'pend/ *v.i.* (a) ~ [up]on abhängen von; **it/that ~s** es kommt drauf an (b) (rely, trust) ~ [up]on sich verlassen auf (+ *Akk.*); (have to rely on) angewiesen sein auf (+ *Akk.*)

dependable /dɪ'pendəbl/ *adj.* zuverlässig

dependant /dɪ'pendənt/ *n.* Abhängige, *der/die*

dependence /dɪ'pendəns/ *n.* Abhängigkeit, *die*

dependent /dɪ'pendənt/ 1 *n.*
▶ DEPENDANT
2 *adj.* abhängig

depict /dɪ'pɪkt/ *v.t.* darstellen

deplete /dɪ'pliːt/ *v.t.* erheblich verringern

deplorable /dɪ'plɔːrəbl/ *adj.* beklagenswert

deplore /dɪ'plɔː(r)/ *v.t.* (a) (disapprove of) verurteilen (b) (regret) beklagen

deploy /dɪ'plɔɪ/ *v.t.* einsetzen

deport /dɪ'pɔːt/ *v.t.* ausweisen

deportation /diːpɔː'teɪʃn/ *n.* Ausweisung, *die*

depose /dɪ'pəʊz/ *v.t.* absetzen

deposit /dɪ'pɒzɪt/ 1 *n.* (a) (in bank) Depot, *das;* (credit) Guthaben, *das;* (Brit.: at interest) Sparguthaben, *das* (b) (first instalment) Anzahlung, *die;* **put down a ~ on sth.** eine Anzahlung für etw. leisten (c) (on bottle) Pfand, *das*
2 *v.t.* (a) (lay down) ablegen; abstellen ‹*etw. Senkrechtes*› (b) (in bank) deponieren

de'posit account *n.* (Brit.) Sparkonto, *das*

depot /'depəʊ/ *n.* Depot, *das*

depraved /dɪ'preɪvd/ *adj.* verdorben

depravity /dɪ'prævɪtɪ/ *n.* Verdorbenheit, *die*

depreciate /dɪ'priːʃɪeɪt/ *v.i.* an Wert verlieren

depreciation /dɪpriːʃɪ'eɪʃn/ *n.* Wertverlust, *der*

depress /dɪ'pres/ *v.t.* (a) (deject) deprimieren (b) (push down) herunterdrücken

depressed /dɪ'prest/ *adj.* deprimiert

de'pressing *adj.,* **de'pressingly** *adv.* deprimierend

depression /dɪ'preʃn/ *n.* (a) Depression, *die* (b) (sunk place) Vertiefung, *die* (c) (Meteorol.) Tief[druckgebiet], *das* (d) (Econ.) Wirtschaftskrise, *die*

deprivation /deprɪ'veɪʃn/ *n.* Entbehrung, *die*

deprive /dɪ'praɪv/ *v.t.* ~ **sb. of sth.** jmdm. etw. nehmen; (prevent from having) jmdm. etw. vorenthalten

deprived /dɪ'praɪvd/ *adj.* benachteiligt ‹*Kind, Familie usw.*›

depth /depθ/ *n.* Tiefe, *die;* **in ~:** gründlich; **in the ~s of winter** im tiefsten Winter

'depth charge *n.* Wasserbombe, *die*

deputation /depjʊ'teɪʃn/ *n.* Abordnung, *die*

deputize /'depjʊtaɪz/ *v.i.* ~ **for sb.** jmdn. vertreten

deputy /'depjʊtɪ/ *n.* [Stell]vertreter, *der/*-vertreterin, *die; attrib.* stellvertretend

derail /dɪ'reɪl/ *v.t.* **be ~ed** entgleisen

de'railment *n.* Entgleisung, *die*

deranged /dɪ'reɪndʒd/ *adj.* [mentally] ~: geistesgestört

deregulate /diː'regjʊleɪt/ *v.t.* deregulieren (fachspr.); dem freien Wettbewerb überlassen

deregulation /diːregjʊ'leɪʃn/ *n.* Deregulation, *die* (fachspr.); Deregulierung, *die* (fachspr.)

derelict /'derɪlɪkt/ 1 *adj.* verlassen und verfallen
2 *n.* Ausgestoßene, *der/die*

deride /dɪˈraɪd/ v.t. sich lustig machen über (+ Akk.)

derision /dɪˈrɪʒn/ n. Spott, der

derisive /dɪˈraɪsɪv/ adj. (ironical) spöttisch; (scoffing) verächtlich

derisory /dɪˈraɪzərɪ/ adj. (ridiculously inadequate) lächerlich

derivation /derɪˈveɪʃn/ n. Ableitung, die

derivative /dɪˈrɪvətɪv/ [1] adj. abgeleitet; (lacking originality) nachahmend
[2] n. Ableitung, die

derive /dɪˈraɪv/ [1] v.t. ~ sth. from sth. etw. aus etw. gewinnen; ~ pleasure from sth. Freude an etw. (Dat.) haben
[2] v.i. ~ from beruhen auf (+ Dat.)

derogatory /dɪˈrɒgətərɪ/ adj. abfällig

derrick /ˈderɪk/ n. [Derrick]kran, der

derv /dɜːv/ n. Diesel[kraftstoff], der

descale /diːˈskeɪl/ v.t. entkalken

descend /dɪˈsend/ [1] v.i. (a) (go down) hinuntergehen/-steigen/-klettern/-fahren; (come down) herunterkommen; ⟨Fallschirm, Flugzeug:⟩ niedergehen
(b) (slope downwards) abfallen
(c) ~ on sb. jmdn. überfallen
[2] v.t. (go/come down) hinunter-/ heruntergehen/-steigen/-klettern/-fahren

descendant /dɪˈsendənt/ n. Nachkomme, der

de'scended adj. be ~ from sb. von jmdm. abstammen

descent /dɪˈsent/ n. (a) Abstieg, der; (of parachute, plane) Niedergehen, das
(b) (lineage) Herkunft, die; be of Russian ~: russischer Abstammung sein

describe /dɪˈskraɪb/ v.t. beschreiben

description /dɪˈskrɪpʃn/ n. (a) Beschreibung, die
(b) (sort, class) Art, die

descriptive /dɪˈskrɪptɪv/ adj. beschreibend; (vivid) anschaulich; a purely ~ report ein reiner Tatsachenbericht

desecrate /ˈdesɪkreɪt/ v.t. entweihen

desert[1] /ˈdezət/ n. Wüste, die

desert[2] /dɪˈzɜːt/ [1] v.t. verlassen
[2] v.i. ⟨Soldat:⟩ desertieren

de'serted adj. verlassen

de'serter n. Deserteur, der

desertion /dɪˈzɜːʃn/ n. Desertion, die

desert 'island /dezət ˈaɪlənd/ n. einsame Insel

deserts /dɪˈzɜːts/ n. pl. get one's [just] ~: das bekommen, was man verdient hat

deserve /dɪˈzɜːv/ v.t. verdienen

deserving /dɪˈzɜːvɪŋ/ adj. verdienstvoll; a ~ cause ein guter Zweck

design /dɪˈzaɪn/ [1] n. Entwurf, der; (pattern) Muster, das; (established form of machine, engine, etc.) Bauweise, die; (general idea, construction) Konstruktion, die
[2] v.t. entwerfen; be ~ed to do sth. etw. tun sollen

designate /ˈdezɪgneɪt/ v.t. (a) bezeichnen
(b) (appoint) designieren (geh.)

designation /dezɪgˈneɪʃn/ n. Bezeichnung, die

'designer n. Designer, der/Designerin, die; (of machines) Konstrukteur, der/ Konstrukteurin, die; attrib. Modell⟨-kleidung, -jeans⟩

desirability /dɪzaɪərəˈbɪlɪtɪ/ n. Wunschbarkeit, die

desirable /dɪˈzaɪərəbl/ adj. wünschenswert

desire /dɪˈzaɪə(r)/ [1] n. Wunsch, der (for nach); (longing) Sehnsucht, die (for nach)
[2] v.t. sich (Dat.) wünschen; (long for) sich sehnen nach

desist /dɪˈzɪst/ v.i. (literary) einhalten (geh.); ~ from sth. von etw. ablassen (geh.)

desk /desk/ n. (a) Schreibtisch, der; (in school) Tisch, der
(b) (cash ~) Kasse, die; (reception ~) Rezeption, die

desk: ~-bound adj. an den Schreibtisch gefesselt (fig.); ~ calendar, ~ diary ns. Tischkalender, der; ~ editor n. Manuskriptbearbeiter, der/-bearbeiterin, die; Lektor, der/Lektorin, die; ~ lamp n. Schreibtischlampe, die; ~top adj. ~top publishing Desktoppublishing, das; ~top computer Tischcomputer, der

desolate /ˈdesələt/ adj. trostlos

desolation /desəˈleɪʃn/ n. Trostlosigkeit, die

despair /dɪˈspeə(r)/ [1] n. Verzweiflung, die; be the ~ of sb. jmdn. zur Verzweiflung bringen
[2] v.i. verzweifeln

desperate /ˈdespərət/ adj. verzweifelt; extrem ⟨Maßnahmen:⟩; be ~ for sth. etw. dringend brauchen

desperation /despəˈreɪʃn/ n. Verzweiflung, die

despicable /dɪˈspɪkəbl/ adj. verabscheuungswürdig

despise /dɪˈspaɪz/ v.t. verachten

despite /dɪˈspaɪt/ prep. trotz

despondent /dɪˈspɒndənt/ adj. bedrückt

despot /ˈdespɒt/ n. Despot, der

dessert /dɪˈzɜːt/ n. Nachtisch, der

dessert: ~spoon n. Esslöffel, der; ~spoonful n. Esslöffel, der; ~ wine n. Dessertwein, der

destabilize /diːˈsteɪbɪlaɪz/ v.t. (Polit.) destabilisieren

destination /destɪˈneɪʃn/ n. Reiseziel, das; (of goods) Bestimmungsort, der; (of train, bus) Zielort, der

destine /ˈdestɪn/ v.t. bestimmen; be ~d to do sth. dazu bestimmt sein, etw. zu tun

destiny /ˈdestɪnɪ/ n. Schicksal, das

destitute /ˈdestɪtjuːt/ adj. mittellos

destroy /dɪˈstrɔɪ/ v.t. zerstören

de'stroyer n. (also Naut.) Zerstörer, der

destruction /dɪ'strʌkʃn/ n. Zerstörung, *die*

destructive /dɪ'strʌktɪv/ adj. zerstörerisch; verheerend ⟨*Sturm, Feuer*⟩

desultory /'desəltəri/ adj. sprunghaft; zwanglos, ungezwungen ⟨*Gespräch*⟩

detach /dɪ'tætʃ/ v.t. entfernen; abnehmen ⟨*wieder zu Befestigendes*⟩; herausnehmen ⟨*innen Befindliches*⟩

detachable /dɪ'tætʃəbl/ adj. abnehmbar

detached /dɪ'tætʃt/ adj. **(a)** (impartial) unvoreingenommen; (unemotional) unbeteiligt **(b)** a ∼ **house** ein Einzelhaus

de'tachment n. **(a)** ▶ DETACH: Entfernen, *das;* Abnehmen, *das;* Herausnehmen, *das* **(b)** (Mil.) Abteilung, *die*

detail /'di:teɪl/ ⟨**1**⟩ n. Einzelheit, *die;* Detail, *das;* in ∼: Punkt für Punkt; **go into** ∼[s] ins Detail gehen
⟨**2**⟩ v.t. **(a)** einzeln ausführen **(b)** (Mil.) abkommandieren

detailed /'di:teɪld/ adj. detailliert; eingehend ⟨*Studie*⟩

detain /dɪ'teɪn/ v.t. **(a)** festhalten; (take into confinement) verhaften **(b)** (delay) aufhalten

detainee /di:teɪ'ni:/ n. Verhaftete, *der/die*

detect /dɪ'tekt/ v.t. entdecken; wahrnehmen ⟨*Bewegung*⟩; aufdecken ⟨*Irrtum, Verbrechen*⟩

detection /dɪ'tekʃn/ n. Entdeckung, *die;* (of error, crime) Aufdeckung, *die*

detective /dɪ'tektɪv/ n. Detektiv, *der;* **private** ∼: Privatdetektiv, *der;* ∼ **work** Ermittlungsarbeit, *die;* ∼ **story** Detektivgeschichte, *die*

detector /dɪ'tektə(r)/ n. Detektor, *der*

detention /dɪ'tenʃn/ n. **(a)** Festnahme, *die;* (confinement) Haft, *die* **(b)** (Sch.) Nachsitzen, *das*

de'tention centre n. (Brit.) Jugendstrafanstalt, *die*

deter /dɪ'tɜ:(r)/ v.t., **-rr-** abschrecken

detergent /dɪ'tɜ:dʒənt/ n. Waschmittel, *das*

deteriorate /dɪ'tɪərɪəreɪt/ v.i. sich verschlechtern; ⟨*Haus.*⟩ verfallen

deterioration /dɪtɪərɪə'reɪʃn/ n. ▶ DETERIORATE: Verschlechterung, *die;* Verfall, *der*

determination /dɪtɜ:mɪ'neɪʃn/ n. Entschlossenheit, *die*

determine /dɪ'tɜ:mɪn/ v.t. **(a)** (decide) beschließen **(b)** (be a decisive factor for) bestimmen **(c)** (ascertain) feststellen

determined /dɪ'tɜ:mɪnd/ adj. **(a)** be ∼ to do sth. etw. unbedingt tun wollen **(b)** (resolute) entschlossen

deterrent /dɪ'terənt/ n. Abschreckungsmittel, *das* (**to** für)

detest /dɪ'test/ v.t. verabscheuen

detestable /dɪ'testəbl/ adj. verabscheuenswert

detonate /'detəneɪt/ ⟨**1**⟩ v.t. zünden ⟨**2**⟩ v.i. detonieren

detonation /detə'neɪʃn/ n. Detonation, *die*

detonator /'detəneɪtə(r)/ n. Sprengkapsel, *die*

detour /'di:tʊə(r)/ n. Umweg, *der;* (diversion) Umleitung, *die*

detoxify /di:'tɒksɪfaɪ/ v.t. entgiften; unschädlich machen ⟨*Gift usw.*⟩

detract /dɪ'trækt/ v.i. ∼ **from sth.** etw. beeinträchtigen

detriment /'detrɪmənt/ n. **to the** ∼ **of sth.** zum Nachteil einer Sache (*Gen.*)

detrimental /detrɪ'mentl/ adj. schädlich; be ∼ **to sth.** einer Sache (*Dat.*) schaden

deuce /dju:s/ n. (Tennis) Einstand, *der*

devaluation /di:vælju:'eɪʃn/ n. Abwertung, *die*

devalue /di:'vælju:/ v.t. abwerten

devastate /'devəsteɪt/ v.t. verwüsten; (fig.) niederschmettern

devastating /'devəsteɪtɪŋ/ adj. verheerend; (fig.) niederschmetternd

devastation /devə'steɪʃn/ n. Verwüstung, *die*

develop /dɪ'veləp/ ⟨**1**⟩ v.t. entwickeln; erschließen ⟨*natürliche Ressourcen*⟩; bekommen ⟨*Krankheit, Fieber, Lust*⟩; ∼ **a taste for sth.** Geschmack an etw. (*Akk.*) finden
⟨**2**⟩ v.i. sich entwickeln (**from** aus; **into** zu)

de'veloper n. **(a)** (Photog.) Entwickler, *der* **(b)** (of land) Bauunternehmer, *der*

developing: ∼ **country** n. Entwicklungsland, *das;* ∼ **world** n. Entwicklungsländer *Pl.*

de'velopment n. Entwicklung, *die* (**from** aus; **into** zu); (of natural resources etc.) Erschließung, *die*

de'velopment area n. (Brit.) Entwicklungsgebiet, *das*

deviant /'di:vɪənt/ adj. abweichend

deviate /'di:vɪeɪt/ v.i. abweichen

deviation /di:vɪ'eɪʃn/ n. Abweichung, *die*

device /dɪ'vaɪs/ n. Gerät, *das;* (as part of sth.) Vorrichtung, *die;* **leave sb. to his own** ∼s jmdn. sich (*Dat.*) selbst überlassen

devil /'devl/ n. Teufel, *der;* **the D**∼: der Teufel

'devilish adj. teuflisch

devious /'di:vɪəs/ adj. **(a)** (winding) verschlungen; ∼ **route** Umweg, *der* **(b)** (unscrupulous, insincere) hinterhältig

devise /dɪ'vaɪz/ v.t. entwerfen; schmieden ⟨*Pläne*⟩

devoid /dɪ'vɔɪd/ adj. ∼ **of sth.** (lacking) ohne etw.; (free from) frei von etw.

devolution /di:və'lu:ʃn/ n. (Polit.) Dezentralisierung, *die*

devote /dɪ'vəʊt/ v.t. widmen (**to** *Dat.*) ····⟩

de'voted adj. treu; aufrichtig
⟨Freundschaft, Liebe, Verehrung⟩; be ~ to sb.
jmdn. innig lieben

devotion /dɪˈvəʊʃn/ n. ~ to sb./sth.
Hingabe an jmdn./etw.

devour /dɪˈvaʊə(r)/ v.t. verschlingen

devout /dɪˈvaʊt/ adj. fromm

dew /djuː/ n. Tau, der

'dewdrop n. Tautropfen, der

dexterity /dekˈsterɪtɪ/ n. Geschicklichkeit,
die

dextrous /ˈdekstrəs/ adj. geschickt

diabetes /daɪəˈbiːtiːz/ n. Zuckerkrankheit,
die

diabetic /daɪəˈbetɪk/ ① adj. zuckerkrank
⟨Person⟩
② n. Diabetiker, der/Diabetikerin, die

diabolical /daɪəˈbɒlɪkl/ adj. teuflisch

diagnose /daɪəgˈnəʊz/ v.t. diagnostizieren;
feststellen ⟨Fehler⟩

diagnosis /daɪəgˈnəʊsɪs/ n., pl. **diagnoses**
/daɪəgˈnəʊsiːz/ Diagnose, die; make a ~: eine
Diagnose stellen

diagonal /daɪˈægənl/ ① adj. diagonal
② n. Diagonale, die

di'agonally adv. diagonal

diagram /ˈdaɪəgræm/ n. Diagramm, das

dial /ˈdaɪəl/ ① n. (of clock or watch) Zifferblatt,
das; (of gauge, meter, etc.) Skala, die; (Teleph.)
Wählscheibe, die
② v.t. & i., (Brit.) **-ll-** (Teleph.) wählen; ~ direct
selbst wählen; (dial extension) durchwählen

dialect /ˈdaɪəlekt/ n. Dialekt, der

dialling (Amer.), **dialing:** ~ **code** n.
Vorwahl, die; ~ **tone** Wählton, der

dialogue /ˈdaɪəlɒg/ n. Dialog, der

'dialogue box n. (Comp.) Dialogbox, die;
Dialogfenster, das

'dial tone n. (Amer.) Wählton, der

dialysis /daɪˈælɪsɪs/ n. [Hämo]dialyse, die
(fachspr.); Blutwäsche, die; ~ **machine**
Dialyseapparat, der

diameter /daɪˈæmɪtə(r)/ n. Durchmesser,
der

diametrical /daɪəˈmetrɪkl/ adj.,
dia'metrically adv. diametral

diamond /ˈdaɪəmənd/ n. (a) Diamant, der
(b) (figure) Raute, die
(c) (Cards) Karo, das; see also CLUB 1C

diaper /ˈdaɪəpə(r)/ n. (Amer.) Windel, die

diaphragm /ˈdaɪəfræm/ n. Diaphragma,
das (Fachspr.); ⟨Anat. also⟩ Zwerchfell, das;
⟨Photog. also⟩ Blende, die

diarrhoea (Amer.: **diarrhea**) /daɪəˈriːə/
n. Durchfall, der

diary /ˈdaɪərɪ/ n. (a) Tagebuch, das
(b) (for appointments) Terminkalender, der

dice /daɪs/ ① n. Würfel, der
② v.t. (Cooking) würfeln

dicey /ˈdaɪsɪ/ adj. (coll.) riskant

Dictaphone ® /ˈdɪktəfəʊn/ n. Diktaphon,
das (fachspr.); Diktiergerät, das

dictate /dɪkˈteɪt/ v.t. & i. diktieren;
(prescribe) vorschreiben; ~ to Vorschriften
machen (+ Dat.)

dic'tating machine n. Diktiergerät, das

dictation /dɪkˈteɪʃn/ n. Diktat, das

dictator /dɪkˈteɪtə(r)/ n. Diktator, der

dictatorial /dɪktəˈtɔːrɪəl/ adj. diktatorisch

dic'tatorship n. Diktatur, die

dictionary /ˈdɪkʃənərɪ/ n. Wörterbuch, das

did ▶ DO

diddle /ˈdɪdl/ v.t. (coll.) übers Ohr hauen
(ugs.)

didn't /ˈdɪdnt/ (coll.) = **did not;** ▶ DO

die /daɪ/ v.i., **dying** /ˈdaɪɪŋ/ sterben (of, from
an + Dat.); ⟨Tier, Pflanze:⟩ eingehen; be
dying to do sth. darauf brennen, etw. zu tun;
be dying for sth. etw. unbedingt brauchen
■ **die 'down** v.i. ⟨Sturm, Wind, Protest:⟩
sich legen; ⟨Flammen:⟩ kleiner werden;
⟨Feuer:⟩ herunterbrennen; ⟨Lärm:⟩ leiser
werden
■ **die 'out** v.i. aussterben

'diehard n. Ewiggestrige, der/die

diesel /ˈdiːzl/ n. ~ **[engine]** Diesel[motor],
der; ~ **[fuel]** Diesel[kraftstoff], der

diet /ˈdaɪət/ ① n. Diät, die; be/go on a ~:
eine Schlankheitskur machen
② v.i. eine Schlankheitskur machen

'diet sheet n. Diätplan, der

differ /ˈdɪfə(r)/ v.i. (be different) sich
unterscheiden

difference /ˈdɪfərəns/ n. (a) Unterschied,
der; make no ~ [to sb.] [jmdm.] nichts
ausmachen; it makes a ~: es ist eine od. (ugs.)
macht einen Unterschied
(b) (disagreement) Meinungsverschiedenheit,
die

different /ˈdɪfərənt/ adj. verschieden;
(pred. also) anders; (attrib. also) ander...; be
~ from or (esp. Brit.) to or (Amer.) than ...:
anders sein als ...

differentiate /dɪfəˈrenʃɪeɪt/ v.t. & i.
unterscheiden (between zwischen + Dat.)

'differently adv. anders (from, esp. Brit. to
als)

difficult /ˈdɪfɪkəlt/ adj. schwierig

'difficulty n. Schwierigkeit, die; with [great]
~: [sehr] mühsam; get into difficulties in
Schwierigkeiten kommen

diffident /ˈdɪfɪdənt/ adj. zaghaft; (modest)
zurückhaltend

diffuse ① /dɪˈfjuːz/ v.t. verbreiten
② v.i. sich ausbreiten (through in + Dat.)
③ /dɪˈfjuːs/ adj. diffus

dig /dɪg/ ① v.i., **-gg-**, **dug** /dʌg/ graben (for
nach)
② v.t., **-gg-**, **dug** graben; umgraben ⟨Erde,
Garten⟩
■ **dig 'out** v.t. ausgraben

■ **dig 'up** v.t. ausgraben; umgraben ⟨Garten⟩; aufreißen ⟨Straße⟩

digest /dɪ'dʒest, daɪ'dʒest/ v.t. verdauen

digestion /dɪ'dʒestʃn, daɪ'dʒestʃn/ n. Verdauung, die

'**digger** n. Bagger, der

digit /'dɪdʒɪt/ n. Ziffer, die

digital /'dɪdʒɪtl/ adj. Digital-; ∼ **audio tape** Digitaltonband, das; ∼ **camera** Digitalkamera, die; ∼ **television** Digitalfernsehen, das; ∼ **video disc** DVD, die; Digital Video Disc, die

dignified /'dɪgnɪfaɪd/ adj. würdig; (stately) würdevoll

dignify /'dɪgnɪfaɪ/ v.t. Würde verleihen (+ Dat.)

dignitary /'dɪgnɪtərɪ/ n. Würdenträger, der; dignitaries (prominent people) Honoratioren Pl.

dignity /'dɪgnɪtɪ/ n. Würde, die

digress /daɪ'gres/ v.i. abschweifen

digression /daɪ'greʃn/ n. Abschweifung, die

dike /daɪk/ n. Deich, der

dilapidated /dɪ'læpɪdeɪtɪd/ adj. verfallen ⟨Gebäude⟩; verwahrlost ⟨Erscheinung⟩

dilate /daɪ'leɪt/ ① v.i. sich weiten ② v.t. ausdehnen

dilemma /dɪ'lemə, daɪ'lemə/ n. Dilemma, das

diligence /'dɪlɪdʒəns/ n. Fleiß, der

diligent /'dɪlɪdʒənt/ adj., **diligently** adv. fleißig

dilute ① /daɪ'lju:t, 'daɪlju:t/ adj. verdünnt ② /daɪ'lju:t/ v.t. verdünnen

dim /dɪm/ ① adj. (a) schwach ⟨Licht, Flackern⟩; dunkel ⟨Zimmer⟩; verschwommen ⟨Gestalt⟩ (b) (vague) verschwommen (c) (coll.: stupid) beschränkt ② v.i. schwächer werden

dime /daɪm/ n. (Amer. coll.) Zehncentstück, das

dimension /dɪ'menʃn, daɪ'menʃn/ n. Dimension, die; ∼s (measurements) Abmessungen; Maße

diminish /dɪ'mɪnɪʃ/ ① v.i. nachlassen; ⟨Vorräte, Einfluss:⟩ abnehmen; ⟨Wert, Ansehen:⟩ geringer werden ② v.t. verringern; schmälern ⟨Ansehen, Ruf⟩

dimple /'dɪmpl/ n. Grübchen, das

dim: ∼**wit** n. (coll.) Dummkopf, der (ugs.); ∼-**witted** /'dɪmwɪtɪd/ adj. (coll.) dusselig (salopp)

din /dɪn/ n. Lärm, der

dine /daɪn/ v.i. [zu Mittag/zu Abend] essen

'**diner** n. Gast, der

dinghy /'dɪŋgɪ, 'dɪŋɪ/ n. Ding[h]i, das; (inflatable) Schlauchboot, das

dingy /'dɪndʒɪ/ adj. schmuddelig

dining /'daɪnɪŋ/**:** ∼ **area** n. ≈ Essecke,

die; ∼ **car** n. Speisewagen, der; ∼ **room** n. Esszimmer, das; (in hotel etc.) Speisesaal, der; ∼ **table** n. Esstisch, der

dinner /'dɪnə(r)/ n. (at midday) Mittagessen, das; (in the evening) Abendessen, das; (formal) Diner, das

dinner: ∼ **jacket** n. (Brit.) Dinnerjacket, das; ∼ **party** n. Abendeinladung, das (mit Essen); (more formal) Abendgesellschaft, die; ∼ **plate** n. flacher Teller; Essteller, der; ∼ **table** n. Esstisch, der; ∼ **time** n. Essenszeit, die; at ∼ **time** zur Essenszeit; (12-2 p.m.) mittags

dinosaur /'daɪnəsɔ:(r)/ n. Dinosaurier, der

dint /dɪnt/ n. by ∼ of durch; by ∼ of doing sth. indem jmd. etw. tut

dip /dɪp/ ① v.t., -pp-: (a) [ein]tauchen (in in + Akk.) (b) ∼ one's headlights abblenden ② v.i. sinken; (incline) abfallen ③ n. (a) (in road) Senke, die (b) (bathe) [kurzes] Bad

diphtheria /dɪf'θɪərɪə/ n. Diphtherie, die

diphthong /'dɪfθɒŋ/ n. Diphthong, der

diploma /dɪ'pləʊmə/ n. Diplom, das

diplomacy /dɪ'pləʊməsɪ/ n. Diplomatie, die

diplomat /'dɪpləmæt/ n. Diplomat, der/ Diplomatin, die

diplomatic /dɪplə'mætɪk/ adj., **diplo'matically** adv. diplomatisch

diplo'matic service n. diplomatischer Dienst

'**dipstick** n. (Öl-/Benzin)messstab, der

dire /'daɪə(r)/ adj. furchtbar

direct /dɪ'rekt, daɪ'rekt/ ① v.t. (a) (turn) richten (to[wards] auf + Akk.); ∼ sb. to a place jmdn. den Weg zu einem Ort weisen (b) (control) leiten; regeln ⟨Verkehr⟩ (c) (order) anweisen (d) (Theatre, Cinemat., etc.) Regie führen bei ② adj. direkt; durchgehend ⟨Zug⟩; unmittelbar ⟨Ursache, Auswirkung, Erfahrung, Verantwortung⟩; genau ⟨Gegenteil⟩; direkt ⟨Widerspruch⟩; diametral ⟨Gegensatz⟩; ∼ speech direkte Rede ③ adv. direkt

direct: ∼ '**current** n. (Electr.) Gleichstrom, der; ∼ '**debit** n. (Brit.) Lastschriftverfahren, das; ∼ '**dialling** n. Durchwahl, die; we will soon have ∼ dialling wir werden bald ein Durchwahlsystem haben; ∼ '**flight** n. Direktflug, der; ∼ '**hit** n. Volltreffer, der

direction /dɪ'rekʃn, daɪ'rekʃn/ n. (a) Richtung, die; in the ∼ of London in Richtung London (b) (guidance) Führung, die; (Theatre, Cinemat., etc.) Regie, die; Spielleitung, die (c) usu. in pl. (order) Anordnung, die; ∼s [for use] Gebrauchsanweisung, die

di'rectly adv. (a) direkt; unmittelbar ⟨folgen, verantwortlich sein⟩ ⋯⫶

(b) (exactly) genau
(c) (at once) umgehend
(d) (shortly) gleich
di'rect object n. direktes Objekt
director /daɪˈrektə(r), dɪˈrektə(r)/ n. (a) (Commerc.) Direktor, der/Direktorin, die; board of ~s Aufsichtsrat, der
(b) (Theatre, Cinemat., etc.) Regisseur, der/Regisseurin, die
directory /daɪˈrektərɪ, dɪˈrektərɪ/ n. (telephone ~) Telefonbuch, das; (of tradesmen etc.) Branchenverzeichnis, das; (Comp.) Verzeichnis, das; ~ enquiries (Brit.), ~ information (Amer.) [Fernsprech]auskunft, die
dirt /dɜːt/ n. Schmutz, der; ~ cheap (coll.) spottbillig
'dirty ① adj. schmutzig; get sth. ~: etw. schmutzig machen
② v.t. schmutzig machen
disa'bility n. Behinderung, die
disa'bility allowance n. Erwerbsunfähigkeitsentschädigung, die
disabled /dɪsˈeɪbld/ adj. behindert
disad'vantage n. Nachteil, der; at a ~: im Nachteil
disad'vantaged adj. benachteiligt
disa'gree v.i. anderer Meinung sein; ~ with sb./sth. mit jmdm./etw. nicht übereinstimmen; ~ [with sb.] about or over sth. sich [mit jmdm.] über etw. (Akk.) nicht einig sein
disa'greeable adj. unangenehm
disa'greement n. (a) (difference of opinion) Uneinigkeit, die; be in ~ with sb./sth. mit jmdm./etw. nicht übereinstimmen
(b) (quarrel) Meinungsverschiedenheit, die
(c) (discrepancy) Diskrepanz, die
disal'low v.t. verbieten; (Sport) nicht geben ⟨Tor⟩
disap'pear v.i. verschwinden; ⟨Brauch, Tierart:⟩ aussterben
disap'pearance n. Verschwinden, das
disap'point v.t. enttäuschen
disap'pointed adj. enttäuscht
disap'pointing adj. enttäuschend
disap'pointment n. Enttäuschung, die
disap'proval n. Missbilligung, die
disap'prove v.i. dagegen sein; ~ of sb./sth. jmdn. ablehnen/etw. missbilligen
dis'arm v.t. entwaffnen
disarmament /dɪsˈɑːməmənt/ n. Abrüstung, die
disarray /dɪsəˈreɪ/ n. Unordnung, die; in ~: in Unordnung
disaster /dɪˈzɑːstə(r)/ n. Katastrophe, die; ~ area Katastrophengebiet, das; ~ fund Nothilfefonds, der
disastrous /dɪˈzɑːstrəs/ adj. katastrophal; verhängnisvoll ⟨Irrtum, Entscheidung, Politik⟩
dis'band ① v.t. auflösen

② v.i. sich auflösen
disbe'lief n. Unglaube, der; in ~: ungläubig
disbe'lieve v.t. ~ sb./sth. jmdm./etw. nicht glauben
disc /dɪsk/ n. (a) Scheibe, die; (record) Platte, die
(b) (Comp.) ▶ DISK A
discard /dɪsˈkɑːd/ v.t. wegwerfen; fallenlassen ⟨Vorschlag, Idee⟩
'disc brake n. Scheibenbremse, die
discern /dɪˈsɜːn/ v.t. wahrnehmen
discernible /dɪˈsɜːnɪbl/ adj. erkennbar
di'scerning adj. kritisch
discharge ① /dɪsˈtʃɑːdʒ/ v.t. (a) entlassen (from aus); freisprechen ⟨Angeklagte⟩
(b) ablassen ⟨Flüssigkeit, Gas⟩
② /ˈdɪstʃɑːdʒ/ n. (a) Entlassung, die (from aus); (of defendant) Freispruch, der
(b) (emission) Ausfluss, der
disciple /dɪˈsaɪpl/ n. (a) (Relig.) Jünger, der
(b) (follower) Anhänger, der/Anhängerin, die
disciplinary /dɪsɪˈplɪnərɪ/ adj. disziplinarisch; ~ action Disziplinarmaßnahmen Pl.
discipline /ˈdɪsɪplɪn/ ① n. Disziplin, die
② v.t. disziplinieren; (punish) bestrafen
disciplined /ˈdɪsɪplɪnd/ adj. diszipliniert
'disc jockey n. Diskjockey, der
dis'claim v.t. abstreiten
dis'claimer n. Gegenerklärung, die; (Law) Verzichterklärung, die
disclose /dɪsˈkləʊz/ v.t. enthüllen; bekannt geben ⟨Information, Nachricht⟩
dis'closure n. Enthüllung, die; (of information, news) Bekanntgabe, die
disco /ˈdɪskəʊ/ n., pl. ~s (coll.) Disko, die
'disco dancing n. Diskotanz, der
dis'colour (Brit.; Amer.: **discolor**) v.t. verfärben
dis'comfort n. (a) no pl. (slight pain) Beschwerden Pl.
(b) (hardship) Unannehmlichkeit, die
'disco music n. Diskomusik, die
disconcert /dɪskənˈsɜːt/ v.t. irritieren
discon'nect v.t. abtrennen; abstellen ⟨Telefon⟩
disconsolate /dɪsˈkɒnsələt/ adj. (a) (unhappy) unglücklich
(b) (inconsolable) untröstlich
discon'tent n. Unzufriedenheit, die
discon'tented adj. unzufrieden
discon'tinue v.t. einstellen
discord /ˈdɪskɔːd/ n. (a) Zwietracht, die
(b) (Mus.) Dissonanz, die
discordant /dɪsˈkɔːdənt/ adj. (a) (conflicting) gegensätzlich
(b) a ~ note ein Misston
discothèque /ˈdɪskətek/ n. Diskothek, die
discount ① /ˈdɪskaʊnt/ n. (Commerc.) Rabatt, der (on auf + Akk.)

2 /dɪˈskaʊnt/ *v.t.* (disbelieve) unberücksichtigt lassen

discourage /dɪˈskʌrɪdʒ/ *v.t.* **(a)** entmutigen **(b)** (advise against) abraten

di'scouragement *n.* **(a)** Entmutigung, *die* **(b)** (depression) Mutlosigkeit, *die*

discouraging /dɪˈskʌrɪdʒɪŋ/ *adj.* entmutigend

dis'courteous *adj.* unhöflich

dis'courtesy *n.* Unhöflichkeit, *die*

discover /dɪˈskʌvə(r)/ *v.t.* entdecken; (by search) herausfinden

di'scovery *n.* Entdeckung, *die*

dis'credit 1 *n.* Misskredit, *der;* **bring** ∼ **on sb./sth., bring sb./sth. into** ∼: jmdn./ etw. in Misskredit bringen 2 *v.t.* in Misskredit bringen

discreet /dɪˈskriːt/ *adj.,* **di'screetly** *adv.* diskret

discrepancy /dɪˈskrepənsɪ/ *n.* Diskrepanz, *die*

discrepant /dɪˈskrepənt/ *adj.* [voneinander] abweichend

discretion /dɪˈskreʃn/ *n.* (prudence) Umsicht, *die*

discriminate /dɪˈskrɪmɪneɪt/ *v.i.* **(a)** unterscheiden **(b)** ∼ **against/in favour of sb.** jmdn. diskriminieren/bevorzugen

discrimination /dɪskrɪmɪˈneɪʃn/ *n.* **(a)** Unterscheidung, *die* **(b)** Diskriminierung, *die* (**against** *Gen.*); ∼ **in favour of** Bevorzugung (+ *Gen.*)

discus /ˈdɪskəs/ *n.* Diskus, *der*

discuss /dɪˈskʌs/ *v.t.* besprechen; (debate) diskutieren über (+ *Akk.*)

discussion /dɪˈskʌʃn/ *n.* Gespräch, *das;* (debate) Diskussion, *die*

disdain /dɪsˈdeɪn/ 1 *n.* Verachtung, *die* 2 *v.t.* verachten; ∼ **to do sth.** zu stolz sein, etw. zu tun

disdainful /dɪsˈdeɪnfl/ *adj.* verächtlich

disease /dɪˈziːz/ *n.* Krankheit, *die*

diseased /dɪˈziːzd/ *adj.* krank

disem'bark *v.i.* von Bord gehen

disen'chant *v.t.* ernüchtern; **he became** ∼**ed with her/it** sie/es hat ihn desillusioniert

disen'gage *v.t.* lösen (**from** aus, von); ∼ **the clutch** auskuppeln

disen'tangle *v.t.* entwirren; (extricate) befreien (**from** aus)

dis'figure *v.t.* entstellen

disgrace /dɪsˈgreɪs/ 1 *n.* Schande, *die* (**to** für) 2 *v.t.* Schande machen (+ *Dat.*); ∼ **oneself** sich blamieren

di'sgraceful /dɪsˈgreɪsfl/ *adj.* skandalös; **it's** ∼: es ist ein Skandal

disgruntled /dɪsˈgrʌntld/ *adj.* verstimmt

disguise /dɪsˈgaɪz/ 1 *v.t.* verkleiden ⟨*Person*⟩; verstellen ⟨*Stimme*⟩; tarnen ⟨*Gegenstand*⟩ 2 *n.* Verkleidung, *die*

disgust /dɪsˈgʌst/ 1 *n.* (nausea) Ekel, *der* (**at** vor + *Dat.*); (revulsion) Abscheu, *der* (**at** vor + *Dat.*); (indignation) Empörung, *die* (**at** über + *Akk.*) 2 *v.t.* anwidern; (fill with nausea) ekeln; (fill with indignation) empören

dis'gusted *adj.* angewidert; (nauseated) angeekelt; (indignant) empört

dis'gusting *adj.* widerlich

dish /dɪʃ/ *n.* **(a)** Schale, *die;* (deeper) Schüssel, *die;* ∼**es** (crockery) Geschirr, *das;* **wash** *or* (coll.) **do the** ∼**es** Geschirr spülen **(b)** (type of food) Gericht, *das* ▪ **dish 'out** *v.t.* **(a)** austeilen ⟨*Essen*⟩ **(b)** (coll.: distribute) verteilen ▪ **dish 'up** *v.t.* auftragen

'dishcloth *n.* Spültuch, *das*

dis'hearten *v.t.* entmutigen

dishevelled (*Amer.:* **disheveled**) /dɪˈʃevld/ *adj.* zerzaust ⟨*Haar*⟩; ungepflegt ⟨*Erscheinung*⟩

dis'honest *adj.,* **dis'honestly** *adv.* unehrlich

dis'honesty *n.* Unehrlichkeit, *die*

dis'honour 1 *n.* Unehre, *die* 2 *v.t.* beleidigen

dishonourable /dɪsˈɒnərəbl/ *adj.* unehrenhaft

dish: ∼ **rack** *n.* Abtropfgestell, *das;* (in dishwasher) Geschirrwagen, *der;* ∼**washer** *n.* Geschirrspülmaschine, *die*

disil'lusion 1 *v.t.* ernüchtern 2 *n.* Desillusion, *die* (**with** über + *Akk.*)

disil'lusionment *n.* Desillusionierung, *die*

disincentive /dɪsɪnˈsentɪv/ *n.* Hemmnis, *das;* **act as** *or* **be a** ∼ **to sb. to do sth.** jmdn. davon abhalten, etw. zu tun

disin'fect *v.t.* desinfizieren

disinfectant /dɪsɪnˈfektənt/ 1 *adj.* desinfizierend 2 *n.* Desinfektionsmittel, *das*

disinformation /dɪsɪnfəˈmeɪʃn/ *n.* Desinformation, *die*

disingenuous /dɪsɪnˈdʒenjʊəs/ *adj.* unaufrichtig

dis'integrate *v.i.* zerfallen

disinte'gration *n.* Zerfall, *der*

dis'interested *adj.* **(a)** (impartial) unvoreingenommen **(b)** (coll.: uninterested) desinteressiert

disjointed /dɪsˈdʒɔɪntɪd/ *adj.* unzusammenhängend

disk *n.* **(a)** (Comp.) [floppy] ∼: Floppydisk, *die;* Diskette, *die;* [hard] ∼ (exchangeable) [harte] Magnetplatte; (fixed) Festplatte, *die* **(b)** ▶ DISC A

'disk drive n. (Comp.) Diskettenlaufwerk, *das*

diskette /dɪ'skeɪt/ n. Diskette, *die*

dis'like ⊞ v.t. nicht mögen; ~ doing sth. etw. ungern tun
⊡ n. Abneigung, *die* (**of, for** gegen); **take a** ~ **to sb./sth.** eine Abneigung gegen jmdn./ etw. empfinden

dislocate /'dɪsləkeɪt/ v.t. ausrenken; auskugeln ⟨Schulter, Hüfte⟩

dis'lodge v.t. entfernen (**from** aus)

dis'loyal adj. illoyal (**to** gegenüber)

dis'loyalty n. Illoyalität, *die* (**to** gegenüber)

dismal /'dɪzməl/ adj. trist

dismantle /dɪs'mæntl/ v.t. demontieren; abbauen ⟨Schuppen, Gerüst⟩

dismay /dɪs'meɪ/ ⊞ v.t. bestürzen
⊡ n. Bestürzung, *die* (**at** über + *Akk.*)

dismiss /dɪs'mɪs/ v.t. entlassen; (reject) ablehnen

dismissal /dɪs'mɪsl/ n. Entlassung, *die*

dismissive /dɪs'mɪsɪv/ adj. abweisend; (disdainful) abschätzig

dis'mount v.i. absteigen

diso'bedience n. Ungehorsam, *der*

diso'bedient adj. ungehorsam

diso'bey v.t. nicht gehorchen (+ *Dat.*); nicht befolgen ⟨Befehl⟩

dis'order n. (a) Durcheinander, *das*
(b) (Med.) Störung, *die*

dis'orderly adj. (untidy) unordentlich; ~ **conduct** ungebührliches Benehmen

dis'organized adj. chaotisch

dis'orientated, dis'oriented adjs. desorientiert

dis'own v.t. verleugnen

disparage /dɪ'spærɪdʒ/ v.t. herabsetzen

disparaging /dɪ'spærɪdʒɪŋ/ adj. abschätzig

disparity /dɪ'spærɪtɪ/ n. Ungleichheit, *die*

dispatch /dɪ'spætʃ/ ⊞ v.t. (a) schicken
(b) (kill) töten
⊡ n. Bericht, *der*

di'spatch note n. Versandanzeige, *die*

dispel /dɪ'spel/ v.t., -ll- vertreiben; zerstreuen ⟨Besorgnis, Befürchtung⟩

dispensable /dɪ'spensəbl/ adj. entbehrlich

dispensary /dɪ'spensərɪ/ n. Apotheke, *die*

dispense /dɪ'spens/ v.i. ~ **with** verzichten auf (+ *Akk.*)

dispensing 'chemist n. Apotheker, *der*/ Apothekerin, *die*

dispersal /dɪ'spɜːsl/ n. Zerstreuung, *die*

disperse /dɪ'spɜːs/ ⊞ v.t. zerstreuen
⊡ v.i. sich zerstreuen

dispirited /dɪ'spɪrɪtɪd/ adj. entmutigt

dis'place v.t. verschieben; (supplant) ersetzen

displaced 'person n. Vertriebene, *der*/ *die*

display /dɪ'spleɪ/ ⊞ v.t. (a) zeigen; ausstellen ⟨Waren⟩

(b) (Comp.) anzeigen
⊡ n. (a) Ausstellung, *die*; (of goods) Auslage, *die*; (ostentatious show) Zurschaustellung, *die*
(b) (Comp. etc.) Display, *das*; Anzeige, *die*

dis'please v.t. ~ **sb.** jmds. Missfallen erregen

dis'pleasure n. Missfallen, *das*

disposable /dɪ'spəʊzəbl/ adj. Wegwerf-

disposal /dɪ'spəʊzl/ n. Beseitigung, *die*; **have sth./sb. at one's** ~: etw./jmdn. zur Verfügung haben; **be at sb.'s** ~: jmdm. zur Verfügung stehen

dispose /dɪ'spəʊz/ v.t. ~ **sb. to sth.** jmdn. zu etw. veranlassen; ~ **sb. to do sth.** jmdn. dazu veranlassen, etw. zu tun

■ **di'spose of** v.t. beseitigen; (settle) erledigen

disposed /dɪ'spəʊzd/ adj. **be** ~ **to do sth.** dazu neigen, etw. zu tun; **be well** ~ **towards sb./sth.** jmdm. wohl gesinnt sein/einer Sache (*Dat.*) positiv gegenüberstehen

disposition /dɪspə'zɪʃn/ n. Veranlagung, *die*; (nature) Art, *die*

dis'prove v.t. widerlegen

disputable /dɪ'spjuːtəbl, 'dɪspjʊtəbl/ adj. strittig

dispute /dɪ'spjuːt/ ⊞ n. Streit, *der* (**over** um)
⊡ v.t. (a) (discuss) sich streiten über (+ *Akk.*)
(b) (oppose) bestreiten

disqualifi'cation n. Ausschluss, *der*; (Sport) Disqualifikation, *die*

dis'qualify v.t. ausschließen (**from** von); (Sport) disqualifizieren

disre'gard ⊞ v.t. ignorieren
⊡ n. Missachtung, *die* (**of, for** *Gen.*); (of wishes, feelings) Gleichgültigkeit, *die* (**for, of** gegenüber)

dis'reputable adj. verrufen

disrepute /dɪsrɪ'pjuːt/ n. Verruf, *der*; **bring sb./sth. into** ~: jmdn./etw. in Verruf bringen

disre'spect n. Missachtung, *die*; **show** ~ **for sb./sth.** keine Achtung vor jmdm./etw. haben

disre'spectful adj. respektlos

disrupt /dɪs'rʌpt/ v.t. stören

disruption /dɪs'rʌpʃn/ n. Störung, *die*

disruptive /dɪs'rʌptɪv/ adj. störend

dissatis'faction n. Unzufriedenheit, *die*

dis'satisfied adj. unzufrieden

dissect /dɪ'sekt/ v.t. sezieren

disseminate /dɪ'semɪneɪt/ v.t. verbreiten

dissent /dɪ'sent/ ⊞ v.i. (a) (refuse to assent) nicht zustimmen; ~ **from sth.** mit etw. nicht übereinstimmen
(b) (disagree) ~ **from sth.** von etw. abweichen
⊡ n. Ablehnung, *die*; (from majority) Abweichung, *die*

dissertation /dɪsə'teɪʃn/ n. Dissertation, *die*

dis'service n. **do sb. a** ~: jmdm. einen schlechten Dienst erweisen

dissident /'dɪsɪdənt/ n. Dissident, der/ Dissidentin, die

dis'similar adj. unähnlich (**to** Dat.)

dissociate /dɪ'səʊʃɪeɪt/ v.t. trennen; **∼ oneself** sich distanzieren (**from** von)

dissolve /dɪ'zɒlv/ ① v.t. auflösen ② v.i. sich auflösen

dissuade /dɪ'sweɪd/ v.t. abbringen (**from** von)

distance /'dɪstəns/ n. **(a)** Entfernung, die (**from** zu)
(b) (way to cover) Strecke, die; **from a ∼:** von weitem; **in/into the ∼:** in der/die Ferne

'distance learning n. Fernstudium, das

distant /'dɪstənt/ adj. **(a)** fern; entfernt ⟨Ähnlichkeit, Verwandtschaft, Verwandte⟩
(b) (reserved) distanziert

dis'taste n. Abneigung, die (**for** gegen)

dis'tasteful adj. unangenehm

distend /dɪ'stend/ v.t. erweitern

distil, (Amer.) **distill** /dɪ'stɪl/ v.t. destillieren; brennen ⟨Branntwein⟩

distillation /dɪstɪ'leɪʃn/ n. Destillation, die

distillery /dɪ'stɪlərɪ/ n. Brennerei, die

distinct /dɪ'stɪŋkt/ adj. deutlich; (different) verschieden

distinction /dɪ'stɪŋkʃn/ n. Unterschied, der

distinctive /dɪ'stɪŋktɪv/ adj. unverwechselbar

dis'tinctly adv. deutlich

distinguish /dɪ'stɪŋgwɪʃ/ ① v.t. **(a)** (make out) erkennen
(b) (differentiate) unterscheiden
(c) (characterize) kennzeichnen
(d) ∼ oneself [by sth.] sich [durch etw.] hervortun
② v.i. unterscheiden; **∼ between** auseinander halten

distinguished /dɪ'stɪŋgwɪʃt/ adj. angesehen; glänzend ⟨Laufbahn⟩; vornehm ⟨Aussehen⟩

distort /dɪ'stɔːt/ v.t. verzerren; (fig.) verdrehen

distortion /dɪ'stɔːʃn/ n. Verzerrung, die; (fig.) Verdrehung, die

distract /dɪ'strækt/ v.t. ablenken; **∼ sb.['s attention from sth.]** jmdn. [von etw.] ablenken

di'stracted adj. von Sinnen nachgestellt; (mentally far away) abwesend

distraction /dɪ'strækʃn/ n. **(a)** (diversion) Ablenkung, die; (interruption) Störung, die
(b) drive sb. to ∼: jmdn. zum Wahnsinn treiben

distraught /dɪ'strɔːt/ adj. aufgelöst (**with** vor + Dat.); verstört ⟨Blick⟩

distress /dɪ'stres/ ① n. **(a)** Kummer, der (**at** über + Akk.)
(b) (pain) Qualen Pl.
(c) an aircraft/ship in ∼: ein Flugzeug in Not/ein Schiff in Seenot
② v.t. nahe gehen (+ Dat.)

di'stressing adj. erschütternd

di'stress signal n. Notsignal, das

distribute /dɪ'strɪbjuːt/ v.t. verteilen (**to** an + Akk.; **among** unter + Akk.); (Commerc.) vertreiben

distribution /dɪstrɪ'bjuːʃn/ n. Verteilung, die; (Commerc.) Vertrieb, der

distributor /dɪ'strɪbjʊtə(r)/ n. Verteiler, der/Verteilerin, die; (Commerc.) Vertreiber, der

district /'dɪstrɪkt/ n. Gegend, die; (Admin.) Bezirk, der

district: ∼ at'torney n. (Amer. Law) [Bezirks]staatsanwalt, der/-anwältin, die; **∼ 'nurse** n. (Brit.) Gemeindeschwester, die

dis'trust /dɪs'trʌst/ ① n. Misstrauen, das (**of** gegen)
② v.t. misstrauen (+ Dat.)

dis'trustful adj. misstrauisch

disturb /dɪ'stɜːb/ v.t. **(a)** stören; **'do not ∼!'** „bitte nicht stören!"
(b) (worry) beunruhigen

disturbance /dɪ'stɜːbəns/ n. Störung, die; **political ∼s** politische Unruhen

disturbed /dɪ'stɜːbd/ adj. besorgt; **[mentally] ∼:** geistig gestört

disturbing /dɪs'tɜːbɪŋ/ adj. bestürzend

disuse /dɪs'juːs/ n. **fall into ∼:** außer Gebrauch kommen

disused /dɪs'juːzd/ adj. stillgelegt; leer stehend ⟨Gebäude⟩

ditch /dɪtʃ/ ① n. Graben, der
② v.t. (coll.) sausen lassen ⟨Plan⟩; sitzen lassen ⟨Familie, Freund⟩

dither /'dɪðə(r)/ v.i. schwanken

ditto /'dɪtəʊ/ n., pl. **∼s** ebenso; ditto; **∼ marks** Unterführungszeichen, das

divan /dɪ'væn/ n. [Polster]liege, die

dive /daɪv/ ① v.i., **dived** or (Amer.) **dove** /dəʊv/ **(a)** einen Kopfsprung machen; (when already in water) tauchen
(b) ⟨Vogel, Flugzeug usw.⟩ einen Sturzflug machen
② n. **(a)** Kopfsprung, der; (of bird, aircraft, etc.) Sturzflug, der
(b) (coll.: place) Spelunke, die

'diver n. **(a)** (Sport) Kunstspringer, der/-springerin, die
(b) (as profession) Taucher, der/Taucherin, die

diverge /daɪ'vɜːdʒ/ v.i. auseinander gehen

divergent /daɪ'vɜːdʒənt/ adj. auseinander gehend

diverse /daɪ'vɜːs/ adj. verschieden

diversify /daɪ'vɜːsɪfaɪ, dɪ'vɜːsɪfaɪ/ v.i. ⟨Firma⟩ sich auf neue Produktions-/Produktbereiche umstellen

diversion /daɪ'vɜːʃn/ n. **(a)** Ablenkung, die; **create a ∼:** ein Ablenkungsmanöver durchführen
(b) (Brit.: alternative route) Umleitung, die

diversity /daɪ'vɜːsɪtɪ/ n. Vielfalt, die

divert /daɪˈvɜːt/ v.t. umleiten ‹Verkehr, Fluss›; ablenken ‹Aufmerksamkeit›

divide /dɪˈvaɪd/ ① v.t. (a) teilen; ~ sth. in two etc. in zwei [Teile] zerteilen (b) (distribute) aufteilen (**among/between** unter + Akk. od. Dat.) (c) (Math.) dividieren (fachspr.), teilen (**by** durch)
② v.i. sich teilen; ~ [**from sth.**] von etw. abzweigen

■ **divide 'out** v.t. aufteilen (**among/between** unter + Akk. od. Dat.); (distribute) verteilen an (+ Akk.)

■ **divide 'up** v.t. aufteilen

dividend /ˈdɪvɪdend/ n. Dividende, die

dividers /dɪˈvaɪdəz/ n. pl. Stechzirkel, der

divine /dɪˈvaɪn/ adj. göttlich

diving /ˈdaɪvɪŋ/ n. Kunstspringen, das

diving: ~ **board** n. Sprungbrett, das; ~ **suit** n. Taucheranzug, der

divinity /dɪˈvɪnɪtɪ/ n. (a) Göttlichkeit, die (b) (god) Gottheit, die

divisible /dɪˈvɪzɪbl/ adj. teilbar (**by** durch)

division /dɪˈvɪʒn/ n. (a) Teilung, die (b) (Math.) Dividieren, das; **do** ~: dividieren; **long** ~: ausführliche Division (mit Aufschreiben der Zwischenprodukte); **short** ~: verkürzte Division (ohne Aufschreiben der Zwischenprodukte) (c) (section, part) Abteilung, die (d) (group) Gruppe, die (e) (Mil. etc.) Division, die (f) (Footb. etc.) Liga, die; Spielklasse, die; (in British football) Division, die

divorce /dɪˈvɔːs/ ① n. [Ehe]scheidung, die ② v.t. ~ one's husband/wife sich von seinem Mann/seiner Frau scheiden lassen

divorcee /dɪvɔːˈsiː/ n. Geschiedene, der/die; **be a** ~: geschieden sein

divorced /dɪˈvɔːst/ adj. geschieden; **get** ~: sich scheiden lassen

divulge /daɪˈvʌldʒ/ v.t. preisgeben

DIY abbr. = **do-it-yourself**

dizzy /ˈdɪzɪ/ adj. schwind[e]lig; **I feel** ~: mir ist schwindlig

DJ /diːˈdʒeɪ/ abbr. = **disc jockey** Diskjockey, der

DNA abbr. = **deoxyribonucleic acid** DNS

do /də, stressed duː/ ① v.t., neg. (coll.) **don't** /dəʊnt/, pres.t. **he does** /dʌz/, neg. (coll.) **doesn't** /ˈdʌznt/, p.t. **did** /dɪd/, neg. (coll.) **didn't** /ˈdɪdnt/, pres.p. **doing** /ˈduːɪŋ/, p.p. **done** /dʌn/ (a) machen ‹Hausaufgaben, Hausarbeit, Examen, Übersetzung, Kopie, Bett, Handstand›; erfüllen ‹Pflicht›; verrichten ‹Arbeit›; vorführen ‹Trick, Nummer, Tanz›; durchführen ‹Test›; schaffen ‹Pensum›; (clean) putzen; (arrange) [zurecht]machen ‹Haare›; schminken ‹Lippen, Augen, Gesicht›; machen (ugs.) ‹Nägel›; (cut) schneiden ‹Nägel›; (paint) machen (ugs.) ‹Zimmer›; streichen ‹Haus,

Möbel›; (repair) in Ordnung bringen; **do the shopping/washing-up/cleaning** einkaufen [gehen]/abwaschen/sauber machen; **what can I do for you?** (in shop) was darfs sein?; **do sth. about sth./sb.** etw. gegen etw./jmdn. unternehmen (b) (cook) braten; **well done** durch[gebraten] (c) (solve) lösen ‹Problem, Rätsel›; machen ‹Puzzle, Kreuzworträtsel› (d) (coll.: swindle) reinlegen (ugs.); **do sb. out of sth.** jmdn. um etw. bringen (e) (satisfy) zusagen (+ Dat.)
② v.i., forms as 1: (a) (act) tun; **do as they do** mach es wie sie (b) (fare) **how are you doing?** wie gehts dir? (c) (get on) vorankommen; (in exams) abschneiden; **do well/badly at school** gut/ schlecht in der Schule sein (d) **how do you do?** (formal) guten Tag/ Morgen/Abend! (e) (serve purpose) es tun; (suffice) [aus]reichen; (be suitable) gehen; **that won't do** das geht nicht; **that will do!** jetzt aber genug!
③ v. substitute, forms as 1: **you mustn't act as he does** du darfst nicht so wie er handeln; **You went to Paris, didn't you? – Yes, I did** Du warst doch in Paris, nicht wahr? – Ja[, stimmt]; **come in, do!** komm doch herein!
④ v. aux. forms as 1: **I do love Greece** Griechenland gefällt mir wirklich gut; **little did he know that ...:** er hatte keine Ahnung, dass ...; **do you know him?** kennst du ihn?; **what does he want?** was will er?; **I don't** or **do not wish to take part** ich möchte nicht teilnehmen; **don't be so noisy!** seid [doch] nicht so laut!
⑤ n. /duː/, pl. **do's** or **dos** /duːz/ (Brit. coll.) Feier, die; Fete, die (ugs.)

■ **do a'way with** v.t. abschaffen

■ **'do for** v.t. (coll.) **do for sb.** jmdn. fertig machen (ugs.); **be done for** erledigt sein

■ **do 'in** v.t. (sl.) kaltmachen (salopp)

■ **do 'up** v.t. (a) (fasten) zumachen; binden ‹Schnürsenkel, Fliege› (b) (wrap) einpacken

■ **'do with** v.t. **I could do with ...:** ich brauche ...

■ **'do without** v.t. **do without sth.** auf etw. (Akk.) verzichten

docile /ˈdəʊsaɪl/ adj. sanft; (submissive) unterwürfig

dock¹ /dɒk/ ① n. (a) Dock, das (b) usu. in pl. (area) Hafen, der ② v.t. [ein]docken ③ v.i. anlegen

dock² n. (in lawcourt) Anklagebank, die; **stand/be in the** ~: ≈ auf der Anklagebank sitzen

'docker n. Hafenarbeiter, der

dock: ~**land** n. das Hafenviertel; ~**yard** n. Schiffswerft, die

doctor /ˈdɒktə(r)/ ① n. (a) Arzt, der/Ärztin, die; as address Herr/Frau Doktor (b) (holder of degree) Doktor, der

② *v.t.* (coll.) verfälschen

doctorate /ˈdɒktərət/ *n.* Doktorwürde, *die*

doctrine /ˈdɒktrɪn/ *n.* Lehre, *die*

document /ˈdɒkjʊmənt/ *n.* (a) Dokument, *das;* Urkunde, *die*
(b) (Comp.) Dokument, *das*

documentary /dɒkjʊˈmentərɪ/ ① *adj.* dokumentarisch
② *n.* (film) Dokumentarfilm, *der*

documentation /dɒkjʊmenˈteɪʃn/ *n.* (material) beweiskräftige Dokumente *Pl.*

dodge /dɒdʒ/ ① *v.i.* ausweichen
② *v.t.* ausweichen (+ *Dat.*) ⟨*Schlag, Hindernis usw.*⟩; entkommen (+ *Dat.*) ⟨*Polizei, Verfolger*⟩
③ *n.* (trick) Trick, *der*

dodgems /ˈdɒdʒəmz/ *n. pl.* [Auto]skooterbahn, *die;* **have a ride/go on the ~:** Autoskooter fahren

dodgy /ˈdɒdʒɪ/ *adj.* (Brit. coll.) (unreliable) unsicher; (risky) gewagt

doe /dəʊ/ *n.* (deer) Damtier, *das;* (rabbit) [Kaninchen]weibchen, *das*

does /dʌz/ ▸ DO

doesn't /ˈdʌznt/ (coll.) = does not; ▸ DO

dog /dɒg/ ① *n.* Hund, *der*
② *v.t.,* -gg- verfolgen; (fig.) heimsuchen

dog: ~ biscuit *n.* Hundekuchen, *der;* **~ collar** *n.* [Hunde]halsband, *das;* (joc.: clerical collar) Kollar, *das;* **~-eared** *adj.* a **~-eared book** ein Buch mit Eselsohren; **~-end** *n.* (coll.) Kippe, *die* (ugs.)

dogged /ˈdɒgɪd/ *adj.* hartnäckig ⟨*Weigerung, Verurteilung*⟩; zäh ⟨*Durchhaltevermögen, Ausdauer*⟩

'dog licence *n.* Hundesteuerbescheinigung, *die*

dogma /ˈdɒgmə/ *n.* Dogma, *das*

dogmatic /dɒgˈmætɪk/ *adj.* dogmatisch

do-gooder /duːˈgʊdə(r)/ *n.* Wohltäter, *der* (iron.)

dog: ~sbody *n.* (Brit. coll.) Mädchen für alles; **~'s life** *n.* a **~'s life** ein Hundeleben; **give** *or* **lead sb. a ~'s life** jmdn. schäbig behandeln; **~'tired** *adj.* hundemüde

doing /ˈduːɪŋ/ *n.* Tun, *das*

do-it-yourself /duːɪtjəˈself/ ① *adj.* Do-it-yourself-
② *n.* Heimwerken, *das*

doldrums /ˈdɒldrəmz/ *n. pl.* **in the ~** (in low spirits) niedergeschlagen; (Econ.) in einer Flaute

dole /dəʊl/ ① *n.* (coll.) **the ~:** Stempelgeld, *das* (ugs.); **be/go on the ~:** stempeln gehen (ugs.)
② *v.t.* ~ **out** [in kleinen Mengen] verteilen

doll /dɒl/ *n.* Puppe, *die*

dollar /ˈdɒlə(r)/ *n.* Dollar, *der*

dollar: ~ 'bill *n.* Dollarnote, *die;* **~ sign** *n.* Dollarzeichen, *das*

dollop /ˈdɒləp/ *n.* (coll.) Klacks, *der* (ugs.)

'doll's house *n.* Puppenhaus, *das*

dolphin /ˈdɒlfɪn/ *n.* Delphin, *der*

domain /dəˈmeɪn/ *n.* (a) Gebiet, *das*
(b) (Comp.) Domäne, *die;* Domain, *die;* **~ name** Domänenname, *der*

dome /dəʊm/ *n.* Kuppel, *die*

domestic /dəˈmestɪk/ *adj.* (a) (household) häuslich; (family) familiär ⟨*Angelegenheit, Reibereien*⟩
(b) (Econ.) inländisch; Binnen-
(c) ~ **animal/cat** Haustier, *das*/-katze, *die*

domesticated /dəˈmestɪkeɪtɪd/ *adj.* gezähmt ⟨*Tier*⟩; (fig.) häuslich

domesticity /dəʊmesˈtɪsɪtɪ, dɒmesˈtɪsɪtɪ/ *n.* (being domestic) Häuslichkeit, *die*

domestic 'science *n.* Hauswirtschaftslehre, *die*

dominant /ˈdɒmɪnənt/ *adj.* vorherrschend

dominate /ˈdɒmɪneɪt/ *v.t.* beherrschen

domination /dɒmɪˈneɪʃn/ *n.* [Vor]herrschaft, *die* (over über + *Akk.*)

domineering /dɒmɪˈnɪərɪŋ/ *adj.* herrisch

domino /ˈdɒmɪnəʊ/ *n.* Domino[stein], *der;* **~es** *sing.* (game) Domino[spiel], *das;* **play ~es** Domino spielen

'domino effect *n.* Dominoeffekt, *der*

don¹ /dɒn/ *v.t.* (Liter.) anlegen (geh.)

don² *n.* (Univ.) Dozent, *der*

donate /dəʊˈneɪt/ *v.t.* spenden; (on large scale) stiften

donation /dəˈneɪʃn/ *n.* Spende, *die* (to für); (large-scale) Stiftung, *die*

done /dʌn/ ▸ DO

donkey /ˈdɒŋkɪ/ *n.* Esel, *der*

donor /ˈdəʊnə(r)/ *n.* Spender, *der*/Spenderin, *die*

don't /dəʊnt/ (coll.) = do not; ▸ DO

doodle /ˈduːdl/ *v.i.* [herum]kritzeln

doom /duːm/ ① *n.* Verhängnis, *das*
② *v.t.* verurteilen; **be ~ed** verloren sein; **be ~ed to fail** *or* **failure** zum Scheitern verurteilt sein

door /dɔː(r)/ *n.* Tür, *die;* (of castle, barn) Tor, *das;* **out of ~s** im Freien; **go out of ~s** nach draußen gehen

door: ~bell *n.* Türklingel, *die;* **~frame** *n.* Türrahmen, *der;* **~ handle** *n.* Türklinke, *die;* **~keeper** *n.* Pförtner, *der;* Portier, *der;* **~knob** *n.* Türknopf, -knauf, *der;* **~man** *n.* Portier, *der;* **~mat** *n.* Fußmatte, *die;* **~step** *n.* Türstufe, *die;* **on one's/the ~step** (fig.) vor jmds. Tür; **~way** *n.* Eingang, *der*

dope /dəʊp/ ① *n.* (a) (sl.: narcotic) Stoff, *der* (salopp)
(b) (coll.: fool) Dussel, *der*
② *v.t.* dopen ⟨*Pferd, Athleten*⟩

dormant /ˈdɔːmənt/ *adj.* ruhend ⟨*Tier, Pflanze*⟩; untätig ⟨*Vulkan*⟩

dormitory /ˈdɔːmɪtərɪ/ *n.* Schlafsaal, *der*

dormouse /ˈdɔːmaʊs/ *n., pl.* **dormice** /ˈdɔːmaɪs/ Haselmaus, *die*

DOS /dɒs/ *abbr.* (Comp.) = **disk operating system** DOS

dosage /'dəʊsɪdʒ/ *n.* (size of dose) Dosis, *die*

dose /dəʊs/ ① *n.* Dosis, *die*
② *v.t.* ~ **sb. with sth.** jmdm. etw. geben

dot /dɒt/ *n.* Punkt, *der;* **on the ~:** auf den Punkt genau

dot.com /'dɒtkɒm/ ① *adj.* Dot-com-
② *n.* Dot-com-Firma, *die*

dote /dəʊt/ *v.i.* ~ **on sb./sth.** jmdn./etw. abgöttisch lieben

'**dot matrix** *n.* (Comp.) Punktmatrix, *die;* ~ **printer** Nadeldrucker, *der*

dotted /'dɒtɪd/ *adj.* gepunktet

dotty /'dɒtɪ/ *adj.* (coll.) (silly) dümmlich; (feeble-minded) vertrottelt (ugs.); (absurd) blödsinnig (ugs.)

double /'dʌbl/ ① *adj.* doppelt; ~ **bed/room** Doppelbett, *das/*-zimmer, *das;* **be ~ the height/width/length** doppelt so hoch/breit/lang sein
② *adv.* doppelt
③ *n.* (a) Doppelte, *das*
(b) (twice as much) doppelt so viel; (twice as many) doppelt so viele
(c) (person) Doppelgänger, *der/*-gängerin, *die*
(d) *in pl.* (Tennis etc.) Doppel, *das*
(e) **at the ~** (Mil.) im Laufschritt; (fig.) ganz schnell
④ *v.t.* verdoppeln
⑤ *v.i.* sich verdoppeln
■ **double 'back** *v.i.* kehrtmachen (ugs.).
■ **double 'up** *v.i.* sich krümmen (**with** vor + *Dat.*)

double: ~ **'agent** *n.* Doppelagent, *der/*-agentin, *die;* ~**-barrelled** (*Amer.:* ~**-barreled**) /'dʌblbærəld/ *adj.* doppelläufig; ~**-barrelled surname** (Brit.) Doppelname, *der;* ~ **'bass** *n.* Kontrabass, *der;* ~ **'bill** *n.* Doppelprogramm, *das;* ~**-breasted** /dʌbl'brestɪd/ *adj.* zwei- od. doppelreihig; ~**-breasted jacket** Zweireiher, *der;* ~**-'check** *v.t.* (verify twice) zweimal kontrollieren; (verify in two ways) zweifach überprüfen; ~ **'chin** *n.* Doppelkinn, *das;* ~**click** (Comp.) ① *v.i.* doppelklicken;
② *v.t.* ~**click sth.** auf etw. (*Dat.*) doppelklicken; ~ **'cream** *n.* Sahne mit hohem Fettgehalt; ~**-'cross** *v.t.* ein Doppelspiel treiben mit; ~**decker** /dʌbl'dekə(r)/ *n.* Doppeldeckerbus, *der*

double entendre /du:bl ã'tãdr/ *n.* Zweideutigkeit, *die*

double: ~**-'glazed** *adj.* Doppel⟨fenster⟩; ~ **'glazing** *n.* Doppelverglasung, *die;* ~**-'jointed** *adj.* sehr gelenkig; ~ **lesson** *n.* Doppelstunde, *die;* ~**'lock** *v.t.* zweimal abschließen; ~ **'meaning** ▶ DOUBLE ENTENDRE; ~**-page 'spread** *n.* the advertisement was a ~**-**page spread die Anzeige war doppelseitig; ~**-'parking** *n.* Parken in der zweiten Reihe; ~ **'room** *n.* Doppelzimmer, *das;* ~ **'standard** *n.* (rule) Doppelmoral, *die;* apply or operate a

~ **standard** *or* ~ **standards** mit zweierlei Maß messen; ~ **'vision** *n.* Doppeltsehen, *das;* ~ **yellow 'lines** *n. pl.:* am Fahrbahnrand verlaufende gelbe Doppellinie, die ein Halteverbot signalisiert

doubly /'dʌblɪ/ *adv.* doppelt

doubt /daʊt/ ① *n.* Zweifel, *der* (about, as to, of an + *Dat.*); ~[s] [about *or* as to sth./as to whether ...] (as to future) Ungewissheit, (as to fact) Unsicherheit [über etw. (*Akk.*)/darüber, ob ...]; **there's no ~ that ...:** es besteht kein Zweifel daran, dass ...; ~[s] (hesitations) Bedenken *Pl.* (about gegen); **no ~** (certainly) gewiss; (probably) sicherlich
② *v.i.* zweifeln
③ *v.t.* zweifeln an (+ *Dat.*); **I don't ~ that** *or* **it ich bezweifle das nicht; I ~ whether** *or* **if** *or* **that ...:** ich bezweifle, dass ...

doubtful /'daʊtfl/ *adj.* skeptisch ⟨Wesen⟩; ungläubig ⟨Blick⟩

doubtless /'daʊtlɪs/ *adv.* (a) (certainly) gewiss
(b) (probably) sicherlich

dough /dəʊ/ *n.* (a) Teig, *der*
(b) (coll.: money) Knete, *die* (salopp)

'**doughnut** *n.* [Berliner] Pfannkuchen, *der*

douse /daʊs/ *v.t.* übergießen; (extinguish) ausmachen

dove¹ /dʌv/ *n.* Taube, *die*

dove² /dəʊv/ ▶ DIVE 1

dovecot, dovecote /'dʌvkɒt/ *n.* Taubenschlag, *der;* **flutter the ~cots** (fig.) für einige Aufregung sorgen

dowdy /'daʊdɪ/ *adj.* unansehnlich; (shabby) schäbig

down¹ /daʊn/ *n.* (feathers) Daunen *Pl.*

down² ① *adv.* (a) (to lower place) herunter/hinunter; (in lift) abwärts
(b) (in lower place, downstairs) unten; ~ **there/here** da/hier unten; **the next floor ~:** ein Stockwerk tiefer; **be ~ with an illness** eine Krankheit haben; **be three points/games ~:** mit drei Punkten/Spielen zurückliegen
② *prep.* herunter/hinunter; **lower ~ the river** weiter unten am Fluss; **walk ~ the hill/road** den Berg/die Straße heruntergehen; **fall ~ the stairs/steps** die Treppe/Stufen herunterstürzen; **fall ~ a hole/ditch** in ein Loch/ einen Graben fallen; **go ~ the pub** in die Kneipe gehen; **live just ~ the road** ein Stück weiter unten in der Straße wohnen; **be ~ the pub/town** in der Kneipe/Stadt sein; **I've got coffee [all] ~ my skirt** mein ganzer Rock ist voll Kaffee
③ *v.t.* (coll.) schlucken (ugs.) ⟨Getränk⟩; ~ **tools** die Arbeit niederlegen

down: ~**-and-'out** *n.* Stadtstreicher, *der/*-streicherin, *die;* ~**cast** *adj.* niedergeschlagen; ~**fall** *n.* Untergang, *der;* ~**-'hearted** *adj.* niedergeschlagen; ~**hill** *adv.* bergab; ~**'load** *v.t.* (Comp.) herunterladen; ~**market** *adj.* weniger anspruchsvoll; ~ **payment** *n.* Anzahlung, *die;* ~**pour** *n.* Regenguss, *der;* ~**right** *adj.*

ausgemacht; glatt ‹*Lüge*›; ∼**size** ①v.t. verschlanken; ②v.i. abspecken; ∼**stairs** ① /'-'-/ adv. die Treppe hinunter‹*gehen, -fallen, -kommen*›; unten ‹*wohnen, sein*›; ② /'--/ adj. im Erdgeschoss nachgestellt; ∼**'stream** adv. flussabwärts; ∼**to-'earth** adj. sachlich; ∼**town** adv. im/ (direction) ins Stadtzentrum; ∼**trodden** adj. unterdrückt; ∼**turn** n. (Econ., Commerc.) Abschwung, der; ∼ **'under** adv. (coll.) in/ (to) nach Australien/Neuseeland

downward /'daʊnwəd/ ① adj. nach unten gerichtet
② adv. abwärts ‹*sich bewegen*›; nach unten ‹*sehen, gehen*›

downwards /'daʊnwədz/ ▶ DOWNWARD 2

dowry /'daʊrɪ/ n. Aussteuer, die

doz. abbr. = **dozen** Dtzd.

doze /dəʊz/ ① v.i. dösen (ugs.)
② n. Nickerchen, das (ugs.)
■ **doze 'off** v.i. eindösen (ugs.)

dozen /'dʌzn/ n. (a) Dutzend, das; half a ∼: sechs
(b) in pl. (coll.: many) Dutzende Pl.

Dr abbr. = **doctor** Dr.

drab /dræb/ adj. langweilig; trostlos ‹*Landschaft*›; eintönig ‹*Leben*›

draft /drɑːft/ ① n. (a) (of speech) Konzept, das; (of treaty, bill) Entwurf, der
(b) (Amer.) ▶ DRAUGHT
② v.t. entwerfen

drafty (Amer.) ▶ DRAUGHTY

drag /dræg/ ① v.t., -gg- schleppen; (Comp.) ziehen; ∼ **and drop** ziehen und ablegen
② v.i., -gg- schleifen; (fig.: pass slowly) sich [hin]schleppen
③ n. (a) (coll.) in ∼: in Frauenkleidung
(b) (coll.: at cigarette) Zug, der
■ **drag 'down** v.t. nach unten ziehen;
∼ **sb. down to one's own level** (fig.) jmdn. auf sein Niveau herabziehen
■ **drag 'on** v.i. sich [da]hinschleppen

dragon /'drægn/ n. Drache, der

'dragonfly n. Libelle, die

drain /dreɪn/ ① n. Abflussrohr, das; (underground) Kanalisationsrohr, das; (grating at roadside) Gully, der; **go down the** ∼ (fig. coll.) für die Katz sein (ugs.)
② v.t. (a) trockenlegen ‹*Teich*›; entwässern ‹*Land*›; ableiten ‹*Wasser*›
(b) (Cookery) abgießen ‹*Wasser, Gemüse*›
(c) austrinken ‹*Glas*›
③ v.i. ‹*Flüssigkeit:*› ablaufen ‹*Geschirr, Gemüse:*› abtropfen

drainage /'dreɪnɪdʒ/ n. Kanalisation, die

'draining board (Brit.; Amer.: **'drainboard**) n. Abtropfbrett, das

'drainpipe n. Regen[abfall]rohr, das

drake /dreɪk/ n. Enterich, der

drama /'drɑːmə/ n. Drama, das

dramatic /drə'mætɪk/ adj. dramatisch

dramatist /'dræmətɪst/ n. Dramatiker, der/Dramatikerin, die

dramatize /'dræmətaɪz/ v.t. dramatisieren

drank ▶ DRINK 2

drape /dreɪp/ ① v.t. drapieren
② n. (Amer.: curtain) Vorhang, der

'draper n. (Brit.) Textilkaufmann, der; ∼**'s** [shop] Textilgeschäft, das

drastic /'dræstɪk/ adj. drastisch

draught /drɑːft/ n. [Luft]zug, der; there's a ∼: es zieht

draught: ∼ **'beer** n. Fassbier, das;
∼ **board** n. (Brit.) Damebrett, das;
∼ **excluder** n. Abdichtvorrichtung, die; Zugluft-Verhinderer, der; ∼**proof** adj. winddicht

draughts /drɑːfts/ n. (Brit.) Damespiel, das

'draughtsman /-mən/ n., pl.
draughtsmen /-mən/ Zeichner, der/ Zeichnerin, die

'draughty adj. zugig

draw /drɔː/ ① v.t., drew /druː/, drawn /drɔːn/ (a) (pull) ziehen; ∼ **the curtains/ blinds** (close) die Vorhänge zuziehen/die Jalousien herunterlassen; ∼ **sth. towards** one etw. zu sich heranziehen
(b) (attract) anlocken; **be** ∼**n to sb.** von jmdm. angezogen werden
(c) (take out) herausziehen; schöpfen ‹*Wasser*›; ∼ **money from the bank** Geld bei der Bank holen/abheben
(d) beziehen ‹*Gehalt, Rente, Arbeitslosenunterstützung*›
(e) ziehen ‹*Strich*›; zeichnen ‹*geometrische Figur, Bild*›
(f) ziehen ‹*Parallele, Vergleich*›; herausstellen ‹*Unterschied*›
② v.i. (a) **drew, drawn:** ∼ **to an end** zu Ende gehen
(b) (Sport) **they drew [three-all]** sie spielten [3 : 3] unentschieden
③ n. (a) (raffle) Tombola, die
(b) (of lottery) Ziehung, die
(c) ([result of] drawn game) Unentschieden, das; **end in a** ∼: mit einem Unentschieden enden
■ **draw 'back** ① v.t. zurückziehen
② v.i. zurückweichen
■ **draw 'in** v.i. einfahren; ‹*Tage:*› kürzer werden
■ **draw 'out** v.i. abfahren; ‹*Tage:*› länger werden
■ **draw 'up** ① v.t. (a) aufsetzen ‹*Vertrag*›; aufstellen ‹*Liste*›
(b) (pull closer) heranziehen
② v.i. [an]halten

draw: ∼**back** n. Nachteil, der; ∼**bridge** n. Zugbrücke, die

drawer /drɔː(r), 'drɔːə(r)/ n. Schublade, die

'drawing n. (sketch) Zeichnung, die

drawing: ∼ **board** n. Zeichenbrett, das;
∼ **pin** n. (Brit.) Reißzwecke, die; ∼ **room** n. Salon, der

drawl /drɔːl/ ① v.i. gedehnt sprechen
② n. gedehntes Sprechen

drawn ▶ DRAW 1, 2

dread /dred/ **1** v.t. sich sehr fürchten vor (+ Dat.); **the ~ed day/moment** der gefürchtete Tag/Augenblick **2** n. Angst, die

dreadful /'dredfl/ adj. schrecklich; (coll.: very bad) fürchterlich; **I feel ~** (unwell) ich fühle mich scheußlich (ugs.)

'**dreadfully** adv. schrecklich; (coll.: very badly) fürchterlich

dream /dri:m/ **1** n. Traum, der; attrib. traumhaft; Traum⟨haus, -auto, -urlaub⟩; **have a ~ about sb./sth.** von jmdm./etw. träumen **2** v.i. & t. dreamt /dremt/ or dreamed träumen

'**dreamer** n. (in sleep) Träumende, der/die; (day~) Träumer, der/Träumerin, die

dreary /'drɪərɪ/ adj. trostlos

dredge /dredʒ/ v.t. ausbaggern

'**dredger** n. Bagger, der

'**dregs** /dregz/ n. pl. [Boden]satz, der

drench /drentʃ/ v.t. durchnässen

dress /dres/ **1** n. Kleid, das; (clothing) Kleidung, die
2 v.t. (a) anziehen; **be well ~ed** gut gekleidet sein; **get ~ed** sich anziehen
(b) verbinden ⟨Wunde⟩
3 v.i. sich anziehen
■ **dress 'up** v.i. sich fein machen

dress: ~ circle n. (Theatre) erster Rang; **~ designer** n. Modeschöpfer, der/-schöpferin, die

'**dresser** n. (a) Anrichte, die
(b) (Amer.) ▶ DRESSING TABLE

'**dressing** n. (a) no pl. Anziehen, das
(b) (Cookery) Dressing, das
(c) (Med.) Verband, der

dressing: ~ gown n. Bademantel, der; **~ room** n. (Sport) Umkleideraum, der; (for actor) Garderobe, die; **~ table** n. Frisierkommode, die

dress: ~maker n. Damenschneider, der/-schneiderin, die; **~making** n. Damenschneiderei, die; **~ rehearsal** n. Generalprobe, die

drew ▶ DRAW 1, 2

dribble /'drɪbl/ v.i. (a) (slobber) sabbern
(b) (Sport) dribbeln

dried /draɪd/ adj. getrocknet; **~ fruit[s]** Dörrobst, das; **~ milk** Trockenmilch, die

drier /'draɪə(r)/ n. (for hair) Trockenhaube, die; (hand-held) Föhn, der; (for laundry) [Wäsche]trockner, der

drift /drɪft/ **1** n. (a) (of snow or sand) Verwehung, die
(b) (gist) **get** or **catch the ~ of sth.** etw im Wesentlichen verstehen
2 v.i. (a) treiben; ⟨Wolke:⟩ ziehen
(b) ⟨Sand, Schnee:⟩ zusammengeweht werden

'**driftwood** n. Treibholz, das

drill /drɪl/ **1** n. (a) (tool) Bohrer, der
(b) (Mil.: training) Drill, der
2 v.t. & i. bohren (**for** nach)

'**drill bit** n. Bohrer, der

drink /drɪŋk/ **1** n. Getränk, das; (alcoholic) Glas, das; (not with food) Drink, der; **have a ~:** [etwas] trinken; (alcoholic) ein Glas trinken
2 v.t. & i. drank /dræŋk/, drunk /drʌŋk/ trinken

drinkable /'drɪŋkəbl/ adj. trinkbar

'**drink-driving** n. Fahren unter Alkoholeinfluss; Alkohol am Steuer; **~ offence** Alkoholdelikt, das

drinker /'drɪŋkə(r)/ n. Trinker, der/Trinkerin, die

drinking /'drɪŋkɪŋ/: **~ fountain** n. Trinkbrunnen, der; **~ water** n. Trinkwasser, das

drip /drɪp/ **1** n. (a) Tropfen, das
(b) (coll.: feeble person) Schlappschwanz, der (salopp)
2 v.i., -pp- tropfen; **be ~ping with water/moisture** triefend nass sein

'**drip-dry** adj. bügelfrei

'**dripping** n. (Cookery) Schmalz, das

drive /draɪv/ **1** n. (a) Fahrt, die
(b) (private road) Zufahrt, die; (entrance) (to small building) Einfahrt, die; (to large building) Auffahrt, die
(c) (energy) Tatkraft, die
(d) (Psych.) Trieb, der
(e) (Motor Veh.) **left-hand/right-hand ~:** Links-/Rechtssteuerung, die
2 v.t., drove /drəʊv/, driven /'drɪvn/ (a) fahren
(b) treiben ⟨Tier⟩
(c) (compel to move) vertreiben (**out of, from** aus)
(d) (fig.) **~ sb. to sth.** jmdn. zu etw. treiben; **~ sb. to do sth.** or **into doing sth.** jmdn. dazu treiben, etw. zu tun
(e) (power) antreiben
3 v.i., drove, driven (a) fahren; **can you ~?** kannst du Auto fahren?
(b) (go by car) mit dem [eigenen] Auto fahren
■ '**drive at** v.t. (fig.) hinauswollen auf (+ Akk.); **what are you driving at?** worauf wollen Sie hinaus?
■ **drive a'way 1** v.i. wegfahren
2 v.t. (a) wegfahren
(b) (chase away) vertreiben
■ **drive 'off** ▶ DRIVE AWAY
■ **drive 'on** v.i. weiterfahren
■ **drive 'up** v.i. vorfahren (**to** vor + Dat.)

'**drive-in** adj. Drive-in-; **~ cinema** or (Amer.) **movie [theater]** Autokino, das

drivel /'drɪvl/ n. Gefasel, das (ugs.); **talk ~:** faseln (ugs.)

driven ▶ DRIVE 2, 3

driver /'draɪvə(r)/ n. (a) Fahrer, der/Fahrerin, die; (of locomotive) Führer, der/Führerin, die; **~'s license** (Amer.) Führerschein, der
(b) (Comp.) Treiber, der

driving /'draɪvɪŋ/ **1** n. Fahren, das
2 adj. peitschend ⟨Regen⟩

driving: ~ force n. treibende Kraft;

Triebfeder, *die;* **the** ∼ **force behind sth.** die
treibende Kraft hinter etw.; ∼ **gloves** *n.*
pl. Autohandschuhe *Pl.;* ∼ **instructor** *n.*
Fahrlehrer, *der/*-lehrerin, *die;* ∼ **lesson** *n.*
Fahrstunde, *die;* ∼ **licence** *n.*
Führerschein, *der;* ∼ **mirror** *n.*
Rückspiegel, *der;* ∼ **school** *n.* Fahrschule,
die; ∼ **test** *n.* Fahrprüfung, *die*

drizzle /'drɪzl/ ⨯1⨯ *n.* Nieseln, *das*
⨯2⨯ *v.i.* **it's drizzling** es nieselt

drone /drəʊn/ ⨯1⨯ *v.i.* (a) ⟨*Biene:*⟩ summen;
⟨*Maschine:*⟩ brummen
(b) ⟨*Rezitator:*⟩ leiern
⨯2⨯ *n.* ▶ 1: Summen, *das;* Brummen, *das;*
Geleier, *das*

drool /druːl/ *v.i.* ∼ **over** eine kindische
Freude haben an (+ *Dat.*)

droop /druːp/ *v.i.* herunterhängen; ⟨*Blume:*⟩
den Kopf hängen lassen

drop /drɒp/ ⨯1⨯ *n.* (a) Tropfen, *der;* **in** ∼**s**
tropfenweise
(b) (decrease) Rückgang, *der*
⨯2⨯ *v.i.,* **-pp-:** (a) (fall) (accidentally)
[herunter]fallen; (deliberately) sich
[hinunter]fallen lassen
(b) (in amount etc.) sinken; ⟨*Preis, Wert:*⟩
sinken, fallen; ⟨*Wind:*⟩ sich legen; ⟨*Stimme:*⟩
sich senken
⨯3⨯ *v.t.,* **-pp-:** (a) fallen lassen; abwerfen
⟨*Bomben, Nachschub*⟩
(b) (discontinue, abandon) fallen lassen; ∼ **out
of university/the course** das Studium
abbrechen *od.* aufgeben
(c) (omit) auslassen
■ **drop 'by, drop 'in** *v.i.* vorbeikommen
■ **drop 'off** ⨯1⨯ *v.i.* (a) (fall off) abfallen
(b) (fall asleep) einnicken
⨯2⨯ *v.t.* absetzen ⟨*Fahrgast*⟩
■ **drop 'out** *v.i.* (a) herausfallen (**of** aus)
(b) (withdraw) aussteigen (ugs.) (**of** aus);
(beforehand) seine Teilnahme absagen

drop: ∼-**down menu** *n.* (Comp.)
Dropdownmenü, *das;* ∼ **handlebars** *n. pl.*
Rennlenker, *der;* ∼ **kick** *n.* (Football)
Dropkick, *der*

droplet /'drɒplɪt/ *n.* Tröpfchen, *das*

dropout /'drɒpaʊt/ *n.* Aussteiger, *der/*
Aussteigerin, *die*

dropper /'drɒpə(r)/ *n.* (esp. Med.) Tropfer,
der

drop shot *n.* (Tennis etc.) Stoppball, *der*

drought /draʊt/ *n.* Dürre, *die*

drove ▶ DRIVE 2, 3

drown /draʊn/ ⨯1⨯ *v.i.* ertrinken
⨯2⨯ *v.t.* ertränken; **be** ∼**ed** ertrinken

drowse /draʊz/ *v.i.* [vor sich hin]dösen

drowsy /'draʊzɪ/ *adj.* schläfrig; (on just
waking) verschlafen

drudgery /'drʌdʒərɪ/ *n.* Schufterei, *die*

drug /drʌɡ/ ⨯1⨯ *n.* (a) (Med.) [Arznei]mittel,
das
(b) (narcotic) Droge, *die;* **be on** ∼**s** Rauschgift
nehmen

⨯2⨯ *v.t.,* **-gg-** betäuben ⟨*Person*⟩; ∼ **sb.'s food/
drink** jmds. Essen/Getränk (*Dat.*) ein
Betäubungsmittel beimischen

drug: ∼ **abuse** *n.* Drogenmissbrauch, *der;*
∼ **abuser** *n.* Drogenmissbrauch
Treibender/Treibende; ∼ **addict** *n.*
Drogensüchtige, *der/die;* ∼ **addiction** *n.*
Drogensucht, *die;* ∼ **dealer** *n.*
Drogenhändler, *der/*-händlerin, *die;* Dealer,
*der/*Dealerin, *die* (Drogenjargon); ∼ **peddler**
▶ DRUG DEALER; ∼-**related** *adj.*
Drogen⟨-tote, -kriminalität, -delikt,
-probleme⟩; ∼ **scene** *n.* Drogenszene, *die;*
∼**store** *n.* (Amer.) Drugstore, *der;*
∼-**taking** *n.* Drogeneinnahme, *die;*
∼ **trafficking** *n.* Drogenhandel, *der;*
∼ **test** *n.* Dopingkontrolle, *die;* Dopingtest,
der; ∼**user** *n.* Drogenkonsument, *der/*
-konsumentin, *die*

drum /drʌm/ ⨯1⨯ *n.* (a) Trommel, *die*
(b) (in jazz or pop) Schlagzeug, *das*
(c) (container) Fass, *das*
⨯2⨯ *v.i.* trommeln
■ **drum 'up** *v.i.* auftreiben

'drum beat *n.* Trommelschlag, *der*

'drummer *n.* Schlagzeuger, *der*

'drumstick *n.* (a) Trommelschlägel, *der*
(b) (Cookery) Keule, *die*

drunk /drʌŋk/ ⨯1⨯ *adj.* **be** ∼: betrunken
sein; **get** ∼: betrunken werden (**on** von);
(intentionally) sich betrinken (**on** mit)
⨯2⨯ *n.* Betrunkene, *der/die*

drunkard /'drʌŋkəd/ *n.* Trinker, *der/*
Trinkerin, *die*

drunken /'drʌŋkn/ *attrib. adj.* betrunken;
(habitually) ständig betrunken; ∼ **driving**
Trunkenheit am Steuer

'drunkenness *n.* Betrunkenheit, *die;*
(habitual) Trunksucht, *die*

dry /draɪ/ ⨯1⨯ *adj.* trocken; trocken, (very ∼)
herb ⟨*Wein*⟩; ausgetrocknet ⟨*Flussbett*⟩; **get**
or **become** ∼: trocknen
⨯2⨯ *v.t.* (a) trocknen ⟨*Haare, Wäsche*⟩;
abtrocknen ⟨*Geschirr, Baby*⟩; ∼ **oneself** sich
abtrocknen; ∼ **one's eyes** *or* **tears/hands**
sich (*Dat.*) die Tränen abwischen/die Hände
abtrocknen
(b) (preserve) trocknen; dörren ⟨*Obst,
Fleisch*⟩
⨯3⨯ *v.i.* trocknen
■ **dry 'out** *v.t. & i.* trocknen
■ **dry 'up** ⨯1⨯ *v.t.* abtrocknen
⨯2⨯ *v.i.* (a) (∼ **the dishes**) abtrocknen
(b) ⟨*Brunnen, Quelle:*⟩ versiegen; ⟨*Fluss,
Teich:*⟩ austrocknen

dry: ∼-**'clean** *v.t.* chemisch reinigen;
∼-**'cleaner's** *n.* chemische Reinigung;
∼-**'cleaning** *n.* chemische Reinigung

'dryer ▶ DRIER

dry: ∼-**eyed** *adj.* ohne Rührung; ∼ **'ice** *n.*
Trockeneis, *das*

drying-'up *n.* Abtrocknen, *das;* **do the** ∼
abtrocknen; *attrib.* ∼ **cloth** Geschirrtuch,
das

'dryness n. Trockenheit, die
dry 'rot n. Trockenfäule, die
dual /'dju:əl/ adj. doppelt
dual: ~ **'carriageway** n. (Brit.) Straße
mit Mittelstreifen; ~ **con'trol** n. (Aeronaut.)
Doppelsteuerung, die; (Motor Veh.) doppelte
Bedienungselemente Pl.; ~**'purpose** adj.
zweifach verwendbar
dub /dʌb/ v.t. -bb- (Cinemat.) synchronisieren
dubious /'dju:bɪəs/ adj. (doubting)
unschlüssig; (suspicious) zweifelhaft
duchess /'dʌtʃɪs/ n. Herzogin, die
duck /dʌk/ ① n. Ente, die
② v.i. sich [schnell] ducken
③ v.t. ~ one's head den Kopf einziehen
duckling /'dʌklɪŋ/ n. Entenküken, das
'duck pond n. Ententeich, der
duct /dʌkt/ n. Rohr, das; (for air) Ventil, das
dud /dʌd/ ① n. (useless thing) Niete, die (ugs.);
(counterfeit) Fälschung, die
② adj. mies (ugs.); schlecht; (fake) gefälscht;
geplatzt ‹Scheck›
dude /dju:d, du:d/ n. (esp. Amer. coll.) Typ, der
(ugs.)
due /dju:/ ① adj. (a) (owed) geschuldet;
zustehend ‹Eigentum, Recht usw.›; there's
sth. ~ to me, I've got sth. ~: mir steht etw.
zu
(b) (immediately payable) fällig
(c) (that it is proper to give or use) gebührend;
angemessen ‹Belohnung›; be ~ to sb. jmdm.
gebühren; with all ~ respect bei allem
gebotenen Respekt
(d) (attributable) the mistake was ~ to
negligence der Fehler war durch
Nachlässigkeit verursacht; it's ~ to her that
we missed the train ihretwegen verpassten
wir den Zug
(e) (scheduled, expected); be ~ to do sth. etw.
tun sollen; be ~ [to arrive] ankommen sollen
(f) (likely to get, deserving) be ~ for sth. etw.
verdienen
② adv. (a) ~ north genau nach Norden
(b) ~ to aufgrund (+ Gen.); auf Grund
(+ Gen.)
③ n. (a) give sb. his ~: jmdm. Gerechtigkeit
widerfahren lassen
(b) ~s (fees) Gebühren Pl.
duel /'dju:əl/ n. Duell, das
duet /dju:'et/ n. (for voices) Duett, das;
(instrumental) Duo, das
duffle /'dʌfl/: ~ **bag** n. Matchbeutel, der;
~ **coat** n. Dufflecoat, der
dug ▶ DIG
duke /dju:k/ n. Herzog, der
dull /dʌl/ ① adj. (a) (stupid) beschränkt; (slow
to understand) begriffsstutzig
(b) (boring) langweilig
(c) (gloomy) trübe ‹Wetter, Tag›
② v.t. abstumpfen ‹Geist, Sinne, Verstand›
duly /'dju:lɪ/ adv. ordnungsgemäß
dumb /dʌm/ adj. (a) stumm
(b) (coll.: stupid) doof (ugs.)

■ **dumb down** v.t. & i. (coll.) verflachen
dumbfounded /dʌm'faʊndɪd/ adj.
sprachlos
dummy /'dʌmɪ/ n. (a) (of tailor)
Schneiderpuppe, die; (in shop)
Schaufensterpuppe, die; (of ventriloquist) Puppe,
die; (stupid person) Dummkopf, der (ugs.); like a
stuffed ~: wie ein Ölgötze (ugs.)
(b) (imitation) Attrappe, die
(c) (esp. Brit.: for baby) Schnuller, der
dump /dʌmp/ ① n. (a) (place) Müllkippe,
die; (heap) Müllhaufen, der; (permanent)
Müllhalde, die
(b) (Mil.) Depot, das
(c) (coll.: town) Kaff, das (ugs.)
② v.t. (dispose of) werfen; (deposit) abladen
‹Sand, Müll usw.›; (leave) lassen; (place)
abstellen
'dumping ground n. Müllkippe, die; (fig.)
Abstellplatz, der
dumpling /'dʌmplɪŋ/ n. Kloß, der
dumps /dʌmps/ n. pl. be or feel down in the
~: ganz down sein (ugs.)
'dump truck n. Kipper, der
dunce /dʌns/ n. Null, die (ugs.)
dune /dju:n/ n. Düne, die
dung /dʌŋ/ n. Dung, der
dungarees /dʌŋgə'ri:z/ n. pl. Latzhose, die
dungeon /'dʌndʒən/ n. Kerker, der
dunk /dʌŋk/ v.t. tunken
dupe /dju:p/ ① v.t. übertölpeln
② n. Dumme, der/die
duplex /'dju:pleks/ adj. (esp. Amer.) (two-
storey) zweistöckig ‹Wohnung›; (two-family)
Zweifamilien‹haus›
duplicate ① /'dju:plɪkət/ adj. (a) (identical)
Zweit-
(b) (twofold) doppelt
② n. Kopie, die; (second copy of letter/document/
key) Duplikat, das; in ~: in doppelter
Ausfertigung
③ /'dju:plɪkeɪt/ v.t. (a) (make a copy of, make in
~) ~ sth. eine zweite Anfertigung von etw.
machen
(b) (on machine) vervielfältigen
(c) (do twice) noch einmal tun
duplicity /dju:'plɪsɪtɪ/ n. Falschheit, die
durability /djʊərə'bɪlɪtɪ/ n. (of friendship,
peace, etc.) Dauerhaftigkeit, die; (of garment,
material) Haltbarkeit, die
durable /'djʊərəbl/ adj. haltbar; dauerhaft
‹Friede, Freundschaft usw.›
duration /djʊə'reɪʃn/ n. Dauer, die
duress /djʊə'res/ n. Zwang, der
during /'djʊərɪŋ/ prep. während; (at a point
in) in (+ Dat.)
dusk /dʌsk/ n. Einbruch der Dunkelheit
dust /dʌst/ ① n. Staub, der
② v.t. abstauben ‹Möbel›; ~ a room/ house
in einem Zimmer/Haus Staub wischen
③ v.i. Staub wischen

dust: ∼bin n. (Brit.) Mülltonne, die; **∼cart** n. (Brit.) Müllwagen, der; **∼ cloth** n. Schonbezug, der; (duster) Staubtuch, das

'duster n. Staubtuch, das

dust: ∼ jacket n. Schutzumschlag, der; **∼man** /-mən/ n., pl. **∼men** /-mən/ (Brit.) Müllmann, der; **∼pan** n. Kehrschaufel, die

'dusty adj. staubig; verstaubt ⟨Bücher, Möbel⟩

Dutch /dʌtʃ/ 1 adj. holländisch; sb. **is ∼:** jmd. ist Holländer/Holländerin 2 n. (a) (language) Holländisch, das; see also ENGLISH 2A (b) **the ∼** pl. die Holländer Pl.

Dutch: ∼ 'courage n. angetrunkener Mut; **∼ 'elm disease** n. Ulmensterben, das; **∼man** /-mən/ n., pl. **∼men** /-mən/ Holländer, der; **∼woman** n. Holländerin, die

dutiful /'djuːtɪfl/ adj., **'dutifully** adv. pflichtbewusst

duty /'djuːtɪ/ n. (a) Pflicht, die; (task) Aufgabe, die; **be on ∼:** Dienst haben; **off ∼:** nicht im Dienst; **be off ∼:** keinen Dienst haben; ⟨ab ... Uhr⟩ dienstfrei sein (b) (tax) Zoll, der; **pay ∼ on sth.** Zoll für etw. bezahlen

'duty-free adj., adv. zollfrei

duvet /'duːveɪ/ n. Federbett, das; **∼ cover** Bettbezug, der

DVD abbr. = **digital video disc** DVD

dwarf /dwɔːf/ n., pl. **∼s** or **dwarves** /'dwɔːvz/ Zwerg, der/Zwergin, die

dwell /dwel/ v.i., dwelt /dwelt/ (literary) wohnen

■ **'dwell [up]on** v.t. (in discussion) sich ausführlich befassen mit; (in thought) in Gedanken verweilen bei

'dwelling n. Wohnung, die

dwelt ▶ DWELL

dwindle /'dwɪndl/ v.i. **∼ [away]** abnehmen; ⟨Unterstützung, Interesse:⟩ nachlassen; ⟨Vorräte:⟩ schrumpfen

dye /daɪ/ 1 n. Färbemittel, das 2 v.t., **∼ing** /'daɪɪŋ/ färben

dying /'daɪɪŋ/ adj. sterbend; absterbend ⟨Baum⟩

dyke ▶ DIKE

dynamic /daɪˈnæmɪk/ adj. dynamisch

dynamism /'daɪnəmɪzm/ n. Dynamik, die

dynamite /'daɪnəmaɪt/ n. Dynamit, das

dynamo /'daɪnəməʊ/ n. Dynamo, der; (in car) Lichtmaschine, die

dynasty /'dɪnəstɪ/ n. Dynastie, die

dysentry /'dɪsəntrɪ/ n. Ruhr, die

Ee

E, e /iː/ n. E, e, das

E. abbr. (a) = **east** O (b) = **eastern** ö

each /iːtʃ/ 1 adj. jeder/jede/jedes; **they cost** or **are a pound ∼:** sie kosten ein Pfund pro Stück 2 pron. (a) jeder/jede/jedes (b) **∼ other** sich

eager /'iːgə(r)/ adj. eifrig; **be ∼ to do sth.** etw. unbedingt tun wollen

'eagerly adv. eifrig; gespannt ⟨warten⟩

eagle /'iːgl/ n. Adler, der

eagle-'eyed adj. adleräugig

ear¹ /ɪə(r)/ n. Ohr, das; **up to one's ∼s in work/debt** bis zum Hals in Arbeit/Schulden; **be[come] all ∼s** [plötzlich] ganz Ohr sein; **play by ∼** (Mus.) nach dem Gehör spielen

ear² n. (Bot.) Ähre, die

ear: ∼ache n. Ohrenschmerzen Pl.; **∼ clip** n. Ohr[en]klipp, der; **∼ drops** n. pl. (a) (Med.) Ohrentropfen Pl.; (b) (earrings) Ohrgehänge, das; **∼drum** n. Trommelfell, das

earl /ɜːl/ n. Graf, der

'ear lobe n. Ohrläppchen, das

early /'ɜːlɪ/ 1 adj. früh 2 adv. früh; **I am a bit ∼:** ich bin etwas zu früh gekommen; **∼ next week** Anfang der nächsten Woche; **∼ in June** Anfang Juni; **from ∼ in the morning till late at night** von früh [morgens] bis spät [nachts]; **∼ on** schon früh

early: ∼ 'closing n. **it is ∼ closing** die Geschäfte haben nachmittags geschlossen; **∼-'closing day** n.: Tag, an dem die Geschäfte nachmittags geschlossen haben

ear: ∼mark v.t. vorsehen; **∼muffs** n. pl. Ohrenschützer Pl.

earn /ɜːn/ v.t. verdienen; (bring in as income or interest) einbringen

earnest /'ɜːnɪst/ 1 adj. ernsthaft 2 n. **in ∼:** mit vollem Ernst

earnings /'ɜːnɪŋz/ n. pl. Verdienst, der; (of business etc.) Ertrag, der

ear: ∼phones n. pl. Kopfhörer, der; **∼piece** n. Hörmuschel, die; **∼-piercing** 1 adj. durch Mark und Bein gehend ⟨Lärm⟩; 2 n. Durchstechen der Ohrläppchen; **∼plug** n. Ohropax, das ⓦ; ····⟩

~**ring** n. Ohrring, der; ~**shot** n. out of/
within ~shot außer/in Hörweite;
~-**splitting** adj. ohrenbetäubend

earth /ɜːθ/ [1] n. (also Brit. Electr.) Erde, die;
how/what etc. on ~ ...? wie/was usw. in aller
Welt ...?
[2] v.t. (Brit. Electr.) erden

earthenware /'ɜːθnweə(r)/ [1] n.
Tonwaren Pl.
[2] adj. Ton-

earthly /'ɜːθlɪ/ adj. irdisch; no ~ use etc.
(coll.) nicht der geringste Nutzen usw.

earth: ~**quake** n. Erdbeben, das;
~ **sciences** n. pl. Geowissenschaften Pl.;
~**worm** n. Regenwurm, der

'**earthy** adj. (a) erdig
(b) (coarse) derb

'**earwax** n. Ohrenschmalz, das

'**earwig** /'ɪəwɪg/ n. Ohrwurm, der

ease /iːz/ [1] n. (a) set sb. at ~: jmdn.
beruhigen; at [one's] ~: entspannt; be or feel
at [one's] ~: sich wohl fühlen; [stand] at ~!
(Mil.) rührt euch!
(b) with ~ (without difficulty) mit Leichtigkeit
[2] v.t. lindern ⟨Schmerz, Kummer⟩;
entspannen ⟨Lage⟩; verringern ⟨Belastung,
Druck, Spannung⟩
[3] v.i. nachlassen

easel /'iːzl/ n. Staffelei, die

easily /'iːzɪlɪ/ adv. leicht

easiness /'iːzɪnɪs/ n. Leichtigkeit, die

east /iːst/ [1] n. (a) Osten, der; in/to[wards]/
from the ~: im/nach/von Osten; to the ~ of
östlich von
(b) usu. E~ (Geog., Polit.) Osten, der
[2] adj. östlich; Ost⟨küste, -wind, -grenze⟩
[3] adv. nach Osten; ~ of östlich von

'**East Ber'lin** pr. n. (Hist.) Ostberlin, das

'**eastbound** adj. ⟨Zug, Verkehr usw.⟩ in
Richtung Osten

Easter /'iːstə(r)/ n. Ostern, das od. Pl.

'**Easter egg** n. Osterei, das

easterly /'iːstəlɪ/ adj. östlich; ⟨Wind⟩ aus
östlichen Richtungen

Easter 'Monday n. Ostermontag, der

eastern /'iːstən/ adj. östlich; Ost⟨grenze,
-hälfte, -seite⟩; ~ Germany Ostdeutschland
(das)

Eastern: ~ '**Europe** pr. n. Osteuropa,
(das); ~ **Euro'pean** [1] adj.
osteuropäisch; [2] n. Osteuropäer, der/
Osteuropäerin, die

Easter 'Sunday n. Ostersonntag, der

East: ~ '**German** (Hist.) [1] adj.
ostdeutsch; he/she is ~ German er ist
Ostdeutscher/sie ist Ostdeutsche; [2] n.
Ostdeutsche, der/die; ~ '**Germany** pr. n.
(Hist.) Ostdeutschland (das); ~ '**Timor**
/'tiːmɔː(r)/ pr. n. Osttimor (das)

eastward(s) /'iːstwəd(z)/ adv. ostwärts

easy /'iːzɪ/ [1] adj. (a) leicht; on ~ terms auf
Raten ⟨kaufen⟩
(b) sorglos ⟨Leben, Zeit⟩

(c) (free from constraint) ungezwungen
[2] adv. leicht; **easier said than done** leichter
gesagt als getan; **take it** ~! (calm down!)
beruhige dich!

easy: ~-**care** attrib. adj. pflegeleicht;
~ **chair** n. Sessel, der; ~-'**going** adj.
gelassen; (lax) nachlässig; ~ '**money** n.
leicht verdientes Geld

eat /iːt/ v.t. & i., ate /et, eɪt/, eaten /'iːtn/
essen; ⟨Tier:⟩ fressen
■ **eat a'way** v.t. ⟨Rost, Säure:⟩ zerfressen
■ **eat 'out** v.i. essen gehen
■ **eat 'up** v.t. aufessen; ⟨Tier:⟩ auffressen

'**eat-by date** n. Verfallsdatum, das

eaten ▶ EAT

eating: ~ **apple** n. Essapfel, der;
~ **disorder** n. Essstörung, die (meist Pl.);
~ **place** n. Essgelegenheit, die

eau-de-Cologne /əʊdəkə'ləʊn/ n.
Kölnischwasser, das

eaves /iːvz/ n. pl. Dachgesims, das

'**eavesdrop** v.i. lauschen; ~ **on** belauschen

'**eavesdropper** n. Lauscher, der/
Lauscherin, die

ebb /eb/ [1] n. Ebbe, die; be at a low ~ (fig.)
⟨Person, Stimmung, Moral:⟩ auf dem
Nullpunkt sein
[2] v.i. zurückgehen; ~ **away** (fig.)
dahinschwinden

'**ebb tide** n. Ebbe, die

ebony /'ebənɪ/ n. Ebenholz, das

EC abbr. = **European Community** EG

eccentric /ɪk'sentrɪk/ [1] adj. exzentrisch
[2] n. Exzentriker, der/Exzentrikerin, die

eccentricity /eksen'trɪsɪtɪ/ n.
Exzentrizität, die

ecclesiastical /ɪkliːzɪ'æstɪkl/ adj.
kirchlich; geistlich ⟨Musik⟩

ECG abbr. = **electrocardiogram** EKG

echo /'ekəʊ/ [1] n. Echo, das
[2] v.t. zurückwerfen; (fig.: repeat) wiederholen

éclair /eɪ'kleə(r)/ n. Eclair, das

eclipse /ɪ'klɪps/ n. (Astron.) Finsternis, die;
~ **of the sun** Sonnenfinsternis, die

'**eco-friendly** adj. umweltfreundlich

ecological /iːkə'lɒdʒɪkl/ adj. ökologisch

eco'logically adv. ökologisch; ~ aware/
sound/harmful umweltbewusst/-gerecht/
-schädlich

ecologist /iː'kɒlədʒɪst/ n. Ökologe, der/
Ökologin, die

ecology /iː'kɒlədʒɪ/ n. Ökologie, die

e-commerce /iː'kɒmɜːs/ n. (Comp.)
elektronischer Handel; E-Commerce, der

economic /iːkə'nɒmɪk/ adj. (a)
Wirtschafts⟨politik, -abkommen, -system,
-krise, -wunder⟩; wirtschaftlich ⟨Entwicklung,
Zusammenbruch⟩
(b) (giving adequate return) wirtschaftlich

economical /iːkə'nɒmɪkl/ adj.
wirtschaftlich; sparsam ⟨Person⟩; be ~ with
sth. mit etw. haushalten

eco'nomically *adv.* wirtschaftlich; (not wastefully) sparsam

economics /i:kə'nɒmɪks/ *n.* Wirtschaftswissenschaft, *die (meist Pl.)*

economist /ɪ'kɒnəmɪst/ *n.* Wirtschaftswissenschaftler, *der*/ -wissenschaftlerin, *die*

economize /ɪ'kɒnəmaɪz/ *v.i.* sparen; ∼ **on sth.** etw. sparen

economy /ɪ'kɒnəmɪ/ *n.* (a) (frugality) Sparsamkeit, *die*
(b) (instance) Einsparung, *die;* **make economies** zu Sparmaßnahmen greifen
(c) (of country etc.) Wirtschaft, *die*

economy: ∼ **class** *n.* Touristenklasse, *die;* Economyklasse, *die;* ∼ **size** *n.* Haushaltspackung, *die*

'ecosystem *n.* Ökosystem, *das*

ecstasy /'ekstəsɪ/ *n.* (a) Ekstase, *die*
(b) E∼ (drug) Ecstasy, *das*

ecstatic /ɪk'stætɪk/ *adj.* ekstatisch

ecu, ECU /'eɪkju:/ *abbr.* = **European currency unit** Ecu, *der od. die*

eddy /'edɪ/ *n.* Strudel, *der*

edge /edʒ/ 1 *n.* (a) (of knife, razor, weapon) Schneide, *die;* **on** ∼ (fig.) nervös *od.* gereizt (**about** wegen)
(b) (of solid, bed, table) Kante, *die;* (of sheet of paper, road, forest, cliff) Rand, *der*
2 *v.i.* sich schieben

edgy /'edʒɪ/ *adj.* nervös

edible /'edɪbl/ *adj.* essbar

edict /'i:dɪkt/ *n.* Erlass, *der*

edit /'edɪt/ *v.t.* herausgeben ⟨Zeitung⟩; redigieren ⟨Buch, Artikel, Manuskript⟩

edition /ɪ'dɪʃn/ *n.* Ausgabe, *die*

editor /'edɪtə(r)/ *n.* Redakteur, *der*/ Redakteurin, *die;* (of particular work) Bearbeiter, *der*/Bearbeiterin, *die;* (of newspaper) Herausgeber, *der*/Herausgeberin, *die*

editorial /edɪ'tɔ:rɪəl/ 1 *n.* Leitartikel, *der* 2 *adj.* redaktionell

EDP *abbr.* = **electronic data processing** EDV

educate /'edjʊkeɪt/ *v.t.* (a) (bring up) erziehen; (train mind and character of) bilden
(b) (provide schooling for) **he was** ∼**d at ...:** er hat seine Ausbildung in ... erhalten

educated /'edjʊkeɪtɪd/ *adj.* gebildet

education /edjʊ'keɪʃn/ *n.* Erziehung, *die;* (system) Erziehungswesen, *das*

educational /edjʊ'keɪʃənl/ *adj.* pädagogisch; Lehr⟨film, -spiele, -anstalt⟩; Erziehungs⟨methoden, -arbeit⟩

edu'cation system *n.* Bildungssystem, *das*

EEC *abbr.* = **European Economic Community** EWG

eel /i:l/ *n.* Aal, *der*

eerie /'ɪərɪ/ *adj.* unheimlich

eff /ef/ *v.i.* (sl.) ∼ **and blind** fluchen

effect /ɪ'fekt/ *n.* (a) Wirkung, *die* (**on** auf + *Akk.*); **the** ∼**s of sth. on sth.** die Auswirkungen einer Sache ⟨Gen.⟩ auf etw. ⟨Akk.⟩; **take** ∼: die erwünschte Wirkung erzielen; **in** ∼: in Wirklichkeit
(b) **come into** ∼: gültig werden; ⟨Gesetz:⟩ in Kraft treten; **put into** ∼: in Kraft setzen ⟨Gesetz⟩; verwirklichen ⟨Plan⟩; **with** ∼ **from 2 November/Monday** mit Wirkung vom 2. November/von Montag
(c) personal ∼s persönliches Eigentum; Privateigentum, *das;* household ∼s Hausrat, *der*

effective /ɪ'fektɪv/ *adj.* (a) wirksam ⟨Mittel, Maßnahmen⟩; **be** ∼ ⟨Arzneimittel:⟩ wirken
(b) (in operation) gültig; ∼ **from/as of** mit Wirkung vom

effectively *adv.* (in fact) effektiv; (with effect) wirkungsvoll

effectual /ɪ'fektjʊəl/ *adj.* wirksam

effeminate /ɪ'femɪnət/ *adj.* unmännlich

effervescent /efə'vesənt/ *adj.* sprudelnd; (fig.) übersprudelnd

effete /e'fi:t/ *adj.* verweichlicht

efficiency /ɪ'fɪʃənsɪ/ *n.* (of person) Fähigkeit, *die;* Tüchtigkeit, *die;* (of machine, factory, engine) Leistungsfähigkeit, *die;* (of organization, method) gutes Funktionieren

efficient /ɪ'fɪʃənt/ *adj.* fähig ⟨Person⟩; tüchtig ⟨Arbeiter, Sekretärin⟩; leistungsfähig ⟨Maschine, Motor, Fabrik⟩; gut funktionierend ⟨Methode, Organisation⟩

efficiently *adv.* gut

effigy /'efɪdʒɪ/ *n.* Bildnis, *das*

effing /'efɪŋ/ *adj.* (sl.) Scheiß- (salopp)

effluent /'eflʊənt/ Abwässer *Pl.*

effort /'efət/ *n.* (a) Anstrengung, *die;* Mühe, *die;* **make an/every** ∼ (physically) sich anstrengen; (mentally) sich bemühen
(b) (attempt) Versuch, *der*

'effortless *adj.* mühelos

effrontery /ɪ'frʌntərɪ/ *n.* Dreistigkeit, *die;* **have the** ∼ **to do sth.** die Stirn besitzen, etw. zu tun

effusive /ɪ'fju:sɪv/ *adj.* überschwänglich; exaltiert (geh.) ⟨Person⟩

EFL *abbr.* = **English as a foreign language**

e.g. /i:'dʒi:/ *abbr.* = **for example** z.B.

egg /eg/ *n.* Ei, *das*
■ **egg 'on** *v.t.* anstacheln

egg: ∼**cup** *n.* Eierbecher, *der;* ∼**plant** *n.* Aubergine, *die;* (fruit also) Eierfrucht, *die;* (plant also) Eierpflanze, *die;* ∼**shell** *n.* Eierschale, *die;* ∼ **timer** *n.* Eieruhr, *die;* ∼ **white** *n.* Eiweiß, *das;* ∼ **yolk** *n.* Eigelb, *das*

ego /'egəʊ, 'i:gəʊ/ *n., pl.* ∼**s** (a) (Psych.) Ego, *das*
(b) (self-esteem) Selbstbewusstsein, *das*

egotism /'egətɪzm/ *n.* (a) Egotismus, *der* (fachspr.); Ichbezogenheit, *die* ⸱⸱⸱⟶

(b) (self-conceit) Egotismus, *der;* Selbstgefälligkeit, *die*

egotist /'egətɪst/ *n.* Egotist, *der*/Egotistin, *die* (fachspr.); (self-centred person) Egozentriker, *der*/Egozentrikerin, *die*

egotistic /egə'tɪstɪk/**, egotistical** /egə'tɪstɪkl/ *adj.* **(a)** ichbezogen ⟨*Rede, Gespräch*⟩
(b) selbstsüchtig, selbstgefällig ⟨*Person*⟩

Egypt /'i:dʒɪpt/ *pr. n.* Ägypten (*das*)

Egyptian /ɪ'dʒɪpʃn/ ① *adj.* ägyptisch; **sb. is ~:** jmd. ist Ägypter/Ägypterin
② *n.* (person) Ägypter, *der*/Ägypterin, *die*

eiderdown /'aɪdədaʊn/ *n.* Federbett, *das*

eight /eɪt/ ① *adj.* acht; **at ~:** um acht; **half past ~:** halb neun; **~ thirty** acht Uhr dreißig; **~ ten/fifty** zehn nach acht/vor neun; (esp. in timetable) acht Uhr zehn/fünfzig; **~-year-old boy** achtjähriger Junge; **an ~-year-old** ein Achtjähriger/eine Achtjährige; **at [the age of] ~, aged ~:** mit acht Jahren; **~ times** achtmal
② *n.* Acht, *die;* **the first/last ~:** die ersten/ letzten acht; **there were ~ of us present** wir waren [zu] acht

eighteen /eɪ'ti:n/ ① *adj.* achtzehn
② *n.* Achtzehn, *die. See also* EIGHT

eighteenth /eɪ'ti:nθ/ ① *adj.* achtzehnt...
② *n.* (fraction) Achtzehntel, *das. See also* EIGHTH

eighth /eɪtθ/ ① *adj.* acht...; **be/come ~:** Achter sein/als Achter ankommen; **~largest** achtgrößt...
② *n.* (in sequence, rank) Achte, *der*/*die*/*das;* (fraction) Achtel, *das;* **the ~ of May** der achte Mai

eightieth /'eɪtɪɪθ/ *adj.* achtzigst...

eighty /'eɪtɪ/ ① *adj.* achtzig
② *n.* Achtzig, *die;* **the eighties** (years) die Achtzigerjahre; **be in one's eighties** in den Achtzigern sein. *See also* EIGHT

Eire /'eərə/ *pr. n.* Irland, *das;* Eire, *das*

either /'aɪðə(r), 'i:ðə(r)/ ① *adj.* **(a)** (each) **at ~ end of the table** an beiden Enden des Tisches
(b) (one or other) [irgend]ein ... [von beiden]; **take ~ one** nimm einen/eine/eins von [den] beiden
② *pron.* **(a)** (each) beide *Pl.;* **I can't cope with ~:** ich kann mit keinem von beiden fertig werden
(b) (one or other) einer/eine/ein[e]s [von beiden]
③ *adv.* auch [nicht]; **'I don't like that ~:** ich mag es auch nicht
④ *conj.* **~ ... or ...:** entweder ... oder ...; (after negation) weder ... noch ...

ejaculate /ɪ'dʒækjʊleɪt/① *v.t.* (utter suddenly) ausstoßen
② *v.i.* (eject semen) ejakulieren

eject /ɪ'dʒekt/ ① *v.t.* **(a)** (from hall, meeting) hinauswerfen (from aus)
(b) ⟨*Gerät:*⟩ auswerfen, ⟨*Person:*⟩ herausholen ⟨*Kassette*⟩

② *v.i.* sich hinauskatapultieren

ejector seat /ɪ'dʒektə si:t/ *n.* Schleudersitz, *der*

eke out /i:k 'aʊt/ *v.t.* strecken; **~ out a living** sich (*Dat.*) seinen Lebensunterhalt notdürftig verdienen

elaborate ① /ɪ'læbərət/ *adj.* kompliziert; kunstvoll [gearbeitet] ⟨*Arrangement, Verzierung*⟩
② /ɪ'læbəreɪt/ *v.i.* mehr ins Detail gehen; **~ on** näher ausführen

elapse /ɪ'læps/ *v.i.* ⟨*Zeit:*⟩ vergehen

elastic /ɪ'læstɪk/ ① *adj.* elastisch
② *n.* (~ band) Gummiband, *das*

elastic 'band *n.* Gummiband, *das*

elated /ɪ'leɪtɪd/ *adj.* freudig erregt; **be** *or* **feel ~:** in Hochstimmung sein

elation /ɪ'leɪʃn/ *n.* freudige Erregung

elbow /'elbəʊ/ ① *n.* Ell[en]bogen, *der*
② *v.t.* **~ sb. aside** jmdn. mit dem Ellenbogen zur Seite stoßen

elbow: ~ grease *n.* (joc.) Muskelkraft, *die;* **~ room** *n.* Ell[en]bogenfreiheit, *die*

elder[1] /'eldə(r)/ ① *attrib. adj.* älter...
② *n.* **(a)** (senior) Ältere, *der*/*die*
(b) (village ~, church ~) Älteste, *der*/*die*

elder[2] *n.* (Bot.) Holunder, *der*

'elderberry *n.* Holunderbeere, *die*

elderly /'eldəlɪ/ ① *adj.* älter
② *n. pl.* **the ~:** ältere Menschen

eldest /'eldɪst/ *adj.* ältest...

elect /ɪ'lekt/ ① *adj. postpos.* gewählt; **the President ~:** der designierte Präsident
② *v.t.* wählen; **~ sb. chairman** jmdn. zum Vorsitzenden wählen

election /ɪ'lekʃn/ *n.* Wahl, *die;* **general ~:** allgemeine Wahlen *Pl.;* **~ results** Wahlergebnisse *Pl.*

e'lection campaign *n.* Wahlkampagne, *die*

electioneer /ɪlekʃə'nɪə(r)/ *v.i.* **be/go ~ing** Wahlkampf machen

elector /ɪ'lektə(r)/ *n.* Wähler, *der*/Wählerin, *die*

electoral /ɪ'lektərl/ *adj.* Wahl-

electoral 'college *n.* Wahlmännergremium, *das;* Wahlausschuss, *der*

electorate /ɪ'lektərət/ *n.* Wähler *Pl.*

electric /ɪ'lektrɪk/ *adj.* elektrisch; Elektro⟨*kabel, -motor, -herd, -kessel*⟩; Strom⟨*versorgung*⟩; (fig.) spannungsgeladen ⟨*Atmosphäre*⟩

electrical /ɪ'lektrɪkl/ *adj.* elektrisch; Elektro⟨*abteilung, -handel, -geräte*⟩

electric: ~ 'blanket *n.* Heizdecke, *die;* **~ 'chair** *n.* elektrischer Stuhl; **~ cooker** *n.* Elektroherd, *der;* **~ 'fire** *n.* [elektrischer] Heizofen; **~ gui'tar** *n.* elektrische Gitarre; E-Gitarre, *die*

electrician /ɪlek'trɪʃn/ *n.* Elektriker, *der*/ Elektrikerin, *die*

electricity /ɪlek'trɪsɪtɪ/ n. Elektrizität, die
electricity: ~ **bill** n. Stromrechnung, die;
~ **man** n. (fitter) Elektroinstallateur, der;
(meter reader, collector) Stromableser, der;
~ **meter** n. Stromzähler, der
electric 'shock n. Stromschlag, der
electrify /ɪ'lektrɪfaɪ/ v.t. elektrifizieren;
(fig.) elektrisieren
electro'cardiogram n.
Elektrokardiogramm, das
electrocute /ɪ'lektrəkju:t/ v.t. durch
Stromschlag töten
electrode /ɪ'lektrəʊd/ n. Elektrode, die
electro'magnet n. Elektromagnet, der
electromag'netic adj.
elektromagnetisch
electron /ɪ'lektrɒn/ n. Elektron, das
electronic /ɪlek'trɒnɪk/ adj. elektronisch
electronic: ~ **'cash** n. elektronisches
Geld; ~ **'mail** n. elektronische Post;
~ **'publishing** n. elektronisches
Publizieren
electronics /ɪlek'trɒnɪks/ n. Elektronik,
die
electron 'microscope n.
Elektronenmikroskop, das
elegance /'elɪɡəns/ n. Eleganz, die
elegant /'elɪɡənt/ adj. elegant
elegy /'elɪdʒɪ/ n. Elegie, die
element /'elɪmənt/ n. (a) Element, das
(b) (Electr.) Heizelement, das
(c) ~s (rudiments) Grundlagen Pl.
elementary /elɪ'mentərɪ/ adj. elementar;
grundlegend ⟨Fakten, Wissen⟩;
Grundschul⟨bildung⟩; Grund⟨kurs,
-ausbildung, -kenntnisse⟩
elementary: ~ **'particle** n. (Phys.)
Elementarteilchen, das; ~ **school** n.
Grundschule, die
elephant /'elɪfənt/ n. Elefant, der; white ~
(fig.) nutzloser Besitz; be a white ~
⟨Gebäude, Einkaufszentrum usw.:⟩ reine
Geldverschwendung sein
elevate /'elɪveɪt/ v.t. [empor]heben
elevation /elɪ'veɪʃn/ n. (a) (height) Höhe,
die
(b) (Archit.) Aufriss, der
elevator /'elɪveɪtə(r)/ n. (Amer.) Aufzug,
der; Fahrstuhl, der
eleven /ɪ'levn/ ①adj. elf
②n. (also Sport) Elf, die. See also EIGHT
elevenses /ɪ'levnzɪz/ n. sing. or pl. (Brit.
coll.) ≈ zweites Frühstück [gegen elf Uhr]
eleventh /ɪ'levnθ/ ①adj. elft...; at the
~ **hour** in letzter Minute
②n. (fraction) Elftel, das. See also EIGHTH
elf /elf/ n., pl. **elves** /elvz/ Elf, der/ Elfe, die
elicit /ɪ'lɪsɪt/ v.t. entlocken (from Dat.);
gewinnen ⟨Unterstützung⟩
eligible /'elɪdʒɪbl/ adj. be ~ for sth. (fit) für
etw. geeignet sein; (entitled) zu etw. berechtigt
sein

eliminate /ɪ'lɪmɪneɪt/ v.t. (a) (remove)
beseitigen; ausschließen ⟨Möglichkeit⟩
(b) (exclude) ausschließen; be ~d (Sport)
ausscheiden
elimination /ɪlɪmɪ'neɪʃn/ n. (a) (removal)
Beseitigung, die; process of ~:
Ausleseverfahren, das
(b) (exclusion) Ausschluss, der; (Sport)
Ausscheiden, das
élite /eɪ'li:t/ n. Elite, die
élitist /eɪ'li:tɪst/adj. elitär; Elite⟨denken⟩
elk /elk/ n., pl. ~s or same (a) (deer) Elch,
der
(b) (moose) Riesenelch, der
ellipse /ɪ'lɪps/ n. Ellipse, die
elliptical /ɪ'lɪptɪkl/ adj. elliptisch
elm /elm/ n. Ulme, die
elocution /elə'kju:ʃn/ n. (art) Sprechkunst,
die
elongated /'i:lɒŋɡeɪtɪd/ adj. lang gestreckt
elope /ɪ'ləʊp/ v.i. durchbrennen (ugs.)
eloquence /'eləkwəns/ n. Beredtheit, die
eloquent /'eləkwənt/ adj. beredt ⟨Person⟩;
gewandt ⟨Stil, Redner⟩
else /els/ adv. (a) (besides) sonst [noch];
somebody/something ~: [noch] jemand
anders/noch etwas; **everybody/everything** ~:
alle anderen/alles andere; **who/what/when/
how** ~? wer/was/wann/wie sonst noch?;
why ~? warum sonst?
(b) (instead) ander...; **sb.** ~'**s hat** der Hut von
jmd. anders; **anybody/anything** ~?
[irgend]jemand anders/[irgend]etwas
anderes?; **somebody/something** ~: jemand
anders/etwas anderes; **everybody/everything**
~: alle anderen/alles andere
(c) (otherwise) sonst; **or** ~: oder aber; **do it or**
~ ...! tun Sie es, sonst ...!
'elsewhere adv. woanders
elude /ɪ'lju:d/ v.t. (avoid) ausweichen
(+ Dat.); (escape from) entkommen (+ Dat.)
elusive /ɪ'lju:sɪv/ adj. schwer zu erreichen
⟨Person⟩; schwer zu fassen ⟨Straftäter⟩;
schwer definierbar ⟨Begriff, Sinn⟩
elves pl. of ELF
emaciated /ɪ'meɪsɪeɪtɪd/ adj. abgezehrt
e-mail /'i:meɪl/ ① n. E-Mail, die; ~ **address**
E-Mail-Adresse, die; ~ **message** E-Mail, die
②v.t. per E-Mail übermitteln ⟨Ergebnisse,
Datei usw.⟩; ~ **sb.** jmdm. eine E-Mail
schicken
emancipated /ɪ'mænsɪpeɪtɪd/ adj.
emanzipiert: **become** ~: sich emanzipieren
emancipation /ɪmænsɪ'peɪʃn/ n.
Emanzipation, die
embalm /ɪm'bɑ:m/ v.t. einbalsamieren
embankment /ɪm'bæŋkmənt/ n. Damm,
der
embargo /em'bɑ:ɡəʊ/ n., pl. ~es Embargo,
das; **put or lay an** ~ **on sth.** etw. mit einem
Embargo belegen

embark /ɪmˈbɑːk/ v.i. (a) sich einschiffen (for nach)
(b) ~ [up]on sth. etw. in Angriff nehmen

embarkation /embɑːˈkeɪʃn/ n. Einschiffung, die

embarrass /ɪmˈbærəs/ v.t. in Verlegenheit bringen

embarrassed /ɪmˈbærəst/ adj. verlegen; feel ~: verlegen sein

em'barrassing adj. peinlich

em'barrassment n. Verlegenheit, die

embassy /ˈembəsɪ/ n. Botschaft, die

embed /ɪmˈbed/ v.t., -dd-: (a) (fix) einlassen; ~ sth. in cement/concrete etw. einzementieren/einbetonieren; ~ded in the mud im Schlamm versunken; ~ded sentence (Ling.) eingeschobener Satz

embellish /emˈbelɪʃ/ v.t. beschönigen ⟨Wahrheit⟩; ausschmücken ⟨Geschichte, Bericht⟩

embers /ˈembəz/ n. pl. Glut, die

embezzle /ɪmˈbezl/ v.t. unterschlagen

embitter /ɪmˈbɪtə(r)/ v.t. verbittern

emblem /ˈembləm/ n. Emblem, das

embody /ɪmˈbɒdɪ/ v.t. verkörpern

embrace /ɪmˈbreɪs/ [1] v.t. umarmen; (fig.: accept, adopt) annehmen
[2] v.i. sich umarmen
[3] n. Umarmung, die

embroider /ɪmˈbrɔɪdə(r)/ v.t. sticken ⟨Muster⟩; besticken ⟨Tuch, Kleid⟩; (fig.) ausschmücken

embroidery /ɪmˈbrɔɪdərɪ/ n. Stickerei, die

embroil /ɪmˈbrɔɪl/ v.t. become/be ~ed in sth. in etw. (Akk.) verwickelt werden/sein

embryo /ˈembrɪəʊ/ n. Embryo, der

embryonic /embrɪˈɒnɪk/ adj. (Biol., fig.) Embryonal⟨entwicklung, -struktur, -zustand, -stadium⟩; unausgereift ⟨Vorstellung⟩

emerald /ˈemərəld/ [1] n. Smaragd, der
[2] adj. smaragdgrün; the E~ Isle die Grüne Insel

emerald 'green n. Smaragdgrün, das

emerge /ɪˈmɜːdʒ/ v.i. auftauchen (from aus, from behind hinter + Dat.); ⟨Wahrheit:⟩ an den Tag kommen; it ~s that ...: es stellt sich heraus, dass ...

emergency /ɪˈmɜːdʒənsɪ/ [1] n. Notfall, der; in an or in case of ~: im Notfall; declare a state of ~: den Ausnahmezustand ausrufen
[2] adj. Not-

emergency: ~ exit n. Notausgang, der; ~ **services** n. pl. Hilfsdienste Pl.

'emery paper n. Schmirgelpapier, das

emetic /ɪˈmetɪk/ (Med.) n. Emetikum, das (fachspr.); Brechmittel, das

emigrant /ˈemɪɡrənt/ n. Auswanderer, der/Auswanderin, die

emigrate /ˈemɪɡreɪt/ v.i. auswandern (to nach, from aus)

emigration /emɪˈɡreɪʃn/ n. Auswanderung, die (to nach, from aus)

eminence /ˈemɪnəns/ n. hohes Ansehen

eminent /ˈemɪnənt/ adj. bedeutend; herausragend

emission /ɪˈmɪʃn/ n. Emission, die (fachspr.); (process also) Abgabe, die

emit /ɪˈmɪt/ v.t., -tt- abgeben, emittieren (fachspr.) ⟨Wärme, Strahlung usw.⟩; ausstoßen ⟨Rauch⟩

emoticon /ɪˈmɒtɪkɒn/ n. (Comp.) Emoticon, das

emotion /ɪˈməʊʃn/ n. Gefühl, das

emotional /ɪˈməʊʃənl/ adj. emotional; Gemüts⟨zustand, -störung⟩; gefühlvoll ⟨Stimme⟩

e'motionally adv. emotional; gefühlvoll ⟨sprechen⟩; ~ disturbed seelisch gestört

emotive /ɪˈməʊtɪv/ adj. emotional

empathize /ˈempəθaɪz/ v.i. ~ with sb. sich in jmdn. hineinversetzen; ~ with sth. etw. nachempfinden

empathy /ˈempəθɪ/ n. Empathie, die (Psych.); Einfühlung, die

emperor /ˈempərə(r)/ n. Kaiser, der

emphasis /ˈemfəsɪs/ n., pl. **emphases** /ˈemfəsiːz/ Betonung, die; lay or place or put ~ on sth. etw. betonen

emphasize /ˈemfəsaɪz/ v.t. betonen

emphatic /ɪmˈfætɪk/ adj. nachdrücklich; demonstrativ ⟨Ablehnung⟩; be ~ that ...: darauf bestehen, dass ...

em'phatically adv. nachdrücklich

empire /ˈempaɪə(r)/ n. Reich, das

empirical /ɪmˈpɪrɪkl/ adj. empirisch

employ /ɪmˈplɔɪ/ v.t. (a) (take on) einstellen; (have working for one) beschäftigen; be ~ed by a company bei einer Firma arbeiten
(b) (use) einsetzen (for, in, on für); anwenden ⟨Methode, List⟩ (for, in, on bei)

employee (Amer.: **employe**) /emplɔɪˈiː, emˈplɔɪiː/ n. Angestellte, der/die

employer /ɪmˈplɔɪə(r)/ n. Arbeitgeber, der/-geberin, die

employment /ɪmˈplɔɪmənt/ n. (a) (work) Arbeit, die
(b) (regular trade or profession) Beschäftigung, die

employment: ~ agency n. Stellenvermittlung, die; ~ **office** n. (Brit.) Arbeitsamt, das

empower /ɪmˈpaʊə(r)/ v.t. (authorize) ermächtigen; (enable) befähigen

empress /ˈempris/ n. Kaiserin, die

emptiness /ˈemptɪnɪs/ n. Leere, die

empty /ˈemptɪ/ [1] adj. leer; frei ⟨Sitz, Parkplatz⟩
[2] v.t. leeren; (pour) schütten (over über + Akk.)
[3] v.i. sich leeren

'empty-handed adj. mit leeren Händen

EMS *abbr.* = **European Monetary System** EWS

emu /'i:mju:/ *n.* (Ornith.) Emu, *der*

EMU *abbr.* = **Economic and Monetary Union** WWU

emulate /'emjʊleɪt/ *v.t.* nacheifern (+ *Dat.*)

emulsion /ɪ'mʌlʃn/ *n.* **(a)** Emulsion, *die*
(b) ▶ EMULSION PAINT

e'mulsion paint *n.* Dispersionsfarbe, *die*

enable /ɪ'neɪbl/ *v.t.* ~ sb. to do sth. es jmdm. ermöglichen; etw. zu tun

enamel /ɪ'næml/ 1 *n.* Email, *das* 2 *v.t.*, (Brit.) -ll- emaillieren

enchant /ɪn'tʃɑ:nt/ *v.t.* verzaubern; (delight) entzücken

en'chanted *adj.* verzaubert

en'chanting *adj.* entzückend

en'chantment *n.* Verzauberung, *die;* (fig.) Zauber, *der*

encircle /ɪn'sɜ:kl/ *v.t.* umgeben

encl. *abbr.* = **enclosed, enclosure[s]** Anl.

enclave /'enkleɪv/ *n.* Enklave, *die*

enclose /ɪn'kləʊz/ *v.t.* **(a)** (surround) umgeben; (shut up or in) einschließen
(b) (with letter) beilegen (**with, in** *Dat.*); please find ~d anbei erhalten Sie

enclosure /ɪn'kləʊʒə(r)/ *n.* **(a)** (in zoo) Gehege, *das*
(b) (with letter) Anlage, *die*

encode /ɪn'kəʊd/ *v.t.* verschlüsseln; chiffrieren

encore /'ɒŋkɔ:(r)/ 1 *int.* Zugabe! 2 *n.* Zugabe, *die*

encounter /ɪn'kaʊntə(r)/ 1 *v.t.* (as adversary) treffen auf (+ *Akk.*); (by chance) begegnen (+ *Dat.*); stoßen auf (+ *Akk.*) ⟨*Problem, Widerstand usw.*⟩ 2 *n.* (chance meeting) Begegnung, *die*

encourage /ɪn'kʌrɪdʒ/ *v.t.* ermutigen; (promote) fördern

encouragement *n.* Ermutigung, *die* (**from** durch)

encroach /ɪn'krəʊtʃ/ *v.i.* ~ **on** eindringen in (+ *Akk.*); in Anspruch nehmen ⟨*Zeit*⟩

encrypt /en'krɪpt/ *v.t.* (Comp.) verschlüsseln ⟨*Daten etc.*⟩

encumber /ɪn'kʌmbə(r)/ *v.t.* belasten

encumbrance /ɪn'kʌmbrəns/ *n.* Belastung, *die*

encyclopaedia /ɪnsaɪklə'pi:dɪə/ *n.* Lexikon, *das;* Enzyklopädie, *die*

encyclopaedic /ɪnsaɪklə'pi:dɪk/ *adj.* enzyklopädisch

end /end/ 1 *n.* **(a)** Ende, *das;* (of nose, hair, finger) Spitze, *die;* **from** ~ **to** ~: von einem Ende zum anderen; **at the** ~ **of** 1987/**March** Ende 1987/März; **in the** ~: schließlich; **come to an** ~: ein Ende nehmen; **be at an** ~: zu Ende sein
(b) (of box, packet, etc.) Schmalseite, *die;* (top/ bottom surface) Ober-/Unterseite, *die;* **on** ~:

hochkant; **make** ~s **meet** (fig.) zurechtkommen; **no** ~ **of** (coll.) unendlich viel/viele
(c) (remnant) Rest, *der;* (of cigarette) Stummel, *der*
(d) (purpose, object) Ziel, *das;* ~ **in itself** Selbstzweck, *der*
2 *v.t.* beenden
3 *v.i.* enden

▪ **end 'up** *v.i.* enden; ~ **up in** (coll.) landen in (+ *Dat.*); ~ **up [as] a teacher** (coll.) schließlich Lehrer werden

endanger /ɪn'deɪndʒə(r)/ *v.t.* gefährden

endear /ɪn'dɪə(r)/ *v.t.* ~ **sb./sth./oneself to sb.** jmdn./etw./sich bei jmdm. beliebt machen

en'dearing *adj.* reizend; gewinnend ⟨*Lächeln, Art*⟩

endeavour (*Brit.; Amer.:* **endeavor**) /ɪn'devə(r)/ 1 *v.i.* ~ **to do sth.** sich bemühen, etw. zu tun 2 *n.* Bemühung, *die;* (attempt) Versuch, *der*

'ending *n.* Schluss, *der;* (of word) Endung, *die*

endive /'endaɪv/ *n.* Endivie, *die*

'endless *adj.* endlos

'endlessly *adv.* unaufhörlich ⟨*streiten, schwatzen*⟩

endorse /ɪn'dɔ:s/ *v.t.* **(a)** indossieren ⟨*Scheck*⟩
(b) beipflichten (+ *Dat.*) ⟨*Meinung*⟩; billigen ⟨*Entscheidung, Handlung*⟩; unterstützen ⟨*Vorschlag*⟩
(c) (Brit. Law) einen Strafvermerk machen auf (+ *Akk. od. Dat.*)

en'dorsement *n.* **(a)** (of cheque) Indossament, *das*
(b) (support) Billigung, *die;* (of proposal) Unterstützung, *die*
(c) (Brit. Law) Strafvermerk, *der*

endow /ɪn'daʊ/ *v.t.* ⟨über Stiftungen⟩ eine Stiftung] finanzieren; stiften ⟨*Preis, Lehrstuhl*⟩; **be** ~**ed with charm/a talent for music** Charme/musikalisches Talent besitzen

en'dowment mortgage *n.* ≈ Tilgungslebensversicherung, *die;*

end: ~ **'product** *n.* Endprodukt, *das;* ~ **re'sult** *n.* Ergebnis, *das;* (consequence) Folge, *die*

endurable /ɪn'djʊərəbl/ *adj.* erträglich

endurance /ɪn'djʊərəns/ *n.* Ausdauer, *die*

en'durance test *n.* Belastungsprobe, *die*

endure /ɪn'djʊə(r)/ *v.t.* ertragen

enema /'enəmə/ *n.* Einlauf, *der*

enemy /'enəmɪ/ 1 *n.* Feind, *der* (**of, to** Gen.) 2 *adj.* feindlich

energetic /enə'dʒetɪk/ *adj.* energiegeladen; (active) tatkräftig

energy /'enədʒɪ/ *n.* Energie, *die*

energy: ~ **consumption** *n.* Energieverbrauch, *der;* ~ **crisis** *n.*   ⋯⋗

Energiekrise, *die;* ~ **resources** *n. pl.*
Energieressourcen *Pl.;* ~**saving** *adj.*
Energie sparend; ~**-saving lamp**
Energiesparlampe, *die*

enforce /ɪn'fɔːs/ *v.t.* durchsetzen; sorgen
für ⟨*Disziplin*⟩; ~**d** erzwungen ⟨*Schweigen*⟩;
unfreiwillig ⟨*Untätigkeit*⟩

ENG *abbr.* = **electronic news-
gathering** elektronische
Berichterstattung; EB

engage /ɪn'geɪdʒ/ **1** *v.t.* (a) (hire) einstellen
⟨*Arbeiter*⟩; engagieren ⟨*Sänger*⟩
(b) wecken ⟨*Interesse*⟩; auf sich (*Akk.*) ziehen
⟨*Aufmerksamkeit*⟩
(c) ~ **the clutch/first gear** einkuppeln/den
ersten Gang einlegen
2 *v.i.* ~ **in** sth. sich an etw. (*Dat.*)
beteiligen; ~ **in politics** sich politisch
engagieren

engaged /ɪn'geɪdʒd/ *adj.* (a) **be** ~ [**to be
married**] [**to sb.**] [mit jmdm.] verlobt sein; **get**
~ [**to be married**] [**to sb.**] sich [mit jmdm.]
verloben
(b) **be** ~ **in** sth./**in doing** sth. mit etw.
beschäftigt sein/damit beschäftigt sein, etw.
zu tun; **be otherwise** ~: etwas anderes
vorhaben
(c) besetzt ⟨*Toilette, [Telefon]anschluss,
Nummer*⟩; ~ **signal** *or* **tone** (Brit.)
Besetztzeichen, *das*

en'gagement *n.* (a) (to be married)
Verlobung, *die* (**to** mit)
(b) (appointment) Verabredung, *die*

en'gagement ring *n.* Verlobungsring,
der

engaging /ɪn'geɪdʒɪŋ/ *adj.* bezaubernd;
einnehmend ⟨*Persönlichkeit, Art*⟩

engine /'endʒɪn/ *n.* (a) Motor, *der;* (rocket/jet
~) Triebwerk, *das*
(b) (locomotive) Lok[omotive], *die*

'engine driver *n.* Lok[omotiv]führer, *der*

engineer /endʒɪ'nɪə(r)/ **1** *n.* (a) Ingenieur,
der/Ingenieurin, *die;* (service ~, installation ~)
Techniker, *der*/Technikerin, *die*
(b) (Amer.: engine driver) Lok[omotiv]führer,
der
2 *v.t.* arrangieren

engi'neering *n.* Technik, *die*

England /'ɪŋglənd/ *pr. n.* England (*das*)

English /'ɪŋglɪʃ/ **1** *adj.* englisch; **he/she is**
~: er ist Engländer/sie ist Engländerin
2 *n.* (a) Englisch, *das;* **say** sth. **in** ~: etw.
auf Englisch sagen; **I cannot** *or* **do not speak**
~: ich spreche kein Englisch; **translate into/
from** [**the**] ~: ins Englische/aus dem
Englischen übersetzen
(b) *pl.* **the** ~: die Engländer *Pl.*

English: ~ **'breakfast** *n.* englisches
Frühstück; ~ **'Channel** *pr. n.* **the**
~ **Channel** der [Ärmel]kanal; ~**man** /-mən/
n., pl. ~**men** /-mən/ Engländer, *der;*
~**woman** *n.* Engländerin, *die*

engrave /ɪn'greɪv/ *v.t.* gravieren;
eingravieren ⟨*Namen, Figur usw.*⟩

engraving /ɪn'greɪvɪŋ/ *n.* Stich, *der;* (from
wood) Holzschnitt, *der*

engross /ɪn'grəʊs/ *v.t.* fesseln; **be** ~**ed in**
sth. in etw. (*Akk.*) vertieft sein; **become** *or*
get ~**ed in** sth. sich in etw. (*Akk.*) vertiefen

engrossing /ɪn'grəʊsɪŋ/ *adj.* fesselnd

engulf /ɪn'gʌlf/ *v.t.* verschlingen

enhance /ɪn'hɑːns/ *v.t.* erhöhen ⟨*Wert,
Aussichten, Schönheit*⟩; verstärken
⟨*Wirkung*⟩; heben ⟨*Aussehen*⟩

enigma /ɪ'nɪgmə/ *n.* Rätsel, *das*

enigmatic /enɪg'mætɪk/ *adj.* rätselhaft

enjoy /ɪn'dʒɔɪ/ **1** *v.t.* (a) **I** ~**ed the book/
work** das Buch/die Arbeit hat mir gefallen;
he ~**s reading/travelling** er liest/reist gern
(b) genießen ⟨*Rechte, Privilegien, Vorteile*⟩
2 *v. refl.* sich amüsieren

enjoyable /ɪn'dʒɔɪəbl/ *adj.* schön;
angenehm ⟨*Empfindung, Arbeit*⟩;
unterhaltsam ⟨*Buch, Film, Stück*⟩

en'joyment *n.* Vergnügen, *das* (**of** an
+ *Dat.*)

enlarge /ɪn'lɑːdʒ/ **1** *v.t.* vergrößern;
verbreitern ⟨*Straße, Durchgang*⟩
2 *v.i.* ~ [**up**]**on** sth. etw. weiter ausführen

en'largement *n.* Vergrößerung, *die;*
(making wider) Verbreiterung, *die*

enlighten /ɪn'laɪtn/ *v.t.* aufklären (**on, as to**
über + *Akk.*).

en'lightenment *n.* Aufklärung, *die*

enlist /ɪn'lɪst/ **1** *v.t.* (obtain) gewinnen
2 *v.i.* ~ [**for the army/navy**] in die Armee/
Marine eintreten; ~ [**as a soldier**] Soldat
werden

enliven /ɪn'laɪvn/ *v.t.* beleben

enmity /'enmɪtɪ/ *n.* Feindschaft, *die*

enormous /ɪ'nɔːməs/ *adj.* enorm; riesig,
gewaltig ⟨*Figur, Tier, Menge*⟩

e'normously *adv.* enorm

enough /ɪ'nʌf/ **1** *adj.* genug; **there's**
~ **room** es ist Platz genug
2 *n.* genug; **be** ~ **to do** sth. genügen, etw.
zu tun; **have had** ~ [**of** sb./sth.] genug [von
jmdm./etw.] haben; **I've had** ~! jetzt reicht's
mir aber!
3 *adv.* genug; **oddly/funnily** ~:
merkwürdigerweise/(ugs.) komischerweise

enquire /ɪn'kwaɪə(r)/ **1** *v.i.* sich
erkundigen (**about, after** nach, **of** bei); ~ **into**
untersuchen
2 *v.t.* sich erkundigen nach ⟨*Weg, Namen*⟩

enquiring /ɪn'kwaɪərɪŋ/ *adj.* fragend;
forschend ⟨*Geist*⟩

enquiry /ɪn'kwaɪərɪ/ *n.* (a) (question)
Erkundigung, *die* (**into** über + *Akk.*); **make
enquiries** Erkundigungen einziehen; ~ **desk,**
~ **office** Auskunft, *die*
(b) (investigation) Untersuchung, *die*

enrage /ɪn'reɪdʒ/ *v.t.* wütend machen; **be**
~**d by** sth. über etw. (*Akk.*) wütend werden

enrich /ɪn'rɪtʃ/ *v.t.* reich machen; (fig.)
bereichern

enrol (*Amer.*: **enroll**) /ɪn'rəʊl/ ⓵ *v.i.*, -ll-
sich einschreiben; ~ **for a course** sich zu
einem Kurs anmelden
  ⓶ *v.t.* einschreiben

en'rolment (*Amer.*: **en'rollment**) *n.*
Einschreibung, *die*

en route /ɑ̃ 'ruːt/ *adv.* unterwegs; ~ **to
Scotland/for Edinburgh** auf dem Weg nach
Schottland/Edinburgh

ensign /'ensaɪn, 'ensn/ *n.* Hoheitszeichen,
das

enslave /ɪn'sleɪv/ *v.t.* versklaven

ensue /ɪn'sjuː/ *v.i.* folgen (**from** aus); **the
discussion which** ~**d** die anschließende
Diskussion

ensure /ɪn'ʃʊə(r)/ *v.t.* ~ **that** ... (see to it
that) gewährleisten, dass ...; ~ **sth.** etw.
gewährleisten

entail /ɪn'teɪl/ *v.t.* mit sich bringen; **sth.** ~**s
doing sth.** etw. bedeutet, dass man etw. tun
muss

entangle /ɪn'tæŋgl/ *v.t.* sich verfangen
lassen; **get** *or* **become** ~**d in** *or* **with sth.**
sich in etw. (*Dat.*) verfangen

enter /'entə(r)/ ⓵ *v.i.* (a) hineingehen;
⟨*Fahrzeug:*⟩ hineinfahren; (come in)
hereinkommen; (into room) eintreten
  (b) (register as competitor) sich zur Teilnahme
anmelden (**for** an + *Dat.*)
  ⓶ *v.t.* (a) [hinein]gehen in (+ *Akk.*);
⟨*Fahrzeug:*⟩ [hinein]fahren in (+ *Akk.*);
betreten ⟨*Gebäude, Zimmer*⟩; einlaufen in
(+ *Akk.*) ⟨*Hafen*⟩; einreisen in (+ *Akk.*)
⟨*Land*⟩; (come into) [herein]kommen in
(+ *Akk.*)
  (b) teilnehmen an (+ *Dat.*) ⟨*Rennen,
Wettbewerb*⟩
  (c) (in book etc.) eintragen (**in** in + *Akk.*)
  (d) (Comp.) eingeben ⟨*Daten usw.*⟩; **press** ~:
'Enter' drücken
  ■ '**enter into** *v.t.* aufnehmen
⟨*Verhandlungen*⟩; eingehen ⟨*Verpflichtung*⟩;
schließen ⟨*Vertrag*⟩
  ■ '**enter [up]on** *v.t.* beginnen

'**enter key** *n.* (Comp.) Entertaste, *die;*
Eingabetaste, *die*

enterprise /'entəpraɪz/ *n.* (a) (undertaking)
Unternehmen, *das;* **free/private** ~: freies/
privates Unternehmertum
  (b) (enterprising spirit) Unternehmungsgeist,
der

enterprising /'entəpraɪzɪŋ/ *adj.*
unternehmungslustig

entertain /entə'teɪn/ *v.t.* (a) (amuse)
unterhalten
  (b) (receive as guest) bewirten
  (c) haben ⟨*Vorstellung*⟩; hegen (geh.) ⟨*Gefühl,
Verdacht, Zweifel*⟩; (consider) in Erwägung
ziehen

enter'tainer *n.* Unterhalter, *der/*
Unterhalterin, *die*

enter'taining *adj.* unterhaltsam

enter'tainment *n.* (a) (amusement)
Unterhaltung, *die*

  (b) (performance, show) Veranstaltung, *die*

enthral (*Amer.*: **enthrall**) /ɪn'θrɔːl/ *v.t.*,
-ll- gefangen nehmen (fig.)

enthuse /ɪn'θjuːz/ ⓵ *v.i.* in Begeisterung
ausbrechen (**about** über + *Akk.*)
  ⓶ *v.t.* begeistern

enthusiasm /ɪn'θjuːzɪæzm/ *n.*
Begeisterung, *die*

enthusiast /ɪn'θjuːzɪæst/ *n.* Enthusiast,
der; (for sports) Fan, *der;* **a great DIY** ~: ein
begeisterter Heimwerker

enthusiastic /ɪnθjuːzɪ'æstɪk/ *adj.*
begeistert; **not be very** ~ **about doing sth.**
keine große Lust haben, etw. zu tun

entice /ɪn'taɪs/ *v.t.* locken (**into** in + *Akk.*);
~ **sb. into doing** *or* **to do sth.** jmdn. dazu
verleiten, etw. zu tun

entire /ɪn'taɪə(r)/ *adj.* (a) (whole) ganz
  (b) (intact) vollständig

en'tirely *adv.* (a) (wholly) völlig
  (b) (solely) ganz ⟨*für sich behalten*⟩; voll
⟨*verantwortlich sein*⟩; **it's up to you** ~: es
liegt ganz bei dir

entirety /ɪn'taɪərətɪ/ *n.* **in its** ~: in seiner/
ihrer Gesamtheit

entitle /ɪn'taɪtl/ *v.t.* berechtigen (**to** zu);
~ **sb. to do sth.** jmdm. das Recht geben, etw.
zu tun; **be** ~**d to [claim] sth.** Anspruch auf
etw. (*Akk.*) haben; **be** ~**d to do sth.** das
Recht haben, etw. zu tun

entomologist /entə'mɒlədʒɪst/ *n.*
Entomologe, *der/*Entomologin, *die*

entomology /entə'mɒlədʒɪ/ *n.*
Entomologie, *die;* Insektenkunde, *die*

entourage /ɒntʊ'rɑːʒ/ *n.* Gefolge, *das*

entrails /'entreɪlz/ *n. pl.* Eingeweide *Pl.*

entrance¹ /ɪn'trɑːns/ *v.t.* hinreißen

entrance² /'entrəns/ *n.* (way in) Eingang,
der (**to** Gen. *od.* zu); (for vehicles) Einfahrt, *die*

entrance /'entrəns/:~ **examination**
n. Aufnahmeprüfung, *die;* ~ **fee** *n.*
Eintrittsgeld, *das;* ~ **hall** *n.* Eingangshalle,
die; ~ **ticket** *n.* Eintrittskarte, *die*

entrant /'entrənt/ *n.* (for competition, race, etc.)
Teilnehmer, *der/*Teilnehmerin, *die* (**for** Gen.,
an + *Dat.*)

entreat /ɪn'triːt/ *v.t.* anflehen

en'treaty *n.* flehentliche Bitte

entrepreneur /ɒntrəprə'nɜː(r)/ *n.*
Unternehmer, *der/*Unternehmerin, *die*

entrepreneurial /ɒntrəprə'nɜːrɪəl/ *adj.*
unternehmerisch

entrust /ɪn'trʌst/ *v.t.* ~ **sb. with sth.** jmdm.
etw. anvertrauen; ~ **sb./sth. to sb./sth.**
jmdn./etw. jmdm./einer Sache anvertrauen;
~ **a task to sb.** jmdn. mit einer Aufgabe
betrauen

entry /'entrɪ/ *n.* (a) Eintritt, *der* (**into** in
+ *Akk.*); (into country) Einreise, *die;* '**no** ~' (for
people) „Zutritt verboten"; (for vehicles)
„Einfahrt verboten"
  (b) (way in) Eingang, *der;* (for vehicle) Einfahrt,
die

 ····❖

(c) (registration, item) Eintragung, *die* (in, into in + *Akk. od. Dat.*); (in dictionary, encyclopaedia) Eintrag, *der*

entry: ~ **fee** *n.* Eintrittsgeld, *das;* ~ **form** *n.* Anmeldeformular, *das;* ~ **visa** *n.* Einreisevisum, *das*

envelop /ɪnˈveləp/ *v.t.* [ein]hüllen (**in** in + *Akk.*); **be** ~**ed in flames** ganz von Flammen umgeben sein

envelope /ˈenvələʊp, ˈɒnvələʊp/ *n.* [Brief]umschlag, *der*

enviable /ˈenvɪəbl/ *adj.* beneidenswert

envious /ˈenvɪəs/ *adj.* neidisch (**of** auf + *Akk.*)

environment /ɪnˈvaɪərənmənt/ *n.* Umwelt, *die;* (surrounding objects, region) Umgebung, *die*

environmental /ɪnvaɪərənˈmentl/ *adj.* Umwelt⟨*verschmutzung, -schutz, -katastrophe*⟩; **for** ~ **reasons** aus Gründen des Umweltschutzes; ~ **group** Umweltschutzorganisation, *die;* ~ **protection** Umweltschutz, *der*

environmental 'health *n.* Umwelthygiene, *die;* ~ **health officer** Umwelthygienebeauftragte, *der/die;* ~ **health department** Umwelthygieneamt, *das*

environ'mentalist *n.* Umweltschützer, *der/*-schützerin, *die*

environ'mentally *adv.* ~ **friendly** umweltfreundlich; ~ **sensitive** ökologisch sensibel; ~ **sound** umweltverträglich; umweltgerecht

envisage /ɪnˈvɪzɪdʒ/, **envision** /ɪnˈvɪʒn/ *v.t.* sich (*Dat.*) vorstellen

envoy /ˈenvɔɪ/ *n.* Gesandte, *der/*Gesandtin, *die*

envy /ˈenvɪ/ ⟨**1**⟩ *n.* Neid, *der;* **you'll be the** ~ **of all your friends** alle deine Freunde werden dich beneiden
⟨**2**⟩ *v.t.* beneiden; ~ **sb. sth.** jmdn. um etw. beneiden

enzyme /ˈenzaɪm/ *n.* Enzym, *das*

ephemeral /ɪˈfemərl/ *adj.* kurzlebig

epic /ˈepɪk/ ⟨**1**⟩ *adj.* episch
⟨**2**⟩ *n.* Epos, *das*

epidemic /epɪˈdemɪk/ ⟨**1**⟩ *adj.* epidemisch
⟨**2**⟩ *n.* Epidemie, *die*

epilepsy /ˈepɪlepsɪ/ *n.* Epilepsie, *die*

epileptic /epɪˈleptɪk/ ⟨**1**⟩ *adj.* epileptisch; ~ **fit** epileptischer Anfall
⟨**2**⟩ *n.* Epileptiker, *der/*Epileptikerin, *die*

Epiphany /ɪˈpɪfənɪ/ *n.* **[Feast of the]** ~: Epiphanias, *das;* Dreikönigsfest, *das;* **at** ~: am Dreikönigstag

episode /ˈepɪsəʊd/ *n.* **(a)** Episode, *die*
(b) (of serial) Folge, *die*

epistle /ɪˈpɪsl/ *n.* Epistel, *die*

epitaph /ˈepɪtɑːf/ *n.* Grab[in]schrift, *die*

epithet /ˈepɪθet/ *n.* Beiname, *der;* (as term of abuse) Schimpfname, *der*

epitome /ɪˈpɪtəmɪ/ *n.* Inbegriff, *der*

epitomize /ɪˈpɪtəmaɪz/ *v.t.* ~ **sth.** der Inbegriff einer Sache (*Gen.*) sein

epoch /ˈiːpɒk/ *n.* Epoche, *die*

'epoch-making *adj.* Epoche machend

equal /ˈiːkwl/ ⟨**1**⟩ *adj.* **(a)** gleich; ~ **in** or **of** ~ **height/size/importance** *etc.* gleich hoch/groß/wichtig *usw.*
(b) **be** ~ **to sth./sb.** (strong, clever, etc. enough) einer Sache/jmdm. gewachsen sein
⟨**2**⟩ *n.* Gleichgestellte, *der/die;* **have no** ~: nicht seines-/ihresgleichen haben
⟨**3**⟩ *v.t.,* (Brit.) **-ll-:** ~ **sb.** es jmdm. gleichtun; **three times four** ~**s twelve** drei mal vier ist [gleich] zwölf

equality /ɪˈkwɒlɪtɪ/ *n.* Gleichheit, *die;* (equal rights) Gleichberechtigung, *die;* ~ **between the sexes** Gleichheit von Mann und Frau

equalize /ˈiːkwəlaɪz/ *v.i.* (Sport) den Ausgleich[streffer] erzielen

'equalizer *n.* (Sport) Ausgleich[streffer], *der*

'equally *adv.* gleich; (just as) ebenso; **in** ~ **gleiche Teile** ⟨*aufteilen*⟩; gleichmäßig ⟨*verteilen*⟩

Equal Oppor'tunities Commission *n.* (Brit.) *Ausschuss für Chancengleichheit;* ≈ Gleichstellungsausschuss, *der*

equal oppor'tunity *n.* Chancengleichheit, *die*

'equals sign *n.* (Math.) Gleichheitszeichen, *das*

equanimity /ekwəˈnɪmɪtɪ/ *n.* Gelassenheit, *die*

equate /ɪˈkweɪt/ *v.t.* gleichsetzen (**with** mit)

equation /ɪˈkweɪʒn/ *n.* (Math.) Gleichung, *die*

equator /ɪˈkweɪtə(r)/ *n.* Äquator, *der*

equilibrium /iːkwɪˈlɪbrɪəm/ *n., pl.* **equilibria** /iːkwɪˈlɪbrɪə/ or ~**s** Gleichgewicht, *das*

equinox /ˈekwɪnɒks/ *n.* Tagundnachtgleiche, *die*

equip /ɪˈkwɪp/ *v.t.,* **-pp-** ausrüsten ⟨*Fahrzeug, Armee*⟩; ausstatten ⟨*Küche*⟩; **fully** ~**ped** komplett ausgerüstet/ausgestattet; ~ **sb./oneself** [**with sth.**] jmdn./sich [mit etw.] ausrüsten

e'quipment *n.* Ausrüstung, *die;* (of kitchen, laboratory) Ausstattung, *die;* (needed for activity) Geräte *Pl.*

equity /ˈekwɪtɪ/ *n.* **(a)** (fairness) Gerechtigkeit, *die;* **with** ~: gerecht
(b) *in pl.* (stocks and shares without fixed interest) [Stamm]aktien *Pl.*
(c) (value of shares) Eigenkapital, *das*
(d) (net value of mortgaged property) *Wert eines Besitzes nach Abzug der Belastungen*

'equity market *n.* (Commerc.) Aktienmarkt, *der*

equivalent /ɪˈkwɪvələnt/ ⟨**1**⟩ *adj.* gleichwertig; **be** ~ **to sth.** einer Sache (*Dat.*) entsprechen
⟨**2**⟩ *n.* **(a)** (thing, person) Pendant, *das;* Gegenstück, *das* (**of** zu)

(b) be the ~ of sth. (have same result) einer Sache (*Dat.*) entsprechen

equivocal /ɪˈkwɪvəkl/ *adj.* zweideutig

er /ɜː(r)/ *int.* äh

era /ˈɪərə/ *n.* Ära, *die*

eradicate /ɪˈrædɪkeɪt/ *v.t.* ausrotten

erase /ɪˈreɪz/ *v.t.* auslöschen; (with rubber, knife) ausradieren; (from tape, also Comp.) löschen

e'raser *n.* **[pencil]** ~: Radiergummi, *der*

erect /ɪˈrekt/ **1** *adj.* aufrecht
2 *v.t.* errichten; aufstellen ⟨*Standbild, Mast, Verkehrsschild, Gerüst, Zelt*⟩

erection /ɪˈrekʃn/ *n.* **(a)** ▶ ERECT 2: Errichtung, *die*; Aufstellen, *das*
(b) (Physiol.) Erektion, *die*

ergonomic /ɜːɡəˈnɒmɪk/ *adj.*, **ergo'nomically** *adv.* ergonomisch

ermine /ˈɜːmɪn/ *n.* Hermelin, *der*

erode /ɪˈrəʊd/ *v.t.* **(a)** ⟨*Säure, Rost:*⟩ angreifen; ⟨*Wasser:*⟩ auswaschen; ⟨*Wind:*⟩ verwittern lassen
(b) (fig.) unterminieren

erosion /ɪˈrəʊʒn/ *n.* **(a)** ▶ ERODE A: Angreifen, *das;* Auswaschung, *die;* Verwitterung, *die*
(b) (fig.) Unterminierung, *die*

erotic /ɪˈrɒtɪk/ *adj.* erotisch

err /ɜː(r)/ *v.i.* sich irren

errand /ˈerənd/ *n.* Botengang, *der;* (shopping) Besorgung, *die;* **go on** or **run an** ~: einen Botengang/eine Besorgung machen

'errand boy *n.* Laufbursche, *der*

erratic /ɪˈrætɪk/ *adj.* unregelmäßig; sprunghaft ⟨*Wesen, Person, Art*⟩; launenhaft ⟨*Verhalten*⟩

erroneous /ɪˈrəʊnɪəs/ *adj.* falsch; irrig ⟨*Schlussfolgerung, Annahme*⟩

error /ˈerə(r)/ *n.* (mistake) Fehler, *der;* (wrong opinion) Irrtum, *der;* **in** ~: irrtümlich[erweise]

'error message *n.* (Comp.) Fehlermeldung, *die*

erudite /ˈeruːdaɪt/ *adj.* gelehrt

erupt /ɪˈrʌpt/ *v.i.* ausbrechen

eruption /ɪˈrʌpʃn/ *n.* Ausbruch, *der*

escalate /ˈeskəleɪt/ *v.i.* **1** sich ausweiten **(into** zu); ⟨*Preise, Kosten:*⟩ [ständig] steigen
2 *v.t.* ausweiten **(into** zu)

escalator /ˈeskəleɪtə(r)/ *n.* Rolltreppe, *die*

escapade /eskəˈpeɪd/ *n.* Eskapade, *die* (geh.)

escape /ɪˈskeɪp/ **1** *n.* Flucht, *die* **(from** aus); **have a narrow** ~: gerade noch einmal davonkommen
2 *v.i.* **(a)** fliehen **(from** aus); (successfully) entkommen **(from** *Dat.*)
(b) ⟨*Gas:*⟩ ausströmen; ⟨*Flüssigkeit:*⟩ auslaufen
3 *v.t.* **(a)** entkommen (+ *Dat.*) ⟨*Verfolger,*

Feind⟩; entgehen (+ *Dat.*) ⟨*Bestrafung, Gefangennahme, Tod*⟩; verschont bleiben von ⟨*Zerstörung, Auswirkungen*⟩
(b) (not be remembered by) entfallen sein (+ *Dat.*)

escape: ~ **artist** ▶ ESCAPOLOGIST; ~ **attempt,** ~ **bid** *ns.* Fluchtversuch, *der;* (from prison) Ausbruchsversuch, *der;* ~ **hatch** *n.* Notausstieg, *der;* (fig.) Rettungsanker, *der;* ~ **key** *n.* (Comp.) Escapetaste, *die;* ~ **road** *n.* Auslaufstrecke, *die;* ~ **route** *n.* Fluchtweg, *der*

escapism /ɪˈskeɪpɪzm/ *n.* Realitätsflucht, *die*

escapologist /eskəˈpɒlədʒɪst/ *n.* (Brit.) Entfesselungskünstler, *der*/-künstlerin, *die*

escarpment /ɪˈskɑːpmənt/ *n.* (Geog.) Steilhang, *der*

escort **1** /ˈeskɔːt/ *n.* **(a)** Begleitung, *die;* (Mil.) Eskorte, *die*
(b) (hired companion) Begleiter, *der*/Begleiterin, *die*
2 /ɪˈskɔːt/ *v.t.* begleiten; (lead) führen; (Mil.) eskortieren

Eskimo /ˈeskɪməʊ/ **1** *adj.* Eskimo-
2 *n., pl.* ~**s** or **same** Eskimo, *der*/Eskimofrau, *die;* **the** ~**[s]** die Eskimos

esoteric /esəʊˈterɪk/ *adj.* esoterisch

especial /ɪˈspeʃl/ *attrib. adj.* [ganz] besonder…

especially /ɪˈspeʃəlɪ/ *adv.* besonders

espionage /ˈespɪənɑːʒ/ *n.* Spionage, *die*

esplanade /espləˈneɪd, espləˈnɑːd/ *n.* Esplanade, *die* (geh.)

espouse /ɪˈspaʊz/ *v.t.* eintreten für

espresso /eˈspresəʊ/ *n., pl.* ~**s** (coffee) Espresso, *der*

e'spresso bar *n.* Espressobar, *die*

Esq. /ɪˈskwaɪə(r)/ *abbr.* = **Esquire** ≈ Hr.; (on letter) ≈ Hrn.; **Jim Smith,** ~: Hr./Hrn. Jim Smith

essay /ˈeseɪ/ *n.* Essay, *der;* Aufsatz, *der* (bes. Schulw.)

essence /ˈesns/ *n.* **(a)** Wesen, *das;* (gist) Wesentliche, *das;* **in** ~: im Wesentlichen
(b) (Cookery) Essenz, *die*

essential /ɪˈsenʃl/ **1** *adj.* **(a)** (fundamental) wesentlich
(b) (indispensable) unentbehrlich; lebensnotwendig ⟨*Versorgungseinrichtungen, Güter*⟩; unabdingbar ⟨*Qualifikation, Voraussetzung*⟩; **it is** ~ **that** …: es ist unbedingt notwendig, dass …
2 *n. pl.* **the** ~**s** (fundamentals) das Wesentliche; (items) das Notwendigste

es'sentially *adv.* im Grunde

establish /ɪˈstæblɪʃ/ *v.t.* **(a)** schaffen ⟨*Einrichtung, Präzedenzfall*⟩; gründen ⟨*Organisation, Institut*⟩; errichten ⟨*Geschäft, System*⟩
(b) (secure acceptance for) etablieren; **become** ~**ed** sich einbürgern
(c) (prove) beweisen   ⋯❖

(d) (discover) feststellen

established /ɪˈstæblɪʃt/ *adj.* bestehend ⟨*Ordnung*⟩; etabliert ⟨*Schriftsteller*⟩; (accepted) üblich; fest ⟨*Brauch*⟩; feststehend ⟨*Tatsache*⟩; **become** ∼: sich durchsetzen

e'stablishment *n.* **(a)** (setting up, foundation) Gründung, *die*
(b) [business] ∼: Unternehmen, *das*

estate /ɪˈsteɪt/ *n.* **(a)** (landed property) Gut, *das*
(b) (Brit.: housing ∼) [Wohn]siedlung, *die*
(c) (of deceased person) Erbmasse, *die*

estate: ∼ **agent** *n.* (Brit.) Grundstücksmakler, *der*/-maklerin, *die;* ∼ **car** *n.* (Brit.) Kombiwagen, *der;* ∼ **duty** (Brit.)**,** **e'state tax** (Amer.) *ns.* Erbschaftssteuer, *die*

esteem /ɪˈstiːm/ ①*n.* Wertschätzung, *die* (geh.) (**for** *Gen.,* für)
②*v.t.* schätzen; **highly** ∼ed hoch geschätzt

estimate ① /ˈestɪmət/ *n.* **(a)** Schätzung, *die;* **at a rough** ∼: grob geschätzt
(b) (Commerc.) Kostenvoranschlag, *der*
② /ˈestɪmeɪt/ *v.t.* schätzen (**at** auf + *Akk.*)

estimation /estɪˈmeɪʃn/ *n.* Schätzung, *die;* **in sb.'s** ∼: nach jmds. Schätzung

Estonia /eˈstəʊnɪə/ *pr. n.* Estland (*das*)

Estonian /eˈstəʊnɪən/ ①*adj.* estländisch; estnisch; **sb. is** ∼: jmd. ist Este/Estin
②*n.* **(a)** (language) Estnisch, *das;* Estländisch, *das; see also* ENGLISH 2 A
(b) (person) Este, *der*/Estin, *die;* Estländer, *der*/Estländerin, *die*

estuary /ˈestjʊərɪ/ *n.* [Trichter]mündung, *die*

ETA *abbr.* = **estimated time of arrival** voraussichtliche Ankunftszeit

etc. *abbr.* = **et cetera** usw.

etch /etʃ/ *v.t.* ätzen (**on** auf + *Akk.*); (on metal also) ⟨*bes. Künstler:*⟩ radieren; (fig.) einprägen (**in, on** *Dat.*)

'etching *n.* (Art) Radierung, *die*

eternal /ɪˈtɜːnl/ *adj.,* **e'ternally** *adv.* ewig

eternity /ɪˈtɜːnɪtɪ/ *n.* Ewigkeit, *die*

ether /ˈiːθə(r)/ *n.* Äther, *der*

ethereal /ɪˈθɪərɪəl/ *adj.* ätherisch

ethical /ˈeθɪkl/ *adj.* ethisch

ethics /ˈeθɪks/ *n.* **(a)** Moral, *die;* (moral philosophy) Ethik, *die*
(b) *usu. constr. as pl.* (moral code) Ethik, *die* (geh.)

Ethiopia /iːθɪˈəʊpɪə/ *pr. n.* Äthiopien (*das*)

Ethiopian /iːθɪˈəʊpɪən/ ①*adj.* äthiopisch; **sb. is** ∼: jmd. ist Äthiopier/Äthiopierin
②*n.* Äthiopier, *der*/Äthiopierin, *die*

ethnic /ˈeθnɪk/ *adj.* ethnisch; ∼ **minority** ethnische Minderheit

ethnic 'cleansing *n.* ethnische Säuberung

ethnology /eθˈnɒlədʒɪ/ *n.* Ethnologie, *die*

ethos /ˈiːθɒs/ *n.* (guiding beliefs) Gesinnung, *die;* (fundamental values) Ethos, *das* (geh.); (characteristic spirit) Geist, *der*

etiquette /ˈetɪket/ *n.* Etikette, *die*

etymology /etɪˈmɒlədʒɪ/ *n.* Etymologie, *die*

EU *abbr.* = **European Union** EU

eulogy /ˈjuːlədʒɪ/ *n.* Lobrede, *die*

euphemism /ˈjuːfəmɪzm/ *n.* Euphemismus, *der*

euphemistic /juːfəˈmɪstɪk/ *adj.* verhüllend

euphoria /juːˈfɔːrɪə/ *n.* Euphorie, *die* (geh.)

Euro- /ˈjʊərəʊ/ *in comb.* euro-/Euro-

Euro: ∼**cheque** *n.* Euroscheck, *der;* ∼**land** *n.* Euroland, *das;* ∼**-MP** *n.* Europaabgeordnete, *der/die*

Europe /ˈjʊərəp/ *pr. n.* Europa (*das*)

European /jʊərəˈpiːən/ ①*adj.* europäisch; **sb. is** ∼: jmd. ist Europäer/Europäerin; ∼ [**Economic**] **Community** Europäische [Wirtschafts]gemeinschaft
②*n.* Europäer, *der*/Europäerin, *die*

European: ∼ **Central 'Bank** *n.* Europäische Zentralbank; ∼ **Com'mission** *n.* Europäische Kommission; ∼ **'Council** *n.* Europäischer Rat; ∼ **Court of 'Justice** *n.* Europäischer Gerichtshof; ∼ **'Cup** *n.* (Footb.) Europacup, *der;* Europapokal, *der;* ∼ **'currency unit** *n.* Europäische Währungseinheit; ∼ **'Monetary System** *n.* Europäisches Währungssystem; ∼ **Monetary 'Union** *n.* Europäische Währungsunion; ∼ **'Parliament** *n.* Europäisches Parlament; ∼ **'Union** *n.* Europäische Union

Euro-: ∼**rebel** *n.* (esp. Brit.) [innerparteilicher] Europagegner/ [innerparteiliche] Europagegnerin; ∼**sceptic** *n.* Euroskeptiker, *der*/ -skeptikerin, *die;* ∼**star** ® *n.* Eurostar, *der;* **go by** ∼**star** mit dem Eurostar fahren

euthanasia /juːθəˈneɪzɪə/ *n.* Euthanasie, *die*

evacuate /ɪˈvækjʊeɪt/ *v.t.* evakuieren (**from** aus)

evacuation /ɪvækjʊˈeɪʃn/ *n.* Evakuierung, *die* (**from** aus)

evade /ɪˈveɪd/ *v.t.* ausweichen (+ *Dat.*) ⟨*Angriff, Angreifer, Schlag, Problem, Frage*⟩; sich entziehen (+ *Dat.*) ⟨*Verhaftung, Verantwortung*⟩; entkommen (+ *Dat.*) ⟨*Verfolger, Verfolgung*⟩; hinterziehen ⟨*Steuern*⟩; ∼ **doing sth.** vermeiden, etw. zu tun

evaluate /ɪˈvæljʊeɪt/ *v.t.* einschätzen; bewerten ⟨*Daten*⟩

evangelical /iːvænˈdʒelɪkl/ *adj.* missionarisch (fig.); (Protestant) evangelikal

evangelist /ɪˈvændʒəlɪst/ *n.* Evangelist, *der*

evaporate /ɪˈvæpəreɪt/ ①*v.i.* verdunsten
②*v.t.* verdunsten lassen

evaporated 'milk *n.* Kondensmilch, *die*

evaporation /ɪˌvæpəˈreɪʃn/ n.
Verdunstung, die

evasion /ɪˈveɪʒn/ n. Umgehung, die; (of responsibility, question) Ausweichen, das (of vor + Dat.); tax ~: Steuerhinterziehung, die

evasive /ɪˈveɪsɪv/ adj. (a) be/become ~: ausweichen
(b) ausweichend ⟨Antwort⟩

eve /iːv/ n. Vorabend, der (of Gen.); (day) Vortag, der (of Gen.)

even /ˈiːvn/ [1] adj. (a) eben ⟨Boden, Fläche⟩; gleich hoch ⟨Stapel, Stuhl-, Tischbein⟩; be of ~ height/length gleich hoch/lang sein
(b) gerade ⟨Zahl, Seite, Hausnummer⟩
(c) be or get ~ with sb. (quits) es jmdm. heimzahlen; break ~: die Kosten decken
[2] adv. sogar; selbst; sogar noch ⟨weniger, schlimmer usw.⟩; ~ if selbst wenn; ~ so [aber] trotzdem; not or never ~ ...: [noch] nicht einmal ...

■ **even 'up** v.t. ausgleichen

evening /ˈiːvnɪŋ/ n. Abend, der; this/ tomorrow ~: heute/morgen Abend; in the ~: am Abend; (regularly) abends

evening: ~ **class** n. Abendkurs, der; ~ **dress** n. Abendkleidung, die; ~ '**meal** n. Abendessen, das; ~ '**paper** n. Abendzeitung, die

'**evenly** adv. gleichmäßig

'**even-numbered** adj. gerade

event /ɪˈvent/ n. (a) in the ~ of his dying or death im Falle seines Todes; in the ~: letzten Endes; in the ~ of rain bei Regenwetter
(b) (occurrence) Ereignis, das
(c) (planned public or social occasion) Veranstaltung, die

e'ventful adj. ereignisreich

eventual /ɪˈventjʊəl/ adj. predict sb.'s ~ downfall vorhersagen, dass jmd. schließlich zu Fall kommen wird; the career of Napoleon and his ~ defeat der Aufstieg Napoleons und schließlich seine Niederlage

eventuality /ɪventjʊˈælɪtɪ/ n. Eventualität, die

e'ventually adv. schließlich

ever /ˈevə(r)/ adv. (a) (always) immer; for ~: für immer; ewig ⟨lieben, da sein, leben⟩; ~ since [then] seit [dieser Zeit]
(b) (at any time) je[mals]; hardly ~: so gut wie nie; as ~: wie gewöhnlich
(c) in comb. with compar. adj. or adv. noch; ~-increasing ständig zunehmend
(d) what ~ does he want? was will er nur?; why ~ not? warum denn nicht?

'**ever:** ~**green** [1] adj. immergrün;
[2] n. immergrüne Pflanze; ~**lasting** adj.
(a) (eternal) immer während; ewig ⟨Leben⟩; unvergänglich ⟨Ruhm, Ehre⟩; (b) (incessant) endlos

every /ˈevrɪ/ adj. (a) jeder/jede/jedes;
~ one jeder/jede/jedes [einzelne]; your ~ wish all[e] deine Wünsche; she comes ~ day sie kommt jeden Tag; ~ three/few days alle drei/paar Tage; ~ other (~ second, almost ~) jeder/jede/jedes zweite
(b) (the greatest possible) all ⟨Respekt, Aussicht⟩

every: ~**body** n. & pron. jeder; ~**body else** alle anderen; ~**day** attrib. adj. alltäglich; Alltags⟨kleidung, -sprache⟩; in ~**day life** im Alltag; ~**one** ▶ ~BODY; ~**place** (Amer.) ▶ ~WHERE; ~**thing** n. & pron. alles; ~**where** adv. überall; ~**where you go/look** wohin man auch geht/sieht

evict /ɪˈvɪkt/ v.t. ~ sb. [from his home] jmdn. zur Räumung [seiner Wohnung] zwingen

eviction /ɪˈvɪkʃn/ n. Zwangsräumung, die; the ~ of the tenant die zwangsweise Vertreibung des Mieters

evidence /ˈevɪdəns/ n. (a) Beweis, der; (indication) Anzeichen, das; be ~ of sth. etw. beweisen
(b) (Law) Beweismaterial, das; give ~: aussagen

evident /ˈevɪdənt/ adj. offensichtlich; be ~ to sb. jmdm. klar sein; it soon became ~ that ...: es stellte sich bald heraus, dass ...

'**evidently** adv. offensichtlich

evil /ˈiːvl, ˈiːvɪl/ [1] adj. böse; schlecht ⟨Charakter, Einfluss, System⟩
[2] n. (a) Böse, das
(b) (bad thing) Übel, das

evocative /ɪˈvɒkətɪv/ adj. be ~ of sth. etw. heraufbeschwören

evoke /ɪˈvəʊk/ v.t. heraufbeschwören; hervorrufen ⟨Bewunderung, Überraschung⟩; erregen ⟨Interesse⟩

evolution /iːvəˈluːʃn/ n. Entwicklung, die; (Biol.) Evolution, die

evolve /ɪˈvɒlv/ [1] v.i. sich entwickeln (from aus, into zu)
[2] v.t. entwickeln

ewe /juː/ n. Mutterschaf, das

ex¹ /eks/ n. (coll.) Verflossene, der/die (ugs.)

ex² prep. (Commerc.) ex works/store ⟨Güter⟩ ab Werk/Lager

ex- pref. Ex-⟨Freundin, Präsident, Champion⟩; Alt⟨bundes⟩kanzler⟩

exacerbate /ekˈsæsəbeɪt/ v.t. verschärfen ⟨Lage⟩; verschlechtern ⟨Zustand⟩

exact /ɪgˈzækt/ [1] adj. genau
[2] v.t. fordern; erheben ⟨Gebühr⟩

exacting /ɪgˈzæktɪŋ/ n. anspruchsvoll; hoch ⟨Anforderung⟩

exactitude /ɪgˈzæktɪtjuːd/ Genauigkeit, die

exactly /ɪgˈzæktlɪ/ adv. genau; not ~ (coll. iron.) nicht gerade

exactness /ɪgˈzæktnɪs/ n. Genauigkeit, die

exaggerate /ɪgˈzædʒəreɪt/ v.t. übertreiben

exaggeration /ɪgzædʒəˈreɪʃn/ n. Übertreibung, die

exam /ɪgˈzæm/ (coll.) ▶ EXAMINATION B

examination /ɪgzæmɪˈneɪʃn/ n. (a)
(inspection; Med.) Untersuchung, die
(b) (Sch. etc.) Prüfung, die; (final ~ at university)
Examen, das

exami'nation paper n. (a) ~[s]
schriftliche Prüfungsaufgaben Pl.
(b) (with candidate's answers) ≈ Klausurarbeit,
die

examine /ɪgˈzæmɪn/ v.t. (a) (inspect; Med.)
untersuchen (for auf + Akk.); prüfen
⟨Dokument, Gewissen⟩; kontrollieren
⟨Ausweis, Gepäck⟩
(b) (Sch. etc.) prüfen (in in + Dat.)
(c) (Law) verhören

examiner /ɪgˈzæmɪnə(r)/ n. Prüfer, der/
Prüferin, die

example /ɪgˈzɑːmpl/ n. Beispiel, das; for ~:
zum Beispiel; **make an ~ of sb.** ein Exempel
an jmdm. statuieren

exasperate /ɪgˈzæspəreɪt/ v.t. (irritate)
verärgern; (infuriate) zur Verzweiflung bringen

exasperation /ɪgˌzæspəˈreɪʃn/ n.
▸ EXASPERATE: Ärger, der/Verzweiflung, die
(with über + Akk.); in ~: verärgert/
verzweifelt

excavate /ˈekskəveɪt/ v.t. (a)
ausschachten; (with machine) ausbaggern
(b) (Archaeol.) ausgraben

excavation /ekskəˈveɪʃn/ n. (a)
Ausschachtung, die; (with machine)
Ausbaggerung, die
(b) (Archaeol.) Ausgrabung, die

excavator /ˈekskəveɪtə(r)/ n. Bagger, der

exceed /ɪkˈsiːd/ v.t. (a) (be greater than)
übertreffen (in an + Dat.); ⟨Kosten, Summe,
Anzahl:⟩ übersteigen (by um)
(b) (go beyond) überschreiten; hinausgehen
über (+ Akk.) ⟨Auftrag, Befehl⟩

ex'ceedingly adv. äußerst; ausgesprochen
⟨hässlich, dumm⟩

excel /ɪkˈsel/ 1 v.t., -ll- übertreffen;
~ **oneself** (lit. or iron.) sich selbst übertreffen
2 v.i., -ll- sich hervortun (at, in in + Dat.)

excellence /ˈeksələns/ n. hervorragende
Qualität

excellent /ˈeksələnt/ adj. hervorragend

except /ɪkˈsept/ 1 prep. ~ [for] außer
(+ Dat.); ~ **for** (in all respects other than)
abgesehen von
2 v.t. ausnehmen (from bei); ~ed
ausgenommen

ex'cepting prep. außer (+ Dat.)

exception /ɪkˈsepʃn/ n. Ausnahme, die;
take ~ to Anstoß nehmen an (+ Dat.)

exceptional /ɪkˈsepʃənl/ adj.
außergewöhnlich

ex'ceptionally adv. (a) (as an exception)
ausnahmsweise
(b) (remarkably) ungewöhnlich

excerpt /ˈeksɜːpt/ n. Auszug, der (from aus)

excess /ɪkˈses/ n. (a) Übermaß, das (of an
+ Dat.); **eat/drink to ~:** übermäßig essen/
trinken

(b) esp. in pl. (over-indulgence) Exzess, der
(c) **be in ~ of sth.** etw. übersteigen
(d) (surplus) Überschuss, der

excess /ˈekses/: ~ **'baggage** n.
Mehrgepäck, das; ~ **'fare** n. Mehrpreis,
der; **pay the ~ fare** nachlösen

excessive /ɪkˈsesɪv/ adj. übermäßig;
übertrieben ⟨Forderung, Lob, Ansprüche⟩;
unmäßig ⟨Esser, Trinker⟩

ex'cessively adv. übertrieben; unmäßig
⟨essen, trinken⟩

excess: ~ **'luggage** ▸ ~ BAGGAGE;
~ **'postage** n. Nachgebühr, die

exchange /ɪksˈtʃeɪndʒ/ 1 v.t. (a) tauschen
⟨Plätze, Ringe, Küsse⟩; umtauschen ⟨Geld⟩;
wechseln ⟨Blicke, Worte⟩; ~ **insults** sich
beleidigen
(b) (give in place of another) eintauschen (for
für, gegen); umtauschen ⟨[gekaufte] Ware⟩
(for gegen)
2 n. (a) Tausch, der; in ~: dafür; in ~ for
sth. für etw.
(b) (Educ.) Austausch, der; an ~ **student** ein
Austauschstudent/eine Austauschstudentin
(c) (of money) Umtausch, der; ~ **rate, rate of**
~: Wechselkurs, der
(d) (Teleph.) Fernmeldeamt, das

exchequer /ɪksˈtʃekə(r)/ n. (Brit.)
Schatzamt, das

excise /ˈeksaɪz/ n. Verbrauchsteuer, die;
Customs and E~ (Brit.) Amt für Zölle und
Verbrauchsteuer

excitable /ɪkˈsaɪtəbl/ adj. leicht erregbar

excite /ɪkˈsaɪt/ v.t. (a) (thrill) begeistern
(b) (agitate) aufregen

ex'cited adj. aufgeregt (at über + Akk.); **get**
~: sich aufregen

ex'citement n. Aufregung, die; (enthusiasm)
Begeisterung, die

exciting /ɪkˈsaɪtɪŋ/ adj. aufregend; (full of
suspense) spannend

exclaim /ɪkˈskleɪm/ 1 v.t. ausrufen
2 v.i. aufschreien

exclamation /ekskləˈmeɪʃn/ n. Ausruf,
der

excla'mation mark, (Amer.)
excla'mation point ns. Ausrufezeichen,
das

exclude /ɪkˈskluːd/ v.t. ausschließen

excluding /ɪkˈskluːdɪŋ/ prep. ~ **drinks/VAT**
Getränke ausgenommen/ohne
Mehrwertsteuer

exclusion /ɪkˈskluːʒn/ n. Ausschluss, der

exclusive /ɪkˈskluːsɪv/ adj. (a) alleinig
⟨Besitzer, Kontrolle⟩; Allein⟨eigentum⟩; (Journ.)
Exklusiv⟨bericht, -interview⟩
(b) (select) exklusiv
(c) ~ **of** ohne

ex'clusively adv. ausschließlich

excommunicate /ekskəˈmjuːnɪkeɪt/ v.t.
exkommunizieren

excrement /ˈekskrɪmənt/ n. Kot, der (geh.)

excrete /ɪkˈskriːt/ v.t. ausscheiden

excruciating /ɪkˈskruːˈʃɪeɪtɪŋ/ *adj.*
unerträglich

excursion /ɪkˈskɜːʃn/ *n.* Ausflug, *der*

excusable /ɪkˈskjuːzəbl/ *adj.*
entschuldbar; verzeihlich

excuse ① /ɪkˈskjuːz/ *v.t.* (a)
entschuldigen; **~ oneself** sich
entschuldigen; **~ me** Entschuldigung
(b) (release, exempt) befreien **(from** von)
② /ɪkˈskjuːs/ *n.* Entschuldigung, *die*

ex-diˈrectory *adj.* (Brit. Teleph.)
Geheim⟨nummer, -anschluss⟩; **be ~:** nicht
im Telefonbuch stehen

execute /ˈeksɪkjuːt/ *v.t.* (a) hinrichten
(b) (put into effect) ausführen

execution /eksɪˈkjuːʃn/ *n.* (a)
Hinrichtung, *die*
(b) (putting into effect) Ausführung, *die*

exeˈcutioner *n.* Scharfrichter, *der*

executive /ɪgˈzekjʊtɪv/ ① *n.* leitender
Angestellter/leitende Angestellte
② *adj.* leitend ⟨Stellung, Funktion⟩

executive: ~ ˈstress *n.* Managerstress,
der; **~ ˈtoy** *n.* Managerspielzeug, *das*

executor /ɪgˈzekjʊtə(r)/ *n.* (Law)
Testamentsvollstrecker, *der*

exemplary /ɪgˈzemplərɪ/ *adj.* (a) (model)
vorbildlich
(b) (deterrent) exemplarisch

exemplify /ɪgˈzemplɪfaɪ/ *v.t.*
veranschaulichen

exempt /ɪgˈzempt/ ① *adj.* [be] **~ [from**
sth.] [von etw.] befreit [sein]
② *v.t.* befreien

exemption /ɪgˈzempʃn/ *n.* Befreiung, *die*

exercise /ˈeksəsaɪz/ ① *n.* (a) Übung, *die*
(b) *no pl.* (physical exertion) Bewegung, *die;*
take ~: sich (Dat.) Bewegung schaffen
② *v.t.* ausüben ⟨Recht, Macht, Einfluss⟩;
walten lassen ⟨Vorsicht⟩
③ *v.i.* sich (Dat.) Bewegung schaffen

exercise: ~ bicycle, (coll.) **~bike** *ns.*
Heimtrainer, *der;* **~ book** *n.* [Schul]heft,
das

exert /ɪgˈzɜːt/ ① *v.t.* aufbieten ⟨Kraft⟩;
ausüben ⟨Einfluss, Druck⟩
② *v. refl.* sich anstrengen

exertion /ɪgˈzɜːʃn/ *n.* (a) (of strength, force)
Aufwendung, *die;* (of influence, pressure)
Ausübung, *die*
(b) (effort) Anstrengung, *die*

exhale /eksˈheɪl/ *v.t. & i.* ausatmen

exhaust /ɪgˈzɔːst/ ① *v.t.* erschöpfen;
erschöpfend behandeln ⟨Thema⟩
② *n.* (Motor Veh.) Auspuff, *der;* (gases)
Auspuffgase *Pl.;* **~ emissions** Auspuffabgase
Pl.; **~ emissions test** Abgasuntersuchung,
die

exˈhausted *adj.* erschöpft

exˈhausting *adj.* anstrengend

exhaustion /ɪgˈzɔːstʃn/ *n.* Erschöpfung,
die

exhaustive /ɪgˈzɔːstɪv/ *adj.* umfassend

exˈhaust pipe *n.* Auspuffrohr, *das*

exhibit /ɪgˈzɪbɪt/ ① *v.t.* ausstellen; zeigen
⟨Mut, Symptome, Angst usw.⟩
② *n.* Ausstellungsstück, *das*

exhibition /eksɪˈbɪʃn/ *n.* Ausstellung, *die;*
make an ~ of oneself sich unmöglich
aufführen

exhibitionism /eksɪˈbɪʃənɪzm/ *n.*
Exhibitionismus, *der*

exhibitionist /eksɪˈbɪʃənɪst/ *n.*
Exhibitionist, *der*/Exhibitionistin, *die*

exhibitor /ɪgˈzɪbɪtə(r)/ *n.* Aussteller, *der*/
Ausstellerin, *die*

exhilarated /ɪgˈzɪləreɪtɪd/ *adj.* belebt

exhilarating /ɪgˈzɪləreɪtɪŋ/ *adj.* belebend

exhilaration /ɪgzɪləˈreɪʃn/ *n.* **[feeling of]**
~: Hochgefühl, *das*

exhort /ɪgˈzɔːt/ *v.t.* ermahnen

exile /ˈeksaɪl/ ① *n.* (a) Exil, *das;* **in/into ~:**
im/ins Exil
(b) (person) Verbannte, *der/die*
② *v.t.* verbannen

exist /ɪgˈzɪst/ *v.i.* existieren; ⟨Zweifel,
Gefahr, Problem, Einrichtung:⟩ bestehen;
~ on sth. von etw. leben

existence /ɪgˈzɪstəns/ *n.* Existenz, *die;*
(mode of living) Dasein, *das;* **be in/come into**
~: existieren/entstehen

exit /ˈeksɪt/ *n.* (way out) Ausgang, *der* **(from**
aus); (for vehicle) Ausfahrt, *die*

exit: ~ permit *n.* Ausreiseerlaubnis, *die;*
~ poll *n.: Befragung der ein Wahllokal*
verlassenden Wähler; **~ visa** *n.*
Ausreisevisum, *das*

exonerate /ɪgˈzɒnəreɪt/ *v.t.* entlasten

exorbitant /ɪgˈzɔːbɪtənt/ *adj.* [maßlos]
überhöht

exorcize /ˈeksɔːsaɪz/ *v.t.* austreiben

exotic /ɪgˈzɒtɪk/ *adj.* exotisch

expand /ɪkˈspænd/ ① *v.i.* (a) sich
ausdehnen; (Commerc.) expandieren
(b) **~ on** weiter ausführen
② *v.t.* ausdehnen; (Commerc.) erweitern

expanse /ɪkˈspæns/ *n.* [weite] Fläche

expansion /ɪkˈspænʃn/ *n.* Ausdehnung,
die; (Commerc.) Expansion, *die*

expect /ɪkˈspekt/ *v.t.* (a) erwarten; **~ to do**
sth. damit rechnen, etw. zu tun; **~ sb. to do**
sth. damit rechnen, dass jmd. etw. tut;
(require) von jmdm. erwarten, dass er etw. tut
(b) (coll.: think, suppose) glauben; **I ~ so** ich
glaube schon

expectancy /ɪkˈspektənsɪ/ *n.* Erwartung,
die

expectant /ɪkˈspektənt/ *adj.*
erwartungsvoll; **~ mother** werdende Mutter

exˈpectantly *adv.* erwartungsvoll;
gespannt ⟨warten⟩

expectation /ekspekˈteɪʃn/ *n.* Erwartung,
die

expedient /ɪkˈspiːdɪənt/ ① *adj.*
angebracht

 ⋯⟶

2 *n.* Mittel, *das*
expedition /ekspɪ'dɪʃn/ *n.* Expedition, *die*
expel /ɪk'spel/ *v.t.,* -II- ausweisen (**from** aus);
～ **sb. from school** jmdn. von der Schule
verweisen
expend /ɪk'spend/ *v.t.* (a) aufwenden
([up]on für)
(b) (use up) aufbrauchen ([up]on für)
expendable /ɪk'spendəbl/ *adj.*
entbehrlich; **be** ～: geopfert werden können
expenditure /ɪk'spendɪtʃə(r)/ *n.* (a)
(amount spent) Ausgaben *Pl.* (**on** für)
(b) (spending) Ausgabe, *die*
expense /ɪk'spens/ *n.* (a) Kosten *Pl.;* **at**
sb.'s ～: auf jmds. Kosten (*Akk.*); **at one's**
own ～: auf eigene Kosten
(b) *usu. in pl.* (Commerc. etc.: amount spent [and
repaid]) Spesen *Pl.*
(c) (fig.) [**be**] **at the** ～ **of sth.** auf Kosten von
etw. [gehen]
ex'pense account *n.* Spesenabrechnung,
die; **put sth. on one's** ～: etw. als Spesen
abrechnen
expensive /ɪk'spensɪv/ *adj.,*
ex'pensively *adv.* teuer
experience /ɪk'spɪərɪəns/ 1 *n.*
Erfahrung, *die;* (incident) Erlebnis, *das*
2 *v.t.* erleben; haben ⟨Schwierigkeiten⟩;
verspüren ⟨Kälte, Schmerz, Gefühl⟩
ex'perienced *adj.* erfahren
experiment /ɪk'sperɪmənt/ 1 *n.* (a)
Experiment, *das,* Versuch, *der* (**on** an + *Dat.*)
(b) (fig.) Experiment, *das*
2 /ɪk'sperɪment/ *v.i.* Versuche anstellen (**on**
an + *Dat.*)
experimental /ɪksperɪ'mentl/ *adj.*
experimentell; Experimentier⟨theater, -kino⟩
expert /'eksp3ːt/ 1 *adj.* ausgezeichnet; **be**
～ **in** *or* **at sth.** Fachmann *od.* Experte für
etw. sein; **be** ～ **in** *or* **at doing sth.** etw.
ausgezeichnet können
2 *n.* Fachmann, *der;* Experte, *der*/Expertin,
die; **be an** ～ **in** *or* **at/on sth.** Fachmann *od.*
Experte in etw. (*Dat.*)/für etw. sein
expertise /eksp3ː'tiːz/ *n.* Fachkenntnisse
Pl.; (skill) Können, *das*
expert: ～ **system** *n.* (Comp.)
Expertensystem, *das;* ～ **'witness** *n.*
sachverständiger Zeuge
expire /ɪk'spaɪə(r)/ *v.i.* ablaufen
expiry /ɪk'spaɪərɪ/ *n.* Ablauf, *der*
explain /ɪk'spleɪn/ 1 *v.t., also abs.*
erklären
2 *v. refl., often abs.* **please** ～ [**yourself**] bitte
erklären Sie mir das
■ **explain a'way** *v.t.* eine [plausible]
Erklärung finden für
explanation /eksplə'neɪʃn/ *n.* Erklärung,
die; **need** ～: einer Erklärung bedürfen
explanatory /ɪk'splænətərɪ/ *adj.*
erklärend; erläuternd ⟨Bemerkung⟩
explicable /ɪk'splɪkəbl/ *adj.* erklärbar

explicit /ɪk'splɪsɪt/ *adj.* klar; ausdrücklich
⟨Zustimmung, Erwähnung⟩
ex'plicitly *adv.* ausdrücklich; deutlich
⟨beschreiben, ausdrücken⟩
explode /ɪk'spləʊd/ 1 *v.i.* explodieren
2 *v.t.* zur Explosion bringen
exploit 1 /'eksplɔɪt/ *n.* Heldentat, *die*
2 /ɪk'splɔɪt/ *v.t.* ausbeuten ⟨Arbeiter usw.⟩;
ausnutzen ⟨Gutmütigkeit, Freund,
Unwissenheit⟩
exploitation /eksplɔɪ'teɪʃn/ *n.* ▶ EXPLOIT 2:
Ausbeutung, *die;* Ausnutzung, *die*
exploration /eksplə'reɪʃn/ *n.* Erforschung,
die; (fig.) Untersuchung, *die*
exploratory /ɪk'splɒrətərɪ/ *adj.*
Forschungs-
explore /ɪk'splɔː(r)/ *v.t.* erforschen; (fig.)
untersuchen
ex'plorer *n.* Entdeckungsreisende, *der/die*
explosion /ɪk'spləʊʒn/ *n.* Explosion, *die*
explosive /ɪk'spləʊzɪv/ 1 *adj.* explosiv
2 *n.* Sprengstoff, *der*
export 1 /ɪk'spɔːt, 'ekspɔːt/ *v.t.*
exportieren; ausführen
2 /'ekspɔːt/ *n.* Export, *der*
export /'ekspɔːt/ : ～ **drive** *n.*
Exportkampagne, *die;* ～ **duty** *n.* Exportzoll,
der
ex'porter *n.* Exporteur, *der*
export /'ekspɔːt/ : ～ **licence** *n.*
Ausfuhrlizenz, *die;* ～ **market** *n.*
Exportmarkt, *der;* ～ **permit** *n.*
Exporterlaubnis, *die;* Ausfuhrerlaubnis, *die*
expose /ɪk'spəʊz/ *v.t.* (a) (uncover) freilegen;
entblößen ⟨Haut, Körper⟩
(b) offenbaren ⟨Schwäche⟩; aufdecken
⟨Missstände, Verbrechen⟩; entlarven ⟨Täter,
Spion⟩
(c) (subject) ～ **to sth.** einer Sache (*Dat.*)
aussetzen
(d) (Photog.) belichten
exposed /ɪk'spəʊzd/ *adj.* (unprotected)
ungeschützt; ～ **position** exponierte Stellung
exposure /ɪk'spəʊʒə(r)/ *n.* (a) (to cold etc.)
die of/suffer from ～: an Unterkühlung (*Dat.*)
sterben/leiden
(b) (Photog.) (exposing time) Belichtung, *die;*
(picture) Aufnahme, *die*
ex'posure meter *n.* Belichtungsmesser,
der
expound /ɪk'spaʊnd/ *v.t.* darlegen
express /ɪk'spres/ 1 *v.t.* ausdrücken;
äußern ⟨Meinung, Wunsch, Dank, Bedauern⟩;
～ **oneself** sich ausdrücken
2 *attrib. adj.* (a) Eil⟨brief, -bote usw.⟩;
Schnell⟨paket, -sendung⟩
(b) ausdrücklich ⟨Wunsch, Absicht⟩
3 *adv.* als Eilsache ⟨senden⟩
4 *n.* (train) Schnellzug, *der*
express de'livery *n.* Eilzustellung, *die*
expression /ɪk'spreʃn/ *n.* Ausdruck, *der*
expressive /ɪk'spresɪv/ *adj.* ausdrucksvoll

express: ~ **'letter** n. Eilbrief, der;
~ **'lift** n. Schnellaufzug, der

ex'pressly adv. ausdrücklich

express: ~ **'train** n. D-Zug, der; ~**way**
n. (Amer.) Schnellstraße, die

expulsion /ɪk'spʌlʃn/ n. Ausweisung, die
(from aus); (from school) Verweisung, die
(from von)

exquisite /'ekskwɪzɪt, ɪk'skwɪzɪt/ adj.
erlesen

ex'quisitely adv. vorzüglich; kunstvoll
⟨verziert, geschnitzt⟩

extend /ɪk'stend/ **1** v.t. verlängern;
ausstrecken ⟨Arm, Bein, Hand⟩; ausziehen
⟨Leiter, Teleskop⟩; verlängern lassen
⟨Leihbuch, Visum⟩; ausdehnen ⟨Einfluss,
Macht⟩; vergrößern ⟨Haus, Geschäft,
Fabrik⟩; gewähren ⟨[Gast]freundschaft, Hilfe,
Kredit⟩ (**to** Dat.); ~ **the time limit** den
Termin hinausschieben
2 v.i. sich erstrecken; **the season** ~**s from
November to March** die Saison geht von
November bis März

extended 'family n. Großfamilie, die

extension /ɪk'stenʃn/ n. **(a)** Verlängerung,
die
(b) (part of house) Anbau, der
(c) (telephone) Nebenanschluss, der; (number)
Apparat, der

extension: ~ **cord** (Amer.) ▶ ~ LEAD;
~ **ladder** n. Ausziehleiter, die; ~ **lead** n.
(Brit.) Verlängerungsschnur, die

extensive /ɪk'stensɪv/ adj. ausgedehnt;
umfangreich ⟨Reparatur, Wissen,
Nachforschungen⟩; beträchtlich ⟨Schäden⟩;
weit reichend ⟨Änderungen⟩

ex'tensively adv. beträchtlich ⟨ändern,
beschädigen⟩; ausführlich ⟨berichten,
schreiben⟩

extent /ɪk'stent/ n. Ausdehnung, die;
(scope) Umfang, der; (of damage) Ausmaß, das;
to what ~? inwieweit?

exterior /ɪk'stɪərɪə(r)/ **1** adj. äußer...;
Außen⟨fläche, -wand⟩
2 n. Äußere, das; (of house) Außenwände Pl.

exterminate /ɪk'stɜːmɪneɪt/ v.t. ausrotten
⟨Nation, Volk⟩; vertilgen ⟨Ungeziefer⟩;
liquidieren ⟨Person⟩

extermination /ɪkstɜːmɪ'neɪʃn/ n.
Ausrottung, die; (of pests) Vertilgung, die

extermi'nation camp n.
Vernichtungslager, das

external /ɪk'stɜːnl/ adj. äußer...;
Außen⟨fläche, -abmessungen⟩; **purely** ~:
rein äußerlich; **for** ~ **use only** nur äußerlich
anzuwenden

extinct /ɪk'stɪŋkt/ adj. erloschen ⟨Vulkan⟩;
ausgestorben ⟨Art, Rasse, Gattung⟩

extinction /ɪk'stɪŋkʃn/ n. Aussterben, das

extinguish /ɪk'stɪŋgwɪʃ/ v.t. löschen

ex'tinguisher n. Feuerlöscher, der

extol /ɪk'stɒl/ v.t., **-ll-** rühmen; preisen

extort /ɪk'stɔːt/ v.t. erpressen (**out of** von)

extortion /ɪk'stɔːʃn/ n. Erpressung, die

extortionate /ɪk'stɔːʃənət/ adj.
Wucher⟨preis, -zinsen usw.⟩; maßlos
überzogen ⟨Forderung⟩

extra /'ekstrə/ **1** adj. zusätzlich;
Mehr⟨arbeit, -kosten, -ausgaben⟩;
Sonder⟨bus, -zug⟩
2 adv. **(a)** (more than usually) besonders; extra
⟨lang, stark, fein⟩
(b) (additionally) extra; **packing and postage**
~: zuzüglich Verpackung und Porto
3 n. **(a)** (added to services, salary, etc.)
zusätzliche Leistung; (on car etc.) Extra, das
(b) (in play, film, etc.) Statist, der/Statistin, die

extract 1 /'ekstrækt/ n. **(a)** Extrakt, der
(fachspr. auch: das)
(b) (from book, music, etc.) Auszug, der
2 /ɪk'strækt/ v.t. ziehen ⟨Zahn⟩;
herausziehen ⟨Dorn, Splitter usw.⟩

extraction /ɪk'strækʃn/ n. (of tooth)
Extraktion, die; (of thorn, splinter, etc.)
Herausziehen, das

ex'tractor fan n. Entlüfter, der

extra-curricular /ekstrəkə'rɪkjʊlə(r)/
adj. extracurricular (fachspr.); ⟨Aktivität⟩
außerhalb des Lehrplans

extradite /'ekstrədaɪt/ v.t. ausliefern

extradition /ekstrə'dɪʃn/ n. Auslieferung,
die

extra'marital adj. außerehelich

extraordinary /ɪk'strɔːdɪnərɪ/ adj.
außergewöhnlich; merkwürdig ⟨Benehmen⟩;
how ~! wie seltsam!

extravagance /ɪk'strævəgəns/ n. **(a)**
Extravaganz, die
(b) (extravagant thing) Luxus, der

extravagant /ɪk'strævəgənt/ adj.
verschwenderisch; aufwendig ⟨Lebensstil⟩;
teuer ⟨Geschmack⟩

extreme /ɪk'striːm/ **1** adj. **(a)** äußerst...
⟨Spitze, Rand, Ende⟩; extrem ⟨Gegensätze,
Hitze, Kälte⟩; höchst... ⟨Gefahr⟩; äußerst...
stärkst... ⟨Schmerzen⟩; größt... ⟨Wichtigkeit⟩;
at the ~ **edge/left** ganz am Rand/ganz links
(b) (not moderate) extrem; drastisch
⟨Maßnahme⟩
2 n. Extrem, das; **go to** ~**s** vor nichts
zurückschrecken; **go from one** ~ **to the
other** von einem Extrem ins andere fallen

ex'tremely adv. äußerst

extremist /ɪk'striːmɪst/ n. Extremist, der/
Extremistin, die; attrib. extremistisch

extremity /ɪk'stremɪtɪ/ n. äußerstes Ende

extricate /'ekstrɪkeɪt/ v.t. ~ **sth. from sth.**
etw. aus etw. herausziehen; ~ **oneself/sb.
from sth.** sich/jmdn. aus etw. befreien

extrovert /'ekstrəvɜːt/ **1** n.
extravertierter Mensch; **be an** ~:
extravertiert sein
2 adj. extravertiert

exuberant /ɪg'zjuːbərənt/ adj. **be** ~: sich
überschwänglich freuen

exude /ɪg'zjuːd/ *v.t.* absondern; (fig.)
ausstrahlen

exult /ɪg'zʌlt/ *v.i.* jubeln (**in**, **at**, **over** über +
Akk.)

eye /aɪ/ ① *n.* **(a)** Auge, *das;* **keep an ~ on
sb./sth.** auf jmdn./etw. aufpassen; **see ~ to
~:** einer Meinung sein; **with one's ~s shut**
(fig.) blind; (easily) im Schlaf; **be up to one's
~s in work/debt** bis über beide Ohren in
Arbeit/Schulden stecken (ugs.)
(b) (of needle) Öhr, *das;* (metal loop) Öse, *die*
② *v.t.*, beäugen; **~ sb. up and down** jmdn.
von oben bis unten mustern

eye: ~ball *n.* Augapfel, *der;* **~brow** *n.*
Augenbraue, *die;* **~catching** *adj.* ins
Auge springend *od.* fallend ⟨*Inserat, Plakat,*

Buchhülle usw.⟩; **be [very] ~-catching** ein
[wirkungsvoller] Blickfang sein; **~ drops**
n. pl. (Med.) Augentropfen *Pl.;* **~ hospital**
n. Augenklinik, *die;* **~lash** *n.*
Augenwimper, *die;* **~ level** *n.* Augenhöhe,
die; **~-level** *attrib.* in Augenhöhe *nachgestellt;*
at ~ level in Augenhöhe; **~lid** *n.* Augenlid,
das; **~ make-up** *n.* Augen-Make-up, *das;*
~shadow *n.* Lidschatten, *der;* **~sight** *n.*
Sehkraft, *die;* **have good ~sight** gute Augen
haben; **his ~sight is poor** er hat schlechte
Augen; **~sore** *n.* Schandfleck, *der;* **~wash**
n. **(a)** (Med.: lotion) Augenwasser, *das;* **(b)** (coll.)
(nonsense) Gewäsch, *das* (ugs.); (concealment)
Augen[aus]wischerei, *die* (ugs.); **~witness**
n. Augenzeuge, *der/*-zeugin, *die*

Ff

F, f /ef/ *n.* F, f, *das*

fable /'feɪbl/ *n.* Fabel, *die;* (myth, lie)
Märchen, *das*

fabric /'fæbrɪk/ *n.* Gewebe, *das*

fabricate /'fæbrɪkeɪt/ *v.t.* (invent) erfinden

fabrication /fæbrɪˈkeɪʃn/ *n.* Erfindung, *die*

'fabric softener /'sɒfənə(r)/ *n.*
Weichspülmittel, *das;* Weichspüler, *der*

fabulous /'fæbjʊləs/ *adj.* **(a)** sagenhaft
(b) (coll.: marvellous) fabelhaft (ugs.)

façade /fəˈsɑːd/ *n.* (lit. or fig.) Fassade, *die;*
that's just a ~ (fig.) das ist alles nur Fassade

face /feɪs/ ① *n.* **(a)** Gesicht, *das;* **lie
~ down[ward]** ⟨*Person/Buch:*⟩ auf dem
Bauch/Gesicht liegen; **make** *or* **pull a ~/~s**
Grimassen schneiden; **on the ~ of it** dem
Anschein nach; **in the ~ of sth.** trotz etw.
(*Gen.*)
(b) (of mountain, cliff) Wand, *die;* (of clock, watch)
Zifferblatt, *das;* (of dice) Seite, *die;* (of coin,
playing card) Vorderseite, *die*
② *v.t.* **(a)** sich wenden zu; [stand] **facing one
another** sich (*Dat.*) gegenüber[stehen]
(b) (fig.) ins Auge sehen (+ *Dat.*) ⟨*Tod,
Vorstellung*⟩; stehen vor (+ *Dat.*) ⟨*Ruin,
Entscheidung*⟩; **~ the facts** den Tatsachen ins
Gesicht sehen; **be ~d with sth.** sich einer
Sache (*Dat.*) gegenübersehen
(c) (coll.: bear) verkraften
③ *v.i.* (in train etc.) **~ backwards/forwards**
⟨*Person:*⟩ entgegen der/in Fahrtrichtung
sitzen
∎ **face 'up to** *v.t.* ins Auge sehen (+ *Dat.*);
sich abfinden mit ⟨*Möglichkeit*⟩

face: ~ cream *n.* Gesichtscreme, *die;*
~ flannel *n.* (Brit.) Waschlappen, *der;*
~less /'feɪslɪs/ *adj.* (anonymous) anonym
(fig.); **~lift** *n.* **(a)** Facelifting, *das;* **have** *or*

get a ~lift sich liften lassen; **(b)** (fig.)
Verschönerung, *die;* **~ pack** *n.*
[Gesichts]maske, *die;* **~-saving** *adj.* zur
Wahrung des Gesichts *nachgestellt*

facet /'fæsɪt/ *n.* Facette, *die;* (fig.) Aspekt,
der

facetious /fəˈsiːʃəs/ *adj.* [gewollt] witzig

face: ~-to-~ *adj.* persönlich ⟨*Gespräch,
Treffen*⟩; **~ value** *n.* Nennwert, *der;* **accept
sth. at [its] ~ value** (fig.) etw. für bare Münze
nehmen

facial /'feɪʃl/ *adj.* Gesichts-

facile /'fæsaɪl/ *adj.* nichts sagend

facilities /fəˈsɪlɪtɪz/ *n. pl.* Einrichtungen
Pl.; **cooking/washing ~:** Koch-/
Waschgelegenheit, *die;* **sports ~:**
Sportanlagen *Pl.;* **shopping ~:**
Einkaufsmöglichkeiten *Pl.*

facsimile /fækˈsɪmɪlɪ/ *n.* **(a)** Faksimile, *das*
(b) ▶ FAX 1

fact /fækt/ *n.* Tatsache, *die;* **~s and figures**
Fakten und Zahlen; **the ~ remains that …:**
Tatsache bleibt: …; **the true ~s of the case**
or **matter** der wahre Sachverhalt; **know for a
~ that …:** genau wissen, dass …; **in ~:**
tatsächlich

faction /'fækʃn/ *n.* Splittergruppe, *die*

factor /'fæktə(r)/ *n.* Faktor, *der*

factory /'fæktərɪ/ *n.* Fabrik, *die*

factory: ~ 'farm *n.* [voll]automatisierter
landwirtschaftlicher Betrieb; **~ 'farming**
n. [fabrikmäßige] Massentierhaltung; **the
~ farming of salmon** die massenweise
Lachsproduktion; **~ worker** *n.*
Fabrikarbeiter, *der/*-arbeiterin, *die*

'fact sheet *n.* Infoblatt, *das*

factual /'fæktjʊəl/ *adj.* sachlich

faculty /'fækəltɪ/ n. (a) Fähigkeit, die; **mental ~**: geistige Kraft (b) (Univ.) Fakultät, die

fad /fæd/ n. Marotte, die

fade /feɪd/ v.i. (a) ⟨Blätter, Blumen:⟩ [ver]welken (b) ~ [in colour] [ver]bleichen; **the light ~d** es dunkelte (c) ⟨Laut:⟩ verklingen (d) (fig.) verblassen; ⟨Schönheit:⟩ verblühen; ⟨Hoffnung:⟩ schwinden (e) (blend) übergehen (**into** in + Akk.). ■ **fade a'way** v.i. schwinden; ⟨Laut:⟩ verklingen (**into** in + Dat.)

faded /'feɪdɪd/ adj. welk ⟨Blume, Blatt, Laub⟩; verblichen ⟨Stoff, Farbe⟩

faeces /'fiːsiːz/ n. pl. Fäkalien Pl.

fag /fæg/ n. (a) (Brit. coll.) Schinderei, die (ugs.) (b) (coll.: cigarette) Stäbchen, das (ugs.)

fail /feɪl/ **1** v.i. (a) scheitern; (in examination) nicht bestehen, (ugs.) durchfallen (**in** in + Dat.) (b) (become weaker) ⟨Augenlicht, Gehör, Stärke:⟩ nachlassen (c) (break down, stop) ⟨Versorgung:⟩ zusammenbrechen; ⟨Motor:⟩ aussetzen; ⟨Batterie, Pumpe:⟩ ausfallen; ⟨Bremse:⟩ versagen **2** v.t. (a) ~ **to do sth.** (not succeed in doing) etw. nicht tun [können]; ~ **to achieve one's purpose/aim** seine Absicht/sein Ziel verfehlen (b) (be unsuccessful in) nicht bestehen, (ugs.) durchfallen in (+ Dat.) ⟨Prüfung⟩ (c) (reject) durchfallen lassen (ugs.) ⟨Prüfling⟩ (d) ~ **to do sth.** (not do) etw. nicht tun; (neglect to do) [es] versäumen, etw. zu tun; **not ~ to do sth.** etw. tun (e) **words ~ me** mir fehlen die Worte; **his courage ~ed him** ihn verließ der Mut **3** n. **without ~**: auf jeden Fall

'failing 1 n. Schwäche, die **2** prep. ~ **that** andernfalls

failure /'feɪljə(r)/ n. (a) (omission, neglect) Versäumnis, das (b) (lack of success) Scheitern, das; **end in ~**: scheitern (c) (person or thing) Versager, der; **our plan/ attempt was a ~**: unser Plan/Versuch war fehlgeschlagen

faint /feɪnt/ **1** adj. (a) matt ⟨Licht, Farbe, Stimme, Lächeln⟩; schwach ⟨Geruch, Duft⟩; leise ⟨Flüstern, Geräusch, Stimme⟩; entfernt ⟨Ähnlichkeit⟩; undeutlich ⟨Umriss, Linie, Spur, Fotokopie⟩ (b) (giddy, weak) matt; **she felt ~**: ihr war schwindelig **2** v.i. ohnmächtig werden (**from** vor + Dat.) **3** n. Ohnmacht, die

faint-'hearted adj. hasenherzig; zaghaft ⟨Versuch⟩

'faintly adv. schwach; entfernt ⟨sich ähneln⟩

fair¹ /feə(r)/ n. (fun~) Jahrmarkt, der; (exhibition) Messe, die; **book/trade ~**: Buch-/ Handelsmesse, die

fair² adj. (a) (just) gerecht; begründet ⟨Beschwerde, Annahme⟩; fair ⟨Spiel, Kampf, Prozess, Preis, Beurteilung, Handel⟩; ~ **play** Fairness, die (b) (not bad, pretty good) ganz gut ⟨Bilanz, Anzahl, Chance⟩; ziemlich ⟨Maß, Geschwindigkeit⟩ (c) (blond) blond ⟨Haar, Person⟩; (light) hell ⟨Haut⟩; (~-skinned) hellhäutig ⟨Person⟩ (d) schön ⟨Wetter, Tag⟩

fair: ~ground n. Festplatz, der; **~-haired** adj. blond; **~-haired boy** (Amer. fig.) Liebling, der; Favorit, der

'fairly adv. (a) fair ⟨kämpfen, spielen⟩; gerecht ⟨bestrafen, beurteilen, behandeln⟩ (b) (rather) ziemlich

'fair-minded adj. unvoreingenommen

'fairness n. Gerechtigkeit, die; **in all ~** [**to sb.**] um fair [gegen jmdn.] zu sein

fairy /'feərɪ/ n. Fee, die

fairy: ~ 'godmother n. gute Fee; **~ story**, **~ tale** ns. Märchen, das

faith /feɪθ/ n. (a) (reliance, trust) Vertrauen, das (**in** zu); **have ~ in oneself** Selbstvertrauen haben; **in good ~**: in gutem Glauben (b) (religious belief) Glaube, der

faithful /'feɪθfl/ adj. (a) treu (**to** Dat.) (b) (conscientious) pflichtbewusst; [ge]treu ⟨Diener⟩ (c) (accurate) wahrheitsgetreu; originalgetreu ⟨Wiedergabe, Kopie⟩

'faithfully adv. (a) treu ⟨dienen⟩; pflichtbewusst [wahrheitsgetreu ⟨überbringen, zustellen⟩; hoch und heilig ⟨versprechen⟩ (b) (accurately) wahrheitsgetreu ⟨erzählen⟩; originalgetreu ⟨wiedergeben⟩; genau ⟨befolgen⟩ (c) **yours ~**: hochachtungsvoll

faith: ~ healer n. Gesundbeter, der/ -beterin, die; **~ healing** n. Gesundbeten, das

fake /feɪk/ **1** adj. unecht; gefälscht ⟨Dokument, Banknote, Münze⟩ **2** n. (a) Imitation, die; (painting) Fälschung, die (b) (person) Schwindler, der/Schwindlerin, die **3** v.t. fälschen ⟨Unterschrift⟩; vortäuschen ⟨Krankheit, Unfall⟩

falcon /'fɔːlkn/ n. Falke, der

fall /fɔːl/ **1** n. (a) Fallen, das; (of person) Sturz, der; ~ **of snow/rain** Schnee-/ Regenfall, der; **have a ~**: stürzen (b) (collapse, defeat) Fall, der; (of dynasty, empire) Untergang, der (c) (decrease) Rückgang, der (d) (Amer.: autumn) Herbst, der **2** v.i., **fell** /fel/, **fallen** /'fɔːln/ (a) fallen; ⟨Baum:⟩ umstürzen; ⟨Pferd:⟩ stürzen; ~ **off sth.**, ~ **down from sth.** von etw. ┄┄>

[herunter]fallen; ~ **down** [into] sth. in etw.
(Akk.). [hinein]fallen; ~ **to the ground** auf
den Boden fallen; ~ **down the stairs** or
downstairs die Treppe herunter-/
hinunterfallen
(b) ⟨Nacht, Dunkelheit:⟩ hereinbrechen;
⟨Abend:⟩ anbrechen
(c) ⟨Blätter:⟩ [ab]fallen
(d) (sink) sinken; ⟨Barometer:⟩ fallen; ⟨Absatz,
Verkauf:⟩ zurückgehen; ~ **by 10 per cent/
from 10**[°**C**] **to 0**[°**C**] um 10%/von 10[°C] auf
0[°C] sinken
(e) (be killed) ⟨Soldat:⟩ fallen
(f) (collapse) einstürzen; ~ **to pieces,** ~ **apart**
auseinander fallen
(g) (occur) fallen (on auf + Akk.)
■ **fall 'back** v.i. zurückweichen
■ **fall 'back on** v.t. zurückgreifen auf
(+ Akk.)
■ **fall 'down** v.i. (a) ▶ FALL 2A
(b) ⟨Brücke, Gebäude:⟩ einstürzen
■ **'fall for** v.t. (coll.) ~ **for sb.** sich in jmdn.
verknallen (ugs.); ~ **for sth.** auf etw. (Akk.)
hereinfallen (ugs.)
■ **fall 'in** v.i. (a) hineinfallen
(b) (Mil.) antreten; ~ **in!** angetreten!
(c) ⟨Gebäude, Wand usw.:⟩ einstürzen
■ **fall 'off** v.i. (a) herunterfallen
(b) (diminish) nachlassen
■ **fall 'out** v.i. (a) herausfallen; ⟨Haare,
Federn:⟩ ausfallen
(b) (quarrel) ~ **out** [**with sb.**] sich [mit jmdm.]
streiten
■ **fall 'over** v.i. umfallen; ⟨Person:⟩
[hin]fallen
■ **fall 'through** v.i. (fig.) ins Wasser fallen
(ugs.)
fallacy /'fæləsɪ/ n. Irrtum, der
fallen ▶ FALL 2
fallible /'fælɪbl/ adj. nicht unfehlbar;
fehlbar ⟨Person⟩
'fallout n. radioaktiver Niederschlag
fallow /'fæləʊ/ adj. brachliegend; ~ **ground/
land** Brache, die/Brachland, das; **lie** ~:
brachliegen
false /fɔːls, fɒls/ adj. falsch; gefälscht
⟨Urkunde, Dokument⟩; künstlich ⟨Wimpern⟩;
under a ~ **name** unter falschem Namen
false 'alarm n. blinder Alarm
'falsely adv. falsch; fälschlich[erweise]
⟨annehmen, glauben, behaupten,
beschuldigen⟩
false: ~ **'move** ▶ FALSE STEP;
~ **pre'tences** n. pl. Vorspiegelung
falscher Tatsachen; ~ **'start** n. Fehlstart,
der; ~ **'step** n. (lit. or fig.) falscher Schritt;
make a ~ **step** einen falschen Schritt tun;
~ **'teeth** n. pl. [künstliches] Gebiss
falsify /'fɔːlsɪfaɪ/ v.t. (alter) fälschen;
(misrepresent) verfälschen ⟨Tatsachen,
Wahrheit⟩
falter /'fɔːltə(r)/ v.i. stocken
fame /feɪm/ n. Ruhm, der

familiar /fə'mɪljə(r)/ adj. (a) vertraut;
bekannt ⟨Gesicht, Name, Lied⟩; **he looks** ~:
er kommt mir bekannt vor
(b) (informal) ungezwungen ⟨Sprache, Art⟩
familiarity /fəmɪlɪ'ærɪtɪ/ n. Vertrautheit,
die
familiarize /fə'mɪljəraɪz/ v.t. vertraut
machen (with mit)
family /'fæməlɪ/ n. Familie, die
family: ~ **'doctor** n. Hausarzt, der;
~ **name** n. Familienname, der;
~ **'planning** n. Familienplanung, die;
~ **'tree** n. Stammbaum, der
famine /'fæmɪn/ n. Hungersnot, die
famished /'fæmɪʃt/ adj. ausgehungert; **I'm
absolutely** ~ (coll.) ich sterbe vor Hunger
(ugs.)
famous /'feɪməs/ adj. berühmt
fan[1] /fæn/ ① n. Fächer, der; (apparatus)
Ventilator, der
② v.t., **-nn-** fächeln ⟨Gesicht⟩; anfachen
⟨Feuer⟩; ~ **oneself/sb.** sich/jmdm. Luft
zufächeln
■ **fan 'out** v.i. fächern; ⟨Soldaten:⟩
ausfächern
fan[2] n. (devotee) Fan, der
fanatic /fə'nætɪk/ n. Fanatiker, der/
Fanatikerin, die
fanatical /fə'nætɪkl/ adj. fanatisch
fanaticism /fə'nætɪsɪzm/ n. Fanatismus,
der
'fan belt n. Keilriemen, der
fanciful /'fænsɪfl/ adj. überspannt
⟨Vorstellung, Gedanke⟩; fantastisch ⟨Gemälde,
Design⟩
'fan club n. Fanklub, der
fancy /'fænsɪ/ ① n. (a) (taste, inclination) **he
has taken a** ~ **to a new car/her** ein neues
Auto/sie hat es ihm angetan; **take** or **catch
sb.'s** ~: jmdm. gefallen
(b) (whim) Laune, die; **tickle sb.'s** ~: jmdn.
reizen
② attrib. adj. kunstvoll ⟨Arbeit, Muster⟩;
fein[st...] ⟨Kuchen, Spitzen⟩
③ v.t. (a) (imagine) sich (Dat.) einbilden;
~ **that!** (coll.) sieh mal einer an!
(b) (suppose) glauben
(c) (wish to have) mögen; **what do you** ~ **for
dinner?** was hättest du gern zum
Abendessen?; **do you think she fancies him?**
glaubst du, sie mag ihn?
fancy 'dress n. [Masken]kostüm, das; **in**
~: kostümiert; **fancy-dress party** Kostümfest,
das; **fancy-dress ball** Maskenball, der
fanfare /'fænfeə(r)/ n. Fanfare, die
fang /fæŋ/ n. Reißzahn, der; (of snake)
Giftzahn, der
fan: ~ **heater** n. Heizlüfter, der; ~**light**
n. Oberlicht, das; ~ **mail** n. Fanpost, die;
~ **oven** n. Heißluftofen, der
fantastic /fæn'tæstɪk/ adj. (a) (grotesque,
quaint) bizarr
(b) (coll.: excellent) fantastisch (ugs.)

fantasy /'fæntəzɪ/ n. Fantasie, die; (mental image) Fantasiegebilde, das

FAQ /fæk/ abbr. (Comp.) FAQ

far /fɑː(r)/ [1] adv. weit; ~ **above/below** hoch über/tief unter (+ Dat.); hoch oben/tief unten; **as ~ as Munich/the church** bis [nach] München/bis zur Kirche; ~ **and wide** weit und breit; **from ~ and wide** von fern und nah; ~ **too** viel zu; ~ **longer/better** weit[aus] länger/besser; **as ~ as I remember/know** soweit ich mich erinnere/weiß; **go so ~ as to do sth.** so weit gehen und etw. tun; **so ~** (until now) bisher; **so ~ so good** so weit, so gut; **by ~:** bei weitem; ~ **from easy/good** alles andere als leicht/gut
[2] adj. (a) (remote) weit entfernt; (in time) fern; **in the ~ distance** in weiter Ferne (b) (more remote) weiter entfernt; **the ~ bank of the river/side of the road** das andere Flussufer/die andere Straßenseite; **the ~ door/wall** etc. die hintere Tür/Wand usw.

farce /fɑːs/ n. Farce, die

farcical /'fɑːsɪkl/ adj. (absurd) farcenhaft

fare /feə(r)/ n. (a) (price) Fahrpreis, der; (money) Fahrgeld, das; **what or how much is the ~?** was kostet die Fahrt? (b) (food) Kost, die

Far: ~ **'East** n. **the ~ East** der Ferne Osten; ~ **'Eastern** adj. fernöstlich; des Fernen Ostens nachgestellt

farewell /feə'wel/ [1] int. leb[e] wohl (veralt.)
[2] n. attrib. ~ **speech/gift** Abschiedsrede, die/-geschenk, das

far-'fetched adj. weit hergeholt

farm /fɑːm/ [1] n. [Bauern]hof, der; (larger) Gut, das; ~ **animals** Nutzvieh, das
[2] v.t. bebauen ⟨Land⟩
[3] v.i. Landwirtschaft treiben

'farmer n. Landwirt, der/-wirtin, die

farm: ~**hand** n. Landarbeiter, der/ -arbeiterin, die; ~**house** n. Bauernhaus, das; (larger) Gutshaus, das

'farming n. Landwirtschaft, die

farm: ~**land** n. Acker- und Weideland, das; ~**worker** n. Landarbeiter, der/ -arbeiterin, die; ~**yard** n. Hof, der

far: ~**'reaching** adj. weit reichend; ~**sighted** adj. (a) (fig.) weit blickend; (b) (Amer.: long-sighted) weitsichtig

fart /fɑːt/ (coarse) [1] v.i. furzen (derb)
[2] n. Furz, der (derb)

farther /'fɑːðə(r)/ ▶ FURTHER 1A, 2

farthest /'fɑːðɪst/ ▶ FURTHEST

fascinate /'fæsɪneɪt/ v.t. fesseln; bezaubern

fascinated /'fæsɪneɪtɪd/ adj. fasziniert

fascinating /'fæsɪneɪtɪŋ/ adj. faszinierend (geh.); bezaubernd; hochinteressant ⟨Thema, Faktum, Meinung⟩; spannend, fesselnd ⟨Buch⟩

fascination /fæsɪ'neɪʃn/ n. Zauber, der; **have a ~ for sb.** einen besonderen Reiz auf jmdn. ausüben

fascism /'fæʃɪzm/ n. Faschismus, der

fascist /'fæʃɪst/ [1] n. Faschist, der/ Faschistin, die
[2] adj. faschistisch

fashion /'fæʃn/ [1] n. (a) Mode, die (b) (manner) Art [und Weise]; **talk/behave in a peculiar ~:** merkwürdig sprechen/sich merkwürdig verhalten
[2] v.t. formen (out of, from aus; [in]to zu)

fashionable /'fæʃənəbl/ adj. modisch; vornehm ⟨Hotel, Restaurant⟩; Mode⟨farbe, -autor⟩

fashionably /'fæʃənəblɪ/ adv. modisch

fashion: ~**-conscious** adj. modebewusst; ~ **designer** n. Modeschöpfer, der/-schöpferin, die; ~ **parade,** ~ **show** ns. Mode[n]schau, die

fast¹ /fɑːst/ [1] v.i. fasten
[2] n. Fasten, das

fast² [1] adj. (a) (fixed, attached) fest; **make [the boat] ~:** das Boot festmachen; **hard and ~:** fest; bindend ⟨Regel⟩; klar ⟨Entscheidung⟩ (b) (rapid) schnell; ~ **train** Schnellzug, der; D-Zug, der (c) **be [ten minutes] ~** ⟨Uhr:⟩ [zehn Minuten] vorgehen
[2] adv. (a) **be ~ asleep** fest schlafen; (when one should be awake) fest eingeschlafen sein (b) (quickly) schnell

'fastback n. (back of car) Fließheck, das; Fastback, das; (car) Wagen mit Fließheck; Fastback, das

fasten /'fɑːsn/ v.t. befestigen (on, to an + Dat.); zumachen ⟨Kleid, Spange, Jacke⟩; [ab]schließen ⟨Tür⟩; anstecken ⟨Brosche⟩ (to an + Akk.); ~ **one's seat belt** sich anschnallen

'fastener, 'fastening ns. Verschluss, der

fast: ~ **'food** n.: im Schnellrestaurant angebotenes Essen; Fastfood, das; attrib. ~**food restaurant** Schnellrestaurant, das; ~ **'forward** n. schneller Vorlauf; (playback) Zeitrafferwiedergabe, die; ~**forward** [1] attrib. adj. Vorspul⟨taste, -funktion⟩; [2] v.t. & i. vorspulen

fastidious /fæ'stɪdɪəs/ adj. wählerisch; (hard to please) heikel

fast: ~ **lane** n. Überholspur, die; **life in the ~ lane** (fig.) Leben auf vollen Touren (ugs.); ~ **track** n. Überholspur, die; **a career on the ~ track** eine Blitzkarriere; **be on the ~ track** eine Blitzkarriere machen; ~**track** [1] v.t. beschleunigen ⟨Projekt⟩; [2] attrib. adj. Schnell-

fat /fæt/ [1] adj. dick; rund ⟨Wangen, Gesicht⟩
[2] n. Fett, das; **animal/vegetable ~:** tierisches/pflanzliches Fett

fatal /'feɪtl/ adj. (a) (disastrous) verheerend (to für); **it would be ∼:** das wäre das Ende (b) (deadly) tödlich ⟨Unfall, Verletzung⟩

fatality /fə'tælɪtɪ/ n. Todesopfer, das

'**fatally** adv. tödlich; **be ∼ ill** todkrank sein

fate /feɪt/ n. Schicksal, das

fat-free adj. fettfrei

'**fathead** n. Dummkopf, der (ugs.)

father /'fɑ:ðə(r)/ n. Vater, der

father: F∼ '**Christmas** n. der Weihnachtsmann; **∼ figure** n. Vaterfigur, die

fatherhood /'fɑ:ðəhʊd/ n. Vaterschaft, die

'**father-in-law** n., pl. **∼s-in-law** Schwiegervater, der

'**fatherly** adj. väterlich

'**Father's Day** n. Vatertag, der

fathom /'fæðəm/ ① n. (Naut.) Faden, der ② v.t. (comprehend) verstehen; **∼ sb./sth. out** jmdn./etw. ergründen

fatigue /fə'ti:g/ ① n. Ermüdung, die ② v.t. ermüden

'**fatness** n. Dicke, die

fatten /'fætn/ v.t. herausfüttern ⟨Person⟩; mästen ⟨Tier⟩

'**fattening** adj. **be ∼:** dick machen

fatty /'fætɪ/ adj. fett ⟨Fleisch, Soße⟩; fetthaltig ⟨Speise, Nahrungsmittel⟩

faucet /'fɔ:sɪt/ n. (Amer.) Wasserhahn, der

fault /fɔ:lt, fɒlt/ n. (a) Fehler, der (b) (responsibility) Schuld, die; **it's your ∼:** du bist schuld; **it isn't my ∼:** ich habe keine Schuld; **be at ∼:** im Unrecht sein (c) (in machinery; also Electr.) Defekt, der

'**faultless** adj. einwandfrei

'**faulty** adj. fehlerhaft; defekt ⟨Gerät, usw.⟩

fauna /'fɔ:nə/ n., pl. **∼ė** /'fɔ:ni:/ or **∼s** Fauna, die

favor etc. (Amer.) ▶ FAVOUR etc.

favour /'feɪvə(r)/ ① n. (a) Gunst, die (b) (kindness) Gefallen, der; **ask sb. a ∼, ask a ∼ of sb.** jmdn. um einen Gefallen bitten; **do sb. a ∼, do a ∼ for sb.** jmdm. einen Gefallen tun; **as a ∼:** aus Gefälligkeit (c) **be in ∼ of sth.** für etw. sein ② v.t. bevorzugen

favourable /'feɪvərəbl/ adj. (Brit.) (a) günstig ⟨Eindruck, Licht⟩; gewogen ⟨Haltung, Einstellung⟩; freundlich ⟨Erwähnung⟩; positiv ⟨Bericht[erstattung], Bemerkung⟩ (b) (helpful) günstig (to für) ⟨Wetter, Wind, Umstand⟩

favourably /'feɪvərəblɪ/ adv. (Brit.) wohlwollend; **be ∼ disposed towards sb./sth.** jmdm./einer Sache positiv gegenüberstehen

favourite /'feɪvərɪt/ (Brit.) ① adj. Lieblings- ② n. (a) Liebling, der; (food/country etc.) Lieblingsessen, das/-land, das usw.; **this/he is my ∼:** das/ihn mag ich am liebsten (b) (Sport) Favorit, der/Favoritin, die

favouritism /'feɪvərɪtɪzm/ n. (Brit.) Begünstigung, die; (when selecting sb. for a post etc.) Günstlingswirtschaft, die

fawn /fɔ:n/ ① n. (a) (colour) Rehbraun, das (b) (young deer) [Dam]kitz, das ② adj. rehfarben

fax /fæks/ ① n. [Tele]fax, das ② v.t. faxen

fax: ∼ machine n. Faxgerät, das; **∼ modem** n. (Comp.) Faxmodem, das; **∼ number** n. Faxnummer, die

FBI abbr. (Amer.) = **Federal Bureau of Investigation** FBI, das

fear /fɪə(r)/ ① n. Angst, die (of vor + Dat.); (instance) Befürchtung, die; **∼ of death** or **dying/heights** Todes-/Höhenangst, die; **∼ of doing sth.** Angst davor, etw. zu tun; **in ∼:** angstvoll; **no ∼!** (coll.) keine Bange! (ugs.) ② v.t. (a) **∼ sb./sth.** vor jmdm./etw. Angst haben; **∼ to do** or **doing sth.** Angst haben, etw. zu tun (b) (be worried about) befürchten; **∼ [that ...]** fürchten[, dass ...]

fearful /'fɪəfl/ adj. (a) (terrible) furchtbar (b) (frightened) ängstlich; **be ∼ of sth./sb.** vor etw./jmdm. Angst haben

'**fearless** adj., '**fearlessly** adv. furchtlos

feasibility /fi:zɪ'bɪlɪtɪ/ n. Durchführbarkeit, die

feasible /'fi:zɪbl/ adj. durchführbar

feast /fi:st/ ① n. (a) (Relig.) Fest, das (b) (banquet) Festessen, das ② v.i. schlemmen; **∼ on sth.** sich an etw. (Dat.) gütlich tun

feat /fi:t/ n. Meisterleistung, die

feather /'feðə(r)/ n. Feder, die

feather: ∼ 'bed n. mit Federn gefüllte Matratze; **∼ 'duster** n. Flederwisch, der; **∼weight** n. (Boxing) Federgewicht, das

feature /'fi:tʃə(r)/ ① n. (a) usu. in pl. (of face) Gesichtszug, der (b) (characteristic) [charakteristisches] Merkmal; **be a ∼ of sth.** charakteristisch für etw. sein (c) (Journ.) Feature, das (d) (Cinemat.) **∼ [film]** Hauptfilm, der ② v.t. vorrangig vorstellen; (in film) in der Hauptrolle zeigen ③ v.i. vorkommen; **∼ in** (be important) eine bedeutende Rolle haben bei

Feb. abbr. = **February** Febr.

February /'febrʊərɪ/ n. Februar, der

feces (Amer.) ▶ FAECES

fed /fed/ ① ▶ FEED 1, 2 ② pred. adj. (coll.) **be/get ∼ up with sb./sth.** jmdn./etw. satt haben/kriegen (ugs.); **I'm ∼ up** ich hab die Nase voll (ugs.)

federal /'fedərl/ adj. Bundes-; föderativ ⟨System⟩

federation /fedə'reɪʃn/ n. Föderation, die

fee /fi:/ n. Gebühr, die; (of doctor, lawyer, etc.) Honorar, das

feeble /'fiːbl/ adj. schwach; wenig überzeugend ⟨Entschuldigung⟩; zaghaft ⟨Versuch⟩; lahm (ugs.) ⟨Witz⟩

feed /fiːd/ ① v.t., fed /fed/ (a) füttern; ~ sb./an animal with sth. jmdm. etw. zu essen/einem Tier [etw.] zu fressen geben (b) (provide food for) ernähren (on, with mit) ② v.i., fed ⟨Tier:⟩ fressen (from aus); ⟨Person:⟩ essen (off von); ~ on sth. ⟨Tier:⟩ etw. fressen ③ n. (a) (for baby) Mahlzeit, die (b) (fodder) Futter, das

'feedback n. Reaktion, die

feel /fiːl/ ① v.t., felt /felt/ (a) (explore by touch) befühlen (b) (perceive by touch) fühlen; (become aware of) bemerken; (have sensation of) spüren (c) (experience) empfinden; verspüren ⟨Drang⟩; ~ the cold/heat unter der Kälte/Hitze leiden; ~ [that] …: das Gefühl haben, dass …; (think) glauben, dass … ② v.i., felt: (a) ~ [about] in sth. [for sth.] in etw. (Dat.) [nach etw.] [herum]suchen (b) (be conscious that one is) sich … fühlen; ~ angry/sure/disappointed böse/sicher/enttäuscht sein; ~ like sth./doing sth. auf etw. (Akk.) Lust haben/Lust haben, etw. zu tun (c) (be consciously perceived as) sich … anfühlen ∎ **'feel for** v.t. ~ for sb. mit jmdm. Mitleid haben

'feeler n. Fühler, der

'feeling n. (a) Gefühl, das; (sense of touch) [sense of] ~: Tastsinn, der; hurt sb.'s ~s jmdn. verletzen (b) (opinion) Ansicht, die

feet pl. of FOOT

feign /fein/ v.t. vortäuschen; ~ to do sth. vorgeben, etw. zu tun

feline /'fiːlain/ adj. (of cat[s]) Katzen-; (catlike) katzenartig; katzenhaft

fell[1] ▸ FALL 2

fell[2] /fel/ v.t. fällen ⟨Baum⟩

fell[3] adj. in one ~ swoop auf einen Schlag

fellow /'feləʊ/ ① n. (a) (comrade) Kamerad, der (b) (Brit. Univ.) Fellow, der (c) (of academy or society) Mitglied, das (d) (coll.: man, boy) Kerl, der (ugs.) ② attrib. adj. Mit-; ~ man or human being Mitmensch, der

fellowship /'feləʊʃɪp/ n. (companionship) Gesellschaft, die

felt[1] /felt/ n. Filz, der

felt[2] ▸ FEEL

felt[-tipped] 'pen n. Filzstift, der

female /'fiːmeil/ ① adj. weiblich; Frauen⟨stimme, -chor, -verein⟩ ② n. Frau, die; (foetus, child) Mädchen, das; (animal) Weibchen, das

feminine /'femɪnɪn/ adj. weiblich; Frauen⟨angelegenheit, -leiden⟩; (womanly) feminin

femininity /femɪ'nɪnɪti/ n. Weiblichkeit, die

feminism /'femɪnɪzm/ n. Feminismus, der

feminist /'femɪnɪst/ ① adj. feministisch; Feministen⟨bewegung, -gruppe⟩ ② n. Feministin, die/Feminist, der

fence /fens/ ① n. Zaun, der ② v.i. (Sport) fechten ③ v.t. ~ [in] einzäunen

'fencer n. Fechter, der/Fechterin, die

fencing /'fensɪŋ/ n. (Sport) Fechten, das

fend /fend/ v.i. ~ for oneself für sich selbst sorgen; (in hostile surroundings) sich allein durchschlagen ∎ **fend 'off** v.t. abwehren

fender /'fendə(r)/ n. (a) (for fire) Kaminschutz, der (b) (Amer.) (car bumper) Stoßstange, die; (car mudguard) Kotflügel, der

ferment /fə'ment/ ① v.i. gären ② v.t. zur Gärung bringen

fermentation /fɜːmen'teiʃn/ n. Gärung, die

fern /fɜːn/ n. Farnkraut, das

ferocious /fə'rəʊʃəs/ adj. wild

ferocity /fə'rɒsɪti/ n. Wildheit, die

ferret /'ferɪt/ n. Frettchen, das

ferrous /'ferəs/ adj. (containing iron) eisenhaltig; Eisen-

ferry /'feri/ ① n. Fähre, die; (service) Fährverbindung, die ② v.t. (in boat) ~ [across or over] übersetzen

'ferry service n. (a) Fährverbindung, die (b) (business) Fährbetrieb, der

fertile /'fɜːtail/ adj. (fruitful) fruchtbar; (capable of developing) befruchtet

fertility /fɜː'tɪlɪti/ n. Fruchtbarkeit, die

fer'tility drug n. Hormonpräparat, das (zur Steigerung der Fruchtbarkeit)

fertilization /fɜːtɪlai'zeiʃn/ n. (a) (Biol.) Befruchtung, die (b) (Agric.) Düngung, die

fertilize /'fɜːtɪlaiz/ v.t. befruchten

'fertilizer n. Dünger, der

fervent /'fɜːvənt/ adj. leidenschaftlich; inbrünstig ⟨Gebet, Wunsch, Hoffnung⟩

fervour (Brit.; Amer.: **fervor**) /'fɜːvə(r)/ n. Leidenschaftlichkeit, die

fester /'festə(r)/ v.i. eitern

festival /'festɪvl/ n. (a) (feast day) Fest, das (b) (of music etc.) Festival, das

festive /'festɪv/ adj. festlich; fröhlich; the ~ season die Weihnachtszeit

festivity /fe'stɪvɪti/ n. (a) (gaiety) Feststimmung, die (b) (celebration) Feier, die; **festivities** Feierlichkeiten Pl.

festoon /fe'stuːn/ ① n. Girlande, die ② v.t. schmücken (with mit)

fetch /fetʃ/ *v.t.* (a) holen; (collect) abholen
(from von); ∼ sb. sth., ∼ sth. for sb. jmdm.
etw. holen
(b) (be sold for) erzielen ⟨*Preis*⟩

'fetching *adj.* einnehmend

fête /feɪt/ *n.* [Wohltätigkeits]basar, *der*

fetish /'fetɪʃ/ *n.* Fetisch, *der*

fetishism /'fetɪʃɪzm/ *n.* Fetischismus, *der*

fetishist /'fetɪʃɪst/ *n.* Fetischist, *der*/
Fetischistin, *die*

fetter /'fetə(r)/ *v.t.* fesseln

fetus (Amer.) ▶ FOETUS

feud /fjuːd/ *n.* Fehde, *die*

feudal /'fjuːdl/ *adj.* Feudal-; feudalistisch;
∼ **system** Feudalsystem, *das*

fever /'fiːvə(r)/ *n.* (a) (high temperature) Fieber,
das; have a [high] ∼: [hohes] Fieber haben
(b) (disease) Fieberkrankheit, *die*

'feverish *adj.* (a) (Med.) fiebrig; be ∼:
Fieber haben
(b) (excited) fiebrig

'fever pitch *n.* Siedepunkt, *der* (fig.); reach
∼: auf dem Siedepunkt angelangt sein; at ∼:
auf dem Siedepunkt

few /fjuː/ [1] *adj.* (a) (not many) wenige; *abs.*
nur wenige; with very ∼ exceptions mit ganz
wenigen Ausnahmen; his ∼ belongings seine
paar Habseligkeiten; a ∼ ...: wenige ...
(b) (some) wenige; a ∼ ...: ein paar ...; a
∼ more ...: noch ein paar ...
[2] *n.* (a) (not many) wenige; a ∼: wenige; just
a ∼ of you/her friends nur ein paar von
euch/ihrer Freunde
(b) (some) with a ∼ of our friends mit einigen
unserer Freunde; quite a ∼: ziemlich viele

fiancé /fɪ'ɒseɪ/ *n.* Verlobte, *der*

fiancée /fɪ'ɒseɪ/ *n.* Verlobte, *die*

fiasco /fɪ'æskəʊ/ *n., pl.* ∼s Fiasko, *das*

fib /fɪb/ [1] *n.* Flunkerei, *die* (ugs.); tell ∼s
flunkern (ugs.).
[2] *v.i.*, -bb- flunkern (ugs.)

fibre (Brit.; Amer.: **fiber**) /'faɪbə(r)/ *n.* (a)
Faser, *die*
(b) (material) [Faser]gewebe, *das*

fibre: ∼**glass** *n.* (plastic)
glasfaserverstärkter Kunststoff; ∼ **optic**
'**cable** *n.* Glasfaserkabel, *das;* ∼ '**optics**
n. Faseroptik, *die*

fibrous /'faɪbrəs/ *adj.* faserig ⟨*Aufbau,
Beschaffenheit, Eigenschaft*⟩; Faser⟨*gewebe,
-holz, -stoff*⟩

fiche /fiːʃ/ *n., pl.* same or ∼s Mikrofiche,
das od. der

fickle /'fɪkl/ *adj.* unberechenbar

fiction /'fɪkʃn/ *n.* erzählende Literatur; a ∼/
∼s eine Erfindung

fictional /'fɪkʃənl/ *adj.* erfunden
⟨*Geschichte*⟩; fiktiv ⟨*Figur*⟩

'fiction writer *n.* Belletrist, *der*/
Belletristin, *die*

fictitious /fɪk'tɪʃəs/ *adj.* fingiert; falsch
⟨*Name, Identität*⟩

fiddle /'fɪdl/ [1] *n.* (a) (Mus.) (coll./derog.)
Fiedel, *die;* (violin for traditional music) Geige, *die;*
[as] fit as a ∼: kerngesund
(b) (coll.: swindle) Gaunerei, *die*
[2] *v.t.* (coll.) frisieren (ugs.) ⟨*Bücher,
Rechnungen*⟩
[3] *v.i.* herumspielen (with mit)

fiddler /'fɪdlə(r)/ *n.* Geiger, *der*/Geigerin, *die*

fiddly /'fɪdlɪ/ *adj.* (coll.) knifflig

fidelity /fɪ'delɪtɪ/ *n.* Treue, *die* (to zu)

fidget /'fɪdʒɪt/ [1] *v.i.* ∼ [about]
herumrutschen
[2] *n.* (person) Zappelphilipp, *der* (ugs.)

'fidgety *adj.* unruhig; zappelig ⟨*Kind*⟩

field /fiːld/ *n.* (a) Feld, *das*
(b) (for game) Platz, *der;* [Spiel]feld, *das*
(c) (subject area) [Fach]gebiet, *das;* in the ∼ of
medicine auf dem Gebiet der Medizin; that is
outside my ∼: das fällt nicht in mein Fach

field: ∼ **day** *n.* have a ∼ day seinen großen
Tag haben; ∼ **events** *n. pl.* technische
Disziplinen *Pl.* ∼ **glasses** *n. pl.*
Feldstecher, *der;* **F**∼ '**Marshal** *n.* (Brit. Mil.)
Feldmarschall, *der;* ∼ **mouse** *n.*
Brandmaus, *die;* ∼ **trip** *n.* Exkursion, *die*

fiend /fiːnd/ *n.* (a) (wicked person) Scheusal,
das
(b) (evil spirit) böser Geist

'fiendish *adj.* (a) (wicked) teuflisch
(b) (very awkward) höllisch

fierce /fɪəs/ *adj.* wild; erbittert ⟨*Widerstand,
Kampf*⟩; scharf ⟨*Kritik*⟩

'fiercely *adv.* heftig ⟨*angreifen, Widerstand
leisten*⟩; wütend ⟨*brüllen*⟩; aufs heftigste
⟨*kritisieren, bekämpfen*⟩

fiery /'faɪərɪ/ *adj.* glühend; (looking like fire)
feurig; (blazing red) feuerrot

fifteen /fɪf'tiːn/ [1] *adj.* fünfzehn
[2] *n.* Fünfzehn, *die.* See also EIGHT

fifteenth /fɪf'tiːnθ/ [1] *adj.* fünfzehnt-...
[2] *n.* (fraction) Fünfzehntel, *das.* See also
EIGHTH

fifth /fɪfθ/ [1] *adj.* fünft-...
[2] *n.* (in sequence, rank) Fünfte, *der/die/das;*
(fraction) Fünftel, *das.* See also EIGHTH

fiftieth /'fɪftɪɪθ/ *adj.* fünfzigst-...

fifty /'fɪftɪ/ [1] *adj.* fünfzig
[2] *n.* Fünfzig, *die.* See also EIGHT; EIGHTY 2

fig /fɪg/ *n.* Feige, *die*

fig. *abbr.* = figure Abb.

fight /faɪt/ [1] *v.i.*, fought /fɔːt/ (a) kämpfen;
(with fists) sich schlagen
(b) (squabble) [sich] streiten (about wegen)
[2] *v.t.*, fought: (a) ∼ sb./sth. gegen jmdn./
etw. kämpfen; (using fists) ∼ sb. sich mit
jmdm. schlagen
(b) (seek to overcome) bekämpfen; (resist)
∼ sb./sth. gegen jmdn./etw. ankämpfen
(c) ∼ a battle einen Kampf austragen
(d) (contest) kandidieren bei ⟨*Wahl*⟩
[3] *n.* Kampf, *der* (for um)

■ **'fight against** *v.t.* kämpfen gegen;
ankämpfen gegen ⟨*Wellen, Wind*⟩

■ **fight 'back** ① *v.i.* zurückschlagen
② *v.t.* (suppress) zurückhalten
■ **fight 'off** *v.t.* abwehren
■ **'fight with** *v.t.* (a) kämpfen mit
(b) (squabble with) [sich] streiten mit
'fighter *n.* Kämpfer, *der*/Kämpferin, *die;*
(aircraft) Kampfflugzeug, *das*
'fighting *n.* Kämpfe *Pl.*
fighting 'chance *n.* have a ~ of
succeeding/of doing sth. Aussicht auf Erfolg
haben/gute Chancen haben, etw. zu tun
'fig leaf *n.* (lit. or fig.) Feigenblatt, *das*
figment /'fɪɡmənt/ *n.* a ~ of one's *or* the
imagination pure Einbildung
'fig tree *n.* Feigenbaum, *der*
figurative /'fɪɡərətɪv/ *adj.* übertragen
figure /'fɪɡə(r)/ ① *n.* (a) (shape) Form, *die*
(b) (carving, sculpture, one's bodily shape) Figur,
die
(c) (illustration) Abbildung, *die*
(d) (person as seen) Gestalt, *die;* (literary ~)
Figur, *die*
(e) (numerical symbol) Ziffer, *die;* (number) Zahl,
die; (amount of money) Betrag, *der*
(f) ~ of speech Redewendung, *die*
② *v.i.* (a) vorkommen
(b) that ~s (coll.) das kann gut sein
■ **figure 'out** *v.t.* (a) (by arithmetic)
ausrechnen
(b) (understand) verstehen
figure: ~head *n.* (lit. or fig.) Galionsfigur,
die; ~ **skating** *n.* Eiskunstlauf, *der*
filament /'fɪləmənt/ *n.* (a) Faden, *der*
(b) (Electr.) Glühfaden, *der*
filch /'fɪltʃ/ *v.t.* stibitzen (ugs.)
file¹ /faɪl/ ① *n.* Feile, *die*
② *v.t.* feilen ⟨*Fingernägel*⟩; mit der Feile
bearbeiten ⟨*Holz, Eisen*⟩
file² ① *n.* (a) (holder) Ordner, *der;* (box)
Kassette, *die*
(b) (papers) Ablage, *die;* (cards) Kartei, *die*
② *v.t.* (a) [in die Kartei] einordnen/[in die
Akten] aufnehmen
(b) einreichen ⟨*Antrag*⟩
file³ ① *n.* (Mil. etc.) Reihe, *die;* [in] single *or*
Indian ~: [im] Gänsemarsch
② *v.i.* ~ [in/out] in einer Reihe [hinein-/
hinaus]gehen
file copy *n.* Belegexemplar, *das;* (of letter)
Kopie für die Akten
filigree /'fɪlɪɡriː/ *n.* Filigran, *das*
'filing cabinet *n.* Aktenschrank, *der*
filings /'faɪlɪŋz/ *n. pl.* Späne *Pl.*
fill /fɪl/ ① *v.t.* (a) füllen; besetzen
⟨*Sitzplätze*⟩; (fig.) ausfüllen ⟨*Gedanken, Zeit*⟩;
(pervade) erfüllen; ~ed with voller ⟨*Reue,
Bewunderung, Neid usw.*⟩
(b) (appoint sb. to) besetzen ⟨*Posten*⟩
② *v.i.* ~ [with sth.] sich [mit etw.] füllen
③ *n.* eat/drink one's ~: sich satt essen/
trinken
■ **fill 'in** ① *v.t.* (a) füllen; zuschütten
⟨*Erdloch*⟩

(b) (complete) ausfüllen
(c) ~ sb. in [on sth.] (coll.) jmdn. [über etw.
⟨*Akk.*⟩] ins Bild setzen
② *v.i.* ~ in for sb. für jmdn. einspringen
■ **fill 'out** *v.t.* ausfüllen
■ **fill 'up** *v.t.* (a) füllen (with mit)
(b) (put petrol into) ~ up the tank tanken; ~
her up! (coll.) voll [tanken]!
fillet /'fɪlɪt/ ① *n.* Filet, *das*
② *v.t.* entgräten ⟨*Fisch*⟩
'filling *n.* (a) (for teeth) Füllung, *die*
(b) (for pancakes etc.) Füllung, *die;* (for
sandwiches etc.) Belag, *der;* (for spreading)
Aufstrich, *der*
'filling station *n.* Tankstelle, *die*
filly /'fɪlɪ/ *n.* junge Stute
film /fɪlm/ ① *n.* (a) Film, *der*
(b) (thin layer) Schicht, *die*
② *v.t.* filmen; drehen ⟨*Kinofilm, Szene*⟩
film: ~ **crew** *n.* Kamerateam, *das;*
~ **director** *n.* Filmregisseur, *der*/
-regisseurin, *die;* ~ **industry** *n.*
Filmindustrie, *die;* ~ **music** *n.*
Filmmusik, *die;* ~ **poster** *n.* Filmplakat,
das; ~ **projector** *n.* Projektor, *der;*
~ **script** *n.* Drehbuch, *das;* ~ **set** *n.*
Dekoration, *die;* ~ **star** *n.* Filmstar, *der;*
~**strip** *n.* Filmstreifen, *der;* ~ **studio** *n.*
Filmstudio, *das*
Filofax ® /'faɪləʊfæks/ *n.* ≈ Terminplaner,
der
filter /'fɪltə(r)/ ① *n.* Filter, *der*
② *v.t.* filtern
■ **filter 'through** *v.t.* durchsickern
filter: ~ **ciga'rette** *n.* Filterzigarette, *die;*
~ **coffee** *n.* Filterkaffee, *der;* ~ **lane** *n.*
Abbiegespur, *die;* ~**tip** *n.* (a) Filter, *der;*
(b) ~-**tip** [**cigarette**] Filterzigarette, *die*
filth /fɪlθ/ *n.* Dreck, *der*
'filthy *adj.* dreckig (ugs.); schmutzig
fin /fɪn/ *n.* Flosse, *die*
final /'faɪnl/ ① *adj.* letzt...; End⟨*spiel,
-stadium, -stufe, -ergebnis*⟩; endgültig
⟨*Entscheidung*⟩
② *n.* (a) (Sport etc.) Finale, *das*
(b) ~s *pl.* (university examination) Examen, *das*
finale /fɪ'nɑːlɪ/ *n.* Finale, *das*
finalist /'faɪnəlɪst/ *n.* Teilnehmer/
Teilnehmerin in der Endausscheidung;
(Sport) Finalist, *der*/Finalistin, *die*
finality /faɪ'nælɪtɪ/ *n.* Endgültigkeit, *die;* (of
tone of voice) Entschiedenheit, *die*
finalize /'faɪnəlaɪz/ *v.t.* [endgültig]
beschließen; (complete) zum Abschluss
bringen
finally /'faɪnəlɪ/ *adv.* (a) (in the end)
schließlich; (expressing impatience etc.) endlich
(b) (in conclusion) abschließend
(c) (conclusively) entschieden ⟨*sagen*⟩
finance /faɪ'næns, 'faɪnæns/ ① *n.* (a) in *pl.*
(resources) Finanzen *Pl.*
(b) (management of money) Geldwesen, *das*
(c) (support) Geldmittel *Pl.* ⋯⋯

2 *v.t.* finanzieren

'**finance company** *n.*
Finanzierungsgesellschaft, *die*

financial /faɪˈnænʃl/ *adj.* finanziell;
Finanz⟨mittel, -experte, -lage⟩; **~ year**
Geschäftsjahr, *das*

fiˈnancially *adv.* finanziell

financier /faɪˈnænsɪə(r)/ *n.* Finanzexperte,
der/-expertin, *die*

finch /fɪntʃ/ *n.* Fink[envogel], *der*

find /faɪnd/ **1** *v.t.*, **found** /faʊnd/ finden;
(come across unexpectedly) entdecken;
auftreiben ⟨Geld, Gegenstand⟩; aufbringen
⟨Kraft, Energie⟩; **want to ~**: suchen; **~ that**
...: herausfinden, dass ...; **~ sth. necessary**
etw. für nötig erachten; **~ sth./sb. to be ...**:
herausfinden, dass etw./jmd. ... ist/war; **you
will ~ [that]** ...: Sie werden sehen, dass ...
2 *n.* Fund, *der*

■ **find 'out** *v.t.* herausfinden

'**finder** *n.* Finder, *der*/Finderin, *die*

'**findings** *n. pl.* Ergebnisse *Pl.*

fine[1] /faɪn/ **1** *n.* Geldstrafe, *die*
2 *v.t.* mit einer Geldstrafe belegen

fine[2] *adj.* (a) hochwertig ⟨Qualität,
Lebensmittel⟩; fein ⟨Gewebe, Spitze⟩; edel
⟨Holz, Wein⟩
(b) (delicate) fein; zart ⟨Porzellan⟩; (thin)
hauchdünn; **cut** *or* **run it ~**: knapp
kalkulieren
(c) (in small particles) [hauch]fein ⟨Sand,
Staub⟩; **~ rain** Nieselregen, *der*
(d) (sharp) scharf ⟨Spitze, Klinge⟩; spitz
⟨Nadel, Schreibfeder⟩
(e) (excellent) ausgezeichnet ⟨Sänger,
Schauspieler⟩
(f) (satisfactory) schön; **that's ~ by** *or* **with me**
ja, ist mir recht
(g) (in good health or state) gut; **feel ~**: sich
wohl fühlen
(h) schön ⟨Wetter⟩

fine 'arts *n. pl.* schöne Künste *Pl.*

finery /ˈfaɪnərɪ/ *n.* Pracht, *die*; (garments etc.)
Staat, *der*

finger /ˈfɪŋgə(r)/ **1** *n.* Finger, *der*
2 *v.t.* berühren; (meddle with) befingern

finger: ~mark *n.* Fingerabdruck, *der*;
~nail *n.* Fingernagel, *der*; **~print** *n.*
Fingerabdruck, *der*; **~tip** *n.* Fingerspitze,
die; **have sth. at one's ~tips** (fig.) etw. im
kleinen Finger haben (ugs.)

finish /ˈfɪnɪʃ/ **1** *v.t.* (a) beenden
⟨Unterhaltung⟩; erledigen ⟨Arbeit⟩;
abschließen ⟨Kurs, Ausbildung⟩; **have ~ed**
sth. etw. fertig haben; **~ writing/reading sth.**
etw. zu Ende schreiben/lesen
(b) aufessen ⟨Mahlzeit⟩; auslesen ⟨Buch,
Zeitung⟩; austrinken ⟨Flasche, Glas⟩
2 *v.i.* (a) aufhören; **have you ~ed?** sind Sie
fertig?; **when does the concert ~?** wann ist
das Konzert aus?; **have you ~ed with the**
sugar? brauchen Sie den Zucker noch?; **~**
with one's boyfriend/girlfriend mit seinem
Freund/seiner Freundin Schluss machen

(b) (in race) das Ziel erreichen
3 *n.* (a) Ende, *das*
(b) (~ing line) Ziel, *das*

■ **finish 'off** *v.t.* abschließen

finishing: ~ post *n.* Zielpfosten, *der*;
~ 'touch *n.* **as a ~ touch to sth.** zur
Vollendung od. Vervollkommnung einer
Sache; **put the ~ touches to sth.** einer Sache
(*Dat.*) den letzten Schliff geben

finite /ˈfaɪnaɪt/ *adj.* begrenzt

Finland /ˈfɪnlənd/ *pr. n.* Finnland (*das*)

Finn /fɪn/ *n.* Finne, *der*/Finnin, *die*

Finnish /ˈfɪnɪʃ/ **1** *adj.* finnisch; **sb. is ~**:
jmd. ist Finne/Finnin
2 *n.* Finnisch, *das; see also* ENGLISH 2A

fiord /ˈfiːɔːd/ *n.* Fjord, *der*

fir /fɜː(r)/ *n.* Tanne, *die*

fire /ˈfaɪə(r)/ **1** *n.* (a) Feuer, *das*; **be on ~**:
brennen; **catch ~**: Feuer fangen; ⟨Wald,
Gebäude:⟩ in Brand geraten; **set ~ to sth.**
etw. anzünden
(b) (in grate) [offenes] Feuer; (electric or gas **~**)
Heizofen, *der*; **light the ~**: den Ofen
anstecken; (in grate) das [Kamin]feuer
anmachen
(c) (destructive burning) Brand, *der*
(d) (of guns) **come/be under ~**: unter
Beschuss geraten/beschossen werden
2 *v.t.* (a) abschießen ⟨Gewehr⟩; abfeuern
⟨Kanone⟩; abgeben ⟨Schuss⟩; **~ one's gun/**
pistol/rifle at sb. auf jmdn. schießen; **two**
shots were ~d es fielen zwei Schüsse;
~ questions at sb. jmdn. mit Fragen
bombardieren
(b) (coll.: dismiss) feuern (ugs.)
3 *v.i.* feuern; **~ at/on** schießen auf (+ *Akk.*);
~! Feuer!

fire: ~ alarm *n.* Feuermelder, *der*; **~arm**
n. Schusswaffe, *die;* **~bomb** *n.* Brandsatz,
der; (aerial bomb) Brandbombe, *die;*
~ brigade (Brit.)**, ~ department** (Amer.)
ns. Feuerwehr, *die;* **~ drill** *n.*
Probe[feuer]alarm, *der;* **~ engine** *n.*
Löschfahrzeug, *das;* **~ escape** *n.* (staircase)
Feuertreppe, *die;* **~ exit** *n.* Notausgang,
der; **~ extinguisher** *n.* Feuerlöscher, *der;*
~fighter *n.* Feuerwehrmann, *der*/-frau, *die;*
~fighting *n.* Feuerbekämpfung, *die;*
Brandbekämpfung, *die;* **~ hazard** *n.*
Brandrisiko, *das;* **~lighter** *n.* (Brit.)
Feueranzünder, *der;* **~man** /ˈfaɪəmən/ *n.,*
pl. **~men** /-mən/ Feuerwehrmann, *der;*
~place *n.* Kamin, *der;* **~ precautions**
n. pl. Feuerschutz, *der;* **~proof** **1** *adj.*
feuerfest; **2** *v.t.* feuerfest machen;
~resistant *adj.* feuerbeständig; **~ risk**
► **~ HAZARD;** **~side** *n.* **at** *or* **by the ~side**
am Kamin; **~ station** *n.* Feuerwache, *die;*
~ tongs *n. pl.* Feuerzange, *die;* **a pair of**
~ tongs eine Feuerzange; **~wood** *n.*
Brennholz, *das;* **~work** *n.*
Feuerwerkskörper, *der;* **~works** (display)
Feuerwerk, *das*

firm[1] /fɜːm/ *n.* Firma, *die*

firm² adj. (a) fest; stabil ⟨Konstruktion, Stuhl⟩
(b) (resolute, strict) bestimmt

'firmly adv. (a) fest
(b) (resolutely, strictly) bestimmt

first /fɜːst/ [1] adj. erst...; **he was ~ to arrive** er kam als Erster an
[2] adv. (a) (before anyone else) zuerst; als Erster/Erste ⟨sprechen, ankommen⟩; (before anything else) an erster Stelle ⟨stehen, kommen⟩; **~ come ~ served** wer zuerst kommt, mahlt zuerst (Spr.)
(b) (beforehand) vorher
(c) (for the ~ time) zum ersten Mal
(d) **~ of all** zuerst; (in importance) vor allem
[3] n. (a) **the ~** (in sequence, rank) der/die/das Erste; pl. die Ersten
(b) **at ~:** zuerst; **from the ~:** von Anfang an

first: ~ 'aid n. erste Hilfe; **~-aid box/kit** Verbandkasten, der/Erste-Hilfe-Ausrüstung, die; **~-class** [1] /'--/ adj. (a) erster Klasse nachgestellt; Erste[r]-Klasse-⟨Fahrkarte, Abteil, Post, Brief usw.⟩; (b) (excellent) erstklassig; [2] /-'-/ adv. erster Klasse ⟨reisen⟩

'firstly adv. zunächst [einmal]; (followed by 'secondly') erstens

first: ~ name n. Vorname, der; **~ 'night** n. (Theatre) Premiere, die; **~ offender** n. Ersttäter, der/-täterin, die; **~-rate** adj. erstklassig; **~ school** n. (Brit.) ≈ Grundschule, die

'fir tree n. Tanne, die

fish /fɪʃ/ [1] n. Fisch, der
[2] v.i. fischen; (with rod) angeln; **go ~ing** fischen/angeln gehen
■ **fish 'out** v.t. (coll.) herausfischen (ugs.)

fish: ~ bone n. [Fisch]gräte, die; **~ cake** n. Fischfrikadelle, die

fisherman /'fɪʃəmən/ n., pl. **fishermen** /'fɪʃəmən/ Fischer, der; (angler) Angler, der

fish: ~eye lens n. Fischaugenobjektiv, das; **~ farm** n. Fischzucht[anlage], die; **~ farming** n. Fischzucht, die; **~ 'finger** n. Fischstäbchen, das; **~ hook** n. Angelhaken, der

'fishing n. Fischen, das; (with rod) Angeln, das

fishing: ~ boat n. Fischerboot, das; **~ industry** n. Fischerei[industrie], die; **~ net** n. Fischernetz, das; **~ rod** n. Angelrute, die **~ tackle** n. Angelgeräte Pl.; **~ vessel** n. Fischereifahrzeug, das; **~ village** n. Fischerdorf, das

fish: ~ kettle n. Fischkessel, der; **~monger** /'fɪʃmʌŋɡə(r)/ n. (Brit.) Fischhändler, der/-händlerin, die; **~ pond** n. Fischteich, der; **~ shop** n. Fischgeschäft, das; **~ slice** n. Wender, der; **~ tank** n. Fischkasten, der; Fischbehälter, der

'fishy adj. (a) fischartig; Fisch⟨geschmack, -geruch⟩
(b) (coll.: suspicious) verdächtig

fist /fɪst/ n. Faust, die

fit¹ /fɪt/ n. Anfall, der; (fig.) [plötzliche] Anwandlung; **be in ~s of laughter** sich vor Lachen biegen; **in a ~ of ...:** in einem Anfall von ...

fit² [1] adj. (a) (suitable) geeignet; **~ to eat** essbar
(b) (worthy) würdig; wert
(c) (proper) richtig; **see** or **think ~ [to do sth.]** es für richtig halten[, etw. zu tun]
(d) (healthy) fit (ugs.); **keep ~:** sich fit halten
[2] n. Passform, die; **it is a good/bad ~:** es sitzt od. passt gut/nicht gut
[3] v.t., **-tt-:** (a) ⟨Kleider:⟩ passen (+ Dat.); ⟨Deckel, Bezug:⟩ passen auf (+ Akk.)
(b) (put into place) anbringen (**to** an + Dat. od. Akk.); einbauen ⟨Motor, Ersatzteil⟩
[4] v.i., **-tt-** passen
■ **fit 'in** [1] v.t. unterbringen
[2] v.i. (a) ⟨Person:⟩ sich anpassen (**with** an + Akk.)
(b) (be in accordance with) **~ in with sth.** mit etw. übereinstimmen

fitful /'fɪtfl/ adj. unbeständig; unruhig ⟨Schlaf⟩; launisch ⟨Brise⟩

'fitment n. Einrichtung, die

'fitness n. (a) (physical) Fitness, die
(b) (suitability) Eignung, die

'fitness studio n. Fitnessstudio, das

'fitted adj. (a) (suited) geeignet (**for** für, zu)
(b) (shaped) tailliert ⟨Kleider⟩; Einbau⟨küche, schrank⟩; **~ carpet** Teppichboden, der

'fitter n. Monteur, der; (of pipes) Installateur, der; (of machines) Maschinenschlosser, der

'fitting [1] adj. (appropriate) passend; (becoming) schicklich (geh.) ⟨Benehmen⟩
[2] n. (a) usu. in pl. (fixture) Anschluss, der; **~s** (furniture) Ausstattung, die
(b) (Brit.: size) Größe, die

'fitting-room n. Anprobe, die

five /faɪv/ [1] adj. fünf
[2] n. Fünf, die. See also EIGHT

fiver /'faɪvə(r)/ n. (Brit. coll.) Fünfpfundschein, der

five: ~-star adj. Fünf-Sterne-⟨Hotel, General⟩; (fig.) ausgezeichnet; **~-'year plan** n. Fünfjahresplan, der

fix /fɪks/ [1] v.t. (a) befestigen
(b) festsetzen ⟨Termin, Preis, Grenze⟩; (agree on) ausmachen
(c) (repair) reparieren
(d) (arrange) arrangieren
[2] n. (coll.: predicament) Klemme, die (ugs.); **be in a ~:** in der Klemme sitzen
■ **fix 'up** v.t. (a) (arrange) arrangieren; festsetzen ⟨Termin, Treffpunkt⟩
(b) (provide) versorgen; **~ sb. up with sth.** jmdm. etw. verschaffen

fixed: ~ price Festpreis, der; **~-rate** attrib. adj. Festzins-; mit festem Zins nachgestellt

fixture /'fɪkstʃə(r)/ n. (a) (furnishing) eingebautes Teil
(b) (Sport) Veranstaltung, die

fizz /fɪz/ v.i. [zischend] sprudeln

fizzle /'fɪzl/ v.i. zischen

■ **fizzle 'out** v.i. ⟨Kampagne:⟩ im Sande verlaufen

fizzy /'fɪzɪ/ adj. sprudelnd; ~ **lemonade** Brause[limonade], die

flabbergast /'flæbəɡɑːst/ v.t. umhauen (ugs.)

flabby /'flæbɪ/ adj. schlaff

flag[1] /flæɡ/ n. Fahne, die; (national ~, on ship) Flagge, die

flag[2] v.i., **-gg-** ⟨Person:⟩ abbauen; ⟨Kraft, Begeisterung usw.:⟩ nachlassen

flagon /'flæɡn/ n. Kanne, die

'flagpole n. Flaggenmast, der

flagrant /'fleɪɡrənt/ adj. eklatant; flagrant ⟨Verstoß⟩

'flagstone n. Steinplatte, die

flair /fleə(r)/ n. Gespür, das; (special ability) Talent, das

flak /flæk/ n. Flakfeuer, das (Milit.); (gun) Flak, die (Milit.); **get a lot of ~ for sth.** (fig.) wegen etw. [schwer] unter Beschuss geraten

flake /fleɪk/ ① n. Flocke, die; (of dry skin) Schuppe, die
② v.i. abblättern

'flak jacket n. kugelsichere Weste

flaky /'fleɪkɪ/ adj. blättrig ⟨Kruste⟩; ~ **pastry** Blätterteig, der

flamboyant /flæm'bɔɪənt/ adj. extravagant

flame /fleɪm/ n. Flamme, die; **be in ~s** in Flammen stehen

'flameproof nicht entflammbar; flammfest

flan /flæn/ n. [fruit] ~: [Obst]torte, die

flank /flæŋk/ n. Seite, die; (of animal; also Mil.) Flanke, die

flannel /'flænl/ n. (a) (fabric) Flanell, der
(b) (Brit.: for washing) Waschlappen, der

flap /flæp/ ① v.t., **-pp-**: ~ **its wings** mit den Flügeln schlagen
② v.i., **-pp-** ⟨Flügel:⟩ schlagen; ⟨Segel, Fahne, Vorhang:⟩ flattern
③ n. (a) Klappe, die; (envelope seal, of shoe) Lasche, die
(b) (fig. coll.) **in a ~:** furchtbar aufgeregt

flare /fleə(r)/ ① v.i. flackern; (fig.) ausbrechen; **tempers ~d** die Gemüter erhitzten sich
② n. Leuchtsignal, das

■ **flare 'up** v.i. (a) aufflackern
(b) (break out) [wieder] ausbrechen

flash /flæʃ/ ① n. Aufleuchten, das; (as signal) Lichtsignal, das; ~ **of lightning** Blitz, der; **in a ~:** (quickly) im Nu
② v.t. (a) aufleuchten lassen; ~ **one's headlights** die Lichthupe betätigen; ~ **sb. a smile/glance** jmdm. ein Lächeln/einen Blick zuwerfen
(b) (display briefly) kurz zeigen
③ v.i. aufleuchten; ~ **by** or **past** ⟨Zeit, Ferien:⟩ wie im Fluge vergehen

flash: ~back n. Rückblende, die (to auf

+ Akk.); ~ **bulb** n. Blitzbirnchen, das; ~ **cube** n. Blitzwürfel, der; ~ **flood** n. Überschwemmung, die (durch heftige Regenfälle); ~**gun** n. Blitzgerät, das; ~**light** n. (a) (for signals) Blinklicht, das; (b) (Amer.: torch) Taschenlampe, die; ~**point** n. Flammpunkt, der; (fig.) Siedepunkt, der

'flashy adj. auffällig

flask /flɑːsk/ n. (a) ▶ THERMOS
(b) (for wine, oil) [bauchige] Flasche
(c) (Chem.) Kolben, der

flat[1] /flæt/ n. (Brit.) Wohnung, die

flat[2] ① adj. (a) flach; eben ⟨Fläche⟩; platt ⟨Nase, Reifen⟩
(b) (downright) glatt (ugs.) ⟨Absage, Weigerung, Widerspruch⟩
(c) (Mus.) [um einen Halbton] erniedrigt ⟨Note⟩
(d) schal, abgestanden ⟨Bier, Sekt⟩
(e) leer ⟨Batterie⟩
② adv. (Mus.) zu tief

flat: ~chested /flæt'tʃestɪd/ adj. flachbrüstig; flachbusig; ~ **'feet** n. pl. Plattfüße Pl.; ~ **'fish** n. Plattfisch, der; ~**'footed** adj. plattfüßig; ~**heeled** adj. ⟨Schuh⟩ mit flachem Absatz; flach ⟨Schuh⟩

flatlet /'flætlɪt/ n. (Brit.) Appartement, das

'flatly adv. rundweg

flat: ~ mate n. (Brit.) Mitbewohner, der/ Mitbewohnerin, die; **they were ~ mates** sie haben zusammen gewohnt; ~ **'out** adv. (at top speed) **he ran/worked ~ out** er rannte/ arbeitete, so schnell er konnte; ~**pack** adj. ⟨Möbel⟩ zum Selbstbau; ~ **rate** n. Einheitstarif, der; ~ **'spin** n. (Aeronaut.) Flachtrudeln, das; **go into a ~ spin** (fig. coll.) durchdrehen (ugs.)

flatten /'flætn/ ① v.t. flach drücken ⟨Schachtel⟩; dem Erdboden gleichmachen ⟨Stadt, Gebäude⟩
② v. refl. ~ **oneself against sth.** sich flach gegen etw. drücken

flatter /'flætə(r)/ v.t. schmeicheln (+ Dat.)

'flattering adj. schmeichelhaft

'flattery n. Schmeichelei, die

flat 'tyre n. Reifenpanne, die

flatulence /'flætjʊləns/ n. Blähungen Pl.; Flatulenz, die (Med.)

flaunt /flɔːnt/ v.t. zur Schau stellen

flavor etc. (Amer.) ▶ FLAVOUR etc.

flavour /'fleɪvə(r)/ (Brit.) ① n. (a) Geschmack, der
(b) (fig.) Anflug, der
② v.t. abschmecken

'flavouring n. (Brit.) Aroma, das

'flavourless adj. (Brit.) fade

flavoursome /'fleɪvəsəm/ adj. (Brit.) schmackhaft

flaw /flɔː/ n. Fehler, der; (imperfection) Makel, der; (in workmanship or goods) Mangel, der

flax /flæks/ n. Flachs, der

flea /fliː/ n. Floh, der

flea: ~ **bite** n. Flohbiss, der; ~ **market** n. (coll.) Flohmarkt, der

fled ▶ FLEE

flee /fliː/ ① v.i., fled /fled/ fliehen; ~ from sth./sb. aus etw./vor jmdm. flüchten ② v.t., fled fliehen aus

fleece /fliːs/ ① n. [Schaf]fell, das ② v.t. (fig.) ausplündern

fleecy /ˈfliːsɪ/ adj. flauschig

fleet /fliːt/ n. Flotte, die

fleeting /ˈfliːtɪŋ/ adj. flüchtig

flesh /fleʃ/ n. Fleisch, das; (of fruit, plant) [Frucht]fleisch, das

flesh: ~-**coloured** adj. fleischfarben; ~ **wound** n. Fleischwunde, die

'fleshy adj. fett; fleischig ⟨Hände⟩

flew ▶ FLY² 1, 2

flex¹ /fleks/ n. (Brit. Electr.) Kabel, das

flex² v.t. beugen ⟨Arm, Knie⟩; ~ one's muscles seine Muskeln spielen lassen

flexible /ˈfleksɪbl/ adj. (a) biegsam; elastisch (b) (fig.) flexibel; ~ working hours or time gleitende Arbeitszeit

flexitime /ˈfleksɪtaɪm/ (Brit.), **flextime** /ˈflekstaɪm/ (Amer.) ns. Gleitzeit, die; be on or work ~: gleitende Arbeitszeit haben

flick /flɪk/ v.t. schnippen; anknipsen ⟨Schalter⟩; verspritzen ⟨Tinte⟩
■ **'flick through** v.t. durchblättern

flicker /ˈflɪkə(r)/ ① v.i. flackern; ⟨Fernsehapparat:⟩ flimmern ② n. Flackern, das; (of TV) Flimmern, das

'flick knife n. (Brit.) Schnappmesser, das

flight¹ /flaɪt/ n. (a) Flug, der (b) ~ [of stairs or steps] Treppe, die

flight² n. (fleeing) Flucht, die; take ~: die Flucht ergreifen; put to ~: in die Flucht schlagen

flight: ~ **attendant** n. Flugbegleiter, der/-begleiterin, die; ~ **control** n. ≈ Flugsicherung, die; ~ **controller** n. (Aeronaut.) Fluglotse, der; ~ **deck** n. (a) (of aircraft carrier) Flugdeck, das; (b) (of aircraft) Cockpit, das; ~ **number** n. Flugnummer, die; ~ **path** n. (Aeronaut.) Flugweg, der; (Astronaut.) Flugbahn, die; ~ **recorder** n. Flugschreiber, der

flimsy /ˈflɪmzɪ/ adj. (a) dünn; nicht sehr haltbar ⟨Verpackung⟩ (b) (fig.) fadenscheinig ⟨Entschuldigung, Argument⟩

flinch /flɪntʃ/ v.i. zurückschrecken (from vor + Dat.); (wince) zusammenzucken

fling /flɪŋ/ ① n. have a or one's ~: sich ausleben ② v.t., flung /flʌŋ/ werfen; ~ oneself into sth. (fig.) sich in etw. (Akk.) stürzen

flint /flɪnt/ n. Feuerstein, der

flip /flɪp/ v.t., -pp- schnippen; ~ [over] (turn over) umdrehen
■ **'flip through** v.t. durchblättern

flippant /ˈflɪpənt/ adj. leichtfertig

flipper /ˈflɪpə(r)/ n. Flosse, die

'flip side n. B-Seite, die

flirt /flɜːt/ v.i. flirten

flirtation /flɜːˈteɪʃn/ n. Flirt, der

flirtatious /flɜːˈteɪʃəs/ adj. kokett ⟨Blick, Art⟩

flit /flɪt/ v.i. huschen

float /fləʊt/ ① v.i. treiben; (in air) schweben ② n. (for carnival) Festwagen, der ③ v.t. (set afloat) flottmachen; (fig.) lancieren ⟨Plan, Idee⟩

floating: ~ **'dock** n. Schwimmdock, das; ~ **'voter** n. Wechselwähler, der/-wählerin, die

flock /flɒk/ ① n. (a) Herde, die; (of birds) Schwarm, der (b) (of people) Schar, die ② v.i. strömen; ~ round sb. sich um jmdn. scharen

flog /flɒg/ v.t., -gg-: (a) auspeitschen (b) (Brit. coll.: sell) verscheuern (salopp)

flood /flʌd/ ① n. Überschwemmung, die; the F~ (Bibl.) die Sintflut ② v.i. ⟨Fluss:⟩ über die Ufer treten; (fig.) strömen ③ v.t. überschwemmen

flood: ~ **damage** n. Hochwasserschaden, der; the area suffered extensive ~ damage in dem Gebiet gab es beträchtliche Hochwasserschäden; ~**gate** n. (Hydraulic Engin.) Schütze, die; open the ~**gates** to sth. (fig.) einer Sache (Dat.) Tür und Tor öffnen; ~**light** ① n. Scheinwerfer, der. ② v.t., **floodlit** /ˈflʌdlɪt/ anstrahlen; ~ **tide** n. Flut, die; ~ **warning** n. Hochwasserwarnung, die; ~ **water** n. Hochwasser, das

floor /flɔː(r)/ ① n. (a) Boden, der (b) (storey) Stockwerk, das; first ~ (Amer.) Erdgeschoss, das; first ~ (Brit.), second ~ (Amer.) erster Stock; ground ~: Erdgeschoss, das; Parterre, das ② v.t. (a) (confound) überfordern (b) (knock down) zu Boden schlagen

floor: ~**board** n. Dielenbrett, das; ~**cloth** n. (Brit.) Scheuertuch, das; ~ **polish** n. Bohnerwachs, das; ~ **show** n. ≈ Unterhaltungsprogramm, das

flop /flɒp/ ① v.i., -pp-: (a) plumpsen (b) (coll.: fail) fehlschlagen; ⟨Theaterstück, Show:⟩ durchfallen ② n. (coll.: failure) Reinfall, der (ugs.)

floppy /ˈflɒpɪ/ adj. weich und biegsam

floppy disk n. (comp.) Floppy Disk, die; Diskette, die

flora /ˈflɔːrə/ n. Flora, die

floral /ˈflɔːrl, ˈflɒrl/ adj. geblümt ⟨Kleid, Stoff⟩; Blumen⟨muster⟩

Florence /ˈflɒrəns/ pr. n. Florenz (das)

florid /ˈflɒrɪd/ adj. blumig ⟨Stil, Redeweise⟩; gerötet ⟨Teint⟩

florist /ˈflɒrɪst/ n. Florist, der/Floristin, die

flotsam /ˈflɒtsəm/ n. ~ [and jetsam] Treibgut, das

flounder /ˈflaʊndə(r)/ v.i. taumeln

flour /ˈflaʊə(r)/ n. Mehl, das

flourish /ˈflʌrɪʃ/ ①v.i. gedeihen; ⟨Geschäft:⟩ florieren, gut gehen ②v.t. schwingen ③n. do sth. with a ~: etw. schwungvoll tun

flout /flaʊt/ v.t. missachten

flow /fləʊ/ ①v.i. fließen; ⟨Körner, Sand:⟩ rinnen, rieseln; ⟨Gas:⟩ strömen ②n. (a) Fließen, das; ~ of water/people Wasser-/Menschenstrom, der; ~ of information Informationsfluss, der (b) (of tide, river) Flut, die

'flow chart n. Flussdiagramm, das

flower /ˈflaʊə(r)/ ①n. (blossom) Blüte, die; (plant) Blume, die; come into ~: zu blühen beginnen ②v.i. blühen

'flower bed n. Blumenbeet, das

flowering /ˈflaʊərɪŋ/ adj. ~ cherry/shrub Zierkirsche, die/Blütenstrauch, der

'flowerpot n. Blumentopf, der

flowery adj. geblümt ⟨Stoff, Muster⟩; (fig.) blumig ⟨Sprache⟩

'flowing adj. fließend; wallend ⟨Haar⟩

flown ▶ FLY² 1, 2

flu /fluː/ n. (coll.) Grippe, die

fluctuate /ˈflʌktjʊeɪt/ v.i. schwanken

fluctuation /flʌktjʊˈeɪʃn/ n. Schwankung, die

fluency /ˈfluːənsɪ/ n. Gewandtheit, die; (spoken) Redegewandtheit, die

fluent /ˈfluːənt/ adj. gewandt ⟨Stil, Redeweise, Redner, Schreiber⟩; be ~ in Russian, speak ~ Russian fließend Russisch sprechen

fluff /flʌf/ n. Flusen Pl.; Fusseln Pl.

fluffy /ˈflʌfɪ/ adj. [flaum]weich ⟨Kissen, Küken⟩; flauschig ⟨Spielzeug, Decke⟩

fluid /ˈfluːɪd/ ①n. Flüssigkeit, die ②adj. flüssig

fluke /fluːk/ n. (piece of luck) Glücksfall, der

flung ▶ FLING 2

fluorescent /flʊəˈresənt/ adj. fluoreszierend

fluorescent 'light n. Leuchtstofflampe, die

fluoride /ˈflʊəraɪd/ n. Fluorid, das; ~ toothpaste fluorhaltige Zahnpasta

flurry /ˈflʌrɪ/ n. (a) Aufregung, die (b) (of rain/snow) [Regen-/Schnee]schauer, der

flush¹ /flʌʃ/ ①v.i. rot werden ②v.t. ausspülen ⟨Becken⟩; ~ the toilet or lavatory spülen ③n. Rotwerden, das

flush² adj. (level) bündig; be ~ with sth. mit etw. bündig abschließen

flush 'toilet n. Toilette mit Wasserspülung

fluster /ˈflʌstə(r)/ v.t. aus der Fassung bringen

flustered /ˈflʌstəd/ adj. nervös

flute /fluːt/ n. Flöte, die

flutter /ˈflʌtə(r)/ ①v.i. flattern ②v.t. flattern mit ⟨Flügel⟩

flux /flʌks/ n. in a state of ~: im Fluss

fly¹ /flaɪ/ n. Fliege, die

fly² ①v.i., flew /fluː/, flown /fləʊn/ (a) fliegen; ~ away or off wegfliegen (b) (fig.) ~ [by or past] wie im Fluge vergehen (c) ⟨Fahne:⟩ gehisst sein ②v.t., flew, flown fliegen ⟨Flugzeug, Fracht, Einsatz usw.⟩; fliegen über (+ Akk.) ⟨Strecke⟩ ③n. in sing. or pl. (on trousers) Hosenschlitz, der

■ **fly 'in** v.i. [mit dem Flugzeug] eintreffen (from aus)

■ **fly 'out** v.i. abfliegen (of von)

'fly-fishing n. Fliegenfischerei, die

flying /ˈflaɪɪŋ/: ~ 'doctor n.: Arzt, der seine Krankenbesuche mit dem Flugzeug macht; ~ 'saucer n. fliegende Untertasse; ~ 'start n. (Sport) fliegender Start; ~ 'visit n. Stippvisite, die (ugs.)

fly: ~**leaf** n. Vorsatzblatt, das; ~**over** n. (Brit.) [Straßen]überführung, die; ~ **spray** n. Insektenspray, der od. das; ~ **swatter** n. Fliegenklappe, die; Fliegenklatsche, die

foal /fəʊl/ n. Fohlen, das

foam /fəʊm/ ①n. Schaum, der ②v.i. schäumen

foam: ~**-backed** adj. schaumstoffverstärkt; ~ 'mattress n. Schaumgummimatratze, die; ~ 'rubber n. Schaumgummi, der

fob /fɒb/ v.t., -bb-: ~ sb. off with sth. jmdn. mit etw. abspeisen (ugs.)

'focal point n. Brennpunkt, der (auch fig.)

focus /ˈfəʊkəs/ ①n., pl. ~es or foci /ˈfəʊsaɪ/ Brennpunkt, der; out of/in ~: unscharf/scharf eingestellt; unscharf/scharf ⟨Foto, Film usw.⟩; (fig.) be the ~ of attention im Brennpunkt des Interesses stehen ②v.t., -s- or -ss- einstellen (on auf + Akk.); bündeln ⟨Licht, Strahlen⟩ ③v.i., -s- or -ss- (fig.) sich konzentrieren (on auf + Akk.)

'focus group n. Fokusgruppe, die

fodder /ˈfɒdə(r)/ n. [Vieh]futter, das

foe /fəʊ/ n. (poet./rhet.) Feind, der

foetus /ˈfiːtəs/ n. Fötus, der

fog /fɒg/ n. Nebel, der

'foglight n. Nebelscheinwerfer, der

foggy /ˈfɒgɪ/ adj. neblig

fogy /ˈfəʊgɪ/ n. [old] ~: [alter] Opa (salopp)/ [alte] Oma (salopp)

foible /ˈfɔɪbl/ n. Eigenheit, die

foil¹ /fɔɪl/ n. Folie, die

foil² v.t. vereiteln

foist /fɔɪst/ v.t. ~ [off] on to sb. jmdm. andrehen (ugs.); auf jmdn. abwälzen ⟨Probleme, Verantwortung⟩

fold /fəʊld/ ① *v.t.* [zusammen]falten;
~ **one's arms** die Arme verschränken
② *v.i.* **(a)** (become ~ed) sich zusammenfalten
(b) (be able to be ~ed) sich falten lassen
(c) (go bankrupt) fold
③ *n.* Falte, *die;* (line made by ~ing) Kniff, *der*
■ **fold 'up** *v.t.* zusammenfalten ⟨*Laken*⟩;
zusammenklappen ⟨*Stuhl*⟩
'**folder** *n.* **(a)** Mappe, *die*
(b) (Comp.) Ordner, *der*
foliage /'fəʊlɪɪdʒ/ *n.* Blätter *Pl.;* (of tree also)
Laub, *das*
folk /fəʊk/ *n.* **(a)** Volk, *das*
(b) *in pl.* ~[s] (people) Leute *Pl.*
folk: ~ **dance** *n.* Volkstanz, *der;* ~ **hero**
n. Volksheld, *der;* ~**lore** /-lɔ:(r)/ *n.*
Folklore, *die;* ~ **music** *n.* Volksmusik, *die;*
~ **singer** *n.* Sänger/Sängerin von
Volksliedern; (modern) Folksänger, *der/*
-sängerin, *die;* ~ **song** Volkslied, *das;*
(modern) Folksong, *der*
follow /'fɒləʊ/ ① *v.t.* **(a)** folgen (+ *Dat.*)
(b) entlanggehen/-fahren ⟨*Straße usw.*⟩
(c) (come after) folgen auf (+ *Akk.*)
(d) (result from) die Folge sein von
(e) (treat or take as guide) sich orientieren an
(+ *Dat.*)
(f) folgen (+ *Dat.*) ⟨*Prinzip, Instinkt, Trend*⟩;
verfolgen ⟨*Politik*⟩; befolgen ⟨*Regel,
Vorschrift, Rat, Warnung*⟩; sich halten an
(+ *Akk.*) ⟨*Konventionen, Diät*⟩
(g) (grasp meaning of) folgen (+ *Dat.*); do you
~ me? verstehst du, was ich meine?
② *v.i.* **(a)** (go, come) ~ after sb./sth. jmdm./
einer Sache folgen
(b) (come next in order or time) folgen; as ~s
wie folgt
(c) ~ from sth. (result) die Folge von etw.
sein; (be deducible) aus etw. folgen
■ **follow 'on** *v.i.* (continue) ~ on from sth.
die Fortsetzung von etw. sein
■ **follow 'up** *v.t.* **(a)** ausbauen ⟨*Erfolg,
Sieg*⟩
(b) nachgehen (+ *Dat.*) ⟨*Hinweis*⟩
'**follower** *n.* Anhänger, *der/*Anhängerin,
die
'**following** ① *adj.* folgend; the ~:
Folgendes
② *prep.* nach
③ *n.* Anhängerschaft, *die*
folly /'fɒlɪ/ *n.* Torheit, *die* (geh.)
fond /fɒnd/ *adj.* liebevoll; lieb ⟨*Erinnerung*⟩;
be ~ of sb. jmdn. mögen; be ~ of doing sth.
etw. gern tun
fondle /'fɒndl/ *v.t.* streicheln
'**fondness** *n.* Liebe, *die;* ~ for sth. Vorliebe
für etw.
font¹ /fɒnt/ *n.* Taufstein, *der*
font² *n.* (Comp., Printing) Schrift, *die;* Font, *der*
(fachspr.); ~ size Schriftgröße, *die;* Fontgröße,
die
food /fu:d/ *n.* **(a)** Nahrung, *die;* (for animals)
Futter, *das*
(b) (as commodity) Lebensmittel *Pl.*

(c) (in solid form) Essen, *das*
(d) (particular kind) Nahrungsmittel, *das;* Kost,
die
food: ~ **chain** *n.* Nahrungskette, *die;*
~ **poisoning** *n.* Lebensmittelvergiftung,
die; ~ **processor** *n.* Küchenmaschine,
die; ~ **shop,** ~ **store** *ns.*
Lebensmittelgeschäft, *das;* ~**stuff** *n.*
Nahrungsmittel, *das;* perishable ~stuffs
leicht verderbliche Lebensmittel
fool /fu:l/ ① *n.* Dummkopf, *der* (ugs.)
② *v.t.* ~ sb. into doing sth. jmdn. [durch
Tricks] dazu bringen, etw. zu tun
■ **fool a'bout, fool a'round** *v.i.* Unsinn
machen
foolhardy /'fu:lhɑ:dɪ/ *adj.* tollkühn
'**foolish** *adj.* töricht; verrückt (ugs.) ⟨*Idee,
Vorschlag*⟩
'**foolproof** *adj.* (infallible) absolut sicher
foot /fʊt/ ① *n., pl.* feet /fi:t/ **(a)** Fuß, *der;* on
~: zu Fuß; put one's ~ in it (fig. coll.) ins
Fettnäpfchen treten (ugs.)
(b) (far end) unteres Ende; (of bed) Fußende,
das
(c) (measure) Fuß, *der* (30,48 cm)
② *v.t.* ~ the bill die Rechnung bezahlen
football /'fʊtbɔ:l/ *n.* (game, ball) Fußball, *der*
'**football boot** *n.* Fußballschuh, *der*
'**footballer** *n.* Fußballspieler, *der/*
-spielerin, *die*
football: ~ **pitch** *n.* Fußballplatz, *der;*
~ **pools** *n. pl.* the ~ pools das Fußballtoto
foot: ~ **brake** *n.* Fußbremse, *die;*
~ **bridge** *n.* Fußgängerbrücke, *die;*
~**hold** *n.* Halt, *der*
'**footing** *n.* **(a)** (fig.) be on an equal ~ [with
sb.] [jmdm.] gleichgestellt sein
(b) (foothold) Halt, *der*
foot: ~**note** *n.* Fußnote, *die;*
~ **passenger** *n.* Fußpassagier, *der;*
~**path** *n.* Fußweg, *der;* ~**print** *n.*
Fußabdruck, *der;* ~**rest** *n.* Fußstütze, *die;*
(on bicycle or motorcycle) Fußraste, *die;* ~**step**
n. Schritt, *der;* follow in sb.'s ~steps (fig.) in
jmds. Fußstapfen (*Akk.*) treten; ~**stool** *n.*
Fußbank, *die;* Fußschemel, *der;* ~**wear** *n.*
Schuhe *Pl.;* ~**work** *n.* (Sport, Dancing)
Beinarbeit, *die*
for /fə(r), *stressed* fɔ:(r)/ ① *prep.* **(a)** für;
what is it ~? wofür ist das?; reason ~ living
Grund zu leben; a request ~ help eine Bitte
um Hilfe; study ~ a university degree auf
einen Hochschulabschluss hin studieren;
take sb. ~ a walk mit jmdm. einen
Spaziergang machen; be '~ doing sth. (in
favour) dafür sein, etw. zu tun; cheque/bill
~ £5 Scheck/Rechnung über 5 Pfund; what
have you got ~ a cold? was haben Sie
gegen Erkältungen da?
(b) (on account of, as penalty of) wegen; were it
not ~ you/ your help ohne dich/deine Hilfe;
~ fear of aus Angst vor (+ *Dat.*)
(c) (in spite of) ~ all ...: trotz ...; ~ all that,
...: trotzdem ... ⋯⟩

(d) ~ all I know/care ...: möglicherweise/was mich betrifft, ...; ~ one thing, ...: zunächst einmal ...

(e) (during) stay ~ a week eine Woche bleiben; we've/we haven't been here ~ three years wir sind seit drei Jahren hier/nicht mehr hier gewesen

(f) walk ~ 20 miles 20 Meilen gehen
2 *conj.* denn

forage /'forɪdʒ/ 1 *n.* Futter, *das*
2 *v.i.* ~ for sth. auf der Suche nach etw. sein

forbad, forbade ▶ FORBID

forbid /fə'bɪd/ *v.t.*, **-dd-**, **forbad** /fə'bæd/ *or* **forbade** /fə'bæd, fə'beɪd/, **forbidden** /fə'bɪdn/ ~ sb. to do sth. jmdm. verbieten, etw. zu tun; ~ [sb.] sth. [jmdm.] etw. verbieten; **it is** ~**den [to do sth.]** es ist verboten[, etw. zu tun]

forbidden ▶ FORBID

for'bidding *adj.* Furcht einflößend

force /fɔːs/ 1 *n.* **(a)** (strength, power) Stärke, *die;* (of explosion, storm) Wucht, *die;* (Phys.; physical strength) Kraft, *die;* **in** ~: mit einem großen Aufgebot
(b) (validity) Kraft, *die;* **in** ~: in Kraft; **come into** ~ ⟨*Gesetz usw.*⟩ in Kraft treten
(c) (violence) Gewalt, *die;* **by** ~: gewaltsam
(d) (group) (of workers) Kolonne, *die;* Trupp, *der;* (Mil.) Armee, *die;* **the** ~ (Police) die Polizei; **the** ~**s** die Armee; **be in the** ~**s** beim Militär sein
2 *v.t.* **(a)** zwingen; ~ sth. [up]on sb. jmdm. etw. aufzwingen
(b) ~ [open] aufbrechen; ~ one's way in sich (*Dat.*) mit Gewalt Zutritt verschaffen

forced /fɔːst/ *adj.* **(a)** (contrived, unnatural) gezwungen
(b) (compelled by force) erzwungen; Zwangs⟨*arbeit*⟩

forced 'landing *n.* Notlandung, *die*

'force-feed *v.t.* zwangsernähren

forceful /'fɔːsfl/ *adj.* stark ⟨*Persönlichkeit, Charakter*⟩; energisch ⟨*Person, Art*⟩; eindrucksvoll ⟨*Sprache*⟩

forceps /'fɔːseps/ *n., pl. same* [pair of] ~: Zange, *die*

forcible /'fɔːsɪbl/ *adj.*, **forcibly** /'fɔːsɪblɪ/ *adv.* gewaltsam

ford /fɔːd/ 1 *n.* Furt, *die*
2 *v.t.* durchqueren; (wade through) durchwaten

fore /fɔː(r)/ 1 *adj., esp. in comb.* vorder...; Vorder⟨*teil, -front usw.*⟩
2 *n.* **to the** ~: im Vordergrund

'forearm *n.* Unterarm, *der*

foreboding /fɔː'bəʊdɪŋ/ *n.* Vorahnung, *die*

'forecast 1 *v.t.*, **forecast** *or* **forecasted** vorhersagen
2 *n.* Voraussage, *die*

'forecaster *n.* Meteorologe, *der/* Meteorologin, *die*

'forecourt *n.* Vorhof, *der*

'forefather *n., usu. in pl.* Vorfahr, *der*

'forefinger *n.* Zeigefinger, *der*

'forefront *n.* **[be] in the** ~ **of** in vorderster Linie (+ *Gen.*) [stehen]

foregone *adj.* **be a** ~ **conclusion** von vornherein feststehen; (be certain) so gut wie sicher sein

'foreground *n.* Vordergrund, *der*

forehead /'forɪd, 'fɔːhed/ *n.* Stirn, *die*

foreign /'forɪn/ *adj.* **(a)** (from abroad) ausländisch; Fremd⟨*kapital, -sprache*⟩; **he is** ~: er ist Ausländer
(b) (abroad) fremd; Außen⟨*politik, -handel*⟩; **from a** ~ **country** aus einem anderen Land; aus dem Ausland; ~ **countries** Ausland, *das*
(c) (from outside) fremd; ~ **body/substance** Fremdkörper, *der*

foreign corre'spondent *n.* (Journ.) Auslandskorrespondent, *der/* -korrespondentin, *die*

'foreigner *n.* Ausländer, *der/*Ausländerin, *die*

foreign: ~ **ex'change** *n.* Devisen *Pl.;* ~ **'language** *n.* Fremdsprache, *die;* ~**-language assistant** Fremdsprachenassistent, *der/*-assistentin, *die;* ~**-language newspaper/broadcast** fremdsprachige Zeitung/Rundfunksendung; ~**-language teaching** Fremdsprachenunterricht, *der;* **F**~ **'Minister** *n.* Außenminister, *der/* -ministerin, *die;* **F**~ **'Ministry** *n.* Außenministerium, *das;* **F**~ **Office** *n.* (Brit. Hist./coll.) Außenministerium, *das;* ~ **policy** *n.* Außenpolitik, *die;* **F**~ **'Secretary** *n.* (Brit.) Außenminister, *der/*-ministerin, *die;* ~ **trade** *n.* Außenhandel, *der*

foreman /'fɔːmən/ *n., pl.* **foremen** /'fɔːmən/ Vorarbeiter, *der*

foremost /'fɔːməʊst, 'fɔːməst/ 1 *adj.* **(a)** vorderst...
(b) (fig.) führend
2 *adv.* **first and** ~: zunächst einmal

'forename *n.* Vorname, *der*

forensic /fə'rensɪk/ *adj.* ~ **medicine** Gerichtsmedizin, *die;* ~ **science** Kriminaltechnik, *die*

'foreplay *n.* Vorspiel, *das*

'forerunner *n.* Vorläufer, *der/*Vorläuferin, *die*

foresaw ▶ FORESEE

foresee /fɔː'siː/ *v.t., forms as* SEE voraussehen

foreseeable /fɔː'siːəbl/ *adj.* vorhersehbar; **in the** ~ **future** in nächster Zukunft

foreseen ▶ FORESEE

'foresight *n.* Weitblick, *der*

foreskin *n.* (Anat.) Vorhaut, *die*

forest /'forɪst/ *n.* Wald, *der;* (commercially exploited) Forst, *der*

fore'stall *v.t.* zuvorkommen (+ *Dat.*)

forested /'forɪstɪd/ *adj.* bewaldet

forestry /ˈfɒrɪstrɪ/ n. Forstwirtschaft, *die*

ˈforetaste n. Vorgeschmack, *der*

foreˈtell v.t., foreˈtold voraussagen

ˈforethought n. (prior deliberation) [vorherige] Überlegung; (care for the future) Vorausdenken, *das*

forever /fəˈrevə(r)/ adv. (constantly) ständig

foreˈwarn v.t. vorwarnen

foreˈwarning n. Vorwarnung, *die*

ˈforeword n. Vorwort, *das*

forfeit /ˈfɔːfɪt/ ① v.t. verlieren; verwirken (geh.) ⟨Recht, jmds. Gunst⟩
② n. Strafe, *die;* (games) Pfand, *das*

forgave ▶ FORGIVE

forge¹ /fɔːdʒ/ ① n. (a) (workshop) Schmiede, *die*
(b) (blacksmith's hearth) Esse, *die*
② v.t. (a) schmieden (into zu)
(b) (fig.) schmieden ⟨Plan⟩; schließen ⟨Vereinbarung, Freundschaft⟩
(c) (counterfeit) fälschen

forge² v.i. ~ ahead [das Tempo] beschleunigen; (fig.) Fortschritte machen

ˈforger n. Fälscher, *der*/Fälscherin, *die*

forgery /ˈfɔːdʒərɪ/ n. Fälschung, *die*

forget /fəˈget/ ① v.t., -tt-, forgot /fəˈgɒt/, forgotten /fəˈgɒtn/ vergessen; (~ learned ability) verlernen
② v.i., -tt-, forgot, forgotten es vergessen; ~ about sth. etw. vergessen; ~ about it! (coll.) schon gut!

forgettable /fəˈgetəbl/ adj. easily ~: leicht zu vergessen

forgetful /fəˈgetfl/ adj. vergesslich

forˈgetfulness n. Vergesslichkeit, *die*

forˈget-me-not n. (Bot.) Vergissmeinnicht, *das*

forgive /fəˈgɪv/ v.t., forgave /fəˈgeɪv/, forgiven /fəˈgɪvn/ verzeihen; vergeben ⟨Sünden⟩; ~ sb. [sth. or for sth.] jmdm. [etw.] verzeihen

forˈgiveness n. Verzeihung, *die;* (of sins) Vergebung, *die*

forˈgiving /fəˈgɪvɪŋ/ adj. versöhnlich

forgo /fɔːˈgəʊ/ v.t., forms as GO: verzichten auf (+ Akk.)

forgone ▶ FORGO

forgot, forgotten ▶ FORGET

fork /fɔːk/ ① n. (a) Gabel, *die;* knives and ~s Besteck, *das*
(b) (in road) Gabelung, *die;* (one branch) Abzweigung, *die*
② v.i. (divide) sich gabeln; (turn) abbiegen; ~ left links abbiegen
∎ **fork ˈout** v.i. (coll.) blechen (ugs.)

forked ˈlightning n., no indef. art. Linienblitz, *der*

ˈforklift truck n. Gabelstapler, *der*

forlorn /fəˈlɔːn/ adj. (a) (desperate) verzweifelt
(b) (forsaken) verlassen

form /fɔːm/ ① n. (a) (shape, type, style) Form, *die;* take ~: Gestalt annehmen
(b) (printed sheet) Formular, *das*
(c) (Brit. Sch.) Klasse, *die*
(d) (bench) Bank, *die*
(e) (Sport: physical condition) Form, *die;* (fig.) true to ~: wie üblich
② v.t. (a) bilden
(b) (shape) formen, gestalten (into zu)
(c) sich ⟨Dat.⟩ bilden ⟨Meinung, Urteil⟩; gewinnen ⟨Eindruck⟩; fassen ⟨Plan⟩; entwickeln ⟨Vorliebe, Gewohnheit⟩; schließen ⟨Freundschaft⟩
(d) (set up) bilden ⟨Regierung⟩; gründen ⟨Bund, Firma, Partei⟩
③ v.i. sich bilden; ⟨Idee:⟩ Gestalt annehmen

formal /ˈfɔːml/ adj. formell; förmlich ⟨Person, Art, Einladung, Begrüßung⟩; (official) offiziell; a ~ 'yes'/'no' eine bindende Zusage/endgültige Absage

formality /fɔːˈmælɪtɪ/ n. (a) (requirement) Formalität, *die*
(b) (being formal) Förmlichkeit, *die*

formalize /ˈfɔːməlaɪz/ v.t. (a) (specify and systematize) formalisieren
(b) (make official) formell bekräftigen

format /ˈfɔːmæt/ n. ① (also Comp.) Format, *das*
② v.t., -tt- (Comp.) formatieren

formation /fɔːˈmeɪʃn/ n. (a) ▶ FORM 2A, D: Bildung, *die;* Gründung, *die*
(b) (Mil., Aeronaut.) Formation, *die*

formative /ˈfɔːmətɪv/ adj. formend, prägend ⟨Einfluss⟩; the ~ years of life die entscheidenden Lebensjahre

former /ˈfɔːmə(r)/ attrib. adj. ehemalig; in ~ times früher; the ~: der/die/das Erstere; pl. die Ersteren

ˈformerly adv. früher

formidable /ˈfɔːmɪdəbl/ adj. gewaltig; gefährlich ⟨Herausforderung, Gegner⟩

formula /ˈfɔːmjʊlə/ n. Formel, *die*

formulate /ˈfɔːmjʊleɪt/ v.t. formulieren; (devise) entwickeln

formulation /fɔːmjʊˈleɪʃn/ n. Formulierung, *die*

forsake /fəˈseɪk/ v.t., forsook /fəˈsʊk/, ~n /fəˈseɪkn/ (a) (give up) verzichten auf (+ Akk.)
(b) (desert) verlassen

forˈsaken adj. verlassen

forsook ▶ FORSAKE

fort /fɔːt/ n. (Mil.) Fort, *das*

forte /ˈfɔːteɪ/ n. Stärke, *die*

forth /fɔːθ/ adv. and so ~: und so weiter; see also BACK 3

forthcoming /ˈ--, ˌ-ˈ-/ adj. (a) (approaching) bevorstehend; in Kürze erscheinend ⟨Buch usw.⟩
(b) pred. be ~ ⟨Geld, Antwort:⟩ kommen; ⟨Hilfe:⟩ geleistet werden; not be ~: ausbleiben
(c) (responsive) mitteilsam ⟨Person⟩

'**forthright** *adj.* direkt

forth'with *adv.* unverzüglich

fortieth /'fɔːtɪɪθ/ *adj.* vierzigst...

fortify /'fɔːtɪfaɪ/ *v.t.* **(a)** (Mil.) befestigen
(b) (strengthen) stärken

fortitude /'fɔːtɪtjuːd/ *n.* innere Stärke

fortnight /'fɔːtnaɪt/ *n.* vierzehn Tage *Pl.*

fortnightly /'fɔːtnaɪtlɪ/ **1** *adj.*
vierzehntäglich; zweiwöchentlich
2 *adv.* alle vierzehn Tage; alle zwei Wochen

fortress /'fɔːtrɪs/ *n.* Festung, *die*

fortuitous /fɔː'tjuːɪtəs/ *adj.*,
for'tuitously *adv.* zufällig

fortunate /'fɔːtʃənət/ *adj.* glücklich

'**fortunately** *adv.* glücklicherweise

fortune /'fɔːtʃən, 'fɔːtʃuːn/ *n.* **(a)** (wealth)
Vermögen, *das*
(b) (luck) Schicksal, *das*; **bad/good** ~: Pech/
Glück, *das*

'**fortune teller** *n.* Wahrsager, *der*/
Wahrsagerin, *die*

forty /'fɔːtɪ/ **1** *adj.* vierzig; **have** ~ '**winks**
ein Nickerchen machen (ugs.).
2 *n.* Vierzig, *die. See also* EIGHT; EIGHTY 2

forum /'fɔːrəm/ *n.* Forum, *das*

forward /'fɔːwəd/ **1** *adv.* **(a)** (in direction
faced) vorwärts
(b) (to the front) nach vorn; vor⟨*laufen,
-rücken, -schieben*⟩
(c) (closer) heran; **he came** ~ **to greet me** er
kam auf mich zu, um mich zu begrüßen
(d) come ~ ⟨*Zeuge, Helfer:*⟩ sich melden
2 *adj.* **(a)** (directed ahead) vorwärts gerichtet
(b) (at or to the front) Vorder-; vorder...
3 *n.* (Sport) Stürmer, *der*/Stürmerin, *die*
4 *v.t.* (send on) nachschicken ⟨*Post*⟩ (**to** an
+ *Akk.*)

forwarding ad'dress /'fɔːwədɪŋ/ *n.*
Nachsendeanschrift, *die*

forward: ~-**looking** *adj.*
vorausschauend; ~ '**planning** *n.*
Vorausplanung, *die*

forwards /'fɔːwədz/ ▶ FORWARD 1A, B

forwent ▶ FORGO

fossil /'fɒsɪl/ *n.* Fossil, *das*; ~ **fuel** fossiler
Brennstoff

foster /'fɒstə(r)/ **1** *v.t.* **(a)** fördern; pflegen
⟨*Freundschaft*⟩
(b) in Pflege haben ⟨*Kind*⟩
2 *adj.* ~: Pflege⟨*kind, -eltern, -sohn usw.*⟩

fought ▶ FIGHT 1, 2

foul /faʊl/ **1** *adj.* **(a)** abscheulich ⟨*Geruch,
Geschmack*⟩
(b) (polluted) verschmutzt ⟨*Wasser, Luft*⟩;
(putrid) faulig ⟨*Wasser*⟩; stickig ⟨*Luft*⟩
(c) (coll.: awful) scheußlich (ugs.); anstößig
⟨*Sprache*⟩
2 *n.* (Sport) Foul, *das*
3 *v.t.* **(a)** beschmutzen; verpesten ⟨*Luft*⟩
(b) (Sport) foulen

foul: ~-**mouthed** /faʊlmaʊðd/ *adj.*
unanständig; unflätig; ~-**smelling** *adj.*
übel riechend

found¹ /faʊnd/ *v.t.* **(a)** (establish) gründen;
stiften ⟨*Krankenhaus, Kloster*⟩; begründen
⟨*Wissenschaft, Religion*⟩
(b) (fig.: base) begründen; **be** ~**ed** [**up**]**on** sth.
[sich] auf etw. (*Akk.*) gründen

found² ▶ FIND 1

foundation /faʊn'deɪʃn/ *n.* **(a)** Gründung,
die; (of hospital, monastery) Stiftung, *die*
(b) *usu. in pl.* ~[**s**] (lit. or fig.) Fundament,
das; **be without** ~ (fig.) unbegründet sein

foundation: ~ **course** *n.* (Univ. etc.)
Grundkurs, *der;* ~ **cream** *n.*
Grundierungscreme, *die;* ~ **stone** *n.* (lit. or
fig.) Grundstein, *der*

'**founder¹** *n.* Gründer, *der*/Gründerin, *die;*
(of hospital) Stifter, *der*/Stifterin, *die*

founder² *v.i.* **(a)** ⟨*Schiff:*⟩ sinken
(b) (fig.: fail) sich zerschlagen

foundry /'faʊndrɪ/ *n.* Gießerei, *die*

fountain /'faʊntɪn/ *n.* Fontäne, *die;* (structure)
Springbrunnen, *der;* (fig.) Quelle, *die*

'**fountain pen** *n.* Füllfederhalter, *der*

four /fɔː(r)/ **1** *adj.* vier
2 *n.* Vier, *die;* **on all** ~**s** auf allen vieren
(ugs.). *See also* EIGHT

four: ~-**by**-~ **1** *adj.* Allrad-; **2** *n.*
Allradler, *der;* Allradfahrzeug, *das;* ~-**door**
attrib. adj. viertürig ⟨*Auto*⟩; ~-**fold**
/'fɔːfəʊld/ *adj., adv.* vierfach; **a** ~-**fold**
increase ein Anstieg auf das Vierfache;
~-**legged** /'fɔːlegɪd, 'fɔːlegd/ *adj.*
vierbeinig; ~-**letter** '**word** *n.* vulgärer
Ausdruck; (expressing anger) ≈ Kraftausdruck,
der; ~-**poster** *n.* Himmelbett, *das;*
~**some** /'fɔːsəm/ *n.* Quartett, *das;* **go in** or
as a ~**some** zu viert gehen; ~-**star** *n.*
~-**star** [**petrol**] Super[benzin], *das*

fourteen /fɔː'tiːn/ **1** *adj.* vierzehn
2 *n.* Vierzehn, *die. See also* EIGHT

fourteenth /fɔː'tiːnθ/ **1** *adj.* vierzehnt...
2 *n.* (fraction) Vierzehntel, *das. See also*
EIGHTH

fourth /fɔːθ/ **1** *adj.* viert...
2 *n.* (in sequence, rank) Vierte, *der/die/das;*
(fraction) Viertel, *das. See also* EIGHTH

'**fourthly** *adv.* viertens

four-wheel '**drive** *n.* (Motor Veh.) Vier- *od.*
Allradantrieb, *der*

fowl /faʊl/ *n.* Haushuhn, *das;* (collectively)
Geflügel, *das*

fox /fɒks/ **1** *n.* Fuchs, *der*
2 *v.t.* verwirren

'**fox-hunting** *n.* Fuchsjagd, *die*

foyer /'fɔɪeɪ/ *n.* Foyer, *das*

fraction /'frækʃn/ *n.* **(a)** (Math.) Bruch, *der*
(b) (small part) Bruchteil, *der*

fracture /'fræktʃə(r)/ **1** *n.* Bruch, *der*
2 *v.t.* brechen

fragile /'frædʒaɪl/ *adj.* zerbrechlich

fragility /frə'dʒɪlɪtɪ/ *n.* Zerbrechlichkeit, *die*

fragment /'frægmənt/ *n.* Bruchstück, *das*

fragmentary /ˈfrægməntərɪ/ *adj.*
bruchstückhaft

fragrance /ˈfreɪgrəns/ *n.* Duft, *der*

fragrant /ˈfreɪgrənt/ *adj.* duftend

frail /freɪl/ *adj.* zerbrechlich; gebrechlich
⟨*Greis, Greisin*⟩

frame /freɪm/ **1** *n.* (a) (of vehicle) Rahmen,
der; (of bed) Gestell, *das*
(b) (border) Rahmen, *der;* [spectacle] ~s
[Brillen]gestell, *das*
2 *v.t.* (a) rahmen
(b) formulieren ⟨*Frage, Antwort*⟩
(c) (coll.: incriminate) ~ sb. jmdm. etwas
anhängen

frame: ~**-up** *n.* (coll.) abgekartetes Spiel
(ugs.); ~**work** *n.* Gerüst, *das*

franc /fræŋk/ *n.* Franc, *der;* (Swiss)
Franken, *der*

France /frɑːns/ *pr. n.* Frankreich (*das*)

franchise /ˈfræntʃaɪz/ *n.* (a) Stimmrecht,
das
(b) (Commerc.) Lizenz, *die*

frank[1] *adj.* offen; freimütig ⟨*Geständnis,
Äußerung*⟩; be ~ with sb. zu jmdm. offen
sein

frank[2] *v.t.* (Post) frankieren

frankfurter /ˈfræŋkfɜːtə(r)/ (*Amer.:*
frankfurt /ˈfræŋkfɜːt/) *n.* Frankfurter
[Würstchen]

'frankly *adv.* offen; (honestly) offen gesagt

frantic /ˈfræntɪk/ *adj.* (a) verzweifelt
⟨*Hilferufe, Gestikulieren*⟩; be ~ with fear/
rage *etc.* außer sich (*Dat.*) sein vor Angst/
Wut *usw.*
(b) hektisch ⟨*Aktivität, Suche*⟩

frantically /ˈfræntɪkəlɪ/, **'frantically** *adv.*
verzweifelt

fraternal /frəˈtɜːnl/ *adj.* brüderlich

fraternize /ˈfrætənaɪz/ *v.i.* ~ [with sb.]
sich verbrüdern [mit jmdm.]

fraud /frɔːd/ *n.* (a) *no pl.* Betrug, *der*
(b) (trick) Schwindel, *der*
(c) (person) Betrüger, *der*/Betrügerin, *die*

fraudulent /ˈfrɔːdjʊlənt/ *adj.* betrügerisch

fraught /frɔːt/ *adj.* be ~ with danger voller
Gefahren sein

fray[1] /freɪ/ *n.* [Kampf]getümmel, *das;* enter
or join the ~: sich in den Kampf stürzen

fray[2] *v.i.* [sich] durchscheuern; ⟨*Hosenbein,
Teppich, Seilende:*⟩ ausfransen; our nerves/
tempers began to ~ (fig.) wir verloren
langsam die Nerven/unsere Gemüter
erhitzten sich

freak /friːk/ *n.* (a) Missgeburt, *die;* attrib.
ungewöhnlich ⟨*Wetter, Ereignis*⟩
(b) (coll.: fanatic) Freak, *der*

freakish /ˈfriːkɪʃ/ *adj.* (capricious) launisch;
verrückt (ugs.); (abnormal) absonderlich

freaky /ˈfriːkɪ/ *adj.*(a) ▸ FREAKISH
(b) (coll.: bizarre) irre (salopp); verrückt (ugs.)

freckle /ˈfrekl/ *n.* Sommersprosse, *die*

'freckled *adj.* sommersprossig

free /friː/ **1** *adj.*, freer /ˈfriːə(r)/, freest
/ˈfriːɪst/ (a) frei; get ~: freikommen; set ~:
freilassen; ~ of charge/cost gebührenfrei/
kostenlos; sb. is ~ to do sth. es steht jmdm.
frei, etw. zu tun; ~ time Freizeit, *die;* he's
~ in the mornings er hat morgens Zeit
(b) (without payment) kostenlos; frei
⟨*Unterkunft, Verpflegung*⟩; Frei⟨*karte,
-exemplar*⟩; Gratis⟨*probe*⟩; 'admission ~'
„Eintritt frei"; for ~ (coll.) umsonst
2 *adv.* gratis; umsonst
3 *v.t.* (set at liberty) freilassen; (disentangle)
befreien (of, from von); ~ sb./oneself from
jmdn./sich befreien aus ⟨*Gefängnis,
Sklaverei*⟩

free 'agent *n.* be a ~: sein eigener Herr
sein

freedom /ˈfriːdəm/ *n.* Freiheit, *die;* ~ of
the press Pressefreiheit, *die;* ~ of action/
speech/movement Handlungs-/Rede-/
Bewegungsfreiheit, *die;* ~ of information
Auskunftsrecht, *das*

'freedom fighter *n.* Freiheitskämpfer,
der/-kämpferin, *die*

free: ~ 'enterprise *n.* freies
Unternehmertum; ~ 'fall *n.* freier Fall;
~**-fall** parachuting Fallschirmspringen mit
freiem Fall; **F~fone** ® /ˈfriːfəʊn/ *n.* ≈
Service 130; phone us on **F~fone** 0800 343
027 rufen Sie uns unter 0800 343 027 zum
Nulltarif an; ~ 'gift *n.* Gratisgabe, *die;*
~**hold** **1** *n.* Besitzrecht, *das;* **2** *adj.*
Eigentums-; ~**holder** *n.* Grundeigentümer,
der; ~ **house** *n.* (Brit.)
brauereiunabhängiges Wirtshaus; ~ 'kick
n. (Footb.) Freistoß, *der;* ~**lance** **1** *n.*
freier Mitarbeiter/freie Mitarbeiterin;
2 *adj.* freiberuflich; ~**lancer**
/ˈfriːlɑːnsə(r)/ ▸ ~LANCE 1

'freely *adv.* (willingly) großzügig; freimütig
⟨*eingestehen*⟩; (without restriction) frei; (frankly)
offen

free: ~ 'market *n.* (Econ.) freier Markt;
F~mason *n.* Freimaurer, *der;*
F~phone ▸ FREEFONE; ~**range** *adj.* frei
laufend ⟨*Huhn*⟩; ~**range eggs** Eier von frei
laufenden Hühnern; ~ **speech** *n.*
Redefreiheit; ~**standing** *adj.* frei
stehend; ~**ware** /ˈfriːweə(r)/ *n., no indef.
art.* (Comp.) Freeware, *die;* kostenlose
Software; ~**way** *n.* (Amer.) Autobahn, *die;*
~**wheel** *v.i.* im Freilauf fahren; ~ 'world
n. freie Welt

freeze /friːz/ **1** *v.i.*, froze /frəʊz/, frozen
/ˈfrəʊzn/ (a) frieren; (become covered with ice)
zufrieren; ⟨*Straße:*⟩ vereisen; ⟨*Flüssigkeit:*⟩
gefrieren; ⟨*Rohr, Schloss:*⟩ einfrieren
(b) (become rigid) steif frieren
2 *v.t.*, froze, frozen (a) (preserve) tiefkühlen
(b) einfrieren ⟨*Kredit, Löhne, Preise usw.*⟩

'freeze-dry *v.t.* gefriertrocknen

'freezer *n.* Tiefkühltruhe, *die;* [upright] ~:
Tiefkühlschrank, *der;* ~ compartment
Tiefkühlfach, *das* ⋯⟶

freezing /'fri:zɪŋ/ ① *adj.* (lit. or fig.) frostig;
it's ∼: es ist eiskalt
② *n.* above/below ∼: über/unter dem/den
Gefrierpunkt

freezing: ∼ **'fog** *n.* gefrierender Nebel;
∼ **point** *n.* Gefrierpunkt, *der*

freight /freɪt/ *n.* Fracht, *die*

'freighter *n.* Frachter, *der*

'freight train *n.* Güterzug, *der*

French /frentʃ/ ① *adj.* französisch; **he/she
is** ∼: er ist Franzose/sie ist Französin
② *n.* **(a)** (language) Französisch, *das; see also*
ENGLISH 2A
(b) the ∼ *pl.* die Franzosen *Pl.*

French: ∼ **'bean** *n.* (Brit.) Gartenbohne,
die; ∼ **'bread** *n.* französisches
[Stangen]weißbrot; ∼ **'dressing** *n.*
Vinaigrette, *die;* ∼ **'fries** *n. pl.* Pommes
frites *Pl.;* ∼ **'kiss** *n.* französischer Kuss
(ugs.); Zungenkuss, *der;* ∼**man** /'frentʃmən/
n., pl. ∼men /'frentʃmən/ Franzose, *der;*
∼ **'polish** *n.* Schellackpolitur, *die;*
∼ **'window** *n.* französisches Fenster;
∼**woman** *n.* Französin, *die*

frenzied /'frenzɪd/ *adj.* rasend

frenzy /'frenzɪ/ *n.* Wahnsinn, *der;* (fury)
Raserei, *die*

frequency /'fri:kwənsɪ/ *n.* **(a)** Häufigkeit,
die
(b) (Phys.) Frequenz, *die*

frequent ① /'fri:kwənt/ *adj.* **(a)** häufig;
become less ∼: seltener werden
(b) (habitual) eifrig
② /frɪ'kwent/ *v.t.* häufig besuchen ⟨Café,
Klub, usw.⟩

frequently /'fri:kwəntlɪ/ *adv.* häufig

fresco /'freskəʊ/ *n. pl.* ∼es *or* ∼s Fresko,
das

fresh /freʃ/ *adj.* frisch; neu ⟨Beweise,
Anstrich, Mut, Energie⟩; ∼ **supplies**
Nachschub, *der* (of an + *Dat.*); **make a**
∼ **start** noch einmal von vorne anfangen;
(fig.) neu beginnen

freshen /'freʃn/ *v.i.* auffrischen
■ **freshen 'up** *v.i.* sich auffrischen

'freshly *adv.* frisch

'freshness *n.* Frische, *die*

fresh 'water *n.* Süßwasser, *das*

fret /fret/ *v.i.,* -tt- sich (*Dat.*) Sorgen machen

fretful /'fretfl/ *adj.* verdrießlich; quengelig
(ugs.)

'fretsaw *n.* Laubsäge, *die*

Fri. *abbr.* = **Friday** Fr.

friar /'fraɪə(r)/ *n.* Ordensbruder, *der*

friction /'frɪkʃn/ *n.* Reibung, *die*

Friday /'fraɪdeɪ, 'fraɪdɪ/ *n.* Freitag, *der;* **on**
∼: [am] Freitag; **on a** ∼, **on** ∼s freitags;
∼ **13 August** Freitag, der 13. August; (at top of
letter etc.) Freitag, den 13. August; **next/last**
∼: [am] nächsten/letzten Freitag; **Good** ∼:
Karfreitag, *der*

fridge /frɪdʒ/ *n.* (Brit. coll.) Kühlschrank, *der*

fried ▶ FRY¹

friend /frend/ *n.* Freund, *der*/Freundin, *die;*
be ∼s **with sb.** mit jmdm. befreundet sein;
make ∼s **[with sb.]** [mit jmdm.] Freundschaft
schließen

friendliness /'frendlɪnɪs/ *n.*
Freundlichkeit, *die*

'friendly ① *adj.* freundlich (**to** zu);
freundschaftlich ⟨Rat, Beziehungen,
Wettkampf⟩
② *n.* (Sport) Freundschaftsspiel, *das*

'friendship *n.* Freundschaft, *die*

fries /fraɪz/ *n. pl.* (Amer.) Pommes frites *Pl.*

frigate /'frɪgət/ *n.* (Naut.) Fregatte, *die*

fright /fraɪt/ *n.* Schreck, *der;* **take** ∼:
erschrecken

frighten /'fraɪtn/ *v.t.* ⟨Explosion, Schuss:⟩
erschrecken; ⟨Gedanke, Drohung:⟩ Angst
machen (+ *Dat.*); **be** ∼**ed** *at or* **by sth.** vor
etw. (*Dat.*) erschrecken

'frightful *adj.,* **'frightfully** *adv.* furchtbar

frigid /'frɪdʒɪd/ *adj.* frostig; (sexually) frigid[e]

frill /frɪl/ *n.* **(a)** Rüsche, *die*
(b) *in pl.* (embellishments) Beiwerk, *das*

'frilly *adj.* mit Rüschen besetzt;
Rüschen⟨kleid, -bluse⟩

fringe /frɪndʒ/ *n.* **(a)** Fransenkante, *die* (**on**
an + *Dat.*)
(b) (hair) [Pony]fransen *Pl.* (ugs.)
(c) (edge) Rand, *der*

frisk /frɪsk/ ① *v.i.* ∼ [**about**]
[herum]springen
② *v.t.* (coll.) filzen (ugs.)

'frisky *adj.* munter

fritter¹ /'frɪtə(r)/ *n.* **apple** *etc.* ∼s
Apfelstücke *usw.* in Pfannkuchenteig

fritter² *v.t.* ∼ **away** vergeuden

frivolity /frɪ'vɒlɪtɪ/ *n.* Oberflächlichkeit, *die*

frivolous /'frɪvələs/ *adj.* **(a)** frivol
(b) (trifling) belanglos

frizzy /'frɪzɪ/ *adj.* kraus

fro /frəʊ/ *adv.* ▶ TO 2

frock /frɒk/ *n.* Kleid, *das*

frog /frɒg/ *n.* Frosch, *der*

frog: ∼**man** /'frɒgmən/ *n., pl.* ∼men
/'frɒgmən/ Froschmann, *der;* ∼**spawn** *n.*
Froschlaich, *der*

frolic /'frɒlɪk/ *v.i.,* -ck- ∼ [**about** *or* **around**]
[herum]springen

from /frəm, *stressed* frɒm/ *prep.* von;
(∼ within; expr. origin) aus; ∼ **Paris** aus Paris; ∼
Paris to Munich von Paris nach München;
be a mile ∼ **sth.** eine Meile von etw. entfernt
sein; **where do you come** ∼?, **where are you**
∼? woher kommen Sie?; **painted** ∼ **life** nach
dem Leben gemalt; **weak** ∼ **hunger** schwach
vor Hunger; ∼ **the year 1972** seit 1972; ∼ [**the
age of**] **18** ab 18 Jahre; ∼ **4 to 6 eggs** 4 bis 6
Eier

front /frʌnt/ ① *n.* **(a)** Vorderseite, *die;* (of
house) Vorderfront, *die;* **in** *or* **at the** ∼ [**of**

sth.] vorn [in etw. *position: Dat., movement: Akk.*]; **to the ~:** nach vorn; **in ~:** vorn[e]; **be in ~ of sth./sb.** vor etw./jmdm. sein
(b) (Mil.) Front, *die*
(c) (at seaside) Strandpromenade, *die*
(d) (Meteerol.) Front, *die*
(e) (bluff) Fassade, *die*
[2] *adj.* vorder...; Vorder⟨*rad, -zimmer, -zahn*⟩; **~ garden** Vorgarten, *der;* **~ row** erste Reihe

frontal /'frʌntl/ *adj.* Frontal-

front 'door *n.* (of flat) Wohnungstür, *die;* (of house) Haustür, *die*

frontier /'frʌntɪə(r)/ *n.* Grenze, *die*

front: ~ 'page *n.* Titelseite, *die;* **~-wheel drive** [1] *n.* Vorderradantrieb, *der;* Frontantrieb, *der;* [2] *adj.* **a ~-wheel drive vehicle** ein Fahrzeug mit Vorderrad- od. Frontantrieb

frost /frɒst/ [1] *n.* Frost, *der;* **ten degrees of ~** (Brit.) zehn Grad minus
[2] *v.t.* **~ed glass** Mattglas, *das*

'frostbite *n.* Erfrierung, *die*

'frosting *n.* (esp. Amer.) Glasur, *die*

'frosty *adj.* frostig

froth /frɒθ/ [1] *n.* Schaum, *der*
[2] *v.i.* schäumen

'frothy *adj.* schaumig

frown /fraʊn/ [1] *v.i.* die Stirn runzeln ([**up**]**on** über + *Akk.*)
[2] *n.* Stirnrunzeln, *das*

froze ▶ FREEZE

frozen /'frəʊzn/ [1] ▶ FREEZE
[2] *adj.* **(a)** zugefroren ⟨*Fluss, See*⟩; eingefroren ⟨*Wasserleitung*⟩; **I'm ~** (fig.) mir ist eiskalt
(b) (to preserve) tiefgekühlt; **~ food** Tiefkühlkost, *die*

frugal /'fru:gl/ *adj.* genügsam ⟨*Lebensweise, Mensch*⟩; frugal ⟨*Mahl*⟩

fruit /fru:t/ *n.* Frucht, *die; collect.* Obst, *das*

'fruit cake *n.* englischer Teekuchen

fruitful /'fru:tfl/ *adj.* fruchtbar

'fruit juice *n.* Obstsaft, *der*

'fruitless *adj.* nutzlos ⟨*Versuch, Gespräch*⟩; fruchtlos ⟨*Verhandlung, Suche*⟩

fruit: ~ machine *n.* (Brit.) Spielautomat, *der;* **~ 'salad** *n.* Obstsalat, *der*

'fruity *adj.* fruchtig ⟨*Geschmack, Wein*⟩

frustrate /frʌ'streɪt/ *v.t.* vereiteln ⟨*Plan, Versuch*⟩; zunichte machen ⟨*Hoffnung, Bemühungen*⟩

'frustrated *adj.* frustriert

frustration /frʌ'streɪʃn/ *n.* Frustration, *die*

fry¹ /fraɪ/ *v.t. & i.,* **fried** /fraɪd/ braten; **fried egg** Spiegelei, *das*

fry² *n.* (fishes) Brut, *die;* **small ~** (fig.) unbedeutende Leute

'frying pan *n.* Bratpfanne, *die*

ft. *abbr.* = **feet, foot** ft.

fuchsia /'fju:ʃə/ *n.* (Bot.) Fuchsie, *die*

fuck /fʌk/ (coarse) [1] *v.t. & i.* ficken (vulg.); [oh,] **~!**, [oh,] **~ it!** [au,] Scheiße! (derb.)
[2] *n.* Fick, *der* (vulg.)

fuddy-duddy /'fʌdɪdʌdɪ/ (coll.) [1] *adj.* verkalkt (ugs.)
[2] *n.* Fossil, *das* (fig.)

fudge /fʌdʒ/ *n.* Karamellbonbon, *der od. das*

fuel /'fju:əl/ *n.* Brennstoff, *der;* (for vehicle) Kraftstoff, *der;* (for ship, aircraft) Treibstoff, *der*

fuel: ~ consumption *n.* (of vehicle) Kraftstoffverbrauch, *der;* **~ gauge** *n.* Kraftstoffanzeiger *der;* **~ injection** *n.* Benzineinspritzung, *die*

fugitive /'fju:dʒɪtɪv/ *n.* Flüchtige, *der/die*

fugue /fju:g/ *n.* (Mus.) Fuge, *die*

fulfil (*Amer.:* **fulfill**) /fʊl'fɪl/ *v.t.,* **-ll-** erfüllen; halten ⟨*Versprechen;*⟩ **~ oneself** sich selbst verwirklichen

ful'filment (*Amer.:* **ful'fillment**) *n.* Erfüllung, *die*

full /fʊl/ [1] *adj.* **(a)** voll; satt ⟨*Person*⟩; **~ of** voller; **be ~ up** voll [besetzt] sein; ⟨*Behälter:*⟩ randvoll sein; ⟨*Flug:*⟩ völlig ausgebucht sein; **I'm ~** [**up**] (coll.) ich bin voll [bis obenhin] (ugs.); **be ~ of oneself** sehr von sich eingenommen sein
(b) ausführlich ⟨*Bericht, Beschreibung*⟩; erfüllt ⟨*Leben*⟩; ganz ⟨*Stunde, Jahr, Monat, Seite*⟩; voll ⟨*Name, Bezahlung, Verständnis*⟩; **~ details** alle Einzelheiten; **at ~ speed** mit Höchstgeschwindigkeit
(c) voll ⟨*Gesicht*⟩; füllig ⟨*Figur*⟩; weit ⟨*Rock*⟩
[2] *n.* **in ~:** vollständig
[3] *adv.* (exactly) genau

full: ~-blown *adj.* ausgewachsen ⟨*Skandal*⟩; ausgereift ⟨*Theorie, Plan, Gedanke*⟩; **~-blown AIDS** Vollbild-Aids, *das;* **~-bodied** *adj.* vollmundig, (fachspr.) körperreich ⟨*Wein*⟩; **~-cream** *adj.* **~-cream milk/cheese** Vollmilch, *die/* Vollfettkäse, *der;* **~ -length** *adj.* lang ⟨*Kleid*⟩; **~ 'moon** *n.* Vollmond, *der;* **~-scale** *adj.* **(a)** in Originalgröße; **(b)** groß angelegt ⟨*Untersuchung, Suchaktion*⟩; **~ 'stop** *n.* Punkt, *der;* **~-time** *adj.* ganztägig; Ganztags⟨*arbeit*⟩; **~-'timer** *n.* Ganztagsbeschäftigte, *der/die*

fully /'fʊlɪ/ *adv.* voll [und ganz]; reich ⟨*belohnt*⟩; ausführlich ⟨*erklären*⟩

fulsome /'fʊlsəm/ *adj.* übertrieben

fumble /'fʌmbl/ *v.i.* **~ at** *or* **with** [herum]fingern an (+ *Dat.*); **~ in one's pockets for sth.** in seinen Taschen nach etw. kramen (ugs.)

fume /fju:m/ [1] *n.* **in** *pl.* **~s** Dämpfe *Pl.;* (from car exhaust) Abgase *Pl.*
[2] *v.i.* vor Wut schäumen

fumigate /'fju:mɪgeɪt/ *v.t.* ausräuchern

fun /fʌn/ *n.* Spaß, *der;* **have ~!** viel Spaß!; **make ~ of sb.** sich über jmdn. lustig machen; **for ~, for the ~ of it** zum Spaß

function /'fʌŋkʃn/ **1** *n.* Aufgabe, *die;*
Funktion, *die;* (formal event) Veranstaltung, *die*
2 *v.i.* ⟨*Maschine, System:*⟩ funktionieren;
~ **as** fungieren als; (serve as) dienen als
functional /'fʌŋkʃənl/ *adj.* **(a)** (useful)
funktionell
(b) (working) funktionsfähig
'function key *n.* (Comp.) Funktionstaste,
die
fund /fʌnd/ **1** *n.* **(a)** (money) Fonds, *der*
(b) (fig.: stock) Fundus, *der* (**of** von, an + *Dat.*)
2 *v.t.* finanzieren
fundamental /fʌndə'mentl/ *adj.*
grundlegend (**to** für); elementar ⟨*Bedürfnisse*⟩
fundamentalism /fʌndə'mentəlɪzm/ *n.*
Fundamentalismus, *der*
fundamentalist /fʌndə'mentəlɪst/ *n.*
Fundamentalist, *der*/Fundamentalistin, *die*
funda'mentally *adv.* grundlegend; von
Grund auf ⟨*verschieden, ehrlich*⟩
fund: ~-raiser /'fʌndreɪzə(r)/ *n.* **(a)**
(person) Geldbeschaffer, *der*/-beschafferin,
die; **(b)** (event) Benefizveranstaltung, *die;*
~-raising /'fʌndreɪzɪŋ/ *n.*
Geldbeschaffung, *die; attrib.* zur
Geldbeschaffung *nachgestellt*
funeral /'fju:nərl/ *n.* Beerdigung, *die.*
~ **director** Bestattungsunternehmer, *der;*
~ **service** Trauerfeier, *die*
'funfair *n.* (Brit.) Jahrmarkt, *der*
fungus /'fʌŋgəs/ *n., pl.* **fungi** /'fʌŋgaɪ,
'fʌndʒaɪ/ *or* **~es** Pilz, *der*
funicular /fju:'nɪkjʊlə(r)/ *adj. & n.*
~ **[railway]** [Stand]seilbahn, *die*
'fun-loving *adj.* lebenslustig
funnel /'fʌnl/ *n.* Trichter, *der;* (of ship etc.)
Schornstein, *der*
funnily /'fʌnɪlɪ/ *adv.* komisch; ~ **enough**
komischerweise
funny /'fʌnɪ/ *adj.* **(a)** komisch; lustig; witzig
⟨*Mensch, Einfall*⟩
(b) (strange) komisch
'funny bone *n.* Musikantenknochen, *der*
fur /fɜ:(r)/ *n.* **(a)** Fell, *das;* (garment) Pelz, *der;*
~ **coat** Pelzmantel, *der*
(b) (in kettle) Kesselstein, *der*
furious /'fjʊərɪəs/ *adj.* wütend; heftig
⟨*Streit*⟩; wild ⟨*Tanz, Tempo, Kampf*⟩; **be**
~ **with sb.** wütend auf jmdn. sein
'furiously *adv.* wütend; wild ⟨*kämpfen*⟩: wie
wild (ugs.) ⟨*arbeiten*⟩
furl /fɜ:l/ *v.t.* einrollen ⟨*Segel, Flagge*⟩
furnace /'fɜ:nɪs/ *n.* Ofen, *der*
furnish /'fɜ:nɪʃ/ *v.t.* **(a)** möblieren
(b) (supply) liefern; ~ **sb. with sth.** jmdm. etw.
liefern
'furnishings *n. pl.*
Einrichtungsgegenstände *Pl.*
furniture /'fɜ:nɪtʃə(r)/ *n.* Möbel *Pl.;* **piece of**
~: Möbel[stück], *das*

furniture: ~ polish *n.* Möbelpolitur, *die;*
~ **van** *n.* Möbelwagen, *der*
furrow /'fʌrəʊ/ *n.* Furche, *die*
furry /'fɜ:rɪ/ *adj.* haarig; ~ **animal** (toy)
Plüschtier, *das*
further /'fɜ:ðə(r)/ **1** *adj.* **(a)** (in space) weiter
entfernt
(b) (additional) weiter...
2 *adv.* weiter
3 *v.t.* fördern
further edu'cation *n.* Weiterbildung, *die;*
(for adults also) Erwachsenenbildung, *die*
further'more *adv.* außerdem
'furthermost *adj.* äußerst...
furthest /'fɜ:ðɪst/ **1** *adj.* am weitesten
entfernt
2 *adv.* am weitesten ⟨*springen, laufen*⟩; am
weitesten entfernt ⟨*sein, wohnen*⟩
furtive /'fɜ:tɪv/ *adj.,* **furtively** *adv.*
verstohlen
fury /'fjʊərɪ/ *n.* Wut, *die;* (of sea, battle) Wüten,
das
fuse¹ /fju:z/ **1** *v.t.* (blend) verschmelzen
(**into** zu)
2 *v.i.* ~ **together** miteinander verschmelzen
fuse² *n.* [time] ~: [Zeit]zünder, *der;* (cord)
Zündschnur, *die*
fuse³ (Electr.) **1** *n.* Sicherung, *die*
2 *v.i.* **the lights have ~d** die Sicherung ist
durchgebrannt
'fuse box *n.* Sicherungskasten, *der*
fuselage /'fju:zəlɑ:ʒ/ *n.* [Flugzeug]rumpf,
der
fusion /'fju:ʒn/ *n.* **(a)** Verschmelzung, *die*
(b) (Phys.) Fusion, *die*
fuss /fʌs/ **1** *n.* Theater, *das* (ugs.); **make a**
~ **[about sth.]** einen Wirbel [um etw.]
machen
2 *v.i.* Wirbel machen; (get agitated) sich
[unnötig] aufregen
'fussy *adj.* (fastidious) eigen; penibel; **I'm not**
~ (I don't mind) ich bin nicht wählerisch
futile /'fju:taɪl/ *adj.* vergeblich ⟨*Versuch,
Bemühung*⟩; zum Scheitern verurteilt ⟨*Plan*⟩
futility /fju:'tɪlɪtɪ/ *n.* (of attempt, effort)
Vergeblichkeit, *die;* (of plan) Zwecklosigkeit,
die
futon /'fu:tɒn/ *n.* Futon, *der*
future /'fju:tʃə(r)/ **1** *adj.* [zu]künftig; **at
some** ~ **date** zu einem späteren Zeitpunkt
2 *n.* **(a)** Zukunft, *die;* **in** ~: in Zukunft;
künftig
(b) (Ling.) Futur, *das;* Zukunft, *die*
(c) *in pl.* (Commerc.) Terminware, *die;*
(contracts) Lieferungsverträge *Pl.*
futuristic /fju:tʃə'rɪstɪk/ *adj.* futuristisch
fuze /fju:z/ ▶ FUSE²
fuzzy /'fʌzɪ/ *adj.* **(a)** (frizzy) kraus
(b) (blurred) verschwommen

Gg

G, g /dʒiː/ *n.* G, g, *das*

gab /gæb/ *n.* (coll.) have the gift of the ∼: reden können

gabble /'gæbl/ *v.i.* brabbeln (ugs.)

gable /'geɪbl/ *n.* Giebel, *der*

gad /gæd/ *v.i.*, -dd- (coll.) ∼ about herumziehen (ugs.)

gadget /'gædʒɪt/ *n.* Gerät, *das*

gadgetry /'gædʒɪtrɪ/ *n.* [hoch technisierte] Ausstattung

Gaelic /'geɪlɪk, 'gælɪk/ ① *adj.* gälisch ② *n.* Gälisch, *das*

gaffe /gæf/ *n.* Fauxpas, *der*

gag /gæg/ ① *n.* (a) Knebel, *der* (b) (joke) Gag, *der* ② *v.t.*, -gg- knebeln

gaiety /'geɪətɪ/ *n.* Fröhlichkeit, *die*

gaily /'geɪlɪ/ *adv.* fröhlich; in leuchtenden Farben ⟨bemalt, geschmückt⟩

gain /geɪn/ ① *n.* (a) Gewinn, *der* (b) (increase) Zunahme, *die* (in an + *Dat.*) ② *v.t.* (a) gewinnen; finden ⟨Zugang, Zutritt⟩; erwerben ⟨Wissen, Ruf⟩; erlangen ⟨Freiheit⟩; erzielen ⟨Vorteil, Punkte⟩; verdienen ⟨Lebensunterhalt, Geldsumme⟩; ∼ weight/five pounds [in weight] zunehmen/ fünf Pfund zunehmen; ∼ speed schneller werden (b) ⟨Uhr:⟩ vorgehen um ③ *v.i.* (a) ∼ by sth. von etw. profitieren (b) ⟨Uhr:⟩ vorgehen

gainful /'geɪnfl/ *adj.* ∼ employment Erwerbstätigkeit, *die*

gainfully /'geɪnfəlɪ/ *adv.* ∼ employed erwerbstätig

gait /geɪt/ *n.* Gang, *der*

gala /'gɑːlə, 'geɪlə/ *n.* Festveranstaltung, *die*; *attrib.* Gala⟨abend, -vorstellung⟩; swimming ∼: Schwimmfest, *das*

galaxy /'gæləksɪ/ *n.* Galaxie, *die*

gale /geɪl/ *n.* Sturm, *der*

gall /gɔːl/ *n.* Unverschämtheit, *die*

gallant /'gælənt/ *adj.* (brave) tapfer; (chivalrous) ritterlich

gallantry /'gæləntrɪ/ *n.* (bravery) Tapferkeit, *die*

'gall bladder *n.* Gallenblase, *die*

gallery /'gælərɪ/ *n.* (a) Galerie, *die* (b) (Theatre) dritter Rang

galley /'gælɪ/ *n.* (a) (ship's kitchen) Kombüse, *die* (b) (Hist.) Galeere, *die*

gallivant /'gælɪvænt/ *v.i.* (coll.) herumziehen (ugs.)

gallon /'gælən/ *n.* Gallone, *die*

gallop /'gæləp/ ① *n.* Galopp, *der* ② *v.i.* ⟨Pferd, Reiter:⟩ galoppieren

gallows /'gæləʊz/ *n. sing.* Galgen, *der*

Gallup poll ® /'gæləp pɒl/ *n.* Meinungsumfrage, *die*

galore /gə'lɔː(r)/ *adv.* im Überfluss; in Hülle und Fülle

galvanize /'gælvənaɪz/ *v.t.* wachrütteln; ∼ sb. into action jmdn. veranlassen, sofort aktiv zu werden

gambit /'gæmbɪt/ *n.* Gambit, *das*

gamble /'gæmbl/ *v.i.* (a) [um Geld] spielen; ∼ at cards/on horses um Geld Karten spielen/auf Pferde wetten (b) (fig.) spekulieren; ∼ on sth. sich auf etw. (*Akk.*) verlassen

gambler /'gæmblə(r)/ *n.* Glücksspieler, *der*

gambling /'gæmblɪŋ/ *n.* Spiel[en], *das*; Glücksspiel, *das*; (on horses, dogs) Wetten, *das*

game¹ /geɪm/ *n.* (a) Spiel, *das*; (of [table] tennis, chess, cards, cricket) Partie, *die* (b) (fig.: scheme) Vorhaben, *das* (c) *in pl.* (athletic contests) Spiele *Pl.*; (in school) (sports) Sport, *der*; (athletics) Leichtathletik, *die* (d) (Hunting, Cookery) Wild, *das*

game² *adj.* mutig; be ∼ to do sth. bereit sein, etw. zu tun

'gamekeeper *n.* Wildheger, *der*

gamma rays /'gæmə/ *n. pl.* (Phys.) Gammastrahlen *Pl.*

gammon /'gæmən/ *n.* Räucherschinken, *der*

gamut /'gæmət/ *n.* Skala, *die*

gander /'gændə(r)/ *n.* Gänserich, *der*

gang /gæŋ/ ① *n.* Bande, *die*; (of workmen, prisoners) Trupp, *der* ② *v.i.* ∼ up against *or* on (coll.) sich verbünden gegen

gangling /'gæŋglɪŋ/ schlaksig (ugs.)

gangster /'gæŋstə(r)/ *n.* Gangster, *der*

'gang warfare *n.* Bandenkrieg, *der*

'gangway *n.* Gangway, *die*; (Brit.: between seats) Gang, *der*

gaol /dʒeɪl/ ▶ JAIL

gap /gæp/ *n.* (a) Lücke, *die* (b) (in time) Pause, *die* (c) (divergence) Kluft, *die*

gape /geɪp/ *v.i.* (a) den Mund aufsperren; ⟨Loch, Abgrund, Wunde:⟩ klaffen (b) (stare) Mund und Nase aufsperren (ugs.); ∼ at sb./sth. jmdn./etw. mit offenem Mund anstarren

g

garage /'gærɪdʒ/ n. Garage, die; (selling petrol) Tankstelle, die; (for repairing cars) [Kfz-]Werkstatt, die

garb /gɑːb/ n. Tracht, die

garbage /'gɑːbɪdʒ/ n. (a) Abfall, der; Müll, der
(b) (coll.: nonsense) Quatsch, der (salopp)

garbage: ~ **can** n. (Amer.) Mülltonne, die; ~ **dis'posal unit,** ~ **disposer** ns. Abfallvernichter, der; Müllwolf, der

garble /'gɑːbl/ v.t. verstümmeln

garden /'gɑːdn/ n. Garten, der

garden: ~ **centre** n. Gartencenter, das; ~ **'city** n. Gartenstadt, die

gardener /'gɑːdnə(r)/ n. Gärtner, der/ Gärtnerin, die

gardening /'gɑːdnɪŋ/ n. Gartenarbeit, die

garden: ~ **'shed** n. Geräteschuppen, der ~ **'waste** n. Gartenabfälle Pl.; Gartenabfall, der

gargle /'gɑːgl/ v.i. gurgeln

gargoyle /'gɑːgɔɪl/ n. (Archit.) Wasserspeier, der

garish /'geərɪʃ/ adj. grell ‹Farbe, Licht›; knallbunt ‹Kleidung›

garland /'gɑːlənd/ n. Girlande, die

garlic /'gɑːlɪk/ n. Knoblauch, der

garment /'gɑːmənt/ n. Kleidungsstück, das; ~s pl. (clothes) Kleidung, die; Kleider Pl.

garnish /'gɑːnɪʃ/ ① v.t. garnieren ② n. Garnierung, die

garret /'gærət/ n. Dachkammer, die

garrison /'gærɪsn/ n. Garnison, die

garter /'gɑːtə(r)/ n. Strumpfband, das

gas /gæs/ ① n. (a) pl. ~es /'gæsɪz/ Gas, das (b) (Amer. coll.: petrol) Benzin, das ② v.t., -ss- mit Gas vergiften

gas: ~ **chamber** n. Gaskammer, die; ~ **'cooker** n. (Brit.) Gasherd, der; ~ **cylinder** n. Gasflasche, die; ~ **'fire** n. Gasofen, der

gash /gæʃ/ ① n. Schnittwunde, die ② v.t. aufritzen ‹Haut›; ~ **one's finger** sich (Dat. od. Akk.) in den Finger schneiden

gas: ~ **heater** n. Gasofen, der; ~ **mask** n. Gasmaske, die; ~ **meter** n. Gaszähler, der

gasoline (gasolene) /'gæsəliːn/ n. (Amer.) Benzin, das

gasometer /gæ'sɒmɪtə(r)/ n. Gasometer, der

gasp /gɑːsp/ ① v.i. nach Luft schnappen (with vor); **he was** ~**ing for air** er rang nach Luft ② v.t. ~ **out** hervorstoßen ③ n. Keuchen, das

'gas station n. (Amer.) Tankstelle, die

gastric: ~ **'flu** (coll.)**,** ~ **influ'enza** ns. Darmgrippe, die; ~ **'ulcer** n. Magengeschwür, das

gastro-enteritis /gæstrəʊentə'raɪtɪs/ n. Gastroenteritis, die (fachspr.); Magen-Darm-Katarrh, der

gastronomy /gæ'strɒnəmɪ/ n. Gastronomie, die

'gasworks n. sing. Gaswerk, das

gate /geɪt/ n. Tor, das; (barrier) Sperre, die; (to field etc.) Gatter, das; (of level crossing) [Bahn]schranke, die; (in airport) Flugsteig, der

gateau /'gætəʊ/ n., pl. ~s or ~x /'gætəʊz/ Torte, die

gate: ~**crasher** /'geɪtkræʃə(r)/ n. ungeladener Gast; ~**way** n. Tor, das

gather /'gæðə(r)/ ① v.t. (a) sammeln; zusammentragen ‹Informationen›; pflücken ‹Obst, Blumen› (b) (infer, deduce) schließen (from aus) (c) ~ **speed/force** schneller/stärker werden ② v.i. sich versammeln; ‹Wolken:› sich zusammenziehen

'gathering n. Versammlung, die

GATT /gæt/ abbr. = **General Agreement on Tariffs and Trade** GATT, das

gauche /gəʊʃ/ adj. linkisch

gaudy /'gɔːdɪ/ adj. protzig; grell ‹Farben›

gauge /geɪdʒ/ n. ① (a) (measure) Maß, das (b) (instrument) Messgerät, das ② v.t. messen; (fig.) beurteilen

gaunt /gɔːnt/ adj. hager

gauntlet /'gɔːntlɪt/ n. Stulpenhandschuh, der

gauze /gɔːz/ n. Gaze, die

gave ▶ GIVE 1, 2

gay /geɪ/ ① adj. (a) fröhlich; (brightly coloured) farbenfroh (b) (coll.: homosexual) schwul (ugs.); Schwulen‹lokal› ② n. (coll.) Schwule, der (ugs.)

gay 'rights n. pl. Schwulenrechte Pl.

gaze /geɪz/ v.i. blicken; (fixedly) starren; ~ **at** sb./sth. jmdn./etw. anstarren

GB abbr. = **Great Britain** GB

GCSE abbr. (Brit.) = **General Certificate of Secondary Education**

gear /gɪə(r)/ ① n. (a) (Motor Veh.) Gang, der; **top/bottom** ~ (Brit.) der höchste/erste Gang; **change** or **shift** ~: schalten; **put the car into** ~: einen Gang einlegen; **out of** ~: im Leerlauf (b) (coll.: clothes) Aufmachung, die (c) (equipment) Gerät, das; Ausrüstung, die ② v.t. ausrichten (**to** auf + Akk.)

gear: ~**box** n. Getriebekasten, der; ~ **lever, (Amer.)** ~ **shift** ns. Schalthebel, der

geese pl. of GOOSE

geezer /'giːzə(r)/ n. (coll.: old man) Opa, der (ugs.)

gel /dʒel/ n. Gel, das

gelatin /'dʒelətɪn/, (Brit.) **gelatine**
/'dʒelətiːn/ n. Gelatine, die

gelignite /'dʒelɪgnaɪt/ n. Gelatinedynamit,
das

gem /dʒem/ n. Edelstein, der

Gemini /'dʒemɪnaɪ, 'dʒemɪnɪ/ n. (Astrol.,
Astron.) Zwillinge Pl.

'gemstone n. Edelstein, der

gender /'dʒendə(r)/ n. (Ling.)
[grammatisches] Geschlecht

gene /dʒiːn/ n. (Biol.) Gen, das

general /'dʒenrl/ [1] adj. allgemein; weit
verbreitet ⟨Ansicht⟩; (true of [nearly] all cases)
allgemein gültig; ungefähr ⟨Vorstellung,
Beschreibung usw.⟩; the ~ public weite
Kreise der Bevölkerung; in ~ use allgemein
verbreitet; as a ~ rule, in ~: im
Allgemeinen
[2] n. (Mil.) General, der

general: ~ e'lection ▸ ELECTION;
~ 'hospital n. Allgemeinkrankenhaus,
das

generalization /dʒenrəlar'zeɪʃn/ n.
Verallgemeinerung, die

generalize /'dʒenrəlaɪz/ [1] v.t.
verallgemeinern
[2] v.i. ~ about sth. etw. verallgemeinern

general 'knowledge n.
Allgemeinwissen, das

generally /'dʒenrəlɪ/ adv. (a) allgemein;
~ available überall erhältlich; ~ speaking
im Allgemeinen
(b) (usually) im Allgemeinen

general: ~ 'manager n. [leitender]
Direktor/[leitende] Direktorin;
~ 'meeting n. Generalversammlung, die;
Hauptversammlung, die; ~ National
Vo'cational Qualification n. (Brit.)
staatliches Berufsausbildungsprogramm;
~ prac'titioner n. (Med.) Arzt/Ärztin für
Allgemeinmedizin

generate /'dʒenəreɪt/ v.t. erzeugen (from
aus); (result in) führen zu

generation /dʒenə'reɪʃn/ n. (a)
Generation, die
(b) (production) Erzeugung, die

generator /'dʒenəreɪtə(r)/ n. Generator,
der

generosity /dʒenə'rɒsɪtɪ/ n.
Großzügigkeit, die

generous /'dʒenərəs/ adj. großzügig;
reichlich ⟨Vorrat, Portion⟩

'generously adv. großzügig

genetic /dʒɪ'netɪk/ adj. genetisch

genetically /dʒɪ'netɪkəlɪ/ adv. genetisch;
~ modified gentechnisch verändert;
~ engineered gentechnisch verändert
⟨Organismen, Pflanzen, Tiere,
Nahrungsmittel⟩; genetisch hergestellt
⟨Medikament, Enzym⟩

genetic engi'neering n.
Gentechnologie, die

genetics /dʒɪ'netɪks/ n. Genetik, die

Geneva /dʒɪ'niːvə/ [1] pr. n. Genf (das)
[2] attrib. adj. Genfer

genial /'dʒiːnɪəl/ adj. freundlich

genitals /'dʒenɪtlz/ n. pl.
Geschlechtsorgane Pl.

genitive /'dʒenɪtɪv/ adj. & n. ~ [case]
Genitiv, der

genius /'dʒiːnɪəs/ n. (a) (person) Genie, das
(b) (ability) Talent, das

genome /'dʒiːnəʊm/ n. (Biol.) Genom, das

genre /'ʒɑ̃rə/ n. Genre, das

gent /dʒent/ n. (a) (coll./joc.) Gent, der (iron.)
(b) the G~s (Brit. coll.) die Herrentoilette

genteel /dʒen'tiːl/ adj. vornehm

gentle /'dʒentl/ adj., ~r /'dʒentlə(r)/, ~st
/'dʒentlɪst/ sanft; liebenswürdig ⟨Person,
Verhalten⟩; leicht, schwach ⟨Brise⟩; leise
⟨Geräusch⟩; gemächlich ⟨Spaziergang,
Tempo⟩; mäßig ⟨Hitze⟩

gentleman /'dʒentlmən/ n., pl. **gentlemen**
/'dʒentlmən/ Herr, der; (well-mannered)
Gentleman, der; Ladies and Gentlemen!
meine Damen und Herren!; 'Gentlemen'
(sign) „Herren"

'gentleness n. Sanftheit, die; (of nature)
Sanftmütigkeit, die

gently /'dʒentlɪ/ adv. (tenderly) zart; zärtlich;
(mildly) sanft; (carefully) behutsam; (quietly, softly)
leise

genuine /'dʒenjʊɪn/ adj. (a) (real) echt
(b) (true) aufrichtig; wahr ⟨Grund, Not⟩

'genuinely adv. wirklich

genus /'dʒiːnəs, 'dʒenəs/ n., pl. **genera**
/'dʒenərə/ (Biol.) Gattung, die

geographical /dʒiːə'græfɪkl/ adj.
geographisch

geography /dʒɪ'ɒɡrəfɪ/ n. Geographie, die;
Erdkunde, die (Schulw.)

geological /dʒiːə'lɒdʒɪkl/ adj. geologisch

geologist /dʒɪ'ɒlədʒɪst/ n. Geologe, der/
Geologin, die

geology /dʒɪ'ɒlədʒɪ/ n. Geologie, die

geometric /dʒiːə'metrɪk/, **geometrical**
/dʒiːə'metrɪkl/ adj. geometrisch

geometry /dʒɪ'ɒmɪtrɪ/ n. Geometrie, die

geranium /dʒə'reɪnɪəm/ n. Geranie, die;
Pelargonie, die

geriatric /dʒerɪ'ætrɪk/ adj. geriatrisch

germ /dʒɜːm/ n. Keim, der

German /'dʒɜːmən/ [1] adj. deutsch; he/she
is ~: er ist Deutscher/sie ist Deutsche
[2] n. (a) (person) Deutsche, der/die
(b) (language) Deutsch, das; see also
ENGLISH 2A

German Democratic Re'public pr. n.
(Hist.) Deutsche Demokratische Republik

Germanic /dʒɜː'mænɪk/ adj. germanisch

German 'measles n. Röteln Pl.

Germany /'dʒɜːmənɪ/ pr. n. Deutschland
(das); Federal Republic of ~:
Bundesrepublik Deutschland, die

germinate /'dʒɜːmɪneɪt/ v.i. keimen

g

germ 'warfare n. Bakterienkrieg, der

gesticulate /dʒe'stɪkjʊleɪt/ v.i. gestikulieren

gesticulation /dʒestɪkjʊ'leɪʃn/ n. Gesten Pl.

gesture /'dʒestʃə(r)/ n. Geste, die

get /get/ [1] v.t., -tt-, got /gɒt/, got or (Amer.) gotten /'gɒtn/ **(a)** (obtain, receive) bekommen; kriegen (ugs.); sich ⟨Dat.⟩ besorgen ⟨Visum, Genehmigung⟩; sich ⟨Dat.⟩ beschaffen ⟨Geld⟩; (find) finden ⟨Zeit⟩; (fetch) holen; (buy) kaufen; **where did you ~ that?** wo hast du das her?; **~ sb. a job/taxi, ~ a job/taxi for sb.** jmdm. einen Job verschaffen/ein Taxi besorgen; **~ oneself sth.** sich ⟨Dat.⟩ etw. zulegen **(b)** ~ **the bus** etc. (be in time for, catch) den Bus usw. erreichen od. (ugs.) kriegen; (travel by) den Bus usw. nehmen **(c)** (prepare) machen (ugs.), zubereiten ⟨Essen⟩ **(d)** (win) bekommen; finden ⟨Anerkennung⟩; erzielen ⟨Tor, Punkt, Treffer⟩; gewinnen ⟨Spiel, Preis, Belohnung⟩; **~ permission** die Erlaubnis erhalten **(e)** finden ⟨Schlaf, Ruhe⟩; bekommen ⟨Einfall, Vorstellung, Gefühl, Kopfschmerzen, Grippe⟩; gewinnen ⟨Eindruck⟩ **(f)** **have got** (coll.: have) haben; **have got a cold** eine Erkältung haben; **have got to do sth.** etw. tun müssen **(g)** (succeed in placing, bringing, etc.) bringen; kriegen (ugs.); **~ a message to sb.** jmdm. eine Nachricht zukommen lassen; **~ things going** or **started** die Dinge in Gang bringen **(h)** **~ everything packed/prepared** alles [ein]packen/vorbereiten; **~ sth. ready/done** etw. fertig machen; **~ one's feet wet** nasse Füße kriegen; **~ one's hands dirty** sich ⟨Dat.⟩ die Hände schmutzig machen; **~ one's hair cut** sich (Dat.) die Haare schneiden lassen; **~ sb. to do sth.** (induce) jmdn. dazu bringen, etw. zu tun **(i)** **~ sb. [on the telephone]** jmdn. [telefonisch] erreichen **(j)** (coll.) (understand) kapieren (ugs.); (hear) mitkriegen (ugs.) [2] v.i., -tt-, got, got or (Amer.) **gotten (a)** (succeed in coming or going) kommen; **~ to London before dark** London vor Einbruch der Dunkelheit erreichen **(b)** (come to be) **~ working** sich an die Arbeit machen; **~ going** or **started** (leave) losgehen; (become lively or operative) in Schwung kommen; **~ going on** or **with sth.** mit etw. anfangen **(c)** **~ to know sb.** jmdn. kennen lernen **(d)** (become) werden; **~ ready/washed** sich fertig machen/waschen; **~ frightened/hungry** Angst/Hunger kriegen

■ **get a'bout** v.i. **(a)** (travel) herumkommen **(b)** ⟨Gerücht:⟩ sich verbreiten

■ **'get at** v.t. **(a)** herankommen an (+ Akk.) **(b)** (find out) [he]rausfinden ⟨Wahrheit usw.⟩; **what are you ~ting at?** worauf wollen Sie hinaus? **(c)** (coll.: attack, taunt) anmachen (salopp)

■ **get a'way** v.i. **(a)** (leave) wegkommen **(b)** (escape) entkommen

■ **get 'back** [1] v.i. zurückkommen; **~ back home** nach Hause kommen [2] v.t. (recover) zurückbekommen; **~ one's own back** (coll.) sich rächen

■ **get 'by** v.i. **(a)** vorbeikommen **(b)** (coll.: manage) über die Runden kommen (ugs.)

■ **get 'down** [1] v.i. hinunter-/heruntersteigen; **~ down to sth.** (start) sich an etw. ⟨Akk.⟩ machen [2] v.t. **(a)** **~ sb./sth. down** jmdn./etw. hinunter-/herunterbringen **(b)** (coll.: depress) fertig machen (ugs.)

■ **get 'in** [1] v.i. (into bus etc.) einsteigen; (arrive) ankommen [2] v.t. (fetch) reinholen

■ **get 'off** [1] v.i. **(a)** (alight) aussteigen; (dismount) absteigen **(b)** (leave) [weg]gehen **(c)** (escape punishment) davonkommen [2] v.t. **(a)** (remove) ausziehen ⟨Kleidung usw.⟩; entfernen ⟨Fleck usw.⟩; abbekommen ⟨Deckel usw.⟩ **(b)** (alight from) aussteigen aus; absteigen von ⟨Fahrrad⟩ **(c)** **~ off the subject** vom Thema abkommen

■ **get 'on** v.i. **(a)** (mount) aufsteigen; (enter vehicle) einsteigen **(b)** (make progress) vorankommen; **he's ~ting on well** es geht ihm gut **(c)** (manage) zurechtkommen

■ **get 'on with** v.t. **(a)** weitermachen mit **(b)** **~ on [well] with sb.** mit jmdm. [gut] auskommen

■ **get 'out** [1] v.i. **(a)** rausgehen/rausfahren **(of aus) (b)** (alight) aussteigen **(c)** (escape) ausbrechen **(of aus)**; (fig.) herauskommen; **~ out of** (avoid) herumkommen um (+ Akk.) [2] v.t. **(a)** (cause to leave) rausbringen **(b)** (withdraw) abheben ⟨Geld⟩ **(of von)**

■ **get 'over** v.t. **(a)** (cross) gehen über (+ Akk.); (climb) klettern über (+ Akk.) **(b)** (recover from) überwinden; hinwegkommen über (+ Akk.)

■ **get 'round** v.i. **~ round to doing sth.** dazu kommen, etw. zu tun

■ **get 'through** v.i. durchkommen

■ **get 'up** v.i. aufstehen

■ **get 'up to** v.t. **~ up to mischief** etwas anstellen

get: **~away** n. Flucht, die; attrib. Flucht⟨plan, -wagen⟩; **make one's ~away** entkommen; **~together** n. (coll.) gemütliches Beisammensein, das; **~-up** n. (coll.) Aufmachung, die

geyser /'giːzə(r)/ n. **(a)** (spring) Geysir, der **(b)** (Brit.) Durchlauferhitzer, der

ghastly /'gɑːstlɪ/ adj. grauenvoll; entsetzlich ⟨Verletzungen⟩; schrecklich ⟨Fehler⟩

gherkin /'gɜːkɪn/ n. Essiggurke, die

ghetto /'getəʊ/ n., pl. ~s Getto, das

ghetto blaster /'getəʊblɑːstə(r)/ n. (coll.) [großer, tragbarer] Radiorekorder

ghost /gəʊst/ n. Geist, der; Gespenst, das

'ghostly adj. gespenstisch

ghost: ~ **story** n. Gespenstergeschichte, die; ~ **writer** n. Ghostwriter, der

giant /'dʒaɪənt/ ⟨1⟩ n. Riese, der ⟨2⟩ attrib. adj. riesig

gibberish /'dʒɪbərɪʃ/ n. Kauderwelsch, das

gibe /dʒaɪb/ n. Stichelei, die

giblets /'dʒɪblɪts/ n. pl. [Geflügel]klein, das

giddiness /'gɪdɪnɪs/ n. Schwindel, der

giddy /'gɪdɪ/ adj. schwind[e]lig

gift /gɪft/ n. (a) Geschenk, das; **make sb. a** ~ **of sth., make a** ~ **of sth. to sb.** jmdm. etw. schenken; **a** ~ **box/pack** eine Geschenkpackung (b) (talent) Begabung, die; **have a** ~ **for languages/ mathematics** sprachbegabt/ mathematisch begabt sein

'gifted adj. begabt (**in, at** für)

gift: ~ **shop** n. Geschenkboutique, die; Geschenkladen, der; ~ **token,** ~ **voucher** ns. Geschenkgutschein, der; ~**-wrap** v.t. als Geschenk einpacken; in Geschenkpapier einpacken

gigantic /dʒaɪˈgæntɪk/ adj. gigantisch; riesig; enorm ⟨Verbesserung, Appetit⟩

giggle /'gɪgl/ ⟨1⟩ n. Kichern, das ⟨2⟩ v.i. kichern

gild /gɪld/ v.t. vergolden

gill /gɪl/ n. Kieme, die

gilt /gɪlt/ ⟨1⟩ n. Goldauflage, die; (paint) Goldfarbe, die ⟨2⟩ adj. vergoldet

gimmick /'gɪmɪk/ n. (coll.) Gag, der

gin /dʒɪn/ n. Gin, der

ginger /'dʒɪndʒə(r)/ n. (a) Ingwer, der (b) (colour) Rötlichgelb, das

ginger: ~ **'beer** n. Ingwerbier, das; ~**bread** n. Pfefferkuchen, der

gingerly /'dʒɪndʒəlɪ/ adv. vorsichtig

gipsy ▶ GYPSY

giraffe /dʒɪ'rɑːf/ n. Giraffe, die

girder /'gɜːdə(r)/ n. Träger, der

girdle /'gɜːdl/ n. Hüfthalter, der

girl /gɜːl/ n. Mädchen, das; (teenager) junges Mädchen

'girlfriend n. Freundin, die

'girlish adj. mädchenhaft

'girl power n. (coll.) Girlpower, die

giro /'dʒaɪərəʊ/ n. (a) Giro, das; attrib. Giro-; **bank** ~: Giroverkehr, der (b) (cheque) Scheck, der

girth /gɜːθ/ n. (a) Umfang, der (b) (for horse) Bauchgurt, der

gismo /'gɪzməʊ/ n. (coll.) Ding, das (ugs.)

gist /dʒɪst/ n. Wesentliche, das; (of tale, question, etc.) Kern, der

give /gɪv/ ⟨1⟩ v.t., gave /geɪv/, given /'gɪvn/ (a) geben (**to** Dat.) (b) (as gift) schenken; ~ **sb. sth.,** ~ **sth. to sb.** jmdm. etw. schenken; ~ **and take** (fig.) Kompromisse eingehen (c) (assign) aufgeben ⟨Hausaufgaben usw.⟩; (grant, award, offer, allow to have) geben; verleihen ⟨Preis, Titel usw.⟩; lassen ⟨Wahl, Zeit⟩; verleihen ⟨Gewicht, Nachdruck⟩; bereiten, machen ⟨Freude, Mühe, Kummer⟩; bieten ⟨Schutz⟩; leisten ⟨Hilfe⟩; gewähren ⟨Unterstützung⟩; **be** ~**n sth.** etw. bekommen; ~**n that** (because) da; (if) wenn; ~ **sb. hope** jmdm. Hoffnung machen (d) (tell) angeben ⟨Namen, Anschrift, Alter, Grund⟩; nennen ⟨Einzelheiten⟩; geben ⟨Rat, Befehl, Anweisung, Antwort⟩; fällen ⟨Urteil, Entscheidung⟩; sagen ⟨Meinung⟩; bekannt geben ⟨Nachricht⟩; ~ **him my best wishes** richte ihm meine besten Wünsche aus (e) (perform, sing, etc.) geben ⟨Vorstellung, Konzert⟩; halten ⟨Vortrag, Seminar⟩ (f) (produce) geben ⟨Licht, Milch⟩; ergeben ⟨Zahlen, Resultat⟩ (g) (make, show) geben ⟨Zeichen, Stoß, Tritt⟩; machen ⟨Satz, Ruck⟩; ausstoßen ⟨Schrei, Seufzer, Pfiff⟩; ~ **sb. a [friendly] look** jmdm. einen [freundlichen] Blick zuwerfen (h) (inflict) versetzen ⟨Schlag, Stoß⟩; **sth.** ~**s me a headache** von etw. bekomme ich Kopfschmerzen (i) geben ⟨Party, Essen usw.⟩ ⟨2⟩ v.i., gave, given (yield) nachgeben; ⟨Knie:⟩ weich werden; ⟨Bett:⟩ federn ⟨3⟩ n. Nachgiebigkeit, die; (elasticity) Elastizität, die

▪ **give a'way** v.t. (a) verschenken (b) (in marriage) dem Bräutigam zuführen (c) (betray) verraten

▪ **give 'back** v.t. zurückgeben

▪ **give in** ⟨1⟩ /'-'/ v.t. abgeben ⟨2⟩ /-'-/ v.i. nachgeben (**to** Dat.)

▪ **give 'off** v.t. ausströmen ⟨Geruch⟩; aussenden ⟨Strahlen⟩

▪ **give 'up** ⟨1⟩ v.i. aufgeben ⟨2⟩ v.t. aufgeben; widmen ⟨Zeit⟩; ~ **sth. up** (abandon habit) sich ⟨Dat.⟩ etw. abgewöhnen; ~ **oneself up** sich stellen

▪ **give 'way** v.i. (a) (yield) nachgeben (b) (in traffic) ~ **way [to traffic from the right]** [dem Rechtsverkehr] die Vorfahrt lassen; **'G**~ **Way** „Vorfahrt beachten" (c) (collapse) einstürzen

given ▶ GIVE 1, 2

'given name n. (Amer.) Vorname, der

give-'way sign n. (Brit.) Vorfahrtsschild, das

gizmo ▶ GISMO

glacier /'glæsɪə(r)/ n. Gletscher, der

glad /glæd/ adj. froh; **be** ~ **of sth.** über etw. (Akk.) froh sein; für etw. dankbar sein

gladden /'glædn/ v.t. erfreuen

glade /gleɪd/ n. Lichtung, die

'gladly adv. gern

glamor (Amer.) ▶ GLAMOUR

glamorous /'glæmərəs/ adj. glanzvoll;
glamourös ‹Filmstar›

glamour /'glæmə(r)/ n. Glanz, der; (of
person) Ausstrahlung, die

glance /glɑːns/ ☐1 n. Blick, der
☐2 v.i. blicken; ~ at sb./sth. jmdn./etw.
anblicken; ~ at one's watch auf seine Uhr
blicken; ~ at the newspaper etc. einen Blick
in die Zeitung usw. werfen; ~ round [the
room] sich [im Zimmer] umsehen

gland /glænd/ n. Drüse, die

glandular /'glændjʊlə(r)/ adj. Drüsen-

glare /gleə(r)/ ☐1 n. (a) grelles Licht
(b) (hostile look) feindseliger Blick; with a ~:
feindselig
☐2 v.i. (glower) [finster] starren; ~ at sb./sth.
jmdn./etw. anstarren

glaring /'gleərɪŋ/ adj. grell; (fig.: conspicuous)
schreiend; grob ‹Fehler›; krass ‹Gegensatz›

glass /glɑːs/ n. (a) (substance) Glas, das;
pieces of/broken ~: Glasscherben Pl.;
(smaller) Glassplitter Pl.
(b) (drinking ~) Glas, das; a ~ of milk ein
Glas Milch
(c) (pane) [Glas]scheibe, die
(d) in pl. (spectacles) [a pair of] ~es eine
Brille

glass 'ceiling n. (fig.) unsichtbare
Barriere

'glassy adj. gläsern

glaze /gleɪz/ ☐1 n. Glasur, die
☐2 v.t. (a) glasieren
(b) (fit with glass) verglasen

glazed /gleɪzd/ adj. glasig ‹Blick›

glazier /'gleɪzɪə(r)/ n. Glaser, der

gleam /gliːm/ ☐1 n. Schein, der; (fainter)
Schimmer, der; ~ of hope
Hoffnungsschimmer, der
☐2 v.i. ‹Licht:› scheinen; ‹Fußboden, Stiefel:›
glänzen; ‹Zähne:› blitzen; ‹Augen:› leuchten

'gleaming adj. glänzend

glean /gliːn/ v.t. zusammentragen
‹Informationen usw.›; ~ sth. from sth. einer
Sache (Dat.) etw. entnehmen

glee /gliː/ n. Freude, die; (gloating joy)
Schadenfreude, die

gleeful /'gliːfl/ adj. freudig; (gloating)
schadenfroh

glen /glen/ n. [schmales] Tal

glib /glɪb/ adj. aalglatt ‹Person›; leicht
dahingesagt ‹Antwort›

glide /glaɪd/ v.i. gleiten; (through the air)
schweben

'glider n. Segelflugzeug, das

glimmer /'glɪmə(r)/ ☐1 n. Schimmer, der (of
von); (of fire) Glimmen, das
☐2 v.i. glimmen

glimpse /glɪmps/ ☐1 n. [kurzer] Blick;
catch or have or get a ~ of sb./sth. jmdn./
etw. [kurz] zu sehen bekommen
☐2 v.t. flüchtig sehen

glint /glɪnt/ ☐1 n. Schimmer, der
☐2 v.i. blinken; glitzern

glisten /'glɪsn/ v.i. glitzern

glitter /'glɪtə(r)/ ☐1 v.i. glitzern; ‹Juwelen,
Sterne:› funkeln
☐2 n. Glitzern, das; (of diamonds) Funkeln, das

glitz /glɪts/ n. Glanz, der

glitzy /'glɪtsɪ/ adj. glanzvoll

gloat /gləʊt/ v.i. ~ over sth. sich hämisch
über etw. (Akk.) freuen

global /'gləʊbl/ adj. weltweit; ~ warming
globaler Temperaturanstieg; the ~ village
das Weltdorf

globalization /gləʊbəlaɪ'zeɪʃn/ n.
Globalisierung, die

globalize /'gləʊbəlaɪz/ v.t. globalisieren

globe /gləʊb/ n. (a) (sphere) Kugel, die
(b) (with map) Globus, der
(c) (world) the ~: der Globus; der Erdball

'globetrotter n. Globetrotter, der;
Weltenbummler, der

gloom /gluːm/ n. (a) (darkness) Dunkel, das
(geh.)
(b) (despondency) düstere Stimmung

'gloomy adj. (a) (dark) düster; finster
(b) (depressing) düster; (depressed) trübsinnig
‹Person›

glorify /'glɔːrɪfaɪ/ v.t. verherrlichen; a
glorified messenger boy ein besserer
Botenjunge

glorious /'glɔːrɪəs/ adj. (a) (illustrious)
ruhmreich ‹Held, Sieg›
(b) (delightful) wunderschön; herrlich

glory /'glɔːrɪ/ ☐1 n. (a) (splendour) Schönheit,
die; (majesty) Herrlichkeit, die
(b) (fame) Ruhm, der
☐2 v.i. ~ in sth. (be proud of) sich einer Sache
(Gen.) rühmen

gloss /glɒs/ n. Glanz, der; ~ paint
Lackfarbe, die

◾ **'gloss over** v.t. bemänteln; beschönigen
‹Fehler›

glossary /'glɒsərɪ/ n. Glossar, das

'glossy ☐1 adj. glänzend; (fig.) glanzvoll
☐2 n. (coll.) (magazine) auf [Hoch]glanzpapier
gedruckte Zeitschrift

glove /glʌv/ n. Handschuh, der

glove: ~ **box** n. (a) ▶ COMPARTMENT; (b)
(for toxic material etc.) Handschuhkasten, der;
~ **compartment** n. Handschuhfach, das;
~ **puppet** n. Handpuppe, die

glow /gləʊ/ v.i. (a) glühen; ‹Lampe,
Leuchtfarbe:› schimmern, leuchten
(b) (fig.) (with warmth or pride) ‹Gesicht,
Wangen:› glühen (with vor + Dat.); (with health
or vigour) strotzen (with vor + Dat.)

glower /'glaʊə(r)/ v.i. finster dreinblicken;
~ at sb. jmdn. finster anstarren

'glowing adj. glühend; begeistert ‹Bericht›

'glow-worm n. Glühwürmchen, das

glucose /'gluːkəʊz/ n. Glucose, die

glue /gluː/ ☐1 n. Klebstoff, der

2 *v.t.* kleben; ∼ sth. to sth. etw. an etw. (*Dat.*) an- *od.* festkleben

'glue-sniffing *n.* Schnüffeln, *das* (ugs.); Sniefen, *das* (ugs.)

glum /glʌm/ *adj.* verdrießlich

glut /glʌt/ *n.* Überangebot, *das* (of an, von + *Dat.*)

glutton /'glʌtən/ *n.* Vielfraß, *der* (ugs.); **a** ∼ **for punishment** (iron.) ein Masochist (fig.)

gluttony /'glʌtənɪ/ *n.* Gefräßigkeit, *die*

glycerine /'glɪsəriːn/ (*Amer.*: **glycerin** /'glɪsərɪn/) *n.* Glyzerin, *das*

GM *abbr.* = **genetically modified**; GM **crops/food** gentechnisch veränderte Feldfrüchte *Pl.*/Nahrungsmittel *Pl.*

gm. *abbr.* = **gram[s]** g

GMO *abbr.* = **genetically modified orgamism** GVO

GMT *abbr.* = **Greenwich Mean Time** GMT; WEZ

gnarled /nɑːld/ *adj.* knorrig; knotig ⟨Hand⟩

gnash /næʃ/ *v.t.* ∼ one's teeth mit den Zähnen knirschen

gnat /næt/ *n.* [Stech]mücke, *die*

gnaw /nɔː/ **1** *v.i.* ∼ [away] at sth. an etw. (*Dat.*) nagen

2 *v.t.* nagen an (+ *Dat.*); abnagen ⟨Knochen⟩

gnome /nəʊm/ *n.* Gnom, *der*

GNVQ *abbr.* = **General National Vocational Qualification**

go /gəʊ/ **1** *v.i.*, *pres.* he goes /gəʊz/, *p.t.* went /went/, *pres. p.* going /'gəʊɪŋ/, *p.p.* gone /gɒn/ **(a)** gehen; ⟨Fahrzeug:⟩ fahren; ⟨Flugzeug:⟩ fliegen; ⟨Vierfüßer:⟩ laufen; (on horseback etc.) reiten; (in lift) fahren; (on outward journey) weg-, abfahren; (travel regularly) ⟨Verkehrsmittel:⟩ verkehren (from ... to zwischen + *Dat.* ... und); **go by bicycle/car/ bus/train** *or* **rail/boat** *or* **sea** *or* **ship** mit dem [Fahr]rad/Auto/Bus/Zug/Schiff fahren; **go by plane** *or* **air** fliegen; **go on foot** zu Fuß gehen; laufen (ugs.); **go on a journey** verreisen; **have far to go** es weit haben; **go to the toilet/cinema/a museum** auf die Toilette/ins Kino/ins Museum gehen; **go to the doctor['s]** *etc.* zum Arzt *usw.* gehen; **go bathing** baden gehen; **go cycling** Rad fahren; **go to see sb.** jmdn. aufsuchen; **go and see whether** ...: nachsehen [gehen], ob ...; **I'll go!** ich geh schon!; (answer phone) ich geh ran *od.* nehme ab; (answer door) ich mache auf **(b)** (start) losgehen; (in vehicle) losfahren **(c)** (pass, circulate) gehen; **a shiver went up** *or* **down my spine** ein Schauer lief mir über den Rücken; **go to** (be given to) ⟨Preis, Gelder, Job:⟩ gehen an (+ *Akk.*); ⟨Titel, Besitz:⟩ übergehen auf (+ *Akk.*); **go towards** (be of benefit to) zugute kommen (+ *Dat.*) **(d)** (act, function effectively) gehen; ⟨Mechanismus, Maschine:⟩ laufen; **keep going** (in movement) weitergehen/-fahren; (in activity) weitermachen; (not fail) sich aufrecht

halten; **keep sth. going** etw. in Gang halten; **make sth. go, get/set sth. going** etw. in Gang bringen
(e) go to work zur Arbeit gehen; **go to school** in die Schule gehen; **go to a comprehensive school** auf eine Gesamtschule gehen
(f) (depart) gehen; ⟨Bus, Zug:⟩ [ab]fahren; ⟨Post:⟩ rausgehen (ugs.)
(g) (cease to function) kaputtgehen; ⟨Sicherung:⟩ durchbrennen; (break) brechen; ⟨Seil usw.:⟩ reißen
(h) (disappear) weggehen; ⟨Mantel, Hut, Fleck:⟩ verschwinden; ⟨Geruch, Rauch:⟩ sich verziehen; ⟨Geld, Zeit:⟩ draufgehen (ugs.) (in, on für)
(i) to go (still remaining) **have sth. [still] to go** [noch] etw. übrig haben; **one week** *etc.* **to go to** ...: noch eine Woche *usw.* bis ...; **there's hours to go** es dauert noch Stunden
(j) (be sold) weggehen (ugs.); verkauft werden; **going! going! gone!** zum Ersten! zum Zweiten! zum Dritten!; **go to sb.** an jmdn. gehen
(k) (run) ⟨Grenze, Straße usw.:⟩ verlaufen, gehen; (lead) gehen; führen; (extend) reichen; **as** *or* **so far as he/it goes** so weit
(l) (turn out, progress) ⟨Projekt, Interview, Abend:⟩ verlaufen; **how did your holiday go?** wie war Ihr Urlaub?; **things have been going well/badly** in der letzten Zeit läuft alles gut/schief
(m) (be, have form or nature) sein; ⟨Sprichwort, Gedicht, Titel:⟩ lauten; **that's the way it goes** so ist es nun mal; **go hungry** hungern; **go without food/water** es ohne Essen/Wasser aushalten
(n) (become) werden; **the tyre has gone flat** der Reifen ist platt
(o) (have usual place) kommen; (belong) gehören; **where does the box go?** wo kommt *od.* gehört die Kiste hin?
(p) (fit) passen; **go in[to] sth.** in etw. (*Akk.*) gehen *od.* [hinein]passen; **go through sth.** durch etw. [hindurch]gehen
(q) (match) passen (with zu)
(r) ⟨Turmuhr, Gong:⟩ schlagen; ⟨Glocke:⟩ läuten
(s) (coll.: be acceptable or permitted) erlaubt sein; **it/that goes without saying** es/das ist doch selbstverständlich. *See also* GOING 2
2 *n., pl.* **goes** /gəʊz/ (coll.) **(a)** (attempt, try) Versuch, *der;* (chance) Gelegenheit, *die;* **have a go** es versuchen; **let me have a go/can I have a go?** lass mich [auch ein]mal/kann ich [auch ein]mal? (ugs.); **it's 'my go** ich bin an der Reihe *od.* dran; **at one go** auf einmal; **at the first go** auf Anhieb
(b) (vigorous activity) **it's all go** es ist alles eine einzige Hetzerei (ugs.); **be on the go** auf Trab sein (ugs.)
(c) (success) **make a go of sth.** mit etw. Erfolg haben
▪ **go a'head** *v.i.* **(a)** (in advance) vorausgehen (of *Dat.*)

 ···❖

(b) (proceed) weitermachen; (make progress) ⟨*Arbeit:*⟩ fortschreiten, vorangehen
■ **go a'long with** *v.i.* **go along with sth.** (agree to) sich einer Sache (*Dat.*) anschließen
■ **go a'way** *v.i.* weggehen; (on holiday or business) verreisen
■ **go 'back** *v.i.* zurückgehen/-fahren; (restart) ⟨*Schule, Fabrik:*⟩ wieder anfangen; (fig.) zurückgehen; **go back to the beginning** noch mal von vorne anfangen
■ **go by** ⟨1⟩ /'--/ *v.t.* **go by sth.** sich nach etw. richten; (adhere to) sich an etw. (*Akk.*) halten ⟨2⟩ /-'-/ *v.i.* ⟨*Zeit:*⟩ vergehen
■ **go 'down** *v.i.* hinuntergehen/-fahren; ⟨*Sonne:*⟩ untergehen; ⟨*Schiff:*⟩ untergehen; (fall to ground) ⟨*Flugzeug usw.:*⟩ abstürzen
■ **'go for** *v.t.* **go for sb./sth.** (go to fetch) jmdn./etw. holen; (apply to) für jmdn./etw. gelten; (like) jmdn./etw. gut finden
■ **go 'in** *v.i.* hineingehen; reingehen (ugs.)
■ **go 'off** ⟨1⟩ *v.i.* **(a)** go off with sb./sth. sich mit jmdm./etw. auf- und davonmachen (ugs.) **(b)** ⟨*Alarm, Schusswaffe:*⟩ losgehen; ⟨*Wecker:*⟩ klingeln; ⟨*Bombe:*⟩ hochgehen **(c)** (turn bad) schlecht werden **(d)** ⟨*Strom:*⟩ ausfallen ⟨2⟩ *v.t.* (begin to dislike) **go off sth.** von etw. abkommen
■ **go 'on** *v.i.* **(a)** weitergehen/-fahren **(b)** (continue) weitermachen **(c)** (happen) passieren
■ **go 'out** *v.i.* ausgehen; **go out to work/for a meal** arbeiten/essen gehen; **go out with sb.** (date sb.) mit jmdm. gehen (ugs.)
■ **go over** ⟨1⟩ /-'-/ *v.i.* hinübergehen ⟨2⟩ /'---, -'-/ *v.t.* (re-examine) durchgehen
■ **go 'round** *v.i.* **(a)** (call) **go round** and *or* **to see sb.** bei jmdm. vorbeigehen (ugs.) **(b)** (look round) sich umschauen **(c)** (suffice) reichen; langen (ugs.) **(d)** (spin) sich drehen
■ **go through** ⟨1⟩ /-'-/ *v.i.* ⟨*Ernennung:*⟩ durchkommen; ⟨*Antrag:*⟩ durchgehen ⟨2⟩ /'---/ **(a)** (rehearse) durchgehen **(b)** (examine) durchsehen **(c)** (endure) durchmachen
■ **go 'through with** *v.t.* zu Ende führen
■ **go 'under** *v.i.* untergehen; (fig.: fail) eingehen
■ **go 'up** *v.i.* **(a)** hinaufgehen/-fahren; ⟨*Ballon:*⟩ aufsteigen; (Theatre) ⟨*Vorhang:*⟩ aufgehen; ⟨*Lichter:*⟩ angehen **(b)** (increase) ⟨*Zahl:*⟩ wachsen; ⟨*Preis, Wert, Niveau:*⟩ steigen; (in price) ⟨*Ware:*⟩ teurer werden
■ **go without** ⟨1⟩ /'---/ *v.t.* verzichten auf (+ *Akk.*) ⟨2⟩ /-'-'/ *v.i.* verzichten

goad /ɡəʊd/ *v.t.* ~ **sb. into sth./doing sth.** jmdn. zu etw. anstacheln/dazu anstacheln, etw. zu tun

'go-ahead ⟨1⟩ *adj.* unternehmungslustig; (progressive) fortschrittlich ⟨2⟩ *n.* **give sb./sth. the** ~: jmdm./einer Sache grünes Licht geben

goal /ɡəʊl/ *n.* **(a)** (aim) Ziel, *das* **(b)** (Footb., Hockey) Tor, *das;* **score/kick a** ~: einen Treffer erzielen
goalie /'ɡəʊlɪ/ *n.* (coll.) Tormann, *der*
goal: ~**keeper** *n.* Torwart, *der;* ~**post** *n.* Torpfosten, *der;* **move the** ~**posts** (fig. coll.) sich nicht an die Spielregeln halten
goat /ɡəʊt/ *n.* Ziege, *die*
gobble /'ɡɒbl/ ⟨1⟩ *v.t.* ~ **[down** *or* **up]** hinunterschlingen ⟨2⟩ *v.i.* schlingen
'go-between *n.* Vermittler, *der*/ Vermittlerin, *die*
goblet /'ɡɒblɪt/ *n.* Kelchglas, *das*
goblin /'ɡɒblɪn/ *n.* Kobold, *der*
god /ɡɒd/ *n.* **(a)** Gott, *der.* **(b)** God (Theol.) Gott
god: ~**child** *n.* Patenkind, *das;* ~-**daughter** *n.* Patentochter, *die*
goddess /'ɡɒdɪs/ *n.* Göttin, *die*
god: ~**father** *n.* Pate, *der;* **G**~-**forsaken** *adj.* gottverlassen; ~**mother** *n.* Patentante, *die;* ~**send** *n.* Gottesgabe, *die;* **be a** ~**send to sb.** für jmdn. ein Geschenk des Himmels sein; ~**son** *n.* Patensohn, *der*
'go-getter *n.* Draufgänger, *der*
'goggle-box *n.* (Brit. coll.) Glotze, *die* (salopp); Glotzkiste, *die* (salopp)
goggles /'ɡɒɡlz/ *n. pl.* Schutzbrille, *die*
going /'ɡəʊɪŋ/ ⟨1⟩ *n.* (progress) Vorankommen, *das;* **while the** ~ **is good** solange es noch geht ⟨2⟩ *adj.* **(a)** (available) erhältlich; **there is sth.** ~: es gibt etw. **(b)** **be** ~ **to do sth.** etw. tun [werden/wollen]; **I was** ~ **to say** ich wollte sagen; **it's** ~ **to snow** es wird schneien; **a** ~ **concern** eine gesunde Firma **(c)** (current) [derzeit/damals/dann] geltend; **the** ~ **rate of exchange** der augenblickliche Wechselkurs **(d)** **a** ~ **concern** eine gesunde Firma
goings-'on *n. pl.* Ereignisse *Pl.*
gold /ɡəʊld/ ⟨1⟩ *n.* Gold, *das* ⟨2⟩ *attrib. adj.* golden; Gold⟨münze, -kette usw.⟩
'gold-digger *n.* Goldgräber, *der;* **she's a** ~-**digger** (fig. coll.) sie ist nur auf das Geld der Männer aus
golden /'ɡəʊldn/ *adj.* golden
golden 'wedding *n.* goldene Hochzeit
gold: ~**fish** *n.* Goldfisch, *der;* ~**fish bowl** *n.* Goldfischglas, *das;* **like being in a** ~**fish bowl** (fig.) wie auf dem Präsentierteller; ~ '**medal** *n.* Goldmedaille, *die;* ~ '**medallist** *n.* Goldmedaillengewinner, *der*/-gewinnerin, *die;* ~ **mine** *n.* Goldmine, *die;* (fig.) Goldgrube, *die;* ~-'**plated** *adj.* vergoldet; ~**smith** *n.* Goldschmied, *der*/-schmiedin, *die*
golf /ɡɒlf/ *n.* Golf, *das*

golf: ~ **ball** n. Golfball, der; ~ **club** n. (a) (implement) Golfschläger, der; (b) (association) Golfklub, der; ~**course** n. Golfplatz, der

'**golfer** n. Golfer, der/Golferin, die

golf links n. Golfplatz, der

gondola /'ɡɒndələ/ n. Gondel, die

gondolier /ɡɒndə'lɪə(r)/ n. Gondoliere, der

gone /ɡɒn/ ⟨1⟩ ▸ GO 1
⟨2⟩ pred. adj. (a) (away) weg; **it's time you were** ~: es ist od. wird Zeit, dass du gehst (b) (of time: after) nach; **it's** ~ **ten o'clock** es ist zehn Uhr vorbei

gong /ɡɒŋ/ n. Gong, der

good /ɡʊd/ ⟨1⟩ adj., **better** /'betə(r)/, **best** /best/ (a) gut; günstig ⟨Gelegenheit, Angebot⟩; ausreichend ⟨Vorrat⟩; ausgiebig ⟨Mahl⟩; **as** ~ **as** so gut wie; **his** ~ **eye/leg** sein gesundes Auge/Bein; **in** ~ **time** frühzeitig; **all in** ~ **time** alles zu seiner Zeit; **be** ~ **at sth.** in etw. (Dat.) gut sein; **too** ~ **to be true** zu schön, um wahr zu sein; **apples are** ~ **for you** Äpfel sind gesund; **be too much of a** ~ **thing** zu viel des Guten sein; ~ **times** eine schöne Zeit; **feel** ~: sich wohl fühlen; **take a** ~ **look round** sich gründlich umsehen; **give sb. a** ~ **beating/scolding** jmdn. tüchtig verprügeln/ausschimpfen; ~ **afternoon/day** guten Tag!; ~ **evening/ morning** guten Abend/Morgen!; ~ **night** gute Nacht!
(b) (enjoyable) schön ⟨Leben, Urlaub, Wochenende⟩; **the** ~ **life** das angenehme[, sorglose] Leben; **have a** ~ **time!** viel Spaß!; **have a** ~ **journey!** gute Reise!
(c) (well-behaved) gut; brav; **be** ~!, **be a** ~ **girl/boy!** sei brav od. lieb!; **[as]** ~ **as gold** ganz artig od. brav
(d) (virtuous) rechtschaffen; (kind) nett; gut ⟨Absicht, Wünsche, Benehmen, Tat⟩; **be** ~ **to sb.** gut zu jmdm. sein; **would you be so** ~ **as to** or ~ **enough to do that?** wären Sie so freundlich od. nett, das zu tun?; **that/it is** ~ **of you** das/es ist nett od. lieb von dir
(e) (commendable) gut; ~ **for 'you** etc. (coll.) bravo!
(f) (attractive) schön ⟨Figur⟩; **look** ~: gut aussehen
(g) (considerable) [recht] ansehnlich ⟨Menschenmenge⟩; ganz schön, ziemlich (ugs.) ⟨Entfernung, Strecke⟩; gut ⟨Preis, Erlös⟩
(h) **make** ~ (succeed) erfolgreich sein; (compensate for) wieder gutmachen; (indemnify) ersetzen
⟨2⟩ n. (a) (use) Nutzen, der; **be some** ~ **to sb./sth.** jmdm./einer Sache nützen; **be no** ~ **to sb./sth.** für jmdn./etw. nicht zu gebrauchen sein; **it is no/not much** ~ **doing sth.** es hat keinen/kaum einen Sinn, etw. zu tun; **what's the** ~ **of ...?, what** ~ **is ...?** was nützt ...?
(b) (benefit) **for your/his** etc. **own** ~: zu deinem/seinem usw. Besten; **do no/little** ~: nichts/wenig helfen od. nützen; **do sb./sth.**

~: jmdm./einer Sache nützen; ⟨Ruhe, Erholung:⟩ jmdm./einer Sache gut tun; ⟨Arznei:⟩ jmdm./einer Sache helfen
(c) (goodness) Gute, das; **be up to no** ~: nichts Gutes im Sinn haben
(d) **for** ~ (finally) ein für alle Mal; (permanently) für immer
(e) **in** pl. (wares etc.) Waren Pl.; (belongings) Habe, die; (Brit. Railw.) Fracht, die; attrib. Güter⟨wagen, -zug⟩

good: ~'**bye** (Amer.: ~'**by**) int. auf Wiedersehen!; (on telephone) auf Wiederhören!; ⟨2⟩ n. Taugenichts, der; ~**-for-nothing** ⟨1⟩ adj. nichtsnutzig; ⟨2⟩ n. Taugenichts, der; ~'**looking** adj. gut aussehend

'**goodness** ⟨1⟩ n. Güte, die
⟨2⟩ int. **[my]** ~! meine Güte! (ugs.)

good: ~**s train** n. (Brit.) Güterzug, der; ~'**tempered** adj. ausgeglichen; verträglich ⟨Person⟩; gut; guter Wille; attrib. Goodwill⟨botschaft, -reise usw.⟩

'**goody** n. (coll.: hero) Gute, der/die

gooey /'ɡuːɪ/ adj., **gooier** /'ɡuːɪə(r)/, **gooiest** /'ɡuːɪɪst/ (coll.) klebrig

goose /ɡuːs/ n., pl. **geese** /ɡiːs/ Gans, die

gooseberry /'ɡʊzbərɪ/ n. Stachelbeere, die

goose bumps (Amer.), **goose pimples** ns. pl. **have** ~: eine Gänsehaut haben

gore[1] /ɡɔː(r)/ v.t. [mit den Hörnern] aufspießen od. durchbohren

gore[2] n. Blut, das

gorge /ɡɔːdʒ/ ⟨1⟩ n. Schlucht, die
⟨2⟩ v.i. & refl. ~ **[oneself]** sich voll stopfen (ugs.) (**on** mit)

gorgeous /'ɡɔːdʒəs/ adj. prächtig; hinreißend ⟨Frau, Mann, Lächeln⟩

gorilla /ɡə'rɪlə/ n. Gorilla, der

gormless /'ɡɔːmlɪs/ adj. (Brit. coll.) dämlich (ugs.)

gorse /ɡɔːs/ n. Stechginster, der

gory /'ɡɔːrɪ/ adj. (fig.) blutrünstig

gosh /ɡɒʃ/ int. (coll.) Gott!

'**go-slow** n. (Brit.) Bummelstreik, der

gospel /'ɡɒspl/ n. Evangelium, das

'**gospel singer** n. Gospelsänger, der/ -sängerin, die

gossamer /'ɡɒsəmə(r)/ n. Altweibersommer, der; attrib. hauchdünn

gossip /'ɡɒsɪp/ ⟨1⟩ n. (a) (talk) Klatsch, der (ugs.)
(b) (person) Klatschbase, die (ugs.)
⟨2⟩ v.i. klatschen (ugs.)

gossip: ~ **column** n. Klatschspalte, die (ugs.); ~ **columnist** n. Klatschspaltenkolumnist, der/-kolumnistin, die

got ▸ GET

Gothic /'ɡɒθɪk/ adj. gotisch

gotten ▸ GET

gouge /ɡaʊdʒ/ v.t. aushöhlen

goulash /'ɡuːlæʃ/ n. Gulasch, das od. der

gourmet /'gʊəmeɪ/ n. Gourmet, der

gout /gaʊt/ n. Gicht, die

govern /'gʌvn/ 1 v.t. (a) regieren ⟨Land, Volk⟩; verwalten ⟨Provinz⟩
(b) (dictate) bestimmen
2 v.i. regieren

governess /'gʌvənɪs/ n. Gouvernante, die (veraltet); Hauslehrerin, die

government /'gʌvnmənt/ n. Regierung, die; attrib. Regierungs-

government: ~ **department** n. Regierungsstelle, die; ~-**funded** adj. staatlich finanziert; ~ **official** n. Regierungsbeamte, der/-beamtin, die

governor /'gʌvənə(r)/ n. (a) (of province etc.) Gouverneur, der
(b) (of institution) Direktor, der/Direktorin, die; [board of] ~s Vorstand, der
(c) (coll.: employer) Boss, der (ugs.)

gown /gaʊn/ n. (a) [elegantes] Kleid
(b) (official or uniform robe) Talar, der

GP abbr. = **general practitioner**

grab /græb/ 1 v.t., -bb- greifen nach; (seize) packen; ~ **the chance** die Gelegenheit ergreifen; ~ **hold of sb./sth.** sich (Dat.) jmdn./etw. schnappen (ugs.)
2 v.i., -bb- ~ **at sth.** nach etw. greifen
3 n. make a ~ at or for sb./sth. nach jmdn./etw. greifen

grace /greɪs/ n. (a) (charm) Anmut, die (geh.)
(b) (decency) **have the** ~ **to do sth.** so anständig sein und etw. tun
(c) (delay) Frist, die; **give sb. a day's** ~: jmdm. einen Tag Aufschub gewähren
(d) (prayers) **say** ~: das Tischgebet sprechen

graceful /'greɪsfl/ adj. elegant; graziös ⟨Bewegung, Eleganz⟩

gracious /'greɪʃəs/ 1 adj. (a) liebenswürdig
(b) (merciful) gnädig
2 int. **good** ~! [ach] du meine Güte!

grade /greɪd/ 1 n. (a) Rang, der; (Mil.) Dienstgrad, der
(b) (position) Stufe, die
(c) (Amer. Sch.: class) Klasse, die
(d) (Sch., Univ.: mark) Note, die; Zensur, die
2 v.t. (a) einstufen ⟨Schüler⟩; [nach Größe/ Qualität] sortieren ⟨Eier, Kartoffeln⟩
(b) (mark) benoten

gradient /'greɪdɪənt/ n. (ascent) Steigung, die; (descent) Gefälle, das

gradual /'grædʒʊəl/ adj., **gradually** adv. allmählich

graduate 1 /'grædʒʊət/ n. Graduierte, der/die; (who has left university) Akademiker, der/Akademikerin, die; **university** ~: Hochschulabsolvent, der/-absolventin, die
2 /'grædʒʊeɪt/ v.i. einen akademischen Grad/Titel erwerben; (Amer. Sch.) die [Schul]abschlussprüfung bestehen (from an + Dat.)

graduation /grædʒʊ'eɪʃn/ n. (a) (Univ.) Graduierung, die

(b) (Amer. Sch.) Entlassung, die

graffiti /grə'fi:ti/ n. sing. or pl. Graffiti Pl.; ~ **artist** Graffitikünstler, der/-künstlerin, die

graft /grɑ:ft/ 1 n. (a) (Bot.) Edelreis, das
(b) (Med.) (operation) Transplantation, die; (thing ~ed) Transplantat, das
(c) (Brit. coll.: work) Plackerei, die (ugs.)
2 v.t. (a) (Bot.) pfropfen
(b) (Med.) transplantieren
3 v.i. (Brit. coll.) schuften (ugs.)

grain /greɪn/ n. (a) Korn, das; collect. Getreide, das
(b) (particle) Korn, das
(c) (in wood) Maserung, die; (in paper) Faser, die; (in leather) Narbung, die; **go against the** ~ **[for sb.]** (fig.) jmdm. gegen den Strich gehen (ugs.)

grainy adj. körnig; gemasert ⟨Holz⟩; genarbt ⟨Leder⟩

gram /græm/ n. Gramm, das

grammar /'græmə(r)/ n. Grammatik, die

grammar: ~ **book** n. Grammatik, die; ~ **school** n. (Brit.) ≈ Gymnasium, das

grammatical /grə'mætɪkl/ adj. (a) grammat[ikal]isch richtig od. korrekt
(b) (of grammar) grammatisch

grammatically /grə'mætɪkəlɪ/ adv. grammati[kal]isch ⟨richtig, falsch⟩

gramme ▶ GRAM

gramophone /'græməfəʊn/ n. Plattenspieler, der

gran /græn/ n. (coll./child lang.) Oma, die (Kinderspr./ugs.)

granary /'grænərɪ/ n. Getreidesilo, der od. das; Kornspeicher, der

granary bread n. Ganzkornbrot, das

grand /grænd/ adj. (a) (most or very important) groß; ~ **finale** großes Finale
(b) (splendid) grandios
(c) (coll.: excellent) großartig

grandad /'grændæd/ n. (coll./child lang.); Opa, der (Kinderspr./ugs.)

grand: ~**child** n. Enkel, der/Enkelin, die; Enkelkind, das; ~**dad[dy]** /'grændæd(i)/ ▶ GRANDAD; ~**daughter** n. Enkelin, die

grandeur /'grændʒə(r), 'grændjə(r)/ n. Erhabenheit, die

grandfather n. Großvater, der; ~ **clock** Standuhr, die

grandiose /'grændɪəʊs/ adj. grandios; (pompous) bombastisch

grand: ~**ma** n. (coll./child lang.) Oma, die (Kinderspr./ugs.); ~**mother** n. Großmutter, die; ~**pa** n. (coll./child lang.) Opa, der (Kinderspr./ugs.); ~**parent** n. (male) Großvater, der; (female) Großmutter, die; ~**parents** Großeltern Pl.; ~ **pi'ano** n. [Konzert]flügel, der; ~**son** n. Enkel, der; ~**stand** n. [Haupt]tribüne, der

granite /'grænɪt/ n. Granit, der

granny /'grænɪ/ n. (coll./child lang.) Oma, die (Kinderspr./ugs.)

granny flat n. Einliegerwohnung, die

grant /grɑːnt/ ① v.t. (a) erfüllen ⟨Wunsch⟩; stattgeben (+ Dat.) ⟨Gesuch⟩
(b) (concede, give) gewähren; geben ⟨Zeit⟩; bewilligen ⟨Geldmittel⟩; zugestehen ⟨Recht⟩; erteilen ⟨Erlaubnis⟩
(c) (in argument) zugeben; **take sb./sth. for ∼ed** sich (Dat.) jmds. sicher sein/etw. für selbstverständlich halten
② n. Zuschuss, der; (financial aid [to student]) [Studien]beihilfe, die; (scholarship) Stipendium, das

granulated sugar /ɡrænjʊleɪtɪd 'ʃʊɡə(r)/ n. Kristallzucker, der

granule /ˈɡrænjuːl/ n. Körnchen, das

grape /ɡreɪp/ n. Weintraube, die; **a bunch of ∼s** eine Traube

grape: **∼fruit** n., pl. same Grapefruit, die; **∼ juice** n. Traubensaft, der; **∼vine** n. (fig.) **the ∼vine** die Flüsterpropaganda; **I heard on the ∼vine that …:** es wird geflüstert, dass …

graph /ɡrɑːf/ n. grafische Darstellung; **∼ paper** Diagrammpapier, das

graphic /ˈɡræfɪk/ adj. (a) grafisch
(b) (vivid) plastisch; anschaulich

graphically /ˈɡræfɪkəlɪ/ adv. (a) (vividly) plastisch
(b) (using graphics) grafisch

graphic 'arts n. pl. Grafik, die

graphics /ˈɡræfɪks/ n. (use of diagrams) grafische Darstellung; **computer ∼:** Computergraphik, die

grapple /ˈɡræpl/ v.i. handgemein werden; **∼ with** (fig.) sich auseinander setzen mit

grasp /ɡrɑːsp/ ① v.i. **∼ at** ergreifen; sich stürzen auf (+ Akk.) ⟨Angebot⟩
② v.t. (a) (seize) ergreifen
(b) (hold firmly) festhalten
(c) (understand) verstehen; erfassen ⟨Bedeutung⟩
③ n. (a) (firm hold) Griff, der
(b) (mental ∼) **have a good ∼ of sth.** etw. gut beherrschen

'grasping adj. habgierig

grass /ɡrɑːs/ n. (a) Gras, das
(b) (lawn) Rasen, der
(c) (Brit. sl.: police informer) Spitzel, der

grass: **∼hopper** n. Grashüpfer, der; **∼root[s]** attrib. adj. (Polit.) Basis-; **∼ seed** n. Grassamen, der; (collect.) Grassamen Pl.

grassy /ˈɡrɑːsɪ/ adj. mit Gras bewachsen

grate¹ /ɡreɪt/ n. Rost, der; (recess) Kamin, der

grate² v.t. (a) reiben; (less finely) raspeln
(b) (grind) **∼ one's teeth** mit den Zähnen knirschen

grateful /ˈɡreɪtfl/ adj. dankbar (**to** Dat.)

'gratefully adv. dankbar

'grater n. Reibe, die; Raspel, die

gratify /ˈɡrætɪfaɪ/ v.t. freuen; **be gratified by** or **with** or **at sth.** über etw. (Akk.) erfreut sein

'gratifying adj. erfreulich

grating /ˈɡreɪtɪŋ/ n. Gitter, das

gratitude /ˈɡrætɪtjuːd/ n. Dankbarkeit, die (**to** gegenüber)

gratuitous /ɡrəˈtjuːɪtəs/ adj. (motiveless) grundlos

gratuity /ɡrəˈtjuːɪtɪ/ n. Trinkgeld, das

grave¹ /ɡreɪv/ n. Grab, das

grave² adj. (a) (important, solemn) ernst
(b) (serious) schwer ⟨Fehler, Irrtum⟩; ernst ⟨Situation, Lage⟩; groß ⟨Gefahr⟩; schlimm ⟨Nachricht⟩

'gravedigger n. Totengräber, der

gravel /ˈɡrævl/ n. Kies, der

grave: **∼stone** n. Grabstein, der; **∼yard** n. Friedhof, der

gravity /ˈɡrævɪtɪ/ n. (a) (of mistake, offence) Schwere, die; (of situation) Ernst, der
(b) (Phys., Astron.) Gravitation, die; Schwerkraft, die

gravy /ˈɡreɪvɪ/ n. (a) (juices) Bratensaft, der
(b) (dressing) [Braten]soße, die

gravy: **∼ boat** n. Sauciere, die; Soßenschüssel, die; **∼ train** n. **ride/board the ∼ train** (coll.) leichtes Geld machen (ugs.)

gray etc. (Amer.) ▶ GREY etc.

graze¹ /ɡreɪz/ v.i. grasen; weiden

graze² ① n. Schürfwunde, die
② v.t. (a) (touch lightly) streifen
(b) (scrape) abschürfen ⟨Haut⟩; zerkratzen ⟨Oberfläche⟩

grease /ɡriːs/ ① n. Fett, das; (lubricant) Schmierfett, das
② v.t. einfetten; (lubricate) schmieren

'greaseproof adj. fettdicht; **∼ paper** Pergament- od. Butterbrotpapier, das

greasy /ˈɡriːsɪ/ adj. fettig; fett ⟨Essen⟩; (lubricated) geschmiert; (dirty with lubricant) schmierig

great /ɡreɪt/ adj. (a) groß; **a ∼ many** sehr viele; sehr gut ⟨Freund⟩; (impressive; coll.: splendid) großartig; **be a ∼ one for sth.** etw. sehr gern tun
(b) Groß⟨onkel, -tante, -neffe, -nichte⟩; Ur⟨großmutter, -großvater, -enkel, -enkelin⟩

great: **G∼ 'Bear** n. (Astron.) Großer Bär; **G∼ 'Britain** pr. n. Großbritannien (das)

'greatly adv. sehr; höchst ⟨verärgert⟩; stark ⟨beeinflusst⟩; bedeutend ⟨verbessert⟩

'greatness n. Größe, die

Great 'War n. Erster Weltkrieg

Greece /ɡriːs/ pr. n. Griechenland (das)

greed /ɡriːd/ n. Gier, die (**for** nach); (gluttony) Gefräßigkeit, die

'greedy adj. gierig; (gluttonous) gefräßig

Greek /ɡriːk/ ① adj. griechisch; **sb. is ∼:** jmd. ist Grieche/Griechin
② n. (a) (person) Grieche, der/Griechin, die
(b) (language) Griechisch, das; see also ENGLISH 2A

green /ɡriːn/ ① adj. (a) grün
(b) (environmentally safe) ökologisch ···⊱

(c) (gullible) naiv; (inexperienced) grün
(d) (Polit.) G∼: grün; **the G∼s** die Grünen
2 n. **(a)** (colour) Grün, das
(b) (piece of land) Grünfläche, die; **village ∼:** Dorfanger, der
(c) in pl. (∼ vegetables) Grüngemüse, das

green: ∼ **belt** n. Grüngürtel, der; ∼ **'card** n. (Motor Veh.) grüne Karte

greenery /'griːnərɪ/ n. Grün, das

green: ∼**fly** n. (Brit.) grüne Blattlaus; ∼**gage** /'griːngeɪdʒ/ n. Reineclaude, die; ∼**grocer** n. (Brit.) Obst- und Gemüsehändler, der/-händlerin, die

'greenhouse n. Gewächshaus, das

greenhouse: ∼ **effect** n. Treibhauseffekt, der; ∼ **gas** n. Treibhausgas, das

green: ∼ **light** n. **(a)** grünes Licht; (as signal) Grün, das; **(b)** (fig.) **give sb./get the ∼:** jmdm. grünes Licht geben/grünes Licht erhalten; **G∼ Party** n. (Polit.) die Grünen Pl.

greet /griːt/ v.t. begrüßen; (in passing) grüßen; (receive) empfangen

'greeting n. Begrüßung, die; (in passing) Gruß, der; (words) Grußformel, die

'greetings card n. Grußkarte, die; (for birthday) Glückwunschkarte, die

gregarious /grɪ'geərɪəs/ adj. gesellig

grenade /grɪ'neɪd/ n. Granate, die

grew ▶ GROW

grey /greɪ/ 1 adj. grau
2 n. Grau, das

grey: ∼**haired** adj. grauhaarig; ∼**hound** n. Windhund, der; ∼**hound racing** n. Windhundrennen, das

greyish /'greɪɪʃ/ adj. gräulich

grid /grɪd/ n. **(a)** (grating) Rost, der
(b) (of lines) Gitter[netz], das
(c) (for supply) Versorgungsnetz, das

grid: ∼**lock** n. Verkehrsinfarkt, der; (fig.) völliger Stillstand; ∼**locked** /'grɪdlɒkt/ adj. total verstopft ⟨Straße, Stadt⟩; (fig.) festgefahren

grief /griːf/ n. Kummer, der (over, at über + Akk., um); (at loss of sb.) Trauer, die (for um); **come to ∼** (fail) scheitern

'grief-stricken adj. untröstlich (at über + Akk.)

grievance /'griːvəns/ n. (complaint) Beschwerde, die; (grudge) Groll, der

grieve /griːv/ 1 v.t. betrüben; bekümmern
2 v.i. trauern (for um)

grievous /'griːvəs/ adj. schwer ⟨Verwundung, Krankheit;⟩ ∼ **bodily harm** (Law) schwere Körperverletzung

grill[1] /grɪl/ 1 v.t. (cook) grillen; (fig.: question) in die Mangel nehmen (ugs.)
2 n. **(a)** mixed ∼: gemischte Grillplatte
(b) (on cooker) Grill, der

grille (grill[2]**)** n. **(a)** Gitter, das
(b) (Motor Veh.) [Kühler]grill, der

grim /grɪm/ adj. (stern) streng; grimmig ⟨Lächeln, Schweigen⟩; (unrelenting) erbittert ⟨Widerstand, Kampf⟩; (ghastly) grauenvoll ⟨Aufgabe, Nachricht⟩; trostlos ⟨Aussichten⟩

grimace /grɪ'meɪs/ 1 n. Grimasse, die
2 v.i. Grimassen schneiden; ∼ **with pain** vor Schmerz das Gesicht verziehen

grime /graɪm/ n. Schmutz, der

grimy /'graɪmɪ/ adj. schmutzig

grin /grɪn/ 1 n. Grinsen, das
2 v.i. -nn- grinsen; ∼ **at sb.** jmdn. angrinsen

grind /graɪnd/ 1 v.t., ground /graʊnd/ **(a)** ∼ [up] zermahlen; mahlen ⟨Kaffee, Pfeffer, Getreide⟩
(b) (sharpen) schleifen ⟨Schere, Messer⟩; schärfen ⟨Klinge⟩
(c) (rub harshly) zerquetschen; ∼ **one's teeth** mit den Zähnen knirschen
2 v.i., ground: ∼ **to a halt** ⟨Fahrzeug:⟩ quietschend zum Stehen kommen; (fig.) ⟨Verkehr:⟩ zum Erliegen kommen
3 n. (coll.) Plackerei, die (ugs.)

'grinder n. Schleifmaschine, die; (coffee ∼ etc.) Mühle, die

'grindstone n. Schleifstein, der

grip /grɪp/ 1 n. **(a)** (firm hold) Halt, der; (fig.: power) Umklammerung, die; **have a ∼ on sth.** etw. festhalten; (fig.) etwas im Griff haben; **loosen one's ∼:** loslassen; **lose one's ∼** (fig.) nachlassen
(b) (strength or way of ∼ping) Griff, der
2 v.t., -pp- [fest] halten; ⟨Reifen:⟩ greifen; (fig.) fesseln ⟨Publikum, Aufmerksamkeit⟩
3 v.i., -pp- ⟨Räder, Bremsen usw.:⟩ greifen

gripe /graɪp/ v.i. (coll.) meckern (ugs.) (about über + Akk.)

gripping /'grɪpɪŋ/ adj. (fig.) packend

grisly /'grɪzlɪ/ adj. grausig

gristle /'grɪsl/ n. Knorpel, der

grit /grɪt/ 1 n. **(a)** Sand, der
(b) (coll.: courage) Schneid, der (ugs.)
2 v.t., -tt-: **(a)** streuen ⟨Straßen⟩
(b) ∼ **one's teeth** die Zähne zusammenbeißen (ugs.)

grizzly /'grɪzlɪ/ n. ∼ **[bear]** Grislybär, der

groan /grəʊn/ 1 n. Stöhnen, das; (of thing) Ächzen, das
2 v.i. [auf]stöhnen (at bei); ⟨Tisch, Planken:⟩ ächzen
3 v.t. stöhnen

grocer /'grəʊsə(r)/ n. Lebensmittelhändler, der/-händlerin, die

grocery /'grəʊsərɪ/ n. **(a)** in pl. (goods) Lebensmittel Pl.
(b) **[store]** Lebensmittelgeschäft, das

groggy /'grɒgɪ/ adj. groggy präd. (ugs.)

groin /grɔɪn/ n. Leistengegend, die

groom /gruːm, grʊm/ 1 n. **(a)** (stable boy) Stallbursche, der
(b) (bride∼) Bräutigam, der
2 v.t. striegeln ⟨Pferd⟩; (fig.) vorbereiten (for auf + Akk.)

groove /gru:v/ n. Rille, die

grope /grəʊp/ v.i. tasten (**for** nach)

gross¹ /grəʊs/ adj. (a) (flagrant) grob ⟨Fahrlässigkeit, Fehler⟩
(b) (obese) fett
(c) (total) Brutto-

gross² n., pl. same Gros, das

'grossly adj. (flagrantly) äußerst; grob ⟨übertreiben⟩

grotesque /grəʊ'tesk/ adj. grotesk

grotto /'grɒtəʊ/ n., pl. ∼es or ∼s Grotte, die

grotty /'grɒtɪ/ adj. (Brit. coll.) mies (ugs.)

ground¹ /graʊnd/ ① n. (a) Boden, der; **get off the ∼** (coll.) konkrete Gestalt annehmen
(b) [sports] ∼: Sportplatz, der
(c) in pl. (attached to house) Anlage, die
(d) (reason) Grund, der; **on the ∼[s] of** auf Grund (+ Gen.); **on the ∼[s] that …:** unter Berufung auf die Tatsache, dass …
(e) in pl. (sediment) Satz, der
② v.t. (Aeronaut.) am Boden festhalten

ground² ① ▶ GRIND 1, 2
② adj. gemahlen ⟨Kaffee, Getreide⟩

ground: ∼ control n. (Aeronaut.: personnel, equipment, etc.) Flugsicherungskontrolldienst, der; ∼ **'floor** ▶ FLOOR 1b; ∼ **forces** n. pl. Bodentruppen Pl.; ∼ **frost** n. Bodenfrost, der

'grounding n. Grundkenntnisse Pl.

'groundless adj. unbegründet

ground: ∼sheet n. Bodenplane, die; ∼**sman** /'graʊndzmən/ n., pl. -smen /'graʊndzmən/ (Sport) Platzwart, der; ∼**work** n. Vorarbeiten Pl.

group /gru:p/ ① n. Gruppe, die
② v.t. gruppieren

group: ∼ practice n. Gemeinschaftspraxis, die; ∼ **therapy** n. Gruppentherapie, die

grouse¹ /graʊs/ n., pl. same Raufußhuhn, das; [red] ∼ (Brit.) Schottisches Moorschneehuhn

grouse² v.i. (coll.) meckern (ugs.)

grove /grəʊv/ n. Wäldchen, das

grovel /'grɒvl/ v.i., (Brit.) -ll- (fig.) katzbuckeln

grow /grəʊ/ ① v.i., grew /gru:/, grown /grəʊn/ (a) wachsen; ∼ **out of** or **from sth.** sich aus etw. entwickeln; (from sth. abstract) von etw. herrühren; ∼ **in** gewinnen an (+ Dat.) ⟨Größe, Bedeutung⟩
(b) (become) werden; ∼ **apart** (fig.) sich auseinander leben; ∼ **to love/hate sb./sth.** jmdn./etw. lieben lernen/hassen lernen; ∼ **to like sb./sth.** nach und nach Gefallen an jmdn./etw. finden
② v.t., grew, grown ziehen; (on a large scale) anpflanzen; züchten ⟨Blumen⟩
■ **grow 'up** v.i. (a) aufwachsen; (become adult) erwachsen werden
(b) ⟨Legende:⟩ entstehen

growl /graʊl/ ① n. Knurren, das; (of bear) Brummen, das
② v.i. knurren; ⟨Bär:⟩ [böse] brummen

grown /grəʊn/ ① ▶ GROW
② adj. erwachsen

'grown-up ① n. Erwachsene, der/die
② adj. erwachsen

growth /grəʊθ/ n. (a) Wachstum, das (**of, in** Gen.); (increase) Zunahme, die (**of, in** Gen.)
(b) (Med.) Gewächs, das

growth: ∼ area n. Wachstumsbereich, der; ∼ **industry** n. Wachstumsindustrie, die; ∼ **rate** n. Wachstumsrate, die

grub /grʌb/ n. (a) Larve, die; (maggot) Made, die
(b) (coll.: food) Fressen, das (salopp)

grubby /'grʌbɪ/ adj. schmudd[e]lig (ugs.)

grudge /grʌdʒ/ ① v.t. ∼ **sb. sth.** jmdm. etw. missgönnen; ∼ **doing sth.** etw. ungern tun
② n. Groll, der; **bear sb. a.** ∼ or a ∼ **against sb.** jmdm. gegenüber nachtragend sein

grudging /'grʌdʒɪŋ/ adj. widerwillig; widerwillig gewährt ⟨Zuschuss⟩

'grudgingly adv. widerwillig

gruelling (Amer.: **grueling**) /'gru:əlɪŋ/ adj. aufreibend; strapaziös ⟨Reise⟩

gruesome /'gru:səm/ adj. grausig

gruff /grʌf/ adj. barsch; rau ⟨Stimme⟩

grumble /'grʌmbl/ v.i. murren; ∼ **about** or **over sth.** sich über etw. (Akk.) beklagen

grumpily /'grʌmpɪlɪ/ adv. unleidlich

grumpy /'grʌmpɪ/ adj. unleidlich

grunge /grʌndʒ/ n. Grunge, der

grunt /grʌnt/ ① n. Grunzen, das
② v.i. grunzen

guarantee /gærən'ti:/ ① v.t. (a) garantieren für; [eine] Garantie geben auf (+ Akk.); **the clock is ∼d for a year** die Uhr hat ein Jahr Garantie
(b) (promise) garantieren (ugs.); (ensure) bürgen für ⟨Qualität⟩
② n. (a) (Commerc. etc.) Garantie, die; (document) Garantieschein, der
(b) (promise) Garantie, die (ugs.); **give sb. a** ∼ **that …:** jmdm. garantieren, dass …

guarantor /'gærəntə(r), gærən'tɔ:(r)/ n. Bürge, der/Bürgin, die

guaranty /'gærəntɪ/ n. (basis of security) Garantie, die; Gewähr, die

guard /gɑ:d/ ① n. (a) (guardsman) Wachtposten, der; (group of soldiers) Wache, die; **be on** ∼: Wache haben; **be on [one's]** ∼ (lit. or fig.) sich hüten
(b) (Brit. Railw.) [Zug]schaffner, der/-schaffnerin, die
(c) (Amer.: prison warder) [Gefängnis]wärter, der/-wärterin, die
(d) (safety device) Schutz, der
② v.t. bewachen; hüten ⟨Geheimnis⟩; schützen ⟨Leben⟩; beschützen ⟨Prominenten⟩ ⋯⋗

■ **'guard against** v.t. sich hüten vor (+ Dat.); vorbeugen (+ Dat.) ⟨Krankheit, Irrtum⟩

guard: ~ **dog** n. Wachhund, der; ~ **duty** n. Wachdienst, der

'guarded adj. zurückhaltend

guardian /'gɑːdɪən/ n. (a) Hüter, der; Wächter, der

(b) (Law) Vormund, der

guardian 'angel n. Schutzengel, der

guerrilla /gə'rɪlə/ n. Guerillakämpfer, der/ -kämpferin, die; attrib. Guerilla-

guess /ges/ [1] v.t. (a) (estimate) schätzen; (surmise) raten; (surmise correctly) erraten; raten ⟨Rätsel⟩; ~ **what!** (coll.) stell dir vor!

(b) (esp. Amer.: suppose) **I** ~: ich glaube

[2] v.i. (estimate) schätzen; (make assumption) vermuten; (surmise correctly) es erraten; ~ **at** sth. etw. schätzen; **keep sb.** ~**ing** (coll.) jmdn. im Unklaren lassen

[3] n. Schätzung, die; **make** or **have a** ~: schätzen

'guesswork n. **be** ~: eine Vermutung sein

guesstimate /'gestɪmət/ n. (coll.) grobe Schätzung

guest /gest/ n. Gast, der

guest: ~ **house** n. Pension, die; ~ **list** n. Gästeliste, die; ~ **room** n. Gästezimmer, das; ~ **worker** n. Gastarbeiter, der/ -arbeiterin, die

guffaw /gʌ'fɔː/ [1] n. brüllendes Gelächter

[2] v.i. brüllend lachen

guidance /'gaɪdəns/ n. (a) (leadership) Führung, die; (by teacher etc.) [An]leitung, die

(b) (advice) Rat, der

guide /gaɪd/ [1] n. (a) Führer, der/Führerin, die; (Tourism) [Fremden]führer, der/-führerin, die

(b) (indicator) **be a [good]** ~ **to** sth. ein [guter] Anhaltspunkt für etw. sein; **be no** ~ **to** sth. keine Rückschlüsse auf etw. (Akk.) zulassen

(c) (Brit.) [**Girl**] **G~:** Pfadfinderin, die

(d) (handbook) Handbuch, das

(e) (for tourists) [Reise]führer, der

[2] v.t. führen; (fig.) bestimmen ⟨Handeln, Urteil⟩; **be** ~**d by** sth./sb. sich von etw./ jmdm. leiten lassen

'guidebook n. [Reise]führer, der

guided 'missile n. Lenkflugkörper, der

'guide dog n. Blinden[führ]hund, der

guided 'tour n. Führung, die (of durch)

'guideline n. Richtlinie, die

guild /gɪld/ n. (a) Verein, der

(b) (Hist.) Gilde, die; Zunft, die

guile /gaɪl/ n. Hinterlist, die

guillotine /'gɪlətiːn/ n. Guillotine, die

guilt /gɪlt/ n. (a) Schuld, die (of, for an + Dat.)

(b) (guilty feeling) Schuldgefühle Pl.

'guiltless adj. unschuldig (of an + Dat.)

'guilty adj. (a) schuldig; **be** ~ **of murder** des Mordes schuldig sein; **find sb.** ~/**not** ~ **[of**

sth.] jmdn. [an etw. (Dat.)] schuldig sprechen/[von etw.] freisprechen; **feel** ~ ein schlechtes Gewissen haben

(b) schuldbewusst ⟨Miene, Blick, Verhalten⟩; schlecht ⟨Gewissen⟩

guinea: ~**fowl,** ~ **hen** ns. Perlhuhn, das; ~ **pig** n. (a) (animal) Meerschweinchen, das;

(b) (fig.: subject of experiment) (person) Versuchsperson, die; Versuchskaninchen, das (ugs. abwertend); (thing) Versuchsobjekt, das; **act as** ~ **pig** Versuchskaninchen spielen

guise /gaɪz/ n. Gestalt, die; **in the** ~ **of** in Gestalt (+ Gen.)

guitar /gɪ'tɑː(r)/ n. Gitarre, die

guitarist /gɪ'tɑːrɪst/ n. Gitarrist, der/ Gitarristin, die

gulf /gʌlf/ n. (a) (Geog.) Golf, der

(b) (wide gap) Kluft, die

gull /gʌl/ n. Möwe, die

gullet /'gʌlɪt/ n. (a) Speiseröhre, die

(b) (throat) Kehle, die

gullible /'gʌlɪbl/ adj. leichtgläubig

gully /'gʌlɪ/ n. (artificial channel) Abzugsrinne, die; (drain) Gully, der

gulp /gʌlp/ [1] v.t. hinunterschlingen; hinuntergießen ⟨Getränk⟩

[2] n. (a) Schlucken, das

(b) (large mouthful of drink) kräftiger Schluck

■ **gulp 'down** v.t. hinunterschlingen; hinuntergießen ⟨Getränk⟩

gum¹ /gʌm/ n. (Anat.) ~[**s**] Zahnfleisch, das

gum² [1] n. (a) Gummi, das; (glue) Klebstoff, der

(b) (Amer.) ▸ CHEWING GUM

[2] v.t., -mm-: (a) (smear with ~) mit Klebstoff bestreichen; gummieren ⟨Briefmarken, Etiketten usw.⟩

(b) (fasten with ~) kleben

'gumboot n. Gummistiefel, der

gumption /'gʌmpʃn/ n. (coll.) Grips, der

gun /gʌn/ n. Schusswaffe, die; (rifle) Gewehr, das; (pistol) Pistole, die; (revolver) Revolver, der

■ **gun 'down** v.t. niederschießen

gun: ~**fight** n. (Amer. coll.) Schießerei, die; ~**fire** n. Geschützfeuer, das; ~ **laws** pl. Waffengesetze Pl.; ~**man** /'gʌnmən/ n., pl. ~**men** /'gʌnmən/ bewaffneter Mann; ~**powder** n. Schießpulver, das; ~**shot** n. Schuss, der; ~**shot wound** Schusswunde, die; ~**smith** n. Büchsenmacher, der

gurgle /'gɜːgl/ [1] n. Gluckern, das; (of brook) Plätschern, das

[2] v.i. gluckern; ⟨Bach:⟩ plätschern; ⟨Baby:⟩ lallen; (with delight) glucksen

guru /'goruː/ n. Guru, der

gush /gʌʃ/ [1] n. Schwall, der

[2] v.i. (a) strömen; ~ **out** herausströmen

(b) (fig.: enthuse) schwärmen

'gushing adj. (a) reißend ⟨Strom⟩

(b) (effusive) exaltiert

gust /gʌst/ n. ~ [**of wind**] Bö[e], die

gusto /'gʌstəʊ/ n. Genuss, der; (vitality) Schwung, der

'gusty *adj.* böig

gut /gʌt/ **1** *n.* (a) (material) Darm, *der*
(b) *in pl.* (bowels) Eingeweide *Pl.;* Gedärme
Pl.
(c) *in pl.* (coll.: courage) Schneid, *der* (ugs.)
2 *v.t.,* -tt-: (a) (remove ∼s of) ausnehmen
(b) (remove fittings from) ausräumen; **the house
was ∼ted [by fire]** das Haus brannte aus
3 *attrib. adj.* ∼ **feeling** instinktives Gefühl;
have a ∼ feeling that … es im Gefühl *od.*
(salopp) Urin haben, dass …

gutter /'gʌtə(r)/ *n.* (below edge of roof)
Dachrinne, *die;* (at side of street) Rinnstein,
der; Gosse, *die*

'guttering *n.* (on roof) Dachrinnen *Pl.*

gutter 'press *n.* Sensationspresse, *die*

guttural /'gʌtərl/ *adj.* guttural; kehlig

guy /gaɪ/ *n.* (a) (coll.: man) Typ, *der* (ugs.)
(b) *in pl.* (Amer.: everyone) [**listen,**] **you ∼s!**
[hört mal,] Kinder! (ugs.)

'guy rope *n.* Zelt[spann]leine, *die*

guzzle /'gʌzl/ **1** *v.t.* (eat)
hinunterschlingen; (drink) hinuntergießen

2 *v.i.* schlingen

gym /dʒɪm/ *n.* (coll.) (a) (gymnasium)
Turnhalle, *die*
(b) (gymnastics) Turnen, *das*

gymnasium *n.* /dʒɪm'neɪzɪəm/ *n., pl.* ∼s
or **gymnasia** /dʒɪm'neɪzɪə/ Turnhalle, *die*

gymnast /'dʒɪmnæst/ *n.* Turner, *der/*
Turnerin, *die*

gymnastic /dʒɪm'næstɪk/ *adj.* turnerisch
⟨*Können*⟩; ∼ **equipment** Turngeräte *Pl.*

gymnastics /dʒɪm'næstɪks/ *n.* Gymnastik,
die; (esp. with apparatus) Turnen, *das*

'gymslip *n.* Trägerrock, *der*

gynaecologist /gaɪnɪ'kɒlədʒɪst/ *n.*
Frauenarzt, *der/*-ärztin, *die*

gynaecology /gaɪnɪ'kɒlədʒɪ/ *n.*
Gynäkologie, *die*

gypsy, Gypsy /'dʒɪpsɪ/ *n.* Zigeuner, *der/*
Zigeunerin, *die*

gyrate /dʒaɪə'reɪt/ *v.i.* sich drehen

Hh

H¹, h /eɪtʃ/ *n.* H, h, *das*

haberdashery /'hæbədæʃərɪ/ *n.* (goods)
Kurzwaren *Pl.;* (Amer.: menswear)
Herrenmoden *Pl.*

habit /'hæbɪt/ *n.* (a) (Gewohnheit, *die;* **good/
bad ∼:** gute/schlechte [An]gewohnheit; **get**
or **fall into a** *or* **the ∼ of doing sth.** [es] sich
(*Dat.*) angewöhnen, etw. zu tun
(b) (coll.: addiction) Süchtigkeit, *die*

habitable /'hæbɪtəbl/ *adj.* bewohnbar

habitat /'hæbɪtæt/ *n.* Habitat, *das*

habitation /hæbɪ'teɪʃn/ *n.* **fit/unfit for
human ∼:** bewohnbar/unbewohnbar

habitual /hə'bɪtjʊəl/ *adj.* (a) gewohnt
(b) (given to habit) gewohnheitsmäßig;
Gewohnheits⟨*trinker*⟩

ha'bitually *adv.* (regularly) regelmäßig

hack¹ /hæk/ *v.t.* (a) hacken ⟨*Holz*⟩; ∼ **sth.
to bits** *or* **pieces** etw. in Stücke hacken
(b) (Comp.) eindringen in (+ *Akk.*)
⟨*Computersystem*⟩; ∼ **into sth.** in etw. (*Akk.*)
eindringen
∎ **hack 'off** *v.t.* abhacken
∎ **hack 'out** *v.t.* heraushauen (**from** aus)

hack² *n.* (derog.: writer) Schreiberling, *der*

hacker /'hækə(r)/ *n.* (Comp.) Hacker, *der*

hackneyed /'hæknɪd/ *adj.* abgegriffen;
abgedroschen (ugs.)

'hacksaw *n.* [Metall]bügelsäge, *die*

had ▶ HAVE

haddock /'hædək/ *n., pl. same* Schellfisch,
der

hadn't /'hædnt/ (coll.) = had not; ▶ HAVE

haemoglobin /hi:mə'gləʊbɪn/ *n.*
Hämoglobin, *das*

haemophilia /hi:mə'fɪlɪə/ *n.* Hämophilie,
die (fachspr.); Bluterkrankheit, *die*

haemophiliac /hi:mə'fɪlɪæk/ *n.* Bluter,
*der/*Bluterin, *die*

haemorrhage /'hemərɪdʒ/ *n.* Blutung, *die*

haemorrhoid /'hemərɔɪd/ *n.*
Hämorrhoide, *die*

hag /hæg/ *n.* [alte] Hexe

haggard /'hægəd/ *adj.* ausgezehrt; (with
worry) abgehärmt

haggle /'hægl/ *v.i.* sich zanken (**over, about**
wegen); (over price) feilschen (**over, about** um)

Hague /heɪg/ *pr. n.* **The ∼:** Den Haag (*das*)

hail¹ /heɪl/ **1** *n.* Hagel, *der*
2 *v.i.* **it ∼s** *or* **is ∼ing** es hagelt; ∼ **down**
(fig.) niederprasseln (**on** auf + *Akk.*)

hail² *v.t.* (a) (call out to) anrufen; (signal to)
anhalten ⟨*Taxi*⟩
(b) (acclaim) zujubeln (+ *Dat.*); bejubeln (**as**
als)

'hailstone *n.* Hagelkorn, *das*

hair /heə(r)/ *n.* (a) (one strand) Haar, *das*   ⋯⟶

(b) collect. Haar, das; Haare Pl.; attrib. Haar-;
have or get one's ~ done sich (Dat.) das
Haar od. die Haare machen lassen (ugs.)

hair: ~**brush** n. Haarbürste, die;
~ **conditioner** n. Pflegespülung, die;
~ **cream** n. Haarcreme, die; Pomade, die;
~ **curler** n. Lockenwickler, der; ~**cut** n.
(a) (act) Haareschneiden, das; go for/need a
~cut zum Friseur gehen/müssen; get/have a
~cut sich (Dat.) die Haare schneiden lassen;
(b) (style) Haarschnitt, der; ~**do** n. (style)
Frisur, die; ~**dresser** n. Friseur, der/
Friseurin, die; go to the ~dresser's zum
Friseur gehen; ~ **dye** n. Haarfärbemittel,
das; ~**grip** n. (Brit.) Haarklammer, die;
~**line** n. **(a)** (edge of hair) Haaransatz, der;
his ~line is receding, he has a receding
~line er bekommt eine Stirnglatze; **(b)**
(crack) Haarriss; ~line fracture (Med.) Fissur,
die; ~**pin** n. Haarnadel, die; ~**pin 'bend**
n. Haarnadelkurve, die; ~**raising**
/ˈheəreɪzɪŋ/ adj. haarsträubend; ~**spray** n.
Haarspray, das; ~**style** n. Frisur, die

'**hairy** adj. **(a)** behaart; flauschig ⟨Pullover,
Teppich⟩
(b) (coll.: difficult) haarig

hale /heɪl/ adj. ~ and hearty gesund und
munter

half /hɑːf/ [1] n., pl. halves /hɑːvz/ **(a)** Hälfte,
die; ~ [of sth.] die Hälfte [von etw.]; ~ of
Europe halb Europa; one and a ~ hours, one
hour and a ~: anderthalb od. eineinhalb
Stunden; divide sth. in ~ or into halves etw.
halbieren; she is three and a ~: sie ist
dreieinhalb
(b) (Footb. etc.: period) Halbzeit, die
[2] adj. halb; ~ the house/books/time die
Hälfte des Hauses/der Bücher/der Zeit; ~ an
hour eine halbe Stunde
[3] adv. **(a)** zur Hälfte; halb ⟨schließen,
aufessen, fertig, voll, geöffnet⟩; (almost) fast
⟨ersticken, tot sein⟩; ~ as much/many halb so
viel/viele; only ~ hear what ...: nur zum Teil
hören, was ...
(b) ~ past or (coll.) ~ one/three etc. halb
zwei/drei/vier usw.; ~ past twelve halb eins

half: ~'**board** n. Halbpension, die;
~**caste** n. Mischling, der; ~'**hearted**
adj. halbherzig; ~'**hour** n. halbe Stunde;
~ '**mast** n. be [flown] at ~ mast auf
Halbmast stehen; ~ '**moon** n. Halbmond,
der; ~ **note** n. (Amer. Mus.) halbe Note;
~'**price** [1] n. halber Preis; [2] adj. zum
halben Preis nachgestellt; [3] adv. zum
halben Preis. ~'**term** n. (Brit.) (holiday)
~**term** [holiday/break] Ferien in der Mitte
des Trimesters; ~'**time** n. (Sport) Halbzeit,
die; ~'**way** [1] adj. ~way point Mitte, die;
[2] adv. die Hälfte des Weges ⟨begleiten,
fahren⟩; ~**wit** n. Schwachkopf, der;
(scatterbrain) Schussel, der

halibut /ˈhælɪbət/ n., pl. same Heilbutt, der

hall /hɔːl/ n. **(a)** Saal, der; (building) Halle, die;
school/church ~: Aula, die/Gemeindehaus,
das

(b) (entrance ~) Flur, der
(c) (Univ.) ~ [of residence]
Studentenwohnheim, das

'**hallmark** n. [Feingehalts]stempel, der; (fig.)
Kennzeichen, das

hallo /həˈləʊ/ int. **(a)** (to call attention) hallo
(b) (Brit.) ▶ HELLO

Hallowe'en /hæləʊˈiːn/ n. Halloween, das;
Abend vor Allerheiligen

hallucination /həluːsɪˈneɪʃn/ n.
Halluzination, die

hallucinogen /həˈluːsɪnədʒen/ n. (Med.)
Halluzinogen, das

hallucinogenic /həluːsɪnəˈdʒenɪk/ adj.
(Med.) halluzinogen

'**hallway** n. Flur, der

halo /ˈheɪləʊ/ n., pl. ~es Heiligenschein, der

halt /hɒlt, hɔːlt/ [1] n. **(a)** Pause, die;
(interruption) Unterbrechung, die; call a ~ to
sth. mit etw. Schluss machen
(b) (Brit. Railw.) Haltepunkt, der
[2] v.i. **(a)** stehen bleiben; ⟨Fahrer:⟩ anhalten;
(for a rest) eine Pause machen; (esp. Mil.) Halt
machen; ~, who goes there? (Mil.) halt, wer
da?
(b) (end) eingestellt werden
[3] v.t. anhalten; einstellen ⟨Projekt⟩

'**halting** adj. schleppend; zögernd ⟨Antwort⟩

halve /hɑːv/ v.t. halbieren

halves pl. of HALF

ham /hæm/ n. Schinken, der

hamburger /ˈhæmbɜːgə(r)/ n. Hacksteak,
das; (in roll) Hamburger, der

hamlet /ˈhæmlɪt/ n. Weiler, der

hammer /ˈhæmə(r)/ [1] n. Hammer, der
[2] v.t. hämmern
[3] v.i. hämmern (at an + Dat.)
▪ **hammer 'out** v.t. ausklopfen ⟨Delle,
Beule⟩; (fig.: devise) ausarbeiten

hammock /ˈhæmək/ n. Hängematte, die

hamper[1] /ˈhæmpə(r)/ n. [Deckel]korb, der

hamper[2] v.t. behindern

hamster /ˈhæmstə(r)/ n. Hamster, der

'**hamstring** [1] n. (Anat.) Kniesehne, die
[2] vt. (fig.) lähmen

hand /hænd/ [1] n. **(a)** Hand, die; by ~
(manually) mit der od. von Hand; give or lend
[sb.] a ~ [with or in sth.] [jmdm.] [bei etw.]
helfen
(b) (share) have a ~ in sth. bei etw. seine
Hände im Spiel haben
(c) (worker) Arbeiter, der; (Naut.: seaman)
Matrose, der
(d) (of clock or watch) Zeiger, der
(e) at ~: in der Nähe; on the one ~ ..., [but]
on the other [~] ...: einerseits ...,
andererseits ...
(f) (Cards) Karte, die
[2] v.t. geben; ⟨Überbringer:⟩ übergeben
⟨Sendung, Lieferung⟩
▪ **hand 'in** v.t. abgeben (to, at bei);
einreichen ⟨Petition⟩
▪ **hand 'out** v.t. austeilen

■ **hand 'over** *v.t.* übergeben (**to** *Dat.*)

hand: ∼**bag** *n.* Handtasche, *die;* ∼ **baggage** *n.* Handgepäck, *das;* ∼**book** *n.* Handbuch, *das;* ∼**brake** *n.* Handbremse, *die;* ∼**cuff** ⟨1⟩ *n., usu. in pl.* Handschelle, *die;* ⟨2⟩ *v.t.* ∼**cuff** sb. jmdm. Handschellen anlegen

handful /'hændfʊl/ *n.* Handvoll, *die;* **be a** ∼: (fig. coll.) einen ständig auf Trab halten (ugs.)

hand: ∼ **grenade** *n.* Handgranate, *die;* ∼**gun** *n.* Faustfeuerwaffe, *die;* ∼**-held** *adj.* ∼**-held camera** Handkamera, *die*

handicap /'hændɪkæp/ ⟨1⟩ *n.* (a) (Sport, also fig.) Handikap, *das* (b) (physical) Behinderung, *die* ⟨2⟩ *v.t.*, -pp- benachteiligen

handicapped /'hændɪkæpt/ *adj.* [mentally/physically] ∼: [geistig/körperlich] behindert

handicraft /'hændɪkrɑːft/ *n.* [Kunst]handwerk, *das;* (needlework, knitting, etc.) Handarbeit, *die*

handiwork /'hændɪwɜːk/ *n.* handwerkliche Arbeit; **it's all his own** ∼: das hat er selbst gemacht

handkerchief /'hæŋkətʃɪf/ *n., pl.* ∼s or **handkerchieves** /'hæŋkətʃiːvz/ Taschentuch, *das*

handle /'hændl/ ⟨1⟩ *n.* (a) (of door) Griff, *der;* Klinke, *die;* (of axe, brush, comb, broom, saucepan) Stiel, *der;* (of cup, jug) Henkel, *der* ⟨2⟩ *v.t.* (a) (touch, feel) anfassen (b) (control) handhaben ⟨*Fahrzeug, Flugzeug*⟩ (c) (deal/cope with) umgehen/fertig werden mit

'handlebars *n. pl.* Lenkstange, *die*

'handling charge /'hændlɪŋ/ *n.* (Commerc.) Bearbeitungsgebühr, *die*

hand: ∼ **lotion** *n.* Handlotion, *die;* ∼ **luggage** *n.* Handgepäck, *das;* ∼**made** *adj.* handgearbeitet; ∼**over** *n.* Übergabe, *die;* ∼**-painted** *adj.* handbemalt; ∼**picked** *adj.* sorgfältig ausgewählt; ∼**shake** *n.* Händedruck, *der*

handsome /'hænsəm/ *adj.* gut aussehend

hand: ∼**s-'on** *adj.* praktisch; ∼**stand** *n.* Handstand, *der;* ∼ **towel** *n.* [Hände]handtuch, *das;* ∼**writing** *n.* [Hand]schrift, *die;* ∼**written** *adj.* handgeschrieben; handschriftlich

handy /'hændɪ/ *adj.* greifbar; **keep/have** sth. ∼: etw. greifbar haben

'handyman *n.* Handwerker, *der;* [home] ∼: Heimwerker, *der*

hang /hæŋ/ ⟨1⟩ *v.t.* (a) *p.t., p.p.* hung /hʌŋ/ hängen; aufhängen ⟨*Bild, Gardinen*⟩; ankleben ⟨*Tapete*⟩ (b) *p.t., p.p.* hanged (execute) hängen (**for** wegen); ∼ **oneself** sich erhängen ⟨2⟩ *v.i.,* hung (a) (hang down) hängen; ⟨*Kleid usw.:*⟩ fallen (b) (be executed) hängen ⟨3⟩ *n.* **get the** ∼ **of** sth. (coll.) mit etw. klarkommen (ugs.)

■ **hang a'bout, hang a'round** *v.i.* (a) (loiter) herumlungern (salopp) (b) (coll.: wait) warten

■ **hang 'on** *v.i.* (a) sich festhalten (**to an** + *Dat.*) (b) (coll.: wait) warten (c) ∼ **on to** (coll.: keep) behalten

■ **hang 'out** ⟨1⟩ *v.t.* aufhängen ⟨*Wäsche*⟩ ⟨2⟩ *v.i.* (a) heraushängen (b) (coll.) (live) wohnen; (be often present) sich herumtreiben (ugs.)

■ **hang 'up** *v.t.* ⟨1⟩ aufhängen ⟨2⟩ *v.i.* (Teleph.) auflegen

hangar /'hæŋə(r)/ *n.* Hangar, *der*

'hanger *n.* Bügel, *der*

hang: ∼**glider** *n.* Hängegleiter, *der;* Drachen, *der;* ∼**glider pilot** Drachenflieger, *der*/-fliegerin, *die;* ∼**gliding** *n.* Drachenfliegen, *das*

'hanging ⟨1⟩ *n.* (execution) Hinrichtung, *die* [durch den Strang] ⟨2⟩ *adj.* ∼ **basket** Hängekorb, *der*

hang: ∼**man** /'hæŋmən/ *n., pl.* ∼**men** /'hæŋmən/ Henker, *der;* ∼**over** *n.* Kater, *der* (ugs.); ∼**-up** *n.* (coll.) Macke, *die* (ugs.)

hanker /'hæŋkə(r)/ *v.i.* ∼ **after** ein heftiges Verlangen haben nach

hanky /'hæŋkɪ/ *n.* (coll.) Taschentuch, *das*

Hanover /'hænəʊvə(r)/ *pr. n.* Hannover (*das*)

haphazard /hæp'hæzəd/ *adj.,* **hap'hazardly** *adv.* willkürlich

happen /'hæpn/ *v.i.* geschehen; ⟨*Vorhergesagtes:*⟩ eintreffen; ∼ **to sb.** jmdm. passieren; ∼ **to do** sth./**be** sb. zufällig etw. tun/jmd. sein; **as it** ∼s or **it so** ∼s **I have** ...: zufällig habe ich ...

'happening *n.* Ereignis, *das*

happily /'hæpɪlɪ/ *adv.* (a) glücklich ⟨*lächeln*⟩; vergnügt ⟨*spielen, lachen*⟩ (b) (gladly) mit Vergnügen

happiness /'hæpɪnɪs/ *n.* ▶ HAPPY A: Glück, *das;* Heiterkeit, *die;* Zufriedenheit, *die*

happy /'hæpɪ/ *adj.* (a) (joyful) glücklich; heiter ⟨*Bild, Veranlagung*⟩; erfreulich ⟨*Erinnerung, Szene*⟩; froh ⟨*Ereignis*⟩; (contented) zufrieden (b) **be** ∼ **to do** sth. (glad) etw. gern tun

happy: ∼ **'ending** *n.* Happyend, *das;* ∼**-go-'lucky** *adj.* sorglos

harass /'hærəs/ *v.t.* schikanieren

harassed /'hærəst/ *adj.* geplagt (**with** von); gequält ⟨*Blick, Ausdruck*⟩

'harassment *n.* Schikanierung, *die;* **sexual** ∼: [sexuelle] Belästigung

harbour (Brit.; Amer.: **harbor**) /'hɑːbə(r)/ ⟨1⟩ *n.* Hafen, *der;* **in** ∼: im Hafen ⟨2⟩ *v.t.* Unterschlupf gewähren (+ *Dat.*) ⟨*Verbrecher, Flüchtling*⟩; hegen (geh.) ⟨*Groll, Verdacht*⟩

hard /hɑːd/ ⟨1⟩ *adj.* (a) hart; fest ⟨*Gelee*⟩; stark ⟨*Regen*⟩; streng ⟨*Frost, Winter*⟩; gesichert ⟨*Beweis, Daten*⟩   ····≫

(b) (difficult) schwer; **this is ~ to believe** das ist kaum zu glauben; **do sth. the ~ way** es sich (*Dat.*) bei etw. unnötig schwer machen **(c)** (strenuous) hart **(d)** (vigorous) kräftig ⟨*Schlag, Stoß, Tritt*⟩ **(e)** (harsh) hart ▢2 *adv.* **(a)** (strenuously) hart ⟨*arbeiten, trainieren*⟩; fleißig ⟨*studieren, üben*⟩; genau ⟨*überlegen*⟩; gut ⟨*aufpassen, zuhören*⟩; **try ~:** sich sehr bemühen **(b)** (vigorously) heftig; fest ⟨*schlagen, drücken, klopfen*⟩ **(c)** (severely) hart; **be ~ up** knapp bei Kasse sein (ugs.); **feel ~ done by** sich schlecht behandelt fühlen

hard: ~back *n.* gebundene Ausgabe; **~board** *n.* Hartfaserplatte, *die;* **~-boiled** *adj.* **(a)** hart gekocht ⟨*Ei*⟩; **(b)** (tough) hartgesotten; **~ 'cash** *n.* **in ~** cash in bar ⟨*bezahlen*⟩; **~ copy** *n.* (Comp.) Hardcopy, *die;* **~-core** *attrib. adj.* hart ⟨*Pornographie*⟩; **~ court** *n.* (Tennis) Hartplatz, *der;* **~ 'currency** *n.* harte Währung; **~ 'disk** ▸ DISK A; **~ drug** *n.* harte Droge; **~-earned** *adj.* schwer verdient

harden /'hɑːdn/ ▢1 *v.t.* härten; (fig.) abhärten (**to** gegen) ▢2 *v.i.* hart werden; (become confirmed) sich verhärten

hardened /'hɑːdnd/ *adj.* abgehärtet (**to** gegen); hartgesotten ⟨*Verbrecher*⟩

hard: ~ 'hat *n.* Schutzhelm, *der;* **~-headed** *adj.* nüchtern; **~-hearted** *adj.* hartherzig (**towards** gegenüber); **~-'hitting** *adj.* (fig.) aggressiv ⟨*Rede, Politik, Kritik*⟩; **~ 'labour** *n.* Zwangsarbeit, *die*

hardly /'hɑːdlɪ/ *adv.* kaum; **~ anyone** *or* **anybody/anything** fast niemand/nichts; **~ ever** so gut wie nie; **~ at all** fast überhaupt nicht

'hardness *n.* Härte, *die*

hard: ~ porn (coll.)**, ~ pornography** *ns.* harte Pornographie; harte Pornos *Pl.* (ugs.); **~ 'pressed** *adj.* hart bedrängt; **be ~ pressed** große Schwierigkeiten haben; **~ sell** *n.* aggressive Verkaufsmethoden *Pl.*

'hardship *n.* **(a)** Not, *die;* Elend, *das* **(b)** (instance) Notlage, *die*

hard: ~ 'shoulder *n.* (Brit.) Standspur, *die;* **~ware** *n.* **(a)** (goods) Eisenwaren *Pl.; attrib.* Eisenwaren⟨*geschäft*⟩; **(b)** (Comp.) Hardware, *die;* **~-wearing** *adj.* strapazierfähig; **~-working** *adj.* fleißig; **~wood** *n.* Hartholz, *das*

hardy /'hɑːdɪ/ *adj.* abgehärtet; zäh ⟨*Rasse*⟩; winterhart ⟨*Pflanze*⟩

hare /heə(r)/ *n.* Hase, *der*

harem /'hɑːriːm, hɑːˈriːm/ *n.* Harem, *der*

hark /hɑːk/ *v.i.* [just] **~ at him** hör ihn dir/hört ihn euch nur an!; **~ back to** zurückkommen auf (+ *Akk.*)

harm /hɑːm/ ▢1 *n.* Schaden, *der;* **do sb. ~, do ~ to sb.** jmdm. schaden ▢2 *v.t.* etwas [zuleide] tun (+ *Dat.*); schaden (+ *Dat.*) ⟨*Beziehungen, Land, Ruf*⟩

harmful /'hɑːmfl/ *adj.* schädlich (**to** für)

'harmless *adj.* harmlos

harmonica /hɑːˈmɒnɪkə/ *n.* Mundharmonika, *die*

harmonious /hɑːˈməʊnɪəs/ *adj.* harmonisch

harmonize /'hɑːmənaɪz/ ▢1 *v.t.* aufeinander abstimmen ▢2 *v.i.* harmonieren (**with** mit)

harmony /'hɑːmənɪ/ *n.* Harmonie, *die;* **be in ~:** harmonieren

harness /'hɑːnɪs/ ▢1 *n.* Geschirr, *das* ▢2 *v.t.* anschirren; (fig.) nutzen

harp /hɑːp/ ▢1 *n.* Harfe, *die* ▢2 *v.i.* **~ on [about]** sth. immer wieder von etw. reden; (critically) auf etw. (*Dat.*) herumreiten (salopp)

harpoon /hɑːˈpuːn/ *n.* Harpune, *die*

harpsichord /'hɑːpsɪkɔːd/ *n.* Cembalo, *das*

harrowing /'hærəʊɪŋ/ *adj.* entsetzlich; grauenhaft ⟨*Anblick, Geschichte*⟩

harsh /hɑːʃ/ *adj.* **(a)** rau ⟨*Gewebe, Klima*⟩; schrill ⟨*Ton, Stimme*⟩; grell ⟨*Licht*⟩; hart ⟨*Bedingungen, Leben*⟩ **(b)** (excessively severe) [sehr] hart; [äußerst] streng ⟨*Disziplin*⟩; rücksichtslos ⟨*Tyrann, Herrscher, Politik*⟩

'harshly *adv.* [sehr] hart

harvest /'hɑːvɪst/ ▢1 *n.* Ernte, *die* ▢2 *v.t.* ernten

harvest 'festival *n.* Erntedankfest, *das*

has ▸ HAVE

has-been /'hæzbiːn/ *n.* (coll.) **be a ~:** seine besten Jahre hinter sich haben

hash /hæʃ/ *n.* **(a)** (Cookery) Haschee, *das* **(b) make a ~ of sth.** (coll.) etw. verpfuschen (ugs.)

'hash browns *n. pl.:* Bratkartoffeln mit Zwiebeln; ≈ Rösti mit Zwiebeln

hashish /'hæʃɪʃ/ *n.* Haschisch, *das*

hasn't /'hæznt/ = **has not;** ▸ HAVE

hassle /'hæsl/ (coll.) ▢1 *n.* Ärger, *der* ▢2 *v.t.* schikanieren

haste /heɪst/ *n.* Eile, *die;* (rush) Hast, *die;* **make ~:** sich beeilen

hasten /'heɪsn/ ▢1 *v.t.* beschleunigen ▢2 *v.i.* eilen

hastily /'heɪstɪlɪ/ *adv.* (hurriedly) eilig; (rashly) übereilt

hasty /'heɪstɪ/ *adj.* eilig; flüchtig ⟨*Skizze, Blick*⟩; (rash) übereilt

hat /hæt/ *n.* Hut, *der*

hatch¹ /hætʃ/ *n.* Luke, *die;* (serving ~) Durchreiche, *die*

hatch² ▢1 *v.t.* ausbrüten ▢2 *v.i.* [aus]schlüpfen

■ **hatch 'out** ▢1 *v.i.* ausschlüpfen ▢2 *v.t.* ausbrüten

'**hatchback** n. (car) Schräghecklimousine, die

hatchet /'hætʃɪt/ n. Beil, das; bury the ∼ (fig.) das Kriegsbeil begraben

hate /heɪt/ ① n. Hass, der
② v.t. hassen; I ∼ to say this (coll.) ich sage das nicht gern

hateful /'heɪtfl/ adj. abscheulich

'**hate mail** n. hasserfüllte Briefe Pl.

'**hatpin** n. Hutnadel, die

hatred /'heɪtrɪd/ n. Hass, der

hat: ∼**stand** n. Hutständer, der; ∼ **trick** n. Hattrick, der

haughty /'hɔːtɪ/ adj. hochmütig

haul /hɔːl/ ① v.i. & t. ziehen
② n. (a) Ziehen, das
(b) (catch) Fang, der; (fig.) Beute, die

haulage /'hɔːlɪdʒ/ n. Transport, der

haunch /hɔːntʃ/ n. sit on one's/its ∼es auf seinem Hinterteil sitzen

haunt /hɔːnt/ v.t. ∼ a house/castle in einem Haus/Schloss spuken; a ∼ed house ein Haus, in dem es spukt

'**haunting** adj. sehnsüchtig

have ① /hæv/ v.t., pres. he has /hæz/, p.t. & p.p. had /hæd/ haben; (obtain) bekommen; (take) nehmen; bekommen ⟨Kind⟩;
∼ breakfast/dinner/lunch frühstücken/zu Abend/zu Mittag essen; ∼ a cup of tea eine Tasse Tee trinken; ∼ sb. to stay jmdn. zu Besuch haben; you've had it now (coll.) jetzt ist es aus (ugs.); ∼ a game of football Fußball spielen
② /həv, əv, stressed hæv/ v. aux., he has /həz, əz, stressed hæz/, had /həd, əd, stressed hæd/ ∼/I had read ich habe/hatte gelesen; I ∼/I had gone ich bin/war gegangen; if I had known ...: wenn ich gewusst hätte ...; ∼ sth. made etw. machen lassen; ∼ to müssen
■ **have 'on** v.t. (a) (wear) tragen
(b) (Brit. coll.: deceive) ∼ sb. on jmdn. auf den Arm nehmen (ugs.)
■ **have 'out** v.t. (a) ∼ a tooth/one's tonsils out sich (Dat.) einen Zahn ziehen lassen/ sich (Dat.) die Mandeln herausnehmen lassen
(b) ∼ it out with sb. mit jmdm. offen sprechen

haven /'heɪvn/ n. geschützte Anlegestelle, die; (fig.) Zufluchtsort, der

haven't /'hævnt/ = have not; ▶ HAVE

haversack /'hævəsæk/ n. Brotbeutel, der

havoc /'hævək/ n. (a) (devastation) Verwüstungen Pl.; cause or wreak ∼: Verwüstungen anrichten
(b) (confusion) Chaos; play ∼ with sth. etw. völlig durcheinander bringen

hawk¹ /hɔːk/ n. Falke, der

hawk² v.t. hausieren mit

'**hawker** n. Hausierer, der/Hausiererin, die

hawthorn /'hɔːθɔːn/ n. (Bot.) (white) Weißdorn, der; (red) Rotdorn, der

hay /heɪ/ n. Heu, das

hay: ∼ **fever** n. Heuschnupfen, der; ∼**making** n. Heuernte, die; ∼**stack** n. Heuschober, der (südd.); Heudieme, die (nordd.); ∼**wire** adj. (coll.) go ∼**wire** ⟨Instrument:⟩ verrückt spielen (ugs.)

hazard /'hæzəd/ ① n. Gefahr, die
② v.t. ∼ a guess es mit Raten probieren

'**hazard lights** n. pl. Warnblinkanlage, die

hazardous /'hæzədəs/ adj. gefährlich; ∼ waste Sondermüll, der

hazard 'warning lights ▶ HAZARD LIGHTS

haze /heɪz/ n. Dunst[schleier], der

hazel /'heɪzl/ adj. haselnussbraun

hazelnut /'heɪzlnʌt/ n. Haselnuss, die

hazy /'heɪzɪ/ adj. dunstig; (fig.) vage

HDTV abbr. = **high-definition television** HDTV

he /hɪ, stressed hiː/ pron. er

head /hed/ ① n. (a) Kopf, der; ∼ first mit dem Kopf voran; ∼ over heels kopfüber; keep/lose one's ∼: einen klaren Kopf behalten/den Kopf verlieren; in one's ∼: im Kopf; enter sb.'s ∼: jmdm. in den Sinn kommen; use your ∼: gebrauch deinen Verstand; a or per ∼: pro Kopf
(b) in pl. (on coin) ∼s Kopf; ∼s or tails? Kopf oder Zahl?
(c) (leader) Leiter, der/Leiterin, die
(d) (on beer) Blume, die
② attrib. adj. ∼ waiter Oberkellner, der; ∼ office Hauptverwaltung, die; ∼ boy/girl ≈ Schulsprecher, der/-sprecherin, die (vom Lehrkörper eingesetzt)
③ v.t. (a) (stand at top of) anführen ⟨Liste⟩; (lead) leiten; führen ⟨Bewegung⟩
(b) (Football) köpfen
④ v.i. steuern; ∼ for London ⟨Flugzeug, Schiff:⟩ Kurs auf London nehmen; ⟨Auto:⟩ in Richtung London fahren; you're ∼ing for trouble du wirst Ärger bekommen

head: ∼**ache** n. Kopfschmerzen Pl.; ∼**band** n. Stirnband, das; ∼**board** n. Kopfende, das; ∼ **count** n. Kopfzahl, die

'**header** n. (Footb.) Kopfball, der

'**headgear** n. Kopfbedeckung, die

'**heading** n. Überschrift, die

head: ∼**lamp** n. Scheinwerfer, der; ∼**land** n. Landspitze, die; ∼**light** n. Scheinwerfer, der; ∼**line** n. Schlagzeile, die; be ∼line news, make [the] ∼lines, hit the ∼lines Schlagzeilen machen; ∼**long** adv. kopfüber; ∼'**master** n. Schulleiter, der; ∼'**mistress** n. Schulleiterin, die; ∼ '**office** n. Hauptsitz, der; ∼**-on** ① /'··/ adj. frontal; Frontal⟨zusammenstoß⟩; ② /·'·/ adv. frontal; ∼**phones** n. pl. Kopfhörer, der; ∼'**quarters** n. sing. or pl. Hauptquartier, das; ∼**rest** n. Kopfstütze, die; ∼**room** n. [lichte] Höhe, die; ∼**scarf** n. Kopftuch, das; ∼**set** n. Kopfhörer, der; ∼**stone** n. (a) (gravestone) Grabstein, der; (b) (of building) Grundstein, der; (fig.) Grundpfeiler, der; ∼**strong** adj.   ····⟶

eigensinnig; ~ **'teacher** ▶ ~MASTER;
~MISTRESS; ~**way** n. make ~way
Fortschritte machen; ~ **wind** n.
Gegenwind, der

heady /'hedı/ adj. berauschend

heal /hiːl/ [1] v.t. heilen
[2] v.i. ~ [up] [ver]heilen

healer /'hiːlə(r)/ n. (person) Heilkundige,
der/die

health /helθ/ n. Gesundheit, die; in good/
very good ~: bei guter/bester Gesundheit;
good or your ~! auf deine Gesundheit!

health: ~ **care** n. Gesundheitsfürsorge,
die; ~ care worker im Gesundheitswesen
Beschäftigte, der/die; inadequate ~ care
unzureichende medizinische Versorgung;
~ **centre** n. Poliklinik, die;
~ **certificate** n. Gesundheitszeugnis, das;
~ **check** n. Gesundheitsuntersuchung, die;
~ **farm** n. Gesundheitsfarm, die (ugs.);
~ **food** n. Reformhauskost, die; ~ food
shop Reformhaus, das; ~ **hazard** n.
Gesundheitsrisiko, das

healthily /'helθɪlı/ adv. gesund

health: ~ **insurance** n.
Krankenversicherung, die; ~ **resort** n.
Kurort, der; ~ **service** n.
Gesundheitsdienst, der; ~ **visitor** n.
Krankenschwester/-pfleger im Sozialdienst;
~ **warning** n. Warnhinweis, der; Hinweis
auf die Gesundheitsgefährdung

healthy /'helθı/ adj. gesund

heap /hiːp/ [1] n. Haufen, der; ~s of (coll.)
jede Menge (ugs.)
[2] v.t. aufhäufen

hear /hɪə(r)/ [1] v.t., heard /hɜːd/ (a) hören
(b) (understand) verstehen
[2] v.i., heard: ~ about sb./sth. von jmdm./
etw. [etwas] hören; he wouldn't ~ of it er
wollte nichts davon hören
[3] int. H~! H~! bravo!; richtig!
■ **hear 'out** v.t. ausreden lassen

heard ▶ HEAR 1, 2

'hearing n. Gehör, das; be hard of ~:
schwerhörig sein

'hearing aid n. Hörgerät, das

hearsay /'hɪəseɪ/ n. Gerücht, das; it's only
~: es ist nur ein Gerücht

hearse /hɜːs/ n. Leichenwagen, der

heart /hɑːt/ n. (also Cards) Herz, das; by ~:
auswendig; at ~: im Grunde seines/ihres
Herzens; take/lose ~: Mut schöpfen/
verlieren; my ~ sank mein Mut sank; the
~ of the matter der wahre Kern der Sache;
see also CLUB 1C

heart: ~**ache** n. [seelische] Qual;
~ **attack** n. Herzanfall, der; (fatal)
Herzschlag, der; ~**beat** n. Herzschlag, der;
~**breaking** adj. herzzerreißend;
~**broken** adj. she was ~broken ihr Herz
war gebrochen; ~**burn** n. Sodbrennen, das;
~ **disease** n. Herzkrankheiten Pl.

hearten /'hɑːtn/ v.t. ermutigen

'heartening adj. ermutigend

heart: ~ **failure** n. Herzversagen, das;
~**felt** adj. tief empfunden ⟨Beileid⟩;
aufrichtig ⟨Dankbarkeit⟩

hearth /hɑːθ/ n.: Platz vor dem Kamin

'hearthrug n. Kaminvorleger, der

heartily /'hɑːtɪlı/ adv. von Herzen; eat ~:
tüchtig essen

'heartless adj. herzlos

heart: ~ **rate** n. Herzfrequenz, die;
~**-shaped** adj. herzförmig; ~**-throb** n.
Idol, das; ~ **transplant** n.
Herztransplantation, die (fachspr.);
~**-warming** adj. herzerfreuend

hearty /'hɑːtı/ adj. herzlich; ungeteilt
⟨Zustimmung⟩; herzhaft ⟨Mahlzeit⟩

heat /hiːt/ [1] n. (a) (hotness) Hitze, die
(b) (Phys.) Wärme, die
(c) (Sport) Vorlauf, der
[2] v.t. heizen
■ **heat 'up** v.t. heiß machen

'heated adj. (angry) hitzig

'heater n. Ofen, der; (for water) Boiler, der

heath /hiːθ/ n. Heide, die

heathen /'hiːðn/ [1] adj. heidnisch
[2] n. Heide, der/Heidin, die

heather /'heðə(r)/ n. Heidekraut, das

'heating n. Heizung, die

heat: ~**proof** adj. feuerfest; ~ **rash** n.
Hitzebläschen Pl.; ~**-resistant** adj.
hitzebeständig; ~**-stroke** n. Hitzschlag, der;
~ **treatment** n. (Med.) Wärmebehandlung,
die; ~**wave** n. Hitzewelle, die

heave /hiːv/ [1] v.t. (a) heben
(b) (coll.: throw) schmeißen (ugs.)
(c) ~ a sigh aufseufzen
[2] v.i. (pull) ziehen
[3] n. Zug, der

heaven /'hevn/ n. Himmel, der; in ~: im
Himmel; for H~'s sake! um Gottes willen!

'heavenly adj. himmlisch

heavily /'hevɪlı/ adj. schwer; (to a great
extent) stark; schwer ⟨bewaffnet⟩; tief
⟨schlafen⟩; dicht ⟨bevölkert⟩; smoke/drink ~:
ein starker Raucher/Trinker sein; it rained/
snowed ~: es regnete/schneite stark

heavy /'hevı/ adj. schwer; unmäßig
⟨Trinken, Rauchen⟩; a ~ smoker/drinker ein
starker Raucher/Trinker; be a ~ sleeper
sehr fest schlafen

heavy: ~**-duty** adj. strapazierfähig
⟨Kleidung, Material⟩; schwer ⟨Werkzeug,
Maschine⟩; ~ **'goods vehicle** n. (Brit.)
Schwerlastwagen, der; ~**-'handed** adj.
(clumsy) ungeschickt ⟨Person⟩; ~ **'industry**
n. Schwerindustrie, die; ~ **'metal** n. (a)
Schwermetall, das; (b) (Mus.) Heavy metal,
das; ~**weight** n. Schwergewicht, das

Hebrew /'hiːbruː/ [1] adj. hebräisch
[2] n. (language) Hebräisch, das

heckle /'hekl/ v.t. durch Zwischenrufe
unterbrechen

heckler /'heklə(r)/ *n.* Zwischenrufer, *der*/ Zwischenruferin, *die*

hectic /'hektɪk/ *adj.* hektisch

he'd /hɪd, *stressed* hi:d/ **(a)** = **he had**;
(b) = **he would**

hedge /hedʒ/ ① *n.* Hecke, *die*
② *v.t.* ~ one's bets (fig.) nicht alles auf eine Karte setzen
③ *v.i.* sich nicht festlegen

'hedge clippers *n. pl.* Heckenschere, *die*

hedgehog /'hedʒhɒg/ *n.* Igel, *der*

'hedgerow *n.* Hecke, *die* [als Feldbegrenzung]

hedonism /'hi:dənɪzm/ *n.* Hedonismus, *der*

hedonist /'hi:dənɪst/ *n.* Hedonist, *der*/ Hedonistin, *die*

heed /hi:d/ ① *v.t.* beachten; beherzigen ⟨*Rat, Lektion*⟩; ~ **the danger/risk** sich (*Dat.*) der Gefahr/des Risikos bewusst sein
② *n.* **give** *or* **pay** ~ **to, take** ~ **of** Beachtung schenken (+ *Dat.*)

'heedless *adj.* unachtsam; **be** ~ **of sth.** auf etw. (*Akk.*) nicht achten

heel /hi:l/ *n.* Ferse, *die;* (of shoe) Absatz, *der;* **Achilles'** ~ (fig.) Achillesferse, *die;* **down at** ~ (fig.) heruntergekommen; **take to one's** ~**s** Fersengeld geben (ugs.)

hefty /'heftɪ/ *adj.* kräftig; (heavy) schwer

height /haɪt/ *n.* **(a)** Höhe, *die;* (of person, animal, building) Größe, *die*
(b) (fig.: highest point) Höhepunkt, *der*

heighten /'haɪtn/ *v.t.* aufstocken; (fig.) verstärken

heir /eə(r)/ *n.* Erbe, *der*/Erbin, *die*

heiress /'eərɪs/ *n.* Erbin, *die*

heirloom /'eəlu:m/ *n.* Erbstück, *das*

held ▶ HOLD² 1, 2

helicopter /'helɪkɒptə(r)/ *n.* Hubschrauber, *der*

heliport /'helɪpɔ:t/ *n.* Heliport, *der*

helium /'hi:lɪəm/ *n.* Helium, *das*

hell /hel/ *n.* **(a)** Hölle, *die*
(b) (coll.) **[oh]** ~! verdammter Mist! (ugs.); **what the** ~! ach, zum Teufel! (ugs.); **run like** ~: wie der Teufel rennen (ugs.)

he'll /hɪl, *stressed* hi:l/ = **he will**

hello /hə'ləʊ, he'ləʊ/ *int.* (greeting) hallo; (surprise) holla

hell's 'angel *n.* Rocker, *der*

helm /helm/ *n.* (Naut.) Ruder, *das*

helmet /'helmɪt/ *n.* Helm, *der*

help /help/ ① *v.t.* **(a)** ~ **sb.** [**to do sth.**] jmdm. helfen[, etw. zu tun]; **can I** ~ **you?** (in shop) was möchten Sie bitte?
(b) (serve) ~ **oneself** sich bedienen; ~ **oneself to sth.** sich (*Dat.*) etw. nehmen; (coll.: steal) etw. mitgehen lassen (ugs.)
(c) (avoid) **if I/you can** ~ **it** wenn es irgend zu vermeiden ist; (remedy) **I can't** ~ **it** ich kann nichts dafür (ugs.); **it can't be** ~**ed** es lässt sich nicht ändern
(d) (refrain from) **I can't** ~ **thinking** *or* **can't**

~ **but think that** …: ich kann mir nicht helfen, ich glaube, …; **I can't** ~ **laughing** ich muss einfach lachen
② *n.* Hilfe, *die;* **with the** ~ **of** …: mit Hilfe … (+ *Gen.*); **be of [some]/no/much** ~ **to sb.** jmdm. eine gewisse/keine/eine große Hilfe sein

■ **help 'out** ① *v.i.* aushelfen
② *v.t.* ~ **sb. out** jmdm. helfen

'help desk *n.* Help Desk, *das* (fachspr.); *Auskunftsstelle für Computerbenutzer*

'helper *n.* Helfer, *der*/Helferin, *die*

helpful /'helpfl/ *adj.* (willing) hilfsbereit; (useful) hilfreich; nützlich

'helping ① *adj.* **lend [sb.] a** ~ **hand [with sth.]** (fig.) [jmdm.] [bei etw.] helfen
② *n.* Portion, *die*

'helpless *adj.,* **'helplessly** *adv.* hilflos

'helpline *n.* Hotline, *die*

helter-skelter /heltə'skeltə(r)/ *n.* [spiralförmige] Rutschbahn

hem /hem/ ① *n.* Saum, *der*
② *v.t.,* **-mm-** säumen

■ **hem 'in** *v.t.* einschließen; **feel** ~**med in** sich eingeengt fühlen

hemisphere /'hemɪsfɪə(r)/ *n.* Halbkugel, *die*

'hemline *n.* Saum, *der*

hemo- (*Amer.*) ▶ HAEMO-

hemp /hemp/ *n.* Hanf, *der*

hen /hen/ *n.* Huhn, *das;* Henne, *die*

hence /hens/ *adv.* (therefore) daher

hence'forth *adv.* von nun an

henchman /'hentʃmən/ *n., pl.* **henchmen** /'hentʃmən/ Handlanger, *der*

hen: ~ **party** *n.* (coll.) [Damen]kränzchen, *das;* ~**pecked** /'henpekt/ *adj.* **a** ~ **husband** ein Pantoffelheld, *der* (ugs.)

hepatitis /hepə'taɪtɪs/ *n.* (Med.) Leberentzündung, *die*

her¹ /hə(r), *stressed* hɜ:(r)/ *pron.* sie; *as indirect object* ihr; **it was** ~: sie wars

her² *poss. pron. attr.* ihr

herald /'herəld/ ① *n.* Herold, *der*
② *v.t.* ankündigen

heraldic /he'rældɪk/ *adj.* heraldisch

heraldry /'herəldrɪ/ *n.* Heraldik, *die*

herb /hɜ:b/ *n.* Kraut, *das*

herbaceous /hɜ:'beɪʃəs/ *adj.* krautartig; ~ **border** Staudenrabatte, *die*

herbal /'hɜ:bl/ *attrib. adj.* Kräuter-

herbivore /'hɜ:bɪvɔ:(r)/ *n.* Pflanzenfresser, *der*

'herb tea *n.* Kräuteraufguss, *der*

herd /hɜ:d/ ① *n.* Herde, *die;* (of wild animals) Rudel, *das*
② *v.t.* **(a)** treiben; ~ **people together** Menschen zusammenpferchen
(b) (tend) hüten

here /hɪə(r)/ ① *adv.* **(a)** (in or at this place) hier; **down/in/up** ~: hier unten/drin/oben; ~ **you are** (coll.: giving sth.) hier

⋯⊹

(b) (to this place) hierher; in[to] ~: hierherein; come/bring ~: hierher kommen/bringen 2 *int.* (attracting attention) he

here'by *adv.* (formal) hiermit

hereditary /hɪˈredɪtərɪ/ *adj.* **(a)** erblich ⟨*Titel, Amt*⟩ **(b)** (Biol.) angeboren

heresy /ˈherɪsɪ/ *n.* Ketzerei, *die*

heretic /ˈherɪtɪk/ *n.* Ketzer, *der*/Ketzerin, *die*

heretical /hɪˈretɪkl/ *adj.* ketzerisch

here'with *adv.* in der Anlage

heritage /ˈherɪtɪdʒ/ *n.* Erbe, *das*

hermetic /hɜːˈmetɪk/ *adj.* luftdicht

hermetically /hɜːˈmetɪkəlɪ/ *adv.* hermetisch

hermit /ˈhɜːmɪt/ *n.* Einsiedler, *der*/ Einsiedlerin, *die*

hernia /ˈhɜːnɪə/ *n.* Bruch, *der*

hero /ˈhɪərəʊ/ *n.*, *pl.* ~es Held, *der*

heroic /hɪˈrəʊɪk/ *adj.* heldenhaft

heroin /ˈherəʊɪn/ *n.* Heroin, *das*

heroine /ˈherəʊɪn/ *n.* Heldin, *die*

heroism /ˈherəʊɪzm/ *n.* Heldentum, *das*

heron /ˈhern/ *n.* Reiher, *der*

herpes /ˈhɜːpiːz/ *n.* (Med.) Herpes, *der*

herring /ˈherɪŋ/ *n.* Hering, *der*

hers /hɜːz/ *poss. pron. pred.* ihrer/ihre/ihres; **the book is ~:** das Buch gehört ihr

her'self *pron.* **(a)** *emphat.* selbst; [all] by ~: [ganz] allein[e] **(b)** *refl.* sich; allein[e] ⟨*tun, wählen*⟩; **younger than/as heavy as ~:** jünger als/so schwer wie sie selbst

he's /hɪz, *stressed* hiːz/ **(a)** = he is; **(b)** = he has

hesitant /ˈhezɪtənt/ *adj.* zögernd ⟨*Reaktion*⟩; stockend ⟨*Rede*⟩

hesitate /ˈhezɪteɪt/ *v.i.* zögern; (falter) ins Stocken geraten; ~ **to do sth.** Bedenken haben, etw. zu tun

hesitation /hezɪˈteɪʃn/ *n.* **(a)** (indecision) Unentschlossenheit, *die;* **without ~:** ohne zu zögern **(b)** (instance of faltering) Unsicherheit, *die* **(c)** (reluctance) Bedenken *Pl.*

hetero /ˈhetərəʊ/ *n.* (coll.) *n.* Hetero *der*/*die*

heterosexual /hetərəʊˈseksjʊəl/ 1 *adj.* heterosexuell 2 *n.* Heterosexuelle, *der*/*die*

het up /het ˈʌp/ *adj.* aufgeregt

hew /hjuː/ *v.t., p.p.* **hewn** /hjuːn/ *or* **hewed** /hjuːd/ hacken ⟨*Holz*⟩; losschlagen ⟨*Kohle, Gestein*⟩

hewn ▶ HEW

hexagon /ˈheksəgən/ *n.* Sechseck, *das*

hey /heɪ/ *int.* he; ~ **presto!** simsalabim!

heyday /ˈheɪdeɪ/ *n.* Blütezeit, *die*

HGV *abbr.* (Brit.) = **heavy goods vehicle**

hi /haɪ/ *int.* hallo (ugs.)

hiatus /haɪˈeɪtəs/ *n.* Unterbrechung, *die*

hibernate /ˈhaɪbəneɪt/ *v.i.* Winterschlaf halten

hibernation /haɪbəˈneɪʃn/ *n.* Winterschlaf, *der*

hiccup /ˈhɪkʌp/ 1 *n.* **(a)** Schluckauf, *der;* **have/get [the] ~s** den Schluckauf haben/ bekommen **(b)** (fig.: stoppage) Störung, *die* 2 *v.i.* schlucksen (ugs.)

hid ▶ HIDE¹

hidden ▶ HIDE¹

hide¹ /haɪd/ 1 *v.t.,* **hid** /hɪd/, **hidden** /ˈhɪdn/ **(a)** verstecken ⟨*Gegenstand, Person usw.*⟩ (from vor + *Dat.*); verbergen ⟨*Gefühle, Sinn usw.*⟩ (from vor + *Dat.*); verheimlichen ⟨*Tatsache, Absicht usw.*⟩ (from *Dat.*) **(b)** (obscure) verdecken 2 *v.i.,* **hid**, **hidden** sich verstecken (from vor + *Dat.*)

hide² *n.* Haut, *die;* (of furry animal) Fell, *das;* (dressed) Leder, *das*

hide-and-'seek *n.* Versteckspiel, *das;* **play ~:** Verstecken spielen

hideous /ˈhɪdɪəs/ *adj.* scheußlich

'hideout *n.* Versteck, *das*

hiding¹ /ˈhaɪdɪŋ/ *n.* **go into ~:** sich verstecken; (to avoid police, public attention) untertauchen; **be in ~:** sich versteckt halten; (to avoid police, public attention) untergetaucht sein

hiding² *n.* (coll.: beating) Tracht Prügel; **give sb. a [good] ~:** jmdm. eine [ordentliche] Tracht Prügel verpassen (ugs.)

'hiding place *n.* Versteck, *das*

hierarchic /haɪəˈrɑːkɪk/, **hierarchical** /haɪəˈrɑːkɪkl/ *adj.* hierarchisch

hierarchy /ˈhaɪərɑːkɪ/ *n.* Hierarchie, *die*

hi-fi /ˈhaɪfaɪ/ (coll.) 1 *adj.* Hi-Fi- 2 *n.* Hi-Fi-Anlage, *die*

high /haɪ/ 1 *adj.* **(a)** hoch; groß ⟨*Höhe*⟩; stark ⟨*Wind*⟩ **(b)** (coll.: on a drug) high (ugs.) **(c)** it's ~ **time you left** es ist höchste Zeit, dass du gehst 2 *adv.* hoch; **search** *or* **look ~ and low** überall suchen 3 *n.* **(a)** (~est level/figure) Höchststand, *der* **(b)** (Meteorol.) Hoch, *das* **(c)** (coll.: drug-induced euphoria) Rausch[zustand], *der;* **give sb. a ~** ⟨*Droge:*⟩ jmdn. high machen (ugs.)

high: ~**brow** 1 *n.* Intellektuelle, *der*/*die;* 2 *adj.* intellektuell ⟨*Person, Gerede usw.*⟩; hochgestochen (abwertend) ⟨*Person, Musik, Literatur usw.*⟩; ~ **chair** *n.* Hochstuhl, *der;* ~**definition 'television** *n.* hoch auflösendes Fernsehen

higher edu'cation *n.* Hochschulbildung, *die*

high: ~ **fi'nance** *n.* Hochfinanz, *die;* ~**-'flier**, ~**-'flyer** *n.* (successful person) Senkrechtstarter, *der;* (person with great

potential) Hochbegabte, *der/die;*
~ **'frequency** *n.* Hochfrequenz, *die;*
~-**'handed** *adj.* selbstherrlich;
~-**heeled** /haɪ'hiːld/ *adj.* ⟨*Schuhe*⟩ mit hohen Absätzen; ~-**income** *adj.* einkommensstark; ~ **jump** *n.* Hochsprung, *der;* ~**land** *n.* Hochland, *das;*
~**light** ① *n.* (a) Höhepunkt, *der;* (b) (bright area) Licht, *das;* ② *v.t.* ~lighted ein Schlaglicht werfen auf (+ *Akk.*) ⟨*Probleme usw.*⟩

'highly *adv.* sehr; hoch ⟨*angesehen, bezahlt*⟩; hoch⟨*interessant, -gebildet*⟩; leicht ⟨*entzündlich*⟩; stark ⟨*gewürzt*⟩; **think ~ of sb./sth.** eine hohe Meinung von jmdm./etw. haben; **speak ~ of sb./sth.** jmdn./etw. sehr loben

highly-strung /'haɪlɪstrʌŋ/ *adj.* übererregbar

Highness /'haɪnɪs/ *n.* **His/her** *etc.* ~: Seine/Ihre *usw.* Hoheit

high: ~-**pitched** /'haɪpɪtʃt/ *adj.* hoch ⟨*Ton, Stimme*⟩; ~-**powered** /'haɪpaʊəd/ *adj.* (forceful) dynamisch ⟨*Geschäftsmann*⟩;
~ **'pressure** *n.* (a) (Meteorol.) Hochdruck, *der;* (b) (Mech. Engin.) Überdruck, *der;*
~-**rise** *adj.* ~-rise building Hochhaus, *das;* ~-rise block of flats/office block Wohn-/Bürohochhaus, *das;* ~-**risk** *attrib. adj.* risikoreich; Risiko⟨*gruppe, -sportart*⟩; **a** ~-risk investment eine Geldanlage mit hohem Risiko; ~ **school** *n.* ≈ Oberschule, *die;* **'seas** *n. pl.* **the** ~ **seas** die hohe See; ~ **season** *n.* Hochsaison, *die;*
~-**speed** *adj.* ~-speed train Hochgeschwindigkeitszug, *der;* ~ **street** *n.* Hauptstraße, *die;* ~ **'tech** (coll.)
▶ ~ TECHNOLOGY; ~-**tech** *adj.* (coll.) Hightech-; ~ **tech'nology** *n.* Spitzentechnologie, *die;* Hochtechnologie, *die;* ~-**'voltage** *adj.* Hochspannungs-;
~**way** *n.* öffentliche Straße

hijack /'haɪdʒæk/ *v.t.* entführen
'hijacker *n.* Entführer, *der;* (of aircraft) Hijacker, *der*

hike /haɪk/ *n.* Wanderung, *die*
'hiker *n.* Wanderer, *der*/Wanderin, *die*

hilarious /hɪ'leərɪəs/ *adj.* urkomisch

hill /hɪl/ *n.* Hügel, *der;* (higher) Berg, *der;* (slope) Hang, *der*

hill: ~**billy** /'hɪlbɪlɪ/ *n.* (Amer.) Hinterwäldler, *der*/Hinterwäldlerin, *die;*
~**side** *n.* Hang, *der;* ~**top** *n.* [Berg]gipfel, *der*

'hilly *adj.* hüg[e]lig

hilt /hɪlt/ *n.* Griff, *der;* **[up] to the** ~ (fig.) voll und ganz

him /ɪm, *stressed* hɪm/ *pron.* ihn; *as indirect object* ihm; **it was** ~: er war's

Himalayas /hɪmə'leɪəz/ *pr. n. pl.* Himalaya, *der*

him'self *pron.* (a) *emphat.* selbst
(b) *refl.* sich. See *also* HERSELF

hind /haɪnd/ *adj.* hinter…; ~ **legs** Hinterbeine *Pl.*

hinder /'hɪndə(r)/ *v.t.* (impede) behindern; (delay) verzögern ⟨*Vollendung einer Arbeit, Vorgang*⟩; aufhalten ⟨*Person*⟩; ~ **sb. from doing sth.** jmdn. daran hindern, etw. zu tun

'hindquarters *n. pl.* Hinterteil, *das*

hindrance /'hɪndrəns/ *n.* Hindernis, *das* (**to** für)

'hindsight *n.* **with [the benefit of]** ~: im Nachhinein

Hindu /'hɪnduː, hɪn'duː/ ① *n.* Hindu, *der*
② *adj.* hinduistisch; Hindu⟨*gott, -tempel*⟩

Hinduism /'hɪnduːɪzm/ *n.* Hinduismus, *der*

hinge /hɪndʒ/ ① *n.* Scharnier, *das*
② *v.t.* mit Scharnieren versehen
③ *v.i.* (depend) abhängen ([up]on von)

hint /hɪnt/ ① *n.* (a) (suggestion) Wink, *der*
(b) (slight trace) Spur, *die* (of von); **the** ~/**no** ~ **of a smile** der Anflug/nicht die Spur eines Lächelns
(c) (information) Tipp, *der* (on für)
② *v.i.* ~ **at** andeuten

hip /hɪp/ *n.* Hüfte, *die*

hip: ~ **bone** *n.* Hüftbein, *das;* ~ **flask** *n.* Taschenflasche, *die;* ~ **joint** *n.* Hüftgelenk, *das*

hippie /'hɪpɪ/ *n.* (coll.) Hippie, *der*

hippopotamus /hɪpə'pɒtəməs/ *n.* Nilpferd, *das*

hippy ▶ HIPPIE

hire /haɪə(r)/ ① *n.* Mieten, *das;* **be on** ~ [**to sb.**] [an jmdn.] vermietet sein; **for** ~: zu vermieten
② *v.t.* (a) (employ) anwerben; engagieren ⟨*Anwalt, Berater usw.*⟩
(b) (obtain use of) mieten; ~ **sth. from sb.** etw. bei jmdm. mieten
(c) (grant use of) ~ [**out**] vermieten; ~ **sth.** [**out**] **to sb.** etw. jmdm. *od.* an jmdn. vermieten

hire: ~ **car** *n.* Mietwagen, *der*; ~ **'purchase** *n.* (Brit.) Ratenkauf, *der; attrib.* Raten-; **pay for/buy sth. on** ~ **purchase** etw. in Raten bezahlen/auf Raten kaufen

his /ɪz, *stressed* hɪz/ *poss. pron.* (a) *attrib.* sein
(b) *pred.* seiner/seine/sein[e]s; *see also* HERS

hiss /hɪs/ ① *n.* Zischen, *das*
② *v.i.* zischen

historian /hɪ'stɔːrɪən/ *n.* Historiker, *der*/Historikerin, *die*

historic /hɪ'stɒrɪk/ *adj.* historisch

historical /hɪ'stɒrɪkl/ *adj.* historisch; geschichtlich ⟨*Belege, Hintergrund*⟩

history /'hɪstərɪ/ *n.* Geschichte, *die*

hit /hɪt/ ① *v.t.,* -tt-, hit schlagen; (with missile) treffen; ⟨*Geschoss, Ball usw.*⟩ treffen; ⟨*Fahrzeug:*⟩ prallen gegen; ⟨*Schiff:*⟩ laufen gegen; ~ **one's head on sth.** mit dem Kopf gegen etw. stoßen; ~ **it off with sb.** gut mit jmdm. auskommen
② *v.i.,* -tt-, hit schlagen

⋯⟡

③ *n.* (a) (blow) Schlag, *der;* (shot or bomb striking target) Treffer, *der*
(b) (success) Erfolg, *der;* (in entertainment) Schlager, *der;* Hit, *der* (ugs.)
■ **hit 'back** *v.t. & i.* zurückschlagen
■ **'hit [up]on** *v.t.* kommen auf (+ *Akk.*) ⟨*Idee*⟩; finden ⟨*richtige Antwort, Methode*⟩
hit-and-'run *adj.* unfallflüchtig ⟨*Fahrer*⟩; ~ **accident** Unfall mit Fahrerflucht
hitch /hɪtʃ/ ① *v.t.* (a) binden ⟨*Seil*⟩ (round um + *Akk.*); [an]koppeln ⟨*Anhänger usw.*⟩ (to an + *Akk.*); spannen ⟨*Zugtier usw.*⟩ (to vor + *Akk.*)
(b) ~ a lift *or* ride (coll.) per Anhalter fahren
② *n.* (problem) Problem, *das*
■ **hitch 'up** *v.t.* hochheben ⟨*Rock*⟩
'hitch-hike *v.i.* per Anhalter fahren
'hitch-hiker *n.* Anhalter, *der*/Anhalterin, *die*
hit: ~ **man** *n.* (Amer.) Killer, *der* (salopp); ~**-or-'miss** *adj.* (coll.: random) unsicher, unzuverlässig ⟨*Methode*⟩; ~ **parade** *n.* Hitparade, *die;* ~ **'record** *n.* Hit, *der* (ugs.)
HIV *abbr.* = **human immunodeficiency virus** HIV; ~**-positive/-negative** HIV-positiv/-negativ
hive /haɪv/ *n.* [Bienen]stock, *der*
HMS *abbr.* (Brit.) = **Her/His Majesty's Ship** H.M.S.
hoard /hɔːd/ ① *n.* Vorrat, *der*
② *v.t.* ~ [up] horten; hamstern ⟨*Lebensmittel*⟩
hoarding /'hɔːdɪŋ/ *n.* (fence) Bauzaun, *der;* (Brit.: for advertisements) Reklamewand, *die*
hoar frost /'hɔːfrɒst/ *n.* [Rau]reif, *der*
hoarse /hɔːs/ *adj.* heiser
hoax /həʊks/ ① *v.t.* anführen (ugs.); foppen
② *n.* (deception) Schwindel, *der;* (practical joke) Streich, *der;* (false alarm) blinder Alarm
hob /hɒb/ *n.* [Koch]platte, *die*
hobble /'hɒbl/ *v.i.* ~ [about] [herum]humpeln
hobby /'hɒbɪ/ *n.* Hobby, *das*
'hobby horse *n.* Steckenpferd, *das*
hobnailed /'hɒbneɪld/ *adj.* Nagel⟨*schuh, -stiefel*⟩
hobo /'həʊbəʊ/ *n., pl.* -es (Amer.) Landstreicher, *der*/-streicherin, *die*
hockey /'hɒkɪ/ *n.* Hockey, *das*
'hockey stick *n.* Hockeyschläger, *der*
hoe /həʊ/ ① *n.* Hacke, *die*
② *v.t. & i.* hacken
hog /hɒg/ ① *n.* [Mast]schwein, *das*
② *v.t.*, -gg- (coll.) mit Beschlag belegen
hoist /hɔɪst/ ① *v.t.* hochziehen, hissen ⟨*Flagge usw.*⟩; hieven ⟨*Last*⟩; setzen ⟨*Segel*⟩
② *n.* [Lasten]aufzug, *der*
hold¹ /həʊld/ *n.* (of ship) Laderaum, *der;* (of aircraft) Frachtraum, *der*
hold² ① *v.t.*, held /held/ (a) halten; (carry)

tragen; (keep fast) festhalten; ~ **the door open for sb.** jmdm. die Tür aufhalten; ~ **sth. in place** etw. halten
(b) (contain) enthalten; (be able to contain) fassen ⟨*Liter, Personen usw.*⟩
(c) (possess) besitzen; haben
(d) (keep possession of) halten ⟨*Stützpunkt, Stadt, Stellung*⟩; ~ **the line** (Teleph.) am Apparat bleiben; ~ **one's own** sich behaupten
(e) (cause to take place) stattfinden lassen; abhalten ⟨*Veranstaltung, Konferenz, Gottesdienst, Sitzung*⟩; veranstalten ⟨*Festival, Auktion*⟩; austragen ⟨*Meisterschaften*⟩; führen ⟨*Unterhaltung, Gespräch*⟩; durchführen ⟨*Untersuchung*⟩; halten ⟨*Vortrag, Rede*⟩
(f) (think, believe) ~ **a view** *or* **an opinion** eine Ansicht haben (on über + *Akk.*); ~ **that ...:** der Ansicht sein, dass ...; ~ **oneself responsible for sth.** sich für etw. verantwortlich fühlen; ~ **sth. against sb.** jmdm. etw. vorwerfen
② *v.i.*, held halten; ⟨*Wetter:*⟩ sich halten
③ *n.* (a) (grasp) Griff, *der;* **grab** *or* **seize** ~ **of sth.** etw. ergreifen; **get** *or* **lay** *or* **take** ~ **of sth.** etw. fassen *od.* packen; **keep** ~ **of sth.** etw. festhalten; **get** ~ **of sth.** (fig.) etw. auftreiben; **get** ~ **of sb.** (fig.) jmdn. erreichen
(b) (influence) Einfluss, *der* (on, over auf + *Akk.*)
(c) (Sport) Griff, *der*
■ **hold 'back** ① *v.t.* zurückhalten
② *v.i.* zögern
■ **hold 'on** ① *v.t.* [fest]halten
② *v.i.* (a) sich festhalten; ~ **on to** sich festhalten an (+ *Dat.*); (keep) behalten
(b) (coll.: wait) warten
■ **hold 'out** ① *v.t.* ausstrecken ⟨*Hand, Arm usw.*⟩; hinhalten ⟨*Tasse, Teller*⟩
② *v.i.* (resist) sich halten
■ **hold 'up** *v.t.* (a) (raise) hochhalten; heben ⟨*Hand, Kopf*⟩
(b) (delay) aufhalten
(c) (rob) überfallen
■ **'hold with** *v.t.* **not** ~ **with sth.** etw. ablehnen
'holdall *n.* Reisetasche, *die*
'holder *n.* (a) (of post, title) Inhaber, *der*/Inhaberin, *die*
(b) ⟨*Zigaretten*⟩spitze, *die;* ⟨*Papier-, Zahnputzglas*⟩halter, *der*
'hold-up *n.* (a) (robbery) [Raub]überfall, *der*
(b) (delay) Verzögerung, *die*
hole /həʊl/ *n.* Loch, *das;* (of fox, badger, rabbit) Bau, *der;* **pick** ~**s in** (fig.) zerpflücken (ugs.)
holiday /'hɒlɪdeɪ/ *n.* (a) [arbeits]freier Tag; (public ~) Feiertag, *der*
(b) *in sing. or pl.* (Brit.: vacation) Urlaub, *der;* (Sch.) [Schul]ferien *Pl.*
holiday: ~ **home** *n.* Feriendomizil, *das;* ~ **job** *n.* Ferienjob, *der;* ~**maker** *n.* Urlauber, *der*/Urlauberin, *die;* ~ **resort** *n.* Ferienort, *der;* ~ **season** *n.* Urlaubszeit, *die*
Holland /'hɒlənd/ *pr. n.* Holland ⟨*das*⟩

hollow /'hɒləʊ/ **1** *adj.* hohl; eingefallen ⟨Wangen, Schläfen⟩; (fig.) leer ⟨Versprechen⟩ **2** *n.* [Boden]senke, *die* **3** *v.t.* ∼ **out** aushöhlen

holly /'hɒlɪ/ *n.* Stechpalme, *die*

holocaust /'hɒləkɔːst/ *n.* (destruction) Massenvernichtung, *die;* **the H**∼: der Holocaust

hologram /'hɒləgræm/ *n.* Hologramm, *der*

holster /'həʊlstə(r)/ *n.* [Pistolen]halfter, *die od. das*

holy /'həʊlɪ/ *adj.* heilig

Holy: H∼ **'Bible** *n.* Heilige Schrift; ∼ **'Ghost ▸** ∼ SPIRIT; ∼ **Land** *n.* the ∼ **Land** das Heilige Land; ∼ **'Spirit** *n.* Heiliger Geist

homage /'hɒmɪdʒ/ *n.* Huldigung, *die* **(to** an + *Akk.*)**; pay** *or* **do** ∼ **to** sb./sth. jmdm./einer Sache huldigen

home /həʊm/ **1** *n.* **(a)** Heim, *das;* (flat) Wohnung, *die;* (house) Haus, *das;* (household) [Eltern]haus, *das;* (native country) Heimat, *die;* **at** ∼: zu Hause; **be/feel at** ∼ (fig.) sich wohl fühlen; **make yourself at** ∼: fühl dich wie zu Hause **(b)** (institution) Heim, *das* **2** *adj.* **(a)** Haus- **(b)** (Sport) Heim-; ∼ **match** Heimspiel, *das* **3** *adv.* nach Hause

home: ∼ **address** *n.* Privatanschrift, *die;* ∼ **'banking** *n.* Homebanking, *das;* ∼**-based** /'həʊmbeɪst/ *adj.* zu Hause arbeitend; **be** ∼**-based** zu Hause arbeiten; seinen Arbeitsplatz zu Hause haben; ∼**coming** *n.* Heimkehr, *die;* ∼ **com'puter** *n.* Heimcomputer, *der;* ∼ **'ground** *n.* **on** ∼ **ground** auf heimischem Boden; (fig.) zu Hause (ugs.); ∼**-grown** *adj.* selbst gezogen; ∼**land** *n.* Heimat, *die*

'homeless 1 *adj.* obdachlos **2** *n. pl.* **the** ∼: die Obdachlosen *Pl.*

'homelessness *n.* Obdachlosigkeit, *die*

homely /'həʊmlɪ/ *adj.* wohnlich ⟨Zimmer usw.⟩; behaglich ⟨Atmosphäre⟩

home: ∼**-made** *adj.* selbst gemacht; selbst gebacken ⟨Brot⟩; hausgemacht ⟨Lebensmittel⟩; **H**∼ **Office** *n.* (Brit.) Innenministerium, *das*

homeopathic *etc.* (Amer.) **▸** HOMOEO-

home: ∼**owner** *n.* Eigenheimbesitzer, *der*/-besitzerin, *die;* ∼ **page** *n.* (Comp.) Homepage, *die;* ∼ **Secretary** *n.* (Brit.) Innenminister, *der;* ∼ **'shopping** *n.* Teleshopping, *das;* ∼**sick** *adj.* heimwehkrank; **become/be** ∼**sick** Heimweh bekommen/haben; ∼**sickness** *n.* Heimweh, *das;* ∼ **'town** *n.* Heimatstadt, *die;* ∼**work** *n.* Hausaufgaben *Pl.;* **piece of** ∼**work** Hausaufgabe, *die*

homicide /'hɒmɪsaɪd/ *n.* Tötung, *die;* (manslaughter) Totschlag, *der*

homoeopathic /həʊmɪə'pæθɪk, hɒmɪə'pæθɪk/ *adj.* homöopathisch

homoeopathy /həʊmɪ'ɒpəθɪ, hɒmɪ'ɒpəθɪ/ *n.* Homöopathie, *die*

homosexual /həʊməʊ'seksjʊəl/ **1** *adj.* homosexuell **2** *n.* Homosexuelle, *der/die*

homosexu'ality *n.* Homosexualität, *die*

hone /həʊn/ *v.t.* wetzen

honest /'ɒnɪst/ *adj.* ehrlich

'honestly *adv.* ehrlich; redlich ⟨handeln⟩; ∼! ehrlich!; (annoyed) also wirklich!

honesty /'ɒnɪstɪ/ *n.* Ehrlichkeit, *die*

honey /'hʌnɪ/ *n.* Honig, *der*

honey: ∼ **bee** *n.* Honigbiene, *die;* ∼**comb** *n.* Honigwabe, *die;* ∼**moon** *n.* Flitterwochen *Pl.;* (journey) Hochzeitsreise, *die;* ∼**suckle** *n.* Geißblatt, *das*

honk /hɒŋk/ **1** *v.i.* ⟨Fahrzeug, Fahrer:⟩ hupen **2** *n.* Hupen, *das*

honor, honorable (Amer.) **▸** HONOUR, HONOURABLE

honorary /'ɒnərərɪ/ *adj.* Ehren⟨mitglied, -präsident, -doktor, -bürger⟩

honour /'ɒnə(r)/ (Brit.) **1** *n.* **(a)** Ehre, *die* **(b)** (distinction) Auszeichnung, *die* **2** *v.t.* ehren; (Commerc.) honorieren

honourable /'ɒnərəbl/ *adj.* (Brit.) ehrenwert (geh.)

'honours degree *n.* Examen mit Auszeichnung

hood /hʊd/ *n.* **(a)** Kapuze, *die* **(b)** (Amer. Motor Veh.) Motorhaube, *die* **(c)** (of pram) Verdeck, *das*

hoodlum /'huːdləm/ *n.* Rowdy, *der*

hoodwink /'hʊdwɪŋk/ *v.t.* hinters Licht führen

hoof /huːf/ *n., pl.* ∼**s** *or* **hooves** /huːvz/ Huf, *der*

hook /hʊk/ **1** *n.* Haken, *der;* **by** ∼ **or by crook** mit allen Mitteln **2** *v.t.* **(a)** (grasp) mit Haken/mit einem Haken greifen **(b)** (fasten) mit Haken/mit einem Haken befestigen **(to** an + *Dat.*) **(c) be** ∼**ed [on** sth.] (addicted) [von etw.] abhängig sein; (harmlessly) auf etw. (*Akk.*) stehen (ugs.)

■ **hook 'up** *v.t.* festhaken **(to** an + *Akk.*)

hooligan /'huːlɪgən/ *n.* Rowdy, *der*

hooliganism /'huːlɪgənɪzm/ *n.* Rowdytum, *das*

hoop /huːp/ *n.* Reifen, *der*

hooray /hʊ'reɪ/ *int.* hurra

hoot /huːt/ **1** *v.i.* **(a)** (call out) johlen **(b)** ⟨Eule:⟩ schreien **(c)** ⟨Fahrzeug, Fahrer:⟩ hupen **2** *n.* **(a)** (shout) ∼**s of derision** verächtliches Gejohle **(b)** (of owl) Schrei, *der* **(c)** (of vehicle) Hupen, *das*

'hooter n. (Brit.: siren) Sirene, *die*

hoover /'huːvə(r)/ (Brit.) **1** n. **(a)** H~ ®
[Hoover]staubsauger, *der*
(b) (made by any company) Staubsauger, *der*
2 v.t. staubsaugen

hooves pl. of HOOF

hop¹ /hɒp/ n. **(a)** (plant) Hopfen, *der*
(b) in pl. (Brewing) Hopfen, *der*

hop² **1** v.i., -pp-: **(a)** hüpfen; ⟨Hase:⟩
hoppeln
(b) (fig. coll.) ~ out of bed aus dem Bett
springen; ~ into the car/on [to] the bus/train
sich ins Auto/in den Bus/Zug schwingen
(ugs.)
2 v.t., -pp- (Brit. coll.) ~ it sich verziehen
(ugs.)
3 n. **(a)** Hüpfer, *der*
(b) (Brit. coll.) catch sb. on the ~: jmdn.
überraschen

hope /həʊp/ **1** n. Hoffnung, *die*; sb.'s ~[s]
of sth. jmds. Hoffnung auf etw. (Akk.); raise
sb.'s ~s jmdm. Hoffnung machen
2 v.i. & t. hoffen (for auf + Akk.); I ~ so/not
hoffentlich/hoffentlich nicht; ~ for the best
das Beste hoffen

hopeful /'həʊpfl/ adj. **(a)** zuversichtlich; be
~ of sth./of doing sth. auf etw. (Akk.) hoffen/
voller Hoffnung sein, etw. zu tun
(b) (promising) viel versprechend

'hopefully adv. **(a)** (expectantly) voller
Hoffnung
(b) (coll.: it is hoped that) hoffentlich

'hopeless adj., **'hopelessly** adv. **(a)**
hoffnungslos
(b) (inadequate) miserabel

'hopelessness n. Hoffnungslosigkeit, *die*

hopscotch /'hɒpskɒtʃ/ n. Himmel-und-
Hölle-Spiel, *das*

horde /hɔːd/ n. Horde, *die*

horizon /hə'raɪzn/ n. Horizont, *der*; on the
~: am Horizont; (fig.) broaden one's/sb.'s ~s
seinen/jmds. Horizont erweitern

horizontal /hɒrɪ'zɒntl/ adj. horizontal;
waagerecht

hori'zontally adv. horizontal; (flat)
waagerecht

hormone /'hɔːməʊn/ n. Hormon, *das*

hormone re'placement therapy n.
Hormonsubstitutionstherapie, *die*

horn /hɔːn/ n. Horn, *das*; (of vehicle) Hupe, *die*

hornet /'hɔːnɪt/ n. Hornisse, *die*

'horny adj. (hard) hornig

horoscope /'hɒrəskəʊp/ n. Horoskop, *das*

horrendous /hə'rendəs/ adj. (coll.)
schrecklich (ugs.)

horrible /'hɒrɪbl/ adj. grauenhaft; grausig
⟨Monster⟩; grauenvoll ⟨Verbrechen,
Albtraum⟩

horrid /'hɒrɪd/ adj. scheußlich

horrific /hə'rɪfɪk/ adj. schrecklich

horrify /'hɒrɪfaɪ/ v.t. mit Schrecken
erfüllen; be horrified (shocked, scandalized)
entsetzt sein (at, by über + Akk.)

'horrifying adj. grauenhaft

horror /'hɒrə(r)/ **1** n. Entsetzen, *das* (at
über + Akk.); (repugnance) Grausen, *das*;
(horrifying thing) Gräuel, *der*
2 attrib. adj. Horror-; ~ film/story
Horrorfilm, der/-geschichte, *die*

'horror-stricken, 'horror-struck adjs.
von Entsetzen gepackt

hors d'œuvre /ɔː'dɜːvr/ n. Horsd'œuvre,
das; ≈ Vorspeise, *die*

horse /hɔːs/ n. Pferd, *das*

horse: ~back n. on ~back zu Pferd;
~ 'chestnut n. Rosskastanie, *die*; ~fly n.
Pferdebremse, *die*; ~man /'hɔːsmən/ n., pl.
~men /'hɔːsmən/ ([skilled] rider) [guter] Reiter;
~play n. Balgerei, *die*; ~power n., pl.
same (Mech.) Pferdestärke, *die*; ~racing n.
Pferderennsport, *der*; ~radish n.
Meerrettich, *der*; ~shoe n. Hufeisen, *das*

horticulture /'hɔːtɪkʌltʃə(r)/ n. Gartenbau,
der

hose /həʊz/, **'hosepipe** ns. Schlauch, *der*

hospice /'hɒspɪs/ n. (Brit.: for the terminally ill)
Sterbehospiz, *das*

hospitable /hɒ'spɪtəbl/ adj. gastfreundlich
⟨Person, Wesensart⟩; be ~ to sb. jmdn.
gastfreundlich aufnehmen

hospital /'hɒspɪtl/ n. Krankenhaus, *das*; in
~ (Brit.), in the ~ (Amer.) im Krankenhaus

'hospital bed n. Krankenhausbett, *das*

hospitality /hɒspɪ'tælɪtɪ/ n.
Gastfreundschaft, *die*

'hospital nurse n. ≈ Krankenschwester,
die

host¹ /həʊst/ n. (large number) Menge, *die*; a
~ of people/children eine Menge Leute/eine
Schar von Kindern

host² n. Gastgeber, *der*/-geberin, *die*

hostage /'hɒstɪdʒ/ n. Geisel, *die*

'host country n. Gastland, *das*

hostel /'hɒstl/ n. (Brit.) Wohnheim, *das*

hostess /'həʊstɪs/ n. Gastgeberin, *die*; (in
nightclub) Animierdame, *die*

hostile /'hɒstaɪl/ adj. **(a)** feindlich
(b) (unfriendly) feindselig (to[wards])
gegenüber); be ~ to sth. etw. ablehnen

hostility /hɒ'stɪlɪtɪ/ n. Feindseligkeit, *die*

hot /hɒt/ adj. **(a)** heiß; warm ⟨Mahlzeit,
Essen⟩; I am/feel ~: mir ist heiß
(b) (pungent) scharf ⟨Gewürz, Senf usw.⟩;
scharf gewürzt ⟨Essen⟩
(c) (recent) noch warm ⟨Nachrichten⟩
(d) (coll.: illegally obtained) heiß ⟨Ware, Geld⟩

hot: ~ 'air n. (coll.) leeres Gerede (ugs.);
~bed n. (Hort.) Mistbeet, *das*; (fig.: of vice,
corruption) Brutstätte, *die* (of für)

hotchpotch /'hɒtʃpɒtʃ/ n. Mischmasch,
der (ugs.) (of aus)

hot: ~desking n.: Mehrfachnutzung von
Arbeitsplätzen; ~ dog n. (coll.) Hotdog, *der*
od. *das*

hotel /həʊ'tel/ n. Hotel, *das*

hotelier /hə'telɪə(r)/ n. Hotelier, der

ho'tel room n. Hotelzimmer, das

hot: ~**head** n. Hitzkopf, der; ~**house** n. Treibhaus, das; ~ **line** n. Hotline, die; (Polit.) heißer Draht

'**hotly** adv. heftig

hot: ~**plate** n. Kochplatte, die; (to keep food ~) Warmhalteplatte, die; ~ **seat** n. (coll.) be in the ~ seat den Kopf hinhalten müssen (ugs.); ~**tempered** adj. heißblütig; ~'**water bottle** n. Wärmflasche, die

hound /haʊnd/ [1] n. Jagdhund, der [2] v.t. verfolgen

hour /'aʊə(r)/ n. (a) Stunde, die; half an ~: eine halbe Stunde; an ~ and a half anderthalb Stunden; be paid by the ~: stundenweise bezahlt werden; the 24-~ clock die Vierundzwanzigstundenuhr (b) (time o'clock) Zeit, die; the small ~s [of the morning] die frühen Morgenstunden; 0100/0200/1700/1800 ~s (on 24-~ clock) 1.00/2.00/17.00/18.00 Uhr

'**hourly** adj., adv. stündlich; be paid ~: stundenweise bezahlt werden

house [1] /haʊs/ n., pl. ~s /'haʊzɪz/ Haus, das; to/at my ~: zu mir [nach Hause]/bei mir [zu Hause] [2] /haʊz/ v.t. (a) ein Heim geben (+ Dat.) (b) (keep, store) unterbringen

house/haʊs/: ~ **arrest** n. Hausarrest, der; ~**boat** n. Hausboot, das; ~**bound** adj. ans Haus gefesselt

household /'haʊshəʊld/ n. Haushalt, der; attrib. Haushalts-

'**householder** n. Wohnungsinhaber, der/-inhaberin, die

household 'name n. geläufiger Name; be a ~: ein Begriff sein

house /haʊs/: ~ **husband** n. Hausmann, der; ~**keeper** n. Haushälterin, die; ~**keeping** n. Hauswirtschaft, die; ~ **plant** n. Zimmerpflanze, die; ~**proud** adj. he/she is ~-proud Ordnung und Sauberkeit [im Haushalt] gehen ihm/ihr über alles; ~**sit** v.i. das Haus hüten; ~**sitter** n. Housesitter, der (ugs.); Person, die für jemanden das Haus hütet; ~**trained** adj. (Brit.) stubenrein ‹Hund, Katze›; ~**warming** n. ~-warming [party] Einzugsfeier, die; ~**wife** n. Hausfrau, die; ~**work** n. Hausarbeit, die

housing /'haʊzɪŋ/ n. (dwellings) Wohnungen Pl.; (provision of dwellings) Wohnungsbeschaffung, die

housing: ~ **association** n. (Brit.) Gesellschaft für sozialen Wohnungsbau; ~ **benefit** n. (Brit.) Wohngeld, das; ~ **estate** n. (Brit.) Wohnsiedlung, die; ~ **shortage** n. Wohnraummangel, der

hovel /'hɒvl/ n. [armselige] Hütte

hover /'hɒvə(r)/ v.i. (a) schweben (b) (linger) sich herumdrücken (ugs.)

'**hovercraft** n., pl. same Hovercraft, das; Luftkissenfahrzeug, das

'**hover mower** n. Luftkissenmäher, der

how /haʊ/ adv. wie; **learn** ~ **to ride a bike**/**swim** Rad fahren/schwimmen lernen; ~ '**are you?** wie geht es dir?; (greeting) guten Morgen/Tag/Abend!; ~ **do you 'do?** (formal) guten Morgen/Tag/Abend!; ~ **much?** wieviel?; ~ **many?** wie viel?; wie viele?

however /haʊ'evə(r)/ adv. (a) wie … auch (b) (nevertheless) jedoch; aber

howl /haʊl/ [1] n. (of animal) Heulen, das; (of distress) Schrei, der; ~s **of laughter** brüllendes Gelächter [2] v.i. ‹Tier, Wind:› heulen; (with distress) schreien [3] v.t. [hinaus]schreien

howler /'haʊlə(r)/ n. (coll.: blunder) Schnitzer, der (ugs.)

HP abbr. (Brit.) = **hire purchase**

HQ abbr. = **headquarters** HQ

HTML abbr. (Comp.) = **hypertext markup language** HTML

hub /hʌb/ n. [Rad]nabe, die; (fig.) Mittelpunkt, der

hubbub /'hʌbʌb/ n. Lärm, der; a ~ **of voices** ein Stimmengewirr

hub: ~**cap** n. Radkappe, die; ~ **dynamo** n. Nabendynamo, der; ~ **gear** n. Nabenschaltung, die

huddle /'hʌdl/ v.i. sich drängen; ~ **together** sich zusammendrängen

◾ **huddle 'up** v.i. (nestle up) sich zusammenkauern; (crowd together) sich [zusammen]drängen

hue[1] /hju:/ n. Farbton, der

hue[2] n. ~ **and cry** lautes Geschrei; (protest) Gezeter, das

huff /hʌf/ [1] v.i. ~ **and puff** schnaufen und keuchen [2] n. **in a** ~: beleidigt

hug /hʌg/ [1] n. Umarmung, die; **give sb. a** ~: jmdn. umarmen [2] v.t., -gg- umarmen

huge /hju:dʒ/ adj. riesig; gewaltig ‹Unterschied, Verbesserung, Interesse›

hulking /'hʌlkɪŋ/ adj. (coll.) ~ **great** klobig

hull /hʌl/ n. (Naut.) Schiffskörper, der

hum /hʌm/ [1] v.i., -mm-: (a) summen; ‹Maschine:› brummen (b) ~ **and haw** (coll.) herumdrucksen (ugs.) [2] v.t., -mm- summen [3] n. (a) Summen, das; (of machinery) Brummen, das (b) (of voices, conversation) Gemurmel, das; (of traffic) Brausen, das

human /'hju:mən/ [1] adj. menschlich; **the** ~ **race** die menschliche Rasse [2] n. Mensch, der

human 'being n. Mensch, der

humane /hju:'meɪn/ adj. human

humanitarian /hju:mænɪ'teərɪən/ adj. humanitär

humanity /hjuːˈmænɪtɪ/ n. (a) (mankind) Menschheit, die; (people collectively) Menschen Pl.
(b) (being humane) Humanität, die
human 'rights n. pl. Menschenrechte Pl.; ∼ rights group Menschenrechtsorganisation, die
humble /ˈhʌmbl/ 1 adj. (a) demütig
(b) (modest) bescheiden
(c) (low-ranking) einfach; niedrig ⟨Status, Rang usw.⟩
2 v.t. (a) demütigen; ∼ oneself sich demütigen od. erniedrigen
(b) (defeat decisively) [vernichtend] schlagen
humbly /ˈhʌmblɪ/ adv. demütig
humdrum /ˈhʌmdrʌm/ adj. alltäglich; eintönig ⟨Leben⟩
humid /ˈhjuːmɪd/ adj. feucht
humidifier /hjuːˈmɪdɪfaɪə(r)/ n. Luftbefeuchter, der
humidify /hjuːˈmɪdɪfaɪ/ v.t. befeuchten
humidity /hjuːˈmɪdɪtɪ/ n. Feuchtigkeit, die
humiliate /hjuːˈmɪlɪeɪt/ v.t. demütigen
humiliation /hjuːmɪlɪˈeɪʃn/ n. Demütigung, die
humility /hjuːˈmɪlɪtɪ/ n. Demut, die
humor (Amer.) ▶ HUMOUR
humorous /ˈhjuːmərəs/ adj. lustig, komisch ⟨Geschichte, Name, Situation⟩; witzig ⟨Bemerkung⟩
humour /ˈhjuːmə(r)/ (Brit.) 1 n. (a) Humor, der; sense of ∼: Sinn für Humor; have no sense of ∼: keinen Humor haben
(b) (mood) Laune, die
2 v.t. ∼ sb. jmdm. seinen Willen lassen
hump /hʌmp/ 1 n. (a) (of person) Buckel, der; (of animal) Höcker, der
(b) (mound) Hügel, der
2 v.t. (Brit. coll.: carry) schleppen
humpback 'bridge n. gewölbte Brücke
hunch¹ /hʌntʃ/ v.t. ∼ [up] hochziehen
hunch² n. (feeling) Gefühl, das
'hunchback n. (back) Buckel, der; (person) Bucklige, der/die; be a ∼: einen Buckel haben
hundred /ˈhʌndrəd/ 1 adj. hundert; a or one ∼: [ein]hundert; two/several ∼: zweihundert/mehrere hundert; a or one ∼ and one [ein]hundert[und]eins
2 n. (a) (number) hundert; a or one/two ∼: [ein]hundert/zweihundert
(b) (written figure; group) Hundert, das
(c) (indefinite amount) ∼s Hunderte. See also EIGHT
hundredth /ˈhʌndrədθ/ 1 adj. hundertst...; a ∼ part ein Hundertstel
2 n. (fraction) Hundertstel, das; (in sequence, rank) Hundertste, der/die/das
'hundredweight n., pl. same (Brit.) 50,8 kg; ≈ Zentner, der
hung ▶ HANG 1, 2
Hungarian /hʌŋˈgeərɪən/ 1 adj. ungarisch; sb. is ∼: jmd. ist Ungar/Ungarin

2 n. (a) (person) Ungar, der/Ungarin, die
(b) (language) Ungarisch, das; see also ENGLISH 2A
Hungary /ˈhʌŋgərɪ/ pr. n. Ungarn (das)
hunger /ˈhʌŋgə(r)/ 1 n. Hunger, der
2 v.i. ∼ after or for sb./sth. [heftiges] Verlangen nach jmdm./etw. haben
'hunger strike n. Hungerstreik, der; go on ∼: in den Hungerstreik treten
hung 'over adj. (coll.) verkatert (ugs.)
hungry /ˈhʌŋgrɪ/ adj. hungrig; be ∼: Hunger haben; go ∼: hungern
hunk /hʌŋk/ n. [großes] Stück
hunt /hʌnt/ 1 n. Jagd, die; (search) Suche, die
2 v.t. jagen; (search for) Jagd machen auf (+ Akk.) ⟨Mörder usw.⟩
3 v.i. jagen; go ∼ing auf die Jagd gehen; ∼ after or for Jagd machen auf (+ Akk.); (seek) suchen
'hunter n. Jäger, der
'hunting n. die Jagd (of auf + Akk.); (searching) Suche, die (for nach)
hurdle /ˈhɜːdl/ n. Hürde, die
hurl /hɜːl/ v.t. werfen; (violently) schleudern; ∼ insults at sb. jmdm. Beleidigungen ins Gesicht schleudern
hurly-burly /ˈhɜːlɪbɜːlɪ/ n. Tumult, der; the ∼ of city life der Großstadtrummel (ugs.)
hurrah /hʊˈrɑː/, **hurray** /hʊˈreɪ/ int. hurra
hurricane /ˈhʌrɪkən/ n. (tropical cyclone) Hurrikan, der; (storm, lit. or fig.) Orkan, der
hurried /ˈhʌrɪd/ adj. eilig; überstürzt ⟨Abreise⟩; in Eile ausgeführt ⟨Arbeit⟩
hurry /ˈhʌrɪ/ 1 n. Eile, die; in a ∼: eilig; be in a ∼: es eilig haben; there's no ∼: es eilt nicht
2 v.t. antreiben ⟨Person⟩; hinunterschlingen ⟨Essen⟩; ∼ one's work seine Arbeit in zu großer Eile erledigen
3 v.i. sich beeilen; (to or from place) eilen
■ **hurry 'up** 1 v.i. sich beeilen
2 v.t. antreiben
hurt /hɜːt/ 1 v.t., hurt (a) wehtun (+ Dat.); (injure) verletzen; ∼ oneself sich (Dat.) weh tun; (injure oneself) sich verletzen; ∼ one's arm/back sich (Dat.) am Arm/Rücken wehtun; (injure) sich (Dat.) den Arm/am Rücken verletzen
(b) (damage, be detrimental to) schaden (+ Dat.)
(c) (upset) verletzen ⟨Person, Stolz⟩
2 v.i., hurt (a) wehtun
(b) (cause damage, be detrimental) schaden
3 adj. gekränkt ⟨Tonfall, Miene⟩
4 n. (emotional pain) Schmerz, der
hurtful /ˈhɜːtfl/ adj. verletzend
hurtle /ˈhɜːtl/ v.i. rasen (ugs.)
husband /ˈhʌzbənd/ n. Ehemann, der; my/your/her ∼: mein/dein/ihr Mann; ∼ and wife Mann und Frau
hush /hʌʃ/ 1 n. (silence) Schweigen, das; (stillness) Stille, die

2 *v.t.* (silence) zum Schweigen bringen; (still) beruhigen

3 *v.i.* still sein; ~! still!

■ **hush 'up** *v.t.* vertuschen

husk /hʌsk/ *n.* Spelze, *die*

husky¹ /'hʌskɪ/ *adj.* heiser

husky² *n.* Eskimohund, *der*

hustle /'hʌsl/ 1 *v.t.* drängen (**into** zu)

2 *n.* ~ **and bustle** geschäftiges Treiben

hut /hʌt/ *n.* Hütte, *die*

hutch /hʌtʃ/ *n.* Stall, *der*

hyacinth /'haɪəsɪnθ/ *n.* Hyazinthe, *die*

hybrid /'haɪbrɪd/ 1 *n.* Hybride, *die od. der* (**between** aus); (fig.: mixture) Mischung, *die*

2 *adj.* hybrid ‹Züchtung›

hydrangea /haɪ'dreɪndʒə/ *n.* Hortensie, *die*

hydrant /'haɪdrənt/ *n.* Hydrant, *der*

hydraulic /haɪ'drɔːlɪk/ *adj.* hydraulisch

hydrochloric acid /haɪdrəklɔːrɪk 'æsɪd/ *n.* Salzsäure, *die*

hydroelectric /haɪdrəʊɪ'lektrɪk/ *adj.* hydroelektrisch; ~ **power station** Wasserkraftwerk, *das*

hydrofoil /'haɪdrəfɔɪl/ *n.* Tragflächenboot, *das*

hydrogen /'haɪdrədʒən/ *n.* Wasserstoff, *der*

'hydrogen bomb *n.* Wasserstoffbombe, *die*

hyena /haɪ'iːnə/ *n.* Hyäne, *die*

hygiene /'haɪdʒiːn/ *n.* Hygiene, *die*

hygienic /haɪ'dʒiːnɪk/ *adj.* hygienisch

hymn /hɪm/ *n.* Hymne, *die*; (sung in service) Kirchenlied, *das*

'hymn book *n.* Gesangbuch, *das*

hyper /'haɪpə(r)/ *adj.* (coll.) aufgedreht (ugs.)

hyperactive /haɪpə'ræktɪv/ *adj.* überaktiv

hyperbole /haɪ'pɜːbəlɪ/ *n.* Hyperbel, *die*

hyper: ~**link** *n.* (Comp.) Hyperlink, *der*; ~**market** *n.* (Brit.) Verbrauchermarkt, *der*; ~**text** *n.* (Comp.) Hypertext, *der*; ~**'ventilate** *v.i.* hyperventilieren

hyphen /'haɪfn/ 1 *n.* Bindestrich, *der*

2 *v.t.* mit Bindestrich schreiben

hyphenate /'haɪfəneɪt/ ▶ HYPHEN 2

hyphenation /haɪfə'neɪʃn/ *n.* Kopplung, *die*

hypnosis /hɪp'nəʊsɪs/ *n., pl.* **hypnoses** /hɪp'nəʊsiːz/ Hypnose, *die*; (act, process) Hypnotisierung, *die*; **under** ~: in Hypnose (*Dat.*)

hypnotic /hɪp'nɒtɪk/ *adj.* hypnotisch

hypnotism /'hɪpnətɪzm/ *n.* Hypnotik, *die*; (act) Hypnotisieren, *das*

hypnotist /'hɪpnətɪst/ *n.* Hypnotiseur, *der*/ Hypnotiseurin, *die*

hypnotize /'hɪpnətaɪz/ *v.t.* hypnotisieren

hypochondria /haɪpə'kɒndrɪə/ *n.* Hypochondrie, *die*

hypochondriac /haɪpə'kɒndrɪæk/ *n.* Hypochonder, *der*

hypocrisy /hɪ'pɒkrɪsɪ/ *n.* Heuchelei, *die*

hypocrite /'hɪpəkrɪt/ *n.* Heuchler, *der*/ Heuchlerin, *die*

hypocritical /hɪpə'krɪtɪkl/ *adj.* heuchlerisch

hypodermic /haɪpə'dɜːmɪk/ *adj. & n.* ~ **[syringe]** Injektionsspritze, *die*

hypotenuse /haɪ'pɒtənjuːz/ *n.* Hypotenuse, *die*

hypothermia /haɪpə'θɜːmɪə/ *n.* (Med.) Hypothermie, *die* (fachspr.); Unterkühlung, *die*

hypothesis /haɪ'pɒθɪsɪs/ *n., pl.* **hypotheses** /haɪ'pɒθɪsiːz/ Hypothese, *die*

hypothetical /haɪpə'θetɪkl/ *adj.* hypothetisch

hysterectomy /hɪstə'rektəmɪ/ *n.* (Med.) Hysterektomie, *die* (fachspr.)

hysteria /hɪ'stɪərɪə/ *n.* Hysterie, *die*

hysterical /hɪ'sterɪkl/ *adj.* hysterisch

hysterics /hɪ'sterɪks/ *n. pl.* (laughter) hysterischer Lachanfall; (crying) hysterischer Weinkrampf; **have** ~: hysterisch lachen/ weinen

Ii

I¹, i /aɪ/ *n.* I, i, *das*

I² *pron.* ich

ice /aɪs/ 1 *n.* (a) Eis, *das*; **feel/be like** ~ (be very cold) eiskalt sein

(b) (~ cream) [Speise]eis, *das*; **an** ~/**two** ~**s** ein/zwei Eis

2 *v.t.* glasieren ‹Kuchen›

■ **ice 'over, ice 'up** *v.i.* ‹Gewässer:› zufrieren

'ice age *n.* Eiszeit, *die*

iceberg /'aɪsbɜːg/ *n.* Eisberg, *der*

ice: ~**box** *n.* (Amer.) Kühlschrank, *der*; ~ **bucket** *n.* Eisbehälter, *der*; ~**cold** *adj.* eiskalt; ~ **'cream** *n.* Eis, *das*; Eiscreme, *die*; **one** ~ **cream/two/too many** ~ **creams** ein/zwei/zu viel Eis; ~ **'cream parlour** *n.* Eisdiele, *die*; ~ **cube** *n.* ···ᐳ

Eiswürfel, *die;* ~ **hockey** *n.* Eishockey, *das*

Iceland /'aɪslənd/ *pr. n.* Island (*das*)

Icelandic /aɪs'lændɪk/ ⚀ *adj.* isländisch ⚁ *n.* Isländisch, *das; see also* ENGLISH 2A

ice: ~ **'lolly** *n.* Eis am Stiel; ~ **rink** *n.* Eisbahn, *die;* ~ **skate** *n.* Schlittschuh, *der;* ~**-skate** *v.i.* Schlittschuh laufen; ~ **skating** *n.* Schlittschuhlaufen, *das*

icicle /'aɪsɪkl/ *n.* Eiszapfen, *der*

icing /'aɪsɪŋ/ *n.* Zuckerguss, *der*

'icing sugar *n.* (Brit.) Puderzucker, *der*

icon /'aɪkɒn/ *n.* (a) Ikone, *die* (b) (Comp.) Icon, *das*

icy /'aɪsɪ/ *adj.* (a) vereist ⟨*Berge, Landschaft, Straße*⟩; eisreich ⟨*Region, Land*⟩; in ~ **conditions** bei Eis (b) (very cold) eiskalt; eisig; (fig.) frostig

I'd /aɪd/ (a) = I had; (b) = I would

idea /aɪ'dɪə/ *n.* Idee, *die;* Gedanke, *der;* (mental picture) Vorstellung, *die;* (vague notion) Ahnung, *die;* **have you any** ~ **[of] how ...?** weißt du ungefähr, wie ...?; **have no** ~ **[of] where ...:** keine Ahnung haben, wo ...; **not have the slightest** *or* **faintest** ~: nicht die leiseste Ahnung haben

ideal /aɪ'dɪəl/ ⚀ *adj.* ideal; vollendet ⟨*Ehemann, Gastgeber*⟩; vollkommen ⟨*Welt*⟩ ⚁ *n.* Ideal, *das*

idealism /aɪ'dɪəlɪzm/ *n.* Idealismus, *der*

idealist /aɪ'dɪəlɪst/ *n.* Idealist, *der*/ Idealistin, *die*

idealistic /aɪdɪə'lɪstɪk/ *adj.* idealistisch

idealize /aɪ'dɪəlaɪz/ *v.t.* idealisieren

ideally /aɪ'dɪəlɪ/ *adv.* ideal; ~, ...: idealerweise *od.* im Idealfall ...

identical /aɪ'dentɪkl/ *adj.* identisch; **be** ~: sich (*Dat.*) völlig gleichen; ~ **twins** eineiige Zwillinge

identification /aɪdentɪfɪ'keɪʃn/ *n.* Identifizierung, *die;* (of plants, animals) Bestimmung, *die*

identifi'cation parade *n.* (Brit.) Gegenüberstellung [zur Identifizierung], *die*

identify /aɪ'dentɪfaɪ/ ⚀ *v.t.* identifizieren; bestimmen ⟨*Pflanze, Tier*⟩ ⚁ *v.i.* ~ **with sb.** sich mit jmdm. identifizieren

Identikit ® /aɪ'dentɪkɪt/ *n.* Phantombild, *das*

identity /aɪ'dentɪtɪ/ *n.* Identität, *die;* **proof of** ~: Identitätsnachweis, *der;* [**case of**] **mistaken** ~: [Personen]verwechslung, *die*

identity: ~ **card** *n.* [Personal]ausweis, *der;* ~ **crisis** *n.* Identitätskrise, *die;* ~ **parade** ▶ IDENTIFICATION PARADE

ideological /aɪdɪə'lɒdʒɪkl/ *adj.* ideologisch

ideology /aɪdɪ'ɒlədʒɪ/ *n.* Ideologie, *die*

idiocy /'ɪdɪəsɪ/ *n.* Idiotie, *die*

idiom /'ɪdɪəm/ *n.* [Rede]wendung, *die*

idiomatic /ɪdɪə'mætɪk/ *adj.* idiomatisch

idiosyncrasy /ɪdɪə'sɪŋkrəsɪ/ *n.* Eigentümlichkeit, *die*

idiosyncratic /ɪdɪəsɪŋ'krætɪk/ *adj.* eigenwillig

idiot /'ɪdɪət/ *n.* Idiot, *der* (ugs.)

idiotic /ɪdɪ'ɒtɪk/ *adj.* idiotisch (ugs.)

idle /'aɪdl/ ⚀ *adj.* (a) (lazy) faul (b) (not in use) außer Betrieb *nachgestellt;* **be** ~ ⟨*Maschinen, Fabrik:*⟩ stillstehen (c) bloß ⟨*Neugier, Spekulation*⟩; leer ⟨*Geschwätz*⟩ ⚁ *v.i.* ⟨*Motor:*⟩ leer laufen

▪ **idle a'way** *v.t.* vertun

'idleness *n.* Faulheit, *die*

idol /'aɪdl/ *n.* Idol, *das*

idolize /'aɪdəlaɪz/ *v.t.* vergöttern

idyllic /ɪ'dɪlɪk/ *adj.* idyllisch

i.e. /aɪ'iː/ *abbr.* = **that is** d.h.; i.e.

if /ɪf/ *conj.* (a) wenn; if anyone should ask ...: falls jemand fragt, ...; **if I knew what to do ...:** wenn ich wüsste, was ich tun soll ...; **if I were you** an deiner Stelle; **if so/not** wenn ja/ nein *od.* nicht; **if then/that/at all** wenn überhaupt; **as if** als ob; **if I only knew, if only I knew!** wenn ich das nur wüsste!; **if it isn't Ronnie!** das ist doch Ronnie! (b) (whenever) [immer] wenn (c) (whether) ob (d) (though) auch *od.* selbst wenn (e) (despite being) wenn auch

iffish /'ɪfɪʃ/, **iffy** /'ɪfɪ/ *adjs.* (coll.) ungewiss; zweifelhaft

igloo /'ɪgluː/ *n.* Iglu, *der od. das*

ignite /ɪg'naɪt/ ⚀ *v.t.* anzünden ⚁ *v.i.* sich entzünden

ignition /ɪg'nɪʃn/ *n.* (a) (igniting) Zünden, *das* (b) (Motor Veh.) Zündung, *die;* ~ **key** Zündschlüssel, *der*

ignorance /'ɪgnərəns/ *n.* Unwissenheit, *die;* **keep sb. in** ~ **of sth.** jmdn. in Unkenntnis über etw. (*Akk.*) lassen

ignorant /'ɪgnərənt/ *adj.* unwissend; **be** ~ **of sth.** (uninformed) über etw. (*Akk.*) nicht informiert sein

ignore /ɪg'nɔː(r)/ *v.t.* ignorieren; nicht befolgen ⟨*Befehl, Rat*⟩; übergehen ⟨*Frage, Bemerkung*⟩

ill /ɪl/ ⚀ *adj.,* **worse** /wɜːs/, **worst** /wɜːst/ krank; **fall** ~: krank werden ⚁ *adv.* **be** ~ **at ease** sich nicht wohl fühlen ⚂ *n.* Übel, *das*

I'll /aɪl/ (a) = I shall (b) = I will

ill-ad'vised *adj.* unklug

illegal /ɪ'liːgl/ *adj.,* **il'legally** *adv.* illegal

il'legal immigrant *n.* illegaler Einwanderer/illegale Einwanderin

illegality /ɪlɪ'gælɪtɪ/ *n.* Ungesetzlichkeit, *die*

illegible /ɪ'ledʒɪbl/ *adj.* unleserlich

illegitimate /ɪlɪ'dʒɪtɪmət/ *adj.* unehelich ⟨*Kind*⟩

ill 'health n. schwache Gesundheit

illicit /ɪˈlɪsɪt/ adj. unerlaubt ⟨Beziehung, [Geschlechts]verkehr⟩; Schwarz⟨handel, -verkauf, -arbeit⟩

'ill-informed adj. schlecht informiert

illiteracy /ɪˈlɪtərəsɪ/ n. Analphabetentum, das

illiterate /ɪˈlɪtərət/ adj. des Lesens und Schreibens unkundig; analphabetisch ⟨Bevölkerung⟩

illness /ˈɪlnɪs/ n. Krankheit, die

illogical /ɪˈlɒdʒɪkl/ adj. unlogisch

ill-'treat v.t. misshandeln

ill-'treatment n. Misshandlung, die

illuminate /ɪˈluːmɪneɪt/ v.t. beleuchten

illuminating /ɪˈluːmɪneɪtɪŋ/ adj. aufschlussreich

illumination /ɪluːmɪˈneɪʃn/ n. Beleuchtung, die

illusion /ɪˈluːʒn/ n. Illusion, die; be under the ~ that ...: sich (Dat.) einbilden, dass ...

illusory /ɪˈluːsərɪ/ adj. illusorisch

illustrate /ˈɪləstreɪt/ v.t. (a) (serve as example of) veranschaulichen
(b) illustrieren ⟨Buch, Erklärung⟩

illustration /ɪləˈstreɪʃn/ n. (a) (example) Beispiel, das (of für)
(b) (picture) Abbildung, die

illustrious /ɪˈlʌstrɪəs/ adj. berühmt ⟨Person⟩

ill 'will n. Böswilligkeit, die

I'm /aɪm/ = I am

image /ˈɪmɪdʒ/ n. (a) Bildnis, das (geh.)
(b) (Optics) Bild, das
(c) [public] ~: Image, das

'image-conscious adj. imagebewusst

imaginable /ɪˈmædʒɪnəbl/ adj. the best solution ~: die denkbar beste Lösung

imaginary /ɪˈmædʒɪnərɪ/ adj. imaginär (geh.); eingebildet ⟨Krankheit⟩

imagination /ɪmædʒɪˈneɪʃn/ n. (a) Fantasie, die
(b) (fancy) Einbildung, die

imaginative /ɪˈmædʒɪnətɪv/ adj. fantasievoll; (showing imagination) einfallsreich

imagine /ɪˈmædʒɪn/ v.t. (a) sich (Dat.) vorstellen
(b) (suppose) glauben
(c) (get the impression) ~ that ...: sich (Dat.) einbilden[, dass ...]

imbalance /ɪmˈbæləns/ n. Unausgeglichenheit, die

imbecile /ˈɪmbɪsiːl/ n. Idiot, der (ugs.)

IMF abbr. = **International Monetary Fund** IWF, der

imitate /ˈɪmɪteɪt/ v.t. nachahmen

imitation /ɪmɪˈteɪʃn/ n. (a) Nachahmung, die
(b) (counterfeit) Imitation, die

immaculate /ɪˈmækjʊlət/ adj. (spotless) makellos; (faultless) tadellos

immaterial /ɪməˈtɪərɪəl/ adj. unerheblich

immature /ɪməˈtjʊə(r)/ adj. unreif; noch nicht voll entwickelt ⟨Lebewesen⟩

immaturity /ɪməˈtjʊərɪtɪ/ n. Unreife, die

immediate /ɪˈmiːdjət/ adj. (a) unmittelbar; (nearest) nächst... ⟨Nachbar[schaft], Umgebung, Zukunft⟩; engst... ⟨Familie⟩
(b) (occurring at once) prompt; unverzüglich ⟨Handeln, Maßnahmen⟩; umgehend ⟨Antwort⟩

im'mediately ① adv. (a) unmittelbar
(b) (without delay) sofort
② conj. sobald

immemorial /ɪmɪˈmɔːrɪəl/ adj. from time ~: seit undenklichen Zeiten

immense /ɪˈmens/ adj. (a) ungeheuer
(b) (coll.: great) enorm

im'mensely adv. (a) ungeheuer
(b) (coll.: very much) unheimlich (ugs.)

immerse /ɪˈmɜːs/ v.t. [ein]tauchen; be ~d in thought/one's work in Gedanken versunken/in seine Arbeit vertieft sein

immersion /ɪˈmɜːʃn/ n. Eintauchen, das

im'mersion heater n. Heißwasserbereiter, der

immigrant /ˈɪmɪgrənt/ ① n. Einwanderer, der/Einwanderin, die
② adj. Einwanderer-; ~ workers ausländische Arbeitnehmer Pl.

immigration /ɪmɪˈgreɪʃn/ n. Einwanderung die (into nach, from aus); attrib. Einwanderungs⟨kontrolle, -gesetz⟩; ~ officer Beamter/Beamtin der Einwanderungsbehörde; ~ authorities Einwanderungsbehörden Pl.; go through ~: durch die Passkontrolle gehen

imminent /ˈɪmɪnənt/ adj. unmittelbar bevorstehend; drohend ⟨Gefahr⟩; be ~: unmittelbar bevorstehen/drohen

immobile /ɪˈməʊbaɪl/ adj. (immovable) unbeweglich

immobilize /ɪˈməʊbɪlaɪz/ v.t. verankern; (fig.) lähmen

immobilizer /ɪˈməʊbɪlaɪzə(r)/ n. (Motor Veh.) Wegfahrsperre, die

immodest /ɪˈmɒdɪst/ adj. unbescheiden; (improper) unanständig

immoral /ɪˈmɒrəl/ adj. unmoralisch; (in sexual matters) sittenlos

immorality /ɪməˈrælɪtɪ/ n. Unmoral, die; (in sexual matters) Sittenlosigkeit, die

immortal /ɪˈmɔːtl/ adj. unsterblich

immortality /ɪmɔːˈtælɪtɪ/ n. Unsterblichkeit, die

immortalize /ɪˈmɔːtəlaɪz/ v.t. unsterblich machen

immovable /ɪˈmuːvəbl/ adj. unbeweglich; be ~: sich nicht bewegen lassen

immune /ɪˈmjuːn/ adj. (a) (exempt) sicher (from vor + Dat.)
(b) (not susceptible) unempfindlich (to gegen) ···⁃

(c) (Med.) immun (**to** gegen); ∼ **system** Immunsystem, *das*

immunity /ɪ'mju:nɪtɪ/ *n.* **(a)** diplomatic ∼: diplomatische Immunität
(b) (Med.) Immunität, *die*

immunization /ɪmjʊnaɪ'zeɪʃn/ *n.* Immunisierung, *die*

immunize /'ɪmjʊnaɪz/ *v.t.* immunisieren

immunodeficiency /ɪ'mju:nəʊdɪfɪʃənsɪ/ *n.* Immunschwäche, *die*

immunology /ɪmjʊ'nɒlədʒɪ/ *n.* Immunologie, *die*

immutable /ɪ'mju:təbl/ *adj.* unveränderlich

imp /ɪmp/ *n.* **(a)** Kobold, *der* **(b)** (fig.: child) Racker, *der* (fam.)

impact /'ɪmpækt/ *n.* **(a)** Aufprall, *der* (**on**, **against** auf + *Akk.*); (collision) Zusammenprall, *der*
(b) (fig.) Wirkung, *die*

impair /ɪm'peə(r)/ *v.t.* beeinträchtigen; schaden (+ *Dat.*) ⟨*Gesundheit*⟩

impale /ɪm'peɪl/ *v.t.* aufspießen

impart /ɪm'pɑ:t/ *v.t.* **(a)** (give) [ab]geben (**to** an + *Akk.*)
(b) (communicate) kundtun (geh.) (**to** *Dat.*); vermitteln ⟨*Kenntnisse*⟩ (**to** *Dat.*)

impartial /ɪm'pɑ:ʃl/ *adj.* unparteiisch; gerecht ⟨*Entscheidung, Urteil*⟩

impassable /ɪm'pɑ:səbl/ *adj.* unpassierbar (**to** für); (to vehicles) unbefahrbar (**to** für)

impasse /'æmpɑ:s/ *n.* Sackgasse, *die*

impassive /ɪm'pæsɪv/ *adj.* ausdruckslos

impatience /ɪm'peɪʃəns/ *n.* Ungeduld, *die* (**at** über + *Akk.*)

impatient /ɪm'peɪʃənt/ *adj.* ungeduldig; ∼ **at sth./with sb.** ungeduldig über etw. (*Akk.*)/mit jmdm.

im'patiently *adv.* ungeduldig

impeccable /ɪm'pekəbl/ *adj.* makellos; tadellos ⟨*Manieren*⟩

impeccably /ɪm'pekəblɪ/ *adv.* tadellos; makellos ⟨*rein*⟩

impede /ɪm'pi:d/ *v.t.* behindern

impediment /ɪm'pedɪmənt/ *n.* **(a)** Hindernis, *das* (**to** für)
(b) (speech defect) Sprachfehler, *der*

impel /ɪm'pel/ *v.t.*, **-ll-** treiben; **feel** ∼**led to do sth.** sich genötigt *od.* gezwungen fühlen, etw. zu tun

impending /ɪm'pendɪŋ/ *adj.* bevorstehend

impenetrable /ɪm'penɪtrəbl/ *adj.* undurchdringlich (**by, to** für)

imperative /ɪm'perətɪv/ 1 *adj.* dringend erforderlich
2 *n.* (Ling.) Imperativ, *der*

imperceptible /ɪmpə'septɪbl/ *adj.* nicht wahrnehmbar; (very slight or gradual) unmerklich

imperfect /ɪm'pɜ:fɪkt/ 1 *adj.* **(a)** (incomplete) unvollständig
(b) (faulty) mangelhaft

2 *n.* (Ling.) Imperfekt, *das*

imperfection /ɪmpə'fekʃn/ *n.* **(a)** (incompleteness) Unvollständigkeit, *die*
(b) (fault) Mangel, *der*

im'perfectly *adv.* **(a)** (incompletely) unvollständig
(b) (faultily) fehlerhaft

imperial /ɪm'pɪərɪəl/ *adj.* kaiserlich

imperialism /ɪm'pɪərɪəlɪzm/ *n.* Imperialismus, *der*

imperil /ɪm'perɪl/ *v.t.*, (Brit.) **-ll-** gefährden

imperious /ɪm'pɪərɪəs/ *adj.* herrisch

impermeable /ɪm'pɜ:mɪəbl/ *adj.* undurchlässig

impersonal /ɪm'pɜ:sənl/ *adj.* unpersönlich

impersonate /ɪm'pɜ:səneɪt/ *v.t.* sich ausgeben als; (to entertain) imitieren; nachahmen

impersonator /ɪm'pɜ:səneɪtə(r)/ *n.* (entertainer) Imitator, *der*/Imitatorin, *die*

impertinence /ɪm'pɜ:tɪnəns/ *n.* Unverschämtheit, *die*

impertinent /ɪm'pɜ:tɪnənt/ *adj.* unverschämt

imperturbable /ɪmpə'tɜ:bəbl/ *adj.* gelassen; **be completely** ∼: durch nichts zu erschüttern sein

impervious /ɪm'pɜ:vɪəs/ *adj.* undurchlässig; **be** ∼ **to sth.** (fig.) unempfänglich für etw. sein

impetuous /ɪm'petjʊəs/ *adj.* unüberlegt; impulsiv ⟨*Person*⟩

impetus /'ɪmpɪtəs/ *n.* **(a)** Kraft, *die* **(b)** (fig.) Motivation, *die*

impinge /ɪm'pɪndʒ/ *v.i.* ∼ **on sth.** auf etw. (*Akk.*) Einfluss nehmen

'impish *adj.* lausbübisch

implacable /ɪm'plækəbl/ *adj.* unversöhnlich; erbittert ⟨*Gegner*⟩

implausible /ɪm'plɔ:zɪbl/ *adj.* unglaubwürdig

implement 1 /'ɪmplɪmənt/ *n.* Gerät, *das*
2 /'ɪmplɪment/ *v.t.* [in die Tat] umsetzen ⟨*Politik, Plan usw.*⟩

implicate /'ɪmplɪkeɪt/ *v.t.* belasten; **be** ∼**d in a scandal** in einen Skandal verwickelt sein

implication /ɪmplɪ'keɪʃn/ *n.* Implikation, *die*; **by** ∼: implizit

implicit /ɪm'plɪsɪt/ *adj.* **(a)** (implied) implizit (geh.); unausgesprochen ⟨*Drohung, Zweifel*⟩
(b) (resting on authority) unbedingt; blind ⟨*Vertrauen*⟩

implicitly /ɪm'plɪsɪtlɪ/ *adv.* **(a)** (by implication) implizit (geh.)
(b) (unquestioningly) blind ⟨*vertrauen, gehorchen usw.*⟩

implode /ɪm'pləʊd/ *v.i.* implodieren

implore /ɪm'plɔ:(r)/ *v.t.* anflehen (**for** um)

imply /ɪm'plaɪ/ *v.t.* **(a)** implizieren (geh.); (say indirectly) hindeuten auf (+ *Akk.*)
(b) (insinuate) unterstellen

impolite ···⁖· in ····

impolite /ɪmpə'laɪt/ *adj.* unhöflich

import [1] /ɪm'pɔːt/ *v.t.* importieren, einführen ⟨*Waren*⟩ (**from** aus, **into** nach) [2] /'ɪmpɔːt/ *n.* **(a)** (process) Import, *der*
(b) (article) Importgut, *das*

importance /ɪm'pɔːtəns/ *n.* Wichtigkeit, *die* (**to** für); (significance) Bedeutung, *die;* **be of ~:** wichtig sein; **full of one's own ~:** von seiner eigenen Wichtigkeit überzeugt

important /ɪm'pɔːtənt/ *adj.* wichtig (**to** für); (significant) bedeutend

'**import duty** *n.* Einfuhrzoll, *der*

im'porter *n.* Importeur, *der*

impose /ɪm'pəʊz/ *v.t.* auferlegen (geh.) ⟨*Bürde, Verpflichtung*⟩ ([**up**]**on** *Dat.*); erheben ⟨*Steuer*⟩ (**on** auf + *Akk.*); verhängen ⟨*Kriegsrecht*⟩; anordnen ⟨*Rationierung*⟩
■ **im'pose on** *v.t.* ausnutzen ⟨*Gutmütigkeit, Toleranz usw.*⟩; **~ on sb.** sich jmdm. aufdrängen

imposing /ɪm'pəʊzɪŋ/ *adj.* imposant

imposition /ɪmpə'zɪʃn/ *n.* **(a)** Auferlegung, *die;* (of tax) Erhebung, *die*
(b) (unreasonable demand) Zumutung, *die*

impossibility /ɪmpɒsɪ'bɪlɪti/ *n.* Unmöglichkeit, *die*

impossible /ɪm'pɒsɪbl/ *adj.*, **impossibly** /ɪm'pɒsɪblɪ/ *adv.* unmöglich

impostor /ɪm'pɒstə(r)/ *n.* Hochstapler, *der*/-staplerin, *die;* (swindler) Betrüger, *der*/ Betrügerin, *die*

impotence /'ɪmpətəns/ *n.* **(a)** (powerlessness) Machtlosigkeit, *die*
(b) (lack of sexual power) Impotenz, *die*

impotent /'ɪmpətənt/ *adj.* **(a)** (powerless) machtlos
(b) (lacking in sexual power; in popular use: sterile) impotent

impound /ɪm'paʊnd/ *v.t.* beschlagnahmen

impoverished /ɪm'pɒvərɪʃt/ *adj.* **be**/ **become ~:** verarmt sein/verarmen

impracticable /ɪm'præktɪkəbl/ *adj.* undurchführbar

impractical /ɪm'præktɪkl/ *adj.* **(a)** (unpractical) unpraktisch
(b) ▶ IMPRACTICABLE

imprecise /ɪmprɪ'saɪs/ *adj.* ungenau

impregnable /ɪm'pregnəbl/ *adj.* uneinnehmbar ⟨*Festung, Bollwerk*⟩; (fig.) unanfechtbar ⟨*Ruf, Stellung*⟩

impregnate /'ɪmpregneɪt/ *v.t.* imprägnieren

impress /ɪm'pres/ *v.t.* beeindrucken; *abs.* Eindruck machen; **be ~ed by** *or* **with sth.** von etw. beeindruckt sein
■ **im'press** [**up**]**on** *v.t.* einschärfen (+ *Dat.*); **~ sth.** [**up**]**on sb.'s memory** jmdm. etw. einschärfen

impression /ɪm'preʃn/ *n.* **(a)** Eindruck, *der;* **form an ~ of sb.** sich (*Dat.*) ein Bild von jmdm. machen
(b) (impersonation) **do an ~ of sb.** jmdn. imitieren; **do ~s** andere Leute imitieren

impressionable *adj.* beeinflussbar

impressionist /ɪm'preʃənɪst/ *n.* Impressionist, *der*/Impressionistin, *die*

impressive /ɪm'presɪv/ *adj.* beeindruckend; imponierend

imprint [1] /'ɪmprɪnt/ *n.* Abdruck, *der;* (fig.) Stempel, *der*
[2] /ɪm'prɪnt/ *v.t.* aufdrucken; (fig.) einprägen (**on** *Dat.*)

imprison /ɪm'prɪzn/ *v.t.* in Haft nehmen; **be ~ed** sich in Haft befinden

im'prisonment *n.* Haft, *die;* **a long term of ~:** eine lange Haftstrafe

improbable /ɪm'prɒbəbl/ *adj.* unwahrscheinlich

impromptu /ɪm'prɒmptjuː/ [1] *adj.* improvisiert; **an ~ speech** eine Stegreifrede [2] *adv.* aus dem Stegreif

improper /ɪm'prɒpə(r)/ *adj.* **(a)** (wrong) unrichtig
(b) (unseemly) unpassend; (indecent) unanständig

im'properly *adv.* ▶ IMPROPER: unrichtig; unpassend; unanständig

improvable /ɪm'pruːvəbl/ *adj.* verbesserungsfähig

improve /ɪm'pruːv/ [1] *v.i.* besser werden; ⟨*Person, Wetter:*⟩ sich bessern
[2] *v.t.* verbessern
[3] *v. refl.* **~ oneself** sich weiterbilden
■ **im'prove** [**up**]**on** *v.t.* überbieten ⟨*Rekord, Angebot*⟩; verbessern ⟨*Leistung*⟩

improvement /ɪm'pruːvmənt/ *n.* Verbesserung, *die* (**on, over** gegenüber); **make ~s to sth.** Verbesserungen an etw. (*Dat.*) vornehmen

improvisation /ɪmprəvaɪ'zeɪʃn/ *n.* Improvisieren, *das*

improvise /'ɪmprəvaɪz/ *v.t.* improvisieren

imprudent /ɪm'pruːdənt/ *adj.* unklug; (showing rashness) unbesonnen

impudence /'ɪmpjʊdəns/ *n.* Unverschämtheit, *die;* (brazenness) Dreistigkeit, *die*

impudent /'ɪmpjʊdənt/ *adj.*, **impudently** *adv.* unverschämt; (brazen[ly]) dreist

impulse /'ɪmpʌls/ *n.* Impuls, *der;* **on** [**an**] **~:** impulsiv

'**impulse buying** *n.* Spontankäufe *Pl.*

impulsive /ɪm'pʌlsɪv/ *adj.* impulsiv

impunity /ɪm'pjuːnɪti/ *v.t.* **with ~:** ungestraft

impure /ɪm'pjʊə(r)/ *adj.* unrein

impurity /ɪm'pjʊərɪti/ *n.* Unreinheit, *die;* (foreign body) Fremdstoff, *der*

impute /ɪm'pjuːt/ *v.t.* zuschreiben (**to** *Dat.*)

in /ɪn/ [1] *prep.* (position; also fig.) in (+ *Dat.*); (into) in (+ *Akk.*); **in this heat** bei dieser Hitze; **two feet in diameter** mit einem Durchmesser von zwei Fuß; **there are three feet in a yard** ein Yard hat drei Fuß; **draw in** ···⁖

crayon/ink mit Kreide/Tinte zeichnen; **pay in pounds/dollars** in Pfund/Dollars bezahlen; **in fog/rain** *etc.* bei Nebel/Regen *usw.;* **in the 20th century** im 20. Jahrhundert; **4 o'clock in the morning/afternoon** 4 Uhr morgens/abends; **in 1990** [im Jahre] 1990; **in three minutes/years** in drei Minuten/Jahren; **in doing this, he** ...: indem er das tut/tat, ... er ...; **in that** ...: insofern als...

2 *adv.* (a) (inside) hinein⟨gehen *usw.*⟩; herein⟨kommen *usw.*⟩

(b) (at home, work, etc.) **be in** da sein

(c) **have it in for sb.** es auf jmdn. abgesehen haben (ugs.); **sb. is in for sth.** (about to undergo) jmdm. steht etw. bevor

3 *adj.* (coll.: in fashion) in (ugs.)

4 *n.* **know the ins and outs of sth.** sich in einer Sache genau auskennen

in. *abbr.* = **inch**[es]

ina'bility *n.* Unfähigkeit, *die*

inaccessible /mək'sesɪbl/ *adj.* unzugänglich

in'accuracy *n.* (a) (incorrectness) Unrichtigkeit, *die*

(b) (imprecision) Ungenauïgkeit, *die*

in'accurate *adj.* (a) (incorrect) unrichtig

(b) (imprecise) ungenau

in'active *adj.* untätig

inac'tivity *n.* Untätigkeit, *die*

inadequacy /ɪn'ædɪkwəsɪ/ *n.* (a) Unzulänglichkeit, *die*

(b) (incompetence) mangelnde Eignung

in'adequate *adj.* unzulänglich; (incompetent) ungeeignet; **feel ∼:** sich überfordert fühlen

inadvertent /ɪnəd'vɜːtənt/ *adj.,* **inad'vertently** *adv.* versehentlich

inad'visable *adj.* nicht ratsam

inane /ɪ'neɪn/ *adj.* dümmlich

in'animate *adj.* unbelebt

inap'plicable *adj.* nicht zutreffend

inap'propriate *adj.* unpassend

in'apt *adj.* unpassend

inar'ticulate *adj.* (a) **she's rather/very ∼:** sie kann sich ziemlich schlecht/sehr schlecht ausdrücken

(b) (indistinct) unverständlich

inat'tentive *adj.* unaufmerksam (**to** gegenüber)

in'audible *adj.* unhörbar

inau'spicious *adj.* (ominous) unheilvoll; (unlucky) unglücklich

'inborn *adj.* angeboren (**in** *Dat.*)

'in-box *n.* (Comp.) Inbox, *die;* Posteingang, *der*

in'bred *adj.* **they are/have become ∼:** bei ihnen herrscht Inzucht

in'breeding *n.* Inzucht, *die*

'inbuilt *adj.* jmdm./einer Sache eigen

Inc. *abbr.* (Amer.) = **Incorporated** e. G.

incalculable /ɪn'kælkjʊləbl/ *adj.* (very great) unermesslich

in'capable *adj.* (a) **be ∼ of doing sth.** außerstande sein, etw. zu tun; **be ∼ of sth.** zu etw. unfähig sein

(b) **be ∼ of** nicht zulassen ⟨Beweis, Messung *usw.*⟩

incapacitate /ɪnkə'pæsɪteɪt/ *v.t.* unfähig machen

incarcerate /ɪn'kɑːsəreɪt/ *v.t.* einkerkern (geh.)

incarceration /ɪnkɑːsə'reɪʃn/ *n.* Einkerkerung, *die* (geh.)

incendiary /ɪn'sendɪərɪ/ *adj. & n.* **∼ device** Brandsatz, *der;* **∼ [bomb]** Brandbombe, *die*

incense[1] /'ɪnsens/ *n.* Weihrauch, *der*

incense[2] /ɪn'sens/ *v.t.* erzürnen

incentive /ɪn'sentɪv/ *n.* Anreiz, *der*

incessant /ɪn'sesənt/ *adj.,* **in'cessantly** *adv.* unablässig

incest /'ɪnsest/ *n.* Inzest, *der*

incestuous /ɪn'sestjʊəs/ *adj.* inzestuös

inch /ɪntʃ/ **1** *n.* Inch, *der;* Zoll, *der* (veralt.)

2 *v.t. & i.* **∼ [one's way] forward** sich Zoll für Zoll vorwärts bewegen

incident /'ɪnsɪdənt/ *n.* (a) (notable event) Vorfall, *der*

(b) (clash) Zwischenfall, *der*

incidental /ɪnsɪ'dentl/ *adj.* beiläufig ⟨Bemerkung⟩; Neben⟨ausgaben, -einnahmen⟩

incidentally /ɪnsɪ'dentəlɪ/ *adv.* nebenbei [bemerkt]

inci'dental music *n.* Begleitmusik, *die*

incinerate /ɪn'sɪnəreɪt/ *v.t.* verbrennen

incinerator /ɪn'sɪnəreɪtə(r)/ *n.* Verbrennungsofen, *der*

incision /ɪn'sɪʒn/ *n.* Einschnitt, *der*

incisive /ɪn'saɪsɪv/ *adj.* schneidend ⟨Ton⟩; scharf ⟨Verstand⟩; scharfsinnig ⟨Kritik, Frage, Bemerkung, Argument⟩

incite /ɪn'saɪt/ *v.t.* anstiften; aufstacheln ⟨Massen, Volk⟩

in'citement *n.* Anstiftung, *die*/ Aufstachelung, *die*

incl. *abbr.* = **including** inkl.

inclination /ɪnklɪ'neɪʃn/ *n.* Neigung, *die*

incline **1** /ɪn'klaɪn/ *v.t.* (a) (bend) neigen

(b) (dispose) veranlassen

2 *v.i.* (be disposed) neigen (**to**[**wards**] zu)

3 /'ɪnklaɪn/ *n.* Steigung, *die*

inclined /ɪn'klaɪnd/ *adj.* geneigt; **they are ∼ to be slow** sie neigen zur Langsamkeit; **if you feel** [**so**] **∼:** wenn Sie Lust [dazu] haben

include /ɪn'kluːd/ *v.t.* einschließen; (contain) enthalten; **∼d in the price** im Preis inbegriffen

including /ɪn'kluːdɪŋ/ *prep.* einschließlich (+ *Gen.*); **∼ VAT** inklusive Mehrwertsteuer

inclusion /ɪn'kluːʒn/ *n.* Aufnahme, *die*

inclusive /ɪn'kluːsɪv/ *adj.* einschließlich; **be ∼ of sth.** etw. einschließen; **from 2 to 6 January ∼:** vom 2. bis einschließlich 6. Januar; **cost £50 ∼:** 50 Pfund kosten, alles inbegriffen

incognito /ɪnkɒgˈniːtəʊ/ adj., adv.
inkognito

inco'herent adj. zusammenhanglos

income /ˈɪnkəm/ n. Einkommen, das

income: ∼ **bracket,** ∼ **group** ns.
Einkommensklasse, die; ∼ **sup'port** n.
(Brit.) zusätzliche Hilfe zum Lebensunterhalt;
∼ **tax** n. Einkommensteuer, die; (on wages,
salary) Lohnsteuer, die

'incoming adj. ankommend; landend
⟨Flugzeug⟩; einfahrend ⟨Zug⟩; eingehend
⟨Telefongespräch, Auftrag⟩

incomings /ˈɪnkʌmɪŋz/ n. pl. (revenue,
income) Einnahmen Pl.

in'comparable adj. unvergleichlich

incom'patible adj. unvereinbar; be ∼
⟨Menschen:⟩ nicht zueinander passen

in'competence /ɪnˈkɒmpɪtəns/ n.
Unfähigkeit, die; Unvermögen, das

in'competent adj. unfähig

incom'plete adj. unvollständig

incompre'hensible adj. unbegreiflich;
unverständlich ⟨Rede, Argument⟩

incon'ceivable adj. unvorstellbar

incon'clusive adj. ergebnislos; nicht
schlüssig ⟨Beweis, Argument⟩

incongruous /ɪnˈkɒŋgrʊəs/ adj.
unpassend

inconsequential /ɪnkɒnsɪˈkwenʃl/ adj.
belanglos

incon'siderate adj. rücksichtslos

incon'sistency n. ▸ INCONSISTENT:
Widersprüchlichkeit, die; Inkonsequenz, die;
Unbeständigkeit, die

incon'sistent adj. widersprüchlich;
(illogical) inkonsequent; (irregular) unbeständig

inconsolable /ɪnkənˈsəʊləbl/ adj.
untröstlich

incon'spicuous adj. unauffällig

incontinence /ɪnˈkɒntɪnəns/ n. (Med.)
Inkontinenz, die

incontinent /ɪnˈkɒntɪnənt/ adj. (Med.)
inkontinent; be ∼: an Inkontinenz leiden

incontrovertible /ɪnkɒntrəˈvɜːtəbl/ adj.
unbestreitbar; unwiderlegbar ⟨Beweis⟩

incon'venience ⓵ n.
Unannehmlichkeiten Pl. (to für); put sb. to a
lot of ∼: jmdm. große Unannehmlichkeiten
bereiten
⓶ v.t. Unannehmlichkeiten bereiten
(+ Dat.); (disturb) stören

incon'venient adj. unbequem; ungünstig
⟨Lage, Standort⟩; come at an ∼ time zu
ungelegener Zeit kommen; be ∼ for sb.
jmdm. nicht passen

incorporate /ɪnˈkɔːpəreɪt/ v.t. aufnehmen
(in[to], with in + Akk.)

incorporated /ɪnˈkɔːpəreɪtɪd/ adj.
eingetragen ⟨Handels⟩gesellschaft⟩

incor'rect adj. (a) unrichtig; be ∼: nicht
stimmen; it is ∼ to say that ...: es stimmt
nicht, dass ...

(b) (improper) inkorrekt

incor'rectly adv. (a) unrichtigerweise;
falsch ⟨beantworten, aussprechen⟩
(b) (improperly) inkorrekt

incorrigible /ɪnˈkɒrɪdʒɪbl/ adj.
unverbesserlich

increase ⓵ /ɪnˈkriːs/ v.i. zunehmen;
⟨Lärm:⟩ größer werden; ⟨Preise, Nachfrage:⟩
steigen; ∼ in weight/size/price schwerer/
größer/teurer werden
⓶ v.t. (a) (make greater) erhöhen
(b) (intensify) verstärken
⓷ /ˈɪnkriːs/ n. Zunahme, die (in Gen.); be on
the ∼: ständig zunehmen

increasing /ɪnˈkriːsɪŋ/ adj. steigend; an
∼ number of people mehr und mehr
Menschen

in'creasingly adv. in zunehmendem
Maße; become ∼ apparent immer deutlicher
werden

in'credible adj. (also coll.: remarkable)
unglaublich

in'credibly adv. (also coll.: remarkably)
unglaublich

incredulity /ɪnkrɪˈdjuːlɪtɪ/ n.
Ungläubigkeit, die

incredulous /ɪnˈkredjʊləs/ adj. ungläubig

increment /ˈɪnkrɪmənt/ n. Erhöhung, die;
(amount of growth) Zuwachs, der

incriminate /ɪnˈkrɪmɪneɪt/ v.t. belasten

incubate /ˈɪnkjʊbeɪt/ v.t. bebrüten; (to
hatching) ausbrüten

incubation /ɪnkjʊˈbeɪʃn/ n. Bebrütung, die

incubator /ˈɪnkjʊbeɪtə(r)/ n. Inkubator,
der; (for babies also) Brutkasten, der

incur /ɪnˈkɜː(r)/ v.t., -rr- sich (Dat.) zuziehen
⟨Unwillen, Ärger⟩; ∼ debts/expenses/risks
Schulden machen/Ausgaben haben/Risiken
eingehen

in'curable adj. unheilbar

incurably /ɪnˈkjʊərəblɪ/ adv. unheilbar
⟨krank⟩

incursion /ɪnˈkɜːʃn/ n. Eindringen, das; (by
sudden attack) Einfall, der

indebted /ɪnˈdetɪd/ pred. adj. be [much]
∼ to sb. for sth. jmdm. für etw. [sehr] zu
Dank verpflichtet sein

in'decency n. Unanständigkeit, die

in'decent adj., **in'decently** adv.
unanständig

indecipherable /ɪndɪˈsaɪfərəbl/ adj.
unentzifferbar

inde'cision n. Unentschlossenheit, die

inde'cisive adj. (a) ergebnislos ⟨Streit,
Diskussion⟩; nichtssagend ⟨Ergebnis⟩
(b) (hesitating) unentschlossen

indeed /ɪnˈdiːd/ adv. (a) in der Tat; thank
you very much ∼: haben Sie vielen
herzlichen Dank; ∼ it is in der Tat
(b) (in fact) ja sogar; ∼, he can ...: ja, er
kann sogar ...
(c) (admittedly) zugegebenermaßen

indefatigable /ɪndɪˈfætɪgəbl/ adj. unermüdlich

indefensible /ɪndɪˈfensɪbl/ adj. (intolerable) unverzeihlich

in'definite adj. (a) (vague) unbestimmt (b) (unlimited) unbegrenzt

in'definitely adv. (a) (vaguely) unbestimmt (b) (unlimitedly) unbegrenzt; auf unbestimmte Zeit ⟨verschieben⟩

indelible /ɪnˈdelɪbl/ adj. unauslöschlich; ∼ ink Wäschetinte, die

indelibly /ɪnˈdelɪblɪ/ adv. unauslöschlich

indemnify /ɪnˈdemnɪfaɪ/ v.t. absichern (against gegen); (compensate) entschädigen

indemnity /ɪnˈdemnɪtɪ/ n. Absicherung, die; (compensation) Entschädigung, die

indentation /ɪndenˈteɪʃn/ n. (a) (indenting, notch) Einkerbung, die (b) (recess) Einschnitt, der

inde'pendence n. Unabhängigkeit, die

inde'pendent adj., **inde'pendently** adv. unabhängig (of von)

indescribable /ɪndɪˈskraɪbəbl/ adj. unbeschreiblich

indestructible /ɪndɪˈstrʌktɪbl/ adj. unzerstörbar

indeterminable /ɪndɪˈtɜːmɪnəbl/ adj. unbestimmbar

indeterminate /ɪndɪˈtɜːmɪnət/ adj. unbestimmt; unklar ⟨Konzept⟩

index /ˈɪndeks/ **1** n. Register, das **2** v.t. mit einem Register versehen

index: ∼**card** n. Karteikarte, die; ∼ **finger** n. Zeigefinger, der; ∼ **gears** pl. Indexschaltung, die; ∼**linked** adj. (Econ.) indexiert; dynamisch ⟨Rente⟩; ∼ **number** n. Indexzahl, die

India /ˈɪndɪə/ n. Indien (das)

Indian /ˈɪndɪən/ **1** adj. (a) indisch; sb. is ∼: jmd. ist Inder/Inderin (b) [American] ∼: indianisch **2** n. (a) Inder, der/Inderin, die (b) [American] ∼: Indianer, der/Indianerin, die

Indian: ∼ **'Ocean** pr. n. Indischer Ozean; ∼ **'summer** n. Altweibersommer, der

indicate /ˈɪndɪkeɪt/ **1** v.t. (a) (be a sign of) erkennen lassen (b) (state briefly) andeuten (c) (mark, point out) anzeigen (d) (suggest, make evident) zum Ausdruck bringen (to gegenüber) **2** v.i. (Motor Veh.) blinken

indication /ɪndɪˈkeɪʃn/ n. [An]zeichen, das (of Gen., für)

indicative /ɪnˈdɪkətɪv/ **1** adj. (a) be ∼ of sth. auf etw. (Akk.) schließen lassen (b) (Ling.) indikativisch **2** n. (Ling.) Indikativ, der

indicator /ˈɪndɪkeɪtə(r)/ n. (on vehicle) Blinker, der

indict /ɪnˈdaɪt/ v.t. anklagen (for, on a charge of Gen.)

indie /ˈɪndɪ/ (coll.) **1** adj. Indie-⟨Gruppe, Szene, Charts etc.⟩ **2** n. (record company) Indie-Label, das; (band) Indie-Band, die

in'difference n. Gleichgültigkeit, die (to[wards] gegenüber)

in'different adj. (a) gleichgültig (b) (not good) mittelmäßig

indigenous /ɪnˈdɪdʒɪnəs/ adj. einheimisch; eingeboren ⟨Bevölkerung⟩

indigestible /ɪndɪˈdʒestɪbl/ adj. (lit. or fig.) unverdaulich

indi'gestion n. Magenverstimmung, die; (chronic) Verdauungsstörungen Pl.

indignant /ɪnˈdɪgnənt/ adj. entrüstet (at, over, about über + Akk.); indigniert ⟨Blick, Geste⟩

in'dignantly adv. entrüstet; indigniert

indignation /ɪndɪgˈneɪʃn/ n. Entrüstung, die (about, at, against, over über + Akk.)

in'dignity n. Demütigung, die

indigo /ˈɪndɪgəʊ/ **1** adj. ∼ [blue] indigoblau **2** n. ∼ [blue] Indigoblau, das

indi'rect adj. indirekt; ∼ **speech** indirekte Rede

indi'rectly adv. indirekt

indirect 'object n. indirektes Objekt; (in German) Dativobjekt, das

indiscipline /ɪnˈdɪsɪplɪn/ n., no indef. art. Disziplinlosigkeit, die

indi'screet adj. indiskret

indi'scretion n. Indiskretion, die

indiscriminate /ɪndɪˈskrɪmɪnət/ adj. (lacking judgement) unkritisch; (random, unrestrained) wahllos

indi'spensable adj. unentbehrlich (to für); unabdingbar ⟨Voraussetzung⟩

indisposed /ɪndɪˈspəʊzd/ adj. (unwell) unpässlich; indisponiert ⟨Sänger, Schauspieler⟩

indisputable /ɪndɪˈspjuːtəbl/ adj., **indisputably** /ɪndɪˈspjuːtəblɪ/ adv. unbestreitbar

indi'stinct adj., **indi'stinctly** adv. undeutlich

indi'stinguishable adj. nicht unterscheidbar

individual /ɪndɪˈvɪdjʊəl/ **1** adj. (a) einzeln (b) (distinctive, characteristic) individuell **2** n. Einzelne, der/die

individualist /ɪndɪˈvɪdjʊəlɪst/ n. Individualist, der/Individualistin, die

individualistic /ɪndɪvɪdjʊəˈlɪstɪk/ adj. individualistisch

individuality /ɪndɪvɪdjʊˈælɪtɪ/ n. (character) eigene Persönlichkeit

indi'vidually adv. einzeln

indi'visible adj. unteilbar

indoctrinate /ɪnˈdɒktrɪneɪt/ v.t. indoktrinieren

indoctrination /ɪndɒktrɪˈneɪʃn/ n. Indoktrination, die

indolence /ˈɪndələns/ n. Trägheit, die
indolent /ˈɪndələnt/ adj. träge
indomitable /ɪnˈdɒmɪtəbl/ adj.
unbeugsam
Indonesia /ɪndəˈniːzɪə/ pr. n. Indonesien
(das)
'indoor adj. ∼ **swimming pool/sports**
Hallenbad, das/-sport, der; ∼ **plants**
Zimmerpflanzen; ∼ **games** Spiele im Haus;
(Sport) Hallenspiele
indoors /ɪnˈdɔːz/ adv. drinnen; im Haus;
go/come ∼: nach drinnen gehen/kommen
indubitable /ɪnˈdjuːbɪtəbl/ adj.
unzweifelhaft
indubitably /ɪnˈdjuːbɪtəblɪ/ adv.
zweifellos; zweifelsohne
induce /ɪnˈdjuːs/ v.t. ∼ sb. to do sth. jmdn.
dazu bringen, etw. zu tun
in'ducement n. (incentive) Anreiz, der
induction /ɪnˈdʌkʃn/ n. Amtseinführung,
die; ∼ **course** Einführungskurs[us], der
indulge /ɪnˈdʌldʒ/ **1** v.t. **(a)** nachgeben
(+ Dat.) ⟨Wunsch, Verlangen, Verlockung⟩;
frönen (geh.) (+ Dat.) ⟨Leidenschaft⟩
(b) (please) verwöhnen
2 v.i. ∼ in frönen (geh.) (+ Dat.)
⟨Leidenschaft⟩
indulgence /ɪnˈdʌldʒəns/ n. **(a)**
Nachsicht, die; (humouring) Nachgiebigkeit,
die (with gegenüber)
(b) (thing indulged in) Luxus, der
indulgent /ɪnˈdʌldʒənt/ adj. nachsichtig
(with, to[wards] gegenüber)
industrial /ɪnˈdʌstrɪəl/ adj. industriell;
Arbeits⟨unfall, -medizin, -psychologie⟩
industrial: ∼ **'action** n.
Arbeitskampfmaßnahmen Pl.; take ∼ action
in den Ausstand treten; ∼ **area** n.
Industriegebiet, das; ∼ **di'sease** n.
Berufskrankheit, die; ∼ **dispute** n.
Arbeitskonflikt, der; ∼ **'espionage** n.
Industriespionage, die; ∼ **estate** n.
Industriegebiet, das ∼ **'injury** n.
Arbeitsverletzung, die
industrialist /ɪnˈdʌstrɪəlɪst/ n.
Industrielle, der/die
industrialization /ɪndʌstrɪəlaɪˈzeɪʃn/ n.
Industrialisierung, die
industrialize /ɪnˈdʌstrɪəlaɪz/ v.t.
industrialisieren
industrial: ∼ **park** n. Industriegebiet,
das; ∼ **plant** n. Industrieanlage, die;
∼ **re'lations** n. pl. Industrialrelations Pl.;
∼ **town** n. Industriestadt, die;
∼ **tribunal** n. Arbeitsgericht, das;
∼ **'waste** n. Industriemüll, der
industrious /ɪnˈdʌstrɪəs/ adj. fleißig;
(busy) emsig
industry /ˈɪndəstrɪ/ n. **(a)** Industrie, die
(b) ▶ INDUSTRIOUS: Fleiß, der; Emsigkeit, die
inebriated /ɪˈniːbrɪeɪtɪd/ adj. betrunken
inebriation /iniːbrɪˈeɪʃn/ n.
Betrunkenheit, die; betrunkener Zustand

in'edible adj. ungenießbar
ineffective /ɪnɪˈfektɪv/ adj. unwirksam; fruchtlos
⟨Anstrengung, Versuch⟩
ineffectual /ɪnɪˈfektjʊəl/ adj. unwirksam;
fruchtlos ⟨Versuch, Bemühung⟩; ineffizient
⟨Methode, Person⟩
inefficiency n. Leistungsschwäche, die;
(of organization, method) schlechtes
Funktionieren
inefficient adj. leistungsschwach;
schlecht funktionierend ⟨Organisation,
Methode⟩
in'elegant adj. unelegant
in'eligible adj. ungeeignet; **be** ∼ **for** nicht
infrage kommen für ⟨Beförderung, Position⟩;
nicht berechtigt sein zu ⟨Leistungen des
Staats usw.⟩
inept /ɪˈnept/ adj. unbeholfen
ineptitude /ɪˈneptɪtjuːd/ n.
Unbeholfenheit, die
ine'quality n. Ungleichheit, die
inert /ɪˈnɜːt/ adj. **(a)** reglos; (sluggish) träge
(b) (Chem.) inert; ∼ **gas** Edelgas, das
inertia /ɪˈnɜːʃə/ n. Trägheit, die
inertia reel 'seat belt n.
Automatikgurt, der
inescapable /ɪnɪˈskeɪpəbl/ adj.
unausweichlich
ines'sential adj. unwesentlich;
(dispensable) entbehrlich
inestimable /ɪnˈestɪməbl/ adj.
unschätzbar
inevitable /ɪnˈevɪtəbl/ adj. unvermeidlich;
unabwendbar ⟨Ereignis, Krieg, Schicksal⟩;
zwangsläufig ⟨Ergebnis, Folge⟩
inevitably /ɪnˈevɪtəblɪ/ adv. zwangsläufig
ine'xact adj. ungenau
inex'cusable adj. unverzeihlich
inexhaustible /ɪnɪɡˈzɔːstɪbl/ adj.
unerschöpflich; unverwüstlich ⟨Person⟩
inexorable /ɪnˈeksərəbl/ adj. unerbittlich
inex'pensive adj. preisgünstig
inex'perience n. Unerfahrenheit, die
inex'perienced adj. unerfahren; ∼ in
sth. wenig vertraut mit etw.
inexpert /ɪnˈekspɜːt/ adj. unerfahren
inex'plicable adj. unerklärlich
inexpressive /ɪnɪkˈspresɪv/ adj.
ausdruckslos ⟨Gesicht, Augen⟩; trocken
⟨Ausdrucksweise, Sprache⟩
inextricably /ɪnˈekstrɪkəblɪ/ adv. become
∼ **entangled** sich vollkommen verheddern
(ugs.); [be] ∼ **linked** untrennbar verbunden
[sein]
infallibility /ɪnfælɪˈbɪlɪtɪ/ n. Unfehlbarkeit,
die
in'fallible adj. unfehlbar
infamous /ˈɪnfəməs/ adj. berüchtigt
infancy /ˈɪnfənsɪ/ n. frühe Kindheit; be in
its ∼ (fig.) noch in den Anfängen stecken
infant /ˈɪnfənt/ n. kleines Kind   ⋯⟶

infantile /'ɪnfəntaɪl/ adj. kindlich; (childish) kindisch

infant mor'tality n. Säuglingssterblichkeit, die

infantry /'ɪnfəntrɪ/ n. Infanterie, die

'infant school n. (Brit.) ≈ Vorschule, die

infatuated /ɪn'fætjʊeɪtɪd/ adj. be ~ with sb. in jmdn. vernarrt sein

infect /ɪn'fekt/ v.t. anstecken; infizieren; **the wound became ~ed** die Wunde entzündete sich

infection /ɪn'fekʃn/ n. Infektion, die; **throat/ear/eye ~:** Hals-/Ohren-/ Augenentzündung, die

infectious /ɪn'fekʃəs/ adj. ansteckend; **be ~** ⟨Person:⟩ eine ansteckende Krankheit haben

infer /ɪn'fɜː(r)/ v.t., **-rr-** schließen (from aus); ziehen ⟨Schlussfolgerung⟩

inference /'ɪnfərəns/ n. [Schluss]folgerung, die

inferior /ɪn'fɪərɪə(r)/ [1] adj. (of lower quality) minderwertig ⟨Ware⟩; minder... ⟨Qualität⟩; unterlegen ⟨Gegner⟩; **~ to sth.** schlechter als etw.; **feel ~:** Minderwertigkeitsgefühle haben [2] n. Untergebene, der/die

inferiority /ɪnfɪərɪ'ɒrɪtɪ/ n. Minderwertigkeit, die; (of opponent) Unterlegenheit, die

inferi'ority complex n. Minderwertigkeitskomplex, der

infernal /ɪn'fɜːnl/ adj. (a) (of hell) höllisch (b) (coll.) verdammt (salopp)

inferno /ɪn'fɜːnəʊ/ n. Inferno, das

in'fertile adj. unfruchtbar

infer'tility n. Unfruchtbarkeit, die

infest /ɪn'fest/ v.t. ⟨Ungeziefer:⟩ befallen; ⟨Unkraut:⟩ überwuchern; **~ed with** befallen/ überwuchert von

infestation /ɪnfes'teɪʃn/ n. **~ of rats/ insects** Ratten-/Insektenplage, die

infidelity /ɪnfɪ'delɪtɪ/ n. Untreue, die (to gegenüber)

'infighting n. (in organization) interne Machtkämpfe Pl.

infiltrate /'ɪnfɪltreɪt/ v.t. (a) infiltrieren; unterwandern ⟨Partei, Organisation⟩ (b) einschleusen ⟨Agenten⟩

infinite /'ɪnfɪnɪt/ adj. (a) (endless) unendlich (b) (very great) ungeheuer

infinitesimal /ɪnfɪnɪ'tesɪml/ adj. (a) (Math.) infinitesimal (b) (very small) äußerst gering; winzig ⟨Menge⟩

infinitive /ɪn'fɪnɪtɪv/ n. Infinitiv, der

infinity /ɪn'fɪnɪtɪ/ n. Unendlichkeit, die

infirm /ɪn'fɜːm/ adj. gebrechlich

infirmary /ɪn'fɜːmərɪ/ n. (hospital) Krankenhaus, das

infirmity /ɪn'fɜːmɪtɪ/ n. Gebrechlichkeit, die; (malady) Gebrechen, das

inflamed /ɪn'fleɪmd/ adj. (Med.) be/become ~: entzündet sein/sich entzünden

inflammable /ɪn'flæməbl/ adj. feuergefährlich

inflammation /ɪnflə'meɪʃn/ n. (Med.) Entzündung, die

inflammatory /ɪn'flæmətərɪ/ adj. aufrührerisch; **an ~ speech** eine Hetzrede

inflatable /ɪn'fleɪtəbl/ adj. aufblasbar; **~ dinghy** Schlauchboot, das

inflate /ɪn'fleɪt/ v.t. aufblasen; (with pump) aufpumpen

inflated /ɪn'fleɪtɪd/ adj. (lit or fig.) aufgeblasen

inflation /ɪn'fleɪʃn/ n. (Econ.) Inflation, die

in'flexible adj. (a) (stiff) unbiegsam (b) (obstinate) [geistig] unbeweglich

inflict /ɪn'flɪkt/ v.t. zufügen ⟨Leid, Schmerzen⟩; beibringen ⟨Wunde⟩; versetzen ⟨Schlag⟩ (on Dat.)

infliction /ɪn'flɪkʃn/ n. ▶ INFLICT: Zufügen, das; Beibringen, das; Versetzen, das

'in-flight adj. Bord⟨verpflegung, -programm⟩

influence /'ɪnflʊəns/ [1] n. Einfluss, der; **be a good/bad ~ [on sb.]** einen guten/ schlechten Einfluss [auf jmdn.] ausüben [2] v.t. beeinflussen

influential /ɪnflʊ'enʃl/ adj. einflussreich

influenza /ɪnflʊ'enzə/ n. Grippe, die

influx /'ɪnflʌks/ n. Zustrom, der

info /'ɪnfəʊ/ n. (coll.) Infos Pl. (ugs.)

inform /ɪn'fɔːm/ [1] v.t. informieren (of über + Akk.); **keep sb. ~ed** jmdn. auf dem Laufenden halten [2] v.i. **~ against or on sb.** jmdn. denunzieren (to bei)

in'formal adj. (a) zwanglos (b) (unofficial) informell

infor'mality n. Zwanglosigkeit, die

informant /ɪn'fɔːmənt/ n. Informant, der/ Informantin, die

information /ɪnfə'meɪʃn/ n. Informationen Pl.; **give ~ on sth.** Auskunft über etw. (Akk.) erteilen; **piece or bit of ~:** Information, die

information: ~ bureau, ~ centre ns. Auskunftsbüro, das; ~ **desk** n. Informationsschalter, der; ~ **explosion** n. Informationsflut, die; ~ **highway** n. (Comp.) Datenautobahn, die; ~ **office** ▶ ~ BUREAU; ~ **pack** n. Informationspaket, das; (folder etc.) Informationsmappe, die; ~ **retrieval** n. (Comp.) Retrieval, das; ~ **science** n. Informatik, die; ~ **superhighway** n. (Comp.) Datenautobahn, die; Datensuperhighway, der; ~ **system** n. Informationssystem, das; ~ **technology** n. Informationstechnologie, die

informative /ɪn'fɔːmətɪv/ adj. informativ; **not very ~:** nicht sehr aufschlussreich ⟨Dokument, Schriftstück⟩

informed /ɪn'fɔːmd/ adj. informiert

in'former *n.* Denunziant, *der/* Denunziantin, *die*

infra-red /ɪnfrə'red/ *adj.* infrarot

infrastructure /'ɪnfrəstrʌktʃə(r)/ *n.* Infrastruktur, *die*

infrequency /ɪn'fri:kwənsɪ/ *n.* Seltenheit, *die*

in'frequent *adj.,* **in'frequently** *adv.* selten

infringe /ɪn'frɪndʒ/ *v.t. & i.* ~ [on] verstoßen gegen

in'fringement *n.* Verstoß, *der* (of gegen)

infuriate /ɪn'fjʊərɪeɪt/ *v.t.* wütend machen; **be** ~d wütend sein (by über + *Akk.*)

infuriating /ɪn'fjʊərɪeɪtɪŋ/ *adj.* ärgerlich

ingenious /ɪn'dʒi:nɪəs/ *adj.* einfallsreich; genial ⟨*Methode, Idee*⟩; raffiniert ⟨*Spielzeug, Maschine*⟩

ingenuity /ɪndʒɪ'nju:ɪtɪ/ *n.* Genialität, *die*

ingot /'ɪŋɡət/ *n.* Ingot, *der*

ingratiate /ɪn'greɪʃɪeɪt/ *v. refl.* ~ oneself **with sb.** sich bei jmdm. einschmeicheln

in'gratitude *n.* Undankbarkeit, *die* (to[wards] gegenüber)

ingredient /ɪn'gri:dɪənt/ *n.* Zutat, *die*

ingrowing /'ɪngrəʊɪŋ/ *adj.* eingewachsen ⟨*Zehennagel usw.*⟩

inhabit /ɪn'hæbɪt/ *v.t.* bewohnen

inhabitable /ɪn'hæbɪtəbl/ *adj.* bewohnbar

inhabitant /ɪn'hæbɪtənt/ *n.* Bewohner, *der/*Bewohnerin, *die*

inhale /ɪn'heɪl/ *v.t. & i.* einatmen; inhalieren (ugs.) ⟨*Zigarettenrauch usw.*⟩

inherent /ɪn'hɪərənt, ɪn'herənt/ *adj. adj.* (belonging by nature) innewohnend (geh.); natürlich ⟨*Anmut, Eleganz*⟩

inherit /ɪn'herɪt/ *v.t.* erben

inheritance /ɪn'herɪtəns/ *n.* Erbe, *das;* (inheriting) Erbschaft, *die*

in'heritance tax *n.* Erbschaftssteuer, *die*

inhibit /ɪn'hɪbɪt/ *v.t.* hemmen

in'hibited *adj.* gehemmt

inhibition /ɪnhɪ'bɪʃn/ *n.* Hemmung, *die*

inho'spitable *adj.* ungastlich ⟨*Person, Verhalten*⟩; unwirtlich ⟨*Gegend, Klima*⟩

'in-house *adj.* hausintern

in'human *adj.* unmenschlich

inhumane /ɪnhju:'meɪn/ *adj.* unmenschlich

initial /ɪ'nɪʃl/ ⒈ *adj.* anfänglich; Anfangs⟨*stadium, -schwierigkeiten*⟩ ⒉ *n. esp. in pl.* Initiale, *die* ⒊ *v.t.,* (Brit.) **-ll-** abzeichnen ⟨*Scheck, Quittung*⟩; paraphieren ⟨*Vertrag, Abkommen usw.*⟩

initial 'letter *n.* Anfangsbuchstabe, *der*

i'nitially *adv.* anfangs; am Anfang

initiate /ɪ'nɪʃɪeɪt/ *v.t.* **(a)** (introduce) einführen (**into** in + *Akk.*); (into knowledge, mystery) einweihen (**into** in + *Akk.*) **(b)** (begin) einleiten

initiation /ɪnɪʃɪ'eɪʃn/ *n.* **(a)** (introduction) Einführung, *die* **(b)** (into knowledge, mystery) Einweihung, *die*

initiative /ɪ'nɪʃətɪv/ *n.* Initiative, *die;* **lack** ~: keine Initiative haben

inject /ɪn'dʒekt/ *v.t.* [ein]spritzen; injizieren (Med.)

injection /ɪn'dʒekʃn/ *n.* Spritze, *die;* Injektion, *die*

injure /'ɪndʒə(r)/ *v.t.* **(a)** verletzen; **his leg was** ~d er wurde/(state) war am Bein verletzt **(b)** (impair) schaden (+ *Dat.*)

injured /'ɪndʒəd/ *adj.* verletzt; verwundet ⟨*Soldat*⟩

injury /'ɪndʒərɪ/ *n.* Verletzung, *die* (to *Gen.*)

'injury time *n.* (Brit. Footb.) Nachspielzeit, *die;* **be into/play** ~: nachspielen

in'justice *n.* Ungerechtigkeit, *die*

ink /ɪŋk/ *n.* Tinte, *die*

'ink-jet printer *n.* Tintenstrahldrucker, *der*

inkling /'ɪŋklɪŋ/ *n.* Ahnung, *die;* **have an** ~ **of sth.** etw. ahnen

'ink pad *n.* Stempelkissen, *das*

inland /'ɪnlənd, 'ɪnlænd/ *adj.* Binnen-; binnenländisch

Inland 'Revenue *n.* (Brit.) ≈ Finanzamt, *das*

'in-laws *n. pl.* (coll.) Schwiegereltern *Pl.*

inlet /'ɪnlət/ *n.* [schmale] Bucht

'inmate *n.* Insasse, *der/*Insassin, *die*

inn /ɪn/ *n.* (hotel) Gasthof, *der;* (pub) Wirtshaus, *das*

innate /ɪ'neɪt/ *adj.* angeboren

inner /'ɪnə(r)/ *adj.* inner...; Innen⟨*hof, -tür, -fläche, -seite usw.*⟩; ~ **tube** Schlauch, *der*

inner 'city *n.* Innenstadt, *die;* ~ **areas** Innenbezirke

innermost /'ɪnəməʊst/ *adj.* innerst...

'innkeeper *n.* [Gast]wirt, *der/*-wirtin, *die*

innocence /'ɪnəsəns/ *n.* **(a)** Unschuld, *die* **(b)** (naïvity) Naivität, *die*

innocent /'ɪnəsənt/ *adj.* **(a)** unschuldig (of an + *Dat.*) **(b)** (naïve) naiv

innocuous /ɪ'nɒkjʊəs/ *adj.* harmlos

innovation /ɪnə'veɪʃn/ *n.* Innovation, *die;* (thing, change) Neuerung, *die*

innovative /'ɪnəvətɪv/ *adj.* innovativ

innuendo /ɪnjuː'endəʊ/ *n., pl.* ~**es** *or* ~**s** versteckte Andeutung

innumerable /ɪ'nju:mərəbl/ *adj.* unzählig

innumeracy /ɪ'nju:mərəsɪ/ *n.* Nicht-Rechnen-Können, *das*

innumerate /ɪ'nju:mərət/ *adj.* **be** ~: nicht rechnen können

inoculate /ɪ'nɒkjʊleɪt/ *v.t.* impfen

inoculation /ɪnɒkjʊ'leɪʃn/ *n.* Impfung, *die*

inof'fensive *adj.* harmlos

inoperable /ɪn'ɒpərəbl/ adj. (Surg.) inoperabel (fachspr.)

inoperative /ɪn'ɒpərətɪv/ adj. ungültig

in'opportune adj. unpassend; unangebracht ⟨Bemerkung⟩

inordinate /ɪ'nɔːdɪnət/ adj. unmäßig; ungeheuer ⟨Menge⟩

inor'ganic adj. anorganisch

'inpatient n. stationär behandelter Patient/ behandelte Patientin

'input n. Input, der od. das

inquest /'ɪŋkwest/ n. gerichtliche Untersuchung der Todesursache

inquire, inquiry ▶ ENQUIR-

inquisitive /ɪn'kwɪzɪtɪv/ adj. neugierig

'inroad n. Eingriff, der (on, into in + Akk.); **make ~s into sb.'s savings** jmds. Ersparnisse angreifen

in'sane adj. geisteskrank

in'sanitary adj. unhygienisch

in'sanity n. Geisteskrankheit, die

insatiable /ɪn'seɪʃəbl/ adj. unersättlich; unstillbar ⟨Verlangen⟩

inscribe /ɪn'skraɪb/ v.t. schreiben; (on stone, rock) einmeißeln; mit einer Inschrift versehen ⟨Denkmal, Grabstein⟩

inscription /ɪn'skrɪpʃn/ n. Inschrift, die; (on coin) Aufschrift, die

inscrutable /ɪn'skruːtəbl/ adj. unergründlich; undurchdringlich ⟨Miene⟩

insect /'ɪnsekt/ n. Insekt, das

insect: ~ bite n. Insektenstich, der; **~-borne** adj. durch Insekten übertragen ⟨Krankheit⟩

insecticide /ɪn'sektɪsaɪd/ n. Insektizid, das

'insect repellent n. Insektenschutzmittel, das

inse'cure adj. unsicher

inse'curity n. Unsicherheit, die

insemination /ɪnsemɪ'neɪʃn/ n. (of woman) Befruchtung, die; (of animal) Besamung, die

in'sensitive adj. (a) gefühllos ⟨Person, Art⟩; (unappreciative) unempfänglich (to für) (b) (physically) unempfindlich (to gegen)

in'separable adj. untrennbar; (fig.) unzertrennlich

insert /ɪn'sɜːt/ v.t. (a) einlegen ⟨Film⟩; einwerfen ⟨Münze⟩; hineinstecken ⟨Schlüssel⟩; einstechen ⟨Nadel⟩ (b) (Comp.) einfügen; **~ key** Einfügetaste, die

insertion /ɪn'sɜːʃn/ n. ▶ INSERT: Einlegen, das; Einwerfen, das; Hineinstecken, das; Einstechen, das; Einfügen, das

'inset n. (small map) Nebenkarte, die; (small photograph, diagram) Nebenbild, das

inside 1 /-'-, '--/ n. (a) (internal side) Innenseite, die; **on the ~:** innen; **to/from the ~:** nach/von innen (b) (inner part) Innere, das 2 /'--/ adj. inner...; Innen⟨wand, -einrichtung, -ansicht⟩; (fig.) intern

3 /-'-/ adv. (on or in the ~) innen; (to the ~) nach innen hinein/herein; (indoors) drinnen; **come ~:** hereinkommen; **go ~:** hineingehen; (ins Haus) hineingehen; **turn a jacket ~ out** eine Jacke nach links wenden; **know sth. ~ out** etw. in- und auswendig kennen

4 /-'-/ prep. (position) in (+ Dat.); (direction) in (+ Akk.) hinein

inside-'leg adj. **~ measurement** Schrittlänge, die

insidious /ɪn'sɪdɪəs/ adj. heimtückisch

'insight n. (discernment) Verständnis, das; **gain an ~ into sth.** Einblick in etw. (Akk.) gewinnen

insig'nificant adj. unbedeutend; geringfügig ⟨Summe⟩

insin'cere adj. unaufrichtig

insin'cerity n. Unaufrichtigkeit, die

insinuate /ɪn'sɪnjʊeɪt/ v.t. andeuten (to sb. jmdm. gegenüber)

insinuation /ɪnsɪnjʊ'eɪʃn/ n. Anspielung, die (about auf + Akk.)

insipid /ɪn'sɪpɪd/ adj. fade

insist /ɪn'sɪst/ v.i. bestehen ([up]on auf + Dat.); **~ on doing sth./on sb.'s doing sth.** darauf bestehen, etw. zu tun/dass jmd. etw. tut; **if you ~:** wenn du darauf bestehst

insistence /ɪn'sɪstəns/ n. Bestehen, das (on auf + Dat.)

insistent /ɪn'sɪstənt/ adj. **be ~ that ...:** darauf bestehen, dass ...

insolence /'ɪnsələns/ n. Unverschämtheit, die; Frechheit, die

insolent /'ɪnsələnt/ adj., **'insolently** adv. unverschämt; frech

in'soluble adj. (a) (esp. Chem.) unlöslich (b) (not solvable) unlösbar

insolvency /ɪn'sɒlvənsɪ/ n. Zahlungsunfähigkeit, die

in'solvent adj. zahlungsunfähig

insomnia /ɪn'sɒmnɪə/ n. Schlaflosigkeit, die

insomniac /ɪn'sɒmnɪæk/ n. **be an ~:** an Schlaflosigkeit leiden

inspect /ɪn'spekt/ v.t. prüfend betrachten; (examine officially) überprüfen; kontrollieren ⟨Räumlichkeiten⟩

inspection /ɪn'spekʃn/ n. Überprüfung, die; (of premises) Kontrolle, die; Inspektion, die; **on [closer] ~:** bei näherer Betrachtung

inspector /ɪn'spektə(r)/ n. (a) (on bus, train, etc.) Kontrolleur, der/Kontrolleurin, die (b) (Brit.) ≈ Polizeiinspektor, der

inspiration /ɪnspə'reɪʃn/ n. Inspiration, die (geh.)

inspire /ɪn'spaɪə(r)/ v.t. (a) inspirieren (geh.) ⟨Person⟩ (b) (instil) einflößen (in Dat.)

inspiring /ɪn'spaɪərɪŋ/ adj. inspirierend (geh.)

insta'bility n. Instabilität, die; (of person) Labilität, die

install /ɪnˈstɔːl/ v.t. installieren; einbauen ‹*Badezimmer*›; anschließen ‹*Telefon, Herd*›; ~ **oneself** sich installieren

installation /ɪnstəˈleɪʃn/ n. **(a)** Installation, die; (of bathroom) Einbau, der; (of telephone, cooker) Anschluss, der **(b)** (apparatus etc. installed) Anlage, die

instalment (*Amer.*: **installment**) /ɪnˈstɔːlmənt/ n. **(a)** (part payment) Rate, die; **pay by** or **in ~s** in Raten zahlen **(b)** (of serial, novel) Fortsetzung, die; (Radio, Telev.) Folge, die

instance /ˈɪnstəns/ n. (example) Beispiel, das (of für); **for ~**: zum Beispiel; **in many ~s** (cases) in vielen Fällen; **in the first ~**: zunächst einmal

instant /ˈɪnstənt/ **1** adj. unmittelbar; sofortig ‹*Wirkung, Linderung, Ergebnis*›; ~ **coffee/tea** Pulverkaffee/Instanttee, der; ~ **potatoes** fertiger Kartoffelbrei **2** n. Augenblick, der; **at that very ~**: genau in dem Augenblick; **come here this ~**: komm sofort her; **in an ~**: augenblicklich

instantaneous /ɪnstənˈteɪnɪəs/ adj. unmittelbar; **his reaction was ~**: er reagierte sofort

'instantly adv. sofort

instead /ɪnˈsted/ adv. stattdessen; ~ **of doing sth.** [an]statt etw. zu tun; ~ **of sth.** anstelle einer Sache (*Gen.*); **I will go ~ of you** ich gehe an deiner Stelle

'instep n. (of foot) Spann, der; Fußrücken, der; (of shoe) Blatt, das

instigate /ˈɪnstɪɡeɪt/ v.t. anstiften (**to** zu); initiieren (geh.) ‹*Reformen, Projekt usw.*›

instigation /ɪnstɪˈɡeɪʃn/ n. Anstiftung, die; (of reforms, project, etc.) Initiierung, die; **at sb.'s ~**: auf jmds. Betreiben (*Akk.*)

instil (*Amer.*: **instill**) /ɪnˈstɪl/ v.t., **-ll-** einflößen (**in** *Dat.*); beibringen ‹*gutes Benehmen, Wissen*› (**in** *Dat.*)

instinct /ˈɪnstɪŋkt/ n. Instinkt, der

instinctive /ɪnˈstɪŋktɪv/ adj., **in'stinctively** adv. instinktiv

institute /ˈɪnstɪtjuːt/ **1** n. Institut, das **2** v.t. einführen; einleiten ‹*Suche, Verfahren*›; anstrengen ‹*Prozess*›

institution /ɪnstɪˈtjuːʃn/ n. Institution, die; (home) Heim, das; Anstalt, die

instruct /ɪnˈstrʌkt/ v.t. **(a)** (teach) unterrichten ‹*Klasse, Fach*› **(b)** (direct, command) anweisen

instruction /ɪnˈstrʌkʃn/ n. **(a)** (teaching) Unterricht, der **(b)** esp. in pl. (direction, order) Anweisung, die; ~ **manual/~s for use** Gebrauchsanleitung, die

instructive /ɪnˈstrʌktɪv/ adj. aufschlussreich; lehrreich ‹*Erfahrung, Buch*›

instructor /ɪnˈstrʌktə(r)/ n. Lehrer, der/ Lehrerin, die; (Mil.) Ausbilder, der

instrument /ˈɪnstrʊmənt/ n. Instrument, das

instrumental /ɪnstrəˈmentl/ adj. **(a)** (Mus.) Instrumental- **(b)** (helpful) dienlich (**to** *Dat.*); **he was ~ in finding me a job** er hat mir zu einer Stelle verholfen

instrumentalist /ɪnstrʊˈmentəlɪst/ n. Instrumentalist, der/Instrumentalistin, die

insubordinate /ɪnsəˈbɔːdɪnət/ adj. aufsässig

insubordination /ɪnsəbɔːdɪˈneɪʃn/ n. Aufsässigkeit, die

insubstantial /ɪnsəbˈstænʃl/ adj. wenig substanziell (geh.)

insufferable /ɪnˈsʌfərəbl/ adj. (unbearably arrogant) unausstehlich

insuf'ficient adj. nicht genügend; unzulänglich ‹*Beweise*›; unzureichend ‹*Versorgung, Beleuchtung*›

insuf'ficiently adv. ungenügend

insular /ˈɪnsjʊlə(r)/ adj. **(a)** Insel-; insular (fachspr.) **(b)** (fig.: narrow-minded) provinziell (abwertend)

insulate /ˈɪnsjʊleɪt/ v.t. isolieren (**against, from** gegen); **insulating tape** Isolierband, das

insulation /ɪnsjʊˈleɪʃn/ n. Isolierung, die

insulin /ˈɪnsjʊlɪn/ n. Insulin, das

insult **1** /ˈɪnsʌlt/ n. Beleidigung, die (**to** *Gen.*) **2** /ɪnˈsʌlt/ v.t. beleidigen

insulting /ɪnˈsʌltɪŋ/ adj. beleidigend

insuperable /ɪnˈsuːpərəbl/ adj. unüberwindlich

insupportable /ɪnsəˈpɔːtəbl/ adj. (unendurable) unerträglich

insurance /ɪnˈʃʊərəns/ n. Versicherung, die; (fig.) Sicherheit, die; **take out ~ against/ on sth.** eine Versicherung gegen etw. abschließen/etw. versichern lassen; **travel ~**: Reisegepäck- und -unfallversicherung, die

insurance: ~ **agent** n. Versicherungsvertreter, der/-vertreterin, die; ~ **broker** n. Versicherungsmakler, der/ -maklerin, die; ~ **claim** n. Versicherungsanspruch, der; ~ **company** n. Versicherungsgesellschaft, die; ~ **stamp** n. (Brit.) Versicherungsmarke, die

insure /ɪnˈʃʊə(r)/ v.t. versichern ‹*Person*›; versichern lassen ‹*Gepäck, Gemälde usw.*›; ~ **[oneself] against sth.** [sich] gegen etw. versichern

insurer /ɪnˈʃʊərə(r)/ n. Versicherer, der

insurmountable /ɪnsəˈmaʊntəbl/ adj. unüberwindlich

intact /ɪnˈtækt/ adj. **(a)** (entire) unbeschädigt; intakt ‹*Uhr, Maschine usw.*› **(b)** (unimpaired) unversehrt

'intake n. **(a)** (action) Aufnahme, die **(b)** (persons, things) Neuzugänge Pl.; (amount) aufgenommene Menge

in'tangible *adj.* nicht greifbar; (mentally) unbestimmbar

integral /'ɪntɪgrl/ *adj.* (a) wesentlich ⟨*Bestandteil*⟩
(b) (whole) vollständig

integrate /'ɪntɪgreɪt/ *v.t.* integrieren (into in + *Akk.*)

integration /ɪntɪ'greɪʃn/ *n.* Integration, *die* (into in + *Akk.*)

integrity /ɪn'tegrɪtɪ/ *n.* Redlichkeit, *die*

intellect /'ɪntəlekt/ *n.* Verstand, *der;* Intellekt, *der*

intellectual /ɪntə'lektjʊəl/ ①*adj.* intellektuell; geistig anspruchsvoll ⟨*Person, Publikum*⟩
②*n.* Intellektuelle, *der/die*

intelligence /ɪn'telɪdʒəns/ *n.* (a) Intelligenz, *die*
(b) (information) Informationen *Pl.*
(c) military ∼ (organization) militärischer Geheimdienst

intelligence: ∼ **quotient** *n.* Intelligenzquotient, *der;* ∼ **test** *n.* Intelligenztest, *der*

intelligent /ɪn'telɪdʒənt/ *adj.* intelligent

intelligible /ɪn'telɪdʒɪbl/ *adj.* verständlich (to für)

intend /ɪn'tend/ *v.t.* beabsichtigen; it was ∼ed as a joke das sollte ein Witz sein

in'tended *adj.* beabsichtigt ⟨*Wirkung*⟩; be ∼ for sb./sth. für jmdn./etw. gedacht sein

intense /ɪn'tens/ *adj.* (a) intensiv; groß ⟨*Hitze, Belastung, Interesse*⟩; stark ⟨*Schmerzen*⟩
(b) (earnest) ernst

in'tensely *adv.* äußerst; intensiv ⟨*studieren, fühlen*⟩

intensify /ɪn'tensɪfaɪ/ ①*v.t.* intensivieren
②*v.i.* zunehmen

intensity /ɪn'tensɪtɪ/ *n.* ▶ INTENSE A: Intensität, *die;* Größe, *die;* Stärke, *die*

intensive /ɪn'tensɪv/ *adj.* intensiv; Intensiv⟨*kurs*⟩; be in ∼ care auf der Intensivstation sein

in'tensively *adv.* intensiv

intent /ɪn'tent/ ①*n.* Absicht, *die;* to all ∼s and purposes im Grunde
②*adj.* be ∼ on achieving sth. etw. unbedingt erreichen wollen

intention /ɪn'tenʃn/ *n.* Absicht, *die*

intentional /ɪn'tenʃənl/ *adj.,* **in'tentionally** *adv.* absichtlich

in'tently *adv.* aufmerksam

interact /ɪntər'ækt/ *v.i.* interagieren

interaction /ɪntər'ækʃn/ *n.* Interaktion, *die*

interactive /ɪntər'æktɪv/ *adj.* (Sociol., Psych., Comp.) interaktiv; ∼ television interaktives Fernsehen

intercede /ɪntə'siːd/ *v.i.* sich einsetzen (with bei; for, on behalf of für)

intercept /ɪntə'sept/ *v.t.* abfangen

interchange ①/'ɪntətʃeɪndʒ/ *n.* (a) Austausch, *der*
(b) (road junction) [Autobahn]kreuz, *das*
②/ɪntə'tʃeɪndʒ/ *v.t.* austauschen

interchangeable /ɪntə'tʃeɪndʒəbl/ *adj.* austauschbar

inter-city /ɪntə'sɪtɪ/ *adj.* Intercity-; ∼ **train** Intercity[-Zug], *der*

intercom /'ɪntəkɒm/ *n.* (coll.) Gegensprechanlage, *die*

interconnect /ɪntəkə'nekt/ ①*v.t.* miteinander verbinden
②*v.i.* miteinander in Zusammenhang stehen

intercontinental /ɪntəkɒntɪ'nentl/ *adj.* interkontinental

intercourse /'ɪntəkɔːs/ *n.* (sexual) [Geschlechts]verkehr, *der*

interest /'ɪntrəst/ ①*n.* (a) Interesse, *das;* take *or* have an ∼ in sb./sth. sich für jmdn./etw. interessieren; [just] for *or* out of ∼: [nur] interessehalber; with ∼: interessiert; act in one's own/sb.'s ∼[s] im eigenen/in jmds. Interesse handeln; be of ∼: interessant sein (to für)
(b) (Finance) Zinsen *Pl.*
②*v.t.* interessieren; be ∼ed sich interessieren (in für)

interest-'free *adj., adv.* unverzinslich ⟨*Schuldverschreibung*⟩; zinsfrei ⟨*Darlehen*⟩

'interesting *adj.* interessant

'interest rate *n.* Zinssatz, *der;* Zinsfuß, *der*

interface /'ɪntəfeɪs/ *n.* (Comp.) Schnittstelle, *die*

interfere /ɪntə'fɪə(r)/ *v.i.* sich einmischen (in in + *Akk.*); ∼ with sth. sich (*Dat.*) an etw. (*Dat.*) zu schaffen machen

interference /ɪntə'fɪərəns/ *n.* (a) (interfering) Einmischung, *die*
(b) (Radio, Telev.) Störung, *die*

interim /'ɪntərɪm/ ①*n.* in the ∼: in der Zwischenzeit
②*adj.* vorläufig

interior /ɪn'tɪərɪə(r)/ ①*adj.* inner...; Innen⟨*fläche, -wand*⟩
②*n.* Innere, *das*

interior: ∼ **deco'ration** *n.* Raumgestaltung, *die;* ∼ **'decorator** *n.* Raumgestalter, *der*/-gestalterin, *die;* ∼ **de'sign** *n.* Innenarchitektur, *die;* ∼ **de'signer** *n.* Innenarchitekt, *der*/-architektin, *die*

interject /ɪntə'dʒekt/ *v.t.* einwerfen

interjection /ɪntə'dʒekʃn/ *n.* Ausruf, *der*

interloper /'ɪntələʊpə(r)/ *n.* Eindringling, *der*

interlude /'ɪntəluːd/ *n.* Pause, *die;* (music) Zwischenspiel, *das*

intermediary /ɪntə'miːdɪərɪ/ *n.* Vermittler, *der*/Vermittlerin, *die*

intermediate /ɪntə'miːdjət/ *adj.* Zwischen-

interminable /ɪn'tɜːmɪnəbl/ *adj.* endlos

intermingle /ɪntə'mɪŋgl/ v.i. sich vermischen

intermission /ɪntə'mɪʃn/ n. Pause, die

intermittent /ɪntə'mɪtənt/ adj. in Abständen auftretend

inter'mittently adv. in Abständen

intern /ɪn'tɜːn/ v.t. gefangen halten

internal /ɪn'tɜːnl/ adj. inner...; Innen⟨fläche, -abmessungen⟩

internalize (internalise) /ɪn'tɜːnəlaɪz/ v.t. (Psych.) verinnerlichen

internally /ɪn'tɜːnəlɪ/ adv. innerlich

international /ɪntə'næʃənl/ [1] adj. international
  [2] n. (a) (Sport) (contest) Länderspiel, das
  (b) (participant) Nationalspieler, der/ -spielerin, die

international: ~ **call** n. Auslandsgespräch, das; ~ **'law** n. Völkerrecht, das

inter'nationally adv. international

International 'Monetary Fund n. Internationaler Währungsfonds

internee /ɪntɜː'niː/ n. Internierte, der/die

Internet /'ɪntənet/ n. the ~ das Internet; on the ~: im Internet

Internet 'Service Provider n. (Comp.) Internetprovider, der

in'ternment n. Internierung, die

interplay /'ɪntəpleɪ/ n. Zusammenspiel, das

interpret /ɪn'tɜːprɪt/ [1] v.t. (a) interpretieren; deuten ⟨Traum, Zeichen⟩
  (b) (between languages) dolmetschen
  [2] v.i. dolmetschen

interpretation /ɪntɜːprɪ'teɪʃn/ n. Interpretation, die; (of dream, symptoms) Deutung, die

in'terpreter n. Dolmetscher, der/ Dolmetscherin, die

interrogate /ɪn'terəgeɪt/ v.t. verhören; ausfragen ⟨Freund, Kind usw.⟩

interrogation /ɪnterə'geɪʃn/ n. Verhör, das

interrogative /ɪntə'rɒgətɪv/ adj. (Ling.) Interrogativ-

interrogator /ɪn'terəgeɪtə(r)/ n. Vernehmer, der

interrupt /ɪntə'rʌpt/ [1] v.t. unterbrechen; don't ~ me when I'm busy stör mich nicht, wenn ich zu tun habe
  [2] v.i. unterbrechen; stören

interruption /ɪntə'rʌpʃn/ n. Unterbrechung, die; Störung, die

intersect /ɪntə'sekt/ v.i. (a) ⟨Straßen:⟩ sich kreuzen
  (b) (Geom.) sich schneiden

intersection /ɪntə'sekʃn/ n. (a) (road junction) Kreuzung, die
  (b) (Geom.) Schnittpunkt, der

intersperse /ɪntə'spɜːs/ v.t. be ~d with durchsetzt sein mit

interval /'ɪntəvl/ n. (a) [Zeit]abstand, der; at ~s in Abständen
  (b) (break; also Brit. Theatre etc.) Pause, die; sunny ~s Aufheiterungen Pl.

intervene /ɪntə'viːn/ v.i. (a) [vermittelnd] eingreifen (in in + Akk.)
  (b) the intervening years die dazwischenliegenden Jahre

intervention /ɪntə'venʃn/ n. Eingreifen, das; Intervention, die (bes. Politik)

interview /'ɪntəvjuː/ [1] n. (a) (for job) Vorstellungsgespräch, das
  (b) (Journ., Radio, Telev.) Interview, das
  [2] v.t. ein Vorstellungsgespräch führen mit; interviewen ⟨Politiker, Filmstar usw.⟩

'interviewer n. Interviewer, der/ Interviewerin, die

intestine /ɪn'testɪn/ n. Darm, der

intimacy /'ɪntɪməsɪ/ n. (a) Vertrautheit, die
  (b) (sexual) Intimität, die

intimate [1] /'ɪntɪmət/ adj. (a) eng ⟨Freund, Verhältnis⟩; genau, (geh.) intim ⟨Kenntnis⟩
  (b) (sexually) intim
  [2] /'ɪntɪmeɪt/ v.t. (imply) andeuten

intimately /'ɪntɪmətlɪ/ adv. genau[estens] ⟨kennen⟩; eng ⟨verbinden⟩

intimidate /ɪn'tɪmɪdeɪt/ v.t. einschüchtern

intimidation /ɪntɪmɪ'deɪʃn/ n. Einschüchterung, die

into /before vowel 'ɪntʊ, before consonant 'ɪntə/ prep. in (+ Akk.); (against) gegen; I went out ~ the street ich ging auf die Straße hinaus; translate sth. ~ English etw. ins Englische übersetzen

in'tolerable adj. unerträglich

in'tolerance n. Intoleranz, die

in'tolerant adj. intolerant (of gegenüber)

intonation /ɪntə'neɪʃn/ n. Intonation, die

intoxicant /ɪn'tɒksɪkənt/ n. Rauschmittel, das

intoxicate /ɪn'tɒksɪkeɪt/ v.t. betrunken machen

intoxication /ɪntɒksɪ'keɪʃn/ n. Rausch, der

intractable /ɪn'træktəbl/ adj. hartnäckig ⟨Problem⟩

intransigent /ɪn'trænsɪdʒənt/ adj. unnachgiebig

in'transitive adj. (Ling.) intransitiv

intra-uterine /ɪntrə'juːtəraɪn/ adj. (Med.) intrauterin; ~ [contraceptive] device Intrauterinpessar, das

intravenous /ɪntrə'viːnəs/ adj. (Med.) intravenös

'in-tray n. Eingangskorb, der

intrepid /ɪn'trepɪd/ adj. unerschrocken

intricacy /'ɪntrɪkəsɪ/ n. Kompliziertheit, die

intricate /'ɪntrɪkət/ adj. kompliziert

intrigue /ɪn'triːg/ v.t. faszinieren ···⟩

intriguing /ɪn'triːɡɪŋ/ adj. faszinierend

intrinsic /ɪn'trɪnsɪk/ adj. innewohnend; inner...; ~ **value** innerer Wert

intrinsically /ɪn'trɪnsɪkəlɪ/ adv. im Wesentlichen

intro /'ɪntrəʊ/ n., pl. ~**s** (coll.) (presentation) Vorstellung, die; (Mus.) Einleitung, die

introduce /ɪntrə'djuːs/ v.t. einführen; ~ **oneself/sb.** [to sb.] sich/jmdn. [jmdm.] vorstellen

introduction /ɪntrə'dʌkʃn/ n. Einführen, das; Einführung, die; (to person) Vorstellung, die; (to book) Einleitung, die

intro'duction agency n. Partnervermittlung[sagentur], die

introductory /ɪntrə'dʌktərɪ/ adj. einleitend; Einführungs⟨kurs, -vortrag⟩

introspective /ɪntrə'spektɪv/ adj. in sich (Akk.) gerichtet

introvert /'ɪntrəvɜːt/ 1 n. Introvertierte, der/die; **be an** ~: introvertiert sein 2 adj. introvertiert

introverted /'ɪntrəvɜːtɪd/ adj. introvertiert

intrude /ɪn'truːd/ v.i. stören

in'truder n. Eindringling, der

in'truder alarm n. Einbruchmeldeanlage, die

intrusion /ɪn'truːʒn/ n. Störung, die

intrusive /ɪn'truːsɪv/ adj. aufdringlich

intuition /ɪntjuː'ɪʃn/ n. Intuition, die

intuitive /ɪn'tjuːɪtɪv/ adj., **in'tuitively** adv. intuitiv

inundate /'ɪnəndeɪt/ v.t. überschwemmen

inure /ɪ'njʊə(r)/ v.t. gewöhnen (**to** an + Akk.)

invade /ɪn'veɪd/ v.t. einfallen in (+ Akk.)

in'vader n. Angreifer, der

invalid[1] /'ɪnvəlɪd/ (Brit.) 1 n. Kranke, der/die; (disabled) Körperbehinderte, der/die 2 adj. körperbehindert

invalid[2] /ɪn'vælɪd/ adj. nicht schlüssig ⟨Argument, Theorie⟩; ungültig ⟨Fahrkarte, Garantie, Vertrag⟩

invalidate /ɪn'vælɪdeɪt/ v.t. aufheben; widerlegen ⟨Theorie, These⟩

in'valuable adj. unersetzlich ⟨Person⟩; unschätzbar ⟨Dienst, Hilfe⟩; außerordentlich wichtig ⟨Rolle⟩

in'variable adj. unveränderlich

invariably /ɪn'veərɪəblɪ/ adv. immer; ausnahmslos ⟨falsch, richtig⟩

invasion /ɪn'veɪʒn/ n. Invasion, die

invective /ɪn'vektɪv/ n. Beschimpfungen Pl.

invent /ɪn'vent/ v.t. erfinden

invention /ɪn'venʃn/ n. Erfindung, die

inventive /ɪn'ventɪv/ adj. (a) schöpferisch ⟨Person, Begabung⟩ (b) (original) originell

inventor /ɪn'ventə(r)/ n. Erfinder, der/Erfinderin, die

inventory /'ɪnvəntərɪ/ n. Bestandsliste, die; **make** or **take an** ~ **of sth.** von etw. ein Inventar aufstellen

inverse /ɪn'vɜːs/ adj. umgekehrt

invert /ɪn'vɜːt/ v.t. umstülpen

in'vertebrate n. wirbelloses Tier

inverted 'commas n. pl. (Brit.) Anführungszeichen Pl.

invest /ɪn'vest/ v.t. (a) (Finance) anlegen (in in + Dat.); investieren (in in + Dat. od. Akk.) (b) (fig.) investieren; ~ **sb. with sth.** jmdm. etw. übertragen; ~ **sth. with sth.** einer Sache (Dat.) etw. verleihen

investigate /ɪn'vestɪɡeɪt/ v.t. untersuchen

investigation /ɪnvestɪ'ɡeɪʃn/ n. Untersuchung, die

investigative /ɪn'vestɪɡətɪv/ adj. detektivisch; ~ **journalism** Enthüllungsjournalismus, der

investigator /ɪn'vestɪɡeɪtə(r)/ n. [private] ~: [Privat]detektiv, der/-detektivin, die

in'vestment n. Investition, die; (money invested) angelegtes Geld; **be a good** ~ (fig.) sich bezahlt machen

investor /ɪn'vestə(r)/ n. [Kapital]anleger, der/-anlegerin, die

inveterate /ɪn'vetərət/ adj. eingefleischt ⟨Trinker, Raucher⟩; unverbesserlich ⟨Lügner⟩

invigilate /ɪn'vɪdʒɪleɪt/ v.i. (Brit.: in examination) Aufsicht führen

invigilator /ɪn'vɪdʒɪleɪtə(r)/ n. (Brit.) Aufsichtsperson, die

invigorate /ɪn'vɪɡəreɪt/ v.t. stärken; (physically) kräftigen

invigorating /ɪn'vɪɡəreɪtɪŋ/ adj. kräftigend ⟨Getränk, Klima⟩

invincible /ɪn'vɪnsɪbl/ adj. unbesiegbar

in'visible adj. unsichtbar

invitation /ɪnvɪ'teɪʃn/ n. Einladung, die; **at sb.'s** ~: auf jmds. Einladung (Akk.)

invite /ɪn'vaɪt/ v.t. (a) (request to come) einladen (b) (request to do sth.) auffordern (c) (bring on) herausfordern ⟨Kritik, Verhängnis⟩

inviting /ɪn'vaɪtɪŋ/ adj. einladend; verlockend ⟨Gedanke, Vorstellung⟩

in-vitro fertili'zation /ɪn'viːtrəʊ fɜːtɪlaɪ'zeɪʃn/ n. künstliche Befruchtung [im Reagenzglas]; In-vitro-Fertilisation, die (fachspr.)

invoice /'ɪnvɔɪs/ 1 n. (bill) Rechnung, die 2 v.t. ~ **sb.** jmdm. eine Rechnung schicken; ~ **sb. for sth.** jmdm. etw. in Rechnung stellen

invoke /ɪn'vəʊk/ v.t. anrufen

in'voluntarily adv., **in'voluntary** adj. unwillkürlich

involve /ɪn'vɒlv/ v.t. (a) (implicate) verwickeln

(b) become *or* **get** ~d **in** a fight in eine Schlägerei verwickelt werden; **get** ~d **with sb.** sich mit jmdm. einlassen
(c) (entail) mit sich bringen
involved /ɪnˈvɒlvd/ *adj.* verwickelt; (complicated) kompliziert
invulnerable /ɪnˈvʌlnərəbl/ *adj.* unverwundbar; (fig.) unantastbar
inward /ˈɪnwəd/ ① *adj.* inner...
② *adv.* einwärts ⟨gerichtet, gebogen⟩; **open** ~: nach innen öffnen
'inwardly *adv.* im Inneren; innerlich
inwards /ˈɪnwədz/ ▶ INWARD 2
iodine /ˈaɪədiːn/ *n.* Jod, *das*
ion /ˈaɪən/ *n.* Ion, *das*
iota /aɪˈəʊtə/ *n.* **not one** *or* **an** ~: nicht ein Jota (geh.)
IOU /aɪəʊˈjuː/ *n.* Schuldschein, *der*
IQ *abbr.* = **intelligence quotient** IQ, *der;* **IQ-test** IQ-Test, *der*
IRA *abbr.* = **Irish Republican Army** IRA, *die*
Iran /ɪˈrɑːn/ *pr. n.* Iran, *der od.* (*das*)
Iraq /ɪˈrɑːk/ *pr. n.* Irak, *der od.* (*das*)
irate /aɪˈreɪt/ *adj.* wütend
Ireland /ˈaɪələnd/ *pr. n.* Irland (*das*)
iris /ˈaɪərɪs/ *n.* (Bot., Anat.) Iris, *die*
Irish /ˈaɪərɪʃ/ ① *adj.* irisch; **sb. is** ~: jmd. ist Ire/Irin
② *n.* **(a)** (language) Irisch, *das; see also* ENGLISH 2A
(b) *constr. as pl.* **the** ~: die Iren *Pl.*
Irish: ~**man** /ˈaɪərɪʃmən/ *n., pl.* ~**men** /ˈaɪərɪʃmən/ Ire, *der;* ~ **Re'public** *pr. n.* Irische Republik; ~ **'Sea** *pr. n.* Irische See; ~**woman** *n.* Irin, *die*
irk /ɜːk/ *v.t.* ärgern
irksome /ˈɜːksəm/ *adj.* lästig
iron /ˈaɪən/ ① *n.* **(a)** (metal) Eisen, *das*
(b) (for smoothing) Bügeleisen, *das*
② *attrib. adj.* eisern; Eisen⟨platte *usw.*⟩
③ *v.t. & i.* bügeln
■ **iron 'out** *v.t.* herausbügeln; (fig.) aus dem Weg räumen
Iron 'Curtain *n.* (Hist.) Eiserner Vorhang
ironic /aɪˈrɒnɪk/, **ironical** /aɪˈrɒnɪkl/ *adj.* ironisch
ironing /ˈaɪənɪŋ/ *n.* Bügeln, *das;* (items) Bügelwäsche, *die;* **do the** ~: bügeln
'ironing board *n.* Bügelbrett, *das*
ironmonger /ˈaɪənmʌŋgə(r)/ *n.* (Brit.) Eisenwarenhändler, *der/*-händlerin, *die*
irony /ˈaɪrənɪ/ *n.* Ironie, *die;* **the** ~ **was that** ...: die Ironie lag darin, dass ...
irradiate /ɪˈreɪdɪeɪt/ *v.t.* bestrahlen
irrational /ɪˈræʃənl/ *adj.* irrational
irreconcilable /ɪˈrekənsaɪləbl/ *adj.* (incompatible) unvereinbar
irrefutable /ɪrɪˈfjuːtəbl/ *adj.* unwiderlegbar

irregular /ɪˈregjʊlə(r)/ *adj.* unregelmäßig; unkorrekt ⟨*Verhalten, Handlung usw.*⟩
irregularity /ɪregjʊˈlærɪtɪ/ *n.* ▶ IRREGULAR: Unregelmäßigkeit, *die;* Unkorrektheit, *die*
irrelevance /ɪˈrelɪvəns/, **irrelevancy** /ɪˈrelɪvənsɪ/ *ns.* Belanglosigkeit, *die;* Irrelevanz, *die* (geh.)
irrelevant /ɪˈrelɪvənt/ *adj.* belanglos; irrelevant (geh.)
irreparable /ɪˈrepərəbl/ *adj.* nicht wieder gutzumachen *nicht präd.;* irreparabel (geh., Med.)
irreplaceable /ɪrɪˈpleɪsəbl/ *adj.* unersetzlich
irrepressible /ɪrɪˈpresɪbl/ *adj.* nicht zu unterdrückend *nicht präd.;* **she is** ~: sie ist nicht unterzukriegen (ugs.)
irreproachable /ɪrɪˈprəʊtʃəbl/ *adj.* untadelig

irresistible /ɪrɪˈzɪstɪbl/ *adj.* unwiderstehlich; bestechend ⟨*Argument*⟩
irresolute /ɪˈrezəluːt/ *adj.* unentschlossen
irrespective /ɪrɪˈspektɪv/ *adj.* ~ **of** ungeachtet (+ *Gen.*)
irresponsible /ɪrɪˈspɒnsɪbl/ *adj.* verantwortungslos ⟨*Person*⟩; unverantwortlich ⟨*Benehmen*⟩
irretrievable /ɪrɪˈtriːvəbl/ *adj.* nicht mehr wiederzubekommen *nicht attr.*
irreverence /ɪˈrevərəns/ *n.* Respektlosigkeit, *die*
irreverent /ɪˈrevərənt/ *adj.* respektlos
irreversible /ɪrɪˈvɜːsɪbl/, **irrevocable** /ɪˈrevəkəbl/ *adjs.* unwiderruflich
irrigate /ˈɪrɪgeɪt/ *v.t.* bewässern
irrigation /ɪrɪˈgeɪʃn/ *n.* Bewässerung, *die*
irritable /ˈɪrɪtəbl/ *adj.* (quick to anger) reizbar; (temporarily) gereizt
irritant /ˈɪrɪtənt/ *n.* Reizstoff, *der*
irritate /ˈɪrɪteɪt/ *v.t.* **(a)** ärgern; **get** ~**d** ärgerlich werden; **be** ~**d by sth.** sich über etw. (*Akk.*) ärgern
(b) (Med.) reizen
irritating /ˈɪrɪteɪtɪŋ/ *adj.* lästig
irritation /ɪrɪˈteɪʃn/ *n.* **(a)** Ärger, *der*
(b) (Med.) Reizung, *die*
is ▶ BE
Islam /ˈɪzlɑːm/ *n.* Islam, *der*
island /ˈaɪlənd/ *n.* Insel, *die*
'islander *n.* Inselbewohner, *der/* -bewohnerin, *die*
island: ~**hop** *v.i.* **go** ~**hopping** eine Inselhoppingtour machen; ~**hopping** *n.* Inselhopping, *das*
isle /aɪl/ *n.* Insel, *die*
isn't /ˈɪznt/ (coll.) = **is not;** ▶ BE
isolate /ˈaɪsəleɪt/ *v.t.* isolieren
isolated /ˈaɪsəleɪtɪd/ *adj.* **(a)** (single) einzeln; ~ **cases/instances** Einzelfälle
(b) (remote) abgelegen ···⊹

isolation /ˌaɪsəˈleɪʃn/ *n.* (a) (act) Isolierung, *die*
(b) (state) Isolation, *die*

ISP *abbr.* = **Internet service provider** ISP

Israel /ˈɪzreɪl/ *pr. n.* Israel (*das*)

Israeli /ɪzˈreɪlɪ/ ① *adj.* israelisch; **sb. is ∼:** jmd. ist Israeli
② *n.* Israeli, *der/die*

issue /ˈɪʃuː, ˈɪsjuː/ ① *n.* (a) (point in question) Frage, *die;* **make an ∼ of sth.** etw. aufbauschen; **evade** *or* **dodge the ∼:** ausweichen
(b) (of magazine etc.) Ausgabe, *die*
(c) (result, outcome) Ergebnis, *das*
② *v.t.* (a) (give out) ausgeben; ausstellen ⟨*Pass*⟩; erteilen ⟨*Lizenz, Befehl*⟩; **∼ sb. with sth.** etw. an jmdn. austeilen
(b) (publish) herausgeben ⟨*Publikation*⟩

it /ɪt/ *pron.* (a) es; **I can't cope with it any more** ich halte das nicht mehr länger aus; **what is it?** was ist los?
(b) (the thing, animal, young child previously mentioned) er/sie/es; *as direct obj.* ihn/sie/es; *as indirect obj.* ihm/ihr/ihm
(c) (the person in question) **who is it?** wer ist da?; **it was the children** es waren die Kinder; **is it you, Dad?** bist du es, Vater?

IT *abbr.* = **information technology** IT

Italian /ɪˈtæljən/ ① *adj.* italienisch; **sb. is ∼:** jmd. ist Italiener/Italienerin
② *n.* (a) (person) Italiener, *der/*Italienerin, *die*
(b) (language) Italienisch, *das; see also* Eɴɢʟɪsʜ 2ᴀ

italic /ɪˈtælɪk/ ① *adj.* kursiv
② *n. in pl.* Kursivschrift, *die;* **in ∼s** kursiv

Italy /ˈɪtəlɪ/ *pr. n.* Italien (*das*)

itch /ɪtʃ/ ① *n.* Juckreiz, *der;* **I have an ∼:** es juckt mich
② *v.i.* (a) einen Juckreiz haben; **it ∼es** es juckt
(b) **∼** *or* **be ∼ing to do sth.** darauf brennen, etw. zu tun

'itchy *adj.* kratzig; **be ∼** ⟨*Körperteil:*⟩ jucken

it'd /ˈɪtəd/ (coll.) (a) = **it had**
(b) = **it would**

item /ˈaɪtəm/ *n.* (a) Ding, *das;* Sache, *die;* (in shop, catalogue) Artikel, *der;* (on radio, TV) Nummer, *die;* **∼ of clothing** Kleidungsstück, *das*
(b) **∼** [of news] Nachricht, *die*

itemize /ˈaɪtəmaɪz/ *v.t.* einzeln aufführen

itinerary /aɪˈtɪnərərɪ/ *n.* Reiseroute, *die*

it'll /ɪtl/ (coll.) = **it will**

its /ɪts/ *poss. pron. attrib.* sein/ihr/sein

it's /ɪts/ (a) = **it is**
(b) = **it has**

itself /ɪtˈself/ *pron.* (a) *emphat.* selbst
(b) *refl.* sich

IUD *abbr.* = **intrauterine device** IUP

I've /aɪv/ = **I have**

IVF *abbr.* = **in-vitro fertilization** IVF

ivory /ˈaɪvərɪ/ *n.* Elfenbein, *das; attrib.* elfenbeinern; Elfenbein-

ivy /ˈaɪvɪ/ *n.* Efeu, *der*

J j

J, j /dʒeɪ/ *n.* J, j, *das*

jab /dʒæb/ ① *v.t.,* **-bb-** stoßen
② *n.* (a) Stoß, *der;* (with needle) Stich, *der*
(b) (Brit. coll.: injection) Spritze, *die*

jabber /ˈdʒæbə(r)/ *v.i.* plappern (ugs.)

jack /dʒæk/ *n.* (a) (for car) Wagenheber, *der*
(b) (Cards) Bube, *der*

jackal /ˈdʒækl/ *n.* Schakal, *der*

jackdaw /ˈdʒækdɔː/ *n.* Dohle, *die*

jacket /ˈdʒækɪt/ *n.* (a) Jacke, *die;* (of suit) Jackett, *das; sports* **∼:** Sakko, *der*
(b) (of book) Schutzumschlag, *der*
(c) **∼ potatoes** in der Schale gebackene Kartoffeln

jack: ∼-knife *v.i.* **the lorry ∼-knifed** der Anhänger des Lastwagens stellte sich quer; **∼pot** *n.* Jackpot, *der;* **hit the ∼pot** (fig.) das große Los ziehen

jacuzzi (Amer.: ®) /dʒəˈkuːzɪ/ *n.* ≈ Whirlpool, *der*

jaded /ˈdʒeɪdɪd/ *adj.* abgespannt

jagged /ˈdʒægɪd/ *adj.* gezackt

jaguar /ˈdʒægjʊə(r)/ *n.* Jaguar, *der*

jail /dʒeɪl/ ① *n.* Gefängnis, *das*
② *v.t.* ins Gefängnis bringen

jail: ∼bird Knastbruder, *der* (ugs.); **∼break** *n.* Gefängnisausbruch, *der*

jailer, jailor /ˈdʒeɪlə(r)/ *n.* Gefängniswärter, *der/*-wärterin, *die*

jam¹ /dʒæm/ ① *v.t.,* **-mm-:** (a) (between two surfaces) einklemmen
(b) (make immovable) blockieren; (fig.) lähmen
② *v.i.,* **-mm-:** (a) (become wedged) sich verklemmen
(b) ⟨*Maschine:*⟩ klemmen
③ *n.* (a) (crush, stoppage) Blockierung, *die*

(b) (coll.: dilemma) be in a ∼: in der Klemme stecken (ugs.)

■ **jam 'on** *v.t.* ∼ **the brakes [full] on** [voll] auf die Bremse steigen (ugs.)

jam² *n.* Marmelade, *die*

Jamaica /dʒə'meɪkə/ *pr. n.* Jamaika *(das)*

jamb /dʒæm/ *n.* (of doorway, window) Pfosten, *der*

'jam-packed *adj.* (coll.) knallvoll (ugs.), proppenvoll (ugs.) **(with** von)

Jan. *abbr.* = **January** Jan.

jangle /'dʒæŋgl/ ① *v.i.* klimpern; ⟨*Klingel:*⟩ bimmeln
② *v.t.* rasseln mit

janitor /'dʒænɪtə(r)/ *n.* Hausmeister, *der*

January /'dʒænjʊərɪ/ *n.* Januar, *der; see also* AUGUST

Japan /dʒə'pæn/ *n.* Japan *(das)*

Japanese /dʒæpə'niːz/ ① *adj.* japanisch; **sb. is** ∼ jmd. ist Japaner/Japanerin
② *n., pl. same* **(a)** (person) Japaner, *der*/ Japanerin, *die*
(b) (language) Japanisch, *das; see also* ENGLISH 2A

jar¹ /dʒɑː(r)/ ① *v.i.,* **-rr-** quietschen; (fig.) ∼ **on sb./sb.'s nerves** jmdm. auf die Nerven gehen
② *v.t.,* **-rr-** erschüttern

jar² *n.* Topf, *der;* (glass ∼) Glas, *das*

jargon /'dʒɑːgən/ *n.* Jargon, *der*

jasmin[e] /'dʒæsmɪn/ *n.* Jasmin, *der*

jaundice /'dʒɔːndɪs/ *n.* (Med.) Gelbsucht, *die*

jaundiced /'dʒɔːndɪst/ *adj.* (fig.) verbittert

jaunt /dʒɔːnt/ *n.* Ausflug, *der*

jaunty /'dʒɔːntɪ/ *adj.* unbeschwert; keck ⟨*Hut*⟩; **he wore his hat at a** ∼ **angle** er hatte sich *(Dat.)* den Hut keck aufs Ohr gesetzt

javelin /'dʒævlɪn/ *n.* **(a)** Speer, *der*
(b) (Sport: event) Speerwerfen, *das*

jaw /dʒɔː/ *n.* Kiefer, *der*

'jawbone *n.* Kieferknochen, *der*

jay /dʒeɪ/ *n.* Eichelhäher, *der*

'jay-walk *v.i.* als Fußgänger im Straßenverkehr unachtsam sein

jazz /dʒæz/ ① *n.* Jazz, *der; attrib.* Jazz-
② *v.t.* ∼ **up** aufpeppen (ugs.)

jazz: ∼ **band** *n.* Jazzband, *die;* ∼ **dance** *n.* Jazztanz, *der;* ∼ **'rock** *n.* Jazzrock, *der*

jazzy /'dʒæzɪ/ *adj.* poppig; **a** ∼ **sports car** ein aufgemotzter Sportwagen (ugs.)

jealous /'dʒeləs/ *adj.* eifersüchtig **(of** auf + *Akk.*)

'jealousy *n.* Eifersucht, *die*

jeans /dʒiːnz/ *n. pl.* Jeans *Pl.*

Jeep ® /dʒiːp/ *n.* Jeep Ⓦⓩ, *der*

jeer /dʒɪə(r)/ *v.i.* höhnen (geh.); ∼ **at sb.** jmdn. verhöhnen

jelly /'dʒelɪ/ *n.* Gelee, *das;* (dessert) Götterspeise, *die*

'jellyfish *n.* Qualle, *die*

jeopardize /'dʒepədaɪz/ *v.t.* gefährden

jeopardy /'dʒepədɪ/ *n.* **in** ∼: in Gefahr; gefährdet

jerk /dʒɜːk/ ① *n.* Ruck, *der*
② *v.t.* reißen an (+ *Dat.*)
③ *v.i.* zucken

jersey /'dʒɜːzɪ/ *n.* Pullover, *der;* (Sport) Trikot, *das*

jest /dʒest/ ① *n.* Scherz, *der;* **in** ∼: im Scherz
② *v.i.* scherzen

Jesus /'dʒiːzəs/ *pr. n.* Jesus *(der)*

jet /dʒet/ *n.* **(a)** (stream) Strahl, *der*
(b) (nozzle) Düse, *die*
(c) (aircraft) Düsenflugzeug, *das;* Jet, *der*

jet: ∼**black** *adj.* pechschwarz;
∼ **engine** *n.* Düsentriebwerk, *das;* ∼**foil** *n.* [Jetfoil-]Tragflügelboot, *das;* ∼ **lag** *n.* Jetlag, *der;* ∼**lagged** *adj.* **sb. is** ∼**lagged** jmdm. macht der Jetlag zu schaffen;
∼ **plane** *n.* Düsenflugzeug, *das;*
∼**-propelled** *adj.* düsengetrieben;
∼ **pro'pulsion** *n.* Düsen- *od.* Strahlantrieb, *der*

jetsam /'dʒetsəm/ *n.* ▶ FLOTSAM

jet: ∼ **set** *n.* Jet-set, *der;* ∼ **ski** *n.* Jetski, *der*

jettison /'dʒetɪsən/ *v.t.* über Bord werfen; (discard) wegwerfen

jetty /'dʒetɪ/ *n.* Landungsbrücke, *die*

Jew /dʒuː/ *n.* Jude, *der*/Jüdin, *die*

jewel /'dʒuːəl/ *n.* Juwel, *das od. der*

'jewel box, 'jewel case *ns.* Schmuckkasten, *der*

jeweller (*Amer.:* **jeweler**) /'dʒuːələ(r)/ *n.* Juwelier, *der*

jewellery (Brit.), **jewelry** /'dʒuːəlrɪ/ *n.* Schmuck, *der*

Jewish /'dʒuːɪʃ/ *adj.* jüdisch; **he/she is** ∼: er ist Jude/sie ist Jüdin

jib /dʒɪb/ *v.i.,* **-bb-** sich sträuben **(at** gegen)

jibe ▶ GIBE

jiffy /'dʒɪfɪ/ *n.* (coll.) **in a** ∼: sofort

'Jiffy bag ® *n.* gefütterte Versandtasche

jig /dʒɪg/ *n.* Jig, *der*

'jigsaw *n.* **(a)** Dekupiersäge, *die;* (electric) Stichsäge, *die*
(b) ∼ **[puzzle]** Puzzle, *das*

jilt /dʒɪlt/ *v.t.* sitzenlassen (ugs.)

jingle /'dʒɪŋgl/ ① *n.* (Commerc.) Werbespruch, *der;* Jingle, *der* (Werbespr.)
② *v.i.* klimpern; ⟨*Glöckchen:*⟩ bimmeln
③ *v.t.* klimpern mit ⟨*Münzen, Schlüsseln*⟩

jinx /dʒɪŋks/ (coll.) ① *n.* Fluch, *der*
② *v.t.* verhexen

jitters /'dʒɪtəz/ *n. pl.* (coll.) großes Zittern

jittery /'dʒɪtərɪ/ *adj.* (coll.) (nervous) nervös; (frightened) verängstigt

job /dʒɒb/ *n.* **(a)** (piece of work) Arbeit, *die;* **I have a** ∼ **for you** ich habe eine Aufgabe für dich
(b) (employment) Stelle, *die;* Job, *der* (ugs.)

job: ~ **advert** n. Stellenanzeige, die;
~**centre** n. (Brit.)
Arbeitsvermittlungsstelle, die; ~ **creation**
scheme n. Beschäftigungsprogramm, das;
Arbeitsbeschaffungsprogramm, das;
~ **description** n.
Arbeitsplatzbeschreibung, die;
~ **evaluation** n. Arbeitsbewertung, die;
~**hunt** v.i. go/be ~-hunting auf Arbeits-
od. Stellensuche gehen/sein; ~**hunter** n.
Stellen- od. Arbeitssuchende, der/die;
~**hunting** n. Arbeitssuche, die;
Stellensuche, die
'jobless adj. arbeitslos
job: ~ **market** n. Arbeitsmarkt, der;
Stellenmarkt, der; ~ **offer** n.
Stellenangebot, das; ~ **satisfaction** n.
Arbeitszufriedenheit, die; ~ **security** n.
Arbeitsplatzsicherheit, die; ~**share** ① n.
geteilter Arbeitsplatz; ② v.i. sich (Dat.)
einen Arbeitsplatz teilen (with mit)
~**sharing** n. Jobsharing, das
jockey /'dʒɒkɪ/ n. Jockei, der
jockey shorts n. pl. (Amer.) Unterhose,
die; Unterhosen Pl.
jocular /'dʒɒkjʊlə(r)/ adj. lustig
jodhpurs /'dʒɒdpəz/ n. pl. Reithose, die
jog /dʒɒg/ ① v.t., -gg-: (a) (shake) rütteln
(b) (nudge) [an]stoßen
(c) ~ sb.'s memory jmds. Gedächtnis (Dat.)
auf die Sprünge helfen
② v.i., -gg-: (a) (up and down) auf und ab
hüpfen
(b) (trot) ⟨Pferd:⟩ [dahin]trotten
(c) (Sport) joggen
③ n. go for a ~: joggen gehen
jogger /'dʒɒgə(r)/ n. Jogger, der/Joggerin,
die
'jogging n. Jogging, das
'jogtrot n. (lit. or fig.) Trott, der
john /dʒɒn/ n. (Amer. sl.: lavatory) Lokus, der
(salopp)
join /dʒɔɪn/ ① v.t. (a) (connect) verbinden (to
mit)
(b) (come into company of) sich gesellen zu
(c) eintreten in (+ Akk.) ⟨Armee, Firma,
Verein, Partei⟩
② v.i. ⟨Straßen:⟩ zusammenlaufen
■ **join in** ① /-'-/ v.i. mitmachen (with bei)
② /'-'-/ v.t. mitmachen bei
■ **join 'up** ① v.i. (Mil.) einrücken
② v.t. miteinander verbinden
'joiner n. Tischler, der/Tischlerin, die
joinery /'dʒɔɪnərɪ/ n., no art. (craft)
Tischlerei, die; Tischlerhandwerk, das
joint /dʒɔɪnt/ ① n. (a) (Building) Fuge, die
(b) (Anat.) Gelenk, das
(c) a ~ [of meat] ein Stück Fleisch; (for
roasting) ein Braten
(d) (coll.: place) Laden, der
(e) (sl.: marijuana cigarette) Joint, der
② adj. (a) (of two or more) gemeinsam
(b) Mit⟨autor, -erbe, -besitzer⟩
'jointly adv. gemeinsam

joint 'venture n. (Commerc.) Jointventure,
das
joist /dʒɔɪst/ n. (Building) Deckenbalken, der;
(steel) [Decken]träger, der
joke /dʒəʊk/ ① n. Witz, der; Scherz, der
② v.i. scherzen, Witze machen (about über
+ Akk.); **joking apart** Scherz beiseite!
'joker n. (a) Spaßvogel, der
(b) (Cards) Joker, der
jollity /'dʒɒlɪtɪ/ n. Fröhlichkeit, die;
(merrymaking) Festlichkeit, die
jolly /'dʒɒlɪ/ ① adj. fröhlich
② adv. (Brit. coll.) ganz schön (ugs.); ~ good!
ausgezeichnet!
jolt /dʒəʊlt/ ① v.t. ⟨Fahrzeug:⟩ durchrütteln
② v.i. ⟨Fahrzeug:⟩ holpern
③ n. (a) (jerk) Stoß, der; Ruck, der
(b) (fig.: shock) Schock, der
Jordan /'dʒɔːdn/ pr. n. Jordanien (das)
jostle /'dʒɒsl/ ① v.i. ~ [against each other]
aneinander stoßen
② v.t. stoßen
jot /dʒɒt/ n. [not] a ~: [k]ein bisschen
■ **jot 'down** v.t. [rasch] aufschreiben
jotter /'dʒɒtə(r)/ n. Notizblock, der
journal /'dʒɜːnl/ n. Zeitschrift, die
journalism /'dʒɜːnəlɪzm/ n. Journalismus,
der
journalist /'dʒɜːnəlɪst/ n. Journalist, der/
Journalistin, die
journey /'dʒɜːnɪ/ n. (a) Reise, die
(b) (of vehicle) Fahrt, die
jovial /'dʒəʊvɪəl/ adj. herzlich ⟨Gruß⟩;
fröhlich ⟨Person⟩
jowl /dʒaʊl/ n. (jaw) Unterkiefer, der; (lower
part of face) Kinnbacken Pl.; (double chin)
Doppelkinn, das
joy /dʒɔɪ/ n. Freude, die
joyful /'dʒɔɪfl/ adj. froh [gestimmt] ⟨Person⟩;
freudig ⟨Blick, Ereignis, Gesang⟩
joy: ~**ride** n. (coll.) Spritztour, die [im
gestohlenen Auto]; ~**stick** n. (a) (Aeronaut.)
Knüppel, der; (b) (on computer etc.) Hebel, der;
Joystick, der
JP abbr. = **Justice of the Peace**
jubilant /'dʒuːbɪlənt/ adj. jubelnd; be ~
⟨Person:⟩ frohlocken
jubilation /dʒuːbɪ'leɪʃn/ n. Jubel, der
jubilee /'dʒuːbɪliː/ n. Jubiläum, das
Judaism /'dʒuːdeɪɪzm/ n., no art.
Judentum, das; Judaismus, der
judge /dʒʌdʒ/ ① n. (a) Richter, der/
Richterin, die
(b) (in contest) Preisrichter, der/-richterin, die
(c) (fig.: critic) Kenner, der/Kennerin, die
② v.t. (a) (sentence) richten (geh.)
(b) (form opinion about) [be]urteilen
'judg[e]ment n. (a) Urteil, das
(b) (critical faculty) Urteilsvermögen, das
judicial /dʒuː'dɪʃl/ adj. gerichtlich
judiciary /dʒuː'dɪʃərɪ/ n. Richterschaft, die
judicious /dʒuː'dɪʃəs/ adj. klar blickend

judo /'dʒuːdəʊ/ n. Judo, das

jug /dʒʌg/ n. Krug, der; (with lid, water ∼) Kanne, die

juggernaut /'dʒʌgənɔːt/ n. (Brit.: lorry) schwerer Brummer (ugs.)

juggle /'dʒʌgl/ v.i. jonglieren

juggler /'dʒʌglə(r)/ n. Jongleur, der/ Jongleurin, die

juice /dʒuːs/ n. Saft, der

juicy /'dʒuːsɪ/ adj. saftig

jukebox /'dʒuːkbɒks/ n. Jukebox, die; Musikbox, die

Jul. abbr. = **July** Jul.

July /dʒʊ'laɪ/ n. Juli, der; see also AUGUST

jumble /'dʒʌmbl/ ① v.t. ∼ **up** durcheinander bringen ② n. Durcheinander, das

'jumble sale n. (Brit.) Trödelmarkt, der

jumbo jet /dʒʌmbəʊ 'dʒet/ n. Jumbojet, der

jump /dʒʌmp/ ① n. (a) Sprung, der (b) (in prices) sprunghafter Anstieg ② v.i. (a) springen; ∼ **for joy** einen Freudensprung machen (b) ∼ **to conclusions** voreilige Schlüsse ziehen ③ v.t. (a) überspringen (b) ∼ **the queue** (Brit.) sich vordrängeln ■ **jump a'bout, jump a'round** v.i. herumspringen (ugs.)
■ **'jump at** v.t. (fig.) sofort zugreifen bei ⟨Angebot, Gelegenheit⟩

jumped-up /'dʒʌmptʌp/ adj. (coll.) emporgekommen

'jumper n. Pullover, der

jump: ∼ **jet** n. Senkrechtstarter, der; ∼ **leads** n. pl. (Brit. Motor Veh.) Starthilfekabel Pl. ; ∼**start** ① v.t. Starthilfe geben, (+ Dat.) ⟨Auto⟩; (fig.) [wieder] in Gang bringen; [wieder] ankurbeln ⟨Wirtschaft, Industrie⟩; ② n. Start durch Starthilfe; (fig.) neuer Impuls od. Auftrieb; ∼**suit** n. Overall, der

jumpy /'dʒʌmpɪ/ adj. nervös

Jun. abbr. = **June** Jun.

junction /'dʒʌŋkʃn/ n. (a) (of railway lines, roads) ≈ Einmündung, die (b) (crossroads) Kreuzung, die

'junction box n. (Electr.) Verteilerkasten, der

juncture /'dʒʌŋktʃə(r)/ n. **at this** ∼: zu diesem Zeitpunkt

June /dʒuːn/ n. Juni, der; see also AUGUST

jungle /'dʒʌŋgl/ n. Dschungel, der

junior /'dʒuːnɪə(r)/ adj. (a) (in age) jünger; ∼ **team** (Sport) Juniorenmannschaft, die (b) (in rank) rangniedriger ⟨Person⟩; niedriger ⟨Rang⟩

junior: ∼ **'partner** n. Juniorpartner, der/ -partnerin, die; ∼ **school** n. (Brit.) Grundschule, die

junk /dʒʌŋk/ n. Trödel, der (ugs.); (trash) Ramsch, der (ugs.)

'junk food n. minderwertige Kost

junkie /'dʒʌŋkɪ/ n. (sl.) Junkie, der (Drogenjargon)

junk: ∼ **mail** n. Postwurfsendungen Pl.; Reklame, die; ∼ **shop** n. Trödelladen, der (ugs.)

Jupiter /'dʒuːpɪtə(r)/ pr. n. (Astron.) Jupiter, der

jurisdiction /dʒʊərɪs'dɪkʃn/ n. Gerichtsbarkeit, die

juror /'dʒʊərə(r)/ n. Geschworene, der/die

jury /'dʒʊərɪ/ n. (a) (in court) **the** ∼: die Geschworenen Pl. (b) (in competition) Jury, die

just /dʒʌst/ ① adj. (morally right) gerecht ② adv. (a) (exactly) genau; ∼ **then/enough** gerade da/genug; ∼ **as** (exactly as) genauso wie; (when) gerade, als; ∼ **as you like** or **please** ganz wie Sie wünschen/du magst; ∼ **as good** etc. genauso gut usw. (b) (barely) gerade [eben]; (with little time to spare) gerade noch; (no more than) nur; ∼ **under £10** nicht ganz zehn Pfund (c) (at this moment) gerade; **not** ∼ **now** im Moment nicht (d) (coll.) (simply) einfach; (only) nur; esp. with imper. mal [eben]; ∼ **look at that!** guck dir das mal an!; ∼ **a moment** einen Moment mal; ∼ **in case** für alle Fälle

justice /'dʒʌstɪs/ n. (a) Gerechtigkeit, die (b) (magistrate) Schiedsrichter, der/-richterin, die; **J**∼ **of the Peace** Friedensrichter, der/ -richterin, die

justifiable /dʒʌstɪ'faɪəbl/ adj. berechtigt

justifiably /dʒʌstɪ'faɪəblɪ/ adv. zu Recht

justification /dʒʌstɪfɪ'keɪʃn/ n. Rechtfertigung, die

justify /'dʒʌstɪfaɪ/ v.t. rechtfertigen; **be justified in doing sth.** etw. zu Recht tun

jut /dʒʌt/ v.i., -tt-: ∼ **[out]** [her]vorragen; herausragen

juvenile /'dʒuːvənaɪl/ ① adj. (a) jugendlich (b) (immature) kindisch ② n. Jugendliche, der/die

juvenile delinquency /dɪ'lɪŋkwənsɪ/ n. Jugendkriminalität, die

juvenile delinquent /dɪ'lɪŋkwənt/ n. jugendlicher Straftäter/jugendliche Straftäterin

juxtapose /dʒʌkstə'pəʊz/ v.t. nebeneinander stellen (**with, to** und)

juxtaposition /dʒʌkstəpə'zɪʃn/ n. Nebeneinanderstellung, die

Kk

K, k /keɪ/ *n.* K, k, *das*

kale /keɪl/ *n.* Grünkohl, *der;* Krauskohl, *der*

kaleidoscope /kə'laɪdəskəʊp/ *n.* Kaleidoskop, *das*

kangaroo /kæŋgə'ruː/ *n.* Känguru, *das*

karaoke /kærɪ'əʊkɪ/ *n., no indef. art.* Karaoke, *das; attrib.* Karaoke-

karate /kə'rɑːtɪ/ *n.* Karate, *das*

kebab /kɪ'bæb/ *n.* Kebab, *der*

keel /kiːl/ *n.* [1] (Naut.) Kiel, *der*
[2] *v.i.* ~ **over** umstürzen; ⟨Schiff:⟩ kentern; ⟨Person:⟩ umkippen

keen /kiːn/ *adj.* (a) (sharp) scharf
(b) (cold) schneidend ⟨Wind, Kälte⟩
(c) (eager) begeistert ⟨Fußballfan, Sportler⟩; lebhaft ⟨Interesse⟩; **be ~ to do sth.** darauf erpicht sein, etw. zu tun; **be ~ on doing sth.** etw. gern[e] tun
(d) (sensitive) scharf ⟨Augen⟩; fein ⟨Sinne⟩

'keenly *adv.* (a) (sharply) scharf
(b) (eagerly) eifrig; brennend ⟨interessiert sein⟩
(c) (acutely) **be ~ aware of sth.** sich ⟨Dat.⟩ einer Sache ⟨Gen.⟩ voll bewusst sein

keep /kiːp/ [1] *v.t., kept /kept/* (a) halten ⟨Versprechen, Schwur, Sabbat, Fasten⟩; einhalten ⟨Verabredung, Vereinbarung⟩; begehen, feiern ⟨Fest⟩
(b) (have charge of) aufbewahren
(c) (retain) behalten; (not lose or destroy) aufheben ⟨Quittung, Rechnung⟩
(d) halten ⟨Bienen, Hund usw⟩
(e) führen ⟨Tagebuch, Geschäft, Ware⟩
(f) (support) versorgen ⟨Familie⟩
(g) (detain) festhalten; ~ **sb. waiting** jmdn. warten lassen; **what kept you?** wo bleibst du denn?
(h) (reserve) aufheben
[2] *v.i., kept* (a) (remain) bleiben; **are you ~ing well?** gehts dir gut?
(b) ~ **[to the] left/right** sich links/rechts halten; ~ **doing sth.** (repeatedly) etw. immer wieder tun; ~ **talking/working** *etc.* **until ...:** weiterreden/-arbeiten *usw.,* bis ...
(c) (remain good) ⟨Lebensmittel:⟩ sich halten
[3] *n.* (a) (maintenance) Unterhalt, *der*
(b) **for ~s** (coll.) auf Dauer
(c) (Hist.: tower) Bergfried, *der*

■ **keep 'back** [1] *v.i.* zurückbleiben
[2] *v.t.* (a) (restrain) zurückhalten ⟨Menschenmenge, Tränen⟩
(b) (withhold) verschweigen ⟨Informationen, Tatsachen⟩ (from *Dat.*)

■ **keep 'down** [1] *v.i.* unten bleiben
[2] *v.t.* (a) niedrig halten ⟨Steuern, Preise *usw.*⟩; ~ **one's weight down** nicht zunehmen
(b) **keep your voice down!** rede nicht so laut!

■ **keep 'off** [1] *v.i.* ⟨Person:⟩ wegbleiben
[2] *v.t.* fern halten; '~ **off the grass'** „Betreten des Rasens verboten"

■ **keep 'on** *v.i.* weitermachen (with *Akk.*); ~ **on doing sth.** etw. [immer] weiter tun; (repeatedly) etw. immer wieder tun

■ **keep 'out** [1] *v.i.* '~**out** „Zutritt verboten"
[2] *v.t.* nicht hereinlassen

■ **keep 'up** [1] *v.i.* ~ **up with sb./sth.** mit jmdm./etw. Schritt halten
[2] *v.t.* aufrechterhalten ⟨Freundschaft, jmds. Moral⟩; ~ **one's strength up** sich bei Kräften halten; ~ **it up!** weiter so!

keep-'fit *n.* Fitnesstraining, *das*

keep-'fit class *n.* Fitnessgruppe, *die;* **go to ~es** zu Fitnessübungen gehen

'keeping *n.* **be in ~ with sth.** einer Sache ⟨Dat.⟩ entsprechen

'keepsake *n.* Andenken, *das*

keg /keg/ *n.* [kleines] Fass

kelp /kelp/ *n.* [See]tang, *der*

kennel /'kenl/ *n.* Hundehütte, *die*

Kenya /'kenjə/ *pr. n.* Kenia (*das*)

kept ▶ KEEP 1, 2

kerb /kɜːb/ *n.* (Brit.) Bordstein, *der*

kerb: ~**-crawling** *n.* (Brit.) ⟨langsames⟩ Fahren am Autostrich zur Kontaktaufnahme mit einer Prostituierten; ~**stone** *n.* (Brit.) Bordstein, *der*

kernel /'kɜːnl/ *n.* Kern, *der*

kerosene, kerosine /'kerəsiːn/ *n.* (Amer., Austral., NZ/as tech. term) Paraffin[öl], *das;* (for jet engines) Kerosin, *das*

kestrel /'kestrəl/ *n.* Turmfalke, *der*

ketch /ketʃ/ *n.* Ketsch, *die*

ketchup /'ketʃʌp/ *n.* Ketschup, *der od. das*

kettle /'ketl/ *n.* [Wasser]kessel, *der*

key /kiː/ [1] *n.* (a) Schlüssel, *der*
(b) (on piano, typewriter, computer, etc.) Taste, *die*
(c) (Mus.) Tonart, *die*
[2] *v.t.* (Comp.) eintasten

key: ~**board** *n.* (of piano etc.) Klaviatur, *die;* (of typewriter, computer, etc.) Tastatur, *die;* ~**board operator** Taster, *der*/Tasterin, *die;* ~**boarder** *n.* Taster, *der*/Tasterin, *die;* ~**boarding** *n.* Tasten, *das;* ~**boarding error** Tastfehler, *der;* ~**hole** *n.* Schlüsselloch, *das;* ~**hole surgery** *n.* Schlüssellochchirurgie, *die;* Knopflochchirurgie, *die*

'keying ▶ KEYBOARDING

key: ~**ring** *n.* Schlüsselring, *der;* ~**stone** *n.* (Archit.) Schlusssstein, *der;* (fig.) Grundpfeiler, *der;* ~**stroke** *n.* Anschlag, *der*

kg. *abbr.* = **kilogram[s]** kg

khaki /'kɑːkɪ/ 1 *adj.* khakifarben
 2 *n.* (cloth) Khaki, *der*

kick /kɪk/ 1 *n.* (a) [Fuß]tritt, *der;* (Footb.)
 Schuss, *der;* **give sb. a ~:** jmdm. einen Tritt
 geben
 (b) (coll.: thrill) do sth. **for ~s** etw. zum Spaß
 tun; **he gets a ~ out of it** er hat Spaß daran
 2 *v.i.* treten; ⟨*Pferd:*⟩ ausschlagen
 3 *v.t.* einen Tritt geben (+ *Dat.*) ⟨*Person,
 Hund*⟩; treten gegen ⟨*Gegenstand*⟩; kicken
 (ugs.), schießen ⟨*Ball*⟩
 ■ **kick a'bout, kick a'round** *v.t.* [in der
 Gegend] herumkicken (ugs.)
 ■ **kick 'off** *v.i.* (Footb.) anstoßen
 ■ **kick 'up** *v.t.* (coll.) **~ up a fuss/row** Krach
 schlagen/anfangen (ugs.)

kick: **~-off** *n.* (Footb.) Anstoß, *der;*
 ~-start 1 *n.* (a) Kickstarter, *der;* (b) (fig.)
 [neuer] Auftrieb; 2 *v.t.* (a) [mit dem
 Kickstarter] starten; (b) (fig.) ankurbeln
 ⟨*Industrie, Wirtschaft*⟩; vorantreiben,
 forcieren ⟨*Friedensprozess, Entwicklung*⟩

kid /kɪd/ 1 *n.* (a) (young goat) Kitz, *das*
 (b) (coll.: child) Kind, *das*
 2 *v.t.,* **-dd-** (coll.) auf den Arm nehmen (ugs.);
 ~ oneself sich (*Dat.*) was vormachen

kiddie /'kɪdɪ/ *n.* (coll.) Kindchen, *das*

kid-'glove *adj.* sanft

kidnap /'kɪdnæp/ *v.t.,* (Brit.) **-pp-** entführen

'kidnapper *n.* Entführer, *der*/Entführerin,
 die

kidney /'kɪdnɪ/ *n.* Niere, *die*

kidney: **~ bean** *n.* Gartenbohne, *die;*
 (scarlet runner bean) Feuerbohne, *die;* **red
 ~ bean** Kidneybohne, *die;* **~ machine** *n.*
 künstliche Niere; **~-shaped** *adj.*
 nierenförmig

kill /kɪl/ *v.t.* (a) töten; (deliberately)
 umbringen; **be ~ed in action** im Kampf
 fallen; **be ~ed in a car crash** bei einem
 Autounfall ums Leben kommen
 (b) **~ time** die Zeit totschlagen

'killer *n.* Mörder, *der*/Mörderin, *die*

'killer whale *n.* Mörderwal, *der*

'killing *n.* (a) Töten, *das*
 (b) **make a ~** (coll.: great profit) einen
 [Mords]reibach machen (ugs.)

'killjoy *n.* Spielverderber, *der*/-verderberin,
 die

kiln /kɪln/ *n.* Brennofen, *der*

kilo /'kiːləʊ/ *n.,* pl. **~s** Kilo, *das*

kilogram, kilogramme /'kɪləgræm/ *n.*
 Kilogramm, *das*

kilometre (Brit.; Amer.: **kilometer**)
 /'kɪləmiːtə(r) (Brit.), kɪ'lɒmɪtə(r)/ *n.*
 Kilometer, *der*

kilowatt *n.* /'kɪləwɒt/ Kilowatt, *das*

kilt /kɪlt/ *n.* Kilt, *der*

kimono /kɪ'məʊnəʊ/ *n.,* pl. **~s** Kimono, *der*

kin /kɪn/ *n.* (relatives) Verwandte *Pl.;* (relative)
 Verwandte, *der*/*die*

kind[1] /kaɪnd/ *n.* (a) (class, sort) Art, *die;*

several ~s of apples mehrere Sorten Äpfel;
 all ~s of things/excuses alles Mögliche/alle
 möglichen Ausreden; **no ... of any ~:**
 keinerlei ...; **what ~ is it?** was für einer/
 eine/eins ist es?; **what ~ of [a] tree is this?**
 was für ein Baum ist das?
 (b) (implying vagueness) **a ~ of ...:** [so] eine
 Art ...; **~ of cute** (coll.) irgendwie niedlich
 (ugs.)

kind[2] *adj.* liebenswürdig; (showing friendliness)
 freundlich; **be ~ to animals** gut zu Tieren
 sein; **how ~!** wie nett [von ihm/Ihnen *usw.*]!

kindergarten /'kɪndəgɑːtn/ *n.*
 Kindergarten, *der*

kind-hearted /kaɪnd'hɑːtɪd/ *adj.*
 gutherzig

kindle /'kɪndl/ (fig.) wecken

kindly /'kaɪndlɪ/ 1 *adv.* (a) freundlich;
 nett
 (b) *in polite request etc.* freundlicherweise;
 thank you ~: herzlichen Dank
 2 *adj.* freundlich; nett; (kind-hearted) gütig

'kindness *n.* (a) *no pl.* (kind nature)
 Freundlichkeit, *die*
 (b) **do sb. a ~** (kind act) jmdm. eine
 Gefälligkeit erweisen

kindred /'kɪndrɪd/ *adj.* verwandt; **~ 'spirit**
 Gleichgesinnte, *der*/*die*

king /kɪŋ/ *n.* König, *der*

kingdom /'kɪŋdəm/ *n.* Königreich, *das*

'kingfisher *n.* Eisvogel, *der*

'king-size[d] *adj.* extragroß; King-size-
 ⟨*Zigaretten*⟩

kink /kɪŋk/ *n.* (in pipe, wire, etc.) Knick, *der;*
 (in hair, wool) Welle, *die*

'kinky *adj.* (coll.) spleenig; (sexually) abartig

kinsman /'kɪnzmən/ *n.,* pl. **kinsmen**
 /'kɪnzmən/ Verwandte, *der*

kinswoman /'kɪnzwʊmn/ *n.* Verwandte,
 die

kiosk /'kiːɒsk/ *n.* (a) Kiosk, *der*
 (b) (telephone booth) [Telefon]zelle, *die*

kip /kɪp/ *n.* (Brit. coll.: sleep) **have a/get some
 ~:** eine Runde pennen (salopp)

kipper /'kɪpə(r)/ *n.* Kipper, *der*

kiss /kɪs/ 1 *n.* Kuss, *der*
 2 *v.t.* küssen; **~ sb. good night/goodbye**
 jmdm. einen Gutenacht-/Abschiedskuss
 geben
 3 *v.i.* **they ~ed** sie küssten sich

kit /kɪt/ *n.* (a) (Brit.: set of items) Set, *das*
 (b) (Brit.: clothing etc.) **sports ~:** Sportzeug,
 das; **riding/skiing ~:** Reit-/Skiausrüstung,
 die

'kitbag *n.* Tornister, *der*

kitchen /'kɪtʃɪn/ *n.* Küche, *die; attrib.*
 Küchen-

kitchen: **~ paper** *n.* Küchenkrepp, *der;*
 ~ roll *n.* Küchenrolle, *die;* (kitchen paper)
 Küchenkrepp, *der;* **~ 'sink** *n.*
 [Küchen]ausguss, *der;* **~ unit** *n.* ⋯⋰

k

Küchenelement, *das;* ~ **units** Küchenmöbel *Pl.;* ~ **utensil** *n.* Küchengerät, *das;* ~**ware** *n.* Küchengeräte *Pl.*

kite /kaɪt/ *n.* Drachen, *der*

kith /kɪθ/ *n.* ~ **and kin** Freunde und Verwandte

kitten /'kɪtn/ *n.* Kätzchen, *das*

kitty /'kɪtɪ/ *n.* (money) Kasse, *die*

kleptomania /kleptə'meɪnɪə/ *n.* Kleptomanie, *die*

kleptomaniac /kleptə'meɪnɪæk/ *n.* Kleptomane, *der*/Kleptomanin, *die*

km. *abbr.* = **kilometre[s]** km

knack /næk/ *n.* Talent, *das;* **get the** ~ [of **doing sth.**] den Bogen rauskriegen [, wie man etw. macht] (ugs.); **have lost the** ~: es nicht mehr zustande bringen

knapsack /'næpsæk/ *n.* Rucksack, *der;* (Mil.) Tornister, *der*

knead /niːd/ *v.t.* kneten

knee /niː/ *n.* Knie, *das*

knee: ~**cap** *n.* Kniescheibe, *die;* ~**deep** *adj.* knietief; ~**high** *adj.* kniehoch; ~**jerk reaction** *n.* (fig.) automatische Reaktion; ~ **joint** *n.* Kniegelenk, *das*

kneel /niːl/ *v.i.,* knelt /nelt/ *or* (esp. Amer.) kneeled /niːld/ *v.i.;* ~ **down** niederknien

knee-length *adj.* knielang

knelt ▶ KNEEL

knew ▶ KNOW

knickers /'nɪkəz/ *n. pl.* (Brit.) [Damen]schlüpfer, *der*

knife /naɪf/ 1 *n., pl.* **knives** /naɪvz/ Messer, *das*
2 *v.t.* (stab) einstechen auf (+ *Akk.*); (kill) erstechen

knife-edge *n.* Schneide, *die;* **be [balanced] on a** ~ (fig.) auf des Messers Schneide stehen

knight /naɪt/ *n.* (a) (Hist.) Ritter, *der* (b) (Chess) Springer, *der*

knighthood *n.* Ritterwürde, *die*

knit /nɪt/ *v.t.,* -tt- stricken; ~ **one's brow** die Stirn runzeln

knitting *n.* Stricken, *das;* (work being knitted) Strickarbeit, *die*

knitting needle *n.* Stricknadel, *die*

knitwear *n.* Strickwaren *Pl.*

knives *pl. of* KNIFE 1

knob /nɒb/ *n.* (a) (on door, walking stick, etc.) Knauf, *der* (b) (control on radio etc.) Knopf, *der* (c) (of butter) Klümpchen, *das*

knock /nɒk/ 1 *v.t.* (a) (strike) (lightly) klopfen an (+ *Akk.*); (forcefully) schlagen gegen *od.* an (+ *Akk.*); ~ **a hole in sth.** ein Loch in etw. (*Akk.*) schlagen (b) (coll.: criticize) herziehen über (+ *Akk.*) (ugs.)
2 *v.i.* klopfen (**at** an + *Akk.*)
3 *n.* Klopfen, *das*

■ **knock 'down** *v.t.* (a) (in car) umfahren (b) (demolish) abreißen

■ **knock 'off** 1 *v.t.* (a) ~ **off work** (coll.: leave) Feierabend machen (b) (deduct) ~ **five pounds off the price** es fünf Pfund billiger machen (c) (coll.: do quickly) aus dem Ärmel schütteln (ugs.) (d) (coll.: steal) klauen (salopp)
2 *v.i.* (coll.) Feierabend machen

■ **knock 'out** *v.t.* (a) (make unconscious) bewusstlos umfallen lassen (b) (Boxing) k.o. schlagen (c) (coll.: exhaust) kaputtmachen (ugs.)

■ **knock 'over** *v.t.* umstoßen; (Fahrer, Fahrzeug:) umfahren ⟨Person⟩

'**knock-down** *adj.* ~ **prices** Schleuderpreise

'**knocker** *n.* [Tür]klopfer, *der*

knock: ~**kneed** /'nɒkniːd/ *adj.* x-beinig ⟨Person⟩; ~**out** *n.* (Boxing) K.-o.-Schlag, *der*

knot /nɒt/ 1 *n.* Knoten, *der*
2 *v.t.,* -tt- knoten ⟨Seil, Faden usw.⟩

'**knotty** *adj.* (fig.: puzzling) verwickelt

know /nəʊ/ *v.t.,* knew /njuː/, known /nəʊn/ (a) (recognize) erkennen (**by** an + *Dat.,* **for** als + *Akk.*) (b) (be able to distinguish) ~ **sth. from sth.** etw. von etw. unterscheiden können (c) (be aware of) wissen (d) (have understanding of) können ⟨ABC, Einmaleins, Deutsch usw.⟩; ~ **how to mend fuses** wissen, wie man Sicherungen repariert; ~ **how to drive a car** Auto fahren können (e) (know) kennen ⟨Person⟩

'**know-all** *n.* Neunmalkluge, *der*/*die*

'**know-how** *n.* praktisches Wissen; (technical expertise) Know-how, *das*

'**knowing** *adj.* (a) wissend ⟨Blick, Lächeln⟩ (b) (cunning) verschlagen

'**knowingly** *adv.* (a) (intentionally) wissentlich (b) viel sagend ⟨lächeln, anblicken⟩

'**knowledge** /'nɒlɪdʒ/ *n.* (a) (familiarity) Kenntnisse *Pl.* (**of** in + *Dat.*) (b) (awareness) Wissen, *das;* **have no** ~ **of sth.** nichts von etw. wissen; keine Kenntnis von etw. haben (geh.) (c) [a] ~ **of languages/French** Sprach-/ Französischkenntnisse *Pl.*

'**knowledgeable** /'nɒlɪdʒəbl/ *adj.* **be** ~ **about** *or* **on sth.** viel über etw. (*Akk.*) wissen

known /nəʊn/ 1 ▶ KNOW
2 *adj.* bekannt

knuckle /'nʌkl/ *n.* [Finger]knöchel, *der*

Koran /kɔː'rɑːn, kə'rɑːn/ *n.* Koran, *der*

Korea /kə'rɪə/ *pr. n.* Korea (*das*)

Korean /kə'riːən/ 1 *adj.* koreanisch; **sb. is** ~: jmd. ist Koreaner/Koreanerin
2 *n.* (a) (person) Koreaner, *der*/Koreanerin, *die* (b) (language) Koreanisch, *das; see also* ENGLISH 2A

kosher /'kəʊʃə(r)/ *adj.* koscher

Kosovan /'kɒsəvən/ 1 adj. ~ town/ immigrant Stadt im Kosovo/Einwanderer aus dem Kosovo; ~ **Albanian** Kosovoalbaner, *der*/-albanerin, *die;* **he/she is ~:** er ist Kosovarer/sie ist Kosovarin
2 n. (person) Kosovare, *der*/Kosovarin, *die*

Kosovo /'kɒsəvə/ *pr. n.* Kosovo, *der od. das od.* (*das*)

kudos /'kju:dɒs/ *n.* Prestige, *das*

Kurd /kɜːd/ *n.* Kurde, *der*/Kurdin, *die*

Kurdish /'kɜːdɪʃ/ 1 adj. kurdisch; **sb. is ~:** jmd. ist Kurde/Kurdin
2 n. (language) Kurdisch, *das*

Kurdistan /kɜːdɪ'stɑːn/ *pr. n.* Kurdistan (*das*)

Kuwait /kʊ'weɪt/ *pr. n.* Kuwait (*das*)

Kuwaiti /kʊ'weɪtɪ/ 1 adj. kuwaitisch; **sb. is ~:** jmd. ist Kuwaiti
2 n. Kuwaiti, *der*/*die*

kW *abbr.* = **kilowatt[s]** kW

Ll

L, l /el/ *n.* L, l, *das*

l. *abbr.* = **litre[s]** l

£ *abbr.* = **pound[s]** £; **cost £5** 5 £ *od.* Pfund kosten

lab /læb/ *n.* (coll.) Labor, *das*

label /'leɪbl/ 1 n. Schildchen, *das;* (on bottles, in clothes) Etikett, *das;* (tied/stuck to an object) Anhänger/Aufkleber, *der*
2 v.t., (Brit.) **-ll-:** (a) etikettieren; auszeichnen ⟨Waren⟩; (write on) beschriften (b) (fig.) ~ **sb./sth. [as] sth.** jmdn./etw. als etw. etikettieren

labor (Amer.) ▶ LABOUR

laboratory /lə'bɒrətərɪ/ *n.* Labor[atorium], *das*

labored, laborer (Amer.) ▶ LABOUR-

laborious /lə'bɔːrɪəs/ *adj.* mühsam

la'boriously *adv.* mühevoll

labour /'leɪbə(r)/ (Brit.) 1 n. (a) Arbeit, *die* (b) (workers) Arbeiterschaft, *die;* **immigrant ~:** ausländische Arbeitskräfte *Pl.* (c) **L~, the L~ Party** (Polit.) die Labour Party (d) (childbirth) Wehen *Pl.;* **be in ~:** in den Wehen liegen
2 v.i. hart arbeiten (**at, on** an + *Dat.*)
3 v.t. ~ **the point** sich lange darüber verbreiten

laboured /'leɪbəd/ *adj.* (Brit.) mühsam; schwerfällig ⟨Stil⟩; **his breathing was ~:** er atmete schwer

'labourer *n.* (Brit.) Arbeiter, *der*/Arbeiterin, *die*

labour: ~ pains *n. pl.* Wehenschmerzen *Pl.;* **~-saving** *adj.* arbeit[s]sparend

laburnum /lə'bɜːnəm/ *n.* (Bot.) Goldregen, *der*

labyrinth /'læbərɪnθ/ *n.* Labyrinth, *das*

lace /leɪs/ 1 n. (a) (for shoe) Schnürsenkel, *der*
(b) (fabric) Spitze, *die; attrib.* Spitzen-
2 v.t. ~ **[up]** [zu]schnüren

lacerate /'læsəreɪt/ *v.t.* aufreißen

'lace-up 1 attrib. adj. Schnür-
2 n. Schnürschuh/-stiefel, *der*

lack /læk/ 1 n. Mangel, *der* (**of** an + *Dat.*)
2 v.t. **sb./sth. ~s sth.** jmdm./einer Sache fehlt es an etw. (*Dat.*)

lackey /'lækɪ/ *n.* Lakai, *der*

'lacking *adj.* **be ~:** fehlen

laconic /lə'kɒnɪk/ *adj.* lakonisch

lacquer /'lækə(r)/ *n.* Lack, *der*

lacrosse /lə'krɒs/ *n.* Lacrosse, *das*

lacy /'leɪsɪ/ *adj.* Spitzen-

lad /læd/ *n.* Junge, *der*

ladder /'lædə(r)/ 1 n. (a) Leiter, *die*
(b) (Brit.: in tights etc.) Laufmasche, *die*
2 v.i. (Brit.) Laufmaschen/eine Laufmasche bekommen
3 v.t. (Brit.) Laufmaschen/eine Laufmasche machen in (+ *Akk.*)

laden /'leɪdn/ beladen (**with** mit)

ladle /'leɪdl/ *n.* Schöpfkelle, *die*

lady /'leɪdɪ/ *n.* (a) Dame, *die;* **~-in-waiting** (Brit.) Hofdame, *die*
(b) '**Ladies'** (WC) „Damen"
(c) (as form of address) **Ladies** meine Damen
(d) (Brit.) (as title) **L~:** Lady

lady: ~bird, (Amer.) **~bug** *ns.* Marienkäfer, *der;* **~like** *adj.* damenhaft

lag[1] /læg/ *v.i.,* **-gg-:** ~ **[behind]** zurückbleiben; (fig.) im Rückstand sein

lag[2] *v.t.,* **-gg-** (insulate) isolieren

lager /'lɑːgə(r)/ *n.* Lagerbier, *das*

'lager lout *n.* Bier trinkender Rüpel

'lagging *n.* Isolierung, *die*

lagoon /lə'guːn/ *n.* Lagune, *die*

laid ▶ LAY[2]

'laid-back *adj.* (coll.) gelassen

lain ▶ LIE[2]

lair /leər/ *n.* (of wild animal) Unterschlupf, *der;* (of pirates, bandits) Schlupfwinkel, *der*

lake /leɪk/ *n.* See, *der*

Lake Constance /leɪk 'kɒnstəns/ *pr. n.* der Bodensee

lama /'lɑːmə/ n. Lama, der
lamb /læm/ n. (a) Lamm, das
(b) (meat) Lamm[fleisch], das
lamb 'chop n. Lammkotelett, das
lambswool /'læmzwʊl/ n. Lambswool, die
lame /leɪm/ adj., **'lamely** adv. lahm
lament /lə'ment/ [1] n. Klage, die (for um)
[2] v.t. ~ that …: beklagen, dass …
[3] v.i. klagen (geh.); ~ over sth. etw.
beklagen (geh.)
lamentable /'læməntəbl/ adj.
beklagenswert
laminated /'læmɪneɪtɪd/ adj. lamelliert;
~ glass Verbundglas, das
lamp /læmp/ n. Lampe, die; (in street)
[Straßen]laterne, die
lamp: ~ **post** n. Laternenpfahl, der;
~**shade** n. Lampenschirm, der
lance /lɑːns/ [1] n. Lanze, die
[2] v.t. (Med.) mit der Lanzette öffnen
lance 'corporal n. Obergefreite, der
land /lænd/ [1] n. Land, das; **have** or **own** ~:
Grundbesitz haben
[2] v.t. (a) (set ashore) [an]landen
(b) (Aeronaut.) landen
(c) ~ **oneself in trouble** sich in
Schwierigkeiten bringen; ~ **sb. with sth.**,
~ **sth. on sb.** jmdm. etw. aufhalsen (ugs.)
[3] v.i. (a) ⟨Boot usw.:⟩ anlegen, landen;
⟨Passagier:⟩ aussteigen (**from** aus); **we** ~**ed at**
Dieppe wir gingen in Dieppe an Land
(b) (Aeronaut.) landen
(c) ~ **on one's feet** (fig.) [wieder] auf die
Füße fallen
'landed adj. ~ **gentry/aristrocracy** Landadel,
der
'landing n. (a) (of ship, aircraft) Landung, die
(b) (on stairs) Treppenabsatz, der; (passage)
Treppenflur, der
landing: ~ **card** n. Landekarte, die;
~ **stage** n. Landesteg, der
land: ~**lady** n. (of rented property)
Vermieterin, die; (b) (of public house)
[Gast]wirtin, die; ~**locked** adj. vom Land
eingeschlossen ⟨Bucht, Hafen⟩; ⟨Staat⟩ ohne
Zugang zum Meer; ~**lord** n. (a) (of rented
property) Vermieter, der; (b) (of public house)
[Gast]wirt, der; ~**mark** n. (a)
Orientierungspunkt, der; (b) (fig.) Markstein,
der; ~ **mass** n. Landmasse, die; ~**mine** n.
Landmine, die; ~**owner** n. Grundbesitzer,
der/-besitzerin, die; ~**scape** /'lændskeɪp/
n. Landschaft, die; ~**scape architect** n.
Landschaftsarchitekt, der/-architektin, die;
~**scape gardener** n.
Landschaftsgärtner, der/-gärtnerin, die;
~**scape gardening** n.
Landschaftsgärtnerei, die; ~**slide** n.
Erdrutsch, der; **a** ~**slide [victory]** (Polit.) ein
Erdrutsch[wahl]sieg
lane /leɪn/ n. (a) (in the country)
Landsträßchen, das; Weg, der
(b) (in town) Gasse, die

(c) (part of road) [Fahr]spur, die; **'get in** ~'
„bitte einordnen"
(d) (Sport) Bahn, die
language /'læŋgwɪdʒ/ n. Sprache, die;
(style) Ausdrucksweise, die
language: ~ **course** n. Sprachkurs[us],
der; ~ **school** n. Sprachenschule; die;
~ **teacher** n. Sprachlehrer, der/-lehrerin,
die
languid /'læŋgwɪd/ adj. träge
languish /'læŋgwɪʃ/ v.i. (a) (lose vitality)
ermatten (geh.)
(b) ~ **under sth.** unter etw. (Dat.)
schmachten (geh.)
lank /læŋk/ adj. (a) hager
(b) glatt herabhängend ⟨Haar⟩
lanky /'læŋkɪ/ adj. schlaksig (ugs.)
lantern /'læntən/ n. Laterne, die
lap¹ /læp/ n. (part of body) Schoß, der
lap² n. (Sport) Runde, die
lap³ [1] v.i., -pp- schlecken
[2] v.t., -pp-: ~ [up] [auf]schlecken
■ **lap 'up** v.t. (fig.) schlucken
'lap belt n. Beckengurt, der
lapel /lə'pel/ n. Revers, das
Lapland /'læplænd/ pr. n. Lappland (das)
lapse /læps/ [1] n. (a) (interval) a/the ~ **of** …:
eine/die Zeitspanne von …
(b) (mistake) Fehler, der; ~ **of memory**
Gedächtnislücke, die
[2] v.i. (a) ⟨Vertrag, usw.:⟩ ungültig werden
(b) ~ **into** verfallen in (+ Akk.)
'laptop [1] adj. tragbar, Laptop⟨gerät, -PC⟩
[2] n. Laptop, der; tragbarer PC
larceny /'lɑːsənɪ/ n. Diebstahl, der
lard /lɑːd/ n. Schweineschmalz, das
larder /'lɑːdə(r)/ n. Speisekammer, die
large /lɑːdʒ/ [1] adj. groß
[2] n. **at** ~ (not in prison etc.) auf freiem Fuß
[3] adv. ▶ BY 2D
'largely adv. weitgehend
larger-than-'life attrib. adj.
überlebensgroß
large: ~**-scale** attrib. adj. groß angelegt;
groß ⟨Erfolg, Misserfolg⟩; ⟨Katastrophe⟩
großen Ausmaßes; ⟨Modell⟩ in großem
Maßstab; ~**-scale manufacture**
Massenproduktion, die; ~**-size[d]** adj. groß
lark¹ /lɑːk/ n. (Ornith.) Lerche, die
lark² (coll.) [1] n. Jux, der (ugs.)
[2] v.i. ~ [**about** or **around**] herumalbern
(ugs.)
larva /'lɑːvə/ n., pl. ~**e** /'lɑːviː/ Larve, die
laryngitis /lærɪn'dʒaɪtɪs/ n.
Kehlkopfentzündung, die
larynx /'lærɪŋks/ n. Kehlkopf, der
lascivious /lə'sɪvɪəs/ adj. lüstern (geh.)
laser /'leɪzə(r)/ n. Laser, der
laser: ~ **beam** n. Laserstrahl, der;
~**disc** n. Laserplatte, die; ~ **printer** n.
Laserdrucker, der

lash /læʃ/ ① *n.* (a) (stroke) [Peitschen]hieb, *der*

(b) (on eyelid) Wimper, *die*

② *v.i.* ⟨*Welle, Regen:*⟩ peitschen (**against** gegen, **on** auf + *Akk.*)

③ *v.t.* (a) (fasten) festbinden (**to** an + *Dat.*)

(b) (as punishment) auspeitschen

■ **lash 'down** ① *v.t.* festbinden

② *v.i.* ⟨*Regen:*⟩ niederprasseln

■ **lash 'out** *v.i.* (a) (hit out) um sich schlagen; **~ out at sb.** nach jmdm. schlagen

(b) **~ out on sth.** (coll.: spend freely) sich (*Dat.*) etw. leisten

lashings /'læʃɪŋz/ *n. pl.* **~ of sth.** Unmengen von etw.

lass /læs/ *n.* Mädchen, *das*

lasso /ləˈsuː/ Lasso, *das*

last¹ /lɑːst/ ① *adj.* letzt...; **be ~ to arrive** als Letzter/Letzte ankommen; **~ night** gestern Nacht/Abend

② *adv.* (a) [ganz] zuletzt; ⟨*als Letzter/Letzte sprechen, ankommen*⟩

(b) (on ~ previous occasion) das letzte Mal; zuletzt

③ *n.* (a) (person or thing) **the ~:** der/die/das Letzte; *pl.* die Letzteren

(b) **at [long] ~:** endlich

last² *v.i.* (a) (continue) dauern; ⟨*Wetter, Ärger:*⟩ anhalten

(b) (suffice) reichen

'**last-ditch** *adj.* **~ attempt** letzter verzweifelter Versuch

'**lasting** *adj.* bleibend; dauerhaft ⟨*Beziehung*⟩; nachhaltig ⟨*Eindruck, Wirkung*⟩

'**lastly** *adv.* schließlich

last: ~-minute *attrib. adj.* in letzter Minute vorgebracht ⟨*Plan, Aufruf, Ergänzung, Gesuch, Bewerbung*⟩; **~ name** *n.* Zuname, *der;* Nachname, *der*

latch /lætʃ/ *n.* Riegel, *der;* **on the ~:** nur eingeklinkt

■ **latch 'on to** *v.t.* (coll.:) kapieren (ugs.)

late /leɪt/ ① *adj.* (a) spät; **am I ~?** komme ich zu spät?; **be ~ for the train** den Zug verpassen; **the train is [an hour] ~:** der Zug hat [eine Stunde] Verspätung; **~ shift** Spätschicht, *die;* **~ summer** Spätsommer, *der*

(b) (dead) verstorben

(c) (former) ehemalig. See also LATER 1; LATEST

② *adv.* (a) (after proper time) verspätet

(b) (at/till a ~ hour) spät; **be up ~:** bis spät in die Nacht aufbleiben; **work ~ at the office** [abends] lange im Büro arbeiten; **[a bit] ~ in the day** (fig. coll.) reichlich spät

③ *n.* **of ~:** in letzter Zeit

latecomer /'leɪtkʌmə(r)/ *n.* Zuspätkommende, *der/die*

'**lately** *adv.* in letzter Zeit

'**lateness** *n.* (a) (delay) Verspätung, *die*

(b) **the ~ of the performance** der späte Beginn der Vorstellung

'**late-night** *attrib. adj.* Spät⟨*programm, -vorstellung*⟩

latent /'leɪtənt/ *adj.* latent

later /'leɪtə(r)/ ① *adv.* **~ [on]** später

② *adj.* später; (more recent) neuer

lateral /'lætərl/ *adj.* seitlich (**to** von); **~ thinking** Querdenken, *das*

latest /'leɪtɪst/ *adj.* (a) (modern) neu[e]st...

(b) (most recent) letzt...

(c) **at [the] ~/the very ~:** spätestens/ allerspätestens

lathe /leɪð/ *n.* Drehbank, *die*

lather /'lɑːðə(r)/ ① *n.* [Seifen]schaum, *der*

② *v.t.* einschäumen

Latin /'lætɪn/ ① *adj.* lateinisch

② *n.* Latein, *das; see also* ENGLISH 2A

Latin A'merica *pr. n.* Lateinamerika (*das*)

Latin-A'merican *adj.* lateinamerikanisch

latitude /'lætɪtjuːd/ *n.* (a) (freedom) Freiheit, *die*

(b) (Geog.) Breite, *die*

latrine /ləˈtriːn/ *n.* Latrine, *die*

latter /'lætə(r)/ *attrib. adj.* letzter...; **the ~:** der/die/das Letztere; *pl.* die Letzteren

'**latterly** *adv.* in letzter Zeit

lattice /'lætɪs/ *n.* Gitter, *das*

laudable /'lɔːdəbl/ *adj.* lobenswert

laugh /lɑːf/ ① *n.* Lachen, *das;* (continuous) Gelächter, *das*

② *v.i.* lachen; **~ out loud** laut auflachen; **~ at sb./sth.** über jmdn./etw. lachen; (jeer) jmdn. auslachen/etw. verlachen

■ **laugh 'off** *v.t.* mit einem Lachen abtun

laughable /'lɑːfəbl/ *adj.* lachhaft; lächerlich

'**laughing** *n.* **be no ~ matter** nicht zum Lachen sein

laughing: ~ gas *n.* Lachgas, *das;* **~ stock** *n.* **make sb. a ~ stock,** make a **~ stock of sb.** jmdn. zum Gespött machen

laughter /'lɑːftə(r)/ *n.* Lachen, *das;* (continuous) Gelächter, *das*

'**laughter lines** *n. pl.* Lachfältchen *Pl.*

launch /lɔːntʃ/ *v.t.* (a) zu Wasser lassen ⟨*Boot*⟩; vom Stapel lassen ⟨*neues Schiff*⟩; abschießen ⟨*Harpune, Torpedo*⟩; schleudern ⟨*Speer*⟩

(b) (fig.) auf den Markt bringen ⟨*Produkt*⟩; vorstellen ⟨*Buch, Schallplatte, Sänger*⟩; **~ an attack** einen Angriff durchführen

■ **launch 'out** *v.i.* (fig.) **~ out into films/a new career/on one's own** sich beim Film versuchen/beruflich etwas ganz Neues anfangen/sich selbstständig machen

'**launching pad, launch pad** *ns.* [Raketen]abschussrampe, *die*

launder /'lɔːndə(r)/ *v.t.* waschen und bügeln

launderette /lɔːndə'ret/**, laundrette** /lɔːn'dret/, (Amer.) **laundromat** /'lɔːndrəmæt/ *ns.* Waschsalon, *der* ⸱⸱⸱⟩

laundry /'lɔːndrɪ/ n. (a) (place) Wäscherei, *die*
(b) (clothes etc.) Wäsche, *die*

'**laundry basket** n. Wäschekorb, *der*

lava /'lɑːvə/ n. Lava, *die*

lavatory /'lævətərɪ/ n. Toilette, *die*

lavender /'lævɪndə(r)/ n. Lavendel, *der*

lavish /'lævɪʃ/ 1 adj. großzügig
2 v.t. ~ sth. on sb. jmdn. mit etw. überhäufen

law /lɔː/ n. (a) Gesetz, *das;* break the ~: gegen das Gesetz verstoßen; take the ~ into one's own hands sich ⟨Dat.⟩ selbst Recht verschaffen; ~ and order Ruhe und Ordnung (b) (of game) Regel, *die*
(c) (as subject) Jura o. Art.

law: ~-**abiding** /'lɔːəbaɪdɪŋ/ adj. gesetzestreu; ~**court** n. Gerichtsgebäude, *das;* (room) Gerichtssaal, *der;* ~ **firm** n. (Amer.) Anwaltskanzlei, *die*

lawful /'lɔːfl/ adj. rechtmäßig ⟨Besitzer, Erbe⟩; legal, gesetzmäßig ⟨Vorgehen, Maßnahme⟩

'**lawless** adj. gesetzlos

lawn /lɔːn/ n. Rasen, *der*

lawn: ~**mower** n. Rasenmäher, *der;* ~ **sprinkler** n. Rasensprenger, *der;* ~ **tennis** n. Rasentennis, *das*

'**law suit** n. Prozess, *der*

lawyer /'lɔːjə(r)/ n. Rechtsanwalt, *der/* Rechtsanwältin, *die*

lax /læks/ adj. lax; be ~ about hygiene/ paying the rent etc. es mit der Hygiene/der Zahlung der Miete *usw.* nicht so genau nehmen

laxative /'læksətɪv/ n. Abführmittel, *das*

laxity /'læksɪtɪ/, '**laxness** ns. Laxheit, *die*

lay¹ /leɪ/ adj. Laien-

lay² v.t., **laid** /leɪd/ (a) legen ⟨Teppichboden, Rohr, Kabel⟩
(b) (impose) auferlegen ⟨Verantwortung, Verpflichtung⟩ (on Dat.); verhängen ⟨Strafe⟩ (on über + Akk.)
(c) ~ the table den Tisch decken
(d) (Biol.) legen ⟨Ei⟩
■ **lay a'side** v.t. beiseite legen
■ **lay 'by** v.t. beiseite legen
■ **lay 'down** v.t. (a) hinlegen
(b) festlegen ⟨Regeln, Bedingungen⟩
■ **lay 'off** 1 v.t. (from work) vorübergehend entlassen
2 v.i. (coll.: stop) aufhören
■ **lay 'out** v.t. (a) (spread out) ausbreiten
(b) anlegen ⟨Garten⟩
■ **lay 'up** v.t. (a) (store) lagern
(b) I was laid up in bed for a week ich musste eine Woche das Bett hüten

lay³ ▶ LIE²

lay: ~**about** n. (Brit.) Gammler, *der* (ugs.); ~-**by** n., pl. ~-**bys** (Brit.) Parkbucht, *die;* Haltebucht, *die*

layer /'leɪə(r)/ n. Schicht, *die*

layette /leɪ'et/ n. [baby's] ~: Babyausstattung, *die*

lay: ~**man** /'leɪmən/ n., pl. ~**men** /'leɪmən/ Laie, *der;* ~**out** n. (of garden, park) Anlage, *die;* (of book, advertisement, etc.) Layout, *das*

laze /leɪz/ v.i. faulenzen; ~ around or about herumfaulenzen (ugs.)

lazily /'leɪzɪlɪ/ adv. faul

laziness /'leɪzɪnɪs/ n. Faulheit, *die*

lazy /'leɪzɪ/ adj. faul

'**lazybones** n. sing. Faulpelz, *der*

lb. abbr. = **pound[s]** ≈ Pfd.

LCD abbr. = **liquid crystal display** LCD

lead¹ /led/ 1 n. (a) (metal) Blei, *das*
(b) (in pencil) [Bleistift]mine, *die*
2 attrib. adj. Blei-
3 v.t. (a) in Blei fassen ⟨Fenster⟩; ~ed bleigefasst
(b) ~ed petrol bleihaltiges Benzin

lead² /liːd/ 1 v.t., **led** /led/ (a) führen; ~ sb. to do sth. (fig.) jmdn. dazu bringen, etw. zu tun
(b) (fig.: influence) ~ sb. to do sth. jmdn. veranlassen, etw. zu tun; be easily led sich leicht beeinflussen lassen; he led me to believe that ...: er machte mich glauben, dass ...
(c) (be first in) anführen
(d) (direct) anführen ⟨Bewegung, Abordnung⟩; leiten ⟨Diskussion, Orchester⟩
2 v.i., **led** (a) ⟨Straße usw., Tür:⟩ führen
(b) (be first) führen; (go in front) vorangehen
3 n. (a) (precedent) Beispiel, *das;* (clue) Anhaltspunkt, *der;* follow sb.'s ~: jmds. Beispiel ⟨Dat.⟩ folgen
(b) (first place) Führung, *die;* be in the ~: in Führung liegen
(c) (distance ahead) Vorsprung, *der*
(d) (leash) Leine, *die;* on a ~: an der Leine
(e) (Electr.) Kabel, *das*
(f) (Theatre) Hauptrolle, *die*
■ **lead a'way** v.t. abführen ⟨Gefangenen, Verbrecher⟩
■ **lead 'off** 1 v.t. abführen
2 v.i. beginnen
■ **lead 'on** 1 v.t. ~ sb. on (entice) jmdn. reizen; (deceive) jmdn. auf den Leim führen
2 v.i. ~ on to the next topic etc. zum nächsten Thema *usw.* führen
■ **lead 'up to** v.t. schließlich führen zu

'**leader** n. (a) Führer, *der/*Führerin, *die;* (of political party) Vorsitzende, *der/die;* (of expedition) Leiter, *der/*Leiterin, *die*
(b) (Brit. Journ.) Leitartikel, *der*

'**leadership** n. Führung, *die*

'**leader writer** n. Leitartikelschreiber, *der/*-schreiberin, *die;* Leitartikler, *der/* -artiklerin, *die* (Pressejargon)

lead-free /'ledfriː/ adj. bleifrei

leading /'liːdɪŋ/ adj. führend

leading: ~ '**lady** n. Hauptdarstellerin, *die;* ~ '**man** n. Hauptdarsteller, *der;*

~ '**question** *n.* Suggestivfrage, *die;*
~ **role** *n.* Hauptrolle, *die;* (fig.) führende
Rolle

lead: ~ '**pencil** /led 'pensl/ *n.* Bleistift,
der; ~ **poisoning** /'led pɔɪzənɪŋ/ *n.*
Bleivergiftung, *die;* ~ **singer** /liːd 'sɪŋə(r)/
n. Leadsänger *der*/-sängerin, *die;* ~ **story**
/'liːd stɔːrɪ/ *n.* (Journ.) Titelgeschichte, *die;*
~ **time** /'liːd taɪm/ *n.* (Econ.)
Entwicklungszeit, *die*

leaf /liːf/ *n., pl.* **leaves** /liːvz/ Blatt, *das;* (of
table) Platte *die*
■ **leaf 'through** *v.t.* durchblättern

leaflet /'liːflɪt/ *n.* [Hand]zettel, *der;*
(advertising) Reklamezettel, *der;* (political)
Flugblatt, *das*

'**leafy** *adj.* belaubt

league /liːg/ *n.* (a) (agreement) Bündnis, *das;*
be in ~ with sb. mit jmdm. im Bunde sein
(b) (Sport) Liga, *die*

league: ~ '**football** *n.* Ligafußball, *der;*
~ **match** *n.* Ligaspiel, *das;* ~ **table** *n.*
Tabelle, *die* (Sport); be at the top/bottom of
the ~ table an der Tabellenspitze/am
Tabellenende sein (fig.); an der Spitze
rangieren/das Schlusslicht bilden (ugs.) (of
unter + *Dat.*)

leak /liːk/ 1 *n.* (a) (hole) Leck, *das;* (in roof,
tent; also fig.) undichte Stelle
(b) (escaping gas) durch ein Leck
austretendes Gas
2 *v.i.* (a) (escape) austreten (**from** aus)
(b) ⟨Fass, Tank, Schiff:⟩ lecken; ⟨Rohr,
Leitung, Dach:⟩ undicht sein; ⟨Gefäß, Füller:⟩
auslaufen
(c) (fig.) ~ [**out**] durchsickern
3 *v.t* ~ **sth. to sb.** jmdm. etw. zuspielen

leakage /'liːkɪdʒ/ *n.* Auslaufen, *das;* (of
fluid, gas) Ausströmen, *das;* (fig.: of information)
Durchsickern, *das*

'**leaky** *adj.* undicht; leck ⟨Boot⟩

lean[1] /liːn/ 1 *adj.* mager .
2 *n.* (meat) Magere, *das*

lean[2] *v.i.,* **leaned** /liːnd, lent/ *or* (Brit.)
leant /lent/ (a) sich beugen; ~ **against the
door** sich gegen die Tür lehnen; ~ **down**/
forward sich herab-/vorbeugen; ~ **back** sich
zurücklehnen
(b) (support oneself) ~ **against/on sth.** sich
gegen/an etw ⟨Akk.⟩ lehnen
(c) (be supported) lehnen (**against** an + *Dat.*)
(d) (fig.) ~ [**up**]**on sb.** (rely) auf jmdn. bauen;
~ **to**[**wards**] **sth.** (tend) zu etw. neigen
2 *v.t.,* **leaned** *or* (Brit.) **leant** lehnen (**against**
gegen *od.* an + *Akk.*)
■ **lean 'over** *v.i.* sich hinüberbeugen

'**leaning** *n.* Neigung, *die*

leant ▶ LEAN[2]

leap /liːp/ 1 *v.i.,* **leaped** /liːpt, lept/ *or* **leapt**
/lept/ (a) springen; ⟨Herz:⟩ hüpfen
(b) (fig.) ~ **at the chance** die Gelegenheit
beim Schopf packen
2 *v.t.,* **leaped** *or* **leapt** überspringen

3 *n.* Sprung, *der;* **with** *or* **in one** ~: mit
einem Satz; **by** ~**s and bounds** (fig.) mit
Riesenschritten

'**leapfrog** 1 *n.* Bockspringen, *das*
2 *v.i.,* -**gg**- Bockspringen machen
3 *v.t.* (a) ~**frog sb.** einen Bocksprung über
jmdn. machen
(b) (fig.) übertreffen ⟨Konkurrenz, Kollegen
usw.⟩

leapt ▶ LEAP 1, 2

'**leap year** *n.* Schaltjahr, *das*

learn /lɜːn/ 1 *v.t.,* **learned** /lɜːnd, lɜːnt/ *or*
learnt /lɜːnt/ (a) lernen; ~ **to swim**
schwimmen lernen
(b) (find out) erfahren
2 *v.i.,* **learned** *or* **learnt** (a) lernen; ~ **about**
sth. etwas über etw. ⟨Akk.⟩ lernen
(b) (get to know) erfahren (**of** von)

learned /'lɜːnɪd/ *adj.* gelehrt

'**learner** *n.* (beginner) Anfänger, *der*/
Anfängerin, *die;* ~ [**driver**] Fahrschüler,
der/-schülerin, *die*

'**learning** *n.* (of person) Gelehrsamkeit, *die*

learning: ~ **difficulties** *n. pl.*
Lernschwierigkeiten *Pl.;* ~ **disability** *n.*
Lernbehinderung, *die*

learnt ▶ LEARN

lease /liːs/ 1 *n.* (of land, business premises)
Pachtvertrag, *der;* (of house, flat, office)
Mietvertrag, *der*
2 *v.t.* (a) (grant ~ on) verpachten
⟨Grundstück, Geschäft, Rechte⟩; vermieten
⟨Haus, Wohnung, Büro⟩
(b) (take ~ on) pachten ⟨Grundstück,
Geschäft⟩; mieten ⟨Haus, Wohnung, Büro⟩

'**leasehold** *n.* ▶ LEASE 2: **have the** ~ **of** *or*
on sth. etw. gepachtet/gemietet haben

leash /liːʃ/ *n.* Leine, *die*

least /liːst/ 1 *adj.* (smallest) kleinst…; (in
quantity) wenigst…; (in status) geringst…
2 *n.* Geringste, *das;* **the** ~ **I can do** das
Mindeste, was ich tun kann; **at** ~:
mindestens; (anyway) wenigstens; **at the**
[**very**] ~: [aller]mindestens; **not** [**in**] **the** ~:
nicht im Geringsten
3 *adv.* am wenigsten

leather /'leðə(r)/ 1 *n.* Leder, *das*
2 *adj.* ledern; Leder⟨jacke, -mantel⟩

'**leather goods** *n. pl.* Lederwaren *Pl.*

'**leathery** *adj.* ledern

leave[1] /liːv/ *n.* (a) (permission) Erlaubnis,
die
(b) (from duty or work) Urlaub, *der;* ~ [**of**
absence] Urlaub, *der*
(c) **take one's** ~ sich verabschieden

leave[2] *v.t.,* **left** /left/ (a) (make or let remain)
hinterlassen; ~ **sb. to do sth.** es jmdm.
überlassen, etw. zu tun; (in will) ~ **sb. sth.,**
~ **sth. to sb.** jmdm. etw. hinterlassen
(b) (refrain from doing, using, etc.) stehen lassen
⟨Abwasch, Essen⟩

⋯⟶

(c) (in given state) lassen; ∼ **sb. alone** (allow to be alone) jmdn. allein lassen; (stop bothering) jmdn. in Ruhe lassen

(d) (refer, entrust) ∼ **sth. to sb./sth.** etw. jmdm./einer Sache überlassen

(e) (go away from, quit, desert) verlassen; ∼ **home at 6 a.m.** um 6 Uhr früh von zu Hause weggehen/-fahren; ∼ **Bonn at 6 p.m.** (by car, in train) um 18 Uhr von Bonn abfahren; (by plane) um 18 Uhr in Bonn abfliegen; *abs.* **the train** ∼s **at 8.30 a.m.** der Zug fährt *od.* geht um 8.30 Uhr; ∼ **on the 8 a.m. train/flight** mit dem Achtuhrzug fahren/der Achtuhrmaschine fliegen

▪ **leave a**'**side** *v.t.* beiseite lassen

▪ **leave be**'**hind** *v.t.* zurücklassen; (by mistake) vergessen; liegen lassen

▪ **leave** '**off** *v.t.* (stop) aufhören mit; *abs.* aufhören

▪ **leave** '**out** *v.t.* auslassen

▪ **leave** '**over** *v.t.* be left over übrig [geblieben] sein

leaves *pl. of* LEAF

Lebanon /'lebənən/ *pr. n.* [the] ∼: [der] Libanon

lecherous /'letʃərəs/ *adj.* lüstern (geh.)

lecture /'lektʃə(r)/ ① **(a)** *n.* Vortrag, *der;* (Univ.) Vorlesung, *die*
(b) (reprimand) Strafpredigt, *die* (ugs.)
② *v.i.* ∼ **[to sb.]** [**on sth.**] [vor jmdm.] einen Vortrag/(Univ.) eine Vorlesung [über etw. (*Akk.*)] halten
③ *v.t.* (scold) ∼ **sb.** jmdm. eine Strafpredigt halten

'**lecture hall** *n.* Hörsaal, *der*

'**lecturer** *n.* Vortragende, *der/die;* **senior** ∼: Dozent, *der/*Dozentin, *die*

'**lecture room** *n.* Vortragsraum, *der;* (Univ.) Vorlesungsraum, *der*

lectureship /'lektʃəʃɪp/ *n.* Dozentur, *die*

lecture: ∼ **theatre** *n.* Hörsaal, *der;* ∼ **tour** *n.* Vortragsreise, *die*

led ▶ LEAD² 1, 2

LED *abbr.* = **light-emitting diode** LED

ledge /ledʒ/ *n.* Sims, *der od. das;* (of rock) Vorsprung, *der*

ledger /'ledʒə(r)/ *n.* (Commerc.) Hauptbuch, *das*

lee /liː/ *n.* **(a)** (shelter) Schutz, *der*
(b) ∼ [**side**] (Naut.) Leeseite, *die*

leech /liːtʃ/ *n.* (Blut)egel, *der*

leek /liːk/ *n.* Stange Porree *od.* Lauch; ∼s Porree, *der;* Lauch, *der*

leek '**soup** *n.* Lauch[creme]suppe, *die*

leer /lɪə(r)/ ① *n.* anzüglicher/spöttischer Blick
② *v.i.* ∼ **at sb.** jmdm. einen anzüglichen/ spöttischen [Seiten]blick zuwerfen

leeward /'liːwəd/ ① *adj.* to/on the ∼ side of the ship nach/in Lee
② *n.* Leeseite, *die;* to ∼: leewärts

'**leeway** *n.* **(a)** (Naut.) Leeweg, *der;* Abdrift, *die*

(b) (fig.) Spielraum, *der*

left¹ ▶ LEAVE²

left² /left/ ① *adj.* **(a)** link...; **on the** ∼ **side** auf der linken Seite; links
(b) L∼ (Polit.) link...
② *adv.* nach links
③ *n.* **(a)** (∼-hand side) linke Seite; **on** *or* **to the** ∼ [**of sb./sth.**] links [von jmdm./etw.]
(b) (Polit.) **the L**∼: die Linke

left: ∼'**hand** *adj.* link...; ∼'**handed** ① *adj.* linkshändig; ⟨*Werkzeug*⟩ für Linkshänder; **be** ∼'**handed** Linkshänder/ Linkshänderin sein; ② *adv.* linkshändig; ∼ '**luggage** [**office**] *n.* (Brit. Railw.) Gepäckaufbewahrung, *die;* ∼'**overs** *n. pl.* Reste *Pl.* ∼ '**wing** *n.* linker Flügel; ∼'**wing** *adj.* (Polit.) linksgerichtet; Links⟨*extremist, -intellektueller*⟩; ∼'**winger** *n.* **(a)** (Sport) Linksaußen, *der;* **(b)** (Polit.) Angehöriger/Angehörige des linken Flügels

leg /leg/ *n.* **(a)** Bein, *das;* **pull sb.'s** ∼ (fig.) jmdn. auf den Arm nehmen (ugs.); **stretch one's** ∼s sich (*Dat.*) die Beine vertreten
(b) ∼ **of lamb** Lammkeule, *die*
(c) (of journey) Etappe, *die*

legacy /'legəsɪ/ *n.* Vermächtnis, *das* (Rechtsspr.); Erbschaft, *die*

legal /'liːgl/ *adj.* **(a)** (concerning the law) juristisch; Rechts⟨*beratung, -streit, -experte, -schutz*⟩; gesetzlich ⟨*Vertreter*⟩; rechtlich ⟨*Gründe, Stellung*⟩; Gerichts⟨*kosten*⟩
(b) (required by law) gesetzlich ⟨*Verpflichtung*⟩; gesetzlich verankert ⟨*Recht*⟩
(c) (lawful) legal; rechtsgültig ⟨*Vertrag, Testament*⟩

legal: ∼ '**action** *n.* Gerichtsverfahren, *das;* Prozess, *der;* **take** ∼ **action against sb.** gerichtlich gegen jmdn. vorgehen; ∼ '**aid** *n.* ≈ Prozesskostenhilfe, *die*

legality /lɪ'gælɪtɪ/ *n.* Legalität, *die*

legalization /liːgəlaɪ'zeɪʃn/ *n.* Legalisierung, *die*

legalize /'liːgəlaɪz/ *v.t.* legalisieren

legend /'ledʒənd/ *n.* Sage, *die;* (unfounded belief) Legende, *die*

legendary /'ledʒəndərɪ/ *adj.* legendär

leggings /'legɪŋz/ *n. pl.* Ledergamaschen *Pl.* (veralt.); (of baby) Strampelhose, *die*

legibility /ledʒɪ'bɪlɪtɪ/ *n.* Leserlichkeit, *die*

legible /'ledʒɪbl/ *adj.* leserlich; **easily**/ **scarcely** ∼: leicht/kaum lesbar

legion /'liːdʒn/ *n.* Legion, *die*

legislate /'ledʒɪsleɪt/ *v.i.* Gesetze verabschieden

legislation /ledʒɪs'leɪʃn/ *n.* **(a)** (laws) Gesetze *Pl.*
(b) (legislating) Gesetzgebung, *die*

legislative /'ledʒɪslətɪv/ *adj.* gesetzgebend

legislator /'ledʒɪsleɪtə(r)/ *n.* Gesetzgeber, *der*

legislature /'ledʒɪsleɪtʃə(r)/ *n.* Legislative, *die*

legitimacy /lɪ'dʒɪtɪməsɪ/ n. (a)
Rechtmäßigkeit, die; Legitimität, die
(b) (of child) Ehelichkeit, die

legitimate /lɪ'dʒɪtɪmət/ adj. (a) (lawful)
legitim; rechtmäßig ⟨Besitzer, Regierung⟩
(b) (valid) berechtigt
(c) ehelich ⟨Kind⟩

legitimatize (legitimatise)
/lɪ'dʒɪtɪmətaɪz/, **legitimize (legitimise)**
/lɪ'dʒɪtɪmaɪz/ v.t. legitimieren

leisure /'leʒə(r)/ n. Freizeit, die; attrib.
Freizeit-

'**leisurely** adj. gemächlich

'**leisurewear** n., no indef. art.
Freizeitkleidung, die

lemon /'lemən/ n. Zitrone, die

lemonade /lemə'neɪd/ n.
[Zitronen]limonade, die

lend /lend/ v.t., lent /lent/ leihen; ~ sth. to
sb. jmdm. etw. leihen

'**lender** n. Verleiher, der/Verleiherin, die

length /leŋθ, leŋkθ/ n. (a) (also of time)
Länge, die; be six feet in ~: sechs Fuß lang
sein; a short ~ of time kurze Zeit
(b) at ~ (for a long time) lange; (eventually)
schließlich; (at [great] ~ (in great detail) lang
und breit; at some ~: ziemlich ausführlich
(c) go to any/great ~s alles nur/alles
Erdenkliche tun
(d) (piece of material) Länge, die; Stück, das

lengthen /'leŋθən/ ① v.i. länger werden
② v.t. verlängern; länger machen ⟨Kleid⟩

lengthways /'leŋθweɪz/ adv. der Länge
nach; längs

'**lengthy** adj. überlang

lenient /'li:nɪənt/ adj. nachsichtig

lens /lenz/ n. Linse, die; (of spectacles) Glas,
das

lens cap n. Objektivdeckel, der

lent ▶ LEND

Lent /lent/ n. Fastenzeit, die

lentil /'lentl/ n. Linse, die

Leo /'li:əʊ/ n., pl. ~s (Astrol., Astron.) der
Löwe

leopard /'lepəd/ n. Leopard, der

leotard /'li:ətɑ:d/ n. Turnanzug, der

leper /'lepə(r)/ n. Leprakranke, der/die

leprosy /'leprəsɪ/ n. Lepra, die

lesbian /'lezbɪən/ ① n. Lesbierin, die
② adj. lesbisch

less /les/ ① adj. weniger; of ~ value/
importance weniger wertvoll/wichtig
② adv. weniger; ~ and ~: immer weniger;
~ and ~ [often] immer seltener
③ n. weniger
④ prep. (deducting) ten ~ three zehn weniger
drei

lessen /'lesn/ ① v.t. verringern
② v.i. sich verringern

lesser /'lesə(r)/ attrib. adj. geringer...

lessee /le'si:/ n. Pächter, der/Pächterin,
die; Mieter, der/Mieterin, die

lesson /'lesn/ n. (a) (class)
[Unterrichts]stunde, die
(b) (example, warning) Lehre, die
(c) (Eccl.) Lesung, die

let /let/ ① v.t., -tt-, let (a) (allow to) lassen;
~ sb. do sth. jmdn. etw. tun lassen; ~ alone
(far less) geschweige denn
(b) (cause to) ~ sb. know jmdn. wissen
lassen
(c) (Brit.: rent out) vermieten
② v. aux., -tt-, let lassen; Let's go to the
cinema. – Yes, ~'s/No, ~'s not Komm/
Kommt, wir gehen ins Kino. – Ja, gut/Nein,
lieber nicht; ~ them come in sie sollen
hereinkommen

■ **let 'down** v.t. (a) (lower) herunter-/
hinunterlassen
(b) (Dressm.) auslassen
(c) (disappoint, fail) im Stich lassen

■ **let 'in** v.t. (a) (admit) herein-/hineinlassen
(b) ~ oneself in for sth. sich auf etw. (Akk.)
einlassen
(c) ~ sb. in on a secret/plan etc. jmdn. in
ein Geheimnis/einen Plan usw. einweihen

■ '**let into** v.t. (a) (admit into) lassen in
(+ Akk.)
(b) (fig.: acquaint with) ~ sb. into a secret
jmdn. in ein Geheimnis einweihen

■ **let 'off** v.t. (a) (excuse) laufen lassen (ugs.);
~ sb. off sth. jmdn. etw. erlassen
(b) (allow to alight) aussteigen lassen
(c) abbrennen ⟨Feuerwerk⟩

■ **let 'on** (coll.) ① v.i. don't ~ on! nichts
verraten!
② v.t. sb. ~ on to me that ...: man hat mir
gesteckt, dass ... (ugs.)

■ **let 'out** v.t. (a) ~ sb./an animal out
jmdn./ein Tier heraus-/hinaus lassen
(b) ausstoßen ⟨Schrei⟩; ~ out a groan
aufstöhnen
(c) verraten ⟨Geheimnis⟩
(d) (Dressm.) auslassen
(e) (Brit.: rent out) vermieten

■ **let 'through** v.t. durchlassen

■ **let 'up** v.i. (coll.) nachlassen

'**let-down** n. Enttäuschung, die

lethal /'li:θl/ adj. tödlich

lethargic /lɪ'θɑ:dʒɪk/ adj. träge; (apathetic)
lethargisch

lethargy /'leθədʒɪ/ n. Trägheit, die; (apathy)
Lethargie, die

letter /'letə(r)/ n. (a) Brief, der (to an
+ Akk.)
(b) (of alphabet) Buchstabe, der

letter: ~ **bomb** n. Briefbombe, die;
~ **box** n. Briefkasten, der; ~**head,**
~**heading** ns. Briefkopf, der

'**lettering** n. Typographie, die

letter: ~ **pad** n. Briefblock, der; ~**s
page** n. Leserbriefseite, die

lettuce /'letɪs/ n. [Kopf]salat, der

leukaemia, (Amer.) **leukemia**
/lu:'ki:mɪə/ n. Leukämie, die

level /'levl/ ① n. (a) Höhe, die; (storey)
Etage, die
(b) (fig.: steady state) Niveau, das; be on a
~ [with sb./sth.] auf dem gleichen Niveau
sein [wie jmd./etw.]
(c) (of computer game) Level, der
② adj. (a) waagerecht; eben ⟨Boden, Land⟩
(b) (on a ~) be ~ [with sth./sb.] auf gleicher
Höhe [mit etw./jmdm.] sein
(c) (fig.) keep a ~ head einen kühlen Kopf
bewahren; do one's ~ best (coll.) sein
Möglichstes tun
③ v.t., (Brit.) -ll-: (a) (make ~) ebnen
(b) (aim) richten ⟨Blick, Gewehr⟩ (at auf
+ Akk.); (fig.) richten ⟨Kritik usw.⟩ (at gegen)

level: ~ **'crossing** n. (Brit. Railw.)
[schienengleicher] Bahnübergang;
~-**'headed** adj. besonnen

lever /'li:və(r)/ ① n. Hebel, der
② v.t. ~ **sth. open** etw. aufhebeln

leverage /'li:vərɪdʒ/ n. Hebelwirkung, die

levity /'levɪtɪ/ n. (frivolity) Unernst, der

levy /'levɪ/ ① n. (tax) Steuer, die
② v.t. erheben

lewd /lju:d/ adj. geil; anzüglich ⟨Geste⟩;
schlüpfrig ⟨Witz⟩

lexicon /'leksɪkən/ n. (a) (dictionary)
Wörterbuch, das; Lexikon, das (veralt.)
(b) (vocabulary) Wortschatz, der

liability /laɪə'bɪlɪtɪ/ n. (a) Haftung, die
(b) (handicap) Belastung, die (to für)

liable /'laɪəbl/ pred. adj. (a) (legally bound) be
~ for sth. für etw. haftbar sein od. haften
(b) (prone) be ~ to sth. ⟨Person:⟩ zu etw.
neigen; be ~ to do sth. ⟨Sache:⟩ leicht etw.
tun; ⟨Person:⟩ dazu neigen, etw. zu tun

liaise /lɪ'eɪz/ v.i. eine Verbindung
herstellen; ~ on a project bei einem Projekt
zusammenarbeiten

liaison /lɪ'eɪzɒn/ n. (cooperation)
Zusammenarbeit, die

liar /'laɪə(r)/ n. Lügner, der/Lügnerin, die

libel /'laɪbl/ ① n. Verleumdung, die
② v.t., (Brit.) -ll- verleumden

libellous (Amer.: **libelous**) /'laɪbələs/ adj.
verleumderisch

liberal /'lɪbərl/ ① adj. (a) großzügig
(b) (Polit.) liberal; **the L~ Democrats** (Brit.) die
Liberaldemokraten
② n. **L~** (Polit.) Liberale, der/die

liberate /'lɪbəreɪt/ v.t. befreien (from aus); a
~d woman eine emanzipierte Frau

liberation /lɪbə'reɪʃn/ n. Befreiung, die; see
also WOMEN'S LIBERATION

liberator /'lɪbəreɪtə(r)/ n. Befreier, der/
Befreierin, die

liberty /'lɪbətɪ/ n. Freiheit, die; take the
~ of doing sth. sich (Dat.) die Freiheit
nehmen, etw. zu tun; take liberties with sb.
sich (Dat.) Freiheiten gegen jmdn.
herausnehmen (ugs.)

Libra /'li:brə/ n. (Astrol., Astron.) die Waage

librarian /laɪ'breərɪən/ n. Bibliothekar, der/
Bibliothekarin, die

library /'laɪbrərɪ/ n. Bibliothek, die; **public
~:** öffentliche Bücherei

library: ~ **book** n. Buch aus der
Bibliothek; ~ **ticket** n. Lesekarte, die

Libya /'lɪbɪə/ pr. n. Libyen (das)

lice pl. of LOUSE

licence /'laɪsəns/ ① n. [behördliche]
Genehmigung; Lizenz, die; [driving] ~:
Führerschein, der
② v.t. ▶ LICENSE 1

'licence fee n. Lizenzgebühr, die

license /'laɪsəns/ ① v.t. ermächtigen; **the
restaurant is ~d to sell drinks** das
Restaurant hat eine Schankerlaubnis od.
-konzession; ~d ⟨Händler, Makler,
Buchmacher⟩ mit [einer] Lizenz; **licensing
laws** Schankgesetze; ~d **premises** Gaststätte
mit Schankerlaubnis; **get a car** ~d ≈ die
Kfz-Steuer für ein Auto bezahlen
② n. (Amer.) ▶ LICENCE 1

'license plate n. (Amer.) Nummernschild,
das

licentious /laɪ'senʃəs/ adj. zügellos
⟨Person⟩; unzüchtig ⟨Benehmen⟩

lichen /'laɪkn, 'lɪtʃn/ n. Flechte, die

lick /lɪk/ ① v.t. (a) lecken
(b) (coll.: beat) verdreschen (ugs.)
② n. Lecken, das
■ **lick 'off** v.t. ablecken

lid /lɪd/ n. (a) Deckel, der
(b) (eyelid) Lid, das

lido /'li:dəʊ/ n., pl. ~s Freibad, das

lie¹ /laɪ/ ① n. Lüge, die; **tell** ~s/a ~: lügen
② v.i., **lying** /'laɪɪŋ/ lügen; ~ to sb. jmdn. be-
od. anlügen

lie² v.i., **lying** /'laɪɪŋ/, **lay** /leɪ/, **lain** /leɪn/ (a)
liegen; (assume horizontal position) sich legen
(b) ~ **idle** ⟨Maschine, Fabrik:⟩ stillstehen
■ **lie a'bout, lie a'round** v.i.
herumliegen (ugs.).
■ **lie 'back** v.i. sich zurücklegen; (sitting)
sich zurücklehnen
■ **lie 'down** v.i. sich hinlegen

lie detector /'laɪdɪ'tektə(r)/ n.
Lügendetektor, der

'lie-in n. (coll.) **have a ~:** [sich] ausschlafen

lieu /lju:/ n. **in ~ of sth.** anstelle einer Sache
(Gen.); **get holiday in ~:** stattdessen Urlaub
bekommen

lieutenant /lef'tenənt/ n. (Army)
Oberleutnant, der

life /laɪf/ n., pl. **lives** /laɪvz/ Leben, das; **for
~:** lebenslänglich ⟨inhaftiert⟩; **true to ~:**
wahrheitsgetreu; **get a ~** (coll.) was aus
seinem Leben machen

life: ~-**and-death** adj. ⟨Kampf⟩ auf Leben
und Tod; (fig.) überaus wichtig ⟨Frage, Brief⟩;
~ **assurance** n. (Brit.)
Lebensversicherung, die; ~-**belt** n.
Rettungsring, der; ~-**boat** n. Rettungsboot,
das; ~-**buoy** n. Rettungsring, der; ~ **cycle**

n. Lebenszyklus, *der;* ~ **expectancy** *n.*
Lebenserwartung, *die;* ~**guard** *n.*
Rettungsschwimmer, *der/*-schwimmerin, *die;*
~ **insurance** *n.* Lebensversicherung, *die;*
~ **jacket** *n.* Schwimmweste, *die;* ~**less**
adj. leblos; (fig.) farblos; ~**like** *adj.*
lebensecht; ~**line** *n.* Rettungsleine, *die;* (fig.)
Rettungsanker, *der;* ~**long** *adj.* lebenslang

lifer /'laɪfə(r)/ *n.* (coll.) Lebenslängliche, *der/*
die (ugs.)

life: ~**saving** *n.* Rettungsschwimmen,
das; attrib. Rettungs-; ~ **sciences** *n. pl.*
Biowissenschaften *Pl.;* ~ **sentence** *n.*
lebenslängliche Freiheitsstrafe; ~**size,**
~**sized** *adj.* lebensgroß; in Lebensgröße
nachgestellt; ~**span** *n.* Lebenserwartung,
die; (Biol.) Lebensdauer, *die;* ~**style** *n.*
Lebensstil, *der;* ~**time** *n.* Lebenszeit, *die;*
during my ~**time** während meines Lebens;
once in a ~**time** einmal im Leben; ~ **vest**
n. Schwimmweste, *die*

lift /lɪft/ ① *v.t.* heben; (fig.) erheben ⟨*Gemüt,*
Geist⟩
② *n.* (a) (in vehicle) **get a** ~: mitgenommen
werden; **give sb. a** ~: jmdn. mitnehmen
(b) (Brit.: elevator) Aufzug, *der*
③ *v.i.* ⟨*Nebel:*⟩ sich auflösen
■ **'lift off** *v.t. & i.* abheben
■ **lift 'up** *v.t.* hochheben; heben ⟨*Kopf*⟩

'lift-off *n.* Abheben, *das*

ligament /'lɪɡəmənt/ *n.* Band, *das*

light¹ /laɪt/ ① *n.* (a) Licht, *das;* ~ **of day**
Tageslicht, *das*
(b) (lamp) Licht, *das;* (fitting) Lampe, *die*
(c) (signal to traffic) Ampel, *die;* **as far as the**
~**s** bis zur Ampel
(d) (to ignite) **have you got a** ~? haben Sie
Feuer? **set** ~ **to sth.** etw. anzünden
(e) **bring sth. to** ~: etw. ans [Tages]licht
bringen; **throw** *or* **shed** ~ **[up]on sth.** Licht
in etw. (*Akk.*) bringen
(f) (aspect) **in that** ~: aus dieser Sicht; **seen**
in this ~: so gesehen; **in the** ~ **of** angesichts
(+ *Gen.*); **show sb. in a bad** ~: ein
schlechtes Licht auf jmdn. werfen
② *adj.* hell; ~**blue/brown** *etc.* hellblau/
-braun *usw.*
③ *v.t.,* **lit** /lɪt/ *or* **lighted** (a) (ignite) anzünden
(b) (illuminate) erhellen
■ **light 'up** ① *v.i.* (a) (become lit) erleuchtet
werden
(b) (become bright) aufleuchten (**with** vor)
② *v.t.* (a) (illuminate) erleuchten
(b) anzünden ⟨*Zigarette*⟩

light² ① *adj.* leicht; (mild) mild ⟨*Strafe*⟩
② *adv.* **travel** ~: mit wenig *od.* leichtem
Gepäck reisen

light: ~ **'aircraft** *n.* Leichtflugzeug, *das;*
~**bulb** *n.* Glühbirne, *die*

'lighted *adj.* brennend ⟨*Kerze, Zigarette*⟩;
angezündet ⟨*Streichholz*⟩

light-emitting 'diode /'daɪəʊd/ *n.*
Leuchtdiode, *die*

lighten¹ /'laɪtn/ *v.t.* (make less heavy, difficult)
leichter machen

lighten² ① *v.t.* (make brighter) aufhellen;
heller machen ⟨*Raum*⟩
② *v.i.* sich aufhellen

'lighter *n.* Feuerzeug, *das*

light: ~**'headed** *adj.* leicht benommen;
~**'hearted** *adj.* (a) (humorous)
unbeschwert; (b) (optimistic) unbekümmert;
~**house** *n.* Leuchtturm, *der;*
~ **'industry** *n.* Leichtindustrie, *die*

'lighting *n.* Beleuchtung, *die*

'lightly *adv.* (a) leicht
(b) (without serious consideration) leichtfertig
(c) (cheerfully) leichthin; **not treat sth.** ~: etw.
nicht auf die leichte Schulter nehmen
(d) **get off** ~: glimpflich davonkommen

'light meter *n.* Lichtmesser, *der;* (exposure
meter) Belichtungsmesser, *der*

'lightness¹ *n.* (of weight; also fig.)
Leichtigkeit, *die*

lightness² *n.* (of colour) Helligkeit, *die*

lightning /'laɪtnɪŋ/ *n.* Blitz, *der;* **flash of** ~:
Blitz, *der*

lightning: ~ **conductor** *n.*
Blitzableiter, *der;* ~ **strike** *n.* Blitzschlag,
der

light: ~**weight** ① *adj.* leicht. ② *n.*
Leichtgewicht, *das;* ~ **year** *n.* Lichtjahr,
das

like¹ /laɪk/ ① *adj.* (a) (resembling) wie; **your**
dress is ~ **mine** dein Kleid ist so ähnlich
wie meins; **in a case** ~ **that** in so einem
Fall; **what is sb./sth.** ~? wie ist jmd./etw.?
(b) (characteristic of) typisch für ⟨*dich, ihn*
usw.⟩
(c) (similar) ähnlich
② *prep.* (in the manner of) wie; [**just**] ~ **that**
[einfach] so
③ *n.* (a) (equal) **his/her** ~: seines-/
ihresgleichen
(b) (similar things) **the** ~: so etwas; **and the** ~:
und dergleichen

like² ① *v.t.* (be fond of, wish for) mögen;
~ **vegetables** Gemüse mögen; gern Gemüse
essen; ~ **doing sth.** etw. gern tun; **would you**
~ **a drink?** möchtest du etwas trinken?;
would you ~ **me to do it?** möchtest du, dass
ich es tue?; **how do you** ~ **it?** wie gefällt es
dir?; **if you** ~ *expr. assent* wenn du willst
② *n., in pl.* ~**s and dislikes** Vorlieben und
Abneigungen

likeable /'laɪkəbl/ *adj.* nett; sympathisch

likelihood /'laɪklɪhʊd/ *n.*
Wahrscheinlichkeit, *die*

likely /'laɪklɪ/ ① *adj.* wahrscheinlich; **there**
are ~ **to be** [traffic] hold-ups man muss mit
[Verkehrs]staus rechnen; **they are** [not] ~ **to**
come sie werden wahrscheinlich [nicht]
kommen; **is it** ~ **to rain tomorrow?** wird es
morgen wohl regnen?; **this is not** ~ **to**
happen es ist unwahrscheinlich, dass das
geschieht   ···⟩

② *adv.* wahrscheinlich; **as ~ as not** höchstwahrscheinlich; **not ~!** (coll.) auf keinen Fall!

'like-minded *adj.* gleich gesinnt

liken /'laɪkn/ *v.t.* **~ sth./sb. to sth. etw./** jmdn. mit etw./jmdm. vergleichen

'likeness *n.* Ähnlichkeit, *die* (**to** mit)

likewise /'laɪkwaɪz/ *adv.* ebenso

liking /'laɪkɪŋ/ *n.* Vorliebe, *die;* **take a ~ to sb./sth.** an jmdm./etw. Gefallen finden; **sth. is [not] to sb.'s ~:** etw. ist [nicht] nach jmds. Geschmack

lilac /'laɪlək/ ① *n.* (a) (Bot.) Flieder, *der* (b) (colour) Zartlila, *das* ② *adj.* zartlila; fliederfarben

Lilo ® /'laɪləʊ/ *n.* Luftmatratze, *die*

lily /'lɪlɪ/ *n.* Lilie, *die*

limb /lɪm/ *n.* (a) (Anat.) Glied, *das* (b) **be out on a ~** (fig.) exponiert sein

limber up /lɪmbər 'ʌp/ *v.i.* (loosen up) die Muskeln lockern

lime¹ /laɪm/ *n.* [quick]~: [ungelöschter] Kalk

lime² *n.* (fruit) Limone, *die*

lime³ ▶ LIME TREE

'limelight *n.* **be in the ~:** im Rampenlicht [der Öffentlichkeit] stehen

limerick /'lɪmərɪk/ *n.* Limerick, *der*

lime: ~stone *n.* Kalkstein, *der;* **~ tree** *n.* Linde, *die*

limit /'lɪmɪt/ ① *n.* (a) Grenze, *die;* **set** *or* **put a ~ on sth.** etw. begrenzen; **be over the ~** ⟨*Autofahrer:*⟩ zu viele Promille haben; **lower/ upper ~:** Untergrenze/Höchstgrenze, *die;* **without ~:** unbegrenzt; **within ~s** innerhalb gewisser Grenzen (b) (coll.) **this is the ~!** das ist [doch] die Höhe!; **he/she is the [very] ~:** er/sie ist [einfach] unmöglich ② *v.t.* begrenzen (**to** auf + *Akk.*); einschränken ⟨*Freiheit*⟩

limitation /lɪmɪ'teɪʃn/ *n.* Beschränkung, *die*

'limited *adj.* (a) (restricted) begrenzt (b) (intellectually narrow) beschränkt

'limitless *adj.* grenzenlos

limousine /'lɪmʊziːn/ *n.* Limousine, *die*

limp¹ /lɪmp/ ① *v.i.* hinken ② *n.* Hinken, *das*

limp² *adj.* schlaff

'limply *adv.* schlaff; (weakly) schwach

limpet /'lɪmpɪt/ *n.* (Zool.) Napfschnecke, *die*

limpid /'lɪmpɪd/ *adj.* klar

linctus /'lɪŋktəs/ *n.* Hustensaft, *der*

line¹ /laɪn/ ① *n.* (a) (string, cord, rope, etc.) Leine, *die* (b) (telephone cable) Leitung, *die* (c) (long mark; also Math., Phys.) Linie, *die* (d) (row, series) Reihe, *die;* (Amer.: queue) Schlange, *die;* **bring sb. into ~:** dafür sorgen, dass jmd. nicht aus der Reihe tanzt (ugs.) (e) (row of words on a page) Zeile, *die*

(f) (wrinkle) Falte, *die* (g) (direction, course) Richtung, *die;* **on the ~s of** nach Art (+ *Gen.*); **be on the right/wrong ~s** in die richtige/falsche Richtung gehen; **along** *or* **on the same ~s** in der gleichen Richtung (h) (Railw.) Bahnlinie, *die;* (track) Gleis, *das* (i) (field of activity) Branche, *die* (j) (Commerc.: product) Artikel, *der;* Linie, *die* (fachspr.) ② *v.t.* (a) linieren ⟨*Papier*⟩; **a ~d face** ein faltiges Gesicht (b) säumen (geh.) ⟨*Straße, Strecke*⟩

■ **line 'up** ① *v.t.* antreten lassen ⟨*Gefangene, Soldaten usw.*⟩; [in einer Reihe] aufstellen ⟨*Gegenstände*⟩ ② *v.i.* ⟨*Gefangene, Soldaten:*⟩ antreten; (queue up) sich anstellen

line² *v.t.* füttern ⟨*Kleidungsstück*⟩; ausschlagen ⟨*Schublade usw.*⟩

lineage /'lɪnɪdʒ/ *n.* Abstammung, *die*

linear /'lɪnɪə(r)/ *adj.* linear

line: ~ dance ① *n.* Linedance, *der;* ② *v.i.* Linedance tanzen; **~ dancing** *n.* Linedance-Tanzen, *das;* **~ manager** *n.* [unmittelbarer] Vorgesetzter; Linienmanager, *der*

linen /'lɪnɪn/ ① *n.* (a) Leinen, *das* (b) (shirts, sheets, etc.) Wäsche, *die* ② *adj.* Leinen⟨*faden, -bluse*⟩; Lein⟨*tuch*⟩

linen: ~ basket *n.* (Brit.) Wäschekorb, *der;* **~ cupboard** *n.* Wäscheschrank, *der*

'line printer *n.* (Comp.) Zeilendrucker, *der*

liner /'laɪnə(r)/ Linienschiff, *das*

'line-up *n.* Aufstellung, *die*

linger /'lɪŋɡə(r)/ *v.i.* verweilen (geh.); bleiben

lingerie /'læʒərɪ/ *n.* [women's] **~:** Damenunterwäsche, *die*

lingo /'lɪŋɡəʊ/ *n.* (coll.) Sprache, *die*

linguist /'lɪŋɡwɪst/ *n.* Sprachkundige, *der/ die*

linguistic /lɪŋ'ɡwɪstɪk/ *adj.* (of **~s**) linguistisch; (of language) sprachlich

linguistics /lɪŋ'ɡwɪstɪks/ *n.* Linguistik, *die*

lining /'laɪnɪŋ/ *n.* (of clothes) Futter, *das;* (of objects, machines, etc.) Auskleidung, *die*

'lining paper *n.* Schrankpapier, *das*

link /lɪŋk/ ① *n.* (a) (of chain) Glied, *das* (b) (connection) Verbindung, *die* ② *v.t.* verbinden; **~ arms** sich unterhaken

■ **link 'up** *v.t.* miteinander verbinden

links /lɪŋks/ *n.* [golf] **~:** Golfplatz, *der*

lino /'laɪnəʊ/ *n., pl.* **~s** Linoleum, *das*

linoleum /lɪ'nəʊlɪəm/ *n.* Linoleum, *das*

linseed /'lɪnsiːd/ *n.* Leinsamen, *der*

linseed 'oil *n.* Leinöl, *das*

lint /lɪnt/ *n.* Mull, *der*

lintel /'lɪntl/ *n.* (Archit.) Sturz, *der*

lion /'laɪən/ *n.* Löwe, *der*

lioness /'laɪənɪs/ *n.* Löwin, *die*

lip /lɪp/ *n.* (a) Lippe, *die;* **lower/upper ~:** Unter-/Oberlippe, *die*

(b) (of cup) [Gieß]rand, *der;* (of jug) Schnabel, *der*

liposuction /'laɪpəʊsʌkʃn, 'lɪpəʊsʌkʃn/ *n.* Fettabsaugung, *die*; Liposuktion, *die*

lip: ~**-read** *v.i.* von den Lippen lesen; ~**-reading** *n.* Lippenlesen, *das;* ~ **service** *n.* pay ~ service to sth. ein Lippenbekenntnis zu etw. ablegen; ~**stick** *n.* Lippenstift, *der*

liquefy /'lɪkwɪfaɪ/ ①*v.t.* verflüssigen ② *v.i.* sich verflüssigen

liqueur /lɪ'kjʊə(r)/ *n.* Likör, *der*

liquid /'lɪkwɪd/ ①*adj.* flüssig ② *n.* Flüssigkeit, *die*

liquidate /'lɪkwɪdeɪt/ *v.t.* (Commerc.) liquidieren

liquidation /lɪkwɪ'deɪʃn/ *n.* (Commerc.) Liquidation, *die*

liquid crystal dis'play *n.* Flüssigkristallanzeige, *die*

liquidize /'lɪkwɪdaɪz/ *v.t.* auflösen; (Cookery) [im Mixer] pürieren

'liquidizer *n.* Mixer, *der*

liquid 'measure *n.* Flüssigkeitsmaß, *das*

liquor /'lɪkə(r)/ *n.* (drink) Alkohol, *der*

liquorice /'lɪkərɪs/ *n.* Lakritze, *die*

Lisbon /'lɪzbən/ *pr. n.* Lissabon (*das*)

lisp /lɪsp/ ① *v.i. & t.* lispeln ② *n.* Lispeln, *das*

list¹ /lɪst/ ① *n.* Liste, *die* ② *v.t.* aufführen; auflisten; (verbally) aufzählen

list² *v.i.* (Naut.) Schlagseite haben

listed 'building *n.* (Brit.) Gebäude unter Denkmalschutz

listen /'lɪsn/ *v.i.* zuhören; ~ to music/the radio Musik/Radio hören; they ~ed to his words sie hörten ihm zu

listener /'lɪsnə(r)/ *n.* Zuhörer, *der*/ Zuhörerin, *die*; (to radio) Hörer, *der*/Hörerin, *die*

listless /'lɪstlɪs/ *adj.* lustlos

'list price *n.* Katalogpreis, *der*

lit ▸ LIGHT¹ 3

litany /'lɪtənɪ/ *n.* Litanei, *die*

lite, Lite ® /laɪt/ ① *adj.* kalorienreduziert ⟨Bier, Käse etc.⟩ ② *n.* Leichtbier, *das*

liter (Amer.) ▸ LITRE

literacy /'lɪtərəsɪ/ *n.* Lese- und Schreibfertigkeit, *die*

literal /'lɪtərl/ *adj.* **(a)** wörtlich **(b)** (not exaggerated) buchstäblich

literally /'lɪtərəlɪ/ *adv.* **(a)** wörtlich **(b)** (actually) buchstäblich **(c)** (coll.: with some exaggeration) geradezu

literary /'lɪtərərɪ/ *adj.* literarisch

literary 'agent *n.* Literaturagent, *der*/ -agentin, *die*

literate /'lɪtərət/ *adj.* des Lesens und Schreibens kundig; (educated) gebildet

literature /'lɪtrətʃə(r)/ *n.* Literatur, *die*

lithe /laɪð/ *adj.* geschmeidig

litigation /lɪtɪ'geɪʃn/ *n.* Rechtsstreit, *der*

litre /'liːtə(r)/ *n.* (Brit.) Liter, *der od. das*

litter /'lɪtə(r)/ ① *n.* **(a)** (rubbish) Abfall, *der* **(b)** (of animals) Wurf, *der* ② *v.t.* verstreuen

litter: ~ **basket** *n.* Abfallkorb, *der;* ~ **bin** *n.* Abfalleimer, *der;* ~**bug**, ~ **lout** *ns.* Schmutzfink, *der* (ugs.)

little /'lɪtl/ ① *adj.*, ~r /'lɪtlə(r)/, ~st /'lɪtlɪst/ (*Note: it is more common to use the compar. and superl. forms* smaller, smallest) **(a)** klein; a ~ way ein kurzes Stück; after a ~ while nach kurzer Zeit **(b)** (not much) wenig; there is very ~ tea left es ist kaum noch Tee da; a ~ ... (a small quantity of) etwas ...; ein bisschen ... ② *n.* wenig; a ~ (a small quantity) etwas; (somewhat) ein wenig; ~ by ~: nach und nach

little: ~ 'finger *n.* kleiner Finger; ~**-known** *adj.* wenig bekannt

liturgy /'lɪtədʒɪ/ *n.* Liturgie, *die*

live¹ /laɪv/ ① *adj.* **(a)** attrib. (alive) lebend **(b)** (Radio, Telev.) ~ performance Liveaufführung, *die;* ~ broadcast Livesendung, *die* **(c)** (Electr.) Strom führend ② *adv.* (Radio, Telev.) live ⟨übertragen usw.⟩

live² /lɪv/ ① *v.i.* **(a)** leben **(b)** (make permanent home) wohnen; leben ② *v.t.* leben

▪ **live 'down** *v.t.* Gras wachsen lassen über (+ *Akk.*); he will never be able to ~ it down das wird ihm ewig anhängen

▪ **live on** ① /'--/ *v.t.* leben von ② /-'-/ *v.i.* weiterleben

▪ **live 'up to** *v.t.* gerecht werden (+ *Dat.*)

live-in /'lɪvɪn/ *attrib. adj.* im Haus wohnend ⟨Personal⟩

livelihood /'laɪvlɪhʊd/ *n.* Lebensunterhalt, *der*

liveliness /'laɪvlɪnɪs/ *n.* Lebhaftigkeit, *die*

lively /'laɪvlɪ/ *adj.* lebhaft; lebendig ⟨Schilderung⟩; rege ⟨Handel⟩

liven up /laɪvn 'ʌp/ ① *v.t.* Leben bringen in (+ *Akk.*) ② *v.i.* ⟨Person:⟩ aufleben

liver /'lɪvə(r)/ *n.* Leber, *die*

livery /'lɪvərɪ/ *n.* Livree, *die*

lives *pl. of* LIFE

live /laɪv/**:** ~**stock** *n. pl.* Vieh, *das;* ~ **wire** *n.* (fig.) Energiebündel, *das* (ugs.)

livid /'lɪvɪd/ *adj.* (Brit. coll.) fuchtig (ugs.)

living /'lɪvɪŋ/ ① *n.* **(a)** Leben, *das* **(b)** make a ~: seinen Lebensunterhalt verdienen **(c)** *pl.* the ~: die Lebenden *Pl.* ② *adj.* lebend; within ~ memory seit Menschengedenken

living: ~ **room** *n.* Wohnzimmer, *das;* ~ 'will *n.* Patientenverfügung, *die*

lizard /ˈlɪzəd/ n. Eidechse, die
llama /ˈlɑːmə/ n. Lama, das
load /ləʊd/ ⟦1⟧ n. (burden, weight; also fig.) Last, die; (amount carried) Ladung, die
⟦2⟧ v.t. (a) (put ~ on) beladen; (put as load) ~ **sb. with work** (fig.) jmdm. Arbeit auftragen (b) laden ⟨Gewehr⟩; ~ **a camera** einen Film [in einen Fotoapparat] einlegen
■ **load 'up** v.i. laden (with Akk.)
'loaded adj. a ~ **question** eine suggestive Frage; **be** ~ (coll.: rich) [schwer] Kohle haben (salopp)
'loading bay n. Ladeplatz, der
loaf[1] /ləʊf/ n., pl. **loaves** /ləʊvz/ Brot, das; [Brot]laib, der; **a** ~ **of bread** ein Laib Brot
loaf[2] v.i. ~ **round town/the house** in der Stadt/zu Hause herumlungern (ugs.)
loan /ləʊn/ ⟦1⟧ n. (a) (thing lent) Leihgabe, die; **be out on** ~: ausgeliehen sein; **have sth. on** ~ [**from sb.**] etw. [von jmdm.] geliehen haben
(b) (money lent) Darlehen, das
⟦2⟧ v.t. ~ **sth. to sb.** jmdm. etw. leihen
loan shark n. (coll.) Kredithai, der (ugs.)
loath /ləʊθ/ pred. adj. **be** ~ **to do sth.** etw. ungern tun
loathe /ləʊð/ v.t. verabscheuen
loathing /ˈləʊðɪŋ/ n. Abscheu, der (of, for vor + Dat.)
loathsome /ˈləʊðsəm/ adj. abscheulich; widerlich
loaves pl. of LOAF[1]
lobby /ˈlɒbɪ/ n. (a) (pressure group) Lobby, die (b) (of hotel) Eingangshalle, die; (of theatre) Foyer, das
lobe /ləʊb/ n. (ear~) Ohrläppchen, das
lobster /ˈlɒbstə(r)/ n. Hummer, der
'lobster pot n. Hummerkorb, der
local /ˈləʊkl/ ⟦1⟧ adj. lokal (bes. Zeitungsw.); Kommunal⟨wahl, -abgaben⟩; (of this area) hiesig; (of that area) dortig; ortsansässig ⟨Firma, Familie⟩; ⟨Wein, Produkt, Spezialität⟩ [aus] der Gegend; **she's a** ~ **girl** sie ist von hier/dort
⟦2⟧ n. (a) (person) Einheimische, der/die (b) (Brit. coll.: pub) [Stamm]kneipe, die
local: ~ **anaes'thetic** n. Lokalanästhetikum, das; ~ **au'thority** n. (Brit.) Kommunalverwaltung, die; ~ **call** n. (Teleph.) Ortsgespräch, das; ~ **'government** n. Kommunalverwaltung, die
locality /ləʊˈkælɪtɪ/ n. Ort, der
'locally adv. im/am Ort
locate /ləʊˈkeɪt/ v.t. (a) **be** ~**d** liegen (b) (determine position of) ausfindig machen
location /ləʊˈkeɪʃn/ n. (a) Lage, die (b) (Cinemat.) Drehort, der; **be on** ~: bei Außenaufnahmen sein
loch /lɒx, lɒk/ n. (Scot.) See, der
lock[1] /lɒk/ n. (of hair) [Haar]strähne, die
lock[2] ⟦1⟧ n. (a) (of door etc.) Schloss, das

(b) (on canal etc.) Schleuse, die
⟦2⟧ v.t. zuschließen
⟦3⟧ v.i. ⟨Tür, Kasten usw.:⟩ sich zuschließen lassen
■ **lock a'way** v.t. einschließen; einsperren ⟨Person⟩
■ **lock 'in** v.t. einschließen; (deliberately) einsperren
■ **lock 'out** v.t. aussperren (of aus); ~ **oneself out** sich aussperren
■ **lock 'up** ⟦1⟧ v.i. abschließen
⟦2⟧ v.t. (a) abschließen ⟨Haus, Tür⟩ (b) (imprison) einsperren
locker /ˈlɒkə(r)/ n. Schließfach, das
locket /ˈlɒkɪt/ n. Medaillon, das
lock: ~**jaw** n. (Med.) Kieferklemme, die; ~**out** n. Aussperrung, die; ~**smith** n. Schlosser, der
locomotive /ləʊkəˈməʊtɪv/ n. Lokomotive, die
locust /ˈləʊkəst/ n. Heuschrecke, die
lodge /lɒdʒ/ ⟦1⟧ n. (a) (cottage) Pförtner-/ Gärtnerhaus, das
(b) (porter's room) [Pförtner]loge, die
⟦2⟧ v.t. (a) einlegen ⟨Beschwerde, Protest usw.⟩
(b) einreichen ⟨Klage⟩
⟦3⟧ v.i. [zur Miete] wohnen
'lodger n. Untermieter, der/Untermieterin, die
lodging /ˈlɒdʒɪŋ/ n. [möbliertes] Zimmer
loft /lɒft/ n. (attic) [Dach]boden, der
lofty /ˈlɒftɪ/ adj. (a) (exalted) hoch (b) (haughty) hochmütig
log /lɒg/ n. (a) (timber) [geschlagener] Baumstamm; (as firewood) [Holz]scheit, das (b) ~[**book**] (Naut.) Logbuch, das
■ **log 'in** ▶ LOG ON
■ **log 'off** v.i. (Comp.) sich abmelden
■ **log 'on** v.i. (Comp.) sich anmelden
■ **log 'out** ▶ LOG OFF
log: ~ **'cabin** n. Blockhütte, die; ~ **'fire** n. Holzfeuer, das
loggerheads /ˈlɒgəhedz/ n. pl. **be at** ~ **with sb.** mit jmdm. im Clinch liegen
logic /ˈlɒdʒɪk/ n. Logik, die
logical /ˈlɒdʒɪkl/ adj. logisch; **she has a** ~ **mind** sie denkt logisch
logically /ˈlɒdʒɪkəlɪ/ adv. logisch
logistics /ləˈdʒɪstɪks/ n. pl. Logistik, die
logo /ˈləʊgəʊ/ n., pl. ~**s** Signet, das
loin /lɔɪn/ n. Lende, die
'loincloth n. Lendenschurz, der
loiter /ˈlɔɪtə(r)/ v.i. trödeln; (linger suspiciously) herumlungern
loll /lɒl/ v.i. sich lümmeln (ugs.)
lollipop /ˈlɒlɪpɒp/ n. Lutscher, der
London /ˈlʌndən/ ⟦1⟧ pr. n. London (das)
⟦2⟧ attrib. adj. Londoner
'Londoner n. Londoner, der/Londonerin, die
lone /ləʊn/ attrib. adj. einsam

loneliness /'ləʊnlmɪs/ n. Einsamkeit, die
lonely /'ləʊnlɪ/ adj. einsam
lone 'parent n. allein erziehender Elternteil; **she/he is a ~**: sie/er ist allein erziehend
loner /'ləʊnə(r)/ n. Einzelgänger, der/ -gängerin, die
lonesome /'ləʊnsəm/ adj. einsam
long¹ /lɒŋ/ 1 adj., ~er /'lɒŋgə(r)/, ~est /'lɒŋgɪst/ (a) lang; weit ⟨Reise, Weg⟩ (b) (elongated) länglich; schmal (c) in the '~ run auf die Dauer
2 n. (~ interval) take ~: lange dauern; for ~: lange; (since ~ ago) seit langem; before ~: bald
3 adv., ~er, ~est (a) lang[e]; as or so ~ as solange; you should have finished ~ before now du hättest schon längst fertig sein sollen; much ~er viel länger (b) as or so ~ as (provided that) solange; wenn
long² v.i. ~ for sb./sth. sich nach jmdm./ etw. sehnen; ~ to do sth. sich danach sehnen, etw. zu tun
long-distance 1 /'---/ adj. Fern⟨gespräch, -verkehr usw.⟩; Langstrecken⟨läufer, -flug usw.⟩
2 /-'--/ adv. phone ~: ein Ferngespräch führen
longevity /lɒn'dʒevɪtɪ/ n. Langlebigkeit, die
long: ~-haired adj. langhaarig; Langhaar⟨dackel, -katze⟩; **~-hand** n. Langschrift, die; **~-haul** adj. Fern⟨verkehr, -lastwagen⟩; Langstrecken⟨[flug]verkehr⟩
'longing 1 n. Sehnsucht, die
2 adj. sehnsüchtig
'longingly adv. sehnsüchtig
longitude /'lɒŋgɪtjuːd/ n. (Geog.) Länge, die
long: ~ jump n. (Brit. Sport) Weitsprung, der; **~-lasting** adj. langandauernd; dauerhaft ⟨Beziehung, Freundschaft⟩; **~-legged** adj. langbeinig; ~ 'lens n. Fernobjektiv, das; **~-life** adj. haltbar [gemacht]; **~-life battery** Batterie mit langer Lebensdauer; **~-life milk** H-Milch, die; **~-lived** /'lɒŋlɪvd/ adj. langlebig; **~-playing 'record** n. Langspielplatte, die; **~-range** adj. (a) Langstrecken⟨flugzeug, -rakete usw.⟩; (b) (relating to time) langfristig; **~-sighted** /lɒn'saɪtɪd/ adj. weitsichtig; (fig.) weitblickend; **~-sleeved** /'lɒŋsliːvd/ adj. langärmelig; **~-standing** attrib. adj. seit langem bestehend; alt ⟨Schulden, Streit⟩; **~-suffering** adj. schwer geprüft; **~-term** adj. langfristig; **~ wave** n. (Radio) Langwelle, die; **~-winded** /lɒŋ'wɪndɪd/ adj. langatmig
loo /luː/ n. (Brit. coll.) Klo, das (ugs.)
look /lʊk/ 1 v.i. (a) sehen; gucken (ugs.) (b) (search) nachsehen (c) (face) zugewandt sein (to[wards] Dat.)

(d) (appear) aussehen; **~ well/ill** gut/schlecht aussehen
2 n. (a) Blick, der; **have** or **take a ~ at sb./ sth.** sich ⟨Dat.⟩ jmdn./etw. ansehen (b) (appearance) Aussehen, das; **good ~s** gutes Aussehen
■ **look 'after** v.t. (care for) sorgen für
■ **look a'head** v.i. (fig.) an die Zukunft denken
■ **'look at** v.t. (a) (regard) ansehen (b) (consider) betrachten
■ **look 'back** v.i. (a) sich umsehen (b) ~ **back on** or **to sth.** an etw. (Akk.) zurückdenken
■ **look 'down [up]on** v.t. (a) herunter-/ hinuntersehen auf (+ Akk.) (b) (fig.: despise) herabsehen auf (+ Akk.)
■ **'look for** v.t. (a) (seek) suchen nach (b) (expect) erwarten
■ **look 'out** v.i. (a) hinaus-/heraussehen (of aus) (b) (take care) aufpassen (c) ~ **out on sth.** ⟨Zimmer, Wohnung usw.⟩ zu etw. hin liegen
■ **look 'out for** v.t. (be prepared for) achten auf (+ Akk.); (keep watching for) Ausschau halten nach ⟨Arbeit, Gelegenheit, Sammelobjekt usw.⟩
■ **look 'over** v.t. (a) sehen über (+ Akk.) (b) (survey) sich ⟨Dat.⟩ ansehen ⟨Haus⟩
■ **look 'round** v.i. sich umsehen
■ **'look through** v.t. (a) ~ **through sth.** durch etw. [hindurch] sehen (b) (inspect) durchsehen ⟨Papiere⟩
■ **'look to** v.t. (rely on) ~ **to sb./sth. for sth.** etw. von jmdm./etw. erwarten
■ **look 'up** 1 v.i. (a) aufblicken (b) (improve) besser werden
2 v.t. nachschlagen ⟨Wort⟩; heraussuchen ⟨Telefonnummer, Zugverbindung usw.⟩
■ **look 'up to** v.t. ~ **up to sb.** zu jmdm. aufsehen
'look-alike n. Doppelgänger, der/-gängerin, die
looker-'on n. Zuschauer, der/Zuschauerin, die
'looking glass n. Spiegel, der
'lookout n., pl. ~s (a) (observation post) Ausguck, der (b) (person) Wache, die (c) (Brit. fig.) **that's a bad ~**: das sind schlechte Aussichten; **that's his ~**: das ist sein Problem (d) **keep a ~ [for sb./sth.]** [nach jmdm./etw] Ausschau halten
loom¹ /luːm/ n. (Weaving) Webstuhl, der
loom² v.i. auftauchen
loop /luːp/ 1 n. (a) Schleife, die (b) (cord) Schlaufe, die
2 v.t. zu einer Schlaufe formen
'loophole n. (fig.) Lücke, die
loopy /'luːpɪ/ adj. (coll.) verrückt (ugs.)
loose /luːs/ adj. (a) (not firm) locker ⟨Zahn, Schraube, Knopf⟩

····▷

(b) (not fixed) lose ⟨*Knopf, Buchseite, Brett, Stein*⟩; offen ⟨*Haar*⟩

(c) be at a ∼ end (fig.) nichts zu tun haben

(d) (inexact) ungenau

loose: ∼**-fitting** *adj.* bequem geschnitten; ∼**-leaf** *adj.* Loseblatt-; ∼**-leaf file** Ringbuch, *das;* ∼**-limbed** *adj.* gelenkig

'loosely *adv.* locker; lose ⟨*zusammenhängen*⟩; frei ⟨*übersetzen*⟩

loosen /'luːsn/ *v.t.* lockern

■ **loosen 'up** *v.i.* sich auflockern; (relax) auftauen

'looseness *n.* Lockerheit, *die*

loot /luːt/ ① *v.t.* plündern
② *n.* Beute, *die*

'looter *n.* Plünderer, *der*

lop /lɒp/ *v.t.* ∼ sth. [off *or* away] etw. abbauen *od.* abhacken

lopsided /lɒp'saɪdɪd/ *adj.* schief

loquacious /ləˈkweɪʃəs/ *adj.* redselig

lord /lɔːd/ ① *n.* **(a)** (master) Herr, *der*
(b) L∼ (Relig.) Herr, *der*
(c) (Brit.: as title) Lord, *der;* **the House of L**∼**s** (Brit.) das Oberhaus
② *int.* (coll.) Gott; **oh/good L**∼**!** du lieber Himmel!

'lordship *n.* Lordschaft, *die*

lore /lɔː(r)/ *n.* Überlieferung, *die*

lorry /'lɒrɪ/ *n.* (Brit.) Lastwagen, *der;* Lkw, *der*

'lorry driver *n.* (Brit.) Lastwagenfahrer, *der;* Lkw-Fahrer, *der*

lose /luːz/ ① *v.t.,* lost /lɒst/ **(a)** verlieren; ∼ one's way sich verlaufen/verfahren
(b) ⟨*Uhr:*⟩ nachgehen
(c) (waste) vertun ⟨*Zeit*⟩; (miss) versäumen ⟨*Gelegenheit*⟩
(d) ∼ weight abnehmen
② *v.i.,* lost **(a)** (in match, contest) verlieren
(b) ⟨*Uhr:*⟩ nachgehen

'loser *n.* Verlierer, *der*/Verliererin, *die*

loss /lɒs/ *n.* **(a)** Verlust, *der* (of *Gen.*); **sell at a** ∼: mit Verlust verkaufen
(b) be at a ∼: nicht [mehr] weiterwissen; be at a ∼ for words um Worte verlegen sein; be at a ∼ what to do nicht wissen, was zu tun ist

loss: ∼ **adjuster** *n.* (Finance) Schaden[s]regulierer, *der*/-reguliererin, *die;* ∼**-making** *adj.* mit Verlust arbeitend

lost /lɒst/ ① ▶ LOSE
② *adj.* **(a)** verloren; get ∼ ⟨*Person:*⟩ sich verlaufen/verfahren; get ∼! (coll.) verdufte! (salopp); ∼ cause aussichtslose Sache
(b) (wasted) vertan ⟨*Zeit*⟩; (missed) versäumt ⟨*Gelegenheit*⟩

lot /lɒt/ *n.* **(a)** (destiny) Los, *das*
(b) (set of persons) Haufen, *der;* the ∼: [sie] alle
(c) (set of things) Menge, *die;* the ∼: alle/alles
(d) (coll.: large quantity) ∼s *or* a ∼ of money *etc.* viel *od.* eine Menge Geld *usw.;* sing *etc.* a ∼: viel singen *usw.;* like sth. a ∼: etw. sehr mögen; have ∼s to do viel zu tun haben

(e) (for choosing) Los, *das;* **draw/cast/throw** ∼**s** [for sth.] um etw. losen

lotion /'ləʊʃn/ *n.* Lotion, *die*

lottery /'lɒtərɪ/ *n.* Lotterie, *die*

'lottery number *n.* Lottozahl, *die*

loud /laʊd/ ① *adj.* **(a)** laut; lautstark ⟨*Protest, Kritik*⟩
(b) (flashy, conspicuous) aufdringlich; grell ⟨*Farbe*⟩
② *adv.* laut; laugh out ∼: laut auflachen; say sth. out ∼: etw. aussprechen

loud'hailer *n.* Megaphon, *das*

'loudly *adv.* laut

loud: ∼**mouth** *n.* Großmaul, *das;* ∼**-mouthed** /'laʊdmaʊðd/ *adj.* großmäulig (ugs.)

'loudness *n.* Lautstärke, *die*

loud'speaker *n.* Lautsprecher, *der*

lounge /laʊndʒ/ ① *v.i.* ∼ [about *or* around] [faul] herumliegen/-sitzen/-stehen
② *n.* **(a)** (in hotel) [Hotel]halle, *die;* (at airport) Wartehalle, *die*
(b) (sitting room) Wohnzimmer, *das*

lounger /'laʊndʒə(r)/ *n.* (sunbed) Liege, *die*

'lounge suit *n.* (Brit.) Straßenanzug, *der*

louse /laʊs/ *n., pl.* lice /laɪs/ Laus, *die*

lousy /'laʊzɪ/ *adj.* (coll.) **(a)** (disgusting) ekelhaft
(b) (very poor) lausig (ugs.); feel ∼: sich mies (ugs.) fühlen

lout /laʊt/ *n.* Rüpel, *der;* Flegel, *der*

loutish /'laʊtɪʃ/ *adj.* rüpelhaft; flegelhaft

louver, louvre /'luːvə(r)/ *n.* ∼ **window** Jalousiefenster, *das;* ∼ **door** Jalousietür, *die*

lovable /'lʌvəbl/ *adj.* liebenswert

love /lʌv/ ① *n.* **(a)** Liebe, *die* (of, for zu); in ∼ [with] verliebt [in (+ *Akk.*)]; fall in ∼ [with] sich verlieben [in (+ *Akk.*)]; for ∼: aus Liebe; ∼ from Beth (in letter) herzliche Grüße von Beth; send one's ∼ to sb. jmdn. grüßen lassen
(b) (sweetheart) Geliebte, *der*/*die;* [my] ∼ (coll.: form of address) [mein] Liebling *od.* Schatz
(c) (Tennis) fifteen/thirty ∼: fünfzehn/dreißig null
② *v.t.* **(a)** lieben; our/their ∼d ones unsere/ ihre Lieben
(b) (like) I'd ∼ a cigarette ich hätte sehr gerne eine Zigarette; ∼ to do *or* ∼ doing sth. etw. gern tun

love: ∼ **affair** *n.* Liebesverhältnis, *das;* ∼ **letter** *n.* Liebesbrief, *der;* ∼ **life** *n.* Liebesleben, *das*

loveliness /'lʌvlɪnɪs/ *n.* Schönheit, *die*

lovely /'lʌvlɪ/ *adj.* [wunder]schön; herrlich ⟨*Tag, Essen*⟩

lover /'lʌvə(r)/ *n.* **(a)** Liebhaber, *der;* Geliebte, *der;* (woman) Geliebte, *die;* be ∼s ein Liebespaar sein
(b) (person who likes sth.) Freund, *der*/ Freundin, *die*

love: ∼**sick** *adj.* an Liebeskummer

leidend; liebeskrank (geh.); ∼ **song** n.
Liebeslied, das; ∼ **story** n.
Liebesgeschichte, die

loving /'lʌvɪŋ/ adj. (a) (affectionate) liebend (b) (expressing love) liebevoll

'**lovingly** adv. liebevoll

low /ləʊ/ ① adj. (a) niedrig; tief ausgeschnitten ‹Kleid›; tief ‹Ausschnitt›; tief liegend ‹Grund›
(b) (of humble rank) nieder...; niedrig
(c) (inferior) niedrig; gering ‹Intelligenz, Bildung›
(d) (in pitch) tief; (in loudness) leise
② adv. (a) (to a ∼ position) tief
(b) (not loudly) leise
(c) lie ∼ (hide) untertauchen

low: ∼**-alcohol** adj. alkoholarm ‹Getränk›; ∼**-brow** adj. schlicht ‹Person›; [geistig] anspruchslos ‹Buch, Programm›; ∼**-budget** adj. Lowbudget-, Billig‹film, -produktion usw.›; ∼**-calorie** adj. kalorienarm ‹Kost, Getränk›; ∼**-cost** adj. preiswert; ∼**-cut** adj. [tief] ausgeschnitten ‹Kleid›; ∼**-cut neck** tiefer Ausschnitt; ∼**-cut shoes** Halbschuhe

lower¹ /'ləʊə(r)/ v.t. (a) herab-/hinablassen (b) senken ‹Blick›; auslassen ‹Saum›; senken ‹Preis, Miete, Zins usw.›; ∼ **one's voice** leiser sprechen

lower² ① compar. adj. unter...; Unter‹grenze, -arm, -lippe usw.›
② compar. adv. tiefer

lower 'case ① n. Kleinbuchstaben Pl.; ② adj. klein ‹Buchstabe›

low: ∼**-fat** adj. fettarm; ∼**-flying** adj. tief fliegend; ∼**-flying aircraft** Tiefflieger, der; ∼ '**frequency** n. Niederfrequenz, die; ∼**-grade** adj. minderwertig; ∼**-income** adj. einkommensschwach; ∼**-income families** Familien mit niedrigem Einkommen; ∼**-key** adj. zurückhaltend; unaufdringlich ‹Beleuchtung, Unterhaltung›; unauffällig ‹Einsatz›; ∼**land** /'ləʊlənd/ n. Tiefland, das

lowly /'ləʊlɪ/ adj. (modest) bescheiden

low: ∼**-lying** adj. tief liegend; ∼**-nicotine** adj. nikotinarm; ∼**-paid** adj. niedrig bezahlt; ∼**-paid families** Familien mit geringem Einkommen; ∼ **point** n. Tiefpunkt, der; ∼ **pressure** n. (Meteorol.) Tiefdruck, der; ∼**-priced** adj. preisgünstig; ∼ **season** n. Nebensaison, die; ∼**-tech** adj. Lowtech‹system, -ausrüstung etc.›; ∼**-voltage** adj. Niederspannungs-; ∼**-wage** attrib. adj. schlecht bezahlt; Niedriglohn‹land›

loyal /'lɔɪəl/ adj. treu

loyalty /'lɔɪəltɪ/ n. Treue, die

'**loyalty card** n. Treuekarte, die (für Kunden)

lozenge /'lɒzɪndʒ/ n. Pastille, die

LP abbr. = **long-playing record** LP, die

'**L-plate** n. (Brit.) 'L'-Schild, das; ≈ „Fahrschule"-Schild, das

Ltd. abbr. = **Limited** GmbH

lubricant /'lu:brɪkənt/ n. Schmiermittel, das

lubricate /'lu:brɪkeɪt/ v.t. schmieren

lubrication /lu:brɪ'keɪʃn/ n. Schmierung, die; attrib. Schmier‹system, -vorrichtung›

lucid /'lu:sɪd/ adj. klar

lucidity /lu:'sɪdɪtɪ/ n. Klarheit, die

luck /lʌk/ n. Glück, das; **good** ∼: Glück, das; **bad** or **hard** ∼: Pech, das; **good** ∼! viel Glück!; **be in/out of** ∼: Glück/kein Glück haben; **no such** ∼: schön wärs

luckily /'lʌkɪlɪ/ adv. glücklicherweise

lucky /'lʌkɪ/ adj. (a) glücklich; **be** ∼: Glück haben
(b) (bringing good luck) Glücks‹zahl, -tag usw.›; ∼ **charm** Glücksbringer, der

lucrative /'lu:krətɪv/ adj. einträglich; lukrativ

ludicrous /'lu:dɪkrəs/ adj. lächerlich; lachhaft ‹Angebot, Ausrede›

lug /lʌg/ v.t., **-gg-** (drag) schleppen

luggage /'lʌgɪdʒ/ n. Gepäck, das

luggage: ∼ **locker** n. [Gepäck]schließfach, das; ∼ **rack** n. Gepäckablage, die

lugubrious /lu:'gu:brɪəs/ adj. (mournful) kummervoll; (dismal) düster

lukewarm /'lu:kwɔ:m/ adj. lauwarm

lull /lʌl/ ① v.t. (a) (soothe) lullen
(b) (fig.) einlullen; ∼ **into a false sense of security** jmdn. in einer trügerischen Sicherheit wiegen
② n. Pause, die

lullaby /'lʌləbaɪ/ n. Schlaflied, das

lumbago /lʌm'beɪgəʊ/ n., pl. ∼**s** (Med.) Hexenschuss, der

lumber /'lʌmbə(r)/ ① n. (a) (furniture) Gerümpel, das
(b) (useless material) Kram, der (ugs.)
(c) (Amer.: timber) [Bau]holz, das
② v.t. ∼ **sb. with sth./sb.** jmdm. etw./jmdn. aufhalsen (ugs.)

'**lumbering** adj. schwerfällig

'**lumberjack** /'lʌmbədʒæk/ n. (Amer.) Holzfäller, der

luminous /'lu:mɪnəs/ adj. [hell] leuchtend; Leucht‹anzeige, -zeiger usw.›

lump /lʌmp/ ① n. (a) Klumpen, der; (of sugar, butter, etc.) Stück, das; (of wood) Klotz, der; (of dough) Kloß, der; (of bread) Brocken, der
(b) (swelling) Beule, die
② v.t. ∼ **sth. with sth.** etw. und etw. zusammentun

lump: ∼ '**payment** n. einmalige Zahlung [einer größeren Summe]; ∼ '**sum** n. Pauschalsumme, die

'**lumpy** adj. klumpig ‹Brei›; ‹Kissen, Matratze› mit klumpiger Füllung

lunacy /'lu:nəsɪ/ n. Wahnsinn, der

lunar /'lu:nə(r)/ adj. Mond-

lunatic /'lu:nətɪk/ ⟦1⟧ *adj.* wahnsinnig
⟦2⟧ *n.* Wahnsinnige, *der/die;* Irre, *der/die*
'lunatic asylum *n.* (Hist.) Irrenanstalt, *die*
(veralt., ugs.)
lunch /lʌntʃ/ ⟦1⟧ *n.* Mittagessen, *das;* **have**
or **eat [one's]** ~: zu Mittag essen
⟦2⟧ *v.i.* zu Mittag essen
lunch: ~ **box** *n.* Lunchbox, *die;* ~ **break**
▶ ~ HOUR
luncheon: ~ **meat** *n.* Frühstücksfleisch,
das; ~ **voucher** *n.* (Brit.) Essenmarke, *die*
lunch: ~ **hour** *n.* Mittagspause, *die;*
~**time** *n.* Mittagszeit, *die;* **at** ~**time** mittags
lung /lʌŋ/ *n.* (right *or* left) Lungenflügel, *der;*
~**s** Lunge, *die*
'lung cancer *n.* Lungenkrebs, *der*
lunge /lʌndʒ/ ⟦1⟧ *n.* Sprung nach vorn
⟦2⟧ *v.i.* ~ **at sb. with a knife** jmdn. mit einem
Messer angreifen
lurch[1] /lɜːtʃ/ *n.* **leave sb. in the** ~: jmdn. im
Stich lassen
lurch[2] ⟦1⟧ *n.* Rucken, *das*
⟦2⟧ *v.i.* rucken; ⟨*Betrunkener:*⟩ torkeln
lure /ljʊə(r), lʊə(r)/ ⟦1⟧ *v.t.* locken
⟦2⟧ *n.* Lockmittel, *das*
lurid /'ljʊərɪd, 'lʊərɪd/ *adj.* **(a)** (in colour) grell
(b) (sensational) reißerisch
lurk /lɜːk/ *v.i.* lauern
luscious /'lʌʃəs/ *adj.* köstlich [süß]; saftig
[süß] ⟨*Obst*⟩
lush /lʌʃ/ *adj.* saftig ⟨*Wiese*⟩; grün ⟨*Tal*⟩;
üppig ⟨*Vegetation*⟩

lust /lʌst/ ⟦1⟧ *n.* **(a)** (sexual) Sinnenlust, *die*
(b) (strong desire) Gier, *die* (for nach)
⟦2⟧ *v.i.* ~ **after** [lustvoll] begehren (geh.)
lustful /'lʌstfl/ *adj.* lüstern (geh.)
lustily /'lʌstɪlɪ/ *adv.* kräftig; aus voller
Kehle ⟨*rufen, singen*⟩
lustre /'lʌstə(r)/ *n.* (Brit.) **(a)** Schimmer, *der*
(b) (fig.: splendour) Glanz, *der*
lusty /'lʌstɪ/ *adj.* kräftig
Luxembourg, Luxemburg
/'lʌksəmbɜːg/ *pr. n.* Luxemburg (*das*)
luxuriant /lʌg'zjʊərɪənt/ *adj.* üppig
luxuriate /lʌg'zjʊərɪeɪt/ *v.i.* ~ **in** sich aalen
in (+ *Dat.*)
luxurious /lʌg'zjʊərɪəs/ *adj.* luxuriös
luxury /'lʌkʃərɪ/ *n.* **(a)** Luxus, *der; attrib.*
Luxus-
(b) (article) Luxusgegenstand, *der;* **luxuries**
Luxus, *der*
LW *abbr.* (Radio) = **long wave** LW
lying /'laɪɪŋ/ *adj.* verlogen ⟨*Person*⟩. *See also*
LIE[1] 2
lymph gland *n.* Lymphknoten, *der*
lynch /lɪntʃ/ *v.t.* lynchen
lynx /lɪŋks/ *n.* Luchs, *der*
lyre /'laɪə(r)/ *n.* Lyra, *die*
lyric /'lɪrɪk/ ⟦1⟧ *adj.* lyrisch; ~ **poetry** Lyrik,
die
⟦2⟧ *n. in pl.* (of song) Text, *der*
lyrical /'lɪrɪkl/ *adj.* **(a)** lyrisch
(b) (coll.: enthusiastic) gefühlvoll

M m

M, m /em/ *n.* M, m, *das*
m. *abbr.* **(a)** = **masculine** m.
(b) = **metre[s]** m
(c) = **million[s]** Mill.
(d) = **minute[s]** Min.
MA *abbr.* = **Master of Arts** M.A.
mac /mæk/ *n.* (Brit. coll.) Regenmantel, *der*
macaroni /mækə'rəʊnɪ/ *n.* Makkaroni *Pl.*
Macedonia /mæsɪ'dəʊnɪə/ *pr. n.*
Makedonien (*das*)
machine /mə'ʃiːn/ *n.* Maschine, *die*
machine: ~ **gun** *n.* Maschinengewehr,
das; ~**made** *adj.* maschinell hergestellt;
~ **operator** *n.* [Maschinen]bediener, *der/*
-bedienerin, *die;* ~**readable** *adj.* (Comp.)
maschinenlesbar
machinery /mə'ʃiːnərɪ/ *n.* **(a)** (machines)
Maschinen *Pl.*
(b) (mechanism) Mechanismus, *der*
machine: ~ **tool** *n.* Werkzeugmaschine,

die; ~**wash** *v.t.* in der Waschmaschine
waschen; ~**washable** *adj.*
waschmaschinenfest
machinist /mə'ʃiːnɪst/ *n.* Maschinist, *der/*
Maschinistin, *die;* [sewing] ~:
[Maschinen]näherin, *die/*-näher, *der*
machismo /mə'tʃɪzməʊ, mə'kɪzməʊ/ *n.*
Machismo, *der;* Männlichkeitswahn, *der*
macho /'mætʃəʊ/ *adj.* Macho-; **he is** ~: er
ist ein Macho
mackerel /'mækərl/ *n., pl. same or* ~**s**
Makrele, *die*
mackintosh /'mækɪntɒʃ/ *n.* Regenmantel,
der
macro /'mækrəʊ/ *n.* (Comp.) Makro, *das*
macrobiotic /mækrəʊbaɪ'ɒtɪk/ *adj.*
makrobiotisch
mad /mæd/ *adj.* **(a)** (insane) geisteskrank
(b) (frenzied) wahnsinnig; **drive sb. mad** jmdn.
um den Verstand bringen

(c) (foolish) verrückt (ugs.)
(d) (very enthusiastic) be ∼ about or on sb./sth. auf jmdn./etw. wild sein (ugs.)
(e) (coll.: annoyed) ∼ [with or at sb.] sauer [auf jmdn.] (ugs.)
(f) (with rabies) toll[wütig]; [run etc.] like ∼ (coll.) wie wild [laufen usw.]

madam /'mædəm/ n. gnädige Frau; **Dear M**∼ (in letter) Sehr geehrte Dame

mad 'cow disease n. (coll.) Rinderwahnsinn, der

madden /'mædn/ v.t. (irritate) [ver]ärgern

maddening /'mædənɪŋ/ adj. (irritating) [äußerst] ärgerlich

made ▶ MAKE 1

made-to-'measure attrib. adj. Maß-

'madly adv. (coll.) wahnsinnig (ugs.)

madman /'mædmən/ n., pl. **madmen** /'mædmən/ n. Wahnsinnige, der

'madness n. Wahnsinn, der

magazine /mægə'ziːn/ n. **(a)** Zeitschrift, die
(b) (of firearm) Magazin, das

maggot /'mægət/ n. Made, die

magic /'mædʒɪk/ **1** n. **(a)** Magie, die; work like ∼: wie ein Wunder wirken
(b) (conjuring) Zauberei, die
2 adj. **(a)** magisch; Zauber⟨trank, -baum⟩
(b) (fig.) wunderbar

magical /'mædʒɪkl/ adj. zauberhaft

magician /mə'dʒɪʃn/ n. Magier, der/Magierin, die; (conjurer) Zauberer, der/Zauberin, die

magic 'wand n. Zauberstab, der

magistrate /'mædʒɪstreɪt/ n. Friedensrichter, der/-richterin, die

magnanimity /mægnə'nɪmɪtɪ/ n. Großmut, die

magnanimous /mæg'nænɪməs/ adj. großmütig **(towards** gegen)

magnate /'mægneɪt/ n. Magnat, der/Magnatin, die

magnesium /mæg'niːzɪəm/ n. Magnesium, das

magnet /'mægnɪt/ n. Magnet, der

magnetic /mæg'netɪk/ adj. magnetisch

magnetic: ∼ **'north** magnetisch Nord, das; ∼ **'tape** n. Magnetband, das

magnetism /'mægnɪtɪzm/ n. **(a)** (force, lit. or fig.) Magnetismus, der
(b) (fig.: charm) Anziehungskraft, die

magnetize /'mægnɪtaɪz/ v.t. magnetisieren

magnification /mægnɪfɪ'keɪʃn/ n. Vergrößerung, die

magnificence /mæg'nɪfɪsəns/ n. Pracht, die; (beauty) Herrlichkeit, die; (lavishness) Üppigkeit, die

magnificent /mæg'nɪfɪsənt/ adj. **(a)** prächtig; herrlich ⟨Garten, Kunstwerk, Wetter⟩; (lavish) üppig ⟨Mahl⟩
(b) (coll.: excellent) fabelhaft (ugs.)

magnifier /'mægnɪfaɪə(r)/ n. (Optics) Lupe, die

magnify /'mægnɪfaɪ/ v.t. **(a)** vergrößern
(b) (exaggerate) aufbauschen

'magnifying glass n. Lupe, die

magnitude /'mægnɪtjuːd/ n. **(a)** (size) Größe, die
(b) (importance) Wichtigkeit, die

magnolia /mæg'nəʊlɪə/ n. Magnolie, die

magnum /'mægnəm/ n. (bottle) Magnum, die

magpie /'mægpaɪ/ n. Elster, die

mahogany /mə'hɒgənɪ/ n. Mahagoni[holz], das; attrib. Mahagoni-

maid /meɪd/ n. Dienstmädchen, das

maiden /'meɪdn/ n. **1** n. Jungfrau, die
2 adj. **(a)** (unmarried) unverheiratet
(b) (first) ∼ **voyage/speech** Jungfernfahrt/-rede, die

'maiden name n. Mädchenname, der

mail /meɪl/ **1** n. ▶ POST² 1
2 v.t. abschicken

mail: ∼**bag** n. Postsack, der; ∼**box** n. (Amer.) Briefkasten, der; ∼**ing address** n. Postanschrift, die; ∼**ing list** n. Adressenliste, die; ∼**man** n. (Amer.) Briefträger, der; ∼ **order** n. Bestellung per Post; ∼ **order catalogue** n. Versandhauskatalog, der; ∼ **order firm** n. Versandhaus, das; ∼ **room** n. Poststelle, die

maim /meɪm/ v.t. verstümmeln

main /meɪn/ **1** n. **(a)** (channel, pipe) Hauptleitung, die; ∼**s** (Electr.) Stromnetz, das
(b) in the ∼: im Großen und Ganzen
2 attrib. adj. Haupt-; the ∼ thing is that ...: die Hauptsache ist, dass ...

main: ∼ **beam** n. (Motor Veh.) on ∼ beam aufgeblendet; ∼ **course** n. Hauptgang, der; Hauptgericht, das; ∼**frame** n. (Comp.) Großrechner, der; ∼**land** /'meɪnlənd/ n. Festland, das; ∼ **line** n. (Railw.) Hauptstrecke, die; ∼**line station/train** Fernbahnhof/-zug, der

'mainly adv. hauptsächlich

main: ∼ **'road** n. Hauptstraße, die; ∼**stay** n. [wichtigste] Stütze; ∼ **street** /Brit. -'-, Amer. '-/ n. Hauptstraße, die

maintain /meɪn'teɪn/ v.t. **(a)** (keep up) aufrechterhalten
(b) (provide for) ∼ sb. für jmds. Unterhalt aufkommen
(c) (preserve) instand halten; warten ⟨Maschine⟩
(d) ∼ that ...: behaupten, dass ...

maintenance /'meɪntənəns/ n. **(a)** (keeping up) Aufrechterhaltung, die
(b) (preservation) Instandhaltung, die; (of machinery) Wartung, die
(c) (Law: money paid to support sb.) Unterhalt, der

maintenance-'free adj. wartungsfrei

m

maison[n]ette /meɪzə'net/ *n.* [zweistöckige] Wohnung

maize /meɪz/ *n.* Mais, *der*

majestic /mə'dʒestɪk/ *adj.*, **majestically** /mə'dʒestɪkəlɪ/ *adv.* majestätisch

majesty /'mædʒɪstɪ/ *n.* Majestät, *die* (geh.); Your/Her *etc.* M∼: Eure/Seine *usw.* Majestät

major /'meɪdʒə(r)/ ①*adj.* (a) *attrib.* (greater) größer... (b) *attrib.* (important) bedeutend...; (serious) schwer; ∼ **road** Hauptverkehrsstraße, *die* (c) (Mus.) Dur-; **C** ∼: C-Dur ②*n.* (Mil.) Major, *der* ③*v.i.* (Amer. Univ.) ∼ **in** sth. etw. als Hauptfach haben

Majorca /mə'jɔːkə/ *pr. n.* Mallorca (*das*)

majority /mə'dʒɒrɪtɪ/ *n.* Mehrheit, *die;* **be in the** ∼: in der Mehrzahl sein

majority 'rule *n.* Mehrheitsregierung, *die*

make /meɪk/ ①*v.t.*, **made** /meɪd/ (a) machen (of aus); bauen ⟨*Straße, Flugzeug*⟩; anlegen ⟨*Teich, Weg usw.*⟩; zimmern ⟨*Tisch, Regal*⟩; basteln ⟨*Spielzeug, Vogelhäuschen usw.*⟩; nähen ⟨*Kleider*⟩; (manufacture) herstellen; (prepare) zubereiten ⟨*Mahlzeit*⟩; machen, kochen ⟨*Kaffee, Tee*⟩; backen ⟨*Brot, Kuchen*⟩ (b) (establish, enact) treffen ⟨*Unterscheidung, Übereinkommen*⟩; ziehen ⟨*Vergleich*⟩; erlassen ⟨*Gesetz*⟩; aufstellen ⟨*Regeln, Behauptung*⟩; stellen ⟨*Forderung*⟩; geben ⟨*Bericht*⟩; vornehmen ⟨*Zahlung*⟩; erheben ⟨*Protest, Beschwerde*⟩ (c) (cause to be or become) ∼ **happy/known** *etc.* glücklich/bekannt *usw.* machen; ∼ **sb. captain** jmdn. zum Kapitän machen (d) ∼ **sb. do** sth. (cause) jmdn. dazu bringen, etw. zu tun; (compel) jmdn. zwingen, etw. zu tun; **be made to do** sth. etw. tun müssen (e) (earn) machen ⟨*Profit, Verlust*⟩; verdienen ⟨*Lebensunterhalt*⟩ (f) **what do you** ∼ **of him?** was hältst du von ihm? (g) (arrive at) erreichen; **make it** (succeed in arriving) es schaffen (h) ∼ 'do vorlieb nehmen; ∼ 'do with/ without sth. mit/ohne etw. auskommen ②*n.* (brand) Marke, *die*
■ **make for** *v.t.* zusteuern auf (+ *Akk.*)
■ **make 'off** *v.i.* sich davonmachen
■ **make 'off with** *v.t.* ∼ off with sb./sth. sich mit jmdm./etw. auf und davon machen
■ **make 'out** ①*v.t.* (a) (write) ausstellen; ∼ **out a cheque to sb.** einen Scheck auf jmdn. ausstellen (b) (claim) behaupten (c) (manage to see or hear) ausmachen; (manage to read) entziffern (d) (pretend) vorgeben ②*v.i.* (coll.) zurechtkommen (**at** bei)
■ **make 'over** *v.t.* überschreiben (**to** auf + *Akk.*)
■ **make 'up** ①*v.t.* (a) (assemble) zusammenstellen

(b) (invent) erfinden
(c) (constitute) bilden; **be made up of** ...: bestehen aus ...
(d) (apply cosmetics to) schminken; ∼ **up one's face** sich schminken
②*v.i.* (be reconciled) sich wieder vertragen
■ **make 'up for** *v.t.* wieder gutmachen; ∼ **up for lost time** Versäumtes nachholen

make: ∼**-believe** ①*n.* it's only ∼-believe das ist bloß Fantasie; ②*adj.* nicht echt; ∼**-or-'break** *attrib. adj.* alles entscheidend; ∼**over** *n.* (of a person's appearance) [grundlegende] Verwandlung; (of a building) Umbau, *der*

'maker *n.* (manufacturer) Hersteller, *der*

make: ∼**shift** *adj.* behelfsmäßig; ∼**-up** *n.* Make-up, *das;* ∼**-up bag** Kosmetiktasche, *die*

making /'meɪkɪŋ/ *n.* **in the** ∼: im Entstehen; **have the** ∼**s of a leader** das Zeug zum Führer haben (ugs.)

maladjusted /mælə'dʒʌstɪd/ *adj.* verhaltensgestört

malady /'mælədɪ/ *n.* Leiden, *das*

malaise /mə'leɪz/ *n.* Unbehagen, *das*

malaria /mə'leərɪə/ *n.* Malaria, *die*

Malaysia /mə'leɪzɪə/ *pr. n.* Malaysia (*das*)

male /meɪl/ ①*adj.* männlich; Männer⟨*stimme, -chor, -verein*⟩; ∼ **doctor/ nurse** Arzt, *der*/Krankenpfleger, *der* ②*n.* (person) Mann, *der;* (animal) Männchen, *das*

'male-dominated *adj.* von Männern dominiert

malevolence /mə'levələns/ *n.* Boshaftigkeit, *die*

malevolent /mə'levələnt/ *adj.* boshaft

malfunction /mæl'fʌŋkʃn/ ①*n.* Störung, *die;* (Med.) Funktionsstörung, *die* ②*v.i.* nicht richtig funktionieren

malice /'mælɪs/ *n.* Bosheit, *die*

malicious /mə'lɪʃəs/ *adj.* böse

malign /mə'laɪn/ *v.t.* verleumden

malignant /mə'lɪgnənt/ *adj.* bösartig

malinger /mə'lɪŋgə(r)/ *v.i.* simulieren

ma'lingerer *n.* Simulant, *der*/Simulantin, *die*

malleable /'mælɪəbl/ *adj.* formbar

mallet /'mælɪt/ *n.* Holzhammer, *der*

malnourished /mæl'nʌrɪʃt/ *adj.* unterernährt

malnutrition /mælnjuː'trɪʃn/ *n.* Unterernährung, *die*

malpractice /mæl'præktɪs/ *n.* (Law, Med.) Kunstfehler, *der*

malt /mɔːlt/ *n.* Malz, *das*

Malta /'mɔːltə/ *pr. n.* Malta (*das*)

maltreat /mæl'triːt/ *v.t.* misshandeln

mal'treatment *n.* Misshandlung, *die*

malt 'whisky *n.* Malzwhisky, *der*

mammal /'mæml/ *n.* Säugetier, *das*

mammoth /'mæməθ/ ①*n.* Mammut, *das*

2 adj. Mammut-; gigantisch ‹Vorhaben›

man /mæn/ **1** n. (a) pl. **men** [men] Mann, der

(b) (human race) der Mensch

2 v.t., -nn- bemannen ‹Schiff›; besetzen ‹Büro, Stelle usw.›; bedienen ‹Telefon, Geschütz›

manacle /ˈmænəkl/ **1** n., usu. in pl. [Hand]fessel, die

2 v.t. Handfesseln anlegen (+ Dat.)

manage /ˈmænɪdʒ/ **1** v.t. (a) leiten ‹Geschäft›

(b) (Sport) betreuen ‹Mannschaft›

(c) (cope with) schaffen

(d) ~ to do sth. es fertig bringen, etw. zu tun; **he ~d to do it** es gelang ihm, es zu tun

2 v.i. zurechtkommen; ~ **without sth.** ohne etw. auskommen; **I can** ~: es geht

manageable /ˈmænɪdʒəbl/ adj. leicht frisierbar ‹Haar›; fügsam ‹Person, Tier›; überschaubar ‹Größe, Menge›

'management n. (a) (of a business) Leitung, die

(b) (managers) **the** ~: die Geschäftsleitung

management: ~ **consultancy** n. Unternehmensberatung, die; ~ **consultant** n. Unternehmensberater, der/-beraterin, die

'manager n. (of shop or bank) Filialleiter, der/-leiterin, die; (of football team) [Chef]trainer, der/-trainerin, die; (of restaurant, shop, hotel) Geschäftsführer, der/-führerin, die

manageress /mænɪdʒəˈres/ n. Geschäftsführerin, die

managerial /mænəˈdʒɪərɪəl/ adj. führend, leitend ‹Stellung›; ~ **skills** Führungsqualitäten

managing /ˈmænɪdʒɪŋ/ adj. ~ **director** Geschäftsführer, der/-führerin, die

mandarin[1] /ˈmændərɪn/ n. ~ [orange] Mandarine, die

mandarin[2] n. (bureaucrat) Bürokrat, der/ Bürokratin, die

mandarine /ˈmændəriːn/ ▶ MANDARIN[1]

mandate /ˈmændeɪt/ n. Mandat, das

mandatory /ˈmændətərɪ/ adj. obligatorisch

mandolin[e] /mændəˈlɪn/ n. Mandoline, die

mane /meɪn/ n. Mähne, die

maneuver[able] (Amer.) ▶ MANŒUVR-

manful /ˈmænfl/ adj., **manfully** /ˈmænfəlɪ/ adv. mannhaft

manger /ˈmeɪndʒə(r)/ n. Krippe, die

mangetout /mɑ̃ʒˈtuː/ n. Zuckererbse, die

mangle /ˈmæŋgl/ v.t. verstümmeln ‹Person›; demolieren ‹Sache›

mango /ˈmæŋgəʊ/ n., pl. ~**es** or ~**s** (fruit) Mango[frucht], die

mangy /ˈmeɪndʒɪ/ adj. (a) (Vet. Med.) räudig

(b) (shabby) schäbig

man: ~**handle** v.t. (a) von Hand bewegen ‹Gegenstand›; (b) grob behandeln ‹Person›; ~**hole** n. Mannloch, das

'manhood n. Mannesalter, das

man: ~**hour** n. Arbeitsstunde, die; ~**hunt** n. Verbrecherjagd, die

mania /ˈmeɪnɪə/ n. Manie, die

maniacal /məˈnaɪəkl/ adj. wahnsinnig

manicure /ˈmænɪkjʊə(r)/ **1** n. Maniküre, die

2 v.t. maniküren

manifest /ˈmænɪfest/ **1** adj. offenkundig

2 v.t. (reveal) offenbaren

'manifestly adv. offenkundig

manifesto /mænɪˈfestəʊ/ n., pl. ~**s** Manifest, das

manifold /ˈmænɪfəʊld/ adj. (literary) mannigfaltig (geh.)

manipulate /məˈnɪpjʊleɪt/ v.t. (a) manipulieren

(b) (handle) handhaben

manipulation /mənɪpjʊˈleɪʃn/ n. (a) Manipulation, die

(b) (handling) Handhabung, die

manipulative /məˈnɪpjʊlətɪv/ adj. manipulativ

mankind /mænˈkaɪnd/ n. Menschheit, die

manly /ˈmænlɪ/ adj. männlich

'man-made adj. künstlich; (synthetic) Kunst‹faser, -stoff›

manned /mænd/ adj. bemannt

manner /ˈmænə(r)/ n. (a) Art, die; Weise, die; **in this** ~: auf diese Art und Weise

(b) (general behaviour) Art, die

(c) in pl. Manieren Pl.

mannerism /ˈmænərɪzm/ n. Eigenart, die

manœuvrable /məˈnuːvrəbl/ adj. (Brit.) manövrierfähig

manœuvre /məˈnuːvə(r)/ (Brit.) **1** n. Manöver, das

2 v.t. & i. manövrieren

manor /ˈmænə(r)/ n. (a) (land) [Land]gut, das

(b) ▶ MANOR HOUSE

'manor house n. Herrenhaus, das

'manpower n. Arbeitskräfte Pl.

mansion /ˈmænʃn/ n. Herrenhaus, das

manslaughter /ˈmænslɔːtə(r)/ n. Totschlag, der

mantel: ~**piece** /ˈmæntlpiːs/ n. (a) (above fireplace) Kaminsims, der od. das; (b) (around fireplace) Kamineinfassung, die; ~**shelf** ▶ ~PIECE A

mantle /ˈmæntl/ n. Umhang, der

manual /ˈmænjʊəl/ **1** adj. (a) manuell; ~ **work** Handarbeit; ~ **worker** Handarbeiter, der/-arbeiterin, die

(b) (not automatic) handbetrieben; ‹Bedienung, Schaltung› von Hand

2 n. Handbuch, das

manually /'mænjʊəlɪ/ adv. manuell; a ~ **operated machine** eine handbetriebene Maschine

manufacture /mænjʊ'fæktʃə(r)/ ⓵ n. Herstellung, die ⓶ v.t. herstellen

manu'facturer n. Hersteller, der

manure /mə'njʊə(r)/ ⓵ n. Dung, der ⓶ v.t. düngen

manuscript /'mænjʊskrɪpt/ n. Manuskript, das

many /'menɪ/ ⓵ adj. viele; **how ~ people/ books?** wie viele od. wie viel Leute/Bücher? ⓶ n. viele [Leute]; ~ **of us** viele von uns; a **good/great ~:** eine Menge

map /mæp/ ⓵ n. [Land]karte, die; (street plan) Stadtplan, der ⓶ v.t., **-pp-** kartographieren

■ **map 'out** v.t. im Einzelnen festlegen

maple /'meɪpl/ n. Ahorn, der

'**map-reading** n. Kartenlesen, das

mar /mɑ:(r)/ v.t. verderben

marathon /'mærəθən/ n. (a) Marathon[lauf], der (b) (fig.) Marathon, das

marauder /mə'rɔ:də(r)/ n. Plünderer, der

marble /'mɑ:bl/ n. (a) (stone) Marmor, der (b) (toy) Murmel, die; [game of] ~s Murmelspiel, das

march ⓵ n. Marsch, der; [protest] ~: Protestmarsch, der ⓶ v.i. marschieren

■ **march 'off** v.i. losmarschieren ⓶ v.t. abführen

■ **march 'past** v.i. vorbeimarschieren

March /mɑ:tʃ/ n. März, der; see also AUGUST

'**marcher** n. [protest] ~: Demonstrant, der/ Demonstrantin, die

mare /meə(r)/ n. Stute, die

margarine /mɑ:dʒə'ri:n/, (coll.) **marge** /mɑ:dʒ/ ns. Margarine, die

margin /'mɑ:dʒɪn/ n. (a) (of page) Rand, der (b) (extra amount) Spielraum, der; [profit] ~: [Gewinn]spanne, die; **by a narrow ~:** knapp

marginal /'mɑ:dʒɪnl/ adj., '**marginally** adv. unwesentlich

marigold /'mærɪgəʊld/ n. Ringelblume, die

marijuana /mærɪjʊ'ɑ:nə/ n. Marihuana, das

marina /mə'ri:nə/ n. Jachthafen, der

marinade /mærɪ'neɪd/ ⓵ n. Marinade, die ⓶ ▶ MARINATE

marinate /'mærɪneɪt/ v.t. marinieren

marine /mə'ri:n/ ⓵ adj. Meeres-; See〈versicherung, -recht usw.〉; Schiffs〈ausrüstung, -turbine usw.〉 ⓶ n. (person) Marineinfanterist, der

mariner /'mærɪnə(r)/ n. Seemann, der

marionette /mærɪə'net/ n. Marionette, die

marital /'mærɪtl/ adj. ehelich; ~ **status** Familienstand, der

maritime /'mærɪtaɪm/ adj. See-

mark¹ /mɑ:k/ ⓵ n. (a) (trace) Spur, die; (stain etc.) Fleck, der; (scratch) Kratzer, der (b) (sign) Zeichen, das (c) (Sch.) Note, die (d) (target) Ziel, das ⓶ v.t. (a) (dirty) schmutzig machen; (scratch) zerkratzen (b) (put distinguishing ~ on) kennzeichnen, markieren (with mit) (c) (Sch.) (correct) korrigieren; (grade) benoten (d) ~ **time** auf der Stelle treten

■ **mark 'off** v.t. abgrenzen (**from** von, gegen)

■ **mark 'out** v.t. markieren

mark² n. (monetary unit) Mark, die

marked /mɑ:kt/ adj., **markedly** /'mɑ:kɪdlɪ/ adv. deutlich

'**marker** n. Markierung, die

'**marker pen** n. Markierstift, der

market /'mɑ:kɪt/ ⓵ n. Markt, der ⓶ v.t. vermarkten

market: ~ **day** n. Markttag, der; ~ **e'conomy** n. Marktwirtschaft, die; ~ '**forces** n. pl. Kräfte des freien Marktes; ~ '**gardening** n. (Brit.) Gemüseanbau, der

'**marketing** n. Marketing, das

market: ~ '**leader** n. (company, brand) Marktführer, der; (product) meistverkauftes Produkt; **the company is the ~ leader in its field** die Firma ist marktführend auf ihrem Gebiet; ~ **place** n. Marktplatz, der; (fig.) Markt, der; ~ '**price** n. Marktpreis, der; ~ '**research** n. Marktforschung, die; ~ **share** n. Marktanteil, der; ~ **town** n. Marktort, der; ~ '**value** n. Marktwert, der

'**marking** n. (a) Markierung, die (b) (on animal) Zeichnung, die

marksman /'mɑ:ksmən/ n., pl. **marksmen** /'mɑ:ksmən/ Scharfschütze, der

marmalade /'mɑ:məleɪd/ n. [orange] ~: Orangenmarmelade, die

maroon¹ /mə'ru:n/ ⓵ adj. kastanienbraun ⓶ n. Kastanienbraun, das

maroon² v.t. (a) (Naut.: put ashore) aussetzen (b) 〈Flut, Hochwasser:〉 von der Außenwelt abschneiden

marquee /mɑ:'ki:/ n. Festzelt, das

marquess, marquis /'mɑ:kwɪs/ n. Marquis, der

marquetry /'mɑ:kɪtrɪ/ n. Marketerie, die

marriage /'mærɪdʒ/ n. (a) Ehe, die (**to** mit) (b) (wedding) Hochzeit, die

marriage: ~ **broker** n. Heiratsvermittler, der/-vermittlerin, die; ~ **bureau** n. Eheanbahnungs- od. Ehevermittlungsinstitut, das; ~ **certificate** n. Trauschein, der; (record of civil marriage also) Heiratsurkunde, die; ~ **guidance** n. Eheberatung, die; ~ **licence** n. Heirats- od. Eheerlaubnis, die

married /'mærɪd/ adj. (a) verheiratet; ~ **couple** Ehepaar, das (b) (marital) Ehe〈leben, -name〉

marrow /ˈmærəʊ/ n. (a) [vegetable] ∼:
Speisekürbis, der
(b) (Anat.) [Knochen]mark, das

marry /ˈmærɪ/ ⒈ v.t. (a) heiraten
(b) (join) trauen; **they were** or **got/have got
married** sie haben geheiratet
⒉ v.i. heiraten

Mars /mɑːz/ pr. n. (Astron.) Mars, der

marsh /mɑːʃ/ n. Sumpf, der

marshal /ˈmɑːʃl/ ⒈ n. (a) (officer in army)
Marschall, der
(b) (Sport) Ordner, der
⒉ v.t., (Brit.) **-ll-** aufstellen ⟨Truppen⟩; ordnen
⟨Fakten⟩

'marshalling yard n. Rangierbahnhof,
der

marshmallow /mɑːʃˈmæləʊ/ n. (sweet) ≈
Mohrenkopf, der

'marshy adj. sumpfig

marsupial /mɑːˈsjuːpɪəl/ n. Beuteltier, das

martial /ˈmɑːʃl/ adj. kriegerisch

martial 'law n. Kriegsrecht, das

martyr /ˈmɑːtə(r)/ ⒈ n. Märtyrer, der/
Märtyrerin, die
⒉ v.t. **be** ∼**ed** den Märtyrertod sterben

marvel /ˈmɑːvl/ ⒈ n. Wunder, das
⒉ v.i., (Brit.) **-ll-** (literary) ∼ **at sth.** über etw
⟨Akk.⟩ staunen

marvellous /ˈmɑːvələs/ adj.,
'marvellously adv. wunderbar

marvelous[ly] (Amer.) ▶ MARVELLOUS[LY]

Marxism /ˈmɑːksɪzm/ n. Marxismus, der

Marxist /ˈmɑːksɪst/ ⒈ n. Marxist, der/
Marxistin, die
⒉ adj. marxistisch

marzipan /ˈmɑːzɪpæn/ n. Marzipan, das

mascara /mæˈskɑːrə/ n. Mascara, das

mascot /ˈmæskɒt/ n. Maskottchen, das

masculine /ˈmæskjʊlɪn/ adj. männlich

masculinity /mæskjuˈlɪnɪtɪ/ n.
Männlichkeit, die

mash /mæʃ/ ⒈ n. (a) Brei, der
(b) (Brit. coll.: ∼ed potatoes) Kartoffelbrei, der
⒉ v.t. zerdrücken; ∼**ed potatoes**
Kartoffelbrei, der

mask /mɑːsk/ ⒈ n. Maske, die
⒉ v.t. maskieren

'masking tape n. Abklebeband, das

masochism /ˈmæsəkɪzm/ n.
Masochismus, der

masochist /ˈmæsəkɪst/ n. Masochist, der/
Masochistin, die

masochistic /mæsəˈkɪstɪk/ adj.
masochistisch

mason /ˈmeɪsn/ n. (a) Steinmetz, der
(b) M∼ (Free∼) [Frei]maurer, der

Masonic /məˈsɒnɪk/ adj. [frei]maurerisch;
∼ **lodge** [Frei]maurerloge, die

masonry /ˈmeɪsnrɪ/ n. Mauerwerk, das

masquerade /mæskəˈreɪd, mɑːskəˈreɪd/
⒈ n. Maskerade, die

⒉ v.i. ∼ **as sb./sth.** sich als jmd./etw.
ausgeben

mass¹ /mæs/ n. (Eccl.) Messe, die

mass² ⒈ n. (a) Masse, die
(b) **a** ∼ **of ...**: eine Unmenge von ...
(c) attrib. (for many people) Massen-
⒉ v.t. anhäufen
⒊ v.i. sich ansammeln; ⟨Truppen:⟩ sich
massieren

massacre /ˈmæsəkə(r)/ ⒈ n. Massaker,
das
⒉ v.t. massakrieren

massage /ˈmæsɑːʒ/ ⒈ n. Massage, die
⒉ v.t. massieren

mass communi'cations n. pl.
Massenkommunikation, die

masseur /mæˈsɜː(r)/ n. Masseur, der

masseuse /mæˈsɜːz/ n. fem. Masseurin,
die

mass hy'steria n. Massenhysterie, die

massive /ˈmæsɪv/ adj. massiv; gewaltig
⟨Aufgabe⟩; enorm ⟨Schulden⟩

mass: ∼ **market** attrib. adj. für den
Massenmarkt nachgestellt; ∼ **'media** n. pl.
Massenmedien Pl.; ∼ **'murderer** n.
Massenmörder, der/-mörderin, die;
∼**pro'duced** adj. serienmäßig
produziert; ∼ **pro'duction** n.
Massenproduktion, die

mast /mɑːst/ n. Mast, der

mastectomy /mæˈstektəmɪ/ n. (Med.)
Mastektomie, die

master /ˈmɑːstə(r)/ ⒈ n. (a) Herr, der
(b) (of dog) Herrchen, das; (of ship) Kapitän,
der
(c) (Sch.: teacher) Lehrer, der
(d) (expert, great artist) Meister, der (at in
+ Dat.)
(e) M∼ **of Arts/Science** Magister Artium/
rerum naturalium
⒉ adj. Haupt-
⒊ v.t. (learn) erlernen; **have** ∼**ed a language**
eine Sprache beherrschen

masterful /ˈmɑːstəfl/ adj. (masterly)
meisterhaft

'master key n. Hauptschlüssel, der

masterly /ˈmɑːstəlɪ/ adj. meisterhaft

master: ∼**mind** ⒈ n. führender Kopf;
⒉ v.t. ∼**mind the plot** der Kopf des
Komplotts sein; ∼**piece** n. (work of art)
Meisterwerk, das; ∼ **stroke** n.
Geniestreich, der; **be a** ∼ **stroke** genial sein;
∼ **switch** n. Hauptschalter, der

mastery /ˈmɑːstərɪ/ n. (a) (skill)
Meisterschaft, die
(b) (knowledge) Beherrschung, die (of Gen.)

masturbate /ˈmæstəbeɪt/ v.i. & t.
masturbieren

masturbation /mæstəˈbeɪʃn/ n.
Masturbation, die

mat /mæt/ n. (a) Matte, die
(b) (to protect table etc.) Untersetzer, der

matador /ˈmætədɔː(r)/ n. Matador, der

m

match¹ /mætʃ/ n. **1** n. **(a)** be no ∼ for sb. sich mit jmdm. nicht messen können; meet one's ∼: seinen Meister finden **(b)** be a [good *etc.*] ∼ for sth. [gut *usw.*] zu etw. passen **(c)** (Sport) Spiel, *das;* (Boxing) Kampf, *der* **2** v.t. **(a)** (equal) ∼ sb. at chess es mit jmdm. im Schach aufnehmen [können] **(b)** (harmonize with) passen zu; a handbag and ∼ing shoes eine Handtasche und [dazu] passende Schuhe; ∼ each other zueinander passen **3** v.i. zusammenpassen

match² n. (∼stick) Streichholz, *das*

'matchbox n. Streichholzschachtel, *die*

'matchless adj. unvergleichlich

match: ∼maker n. Ehestifter, *der/* Ehestifterin, *die;* ∼**stick** n. Streichholz, *das*

mate¹ /meɪt/ **1** n. **(a)** Kumpel, *der* (ugs.); **look** *or* **listen, ∼, ...:** jetzt hör [mir] mal gut zu, Freundchen, ... **(b)** (Naut.) ≈ Kapitänleutnant, *der* **(c)** (workman's assistant) Gehilfe, *der* **(d)** (Zool.) (male) Männchen, *das;* (female) Weibchen, *das* **2** v.i. sich paaren **3** v.t. paaren ⟨*Tiere*⟩

mate² (Chess) ▶ CHECKMATE

material /məˈtɪərɪəl/ **1** adj. **(a)** materiell **(b)** (relevant) wesentlich **2** n. **(a)** ∼[s] Material, *das;* **building/writing** ∼**s** Bau-/Schreibmaterial, *das* **(b)** (cloth) Stoff, *der*

materialism /məˈtɪərɪəlɪzm/ n. Materialismus, *der*

materialistic /mətɪərɪəˈlɪstɪk/ adj. materialistisch

materialize /məˈtɪərɪəlaɪz/ v.i. ⟨*Plan, Idee:*⟩ sich verwirklichen; ⟨*Treffen:*⟩ zustande kommen

maternal /məˈtɜːnl/ adj. mütterlich; Mutter⟨*instinkt*⟩

maternity /məˈtɜːnɪtɪ/ n. Mutterschaft, *die*

maternity: ∼ **benefit** n. Mutterschaftsgeld, *das;* ∼ **dress** n. Umstandskleid, *das;* ∼ **hospital** n. Entbindungsheim, *das;* ∼ **leave** n. Mutterschaftsurlaub, *der;* ∼ **nurse** n. Hebamme, *die;* ∼ **pay** n. Mutterschaftsgeld, *das;* ∼ **unit,** ∼ **ward** ns. Entbindungsstation, *die;* ∼ **wear** n. Umstandskleidung, *die*

matey /ˈmeɪtɪ/ adj., **matier** /ˈmeɪtɪə(r)/, **matiest** /ˈmeɪtɪɪst/ (Brit. coll.) kameradschaftlich

math /mæθ/ (Amer. coll.) ▶ MATHS

mathematical /mæθɪˈmætɪkl/ adj., **mathematically** /mæθɪˈmætɪkəlɪ/ adv. mathematisch

mathematician /mæθɪməˈtɪʃn/ n. Mathematiker, *der/* Mathematikerin, *die*

mathematics /mæθɪˈmætɪks/ n. Mathematik, *die*

maths /mæθs/ n. (Brit. coll.) Mathe, *die* (Schülerspr.)

matinée /ˈmætɪneɪ/ n. Nachmittagsvorstellung, *die*

matriarchal /meɪtrɪˈɑːkl/ adj. matriarchalisch

matriarchy /ˈmeɪtrɪɑːkɪ/ n. Matriarchat, *das*

matrices pl. of MATRIX

matriculate /məˈtrɪkjʊleɪt/ **1** v.t. immatrikulieren (in an + *Dat.*) **2** v.i. sich immatrikulieren

matriculation /mətrɪkjʊˈleɪʃn/ n. Immatrikulation, *die*

matrimonial /mætrɪˈməʊnɪəl/ adj. Ehe-

matrimony /ˈmætrɪmənɪ/ n. Ehestand, *der*

matrix /ˈmeɪtrɪks/ n., pl. **matrices** /ˈmeɪtrɪsiːz/ or ∼**es** Matrix, *die*

matron /ˈmeɪtrən/ n. (in school) ≈ Hausmutter, *die;* (in hospital) Oberschwester, *die*

matt /mæt/ adj. matt

'matted adj. verfilzt

matter /ˈmætə(r)/ **1** n. **(a)** (affair) Angelegenheit, *die;* ∼s die Dinge; money ∼s Geldangelegenheiten **(b)** it's a ∼ of taste das ist Geschmackssache; [only] a ∼ of time [nur noch] eine Frage der Zeit **(c)** what's the ∼? was ist [los]? **(d)** (physical material) Materie, *die* **2** v.i. etwas ausmachen; what does it ∼? was macht das schon?; [it] doesn't ∼: [das] macht nichts (ugs.)

'matter-of-fact adj. sachlich

mattress /ˈmætrɪs/ n. Matratze, *die*

mature /məˈtjʊə(r)/ **1** adj. reif; ausgereift ⟨*Stil, Käse, Portwein, Sherry*⟩ **2** v.t. reifen lassen **3** v.i. reifen

maturity /məˈtjʊərɪtɪ/ n. Reife, *die*

Maundy Thursday /mɔːndɪ ˈθɜːzdɪ/ n. Gründonnerstag, *der*

mausoleum /mɔːsəˈliːəm/ n. Mausoleum, *das*

mauve /məʊv/ adj. mauve

mawkish /ˈmɔːkɪʃ/ adj. rührselig

max. abbr. = **maximum** (adj.) max., (n.) Max.

maxim /ˈmæksɪm/ n. Maxime, *die*

maximum /ˈmæksɪməm/ **1** n., pl. **maxima** /ˈmæksɪmə/ Maximum, *das* **2** adj. maximal; Maximal-; ∼ **speed/ temperature** Höchstgeschwindigkeit, *die/* -temperatur, *die*

'maximum-security attrib. adj. Hochsicherheits⟨*gefängnis*⟩trakt⟩

may v. aux., only in pres. **may**, neg. (coll.) **mayn't** /meɪnt/, past **might** /maɪt/, neg. (coll.) **mightn't** /ˈmaɪtnt/ (a) (expr. possibility) können; **it** ∼ **be true** das kann stimmen; **I** ∼ **be wrong** vielleicht irre ich mich; **it** ∼ **not be possible**

das wird vielleicht nicht möglich sein; **he ∼ have missed his train** vielleicht hat er seinen Zug verpasst; **it ∼** or **might rain** es könnte regnen; **we ∼** or **might as well go** wir könnten eigentlich ebenso gut [auch] gehen
(b) (expr. permission) dürfen
(c) (expr. wish) mögen; **∼ the best man win!** auf dass der Beste gewinnt!

May /meɪ/ n. Mai, der; see also AUGUST

maybe /'meɪbiː, 'meɪbɪ/ adv. vielleicht

'May Day n. der Erste Mai; **the ∼ holiday** der Maifeiertag

'mayfly n. Eintagsfliege, die

mayhem /'meɪhem/ n. Chaos, das

mayn't /meɪnt/ (coll.) = may not; ▶ MAY

mayonnaise /meɪə'neɪz/ n. Mayonnaise, die

mayor /meə(r)/ n. Bürgermeister, der

mayoress /'meərɪs/ n. (woman mayor) Bürgermeisterin, die; (mayor's wife) [Ehe]frau des Bürgermeisters

maze /meɪz/ n. Labyrinth, das

MBA abbr. = **Master of Business Administration** Diplom in Betriebswirtschaft

me /mɪ, stressed miː/ pron. mich; as indirect object mir; **who, me?** wer, ich?; **not me** ich nicht; **it's me** ich bins

ME abbr. (Med.) = **myalgic encephalomyelitis**

meadow /'medəʊ/ n. Wiese, die

meagre /'miːɡə(r)/ adj. dürftig

meal /miːl/ n. Mahlzeit, die; **go out for a ∼:** essen gehen; **enjoy your ∼:** guten Appetit!; **∼s on wheels** (Brit.) Essen auf Rädern

meal: ∼ ticket n. Essenmarke, die; (fig. coll.) melkende Kuh (ugs.); **∼time** n. Essenszeit, die; **∼ voucher** n. Essenmarke, die

mean¹ /miːn/ n. **(a)** Mittelweg, der
(b) (Math.) Mittelwert, der

mean² adj. **(a)** (miserly) geizig
(b) (unkind) gemein
(c) (shabby) schäbig

mean³ v.t., **meant** /ment/ **(a)** (intend) beabsichtigen; **∼ to do sth.** etw. tun wollen
(b) (design, destine) **be ∼t to do sth.** etw. tun sollen
(c) (intend to convey) meinen; **I [really] ∼ it** ich meine das ernst; **what do you ∼ by that?** was hast du damit gemeint?
(d) (signify) bedeuten

meander /mɪ'ændə(r)/ v.i. **(a)** ⟨Fluss:⟩ sich winden
(b) ⟨Person:⟩ schlendern

'meaning n. Bedeutung, die; (of text etc., life) Sinn, der

meaningful /'miːnɪŋfl/ adj. bedeutungsvoll ⟨Blick, Ergebnis⟩; sinnvoll ⟨Aufgabe, Gespräch⟩

'meaningless adj. ⟨Wort, Gespräch:⟩ ohne Sinn; sinnlos ⟨Aktivität⟩

means /miːnz/ n. **(a)** Möglichkeit, die; [Art und] Weise; **by this ∼:** hierdurch; **∼ of transport** Transportmittel, das
(b) pl. (resources) Mittel Pl.; **live within/ beyond one's ∼:** seinen Verhältnissen entsprechend/über seine Verhältnisse leben
(c) **by all ∼!** selbstverständlich!; **by no [manner of] ∼:** ganz und gar nicht; **by ∼ of** durch; mit [Hilfe von]

'means test n. Überprüfung der Bedürftigkeit

meant ▶ MEAN³

mean: ∼time 1 n. **in the ∼time** inzwischen; 2 adv. inzwischen; **∼while** adv. inzwischen

measles /'miːzlz/ n. Masern Pl.

measly /'miːzlɪ/ adj. (coll.) pop[e]lig (ugs.)

measurable /'meʒərəbl/ adj. messbar

measure /'meʒə(r)/ 1 n. **(a)** Maß, das; **for good ∼:** sicherheitshalber; (as an extra) zusätzlich; **made to ∼:** maßgeschneidert
(b) (degree) **in some/large ∼:** in gewisser Hinsicht/ in hohem Maße
(c) (for measuring) Maß, das
(d) (step) Maßnahme, die; **take ∼s** Maßnahmen treffen
2 v.t. messen ⟨Größe, Menge usw.⟩; ausmessen ⟨Raum⟩
3 v.i. messen

■ **measure 'up to** v.t. entsprechen (+ Dat.)

'measured /'meʒəd/ adj. gemessen ⟨Schritt, Worte⟩

'measurement n. **(a)** Messung, die
(b) (dimension) Maß, das

'measuring tape n. Bandmaß, das

meat /miːt/ n. Fleisch, das

'meaty adj. **(a)** fleischig
(b) (fig.) gehaltvoll

mechanic /mɪ'kænɪk/ n. Mechaniker, der/ Mechanikerin, die

mechanical /mɪ'kænɪkl/ adj. mechanisch

mechanical engi'neering n. Maschinenbau, der

me'chanically adv. mechanisch

mechanical 'pencil n. (Amer.) Drehbleistift, der

me'chanics n. **(a)** Mechanik, die
(b) pl. (mechanism) Mechanismus, der

mechanism /'mekənɪzm/ n. Mechanismus, der

mechanize /'mekənaɪz/ v.t. mechanisieren

medal /'medl/ n. Medaille, die; (decoration) Orden, der

medallion /mɪ'dæljən/ n. [große] Medaille

medallist /'medəlɪst/ n. Medaillengewinner, der/-gewinnerin, die

meddle /'medl/ v.i. **∼ with sth.** sich (Dat.) an etw. (Dat.) zu schaffen machen; **∼ in sth.** sich in etw. (Akk.) einmischen

media /'miːdɪə/ ▶ MASS MEDIA; MEDIUM 1

mediaeval ▶ MEDIEVAL

'media studies n. sing.
Medienwissenschaft, die; (school subject)
Medienkunde, die

mediate /'mi:dɪeɪt/ v.i. vermitteln

mediator /'mi:dɪeɪtə(r)/ n. Vermittler, der/
Vermittlerin, die

medical /'medɪkl/ adj. medizinisch;
ärztlich ⟨Behandlung, Untersuchung⟩

medical: ~ **certificate** n. Attest, das;
~ **exami'nation** n. ärztliche
Untersuchung; ~ **'history** n. (of person)
Krankengeschichte, die; ~ **insurance** n.
Krankenversicherung, die; **have** ~ **insurance**
krankenversichert sein; ~ **prac'titioner**
n. praktischer Arzt/praktische Ärztin;
~ **report** n. medizinisches Gutachten;
~ **school** n. medizinische Hochschule;
~ **student** n. Medizinstudent, der/
-studentin die

medicament /mɪ'dɪkəmənt, 'medɪkəmənt/
n. Medikament, das

Medicare /'medɪkeə(r)/ n. (Amer.)
[bundes]staatliches
Krankenversicherungssystem für Personen
über 65 Jahre

medicated /'medɪkeɪtɪd/ adj. medizinisch

medication /medɪ'keɪʃn/ n. (medicine)
Medikament, das

medicinal /mɪ'dɪsɪnl/ adj. medizinisch

medicine /'medsən, 'medɪsɪn/ n. **(a)**
(science) Medizin, die
(b) (preparation) Medikament, das

'medicine chest n.
Medikamentenschränkchen, das; (in home)
Hausapotheke, die

medieval /medɪ'i:vl/ adj. mittelalterlich

mediocre /mi:dɪ'əʊkə(r)/ adj. mittelmäßig

mediocrity /mi:dɪ'ɒkrɪtɪ/ n.
Mittelmäßigkeit, die

meditate /'medɪteɪt/ v.i. nachdenken, (esp.
Relig.) meditieren ([up]on über + Akk.)

meditation /medɪ'teɪʃn/ n. **(a)** (act)
Nachdenken, das
(b) (Relig.) Meditation, die

Mediterranean /medɪtə'reɪnɪən/ pr. n. the
~: das Mittelmeer

medium /'mi:dɪəm/ [1] n., pl. media
/'mi:dɪə/ or ~s **(a)** (substance) Medium, das
(b) (means) Mittel, das; **by** or **through the**
~ **of** durch
(c) pl. ~s (Spiritualism) Medium, das
(d) in pl. **media** (mass media) Medien Pl.
[2] adj. mittler ...; medium nur präd. ⟨Steak⟩

medium: ~**range** adj.
Mittelstrecken⟨flugzeug, -rakete⟩; ~**size[d]**
adj. mittelgroß

medley /'medlɪ/ n. **(a)** buntes Gemisch
(b) (Mus.) Potpourri, das

meek /mi:k/ adj. **(a)** (humble) sanftmütig
(b) (submissive) zu nachgiebig

meet /mi:t/ [1] v.t., met /met/ **(a)** treffen;
(collect) abholen

(b) (make the acquaintance of) kennen lernen;
pleased to ~ **you** [sehr] angenehm
(c) (experience) stoßen auf (+ Akk.)
⟨Widerstand, Problem⟩
(d) (satisfy) entsprechen (+ Dat.) ⟨Wunsch,
Bedürfnis, Kritik⟩; einhalten ⟨Termin,
Zeitplan⟩
(e) (pay) decken ⟨Kosten⟩; bezahlen
⟨Rechnung⟩
[2] v.i., met **(a)** (by chance) sich (Dat.)
begegnen; (by arrangement) sich treffen; **we've**
met before wir kennen uns bereits
(b) (assembly) ⟨Komitee, Ausschuss usw.:⟩ tagen
■ **meet 'up** v.i. sich treffen; ~ **up with sb.**
(coll.) sich treffen
■ **'meet with** v.t. **(a)** begegnen (+ Dat.)
(b) (experience) haben ⟨Erfolg, Unfall⟩; stoßen
auf (+ Akk.) ⟨Widerstand⟩

'meeting n. **(a)** Begegnung, die; (by
arrangement) Treffen, das
(b) (assembly) Versammlung, die; (of committee
etc.) Sitzung, die

'meeting place n. Treffpunkt, der

mega /'megə/ (coll.) [1] adj. **(a)** (enormous)
Mega- (Jugendspr.)
(b) (excellent) geil (Jugendspr.)
[2] adv. äußerst; **be** ~ **rich** super- od.
(Jugendspr.) megareich sein

'megabyte n. (Comp.) Megabyte, das

megalomania /megələ'meɪnɪə/ n.
Größenwahn, der

megaphone /'megəfəʊn/ n. Megaphon, das

melancholic /melən'kɒlɪk/ adj.
melancholisch

melancholy /'melənkəlɪ/ [1] n.
Melancholie, die
[2] adj. melancholisch

mellow /'meləʊ/ [1] adj. **(a)** (softened by age
or experience) abgeklärt
(b) (ripe, well-matured) reif
[2] v.i. reifen

melodic /mɪ'lɒdɪk/**, melodious**
/mɪ'ləʊdɪəs/ adjs., **me'lodiously** adv.
melodisch

melodrama /'melədrɑːmə/ n. Melodrama,
das

melodramatic /melədrə'mætɪk/ adj.
melodramatisch

melody /'melədɪ/ n. Melodie, die

melon /'melən/ n. Melone, die

melt /melt/ [1] v.i. schmelzen
[2] v.t. schmelzen; zerlassen ⟨Butter⟩
■ **melt a'way** v.i. [weg]schmelzen
■ **melt 'down** [1] v.i. schmelzen
[2] v.t. einschmelzen

melting: ~ **point** n. Schmelzpunkt, der;
~ **pot** n. (fig.) Schmelztiegel, der

member /'membə(r)/ n. **(a)** Mitglied, das;
be a ~: Mitglied sein; ~ **of a/the family**
Familienangehörige, der/die
(b) M~ **[of Parliament]** (Brit.) Abgeordnete
[des Unterhauses], der/die

'membership n. (a) Mitgliedschaft, *die* (of
in + *Dat.*)
(b) (number of members) Mitgliederzahl, *die*
(c) (members) Mitglieder *Pl.*

'member state n. Mitglied[s]staat, *der*

membrane /'membreɪn/ n. (Biol.)
Membran, *die*

memento /mɪ'mentəʊ/ n., pl. ∼es or ∼s
Andenken, *das* (of an + *Akk.*)

memo /'meməʊ/ n., pl. ∼s (coll.)
▶ MEMORANDUM

memoirs /'memwɑːz/ n. pl. Memoiren *Pl.*

memorable /'memərəbl/ adj. denkwürdig
⟨*Ereignis, Tag*⟩; unvergesslich ⟨*Film, Buch,
Aufführung*⟩

memorandum /memə'rændəm/ n., pl.
memoranda /memə'rændə/ or ∼s
Mitteilung, *die*

memorial /mɪ'mɔːrɪəl/ ① adj. Gedenk-
② n. Denkmal, *das* (**to** für)

memorize /'meməraɪz/ v.t. sich (*Dat.*)
merken od. einprägen; (learn by heart)
auswendig lernen

memory /'memərɪ/ n. (a) Gedächtnis, *das*
(b) (thing remembered, act of remembering)
Erinnerung, *die* (of an + *Akk.*); from ∼: aus
dem Gedächtnis; in ∼ of zur Erinnerung an
(+ *Akk.*)
(c) (Comp.) Speicher, *der*

'memory bank n. Speicherbank, *die*

men pl. of MAN

menace /'menəs/ ① v.t. bedrohen
② n. Plage, *die*

menacing /'menəsɪŋ/ adj. drohend

mend /mend/ ① v.t. reparieren; ausbessern
⟨*Kleidung*⟩; kleben ⟨*Glas, Porzellan*⟩
② v.i. ⟨*Knochen, Bein usw.*⟩ heilen
③ n. be on the ∼: auf dem Wege der
Besserung sein

'menfolk n. pl. Männer *Pl.*

menial /'miːnɪəl/ adj. niedrig;
untergeordnet ⟨*Aufgabe*⟩

meningitis /menɪn'dʒaɪtɪs/ n.
Hirnhautentzündung, *die*

menopause /'menəpɔːz/ n. Wechseljahre
Pl.

menstrual /'menstrʊəl/ adj. menstrual
(fachspr.)

menstruate /'menstrʊeɪt/ v.i.
menstruieren

menstruation /menstrʊ'eɪʃn/ n.
Menstruation, *die*

menswear /'menzweə(r)/ n.
Herrenbekleidung, *die*

mental /'mentl/ adj. (a) (of the mind) geistig;
Geistes⟨*zustand, -störung*⟩
(b) (Brit. coll.: mad) verrückt (salopp)

mental: ∼ a'**rithmetic** n. Kopfrechnen,
das; ∼ '**health** n. seelische Gesundheit;
∼ '**hospital** n. Nervenklinik, *die* (ugs.);
∼ '**illness** n. Geisteskrankheit, *die*

mentality /men'tælɪtɪ/ n. Mentalität, *die*

'mentally adv. geistig

mention /'menʃn/ ① n. Erwähnung, *die*
② v.t. erwähnen (**to** gegenüber); don't ∼ it
keine Ursache

menu /'menjuː/ n. (a) [Speise]karte, *die*
(b) (Comp., Telev.) Menü, *das*

'menu bar n. (Comp.) Menüleiste, *die*

mercenary /'mɜːsɪnərɪ/ ① adj.
gewinnsüchtig
② n. Söldner, *der*

merchandise /'mɜːtʃəndaɪz/ n.
[Handels]ware, *die*

merchant /'mɜːtʃənt/ n. Kaufmann, *der*

merchant: ∼ '**bank** n. Handelsbank, *die;*
∼ '**navy** n. (Brit.) Handelsmarine, *die*

merciful /'mɜːsɪfl/ adj. gnädig

mercifully /'mɜːsɪfəlɪ/ adv. (fortunately)
glücklicherweise

merciless /'mɜːsɪlɪs/ adj., **'mercilessly**
adv. gnadenlos

mercury /'mɜːkjʊrɪ/ ① n. Quecksilber, *das*
② pr. n. M∼ (Astron.) Merkur, *der*

mercy /'mɜːsɪ/ n. Erbarmen, *das* (**on** mit);
show sb. [**no**] ∼: mit jmdm. [kein]
Erbarmen haben; **be at the** ∼ **of sb./sth.**
jmdm./einer Sache [auf Gedeih und
Verderb] ausgeliefert sein

mere /mɪə(r)/ adj., **'merely** adv. bloß

merge /mɜːdʒ/ ① v.t. (a) (combine)
zusammenschließen
(b) (blend gradually) verschmelzen (**with** mit)
② v.i. (a) (combine) fusionieren (**with** mit)
(b) ⟨*Straße:*⟩ zusammenlaufen (**with** mit)

merger /'mɜːdʒə(r)/ n. Fusion, *die*

meringue /mə'ræŋ/ n. Meringe, *die;*
Baiser, *das*

merit /'merɪt/ ① n. (a) (worth) Verdienst,
das
(b) (good feature) Vorzug, *der*
② v.t. verdienen

mermaid /'mɜːmeɪd/ n. Nixe, *die*

merrily /'merɪlɪ/ adv. munter

merriment /'merɪmənt/ n. Fröhlichkeit,
die

merry /'merɪ/ adj. fröhlich; ∼ **Christmas!**
frohe od. fröhliche Weihnachten!

'merry-go-round n. Karussell, *das*

'merrymaking n. Feiern, *das*

mesh /meʃ/ n. (a) Masche, *die*
(b) (netting; also fig.: network) Geflecht, *das;* **wire**
∼: Maschendraht, *der*

mesmerize /'mezməraɪz/ v.t. faszinieren

mess /mes/ n. (a) (dirty/untidy state) [be] a
∼ or in a ∼: schmutzig/unaufgeräumt
[sein]; **what a** ∼! was für ein Dreck (ugs.)/
Durcheinander!
(b) (bad state) **be** [**in**] **a** ∼: sich in einem
schlimmen Zustand befinden; ⟨*Person:*⟩
schlimm dran sein; **get into a** ∼: in
Schwierigkeiten geraten; **make a** ∼ **of**
verpfuschen (ugs.) ⟨*Arbeit, Leben*⟩
(c) (Mil.) Kasino, *das*   ···❖

m

■ **mess a'bout, mess a'round** ⓵ *v.i.*
(potter) herumwerken; (fool about)
herumalbern
⓶ *v.t.* ~ sb. about *or* around mit jmdm.
nach Belieben umspringen
■ **mess 'up** *v.t.* (a) (make dirty) schmutzig
machen; (make untidy) in Unordnung bringen
(b) (bungle) ~ it/things up Mist bauen (ugs.)
message /'mesɪdʒ/ *n.* Nachricht, *die;* give
sb. a ~: jmdm. etwas ausrichten
messenger /'mesɪndʒə(r)/ *n.* Bote, *der/*
Botin, *die*
Messiah /mɪ'saɪə/ *n.* Messias, *der*
Messrs /'mesəz/ *n. pl.* (a) (in name of firm) ≈
Fa.
(b) *pl. of* MR; (in list of names) ~ A and B die
Herren A und B
'**messy** *adj.* (dirty) schmutzig; (untidy)
unordentlich
met ▸ MEET
metabolism /mɪ'tæbəlɪzm/ *n.*
Stoffwechsel, *der*
metal /'metl/ ⓵ *n.* Metall, *das*
⓶ *adj.* Metall-
'**metal detector** *n.* Metallsuchgerät, *das*
metallic /mɪ'tælɪk/ *adj.* metallisch; have a
~ taste nach Metall schmecken
metallurgy /mɪ'tælədʒɪ/ *n.* Metallurgie, *die*
'**metalwork** *n.* (products) Metallarbeiten *Pl.*
metamorphosis /metə'mɔːfəsɪs/ *n., pl.*
metamorphoses /metə'mɔːfəsiːz/
Metamorphose, *die*
metaphor /'metəfə(r)/ *n.* Metapher, *die*
metaphorical /metə'fɒrɪkl/ *adj.,*
metaphorically /metə'fɒrɪkəlɪ/ *adv.*
metaphorisch
meteor /'miːtɪə(r)/ *n.* Meteor, *der*
meteoric /miːtɪ'ɒrɪk/ *adj.* (fig.) kometenhaft
meteorological /miːtɪərə'lɒdʒɪkl/ *adj.*
meteorologisch ⟨*Instrument*⟩; Wetter⟨*ballon,*
-bericht⟩
meteorologist /miːtɪə'rɒlədʒɪst/ *n.*
Meteorologe, *der/*Meteorologin, *die*
meteorology /miːtɪə'rɒlədʒɪ/ *n.*
Meteorologie, *die*
meter¹ /'miːtə(r)/ *n.* (a) Zähler, *der;* (for
coins) Münzzähler, *der*
(b) (parking ~) Parkuhr, *die*
meter² (Amer.) ▸ METRE¹, ²
methane /'miːθeɪn/ *n.* Methan, *das*
method /'meθəd/ *n.* Methode, *die*
methodical /mɪ'θɒdɪkl/ *adj.,*
me'thodically *adv.* systematisch
Methodist /'meθədɪst/ *n.* Methodist, *der/*
Methodistin, *die*
meths /meθs/ *n.* (Brit. coll.) [Brenn]spiritus,
der
methylated spirit[s] /meθɪleɪtɪd
'spɪrɪt(s)/ *n.* [*pl.*] Brennspiritus, *der*
meticulous /mɪ'tɪkjʊləs/ *adj.,*
me'ticulously *adv.* (scrupulous[ly])
sorgfältig; (overscrupulous[ly]) übergenau

metre¹ /'miːtə/ *n.* (Brit.: poetic rhythm)
Metrum, *das*
metre² *n.* (Brit.: unit) Meter, *der od. das*
metric /'metrɪk/ *adj.* metrisch; ~ system
metrisches System
metrication /metrɪ'keɪʃn/ *n.* Umstellung
auf das metrische System
metro /'metrəʊ/ *n., pl.* ~s U-Bahn, *die;* the
Paris M~ die [Pariser] Metro
metronome /'metrənəʊm/ *n.* Metronom,
das
metropolis /mɪ'trɒpəlɪs/ *n.* Metropole, *die*
metropolitan /metrə'pɒlɪtən/ *adj.* ~ New
York der Großraum New York; ~ London
Großlondon (*das*)
Mexican /'meksɪkən/ ⓵ *adj.* mexikanisch;
sb. is ~: jmd. ist Mexikaner/Mexikanerin
⓶ *n.* Mexikaner, *der/*Mexikanerin, *die*
Mexico /'meksɪkəʊ/ *pr. n.* Mexiko (*das*)
miaow /mɪ'aʊ/ ⓵ *v.i.* miauen
⓶ *n.* Miauen, *das*
mice *pl. of* MOUSE
microbe /'maɪkrəʊb/ *n.* Mikrobe, *die*
micro /'maɪkrəʊ/: ~chip *n.* Mikrochip,
der; ~computer *n.* Mikrocomputer, *der;*
~dot *n.* Mikrat, *das;* ~fibre *n.*
Mikrofaser, *die;* ~fiche *n.* Mikrofiche, *das
od. der;* ~film ⓵ *n.* Mikrofilm, *der;* ⓶ *v.t.*
auf Mikrofilm aufnehmen; ~light
['aircraft] *n.* Ultraleichtflugzeug, *das*
microphone /'maɪkrəfəʊn/ *n.* Mikrofon,
das
microprocessor /maɪkrəʊ'prəʊsesə(r)/ *n.*
Mikroprozessor, *der*
microscope /'maɪkrəskəʊp/ *n.* Mikroskop,
das
microscopic /maɪkrə'skɒpɪk/ *adj.*
mikroskopisch; (fig.: very small) winzig
'**microwave** *n.* Mikrowelle, *die;* ~ [oven]
Mikrowellenherd, *der*
mid- /mɪd/ *in comb.* in ~-air in der Luft; in
~-sentence mitten im Satz; ~-July Mitte
Juli; the ~-60s die Mitte der Sechzigerjahre;
a man in his ~-fifties ein Mittfünfziger; be in
one's ~-thirties Mitte dreißig sein
midday /'mɪddeɪ, mɪd'deɪ/ *n.* (a) (noon) zwölf
Uhr
(b) (middle of day) Mittag, *der; attrib.* Mittags-
middle /'mɪdl/ ⓵ *attrib. adj.* mittler...
⓶ *n.* (a) Mitte, *die;* in the ~ of the forest/
night mitten im Wald/in der Nacht
(b) (waist) Taille, *die*
middle: ~ 'age *n.* mittleres [Lebens]alter;
~-aged /'mɪdleɪdʒd/ *adj.* mittleren Alters
nachgestellt; M~ 'Ages *n. pl.* the M~ Ages
das Mittelalter; ~ 'class *n.* Mittelstand,
der; ~-class *adj.* bürgerlich; M~ 'East
pr. n. the M~ East der Nahe [und Mittlere]
Osten; M~ 'Eastern *adj.* nahöstlich;
~man *n.* (Commerc.) Zwischenhändler, *der/*
-händlerin, *die;* (fig.) Vermittler, *der/*

Vermittlerin, *die;* ∼ **'management** *n.*
mittleres Management; ∼ **name** *n.* zweiter
Vorname

middling /'mɪdlɪŋ/ *adj.* mittelmäßig

'midfield *n.* (Footb.) Mittelfeld, *das*

midge /mɪdʒ/ *n.* Stechmücke, *die*

midget /'mɪdʒɪt/ ⓵ *n.* Liliputaner, *der*/
Liliputanerin, *die*
⓶ *adj.* winzig

Midlands /'mɪdləndz/ *n. pl.* the ∼ (Brit.)
Mittelengland (*das*)

midlife crisis /mɪdlaɪf 'kraɪsɪs/ *n.*
Midlifecrisis, *die*

'midnight *n.* Mitternacht, *die*

'midpoint *n.* Mitte, *die*

midriff /'mɪdrɪf/ *n.* Bauch, *der*

midst /mɪdst/ *n.* in the ∼ of sth. mitten in
einer Sache; in our/their/your ∼: in unserer/
ihrer/eurer Mitte

midsummer /'--, -'-/ *n.* die [Zeit der]
Sommersonnenwende

midway /'--, -'-/ *adv.* auf halbem Weg[e]
⟨*sich treffen, sich befinden*⟩

midweek /'mɪdwiːk, mɪd'wiːk/ *n.* in ∼: in
der Wochenmitte

'midwife *n., pl.* **'midwives** Hebamme, *die*

midwifery /'mɪdwɪfrɪ, mɪd'wɪfərɪ/ *n., no
art.* Geburtshilfe, *die*

mid'winter *n.* die [Zeit der]
Wintersonnenwende

might[1] ▸ MAY

might[2] /maɪt/ *n.* (a) (force) Gewalt, *die*
(b) (power) Macht, *die*

mightn't /'maɪtnt/ (coll.) = might not; ▸ MAY

mighty /'maɪtɪ/ ⓵ *adj.* mächtig
⓶ *adv.* (coll.) verdammt (ugs.)

migraine /'miːɡreɪn/ *n.* Migräne, *die*

migrant /'maɪɡrənt/ *n.* (a) Auswanderer,
der/Auswanderin, *die*
(b) (bird) Zugvogel, *der*

migrate /maɪ'ɡreɪt/ *v.i.* (a) (to a town)
abwandern; (to another country) auswandern
(b) ⟨*Vogel:*⟩ fortziehen

migration /maɪ'ɡreɪʃn/ *n.* (a) (to a town)
Abwandern, *das;* (to another country)
Auswandern, *das*
(b) (of birds) Zug, *der*

migratory /maɪ'ɡreɪtərɪ/ *adj.* ∼ bird/fish
Zugvogel, *der*/Wanderfisch, *der*

mike /maɪk/ *n.* (coll.) Mikro, *das*

Milan /mɪ'læn/ *pr. n.* Mailand (*das*)

mild /maɪld/ *adj.* mild; sanft ⟨*Person*⟩

mildew /'mɪldjuː/ *n.* (a) Schimmel, *der*
(b) (on plant) Mehltau, *der*

'mildly *adv.* (a) (gently) mild[e]
(b) (slightly) ein bisschen
(c) to put it ∼: gelinde gesagt

mile /maɪl/ *n.* (a) Meile, *die*
(b) (fig. coll.) ∼s better/too big tausendmal
besser/viel zu groß; be ∼s ahead of sb.
jmdm. weit voraus sein

mileage /'maɪlɪdʒ/ *n.* [Anzahl der] Meilen
Pl.; a low ∼: ein niedriger Meilenstand

'milestone *n.* Meilenstein, *der*

militant /'mɪlɪtənt/ ⓵ *adj.* militant
⓶ *n.* Militante, *der/die*

military /'mɪlɪtərɪ/ ⓵ *adj.* militärisch;
Militär⟨*regierung, -akademie, -uniform,
-parade*⟩; ∼ **service** Militärdienst, *der*
⓶ *n.* the ∼: das Militär

militate /'mɪlɪteɪt/ *v.i.* ∼ against/in favour
of sth. [deutlich] gegen/für etw. sprechen

militia /mɪ'lɪʃə/ *n.* Miliz, *die*

milk /mɪlk/ ⓵ *n.* Milch, *die*
⓶ *v.t.* melken

milk: ∼ **bottle** *n.* Milchflasche, *die;*
∼ **'chocolate** *n.* Milchschokolade, *die;*
∼ **float** *n.* (Brit.) Milchwagen, *der*

milking /'mɪlkɪŋ/ *n.* Melken, *das*

milk: ∼ **jug** *n.* Milchkännchen, *das;*
∼**man** /'mɪlkmən/ *n., pl.* ∼**men** /'mɪlkmən/
Milchmann, *der;* ∼ **shake** *n.* Milchshake,
der; ∼ **tooth** *n.* Milchzahn, der

'milky *adj.* milchig

Milky 'Way *n.* Milchstraße, *die*

mill /mɪl/ ⓵ *n.* (a) Mühle, *die*
(b) (factory) Fabrik, *die*
⓶ *v.t.* (a) mahlen ⟨*Getreide*⟩
(b) fräsen ⟨*Metallgegenstand*⟩

mill a'bout (Brit.), **mill a'round** *v.i.*
durcheinander laufen

millennium /mɪ'lenɪəm/ *n., pl.* ∼s *or*
millennia /mɪ'lenɪə/ Jahrtausend, *das;*
Millennium, *das*

mil'lennium bug *n.* (Comp.)
Jahrtausendvirus, *der od. das*

'miller *n.* Müller, *der*

millet /'mɪlɪt/ *n.* Hirse, *die*

milligram /'mɪlɪɡræm/ *n.* Milligramm, *das*

millilitre (*Brit.; Amer.:* **milliliter**)
/'mɪlɪliːtə(r)/ *n.* Milliliter, *der od. das*

millimetre (*Brit.; Amer.:* **millimeter**)
/'mɪlɪmiːtə(r)/ *n.* Millimeter, *der*

milliner /'mɪlɪnə(r)/ *n.* Modist, *der*/
Modistin, *die*

'millinery *n.* Hutmacherei, *die*

million /'mɪljən/ ⓵ *adj.* a *or* one/two ∼:
eine Million/zwei Millionen; half a ∼: eine
halbe Million
⓶ *n.* (a) Million, *die*
(b) (indefinite amount) ∼s of people eine
Unmenge Leute

millionaire /mɪljə'neə(r)/ *n.* Millionär,
der/Millionärin, *die*

millionth /'mɪljənθ/ ⓵ *adj.* millionst...
⓶ *n.* (fraction) Millionstel, *das*

'millstone *n.* Mühlstein, *der*

mime /maɪm/ ⓵ *n.* (a) (performance)
Pantomime, *die*
(b) (art) Pantomimik, *die*
⓶ *v.i.* pantomimisch agieren
⓷ *v.t.* pantomimisch darstellen

mimic /'mɪmɪk/ ⓵ *n.* Imitator, *der*   ···⟶

2 *v.t.*, **-ck-** nachahmen

min. *abbr.* **(a)** = **minute[s]** Min.
(b) = **minimum** (*adj.*) mind., (*n.*) Min.

mince /mɪns/ 1 *n.* Hackfleisch, *das*
2 *v.t.* durch den [Fleisch]wolf drehen
⟨*Fleisch*⟩

'**mincemeat** *n.* **(a)** Hackfleisch, *das*
(b) (sweet) *süße Pastetenfüllung aus Obst,
Rosinen, Gewürzen, Nierenfett usw.*

mince 'pie *n.* *mit „mincemeat" B gefüllte
Pastete*

'**mincer** *n.* Fleischwolf, *der*

mind /maɪnd/ 1 *n.* **(a)** Geist, *der*
(b) (remembrance) bear *or* keep sth. in ∼: an
etw. (*Akk.*) denken; **have [got]** sb./sth. in ∼:
an jmdn./etw. denken
(c) (opinion) **give one's** ∼ **a piece of one's** ∼:
jmdm. gründlich die Meinung sagen; **to my**
∼: meiner Meinung *od.* Ansicht nach;
change one's ∼: seine Meinung ändern; **I
have a good** ∼ **to do that** ich hätte große
Lust, das zu tun; **make up one's** ∼, **make
one's** ∼ **up** sich entscheiden
(d) ([normal] mental powers) Verstand, *der*; **be
out of one's** ∼: den Verstand verloren haben
(e) frame of ∼: [seelische] Verfassung
2 *v.t.* **(a) I can't afford a bicycle, never** ∼ **a
car** ich kann mir kein Fahrrad leisten,
geschweige denn ein Auto; **we've got some
decorations up, - not many,** ∼ **you** wir haben
etwas dekoriert, allerdings nicht viel
(b) *usu. neg. or interrog.* (object to) **would you**
∼ **opening the door?** würdest du bitte die
Tür öffnen?; **I wouldn't** ∼ **a walk** ich hätte
nichts gegen einen Spaziergang
(c) (take care) ∼ **you don't go too near the
cliff edge!** pass auf, dass du nicht zu nah an
den Felsenrand gehst!; ∼ **how you go!** pass
auf!
(d) (have charge of) aufpassen auf (+ *Akk.*)
3 *v.i.* **(a)** ∼! Vorsicht!; Achtung!
(b) (care, object) **do you** ∼ **if I smoke?** stört es
Sie, wenn ich rauche?
(c) never ∼ (it's not important) macht nichts
■ **mind 'out** *v.i.* aufpassen (**for** auf + *Akk.*);
∼ **out!** Vorsicht!

mind: ∼**-bending,** (coll.) ∼**-blowing**
adjs. bewusstseinsverändernd;
∼**-boggling** /'maɪndbɒglɪŋ/ *adj.* (coll.)
wahnsinnig (ugs.)

'**minded** *adj.* **mechanically** ∼: technisch
veranlagt; **not politically** ∼: unpolitisch

minder /'maɪndə(r)/ *n.* **(a)** (for child) **we need
a** ∼ **for the child** wir brauchen jemanden,
der auf das Kind aufpasst *od.* das Kind
betreut
(b) (sl.: protector of criminal) Gorilla, *der* (salopp)

mindful /'maɪndfl/ *adj.* **be** ∼ **of sth.** etw.
berücksichtigen

'**mindless** *adj.* geistlos ⟨*Person*⟩; sinnlos
⟨*Gewalt*⟩

mine¹ /maɪn/ *n.* **(a)** Bergwerk, *das*
(b) (explosive) Mine, *die*

mine² *poss. pron. pred.* meiner/meine/
mein[e]s; *see also* HERS

mine: ∼**-detector** *n.* Minensuchgerät,
das; ∼**field** *n.* Minenfeld, *das*

'**miner** *n.* Bergmann, *der*

mineral /'mɪnərl/ 1 *adj.* mineralisch;
Mineral⟨*salz, -quelle*⟩
2 *n.* **(a)** Mineral, *das*
(b) (Brit.: soft drink) Erfrischungsgetränk, *das*

'**mineral water** *n.* Mineralwasser, *das*

'**minesweeper** /'maɪnswiːpə(r)/ *n.*
Minensuchboot, *das*

mingle /'mɪŋgl/ 1 *v.t.* [ver]mischen
2 *v.i.* sich [ver]mischen (**with** mit)

mini /'mɪnɪ/ *n.* (coll.) **(a)** (car) **M**∼ ® Mini, *der*
(b) (skirt) Mini, *der* (ugs.)

mini- /'mɪnɪ/ *in comb.* Mini-; Klein⟨*bus,
-wagen, -taxi*⟩

miniature /'mɪnɪtʃə(r)/ 1 *n.* (picture)
Miniatur, *die*
2 *adj.* Miniatur-

mini: ∼**bus** *n.* Kleinbus, *der;* ∼**cab** *n.*
Minicar, *das*

minim /'mɪnɪm/ *n.* (Brit. Mus.) halbe Note

minimal /'mɪnɪml/ *adj.* minimal

minimize /'mɪnɪmaɪz/ *v.t.* **(a)** (reduce) auf
ein Mindestmaß reduzieren
(b) (understate) bagatellisieren

minimum /'mɪnɪməm/ 1 *n., pl.* **minima**
/'mɪnɪmə/ Minimum, *das* (**of** an + *Dat.*)
2 *attrib. adj.* Mindest-

minimum: ∼ '**lending rate** *n.*
Mindestausleihsatz [*der Bank von England*];
≈ Mindestdiskontsatz, *der;* ∼ '**wage** *n.*
Mindestlohn, *der*

mining /'maɪnɪŋ/ *n.* Bergbau, *der; attrib.*
Bergbau-

mining: ∼ **industry** *n.* Bergbau, *der;*
∼ **town** *n.* Bergbaustadt, *die*

minion /'mɪnjən/ *n.* Lakai, *der*

mini: ∼ **roundabout** *n.* (Brit.) *sehr kleiner,
oft nur aufs Pflaster aufgezeichneter
Kreisverkehr;* ∼**skirt** *n.* Minirock, *der*

minister /'mɪnɪstə(r)/ 1 *n.* **(a)** (Polit.)
Minister, *der*/Ministerin, *die*
(b) (Eccl.) Geistliche, *der*/*die*; Pfarrer, *der*/
Pfarrerin, *die*
2 *v.i.* ∼ **to sb.** sich um jmdn. kümmern

ministerial /mɪnɪ'stɪərɪəl/ *adj.* (Polit.)
Minister-; ministeriell

ministry /'mɪnɪstrɪ/ *n.* **(a)** (Polit.)
Ministerium, *das*
(b) (Eccl.) geistliches Amt

mink /mɪŋk/ *n.* Nerz, *der*

minnow /'mɪnəʊ/ *n.* Elritze, *die*

minor /'maɪnə(r)/ 1 *adj.* **(a)** (lesser)
kleiner...
(b) (unimportant) weniger bedeutend; (not
serious) leicht; ∼ **road** kleine Straße
(c) (Mus.) Moll-; **A** ∼: a-Moll
2 *n.* Minderjährige, *der*/*die*

713

minority ⋯⫶ misinterpret ⋯⫶

minority /maɪˈnɒrɪtɪ, mɪˈnɒrɪtɪ/ n.
Minderheit, *die;* **in the ∼:** in der Minderheit
minstrel /ˈmɪnstrl/ n. fahrender Sänger
mint[1] /mɪnt/ [1] n. (place) Münzanstalt, *die*
[2] *adj.* funkelnagelneu (ugs.); **in ∼ condition**
in tadellosem Zustand
[3] *v.t.* prägen
mint[2] n. (a) (plant) Minze, *die*
(b) (peppermint) Pfefferminz, *das; attrib.*
Pfefferminz-
mint 'sauce n. Minzsoße, *die*
minuet /mɪnjʊˈet/ n. Menuett, *das*
minus /ˈmaɪnəs/ *prep.* minus; weniger;
(without) abzüglich (+ *Gen.*)
minuscule /ˈmɪnəskjuːl/ *adj.* winzig
minute[1] /ˈmɪnɪt/ n. (a) Minute, *die;*
(moment) Moment, *der*
(b) ∼s (of meeting) Protokoll, *das;* **take the
∼s of a meeting** bei einer Sitzung [das]
Protokoll führen
minute[2] /maɪˈnjuːt/ *adj.* (tiny) winzig
minute hand /ˈmɪnɪthænd/ n.
Minutenzeiger, *der;* großer Zeiger
minutiae /maɪˈnjuːʃiː, mɪˈnjuːʃiː/ n. pl.
Details Pl.
miracle /ˈmɪrəkl/ n. Wunder, *das*
miraculous /mɪˈrækjʊləs/ *adj.* wunderbar
mirage /ˈmɪrɑːʒ/ n. Fata Morgana, *die*
mire /maɪə(r)/ n. Morast, *der*
mirror /ˈmɪrə(r)/ [1] n. Spiegel, *der*
[2] *v.t.* [wider]spiegeln
mirror 'image n. Spiegelbild, *das*
misadventure /mɪsədˈventʃə(r)/ n.
Missgeschick, *das*
misanthropist /mɪˈzænθrəpɪst/ ns.
Misanthrop, *der* (geh.); Menschenfeind, *der*
misanthropy /mɪˈzænθrəpɪ/ n.
Menschenfeindlichkeit, *die*
misapprehension /mɪsæprɪˈhenʃn/ n.
Missverständnis, *das;* **be under a ∼:** einem
Irrtum unterliegen
misbehave /mɪsbɪˈheɪv/ *v.i. & refl.* sich
schlecht benehmen
misbehaviour (*Amer.:* **misbehavior**)
/mɪsbɪˈheɪvjə(r)/ n. schlechtes Benehmen
miscalculate /mɪsˈkælkjʊleɪt/ [1] *v.t.*
falsch berechnen; (misjudge) falsch
einschätzen
[2] *v.i.* sich verrechnen
miscalculation /mɪskælkjʊˈleɪʃn/ n.
Rechenfehler, *der;* (misjudgement)
Fehleinschätzung, *die*
miscarriage /mɪsˈkærɪdʒ/ n. (a)
Fehlgeburt, *die*
(b) ∼ of justice Justizirrtum, *der*
miscarry /mɪsˈkærɪ/ *v.i.* (a) (Med.) eine
Fehlgeburt haben
(b) (Plan, Vorhaben usw.:) fehlschlagen
miscellaneous /mɪsəˈleɪnɪəs/ *adj.* (a)
[kunter]bunt
(b) *with pl.* n. verschieden

miscellany /mɪˈselənɪ/ n. [bunte]
Sammlung; [buntes] Gemisch
mischief /ˈmɪstʃɪf/ n. (a) Unfug, *der;* **get
up to ∼:** etwas anstellen
(b) (harm) Schaden, *der*
mischievous /ˈmɪstʃɪvəs/ *adj.*
spitzbübisch; schelmisch
misconception /mɪskənˈsepʃn/ n.
falsche Vorstellung (about von); **be
[labouring] under a ∼ about sth.** sich (*Dat.*)
eine falsche Vorstellung von etw. machen
misconduct /mɪsˈkɒndʌkt/ n.
unkorrektes Verhalten
misconstrue /mɪskənˈstruː/ *v.t.*
missverstehen
miscount /mɪsˈkaʊnt/ [1] *v.i.* sich
verzählen
[2] *v.t.* falsch zählen
misdeed /mɪsˈdiːd/ n. Missetat, *die* (veralt.,
scherzh.)
misdemeanour (*Amer.:*
misdemeanor) /mɪsdɪˈmiːnə(r)/ n.
Missetat, *die* (veralt., scherzh.)
misdirect /mɪsdɪˈrekt, mɪsdaɪˈrekt/ *v.t.*
falsch adressieren (Brief); in die falsche
Richtung schicken (Person)
miser /ˈmaɪzə(r)/ n. Geizhals, *der*
miserable /ˈmɪzərəbl/ *adj.* (a)
unglücklich; **feel ∼:** sich elend fühlen
(b) trist (Wetter, Urlaub)
miserably /ˈmɪzərəblɪ/ *adv.* unglücklich;
jämmerlich (versagen); **∼ poor** bettelarm
miserly /ˈmaɪzəlɪ/ *adj.* geizig
misery /ˈmɪzərɪ/ n. (a) Elend, *das*
(b) (coll.: discontented person) ∼ [guts]
Miesepeter, *der* (ugs.)
misfire /mɪsˈfaɪə(r)/ *v.i.* (a) (Motor:)
Fehlzündungen haben
(b) (Plan, Versuch:) fehlschlagen; (Streich,
Witz:) danebengehen
misfit /ˈmɪsfɪt/ n. Außenseiter, *der/*
Außenseiterin, *die*
misfortune /mɪsˈfɔːtʃuːn/ n. Missgeschick,
das
misgiving /mɪsˈɡɪvɪŋ/ n. ∼[s] Bedenken
Pl.
misguided /mɪsˈɡaɪdɪd/ *adj.* töricht
mishandle /mɪsˈhændl/ *v.t.* falsch
behandeln
mishap /ˈmɪshæp/ n. Missgeschick, *das*
mishear /mɪsˈhɪə(r)/ [1] *v.i.,* **misheard**
/mɪsˈhɜːd/ sich verhören
[2] *v.t.,* **misheard** falsch verstehen
mishit [1] /ˈmɪshɪt/ n. Fehlschlag, *der*
[2] /mɪsˈhɪt/ *v.t.,* **-tt-, mishit** verschlagen
mishmash /ˈmɪʃmæʃ/ n. Mischmasch, *der*
(ugs.) (of aus)
misinform /mɪsɪnˈfɔːm/ *v.t.* falsch
informieren
misinterpret /mɪsɪnˈtɜːprɪt/ *v.t.* (make
wrong inference from) falsch deuten; missdeuten ⋯⫶

misinterpretation /mısınt3:prı'teıʃn/ n.
be open to ~: leicht missdeutet werden
können

misjudge /mıs'dʒʌdʒ/ v.t. falsch
einschätzen; falsch beurteilen ⟨Person⟩

misjudgement, misjudgment
/mıs'dʒʌdʒmənt/ n. Fehleinschätzung, die; (of
person) falsche Beurteilung

mislay /mıs'leı/ v.t., mislaid /mıs'leıd/
verlegen

mislead /mıs'li:d/ v.t., misled /mıs'led/
irreführen

mis'leading adj. irreführend

mismanage /mıs'mænıdʒ/ v.t. schlecht
abwickeln ⟨Geschäft, Projekt⟩

mismanagement /mıs'mænıdʒmənt/ n.
schlechte Abwicklung

misnomer /mıs'nəʊmə(r)/ n. unzutreffende
Bezeichnung

misogynist /mı'sɒdʒınıst/ n.
Frauenhasser, der

misplace /mıs'pleıs/ v.t. an den falschen
Platz stellen/legen/setzen usw.

misprint [1] /'mısprınt/ n. Druckfehler, der
[2] /mıs'prınt/ v.t. verdrucken

mispronounce /mısprə'naʊns/ v.t. falsch
aussprechen

misquote /mıs'kwəʊt/ v.t. falsch zitieren;
he was ~d as saying that ...: man
unterstellte ihm, gesagt zu haben, dass ...

misread /mıs'ri:d/ v.t., misread /mıs'red/
falsch lesen

misrepresent /mısreprı'zent/ v.t. falsch
darstellen

misrepresentation /mısreprızen'teıʃn/
n. falsche Darstellung

miss [1] n. Fehlschlag, der; (shot) Fehlschuss,
der; (throw) Fehlwurf, der
[2] v.t. (a) (fail to hit) verfehlen
(b) (let slip) verpassen; ~ an opportunity sich
(Dat.) eine Gelegenheit entgehen lassen
(c) (fail to catch) verpassen ⟨Zug⟩
(d) (fail to take part in) versäumen; ~ school in
der Schule fehlen
(e) (fail to see) übersehen; (fail to hear) nicht
mitbekommen
(f) (feel the absence of) vermissen; she ~es
him er fehlt ihr
[3] v.i. (not hit sth.) danebentreffen
■ **miss 'out** [1] v.t. weglassen
[2] v.i. ~ out on sth. (coll.) sich (Dat.) etw.
entgehen lassen

Miss /mıs/ n. ~ Brown (unmarried woman)
Frau Brown; Fräulein Brown (veralt.); (girl)
Fräulein Brown

misshapen /mıs'ʃeıpn/ adj. missgebildet

missile /'mısaıl/ n. (a) (thrown)
[Wurf]geschoss, das
(b) (Mil.) Rakete, die

'missile base, 'missile site ns.
Raketenbasis, die

'missing adj. fehlend; be ~: fehlen;
⟨Person:⟩ (Mil. etc.) vermisst werden; (not
present) fehlen; ~ person Vermisste, der/die

mission /'mıʃn/ n. (a) Mission, die
(b) (planned operation) Einsatz, der

missionary /'mıʃənərı/ n. Missionar, der/
Missionarin, die

'mission statement n.
Unternehmensleitbild, das

misspell /mıs'spel/ v.t., forms as SPELL[1]
falsch schreiben

mist /mıst/ n. (fog) Nebel, der; (haze) Dunst,
der; (on windscreen etc.) Beschlag, der
■ **mist 'up** v.i. [sich] beschlagen

mistake /mı'steık/ [1] n. Fehler, der; by ~:
versehentlich
[2] v.t., forms as TAKE 1: (a) falsch verstehen
(b) ~ x for y x mit y verwechseln

mistaken /mı'steıkn/ adj. be ~: sich
täuschen; a case of ~ identity eine
Verwechslung

mi'stakenly adv. irrtümlicherweise

mistletoe /'mısltəʊ/ n. Mistel, die

mistook ► MISTAKE 2

mistranslate /mıstræns'leıt/ v.t. falsch
übersetzen

mistreat /mıs'tri:t/ v.t. schlecht behandeln;
(violently) misshandeln

mistreatment /mıs'tri:tmənt/ n. schlechte
Behandlung; (violent) Misshandlung, die

mistress /'mıstrıs/ n. (a) (Brit. Sch.: teacher)
Lehrerin, die
(b) (lover) Geliebte, die

mistrust /mıs'trʌst/ [1] v.t. misstrauen
(+ Dat.)
[2] n. Misstrauen, das (of gegenüber + Dat.)

mistrustful /mıs'trʌstfl/ adj. misstrauisch
(of gegenüber)

'misty adj. dunstig

misunderstand /mısʌndə'stænd/ v.t.,
forms as UNDERSTAND: missverstehen

misunder'standing n. Missverständnis,
das

misuse [1] /mıs'ju:z/ v.t. missbrauchen
[2] /mıs'ju:s/ n. Missbrauch, der

mite /maıt/ n. (a) (Zool.) Milbe, die
(b) (small child) Würmchen, das (fam.); poor
little ~: armes Kleines

miter (Amer.) ► MITRE

mitigate /'mıtıgeıt/ v.t. (a) (reduce) lindern
(b) (make less severe) mildern; mitigating
circumstances mildernde Umstände

mitre /'maıtə(r)/ n. (Brit. Eccl.) Mitra, die

mitten /'mıtn/ n. Fausthandschuh, der

mix /mıks/ [1] v.t. [ver]mischen; verrühren
⟨Zutaten⟩
[2] v.i. (a) (become ~ed) sich vermischen
(b) (be sociable, participate) Umgang mit
anderen [Menschen] haben; ~ with Umgang
haben mit; ~ well kontaktfreudig sein
[3] n. (coll.) Mischung, die; [cake] ~:
Backmischung, die

■ **mix 'up** *v.t.* (a) vermischen
  (b) (muddle) durcheinander bringen; (confuse)
verwechseln
  (c) be/get ∼ed up in sth. in etw. (*Akk.*)
verwickelt sein/werden

mixed /mɪkst/ *adj.* (a) gemischt
  (b) (diverse) unterschiedlich

mixed: ∼ **'bag** *n.* bunte Mischung;
∼ **'blessing** *n.* be a ∼ blessing nicht nur
Vorteile haben; ∼ **'grill** *n.* Mixedgrill, *der*
(Gastr.); gemischte Grillplatte;
∼ **'marriage** *n.* Mischehe, *die;* ∼ **'up** *adj.*
(fig. coll.) verwirrt, konfus ⟨*Person*⟩; be/feel
very ∼ up völlig durcheinander sein

'mixer *n.* (for food) Küchenmaschine, *die;*
hand ∼: Handrührgerät, *das*

mixture /'mɪkstʃə(r)/ *n.* (a) Mischung, *die*
(of aus)
  (b) (Med.) Mixtur, *die*

'mix-up *n.* Durcheinander, *das;*
(misunderstanding) Missverständnis, *das*

mm. *abbr.* = millimetre[s] mm

moan /məʊn/ ① *n.* (a) Stöhnen, *das*
  (b) have a ∼ (complain) jammern
  ② *v.i.* (a) stöhnen (with vor + *Dat.*)
  (b) (complain) jammern (about über + *Akk.*)
  ③ *v.t.* stöhnen

moat /məʊt/ *n.* [castle] ∼: Burggraben, *der*

mob /mɒb/ ① *n.* (a) (rabble) Mob, *der*
  (b) (coll.: group) **Peter and his** ∼: Peter und
seine ganze Blase (salopp)
  ② *v.t.,* **-bb-** belagern (ugs.) ⟨*Star*⟩

mobile /'məʊbaɪl/ ① *adj.* beweglich; (on
wheels) fahrbar; **upwardly** ∼: sozial
aufsteigend
  ② *n.* Mobile, *das;* (∼ phone) Handy, *das*

mobile: ∼ **'home** *n.* transportable
Wohneinheit; ∼ **'phone** *n.* Mobiltelefon,
das

mobility /mə'bɪlɪtɪ/ *n.* Beweglichkeit, *die*

mobilization /məʊbɪlaɪ'zeɪʃn/ *n.*
Mobilisierung, *die*

mobilize /'məʊbɪlaɪz/ *v.t.* mobilisieren

moccasin /'mɒkəsɪn/ *n.* Mokassin, *der*

mocha /'mɒkə/ *n.* Mokka, *der*

mock /mɒk/ ① *v.t.* sich lustig machen über
(+ *Akk.*)
  ② *v.i.* sich lustig machen (at über + *Akk.*)
  ③ *adj.* Schein⟨*kampf, -angriff, -ehe*⟩

mockery /'mɒkərɪ/ *n.* Spott, *der;* **make a**
∼ **of** sth. etw. zur Farce machen

'mock-up *n.* Modell [in Originalgröße]

mode /məʊd/ *n.* (a) Art [und Weise], *die*
  (b) (fashion) Mode, *der*

model /'mɒdl/ ① *n.* (a) Modell, *das*
  (b) (example to be imitated) Vorbild, *das*
  (c) (Art) Modell, *das;* (Fashion) Mannequin,
das; (male) Dressman, *der*
  ② *adj.* (a) (exemplary) Muster-
  (b) (miniature) Modell-
  ③ *v.t.,* (Brit.) **-ll-:** (a) modellieren; ∼ sth. after
or [up]on sth. etw. einer Sache (*Dat.*)
nachbilden

(b) (Fashion) vorführen
  ④ *v.i.* (Fashion) als Mannequin/Dressman
arbeiten; (Art) Modell stehen/sitzen

modem /'məʊdem/ *n.* Modem, *der*

moderate ① /'mɒdərət/ *adj.* (a) gemäßigt
⟨*Ansichten*⟩; maßvoll ⟨*Trinker, Forderungen*⟩
  (b) mittler... ⟨*Größe, Menge, Wert*⟩;
(reasonable) angemessen ⟨*Preis, Summe*⟩
  ② /'mɒdərət/ *n.* Gemäßigte, *der/die*
  ③ /'mɒdəreɪt/ *v.t.* mäßigen
  ④ *v.i.* nachlassen

moderately /'mɒdərətlɪ/ *adv.*
einigermaßen; mäßig ⟨*begeistert, groß,
begabt*⟩

moderation /mɒdə'reɪʃn/ *n.* Mäßigkeit,
die; in ∼: mit Maßen

modern /'mɒdn/ *adj.* modern; heutig
⟨*Zeit[alter], Welt, Mensch*⟩; ∼ **art/music**
moderne Kunst/Musik; ∼ **history** neuere
Geschichte; ∼ **languages** neuere Sprachen

modernize /'mɒdənaɪz/ *v.t.* modernisieren

modest /'mɒdɪst/ *adj.* bescheiden; einfach
⟨*Haus, Kleidung*⟩

'modestly *adv.* bescheiden

'modesty *n.* Bescheidenheit, *die*

modification /mɒdɪfɪ'keɪʃn/ *n.*
[Ab]änderung, *die*

modify /'mɒdɪfaɪ/ *v.t.* [ab]ändern

modulate /'mɒdjʊleɪt/ *v.t. & i.* modulieren

modulation /mɒdjʊ'leɪʃn/ *n.* Modulation,
die

module /'mɒdjuːl/ *n.* (a) Bauelement, *das*
  (b) (Astronaut.) **command** ∼:
Kommandoeinheit, *die*
  (c) (Educ.) Unterrichtseinheit, *die*

mohair /'məʊheə(r)/ *n.* Mohair, *der*

moist /mɔɪst/ *adj.* feucht (with von)

moisten /'mɔɪsn/ *v.t.* anfeuchten

moisture /'mɔɪstʃə(r)/ *n.* Feuchtigkeit, *die*

moisturize /'mɔɪstjʊraɪz, 'mɔɪstʃəraɪz/ *v.t.*
befeuchten; ∼ **the skin** der Haut (*Dat.*)
Feuchtigkeit zuführen; ⟨*Creme:*⟩ der Haut
(*Dat.*) Feuchtigkeit verleihen

moisturizer /'mɔɪstʃəraɪzə(r)/,
moisturizing cream /'mɔɪstʃəraɪzɪŋ
kriːm/ *ns.* Feuchtigkeitscreme, *die*

molar /'məʊlə(r)/ *n.* Backenzahn, *der*

molasses /mə'læsɪz/ *n.* Melasse, *die*

mold (Amer.) ▶ MOULD[1, 2]

molder, molding, moldy (Amer.)
▶ MOULD-

mole[1] /məʊl/ *n.* (on skin) Leberfleck, *der*

mole[2] *n.* (animal) Maulwurf, *der*

molecular /mə'lekjʊlə(r)/ *adj.* molekular

molecule /'mɒlɪkjuːl/ *n.* Molekül, *das*

'molehill *n.* Maulwurfshügel, *der*

molest /mə'lest/ *v.t.* belästigen

mollify /'mɒlɪfaɪ/ *v.t.* besänftigen

mollusc, (Amer.) **mollusk** /'mɒləsk/ *n.*
Weichtier, *das*

m

mollycoddle /'mɒlɪkɒdl/ v.t. [ver]hätscheln

molt (Amer.) ▶ MOULT

molten /'məʊltn/ adj. geschmolzen

mom /mɒm/ (Amer. coll.) ▶ MUM²

moment /'məʊmənt/ n. Augenblick, der; at any ~, (coll.) any ~: jeden Augenblick; one or just a or wait a ~! einen Augenblick!; in a ~ (very soon) sofort; at the ~: im Augenblick; the ~ of truth die Stunde der Wahrheit

momentarily /'məʊməntərɪlɪ/ adv. einen Augenblick lang

momentary /'məʊməntərɪ/ adj. kurz

momentous /mə'mentəs/ adj. (important) bedeutsam; (of consequence) folgenschwer

momentum /mə'mentəm/ n. Schwung, der

Mon. abbr. = **Monday** Mo.

monarch /'mɒnək/ n. Monarch, der/ Monarchin, die

'monarchy n. Monarchie, die

monastery /'mɒnəstrɪ/ n. Kloster, das

monastic /mə'næstɪk/ adj. mönchisch

Monday /'mʌndeɪ, 'mʌndɪ/ n. Montag, der; see also FRIDAY

monetary /'mʌnɪtərɪ/ adj. (a) (of currency) monetär; Währungs⟨politik, -system⟩; ~ union Währungsunion, die (b) (of money) finanziell

money /'mʌnɪ/ n. Geld, das; make ~ ⟨Person:⟩ [viel] Geld verdienen; ⟨Geschäft:⟩ etwas einbringen; for 'my ~: wenn man mich fragt

money: ~ **bag** n. Geldsack, der; ~ **belt** n. Geldgürtel, der; ~ **box** n. Sparbüchse, die; ~**making** adj. Gewinn bringend; ~ **order** n. Postanweisung, die

Mongolia /mɒŋ'gəʊlɪə/ pr. n. Mongolei, die

Mongolian /mɒŋ'gəʊlɪən/ [1] adj. mongolisch; sb. is ~: jmd. ist Mongole/ Mongolin [2] n. (person) Mongole, der/Mongolin, die

mongrel /'mʌŋgrəl/ n. ~ [dog] Promenadenmischung, die

monitor /'mɒnɪtə(r)/ [1] n. (a) (Sch.) Aufsichtsschüler, der/-schülerin, die (b) (Med., Telev., Comp.) Monitor, der [2] v.t. beobachten ⟨Wetter, Flugzeug⟩; abhören ⟨Sendung, Telefongespräch⟩

monk /mʌŋk/ n. Mönch, der

monkey /'mʌŋkɪ/ n. Affe, der

monkey: ~ **business** n. (coll.: mischief) Schabernack, der; ~ **nut** n. Erdnuss, die; ~ **wrench** n. Universalschraubenschlüssel, der

mono /'mɒnəʊ/ adj. Mono⟨platte[nspieler], -wiedergabe⟩

monochrome /'mɒnəkrəʊm/ adj. monochrom (fachspr.); einfarbig; Schwarzweiß- (Ferns.)

monocle /'mɒnəkl/ n. Monokel, das

monogamous /mə'nɒgəməs/ adj. monogam

monogamy /mə'nɒgəmɪ/ n. Monogamie, die; Einehe, die

monogram /'mɒnəgræm/ n. Monogramm, das

monogrammed /'mɒnəgræmd/ adj. monogrammiert; ⟨Taschentuch usw.:⟩ mit Monogramm

monologue (Amer.: **monolog**) /'mɒnəlɒg/ n. Monolog, der

monopolize /mə'nɒpəlaɪz/ v.t. (Econ.) monopolisieren; (fig.) mit Beschlag belegen; ~ the conversation den/die anderen nicht zu Wort kommen lassen

monopoly /mə'nɒpəlɪ/ n. (a) (Econ.) Monopol, das (of auf + Akk.) (b) (exclusive possession) alleiniger Besitz

monotone /'mɒnətəʊn/ n. gleich bleibender Ton

monotonous /mə'nɒtənəs/ adj., **mo'notonously** adv. eintönig

monotony /mə'nɒtənɪ/ n. Eintönigkeit, die

monsoon /mɒn'suːn/ n. Monsun, der

monster /'mɒnstə(r)/ n. (a) (creature) Ungeheuer, das; (huge thing) Ungetüm, das (b) (inhuman person) Unmensch, der

monstrosity /mɒn'strɒsɪtɪ/ n. (a) (outrageous thing) Ungeheuerlichkeit, die (b) (hideous building etc.) Ungetüm, das

monstrous /'mɒnstrəs/ adj. (a) (huge) riesig (b) (outrageous) ungeheuerlich (c) (atrocious) scheußlich

month /mʌnθ/ n. Monat, der; for a ~/~s einen Monat [lang]/monatelang

'monthly [1] adj. monatlich; Monats⟨einkommen, -gehalt⟩ [2] adv. einmal im Monat [3] n. Monatsschrift, die

monument /'mɒnjʊmənt/ n. Denkmal, das

monumental /mɒnjʊ'mentl/ adj. (a) (massive) monumental (b) gewaltig ⟨Misserfolg, Irrtum⟩

moo /muː/ [1] n. Muhen, das [2] v.i. muhen

mooch /muːtʃ/ v.i. (coll.) ~ about or around/ along herumschleichen (ugs.)/zockeln (ugs.)

mood /muːd/ n. (a) Stimmung, die; be in a good/bad ~: [bei] guter/schlechter Laune sein; I'm not in the ~: ich hab keine Lust dazu (b) (bad ~) Verstimmung, die

'moody adj. (a) (sullen) missmutig (b) (subject to moods) launenhaft

moon /muːn/ n. Mond, der

moon: ~**beam** n. Mondstrahl, der; ~**light** [1] n. Mondlicht, das; Mondschein, der; [2] v.i. (coll.) nebenberuflich abends arbeiten; ~**lit** adj. mondbeschienen (geh.)

moor¹ /mʊə(r), mɔ:(r)/ n. (Geog.) [Hoch]moor, das

moor² v.t. & i. festmachen; vertäuen

'moorhen n. [Grünfüßiges] Teichhuhn

'mooring n. ~[s] Anlegestelle, *die*

'mooring post n. Pfahl, *der;*
≈ Duckdalben, *der*

moorland /'mʊələnd, 'mɔːlənd/ n.
Moorland, *das*

moose /muːs/ n., pl. *same* Amerikanischer
Elch

moot /muːt/ 1 adj. umstritten; offen
⟨*Frage*⟩; strittig ⟨*Punkt*⟩
2 v.t. erörtern ⟨*Frage, Punkt*⟩

mop /mɒp/ 1 n. (a) Mopp, *der*
(b) ~ [of hair] Wuschelkopf, *der*
2 v.t., **-pp-** moppen ⟨*Fußboden*⟩; (wipe)
abwischen ⟨*Träne, Schweiß, Stirn*⟩
■ **mop 'up** v.t. aufwischen

mope /məʊp/ v.i. Trübsal blasen

moped /'məʊped/ n. Moped, *das*

moral /'mɒrl/ 1 adj. moralisch; sittlich
⟨*Wert*⟩; Moral⟨*begriff, -prinzip*⟩
(b) (virtuous) moralisch ⟨*Leben, Person*⟩
2 n. (a) Moral, *die*
(b) in pl. (habits) Moral, *die*

morale /mə'rɑːl/ Moral, *die;* **low/high** ~:
schlechte/gute Moral

mo'rale-booster n. be a *or* act as a ~ for
sb. jds. Moral heben *od.* stärken

morality /mə'rælɪtɪ/ n. Moral, *die*

moral sup'port n. moralische
Unterstützung

morbid /'mɔːbɪd/ adj. krankhaft; morbid
(geh.) ⟨*Faszination, Neigung*⟩

more /mɔː(r)/ 1 adj. mehr; **any** *or* **some** ~
(apples, books, etc.) noch welche; **any** *or* **some**
~ (tea, paper, etc.) noch etwas; **any** *or* **some**
~ **apples/tea** noch Äpfel/Tee; **I haven't any**
~ **[apples/tea]** ich habe keine [Äpfel]/keinen
[Tee] mehr; ~ **and** ~: immer mehr
2 n. mehr; ~ **and** ~: immer mehr; **six or**
~: mindestens sechs
3 adv. (a) mehr; ~ **interesting**
interessanter
(b) (nearer, rather) eher
(c) (again) wieder; **no** ~, **not any** ~: nicht
mehr; **once** ~: noch einmal
(d) ~ **and** ~: immer mehr; ~ **and** ~ **absurd**
immer absurder
(e) ~ **or less** (fairly) mehr oder weniger;
(approximately) annähernd

moreish /'mɔːrɪʃ/ adj. (coll.) lecker

more'over adv. und außerdem

morgue /mɔːg/ ▶ MORTUARY

morning /'mɔːnɪŋ/ n. Morgen, *der;* (not
afternoon) Vormittag, *der; attrib.* morgendlich;
Morgen-; **this** ~: heute Morgen; **tomorrow**
~, (coll.) **in the** ~: morgen früh; **[early] in the**
~: am [frühen] Morgen; (regularly)
[früh]morgens

morning: ~ **'after** n. ~-**'after [feeling]**
(coll.: hangover) Katzenjammer, *der;* ~-**'after**
pill n. Pille [für den Morgen] danach;
~ **'star** n. Morgenstern, *der*

Moroccan /mə'rɒkən/ 1 adj.
marokkanisch; **sb. is** ~: jmd. ist
Marokkaner/Marokkanerin
2 n. Marokkaner, *der*/Marokkanerin, *die*

Morocco /mə'rɒkəʊ/ pr. n. Marokko (*das*)

moron /'mɔːrɒn/ n. (coll.) Schwachkopf, *der*
(ugs.)

morose /mə'rəʊs/ adj. verdrießlich

morphine /'mɔːfiːn/ n. Morphin, *das*

Morse [code] /mɔːs ('kəʊd)/ n.
Morsealphabet, *das*

morsel /'mɔːsl/ n. (of food) Bissen, *der*

mortal /'mɔːtl/ 1 adj. (a) sterblich
(b) (fatal) tödlich (**to** für)
2 n. Sterbliche, *der*/*die*

mortality /mɔː'tælɪtɪ/ n. (a) Sterblichkeit,
die
(b) ~ **[rate]** Sterblichkeitsrate, *die*

'mortally adv. tödlich

mortar /'mɔːtə(r)/ n. (a) Mörtel, *der*
(b) (vessel) Mörser, *der*
(c) (weapon) Minenwerfer, *der;* Mörser, *der*

mortgage /'mɔːgɪdʒ/ 1 n. Hypothek, *die*
2 v.t. mit einer Hypothek belasten

mortuary /'mɔːtjʊərɪ/ n. (building)
Leichenschauhaus, *das;* (room)
Leichenkammer, *die*

mosaic /məʊ'zeɪɪk/ n. Mosaik, *das*

Moscow /'mɒskəʊ/ pr. n. Moskau (*das*)

Moselle /məʊ'zel/ pr. n. Mosel, *die*

Moslem /'mɒzləm/ ▶ MUSLIM

mosque /mɒsk/ n. Moschee, *die*

mosquito /mɒs'kiːtəʊ/ n., pl. ~**es**
Stechmücke, *die;* (in tropics) Moskito, *der*

mos'quito net n. Moskitonetz, *das*

moss /mɒs/ n. Moos, *das*

'mossy adj. moosig

most /məʊst/ 1 adj. (in number, majority of)
die meisten; (in amount) meist…; **make the**
~ **mistakes/the** ~ **noise** die meisten Fehler/
den größten Lärm machen; **for the** ~ **part**
größtenteils
2 n. (a) (greatest amount) **the** ~ **it will cost is**
£10 es wird höchstens zehn Pfund kosten;
pay the ~: am meisten bezahlen
(b) (greater part) ~ **of the girls** die meisten
Mädchen; ~ **of his friends** die meisten
seiner Freunde; ~ **of the poem** der größte
Teil des Gedichts; ~ **of the time** die meiste
Zeit
(c) (on ~ occasions) meistens
3 adv. (a) am meisten; **the** ~ **interesting**
book das interessanteste Buch; ~ **often** am
häufigsten
(b) (exceedingly) äußerst

'mostly adv. (most of the time) meistens;
(mainly) größtenteils

MOT ▶ MOT TEST

motel /məʊ'tel/ n. Motel, *das*

moth /mɒθ/ n. Nachtfalter, *der;* (in clothes)
Motte, *die*

m

moth: ~**ball** n. Mottenkugel, *die;*
~**eaten** *adj.* von Motten zerfressen

mother /'mʌðə(r)/ [1] n. Mutter, *die*
[2] *v.t.* (over-protect) bemuttern

'**motherboard** n. (Comp.) Mutterplatine, *die*

'**motherhood** n. Mutterschaft, *die*

Mothering Sunday /'mʌðərɪŋ sʌndɪ/
(Brit. Eccl.) ▶ MOTHER'S DAY

mother: ~**in-law** n., pl. ~**s-in-law**
Schwiegermutter, *die;* ~**land** n. Vaterland,
das

motherly /'mʌðəlɪ/ *adj.* mütterlich; ~ love
Mutterliebe, *die*

mother: ~**of-'pearl** n. Perlmutt, *das;*
M~**'s Day** n. Muttertag, *der;* ~ '**tongue**
n. Muttersprache, *die*

moth: ~ **hole** n. Mottenloch, *das;* ~**proof**
adj. mottenfest

motif /məʊ'tiːf/ n. Motiv, *das*

motion /'məʊʃn/ [1] n. (a) Bewegung, *die*
(b) (proposal) Antrag, *der*
[2] *v.t. & i.* ~ [to] sb. to do sth. jmdm.
bedeuten (geh.), etw. zu tun

'**motionless** *adj.* bewegungslos

motivate /'məʊtɪveɪt/ *v.t.* motivieren

motivation /məʊtɪ'veɪʃn/ n. Motivation,
die

motive /'məʊtɪv/ n. Beweggrund, *der;* the
~ for the crime das Tatmotiv

motley /'mɒtlɪ/ *adj.* bunt gemischt

motor /'məʊtə(r)/ [1] n. (a) Motor, *der*
(b) (Brit.: ~ car) Auto, *das*
[2] *adj.* Motor⟨mäher, -jacht usw.⟩
[3] *v.i.* (Brit.) [mit dem Auto] fahren

motor: ~**bike** n. (coll.) Motorrad, *das;*
~ **boat** n. Motorboot, *das*

motorcade /'məʊtəkeɪd/ n. Fahrzeug- od.
Wagenkolonne, *die*

motor: ~ **car** n. (Brit.) Kraftfahrzeug, *das;*
~ **cycle** n. Motorrad, *das;* ~**cyclist** n.
Motorradfahrer, *der/*-fahrerin, *die*

'**motoring** n. (Brit.) Autofahren, *das*

'**motorist** n. Autofahrer, *der/*-fahrerin, *die*

motorize /'məʊtəraɪz/ *v.t.* motorisieren

motor: ~ **racing** n. Autorennsport, *der;*
~ **show** n. Auto[mobil]ausstellung, *die;*
~ **vehicle** n. Kraftfahrzeug, *das;* ~**way**
n. (Brit.) Autobahn, *die*

MO'T test n. (Brit.) ≈ TÜV, *der*

mottled /'mɒtld/ *adj.* gesprenkelt

motto /'mɒtəʊ/ n., pl. ~**es** Motto, *das*

mould[1] /məʊld/ [1] n. (hollow container) Form,
die
[2] *v.t.* formen (out of, from aus)

mould[2] n. (Bot.) Schimmel, *der*

moulder /'məʊldə(r)/ *v.i.* ~ [away]
[ver]modern

'**moulding** n. (a) Formteil, *das* (of, in aus);
(Archit.) Zierleiste, *die*
(b) (wooden) Leiste, *die*

'**mouldy** *adj.* schimmlig; go ~: schimmeln

moult /məʊlt/ *v.i.* ⟨Vogel:⟩ sich mausern;
⟨Hund, Katze:⟩ sich haaren

mound /maʊnd/ n. (a) (of earth) Hügel, *der*
(b) (heap) Haufen, *der*

mount /maʊnt/ [1] n. (a) M~ Vesuvius/
Everest der Vesuv/der Mount Everest
(b) (animal) Reittier, *das;* (horse) Pferd, *das*
(c) (of picture, photograph) Passepartout, *das*
(d) (for gem) Fassung, *die*
[2] *v.t.* (a) hinaufsteigen ⟨Treppe⟩; steigen auf
(+ Akk.) ⟨Plattform, Reittier, Fahrzeug⟩
(b) aufziehen ⟨Bild⟩; einfassen ⟨Edelstein
usw.⟩
(c) inszenieren ⟨Stück, Oper⟩; organisieren
⟨Ausstellung⟩; durchführen ⟨Angriff,
Operation⟩
[3] *v.i.* ~ [up] (increase) steigen (to auf + Akk.)

mountain /'maʊntɪn/ n. Berg, *der;* in the
~s im Gebirge

mountain: ~ **bike** n. Mountainbike, *das;*
~ **chain** n. Gebirgszug, *der*

mountaineer /maʊntɪ'nɪə(r)/ n.
Bergsteiger, *der/*Bergsteigerin, *die*

mountai'neering n. Bergsteigen, *das*

mountainous /'maʊntɪnəs/ *adj.* (a)
gebirgig
(b) (huge) riesig

mountain: ~ '**range** n. Gebirgszug, *der;*
~**side** n. [Berg][ab]hang, *der;* ~ **top** n.
Berggipfel, *der*

mourn /mɔːn/ [1] *v.i.* trauern; ~ for or over
trauern um ⟨Toten⟩
[2] *v.t.* betrauern

'**mourner** n. Trauernde, *der/die*

mournful /'mɔːnfl/ *adj.* klagend ⟨Stimme,
Ton, Schrei⟩; trauervoll (geh.) ⟨Person⟩

'**mourning** n. Trauer, *die;* be in/go into ~:
Trauer tragen/anlegen

mouse /maʊs/ n., pl. **mice** /maɪs/ Maus, *die*

mouse: ~ **button** n. (Comp.) Maustaste,
die; ~ **click** n. (Comp.) Mausklick, *der;*
~ **mat** n. (Comp.) Mauspad, *das;*
~ **pointer** n. (Comp.) Mauszeiger, *der;*
~**trap** n. Mausefalle, *die*

mousse /muːs/ n. Mousse, *die*

moustache /mə'stɑːʃ/ n. Schnurrbart, *der*

mousy /'maʊsɪ/ *adj.* (a) mattbraun ⟨Haar⟩
(b) (timid) scheu

mouth [1] /maʊθ/ n. (a) (of person) Mund,
der; (of animal) Maul, *das;* with one's ~ open/
full mit offenem/vollem Mund
(b) (harbour entrance) [Hafen]einfahrt, *die;* (of
tunnel, cave) Eingang, *der;* (of river) Mündung,
die
[2] /maʊð/ *v.t.* mit Lippenbewegungen sagen

mouthful /'maʊθfʊl/ n. Mundvoll, *der*

mouth: ~ **organ** n. Mundharmonika, *die;*
~**piece** n. (a) Mundstück, *das;* (b) (fig.)
Sprachrohr, *das*

movable /'muːvəbl/ *adj.* beweglich

move /muːv/ [1] n. (a) (change of home)
Umzug, *der*

(b) (action taken) Schritt, *der;* (Footb. etc.) Spielzug, *der*
(c) (turn in game) Zug, *der;* **make a** ~**:** ziehen; **it's your** ~**:** du bist am Zug
(d) be on the ~ ⟨*Person:*⟩ unterwegs sein
(e) make a ~ (do sth.) etwas tun; (coll.: leave) losziehen (ugs.)
(f) get a ~ **on** (coll.) einen Zahn zulegen (ugs.); **get a** ~ **on!** (coll.) [mach] Tempo! (ugs.)
2 *v.t.* **(a)** (change position of) bewegen; wegräumen ⟨*Hindernis, Schutt*⟩; (transport) befördern; ~ **sth. to a new position** etw. an einen neuen Platz bringen; ~ **house** umziehen
(b) (in game) ziehen
(c) (affect) bewegen; ~ **sb. to tears** jmdn. zu Tränen rühren; **be** ~**d by sth.** über etw. (*Akk.*) gerührt sein
(d) (prompt) ~ **sb. to do sth.** jmdn. dazu bewegen, etw. zu tun
(e) (propose) beantragen
3 *v.i.* **(a)** sich bewegen; (in vehicle) fahren
(b) (in games) ziehen
(c) (do sth.) handeln
(d) (change home) umziehen (**to** nach); ~ **into a flat** in eine Wohnung einziehen; ~ **out of a flat** aus einer Wohnung ausziehen; ~ **to London** nach London ziehen
(e) (change posture or state) sich bewegen; **don't** ~**!** keine Bewegung!
■ **move a'bout** **1** *v.i.* zugange sein; (travel) unterwegs sein
2 *v.t.* herumräumen
■ **move a'long** **1** *v.i.* **(a)** gehen/fahren
(b) ~ **along, please!** gehen/fahren Sie bitte weiter!
2 *v.t.* zum Weitergehen/-fahren auffordern
■ **move 'in** **1** *v.i.* **(a)** (to home etc.) einziehen
(b) ~ **in on** ⟨*Truppen, Polizeikräfte:*⟩ vorrücken gegen
2 *v.t.* hineinbringen
■ **move 'off** *v.i.* sich in Bewegung setzen
■ **move 'on** **1** *v.i.* weitergehen/-fahren; ~ **on to another question** (fig.) zu einer anderen Frage übergehen
2 *v.t.* zum Weitergehen/-fahren auffordern
■ **move 'out** *v.i.* ausziehen (**of** aus)
■ **move 'over** *v.i.* rücken
■ **move 'up** *v.i.* **(a)** rücken
(b) (in queue, hierarchy) aufrücken
'**movement** *n.* **(a)** Bewegung, *die;* (trend, tendency) Tendenz, *die* (**towards** zu)
(b) *in pl.* Aktivitäten *Pl.*
(c) (Mus.) Satz, *der*
movie /'muːvɪ/ *n.* (Amer. coll.) Film, *der;* the ~**s** der Film; **go to the** ~**s** ins Kino gehen
moving /'muːvɪŋ/ *adj.* **(a)** beweglich
(b) (affecting) ergreifend
mow /məʊ/ *v.t., p.p.* **mown** /məʊn/ *or* **mowed** /məʊd/ mähen
■ **mow 'down** *v.t.* (shoot) niedermähen ⟨*Menschen*⟩
'**mower** *n.* Rasenmäher, *der*
mown ▶ MOW

MP *abbr.* = **Member of Parliament**
m.p.g. *abbr.* = **miles per gallon**
m.p.h. *abbr.* = **miles per hour**
MPV *abbr.* = **multi-purpose vehicle**
Mr /'mɪstə(r)/ *n.* Herr; (in an address) Herrn
Mrs /'mɪsɪz/ *n.* Frau
Ms /mɪz/ *n.* Frau
MS *abbr.* (Med.) = **multiple sclerosis** MS
Mt. *abbr.* = **Mount**
much /mʌtʃ/ **1** *adj.,* **more** /mɔː(r)/, **most** /məʊst/ viel; **too** ~**:** zu viel *indekl*
2 *n.* vieles; ~ **of the day** der Großteil des Tages; **not be** ~ **to look at** nicht sehr ansehnlich sein
3 *adv.,* **more, most (a)** viel ⟨*besser, schöner usw.*⟩; ~ **more lively/attractive** viel lebhafter/ attraktiver
(b) mit Abstand ⟨*der/die/das Beste, Klügste usw.*⟩
(c) (greatly) sehr ⟨*lieben, genießen usw.*⟩; (for ~ **of the time**) viel ⟨*lesen, spielen usw.*⟩; (often) oft ⟨*sehen, besuchen usw.*⟩
(d) [**pretty** *or* **very**] ~ **the same** fast [genau] der-/die-/dasselbe
muck /mʌk/ *n.* **(a)** (coll.: something disgusting) Dreck, *der* (ugs.)
(b) (coll.: nonsense) Mist, *der* (ugs.)
■ **muck a'bout, muck a'round** (Brit. coll.) *v.i.* **(a)** herumalbern (ugs.)
(b) (tinker) herumfummeln (**with** an + *Dat.*)
■ **muck 'in** *v.i.* (coll.) mit anpacken (**with** bei)
■ **muck 'up** *v.t.* **(a)** (Brit. coll.: bungle) vermurksen (ugs.)
(b) (make dirty) dreckig machen (ugs.)
(c) (coll.: spoil) vermasseln (salopp)
'**mucky** *adj.* dreckig (ugs.)
mucus /'mjuːkəs/ *n.* Schleim, *der*
mud /mʌd/ *n.* Schlamm, *der*
muddle /'mʌdl/ **1** *n.* Durcheinander, *das*
2 *v.t.* ~ [**up**] durcheinander bringen; ~ **up** (mix up) verwechseln (**with** mit)
■ **muddle a'long, muddle 'on** *v.i.* vor sich (*Akk.*) hin wursteln (ugs.)
■ **muddle 'through** *v.i.* sich durchwursteln (ugs.)
muddy /'mʌdɪ/ *adj.* schlammig; **get** *or* **become** ~**:** verschlammen
'**mudguard** *n.* Schutzblech, *das;* (of car) Kotflügel, *der*
muesli /'mjuːzlɪ/ *n.* Müsli, *das*
muff¹ /mʌf/ *n.* Muff, *der*
muff² *v.t.* verpatzen (ugs.)
muffin /'mʌfɪn/ *n.* Muffin, *der*
muffle /'mʌfl/ *v.t.* **(a)** (envelop) ~ [**up**] einhüllen
(b) dämpfen ⟨*Geräusch*⟩
'**muffler** *n.* **(a)** (wrap, scarf) Schal, *der*
(b) (Amer. Motor Veh.) Schalldämpfer, *der*
mug /mʌg/ **1** *n.* **(a)** Becher, *der* (*meist mit Henkel*); (for beer etc.) Krug, *der*
(b) (coll.: face, mouth) Visage, *die* (salopp)　⋯⟶

(c) (Brit. coll.: gullible person) Trottel, der (ugs.)
2 v.t., -gg- (rob) überfallen und berauben
'**mugger** n. Straßenräuber, der/-räuberin, die
'**mugging** n. Straßenraub, der
muggy /'mʌgɪ/ adj. schwül
mule /mju:l/ n. Maultier, das
multi: ∼**coloured** (Brit.; Amer.: ∼**colored**) adj. mehrfarbig; bunt ⟨Stoff, Kleid⟩; ∼'**cultural** adj. multikulturell; ∼**function button** n. Multifunktionstaste, die; ∼**media** n. sing. Multimedia, das; ∼**millio'naire** n. Multimillionär, der/-millionärin, die; ∼**national** /mʌltɪ'næʃənl/ 1 adj. multinational; 2 n. multinationaler Konzern, der; Multi, der (ugs.)
multiple /'mʌltɪpl/ adj. mehrfach
multiple: ∼'**choice** adj. Multiplechoice⟨test, -frage⟩; ∼ '**store** n. (Brit.) Kettenladen, der
multiplication /mʌltɪplɪ'keɪʃn/ n. Multiplikation, die
multiply /'mʌltɪplaɪ/ 1 v.t. multiplizieren, malnehmen (by mit) 2 v.i. sich vermehren
multi: ∼**-purpose** adj. Mehrzweck-; ∼**-purpose 'vehicle** n. Großraumlimousine, die; '∼**-storey** adj. mehrstöckig; mehrgeschossig; ∼**-storey car park/block of flats** Parkhaus/Wohnhochhaus, das; ∼**track** adj. mehrspurig; Mehrspur⟨aufnahme, -ton, -tonbandgerät⟩
multitude /'mʌltɪtju:d/ n. (crowd) Menge, die; (great number) Vielzahl, die
mum[1] /mʌm/ (coll.) 1 int. ∼'s the word nicht weitersagen! 2 adj. keep ∼: den Mund halten (ugs.)
mum[2] n. (Brit. coll.: mother) Mama, die (fam.)
mumble /'mʌmbl/ v.i. & t. nuscheln (ugs.)
mummy[1] n. (Brit. coll.: mother) Mutti, die (fam.)
mummy[2] /'mʌmɪ/ n. Mumie, die
mumps /mʌmps/ n. Mumps, der
munch /mʌntʃ/ v.t. & i. ∼ [one's food] mampfen (salopp)
mundane /mʌn'deɪn/ adj. (a) (dull) banal (b) (worldly) weltlich
Munich /'mju:nɪk/ pr. n. München ⟨das⟩
municipal /mjʊ'nɪsɪpl/ adj. kommunal; Kommunal⟨politik, -verwaltung⟩
munition /mju:'nɪʃn/ n., usu. in pl. Kriegsmaterial, das; ∼[s] factory Rüstungsbetrieb, der
mural /'mjʊərl/ n. Wandbild, das
murder /'mɜ:də(r)/ 1 n. Mord, der (of an + Dat.) 2 v.t. ermorden
'**murderer** n. Mörder, der/Mörderin, die
murderess /'mɜ:dərɪs/ n. Mörderin, die

murderous /'mɜ:dərəs/ adj. tödlich; Mord⟨absicht, -drohung⟩; mörderisch (ugs.) ⟨Kampf⟩
murk /mɜ:k/ n. Dunkelheit, die
'**murky** adj. (a) (dark) düster (b) (dirty) schmutzig-trüb ⟨Wasser⟩
murmur /'mɜ:mə(r)/ 1 n. (a) (subdued sound) Rauschen, das (b) (expression of discontent) Murren, das (c) (soft speech) Murmeln, das 2 v.t. murmeln 3 v.i. ⟨Person:⟩ murmeln; (complain) murren
muscle /'mʌsl/ n. Muskel, der
muscular /'mʌskjʊlə(r)/ adj. (a) (Anat.) Muskel- (b) (strong) muskulös
muse /mju:z/ (literary) v.i. [nach]sinnen (geh.) (on, over über + Akk.)
museum /mju:'zi:əm/ n. Museum, das
mush /mʌʃ/ n. Brei, der
mushroom /'mʌʃrom, 'mʌʃru:m/ 1 n. Pilz, der; (cultivated) Champignon, der 2 v.i. wie Pilze aus dem Boden schießen
'**mushroom cloud** n. Rauchpilz, der; (after nuclear explosion) Atompilz, der
'**mushy** adj. breiig
music /'mju:zɪk/ n. (a) Musik, die; piece of ∼: Musikstück, das; set sth. to ∼: etw. vertonen (b) (score) Noten Pl.
musical /'mju:zɪkl/ 1 adj. musikalisch; Musik⟨instrument, -verständnis, -notation, -abend⟩ 2 n. Musical, das
'**musical box** n. (Brit.) Spieldose, die
musician /mju:'zɪʃn/ n. Musiker, der/ Musikerin, die
music: ∼ **lesson** n. Musikstunde, die; ∼ **room** n. Musiksaal, der; ∼ **stand** n. Notenständer, der; ∼ **teacher** n. Musiklehrer, der/-lehrerin, die; ∼ **video** n. Musikvideo, das
Muslim /'mʊslɪm, 'mʌzlɪm/ 1 adj. moslemisch 2 n. Moslem, der/Moslime, die
muslin /'mʌzlɪn/ n. Musselin, der
mussel /'mʌsl/ n. Muschel, die
must /məst, stressed mʌst/ 1 v. aux., only in pres., neg. (coll.) mustn't /'mʌsnt/ müssen; with neg. dürfen 2 n. (coll.) Muss, das
mustache ▶ MOUSTACHE
mustard /'mʌstəd/ n. Senf, der
muster /'mʌstə(r)/ 1 n. pass ∼: akzeptabel sein 2 v.t. versammeln; (Mil., Naut.) [zum Appell] antreten lassen; (fig.) zusammennehmen ⟨Kraft, Mut, Verstand⟩ 3 v.i. sich [ver]sammeln ■ **muster 'up** v.t. aufbringen
mustn't /'mʌsnt/ (coll.) = must not; ▶ MUST 1
musty /'mʌstɪ/ adj. muffig

mutant /'mjuːtənt/ 1 *adj.* mutiert
2 *n.* Mutante, *die*
mutation /mjuːˈteɪʃn/ *n.* Mutation, *die*
mute /mjuːt/ 1 *adj.* stumm
2 *n.* Stumme, *der*/*die*
'muted *adj.* gedämpft
mutilate /'mjuːtɪleɪt/ *v.t.* verstümmeln
mutilation /mjuːtɪˈleɪʃn/ *n.*
Verstümmelung, *die*
mutinous /'mjuːtɪnəs/ *adj.* meuternd
mutiny /'mjuːtɪnɪ/ 1 *n.* Meuterei, *die*
2 *v.i.* meutern
mutter /'mʌtə(r)/ *v.i.* & *t.* murmeln
'muttering *n.* Gemurmel, *das*
mutton /'mʌtn/ *n.* Hammelfleisch, *das*
mutual /'mjuːtjʊəl/ *adj.* **(a)** gegenseitig
(b) (coll.: shared) gemeinsam
'mutually *adv.* **(a)** gegenseitig; be
~ **exclusive** sich [gegenseitig] ausschließen
(b) (in common) gemeinsam
muzak /'mjuːzæk/ *n.* (often derog.)
Hintergrundmusik, *die*
muzzle /'mʌzl/ 1 *n.* **(a)** (of dog) Schnauze,
die; (of horse, cattle) Maul, *das*
(b) (of gun) Mündung, *die*
(c) (put over animal's mouth) Maulkorb, *der*
2 *v.t.* **(a)** einen Maulkorb anlegen (+ *Dat.*)
⟨*Hund*⟩
(b) (fig.) mundtot machen (ugs.) (+ *Dat.*)
muzzy /'mʌzɪ/ *adj.* verschwommen; feel ~:
ein dumpfes Gefühl haben
MW *abbr.* (Radio) = **medium wave** MW

my /maɪ/ *poss. pron. attrib.* mein; **my**[**, my**]**!**,
[**my**] **oh my!** [ach du] meine Güte! (ugs.)
myalgic encephalomyelitis
/maɪˈældʒɪk ensefələʊmaɪəˈlaɪtɪs/ *n.* (Med.)
myalgische Enzephalomyelitis
myopia /maɪˈəʊpɪə/ *n.* Kurzsichtigkeit, *die*
(auch fig.)
myopic /maɪˈəʊpɪk/ *adj.* kurzsichtig (auch
fig.)
myself /maɪˈself/ *pron.* **(a)** *emphat.* selbst; I
thought so ~: das habe ich auch gedacht
(b) *refl.* mich/mir. *See also* HERSELF
mysterious /mɪˈstɪərɪəs/ *adj.* rätselhaft;
geheimnisvoll ⟨*Fremder, Orient*⟩
my'steriously *adv.* auf rätselhafte Weise;
geheimnisvoll ⟨*lächeln usw.*⟩
mystery /'mɪstərɪ/ *n.* **(a)** Rätsel, *das*
(b) (secrecy) Geheimnis, *das*
mystery: ~ **tour** *n.* Fahrt ins Blaue (ugs.);
~ **writer** Kriminalschriftsteller, *der*/
-schriftstellerin, *die*
mystic /'mɪstɪk/ 1 *adj.* mystisch
2 *n.* Mystiker, *der*/Mystikerin, *die*
mystical /'mɪstɪkl/ *adj.* mystisch
mysticism /'mɪstɪsɪzm/ *n.* Mystik, *die*
mystify /'mɪstɪfaɪ/ *v.t.* verwirren
myth /mɪθ/ *n.* Mythos, *der*
mythical /'mɪθɪkl/ *adj.* **(a)** (based on myth)
mythisch
(b) (invented) fiktiv
mythological /mɪθəˈlɒdʒɪkl/ *adj.*
mythologisch
mythology /mɪˈθɒlədʒɪ/ *n.* Mythologie, *die*

n

Nn

N, n /en/ *n.* N, n, *das*
N. *abbr.* **(a)** = **north** N
(b) = **northern** n.
NAAFI /'næfɪ/ *abbr.* (Brit.) **Navy, Army and
Air Force Institutes** *Kaufhaus für Angehörige
der britischen Truppen*
nab /næb/ *v.t.,* -bb- (coll.) **(a)** (arrest)
schnappen (ugs.)
(b) (seize) sich (*Dat.*) schnappen
nag /næg/ *v.i.* & *t.* -gg-: ~ [**at**] sb. an jmdm.
herumnörgeln; ~ [**at**] sb. to do sth. jmdm.
zusetzen (ugs.), dass er etw. tut
'nagging 1 *adj.* (persistent) quälend;
bohrend ⟨*Schmerz*⟩
2 *n.* Genörgel, *das*
nail /neɪl/ 1 *n.* Nagel, *der;* hit the ~ on the
head (fig.) den Nagel auf den Kopf treffen
(ugs.)
2 *v.t.* nageln (**to** an + *Akk.*)

■ **nail 'down** *v.t.* festnageln; zunageln
⟨*Kiste*⟩
nail: ~ **brush** *n.* Nagelbürste, *die;*
~ **clippers** *n. pl.* [pair of] ~ clippers
Nagelknipser, *der;* ~ **file** *n.* Nagelfeile, *die;*
~ **polish** *n.* Nagellack, *der;* ~ polish
remover Nagellackentferner, *der;*
~ **scissors** *n. pl.* [pair of] ~ scissors
Nagelschere, *die;* ~ **varnish** (Brit.)
▶ ~ POLISH
naive, naïve /naɪˈiːv/ *adj.,* **na'ively,
na'ïvely** *adv.* naiv
naked /'neɪkɪd/ *adj.* nackt; visible to *or*
with the ~ eye mit bloßem Auge zu
erkennen
'nakedness *n.* Nacktheit, *die*
name /neɪm/ 1 *n.* **(a)** Name, *der;* what's
your ~/the ~ of this place? wie heißt du/
dieser Ort?; my ~ is Jack ich heiße Jack;   ⋯

last ∼: Nachname, *der;* by ∼: namentlich ⟨*erwähnen, aufrufen usw.*⟩; know sb. by ∼: jmdn. mit Namen kennen

(b) (reputation) Ruf, *der;* make a ∼ for oneself sich (*Dat.*) einen Namen machen

(c) call sb. ∼s jmdn. beschimpfen

⟨2⟩ *v.t.* (a) (give ∼ to) einen Namen geben (+ *Dat.*); ∼ sb. John jmdn. John nennen; ∼ sb./sth. after *or* (Amer.) for sb. jmdn./etw. nach jmdm. benennen; be ∼d John John heißen; a man ∼d Smith ein Mann namens Smith

(b) (call by right ∼) benennen

(c) (nominate) ∼ sb. [as] sth. jmdn. zu etw. ernennen

'**name-drop** *v.i.* [scheinbar beiläufig] bekannte Namen fallen lassen

'**nameless** *adj.* namenlos

'**namely** *adv.* nämlich

'**namesake** *n.* Namensvetter, *der/* -schwester, *die*

nanny /'nænɪ/ *n.* (Brit.) Kindermädchen, *das*

nanny: ∼ **goat** *n.* Ziege, *die;* ∼ '**state** *n.* (derog.) Versorgungsstaat, *der*

nap /næp/ ⟨1⟩ *n.* Nickerchen, *das* (fam.); have a ∼: ein Nickerchen halten

⟨2⟩ *v.i.,* -pp- dösen (ugs.); catch sb. ∼ping (fig.) jmdn. überrumpeln

nape /neɪp/ *n.* ∼ [of the neck] Nacken, *der;* Genick, *das*

napkin /'næpkɪn/ *n.* Serviette, *die*

Naples /'neɪplz/ *pr. n.* Neapel (*das*)

nappy /'næpɪ/ *n.* (Brit.) Windel, *die*

narcissistic /nɑːsɪ'sɪstɪk/ *adj.* narzisstisch

narcissus /nɑː'sɪsəs/ *n., pl.* **narcissi** /nɑː'sɪsaɪ/ *or* ∼es Narzisse, *die*

narcotic /nɑː'kɒtɪk/ ⟨1⟩ *n.* (a) (drug) Rauschgift, *das*

(b) (active ingredient) Betäubungsmittel, *das*

⟨2⟩ *adj.* (a) narkotisch; ∼ **drug** Rauschgift, *das*

(b) (causing drowsiness) einschläfernd

narrate /nə'reɪt/ *v.t.* erzählen; kommentieren ⟨*Film*⟩

narration /nə'reɪʃn/ *n.* Erzählung, *die*

narrative /'nærətɪv/ ⟨1⟩ *n.* Erzählung, *die*

⟨2⟩ *adj.* erzählend

narrator /nə'reɪtə(r)/ *n.* Erzähler, *der/* Erzählerin, *die*

narrow /'nærəʊ/ ⟨1⟩ *adj.* (a) schmal; schmal geschnitten ⟨*Rock, Hose, Ärmel usw.*⟩; eng ⟨*Tal, Gasse*⟩

(b) (limited) eng; begrenzt ⟨*Auswahl*⟩

(c) knapp ⟨*Sieg, Mehrheit*⟩; have a ∼ escape mit knapper Not entkommen (from *Dat.*)

(d) (not tolerant) engstirnig

⟨2⟩ *v.i.* sich verschmälern; ⟨*Tal:*⟩ sich verengen

⟨3⟩ *v.t.* verschmälern; (fig.) einengen

■ **narrow 'down** *v.t.* einengen (to auf + *Akk.*)

narrow-'minded *adj.* engstirnig

nasal /'neɪzl/ *adj.* (a) (Anat.) Nasen-

(b) näselnd; speak in a ∼ voice näseln

nastily /'nɑːstɪlɪ/ *adv.* (a) (unpleasantly) scheußlich

(b) (ill-naturedly) gemein; behave ∼: hässlich sein

nasty /'nɑːstɪ/ *adj.* (a) (unpleasant) scheußlich ⟨*Geruch, Geschmack*⟩; gemein ⟨*Trick, Person*⟩; hässlich ⟨*Angewohnheit*⟩; that was a ∼ thing to say/do das war gemein

(b) (ill-natured) böse; be ∼ to sb. hässlich zu jmdm. sein

(c) (serious) übel; schlimm ⟨*Krankheit, Husten, Verletzung*⟩; she had a ∼ fall sie ist übel gefallen

nation /'neɪʃn/ *n.* Nation, *die;* (people) Volk, *das*

national /'næʃənl/ ⟨1⟩ *adj.* national; National⟨*flagge, -held, -theater, -gericht, -charakter*⟩; Staats⟨*sicherheit, -religion*⟩; überregional ⟨*Rundfunkstation, Zeitung*⟩; landesweit ⟨*Streik*⟩

⟨2⟩ *n.* (citizen) Staatsbürger, *der/*-bürgerin, *die;* foreign ∼: Ausländer, *der/*Ausländerin, *die*

national: ∼ '**anthem** *n.* Nationalhymne, *die;* ∼ **call** *n.* (Brit. Teleph.) Inlandsgespräch, *das;* ∼ '**costume** *n.* Nationaltracht, *die;* **N∼** '**Health [Service]** *n.* (Brit.) staatlicher Gesundheitsdienst; **N∼** Health doctor/patient/spectacles ≈ Kassenarzt, *der/* -patient, *der/*-brille, *die;* **N∼** In'surance *n.* (Brit.) Sozialversicherung, *die*

nationalism /'næʃənəlɪzm/ *n.* Nationalismus, *der*

nationalist /'næʃənəlɪst/ ⟨1⟩ *n.* Nationalist, *der/*Nationalistin, *die*

⟨2⟩ *adj.* nationalistisch

nationality /næʃə'nælɪtɪ/ *n.* Staatsangehörigkeit, *die;* what's his ∼? welche Staatsangehörigkeit hat er?

nationalization /næʃənəlaɪ'zeɪʃn/ *n.* Verstaatlichung, *die*

nationalize /'næʃənəlaɪz/ *v.t.* verstaatlichen

'**nationally** *adv.* landesweit

National: **n∼** '**park** *n.* Nationalpark, *der;* ∼ '**Savings** *n. pl.* (Brit.) Staatsschuldverschreibungen *Pl.;* ∼ Savings certificate Sparkassengutschein, *der;* öffentlicher Sparbrief; **n∼** '**service** *n.* (Brit.) Wehrdienst, *der;* do **n∼** service seinen Wehrdienst ableisten; ∼ '**Socialist** *n.* Nationalsozialist, *der/*-sozialistin, *die; attrib.* nationalsozialistisch; ∼ **Vo'cational Qualification** *n.* (Brit.) staatliches Berufsausbildungsprogramm

native /'neɪtɪv/ ⟨1⟩ *n.* (a) (of specified place) a ∼ of Britain ein gebürtiger Brite/eine gebürtige Britin

(b) (person born in a place) Eingeborene, *der/ die*

(c) (local inhabitant) Einheimische, *der/die*

⟨2⟩ *adj.* eingeboren; einheimisch ⟨*Pflanze, Tier*⟩; ∼ **inhabitant** Eingeborene/

Einheimische, *der/die;* ~ **land** Geburts- *od.*
Heimatland, *das;* ~ **language**
Muttersprache, *die*

nativity /nə'tɪvɪtɪ/ *n.* **the N~** [of Christ] die
Geburt Christi

na'tivity play *n.* Krippenspiel, *das*

NATO, Nato /'neɪtəʊ/ *abbr.* = **North
Atlantic Treaty Organization**
NATO, *die*

natter /'nætə(r)/ (Brit. coll.) ⊡ *v.i.* quatschen
(ugs.)
⊡ *n.* **have a ~:** quatschen (ugs.)

natural /'nætʃrəl/ *adj.* natürlich;
Natur⟨zustand, -seide, -gewalt⟩

natural: ~ **'childbirth** *n.* natürliche
Geburt; ~ **'gas** *n.* Erdgas, *das;*
~ **'history** *n.* Naturkunde, *die*

naturalism /'nætʃrəlɪzm/ *n.*
Naturalismus, *der*

naturalist /'nætʃrəlɪst/ *n.* Naturforscher,
der/-forscherin, *die*

naturalization /nætʃrəlaɪ'zeɪʃn/ *n.*
Einbürgerung, *die*

naturalize /'nætʃrəlaɪz/ *v.t.* einbürgern

'naturally *adv.* **(a)** (by nature) von Natur aus
⟨*blass, fleißig usw.*⟩; (in a true-to-life way)
naturgetreu
(b) (of course) natürlich

'naturalness *n.* Natürlichkeit, *die*

nature /'neɪtʃə(r)/ *n.* **(a)** Natur, *die*
(b) (essential qualities) Beschaffenheit, *die;* **in
the ~ of things** naturgemäß
(c) (kind) Art, *die;* **things of this ~:**
derartiges
(d) (character) Wesen, *das;* **be proud/friendly**
etc. **by ~:** ein stolzes/freundliches *usw.*
Wesen haben

nature: ~ **conservation** *n.*
Naturschutz, *der;* ~ **lover** *n.* Naturfreund,
der/-freundin, *die;* ~ **reserve** *n.*
Naturschutzgebiet, *das;* ~ **study** *n.*
Naturkunde, *die;* ~ **trail** *n.* Naturlehrpfad,
der

naturist /'neɪtʃərɪst/ *n.* (nudist) Naturist,
*der/*Naturistin, *die;* FKK-Anhänger, *der/*
FKK-Anhängerin, *die*

naught /nɔːt/ *n.* (arch./dial.) **come to ~:**
zunichte werden

naughtily /'nɔːtɪlɪ/ *adv.* ungezogen

naughtiness /'nɔːtɪnɪs/ *n.* Ungezogenheit,
die

naughty /'nɔːtɪ/ *adj.* ungezogen; **you
~ boy/dog** du böser Junge/Hund

nausea /'nɔːzɪə/ *n.* Übelkeit, *die*

nauseate /'nɔːzɪeɪt/ *v.t.* (disgust) anwidern

'nauseating *adj.* (disgusting) widerlich

nauseous /'nɔːzɪəs/ *adj.* **sb. is** *or* **feels ~:**
jmdm. ist übel

nautical /'nɔːtɪkl/ *adj.* nautisch

nautical 'mile *n.* Seemeile, *die*

naval /'neɪvl/ *adj.* Marine-; See⟨*schlacht,
-macht, -streitkräfte*⟩; ~ **ship** Kriegsschiff,
das

naval: ~ **base** *n.* Flottenstützpunkt, *der;*
~ **officer** *n.* Marineoffizier, *der*

nave /neɪv/ *n.* [Mittel]schiff, *das*

navel /'neɪvl/ *n.* Nabel, *der*

navigate /'nævɪgeɪt/ *v.t.* **(a)** navigieren
⟨*Schiff, Flugzeug*⟩
(b) befahren ⟨*Fluss usw.*⟩

navigation /nævɪ'geɪʃn/ *n.* Navigation, *die*

navigator /'nævɪgeɪtə(r)/ *n.* Navigator,
*der/*Navigatorin, *die*

navy /'neɪvɪ/ ⊡ *n.* **(a)** [Kriegs]marine, *die*
(b) ▶ NAVY BLUE
⊡ *adj.* ▶ NAVY-BLUE

navy: ~ **'blue** *n.* Marineblau, *das;*
~**-blue** *adj.* marineblau

Nazi /'nɑːtsɪ/ ⊡ *n.* Nazi, *der*
⊡ *adj.* nazistisch; Nazi-

NB *abbr.* = **nota bene** NB

NCO *abbr.* = **non-commissioned
officer** Uffz.

NE *abbr.* = **north-east** NO

near /nɪə(r)/ ⊡ *adv.* nah[e]; **stand/live
[quite] ~:** [ganz] in der Nähe stehen/
wohnen; **come** *or* **draw ~/~er** ⟨*Tag,
Zeitpunkt:*⟩ nahen/näher rücken; **get ~er
together** näher zusammenrücken; ~ **at hand**
in Reichweite (*Dat.*); ⟨*Ort:*⟩ ganz in der Nähe;
~ **to** = 2
⊡ *prep.* **(a)** (position) nahe an/bei (+ *Dat.*);
(fig.) in der Nähe (+ *Gen.*); **keep ~ me** halte
dich in meiner Nähe; **it's ~ here** es ist hier
in der Nähe
(b) (motion) nahe an (+ *Akk.*); (fig.) in der
Nähe (+ *Gen.*); **don't come ~ me** komm mir
nicht zu nahe
⊡ *adj.* **(a)** (in space or time) nahe; **in the
~ future** in nächster Zukunft; **the ~est man**
der am nächsten stehende Mann
(b) (in nature) **£30 or ~/~est offer** 30 Pfund
oder nächstbestes Angebot; ~ **escape**
Entkommen mit knapper Not; **that was a
~ miss/thing!** das war knapp!
⊡ *v.t.* sich nähern (+ *Dat.*); **the building is
~ing completion** das Gebäude steht kurz
vor seiner Vollendung
⊡ *v.i.* ⟨*Zeitpunkt:*⟩ näher rücken

'nearby *adj.* nahe gelegen

'nearly *adv.* fast; **be ~ in tears** den Tränen
nahe sein; **it is ~ six o'clock** es ist kurz vor
sechs Uhr; **are you ~ ready?** bist du bald
fertig?

'nearness *n.* Nähe, *die*

'near-sighted *adj.* (Amer.) kurzsichtig

neat /niːt/ *adj.* **(a)** (tidy) ordentlich
(b) (undiluted) pur
(c) (smart) gepflegt ⟨*Erscheinung, Kleidung*⟩
(d) (deft) geschickt

'neatly *adv.* ▶ NEAT A, C, D: ordentlich;
gepflegt; geschickt   ····∳

'neatness n. ▶ NEAT A, C, D: Ordentlichkeit, *die;* Gepflegtheit, *die;* Geschicktheit, *die*

necessarily /nesɪˈserɪlɪ/ adv. zwangsläufig; **it is not ~ true** es muss nicht [unbedingt] stimmen

necessary /ˈnesɪsərɪ/ ①️ adj. nötig; notwendig; **do everything ~:** das Nötige *od.* Notwendige tun
②️ n. **the necessaries of life** das Lebensnotwendige

necessitate /nɪˈsesɪteɪt/ v.t. erforderlich machen

necessity /nɪˈsesɪtɪ/ n. (a) (need, necessary thing) Notwendigkeit, *die;* **do sth. out of** *or* **from ~:** etw. notgedrungen tun; **of ~:** notwendigerweise
(b) (want) Not, *der*

neck /nek/ n. (a) Hals, *der;* **be a pain in the ~** (coll.) jmdm. auf die Nerven gehen (ugs.); **break one's ~** (fig. coll.) sich den Hals brechen; **~ and ~:** Kopf an Kopf
(b) (of garment) Kragen, *der*

neck: ~lace /ˈneklɪs/ n. [Hals]kette, *die;* (with jewels) Kollier, *das;* **~line** n. [Hals]ausschnitt, *der;* **~tie** n. Krawatte, *die*

nectar /ˈnektə(r)/ n. Nektar, *der*

née (*Amer.:* **nee**) /neɪ/ adj. geborene

need /niːd/ ①️ n. (a) Notwendigkeit, *die* (for, of Gen.); (demand) Bedarf, *der* (for, of an + Dat.); **as the ~ arises** nach Bedarf; **if ~ be** nötigenfalls; **there's no ~ for that** [das ist] nicht nötig; **there's no ~ to do sth.** es ist nicht nötig, etw. zu tun; **be in ~ of sth.** etw. brauchen; **there's no ~ for you to come** du brauchst nicht zu kommen
(b) *no pl.* (emergency) Not, *die;* **in case of ~:** im Notfall
(c) (thing) Bedürfnis, *das*
②️ v.t. (a) (require) brauchen; **sth. that urgently ~s doing** etw., was dringend gemacht werden muss; **it ~s a coat of paint** es muss gestrichen werden
(b) (expr. necessity) müssen; **I ~ to do it** ich muss es tun; **it ~s/doesn't ~ to be done** es muss getan werden/es braucht nicht getan zu werden
(c) pres. **he ~,** neg. **~ not** *or* (coll.) **~n't** /ˈniːdnt/ (expr. desirability) müssen; *with neg.* brauchen zu

needle /ˈniːdl/ ①️ n. Nadel, *die*
②️ v.t. (coll.) nerven (ugs.)

needle: ~cord n. (Textiles) Feinkord, *der;* **~craft** n. Nadelarbeit, *die*

needless /ˈniːdlɪs/ adj. unnötig; **~ to add** *or* **say,** …: überflüssig zu sagen, dass …

'needlessly adv. unnötig

'needlework n. Handarbeit, *die;* **do ~:** handarbeiten

needn't /ˈniːdnt/ (coll.) = need not; ▶ NEED 2C

'needy adj. notleidend; bedürftig

negation /nɪˈɡeɪʃn/ n. Verneinung, *die*

negative /ˈneɡətɪv/ ①️ adj. negativ
②️ n. (a) (Photog.) Negativ, *das*
(b) (~ statement) negative Aussage; (answer) Nein, *das*

negative 'equity n. Negativwert, *der*

'negatively adv. negativ

neglect /nɪˈɡlekt/ ①️ v.t. vernachlässigen; **she ~ed to write** sie hat es versäumt zu schreiben
②️ n. Vernachlässigung, *die;* **be in a state of ~** ⟨Gebäude:⟩ verwahrlost sein

neglectful /nɪˈɡlektfl/ adj. gleichgültig (of gegenüber); **be ~ of** sich nicht kümmern um

negligence /ˈneɡlɪdʒəns/ n. Nachlässigkeit, *die;* (Law, Insurance, etc.) Fahrlässigkeit, *die*

negligent /ˈneɡlɪdʒənt/ adj. nachlässig; **be ~ about sth.** sich um etw. nicht kümmern

negligible /ˈneɡlɪdʒɪbl/ adj. unerheblich

negotiable /nɪˈɡəʊʃəbl/ adj. (a) verhandlungsfähig ⟨Forderung, Bedingungen⟩
(b) passierbar ⟨Straße, Fluss⟩

negotiate /nɪˈɡəʊʃɪeɪt/ ①️ v.i. verhandeln (for, on, about über + Akk.)
②️ v.t. (a) (arrange) aushandeln
(b) überwinden ⟨Hindernis⟩; passieren ⟨Straße, Fluss⟩; nehmen ⟨Kurve⟩

negotiation /nɪɡəʊʃɪˈeɪʃn/ n. Verhandlung, *die*

negotiator /nɪˈɡəʊʃɪeɪtə(r)/ n. Unterhändler, *der*/-händlerin, *die*

Negress /ˈniːɡrɪs/ n. Negerin, *die*

Negro /ˈniːɡrəʊ/ ①️ n., pl. **~es** Neger, *der*
②️ adj. Neger-

neigh /neɪ/ ①️ v.i. wiehern
②️ n. Wiehern, *das*

neighbor etc. (Amer.) ▶ NEIGHBOUR etc.

neighbour /ˈneɪbə(r)/ ①️ n. Nachbar, *der*/Nachbarin, *die;* **my next-door ~s** meine Nachbarn von nebenan
②️ v.t. & i. **~ [upon]** grenzen an (+ Akk.)

'neighbourhood n. (district) Gegend, *die;* (neighbours) Nachbarschaft, *die;* [somewhere] **in the ~ of £100** [so] um [die] 100 Pfund

'neighbourhood watch n.: Programm für Verhütung von Straftaten, bes. von Wohnungseinbrüchen, durch erhöhte Wachsamkeit aller in einem Wohngebiet lebenden Menschen

'neighbouring adj. Nachbar-; angrenzend ⟨Felder⟩

neighbourly /ˈneɪbəlɪ/ adj. (a) (characteristic of neighbours) [gut]nachbarlich
(b) (friendly) freundlich

neither /ˈnaɪðə(r), ˈniːðə(r)/ ①️ adj. keiner/keine/keins der beiden
②️ pron. keiner/keine/keins von *od.* der beiden
③️ adv. (also not) auch nicht; **~ am I,** (coll.) **me ~:** ich auch nicht
④️ conj. (not either) weder; **~ … nor …:** weder … noch …

neo'classical adj. klassizistisch

neo'fascist *adj.* neofaszistisch

neon /'niːɒn/ *n.* Neon, *das*

neo-'nazi [1] *n.* Neonazi, *der*
[2] *adj.* neonazistisch; **a ~ group** eine
Neonazigruppe

neon: ~ **'lamp,** ~ **'light** *ns.* Neonlampe,
die; ~ **'sign** *n.* Neonreklame, *die*

nephew /'nevjuː, 'nefjuː/ *n.* Neffe, *der*

nepotism /'nepətɪzm/ *n.*
Vetternwirtschaft, *die*

Neptune /'neptjuːn/ *pr. n.* (Astron.) Neptun,
der

nerve /nɜːv/ *n.* Nerv, *der;* **get on sb.'s ~s**
jmdm. auf die Nerven gehen (ugs.); **lose
one's ~:** die Nerven verlieren; **what** [a] **~!**
[so eine] Frechheit!

nerve: ~ **cell** *n.* Nervenzelle, *die;*
~ **centre** *n.* (fig.) Schaltzentrale, *die;*
~ **gas** *n.* Nervengas, *das;* ~**-racking** *adj.*
nervenaufreibend

nervous /'nɜːvəs/ *adj.* **(a)** (Anat., Med.)
Nerven-; ~ **breakdown**
Nervenzusammenbruch, *der*
(b) (having delicate nerves) nervös; **be a
~ wreck** mit den Nerven völlig am Ende
sein
(c) (Brit.: timid) **be ~ of** *or* **about** Angst haben
vor (+ *Dat.*); **be a ~ person** ängstlich sein

'nervously *adv.* nervös

'nervousness *n.* Ängstlichkeit, *die*

nervy /'nɜːvɪ/ *adj.* **(a)** nervös
(b) (Amer. coll.: impudent) unverschämt

nest [1] *n.* Nest, *das*
[2] *v.i.* nisten

'nest egg *n.* (fig.) Notgroschen, *der*

nestle /'nesl/ *v.i.* **(a)** sich schmiegen **(to, up
against** an + *Akk.*)
(b) (lie half hidden) eingebettet sein

net¹ /net/ [1] *n.* **(a)** Netz, *das*
(b) the Net (Comp.) das Netz
[2] *v.t.,* **-tt-** [mit einem Netz] fangen

net² *adj.* **(a)** netto; Netto‹*einkommen,*
-[verkaufs]preis usw.›; ~ **weight**
Nettogewicht, *das*
(b) (ultimate) End‹*ergebnis, -effekt*›

net: ~**ball** *n.* Netzball, *der;* ~ **'curtain** *n.*
Store, *der*

Netherlands /'neðələndz/ *pr. n. sing. or
pl.* Niederlande *Pl.*

net 'profit *n.* Reingewinn, *der*

'netspeak *n.* Internetjargon, *der*

nett ▶ NET² A

'netting *n.* ([piece of] net) Netz, *das;* **wire ~:**
Maschendraht, *der*

nettle /'netl/ *n.* Nessel, *die*

'network *n.* Netz, *das;* (Comp.) Netzwerk,
das

'network provider *n.* (Comp)
Netzanbieter, *der*

neuralgia /njʊəˈrældʒə/ *n.* Neuralgie, *die*

neurological /njʊərəˈlɒdʒɪkl/ *adj.*
neurologisch

neurologist /njʊəˈrɒlədʒɪst/ *n.* Neurologe,
der/Neurologin, *die*

neurology /njʊəˈrɒlədʒɪ/ *n.* Neurologie, *die*

neurosis /njʊəˈrəʊsɪs/ *n., pl.* **neuroses**
/njʊəˈrəʊsiːz/ Neurose, *die*

neurotic /njʊəˈrɒtɪk/ *adj.* **(a)** nervenkrank
(b) (coll.) neurotisch

neuter /'njuːtə(r)/ *adj.* sächlich

neutral /'njuːtrl/ [1] *adj.* neutral
[2] *n.* (~ gear) Leerlauf, *der*

neutrality /njuːˈtrælɪtɪ/ *n.* Neutralität, *die*

neutralize /'njuːtrəlaɪz/ *v.t.* neutralisieren

neutron /'njuːtrɒn/ *n.* Neutron, *das*

never /'nevə(r)/ *adv.* **(a)** nie; ~**-ending**
endlos
(b) (coll.) **you ~ believed that, did you?** du
hast das doch wohl nicht geglaubt?; **well, I
~** [did]! [na] so was!

neverthe'less *adv.* trotzdem

new /njuː/ *adj.* neu

new: New Age *n.* Newage, *das; attrib.*
Newage-; ~**-born** *adj.* neugeboren;
~**comer** /'njuːkʌmə(r)/ *n.*
Neuankömmling, *der;* ~**fangled**
/'njuːfæŋgld/ *adj.* neumodisch; ~**found**
adj. neu; ~**-laid** *adj.* frisch [gelegt]; **New
'Left** *n.* neue Linke; ~ **'look** *n.* (coll.)
neuer Stil

'newly *adv.* (recently) neu; ~ **married** seit
kurzem verheiratet

'newly-wed *n.* Jungverheiratete, *der*/*die*

new: New 'Man *n.* der neue Mann;
~ **'moon** *n.* Neumond, *der*

'newness *n.* Neuheit, *die*

news /njuːz/ *n.* **(a)** Nachricht, *die;* **be in the
~:** Schlagzeilen machen; **good/bad ~:**
schlechte/gute Nachrichten *Pl.*
(b) (Radio, Telev.) Nachrichten *Pl.*

news: ~ **agency** *n.* Nachrichtenagentur,
die; ~**agent** *n.* Zeitungshändler, *der*/
-händlerin, *die;* ~ **bulletin** *n.* Nachrichten
Pl.; ~**cast** *n.* Nachrichtensendung, *die;*
~**caster** *n.* Nachrichtensprecher, *der*/
-sprecherin, *die;* ~ **desk** *n.*
Nachrichtenredaktion, *die;* **this is Joe Smith
at the ~ desk** (Radio) hier ist Joe Smith mit
den Nachrichten; ~**flash** *n.* Kurzmeldung,
die; ~**group** *n.* (Comp.) Newsgroup, *die;*
~ **'headline** *n.* Schlagzeile, *die;* ~**letter**
n. Rundschreiben, *das;* ~**paper** *n.* **(a)**
Zeitung, *die;* ~**paper boy/girl**
Zeitungsausträger, *der*/-austrägerin, *die;* **(b)**
(material) Zeitungspapier, *das;* ~**reader** *n.*
Nachrichtensprecher, *der*/-sprecherin, *die;*
~**reel** *n.* Wochenschau, *die;* ~**room** *n.*
Nachrichtenredaktion, *die;* ~**sheet** *n.*
Informationsblatt, *das;* ~**stand** *n.*
Zeitungskiosk, *der;* Zeitungsstand, *der;*
~ **summary** *n.* Kurznachrichten *Pl.;*
~ **vendor** *n.* Zeitungsverkäufer, *der*/
-verkäuferin, *die;* ~**worthy** *adj.* [für die
Medien] interessant

newt /njuːt/ *n.* [Wasser]molch, *der*

New: new town n.: mit Unterstützung der Regierung völlig neu entstandene Ansiedlung; **new 'year** n. Neujahr, das; over the new year über Neujahr; **a Happy New Year** ein glückliches od. gutes neues Jahr; ~ **'Year's** (Amer.), ~ **Year's 'Day** ns. Neujahrstag, der; ~ **Year's 'Eve** n. Silvester, der od. das; ~ **Zealand** /-'ziːlənd/ pr. n. Neuseeland (das); ~ **'Zealander** n. Neuseeländer, der /-länderin, die

next /nekst/ **1** adj. nächst...; the ~ but one der/die/das Übernächste; ~ **to** (fig.: almost) fast; nahezu; [the] ~ time das nächste Mal; the ~ best der/die/das Nächstbeste; am I ~? komme ich jetzt dran?

2 adv. (in the ~ place) als Nächstes; (on the ~ occasion) das nächste Mal; it's my turn ~: ich komme als Nächster dran; sit/stand ~ to sb. neben jmdm. stehen/sitzen; place sth. ~ to sb./sth. etw. neben jmdn./etw. stellen

3 n. (a) the week after ~: [die] übernächste Woche

(b) (person) ~ of kin nächster/nächste Angehörige; ~, please! der Nächste, bitte!

'next-door adj. gleich nebenan nachgestellt

NHS abbr. (Brit.) = **National Health Service**

nib /nɪb/ n. Feder, die

nibble /'nɪbl/ v.t. & i. knabbern (at, on an + Dat.)

nice /naɪs/ adj. nett; angenehm ‹Stimme›; schön ‹Wetter›; (iron.: disgraceful, difficult) schön; ~ [and] warm/fast schön warm/schnell; ~-looking gut aussehend

'nicely adv. (coll.) (a) (well) nett; gut ‹arbeiten, sich benehmen, platziert sein› (b) (all right) gut; that will do ~: das reicht völlig

niceties /'naɪsɪtɪz/ n. pl. Feinheiten Pl.

niche /nɪtʃ, niːʃ/ n. (a) (in wall) Nische, die (b) (fig.: suitable place) Platz, der

nick /nɪk/ n. (a) (notch) Kerbe, die (b) (sl. prison) Knast, der (salopp) (c) (Brit.: police station) Wache, die (d) in good/poor ~ (coll.) gut/nicht gut im Schuss (ugs.) (e) in the ~ of time gerade noch rechtzeitig

2 v.t. (a) einkerben (b) (Brit. coll.: arrest) einlochen (salopp) (c) (Brit. coll.: steal) klauen (salopp)

nickel /'nɪkl/ n. (a) Nickel, das (b) (Amer. coll.: coin) Fünfcentstück, das

nickname /'nɪkneɪm/ n. Spitzname, der; (affectionate) Koseform, die

nicotine /'nɪkətiːn/ n. Nikotin, das

'nicotine patch n. Nikotinpflaster, das

niece /niːs/ n. Nichte, die

Nigeria /naɪ'dʒɪərɪə/ pr. n. Nigeria (das)

niggardly /'nɪgədlɪ/ adj. knaus[e]rig (ugs.)

niggling /'nɪglɪŋ/ adj. (a) (petty) belanglos (b) (trivial) nichts sagend (c) (nagging) nagend

night /naɪt/ n. Nacht, die; (evening) Abend, der; the following ~: die Nacht/der Abend darauf; the previous ~: die vorausgegangene Nacht/der vorausgegangene Abend; on Sunday ~: Sonntagnacht/[am] Sonntagabend; for the ~: über Nacht; at ~: nachts/abends; late at ~: spätabends

night: ~bird n. (person) Nachteule, die (ugs. scherzh.); ~ **blindness** n. Nachtblindheit, die; ~**cap** n. (drink) Schlaftrunk, der; ~**clothes** n. pl. Nachtwäsche, die; ~**club** n. Nachtklub, der; ~**dress** n. Nachthemd, das; ~ **duty** n. Nachtdienst, der; be on ~ duty Nachtdienst haben; ~**fall** n. Einbruch der Dunkelheit

nightie /'naɪtɪ/ n. (coll.) Nachthemd, das

nightingale /'naɪtɪŋgeɪl/ n. Nachtigall, die

'nightlife n. Nachtleben, das

nightly /'naɪtlɪ/ **1** adj. (happening every night/evening) allnächtlich/allabendlich

2 adv. (every night) jede Nacht; (every evening) jeden Abend

night: ~mare n. Albtraum, der; ~**marish** /'naɪtmeərɪʃ/ adj. albtraumhaft; ~ **owl** n. (a) (Ornith.) Eule, die; (b) (coll.: person) Nachteule, die (ugs. scherzh.); ~ **porter** n. Nachtportier, der; ~ **safe** n. Nachttresor, der; ~ **school** n. Abendschule, die; ~ **shelter** n. Nachtasyl, das; ~ **shift** n. Nachtschicht, die; ~ **'sky** n. Nachthimmel, der; ~ **'storage heater** n. Nachtspeicherofen, der; ~**time** n. Nacht, die; in the or at ~-time nachts; ~**'watchman** n. Nachtwächter, der; ~**wear** n. sing. ▶ NIGHTCLOTHES

nihilistic /naɪɪ'lɪstɪk, nɪhɪ'lɪstɪk/ adj. nihilistisch

nil /nɪl/ n. null

Nile /naɪl/ pr. n. Nil, der

nimble /'nɪmbl/ adj., **nimbly** /'nɪmblɪ/ adv. flink

nine /naɪn/ **1** adj. neun

2 n. Neun, die. See also EIGHT

nineteen /naɪn'tiːn/ **1** adj. neunzehn

2 n. Neunzehn, die. See also EIGHT

nineteenth /naɪn'tiːnθ/ **1** adj. neunzehnt...

2 n. (fraction) Neunzehntel, das. See also EIGHTH

ninetieth /'naɪntɪɪθ/ adj. neunzigst...

ninety /'naɪntɪ/ **1** adj. neunzig

2 n. Neunzig, die. See also EIGHT; EIGHTY 2

ninth /naɪnθ/ **1** adj. neunt...

2 n. (in sequence, rank) Neunte, der/die/das; (fraction) Neuntel, das. See also EIGHTH

nip **1** v.t., -pp- zwicken

2 v.i., -pp- (Brit. coll.) ~ in hinein-/hereinflitzen (ugs.); ~ out hinaus-/herausflitzen (ugs.)

3 n. (pinch, squeeze) Kniff, der; (bite) Biss, der

'nipper n. (Brit. coll.: child) Balg, das (ugs.)

nipple /'nɪpl/ n. (a) Brustwarze, die (b) (of feeding bottle) Sauger, der

nitrate /'naɪtreɪt/ *n.* **(a)** (salt) Nitrat, *das*
(b) (fertilizer) Nitratdünger, *der*

nitric acid /'naɪtrɪk æsɪd/ *n.*
Salpetersäure, *die*

nitrogen /'naɪtrədʒən/ *n.* Stickstoff, *der*

'nitrogen cycle *n.* Stickstoffkreislauf, *der*

nitwit /'nɪtwɪt/ *n.* (coll.) Trottel, *der* (ugs.)

no /nəʊ/ **①** *adj.* kein
② *adv.* **(a)** (by no amount) nicht; **no less
[than]** nicht weniger [als]; **no more wine?**
keinen Wein mehr?
(b) (as answer) nein
③ *n.*, *pl.* **noes** /nəʊz/ Nein, *das*

No. *abbr.* = **number** Nr.

Noah's ark /nəʊəz 'ɑːk/ *n.* die Arche Noah

Nobel prize /nəʊbel 'praɪz/ *n.* Nobelpreis,
der

nobility /nə'bɪlɪtɪ/ *n.* Adel, *der;* **many of the
∼:** viele Adlige

noble /'nəʊbl/ **①** *adj.* ad[e]lig; edel
⟨Gedanken, Gefühle⟩
② *n.* Adlige, *der/die*

nobleman /'nəʊblmən/ *n.*, *pl.* **noblemen**
/'nəʊblmən/ Adlige, *der*

nobly /'nəʊblɪ/ *adv.* **(a)** edel [gesinnt]
(b) (generously) edelmütig (geh.)

nobody /'nəʊbədɪ/ *n.* & *pron.* niemand;
keiner; (person of no importance) Niemand, *der*

no-'claim[s] bonus *n.* (Insurance)
Schadenfreiheitsrabatt, *der*

nocturnal /nɒk'tɜːnl/ *adj.* nächtlich;
∼ animal/bird Nachttier, *das/*-vogel, *der*

nod /nɒd/ **①** *v.i.*, **-dd-** nicken
② *v.t.*, **-dd-:** **∼ one's head [in greeting]** [zum
Gruß] mit dem Kopf nicken
③ *n.* [Kopf]nicken, *das*
■ **nod 'off** *v.i.* einnicken (ugs.)

nodule /'nɒdjuːl/ *n.* **(a)** Klümpchen, *das*
(b) (Bot.) Knötchen, *das*

no-'fly zone *n.* Flugverbotszone, *die*

no-'go *adj.* Sperr⟨gebiet, -zone⟩

'no-good *adj.* (coll.) nichtsnutzig (abwertend)

no-hoper /nəʊ'həʊpə(r)/ *n.* absoluter
Außenseiter; **be a ∼:** keine Chance haben

nohow /'nəʊhaʊ/ *adv.* (Amer. coll.) in keiner
Weise

noise /nɔɪz/ *n.* Geräusch, *das;* (loud, harsh,
unwanted) Lärm, *der*

'noise abatement *n.* Lärmbekämpfung,
die

'noiseless *adj.*, **'noiselessly** *adv.*
lautlos

noise: ∼ level *n.* Geräuschpegel, *der;* (of
unpleasant noise) Lärmpegel, *der;*
∼ pollution *n.* Lärmbelästigung, *die*

noisily /'nɔɪzɪlɪ/ *adv.*, **noisy** /'nɔɪzɪ/ *adj.*
laut

nomad /'nəʊmæd/ *n.* Nomade, *der*

nomadic /nəʊ'mædɪk/ *adj.* nomadisch;
∼ tribe Nomadenstamm, *der*

'no man's land *n.* Niemandsland, *das*

nominal /'nɒmɪnl/ *adj.* **(a)** (in name only)
nominell
(b) (virtually nothing) äußerst gering

nominally /'nɒmɪnəlɪ/ *adv.* namentlich

nominate /'nɒmɪneɪt/ *v.t.* **(a)** (propose)
nominieren
(b) (appoint) ernennen

nomination /nɒmɪ'neɪʃn/ *n.* ▶ NOMINATE:
Nominierung, *die;* Ernennung, *die*

nominative /'nɒmɪnətɪv/ *adj.* & *n.*
∼ [case] Nominativ, *der*

nominee /nɒmɪ'niː/ *n.* (candidate) Kandidat,
*der/*Kandidatin, *die*

non- /nɒn/ *pref.* nicht-

non-alco'holic *adj.* alkoholfrei

nonchalant /'nɒnʃələnt/ *adj.*
unbekümmert

non-commissioned 'officer *n.*
Unteroffizier, *der*

non-committal /nɒnkə'mɪtl/ *adj.*
unverbindlich; **he was ∼:** er hat sich nicht
klar geäußert

noncon'formist *n.* Nonkonformist, *der/*
Nonkonformistin, *die*

non-con'tributory *adj.* beitragsfrei

nondescript /'nɒndɪskrɪpt/ *adj.*
unscheinbar; undefinierbar ⟨Farbe⟩

'non-drip *adj.* nicht tropfend ⟨Farbe⟩

non-'driver *n.* Nicht[auto]fahrer, *der*

none /nʌn/ **①** *pron.* kein...; **∼ of them**
keiner/keine/keines von ihnen; **∼ of this**
nichts davon
② *adv.* keineswegs; **I'm ∼ the wiser now**
jetzt bin ich um nichts klüger; **∼ the less**
nichtsdestoweniger

nonentity /nɒ'nentɪtɪ/ *n.* Nichts, *das*

non-existent /nɒnɪg'zɪstənt/ *adj.* nicht
vorhanden

non-'fiction *n.* Sachliteratur, *die*

non-'iron *adj.* bügelfrei

non-'member *n.* Nichtmitglied, *das*

'no-no *n.*, *pl.* **∼es** (coll.) **be a ∼:** nicht
infrage kommen (ugs.)

non-'payment *n.* Nichtzahlung, *die*

nonplus /nɒn'plʌs/ *v.t.*, **-ss-** verblüffen

non-'profit[-making] *adj.* nicht auf
Gewinn ausgerichtet

non-prolife'ration *n.* Nichtverbreitung
von Atomwaffen; **∼ treaty**
Atom[waffen]sperrvertrag, *der*

non-re'cyclable *adj.* nicht recycelbar

non-'resident *n.* (outside a country)
Nichtansässige, *der/die;* **the bar is open to
∼s** die Bar ist auch für Gäste geöffnet, die
nicht im Hotel wohnen

nonsense /'nɒnsəns/ **①** *n.* Unsinn, *der*
② *int.* Unsinn

nonsensical /nɒn'sensɪkl/ *adj.* unsinnig

non sequitur /nɒn 'sekwɪtə(r)/ *n.*
unlogische Folgerung

non-'smoker n. (a) (person) Nichtraucher, *der/*-raucherin, *die*
(b) (train compartment) Nichtraucherabteil, *das*
non-'starter n. (fig. coll.) Reinfall, *der* (ugs.)
non-'stick adj. ~ frying pan *etc.* Bratpfanne *usw.* mit Antihaftbeschichtung
non-stop [1] /'--/ adj. durchgehend ⟨Zug, Busverbindung⟩; Nonstop⟨flug, -revue⟩
[2] /-'-/ adv. ohne Unterbrechung ⟨tanzen, reden, reisen, senden⟩⟩; nonstop ⟨fliegen, tanzen, fahren⟩
'non-toxic adj. ungiftig
noodle /'nu:dl/ n., usu. pl. Nudel, *die*
nook /nʊk/ n. Winkel, *der;* Ecke, *die*
noon /nu:n/ n. Mittag, *der;* zwölf Uhr [mittags]; at/before ~: um/vor zwölf [Uhr mittags]
'no one pron. ▸ NOBODY
noose /nu:s/ n. Schlinge, *die*
nor /nɔː(r), stressed nɔː(r)/ conj. noch; **neither/not ... ~ ...:** weder ... noch ...
norm /nɔːm/ n. Norm, *die*
normal /'nɔːml/ [1] adj. normal
[2] n. (a) (~ value) Normalwert, *der* (b) (usual state) normaler Stand; **everything is back to** or **has returned to** ~: es hat sich wieder alles normalisiert
normality /nɔː'mælɪtɪ/ Normalität, *die*
'normally adv. (a) (in normal way) normal (b) (ordinarily) normalerweise
north /nɔːθ/ [1] n. (a) Norden, *der;* in/to[wards]/from the ~: im/nach/von Norden; **to the ~ of** nördlich von (b) usu. N~ (Geog., Polit.) Norden, *der*
[2] adj. nördlich; Nord⟨wind, -küste, -grenze⟩
[3] adv. nach Norden; ~ **of** nördlich von
north: N~ **'Africa** pr. n. Nordafrika (das); N~ **A'merica** pr. n. Nordamerika (das); N~ **A'merican** [1] adj. nordamerikanisch; [2] n. Nordamerikaner, *der/*-amerikanerin, *die;* ~**bound** adj. ⟨Zug, Verkehr usw.⟩ in Richtung Norden; ~-**'east** [1] n. Nordosten, *der;* [2] adj. nordöstlich; Nordost⟨wind, -küste⟩; [3] adv. nordostwärts; nach Nordosten; ~-**'eastern** adj. nordöstlich
northerly /'nɔːðəlɪ/ adj. nördlich; ⟨Wind⟩ aus nördlichen Richtungen
northern /'nɔːðən/ adj. nördlich; Nord⟨grenze, -hälfte, -seite⟩
northern: N~ **'Ireland** pr. n. Nordirland (das); ~ **'lights** n. pl. Nordlicht, *das*
North: ~ **'Germany** pr. n. Norddeutschland (das); ~ **'Pole** pr. n. Nordpol, *der;* ~ **'Sea** pr. n. Nordsee, *die*
northward[s] /'nɔːθwəd(z)/ adv. nordwärts
north: ~-**'west** [1] n. Nordwesten, *der;* [2] adj. nordwestlich; Nordwest⟨wind, -küste⟩; [3] adv. nordwestwärts; nach Nordwesten; ~-**'western** adj. nordwestlich
Norway /'nɔːweɪ/ pr. n. Norwegen (das)
Norwegian /nɔː'wiːdʒn/ [1] adj. norwegisch; **sb. is** ~: jmd. ist Norweger/Norwegerin

[2] n. (a) (person) Norweger, *der/*Norwegerin, *die*
(b) (language) Norwegisch, *das; see also* ENGLISH 2A
Nos. abbr. = **numbers** Nrn.
nose /nəʊz/ [1] n. Nase, *die*
[2] v.t. ~ **one's way** sich (Dat.) vorsichtig seinen Weg bahnen
[3] v.i. sich vorsichtig bewegen
■ **nose a'bout, nose a'round** v.i. (coll.) herumschnüffeln (ugs.)
nose: ~**bleed** n. Nasenbluten, *das;* ~**dive** [1] n. Sturzflug, *der;* [2] v.i. im Sturzflug hinuntergehen
nosey ▸ NOSY
nostalgia /nɒ'stældʒə/ n. Nostalgie, *die;* ~ **for sth.** Sehnsucht nach etw.
nostalgic /nɒ'stældʒɪk/ adj. nostalgisch
nostril /'nɒstrɪl/ n. Nasenloch, *das;* (of horse) Nüster, *die*
nosy /'nəʊzɪ/ adj. (coll.) neugierig
not /nɒt/ adv. nicht; **he is** ~ **a doctor** er ist kein Arzt; ~ **at all** überhaupt nicht; ~ **... but** ...: nicht ..., sondern ...; ~ **a thing** gar nichts
notable /'nəʊtəbl/ adj. bemerkenswert; **be** ~ **for sth.** für etw. bekannt sein
notably /'nəʊtəblɪ/ adv. besonders
notation /nəʊ'teɪʃn/ n. Notierung, *die*
notch /nɒtʃ/ [1] n. Kerbe, *die*
[2] v.t. kerben
■ **notch 'up** v.t. erreichen
note /nəʊt/ [1] n. (a) (Mus.) (sign) Note, *die;* (key of piano) Taste, *die;* (sound) Ton, *der* (b) (jotting) Notiz, *die;* **take** or **make** ~**s** sich (Dat.) Notizen machen; **take** or **make a** ~ **of sth.** sich (Dat.) etw. notieren (c) (comment, footnote) Anmerkung, *die* (d) (short letter) [kurzer] Brief (e) (importance) **a person/something of** ~: eine bedeutende Persönlichkeit/etwas Bedeutendes; **be of** ~: bedeutend sein
[2] v.t. (a) (pay attention to) beachten (b) (notice) bemerken (c) (write) ~ **[down]** [sich (Dat.)] notieren
'notebook n. (a) Notizbuch, *das;* (for lecture notes) Kollegheft, *das*
(b) ~**book [computer]** Notebook, *das*
'noted adj. bekannt (**for** für, wegen)
note: ~**pad** n. Notizblock, *der;* ~**paper** n. Briefpapier, *das;* ~**worthy** adj. bemerkenswert
nothing /'nʌθɪŋ/ n. nichts; ~ **interesting** nichts Interessantes; ~ **much** nichts Besonderes; ~ **more than** nur; ~ **more,** ~ **less** nicht mehr, nicht weniger; **next to** ~: so gut wie nichts; **have [got]** or **be** ~ **to do with sb./sth.** (not concern) nichts zu tun haben mit jmdm./etw.; **have** ~ **to do with sb.** (avoid) jmdm. aus dem Weg gehen
notice /'nəʊtɪs/ [1] n. (a) Anschlag, *der;* (in newspaper) Anzeige, *die*

(b) (warning) **at short/a moment's ∼:** kurzfristig/von einem Augenblick zum andern
(c) (formal notification) Ankündigung, *die;* **until further ∼:** bis auf weiteres
(d) (ending an agreement) Kündigung, *die;* **give sb. a month's ∼:** jmdm. mit einer Frist von einem Monat kündigen; **hand in one's ∼, give ∼** (Brit.), **give one's ∼** (Amer.) kündigen
(e) (attention) **bring sb. to sb.'s ∼:** jmdn. auf jmdn./etw. aufmerksam machen; **take no ∼ of sb./sth.** (disregard) keine Notiz von jmdm./etw. nehmen; **take no ∼:** sich nicht darum kümmern
② *v.t.* bemerken
noticeable /'nəʊtɪsəbl/ *adj.* wahrnehmbar ⟨*Fleck, Schaden, Geruch*⟩; merklich ⟨*Verbesserung*⟩; spürbar ⟨*Mangel*⟩
noticeably /'nəʊtɪsəblɪ/ *adv.* sichtlich ⟨*größer, kleiner*⟩; merklich ⟨*verändern*⟩; spürbar ⟨*kälter*⟩
'noticeboard *n.* (Brit.) Anschlagbrett, *das;* schwarzes Brett
notifiable /'nəʊtɪfaɪəbl/ *adj.* meldepflichtig ⟨*Krankheit*⟩
notification /nəʊtɪfɪ'keɪʃn/ *n.* Mitteilung, *die* (of sth. über etw. [*Akk.*])
notify /'nəʊtɪfaɪ/ *v.t.* **(a)** (make known) ankündigen
(b) (inform) benachrichtigen (of über + *Akk.*)
notion /'nəʊʃn/ *n.* Vorstellung, *die;* **not have the faintest/least ∼ of how/what** *etc.* nicht die blasseste/geringste Ahnung haben, wie/was *usw.*
notoriety /nəʊtə'raɪətɪ/ *n.* traurige Berühmtheit
notorious /nə'tɔːrɪəs/ *adj.* berüchtigt (**for** wegen); notorisch ⟨*Lügner*⟩
nougat /'nuːgɑː/ *n.* Nougat, *das od. der*
nought /nɔːt/ *n.* Null, *die*
noun /naʊn/ *n.* (Ling.) Substantiv, *das*
nourish /'nʌrɪʃ/ *v.t.* ernähren (**on** mit)
'nourishing *adj.* nahrhaft
'nourishment *n.* Nahrung, *die*
Nov. *abbr.* = **November** Nov.
novel /'nɒvl/ **①** *n.* Roman, *der*
② *adj.* neuartig
novelist /'nɒvəlɪst/ *n.* Romanautor, *der*/-autorin, *die*
novella /nə'velə/ *n.* Novelle, *die*
novelty /'nɒvltɪ/ *n.* **(a) be a/no ∼:** etwas/nichts Neues sein
(b) (newness) Neuheit, *die*
(c) (gadget) Überraschung, *die*
November /nə'vembə(r)/ *n.* November, *der; see also* Augus т
novice /'nɒvɪs/ *n.* Anfänger, *der*/Anfängerin, *die*
now /naʊ/ **①** *adv.* jetzt; (nowadays) heutzutage; (immediately) [jetzt] sofort; **just ∼** (very recently) gerade eben; **[every] ∼ and then** *or* **again** hin und wieder; **well ∼:** also; **∼, ∼:** na, na; **∼ then** na (ugs.)

② *conj.* **∼ [that]** …: jetzt, wo …
③ *n.* **before ∼:** früher; **by ∼:** inzwischen; **a week from ∼:** [heute] in einer Woche
nowadays /'naʊədeɪz/ *adv.* heutzutage
nowhere /'nəʊweə(r)/ *adv.* nirgends; nirgendwo; (to no place) nirgendwohin
no-'win *attrib. adj.* Verlierer-
noxious /'nɒkʃəs/ *adj.* giftig
nozzle /'nɒzl/ *n.* Düse, *die*
nuance /'njuːɑ̃s/ *n.* Nuance, *die*
nuclear /'njuːklɪə(r)/ *adj.* Atom-; Kern⟨explosion⟩; atomar ⟨Antrieb, Gefechtskopf, Wettrüsten, Abrüstung⟩; nuklear ⟨Sprengkörper⟩; atomgetrieben ⟨Unterseeboot⟩
nuclear: ∼ 'bomb *n.* Atombombe, *die;* **∼ capa'bility** *n.* nukleares Potenzial; **a missile with ∼ capability** eine nuklearfähige Rakete; **have ∼ capability** nuklearfähig sein; **∼ de'terrent** *n.* atomare od. nukleare Abschreckung; **∼ 'energy** *n.* Atom- od. Kernenergie, *die;* **∼ 'family** *n.* Kernfamilie, *die;* **∼-free** *adj.* atomwaffenfrei ⟨Zone⟩; **∼ 'fuel** *n.* Kernbrennstoff, *der;* **∼ 'physics** *n.* Kernphysik, *die;* **∼ 'power** *n.* **(a)** Atom- od. Kernkraft, *die;* **(b)** (country) Atom- od. Nuklearmacht, *die;* **∼-'powered** *adj.* atomgetrieben; **∼ 'power station** *n.* Atom- od. Kernkraftwerk, *das;* **∼ 'test** *n.* Atom[waffen]test, *der;* **∼ 'testing** *n.* Atomversuche *Pl.;* **∼ 'warfare** *n.* Atomkrieg, *der;* **∼ 'waste** *n.* Atommüll, *der*
nucleus /'njuːklɪəs/ *n., pl.* **nuclei** /'njuːklɪaɪ/ Kern, *der*
nude /njuːd/ **①** *adj.* nackt
② *n.* **(a)** (figure) Akt, *der*
(b) in the ∼: nackt
nudge /nʌdʒ/ **①** *v.t.* anstoßen
② *n.* Stoß, *der*
nudism /'njuːdɪzm/ *n.* Nudismus, *der;* Freikörperkultur, *die*
nudist /'njuːdɪst/ *n.* Nudist, *der*/Nudistin, *die; attrib.* Nudisten-
nudity /'njuːdɪtɪ/ *n.* Nacktheit, *die*
nugget /'nʌgɪt/ *n.* Klumpen, *der;* (of gold) Goldklumpen, *der;* (fig.) **∼s of wisdom** goldene Weisheiten
nuisance /'njuːsəns/ *n.* Ärgernis, *das;* **what a ∼!** so etwas Dummes!
null /nʌl/ *adj.* **∼ and void** null und nichtig
numb /nʌm/ **①** *adj.* gefühllos, taub (**with** vor + *Dat.*); (without emotion) benommen
② *v.t.* betäuben
number /'nʌmbə(r)/ **①** *n.* **(a)** (in series) Nummer, *die;* **you've got the wrong ∼** (Teleph.) Sie sind falsch verbunden; **dial a wrong ∼:** sich verwählen (ugs.)
(b) (esp. Math.: numeral) Zahl, *die*
(c) (sum, total, quantity) [An]zahl, *die;* **a ∼ of people/things** einige Leute/Dinge; **a ∼ of times** mehrmals ····❖

2 *v.t.* (a) (assign ~ to) nummerieren
(b) (amount to, comprise) zählen
(c) (include) zählen (among, with zu)
(d) sb.'s days are ~ed jmds. Tage sind
gezählt
'numbering *n.* Nummerierung, *die*
'numberless *adj.* unzählig; zahllos
'number plate *n.* Nummernschild, *das*
numeracy /'nju:mərəsɪ/ *n.* rechnerische
Fähigkeiten *Pl.*
numeral /'nju:mərl/ *n.* Ziffer, *die*
numerate /'nju:mərət/ *adj.* be ~: rechnen
können
numerical /nju:'merɪkl/ *adj.* numerisch;
Zahlen⟨*wert, -folge*⟩; zahlenmäßig ⟨*Stärke,
Überlegenheit*⟩
numerically /nju:'merɪkəlɪ/ *adv.*
numerisch
numerous /'nju:mərəs/ *adj.* zahlreich
nun /nʌn/ *n.* Nonne, *die*
nurse /nɜːs/ **1** *n.* Krankenschwester, *die*;
[male] ~: Krankenpfleger, *der*
2 *v.t.* (a) pflegen ⟨*Kranke*⟩
(b) (fig.) hegen (geh.) ⟨*Gefühl, Groll*⟩
'nursemaid *n.* (lit. or fig.) Kindermädchen,
das
nursery /'nɜːsərɪ/ *n.* (a) (room)
Kinderzimmer, *das*
(b) (crèche) Kindertagesstätte, *die*
(c) ▶ NURSERY SCHOOL
(d) (for plants) Gärtnerei, *die*
nursery: ~ **rhyme** *n.* Kinderreim, *der*;
~ **school** *n.* Kindergarten, *der*;
~**school teacher** *n.* (female)
Kindergärtnerin, *die*; Erzieherin, *die*; (male)
Erzieher, *der*; ~ **slopes** *n. pl.* (Skiing)
Idiotenhügel, *der* (ugs. scherzh.)

nursing /'nɜːsɪŋ/ *n.* Krankenpflege, *die*;
attrib. Pflege⟨*personal, -beruf*⟩
'nursing home *n.* Pflegeheim, *das*
nurture /'nɜːtʃə(r)/ *v.t.* (rear) aufziehen; (fig.)
nähren
nut /nʌt/ *n.* (a) Nuss, *die*
(b) (Mech. Engin.) [Schrauben]mutter, *die*
(c) (crazy person) Verrückte, *der/die* (ugs.)
nut: ~ **case** *n.* (coll.) Verrückte, *der/die*
(ugs.); ~ **crackers** *n. pl.* Nussknacker, *der*
nutmeg /'nʌtmeg/ *n.* Muskat, *der*
nutrient /'nju:trɪənt/ *n.* Nährstoff, *der*
nutrition /nju:'trɪʃn/ *n.* Ernährung, *die*;
(food) Nahrung, *die*
nutritional /nju:'trɪʃənl/ *adj.* nahrhaft;
~ **value** Nährwert, *der*
nutritionist /nju:'trɪʃənɪst/ *n.*
Ernährungswissenschaftler, *der/*
-wissenschaftlerin, *die*
nutritious /nju:'trɪʃəs/ *adj.* nahrhaft
'nutshell *n.* Nussschale, *die*; in a ~ (fig.)
hurz [gesagt]
nutty /'nʌtɪ/ *adj.* (a) (in taste) nussig
(b) (coll.: crazy) verrückt (ugs.)
nuzzle /'nʌzl/ *v.i.* sich kuscheln (up to,
against an + *Akk.*)
NVQ *abbr.* (Brit.) = **National
Vocational Qualification**
NW *abbr.* = **north-west** NW
nylon /'naɪlɒn/ *n.* (a) Nylon, *das; attrib.*
Nylon-
(b) in *pl.* (stockings) Nylonstrümpfe *Pl.*
nymph /nɪmf/ *n.* Nymphe, *die*
nymphomaniac /nɪmfə'meɪnɪæk/ *n.*
Nymphomanin, *die*
NZ *abbr.* = **New Zealand**

Oo

O, o /əʊ/ *n.* O, o, *das*
oaf /əʊf/ *n.* Stoffel, *der* (ugs.)
oak /əʊk/ *n.* Eiche, *die*
'oak tree *n.* Eiche, *die*
OAP *abbr.* (Brit.) = **old-age pensioner**
Rentner, *der/*Rentnerin, *die*
oar /ɔː(r)/ *n.* Ruder, *das*
oarsman /'ɔːzmən/ *n., pl.* oarsmen
/'ɔːzmən/ Ruderer, *der*
oasis /əʊ'eɪsɪs/ *n., pl.* oases /əʊ'eɪsiːz/ Oase,
die
oat /əʊt/ *n.* ~s Hafer, *der*
'oatcake *n.* [flacher] Haferkuchen
oath /əʊθ/ *n.* (a) Eid, *der;* Schwur, *der;* take
or swear an ~: einen Eid schwören

(b) (swear word) Fluch, *der*
'oatmeal *n.* Hafermehl, *das*
obedience /ə'biːdɪəns/ *n.* Gehorsam, *der*
obedient /ə'biːdɪənt/ *adj.* gehorsam; be
~ to sb./sth. jmdm./einer Sache gehorchen
o'bediently *adv.* gehorsam
obelisk /'ɒbəlɪsk/ *n.* Obelisk, *der*
obese /əʊ'biːs/ *adj.* fettleibig
obesity /əʊ'biːsɪtɪ/ *n.* Fettleibigkeit, *die*
obey /əʊ'beɪ/ **1** *v.t.* gehorchen (+ *Dat.*); sich
halten an (+ *Akk.*) ⟨*Vorschrift, Regel*⟩;
befolgen ⟨*Befehl*⟩
2 *v.i.* gehorchen
obituary /ə'bɪtjʊərɪ/ *n.* Nachruf, *der* (to, of
auf + *Akk.*)

object ① /'ɒbdʒɪkt/ *n.* (a) (thing)
Gegenstand, *der*
(b) (purpose) Ziel, *das*
(c) (obstacle) **money/time** *etc.* **is no ∼**: Geld/
Zeit *usw.* spielt keine Rolle
(d) (Ling.) Objekt, *das*
② /əb'dʒekt/ *v.i.* (a) Einwände/einen
Einwand erheben (**to** gegen)
(b) (have objection or dislike) etwas dagegen
haben; **∼ to sb./sth.** etwas gegen jmdn./etw.
haben
③ /əb'dʒekt/ *v.t.* einwenden

objection /əb'dʒekʃn/ *n.* (a) Einwand, *der;*
raise *or* **make an ∼** [**to sth.**] einen Einwand
[gegen etw.] erheben
(b) (dislike) Abneigung, *die;* **have an/no ∼ to**
sb./sth. etw./nichts gegen jmdn./etw. haben;
have no ∼s nichts dagegen haben

objectionable /əb'dʒekʃənəbl/ *adj.*
unangenehm ⟨*Anblick, Geruch*⟩; anstößig
⟨*Bemerkung, Wort, Benehmen*⟩

objective /əb'dʒektɪv/ ① *adj.* objektiv
② *n.* (goal) Ziel, *das*

ob'jectively *adv.* objektiv

objectivity /ɒbdʒek'tɪvɪtɪ/ *n.* Objektivität,
die

obligation /ɒblɪ'geɪʃn/ *n.* Verpflichtung,
die; **be under an ∼ to sb.** jmdm. verpflichtet
sein; **without ∼**: unverbindlich

obligatory /ə'blɪgətərɪ/ *adj.* obligatorisch;
it has become ∼ to ...: es ist jetzt Pflicht,
zu ...

oblige /ə'blaɪdʒ/ *v.t.* (a) (be binding on) **∼ sb.**
to do sth. jmdm. vorschreiben, etw. zu tun
(b) (compel) zwingen; **be ∼d to do sth.**
gezwungen sein, etw. zu tun; **feel ∼d to do**
sth. sich verpflichtet fühlen, etw. zu tun
(c) (be kind to) **∼ sb. by doing sth.** jmdm. den
Gefallen tun und etw. tun
(d) (grateful) **be much/greatly ∼d to sb.** [**for**
sth.] jmdm. [für etw.] sehr verbunden sein;
much ∼d! besten Dank!

obliging /ə'blaɪdʒɪŋ/ *adj.*
entgegenkommend

oblique /ə'bliːk/ *adj.* schief ⟨*Gerade,*
Winkel⟩; (fig.) indirekt

obliterate /ə'blɪtəreɪt/ *v.t.* auslöschen

oblivion /ə'blɪvɪən/ *n.* Vergessenheit, *die;*
sink *or* **fall into ∼**: in Vergessenheit geraten

oblivious /ə'blɪvɪəs/ *adj.* **be ∼ to** *or* **of sth.**
sich (*Dat.*) einer Sache (*Gen.*) nicht bewusst
sein

oblong /'ɒblɒŋ/ ① *adj.* rechteckig
② *n.* Rechteck, *das*

obnoxious /əb'nɒkʃəs/ *adj.* widerlich

oboe /'əʊbəʊ/ *n.* Oboe, *die*

obscene /əb'siːn/ *adj.* obszön

obscenity /əb'senɪtɪ/ *n.* Obszönität, *die*

obscure /əb'skjʊə(r)/ ① *adj.* (a)
(unexplained) dunkel
(b) (hard to understand) schwer verständlich
⟨*Argument, Dichtung, Autor, Stil*⟩
(c) (unknown) unbekannt

② *v.t.* (a) (make indistinct) verdunkeln;
versperren ⟨*Aussicht*⟩
(b) (make unintelligible) unverständlich machen

obsequious /əb'siːkwɪəs/ *adj.* unterwürfig

observance /əb'zɜːvəns/ *n.* Einhaltung,
die

observant /əb'zɜːvənt/ *adj.* aufmerksam

observation /ɒbzə'veɪʃn/ *n.* (a)
Beobachtung, *die;* **be [kept] under ∼**:
beobachtet werden; (by police) überwacht
werden
(b) (remark) Bemerkung, *die* (**on** über + *Akk.*)

obser'vation post *n.*
Beobachtungsposten, *der*

observatory /əb'zɜːvətərɪ/ *n.* (Astron.)
Sternwarte, *die*

observe /əb'zɜːv/ *v.t.* (a) (watch)
beobachten; (perceive) bemerken
(b) (abide by, keep) einhalten
(c) (say) bemerken

ob'server *n.* Beobachter, *der*/Beobachterin,
die

obsess /əb'ses/ *v.t.* **∼ sb.** von jmdm. Besitz
ergreifen (fig.); **be/become ∼ed with** *or* **by**
sb./sth. von jmdm./etw. besessen sein/
werden

obsession /əb'seʃn/ *n.* Zwangsvorstellung,
die

obsessive /əb'sesɪv/ *adj.* zwanghaft; **be**
∼ about sth. von etw. besessen sein

obsolescent /ɒbsə'lesənt/ *adj.* veraltend

obsolete /'ɒbsəliːt/ *adj.* veraltet

obstacle /'ɒbstəkl/ *n.* Hindernis, *das* (**to**
für)

obstacle: ∼ course *n.*
Hindernisparcours, *der;* **∼ race** *n.*
Hindernisrennen, *das*

obstetrics /ɒb'stetrɪks/ *n.* (Med.)
Obstetrik, *die* (fachspr.)

obstinacy /'ɒbstɪnəsɪ/ *n.* ▶ OBSTINATE:
Starrsinn, *der;* Hartnäckigkeit, *die*

obstinate /'ɒbstɪnət/ *adj.* starrsinnig;
(adhering to particular course of action) hartnäckig

obstruct /əb'strʌkt/ *v.t.* (a) (block)
blockieren; behindern ⟨*Verkehr*⟩; **∼ sb.'s**
view jmdm. die Sicht versperren
(b) (fig.: impede; also Sport) behindern

obstruction /əb'strʌkʃn/ *n.* Blockierung,
die; (of progress; also Sport) Behinderung, *die*

obstructive /əb'strʌktɪv/ *adj.* hinderlich;
obstruktiv ⟨*Politik, Taktik*⟩; **be ∼** ⟨*Person:*⟩
sich quer legen (ugs.)

obtain /əb'teɪn/ *v.t.* bekommen; erzielen
⟨*Resultat, Wirkung*⟩

obtainable /əb'teɪnəbl/ *adj.* erhältlich

obtrusive /əb'truːsɪv/ *adj.* aufdringlich;
(conspicuous) auffällig

obtuse /əb'tjuːs/ *adj.* (a) stumpf ⟨*Winkel*⟩
(b) (stupid) begriffsstutzig

obvious /'ɒbvɪəs/ *adj.* offenkundig; (easily
seen) augenfällig; **be ∼** [**to sb.**] **that ...:**
[jmdm.] klar sein, dass ... ⋯⟶

'obviously *adv.* offenkundig; sichtlich
⟨enttäuschen, überraschen usw.⟩

occasion /əˈkeɪʒn/ **1** *n.* (a) Gelegenheit,
die; **rise to the** ∼: sich der Situation
gewachsen zeigen; **on several** ∼**s** bei
mehreren Gelegenheiten; **on** ∼**[s]**
gelegentlich
(b) (special occurrence) Anlass, *der;* **it was quite
an** ∼: es war ein Ereignis
(c) (reason) Grund, *der* (**for** zu)
2 *v.t.* verursachen

occasional /əˈkeɪʒənl/ *adj.* gelegentlich;
vereinzelt ⟨Regenschauer⟩

oc'casionally *adv.* gelegentlich; [only]
very ∼: gelegentlich einmal

occult /ɒˈkʌlt, ˈɒkʌlt/ *adj.* okkult; **the** ∼:
das Okkulte

occupant /ˈɒkjʊpənt/ *n.* Bewohner, *der/*
Bewohnerin, *die;* (of car, bus, etc.) Insasse, *der/*
Insassin, *die*

occupation /ɒkjʊˈpeɪʃn/ *n.* (a) (Mil.)
Besetzung, *die;* (period) Besatzungszeit, *die*
(b) (activity) Beschäftigung, *die*
(c) (profession) Beruf, *der*

occupational /ɒkjʊˈpeɪʃənl/ *adj.*
Berufs⟨beratung, -risiko⟩; ∼ **therapy**
Beschäftigungstherapie, *die;* ∼ **therapist**
Beschäftigungstherapeut, *der/*-therapeutin,
die

occupier /ˈɒkjʊpaɪə(r)/ *n.* (Brit.) Besitzer,
*der/*Besitzerin, *die;* (tenant) Bewohner, *der/*
Bewohnerin, *die*

occupy /ˈɒkjʊpaɪ/ *v.t.* (a) (Mil.; as
demonstration) besetzen
(b) (live in) bewohnen
(c) (take up, fill) einnehmen; belegen
⟨Zimmer⟩; in Anspruch nehmen ⟨Zeit,
Aufmerksamkeit⟩
(d) (busy, employ) beschäftigen

occur /əˈkɜː(r)/ *v.i.,* **-rr-:** (a) (be met with)
vorkommen; ⟨Gelegenheit:⟩ sich bieten;
⟨Problem:⟩ auftreten
(b) (happen) ⟨Veränderung:⟩ eintreten;
⟨Unfall, Vorfall:⟩ sich ereignen
(c) ∼ **to sb.** (be thought of) jmdm. in den Sinn
kommen; ⟨Idee:⟩ jmdm. kommen

occurrence /əˈkʌrəns/ *n.* (a) (incident)
Ereignis, *das;* Begebenheit, *die*
(b) (occurring) Vorkommen, *das*

ocean /ˈəʊʃn/ *n.* Ozean, *der;* Meer, *das*

o'clock /əˈklɒk/ *adv.* **it is two/six** ∼: es ist
zwei/sechs Uhr; **at two/six** ∼: um zwei/sechs
Uhr; **six** ∼ *attrib.* Sechsuhr⟨zug, -maschine,
-nachrichten⟩

Oct. *abbr.* = **October** Okt.

octagon /ˈɒktəgən/ *n.* Achteck, *das*

octane /ˈɒkteɪn/ *n.* Oktan, *das*

octave /ˈɒktɪv/ *n.* Oktave, *die*

October /ɒkˈtəʊbə(r)/ *n.* Oktober, *der; see
also* AUGUST

octopus /ˈɒktəpəs/ *n.* Tintenfisch, *der*

odd /ɒd/ *adj.* (a) (surplus, spare) übrig ⟨Stück,
Silbergeld⟩; **£25 and a few** ∼ **pence** 25 Pfund
und ein paar Pence
(b) (occasional) gelegentlich; ∼ **job**/∼**-job man**
Gelegenheitsarbeit, *die/*-arbeiter, *der*
(c) (one of pair or group) einzeln; ∼ **socks** nicht
zusammengehörende Socken; **be the** ∼ **man
out** ⟨Gegenstand:⟩ nicht dazu passen
(d) (uneven) ungerade ⟨Zahl, Seite,
Hausnummer⟩
(e) (plus something) **forty** ∼: über vierzig;
twelve pounds ∼: etwas mehr als zwölf
Pfund
(f) (strange, eccentric) seltsam

oddity /ˈɒdɪtɪ/ *n.* (object, event) Kuriosität, *die*

'oddly *adv.* seltsam; ∼ **enough**
seltsamerweise

odd 'man *n.* ∼ **out** Außenseiter, *der/*
Außenseiterin, *die;* **be the** ∼ **out** (extra person)
überzählig sein

'odd-numbered *adj.* ungerade

odds /ɒdz/ *n. pl.* (a) (Betting) Odds *Pl.*
(b) [**the**] ∼ **are that she did it** wahrscheinlich
hat sie es getan; **the** ∼ **are against/in favour
of sb./sth.** jmds. Aussichten/die Aussichten
für etw. sind gering/gut
(c) ∼ **and ends** Kleinigkeiten; (of food) Reste
(d) **be at** ∼ **with sb. over sth.** mit jmdm. in
etw. *(Dat.)* uneinig sein
(e) **it makes no/little** ∼ [**whether** ...] es ist
völlig/ziemlich gleichgültig[, ob ...]

'odds-on **1** *adj.* gut ⟨Chance, Aussicht⟩;
hoch, klar ⟨Favorit⟩
2 *adv.* wahrscheinlich

odious /ˈəʊdɪəs/ *adj.* widerwärtig

odor etc. (Amer.) ▶ ODOUR etc.

odour /ˈəʊdə(r)/ *n.* Geruch, *der*

'odourless *adj.* geruchlos

oedema /ɪˈdiːmə/ *n.* Ödem, *das*

oestrogen /ˈiːstrədʒən/ *n.* Östrogen, *das*

œuvre /ˈɜːvr/ *n.* Œuvre, *das* (geh.); Werk, *das*

of /əv, *stressed* ɒv/ *prep.* von; (indicating material,
substance) aus; **articles of clothing**
Kleidungsstücke; **a friend of mine** ein Freund
von mir; **where's that pencil of mine?** wo ist
mein Bleistift?; **it was clever of you to do
that** es war klug von dir, das zu tun; **the
approval of sb.** jmds. Zustimmung; **the works
of Shakespeare** Shakespeares Werke; **be
made of** ...: aus ... [hergestellt] sein; **the fifth
of January** der fünfte Januar; **his love of his
father** seine Liebe zu seinem Vater; **person of
extreme views** Mensch mit extremen
Ansichten; **a boy of 14 years** ein
vierzehnjähriger Junge; **the five of us** wir
fünf

off /ɒf/ **1** *adv.* (a) (away) **be a few miles** ∼:
wenige Meilen entfernt sein; **the lake is not
far** ∼: der See ist nicht weit [weg]; **I'm**
∼ **now** ich gehe jetzt; ∼ **we go!** los gehts!
(b) (not on or attached or supported) ab; **get the
lid** ∼: den Deckel abbekommen

(c) be ~ (switched or turned ~) ‹*Wasser, Gas, Strom:*› abgestellt sein; **the light/radio** etc. **is ~**: das Licht/Radio usw. ist aus

(d) the meat etc. **is ~**: das Fleisch usw. ist schlecht [geworden]

(e) be ~ (cancelled) abgesagt sein; ‹*Verlobung:*› [auf]gelöst sein; **~ and on** immer mal wieder (ugs.)

(f) (not at work) frei; **on my day ~**: an meinem freien Tag; **have a week ~**: eine Woche Urlaub bekommen

(g) (no longer available) [the] **soup** etc. **is ~**: es gibt keine Suppe usw. mehr

(h) (situated as regards money etc.) **he is badly** etc. **~**: er ist schlecht usw. gestellt

2 prep. von; be ~ **school/work** in der Schule/am Arbeitsplatz fehlen; **be ~ one's food** keinen Appetit haben; **just ~ the square** ganz in der Nähe des Platzes

offal /ˈɒfl/ n. Innereien Pl.

off: **~beat** adj. (fig.: eccentric) unkonventionell; **~'centre** adv. nicht [genau] in der Mitte; **~ 'colour** adj. unwohl; **~cut** n. Rest, der; **~duty** attrib. adj. Freizeit-; ‹*Polizist* usw.›, der dienstfrei hat

offence /əˈfens/ n. (Brit.) **(a)** (hurting of sb.'s feelings) Kränkung, die; **I meant no ~**: ich wollte Sie/ihn usw. nicht kränken

(b) (annoyance) **give ~**: Missfallen erregen; **take ~**: verärgert sein

(c) (crime) Straftat, die; **criminal ~**: strafbare Handlung

offend /əˈfend/ **1** v.i. verstoßen (**against** gegen)

2 v.t. ~ **sb.** bei jmdm. Anstoß erregen; (hurt feelings of) jmdn. kränken

offender n. Straffällige, der/die

offense (Amer.) ▶ OFFENCE

offensive /əˈfensɪv/ **1** adj. **(a)** (aggressive) offensiv; Angriffs‹*waffe*›

(b) (giving offence) ungehörig; (indecent) anstößig

2 n. Offensive, die; **take the** or **go on the ~**: in die od. zur Offensive übergehen

offer /ˈɒfə(r)/ **1** v.t. anbieten; vorbringen ‹*Entschuldigung*›; bieten ‹*Chance*›; aussprechen ‹*Beileid*›; **~ to help** seine Hilfe anbieten; **~ resistance** Widerstand leisten

2 n. Angebot, das; [**have/be**] **on ~**: im Angebot [haben/sein]

'offering n. (thing) Angebot, das; (to a deity) Opfer, das

off'hand **1** adv. **(a)** (without preparation) auf Anhieb ‹*sagen, wissen*›; spontan ‹*beschließen, entscheiden*›

(b) (casually) leichthin

2 adj. **(a)** (without preparation) spontan

(b) (casual) beiläufig; **be ~ with sb.** zu jmdm. kurz angebunden sein

office /ˈɒfɪs/ n. **(a)** Büro, das

(b) (branch) Zweigstelle, die

(c) (position) Amt, das; **hold ~**: amtieren

office: **~ block** n. Bürogebäude, das; **~ hours** n. pl. Dienststunden Pl.; **~ job** n. Bürotätigkeit, die

officer /ˈɒfɪsə(r)/ n. **(a)** (Army etc.) Offizier, der

(b) (official) Beamte, der/Beamtin, die

(c) (constable) Polizeibeamte, der/-beamtin, die

office: **~ technology** n. Bürotechnik, die; **~ worker** n. Büroangestellte, der/die

official /əˈfɪʃl/ **1** adj. offiziell; amtlich ‹*Verlautbarung*›; regulär ‹*Streik*›

2 n. Beamte, der/Beamtin, die; (party, union, or sports ~) Funktionär, der/Funktionärin, die

officialdom /əˈfɪʃldəm/ n., no art. Beamtentum, das; Bürokratie, die

of'ficially adv. offiziell

officious /əˈfɪʃəs/ adj. übereifrig

offing /ˈɒfɪŋ/ n. **be in the ~**: bevorstehen; ‹*Gewitter:*› aufziehen

off: **~licence** n. (Brit.) ≈ Wein- und Spirituosenladen, der; **~line** (Comp.) **1** /'-/ adj. Offline-; **2** /-'-/ adv. offline; **~load** v.t. abladen; **~peak** attrib. adj. offline; **~peak hours** außerhalb der Spitzenlastzeiten; **~peak power** or **electricity** Nachtstrom, der; **~putting** /ˈɒfpʊtɪŋ/ adj. (Brit.) abstoßend; **~print** n. Sonderdruck, der; **~road** attrib. adj. Gelände-, Offroad‹*fahrzeug, -fahrrad, -wagen, -fahrt, -einsatz*›; **~road driving** Fahren im Gelände; **~set** /'-, -'-/ v.t., forms as SET: ausgleichen; **~ season** n. Nebensaison, die; **~shore** adj. küstennah; **~'side** n. Abseits-; **be ~side** abseits sein; **~spring** n., pl. same Nachkommenschaft, die; (of animal) Junge Pl.; **~-the-peg** attrib. adj. Konfektions-; **~-the-shoulder** attrib. adj. schulterfrei ‹*Kleid*›; **~-the-wall** attrib. adj. (esp. Amer. coll.) ausgeflippt (ugs.); **~'white** adj. gebrochen weiß

Oftel /ˈɒftel/ abbr. (Brit.) = **Office of Telecommunications** *Regulierungsbehörde für Telekommunikation*

often /ˈɒfn, ˈɒftn/ adv. oft; **every so ~**: gelegentlich

Ofwat /ˈɒfwɒt/ abbr. (Brit.) = **Office of Water Services** *Regulierungsbehörde für Wasserwirtschaft*

oh /əʊ/ int. oh; expr. pain au

OHP abbr. (Brit.) = **overhead projector** OHP

oil /ɔɪl/ **1** n. Öl, das

2 v.t. ölen

oil: **~burner** n. Ölbrenner, der; **~can** n. Ölkanne, die; **~ change** n. (Motor Veh.) Ölwechsel, der; **~ drum** n. Ölfass, das; **~field** n. Ölfeld, das; **~ lamp** n. Öllampe, die; **~ painting** n. Ölgemälde, das; **~producing** adj. [Erd]öl fördernd ‹*Land*›; **~ refinery** n. [Erd]ölraffinerie, ····﹢

die; ~ **rig** ▶ RIG¹ 1; ~**skins** n. pl. Ölzeug, das; ~ **slick** n. Ölteppich, der; ~ **tanker** n. Öltanker, der; ~ **well** n. Ölquelle, die

oily /'ɔɪlɪ/ adj. ölig; ölverschmiert ⟨Gesicht, Hände⟩

ointment /'ɔɪntmənt/ n. Salbe, die

OK /əʊ'keɪ/ (coll.) [1] adj. in Ordnung; okay (ugs.)
[2] adv. gut
[3] int. okay (ugs.)
[4] v.t. (approve) zustimmen (+ Dat.); be OK'd by sb. von jmdm. das Okay bekommen (ugs.)

okay /əʊ'keɪ/ ▶ OK

old /əʊld/ adj. alt; be [more than] 30 years ~: [über] 30 Jahre alt sein

old: ~ 'age n. [fortgeschrittenes] Alter; ~-**age** attrib. adj. Alters⟨rente, -ruhegeld⟩; ~-**age** pensioner Rentner, der/Rentnerin, die; ~-**fashioned** /əʊld'fæʃnd/ adj. altmodisch; ~ '**people's home** n. Altenheim, das; Altersheim, das; ~ '**wives' tale** n. Ammenmärchen, das

olive /'ɒlɪv/ n. Olive, die

olive 'oil n. Olivenöl, das

Olympic /ə'lɪmpɪk/ adj. olympisch; ~ Games Olympische Spiele

Olympics /ə'lɪmpɪks/ n. pl. Olympiade, die; Winter ~: Winterolympiade, die

omelette (**omelet**) /'ɒmlɪt/ n. Omelett, das

omen /'əʊmən/ n. Vorzeichen, das

ominous /'ɒmɪnəs/ adj. (of evil omen) ominös; (worrying) beunruhigend

omission /ə'mɪʃn/ n. Auslassung, die; (failure to act) Unterlassung, die

omit /ə'mɪt/ v.t., -tt- weglassen; ~ to do sth. es versäumen, etw. zu tun

omnipotence /ɒm'nɪpətəns/ n. Allmacht, die (geh.)

omnipotent /ɒm'nɪpətənt/ adj. allmächtig

on /ɒn/ [1] prep. auf (position: + Dat.; direction: + Akk.); (attached to) an (+ Dat./ Akk.); (concerning, about) über (+ Akk.); (in expressions of time) an ⟨einem Abend, Tag usw.⟩; write sth. on the wall etw. an die Wand schreiben; be hanging on the wall an der Wand hängen; have sth. on one etw. bei sich haben; on the bus/train im Bus/Zug; (by bus/ train) mit dem Bus/Zug; on Oxford 556767 unter der Nummer Oxford 556767; on Sundays sonntags; on [his] arrival bei seiner Ankunft; on entering the room ...: beim Betreten des Zimmers ...; it's just on 9 es ist fast 9 Uhr; the drinks are on me (coll.) die Getränke gehen auf mich
[2] adv. with/without a hat/coat on mit/ohne Hut/Mantel; have a hat on einen Hut aufhaben; on and on immer weiter; speak/ wait/work etc. on weiterreden/-warten/ -arbeiten usw.; from now on von jetzt an; the light/radio etc. is on das Licht/Radio usw. ist an; is Sunday's picnic on? findet das Picknick am Sonntag statt?; what's on at the

cinema? was läuft im Kino?; on and off immer mal wieder (ugs.); on to, onto auf (+ Akk.)

once /wʌns/ [1] adv. (a) einmal; ~ a week/ month/year einmal die Woche/im Monat/im Jahr; ~ again or more noch einmal; ~ [and] for all ein für alle Mal; never/not ~: nicht ein einziges Mal
(b) (multiplied by one) ein mal
(c) (formerly) früher einmal; ~ upon a time there lived a king es war einmal ein König
(d) at ~ (immediately) sofort; (at the same time) gleichzeitig; all at ~ (suddenly) plötzlich; (simultaneously) alle[s] zugleich
[2] conj. wenn; (with past tense) als
[3] n. [just or only] this ~: [nur] dieses eine Mal

'oncoming adj. entgegenkommend ⟨Fahrzeug, Verkehr⟩

one /wʌn/ [1] adj. ein; see also EIGHT 1; (single, only) einzig; no/not ~: kein; the ~ thing das Einzige; at ~ time einmal; ~ morning/night eines Morgens/Nachts
[2] n. (a) eins
(b) (number, symbol) Eins, die
(c) (unit) in ~s einzeln
[3] pron. (a) ein... (of + Gen.); big ~s and little ~s Große und Kleine; the older/younger ~: der/die/das Ältere/Jüngere; this ~: dieser/diese/dieses [da]; that ~: der/die/das [da]; which ~? welcher/welche/welches?; which ~s? welche?; ~ by ~: einzeln; love/ hate ~ another sich lieben/hassen; be kind to ~ another nett zueinander sein
(b) (people in general; coll.: I, we) man; as indirect object einem; as direct object einen; ~'s sein

one: ~-**night 'stand** n. (coll.) [sexuelles] Abenteuer für eine Nacht; ~-**off** (Brit.) [1] n. (article) Einzelstück, das; [2] adj. einmalig; ~-**parent family** n. Einelternfamilie, die

onerous /'əʊnərəs/ adj. schwer

one: ~'**self** pron. (a) emphat. selbst; be ~self man selbst sein; (b) refl. sich; see also HERSELF; ~-**sided** adj. einseitig; ~-**stop shopping** n. Einkaufen in einem Einkaufszentrum [mit Komplettangebot]; ~-**storey** adj. eingeschossig; ~-**touch** adj. ~-**touch dialling** Zielwahl, die; ~-**track** adj. eingleisig; have a ~-**track mind** (be obsessed) nur eins im Kopf haben; ~-**upmanship** /wʌn'ʌpmənʃɪp/ n., no indef. art. die Kunst, den anderen immer um eine Nasenlänge voraus zu sein; ~-**way** adj. (a) in einer Richtung nachgestellt; Einbahn⟨straße, -verkehr⟩; (b) einfach ⟨Fahrpreis, Flug⟩

'ongoing adj. aktuell ⟨Problem, Debatte⟩; andauernd ⟨Situation⟩

onion /'ʌnjən/ n. Zwiebel, die

onion: ~ **skin** n. Zwiebelschale, die; ~ '**soup** n. Zwiebelsuppe, die

online (Comp.) [1] /'--/ adj. Online-
[2] /-'-/ adv. online

'onlooker *n.* Zuschauer, *der*/Zuschauerin, *die*

only /'əʊnlɪ/ ① *attrib. adj.* einzig...; the ~ **person** der/die Einzige; **an** ~ **child** ein Einzelkind

② *adv.* nur; **we had been waiting** ~ **5 minutes when ...**: wir hatten erst 5 Minuten gewartet, als ...; **it's** ~/~ **just 6 o'clock** es ist erst 6 Uhr/gerade erst 6 Uhr vorbei; **he** ~ **just made it** er hat es gerade noch geschafft; ~ **if** nur [dann] ..., wenn; ~ **the other day/week** erst neulich

on-screen *adj.* (Comp., TV) Bildschirm-

'onset *n.* (of winter) Einbruch, *der;* (of disease) Ausbruch, *der*

onslaught /'ɒnslɔːt/ *n.* [heftige] Attacke (fig.)

'on-target *attrib. adj.* ~ **earnings £50,000** Verdienst bei erfolgreicher Tätigkeit 50 000 Pfund

onto ▶ ON 2

onus /'əʊnəs/ *n.* the ~ **is on him to do it** es ist seine Sache, es zu tun

onward[s] /'ɒnwədz/ *adv.* (in space) vorwärts; **from X** ~: von X an; **from that day** ~: von diesem Tag an

onyx /'ɒnɪks/ *n.* Onyx, *der*

ooze /uːz/ ① *v.i.* sickern (**from** aus) ② *v.t.* triefen von *od.* vor (+ *Dat.*); (fig.) ausstrahlen

op /ɒp/ *n.* (coll.) Operation, *die*

opaque /əʊ'peɪk/ *adj.* lichtundurchlässig; opak (fachspr.)

open /'əʊpn/ ① *adj.* (a) offen; (not blocked or obstructed) frei; (available) frei ⟨Stelle⟩; **in the** ~ **air** im Freien; **be** ~ ⟨Laden, Museum, Bank usw.⟩ geöffnet sein; **have an** ~ **mind about** *or* **on sth.** einer Sache gegenüber aufgeschlossen sein

(b) unverhohlen ⟨Bewunderung, Hass, Verachtung⟩

(c) (frank, communicative) offen ⟨Wesen, Streit, Abstimmung, Regierungsstil⟩; (not secret) öffentlich ⟨Wahl⟩

(d) geöffnet ⟨Regenschirm⟩; aufgeblüht ⟨Blume, Knospe⟩; aufgeschlagen ⟨Zeitung, Landkarte⟩

② *n.* **in the** ~ (outdoors) unter freiem Himmel; **[out] in the** ~ (fig.) öffentlich bekannt

③ *v.t.* (a) öffnen

(b) eröffnen ⟨Konferenz, Diskussion, Laden⟩; beginnen ⟨Verhandlungen, Spiel⟩

(c) (unfold, spread out) aufschlagen ⟨Zeitung, Buch, Landkarte⟩; öffnen ⟨Schirm⟩

④ *v.i.* (a) sich öffnen; ~ **into/on to sth.** zu etw. führen

(b) (become ~ to customers) öffnen; (start trading etc.) eröffnet werden

(c) (start) beginnen; ⟨Ausstellung:⟩ eröffnet werden; ⟨Theaterstück:⟩ Premiere haben

■ **open 'up** ① *v.t.* öffnen; (establish) eröffnen ② *v.i.* sich öffnen; ⟨Filiale:⟩ eröffnet werden; ⟨Firma:⟩ sich niederlassen

open: ~**-air** *attrib. adj.* Openair⟨konzert⟩; ~**-air [swimming] pool** Freibad, *das;* ~**-and-'shut case** *n.* (coll.) klarer Fall; ~ **day** *n.* Tag der offenen Tür

'opener *n.* Öffner, *der*

'opening ① *n.* (a) Öffnen, *das;* (becoming open) Sichöffnen, *das;* (of exhibition, new centre) Eröffnen, *das*

(b) (establishment, ceremony) Eröffnung, die

(c) (initial part) Anfang, der

(d) (gap, aperture) Öffnung, die

(e) (opportunity) Möglichkeit, die; (vacancy) freie Stelle

② *adj.* einleitend

opening: ~ **hours** *n. pl.* Öffnungszeiten Pl.; ~ **time** *n.* Öffnungszeit, *die*

'openly *adv.* (a) (publicly) in der Öffentlichkeit; öffentlich ⟨zugeben, verurteilen⟩

(b) (frankly) offen

open: ~ '**market** *n.* offener *od.* freier Markt; ~**-'minded** *adj.* aufgeschlossen

openness /'əʊpnnɪs/ *n.* (frankness) Offenheit, *die*

open: ~**-'plan** *adj.* ~**-plan office** Großraumbüro, *das;* ~ '**prison** *n.* offene Anstalt; ~ '**sandwich** *n.* belegtes Brot

opera /'ɒpərə/ *n.* Oper, *die*

opera: ~ **glasses** *n. pl.* Opernglas, *das;* ~ **house** *n.* Opernhaus, *das;* ~ **singer** *n.* Opernsänger, *der*/-sängerin, *die*

operate /'ɒpəreɪt/ ① *v.i.* (a) (be in action) in Betrieb sein; ⟨Bus, Zug usw.⟩ verkehren

(b) (function) arbeiten; **the torch** ~**s on batteries** die Taschenlampe arbeitet mit Batterien

(c) ~ [**on sb.**] (Med.) [jmdn.] operieren ② *v.t.* bedienen ⟨Maschine⟩; unterhalten ⟨Busverbindung, Telefondienst⟩; betätigen ⟨Hebel, Bremse⟩

operating: ~ **system** *n.* (Comp.) Betriebssystem, *das;* ~ **theatre** *n.* (Brit. Med.) Operationssaal, *der*

operation /ɒpə'reɪʃn/ *n.* (a) (causing to work) (of machine) Bedienung, *die;* (of bus service, telephone service, etc.) Unterhaltung, *die;* (of lever, brake) Betätigung, *die*

(b) **come into** ~ ⟨Gesetz, Gebühr usw.⟩ in Kraft treten; **be in/out of** ~ ⟨Maschine, Gerät usw.⟩ in/außer Betrieb sein

(c) (Med.) Operation, *die;* **have an** ~: operiert werden

operational /ɒpə'reɪʃənl/ *adj.* (esp. Mil.: ready to function) einsatzbereit

operative /'ɒpərətɪv/ *adj.* **become** ~ ⟨Gesetz:⟩ in Kraft treten; **the scheme is** ~: das Programm läuft

operator /'ɒpəreɪtə(r)/ *n.* [Maschinen]bediener, *der*/-bedienerin, *die;* (Teleph.) (at exchange) Vermittlung, *die;* (at switchboard) Telefonist, *der*/Telefonistin, *die*

ophthalmic op'tician /ɒf'θælmɪk/ *n.* (Brit.) Augenoptiker, *der*/-optikerin, *die*

opinion /ə'pɪnjən/ *n.* Meinung, *die* (**on** über ···⋗

+ *Akk.,* zu); **have a high/low** ∼ **of sb.** eine/
keine hohe Meinung von jmdm. haben; **in
my** ∼: meiner Meinung nach

opinionated /ə'pɪnjəneɪtɪd/ *adj.*
rechthaberisch

o'pinion poll *n.* Meinungsumfrage, *die*

opium /'əʊpɪəm/ *n.* Opium, *das*

opponent /ə'pəʊnənt/ *n.* Gegner, *der*/
Gegnerin, *die*

opportune /'ɒpətjuːn/ *adj.* **(a)** (favourable)
günstig
(b) (well-timed) zur rechten Zeit *nachgestellt*

opportunism /ɒpə'tjuːnɪzm/ *n.*
Opportunismus, *der*

opportunist /ɒpə'tjuːnɪst/ *n.* Opportunist,
der/Opportunistin, *die*

opportunity /ɒpə'tjuːnɪtɪ/ *n.* Gelegenheit,
die

oppose /ə'pəʊz/ **1** *v.t.* sich wenden gegen
2 *v.i.* **the opposing team** die gegnerische
Mannschaft

opposed /ə'pəʊzd/ *adj.* **as** ∼ **to** im
Gegensatz zu; **be** ∼ **to sth.** ⟨*Person:*⟩ gegen
etw. sein

opposite /'ɒpəzɪt/ **1** *adj.* gegenüberliegend
⟨*Straßenseite, Ufer*⟩; entgegengesetzt ⟨*Ende,
Weg, Richtung*⟩; **the** ∼ **sex** das andere
Geschlecht
2 *n.* Gegenteil, *das* **(of** von)
3 *adv.* gegenüber
4 *prep.* gegenüber

opposite 'number *n.* (fig.) Pendant, *das*

opposition /ɒpə'zɪʃn/ *n.* **(a)** Opposition,
die; (resistance) Widerstand, *der* **(to** gegen); **in**
∼ **to** entgegen
(b) (Brit. Polit.) **the O**∼: die Opposition

oppress /ə'pres/ *v.t.* unterdrücken; (fig.)
⟨*Gefühl:*⟩ bedrücken

oppression /ə'preʃn/ *n.* Unterdrückung,
die

oppressive /ə'presɪv/ *adj.* repressiv; (fig.)
bedrückend ⟨*Ängste, Atmosphäre*⟩; (hot and
close) drückend ⟨*Wetter, Klima, Tag*⟩

opt /ɒpt/ *v.i.* sich entscheiden **(for** für); ∼ **to
do sth.** sich dafür entscheiden, etw. zu tun;
∼ **out** nicht mitmachen/(stop taking part) nicht
länger mitmachen **(of** bei)

optic /'ɒptɪk/ **1** *adj.* (Anat.) Seh⟨*nerv, -bahn*⟩
2 *n. or* **O**∼ ℗ (Brit.: for spirits) Portionierer,
der

optical /'ɒptɪkl/ *adj.* optisch

optical 'character reader *n.* (Comp.)
Klarschriftleser, *der*

optician /ɒp'tɪʃn/ *n.* Optiker, *der*/
Optikerin, *die*

optics /'ɒptɪks/ *n.* Optik, *die*

optima *pl. of* OPTIMUM

optimise ▶ OPTIMIZE

optimism /'ɒptɪmɪzm/ *n.* Optimismus, *der*

optimist /'ɒptɪmɪst/ *n.* Optimist, *der*/
Optimistin, *die*

optimistic /ɒptɪ'mɪstɪk/ *adj.* optimistisch

optimize /'ɒptɪmaɪz/ *v.t.* (make the most of)
das Beste machen aus

optimum /'ɒptɪməm/ **1** *n., pl.* **optima**
/'ɒptɪmə/ Optimum, *das*
2 *adj.* optimal

option /'ɒpʃn/ *n.* (choice) Wahl, *die;* (thing)
Wahlmöglichkeit, *die*

optional /'ɒpʃənl/ *adj.* nicht zwingend;
∼ **subject** Wahlfach, *das*

opulence /'ɒpjʊləns/ *n.* Wohlstand, *der*

opulent /'ɒpjʊlənt/ *adj.* wohlhabend; feudal
⟨*Auto, Haus usw.*⟩

or /ə(r), *stressed* ɔ:(r)/ *conj.* **(a)** oder; **he
cannot read or write** er kann weder lesen
noch schreiben; **without food or water** ohne
Essen und Wasser; **15 or 20 minutes** 15 bis 20
Minuten; **in a day or two** in ein, zwei Tagen
(b) (introducing explanation) das heißt; **or rather**
beziehungsweise

oracle /'ɒrəkl/ *n.* Orakel, *das*

oral /'ɔ:rəl/ *adj.* mündlich; (Med.) oral

orally /'ɔ:rəlɪ/ *adv.* **take** ∼: einnehmen

orange /'ɒrɪndʒ/ **1** *n.* **(a)** (fruit) Orange, *die;*
Apfelsine, *die*
(b) (colour) Orange, *das*
2 *adj.* orange[farben]

orange: ∼ **juice** *n.* Orangensaft, *der;*
∼ **peel** *n.* Orangenschale, *die;* ∼ **'squash**
n. Orangensaftgetränk, *das*

orator /'ɒrətə(r)/ *n.* Redner, *der*/Rednerin,
die

oratory /'ɒrətərɪ/ *n.* Redekunst, *die*

orb /ɔ:b/ *n.* Kugel, *die*

orbit /'ɔ:bɪt/ **1** *n.* (Astron.) [Umlauf]bahn, *die*
2 *v.i.* kreisen
3 *v.t.* umkreisen

orbital /'ɔ:bɪtl/ *adj.* ∼ **road** Ringstraße, *die*

orchard /'ɔ:tʃəd/ *n.* Obstgarten, *der;*
(commercial) Obstplantage, *die*

orchestra /'ɔ:kɪstrə/ *n.* Orchester, *das*

orchestral /ɔ:'kestrl/ *adj.* Orchester-

orchestrate /'ɔ:kɪstreɪt/ *v.t.* orchestrieren

orchid /'ɔ:kɪd/ *n.* Orchidee, *die*

ordain /ɔ:'deɪn/ *v.t.* **(a)** (Eccl.) ordinieren
(b) (decree) verfügen

ordeal /ɔ:'diːl/ *n.* Qual, *die*

order /'ɔ:də(r)/ **1** *n.* **(a)** (sequence)
Reihenfolge, *die;* **out of** ∼: durcheinander
(b) (regular arrangement, normal state) Ordnung,
die; **be/not be in** ∼: in Ordnung/nicht in
Ordnung sein (ugs.); **be out of/in** ∼ (not in/in
working condition) nicht funktionieren/
funktionieren; **'out of** ∼' „außer Betrieb"; **in
good/bad** ∼: in gutem/schlechtem Zustand
(c) (command) Anweisung, *die;* (Mil.) Befehl,
der
(d) in ∼ **to do sth.** um etw. zu tun
(e) (Commerc.) Auftrag, *der* **(for** über + *Akk.*);
(to waiter, ∼ed goods) Bestellung, *die*
(f) keep ∼: Ordnung [be]wahren; *see also*
LAW B
(g) (religious ∼) Orden, *der*

2 *v.t.* **(a)** (command) befehlen; ⟨*Richter:*⟩ verfügen; ~ **sb. to do sth.** jmdn. anweisen/ (Milit.) jmdm. befehlen, etw. zu tun **(b)** (Commerc.) bestellen (**from** bei) **(c)** (arrange) ordnen

■ **order a'bout, order a'round** *v.t.* herumkommandieren

'**order form** *n.* Bestellformular, *das*

orderly /'ɔːdəlɪ/ 1 *adj.* friedlich; diszipliniert ⟨*Menge*⟩; (methodical) methodisch; (tidy) ordentlich 2 *n.* **(a)** (Mil.) [Offiziers]bursche, *der* **(b) medical ~:** ≈ Krankenpfleger[helfer, *der*

ordinal /'ɔːdɪnl/ *adj. & n.* ~ **[number]** Ordinalzahl, *die*

ordinarily /'ɔːdɪnərɪlɪ/ *adv.* normalerweise; gewöhnlich

ordinary /'ɔːdɪnərɪ/ *adj.* (normal) normal ⟨*Gebrauch*⟩; üblich ⟨*Verfahren*⟩; (not exceptional) gewöhnlich

ordination /ɔːdɪ'neɪʃn/ *n.* (Eccl.) Ordination, *die;* Ordinierung, *die*

ordnance 'survey /'ɔːdnəns/ *n.* (Brit.) amtliche Landesvermessung; ~ **survey map** amtliche topographische Karte

ore /ɔː(r)/ *n.* Erz, *das*

organ /'ɔːgən/ *n.* **(a)** (Mus.) Orgel, *die* **(b)** (Biol.) Organ, *das*

'**organ donor** *n.* Organspender, *der/* -spenderin, *die;* ~ **card** Organspende[r]ausweis, *der*

organic /ɔː'gænɪk/ *adj.* organisch; biologisch-dynamisch ⟨*Ackerbau*⟩; biodynamisch ⟨*Nahrungsmittel*⟩

organically /ɔː'gænɪkəlɪ/ *adv.* **(a)** (also Med.) organisch **(b)** (without chemicals) biologisch

organism /'ɔːgənɪzm/ *n.* Organismus, *der*

organist /'ɔːgənɪst/ *n.* Organist, *der/* Organistin, *die*

organization /ɔːgənaɪ'zeɪʃn/ *n.* Organisation, *die;* ~ **of time/work** Zeit-/ Arbeitseinteilung, *die*

organize /'ɔːgənaɪz/ *v.t.* organisieren; einteilen ⟨*Arbeit, Zeit*⟩; veranstalten ⟨*Konferenz, Festival*⟩; ~ **into groups** in Gruppen einteilen

organized /'ɔːgənaɪzd/ *adj.* organisiert

'**organizer** *n.* Organisator, *der/* Organisatorin, *die;* (of event, festival) Veranstalter, *die/*Veranstalterin, *die*

'**organ transplant** *n.* Organverpflanzung, *die*

orgasm /'ɔːgæzm/ *n.* Orgasmus, *der*

orgy /'ɔːdʒɪ/ *n.* Orgie, *die*

orient 1 /'ɔːrɪənt/ *n.* **the O~:** der Orient 2 /'ɒrɪent/ *v.t.* ausrichten (**towards** nach); ~ **oneself** sich orientieren

oriental /ɒrɪ'entl/ 1 *adj.* orientalisch 2 *n.* Asiat, *der/*Asiatin, *die*

orientate /'ɒrɪənteɪt/ ▶ ORIENT 2

orientation /ɒrɪən'teɪʃn/ *n.* Orientierung, *die*

orienteering /ɒrɪən'tɪərɪŋ/ *n.* (Brit.) Orientierungslauf, *der*

orifice /'ɒrɪfɪs/ *n.* Öffnung, *die*

origin /'ɒrɪdʒɪn/ *n.* (derivation) Herkunft, *die;* (beginnings) Anfänge *Pl.;* (source) Ursprung, *der;* **country of ~:** Herkunftsland, *das;* **have its ~ in sth.** seinen Ursprung in etw. (*Dat.*) haben

original /ə'rɪdʒɪnl/ 1 *adj.* ursprünglich; Ur⟨*text, -fassung*⟩; eigenständig ⟨*Forschung*⟩; (inventive) originell; **an ~ painting** ein Original 2 *n.* Original, *das*

original 'gravity *n.* Stammwürze, *die*

originality /ərɪdʒɪ'nælɪtɪ/ *n.* Originalität, *die*

originally /ə'rɪdʒɪnəlɪ/ *adv.* **(a)** ursprünglich **(b)** originell ⟨*schreiben usw.*⟩

originate /ə'rɪdʒɪneɪt/ *v.i.* ~ **from** entstehen aus; ~ **in** seinen Ursprung haben in (+ *Dat.*)

ornament /'ɔːnəmənt/ *n.* Ziergegenstand, *der*

ornamental /ɔːnə'mentl/ *adj.* dekorativ; Zier⟨*pflanze, -naht usw.*⟩

ornate /ɔː'neɪt/ *adj.* reich verziert; prunkvoll ⟨*Dekoration*⟩

ornithologist /ɔːnɪ'θɒlədʒɪst/ *n.* Ornithologe, *der/*Ornithologin, *die*

ornithology /ɔːnɪ'θɒlədʒɪ/ *n.* Ornithologie, *die*

orphan /'ɔːfn/ 1 *n.* Waise, *die* 2 *v.t.* **be ~ed** [zur] Waise werden

orphanage /'ɔːfənɪdʒ/ *n.* Waisenhaus, *das*

orthodox /'ɔːθədɒks/ *adj.* orthodox

orthopaedic /ɔːθə'piːdɪk/ *adj.* orthopädisch

orthopaedics /ɔːθə'piːdɪks/ *n.* Orthopädie, *die*

oscillate /'ɒsɪleɪt/ *v.i.* schwingen

oscillation /ɒsɪ'leɪʃn/ *n.* Schwingen, *das;* (single ~) Schwingung, *die*

osmosis /ɒz'məʊsɪs/ *n., pl.* **osmoses** /ɒz'məʊsiːz/ Osmose, *die*

ostensible /ɒ'stensɪbl/ *adj.* vorgeschoben

ostensibly /ɒ'stensɪblɪ/ *adv.* vorgeblich

ostentatious /ɒsten'teɪʃəs/ *adj.* prunkhaft ⟨*Kleidung, Schmuck*⟩; prahlerisch ⟨*Art*⟩

osteopath /'ɒstɪəpæθ/ *n.* Osteopath, *der/* Osteopathin, *die*

osteoporosis /ɒstɪəʊpə'rəʊsɪs/ *n.* Osteoporose, *die*

ostrich /'ɒstrɪtʃ/ *n.* Strauß, *der*

other /'ʌðə(r)/ 1 *adj.* **(a)** (not the same) ander...; **the ~ two/three** *etc.* (the remaining) die beiden/drei *usw.* anderen; **the ~ one** der/die/das andere; **some ~ time** ein andermal ⋯⟶

(b) (further) one ~ thing noch eins; some/six ~ people noch ein paar/noch sechs [andere *od.* weitere] Leute; no ~ questions keine weiteren Fragen
(c) ~ than (different from) anders als; (except) außer
(d) the ~ day/evening neulich/neulich abends
☐**2** *n.* anderer/andere/anderes; there are six ~s es sind noch sechs andere da; any ~: irgendein anderer/-eine andere/-ein anderes; not any ~: kein anderer/keine andere/kein anderes; one after the ~: einer/eine/eins nach dem/der/dem anderen
☐**3** *adv.* anders; ~ than that, ...: abgesehen davon, ...

otherwise /'ʌðəwaɪz/ ☐**1** *adv.* **(a)** (in a different way) anders
(b) (or else) anderenfalls
(c) (in other respects) im Übrigen
☐**2** *pred. adj.* anders

otter /'ɒtə(r)/ *n.* [Fisch]otter, *der*

ouch /aʊtʃ/ *int.* autsch

ought /ɔːt/ *v. aux. only in pres. and past ought, neg.* (coll.) oughtn't /'ɔːtnt/ I ~ to do/ have done it (expr. moral duty) ich müsste es tun/hätte es tun müssen; (expr. desirability) ich sollte es tun/hätte es tun sollen; ~ not *or* ~n't you to have left by now? müsstest du nicht schon weg sein?; one ~ not to do it man sollte es nicht tun; he ~ to be hanged/ in hospital er gehört an den Galgen/ins Krankenhaus; that ~ to be enough das dürfte reichen; he ~ to win er müsste [eigentlich] gewinnen

oughtn't /'ɔːtnt/ (coll.) = ought not

ounce /aʊns/ *n.* (measure) Unze, *die*

our /'aʊə(r)/ *poss. pron. attrib.* unser

ours /'aʊəz/ *poss. pron. pred.* unserer/ unsere/unseres; *see also* HERS

ourselves /aʊə'selvz/ *pron.* **(a)** *emphat.* selbst
(b) *refl.* uns. *See also* HERSELF

oust /aʊst/ *v.t.* verdrängen; ~ sb. from his job/from power jmdn. von seinem Arbeitsplatz vertreiben/jmdn. entmachten

out /aʊt/ *adv.* **(a)** (away from place) ~ here/ there hier/da draußen; be ~ in the garden draußen im Garten sein; what's it like ~? wie ist es draußen?; go ~ shopping *etc.* einkaufen *usw.* gehen; be ~ (not at home, not in one's office, etc.) nicht da sein; she was ~ all night sie war eine/die ganze Nacht weg; have a day ~ in London einen Tag in London verbringen; row ~ to ...: hinaus-/ herausrudern zu ...; be ~ at sea auf See sein
(b) (Sport, Games) be ~ ⟨Ball:⟩ aus *od.* im Aus sein; ⟨Mitspieler:⟩ ausscheiden; ⟨Schlagmann:⟩ aus[geschlagen] sein; not ~: nicht aus
(c) be ~ (asleep) weg sein (ugs.); (unconscious) bewusstlos sein
(d) (no longer burning) aus[gegangen]

(e) (in error) be 3% ~ in one's calculations sich um 3% verrechnet haben; this is £5 ~: das stimmt um 5 Pfund nicht
(f) (not in fashion) passee (ugs.); out (ugs.)
(g) say it ~ loud es laut sagen; ~ with it! heraus mit der Sprache; their secret is ~: ihr Geheimnis ist bekannt geworden; [the] truth will ~: die Wahrheit wird an den Tag kommen; the sun/moon is ~: die Sonne/der Mond scheint; the third volume is just ~: der dritte Band ist soeben erschienen; the roses are ~: die Rosen blühen
(h) be ~ for sth./to do sth. auf etw. (*Akk.*) aus sein/darauf aus sein, etw. zu tun; be ~ for trouble Streit suchen
(i) (to or at an end) before the day/month was ~: am selben Tag/vor Ende des Monats. *See also* OUT OF

out: ~**back** *n.* (esp. Austral.) Hinterland, *das;* ~**bid** *v.t.,* ~**bid** überbieten; ~**board** *adj.* ~**board motor** Außenbordmotor, *der;* ~**break** *n.* Ausbruch, *der;* at the ~**break** of war bei Kriegsausbruch; an ~**break** of flu eine Grippeepidemie; ~**building** *n.* Nebengebäude, *das;* ~**burst** *n.* Ausbruch, *der;* an ~**burst** of weeping/laughter ein Weinkrampf/Lachanfall; an ~**burst** of temper ein Wutanfall; ~**cast** *n.* Ausgestoßene, *der/ die;* a social ~**cast** ein Geächteter/eine Geächtete; ~**come** *n.* Ergebnis, *das;* Resultat, *das;* ~**cry** *n.* [Aufschrei der] Empörung; ~**dated** *adj.* überholt; ~**do** *v.t., forms as* DO: überbieten (in an + *Dat.*); ~**door** *adj.* ~**door shoes/things** Straßenschuhe/-kleidung, *die;* ~**door games/ pursuits** Spiele/-Betätigungen im Freien; ~**door swimming pool** Freibad, *das;* ~**'doors** ☐**1** *adv.* draußen; go ~**doors** nach draußen gehen; ☐**2** *n.* the [great] ~**doors** die freie Natur

outer /'aʊtə(r)/ *adj.* äußer...; Außen⟨fläche, -seite, -wand, -tür⟩

outer 'space *n.* Weltraum, *der*

out: ~**fit** *n.* **(a)** (clothes) Kleider *Pl.;* **(b)** (equipment) Ausrüstung, *die;* **(c)** (coll.: organization) Laden, *der* (ugs.); ~**going** ☐**1** *adj.* **(a)** [aus dem Amt] scheidend ⟨Regierung, Präsident⟩; **(b)** (friendly) kontaktfreudig ⟨Person⟩; ☐**2** *n., in pl.* ~**s** (expenditure) Ausgaben *Pl.;* ~**'grow** *v.t., forms as* GROW: herauswachsen aus ⟨Kleider⟩; (leave behind) entwachsen (+ *Dat.*); ~**growth** *n.* Auswuchs, *der;* ~**house** *n.* Nebengebäude, *das*

'outing *n.* Ausflug, *der*

out: ~**landish** /aʊt'lændɪʃ/ *adj.* ausgefallen; ~**last** *v.t.* überdauern; überleben ⟨Person, Jahrhundert⟩; ~**law** ☐**1** *n.* Bandit, *der/*Banditin, *die;* ☐**2** *v.t.* verbieten; ~**lay** *n.* Auslagen *Pl.* (on für); ~**let** /'aʊtlet, 'aʊtlɪt/ *n.* **(a)** Ablauf, Abfluss, *der;* Auslauf, Auslass, *der;* **(b)** (fig.) Ventil, *das;* **(c)** (market) Absatzmarkt, *der;* (shop) Verkaufsstelle, *die;* ~**line** ☐**1** *n.* **(a)** *in sing. or pl.* Umriss, *der;* **(b)** (short account)

Grundriss, *der;* (of topic) Übersicht, die **(of** über + *Akk.*); **2** *v.t.* (describe) umreißen; **∼live** /aʊt'lɪv/ *v.t.* überleben; **∼look** *n.* **(a)** (view) Aussicht, *die* (over über + *Akk.,* on to auf + *Akk.*); (fig.; Meteorol.) Aussichten *Pl.;* **(b)** (mental attitude) Einstellung, *die* (on zu); **∼lying** *adj.* entlegen; **∼ma'nœuvre** *v.t.* überlisten ⟨*Truppen*⟩; **∼moded** /aʊt'məʊdɪd/ *adj.* antiquiert; **∼'number** *v.t.* zahlenmäßig überlegen sein (+ *Dat.*)

'out of *prep.* **(a)** (from within) aus; **go ∼ the door** zur Tür hinausgehen
(b) (not within) **be ∼ the country** im Ausland sein; **be ∼ town/the room** nicht in der Stadt/ im Zimmer sein; **feel ∼ it** *or* **things** sich ausgeschlossen fühlen
(c) (from among) **one ∼ every three smokers** jeder dritte Raucher; **58 ∼ every 100** 58 von hundert
(d) (beyond range of) außer ⟨*Reich-/Hörweite, Sicht, Kontrolle*⟩
(e) (from) aus; **get money ∼ sb.** Geld aus jmdm. herausholen; **do well ∼ sb./sth.** von jmdm./etw. profitieren
(f) aus ⟨*Mitleid, Furcht, Neugier usw.*⟩
(g) (without) **∼ money** ohne Geld; **we're ∼ tea** wir haben keinen Tee mehr
(h) (away from) von … entfernt; **ten miles ∼ London** 10 Meilen außerhalb von London

out: ∼-of-court settlement *n.* (Law) (agreement) außergerichtlicher Vergleich; (payment) Vergleichssumme, *die;* **∼-of-'date** *attrib. adj.* veraltet; (expired) ungültig ⟨*Karte*⟩; **∼-of-'pocket** *attrib. adj.* Bar⟨*auslagen*⟩; **∼-of-'print** *attrib. adj.* vergriffen; **∼-of-work** *attrib. adj.* arbeitslos; **∼patient** *n.* ambulanter Patient/ambulante Patientin; **∼patients[' department]** Poliklinik, *die;* **∼'play** *v.t.* (Sport) besser spielen als; **∼post** *n.* Außenposten, *der;* (of civilization etc.; also Mil.) Vorposten, *der;* **∼pouring** *n.,* *usu. in pl.* Gefühlsäußerung, *die;* **∼put** *n.* **(a)** Produktion, *die;* (of liquid, electricity, etc.) Leistung, *die;* **(b)** (Comp.) Ausgabe, *die*

outrage **1** /'aʊtreɪdʒ/ *n.* **(a)** (deed) Verbrechen, *das;* (during war) Gräueltat, *die;* (against decency) grober Verstoß
(b) (strong resentment) Empörung, *die* (at gegen)
2 /aʊt'reɪdʒ/ *v.t.* empören

outrageous /aʊt'reɪdʒəs/ *adj.* unverschämt; unverschämt hoch ⟨*Preis*⟩; unerhört ⟨*Frechheit, Skandal*⟩

out: ∼right **1** /'-'-/ *adv.* **(a)** ganz, komplett ⟨*kaufen, verkaufen*⟩; **(b)** (openly) freiheraus ⟨*erzählen, sagen, lachen*⟩; **2** /'-'-/ *adj.* ausgemacht ⟨*Unehrlichkeit*⟩; glatt (ugs.) ⟨*Ablehnung, Absage, Lüge*⟩; klar ⟨*Sieg, Niederlage, Sieger*⟩; **∼set** *n.* Anfang, *der;* at **the ∼set** zu Anfang; **from the ∼set** von Anfang an; **∼'shine** *v.t.,* **∼shone** /aʊt'ʃɒn/ (fig.) in den Schatten stellen

outside **1** /-'-, '-'-/ *n.* **(a)** Außenseite, *die;* **on the ∼:** außen; **to/from the ∼:** nach/von außen; **∼ lane** Überholspur, *die*

(b) (external appearance) Äußere, *das*
(c) **at the [very] ∼** äußerstenfalls; höchstens
2 /'--/ *adj.* **(a)** äußer…; Außen⟨*wand, -antenne, -kajüte, -toilette, -durchmesser*⟩; **∼ lane** Überholspur, *die*
(b) **have only an ∼ chance** nur eine sehr geringe Chance haben
3 /-'-/ *adv.* (on the ∼) draußen; (to the ∼) nach draußen
4 /-'-/ *prep.* **(a)** (position) außerhalb (+ *Gen.*); **∼ the door** vor der Tür
(b) (to the ∼ of) aus … hinaus; **go ∼ the house** nach draußen gehen

out'sider *n.* (Sport; also fig.) Außenseiter, *der*

out: ∼size *adj.* überdimensional; **∼size clothes** Kleidung in Übergröße; **∼skirts** *n. pl.* Stadtrand, *der;* **the ∼skirts of the town** die Außenbezirke der Stadt; **∼'smart** *v.t.* (coll.) ausschmieren (ugs.); **∼'spoken** *adj.* freimütig; **be ∼spoken about sth.** sich freimütig über etw. äußern; **∼'standing** *adj.* **(a)** (exceptional) hervorragend; überragend ⟨*Bedeutung*⟩; außergewöhnlich ⟨*Person, Mut, Fähigkeit*⟩; **(b)** (not yet settled) ausstehend ⟨*Schuld, Geldsumme*⟩; unbezahlt ⟨*Rechnung*⟩; ungelöst ⟨*Problem*⟩; **∼'standingly** *adv.* außergewöhnlich; **∼stretched** *adj.* ausgestreckt; (spread out) ausgebreitet; **∼'strip** *v.t.* (pass in running) überholen; (in competition) überflügeln; **∼tray** *n.* Ablage für Ausgänge; **∼'vote** *v.t.* überstimmen

outward /'aʊtwəd/ **1** *adj.* **(a)** (external, apparent) [rein] äußerlich; äußer… ⟨*Erscheinung, Bedingung*⟩
(b) Hin⟨*reise, -fracht*⟩
2 *adv.* nach außen ⟨*aufgehen, richten*⟩

'outwardly *adv.* nach außen hin ⟨*Gefühle zeigen*⟩; öffentlich ⟨*Loyalität erklären*⟩

'outwards ▸ OUTWARD 2

out: ∼'weigh *v.t.* schwerer wiegen als; überwiegen ⟨*Nachteile*⟩; **∼'wit** *v.t.,* -tt- überlisten; **∼'worn** *adj.* veraltet

oval /'əʊvl/ **1** *adj.* oval
2 *n.* Oval, *das*

ovary /'əʊvərɪ/ *n.* (Anat.) Eierstock, *der*

ovation /əʊ'veɪʃn/ *n.* Ovation, *die;* **a standing ∼:** stehende Ovationen *Pl.*

oven /'ʌvn/ *n.* [Back]ofen, *der*

oven: ∼ cloth *n.* Topflappen, *der;* **∼ glove** *n.* Topfhandschuh, *der;* **∼proof** *adj.* feuerfest; **∼-ready** *adj.* backfertig ⟨*Pommes frites, Pastete*⟩; bratfertig ⟨*Geflügel*⟩; **∼ware** *n.* feuerfestes Geschirr

over /'əʊvə(r)/ **1** *adv.* **(a)** (outward and downward) hinüber; **climb/look/jump ∼:** hinüber- *od.* (ugs.) rüberklettern/-sehen/ -springen
(b) (so as to cover surface) **board/cover ∼:** zunageln/-decken
(c) (across a space) hinüber; (towards speaker) herüber; **he swam ∼ to us/the other side** er schwamm zu uns herüber/hinüber zur anderen Seite; **∼ here/there** (direction) hier ⋯◇

herüber/dort hinüber; (location) hier/dort;
[come in, please,] ~ (Radio) übernehmen Sie
bitte; ~ and out (Radio) Ende
(d) (in excess etc.) children of 12 and ~:
Kinder im Alter von zwölf Jahren und
darüber; be [left] ~: übrig [geblieben] sein
(e) (from beginning to end) von Anfang bis
Ende; say sth. twice ~: etw. zweimal sagen;
[all] ~ again, (Amer.) ~: noch einmal [ganz
von vorn]; ~ and ~ [again] immer wieder
(f) (at an end) vorbei; vorüber; be ~: vorbei
sein; ⟨Aufführung:⟩ zu Ende sein; get sth.
~ with etw. hinter sich ⟨Akk.⟩ bringen; be
~ and done with erledigt sein
(g) all ~ (completely finished) aus [und vorbei]; I
ache all ~: mir tut alles weh; be shaking all
~: am ganzen Körper zittern
[2] prep. (a) (above, on, round about) über
⟨position: + Dat.; direction: + Akk.⟩; (across)
über (+ Akk.); look ~ a wall über eine Mauer
sehen; fall ~ a cliff von einem Felsen
stürzen; the pub ~ the road die Wirtschaft
gegenüber; hit sb. ~ the head jmdm. auf den
Kopf schlagen; ~ the page auf der nächsten
Seite
(b) (in or across every part of) [überall] in
(+ Dat.); (to and fro upon) über (+ Akk.); (all
through) durch; all ~ (in or on all parts of)
überall in (+ Dat.); travel all ~ the country
das ganze Land bereisen; all ~ Spain in ganz
Spanien; all ~ the world in der ganzen Welt
(c) (on account of) wegen
(d) (engaged with) bei; take trouble ~ sth. sich
⟨Dat.⟩ mit etw. Mühe geben; be a long time
~ sth. lange für etw. brauchen; ~ work/
dinner bei der Arbeit/beim Essen
(e) (superior to, in charge of) über (+ Akk.); have
command/authority ~ sb. Befehlsgewalt über
jmdn./Weisungsbefugnis gegenüber jmdm.
haben; be ~ sb. (in rank) über jmdm. stehen
(f) (beyond, more than) über (+ Akk.); ~ and
above zusätzlich zu
(g) (throughout, during) über (+ Akk.); ~ the
weekend/summer übers Wochenende/den
Sommer über; ~ the past years in den
letzten Jahren

over: ~'**active** adj. hyperaktiv; ~**all**
[1] n. (Brit.: garment) Arbeitskittel, der; [2] adj.
(a) Gesamt⟨breite, -einsparung, -abmessung⟩;
have an ~all majority die absolute Mehrheit
haben; (b) (general) allgemein; [3] /'---, -'-/
adv. (a) (in all parts) insgesamt; (b) (taken as a
whole) im Großen und Ganzen; ~'**anxious**
adj. be ~anxious to do sth. etw. unbedingt
tun wollen; ~'**awe** v.t. Ehrfurcht einflößen
(+ Dat.); ~'**balance** v.i. das Gleichgewicht
verlieren; ~'**bearing** adj. herrisch;
~'**blown** adj. ⟨past its prime, lit. or fig.⟩
verblühend; ~**board** adv. über Bord; fall
~board über Bord gehen; ~'**cast** adj. trübe;
bewölkt ⟨Himmel⟩; ~'**charge** v.t. (a)
(beyond reasonable price) zu viel abverlangen
(+ Dat.); (b) (beyond right price) zu viel
berechnen (+ Dat.); ~'**coat** n. Mantel, der;
~'**come** v.t., forms as COME: (a)
überwinden; bezwingen ⟨Feind⟩; ⟨Dämpfe:⟩

betäuben; (b) he was ~come by grief/with
emotion Kummer/Rührung überwältigte ihn;
~'**confidence** n. übersteigertes
Selbstvertrauen; ~'**confident** adj.
übertrieben zuversichtlich; ~'**cooked** adj.
verkocht; ~'**critical** adj. zu kritisch;
~'**crowded** adj. überfüllt; ~'**crowding**
n. (of room, bus, train) Überfüllung, die; (of city)
Übervölkerung, die; ~'**do** v.t., forms as DO:
(carry to excess) übertreiben; ~**do it** or **things**
(work too hard) sich übernehmen; ~'**done**
adj. (a) (exaggerated) übertrieben; (b)
(~cooked) verkocht; verbraten ⟨Fleisch⟩;
~**dose** n. [1] Überdosis, die; [2] v.i. ~dose
on heroin eine Überdosis Heroin nehmen;
~**draft** n. Kontoüberziehung, die; have an
~draft of £50 sein Konto um 50 Pfund
überzogen haben; ~'**draw** v.t., forms as
DRAW 1: überziehen ⟨Konto⟩; ~'**drawn** adj.
überzogen ⟨Konto⟩; I am ~drawn [at the
bank] mein Konto ist überzogen; ~**drive** n.
Schongang, der; ~'**due** adj. überfällig; the
train is 15 minutes ~due der Zug hat schon
15 Minuten Verspätung; ~'**eager** adj.
übereifrig; ~'**eat** v.i., forms as EAT: zu viel
essen; ~'**estimate** [1] /-'estɪmət/ v.t.
überschätzen; [2] /-'estɪmət/ n. zu hohe
Schätzung; ~**ex'ert** v. refl. sich
überanstrengen; ~**ex'pose** v.t. (Photog.)
überbelichten; ~'**fill** v.t. zu voll machen;
~**flow** [1] /--'-/ v.t. laufen über (+ Akk.)
⟨Rand⟩; (flow over brim of) überlaufen aus;
~**flow its banks** ⟨Fluss:⟩ über die Ufer treten;
[2] /--'-/ v.i. überlaufen; [3] /'---/ n. ~**flow**
[pipe] Überlauf, der; ~'**full** adj. zu voll;
übervoll; ~'**grown** adj. überwachsen (with
von); ~**hang** [1] /--'-/ v.t., ~hung /əʊvəˈhʌŋ/
⟨Felsen, Stockwerk:⟩ hinausragen über
(+ Akk.); [2] /'---/ n. Überhang, der;
~'**hanging** adj. überhängend; ~**haul**
[1] /--'-/ v.t. überholen; überprüfen ⟨System⟩;
[2] /'---/ n. Überholung, die; ~**head** [1] /--'-/
adv. über mir/ihm/uns usw.; [2] /'---/ adj.
~**head wires** Oberleitung, die; ~**head**
lighting Deckenbeleuchtung, die; [3] /'---/ n.
~**heads**, (Amer.) ~**head** (Commerc.)
Gemeinkosten Pl.; ~'**hear** v.t., forms as
HEAR 1: (accidentally) zufällig [mit]hören;
(intentionally) belauschen; ~'**heat** v.i. zu heiß
werden; ⟨Maschine, Lager:⟩ heißlaufen;
~**in'dulge** v.i. es übertreiben; ~**indulge**
in food and drink sich an Essen und Trinken
mehr als gütlich tun; ~**in'dulgence** n.
übermäßiger Genuss (in von); (towards a
person) zu große Nachgiebigkeit;
~**in'dulgent** adj. unmäßig; (towards a
person) zu nachgiebig

overjoyed /əʊvəˈdʒɔɪd/ adj. überglücklich
(at über + Akk.)

over: ~'**land** [1] /--'-/ adv. auf dem Landweg;
~**lap** [1] /--'-/ v.t. überlappen; [2] /--'-/ v.i.
⟨Flächen, Dachziegel:⟩ sich überlappen;
⟨Aufgaben:⟩ sich überschneiden; [3] n.
Überlappung, die; ~'**leaf** adv. auf der
Rückseite; ~'**load** v.t. überladen; ~'**look**
v.t. (a) ⟨Hotel, Zimmer, Haus:⟩ Aussicht

bieten auf (+ *Akk.*); **(b)** (ignore, not see) übersehen; (allow to go unpunished) hinwegsehen über (+ *Akk.*)

'**overly** *adv.* allzu

over: ~'**man** *v.t.* überbesetzen; ~**manning** *n.* [personelle] Überbesetzung; ~'**modest** *adj.* zu bescheiden; ~'**much** ① *adj.* allzu viel; ② *adv.* allzu sehr; ~**night** ① /--'-/ *adv.* (also fig.: suddenly) über Nacht; **stay ~ night** übernachten; ② /---/ *adj.* ~**night stay** Übernachtung, *die;* **be an** ~**night success** (fig.) über Nacht Erfolg haben; ~'**pay** *v.t., forms as* PAY 2: überbezahlen; ~'**populated** *adj.* überbevölkert; ~**popu'lation** *n.* Übervölkerung, *die;* ~'**power** *v.t.* überwältigen; ~'**powering** *adj.* überwältigend; durchdringend 〈*Geruch*〉; ~'**priced** *adj.* zu teuer; ~'**qualified** *adj.* überqualifiziert; ~'**rate** *v.t.* überschätzen; ~**re'act** *v.i.* unangemessen heftig reagieren (**to** auf + *Akk.*); ~**re'action** *n.* Überreaktion, *die* (**to** auf + *Akk.*); ~'**ride** *v.t. forms as* RIDE 3: sich hinwegsetzen über (+ *Akk.*); ~'**riding** *adj.* vorrangig; **be of** ~**riding importance** wichtiger als alles andere sein; ~'**ripe** *adj.* überreif; ~'**rule** *v.t.* aufheben 〈*Entscheidung*〉; zurückweisen 〈*Einwand, Argument*〉; ~**rule sb.** jmds. Vorschlag ablehnen; ~'**run** *v.t., forms as* RUN 3: **be** ~**run with** überlaufen sein von 〈*Touristen*〉; überwuchert sein von 〈*Unkraut*〉; ~**seas** ① /--'-/ *adv.* in Übersee 〈*leben, sein*〉; nach Übersee 〈*gehen*〉; ② /'---/ *adj.* Übersee-; ~'**see** *v.t., forms as* SEE 1: überwachen; (manage) leiten 〈*Abteilung*〉; ~'**sensitive** *adj.* überempfindlich; ~**-sexed** /əʊvə'sekst/ *adj.* sexbesessen; ~'**shadow** *v.t.* überschatten; ~'**shoot** *v.t., forms as* SHOOT 2: hinausschießen über (+ *Akk.*); ~**shoot [the runway]** 〈*Pilot, Flugzeug:*〉 zu weit kommen; ~**sight** *n.* Versehen, *das;* ~**simplifi'cation** *n.* zu starke Vereinfachung; ~'**simplify** *v.t.* zu stark vereinfachen; ~'**sleep** *v.i., forms as* SLEEP 2: verschlafen; ~'**spend** *v.i., forms as* SPEND: zu viel [Geld] ausgeben; ~**statement** *n.* Übertreibung, *die;* ~'**stay** *v.t.* überziehen 〈*Urlaub*〉; ~'**step** *v.t.* überschreiten; ~'**stretch** *v.t.* überdehnen; (fig.) überfordern

overt /əʊ'vɜːt/ *adj.* unverhohlen

over: ~'**take** *v.t., forms as* TAKE: überholen; '**no** ~**taking**' (Brit.) „Überholen verboten"; ~**-the-top** *adj.* überzogen; ~**throw** ① /--'-/ *v.t., forms as* THROW 1: stürzen; ② /'---/ *n.* Sturz, *der;* ~**time** ① *n.* Überstunden *Pl.;* ② *adv.* **work** ~**time** Überstunden machen; ~'**tire** *v.t.* übermüden; ~**tire oneself** sich übernehmen *od.* überanstrengen

overtly /'əʊvətlɪ, əʊ'vɜːtlɪ/ *adv.* unverhohlen

'**overtone** *n.* (fig.) Unterton, *der*

overture /'əʊvətjʊə(r)/ *n.* (Mus.) Ouvertüre, *die*

over: ~'**turn** ① *v.t.* umstoßen; ② *v.i.* 〈*Auto, Boot:*〉 umkippen; 〈*Boot:*〉 kentern; ~**use** /əʊvə'juːz/ *v.t.* zu oft verwenden

overweening /əʊvə'wiːnɪŋ/ *adj.* maßlos 〈*Ehrgeiz, Gier, Stolz*〉

'**overweight** *adj.* übergewichtig 〈*Person*〉; **be** ~**weight** Übergewicht haben

overwhelm /əʊvə'welm/ *v.t.* überwältigen

over'whelming *adj.* überwältigend

over: ~'**work** ① *v.t.* mit Arbeit überlasten; ② *v.i.* sich überarbeiten; ~'**wrought** *adj.* überreizt

ovulate /'ɒvjʊleɪt/ *v.i.* (Physiol.) ovulieren

ovulation /ɒvjʊ'leɪʃn/ *n.* Ovulation, *die*

owe /əʊ/ *v.t.,* owing /'əʊɪŋ/ schulden; ~ **sb. sth.,** ~ **sth. to sb.** jmdm. etw. schulden; (fig.) jmdm. etw. verdanken

owing /'əʊɪŋ/ *pred. adj.* ausstehend; **be** ~: ausstehen

'**owing to** *prep.* wegen

owl /aʊl/ *n.* Eule, *die*

own /əʊn/ ① *adj.* eigen; **be sb.'s** ~ [property] jmdm. selbst gehören; **a house/ ideas of one's** ~: ein eigenes Haus/eigene Ideen; **on one's/its** ~: allein ② *v.t.* besitzen; **be** ~**ed by sb.** jmdm. gehören

■ **own 'up** *v.i.* gestehen; ~ **up to sth.** etw. zugeben

'**own-brand,** '**own-label** ① *attrib. adjs.* Eigenmarken- ② *n.* Hausmarke, *die*

'**owner** *n.* Besitzer, *der*/Besitzerin, *die;* (of shop, hotel, firm, etc.) Inhaber, *der*/Inhaberin, *die*

owner-'occupier *n.* (Brit.) Eigenheimbesitzer, *der*/-besitzerin, *die*

'**ownership** *n.* Besitz, *der*

own 'goal *n.* (lit. or fig.) Eigentor, *das*

ox /ɒks/ *n., pl.* oxen /'ɒksn/ Ochse, *der*

oxidize (**oxidise**) /'ɒksɪdaɪz/ *v.t. & i.* (Chem.) oxidieren; oxydieren (fachspr.)

oxtail 'soup *n.* Ochsenschwanzsuppe, *die*

oxygen /'ɒksɪdʒən/ *n.* Sauerstoff, *der*

'**oxygen mask** *n.* Sauerstoffmaske, *die*

oyster /'ɔɪstə(r)/ *n.* Auster, *die*

oz. *abbr.* = **ounce[s]**

ozone /'əʊzəʊn/ *n.* Ozon, *das*

ozone: ~ **depletion** *n.* Ozonabbau, *der;* ~**-friendly** *adj.* ozonsicher; (not using CFCs) FCKW-frei; ~ **hole** *n.* Ozonloch, *das* (ugs.); ~ **layer** *n.* Ozonschicht, *die*

O

Pp

P, p /piː/ n. P, p, das
p. abbr. (a) = **page** S.
 (b) (Brit.) = **penny/pence** p
pace /peɪs/ ① n. (a) (step) Schritt, der
 (b) (speed) Tempo, das; keep ~ with Schritt
halten mit
 ② v.i. ~ up and down auf und ab gehen
 ③ v.t. auf und ab gehen in (+ Dat.)
'**pacemaker** n. (Sport, Med.) Schrittmacher,
der
Pacific /pə'sɪfɪk/ ① adj. (Geog.) ~ Ocean
Pazifischer od. Stiller Ozean
 ② n. the ~: der Pazifik
pacifier /'pæsɪfaɪə(r)/ n. (Amer.: dummy)
Schnuller, der
pacifism /'pæsɪfɪzm/ n. Pazifismus, der
pacifist /'pæsɪfɪst/ ① n. Pazifist, der/
Pazifistin, die
 ② adj. pazifistisch
pacify /'pæsɪfaɪ/ v.t. besänftigen
pack /pæk/ ① n. (a) (bundle) Bündel, das;
(Mil.) Tornister, der; (rucksack) Rucksack, der
 (b) (derog.: lot) (people) Bande, die; a ~ of lies/
nonsense ein Sack voll Lügen/eine Menge
Unsinn
 (c) (Brit.) ~ [of cards] [Karten]spiel, das
 (d) (of wolves, wild dogs) Rudel, das; (of hounds)
Meute, die
 (e) (packet) Packung, die
 ② v.t. (a) einpacken; (fill) packen; ~ one's
bags seine Koffer packen
 (b) (cram) voll stopfen (ugs.)
 (c) (wrap) verpacken (in in + Dat. od. Akk.)
 ③ v.i. packen; send sb. ~ing (fig.) jmdn.
rausschmeißen (ugs.)
 ▪ pack 'up ① v.t. zusammenpacken
⟨Sachen, Werkzeug⟩; packen ⟨Paket⟩
 ② v.i. (coll.: stop) aufhören
package /'pækɪdʒ/ ① n. Paket, das
 ② v.t. verpacken
package: ~ **deal** n. Paket, das;
 ~ **holiday**, ~ **tour** ns. Pauschalreise, die
packaging /'pækɪdʒɪŋ/ n. (material)
Verpackung, die
packed /pækt/ adj. (a) gepackt; ~ lunch
Lunchpaket, das
 (b) (crowded) [über]voll; ~ out gerammelt voll
(ugs.)
packet /'pækɪt/ n. Päckchen, das; (box)
Schachtel, die; a ~ of cigarettes ein
Päckchen/eine Schachtel Zigaretten; cost/
earn a ~: ein Heidengeld kosten (ugs.)/ein
Schweinegeld verdienen (ugs.)
packet 'soup n. Instantsuppe, die
'**packing** n. (material) Verpackungsmaterial,
das; postage and ~: Porto und Verpackung

'**packing case** n. [Pack]kiste, die
pact /pækt/ n. Pakt, der
pad¹ /pæd/ ① n. Polster, das; (block of paper)
Block, der
 ② v.t., -dd- polstern ⟨Jacke, Schulter⟩
 ▪ pad 'out v.t. (fig.) auswalzen
pad² v.i., -dd- tappen
padded /'pædɪd/ adj. gepolstert
padded 'envelope n. wattierter
Umschlag
padding /'pædɪŋ/ n., no indef. art.
Polsterung, die; (fig.) Füllsel, das
paddle¹ /'pædl/ ① n. [Stech]paddel, das
 ② v.t. & i. paddeln
paddle² ① v.i. (with feet) planschen
 ② n. have a/go for a ~: ein bisschen
planschen/planschen gehen
paddling pool /'pædlɪŋpuːl/ n.
Planschbecken, das
paddock /'pædək/ n. Koppel, die
'**padlock** ① n. Vorhängeschloss, das
 ② v.t. [mit einem Vorhängeschloss]
verschließen
paediatrician /piːdɪə'trɪʃn/ n. Kinderarzt,
der/-ärztin, die
paediatrics /piːdɪ'ætrɪks/ n. Pädiatrie, die
(fachspr.); Kinderheilkunde, die
paedophile /'piːdəfaɪl/ ① n. Pädophile,
der
 ② adj. pädophil
pagan /'peɪgən/ ① n. Heide, der/Heidin, die
 ② adj. heidnisch
page¹ /peɪdʒ/ n. (boy) Page, der
page² n. (of book etc.) Seite, die
pageant /'pædʒənt/ n. (spectacle)
Schauspiel, das
pageantry /'pædʒəntri/ n. Prunk, der
page: ~ **break** n. (Comp.) Seitenbruch, der;
 ~ **number** n. Seitenzahl, die
pager /'peɪdʒə(r)/ n. Piepser, der (ugs.)
paginate /'pædʒɪneɪt/ v.t. paginieren
pagination /pædʒɪ'neɪʃn/ n. Paginierung,
die
'**paging device** ▶ PAGER
paid /peɪd/ ① ▶ PAY 2, 3
 ② adj. (a) bezahlt ⟨Urlaub, Arbeit⟩
 (b) put ~ to (Brit. coll.) zunichte machen;
kurzen Prozess machen mit (ugs.) ⟨Person⟩
pail /peɪl/ n. Eimer, der
pain /peɪn/ n. (a) (suffering) Schmerzen Pl.;
(mental ~) Qualen Pl.; be in ~: Schmerzen
haben
 (b) (instance) Schmerz, der; I have a ~ in my
knee/stomach mein Knie/Magen tut weh

p

(c) *in pl.* (trouble taken) Mühe, *die;* **take** ~s sich (*Dat.*) Mühe geben (**over** mit, bei)

painful /'peɪnfl/ *adj.* **(a)** schmerzhaft; **be** ~ ⟨*Körperteil:*⟩ wehtun **(b)** (distressing) schmerzlich ⟨*Gedanke, Erinnerung*⟩; traurig ⟨*Pflicht*⟩

'painkiller *n.* schmerzstillendes Mittel

'painless *adj.* schmerzlos; (fig.) unproblematisch

painstaking /'peɪnzteɪkɪŋ/ *adj.* gewissenhaft

paint /peɪnt/ ①*n.* Farbe, *die;* (on car) Lack, *der* ②*v.t.* (cover, colour) [an]streichen; (make picture of, make by ~ing) malen; bemalen ⟨*Wand, Vase, Decke*⟩

paint: ~**box** *n.* Malkasten, *der;* ~**brush** *n.* Pinsel, *der*

'painter *n.* Maler, *der*/Malerin, *die*

'painting *n.* (art) Malerei, *die;* (picture) Gemälde, *das;* Bild, *das*

'painting book *n.* Malbuch, *das*

paint: ~ **stripper** *n.* Abbeizer, *der;* ~**work** *n.* (on walls etc.) Anstrich, *der;* (of car) Lack, *der*

pair /peə(r)/ ①*n.* Paar, *das;* **a** ~ **of gloves/socks/shoes** *etc.* ein Paar Handschuhe/Socken/Schuhe *usw.;* **in** ~**s** paarweise; **a** ~ **of trousers/jeans** eine Hose/Jeans ②*v.t.* paaren

■ **pair 'off** *v.i.* Zweiergruppen bilden

pajamas /pə'dʒɑːməz/ (Amer.) ▶ PYJAMAS

Pakistan /pɑːkɪ'stɑːn/ *pr. n.* Pakistan (*das*)

Pakistani /pɑːkɪ'stɑːnɪ/ ①*adj.* pakistanisch; **sb. is** ~: jmd. ist Pakistani ②*n.* Pakistani, *der/die*

pal /pæl/ *n.* (coll.) Kumpel, *der* (ugs.)

palace /'pælɪs/ *n.* Palast, *der*

palate /'pælət/ *n.* Gaumen, *der*

palatial /pə'leɪʃl/ *adj.* palastartig

pale[1] /peɪl/ *adj.* blass, (nearly white) bleich ⟨*Gesichtsfarbe, Haut, Gesicht*⟩; blass ⟨*Farbe*⟩; fahl ⟨*Licht*⟩; **go** ~: blass/bleich werden; (fig.) ~ **imitation** schlechte Nachahmung

pale[2] *n.* **beyond the** ~: unmöglich

Palestine /'pælɪstaɪn/ *pr. n.* Palästina (*das*)

Palestinian /pælɪ'stɪnɪən/ ①*adj.* palästinensisch; **sb. is** ~ jmd. ist Palästinenser/Palästinenserin ②*n.* Palästinenser, *der*/Palästinenserin, *die*

palette /'pælɪt/ *n.* Palette, *die*

pall[1] /pɔːl/ *n.* **(a)** (over coffin) Sargtuch, *das* **(b)** (fig.) Schleier, *der*

pall[2] *v.i.* ~ **[on sb.]** [jmdm.] langweilig werden

pallor /'pælə(r)/ *n.* Blässe, *die*

palm[1] /pɑːm/ *n.* (tree) Palme, *die*

palm[2] *n.* Handteller, *der*

■ **palm 'off** *v.t.* ~ sth. off on sb., ~ sb. off with sth. jmdm. etw. andrehen (ugs.)

palmistry /'pɑːmɪstrɪ/ *n.* Handlesekunst, *die*

palm: P~ **'Sunday** *n.* Palmsonntag, *der;* ~**top** *n.* ~top **[computer]** Palmtop, *der;* ~ **tree** *n.* Palme, *die*

palpitation /pælpɪ'teɪʃn/ *n. in pl.* (Med.: of heart) Palpitation, *die* (fachspr.); **suffer from** ~s Herzklopfen haben

paltry /'pɔːltrɪ, 'pɒltrɪ/ *adj.* schäbig

pamper /'pæmpə(r)/ *v.t.* verhätscheln; ~ **oneself** sich verwöhnen

pamphlet /'pæmflɪt/ *n.* (leaflet) Prospekt, *der;* (booklet) Broschüre, *die*

pan /pæn/ *n.* [Koch]topf, *der;* (for frying) Pfanne, *die*

panacea /pænə'sɪə/ *n.* Allheilmittel, *das*

Panama /pænə'mɑː/ *pr. n.* Panama (*das*); ~ **Ca'nal** Panamakanal, *der*

'pancake *n.* Pfannkuchen, *der*

pancreas /'pæŋkrɪəs/ *n.* Bauchspeicheldrüse, *die*

panda /'pændə/ *n.* Panda, *der*

pandemonium /pændɪ'məʊnɪəm/ *n.* Chaos, *das;* (uproar) Tumult, *der*

pander /'pændə(r)/ *v.i.* ~ **to** allzu sehr entgegenkommen (+ *Dat.*)

pane /peɪn/ *n.* Scheibe, *die*

panel /'pænl/ *n.* **(a)** Paneel, *das* **(b)** (esp. Telev., Radio, etc.) (quiz team) Rateteam, *das;* (in public discussion) Podium, *das*

panelling /'pænəlɪŋ/ *n.* Täfelung, *die*

panellist /'pænəlɪst/ *n.* (Telev., Radio) (on quiz programme) Mitglied des Rateteams; (on discussion panel) Diskussionsteilnehmer, *der*/-teilnehmerin, *die*

'pan-fry *v.t.* [in der Pfanne] braten

pang /pæŋ/ *n.* (of pain) Stich, *der;* **feel** ~s **of conscience/guilt** Gewissensbisse haben; ~[s] **of hunger** quälender Hunger

panic /'pænɪk/ ①*n.* Panik, *die;* **hit the** ~ **button** (fig. coll.) Alarm schlagen; (~) durchdrehen (ugs.) ②*v.i.,* -ck- in Panik (*Akk.*) geraten; **don't** ~! nur keine Panik!

panic: ~ **attack** *n.* Angstanfall, *der;* ~-**stricken,** ~-**struck** *adjs.* von Panik erfasst

panorama /pænə'rɑːmə/ *n.* Panorama, *das*

pansy /'pænzɪ/ *n.* Stiefmütterchen, *das*

pant /pænt/ *v.i.* keuchen; ⟨*Hund:*⟩ hecheln

panther /'pænθə(r)/ *n.* Panther, *der*

panties /'pæntɪz/ *n. pl.* (coll.) **[pair of]** ~: Schlüpfer, *der*

pantomime /'pæntəmaɪm/ *n.* (Brit.) *Märchenspiel im Varieteestil, das um Weihnachten aufgeführt wird*

pantry /'pæntrɪ/ *n.* Speisekammer, *die*

pants /pænts/ *n. pl.* **(a)** (esp. Amer. coll.: trousers) **[pair of]** ~: Hose, *die* **(b)** (Brit. coll.: underpants) Unterhose, *die*

paparazzo /pæpæ'rɑːtsəʊ/ n., pl. **paparazzi** /pæpæ'rɑːtsi:/ Paparazzo, der

paper /'peɪpə(r)/ ① n. (a) (material) Papier, das

(b) in pl. (documents) Unterlagen Pl.; (to prove identity etc.) Papiere Pl.

(c) (in examination) (Univ.) Klausur, die; (Sch.) Arbeit, die

(d) (newspaper) Zeitung, die

(e) (learned article) Referat, das

② adj. aus Papier nachgestellt; Papier⟨mütze, -taschentuch⟩

③ v.t. tapezieren

paper: ∼**back** ① n. Paperback, das; ② adj. ∼back book Paperback, das; ∼ '**bag** n. Papiertüte, die; ∼ **boy** n. Zeitungsjunge, der; ∼ **clip** n. Büroklammer, die; (larger) Aktenklammer, die; ∼ '**handkerchief** n. Papiertaschentuch, das; ∼ **mill** n. Papierfabrik od. -mühle, die; ∼ **money** n. Papiergeld, das; ∼ '**napkin** n. Papierserviette, die; ∼ **round** n. Zeitungenaustragen, das; ∼ **servi'ette** ▶ ∼ NAPKIN; ∼ '**towel** n. Papierhandtuch, das; ∼**weight** n. Briefbeschwerer, der; ∼**work** n. Schreibarbeit, die

par /pɑː(r)/ n. feel below ∼: nicht ganz auf dem Posten sein (ugs.); be on a ∼ with sth./sth. jmdm./einer Sache gleichkommen

parable /'pærəbl/ n. Gleichnis, das

parachute /'pærəʃuːt/ ① n. Fallschirm, der

② v.i. ⟨Truppen:⟩ abspringen (into über + Dat.)

parade /pə'reɪd/ ① n. (a) (display) Zurschaustellung, die

(b) (Mil.) Appell, der

(c) (procession) Umzug, der; (of troops) Parade, die

② v.t. zur Schau stellen

③ v.i. paradieren

pa'rade ground n. Exerzierplatz, der

paradise /'pærədaɪs/ n. Paradies, das

paradox /'pærədɒks/ n. Paradox[on], das

paradoxical /pærə'dɒksɪkl/ adj. paradox

paraffin /'pærəfɪn/ n. Paraffin, das; (Brit.: fuel) Petroleum, das

paragliding /'pærəglaɪdɪŋ/ n. Paragliding, das

paragon /'pærəgən/ Muster, das (of an + Dat.); ∼ of virtue Tugendheld, der/-heldin, die

paragraph /'pærəgrɑːf/ n. Absatz, der

parallel /'pærəlel/ ① adj. parallel; (fig.: similar) vergleichbar; ∼ bars Barren, die ② n. Parallele, die; ∼ [of latitude] Breitenkreis, der

paralyse /'pærəlaɪz/ v.t. lähmen; (fig.) lahm legen ⟨Verkehr, Industrie⟩

paralysis /pə'rælɪsɪs/ n. Lähmung, die

paralyze (Amer.) ▶ PARALYSE

paramedic /pærə'medɪk/ n. medizinische Hilfskraft; (ambulance worker) Sanitäter, der/Sanitäterin, die

parameter /pə'ræmɪtə(r)/ n. Faktor, der

paramilitary /pærə'mɪlɪtərɪ/ adj. paramilitärisch

paramount /'pærəmaʊnt/ adj. größt… ⟨Wichtigkeit⟩; Haupt⟨überlegung⟩; be ∼: Vorrang haben

paranoia /pærə'nɔɪə/ n. Paranoia, die (Med.); (tendency) Verfolgungswahn, der

paranoid /'pærənɔɪd/ adj. be ∼ ⟨Person:⟩ an Verfolgungswahn leiden

parapet /'pærəpɪt/ n. Brüstung, die

paraphernalia /pærəfə'neɪlɪə/ n. sing. Apparat, der

paraphrase /'pærəfreɪz/ ① n. Umschreibung, die ② v.t. umschreiben

paraplegic /pærə'pliːdʒɪk/ ① adj. doppelseitig gelähmt ② n. doppelseitig Gelähmter/Gelähmte

parasite /'pærəsaɪt/ n. Schmarotzer, der

parasitic /pærə'sɪtɪk/ adj. (a) (Biol.) parasitisch

(b) (fig.) schmarotzerhaft

parasol /'pærəsɒl/ n. Sonnenschirm, der

paratroops /'pærətruːps/ n. pl. Fallschirmjäger Pl.

parcel /'pɑːsl/ n. Paket, das

parched /pɑːtʃt/ adj. ausgedörrt; trocken ⟨Lippen⟩

parchment /'pɑːtʃmənt/ n. Pergament, das

pardon /'pɑːdn/ ① n. Verzeihung, die; beg sb.'s ∼: jmdn. um Entschuldigung bitten; I beg your ∼: entschuldigen Sie bitte ② v.t. (a) ∼ sb. [for] sth. jmdm. etw. verzeihen

(b) (excuse) entschuldigen

pardonable /'pɑːdənəbl/ adj. verzeihlich

pare /peə(r)/ v.t. (trim) schneiden; (peel) schälen

parent /'peərənt/ n. Elternteil, der; ∼s Eltern Pl.

parental /pə'rentl/ adj. Eltern⟨pflicht, -haus, -liebe⟩

parenthesis /pə'renθɪsɪs/ n., pl. **parentheses** /pə'renθɪsiːz/ (bracket) runde Klammer

'parents' evening n. Elternabend, der

'parents-in-law pl. Schwiegeltern Pl.

Paris /'pærɪs/ pr. n. Paris (das)

parish /'pærɪʃ/ n. Gemeinde, die

parish: ∼ '**church** n. Pfarrkirche, die; ∼ '**council** n. (Brit.) Gemeinderat, der

parishioner /pə'rɪʃənə(r)/ n. Gemeinde[mit]glied, das

parish 'priest n. Gemeindepfarrer, der

park /pɑːk/ ① n. Park, der ② v.i. parken ③ v.t. abstellen; parken ⟨Kfz⟩; a ∼ed car ein parkendes Auto

park-and-'ride n. Park-and-ride-System, das; (place) Park-and-ride-Parkplatz, der

'parking n. Parken, das; 'no ∼' „Parken verboten"

parking: ∼ **fine** n. Geldbuße für falsches Parken; ∼ **light** n. Parkleuchte, die; ∼ **lot** n. (Amer.) Parkplatz, der; ∼ **meter** n. Parkuhr, die; ∼ **offence** n. Verstoß gegen das Parkverbot; ∼ **space** n. (a) no pl. Parkraum, der; (b) (single space) Parkplatz, der; ∼ **ticket** n. Strafzettel [für falsches Parken]

'park-keeper n. Parkwächter, der/ -wächterin, die

parliament /'pɑːləmənt/ n. Parlament, das; [Houses of] P∼ (Brit.) Parlament, das

parliamentary /pɑːlə'mentərɪ/ adj. parlamentarisch; Parlaments⟨geschäfte, -wahlen, -reform⟩

parlour (Brit.; Amer.: **parlor**) /'pɑːlə(r)/ n. (dated) Wohnzimmer, das

parochial /pə'rəʊkɪəl/ adj. krähwinklig

parody /'pærədɪ/ ① n. Parodie, die (of auf + Akk.)
② v.t. parodieren

parole /pə'rəʊl/ n. bedingter Straferlass (Rechtsw.); on ∼: auf Bewährung

paroxysm /'pærəksɪzm/ n. Krampf, der; (fit, convulsion) Anfall, der (of von)

parquet /'pɑːkɪ, 'pɑːkeɪ/ n. ∼ [floor/ flooring] Parkett, das

parrot /'pærət/ n. Papagei, der

parry /'pærɪ/ v.t. abwehren ⟨Faustschlag⟩; (Fencing; also fig.) parieren

parsley /'pɑːslɪ/ n. Petersilie, die

parsnip /'pɑːsnɪp/ n. Gemeiner Pastinak, der

parson /'pɑːsn/ n. Pfarrer, der

part /pɑːt/ ① n. (a) Teil, der; the greater ∼: der größte Teil; der Großteil; for the most ∼: größtenteils; in ∼: teilweise; in large ∼: groß[en]teils; in ∼s zum Teil
(b) (of machine) [Einzel]teil, das
(c) (share) Anteil, der
(d) (Theatre) Rolle, die
(e) (Mus.) Part, der; Stimme, die
(f) usu. in pl. (region) Gegend, die; (of continent, world) Teil, der
(g) (side) Partei, die; take sb.'s ∼: jmds. od. für jmdn. Partei ergreifen
(h) take [no] ∼ [in sth.] sich [an etw. (Dat.)] [nicht] beteiligen
(i) take sth. in good ∼: etw. nicht übel nehmen
② adv. teils
③ v.t. (a) (divide into ∼s) teilen; scheiteln ⟨Haar⟩
(b) (separate) trennen
④ v.i. ⟨Seil, Tau, Kette⟩ reißen; ⟨Wege, Personen⟩ sich trennen; ∼ with sich trennen von ⟨Besitz, Geld⟩

part ex'change n. accept sth. in ∼ for sth. etw. für etw. in Zahlung nehmen; sell sth. in ∼: etw. in Zahlung geben

partial /'pɑːʃl/ adj. (a) (biased) voreingenommen
(b) be/not be ∼ to sth. eine Schwäche/keine besondere Vorliebe für etw. haben
(c) partiell ⟨Lähmung, Sonnenfinsternis⟩; a ∼ success ein Teilerfolg

'partially adv. teilweise

participant /pɑː'tɪsɪpənt/ n. Beteiligte, der/die (in an + Dat.)

participate /pɑː'tɪsɪpeɪt/ v.i. sich beteiligen (in an + Dat.); (in arranged event) teilnehmen (in an + Dat.)

participation /pɑːtɪsɪ'peɪʃn/ n. Beteiligung, die (in an + Dat.); (in arranged event) Teilnahme, die (in bei, an + Dat.)

participle /'pɑːtɪsɪpl/ n. Partizip, das

particle /'pɑːtɪkl/ n. Teilchen, das

particular /pə'tɪkjʊlə(r)/ ① adj. (a) besonder...; here in ∼: besonders hier; nothing/anything [in] ∼: nichts/irgendetwas Besonderes
(b) (fastidious) genau; I am not ∼: es ist mir gleich; be ∼ about sth. es mit etw. genau nehmen
② n., in pl. Einzelheiten Pl.; Details Pl.; (of person) Personalien Pl.

par'ticularly adv. besonders

'parting ① n. (a) (final) ∼: Abschied, der
(b) (Brit.: in hair) Scheitel, der
② attrib. adj. Abschieds-

partisan /'pɑːtɪzæn/ n. Partisan, der/ Partisanin, die

partition /pɑː'tɪʃn/ ① n. (a) (Polit.) Teilung, die
(b) (room divider) Trennwand, die
② v.t. (a) (divide) aufteilen ⟨Land, Zimmer⟩
(b) (Polit.) teilen ⟨Land⟩
■ **partition 'off** v.t. abteilen

'partly adv. zum Teil; teilweise

partner /'pɑːtnə(r)/ n. Partner, der/ Partnerin, die

'partnership n. Partnerschaft, die; business ∼: [Personen]gesellschaft, die

'part-owner n. Mitbesitzer, der/ -besitzerin, die

partridge /'pɑːtrɪdʒ/ n., pl. same or ∼s Rebhuhn, das

part: ∼**time** ① /'--/ adj. Teilzeit⟨arbeit, -arbeiter⟩; ② /-'-/ adv. stundenweise, halbtags ⟨arbeiten, studieren⟩; ∼**'timer** n. Teilzeitkraft, die; study as a ∼**timer** halbtags od. stundenweise studieren

party /'pɑːtɪ/ n. (a) (Polit., Law) Partei, die; attrib. Partei-
(b) (group) Gruppe, die
(c) (social gathering) Party, die

party: ∼ **po'litical** adj. parteipolitisch; ∼ **'politics** n. Parteipolitik, die; ∼ **wall** n. Mauer zum Nachbargrundstück/-gebäude

pass /pɑːs/ ① n. (a) (passing of an   ···⟶

examination) bestandene Prüfung; '∼' (mark)
Ausreichend, *das;* **get a ∼ in maths** die
Mathematikprüfung bestehen
(b) (written permission) Ausweis, *der*
(c) (Footb.) Pass, *der* (fachspr.); Ballabgabe, *die*
(d) (in mountains) Pass, *der*
② *v.i.* **(a)** (go by) ⟨*Fußgänger:*⟩ vorbeigehen;
⟨*Fahrer, Fahrzeug:*⟩ vorbeifahren; ⟨*Zeit,
Sekunde:*⟩ vergehen; (by chance) ⟨*Person,
Fahrzeug:*⟩ vorbeikommen
(b) (come to an end) vorbeigehen; ⟨*Gewitter,
Unwetter:*⟩ vorüberziehen
(c) (be accepted) durchgehen **(as** als, **for** für)
(d) (in exam) bestehen
③ *v.t.* **(a)** ⟨*Fußgänger:*⟩ vorbeigehen an
(+ *Dat.*); ⟨*Fahrer, Fahrzeug:*⟩ vorbeifahren an
(+ *Dat.*); (by chance) ⟨*Person, Fahrzeug:*⟩
vorbeikommen an (+ *Dat.*)
(b) (overtake) vorbeifahren an (+ *Dat.*)
(c) bestehen ⟨*Prüfung*⟩
(d) (approve) verabschieden ⟨*Gesetzentwurf*⟩;
annehmen ⟨*Vorschlag*⟩; bestehen lassen
⟨*Prüfungskandidaten*⟩
(e) (Footb. etc.) abgeben **(to** an + *Akk.*)
(f) (spend) verbringen ⟨*Leben, Zeit, Tag*⟩
(g) (hand) ∼ **sb. sth.** jmdm. etw. reichen *od.*
geben
(h) fällen ⟨*Urteil*⟩; machen ⟨*Bemerkung*⟩
(i) ∼ **water** Wasser lassen
∎ **pass a'way** *v.i.* (euphem.) verscheiden
(geh.)
∎ **pass 'off** *v.t.* ∼ **sth. off as sth.** etw. als
etw. ausgeben
∎ **pass 'on** *v.t.* weitergeben **(to** an + *Akk.*)
∎ **pass 'out** *v.i.* ohnmächtig werden
∎ **pass 'up** *v.t.* entgehen lassen
⟨*Gelegenheit*⟩; ablehnen ⟨*Angebot*⟩

passable /'pɑːsəbl/ *adj.* **(a)** (acceptable)
passabel
(b) befahrbar ⟨*Straße*⟩

passage /'pæsɪdʒ/ *n.* **(a)** (voyage) Überfahrt,
die
(b) (way) Durchgang, *der;* (corridor) Korridor,
der
(c) (part of book etc.) Textstelle, *die;* (Mus.)
Stelle, *die*

'passageway *n.* Gang, *der;* (between houses)
Durchgang, *der*

passenger /'pæsɪndʒə(r)/ *n.* Passagier, *der;*
(on train) Reisende, *der/die;* (on bus, in taxi)
Fahrgast, *der;* (in car, on motor cycle) Mitfahrer,
*der/*Mitfahrerin, *die;* (in front seat of car)
Beifahrer, *der/*Beifahrerin, *die*

passenger: ∼ **aircraft** *n.*
Passagierflugzeug, *das;* ∼ **door** *n.*
Beifahrertür, *die;* ∼ **lounge** *n.* Warteraum,
der; ∼ **plane** *n.* Passagierflugzeug, *das;*
∼ **seat** *n.* Beifahrersitz, *der;* ∼ **service**
n. (train) Personenzugverbindung, *die;* (ferry)
Personenfährverbindung, *die*

passer-by /pɑːsəˈbaɪ/ *n.* Passant, *der/*
Passantin, *die*

'passing ① *n.* (of time, years) Lauf, *der;* **in** ∼:
beiläufig ⟨*bemerken usw.*⟩

② *adj.* **(a)** vorbeifahrend ⟨*Zug, Auto*⟩;
vorbeikommend ⟨*Person*⟩
(b) flüchtig ⟨*Blick*⟩; vorübergehend ⟨*Mode,
Interesse*⟩; flüchtig ⟨*Bekanntschaft*⟩

'passing place *n.* Ausweichstelle, *die*

passion /'pæʃn/ *n.* Leidenschaft, *die;*
(enthusiasm) leidenschaftliche Begeisterung;
he has a ∼ **for steam engines** Dampfloks
sind seine Leidenschaft

passionate /'pæʃənət/ *adj.*
leidenschaftlich; heftig ⟨*Verlangen*⟩

passive /'pæsɪv/ ① *adj.* **(a)** passiv
(b) (Ling.) Passiv-
② *n.* (Ling.) Passiv, *das*

pass: ∼ **key** *n.* (master key) Hauptschlüssel,
der; ∼ **mark** *n.* Mindestpunktzahl, *die;*
∼**port** *n.* **(a)** [Reise]pass, *der; attrib.* Pass-;
∼**port control** Passkontrolle, *die;* **(b)** (fig.)
Schlüssel, *der* **(to** zu); ∼**word** *n.* **(a)** Parole,
die; Losung, *die;* **(b)** (Comp.) Passwort, *das*

past /pɑːst/ ① *adj.* **(a)** *pred.* (over) vorbei
(b) *attrib.* (previous) früher; vergangen;
ehemalig ⟨*Präsident, Vorsitzende usw.*⟩
(c) *attrib.* (just gone by) letzt...; vergangen; **in
the** ∼ **few days** während der letzten Tage
(d) (Ling.) ∼ **tense** Vergangenheit, *die*
② *n.* Vergangenheit, *die;* **in the** ∼: früher; **in
der Vergangenheit** ⟨*leben*⟩; **be a thing of the**
∼: der Vergangenheit angehören
③ *prep.* (in time) nach; (in place) hinter
(+ *Dat.*); **half** ∼ **three** halb vier; **five [minutes]**
∼ **two** fünf [Minuten] nach zwei; **gaze/walk**
∼ **sb./sth.** an jmdm./etw. vorbeiblicken/
vorbeigehen; ∼ **repair** nicht mehr zu
reparieren
④ *adv.* vorbei; **hurry** ∼: vorübereilen

pasta /'pæstə/ *n.* Teigwaren *Pl.*

paste /peɪst/ ① *n.* **(a)** Brei, *der*
(b) (glue) Kleister, *der*
(c) (of meat, fish, etc.) Paste, *die*
② *v.t.* **(a)** kleben; ∼ **sth. into sth.** etw. in
etw. (*Akk.*) einkleben
(b) (Comp.) einfügen **(into** in + *Akk.*); *see also*
CUT 1E

pastel /'pæstl/ ① *n.* (crayon) Pastellstift, *der*
② *adj.* pastellfarben; Pastell⟨*farben, -töne,
-zeichnung*⟩

pasteurize /'pɑːstʃəraɪz/ *v.t.*
pasteurisieren

pastille /'pæstɪl/ *n.* Pastille, *die*

pastime /'pɑːstaɪm/ *n.* Zeitvertreib, *der;*
(person's specific) ∼ Hobby, *das*

past 'master *n.* (fig.) Meister, *der*

pastor /'pɑːstə(r)/ *n.* Pfarrer, *der/*Pfarrerin,
die; Pastor, *der/*Pastorin, *die*

pastoral /'pɑːstərl/ *adj.* Weide-; ländlich
⟨*Reiz, Idylle, Umgebung*⟩

pastry /'peɪstrɪ/ *n.* Teig, *der;* (article of food)
Gebäckstück, *das;* **pastries** *collect.*
[Fein]gebäck, *das*

pasture /'pɑːstʃə(r)/ *n.* Weide, *die*

'pastureland *n.* Weideland, *das*

pasty /'pæstɪ/ *n.* Pastete, *die*

pat ⋯ pay ⋯

pat¹ /pæt/ 1 n. (a) (tap) Klaps, *der*
(b) (of butter) Stückchen, *das*
2 v.t., **-tt-** leicht klopfen auf (+ *Akk.*);
tätscheln, (once) einen Klaps geben (+ *Dat.*)
⟨*Person, Hund, Pferd*⟩; ~ sb. on the arm/
head jmdm. den Arm/Kopf tätscheln

pat² adv. have sth. off ~: etw. parat haben

patch /pætʃ/ 1 n. (a) Stelle, *die;* fog ~es
Nebelfelder
(b) (on worn garment) Flicken, *der;* be not a
~ on sth. (fig. coll.) nichts gegen etw. sein
2 v.t. flicken

■ **patch 'up** v.t. reparieren; (fig.) beilegen
⟨*Streit*⟩

patchwork n. Patchwork, *das*

patchy /'pætʃɪ/ adj. uneinheitlich
⟨*Qualität*⟩; ungleichmäßig ⟨*Arbeit*⟩; sehr
lückenhaft ⟨*Wissen*⟩

pâté /'pæteɪ/ n. Pastete, *die*

patent /'peɪtənt, 'pætənt/ 1 adj. (obvious)
offenkundig
2 n. Patent, *das*
3 v.t. patentieren lassen

patent 'leather n. Lackleder, *das;*
~ shoes Lackschuhe *Pl.*

'patently adv. offenkundig; ~ obvious
ganz offenkundig

paternal /pə'tɜːnl/ adj. väterlich

paternity /pə'tɜːnɪtɪ/ n. (fatherhood)
Vaterschaft, *die*

pa'ternity leave n. Vaterschaftsurlaub,
der

path /pɑːθ/ n. Weg, *der;* (line of motion) Bahn,
die

pathetic /pə'θetɪk/ adj. (a) (pitiful) Mitleid
erregend
(b) (contemptible) armselig ⟨*Entschuldigung*⟩;
erbärmlich ⟨*Person, Leistung*⟩

pathogen /'pæθədʒən/ n.
[Krankheits]erreger, *der*

pathological /pæθə'lɒdʒɪkl/ adj. (a)
pathologisch
(b) (fig.: obsessive) krankhaft

pathologist /pə'θɒlədʒɪst/ n. Pathologe,
der/Pathologin, *die*

pathology /pə'θɒlədʒɪ/ n. Pathologie, *die;*
the ~ of a disease das Krankheitsbild

'pathway n. Weg, *der*

patience /'peɪʃəns/ n. Geduld, *die*

patient /'peɪʃənt/ 1 adj. geduldig
2 n. Patient, *der*/Patientin, *die*

'patiently adv. geduldig

patio /'pætɪəʊ/ n., pl. ~s Veranda, *die;*
Terrasse, *die*

patio 'door n. große Glasschiebetür (*zum
Garten*)

patriarch /'peɪtrɪɑːk/ n. (of family)
Familienoberhaupt, *das*

patriarchal /peɪtrɪ'ɑːkl/ adj.
patriarchalisch

patriot /'peɪtrɪət/ n. Patriot, *der*/Patriotin,
die

patriotic /peɪtrɪ'ɒtɪk/ adj. patriotisch

patriotism /'peɪtrɪətɪzm/ n. Patriotismus,
der

patrol /pə'trəʊl/ 1 n. (Police) Streife, *die;*
(Mil.) Patrouille, *die;* be on ~: patrouillieren
2 v.i. **-ll-** patrouillieren; ⟨*Polizei:*⟩ Streife
laufen/fahren
3 v.t., **-ll-** patrouillieren durch (+ *Akk.*);
abpatrouillieren ⟨*Straßen, Gegend, Lager*⟩;
patrouillieren vor (+ *Dat.*) ⟨*Küste, Grenze*⟩;
⟨*Polizei:*⟩ Streife laufen/fahren in (+ *Dat.*)
⟨*Straßen, Stadtteil*⟩

patrol: ~ **boat** n. Patrouillenboot, *das;*
~ **car** n. Streifenwagen, *der*

patron /'peɪtrən/ n. (a) Gönner, *der*/
Gönnerin, *die;* (of institution, campaign)
Schirmherr, *der*/Schirmherrin, *die*
(b) (customer) (of shop) Kunde, *der*/Kundin,
die; (of restaurant, hotel) Gast, *der;* (of theatre,
cinema) Besucher, *der*/Besucherin, *die*
(c) ~ [saint] Schutzheilige, *der*/*die*

patronage /'pætrənɪdʒ/ n. Gönnerschaft,
die; (for campaign, institution) Schirmherrschaft,
die

patronize /'pætrənaɪz/ v.t. (a) (frequent)
besuchen
(b) (condescend to) ~ sb. jmdn. herablassend
behandeln

patronizing /'pætrənaɪzɪŋ/ adj.
gönnerhaft; herablassend

patter /'pætə(r)/ 1 n. (of rain) Prasseln, *das;*
(of feet) Trappeln, *das*
2 v.i. ⟨*Regen:*⟩ prasseln

pattern /'pætən/ n. Muster, *das;* (model)
Vorlage, *die;* (for sewing) Schnittmuster, *das;*
(for knitting) Strickmuster, *das*

paunch /pɔːntʃ/ n. Bauch, *der*

pauper /'pɔːpə(r)/ n. Arme, *der*/*die*

pause /pɔːz/ 1 n. Pause, *die*
2 v.i. eine Pause machen; ⟨*Redner:*⟩
innehalten; (hesitate) zögern

pave /peɪv/ v.t. befestigen; (with stones)
pflastern; ~ the way for sth. (fig.) einer
Sache (*Dat.*) den Weg ebnen

'pavement n. (a) (Brit.: footway) Bürgersteig,
der
(b) (Amer.: roadway) Fahrbahn, *die*

'pavement café n. Straßencafé, *das*

pavilion /pə'vɪljən/ n. Pavillon, *der;* (Brit.
Sport) Klubhaus, *das*

'paving stone n. Platte, *die;* Pflasterstein,
der

paw /pɔː/ n. Pfote, *die;* (of bear, lion, tiger)
Pranke, *die*

pawn¹ /pɔːn/ n. (Chess) Bauer, *der;* (fig.)
Schachfigur, *die*

pawn² /pɔːn/ 1 n. Pfand, *das;* in ~: verpfändet
2 v.t. verpfänden

pawn: ~**broker** n. Pfandleiher, *der*/
-leiherin, *die;* ~**shop** n. Leihhaus, *das*

pay /peɪ/ 1 n. (wages) Lohn, *der;* (salary)
Gehalt, *das;* be in the ~ of sb./sth. für
jmdn./etw. arbeiten ⋯

2 *v.t.*, paid /peɪd/ bezahlen; zahlen ⟨*Geld*⟩; ~ **sb. to do sth.** jmdn. dafür bezahlen, dass er etw. tut; ~ **sb. £10** jmdm. 10 Pfund zahlen

3 *v.i.*, paid (a) zahlen; ~ **for sth./sb.** etw./ für jmdn. bezahlen; **sth.** ~**s for itself** etw. macht sich bezahlt

(b) (be profitable) sich lohnen; ⟨*Geschäft:*⟩ rentabel sein; **it** ~**s to be careful** es lohnt sich, vorsichtig zu sein. *See also* PAID

■ **pay 'back** *v.t.* zurückzahlen; **I'll** ~ **you back later** ich gebe dir das Geld später zurück

■ **pay 'in** *v.t.* einzahlen

■ **pay 'off** *v.t.* auszahlen ⟨*Arbeiter*⟩; abbezahlen ⟨*Schulden*⟩; ablösen ⟨*Hypothek*⟩; befriedigen ⟨*Gläubiger*⟩

■ **pay 'out** *v.t.* auszahlen; (spend) ausgeben

■ **pay 'up** *v.i.* zahlen

payable /'peɪəbl/ *adj.* zahlbar; **be** ~ **to sb.** an jmdn. zu zahlen sein; **make a cheque** ~ **to the Post Office/to sb.** einen Scheck auf die Post/auf jmds. Namen ausstellen

pay: ~ **and display** 1 *n.* Parken mit Parkschein; *attrib.* Parkschein-; 2 *n.* ~ **and display car park** Parkplatz mit Parkscheinautomat; ~ **cheque** *n.* Lohn-/ Gehaltsscheck, *der;* ~ **claim** *n.* Lohn-/ Gehaltsforderung, *die;* ~ **day** *n.* Zahltag, *der;* ~ **increase** ▸ PAY RISE

payee /peɪ'iː/ *n.* Zahlungsempfänger, *der/* -empfängerin, *die*

paying /'peɪɪŋ/: ~ 'guest *n.* zahlender Gast; ~'in slip *n.* (Brit. Banking) Einzahlungsschein, *der*

'**payment** *n.* (a) (of sum, bill, debt, fine) Bezahlung, *die;* (of interest, instalment, tax, fee) Zahlung, *die;* **in** ~ [**for sth.**] als Bezahlung [für etw.]

(b) (amount) Zahlung, *die*

pay: ~ **packet** *n.* (Brit.) Lohntüte, *die;* ~**phone** *n.* Münzfernsprecher, *der;* ~ **rise** *n.* Lohn-/Gehaltserhöhung, *die;* ~**roll** *n.* Lohnliste, *die;* **be on sb.'s** ~**roll** für jmdn. arbeiten; ~**slip** *n.* Lohnstreifen, *der/* Gehaltszettel, *der;* ~ **station** *n.* (Amer.) ▸ ~PHONE

p.c. *abbr.* = **per cent** v. H.

PC *abbr.* (a) (Brit.) = **police constable** Wachtm.

(b) = **personal computer** PC

(c) = **politically correct** politisch korrekt

PE *abbr.* = **physical education**

pea /piː/ *n.* Erbse, *die*

peace /piːs/ *n.* Frieden, *der;* (tranquillity) Ruhe, *die;* ~ **of mind** Seelenfrieden, *der*

peaceable /'piːsəbl/ *adj.* friedfertig; (calm) friedlich

peaceful /'piːsfl/ *adj.* friedlich; friedfertig ⟨*Person, Volk*⟩

'**peacefully** *adv.* friedlich; **die** ~: sanft entschlafen

peace: ~**keeper** *n.* Friedenswächter, *der;* ~**keeping force** Friedenstruppe, *die;*

~**maker** *n.* Friedensstifter, *der/*-stifterin, *die;* ~ **movement** *n.* Friedensbewegung, *die;* ~ **process** *n.* Friedensprozess, *der* ~ **treaty** *n.* Friedensvertrag, *der*

peach /piːtʃ/ *n.* Pfirsich, *der*

'**peacock** *n.* Pfau, *der*

'**pea-green** *adj.* erbsengrün; maigrün

peak /piːk/ 1 *n.* (a) (of cap) Schirm, *der* (b) (of mountain) Gipfel, *der;* (fig.) Höhepunkt, *der* 2 *attrib. adj.* Höchst-, Spitzen⟨*preise,* -*werte*⟩; ~**-hour traffic** Stoßverkehr, *der*

peaked /piːkt/ *adj.* ~ **cap** Schirmmütze, *die*

'**peak season** *n.* Hochsaison, *die*

peal /piːl/ *n.* Läuten, *das;* ~ **of bells** Glockenläuten, *das;* **a** ~/~**s of laughter** schallendes Gelächter

peanut /'piːnʌt/ *n.* Erdnuss, *die;* ~ **butter** Erdnussbutter, *die;* ~**s** (coll.: little money) ein paar Kröten (salopp)

pear /peə(r)/ *n.* Birne, *die*

pearl /pɜːl/ *n.* Perle, *die*

pear: ~**-shaped** *adj.* birnenförmig: ~**tree** *n.* Birnbaum, *der*

peasant /'pezənt/ *n.* [armer] Bauer, *der;* Landarbeiter, *der*

pea 'soup Erbsensuppe, *die*

peat /piːt/ *n.* Torf, *der*

pebble /'pebl/ *n.* Kiesel[stein], *der*

peck /pek/ 1 *v.t.* hacken; picken ⟨*Körner*⟩ 2 *v.i.* picken (at nach); ~ **at one's food** im Essen herumstochern 3 *n.* (kiss) flüchtiger Kuss

'**pecking order** *n.* Hackordnung, *die*

peckish /'pekɪʃ/ *adj.* (coll.) **feel/get** ~: Hunger haben/bekommen

peculiar /pɪ'kjuːlɪə(r)/ *adj.* (a) (strange) seltsam; **I feel [slightly]** ~: mir ist [etwas] komisch

(b) (especial) besonder...

(c) (belonging exclusively) eigentümlich (**to** *Dat.*)

peculiarity /pɪkjuːlɪ'ærɪtɪ/ *n.* (a) (odd trait) Eigentümlichkeit, *die*

(b) (distinguishing characteristic) [charakteristisches] Merkmal

pe'culiarly *adv.* (a) (strangely) seltsam

(b) (especially) besonders

pedal /'pedl/ 1 *n.* Pedal, *das* 2 *v.i.*, (Brit.) -ll- in die Pedale treten

'**pedal bin** *n.* Treteimer, *der*

pedalo /'pedələʊ/ *n., pl.* ~**s** Tretboot, *das*

pedant /'pedənt/ *n.* Pedant, *der/*Pedantin, *die*

pedantic /pɪ'dæntɪk/ *adj.* pedantisch

peddle /'pedl/ *v.t.* auf der Straße verkaufen; (door to door) hausieren mit

pedestal /'pedɪstl/ *n.* Sockel, *der*

pedestrian /pɪ'destrɪən/ 1 *adj.* (uninspired) trocken; langweilig 2 *n.* Fußgänger, *der/*-gängerin, *die*

pedestrian 'crossing *n.* Fußgängerüberweg, *der*

pedestrianize (**pedestrianise**)
/pɪ'destrɪənaɪz/ *v.t.* zur Fußgängerzone
machen; ~**d zone** Fußgängerzone, *die*

pedestrian 'precinct ▶ PRECINCT A

pediatrician *etc.* ▶ PAEDIATRICIAN *etc.*

pedicure /'pedɪkjʊə(r)/ *n., no art.*
Pediküre, *die*

pedigree /'pedɪgriː/ ① *n.* Stammbaum, *der*
② *adj.* mit Stammbaum *nachgestellt*

pedlar /'pedlə(r)/ *n.* Straßenhändler, *der*/
-händlerin, *die;* (door to door) Hausierer, *der*/
Hausiererin, *die*

pee /piː/ (coll.) ① *v.i.* pinkeln (salopp); Pipi
machen (Kinderspr.)
② *n.* **(a) have a** ~: pinkeln (salopp)
(b) (urine) Pipi, *das* (Kinderspr.)

peek /piːk/ ▶ PEEP²

peel /piːl/ ① *v.t.* schälen
② *v.i.* 〈Person, Haut:〉 sich schälen; 〈Farbe:〉
abblättern
③ *n.* Schale, *die*

'peelings *n. pl.* Schalen *Pl.*

peep¹ /piːp/ ① *v.i.* 〈Maus, Vogel:〉 piep[s]en
② *n.* Piepsen, *das;* (coll.: remark etc.) Piep[s],
der

peep² ① *v.i.* gucken (ugs.); (furtively)
verstohlen gucken (ugs.)
② *n.* kurzer/verstohlener Blick

peep: ~**hole** *n.* Guckloch, *das;* ~**ing
'Tom** *n.* Spanner, *der* (ugs.)

peer¹ /pɪə(r)/ *n.* Peer, *der;* (equal)
Gleichgestellte, *der/die*

peer² *v.i.* forschend schauen; (with difficulty)
angestrengt schauen; ~ **at sth./sb.** [sich
(*Dat.*)] etw. genau ansehen/jmdn. forschend
ansehen; (with difficulty) [sich (*Dat.*)] etw./
jmdn. angestrengt ansehen

peerage /'pɪərɪdʒ/ *n.* Peerswürde, *die*

'peer pressure *n.* Gruppenzwang, *der*

peevish /'piːvɪʃ/ *adj.* nörgelig

peg /peg/ *n.* (for holding together) Stift, *der;* (for
tying things to) Pflock, *der;* (for hanging things on)
Haken, *der;* (clothes ~) Wäscheklammer, *die;*
(tent ~) Hering, *der;* **off the** ~ (Brit.: ready-
made) von der Stange (ugs.)

pejorative /pɪ'dʒɒrətɪv/ *adj.*,
pe'joratively *adv.* abwertend

pelican /'pelɪkən/ *n.* Pelikan, *der*

'pelican crossing *n.* (Brit.)
Ampelübergang, *der*

pellet /'pelɪt/ *n.* Kügelchen, *das*

pelmet /'pelmɪt/ *n.* Blende, *die*

pelt¹ /pelt/ *n.* Fell, *das*

pelt² ① *v.t.* ~ **sb. with sth.** jmdn. mit etw.
bewerfen
② *v.i.* **(a)** it was ~ing down [with rain] es
goss wie aus Kübeln (ugs.)
(b) (run fast) rasen (ugs.)

pelvic /'pelvɪk/ *adj.* Becken-

pelvis /'pelvɪs/ *n., pl.* **pelves** /'pelviːz/ *or*
~**es** (Anat.) Becken, *das*

pen¹ /pen/ ① *n.* (enclosure) Pferch, *der*

② *v.t.*, **-nn-:** ~ **sb. in a corner** jmdn. in eine
Ecke drängen
∎ **pen 'in** *v.t.* einpferchen

pen² ① *n.* Federhalter, *der;* (fountain ~)
Füller, *der;* (ball ~) Kugelschreiber, *der;* (felt-
tip ~) Filzstift, *der*
② *v.t.*, **-nn-** schreiben

penal /'piːnl/ *adj.* Straf-

penalize /'piːnəlaɪz/ *v.t.* bestrafen; (Sport)
eine Strafe verhängen gegen

penalty /'penltɪ/ *n.* **(a)** Strafe, *die;* **pay the**
~/**the** ~ **for** *or* **of sth.** dafür/für etw. büßen
[müssen]
(b) (Footb.) Elfmeter, *der*

penalty: ~ **box** *n.* (Footb.) Strafraum, *der;*
(Ice Hockey) Strafbank, *die;* ~ **kick** *n.* (Footb.)
Strafstoß, *der*

penance /'penəns/ *n.* Buße, *die;* **act of** ~:
Bußwerk, *das;* **do** ~: Buße tun

pence ▶ PENNY

pencil /'pensɪl/ ① *n.* Bleistift, *der;* red/
coloured ~: Rot-/Buntstift, *der*
② *v.t.,* (Brit.) **-ll-** mit einem Bleistift/Farbstift
schreiben

pencil: ~ **case** *n.* Griffelkasten, *der;* (of
soft material) Federmäppchen, *das;*
~ **sharpener** *n.* Bleistiftspitzer, *der*

pendant /'pendənt/ *n.* Anhänger, *der*

pending /'pendɪŋ/ ① *adj.* unentschieden
〈Angelegenheit, Sache〉; schwebend
〈Verfahren〉
② *prep.* ~ **his return** bis zu seiner
Rückkehr

pendulum /'pendjʊləm/ *n.* Pendel, *das*

penetrate /'penɪtreɪt/ *v.t.* eindringen in
(+ *Akk.*); (pass through) durchdringen

penetrating /'penɪtreɪtɪŋ/ *adj.*
durchdringend

penetration /penɪ'treɪʃn/ *n.* Eindringen,
das (of in + *Akk.*); (passing through)
Durchdringen, *das*

'penfriend *n.* Brieffreund, *der*/-freundin,
die

penguin /'peŋgwɪn/ *n.* Pinguin, *der*

penicillin /penɪ'sɪlɪn/ *n.* Penizillin, *das*

peninsula /pɪ'nɪnsjʊlə/ *n.* Halbinsel, *die*

penis /'piːnɪs/ *n.* Penis, *der*

penitence /'penɪtəns/ *n.* Reue, *die*

penitent /'penɪtənt/ *adj.* reuevoll (geh.);
reuig (geh.) 〈Sünder〉

penitentiary /penɪ'tenʃərɪ/ *n.* (Amer.)
Straf[vollzugs]anstalt, *die*

pen: ~**knife** *n.* Taschenmesser, *das;*
~ **light** *n.* [Mini]stablampe, *die*

pennant /'penənt/ *n.* Wimpel, *der;* (on official
car etc.) Stander, *der*

penniless /'penɪlɪs/ *adj.* mittellos

penny /'penɪ/ *n., pl. usu.* **pennies** /'penɪz/
(for separate coins), **pence** /pens/ (for sum of
money) Penny, *der;* **fifty pence** fünfzig Pence;
two/fifty pence [piece] Zwei-/
Fünfzigpencestück, *das*

P

pension /'penʃn/ n. Rente, die; (payment to retired civil servant) Pension, die; **widow's ~**: Witwenrente, die /-pension, die; **be on a ~**: eine Rente beziehen

■ **pension 'off** v.t. berenten (Amtsspr.); auf Rente setzen (ugs.); pensionieren ⟨Lehrer, Beamten⟩

'**pensioner** n. Rentner, der/Rentnerin, die; (retired civil servant) Pensionär, der/Pensionärin, die

pensive /'pensɪv/ adj. nachdenklich

pentagon /'pentəgən/ n. Fünfeck, das; **the P~** (Amer. Polit.) das Pentagon

Pentecost /'pentɪkɒst/ n. Pfingsten, das

pent: ~house n. Penthaus, das; **~-up** adj. angestaut ⟨Ärger, Wut⟩; unterdrückt ⟨Sehnsucht, Gefühle⟩

penultimate /pe'nʌltɪmət/ adj. vorletzt...

people /'piːpl/ n. (a) constr. as pl. Leute Pl.; Menschen Pl.; (as opposed to animals) Menschen Pl.; **city/country ~** (inhabitants) Stadt-/Landbewohner Pl.; **local ~**: Einheimische Pl.; **working ~**: arbeitende Menschen; **coloured/white ~**: Farbige/Weiße Pl.; **~ say ...**: man sagt ...; **a crowd of ~**: eine Menschenmenge

(b) (nation) Volk, das

pepper /'pepə(r)/ ⓵ n. (a) Pfeffer, der

(b) (vegetable) Paprikaschote, die; **red/green ~**: roter/grüner Paprika

⓶ v.t. (a) pfeffern

(b) (pelt) bombardieren (ugs.)

pepper: ~corn n. Pfefferkorn, das; **~ mill** n. Pfeffermühle, die; **~mint** n. (sweet) Pfefferminz, das; **~ pot** n. Pfefferstreuer, der

peppery /'pepərɪ/ adj. pfeff[e]rig; (spicy) scharf

per /pə(r), stressed pɜ:(r)/ prep. pro

perceive /pə'siːv/ v.t. wahrnehmen; (with the mind) spüren; **~d** vermeintlich ⟨Bedrohung, Gefahr, Wert⟩

per cent (Brit.; Amer.: **percent**) /pə'sent/ ⓵ adv. **ninety ~ effective** zu 90 Prozent wirksam

⓶ adj. **a 5 ~ increase** ein Zuwachs von 5 Prozent

⓷ n. (a) Prozent, das

(b) ▸ PERCENTAGE

percentage /pə'sentɪdʒ/ n. Prozentsatz, der

per'centage sign n. Prozentzeichen, das

perceptible /pə'septɪbl/ adj. wahrnehmbar

perception /pə'sepʃn/ n. (act) Wahrnehmung, die; (result) Erkenntnis, die; (faculty) Wahrnehmungsvermögen, das

perceptive /pə'septɪv/ adj. einfühlsam ⟨Person, Bemerkung⟩

perch /pɜːtʃ/ ⓵ n. Sitzstange, die

⓶ v.i. (a) sich niederlassen

(b) (be supported) sitzen

⓷ v.t. setzen/stellen/legen

percolate /'pɜːkəleɪt/ v.i. [durch]sickern

percolator /'pɜːkəleɪtə(r)/ n. Kaffeemaschine, die

percussion /pə'kʌʃn/ n. (Mus.) Schlagzeug, das; **~ instrument** Schlaginstrument, das

perennial /pə'renjəl/ ⓵ adj. (a) (Bot.) ausdauernd

(b) immer wieder auftretend ⟨Problem⟩

⓶ n. (Bot.) ausdauernde Pflanze

perfect ⓵ /'pɜːfɪkt/ adj. vollkommen; perfekt ⟨Englisch, Timing⟩; tadellos ⟨Zustand⟩; (coll.: unmitigated) absolut; **a ~ stranger** ein völlig Fremder

⓶ /pə'fekt/ v.t. vervollkommnen

perfection /pə'fekʃn/ n. Perfektion, die; **to ~**: perfekt

perfectionism /pə'fekʃənɪzm/ n. Perfektionismus, der

perfectionist /pə'fekʃənɪst/ n. Perfektionist, der/Perfektionistin, die

'**perfectly** adv. (a) (completely) vollkommen; **be ~ entitled to do sth.** durchaus berechtigt sein, etw. zu tun

(b) (faultlessly) perfekt; tadellos ⟨sich verhalten⟩

perfect 'pitch n. (Mus.) absolutes Gehör

perforate /'pɜːfəreɪt/ v.t. perforieren; (make opening into) durchlöchern

perforation /pɜːfə'reɪʃn/ n. (a) (hole) Loch, das

(b) in pl. **~s** Perforation, die; (in sheets of stamps) Zähnung, die

perform /pə'fɔːm/ ⓵ v.t. ausführen ⟨Arbeit, Operation⟩; erfüllen ⟨Pflicht, Aufgabe⟩; vollbringen ⟨[Helden]tat, Leistung⟩; ausfüllen ⟨Funktion⟩; vollbringen ⟨Wunder⟩; anstellen ⟨Berechnungen⟩; durchführen ⟨Experiment, Sektion⟩; vorführen ⟨Trick⟩; aufführen ⟨Theaterstück, Scharade⟩; vortragen ⟨Lied, Sonate usw.⟩

⓶ v.i. eine Vorführung geben; (sing) singen; (play) spielen

performance /pə'fɔːməns/ n. (a) (of duty, task) Erfüllung, die

(b) ([notable] achievement; Motor Veh.) Leistung, die

(c) (at theatre, cinema, etc.) Vorstellung, die; **her ~ as Desdemona** ihre Darstellung der Desdemona; **the ~ of a play/opera** die Aufführung eines Theaterstücks/einer Oper

performance: ~ art n. Performance-Art, die; **~ artist** n. Performancekünstler, der/-künstlerin, die **~-enhancing** adj. **~-enhancing drug/substance** leistungsfördernde od. -steigernde Droge/Substanz

per'former n. Künstler, der/Künstlerin, die

per'forming attrib. adj. dressiert ⟨Tier⟩

performing 'arts n. pl. darstellende Künste

perfume /'pɜːfjuːm/ n. Duft, der; (fluid) Parfüm, das

perfunctory /pə'fʌŋktəri/ *adj.*
oberflächlich ⟨*Arbeit, Überprüfung*⟩; flüchtig
⟨*Erkundigung, Bemerkung*⟩

perhaps /pə'hæps/ *adv.* vielleicht

peril /'perl/ *n.* Gefahr, *die*

perilous /'perələs/ *adj.* gefahrvoll; **be ~:**
gefährlich sein

perimeter /pə'rɪmɪtə(r)/ *n.* [äußere]
Begrenzung; Grenze, *die*

period /'pɪəriəd/ [1] *n.* **(a)** (of history or life)
Periode, *die;* Zeit, *die;* (any portion of time)
Zeitraum, *der;* **the Classical/Romantic ~:** die
Klassik/Romantik
(b) (Sch.) Stunde, *die;* **chemistry/English ~:**
Chemie-/Englischstunde, *die*
(c) (menstruation) Periode, *die*
(d) (punctuation mark) Punkt, *der*
[2] *adj.* zeitgenössisch ⟨*Tracht, Kostüm*⟩;
antik ⟨*Möbel*⟩

periodic /pɪərɪ'ɒdɪk/ *adj.* regelmäßig;
(intermittent) gelegentlich

periodical /pɪərɪ'ɒdɪkl/ [1] *adj.* ▸ PERIODIC
[2] *n.* Zeitschrift, *die;* **weekly/monthly ~:**
Wochenzeitschrift/Monatsschrift, *die*

peri'odically *adv.* regelmäßig; (intermittently)
gelegentlich

peripheral /pə'rɪfərl/ [1] *adj.* peripher
(geh.); Rand⟨*problem, -erscheinung*⟩
[2] *n.* (Comp.) Peripheriegerät, *das*

periphery /pə'rɪfəri/ *n.* Peripherie, *die*

periscope /'perɪskəʊp/ *n.* Periskop, *das*

perish /'perɪʃ/ *v.i.* **(a)** (die) umkommen
(b) (rot) verderben; ⟨*Gummi:*⟩ altern

perishable /'perɪʃəbl/ *adj.* [leicht]
verderblich

'perishing (coll.) [1] *adj.* mörderisch
⟨*Kälte*⟩; **it's/I'm ~:** es ist bitterkalt/ich
komme um vor Kälte (ugs.)
[2] *adv.* mörderisch ⟨*kalt*⟩

perjury /'pɜːdʒəri/ *n.* Meineid, *der;* **commit
~:** einen Meineid leisten

perk¹ /pɜːk/ (coll.) [1] *v.i.* **~ up** munter
werden
[2] *v.t.* **~ up** aufmuntern

perk² *n.* (Brit. coll.) [Sonder]vergünstigung,
die

perky /'pɜːki/ *adj.* lebhaft; munter

perm /pɜːm/ [1] *n.* Dauerwelle, *die*
[2] *v.t.* **have one's hair ~ed** sich (*Dat.*) eine
Dauerwelle machen lassen

permanence /'pɜːmənəns/ *n.*
Dauerhaftigkeit, *die*

permanent /'pɜːmənənt/ *adj.* fest ⟨*Sitz,
Bestandteil, Mitglied*⟩; ständig ⟨*Wohnsitz,
Adresse, Kampf*⟩; Dauer⟨*stellung, -visum*⟩;
bleibend ⟨*Schaden*⟩

'permanently *adv.* dauernd; auf Dauer
⟨*verhindern, bleiben*⟩

permanent 'wave *n.* Dauerwelle, *die*

permeable /'pɜːmɪəbl/ *adj.* durchlässig; **be
~ to sth.** etw. durchlassen

permeate /'pɜːmɪeɪt/ [1] *v.t.* dringen
durch; **be ~d with** *or* **by sth.** (fig.) von etw.
durchdrungen sein
[2] *v.i.* **~ through sth.** etw. durchdringen

permissible /pə'mɪsɪbl/ *adj.* zulässig; **be
~ to** *or* **for sb.** jmdm. erlaubt sein

permission /pə'mɪʃn/ *n.* Erlaubnis, *die;*
(given by official body) Genehmigung, *die;* **give
sb. ~ to do sth.** jmdm. erlauben, etw. zu tun

permissive /pə'mɪsɪv/ *adj.* **the ~ society**
die permissive Gesellschaft

permit [1] /pə'mɪt/ *v.t.,* **-tt-** zulassen
⟨*Berufung, Einspruch usw.*⟩; **~ sb. sth.**
jmdm. etw. erlauben; **sb. is ~ted to do sth.**
es ist jmdm. erlaubt, etw. zu tun
[2] *v.i.,* **-tt-** es zulassen
[3] /'pɜːmɪt/ *n.* Genehmigung, *die*

pernicious /pə'nɪʃəs/ *adj.* verderblich;
bösartig ⟨*Krankheit*⟩

peroxide /pə'rɒksaɪd/ *n.* Peroxid, *das;*
~ blonde Wasserstoffblondine, *die*

perpendicular /pɜːpən'dɪkjʊlə(r)/ *adj.*
senkrecht

perpetrate /'pɜːpɪtreɪt/ *v.t.* begehen;
verüben ⟨*Gräuel*⟩

perpetual /pə'petjʊəl/ *adj.* **(a)** (eternal) ewig
(b) (continuous; coll.: repeated) ständig

per'petually *adv.* **(a)** (eternally) ewig
(b) (continuously; coll.: repeatedly) ständig

perpetuate /pə'petjʊeɪt/ *v.t.*
aufrechterhalten

perplex /pə'pleks/ *v.t.* verwirren

perplexed /pə'plekst/ *adj.* verwirrt;
(puzzled) ratlos

perplexity /pə'pleksɪti/ *n.* Verwirrung,
die; (puzzlement) Ratlosigkeit, *die*

persecute /'pɜːsɪkjuːt/ *v.t.* verfolgen

persecution /pɜːsɪ'kjuːʃn/ *n.* Verfolgung,
die

persecutor /'pɜːsɪkjuːtə(r)/ *n.* Verfolger,
der/Verfolgerin, *die*

perseverance /pɜːsɪ'vɪərəns/ *n.*
Beharrlichkeit, *die;* Ausdauer, *die*

persevere /pɜːsɪ'vɪə(r)/ *v.i.* ausharren;
~ with *or* **at** *or* **in sth.** bei etw. dabeibleiben

Persian /'pɜːʃn/ *adj.* persisch; Perser⟨*katze,
-teppich*⟩

persist /pə'sɪst/ *v.i.* **(a)** nicht nachgeben;
~ in doing sth. etw. weiterhin [beharrlich]
tun
(b) (continue to exist) anhalten

persistence /pə'sɪstəns/ *n.* Hartnäckigkeit,
die

persistent /pə'sɪstənt/ *adj.* **(a)** hartnäckig
(b) (constantly repeated) dauernd; hartnäckig
⟨*Gerüchte*⟩

per'sistently *adv.* hartnäckig

person /'pɜːsn/ *n.* Mensch, *der;* **in ~:**
persönlich; selbst

personal /'pɜːsənl/ *adj.* persönlich;   ···✦

p

Privat⟨angelegenheit, -leben⟩; ~ **computer**
Personalcomputer, der; ~ **stereo** Walkman,
der; ~ **hygiene** Körperpflege, die
personal: ~ **ad** n. Privatanzeige, die;
(seeking friendship, romance) Kontaktanzeige, die;
~ **as'sistant** n. persönlicher Referent/
persönliche Referentin; ~ **'best** n. (Sport)
persönliche Bestleistung; ~ **call** n. (Brit.
Teleph.) Anruf mit Voranmeldung;
~ **column** n. Rubrik für private
[Klein]anzeigen; ~ **identifi'cation
number** n. persönliche
Identifikationsnummer; Geheimnummer, die
personality /pɜːsə'nælɪtɪ/ n.
Persönlichkeit, die
'personal loan n. Personal- od.
Privatdarlehen, das; Personal- od.
Privatkredit, der
'personally adv. persönlich
personal: ~ **'organizer** n.
Terminplaner, der; ~ **'pension plan** n.
persönlicher Renten[vorsorge]plan;
~ **'property** n. persönliches Eigentum
personification /pəsɒnɪfɪ'keɪʃn/ n.
Verkörperung, die
personify /pə'sɒnɪfaɪ/ v.t. verkörpern; **be
kindness personified** die Freundlichkeit in
Person sein
personnel /pɜːsə'nel/ n. Belegschaft, die; (of
shop, restaurant, etc.) Personal, das; attrib.
Personal-; ~ **department** Personalabteilung,
die
person-to-'person adj. (Amer. Teleph.)
~ **call** Anruf mit Voranmeldung
perspective /pə'spektɪv/ n. Perspektive,
die; (fig.) Blickwinkel, der
perspiration /pɜːspɪ'reɪʃn/ n. Schweiß, der
perspire /pə'spaɪə(r)/ v.i. schwitzen
persuade /pə'sweɪd/ v.t. (a) (convince)
überzeugen (of von); ~ **oneself [that]** ...: sich
(Dat.) einreden, dass ...
(b) (induce) überreden
persuasion /pə'sweɪʒn/ n. Überzeugung,
die; **it didn't take much** ~: es brauchte nicht
viel Überredungskunst
persuasive /pə'sweɪsɪv/ adj.,
per'suasively adv. überzeugend
pert /pɜːt/ adj. keck
pertinent /'pɜːtɪnənt/ adj. relevant (**to** für)
perturb /pə'tɜːb/ v.t. beunruhigen
Peru /pə'ruː/ pr. n. Peru (das)
Peruvian /pə'ruːvɪən/ 1 adj. peruanisch;
sb. is ~: jmd. ist Peruaner/Peruanerin
2 n. Peruaner, der/Peruanerin, die
peruse /pə'ruːz/ v.t. genau durchlesen; (fig.:
examine) untersuchen
pervade /pə'veɪd/ v.t. durchdringen
pervasive /pə'veɪsɪv/ adj. durchdringend
⟨Geruch, Kälte⟩; weit verbreitet ⟨Ansicht⟩;
sich ausbreitend ⟨Gefühl⟩
perverse /pə'vɜːs/ adj. starrköpfig

perversion /pə'vɜːʃn/ n. (a) (sexual)
Perversion, die
(b) ~ **of justice** Rechtsbeugung, die
pervert 1 /pə'vɜːt/ v.t. (morally) verderben
2 /'pɜːvɜːt/ n. perverser Mensch
perverted /pə'vɜːtɪd/ adj. (sexually) pervers
pessimism /'pesɪmɪzm/ n. Pessimismus,
der
pessimist /'pesɪmɪst/ n. Pessimist, der/
Pessimistin, die
pessimistic /pesɪ'mɪstɪk/ adj.
pessimistisch
pest /pest/ n. (thing) Ärgernis, das; (person)
Nervensäge, die (ugs.); (animal) Schädling, der
pester /'pestə(r)/ v.t. belästigen; nerven
(ugs.); ~ **sb. for sth.** jmdm. wegen etw. in den
Ohren liegen
pesticide /'pestɪsaɪd/ n. Pestizid, das
pestle /'pesl/ n. Stößel, der
pet /pet/ 1 n. (a) (animal) Haustier, das
(b) (as term of endearment) Schatz, der
2 adj. (favourite) Lieblings-
3 v.i., -tt- knutschen (ugs.)
petal /'petl/ n. Blütenblatt, das
peter /'piːtə(r)/ v.i. ~ **out** [allmählich] zu
Ende gehen; ⟨Weg:⟩ sich verlieren
'pet food n. Tierfutter, das
petite /pə'tiːt/ adj. zierlich
petition /pə'tɪʃn/ 1 n. Petition, die;
Eingabe, die
2 v.t. eine Eingabe richten an (+ Akk.)
petitioner /pə'tɪʃənə(r)/ n. Antragsteller,
der/Antragstellerin, die
petrify /'petrɪfaɪ/ v.t. **be petrified with fear/
shock** starr vor Angst/Schrecken sein
petrol /'petrl/ n. (Brit.) Benzin, das
petrol: ~ **bomb** n. Benzinbombe, die;
~ **can** n. (Brit.) Benzinkanister, der; ~ **cap**
n. (Brit.) Tankverschluss, der
petroleum /pɪ'trəʊlɪəm/ n. Erdöl, das
petroleum 'jelly n. Vaseline, die
petrol: ~ **pump** n. (Brit.) Zapfsäule, die;
~ **station** n. (Brit.) Tankstelle, die;
~ **tank** n. (Brit.) Benzintank, der;
~ **tanker** n. (Brit.) Benzintankwagen, der
'pet shop n. Tierhandlung, die
petticoat /'petɪkəʊt/ n. Unterrock, der
petty /'petɪ/ adj. kleinlich ⟨Vorschrift,
Einwand⟩; belanglos ⟨Detail, Sorgen⟩;
~ **criminal** Kleinkriminelle, der/die; ~ **theft**
Bagatelldiebstahl, der; ~ **thief** kleiner Dieb/
kleine Diebin
petty 'cash n. kleine Kasse; Portokasse,
die
petulance /'petjʊləns/ n. Bockigkeit, die
petulant /'petjʊlənt/ adj. bockig
pew /pjuː/ n. Kirchenbank, die
pewter /'pjuːtə(r)/ n. Zinn, das
phallic /'fælɪk/ adj. phallisch; ~ **symbol**
Phallussymbol, das
phantom /'fæntəm/ n. Phantom, das

pharmacist /'fɑːməsɪst/ n. Apotheker, der/Apothekerin, die

pharmacy /'fɑːməsɪ/ n. (dispensary) Apotheke, die

phase /feɪz/ n. Phase, die
■ **phase 'in** v.t. stufenweise einführen
■ **phase 'out** v.t. allmählich abschaffen ⟨Verfahrensweise, Methode⟩; (stop producing) [langsam] auslaufen lassen

Ph.D. /piːeɪtʃ'diː/ abbr. = **Doctor of Philosophy** Dr. phil.

pheasant /'fezənt/ n. Fasan, der

phenomenal /fɪ'nɒmɪnl/ adj., **phenomenally** /fɪ'nɒmɪnəlɪ/ adv. phänomenal

phenomenon /fɪ'nɒmɪnən/ n., pl. **phenomena** /fɪ'nɒmɪnə/ Phänomen, das

phew /fjuː/ int. puh

philanderer /fɪ'lændərə(r)/ n. Schürzenjäger, der (spött.)

philanthropist /fɪ'lænθrəpɪst/ n. Philanthrop, der/Philanthropin, die (geh.)

philanthropy /fɪ'lænθrəpɪ/ n. Philanthropie, die (geh.)

Philippines /'fɪlɪpiːnz/ pr. n. pl. Philippinen Pl.

philistine /'fɪlɪstaɪn/ n. Banause, der/ Banausin, die

Phillips /'fɪlɪps/ n. **~ screw** ® Kreuz[schlitz]schraube, die; **~ screwdriver** ® Kreuz[schlitz]schraubenzieher, der

philosopher /fɪ'lɒsəfə(r)/ n. Philosoph, der/Philosophin, die

philosophical /fɪlə'sɒfɪkl/ adj. (a) philosophisch
(b) (resigned) abgeklärt

philosophize (**philosophise**) /fɪ'lɒsəfaɪz/ v.i. philosophieren (about, on über + Akk.)

philosophy /fɪ'lɒsəfɪ/ n. Philosophie, die

phlegm /flem/ n. Schleim, der

phobia /'fəʊbɪə/ n. Phobie, die

phobic /'fəʊbɪk/ adj. phobisch

phone /fəʊn/ n. (coll.) ① n. Telefon, das; **by ~:** telefonisch; **be on the ~:** Telefon haben; (be phoning) telefonieren
② v.t. & i. anrufen
■ **phone 'back** v.t. & i. zurückrufen; (make further call) wieder anrufen
■ **phone 'up** v.t. & i. anrufen

phone: ~ book n. Telefonbuch, das; **~ booth, ~ box** ns. Telefonzelle, die; **~ call** n. Anruf, der; **~ card** n. Telefonkarte, die; **~-in** n. **~-in [programme]** (Radio) Hörersendung, die; (Telev.) Phone-in-Sendung, die (Jargon); **~ number** n. Telefonnummer, die

phonetic /fə'netɪk/ adj. phonetisch

phonetics /fə'netɪks/ n. Phonetik, die

phoney /'fəʊnɪ/ adj. (coll.) (sham) falsch; gefälscht ⟨Brief, Dokument⟩

phonograph /'fəʊnəɡrɑːf/ n. (Amer.) Plattenspieler, der

phony ▶ PHONEY

phosphate /'fɒsfeɪt/ n. Phosphat, das

phosphorus /'fɒsfərəs/ n. Phosphor, der

photo /'fəʊtəʊ/ n., pl. **~s** Foto, das

photo: ~ album n. Fotoalbum, das; **~call** n. Fototermin, der; **~copier** n. Fotokopiergerät, das; **~copy** ① n. Fotokopie, die; ② v.t. fotokopieren

photogenic /fəʊtə'dʒiːnɪk/ adj. fotogen

photograph /'fəʊtəɡrɑːf/ ① n. Fotografie, die; Foto, das; **take a ~** [of sb./sth.] [jmdn./ etw.] fotografieren
② v.t. & i. fotografieren

'photograph album n. Fotoalbum, das

photographer /fə'tɒɡrəfə(r)/ n. Fotograf, der/Fotografin, die

photographic /fəʊtə'ɡræfɪk/ adj. fotografisch; Foto⟨ausrüstung, -apparat, -ausstellung⟩

photography /fə'tɒɡrəfɪ/ n. Fotografie, die

photo: ~ session, ~ shoot ns. Shooting, das; **~'synthesis** n. Photosynthese, die

phrase /freɪz/ ① n. [Rede]wendung, die
② v.t. formulieren

'phrase book n. Sprachführer, der

physical /'fɪzɪkl/ adj. (a) physisch ⟨Gewalt⟩; dinglich ⟨Welt, Universum⟩
(b) (of physics) physikalisch
(c) (bodily) körperlich

physical edu'cation n. (Sch.) Sport, der

'physically adv. (relating to the body) körperlich

physical 'training n. Sport, der; (Sch.) Sport[unterricht], der

physician /fɪ'zɪʃn/ n. Arzt, der/Ärztin, die

physicist /'fɪzɪsɪst/ n. Physiker, der/ Physikerin, die

physics /'fɪzɪks/ n. Physik, die

physiology /fɪzɪ'ɒlədʒɪ/ n. Physiologie, die

physiotherapist /fɪzɪəʊ'θerəpɪst/ n. Physiotherapeut, der/-therapeutin, die

physiotherapy /fɪzɪəʊ'θerəpɪ/ n. Physiotherapie, die

physique /fɪ'ziːk/ n. Körperbau, der

pianist /'piːənɪst/ n. Pianist, der/Pianistin, die

piano /pɪ'ænəʊ/ n., pl. **~s** (upright) Klavier, das; (grand) Flügel, der

piano: ~ ac'cordion n. Akkordeon, das; **~ music** n. Klaviermusik, die; **~ player** n. Klavierspieler, der/-spielerin, die; **~ stool** n. Klavierschemel, der; **~ tuner** n. Klavierstimmer, der/-stimmerin, die

pick¹ /pɪk/ n. (tool) Spitzhacke, die

pick² ① n. (a) (choice) Wahl, die; **take your ~:** du hast die Wahl
(b) (best part) Elite, die; **the ~ of the fruit** die besten Früchte ····⊱

p

2 *v.t.* **(a)** pflücken ⟨*Blumen, Äpfel usw.*⟩; lesen ⟨*Trauben*⟩ **(b)** (select) auswählen; ~ **one's way** sich (*Dat.*) vorsichtig [s]einen Weg suchen **(c)** ~ **one's nose** in der Nase bohren **(d)** ~ **sb.'s pocket** jmdn. bestehlen; **he had his pocket** ~ed er wurde von einem Taschendieb bestohlen **(e)** ~ **a lock** ein Schloss knacken (salopp) **3** *v.i.* ~ **and choose** wählerisch sein ▪ **'pick at** *v.t.* herumstochern in (+ *Dat.*) ⟨*Essen*⟩

▪ **'pick on** *v.t.* (victimize) es abgesehen haben auf (+ *Akk.*)

▪ **pick 'out** *v.t.* **(a)** (choose) auswählen; (for oneself) sich (*Dat.*) aussuchen **(b)** (distinguish) entdecken ⟨*Detail, jmds. Gesicht in der Menge*⟩

▪ **pick up** **1** /'--/ *v.t.* **(a)** [in die Hand] nehmen; hochnehmen ⟨*Baby*⟩; (after dropping) aufheben; aufnehmen ⟨*Masche*⟩; ~ **up the telephone** den [Telefon]hörer abnehmen **(b)** (collect) mitnehmen; (by arrangement) abholen (**at, from** von); (obtain) holen **(c)** (become infected by) sich (*Dat.*) holen (ugs.) ⟨*Virus, Grippe*⟩ **(d)** ⟨*Bus, Autofahrer:*⟩ mitnehmen **(e)** (rescue from the sea) [aus Seenot] bergen **(f)** empfangen ⟨*Signal, Funkspruch usw.*⟩ **(g)** (coll.: make acquaintance of) aufreißen (ugs.) **2** /-'-/ *v.i.* **(a)** sich bessern **(b)** ⟨*Wind:*⟩ auffrischen

'pickaxe (*Amer.:* **'pickax**) ▸ PICK¹

picket /'pɪkɪt/ **1** *n.* Streikposten, *der* **2** *v.i.* Streikposten stehen **3** *v.t.* Streikposten stellen vor (+ *Dat.*)

'picket fence *n.* Palisadenzaun, *der*

'picketing /'pɪkɪtɪŋ/ *n.* Aufstellen von Streikposten

'picket line *n.* Streikpostenkette, *die*

pickle /'pɪkl/ **1** *n.*, usu. in pl. (food) Mixedpickles *Pl.* **2** *v.t.* einlegen ⟨*Gurken, Zwiebeln, Eier*⟩; marinieren ⟨*Hering*⟩

pick: ~**-me-up** *n.* Stärkungsmittel, *das;* ~**pocket** *n.* Taschendieb, *der/*-diebin, *die;* ~**up** *n.* **(a)** ~**up** [**truck**] Kleinlastwagen, *der;* **(b)** (of record player, guitar) Tonabnehmer, *der*

picnic /'pɪknɪk/ **1** *n.* Picknick, *das;* **go for** *or* **on/have a** ~: ein Picknick machen **2** *v.i.,* **-ck-** picknicken; Picknick machen

picnic: ~ **basket** *n.* Picknickkorb, *der;* ~ **site** *n.* Picknickplatz, *der*

pictorial /pɪk'tɔːrɪəl/ *adj.* illustriert ⟨*Bericht, Zeitschrift*⟩; bildlich ⟨*Darstellung*⟩

picture /'pɪktʃə(r)/ **1** *n.* **(a)** Bild, *das;* **get the** ~ (coll.) verstehen[, worum es geht]; **put sb. in the** ~: jmdn. ins Bild setzen **(b)** (film) Film, *der* **(c)** *in pl.* (Brit.: cinema) Kino, *das;* **go to the** ~**s** ins Kino gehen; **what's on at the** ~**s?** was läuft im Kino? **2** *v.t.* ~ [**to oneself**] sich (*Dat.*) vorstellen

picture: ~ **book** *n.* Bilderbuch, *das;* ~ **frame** *n.* Bilderrahmen, *der;* ~ **'postcard** *n.* Ansichtskarte, *die*

picturesque /pɪktʃə'resk/ *adj.* malerisch

pidgin /'pɪdʒɪn/ *n.* Pidgin, *das*

pidgin 'English *n.* Pidginenglisch, *das*

pie /paɪ/ *n.* (of meat, fish, etc.) Pastete, *die;* (of fruit etc.) ≈ Obstkuchen, *der*

piece /piːs/ **1** *n.* **(a)** Stück, *das;* (of broken glass or pottery) Scherbe, *die;* (of jigsaw puzzle, crashed aircraft, etc.) Teil, *der;* (Amer.: distance) [kleines] Stück; **a** ~ **of meat/cake** ein Stück Fleisch/Kuchen; ~ **of furniture/luggage** Möbel-/Gepäckstück, *das;* **a three-**~ **suite** eine dreiteilige Sitzgarnitur; ~ **of luck** Glücksfall, *der;* ~ **of news/gossip/ information** Nachricht, *die*/Klatsch, *der/* Information, *der* **(b)** (Chess) Figur, *die* **(c)** (coin) **gold** ~: Goldstück, *das;* **a 10p** ~: ein 10-Pence-Stück **(d)** (literary or musical composition) Stück, *das;* ~ **of music** Musikstück, *das* **2** *v.t.* ~ **to'gether** zusammenfügen (**from** aus)

piece: ~**meal** *adv., adj.* stückweise; ~**work** *n.* Akkordarbeit, *die*

pie: ~ **chart** *n.* Kreisdiagramm, *das;* ~**crust** *n.* Teigmantel, *der*

pier /pɪə(r)/ *n.* (at seaside) Pier, *der*

pierce /pɪəs/ *v.t.* (prick) durchstechen; (penetrate) [ein]dringen in (+ *Akk.*) ⟨*Körper, Fleisch, Herz*⟩; ~ **a hole in sth.** ein Loch in etw. (*Akk.*) stechen

piercing /'pɪəsɪŋ/ *adj.* durchdringend ⟨*Stimme, Schrei, Blick*⟩

piety /'paɪətɪ/ *n.* Frömmigkeit, *die*

pig /pɪg/ *n.* **(a)** Schwein, *das;* ~**s might fly** (iron.) da müsste schon ein Wunder geschehen **(b)** (coll.: greedy person) Vielfraß, *der* (ugs.)

pigeon /'pɪdʒɪn/ *n.* Taube, *die*

'pigeonhole *n.* [Ablage]fach, *das;* (for letters) Postfach, *das*

piggy /'pɪgɪ/**:** ~**back** *n.* **give sb. a** ~**back** jmdn. huckepack nehmen; ~ **bank** *n.* Sparschwein[chen], *das*

pig'headed *adj.* dickschädelig (ugs.)

piglet /'pɪglɪt/ *n.* Ferkel, *das*

pigment /'pɪgmənt/ *n.* Pigment, *das*

pigmentation /pɪgmən'teɪʃn/ *n.* Pigmentierung, *die*

pig's 'ear *n.* (Brit. coll.) **make a** ~'**s ear of sth.** etw. verpfuschen *od.* (ugs.) vermurksen

pig: ~**sty** *n.* (lit. or fig.) Schweinestall, *der;* ~**tail** *n.* (plaited) Zopf, *der;* ~**tails** (at either side of head) Rattenschwänzchen *Pl.* (ugs.)

pike /paɪk/ *n., pl. same* Hecht, *der*

pilchard /'pɪltʃəd/ *n.* Sardine, *die*

pile¹ /paɪl/ **1** *n.* **(a)** (of dishes, plates) Stapel, *der;* (of paper, books, letters) Stoß, *der;* (of clothes) Haufen, *der* **(b)** (coll.: large quantity) Haufen, *der* (ugs.)

☐ *v.t.* **(a)** (load) [voll] beladen
(b) (heap up) aufstapeln ⟨*Holz, Steine*⟩;
aufhäufen ⟨*Abfall, Schnee*⟩

■ **pile 'in** *v.i.* (seen from outside)
hineindrängen; (seen from inside)
hereindrängen

■ **'pile into** *v.t.* sich zwängen in (+ *Akk.*)
⟨*Auto, Zimmer, Zugabteil*⟩

■ **pile 'on** ☐ *v.i.* ▸ PILE IN
☐ *v.t.* (fig.) ~ on the pressure Druck
machen

■ **'pile on to** *v.t.* drängen in (+ *Akk.*) ⟨*Bus usw.*⟩

■ **pile 'out** *v.i.* nach draußen drängen

■ **pile 'up** ☐ *v.i.* **(a)** ⟨*Waren, Post, Arbeit, Schnee:*⟩ sich auftürmen; ⟨*Verkehr:*⟩ sich
stauen
(b) (crash) aufeinander auffahren
☐ *v.t.* aufstapeln ⟨*Steine, Bücher usw.*⟩;
aufhäufen ⟨*Abfall, Schnee*⟩

pile² *n.* (of fabric etc.) Flor, *der*

pile³ *n.* (stake) Pfahl, *der*

'piledriver *n.* [Pfahl]ramme, *die*

piles /paɪlz/ *n. pl.* (Med.) Hämorrhoiden *Pl.*

'pile-up *n.* Massenkarambolage, *die*

pilfer /'pɪlfə(r)/ *v.t.* stehlen

pilgrim /'pɪlɡrɪm/ *n.* Pilger, *der*/Pilgerin, *die*

pilgrimage /'pɪlɡrɪmɪdʒ/ *n.* Pilgerfahrt, *die*

pill /pɪl/ *n.* **(a)** Tablette, *die*; Pille, *die* (ugs.)
(b) (coll.: contraceptive) the ~ or P-~: die Pille
(ugs.); be on the ~: die Pille nehmen (ugs.)

pillage /'pɪlɪdʒ/ *v.t.* [aus]plündern

pillar /'pɪlə(r)/ *n.* Säule, *die*

'pillar box *n.* (Brit.) Briefkasten, *der*

'pillbox *n.* Pillenschachtel, *die*

pillion /'pɪljən/ *n.* Beifahrersitz, *der*; ride
~: als Beifahrer/Beifahrerin mitfahren

pillow /'pɪləʊ/ *n.* [Kopf]kissen, *das*

'pillowcase, 'pillowslip *ns.*
[Kopf]kissenbezug, *der*

'pill-popping *n.* (coll.) Pillenschluckerei, *die* (ugs.)

pilot /'paɪlət/ ☐ *n.* **(a)** (Aeronaut.) Pilot, *der*/
Pilotin, *die*
(b) (Naut.) Lotse, *der*
☐ *adj.* Pilot⟨*programm, -studie, -projekt usw.*⟩
☐ *v.t.* **(a)** (Aeronaut.) fliegen
(b) (Naut.; fig.) lotsen

'pilot light *n.* Zündflamme, *die*

pimp /pɪmp/ *n.* Zuhälter, *der*

pimple /'pɪmpl/ *n.* Pickel, *der*

pimply /'pɪmplɪ/ *adj.* pick[e]lig

pin ☐ *n.* **(a)** Stecknadel, *die*; ~s and
needles (fig.) Kribbeln, *das*
(b) (peg) Stift, *der*
(c) (Electr.) a two-/three-~ plug ein zwei-/
dreipoliger Stecker
☐ *v.t.*, -nn-: **(a)** nageln ⟨*Knochen, Bein*⟩; ~ a
badge to one's lapel sich (*Dat.*) ein
Abzeichen ans Revers stecken
(b) (fig.) ~ one's hopes on sb./sth. seine

(ganze) Hoffnung auf jmdn./etw. setzen;
~ the blame for sth. on sb. jmdm. die
Schuld an etw. (*Dat.*) zuschieben
(c) ~ sb. against the wall jmdn. an die
Wand drängen

■ **pin 'down** *v.t.* **(a)** (fig.) festnageln (to or
on auf + *Akk.*)
(b) (trap) festhalten

■ **pin 'up** *v.t.* aufhängen ⟨*Bild, Foto*⟩;
anschlagen ⟨*Bekanntmachung, Liste*⟩;
aufstecken ⟨*Haar*⟩; abstecken ⟨*Saum*⟩

PIN /pɪn/ *abbr.* = PIN [number]
▸ PERSONAL IDENTIFICATION NUMBER

pinafore /'pɪnəfɔː(r)/ *n.* Schürze, *die* (mit
Oberteil)

pincers /'pɪnsəz/ *n. pl.* **(a)** [pair of] ~:
Beißzange, *die*
(b) (of crab etc.) Schere, *die*

pinch /pɪntʃ/ ☐ *n.* **(a)** (squeezing) Kniff, *der*;
give sb. a ~ on the arm/cheek jmdn. od.
jmdm. in den Arm/die Backe kneifen
(b) (fig.) feel the ~: knapp bei Kasse sein
(ugs.); at a ~: zur Not
(c) (small amount) Prise, *die*
☐ *v.t.* **(a)** kneifen; ~ sb.'s cheek/bottom
jmdn. in die Wange/den Hintern (ugs.)
kneifen
(b) (coll.: steal) klauen (salopp)

'pincushion *n.* Nadelkissen, *das*

pine¹ /paɪn/ *n.* (tree) Kiefer, *die*

pine² *v.i.* sich [vor Kummer] verzehren
(geh.)

■ **pine a'way** *v.i.* dahinkümmern

pineapple /'paɪnæpl/ *n.* Ananas, *die*

'pine tree *n.* Kiefer, *die*

ping-pong (Amer.: Ping-Pong®)
/'pɪŋpɒŋ/ *n.* Tischtennis, *das*

pinhole 'camera *n.* Lochkamera, *die*;
Camera obscura, *die*

pink /pɪŋk/ ☐ *n.* Rosa, *das*
☐ *adj.* rosa

pinkie /'pɪŋkɪ/ *n.* (Amer., Scot.) kleiner
Finger

'pin money *n.* Taschengeld, *das*

pinnacle /'pɪnəkl/ *n.* Gipfel, *der*; (fig.)
Höhepunkt, *der*

pin: ~point *v.t.* genau festlegen; **~prick**
n. Nadelstich, *der*; **~stripe** *n.*
Nadelstreifen, *der*; **~stripe suit**
Nadelstreifenanzug, *der*

pint /paɪnt/ *n.* Pint, *das*; ≈ halber Liter

pint 'mug *n.* ≈ Halbliterglas, *das od.*
-humpen, *der*

'pin-up (coll.) *n.* **(a)** Pin-up-Girl, *das*; (picture) (of
beautiful girl) Pin-up[-Foto], *das*; (of sports, film or
pop star) Starfoto, *das*

pioneer /paɪə'nɪə(r)/ ☐ *n.* Pionier, *der*
☐ *v.t.* Pionierarbeit leisten für

pious /'paɪəs/ *adj.* fromm

pip /pɪp/ *n.* (seed) Kern, *der*

pipe /paɪp/ ☐ *n.* **(a)** (tube) Rohr, *das*
(b) (Mus.) Pfeife, *die*
(c) [tobacco] ~: [Tabaks]pfeife, *die*   ···⟋·

2 v.t. [durch ein Rohr/durch Rohre] leiten
■ **pipe 'down** v.i. (coll.) ruhig sein
■ **pipe 'up** v.i. (coll.) etwas sagen
pipe: ～ **dream** n. Wunschtraum, der;
Hirngespinst, das (abwertend); ～**line** n.
Pipeline, die; **in the** ～**line** (fig.) in
Vorbereitung

piper /'paɪpə(r)/ n. Pfeifer, der/Pfeiferin, die;
(bagpiper) Dudelsackspieler, der/-spielerin, die
piping hot /'paɪpɪŋ hɒt/ adj. kochend heiß
piquant /'piːkənt/ adj. pikant
pique /piːk/ n. **in a [fit of]** ～: verstimmt
piracy /'paɪrəsɪ/ n. Seeräuberei, die
piranha /pɪ'rɑːnə, pɪ'rɑːnjə/ n. Piranha, der
pirate /'paɪrət/ n. (a) Pirat, der; Seeräuber,
der
(b) (Radio) ～ **radio station** Piratensender, der
Pisces /'paɪsiːz/ n. (Astrol, Astron.) Fische Pl.
piss /pɪs/ (coarse) **1** n. (a) (urine) Pisse, die
(derb)
(b) **have a/go for a** ～: pissen/pissen gehen
(derb)
2 v.i. pissen (derb)
■ '**piss down** v.i. (sl.) ～ **down [with rain]**
schiffen (salopp)
■ **piss 'off** (Brit. sl.) **1** v.i. sich verpissen
(salopp)
2 v.t. ankotzen (derb)
pissed /pɪst/ adj. (sl.) (a) (drunk) voll (salopp)
(b) (Amer.: angry) [stock]sauer (**with** auf
+ *Akk.*) (salopp)
pissed 'off adj. (sl.) stocksauer (**with** auf
+ *Akk.*) (salopp)
'**piss-up** n. (sl.) Sauferei, die (salopp)
pistol /'pɪstl/ n. Pistole, die
piston /'pɪstən/ n. Kolben, der
pit /pɪt/ **1** n. (hole, mine) Grube, die; (natural)
Vertiefung, die
2 v.t., **-tt-:** ～ **one's wits/skill** etc. **against sth.**
seinen Verstand/sein Können usw. an etw.
(*Dat.*) messen
'**pit bull terrier** n. Pitbullterrier, der
pitch¹ /pɪtʃ/ **1** n. (a) (Brit.: usual place)
[Stand]platz, der; (Sport: playing area) Feld, das;
Platz, der
(b) (Mus.) Tonhöhe, die
(c) (slope) Neigung, die
2 v.t. (a) (erect) aufschlagen; ～ **camp/**
das Lager aufschlagen
(b) (throw) werfen
3 v.i. stürzen; ⟨*Schiff:*⟩ stampfen; ～ **forward**
vornüberstürzen
pitch² n. (substance) Pech, das
pitch: ～'**black** adj. pechschwarz;
stockdunkel (ugs.) ⟨*Nacht*⟩; ～'**dark** adj.
stockdunkel (ugs.)
pitcher /'pɪtʃə(r)/ n. [Henkel]krug, der
'**pitchfork** n. Heugabel, die
'**pitfall** n. Fallstrick, der
pith /pɪθ/ n. (a) (of orange etc.) weiße Haut
(b) (fig.) Kern, der
'**pith helmet** n. Tropenhelm, der

'**pithy** adj. (fig.) prägnant
pitiable /'pɪtɪəbl/, **pitiful** /'pɪtɪfl/ adjs. (a)
Mitleid erregend
(b) (contemptible) jämmerlich
pitifully /'pɪtɪfəlɪ/ adv. erbärmlich;
jämmerlich
'**pitiless** adj. unbarmherzig
'**pit stop** n. (Motor racing) Boxenstopp, der
pittance /'pɪtəns/ n. Hungerlohn, der
pity /'pɪtɪ/ **1** n. Mitleid, das; **feel** ～ **for sb.**
Mitgefühl für jmdn. empfinden; **have/take**
～ **on sb.** Erbarmen mit jmdm. haben; **[what**
a] ～! [wie] schade!
2 v.t. bemitleiden; **I** ～ **you** du tust mir leid
pivot /'pɪvət/ **1** n. [Dreh]zapfen, der
2 v.i. sich drehen
pivotal /'pɪvətl/ adj. (fig.: crucial) zentral
pixel /'pɪksl/ n. (Comp. etc.) Bildpunkt, der;
Pixel, das
pixie /'pɪksɪ/ n. Kobold, der
pizza /'piːtsə/ n. Pizza, die
pizzeria /piːtsə'riːə/ n. Pizzeria, die
placard /'plækɑːd/ n. Plakat, das
placate /plə'keɪt/ v.t. beschwichtigen
place /pleɪs/ **1** n. (a) (spot) Stelle,
die; **a [good]** ～ **to park/to stop** ein [guter]
Platz zum Parken/eine [gute] Stelle zum
Halten; **do you know a good/cheap** ～ **to eat?**
weißt du, wo man gut/billig essen kann?;
～ **of worship** Andachtsort, der; **all over the**
～: überall; (coll.: in a mess) ganz
durcheinander (ugs.)
(b) (rank, position) Stellung, die; **put sb. in his**
～: jmdn. in seine Schranken weisen
(c) (country, town) Ort, der; ～ **of birth**
Geburtsort, der; ～ **of residence** Wohnort,
der; '**go** ～**s** (coll.: fig.) es [im Leben] zu was
bringen (ugs.)
(d) (coll.: premises) Bude, die (ugs.); **she is at**
his ～: sie ist bei ihm
(e) (seat etc.) [Sitz]platz, der; **change** ～**s [with**
sb.] [mit jmdm.] die Plätze tauschen; (fig.)
[mit jmdm.] tauschen
(f) (step, stage) **in the first** ～: zuerst; **why**
didn't you say so in the first ～? warum hast
du das nicht gleich gesagt?
(g) (proper ～) Platz, der; **everything fell into**
～ (fig.) alles wurde klar; **out of** ～: nicht am
richtigen Platz; (several things) in Unordnung
(h) (position in competition) Platz, der
2 v.t. (a) (vertically) stellen; (horizontally) legen
(b) **in** p.p. (situated) gelegen
(c) (find situation or home for) unterbringen (**with**
bei)
(d) (class) einordnen; einstufen; **be** ～**d**
second in the race im Rennen den zweiten
Platz belegen
placebo /plə'siːbəʊ/ n., pl. ～**s** Placebo, das
'**place mat** n. Set, der od. das
placement /'pleɪsmənt/ n. Platzierung, die
'**place name** n. Ortsname, der
placenta /plə'sentə/ n., pl. ～**e** /plə'sentiː/
or ～**s** Plazenta, die

'place setting *n.* Gedeck, *das*

placid /'plæsɪd/ *adj.* ruhig

plagiarism /'pleɪdʒərɪzm/ *n.* Plagiat, *das*

plagiarize /'pleɪdʒəraɪz/ *v.t.* plagiieren

plague /pleɪg/ ① *n.* **(a)** (esp. Hist.: epidemic) Seuche, *die;* **the** ~ (bubonic) die Pest
(b) (infestation) ~ **of** rats Rattenplage, *die*
② *v.t.* plagen; ~**d with** *or* **by** sth. von etw. geplagt

plaice /pleɪs/ *n., pl. same* Scholle, *die*

plain /pleɪn/ ① *adj.* **(a)** (clear) klar; (obvious) offensichtlich
(b) (frank) offen; schlicht ⟨Wahrheit⟩; **be** ~ **sailing** (fig.) [ganz] einfach sein
(c) (unsophisticated) einfach; schlicht ⟨Kleidung⟩; unliniert ⟨Papier⟩; ⟨Stoff⟩ ohne Muster
(d) wenig attraktiv ⟨Mädchen⟩
② *adv.* **(a)** (clearly) deutlich
(b) (simply) einfach
③ *n.* Ebene, *die*

plain: ~ **'chocolate** *n.* halbbittere Schokolade; ~ **'clothes** *n. pl.* **in** ~ **clothes** in Zivil

'plainly *adv.* **(a)** (clearly) deutlich
(b) (obviously) offensichtlich; (undoubtedly) eindeutig
(c) (frankly) offen
(d) (simply) schlicht

plaintiff /'pleɪntɪf/ *n.* Kläger, *der*/Klägerin, *die*

plaintive /'pleɪntɪv/ *adj.* klagend

plait /plæt/ ① *n.* Zopf, *der*
② *v.t.* flechten

plan /plæn/ ① *n.* Plan, *der;* [go] **according to** ~: nach Plan [gehen]; planmäßig [verlaufen]
② *v.t.,* **-nn-** planen; (design) entwerfen
③ *v.i.,* **-nn-** planen

plane¹ /pleɪn/ *n.* ~ [tree] Platane, *die*

plane² ① *n.* (tool) Hobel, *der*
② *v.t.* hobeln

plane³ *n.* **(a)** (Geom.: fig.) Ebene, *die*
(b) (aircraft) Flugzeug, *das;* Maschine, *die* (ugs.)

'planeload *n.* Flugzeugladung, *die*

planet /'plænɪt/ *n.* Planet, *der*

planetarium /plænɪ'teərɪəm/ *n., pl.* ~**s** *or* **planetaria** /plænɪ'teərɪə/ Planetarium, *das*

planetary /'plænɪtərɪ/ *adj.* planetarisch

plank /plæŋk/ *n.* Brett, *das;* (thicker) Bohle, *die;* (on ship) Planke, *die*

plankton /'plæŋktən/ *n.* Plankton, *das*

planned e'conomy *n.* Planwirtschaft, *die*

'planner *n.* Planer, *der*/Planerin, *die*

'planning *n.* Planen, *das;* Planung, *die*

plant /plɑːnt/ ① *n.* **(a)** (Bot.) Pflanze, *die*
(b) *no indef. art.* (machinery) Maschinen *Pl.*
(c) (factory) Fabrik, *die;* Werk, *das*
② *v.t.* **(a)** pflanzen

(b) (coll.: conceal) anbringen ⟨Wanze⟩; legen ⟨Bombe⟩; ~ sth. **on** sb. jmdm. etw. unterschieben

plantation /plɑːn'teɪʃn/ *n.* Plantage, *die*

planter /'plɑːntə(r)/ *n.* (container) Pflanzgefäß, *das*

'plant food *n.* Pflanzennahrung, *die*

plaque /plɑːk, plæk/ *n.* **(a)** Platte, *die;* (commemorating sb.) [Gedenk]tafel, *die*
(b) (Dent.) Zahnbelag, *der*

plasma /'plæzmə/ *n.* Plasma, *das*

plaster /'plɑːstə(r)/ ① *n.* **(a)** (for walls etc.) [Ver]putz, *der*
(b) ~ **[of Paris]** Gips, *der;* **have one's leg in** ~: ein Gipsbein haben
(c) ▶ STICKING PLASTER
② *v.t.* **(a)** verputzen ⟨Wand⟩
(b) (daub) ~ sth. **on** sth. etw. dick auf etw. (Akk.) auftragen

plaster: ~**board** *n.* Gipsplatte, *die;* ~ **cast** *n.* (Med.) Gipsverband, *der*

plastered /'plɑːstəd/ *adj.* (sl.: drunk) voll (salopp); **get** ~: sich voll laufen lassen (salopp)

'plasterer *n.* Gipser, *der*

plastic /'plæstɪk/ ① *n.* **(a)** Plastik, *das;* Kunststoff, *der*
(b) (coll.: credit cards etc.) Plastikgeld, *das*
② *adj.* aus Plastik *od.* Kunststoff *nachgestellt;* ~ **bag** Plastiktüte, *die;* ~ **money** (joc.) Kreditkarten *Pl.*

plastic 'bullet *n.* Plastikgeschoss, *das*

Plasticine ® /'plæstɪsiːn/ *n.* Plastilin, *die*

plastic: ~ **'surgeon** *n.* Facharzt für plastische Chirurgie; ~ **'surgery** *n.* plastische Chirurgie

plate /pleɪt/ ① *n.* **(a)** Teller, *der;* (serving ~) Platte, *die*
(b) (metal ~ with name etc.) Schild, *das*
(c) (for printing) Platte, *die;* (illustration) [Bild]tafel, *die*
② *v.t.* ~ sth. **[with gold/silver]** etw. vergolden/versilbern

plateau /'plætəʊ/ *n., pl.* ~**x** /'plætəʊz/ *or* ~**s** Hochebene, *die;* Plateau, *das*

plate: ~ **'glass** *n.* Flachglas, *das;* ~ **rack** *n.* (Brit.) Abtropfständer, *der;* Geschirrablage, *die*

platform /'plætfɔːm/ *n.* **(a)** (Brit. Railw.) Bahnsteig, *der;* ~ **4** Gleis 4
(b) (stage) Podium, *das*

platinum /'plætɪnəm/ *n.* Platin, *das*

platitude /'plætɪtjuːd/ *n.* Plattitüde, *die* (geh.); Gemeinplatz, *der*

platonic /plə'tɒnɪk/ *adj.* platonisch ⟨Liebe, Freundschaft⟩

platoon /plə'tuːn/ *n.* (Mil.) Zug, *der*

plausible /'plɔːzɪbl/ *adj.* plausibel; einleuchtend

play /pleɪ/ ① *n.* **(a)** (Theatre) [Theater]stück, *das;* **television** ~: Fernsehspiel, *das*
(b) (recreation) Spielen, *das;* Spiel, *das;* ~ **on words** Wortspiel, *das*
(c) (Sport) Spiel, *das* ⋯⟫

(d) come into ～, **be brought** *or* **called into**
～**:** ins Spiel kommen
[2] *v.i.* **(a)** spielen; ～ **safe** sichergehen; ～ **for**
time Zeit gewinnen wollen
(b) (Mus.) spielen (**on** auf + *Dat.*)
[3] *v.t.* (also Sport, Theatre, Cards, Mus.) spielen;
abspielen ⟨*Schallplatte, Tonband*⟩; schlagen
⟨*Ball*⟩; spielen gegen ⟨*Mannschaft, Gegner*⟩;
～ **the violin** *etc.* Geige *usw.* spielen; ～ **a**
trick/joke on sb. jmdn. hereinlegen (ugs.)/
jmdm. einen Streich spielen; ～ **one's cards**
right (fig.) es richtig anfassen (fig.)
▪ **play a'bout, play a'round** *v.i.*
spielen; **stop** ～**ing about** *or* **around** hör doch
auf mit dem Unsinn!
▪ **play a'long** *v.i.* mitspielen
▪ **play 'back** *v.t.* abspielen ⟨*Tonband*⟩
▪ **play 'down** *v.t.* herunterspielen
▪ **play 'up** [1] *v.i.* (coll.) ⟨*Kinder:*⟩ nichts als
Ärger machen
[2] *v.t.* (coll.: annoy) ärgern
play: ～**-acting** *n.* Theater, *das* (ugs.);
～ **area** *n.* Spielplatz, *der;* ～**back** *n.*
Wiedergabe, *die;* **listen to the** ～**back** die
Aufnahme anhören; ～**boy** *n.* Playboy, *der*
'**player** *n.* Spieler, *der*/Spielerin, *die*
playful /'pleɪfl/ *adj.* spielerisch; (frolicsome)
verspielt
play: ～**ground** *n.* Spielplatz, *der;* (Sch.)
Schulhof, *der;* ～ **group** *n.* Spielgruppe, *die*
playing: ～ **area** *n.* (Sport) Spielfeld, *das;*
～ **card** *n.* Spielkarte, *die;* ～ **field** *n.*
Sportplatz, *der*
play: ～**mate** *n.* Spielkamerad, *der*/
-kameradin, *die;* ～**off** *n.*
Entscheidungsspiel, *das;* ～**pen** Laufgitter,
das; ～ **school** *n.* Kindergarten, *der;*
～**thing** *n.* Spielzeug, *das;* ～**wright**
/'pleɪraɪt/ *n.* Dramatiker, *der*/Dramatikerin,
die
PLC, plc *abbr.* (Brit.) = **public limited**
company ≈ GmbH
plea /pliː/ *n.* Bitte, *die;* (public appeal) Appell,
der (**for** zu)
plead /pliːd/ [1] *v.i.* **(a)** inständig bitten (**for**
um); (imploringly) flehen (**for** um); ～ **with sb.**
for sth. jmdn. inständig um etw. bitten
(b) (Law; also fig.) plädieren
[2] *v.t.* **(a)** inständig bitten; (imploringly) flehen
(b) (Law) ～ **guilty/not guilty** sich schuldig/
nicht schuldig bekennen
'**pleading** *adj.* flehend
pleasant /'plezənt/ *adj.* angenehm
pleasantry /'plezəntrɪ/ *n.* Nettigkeit, *die*
please /pliːz/ [1] *v.t.* gefallen (+ *Dat.*);
～ **oneself** tun, was man will; ～ **yourself**
ganz wie du willst
[2] *v.i.* **I come and go as I** ～**:** ich komme und
gehe, wie es mir gefällt; **if you** ～**:** bitte schön
[3] *int.* bitte; ～ **do!** aber bitte *od.* gern!
pleased /pliːzd/ *adj.* (satisfied) zufrieden (**by**
mit); (happy) erfreut (**by** über + *Akk.*); **be** ～ **at**
or **about sth.** sich über etw. (*Akk.*) freuen
pleasing /'pliːzɪŋ/ *adj.* gefällig

pleasure /'pleʒə(r)/ *n.* (joy) Freude, *die;*
(enjoyment) Vergnügen, *das;* **have the** ～ **of**
doing sth. das Vergnügen haben, etw. zu tun;
with ～**:** mit Vergnügen
'**pleasure cruise** *n.* Vergnügungsfahrt,
die
pleat /pliːt/ *n.* Falte, *die*
'**pleated** *adj.* gefältelt; Falten⟨*rock*⟩
plebiscite /'plebɪsɪt, 'plebɪsaɪt/ *n.* Plebiszit,
das
pledge /pledʒ/ [1] *n.* Versprechen, *das*
[2] *v.t.* versprechen; geloben ⟨*Treue*⟩
plentiful /'plentɪfl/ *adj.* reichlich; **be** ～**:**
reichlich vorhanden sein
plenty /'plentɪ/ *n.* ～ **of** viel; eine Menge;
(coll.: enough) genug
pleurisy /'plʊərɪsɪ/ *n.* Pleuritis, *die;*
Brustfellentzündung, *die*
pliable /'plaɪəbl/ *adj.* biegsam
plied ▶ PLY
pliers /'plaɪəz/ *n. pl.* [**pair of**] ～**:** Zange, *die*
plight /plaɪt/ *n.* Notlage, *die*
plimsoll /'plɪmsl/ *n.* (Brit.) Turnschuh, *der*
plinth /plɪnθ/ *n.* Sockel, *der*
plod /plɒd/ *v.i.,* **-dd-** trotten
▪ **plod 'on** *v.i.* (fig.) sich weiterkämpfen
plonk /plɒŋk/ *n.* (coll.) [billiger] Wein
plot /plɒt/ [1] *n.* **(a)** (conspiracy)
Verschwörung, *die*
(b) (of play, novel) Handlung, *die*
(c) (of ground) Stück Land
[2] *v.t.,* **-tt-: (a)** [heimlich] planen
(b) (mark on map) einzeichnen
[3] *v.i.,* **-tt-:** ～ **against sb.** sich gegen jmdn.
verschwören
'**plotter** *n.* Verschwörer, *der*/Verschwörerin,
die
plough /plaʊ/ [1] *n.* Pflug, *der*
[2] *v.t.* pflügen
▪ **plough 'back** *v.t.* (Finance) reinvestieren
plow (Amer./arch.) ▶ PLOUGH
ploy /plɔɪ/ *n.* Trick, *der*
pluck /plʌk/ [1] *v.t.* **(a)** pflücken ⟨*Obst*⟩;
～ [**out**] auszupfen ⟨*Federn, Haare*⟩
(b) (pull at) zupfen an (+ *Dat.*)
(c) (strip of feathers) rupfen
[2] *v.i.* ～ **at sth.** an etw. (*Dat.*) zupfen
[3] *n.* Mut, *der*
▪ **pluck 'up** *v.t.* ～ **up** [**one's**] **courage** all
seinen Mut zusammennehmen
pluckily /'plʌkɪlɪ/ *adv.,* '**plucky** *adj.*
tapfer
plug /plʌg/ [1] *n.* **(a)** (filling hole) Pfropfen, *der;*
(in cask) Spund, *der;* (for basin etc.) Stöpsel, *der*
(b) (Electr.) Stecker, *der*
[2] *v.t.,* **-gg-: (a)** ～ [**up**] zustopfen ⟨*Loch usw.*⟩
(b) (coll.: advertise) Schleichwerbung machen
für
▪ **plug 'in** *v.t.* anschließen
'**plughole** *n.* Abfluss, *der*
plum /plʌm/ *n.* **(a)** Pflaume, *die*

plumage ⋯▷ point ⋯⋯

(b) (fig.) Leckerbissen, *der;* **a ~ job** ein Traumjob (ugs.)

plumage /ˈpluːmɪdʒ/ *n.* Gefieder, *das*

plumb¹ /plʌm/ ①*v.t.* [aus]loten ② *adv.* **(a)** lotrecht **(b)** (fig.) genau

plumb² *v.t.* **~ in** fest anschließen

plumber /ˈplʌmə(r)/ *n.* Klempner, *der*

plumbing /ˈplʌmɪŋ/ *n.* **(a)** Klempnerarbeiten *Pl.* **(b)** (waterpipes) Wasserleitungen *Pl.*

'plumb line *n.* Lot, *das*

plume /pluːm/ *n.* Feder, *die;* (ornamental bunch) Federbusch, *der*

plummet /ˈplʌmɪt/ *v.i.* stürzen

plump /plʌmp/ *adj.* mollig; rundlich

■ **'plump for** *v.t.* sich entscheiden für

plunder /ˈplʌndə(r)/ ①*v.t.* [aus]plündern ⟨*Gebäude, Gebiet*⟩ ② *n.* Plünderung, *die;* (booty) Beute, *die*

plunge /plʌndʒ/ ①*v.t.* stecken; (into liquid) tauchen ② *v.i.* **(a)** ~ **into sth.** in etw. (*Akk.*) stürzen **(b)** ⟨*Straße usw.*⟩: steil abfallen ③ *n.* Sprung, *der;* **take the ~** (fig. coll.) den Sprung wagen

plunger /ˈplʌndʒə(r)/ *n.* (suction cup) Stampfer, *der*

plural /ˈplʊərl/ ①*adj.* pluralisch; Plural-; **~ noun** Substantiv im Plural ② *n.* Mehrzahl, *die;* Plural, *der*

pluralism /ˈplʊərəlɪzm/ *n.* Pluralismus, *der*

plus /plʌs/ ①*prep.* plus (+ *Dat.*) ② *n.* (advantage) Pluspunkt, *der*

plush /plʌʃ/ ①*n.* Plüsch, *der* ② *adj.* (coll.) feudal (ugs.)

Pluto /ˈpluːtəʊ/ *pr. n.* (Astron.) Pluto, *der*

plutonium /pluːˈtəʊnɪəm/ *n.* Plutonium, *das*

ply /plaɪ/ ①*v.t.* **(a)** (use) gebrauchen **(b)** nachgehen (+ *Dat.*) ⟨*Handwerk, Arbeit*⟩ **(c)** (supply) ~ **sb. with sth.** jmdn. mit etw. versorgen **(d)** (assail) überhäufen ② *v.i.* ~ **between** zwischen ⟨*Orten*⟩ [hin- und her]pendeln

'plywood *n.* Sperrholz, *das*

PM *abbr.* = **Prime Minister**

p.m. /piːˈem/ *adv.* nachmittags; **one ~:** ein Uhr mittags

PMT *abbr.* = **premenstrual tension** PMS

pneumatic /njuːˈmætɪk/ *adj.* pneumatisch

pneumatic 'drill *n.* Preßluftbohrer, *der*

pneumonia /njuːˈməʊnɪə/ *n.* Lungenentzündung, *die*

PO *abbr.* **(a)** = **postal order** PA **(b)** = **Post Office** PA

poach¹ /pəʊtʃ/ *v.t.* **(a)** (catch illegally) wildern; illegal fangen ⟨*Fische*⟩ **(b)** stehlen, (ugs.) klauen ⟨*Idee*⟩

poach² *v.t.* (Cookery) pochieren ⟨*Ei*⟩; dünsten ⟨*Fisch, Fleisch, Gemüse*⟩; **~ed eggs** verlorene Eier

'poacher *n.* Wilderer, *der*

PO box ▶ POST OFFICE BOX

pocket /ˈpɒkɪt/ ①*n.* **(a)** Tasche, *die* **(b)** (fig.) **be in ~:** Geld verdient haben; **be out of ~:** draufgelegt haben ② *adj.* Taschen⟨*rechner, -uhr, -ausgabe*⟩ ③ *v.t.* **(a)** einstecken **(b)** (steal) in die eigene Tasche stecken (ugs.)

pocket: ~book *n.* (wallet) Brieftasche, *die;* (notebook) Notizbuch, *das;* **~ 'handkerchief** *n.*Taschentuch, *das;* **~ knife** *n.* Taschenmesser, *das;* **~ money** *n.* Taschengeld, *das;* **~size[d]** *adj.* im Taschenformat *nachgestellt*

'pockmarked *adj.* **(a)** pockennarbig ⟨*Gesicht, Haut*⟩ **(b)** **a wall ~ with bullets** eine mit Einschüssen übersäte Wand

pod /pɒd/ *n.* Hülse, *die;* (of pea) Schote, *die*

podgy /ˈpɒdʒɪ/ *adj.* dicklich

poem /ˈpəʊɪm/ *n.* Gedicht, *das*

poet /ˈpəʊɪt/ *n.* Dichter, *der*/Dichterin, *die*

poetic /pəʊˈetɪk/ *adj.* dichterisch

poetry /ˈpəʊɪtrɪ/ *n.* [Vers]dichtung, *die;* Lyrik, *die*

pogrom /ˈpɒgrəm/ *n.* Pogrom, *das od. der*

poignant /ˈpɔɪnjənt/ *adj.* tief ⟨*Bedauern, Trauer*⟩; ergreifend ⟨*Anblick*⟩

point /pɔɪnt/ ①*n.* **(a)** (tiny mark, dot) Punkt, *der* **(b)** (of tool, pencil, etc.) Spitze, *die* **(c)** (single item; unit of scoring) Punkt, *der* **(d)** (stage, degree) **up to a ~:** bis zu einem gewissen Grad; **he gave up at this ~:** an diesem Punkt gab er auf **(e)** (moment) Zeitpunkt, *der;* **be on the ~ of doing sth.** etw. gerade tun wollen **(f)** (distinctive trait) Seite, *die;* **best/strong ~:** starke Seite; Stärke, *die* **(g)** (thing to be discussed) **come to** *or* **get to the ~:** zum Thema kommen; **be beside the ~:** keine Rolle spielen; **make a ~ of doing sth.** [großen] Wert darauf legen, etw. zu tun **(h)** (of story, joke, remark) Pointe, *die* **(i)** (purpose) Zweck, *der;* Sinn, *der;* **there's no ~ in protesting** es hat keinen Sinn *od.* Zweck zu protestieren **(j)** (precise place, spot) Punkt, *der;* Stelle, *die;* **~ of view** (fig.) Standpunkt, *der* **(k)** (Brit.) [power *or* electric] **~:** Steckdose, *die* **(l)** *usu in pl.* (Brit. Railw.) Weiche, *die* ② *v.i.* **(a)** zeigen, weisen (**to, at** auf + *Akk.*) **(b)** ~ **towards** *or* **to** (fig.) [hin]deuten auf (+ *Akk.*) ③ *v.t.* richten ⟨*Waffe, Kamera*⟩ (**at** auf + *Akk.*); ~ **one's finger at sth./sb.** mit dem Finger auf etw./jmdn. zeigen

■ **point 'out** *v.t.* hinweisen auf (+ *Akk.*); ~ **sth./sb. out to sb.** jmdn. auf etw./jmdn. hinweisen

point-'blank 1 *adj.* (lit. or fig.) direkt; glatt
⟨*Weigerung*⟩; ~ **range** kürzeste Entfernung
2 *adv.* (at very close range) aus kürzester
Entfernung

'pointed *adj.* (a) spitz
(b) (fig.) unmissverständlich

'pointer *n.* (a) Zeiger, *der;* (rod) Zeigestock,
der
(b) (coll.: indication) Hinweis, *der* (**to** auf
+ *Akk.*)

'pointless *adj.* sinnlos; belanglos
⟨*Bemerkung, Geschichte*⟩

poise /pɔɪz/ *n.* (composure) Haltung, *die;* (self-
confidence) Selbstvertrauen, *das*

poised /pɔɪzd/ *adj.* selbstsicher

poison /'pɔɪzn/ 1 *n.* Gift, *das*
2 *v.t.* vergiften

'poisoning *n.* Vergiftung, *die*

poisonous /'pɔɪzənəs/ *adj.* giftig

poke 1 *v.t.* (a) ~ sth. [with sth.] [mit etw.]
gegen etw. stoßen; ~ **sth. into sth.** etw. in
etw. (*Akk.*) stoßen; ~ **the fire** das Feuer
schüren
(b) stecken ⟨*Kopf*⟩
2 *v.i.* (a) [herum]stochern (**at, in, among** in
+ *Dat.*)
(b) (pry) schnüffeln (ugs.)
3 *n.* (thrust) Stoß, *der;* **give sb. a** ~ [**in the
ribs**] jmdm. einen [Rippen]stoß versetzen;
give the fire a ~: das Feuer [an]schüren
■ **poke a'bout, poke a'round** *v.i.*
herumschnüffeln (ugs.)

'poker[1] *n.* Schüreisen, *das*

'poker[2] *n.* (Cards) Poker, *das od. der*

'poker-faced *adj.* mit unbewegter Miene
nachgestellt

poky /'pəʊkɪ/ *adj.* winzig

Poland /'pəʊlənd/ *pr. n.* Polen (*das*)

polar /'pəʊlə(r)/ *adj.* polar ⟨*Kaltluft,
Gewässer*⟩; Polar⟨*eis, -gebiet, -fuchs*⟩

polar: ~ **'bear** *n.* Eisbär, *der;* ~ **'cap** *n.*
Polkappe, *die*

pole[1] *n.* (support) Stange, *die;* **drive sb. up the**
~ (Brit. coll.) jmdn. zum Wahnsinn treiben
(ugs.)

pole[2] *n.* (Astron., Geog., Magn., Electr., fig.) Pol,
der

Pole /pəʊl/ *n.* Pole, *der*/Polin, *die*

pole: ~ **star** *n.* Polarstern, *der;* ~**-vault**
n. Stabhochsprung, *der;* ~ **vaulter** *n.*
Stabhochspringer, *der*/-springerin, *die*

police /pə'liːs/ 1 *n. pl.* Polizei, *die;*
(members) Polizisten *Pl.; attrib.* Polizei-
2 *v.t.* [polizeilich] überwachen
⟨*Fußballspiel*⟩; kontrollieren ⟨*Gebiet*⟩

police: ~ **force** *n.* **the** ~ **force** die Polizei;
~**man** /pə'liːsmən/ *n., pl.* -**men** /pə'liːsmən/
Polizist, *der;* ~ **officer** *n.* Polizeibeamte,
der/-beamtin, *die;* ~ **state** *n.* Polizeistaat,
der; ~ **station** *n.* Polizeirevier, *das;*
~**woman** *n.* Polizistin, *die*

policy[1] /'pɒlɪsɪ/ *n.* Politik, *die*

policy[2] *n.* (Insurance) Police, *die*

'policy holder *n.* Versicherte, *der*/*die*

polio /'pəʊlɪəʊ/ *n., no art.* Polio, *die;*
[spinale] Kinderlähmung

polish /'pɒlɪʃ/ 1 *v.t.* (a) polieren; bohnern
⟨*Fußboden*⟩; putzen ⟨*Schuhe*⟩
(b) (fig.) ausfeilen ⟨*Text, Theorie, Stil*⟩
2 *n.* (a) (smoothness) Glanz, *der*
(b) (substance) Politur, *die*
(c) (fig.) Schliff, *der*
■ **polish 'off** *v.t.* (coll.) (a) (consume)
verdrücken (ugs.)
(b) (complete quickly) durchziehen (ugs.)
■ **polish 'up** *v.t.* (a) polieren
(b) ausfeilen ⟨*Stil*⟩; aufpolieren ⟨*Kenntnisse*⟩

Polish /'pəʊlɪʃ/ 1 *adj.* polnisch; **sb. is** ~:
jmd. ist Pole/Polin
2 *n.* Polnisch, *das; see also* ENGLISH 2A

polite /pə'laɪt/ *adj.,* ~**r** /pə'laɪtə(r)/, ~**st**
/pə'laɪtɪst/ höflich

po'liteness *n.* Höflichkeit, *die*

political /pə'lɪtɪkl/ *adj.* politisch

politically /pə'lɪtɪkəlɪ/ *adv.* politisch;
~ **correct** politisch korrekt

political 'prisoner *n.* politischer
Gefangener/politische Gefangene

politician /pɒlɪ'tɪʃn/ *n.* Politiker, *der*/
Politikerin, *die*

politicize (**politicise**) /pə'lɪtɪsaɪz/ *v.t.*
politisieren

politics /'pɒlɪtɪks/ *n.* Politik, *die;* (of
individual) politische Einstellung

polka /'pɒlkə, 'pəʊlkə/ *n.* Polka, *die*

'polka dot *n.* [großer] Tupfen

poll /pəʊl/ 1 *n.* (a) (voting) Abstimmung, *die;*
(to elect sb.) Wahl, *die;* **go to the** ~**s** zur Wahl
gehen
(b) (opinion ~) Umfrage, *die*
2 *v.t.* (a) (take vote[s] of) abstimmen/wählen
lassen
(b) (take opinion of) befragen

pollen /'pɒlən/ *n.* Pollen, *der;* Blütenstaub,
der

'pollen count *n.* Pollenmenge, *die*

pollinate /'pɒlɪneɪt/ *v.t.* bestäuben

pollination /pɒlɪ'neɪʃn/ *n.* Bestäubung, *die*

polling /'pəʊlɪŋ/: ~ **booth** *n.* Wahlkabine,
die; ~ **station** *n.* (Brit.) Wahllokal, *das*

'poll tax *n.* Kopfsteuer, *die*

pollutant /pə'luːtənt/ *n.*
[Umwelt]schadstoff, *der*

pollute /pə'luːt/ *v.t.* verschmutzen ⟨*Luft,
Boden, Wasser*⟩

pollution /pə'luːʃn/ *n.* [environmental] ~:
[Umwelt]verschmutzung, *die;* **noise** ~:
Lärmbelästigung, *die*

polo /'pəʊləʊ/ *n.* Polo, *das*

polo: ~ **neck** *n.* Rollkragen, *der;* ~ **shirt**
n. Polohemd, *das*

poly /'pɒlɪ/ *n., pl.* ~**s** (coll.) Polytechnikum,
das; ≈ TH, *die*

polyester /pɒlɪ'estə(r)/ *n.* Polyester, *der*

polygamy /pə'lɪgəmɪ/ *n.* Polygamie, *die*

polystyrene /ˌpɒlɪˈstaɪriːn/ n. Polystyrol, das; ~ **foam** Styropor ⓌZ, das

polytechnic /ˌpɒlɪˈteknɪk/ n. (Brit.) ≈ technische Hochschule

polythene /ˈpɒlɪθiːn/ n. Polyäthylen, das; ~ **bag** Plastikbeutel, der

polyunsaturated /ˌpɒlɪʌnˈsætʃəreɪtɪd/ adj. mehrfach ungesättigt

polyunsaturates /ˌpɒlɪʌnˈsætjʊrəts/ n. pl. mehrfach ungestättigte Fettsäuren Pl.

pomegranate /ˈpɒmɪɡrænɪt/ n. Granatapfel, der

'pommel horse n. Seitpferd, das

pomp /pɒmp/ n. Pomp, der

pompom /ˈpɒmpɒm/ n. Pompon, der; ~ **hat** Pudelmütze, die

pompous /ˈpɒmpəs/ adj. großspurig; gespreizt ⟨Sprache⟩

pond /pɒnd/ n. Teich, der

ponder /ˈpɒndə(r)/ 1 v.t. nachdenken über (+ Akk.) ⟨Frage, Ereignis⟩; abwägen ⟨Vorteile, Worte⟩ 2 v.i. nachdenken (over, on über + Akk.)

ponderous /ˈpɒndərəs/ adj. schwer

pong /pɒŋ/ (Brit. coll.) 1 n. Mief, der (ugs.) 2 v.i. miefen (ugs.)

pony /ˈpəʊnɪ/ n. Pony, das

pony: ~**tail** n. Pferdeschwanz, der; ~**-trekking** /ˈpəʊnɪtrekɪŋ/ n. (Brit.) Ponyreiten, das

poodle /ˈpuːdl/ n. Pudel, der

pool¹ /puːl/ n. (a) Tümpel, der (b) (temporary) Lache, die; ~ **of blood** Blutlache, die (c) (swimming ~) Schwimmbecken, das; (public) Schwimmbad, das; (in house or garden) Pool, der

pool² 1 n. (a) (Gambling) [gemeinsame Spiel]kasse; **the ~s** (Brit.) das Toto (b) (common supply) Topf, der; **a ~ of experience** ein Erfahrungsschatz (c) (game) Pool[billard], das 2 v.t. zusammenlegen ⟨Geld, Ersparnisse⟩; bündeln ⟨Anstrengungen⟩

'pool table n. Pool[billard]tisch, der

poor /pʊə(r)/ 1 adj. (a) arm (b) (inadequate) schlecht; schwach ⟨Spiel, Gesundheit, Leistung, Rede⟩; dürftig ⟨Kleidung, Essen, Unterkunft⟩; **of ~ quality** minderer Qualität (c) (paltry) schwach ⟨Trost⟩; schlecht ⟨Aussichten⟩ (d) (unfortunate) arm (auch iron.) (e) karg ⟨Boden⟩ (f) (deficient) arm (in an + Dat.); ~ **in vitamins** vitaminarm 2 n. pl. **the** ~: die Armen Pl.

poorly /ˈpʊəlɪ/ adv., pred. adj. schlecht

pop¹ /pɒp/ 1 v.i., -pp-: (a) (make sound) knallen (b) (coll.: go quickly) **let's ~ round to Fred's** komm, wir gehen kurz bei Fred vorbei (ugs.)

2 v.t., -pp-: (a) (coll.: put) ~ **the meat in the fridge** das Fleisch in den Kühlschrank tun (b) platzen ⟨Luftballon⟩ 3 n. (a) Knall, der; Knallen, das (b) (coll.: drink) Brause, die (ugs.) 4 adv. **go** ~: knallen ■ **pop 'out** v.i. hervorschießen; ~ **out to the shops** schnell einkaufen gehen

pop² (coll.) 1 n. Popmusik, die; Pop, der 2 adj. Pop⟨star, -musik usw.⟩

'popcorn n. Popcorn, das

pope /pəʊp/ n. Papst, der/Päpstin, die

poplar /ˈpɒplə(r)/ n. Pappel, die

'pop music n. Popmusik, die

popper /ˈpɒpə(r)/ n. (Brit. coll.) Druckknopf, der

poppy /ˈpɒpɪ/ n. Mohn, der

popular /ˈpɒpjʊlə(r)/ adj. (a) (well liked) beliebt; populär ⟨Entscheidung, Maßnahme⟩ (b) verbreitet ⟨Aberglaube, Irrtum, Meinung⟩; allgemein ⟨Wahl, Unterstützung⟩

popularity /ˌpɒpjʊˈlærɪtɪ/ n. Beliebtheit, die; (of decision, measure) Popularität, die

popularize /ˈpɒpjʊləraɪz/ v.t. (a) (make popular) populär machen (b) (make understandable) breiteren Kreisen zugänglich machen

'popularly adv. allgemein

popular 'music n. Unterhaltungsmusik, die

populate /ˈpɒpjʊleɪt/ v.t. bevölkern; bewohnen ⟨Insel⟩

population /ˌpɒpjʊˈleɪʃn/ n. Bevölkerung, die; **Britain has a ~ of 56 million** Großbritannien hat 56 Millionen Einwohner; ~ **density** Bevölkerungsdichte, die

popu'lation explosion n. Bevölkerungsexplosion, die

'pop-up adj. Stehauf⟨buch, -illustration⟩; ~ **toaster** Toaster mit Auswerfmechanismus; ~ **menu** (Comp.) Pop-up-Menü, das

porcelain /ˈpɔːslɪn/ n. Porzellan, das

porch /pɔːtʃ/ n. Vordach, das; (with side walls) Vorbau, der; (enclosed) Windfang, der

porcupine /ˈpɔːkjʊpaɪn/ n. Stachelschwein, das

pore¹ /pɔː(r)/ n. Pore, die

pore² v.i. ~ **over sth.** etw. [genau] studieren

pork /pɔːk/ n. Schweinefleisch, das; attrib. Schweine-

pork: ~ **'chop** n. Schweinekotelett, das; ~ **'pie** n. Schweinepastete, die

porn /pɔːn/ n. (coll.) Pornographie, die; Pornos Pl. (ugs.)

pornographic /ˌpɔːnəˈɡræfɪk/ adj. pornographisch; Porno- (ugs.)

pornography /pɔːˈnɒɡrəfɪ/ n. Pornographie, die

porous /ˈpɔːrəs/ adj. porös

porridge /ˈpɒrɪdʒ/ n. [Hafer]brei, der

port¹ /pɔːt/ ⟦1⟧ n. (a) Hafen, der
(b) (Naut., Aeronaut.: left side) Backbord, das
⟦2⟧ adj. (Naut., Aeronaut.: left) Backbord-;
backbordseitig

port² n. (wine) Portwein, der

portable /ˈpɔːtəbl/ adj. tragbar

port au'thority n. Hafenbehörde, die

porter¹ /ˈpɔːtə(r)/ n. (Brit.: doorman) Pförtner,
der; (of hotel) Portier, der

porter² n. [Gepäck]träger, der/-trägerin, die;
(in hotel) Hausdiener, der

portfolio /pɔːtˈfəʊlɪəʊ/ n. pl. ~s (a) (Polit.)
Geschäftsbereich, der
(b) (case, contents) Mappe, die

porthole /ˈpɔːthəʊl/ n. (Naut.) Seitenfenster,
das; (round) Bullauge, das

portion /ˈpɔːʃn/ n. (a) (part) Teil, der; (of
ticket) Abschnitt, der
(b) (of food) Portion, die

portly /ˈpɔːtlɪ/ adj. beleibt

portrait /ˈpɔːtrɪt/ n. Porträt, das

portray /pɔːˈtreɪ/ v.t. darstellen; (make
likeness of) porträtieren

Portugal /ˈpɔːtjʊgl/ pr. n. Portugal (das)

Portuguese /pɔːtjʊˈgiːz/ ⟦1⟧ adj.
portugiesisch; **sb. is** ~: jmd. ist Portugiese/
Portugiesin.
⟦2⟧ n., pl. same (a) (person) Portugiese, der/
Portugiesin, die
(b) (language) Portugiesisch, das; see also
ENGLISH 2A

pose /pəʊz/ ⟦1⟧ v.t. aufwerfen ⟨Frage,
Problem⟩; darstellen ⟨Bedrohung⟩; mit sich
bringen ⟨Schwierigkeiten⟩
⟦2⟧ v.i. (a) (assume attitude) posieren; (fig.) sich
geziert benehmen
(b) ~ **as** sich geben als
⟦3⟧ n. Pose, die; **strike a** ~: eine Pose
einnehmen

poser /ˈpəʊzə(r)/ n. (question) knifflige Frage

posh /pɒʃ/ adj. (coll.) vornehm; nobel (spött.);
stinkvornehm (salopp)

position /pəˈzɪʃn/ ⟦1⟧ n. (a) (place occupied)
Platz, der; (of player in team, of plane, ship, etc.)
Position, die; (of hands of clock, words, stars)
Stellung, die; (of building) Lage, die; **be in/out
of** ~: an seinem Platz/nicht an seinem Platz
sein
(b) (Mil.) Stellung, die
(c) (fig.: mental attitude) Standpunkt, der
(d) (fig.: situation) **be in a good** ~ [financially]
[finanziell] gut gestellt sein; **be in a** ~ **of
strength** eine starke Position haben
(e) (rank) Stellung, die
(f) (job) Stelle, die
(g) (posture) Haltung, die
⟦2⟧ v.t. platzieren; postieren ⟨Polizisten,
Wachen⟩; ~ **oneself** sich stellen/(sit) setzen

positive /ˈpɒzɪtɪv/ adj. (a) (also Math.)
positiv; konstruktiv ⟨Vorschlag⟩; (definite)
eindeutig; (convinced) sicher; **I'm** ~ **of it** ich
bin [mir] [dessen] ganz sicher

(b) (Electr.) positiv ⟨Elektrode, Ladung⟩;
Plus⟨platte, -leiter⟩
(c) as intensifier (coll.) echt

positive: ~ **discrimi'nation** n. positive
Diskriminierung; ~ **vetting** n., no indef.
art. (Brit.) Sicherheitsüberprüfung, die

possess /pəˈzes/ v.t. besitzen; (as faculty or
quality) haben; ⟨Furcht usw.⟩ ergreifen; **what
~ed you?** was ist in dich gefahren?

possessed /pəˈzest/ adj. besessen

possession /pəˈzeʃn/ n. (a) (thing possessed)
Besitz, der; **some of my** ~s einige meiner
Sachen
(b) in pl. (property) Besitz, der
(c) (possessing) Besitz, der; **be in** ~ **of sth.** im
Besitz einer Sache ⟨Gen.⟩ sein; **take** ~ **of** in
Besitz nehmen; beziehen ⟨Haus, Wohnung⟩

possessive /pəˈzesɪv/ adj. (a)
besitzergreifend; **be** ~ **about sth./sb.** etw.
eifersüchtig hüten/an jmdn. Besitzansprüche
stellen
(b) (Ling.) possessiv; Possessiv⟨pronomen⟩

possessor /pəˈzesə(r)/ n. Besitzer, der/
Besitzerin, die

possibility /pɒsɪˈbɪlɪtɪ/ n. Möglichkeit, die

possible /ˈpɒsɪbl/ adj. möglich; (likely) [gut]
möglich; **if** ~: wenn möglich; **as ... as** ~: so
... wie möglich; möglichst ...

possibly /ˈpɒsɪblɪ/ adv. (a) **as often as I**
~ **can** sooft ich irgend kann; **I cannot**
~ **commit myself** ich kann mich unmöglich
festlegen
(b) (perhaps) möglicherweise

post¹ /pəʊst/ n. (a) (as support) Pfosten, der
(b) (stake) Pfahl, der
(c) (starting/finishing ~) Start-/Zielpfosten, der

post² ⟦1⟧ n. (a) (Brit.: one dispatch/delivery of
letters) Postausgang, der/Post[zustellung], die;
by return of ~: postwendend
(b) no indef. art. (Brit.: official conveying) Post,
die; **by** ~: mit der Post; per Post
(c) (~ office) Post, die
⟦2⟧ v.t. (a) abschicken
(b) (fig. coll.) **keep sb.** ~ed jmdn. auf dem
Laufenden halten

post³ ⟦1⟧ n. (a) (job) Stelle, die; Posten, der
(b) (Mil.; also fig.) Posten, der
⟦2⟧ v.t. postieren; aufstellen

postage /ˈpəʊstɪdʒ/ n. Porto, das

'postage stamp n. Briefmarke, die

postal /ˈpəʊstl/ adj. Post-; postalisch
⟨Aufgabe, Einrichtung⟩; (by post) per Post
nachgestellt

'postal order n. ≈ Postanweisung, die

post: ~**box** n. (Brit.) Briefkasten, der;
~**card** n. Postkarte, die; ~**code** n. (Brit.)
Postleitzahl, die; ~'**date** v.t. (give later date to)
vordatieren

poster /ˈpəʊstə(r)/ n. Plakat, das

poste restante /pəʊst reˈstãt/ n.
Abteilung/Schalter für postlagernde
Sendungen; **write to sb. [at the]** ~ **in Rome**
jmdm. postlagernd nach Rom schreiben

posterior /pɒˈstɪərɪə(r)/ n. (joc.) Hinterteil, das (ugs.)

posterity /pɒˈsterɪtɪ/ n., no art. Nachwelt, die

postgrad /ˌpəʊstˈɡræd/ (coll.)**, post'graduate** 1 adj. Graduierten-
2 n. Graduierte, der/die

posthumous /ˈpɒstjʊməs/ adj. postum

post: ~**man** /ˈpəʊstmən/, pl. ~**men** /ˈpəʊstmən/ n. Briefträger, der; ~**mark** 1 n. Poststempel, der; 2 v.t. abstempeln; ~'**modern** ▶ ~MODERNIST 1; ~'**modernist** 1 adj. postmodernistisch; 2 n. Postmodernist, der/Postmodernistin, die

postmortem /pəʊstˈmɔːtəm/ n. Obduktion, die

post: ~ **office** n. (a) (organization) the P~ Office die Post; (b) (place) Postamt, das; Post, die; ~ **office box** n. Postfach, das

postpone /pəˈspəʊn/ v.t. verschieben; (for an indefinite period) aufschieben

post'ponement n. Verschiebung, die/ Aufschub, der

'**post room** n. Poststelle, die

postscript /ˈpəʊskrɪpt/ n. Nachschrift, die; (fig.) Nachtrag, der

posture /ˈpɒstʃə(r)/ n. [Körper]haltung, die

'**post-war** adj. Nachkriegs-; der Nachkriegszeit nachgestellt

posy /ˈpəʊzɪ/ n. Sträußchen, das

pot¹ /pɒt/ 1 n. (a) [Koch]topf, der; go to ~ (coll.) den Bach runtergehen (ugs.)
(b) (container, contents) Topf, der; (teapot, coffee pot) Kanne, die
(c) (coll.: large sum) a ~ of/~s of massenweise
2 v.t. ~ [up] eintopfen ⟨Pflanze⟩

pot² n. (sl.: marijuana) Pot, das (Jargon)

potassium /pəˈtæsɪəm/ n. Kalium, das

potato /pəˈteɪtəʊ/ n., pl. ~**es** Kartoffel, die

potato 'salad n. Kartoffelsalat, der

pot: ~**belly** n. Schmerbauch, der (ugs.); ~**boiler** n. (derog.) Fließbandprodukt, das

potent /ˈpəʊtənt/ adj. [hoch]wirksam ⟨Droge⟩; stark ⟨Schnaps usw.⟩; schlagkräftig ⟨Waffe⟩

potential /pəˈtenʃl/ 1 adj. potenziell (geh.); möglich
2 n. Potenzial, das (geh.); Möglichkeiten Pl.

potentially /pəˈtenʃəlɪ/ adv. potenziell (geh.); he's ~ **dangerous** er kann gefährlich werden; a ~ **rich country** ein Land, das reich sein könnte

pot: ~**hole** n. (a) Schlagloch, das; (b) (cave) [tiefe] Höhle; ~**holer** n. Höhlenforscher, der/-forscherin, die; ~ **plant** n. Topfpflanze, die

potpourri /pəʊpʊəˈriː/ n. Duftmischung, die

pot: ~ **roast** n. Schmorbraten, der; ~**shot** n. take a ~**shot** [at sb./sth.] aufs Geratewohl [auf jmdn./etw.] schießen

'**potted** adj. (a) (planted) Topf-
(b) (abridged) kurz [gefasst]

'**potter¹** n. Töpfer, der/Töpferin, die

'**potter²** v.i. ~ [about] [he]rumwerkeln (ugs.)

pottery /ˈpɒtərɪ/ n. (a) Töpferware, die
(b) (workshop, craft) Töpferei, die

potty¹ /ˈpɒtɪ/ adj. (Brit. coll.) verrückt (ugs.) (about, on nach)

potty² n. (Brit. coll.) Töpfchen, das

pouch /paʊtʃ/ n. Beutel, der

pouffe /puːf/ n. Sitzpolster, das

poultry /ˈpəʊltrɪ/ n. Geflügel, das

pounce /paʊns/ v.i. (a) sich auf sein Opfer stürzen; ⟨Raubvogel:⟩ herabstoßen auf (+ Akk.)
(b) (fig.) ~ [up]on/at sich stürzen auf (+ Akk.)

pound¹ /paʊnd/ n. (a) (unit of weight) [britisches] Pfund (453,6 Gramm); two ~[s] of apples 2 Pfund Äpfel
(b) (unit of currency) Pfund, das

pound² n. (enclosure) Pferch, der; (for stray dogs) Zwinger, der; (for cars) Abstellplatz, der

pound³ 1 v.t. (crush) zerstoßen
2 v.i. (a) (make one's way heavily) stampfen
(b) ⟨Herz:⟩ heftig schlagen

'**pound[s] sign** n. Pfundzeichen, das

pour /pɔː(r)/ 1 v.t. gießen; (into cup, glass) einschenken
2 v.i. (a) (flow) strömen; ⟨Rauch:⟩ hervorquellen (from aus); ~ [with rain] in Strömen regnen
(b) (fig.) strömen; ~ in herein-/ hineinströmen; ~ out heraus-/ hinausströmen
■ **pour 'down** v.i. it's ~ing down es gießt [in Strömen] (ugs.)

pout /paʊt/ 1 v.i. einen Schmollmund machen
2 v.t. aufwerfen ⟨Lippen⟩

poverty /ˈpɒvətɪ/ n. Armut, die

poverty: ~ **line** n. Armutsgrenze, die; be on the ~ line an der Armutsgrenze liegen; live below the ~ line unterhalb der Armutsgrenze leben; ~-**stricken** adj. Not leidend

powder /ˈpaʊdə(r)/ 1 n. (a) Pulver, das
(b) (cosmetic) Puder, der
2 v.t. (a) pudern
(b) (reduce to ~) pulverisieren; ~ed **milk** Milchpulver, das

'**powdery** adj. pulv[e]rig

power /ˈpaʊə(r)/ 1 n. (a) (ability) Kraft, die; do all in one's ~ to help sb. alles in seiner Macht Stehende tun, um jmdm. zu helfen
(b) (faculty) Fähigkeit, die
(c) (strength, intensity) Kraft, die; (of blow) Wucht, die   ···⊱

(d) (authority, political ∿) Macht, *die* (over über + *Akk.*); **come into** ∿: an die Macht kommen
(e) (authorization) Vollmacht, *die*
(f) (State) Macht, *die*
(g) (Math.) Potenz, *die*
(h) (Mech., Electr.) Kraft, *die;* (electric current) Strom, *der*
[2] *v.t.* ⟨*Treibstoff, Strom:*⟩ antreiben; ⟨*Batterie:*⟩ mit Energie versorgen
power: ∿-**assisted** *adj.* ∿-assisted steering/brakes Servolenkung, *die/*-bremsen *Pl.;* ∿ **brakes** *n. pl.* Servobremsen *Pl.;* ∿ **cable** *n.* Hochspannungsleitung, *die;* ∿ **cut** *n.* Stromsperre, *die;* ∿ **dressing** *n.: das Tragen betont streng wirkender Kleidung;* ∿ **failure** *n.* Stromausfall, *der*
powerful /'pauəfl/ *adj.* (a) (strong) stark; kräftig ⟨*Tritt, Schlag, Tier*⟩; heftig ⟨*Gefühl, Empfindung*⟩; hell, strahlend ⟨*Licht*⟩
(b) mächtig ⟨*Clique, Person, Herrscher*⟩
powerless *adj.* machtlos
power: ∿ **plant** ▶ ∿ STATION; ∿ **point** *n.* (Brit.) Steckdose, *die;* ∿ **station** *n.* Kraftwerk, *das;* ∿ **steering** *n.* Servolenkung, *die;* ∿ **supply** *n.* Energieversorgung, *die* (to *Gen.*)
pp. *abbr.* = **pages**
p.p. /piː'piː/ *abbr.* = **by proxy** pp[a].
practicable /'præktɪkəbl/ *adj.* durchführbar ⟨*Projekt, Plan*⟩
practical /'præktɪkl/ *adj.* (a) praktisch; praktisch veranlagt ⟨*Person*⟩
(b) (virtual) tatsächlich
(c) (feasible) möglich
practical 'joke *n.* Streich, *der*
practically *adv.* praktisch; (almost) so gut wie; praktisch (ugs.)
practice¹ /'præktɪs/ *n.* (a) (repeated exercise) Übung, *die;* **be out of** ∿: außer Übung sein
(b) (session) Übungen *Pl.;* **piano** ∿: Klavierüben, *das*
(c) (of doctor, lawyer, etc.) Praxis, *die*
(d) (action) **put sth. into** ∿: etw. in die Praxis umsetzen
(e) (custom) Gewohnheit, *die;* **regular** ∿: Brauch, *der*
practice², practiced, practicing (Amer.) ▶ PRACTIS-
practise /'præktɪs/ [1] *v.t.* (a) (apply) anwenden; praktizieren
(b) ausüben ⟨*Beruf, Religion*⟩
(c) trainieren in (+ *Dat.*) ⟨*Sportart*⟩; ∿ **the piano/flute** Klavier/Flöte üben
[2] *v.i.* üben
practised /'præktɪst/ *adj.* geübt
practising /'præktɪsɪŋ/ *adj.* praktizierend ⟨*Arzt, Katholik usw.*⟩
practitioner /præk'tɪʃənə(r)/ *n.* Fachmann, *der; see also* GENERAL PRACTITIONER
pragmatic /præg'mætɪk/ *adj.* pragmatisch
Prague /prɑːg/ *pr. n.* Prag (*das*)

prairie /'preəri/ *n.* Grassteppe, *die;* (in North America) Prärie, *die*
praise /preɪz/ [1] *v.t.* loben; (more strongly) rühmen
[2] *n.* Lob, *das*
praiseworthy *adj.* lobenswert
pram /præm/ *n.* (Brit.) Kinderwagen, *der*
prance /prɑːns/ *v.i.* (a) ⟨*Pferd:*⟩ tänzeln
(b) (fig.) stolzieren; ∿ **about** *or* **around** herumhüpfen
prank /præŋk/ *n.* Streich, *der*
prattle /'prætl/ [1] *v.i.* plappern (ugs.)
[2] *n.* Geplapper, *das* (ugs.)
prawn /prɔːn/ *n.* Garnele, *die*
prawn 'cocktail *n.* Krabbencocktail, *der*
pray /preɪ/ *v.i.* beten (for um)
prayer /preə(r)/ *n.* (a) Gebet, *das*
(b) *no art.* (praying) Beten, *das*
'prayer book *n.* Gebetbuch, *das*
preach /priːtʃ/ [1] *v.i.* predigen (to zu, vor + *Dat.;* on über + *Akk.*)
[2] *v.t.* halten ⟨*Predigt*⟩; predigen ⟨*Evangelium, Botschaft*⟩
'preacher *n.* Prediger, *der/*Predigerin, *die*
pre-arrange /priːə'reɪndʒ/ *v.t.* vorher absprechen; vorher ausmachen ⟨*Treffpunkt, Zeichen*⟩
precarious /prɪ'keərɪəs/ *adj.* (a) (uncertain) labil; prekär; **make a** ∿ **living** eine unsichere Existenz haben
(b) (insecure, dangerous) gefährlich
precaution /prɪ'kɔːʃn/ *n.* Vorsichts-, Schutzmaßnahme, *die;* **as a** ∿: vorsichtshalber
precede /prɪ'siːd/ *v.t.* (in order or time) vorangehen (+ *Dat.*)
precedence /'presɪdəns/ *n.* Priorität, *die* (geh.), Vorrang, *der* (over vor + *Dat.*)
precedent /'presɪdənt/ *n.* Präzedenzfall, *der*
precinct /'priːsɪŋkt/ *n.* (a) [pedestrian] ∿: Fußgängerzone, *die*
(b) (Amer.: district) Bezirk, *der*
precious /'preʃəs/ [1] *adj.* (a) kostbar ⟨*Schmuckstück, Zeit*⟩; Edel⟨*metall, -stein*⟩
(b) (beloved) lieb
(c) (affected) affektiert
[2] *adv.* (coll.) herzlich ⟨*wenig, wenige*⟩
precipice /'presɪpɪs/ *n.* Abgrund, *der*
precipitate [1] /prɪ'sɪpɪtət/ *adj.* eilig ⟨*Flucht*⟩; übereilt ⟨*Entschluss*⟩
[2] /prɪ'sɪpɪteɪt/ *v.t.* (hasten) beschleunigen; (trigger) auslösen
precipitation /prɪsɪpɪ'teɪʃn/ *n.* (Meteorol.) Niederschlag, *der*
precipitous /prɪ'sɪpɪtəs/ *adj.* (a) (steep) sehr steil
(b) ▶ PRECIPITATE 1
précis /'preɪsiː/ *n., pl. same* /'preɪsiːz/ Zusammenfassung, *die*

precise /prɪˈsaɪs/ *adj.* genau; präzise; fein ⟨*Instrument*⟩; förmlich ⟨*Art*⟩; **be [more]** ∼: sich präzise[r] ausdrücken

pre'cisely *adv.* genau

precision /prɪˈsɪʒn/ *n.* Genauigkeit, *die*

precision 'instrument *n.* Präzisions[mess]gerät, *das*

preclude /prɪˈkluːd/ *v.t.* ausschließen

precocious /prɪˈkəʊʃəs/ *adj.* frühreif ⟨*Kind*⟩; altklug ⟨*Äußerung*⟩

preconceived /priːkənˈsiːvd/ *adj.* vorgefasst ⟨*Ansicht, Vorstellung*⟩

preconception /priːkənˈsepʃn/ *n.* vorgefasste Meinung (**of** über + *Akk.*)

precondition /priːkənˈdɪʃn/ *n.* Vorbedingung, *die* (**of** für)

pre-cooked /priːˈkʊkt/ *adj.* vorgekocht

precursor /priːˈkɜːsə(r)/ *n.* Wegbereiter, *der*/-bereiterin, *die*

predator /ˈpredətə(r)/ *n.* Raubtier, *das;* (fish) Raubfisch, *der*

'predatory *adj.* räuberisch; ∼ **animal** Raubtier, *das*

predecessor /ˈpriːdɪsesə(r)/ *n.* Vorgänger, *der*/-gängerin, *die*

predestine /priːˈdestɪn/ *v.t.* von vornherein bestimmen (**to** zu)

predicament /prɪˈdɪkəmənt/ *n.* Dilemma, *das*

predicate /ˈpredɪkət/ *n.* (Ling.) Prädikat, *das*

predicative /prɪˈdɪkətɪv/ *adj.* (Ling.) prädikativ

predict /prɪˈdɪkt/ *v.t.* voraus-, vorhersagen; vorhersehen ⟨*Folgen*⟩

predictable /prɪˈdɪktəbl/ *adj.* voraussagbar; vorhersehbar ⟨*Ereignis, Reaktion*⟩; berechenbar ⟨*Person*⟩

prediction /prɪˈdɪkʃn/ *n.* Vorhersage, *die*

predominance /prɪˈdɒmɪnəns/ *n.* **(a)** (control) Vorherrschaft, *die* (**over** über + *Akk.*); **(b)** (majority) Überzahl, *die* (**of** von)

predominant /prɪˈdɒmɪnənt/ *adj.* (having more power) dominierend; (prevailing) vorherrschend

pre'dominantly *adv.* überwiegend

predominate /prɪˈdɒmɪneɪt/ *v.i.* (be more powerful) dominierend sein; (be more important) vorherrschen

pre-eminent /priːˈemɪnənt/ *adj.* herausragend

pre-empt /priːˈempt/ *v.t.* zuvorkommen (+ *Dat.*)

preen /priːn/ *v.t.* putzen ⟨*Federn*⟩

prefab /ˈpriːfæb/ *n.* (coll.) Fertighaus, *das*

prefabricated /priːˈfæbrɪkeɪtɪd/ *adj.* vorgefertigt

preface /ˈprefəs/ ① *n.* Vorwort, *das* (**to** *Gen.*)
② *v.t.* (introduce) einleiten

prefect /ˈpriːfekt/ *n.* (Sch.) *die Aufsicht führender älterer Schüler/führende ältere Schülerin*

prefer /prɪˈfɜː(r)/ *v.t.,* **-rr-** vorziehen; ∼ **to do sth.** etw. lieber tun; ∼ **sth. to sth.** etw. einer Sache (*Dat.*) vorziehen

preferable /ˈprefərəbl/ *adj.* vorzuziehen *präd.;* vorzuziehend *attr.;* besser (**to** als)

preferably /ˈprefərəblɪ/ *adv.* am besten; (as best liked) am liebsten; **Wine or beer?** – **Wine,** ∼! Wein oder Bier? – Lieber Wein!

preference /ˈprefərəns/ *n.* **(a)** (greater liking) Vorliebe, *die;* **for** ⟹ ▶ PREFERABLY; **have a** ∼ **for sth.** [over sth.] etw. [einer Sache (*Dat.*)] vorziehen; **do sth. in** ∼ **to sth. else** etw. lieber als etw. anderes tun **(b)** (thing preferred) **what are your** ∼**s?** was wäre dir am liebsten? **(c)** **give** ∼ **to sb.** jmdn. bevorzugen

preferential /prefəˈrenʃl/ *adj.* bevorzugt ⟨*Behandlung*⟩

preferred /prɪˈfɜːd/ *adj.* bevorzugt; **my** ∼ **solution** *etc.* die Lösung *usw.,* der ich den Vorzug gebe

prefix /ˈpriːfɪks/ *n.* Präfix, *das*

pregnancy /ˈpregnənsɪ/ *n.* (of woman) Schwangerschaft, *die;* (of animal) Trächtigkeit, *die*

'pregnancy test *n.* Schwangerschaftstest, *der*

pregnant /ˈpregnənt/ *adj.* schwanger ⟨*Frau*⟩; trächtig ⟨*Tier*⟩

preheat /priːˈhiːt/ *v.t.* vorheizen ⟨*Backofen*⟩; vorwärmen ⟨*Geschirr, Essen*⟩

prehistoric /priːhɪˈstɒrɪk/ *adj.* prähistorisch

prehistory /priːˈhɪstərɪ/ Vorgeschichte, *die*

prejudge /priːˈdʒʌdʒ/ *v.t.* vorschnell urteilen über (+ *Akk.*)

prejudice /ˈpredʒʊdɪs/ ① *n.* Vorurteil, *das* ② *v.t.* beeinflussen

prejudiced /ˈpredʒʊdɪst/ *adj.* voreingenommen (**about** gegenüber, **against** gegen)

preliminary /prɪˈlɪmɪnərɪ/ ① *adj.* Vor-; vorbereitend ⟨*Forschung, Maßnahme*⟩ ② *n., usu. in pl.* **preliminaries** Präliminarien *Pl.;* **as a** ∼ **to sth.** als Vorbereitung auf etw. (*Akk.*)

prelude /ˈpreljuːd/ *n.* **(a)** (introduction) Anfang, *der* (**to** *Gen.*) **(b)** (Theatre, Mus.) Vorspiel, *das*

premature /ˈpremətjʊə(r)/ *adj.* **(a)** (hasty) übereilt **(b)** (early) vorzeitig ⟨*Altern, Ankunft*⟩; verfrüht ⟨*Bericht, Eile*⟩; ∼ **baby** Frühgeburt, *die*

prema'turely *adv.* (early) vorzeitig; zu früh ⟨*geboren werden*⟩; (hastily) übereilt

premeditated /priːˈmedɪteɪtɪd/ *adj.* vorsätzlich

premeditation /priːmedɪˈteɪʃn/ *n.* Vorsatz, *der*

P

premenstrual /pri:'menstruəl/ *adj.*
prämenstruell; ~ **tension** prämenstruelles
Syndrom

premier /'premɪə(r)/ *n.* Premier[minister],
der/Premierministerin, *die*

première /'premjeɑ(r)/ *n.* Premiere, *die;*
Erstaufführung, *die*

premise /'premɪs/ *n.* (a) ~s *pl.* (building)
Gebäude, *das;* (buildings and land) Gelände, *das;*
(rooms) Räumlichkeiten *Pl.*
(b) ▶ PREMISS

premiss /'premɪs/ *n.* Prämisse, *die*

premium /'pri:mɪəm/ *n.* Prämie, *die;* **be at
a** ~ (fig.) sehr gefragt sein

'**Premium Bond** *n.* (Brit.) Prämienanleihe,
die; Losanleihe, *die*

premonition /premə'nɪʃn/ *n.* Vorahnung,
die

pre-natal /pri:'neɪtl/ *adj.* pränatal (fachspr.);
~ **care** Schwangerschaftsfürsorge, *die*

preoccupation /prɪɒkjʊ'peɪʃn/ *n.* Sorge,
die (with um)

preoccupied /prɪ'ɒkjʊpaɪd/ *adj.* (lost in
thought) gedankenverloren; (concerned) besorgt
(with um)

pre-'packed *adj.* abgepackt

prepaid /pri:'peɪd/ *adj.* ~ **envelope**
frankierter Umschlag

preparation /prepə'reɪʃn/ *n.* Vorbereitung,
die; ~s *pl.* Vorbereitungen *Pl.* (for für)

preparatory /prɪ'pærətərɪ/ ① *adj.*
vorbereitend ⟨Maßnahme, Schritt⟩; ~ **work**
Vorarbeiten *Pl.*
② *adv.* ~ **to sth.** vor etw. (*Dat.*)

prepare /prɪ'peə(r)/ ① *v.t.* (a) vorbereiten;
ausarbeiten ⟨Plan, Rede⟩; vorbereiten
⟨Person⟩ (for auf + *Akk.*); **be** ~**d to do sth.**
(be willing) bereit sein, etw. zu tun
(b) herstellen ⟨Chemikalie usw.⟩; zubereiten
⟨Essen⟩
② *v.i.* sich vorbereiten (for auf + *Akk.*)

preponderance /prɪ'pɒndərəns/ *n.*
Überlegenheit, *die* (over über + *Akk.*)

preposition /prepə'zɪʃn/ *n.* (Ling.)
Präposition, *die*

prepossessing /pri:pə'zesɪŋ/ *adj.*
einnehmend

preposterous /prɪ'pɒstərəs/ *adj.* absurd;
grotesk ⟨Äußeres, Kleidung⟩

'**pre-program** *v.t.*, **-mm-**
[vor]programmieren

prerequisite /pri:'rekwɪzɪt/ ① *n.*
[Grund]voraussetzung, *die*
② *adj.* unbedingt erforderlich

prerogative /prɪ'rɒgətɪv/ *n.* Privileg, *das;*
Vorrecht, *das*

Presbyterian /prezbɪ'tɪərɪən/ ① *adj.*
presbyterianisch
② *n.* Presbyterianer, *der*/Presbyterianerin,
die

prescribe /prɪ'skraɪb/ *v.t.* (a) (impose)
vorschreiben
(b) (Med.; also fig.) verschreiben

prescription /prɪ'skrɪpʃn/ *n.* (a)
Vorschreiben, *das*
(b) (Med.) Rezept, *das*

pre'scription charge *n.* Rezeptgebühr,
die

presence /'prezəns/ *n.* (a) (of person)
Anwesenheit, *die;* (of things) Vorhandensein,
das; **in the** ~ **of** in Anwesenheit (+ *Gen.*)
(b) ~ **of mind** Geistesgegenwart, *die*

present¹ /'prezənt/ ① *adj.* (a) anwesend
(at bei); **all those** ~: alle Anwesenden
(b) (existing now) gegenwärtig; jetzig ⟨Bischof,
Chef usw.⟩
(c) (Ling.) ~ **tense** Präsens, *das;* Gegenwart,
die
② *n.* (a) **the** ~: die Gegenwart; **at** ~:
zurzeit; **for the** ~: vorläufig
(b) (Ling.) Präsens, *das;* Gegenwart, *die*

present² ① /'prezənt/ *n.* (gift) Geschenk,
das
② /prɪ'zent/ *v.t.* (a) schenken; überreichen
⟨Preis, Medaille, Geschenk⟩; ~ **sth. to sb.** *or*
sb. with sth. jmdm. etw. schenken/
überreichen; ~ **sb. with difficulties/a
problem** jmdn. vor Schwierigkeiten/ein
Problem stellen
(b) überreichen ⟨Gesuch⟩ (to bei); vorlegen
⟨Scheck, Bericht, Rechnung⟩ (to *Dat.*);
~ **one's case** seinen Fall darlegen
(c) (exhibit) zeigen; bereiten ⟨Schwierigkeit⟩
(d) (introduce) vorstellen (to *Dat.*); vorlegen
⟨Abhandlung⟩; moderieren ⟨Sendung⟩
③ *v. refl.* ⟨Problem:⟩ auftreten; ⟨Möglichkeit:⟩
sich ergeben; ~ **oneself for an interview** zu
einem Gespräch erscheinen

presentable /prɪ'zentəbl/ *adj.* ansehnlich;
I'm not ~: ich kann mich nicht so zeigen

presentation /prezən'teɪʃn/ *n.* (a) (giving)
Schenkung, *die;* (of prize, medal) Überreichung,
die
(b) (ceremony) Verleihung, *die*
(c) (of petition) Überreichung, *die;* (of cheque,
report, account) Vorlage, *die;* (of case)
Darlegung, *die*

present-day /'prezənt'deɪ/ *adj.* heutig

presenter /prɪ'zentə(r)/ *n.* (Radio, Telev.)
Moderator, *der*/Moderatorin, *die*

presentiment /prɪ'zentɪmənt/ *n.*
Vorahnung, *die*

presently /'prezəntlɪ/ *adv.* bald; (Amer.,
Scot.: now) zurzeit

preservation /prezə'veɪʃn/ *n.* Erhaltung,
die; (of leather, wood, etc.) Konservierung, *die*

preservative /prɪ'zɜ:vətɪv/ *n.*
Konservierungsmittel, *das*

preserve /prɪ'zɜ:v/ ① *n.* (a) in sing. or pl.
(fruit) Eingemachte, *das*
(b) (fig.: special sphere) Domäne, *die* (geh.)
(c) wildlife/game ~: Tierschutzgebiet, *das*/
Wildpark, *der*
② *v.t.* (a) (keep safe) schützen (**from** vor
z+ *Dat.*)
(b) bewahren ⟨Brauch⟩; wahren ⟨Anschein,
Reputation⟩

p

(c) (keep from decay) konservieren; einmachen ⟨*Obst, Gemüse*⟩

(d) (protect) hegen ⟨*Tierart, Wald*⟩

preside /prɪ'zaɪd/ *v.i.* präsidieren, vorsitzen (**over** *Dat.*); (at meeting etc.) den Vorsitz haben (**at** bei)

presidency /'prezɪdənsɪ/ *n.* **(a)** Präsidentschaft, *die*

(b) (of society) Vorsitz, *der*

president /'prezɪdənt/ *n.* **(a)** Präsident, *der*/Präsidentin, *die*

(b) (of society) Vorsitzende, *der*/*die*

presidential /prezɪ'denʃl/ *adj.* Präsidenten-

press¹ /pres/ **1** *n.* **(a)** (newspapers etc.) Presse, *die; attrib.* Presse-

(b) ▶ PRINTING PRESS

(c) (for flattening, compressing, etc.) Presse, *die*

2 *v.t.* **(a)** drücken; drücken auf (+ *Akk.*) ⟨*Klingel, Knopf*⟩; treten auf (+ *Akk.*) ⟨*Gas-, Brems-, Kupplungspedal usw.*⟩

(b) (urge) drängen ⟨*Person*⟩; (force) aufdrängen (**[up]on** *Dat.*); nachdrücklich vorbringen ⟨*Forderung, Argument*⟩; **he did not ~ the point** er ließ die Sache auf sich beruhen

(c) (compress) pressen; auspressen ⟨*Orangen, Saft*⟩; keltern ⟨*Trauben, Äpfel*⟩

(d) (iron) bügeln

(e) be ~**ed for time/money** zu wenig Zeit/ Geld haben

3 *v.i.* **(a)** (exert pressure) drücken

(b) (be urgent) drängen

(c) (make demand) ~ **for sth.** auf etw. (*Akk.*) drängen

■ **press a'head, press 'on** *v.i.* (continue) [zügig] weitermachen; (continue travelling) [zügig] weitergehen/-fahren; ~ **on with one's work** sich mit der Arbeit ranhalten (ugs.)

press² *v.t.* ~ **into service/use** in Dienst nehmen; einsetzen

press: ~ **agent** *n.* Presseagent, *der*/ -agentin, *die;* ~ **conference** *n.* Pressekonferenz, *die;* ~ **coverage** *n.* Berichterstattung in der Presse; ~ **cutting** *n.* (Brit.) Zeitungsausschnitt, *der*

'pressing *adj.* (urgent) dringend

press: ~**man** *n.* (Brit.: journalist) Journalist, *der;* ~ **release** *n.* Presseinformation, *die;* ~ **stud** *n.* (Brit.) Druckknopf, *der;* ~-**up** *n.* Liegestütz, *der*

pressure /'preʃə(r)/ **1** *n.* Druck, *der;* put ~ **on sb.** jmdn. unter Druck setzen; **atmospheric ~:** Luftdruck, *der*

2 *v.t.* unter Druck setzen ⟨*Person*⟩; ~ **sb. into doing sth.** jmdn. [dazu] drängen, etw. zu tun

pressure: ~ **cooker** *n.* Schnellkochtopf, *der;* ~ **group** *n.* Pressuregroup, *die*

pressurize /'preʃəraɪz/ *v.t.* **(a)** ▶ PRESSURE 2

(b) ~**d cabin** Druckkabine, *die*

prestige /pre'stiːʒ/ *n.* Prestige, *das*

prestigious /pre'stɪdʒəs/ *adj.* angesehen

presumably /prɪ'zjuːməblɪ/ *adv.* vermutlich

presume /prɪ'zjuːm/ **1** *v.t.* **(a)** ~ **to do sth.** sich (*Dat.*) anmaßen, etw. zu tun; (take the liberty) sich (*Dat.*) erlauben, etw. zu tun

(b) (suppose) annehmen

2 *v.i.* [**up**]**on sth.** etw. ausnützen

presumption /prɪ'zʌmpʃn/ *n.* **(a)** (arrogance) Anmaßung, *die*

(b) (assumption) Annahme, *die*

presumptuous /prɪ'zʌmptjʊəs/ *adj.* anmaßend

presuppose /priːsə'pəʊz/ *v.t.* voraussetzen

pre-teen /'priːtiːn/ *adj.* ≈ zehn- bis zwölfjährig

pretence /prɪ'tens/ *n.* (Brit.) **(a)** (pretext) Vorwand, *der*

(b) *no art.* (make-believe, insincere behaviour) Verstellung, *die;* **it is all** *or* **just a ~:** das ist alles nicht echt

pretend /prɪ'tend/ **1** *v.t.* **(a)** vorgeben; **she ~ed to be asleep** sie tat, als ob sie schlief[e]

(b) (imagine in play) ~ **to be sth.** so tun, als ob man etw. sei

2 *v.i.* sich verstellen; **she's only ~ing** sie tut nur so

pretense (Amer.) ▶ PRETENCE

pretension /prɪ'tenʃn/ *n.* **(a)** Anspruch, *der* (**to** auf + *Akk.*)

(b) (pretentiousness) Überheblichkeit, *die*

pretentious /prɪ'tenʃəs/ *adj.* hochgestochen; wichtigtuerisch ⟨*Person*⟩; (ostentatious) großspurig

pretext /'priːtekst/ *n.* Vorwand, *der;* [up]on *or* under the ~ of doing sth. unter dem Vorwand, etw. tun zu wollen

prettily /'prɪtɪlɪ/ *adv.* hübsch; sehr schön ⟨*singen, tanzen*⟩

pretty /'prɪtɪ/ **1** *adj.* (also iron.) hübsch

2 *adv.* ziemlich; **I am ~ well** es geht mir ganz gut

prevail /prɪ'veɪl/ *v.i.* **(a)** die Oberhand gewinnen (**against, over** über + *Akk.*); ~ [**up**]**on sb. to do sth.** jmdn. dazu bewegen, etw. zu tun

(b) (predominate) ⟨*Zustand, Bedingung:*⟩ vorherrschen

(c) (be current) herrschen

prevalence /'prevələns/ *n.* Vorherrschen, *das*

prevalent /'prevələnt/ *adj.* **(a)** (existing) herrschend; weit verbreitet ⟨*Krankheit*⟩

(b) (predominant) vorherrschend

prevent /prɪ'vent/ *v.t.* (hinder) verhindern; (forestall) vorbeugen; ~ **sb. from doing sth.,** ~ **sb.'s doing sth.,** (coll.) ~ **sb. doing sth.** jmdn. daran hindern, etw. zu tun

preventable /prɪ'ventəbl/ *adj.* vermeidbar

prevention /prɪ'venʃn/ *n.* Verhinderung, *die;* (forestalling) Vorbeugung, *die* ····:̈·

p

preventive /prɪ'ventɪv/ adj. vorbeugend;
Präventiv⟨maßnahme⟩
preventive 'medicine n.
Präventivmedizin, die
preview /'priːvjuː/ n. (of film, play)
Voraufführung, die; (of exhibition) Vernissage,
die (geh.)
previous /'priːvɪəs/ ① adj. (a) früher
⟨Anstellung, Gelegenheit⟩; vorherig ⟨Abend⟩;
vorig ⟨Besitzer, Wohnsitz⟩; **the ~ page** die
Seite davor
(b) (prior) ~ **to** vor (+ Dat.)
② adv. ~ **to** vor (+ Dat.)
'previously adv. vorher
pre-war /'priːwɔː(r)/ adj. Vorkriegs-
prey /preɪ/ ① n., pl. same (a) (animal[s])
Beute, die; **beast/bird of ~**: Raubtier, das/
-vogel, der
(b) (victim) Opfer, das
② v.i. ~ **[up]on** ⟨Raubtier, Raubvogel:⟩
schlagen; (plunder) ausplündern ⟨Person⟩;
Jagd machen auf (+ Akk.); ~ **[up]on sb.'s
mind** jmdm. keine Ruhe lassen
price /praɪs/ n. (lit. or fig.) Preis, der; **at a
~ of** zum Preis von; **what is the ~ of this?**
was kostet das?; **at/not at any ~**: um jeden/
keinen Preis
price: ~ bracket ▶ ~ RANGE; **~ cut** n.
Preissenkung, die; **~-cutting** n.
Preisschleuderei, die; **~ increase** n.
Preiserhöhung, die
'priceless adj. (a) (invaluable) unbezahlbar;
(b) (coll.: amusing) köstlich
price: ~ list n. Preisliste, die; **~ range**
n. Preisspanne, die; **~ rise** n. Preisanstieg,
der; **~ tag** n. Preisschild, das; **~ war** n.
Preiskrieg, der
pricey /'praɪsɪ/ adj. (Brit. coll.) teuer
prick /prɪk/ ① v.t. stechen; stechen in
⟨Ballon⟩; aufstechen ⟨Blase⟩
② v.i. stechen
③ n. Stich, der
■ **'prick up** v.t. aufrichten ⟨Ohren⟩; **~ up
one's/its ears** die Ohren spitzen
prickle /'prɪkl/ ① n. (a) Dorn, der
(b) (Zool., Bot.) Stachel, der
② v.i. kratzen
prickly /'prɪklɪ/ adj. dornig; stachelig; (fig.)
empfindlich
pride /praɪd/ ① n. (a) Stolz, der; (arrogance)
Hochmut, der; **take [a] ~ in sb./sth.** auf
jmdn./etw. stolz sein; **sb's ~ and joy** jmds.
ganzer Stolz
(b) (of lions) Rudel, das
② v. refl. ~ **oneself [up]on sth.** auf etw.
(Akk.) stolz sein
pried ▶ PRY
priest /priːst/ n. Priester, der
'priesthood n. geistliches Amt
prig /prɪg/ n. Tugendbold, der (ugs., iron.)
priggish /'prɪgɪʃ/ adj. übertrieben
tugendhaft
prim /prɪm/ adj. spröde; (prudish) zimperlich

primarily /'praɪmərɪlɪ/ adv. in erster Linie
primary /'praɪmərɪ/ ① adj. (a) (first) primär
(geh.); grundlegend
(b) (chief) Haupt⟨rolle, -ziel, -zweck⟩
② n. (Amer.: election) Vorwahl, die
'primary school n. Grundschule, die
primate /'praɪmeɪt/ n. (a) (Eccl.) Primas, der
(b) (Zool.) Primat, der
prime¹ /praɪm/ ① n. Höhepunkt, der; **be in
one's ~**: in den besten Jahren sein
② adj. (a) Haupt-; hauptsächlich
(b) (excellent) erstklassig; vortrefflich
⟨Beispiel⟩
prime² v.t. (a) (equip) vorbereiten; ~ **sb.
with information/advice** jmdn. instruieren/
jmdm. Ratschläge erteilen
(b) grundieren ⟨Wand, Decke⟩
(c) schärfen ⟨Sprengkörper⟩
prime: ~ 'minister n. Premierminister,
der/-ministerin, die; **~ 'number** n. (Math.)
Primzahl, die
'primer n. (a) (explosive) Zündvorrichtung,
die
(b) (paint) Grundierlack, der
'prime time n. Hauptsendezeit, die; **~-time**
TV Hauptsendezeit im Fernsehen
primeval /praɪ'miːvl/ adj. urzeitlich;
Ur⟨zeiten, -wälder⟩
primitive /'prɪmɪtɪv/ adj. primitiv;
(prehistoric) urzeitlich ⟨Mensch⟩
primrose /'prɪmrəʊz/ n. gelbe
Schlüsselblume
Primus ® /'praɪməs/ n. ~ **[stove]**
Primuskocher, der
prince /prɪns/ n. Prinz, der
'princely adj. fürstlich
princess /prɪn'ses/ n. Prinzessin, die
principal /'prɪnsɪpl/ ① adj. Haupt-; (most
important) wichtigst...
② n. (of college) Rektor, der/Rektorin, die
principality /prɪnsɪ'pælɪtɪ/ n. Fürstentum,
das
'principally adv. in erster Linie
principle /'prɪnsɪpl/ n. Prinzip, das; **on the
~ that ...**: nach dem Grundsatz, dass ...; **in
~**: im Prinzip; **do sth. on ~** or **as a matter of
~**: etw. prinzipiell od. aus Prinzip tun
print /prɪnt/ ① n. (a) (impression) Abdruck,
der; (finger~) Fingerabdruck, der
(b) (~ed lettering) Gedruckte, das; (typeface)
Druck, der
(c) **be in/out of ~** ⟨Buch:⟩ erhältlich/
vergriffen sein
(d) (~ed picture or design) Druck, der
(e) (Photog.) Abzug, der
② v.t. (a) drucken ⟨Buch, Zeitschrift usw.⟩
(b) (write) in Druckschrift schreiben
■ **print 'out** v.t. (Comp.) ausdrucken
'printed adj. (a) gedruckt
(b) (published) veröffentlicht
'printed matter n. (Post) Drucksachen Pl.
'printer n. (a) (worker) Drucker, der/
Druckerin, die; (firm) Druckerei, die

(b) (Comp.) Drucker, *der*

'printing *n.* **(a)** Drucken, *das*
(b) (writing like print) Druckschrift, *die*
(c) (edition) Auflage, *die*

'printing press *n.* Druckerpresse, *die*

print: ~**out** *n.* (Comp.) Ausdruck, *der;*
~ **run** *n.* (Publishing) Auflage, die; **what is
the** ~ **run?** wie hoch ist die Auflage?

prion /'pri:ɒn/ *n.* (Biol.) Prion, *das*

prior /'praɪə(r)/ [1] *adj.* vorherig ⟨Warnung,
Zustimmung usw.⟩; früher ⟨Verabredung⟩;
Vor⟨geschichte, -kenntnis⟩
[2] *adv.* ~ **to** vor (+ *Dat.*); ~ **to doing sth.**
bevor man etw. tut/tat; ~ **to that** vorher

priority /praɪ'ɒrɪtɪ/ *n.* **(a)** (precedence)
Vorrang, *der; attrib.* vorrangig; **have** *or* **take**
~: Vorrang haben (**over** vor + *Dat.*); **have** ~
(on road) Vorfahrt haben; **give** ~ **to sb./sth.**
jmdm./einer Sache den Vorrang geben; **give
top** ~ **to sth.** einer Sache (*Dat.*) höchste
Priorität einräumen
(b) (matter) vordringliche Angelegenheit

prioritize (**prioritise**) /praɪ'ɒrɪtaɪz/ *v.t.*
nach Vordringlichkeit ordnen

prism /'prɪzm/ *n.* Prisma, *das*

prison /'prɪzn/ *n.* **(a)** Gefängnis, *das; attrib.*
Gefängnis-
(b) (custody) Haft, *die;* in ~: im Gefängnis; **go
to** ~: ins Gefängnis gehen

'prison camp *n.* Gefangenenlager, *das*

'prisoner *n.* Gefangene, *der/die;* **take sb.** ~:
jmdn. gefangen nehmen

prisoner of 'war *n.* Kriegsgefangene,
der/die

prison: ~ **sentence** *n.* Gefängnisstrafe,
die; ~ **service** *n.* Strafvollzugsbehörde,
die

pristine /'prɪsti:n/ *adj.* unberührt; **in**
~ **condition** in tadellosem Zustand

privacy /'prɪvəsɪ/ *n.* Privatsphäre, *die;*
(being undisturbed) Ungestörtheit, *die;* **invasion
of** ~: Eindringen in die Privatsphäre; **in the
strictest** ~: unter strengster Geheimhaltung

private /'praɪvət/ [1] *adj.* **(a)** (outside State
system) privat; Privat⟨schule, -industrie,
-klinik usw.⟩
(b) persönlich ⟨Dinge, Meinung, Interesse⟩;
nichtöffentlich ⟨Versammlung, Sitzung⟩;
privat ⟨Telefongespräch, Vereinbarung⟩;
Privat⟨strand, -parkplatz, -leben⟩; geheim
⟨Verhandlung, Geschäft⟩; persönlich
⟨Gründe⟩; (confidential) vertraulich
[2] *n.* **(a)** (Brit. Mil.) einfacher Soldat
(b) in ~: privat; in kleinem Kreis ⟨feiern⟩;
(confidentially) ganz im Vertrauen

private: ~ **de'tective** *n.*
[Privat]detektiv, *der/*-detektivin, *die;*
~ **'enterprise** *n.* das freie
Unternehmertum; [spirit of] ~ **enterprise**
(fig.) Unternehmungsgeist, *der;* ~ **'income**
n. private Einkünfte *Pl.;* ~ **investigator**
n. Privatdetektiv, *der/*-detektivin, *die*

'privately *adv.* privat ⟨erziehen, zugeben⟩;
vertraulich ⟨jmdn. sprechen⟩; insgeheim
⟨denken, glauben⟩; ~ **owned** in Privatbesitz

private: ~ **'parts** *n. pl.* Geschlechtsteile
Pl.; ~ **'practice** *n.* (Med.) Privatpraxis,
die; ~ **'property** *n.* Privateigentum, *das;*
~ **'view[ing]** *n.* (Art) Vernissage, *die*

privation /praɪ'veɪʃn/ *n.* Not, *die;* **suffer
many** ~**s** viele Entbehrungen erleiden

privatize /'praɪvətaɪz/ *v.t.* privatisieren

privet /'prɪvɪt/ *n.* Liguster, *der*

privilege /'prɪvɪlɪdʒ/ *n.* (right, immunity)
Privileg, *das;* (special benefit) Sonderrecht,
das; (honour) Ehre, *die*

'privileged *adj.* privilegiert

privy /'prɪvɪ/ *adj.* **be** ~ **to sth.** in etw. (*Akk.*)
eingeweiht sein

prize[1] /praɪz/ [1] *n.* **(a)** (reward, money) Preis,
der; **win** *or* **take first** ~: den ersten Preis
gewinnen
(b) (in lottery) Gewinn, *der*
[2] *v.t.* ~ **sth.** [highly] etw. hoch schätzen

prize[2] *v.t.* ~ **[open]** aufstemmen

prize: ~**-giving** *n.* Preisverleihung, *die;*
~ **money** *n.* Geldpreis, *der;* (Sport)
Preisgeld, *das;* ~**winner** *n.* Preisträger,
der/-trägerin, *die;* (in lottery) Gewinner, *der/*
Gewinnerin, *die*

pro /prəʊ/ *n.* **in pl. the** ~**s and cons** das Pro
und Kontra

proactive /prəʊ'æktɪv/ *adj.* aktiv
⟨Haltung, Rolle⟩; **be** ~ ⟨Person:⟩ [selbst] die
Initiative ergreifen

probability /prɒbə'bɪlɪtɪ/ *n.*
Wahrscheinlichkeit, *die;* **in all** ~: aller
Wahrscheinlichkeit nach

probable /'prɒbəbl/ *adj.* wahrscheinlich;
highly ~: höchstwahrscheinlich

probably /'prɒbəblɪ/ *adv.* wahrscheinlich

probation /prə'beɪʃn/ *n.* **(a)** Probezeit, *die*
(b) (Law) Bewährung, *die;* **on** ~: auf
Bewährung

probationary /prə'beɪʃənərɪ/ *adj.* Probe-;
~ **period** Probezeit, *die*

pro'bation officer *n.* Bewährungshelfer,
der/-helferin, *die*

probe /prəʊb/ [1] *n.* **(a)** (into *Gen.*) Untersuchung, *die*
(into *Gen.*)
(b) (Med., Astron.) Sonde, *die*
[2] *v.t.* untersuchen

problem /'prɒbləm/ *n.* Problem, *das;*
(puzzle) Rätsel, *das;* **what's the** ~**?** (coll.) wo
fehlts denn?; **the** ~ **about** *or* **with sb./sth.**
das Problem mit jmdm./bei etw.

problematic /prɒblə'mætɪk/**,
problematical** /prɒblə'mætɪkl/ *adj.*
problematisch

procedure /prə'si:djə(r)/ *n.* Verfahren, *das*

proceed /prə'si:d/ *v.i.* (formal) **(a)** (on foot)
gehen; (as or by vehicle) fahren; (after
interruption) weitergehen/-fahren ⸱⸱⸱⟶

(b) (begin and carry on) beginnen; (after interruption) fortfahren; ~ **in** or **with sth.** (begin) [mit] etw. beginnen; (continue) etw. fortsetzen **(c)** (be under way) ⟨*Verfahren:*⟩ laufen; (be continued after interruption) fortgesetzt werden

pro'ceedings *n. pl.* **(a)** (events) Vorgänge *Pl.*
(b) (Law) Verfahren, *das;* **legal** ~: Gerichtsverfahren, *das;* **start/take [legal]** ~: gerichtlich vorgehen (**against** gegen)

proceeds /'prəʊsiːdz/ *n. pl.* Erlös, *der* (**from** aus)

process¹ /'prəʊses/ 1 *n.* **(a)** (of time or history) Lauf, *der;* **he learnt a lot in the** ~: er lernte eine Menge dabei; **be in the** ~ **of doing sth.** gerade etw. tun
(b) (proceeding, natural operation) Vorgang, *der*
(c) (method) Verfahren, *das*
2 *v.t.* verarbeiten ⟨*Rohstoff, Signal, Daten*⟩; bearbeiten ⟨*Antrag, Akte*⟩; (Photog.) entwickeln ⟨*Film*⟩

process² /prəʊ'ses/ *v.i.* ziehen

'process cheese (Amer.)**, 'processed cheese** *ns.* Schmelzkäse, *der*

procession /prə'seʃn/ *n.* Zug, *der;* (religious) Prozession, *die;* (festive) Umzug, *der;* **go/ march in** ~: ziehen

proclaim /prə'kleɪm/ *v.t.* erklären ⟨*Absicht*⟩; geltend machen ⟨*Recht, Anspruch*⟩; verkünden ⟨*Amnestie*⟩; ausrufen ⟨*Republik*⟩

proclamation /prɒklə'meɪʃn/ *n.* **(a)** (proclaiming) Verkündung, *die*
(b) (notice) Bekanntmachung, *die;* (decree) Erlass, *der*

procreation /prəʊkrɪ'eɪʃn/ *n.* Fortpflanzung, *die*

procure /prə'kjʊə(r)/ *v.t.* beschaffen

prod /prɒd/ 1 *v.t.,* **-dd-** (poke) stupsen (ugs.); stoßen mit ⟨*Stock, Finger usw.*⟩; ~ **sb. gently** jmdn. anstupsen
2 *n.* Stupser, *der;* **give sb. a** ~: jmdm. einen Stupser geben

prodigal /'prɒdɪgl/ *adj.* verschwenderisch; ~ **son** verlorener Sohn

prodigious /prə'dɪdʒəs/ *adj.* ungeheuer

prodigy /'prɒdɪdʒɪ/ *n.* [außergewöhnliches] Talent; **child** ~: Wunderkind, *das*

produce 1 /'prɒdjuːs/ *n.* Produkte *Pl.;* Erzeugnisse *Pl.*
2 /prə'djuːs/ *v.t.* **(a)** vorzeigen ⟨*Pass, Fahrkarte*⟩
(b) produzieren ⟨*Show, Film*⟩; inszenieren ⟨*Theaterstück, Hörspiel*⟩; herausgeben ⟨*Schallplatte, Buch*⟩
(c) (manufacture) herstellen; (in nature; Agric.) produzieren
(d) (cause) hervorrufen; bewirken ⟨*Änderung*⟩
(e) (bring into being) erzeugen; führen zu ⟨*Situation*⟩
(f) (yield) geben ⟨*Milch*⟩; legen ⟨*Eier*⟩
(g) ⟨*Baum, Blume:*⟩ tragen ⟨*Früchte, Blüten*⟩; entwickeln ⟨*Triebe*⟩; bilden ⟨*Keime*⟩

producer /prə'djuːsə(r)/ *n.* **(a)** (Cinemat., Theatre, Radio, Telev.) Produzent, *der/* Produzentin, *die*
(b) (Brit. Theatre/Radio/Telev.) Regisseur, *der/* Regisseurin, *die*

product /'prɒdʌkt/ *n.* **(a)** Produkt, *das;* (of industrial process) Erzeugnis, *das;* (of art or intellect) Werk, *das*
(b) (result) Folge, *die*
(c) (Math.) Produkt, *das* (**of** aus)

production /prə'dʌkʃn/ *n.* **(a)** (Cinemat.) Produktion, *die;* (Theatre) Inszenierung, *die;* (of record, book) Herausgabe, *die*
(b) (making) Produktion, *die;* (manufacturing) Herstellung, *die;* (thing produced) Produkt, *das;* (thing created) Werk, *das*
(c) (yielding) Produktion, *die;* (yield) Ertrag, *der*

production: ~ **line** *n.* Fertigungsstraße, *die;* ~ **manager** *n.* Produktionsleiter, *der/*-leiterin, *die*

productive /prə'dʌktɪv/ *adj.* leistungsfähig ⟨*Betrieb, Bauernhof*⟩; fruchtbar ⟨*Gespräch, Verhandlungen*⟩

productivity /prɒdʌk'tɪvɪtɪ/ *n.* Produktivität, *die*

'product range *n.* Produktpalette, *die*

Prof. /prɒf/ *abbr.* = **Professor** Prof.

profane /prə'feɪn/ *adj.* **(a)** (irreligious) gotteslästerlich
(b) (secular) weltlich
(c) (irreverent) respektlos ⟨*Bemerkung*⟩; profan ⟨*Sprache*⟩

profess /prə'fes/ *v.t.* **(a)** (declare openly) bekunden ⟨*Vorliebe, Abneigung*⟩; ~ **to be/do sth.** erklären, etw. zu sein/tun
(b) (claim) vorgeben; ~ **to be/do sth.** behaupten, etw. zu sein/tun

profession /prə'feʃn/ *n.* **(a)** Beruf, *der;* **be a pilot by** ~: von Beruf Pilot sein
(b) (body of people) Berufsstand, *der*

professional /prə'feʃənl/ 1 *adj.* **(a)** Berufs⟨*ausbildung, -leben*⟩; beruflich ⟨*Qualifikation*⟩
(b) (worthy of profession) (in technical expertise) fachmännisch; (in attitude) professionell; (in experience) routiniert
(c) ~ **people** Angehörige *Pl.* hoch qualifizierter Berufe
(d) (by profession) gelernt; (not amateur) Berufs⟨*musiker, -sportler*⟩; Profi⟨*sportler*⟩
(e) (paid) Profi⟨*sport, -boxen*⟩
2 *n.* (trained person) Fachmann, *der/*Fachfrau, *die;* (non-amateur; also Sport) Profi, *der*

professor /prə'fesə(r)/ *n.* **(a)** (Univ.) Professor, *der/*Professorin, *die* (**of** für)
(b) (Amer.: teacher at university) Dozent, *der/* Dozentin, *die*

proficiency /prə'fɪʃənsɪ/ *n.* Können, *das*

proficient /prə'fɪʃənt/ *adj.* fähig; gut ⟨*Pianist, Reiter usw.*⟩; geschickt ⟨*Radfahrer, Handwerker*⟩; **be** ~ **at** or **in maths** viel von Mathematik verstehen

profile /'prəʊfaɪl/ *n.* **(a)** (side aspect) Profil, *das*

(b) (biographical sketch) Porträt, *das*
(c) (fig.) keep a low ∼: sich zurückhalten

profit /'prɒfɪt/ *n.* Gewinn, *der;* Profit, *der;*
make a ∼ from *or* out of sth. mit etw. Geld
verdienen; make [a few pence] ∼ on sth.
[ein paar Pfennige] an etw. (*Dat.*) verdienen;
∼ and loss Gewinn und Verlust; ∼-and-loss
account Gewinn-und-Verlust-Rechnung, *die*
■ 'profit by *v.t.* profitieren von; Nutzen
ziehen aus ⟨*Fehler, Erfahrung*⟩
■ 'profit from *v.t.* profitieren von

profitable /'prɒfɪtəbl/ *adj.* rentabel;
einträglich; (fruitful) nützlich

profiteer /prɒfɪ'tɪə(r)/ ①*n.* Profitmacher,
der/-macherin, *die*
②*v.i.* sich bereichern

profi'teering *n.* Wucher, *der*

profit: ∼ margin *n.* Gewinnspanne, *die;*
∼-sharing *n.* Gewinnbeteiligung, *die*

profligate /'prɒflɪgət/ *adj.*
verschwenderisch; be ∼ of *or* with sth.
verschwenderisch umgehen mit etw.

profound /prə'faʊnd/ *adj.* tief; nachhaltig
⟨*Wirkung, Einfluss*⟩; tief greifend ⟨*Wandel,
Veränderung*⟩; tief empfunden ⟨*Beileid,
Mitgefühl*⟩; tief sitzend ⟨*Misstrauen*⟩

prognosis /prɒg'nəʊsɪs/ *n.,* pl. prognoses
/prɒg'nəʊsiːz/ Prognose, *die*

program /'prəʊgræm/ ①*n.* **(a)** (Amer.)
▶ PROGRAMME 1
(b) (Comp.) Programm, *das;* ∼ file
Programmdata, *die*
②*v.t.,* -mm- (Comp.) programmieren

programme /'prəʊgræm/ *n.* **(a)** ([notice of]
events) Programm, *das*
(b) (Radio, Telev.) Sendung, *die*
(c) (plan, instructions for machine) Programm,
das

programmer /'prəʊgræmə(r)/ *n.* (Comp.)
Programmierer, *der/*Programmiererin, *die*

progress ①/'prəʊgres/ *n.* **(a)** no pl., no
indef. art. (onward movement)
[Vorwärts]bewegung, *die*
(b) (advance) Fortschritt, *der;* make ∼:
vorankommen; ⟨*Student, Patient:*⟩
Fortschritte machen; in ∼: im Gange
②/prə'gres/ *v.i.* **(a)** (move forward)
vorankommen
(b) (be carried on, develop) Fortschritte machen

progression /prə'greʃn/ *n.* **(a)**
(development) Fortschritt, *der*
(b) (succession) Folge, *die*

progressive /prə'gresɪv/ *adj.* **(a)**
fortschreitend ⟨*Verbesserung,
Verschlechterung*⟩; schrittweise ⟨*Reform*⟩;
allmählich ⟨*Veränderung*⟩
(b) (favouring reform; in culture) fortschrittlich;
progressiv

pro'gressively *adv.* immer ⟨*schlechter,
weiter*⟩

prohibit /prə'hɪbɪt/ *v.t.* (forbid) verbieten;
∼ sb.'s doing sth., ∼ sb. from doing sth.
jmdm. verbieten, etw. zu tun

prohibition /prəʊhɪ'bɪʃn, prəʊɪ'bɪʃn/ *n.*
Verbot, *das*

prohibitive /prə'hɪbɪtɪv/ *adj.*
unerschwinglich ⟨*Preis, Miete*⟩; untragbar
⟨*Kosten*⟩

project ①/prə'dʒekt/ *v.t.* werfen ⟨*Schein*⟩;
senden ⟨*Strahl*⟩; (Cinemat.) projizieren
②/prə'dʒekt/ *v.i.* (jut out) ⟨*Felsen:*⟩
vorspringen; ⟨*Zähne, Brauen:*⟩ vorstehen
③/'prɒdʒekt/ *n.* Projekt, *das*

projectile /prə'dʒektaɪl/ *n.* Geschoss, *das*

projection /prə'dʒekʃn/ *n.* **(a)** (protruding
thing) Vorsprung, *der*
(b) (estimate) Hochrechnung, *die;* (forecast)
Voraussage, *die*

projectionist /prə'dʒekʃənɪst/ *n.* (Cinemat.)
Filmvorführer, *der/*-vorführerin, *die*

pro'jection room *n.* (Cinemat.)
Vorführrraum, *der*

projector /prə'dʒektə(r)/ *n.* Projektor, *der*

proletarian /prəʊlɪ'teərɪən/①*adj.*
proletarisch
②*n.* Proletarier, *der/*Proletarierin, *die*

'pro-life *adj.* Lebensschutz-

'pro-lifer *n.* Verfechter, *der/*Verfechterin,
die des Rechts auf Leben

proliferate /prə'lɪfəreɪt/ *v.i.* (increase) sich
ausbreiten

proliferation /prəlɪfə'reɪʃn/ *n.* starke
Zunahme

prolific /prə'lɪfɪk/ *adj.* **(a)** (fertile) fruchtbar
(b) (productive) produktiv

prologue (*Amer.:* **prolog**) /'prəʊlɒg/ *n.*
Prolog, *der* (to zu)

prolong /prə'lɒŋ/ *v.t.* verlängern

prolonged /prə'lɒŋd/ *adj.* lang; lang
anhaltend ⟨*Beifall*⟩

promenade /prɒmə'nɑːd/ *n.* Promenade,
die

prominence /'prɒmɪnəns/ *n.* **(a)**
(conspicuousness) Auffälligkeit, *die*
(b) (distinction) Bekanntheit, *die*

prominent /'prɒmɪnənt/ *adj.* **(a)**
(conspicuous) auffallend
(b) (foremost) herausragend; he was ∼ in
politics er war ein prominenter Politiker
(c) (projecting) vorspringend; vorstehend
⟨*Backenknochen, Brauen*⟩

promiscuity /prɒmɪ'skjuːɪtɪ/ *n.*
Promiskuität, *die* (geh.)

promiscuous /prə'mɪskjʊəs/ *adj.*
promiskuitiv (geh.); a ∼ man ein Mann, der
häufig die Partnerin wechselt

promise ①/'prɒmɪs/①*n.* **(a)** Versprechen,
das; sb.'s ∼s jmds. Versprechungen; give *or*
make a ∼ [to sb.] [jmdm.] ein Versprechen
geben; give *or* make a ∼ [to sb.] to do sth.
[jmdm.] versprechen, etw. zu tun
(b) (fig.: reason for expectation) Hoffnung, *die;* a
painter of *or* with ∼: ein viel versprechender
Maler
②*v.t.* **(a)** versprechen; ∼ sth. to sb., ∼ sb.
sth. jmdm. etw. versprechen ····➔

(b) (fig.: give reason for expectation of) verheißen
(geh.); ~ **sb. sth.** jmdm. etw. in Aussicht
stellen

③ *v.i.* ~ **well** *or* **favourably** viel
versprechend sein; **I can't** ~: ich kann es
nicht versprechen

promising /'prɒmɪsɪŋ/ *adj.* viel
versprechend

promote /prə'məʊt/ *v.t.* **(a)** (to more senior
job) befördern
(b) (encourage) fördern
(c) (publicize) Werbung machen für
(d) (Footb.) **be** ~**d** aufsteigen

pro'moter *n.* Veranstalter, *der*/
Veranstalterin, *die*

promotion /prə'məʊʃn/ *n.* **(a)** Beförderung,
die; **win** *or* **gain** ~: befördert werden
(b) (furtherance) Förderung, *die*
(c) (publicization) Werbung, *die;* (instance)
Werbekampagne, *die*
(d) (Footb.) Aufstieg, *der*

promotional /prə'məʊʃənl/ *adj.*
Werbe⟨*kampagne, -broschüre usw.*⟩

prompt /prɒmpt/ ① *adj.* **(a)** (ready to act)
bereitwillig; **be** ~ **in doing sth.** *or* **to do sth.**
etw. unverzüglich tun
(b) (done readily) sofortig; **her** ~ **answer** ihre
prompte Antwort; **take** ~ **action** sofort
handeln
(c) (punctual) pünktlich
② *adv.* pünktlich; **at 6 o'clock** ~: Punkt
6 Uhr
③ *v.t.* **(a)** (incite) veranlassen
(b) (supply with words) soufflieren (+ *Dat.*); (give
suggestion to) weiterhelfen (+ *Dat.*)
(c) hervorrufen ⟨*Kritik*⟩; provozieren
⟨*Antwort*⟩

'**promptly** *adv.* **(a)** (quickly) prompt
(b) (punctually) pünktlich

prone /prəʊn/ *adj.* (liable) **be** ~ **to** anfällig
sein für ⟨*Krankheiten*⟩; **be** ~ **to do sth.** dazu
neigen, etw. zu tun

prong /prɒŋ/ *n.* (of fork) Zinke, *die*

pronoun /'prəʊnaʊn/ *n.* (Ling.) Pronomen,
das; Fürwort, *das*

pronounce /prə'naʊns/ ① *v.t.* **(a)** (declare)
verkünden; ~ **sb./sth.** [**to be**] **sth.** jmdn./etw.
für etw. erklären; ~ **sb. fit for work** jmdn.
für arbeitsfähig erklären
(b) aussprechen ⟨*Wort, Buchstaben usw.*⟩
② *v.i.* ~ **on sth.** zu etw. Stellung nehmen;
~ **for** *or* **in favour of/against sth.** sich für/
gegen etw. aussprechen

pronounced /prə'naʊnst/ *adj.* (marked)
ausgeprägt

pro'nouncement *n.* Erklärung, *die;* **make
a** ~ [**about sth.**] eine Erklärung [zu etw.]
abgeben

pronunciation /prənʌnsɪ'eɪʃn/ *n.*
Aussprache, *die;* **what is the** ~ **of this word?**
wie wird dieses Wort ausgesprochen?

proof /pruːf/ ① *n.* **(a)** (fact, evidence) Beweis,
der
(b) *no indef. art.* (Law) Beweismaterial, *das*

(c) (proving) **in** ~ **of** zum Beweis (+ *Gen.*)
(d) *no art.* (standard of strength) Proof *o. Art.;*
100° ~ (Brit.), **128°** ~ (Amer.) 64 Vol.-%
Alkohol
(e) (Printing) [Korrektur]abzug, *der*
② *adj.* **(a)** **be** ~ **against sth.** unempfindlich
gegen etw. sein; (fig.) gegen etw. immun sein
(b) *in comb.* ⟨*kugel-, einbruch-,
idioten*⟩sicher; ⟨*schall-, wasser*⟩dicht; **flame-**
~: nicht brennbar

proof ~**read** *v.t.* Korrektur lesen;
~**-reader** *n.* Korrektor, *der*/Korrektorin,
die

prop¹ /prɒp/ ① *n.* Stütze, *die;* (Mining)
Strebe, *die*
② *v.t.,* **-pp-** stützen; **the ladder was** ~**ped
against the house** die Leiter war gegen das
Haus gelehnt
■ **prop 'up** *v.t.* stützen; (fig.) vor dem
Konkurs bewahren ⟨*Firma*⟩; stützen
⟨*Regierung*⟩

prop² *n.* (Theatre, Cinemat.: also fig.) Requisit,
das

propaganda /prɒpə'gændə/ *n.*
Propaganda, *die*

propagate /'prɒpəgeɪt/ ① *v.t.* **(a)** (Hort.,
Agric.) vermehren (**from, by** durch)
(b) (spread) verbreiten
② *v.i.* **(a)** (Bot.) sich vermehren
(b) (spread) sich ausbreiten

propagation /prɒpə'geɪʃn/ *n.* **(a)** (Hort.,
Agric.) Züchtung, *die*
(b) (Bot.) Vermehrung, *die*
(c) (spreading) Verbreitung, *die*

propel /prə'pel/ *v.t.,* **-ll-** antreiben

propellant /prə'pelənt/ *n.* **(a)** Treibstoff,
der
(b) (of aerosol spray) Treibgas, *das*

pro'peller *n.* Propeller, *der*

propelling 'pencil *n.* (Brit.) Drehbleistift,
der

propensity /prə'pensɪtɪ/ *n.* **have a** ~ **to do
sth.** *or* **for doing sth.** dazu neigen, etw. zu
tun

proper /'prɒpə(r)/ *adj.* **(a)** (accurate) richtig;
zutreffend ⟨*Beschreibung*⟩; eigentlich
⟨*Wortbedeutung*⟩
(b) (genuine, strictly so called) im engeren Sinn
nachgestellt; **in London** ~: in London selbst
(c) (genuine) echt; richtig ⟨*Wirbelsturm,
Schauspieler*⟩
(d) (satisfactory) richtig; zufrieden stellend
⟨*Antwort*⟩
(e) (suitable) angemessen; (morally fitting)
gebührend; **do sth. the** ~ **way** etw. richtig
machen
(f) *attrib.* (coll.: thorough) richtig

'**properly** *adv.* richtig; (rightly) zu Recht;
~ **speaking** genau genommen

proper 'name, proper 'noun *ns.* (Ling.)
Eigenname, *der*

property /'prɒpətɪ/ *n.* **(a)** (possession[s])
Eigentum, *das;* **lost** ~ [**department** *or* **office**]
Fundbüro, *das*

(b) (estate) Besitz, *der;* Immobilie, *die* (fachspr.)

(c) (attribute) Eigenschaft, *die;* (effect, special power) Wirkung, *die*

'property developer *n.* ≈ Bauunternehmer, *der*/-unternehmerin, *die*

prophecy /'prɒfɪsɪ/ *n.* (prediction) Vorhersage, *die;* (prophetic utterance) Prophezeiung, *die*

prophesy /'prɒfɪsaɪ/ *v.t.* (predict) vorhersagen; (fig.) prophezeien ⟨*Unglück*⟩; (as fortune teller) weissagen

prophet /'prɒfɪt/ *n.* Prophet, *der*

prophetic /prə'fetɪk/ *adj.* prophetisch

proportion /prə'pɔ:ʃn/ ⟨1⟩ *n.* **(a)** (portion) Teil, *der*

(b) (ratio) Verhältnis, *das;* **the ~ of sth. to sth.** das Verhältnis von etw. zu etw.

(c) (correct relation; Math.) Proportion, *die;* **be in ~ [to** *or* **with sth.]** im richtigen Verhältnis [zu *od.* mit etw.] stehen; **keep things in ~** (fig.) die Dinge im richtigen Licht sehen; **be out of ~/all** *or* **any ~ [to** *or* **with sth.]** in keinem/keinerlei Verhältnis zu etw. stehen

(d) *in pl.* (size) Dimensionen *Pl.*

⟨2⟩ *v.t.* proportionieren

proportional /prə'pɔ:ʃənl/ *adj.* **(a)** (in proportion) entsprechend; **be ~ to sth.** einer Sache (*Dat.*) entsprechen

(b) (Math.) **be directly/indirectly ~ to sth.** einer Sache (*Dat.*) direkt/umgekehrt proportional sein

proportionate /prə'pɔ:ʃənət/ ▶ PROPORTIONAL A

proposal /prə'pəʊzl/ *n.* Vorschlag, *der;* (offer) Angebot, *das;* **~ [of marriage]** [Heirats]antrag, *der*

propose /prə'pəʊz/ ⟨1⟩ *v.t.* **(a)** vorschlagen; **~ sth. to sb.** jmdm. etw. vorschlagen; **~ marriage [to sb.]** [jmdm.] einen Heiratsantrag machen

(b) (nominate) **~ sb. as/for sth.** jmdn. als/für etw. vorschlagen

(c) (intend) **~ doing** *or* **to do sth.** beabsichtigen, etw. zu tun

⟨2⟩ *v.i.* (offer marriage) **~ [to sb.]** jmdm. einen Heiratsantrag machen

proposition /prɒpə'zɪʃn/ *n.* **(a)** (proposal) Vorschlag, *der;* **make** *or* **put a ~ to sb.** jmdm. einen Vorschlag machen

(b) (statement; Logic) Aussage, *die*

propound /prə'paʊnd/ *v.t.* darlegen

proprietary /prə'praɪətərɪ/ *adj.* **~ name** *or* **term** Markenname, *der*

proprietor /prə'praɪətə(r)/ *n.* Inhaber, *der*/ Inhaberin, *die*

propriety /prə'praɪətɪ/ *n.* Anstand, *der;* **breach of ~:** Verstoß gegen die guten Sitten

propulsion /prə'pʌlʃn/ *n.* Antrieb, *der*

prosaic /prə'zeɪɪk/ *adj.* prosaisch (geh.); nüchtern

proscribe /prə'skraɪb/ *v.t.* verbieten

prose /prəʊz/ *n.* Prosa, *die; attrib.* Prosa⟨*werk, -stil*⟩

prosecute /'prɒsɪkju:t/ ⟨1⟩ *v.t.* strafrechtlich verfolgen; **~ sb. for sth./doing sth.** jmdn. wegen etw. strafrechtlich verfolgen/jmdn. strafrechtlich verfolgen, weil *or* etw. tut/getan hat

⟨2⟩ *v.i.* Anzeige erstatten

prosecution /prɒsɪ'kju:ʃn/ *n.* (bringing to trial) [strafrechtliche] Verfolgung; (court procedure) Anklage, *die;* (prosecuting party) Anklage[vertretung], *die;* **the ~:** die Anklage

prosecutor /'prɒsɪkju:tə(r)/ *n.* Ankläger, *der*/Anklägerin, *die;* **public ~** ≈ Generalstaatsanwalt, *der*/-anwältin, *die*

prospect ⟨1⟩ /'prɒspekt/ *n.* **(a)** (expectation) Erwartung, *die* (of hinsichtlich); **[at the] ~ of sth./doing sth.** beim [Gedanken an] etw. (*Akk.*)/[darauf], etw. zu tun

(b) *in pl.* (hope of success) Zukunftsaussichten *Pl.;* **a man with [good] ~s** ein Mann mit Zukunft; **sb.'s ~s of sth./doing sth.** jmds. Chancen auf etw. (*Akk.*)/darauf, etw. zu tun; **the ~s for sb./sth.** die Aussichten für jmdn./ etw.

⟨2⟩ /prə'spekt/ *v.i.* nach Bodenschätzen suchen

prospective /prə'spektɪv/ *adj.* voraussichtlich; zukünftig ⟨*Erbe, Braut*⟩; potenziell ⟨*Käufer, Kandidat*⟩

prospector /prə'spektə(r)/ *n.* Prospektor, *der;* (for gold) Goldsucher, *der*

prospectus /prə'spektəs/ *n.* Prospekt, *der;* (Brit. Univ.) Studienführer, *der*

prosper /'prɒspə(r)/ *v.i.* gedeihen; ⟨*Geschäft:*⟩ florieren; ⟨*Berufstätiger:*⟩ Erfolg haben

prosperity /prɒ'sperɪtɪ/ *n.* Wohlstand, *der*

prosperous /'prɒspərəs/ *adj.* wohlhabend; florierend ⟨*Unternehmen*⟩

prostitute /'prɒstɪtju:t/ *n.* Prostituierte, *die*

prostitution /prɒstɪ'tju:ʃn/ *n.* Prostitution, *die*

prostrate ⟨1⟩ /'prɒstreɪt/ *adj.* [auf dem Bauch] ausgestreckt

⟨2⟩ /prə'streɪt/ *v. refl.* **~ oneself [at sth./ before sb.]** sich [vor etw./jmdm.] niederwerfen

protagonist /prəʊ'tægənɪst/ *n.* (Lit.) Protagonist, *der*/Protagonistin, *die*

protect /prə'tekt/ *v.t.* **(a)** schützen (from vor + *Dat.*, against gegen)

(b) (preserve) unter [Natur]schutz stellen ⟨*Pflanze, Tier*⟩

protection /prə'tekʃn/ *n.* Schutz, *der* (from vor + *Dat.*, against gegen)

protective /prə'tektɪv/ *adj.* schützend; Schutz⟨*hülle, -anstrich, -vorrichtung, -maske*⟩; **be ~ towards sb.** fürsorglich gegenüber jmdm. sein

protein /'prəʊti:n/ *n.* Protein, *das* (fachspr.); Eiweiß, *das*

protest ① /'prəʊtest/ n. (a) Beschwerde, die; make or lodge a ~ [against sb./sth.] eine Beschwerde [gegen jmdn./etw.] einreichen (b) (gesture of disapproval) ~[s] Protest, der; under ~: unter Protest; in ~ [against sth.] aus Protest [gegen etw.] (c) no art. (dissent) Protest, der ② /prə'test/ v.t. (affirm) beteuern ③ /prə'test/ v.i. protestieren (about gegen); (make written or formal ~) Protest einlegen (to bei)

Protestant /'prɒtɪstənt/ ① n. Protestant, der/Protestantin, die ② adj. protestantisch; evangelisch

Protestantism /'prɒtɪstəntɪzm/ n., no art. Protestantismus, der

pro'tester n. Protestierende, der/die; (at demonstration) Demonstrant, der/ Demonstrantin, die

protocol /'prəʊtəkɒl/ n. Protokoll, das

proton /'prəʊtən/ n. Proton, das

prototype /'prəʊtətaɪp/ n. Prototyp, der

protract /prə'trækt/ v.t. verlängern

protractor /prə'træktə(r)/ n. (Geom.) Winkelmesser, der

protrude /prə'truːd/ v.i. herausragen (from aus); ⟨Zähne⟩ vorstehen

protuberance /prə'tjuːbərəns/ n. Auswuchs, der

proud /praʊd/ ① adj. (a) stolz; ~ to do sth. or to be doing sth. stolz darauf, etw. zu tun; ~ of sb./sth./doing sth. stolz auf jmdn./etw./ darauf, etw. zu tun (b) (arrogant) hochmütig ② adv. (Brit. coll.) do sb. ~: jmdn. verwöhnen

'proudly adv. (a) stolz (b) (arrogantly) hochmütig

provable /'pruːvəbl/ adj. beweisbar

prove /pruːv/ ① v.t., p.p. ~d or proven /'pruːvn/ beweisen; nachweisen ⟨Identität⟩; ~ sb. right/wrong ⟨Ereignis:⟩ jmdm. recht/unrecht geben; be ~d wrong or to be false ⟨Theorie:⟩ widerlegt werden; ~ one's/ sb.'s case or point beweisen, dass man recht hat/jmdm. recht geben ② v. refl., p. p. proved or proven: ~ oneself sich bewähren ③ v.i., p. p. proved or proven: ~ [to be] sich erweisen als

proven ▸ PROVE

proverb /'prɒvɜːb/ n. Sprichwort, das

proverbial /prə'vɜːbɪəl/ adj. sprichwörtlich

provide /prə'vaɪd/ v.t. (a) besorgen; liefern ⟨Beweis⟩; bereitstellen ⟨Dienst, Geld⟩; ~ a home/a car for sb. jmdm. Unterkunft/ein Auto [zur Verfügung] stellen (b) ⟨Vertrag, Gesetz:⟩ vorsehen

■ **pro'vide for** v.t. (a) (make provision for) vorsorgen für; ⟨Plan, Gesetz:⟩ vorsehen (b) (maintain) sorgen für, versorgen ⟨Familie, Kind⟩

pro'vided conj. ~ [that] ...: vorausgesetzt, [dass] ...

providence /'prɒvɪdəns/ n. (a) [divine] ~: die [göttliche] Vorsehung (b) P~ (God) der Himmel

province /'prɒvɪns/ n. (a) Provinz, die (b) the ~s (regions outside capital) die Provinz (c) (sphere of action) [Tätigkeits]bereich, der; (area of responsibility) Zuständigkeitsbereich, der

provincial /prə'vɪnʃl/ adj. Provinz-

provision /prə'vɪʒn/ n. (a) (providing) Bereitstellung, die; make ~ for vorsorgen od. Vorsorge treffen für ⟨Notfall⟩ (b) ~s pl. (food) Lebensmittel Pl.

provisional /prə'vɪʒənl/ adj., **provisionally** /prə'vɪʒənəlɪ/ adv. vorläufig; provisorisch

proviso /prə'vaɪzəʊ/ n., pl. ~s Vorbehalt, der

provocation /prɒvə'keɪʃn/ n. Provokation, die

provocative /prə'vɒkətɪv/ adj. provozierend; (sexually) aufreizend

provoke /prə'vəʊk/ v.t. (a) provozieren ⟨Person⟩; reizen ⟨Person, Tier⟩; ~ sb. into doing sth. jmdn. so sehr provozieren, dass er etw. tut (b) (give rise to) hervorrufen; erregen

prow /praʊ/ n. (Naut.) Bug, der

prowl /praʊl/ ① v.i. streifen ② v.t. durchstreifen ③ n. be on the ~: auf einem Streifzug sein

proximity /prɒk'sɪmɪtɪ/ n. Nähe, die

proxy /'prɒksɪ/ n. by ~: durch einen Bevollmächtigten/eine Bevollmächtigte

prude /pruːd/ n. prüder Mensch

prudence /'pruːdəns/ n. Besonnenheit, die

prudent /'pruːdənt/ adj. (a) (careful) besonnen (b) (circumspect) vorsichtig

prudish /'pruːdɪʃ/ adj. prüde

prune¹ /pruːn/ n. Backpflaume, die

prune² v.t. (a) (trim) [be]schneiden (b) (fig.) reduzieren

pry /praɪ/ v.i. neugierig sein

■ **'pry into** v.t. seine Nase stecken in (+ Akk.) (ugs.) ⟨Angelegenheit⟩

PS abbr. = **postscript** PS

psalm /sɑːm/ n. Psalm, der

pseudo /'sjuːdəʊ/ ① adj. (a) (sham) unecht (b) (insincere) verlogen ② n., pl. ~s (pretentious person) Möchtegern, der (ugs. spött.)

pseudonym /'sjuːdənɪm/ n. Pseudonym, das

psychiatric /saɪkɪ'ætrɪk/ adj. psychiatrisch

psychiatrist /saɪ'kaɪətrɪst/ n. Psychiater, der/Psychiaterin, die

psychiatry /saɪ'kaɪətrɪ/ n. Psychiatrie, die

psychic /'saɪkɪk/ *adj.* be ~: übernatürliche Fähigkeiten haben

psychoanalyse /saɪkəʊ'ænəlaɪz/ *v.t.* psychoanalysieren

psychoa'nalysis *n.* Psychoanalyse, *die*

psycho'analyst *n.* Psychoanalytiker, *der*/-analytikerin, *die*

psychological /saɪkə'lɒdʒɪkl/ *adj.* psychologisch; psychisch ‹*Problem*›

psychologist /saɪ'kɒlədʒɪst/ *n.* Psychologe, *der*/Psychologin, *die*

psychology /saɪ'kɒlədʒɪ/ *n.* Psychologie, *die*

psychopath /'saɪkəpæθ/ *n.* Psychopath, *der*/Psychopathin, *die*

psychopathic /saɪkə'pæθɪk/ *adj.* psychopathisch

psychosis /saɪ'kəʊsɪs/ *n.*, *pl.* **psychoses** /saɪ'kəʊsiːz/ Psychose, *die*

psychotherapist /saɪkəʊ'θerəpɪst/ *n.* Psychotherapeut, *der*/-therapeutin, *die*

psycho'therapy *n.* Psychotherapie, *die*

psychotic /saɪ'kɒtɪk/ *adj.* psychotisch

PTO *abbr.* = **please turn over** b.w.

pub /ʌb/ *n.* (Brit. coll.) Kneipe, *die* (ugs.)

'pub crawl *n.* (Brit. coll.) Zechtour, *die* (ugs.)

puberty /'pjuːbətɪ/ *n.*, *no art.* Pubertät, *die*

'pub grub *n.* (Brit. coll.) Kneipenessen, *das* (ugs.)

pubic /'pjuːbɪk/ *adj.* Scham-

public /'pʌblɪk/ **1** *adj.* öffentlich; **make sth. ~:** etw. bekannt machen **2** *n.*, *sing. or pl.* **(a)** (the people) Öffentlichkeit, *die* **(b)** (section of community) Publikum, *das* **(c)** in ~: öffentlich

publican /'pʌblɪkən/ *n.* (Brit.) [Gast]wirt, *der*/-wirtin, *die*

publication /pʌblɪ'keɪʃn/ *n.* Veröffentlichung, *die*

public: ~ **'building** *n.* öffentliches Gebäude; ~ **con'venience** *n.* öffentliche Toilette; ~ **'figure** *n.* Persönlichkeit des öffentlichen Lebens; ~ **'footpath** *n.* öffentlicher Fußweg; ~ **'holiday** *n.* gesetzlicher Feiertag; ~ **'house** *n.* (Brit.) Gastwirtschaft, *die;* Gaststätte, *die*

publicity /pʌb'lɪsɪtɪ/ *n.* Publicity, *die;* (advertising) Werbung, *die;* ~ **campaign** Werbekampagne, *die*

pub'licity agent *n.* Publicitymanager, *der*/-managerin, *die*

publicize /'pʌblɪsaɪz/ *v.t.* publik machen ‹*Ungerechtigkeit*›; werben für, Reklame machen für ‹*Produkt*›

public: ~ **'library** *n.* öffentliche Bücherei; ~ **limited company** *n.* (Brit.) ≈ Aktiengesellschaft, *die*

'publicly *adv.* öffentlich; ~ **owned** staatseigen

public: ~ **property** *n.* Staatsbesitz, *der;* ~ **re'lations** *n.*, *sing. or pl.*

Publicrelations *Pl.;* ~ **school** *n.* **(a)** (Brit.) Privatschule, *die;* **(b)** (Scot., Amer.) staatliche *od.* öffentliche Schule; ~ **'servant** *n.* Inhaber/Inhaberin eines öffentlichen Amtes; ~ **'transport** *n.* öffentlicher Personenverkehr

publish /'pʌblɪʃ/ *v.t.* ‹*Verlag:*› verlegen ‹*Buch, Zeitschrift, Musik usw.*›; ‹*Autor:*› veröffentlichen ‹*Text*›

'publisher *n.* Verleger, *der*/Verlegerin, *die;* ~[s] (company) Verlag, *der*

'publishing *n.*, *no art.* Verlagswesen, *das*

puck /pʌk/ *n.* (Ice Hockey) Puck, *der*

pucker /'pʌkə(r)/ **1** *v.t.* ~ [up] runzeln ‹*Brauen, Stirn*›; kräuseln ‹*Lippen*› **2** *v.i.* ~ [up] ‹*Stoff:*› sich kräuseln

pudding /'pʊdɪŋ/ *n.* **(a)** Pudding, *der* **(b)** (dessert) süße Nachspeise

puddle /'pʌdl/ *n.* Pfütze, *die*

puerile /'pjʊəraɪl/ *adj.* kindisch

puff /pʌf/ **1** *n.* **(a)** Stoß, *der;* ~ **of breath/wind** Atem-/Windstoß, *der* **(b)** ~ **of smoke** Rauchstoß, *der* **(c)** (pastry) Blätterteigteilchen, *das* **2** *v.i.* **(a)** ~ **[and blow]** schnaufen [und keuchen] **(b)** (~ cigarette smoke etc.) paffen (ugs.) (**at an** + *Dat.*) **(c)** ‹*Person:*› keuchen; ‹*Zug, Lokomotive:*› schnaufend fahren **3** *v.t.* blasen ‹*Rauch*›; stäuben ‹*Puder*›

■ **puff 'out** *v.t.* **(a)** bauschen ‹*Segel*› **(b)** (put out of breath) außer Atem bringen ‹*Person*›; **be** ~**ed [out]** außer Atem sein

puff 'pastry *n.* Blätterteig, *der*

puffy /'pʌfɪ/ *adj.* verschwollen

pugnacious /pʌɡ'neɪʃəs/ *adj.* kampflustig

puke /pjuːk/ (coarse) **1** *v.i.* kotzen (salopp) **2** *n.* Kotze, *die* (salopp)

pull /pʊl/ **1** *v.t.* **(a)** (draw, tug) ziehen an (+ *Dat.*); ziehen ‹*Hebel*›; ~ **sb.'s** *or* **sb. by the hair/ears/sleeve** jmdn. an den Haaren/Ohren/am Ärmel ziehen; ~ **sth. over one's ears/head** sich (*Dat.*) etw. über die Ohren/den Kopf ziehen; ~ **to pieces** in Stücke reißen; (fig.) zerpflücken ‹*Argument usw.*› **(b)** (extract) [her]ausziehen; [heraus]ziehen ‹*Zahn*› **(c)** (strain) sich (*Dat.*) zerren ‹*Muskel*› **2** *v.i.* **(a)** ziehen; **'P~' '**„Ziehen" **(b)** ~ **[to the left/right]** ‹*Auto, Boot:*› [nach links/rechts] ziehen **(c)** (pluck) ~ **at** ziehen an (+ *Dat.*); ~ **at sb.'s sleeve** jmdn. am Ärmel ziehen **3** *n.* **(a)** Zug, *der* **(b)** (influence) Einfluss, *der* (**with** auf + *Akk.,* bei)

■ **pull a'part** *v.t.* **(a)** (take to pieces) auseinander nehmen **(b)** (fig.: criticize) zerpflücken; verreißen ‹*Buch, [literarisches] Werk*›

■ **pull 'down** *v.t.* **(a)** herunterziehen **(b)** (demolish) abreißen

■ **pull 'in** **1** *v.t.* hereinziehen   ⋯⊹

$\boxed{2}$ *v.i.* (a) ⟨*Zug:*⟩ einfahren
(b) (move to side of road) an die Seite fahren; (stop) anhalten
■ **pull 'off** *v.t.* (a) (remove) abziehen; (violently) abreißen
(b) (accomplish) an Land ziehen (ugs.)
■ **pull 'out** $\boxed{1}$ *v.t.* herausziehen
$\boxed{2}$ *v.i.* (a) (depart) abfahren
(b) (away from roadside) ausscheren
■ **pull 'through** *v.i.* ⟨*Patient:*⟩ durchkommen
■ **pull to'gether** *v. refl.* sich zusammennehmen
■ **pull 'up** $\boxed{1}$ *v.t.* (a) hochziehen
(b) [he]rausziehen ⟨*Unkraut, Pflanze*⟩
(c) (reprimand) zurechtweisen
$\boxed{2}$ *v.i.* (stop) anhalten
'**pull-down menu** *n.* (Comp.) Pull-down-Menü, *das*
pulley /'pʊlɪ/ *n.* Rolle, *die*
pullover /'pʊləʊvə(r)/ *n.* Pullover, *der*
pulp /pʌlp/ $\boxed{1}$ *n.* Brei, *der*
$\boxed{2}$ *v.t.* zerdrücken ⟨*Rübe*⟩; einstampfen ⟨*Druckerzeugnis*⟩
pulpit /'pʊlpɪt/ *n.* Kanzel, *die*
pulsate /pʌl'seɪt/ *v.i.* pulsieren
pulse¹ /pʌls/ *n.* Puls, *der;* (single beat) Pulsschlag, *der*
pulse² *n.* (Cookery) Hülsenfrucht, *die*
'**pulse rate** *n.* Pulsfrequenz, *die*
pulverize /'pʌlvəraɪz/ *v.t.* pulverisieren
puma /'pju:mə/ *n.* Puma, *der*
pumice /'pʌmɪs/ *n.* ~ [stone] Bimsstein, *der*
pummel /'pʌml/ *v.t.,* (Brit) -ll- einschlagen auf (+ *Akk.*)
pump /pʌmp/ $\boxed{1}$ *n.* Pumpe, *die*
$\boxed{2}$ *v.i.* pumpen
$\boxed{3}$ *v.t.* pumpen; ~ sth. dry etw. leer pumpen; ~ sb. for information Auskünfte aus jmdm. herausholen; ~ up aufpumpen
'**pump-action** *adj.* ~ spray Pumpspray, *das od. der*
pumpkin /'pʌmpkɪn/ *n.* Kürbis, *der*
pun /pʌn/ *n.* Wortspiel, *das*
punch¹ /pʌntʃ/ $\boxed{1}$ *v.t.* (with fist) boxen
(b) (pierce) lochen; ~ a hole ein Loch stanzen; ~ a hole/holes in sth. etw. lochen
$\boxed{2}$ *n.* (a) (blow) Faustschlag, *der*
(b) (for making holes) (in leather, tickets) Lochzange, *die;* (in paper) Locher, *der*
punch² *n.* (drink) Punsch, *der*
punch: ~ **line** *n.* Pointe, *die;* ~**-up** *n.* (Brit. coll.) Prügelei, *die*
punctual /'pʌŋktjʊəl/ *adj.* pünktlich
punctuality /pʌŋktjʊ'ælɪtɪ/ *n.* Pünktlichkeit, *die*
'**punctually** *adv.* pünktlich
punctuate /'pʌŋktjʊeɪt/ *v.t.* mit Satzeichen versehen
punctuation /pʌŋktjʊ'eɪʃn/ *n.* Zeichensetzung, *die*

punctu'ation mark *n.* Satzzeichen, *das*
puncture /'pʌŋktʃə(r)/ $\boxed{1}$ *n.* (a) (flat tyre) Reifenpanne, *die*
(b) (hole) Loch, *das*
$\boxed{2}$ *v.t.* durchstechen; be ~d ⟨*Reifen:*⟩ platt sein
pundit /'pʌndɪt/ *n.* Experte, *der*/Expertin, *die*
pungent /'pʌndʒənt/ *adj.* beißend, ätzend ⟨*Rauch*⟩; scharf ⟨*Soße*⟩; stechend riechend ⟨*Gas*⟩
punish /'pʌnɪʃ/ *v.t.* bestrafen
punishable /'pʌnɪʃəbl/ *adj.* strafbar
'**punishment** *n.* (a) (punishing) Bestrafung, *die*
(b) (penalty) Strafe, *die*
punitive /'pju:nɪtɪv/ *adj.* (a) (penal) Straf-
(b) (severe) [allzu] rigoros
punk /pʌŋk/ *n.* (a) (Amer. sl.: worthless person) Dreckskerl, *der* (salopp)
(b) (admirer of ~ rock) Punk, *der;* (performer) Punk[rock]er, *der*/-[rock]erin, *die*
(c) (music) Punkrock, *der*
punnet /'pʌnɪt/ *n.* (Brit.) Körbchen, *das*
punt /pʌnt/ *n.* Stechkahn, *der*
punter *n.* (coll.) the ~s (customers) die Leutchen (ugs.)
puny /'pju:nɪ/ *adj.* (a) (undersized) zu klein ⟨*Baby, Junge*⟩
(b) (feeble) gering ⟨*Kraft*⟩; schwach ⟨*Waffe, Person*⟩
pup /pʌp/ *n.* Welpe, *der*
pupa /'pju:pə/ *n., pl.* ~e /'pju:pi:/ Puppe, *die*
pupate /pju:'peɪt/ *v.i.* sich verpuppen
pupil /'pju:pɪl/ *n.* (a) Schüler, *der*/Schülerin, *die*
(b) (Anat.) Pupille, *die*
puppet /'pʌpɪt/ *n.* Puppe, *die;* (marionette; also fig.) Marionette, *die*
puppy /'pʌpɪ/ *n.* Hundejunge, *das;* Welpe, *der*
puppy: ~ **fat** *n.* (Brit.) Babyspeck, *der;* ~ **love** *n.* Jugendschwärmerei, *die*
purchase /'pɜ:tʃəs/ $\boxed{1}$ *n.* (a) Kauf, *der;* **make a ~:** etwas kaufen
(b) (hold) Halt, *der;* (leverage) Hebelwirkung, *die*
$\boxed{2}$ *v.t.* kaufen
'**purchase price** *n.* Kaufpreis, *der*
'**purchaser** *n.* Käufer, *der*/Käuferin, *die*
'**purchasing power** *n.* Kaufkraft, *die*
pure /pjʊə(r)/ *adj.* rein
purée /'pjʊəreɪ/ *n.* Püree, *das*
'**purely** *adv.* (a) (solely) rein
(b) (merely) lediglich
purgatory /'pɜːgətərɪ/ *n.* it was ~ (fig.) es war eine Strafe
purge /pɜːdʒ/ $\boxed{1}$ *v.t.* (a) (cleanse) reinigen (of von)
(b) (remove) entfernen
(c) (rid) säubern ⟨*Partei*⟩ (of von)
$\boxed{2}$ *n.* Säuberung[saktion], *die*

purification /pjʊərɪfɪˈkeɪʃn/ *n.* Reinigung, *die*

purify /ˈpjʊərɪfaɪ/ *v.t.* reinigen

purist /ˈpjʊərɪst/ *n.* Purist, *der*/Puristin, *die*

puritan, (Hist.) **Puritan** /ˈpjʊərɪtn/ *n.* Puritaner, *der*/Puritanerin, *die*

puritanical /pjʊərɪˈtænɪkl/ *adj.* puritanisch

purity /ˈpjʊərɪtɪ/ *n.* Reinheit, *die*

purl /pɜːl/ ① *n.* linke Masche
② *v.t.* links stricken; ∼ **three** [**stitches**] drei linke Maschen stricken

purple /ˈpɜːpl/ ① *adj.* lila; violett
② *n.* Lila, *das;* Violett, *das*

purport /pəˈpɔːt/ *v.t.* ∼ **to do sth.** (profess) [von sich] behaupten, etw. zu tun; (be intended to seem) den Anschein erwecken sollen, etw. zu tun

purpose /ˈpɜːpəs/ *n.* (a) (object) Zweck, *der;* (intention) Absicht, *die;* **what is the** ∼ **of doing that?** was hat es für einen Zweck, das zu tun?; **on** ∼: mit Absicht; absichtlich
(b) (effect) **to no** ∼: ohne Erfolg; **to some/ good** ∼: mit einigem/gutem Erfolg
(c) (determination) Entschlossenheit, *die*

'purpose-built *adj.* [eigens] zu diesem Zweck errichtet ⟨*Gebäude*⟩

purposeful /ˈpɜːpəsfl/ *adj.* zielstrebig; (with specific aim) entschlossen

'purposely *adv.* absichtlich

'purpose-made *adj.* spezialgefertigt

purr /pɜː(r)/ ① *v.i.* schnurren
② *n.* Schnurren, *das*

purse /pɜːs/ ① *n.* Portemonnaie, *das*
② *v.t.* kräuseln ⟨*Lippen*⟩

purser /ˈpɜːsə(r)/ *n.* Zahlmeister, *der*/ -meisterin, *die*

pursue /pəˈsjuː/ *v.t.* (a) (chase) verfolgen
(b) (look into) nachgehen (+ *Dat.*)
(c) (engage in) betreiben

pursuer /pəˈsjuːə(r)/ *n.* Verfolger, *der*/ Verfolgerin, *die*

pursuit /pəˈsjuːt/ *n.* (a) Verfolgung, *die;* (of knowledge, truth, etc.) Streben, *das* (of nach); **in** ∼ **of** auf der Jagd nach ⟨*Wild, Dieb usw.*⟩; in Ausführung (+ *Gen.*) ⟨*Beschäftigung*⟩; **with the police in** [**full**] ∼: mit der Polizei [dicht] auf den Fersen
(b) (pastime) Beschäftigung, *die*

pus /pʌs/ *n.* Eiter, *der*

push /pʊʃ/ ① *v.t.* (a) schieben; (make fall) stoßen; drücken gegen ⟨*Tür*⟩; ∼ **one's way through/into/on to** *etc.* **sth.** sich ⟨*Dat.*⟩ einen Weg durch/in/auf *usw.* etw. (*Akk.*) bahnen
(b) (fig.: impel) drängen
(c) (tax) ∼ **sb.** [**hard**] jmdn. [stark] fordern; **be** ∼**ed for sth.** (coll.: find it difficult to provide sth.) mit etw. knapp sein; **be** ∼**ed for money** *or* **cash** knapp bei Kasse sein (ugs.)
(d) (sell illegally, esp. drugs) pushen (Drogenjargon)

② *v.i.* (a) schieben; (in queue) drängeln; (at door) drücken; ∼ **and shove** schubsen und drängeln
(b) (make demands) ∼ **for sth.** etw. fordern
(c) (make one's way) **he** ∼**ed between us** er drängte sich zwischen uns; ∼ **through the crowd** sich durch die Menge drängeln

③ *n.* (a) Stoß, *der;* **give sth. a** ∼: etw. schieben
(b) (effort) Anstrengungen *Pl.;* (Mil.: attack) Vorstoß, *der*
(c) (crisis) **when it comes to the** ∼, (Amer. coll.) **when** ∼ **comes to shove** wenn es ernst wird
(d) (Brit. coll.: dismissal) **get the** ∼: rausfliegen (ugs.)

■ **push a'head** *v.i.* ∼ **ahead with sth.** etw. vorantreiben

■ **push 'in** *v.i.* sich hineindrängen

■ **push 'off** *v.i.* (a) (Boating) abstoßen
(b) (coll.: leave) abhauen (salopp)

■ **push 'on** ① *v.i.* (with plans etc.) weitermachen
② *v.t.* draufdrücken ⟨*Deckel usw.*⟩

■ **push 'up** *v.t.* hochschieben; (fig.) hochtreiben

push: ∼**bike** *n.* (Brit. coll.) Fahrrad, *das;* ∼**button** *n.* [Druck]knopf, *der;* Drucktaste, *die;* ∼**chair** *n.* (Brit.) Sportwagen, *der*

pusher /ˈpʊʃə(r)/ *n.* (seller of drugs) Dealer, *der*/Dealerin, *die*

'pushover *n.* (coll.) Kinderspiel, *das*

pushy /ˈpʊʃɪ/ *adj.* (coll.) [übermäßig] ehrgeizig ⟨*Person*⟩

pussy /ˈpʊsɪ/ *n.* (child lang.: cat) Miezekatze, *die* (fam.)

put /pʊt/ ① *v.t.*, **-tt-**, **put** (a) (place) tun; (vertically) stellen; (horizontally) legen; ∼ **plates on the table** Teller auf den Tisch stellen; ∼ **a stamp on the letter** eine Briefmarke auf den Brief kleben; ∼ **the letter in an envelope/the letter box** den Brief in einen Umschlag/in den Briefkasten stecken; ∼ **sth. in one's pocket** etw. in die Tasche stecken; ∼ **petrol in the tank** Benzin in den Tank füllen; ∼ **the car in**[**to**] **the garage** das Auto in die Garage stellen; ∼ **the plug in the socket** den Stecker in die Steckdose stecken; ∼ **one's hands over one's eyes** sich ⟨*Dat.*⟩ die Hände auf die Augen legen; **where shall I** ∼ **it?** wo soll ich es hintun (ugs.)/-stellen/-legen *usw.*?; (fig.) **be** ∼ **in a difficult position** in eine schwierige Lage geraten; ∼ **sb. on to sth.** jmdn. auf etw. (*Akk.*) hinweisen; ∼ **sb. to work** jmdn. arbeiten lassen; ∼ **sb. on antibiotics** jmdn. auf Antibiotika setzen; ∼ **oneself in sb.'s place or situation** sich in jmds. Lage (*Akk.*) versetzen
(b) (submit) unterbreiten ⟨*Vorschlag, Plan*⟩ (to *Dat.*)
(c) (express) ausdrücken; **let's** ∼ **it like this: ...:** sagen wir so: ...; ∼ **sth. into English** *etc.* etw. ins Englische *usw.* übertragen; ∼ **sth. into words** etw. in Worte fassen
(d) (write) schreiben; ∼ **one's name on the** ⋯⯈

list seinen Namen auf die Liste setzen;
~ **sth. on the bill** etw. auf die Rechnung
setzen
(e) (stake) setzen (**on** auf + *Akk.*)
(f) (estimate) ~ **sb./sth. at** jmdn./etw.
schätzen auf (+ *Akk.*)
[2] *v.i.* -tt-, put (Naut.) ~ [out] to sea in See
stechen
■ **put a'cross** *v.t.* **(a)** (communicate)
vermitteln (**to** *Dat.*)
(b) (make acceptable) ankommen mit
■ **put a'way** *v.t.* **(a)** wegräumen; reinstellen
⟨*Auto*⟩; (in file) abheften
(b) (save) beiseite legen
(c) (coll.) (eat) verdrücken (ugs.); (drink)
runterkippen (ugs.)
(d) (coll.: confine) einsperren (ugs.)
■ **put 'back** *v.t.* **(a)** ~ **the book back** das
Buch zurücktun
(b) ~ **the clock back** die Uhr zurückstellen
(c) (postpone) verschieben
■ **put 'down** *v.t.* **(a)** (set down) (vertically)
hinstellen; (horizontally) hinlegen; auflegen
⟨*Hörer*⟩
(b) (suppress) niederwerfen
(c) (humiliate) herabsetzen
(d) (kill) töten
(e) (write) notieren
(f) (attribute) ~ **sth. down to sth.** etw. auf etw.
(*Akk.*) zurückführen
■ **put 'forward** *v.t.* **(a)** (propose) aufwarten
mit
(b) (nominate) vorschlagen
(c) ~ **the clock forward** die Uhr vorstellen
■ **put 'in** [1] *v.t.* **(a)** (install) einbauen
(b) (submit) stellen ⟨*Forderung*⟩; einreichen
⟨*Bewerbung*⟩
(c) (devote) aufwenden ⟨*Mühe*⟩; (perform)
einlegen ⟨*Sonderschicht, Überstunden*⟩
[2] *v.i.* ~ **in for** sich bewerben um ⟨*Stellung*⟩;
beantragen ⟨*Urlaub*⟩
■ **put 'off** *v.t.* **(a)** (postpone) verschieben
(**until** auf + *Akk.*); (postpone engagement with)
vertrösten (**until** auf + *Akk.*)
(b) (switch off) ausmachen
(c) (repel) abstoßen; ~ **sb. off sth.** jmdm. etw.
verleiden
(d) (distract) stören
(e) (dissuade) ~ **sb. off doing sth.** jmdn.
davon abbringen, etw. zu tun
■ **put 'on** *v.t.* **(a)** anziehen ⟨*Kleidung, Hose
usw.*⟩; aufsetzen ⟨*Hut, Brille*⟩; draufsetzen
⟨*Deckel*⟩; ~ **it on** (coll.) [nur] Schau machen
(ugs.)
(b) anmachen ⟨*Radio, Licht*⟩; aufsetzen
⟨*Wasser, Kessel*⟩

(c) (gain) ~ **on weight** zunehmen
(d) (stage) spielen ⟨*Stück*⟩; zeigen ⟨*Film*⟩
■ **put 'out** *v.t.* **(a)** rausbringen
(b) ausmachen ⟨*Licht*⟩; löschen ⟨*Feuer*⟩
(c) (inconvenience) in Verlegenheit bringen
■ **put 'through** *v.t.* **(a)** (carry out)
durchführen ⟨*Plan, Programm*⟩
(b) (Teleph.) verbinden (**to** mit)
■ **put 'up** [1] *v.t.* **(a)** heben ⟨*Hand*⟩; errichten
⟨*Gebäude, Denkmal*⟩; aufstellen ⟨*Gerüst*⟩
(b) (display) aushängen
(c) hochnehmen ⟨*Fäuste*⟩; leisten
⟨*Widerstand, Gegenwehr*⟩
(d) (propose) vorschlagen; (nominate) aufstellen
(e) (incite) ~ **sb. up to sth.** jmdn. zu etw.
anstiften
(f) (accommodate) unterbringen
(g) (increase) [he]raufsetzen ⟨*Preis, Miete*⟩
[2] *v.i.* (lodge) übernachten
■ **put 'up with** *v.t.* sich (*Dat.*) bieten lassen
⟨*Beleidigung, Benehmen*⟩; sich abfinden mit
⟨*Lärm, Elend*⟩; sich abgeben mit ⟨*Person*⟩

'**put-down** *n.* Herabsetzung, *die;* (snub)
Abfuhr, *die*

putrefaction /pjuːtrɪˈfækʃn/ *n., no indef.
art.* Zersetzung, *die*

putrefy /ˈpjuːtrɪfaɪ/ *v.i.* sich zersetzen

putrid /ˈpjuːtrɪd/ *adj.* (rotten) faul; ~ **smell**
Fäulnisgeruch, *der*

putt /pʌt/ (Golf) [1] *v.i. & t.* putten
[2] *n.* Putt, *der*

'**putter** *n.* Putter, *der*

putty /ˈpʌtɪ/ *n.* Kitt, *der*

'**put-up** *adj.* **a** ~ **job** ein abgekartetes Spiel
(ugs.)

puzzle /ˈpʌzl/ [1] *n.* (problem, enigma) Rätsel,
das; (toy) Geduldsspiel, *das*
[2] *v.t.* rätselhaft *od.* ein Rätsel sein (+ *Dat.*)
[3] *v.i.* ~ **over** *or* **about sth.** sich (*Dat.*) über
etw. den Kopf zerbrechen

puzzled /ˈpʌzld/ *adj.* ratlos

puzzling /ˈpʌzlɪŋ/ *adj.* rätselhaft

PVC *abbr.* = **polyvinyl chloride** PVC,
das

pygmy /ˈpɪgmɪ/ *n.* Pygmäe, *der*

pyjamas /pɪˈdʒɑːməz/ *n. pl.* [**pair of**] ~:
Schlafanzug, *der*

pylon /ˈpaɪlən/ *n.* Mast, *der*

pyramid /ˈpɪrəmɪd/ *n.* Pyramide, *die*

Pyrenees /pɪrəˈniːz/ *pr. n. pl.* **the** ~: die
Pyrenäen

python /ˈpaɪθən/ *n.* Python, *der*

Qq

Q, q /kjuː/ n. Q, q, das

quack /kwæk/ [1] v.i. ‹Ente:› quaken
[2] n. Quaken, das

quadrangle /'kwɒdræŋgl/ n. [viereckiger] Innenhof

quadruped /'kwɒdrʊped/ n. Vierfüßler, der

quadruple /'kwɒdrʊpl/ [1] adj. vierfach
[2] v.t. vervierfachen
[3] v.i. sich vervierfachen

quagmire /'kwæɡmaɪə(r)/ n. Sumpf, der; Morast, der

quail[1] /kweɪl/ n. (Ornith.) Wachtel, die

quail[2] v.i. ‹Person:› [ver]zagen

quaint /kweɪnt/ adj. drollig ‹Häuschen, Einrichtung›; malerisch ‹Ort›; (odd) kurios ‹Bräuche, Anblick›

quake /kweɪk/ [1] n. (coll.) [Erd]beben, das
[2] v.i. beben; ~ with fear vor Angst zittern

Quaker /'kweɪkə(r)/ n. Quäker, der/ Quäkerin, die

qualification /ˌkwɒlɪfɪ'keɪʃn/ n. (a) Qualifikation, die; (condition) Voraussetzung, die
(b) (limitation) Vorbehalt, der; **without** ~: vorbehaltlos

qualified /'kwɒlɪfaɪd/ adj. (a) qualifiziert; (by training) ausgebildet
(b) (restricted) nicht uneingeschränkt; **a ~ success** kein voller Erfolg; **~ acceptance** bedingte Annahme

qualify /'kwɒlɪfaɪ/ [1] v.t. (a) (make competent) berechtigen (**for** zu)
(b) (modify) einschränken
[2] v.i. (a) ~ **in law/medicine** seinen [Studien]abschluss in Jura/Medizin machen; ~ **as a doctor/lawyer** sein Examen als Arzt/ Anwalt machen
(b) (fulfil a condition) in Frage kommen (**for** für)
(c) (Sport) sich qualifizieren

qualifying /'kwɒlɪfaɪŋ/ adj. (Sport) ~ **match** Qualifikationsspiel, das

quality /'kwɒlɪtɪ/ [1] n. (a) Qualität, die
(b) (characteristic) Eigenschaft, die
[2] adj. Qualitäts-

quality: ~ **control** n. Qualitätskontrolle, die; ~ **time** n.: ganz dem Miteinander gewidmete Zeit

qualm /kwɑːm/ n. Bedenken, das (**over, about** gegen)

quandary /'kwɒndərɪ/ n. Dilemma, das

quantify /'kwɒntɪfaɪ/ v.t. quantifizieren

quantity /'kwɒntɪtɪ/ n. (a) Quantität, die
(b) (amount, sum) Menge, die

'quantity surveyor n. Baukostenkalkulator, der/-kalkulatorin, die

quantum: ~ **jump,** ~ **leap** ns. (Phys.; also fig.) Quantensprung, der; ~ **me'chanics** n. Quantenmechanik, die

quarantine /'kwɒrəntiːn/ n. Quarantäne, die; **be in** ~: unter Quarantäne stehen

quarrel /'kwɒrl/ [1] n. (a) Streit, der; **have/ pick a** ~ **with sb.** [about/over sth.] sich mit jmdm. [über etw. ‹Akk.›] streiten/mit jmdm. [wegen etw.] Streit anfangen
(b) (cause of complaint) Einwand, der (**with** gegen)
[2] v.i., (Brit.) -ll- [sich] streiten (**over** um, **about** über + Akk.); ~ **with each other** [sich] [miteinander] streiten; (fall out) sich [zer]streiten (**over** um, **about** über + Akk.)

quarrelsome /'kwɒrlsəm/ adj. streitsüchtig

quarry[1] /'kwɒrɪ/ n. Steinbruch, der

quarry[2] n. (prey) Beute, die

quart /kwɔːt/ n. Quart, das

quarter /'kwɔːtə(r)/ [1] n. (a) Viertel, das; **a or one** ~ **of** ein Viertel (+ Gen.); **a** ~ **of a mile/an hour** eine Viertelmeile/-stunde
(b) (of year) Quartal, das; Vierteljahr, das
(c) [a] ~ **to/past six** Viertel vor/nach sechs
(d) (direction) Richtung, die
(e) (area of town) [Stadt]viertel, das
(f) ~**s** pl. (lodgings) Quartier, das (bes. Milit.); Unterkunft, die
(g) (Amer. coin) Vierteldollar, der
[2] v.t. (a) (divide) vierteln
(b) (lodge) einquartieren ‹Soldaten›

quarter-'final n. Viertelfinale, das

'quarterly [1] adj. vierteljährlich
[2] n. Vierteljahr[e]sschrift, die

quarter-'pounder n. Viertelpfünder, der

quartet /kwɔː'tet/ n. Quartett, das

quartz /kwɔːts/ n. Quarz, der

quash /kwɒʃ/ v.t. (a) (annul) aufheben
(b) (suppress) niederschlagen

quaver /'kweɪvə(r)/ [1] n. (Brit. Mus.) Achtelnote, die
[2] v.i. (vibrate) zittern

quay /kiː/, **'quayside** ns. Kai, der

queasy /'kwiːzɪ/ adj. unwohl

queen /kwiːn/ n. (a) Königin, die
(b) (Chess, Cards) Dame, die

queen: ~ **bee** n. Bienenkönigin, die; ~ **'mother** n. Königinmutter, die

queer /kwɪə(r)/ [1] adj. (a) (strange) sonderbar; (eccentric) verschroben
(b) (shady) merkwürdig
(c) (Brit. coll. dated: out of sorts) unwohl ⋯⃗

(d) (sl. derog.: homosexual) schwul (ugs.)
2 *n.* (sl. derog.: homosexual) Schwule, *der* (ugs.)
quell /kwel/ *v.t.* (literary) niederschlagen
⟨*Aufstand*⟩; zügeln ⟨*Furcht*⟩
quench /kwentʃ/ *v.t.* löschen
query /'kwɪərɪ/ **1** *n.* Frage, *die*
2 *v.t.* in Frage stellen ⟨*Anweisung,
Glaubwürdigkeit*⟩; beanstanden ⟨*Rechnung*⟩
quest /kwest/ *n.* Suche, *die* (**for** nach)
question /'kwestʃn/ **1** *n.* **(a)** Frage, *die*;
ask sb. a ∼: jmdm. eine Frage stellen
(b) (doubt, objection) Zweifel, *der* (**about** an
+ *Dat.*); **there is no** ∼ **about sth.** es besteht
kein Zweifel an etw. (*Dat.*); **beyond all** *or*
without ∼: ohne Frage
(c) (problem, concern) Frage, *die*; **sth./it is only
a** ∼ **of time** etw./es ist [nur] eine Frage der
Zeit; **it is [only] a** ∼ **of doing sth.** es geht
[nur] darum, etw. zu tun; **the person/thing in**
∼: die fragliche Person/Sache; **sth./it is out
of the** ∼: etw./es ist ausgeschlossen
2 *v.t.* **(a)** befragen; ⟨*Polizei, Gericht usw.*:⟩
vernehmen
(b) (throw doubt upon, raise objections to)
bezweifeln
questionable /'kwestʃənəbl/ *adj.*
fragwürdig
'question mark *n.* Fragezeichen, *das*
questionnaire /kwestʃə'neə(r)/ *n.*
Fragebogen, *der*
queue /kjuː/ **1** *n.* Schlange, *die*; **join the** ∼:
sich anstellen
2 *v.i.* ∼ **[up]** Schlange stehen
'queue-jumping *n.* (Brit.) Vordrängen, *das*
quibble /'kwɪbl/ **1** *n.* Spitzfindigkeit, *die*
2 *v.i.* streiten
quibbling /'kwɪblɪŋ/ *adj.* spitzfindig
quiche /kiːʃ/ *n.* Quiche, *die*
quick /kwɪk/ **1** *adj.* schnell; kurz ⟨*Rede,
Pause*⟩; flüchtig ⟨*Kuss, Blick*⟩; **be** ∼! mach
schnell! (ugs.); **be** ∼ **to do sth.** etw. schnell
tun; **a** ∼ **temper** ein aufbrausendes Wesen
2 *adv.* schnell
3 *n.* empfindliches Fleisch; **be cut to the** ∼
(fig.) tief getroffen sein
quicken /'kwɪkn/ **1** *v.t.* beschleunigen
2 *v.i.* sich beschleunigen
'quickly *adv.* schnell
'quickness *n.* **(a)** (speed) Schnelligkeit, *die*
(b) (∼ of perception) Schärfe, *die*
quick: ∼**sand** *n.* Treibsand, *der*;
∼**-tempered** /-'tempəd/ *adj.* hitzig; **be**
∼**-tempered** leicht aufbrausen; ∼**-witted**
adj. geistesgegenwärtig
quid /kwɪd/ *n., pl. same* (Brit. coll.) Pfund, *das*
quiet /'kwaɪət/ **1** *adj.*, ∼**er** /'kwaɪətə(r)/,
∼**est** /'kwaɪətɪst/ **(a)** (silent) still; (not loud)
leise; **keep** ∼ **about sth.** (fig.) etw. geheim
halten
(b) (peaceful, not busy) ruhig
(c) (not overt) versteckt; **on the** ∼: still und
heimlich
2 *n.* Ruhe, *die*; (silence, stillness) Stille, *die*

quieten /'kwaɪətn/ *v.t.* beruhigen
■ **quieten 'down** *v.i.* sich beruhigen
'quietly *adv.* **(a)** (silently) still; (not loudly) leise
(b) (peacefully) ruhig
'quietness *n.* (absence of noise) Stille, *die*;
(peacefulness) Ruhe, *die*
quill /kwɪl/ *n.* (feather) Kielfeder, *die*; (of
porcupine) Stachel, *der*
quilt /kwɪlt/ **1** *n.* Schlafdecke, *die*
2 *v.t.* wattieren
quince /kwɪns/ *n.* Quitte, *die*
quintessential /kwɪntɪ'senʃl/ *adj.*
typisch; wesentlich
quintet /kwɪn'tet/ *n.* Quintett, *das*
quip /kwɪp/ **1** *n.* Witzelei, *die*
2 *v.i.*, **-pp-** witzeln (**at** über + *Akk.*)
quirk /kwɜːk/ *n.* Marotte, *die*; **a** ∼ **of fate**
eine Laune des Schicksals
quirky /'kwɜːkɪ/ *adj.* schrullig (ugs.)
quit /kwɪt/ *v.t.*, **-tt-**, (Amer.) **quit (a)** (give up)
aufgeben; (stop) aufhören mit; ∼ **doing sth.**
aufhören, etw. zu tun; **they were given notice
to** ∼ **[the flat]** ihnen wurde [die Wohnung]
gekündigt
(b) (Comp.) beenden
quite /kwaɪt/ *adv.* **(a)** (entirely) ganz; völlig;
fest ⟨*entschlossen*⟩; ∼ **[so]!** [ja,] genau!
(b) (to some extent) ziemlich; ganz ⟨*gern*⟩; ∼ **a
few** ziemlich viele
quits /kwɪts/ *pred. adj.* **be** ∼ **[with sb.]** [mit
jmdm.] quitt sein (ugs.)
quiver[1] /'kwɪvə(r)/ *v.i.* zittern (**with** vor
+ *Dat.*); ⟨*Stimme, Lippen:*⟩ beben (geh.); ⟨*Lid:*⟩
zucken
quiver[2] *n.* (for arrows) Köcher, *der*
quiz /kwɪz/ **1** *n., pl.* ∼**zes** Quiz, *das*
2 *v.t.*, **-zz-** ausfragen (**about sth.** nach etw.,
about sb. über jmdn.)
quizzical /'kwɪzɪkl/ *adj.* fragend
'quiz programme, 'quiz show *ns.*
(Radio, Telev.) Quizsendung, *die*
quoit /kɔɪt/ *n.* [Gummi]ring, *der*
quorum /'kwɔːrəm/ *n.* Quorum, *das*
quota /'kwəʊtə/ *n.* **(a)** (share) Anteil, *der*
(b) (goods to be produced)
Produktionsmindestquote, *die*
(c) (maximum number) Höchstquote, *die*
quotation /kwəʊ'teɪʃn/ *n.* **(a)** Zitieren, *das*;
(passage) Zitat, *das*
(b) (estimate) Kosten[vor]anschlag, *der*
quo'tation marks *n. pl.*
Anführungszeichen *Pl.*
quote /kwəʊt/ **1** *v.t. also abs.* zitieren
(**from** aus); zitieren aus ⟨*Buch, Text*⟩; (mention)
anführen; nennen ⟨*Preis*⟩
2 *n.* (coll.) **(a)** (passage) Zitat, *das*
(b) (estimate) Kosten[vor]anschlag, *der*
(c) *usu. in pl.* (quotation mark)
Anführungszeichen, *das*
quotient /'kwəʊʃnt/ *n.* (Math.) Quotient, *der*;
see also INTELLIGENCE QUOTIENT

q

Rr

R, r /ɑ:(r)/ *n.* R, r, *das*

R. *abbr.* = **River** Fl.

rabbi /'ræbaɪ/ *n.* Rabbi[ner], *der;* (as title) Rabbi, *der*

rabbit /'ræbɪt/ *n.* Kaninchen, *das*

rabbit: ∼ **burrow** *n.* Kaninchenbau, *der;* ∼ **hutch** *n.* (also fig.) Kaninchenstall, *der;* ∼ **warren** *n.* Kaninchengehege, *das;* (fig.) Labyrinth, *das*

rabble /'ræbl/ *n.* Mob, *der*

rabid /'ræbɪd/ *adj.* **(a)** tollwütig **(b)** (extreme) fanatisch

rabies /'reɪbi:z/ *n.* Tollwut, *die*

race¹ /reɪs/ **1** *n.* Rennen, *das;* (fig.) a ∼ **against time** ein Wettlauf mit der Zeit **2** *v.i.* **(a)** (in swimming, running, etc.) um die Wette schwimmen/laufen *usw.* (**with, against mit**) **(b)** ⟨*Motor:*⟩ durchdrehen; ⟨*Puls:*⟩ jagen **(c)** (rush) sich sehr beeilen; ∼ **after sb.** jmdn. hinterherhetzen **3** *v.t.* um die Wette schwimmen/laufen *usw.* mit

race² *n.* (Anthrop., Biol.) Rasse, *die;* **the human** ∼: die Menschheit

race: ∼**course** *n.* Rennbahn, *die;* ∼ **hatred** *n.* Rassenhass, *der;* ∼**horse** *n.* Rennpferd, *das;* ∼ **meeting** *n.* Renntag, *der;* (on successive days) Renntage *Pl.* ∼ **relations** *n. pl.* Beziehung zwischen den Rassen; ∼ **riot** *n.* Rassenkrawall, *der;* ∼**track** *n.* Rennbahn, *die*

racial /'reɪʃl/ *adj.* Rassen⟨*diskriminierung, -konflikt, -gleichheit, -spannung, -vorurteil*⟩; rassisch ⟨*Gruppe, Minderheit*⟩

racialism /'reɪʃəlɪzm/ *n.* Rassismus, *der*

racialist /'reɪʃəlɪst/ **1** *n.* Rassist, *der*/ Rassistin, *die* **2** *adj.* rassistisch

racially /'reɪʃəlɪ/ *adv.* rassisch; **be** ∼ **prejudiced** Rassenvorurteile haben

racing /'reɪsɪŋ/ *n.* Rennsport, *der;* (with horses) Pferdesport, *der*

racing: ∼ **bicycle** *n.* Rennrad, *das;* Rennmaschine, *die;* ∼ **car** *n.* Rennwagen, *der;* ∼ **driver** *n.* Rennfahrer, *der*/-fahrerin, *die*

racism /'reɪsɪzm/ *n.* Rassismus, *der*

racist /'reɪsɪst/ **1** *n.* Rassist, *der*/Rassistin, *die* **2** *adj.* rassistisch

rack /ræk/ **1** *n.* (for luggage) Ablage, *die;* (for toast, plates) Ständer, *der;* (on bicycle, motor cycle) Gepäckträger, *der*

2 *v.t.* ∼ **one's brain[s]** (fig.) sich (*Dat.*) den Kopf zerbrechen (ugs.)

racket¹ /'rækɪt/ *n.* Schläger, *der*

racket² *n.* **(a)** (disturbance) Lärm, *der;* Krach, *der* **(b)** (scheme) Schwindelgeschäft, *das* (ugs.)

racketeer /rækɪ'tɪə(r)/ *n.* Ganove, *der;* (profiteer) Wucherer, *der*

racketeering /rækɪ'tɪərɪŋ/ *n.* kriminelle Geschäfte *Pl.*

racoon /rə'ku:n/ *n.* Waschbär, *der*

racy /'reɪsɪ/ *adj.* flott (ugs.) ⟨*Stil*⟩

radar /'reɪdɑ:(r)/ *n.* Radar, *das od. der*

'radar screen *n.* Radarschirm, *der*

radiant /'reɪdɪənt/ *adj.* strahlend; fröhlich ⟨*Stimmung*⟩; **be** ∼: strahlen (**with vor** + *Dat.*)

radiate /'reɪdɪeɪt/ **1** *v.i.* **(a)** ⟨*Hitze, Wärme:*⟩ ausstrahlen; ⟨*Schein, Wellen:*⟩ ausgehen (**from von**) **(b)** (from central point) strahlenförmig ausgehen (**from von**) **2** *v.t.* ausstrahlen ⟨*Licht, Wärme; Glück, Liebe*⟩; aussenden ⟨*Strahlen, Wellen*⟩

radiation /reɪdɪ'eɪʃn/ *n.* (of energy) Emission, *die;* (of signals) Ausstrahlung, *die;* (energy transmitted) Strahlung, *die*

radiator /'reɪdɪeɪtə(r)/ *n.* **(a)** (for heating) Heizkörper, *der* **(b)** (Motor Veh.) Kühler, *der*

'radiator cap *n.* Kühlverschraubung, *die*

radical /'rædɪkl/ *adj.* **1 (a)** (thorough; also Polit.) radikal; drastisch ⟨*Maßnahme*⟩ **(b)** (progressive) radikal **(c)** (fundamental) grundlegend **2** *n.* (Polit.) Radikale, *der*/*die*

radio /'reɪdɪəʊ/ **1** *n., pl.* ∼**s (a)** *no indef. art.* Funk, *der;* (for private communication) Sprechfunk, *der* **(b)** *no indef. art.* (Broadcasting) Rundfunk, *der;* **on the** ∼: im Radio **(c)** (apparatus) Radio, *das* **2** *attrib. adj.* (Broadcasting) Rundfunk-; Radio⟨*welle, -teleskop*⟩; Funk⟨*mast, -turm, -taxi*⟩ **3** *v.t.* funken

radio: ∼'**active** *adj.* radioaktiv; ∼**ac'tivity** *n.* Radioaktivität, *die;* ∼ **cas'sette player** *n.* Kassettenradio, *das;* Radio mit Kassettenteil; ∼**con'trolled** *adj.* funkgesteuert; ∼ **frequency** *n.* Hochfrequenz, *die; attrib.* ∼**frequency** Hochfrequenz-; ∼ **play** *n.* Hörspiel, *das;* ∼ **station** *n.* Rundfunkstation, *die;* Rundfunk- *od.* ┄┅▸

Radiosender, *der;* ∼ **'telescope** *n.*
Radioteleskop, *das;* ∼**'therapy** *n.*
Strahlentherapie, *die*

radish /'rædɪʃ/ *n.* Rettich, *der;* (small, red)
Radieschen, *das*

radius /'reɪdɪəs/ *n., pl.* radii /'reɪdɪaɪ/ *or*
∼es (Math.) Radius, *der;* (fig.) Umkreis, *der*

RAF /ɑːreɪˈef, (coll.) ræf/ *abbr.* = **Royal Air Force**

raffle /'ræfl/ ① *n.* Tombola, *die;* ∼ **ticket**
Los, *das*
② *v.t.* ∼ [off] verlosen

raft /rɑːft/ *n.* Floß, *das*

rafter /'rɑːftə(r)/ *n.* Sparren, *der*

rag[1] /ræg/ *n.* (a) [Stoff]fetzen, *der*
(b) *in pl.* (old and torn clothes) Lumpen *Pl.*
(c) (derog.: newspaper) Käseblatt, *das* (salopp)

rag[2] *v.t.,* -gg- (tease) aufziehen

rag: ∼**bag** *n.* (fig.) Sammelsurium, *das;*
∼ **doll** *n.* Stoffpuppe, *die*

rage /reɪdʒ/ ① *n.* (a) (violent anger) Wut, *die;*
(fit of anger) Wutausbruch, *der*
(b) sth. is [all] the ∼: etw. ist [ganz] groß in
Mode
② *v.i.* (a) (rave) toben; ∼ at *or* against sth./
sb. gegen etw./jmdn. wüten
(b) (be violent, unchecked) toben; ⟨Krankheit:⟩
wüten

ragged /'rægɪd/ *adj.* zerrissen

'rag trade *n.* (coll.) Modebranche, *die* (ugs.)

raid /reɪd/ ① *n.* Einfall, *der;* Überfall, *der;*
(Mil.) Überraschungsangriff, *der;* (by police)
Razzia, *die* (on in + *Dat.*)
② *v.t.* ⟨Polizei:⟩ eine Razzia machen auf
(+ *Akk.*); ⟨Räuber, Soldaten:⟩ überfallen

'raider *n.* Räuber, *der/*Räuberin, *die*

rail[1] /reɪl/ *n.* (a) Stange, *die;* (on ship) Reling,
die; (as protection against contact) Barriere, *die*
(b) (Railw.: of track) Schiene, *die*
(c) (∼way) [Eisen]bahn, *die; attrib.* Bahn-; by
∼: mit der Bahn

'rail card *n.* Bahnkarte, *die*

railing /'reɪlɪŋ/ *n.* (round park) Zaun, *der;* (on
staircase) Geländer, *das*

rail: ∼**road** (Amer.) ▶ ∼WAY; **R**∼**track** *n.,*
no art. (Brit.) *Betreibergesellschaft des
britischen Schienennetzes;* ∼**way** *n.* (a)
(track) Bahnlinie, *die;* Bahnstrecke, *die;* (b)
(system) [Eisen]bahn, *die*

railway: ∼ **carriage** *n.* Eisenbahnwagen,
der; ∼ **crossing** *n.* Bahnübergang, *der;*
∼ **engine** *n.* Lokomotive, *die;* ∼ **line** *n.*
[Eisen]bahnlinie, *die;* ∼ **station** *n.*
Bahnhof, *der;* ∼ **worker** *n.* Bahnarbeiter,
der/-arbeiterin, *die*

rain /reɪn/ ① *n.* (a) Regen, *der*
(b) (fig.: of arrows, blows, etc.) Hagel, *der*
② *v.i. impers.* it is ∼ing es regnet
③ *v.t.* hageln lassen ⟨Schläge, Hiebe⟩

rain: ∼**bow** /'reɪnbəʊ/ *n.* Regenbogen, *der;*
∼ **check** *n.* (Amer. fig.) take a ∼ check on
sth. auf etw. (*Akk.*) später wieder
zurückkommen; ∼ **cloud** *n.* Regenwolke,

die; ∼**coat** *n.* Regenmantel, *der;* ∼**fall** *n.*
Niederschlag, *der;* ∼**forest** *n.* Regenwald,
der; ∼**proof** *adj.* regendicht; ∼**water** *n.*
Regenwasser, *das;* ∼**wear** *n.*
Regenkleidung, *die*

'rainy *adj.* regnerisch ⟨Tag, Wetter⟩;
regenreich ⟨Gebiet, Sommer⟩; ∼ **season**
Regenzeit, *die;* keep sth. for a ∼ day (fig.) sich
(*Dat.*) etw. für schlechte Zeiten aufheben

raise /reɪz/ *v.t.* (a) (lift up) heben; erhöhen
⟨Temperatur, Miete, Gehalt⟩; hochziehen
⟨Fahne⟩; aufziehen ⟨Vorhang⟩; hochheben
⟨Arm⟩; ∼ one's glass to sb. das Glas auf
jmdn. erheben
(b) (set upright) aufrichten; erheben ⟨Banner⟩;
∼ sb.'s spirits jmds. Stimmung heben
(c) erheben ⟨Forderungen, Einwände⟩;
aufwerfen ⟨Frage⟩; zur Sprache bringen
⟨Thema, Problem⟩
(d) aufziehen ⟨Vieh, [Haus]tiere⟩; großziehen
⟨Familie, Kinder⟩
(e) aufbringen ⟨Geld, Betrag⟩
(f) aufheben ⟨Belagerung, Blockade,
Embargo, Verbot⟩

raisin /'reɪzn/ *n.* Rosine, *die*

rake /reɪk/ ① *n.* Rechen, *der;* Harke, *die*
② *v.t.* (a) harken
(b) ∼ the fire die Asche entfernen
(c) (with eyes, shots) bestreichen
■ **rake 'in** *v.t.* (coll.) scheffeln (ugs.).
■ **rake 'up** *v.t.* zusammenharken; (fig.)
wieder ausgraben

'rake-off *n.* (coll.) [Gewinn]anteil, *der*

rakish /'reɪkɪʃ/ *adj.* flott; keß

rally /'rælɪ/ ① *v.i.* (regain health) sich wieder
[ein wenig] erholen
② *v.t.* (a) (reassemble) wieder zusammenrufen
(b) einigen ⟨Partei, Kräfte⟩; sammeln
⟨Anhänger⟩
③ *n.* (a) (mass meeting) Versammlung, *die*
(b) [motor] ∼: Rallye, *die*
(c) (Tennis) Ballwechsel, *der*

ram /ræm/ ① *n.* (Zool.) Schafbock, *der;*
Widder, *der*
② *v.t.,* -mm-: (a) (force) stopfen; ∼ a post into
the ground einen Pfosten in die Erde
rammen; ∼ sth. home to sb. jmdm. etw.
deutlich vor Augen führen
(b) (collide with) rammen

RAM /ræm/ *abbr.* (Comp.) = **random
access memory** RAM

ramble /'ræmbl/ ① *n.* [nature] ∼:
Wanderung, *die*
② *v.i.* (a) (walk) umherstreifen (through, in in
+ *Dat.*)
(b) (in talk) zusammenhangloses Zeug reden;
keep rambling on about sth. sich endlos über
etw. (*Akk.*) auslassen

rambler /'ræmblə(r)/ *n.* Wanderer, *der/*
Wanderin, *die*

rambling /'ræmblɪŋ/ ① *n.* Wandern, *das*
② *adj.* (a) (irregularly arranged) verschachtelt;
verwinkelt ⟨Straßen⟩

(b) (incoherent) unzusammenhängend ⟨*Erklärung*⟩

(c) ~ **rose** Kletterrose, *die*

ramp /ræmp/ *n.* Rampe, *die*

rampage ⟨1⟩ /'ræmpeɪdʒ/ *n.* Randale, *die* (ugs.); **be/go on the** ~ (coll.) randalieren ⟨2⟩ /ræm'peɪdʒ/ *v.i.* randalieren

rampant /'ræmpənt/ *adj.* zügellos ⟨*Gewalt, Rassismus*⟩; steil ansteigend ⟨*Inflation*⟩; üppig ⟨*Wachstum*⟩

rampart /'ræmpɑːt/ *n.* Wehrgang, *der*

ram: ~ **raid** ⟨1⟩ *v.t.* [durch Rammen mit einem Fahrzeug] einbrechen in (+ *Akk.*); ⟨2⟩ *n.* [durch Rammen eines Gebäudes verübter] Einbruch; ~**-raider** *n.*: *Einbrecher, der sich durch Einrammen bes. eines Schaufensters mit einem Fahrzeug Zutritt verschafft*

'ramshackle *adj.* klapprig ⟨*Auto*⟩; verkommen ⟨*Gebäude*⟩

ran ▶ RUN 2, 3

ranch /rɑːntʃ/ *n.* Ranch, *die*

'ranch hand *n.* Farmarbeiter, *der*/-arbeiterin, *die*

rancid /'rænsɪd/ *adj.* ranzig

rancour (*Brit.; Amer.:* **rancor**) /'ræŋkə(r)/ *n.* [tiefe] Verbitterung

R&B *abbr.* = **rhythm and blues** R&B

R&D *abbr.* = **research and development** F&E

random /'rændəm/ ⟨1⟩ *n.* **at** ~: wahllos; willkürlich; (aimlessly) ziellos; **choose at** ~: aufs Geratewohl wählen ⟨2⟩ *adj.* willkürlich

random 'access memory *n.* (Comp.) Schreib-Lese-Speicher, *der*

randy /'rændɪ/ *adj.* geil; scharf (ugs.)

rang ▶ RING[2] 2, 3

range /reɪndʒ/ ⟨1⟩ *n.* **(a)** ~ **of mountains** Bergkette, *die* **(b)** (of subjects) Palette, *die;* (of knowledge, voice) Umfang, *der* **(c)** (of missile etc.) Reichweite, *die;* **at a** ~ **of 200 metres** auf eine Entfernung von 200 Metern **(d)** (series, selection) Kollektion, *die* **(e)** (stove) Herd, *der* ⟨2⟩ *v.i.* ⟨*Preise, Temperaturen:*⟩ schwanken, sich bewegen (**from** ... **to** zwischen [+ *Dat.*] ... und)

'ranger *n.* Förster, *der*/Försterin, *die*

rank[1] /ræŋk/ ⟨1⟩ *n.* **(a)** (position in hierarchy) Rang, *der;* (Mil. also) Dienstgrad, *der* **(b)** (social position) [soziale] Stellung **(c)** (row) Reihe, *die;* **the** ~ **and file** (fig.) die breite Masse; **the** ~**s** (enlisted men) die Mannschaften und Unteroffiziere ⟨2⟩ *v.t.* ~ **among** zählen zu ⟨3⟩ *v.i.* ~ **among** zählen zu

rank[2] *adj.* **(a)** krass ⟨*Außenseiter*⟩ **(b)** ~ **weeds** [wild]wucherndes Unkraut

rankings /'ræŋkɪŋz/ *n. pl.* (Sport) Rangliste,

die; the team has fallen in the ~: die Mannschaft ist in der Tabelle nach unten gerutscht

ransack /'rænsæk/ *v.t.* **(a)** (search) durchsuchen (**for** nach) **(b)** (pillage) plündern

ransom /'rænsəm/ *n.* ~ **[money]** Lösegeld, *das;* **hold to** ~: als Geisel festhalten

rant /rænt/ *v.i.* ~ **[and rave]** wettern (ugs.) (**about** über + *Akk.*)

rap /ræp/ ⟨1⟩ *n.* [energisches] Klopfen ⟨2⟩ *v.t.,* **-pp-** klopfen ⟨3⟩ *v.i.,* **-pp-** klopfen (**on** an + *Akk.*)

rape[1] /reɪp/ ⟨1⟩ *n.* Vergewaltigung, *die* ⟨2⟩ *v.t.* vergewaltigen

rape[2] *n.* (Bot., Agric.) Raps, *der*

rape: ~**seed** *n.* Rapssamen, *der;* ~**seed oil** *n.* Rapsöl, *das*

rapid /'ræpɪd/ ⟨1⟩ *adj.* schnell ⟨*Bewegung, Wachstum, Puls*⟩; rasch ⟨*Fortschritt, Ausbreitung*⟩ ⟨2⟩ *n.* **in** *pl.* Stromschnellen *Pl.*

rapid-'fire *adj.* Schnellfeuer⟨*waffe, -schießen*⟩; (fig.) schnell aufeinander folgend ⟨*Wiederholung*⟩; Schnellfeuer⟨*witze, -fragen*⟩

rapidity /rə'pɪdɪtɪ/ *n.* Schnelligkeit, *die*

'rapidly *adv.* schnell

rapist /'reɪpɪst/ *n.* Vergewaltiger, *der*

rapport /ræ'pɔː(r)/ *n.* [harmonisches] Verhältnis

rapt /ræpt/ *adj.* gespannt ⟨*Miene*⟩

rapture /'ræptʃə(r)/ *n.* **[state of]** ~: Verzückung, *die*

rapturous /'ræptʃərəs/ *adj.* begeistert

rare[1] /reə(r)/ *adj.,* **rarely** *adv.* selten

rare[2] *adj.* (Cookery) englisch gebraten

rarefied /'reərɪfaɪd/ *adj.* dünn ⟨*Luft*⟩; (fig.) exklusiv

rarity /'reərɪtɪ/ *n.* Seltenheit, *die*

rash[1] /ræʃ/ *n.* [Haut]ausschlag, *der*

rash[2] *adj.* voreilig ⟨*Urteil, Entscheidung*⟩; überstürzt ⟨*Versprechung*⟩

rasher /'ræʃə(r)/ *n.* Speckscheibe, *die*

'rashly *adv.* voreilig

rasp /rɑːsp/ ⟨1⟩ *n.* (tool) Raspel, *die* ⟨2⟩ *v.t.* (say gratingly) schnarren

raspberry /'rɑːzbərɪ/ *n.* Himbeere, *die*

rat /ræt/ *n.* **(a)** Ratte, *die;* **smell a** ~ (fig.) Lunte riechen (ugs.) **(b)** (coll. derog.: person) Ratte, *die* (derb)

ratchet /'rætʃɪt/ *n.* **(a)** (Mech. Engin.) (set of teeth) Zahnkranz, *der* **(b)** ~ **[wheel]** Klinkenrad, *das*

'ratchet screwdriver *n.* Drillschraubenzieher, *der*

rate /reɪt/ ⟨1⟩ *n.* **(a)** (proportion) Rate, *die;* ~ **of inflation** Inflationsrate, *die* **(b)** (tariff) Satz, *der;* ~ **[of pay]** Lohnsatz, *der* **(c)** (speed) Geschwindigkeit, *die;* Tempo, *das* **(d)** (Brit.: levy) **[local** *or* **council]** ~**s** Gemeindeabgaben *Pl.* **(e)** (coll.) **at any** ~ (at least) zumindest; ···>

r

wenigstens; (whatever happens) auf jeden Fall;
at this ~ we won't get any work done so
kriegen wir gar nichts fertig (ugs.)
2 *v.t.* **(a)** einschätzen ⟨Intelligenz, Leistung⟩
(b) (consider) betrachten; rechnen **(among** zu)
3 *v.i.* ~ **as** gelten als
'**ratepayer** *n.* (Brit.) Realsteuerpflichtige,
der/die
rather /'rɑːðə(r)/ *adv.* **(a)** (by preference)
lieber
(b) (somewhat) ziemlich; **I** ~ **think that ...**: ich
bin ziemlich sicher, dass ...
(c) (more truly) vielmehr; **or** ~:
beziehungsweise
ratification /rætɪfɪ'keɪʃn/ *n.* Ratifizierung,
die
ratify /'rætɪfaɪ/ *v.t.* ratifizieren
rating /'reɪtɪŋ/ *n.* **(a)** (estimated standing)
Einschätzung, *die*
(b) (Radio, Telev.) [popularity] ~:
Einschaltquote, *die*
(c) (Brit. Navy) Matrose, *der*
ratio /'reɪʃɪəʊ/ *n., pl.* ~**s** Verhältnis, *das*
ration /'ræʃn/ **1** *n.* ~[**s**] Ration, *die* (of an
+ *Dat.*)
2 *v.t.* rationieren ⟨Benzin, Zucker usw.⟩
rational /'ræʃənl/ *adj.* (having reason)
rational ⟨Wesen⟩; (sensible) vernünftig ⟨Person,
Art usw.⟩
rationalist /'ræʃənəlɪst/ *n.* Rationalist,
*der/*Rationalistin, *die*
rationalize /'ræʃənəlaɪz/ *v.t.*
rationalisieren
rationing /'ræʃənɪŋ/ *n.* Rationierung, *die*
rat: ~ **poison** *n.* Rattengift, *das;* ~ **race**
n. erbarmungsloser Konkurrenzkampf;
~ **run** *n.* (Brit. coll.) Schleichweg, *der*
rattle /'rætl/ **1** *v.i.* **(a)** ⟨Fenster:⟩ klappern;
⟨Flaschen:⟩ klirren; ⟨Kette:⟩ rasseln
(b) ⟨Zug, Bus:⟩ rattern
2 *v.t.* **(a)** klappern mit ⟨Würfel, Geschirr⟩;
klirren lassen ⟨Fenster[scheiben]⟩; rasseln
mit ⟨Kette⟩
(b) (coll.: disconcert) ~ **sb.**, **get sb.** ~**d** jmdn.
durcheinander bringen
3 *n.* **(a)** (of baby) Rassel, *die*
(b) (sound) Klappern, *das*
■ **rattle** '**off** *v.t.* (coll.) herunterrasseln (ugs.)
'**rattlesnake** *n.* Klapperschlange, *die*
raucous /'rɔːkəs/ *adj.* rau
raunchy /'rɔːntʃɪ/ *adj.* (lewd) vulgär;
(suggestive) scharf (salopp)
ravage /'rævɪdʒ/ **1** *v.t.* heimsuchen
⟨Gebiet, Stadt⟩
2 *n. in pl.* verheerende Wirkung
rave /reɪv/ **1** *v.i.* **(a)** (talk wildly) irrereden
(b) (speak admiringly) schwärmen (**about** von)
2 *attrib. adj.* (coll.) begeistert ⟨Kritik⟩
3 *n.* (coll.: dancing party) Rave, *der od. das*
raven /'reɪvn/ *n.* Rabe, *der*
ravenous /'rævənəs/ *adj.* **I'm** ~: ich habe
einen Bärenhunger (ugs.)
'**rave-up** *n.* (Brit. coll.) [wilde] Fete (ugs.)

ravine /rə'viːn/ *n.* Schlucht, *die*
raving /'reɪvɪŋ/ **1** *adj.* irreredend ⟨Idiot⟩
2 *adv.* **be** ~ **mad** völlig verrückt sein (ugs.)
ravish /'rævɪʃ/ *v.t.* (charm) entzücken
'**ravishing** *adj.* bildschön ⟨Anblick, Person⟩;
hinreißend ⟨Schönheit⟩
raw /rɔː/ *adj.* **(a)** (uncooked) roh
(b) (inexperienced) unerfahren
(c) (stripped of skin) blutig ⟨Fleisch⟩; offen
⟨Wunde⟩
(d) (chilly) nasskalt
raw ma'terial *n.* Rohstoff, *der*
Rawlplug ® /'rɔːlplʌg/ *n.* Dübel, *der*
ray /reɪ/ *n.* Strahl, *der;* ~ **of sunshine/light**
Sonnen-/Lichtstrahl, *der*
raze /reɪz/ *v.t.* ~ **to the ground** dem
Erdboden gleichmachen
razor /'reɪzə(r)/ *n.* Rasiermesser, *das;*
[electric] ~: [elektrischer] Rasierapparat
razor: ~ **blade** *n.* Rasierklinge, *die;*
~-**sharp** *adj.* sehr scharf ⟨Messer⟩; (fig.)
messerscharf ⟨Verstand, Intellekt⟩;
scharfsinnig ⟨Person⟩
RC *abbr.* = **Roman Catholic** r.-k.;
röm.-kath.
Rd. *abbr.* = **Road** Str.
re /riː/ *prep.* (Commerc.) betreffs
RE *abbr.* (Brit.) = **Religious Education**
Religionslehre, *die*
reach /riːtʃ/ **1** *v.t.* **(a)** (arrive at) erreichen;
ankommen in (+ *Dat.*) ⟨Stadt, Land⟩;
erzielen ⟨Übereinstimmung⟩; kommen zu
⟨Entscheidung; Ausgang, Eingang⟩; **you can**
~ **her at this number** du kannst sie unter
dieser Nummer erreichen
(b) (extend to) ⟨Straße:⟩ führen bis zu; ⟨Leiter,
Haar:⟩ reichen bis zu
2 *v.i.* **(a)** (stretch out hand) ~ **for sth.** nach
etw. greifen; ~ **across the table** über den
Tisch langen
(b) (be long/tall enough) **sth. will/won't** ~: etw.
ist/ist nicht lang genug; **I can't** ~: ich
komme nicht daran
(c) (go as far as) ⟨Wasser, Gebäude, Besitz:⟩
reichen ([up] **to** bis [hinauf] zu)
3 *n.* Reichweite, *die;* **be within easy** ~ ⟨Ort:⟩
leicht erreichbar sein; **be out of** ~ ⟨Ort:⟩
nicht erreichbar sein; ⟨Gegenstand:⟩ außer
Reichweite sein
■ **reach** '**out** *v.i.* die Hand ausstrecken (**for**
nach)
react /rɪ'ækt/ *v.i.* reagieren (**to** auf + *Akk.*)
reaction /rɪ'ækʃn/ *n.* Reaktion, *die* (**to** auf
+ *Akk.*)
reactionary /rɪ'ækʃənərɪ/ (Polit.) **1** *adj.*
reaktionär
2 *n.* Reaktionär, *der/*Reaktionärin, *die*
reactor /rɪ'æktə(r)/ *n.* [nuclear] ~:
Kernreaktor, *der*
read /riːd/ **1** *v.t.*, **read** /red/ **(a)** lesen; ~ **sb.**
sth., ~ **sth. to sb.** jmdm. etwas vorlesen;
~ **the gas meter** das Gas ablesen

(b) (interpret) deuten; **~ between the lines** zwischen den Zeilen lesen
(c) (study) studieren
[2] *v.i.*, **read (a)** lesen; **~ to sb.** jmdm. vorlesen
(b) (convey meaning) lauten; **the contract ~s as follows** der Vertrag hat folgenden Wortlaut
■ **read 'out** *v.t.* laut vorlesen
■ **read 'over, read 'through** *v.t.* durchlesen
■ **read 'up** *v.t.* sich informieren (**on** über + *Akk.*)

readable /'riːdəbl/ *adj.* **(a)** (pleasant to read) lesenswert
(b) (legible) leserlich

'reader *n.* **(a)** Leser, *der*/Leserin, *die*
(b) (book) Lesebuch, *das*

'readership *n.* Leserschaft, *die*

readily /'redɪlɪ/ *adv.* **(a)** (willingly) bereitwillig
(b) (easily) ohne weiteres

readiness /'redɪnɪs/ *n.* Bereitschaft, *die;* **be in ~:** bereit sein (**for** für)

'reading *n.* **(a)** Lesen, *das*
(b) (figure shown) Anzeige, *die*
(c) (recital) Lesung, *die* (**from** aus)
(d) (Parl.) Lesung, *die*

reading: ~ glasses *n. pl.* Lesebrille, *die;*
~ lamp, ~ Leselampe, *die;*
~ matter *n.* Lesestoff, *der;* Lektüre, *die*

readjust /riːə'dʒʌst/ [1] *v.t.* neu einstellen; neu anpassen ‹*Gehalt, Zinssatz*›
[2] *v. refl. & i.* **~ [oneself] to** sich wieder gewöhnen an (+ *Akk.*)

read /riːd/**: ~-'only memory** *n.* (Comp.) Fest[wert]speicher, *der;* **~-out** *n.* (Comp.) Ausgabe, *die;* **~-write** *n. attrib.* (Comp.) Schreib-Lese-; **~-write head** Schreib-Lese-Kopf, *der*

ready /'redɪ/ [1] *adj.* **(a)** (prepared) fertig; **be ~ to do sth.** bereit sein, etw. zu tun; **get ~:** sich fertig machen
(b) (willing) bereit
(c) (within reach) griffbereit
[2] *adv.* fertig
[3] *n.* **at the ~** ‹*Schusswaffe*› im Anschlag

ready: ~ 'cash ▶~ MONEY; **~-cooked** *adj.* vorgekocht; **~-cooked meal** Fertiggericht, *das;* Fertigmahlzeit, *die;* **~-'made** *adj.* **(a)** Konfektions‹*anzug, -kleidung*›; **(b)** (fig.) vorgefertigt; **~ 'money** *n.* Bargeld, *das;* **~-to-eat** *adj.* Fertig‹*mahlzeit, -dessert*›; **~-to-serve** *adj.* tischfertig; **~-to-wear** *adj.* Konfektions‹*anzug, -kleidung*›

real /rɪəl/ *adj.* **(a)** (actually existing) real ‹*Ereignis, Lebewesen*›; wirklich ‹*Macht*›
(b) (genuine) echt ‹*Interesse, Gold, Seide*›
(c) (complete) total (ugs.) ‹*Desaster, Enttäuschung*›

(d) (true) wahr ‹*Grund, Name, Glück*›; echt ‹*Mitleid, Sieg*›; **the ~ thing** der/die/das Echte
(e) be for ~ (coll.) echt sein

'real estate *n.* (Amer.) Immobilien *Pl.*

realism /'rɪəlɪzm/ *n.* Realismus, *der*

'realist *n.* Realist, *der*/Realistin, *die*

realistic /rɪə'lɪstɪk/ *adj.* realistisch

reality /rɪ'ælɪtɪ/ *n.* Realität, *die;* **in ~:** in Wirklichkeit

realization /rɪəlaɪ'zeɪʃn/ *n.* Erkenntnis, *die*

realize /'rɪəlaɪz/ *v.t.* **(a)** (be aware of) bemerken; erkennen ‹*Fehler*›; **I didn't ~** *abs.* ich habe es nicht gewusst; **~ [that]** …: merken, dass …
(b) (make happen) verwirklichen
(c) erbringen ‹*Summe, Preis*›

real-life *attrib. adj.* real

really /'rɪəlɪ/ *adv.* wirklich; **not ~:** eigentlich nicht; **[well,] ~!** [also] so was!

realm /relm/ *n.* Reich, *das*

realtor /'riːəltə(r)/ (Amer.) Grundstücksmakler, *der*

reap /riːp/ *v.t.* (cut) schneiden ‹*Getreide*›; (gather in) einfahren ‹*Getreide, Ernte*›

reappear /riːə'pɪə(r)/ *v.i.* wieder auftauchen; (come back) [wieder] zurückkommen

rear[1] /rɪə(r)/ [1] *n.* **(a)** (back part) hinterer Teil
(b) (back) Rückseite, *die*
(c) (Mil.) Rücken, *der*
[2] *adj.* hinter…; **~ axle** Hinterachse, *die*

rear[2] [1] *v.t.* großziehen ‹*Kind, Familie*›; halten ‹*Vieh*›
[2] *v.i.* ‹*Pferd:*› sich aufbäumen

rear: ~guard *n.* (Mil.) Nachhut, *die;* **~ light** *n.* Rücklicht, *das;* **~-wheel drive** [1] *n.* Hinterradantrieb, *der;* [2] *adj.* a **~-wheel drive vehicle** ein Fahrzeug mit Hinterradantrieb

rearm /riː'ɑːm/ *v.i. & t.* wieder aufrüsten

rearrange /riːə'reɪndʒ/ *v.t.* umräumen ‹*Möbel*›; verlegen ‹*Spiel*› (**for** auf + *Akk.*); ändern ‹*Programm*›

rear-view 'mirror *n.* Rückspiegel, *der*

reason /'riːzn/ [1] *n.* **(a)** (cause) Grund, *der;* **have no ~ to complain** sich nicht beklagen können; **for that [very] ~:** aus [eben] diesem Grund
(b) (power to understand; sense) Vernunft, *die;* (power to think) Verstand, *der;* **in** or **within ~:** innerhalb eines vernünftigen Rahmens; **it stands to ~ that** …: es ist unzweifelhaft, dass …
[2] *v.i.* **(a)** schlussfolgern (**from** aus)
(b) **~ with** diskutieren mit (**about, on** über + *Akk.*); **you can't ~ with her** mit ihr kann man nicht vernünftig reden
[3] *v.t.* schlussfolgern

reasonable /'riːzənəbl/ *adj.* **(a)** vernünftig
(b) (inexpensive) günstig ⫶⫶⫶⫶

r

reasonably /ˈriːzənəblɪ/ adv. (a) (within reason) vernünftig

(b) (fairly) ganz ⟨gut⟩; ziemlich ⟨gesund⟩

reasoned /ˈriːznd/ adj. durchdacht

reasoning /ˈriːzənɪŋ/ n. logisches Denken

reassurance /riːəˈʃʊərəns/ n. (a) (calming) give sb. ~: jmdn. beruhigen

(b) (confirmation) Bestätigung, die

reassure /riːəˈʃʊə(r)/ v.t. beruhigen; ~ sb. about his health. jmdm. versichern, dass er gesund ist

reassuring /riːəˈʃʊərɪŋ/ adj. beruhigend

rebate /ˈriːbeɪt/ n. (a) (refund) Rückzahlung, die

(b) (discount) Preisnachlass, der (on auf + Akk.)

rebel ① /ˈrebl/ n. Rebell, der/Rebellin, die

② attrib. adj. Rebellen-

③ /rɪˈbel/ v.i., -ll- rebellieren

rebellion /rɪˈbeljən/ n. Rebellion, die

rebellious /rɪˈbeljəs/ adj. rebellisch

rebirth /riːˈbɜːθ/ n. (revival) Wiederaufleben, das

reboot /riːˈbuːt/ (Comp.) v.t. & i. neu booten

rebound ① /rɪˈbaʊnd/ v.i. (a) (spring back) abprallen (**from** von)

(b) (fig.) zurückfallen (**upon** auf + Akk.)

② /ˈriːbaʊnd/ n. Abprall, der

rebuff /rɪˈbʌf/ ① n. [schroffe] Abweisung

② v.t. [schroff] zurückweisen

rebuild /riːˈbɪld/ v.t., rebuilt /riːˈbɪlt/ wieder aufbauen

rebuke /rɪˈbjuːk/ ① v.t. tadeln, rügen (**for** wegen)

② n. Rüge, die

recall ① /rɪˈkɔːl/ v.t. (a) (remember) sich erinnern an (+ Akk.)

(b) (serve as reminder of) erinnern an (+ Akk.)

(c) abberufen ⟨Botschafter⟩

② /rɪˈkɔːl, ˈriːkɔːl/ n. (a) [**powers of**] ~: Gedächtnis, das

(b) **beyond** ~: unwiderruflich

recant /rɪˈkænt/ v.i. [öffentlich] widerrufen

recap /ˈriːkæp/ v.t. & i., -pp- (coll.) rekapitulieren

recapitulate /riːkəˈpɪtjʊleɪt/ v.t. & i. rekapitulieren

recapture /riːˈkæptʃə(r)/ v.t. wieder ergreifen ⟨Gefangenen⟩; wieder einfangen ⟨Tier⟩

recede /rɪˈsiːd/ v.i. ⟨Hochwasser, Flut:⟩ zurückgehen; ~ [**into the distance**] in der Ferne verschwinden

receding /rɪˈsiːdɪŋ/ adj. fliehend ⟨Kinn, Stirn⟩

receipt /rɪˈsiːt/ n. (a) (receiving) Empfang, der

(b) (written acknowledgement) Quittung, die

(c) in pl. (amount received) Einnahmen Pl. (**from** aus)

receive /rɪˈsiːv/ v.t. (a) (get) erhalten; beziehen ⟨Gehalt, Rente⟩

(b) (accept) entgegennehmen ⟨Strauß Lieferung⟩

(c) (entertain) empfangen ⟨Gast⟩

re'ceiver n. (a) Empfänger, der/ Empfängerin, die

(b) (Teleph.) [Telefon]hörer, der

(c) (of stolen goods) Hehler, der/Hehlerin, die

recent /ˈriːsənt/ adj. jüngst... ⟨Ereignisse, Vergangenheit usw.⟩; **the ~ closure of the factory** die kürzlich erfolgte Schließung der Fabrik

'recently adv. (a short time ago) vor kurzem; (in the recent past) in der letzten Zeit

receptacle /rɪˈseptəkl/ n. Behälter, der; Gefäß, das

reception /rɪˈsepʃn/ n. (a) (welcome) Aufnahme, die

(b) (party) Empfang, der

(c) (Brit.: foyer) die Rezeption

reception: ~ com'mittee n. Empfangskomitee, das; **~ desk** n. Rezeption, die

re'ceptionist n. (in hotel) Empfangschef, der/-dame, die; (at doctor's) Sprechstundenhilfe, die

receptive /rɪˈseptɪv/ adj. aufgeschlossen, empfänglich (**to** für)

recess /rɪˈses, ˈriːses/ n. (a) (alcove) Nische, die

(b) (Brit. Parl.; Amer.: short vacation) Ferien Pl.; (Amer. Sch.; between classes) Pause, die

recession /rɪˈseʃn/ n. (Econ.) Rezession, die (fachspr.); Konjunkturrückgang, der

recharge /riːˈtʃɑːdʒ/ v.t. aufladen ⟨Batterie⟩

rechargeable /riːˈtʃɑːdʒəbl/ adj. wieder aufladbar

recipe /ˈresɪpɪ/ n. Rezept, das

recipient /rɪˈsɪpɪənt/ n. Empfänger, der/ Empfängerin, die

reciprocal /rɪˈsɪprəkl/ adj. gegenseitig ⟨Abkommen, Zuneigung⟩

reciprocate /rɪˈsɪprəkeɪt/ v.t. erwidern

recital /rɪˈsaɪtl/ n. (performance) [Solisten]konzert, das; (of literature also) Rezitation, die

recitation /resɪˈteɪʃn/ n. Rezitation, die

recite /rɪˈsaɪt/ v.t. (a) rezitieren ⟨Gedicht⟩

(b) (list) aufzählen

reckless /ˈreklɪs/ adj. unbesonnen; rücksichtslos ⟨Fahrweise⟩; **~ of the dangers/ consequences** ungeachtet der Gefahren/ Folgen

reckon /ˈrekn/ v.t. (a) (work out) ausrechnen ⟨Kosten⟩; bestimmen ⟨Position⟩

(b) (consider) halten (**as** für)

(c) (estimate) schätzen

▪ **'reckon on** v.t. (a) (rely on) zählen auf (+ Akk.)

(b) (expect) rechnen mit

▪ **'reckon with** v.i. rechnen mit

'reckoning n. Berechnung, die; **by my ~:** nach meiner Rechnung

reclaim /rɪˈkleɪm/ v.t. **(a)** zurückbekommen ‹Steuern›
(b) urbar machen ‹Land›

recline /rɪˈklaɪn/ v.i. liegen; **reclining seat** Liegesitz, der

recluse /rɪˈkluːs/ n. Einsiedler, der/ Einsiedlerin, die

recognition /rekəgˈnɪʃn/ n. **(a)** Wiedererkennen, das; **be beyond all ~:** nicht wieder zu erkennen sein
(b) (acknowledgement) Anerkennung, die; **in ~ of** als Anerkennung für

recognize /ˈrekəgnaɪz/ v.t. **(a)** (know again) wieder erkennen **(by an + Dat., from** durch)
(b) (acknowledge) anerkennen ‹Gültigkeit, Land›; **be ~d as** gelten als

recoil [1] /rɪˈkɔɪl/ v.i. zurückfahren
[2] /ˈriːkɔɪl, rɪˈkɔɪl/ n. Rückstoß, der

recollect /rekəˈlekt/ [1] v.t. sich erinnern **an** (+ Akk.)
[2] v.i. sich erinnern

recollection /rekəˈlekʃn/ n. Erinnerung, die

recommend /rekəˈmend/ v.t. empfehlen

recommendation /rekəmenˈdeɪʃn/ n. Empfehlung, die; **on sb.'s ~:** auf jmds. Empfehlung (Akk.)

recompense /ˈrekəmpens/ [1] v.t. entschädigen
[2] n. Entschädigung, die

reconcile /ˈrekənsaɪl/ v.t. **(a)** (restore to friendship) versöhnen
(b) ~ oneself to sth. sich mit etw. versöhnen

reconciliation /rekənsɪlɪˈeɪʃn/ n. Versöhnung, die

recondition /riːkənˈdɪʃn/ v.t. [general]überholen; **~ed engine** Austauschmotor, der

reconnaissance /rɪˈkɒnɪsəns/ n. (Mil.) Aufklärung, die

reconnoitre (Brit.; Amer.: **reconnoiter**) /rekəˈnɔɪtə(r)/ v.i. auf Erkundung [aus]gehen

reconsider /riːkənˈsɪdə(r)/ v.t. [noch einmal] überdenken

reconstruct /riːkənˈstrʌkt/ v.t. wieder aufbauen; (fig.) rekonstruieren

reconstruction /riːkənˈstrʌkʃn/ n. Wiederaufbau, der; (thing reconstructed) Rekonstruktion, die

record [1] /ˈrekɔːd/ v.t. **(a)** aufzeichnen; **~ a new CD** eine neue CD aufnehmen
(b) (register officially) dokumentieren; protokollieren ‹Verhandlung›
[2] /ˈrekɔːd/ n. **(a) be on ~** ‹Prozess, Verhandlung, Besprechung:› protokolliert sein; **have sth. on ~:** etw. dokumentiert haben
(b) (report) Protokoll, das
(c) (document) Dokument, das; **[strictly] off the ~:** [ganz] inoffiziell
(d) (for ~ player) [Schall]platte, die

(e) have a [criminal/police] ~: vorbestraft sein
(f) (Sport) Rekord, der

record /ˈrekɔːd/**: ~-breaking** adj. Rekord-; **~ deck** n. Plattenspieler, der

recorded /rɪˈkɔːdɪd/ adj. aufgezeichnet ‹Konzert, Rede›; **~ music** Musikaufnahmen Pl.

recorded de'livery n. (Brit. Post.) eingeschriebene Sendung (ohne Versicherung)

recorder /rɪˈkɔːdə(r)/ n. (Mus.) Blockflöte, die

'record holder n. (Sport) Rekordhalter, der/-halterin, die

recording /rɪˈkɔːdɪŋ/ n. **(a)** (process) Aufzeichnung, die
(b) (what is recorded) Aufnahme, die

recording: ~ head n. Aufnahmekopf, der; **~ studio** n. Tonstudio, das

record /ˈrekɔːd/**: ~ player** n. Plattenspieler, der; **~ sleeve** n. Plattenhülle, die; **~ token** n. [Schall]plattengutschein, der

re-count [1] /riːˈkaʊnt/ v.t. [noch einmal] nachzählen
[2] /ˈriːkaʊnt/ n. Nachzählung, die

recoup /rɪˈkuːp/ v.t. [wieder] hereinbekommen ‹[Geld]einsatz›

recourse /rɪˈkɔːs/ n. **have ~ to sb./sth.** bei jmdm./zu etw. Zuflucht nehmen

recover /rɪˈkʌvə(r)/ [1] v.t. zurückbekommen
[2] v.i. **~ from sth.** sich von etw. [wieder] erholen; **be [fully] ~ed** [völlig] wiederhergestellt sein

recovery /rɪˈkʌvərɪ/ n. Erholung, die; **make a quick/good ~:** sich schnell/gut erholen

recovery: ~ position n. (Med.) stabile Seitenlage; **~ vehicle** n. Bergungsfahrzeug, das

recreation /rekrɪˈeɪʃn/ n. Freizeitbeschäftigung, die; Hobby, das

recreational /rekrɪˈeɪʃənl/ adj. Freizeit-

recreational: ~ 'drug n. Freizeitdroge, die; **~ 'vehicle** n. (Amer.) Wohnmobil, das

recre'ation centre n. Freizeitzentrum, das

recrimination /rɪkrɪmɪˈneɪʃn/ n. Gegenbeschuldigung, die

recruit /rɪˈkruːt/ [1] n. **(a)** (Mil.) Rekrut, der
(b) (new member) neues Mitglied
[2] v.t. (Mil.: enlist) anwerben; (into party etc.) werben ‹Mitglied›; einstellen ‹neuen Mitarbeiter›

re'cruitment n. (Mil.) Anwerbung, die; (of new staff) Neueinstellung, die; **~ of members** Mitgliederwerbung, die

rectangle /ˈrektæŋgl/ n. Rechteck, das

rectangular /rekˈtæŋjʊlə(r)/ adj. rechteckig

rector /ˈrektə(r)/ n. **(a)** Pfarrer, der
(b) (Univ.) Rektor, der/Rektorin, die

···✦

rectory /'rektərɪ/ n. Pfarrhaus, das

recuperate /rɪ'kju:pəreɪt/ v.i. sich erholen

recuperation /rɪkju:pə'reɪʃn/ n. Erholung, die

recur /rɪ'kɜ:(r)/ v.i., -rr- sich wiederholen; 〈Krankheit:〉 wiederkehren; 〈Symptom:〉 wieder auftreten

recurrence /rɪ'kʌrəns/ n. Wiederholung, die; (of illness, thought, feeling) Wiederkehr, die; (of symptom) Wiederauftreten, das

recurrent /rɪ'kʌrənt/ adj. immer wiederkehrend

recycle /ri:'saɪkl/ v.t. wieder verwerten; ∼d paper Recyclingpapier, das

recyclable /ri:'saɪkləbl/ adj. recycelbar

recycling /ri:'saɪklɪŋ/ n. Recycling, das

red /red/ **1** adj. rot

2 n. **(a)** Rot, das **(b)** (debt) [be] in the ∼: in den roten Zahlen [sein]

red: ∼ **'card** n. (Footb.) rote Karte, die; **Red 'Cross** n. Rotes Kreuz; ∼'**currant** n. [rote] Johannisbeere

redden /'redn/ v.i. 〈Gesicht, Himmel:〉 sich röten; 〈Person:〉 rot werden

reddish /'redɪʃ/ adj. rötlich

redecorate /ri:'dekəreɪt/ v.t. renovieren; (with wallpaper) neu tapezieren; (with paint) neu streichen

redeem /rɪ'di:m/ v.t. **(a)** [wieder] einlösen 〈Pfand〉; einlösen 〈Gutschein, Coupon〉 **(b)** (save) retten

redemption /rɪ'dempʃn/ n. (from sin) Erlösung, die

redeploy /ri:dɪ'plɔɪ/ v.t. woanders einsetzen 〈Arbeitskräfte〉

red: ∼-'handed adj. catch sb. ∼-handed jmdn. auf frischer Tat ertappen; ∼ 'herring n. (fig.) Ablenkungsmanöver, das; ∼-**hot** adj. [rot] glühend

redial **1** /ri:'daɪəl/ v.t. noch einmal wählen 〈Telefonnummer〉 **2** /'ri:daɪəl/ n. Wahlwiederholung, die; ∼ button Wahlwiederholungstaste, die

Red 'Indian (Brit.) **1** n. Indianer, der/ Indianerin, die **2** adj. Indianer-

redirect /ri:daɪ'rekt/ v.t. nachsenden 〈Post, Brief usw.〉; umleiten 〈Verkehr〉

rediscover /ri:dɪ'skʌvə(r)/ v.t. wieder entdecken

redistribute /ri:dɪ'strɪbju:t/ v.t. umverteilen 〈Besitz, Einkommen〉

redistribution /ri:dɪstrɪ'bju:ʃn/ n. (of land, wealth) Umverteilung, die

red: ∼-'letter day n. großer Tag; ∼ 'light n. rotes Warnlicht; (traffic light) rote Ampel; **drive through a** ∼ **light** bei Rot über die Ampel fahren; ∼-'**light district** n. Strich, der (salopp); ∼ **meat** n. dunkles Fleisch (z.B. vom Rind)

redo /ri:'du:/ v.t. forms as DO: noch einmal machen 〈Bett, Hausaufgabe〉; neu frisieren 〈Haare〉

redouble /ri:'dʌbl/ v.t. verdoppeln

red 'pepper n. rote Paprika[schote]

redress /rɪ'dres/ **1** n. Entschädigung, die **2** v.t. wieder gutmachen; ∼ **the balance** das Gleichgewicht wiederherstellen

reduce /rɪ'dju:s/ v.t. **(a)** senken 〈Preis, Gebühr, Fieber, Aufwendungen, Blutdruck usw.〉; reduzieren 〈Geschwindigkeit, Gewicht〉; **at** ∼**d prices** zu herabgesetzten Preisen **(b)** ∼ **to silence/tears** verstummen lassen/ zum Weinen bringen

reduction /rɪ'dʌkʃn/ n. (in price, costs, speed, etc.) Senkung, die (in Gen.); ∼ **in wages/ weight** Lohnsenkung, die/Gewichtsabnahme, die

redundancy /rɪ'dʌndənsɪ/ n. (Brit.) Arbeitslosigkeit, die; **redundancies** Entlassungen Pl.; **take** or **accept voluntary** ∼: seiner betriebsbedingten Kündigung zustimmen

re'dundancy payment n. Abfindung, die

redundant /rɪ'dʌndənt/ adj. (Brit.) arbeitslos; **be made** ∼: den Arbeitsplatz verlieren; **make** ∼: entlassen

red 'wine n. Rotwein, der

reed /ri:d/ n. Schilf[rohr], das

re-educate /ri:'edjʊkeɪt/ v.t. umerziehen

reef /ri:f/ n. Riff, das

'reef knot n. Kreuzknoten, der

reek /ri:k/ v.i. stinken (of nach)

reel /ri:l/ **1** n. 〈Garn-, Angel〉rolle, die; 〈Film-, Tonband〉spule, die **2** v.i. **(a)** (be in a whirl) sich drehen **(b)** (sway) torkeln

re-establish /ri:ɪ'stæblɪʃ/ v.t. wiederherstellen

re-examine /ri:ɪg'zæmɪn/ v.t. (scrutinize) erneut überprüfen

ref /ref/ n. (Sport coll.) Schiri, der (Sportjargon)

ref. abbr. = **reference** Verw.; **your/our ref.** Ihr/unser Zeichen

refashion /ri:'fæʃn/ v.t. umgestalten

refectory /rɪ'fektərɪ/ n. Mensa, die

refer /rɪ'fɜ:(r)/ **1** v.i., -rr-: **(a)** ∼ **to** (allude to) sich beziehen auf (+ Akk.) 〈Buch, Person usw.〉; (speak of) sprechen von 〈Person, Problem usw.〉 **(b)** ∼ **to** (apply to, relate to) betreffen **(c)** ∼ **to** (consult, cite as proof) nachsehen in (+ Dat.) **2** v.t., -rr-: ∼ **sb./sth. to sb./sth.** jmdn./etw. an jmdn./auf etw. (Akk.) verweisen

referee /refə'ri:/ **1** n. (Sport) (umpire) Schiedsrichter, der/-richterin, die; (Boxing) Ringrichter, der **2** v.t. als Schiedsrichter/-richterin leiten

reference /'refrəns/ n. (a) (allusion)
Hinweis, der (to auf + Akk.); **make no ~ to
sth.** etw. nícht ansprechen
(b) (testimonial) Zeugnis, das
reference: ~ book n. Nachschlagewerk,
das; **~ number** n. [Kenn]nummer, die;
~ point n. Bezugspunkt, der
referendum /refə'rendəm/ n.
Volksentscheid, der
refill ⓵ /ri:'fɪl/ v.t. nachfüllen; **~ the
glasses** nachschenken
⓶ /'ri:fɪl/ n. (for ball pen) Ersatzmine, die
refine /rɪ'faɪn/ v.t. (a) (purify) raffinieren
(b) (make cultured) kultivieren
(c) (improve) verbessern; verfeinern ‹Stil,
Technik›
refined /rɪ'faɪnd/ adj. kultiviert
re'finement n. Kultiviertheit, die;
(improvement) Verbesserung, die
refinery /rɪ'faɪnərɪ/ n. Raffinerie, die
reflate /ri:'fleɪt/ v.t. (Econ.) ankurbeln
reflation /ri:'fleɪʃn/ n. (Econ.) Reflation, die
reflect /rɪ'flekt/ v.t. (a) reflektieren
(b) (fig.) widerspiegeln ‹Ansichten›
(c) (contemplate) nachdenken über (+ Akk.);
~ what/how …: überlegen, was/wie …
■ **re'flect [up]on** v.t. (a) (consider)
nachdenken über (+ Akk.)
(b) **~ badly [up]on sb./sth.** auf jmdn./etw.
ein schlechtes Licht werfen
reflection /rɪ'flekʃn/ n. (a) Reflexion, die;
(by surface of water) Spiegelung, die
(b) (image) Spiegelbild, das
(c) (consideration) Nachdenken, das (**upon**
über + Akk.); **on ~:** bei weiterem
Nachdenken
reflective /rɪ'flektɪv/ adj. (a) reflektierend
(b) (thoughtful) nachdenklich
reflector /rɪ'flektə(r)/ n. Rückstrahler, der
reflex /'ri:fleks/ ⓵ n. Reflex, der
⓶ adj. **~ action** Reflexhandlung, die
reflexive /ri'fleksɪv/ adj. (Ling.) reflexiv
reforestation /ri:forɪ'steɪʃn/ n.
Wiederaufforstung, die
reform /rɪ'fɔ:m/ ⓵ v.t. (make better) bessern
‹Person›; reformieren ‹Institution›
⓶ n. Reform, die (**in** Gen.)
reformation /refə'meɪʃn/ n. (of character)
Wandlung, die; **the R~** (Hist.) die
Reformation
re'former n. [political] ~: Reformpolitiker,
der/-politikerin, die
refract /rɪ'frækt/ v.t. (Phys.) brechen
refrain[1] /rɪ'freɪn/ n. Refrain, der
refrain[2] v.i. **~ from doing sth.** es
unterlassen, etw. zu tun
refresh /rɪ'freʃ/ v.t. erfrischen
re'fresher course n. Auffrischungskurs,
der
re'freshing adj. erfrischend; wohltuend
‹Abwechslung›
re'freshment n. Erfrischung, die

refrigerate /rɪ'frɪdʒəreɪt/ v.t. (a) kühl
lagern ‹Lebensmittel›
(b) (chill) kühlen; (freeze) einfrieren
refrigeration /rɪfrɪdʒə'reɪʃn/ n. kühle
Lagerung; (chilling) Kühlung, die; (freezing)
Einfrieren, das
refrigerator /rɪ'frɪdʒəreɪtə(r)/ n.
Kühlschrank, der
refuel /ri:'fju:əl/, (Brit.) -ll-: ⓵ v.t. auftanken
⓶ v.i. [auf]tanken
refuge /'refju:dʒ/ n. Zuflucht, die; **take ~ in**
Schutz od. Zuflucht suchen in (+ Dat.) (**from**
vor + Dat.); **women's ~:** Frauenhaus, das
refugee /refjʊ'dʒi:/ n. Flüchtling, der
refu'gee camp n. Flüchtlingslager, das
refund ⓵ /ri:'fʌnd/ v.t. (pay back)
zurückzahlen ‹Geld›; erstatten ‹Kosten›
⓶ /'ri:fʌnd/ n. Rückzahlung, die; (of
expenses) [Rück]erstattung, die
refundable /ri:'fʌndəbl/ adj. **be ~:**
zurückerstattet werden
refurbish /ri:'fɜ:bɪʃ/ v.t. renovieren ‹Haus›
refurnish /ri:'fɜ:nɪʃ/ v.t. neu einrichten
refusal /rɪ'fju:zl/ n. Ablehnung, die; (after a
period of time) Absage, die; **~ to do sth.**
Weigerung, etw. zu tun
refuse[1] /rɪ'fju:z/ ⓵ v.t. ablehnen;
verweigern ‹Zutritt, Einreise, Erlaubnis›;
~ sb. admittance/entry/permission jmdm.
den Zutritt/die Einreise/die Erlaubnis
verweigern; **~ to do sth.** sich weigern, etw.
zu tun
⓶ v.i. ablehnen; (after request) sich weigern
refuse[2] /'refju:s/ n. Abfall, der
refuse /'refju:s/**: ~ collection** n.
Müllabfuhr, die; **~ collector** n.
Müllwerker, der; **~ disposal** n.
Abfallbeseitigung, die
refute /rɪ'fju:t/ v.t. widerlegen
regain /rɪ'geɪn/ v.t. zurückgewinnen
‹Zuversicht, Vertrauen, Augenlicht›; **~ one's
strength** wieder zu Kräften kommen
regal /'ri:gl/ adj. majestätisch
regalia /rɪ'geɪlɪə/ n. pl. (of royalty)
Krönungsinsignien Pl.
regard /rɪ'gɑ:d/ ⓵ v.t. (a) (look at)
betrachten
(b) (give heed to) beachten
(c) (fig.: look upon, contemplate) betrachten;
~ sb. as a friend/fool/genius jmdn. als
Freund betrachten/für einen Dummkopf/ein
Genie halten; **be ~ed as** gelten als
(d) (concern, have relation to) betreffen; **as ~s
sb./sth., ~ing sb./sth.** was jmdn./etw.
angeht od. betrifft
⓶ n. (a) (attention) **pay** or **have ~ to sb./sth.**
jmdm./etw. Beachtung schenken; **without
~ to** ohne Rücksicht auf (+ Akk.)
(b) (esteem) Achtung, die; **hold sb./sth. in
high ~:** jmdn./etw. sehr schätzen
(c) in pl. Grüße Pl.; **give her my ~s** grüße
sie von mir; **with kind[est] ~s** mit
herzlich[st]en Grüßen
                    ···⟫

re'gardless *adj.* ohne Rücksicht (**of** auf + *Akk.*)

regatta /rɪ'gætə/ *n.* Regatta, *die*

regenerate /rɪ'dʒenəreɪt/ *v.t.* erneuern

reggae /'regeɪ/ *n.* Reggae, *der*

regime, régime /reɪ'ʒiːm/ *n.* [Regierungs]system, *das*

regiment /'redʒɪmənt/ *n.* Regiment, *das*

regimental /redʒɪ'mentl/ *adj.* Regiments-

region /'riːdʒn/ *n.* (a) (area) Gebiet, *das* (b) (administrative division) Bezirk, *der*; **in the ~ of** (fig.) ungefähr

regional /'riːdʒənl/ *adj.* regional

regionalism /'riːdʒənəlɪzm/ *n.* (Polit., Ling.) Regionalismus, *der*

regionalize /'riːdʒənəlaɪz/ *v.t.* regionalisieren

register /'redʒɪstə(r)/ [1] *n.* Register, *das*; (at school) Klassenbuch, *das* [2] *v.t.* (a) (enter) registrieren; (cause to be entered) registrieren lassen; anmelden ⟨*Auto, Patent*⟩; (at airport) einchecken ⟨*Gepäck*⟩; *abs.* (at hotel) sich ins Fremdenbuch eintragen; **~ with the police** sich polizeilich anmelden (b) (enrol) anmelden; (Univ.) sich einschreiben (c) zum Ausdruck bringen ⟨*Überraschung*⟩; **~ a protest** Protest anmelden

registered /'redʒɪstəd/ *adj.* eingetragen ⟨*Firma*⟩; eingeschrieben ⟨*Student, Brief*⟩; **~ trade mark** eingetragenes Warenzeichen; **by ~ post** per Einschreiben

registrar /'redʒɪstrɑː(r)/ *n.* Standesbeamte, *der*/-beamtin, *die*

registration /redʒɪ'streɪʃn/ *n.* Registrierung, *die*; (enrolment) Anmeldung, *die*; (of students) Einschreibung, *die*

registration: ~ document *n.* (Brit.) Kraftfahrzeugbrief, *der*; **~ form** *n.* Anmeldeformular, *das*; **~ number** *n.* amtliches Kennzeichen; **~ plate** *n.* (Motor Veh.) Nummernschild, *das*

registry /'redʒɪstrɪ/ *n.* **~ [office]** Standesamt, *das*

regret /rɪ'gret/ [1] *v.t.*, **-tt-** bedauern; **I ~ to say that …:** ich muss leider sagen, dass … [2] *n.* Bedauern, *das*; **have no ~s** nichts bereuen

regretfully /rɪ'gretfəlɪ/ *adv.* mit Bedauern

regrettable /rɪ'gretəbl/ *adj.* bedauerlich

regrettably /rɪ'gretəblɪ/ *adv.* bedauerlicherweise

regroup /riː'gruːp/ [1] *v.t.* umgruppieren [2] *v.i.* (a) (form new group) sich neu gruppieren (b) (Mil.) sich neu formieren

regular /'regjʊlə(r)/ [1] *adj.* regelmäßig; geregelt ⟨*Arbeit*⟩; fest ⟨*Anstellung*⟩; **~ customer** Stammkunde, *der*/-kundin, *die*; **~ army** reguläre Armee [2] *n.* (coll.: ~ customer) Stammkunde, *der*/-kundin, *die*; (in pub) Stammgast, *der*

regularity /regjʊ'lærɪtɪ/ *n.* Regelmäßigkeit, *die*

'regularly *adv.* regelmäßig

regulate /'regjʊleɪt/ *v.t.* (control) regeln; (restrict) begrenzen; (adjust) regulieren

regulation /regjʊ'leɪʃn/ *n.* (a) ▶ REGULATE: Regelung, *die*; Begrenzung, *die*; Regulierung, *die* (b) (rule) Vorschrift, *die*

rehabilitate /riːhə'bɪlɪteɪt/ *v.t.* rehabilitieren; **~ [back into society]** wieder [in die Gesellschaft] eingliedern

rehabilitation /riːhəbɪlɪ'teɪʃn/ *n.* **~ [in society]** Wiedereingliederung, *die* [in die Gesellschaft]

rehash [1] /riː'hæʃ/ *v.t.* aufwärmen [2] /'riːhæʃ/ *n.* Aufguss, *der*

rehearsal /rɪ'hɜːsl/ *n.* Probe, *die*

rehearse /rɪ'hɜːs/ *v.t.* proben

reheat /riː'hiːt/ *v.t.* wieder erwärmen; aufwärmen ⟨*Essen*⟩

rehouse /riː'haʊz/ *v.t.* umquartieren

reign /reɪn/ [1] *n.* Herrschaft, *die* [2] *v.i.* herrschen (**over** über + *Akk.*)

reimburse /riːɪm'bɜːs/ *v.t.* [zurück]erstatten ⟨[*Un*]*kosten, Spesen*⟩; entschädigen ⟨*Person*⟩

rein /reɪn/ *n.* Zügel, *der*

reincarnation /riːɪnkɑː'neɪʃn/ *n.* (Relig.) Reinkarnation, *die*

reindeer /'reɪndɪə(r)/ *n., pl. same* Ren[tier], *das*

reinforce /riːɪn'fɔːs/ *v.t.* verstärken; **~d concrete** Stahlbeton, *der*

rein'forcement *n.* Verstärkung, *die*; **~[s]** (additional men etc.) Verstärkung, *die*

reinstate /riːɪn'steɪt/ *v.t.* (in job) wieder einstellen

reintegrate /riː'ɪntɪgreɪt/ [1] *v.t.* wieder eingliedern (**into** in + *Akk.*) [2] *v. refl.* sich wieder eingliedern (**into** in + *Akk.*)

reintegration /riːɪntɪ'greɪʃn/ *n.* Wiedereingliederung, *die* (**into** in + *Akk.*)

reinvigorate /riːɪn'vɪgəreɪt/ *v.t.* neu beleben; **feel ~d** sich gestärkt fühlen

reissue /riː'ɪʃuː/ *v.t.* neu herausbringen

reiterate /riː'ɪtəreɪt/ *v.t.* wiederholen

reject [1] /rɪ'dʒekt/ *v.t.* ablehnen; zurückweisen ⟨*Bitte, Annäherungsversuch*⟩ [2] /'riːdʒekt/ (thing) Ausschuss, *der*

rejection /rɪ'dʒekʃn/ *n.* Ablehnung, *die*/ Zurückweisung, *die*

re'jection slip *n.* Absage, *die*

rejoice /rɪ'dʒɔɪs/ *v.i.* sich freuen (**over, at** über + *Akk.*)

rejoin¹ /rɪ'dʒɔɪn/ *v.t.* (reply) erwidern (**to** auf + *Akk.*)

rejoin² /riː'dʒɔɪn/ *v.t.* wieder eintreten in (+ *Akk.*) ⟨*Partei, Verein*⟩

rejoinder /rɪ'dʒɔɪndə(r)/ *n.* Erwiderung, *die* (**to** auf + *Akk.*)

rejuvenate /rɪ'dʒuːvəneɪt/ *v.t.* verjüngen

rekindle /riːˈkɪndl/ *v.t.* wieder anfachen; wieder aufleben lassen ‹*Verlangen, Hoffnungen*›

relapse /rɪˈlæps/ ① *v.i.* ‹*Kranker:*› einen Rückfall bekommen
② *n.* Rückfall, *der*

relate /rɪˈleɪt/ ① *v.t.* (a) erzählen ‹*Geschichte*›; erzählen von ‹*Abenteuer*›
(b) (bring into relation) in Zusammenhang bringen (**to, with** mit)
② *v.i.* (a) ~ **to** (have reference) in Zusammenhang stehen mit; betreffen ‹*Person*›
(b) ~ **to** (feel involved with) eine Beziehung haben zu

re'lated *adj.* verwandt (**to** mit)

relation /rɪˈleɪʃn/ *n.* (a) (connection) Beziehung, *die,* Zusammenhang, *der* (**of …** and zwischen … und); **in** *or* **with** ~ **to** in Bezug auf (+ *Akk.*)
(b) **in** *pl.* (dealings) Verhältnis, *das* (**with** zu)
(c) (relative) Verwandte, *der*/*die*

re'lationship *n.* (a) (mutual tie) Beziehung, *die* (**with** zu)
(b) (kinship) Verwandtschaftsverhältnis, *das*
(c) (connection) Beziehung, *die;* (between cause and effect) Zusammenhang, *der*
(d) (sexual) Verhältnis, *das*

relative /ˈrelətɪv/ ① *n.* Verwandte, *der*/*die*
② *adj.* relativ; Relativ‹*satz, -pronomen*›

'relatively *adv.* relativ; verhältnismäßig

relative 'pronoun *n.* (Ling.) Relativpronomen, *das*

relax /rɪˈlæks/ ① *v.t.* (a) entspannen ‹*Muskel, Körper*[*teil*]›; lockern ‹*Griff*›
(b) (make less strict) lockern ‹*Gesetz, Disziplin*›
② *v.i.* sich entspannen

relaxation /riːlækˈseɪʃn/ *n.* Entspannung, *die;* **for** ~: zur Entspannung

relaxed /rɪˈlækst/ *adj.* entspannt, gelöst ‹*Atmosphäre, Person*›

re'laxing *adj.* entspannend

relay ① /ˈriːleɪ/ *n.* (a) (race) Staffel, *die*
(b) (gang) Schicht, *die;* **work in** ~**s** schichtweise arbeiten
(c) (Electr.) Relais, *das*
② /riːˈleɪ/ *v.t.* (a) weiterleiten
(b) (Radio, Telev.) übertragen

'relay race *n.* Staffellauf, *der;* (Swimming) Staffelschwimmen, *das*

release /rɪˈliːs/ ① *v.t.* (a) (free) freilassen ‹*Tier, Häftling, Sklaven*›; (from jail) entlassen (**from** aus)
(b) (let go) loslassen; lösen ‹*Handbremse*›
(c) (make known) veröffentlichen ‹*Erklärung, Nachricht*›; (issue) herausbringen ‹*Film, Schallplatte*›
② *n.* (a) ▶ 1ᴀ: Freilassung, *die;* Entlassung, *die*
(b) (of published item) Veröffentlichung, *die*
(c) (handle, lever, button) Auslöser, *der*

relegate /ˈrelɪgeɪt/ *v.t.* (a) ~ **sb. to the position of …**: jmdn. zu … degradieren

(b) (Sport) absteigen lassen; **be** ~**d** absteigen (**to** in + *Akk.*)

relegation /relɪˈgeɪʃn/ *n.* (Sport) Abstieg, *der*

relent /rɪˈlent/ *v.i.* nachgeben

re'lentless *adj.,* **re'lentlessly** *adv.* unerbittlich

relevance /ˈrelɪvəns/ *n.* Relevanz, *die* (**to** für)

relevant /ˈrelɪvənt/ *adj.* relevant (**to** für); wichtig ‹*Information*›

reliability /rɪlaɪəˈbɪlɪti/ *n.* Zuverlässigkeit, *die*

reliable /rɪˈlaɪəbl/ *adj.,* **reliably** /rɪˈlaɪəbli/ *adv.* zuverlässig

reliance /rɪˈlaɪəns/ *n.* Abhängigkeit, *die* (**on** von)

reliant /rɪˈlaɪənt/ *adj.* **be** ~ **on** sb./sth. auf jmdn./etw. angewiesen sein

relief[1] /rɪˈliːf/ *n.* (a) Erleichterung, *die;* **give** [**sb.**] ~ [**from pain**] [jmdm.] [Schmerz]linderung verschaffen; **what a** ~!, **that's a** ~! da bin ich aber erleichtert!
(b) (assistance) Hilfe, *die*

relief[2] *n.* (Art) Relief, *das*

relief: ~ **bus** *n.* Entlastungsbus, *der;* (as replacement) Ersatzbus, *der;* ~ **map** *n.* Reliefkarte, *die;* ~ **road** *n.* Entlastungsstraße, *die;* ~ **worker** *n.* Helfer, *der*

relieve /rɪˈliːv/ *v.t.* (a) erleichtern; unterbrechen ‹*Eintönigkeit*›; abbauen ‹*Anspannung*›; stillen ‹*Schmerzen*›; **I am** *or* **feel** ~**d to hear that …**: es erleichtert mich zu hören, dass …
(b) ablösen ‹*Wache, Truppen*›

religion /rɪˈlɪdʒn/ *n.* Religion, *die*

religious /rɪˈlɪdʒəs/ *adj.* religiös; Religions‹*freiheit, -unterricht*›

re'ligiously *adv.* (conscientiously) gewissenhaft

relinquish /rɪˈlɪŋkwɪʃ/ *v.t.* (a) (give up) aufgeben
(b) ~ **one's hold** *or* **grip on sb./sth.** jmdn./etw. loslassen

relish /ˈrelɪʃ/ ① *n.* (a) (liking) Vorliebe, *die;* **do sth. with** [**great**] ~: etw. mit [großem] Genuss tun
(b) (condiment) Relish, *das*
② *v.t.* genießen

relive /riːˈlɪv/ *n.* noch einmal durchleben

reload /riːˈləʊd/ *v.t.* nachladen ‹*Schusswaffe*›

relocate /riːləˈkeɪt/ ① *v.t.* verlegen ‹*Fabrik, Büro*›; versetzen ‹*Angestellten*›
② *v.i.* (settle) sich niederlassen

relocation /riːləˈkeɪʃn/ *n.* (of factory, office) Verlegung, *die;* (of employee) Versetzung, *die;* ~ **expenses** Umzugskosten *Pl.*

reluctance /rɪˈlʌktəns/ *n.* Widerwille, *der;* **have a** [**great**] ~ **to do sth.** etw. nur mit Widerwillen tun

reluctant /rɪˈlʌktənt/ *adj.* unwillig; be ~ to do sth. etw. nur ungern tun

re'luctantly *adv.* nur ungern

rely /rɪˈlaɪ/ *v.i.* (have trust) sich verlassen/(be dependent) angewiesen sein ([up]on auf + *Akk.*)

remain /rɪˈmeɪn/ *v.i.* (a) (be left over) übrigbleiben
(b) (stay) bleiben; ~ **behind** noch dableiben
(c) (continue to be) bleiben; it ~s to be seen es wird sich zeigen

remainder /rɪˈmeɪndə(r)/ *n.* Rest, *der*

re'maining *adj.* restlich

re'mains *n. pl.* (a) Reste *Pl.*
(b) (human) sterbliche [Über]reste *Pl.* (verhüll.)

remand /rɪˈmɑːnd/ [1] *v.t.* ~ **sb.** [in custody] jmdn. in Untersuchungshaft behalten
[2] *n.* on ~: in Untersuchungshaft

remark /rɪˈmɑːk/ [1] *v.t.* bemerken (to gegenüber)
[2] *v.i.* eine Bemerkung machen ([up]on zu, über + *Akk.*)
[3] *n.* Bemerkung, *die* (on über + *Akk.*)

remarkable /rɪˈmɑːkəbl/ *adj.* (a) (notable) bemerkenswert
(b) (extraordinary) außergewöhnlich

remarkably /rɪˈmɑːkəblɪ/ *adv.* (a) (notably) bemerkenswert
(b) (exceptionally) außergewöhnlich

remarry /riːˈmærɪ/ *v.i. & t.* wieder heiraten

remedy /ˈremɪdɪ/ [1] *n.* [Heil]mittel, *das* (for gegen)
[2] *v.t.* beheben ‹*Problem*›; retten ‹*Situation*›

remember /rɪˈmembə(r)/ *v.t.* (a) sich erinnern an (+ *Akk.*); I ~ed to bring the book ich habe daran gedacht, das Buch mitzubringen; an evening to ~: ein unvergesslicher Abend
(b) (convey greetings) ~ me to them grüße sie von mir

remembrance /rɪˈmembrəns/ *n.* Gedenken, *das*; in ~ of sb. zu jmds. Gedächtnis

Remembrance Day, Remembrance Sunday *ns.* (Brit.) ≈ Volkstrauertag, *der*

remind /rɪˈmaɪnd/ *v.t.* erinnern (of an + *Akk.*); ~ sb. to do sth. jmdn. daran erinnern, etw. zu tun; that ~s me, ...: dabei fällt mir ein, ...

re'minder *n.* Erinnerung, *die* (of an + *Akk.*); (letter) Mahnung, *die*; Mahnbrief, *der*

reminisce /remɪˈnɪs/ *v.i.* sich in Erinnerungen (*Dat.*) ergehen (about an + *Akk.*)

reminiscences /remɪˈnɪsənsɪz/ *n. pl.* Erinnerungen *Pl.*; (memoirs) [Lebens]erinnerungen *Pl.*

reminiscent /remɪˈnɪsənt/ *adj.* be ~ of sth. an etw. (*Akk.*) erinnern

remiss /rɪˈmɪs/ *adj.* nachlässig (of von)

remission /rɪˈmɪʃn/ *n.* (a) (of debt, punishment) Erlass, *der*

(b) (of prison sentence) Straferlass, *der*

remit /rɪˈmɪt/ *v.t.,* -tt- (send) überweisen ‹*Geld*›

remittance /rɪˈmɪtəns/ *n.* Überweisung, *die*

remnant /ˈremnənt/ *n.* Rest, *der*

remonstrate /ˈremənstreɪt/ *v.i.* protestieren (against gegen); ~ with sb. jmdm. Vorhaltungen machen (about, on wegen)

remorse /rɪˈmɔːs/ *n.* Reue, *die* (for, about über + *Akk.*)

re'morseful /rɪˈmɔːsfl/ *adj.* reumütig

re'morseless *adj.* unerbittlich

remote /rɪˈməʊt/ *adj.,* ~r /rɪˈməʊtə(r)/, ~st /rɪˈməʊtɪst/ (a) fern ‹*Vergangenheit, Zukunft, Zeit*›; abgelegen ‹*Ort, Gebiet*›; ~ from weit entfernt von
(b) (slight) gering ‹*Chance*›

remote: ~ con'trol *n.* (of vehicle) Fernlenkung, *die;* (for TV set) Fernbedienung, *die;* ~**-con'trol[led]** *adj.* ferngelenkt; fernbedient ‹*Anlage*›

re'motely *adv.* entfernt ‹*verwandt*›; they are not ~ alike sie haben nicht die entfernteste Ähnlichkeit miteinander

removable /rɪˈmuːvəbl/ *adj.* abnehmbar; entfernbar ‹*Trennwand*›; herausnehmbar ‹*Futter*›

removal /rɪˈmuːvl/ *n.* (a) Entfernung, *die;* (of obstacle, problem) Beseitigung, *die*
(b) (transfer of furniture) Umzug, *der*

removal: ~ expenses *n. pl.* Umzugskosten *Pl.;* ~ **firm** *n.* Spedition, *die;* ~ **man** *n.* Möbelpacker, *der;* ~ **van** *n.* Möbelwagen, *der*

remove /rɪˈmuːv/ *v.t.* entfernen; beseitigen ‹*Spur, Hindernis*›; (take off) abnehmen; ausziehen ‹*Kleidungsstück*›; ~ a book from the shelf ein Buch vom Regal nehmen

re'mover *n.* (a) (of paint/varnish/hair/rust) Farb-/Lack-/Haar-/Rostentferner, *der*
(b) (man) Möbelpacker, *der;* [firm of] ~s Spedition[sfirma], *die*

remunerate /rɪˈmjuːnəreɪt/ *v.t.* bezahlen

remuneration /rɪmjuːnəˈreɪʃn/ *n.* Bezahlung, *die*

Renaissance /rəˈneɪsəns, rɪˈneɪsəns/ *n.* (Hist.) Renaissance, *die*

rename /riːˈneɪm/ *v.t.* umbenennen

render /ˈrendə(r)/ *v.t.* (a) (make) machen
(b) erweisen ‹*Dienst*›
(c) (translate) übersetzen (by mit)

'rendering *n.* (translation) Übersetzung, *die*

rendezvous /ˈrɒndeɪvuː/ *n., pl. same* /ˈrɒndeɪvuːz/ (a) (meeting place) Treffpunkt, *der*
(b) (meeting) Verabredung, *die*

renegade /ˈrenɪgeɪd/ [1] *n.* Abtrünnige, *der/die*
[2] *adj.* abtrünnig

renegotiate /riːnɪˈgəʊʃɪeɪt/ *v.t.* neu aushandeln

renew /rɪ'nju:/ v.t. erneuern; fortsetzen ⟨Angriff, Bemühungen⟩; (extend) erneuern ⟨Vertrag, Ausweis usw.⟩; ~ a library book ⟨Bibliothekar/Benutzer:⟩ ein Buch [aus der Bücherei] verlängern/verlängern lassen

re'newable /rɪ'nju:əbl/ adj. regenerationsfähig ⟨Energiequelle⟩; verlängerbar ⟨Vertrag, Genehmigung, Ausweis⟩

renewal /rɪ'nju:əl/ n. Erneuerung, die

renounce /rɪ'naʊns/ v.t. verzichten auf (+ Akk.); verstoßen ⟨Person⟩; ~ the devil/ one's faith dem Teufel/seinem Glauben abschwören

renovate /'renəveɪt/ v.t. renovieren ⟨Gebäude⟩; restaurieren ⟨Möbel usw.⟩

renovation /renə'veɪʃn/ n. ▶ RENOVATE: Renovierung, die; Restaurierung, die

renown /rɪ'naʊn/ n. Renommee, das

renowned /rɪ'naʊnd/ adj. berühmt (for wegen, für)

rent /rent/ ① n. (for house etc.) Miete, die; (for land) Pacht, die
② v.t. (a) (use) mieten ⟨Haus, Wohnung usw.⟩; pachten ⟨Land⟩; mieten ⟨Auto⟩ (b) (let) vermieten ⟨Haus, Auto usw.⟩ (to Dat., an + Akk.); verpachten ⟨Land⟩ (to Dat., an + Akk.)
∎ **rent 'out** v.t. ▶ RENT 2B

rental /'rentl/ n. Miete, die

rent: ~ **boy** n. (coll.) Strichjunge, der (salopp); ~ **rebate** n. Mietermäßigung, die; ~ **tribunal** n. Mietgericht, das

renunciation /rɪnʌnsɪ'eɪʃn/ n. ▶ RENOUNCE: Verzicht, der; Verstoßung, die

reopen /riː'əʊpn/ ① v.t. wieder öffnen; wieder aufmachen; wieder eröffnen ⟨Geschäft, Lokal usw.⟩; wieder aufnehmen ⟨Diskussion, Verhandlung⟩
② v.i. ⟨Geschäft, Lokal usw.:⟩ wieder öffnen

reorder /riː'ɔːdə(r)/ v.t. (a) (Commerc.) nachbestellen ⟨Ware⟩ (b) (rearrange) umordnen

reorganization /riːɔːgənaɪ'zeɪʃn/ n. Umorganisation, die; (of time, work) Neueinteilung, die

reorganize /riː'ɔːgənaɪz/ v.t. umorganisieren; neu einteilen ⟨Zeit, Arbeit⟩

rep /rep/ n. (coll.: representative) Vertreter, der/ Vertreterin, die

repaid ▶ REPAY

repair /rɪ'peə(r)/ ① v.t. (mend) reparieren; ausbessern ⟨Kleidung, Straße⟩
② n. Reparatur, die; **be in good/bad** ~: in gutem/schlechtem Zustand sein

repair: ~ **man** n. Mechaniker, der; (in house) Handwerker, der; ~ **shop** n. Reparaturwerkstatt, die

repaper /riː'peɪpə(r)/ v.t. neu tapezieren

repatriate /riː'pætrɪeɪt/ v.t. repatriieren

repatriation /riːpætrɪ'eɪʃn/ n. Repatriierung, die

repay /riː'peɪ/ v.t., repaid /riː'peɪd/

zurückzahlen ⟨Schulden usw.⟩; erwidern ⟨Besuch, Gruß, Freundlichkeit⟩; ~ sb. for sth. jmdm. etw. vergelten

re'payment n. Rückzahlung, die

re'payment mortgage n. Tilgungshypothek, die

repeal /rɪ'piːl/ ① v.t. aufheben ⟨Gesetz, Erlass usw.⟩
② n. Aufhebung, die

repeat /rɪ'piːt/ ① n. Wiederholung, die
② v.t. wiederholen; **please ~ after me:** ...: sprich/sprecht/sprechen Sie mir bitte nach: ...

re'peated adj. wiederholt; (several) mehrere; **make ~ efforts to ...:** wiederholt od. mehrfach versuchen, ...zu...

re'peatedly adv. mehrmals

repel /rɪ'pel/ v.t., -ll-: (a) (drive back) abwehren (b) (be repulsive to) abstoßen

repellent /rɪ'pelənt/ ① adj. abstoßend
② n. [insect] ~: Insektenschutzmittel, das

repent /rɪ'pent/ v.i. bereuen (of Akk.)

repentance /rɪ'pentəns/ n. Reue, die

repentant /rɪ'pentənt/ adj. reuig

repercussion /riːpə'kʌʃn/ n., usu. in pl. Auswirkung, die ([up]on auf + Akk.)

repertoire /'repətwɑː(r)/ n. Repertoire, das

repertory /'repətərɪ/ n. (Theatre) Repertoiretheater, das

'repertory company n. Repertoiretheater, das

repetition /repɪ'tɪʃn/ n. Wiederholung, die

repetitious /repɪ'tɪʃəs/ adj. sich immer wiederholend attr.

repetitive /rɪ'petɪtɪv/ adj. eintönig

repetitive 'strain injury n. chronisches Überlastungssyndrom

rephrase /riː'freɪz/ v.t. umformulieren; **I'll ~ that** ich will es anders ausdrücken

replace /rɪ'pleɪs/ v.t. (a) (vertically) zurückstellen; (horizontally) zurücklegen (b) (take place of) ersetzen; ~ A with or by B A durch B ersetzen (c) (exchange) austauschen, auswechseln ⟨Maschinen[teile] usw.⟩

re'placement n. (a) ▶ REPLACE A: Zurückstellen, das; Zurücklegen, das (b) (provision of substitute for) Ersatz, der; attrib. Ersatz- (c) (substitute) Ersatz, der; ~ [part] Ersatzteil, das

replay ① /riː'pleɪ/ v.t. wiederholen ⟨Spiel⟩; nochmals abspielen ⟨Tonband usw.⟩
② /'riːpleɪ/ n. Wiederholung, die; (match) Wiederholungsspiel, das

replenish /rɪ'plenɪʃ/ v.t. auffüllen

replica /'replɪkə/ n. Nachbildung, die

reply /rɪ'plaɪ/ ① v.i. ~ [to sb./sth.] [jmdm./ auf etw. (Akk.)] antworten
② v.t. ~ that ...: antworten, dass ...
③ n. Antwort, die (to auf + Akk.)

r

re'ply-paid *adj.* ~-paid telegram
RP-Telegramm, *das;* ~-paid envelope
Freiumschlag, *der*

repopulate /riː'pɒpjʊleɪt/ *v.t.* neu
besiedeln

report /rɪ'pɔːt/ [1] *v.t.* (a) (relate) berichten;
(in writing) einen Bericht schreiben über
(+ *Akk.*); (state formally also) melden
(b) (name to authorities) melden (to *Dat.*); (for
prosecution) anzeigen (to bei)
[2] *v.i.* (a) Bericht erstatten (on über + *Akk.*);
berichten (on über + *Akk.*)
(b) (present oneself) sich melden (to bei)
[3] *n.* (a) (account) Bericht, *der* (on, about
über + *Akk.*)
(b) (Sch.) Zeugnis, *das*
(c) (of gun) Knall, *der*

reportedly /rɪ'pɔːtɪdlɪ/ *adv.* wie verlautet

reported 'speech *n.* indirekte Rede

re'porter *n.* Reporter, *der*/Reporterin, *die*

repossess /riːpə'zes/ *v.t.* wieder in Besitz
nehmen

reprehensible /reprɪ'hensɪbl/ *adj.*
tadelnswert

represent /reprɪ'zent/ *v.t.* (a) darstellen
(as als)
(b) (act for) vertreten

representation /reprɪzen'teɪʃn/ *n.* (a)
(depicting, image) Darstellung, *die*
(b) (acting for sb.) Vertretung, *die*
(c) make ~s to sb. bei jmdm. Protest
einlegen

representative /reprɪ'zentətɪv/ [1] *n.* (a)
(Commerc.) Vertreter, *der*/Vertreterin, *die*
(b) R~ (Amer. Polit.) Abgeordnete, *der/die*
[2] *adj.* (typical) repräsentativ (of für)

repress /rɪ'pres/ *v.t.* (a) unterdrücken
(Aufruhr, Gefühle, Lachen usw.)
(b) (Psych.) verdrängen (Gefühle) (from aus)

repressed /rɪ'prest/ *adj.* unterdrückt;
(Psych.) verdrängt

repression /rɪ'preʃn/ *n.* Unterdrückung,
die

repressive /rɪ'presɪv/ *adj.* repressiv

reprieve /rɪ'priːv/ [1] *v.t.* ~ sb. (postpone
execution) jmdm. Strafaufschub gewähren;
(remit execution) jmdn. begnadigen
[2] *n.* Strafaufschub, *der* (of für)/
Begnadigung, *die;* (fig.) Gnadenfrist, *die*

reprimand /'reprɪmɑːnd/ [1] *n.* Tadel, *der*
[2] *v.t.* tadeln

reprint [1] /riː'prɪnt/ *v.t.* wieder abdrucken
[2] /'riːprɪnt/ *n.* Nachdruck, *der*

reprisal /rɪ'praɪzl/ *n.* Vergeltungsakt, *der*
(for gegen)

reproach /rɪ'prəʊtʃ/ [1] *v.t.* ~ sb. jmdm.
Vorwürfe machen
[2] *n.* Vorwurf, *der*

reproachful /rɪ'prəʊtʃfl/ *adv.* vorwurfsvoll

reproduce /riːprə'djuːs/ [1] *v.t.*
wiedergeben
[2] *v.i.* (multiply) sich fortpflanzen

reproduction /riːprə'dʌkʃn/ *n.* (a)
Wiedergabe, *die*
(b) (producing offspring) Fortpflanzung, *die*
(c) (copy) Reproduktion, *die*

reproductive /riːprə'dʌktɪv/ *adj.*
Fortpflanzungs-

reprove /rɪ'pruːv/ *v.t.* tadeln

reptile /'reptaɪl/ *n.* Reptil, *das*

republic /rɪ'pʌblɪk/ *n.* Republik, *die*

republican /rɪ'pʌblɪkən/ [1] *adj.*
republikanisch
[2] *n.* R~ (Amer. Polit.) Republikaner, *der*/
Republikanerin, *die*

repudiate /rɪ'pjuːdɪeɪt/ *v.t.* zurückweisen

repugnance /rɪ'pʌgnəns/ *n.* Abscheu, *der*
(to[wards] vor + Dat.)

repugnant /rɪ'pʌgnənt/ *adj.* widerlich (to
Dat.)

repulse /rɪ'pʌls/ *v.t.* abwehren

repulsion /rɪ'pʌlʃn/ *n.* (disgust) Widerwille,
der (towards gegen)

repulsive /rɪ'pʌlsɪv/ *adj.* abstoßend

reputable /'repjʊtəbl/ *adj.* angesehen
(Person, Beruf, Zeitung usw.); anständig
(Verhalten); seriös (Firma)

reputably /'repjʊtəblɪ/ *adv.* anständig

reputation /repjʊ'teɪʃn/ *n.* (a) Ruf, *der;*
have a ~ for or of doing/being sth. in dem
Ruf stehen, etw. zu tun/sein
(b) (good name) Name, *der*

repute /rɪ'pjuːt/ [1] *v.t. in pass.* be ~d [to
be] sth. als etw. gelten; she is ~d to have/
make ...: man sagt, dass sie ... hat/macht
[2] *n.* Ruf, *der*

reputed /rɪ'pjuːtɪd/ *adj.*, **re'putedly** *adv.*
angeblich

request /rɪ'kwest/ [1] *v.t.* bitten; ~ sth. of
or from sb. jmdn. um etw. bitten
[2] *n.* Bitte, *die* (for um); at sb.'s ~: auf jmds.
Bitte (*Akk.*) [hin]

re'quest stop *n.* (Brit.) Bedarfshaltestelle,
die

require /rɪ'kwaɪə(r)/ *v.t.* (a) (need) brauchen
(b) (order, demand) verlangen (of von); be ~d
to do sth. etw. tun müssen

re'quirement *n.* (a) (need) Bedarf, *der*
(b) (condition) Erfordernis, *das*

requisite /'rekwɪzɪt/ [1] *adj.* notwendig (to,
for für)
[2] *n. in pl.* toilet/travel ~s Toiletten-/
Reiseartikel Pl.

requisition /rekwɪ'zɪʃn/ [1] *n.* (order for sth.)
Anforderung, *die* (for Gen.)
[2] *v.t.* anfordern

rescind /rɪ'sɪnd/ *v.t.* für ungültig erklären

rescue /'reskjuː/ [1] *v.t.* retten (from aus)
[2] *n.* Rettung, *die; attrib.* Rettungs(dienst,
-mannschaft); go/come to the/sb.'s ~: jmdm.
zu Hilfe kommen

rescuer /'reskjuːə(r)/ *n.* Retter, *der*/
Retterin, *die*

'rescue worker n. [Einsatz]helfer, der/
-helferin, die

research /rɪ'sɜːtʃ, 'riːsɜːtʃ/ **1** n.
Forschung, die (**into, on** über + Akk.)
2 v.i. forschen; ~ **into** sth. etw. erforschen

research as'sistant n.
wissenschaftlicher Assistent/
wissenschaftliche Assistentin

researcher /-'--, '---/ n. Forscher, der/
Forscherin, die

research: ~ **student** n. ≈ Doktorand,
der/Doktorandin, die; ~ **work** n.
Recherchen Pl.; (medical, scientific)
Forschungsarbeit, die; ~ **worker** n.
≈ Rechercheur, der/Rechercheurin, die;
(medical, scientific) Forscher, der/Forscherin,
die

resell /riː'sel/ v.t., **resold** /riː'səʊld/
weiterverkaufen (**to** an + Akk.)

resemblance /rɪ'zembləns/ n.
Ähnlichkeit, die (**to** mit)

resemble /rɪ'zembl/ v.t. ähneln, gleichen
(+ Dat.)

resent /rɪ'zent/ v.t. übel nehmen

resentful /rɪ'zentfl/ adj. übelnehmerisch,
nachtragend ⟨Person, Art⟩; **be** ~ **of** or **feel**
~ **about** sth. etw. übel nehmen

re'sentment n. Groll, der (geh.); **feel**
~ **towards** or **against** sb. einen Groll auf
jmdn. haben

reservation /rezə'veɪʃn/ n. **(a)**
Reservierung, die; **have a** ~ [**for a room**] ein
Zimmer reserviert haben
(b) (doubt) Vorbehalt, der (**about** gegen);
Bedenken (**about** bezüglich + Gen.); **without**
~: ohne Vorbehalt

reserve /rɪ'zɜːv/ **1** v.t. reservieren lassen
⟨Zimmer, Tisch, Platz⟩; (set aside)
reservieren; ~ **the right to do** sth. sich
(Dat.) [das Recht] vorbehalten, etw. zu tun
2 n. **(a)** (extra amount) Reserve, die (**of** an
+ Dat.) **have/hold** or **keep** sth. **in** ~: etw. in
Reserve haben/halten
(b) (place set apart) Reservat, das
(c) (Sport) Reservespieler, der/-spielerin, die;
the R~s die Reserve
(d) (reticence) Zurückhaltung, die

reserved /rɪ'zɜːvd/ adj. (reticent) reserviert

reservoir /'rezəvwɑː(r)/ n. [(artificial) lake)
Reservoir, das

reshape /riː'ʃeɪp/ v.t. umgestalten

reshuffle /riː'ʃʌfl/ **1** v.t. **(a)** umbilden
⟨Kabinett⟩
(b) (Cards) neu mischen
2 n. Umbildung, die

reside /rɪ'zaɪd/ v.i. (formal) wohnen;
wohnhaft sein (Amtsspr.)

residence /'rezɪdəns/ n. **(a)** (abode)
Wohnsitz, der; (of ambassador etc.) Residenz,
die
(b) (stay) Aufenthalt, der

'residence permit n.
Aufenthaltsgenehmigung, die

resident /'rezɪdənt/ **1** adj. wohnhaft; **be**
~ **in England** seinen Wohnsitz in England
haben
2 n. (inhabitant) Bewohner, der/Bewohnerin,
die; (at hotel) Hotelgast, der

residential /rezɪ'denʃl/ adj. Wohn⟨gebiet,
-siedlung, -straße⟩; ~ **hotel** Hotel für
Dauergäste

residential 'care n. stationäre Pflege

resident's 'parking n. Parken nur für
Anlieger

residual /rɪ'zɪdjʊəl/ adj. zurückgeblieben

residue /'rezɪdjuː/ n. **(a)** Rest, der
(b) (Chem.) Rückstand, der

resign /rɪ'zaɪn/ **1** v.t. zurücktreten von
⟨Amt⟩
2 v. refl. ~ **oneself to** sth./**to doing** sth.
sich mit etw. abfinden/sich damit abfinden,
etw. zu tun
3 v.i. ⟨Arbeitnehmer:⟩ kündigen;
⟨Regierungsbeamter:⟩ zurücktreten (**from**
von)

resignation /rezɪg'neɪʃn/ n. **(a)** ▶ RESIGN
3: Kündigung, die; Rücktritt, der; **tender**
one's ~: seine Kündigung/seinen Rücktritt
einreichen
(b) (being resigned) Resignation, die; **with** ~:
resigniert

resigned /rɪ'zaɪnd/ adj. resigniert; **be** ~ **to**
sth. sich mit etw. abgefunden haben

resilience /rɪ'zɪlɪəns/ n. **(a)** Elastizität, die
(b) (fig.) Unverwüstlichkeit, die

resilient /rɪ'zɪlɪənt/ adj. elastisch; (fig.)
unverwüstlich

resin /'rezɪn/ n. Harz, das

resist /rɪ'zɪst/ **1** v.t. **(a)** standhalten
(+ Dat.) ⟨Frost, Hitze, Feuchtigkeit usw.⟩
(b) (oppose) sich widersetzen (+ Dat.);
widerstehen (+ Dat.) ⟨Versuchung⟩
2 v.i. ▶ 1B: sich widersetzen; widerstehen

resistance /rɪ'zɪstəns/ n. Widerstand, der
(**to** gegen)

re'sistance movement n.
Widerstandsbewegung, die

resistant /rɪ'zɪstənt/ adj. **(a)** (opposed) **be**
~ **to** sich widersetzen (+ Dat.)
(b) (having power to resist) widerstandsfähig (**to**
gegen)

reskill /riː'skɪl/ v.t. fort- od. weiterbilden;
umschulen ⟨Arbeitslose⟩

resold ▶ RESELL

resolute /'rezəluːt/ adj. resolut, energisch
⟨Person⟩; entschlossen ⟨Tat⟩

resolution /rezə'luːʃn/ n. **(a)** (firmness)
Entschlossenheit, die
(b) (decision) Entschließung, die; (Polit. also)
Resolution, die
(c) (resolve) Vorsatz, der; **make a** ~: einen
Vorsatz fassen

resolve /rɪ'zɒlv/ **1** v.t. **(a)** lösen ⟨Problem,
Rätsel⟩; ausräumen ⟨Schwierigkeit⟩
(b) (decide) beschließen   ⋯⋗

(c) (settle) beilegen ⟨*Streit*⟩; regeln
⟨*Angelegenheit*⟩
2 *n.* **(a)** Vorsatz, *der*
(b) (resoluteness) Entschlossenheit, *die*
resolved /rɪˈzɒlvd/ *adj.* ∼ **[to do sth.]**
entschlossen[, etw. zu tun]
resonant /ˈrezənənt/ *adj.* hallend ⟨*Ton,
Klang*⟩
resort /rɪˈzɔːt/ **1** *n.* **(a)** ⟨place⟩
Aufenthalt[sort], *der;* [holiday] ∼: Ferienort,
der; **ski** ∼: Skiurlaubsort, *der;* **seaside** ∼:
Seebad, *das*
(b) (recourse) **as a last** ∼: als letzter Ausweg
2 *v.i.* ∼ **to sth./sb.** zu etw. greifen/sich an
jmdn. wenden **(for** um)
resound /rɪˈzaʊnd/ *v.i.* widerhallen
re'sounding *adj.* hallend ⟨*Lärm*⟩;
überwältigend ⟨*Sieg, Erfolg*⟩
resource /rɪˈsɔːs, rɪˈzɔːs/ *n. usu. in pl.*
(stock) Mittel *Pl.;* Ressource, *die*
resourceful /rɪˈsɔːsfl, rɪˈzɔːsfl/ *adj.* findig
⟨*Person*⟩
respect /rɪˈspekt/ **1** *n.* **(a)** (esteem)
Respekt, *der,* Achtung, *die* **(for** vor + *Dat.*);
show ∼ **for sb./sth.** Respekt vor jmdm./etw.
zeigen
(b) (aspect) Hinsicht, *die;* **in some** ∼**s** in
mancher Hinsicht
(c) with ∼ **to …:** in Bezug auf … (*Akk.*); was
… [an]betrifft
2 *v.t.* respektieren; achten
respectable /rɪˈspektəbl/ *adj.* angesehen
⟨*Bürger usw.*⟩; ehrenwert ⟨*Motive*⟩; (decent)
ehrbar (geh.) ⟨*Leute, Kaufmann*⟩; anständig,
respektabel ⟨*Beschäftigung usw.*⟩
respectful /rɪˈspektfl/ *adj.* respektvoll
(to[wards] gegenüber)
re'spectfully *adv.* respektvoll
respective /rɪˈspektɪv/ *adj.* jeweilig
re'spectively *adv.* beziehungsweise
respiration /respɪˈreɪʃn/ *n.* Atmung, *die*
respiratory /ˈrespərətərɪ/ *adj.*
Atmungs⟨*system, -organ, -funktion*⟩
respite /ˈrespaɪt/ *n.* Ruhepause, *die;* (delay)
Aufschub, *der;* **without** ∼: ohne Pause
resplendent /rɪˈsplendənt/ *adj.* prächtig
respond /rɪˈspɒnd/ **1** *v.i.* **(a)** (answer)
antworten **(to** auf + *Akk.*)
(b) (react) reagieren **(to** auf + *Akk.*); ⟨*Patient,
Bremsen:*⟩ ansprechen **(to** auf + *Akk.*)
2 *v.t.* antworten; erwidern
response /rɪˈspɒns/ *n.* **(a)** (answer) Antwort,
die **(to** auf + *Akk.*); **in** ∼ **[to]** als Antwort [auf
(+ *Akk.*)]
(b) (reaction) Reaktion, *die*
responsibility /rɪspɒnsɪˈbɪlɪtɪ/ *n.* **(a)** (being
responsible) Verantwortung, *die*
(b) (duty) Verpflichtung, *die*
responsible /rɪˈspɒnsɪbl/ *adj.* **(a)**
verantwortlich; **be** ∼ **to sb.** jmdm.
gegenüber verantwortlich sein **(for** für)
(b) (trustworthy) verantwortungsvoll

responsibly /rɪˈspɒnsɪblɪ/ *adv.*
verantwortungsbewusst
responsive /rɪˈspɒnsɪv/ *adj.*
aufgeschlossen ⟨*Person*⟩; **be** ∼ **to sth.** auf
etw. (*Akk.*) reagieren
rest[1] /rest/ **1** *v.i.* ruhen; ∼ **on** ruhen auf
(+ *Dat.*); ∼ **from sth.** sich von etw. ausruhen;
∼ **assured that …:** seien Sie versichert, dass
…; ∼ **with sb.** ⟨*Verantwortung:*⟩ bei jmdm.
liegen
2 *v.t.* **(a)** ∼ **sth. against sth.** etw. an etw.
(*Akk.*) lehnen
(b) ausruhen ⟨*Augen*⟩
3 *n.* **(a)** (repose) Ruhe, *die*
(b) (break, relaxation) Ruhe[pause], *die;*
Erholung, *die* **(from** von); **take a** ∼: sich
ausruhen **(from** von); **give it a** ∼! (coll.) hör
jetzt mal auf damit!
(c) (pause) **have a** ∼: [eine] Pause machen;
∼ **period** [Ruhe]pause, *die*
rest[2] *n.* **the** ∼: der Rest; **we'll do the** ∼:
alles Übrige erledigen wir
restaurant /ˈrestərɒnt/ *n.* Restaurant, *das*
'restaurant car *n.* (Brit. Railw.)
Speisewagen, *der*
rest: ∼ **cure** *n.* Erholungskur, *die;* ∼ **day**
n. Ruhetag, *der*
'rested *adj.* ausgeruht
restful /ˈrestfl/ *adj.* ruhig ⟨*Tag, Woche*⟩
'rest home *n.* Pflegeheim, *das*
restive /ˈrestɪv/ *adj.* unruhig
'restless *adj.* unruhig ⟨*Nacht, Schlaf,
Bewegung*⟩; ruhelos ⟨*Person*⟩
restoration /restəˈreɪʃn/ *n.* **(a)** (of peace,
health) Wiederherstellung, *die;* (of work of art,
building) Restaurierung, *die*
(b) the R∼ (Brit. Hist.) die Restauration
restore /rɪˈstɔː(r)/ *v.t.* **(a)** (give back)
zurückgeben
(b) restaurieren ⟨*Bauwerk, Kunstwerk usw.*⟩;
∼ **sb. to health** jmdn. wiederherstellen
(c) wiederherstellen ⟨*Ordnung, Ruhe*⟩
restrain /rɪˈstreɪn/ *v.t.* zurückhalten
⟨*Gefühl, Lachen, Person*⟩; bändigen
⟨*unartiges Kind, Tier*⟩; ∼ **sb./oneself from
doing sth.** jmdn. davon abhalten/sich
zurückhalten, etw. zu tun
restrained /rɪˈstreɪnd/ *adj.* zurückhaltend
⟨*Wesen, Kritik*⟩; beherrscht ⟨*Reaktion, Worte*⟩
restraint /rɪˈstreɪnt/ *n.* **(a)** (restriction)
Einschränkung, *die*
(b) (reserve) Zurückhaltung, *die*
(c) (self-control) Selbstbeherrschung, *die*
restrict /rɪˈstrɪkt/ *v.t.* beschränken **(to** auf
+ *Akk.*)
re'stricted *adj.* beschränkt
restriction /rɪˈstrɪkʃn/ *n.* Beschränkung,
die **(on** *Gen.*)
restrictive /rɪˈstrɪktɪv/ *adj.* restriktiv
'rest room *n.* (esp. Amer.) Toilette, *die*
restyle /riːˈstaɪl/ *v.t.* neu stylen; ∼ **sb.'s
hair** jmdm. eine neue Frisur machen

result /rɪˈzʌlt/ ① *v.i.* (a) (follow) ~ **from** sth. die Folge einer Sache ⟨*Gen.*⟩ sein (b) (end) ~ **in** sth. in etw. ⟨*Dat.*⟩ resultieren ② *n.* Ergebnis, *das;* **be the** ~ **of** sth. die Folge einer Sache ⟨*Gen.*⟩ sein; **as a** ~ [**of this**] infolgedessen

reˈsultant /rɪˈzʌltənt/ *attrib. adj.* daraus resultierend

resume /rɪˈzjuːm/ *v.t.* wieder aufnehmen; fortsetzen ⟨*Reise*⟩

résumé /ˈrezʊmeɪ/ *n.* (a) (summary) Zusammenfassung, *die* (b) (Amer.: curriculum vitae) Lebenslauf, *der*

resumption /rɪˈzʌmpʃn/ *n.* Wiederaufnahme, *die*

resurface /riːˈsɜːfɪs/ ① *v.t.* ~ **a road** den Belag einer Straße erneuern ② *v.i.* (lit. or fig.) wieder auftauchen

resurgence /rɪˈsɜːdʒəns/ *n.* Wiederaufleben, *das*

resurrection /rezəˈrekʃn/ *n.* Auferstehung, *die*

resuscitate /rɪˈsʌsɪteɪt/ *v.t.* wieder beleben

resuscitation /rɪsʌsɪˈteɪʃn/ *n.* Wiederbelebung, *die*

retail /ˈriːteɪl/ ① *adj.* Einzel⟨*handel*⟩; Einzelhandels⟨*geschäft, -preis*⟩ ② *adv.* **buy/sell** ~: en détail kaufen/ verkaufen

ˈretailer *n.* Einzelhändler, *der*/-händlerin, *die*

ˈretailing /ˈriːteɪlɪŋ/ *n., no art.* Einzelhandel, *der*

retail ˈprice index *n.* (Brit.) Preisindex des Einzelhandels

retain /rɪˈteɪn/ *v.t.* behalten; ein-, zurückbehalten ⟨*Gelder*⟩

retaining: ~ **fee** *n.* Honorarvorschuss, *der;* ~ **wall** *n.* Böschungsmauer, *die*

retaliate /rɪˈtælɪeɪt/ *v.i.* Vergeltung üben (**against** an + *Dat.*)

retaliation /rɪtælɪˈeɪʃn/ *n.* Vergeltung, *die;* **in** ~ **for** als Vergeltung für

retarded /rɪˈtɑːdɪd/ *adj.* [**mentally**] ~: [geistig] zurückgeblieben

retch /retʃ/ *v.i.* würgen

retentive /rɪˈtentɪv/ *adj.* gut ⟨*Gedächtnis*⟩

rethink /riːˈθɪŋk/ *v.t.,* **rethought** /riːˈθɔːt/ noch einmal überdenken

reticence /ˈretɪsəns/ *n.* Zurückhaltung, *die*

reticent /ˈretɪsənt/ *adj.* zurückhaltend (**on, about** in Bezug auf + *Akk.*)

retina /ˈretɪnə/ *n.* Netzhaut, *die*

retinue /ˈretɪnjuː/ *n.* Gefolge, *das*

retire /rɪˈtaɪə(r)/ *v.i.* (a) ⟨*Angestellter, Arbeiter:*⟩ in Rente ⟨*Akk.*⟩ gehen; ⟨*Beamter, Militär:*⟩ in Pension *od.* den Ruhestand gehen (b) (withdraw) sich zurückziehen (**to** in + *Akk.*)

retired /rɪˈtaɪəd/ *adj.* aus dem Berufsleben ausgeschieden; ⟨*Beamter, Soldat*⟩ im Ruhestand, pensioniert

reˈtirement *n.* Ruhestand, *der;* **take early** ~ ⟨*Selbständiger:*⟩ sich vorzeitig zur Ruhe setzen; ⟨*Angestellter, Arbeiter:*⟩ vorzeitig in Rente ⟨*Akk.*⟩ gehen; ⟨*Beamter, Militär:*⟩ sich vorzeitig pensionieren lassen

retirement: ~ **age** *n.* Altersgrenze, *die;* ~ **home** *n.* (a) (house, flat) Alters- *od.* Ruhesitz, *der;* (b) (institution) Alters- *od.* Altenheim, *das;* ~ **pay,** ~ **pension** *ns.* [Alters]rente, *die*

retiring /rɪˈtaɪərɪŋ/ *adj.* (shy) zurückhaltend

retort /rɪˈtɔːt/ ① *n.* Entgegnung, *die* (**to** auf + *Akk.*) ② *v.t.* entgegnen

retrace /rɪˈtreɪs/ *v.t.* zurückverfolgen; ~ **one's steps** denselben Weg noch einmal zurückgehen

retract /rɪˈtrækt/ *v.t.* zurücknehmen

retrain /riːˈtreɪn/ ① *v.i.* [sich] umschulen [lassen] ② *v.t.* umschulen

reˈtraining *n.* Umschulung, *die*

retreat /rɪˈtriːt/ ① *n.* (a) (withdrawal) Rückzug, *der;* **beat a** ~ (fig.) das Feld räumen (b) (place) Zufluchtsort, *der* ② *v.i.* sich zurückziehen

retribution /retrɪˈbjuːʃn/ *n.* Vergeltung, *die*

retrieval /rɪˈtriːvl/ *n.* (a) (of situation) Rettung, *die;* **beyond** *or* **past** ~: hoffnungslos (b) (rescue) Rettung, *die;* (from wreckage) Bergung, *die*

retrieve /rɪˈtriːv/ *v.t.* (a) (rescue) retten (**from** aus); (from wreckage) bergen (**from** aus) (b) (recover) zurückholen ⟨*Brief*⟩; wiederholen ⟨*Ball*⟩; wiederbekommen ⟨*Geld*⟩ (c) (Comp.) wieder auffinden ⟨*Informationen*⟩ (d) ⟨*Hund:*⟩ apportieren (e) retten ⟨*Situation*⟩

reˈtriever *n.* Apportierhund, *der;* (breed) Retriever, *der*

retrospect /ˈretrəspekt/ *n.* **in** ~: im Nachhinein

retrospective /retrəˈspektɪv/ ① *adj.* retrospektiv (geh.) ② *n.* (Art) Retrospektive, *die* (geh.)

retrovirus /ˈretrəʊvaɪrəs/ *n.* Retrovirus, *das od. der*

returf /riːˈtɜːf/ *v.t.* neuen Rasen verlegen auf (+ *Dat.*)

return /rɪˈtɜːn/ ① *v.i.* (come back) zurückkommen; (go back) zurückgehen; (by vehicle) zurückfahren ② *v.t.* (a) (bring back) zurückbringen; zurückgeben ⟨*geliehenen/gestohlenen Gegenstand*⟩; ~**ed with thanks** mit Dank zurück   ····ᐳ

(b) erwidern ‹Besuch, Gruß, Liebe›; sich revanchieren für (ugs.) ‹Freundlichkeit, Gefallen›
(c) (elect) wählen ‹Kandidaten›
(d) ~ a verdict of guilty/not guilty ‹Geschworene:› auf „schuldig"/„nicht schuldig" erkennen
3 n. **(a)** Rückkehr, die; many happy ~s [of the day]! herzlichen Glückwunsch [zum Geburtstag]!
(b) by ~ [of post] postwendend
(c) (ticket) Rückfahrkarte, die; (for flight) Rückflugschein, der
(d) ~[s] (proceeds) Gewinn, der (on, from aus)
(e) (bringing back) Zurückbringen, das; (of property, goods, book) Rückgabe, die (to an + Akk.); receive/get sth. in ~ [for sth.] etw. [für etw.] bekommen

returnable /rɪˈtɜːnəbl/ adj. Mehrweg‹behälter, -flasche usw.›; rückzahlbar ‹Gebühr, Kaution›; ~ bottle Pfandflasche, die; ~ deposit Pfand, der

return: ~ 'fare n. Preis für eine Rückfahrkarte/(for flight) einen Rückflugschein; ~ 'flight n. Rückflug, der; ~ 'journey n. Rückreise, die; Rückfahrt, die; ~ 'match n. Rückspiel, das; ~ 'ticket n. (Brit.) Rückfahrkarte, die; (for flight) Rückflugschein, der; ~ 'trip n. **(a)** (trip back) Rückweg, der; Rückfahrt, die; **(b)** (trip out and back) Hin- und Rückfahrt, die; Hin- und Rückreise, die

retype /riːˈtaɪp/ v.t. neu tippen
reunification /riːjuːnɪfɪˈkeɪʃn/ n. Wiedervereinigung, die
reunify /riːˈjuːnɪfaɪ/ v.t. wieder vereinigen
reunion /riːˈjuːnjən/ n. (gathering) Treffen, das
reunite /riːjʊˈnaɪt/ v.t. wieder zusammenführen
reusable /riːˈjuːzəbl/ adj. wieder verwendbar
reuse **1** /riːˈjuːz/ v.t. wieder verwenden **2** /riːˈjuːs/ n. Wiederverwendung, die
rev /rev/ (coll.) **1** n., usu. in pl. Umdrehung, die
2 v.i., **-vv-** hochtourig laufen
3 v.t., **-vv-** aufheulen lassen
▪ **rev 'up** v.t. aufheulen lassen
Rev. /ˈrevərənd, (coll.) rev/ abbr. = **Reverend** Rev.
reveal /rɪˈviːl/ v.t. enthüllen (geh.); be ~ed ‹Wahrheit:› ans Licht kommen
re'vealing adj. aufschlussreich
revel /ˈrevl/ v.i., (Brit.) **-ll-** genießen (in Akk.); ~ in doing sth. es [richtig] genießen, etw. zu tun
revelation /revəˈleɪʃn/ n. **(a)** Enthüllung, die (geh.); be a ~: einem die Augen öffnen **(b)** (Relig.) Offenbarung, die
reveller /ˈrevələ(r)/ n. Feiernde, der/die
revelry /ˈrevlrɪ/ n. Feiern, das

revenge /rɪˈvendʒ/ **1** v.t. rächen ‹Person, Tat›
2 n. (action) Rache, die; take ~ or have one's ~ [on sb.] [for sth.] Rache [an jmdm.] [für etw.] nehmen; in ~ for sth. als Rache für etw
revengeful /rɪˈvendʒfl/ adj. rachsüchtig (geh.)
revenue /ˈrevənjuː/ n. ~[s] Einnahmen Pl.
revere /rɪˈvɪə(r)/ v.t. verehren
reverence /ˈrevərəns/ n. Ehrfurcht, die
Reverend /ˈrevərənd/ adj. the ~ John Wilson Hochwürden John Wilson
reverent /ˈrevərənt/ adj. ehrfürchtig
reverie /ˈrevərɪ/ n. Träumerei, die
reversal /rɪˈvɜːsl/ n. Umkehrung, die
reverse /rɪˈvɜːs/ **1** adj. entgegengesetzt ‹Richtung›; Rück‹seite›; umgekehrt ‹Reihenfolge›
2 n. **(a)** (contrary) Gegenteil, das **(b)** (Motor Veh.) Rückwärtsgang, der; put the car into ~, go into ~: den Rückwärtsgang einlegen
3 v.t. **(a)** umkehren ‹Reihenfolge›; ~ the charge[s] (Brit.) ein R-Gespräch anmelden **(b)** zurücksetzen ‹Fahrzeug›
4 v.i. zurücksetzen; rückwärts fahren
reverse: ~·'charge adj. (Brit.) make a ~-charge call ein R-Gespräch führen; ~ 'gear n. (Motor Veh.) Rückwärtsgang, der; see also GEAR 1A
reversible /rɪˈvɜːsɪbl/ adj. beidseitig tragbar ‹Kleidungsstück›; Wende‹mantel, -jacke›
re'versing light n. Rückfahrscheinwerfer, der
revert /rɪˈvɜːt/ v.i. ~ to zurückkommen auf (+ Akk.) ‹Thema, Frage›; ~ to savagery in den Zustand der Wildheit zurückfallen
review /rɪˈvjuː/ **1** n. **(a)** (survey) Überblick, der (of über + Akk.)
(b) (re-examination) [nochmalige] Überprüfung **(c)** (of book, play, etc.) Kritik, die; Rezension, die
2 v.t. **(a)** (survey) untersuchen; prüfen **(b)** (re-examine) überprüfen **(c)** (Mil.) inspizieren **(d)** (write a criticism of) rezensieren
re'viewer n. Rezensent, der/Rezensentin, die
revile /rɪˈvaɪl/ v.t. schmähen (geh.)
revise /rɪˈvaɪz/ v.t. **(a)** (check over) durchsehen ‹Manuskript› **(b)** (for exam) wiederholen; abs. lernen
revision /rɪˈvɪʒn/ n. **(a)** (checking over) Durchsicht, die **(b)** (amended version) revidierte Fassung **(c)** (for exam) Wiederholung, die
revisit /riːˈvɪzɪt/ v.t. wieder besuchen
revitalize /riːˈvaɪtəlaɪz/ v.t. neu beleben
revival /rɪˈvaɪvl/ n. Neubelebung, die
revive /rɪˈvaɪv/ **1** v.i. (come back to consciousness) wieder zu sich kommen; (be reinvigorated) zu neuem Leben erwachen

2 *v.t.* **(a)** (restore to consciousness) wieder beleben; (reinvigorate) wieder zu Kräften kommen lassen
(b) wieder wecken ⟨*Lebensgeister, Interesse*⟩

revoke /rɪ'vəʊk/ *v.t.* aufheben ⟨*Entscheidung*⟩; widerrufen ⟨*Befehl, Erlaubnis, Genehmigung*⟩

revolt /rɪ'vəʊlt/ **1** *v.i.* revoltieren (**against** gegen)
2 *v.t.* mit Abscheu erfüllen
3 *n.* Revolte, *die* (auch fig.); Aufstand, *der*

re'volting *adj.* abscheulich; (unpleasant) widerlich

revolution /revə'lu:ʃn/ *n.* Revolution, *die*

revolutionary /revə'lu:ʃənərɪ/ **1** *adj.* revolutionär
2 *n.* Revolutionär, *der*/Revolutionärin, *die*

revolve /rɪ'vɒlv/ **1** *v.t.* drehen
2 *v.i.* sich drehen (**round, about, on** um)

revolver /rɪ'vɒlvə(r)/ *n.* [Trommel]revolver, *der*

revolving /rɪ'vɒlvɪŋ/ *attrib. adj.* Dreh⟨*bühne, -tür*⟩

revue /rɪ'vju:/ *n.* Kabarett, *das;* (musical show) Revue, *die*

revulsion /rɪ'vʌlʃn/ *n.* Abscheu, *der* (**at** vor + *Dat.,* gegen)

reward /rɪ'wɔːd/ **1** *n.* Belohnung, *die*
2 *v.t.* belohnen

re'warding *adj.* lohnend; **be ~/financially ~**: sich lohnen/einträglich sein

rewind /ri:'waɪnd/ *v.t.,* **rewound** /ri:'waʊnd/
(a) wieder aufziehen ⟨*Uhr*⟩
(b) zurückspulen ⟨*Film, Band*⟩

'rewind button *n.* (on camera) Rückspulknopf, *der;* (on cassette recorder etc.) Rücklauftaste, *die*

reword /ri:'wɜːd/ *v.t.* umformulieren

rewrite /ri:'raɪt/ *v.t.,* **rewrote** /ri:'rəʊt/, **rewritten** /ri:'rɪtn/ noch einmal [neu] schreiben; (write differently) umschreiben

rhetoric /'retərɪk/ *n.* **[art of] ~**: Redekunst, *die;* Rhetorik, *die*

rhetorical /rɪ'tɒrɪkl/ *adj.* rhetorisch

rheumatic /ru:'mætɪk/ *adj.* rheumatisch

rheumatism /'ru:mətɪzm/ *n.* Rheumatismus, *der;* Rheuma, *das* (ugs.)

Rhine /raɪn/ *pr. n.* Rhein, *der*

rhino /'raɪnəʊ/ *n., pl.* **same** *or* **~s** (coll.), **rhinoceros** /raɪ'nɒsərəs/ *n., pl.* **same** *or* **~es** Nashorn, *das;* Rhinozeros, *das*

rhododendron /rəʊdə'dendrən/ *n.* Rhododendron, *der*

rhubarb /'ru:bɑːb/ *n.* Rhabarber, *der*

rhyme /raɪm/ **1** *n.* Reim, *der;* **without ~ or reason** ohne Sinn und Verstand
2 *v.i.* sich reimen (**with** auf + *Akk.*)

rhythm /'rɪðm/ *n.* Rhythmus, *der*

rhythmic /'rɪðmɪk/**, rhythmical** /'rɪðmɪkl/ *adj.* rhythmisch

rib /rɪb/ **1** *n.* Rippe, *die*
2 *v.t.,* **-bb-** (coll.) aufziehen (ugs.)

ribald /'rɪbəld/ *adj.* zotig

ribbon /'rɪbn/ *n.* Band, *das;* (on typewriter) [Farb]band, *das*

'ribcage *n.* Brustkorb, *der*

rice /raɪs/ *n.* Reis, *der*

rice: ~ 'pudding *n.* Milchreis, *der;* **~ wine** *n.* Reiswein, *der*

rich /rɪtʃ/ **1** *adj.* **(a)** reich (**in** an + *Dat.*); (fertile) fruchtbar ⟨*Land, Boden*⟩
(b) (splendid) prachtvoll
(c) (containing much fat, oil, eggs, etc.) gehaltvoll
(d) (deep, full) voll[tönend] ⟨*Stimme*⟩; voll ⟨*Ton*⟩; satt ⟨*Farbe, Farbton*⟩
2 *n. pl.* **the ~**: die Reichen *Pl.;* **~ and poor** Arm und Reich

riches /'rɪtʃɪz/ *n. pl.* Reichtum, *der*

'richly *adv.* **(a)** (splendidly) reich; üppig ⟨*ausgestattet*⟩; prächtig ⟨*gekleidet*⟩
(b) (fully) voll und ganz; **~ deserved** wohlverdient

'richness *n.* **(a)** (of food) Reichhaltigkeit, *die*
(b) (of voice) voller Klang; (of colour) Sattheit, *die*

rickets /'rɪkɪts/ *n.* Rachitis, *die*

rickety /'rɪkɪtɪ/ *adj.* wack[e]lig

ricochet /'rɪkəʃeɪ/ **1** *n.* **(a)** Abprallen, *das*
(b) (hit) Abpraller, *der*
2 *v.i.,* **~ed** /'rɪkəʃeɪd/ abprallen (**off** von)

rid /rɪd/ *v.t.,* **-dd-, rid: ~ sth. of sth.** etw. von etw. befreien; **~ oneself of sb./sth.** sich von jmdm./etw. befreien; **be ~ of sb./sth.** jmdn./etw. los sein (ugs.); **get ~ of sb./sth.** jmdn./etw. loswerden

riddance /'rɪdəns/ *n.* **good ~!** Gott sei Dank ist er/es usw. weg!

ridden ▶ RIDE 2, 3

riddle¹ /'rɪdl/ *n.* Rätsel, *das*

riddle² *v.t.* durchlöchern; **~d with bullets** von Kugeln durchsiebt

ride /raɪd/ **1** *n.* (on horseback) [Aus]ritt, *der;* (in vehicle, at fair) Fahrt, *die;* **~ in a train/coach** Zug-/Busfahrt, *die;* **go for a ~:** ausreiten; **go for a [bi]cycle ~:** Rad fahren; **go for a ~ [in the car]** [mit dem Auto] wegfahren; **take sb. for a ~** (fig. coll.: deceive) jmdn. reinlegen (ugs.)
2 *v.i.,* **rode** /rəʊd/, **ridden** /'rɪdn/ (on horse) reiten; (on bicycle, in vehicle) fahren; **~ to town on one's bike/in one's car/on the train** mit dem Rad/Auto/Zug in die Stadt fahren
3 *v.t.,* **rode, ridden** reiten ⟨*Pferd usw.*⟩; fahren mit ⟨*Fahrrad*⟩
■ **ride a'way, ride 'off** *v.i.* wegreiten/-fahren

'rider *n.* **(a)** Reiter, *der*/Reiterin, *die;* (of cycle) Fahrer, *der*/Fahrerin, *die*
(b) (addition) Zusatz, *der*

ridge /rɪdʒ/ *n.* **(a)** (of roof) First, *der*
(b) (long hilltop) Kamm, *der*
(c) (Meteorol.) **~ [of high pressure]** lang gestrecktes Hoch

ridicule /'rɪdɪkjuːl/ **1** *n.* Spott, *der*   ···❖

r

2 _v.t._ verspotten

ridiculous /rɪ'dɪkjʊləs/ _adj._ lächerlich

riding /'raɪdɪŋ/ _n._ Reiten, _das_

riding: ~ **lesson** _n._ Reitstunde, _die;_ ~ **school** _n._ Reitschule, _die_

rife /raɪf/ _pred. adj._ weit verbreitet

riff-raff /'rɪfræf/ _n._ Gesindel, _das_

rifle /'raɪfl/ 1 _n._ Gewehr, _das_ 2 _v.t._ durchwühlen 3 _v.i._ ~ **through sth.** etw. durchwühlen

rift /rɪft/ _n._ Unstimmigkeit, _die_

rig¹ /rɪɡ/ _n._ (for oil well) [Öl]förderturm, _der;_ (off shore) Förderinsel, _die_ ▪ **rig 'out** _v.t._ ausstaffieren ▪ **rig 'up** _v.t._ aufbauen

rig² _v.t.,_ **-gg-** manipulieren ‹[_Wahl_]_ergebnis_›; fälschen ‹_Wahl_›

rigging /'rɪɡɪŋ/ _n._ Takelung, _die_

right /raɪt/ 1 _adj._ (a) (just, morally good, sound) richtig (b) (correct, true) richtig; **you're [quite]** ~: du hast [völlig] recht; **be** ~ **in sth.** Recht mit etw. haben; **is that clock** ~? geht die Uhr da richtig?; **put** _or_ **set** ~: richtig stellen ‹_Irrtum, Behauptung_›; wieder gutmachen ‹_Unrecht_›; berichtigen ‹_Fehler_›; richtig stellen ‹_Uhr_›; **put** _or_ **set sb.** ~: jmdn. berichtigen; **that's** ~: ja[wohl]; so ist es; **is that** ~? stimmt das?; (indeed?) aha!; **[am I]** ~? nicht [wahr]? (c) (preferable, most suitable) richtig; recht; **do sth. the** ~ **way** etw. richtig machen (d) (opposite of left) recht...; **on the** ~ **side** rechts (e) **R**~ (Polit.) recht... 2 _v.t._ aus der Welt schaffen ‹_Unrecht_› 3 _n._ (a) (fair claim, authority) Recht, _das;_ **have a/no** ~ **to sth.** ein/kein Anrecht _od._ Recht auf etw. (_Akk._) haben; **in one's own** ~: aus eigenem Recht; ~ **of way** Vorfahrtsrecht, _das;_ **have** ~ **of way** Vorfahrt haben (b) (what is just) Recht, _das;_ **by** ~[s] von Rechts wegen; **in the** ~: im Recht (c) (~-hand side) rechte Seite; **on** _or_ **to the** ~ [**of sb./sth.**] rechts [von jmdm./etw.] (d) (Polit.) **the R**~: die Rechte 4 _adv._ (a) (correctly) richtig (b) (to the ~-hand side) nach rechts (c) (completely) ganz (d) (exactly) genau; ~ '**now** im Moment; jetzt sofort ‹_handeln_› (e) (straight) direkt

'**right angle** _n._ rechter Winkel; **at** ~**s to sth.** rechtwinklig zu etw.

righteous /'raɪtʃəs/ _adj._ rechtschaffen

rightful /'raɪtfl/ _adj._ rechtmäßig ‹_Besitzer, Herrscher_›

right: ~'**hand** _adj._ recht...; ~'**handed** 1 _adj._ rechtshändig; ‹_Werkzeug_› für Rechtshänder; **be** ~**handed** ‹_Person_:› Rechtshänder/Rechtshänderin sein; 2 _adv._ rechtshändig; ~-**hand 'man** _n._ rechte Hand

'**rightly** _adv._ zu Recht

right: ~'**minded** _adj._ gerecht denkend; ~**-to-'life** _attrib. adj._ Recht-auf-Leben-; ~ '**wing** _n._ rechter Flügel; ~**-wing** _adj._ (Polit.) rechtsgerichtet; Rechts‹_extremist, -intellektueller_›; ~**-winger** _n._ (a) (Sport) Rechtsaußen, _der;_ (b) (Polit.) Rechte, _der/die_

rigid /'rɪdʒɪd/ _adj._ (a) starr; (stiff) steif (b) (strict) streng; unbeugsam ‹_System_›

rigidity /rɪ'dʒɪtɪ/ _n._ ▶ RIGID: Starrheit, _die;_ Steifheit, _die;_ Strenge, _die_

rigmarole /'rɪɡmərəʊl/ _n._ (a) (talk) langatmiges Geschwafel (ugs.) (b) (procedure) Zirkus, _der_

rigor /'rɪɡə(r)/ (Amer.) ▶ RIGOUR

rigor mortis /rɪɡə 'mɔːtɪs/ _n._ Totenstarre, _die_

rigorous /'rɪɡərəs/ _adj._ streng

rigour /'rɪɡə(r)/ _n._ (Brit.) Strenge, _die_

rile /raɪl/ _v.t._ (coll.) ärgern

rim /rɪm/ _n._ Rand, _der;_ (of wheel) Felge, _die_

rind /raɪnd/ _n._ (of fruit) Schale, _die;_ (of cheese) Rinde, _die;_ (of bacon) Schwarte, _die_

ring¹ /rɪŋ/ 1 _n._ (a) Ring, _der_ (b) (Boxing) Ring, _der;_ (in circus) Manege, _die_ 2 _v.t._ (surround) umringen; einkreisen ‹_Wort usw._›

ring² /rɪŋ/ 1 _n._ (a) (act of sounding bell) Läuten, _das;_ Klingeln, _das_ (b) (Brit. coll.: telephone call) Anruf, _der;_ **give sb. a** ~: jmdn. anrufen (c) (fig.: impression) **have the** ~ **of truth [about it]** glaubhaft klingen 2 _v.i.,_ **rang** /ræŋ/, **rung** /rʌŋ/ (a) (sound clearly) [er]schallen; ‹_Hammer_:› [er]dröhnen (b) (be sounded) ‹_Glocke, Klingel, Telefon_:› läuten; ‹_Wecker, Telefon, Kasse_:› klingeln; **the doorbell rang** es klingelte (c) (~ bell) läuten (**for** nach) (d) (Brit.: make telephone call) anrufen 3 _v.t.,_ **rang, rung** (a) läuten ‹_Glocke_›; ~ **the [door]bell** läuten; klingeln; **it** ~**s a bell** (fig. coll.) es kommt mir [irgendwie] bekannt vor (b) (Brit.: telephone) anrufen ▪ **ring 'back** (Brit.) _v.t. & i._ (a) (again) wieder anrufen (b) (in return) zurückrufen ▪ **ring 'off** _v.i._ (Brit.) auflegen ▪ **ring 'out** _v.i._ ertönen ▪ **ring 'up** _v.t._ (Brit.: telephone) anrufen

ring: ~ **binder** _n._ Ringbuch, _das;_ ~ **finger** _n._ Ringfinger, _der_

ringing /'rɪŋɪŋ/ _n._ Läuten, _das;_ (Brit. Teleph.) ~ **tone** Freiton, _der_

'**ringleader** _n._ Anführer, _der_/Anführerin, _die_

ringlet /'rɪŋlɪt/ _n._ [Ringel]löckchen, _das_

'**ring road** _n._ Ringstraße, _die_

rink /rɪŋk/ _n._ (for ice skating) Eisbahn, _die;_ (for roller skating) Rollschuhbahn, _die_

rinse /rɪns/ 1 _v.t._ (a) (wash out) ausspülen ‹_Mund, Gefäß usw._›; (b) [aus]spülen ‹_Wäsche usw._›; abspülen ‹_Hände, Geschirr_›

2 *n.* Spülen, *das;* **give sth. a [good/quick]** ∼: etw. [gut/schnell] ausspülen/abspülen/ spülen

■ **rinse 'out** *v.t.* ausspülen

riot /'raɪət/ 1 *n.* Aufruhr, *der;* ∼s Unruhen *Pl.;* **run** ∼: randalieren

2 *v.i.* randalieren

'**rioter** *n.* Randalierer, *der*

'**riot gear** *n.* Schutzkleidung *od.* -ausrüstung

riotous /'raɪətəs/ *adj.* (a) gewalttätig (b) (unrestrained) wild

rip /rɪp/ 1 *n.* Riss, *der*

2 *v.t.*, **-pp-** zerreißen; ∼ **open** aufreißen

■ **rip 'off** *v.t.* (a) (remove from) reißen von; (remove) abreißen

(b) (coll.: defraud) übers Ohr hauen (ugs.)

■ **rip 'out** *v.t.* herausreißen (of aus)

RIP *abbr.* = **rest in peace** R.I.P.

'**ripcord** *n.* Reißleine, *die*

ripe /raɪp/ *adj.* reif (**for** zu)

ripen /'raɪpn/ 1 *v.t.* zur Reife bringen

2 *v.i.* reifen

'**ripeness** *n.* Reife, *die*

'**rip-off** *n.* (coll.) Nepp, *der* (ugs.)

riposte /rɪ'pɒst/ 1 *n.* (retort) [rasche] Entgegnung

2 *v.i.* [rasch] antworten

ripple /'rɪpl/ 1 *n.* kleine Welle

2 *v.i.* ⟨See:⟩ sich kräuseln; ⟨Welle:⟩ plätschern

3 *v.t.* kräuseln

rise /raɪz/ 1 *n.* (a) (advancement) Aufstieg, *der*

(b) (in value, price, cost) Steigerung, *die;* (in population, temperature) Zunahme, *die*

(c) (Brit.) [**pay**] ∼ (in wages) Lohnerhöhung, *die;* (in salary) Gehaltserhöhung, *die*

(d) (hill) Anhöhe, *die*

(e) **give** ∼ **to** führen zu; Anlass geben zu ⟨*Spekulation*⟩

2 *v.i.*, **rose** /rəʊz/, **risen** /'rɪzn/ (a) (go up) aufsteigen

(b) ⟨Sonne, Mond:⟩ aufgehen

(c) (increase, reach higher level) steigen

(d) (advance) ⟨Person:⟩ aufsteigen

(e) ⟨Teig, Kuchen:⟩ aufgehen

(f) (Theatre) ⟨Vorhang:⟩ aufgehen

(g) ⟨Fluss:⟩ entspringen

■ **rise 'up** *v.i.* (a) ∼ **up** [**in revolt**] aufbegehren (geh.)

(b) ⟨Berg:⟩ aufragen

risen ▶ RISE 2

'**riser** *n.* **early** ∼: Frühaufsteher, *der/* Frühaufsteherin, *die*

rising /'raɪzɪŋ/ 1 *n.* (of sun, moon, etc.) Aufgang, *der*

2 *adj.* (a) aufgehend ⟨Sonne, Mond usw.⟩

(b) steigend ⟨Kosten, Temperatur, Wasser, Flut⟩

(c) (sloping upwards) ansteigend

risk /rɪsk/ 1 *n.* Gefahr, *die;* (chance taken) Risiko, *das;* **at one's own** ∼: auf eigene

Gefahr *od.* eigenes Risiko; **take the** ∼ **of doing sth.** es riskieren, etw. zu tun; **be at** ∼ ⟨*Zukunft, Plan:*⟩ gefährdet sein

2 *v.t.* riskieren; **I'll** ∼ **it** ich lasse es darauf ankommen

'**risky** *adj.* gefährlich; gewagt ⟨*Experiment, Projekt*⟩

risotto /rɪ'zɒtəʊ/ *n., pl.* ∼s Risotto, *der od. das*

risqué /'rɪskeɪ/ *adj.* gewagt

rissole /'rɪsəʊl/ *n.* Frikadelle, *die*

rite /raɪt/ *n.* Ritus, *der*

ritual /'rɪtʃʊəl/ 1 *adj.* rituell; Ritual⟨mord, -tötung⟩

2 *n.* Ritual, *das*

rival /'raɪvl/ 1 *n.* (competitor) Rivale, *der/* Rivalin, *die;* **business** ∼s Konkurrenten *Pl.*

2 *v.t.*, (Brit.) **-ll-** nicht nachstehen (+ *Dat.*)

rivalry /'raɪvlrɪ/ *n.* Rivalität, *die* (geh.)

river /'rɪvə(r)/ *n.* Fluss, *das*

river: ∼ **bank** Flussufer, *der;* ∼ **basin** *n.* Stromgebiet, *das;* ∼ **bed** *n.* Flussbett, *das* ∼**side** 1 *n.* Flussufer, *das;* 2 *attrib. adj.* am Fluss gelegen; am Fluss *nachgestellt*

rivet /'rɪvɪt/ 1 *n.* Niete, *die*

2 *v.t.* (a) [ver]nieten

(b) (fig.) fesseln

'**riveting** *adj.* fesselnd

rivulet /'rɪvjʊlɪt/ *n.* Bach, *der*

RN *abbr.* (Brit.) = **Royal Navy** Königl. Mar.

road /rəʊd/ *n.* Straße, *die;* **across** *or* **over the** ∼ [**from us**] [bei uns] gegenüber; **by** ∼ (by car/bus/lorry) per Auto/Bus/Lkw; **be on the** ∼: auf Reisen *od.* unterwegs sein; ⟨*Theaterensemble usw.:*⟩ auf Tournee *od.* Tour sein

road: ∼ **accident** *n.* Verkehrsunfall, *der;* ∼ **atlas** *n.* Autoatlas, *der;* ∼**block** *n.* Straßensperre, *die;* ∼ **bridge** *n.* Straßenbrücke, *die;* ∼ **haulage** *n.* Gütertransport auf der Straße; ∼ **hog** *n.* Verkehrsrowdy, *der;* ∼ **hump** ▶ SPEED BUMP

roadie /'rəʊdɪ/ *n.* (coll.) Roadie, *der*

road: ∼ **manager** *n.* Roadmanager, *der;* ∼ **map** *n.* Straßenkarte, *die;* ∼**mender** *n.* Straßen[bau]arbeiter, *der/*-arbeiterin, *die;* ∼ **rage** *n.:* häufig zu gewalttätigen *Ausbrüchen führende Wut eines Autofahrers;* ∼ **safety** *n.* Verkehrssicherheit, *die;* ∼ **sense** *n.* Gespür für Verkehrssituationen; ∼**side** *n.* Straßenrand, *der;* **at** *or* **by/along the** ∼**side** am Straßenrand; ∼ **sign** *n.* Verkehrszeichen, *das;* Straßenschild, *das* (ugs.); ∼ **sweeper** *n.* Straßenkehrer, *der/* -kehrerin, *die;* ∼ **tax** *n.* (Brit.) Kraftfahrzeugsteuer, *die;* Kfz-Steuer, *die;* ∼ **transport** *n.* Personen- und Güterförderung auf der Straße; **form of** ∼ **transport** Verkehrsmittel der Straße; ∼ **user** *n.* Verkehrsteilnehmer, *der/* ⋯⟩

-teilnehmerin, *die;* ~**way** *n.* Fahrbahn, *die;*
~**works** *n. pl.* Straßenbauarbeiten *Pl.;*
~**worthy** *adj.* fahrtüchtig

roam /rəʊm/ [1] *v.i.* umherstreifen
[2] *v.t.* streifen durch

roar /rɔː(r)/ [1] *n.* (of wild beast) Gebrüll, *das;*
(of applause) Tosen, *das;* (of engine, traffic)
Dröhnen, *das;* ~s/a ~ [of laughter]
dröhnendes Gelächter
[2] *v.i.* brüllen (**with** vor + *Dat.*); ⟨*Motor.*⟩
dröhnen

'**roaring** *adj.* (a) bullernd (ugs.) ⟨*Feuer*⟩
(b) a ~ **success** ein Bombenerfolg; do a
~ **trade** ein Bombengeschäft machen

roast /rəʊst/ [1] *v.t.* braten; rösten
⟨*Kaffeebohnen, Kastanien*⟩
[2] *attrib. adj.* gebraten ⟨*Fleisch, Ente usw.*⟩;
Brat⟨*hähnchen, -kartoffeln*⟩; Röst⟨*kastanien*⟩;
~ **beef** (sirloin) Roastbeef, *das*
[3] *n.* Braten, *der*

rob /rɒb/ *v.t.,* -**bb**- ausrauben ⟨*Bank, Safe,
Kasse*⟩; berauben ⟨*Person*⟩

robber /'rɒbə(r)/ *n.* Räuber, *der*/Räuberin,
die

robbery /'rɒbərɪ/ *n.* Raub, *der;* **robberies**
Raubüberfälle *Pl.*

robe /rəʊb/ *n.* Gewand, *das* (*geh.*); (of judge,
vicar) Talar, *der*

robin /'rɒbɪn/ *n.* ~ [**redbreast**] Rotkehlchen,
das

robot /'rəʊbɒt/ *n.* Roboter, *der*

robotics /rəʊ'bɒtɪks/ *n.* Robotertechnik,
die; Robotik, *die*

robust /rəʊ'bʌst/ *adj.* robust

rock[1] /rɒk/ *n.* (a) (piece of ~) Fels, *der,*
(b) (large ~, hill) Felsen, *der*
(c) (substance) Fels, *der;* (esp. Geol.) Gestein,
das
(d) (boulder) Felsbrocken, *der;* (Amer.: stone)
Stein, *der*
(e) stick of ~: Zuckerstange, *die*
(f) be on the ~s (fig. coll.) ⟨*Ehe, Firma*⟩
kaputt sein (ugs.)

rock[2] [1] *v.t.* wiegen; (in cradle) schaukeln
[2] *v.i.* (a) schaukeln
(b) (sway) schwanken
[3] *n.* (Mus.) Rock, *der; attrib.* Rock-; ~ **and or**
'**n' roll** [**music**] Rock and Roll, *der*

rock: ~-'**bottom** (coll.) [1] *adj.* ~-**bottom**
prices Schleuderpreise *Pl.* (ugs.); [2] *n.* **reach**
or **touch** ~-**bottom** ⟨*Handel, Preis*⟩ in den
Keller fallen (ugs.); **her spirits reached**
~-**bottom** ihre Stimmung war auf dem
Tiefpunkt; ~ **climber** *n.* Kletterer, *der*/
Kletterin, *die;* ~ **climbing** *n.*
[Fels]klettern, *das*

rocker /'rɒkə(r)/ *n.* **be off one's** ~ (fig. coll.)
übergeschnappt *od.* durchgedreht sein (ugs.)

rockery /'rɒkərɪ/ *n.* Steingarten, *der*

rocket /'rɒkɪt/ [1] *n.* Rakete, *die*
[2] *v.i.* ⟨*Preise*⟩ in die Höhe schnellen

rocket: ~ **base** *n.* (Mil.)

Raketen[abschuss]basis, *die;* ~ **launcher**
n. Raketenwerfer, *der;* ~-**propelled** *adj.*
raketengetrieben

rock: ~ **face** *n.* Felswand, *die;* ~**fall** *n.*
Steinschlag, *der;* ~ **formation** *n.*
Gesteinsformation, *die;* ~ **garden** *n.*
Steingarten, *der;* ~-**hard** *adj.* steinhart

rocking: ~ **chair** *n.* Schaukelstuhl, *der;*
~ **horse** *n.* Schaukelpferd, *das*

rock: ~ **plant** *n.* Felsenpflanze, *die;* (Hort.)
Steingartengewächs, *das;* ~ **salt** *n.*
Steinsalz, *das*

'**rocky** *adj.* (a) felsig
(b) (coll.: unsteady) wackelig (ugs.)

rod /rɒd/ *n.* Stange, *die;* (for punishing) Rute,
die; (for fishing) [Angel]rute, *die*

rode ▶ RIDE 2, 3

rodent /'rəʊdənt/ *n.* Nagetier, *das*

rodeo /'rəʊdɪəʊ, rəʊ'deɪəʊ/ *n., pl.* ~**s** Rodeo,
der od. das

roe[1] /rəʊ/ *n.* (of fish) [**hard**] ~: Rogen, *der;*
[**soft**] ~: Milch, *die*

roe[2] *n.* ~ [**deer**] Reh, *das*

rogue /rəʊg/ *n.* Gauner, *der*

role, rôle /rəʊl/ *n.* Rolle, *die*

role: ~ **model** *n.* Leitbild, *das;*
~ **playing** *n.* Rollenspiel, *das;*
~ **reversal** *n.* Rollentausch, *der*

roll[1] /rəʊl/ *n.* (a) Rolle, *die;* (of cloth etc.)
Ballen, *der;* ~ **of film** Rolle Film
(b) [**bread**] ~: Brötchen, *das*
(c) **be on a** ~ (coll.) eine Glückssträhne
haben

roll[2] [1] *n.* (of drum) Wirbel, *der*
[2] *v.t.* (a) rollen; (between surfaces) drehen
(b) (shape by ~ing) rollen; drehen ⟨*Zigarette*⟩
(c) walzen ⟨*Rasen, Metall usw.*⟩; ausrollen
⟨*Teig*⟩
[3] *v.i.* (a) rollen
(b) ⟨*Maschine*⟩ laufen; **get sth.** ~**ing** (fig.)
etw. ins Rollen bringen
(c) **be** ~**ing in money** *or* **in it** (coll.) im Geld
schwimmen (ugs.)
■ **roll a'bout** *v.i.* herumrollen; ⟨*Schiff*⟩
schlingern; ⟨*Kind, Hund*⟩ sich wälzen
■ **roll 'back** *v.t.* zurückrollen
■ **roll 'by** *v.i.* ⟨*Zeit*⟩ vergehen
■ **roll 'in** *v.i.* (coll.) ⟨*Briefe, Geldbeträge*⟩
eingehen
■ **roll 'out** *v.t.* ausrollen ⟨*Teig, Teppich*⟩
■ **roll 'over** *v.i.* ⟨*Person*⟩ sich umdrehen, (to
make room) sich zur Seite rollen
■ **roll 'up** [1] *v.t.* aufrollen ⟨*Teppich*⟩;
zusammenrollen ⟨*Landkarte, Dokument
usw.*⟩; hochkrempeln ⟨*Ärmel*⟩
[2] *v.i.* (coll.: arrive) aufkreuzen (salopp)

'**roll-call** *n.* Ausrufen aller Namen; (Mil.)
Zählappell, *der*

rolled 'oats *n. pl.* Haferflocken *Pl.*

'**roller** *n.* (a) Rolle, *die;* (for lawn, road, etc.)
Walze, *die*
(b) (for hair) Lockenwickler, *der*

roller: R~**blade** ® *n.* Rollerblade, *der;*

Inliner, der; ~**blade** v.i. Rollerblades
fahren; ~ **blind** n. Rouleau, das;
~ **coaster** n. Achterbahn, die; ~ **skate**
n. Rollschuh, der; ~**skate** v.i. Rollschuh
laufen; ~ **skating** n. Rollschuhlaufen, das

'**roll film** n. Rollfilm, der

'**rolling** adj. wellig ‹Gelände›; ~ **hills** sanfte
Hügel Pl.

rolling: ~ **pin** n. Teigrolle, die; ~ **stock**
n. (Brit. Railw.) Fahrzeugbestand, der

roll: ~**neck** ① n. Rollkragen, der; ② adj.
Rollkragen-; ~**on** ~**off** adj. ~-on ~-off
ship/ferry Roll-on-roll-off-Schiff, das/-Fähre,
die; ~**over** n. (von Auslosung zu
Auslosung) aufgestockter Jackpot; ~**up**
(Brit. coll.), ~**your-own** (esp. Amer. coll.) ns.
Selbstgedrehte, die

ROM /rɒm/ abbr. (Comp.) = **read only
memory** ROM

Roman /'rəʊmən/ ① n. Römer, der/
Römerin, die
② adj. römisch

Roman 'Catholic ① adj. römisch-
katholisch
② n. Katholik, der/Katholikin, die; **sb. is a**
~: jmd. ist römisch-katholisch

romance /rə'mæns/ n. (a) (love affair)
Romanze, die
(b) (love story) [romantische]
Liebesgeschichte

Romania /rəʊ'meɪnɪə/ pr. n. Rumänien
(das)

Romanian /rəʊ'meɪnɪən/ ① adj.
rumänisch; **sb. is** ~: jmd. ist Romäne/
Romänin
② n. (a) (person) Rumäne, der/Rumänin, die
(b) (language) Rumänisch, das; see also
ENGLISH 2A

Roman 'numeral n. römische Ziffer

romantic /rəʊ'mæntɪk/ adj. romantisch

romanticism /rəʊ'mæntɪsɪzm/ n. (Lit., Art.,
Mus.) Romantik, die

romanticize /rəʊ'mæntɪsaɪz/ v.t.
romantisieren

'**roman type** n. (Printing) Antiquaschrift,
die

Romany /'rəʊmənɪ/ ① (a) (person) Rom,
der
(b) (language) Romani, das
② adj. Roma-; (Ling.) Romani-

Rome /rəʊm/ pr. n. Rom (das)

romp /rɒmp/ ① v.i. (a) [herum]tollen
(b) ~ **home** or **in** (coll.: win easily) spielend
gewinnen
② n. Tollerei, die

rompers /'rɒmpəz/ n. pl. Spielhöschen, das

roof /ruːf/ ① n. (a) Dach, das
(b) ~ **of the mouth** Gaumen, der
② v.t. bedachen

'**roof garden** Dachgarten, der

'**roofing** n. (material) Deckung, die

'**roof:** ~ **rack** n. Dachgepäckträger, der;
~**top** n. Dach, das

rook[1] /rʊk/ n. (Ornith.) Saatkrähe, die

rook[2] n. (Chess) Turm, der

rookery /'rʊkərɪ/ n. Saatkrähenkolonie, die

room /ruːm, rʊm/ n. (a) (in building) Zimmer,
das; (for function) Saal, der
(b) (space) Platz, der; **make** ~ **[for sb./sth.]**
[jmdm./einer Sache] Platz machen; **there is
still** ~ **for improvement in his work** seine
Arbeit ist noch verbesserungsfähig

room: ~**mate** n. Zimmergenosse, der/
-genossin, die; ~ **service** n.
Zimmerservice, der; ~ **temperature** n.
Zimmertemperatur, die

roomy /'ruːmɪ/ adj. geräumig

roost /ruːst/ ① n. [Sitz]stange, die
② v.i. ‹Vogel:› sich [zum Schlafen]
niederlassen

root[1] /ruːt/ ① n. Wurzel, die; **put down** ~s/
take ~: Wurzeln schlagen
② v.i. ‹Pflanze:› wurzeln
③ v.t. **stand** ~**ed to the spot** wie
angewurzelt dastehen
▪ **root 'out** v.t. ausrotten

root[2] v.i. (a) (turn up ground) wühlen (for
nach)
(b) (coll.) ~ **for** (cheer) anfeuern

'**root crop[s]** n. [pl.] Hackfrüchte Pl.

'**rooted** adj. eingewurzelt

'**rootless** adj. wurzellos

'**root vegetable** n. Wurzelgemüse, das

rope /rəʊp/ ① n. (a) (cord) Seil, das
(b) **know the** ~s sich auskennen
② v.t. festbinden
▪ **rope 'in** v.t. (fig.) einspannen (ugs.)

rope 'ladder n. Strickleiter, die

ro-ro /'rəʊrəʊ/ adj. Ro-Ro-‹Schiff, Fähre›

rosary /'rəʊzərɪ/ n. Rosenkranz, der

rose[1] /rəʊz/ n. (a) (plant, flower) Rose, die
(b) (colour) Rosa, das

rose[2] ► RISE 2

rosé /'rəʊzeɪ, 'rəʊzeɪ/ n. Rosé, der

rose: ~ **bed** n. Rosenbeet, das; ~**bud** n.
Rosenknospe, die; ~ **bush** n. Rosenstrauch,
der; ~ **hip** n. Hagebutte, die

rosemary /'rəʊzmərɪ/ n. Rosmarin, der

'**rose petal** n. Rosen[blüten]blatt, das

rosette /rəʊ'zet/ n. Rosette, die

roster /'rɒstə(r)/ n. Dienstplan, der

rostrum /'rɒstrəm/ n., pl. **rostra** /'rɒstrə/
or ~s Podium, das

rosy /'rəʊzɪ/ adj. rosig

rot /rɒt/ ① n. (a) ► 2: Verrottung, die;
Fäulnis, die; (fig.: deterioration) Verfall, der;
stop the ~ (fig.) dem Verfall Einhalt gebieten
(b) (coll.: nonsense) Quark, der (salopp)
② v.i., -tt- verrotten; ‹Fleisch, Gemüse,
Obst:› verfaulen
③ v.t., -tt- verrotten lassen; verfaulen lassen
‹Fleisch, Gemüse, Obst›; zerstören ‹Zähne›

rota /'rəʊtə/ n. (Brit.) (order of rotation) Turnus,
der; (list) Arbeitsplan, der

rotary /'rəʊtərɪ/ adj. rotierend

r

rotate /rəʊ'teɪt/ ① *v.i.* (revolve) rotieren; sich drehen
② *v.t.* in Rotation versetzen
rotation /rəʊ'teɪʃn/ *n.* (a) Rotation, *die,* Drehung, *die* (about um)
(b) (succession) turnusmäßiger Wechsel; **in** *or* **by ~:** im Turnus
rote /rəʊt/ *n.* **by ~:** auswendig
rotten /'rɒtn/ *adj.,* **~er** /'rɒtənə(r)/, **~est** /'rɒtənɪst/ (a) (decayed) verrottet; verfault ⟨*Obst, Gemüse*⟩; faul ⟨*Ei, Holz, Zähne*⟩; **~ to the core** (fig.) verdorben bis ins Mark
(b) (corrupt) verdorben
(c) (coll.: bad) mies (ugs.)
rotund /rəʊ'tʌnd/ *adj.* (a) (round) rund
(b) (plump) rundlich
rouble /'ru:bl/ *n.* Rubel, *der*
rouge /ru:ʒ/ *n.* Rouge, *das*
rough /rʌf/ ① *adj.* (a) (coarse, uneven) rau; holp[e]rig ⟨*Straße usw.*⟩; uneben ⟨*Gelände*⟩; unruhig ⟨*Überfahrt*⟩
(b) (violent) grob ⟨*Person, Worte, Behandlung*⟩
(c) (trying) hart; **this is ~ on him** das ist hart für ihn; **sth. is ~ going** etw. ist nicht einfach
(d) (approximate) grob ⟨*Skizze, Schätzung*⟩; vag ⟨*Vorstellung*⟩; **~ paper/notebook** Konzeptpapier, *das*/Kladde, *die*
(e) (coll.: ill) angeschlagen (ugs.)
② *n.* [**be**] **in ~:** [sich] im Rohzustand [befinden]
③ *adv.* rau ⟨*spielen*⟩; **sleep ~:** im Freien schlafen
④ *v.t.* **~ it** primitiv leben
■ **rough 'out** *v.t.* grob entwerfen
■ **rough 'up** *v.t.* (coll.) zusammenschlagen
roughage /'rʌfɪdʒ/ *n.* Ballaststoffe *Pl.*
rough: ~and-ready *adj.* provisorisch; **~ and 'tumble** *n.* [milde] Rauferei; **~ copy, ~ draft** *ns.* grobe Skizze; grober Entwurf; **~ 'diamond** *n.* (fig.) ungehobelter, aber guter Mensch
roughen /'rʌfn/ *v.t.* aufrauen
rough: ~ 'justice *n.* ziemlich willkürliche Urteile *Pl.;* **~ 'luck** *n.* Pech, *das*
'roughly *adv.* (a) (violently) roh; grob
(b) (crudely) leidlich; grob ⟨*skizzieren, bearbeiten, bauen*⟩
(c) (approximately) ungefähr; grob ⟨*geschätzt*⟩
'roughness *n.* (a) Rauheit, *die;* (unevenness) Unebenheit, *die*
(b) (violence) Rohheit, *die*
'roughshod *adj.* **ride ~ over sb./sth.** jmdn./etw. mit Füßen treten
roulette /ru:'let/ *n.* Roulette, *das*
round /raʊnd/ ① *adj.* rund; **in ~ figures** rund gerechnet
② *n.* (a) (recurring series) Serie, *die;* **~ of talks/negotiations** Gesprächs-/Verhandlungsrunde, *die;* **the daily ~:** der Alltag
(b) (of ammunition) Ladung, *die;* **50 ~s [of ammunition]** 50 Schuss Munition
(c) (of game or contest) Runde, *die*
(d) (burst) **~ of applause** Beifallssturm, *der*
(e) **~ [of drinks]** Runde, *die*

(f) (regular calls) Runde, *die;* Tour, *die;* **go [on]** *or* **make one's ~s** seine Runden machen
(g) **a ~ of toast/sandwiches** eine Scheibe Toast/eine Portion Sandwiches
③ *adv.* (a) **all the year ~:** das ganze Jahr hindurch; **the third time ~:** beim dritten Mal; **have a look ~:** sich umsehen; **ask sb. ~ [for a drink]** jmdn. [zu einem Gläschen zu sich] einladen
(b) (by indirect way) herum; **walk ~:** außen herum gehen
(c) (here) hier; (there) dort; **I'll go ~ tomorrow** ich gehe morgen hin
④ *prep.* (a) um [… herum]; **travel ~ England** durch England reisen; **run ~ the streets** durch die Straßen rennen; **walk ~ and ~ sth.** immer wieder um etw. herumgehen
(b) (in various directions from) um [… herum]; rund um ⟨*einen Ort*⟩
⑤ *v.t.* **a bend** um eine Kurve fahren/gehen/kommen *usw*
■ **round 'off** *v.t.* abrunden
■ **round 'up** *v.t.* verhaften ⟨*Verdächtige*⟩; zusammentreiben ⟨*Vieh*⟩
round: ~ a'bout *adv.* (on all sides) ringsum; **~about** ① *n.* (a) (Brit.: merry-go-round) Karussell, *das;* (b) (Brit.: road junction) Kreisverkehr, *der.* ② *adj.* umständlich; **~ 'brackets** *n. pl.* runde Klammern *Pl.*
rounded /'raʊndɪd/ *adj.* (a) rund
(b) harmonisch ⟨*Person*⟩
rounders /'raʊndəz/ *n. sing.* (Brit.) Rounders, *das;* ≈ Schlagball, *der*
round: ~ 'number *n.* runde Zahl; **~ 'robin** *n.* Petition, *die;* **~-shouldered** /raʊnd'ʃəʊldəd/ *adj.* ⟨*Person*⟩ mit einem Rundrücken; **~-the-'clock** *adj.* rund um die Uhr *nachgestellt;* **~ 'trip** *n.* Rundreise, *die;* **~-up** *n.* (a) (of animals) Zusammentreiben, *das;* (b) (summary) Zusammenfassung, *die*
rouse /raʊz/ *v.t.* wecken (**from** aus)
rousing /'raʊzɪŋ/ *adj.* mitreißend ⟨*Lied*⟩; leidenschaftlich ⟨*Rede*⟩
rout /raʊt/ ① *n.* [wilde] Flucht; (defeat) verheerende Niederlage
② *v.t.* aufreiben ⟨*Feind, Truppen*⟩; vernichtend schlagen ⟨*Gegner*⟩
route /ru:t/ *n.* Route, *die;* Weg, *der*
'route march *n.* (Mil.) Übungsmarsch, *der*
routine /ru:'ti:n/ ① *n.* (a) Routine, *die*
(b) (coll.: set speech) Platte, *die* (ugs.)
(c) (Theatre) Nummer, *die;* (Dancing, Skating) Figur, *die*
② *adj.* routinemäßig; Routine⟨*arbeit*⟩
roux /ru:/ *n.* Mehlschwitze, *die*
row¹ /raʊ/ ① (coll.) *n.* (a) (noise) Krach, *der;* **make a ~:** Krach machen
(b) (quarrel) Krach, *der* (ugs.); **have/start a ~:** Krach haben/anfangen (ugs.)
② *v.i.* sich streiten
row² /rəʊ/ *n.* Reihe, *die;* **in a ~:** in einer Reihe
row³ /rəʊ/ *v.i. & t.* (with oars) rudern

rowan /'rəʊən/ n. ~ [tree] Eberesche, *die*
rowboat /'rəʊbəʊt/ n. (Amer.) Ruderboot, *das*
rowdy /'raʊdɪ/ 1 adj. rowdyhaft; **the party was** ~: auf der Party ging es laut zu 2 n. Krawallmacher, *der*
rower /'rəʊə(r)/ n. Ruderer, *der*/Ruderin, *die*
rowing /'rəʊɪŋ/ n. Rudern, *das*
rowing: ~ **boat** n. (Brit.) Ruderboot, *das;* ~ **machine** n. Rudergerät, *das*
royal /'rɔɪəl/ adj. königlich
royal: R~ **'Air Force** n. (Brit.) Königliche Luftwaffe; ~ **'blue** n. (Brit.) Königsblau, *das;* ~ **'family** n. königliche Familie; **R**~ **'Navy** n. (Brit.) Königliche Kriegsmarine
royalty /'rɔɪəltɪ/ n. (a) (payment) Tantieme, *die* (on für)
(b) collect. (royal persons) Mitglieder *Pl.* des Königshauses
RSI abbr. = **repetitive strain injury**
RSPCA abbr. (Brit.) = **Royal Society for the Prevention of Cruelty to Animals** *britischer Tierschutzverein*
rub /rʌb/ 1 v.t., **-bb-** reiben (**on, against** an + Dat.); (to remove dirt etc.) abreiben; (to dry) trockenreiben; ~ **sth. off sth.** etw. von etw. [ab]reiben
2 v.i., **-bb-** reiben ([up]**on, against** an + Dat.)
3 n. give it a ~: reib es ab; there's the ~ (fig.) da liegt der Haken [dabei] (ugs.)
▪ **rub 'down** v.t. abreiben
▪ **rub 'in** v.t. einreiben; **there's no need to** or **don't** ~ **it in** (fig.) reib es mir nicht [dauernd] unter die Nase
▪ **rub 'off** v.t. wegreiben; wegwischen
▪ **rub 'out** 1 v.t. ausreiben; (using eraser) ausradieren
2 v.i. sich ausreiben/sich ausradieren lassen
rubber /'rʌbə(r)/ n. (a) Gummi, *das od. der*
(b) (eraser) Radiergummi, *der*
rubber: ~ **'band** n. Gummiband, *das;* ~ **'glove** n. Gummihandschuh, *der;* ~ **'plant** n. Gummibaum, *der;* ~ **'stamp** n. Gummistempel, *der;* ~**-stamp** v.t. (fig.) absegnen (ugs.)
rubbery /'rʌbərɪ/ adj. gummiartig; (tough) zäh
rubbish /'rʌbɪʃ/ 1 n. (a) (refuse) Abfall, *der;* (to be collected and dumped) Müll, *der*
(b) (worthless material) Plunder, *der* (ugs.); **be** ~: nichts taugen
(c) (nonsense) Quatsch, *der* (ugs.)
2 int. Quatsch (ugs.)
rubbish: ~ **bin** n. Abfall-/Mülleimer, *der;* (in factory) Abfall-/Mülltonne, *die;* ~ **chute** n. Müllschlucker, *der;* ~ **collection** n. Müllabfuhr, *die;* ~ **dump** n. Müllkippe, *die;* ~ **heap** n. Müllhaufen, *der;* ~ **tip** n. Müllabladeplatz, *der*

rubbishy /'rʌbɪʃɪ/ adj. mies (ugs.)
rubble /'rʌbl/ n. Trümmer *Pl.*
rubella /rʊ'belə/ n. (Med.) Röteln *Pl.*
ruby /'ruːbɪ/ n. Rubin, *der*
ruby 'wedding n. Rubinhochzeit, *die*
rucksack /'rʌksæk, 'rʊksæk/ n. Rucksack, *der*
rudder /'rʌdə(r)/ n. [Steuer]ruder, *das*
ruddy /'rʌdɪ/ adj. (a) (reddish) rötlich
(b) (Brit. coll.: bloody) verdammt (salopp)
rude /ruːd/ adj. (a) unhöflich; (stronger) rüde; **be** ~ **to sb.** zu jmdm. grob unhöflich sein/jmdn. rüde behandeln
(b) (abrupt) unsanft; ~ **awakening** böses Erwachen
'rudely adv. (a) (impolitely) unhöflich; rüde
(b) (abruptly) jäh (geh.)
'rudeness n. (bad manners) ungehöriges Benehmen
rudimentary /ruːdɪ'mentərɪ/ elementar; primitiv ‹Gebäude›
rudiments /'ruːdɪmənts/ n. pl. Grundlagen *Pl.*
rueful /'ruːfl/ adj. reumütig
ruffian /'rʌfɪən/ n. Rohling, *der*
ruffle /'rʌfl/ v.t. (a) kräuseln; ~ **sb.'s hair** jmdm. durch die Haare fahren
(b) (upset) aus der Fassung bringen
rug /rʌg/ n. (a) [kleiner, dicker] Teppich; **Persian** ~: Perserbrücke, *die*
Rugby /'rʌgbɪ/ n. Rugby, *das*
Rugby: ~ **ball** n. Rugbyball, *der;* ~ **tackle** n. tiefes Fassen; **the policeman brought him down with a** ~ **tackle** der Polizist warf sich auf ihn und riss ihn zu Boden
rugged /'rʌgɪd/ adj. (a) (uneven) zerklüftet; unwegsam ‹Land›; zerfurcht ‹Gesicht›
(b) (sturdy) robust
ruin /'ruːɪn/ 1 n. (a) in sing. or pl. (remains) Ruine, *die;* **in** ~**s** in Trümmern
(b) (downfall) Ruin, *der*
2 v.t. ruinieren; verderben ‹Urlaub, Abend›; ~**ed** (reduced to ruins) verfallen; **a** ~**ed castle/church** eine Burg-/Kirchenruine
ruinous /'ruːɪnəs/ adj. ruinös
rule /ruːl/ 1 n. (a) Regel, *die;* **the** ~**s of the game** die Spielregeln; **be against the** ~**s** regelwidrig sein; (fig.) gegen die Spielregeln verstoßen; **as a** ~: in der Regel; ~ **of thumb** Faustregel, *die*
(b) no pl. (government) Herrschaft, *die* (**over** über + Akk.)
2 v.t. (a) (control) beherrschen
(b) (be the ruler of) regieren; ‹Monarch, Diktator usw.:› herrschen über (+ Akk.)
3 v.i. (a) (govern) herrschen
(b) (decide) entscheiden (**against** gegen; **in favour of** für)
▪ **rule 'out** v.t. ausschließen; (prevent) unmöglich machen
'rule book n. Regeln *Pl.*
ruled /ruːld/ adj. liniert ‹Papier›

r

ruler /'ruːlə(r)/ *n.* **(a)** (person) Herrscher,
der/Herrscherin, *die*
  (b) (for measuring) Lineal, *das*

ruling /'ruːlɪŋ/ **1** *adj.* herrschend ⟨*Klasse*⟩;
regierend ⟨*Partei*⟩
  2 *n.* Entscheidung, *die*

rum /rʌm/ *n.* Rum, *der*

Rumania *etc.* /ruːˈmeɪnɪə/ ▶ ROMANIA *etc.*

rumble /'rʌmbl/ **1** *n.* Grollen, *das*
  2 *v.i.* **(a)** grollen; ⟨*Magen:*⟩ knurren
  (b) ⟨*Fahrzeug:*⟩ rumpeln (ugs.)

ruminate /'ruːmɪneɪt/ *v.i.* ~ on *or* over sth.
über etw. (*Akk.*) grübeln

rummage /'rʌmɪdʒ/ *v.i.* wühlen; ~ through
sth. etw. durchwühlen (ugs.)

rummy /'rʌmɪ/ *n.* Rommé, *das*

rumour (*Brit.; Amer.:* **rumor**) /'ruːmə(r)/
1 *n.* Gerücht, *das;* there is a ~ that …: es
geht das Gerücht, dass …
  2 *v.t.* it is ~ed that …: es geht das Gerücht,
dass …

rump /rʌmp/ *n.* **(a)** (buttocks) Hinterteil, *das*
(ugs.)
  (b) (remnant) Rest, *der*

rumple /'rʌmpl/ *v.t.* **(a)** (crease) zerknittern
  (b) (tousle) zerzausen

'rump steak *n.* Rumpsteak, *das*

rumpus /'rʌmpəs/ *n.* (coll.) Krach, *der* (ugs.);
kick up *or* make a ~: einen Spektakel
veranstalten (ugs.)

'rumpus room *n.* (Amer.) Spielzimmer, *das*

run /rʌn/ **1** *n.* **(a)** Lauf, *der;* go for a ~:
laufen gehen; on the ~ (fleeing) auf der
Flucht
  (b) (trip in vehicle) Fahrt, *die;* (for pleasure)
Ausflug, *der*
  (c) (continuous stretch) Länge, *die*
  (d) (spell) she has had a long ~ of success
sie war lange [Zeit] erfolgreich; have a long
~ ⟨*Stück, Show:*⟩ viele Aufführungen
erleben
  (e) (succession) Serie, *die;* (Cards) Sequenz, *die;*
a ~ of victories eine Siegesserie
  (f) (use) have the ~ of sth. etw. zu seiner
freien Verfügung haben
  (g) (enclosure) Auslauf, *der*
  (h) (in stocking etc.) Laufmasche, *die*
  2 *v.i.,* -nn-, ran /ræn/, run **(a)** laufen; ~ for
the bus laufen, um den Bus zu kriegen (ugs.);
~ to help sb. jmdm. zu Hilfe eilen
  (b) (roll, slide) laufen; ⟨*Ball, Kugel:*⟩ rollen,
laufen; ⟨*Schlitten,* [*Schiebe*]*tür:*⟩ gleiten
  (c) ⟨*Rad, Maschine:*⟩ laufen
  (d) (operate on a schedule) fahren; ~ between
two places ⟨*Zug, Bus:*⟩ zwischen zwei Orten
verkehren
  (e) (flow) laufen; ⟨*Fluss:*⟩ fließen; ⟨*Augen:*⟩
tränen; his nose was ~ning ihm lief die
Nase
  (f) ⟨*Vertrag, Theaterstück:*⟩ laufen
  (g) (have wording) lauten; ⟨*Geschichte:*⟩ gehen
(fig.)
  (h) ⟨*Butter, Eis:*⟩ zerlaufen; ⟨*Farben:*⟩
auslaufen

  (i) (in election) kandidieren
  3 *v.t.,* -nn-, ran, run **(a)** laufen lassen; (drive)
fahren; ~ one's hand/fingers through/along
or over sth. mit der Hand/den Fingern durch
etw. fahren/über etw. (*Akk.*) streichen; ~ an
or one's eye along *or* down *or* over sth. (fig.)
etw. überfliegen
  (b) (cause to flow) [ein]laufen lassen; ~ a bath
ein Bad einlaufen lassen
  (c) (organize, manage) führen, leiten ⟨*Geschäft
usw.*⟩; veranstalten ⟨*Wettbewerb*⟩
  (d) (operate) bedienen ⟨*Maschine*⟩; verkehren
lassen ⟨*Verkehrsmittel*⟩; einsetzen
⟨*Sonderbus, -zug*⟩; laufen lassen ⟨*Motor*⟩
  (e) (own and use) sich (*Dat.*) halten ⟨*Auto*⟩
  (f) ~ sb. into town *etc.* jmdn. in die Stadt
usw. fahren
■ **run a'cross** *v.t.* ~ across sb./sth. jmdn.
treffen/auf etw. (*Akk.*) stoßen
■ **run a'way** *v.i.* **(a)** (flee) weglaufen;
fortlaufen
  (b) (abscond) ~ away [from home] [von zu
Hause] weglaufen
■ **run 'down** **1** *v.t.* **(a)** (collide with)
überfahren
  (b) (criticize) heruntermachen (ugs.)
  (c) (reduce) abbauen
  2 *v.i.* **(a)** hin-/herunterlaufen
  (b) (decline) sich verringern
  (c) ⟨*Uhr, Spielzeug:*⟩ ablaufen; ⟨*Batterie*⟩ leer
werden
■ **run 'into** *v.t.* **(a)** ~ into a tree gegen einen
Baum fahren
  (b) (meet) ~ into sb. jmdm. in die Arme
laufen (ugs.)
  (c) stoßen auf (+ *Akk.*) ⟨*Schwierigkeiten,
Widerstand usw.*⟩
  (d) (amount to) ~ into thousands in die
tausende gehen
■ **run 'off** **1** *v.i.* weglaufen
  2 *v.t.* abziehen ⟨*Kopien*⟩
■ **run 'out** *v.i.* **(a)** hin-/herauslaufen
  (b) ⟨*Vorräte, Bestände:*⟩ zu Ende gehen
■ **run 'out of** *v.t.* ~s out of sth. jmdm.
geht etw. aus; I'm ~ning out of patience
meine Geduld geht zu Ende
■ **run 'over** **1** /'---/ *v.t.* (knock down)
überfahren
  2 /-'--/ *v.i.* überlaufen
■ **'run through** *v.t.* durchspielen
⟨*Theaterstück*⟩; durchgehen ⟨*Plan*⟩
■ **'run to** *v.t.* **(a)** (amount to) sich belaufen auf
(*Akk.*)
  (b) (be sufficient for) sth. will ~ to sth. etw.
reicht für etw.
■ **run 'up** **1** *v.i.* hinlaufen; come ~ning up
hingelaufen kommen
  2 *v.t.* **(a)** rasch nähen ⟨*Kleidungsstück*⟩
  (b) zusammenkommen lassen ⟨*Schulden,
Rechnung*⟩
■ **run 'up against** *v.t.* stoßen auf (+ *Akk.*)
⟨*Probleme, Widerstand usw.*⟩

run: ~**about** *n.* (coll.) [little] ~**about**
Kleinwagen, *der;* ~**around** *n.* (coll.) **give sb.
the** ~**around** jmdn. an der Nase
herumführen (ugs.); ~**away** **1** *n.*

Ausreißer, *der*/Ausreißerin, *die* (ugs.);
2 *attrib. adj.* durchgegangen ⟨*Pferd*⟩; außer
Kontrolle geraten ⟨*Fahrzeug, Preise*⟩;
galoppierend ⟨*Inflation*⟩; **~down** /'-'-/ *n.*
(coll.: briefing) Übersicht, *die* (on über + *Akk.*);
~-down /-'-'-/ *adj.* (tired) mitgenommen
rung¹ /rʌŋ/ *n.* Sprosse, *die*
rung² ▸ RING² 2, 3
'**runner** *n.* (a) Läufer, *der*/Läuferin, *die*
(b) (Bot.) Ausläufer, *der*
(c) (on sledge) Kufe, *die*
'**runner bean** *n.* (Brit.) Stangenbohne, *die*
runner-'up *n.* Zweite, *der*/*die;* **the runners-**
up die Platzierten *Pl.*
'**running** **1** *n.* (a) (management) Leitung, *die*
(b) (action) Laufen, *das;* **in/out of the ~:** im/
aus dem Rennen
2 *adj.* (in succession) hintereinander; **win for**
the third year ~: schon drei Jahre
hintereinander gewinnen
running: ~ '**commentary** *n.*
(Broadcasting; also fig.) Livekommentar, *der;*
~ **costs** *n. pl.* Betriebskosten *Pl.;*
~ **shoe** *n.* Rennschuh, *der;* ~ '**total** *n.*
fortlaufende Summe; ~ **track** *n.*
Aschenbahn, *die;* ~ '**water** *n.* **hot and cold**
~ **water** fließendes kaltes und warmes
Wasser
runny /'rʌnɪ/ *adj.* (a) laufend ⟨*Nase*⟩
(b) zu dünn ⟨*Farbe, Marmelade*⟩
run: ~**-of-the-'mill** *adj.* ganz gewöhnlich;
~**-up** *n.* (a) during *or* in the ~**-up to an**
event im Vorfeld eines Ereignisses; (b)
(Sport) Anlauf, *der;* ~**way** *n.* (for take-off)
Startbahn, *die;* (for landing) Landebahn, *die*
rupture /'rʌptʃə(r)/ **1** *n.* Bruch, *der*
2 *v.t.* ~ **oneself** sich (*Dat.*) einen Bruch
zuziehen
rural /'rʊərl/ *adj.* ländlich
ruse /ruːz/ *n.* List, *die*
rush¹ /rʌʃ/ *n.* (Bot.) Binse, *die*
rush² **1** *n.* (a) (hurry) Eile, *die;* **what's all the**
~**?** wozu diese Hast?; **be in a [great] ~:** in
[großer] Eile sein

(c) (period of great activity) Hochbetrieb, *der;*
(~ hour) Stoßzeit, *die*
(c) **make a ~ for sth.** sich auf etw. (*Akk.*)
stürzen
2 *v.t.* (a) ~ **sb./sth. somewhere** jmdn./etw.
auf schnellstem Wege irgendwohin bringen;
be ~ed (have to hurry) in Eile sein; ~ **sb. into**
doing sth. jmdn. dazu drängen, etw. zu tun
(b) (perform quickly) auf die Schnelle
erledigen; ~ **it** zu schnell machen
3 *v.i.* (a) (move quickly) eilen; ⟨*Hund, Pferd:*⟩
laufen; ~ **to help sb.** jmdm. zu Hilfe eilen
(b) (hurry unduly) sich zu sehr beeilen; **don't**
~**!** nur keine Eile!
■ **rush a'bout, rush a'round** *v.i.*
herumhetzen
rush: ~ **hour** *n.* Stoßzeit, *die;* ~ **job** *n.*
eilige Arbeit
rusk /rʌsk/ *n.* Zwieback, *der*
Russia /'rʌʃə/ *pr. n.* Russland (*das*)
Russian /'rʌʃn/ **1** *adj.* russisch; **sb. is ~:**
jmd. ist Russe/Russin
2 *n.* (a) (person) Russe, *der*/Russin, *die*
(b) (language) Russisch, *das; see also* ENGLISH
2A
rust /rʌst/ **1** *n.* Rost, *der*
2 *v.i.* rosten
rustic /'rʌstɪk/ *adj.* (a) ländlich
(b) rustikal ⟨*Mobiliar*⟩
rustle /'rʌsl/ **1** *n.* Rascheln, *das*
2 *v.i.* rascheln
3 *v.t.* (a) rascheln lassen
(b) (Amer.: steal) stehlen
■ **rustle 'up** *v.t.* zusammenzaubern
⟨*Mahlzeit*⟩
'**rustproof** *adj.* rostfrei
'**rusty** *adj.* rostig
rut /rʌt/ *n.* Spurrille, *die;* **be in a ~** (fig.) aus
dem [Alltags]trott nicht mehr
herauskommen
ruthless /'ruːθlɪs/ *adj.* rücksichtslos
RV *abbr.* (Amer.) = **recreational**
vehicle
rye /raɪ/ *n.* Roggen, *der*
'**rye bread** *n.* Roggenbrot, *das*

Ss

S, s /es/ *n.* S, s, *das*
S. *abbr.* (a) = **south** S
(b) = **southern** s.
sabbath /'sæbəθ/ *n.* Sabbat, *der*
sabbatical /sə'bætɪkl/ **1** *adj.* ~ **term/year**
Forschungssemester/-jahr, *das*
2 *n.* Forschungsurlaub, *der*
sabotage /'sæbətɑːʒ/ **1** *n.* Sabotage, *die*

2 *v.t.* einen Sabotageakt verüben auf
(+ *Akk.*); (fig.) sabotieren
saboteur /sæbə'tɜː(r)/ *n.* Saboteur, *der*
saccharin /'sækərɪn/ *n.* Saccharin, *das*
sachet /'sæʃeɪ/ *n.* Beutel, *der;* (cushion-
shaped) Kissen, *das*
sack /sæk/ **1** *n.* (a) Sack, *der* ┄┄┅⟶

(b) (coll.: dismissal) Rausschmiss, *der* (ugs.); **get the ∼:** rausgeschmissen werden (ugs.); **give sb. the ∼:** jmdn. rausschmeißen (ugs.)
[2] *v.t.* (coll.) rausschmeißen (ugs.) **(for wegen)**

sacking /'sækɪŋ/ *n.***(a)** (coll.: dismissal) Rausschmiss, *der* (ugs.)
(b) (coarse fabric) Sackleinen, *das*

sacrament /'sækrəmənt/ *n.* Sakrament, *das*

sacred /'seɪkrɪd/ *adj.* heilig

sacrifice /'sækrɪfaɪs/ [1] *n.* Opfer, *das*
[2] *v.t.* opfern

sacrilege /'sækrɪlɪdʒ/ *n.* **[act of]** ∼: Sakrileg, *das*

sad /sæd/ *adj.* traurig **(at, about über + *Akk.*)**; schmerzlich ⟨*Tod, Verlust*⟩; **feel ∼:** traurig sein

sadden /'sædn/ *v.t.* traurig stimmen

SAD *abbr.* = **seasonal affective disorder**

saddle /'sædl/ [1] *n.* Sattel, *der*
[2] *v.t.* **(a)** satteln ⟨*Pferd usw.*⟩
(b) (fig.) ∼ **sb. with sth.** jmdm. etw. aufbürden (geh.)

'saddlebag *n.* Satteltasche, *die*

sadism /'seɪdɪzm/ *n.* Sadismus, *der*

sadist /'seɪdɪst/ *n.* Sadist, *der*/Sadistin, *die*

sadistic /sə'dɪstɪk/ *adj.,* **sa'distically** *adv.* sadistisch

'sadly *adv.* **(a)** (with sorrow) traurig
(b) (unfortunately) leider

'sadness *n.* Traurigkeit, *die*

sadomasochism /seɪdəʊ'mæsəkɪzm/ *n.* Sadomasochismus, *der*

s.a.e. /eseɪ'iː/ *abbr.* = **stamped addressed envelope** adressierter Freiumschlag

safari /sə'fɑːrɪ/ *n.* Safari, *die;* **on ∼:** auf Safari

safe /seɪf/ [1] *n.* Safe, *der;* Geldschrank, *der*
[2] *adj.* **(a)** (out of danger) sicher **(from vor + *Dat.*)**; **he's ∼:** er ist in Sicherheit; ∼ **and sound** sicher und wohlbehalten
(b) (free from danger) ungefährlich; sicher ⟨*Ort, Hafen*⟩; **wish sb. a ∼ journey** jmdm. eine gute Reise wünschen; **to be on the ∼ side** zur Sicherheit
(c) (reliable) sicher ⟨*Methode, Investition*⟩

safe: ∼**guard** [1] *n.* Schutz, *der;* [2] *v.t.* schützen; ∼ **'haven** *n.* **(a)** (safe place) Zuflucht, *die;* **(b)** (Polit.) Schutzzone, *die*

safely /'seɪflɪ/ *adv.* sicher; **did the parcel arrive ∼?** ist das Paket heil angekommen?

safe 'sex Safersex, *der*

safety: ∼ **belt** *n.* Sicherheitsgurt, *der;* ∼ **catch** *n.* (of gun) Sicherungshebel, *der;* ∼ **helmet** *n.* Schutzhelm, *der;* ∼ **margin** *n.* Spielraum, *der;* ∼ **pin** *n.* Sicherheitsnadel, *die;* ∼ **valve** *n.* Sicherheitsventil, *das;* (fig.) Ventil, *das*

'safe zone *n.* (Polit.) Schutzzone, *die*

saffron /'sæfrən/ *n.* Safran, *der*

sag /sæg/ *v.i.,* **-gg-** durchhängen; (sink) sich senken

saga /'sɑːgə/ *n.* **(a)** (story of adventure) Heldenepos, *das;* (medieval narrative) Saga, *die*
(b) (long involved story) [ganzer] Roman (fig.)

sage[1] /seɪdʒ/ *n.* (Bot.) Salbei, *der od. die*

sage[2] [1] *adj.* weise
[2] *n.* Weise, *der*

Sagittarius /sædʒɪ'teərɪəs/ *n.* (Astrol; Astron.) der Schütze

Sahara /sə'hɑːrə/ *pr. n.* **the ∼ [Desert]** die [Wüste] Sahara

said ▸ SAY 1

sail /seɪl/ [1] *n.* **(a)** Segelfahrt, *die*
(b) (piece of canvas) Segel, *das*
[2] *v.i.* **(a)** (travel on water) fahren; (in sailing boat) segeln
(b) (start voyage) auslaufen **(for nach)**
[3] *v.t.* **(a)** steuern ⟨*Boot, Schiff*⟩; segeln mit ⟨*Segeljacht, -schiff*⟩
(b) durchfahren/⟨*Segelschiff:*⟩ durchsegeln ⟨*Meer*⟩

sail: ∼**board** *n.* Surfbrett, *das* **(zum Windsurfen);** ∼**boarding** *n.* Windsurfen, *das;* ∼**boat** *n.* (Amer.) Segelboot, *das*

'sailing *n.* Segeln, *das*

sailing: ∼ **boat** *n.* Segelboot, *das;* ∼ **ship** *n.* Segelschiff, *das*

sailor /'seɪlə(r)/ *n.* Seemann, *der;* (in navy) Matrose, *der*

saint [1] /sənt/ *adj.* **S∼ Michael** der heilige Michael; Sankt Michael
[2] /seɪnt/ *n.* Heilige, *der/die*

'saintly /'seɪntlɪ/ *adj.* heilig

sake /seɪk/ *n.* **for the ∼ of** um ... (*Gen.*) willen; **for my** *etc.* ∼: um meinetwillen *usw.;* mir *usw.* zuliebe

salad /'sæləd/ *n.* Salat, *der*

salad: ∼ **cream** *n.* ≈ Mayonnaise, *die;* ∼ **dressing** *n.* Salatsoße, *die;* ∼ **servers** *n. pl.* Salatbesteck, *das*

salary /'sælərɪ/ *n.* Gehalt, *das*

sale /seɪl/ *n.* **(a)** Verkauf, *der;* (at reduced prices) Ausverkauf, *der;* (at end of season) Schlußverkauf, *der;* **[up] for ∼:** zu verkaufen
(b) ∼**s** (amount sold) Verkaufszahlen *Pl.* **(of für)**; Absatz, *der*
(c) [jumble *or* rummage] ∼: [Wohltätigkeits]basar, *der*

'sale price *n.* **(a)** (retail price) Verkaufspreis, *der*
(b) (price in sale) Ausverkaufspreis, *der*

sales: ∼ **assistant** (Brit.), ∼ **clerk** (Amer.) *ns.* Verkäufer, *der*/Verkäuferin, *die;* ∼**man** /'seɪlzmən/ *n., pl.* ∼**men** /'seɪlzmən/ Verkäufer, *der*

'salesmanship *n.* Kunst des Verkaufens

sales: ∼ **rep** (coll.), ∼ **representative** *ns.* [Handels]vertreter, *der*/-vertreterin, *die;* ∼**woman** *n.* Verkäuferin, *die*

salient /'seɪlɪənt/ *adj.* auffallend

saliva /sə'laɪvə/ *n.* Speichel, *der*

sallow /'sæləʊ/ adj. blassgelb

salmon /'sæmən/ n. Lachs, der

saloon /sə'luːn/ n. (a) (Brit.) ~ [bar] *separater Teil eines Pubs mit mehr Komfort* (b) (Brit.) ~ [car] Limousine, die

salt /sɔːlt, sɒlt/ ① n. [common] ~: [Koch]salz, das
  ② adj. (containing or tasting of ~) salzig; (preserved with ~) gepökelt ⟨Fleisch⟩; gesalzen ⟨Butter⟩
  ③ v.t. (a) salzen
  (b) (cure) [ein]pökeln
  (c) ~ the roads Salz auf die Straßen streuen

salt: ~ **cellar** n. Salzfässchen, das; ~ '**water** n. Salzwasser, das

'**salty** adj. salzig

salute /sə'luːt/ ① v.t. grüßen
  ② v.i. (Mil., Navy) [militärisch] grüßen
  ③ n. Salut, der; militärischer Gruß

salvage /'sælvɪdʒ/ ① n. Bergung, die
  ② v.t. bergen

salvation /sæl'veɪʃn/ n. Erlösung, die

Salvation 'Army n. Heilsarmee, die

salvo /'sælvəʊ/ n. Salve, die

Samaritan /sə'mærɪtən/ n. good ~: [barmherziger] Samariter; the ~s (organization) ≈ die Telefonseelsorge

same /seɪm/ ① adj. the ~: der/die/das gleiche; the ~ [thing] (identical) der-/die-/ dasselbe
  ② adv. all or just the ~: trotzdem

sample /'sɑːmpl/ ① n. (example) [Muster]beispiel, das; (specimen) Probe, die; [commercial] ~: Muster, das
  ② v.t. probieren

'**sample letter** n. Musterbrief, der

sampler /'sɑːmplə(r)/ n. (trial pack) Probe[packung], die

sanatorium /sænə'tɔːrɪəm/ n. Sanatorium, das

sanctify /'sæŋktɪfaɪ/ v.t. heiligen

sanctimonious /sæŋktɪ'məʊnɪəs/ adj. scheinheilig

sanction /'sæŋkʃn/ ① n. Sanktion, die
  ② v.t. sanktionieren

sanctity /'sæŋktɪtɪ/ n. Heiligkeit, die

sanctuary /'sæŋktʃʊərɪ/ n. (a) (holy place) Heiligtum, das
  (b) (refuge) Zufluchtsort, der
  (c) (for animals) Naturschutzgebiet, das

sand /sænd/ ① n. Sand, der
  ② v.t. ~ sth. [down] etw. [ab]schmirgeln

sandal /'sændl/ n. Sandale, die

sandalwood n. Sandelholz, das

sand: ~**bag** ① n. Sandsack, der; ② v.t. mit Sandsäcken schützen; ~**bank** n. Sandbank, die; ~**castle** n. Sandburg, die; ~ **dune** n. Düne, die; ~**paper** ① n. Sandpapier, das; ② v.t. [mit Sandpapier] [ab]schmirgeln; ~**pit** n. Sandkasten, der; ~**stone** n. Sandstein, der

sandwich /'sænwɪdʒ/ ① n. Sandwich, der od. das; ≈ [zusammengeklapptes] belegtes Brot; cheese ~: Käsebrot, das
  ② v.t. einschieben (between zwischen + Akk.; into in + Akk.)

'**sandy** adj. (a) sandig; Sand⟨boden, -strand⟩
  (b) rotblond ⟨Haar⟩

sane /seɪn/ adj. (a) geistig gesund
  (b) (sensible) vernünftig

sang ▸ SING

sanitary /'sænɪtərɪ/ adj. sanitär ⟨Verhältnisse, Anlagen⟩

'**sanitary napkin** (Amer.), '**sanitary towel** (Brit.) ns. Damenbinde, die

sanitation /sænɪ'teɪʃn/ n. Kanalisation und Abfallbeseitigung

sanitize (**sanitise**) /'sænɪtaɪz/ v.t. (fig.) entschärfen

sanity /'sænɪtɪ/ n. geistige Gesundheit; lose one's ~: den Verstand verlieren

sank ▸ SINK 2, 3

Santa Claus /'sæntə klɔːz/ n. der Weihnachtsmann

sap /sæp/ ① n. Saft, der
  ② v.t., -pp- zehren an (+ Dat.)

sapling /'sæplɪŋ/ n. junger Baum

sapphire /'sæfaɪə(r)/ n. Saphir, der

sarcasm /'sɑːkæzm/ n. Sarkasmus, der

sarcastic /sɑː'kæstɪk/ adj. sarkastisch

sardine /sɑː'diːn/ n. Sardine, die

Sardinia /sɑː'dɪnɪə/ pr. n. Sardinien (das)

sardonic /sɑː'dɒnɪk/ adj. höhnisch; sardonisch ⟨Lächeln⟩

sash /sæʃ/ n. Schärpe, die

sash 'window n. Schiebefenster, das

sat ▸ SIT

Sat. abbr. = **Saturday** Sa.

Satan /'seɪtən/ pr. n. Satan, der

satanic /sə'tænɪk/ adj. satanisch

satchel /'sætʃl/ n. [Schul]ranzen, der

satellite /'sætəlaɪt/ n. Satellit, der

satellite: ~ '**broadcasting** n. Satellitenfunk, der; ~ **dish** n. Satellitenschüssel, die; ~ **receiver** n. Satellitenempfänger, der; ~ **technology** n. Satellitentechnik, die; ~ '**television** n. Satellitenfernsehen, das; ~ **town** n. Satelliten- od. Trabantenstadt, die

satin /'sætɪn/ n. Satin, der

satire /'sætaɪə(r)/ n. Satire, die (on auf + Akk.)

satirical /sə'tɪrɪkl/ adj. satirisch

satisfaction /sætɪs'fækʃn/ n. Befriedigung, die (at, with über + Akk.); meet with sb.'s [complete] ~: jmdn. [in jeder Weise] zufrieden stellen

satisfactory /sætɪs'fæktərɪ/ adj. zufrieden stellend

satisfied /'sætɪsfaɪd/ adj. (a) (contented) zufrieden
  (b) (convinced) überzeugt (of von)

S

satisfy /'sætɪsfaɪ/ v.t. (a) befriedigen; zufrieden stellen ⟨Kunden⟩; stillen ⟨Hunger, Durst⟩
(b) (convince) ~ sb. [of sth.] jmdn. [von etw.] überzeugen

'**satisfying** adj. befriedigend; sättigend ⟨Gericht, Speise⟩

saturate /'sætʃəreɪt/ v.t. durchnässen; [mit Feuchtigkeit durch]tränken ⟨Boden, Erde⟩

saturated /'sætʃəreɪtɪd/ adj. durchnässt

saturation /sætʃə'reɪʃn/ n. Durchnässung, die

Saturday /'sætədeɪ, 'sætədɪ/ n. Samstag, der; see also FRIDAY

'**Saturday job** n. Samstagsjob, der (ugs.)

Saturn /'sætən/ pr. n. (Astron.) Saturn, der

sauce /sɔːs/ n. (a) Soße, die
(b) (impudence) Frechheit, die

sauce: ~ **boat** n. Sauciere, die; ~**pan** /'sɔːspən/ n. Kochtopf, der; (with straight handle) [Stiel]kasserolle, die

saucer /'sɔːsə(r)/ n. Untertasse, die

saucy /'sɔːsɪ/ adj. (a) (rude) frech
(b) (pert, jaunty) keck

Saudi Arabia /saʊdɪ ə'reɪbɪə/ pr. n. Saudi-Arabien (das)

sauna /'sɔːnə, 'saʊnə/ n. Sauna, die

saunter /'sɔːntə(r)/ v.i. schlendern

sausage /'sɒsɪdʒ/ n. Wurst, die

sausage: ~ **meat** n. Wurstmasse, die; ~ '**roll** n.: Blätterteig mit Wurstfüllung

savage /'sævɪdʒ/ ①adj. (a) (uncivilized) primitiv; wild ⟨Volksstamm⟩; unzivilisiert ⟨Land⟩
(b) (fierce) brutal; wild ⟨Tier⟩
②n. Wilde, der/die (veralt.)

savagery /'sævɪdʒrɪ/ n. Brutalität, die

save /seɪv/ ①v.t. (a) (rescue) retten (from vor + Dat.); ~ oneself from falling sich [beim Hinfallen] fangen
(b) (put aside) aufheben; sparen ⟨Geld⟩; sammeln ⟨Briefmarken usw.⟩; (conserve) sparsam umgehen mit
(c) (make unnecessary) sparen ⟨Geld, Zeit, Energie⟩; ~ sb./oneself sth. jmdm./sich etw. ersparen
(d) (Sport) abwehren ⟨Schuss, Ball;⟩
(e) (Comp.) speichern; sichern; ~ sth. on [to] a disk etw. auf Diskette abspeichern
②v.i. sparen (on Akk.)
③n. (Sport) Abwehr, die
∎ **save 'up** ①v.t. sparen
②v.i. sparen (for für, auf + Akk.)

'**saver** n. Sparer, der/Sparerin, die

saving /'seɪvɪŋ/ ①n. in pl. Ersparnisse Pl.
②adj. ⟨kosten-, benzin⟩sparend

savings: ~ **account** n. Sparkonto, das; ~ **bank** n. Sparkasse, die

saviour /'seɪvjə(r)/ n. (a) Retter, der/Retterin, die
(b) (Relig.) the S~: der Heiland

savor etc. (Amer.) ▶ SAVOUR etc.

savour /'seɪvə(r)/ (Brit.) ①n. (flavour) Geschmack, der
②v.t. genießen

savoury /'seɪvərɪ/ (Brit.) ①adj. (a) pikant; salzig
(b) (appetizing) appetitanregend
②n. [pikantes] Häppchen

saw¹ /sɔː/ ①n. Säge, die
②v.t., p.p. sawn /sɔːn/ or sawed [zer]sägen; ~ in half in der Mitte durchsägen
③v.i., p.p. sawn or sawed sägen; ~ through sth. etw. durchsägen

saw² ▶ SEE

saw: ~**dust** n. Sägemehl, das; ~**mill** n. Sägemühle, die

sawn ▶ SAW¹ 2, 3

'**sawn-off** adj. (Brit.) ⟨Gewehr⟩ mit abgesägtem Lauf

saxophone /'sæksəfəʊn/ n. Saxophon, das

saxophonist /sæk'sɒfənɪst/ n. Saxophonist, der/Saxophonistin, die

say /seɪ/ ①v.t. pres. t. he says /sez/, p.t. & p.p. said /sed/ (a) sagen; that is to ~: das heißt; do as or what I ~: tun Sie, was ich sage; when all is said and done letzten Endes; go without ~ing sich von selbst verstehen; she is said to be clever/to have done it man sagt, sie sei klug/habe es getan
(b) (recite) sprechen ⟨Gebet, Text⟩
(c) (have specified wording or reading) sagen; ⟨Zeitung:⟩ schreiben; ⟨Uhr:⟩ zeigen ⟨Uhrzeit⟩; what does it ~ here? was steht hier?
②n. have a or some ~: ein Mitspracherecht haben (in bei); have no ~: nichts zu sagen haben; have one's ~: seine Meinung sagen

'**saying** n. Redensart, die

scab /skæb/ n. [Wund]schorf, der

scaffold /'skæfəld/ n. Schafott, das

'**scaffolding** n. Gerüst, das

'**scaffolding pole** n. Gerüststange, die

scald /skɔːld, skɒld/ ①n. Verbrühung, die
②v.t. verbrühen

scale¹ /skeɪl/ n. (a) (of fish, reptile, etc.) Schuppe, die
(b) (in kettle etc.) Kesselstein, der; (on teeth) Zahnstein, der

scale² n. (a) in sing. or pl. (weighing instrument) ~[s] Waage, die
(b) (dish of balance) Waagschale, die

scale³ ①n. (a) (series of degrees) Skala, die
(b) (Mus.) Tonleiter, die
(c) (dimensions) Ausmaß, das; be on a small ~: bescheidenen Umfang haben
(d) (ratio of reduction) Maßstab, der; what is the ~ of the map? welchen Maßstab hat diese Karte?
(e) (indication) (on map) Maßstab, der; (on thermometer) [Anzeige]skala, die
②v.t. ersteigen ⟨Mauer, Leiter, Gipfel⟩
∎ **scale 'down** v.t. [entsprechend] drosseln ⟨Produktion⟩; Abstriche machen bei ⟨Planungen⟩

scalp /skælp/ n. Kopfhaut, die

scalpel /'skælpl/ n. Skalpell, *das*

scam /skæm/ n. (coll.) Masche, *die* (ugs.)

scamper /'skæmpə(r)/ v.i. ‹Person:› flitzen; ‹Tier:› huschen

scampi /'skæmpɪ/ n. pl. Scampi Pl.

scan /skæn/ v.t., **-nn-:** (a) (search thoroughly) absuchen (**for** nach)
(b) (look over cursorily) flüchtig ansehen; überfliegen ‹Zeitung, Liste usw.› (**for** auf der Suche nach)
(c) (Med.) szintigraphisch untersuchen
(d) (Comp.) scannen
[2] v.i., **-nn-** ‹Vers[zeile]:› das richtige Versmaß haben
[3] n. (Med.) szintigraphische Untersuchung, *die;* (image) Szintigramm, *das*

scandal /'skændl/ n. (a) Skandal, *der* (**about/of** um); (story) Skandalgeschichte, *die*
(b) (outrage) Empörung, *die*
(c) (gossip) Klatsch, *der* (ugs.)

scandalize /'skændəlaɪz/ v.t. schockieren

scandalous /'skændələs/ adj. skandalös; schockierend ‹Bemerkung›

Scandinavia /skændɪ'neɪvɪə/ pr. n. Skandinavien (*das*)

Scandinavian /skændɪ'neɪvɪən/ [1] adj. skandinavisch; **sb. is ∼:** jmd. ist Skandinavier/Skandinavierin
[2] n.(a) (person) Skandinavier, *der*/ Skandinavierin, *die*
(b) (Ling.) skandinavische Sprachen Pl.

scant /skænt/ adj. wenig

scanty /'skæntɪ/ adj. spärlich; knapp ‹Bikini›

scapegoat /'skeɪpgəʊt/ n. Sündenbock, *der;* **make sb. a ∼:** jmdn. zum Sündenbock machen

scar /skɑ:(r)/ [1] n. Narbe, *die*
[2] v.t., **-rr-:** ∼ **sb./sb.'s face** bei jmdm./in jmds. Gesicht (*Dat.*) Narben hinterlassen

scarce /skeəs/ adj. (a) (insufficient) knapp
(b) (rare) selten; **make oneself ∼** (coll.) sich aus dem Staub machen (ugs.)

'scarcely adv. kaum

scarcity /'skeəsɪtɪ/ n. Knappheit, *die* (**of** an + *Dat.*)

scare /skeə(r)/ [1] n. (a) (sensation of fear) Schreck[en], *der;* **give sb. a ∼:** jmdm. einen Schreck[en] einjagen
(b) (general alarm) [allgemeine] Hysterie; **bomb ∼:** Bombendrohung, *die*
[2] v.t. (frighten) Angst machen (+ *Dat.*); (startle) erschrecken
■ **scare a'way, scare 'off** v.t. verscheuchen

'scarecrow n. Vogelscheuche, *die*

scared /skeəd/ adj. **be ∼ of sb./sth.** vor jmdm./etw. Angst haben; **be ∼ of doing/to do sth.** sich nicht [ge]trauen, etw. zu tun

scaremongering /'skeəmʌŋgərɪŋ/ n. Panikmache, *die*

scarf /skɑ:f/ n., pl. **∼s** or **scarves** /skɑ:vz/ Schal, *der;* (square) Halstuch, *das;* (worn over hair) Kopftuch, *das*

scarlet /'skɑ:lɪt/ [1] n. Scharlach, *der*
[2] adj. scharlachrot

scarlet 'fever n. Scharlach, *der*

scarves ▶ SCARF

scary /'skeərɪ/ adj. Furcht erregend ‹Anblick›; schaurig ‹Film, Geschichte›

scathing /'skeɪðɪŋ/ adj. bissig ‹Person, Humor, Bemerkung›

scatter /'skætə(r)/ [1] v.t. (a) vertreiben; auseinander treiben ‹Menge›
(b) (distribute irregularly) verstreuen
[2] v.i. sich auflösen; ‹Menge:› sich zerstreuen; (in fear) auseinander stieben

scattered /'skætəd/ adj. verstreut; vereinzelt ‹Regenschauer›

scatty /'skætɪ/ adj. (Brit. coll.) dusslig (salopp)

scavenge /'skævɪndʒ/ v.i. **∼ for sth.** nach etw. suchen

'scavenger n. (animal) Aasfresser, *der;* (fig. derog.: person) Aasgeier, *der* (ugs.)

scenario /sɪ'nɑ:rɪəʊ/ n., pl. **∼s** Szenario, *das*

scene /si:n/ n. (a) (place of event) Schauplatz, *der;* **∼ of the crime** Tatort, *der*
(b) (division of act) Auftritt, *der*
(c) (view) Anblick, *der*
(d) **behind the ∼s** hinter den Kulissen
(e) **the political/drug/artistic ∼:** die politische/Drogen-/Kunstszene

scenery /'si:nərɪ/ n. (a) Landschaft, *die*
(b) (Theatre) Bühnenbild, *das*

scenic /'si:nɪk/ adj. landschaftlich schön

scent /sent/ [1] n. (a) (smell) Duft, *der*
(b) (Hunting; also fig.: trail) Fährte, *die;* **be on the ∼ of sb./sth.** (fig.) jmdm./einer Sache auf der Spur sein
(c) (Brit.: perfume) Parfüm, *das*
[2] v.t. wittern

scented /'sentɪd/ adj.(a) (having smell) duftend
(b) (perfumed) parfümiert

sceptic /'skeptɪk/ n. Skeptiker, *der*/ Skeptikerin, *die*

sceptical /'skeptɪkl/ adj. skeptisch; **be ∼ about** or **of sb./sth.** jmdm./einer Sache skeptisch gegenüberstehen

scepticism /'skeptɪsɪzm/ n. Skepsis, *die*

schedule /'ʃedju:l/ [1] n. (a) (list) Tabelle, *die;* (for event) Programm, *das*
(b) (of work) Zeitplan, *der*
(c) **on ∼:** plangemäß
[2] v.t. zeitlich planen

'scheduled flight n. Linienflug, *der*

scheme /ski:m/ n. (a) (arrangement) Anordnung, *die*
(b) (plan) Programm, *das;* (project) Projekt, *das*
(c) (dishonest plan) Intrige, *die*

schizophrenia /skɪtsə'fri:nɪə/ n. Schizophrenie, *die* ┅┅╌┇

schizophrenic /ˌskɪtsəˈfrenɪk, ˌskɪtsəˈfriːnɪk/ *adj.* schizophren

scholar /ˈskɒlə(r)/ *n.* Gelehrte, *der/die*

'scholarly *adj.* wissenschaftlich; gelehrt ⟨*Person*⟩

'scholarship *n.* (a) (award) Stipendium, *das* (b) (scholarly work) Gelehrsamkeit, *die*

school /skuːl/ *n.* Schule, *die;* (Amer.: college) Hochschule, *die;* **be at** *or* **in** ∼: in der Schule sein; (attend) ∼) zur Schule gehen; **go to** ∼: zur Schule gehen; ∼ **holidays/exchange** Schulferien *Pl.*/Schüleraustausch, *der*

school: ∼ **age** *n.* Schulalter, *das;* ∼**bag** *n.* Schultasche, *die;* ∼**boy** *n.* Schüler, *der;* ∼**child** *n.* Schulkind, *das;* ∼ **friend** *n.* Schulfreund, *der*/-freundin, *die;* ∼**girl** *n.* Schülerin, *die;* ∼ **'governor** *n.:* Mitglied des Schulbeirats; ∼**kid** *n.* (coll.) Schulkind, *das;* ∼ **leaver** *n.* (Brit.) Schulabgänger, *der*/-abgängerin, *die;* ∼**master** *n.* Lehrer, *der;* ∼**mistress** *n.* Lehrerin, *die;* ∼ **'rule** *n.* Schulvorschrift, *die;* Schulregel, *die;* **it is a** ∼ **rule that** ...: an der Schule ist es Vorschrift, dass ...; ∼**teacher** *n.* Lehrer, *der*/Lehrerin, *die;* ∼ **'uniform** *n.* Schuluniform, *die;* ∼ **work** *n.* Schularbeiten *Pl.;* ∼ **'year** *n.* Schuljahr, *das*

sciatica /saɪˈætɪkə/ *n.* Ischias, *der od. das*

science /ˈsaɪəns/ *n.* Wissenschaft, *die*

science 'fiction *n.* Sciencefiction, *die*

scientific /saɪənˈtɪfɪk/ *adj.* wissenschaftlich

scientist /ˈsaɪəntɪst/ *n.* Wissenschaftler, *der*/Wissenschaftlerin, *die*

sci-fi /ˈsaɪfaɪ/ *n.* (coll.) Sciencefiction, *die*

scintillating /ˈsɪntɪleɪtɪŋ/ *adj.* (fig.) geistsprühend

scissors /ˈsɪzəz/ *n. pl.* [pair of] ∼: Schere, *die*

scoff¹ /skɒf/ *v.i.* (mock) spotten; ∼ **at** sich lustig machen über (+ *Akk.*)

scoff² *v.t.* (coll.: eat greedily) verschlingen

scold /skəʊld/ *v.t.* ausschimpfen (**for** wegen); **she** ∼**ed him for being late** sie schimpfte ihn aus, weil er zu spät kam

scone /skɒn, skəʊn/ *n.: weicher, oft zum Tee gegessener kleiner Kuchen*

scoop /skuːp/ 1 *n.* (a) Schaufel, *die;* (for ice cream etc.) Portionierer, *der* (b) (Journ.) Knüller, *der* (ugs.) 2 *v.t.* schaufeln ⟨*Kohlen, Zucker*⟩; schöpfen ⟨*Flüssigkeit*⟩

■ **scoop 'out** *v.t.* (a) (hollow out) aushöhlen; schaufeln ⟨*Loch, Graben*⟩ (b) [her]ausschöpfen ⟨*Flüssigkeit*⟩; auslöffeln ⟨*Fruchtfleisch*⟩; (with a knife) herausschneiden ⟨*Gehäuse, Fruchtfleisch*⟩

■ **scoop 'up** *v.t.* schöpfen ⟨*Flüssigkeit, Suppe*⟩; schaufeln ⟨*Erde*⟩

scooter /ˈskuːtə(r)/ *n.* (a) (toy) Roller, *der* (b) [motor] ∼: [Motor]roller, *der*

scope /skəʊp/ *n.* (a) Bereich, *der;* (of discussion etc.) Rahmen, *der* (b) (opportunity) Entfaltungsmöglichkeiten *Pl.*

scorch /skɔːtʃ/ *v.t.* versengen

scorched 'earth policy *n.* Politik der verbrannten Erde

scorching /ˈskɔːtʃɪŋ/ *adj.* glühend heiß

score /skɔː(r)/ 1 *n.* (a) (points) [Spiel]stand, *der;* (made by one player) Punktzahl, *die;* **keep** [the] ∼: zählen (b) (Mus.) Partitur, *die;* (Cinemat.) [Film]musik, *die* (c) *pl. same or* ∼**s** (group of 20) zwanzig (d) *in pl.* (great numbers) ∼**s** [and ∼**s**] of zig (ugs.); Dutzende [von] (e) **on that** ∼: was das betrifft (f) **pay off** *or* **settle an old** ∼ (fig.) eine alte Rechnung begleichen 2 *v.t.* erzielen ⟨*Erfolg, Punkt usw.*⟩; ∼ **a goal** ein Tor schießen 3 *v.i.* (a) (make ∼) Punkte/einen Punkt erzielen; (∼ goal/goals) ein Tor/Tore schießen/werfen (b) (keep ∼) aufschreiben

'scoreboard *n.* Anzeigetafel, *die*

'scorer *n.* (a) (recorder) Anschreiber, *der*/Anschreiberin, *die* (b) (Footb.) Torschütze, *der*/-schützin, *die*

'scoresheet *n.* Anschreibebogen, *der*

scorn /skɔːn/ 1 *n.* Verachtung, *die* 2 *v.t.* verachten; in den Wind schlagen ⟨*Rat*⟩; ausschlagen ⟨*Angebot*⟩

scornful /ˈskɔːnfl/ *adj.* verächtlich ⟨*Lächeln, Blick*⟩; **be** ∼ **of sth.** für etw. nur Verachtung haben

Scorpio /ˈskɔːpɪəʊ/ *n.* (Astrol; Astron.) der Skorpion

scorpion /ˈskɔːpɪən/ *n.* Skorpion, *der*

Scot /skɒt/ *n.* Schotte, *der*/Schottin, *die*

scotch *v.t.* den Boden entziehen (+ *Dat.*) ⟨*Gerücht*⟩; zunichte machen ⟨*Plan*⟩

Scotch /skɒtʃ/ 1 *adj.* ▶ SCOTTISH 2 *n.* Scotch, *der;* schottischer Whisky

Scotch: ∼ **'egg** *n.: hart gekochtes Ei in Wurstbrät;* ∼ **'whisky** *n.* schottischer Whisky

scot-free *adj.* [get off/go] ∼: ungeschoren [davonkommen *od.* bleiben]

Scotland /ˈskɒtlənd/ *pr. n.* Schottland (*das*)

Scots /skɒts/ 1 *adj.* (esp. Scot.) schottisch; **sb. is** ∼: jmd. ist Schotte/Schottin 2 *n.* (dialect) Schottisch, *das*

Scotsman /ˈskɒtsmən/ *n., pl.* **Scotsmen** /ˈskɒtsmən/ Schotte, *der*

'Scotswoman *n.* Schottin, *die*

Scottish /ˈskɒtɪʃ/ *adj.* schottisch; **sb. is** ∼: jmd. ist Schotte/Schottin

scoundrel /ˈskaʊndrl/ *n.* Schuft, *der*

scour¹ /ˈskaʊə(r)/ *v.t.* (search) durchkämmen (**for** nach)

scour² *v.t.* scheuern ⟨*Topf, Metall*⟩

'scourer *n.* Topfreiniger, *der*

scourge /skɜːdʒ/ n. Geißel, die

scout /skaʊt/ ① n. (a) [Boy] S~:
Pfadfinder, der
(b) (Mil.) Späher, der
② v.i. ~ **for** Ausschau halten nach

scowl /skaʊl/ ① v.i. ein mürrisches
Gesicht machen
② n. mürrischer [Gesichts]ausdruck

scram /skræm/ v.i., **-mm-** (coll.) abhauen
(salopp)

scramble /'skræmbl/ ① v.i. (a) (clamber)
klettern; ~ **through a hedge** sich durch eine
Hecke zwängen
(b) (move hastily) rennen (ugs.); ~ **for sth.** um
etw. rangeln
② v.t. (Teleph., Radio) verschlüsseln

scrambled 'egg n. Rührei, das

scrap¹ /skræp/ ① n. (a) (of paper) Fetzen,
der; (of food) Bissen, der
(b) in pl. (odds and ends) (of food) Reste Pl.
(c) (smallest amount) **not a** ~ **of** kein bisschen;
(of sympathy, truth also) nicht ein Fünkchen;
not a ~ **of evidence** nicht die Spur eines
Beweises
(d) ~ [metal] Schrott, der; ~ **iron** Alteisen,
das
② v.t., **-pp-** wegwerfen; (send for ~)
verschrotten; (fig.) aufgeben

scrap² (coll.) ① n. (fight) Rauferei, die
② v.i., **-pp-** sich raufen

'scrapbook n. [Sammel]album, das

scrape /skreɪp/ ① v.t. (a) (make smooth)
schaben 〈Häute, Möhren, Kartoffeln usw.〉;
abziehen 〈Holz〉; (damage) verschrammen
〈Fußboden, Auto〉
(b) (remove) [ab]kratzen 〈Farbe, Schmutz,
Rost〉 (**off, from** von)
(c) (draw along) schleifen
(d) ~ **together** (raise) zusammenkratzen
(ugs.); (save up) zusammensparen
② v.i. (a) (move with sound) schleifen
(b) (emit scraping noise) ein schabendes
Geräusch machen
(c) (rub) streifen (**against, over** Akk.)
③ n. (a) (act, sound) Kratzen, das (**against** an
+ Dat.)
(b) (predicament) Schwulitäten Pl. (ugs.)
∎ **scrape 'by** v.i. (fig.) sich über Wasser
halten (**on** mit)
∎ **scrape 'out** v.t. (a) (excavate) buddeln
(ugs.); scharren
(b) (clean) auskratzen
∎ **scrape through** ① /'--/ v.t. sich
zwängen durch; (fig.) mit Hängen und
Würgen kommen durch 〈Prüfung〉
② /-'-/ v.i. sich durchzwängen; (fig.: in
examination) mit Hängen und Würgen
durchkommen

'scraper n. (for shoes) Kratzeisen, das; (grid)
Abtreter, der; (tool, kitchen utensil) Schaber,
der; (for removing ice from car windows)
[Eis]kratzer, der

scrap: ~ **heap** n. Schrotthaufen, der;

~ **merchant** n. Schrotthändler, der/
-händlerin, die; ~ **'paper** n.
Schmierpapier, das

scrappy /'skræpɪ/ adj. lückenhaft

'scrapyard n. Schrottplatz, der

scratch /skrætʃ/ ① v.t. (a) (score surface of)
zerkratzen; (score skin of) kratzen
(b) (get scratch[es] on) ~ **oneself/one's hands**
etc. sich schrammen/sich (Dat.) die Hände
usw. zerkratzen
(c) (scrape without marking) kratzen; kratzen an
(+ Dat. 〈Insektenstich usw.〉; ~ **oneself/**
one's arm sich kratzen/sich (Dat.) den Arm
od. am Arm kratzen
② v.i. kratzen; (~ oneself) sich kratzen
③ n. (a) (mark, wound) Kratzer, der (ugs.);
Schramme, die
(b) (sound) Kratzen, das
(c) **have a** [**good**] ~: sich [ordentlich]
kratzen
(d) **start from** ~: bei Null anfangen (ugs.); **be**
up to ~ 〈Arbeit, Leistung:〉 nichts zu
wünschen übrig lassen; 〈Person:〉 den
Anforderungen genügen
∎ **scratch a'bout, scratch a'round**
v.i. scharren; (fig.: search) suchen (**for** nach)

'scratch card n. Rubbellos, das

scrawl /skrɔːl/ ① v.t. hinkritzeln
② v.i. kritzeln
③ n. Gekritzel, das; (handwriting) Klaue, die
(salopp)

scrawny /'skrɔːnɪ/ adj. hager; dürr

scream /skriːm/ ① v.i. schreien (**with** vor
+ Dat.)
② v.t. schreien
③ n. Schrei, der; (of jet engine) Heulen, das;
~**s of pain** Schmerzensschreie Pl.

screech /skriːtʃ/ ① v.i. & t. kreischen
② n. Kreischen, das

screen /skriːn/ ① n. (a) (partition)
Trennwand, die; (piece of furniture)
Wandschirm, der
(b) (of trees, persons, fog) Wand, die
(c) (Cinemat.) Leinwand, die; [**TV**] ~:
Bildschirm, der
② v.t. (a) (shelter) schützen (**from** vor
+ Dat.); (conceal) verdecken
(b) vorführen 〈Film〉
(c) (for disease) untersuchen

screening /'skriːnɪŋ/ n. (a) (in cinema)
Vorführung, die; (on TV) Sendung, die
(b) (Med.) Untersuchung, die

screen: ~**play** n. Drehbuch, das;
~ **saver** n. (Comp.) Bildschirmschoner, der;
~**writer** n. Filmautor, der/-autorin, die

screw /skruː/ ① n. Schraube, die; **he has a**
~ **loose** (coll. joc.) bei ihm ist eine Schraube
locker od. lose (salopp)
② v.t. (a) schrauben (**to** an + Akk.);
~ **together** zusammenschrauben; ~ **down**
festschrauben
(b) ~ **you!** (coarse) leck mich am Arsch!
(salopp)   ····‡

■ **screw 'up** v.t. (a) (crumple up) zusammenknüllen ‹Blatt Papier›
(b) verziehen ‹Gesicht›; zusammenkneifen ‹Augen, Mund›
(c) (sl.: bungle) vermurksen (salopp); ∼ **it/ things up** Mist bauen (salopp)

screw: ∼ **cap** n. Schraubverschluss, der; ∼**driver** n. Schraubenzieher, der

'**screwed-up** adj. (fig. coll.) neurotisch

'**screw top** ▶ ∼ CAP

screwy /'skruːɪ/ adj. (coll.) spinnig (ugs.)

scribble /'skrɪbl/ ① v.t. hinkritzeln
② v.i. kritzeln
③ n. Gekritzel, das

script /skrɪpt/ n. (a) (handwriting) Handschrift, die
(b) (of play) Regiebuch, das; (of film) [Dreh]buch, das
(c) (for broadcaster) Manuskript, das

scripture /'skrɪptʃə(r)/ n. (a) [Holy] S∼, the [Holy] S∼s die [Heilige] Schrift
(b) (Sch.) Religion, die

'**scriptwriter** n. (of film) Drehbuchautor, der/-autorin, die

scroll /skrəʊl/ ① n. (roll) Rolle, die
② v.t. (Comp.) scrollen

scrollable /'skrəʊləbl/ adj. (Comp.) scrollbar

'**scroll bar** n. (Comp.) Rollballen, der

scrounge /skraʊndʒ/ (coll.) ① v.t. schnorren (ugs.) (**off, from** von)
② v.i. schnorren (ugs.) (**from** bei)

'**scrounger** n. (coll.) Schnorrer, der/ Schnorrerin, die (ugs.)

scrub¹ /skrʌb/ ① v.t. -bb-: (a) schrubben (ugs.); scheuern
(b) (coll.: cancel) zurücknehmen ‹Befehl›; sausen lassen (ugs.) ‹Plan›
② v.i. -bb- schrubben (ugs.); scheuern
③ n. give sth. a ∼: etw. schrubben (ugs.) od. scheuern

scrub² n. (brushwood) Buschwerk, das; (area) Buschland, das

scruff¹ /skrʌf/ n. by the ∼ of the neck beim Genick

scruff² n. (Brit. coll.) (man) vergammelter Typ (ugs.); (woman, girl) Schlampe, die

'**scruffy** adj. vergammelt (ugs.)

scrum /skrʌm/ n. Gedränge, das

scruple /'skruːpl/ n. Skrupel, der; **have no** ∼**s about doing sth.** keine Skrupel haben, etw. zu tun

scrupulous /'skruːpjʊləs/ adj. gewissenhaft ‹Person›; unbedingt ‹Ehrlichkeit›; peinlich ‹Sorgfalt›

scrutinize /'skruːtɪnaɪz/ v.t. [genau] untersuchen ‹Forschungs]gegenstand›; [über]prüfen ‹Rechnung, Pass, Fahrkarte›; mustern ‹Person›

scrutiny /'skruːtɪnɪ/ n. (a) (critical gaze) musternder Blick
(b) (examination) (of recruit) Musterung, die; (of bill, passport, ticket) [Über]prüfung, die

scuff /skʌf/ ① v.t. streifen; verschrammen ‹Schuhe, Fußboden›
② n. Schramme, die

scuffle /'skʌfl/ ① n. Handgreiflichkeiten Pl.
② v.i. handgreiflich werden (**with** gegen)

scullery /'skʌlərɪ/ n. Spülküche, die

sculptor /'skʌlptə(r)/ n. Bildhauer, der/ -hauerin, die

sculpture /'skʌlptʃə(r)/ n. (a) (art) Bildhauerei, die
(b) (piece of work) Skulptur, die; Plastik, die; (pieces collectively) Skulpturen Pl.

scum /skʌm/ n. (a) Schmutzschicht, die; (film) Schmutzfilm, der
(b) (fig. derog.) Abschaum, der

'**scumbag** n. (sl. derog.) Schwein, das (salopp)

scurry /'skʌrɪ/ v.i. huschen

scuttle¹ /'skʌtl/ n. Kohlenfüller, der

scuttle² (Naut.) v.t. versenken

scuttle³ v.i. rennen; flitzen (ugs.); ‹Maus, Krabbe:› huschen

scythe /saɪð/ n. Sense, die

SE abbr. = **south-east** SO

sea /siː/ n. (a) Meer, das; **the** ∼: das Meer; die See; **by** ∼: mit dem Schiff; **by the** ∼: am Meer; **at** ∼: auf See (Dat.); **be all at** ∼ (fig.) nicht mehr weiter wissen; **put [out] to** ∼: in See (Akk.) gehen
(b) (specific tract of water) Meer, das

sea: ∼ '**air** n. Seeluft, die; ∼'**bed** n. Meeresboden, der; ∼**bird** n. Seevogel, der; ∼ **breeze** n. Seewind, der; ∼**food** n. Meeresfrüchte Pl.; attrib. Fisch‹restaurant›; ∼**gull** n. [See]möwe, die

seal¹ /siːl/ n. (Zool.) Robbe, die; [common] ∼: [Gemeiner] Seehund

seal² ① n. (wax etc., stamp, impression) Siegel, das
② v.t. (a) (stamp, affix ∼ to) siegeln ‹Dokument›; (fasten with ∼) verplomben ‹Tür, Stromzähler›
(b) (close securely) abdichten ‹Behälter, Rohr usw.›; zukleben ‹Umschlag, Paket›
(c) (stop up) verschließen; abdichten ‹Leck›; verschmieren ‹Riss›

■ **seal 'off** v.t. abriegeln

sea: ∼ **lane** n. See[schifffahrts]straße, die; ∼ **legs** n. pl. Seebeine Pl. (Seemannsspr.); **get** or **find one's** ∼ **legs** sich (Dat.) Seebeine wachsen lassen; ∼**level** n. Meeresspiegel, der

'**sealing wax** n. Siegellack, der

'**sea lion** n. Seelöwe, der

seam /siːm/ n. (a) Naht, die
(b) (of coal) Flöz, das

sea: ∼**man** /'siːmən/ n., pl. ∼**men** /'siːmən/ Matrose, der; ∼ **mist** n. Küstennebel, der

'**seamless** adj. nahtlos

'**seamy** adj. the ∼ **side** (of life etc.] (fig.) die Schattenseite[n] [des Lebens usw.]

seance /'seɪəns/, **séance** /'seɪɑ̃s/ n. Séance, die

sea: ~plane *n.* Wasserflugzeug, *das;*
~port *n.* Seehafen, *der;* **~ power** *n.*
Seemacht, *die*

sear /'sɪə(r)/ *v.t.* versengen

search /sɜːtʃ/ [1] *v.t.* durchsuchen (for
nach); absuchen ‹*Gebiet, Fläche*› (for nach);
(fig.: probe) erforschen ‹*Herz, Gewissen*›;
suchen in (+ *Dat.*) ‹*Gedächtnis*› (for nach)
[2] *v.i.* suchen (for nach)
[3] *n.* Suche, *die* (for nach); (of building, room,
etc.) Durchsuchung, *die;* in ~ of sb./sth. auf
der Suche nach jmdm./etw

'search engine *n.* (Comp.) Suchmaschine,
die

'searching *adj.* prüfend, forschend ‹*Blick*›;
bohrend ‹*Frage*›

search: ~light *n.* Suchscheinwerfer, *der;*
~ party *n.* Suchtrupp, *der;* **~ warrant**
n. Durchsuchungsbefehl, *der*

sea: ~ salt *n.* Meersalz, *das;* Seesalz, *das;*
~shore *n.* [Meeres]küste, *die;* (beach)
Strand, *der;* **~sick** *adj.* seekrank;
~sickness *n.* Seekrankheit, *die;* **~side**
n. [Meeres]küste, *die;* by/to/at the **~side** am/
ans/am Meer; **~side town** Seestadt, *die*

season /'siːzn/ [1] *n.* **(a)** Jahreszeit, *die;*
nesting **~:** Nistzeit, *die*
(b) (period of social activity) [opera/football] **~:**
[Opern-/Fußball]saison, *die;* holiday *or*
(Amer.) vacation **~:** Urlaubszeit, *die;* tourist
~: Reisezeit, *die*
(c) raspberries are in/out of *or* not in **~:**
jetzt ist die/nicht die Saison *od.* Zeit für
Himbeeren; be in **~** (on heat) brünstig sein
(d) ▶ SEASON TICKET
[2] *v.t.* würzen ‹*Fleisch, Rede*›

seasonable /'siːzənəbl/ *adj.* der
Jahreszeit gemäß

seasonal /'siːzənl/ *adj.* Saison‹*arbeit,*
-geschäft›; saisonabhängig ‹*Preise*›

seasonal affective disorder /siːzənl
ə'fektɪv dɪsɔːdə(r)/ *n.* (Med.) saisonabhängige
Depression

'seasoned *adj.* (fig.) erfahren

'seasoning *n.* Gewürze *Pl.;* Würze, *die*

'season ticket *n.* Dauerkarte, *die*

seat /siːt/ [1] *n.* **(a)** Sitzgelegenheit, *die;* (in
vehicle, cinema, etc.) Sitz, *der;* (of toilet)
[Klosett]brille, *die* (ugs.)
(b) (place) Platz, *der;* (in vehicle) [Sitz]platz,
der; have *or* take a **~:** sich [hin]setzen
(c) (part of chair) Sitzfläche, *die*
(d) (buttocks) Gesäß, *das;* (part of clothing)
Gesäßpartie, *die;* (of trousers) Sitz, *der*
[2] *v.t.* **(a)** (cause to sit) setzen;
‹*Platzanweiser:*› einen Platz anweisen
(+ *Dat.*); **~** oneself sich setzen
(b) (have **~**s for) Sitzplätze bieten (+ *Dat.*);
~ 500 people 500 Sitzplätze haben

'seat belt *n.* Sicherheitsgurt, *der*

'seat-belt tensioner /'tenʃnə(r)/ *n.*
Gurtstraffer, *der*

'seated *adj.* sitzend; remain **~:** sitzen
bleiben

'seating *n.* Sitzplätze *Pl.;* attrib.
Sitz‹*ordnung, -plan*›

sea: ~ urchin *n.* Seeigel, *der;* **~ wall** *n.*
Strandmauer, *die;* **~ water** *n.*
Meerwasser, *das;* **~weed** *n.* [See]tang, *der;*
~worthy *adj.* seetüchtig

secateurs /sekə'tɜːz/ *n. pl.* (Brit.)
Gartenschere, *die*

secluded /sɪ'kluːdɪd/ *adj.* (hidden)
versteckt; (isolated) abgelegen; zurückgezogen
‹*Leben*›

seclusion /sɪ'kluːʒn/ *n.* (remoteness)
Abgelegenheit, *die;* (privacy)
Zurückgezogenheit, *die*

second¹ /'sekənd/ [1] *adj.* zweit...;
~ largest/highest *etc.* zweitgrößt.../-höchst...
usw.; come/be **~:** Zweiter/Zweite werden/
sein
[2] *n.* **(a)** (unit of time or angle) Sekunde, *die*
(b) (coll.: moment) Sekunde, *die* (ugs.); wait a
few **~**s einen Moment warten; in a **~**
(immediately) sofort (ugs.); (very quickly) im Nu
(ugs.); just a **~!** (coll.) einen Moment!
(c) the **~** (in sequence, rank) der/die/das
Zweite
(d) *in pl.* (helping of food) zweite Portion
[3] *v.t.* (support) unterstützen

second² /sɪ'kɒnd/ *v.t.* (transfer)
vorübergehend versetzen

secondary /'sekəndərɪ/ *adj.* (of less
importance) zweitrangig; Neben‹*sache*›; be
~ to sth. einer Sache (*Dat.*) untergeordnet
sein

'secondary school *n.* höhere Schule

second: ~best [1] /'---/ *adj.* zweitbest...;
[2] /-'-/ *n.* Zweitbeste, *der/die/das;* **~class**
[1] /'--/ *adj.* (of lower class) zweiter Klasse
nachgestellt; Zweite[r]-Klasse-‹*Fahrkarte,*
Abteil, Post, Brief usw.›; **~-class stamp**
Briefmarke für einen Zweiter-Klasse-Brief;
[2] /-'-/ *adv.* zweiter Klasse ‹*fahren*›;
~ 'floor ▶ FLOOR 1B; **~ hand** *n.*
Sekundenzeiger, *der;* **~-hand** [1] /'---/ *adj.*
(a) gebraucht ‹*Kleidung, Auto usw.*›;
antiquarisch ‹*Buch*›; **(b)** (selling used goods)
Gebrauchtwaren-; Secondhand‹*laden*›; **(c)**
‹*Nachrichten, Bericht*› aus zweiter Hand;
[2] /-'-/ *adv.* aus zweiter Hand; **~ 'home** *n.*
Zweitwohnung, *die*

'secondly *adv.* zweitens

second: ~ name *n.* Nachname, *der;*
~-'rate *adj.* zweitklassig; **~ 'thoughts**
n. pl. have **~** thoughts es sich (*Dat.*) anders
überlegen (about mit); we've had
~ thoughts about buying it wir wollen es
nun doch nicht kaufen; but on **~ thoughts**
...: wenn ich's mir [noch mal] überlege, ...

secrecy /'siːkrɪsɪ/ *n.* **(a)** (keeping of secret)
Geheimhaltung, *die*
(b) (secretiveness) Heimlichtuerei, *die*
(c) in **~:** im Geheimen

secret /'siːkrɪt/ [1] *adj.* geheim; ⋯❖

S

Geheim⟨*fach, -tür, -abkommen, -kode*⟩;
heimlich ⟨*Trinker, Liebhaber*⟩; **keep sth. ∼:**
etw. geheim halten (**from** vor + *Dat.*)
2 *n.* (a) Geheimnis, *das;* **make no ∼ of sth.**
kein Geheimnis aus etw. machen; (fig.)
keinen Hehl aus etw. machen; **keep ∼s/ a ∼:**
schweigen (fig.)
(b) **in ∼:** im Geheimen
secret 'agent *n.* Geheimagent, *der/*
-agentin, *die*
secretarial /sekrə'teərɪəl/ *adj.*
Sekretärinnen⟨*kursus, -tätigkeit*⟩; ⟨*Arbeit*⟩ als
Sekretärin
secretary /'sekrətərɪ/ *n.* Sekretär, *der/*
Sekretärin, *die*
secret 'ballot *n.* geheime Abstimmung
secretive /'si:krɪtɪv/ *adj.* verschlossen
⟨*Person*⟩: **be ∼:** geheimnisvoll tun (**about**
mit)
'secretly *adv.* heimlich; insgeheim ⟨*etw.*
glauben⟩
sect /sekt/ *n.* Sekte, *die*
section /'sekʃn/ *n.* (a) (part cut off)
Abschnitt, *der;* Stück, *das;* (part of divided
whole) Teil, *der*
(b) (of firm) Abteilung, *die;* (of organization)
Sektion, *die*
(c) (of chapter, book) Abschnitt, *der;* (of statute
etc.) Paragraph, *der*
sector /'sektə(r)/ *n.* Sektor, *der*
secular /'sekjʊlə(r)/ *adj.* weltlich
secure /sɪ'kjʊə(r)/ **1** *adj.* sicher; (firmly
fastened) fest; **∼ against burglars** gegen
Einbruch geschützt
2 *v.t.* (a) sichern (**for** *Dat.*); beschaffen
⟨*Auftrag*⟩ (**for** *Dat.*); (for oneself) sich (*Dat.*)
sichern
(b) (fasten) sichern
se'curely *adv.* (firmly) fest ⟨*verriegeln,*
zumachen⟩; sicher ⟨*befestigen, untergebracht*
sein⟩
security /sɪ'kjʊərɪtɪ/ *n.* (a) Sicherheit, *die;*
∼ [measures] Sicherheitsmaßnahmen *Pl.*
(b) (Finance) **securities** *pl.* Wertpapiere *Pl.*
security: ∼ check *n.*
Sicherheitskontrolle, *die;* **∼ forces** *n. pl.*
Sicherheitskräfte *Pl.;* **∼ guard** *n.* Wächter,
*der/*Wächterin, *die;* **∼ risk** *n.*
Sicherheitsrisiko, *das;* **∼ van** *n.*
gepanzerter Transporter; (for money)
Geldtransporter, *der*
sedan /sɪ'dæn/ *n.* (Amer. Motor Veh.)
Limousine, *die*
sedate /sɪ'deɪt/ **1** *adj.* bedächtig; gesetzt
⟨*alte Dame*⟩; gemächlich ⟨*Tempo, Leben*⟩
2 *v.t.* sedieren
sedation /sɪ'deɪʃn/ *n.* Sedation, *die;* **be**
under ∼: sediert sein
sedative /'sedətɪv/ **1** *n.*
Beruhigungsmittel, *das*
2 *adj.* sedativ
sedentary /'sedəntərɪ/ *adj.* sitzend

sediment /'sedɪmənt/ *n.* Ablagerung, *die;*
(of tea, coffee, etc.) Bodensatz, *der*
seduce /sɪ'dju:s/ *v.t.* verführen
seduction /sɪ'dʌkʃn/ *n.* Verführung, *die*
seductive /sɪ'dʌktɪv/ *adj.* verführerisch;
verlockend ⟨*Angebot*⟩
see /si:/ **1** *v.t.,* saw /sɔ:/, seen /si:n/ (a)
sehen; **I can ∼ it's hard for you** ich verstehe,
dass es nicht leicht für dich ist; **I ∼ what**
you mean ich verstehe[, was du meinst]
(b) (meet [with]) sehen; treffen; (meet socially)
sich treffen mit; **I'll ∼ you there/at five** wir
sehen uns dort/um fünf; **∼ you!, [I'll be]**
∼ing you! (coll.) bis bald! (ugs.)
(c) (speak to) sprechen ⟨*Person*⟩ (**about**
wegen); (visit) gehen zu ⟨*Arzt, Anwalt usw.*⟩;
(receive) empfangen
(d) (find out) feststellen; (by looking) nachsehen
(e) (make sure) **∼ [that]** ...: darauf achten,
dass ...
(f) (imagine) sich (*Dat.*) vorstellen
(g) (escort) begleiten
2 *v.i.,* saw, seen (a) sehen
(b) (make sure) nachsehen
(c) **I ∼:** ich verstehe; **you ∼:** weißt du/wisst
ihr/wissen Sie
■ **'see about** *v.t.* sich kümmern um
■ **see 'off** *v.t.* (a) (say goodbye to)
verabschieden
(b) (chase away) vertreiben
■ **see 'out** *v.t.* (escort) hinausbegleiten (**of**
aus); **∼ oneself out** allein hinausfinden
■ **see through** *v.t.* (a) /'--/ hindurchsehen
durch; (fig.) durchschauen
(b) /-'-/ (not abandon) zu Ende bringen
■ **'see to** *v.t.* sich kümmern um
seed /si:d/ **1** *n.* (a) Samen, *der;* (of grape
etc.) Kern, *der*
(b) *no pl., no indef. art.* (**∼s** collectively)
Samen[körner] *Pl.;* (as collected for sowing)
Saatgut, *das;* (for birds) Körner *Pl.;* **go** *or* **run**
to ∼: Samen bilden; (fig.) herunterkommen
(ugs.)
(c) (Sport) gesetzter Spieler/gesetzte Spielerin
2 *v.t.* (a) (place **∼s** in) besäen
(b) (Sport) setzen ⟨*Spieler*⟩; **be ∼ed number**
one als Nummer eins gesetzt werden/sein
'seed bed *n.* [Saat]beet, *das*
'seedless *adj.* kernlos
seedling /'si:dlɪŋ/ *n.* Sämling, *der*
'seedy *adj.* (a) (coll.: unwell) **feel ∼:** sich
[leicht] angeschlagen fühlen
(b) (shabby) schäbig, (ugs.) vergammelt
⟨*Aussehen*⟩; heruntergekommen ⟨*Stadtteil*⟩
(c) (disreputable) zweifelhaft
'seeing *conj.* **∼ [that]** ...: in Anbetracht
dessen, dass ...
seek /si:k/ *v.t.,* sought /sɔ:t/ suchen;
anstreben ⟨*Posten, Amt*⟩; sich bemühen um
⟨*Anerkennung, Interview, Einstellung*⟩; (try to
reach) aufsuchen
seem /si:m/ *v.i.* scheinen; **you ∼ tired** du
wirkst müde; **she ∼s nice** sie scheint nett zu
sein

'seeming adj. scheinbar

'seemingly adv. **(a)** (evidently) offensichtlich
(b) (to outward appearance) scheinbar

seemly /'siːmlɪ/ adj. schicklich

seen ▶ SEE

seep /siːp/ v.i. ~ [away] [ab]sickern

'see-saw n. Wippe, die

seethe /siːð/ v.i. **(a)** ~ [with anger/ inwardly] vor Wut/innerlich schäumen
(b) ⟨Straßen usw.:⟩ wimmeln (with von)

'see-through adj. durchsichtig

segment /'segmənt/ n. (of orange, pineapple, etc.) Scheibe, die

segregate /'segrɪgeɪt/ v.t. trennen; (racially) absondern

segregation /segrɪ'geɪʃn/ n. Trennung, die; [racial] ~: Rassentrennung, die

seismic /'saɪzmɪk/ adj. seismisch

seize /siːz/ **1** v.t. **(a)** ergreifen; ~ power die Macht ergreifen; ~ sb. by the arm/collar jmdn. am Arm/Kragen packen; ~ the opportunity [to do sth.] die Gelegenheit ergreifen [und etw. tun]; ~ any/a or the chance [to do sth.] jede/die Gelegenheit nutzen[, um etw. zu tun]; be ~d with remorse/panic von Gewissensbissen geplagt/ von Panik ergriffen werden
(b) (capture) gefangen nehmen ⟨Person⟩; kapern ⟨Schiff⟩; mit Gewalt übernehmen ⟨Flugzeug, Gebäude⟩; einnehmen ⟨Festung, Brücke⟩
(c) (confiscate) beschlagnahmen
2 v.i. ▶ ~ UP
■ **'seize on** v.t. sich (Dat.) vornehmen ⟨Einzelheit, Aspekt, Schwachpunkt⟩; aufgreifen ⟨Idee, Vorschlag⟩
■ **seize 'up** v.i. sich festfressen

seizure /'siːʒə(r)/ n. **(a)** ▶ SEIZE 1B, C: Gefangennahme, die; Kapern, das; Übernahme, die; Einnahme, die; Beschlagnahme, die
(b) (Med.) Anfall, der

seldom /'seldəm/ adv. selten

select /sɪ'lekt/ **1** adj. ausgewählt
2 v.t. auswählen

selection /sɪ'lekʃn/ n. **(a)** (what is selected [from]) Auswahl, die (of an + Dat., from aus)
(b) (act of choosing) [Aus]wahl, die

selective /sɪ'lektɪv/ adj. (using selection) selektiv; (careful in one's choice) wählerisch

self /self/ n., pl. **selves** [selvz] Selbst, das (geh.); Ich, das

self- pref. selbst-/Selbst-

self: ~-**ab'sorbed** adj. mit sich selbst beschäftigt; ~-**ad'dressed** adj.
~-addressed envelope adressierter Rückumschlag; ~-**ad'hesive** adj. selbstklebend; ~-**ap'pointed** adj. selbst ernannt; ~-**as'surance** n. Selbstsicherheit, die; ~-**as'sured** adj. selbstsicher; ~-**a'wareness** n. Selbsterkenntnis, die; ~-**'catering** **1** adj.

mit Selbstversorgung nachgestellt; **2** n. Selbstversorgung, die; ~-**'centred** adj. egozentrisch; ~-**con'fessed** adj. erklärt; ~-**'confidence** n. Selbstbewusstsein, das; ~-**'confident** adj. selbstbewusst; ~-**'conscious** adj. unsicher; ~-**'consciousness** n. Unsicherheit, die; ~-**con'tained** adj. abgeschlossen ⟨Wohnung⟩; ~-**con'trol** n. Selbstbeherrschung, die; ~-**con'trolled** adj. voller Selbstbeherrschung nachgestellt; ~-**'critical** adj. selbstkritisch; ~-**de'ception** n. Selbsttäuschung, die; ~-**de'feating** adj. unsinnig; ~-**de'fence** n. Notwehr, die; in ~-defence aus Notwehr; ~-**de'lusion** n. Selbsttäuschung, die; ~-**de'nial** n. Selbstverleugnung, die; ~-**de'structive** adj. selbstzerstörerisch; ~-**'discipline** n. Selbstdisziplin, die; ~-**drive** adj. ~-drive hire [company] Autovermietung, die; ~-drive vehicle Mietwagen, der; ~-**em'ployed** adj. selbstständig; ~-**e'steem** n. Selbstachtung, die; ~-**'evident** adj. offenkundig; ~-**ex'planatory** adj. ohne weiteres verständlich; be ~-explanatory für sich selbst sprechen; ~-**ful'filling** adj. zur eigenen Bestätigung mit beitragend; ~-**'help** n. Selbsthilfe, die; ~-**im'portant** adj. eingebildet; ~-**in'dulgent** adj. maßlos; ~-**in'flicted** adj. selbst beigebracht ⟨Wunde⟩; selbst auferlegt ⟨Strafe⟩; ~-**'interest** n. Eigeninteresse, das

'selfish adj., **'selfishly** adv. selbstsüchtig

'selfishness n. Selbstsucht, die

self-'knowledge n. Selbsterkenntnis, die

selfless /'selflɪs/ adj. selbstlos

self: ~-**'motivated** adj. von sich aus motiviert; ~-**ob'sessed** adj. ichbesessen; ~-**o'pinionated** adj. eingebildet; ~-**'pity** n. Selbstmitleid, das; ~-**'portrait** n. Selbstporträt, das; ~-**pos'sessed** adj. selbstbeherrscht; ~-**preser'vation** n. Selbsterhaltung, die; ~-**'raising flour** n. (Brit.) mit Backpulver versetztes Mehl; ~-**re'liant** adj. selbstbewusst; ~-**re'spect** n. Selbstachtung, die; ~-**re'specting** adj. no ~-respecting person ...: niemand, der etwas auf sich hält, ...; ~-**'righteous** adj. selbstgerecht; ~-**'sacrifice** n. Selbstaufopferung, die; ~-**'satisfied** adj. selbstzufrieden; (smug) selbstgefällig; ~-**'service** n. Selbstbedienung, die; attrib. Selbstbedienungs-; ~-**'sufficient** adj. unabhängig; selbstständig ⟨Person⟩; ~-**'taught** adj. autodidaktisch; ~-taught person Autodidakt, der/Autodidaktin, die; ~-**'willed** adj. eigenwillig

sell /sel/ **1** v.t., sold /səʊld/ ~ sth. to sb., ~ sb. sth. jmdm. etw. verkaufen; be sold out ausverkauft sein
2 v.i., sold sich verkaufen ⟨Person:⟩ verkaufen   ⋯⟩

■ **sell 'off** *v.t.* verkaufen

■ **sell 'out** ① *v.t.* **(a)** ausverkaufen
(b) (coll.: betray) verraten
② *v.i.* **we have** *or* **are sold out** wir sind
ausverkauft

'**sell-by date** *n.* ≈
Mindesthaltbarkeitsdatum, *das*

'**seller** *n.* **(a)** Verkäufer, *der*/Verkäuferin,
die
(b) (product) **be a good/slow ~:** sich gut/nur
langsam verkaufen

'**selling point** *n.* **a [good] ~ point** (fig.) ein
Pluspunkt

'**sellotape** *v.t.* mit Tesafilm kleben

Sellotape ® /'seləteɪp/ *n.* ≈ Tesafilm, *der*
Ⓦⓩ

'**sell-out** *n.* **be a ~:** ausverkauft sein; (coll.:
betrayal) Verrat sein

selves *pl. of* SELF

semaphore /'seməfɔː(r)/ ① *n.* (system)
Winken, *das*
② *v.i.* **~ to sb.** jmdm. ein Winksignal
übermitteln

semblance /'sembləns/ *n.* Anschein, *der*

semen /'siːmən/ *n.* Samen, *der*

semester /sɪ'mestə(r)/ *n.* Semester, *das*

semi- /semɪ/ *pref.* halb-/Halb-

semi: ~bold *adj.* (Printing) halbfett;
~breve *n.* (Brit. Mus.) ganze Note; **~circle**
n. Halbkreis, *der;* **~'circular** *adj.*
halbkreisförmig; **~'colon** *n.* Semikolon,
das; **~de'tached** *adj.* & *n.* **~-detached**
[house] Doppelhaushälfte, *die;* **~'final** *n.*
Halbfinale, *das*

seminar /'semɪnaː(r)/ *n.* Seminar, *das*

semi: ~'precious *adj.* **~-precious stone**
Halbedelstein, *der;* **~skimmed** ① *adj.*
teilentrahmt; ② *n.* teilentrahmte Milch;
~tone *n.* (Mus.) Halbton, *der*

semolina /semə'liːnə/ *n.* Grieß, *der*

senate /'senət/ *n.* Senat, *der*

senator /'senətə(r)/ *n.* Senator, *der*

send /send/ *v.t.,* **sent** [sent] schicken;
senden (geh.)

■ **send a'way** ① *v.t.* wegschicken
② *v.i.* **~ away [to sb.] for sth.** etw. [bei
jmdm.] anfordern

■ **send 'back** *v.t.* zurückschicken

■ '**send for** *v.t.* **(a)** (tell to come) holen lassen;
rufen ⟨Polizei, Arzt usw.⟩
(b) (order from elsewhere) anfordern

■ **send 'off** *v.t.* ① **(a)** (dispatch) abschicken
⟨Sache⟩
(b) (Sport) vom Platz stellen
② *v.i.* ▶ SEND AWAY 2

■ **send 'up** *v.t.* (Brit. coll.: parody) parodieren

'**sender** *n.* Absender, *der*

'**send-off** *n.* Verabschiedung, *die*

senile /'siːnaɪl/ *adj.* senil

senile de'mentia *n.* senile Demenz

senility /sɪ'nɪlɪtɪ/ *n.* Senilität, *die*

senior /'siːnɪə(r)/ ① *adj.* **(a)** (older) älter
(b) höher ⟨Rang, Beamter, Stellung⟩; leitend
⟨Angestellter, Stellung⟩; **~ manager** obere
Führungskraft; **~ management** oberer
Führungskreis
② *n.* (older) Ältere, *der*/*die;* (of higher rank)
Vorgesetzte, *der*/*die*

senior 'citizen *n.* Senior, *der*/Seniorin,
die

seniority /siːnɪ'ɒrɪtɪ/ *n.* (greater length of
service) höheres Dienstalter; (higher rank)
höherer Rang

senior 'partner *n.* Seniorpartner, *der*/
-partnerin, *die*

sensation /sen'seɪʃn/ *n.* **(a)** (feeling) Gefühl,
das
(b) (person, event, etc.) Sensation, *die*

sensational /sen'seɪʃənl/ *adj.* sensationell

sensationalise ▶ SENSATIONALIZE

sensationalism /sen'seɪʃənəlɪzm/ *n.*
Sensationshascherei, *die*

sensationalist /sen'seɪʃənəlɪst/ *adj.*
sensationslüstern

sensationalize /sen'seɪʃənəlaɪz/ *v.t.*
~ sth. etw. zur Sensation aufbauschen

sense /sens/ ① *n.* **(a)** (faculty) Sinn, *der;*
~ of smell/touch/taste Geruchs-/Tast-/
Geschmackssinn, *der;* **come to one's ~s** das
Bewusstsein wiedererlangen
(b) *in pl.* (normal state of mind) Verstand, *der;*
have taken leave of one's ~s den Verstand
verloren haben
(c) (consciousness) Gefühl, *das;* **~ of
responsibility/guilt** Verantwortungs-/
Schuldgefühl, *das*
(d) (practical wisdom) Verstand, *der;* **sound** *or*
good ~: [gesunder Menschen]verstand; **not
have the ~ to do sth.** nicht so schlau sein,
etw. zu tun; **there is no ~ in doing that** es
hat keinen Sinn, das zu tun
(e) (meaning) Sinn, *der;* (of word) Bedeutung,
die; **make ~:** einen Sinn ergeben; **in a** *or* **one
~:** in gewisser Hinsicht; **make ~ of sth.** etw.
verstehen
② *v.t.* spüren

'**senseless** *adj.* **(a)** (unconscious) bewusstlos
(b) (purposeless) sinnlos

sensible /'sensɪbl/ *adj.* **(a)** (reasonable)
vernünftig
(b) (practical) zweckmäßig

sensibly /'sensɪblɪ/ *adv.* **(a)** (reasonably)
vernünftig
(b) (practically) zweckmäßig

sensitive /'sensɪtɪv/ *adj.* empfindlich; **be
~ to sth.** empfindlich auf etw. (*Akk.*)
reagieren

sensitivity /sensɪ'tɪvɪtɪ/ *n.*
Empfindlichkeit, *die*

sensory /'sensərɪ/ *adj.* Sinnes-

sensual /'sensjʊəl/ *adj.* sinnlich

sensuous /'sensjʊəs/ *adj.* sinnlich

sent ▶ SEND

sentence /'sentəns/ ① *n.* **(a)** (Law)
[Straf]urteil, *das*

(b) (Ling.) Satz, *der*
2 *v.t.* verurteilen (**to** zu)
sentiment /'sentɪmənt/ *n.* **(a)** Gefühl, *das*
(b) (sentimentality) Sentimentalität, *die*
(c) (thought) Gedanke, *der*
sentimental /sentɪ'mentl/ *adj.*
sentimental
sentimentality /sentɪmen'tælɪtɪ/ *n.*
Sentimentalität, *die*
sentimentalize /sentɪ'mentəlaɪz/ *v.t.*
sentimental darstellen
sentry /'sentrɪ/ *n.* Wache, *die*
separable /'sepərəbl/ *adj.* trennbar
separate **1** /'sepərət/ *adj.* verschieden
⟨*Fragen, Probleme, Gelegenheiten*⟩; gesondert
⟨*Teil*⟩; separat ⟨*Eingang, Toilette, Blatt
Papier, Abteil*⟩; (one's own, individual) eigen
⟨*Zimmer, Identität, Organisation*⟩; **keep two
things** ~: zwei Dinge auseinander halten
2 /'sepəreɪt/ *v.t.* trennen; **they are** ~**d** (no
longer live together) sie leben getrennt
3 *v.i.* **(a)** (disperse) sich trennen
(b) ⟨*Ehepaar:*⟩ sich trennen
separately /'sepərətlɪ/ *adv.* getrennt
separation /sepə'reɪʃn/ *n.* Trennung, *die*
Sept. *abbr.* = **September** Sept.
September /sep'tembə(r)/ *n.* September,
der; see also AUGUST
septic /'septɪk/ *adj.* septisch; **go** ~: eitrig
werden
sequel /'si:kwl/ *n.* **(a)** (consequence, result)
Folge, *die* (**to** von)
(b) (continuation) Fortsetzung, *die*
sequence /'si:kwəns/ *n.* **(a)** Reihenfolge,
die
(b) (part of film) Sequenz, *die*
sequin /'si:kwɪn/ *n.* Paillette, *die*
Serbia /'sɜːbɪə/ *pr. n.* Serbien, *das*
Serbian /'sɜːbɪən/ **1** *adj.* serbisch; **sb. is**
~: jmd. ist Serbe/Serbin
2 *n.* **(a)** (Ling.) serbischer Dialekt
(b) (person) Serbe, *der*/Serbin, *die. See also*
ENGLISH 2A
serenade /serə'neɪd/ **1** *n.* Ständchen, *das*
2 *v.t.* ~ **sb.** jmdm. ein Ständchen bringen
serene /sɪ'riːn/ *adj.* gelassen
serenity /sɪ'renɪtɪ/ *n.* Gelassenheit, *die*
sergeant /'sɑːdʒənt/ *n.* (Mil.) Unteroffizier,
der; (police officer) ≈ Polizeimeister, *der*
sergeant 'major *n.* ≈
[Ober]stabsfeldwebel, *der*
serial /'sɪərɪəl/ *n.* Fortsetzungsgeschichte,
die; (Radio, Telev.) Serie, *die*
serialize /'sɪərɪəlaɪz/ *v.t.* in Fortsetzungen
veröffentlichen; (Radio, Telev.) in
Fortsetzungen senden
'serial killer *n.* Serienmörder, *der*
series /'sɪərɪːz, 'sɪərɪz/ *n., pl. same* **(a)**
(sequence) Reihe, *die;* (of events, misfortunes)
Folge, *die*
(b) (set of successive issues) Serie, *die;* **radio/TV**
~: Hörfunkreihe/Fernsehserie, *die*

(c) (set of books) Reihe, *die*
serious /'sɪərɪəs/ *adj.* **(a)** (earnest) ernst
(b) (important, grave) ernst ⟨*Angelegenheit,
Lage, Problem, Zustand*⟩; ernsthaft ⟨*Frage,
Einwand, Kandidat*⟩; schwer ⟨*Krankheit,
Unfall, Fehler, Niederlage*⟩; ernst zu
nehmend ⟨*Rivale*⟩; ernstlich ⟨*Gefahr,
Bedrohung*⟩; bedenklich ⟨*Mangel*⟩
'seriously *adv.* **(a)** (earnestly) ernst; **take
sth./sb.** ~: etw./jmdn. ernst nehmen
(b) (severely) ernstlich; schwer ⟨*verletzt*⟩
'seriousness *n.* Ernst, *der; in all* ~: ganz
im Ernst
sermon /'sɜːmən/ *n.* Predigt, *die*
serpent /'sɜːpənt/ *n.* Schlange, *die*
serrated /se'reɪtɪd/ *adj.* gezackt; ~ **knife**
Sägemesser, *das*
serum /'sɪərəm/ *n.* Serum, *das*
servant /'sɜːvənt/ *n.* Diener, *der*/Dienerin,
die
serve /sɜːv/ **1** *v.t.* **(a)** (work for) dienen
(+ *Dat.*)
(b) (be useful to) dienlich sein (+ *Dat.*)
(c) (meet needs of) nutzen (+ *Dat.*); ~ **a/no
purpose** einen Zweck erfüllen/keinen Zweck
haben
(d) durchlaufen ⟨*Lehre*⟩; verbüßen
⟨*Haftstrafe*⟩
(e) (dish up) servieren; (pour out) einschenken
(**to** *Dat.*)
(f) ~[**s**] *or* **it** ~**s him right!** [das] geschieht
ihm recht!
2 *v.i.* **(a)** dienen; ~ **as chairman** das Amt
des Vorsitzenden innehaben; ~ **as a Member
of Parliament** Mitglied des Parlaments sein;
~ **on a jury** Geschworener/Geschworene
sein
(b) (be of use) ~ **to do sth.** dazu dienen, etw.
zu tun; ~ **to show sth.** etw. zeigen; ~ **for** *or*
as dienen als
(c) (Sport) aufschlagen
3 *n.* ▶ SERVICE 1G
◼ **serve 'up** *v.t.* **(a)** servieren
(b) (offer for consideration) auftischen (ugs.)
server /'sɜːvə(r)/ *n.* (Comp.) Server, *der*
service /'sɜːvɪs/ **1** *n.* **(a)** Dienst, *der; do
sb. a* ~: jmdm. einen guten Dienst erweisen
(b) (Eccl.) Gottesdienst, *der*
(c) (attending to customer) Service, *der;* (in shop,
garage, etc.) Bedienung, *die*
(d) (system of transport) Verbindung, *die;* **there
is no [bus]** ~ **on Sundays** sonntags
verkehren keine Busse
(e) (provision of maintenance) [after-sale] ~:
Kundendienst, *der; take one's car in for a* ~:
sein Auto zur Inspektion bringen
(f) (operation) Betrieb, *der; out of* ~: außer
Betrieb
(g) (Sport) Aufschlag, *der; whose* ~ *is it?*
wer hat Aufschlag?
(h) (crockery set) Service, *das*
(i) (assistance) **can I be of** ~ [**to you**]? kann
ich Ihnen behilflich sein?; **I'm at your** ~: ich
stehe zu Ihren Diensten ···>

S

(j) (Mil.) the [armed *or* fighting] ~s die Streitkräfte *PL.*; in the ~s beim Militär
(k) [motorway] ~s [Autobahn]raststätte, *die* 〔2〕 *v.t.* warten 〈*Wagen, Waschmaschine, Heizung*〉

serviceable /'sɜːvɪsəbl/ *adj.* **(a)** (useful) nützlich
(b) (durable) haltbar

service: ~ **area** *n.* Raststätte, *die;* ~ **charge** *n.* Bedienungsgeld, *das;* ~ **hatch** *n.* Durchreiche, *die;* ~ **industry** *n.* Dienstleistungsbetrieb, *der;* ~**man** *n.* /'sɜːvɪsmən/ *n.,* *Pl.* ~**men** /'sɜːvɪsmən/ Militärangehörige, *der;* ~ **provider** *n.* (Comp.) Provider, *der;* Internet ~ provider Internetanbieter, *der;* ~ **station** *n.* Tankstelle, *die*

serviette /sɜːvɪˈet/ *n.* (Brit.) Serviette, *die*

servile /'sɜːvaɪl/ *adj.* unterwürfig

servility /sɜːˈvɪlɪtɪ/ *n.* Unterwürfigkeit, *die*

serving /'sɜːvɪŋ/ *n.* Portion, *die*

'serving spoon *n.* Vorlegelöffel, *der*

servitude /'sɜːvɪtjuːd/ *n.* Knechtschaft, *die*

sesame /'sesəmɪ/ *n.* ~ [**seed**] Sesamkorn, *das*

session /'seʃn/ *n.* (meeting) Sitzung, *die;* be in ~: tagen

set /set/ 〔1〕 *v.t.,* -tt-, set **(a)** (put) (horizontally) legen; (vertically) stellen; ~ **sth. ashore** jmdn. an Land setzen; ~ **sth./things right** *or* **in order** etw./die Dinge in Ordnung bringen
(b) (apply) setzen; ~ **a match to sth.** ein Streichholz an etw. (*Akk.*) halten; *see also* FIRE 1A; LIGHT[1] 1D
(c) (adjust) einstellen (at auf + *Akk.*); aufstellen 〈*Falle*〉; stellen 〈*Uhr*〉; ~ **the alarm for 5.30 a.m.** den Wecker auf 5.30 Uhr stellen
(d) be ~ 〈*Buch, Film:*〉 spielen (in in + *Dat.*)
(e) (specify) festlegen 〈*Bedingungen*〉; festsetzen 〈*Termin, Ort usw.*〉 (for auf + *Akk.*); ~ **limits** Grenzen setzen
(f) ~ **sb. thinking that …**: jmdn. auf den Gedanken bringen, dass …
(g) (put forward) stellen 〈*Frage, Aufgabe*〉; aufgeben 〈*Hausaufgabe*〉; aufstellen 〈*Rekord*〉; (compose) zusammenstellen 〈*Rätsel, Fragen*〉; ~ **sb. an example,** ~ **an example to sb.** jmdm. ein Beispiel geben; ~ **sb. a task/problem** jmdm. eine Aufgabe stellen/jmdn. vor ein Problem stellen; ~ [**sb./oneself**] **a target** [jmdm./sich] ein Ziel setzen
(h) (Med.: put into place) [ein]richten; einrenken 〈*verrenktes Gelenk*〉
(i) legen 〈*Haare*〉
(j) decken 〈*Tisch*〉; auflegen 〈*Gedeck*〉
(k) fassen 〈*Edelstein*〉
〔2〕 *v.i.,* -tt-, set **(a)** (solidify) fest werden
(b) (go down) 〈*Sonne, Mond:*〉 untergehen
〔3〕 *n.* **(a)** (group) Satz, *der;* ~ [**of two**] Paar, *das;* a ~ **of chairs** eine Sitzgruppe
(b) (radio, TV) Gerät, *das*
(c) (Tennis) Satz, *der*
(d) (of hair) Legen, *das*

(e) (Theatre: scenery) Bühnenbild, *das;* (*area of performance*) (*of film*) Drehort, *der;* (of play) Bühne, *die*
(f) (of people) Kreis, *der*
(g) (Math.) Menge, *die*
〔4〕 *adj.* **(a)** (fixed) fest 〈*Absichten, Zielvorstellungen, Zeitpunkt*〉; be ~ **in one's ways** *or* **habits** in seinen Gewohnheiten festgefahren sein; ~ **meal** *or* **menu** Menü, *das*
(b) vorgeschrieben 〈*Buch, Lektüre*〉
(c) (ready) be [all] ~ **for sth.** zu etw. bereit sein; be [all] ~ **to do sth.** bereit sein, etw. zu tun
(d) (determined) be ~ **on sth./doing sth.** zu etw. entschlossen sein/entschlossen sein, etw. zu tun
■ **'set about** *v.t.* ~ **about sth.** sich an etw. (*Akk.*) machen; ~ **about doing sth.** sich daranmachen, etw. zu tun
■ **set a'side** *v.t.* **(a)** beiseite legen
(b) aufheben 〈*Urteil, Entscheidung*〉
■ **set 'back** *v.t.* **(a)** aufhalten 〈*Entwicklung*〉; zurückwerfen 〈*Projekt, Programm*〉
(b) (coll.: cost) kosten 〈*Person*〉
(c) (place at a distance) zurücksetzen
■ **set 'down** *v.t.* **(a)** absetzen 〈*Fahrgast*〉
(b) (record) niederschreiben
■ **set 'off** 〔1〕 *v.i.* (begin journey) aufbrechen; (start to move) loslaufen; 〈*Fahrzeug:*〉 losfahren
〔2〕 *v.t.* **(a)** (cause to explode) explodieren lassen; abbrennen 〈*Feuerwerk*〉
(b) auslösen 〈*Reaktion, Alarmanlage*〉
■ **set 'out** 〔1〕 *v.i.* **(a)** (begin journey) aufbrechen (for nach/zu)
(b) ~ **out to do sth.** sich (*Dat.*) vornehmen, etw. zu tun
〔2〕 *v.t.* darlegen
■ **set 'up** 〔1〕 *v.t.* **(a)** errichten 〈*Straßensperre, Denkmal*〉; aufbauen 〈*Zelt, Klapptisch*〉
(b) (establish) gründen 〈*Firma, Organisation*〉; einrichten 〈*Büro*〉
〔2〕 *v.i.* ~ **up in business** ein Geschäft aufmachen

'setback *n.* Rückschlag, *der*

settee /seˈtiː/ *n.* Sofa, *das*

'setting *n.* **(a)** (Mus.) Vertonung, *die*
(b) (surroundings) Rahmen, *der;* (of novel etc.) Schauplatz, *der*

'setting lotion *n.* Haarfestiger, *der*

settle /'setl/ 〔1〕 *v.t.* **(a)** (horizontally) [sorgfältig] legen; (vertically) [sorgfältig] stellen; (at an angle) [sorgfältig] lehnen
(b) (determine, resolve) sich einigen auf 〈*Preis*〉; beilegen 〈*Streit, Konflikt, Meinungsverschiedenheit*〉; ausräumen 〈*Zweifel*〉; entscheiden 〈*Frage, Spiel*〉
(c) bezahlen 〈*Rechnung, Betrag*〉; erfüllen 〈*Forderung, Anspruch*〉; ausgleichen 〈*Konto*〉
〔2〕 *v.i.* **(a)** (become established) sich niederlassen; (as colonist) sich ansiedeln
(b) (pay) abrechnen
(c) (in chair, in front of fire, etc.) sich

settlement ··→ shadow ····

niederlassen; (to work etc.) sich konzentrieren (**to auf** + *Akk.*); (into way of life, retirement, etc.) sich gewöhnen (**into an** + *Akk.*)
(**d**) (subside) ⟨*Haus, Fundament, Boden:*⟩ sich senken
(**e**) ⟨*Schnee:*⟩ liegen bleiben
■ **settle 'down** 1 *v.i.* (**a**) (make oneself comfortable) sich niederlassen (**in in** + *Dat.*)
(**b**) (in town or house) heimisch werden
2 *v.t.* (**a**) ~ oneself down sich [gemütlich] hinsetzen
(**b**) (calm down) beruhigen
■ '**settle for** *v.t.* (agree to) sich zufrieden geben mit
■ **settle 'in** *v.i.* (in new home) sich einleben
■ **settle on** *v.t.* (decide on) sich entscheiden für
■ **settle 'up** *v.i.* abrechnen; ~ **up with the waiter** beim Kellner bezahlen
'**settlement** *n.* (**a**) (of argument, conflict, dispute, differences) Beilegung, *die;* (of question) Klärung, *die;* (of bill, account) Bezahlung, *die;* (of court case) Vergleich, *der*
(**b**) (colony) Siedlung, *die*
settler /'setlə(r)/ *n.* Siedler, *der*/Siedlerin, *die*

set: ~**to** *n., pl.* ~**tos: have a** ~**to** Streit haben; (with fists) sich prügeln; ~**up** *n.* System, *das*
seven /'sevn/ 1 *adj.* sieben
2 *n.* Sieben, *die.* See also EIGHT
seventeen /sevn'tiːn/ 1 *adj.* siebzehn
2 *n.* Siebzehn, *die.* See also EIGHT
seventeenth /sevn'tiːnθ/ 1 *adj.* siebzehnt...
2 *n.* (fraction) Siebzehntel, *das.* See also EIGHTH
seventh /'sevnθ/ 1 *adj.* sieb[en]t...
2 *n.* (in sequence, rank) Sieb[en]te, *der/die/das;* (fraction) Sieb[en]tel, *das.* See also EIGHTH
seventieth /'sevntiθ/ *adj.* siebzigst...
seventy /'sevnti/ 1 *adj.* siebzig
2 *n.* Siebzig, *die.* See also EIGHT; EIGHTY 2
sever /'sevə(r)/ *v.t.* (**a**) (cut) durchtrennen; (fig.) abbrechen ⟨*Beziehungen*⟩
(**b**) (separate) abtrennen; (with axe etc.) abhacken
several /'sevrl/ 1 *adv.* mehrere; einige; ~ **times** mehrmals
2 *pron.* einige; ~ **of us** einige von uns; ~ **of the buildings** einige *od.* mehrere [der] Gebäude
severe /sɪ'vɪə(r)/ *adj.,* ~**r** /sɪ'vɪərə(r)/, ~**st** /sɪ'vɪərɪst/ hart ⟨*Urteil, Strafe, Kritik, Test, Prüfung*⟩; streng ⟨*Frost, Stil, Schönheit*⟩; schwer ⟨*Dürre, Verlust, Behinderung, Verletzung, Krankheit*⟩; rau ⟨*Wetter*⟩; heftig ⟨*Anfall, Schmerz*⟩; bedrohlich ⟨*Mangel, Knappheit*⟩; stark ⟨*Blutung*⟩
se'verely *adv.* hart; schwer ⟨*verletzt, behindert*⟩

severity /sɪ'verɪtɪ/ *n.* Strenge, *die;* (of drought, shortage) großes Ausmaß; (of criticism) Schärfe, *die*
sew /səʊ/ *v.t. & i., p.p.* **sewn** /səʊn/ *or* **sewed** /səʊd/ nähen
■ **sew 'on** *v.t.* annähen ⟨*Knopf*⟩; aufnähen ⟨*Abzeichen, Band*⟩
■ **sew 'up** *v.t.* nähen ⟨*Saum, Naht, Wunde*⟩
sewage /'sjuːɪdʒ/ *n.* Abwasser, *das*
'**sewage disposal** *n.* Abwasserbeseitigung, *die*
sewer /'sjuːə(r), 'suːə(r)/ *n.* (tunnel) Abwasserkanal, *der;* (pipe) Abwasserleitung, *die*
'**sewing** *n.* Näharbeit, *die*
'**sewing machine** *n.* Nähmaschine, *die*
sewn ▶ SEW
sex /seks/ *n.* (**a**) Geschlecht, *das*
(**b**) (sexuality; coll.: intercourse) Sex, *der* (ugs.); **have** ~ **with sb.** (coll.) mit jmdm. schlafen; Sex mit jmdm. haben (salopp)
sex: ~ **appeal** *n.* Sexappeal, *der;* ~ **change** *n.* Geschlechtsumwandlung, *die;* ~ **discrimination** *n.* sexuelle Diskriminierung; ~ **education** *n.* Sexualerziehung, *die*
sexism /'seksɪzm/ *n.* Sexismus, *der*
sexist /'seksɪst/ *adj.* sexistisch
sex: ~ **life** *n.* Geschlechtsleben, *das;* Sexualleben, *das;* ~ **maniac** *n.* Triebverbrecher, *der;* **you** ~ **maniac!** (coll.) du geiler Bock! (ugs.); ~ **offender** *n.* Sexual[straf]täter, *der*/-täterin, *die*
sexploitation /seksplɔɪ'teɪʃn/ *n.* [kommerzielle] Ausbeutung der Sexualität
sex: ~ **shop** *n.* Sexshop, *der;* ~ **symbol** *n.* Sexidol, *das*
sexual /'seksʊəl/ *adj.* sexuell
sexual: ~ **a'buse** *n.* sexueller Missbrauch; ~ '**harassment** *n.* sexuelle Belästigung; ~ '**intercourse** *n.* Geschlechtsverkehr, *der*
sexuality /seksʊ'ælɪtɪ/ *n.* Sexualität, *die*
sexual: ~ '**organs** *n. pl.* Geschlechtsorgane *Pl.;* ~ '**partner** *n.* Sexualpartner, *der*/-partnerin, *die*
'**sexy** *adj.* sexy (ugs.)
sh /ʃ/ *int.* sch; pst
shabbily /'ʃæbɪlɪ/ *adv.,* **shabby** /'ʃæbɪ/ *adj.* schäbig
shack /ʃæk/ *n.* [armselige] Hütte
shackle /'ʃækl/ 1 *n., usu. in pl.* Fessel, *die*
2 *v.t.* anketten (**to an** + *Akk.*)
shade /ʃeɪd/ 1 *n.* (**a**) Schatten, *der*
(**b**) (colour) Ton, *der;* (fig.) Schattierung, *die*
(**c**) (lamp~) [Lampen]schirm, *der*
2 *v.t.* (**a**) (screen) beschatten
(**b**) (darken with lines) ~ **[in]** [ab]schattieren
3 *v.i.* übergehen (**into in** + *Akk.*)
shadow /'ʃædəʊ/ 1 *n.* Schatten, *der*
2 *v.t.* (follow) beschatten ····→

S

'**shadowy** *adj.* (indistinct) schattenhaft

shady /'ʃeɪdɪ/ *adj.* (a) schattig
(b) (disreputable) zwielichtig

shaft /ʃɑːft/ *n.* (a) (of tool, golf club) Schaft,
der
(b) (Mech. Engin.) Welle, *die*
(c) (of mine, lift) Schacht, *der*
(d) (of light, lightning) Strahl, *der*

shaggy /'ʃægɪ/ *adj.* zottelig

shake /ʃeɪk/ ①*n.* Schütteln, *das;* give sb./
sth. a ∼: jmdn./etw. schütteln
②*v.t.,* **shook** /ʃʊk/, **shaken** /'ʃeɪkn/ (a) (move
violently) schütteln; ∼ one's fist/a stick at sb.
jmdm. mit der Faust/einem Stock drohen;
∼ hands sich (*Dat.*) die Hand geben
(b) (cause to tremble) erschüttern ⟨*Gebäude
usw.*⟩; ∼ one's head den Kopf schütteln
(c) (shock) erschüttern
③*v.i.,* **shook, shaken** wackeln ⟨*Boden,
Stimme:*⟩ beben; ⟨*Hand:*⟩ zittern
■ **shake 'off** *v.t.* abschütteln
■ **shake 'up** *v.t.* (a) (upset, shock) einen
Schrecken einjagen (+ *Dat.*)
(b) (reorganize) umkrempeln (ugs.)

shaken ▸ SHAKE 2, 3

shaky /'ʃeɪkɪ/ *adj.* wack[el]ig ⟨*Möbelstück,
Leiter:*⟩; zittrig ⟨*Hand, Stimme, Greis:*⟩; feel ∼:
sich zittrig fühlen

shall /ʃl, *stressed* ʃæl/ *v. aux. only in pres.*
shall, *neg.* (coll.) shan't /ʃɑːnt/, *past* should
/ʃəd, *stressed* ʃʊd/, *neg.* (coll.) shouldn't
/'ʃʊdnt/ (a) (expr. simple future) werden
(b) should (expr. conditional) würde/würdest/
würden/würdet; I should have been killed if I
had let go sie ich wäre getötet worden, wenn ich
losgelassen hätte; if we should be defeated
falls wir unterliegen [sollten]
(c) (expr. will or intention) what ∼ we do? was
sollen wir tun?; let's go in, ∼ we? gehen wir
doch hinein, oder?; we should be safe by
now jetzt dürften wir in Sicherheit sein; he
shouldn't do things like that! er sollte so
etwas nicht tun!

shallot /ʃə'lɒt/ *n.* Schalotte, *die*

shallow /'ʃæləʊ/ *adj.* seicht ⟨*Wasser, Fluss*⟩;
flach ⟨*Schüssel, Teller, Wasser*⟩; (fig.) flach
⟨*Person*⟩

sham /ʃæm/ ①*adj.* unecht; imitiert ⟨*Leder,
Holz, Pelz*⟩
②*n.* (pretence) Heuchelei, *die;* (person)
Heuchler, *der/*Heuchlerin, *die*
③*v.t.,* -mm- vortäuschen
④*v.i.,* -mm- simulieren

shambles /'ʃæmblz/ *n.* (coll.) Chaos, *das;*
the room was a ∼: das Zimmer glich einem
Schlachtfeld

shambolic /ʃæm'bɒlɪk/ *adj.* (coll.)
chaotisch

shame /ʃeɪm/ *n.* (a) Scham, *die*
(b) (state of disgrace) Schande, *die;* put sb./sth.
to ∼: jmdn. beschämen/etw. in den Schatten
stellen
(c) what a ∼! wie schade!

'**shamefaced** *adj.* betreten

shameful /'ʃeɪmfl/ *adj.* beschämend

'**shameless** *adj.* schamlos

shampoo /ʃæm'puː/ ①*v.t.* schamponieren
②*n.* Shampoo[n], *das*

shamrock /'ʃæmrɒk/ *n.* Klee, *der*

shandy /'ʃændɪ/ *n.* Bier mit Limonade;
Radlermaß, *die* (bes. südd.)

shan't /ʃɑːnt/ (coll.) = shall not

shanty[1] /'ʃæntɪ/ *n.* (hut) [armselige] Hütte

shanty[2] *n.* (song) Shanty, *das*

'**shanty town** *n.* Bidonville, *das*

shape /ʃeɪp/ ①*v.t.* formen; bearbeiten
⟨*Holz, Stein*⟩ (into zu)
②*n.* Form, *die;* take ∼: Gestalt annehmen
■ **shape 'up** *v.i.* sich entwickeln

'**shapeless** *adj.* formlos; unförmig ⟨*Kleid,
Person*⟩

shapely /'ʃeɪplɪ/ *adj.* wohlgeformt ⟨*Beine,
Busen*⟩; gut ⟨*Figur*⟩

share /ʃeə(r)/ ①*n.* (a) (portion) Teil, *der od.
das;* [fair] ∼: Anteil, *der;* fair ∼s gerechte
Teile; do more than one's [fair] ∼ of the work
mehr als seinen Teil zur Arbeit beitragen
(b) (Commerc.) Aktie, *die*
②*v.t.* teilen; gemeinsam tragen
⟨*Verantwortung*⟩
③*v.i.* ∼ in teilnehmen an (+ *Dat.*); beteiligt
sein an (+ *Dat.*) ⟨*Gewinn*⟩; teilen ⟨*Freude,
Erfahrung*⟩
■ **share 'out** *v.t.* aufteilen (**among** unter
+ *Akk.*)

share: ∼ **certificate** *n.* Aktienurkunde,
die; ∼**holder** *n.* Aktionär, *der/*Aktionärin,
die; ∼ **index** *n.* Aktienindex, *der;* ∼**-out**
n. Aufteilung, *die;* ∼**ware** *n.* (Comp.)
Shareware, *die*

shark /ʃɑːk/ *n.* Hai[fisch], *der*

sharp /ʃɑːp/ ①*adj.* (a) scharf; spitz ⟨*Nadel,
Bleistift, Gipfel, Winkel*⟩; deutlich
⟨*Unterscheidung*⟩; sauer ⟨*Apfel*⟩; herb ⟨*Wein*⟩;
(shrill, piercing) schrill ⟨*Schrei, Pfiff*⟩; heftig
⟨*Schmerz, Krampf, Kampf*⟩; begabt ⟨*Schüler,
Student*⟩
(b) (derog.: dishonest) gerissen
(c) (Mus.) [um einen Halbton] erhöht ⟨*Note*⟩
②*adv.* (a) (punctually) at six o'clock ∼: Punkt
sechs Uhr
(b) turn ∼ right/left scharf nach rechts/links
abbiegen
(c) look ∼! halt dich ran! (ugs.)
(d) (Mus.) zu hoch ⟨*singen, spielen*⟩

sharpen /'ʃɑːpn/ *v.t.* schärfen; [an]spitzen
⟨*Bleistift*⟩

'**sharpener** *n.* (for pencils) Spitzer, *der* (ugs.)

'**sharp-eyed** *adj.* scharfäugig; be ∼:
scharfe Augen haben

'**sharpish** *adv.* (coll.) (quickly) rasch; (promptly)
unverzüglich; sofort

'**sharply** *adv.* scharf; in scharfem Ton
⟨*antworten*⟩

'**sharpness** *n.* Schärfe, *die;* (fineness of point)
Spitzheit, *die*

'**sharp-witted** *adj.* scharfsinnig

shatter /'ʃætə(r)/ **1** v.t. zertrümmern; zerbrechen ‹Glas, Fenster›; zerschlagen ‹Hoffnungen›
2 v.i. zerbrechen

shattered /'ʃætəd/ adj. (a) zerbrochen ‹Glas, Fenster›; (fig.) zerstört ‹Hoffnungen›; zerrüttet ‹Nerven›
(b) (coll.: greatly upset) she was ∼ by the news die Nachricht hat sie schwer mitgenommen; I'm ∼! ich bin ganz erschüttert!; (Brit. coll.: exhausted) ich bin kaputt! (ugs.)

'**shattering** adj. verheerend ‹Wirkung›; vernichtend ‹Schlag, Niederlage›

shave /ʃeɪv/ **1** v.t. rasieren; abrasieren ‹Haare›
2 v.i. sich rasieren
3 n. Rasur, die; have a ∼: sich rasieren
■ **shave 'off** v.t. abrasieren

'**shaven** /'ʃeɪvn/ adj. rasiert; [kahl] geschoren ‹Kopf›

'**shaver** n. Rasierapparat, der

'**shaver point** n. Anschluss, der für den Rasierapparat

shaving /'ʃeɪvɪŋ/ n. (a) Rasieren, das
(b) in pl. (of wood, metal, etc.) Späne Pl.

shaving: ∼ **brush** n. Rasierpinsel, der; ∼ **cream** n. Rasiercreme, die; ∼ **foam** n. Rasierschaum, der ∼ **soap** n. Rasierseife, die; ∼ **stick** n. Stangenrasierseife, die

shawl /ʃɔːl/ n. Schultertuch, das

she /ʃɪ, stressed ʃiː/ pron. sie

sheaf /ʃiːf/ n., pl. **sheaves** /ʃiːvz/ (of corn etc.) Garbe, die; (of paper, arrows, etc.) Bündel, das

shear /ʃɪə(r)/ v.t., p.p. **shorn** /ʃɔːn/ or **sheared** (clip) scheren

shears /ʃɪəz/ n. pl. [pair of] ∼: Schere, die; garden ∼: Gartenschere, die

sheath /ʃiːθ/ n., pl. ∼s /ʃiːðz, ʃɪːθs/ (a) (for knife, sword, etc.) Scheide, die
(b) (condom) Gummischutz, der

sheaves pl. of SHEAF

shebang /ʃɪ'bæŋ/ n. (Amer. coll.) the whole ∼: der ganze Kram (ugs.)

shed¹ /ʃed/ v.t., -dd-, shed (a) verlieren; abwerfen ‹Laub, Geweih›
(b) vergießen ‹Blut, Tränen›
(c) verbreiten ‹Licht›

shed² n. Schuppen, der

she'd /ʃɪd, stressed ʃiːd/ (a) = she had;
(b) = she would

sheen /ʃiːn/ n. Glanz, der

sheep /ʃiːp/ n., pl. same Schaf, das

sheep: ∼ **dip** n. Desinfektionsbad für Schafe; ∼**dog** n. Hütehund, der; Schäferhund, der; Old English S∼dog Bobtail, der

sheepish /'ʃiːpɪʃ/ adj. verlegen

sheep: ∼ **shearer** /'ʃiːp ʃɪərə(r)/ n. Schafscherer, der; ∼**shearing** n. Schafschur, die; ∼**skin** n. Schaffell, das

sheer /ʃɪə(r)/ adj. (a) rein; blank ‹Unsinn, Gewalt›; by ∼ chance rein zufällig
(b) schroff ‹Felsen, Abfall›

sheet /ʃiːt/ n. (a) Laken, das
(b) (of thin metal or plastic) Folie, die; (of iron, tin) Blech, das; (of glass) Platte, die; (of paper) Bogen, der; Blatt, das
(c) ‹Eis-, Nebel›decke, die

sheet: ∼ **lightning** n. Flächenblitz, der; ∼ **music** n. Notenblätter Pl.

sheik[h] /ʃeɪk, ʃiːk/ n. Scheich, der

shelf /ʃelf/ n., pl. **shelves** /ʃelvz/ Brett, das; Bord, das; **shelves** (set) Regal, das

'**shelf life** n. Lagerfähigkeit, die

shell /ʃel/ **1** n. (a) Schale, die; (of snail) Haus, das; (of turtle, tortoise) Panzer, der; (on beach) Muschel, die
(b) (Mil.) (bomb) Granate, die
2 v.t. (a) (take out of ∼) schälen
(b) (Mil.) [mit Artillerie] beschießen
■ **shell 'out** v.t. & i. (coll.) blechen (ugs.) (on für)

she'll /ʃɪl, stressed ʃiːl/ = she will

shell: ∼**fish** n., pl. same (a) Schal[en]tier, das; (oyster, clam) Muschel, die; (crustacean) Krebstier, das; (b) in pl. (Gastr.) Meeresfrüchte Pl.; ∼ **shock** n. Kriegsneurose, die; ∼ **suit** n. Trilobalanzug, der

shelter /'ʃeltə(r)/ **1** n. (a) (shield) Schutz, der (against vor + Dat., gegen); **bomb** or air-**raid** ∼: Luftschutzraum, der; get under ∼: sich unterstellen
(b) no pl. (place of safety) Zuflucht, die
2 v.t. schützen (from vor + Dat.); Unterschlupf gewähren (+ Dat.) ‹Flüchtling›
3 v.i. Schutz suchen (from vor + Dat.)

'**sheltered** /'ʃeltəd/ adj. geschützt; behütet ‹Leben›; live in ∼ housing in einer Altenwohnung/in Altenwohnungen leben

shelve /ʃelv/ **1** v.t. (defer) auf Eis legen (ugs.)
2 v.i. (slope) abfallen

shelves pl. of SHELF

'**shelving** n. Regale Pl.

shepherd /'ʃepəd/ **1** n. Schäfer, der
2 v.t. führen

'**shepherdess** n. Schäferin, die

shepherd: ∼'s '**crook** n. Schäferstock, der; ∼'s '**pie** n: Auflauf aus Hackfleisch mit einer Schicht Kartoffelbrei darüber

sheriff /'ʃerɪf/ n. Sheriff, der

sherry /'ʃerɪ/ n. Sherry, der

she's /ʃɪz, stressed ʃiːz/ (a) = she is;
(b) = she has

shield /ʃiːld/ **1** n. Schild, der
2 v.t. schützen (from vor + Dat.)

shift /ʃɪft/ **1** v.t. (a) (move) umstellen ‹Möbel›; wegnehmen ‹Arm, Hand, Fuß›; wegräumen ‹Schutt›; entfernen ‹Schmutz, Fleck›; ∼ the responsibility/blame on to sb. die Verantwortung/Schuld auf jmdn. schieben

⋯⫸

(b) (Amer. Motor Veh.) ~ **gears** schalten
[2] *v.i.* (a) ⟨Wind:⟩ drehen (**to** nach);
⟨Ladung:⟩ verrutschen
(b) (coll.: move quickly) rasen
[3] *n.* (a) a ~ **in emphasis** eine Verlagerung
des Akzents; a ~ **in public opinion** ein
Umschwung der öffentlichen Meinung
(b) (for work) Schicht, *die;* **eight-hour/late** ~:
Achtstunden-/Spätschicht, *die;* **do** *or* **work**
the late ~: Spätschicht haben
'**shift work** *n.* Schichtarbeit, *die*
shifty /'ʃɪftɪ/ *adj.* verschlagen
shilling /'ʃɪlɪŋ/ *n.* (Hist.) Shilling, *der*
shilly-shally /'ʃɪlɪʃælɪ/ *v.i.* zaudern; **stop**
~**ing!** entschließ dich endlich!
shimmer /'ʃɪmə(r)/ [1] *v.i.* schimmern
[2] *n.* Schimmer, *der*
shin /ʃɪn/ [1] *n.* Schienbein, *das*
[2] *v.i.,* -**nn**-: ~ **up/down a tree** *etc.* einen
Baum *usw.* hinauf-/hinunterklettern
'**shin bone** *n.* Schienbein, *das*
shine /ʃaɪn/ [1] *v.i.,* shone /ʃɒn/ ⟨Lampe,
Licht, Stern:⟩ leuchten; ⟨Sonne, Mond:⟩
scheinen; (reflect light) glänzen
[2] *v.t.,* shone: ~ **a light on sth./in sb.'s eyes**
etw. anleuchten/jmdm. in die Augen
leuchten
[3] *n.* Glanz, *der*
shingle /'ʃɪŋɡl/ *n.* (pebbles) Kies, *der*
'**shingles** *n.* (Med.) Gürtelrose, *die*
shin: ~ **guard,** ~ **pad** *ns.*
Schienbeinschutz, *der*
shiny /'ʃaɪnɪ/ *adj.* glänzend
ship /ʃɪp/ [1] *n.* Schiff, *das*
[2] *v.t.,* -**pp**- (transport by sea) verschiffen; (send
by road, train, or air) verschicken ⟨Waren⟩
'**shipbuilding** *n.* Schiffbau, *der*
'**shipment** *n.* (a) Versand, *der;* (by sea)
Verschiffung, *die*
(b) (amount) Sendung, *die*
'**shipowner** *n.* Schiffseigentümer, *der/*
-eigentümerin, *die;* (of several ships) Reeder,
*der/*Reederin, *die*
'**shipper** *n.* Spediteur, *der/*Spediteurin, *die;*
(company) Spedition, *die*
'**shipping** *n.* (a) (ships) Schiffe *Pl.;* (traffic)
Schifffahrt, *die*
(b) (transporting) Versand, *der*
shipping: ~ **agent** *n.* Schiffsagent, *der;*
~ **forecast** *n.* Seewetterbericht, *der;*
~ **lane** *n.* Schifffahrtsweg, *der*
ship: ~**shape** *adj.* in bester Ordnung;
~**wreck** [1] *n.* Schiffbruch, *der;* [2] *v.t.* be
~**wrecked** Schiffbruch erleiden; ~**yard** *n.*
[Schiffs]werft, *die*
shirk /ʃɜːk/ *v.t.* sich drücken vor (+ *Dat.*)
'**shirker** *n.* Drückeberger, *der/*
Drückebergerin, *die* (ugs.)
shirt /ʃɜːt/ *n.* [man's] ~: [Herren- *od.*
Ober]hemd, *das;* [woman's] ~: Hemdbluse,
die
'**shirtsleeve** *n.* Hemdsärmel, *der;* **in** ~**s** in
Hemdsärmeln

shit /ʃɪt/ (coarse) [1] *v.i.,* -**tt**-, shitted *or* shit
scheißen (derb)
[2] *n.* (a) Scheiße, *die* (derb); **have** (Brit.) *or*
(Amer.) **take a** ~: scheißen (derb)
(b) (person) Scheißkerl, *der* (derb)
(c) (nonsense) Scheiß, *der* (salopp)
shiver /'ʃɪvə(r)/ [1] *v.i.* zittern (**with** vor
+ *Dat.*)
[2] *n.* Schau[d]er, *der* (geh.)
shoal /ʃəʊl/ *n.* (of fish) Schwarm, *der*
shock /ʃɒk/ [1] *n.* (a) Schock, *der;* **give sb. a**
~: jmdm. einen Schock versetzen
(b) (violent impact) Erschütterung, *die* (**of**
durch)
(c) (Electr.) Schlag, *der*
(d) (Med.) Schock, *der*
[2] *v.t.* ~ **sb.** [deeply] ein [schwerer] Schock
für jmdn. sein; (scandalize) jmdn. schockieren
'**shock absorber** *n.* Stoßdämpfer, *der*
'**shocking** *adj.* (a) schockierend
(b) (coll.: very bad) fürchterlich (ugs.)
shock: ~ **jock** *n.* (coll.) Skandal-DJ, *der;*
~**proof** *adj.* stoßfest; ~ **wave** *n.*
Druckwelle, *die* (**from** *Gen.*); (of earthquake)
Erschütterungswelle, *die* (**from** *Gen.*)
shod ▶ SHOE 2
shoddy /'ʃɒdɪ/ *adj.* schäbig; minderwertig
⟨Arbeit, Stoff, Artikel⟩
shoe /ʃuː/ [1] *n.* Schuh, *der;* (of horse)
[Huf]eisen, *das;* **put oneself into sb.'s** ~**s** (fig.)
sich in jmds. Lage (*Akk.*) versetzen
[2] *v.t.,* ~**ing,** shod /ʃɒd/ beschlagen ⟨Pferd⟩
shoe: ~**cream** *n.* Schuhcreme, *die;*
~**horn** *n.* Schuhlöffel, *der;* ~**lace** *n.*
Schnürsenkel, *der;* ~**maker** *n.*
Schuhmacher, *der;* ~ **polish** *n.*
Schuhcreme, *die;* ~ **shop** *n.* Schuhgeschäft,
das; ~**string** *n.* **on a** ~**string** (coll.) mit ganz
wenig Geld
shone ▶ SHINE 1, 2
shoo /ʃuː/ [1] *int.* sch
[2] *v.t.* scheuchen; ~ **away** fortscheuchen
shook ▶ SHAKE 2, 3
shoot /ʃuːt/ [1] *v.i.,* shot /ʃɒt/ (a) schießen
(**at** auf + *Akk.*)
(b) (move rapidly) schießen (ugs.)
[2] *v.t.,* shot (a) (wound) anschießen; (kill)
erschießen; (hunt) schießen; ~ **sb. dead** jmdn.
erschießen
(b) schießen mit ⟨Bogen, Munition, Pistole⟩;
abschießen ⟨Pfeil, Kugel⟩ (**at** auf + *Akk.*)
(c) (Cinemat.) drehen ⟨Film, Szene⟩
[3] *n.* (Bot.) Trieb, *der*
▪ **shoot 'down** *v.t.* niederschießen
⟨Person⟩; abschießen ⟨Flugzeug⟩
▪ **shoot 'out** *v.i.* hervorschießen
▪ **shoot 'up** *v.i.* in die Höhe schießen;
⟨Preise, Kosten, Temperatur:⟩ in die Höhe
schnellen
shooting: ~ **range** *n.* Schießstand, *der;*
~ '**star** *n.* Sternschnuppe, *die;* ~ **stick** *n.*
Jagdstock, *der*
'**shoot-out** *n.* Schießerei, *die*

shop /ʃɒp/ **1** n. Laden, der; Geschäft, das; **go to the ~s** einkaufen gehen; **talk ~:** fachsimpeln (ugs.)
2 v.i., -pp- einkaufen; **go ~ping** einkaufen gehen
■ **shop a'round** v.i. sich umsehen (**for** nach)

shopaholic /ˈʃɒpəhɒlɪk/ n. Kaufsüchtige, der|die

shop: **~ assistant** n. (Brit.) Verkäufer, der/Verkäuferin, die; **~front** n. Schaufensterfront, die; **~keeper** n. Ladenbesitzer, der/-besitzerin, die; **~lifter** n. Ladendieb, der/-diebin, die; **~lifting** n. Ladendiebstahl, der; **~owner** ▶ ~KEEPER

'shopper n. Käufer, der/Käuferin, die

'shopping n. (a) Einkaufen, das; **do the/one's ~:** einkaufen/[seine] Einkäufe machen
(b) (items bought) Einkäufe Pl.

shopping: **~ bag** n. Einkaufstasche, die; **~ basket** n. Einkaufskorb, der; **~ centre** n. Einkaufszentrum, das; **~ list** n. Einkaufszettel, der; **~ mall** /-mæl/ n. Einkaufszentrum, das; **~ precinct** n. Einkaufs- od. Geschäftsviertel, das; **~ street** n. Geschäftsstraße, die; **~ trolley** n. (in supermarket) Einkaufswagen, der; (personal) Einkaufsroller, der

shop: **~-soiled** adj. (Brit.) (slightly damaged) leicht beschädigt; (slightly dirty) angeschmutzt; **~ steward** n. [gewerkschaftlicher] Vertrauensmann; **~ 'window** n. Schaufenster, das

shore /ʃɔː(r)/ n. Ufer, das; (beach) Strand, der
■ **shore 'up** v.t. abstützen ‹Mauer, Haus›; (fig.) stützen

shorn ▶ SHEAR

short /ʃɔːt/ **1** adj. (a) kurz; **in a ~ time** or **while** (soon) bald; **in Kürze; a ~ time** or **while ago/later** vor kurzem/kurze Zeit später; **in ~, ...:** kurz, ...
(b) klein ‹Person, Wuchs›
(c) (deficient, scanty) knapp; **go ~ [of sth.]** [an etw. (Dat.)] Mangel leiden; **sb. is ~ of sth.** jmdm. fehlt es an etw. (Dat.); **time is getting/is ~:** die Zeit wird/ist knapp; **be in ~ supply** knapp sein; **be ~ [of cash]** knapp [bei Kasse] sein (ugs.)
2 adv. (a) (abruptly) plötzlich; **stop ~:** plötzlich abbrechen; **stop sb. ~:** jmdm. ins Wort fallen
(b) **stop ~ of doing sth.** nicht so weit gehen, etw. zu tun

shortage /ˈʃɔːtɪdʒ/ n. Mangel, der (**of** an + Dat.); **~ of fruit/teachers** Obstknappheit, die/Lehrermangel, der

short: **~bread** n. Shortbread, das; Kekse aus Butterteig; **~ 'circuit** n. (Electr.) Kurzschluss, der; **~coming** n., usu. in pl.

Unzulänglichkeit, die; **~ 'cut** n. Abkürzung, die; **take a ~ cut** den Weg abkürzen

shorten /ˈʃɔːtn/ **1** v.i. kürzer werden
2 v.t. kürzen; verkürzen ‹Besuch, Wartezeit›

short: **~fall** n. Fehlmenge, die; **~-haired** adj. kurzhaarig; Kurzhaar‹dackel, -katze›; **~hand** n. Stenografie, die; **~hand typist** Stenotypist, der/-typistin, die; **~ list** n. (Brit.) engere Auswahl; **be on/put sb. on the ~ list** in der engeren Auswahl sein/jmdn. in die engere Auswahl nehmen; **~-list** v.t. in die engere Auswahl nehmen; **~-lived** adj. kurzlebig

'shortly adv. in Kürze; demnächst; **~ before/after sth.** kurz vor/nach etw.

short: **~ 'pastry** n. Mürbeteig, der; **~-range** adj. (a) Kurzstrecken‹flugzeug, -rakete usw.›; (b) (relating to time) kurzfristig

shorts /ʃɔːts/ n. pl. (a) (trousers) kurze Hose[n Pl.]; Shorts Pl.
(b) (Amer.: underpants) Unterhose, die

short: **~'sighted** adj. kurzsichtig; **~-sleeved** /-sliːvd/ adj. kurzärm[e]lig; **~-staffed** /-staːft/ adj. **be [very] ~-staffed** [viel] zu wenig Personal haben; **~ 'story** n. Kurzgeschichte, die; **~'tempered** adj. aufbrausend; **~-term** adj. kurzfristig; (provisional) vorläufig ‹Lösung›; befristet ‹Vertrag›; **~ 'trousers** n. pl. kurze Hose[n Pl.]; **~ wave** n. (Radio) Kurzwelle, die

shot /ʃɒt/ **1** n. (a) Schuss, der; **fire a ~:** einen Schuss abgeben (**at** auf + Akk.); **like a ~** (fig.) wie der Blitz (ugs.); **I'd do it like a ~:** ich würde es auf der Stelle tun
(b) (Athletics) **put the ~:** die Kugel stoßen; **[putting] the ~:** Kugelstoßen, das
(c) (Sport: stroke, kick, throw) Schuss, der
(d) (Photog.) Aufnahme, die; (Cinemat.) Einstellung, die
2 ▶ SHOOT 1, 2
3 adj. **be/get ~ of** (coll.) los sein/loswerden

'shotgun n. [Schrot]flinte, die

should ▶ SHALL

shoulder /ˈʃəʊldə(r)/ **1** n. Schulter, die
2 v.t. schultern; (fig.) übernehmen

shoulder: **~ bag** n. Umhängetasche, die; **~ blade** n. Schulterblatt, das; **~ joint** n. Schultergelenk, das; **~-length** adj. schulterlang; **~ pad** n. Schulterpolster, das; **~ strap** n. (on garment) Schulterklappe, die; (on bag) Trageriemen, der

shouldn't /ˈʃʊdnt/ (coll.) = should not; ▶ SHALL

shout /ʃaʊt/ **1** n. Ruf, der; (inarticulate) Schrei, der
2 v.i. & t. schreien
■ **shout 'down** v.t. niederschreien
■ **shout 'out** **1** v.i. aufschreien
2 v.t. [laut] rufen

'shouting n. Geschrei, das

shove /ʃʌv/ **1** n. Stoß, der
2 v.t. stoßen; schubsen (ugs.); (coll.: put) tun ⋯✦

S

■ **shove a'way** v.t. (coll.) wegschubsen (ugs.)

■ **shove 'off** v.i. (coll.: leave) abschieben (ugs.)

shovel /'ʃʌvl/ 1 n. Schaufel, die 2 v.t., (Brit.) -ll- schaufeln

show /ʃəʊ/ 1 n. (a) (entertainment, performance) Show, die; (Theatre) Vorstellung, die; (Radio, Telev.) [Unterhaltungs]sendung, die (b) (exhibition) Ausstellung, die; Schau, die; put sth. on ~: etw. ausstellen; be on ~: ausgestellt sein (c) (appearance) Anschein, der; be for ~: reine Angeberei sein (ugs.) 2 v.t., p.p. shown /ʃəʊn/ (a) zeigen; vorzeigen ⟨Pass, Fahrschein usw.⟩; ~ sb. sth., ~ sth. to sb. jmdm. etw. zeigen (b) beweisen ⟨Mut, Urteilsvermögen usw.⟩; ~ sb. that ...: jmdm. beweisen, dass ...; ~ [sb.] kindness/mercy freundlich [zu jmdm.] sein/Erbarmen [mit jmdm.] haben (c) ⟨Thermometer, Uhr usw.⟩ anzeigen (d) (exhibit in a show) ausstellen; zeigen ⟨Film⟩ 3 v.i., p.p. shown (a) (be visible) sichtbar od. zu sehen sein; (come into sight) sich zeigen (b) (be ~n) ⟨Film:⟩ laufen; ⟨Künstler:⟩ ausstellen

■ **show 'in** v.t. hinein-/hereinführen

■ **show 'off** v.i. angeben (ugs.); prahlen

■ **show 'out** v.t. hinausführen

■ **show 'round** v.t. herumführen

■ **show 'through** v.i. durchscheinen

■ **show 'up** 1 v.t. (a) (make visible) [deutlich] sichtbar machen (b) (coll.: embarrass) blamieren 2 v.i. (a) (be visible) [deutlich] zu sehen sein (b) (coll.: arrive) sich blicken lassen (ugs.)

show: ~ biz (coll.)**, ~ business** ns., no art. Schaugeschäft, das; **~case** n. Vitrine, die; (fig.) Schaufenster, das; '**~down** n. (fig.) Kraftprobe, die; **have a ~down [with sb.]** sich [mit jmdm.] auseinander setzen

shower /'ʃaʊə(r)/ 1 n. (a) Schauer, der; ~ **of rain/hail** Regen-/Hagelschauer, der (b) (for washing) Dusche, die; **have** or **take a [cold/quick] ~:** [kalt/schnell] duschen 2 v.t. (lavish) ~ **sth. [up]on sb., ~ sb. with sth.** jmdn. mit etw. überhäufen 3 v.i. (have a ~) duschen

shower: ~ cap n. Duschhaube, die; ~ **curtain** n. Duschvorhang, der; ~ **gel** n. Duschgel, das; **~proof** adj. (bedingt) regendicht

'**showery** adj. **it is ~:** es gibt immer wieder kurze Schauer; **a ~ day** ein Tag mit Schauerwetter

'**showjumping** n. Springreiten, das

shown ▸ SHOW 2, 3

show: ~off n. (coll.) Angeber, der/ Angeberin, die; **~piece** n. (of exhibition, collection) Schaustück, das; (highlight) Paradestück, das; **~room** n. Ausstellungsraum, der; ~ **trial** n. Schauprozess, der

'**showy** adj. protzig (ugs.)

shrank ▸ SHRINK

shred /ʃred/ 1 n. Fetzen, der; (fig.) Spur, die; **tear sth. to ~s** etw. zerfetzen; (fig.) etw. zerpflücken 2 v.t., -dd- [im Reißwolf] zerkleinern

shredder /'ʃredə(r)/ n. (for paper) Reißwolf, der

shrew /ʃruː/ n. (Zool.) Spitzmaus, die

shrewd /ʃruːd/ adj. klug; genau ⟨[Ein]schätzung⟩

shriek /ʃriːk/ 1 n. [Auf]schrei, der 2 v.i. [auf]schreien 3 v.t. schreien

shrift /ʃrɪft/ n. **give sb. short ~:** jmdn. kurz abfertigen (ugs.); **get short ~** kurz abgefertigt werden (ugs.)

shrill /ʃrɪl/ adj. schrill

shrimp /ʃrɪmp/ n. Garnele, die

shrine /ʃraɪn/ n. (tomb) Grab, das

shrink /ʃrɪŋk/ 1 v.i., shrank /ʃræŋk/, shrunk /ʃrʌŋk/ (a) schrumpfen; ⟨Kleidung, Stoff:⟩ einlaufen; ⟨Metall, Holz:⟩ sich zusammenziehen (b) (recoil) ~ **from sb./sth.** vor jmdm. zurückweichen/vor etw. (Dat.) zurückschrecken; ~ **from doing sth.** sich scheuen, etw. zu tun 2 v.t., shrank, shrunk einlaufen lassen ⟨Textilien⟩

shrinkage /'ʃrɪŋkɪdʒ/ n. (of clothing) Einlaufen, das

shrink: ~-proof, ~-resistant adjs. schrumpffrei; **be ~-proof** nicht einlaufen; **~-wrap** v.t. in einer Schrumpffolie verpacken

shrivel /'ʃrɪvl/ v.i., (Brit.) -ll- ~ **[up]** verschrumpeln; ⟨Pflanze, Blume:⟩ welk werden

shroud /ʃraʊd/ 1 n. Leichentuch, das 2 v.t. ~ **sth. in sth.** etw. in etw. (Akk.) hüllen

Shrove 'Tuesday /ʃrəʊv/ n. Fastnachtsdienstag, der

shrub /ʃrʌb/ n. Strauch, der

shrubbery /'ʃrʌbərɪ/ n. Gesträuch, das

shrug /ʃrʌg/ 1 v.t. & i., -gg- ~ **[one's shoulders]** die Achseln zucken 2 n. ~ **[of one's** or **the shoulders]** Achselzucken, das

■ **shrug 'off** v.t. in den Wind schlagen

shrunk ▸ SHRINK

shrunken /'ʃrʌŋkn/ adj. verhutzelt (ugs.) ⟨Person⟩; schrump[e]lig ⟨Apfel⟩

shudder /'ʃʌdə(r)/ 1 v.i. zittern (with vor + Dat.) 2 n. Zittern, das

shuffle /'ʃʌfl/ 1 n. (a) Schlurfen, das; **walk with a ~:** schlurfen (b) (Cards) Mischen, das; **give the cards a [good] ~:** die Karten [gut] mischen 2 v.t. (a) (Cards) mischen

(b) ~ **one's feet** von einem Fuß auf den anderen treten

shun /ʃʌn/ *v.t.*, **-nn-** meiden

shunt /ʃʌnt/ *v.t.* (Railw.) rangieren

shush /ʃʊʃ/ *int.* still

shut /ʃʌt/ ① *v.t.*, **-tt-**, **shut** zumachen; schließen; zusammenklappen ⟨*Klappmesser, Fächer*⟩; ~ **one's finger in the door** sich ⟨*Dat.*⟩ den Finger in der Tür einklemmen ② *v.i.*, **-tt-**, **shut** schließen; ⟨*Blüte:*⟩ sich schließen

■ **shut 'down** ① *v.t.* **(a)** schließen, zumachen ⟨*Deckel*⟩
(b) stilllegen ⟨*Fabrik*⟩; abschalten ⟨*Kernreaktor*⟩
② *v.i.* ⟨*Laden, Fabrik:*⟩ geschlossen werden

■ **shut 'out** *v.t.* aussperren

■ **shut 'up** ① *v.t.* abschließen; einsperren ⟨*Tier, Person*⟩
② *v.i.* (coll.: be quiet) den Mund halten

shutter /'ʃʌtə(r)/ *n.* **(a)** [Fenster]laden, *der*
(b) (Photog.) Verschluss, *der;* ~ **release** Auslöser, *der;* ~ **speed** Verschlusszeit, *die*

shuttle /'ʃʌtl/ ① *n.* (in loom) Schiffchen, *das*
② *v.i.* pendeln

shuttle: ~**cock** *n.* Federball, *der;*
'~ **service** *n.* Pendelverkehr, *der*

shy /ʃaɪ/ *adj.*, ~**er** or **shier** /'ʃaɪə(r)/, ~**est** or **shiest** /'ʃaɪɪst/ scheu; (diffident) schüchtern

■ **shy a'way** *v.i.* ~ **away from sth./doing sth.** etw. scheuen/sich scheuen, etw. zu tun

'**shyness** *n.* Scheuheit, *die;* (diffidence) Schüchternheit, *die*

Siamese /saɪə'miːz/ ~ '**cat** *n.* Siamkatze, *die;* ~ '**twins** *n. pl.* siamesische Zwillinge *Pl.*

Siberia /saɪ'bɪərɪə/ *pr. n.* Sibirien (*das*)

sibling /'sɪblɪŋ/ *n.* (male) Bruder, *der;* (female) Schwester, *die; in pl.* Geschwister *Pl.*

Sicily /'sɪsɪlɪ/ *pr. n.* Sizilien (*das*)

sick /sɪk/ ① *adj.* **(a)** (ill) krank; **be off** ~: krank [gemeldet] sein
(b) (Brit.: vomiting or about to vomit) **be** ~: sich erbrechen; **I'm going to be** ~: ich muss mich erbrechen; **sb. gets/feels** ~: jmdm. wird/ist [es] übel *od.* schlecht; **be/get** ~ **of sb./sth.** (fig.) jmdn./etw. satt haben/ allmählich satt haben; **make sb.** ~ (disgust) jmdn. anekeln
② *n. pl.* **the** ~: die Kranken *Pl.*

sick 'building syndrome *n.* Sickbuildingsyndrom, *das*

'**sicken** /'sɪkn/ ① *v.i.* **be** ~**ing for sth.** (Brit.) krank werden; etw. ausbrüten (ugs.)
② *v.t.* (disgust) anwidern

'**sickening** *adj.* Ekel erregend, widerlich ⟨*Anblick, Geruch*⟩

sickle /'sɪkl/ *n.* Sichel, *die*

sick: ~ **leave** *n.* Urlaub wegen Krankheit; **be on** ~ ≈ krank geschrieben sein; ~ **list** *n.* Liste der Kranken, *die;* **on the** ~ **list:** krank [gemeldet/geschrieben]

'**sickly** *adj.* kränklich

'**sickness** *n.* Krankheit, *die;* (nausea) Übelkeit, *die*

sick: ~ **pay** *n.* Entgeltfortzahlung im Krankheitsfalle; (paid by insurance) Krankengeld, *das;* ~**room** *n.* Krankenzimmer, *das*

side /saɪd/ ① *n.* **(a)** Seite, *die;* ~ **of beef** Rinderhälfte, *die;* ~ **of bacon** Speckseite, *die;* **walk/stand** ~ **by** ~: nebeneinander gehen/stehen; **work/fight** ~ **by** ~ [**with sb.**] Seite an Seite [mit jmdm.] arbeiten/ kämpfen; **live** ~ **by** ~ [**with sb.**] in [jmds.] unmittelbarer Nachbarschaft leben; **to one** ~: zur Seite; **on one** ~: an der Seite; **on the** ~ (as ~line) nebenbei; **take** ~**s** [**with/against sb.**] [für/gegen jmdn.] Partei ergreifen
(b) (Sport: team) Mannschaft, *die*
② *v.i.* ~ **with sb.** sich auf jmds. Seite (*Akk.*) stellen
③ *adj.* Seiten-

side: ~**board** *n.* Anrichte, *die;* ~**boards** (coll.), ~**burns** *ns. pl.* (on cheeks) Backenbart, *der;* (in front of the ears) Koteletten *Pl.;* ~**car** *n.* Beiwagen, *der;* ~ **dish** *n.* Beilage, *die;* ~ **door** *n.* Seitentür, *die;* ~ **effect** *n.* Nebenwirkung, *die;* ~ **entrance** *n.* Seiteneingang, *der;* ~ **exit** *n.* Seitenausgang, *der;* ~ **issue** *n.* Randproblem, *das;* ~**kick** *n.* (coll.) Kumpan, *der;* ~**light** *n.* Begrenzungsleuchte, *die;* **drive on** ~**lights** mit Standlicht fahren; ~**line** *n.* (occupation) Nebenbeschäftigung, *die;* ~**long** *adj.* a ~**long look/glance** ein Seitenblick; ~ **plate** *n.* kleiner Teller (neben dem Teller für das Hauptgericht); ~ **road** *n.* Seitenstraße, *die;* ~**saddle** *adv.* ride ~**saddle** im Damensitz reiten; ~ **salad** *n.* Salat [als Beilage]; **steak with chips and a** ~ **salad** Steak mit Pommes frites und dazu ein Salat; ~**show** *n.* Nebenattraktion, *die;* ~**step** ① *n.* Schritt zur Seite; ② *v.t.* ausweichen (+ *Dat.*); ~ **street** *n.* Seitenstraße, *die;* ~ **table** *n.* Beistelltisch, *der;* ~**track** *v.t.* get ~**tracked** abgelenkt werden; ~**walk** *n.* (Amer.) Bürgersteig, *der;* ~**ways** /'saɪdweɪz/ ① *adv.* **look at sb./sth.** ~**ways** jmdn./etw. von der Seite ansehen; ② *adj.* seitlich; ~ **wind** *n.* Seitenwind, *der*

siding /'saɪdɪŋ/ *n.* Abstellgleis, *das*

sidle /'saɪdl/ *v.i.* schleichen [**up to** zu]

siege /siːdʒ/ *n.* Belagerung, *die;* (by police) Umstellung, *die;* **lay** ~ **to sth.** etw. belagern

siesta /sɪ'estə/ *n.* Siesta, *die*

sieve /sɪv/ ① *n.* Sieb, *das*
② *v.t.* sieben

sift /sɪft/ *v.t.* sieben; ~ **sth. from sth.** etw. von etw. trennen

■ **sift 'out** *v.t.* aussieben

sigh /saɪ/ ① *n.* Seufzer, *der;* **breathe** *or* **give** *or* **heave a** ~: einen Seufzer ausstoßen; ~ **of relief/contentment** Seufzer der Erleichterung/Zufriedenheit
② *v.i.* seufzen; ~ **with relief/despair** erleichtert/verzweifelt seufzen

sight /saɪt/ ⟨1⟩ *n.* (a) (faculty) Sehvermögen, *das;* **know sb. by ~:** jmdn. vom Sehen kennen

(b) (act of seeing; spectacle) Anblick, *der;* **catch/ lose ~ of sb./sth.** jmdn./etw. erblicken/aus dem Auge verlieren; **at first ~:** auf den ersten Blick

(c) *in pl.* **~s** (places of interest) Sehenswürdigkeiten *Pl.;* **see the ~s** die Sehenswürdigkeiten besichtigen

(d) (range) Sichtweite, *die;* **in ~:** in Sicht; **within** *or* **in ~ of sb./sth.** (able to see) in jmds. Sichtweite (*Dat.*)/in Sichtweite einer Sache; **out of ~:** außer Sicht

(e) (of gun) Visier, *das;* **set/have [set] one's ~s on sth.** (fig.) etw. anpeilen

⟨2⟩ *v.t.* sichten ⟨*Land, Schiff, Flugzeug*⟩; sehen ⟨*Entflohenen, Vermissten*⟩

sighted /ˈsaɪtɪd/ *adj.* sehend; **partially ~:** [hochgradig] sehbehindert

'sighting *n.* Beobachtung, *die*

sight-read (Mus.) *v.t. & i.* ⟨*Pianist usw.:*⟩ vom Blatt spielen; ⟨*Sänger:*⟩ vom Blatt singen

'sightseeing *n.* **go ~:** Besichtigungen machen

sightseer /ˈsaɪtsiːə(r)/ *n.* Tourist (*der die Sehenswürdigkeiten besichtigt*)

sign /saɪn/ ⟨1⟩ *n.* (a) (symbol, signal, indication) Zeichen, *das;* (of future event) Anzeichen, *das;* **as a ~ of** als Zeichen (+ *Gen.*)

(b) (Astrol.) **~ [of the zodiac]** Sternzeichen, *das*

(c) (notice; on shop etc.) Schild, *das*

⟨2⟩ *v.t. & i.* unterschreiben; **~ one's name** [mit seinem Namen] unterschreiben

▪ **sign 'on** *v.i.* (as unemployed) sich arbeitslos melden

▪ **sign 'up** *v.i.* sich [vertraglich] verpflichten (**with** bei); (for course) sich einschreiben

signal /ˈsɪgnl/ ⟨1⟩ *n.* Signal, *das;* **a ~ for sth./to sb.** ein Zeichen zu etw./für jmdn

⟨2⟩ *v.i.,* (Brit.) **-ll-** signalisieren; Signale geben; ⟨*Kraftfahrer:*⟩ blinken; (with hand) anzeigen; **~ to sb. [to do sth.]** jmdm. ein Zeichen geben[, etw. zu tun]

signal: ~ box *n.* Stellwerk, *das;* **~ man** /-mən/ *n.* Bahnwärter, *der*

signature /ˈsɪgnətʃə(r)/ *n.* Unterschrift, *die;* (on painting) Signatur, *die*

'signature tune *n.* Erkennungsmelodie, *die*

'signboard *n.* Schild, *das*

signet ring /ˈsɪgnɪt rɪŋ/ *n.* Siegelring, *der*

significance /sɪgˈnɪfɪkəns/ *n.* Bedeutung, *die;* **be of [no] ~:** [nicht] von Bedeutung sein

significant /sɪgˈnɪfɪkənt/ *adj.* (a) (noteworthy, important) bedeutend

(b) (full of meaning) bedeutsam

sig'nificantly *adv.* (a) (meaningfully) bedeutungsvoll; **~ [enough]** bedeutsamerweise

(b) (notably) bedeutend

signify /ˈsɪgnɪfaɪ/ *v.t.* bedeuten

sign: ~ language *n.* Zeichensprache, *die;* **~post** *n.* Wegweiser, *der;* **~writer** *n.* Schildermaler, *der*

Sikh /siːk, sɪk/ *n.* Sikh, *der*

silence /ˈsaɪləns/ ⟨1⟩ *n.* Schweigen, *das;* (keeping a secret) Verschwiegenheit, *die;* (stillness) Stille, *die;* **there was ~:** es herrschte Schweigen/Stille; **in ~:** schweigend

⟨2⟩ *v.t.* zum Schweigen bringen; (fig.) ersticken ⟨*Proteste*⟩; mundtot machen ⟨*Gegner*⟩

'silencer *n.* (on gun; Brit. Motor Veh.) Schalldämpfer, *der*

silent /ˈsaɪlənt/ *adj.* stumm; (noiseless) unhörbar; (still) still; **be ~** (say nothing) schweigen; **~ film** Stummfilm, *der*

'silently *adv.* schweigend; stumm ⟨*weinen, beten*⟩; (noiselessly) lautlos

silent ma'jority *n.* schweigende Mehrheit

silhouette /sɪlʊˈet/ ⟨1⟩ *n.* (a) (picture) Schattenriss, *der*

(b) (appearance against the light) Silhouette, *die*

⟨2⟩ *v.t.* **be ~d against sth.** sich als Silhouette gegen etw. abheben

silicon /ˈsɪlɪkən/ *n.* Silicium, *das;* **~ chip** Siliciumchip, *der*

silicone /ˈsɪlɪkəʊn/ *n.* Silikon, *das;* **~ [breast] implant** Silikon[brust]implantat, *das*

silk /sɪlk/ ⟨1⟩ *n.* Seide, *die*

⟨2⟩ *attrib. adj.* seiden; Seiden-

'silkworm *n.* Seidenraupe, *die*

'silky *adj.* seidig

sill /sɪl/ *n.* (of door) [Tür]schwelle, *die;* (of window) Fensterbank, *die*

silly /ˈsɪlɪ/ *adj.* dumm; (imprudent, unwise) töricht; (childish) albern

silo /ˈsaɪləʊ/ *n., pl.* **~s** Silo, *der*

silt /sɪlt/ *n.* Schlamm, *der;* Schlick, *der*

silver /ˈsɪlvə(r)/ ⟨1⟩ *n.* Silber, *das*

⟨2⟩ *attrib. adj.* silbern; Silber⟨*pokal, -münze*⟩

silver: ~ 'jubilee *n.* silbernes Jubiläum; **~ 'medal** *n.* Silbermedaille, *die;* **~ 'paper** *n.* Silberpapier, *das;* **~-plated** *adj.* versilbert; **~smith** *n.* Silberschmied, *der*/-schmiedin, *die;* **~ 'wedding** *n.* Silberhochzeit, *die*

similar /ˈsɪmɪlə(r)/ *adj.* ähnlich (**to** *Dat.*)

similarity /sɪmɪˈlærɪtɪ/ *n.* Ähnlichkeit, *die* (**to** mit)

'similarly *adv.* ähnlich; (in exactly the same way) ebenso

simile /ˈsɪmɪlɪ/ *n.* Vergleich, *der*

simmer /ˈsɪmə(r)/ ⟨1⟩ *v.i.* ⟨*Flüssigkeit:*⟩ sieden; ziehen

⟨2⟩ *v.t.* köcheln *od.* ziehen lassen

▪ **simmer 'down** *v.i.* sich abregen (ugs.)

simper /ˈsɪmpə(r)/ *v.i.* affektiert *od.* gekünstelt lächeln

simple /ˈsɪmpl/ *adj.* einfach; (unsophisticated, not elaborate) schlicht ⟨*Mobiliar, Schönheit,*

Kunstwerk, Kleidung⟩; **it was a**
~ misunderstanding es war [ganz] einfach
ein Missverständnis
'simple-minded *adj.* **(a)** (unsophisticated)
schlicht
(b) (unintelligent) beschränkt
simpleton /'sɪmpltən/ *n.* Einfaltspinsel,
der (ugs.)
simplicity /sɪm'plɪsɪtɪ/ *n.* Einfachheit, *die;*
(unpretentiousness, lack of sophistication)
Schlichtheit, *die*
simplification /sɪmplɪfɪ'keɪʃn/ *n.*
Vereinfachung, *die*
simplify /'sɪmplɪfaɪ/ *v.t.* vereinfachen
simplistic /sɪm'plɪstɪk/ *adj.* [all]zu simpel
simply /'sɪmplɪ/ *adv.* einfach; (in an
unsophisticated manner) schlicht; (merely) nur; **it**
~ isn't true es ist einfach nicht wahr; **I was**
~ trying to help ich wollte nur helfen
simulate /'sɪmjʊleɪt/ *v.t.* **(a)** (feign)
vortäuschen
(b) simulieren ⟨*Bedingungen, Wetter usw.*⟩
simulation /sɪmjʊ'leɪʃn/ *n.* **(a)** (feigning)
Vortäuschung, *die*
(b) (imitation of conditions) Simulation, *die*
(c) (simulated object) Imitation, *die*
simulator /'sɪmjʊleɪtə(r)/ *n.* Simulator, *der*
simultaneous /sɪml'teɪnɪəs/ *adj.,*
simul'taneously *adv.* gleichzeitig
sin /sɪn/ ① *n.* Sünde, *die*
② *v.i.,* **-nn-** sündigen
since /sɪns/ ① *adv.* seitdem
② *prep.* seit; **I have/had been waiting ~**
8 o'clock ich warte/wartete [schon] seit
8 Uhr; **he has lived here ~ his childhood** er
wohnt seit seiner Kindheit hier; **~ seeing**
you ...: seit ich dich gesehen habe; **~ then/**
that time inzwischen
③ *conj.* **(a)** seit; **it is a long time/so long/not**
so long ~ ...: es ist lange/so lange/gar nicht
lange her, dass ...
(b) (seeing that, as) da
sincere /sɪn'sɪə(r)/ *adj.,* **~r** /sɪn'sɪərə(r)/,
~st /sɪn'sɪərɪst/ aufrichtig; herzlich ⟨*Grüße,*
Glückwünsche usw.⟩
sin'cerely *adv.* aufrichtig; **yours ~**: mit
freundlichen Grüßen
sincerity /sɪn'serɪtɪ/ *n.* Aufrichtigkeit, *die*
sinew /'sɪnjuː/ *n.* Sehne, *die*
sinful /'sɪnfl/ *adj.* sündig; (reprehensible)
sündhaft; **it is ~ to ...**: es ist eine Sünde,
zu ...
sing /sɪŋ/ *v.i. & t.,* **sang** /sæŋ/, **sung** /sʌŋ/
singen
▪ **sing 'up** *v.i.* lauter singen
singe /sɪndʒ/ *v.t. & i.,* **~ing** versengen
singer /'sɪŋə(r)/ *n.* Sänger, *der*/Sängerin,
die
single /'sɪŋgl/ ① *adj.* **(a)** einfach; (sole)
einzig; (separate, individual, isolated) einzeln; **not**
a ~ one kein Einziger/keine Einzige/kein

Einziges; **every ~ one** jeder/jede/jedes
Einzelne; **every ~ day** jeden Tag; **~ ticket**
(Brit.) einfache Fahrkarte
(b) (for one person) Einzel⟨*bett, -zimmer*⟩
(c) (unmarried) ledig; **a ~ man/woman** ein
Lediger/eine Ledige; **~ people** Ledige *Pl.*;
~ parent allein erziehender Elternteil;
~ mother allein erziehende *od.* stehende
Mutter
② *n.* **(a)** (Brit.: ticket) einfache Fahrkarte; **[a]**
~/two ~s to Manchester, please einmal/
zweimal einfach nach Manchester, bitte
(b) (record) Single, *die*
(c) *in pl.* (Tennis etc.) Einzel, *das*
▪ **single 'out** *v.t.* **~ sb./sth. out as/for sth.**
jmdn./etw. als/für etw. auswählen
single: ~ cream *n.* [einfache] Sahne;
~ 'currency *n.* Einheitswährung, *die;*
~-decker ① *n.* Bus/Straßenbahn mit nur
einem Deck; **be a ~-decker** ⟨*Bus,*
Straßenbahn:⟩ nur ein Deck haben; ② *adj.*
~-decker bus/tram Bus/Straßenbahn mit
[nur] einem Deck; **~ [European]**
market *n.* [europäischer] Binnenmarkt;
~'handed *adv.* allein; **~lens 'reflex**
camera *n.* (Photog.) einäugige
Spiegelreflexkamera; **~-minded** *adj.*
zielstrebig; **~-mindedly** /sɪŋgl'maɪndɪdlɪ/
adv. zielstrebig; **~-sex** *adj.* **~ school** reine
Mädchen-/Jungenschule
'singles bar *n.* Singlekneipe, *die*
'single-storey *adj.* eingeschossig
singlet /'sɪŋglɪt/ *n.* (Brit.) (vest) Unterhemd,
das; (Sport) Trikot, *das*
singly /'sɪŋglɪ/ *adv.* einzeln
singular /'sɪŋgjʊlə(r)/ ① *adj.* **(a)** (Ling.)
singularisch; Singular-; **~ noun** Substantiv
im Singular
(b) (extraordinary) einmalig
② *n.* (Ling.) Einzahl, *die;* Singular, *der*
'singularly *adv.* (extraordinarily)
außerordentlich
sinister /'sɪnɪstə(r)/ *adj.* finster; (of evil
omen) Unheil verkündend
sink /sɪŋk/ ① *n.* Spülbecken, *das*
② *v.i.,* **sank** /sæŋk/ *or* **sunk** /sʌŋk/, **sunk**
sinken
③ *v.t.,* **sank** *or* **sunk**, **sunk (a)** versenken
⟨*Schiff*⟩
(b) niederbringen ⟨*Schacht*⟩
▪ **sink 'in** *v.i.* (fig.) jmdm. ins Bewusstsein
dringen; ⟨*Warnung, Lektion:*⟩ verstanden
werden
'sink unit *n.* Spüle, *die*
'sinner *n.* Sünder, *der*/Sünderin, *die*
sinus /'saɪnəs/ *n.* Nebenhöhle, *die*
sinusitis /saɪnə'saɪtɪs/ *n.*
Nebenhöhlenentzündung, *die*
sip /sɪp/ ① *v.t.,* **-pp-**: **~ [up]** schlürfen
② *v.i.,* **-pp-**: **~ at/from sth.** an etw. (*Dat.*)
nippen
③ *n.* Schlückchen, *das*
siphon /'saɪfn/ ① *n.* Siphon, *der*   ⋯⟩

S

2 *v.t.* [durch einen Saugheber] laufen lassen

sir /sɜ:(r)/ *n.* (a) (formal address) der Herr; (to teacher) Herr Meier/Schmidt *usw.*

(b) (in letter) **Dear Sir** Sehr geehrter Herr; **Dear Sirs** Sehr geehrte [Damen und] Herren; **Dear Sir or Madam** Sehr geehrte Dame/Sehr geehrter Herr

(c) Sir /sə(r)/ (title of knight etc.) Sir

siren /'saɪrən/ *n.* Sirene, *die*

sirloin /'sɜ:lɔɪn/ *n.* (a) (Brit.) Roastbeef, *das;* ∼ **steak** Rumpsteak, *das*

(b) (Amer.) Rumpsteak, *das*

sissy /'sɪsɪ/ 1 *n.* Waschlappen, *der* 2 *adj.* feige

sister /'sɪstə(r)/ *n.* (a) Schwester, *die*

(b) (Brit.: nurse) Oberschwester, *die*

'sister-in-law *n., pl.* **sisters-in-law** Schwägerin, *die*

sisterly /'sɪstəlɪ/ *adj.* schwesterlich

sit /sɪt/ 1 *v.i.,* -tt-, sat /sæt/ (a) (become seated) sich setzen; ∼ **on** *or* **in a chair/in an armchair** sich auf einen Stuhl/in einen Sessel setzen

(b) (be seated) sitzen

2 *v.t.,* -tt-, sat (a) setzen

(b) (Brit.) machen ⟨*Prüfung*⟩

■ **sit 'back** *v.i.* sich zurücklehnen; (fig.) sich im Sessel zurücklehnen

■ **sit 'down** *v.i.* (a) (become seated) sich setzen (on/in auf/in + *Akk.*)

(b) (be seated) sitzen

■ **sit 'up** *v.i.* (a) (rise) sich aufsetzen

(b) (be sitting erect) [aufrecht] sitzen

(c) (stay up) aufbleiben

2 *v.t.* aufsetzen

sitcom /'sɪtkɒm/ (coll.) ▶ SITUATION COMEDY

site /saɪt/ 1 *n.* (a) (land) Grundstück, *das*

(b) (location) Sitz, *der;* (of new factory etc.) Standort, *der*

2 *v.t.* stationieren ⟨*Raketen*⟩; ∼ **a factory in London** London als Standort einer Fabrik wählen; **be** ∼**d** gelegen sein

siting /'saɪtɪŋ/ *n.* Standortwahl, *die* (of für); (position) Lage, *die*

sitter /'sɪtə(r)/ ▶ BABYSITTER

'sitting *n.* Sitzung, *die;* **the first** ∼ **[for lunch]** der erste Schub [zum Mittagessen]

sitting: ∼ **'duck** *n.* (fig.) leichtes Ziel; ∼ **room** *n.* Wohnzimmer, *das;* ∼ **'target** ▶ ∼ DUCK

situate /'sɪtjʊeɪt/ *v.t.* legen

'situated *adj.* gelegen; **be** ∼: liegen

situation /sɪtjʊ'eɪʃn/ *n.* (a) (location) Lage, *die*

(b) (circumstances) Situation, *die*

(c) (job) Stelle, *die*

situation 'comedy *n.* Situationskomödie, *die*

six /sɪks/ 1 *adj.* sechs

2 *n.* Sechs, *die. See also* EIGHT

six: ∼**-'footer** *n.* (person) Zweimetermann, *der/*-frau, *die;* ∼**-pack** *n.* Sechserpack, *der*

sixteen /sɪks'ti:n/ 1 *adj.* sechzehn

2 *n.* Sechzehn, *die. See also* EIGHT

sixteenth /sɪks'ti:nθ/ 1 *adj.* sechzehnt...

2 *n.* (fraction) Sechzehntel, *das. See also* EIGHTH

sixth /sɪksθ/ 1 *adj.* sechst...

2 *n.* (in sequence, rank) Sechste, *der/die/das;* (fraction) Sechstel, *das. See also* EIGHTH

sixth: ∼ **form** *n.* (Brit. Sch.) ≈ zwölfte/dreizehnte Klasse; ∼**-form college** *n.* (Brit. Sch.) ≈ Oberstufenzentrum, *das; College, das nur Schüler der zwölften/dreizehnten Klasse aufnimmt;* ∼**-former** *n.* (Brit. Sch.) Schüler/Schülerin der zwölften/dreizehnten Klasse; ∼ **'sense** *n.* sechster Sinn

sixtieth /'sɪkstɪɪθ/ *adj.* sechzigst...

sixty /'sɪkstɪ/ 1 *adj.* sechzig

2 *n.* Sechzig, *die. See also* EIGHT; EIGHTY 2

size /saɪz/ *n.* Größe, *die;* (of paper) Format, *das;* **be twice the** ∼ **of sth.** zweimal so groß wie etw. sein; **a** ∼ **8 dress** ein Kleid [in] Größe 8; **be** ∼ **8** ⟨Person:⟩ Größe 8 haben

■ **size 'up** *v.t.* taxieren ⟨*Lage*⟩

sizeable /'saɪzəbl/ *adj.* ziemlich groß; beträchtlich ⟨Summe, Einfluss⟩

sizzle /'sɪzl/ *v.i.* zischen

skate /skeɪt/ 1 *n.* (ice ∼) Schlittschuh, *der;* (roller ∼) Rollschuh, *der*

2 *v.i.* (ice-∼) Schlittschuh laufen; (roller-∼) Rollschuh laufen

'skateboard 1 *n.* Skateboard, *das;* Rollerbrett, *das*

2 *v.i.* Skateboard fahren

'skateboarder *n.* Skateboardfahrer, *der/* -fahrerin, *die*

'skateboarding *n.* Skateboardfahren, *das*

'skater *n.* (ice ∼) Eisläufer, *der/*-läuferin, *die;* (roller ∼) Rollschuhläufer, *der/*-läuferin, *die*

skating /'skeɪtɪŋ/ *n.* (ice ∼) Schlittschuhlaufen, *das;* (roller ∼) Rollschuhlaufen, *das*

'skating rink *n.* (ice) Eisbahn, *die;* (for roller skating) Rollschuhbahn, *die*

skeleton /'skelɪtn/ *n.* Skelett, *das*

skeleton: ∼ **'key** *n.* Dietrich, *der;* ∼ **'staff** *n.* Minimalbesetzung, *die*

skeptic *etc.* (Amer.) ▶ SCEPTIC *etc.*

sketch /sketʃ/ 1 *n.* (a) (drawing) Skizze, *die*

(b) (play) Sketch, *der*

2 *v.t.* skizzieren

sketch: ∼**book** *n.* Skizzenbuch, *das;* ∼ **map** *n.* Faustskizze, *die*

'sketchy *adj.* skizzenhaft; lückenhaft ⟨Informationen, Bericht⟩

skew /skju:/ 1 *adj.* schräg

2 *n.* **on the** ∼: schief

skewer /'skju:ə(r)/ 1 *n.* Bratspieß, *der*

2 *v.t.* aufspießen

ski /ski:/ 1 *n.* (a) Ski, *der*

(b) (on vehicle) Kufe, *die*

2 *v.i.* Ski laufen *od.* fahren

'ski boot *n.* Skistiefel, *der*

skid /skɪd/ ⏺1 *v.i.*, **-dd-** schlittern; (from one side to the other; spinning round) schleudern
⏺2 *n.* Schlittern/Schleudern, *das*

'skid marks *n. pl.* Schleuderspur, *die*

skier /'skiːə(r)/ *n.* Skiläufer, *der*/-läuferin, *die*

skiing /'skiːɪŋ/ *n.* Skilaufen, *das;* (Sport) Skisport, *der*

'ski jumping *n.* Skispringen, *das*

skilful /'skɪlfl/ *adj.* geschickt; gewandt ⟨Redner⟩; gut ⟨Beobachter, Lehrer⟩

'ski lift *n.* Skilift, *der*

skill /skɪl/ *n.* **(a)** (expertness) Geschick, *das;* (of artist) Können, *das*
(b) (technique) Fertigkeit, *die;* (of weaving, bricklaying) Technik, *die*

skilled /skɪld/ *adj.* **(a)** ▶ SKILFUL
(b) qualifiziert ⟨Arbeit, Tätigkeit⟩; ~ trade Ausbildungsberuf, *der*
(c) (trained) ausgebildet

'skillful (Amer.) ▶ SKILFUL

skim /skɪm/ *v.t.*, **-mm-**: **(a)** (remove) abschöpfen
(b) abrahmen ⟨Milch⟩
(c) ▶ ~ THROUGH
■ **skim 'off** *v.t.* abschöpfen
■ **'skim through** *v.t.* überfliegen ⟨Buch, Zeitung⟩

skimmed 'milk *n.* entrahmte Milch

skimp /skɪmp/ ⏺1 *v.t.* sparen an (+ *Dat.*)
⏺2 *v.i.* sparen (with, on an + *Dat.*)

'skimpy *adj.* winzig ⟨Badeanzug⟩; spärlich ⟨Wissen⟩

skin /skɪn/ ⏺1 *n.* **(a)** Haut, *die*
(b) (fur) Fell, *das*
(c) (peel) Schale, *die*
⏺2 *v.t.*, **-nn-** häuten; schälen ⟨Frucht⟩

skin: ~ **cancer** *n.* Hautkrebs, *der;* ~ **colour** *n.* Hautfarbe, *die;* ~ **cream** *n.* Hautcreme, *die;* ~**-'deep** *adj.* (fig.) oberflächlich; ~ **disease** *n.* Hautkrankheit, *die;* ~ **diver** *n.* Taucher, *der*/Taucherin, *die;* ~ **diving** *n.* Tauchen, *das;* ~**flint** *n.* Geizhals, *der;* ~ **graft** *n.* Hauttransplantation, *die;* ~**head** *n.* Skinhead, *der*

skinny /'skɪnɪ/ *adj.* mager

skint /skɪnt/ *adj.* (Brit. coll.) be ~: blank *od.* pleite sein (ugs.)

'skin-tight *adj.* hauteng

skip¹ /skɪp/ ⏺1 *v.i.*, **-pp-**: **(a)** hüpfen
(b) (with skipping rope) seilspringen
⏺2 *v.t.*, **-pp-** (omit) überspringen; ~ **breakfast/ lunch** das Frühstück/Mittagessen auslassen
⏺3 *n.* Hüpfer, *der*

skip² *n.* (Building) Container, *der*

ski: ~ **pass** *n.* Skipass, *der;* ~ **pole** *n.* Skistock, *der*

skipper /'skɪpə(r)/ *n.* Kapitän, *der*

'skipping rope (Brit.**)**, **'skip rope** (Amer.) *ns.* Sprungseil, *das*

'ski resort *n.* Skiurlaubsort, *der*

skirmish /'skɜːmɪʃ/ *n.* (Mil.) Gefecht, *das*

skirt /skɜːt/ ⏺1 *n.* Rock, *der*
⏺2 *v.t.* herumgehen um
■ **skirt 'round** *v.t.* herumgehen um; (fig.) umgehen

'skirting *n.* ~ **[board]** (Brit.) Fußleiste, *die*

ski: ~ **run** *n.* Skihang, *der;* (prepared) [Ski]piste, *die;* ~**stick** *n.* Skistock, *der*

skittle /'skɪtl/ *n.* **(a)** Kegel, *der*
(b) ~s *sing.* (game) Kegeln, *das*

skive /skaɪv/ *v.i.* (Brit. coll.) sich drücken (ugs.)
■ **skive 'off** (Brit. coll.) ⏺1 *v.i.* sich verdrücken (ugs.)
⏺2 *v.t.* schwänzen (ugs.)

skulk /skʌlk/ *v.i.* lauern

skull /skʌl/ *n.* Schädel, *der*

skunk /skʌŋk/ *n.* Stinktier, *das*

sky /skaɪ/ *n.* Himmel, *der;* in the ~: am Himmel

sky: ~**diving** *n.* Fallschirmspringen, *das* (als Sport); Fallschirmsport, *der;* ~**high** ⏺1 *adj.* himmelhoch; astronomisch (ugs.) ⟨Preise usw.⟩; ⏺2 *adv.* go ~-high ⟨Preise usw.⟩ in astronomische Höhen klettern (ugs.); ~**light** *n.* Dachfenster, *das;* ~**line** *n.* Silhouette, *die;* (characteristic of certain town) Skyline, *die;* ~**scraper** *n.* Wolkenkratzer, *der*

slab /slæb/ *n.* **(a)** (flat stone etc.) Platte, *die*
(b) (thick slice) [dicke] Scheibe; (of cake) [dickes] Stück; (of chocolate, toffee) Tafel, *die*

slack /slæk/ ⏺1 *adj.* **(a)** (lax) nachlässig; schlampig (ugs.)
(b) (loose) schlaff; locker ⟨Verband⟩
⏺2 *n.* take in *or* up the ~: das Seil/die Schnur *usw.* straffen
⏺3 *v.i.* (coll.) bummeln (ugs.)

slacken /'slækn/ ⏺1 *v.i.* **(a)** (loosen) sich lockern
(b) (diminish) nachlassen; ⟨Geschwindigkeit⟩ sich verringern
⏺2 *v.t.* **(a)** (loosen) lockern
(b) (diminish) verringern

slacker /'slækə(r)/ *n.* (derog.) Faulenzer, *der*/Faulenzerin, *die*

slacks /slæks/ *n. pl.* [pair of] ~: lange Hose; Slacks *Pl.*

slag /slæg/ *n.* Schlacke, *die*

slain ▶ SLAY

slake /sleɪk/ *v.t.* löschen, stillen ⟨Durst⟩

slam /slæm/ ⏺1 *v.t.*, **-mm-**: **(a)** (shut) zuschlagen
(b) (put violently) knallen (ugs.)
⏺2 *v.i.*, **-mm-** zuschlagen

slander /'slɑːndə(r)/ ⏺1 *n.* Verleumdung, *die* (on Gen.)
⏺2 *v.t.* verleumden

slanderous /'slɑːndərəs/ *adj.* verleumderisch

S

slang /slæŋ/ n. Slang, der; ‹Theater-, Soldaten-, Juristen›jargon, der; attrib. Slang‹wort, -ausdruck›

'slanging match n. gegenseitige [lautstarke] Beschimpfung

slangy /'slæŋɪ/ adj. Slang‹ausdruck, -wort›; salopp ‹Wortwahl, Redeweise›

slant /slɑːnt/ 1 v.i. ‹Fläche:› sich neigen; ‹Linie:› schräg verlaufen. 2 v.t. (a) abschrägen. (b) (fig.: bias) [so] hinbiegen (ugs.) ‹Meldung, Bemerkung›. 3 n. Schräge, die; on the or a ~: schräg

slanting /'slɑːntɪŋ/ adj. schräg

slap /slæp/ 1 v.t., -pp-: (a) schlagen. (b) (put) knallen (ugs.). 2 v.i., -pp- schlagen; klatschen. 3 n. Schlag, der. 4 adv. voll; ~ in the middle genau in der Mitte

'slapdash adj. schludrig (ugs.)

'slap-up attrib. adj. (coll.) ‹Essen› mit allen Schikanen (ugs.)

slash /slæʃ/ 1 v.t. (a) aufschlitzen. (b) (fig.) [drastisch] reduzieren; [drastisch] kürzen ‹Gehalt, Umfang›. 2 n. (a) (slit) Schlitz, der. (b) (~ing stroke) Hieb, der

slat /slæt/ n. Latte, die

slate /sleɪt/ 1 n. (a) (Geol.) Schiefer, der. (b) (Building) Schieferplatte, die. 2 v.t. (Brit. coll.: criticize) in der Luft zerreißen (ugs.)

slaughter /'slɔːtə(r)/ 1 n. Schlachten, das; (massacre) Gemetzel, das. 2 v.t. schlachten; (massacre) abschlachten

slave /sleɪv/ 1 n. Sklave, der/Sklavin, die. 2 v.i. ~ [away] schuften (ugs.); sich abplagen (at mit)

'slave driver n. (fig.) Sklaventreiber, der/ -treiberin, die

slavery /'sleɪvərɪ/ n. Sklaverei, die

slavish /'sleɪvɪʃ/ adj. sklavisch

slay /sleɪ/ v.t., slew /sluː/, slain /sleɪn/ (literary) ermorden

sleaze /sliːz/ n. (derog.) Korruption, die

'sleazebag, 'sleazeball ns. (sl. derog.) Drecksack, der (derb abwertend)

sleazy /'sliːzɪ/ adj. schäbig; (disreputable) anrüchig

sled /sled/, **sledge** /sledʒ/ ns. Schlitten, der

'sledgehammer n. Vorschlaghammer, der

sleek /sliːk/ adj. (glossy) seidig

sleep /sliːp/ 1 n. Schlaf, der; get/go to ~: einschlafen; **put to ~**: einschläfern ‹Tier›. 2 v.i., slept /slept/ schlafen. 3 v.t. slept: the hotel ~s 80 das Hotel hat 80 Betten

■ **sleep a'round** v.i. (coll.) herumschlafen (ugs.)

■ **sleep 'in** v.i. im Bett bleiben

■ **sleep 'off** v.t. ausschlafen; ~ **it off** seinen Rausch ausschlafen

■ **sleep 'over** v.i. [auswärts] übernachten; **our cousin was ~ing over** unser Cousin übernachtete bei uns

■ **sleep together** v.i. (also coll. euphem.) miteinander schlafen

■ **sleep with** v.t. ~ **with sb.** (coll. euphem.) mit jmdm. schlafen

'sleeper n. (a) **be a heavy/light ~**: einen tiefen/leichten Schlaf haben. (b) (Brit. Railw.: support) Schwelle, die. (c) (Railw.) (coach) Schlafwagen, der; (train) [night] ~: Nachtzug mit Schlafwagen

sleeping: ~ **accommodation** n. Übernachtungsmöglichkeit, die; ~ **bag** n. Schlafsack, der; ~ **car** n. Schlafwagen, der; ~ **'partner** n. (Commerc.) stiller Teilhaber; ~ **pill, ~ tablet** ns. Schlaftablette, die

sleep: ~**less** adj. schlaflos; ~**walk** v.i. schlafwandeln; ~**walker** n. Schlafwandler, der/-wandlerin, die

'sleepover n. Übernachtung außer Haus od. bei anderen Leuten

'sleepy adj. schläfrig

sleet /sliːt/ 1 n. Schneeregen, der. 2 v.i. impers. **it is ~ing** es gibt Schneeregen

sleeve /sliːv/ n. (a) Ärmel, der; (fig.) **have sth. up one's ~**: etw. in petto haben (ugs.); **roll up one's ~s** die Ärmel hochkrempeln (ugs.). (b) (for record) Hülle, die

'sleeveless adj. ärmellos

sleigh /sleɪ/ n. Schlitten, der

sleight of 'hand /slaɪt/ n. Fingerfertigkeit, die

slender /'slendə(r)/ adj. (a) (slim) schlank; schmal ‹Buch, Band›. (b) gering ‹Chance, Mittel, Hoffnung›

slept ► SLEEP 2, 3

sleuth /sluːθ/ n. Detektiv, der

slew¹ /sluː/ v.i. & t. schwenken

slew² ► SLAY

slice /slaɪs/ 1 n. Scheibe, die; (of apple, melon, peach, cake, pie) Stück, das; **a ~ of cake** ein Stück Kuchen. 2 v.t. in Scheiben schneiden; in Stücke schneiden ‹Bohnen, Apfel, Kuchen usw.›; ~**d bread** Schnittbrot, das

slick /slɪk/ 1 adj. (a) (dexterous) professionell. (b) (pretentiously dexterous) clever (ugs.). 2 n. [oil] ~: Ölteppich, der

slid ► SLIDE 1, 2

slide /slaɪd/ 1 v.i., slid /slɪd/ rutschen; ‹Kolben, Schublade, Feder:› gleiten. 2 v.t., slid schieben. 3 n. (a) (children's ~) Rutschbahn, die. (b) (Photog.) Dia[positiv], das

slide: ~ **film** n. Diafilm, der; ~ **projector** n. Diaprojektor, der; ~ **show** n. Diashow, die

sliding door /'slaɪdɪŋ/ n. Schiebetür, die

slight /slaɪt/ **1** *adj.* leicht; schwach ⟨*Hoffnung, Aussichten, Wirkung*⟩; **not in the ~est** nicht im Geringsten
2 *n.* Verunglimpfung, *die* (**on** *Gen.*); (lack of courtesy) Affront, *der* (**on** gegen)

'**slightly** *adv.* ein bisschen; leicht ⟨*verletzen, riechen nach, gewürzt sein, ansteigen*⟩; flüchtig ⟨*jmdn. kennen*⟩; oberflächlich ⟨*etw. kennen*⟩

slim /slɪm/ **1** *adj.* schlank; schmal ⟨*Band, Buch*⟩; schwach ⟨*Aussicht, Hoffnung*⟩; gering ⟨*Gewinn, Chancen*⟩
2 *v.i.* -mm- abnehmen

slime /slaɪm/ *n.* Schleim, *der*

slimmer /'slɪmə(r)/ *n.* (Brit.) *jmd., der etwas für die schlanke Linie tut;* **advice/a diet for ~s** Ratschläge *Pl.*/eine Diät zum Abnehmen

slimming /'slɪmɪŋ/ **1** *n.* Abnehmen, *das; attrib.* Schlankheits-
2 *adj.* schlank machend

slimy /'slaɪmɪ/ *adj.* schleimig

sling /slɪŋ/ **1** *n.* (Med.) Schlinge, *die*
2 *v.t.* slung /slʌŋ/ (coll.: throw) schmeißen (ugs.)

sling 'out *v.t.* (coll.) wegschmeißen (ugs.); **~ sb. out** jmdn. rausschmeißen (ugs.)

slink /slɪŋk/ *v.i.*, slunk /slʌŋk/ schleichen
■ **slink a'way, slink 'off** *v.i.* davonschleichen

slip /slɪp/ **1** *v.i.*, -pp-: (a) (slide) rutschen; ⟨*Messer:*⟩ abrutschen; (and fall) ausrutschen
(b) (escape) schlüpfen
(c) (go) **~ to the butcher's** *etc.* [rasch] zum Fleischer *usw.* rüberspringen (ugs.)
2 *v.t.*, -pp-: (a) stecken; **~ the dress over one's head** das Kleid über den Kopf streifen
(b) **~ sb.'s mind** *or* **memory** jmdm. entfallen
3 *n.* (a) (fall) **after his ~:** nachdem er ausgerutscht [und gestürzt] war
(b) (mistake) Versehen, *das;* **~ of the tongue** Versprecher, *der*
(c) (underwear) Unterrock, *der*
(d) (piece of paper) Zettel, *der*
(e) **give sb. the ~:** jmdm. entwischen (ugs.)
■ **slip a'way** *v.i.* (a) ⟨*Person:*⟩ sich fortschleichen
(b) ⟨*Zeit:*⟩ verfliegen
■ **slip 'down** *v.i.* runterrutschen (ugs.)
■ **slip 'in** *v.i.* ⟨*Person:*⟩ sich hineinschleichen
■ '**slip into** *v.t.* schlüpfen in (+ *Akk.*) ⟨*Kleidungsstück*⟩
■ **slip 'off** **1** *v.i.* (a) runterrutschen (ugs.)
(b) ▶ SLIP AWAY A
2 *v.t.* abstreifen ⟨*Schmuck, Handschuh*⟩; schlüpfen aus ⟨*Kleid, Schuh*⟩
■ **slip 'on** *v.t.* überstreifen ⟨*Handschuh, Ring*⟩; schlüpfen in (+ *Akk.*) ⟨*Kleid, Schuh*⟩
■ **slip 'out** *v.i.* ⟨*Person:*⟩ sich hinausschleichen
■ **slip 'over** *v.i.* (fall) ausrutschen
■ **slip 'up** *v.i.* (coll.) einen Schnitzer machen (ugs.)

slipped 'disc /slɪpt/ *n.* Bandscheibenvorfall, *der*

'**slipper** *n.* Hausschuh, *der*

slippery /'slɪpərɪ/ *adj.* schlüpfrig

slippy /'slɪpɪ/ (coll.) ▶ SLIPPERY

slip: ~ road *n.* (Brit.) (to motorway) Auffahrt, *die;* (from motorway) Ausfahrt, *die;* **~shod** *adj.* schludrig (ugs.); **~-up** *n.* (coll.) Schnitzer, *der*

slit /slɪt/ **1** *n.* Schlitz, *der*
2 *v.t.*, -tt-, slit aufschlitzen; **~ sb.'s throat** jmdm. die Kehle durchschneiden

slither /'slɪðə(r)/ *v.i.* rutschen

sliver /'slɪvə(r)/ *n.* Splitter, *der*

slob /slɒb/ *n.* (coll.) Schwein, *das* (derb)

slobber /'slɒbə(r)/ *v.i.* sabbern (ugs.)

slog /slɒg/ **1** *v.t.*, -gg- (in boxing, fight) voll treffen
2 *v.i.*, -gg- (work) schuften (ugs.)
3 *n.* (a) (hit) wuchtiger Schlag
(b) (work) Plackerei, *die* (ugs.)

slogan /'sləʊgən/ *n.* Slogan, *der;* (advertising ~) Werbeslogan, *der*

slop /slɒp/ **1** *v.i.* schwappen (**out of, from** aus)
2 *v.t.* schwappen; (intentionally) kippen
■ **slop 'over** *v.i.* überschwappen

slope /sləʊp/ **1** *n.* (a) (slant) Neigung, *die*
(b) (slanting ground) Hang, *der*
2 *v.i.* (slant) sich neigen; ⟨*Boden, Garten:*⟩ abschüssig sein; **~ downwards/upwards** ⟨*Straße:*⟩ abfallen/ansteigen
■ **slope a'way** *v.i.* abfallen
■ **slope 'off** *v.i.* (coll.) sich verdrücken (ugs.)

sloppy /'slɒpɪ/ *adj.* schludrig (ugs.)

slosh /slɒʃ/ *adj.* **1** *v.i.* platschen (ugs.); ⟨*Flüssigkeit:*⟩ schwappen
2 *v.t.* (coll.: pour clumsily) schwappen

sloshed /slɒʃt/ *adj.* (Brit. coll.) blau (ugs.)

slot /slɒt/ **1** *n.* (a) (hole) Schlitz, *der*
(b) (groove) Nut, *die*
2 *v.t.*, -tt-: **~ sth. into place/sth.** etw. einfügen/in etw. (*Akk.*) einfügen
■ **slot 'in** **1** *v.t.* einfügen
2 *v.i.* sich einfügen
■ **slot to'gether** **1** *v.t.* zusammenfügen
2 *v.i.* (lit. or fig.) sich zusammenfügen

sloth /sləʊθ/ *n.* (a) (lethargy) Trägheit, *die*
(b) (Zool.) Faultier, *das*

'**slot machine** *n.* Automat, *der;* (for gambling) Spielautomat, *der*

slouch /slaʊtʃ/ *v.i.* sich schlecht halten

Slovak /'sləʊvæk/ **1** *adj.* slowakisch; **sb. is ~:** jmd. ist Slowake/Slowakin
2 *n.* (a) (person) Slowake, *der*/Slowakin, *die*
(b) (language) Slowakisch, *das; see also* ENGLISH 2A

Slovakia /slə'vɑ:kɪə/ *pr. n.* Slowakei, *die*

Slovene /'sləʊvi:n/ **1** *adj.* slowenisch; **sb. is ~:** jmd. ist Slowene/Slowenin
2 *n.* (a) (person) Slowene, *der*/Slowenin, *die*
(b) (language) Slowenisch, *das*

Slovenia /slə'vi:nɪə/ *pr. n.* Slowenien (*das*)

S

Slovenian /slə'viːnɪən/ ▶ SLOVENE

slovenly /'slʌvnlɪ/ *adj.* schlampig (ugs.)

slow /sləʊ/ ⟦1⟧ *adj.* langsam; langwierig ⟨*Arbeit*⟩; **be [ten minutes]** ~ ⟨*Uhr:*⟩ [zehn Minuten] nachgehen
⟦2⟧ *adv.* langsam
⟦3⟧ *v.i.* langsamer werden; ~ **to a halt** anhalten
■ **slow 'down, slow 'up** *v.i.* langsamer werden

'slowcoach *n.* Trödler, *der*/Trödlerin, *die* (ugs.)

'slowly *adv.* langsam

slow 'motion *n.* **in** ~: in Zeitlupe

slowness *n.* Langsamkeit, *die*

slow: ~ **'puncture** *n.* winziges Loch; ~ **train** *n.* Bummelzug, *der* (ugs.); ~**-witted** /sləʊ'wɪtɪd/ *adj.* [geistig] schwerfällig

sludge /slʌdʒ/ *n.* Schlamm, *der*

slug /slʌg/ *n.* Nacktschnecke, *die*

sluggish /'slʌgɪʃ/ *adj.* träge; schleppend ⟨*Nachfrage*⟩

sluice /sluːs/ ⟦1⟧ *n.* Schütz, *das*
⟦2⟧ *v.t.* ~ **[down]** abspritzen

'sluice gate *n.* Schütz, *das*

slum /slʌm/ *n.* Slum, *der;* (single house or apartment) Elendsquartier, *das*

slumber /'slʌmbə(r)/ (poet./rhet.) ⟦1⟧ *n.* ~**[s]** Schlummer, *der* (geh.)
⟦2⟧ *v.i.* schlummern (geh.)

slump /slʌmp/ ⟦1⟧ *n.* Sturz, *der* (fig.); (in demand, investment, sales) starker Rückgang (in *Gen.*); (economic depression) Depression, *die*
⟦2⟧ *v.i.* (a) (Commerc.) stark zurückgehen; ⟨*Preise, Kurse:*⟩ stürzen
(b) (collapse) ⟨*Person:*⟩ fallen; ~**ed in a chair** in einem Sessel zusammengesunken

slung ▶ SLING 2

slunk ▶ SLINK

slur /slɜː(r)/ ⟦1⟧ *v.t.*, **-rr-:** ~ **one's words/ speech** undeutlich sprechen
⟦2⟧ *n.* Beleidigung, *die* (on für)

slurp /slɜːp/ (coll.) ⟦1⟧ *v.t.* ~ **[up]** schlürfen
⟦2⟧ *n.* Schlürfen, *das*

slush /slʌʃ/ *n.* Schneematsch, *der*

'slush fund *n.* Fonds, *der* für Bestechungsgelder

'slushy *adj.* (a) matschig
(b) (sloppy) sentimental

slut /slʌt/ *n.* Schlampe, *die* (ugs.)

sly /slaɪ/ ⟦1⟧ *adj.* schlau; gerissen (ugs.) ⟨*Geschäftsmann, Trick*⟩; verschlagen ⟨*Blick*⟩
⟦2⟧ *n.* **on the** ~: heimlich

smack¹ /smæk/ ⟦1⟧ *n.* (a) (sound) Klatsch, *der*
(b) (blow) Schlag, *der;* (on child's bottom) Klaps, *der* (ugs.)
⟦2⟧ *v.t.* (a) [mit der flachen Hand] schlagen
(b) ~ **one's lips** [mit den Lippen] schmatzen
⟦3⟧ *adv.* (coll.) direkt

smack² *v.i.* ~ **of** schmecken nach; (fig.) riechen nach (ugs.)

small /smɔːl/ ⟦1⟧ *adj.* klein; gering ⟨*Wirkung, Appetit, Fähigkeit*⟩; schmal ⟨*Taille*⟩; dünn ⟨*Stimme*⟩; **make sb. feel** ~: jmdn. beschämen
⟦2⟧ *n.* ~ **of the back** Kreuz, *das*
⟦3⟧ *adv.* klein

small: ~ **ad** *n.* (coll.) Kleinanzeige, *die;* ~ **'change** *n.* Kleingeld, *das;* ~**holding** *n.* landwirtschaftlicher Kleinbetrieb; ~**-'minded** *adj.* kleinlich; ~**pox** *n.* Pocken *Pl.;* ~ **'print** *n.* (lit. or fig.) Kleingedruckte, *das*

smalls /smɔːlz/ *n. pl.* (Brit. coll.) Unterwäsche, *die*

small: ~ **'screen** *n.* (Telev.) Bildschirm, *der;* ~ **talk** *n.* leichte Unterhaltung; (at parties) Smalltalk, *der;* **make** ~ **talk [with sb.]** [mit jmdm.] Konversation machen

smarmy /'smɑːmɪ/ *adj.* (coll.) kriecherisch

smart /smɑːt/ ⟦1⟧ *adj.* (a) (clever) clever; (ingenious) raffiniert
(b) (neat) schick; schön ⟨*Haus, Garten, Auto*⟩
(c) *attrib.* (fashionable) elegant; smart
⟦2⟧ *v.i.* schmerzen

smart: ~ **alec[k]** /smɑːt 'ælɪk/ *n.* (coll.) Besserwisser, *der*/Besserwisserin, *die;* ~ **bomb** *n.* intelligente Bombe; ~ **card** *n.* Chipkarte, *die;* ~ **drug** *n.* Nootropikum, *das*

smarten /'smɑːtn/ *v.t.* herrichten; ~ **oneself [up]** auf sein Äußeres achten

'smartly *adv.* (a) (cleverly) clever
(b) (neatly) schmuck ⟨[an]gestrichen⟩; smart, flott ⟨gekleidet, geschnitten⟩

'smart money *n.* **the** ~ **is on** … Experten setzen auf …

smash /smæʃ/ ⟦1⟧ *v.t.* (a) zerschlagen
(b) ~ **sb. in the face/mouth** jmdm. [hart] ins Gesicht/auf den Mund schlagen
(c) (Tennis etc.) schmettern
⟦2⟧ *v.i.* (a) zerbrechen
(b) (crash) krachen (**into** gegen)
⟦3⟧ *n.* (a) (sound) Krachen, *das*
(b) ▶ SMASH-UP
(c) (Tennis) Schmetterball, *der*
■ **smash 'in** *v.t.* zerschmettern; einschlagen ⟨*Tür, Schädel*⟩
■ **smash 'up** *v.t.* zertrümmern

smash-and-'grab [raid] *n.* (coll.) Schaufenstereinbruch, *der*

smashed /smæʃt/ *adj.* (sl.) (a) (drunk) **get** ~ **on sth.** von etw. besoffen werden (derb); **be** ~ **out of one's head** *or* **mind** *or* **brains** sturzbetrunken (ugs.) *od.* (derb) sturzbesoffen sein
(b) (on drugs) stoned (Drogenjargon)

'smashing *adj.* (coll.) toll (ugs.)

'smash-up *n.* schwerer Zusammenstoß

smattering /'smætərɪŋ/ *n.* [have] **a** ~ **of** German *etc.* ein paar Brocken Deutsch *usw.* [können]

smear /smɪə(r)/ ①v.t. (a) (daub) beschmieren; (put on or over) schmieren (b) (smudge) verwischen (c) (fig.) in den Schmutz ziehen ②n. (a) (blotch) [Schmutz]fleck, der (b) (fig.) Beschmutzung, die (on Gen.)

smear: ~ **campaign** n. Schmutzkampagne, die; ~ **tactics** n. pl. schmutzige Mittel Pl.; ~ **test** n. (Med.) Abstrich, der

smell /smel/ ①n. (a) have a good/bad sense of ~: einen guten/schlechten Geruchssinn haben (b) (odour) Geruch, der (of nach); (pleasant also) Duft, der (of nach); a ~ of burning/gas ein Brand-/Gasgeruch (c) (stink) Gestank, der ②v.t., smelt /smelt/ or smelled /smeld/ (a) (perceive) riechen (b) (inhale ~ of) riechen an (+ Dat.) ③v.i., smelt or smelled (a) (emit ~) riechen; (pleasantly also) duften (b) ~ of sth. (lit. or fig.) nach etw. riechen (c) (stink) riechen

'smelly adj. stinkend; be ~: stinken

smelt ▶ SMELL 2, 3

smile /smaɪl/ ①n. Lächeln, das; give sb. a ~: jmdn. anlächeln ②v.i. lächeln; ~ at sb./sth. jmdn. anlächeln/über etw. (Akk.) lächeln

smirk /smɜːk/ ①v.t. grinsen ②n. Grinsen, das

smith /smɪθ/ n. Schmied, der

smithereens /smɪðə'riːnz/ n. pl. blow/ smash sth. to ~: etw. in tausend Stücke sprengen/schlagen

smock /smɒk/ n. Kittel, der

smog /smɒg/ n. Smog, der

smoke /sməʊk/ ①n. Rauch, der ②v.i. & t. rauchen

smoked /sməʊkt/ adj. (Cookery) geräuchert

'smoke detector n. Rauchmelder, der

'smokeless adj. rauchlos; rauchfrei ⟨Zone⟩

smoker /'sməʊkə(r)/ n. (a) Raucher, der/ Raucherin, die; ~'s cough Raucherhusten, der (b) (Railw.) Raucherabteil, das

'smokescreen n. [künstliche] Nebelwand; (fig.) Vernebelung die (for Gen.)

smoking /'sməʊkɪŋ/ n. (a) Rauchen, das; 'no ~' „Rauchen verboten" (b) (seating area) [do you want to sit in] ~ or non-~? möchten Sie für Raucher oder Nichtraucher?

'smoking compartment n. (Railw.) Raucherabteil, das

smoky /'sməʊkɪ/ adj. (emitting smoke) rauchend; (smoke-filled) verräuchert

smooth /smuːð/ ①adj. (a) (even) glatt; eben ⟨Straße, Weg⟩ (b) (mild) weich

(d) (not jerky) geschmeidig ⟨Bewegung⟩; ruhig ⟨Fahrt, Flug⟩; weich ⟨Landung⟩ (d) (without problems) reibungslos ②v.t. glätten

smoothie /'smuːðɪ/ n. (coll. derog.) aalglatter Typ (ugs.)

'smoothly adv. (a) (evenly) glatt (b) (not jerkily) geschmeidig ⟨sich bewegen⟩; weich ⟨landen⟩; reibungslos ⟨funktionieren⟩

smother /'smʌðə(r)/ v.t. ersticken; (fig.) unterdrücken ⟨Gähnen⟩; ersticken ⟨Gelächter, Schreie⟩

smoulder /'sməʊldə(r)/ v.i. schwelen; she was ~ing with rage Zorn schwelte in ihr

smudge /smʌdʒ/ ①v.t. verwischen ②v.i. schmieren ③n. Fleck, der

smug /smʌg/ adj. selbstgefällig

smuggle /'smʌgl/ v.t. schmuggeln ■ **smuggle 'in** v.t. einschmuggeln; hinein-/ hereinschmuggeln ⟨Person⟩ ■ **smuggle 'out** v.t. hinaus-/ herausschmuggeln

smuggler /'smʌglə(r)/ n. Schmuggler, der/ Schmugglerin, die

smuggling /'smʌglɪŋ/ n. Schmuggel, der

smutty /'smʌtɪ/ adj. (lewd) schmutzig

snack /snæk/ n. Imbiss, der

'snackbar n. Schnellimbiss, der

snag /snæg/ n. (problem) Haken, der; what's the ~? wo klemmt es? (ugs.)

snail /sneɪl/ n. Schnecke, die; at [a] ~'s pace im Schneckentempo (ugs.)

'snail mail n. (coll. joc.) Schneckenpost, die

snake /sneɪk/ n. Schlange, die

snap /snæp/ ①v.t., -pp-: (a) (break) zerbrechen; ~ sth. in two or in half etw. in zwei Stücke brechen (b) ~ one's fingers mit den Fingern schnalzen (c) ~ sth. home or into place etw. einschnappen lassen; ~ shut zuschnappen lassen ⟨Portemonnaie, Schloss⟩; zuklappen ⟨Buch, Etui⟩; ~ sth. open etw. aufschnappen lassen (d) (take photograph of) knipsen (e) (say sharply) fauchen; (speak crisply or curtly) bellen ②v.i., -pp-: (a) (break) brechen (b) (fig.: give way under strain) ausrasten (ugs.); my patience has finally ~ped nun ist mir der Geduldsfaden aber gerissen ③n. (Photog.) Schnappschuss, der ■ **snap at** v.t. (speak sharply to) anfauchen (ugs.) ■ **snap 'off** v.t. & i. abbrechen ■ **snap 'up** v.t. (fig. coll.) [sich (Dat.)] schnappen (ugs.)

'snapshot n. Schnappschuss, der

snare /sneə(r)/ ①n. Schlinge, die ②v.t. [in einer Schlinge] fangen

snarl¹ /snɑːl/ ①v.i. knurren ②n. Knurren, das

snarl² n. (tangle) Knoten, der
■ **snarl 'up** v.t. (bring to a halt) zum Erliegen bringen; **get ~ed up in the traffic** im Verkehr stecken bleiben
'snarl-up n. Stau, der
snatch /snætʃ/ ① v.t. (a) (grab) schnappen; **~ sth. from sb.** jmdm. etw. wegreißen; **~ some sleep** ein bisschen schlafen
(b) (steal) klauen (ugs.)
② v.i. einfach zugreifen
③ n. **~es of talk/conversation** Gesprächsfetzen Pl.
snazzy /'snæzɪ/ adj. (coll.) [super]schick (ugs.)
sneak /sniːk/ ① v.t. schmuggeln; **~ a look at** schielen nach
② v.i. (a) schleichen
(b) (Brit. Sch. coll.: tell tales) petzen (Schülerspr.)
③ n. (Brit. Sch. coll.) Petze, die (Schülerspr.)
■ **sneak 'out** v.i. [sich] hinausschleichen
'sneaker (Amer.) Turnschuh, der
'sneaking attrib. adj. heimlich; leise ‹Verdacht›
'sneak thief n. Einschleichdieb, der
'sneaky adj. (a) (underhand) hinterhältig
'(b) **have a ~ feeling that …**: so ein leises Gefühl haben, dass …
sneer /snɪə(r)/ v.i. höhnisch lächeln/grinsen
■ **sneer at** v.t. höhnisch anlächeln/angrinsen; (scorn) verhöhnen
sneeze /sniːz/ ① v.i. niesen
② n. Niesen, das
snicker /'snɪkə(r)/ ▶ SNIGGER
snide /snaɪd/ adj. abfällig
sniff /snɪf/ ① n. Schnuppern, das; (with running nose, while crying) Schniefen, das
② v.i. schniefen; (to detect a smell) schnuppern
③ v.t. riechen od. schnuppern an (+ Dat.); **~ glue/cocaine** Klebstoff schnüffeln/Kokain sniffen (Drogenjargon)
■ **'sniff at** v.t. (a) ▶ SNIFF 3
(b) (show contempt for) die Nase rümpfen über
sniffer dog /'snɪfə dɒɡ/ n. Spürhund, der
snigger /'snɪɡə(r)/ ① v.i. [boshaft] kichern
② n. [boshaftes] Kichern
snip /snɪp/ ① v.t., -pp- schnippeln (ugs.), schneiden ‹Loch›; schnippeln (ugs.) od. schneiden an (+ Dat.) ‹Tuch, Haaren, Hecke›; (cut off) abschnippeln (ugs.); abschneiden
② n. (cut) Schnitt, der; Schnipser, der (ugs.)
snipe /snaɪp/ v.i. **~ at** aus dem Hinterhalt beschießen
'sniper n. Heckenschütze, der
snippet /'snɪpɪt/ n. (of information in newspaper) Notiz, die; (of conversation) Gesprächsfetzen, der; **useful ~s of information** nützliche Hinweise
snivel /'snɪvl/ v.i., (Brit.) -ll- schniefen
'snivelling (Amer.: **sniveling**) (fig.) attrib. adj. heulend
snob /snɒb/ n. Snob, der
snobbery /'snɒbərɪ/ n. Snobismus, der
snobbish /'snɒbɪʃ/ adj. snobistisch

snog /snɒɡ/ (Brit. coll.) ① v.i., -gg- knutschen (ugs.)
② n. Knutschen, das (ugs.)
snooker /'snuːkə(r)/ n. Snooker, das
snoop /snuːp/ v.i. schnüffeln (ugs.)
snooty /'snuːtɪ/ adj. (coll.) hochnäsig (ugs.)
snooze /snuːz/ (coll.) ① v.i. dösen (ugs.)
② n. Nickerchen, das (fam.)
'snooze button n. Schlummertaste, die
snore /snɔː(r)/ ① v.i. schnarchen
② n. Schnarcher, der (ugs.); **~s** Schnarchen, das
snorkel /'snɔːkl/ n. Schnorchel, der
snort /snɔːt/ v.i. schnauben (with, in vor + Dat.); (sl.: take) **~ [coke]** [Koks] sniffen (Drogenjargon)
snot /snɒt/ n. (sl.) Rotz, der (derb)
snotty adj. rotznäsig (salopp); **~ child/nose** Rotznase, die (salopp)
snout /snaʊt/ n. Schnauze, die; (of pig) Rüssel, der
snow /snəʊ/ ① n. Schnee, der
② v.i. impers. **it ~s/is ~ing** es schneit
■ **snow 'in** v.t. **they are ~ed in** sie sind eingeschneit
■ **snow 'under** v.t. **be ~ed under** (with work) erdrückt werden; (with gifts, mail) überschüttet werden
snow: **~ball** ① n. Schneeball, der; ② v.i. (fig.) lawinenartig zunehmen; **~blindness** n. Schneeblindheit, die; **~board** ① n. Snowboard, das; ② v.i. Snowboard fahren; **~boarder** n. Snowboarder, der/Snowboarderin, die; **~boarding** n. Snowboardfahren, das; Snowboarden, das; **~bound** adj. eingeschneit; **~capped** adj. schneebedeckt; **~ chains** n. pl. Schneeketten Pl.; **~drift** n. Schneewehe, die; **~drop** n. Schneeglöckchen, das; **~fall** n. Schneefall, der; **~flake** n. Schneeflocke, die; **~man** n. Schneemann, der; **~plough** n. Schneepflug, der; **~storm** n. Schneesturm, der
'snowy adj. schneereich ‹Gegend›; schneebedeckt ‹Berge›
snub /snʌb/ ① v.t., -bb-: (a) (rebuff) brüskieren
(b) (reject) ablehnen
② n. Abfuhr, die
snub-'nosed adj. stupsnasig
snuff¹ /snʌf/ n. Schnupftabak, der; **take a pinch of ~:** eine Prise schnupfen
snuff² v.t. **~ [out]** löschen ‹Kerze›
snuffle /'snʌfl/ v.i. schnüffeln
snug /snʌɡ/ adj. gemütlich; behaglich; **be a ~ fit** genau passen
snuggle /'snʌɡl/ v.i. **~ up to sb.** sich an jmdn. kuscheln; **~ together** sich aneinander kuscheln; **~ up** or **down in bed** sich ins Bett kuscheln
so /səʊ/ ① adv. (a) so; **as winter draws near, so it gets darker** je näher der Winter rückt, desto dunkler wird es; **so … as so … wie; so**

far bis hierher; (until now) bisher; (to such a distance) so weit; **so much the better** um so besser; **so long!** bis dann! (ugs.); **and so on** [**and so forth**] und so weiter [und so fort]; **so as to** um … zu; **so [that]** damit; **I'm so glad/ tired!** ich bin ja so froh/müde!; **It's a rainbow! – So it is!** Es ist ein Regenbogen! – Ja, wirklich!; **'You suggested it. – So I did** Du hast es vorgeschlagen. – Das stimmt; **is that so?** so? (ugs.); **wirklich?**; **so am/have/ would/could/will/do I** ich auch

(b) *pron.* he suggested that I take the train, and if I had done so, …: er riet mir, den Zug zu nehmen, und wenn ich es getan hätte, …; **I'm afraid so** leider ja; **I told you so** ich habe es dir [ja] gesagt; **a week or so** etwa eine Woche; **very much so** in der Tat

2 *conj.* (therefore) daher; **so there you 'are!** ich habe also recht!; **so 'there!** [und] fertig!; **so?** na und?; **so you see** …: du siehst also …; **so where have you been?** wo warst du denn?

soak /səʊk/ **1** *v.t.* (a) einweichen ⟨*Wäsche in Lauge*⟩; eintauchen ⟨*Brot in Milch*⟩
(b) (wet) nass machen
2 *v.i.* (a) (steep) **put sth. in sth. to** ~: etw. in etw. (*Dat.*) einweichen
(b) (drain) ⟨*Feuchtigkeit, Nässe:*⟩ sickern

'soaking *adj. & adv.* ~ [**wet**] völlig durchnässt

'so-and-so *n., pl.* ~'s (a) (person not named) [Herr/Frau] Soundso
(b) (coll.: disliked person) Biest, *das* (ugs.)

soap /səʊp/ *n.* (a) Seife, *die;* **with** ~ **and water** mit Wasser und Seife
(b) (coll.) ▶ SOAP OPERA

soap: ~ **flakes** *n. pl.* Seifenflocken *Pl.;* ~ **opera** *n.* Seifenoper, *die* (ugs.); ~ **powder** *n.* Seifenpulver, *das;* ~**suds** *n. pl.* Seifenschaum, *der*

'soapy *adj.* seifig; ~ **water** Seifenlauge, *die*

soar /sɔː(r)/ *v.i.* aufsteigen; (fig.) ⟨*Preise, Kosten usw.:*⟩ in die Höhe schießen (ugs.)

sob /sɒb/ **1** *v.i.,* -bb- schluchzen (**with** vor + *Dat.*)
2 *n.* Schluchzer, *der*

sober /'səʊbə(r)/ *adj.* (a) (not drunk) nüchtern
(b) (serious) ernst

■ **sober 'up 1** *v.i.* nüchtern werden
2 *v.t.* ausnüchtern

'sobering *adj.* ernüchternd

so-called /'səʊkɔːld/ *adj.* so genannt; (alleged) angeblich

soccer /'sɒkə(r)/ *n.* Fußball, *der*

sociable /'səʊʃəbl/ *adj.* gesellig

social /'səʊʃl/ *adj.* (a) sozial; gesellschaftlich
(b) (of ~ life) gesellschaftlich; gesellig ⟨*Abend, Beisammensein*⟩

'social club *n.* Klub für geselliges Beisammensein

socialism /'səʊʃəlɪzm/ *n.* Sozialismus, *der*

socialist /'səʊʃəlɪst/ **1** *n.* Sozialist, *der*/ Sozialistin, *die*
2 *adj.* sozialistisch

socialize /'səʊʃəlaɪz/ *v.i.* geselligen Umgang pflegen; ~ **with sb.** (chat) sich mit jmdm. unterhalten

'social life *n.* gesellschaftliches Leben; **not have much** ~ ⟨*Person:*⟩ nicht viel ausgehen

'socially *adv.* **meet** ~: sich privat treffen; ~ **deprived** sozial benachteiligt

social: ~ **'science** *n.* Sozialwissenschaften *Pl.;* Gesellschaftswissenschaften *Pl.;* ~ **se'curity** *n.* (a) (Brit.: benefit) Sozialhilfe, *die;* (b) (system) soziale Sicherheit; ~ **'service** *n.* staatliche Sozialleistung; ~ **'services** *n. pl.* Sozialdienste *Pl.;* ~ **work** *n.* Sozialarbeit, *die;* ~ **worker** *n.* Sozialarbeiter, *der*/-arbeiterin, *die*

society /sə'saɪətɪ/ *n.* (a) Gesellschaft, *die;* **high** ~: Highsociety, *die*
(b) (club, association) Verein, *der*

socio-eco'nomic *adj.* sozioökonomisch

sociological /səʊsɪə'lɒdʒɪkl/ *adj.* soziologisch

sociologist /səʊsɪ'ɒlədʒɪst/ *n.* Soziologe, *der*/Soziologin, *die*

sociology /səʊsɪ'ɒlədʒɪ/ *n.* Soziologie, *die*

sock[1] /sɒk/ *n.* Socke, *die*

sock[2] *v.t.* (coll.: hit) hauen (ugs.)

socket /'sɒkɪt/ *n.* (a) (Anat.) (of eye) Höhle, *die;* (of joint) Pfanne, *die*
(b) (Electr.) Steckdose, *die*

soda /'səʊdə/ *n.* Soda, *das*

'soda water *n.* Soda[wasser], *das*

sodden /'sɒdn/ *adj.* durchnässt (**with** von)

sodium /'səʊdɪəm/ *n.* Natrium, *das*

sodium: ~ **bi'carbonate** *n.* doppeltkohlensaures Natrium; Natriumhydrogenkarbonat, *das;* ~ **'chloride** *n.* Natriumchlorid, *das*

sofa /'səʊfə/ *n.* Sofa, *das*

soft /sɒft/ *adj.* weich; (quiet) leise; (gentle) sanft; **have a** ~ **spot for sb.** eine Vorliebe für jmdn. haben

soft: ~**-boiled** *adj.* weich gekocht ⟨*Ei*⟩; ~**-centred** *adj.* ⟨*Praline usw.*⟩ mit weicher Füllung; ~ **copy** *n.* (Comp.) Softcopy, *die;* ~ **cover** *n.* book with a ~ cover Buch mit einem Softcover (Verlagsw.) od. mit einem flexiblen Einband; ~ **drink** *n.* alkoholfreies Getränk; ~ **drug** *n.* weiche Droge

soften /'sɒfn/ **1** *v.i.* weicher werden
2 *v.t.* aufweichen ⟨*Boden*⟩; enthärten ⟨*Wasser*⟩; mildern ⟨*Farbe*⟩

soft: ~ **'furnishings** *n. pl.* (Brit.) Raumtextilien *Pl.;* ~**'hearted** /sɒft'hɑːtɪd/ *adj.* weichherzig

'softly *adv.* (quietly) leise; (gently) sanft

soft: ~ **option** *n.* Weg des geringsten Widerstandes; ~ **'porn** (coll.), ~ **por'nography** *ns.* Softpornographie, ⋯⟩

die; ~**spoken** *adj.* leise sprechend ⟨*Person*⟩; ~ **top** *n.* **(a)** (roof) Stoffverdeck, *das;* **(b)** (car) Cabrio, *das;* ~ **'toy** *n.* Stoffspielzeug, *das;* (toy animal) Stofftier, *das;* ~ **verge** *n.* (Brit.) Grünstreifen, *der;* ~**ware** *n.* (Comp.) Software, *die*

soggy /'sɒgı/ *adj.* aufgeweicht

soil¹ /sɔıl/ *n.* Erde, *die;* Boden, *der*

soil² *v.t.* beschmutzen

solace /'sɒləs/ *n.* Trost, *der;* **take** *or* **find** ~ **in sth.** Trost in etw. (*Dat.*) finden

solar /'səʊlə(r)/ *adj.* Sonnen-

solar: ~ **e'clipse** *n.* Sonnenfinsternis, *die;* ~ **'energy** *n.* Sonnenenergie, *die;* ~ **'panel** *n.* Sonnenkollektor, *der;* (on satellite) Sonnensegel, *das;* ~**powered** *adj.* mit Sonnenenergie betrieben; ~ **system** *n.* Sonnensystem, *das*

sold ▶ SELL

solder /'səʊldə(r)/ ① *n.* Lot, *das* ② *v.t.* löten

soldering iron /'səʊldərıŋaıən/ *n.* Lötkolben, *der*

soldier /'səʊldʒə(r)/ *n.* Soldat, *der*

sole¹ /səʊl/ *n.* (of foot/shoe) Sohle, *die*

sole² *adj.* einzig; alleinig ⟨*Verantwortung, Recht*⟩; Allein⟨*erbe, -eigentümer*⟩

'solely *adv.* einzig und allein

solemn /'sɒləm/ *adj.* feierlich; ernst ⟨*Anlass, Gespräch*⟩

solicitor /sə'lısıtə(r)/ *n.* (Brit.: lawyer) Rechtsanwalt, *der*/-anwältin, *die*

solid /'sɒlıd/ ① *adj.* **(a)** (rigid) fest **(b)** (of the same substance all through) massiv **(c)** (well-built) stabil; solide gebaut ⟨*Haus, Mauer usw.*⟩ **(d)** (complete) ganz; **a good** ~ **meal** eine kräftige Mahlzeit ② *n.* fester Körper

solidarity /sɒlı'dærıtı/ *n.* Solidarität, *die*

solid: ~ **'fuel** *n.* fester Brennstoff; ~**'fuel** *attrib. adj.* Festbrennstoff-; ~**-fuel rocket** *n.* Feststoffrakete, *die*

solidify /sə'lıdıfaı/ *v.i.* fest werden

solitary /'sɒlıtərı/ *adj.* **(a)** einsam; ~ **confinement** Einzelhaft, *die* **(b)** (sole) einzig

solitude /'sɒlıtjuːd/ *n.* Einsamkeit, *die*

solo /'səʊləʊ/ ① *n.,* pl. ~**s** (Mus.) Solo, *das* ② *adj.* **(a)** (Mus.) Solo- **(b)** ~ **flight** Alleinflug, *der* ③ *adv.* **(a)** (Mus.) solo **(b)** **go**/**fly** ~ (Aeronaut.) einen Alleinflug machen

soloist /'səʊləʊıst/ *n.* (Mus.) Solist, *der*/Solistin, *die*

solstice /'sɒlstıs/ *n.* Sonnenwende, *die*

soluble /'sɒljʊbl/ *adj.* **(a)** (esp. Chem.) löslich **(b)** (solvable) lösbar

solution /sə'luːʃn/ *n.* **(a)** (esp. Chem.) Lösung, *die*

(b) ([result of] solving) Lösung, *die* (**to** *Gen.*); **find a** ~ **to sth.** eine Lösung für etw. finden; etw. lösen

solvable /'sɒlvəbl/ *adj.* lösbar

solve /sɒlv/ *v.t.* lösen

solvent /'sɒlvənt/ ① *adj.* **(a)** (esp. Chem.) lösend **(b)** (Finance) solvent ② *n.* Lösungsmittel, *das*

sombre (*Amer.:* **somber**) /'sɒmbə(r)/ *adj.* dunkel; düster ⟨*Stimmung, Atmosphäre*⟩

some /sʌm, *stressed* sʌm/ ① *adj.* **(a)** (one or other) [irgend]ein; ~ **day** eines Tages **(b)** (a considerable quantity of) einig... **(c)** (a small quantity of) ein bisschen; **would you like** ~ **wine/cherries?** möchten Sie [etwas] Wein/[ein paar] Kirschen?; **do** ~ **shopping/reading** einkaufen/lesen **(d)** (to a certain extent) ~ **guide** eine gewisse Orientierungshilfe ② *pron.* einig...; **would you like** ~? möchtest du etwas/(plural) welche?; ~ ..., **others** ...: manche ..., andere ...

somebody /'sʌmbədı/ *n. & pron.* jemand; ~ **or other** irgendjemand

'somehow *adv.* ~ **[or other]** irgendwie

someone /'sʌmwʌn/ ▶ SOMEBODY

somersault /'sɒməsɔːlt/ *n.* Purzelbaum, *der* (ugs.); Salto, *der* (Sport); **turn a** ~: einen Purzelbaum schlagen (ugs.)/einen Salto springen

'something *n. & pron.* etwas; ~ **new** etwas Neues; ~ **or other** irgendetwas; **see** ~ **of sb.** jmdn. sehen

'sometime ① *adj.* ehemalig ② *adv.* irgendwann

'sometimes *adv.* manchmal

'somewhat *adv.* ziemlich

'somewhere ① *adv.* **(a)** (in a place) irgendwo **(b)** (to a place) irgendwohin ② *n.* **look for** ~ **to stay** sich nach einer Unterkunft umsehen

son /sʌn/ *n.* Sohn, *der*

sonata /sə'nɑːtə/ *n.* Sonate, *die*

song /sɒŋ/ *n.* **(a)** Lied, *das* **(b)** (bird cry) Gesang, *der*

song: ~**bird** *n.* Singvogel, *der;* ~**book** *n.* Liederbuch, *das*

sonic /'sɒnık/ *attrib. adj.* Schall-; ~ **bang** *or* **boom** Überschallknall, *der*

'son-in-law *n.,* pl. **sons-in-law** Schwiegersohn, *der*

soon /suːn/ *adv.* **(a)** bald; (quickly) schnell **(b)** (early) früh; **none too** ~: keinen Augenblick zu früh; ~**er or later** früher oder später **(c)** **we'll set off as** ~ **as he arrives** sobald er ankommt, machen wir uns auf den Weg; **as** ~ **as possible** so bald wie möglich **(d)** (willingly) **just as** ~ **[as** ...] genauso gern [wie ...]; **she would** ~**er die than** ...: sie würde lieber sterben, als ...

soot /sʊt/ n. Ruß, der

soothe /suːð/ v.t. **(a)** (calm) beruhigen
(b) lindern ⟨Schmerz⟩

soothing /'suːðɪŋ/ adj. beruhigend;
wohltuend ⟨Bad, Creme, Massage⟩

'**sooty** adj. verrußt; rußig

sophisticated /sə'fɪstɪkeɪtɪd/ adj. **(a)**
(cultured) kultiviert
(b) (elaborate, complex) hoch entwickelt; subtil
⟨Argument, System⟩

soporific /sɒpə'rɪfɪk/ adj. einschläfernd

sopping /'sɒpɪŋ/ adj. & adv. ~ [wet] völlig
durchnässt

soppy /'sɒpɪ/ adj. (Brit. coll.) rührselig;
sentimental ⟨Person⟩

soprano /sə'prɑːnəʊ/ n. Sopran, der; (female
also) Sopranistin, die

sorbet /'sɔːbɪt, 'sɔːbeɪ/ n. Sorbet, das

sorcerer /'sɔːsərə(r)/ n. Zauberer, der

sorcery /'sɔːsərɪ/ n. Zauberei, die

sordid /'sɔːdɪd/ adj. dreckig; unerfreulich
⟨Detail, Geschichte⟩

sore /sɔː(r)/ **1** adj. weh; (inflamed or injured)
wund; **a ~ throat** Halsschmerzen Pl.; **sb. has
a ~ back/foot** etc. jmdm. tut der Rücken/
Fuß usw. weh
2 n. wunde Stelle

'**sorely** adv. sehr; dringend ⟨nötig⟩;
~ **tempted** stark versucht

sorrow /'sɒrəʊ/ n. Kummer, der

sorry /'sɒrɪ/ adj. **(a)** sb. is ~ **that** ...: es tut
jmdm. Leid, dass ...; **sb. is ~ about sth.**
jmdm. tut etwas Leid; **I am** or **feel ~ for him**
er tut mir Leid; **sb. is** or **feels ~ for sth.**
jmd. bedauert etw.; ~! Entschuldigung!; ~?
wie bitte?; **I'm ~ to say** leider; **you'll be ~!**
das wird dir noch Leid tun
(b) (wretched) traurig

sort /sɔːt/ **1** n. **(a)** Art, die; (type) Sorte, die;
a new ~ of bicycle ein neuartiges Fahrrad;
all ~s of ...: alle möglichen ...; **there are all
~s of things to do** es gibt alles Mögliche od.
allerlei zu tun; ~ **of** (coll.: more or less) mehr
oder weniger; **nothing of the ~:** nichts
dergleichen
(b) be out of ~s nicht in Form sein
2 v.t. sortieren

■ **sort 'off** v.t. **(a)** (settle) klären; schlichten
⟨Streit⟩; beenden ⟨Verwirrung⟩
(b) (select) aussuchen

'**sort code** n. Bankleitzahl, die

sortie /'sɔːtɪ/ n. Ausfall, der; (flight) Einsatz,
der

'**sorting office** n. Postverteilstelle, die

SOS n. SOS, das

'**so so**, '**so-so** adj., adv. so lala (ugs.)

soufflé /'suːfleɪ/ n. Soufflé, das

sought ▶ SEEK

soul /səʊl/ n. Seele, die; **not a ~:** keine
Menschenseele

'**soul-destroying** adj. **(a)** (boring)
nervtötend

(b) (depressing) deprimierend

soulful /'səʊlfl/ adj. gefühlvoll; (sad)
schwermütig

soul: ~ **mate** n. Seelenverwandte, der/die;
~-**searching** n. Gewissenskampf, der

sound¹ /saʊnd/ **1** adj. **(a)** (healthy) gesund;
intakt ⟨Gebäude, Mauerwerk⟩; **of ~ mind** im
Vollbesitz seiner geistigen Kräfte
(b) (well-founded) vernünftig ⟨Argument, Rat⟩;
klug ⟨Wahl⟩; **it makes ~ sense** es ist sehr
vernünftig
(c) (Finance: secure) gesund, solide ⟨Basis⟩;
klug ⟨Investition⟩
2 adv. fest, tief ⟨schlafen⟩

sound² **1** n. **(a)** (Phys.) Schall, der
(b) (noise) Laut, der; (of wind, sea, car, footsteps,
breaking glass or twigs) Geräusch, das; (of voices,
laughter, bell) Klang, der; **do sth. without a ~:**
etw. lautlos tun
(c) (Radio, Telev., Cinemat.) Ton, der
(d) (fig.: impression) **I like the ~ of your plan**
ich finde, Ihr Plan hört sich gut an; **I don't
like the ~ of this** das hört sich nicht gut an
2 v.i. klingen; **it ~s as if .../like ...:** es
klingt, als .../wie ...; **that ~s a good idea to
me** ich finde, die Idee hört sich gut an; **that
~s odd to me** das hört sich seltsam an, finde
ich; **~s good to me!** klingt gut! (ugs.)
3 v.t. **(a)** ertönen lassen
(b) (utter) ~ **a note of caution** zur Vorsicht
mahnen

■ **sound 'off** v.i. tönen (ugs.),
schwadronieren (**on, about,** von)

■ **sound 'out** v.i. ausfragen ⟨Person⟩; ~ **sb.
out on sth.** bei jmdm. wegen etw. vorfühlen

sound: ~ **barrier** n. Schallmauer, die;
~ **bite** n. kurzes, prägnantes Zitat;
~ **card** n. (Comp.) Soundkarte, die;
~ **effect** n. Geräuscheffekt, der;
~ **engineer** n. Toningenieur, der/
-ingenieurin, die

'**sounding board** n. **(a)** (Mus.) Decke, die
(b) (fig.: trial audience) ≈ Testgruppe, die

'**soundless** adj. lautlos

'**soundly** adv. **(a)** (solidly) stabil, solide
⟨bauen⟩
(b) (deeply) tief, fest ⟨schlafen⟩
(c) (thoroughly) ordentlich (ugs.) ⟨verhauen⟩;
vernichtend ⟨schlagen, besiegen⟩

sound: ~**proof** **1** adj. schalldicht; **2** v.t.
schalldicht machen; ~ **system** n.
Tonanlage, die; ~-**track** n. Soundtrack, der;
~ **wave** n. Schallwelle, die

soup /suːp/ n. Suppe, die; **be/land in the ~**
(fig. coll.) in der Patsche sitzen/landen (ugs.)

souped-up /'suːptʌp/ attrib. adj. (Motor Veh.
coll.) frisiert (ugs.)

soup: ~ **plate** n. Suppenteller, der;
~ **spoon** n. Suppenlöffel, der

sour /'saʊə(r)/ adj. **(a)** sauer
(b) (morose) griesgrämig; säuerlich ⟨Blick⟩
(c) (unpleasant) bitter

S

source /sɔːs/ n. Quelle, die; ~ of income/ infection Einkommensquelle, die/ Infektionsherd, der; at ~: an der Quelle

sour 'cream n. saure Sahne; Sauerrahm, der

south /saʊθ/ 1 n. (a) Süden, der; in/ to[wards]/from the ~: im/nach/von Süden; to the ~ of südlich von
(b) usu. S~ (Geog., Polit.) Süden, der
2 adj. südlich; Süd⟨küste, -wind, -grenze⟩
3 adv. nach Süden; ~ of südlich von

South: ~ **'Africa** pr. n. Südafrika ⟨das⟩; ~ **'African** adj. südafrikanisch; ~ **A'merica** pr. n. Südamerika ⟨das⟩; ~ **A'merican** adj. südamerikanisch; **s~bound** adj. ⟨Zug, Verkehr usw.⟩ in Richtung Süden; **s~-'east** 1 n. Südosten, der; 2 adj. südöstlich; Südost⟨wind, -küste⟩; 3 adv. südostwärts; nach Südosten; **s~-'eastern** adj. südöstlich

southerly /ˈsʌðəlɪ/ adj. südlich; ⟨Wind⟩ aus südlichen Richtungen

southern /ˈsʌðən/ adj. südlich; Süd⟨grenze, -hälfte, -seite⟩

Southern Europe pr. n. Südeuropa ⟨das⟩

South: ~ **'Germany** pr. n. Süddeutschland ⟨das⟩; ~ **'Pole** pr. n. Südpol, der

southward[s] /ˈsaʊθwəd(s)/ adv. südwärts

south: ~**-'west** 1 n. Südwesten, der; 2 adj. südwestlich; Südwest⟨wind, -küste⟩; 3 adv. südwestwärts; nach Südwesten; ~**-'western** adj. südwestlich

souvenir /suːvəˈnɪə(r)/ n. Souvenir, das ⟨of aus⟩; Andenken, das

sovereign /ˈsɒvrɪn/ n. (ruler) Souverän, der

sovereignty /ˈsɒvrɪntɪ/ n. Souveränität, die

Soviet /ˈsəʊvɪət, ˈsɒvɪət/ adj. (Hist.) sowjetisch; Sowjet⟨bürger, -literatur⟩

Soviet 'Union pr. n. (Hist.) Sowjetunion, die

sow[1] /səʊ/ v.t., p.p. **sown** /səʊn/ or **sowed** /səʊd/ (a) ⟨plant⟩ [aus]säen
(b) einsäen ⟨Feld, Boden⟩

sow[2] /saʊ/ n. (female pig) Sau, die

sown ▸ sow[1]

soya [bean] /ˈsɔɪə (biːn)/ n. Sojabohne, die

soy sauce /ˈsɔɪ sɔːs/ n. Sojasoße, die

sozzled /ˈsɒzld/ adj. (coll.) voll (ugs.)

spa /spɑː/ n. (a) ⟨place⟩ Bad, das; Badeort, der
(b) (spring) Mineralquelle, die

space /speɪs/ n. (a) Raum, der
(b) (interval between points) Platz, der; **clear a ~:** Platz schaffen
(c) **the wide open ~s** das weite, flache Land
(d) (Astron.) Weltraum, der
(e) (blank between words) Zwischenraum, der
(f) (interval of time) Zeitraum, der; **in the ~ of a minute/an hour** innerhalb einer Minute/ Stunde; **in a short ~ of time he was back** nach kurzer Zeit war er zurück

■ **space 'out** v.t. verteilen

space: ~ **age** n. [Welt]raumzeitalter, das; ~ **bar** n. Leertaste, die; ~**craft** n. Raumfahrzeug, das; ~**saving** adj. Platz sparend; ~**ship** n. Raumschiff, das; ~**suit** n. Raumanzug, der; ~ **travel** n. Raumfahrt, die

spacious /ˈspeɪʃəs/ adj. geräumig

spade /speɪd/ n. (a) Spaten, der
(b) (Cards) Pik, das; see also CLUB 1c

spaghetti /spəˈgetɪ/ n. Spaghetti Pl.

Spain /speɪn/ pr. n. Spanien ⟨das⟩

spam /spæm/ n. (Comput.) Spam, der

span /spæn/ 1 n. (a) Spanne, die; Zeitspanne, die
(b) (of bridge) Spannweite, die
2 v.t., -nn- überspannen ⟨Fluss⟩; umfassen ⟨Zeitraum⟩

Spaniard /ˈspænjəd/ n. Spanier, der/ Spanierin, die

Spanish /ˈspænɪʃ/ 1 adj. spanisch; **sb. is ~:** jmd. ist Spanier/Spanierin
2 n. (a) (language) Spanisch, das; see also ENGLISH 2A
(b) **the ~** pl. die Spanier Pl.

spank /spæŋk/ 1 n. ≈ Klaps, der (ugs.)
2 v.t. ~ **sb.** jmdm. einen Klaps geben (ugs.)

spanner /ˈspænə(r)/ n. (Brit.) Schraubenschlüssel, der

spar /spɑː(r)/ v.i., -rr-: (a) (Boxing) sparren
(b) (fig.: argue) [sich] zanken

spare /speə(r)/ 1 adj. (a) (not in use) übrig; ~ **time/moment** Freizeit, die/freier Augenblick; **there is one ~ seat** ein Platz ist noch frei
(b) (for use when needed) zusätzlich, Extra⟨bett, -tasse⟩; ~ **room** Gästezimmer, das
2 n. Ersatzteil, das/-reifen, der usw
3 v.t. (a) entbehren; **we arrived with ten minutes to ~:** wir kamen zehn Minuten früher an
(b) (not inflict on) ~ **sb. sth.** jmdm. etw. ersparen
(c) (not hurt) [ver]schonen
(d) (fail to use) **not ~ any expense/pains** or **efforts** keine Kosten/Mühe scheuen; **no expense ~d** an nichts gespart

spare: ~ **'part** n. Ersatzteil, das; ~ **'tyre** n. Reserve-, Ersatzreifen, der; ~ **'wheel** n. Ersatzrad, das

sparing /ˈspeərɪŋ/ adj., **'sparingly** adv. sparsam

spark /spɑːk/ 1 n. (a) Funke, der; (fig.) a ~ **of generosity/decency** ein Funke[n] Großzügigkeit/Anstand
(b) **a bright ~** (coll.: person, also iron.) ein schlauer Kopf
2 v.t. ~ **[off]** zünden; (fig.) auslösen

sparkle /ˈspɑːkl/ 1 v.i. (a) ⟨Diamant:⟩ glitzern; ⟨Augen:⟩ funkeln
(b) (be lively) sprühen (**with** vor + Dat.)
2 n. Funkeln, das

sparkling /'spɑ:klɪŋ/ *adj.* glitzernd ⟨*Diamant*⟩; funkelnd ⟨*Augen*⟩

sparkling 'wine *n.* Schaumwein, *der*

'spark plug *n.* Zündkerze, *die*

sparrow /'spærəʊ/ *n.* Spatz, *der*

sparse /spɑ:s/ *adj.* spärlich; dünn ⟨*Besiedlung*⟩

spasm /'spæzm/ *n.* Krampf, *der*

spasmodic /spæz'mɒdɪk/ *adj.* **(a)** (marked by spasms) krampfartig
(b) (intermittent) sporadisch

spastic /'spæstɪk/ ⟦1⟧ *n.* Spastiker, *der*/ Spastikerin, *die*
⟦2⟧ *adj.* spastisch

spat ▶ SPIT 1, 2

spate /speɪt/ *n.* **(a)** the river is in [full] ∼: der Fluss führt Hochwasser
(b) (fig.) a ∼ of sth. eine Flut von etw.; a ∼ of burglaries eine Einbruchsserie

spatial /'speɪʃl/ *adj.* räumlich

spatter /'spætə(r)/ *v.t.* spritzen; ∼ sb./sth. with sth. jmdn./etw. mit etw. bespritzen

spatula /'spætjʊlə/ *n.* Spachtel, *der od. die*

spawn /spɔ:n/ ⟦1⟧ *v.t.* (fig.) hervorbringen
⟦2⟧ *v.i.* (Zool.) laichen
⟦3⟧ *n.* (Zool.) Laich, *der*

speak /spi:k/ ⟦1⟧ *v.i.*, spoke /spəʊk/, spoken /'spəʊkn/ **(a)** sprechen; ∼ [with sb.] on *or* about sth. [mit jmdm.] über etw. ⟨*Akk.*⟩ sprechen; ∼ for/against sth. sich für/gegen etw. aussprechen
(b) (on telephone) Is Mr Grant there? – S∼ing! Ist Mister Grant da? – Am Apparat!; who is ∼ing, please? wer ist am Apparat, bitte?
⟦2⟧ *v.t.*, spoke, spoken sprechen ⟨*Satz, Wort, Sprache*⟩; sagen ⟨*Wahrheit*⟩; ∼ one's mind sagen, was man denkt
▪ **'speak for** *v.t.* sprechen für; sth. is spoken for (reserved) etw. ist schon vergeben
▪ **'speak of** *v.t.* sprechen von; ∼ing of Mary da wir gerade von Mary sprechen; nothing to ∼ of nichts Besonderes
▪ **'speak to** *v.t.* sprechen mit; reden mit
▪ **speak 'up** *v.i.* lauter sprechen

'speaker *n.* **(a)** (in public) Redner, *der*/ Rednerin, *die*
(b) (of a language) Sprecher *der*/Sprecherin, *die;* be a 'French ∼: Französisch sprechen
(c) (loudspeaker) Lautsprecher, *der*

'speaking ⟦1⟧ *n.* Sprechen, *das;* ∼ clock (Brit.) telefonische Zeitansage
⟦2⟧ *adv.* strictly/generally ∼: genau genommen/im Allgemeinen

spear /spɪə(r)/ *n.* Speer, *der*

'spearhead ⟦1⟧ *n.* (fig.) Speerspitze, *die*
⟦2⟧ *v.t.* (fig.) anführen

'spearmint *n.* Grüne Minze; ∼ chewing gum Pfefferminzkaugummi, *der od. das*

spec¹ /spek/ (coll.) ▶ SPECIFICATION

spec² /spek/ *n.* (coll.: speculation) on ∼: auf gut Glück; auf Verdacht (ugs.)

special /'speʃl/ *adj.* speziell; besonder...; nobody ∼: niemand Besonderes

special de'livery *n.* (Post) Eilzustellung, *die*

special effects *n. pl.* (Cinemat.) Special effects *Pl.*

specialist /'speʃəlɪst/ *n.* **(a)** Spezialist, *der*/Spezialistin, *die* (in für)
(b) (Med.) Facharzt, *der*/-ärztin, *die*

speciality /speʃɪ'ælɪtɪ/ *n.* Spezialität, *die*

specialization /speʃəlaɪ'zeɪʃn/ *n.* Spezialisierung, *die*

specialize /'speʃəlaɪz/ *v.i.* sich spezialisieren (in auf + *Akk.*)

specialized /'speʃəlaɪzd/ *adj.* **(a)** (requiring detailed knowledge) speziell; Spezial⟨*kenntnisse, -gebiet*⟩
(b) (concentrating on small area) spezialisiert

'specially *adv.* **(a)** speziell; make sth. ∼: etw. speziell *od.* extra anfertigen
(b) (especially) besonders

special: ∼ 'needs *n.* children with ∼ needs Kinder, die besonders betreut werden müssen; ∼ needs teacher Förderlehrer, *der*/-lehrerin, *die;* ∼ 'offer *n.* Sonderangebot, *das;* on ∼ offer im Sonderangebot; ∼ school *n.* Sonderschule, *die*

specialty /'speʃltɪ/ (esp. Amer.) ▶ SPECIALITY

species /'spi:ʃi:z/ *n., pl. same* Art, *die*

specific /spɪ'sɪfɪk/ *adj.* bestimmt; could you be more ∼? kannst du dich genauer ausdrücken?

specifically /spɪ'sɪfɪkəlɪ/ *adv.* ausdrücklich; eigens; extra (ugs.)

specification /spesɪfɪ'keɪʃn/ *n., often pl.* (details) technische Daten *Pl.*; (for building) Baubeschreibung, *die*

specify /'spesɪfaɪ/ *v.t.* ausdrücklich sagen; unless otherwise specified wenn nicht anders angegeben

specimen /'spesɪmən/ *n.* **(a)** (example) Exemplar, *das*
(b) (sample) Probe, *die*

speck /spek/ *n.* **(a)** (spot) Fleck, *der*
(b) (particle) Teilchen, *das;* ∼ of soot/dust Rußflocke, *die*/Staubkörnchen, *das*

specs /speks/ *n. pl.* (coll.: spectacles) Brille, *die*

spectacle /'spektəkl/ *n.* **(a)** *in pl.* [pair of] ∼s Brille, *die*
(b) (public show) Spektakel, *das*
(c) (object of attention) Anblick, *der*

'spectacle case *n.* Brillenetui, *das*

spectacular /spek'tækjʊlə(r)/ *adj.* spektakulär

spectator /spek'teɪtə(r)/ *n.* Zuschauer, *der*/Zuschauerin, *die*

spec'tator sport *n.* Publikumssport, *der*

specter (Amer.) ▶ SPECTRE

spectra *pl. of* SPECTRUM

spectre /'spektə(r)/ *n.* (Brit.) **(a)** (ghost) Gespenst, *das*
(b) (fig.) Schreckgespenst, *das*

S

spectrum /'spektrəm/ n., pl. **spectra** /'spektrə/ Spektrum, *das*

speculate /'spekjʊleɪt/ v.i. spekulieren (about, on über + *Akk.*)

speculation /spekjʊ'leɪʃn/ n. Spekulation, *die* (over über + *Akk.*)

speculative /'spekjʊlətɪv/ adj. spekulativ

speculator /'spekjʊleɪtə(r)/ n. Spekulant, *der*/Spekulantin, *die*

sped ▶ SPEED 2

speech /spiːtʃ/ n. (a) (public address) Rede, *die;* make *or* deliver *or* give a ~: eine Rede halten
(b) (faculty or manner of speaking) Sprache, *die*

'speechless adj. sprachlos (with vor + *Dat.*)

speed /spiːd/ ①① n. Geschwindigkeit, *die;* Schnelligkeit, *die;* at a ~ of ...: mit einer Geschwindigkeit von ...
②② v.i. (a) p.t. & p.p.p. **sped** /sped/ *or* **speeded** schnell fahren; rasen (ugs.)
(b) p.t.&p.p. **speeded** (go too fast) zu schnell fahren; rasen (ugs.)

speed: ~**boat** n. Rennboot, *das;* ~ **bump** n. Bodenschwelle, *die;* ~ **camera** n. Geschwindigkeitsüberwachungskamera, *die*

'speeding n. Geschwindigkeitsüberschreitung, *die*

'speed limit n. Geschwindigkeitsbeschränkung, *die*

speedo /'spiːdəʊ/ n., pl. ~s (Brit. coll.) Tacho, *der* (ugs.)

speedometer /spiː'dɒmɪtə(r)/ n. Tachometer, *der* od. *das*

speed: ~ **ramp** n. Bodenschwelle, *die;* ~**way** n. Speedwayrennen, *das*

'speedy adj. schnell; umgehend, prompt ‹*Antwort*›

spell¹ /spel/ ①① v.t., **spelt** /spelt/ (Brit.) *or* **spelled** (a) schreiben; (aloud) buchstabieren
(b) (fig.: mean) bedeuten
②② v.i., **spelt** (Brit.) *or* **spelled** (say) buchstabieren; (write) richtig schreiben

spell² n. (period) Weile, *die;* a cold ~: eine Kälteperiode

spell³ n. (a) (magic charm) Zauberspruch, *der;* cast a ~ on sb. jmdn. verzaubern
(b) (fascination) Zauber, *der;* break the ~: den Bann brechen

'spellbound adj. verzaubert

'spell checker ▶ SPELLING CHECKER

'spelling n. Rechtschreibung, *die*

spelling: ~ **checker** n. Rechtschreibprogramm, *das;* ~ **mistake** n. Rechtschreibfehler, *der*

spelt ▶ SPELL¹

spend /spend/ v.t., **spent** /spent/ (a) (pay out) ausgeben; ~ a penny (fig. coll.) mal verschwinden (ugs.)
(b) verbringen ‹*Zeit*›

'spendthrift n. Verschwender, *der*/ Verschwenderin, *die*

spent ①① ▶ SPEND
②② adj. (a) (used up) verbraucht
(b) (drained of energy) erschöpft

sperm /spɜːm/ n. pl. ~s *or same* Sperma, *der*

sperm: ~ **bank** n. Samenbank, *die;* ~ **count** n. Spermienzahl, *die*

spew /spjuː/ v.t. spucken

sphere /sfɪə(r)/ n. (a) (field of action) Bereich, *der;* Sphäre, *die* (geh.)
(b) (Geom.) Kugel, *die*

spherical /'sferɪkl/ adj. kugelförmig

spice /spaɪs/ ①① n. Gewürz, *das;* (fig.) Würze, *die*
②② v.t. würzen

'spice rack n. Gewürzregal, *das*

spicy /'spaɪsɪ/ adj. pikant; würzig

spider /'spaɪdə(r)/ n. Spinne, *die*

spider: ~ **plant** n. Grünlilie, *die;* ~**'s web** (*Amer.:* ~ **web**) Spinnennetz, *das;* (fig.) Netz, *das*

spike /spaɪk/ n. Stachel, *der*

spiky /'spaɪkɪ/ adj. stachelig

spill /spɪl/ ①① v.t., **spilt** /spɪlt/ *or* **spilled** verschütten ‹*Flüssigkeit*›; ~ sth. on sth. etw. auf etw. (*Akk.*) schütten; ~ the beans aus der Schule plaudern
②② v.i., **spilt** *or* **spilled** überlaufen

spilt ▶ SPILL

spin /spɪn/ ①① v.t., **-nn-**, **spun** /spʌn/ (a) spinnen; ~ **yarn** Garn spinnen
(b) (in washing machine etc.) schleudern
②② v.i., **-nn-**, **spun** sich drehen; my head is ~ning (fig.) mir schwirrt der Kopf
▪ **spin 'out** v.t. (prolong) in die Länge ziehen

spinach /'spɪnɪdʒ/ n. Spinat, *der*

spinal /'spaɪnl/ adj. Wirbelsäulen-; Rückgrat[s]-

spinal: ~ '**column** n. Wirbelsäule, *die;* ~ '**cord** n. Rückenmark, *das*

spindle /'spɪndl/ n. Spindel, *die*

spindly /'spɪndlɪ/ adj. spindeldürr

spin: ~ **doctor** n. (coll.) Spin-Doktor, *der;* ~ '**drier** n. Wäscheschleuder, *die;* ~ -'**dry** v.t. schleudern

spine /spaɪn/ n. (a) (backbone) Wirbelsäule, *die*
(b) (Bot., Zool.) Stachel, *der*

'spineless adj. (fig.) rückgratlos

'spin-off n. Nebenprodukt, *das*

spinster /'spɪnstə(r)/ n. ledige Frau

spiny /'spaɪnɪ/ adj. stachelig

spiral /'spaɪrl/ ①① adj. spiralförmig
②② n. Spirale, *die*
③③ v.i., (Brit.) **-ll-** ‹*Weg:*› sich hochwinden; ‹*Kosten:*› in die Höhe klettern; ‹*Rauch:*› in einer Spirale aufsteigen

spiral 'staircase n. Wendeltreppe, *die*

spire /'spaɪə(r)/ n. Turmspitze, *die*

spirit /'spɪrɪt/ n. **(a)** in pl. (distilled liquor) Spirituosen Pl.
(b) (mental attitude) Geisteshaltung, die; in the right/wrong ~: mit der richtigen/falschen Einstellung; take sth. in the wrong ~: etw. falsch auffassen
(c) (courage) Mut, der
(d) (mental tendency) Geist, der; high ~s gehobene Stimmung; in poor or low ~s niedergedrückt

'**spirited** adj. beherzt

'**spirit level** n. Wasserwaage, die

spiritual /'spɪrɪtʃʊəl/ adj. spirituell (geh.)

spit /spɪt/ 1 v.i., -tt-, spat /spæt/ or spit spucken
2 v.t., -tt-, spat or spit spucken
3 n. Spucke, die
■ **spit 'out** v.t. ausspucken

spite /spaɪt/ 1 n. **(a)** Boshaftigkeit, die
(b) in ~ of trotz; in ~ of oneself obwohl man es eigentlich nicht will
2 v.t. ärgern

spiteful /'spaɪtfl/ adj. gehässig

spitting 'image n. be the ~ of sb. jmdm. wie aus dem Gesicht geschnitten sein

spittle /'spɪtl/ n. Spucke, die

splash /splæʃ/ 1 v.t. spritzen; ~ sth. on [to] or over sb./sth. jmdn./etw. mit etw. bespritzen
2 v.i. **(a)** spritzen
(b) (in water) platschen (ugs.)
3 n. **(a)** (liquid) Spritzer, der
(b) (noise) Plätschern, das
■ **splash 'out** vi. (coll.) ~ out on sth. für etw. unbekümmert Geld ausgeben

splendid /'splendɪd/ adj. (excellent) großartig; (magnificent) prächtig

splendour (Brit.; Amer.: **splendor**) /'splendə(r)/ n. Pracht, die

splint /splɪnt/ n. Schiene, die

splinter /'splɪntə(r)/ n. Splitter, der

split /splɪt/ 1 n. **(a)** (tear) Riss, der
(b) (division into parts) [Auf]teilung, die; (fig.) Spaltung, die
2 adj. gespalten; be ~ on a question [sich (Dat.)] in einer Frage uneins sein
3 v.t., -tt-, split **(a)** (tear) zerreißen
(b) (divide) teilen
4 v.i., -tt-, split **(a)** ⟨Holz:⟩ splittern; ⟨Stoff, Seil:⟩ reißen; ~ apart zersplittern
(b) (divide into parts) sich teilen
■ **split 'up** 1 v.t. aufteilen
2 v.i. (coll.) sich trennen; ~ up with sb. sich von jmdm. trennen

split: ~-level adj. mit Zwischengeschoss nachgestellt; auf zwei Ebenen nachgestellt; a ~-level lounge ein Wohnraum auf zwei Ebenen; ~-level cooker Einbauherd, bei dem Kochplatten und Backofen getrennt sind; ~ **'pea** n. getrocknete [halbe] Erbse; ~ **perso'nality** n. gespaltene Persönlichkeit; ~ **'second** n. in a ~ second im Bruchteil einer Sekunde; ~-**second timing** [zeitliche] Abstimmung auf die Sekunde genau

splitting /'splɪtɪŋ/ adj. a ~ headache rasende Kopfschmerzen Pl.

splutter /'splʌtə(r)/ v.i. ⟨Person:⟩ prusten; ⟨Motor:⟩ stottern

spoil /spɔɪl/ 1 v.t., spoilt /spɔɪlt/ or spoiled **(a)** (impair) verderben
(b) (pamper) verwöhnen; be ~t for choice die Qual der Wahl haben
2 v.i., spoilt or spoiled **(a)** verderben
(b) be ~ing for a fight Streit suchen
3 n. ~[s pl.] Beute, die

'**spoiler** n. (of car, aircraft) Spoiler, der

'**spoilsport** n. Spielverderber, der/ -verderberin, die

spoilt ▶ SPOIL 1, 2

spoke[1] /spəʊk/ n. Speiche, die

spoke[2], **spoken** ▶ SPEAK

spokesman /'spəʊksmən/ n., pl. spokesmen /'spəʊksmən/ Sprecher, der

sponge /spʌndʒ/ 1 n. Schwamm, der
2 v.t. mit einem Schwamm waschen
■ '**sponge on** v.t. ~ on sb. bei od. von jmdm. schnorren (ugs.)

sponge: ~ bag n. (Brit.) Kulturbeutel, der; ~ **cake** n. Biskuitkuchen, der

sponger /'spʌndʒə(r)/ n. Schmarotzer, der/ Schmarotzerin, die

spongy /'spʌndʒɪ/ adj. schwammig

sponsor /'spɒnsə(r)/ 1 n. Sponsor, der
2 v.t. **(a)** sponsern
(b) (Polit.) ~ sb. jmds. Kandidatur unterstützen

spontaneity /spɒntə'ni:ɪtɪ/ n. Spontaneität, die

spontaneous /spɒn'teɪnɪəs/ adj. spontan

spooky /'spu:kɪ/ adj. gespenstisch

spool /spu:l/ n. Spule, die

spoon /spu:n/ n. **(a)** Löffel, der
(b) (amount) ▶ SPOONFUL

'**spoon-feed** v.t. (fig.) ~ sb. jmdm. alles vorkauen (ugs.)

spoonful /'spu:nfʊl/ n. a ~ of sugar ein Löffel [voll] Zucker

sporadic /spə'rædɪk/ adj. sporadisch

sporadically /spə'rædɪkəlɪ/ adv. hin und wieder

spore /spɔ:(r)/ n. Spore, die

sport /spɔ:t/ 1 n. **(a)** Sport, der; ~s Sportarten Pl.; water/indoor ~: Wasser-/ Hallensport, der
(b) (fun) Spaß, der
(c) be a [real] ~ (coll.) ein prima Kerl sein (ugs.); be a ~! sei kein Spielverderber!
2 v.t. stolz tragen

'**sporting** adj. **(a)** sportlich
(b) give sb. a ~ chance jmdm. eine [faire] Chance geben

sports: ~ bra n. Sport-BH, der; ~ **car** n. Sportwagen, der; ~ **centre** n. ⋯⋗

Sportzentrum, *das;* ~ **channel** *n.*
Sportkanal, *der;* ~ **commentator** *n.*
Sportberichterstatter, *der*/-berichterstatterin,
die; ~ **complex** *n.* Sportzentrum, *das;*
~ **field** *n.* Sportplatz, *der;* ~ **hall** *n.*
Sporthalle, *die;* ~ **jacket** *n.* sportlicher
Sakko; ~**man** /'spɔ:tsmən/ *n., pl.* ~**men**
/'spɔ:tsmən/ *Sportler, der;* ~**manship**
/'spɔ:tsmənʃɪp/ *n.* (fairness) [sportliche]
Fairness, *die;* ~ **page** *n.* (Journ.) Sportseite, *die;*
~ **section** *n.* (Journ.) Sportteil, *der;*
~**wear** *n.* Sport[be]kleidung, *die;*
~**woman** *n.* Sportlerin, *die*

'sporty *adj.* sportlich

spot /spɒt/ [1] *n.* (a) (precise place) Stelle, *die;*
on this ~: an dieser Stelle; be in a tight ~
(fig. coll.) in der Klemme sitzen (ugs.); put sb.
on the ~ (fig. coll.) jmdn. in Verlegenheit
bringen
(b) (suitable area) Platz, *der*
(c) (dot) Tupfen, *der*
(d) (stain) ~ **[of blood/grease/ink]** [Blut-/Fett-/
Tinten]fleck, *der*
(e) (Brit. coll.: small amount) do a ~ of work/
sewing ein bisschen arbeiten/nähen
(f) (drop) a ~ or a few ~s of rain ein paar
Regentropfen
(g) (Med.) Pickel, *der*
[2] *v.t.,* -tt- (detect) entdecken; erkennen
⟨*Gefahr*⟩

spot: ~ **'check** *n.* Stichprobe, *die;* ~**less**
adj. fleckenlos; her house is absolutely ~**less**
(fig.) ihr Haus ist makellos sauber; ~**light**
n. Scheinwerfer, *der;* be in the ~**light** (fig.) im
Rampenlicht stehen

spotted /'spɒtɪd/ *adj.* gepunktet

'spotty *adj.* (pimply) picklig

spouse /spaʊs/ *n.* [Ehe]gatte, *der*/-gattin,
die

spout /spaʊt/ [1] *n.* Schnabel, *der;* (of tap)
Ausflussrohr, *das*
[2] *v.i.* (gush) schießen (from aus)

sprain /spreɪn/ [1] *v.t.* verstauchen
[2] *n.* Verstauchung, *die*

sprang ▶ SPRING 2, 3

sprawl /sprɔ:l/ *v.i.* (a) sich ausstrecken;
(fall) der Länge nach hinfallen
(b) (straggle) sich ausbreiten

'sprawling *attrib. adj.* wuchernd
⟨*Großstadt*⟩

spray[1] /spreɪ/ (bouquet) Strauß, *der*

spray[2] [1] *v.t.* spritzen; sprühen ⟨*Parfüm*⟩;
besprühen ⟨*Haar, Pflanze*⟩
[2] *n.* (a) (drops) Sprühnebel, *der*
(b) (liquid) Spray, *der od. das*

spray: ~ **can** ▶ AEROSOL A; ~ **gun** *n.*
Spritzpistole, *die*

spread /spred/ [1] *v.t.,* spread (a)
ausbreiten ⟨*Tuch, Landkarte*⟩ (on auf
+ *Dat.*); streichen ⟨*Butter, Farbe, Marmelade*⟩
(b) (extend range of) verbreiten
(c) (distribute) verteilen
[2] *v.i.,* spread sich ausbreiten

[3] *n.* (a) Verbreitung, *die;* (of city, poverty)
Ausbreitung, *die*
(b) (coll.: meal) Festessen, *das*
(c) (paste) Brotaufstrich, *der*
(d) (Printing) the advertisement was a full-
page/double-page ~: die Anzeige war
ganzseitig/doppelseitig
■ **spread 'out** [1] *v.t.* ausbreiten
[2] *v.i.* sich verteilen

'spreadsheet *n.* (Comp.) Arbeitsblatt, *das*

spree /spri:/ *n.* go on a shopping ~: ganz
groß einkaufen gehen

'spree killer *n.* Amokläufer, *der*

sprig /sprɪg/ *n.* Zweig, *der*

sprightly /'spraɪtlɪ/ *adj.* munter

spring /sprɪŋ/ [1] *n.* (a) (season) Frühling,
der; in [the] ~: im Frühling od. Frühjahr
(b) (water) Quelle, *die*
(c) (Mech.) Feder, *die*
(d) (jump) Sprung, *der*
[2] *v.i.,* sprang /spræŋ/ or (Amer.) sprung
/sprʌŋ/, sprung (a) (jump) springen; ~ to life
(fig.) [plötzlich] zum Leben erwachen
(b) (arise) entspringen (from *Dat.*)
[3] *v.t.,* sprang or (Amer.) sprung, sprung:
~ sth. on sb. jmdn. mit etw. überfallen

spring: ~**board** *n.* Sprungbrett, *das;*
~ **'chicken** *n.* be no ~ chicken nicht
mehr der/die Jüngste sein (ugs.); ~**'clean**
[1] *n.* Frühjahrsputz, *der;* [2] *v.t.*
Frühjahrsputz machen in (+ *Dat.*):
~**loaded** *adj.* mit Sprungfeder
nachgestellt; ~ **'onion** *n.* Frühlingszwiebel,
die; ~**time** *n.* Frühling, *der*

springy /'sprɪŋɪ/ *adj.* elastisch; federnd
⟨*Schritt, Brett, Boden*⟩

sprinkle /'sprɪŋkl/ *v.t.* streuen; sprengen
⟨*Flüssigkeit*⟩

sprinkler /'sprɪŋklə(r)/ *n.* (Hort.) Sprinkler,
der

sprinkling /'sprɪŋklɪŋ/ *n.* a ~ of snow/
sugar/dust eine dünne Schneedecke/Zucker-/
Staubschicht

sprint /sprɪnt/ [1] *v.t. & i.* rennen; sprinten
(bes. Sport)
[2] *n.* Sprint, *der*

sprout /spraʊt/ [1] *n.* (a) Brussels ~s
Rosenkohl, *der*
(b) (Bot.) Trieb, *der*
[2] *v.i.* sprießen (geh.)

spruce /spru:s/ [1] *adj.* gepflegt
[2] *n.* Fichte, *die*

sprung /sprʌŋ/ [1] ▶ SPRING 2, 3
[2] *attrib. adj.* gefedert

spry /spraɪ/ *adj.* rege

spud /spʌd/ *n.* (coll.) Kartoffel, *die*

spun ▶ SPIN

spunk /spʌŋk/ *n.* (coll.: courage) Mumm, *der*
(ugs.)

spur /spɜ:(r)/ [1] *n.* Sporn, *der;* (fig.) Ansporn,
der; on the ~ of the moment ganz spontan
[2] *v.t.,* -rr- (fig.) anspornen

spurious /'spjʊərɪəs/ *adj.* gespielt ⟨*Interesse*⟩; unberechtigt ⟨*Anspruch, Anklage*⟩

spurn /spɜːn/ *v.t.* zurückweisen

spurt¹ /spɜːt/ *n.* Spurt, *der;* **put on a** ∼: einen Spurt einlegen

spurt² ⨐ *v.i.* ∼ **out** [**from** *or* **of**] herausspritzen [aus]
⨑ *n.* Strahl, *der*

spy /spaɪ/ ⨐ *n.* Spion, *der*/Spionin, *die*
⨑ *v.i.* spionieren; ∼ **on sb.** jmdm. nachspionieren

spy: ∼**master** *n.* Chef, *der* eines Spionagerings; ∼ **ring** *n.* Spionagering, *der;* ∼ **story** *n.* Spionagegeschichte, *die*

squabble /'skwɒbl/ ⨐ *n.* Streit, *der*
⨑ *v.i.* sich zanken (**over, about** wegen)

squad /skwɒd/ *n.* (a) (Mil.) Gruppe, *die*
(b) (group) Mannschaft, *die*

squadron /'skwɒdrən/ *n.* (a) (Navy) Geschwader, *das*
(b) (Air Force) Staffel, *die*

squalid /'skwɒlɪd/ *adj.* (a) (dirty) schmutzig
(b) (poor) schäbig

squall /skwɔːl/ *n.* (gust) Bö, *die*

squalor /'skwɒlə(r)/ *n.* Schmutz, *der*

squander /'skwɒndə(r)/ *v.t.* vergeuden

square /skweə(r)/ ⨐ *n.* (a) (Geom.) Quadrat, *das*
(b) (open area) Platz, *der*
⨑ *adj.* (a) quadratisch
(b) **a** ∼ **metre/mile** ein Quadratmeter/eine Quadratmeile
(c) **be all** ∼: [völlig] quitt sein (*ugs.*)
⨒ *v.t.* (a) (Math.) quadrieren
(b) ∼ **it with sb.** es mit jmdm. klären
⨓ *v.i.* (agree) übereinstimmen
▪ **square 'up** *v.i.* (settle up) abrechnen

square: ∼ **'brackets** *n. pl.* eckige Klammern *Pl.;* ∼ **'meal** *n.* anständige Mahlzeit (ugs.); ∼ **'root** *n.* Quadratwurzel, *die*

squash /skwɒʃ/ ⨐ *v.t.* (crush) zerquetschen; ∼ **sth. flat** etw. platt drücken
⨑ *n.* (a) Fruchtsaftgetränk, *das*
(b) (Sport) Squash, *das*

squash: ∼ **court** *n.* Squashfeld, *das;* ∼ **racket** *n.* Squashschläger, *der*

squat /skwɒt/ *v.i.*, **-tt-:** (a) (crouch) hocken
(b) ∼ **in a house** ein Haus besetzen

'squatter *n.* Hausbesetzer, *der*/-besetzerin, *die*

squawk /skwɔːk/ *v.i.* ⟨*Krähe:*⟩ krähen; ⟨*Huhn:*⟩ kreischen

squeak /skwiːk/ ⨐ *n.* (a) (of animal) Quieken, *das*
(b) (of brakes, hinge, etc.) Quietschen, *das*
⨑ *v.i.* (a) ⟨*Tier:*⟩ quieken
(b) ⟨*Scharnier, Tür, Bremse, Schuh usw.:*⟩ quietschen

squeaky /'skwiːkɪ/ *adj.* quietschend

squeal /skwiːl/ ⨐ *v.i.* (a) ∼ **with pain/in**

fear ⟨*Person:*⟩ vor Schmerz/Angst aufschreien; ⟨*Tier:*⟩ vor Schmerz/Angst laut quieken
(b) ⟨*Bremsen, Räder:*⟩ kreischen; ⟨*Reifen:*⟩ quietschen
⨑ *n.* Kreischen, *das;* (of tyres) Quietschen, *das;* (of animal) Quieken, *das*

squeamish /'skwiːmɪʃ/ *adj.* **be** ∼: zart besaitet sein

squeeze /skwiːz/ ⨐ *n.* Druck, *der;* **give sth. a small** ∼: etw. [leicht] drücken
⨑ *v.t.* (a) (press) drücken; drücken auf (+ *Akk.*) ⟨*Tube, Plastikflasche*⟩; (to get juice) auspressen
(b) (extract) drücken (**out of** aus); ∼ **out sth.** etw. herausdrücken
(c) (force) zwängen

squelch /skweltʃ/ *v.i.* quatschen (ugs.)

squid /skwɪd/ *n.* Kalmar, *der*

squiggle /'skwɪgl/ *n.* Schnörkel, *der*

squint /skwɪnt/ ⨐ *n.* Schielen, *das*
⨑ *v.i.* (a) (Med.) schielen
(b) (with half-closed eyes) blinzeln

squire /'skwaɪə(r)/ *n.* ≈ Gutsherr, *der*

squirm /skwɜːm/ *v.i.* sich winden (**with** vor + *Dat.*)

squirrel /'skwɪrl/ *n.* Eichhörnchen, *das*

squirt /skwɜːt/ ⨐ *v.t.* spritzen; sprühen ⟨*Spray, Puder*⟩; ∼ **sth. at sb.** jmdn. mit etw. bespritzen/besprühen
⨑ *v.i.* spritzen
⨒ *n.* Spritzer, *der*

st. *abbr.* (Brit.: unit of weight) = **stone**

St *abbr.* = **Saint** St.

St. *abbr.* = **Street** Str.

stab /stæb/ ⨐ *v.t.*, **-bb-** stechen; ∼ **sb. in the chest** jmdm. in die Brust stechen
⨑ *v.i.*, **-bb-** stechen
⨒ *n.* (a) Stich, *der*
(b) (coll.: attempt) **make** *or* **have a** ∼ [**at it**] [es] probieren

stability /stə'bɪlɪtɪ/ *n.* Stabilität, *die*

stabilize /'steɪbɪlaɪz/ ⨐ *v.t.* stabilisieren
⨑ *v.i.* sich stabilisieren

stable¹ /'steɪbl/ *adj.* stabil; gefestigt ⟨*Person*⟩

stable² *n.* Stall, *der*

stack /stæk/ ⨐ *n.* (a) (pile) Stoß, *der;* Stapel, *der*
(b) (coll.: large amount) Haufen, *der* (ugs.)
(c) [chimney] ∼: Schornstein, *der*
⨑ *v.t.* ∼ [**up**] [auf]stapeln

stadium /'steɪdɪəm/ *n.* Stadion, *das*

staff /stɑːf/ ⨐ *n.* (a) (stick) Stock, *der*
(b) (personnel) Personal, *das;* (of school) Lehrerkollegium, *das*
⨑ *v.t.* mit Personal ausstatten

staff: ∼ **meeting** *n.* [Lehrer]konferenz, *die;* ∼**room** *n.* Lehrerzimmer, *das*

stag /stæg/ *n.* Hirsch, *der*

stage /steɪdʒ/ ⨐ *n.* (a) (Theatre) Bühne, *die*
(b) (part of process) Stadium, *das;* **at this** ∼: ⋯⟩

in diesem Stadium; **do** sth. **by** ∼**s** etw.
abschnittsweise tun; **in the final** ∼**s** in der
Schlussphase
(c) (distance) Etappe, *die*
2 *v.t.* (a) (present) inszenieren
(b) (arrange) veranstalten

stage: ∼**coach** *n.* Postkutsche, *die;*
∼ **door** *n.* Bühneneingang, *der;* ∼ **effect**
n. Bühneneffekt, *der;* ∼ **fright** *n.*
Lampenfieber, *das;* ∼**hand** *n.*
Bühnenarbeiter, *der/*-arbeiterin, *die;*
∼-**manage** *v.t.* (fig.) veranstalten;
∼ **name** *n.* Künstlername, *der*

stagger /'stægə(r)/ 1 *v.i.* schwanken
2 *v.t.* (astonish) die Sprache verschlagen
(+ *Dat.*)

stagnant /'stægnənt/ *adj.* (a) stehend
‹*Gewässer*›
(b) (Econ.) stagnierend

stagnate /stæg'neɪt/ *v.i.* (a) ‹*Wasser:*›
abstehen
(b) ‹*Wirtschaft, Geschäft:*› stagnieren;
‹*Person:*› abstumpfen

stagnation /stæg'neɪʃn/ *n.* (a) (of water)
Stehen, *das*
(b) (Econ.) Stagnation, *die*

stag: ∼ **night** *n.*: Zechabend des
Bräutigams mit seinen Freunden kurz vor
seiner Hochzeit; ∼ **party** *n.* Herrenabend,
der

staid /steɪd/ *adj.* gesetzt

stain /steɪn/ 1 *v.t.* (a) verfärben; (make ∼s
on) Flecken hinterlassen auf (+ *Dat.*)
(b) (colour) beizen ‹*Holz*›
2 *n.* Fleck, *der*

stained 'glass *n.* farbiges Glas;
∼ 'window Fenster mit Glasmalerei

'**stainless** *adj.* fleckenlos

stainless 'steel *n.* Edelstahl, *der*

'**stain remover** *n.* Fleck[en]entferner, *der*

stair /steə(r)/ *n.* (step) [Treppen]stufe, *die;*
∼s Treppe, *die*

stair: ∼**case** *n.* Treppenhaus, *das;* ∼**way**
n. Treppe, *die*

stake /steɪk/ *n.* (a) (pointed stick) Pfahl, *der*
(b) (wager) Einsatz, *der;* **be at** ∼: auf dem
Spiel stehen

stale /steɪl/ *adj.* alt; muffig; abgestanden
‹*Luft*›; alt[backen] ‹*Brot*›; schal ‹*Bier, Wein
usw.*›

'**stalemate** *n.* Patt, *das*

stalk[1] /stɔːk/ *v.t.* (a) sich heranpirschen an
(+ *Akk.*)
(b) (follow obsessively) ∼ sb. jmdm. nachstellen

stalk[2] *n.* (Bot.) (main stem) Stängel, *der;* (of
leaf, flower, fruit) Stiel, *der*

stalker /'stɔːkə(r)/ *n.* (obsessive pursuer)
[lästiger] Verfolger

stall /stɔːl/ 1 *n.* (a) Stand, *der*
(b) (Brit. Theatre) ∼s Parkett, *das*
2 *v.t.* abwürgen (ugs.) ‹*Motor*›
3 *v.i.* ‹*Motor:*› stehen bleiben

'**stallholder** *n.* Standinhaber, *der/*
-inhaberin, *die*

stallion /'stæljən/ *n.* Hengst, *der*

stalwart /'stɔːlwət/ *adj.* (determined)
entschieden; (loyal) treu

stamen /'steɪmən/ *n.* Staubblatt, *das*

stamina /'stæmɪnə/ *n.* Ausdauer, *die*

stammer /'stæmə(r)/ 1 *v.i.* stottern
2 *v.t.* stammeln
3 *n.* Stottern, *das*

stamp /stæmp/ 1 *v.t.* (a) (impress, imprint sth.
on) [ab]stempeln
(b) ∼ **one's foot** mit dem Fuß stampfen
(c) (put postage ∼ on) frankieren; ∼**ed
addressed envelope** frankierter
Rückumschlag
(d) **become** or **be** ∼**ed on** sb.'s **memory** or
mind sich jmdm. fest einprägen
2 *v.i.* aufstampfen
3 *n.* Marke, *die;* (postage ∼) Briefmarke, *die;*
(instrument for ∼ing) Stempel, *der*
■ '**stamp on** *v.t.* (a) zertreten ‹*Insekt*›;
∼ **on** sb's **foot** jmdm. auf den Fuß treten
(b) (suppress) durchgreifen gegen
■ **stamp 'out** *v.t.* [aus]stanzen; (fig.)
ausmerzen

stamp: ∼ **album** *n.* Briefmarkenalbum,
das; ∼ **collecting** *n.*
Briefmarkensammeln, *das;* ∼ **collection**
n. Briefmarkensammlung, *die;* ∼ **duty** *n.*
Stempelsteuer, *die*

stampede /stæm'piːd/ *n.* Stampede, *die*

stance /stɑːns/ *n.* (posture; fig.: attitude)
Haltung, *die*

stanch /stɑːnʃ/ *v.t.* stillen ‹*Blut*›; abbinden
‹*Wunde*›

stand /stænd/ 1 *v.i.*, **stood** /stʊd/ (a)
stehen
(b) **my offer/promise still** ∼**s** mein Angebot/
Versprechen gilt nach wie vor; **as it** ∼**s,** as
things ∼: wie die Dinge [jetzt] liegen; **I'd like
to know where I** ∼ (fig.) ich möchte wissen,
wo ich dran bin
(c) (be candidate) kandidieren
(d) [not] ∼ **in** sb.'s **way** (fig.) jmdm. [keine]
Steine in den Weg legen
(e) (be likely) ∼ **to win** or **gain/lose** sth. etw.
gewinnen/verlieren können
2 *v.t.*, **stood** (a) (set in position) stellen
(b) (endure) ertragen; **I cannot** ∼ [**the sight of**]
him/her ich kann ihn/sie nicht ausstehen; **he
can't** ∼ **the pressure/strain** er ist dem Druck/
den Strapazen nicht gewachsen; **I can't** ∼ **it
any longer!** ich halte es nicht mehr aus!
(c) (buy) ∼ sb. sth. jmdm. etw. spendieren
3 *n.* (a) (support) Ständer, *der*
(b) (stall; at exhibition) Stand, *der*
(c) (raised structure) Tribüne, *die*
■ **stand a'bout, stand a'round** *v.i.*
herumstehen
■ **stand a'side** *v.i.* zur Seite treten
■ **stand 'back** *v.i.* (a) ∼ [**well**] **back [from**
sth.] [ein gutes Stück] [von etw.] entfernt
stehen

(b) (fig.: distance oneself) zurücktreten

■ '**stand between** *v.t.* sth. ~s between sb. and sth. (fig.) etw. steht jmdm. bei etw. im Wege

■ **stand by** ① /-'-/ *v.i.* **(a)** (be near) daneben stehen
(b) (be ready) sich zur Verfügung halten
② /'-'-/ *v.t.* **(a)** (support) ~ by sb./one another jmdm./sich [gegenseitig] beistehen
(b) (adhere to) ~ by sth. zu etw. stehen

■ **stand 'down** *v.i.* verzichten

■ '**stand for** *v.t.* **(a)** (signify) bedeuten
(b) (coll.: tolerate) sich (*Dat.*) bieten lassen

■ '**stand 'in** *v.i.* aushelfen; ~ in for sb. für jmdn. einspringen

■ **stand 'out** *v.i.* (be prominent) herausragen;
~ out a mile (fig.) nicht zu übersehen sein

■ '**stand over** *v.t.* beaufsichtigen

■ **stand 'up** *v.i.* **(a)** aufstehen; ~ up straight sich aufrecht hinstellen
(b) ~ up well [in comparison with sb./sth.] [im Vergleich zu jmdm./etw.] gut abschneiden; ~ up for sb./sth. für jmdn./ etw. Partei ergreifen; ~ up to sb. sich jmdm. entgegenstellen

stand-alone /'stændə'ləʊn/ *adj.* (Comp.) selbstständig

standard /'stændəd/ ① *n.* **(a)** Maßstab, *der;* **safety** ~s Sicherheitsnormen *Pl.;* **above/below/up to** ~: überdurchschnittlich [gut]/unter dem Durchschnitt/der Norm entsprechend
(b) (degree) Niveau, *das;* ~ of living Lebensstandard, *der*
(c) ~s (morals) Prinzipien *Pl.*
(d) (flag) Standarte, *die*
② *adj.* Standard-; be ~ practice allgemein üblich sein

standardize /'stændədaɪz/ *v.t.* standardisieren

'**standard lamp** *n.* Stehlampe, *die*

stand: ~**-by** ① *n.* be on ~**-by** einsatzbereit sein; ② *adj.* Ersatz-; ~**-in** ① *n.* Ersatz, *der;* ② *adj.* Ersatz-

'**standing** ① *n.* **(a)** (repute) Ansehen, *das*
(b) (duration) of long/short ~: von langer/ kurzer Dauer
② *adj.* **(a)** (erect) stehend
(b) fest ‹Regel, Brauch›

standing: ~ '**order** *n.* Dauerauftrag, *der;*
~ o'**vation** *n.* stürmischer Beifall;
~ **room** *n.* Stehplätze *Pl.*

stand-offish /stænd'ɒfɪʃ/ *adj.* reserviert

stand: ~**pipe** *n.* Standrohr, *das;* ~**point** *n.* (fig.) Standpunkt, *der;* ~**still** *n.* Stillstand, *der;* be at a ~**still** stillstehen; come to a ~**still** zum Stehen kommen

stank ▶ STINK 1

staple[1] /'steɪpl/ ① *n.* [Heft]klammer, *die*
② *v.t.* heften (**on to** an + *Akk.*)

staple[2] ① *attrib. adj.* **(a)** Grund-; a ~ **diet** ein Grundnahrungsmittel
(b) (Commerc.) grundlegend; ~ **goods** Haupthandelsartikel *Pl.*

② *n.* (Commerc.: major item) Haupterzeugnis, *das*

stapler /'steɪplə(r)/ *n.* [Draht]hefter, *der*

star /stɑː(r)/ ① *n.* **(a)** Stern, *der*
(b) (prominent person) Star, *der*
② *v.i.* ~ **in a film** in einem Film die Hauptrolle spielen

starboard /'stɑːbəd/ *n.* Steuerbord, *das*

starch /stɑːtʃ/ *n.* Stärke, *die*

starchy /'stɑːtʃɪ/ *adj.* stärkehaltig ‹Nahrungsmittel›; (fig.: prim) steif

stardom /'stɑːdəm/ *n.* Starruhm, *der*

stare /steə(r)/ *v.i.* starren; ~ **at** sb./sth. jmdn./etw. anstarren

'**starfish** *n.* Seestern, *der*

stark /stɑːk/ ① *adj.* scharf ‹Kontrast, Umriss›
② *adv.* völlig; ~ **naked** splitternackt (ugs.)

'**starless** *adj.* stern[en]los

starlet /'stɑːlɪt/ *n.* Starlet[t], *das*

starling /'stɑːlɪŋ/ *n.* Star, *der*

'**starlit** *adj.* sternhell

starry /'stɑːrɪ/ *adj.* sternklar

star: ~ **sign** *n.* Sternzeichen, *das;*
~**-studded** *adj.* ‹Show, Film, Besetzung› mit großem Staraufgebot

start /stɑːt/ ① *v.i.* **(a)** (begin) anfangen;
~ **on sth.** etw. beginnen
(b) (set out) aufbrechen
(c) (begin to function) anlaufen ‹Auto, Motor usw.›: anspringen
② *v.t.* **(a)** (begin) beginnen [mit]; ~ **doing** or **to do sth.** [damit] anfangen, etw. zu tun
(b) (cause) auslösen; anfangen ‹Streit, Schlägerei›; legen/(accidentally) verursachen ‹Brand›
(c) (set up) ins Leben rufen ‹Organisation, Projekt›
(d) (switch on) einschalten; anlassen ‹Motor, Auto›
③ *n.* **(a)** Anfang, *der;* Beginn, *der;* (of race) Start, *der;* **from the** ~: von Anfang an; **from** ~ **to finish** von Anfang bis Ende; **make a** ~: anfangen (**on** mit); (on journey) aufbrechen
(b) (Sport) ~**ing place**) Start, *der*

'**starter** *n.* **(a)** (food) Vorspeise, *die*
(b) (Sport) Starter, *der*

starting /'stɑːtɪŋ/**:** ~ **point** *n.* (lit. or fig.) Ausgangspunkt, *der;* ~ **post** *n.* (Sport) Startpfosten, *der;* ~ **salary** *n.* Anfangsgehalt, *das*

startle /'stɑːtl/ *v.t.* erschrecken; be ~d by sth. über etw. (*Akk.*) erschrecken

startling /'stɑːtlɪŋ/ *adj.* erstaunlich

starvation /stɑː'veɪʃn/ *n.* Verhungern, *das*

starve /stɑːv/ *v.i.* ~ [**to death**] verhungern

stash /stæʃ/ (coll.) ① *v.t.* ~ [**away**] verstecken
② *n.* [geheimes] Lager

state /steɪt/ ① *n.* **(a)** (condition) Zustand, *der*
(b) (nation) Staat, *der*
(c) be in a ~: aufgeregt sein
(d) lie in ~: aufgebahrt sein ⋯⇨

S

2 v.t. (express) erklären; angeben ⟨Alter usw.⟩

stately /'steɪtlɪ/ adj. majestätisch; stattlich ⟨Körperbau, Gebäude⟩

stately 'home n. Herrensitz, der

'statement n. (a) (stating, account) Aussage, die; (declaration) Erklärung, die
(b) [bank] ∼: Kontoauszug, der

state: ∼-of-the-'art adj. auf dem neuesten Stand der Technik nachgestellt; ∼ **school** n. (Brit.) staatliche Schule; ∼**-owned** adj. staatlich

statesman /'steɪtsmən/ n., pl. **statesmen** /'steɪtsmən/ Staatsmann, der

static /'stætɪk/ adj. statisch

static elec'tricity n. statische Elektrizität

station /'steɪʃn/ **1** n. (a) ▶ RAILWAY STATION
(b) (status) Rang, der
2 v.t. aufstellen ⟨Wache⟩

stationary /'steɪʃənərɪ/ adj. stehend; be ∼: stehen

stationer /'steɪʃənə(r)/ n. ∼'s [shop] Schreibwarengeschäft, das

stationery /'steɪʃənərɪ/ n. (a) (writing materials) Schreibwaren Pl.
(b) (writing paper) Briefpapier, das

'station wagon n. (Amer.) Kombiwagen, der

statistic /stə'tɪstɪk/ n. statistische Tatsache

statistical /stə'tɪstɪkl/ attrib. adj., **statistically** /stə'tɪstɪkəlɪ/ adv. statistisch

statistics /stə'tɪstɪks/ n. Statistik, die

statue /'stætʃuː, 'stætjuː/ n. Statue, die

statuesque /stætjʊ'esk/ adj. statuenhaft; (imposing) stattlich

stature /'stætʃə(r)/ n. Statur, die; (fig.) Format, das

status /'steɪtəs/ n. Rang, der; social ∼: [gesellschaftlicher] Status

'status symbol n. Statussymbol, das

statute /'stætjuːt/ n. Gesetz, das

statutory /'stætjʊtərɪ/ adj. gesetzlich

staunch /stɔːntʃ/ adj. treu ⟨Freund⟩; überzeugt ⟨Katholik usw.⟩

stave /steɪv/ v.t. ∼ 'off abwenden; stillen ⟨Hunger⟩

stay /steɪ/ **1** n. Aufenthalt, der; (visit) Besuch, der; come/go for a short ∼ with sb. jmdn. kurz besuchen
2 v.i. bleiben; ∼ put (coll.) ⟨Person:⟩ bleiben[, wo man ist]; ∼ the night in a hotel die Nacht in einem Hotel verbringen
3 v.t. ∼ the course (fig.) durchhalten
■ **stay a'head** v.i. die Führung halten
■ **stay a'way** v.i. wegbleiben
■ **stay be'hind** v.i. zurückbleiben
■ **stay 'in** v.i. zu Hause bleiben
■ **stay 'out** v.i. (a) (not go home) wegbleiben (ugs.)
(b) (remain outside) draußen bleiben

■ **stay 'over** v.i. (coll.) über Nacht bleiben
■ **stay 'up** v.i. aufbleiben

'staying power n. Durchhaltevermögen, das

stead /sted/ n. (a) in sb.'s ∼: an jmds. Stelle (Dat.)
(b) stand sb. in good ∼: jmdm. zustatten kommen

steadfast /'stedfɑːst/ adj. standhaft; zuverlässig ⟨Freund⟩

steadily /'stedɪlɪ/ adv. (a) (stably) fest
(b) (continuously) stetig

steady /'stedɪ/ **1** adj. (a) (stable) stabil; (not wobbling) standfest
(b) (still) ruhig
(c) (regular, constant) stetig; gleichmäßig ⟨Arbeit, Tempo⟩; stabil ⟨Preis, Lohn⟩; gleich bleibend ⟨Temperatur⟩; we had ∼ rain/drizzle wir hatten Dauerregen/es nieselte [bei uns] ständig
(d) a ∼ job eine feste Stelle; a ∼ boyfriend ein fester Freund
2 v.t. festhalten ⟨Leiter⟩; beruhigen ⟨Nerven⟩

steak /steɪk/ n. Steak, das

'steak knife n. Messer mit Sägezahnung

steal /stiːl/ **1** v.t., stole /stəʊl/, stolen /'stəʊln/ stehlen (from Dat.)
2 v.i., stole, stolen (a) stehlen; ∼ from sb. jmdn. bestehlen
(b) ∼ in/out sich hinein-/hinausstehlen

stealth /stelθ/ n. Heimlichkeit, die; by ∼: heimlich

stealthy /'stelθɪ/ adj. heimlich

steam /stiːm/ **1** n. Dampf, der; let off ∼ (fig.) Dampf ablassen (ugs.); run out of ∼ (fig.) den Schwung verlieren; under one's own ∼ (fig.) aus eigener Kraft
2 v.t. (Cookery) dämpfen; dünsten
3 v.i. dämpfen; ∼ing hot dampfend heiß
■ **steam a'head** v.i. (fig. coll.) rasche Fortschritte machen
■ **steam 'up** v.i. beschlagen

steam: ∼boat n. Dampfschiff, das; (small) Dampfboot, das; ∼ **engine** n. Dampflok[omotive], die; (stationary) Dampfmaschine, die

'steamer n. Dämpfer, der

steam: ∼ iron n. Dampfbügeleisen, das; ∼**roller** n. Dampfwalze, die; ∼ **train** n. Dampfzug, der

'steamy adj. dunstig; beschlagen ⟨Glas⟩

steel /stiːl/ **1** n. Stahl, der
2 attrib. adj. stählern; Stahl⟨helm, -block, -platte⟩
3 v.t. ∼ oneself for/against sth. sich für/ gegen etw. wappnen (geh.); ∼ oneself to do sth. allen Mut zusammennehmen, um etw. zu tun

steel: ∼ 'band n. (Mus.) Steelband, die; ∼ 'drum** n. (Mus.) Steeldrum, die; ∼ **industry** n. Stahlindustrie, die; ∼ 'wool** n. Stahlwolle, die; ∼**works** n. sing. or pl. Stahlwerk, das

steep¹ /sti:p/ adj. (a) steil
(b) (coll.: excessive) happig (ugs.); **the bill is [a bit] ~:** die Rechnung ist [ziemlich] gesalzen (ugs.)

steep² v.t. (soak) einweichen

steeped /sti:pt/ adj. durchdrungen (in von)

steeple /'sti:pl/ n. Kirchturm, der

steer /stɪə(r)/ ① v.t. steuern; lenken
② v.i. steuern; **~ clear of sb./sth.** (fig. coll.) jmdm./einer Sache aus dem Weg[e] gehen

'steering n. (Motor Veh.) Lenkung, die

steering: ~ column n. Lenksäule, die; **~ lock** n. Lenkradschloss, das; **~ wheel** n. Lenkrad, das

stem¹ /stem/ ① n. (a) (Bot.) Stiel, der
(b) (Ling.) Stamm, der
② v.i., -mm-: **~ from sth.** auf etw. (Akk.) zurückzuführen sein

stem² v.t., -mm- (check, dam up) aufhalten; eindämmen ⟨Flut⟩; stillen ⟨Blutung⟩

stench /stentʃ/ n. Gestank, der

stencil /'stensl/ n. Schablone, die; (for duplicating) Matrize, die

step /step/ ① n. (a) Schritt, der; **take a ~ back/forwards** einen Schritt zurücktreten/ nach vorn treten
(b) (stair) Stufe, die; **a flight of ~s** eine Treppe; [pair of] **~s** (ladder) Stehleiter, die
(c) **be in ~:** im Schritt sein; (with music) im Takt sein
(d) **take ~s to do sth.** Schritte unternehmen, um etw. zu tun
(e) (stage) **~ by ~:** Schritt für Schritt; **what is the next ~?** wie geht es weiter?
(f) (grade) Stufe, die
② v.i., -pp- treten; **~ inside** eintreten; **~ into sb's shoes** (fig.) an jmds. Stelle treten; **~ over sb./sth.** über jmdn./etw. steigen

■ **step 'back** v.i. zurücktreten
■ **step 'in** v.i. (a) eintreten
(b) (fig.) (take sb.'s place) einspringen; (intervene) eingreifen
■ **step 'up** ① v.i. (ascend) hinaufsteigen
② v.t. erhöhen; verstärken ⟨Anstrengungen⟩

step: ~ aerobics n. Stepaerobic, das; **~child** n. Stiefkind, das; **~daughter** n. Stieftochter, die; **~father** n. Stiefvater, der; **~ladder** n. Stehleiter, die; **~mother** n. Stiefmutter, die

'stepping stone n. Trittstein, der; (fig.) Sprungbrett, das (**to** für)

stereo /'sterɪəʊ/ ① n. Stereo, das; (equipment) Stereoanlage, die
② adj. stereo; Stereo⟨aufnahme, -platte⟩

stereophonic /sterɪə'fɒnɪk/ adj. stereophon

stereotype /'sterɪətaɪp/ ① n. Stereotyp, das
② v.t. in ein Klischee zwängen; **~d** stereotyp

sterile /'steraɪl/ adj. steril

sterility /stə'rɪlɪtɪ/ n. Sterilität, die

sterilization /sterɪlaɪ'zeɪʃn/ n. Sterilisation, die

sterilize /'sterɪlaɪz/ v.t. sterilisieren

sterling /'stɜ:lɪŋ/ ① n. Sterling, der; **in ~:** in Pfund [Sterling]
② attrib. adj. (a) **~ silver** Sterlingsilber, das
(b) (fig.) gediegen

stern¹ /stɜ:n/ adj. streng; ernst ⟨Warnung⟩

stern² n. (Naut.) Heck, das

'sternly adv. streng

steroid /'steroɪd/ n. Steroid, das

stethoscope /'steθəskəʊp/ n. Stethoskop, das

stew /stju:/ ① n. Eintopf, der
② v.t. schmoren [lassen]

steward /'stju:əd/ n. (a) (on ship, plane) Steward, der
(b) (at public meeting etc.) Ordner, der

'stewardess n. Stewardess, die

stewed /stju:d/ adj. (Cookery) geschmort

'stewing steak n. [Rinder]schmorfleisch, das

stick /stɪk/ ① v.t., stuck /stʌk/ (a) (thrust point of) stecken; **~ sth. in[to] sth.** mit etw. in etw. (Akk.) stechen
(b) (coll.: put) stecken; **~ a picture on the wall/a vase on the shelf** ein Bild an die Wand hängen/eine Vase aufs Regal stellen; **~ sth. in the kitchen** etw. in die Küche tun (ugs.)
(c) (with glue etc.) kleben
(d) **the car is stuck in the mud** das Auto ist im Schlamm stecken geblieben; **the door is stuck** die Tür klemmt [fest]
② v.i., stuck (a) (be fixed by point) stecken
(b) (adhere) kleben; **~ to sth.** an etw. (Dat.) kleben
(c) (become immobile) ⟨Auto, Räder:⟩ stecken bleiben; ⟨Schublade, Tür, Griff, Bremse:⟩ klemmen; ⟨Schlüssel:⟩ feststecken
③ n. Stock, der; **a ~ of chalk** ein Stück Kreide; **a ~ of celery/rhubarb** eine Stange Sellerie/Rhabarber

■ **stick a'bout, stick a'round** v.i. (coll.) dableiben; (wait) warten
■ **'stick by** v.t. (fig.) stehen zu
■ **stick 'on** v.t. (glue on) aufkleben
■ **stick 'out** ① v.t. (a) herausstrecken ⟨Zunge⟩
(b) **~ it out** (coll.) durchhalten
② v.i. (a) ⟨Bauch:⟩ vorstehen; **his ears ~ out** er hat abstehende Ohren
(b) (fig.: be obvious) sich abheben; **~ out a mile** (coll.) [klar] auf der Hand liegen; **~ out like a sore thumb** (coll.) ins Auge springen
■ **'stick to** v.t. (a) (be faithful to) halten ⟨Versprechen⟩; bleiben bei ⟨Entscheidung⟩
(b) **~ to the point** beim Thema bleiben
■ **stick to'gether** v.i. zusammenkleben; (fig.) zusammenhalten
■ **stick 'up** ① v.t. (a) (coll.) anschlagen ⟨Poster⟩; **~ up one's hand** die Hand heben ⋯⋗

S

(b) (seal) zukleben

2 *v.i.* ~ up for sb./sth. für jmdn./etw. eintreten; ~ up for yourself! setz dich zur Wehr!

stick de'odorant *n.* Deo[dorant]stift, *der*

'**sticker** *n.* Aufkleber, *der*

'**sticking plaster** *n.* Heftpflaster, *das*

stickler /'stɪklə(r)/ *n.* **be a ~ for tidiness/ authority** es mit der Sauberkeit sehr genau nehmen/in puncto Autorität keinen Spaß verstehen

'**stick-up** *n.* (coll.) bewaffneter Raubüberfall

'**sticky** *adj.* (a) klebrig; ~ **label** Aufkleber, *der*

(b) (humid) schwül ⟨*Klima, Luft*⟩

stiff /stɪf/ *adj.* (a) (rigid) steif; hart ⟨*Bürste, Stock*⟩; **be frozen ~:** steif vor Kälte sein

(b) (intense, severe) hartnäckig

(c) (formal) steif

(d) (difficult) hart ⟨*Test*⟩; schwer ⟨*Frage, Prüfung*⟩

(e) (coll.) **be bored/scared ~:** sich zu Tode langweilen/eine wahnsinnige Angst haben (ugs.)

stiffen /'stɪfn/ 1 *v.t.* steif machen

2 *v.i.* steifer werden; ⟨*Person:*⟩ erstarren

'**stiffness** *n.* Steifheit, *die*

stifle /'staɪfl/ 1 *v.t.* ersticken; (fig.) unterdrücken

2 *v.i.* ersticken

stifling /'staɪflɪŋ/ *adj.* stickig; drückend ⟨*Hitze*⟩

stigma /'stɪgmə/ *n.* Stigma, *das* (geh.)

stile /staɪl/ *n.* Zauntritt, *der*

stiletto /stɪ'letəʊ/ *n.* ~ [**heel**] Stöckelabsatz, *der*

still[1] /stɪl/ 1 *pred. adj.* still; **be ~:** [still] stehen; **hold sth. ~:** etw. ruhig halten; **keep** *or* **stay ~:** stillhalten; **stand ~:** stillstehen

2 *adv.* (a) (without change) noch; *expr. surprise or annoyance* immer noch

(b) (nevertheless) trotzdem

(c) *with comparative* (even) noch

still[2] *n.* Destillierapparat, *der*

still: ~ **birth** *n.* Totgeburt, *die;* ~**born** *adj.* tot geboren; ~ '**life** *n.* (Art) Stilleben, *das*

stilt /stɪlt/ *n.* Stelze, *die*

'**stilted** *adj.* gestelzt

stimulant /'stɪmjʊlənt/ *n.* Stimulans, *das*

stimulate /'stɪmjʊleɪt/ *v.t.* anregen

stimulation /stɪmjʊ'leɪʃn/ *n.* Anregung, *die*

stimulus /'stɪmjʊləs/ *n., pl.* **stimuli** /'stɪmjʊlaɪ/ Ansporn, *der*

sting /stɪŋ/ 1 *n.* (a) (wounding) Stich, *der;* (by jellyfish, nettles) Verbrennung, *die*

(b) (from ointment, wind) Brennen, *das*

2 *v.t.*, **stung** /stʌŋ/ stechen

3 *v.i.*, **stung** brennen

'**stinging nettle** *n.* Brennnessel, *die*

stingy /'stɪndʒɪ/ *adj.* geizig; knaus[e]rig (ugs.)

stink /stɪŋk/ 1 *v.i.*, **stank** /stæŋk/ *or* **stunk** /stʌŋk/, **stunk** stinken (**of** nach)

2 *n.* Gestank, *der*

'**stink bomb** *n.* Stinkbombe, *die*

stint /stɪnt/ 1 *v.i.* ~ **on sth.** an etw. (*Dat.*) sparen

2 *n.* [Arbeits]pensum, *das*

stipulate /'stɪpjʊleɪt/ *v.t.* (demand) fordern; (lay down) festlegen

stipulation /stɪpjʊ'leɪʃn/ *n.* (condition) Bedingung, *die*

stir /stɜː(r)/ 1 *v.t.*, **-rr-:** (a) (mix) rühren; umrühren ⟨*Tee, Kaffee*⟩

(b) (move) bewegen

2 *v.i.*, **-rr-** (move) sich rühren

3 *n.* Aufregung, *die*

▪ **stir 'in** *v.t.* einrühren

▪ **stir 'up** *v.t.* (a) (disturb) aufrühren

(b) (fig.: arouse) wecken ⟨*Interesse, Leidenschaft*⟩

stirring /'stɜːrɪŋ/ *adj.* bewegend ⟨*Musik, Poesie*⟩; mitreißend ⟨*Rede*⟩

stirrup /'stɪrəp/ *n.* Steigbügel, *der*

stitch /stɪtʃ/ 1 *n.* (a) (Sewing) Stich, *der;* (Knitting) Masche, *die*

(b) (pain) **have a ~:** Seitenstechen haben

2 *v.t.* nähen

▪ **stitch 'up** *v.t.* (a) nähen; vernähen ⟨*Loch, Riss, Wunde*⟩

(b) (Brit. fig. coll.: betray, cheat) reinlegen (ugs.); linken (salopp)

'**stitching** *n.* (a) Naht, *die*

(b) (ornamental stitches) Stickerei, *die*

stoat /stəʊt/ *n.* Hermelin, *das*

stock /stɒk/ 1 *n.* (a) (origin, family, breed) Abstammung, *die*

(b) (supply, store) Vorrat, *der;* (in shop etc.) Warenbestand, *der;* **be in/out of ~** ⟨*Ware:*⟩ vorrätig/nicht vorrätig sein; **have sth. in ~:** etw. auf Lager haben; **take ~ of sth.** (fig.) über etw. (*Akk.*) Bilanz ziehen

(c) (Cookery) Brühe, *die*

2 *v.t.* (a) (supply with ~) beliefern

(b) (Commerc.: keep in ~) auf Lager haben

3 *attrib. adj.* Standard-

stock: ~**broker** Effektenmakler, *der/* -maklerin, *die;* ~ **cube** *n.* Brühwürfel, *der;* ~ **exchange** *n.* Börse, *die.*

stocking /'stɒkɪŋ/ *n.* Strumpf, *der*

'**stockist** *n.* Fachhändler, *der/*-händlerin, *die*

stock: ~ **market** *n.* (a) Börse, *die;* (b) (trading) Börsengeschäft, *das;* ~ **market crash** Börsenkrach, *der;* ~**pile** 1 *n.* Vorrat, *der;* (weapons) Arsenal, *das;* 2 *v.t.* horten; anhäufen ⟨*Waffen*⟩; ~**pot** *n.* Suppentopf, *der;* ~**room** *n.* Lager, *das;* ~-'**still** *pred. adj.* bewegungslos; ~**taking** *n.* Inventur, *die*

stocky /'stɒkɪ/ *adj.* stämmig

stodgy /'stɒdʒɪ/ *adj.* pappig

S

stoical /'stəʊɪkl/ *adj.* stoisch

stoicism /'stəʊɪsɪzm/ *n.* Stoizismus, *der*

stoke /stəʊk/ *v.t.* heizen ‹*Ofen, Kessel*›; unterhalten ‹*Feuer*›

stole ▶ STEAL

stolen /'stəʊln/ [1] ▶ STEAL
[2] *attrib. adj.* heimlich ‹*Vergnügen, Kuss*›

stolid /'stɒlɪd/ *adj.* stur (ugs.)

stomach /'stʌmək/ [1] *n.* (a) Magen, *der*
(b) (abdomen) Bauch, *der*
[2] *v.t.* (fig.: tolerate) ausstehen

stomach: ~ **ache** *n.* Magenschmerzen *Pl.;* have a ~ ache Magenschmerzen haben; ~ **upset** *n.* Magenverstimmung, *die*

stone /stəʊn/ [1] *n.* (a) Stein, *der;* a ~'s throw [away] (fig.) nur einen Steinwurf weit entfernt; be written *or* carved *or* set in ~ (fig.) unverrückbar sein
(b) (Brit.: weight unit) *Gewicht von 6,35 kg*
[2] *adj.* steinern; Stein‹*mauer, -brücke*›
[3] *v.t.* mit Steinen bewerfen

stone: S~ **Age** *n.* Steinzeit, *die;* ~-**cold** *adj.* eiskalt

stoned /stəʊnd/ *adj.* (sl.) stoned (Drogenjargon); (drunk) voll zu (salopp)

stone: ~-'**dead** *pred. adj.* mausetot (fam.); kill sth. ~-dead (fig.) etw. völlig zunichte machen; ~-'**deaf** *adj.* stocktaub (ugs.); ~**mason** *n.* Steinmetz, *der;* ~-'**wall** (Brit.) *v.i.* mauern (fig.); ~**ware** *n., no pl.* Steingut, *das; attrib.* ‹*Krug, Vase*› aus Steingut; ~**washed** *adj.* mit Steinen ausgewaschen; ~**work** *n.* Mauerwerk, *das*

stony /'stəʊnɪ/ *adj.* steinig

stood ▶ STAND 1, 2

stool /stuːl/ *n.* Hocker, *der*

stoop /stuːp/ [1] *v.i.* ~ [down] sich bücken
[2] *n.* walk with a ~: gebeugt gehen

stop /stɒp/ [1] *v.t., -pp-:* (a) anhalten ‹*Person, Fahrzeug*›; aufhalten ‹*Fortschritt, Verkehr, Feind*›
(b) (not let continue) unterbrechen ‹*Redner, Spiel, Gespräch*›; beenden ‹*Krieg, Arbeit*›; stoppen ‹*Produktion, Uhr*›; einstellen ‹*Zahlung, Lieferung*›; ~ that! hör damit auf; ~ smoking/crying aufhören zu rauchen/ weinen
(c) (not let happen) verhindern ‹*Verbrechen, Unfall*›; ~ sth. [from] happening verhindern, dass etw. geschieht
(d) (switch off) abstellen ‹*Maschine*›
(e) (block up) zustopfen ‹*Loch*›; verschließen ‹*Wasserhahn, Flasche*›
(f) ~ a cheque einen Scheck sperren lassen
[2] *v.i., -pp-:* (a) (not extend further) aufhören; ‹*Zahlungen, Lieferungen*› eingestellt werden
(b) (not move further) ‹*Fahrzeug, Fahrer*› halten; ‹*Maschine, Motor*› stillstehen; ‹*Uhr, Fußgänger, Herz*› stehen bleiben
[3] *n.* (a) (halt) Halt, *der;* bring to a ~: zum Stehen bringen ‹*Fahrzeug*›; zum Erliegen bringen ‹*Verkehr*›; unterbrechen ‹*Arbeit*›; come to a ~: stehen bleiben ‹*Fahrzeug*›;

zum Stehen kommen; ‹*Arbeit, Verkehr*› zum Erliegen kommen; put a ~ to abstellen ‹*Missstände, Unsinn*›
(b) (place) Haltestelle, *die*

■ **stop 'by** *v.i.* (Amer.) vorbeischauen (ugs.)
■ **stop 'out** *v.i.* (coll.) draußen bleiben
■ **stop 'over** *v.i.* (coll.) übernachten (at bei)
■ **stop 'up** [1] *v.t.* zustopfen ‹*Loch, Öffnung*›
[2] *v.i.* (coll.) ▶ STAY UP

stop: ~ **button** *n.* Stopptaste, *die;* ~**cock** *n.* Abstellhahn, *der;* ~**gap** *n.* Notlösung, *die;* ~ **light** *n.* (traffic light) rotes Licht; ~**over** *n.* Stopover, *der*

stoppage /'stɒpɪdʒ/ *n.* (a) (halt) Stillstand, *der;* (strike) Streik, *der*
(b) (deduction) Abzug, *der*

stopper /'stɒpə(r)/ *n.* Stöpsel, *der*

stopping /'stɒpɪŋ/: ~ **distance** *n.* Anhalteweg, *der;* ~ **place,** ~ **point** *ns.* Station, *die*

stop: ~**press** *n.* letzte Meldung/ Meldungen *Pl.;* ~ **sign** *n.* Stoppschild, *das;* ~ **signal** *n.* Haltesignal, *das;* ~**watch** *n.* Stoppuhr, *die*

storage /'stɔːrɪdʒ/ *n.* Lagerung, *die;* (of films, books, documents) Aufbewahrung, *die;* (of data, water, electricity) Speicherung, *die*

storage: ~ **capacity** *n.* (Comp.) Speicherkapazität, *die;* ~ **device** *n.* (Comp.) Speichermedium, *das;* ~ **heater** *n.* [Nacht]speicherofen, *der;* ~ **space** *n.* Lagerraum, *der;* (in house) Platz [zum Aufbewahren]; ~ **tank** *n.* Sammelbehälter, *der*

store /stɔː(r)/ [1] *n.* (a) (Amer.: shop) Laden, *der*
(b) (Brit.: large general shop) Kaufhaus, *das*
(c) (warehouse) Lager, *das;* put sth. in ~: etw. einlagern
(d) (stock) Vorrat, *der* (of an + *Dat.*); be *or* lie in ~ for sb. jmdn. erwarten
(e) set [great] ~ by *or* on sth. [großen] Wert auf etw. (*Akk.*) legen
[2] *v.t.* einlagern; speichern ‹*Getreide, Energie, Wissen, Daten*›

■ **store 'up** *v.t.* speichern; ~ up provisions sich (*Dat.*) Vorräte anlegen

store: ~ **detective** *n.* Kaufhausdetektiv, *der;* ~**house** *n.* Lager[haus], *das;* ~**keeper** *n.* (Amer.: shopkeeper) Besitzer eines Einzelhandelsgeschäftes; ~**room** *n.* Lagerraum, *der*

storey /'stɔːrɪ/ *n.* Stockwerk, *das*

stork /stɔːk/ *n.* Storch, *der*

storm /stɔːm/ [1] *n.* Unwetter, *das;* (thunder~) Gewitter, *das*
[2] *v.t. & i.* stürmen

'**storm damage** *n.* Sturmschaden, *der* (meist *Pl.*)

'**stormy** *adj.* stürmisch

story[1] /'stɔːrɪ/ *n.* (a) Geschichte, *die*
(b) (news item) Bericht, *der*
(c) (coll.: lie) Märchen, *das*

story[2] (Amer.) ▶ STOREY

S

'**story book** n. Geschichtenbuch, das; (with fairy tales) Märchenbuch, das

stout /staʊt/ adj. (a) (strong) fest (b) (fat) beleibt

stove /stəʊv/ n. Ofen, der; (for cooking) Herd, der

stow /stəʊ/ v.t. verstauen (**into** in + Dat.)
■ **stow a'way** ① v.t. verwahren
② v.i. als blinder Passagier reisen

straddle /'strædl/ v.t. ~ **a fence/chair** rittlings auf einem Zaun/Stuhl sitzen

straggle /'strægl/ v.i. ~ [**along**] **behind the others** den anderen hinterherzockeln (ugs.)

straggler /'stræglə(r)/ n. Nachzügler, der

straggly /'stræglɪ/ zottig ⟨Haar, Bart⟩

straight /streɪt/ ① adj. (a) gerade; glatt ⟨Haar⟩; **in a** ~ **line** in gerader Linie
(b) (undiluted) **drink whisky** ~: Whisky pur trinken
(c) (direct) direkt ⟨Blick, Schuss, Weg⟩; **be** ~ **with sb.** zu jmdm. offen sein; **get sth.** ~ (fig.) etw. genau verstehen; **put** or **set the record** ~: die Sache richtig stellen
② adv. (a) gerade
(b) (directly) geradewegs; ~ **after** sofort nach; **come** ~ **to the point** direkt zur Sache kommen; **look sb.** ~ **in the eye** jmdm. direkt in die Augen blicken; ~ **ahead** or **on** immer geradeaus
(c) (frankly) aufrichtig
(d) (clearly) klar ⟨sehen, denken⟩

straight a'way adv. sofort

straighten /'streɪtn/ ① v.t. (a) gerade ziehen ⟨Teppich⟩; glätten ⟨Kleidung, Haare⟩
(b) (put in order) aufräumen
② v.i. gerade werden
■ **straighten 'out** ① v.t. (a) gerade biegen; glätten ⟨Decke, Teppich⟩
(b) (clear up) klären
② v.i. gerade werden
■ **straighten 'up** ① v.t. ▶ TIDY UP
② v.i. sich aufrichten

straight: ~ '**face** n. **with a** ~ **face** ohne eine Miene zu verziehen; **keep a** ~ **face** keine Miene verziehen; ~**-faced** adj. mit unbewegter Miene nachgestellt; ~'**forward** adj. (a) (frank) freimütig; schlicht ⟨Stil, Sprache, Bericht⟩; klar ⟨Anweisung, Vorstellungen⟩; (b) (simple) einfach

strain /streɪn/ ① n. (a) (pull) Belastung, die; (on rope) Spannung, die
(b) (tension) Stress, der; **be under** [**a great deal of**] ~: unter großem Stress stehen
(c) (person, thing) **be a** ~ **on sb./sth.** jmdn./ etw. belasten
(d) (muscular injury) Zerrung, die
② v.t. (a) (overexert) überanstrengen; zerren ⟨Muskel⟩
(b) (stretch tightly) [fest] spannen
(c) (filter) durchseihen; seihen (**through** durch)
③ v.i. (strive intensely) sich anstrengen

strained /streɪnd/ adj. gezwungen ⟨Lächeln⟩; ~ **relations** gespannte Beziehungen Pl.

'**strainer** n. Sieb, das

strait /streɪt/ n. (a) in sing. or pl. (Geog.) Meerenge, die
(b) usu. in pl. (distress, difficulty) Schwierigkeiten Pl.

strait: ~**jacket** n. Zwangsjacke, die; ~**-laced** /streɪt'leɪst/ adj. puritanisch

strand¹ /strænd/ n. (thread) Faden, der; (of beads) Kette, die; (of hair) Strähne, die; (of rope) Strang, der

strand² v.t. (leave behind) trockensetzen; **be** [**left**] ~**ed** festsitzen; (fig.) seinem Schicksal überlassen sein

strange /streɪndʒ/ adj. (peculiar) seltsam; sonderbar; ~ **to say** seltsamerweise; **feel** ~: sich komisch fühlen

strangely /'streɪndʒlɪ/ adv. seltsam

stranger /'streɪndʒə(r)/ n. Fremde, der/die; **he is a** ~ **here/to the town** er ist hier/in der Stadt fremd; **be a/no** ~ **to sth.** etw. nicht gewöhnt sein/etw. gewöhnt sein

strangle /'stræŋgl/ v.t. erwürgen

'**stranglehold** n. Würgegriff, der

strangulation /stræŋgjʊ'leɪʃn/ n. Erwürgen, das

strap /stræp/ ① n. (a) (leather) Riemen, der; (textile) Band, das; (shoulder ~) Träger, der; (for watch) Armband, das
(b) (to grasp in vehicle) Halteriemen, der
② v.t., -**pp**-: ~ [**into position**]/**down** festschnallen; ~ **oneself in** sich anschnallen

'**strapless** adj. trägerlos

strapping /'stræpɪŋ/ adj. stramm

strata pl. of STRATUM

strategic /strə'tiːdʒɪk/ adj. strategisch

strategically /strə'tiːdʒɪkəlɪ/ adv. strategisch

strategist /'strætɪdʒɪst/ n. Stratege, der/ Strategin, die

strategy /'strætɪdʒɪ/ n. Strategie, die

stratosphere /'strætəsfɪə(r)/ n. Stratosphäre, die

stratum /'strɑːtəm/ n., pl. **strata** /'strɑːtə/ Schicht, die

straw /strɔː/ n. (a) no pl. Stroh, das
(b) (single stalk) Strohhalm, der; **that's the last** or **final** ~: jetzt reichts aber
(c) [drinking] ~: Strohhalm, der

strawberry /'strɔːbərɪ/ n. Erdbeere, die

stray /streɪ/ ① v.i. (a) (wander) streunen
(b) (deviate) abweichen (**from** von)
② n. (animal) streunendes Tier
③ adj. (a) streunend
(b) (occasional) vereinzelt

streak /striːk/ n. Streifen, der; (in hair) Strähne, die; **have a jealous/cruel** ~: zur Eifersucht/Grausamkeit neigen

'**streaky** adj. streifig; ~ **bacon** durchwachsener Speck

stream /striːm/ **1** n. (of water) Wasserlauf, der; (brook) Bach, der
2 v.i. strömen; ⟨Sonnenlicht:⟩ fluten; **have a ∼ing cold** einen schlimmen Schnupfen haben

streamer /ˈstriːmə(r)/ n. (ribbon) Band, das; (of paper) Luftschlange, die

'streamline v.t. [eine] Stromlinienform geben (+ Dat.); **be ∼lined** eine Stromlinienform haben

street /striːt/ n. Straße, die; **in the ∼:** auf der Straße; **in** (Brit.) **or on ... Street** in der ...straße

street: ∼**car** n. (Amer.) Straßenbahn, die; ∼ **cred** /ˈstriːt kred/ (coll.)**,** ∼ **credibility** ns. [glaubwürdiges] Image; ∼ **crime** n., no indef. art. Straßenkriminalität, die; ∼ **lamp** n. Straßenlaterne, die; ∼ **lighting** n. Straßenbeleuchtung, die; ∼ **map** n. Stadtplan, der; ∼ **market** n. Straßenmarkt, der; ∼ **plan** n. Stadtplan, der; ∼ **sweeper** n. (a) (person) Straßenfeger, der/-fegerin, die (bes. nordd.); Straßenkehrer, der/-kehrerin, die (bes. südd.); (b) (vehicle) Straßenkehrmaschine, die; ∼ **vendor** n. Straßenhändler, der/-händlerin, die; ∼**-wise** adj. (coll.) **be ∼-wise** wissen, wo es langgeht

strength /streŋθ/ n. (power) Kraft, die; (strong point, force, intensity, amount of ingredient) Stärke, die; (of poison, medicine) Wirksamkeit, die; **not know one's own ∼:** nicht wissen, wie stark man ist; **give sb. ∼:** jmdn. stärken; **go from ∼ to ∼:** immer erfolgreicher werden; **on the ∼ of sth./that** aufgrund einer Sache (Gen.)/dessen; **in full ∼:** in voller Stärke; **the police were there in ∼:** ein starkes Polizeiaufgebot war da

strengthen /ˈstreŋθən/ v.t. stärken; (reinforce, intensify) verstärken

strenuous /ˈstrenjʊəs/ adj. (a) (energetic) energisch; gewaltig ⟨Anstrengung⟩; (b) (requiring exertion) anstrengend

stress /stres/ **1** n. (a) (strain) Stress, der; **be under ∼:** unter Stress (Dat.) stehen; (b) (emphasis) Betonung, die **2** v.t. (emphasize) betonen

'stressed out adj. (coll.) [völlig] gestresst

stressful /ˈstresfl/ adj. anstrengend

stress: ∼ **mark** n. Betonungszeichen, das; ∼**-related** adj. stressbedingt

stretch /stretʃ/ **1** v.t. (a) (lengthen) strecken ⟨Arm, Hand⟩; recken ⟨Hals⟩; dehnen ⟨Gummiband⟩; (tighten) spannen (b) (widen) dehnen **2** (a) v.i. (extend in length) sich dehnen (b) ∼ **to sth.** (be sufficient for) für etw. reichen **3** v. refl. sich strecken **4** n. (a) **have a ∼:** sich strecken (b) **at a ∼** (fig.) wenn es sein muss (c) (expanse) Abschnitt, der; **a ∼ of road** ein Stück Straße

(d) (period) **a four-hour ∼:** eine [Zeit]spanne von vier Stunden; **at a ∼:** ohne Unterbrechung
5 adj. Stretch⟨hose, -gewebe⟩

stretcher /ˈstretʃə(r)/ n. [Trag]bahre, die

stretch: ∼ **marks** n. pl. Schwangerschaftsstreifen Pl.; ∼ **pants** n. pl. Stretchhose, die

stretchy /ˈstretʃɪ/ adj. (coll.) dehnbar

strew /struː/ v.t., p.p. **strewed** /struːd/ or **strewn** /struːn/ streuen

stricken /ˈstrɪkn/ adj. (afflicted) heimgesucht; havariert ⟨Schiff⟩; **be ∼ with fear/grief** angsterfüllt/gramgebeugt

strict /strɪkt/ adj. (a) (firm) streng; **in ∼ confidence** streng vertraulich (b) (precise) streng

'strictly adv. streng; ∼ **[speaking]** streng genommen

stride /straɪd/ **1** n. Schritt, der; **put sb. off his ∼** (fig.) jmdn. aus dem Konzept bringen; **take sth. in one's ∼** (fig.) mit etw. gut fertig werden
2 v.i., **strode** /strəʊd/, **stridden** /ˈstrɪdn/ [mit großen Schritten] gehen

strident /ˈstraɪdənt/ adj. schrill

strife /straɪf/ n. Streit, der

strike /straɪk/ **1** n. (Industry) Streik, der; Ausstand, der; **be on/go [out] or come out on ∼:** in den Streik getreten sein/in den Streik treten
2 v.t., **struck** /strʌk/ (a) (hit) schlagen ⟨Schlag, Geschoss:⟩ treffen; ⟨Blitz:⟩ [ein]schlagen in (+ Akk.) (b) (delete) streichen (**from, off** aus) (c) (ignite) anzünden ⟨Streichholz⟩ (d) (chime) schlagen (e) (impress) beeindrucken; ∼ **sb. as [being]** silly jmdm. dumm erscheinen; **it ∼s sb. that ...:** es scheint jmdm., dass ... (f) (occur to) einfallen (+ Dat.)
3 v.i., **struck** (a) (deliver a blow) zuschlagen; ⟨Blitz:⟩ einschlagen; ⟨Unheil, Katastrophe:⟩ hereinbrechen (geh.); (hit) schlagen (**against** gegen, **[up]on** auf + Akk.) (b) (ignite) zünden (c) (chime) schlagen (d) (Industry) streiken

■ **strike 'back** v.i. zurückschlagen
■ **strike 'off** v.t. (∼ off list) streichen ⟨Namen⟩; (from professional body) die Zulassung entziehen (+ Dat.)
■ **'strike through** v.t. durchstreichen ⟨Wort⟩; (on list also) ausstreichen
■ **'strike up** v.t. beginnen ⟨Unterhaltung⟩; schließen ⟨Freundschaft⟩

strike: ∼ **action** n. Streikaktionen Pl.; ∼ **pay** n. Streikgeld, das

'striker n. (a) (worker on strike) Streikende, der/die (b) (Footb.) Stürmer, der/Stürmerin, die

striking /ˈstraɪkɪŋ/ adj. auffallend; erstaunlich ⟨Ähnlichkeit⟩; schlagend ⟨Beispiel⟩

S

'**striking distance** n. Reichweite, *die*

string /strɪŋ/ ⟦1⟧ n. **(a)** (thin cord) Schnur, *die;* (to tie up parcels etc. also) Bindfaden, *der;* **pull [a few or some] ~s** (fig.) seine Beziehungen spielen lassen; **with no ~s attached** ohne Bedingung[en]

(b) (of bow) Sehne, *die;* (of racket, musical instrument) Saite, *die*

⟦2⟧ *v.t.,* **strung** /strʌŋ/ (thread) auffädeln

■ **string a'long** v.t. (deceive) an der Nase herumführen (ugs.)

■ **string to'gether** v.t. auffädeln; miteinander verknüpfen ⟨*Wörter*⟩

■ **string 'up** v.t. aufhängen

string: **~ bag** n. [Einkaufs]netz, *das;* **~ 'bean** n. (Amer.) Stangenohne, *die*

stringed /strɪŋd/ attrib. adj. (Mus.) Saiten-

stringent /'strɪndʒənt/ adj. streng

string 'vest n. Netzhemd, *das*

strip[1] /strɪp/ ⟦1⟧ v.t., **-pp-** ausziehen ⟨*Person*⟩ ⟦2⟧ v.i., **-pp-** sich ausziehen

strip[2] n. (narrow piece) Streifen, *der*

strip: **~ cartoon** n. Comic[strip], *der;* **~ club** n. Stripteaselokal, *das*

stripe /straɪp/ n. Streifen, *der*

striped /straɪpt/ adj. gestreift

strip: **~ light** n. Neonröhre, *die;* **~ lighting** n. Neonbeleuchtung, *die*

stripped pine /strɪpt 'paɪn/ n. abgebeizte Kiefer

stripper /'strɪpə(r)/ n. Stripper, *der/* Stripperin, *die* (ugs.)

strip'tease n. Striptease, *der*

stripy /'straɪpɪ/ adj. gestreift; Streifen⟨*muster*⟩

strive /straɪv/ v.i., **strove** /strəʊv/, **striven** /'strɪvn/ sich bemühen; **~ after or for sth.** nach etw. streben

strode ▶ STRIDE 2

stroke[1] /strəʊk/ n. **(a)** (act of striking) Schlag, *der*

(b) (Med.) Schlaganfall, *der*

(c) (sudden impact) **~ of lightning** Blitzschlag, *der;* **~ of [good] luck** Glücksfall, *der*

(d) **at a or one ~:** auf einen Schlag; **not do a ~ [of work]** keinen [Hand]schlag tun; **~ of genius** genialer Einfall

(e) (in swimming) Zug, *der*

(f) (of clock) Schlag, *der;* **on the ~ of nine** Punkt neun [Uhr]

stroke[2] ⟦1⟧ v.t. streicheln ⟦2⟧ n. **give sb./sth. a ~:** jmdn./etw. streicheln

stroll /strəʊl/ ⟦1⟧ v.i. spazieren gehen ⟦2⟧ n. **go for a ~:** einen Spaziergang machen

strong /strɒŋ/ adj., **~er** /'strɒŋgə(r)/, **~est** /'strɒŋgɪst/ stark; fest ⟨*Fundament, Schuhe*⟩; robust ⟨*Konstitution, Magen*⟩; kräftig ⟨*Arme, Muskeln, Tritt, Zähne*⟩; leistungsfähig ⟨*Wirtschaft*⟩; gut, handfest ⟨*Grund, Beispiel, Argument*⟩; glühend ⟨*Anhänger*⟩; kräftig ⟨*Geruch, Geschmack, Stimme*⟩; **there is a**

~ possibility that ...: es ist sehr wahrscheinlich, dass ...; **take ~ measures/ action** energisch vorgehen

strong: **~hold** n. Festung, *die;* (fig.) Hochburg, *die;* **~ 'language** n. derbe Ausdrucksweise

'**strongly** adv. stark; solide ⟨*gearbeitet*⟩; energisch ⟨*protestieren, bestreiten*⟩; nachdrücklich ⟨*unterstützen*⟩; dringend ⟨*raten*⟩; fest ⟨*glauben*⟩

strong: **~man** n. Muskelmann, *der* (ugs.); **~'minded** adj. willensstark; **~room** n. Tresorraum, *der;* **~'willed** adj. willensstark

stroppy /'strɒpɪ/ adj. (Brit. coll.) pampig (salopp)

strove ▶ STRIVE

struck ▶ STRIKE 2, 3

structural /'strʌktʃərl/ adj. baulich

structure /'strʌktʃə(r)/ n. **(a)** Struktur, *die* **(b)** (something constructed) Konstruktion, *die;* (building) Bauwerk, *das*

structured /'strʌktʃəd/ adj. strukturiert; geregelt ⟨*Leben*⟩

struggle /'strʌgl/ ⟦1⟧ v.i. kämpfen; **~ to do sth.** sich abmühen, etw. zu tun; **~ against or with sb./sth.** mit jmdm./etw. od. gegen jmdn./ etw. kämpfen; **~ with sth.** (try to cope) mit etw. kämpfen ⟦2⟧ n. Kampf, *der*

strum /strʌm/ ⟦1⟧ v.i., **-mm-** klimpern (ugs.) (on auf + *Dat.*) ⟦2⟧ v.t., **-mm-** klimpern (ugs.) auf (+ *Dat.*)

strung ▶ STRING 2

strut[1] /strʌt/ ⟦1⟧ v.i., **-tt-** stolzieren ⟦2⟧ n. stolzierender Gang

strut[2] n. (support) Strebe, *die*

stub /stʌb/ ⟦1⟧ n. **(a)** (remaining portion) Stummel, *der;* (of cigarette) Kippe, *die* **(b)** (counterfoil) Abschnitt, *der* ⟦2⟧ v.t., **-bb-:** **(a)** **~ one's toe [against or on sth.]** sich ⟨*Dat.*⟩ den Zeh [an etw. ⟨*Dat.*⟩] stoßen **(b)** ausdrücken ⟨*Zigarette*⟩

■ **stub 'out** v.t. ausdrücken

stubble /'stʌbl/ n. Stoppeln Pl.

stubbly /'stʌblɪ/ adj. stopp[e]lig

stubborn /'stʌbən/ adj. **(a)** (obstinate) starrköpfig; störrisch ⟨*Tier, Gesicht, Haltung*⟩ **(b)** (resolute) hartnäckig

'**stubbornness** n. ▶ STUBBORN: Starrköpfigkeit, *die;* Hartnäckigkeit, *die*

stuck ▶ STICK 1, 2

'**stuck up** adj. (conceited) eingebildet

student /'stjuːdənt/ n. Student, *der/* Studentin, *die;* (in school or training establishment) Schüler, *der/*Schülerin, *die;* **be a ~ of sth.** etw. studieren

studio /'stjuːdɪəʊ/ n., pl. **~s** **(a)** (workroom) Atelier, *das* **(b)** (Cinemat., Radio, Telev.) Studio, *das*

studio: **~ apartment** (Amer.) ▶ **~ FLAT;**

~ **'audience** n. (Radio, Telev.) Publikum im Studio; ~ **flat** n. (Brit.) (a) Atelier, das; (b) (one-room flat) Einzimmerwohnung, die

studious /'stju:dɪəs/ adj. lerneifrig

study /'stʌdɪ/ ①n. (a) Studium, das (b) (room) Arbeitszimmer, das ② v.t. studieren; sich (Dat.) [sorgfältig] durchlesen ⟨Prüfungsfragen, Bericht⟩

'study group n. Arbeitsgruppe, die

stuff /stʌf/ ①n. (material[s]) Zeug, das (ugs.) ② v.t. (a) stopfen; zustopfen ⟨Loch, Ohren⟩; (Cookery) füllen; ~ sth. with or full of sth. etw. mit etw. voll stopfen (ugs.) (b) (sl.) ~ him! zum Teufel mit ihm!

stuffed 'shirt n. (coll. derog.) Spießer, der (ugs. abwertend)

'stuffing n. (a) (material) Füllmaterial, das (b) (Cookery) Füllung, die

stuffy /'stʌfɪ/ adj. stickig

stumble /'stʌmbl/ v.i. stolpern (**over** über + Akk.)

stumbling block /'stʌmblɪŋblɒk/ n. Stolperstein, der

stump /stʌmp/ ①n. (of tree, branch, tooth) Stumpf, der; (of cigar, pencil) Stummel, der ② v.t. verwirren; **be** ~**ed** ratlos sein

'stumpy adj. gedrungen; ~ **tail** Stummelschwanz, der

stun /stʌn/ v.t., **-nn-** (knock senseless) betäuben; **be** ~**ned at** or **by** sth. (fig.) von etw. wie betäubt sein

stung ▸ STING 2, 3

stunk ▸ STINK 1

stunner /'stʌnə(r)/ n. (coll.) **be a** ~: Spitze sein (ugs.)

stunning /'stʌnɪŋ/ adj. (coll.) (a) (splendid) hinreißend (b) (shocking) bestürzend ⟨Nachricht⟩; (amazing) sensationell

stunt¹ /stʌnt/ v.t. hemmen

stunt² n. halsbrecherisches Kunststück; (Cinemat.) Stunt, der

'stunt man n. Stuntman, der

stupefying /'stju:pɪfaɪɪŋ/ adj. die Sinne betäubend ⟨Hitze⟩; (fig.: astonishing) unfassbar

stupendous /stju:'pendəs/ adj. gewaltig

stupid /'stju:pɪd/ adj. dumm; (ridiculous) lächerlich; **it would be** ~ **to do sth.** es wäre töricht, etw. zu tun

stupidity /stju:'pɪdɪtɪ/ n. Dummheit, die

'stupidly adv. dumm

stupor /'stju:pə(r)/ n. Benommenheit, die; **in a drunken** ~: sinnlos betrunken

sturdy /'stɜ:dɪ/ adj. kräftig; stämmig ⟨Beine, Arme⟩

stutter /'stʌtə(r)/ ①v.i. stottern ②n. Stottern, das

sty¹ /staɪ/ ▸ PIGSTY

sty², **stye** /staɪ/ n. (Med.) Gerstenkorn, das

style /staɪl/ n. Stil, der; [hair]~: Frisur, die; **dress in the latest** ~: sich nach der neuesten Mode kleiden

styli pl. of STYLUS

stylish /'staɪlɪʃ/ adj. stilvoll; elegant ⟨Kleidung, Auto, Person⟩

stylist /'staɪlɪst/ n. (hair~) Haarstylist, der/ -stilistin, die

stylus /'staɪləs/ n., pl. **styli** /'staɪlaɪ/ or ~**es** [Abtast]nadel, die

suave /swɑ:v/ adj. gewandt

sub- /sʌb/ pref. unter-; sub-

sub'conscious ① adj. unterbewusst ② n. Unterbewusstsein, das

sub'continent n. Subkontinent, der

'subcontract v.t. an einen Subunternehmer vergeben

subcon'tractor n. Subunternehmer, der/ -unternehmerin, die

'subculture n. Subkultur, die

subdivide /'---, --'-/ v.t. unterteilen

subdue /səb'dju:/ v.t. bändigen ⟨Kind, Tier⟩; dämpfen ⟨Zorn, Lärm, Licht⟩

subdued /səb'dju:d/ adj. gedämpft

'subgroup n. Untergruppe, die

'subheading n. Untertitel, der

sub'human adj. unmenschlich

subject ① /'sʌbdʒɪkt/ n. (a) Staatsbürger, der/-bürgerin, die; (to monarch) Untertan, der/ Untertanin, die (b) (topic) Thema, das; (of study) Fach, das; **change the** ~: das Thema wechseln ② /'sʌbdʒɪkt/ adj. **be** ~ **to sth.** von etw. abhängen ③ /səb'dʒekt/ v.t. unterwerfen (**to** Dat.); (expose) ~ **sb./sth. to sth.** jmdn./etw. einer Sache (Dat.) aussetzen

subjective /səb'dʒektɪv/ adj.,

sub'jectively adv. subjektiv

'subject matter n., no indef. art. Gegenstand, der

subjugate /'sʌbdʒʊgeɪt/ v.t. unterjochen (**to** unter + Akk.)

subjugation /sʌbdʒʊ'geɪʃn/ n. Unterjochung, die

subjunctive /səb'dʒʌŋktɪv/ n. Konjunktiv, der

sub'let v.t., **-tt-, sublet** untervermieten

sublime /sə'blaɪm/ adj. erhaben

submarine /sʌbmə'ri:n/ n. Unterseeboot, das; U-Boot, das

submerge /səb'mɜ:dʒ/ v.t. (a) ~ **sth. [in the water]** etw. eintauchen (b) (flood) ⟨Wasser:⟩ überschwemmen; **be** ~**d in water** unter Wasser stehen

submerged /səb'mɜ:dʒd/ adj. versunken

submission /səb'mɪʃn/ n. (a) (surrender, meekness) Unterwerfung, die (b) (presentation) Einreichung, die (**to** bei)

submissive /səb'mɪsɪv/ adj. gehorsam

submit /səb'mɪt/ v.t., **-tt-** (present) einreichen; vorbringen ⟨Vorschlag⟩; ~ **sth. to sb.** jmdm. etw. vorlegen

S

subordinate ⊞ /sə'bɔːdɪmət/ *adj.*
untergeordnet

⊡ /sə'bɔːdɪmət/ *n.* Untergebene, *der*/*die*

⊟ /sə'bɔːdɪmeɪt/ *v.t.* unterordnen (to *Dat.*)

subscribe /səb'skraɪb/ *v.i.* (a) (support) ~ to
sth. sich einer Sache anschließen

(b) (make contribution) ~ to sth. eine Spende
für etw. zusichern

(c) ~ to a newspaper eine Zeitung
abonnieren

sub'scriber *n.* (to newspaper etc.) Abonnent,
der/Abonnentin, *die* (to *Gen.*)

subscription /səb'skrɪpʃn/ *n.* (membership
fee) Mitgliedsbeitrag, *der* (to für); (to
newspaper etc.) Abonnement, *das*

subsequent /'sʌbsɪkwənt/ *adj.* folgend;
später ⟨Gelegenheit⟩

'subsequently *adv.* später; danach

subservient /səb'sɜːvɪənt/ *adj.*
untergeordnet (to *Dat.*); (servile) unterwürfig

subside /səb'saɪd/ *v.i.* (a) (sink lower) ⟨Flut,
Fluss:⟩ sinken; ⟨Boden, Haus:⟩ sich senken

(b) (abate) nachlassen

subsidence /səb'saɪdəns/ *n.* (of ground,
structure) Senkung, *die*

subsidiary /səb'sɪdɪərɪ/ ⊞ *adj.*
untergeordnet ⟨Funktion, Stellung⟩;
Neben⟨fach, -aspekt⟩

⊡ *n.* (Commerc.) Tochtergesellschaft, *die*

subsidize /'sʌbsɪdaɪz/ *v.t.* subventionieren

subsidy /'sʌbsɪdɪ/ *n.* Subvention, *die*

subsist /səb'sɪst/ *v.i.* ~ on sth. von etw.
leben

subsistence /səb'sɪstəns/ *n.* [Über]leben,
das

'subsoil *n.* Untergrund, *der*

substance /'sʌbstəns/ *n.* (a) Stoff, *der*

(b) (solidity) Substanz, *die*

(c) (content) Inhalt, *der*

'substance abuse *n.* Drogen- und
Genussmittelmissbrauch, *der*

sub'standard *adj.* unzulänglich

substantial /səb'stænʃl/ *adj.* (a)
(considerable) beträchtlich

(b) gehaltvoll ⟨Essen⟩

(c) (solid) solide ⟨Möbel, Haus⟩; wesentlich
⟨Unterschied⟩

sub'stantially *adv.* (a) (considerably)
wesentlich

(b) (solidly) solide

(c) (essentially) im Wesentlichen

substitute /'sʌbstɪtjuːt/ ⊞ *n.* (a) ~[s *pl.*]
Ersatz, *der*

(b) (Sport) Ersatzspieler, *der*/-spielerin, *die*

⊡ *v.t.* ~ A for B B durch A ersetzen

substitution /sʌbstɪ'tjuːʃn/ *n.* Ersetzung,
die; **make a** ~ (Sport) [einen Spieler]
auswechseln

subterfuge /'sʌbtəfjuːdʒ/ *n.*
Täuschungsmanöver *Pl.*

'subtitle *n.* Untertitel, *der*

subtle /'sʌtl/ *adj.* subtil (geh.); zart ⟨Duft,
Parfüm, Hinweis⟩; fein ⟨Geschmack,
Unterschied, Humor⟩

'subtotal *n.* Zwischensumme, *die*

subtract /səb'trækt/ *v.t.* abziehen

subtraction /səb'trækʃn/ *n.* Subtraktion,
die

sub'tropical *adj.* subtropisch

suburb /'sʌbɜːb/ *n.* Vorort, *der*

suburban /sə'bɜːbən/ *adj.* Vorort-; ⟨Leben,
Haus⟩ am Stadtrand

suburbia /sə'bɜːbɪə/ *n.* (derog.) die
[eintönigen] Vororte *Pl.*

subversive /səb'vɜːsɪv/ *adj.* subversiv

'subway *n.* (a) (passage) Unterführung, *die*

(b) (Amer.: railway) Untergrundbahn, *die;*
U-Bahn, *die*

sub-'zero *adj.* ~ temperatures/conditions
Temperaturen unter Null

succeed /sək'siːd/ ⊞ *v.i.* (a) Erfolg haben;
sb. ~s in sth. jmdm. gelingt etw.; jmd.
schafft etw.; sb. ~s in doing sth. es gelingt
jmdm., etw. zu tun; jmd. schafft es, etw. zu
tun; ~ in business/college geschäftlich/im
Studium erfolgreich sein; I did not ~ in
doing it ich habe es nicht geschafft

(b) (come next) die Nachfolge antreten

⊡ *v.t.* (take place of) ablösen

success /sək'ses/ *n.* Erfolg, *der;* **make a**
~ **of sth.** bei etw. Erfolg haben

successful /sək'sesfl/ *adj.* erfolgreich; be
~ in sth./doing sth. Erfolg bei etw. haben/
dabei haben, etw. zu tun

suc'cessfully *adv.* erfolgreich

succession /sək'seʃn/ *n.* (a) Folge, *die;* in
~: hintereinander

(b) (series) Serie, *die*

(c) (to throne) Erbfolge, *die*

successive /sək'sesɪv/ *adj.* aufeinander
folgend

suc'cessively *adv.* hintereinander

successor /sək'sesə(r)/ *n.* Nachfolger, *der*/
Nachfolgerin, *die*

suc'cess story *n.* Erfolgsstory, *die* (ugs.)

succinct /sək'sɪŋkt/ *adj.* (a) (terse) knapp

(b) (clear) prägnant

succulent /'sʌkjʊlənt/ *adj.* saftig

succumb /sə'kʌm/ *v.i.* unterliegen; ~ to
sth. einer Sache (*Dat.*) erliegen

such /sʌtʃ/ ⊞ *adj.* (a) (of that kind) solch…;
~ a person ein solcher Mensch; ~ a book
ein solches Buch; ~ people solche Leute;
~ things so etwas; I said no ~ thing ich
habe nichts dergleichen gesagt; there is no
~ bird einen solchen Vogel gibt es nicht; or
some ~ thing oder so etwas; you'll do no
~ thing das wirst du nicht tun; experiences
~ as these solche Erfahrungen

(b) (so great) solch…; derartig; I got ~ a fright
that …: ich bekam einen derartigen *od.* (ugs.)
so einen Schrecken, dass …; ~ was the force
of the explosion that …: die Explosion war
so stark, dass …; to ~ an extent dermaßen

(c) *with adj.* so; ~ **a big house** ein so großes Haus; ~ **a long time** so lange

2 *pron.* **as ~:** als solcher/solche/solches; (strictly speaking) im Grunde genommen; an sich; ~ **as** wie [zum Beispiel]; ~ **is life** so ist das Leben

such-and-such /'sʌtʃənsʌtʃ/ *adj.* **at ~ a time** um die und die Zeit

'suchlike *pron.* derlei

suck /sʌk/ **1** *v.t.* saugen (**out of** aus); lutschen ‹*Bonbon*›

2 *sth.* ~**s** (esp. Amer. sl.) etw. ist Scheiße (derb)

■ **suck 'up** **1** *v.t.* aufsaugen

2 *v.i.* ~ **up to sb.** (coll.) jmdm. in den Hintern kriechen (salopp)

'sucker *n.* **(a)** (suction pad) Saugfuß, *der;* (Zool.) Saugnapf, *der*
(b) (coll.: dupe) Dumme, *der/die*

suckle /'sʌkl/ *v.t.* säugen

suction /'sʌkʃn/ *n.* Saugwirkung, *die*

Sudan /suː'dɑːn/ *pr. n.* **[the] ~:** [der] Sudan

sudden /'sʌdn/ **1** *adj.* **(a)** (unexpected) plötzlich
(b) (abrupt) jäh ‹*Abgrund, Übergang, Ruck*›; **there was a ~ bend in the road** plötzlich machte die Straße eine Biegung

2 *n.* **all of a ~:** plötzlich

'suddenly *adv.* plötzlich

'suddenness *n.* Plötzlichkeit, *die*

suds /sʌdz/ *n. pl.* **[soap]~:** [Seifen]lauge, *die;* (froth) Schaum, *der*

sue /suː/ **1** *v.t.* verklagen (**for** auf + *Akk.*)
2 *v.i.* klagen (**for** auf + *Akk.*)

suede /sweɪd/ *n.* Wildleder, *das*

suet /'suːɪt/ *n.* Talg, *der*

Suez /'suːɪz, 'sjuːɪz/ *pr. n.* Suez (*das*); ~ **Canal** Suez-Kanal, *der*

suffer /'sʌfə(r)/ **1** *v.t.* erleiden; durchmachen ‹*Schweres, Kummer*›; dulden ‹*Unverschämtheit*›

2 *v.i.* leiden

■ **'suffer from** *v.t.* leiden unter (+ *Dat.*); leiden an (+ *Dat.*) ‹*Krankheit*›

sufferance /'sʌfərəns/ *n.* Duldung, *die;* **he remains here on ~ only** er ist hier bloß geduldet

'suffering *n.* Leiden, *das*

suffice /sə'faɪs/ **1** *v.i.* genügen; ~ **it to say** ...: nur so viel sei gesagt: ...

2 *v.t.* genügen (+ *Dat.*)

sufficiency /sə'fɪʃənsɪ/ *n.* Zulänglichkeit, *die*

sufficient /sə'fɪʃənt/ *adj.* genug; ~ **money/ food** genug Geld/genug zu essen; **be ~:** genügen; ~ **reason** Grund genug; **have you had ~?** (food, drink) haben Sie schon genug?

sufficiently *adv.* genug; (adequately) ausreichend; ~ **large** groß genug; **a ~ large number** eine genügend große Zahl

suffix /'sʌfɪks/ *n.* Nachsilbe, *die*

suffocate /'sʌfəkeɪt/ **1** *v.t.* ersticken; **he was ~d by the smoke** der Rauch erstickte ihn

2 *v.i.* ersticken

suffocation /sʌfə'keɪʃn/ *n.* Erstickung, *die;* **a feeling of ~:** das Gefühl, zu ersticken

sugar /'ʃʊgə(r)/ **1** *n.* Zucker, *der;* **two ~s, please** (lumps) zwei Stück Zucker, bitte; (spoonfuls) zwei Löffel Zucker, bitte

2 *v.t.* zuckern

sugar: ~ **basin ▶ ~ BOWL;** ~ **beet** *n.* Zuckerrübe, *die;* ~ **bowl** *n.* Zuckerschale, *die;* (covered) Zuckerdose, *die;* ~ **cane** *n.* Zuckerrohr, *das;* ~**-coated** *adj.* gezuckert; mit Zucker überzogen ‹*Dragee usw.*›; ~ **daddy** *n.* (coll.) *spendabler älterer Mann, der ein junges Mädchen aushält;* ~ **lump** *n.* Zuckerstück, *das;* (when counted) Stück Zucker; ~ **tongs** *n. pl.* Zuckerzange, *die*

'sugary *adj.* süß; (fig.) süßlich

suggest /sə'dʒest/ *v.t.* **(a)** (propose) vorschlagen; ~ **sth. to sb.** jmdm. etw. vorschlagen; **he ~ed going to the cinema** er schlug vor, ins Kino zu gehen
(b) (assert) **are you trying to ~ that he is lying** wollen Sie damit sagen, dass er lügt?
(c) (make one think of) suggerieren; ‹*Symptome, Tatsachen:*› schließen lassen auf (+ *Akk.*)

suggestion /sə'dʒestʃn/ *n.* **(a)** Vorschlag, *der;* **at** *or* **on sb.'s ~:** auf jmds. Vorschlag (*Akk.*)
(b) (insinuation) Andeutungen *Pl.*
(c) (fig.: trace) Spur, *die*

suggestive /sə'dʒestɪv/ *adj.* **(a) be ~ of sth.** auf etw. (*Akk.*) schließen lassen
(b) (indecent) anzüglich

suicidal /suːɪ'saɪdl/ *adj.* selbstmörderisch; **I felt** *or* **was quite ~:** ich hätte mich am liebsten gleich umgebracht

suicide /'suːɪsaɪd/ *n.* Selbstmord, *der*

'suicide attempt *n.* Selbstmordversuch, *der*

suit /suːt/ **1** *n.* **(a)** (for men) Anzug, *der;* (for women) Kostüm, *das*
(b) (Law) ~ **[at law]** Prozess, *der*
(c) (Cards) Farbe, *die;* **follow ~** (fig.) das Gleiche tun

2 *v.t.* **(a)** anpassen (**to** *Dat.*)
(b) be ~ed [to sth./one another] [zu etw./ zueinander] passen
(c) (satisfy needs of) passen (+ *Dat.*); **will Monday ~ you?** passt Ihnen Montag?; **does the climate ~ you?** bekommt Ihnen das Klima?
(d) (go well with) passen zu; **does this hat ~ me?** steht mir dieser Hut?; **black ~s her** Schwarz steht ihr gut

3 *v. refl.* ~ **oneself** tun, was man will; ~ **yourself!** [ganz] wie du willst!

suitability /suːtə'bɪlɪtɪ/ *n.* Eignung, *die* (**for** für)

suitable /'suːtəbl/ *adj.* geeignet; angemessen ‹*Kleidung*›; (convenient) passend; ···⟶

∼ **for children** für Kinder geeignet; **Monday is the most** ∼ **day [for me]** Montag passt [mir] am besten

suitably /'suːtəblɪ/ adv. angemessen; entsprechend 〈gekleidet〉

'suitcase n. Koffer, der

suite /swiːt/ n. **(a)** (of furniture) Garnitur, die; **three-piece** ∼: Polstergarnitur, die **(b)** (of rooms) Suite, die

suitor /'suːtə(r)/ n. Freier, der

sulfur, sulfuric (Amer.) ▶ SULPH-

sulk /sʌlk/ v.i. schmollen

'sulky adj. schmollend; eingeschnappt (ugs.)

sullen /'sʌlən/ adj. mürrisch

sulphur /'sʌlfə(r)/ n. Schwefel, der

sulphuric /sʌl'fjʊərɪk/ adj. ∼ **acid** Schwefelsäure, die

sultan /'sʌltən/ n. Sultan, der

sultana /sʌl'tɑːnə/ n. Sultanine, die

sultry /'sʌltrɪ/ adj. schwül

sum /sʌm/ n. **(a)** Summe, die (of aus); ∼ **[total]** Ergebnis, das **(b)** (Arithmetic) Rechenaufgabe, die; **do** ∼**s** rechnen; **she is good at** ∼**s** sie kann gut rechnen

■ **sum 'up** ⃞1 v.t. **(a)** zusammenfassen **(b)** (Brit.: assess) einschätzen ⃞2 v.i. ein Fazit ziehen

summarily /'sʌmərɪlɪ/ adv. summarisch; ∼ **dismissed** fristlos entlassen

summarize /'sʌməraɪz/ v.t. zusammenfassen

summary /'sʌmərɪ/ ⃞1 adj. summarisch; fristlos 〈Entlassung〉 ⃞2 n. Zusammenfassung, die

summer /'sʌmə(r)/ n. Sommer, der; **in [the]** ∼: im Sommer

summer: ∼ **house** n. [Garten]laube, die; ∼ **school** n. Sommerkurs, der; ∼ **term** n. Sommerhalbjahr, das; ∼**time** n. Sommer, der

'summery adj. sommerlich

summing 'up n. Zusammenfassung, die

summit /'sʌmɪt/ n. Gipfel, der; ∼ **conference/meeting** Gipfelkonferenz, die/-treffen, das

summon /'sʌmən/ v.t. **(a)** rufen (to zu); holen 〈Hilfe〉 **(b)** (Law) vorladen

■ **summon 'up** v.t. aufbringen

summons /'sʌmənz/ n. Vorladung, die

sump /sʌmp/ n. Ölwanne, die

sumptuous /'sʌmptjʊəs/ adj. üppig; luxuriös 〈Möbel, Kleidung〉

sun /sʌn/ ⃞1 n. Sonne, die; **catch the** ∼ (be in sunny position) viel Sonne abbekommen; (get ∼**burnt**) einen Sonnenbrand bekommen ⃞2 v. refl., -**nn**- sich sonnen

Sun. abbr. = **Sunday** So.

sun: ∼**baked** adj. an der Sonne getrocknet 〈Ziegel〉; ausgedörrt 〈Landschaft, Prärie usw.〉; ∼**bathe** v.i. sonnenbaden;

∼**bathing** n. Sonnenbaden, das; ∼**beam** n. Sonnenstrahl, der; ∼**bed** n. (with UV lamp) Sonnenbank, die; (in garden) Gartenliege, die; ∼**block** n. Sonnenschutzcreme, die [mit hohem Lichtschutzfaktor]; ∼**burn** n. Sonnenbrand, der; ∼**burnt** adj. be/get ∼**burnt** einen Sonnenbrand haben/ bekommen; ∼**cream** n. Sonnencreme, die

sundae /'sʌndeɪ/ n. [ice cream] ∼: Eisbecher, der

Sunday /'sʌndeɪ, 'sʌndɪ/ n. Sonntag, der; ∼ **opening** die sonntägliche Öffnung; ∼ **trading** sonntägliche Ladenöffnung; see also FRIDAY

sun: ∼**deck** n. Sonnendeck, das; ∼**dial** n. Sonnenuhr, die; ∼**drenched** adj. sonnenüberflutet (geh.); ∼**dress** n. Strandod. Sonnenkleid, das; ∼**dried** adj. an der Sonne getrocknet

sundry /'sʌndrɪ/ ⃞1 adj. verschieden ⃞2 n. in pl. Verschiedenes

'sunflower n. Sonnenblume, die

sung ▶ SING

sun: ∼**glasses** n. pl. Sonnenbrille, die; ∼**hat** n. Sonnenhut, der

sunk ▶ SINK 2, 3

sun: ∼**lamp** n. Höhensonne, die; ∼**lit** adj. sonnenbeschienen; ∼**light** n. Sonnenlicht, das

sunny /'sʌnɪ/ adj. sonnig; ∼ **intervals** Aufheiterungen

sun: ∼ **protection factor** n. Lichtschutzfaktor, der; ∼**ray** n. Sonnenstrahl, der; ∼**rise** n. Sonnenaufgang, der; ∼**roof** n. (Motor Veh.) Schiebedach, das; ∼**set** n. Sonnenuntergang, der; ∼**shade** n. Sonnenschirm, der; ∼**shine** n. Sonnenschein, der; ∼**stroke** n. Sonnenstich, der; ∼**tan** n. [Sonnen]bräune, die; **get a** ∼**tan** braun werden; ∼**tan lotion** n. Sonnencreme, die; ∼**tanned** adj. braun [gebrannt]; ∼**tan oil** n. Sonnenöl, das; ∼**trap** n. sonniges Plätzchen; ∼ **worshipper** n. (lit./joc.) Sonnenanbeter, der/-anbeterin, die

super /'suːpə(r)/ adj. (coll.) super (ugs.)

superb /suː'pɜːb/ adj. einzigartig; erstklassig 〈Essen〉

superbug /'suːpəbʌg/ n. multiresistenter Erreger

supercilious /suːpə'sɪlɪəs/ adj. hochnäsig

supercomputer /'suːpəkəmpjuːtə(r)/ n. Supercomputer, der

superficial /suːpə'fɪʃl/ adj. oberflächlich

superficiality /suːpəfɪʃɪ'ælɪtɪ/ n. Oberflächlichkeit, die

superfluous /suː'pɜːfluəs/ adj. überflüssig

super: ∼**glue** n. Sekundenkleber, der; ∼**human** adj. übermenschlich; ∼**highway** n. **(a)** (Amer.) Autobahn, die; **(b)** (Comp.) Datenautobahn, die

superintendent /suːpərɪn'tendənt/ n. (Brit. Police) Kommissar, der/Kommissarin, die

superior /suːˈpɪərɪə(r)/ **1** *adj.* **(a)** (of higher quality) besonders gut ‹*Restaurant, Qualität, Stoff*›; überlegen ‹*Technik, Intelligenz*›; **he thinks he is ~ to us** er hält sich für besser als wir **(b)** (having higher rank) höher...; **be ~ to sb.** einen höheren Rang als jmd. haben **2** *n.* Vorgesetzte, *der/die*

superiority /suːpɪərɪˈɒrɪtɪ/ *n.* Überlegenheit, *die* (**to** über + *Akk.*)

superlative /suːˈpɜːlətɪv/ **1** *adj.* **(a)** unübertrefflich **(b)** (Ling.) **a ~ adjective/adverb** ein Adjektiv/ Adverb im Superlativ **2** *n.* (Ling.) Superlativ, *der*

super: ~market *n.* Supermarkt, *der;* **~model** *n.* Supermodel, *das;* **~natural** *adj.* übernatürlich; **~power** *n.* (Polit.) Supermacht, *die*

supersede /suːpəˈsiːd/ *v.t.* ablösen (by durch)

supersonic /suːpəˈsɒnɪk/ *adj.* Überschall-

superstar /ˈsuːpəstɑː(r)/ *n.* Superstar, *der*

superstition /suːpəˈstɪʃn/ *n.* Aberglaube, *der*

superstitious /suːpəˈstɪʃəs/ *adj.* abergläubisch

superstore /ˈsuːpəstɔː(r)/ *n.* Großmarkt, *der*

supervise /ˈsuːpəvaɪz/ *v.t.* beaufsichtigen

supervision /suːpəˈvɪʒn/ *n.* Aufsicht, *die*

supervisor /ˈsuːpəvaɪzə(r)/ *n.* Aufseher, *der*/Aufseherin, *die*

supper /ˈsʌpə(r)/ *n.* Abendessen, *das;* **have [one's] ~:** zu Abend essen

'suppertime *n.* Abendbrotzeit, *die;* **it's ~:** es ist Zeit zum Abendessen

supplant /səˈplɑːnt/ *v.t.* ablösen, ersetzen (by durch)

supple /ˈsʌpl/ *adj.* geschmeidig

supplement /ˈsʌplɪmənt/ **1** *n.* **(a)** Ergänzung, *die* (**to** + *Gen.*); (addition) Zusatz, *der* **(b)** (of book) Nachtrag, *der;* (of newspaper) Beilage, *die* **(c)** (to fare) Zuschlag, *der* **2** *v.t.* ergänzen

supplementary /sʌplɪˈmentərɪ/ *adj.* zusätzlich; **~ fare/charge** Zuschlag, *der*

supplier /səˈplaɪə(r)/ *n.* (Commerc.) Lieferant, *der*/Lieferantin, *die*

supply /səˈplaɪ/ **1** *v.t.* liefern ‹*Waren usw.*›; beliefern ‹*Kunden, Geschäft*›; **~ sth. to sb., ~ sb. with sth.** jmdn. mit etw. versorgen/ (Commerc.) beliefern **2** *n.* Vorräte *Pl.;* **military/medical supplies** militärischer/medizinischer Nachschub; **~ and demand** (Econ.) Angebot und Nachfrage

sup'ply teacher *n.* Vertretung, *die*

support /səˈpɔːt/ **1** *v.t.* **(a)** (hold up) stützen ‹*Mauer, Verletzten*›; (bear weight of) tragen

(b) unterstützen ‹*Politik, Verein*›; (Footb.) **~ Spurs** Spurs-Fan sein **(c)** (provide for) ernähren ‹*Familie, sich selbst*› **(d)** (speak in favour of) befürworten **2** *n.* **(a)** Unterstützung, *die;* **in ~:** zur Unterstützung; **speak in ~ of sb./sth.** jmdn. unterstützen/etw. befürworten **(b)** (money) Unterhalt, *der* **(c)** (sb./sth. that ~s) Stütze, *die*

sup'porter *n.* Anhänger, *der*/Anhängerin, *die;* **football ~:** Fußballfan, *der*

sup'porting *adj.* (Cinemat., Theatre) **~ role** Nebenrolle, *die;* **~ actor/actress** Schauspieler/-spielerin in einer Nebenrolle; **~ film** Vorfilm, *der*

supportive /səˈpɔːtɪv/ *adj.* hilfreich; **be very ~ [to sb.]** [jmdm.] eine große Hilfe *od.* Stütze sein

suppose /səˈpəʊz/ *v.t.* **(a)** (assume) annehmen; **~ or supposing [that] he ...:** angenommen, [dass] er ... **(b)** (presume) vermuten; **I ~ so** (doubtfully) ja, vermutlich; (more confidently) ich glaube schon **(c)** **be ~d to do/be sth.** (be generally believed to do/be sth.) etw. tun/sein sollen **(d)** (allow) **you are not ~d to do that** das darfst du eigentlich nicht; **I'm not ~d to be here** ich dürfte eigentlich gar nicht hier sein

supposed /səˈpəʊzd/ *attrib. adj.* mutmaßlich

supposedly /səˈpəʊzɪdlɪ/ *adv.* angeblich

supposition /sʌpəˈzɪʃn/ *n.* Annahme, *die;* Vermutung, *die*

suppress /səˈpres/ *v.t.* unterdrücken

suppression /səˈpreʃn/ *n.* Unterdrückung, *die*

supremacy /suːˈpreməsɪ/ *n.* **(a)** (supreme authority) Souveränität, *die* **(b)** (superiority) Überlegenheit, *die*

supreme /suːˈpriːm/ *adj.* höchst...

Supt. *abbr.* = **Superintendent**

surcharge /ˈsɜːtʃɑːdʒ/ *n.* Zuschlag, *der*

sure /ʃʊə(r)/ **1** *adj.* sicher; **be ~ of sth.** sich (*Dat.*) einer Sache (*Gen.*) sicher sein; **~ of oneself** selbstsicher; **don't be too ~:** da wäre ich mir nicht so sicher; **there is a ~ to be a petrol station** es gibt bestimmt eine Tankstelle; **don't worry, it's ~ to turn out well** keine Sorge, es wird schon alles gut gehen; **for ~** (coll.) auf jeden Fall; **make ~ [of sth.]** sich [einer Sache] vergewissern; **make or be ~ you do it, be ~ to do it** (do not fail to do it) sieh zu, dass du es tust; (do not forget) vergiss nicht, es zu tun; **a ~ winner** ein todsicherer Tipp (ugs.) **2** *adv.* **~ enough** tatsächlich **3** *int.* **~!, ~ thing!** (Amer.) na klar! (ugs.)

sure: ~-fire *attrib. adj.* (Amer. coll.) todsicher; **~-footed** *adj.* trittsicher

'surely **1** *adv.* **(a)** as sentence-modifier doch; **~ we've met before?** wir kennen uns doch, oder?

····❖

(b) (steadily) sicher; **slowly but ~**: langsam, aber sicher
(c) (certainly) sicherlich
[2] *int.* (Amer.) natürlich

surf /sɜːf/ *n.* [1] Brandung, *die*
[2] *v.i.* **(a)** surfen
(b) (Comp.) surfen; (TV) zappen (ugs.)
[3] *v.t.* (Comp., TV) **~ the Internet** im Internet surfen; **~ the channels** sich durch die Kanäle zappen (ugs.)

surface /'sɜːfɪs/ [1] *n.* Oberfläche, *die;* **outer ~**: Außenfläche, *die;* **the earth's ~**: die Erdoberfläche; **on the ~**: an der Oberfläche; (fig.) oberflächlich betrachtet
[2] *v.i.* auftauchen; (fig.) hochkommen

surface: ~ area *n.* Oberfläche, *die;* **~ mail** *n.* gewöhnliche Post

'surfboard *n.* Surfbrett, *das*

surfeit /'sɜːfɪt/ *n.* Übermaß, *das*

'surfer *n.* Surfer, *der*/Surferin, *die*

'surfing *n.* Surfen, *das*

surge /sɜːdʒ/ *v.i.* ⟨Wellen:⟩ branden; **the crowd ~d forward** die Menschenmenge drängte nach vorn

surgeon /'sɜːdʒən/ *n.* Chirurg, *der*/Chirurgin, *die*

surgery /'sɜːdʒərɪ/ *n.* **(a)** Chirurgie, *die;* **undergo ~**: sich einer Operation (*Dat.*) unterziehen
(b) (Brit.: place) Praxis, *die;* **doctor's/dental ~**: Arzt-/Zahnarztpraxis, *die*
(c) (Brit.: time) Sprechstunde, *die*

surgical /'sɜːdʒɪkl/ *adj.* chirurgisch; **~ treatment** Operation, *die*/Operationen *Pl.*

surly /'sɜːlɪ/ *adj.* mürrisch

surmise /sə'maɪz/ [1] *n.* Vermutung, *die*
[2] *v.t.* mutmaßen

surmount /sə'maʊnt/ *v.t.* überwinden

surmountable /sə'maʊntəbl/ *adj.* überwindbar

surname /'sɜːneɪm/ *n.* Nachname, *der;* Zuname, *der*

surpass /sə'pɑːs/ *v.t.* übertreffen; **~ oneself** sich selbst übertreffen

surplus /'sɜːpləs/ [1] *n.* Überschuss, *der* (of an + *Dat.*)
[2] *adj.* überschüssig; **be ~ to sb.'s requirements** von jmdm. nicht benötigt werden

surprise /sə'praɪz/ [1] *n.* **(a)** Überraschung, *die;* **take sb. by ~**: jmdn. überrumpeln; **to my great ~, much to my ~**: zu meiner großen Überraschung; **it came as a ~ to us** es war für uns eine Überraschung
(b) *attrib.* überraschend, unerwartet ⟨*Besuch*⟩; **a ~ attack** ein Überraschungsangriff
[2] *v.t.* überraschen; überrumpeln ⟨*Feind*⟩; **I shouldn't be ~d if ...**: es würde mich nicht wundern, wenn ...; **be ~d at sb./sth.** sich über jmdn./etw. wundern

surprising /sə'praɪzɪŋ/ *adj.* überraschend

surprisingly *adv.* überraschend; **~ [enough], he was ...**: überraschenderweise war er ...

surreal /sə'rɪːəl/ *adj.* surrealistisch

surrealism /sə'rɪːəlɪzm/ *n.* Surrealismus, *der*

surrender /sə'rendə(r)/ [1] *n.* (to enemy) Kapitulation, *die;* (of possession) Aufgabe, *die*
[2] *v.i.* kapitulieren
[3] *v.t.* aufgeben

surreptitious /sʌrəp'tɪʃəs/ *adj.* heimlich; verstohlen ⟨*Blick*⟩

surrogate /'sʌrəgət/ *n.* Ersatz, *der*

surrogate 'mother *n.* Leihmutter, *die*

surround /sə'raʊnd/ *v.t.* **(a)** (come or be all round) umringen; ⟨*Truppen, Heer:*⟩ umzingeln ⟨*Stadt, Feind*⟩
(b) (encircle) umgeben; **be ~ed by** or **with sth.** von etw. umgeben sein

sur'rounding *adj.* umliegend; **the ~ countryside** die [Landschaft in der] Umgebung

sur'roundings *n. pl.* Umgebung, *die*

surveillance /sə'veɪləns/ *n.* Überwachung, *die;* **be under ~**: überwacht werden

survey [1] /sə'veɪ/ *v.t.* betrachten; überblicken ⟨*Landschaft*⟩; inspizieren ⟨*Gebäude*⟩; bewerten ⟨*Situation*⟩
[2] /'sɜːveɪ/ *n.* Überblick, *der* (of über + *Akk.*); (poll) Umfrage, *die;* (Surv.) Vermessung, *die*

surveyor /sə'veɪə(r)/ *n.* (of building) Gutachter, *der*/Gutachterin, *die;* (of land) Landvermesser, *der*/-vermesserin, *die*

survival /sə'vaɪvl/ *n.* Überleben, *das;* **fight for ~**: Existenzkampf, *der*

sur'vival kit *n.* Notausrüstung, *die*

survive /sə'vaɪv/ [1] *v.t.* überleben
[2] *v.i.* ⟨*Person:*⟩ überleben; ⟨*Schriften, Traditionen:*⟩ erhalten bleiben

survivor /sə'vaɪvə(r)/ *n.* Überlebende, *der*/*die*

sus /sʌs/ (Brit. coll.) *v.t.*, **-ss-** spitzkriegen (ugs.); **get sb. ~sed** jmdn. durchschauen (ugs.)
■ **sus 'out** *v.t.* (coll.) checken (ugs.); spannen (ugs.)

susceptible /sə'septɪbl/ *adj.* empfänglich (to für); (to illness) anfällig (to für)

suspect [1] /sə'spekt/ *v.t.* **(a)** (imagine to be likely) vermuten; **~ the worst** das Schlimmste befürchten; **~ sb. to be sth., ~ that sb. is sth.** glauben *od.* vermuten, dass jmd. etw. ist
(b) (mentally accuse) verdächtigen; **~ sb. of sth./of doing sth.** jmdn. einer Sache verdächtigen/jmdn. verdächtigen, etw. zu tun
[2] /'sʌspekt/ *adj.* fragwürdig; verdächtig ⟨*Stoff, Paket*⟩
[3] /'sʌspekt/ *n.* Verdächtige, *der*/*die*

suspend /sə'spend/ *v.t.* **(a)** (hang up) [auf]hängen
(b) (stop) suspendieren

(c) (from work) ausschließen **(from** von); sperren ⟨*Sportler*⟩

suspended 'sentence n. (Law) Strafe mit Bewährung

suspender belt /sə'spendə belt/ n. (Brit.) Strumpfbandgürtel, *der*

suspenders /sə'spendəz/ n. pl. **(a)** (Brit.: for stockings) Strumpfbänder *Pl.*
(b) (Amer.: for trousers) Hosenträger *Pl.*

suspense /sə'spens/ n. Spannung, *die;* **keep sb. in** ∼: jmdn. auf die Folter spannen

suspension /sə'spenʃn/ n. (Motor Veh.) Federung, *die*

su'spension bridge n. Hängebrücke, *die*

suspicion /sə'spɪʃn/ n. **(a)** (uneasy feeling) Misstrauen, *das* (of gegenüber); (unconfined belief) Verdacht, *der;* **have a** ∼ **that** ...: den Verdacht haben, dass ...
(b) (suspecting) Verdacht, *der* (of auf + *Akk.*); **on** ∼ **of murder** wegen Mordverdachts; **be under** ∼: verdächtigt werden

suspicious /sə'spɪʃəs/ adj. **(a)** (tending to suspect) misstrauisch (of gegenüber); **be** ∼ **of sb./sth.** jmdm./einer Sache misstrauen
(b) (arousing suspicion) verdächtig

sustain /sə'steɪn/ v.t. **(a)** (support) tragen ⟨*Gewicht*⟩; (fig.) aufrechterhalten
(b) erleiden ⟨*Verlust, Verletzung*⟩

sustainable /sʌ'steɪnəbl/ adj. (Ecology) nachhaltig

sustenance /'sʌstɪnəns/ n. Nahrung, *die*

SW abbr. **(a)** = **south-west** SW
(b) (Radio) = **short wave** KW

swab /swɒb/ n. (Med.: pad) Tupfer, *der*

swagger /'swægə(r)/ v.i. großspurig stolzieren

swallow[1] /'swɒləʊ/ **1** v.t. schlucken; (by mistake) verschlucken
2 v.i. schlucken
3 n. Schluck, *der*
∎ **swallow 'up** v.t. verschlucken

swallow[2] n. Schwalbe, *die*

swam ▶ SWIM 1

swamp /swɒmp/ **1** n. Sumpf, *der*
2 v.t. überschwemmen

'swampy adj. sumpfig

swan /swɒn/ n. Schwan, *der*

'swansong n. (fig.) Schwanengesang, *der*

swap /swɒp/ **1** v.t., **-pp-** tauschen (for gegen)
2 v.i., **-pp-** tauschen
3 n. Tausch, *der*

swarm /swɔːm/ **1** n. Schwarm, *der*
2 v.i. schwärmen; (teem) wimmeln (with von)

swarthy /'swɔːðɪ/ adj. dunkel

swastika /'swɒstɪkə/ n. Hakenkreuz, *das*

swat /swɒt/ v.t., **-tt-** totschlagen

sway /sweɪ/ **1** v.i. [hin und her] schwanken; (gently) sich wiegen
2 v.t. **(a)** wiegen
(b) (influence) beeinflussen

3 n. (fig.) Herrschaft, *die;* **hold** ∼ **over sb.** über jmdn. herrschen

swear /sweə(r)/ **1** v.t., swore /swɔː(r)/, sworn /swɔːn/ schwören ⟨*Eid usw.*⟩
2 v.i., swore, sworn (a) fluchen
(b) ∼ **to sth.** etw. beschwören
∎ **'swear at** v.t. beschimpfen
∎ **'swear by** v.t. (coll.) schwören auf (+ *Akk.*)

'swear word n. Kraftausdruck, *der*

sweat /swet/ **1** n. Schweiß, *der*
2 v.i. schwitzen

'sweatband n. Schweißband, *das*

sweater /'swetə(r)/ n. Pullover, *der*

sweat: ∼**shirt** n. Sweatshirt, *das;* ∼**shop** n. ausbeuterische [kleine] Klitsche (ugs.)

'sweaty adj. schweißig

swede n. Kohlrübe, *die*

Swede /swiːd/ n. Schwede, *der*/Schwedin, *die*

Sweden /'swiːdn/ pr. n. Schweden (*das*)

Swedish /'swiːdɪʃ/ **1** adj. schwedisch; **sb. is** ∼: jmd. ist Schwede/Schwedin
2 n. Schwedisch, *das; see also* ENGLISH 2A

sweep /swiːp/ **1** v.t., swept /swept/ **(a)** fegen; kehren
(b) ∼ **the country** ⟨*Epidemie, Mode:*⟩ das Land überrollen
2 v.i., swept **(a)** fegen; kehren
(b) (go fast) ⟨*Person, Auto:*⟩ rauschen; ⟨*Wind usw.:*⟩ fegen
3 n. **(a)** **give sth. a** ∼: etw. fegen od. kehren
(b) (curve) Bogen, *der*
∎ **sweep 'up** v.t. zusammenfegen; zusammenkehren

'sweeping adj. pauschal; weit reichend ⟨*Einsparung*⟩; umwälzend ⟨*Veränderung*⟩

sweet /swiːt/ **1** adj. süß ⟨*Wesen, Gesicht, Mädchen*⟩; **have a** ∼ **tooth** gern Süßes mögen; **how** ∼ **of you!** wie nett od. lieb von dir!
2 n. (Brit.) **(a)** (candy) Bonbon, *das od. der*
(b) (dessert) Nachtisch, *der*

sweet: ∼**-and-'sour** attrib. adj. süßsauer; ∼ **corn** n. Zuckermais, *der*

sweeten /'swiːtn/ v.t. süßen

'sweetener n. Süßstoff, *der*

'sweetheart n. Schatz, *der*

'sweetness n. Süße, *die*

sweet: ∼ **'pea** n. Wicke, *die;* ∼ **po'tato** n. Batate, *die;* ∼**shop** n. (Brit.) Süßwarengeschäft, *das;* ∼ **talk** (Amer.) n. Süßholzgeraspel, *das* (ugs.); ∼**-talk** v.t. ∼**-talk sb.** [into doing sth.] jmdn. beschwatzen[, etw. zu tun]

swell /swel/ **1** v.t., swelled, swollen /'swəʊlən/ or swelled anschwellen lassen
2 v.i., swelled, swollen or swelled **(a)** (expand) ⟨*Körperteil:*⟩ anschwellen; ⟨*Segel:*⟩ sich blähen; ⟨*Material:*⟩ aufquellen
(b) ⟨*Anzahl:*⟩ zunehmen ⋯⋙

S

'**swelling** *n.* Schwellung, *die*

swelter /'sweltə(r)/ *v.i.* ~ **in the heat** in der Hitze schmoren (ugs.); ~**ing** glühend heiß ⟨*Tag, Wetter*⟩; ~**ing heat** Bruthitze, *die*

swept ▸ SWEEP 1, 2

swerve /swɜːv/ [1] *v.i.* einen Bogen machen; ~ **to the right/left** nach rechts/links [aus]schwenken
[2] *n.* Bogen, *der*

swift /swɪft/ [1] *adj.* schnell
[2] *n.* Mauersegler, *der*

'**swiftly** *adv.* schnell

swig /swɪg/ (coll.) Schluck, *der*

swill /swɪl/ *v.t.* ~ [**out**] [aus]spülen

swim /swɪm/ [1] *v.i.*, -mm-, **swam** /swæm/, **swum** /swʌm/ schwimmen; **my head was** ~**ming** mir war schwindelig
[2] *n.* **have a/go for a** ~: schwimmen/ schwimmen gehen

'**swimmer** *n.* Schwimmer, *der*/ Schwimmerin, *die*; **be a good/poor** ~: gut/ schlecht schwimmen können

'**swimming** *n.* Schwimmen, *das*

swimming: ~ **baths** *n. pl.* Schwimmbad, *das*; ~ **costume** *n.* Badeanzug, *der*; ~ **lesson** *n.* Schwimmstunde, *die*; ~ **lessons** Schwimmunterricht, *der*; ~ **pool** *n.* Schwimmbecken, *das*; (building) Schwimmbad, *das*; ~ **trunks** *n. pl.* Badehose, *die*

'**swimsuit** *n.* Badeanzug, *der*

swindle /'swɪndl/ [1] *v.t.* betrügen; ~ **sb. out of sth.** jmdn. um etw. betrügen
[2] *n.* Schwindel, *der*; Betrug, *der*

swindler /'swɪndlə(r)/ *n.* Schwindler, *der*/ Schwindlerin, *die*

swine /swaɪn/ *n.* Schwein, *das*

swing /swɪŋ/ [1] *n.* (a) Schaukel, *die*
(b) (~ing) Schaukeln, *das*; **in full** ~ (fig.) in vollem Gang[e]
[2] *v.i.*, **swung** /swʌŋ/ (a) schwingen; (in wind) schaukeln
(b) (go in sweeping curve) schwenken
[3] *v.t.*, **swung** schwingen

swing: ~**bin** *n.* Schwingdeckel[müll]eimer, *der*; ~ '**door** *n.* Pendeltür, *die*

swipe /swaɪp/ (coll.) [1] *v.t.* (a) (hit) knallen (ugs.)
(b) (coll.: steal) klauen (ugs.)
(c) ~ **the card through the swipe reader** die Karte durch das [Karten]lesegerät ziehen
[2] *n.* (device) ~ [**reader**] [Karten]lesegerät, *das*

'**swipe card** *n.* Magnetkarte, *die*

swirl /swɜːl/ [1] *v.i.* wirbeln
[2] *v.t.* umherwirbeln
[3] *n.* Spirale, *die*

swish /swɪʃ/ [1] *v.i.* zischen
[2] *n.* Zischen, *das*
[3] *adj.* (coll.) schick (ugs.)

Swiss /swɪs/ [1] *adj.* Schweizer; schweizerisch; **sb. is** ~: jmd. ist Schweizer/ Schweizerin

[2] *n.* Schweizer, *der*/Schweizerin, *die*; **the** ~ *pl.* die Schweizer *Pl.*

Swiss 'roll *n.* Biskuitrolle, *die*

switch /swɪtʃ/ [1] *n.* (a) (esp. Electr.) Schalter, *der*
(b) (change) Wechsel, *der*
[2] *v.t.* (a) (change) ~ **sth.** [**over**] **to sth.** etw. auf etw. (*Akk.*) umstellen *od.* (Electr.) umschalten
(b) (exchange) tauschen
[3] *v.i.* wechseln; ~ [**over**] **to sth.** auf etw. (*Akk.*) umstellen *od.* (Electr.) umschalten
■ **switch 'off** *v.t. & i.* ausschalten; (also fig. coll.) abschalten
■ **switch 'on** [1] *v.t.* einschalten; anschalten
[2] *v.i.* sich anschalten

switch: ~**back** *n.* Achterbahn, *die*; ~**blade** *n.* Springmesser, *das*; ~**board** *n.* [Telefon]zentrale, *die*

Switzerland /'swɪtsələnd/ *pr. n.* die Schweiz

swivel /'swɪvl/ [1] *v.i.*, -ll- sich drehen
[2] *v.t.*, -ll- drehen

'**swivel chair** *n.* Drehstuhl, *der*

swollen /'swəʊlən/ [1] ▸ SWELL
[2] *adj.* geschwollen; angeschwollen ⟨*Fluss*⟩

swoon /swuːn/ (literary) *v.i.* ohnmächtig werden

swoop /swuːp/ [1] *n.* (a) Sturzflug, *der*
(b) (coll.: raid) Razzia, *die*
[2] *v.i.* herabstoßen; ~ **on sb.** sich auf jmdn. stürzen

swop ▸ SWAP

sword /sɔːd/ *n.* Schwert, *das*

'**swordfish** *n.* Schwertfisch, *der*

swore, sworn ▸ SWEAR

swot /swɒt/ (Brit. coll.) [1] *n.* Streber, *der*/ Streberin, *die*
[2] *v.i.*, -tt- büffeln (ugs.)

swum ▸ SWIM 1

swung ▸ SWING 2, 3

'**swung dash** *n.* Tilde, *die*

sycamore /'sɪkəmɔː(r)/ *n.* Bergahorn, *der*

sycophant /'sɪkəfænt/ *n.* Kriecher, *der*

syllable /'sɪləbl/ *n.* Silbe, *die*

syllabus /'sɪləbəs/ *n.* Lehrplan, *der*; (for exam) Studienplan, *der*

symbol /'sɪmbl/ *n.* Symbol, *das* (**of** für)

symbolic /sɪm'bɒlɪk/, **symbolical** /sɪm'bɒlɪkl/ *adj.* symbolisch

symbolism /'sɪmbəlɪzm/ *n.* Symbolik, *die*

symbolize /'sɪmbəlaɪz/ *v.t.* symbolisieren

symmetrical /sɪ'metrɪkl/ *adj.* symmetrisch

symmetry /'sɪmɪtrɪ/ *n.* Symmetrie, *die*

sympathetic /sɪmpə'θetɪk/ *adj.* mitfühlend

sympathize /'sɪmpəθaɪz/ *v.i.* (a) ~ **with sb.** mit jmdm. [mit]fühlen
(b) ~ **with** (understand) Verständnis haben für

sympathy /'sɪmpəθɪ/ *n.* Mitgefühl, *das;* in deepest ∼: mit aufrichtigem Beileid

symphonic /sɪm'fɒnɪk/ *adj.* sinfonisch

symphony /'sɪmfənɪ/ *n.* Sinfonie, *die*

'symphony orchestra *n.* Sinfonieorchester, *das*

symposium /sɪm'pəʊzɪəm/ *n., pl.* symposia /sɪm'pəʊzɪə/ Symposion, *das*

symptom /'sɪmptəm/ *n.* Symptom, *das*

symptomatic /sɪmptə'mætɪk/ *adj.* symptomatisch (of für)

synagogue (*Amer.:* **synagog**) /'sɪnəgɒg/ *n.* Synagoge, *die*

sync /sɪŋk/ (coll.) *n.* be in ∼/out of ∼: harmonieren/nicht harmonieren (with mit)

synchromesh /'sɪŋkrəmeʃ/ *n.* (Motor Veh.) Synchrongetriebe, *das*

synchronize /'sɪŋkrənaɪz/ *v.t.* synchronisieren; gleichstellen ⟨Uhren⟩

syndicate /'sɪndɪkət/ *n.* Syndikat, *das*

syndrome /'sɪndrəʊm/ *n.* Syndrom, *das*

synonym /'sɪnənɪm/ *n.* Synonym, *das*

synonymous /sɪ'nɒnɪməs/ *adj.* (a) (Ling.) synonym (with mit) (b) ∼ with (fig.) gleichbedeutend mit

synopsis /sɪ'nɒpsɪs/ *n., pl.* synopses /sɪ'nɒpsiːz/ Inhaltsangabe, *die*

syntactic /sɪn'tæktɪk/ *adj.* syntaktisch

syntax /'sɪntæks/ *n.* Syntax, *die*

synthesis /'sɪnθɪsɪs/ *n., pl.* **syntheses** /'sɪnθɪsiːz/ Synthese, *die*

synthesize /'sɪnθɪsaɪz/ *v.t.* zur Synthese bringen; (Chem.) synthetisieren

synthesizer /'sɪnθɪsaɪzə(r)/ *n.* (Mus.) Synthesizer, *der*

synthetic /sɪn'θetɪk/ *adj.* synthetisch

syphilis /'sɪfɪlɪs/ *n.* Syphilis, *die*

syphon ▸ SIPHON

Syria /'sɪrɪə/ *pr. n.* Syrien (*das*)

syringe /sɪ'rɪndʒ/ **1** *n.* Spritze, *die* **2** *v.t.* spritzen; ausspritzen ⟨Ohr⟩

syrup /'sɪrəp/ *n.* Sirup, *der*

system /'sɪstəm/ *n.* System, *das*

systematic /sɪstə'mætɪk/ *adj.,* **systematically** /sɪstə'mætɪkəlɪ/ *adv.* systematisch

systematize /'sɪstəmətaɪz/ *v.t.* systematisieren

system: ∼ **disk** *n.* (Comp.) Systemdiskette, *die;* ∼ **error** *n.* (Comp.) Systemfehler, *der;* ∼**s analyst** *n.* Systemanalytiker, *der*/-analytikerin, *die;* ∼ **software** *n.* (Comp.) Systemsoftware, *die*

Tt

T, t /tiː/ *n.* T, t, *das;* **to a T** ganz genau; **T-junction** Einmündung, *die;* **T-bone steak** T-Bone-Steak, *das;* **T-shirt** T-Shirt, *das*

ta /tɑː/ *int.* (Brit. coll.) danke

tab /tæb/ **1** *n.* (a) (projecting flap) Zunge, *die;* (on clothing) Etikett, *das;* (with name) Namensschild, *das* (b) pick up the ∼ (Amer. coll.) die Zeche bezahlen (c) keep ∼s *or* a ∼ on (watch) [genau] beobachten (d) (Comp.) Tabulator, *der* **2** *v.t.* (Comp.) tabellarisieren

tabby /'tæbɪ/ *n.* ∼ [cat] Tigerkatze, *die*

'tab key *n.* (Comp.) Tabulatortaste, *die*

table /'teɪbl/ **1** *n.* (a) Tisch, *der* (b) (list) Tabelle, *die;* ∼ of contents Inhaltsverzeichnis, *das* **2** *v.t.* einbringen

tableau /'tæbləʊ/ *n., pl.* ∼**x** /'tæbləʊz/ Tableau, *das*

table: ∼**cloth** *n.* Tischdecke, *die;* ∼ **leg** *n.* Tischbein, *das;* ∼ **linen** *n.* Tischwäsche, *die;* ∼ **manners** *n. pl.* Tischmanieren *Pl.;* ∼ **mat** *n.* Set, *das;*

∼ **salt** *n.* Tafelsalz, *das;* ∼**spoon** *n.* Serivlöffel, *der;* ∼**spoonful** *n.* Serivlöffel [voll]

tablet /'tæblɪt/ *n.* (a) Tablette, *die* (b) (of soap) Stück, *das*

table: ∼ **tennis** *n.* Tischtennis, *das;* ∼ **tennis bat** Tischtennisschläger, *der;* ∼ **wine** *n.* Tischwein, *der*

tabloid /'tæblɔɪd/ *n.* Boulevardzeitung, *die;* the ∼s (derog.) die Boulevardpresse; ∼ **journalism** Sensationsjournalismus, *der*

taboo, tabu /tə'buː/ **1** *n.* Tabu, *das* **2** *adj.* Tabu⟨wort⟩; be ∼: tabu sein

tabulate /'tæbjʊleɪt/ *v.t.* tabellarisch darstellen

tabulator /'tæbjʊleɪtə(r)/ *n.* Tabulator, *der*

tacit /'tæsɪt/ *adj.,* **'tacitly** *adv.* stillschweigend

taciturn /'tæsɪtɜːn/ *adj.* schweigsam; wortkarg

tack /tæk/ **1** *n.* (a) (nail) kleiner Nagel (b) (stitch) Heftstich, *der* (c) (Naut., also fig.) Kurs, *der* **2** *v.t.* (a) (nail) festnageln (b) (stitch) heften

 ···❖

③ *v.i.* (Naut.) kreuzen

tackle /'tækl/ ① *v.t.* (a) angehen ⟨*Problem usw.*⟩; ~ **sb. about/on/over sth.** jmdn. auf etw. (*Akk.*) ansprechen; (ask for sth.) jmdn. um etw. angehen
(b) (Sport) angreifen ⟨*Spieler*⟩; (Amer. Footb.; Rugby) fassen
② *n.* (a) (equipment) Ausrüstung, *die*
(b) (Sport) Angriff, *der;* (sliding ~) Tackling, *das;* (Amer. Footb.; Rugby) Fassen und Halten

tacky /'tækɪ/ *adj.* (a) (sticky) klebrig
(b) (coll. derog.: tasteless) geschmacklos

tact /tækt/ *n.* Takt, *der;* **he has no ~:** er hat kein Taktgefühl

tactful /'tæktfl/ *adj.,* '**tactfully** *adv.* taktvoll

tactical /'tæktɪkl/ *adj.* taktisch

tactics /'tæktɪks/ *n. pl.* Taktik, *die*

'**tactless** *adj.,* '**tactlessly** *adv.* taktlos

tadpole /'tædpəʊl/ *n.* Kaulquappe, *die*

tag¹ /tæg/ ① *n.* (a) Schild, *das*
(b) (electronic device) (on person) elektronische Fessel; (on goods) Sicherungsetikett, *das*
(c) (Comp.) Tag, *das;* Markierung, *die*
② *v.t.,* **-gg-:** (Comp.) taggen; markieren
▪ **tag a'long** *v.i.* mitkommen

tag² *n.* (game) Fangen, *das*

tail /teɪl/ ① *n.* (a) Schwanz, *der*
(b) *in pl.* (on coin) ~s [**it is**] Zahl
② *v.t.* (coll.: follow) beschatten
▪ **tail 'back** *v.i.* sich stauen
▪ **tail 'off** *v.i.* (a) zurückgehen
(b) (into silence) verstummen

tail: ~**back** *n.* (Brit.) Rückstau, *der;* ~ **end** *n.* Ende, *das;* ~**gate** ① *n.* (Motor Veh.) Heckklappe, *die;* ② *v.i.* zu dicht auffahren; ~ **light** *n.* Rücklicht, *das*

tailor /'teɪlə(r)/ *n.* Schneider, *der/* Schneiderin, *die*

tailored /'teɪləd/**,** '**tailor-made** *adjs.* maßgeschneidert

'**tail wind** *n.* Rückenwind, *der*

taint /teɪnt/ *v.t.* verderben; **be** ~**ed with sth.** mit etw. behaftet sein (geh.)

Taiwan /taɪˈwɑːn/ *pr. n.* Taiwan (*das*)

take /teɪk/ ① *v.t.,* **took** /tʊk/, **taken** /'teɪkn/
(a) (get hold of, grasp, seize) nehmen
(b) (capture) einnehmen ⟨*Stadt, Festung*⟩; machen ⟨*Gefangenen*⟩
(c) (gain, earn) ⟨*Laden:*⟩ einbringen; ⟨*Person:*⟩ einnehmen; ⟨*Film, Stück:*⟩ einspielen; (win) gewinnen ⟨*Satz, Spiel, Preis, Titel*⟩
(d) (~ away with one) mitnehmen; (steal) mitnehmen (verhüll.); ~ **place** stattfinden; (spontaneously) sich ereignen; ⟨*Wandlung:*⟩ sich vollziehen
(e) (avail oneself of, use) nehmen; machen ⟨*Pause, Ferien, Nickerchen*⟩; ~ **the opportunity to do/of doing sth.** die Gelegenheit dazu benutzen, etw. zu tun
(f) (carry, guide, convey) bringen; ~ **sb. to visit sb.** jmdn. zu Besuch bei jmdm. mitnehmen;

~ **home** mit nach Hause nehmen; (earn) nach Hause bringen ⟨*Geld*⟩; (accompany) nach Hause bringen
(g) (remove) nehmen; (deduct) abziehen; ~ **sth./sb. from sb.** jmdn. etw./jmdm. wegnehmen
(h) (make) machen ⟨*Foto, Kopie*⟩; (photograph) aufnehmen; aufnehmen ⟨*Brief, Diktat*⟩; machen ⟨*Prüfung, Sprung, Spaziergang, Reise*⟩; ablegen ⟨*Gelübde, Eid*⟩; treffen ⟨*Entscheidung*⟩
(i) (conduct) halten ⟨*Gottesdienst, Unterricht*⟩; **Ms X** ~**s us for maths** in Mathe haben wir Frau X
(j) (eat, drink) nehmen ⟨*Zucker, Milch, Tabletten, Überdosis*⟩; trinken ⟨*Tee, Kaffee, Kognak usw.*⟩
(k) (need, require) brauchen ⟨*Platz, Zeit*⟩; haben ⟨*Objekt, Plural-s*⟩; gebraucht werden mit ⟨*Kasus*⟩; **sth.** ~**s an hour/a year/all day** etw. dauert eine Stunde/ein Jahr/einen ganzen Tag
(l) (ascertain and record) notieren ⟨*Namen, Adresse, Autonummer usw.*⟩; fühlen ⟨*Puls*⟩; messen ⟨*Temperatur, Größe usw.*⟩
(m) (assume) ~ **it** [**that**] ...: annehmen, dass ...; ~ **sb./sth. for/to be sth.** jmdn./etw. für etw. halten
(n) (react to) aufnehmen; ~ **sth. well/badly** etw. gut/nur schwer verkraften; ~ **sth. calmly** *or* **coolly** etw. gelassen [auf]nehmen
(o) (accept) annehmen
(p) (adopt, choose) ergreifen ⟨*Maßnahmen*⟩; unternehmen ⟨*Schritte*⟩; ~ **the wrong road** die falsche Straße fahren/gehen
(q) **be** ~**n ill** krank werden
(r) ~ **sth. to bits** *or* **pieces** etw. auseinander nehmen
② *v.i.,* **took, taken** (a) ⟨*Transplantat:*⟩ vom Körper angenommen werden; ⟨*Sämling, Pflanze:*⟩ angehen
(b) (detract) ~ **from sth.** etw. schmälern
▪ '**take after** *v.t.* ~ **after sb.** (resemble) jmdm. ähnlich sein; (~ **as one's example**) es jmdm. gleichtun
▪ **take a'way** *v.t.* (a) (remove) wegnehmen; (to a distance) mitnehmen; ~ **sth. away from sb.** jmdm. etw. abnehmen; **to** ~ **away** ⟨*Pizza, Snack usw.*⟩ zum Mitnehmen
(b) (Math.: deduct) abziehen
▪ **take a'way from** *v.t.* schmälern
▪ **take 'back** *v.t.* zurücknehmen; (return) zurückbringen
▪ **take 'down** *v.t.* (a) (carry or lead down) hinunterbringen
(b) abnehmen ⟨*Bild, Ankündigung, Weihnachtsschmuck*⟩; herunterziehen ⟨*Hose*⟩; ~ **sth. down from a shelf** etw. von einem Regal herunternehmen
(c) (write down) aufnehmen
▪ **take 'in** *v.t.* (a) (bring into) hineinbringen; (bring indoors) hereinholen
(b) enger machen ⟨*Kleidungsstück*⟩
(c) (understand) begreifen
(d) (cheat) hereinlegen (ugs.); (deceive) täuschen

■ **take 'off** ① *v.t.* (a) abnehmen ‹Deckel, Hut, Tischtuch, Verband›; abziehen ‹Kissenbezug›; ausziehen ‹Schuhe, Handschuhe›; ablegen ‹Mantel, Schmuck› **(b)** (deduct) abziehen; ~ sth. off sth. etw. von etw. abziehen **(c)** ~ a day *etc.* off sich (*Dat.*) einen Tag *usw.* frei nehmen (ugs.) **(d)** (mimic) nachahmen ② *v.i.* (Aeronaut.) starten

■ **take 'on** *v.t.* (a) (undertake) übernehmen; auf sich (*Akk.*) nehmen ‹Bürde› **(b)** (employ) einstellen **(c)** (as opponent) es aufnehmen mit; (Sport: meet) antreten gegen

■ **take 'out** *v.t.* (a) (remove) herausnehmen; ziehen ‹Zahn›; ~ sth. out of sth. etw. aus etw. [heraus]nehmen **(b)** (withdraw) abheben ‹Geld› **(c)** (go out with) ~ sb. out mit jmdm. ausgehen; ~ sb. out to *or* for lunch jmdn. zum Mittagessen einladen **(d)** (get issued) abschließen ‹Versicherung›; ausleihen ‹Bücher›; ~ out a subscription to sth. etw. abonnieren **(e)** ~ it out on sb. seine Wut an jmdm. auslassen

■ **take 'over** ① *v.t.* übernehmen ② *v.i.* übernehmen; ‹Manager, Firmenleiter:› die Geschäfte übernehmen; ‹Regierung, Präsident:› die Amtsgeschäfte übernehmen; ~ over from sb. jmdn. ersetzen; (temporarily) jmdn. vertreten

■ **'take to** *v.t.* (a) (get into habit of) ~ to doing sth. es sich (*Dat.*) angewöhnen, etw. zu tun **(b)** (like) sich hingezogen fühlen zu ‹Person›; sich erwärmen für ‹Sache›

■ **take 'up** ① *v.t.* (a) (lift up) hochheben; (pick up) aufheben; herausreißen ‹Dielen›; aufreißen ‹Straße› **(b)** (carry or lead up) hinaufbringen **(c)** in Anspruch nehmen ‹Zeit›; brauchen/ (undesirably) wegnehmen ‹Platz› **(d)** (start) ergreifen ‹Beruf›; anfangen ‹Tennis, Schach, Gitarre usw.›; aufnehmen ‹Arbeit, Kampf›; antreten ‹Stelle›; ~ up a hobby sich (*Dat.*) ein Hobby zulegen **(e)** (pursue further) ~ sth. up with sb. sich in einer Sache an jmdn. wenden ② *v.i.* ~ up with sb. (coll.) sich mit jmdm. einlassen

'takeaway *n.* (meal) Essen zum Mitnehmen; (restaurant) Restaurant mit Straßenverkauf

taken ▶ TAKE

take: ~**off** *n.* (a) (Aeronaut.) Start, *der;* (b) (coll.: caricature) Parodie, *die;* ~**over** *n.* Übernahme, *die*

takings /'teɪkɪŋz/ *n. pl.* Einnahmen *Pl.*

talc /tælk/ *n.* Talkum, *das*

talcum /'tælkəm/ *n.* ~ [powder] Körperpuder, *der*

tale /teɪl/ *n.* Erzählung, *die;* Geschichte, *die* (of von, about über + *Akk.*)

talent /'tælənt/ *n.* Talent, *das;* have [great/ no *etc.*] ~ [for sth.] [viel/kein *usw.*] Talent [zu *od.* für etw.] haben

'talented *adj.* talentiert

'talent-spotting *n.* Talentsuche, *die*

talk /tɔːk/ ① *n.* (a) (discussion) Gespräch, *das;* have a ~ [with sb.] [about sth.] [mit jmdm.] [über etw. (*Akk.*)] sprechen; have *or* hold ~s [with sb.] [mit jmdm.] Gespräche führen; there is [much/some] ~ of …: man hört [häufig/öfter] von … **(b)** (speech, lecture) Vortrag, *der* ② *v.i.* sprechen (with, to mit); (lecture) sprechen; (converse) sich unterhalten; (have ~s) Gespräche führen; (gossip) reden; ~ on the phone telefonieren ③ *v.t.* reden; ~ sb. into/out of sth. jmdn. zu etw. überreden/jmdm. etw. ausreden

■ **talk 'over** *v.t.* besprechen

■ **talk 'round** *v.t.* ~ sb. round jmdn. überreden

talkative /'tɔːkətɪv/ *adj.* gesprächig

talking: ~ point *n.* Gesprächsthema, *das;* ~**-to** *n.* (coll.) Standpauke, *die* (ugs.)

'talk show *n.* Talkshow, *die*

tall /tɔːl/ *adj.* hoch; groß ‹Person, Tier›; that's a ~ order das ist ziemlich viel verlangt; ~ story unglaubliche Geschichte

tally /'tælɪ/ ① *n.* keep a ~ of sth. über etw. (*Akk.*) Buch führen ② *v.i.* übereinstimmen

talon /'tælən/ *n.* Klaue, *die*

tambourine /tæmbə'riːn/ *n.* Tamburin, *das*

tame /teɪm/ ① *adj.* zahm; (fig.: spiritless) lahm (ugs.) ② *v.t.* zähmen

tamper /'tæmpə(r)/ *v.i.* ~ with sich (*Dat.*) zu schaffen machen an (+ *Dat.*)

tampon /'tæmpɒn/ *n.* Tampon, *der*

tan /tæn/ ① *v.t.,* -nn- gerben ‹Tierhaut, Fell› ② *v.i.,* -nn- braun werden ③ *n.* (a) (colour) Gelbbraun, *das* **(b)** (sun~) Bräune, *die;* have/get a ~: braun sein/werden ④ *adj.* gelbbraun

tandem /'tændəm/ *n.* ~ [bicycle] Tandem, *das*

tang /tæŋ/ *n.* (taste) Geschmack, *der;* (smell) Geruch, *der*

tangent /'tændʒənt/ *n.* Tangente, *die;* go off at a ~ (fig.) plötzlich vom Thema abschweifen

tangerine /tændʒə'riːn/ *n.* (fruit) ~ [orange] Tangerine, *die*

tangible /'tændʒɪbl/ *adj.* greifbar; spürbar ‹Unterschied, Verbesserung›; handfest ‹Beweis›

tangle /'tæŋgl/ ① *n.* Gewirr, *das;* (in hair) Verfilzung, *die* ② *v.t.* verheddern (ugs.); verfilzen ‹Haar›

■ **tangle 'up** *v.t.* verheddern (ugs.)

tango /ˈtæŋɡəʊ/ n., pl. ∼s Tango, der

tank /tæŋk/ n. (a) Tank, der
(b) (Mil.) Panzer, der

tankard /ˈtæŋkəd/ n. Krug, der

tanker /ˈtæŋkə(r)/ n. (ship) Tanker, der;
(vehicle) Tank[last]wagen, der

tanned /tænd/ adj. braun gebrannt

tantalize /ˈtæntəlaɪz/ v.t. reizen

tantalizing /ˈtæntəlaɪzɪŋ/ adj. verlockend

tantamount /ˈtæntəmaʊnt/ adj. be ∼ to
sth. gleichbedeutend mit etw. sein

tantrum /ˈtæntrəm/ n. Wutanfall, der; (of
child) Trotzanfall, der; **throw a** ∼: einen
Wutanfall/Trotzanfall bekommen

tap¹ /tæp/ ① n. Hahn, der; **hot/cold[-water]**
∼: Warm-/Kaltwasserhahn, der; **be on** ∼ (fig.)
zur Verfügung stehen
② v.t., **-pp-**: (a) erschließen ⟨Reserven,
Markt⟩
(b) (Teleph.) abhören; anzapfen (ugs.)

tap² ① v.t., **-pp-** klopfen an (+ Akk.); (on
upper surface) klopfen auf (+ Akk.)
② v.i., **-pp-**: ∼ **at/on sth.** an etw. (Akk.)
klopfen; (on upper surface) auf etw. (Akk.)
klopfen
③ n. Klopfen, das

'tap dance ① n. Stepp[tanz], der
② v.i. Stepp tanzen; steppen

tape /teɪp/ ① n. (a) Band, das; **adhesive** or
(coll.) **sticky** ∼: Klebeband, das
(b) (for recording) [Ton]band, das (of mit);
make a ∼ **of sth.** etw. auf Band aufnehmen
② v.t. (a) (record on ∼) [auf Band] aufnehmen
(b) (bind with ∼) [mit Klebeband] zukleben
(c) **have got sb./sth.** ∼d (coll.) jmdn.
durchschaut haben/etw. im Griff haben

tape: ∼ **cassette** n. Tonbandkassette,
die; ∼ **deck** n. Tapedeck, das;
∼ **measure** n. Bandmaß, das

taper /ˈteɪpə(r)/ ① v.i. sich verjüngen; ∼ [to
a point] spitz zulaufen
② n. [wax] ∼: Wachsstock, der

tape: ∼ **recorder** n. Tonbandgerät, das;
∼ **recording** n. Tonbandaufnahme, die

tapestry /ˈtæpɪstrɪ/ n. Gobelingewebe, das;
(wall-hanging) Bildteppich, der

'tapeworm n. Bandwurm, der

'tap water n. Leitungswasser, das

tar /tɑː(r)/ ① n. Teer, der; **high-**∼**/low-**∼
cigarette Zigarette mit hohem/niedrigem
Teergehalt
② v.t., **-rr-** teeren

target /ˈtɑːɡɪt/ ① n. (a) Ziel, das; **hit/miss**
the/its ∼: [das Ziel] treffen/das Ziel
verfehlen; **production/export/savings** ∼:
Produktions-/Export-/Sparziel, das; **be**
above/below ∼ (fig.) das Ziel über-/
unterschritten haben
(b) (Sport) Zielscheibe, die
② v.t. (fig.) zielen auf ⟨Käufergruppe⟩

target: ∼ **date** n. vorgesehener Termin;
∼ **figure** n. (esp. Commerc.) Ziel, das

tariff /ˈtærɪf/ n. (a) (tax) Zoll, der

(b) (list of charges) Tarif, der

tarnish /ˈtɑːnɪʃ/ ① v.t. stumpf werden
lassen ⟨Metall⟩; (fig.) beflecken ⟨Ruf⟩
② v.i. stumpf werden

tarpaulin /tɑːˈpɔːlɪn/ n. Plane, die

tart¹ /tɑːt/ adj. herb; sauer ⟨Obst⟩; (fig.)
scharfzüngig

tart² n. (a) (Brit.) (filled pie) ≈ Obstkuchen,
der; (small pastry) Obsttörtchen, das
(b) (sl.: prostitute) Nutte, die (salopp)
■ **tart 'up** v.t. (Brit. coll.) ∼ **oneself up, get**
∼**ed up** sich auftakeln (ugs.)

tartan /ˈtɑːtən/ ① n. Schotten[stoff], der
② adj. Schotten⟨rock, -jacke⟩

tartar /ˈtɑːtə(r)/ n. Zahnstein, der

tartar sauce /ˈtɑːtə ˈsɔːs/ n.
Remoulade[nsoße], die

task /tɑːsk/ n. Aufgabe, die; **take sb. to** ∼:
jmdm. eine Lektion erteilen

task: ∼**bar** n. (Comp.) Taskleiste, die;
∼ **force** n. Sonderkommando, das

tassel /ˈtæsl/ n. Quaste, die

taste /teɪst/ ① v.t. (a) schmecken; (try a little)
probieren
(b) (recognize flavour of) [heraus]schmecken
② v.i. schmecken (of nach); **not** ∼ **of**
anything nach nichts schmecken
③ n. (a) (flavour) Geschmack, der; [sense of]
∼: Geschmack[ssinn], der
(b) (discernment) Geschmack, der
(c) (sample) Kostprobe, die

tasteful /ˈteɪstfl/ adj., **'tastefully** adv.
geschmackvoll

'tasteless adj. geschmacklos

tasty /ˈteɪstɪ/ adj. lecker

tat /tæt/ n. ▶ TIT²

tattered /ˈtætəd/ adj. zerlumpt ⟨Kleidung⟩;
zerfleddert ⟨Buch⟩

tatters /ˈtætəz/ n. pl. Fetzen Pl.; **be in** ∼: in
Fetzen sein; (fig.) ruiniert sein

tattoo /təˈtuː/ ① v.t. tätowieren
② n. Tätowierung, die

tattooer /təˈtuːə(r)/, **tattooist** /təˈtuːɪst/
ns. Tätowierer, der/Tätowiererin, die

tatty /ˈtætɪ/ adj. (coll.) schäbig

taught ▶ TEACH

taunt /tɔːnt/ ① v.t. verspotten (about
wegen)
② n. spöttische Bemerkung

Taurus /ˈtɔːrəs/ n. (Astrol., Astron.) der Stier

taut /tɔːt/ adj. straff ⟨Seil, Kabel⟩; gespannt
⟨Muskel⟩

tavern /ˈtævən/ n. Schenke, die

tawny /ˈtɔːnɪ/ adj. gelbbraun

tax /tæks/ ① n. Steuer, die; **before/after** ∼:
vor Steuern/nach Abzug der Steuern; **for**
∼ **reasons** aus steuerlichen Gründen
② v.t. (a) besteuern; versteuern
⟨Einkommen⟩
(b) (fig.) strapazieren ⟨Kräfte, Geduld⟩

taxable /ˈtæksəbl/ adj. steuerpflichtig

tax: ∼ **allowance** n. Steuerfreibetrag, der; ∼ **assessment** n. Steuerbescheid, der

taxation /tæk'seɪʃn/ n. Besteuerung, die; (taxes payable) Steuern Pl.

tax: ∼ **avoidance** n. Steuerumgehung, die; ∼ **bill** n. Steuerbescheid, der; (amount) Steuerschuld, die; ∼ **bracket** n. Stufe im Steuertarif; ∼-**deductible** adj. steuerabzugsfähig; [steuerlich] absetzbar; ∼ **demand** n. Steuerforderung, die; ∼ **disc** n. (Motor Veh.) Steuerplakette, die; ∼ **evasion** n. Steuerhinterziehung, die; ∼ **exile** n. (person) Steuerflüchtling, der; ∼ **form** n. Steuerformular, das; ∼-**free** adj. steuerfrei; ∼ **haven** n. Steueroase, die (ugs.)

taxi /'tæksɪ/ [1] n. Taxi, das
[2] v.i., ∼ing or taxying ⟨Flugzeug:⟩ rollen

'taxi driver n. Taxifahrer, der/-fahrerin, die

tax: ∼ **incentive** n. steuerlicher Anreiz; ∼ **inspector** n. Steuerinspektor, der/ -inspektorin, die

taxi: ∼ **rank** (Brit.), ∼ **stand** (Amer.) ns. Taxistand, der

tax: ∼**man** n. (coll.) Finanzbeamte, der/ -beamtin, die; ∼ **office** n. Finanzamt, das ∼**payer** n. Steuerzahler, der/-zahlerin, die; ∼ **return** n. Steuererklärung, die; ∼ **relief** n. Steuererleichterung, die; ∼ **year** n. Steuerjahr, das

TB abbr. = **tuberculosis** Tb, die

tbsp. abbr., pl. same or ∼s: **tablespoon**

tea /tiː/ n. (a) Tee, der
(b) (meal) [high] ≈ Abendessen, das

tea: ∼ **bag** n. Teebeutel, der; ∼ **break** n. (Brit.) Teepause, die; ∼ **caddy** n. Teebüchse, die

teach /tiːtʃ/ [1] v.t., taught /tɔːt/ unterrichten; (at university) lehren; ∼ sb./ oneself/an animal sth. jmdm./sich/einem Tier etw. beibringen; ∼ sb. to ride jmdm. das Reiten beibringen
[2] v.i., taught unterrichten

'teacher n. Lehrer, der/Lehrerin, die

teacher: ∼ **training** n. Lehrerausbildung, die; ∼-**training college** n. ≈ pädagogische Hochschule

'teaching profession n. Lehrberuf, der

tea: ∼ **cloth** n. Geschirrtuch, das; ∼ **cosy** n. Teewärmer, der; ∼**cup** n. Teetasse, die

teak /tiːk/ n. Teak[holz], das

'tea leaf n. Teeblatt, das

team /tiːm/ n. Team, das; (Sport also) Mannschaft, die
■ **team 'up** v.i. sich zusammentun (ugs.)

team: ∼ **effort** n. Team- od. Gemeinschaftsarbeit, die; ∼ **game** n. Mannschaftsspiel, das; ∼ **leader** n. Gruppenleiter, der/-leiterin, die; ∼**mate** n. Mannschaftskamerad, der/-kameradin, die;

∼ **'spirit** n. Teamgeist, der; (Sport also) Mannschaftsgeist, der; ∼**work** n. Teamarbeit, die

'teapot n. Teekanne, die

tear¹ /teə(r)/ [1] n. Riss, der
[2] v.t., tore /tɔː(r)/, torn /tɔːn/ (a) (rip) zerreißen; (pull apart) auseinander reißen; (damage) aufreißen; ∼ open aufreißen ⟨Brief, Paket⟩
(b) ∼ sth. out of sb.'s hands jmdm. etw. aus der Hand reißen
[3] v.i., tore, torn (a) (rip) [zer]reißen
(b) (move hurriedly) rasen (ugs.)
■ **tear a'way** v.t. wegreißen; ∼ oneself away (fig.) sich losreißen
■ **tear 'up** v.t. zerreißen

tear² /tɪə(r)/ n. Träne, die

tearful /'tɪəfl/ adj. weinend

tear /tɪə(r)/: ∼**drop** n. Träne, die; ∼ **gas** n. Tränengas, das

tease /tiːz/ [1] v.t. necken (about wegen); aufziehen (ugs.) (about mit)
[2] v.i. seine Späße machen

tea: ∼ **service,** ∼**set** ns. Teeservice, das; ∼ **shop** n. (Brit.) ≈ Café, das; ∼**spoon** n. Teelöffel, der; ∼ **strainer** n. Teesieb, das

teat /tiːt/ n. (a) Zitze, die
(b) (of rubber or plastic) Sauger, der

tea: ∼**time** n. Teezeit, die; ∼ **towel** n. Geschirrtuch, das; ∼ **trolley** n. Teewagen, der; ∼ **urn** n. Teebehälter, der

techie /'tekɪ/ n. (coll.) Technikfreak, der; (computer expert) Computerfreak, der

technical /'teknɪkl/ adj. technisch ⟨Problem, Daten, Fortschritt⟩; Fach⟨kenntnis, -sprache, -begriff, -wörterbuch⟩; ∼ **college** n. Fachhochschule, die; ∼ **term** Fachbegriff, der; Fachausdruck, der

technicality /teknɪ'kælɪtɪ/ n. technisches Detail

technician /tek'nɪʃn/ n. Techniker, der/ Technikerin, die

technique /tek'niːk/ n. Technik, die; (procedure) Methode, die

techno [1] adj. Techno-
[2] n. Techno, der od. das

technological /teknə'lɒdʒɪkl/ adj. technisch; technologisch

technology /tek'nɒlədʒɪ/ n. Technik, die; (application of science) Technologie, die

technophobe /'teknəʊfəʊb/ n. Mensch mit einer Technikphobie

teddy /'tedɪ/ n. ∼ [**bear**] Teddy[bär], der

tedious /'tiːdɪəs/ adj. langwierig ⟨Reise, Arbeit⟩; (uninteresting) langweilig

tee /tiː/ (Golf) Tee, das

teem /tiːm/ v.i. wimmeln (with von)

teen /tiːn/ adj. Teenager-

teenage[d] /'tiːneɪdʒ(d)/ attrib. adj. im Teenageralter nachgestellt ⋯⋗

teenager /'ti:neɪdʒə(r)/ n. Teenager, der; (loosely) Jugendliche, der/die

teens /ti:nz/ n. pl. Teenagerjahre Pl.

'tee shirt n. T-Shirt, das

teeter /'ti:tə(r)/ v.i. wanken; ~ **on the edge of sth.** schwankend am Rande einer Sache (Gen.) stehen

teeth pl. of TOOTH

teething troubles /'ti:ðɪŋ trʌblz/ n. pl. have ~ (fig.) Anfangsschwierigkeiten haben

teetotal /ti:'təʊtl/ adj. abstinent lebend

teetotaller /ti:'təʊtələ(r)/ n. Abstinenzler, der/Abstinenzlerin, die

TEFL /'tefl/ abbr. = **teaching of English as a foreign language**

Teflon ® /'teflɒn/ n. Teflon ⓌⓏ, das

Tel., tel. abbr. = **telephone** Tel.

telebanking /'telɪbæŋkɪŋ/ n. Telebanking, das

telecommunications /telɪkəmju:nɪ'keɪʃnz/ n. pl. Fernmelde- od. Nachrichtentechnik, die

telecommute /'telɪkəmju:t/ v.i. Telearbeit verrichten

telecommuting /'telɪkəmju:tɪŋ/ n. Telearbeit, die

teleconference /'telɪkɒnfərəns/ n. Telekonferenz, die

telecottage /'telɪkɒtɪdʒ/ n.: jedermann zugängliche Einrichtung, die bes. Telearbeitern Zugang zu einem ans Internet angeschlossenen Computer bietet

telegram /'telɪɡræm/ n. Telegramm, das

telegraph /'telɪɡrɑ:f/ n. Telegraf, der; ~ **pole** Telegrafenmast, der

telemarketing /'telmɑ:kɪtɪŋ/ n. Telefonmarketing, das

telepathy /tɪ'lepəθɪ/ n. Telepathie, die

telephone /'telɪfəʊn/ 〔1〕 n. Telefon, das; attrib. Telefon-; **answer the** ~: Anrufe entgegennehmen; (on one occasion) ans Telefon gehen; (speak) sich melden; **be on the** ~: Telefon haben; (be speaking) telefonieren (**to** mit)
〔2〕 v.t. anrufen
〔3〕 v.i. anrufen; ~ **for a taxi** nach einem Taxi telefonieren

telephone: ~ **'answering machine** n. Anrufbeantworter, der; ~ **'banking** n. Telefonbanking, das; ~ **book** n. Telefonbuch, das; ~ **booth,** (Brit.) ~ **box** ns. Telefonzelle, die; ~ **call** n. Telefongespräch, das; ~ **connection** n. Telefonverbindung, die; ~ **directory** n. Telefonverzeichnis, das; ~ **exchange** n. Fernmeldeamt, das; ~ **number** n. Telefonnummer, die; ~ **operator** n. Telefonist, der/Telefonistin, die

telephonist /tɪ'lefənɪst/ n. Telefonist, der/ Telefonistin, die

telephoto /telɪ'fəʊtəʊ/ adj. ~ **lens** Teleobjektiv, das

teleprinter /'telɪprɪntə(r)/ n. Fernschreiber, der

'telesales n. pl. Telefonverkauf, der; Verkauf per Telefon

telescope /'telɪskəʊp/ n. Teleskop, das; Fernrohr, das

telescopic /telɪ'skɒpɪk/ adj. (collapsible) ausziehbar; Teleskop⟨antenne⟩

Teletex ® /'telɪteks/ n. Teletex, das

teletext /'telɪtekst/ n. Teletext, der

televise /'telɪvaɪz/ v.t. im Fernsehen senden od. übertragen

television /'telɪvɪʒn, telɪ'vɪʒn/ n. (a) no art. das Fernsehen; **on** ~: im Fernsehen; **watch** ~: fernsehen
(b) (~ set) Fernsehapparat, der; Fernseher, der (ugs.)

television: ~ **aerial** n. Fernsehantenne, die; ~ **channel** n. [Fernseh]kanal, der; ~ **coverage** n. Fernsehberichterstattung, die; ~ **licence** n. (Brit.) Fernsehgenehmigung, die (die jährlich gegen Zahlen der Gebühren erneuert wird); ~ **licence fee** Fernsehgebühren Pl.; ~ **lounge** n. Fernsehraum, der; ~ **personality** n. Fernsehgröße, die (ugs.); ~ **picture** n. Fernsehbild, das; ~ **programme** n. Fernsehsendung, die; ~ **screen** n. Bildschirm, der; ~ **serial** n. Fernsehserie, die; ~ **set** n. Fernsehgerät, das; ~ **studio** n. Fernsehstudio, das; ~ **viewer** n. Fernsehzuschauer, der/ -zuschauerin, die

teleworking /'telɪwɜ:kɪŋ/ n. Telearbeit, die

telex /'teleks/ 〔1〕 n. Telex, das
〔2〕 v.t. ein Telex schicken (+ Dat.); telexen ⟨Nachricht⟩

tell /tel/ 〔1〕 v.t., **told** /təʊld/ (a) (relate) erzählen; (make known) sagen ⟨Name, Adresse⟩; anvertrauen ⟨Geheimnis⟩; ~ **sb. sth.** or **sth. to sb.** jmdm. etw. erzählen/sagen/ anvertrauen; ~ **sb. the way to the station** jmdm. den Weg zum Bahnhof beschreiben; ~ **sb. the time** jmdm. die Uhrzeit sagen; ~ **tales** (lie) Lügengeschichten erzählen; (gossip) tratschen (ugs.)
(b) (instruct) sagen; ~ **sb.** [**not**] **to do sth.** jmdm. sagen, er soll[e] etw. [nicht] tun
(c) (determine) feststellen; (see, recognize) erkennen (**by** an + Dat.); (with reference to future) [vorher]sagen
(d) (distinguish) unterscheiden
(e) **all told** insgesamt
〔2〕 v.i., **told** (a) (determine) **how can you** ~? wie kann man das feststellen od. wissen?; **you never can** ~: man kann nie wissen
(b) (give information) erzählen (**of, about** von)
(c) (reveal secret) es verraten; **time will** ~: das wird sich zeigen
(d) (produce an effect) sich auswirken
▪ **tell a'part** v.t. auseinander halten
▪ **tell 'off** v.t. (coll.) ~ **sb. off** [**for sth.**] jmdn. [für od. wegen etw.] ausschimpfen

teller /'telə(r)/ n. (a) (in bank) ▸ CASHIER

(b) (counting votes) Stimmenzähler, *der/* -zählerin, *die*

telly /'telɪ/ *n.* (Brit. coll.) Fernseher, *der* (ugs.); **on ~:** im Fernsehen; **watch ~ :** Fernsehen gucken (ugs.)

temp /temp/ *n.* (Brit. coll.) Zeitarbeitskraft, *die*

temper /'tempə(r)/ 1 *n.* **(a)** Naturell, *das;* **be in a good/bad ~:** gute/schlechte Laune haben; **keep/lose one's ~:** sich beherrschen/die Beherrschung verlieren **(b)** (anger) **fit of ~:** Wutanfall, *der;* **have a ~:** jähzornig sein 2 *v.t.* mäßigen; mildern ⟨*Kritik*⟩

temperament /'temprəmənt/ *n.* (nature) Veranlagung, *die;* Natur, *die;* (disposition) Temperament, *das*

temperamental /temprə'mentl/ *adj.* launenhaft

temperate /'tempərət/ *adj.* gemäßigt

temperature /'temprɪtʃə(r)/ *n.* Temperatur, *die;* **have or run a ~** (coll.) Temperatur *od.* Fieber haben

template /'templɪt/ *n.* **(a)** Schablone, *die* **(b)** (Comp.) Schablone, *die;* Template, *das*

temple¹ /'templ/ *n.* Tempel, *der*

temple² *n.* (Anat.) Schläfe, *die*

tempo /'tempəʊ/ *n., pl.* **~s** *or* **tempi** /'tempiː/ Tempo, *das*

temporarily /'tempərərɪlɪ/ *adv.* vorübergehend

temporary /'tempərərɪ/ 1 *adj.* vorübergehend; provisorisch ⟨*Gebäude, Büro;*⟩ **~ job** Aushilfstätigkeit, *die* 2 *n.* Aushilfe, *die;* Aushilfskraft, *die*

tempt /tempt/ *v.t.* **(a)** **~ sb. to do sth.** jmdn. geneigt machen, etw. zu tun; **be ~ed to do sth.** versucht sein, etw. zu tun; **~ sb. out** jmdn. hinauslocken **(b)** (provoke) herausfordern; **~ fate** das Schicksal herausfordern

temptation /temp'teɪʃn/ *n.* **(a)** *no pl.* (attracting) Verlockung, *die;* (being attracted) Versuchung, *die* **(b)** (thing) Verlockung, *die*

'tempting *adj.* verlockend

ten /ten/ 1 *adj.* zehn 2 *n.* Zehn, *die.* See also EIGHT

tenable /'tenəbl/ *adj.* haltbar ⟨*Theorie*⟩; vertretbar ⟨*Standpunkt*⟩

tenacious /tɪ'neɪʃəs/ *adj.* hartnäckig

tenacity /tɪ'næsɪtɪ/ *n.* Hartnäckigkeit, *die*

tenant /'tenənt/ *n.* (of flat, residential building) Mieter, *der/*Mieterin, *die;* (of farm, shop) Pächter, *der/*Pächterin, *die*

tend¹ /tend/ *v.i.* **~ to do sth.** dazu neigen *od.* tendieren, etw. zu tun; **~ to sth.** zu etw. neigen; **he ~s to get upset if ...:** er regt sich leicht auf, wenn ...

tend² *v.t.* sich kümmern um; hüten ⟨*Schafe*⟩; bedienen ⟨*Maschine*⟩

tendency /'tendənsɪ/ *n.* (inclination) Tendenz, *die;* **have a ~ to do sth.** dazu neigen, etw. zu tun

tender¹ /'tendə(r)/ *adj.* **(a)** (not tough) zart **(b)** (loving) zärtlich **(c)** (sensitive) empfindlich

tender² 1 *v.t.* **(a)** (present) einreichen ⟨*Rücktritt*⟩; vorbringen ⟨*Entschuldigung*⟩ **(b)** (offer as payment) anbieten 2 *n.* Angebot, *das*

'tenderly *adv.* (gently) behutsam; (lovingly) zärtlich

'tenderness *n.* ▶ TENDER¹: Zartheit, *die;* Zärtlichkeit, *die;* Empfindlichkeit, *die*

tendon /'tendən/ *n.* (Anat.) Sehne, *die*

tenement /'tenɪmənt/ *n.* Mietshaus, *das*

tenet /'tenɪt/ *n.* Grundsatz, *der*

tenner /'tenə(r)/ *n.* (Brit. coll.) Zehnpfundschein, *der*

tennis /'tenɪs/ *n.* Tennis, *das*

tennis: ~ ball *n.* Tennisball, *der;* **~ club** *n.* Tennisverein, *der;* **~ court** *n.* (for lawn ~) Tennisplatz, *der;* (indoor) Tennishalle, *die;* **~ 'elbow** *n., no art.* (Med.) Tennisell[en]bogen, *der;* **~ match** *n.* Tennismatch, *das;* Tennisspiel, *das;* **~ racket** *n.* Tennisschläger, *der;* **~ shoe** *n.* Tennisschuh, *der*

tenor /'tenə(r)/ *n.* (Mus.) Tenor, *der*

tense¹ /tens/ *n.* (Ling.) Zeit, *die;* **in the present/future etc. ~:** im Präsens/Futur *usw.*

tense² 1 *adj.* gespannt 2 *v.i.* **sb. ~s** jmds. Muskeln spannen sich an 3 *v.t.* anspannen

tension /'tenʃn/ *n.* **(a)** Spannung, *die* **(b)** (mental strain) Anspannung, *die*

tent /tent/ *n.* Zelt, *das*

tentacle /'tentəkl/ *n.* Tentakel, *der od. das*

tentative /'tentətɪv/ *adj.* **(a)** (not definite) vorläufig **(b)** (hesitant) zaghaft

tenterhooks /'tentəhʊks/ *n. pl.* **be on ~:** [wie] auf glühenden Kohlen sitzen

tenth /tenθ/ 1 *adj.* zehnt... 2 *n.* (in sequence, rank) Zehnte, *der/die/das;* (fraction) Zehntel, *das. See also* EIGHTH

tent: ~ peg *n.* Zeltpflock, *der;* **~ pole** *n.* Zeltstange, *die*

tenuous /'tenjʊəs/ *adj.* dünn ⟨*Atmosphäre*⟩; dürftig ⟨*Argument*⟩; unbegründet ⟨*Anspruch*⟩

tepid /'tepɪd/ *adj.* lauwarm

term /tɜːm/ 1 *n.* **(a)** [Fach]begriff, *der* **(b)** *in pl.* (conditions) Bedingungen *Pl.;* **come to ~s with sth.** mit etw. zurechtkommen; (resign oneself to sth.) sich mit etw. abfinden **(c)** *in pl.* (charges) Konditionen *Pl.* **(d)** **in the short/long/medium ~:** kurz-/lang-/ mittelfristig **(e)** (Sch.) Halbjahr, *das;* (Univ.: one of two/three divisions per year) Semester, *das/*Trimester, *das* ⸱⸱⸱⧫

(f) (limited period) Zeitraum, *der;* ∼ **[of office]** Amtszeit, *die*

(g) *in pl.* (mode of expression) Worte *Pl.*

(h) *in pl.* (relations) **be on good/bad** ∼**s with sb.** mit jmdm. auf gutem/schlechtem Fuß stehen

2 *v.t.* nennen

terminal /'tɜːmɪnl/ 1 *n.* **(a)** (for train or bus) Bahnhof, *der;* (for airline passengers) Terminal, *der od. das*

(b) (Teleph., Comp.) Terminal, *das*

2 *adj.* (Med.) unheilbar

terminally /'tɜːmɪnəlɪ/ *adv.* ∼ **ill** unheilbar krank

terminate /'tɜːmɪneɪt/ *v.t.* **(a)** beenden; lösen ⟨*Vertrag*⟩

(b) (Med.) unterbrechen ⟨*Schwangerschaft*⟩

termination /tɜːmɪ'neɪʃn/ *n.* **(a)** *no pl.* Beendigung, *die;* (of lease) Ablauf, *der*

(b) (Med.) Schwangerschaftsabbruch, *der*

termini *pl. of* TERMINUS

terminology /tɜːmɪ'nɒlədʒɪ/ *n.* Terminologie, *die*

terminus /'tɜːmɪnəs/ *n., pl.* ∼**es** *or* **termini** /'tɜːmɪnaɪ/ Endstation, *die*

terrace /'terəs, 'terɪs/ *n.* Terrasse, *die; (row of houses)* Häuserreihe, *die*

terraced house /'terəst haʊs, 'terɪst haʊs/ *n.* Reihenhaus, *das*

terracotta /terə'kɒtə/ *n., no indef. art.* Terrakotta, *die*

terrain /te'reɪn/ *n.* Gelände, *das*

terrestrial /tə'restrɪəl/ *adj.* terrestrisch ⟨*Raumschiff, Fernsehen, Bevölkerung*⟩; Erd⟨*satellit, -bevölkerung*⟩

terrible /'terɪbl/ *adj.* **(a)** (coll.: very great or bad) schrecklich (ugs.)

(b) (coll.: incompetent) schlecht

(c) (causing terror) furchtbar

terribly /'terɪblɪ/ *adv.* **(a)** (coll.: very) unheimlich (ugs.)

(b) (coll.: appallingly) furchtbar (ugs.)

(c) (coll.: incompetently) schlecht

(d) (fearfully) auf erschreckende Weise

terrier /'terɪə(r)/ *n.* Terrier, *der*

terrific /tə'rɪfɪk/ *adj.* (coll.) **(a)** (great, intense) irrsinnig (ugs.)

(b) (magnificent) sagenhaft (ugs.)

(c) (highly expert) klasse (ugs.)

terrify /'terɪfaɪ/ *v.t.* **(a)** Angst machen (+ *Dat.*); **be terrified that ...:** Angst haben, dass ...

(b) (scare) Angst einjagen (+ *Dat.*)

'terrifying *adj.* entsetzlich ⟨*Erlebnis, Buch*⟩; Furcht erregend ⟨*Anblick*⟩; beängstigend ⟨*Geschwindigkeit*⟩

terrine /tə'riːn/ *n.* **(a)** (dish) Steinguttopf, *der*

(b) (Gastr.) Terrine, *die*

territorial /terɪ'tɔːrɪəl/ *adj.* territorial; Gebiets⟨*anspruch usw.*⟩

territory /'terɪtrɪ/ *n.* Gebiet, *das*

terror /'terə(r)/ *n.* [panische] Angst; Schrecken, *der*

terrorism /'terərɪzm/ *n.* Terrorismus, *der;* (terrorist acts) Terror, *der*

'terrorist *n.* Terrorist, *der*/Terroristin, *die*

terrorize /'terəraɪz/ *v.t.* **(a)** (frighten) in [Angst und] Schrecken versetzen

(b) (coerce) terrorisieren

terse /tɜːs/ *adj.* **(a)** (concise) kurz und bündig

(b) (curt) knapp

test /test/ 1 *n.* **(a)** (Sch.) Klassenarbeit, *die;* (Univ.) Klausur, *die;* **put sb./sth. to the** ∼: jmdn./etw. erproben

(b) (analysis) Test, *der*

2 *v.t.* untersuchen ⟨*Wasser, Augen*⟩; testen ⟨*Gehör, Augen*⟩; prüfen ⟨*Schüler*⟩; ∼ **sb. for Aids** jmdn. auf Aids untersuchen

▪ **'test out** *v.t.* ausprobieren ⟨*Produkte*⟩ (**on** an + *Dat.*); erproben ⟨*Theorie, Idee*⟩

Testament /'testəmənt/ *n.* **Old/New** ∼ (Bibl.) Altes/Neues Testament

test: ∼ **ban** *n.* Atom[waffen]teststopp, *der;* ∼ **ban treaty** *n.* [Atom]teststopp-Abkommen, *das;* ∼ **drive** *n.* Probefahrt, *die;* ∼**drive** *v.t.* Probe fahren

testicle /'testɪkl/ *n.* Testikel, *der* (fachspr.); Hoden, *der*

testify /'testɪfaɪ/ 1 *v.i.* **(a)** ∼ **to sth.** etw. bezeugen

(b) (Law) ∼ **against sb.** gegen jmdn. aussagen

2 *v.t.* bestätigen

testimonial /testɪ'məʊnɪəl/ *n.* Zeugnis, *das;* Referenz, *die*

testimony /'testɪmənɪ/ *n.* Aussage, *die*

test: ∼ **pilot** *n.* Testpilot, *der*/-pilotin, *die;* ∼ **tube** *n.* Reagenzglas, *das;* ∼**tube baby** *n.* (coll.) Retortenbaby, *das* (ugs.)

testy /'testɪ/ *adj.* leicht reizbar ⟨*Person*⟩; gereizt ⟨*Antwort*⟩

tetanus /'tetənəs/ *n.* Tetanus, *der*

tetchy /'tetʃɪ/ *adj.* leicht reizbar; gereizt

tether /'teðə(r)/ 1 *n.* **be at the end of one's** ∼: am Ende [seiner Kraft] sein

2 *v.t.* anbinden (**to** an + *Dat. od. Akk.*)

text /tekst/ *n.* Text, *der*

text: ∼**book** *n.* Lehrbuch, *das;* ∼**book case** Paradefall, *der;* ∼ **file** *n.* (Comp.) Textdatei, *die*

textile /'tekstaɪl/ *n.* Stoff, *der;* ∼**s** Textilien *Pl.*

'text processing *n.* (Comp.) Textverarbeitung, *die*

texture /'tekstʃə(r)/ *n.* Beschaffenheit, *die;* (of fabric) Struktur, *die*

Thai /taɪ/ 1 *adj.* thailändisch; **sb. is** ∼: jmd. ist Thai

2 *n.* **(a)** *pl. same or* ∼**s** Thai, *der*/*die*

(b) (language) Thai, *das*

Thailand /'taɪlænd/ *pr. n.* Thailand (*das*)

Thames /temz/ *pr. n.* Themse, *die*

than /ðən, *stressed* ðæn/ *conj.* als; **I know you better** ∼ **[I do] him** ich kenne dich besser als ihn

thank /θæŋk/ *v.t.* ~ sb. [for sth.] jmdm. [für etw.] danken; ~ **God** *or* **goodness** *or* **heaven[s]** Gott sei Dank; [I] ~ **you** danke; **no,** ~ **you** nein, danke; **yes,** ~ **you** ja, bitte; ~ **you very much** vielen herzlichen Dank

thankful /'θæŋkfl/ *adj.* dankbar

thankfully /'θæŋkfəlɪ/ *adv.* **(a)** (gratefully) dankbar
(b) (as sentence-modifier: fortunately) glücklicherweise

'**thankless** *adj.* undankbar

thanks /θæŋks/ *n. pl.* **(a)** (gratitude) Dank, *der;* ~ **to** (with the help of) dank; (on account of the bad influence of) wegen
(b) (formula expr. gratitude) danke; **no,** ~: nein, danke; **yes,** ~: ja, bitte; **many** ~ (coll.) vielen Dank

thanksgiving /'θæŋksgɪvɪŋ/ *n.* **T**~ **[Day]** (Amer.) [amerikanisches] Erntedankfest; Thanksgiving Day, *der*

'**thank-you** *n.* (coll.) Dankeschön, *das*

that [1] /ðæt/ *adj., pl.* **those** /ðəʊz/ **(a)** dieser/diese/dieses
(b) (coupled or contrasted with 'this') der/die/das
[2] /ðæt/ *pron., pl.* **those (a)** der/die/das; **what bird is** ~? was für ein Vogel ist das?; **like** ~: so; **[just] like** ~ (without effort, thought) einfach so; ~'**s right!** gut *od.* recht so; (iron.) nur so weiter!; ~ **will do** das reicht
(b) (Brit.) **who is** ~? wer ist da?; (on telephone) wer ist am Apparat?
[3] /ðət/ *rel. pron., pl.* **same** der/die/das; **everyone** ~ **I know** jeder, den ich kenne; **this is all [the money]** ~ **I have** das ist alles [Geld], was ich habe
[4] /ðæt/ *adv.* (coll.) so
[5] /ðət/ *rel. adv.* der/die/das; **the day** ~ **I first met her** der Tag, an dem ich sie zum ersten Mal sah
[6] /ðət, stressed ðæt/ *conj.* dass; **[in order]** ~: damit

thatch /θætʃ/ *n.* (of straw) Strohdach, *das;* (of reeds) Schilfdach, *das;* (roofing) Dachbedeckung, *die*

thatched /θætʃt/ *adj.* stroh-/schilfgedeckt

thaw /θɔː/ [1] *n.* Tauwetter, *das*
[2] *v.i.* **(a)** tauen
(b) (melt) auftauen
[3] *v.t.* auftauen
■ **thaw 'out** ▶ THAW 2, 3

the /before vowel ðɪ, before consonant ðə, when stressed ðiː/ [1] *def. art.* der/die/das
[2] *adv.* ~ **more I practise** ~ **better I play** je mehr ich übe, desto *od.* umso besser spiele ich; **so much** ~ **worse for sb./sth.** umso schlimmer für jmdn./etw

theatre (Amer.: **theater**) /'θɪətə(r)/ *n.* **(a)** Theater, *das*
(b) (lecture ~) Hörsaal, *der*
(c) (Brit. Med.) ▶ OPERATING THEATRE

theatrical /θɪ'ætrɪkl/ *adj.* **(a)** schauspielerisch
(b) (showy) theatralisch

theft /θeft/ *n.* Diebstahl, *der*

their /ðeə(r)/ *poss. pron. attrib.* ihr

theirs /ðeəz/ *poss. pron. pred.* ihrer/ihre/ ihres

them /ðəm, stressed ðem/ *pron.* sie; (as indirect object) ihnen; *see also* HER[1]

theme /θiːm/ *n.* Thema, *das*

theme: ~ **music** *n.* Titelmelodie, *die;* ~ **park** *n.*: Freizeitpark, dessen Attraktionen und Einrichtungen auf ein bestimmtes Thema bezogen sind; ~ **song** *n.* Erkennungssong, *der;* ~ **tune** Erkennungsmelodie, *die*

themselves /ðəm'selvz/ *pron.* **(a)** *emphat.* selbst
(b) *refl.* sich ⟨waschen usw.⟩; sich selbst ⟨die Schuld geben, regieren⟩. *See also* HERSELF

then /ðen/ [1] *adv.* **(a)** (at that time) damals; ~ **and there** auf der Stelle
(b) (after that) dann; ~ **[again]** (and also) außerdem; **but** ~ (after all) aber schließlich
(c) (in that case) dann; **but** ~ **again** aber andererseits
[2] *n.* **before** ~: vorher; davor; **from** ~ **on** von da an; **since** ~: seitdem
[3] *adj.* damalig

theological /θiːə'lɒdʒɪkl/ *adj.* theologisch; Theologie⟨student⟩

theology /θɪ'ɒlədʒɪ/ *n.* Theologie, *die*

theoretical /θɪə'retɪkl/ *adj.* theoretisch

theory /'θɪərɪ/ *n.* Theorie, *die;* **in** ~: theoretisch

therapeutic /θerə'pjuːtɪk/ *adj.* therapeutisch

therapist /'θerəpɪst/ *n.* Therapeut, *der/* Therapeutin, *die*

therapy /'θerəpɪ/ *n.* Therapie, *die*

there /ðeə(r)/ [1] *adv.* **(a)** (in/at that place) da; dort; (fairly close) da; **be down/in/up** ~: da unten/drin/oben sein
(b) (calling attention) **hello** *or* **hi** ~! hallo!; **you** ~! Sie da!
(c) (in that respect) da; **so** ~! und damit basta (ugs.)
(d) (to that place) dahin, dorthin ⟨gehen, fahren, rücken⟩; **down/up** ~: dort hinunter/ hinauf
(e) /ðə(r), stressed ðeə(r)/ **was** ~ **anything in it?** war da irgendwas drin?; ~ **was once** es war einmal; ~ **is enough food** es gibt genug zu essen
[2] *int.* ~, ~: na, na (ugs.); ~ **[you are]!** da, siehst du!
[3] *n.* da; dort; **near** ~: da *od.* dort in der Nähe

thereabouts /'ðeərəbaʊts/ *adv.* **(a)** da [in der Nähe]
(b) (near that number) ungefähr

therefore /'ðeəfɔː(r)/ *adv.* deshalb; also

thermal /'θɜːml/ *adj.* thermisch; ~ **underwear** kälteisolierende Unterwäsche

thermal imaging /θɜːml 'ɪmɪdʒɪŋ/ *n.* Thermographie, *die*

t

thermometer /θə'mɒmɪtə(r)/ n.
Thermometer, das

Thermos, thermos ® /'θɜːməs/ n.
~ [flask/jug/bottle] Thermosflasche, die (Wz)

thermostat /'θɜːməstæt/ n. Thermostat,
der

these pl. of THIS

thesis /'θiːsɪs/ n., pl. **theses** /'θiːsiːz/ (a)
(proposition) These, die
(b) (dissertation) Dissertation, die (on über
+ Akk.)

they /ðeɪ/ pron. (a) sie
(b) (people in general) man

they'd /ðeɪd/ (a) = they would
(b) = they had

they'll /ðeɪl/ = they will

they're /ðeə(r)/ = they are

they've /ðeɪv/ = they have

thick /θɪk/ ❶ adj. (a) dick; a rope two
inches ~, a two-inch ~ rope ein zwei Zoll
starkes od. dickes Seil
(b) (dense) dicht ‹Haar, Nebel, Wolken usw.›
(c) (filled) ~ with voll von
(d) dickflüssig ‹Sahne›; dick ‹Suppe,
Schlamm, Kleister›
(e) (stupid) dumm
❷ n. in the ~ of mitten in (+ Dat.)

thick 'ear n. give sb. a ~ (Brit. coll.) jmdm.
ein paar hinter die Ohren geben (ugs.)

thicken /'θɪkn/ ❶ v.t. dicker machen;
eindicken ‹Sauce›
❷ v.i. (a) dicker werden
(b) ‹Nebel:› dichter werden
(c) the plot ~s die Sache wird kompliziert

'thickly adv. (a) (in a thick layer) dick
(b) (densely) dicht

'thickness n. (a) Dicke, die; be two metres
in ~: zwei Meter dick sein
(b) (denseness) Dichte, die

thick: ~set adj. gedrungen; **~-skinned**
adj. (fig.) dickfellig (ugs.)

thief /θiːf/ n., pl. **thieves** /θiːvz/ Dieb, der/
Diebin, die

thieve /θiːv/ v.i. stehlen

thieves pl. of THIEF

thigh /θaɪ/ n. Oberschenkel, der

thimble /'θɪmbl/ n. Fingerhut, der

thin /θɪn/ ❶ adj. (a) dünn; a tall, ~ man ein
großer, hagerer Mann
(b) (sparse) dünn, schütter ‹Haar›
❷ adv. dünn
❸ v.t., -nn-: (a) dünner machen
(b) (dilute) verdünnen

■ **thin 'out** v.i. ‹Menschenmenge:› sich
verlaufen; ‹Verkehr:› abnehmen

thing /θɪŋ/ n. (a) Sache, die; Ding, das;
what's that ~ in your hand? was hast du da
in der Hand?; be a rare ~: etwas Seltenes
sein
(b) (action) it was the right ~ to do es war das
einzig Richtige; that was a foolish/friendly
~ to do das war eine große Dummheit/das
war sehr freundlich

(c) (fact) [Tat]sache, die; it's a strange ~ that
…: es ist seltsam, dass …; the best/worst
~ about her das Beste/Schlimmste an ihr
(d) (idea) say the first ~ that comes into
one's head das sagen, was einem gerade so
einfällt; what a ~ to say! wie kann man nur
so etwas sagen!
(e) (task) she has a reputation for getting ~s
done sie ist für ihre Tatkraft bekannt; a big
~ to undertake ein großes Unterfangen
(f) (affair) Sache, die; Angelegenheit, die
(g) (circumstance) take ~s too seriously alles
zu ernst nehmen; how are ~s? wie gehts
[dir]?
(h) (individual, creature) Ding, das
(i) in pl. (personal belongings, clothes) Sachen Pl.
(j) (product of work) Sache, die; the latest ~:
der letzte Schrei
(k) (what is important or proper) das Richtige; the
~ is … (question) die Frage ist …

thingamy /'θɪŋəmɪ/, **thingumabob**
/'θɪŋəməbɒb/, **thingumajig** /'θɪŋəmədʒɪg/,
thingummy /'θɪŋəmɪ/, **thingy** /'θɪŋɪ/ ns.
(coll.) Dings, der/die/das (salopp); Dingsbums,
der/die/das (ugs.)

think /θɪŋk/ ❶ v.t., thought /θɔːt/ (a)
(consider) meinen; we ~ [that] he will come
wir denken od. glauben, dass er kommt;
what do you ~? was meinst du? do you
really ~ so? findest du wirklich?; what do
you ~ of him/it? was hältst du von ihm/
davon?; …, don't you ~? …, findest od.
meinst du nicht auch?; I ~ so/not ich glaube
schon/nicht; I ~ I'll try ich glaube, ich werde
es versuchen
(b) (imagine) sich (Dat.) vorstellen
❷ v.i., thought [nach]denken; I need time to
~: ich muss es mir erst überlegen; I've been
~ing ich habe nachgedacht; ~ twice es sich
(Dat.) zweimal überlegen

■ **'think of** v.t. (a) denken an (+ Akk.); he
~s of everything er denkt einfach an alles
(b) (have as idea) we'll ~ of something wir
werden uns etwas einfallen lassen; can you
~ of anyone who …? fällt dir jemand ein,
der …?
(c) (remember) sich erinnern an (+ Akk.); I
just can't ~ of her name ich komme einfach
nicht auf ihren Namen
(d) ~ little/nothing of sb./sth. (consider
contemptible) wenig/nichts von jmdm./etw.
halten; not ~ much of sb./sth. nicht viel von
jmdm./etw. halten

■ **think 'over** v.t. sich (Dat.) überlegen

■ **think 'through** v.t. [gründlich]
durchdenken

■ **think 'up** v.t. (coll.) sich (Dat.) ausdenken

'thinker n. Denker, der/Denkerin, die

'think tank n. Beraterstab, der

'thin-skinned adj. (fig.) empfindlich;
dünnhäutig (geh.)

third /θɜːd/ ❶ adj. dritt…
❷ n. (in sequence, rank) Dritte, der/die/das;
(fraction) Drittel, das. See also EIGHTH

'thirdly adv. drittens

third: ~ '**party** n. attrib. ~-**party insurance** Haftpflichtversicherung, die; ~-**rate** adj. drittklassig; **T**~ '**World** n. Dritte Welt; **countries of the T**~ **World, T**~ **World countries** Länder der Dritten Welt

thirst /θɜːst/ 1 n. Durst, der; **die of** ~: verdursten
2 v.i. ~ **for revenge/knowledge** nach Rache/Wissen dürsten (geh.)

'**thirsty** adj. durstig; **be** ~: Durst haben

thirteen /θɜː'tiːn/ 1 adj. dreizehn
2 n. Dreizehn, die. See also EIGHT

thirteenth /θɜː'tiːnθ/ adj. dreizehnt… See also EIGHTH

thirtieth /'θɜːtɪɪθ/ 1 adj. dreißigst…
2 n. (fraction) Dreißigstel, das. See also EIGHTH

thirty /'θɜːtɪ/ 1 adj. dreißig
2 n. Dreißig, die. See also EIGHT; EIGHTY 2

'**thirty-something** 1 adj. **be** ~: in den Dreißigern sein
2 n. Dreißiger, der/-in, die

this /ðɪs/ 1 adj., pl. **these** /ðiːz/ dieser/ diese/dieses; (with less emphasis) der/die/das; **at** ~ **time** zu dieser Zeit; **by** ~ **time** inzwischen; mittlerweile; **these days** heut[zutage]; **before** ~ **time** vorher; zuvor; **all** ~ **week** die[se] ganze Woche; ~ **morning/ evening** etc. heute Morgen/Abend usw.; **these last three weeks** die letzten drei Wochen; ~ **Monday (to come)** nächsten Montag
2 pron., pl. **these (a) what's** ~ **?** was ist [denn] das?; **fold it like** ~: falte es so!
(b) (the present) **before** ~: bis jetzt
(c) (Brit. Teleph.: person speaking) ~ **is Andy** hier [spricht od. ist] Andy; (Amer. Teleph.) **who did you say** ~ **was?** wer ist am Apparat?
(d) ~ **and that** dies und das

thistle /'θɪsl/ n. Distel, die

thorn /θɔːn/ n. **(a)** (part of plant) Dorn, der
(b) (plant) Dornenstrauch, der

'**thorny** adj. **(a)** dornig
(b) (fig.) heikel

thorough /'θʌrə/ adj. gründlich

thorough: ~**bred** n. reinrassiges Tier; (horse) Rassepferd, das; ~-**fare** n. Durchfahrtsstraße, die; '**no** ~**fare**' „Durchfahrt verboten"; (on foot) „kein Durchgang"

'**thoroughly** adv. gründlich ⟨untersuchen⟩; gehörig ⟨erschöpft⟩; so richtig ⟨genießen⟩; zutiefst ⟨beschämt⟩; total ⟨verdorben, verwöhnt⟩; **be** ~ **fed up with sth.** (coll.) von etw. die Nase gestrichen voll haben (ugs.)

'**thoroughness** n. Gründlichkeit, die

those ▶ THAT 1, 2

though /ðəʊ/ 1 conj. **(a)** (despite the fact that) obwohl; **late** ~ **it was** obwohl es so spät war;

---

the car, ~ **powerful, is also economical** der Wagen ist zwar stark, aber [zugleich] auch wirtschaftlich
(b) (but nevertheless) aber; **a slow** ~ **certain method** eine langsame, aber od. wenn auch sichere Methode
(c) (even if) [even] ~: auch wenn
(d) (and yet) ~ **you never know** obwohl man nie weiß
2 adv. (coll.) trotzdem

thought /θɔːt/ 1 ▶ THINK
2 n. **(a)** no pl. Denken, das
(b) no pl., no art. (reflection) Überlegung, die; Nachdenken, das
(c) (consideration) Rücksicht, die (**for** auf + Akk.)
(d) (idea, conception) Gedanke, der; **it's the** ~ **that counts** der gute Wille zählt; **give up all** ~[**s**] **of sth.** sich (Dat.) etw. aus dem Kopf schlagen

thoughtful /'θɔːtfl/ adj. **(a)** nachdenklich
(b) (considerate) rücksichtsvoll; (helpful) aufmerksam

'**thoughtfully** adv. **(a)** nachdenklich
(b) (considerately) rücksichtsvollerweise

'**thoughtless** adj. **(a)** gedankenlos
(b) (inconsiderate) rücksichtslos

'**thoughtlessly** adv. **(a)** gedankenlos
(b) (inconsiderately) aus Rücksichtslosigkeit

thought: ~ **process** n. Denkprozess, der; ~-**provoking** adj. nachdenklich stimmend; **be** ~-**provoking** nachdenklich stimmen

thousand /'θaʊznd/ 1 adj. **(a)** tausend; **a** or **one** ~: eintausend; **two/several** ~: zweitausend/mehrere tausend; **a** or **one** ~ **and one** [ein]tausend[und]eins
(b) a ~ [**and one**] (fig.: innumerable) tausend (ugs.)
2 n. **(a)** (number) tausend; **a** or **one/two** ~: ein-/zweitausend
(b) (written figure; group) Tausend, das
(c) (indefinite amount) ~**s** tausende

thousandth /'θaʊzndθ/ 1 adj. tausendst…
2 n. (fraction) Tausendstel, das; (in sequence) Tausendste, der/die/das

thrash /θræʃ/ v.t. **(a)** verprügeln
(b) (defeat) vernichtend schlagen
■ **thrash 'out** v.t. ausdiskutieren

thrashing /'θræʃɪŋ/ n. (beating) Prügel Pl.; **give sb. a** ~: jmdm. eine Tracht Prügel verpassen (ugs.)

thread /θred/ 1 n. **(a)** Faden, der
(b) (of screw) Gewinde, das
2 v.t. **(a)** einfädeln; auffädeln ⟨Perlen⟩
(b) ~ **one's way through sth.** sich durch etw. schlängeln

'**threadbare** adj. abgenutzt; abgetragen ⟨Kleidung⟩; (fig.) abgedroschen ⟨Argument⟩

threat /θret/ n. Drohung, die

threaten /'θretn/ v.t. **(a)** bedrohen; ~ **sb. with sth.** jmdm. etw. androhen
(b) ~ **to do sth.** damit drohen, etw. zu tun
(c) drohen mit ⟨Gewalt, Rache usw.⟩

t

threatening /'θretnɪŋ/ adj. drohend

three /θriː/ [1] adj. drei
[2] n. Drei, die. See also EIGHT

three: ~**dimensional** /θriːdɪ'menʃənl/ adj. dreidimensional; ~**fold** adj., adv. dreifach; **a** ~**fold increase** ein Anstieg auf das Dreifache; ~**lane** adj. dreispurig; ~**pin** ▶ PIN 1 C; ~**quarters** [1] n. drei Viertel pl. (**of** + Gen.); ~**quarters of an hour** eine Dreiviertelstunde; [2] adv. drei viertel ⟨voll⟩; ~**some** /'θriːsəm/ n. Dreigespann, das; Trio, das

thresh /θreʃ/ v.t. dreschen

threshold /'θreʃəʊld/ n. Schwelle, die

threw ▶ THROW 1

thrift /θrɪft/ n. Sparsamkeit, die

'thrifty adj. sparsam

thrill /θrɪl/ [1] v.t. (a) (excite) faszinieren (b) (delight) begeistern
[2] n. (a) Erregung, die (b) (exciting experience) aufregendes Erlebnis

'thriller n. Thriller, der

'thrilling adj. aufregend; spannend ⟨Buch, Film⟩

thrive /θraɪv/ v.i., **thrived** or **throve** /θrəʊv/, **thrived** or **thriven** /'θrɪvn/ (a) ⟨Pflanze:⟩ wachsen und gedeihen (b) (prosper) aufblühen (**on** bei)

throat /θrəʊt/ n. Hals, der; (esp. inside) Kehle, die; **a [sore]** ~: Halsschmerzen Pl.

throb /θrɒb/ [1] v.i., **-bb-** pochen; ⟨Motor:⟩ dröhnen
[2] n. Pochen, das; (of engine) Dröhnen, das

throes /θrəʊz/ n. pl. Qual, die; **be in the** ~ **of sth.** (fig.) mitten in etw. (Dat.) stecken (ugs.)

thrombosis /θrɒm'bəʊsɪs/ n., pl. **thromboses** /θrɒm'bəʊsiːz/ Thrombose, die

throne /θrəʊn/ n. Thron, der

throng /θrɒŋ/ n. [Menschen]menge, die

throttle /'θrɒtl/ v.t. erdrosseln

through /θruː/ [1] prep. (a) durch (b) (Amer.: up to and including) bis [einschließlich] (c) (by reason of) durch; infolge von ⟨Vernachlässigung, Einflüssen⟩
[2] adv. (a) **let sb.** ~: jmdn. durchlassen (b) (Teleph.) **be** ~: durch sein (ugs.); **be** ~ **to sb.** mit jmdm. verbunden sein
[3] attrib. adj. durchgehend ⟨Zug⟩

through'out [1] prep. ~ **the war/period** den ganzen Krieg/die ganze Zeit hindurch; ~ **the country** im ganzen Land
[2] adv. (entirely) ganz; (always) stets; die ganze Zeit [hindurch]

throve ▶ THRIVE

throw /θrəʊ/ [1] v.t., **threw** /θruː/, **thrown** /θrəʊn/ (a) werfen; ~ **sth. to sb.** jmdm. etw. zuwerfen; ~ **sth. at sb.** etw. nach jmdm. werfen (b) (bring to the ground) zu Boden werfen; abwerfen ⟨Reiter⟩

(c) (coll.: disconcert) ⟨Frage:⟩ aus der Fassung bringen
[2] n. Wurf, der

■ **throw a'way** v.t. (a) wegwerfen (b) (lose by neglect) verschenken ⟨Vorteil, Spiel usw.⟩

■ **throw 'up** [1] v.t. (a) hochwerfen ⟨Arme, Hände⟩ (b) (produce) hervorbringen ⟨Ideen usw.⟩
[2] v.i. (coll.) brechen (ugs.)

'throwaway adj. (a) Wegwerf-; Einweg- (b) beiläufig ⟨Bemerkung⟩

thrown ▶ THROW 1

thrush /θrʌʃ/ n. (Ornith.) Drossel, die

thrust /θrʌst/ [1] v.t., **thrust** stoßen; ~ **aside** (fig.) beiseite schieben
[2] n. Stoß, der

thud /θʌd/ n. dumpfer Schlag

thug /θʌg/ n. Schläger, der; **football** ~**s** Fußballrowdys Pl.

thuggish /'θʌgɪʃ/ adj. aggressiv ⟨Verhalten, Fußballfan⟩

thumb /θʌm/ [1] n. Daumen, der; **get the** ~**s up** ⟨Person, Projekt:⟩ akzeptiert werden; **be under sb.'s** ~: unter jmds. Fuchtel stehen
[2] v.t. ~ **a lift** per Anhalter fahren

■ **'thumb through** v.t. durchblättern

thumb: ~**index** n. Daumenregister, das; ~**nail** n. Daumennagel, der; ~**tack** n. (Amer.) Reißzwecke, die

thump /θʌmp/ [1] v.t. [mit Wucht] schlagen
[2] v.i. (a) hämmern (**at, on** gegen) (b) ⟨Herz:⟩ heftig pochen
[3] n. (blow) Schlag, der; (sound) Bums, der (ugs.); dumpfer Schlag

thunder /'θʌndə(r)/ [1] n. Donner, der
[2] v.i. donnern

thunder: ~**clap** n. Donnerschlag, der; ~**storm** n. Gewitter, das

thundery /'θʌndərɪ/ adj. gewittrig

Thurs. abbr. = **Thursday** Do.

Thursday /'θɜːzdeɪ, 'θɜːzdɪ/ n. Donnerstag, der; see also FRIDAY

thus /ðʌs/ adv. so

thwart /θwɔːt/ v.t. durchkreuzen ⟨Pläne⟩; vereiteln ⟨Versuch⟩; ~ **sb.** jmdm. einen Strich durch die Rechnung machen

thyme /taɪm/ n. Thymian, der

thyroid /'θaɪrɔɪd/ n. Schilddrüse, die

tiara /tɪ'ɑːrə/ n. Diadem, das

tick /tɪk/ [1] v.i. ticken
[2] v.t. (a) mit einem Häkchen versehen (b) ▶ ~ OFF A
[3] n. (a) (of clock etc.) Ticken, das (b) (mark) Häkchen, das

■ **tick 'off** v.t. (a) (cross off) abhaken (b) (coll.: reprimand) rüffeln (ugs.)

ticket /'tɪkɪt/ n. Karte, die; (for bus, train) Fahrschein, der; (for aeroplane) Flugschein, der; (for lottery, raffle) Los, das; (for library) Ausweis, der; **price** ~: Preisschild, das

ticket: ~**agency** n. Kartenvorverkaufsstelle, die; ~**agent** n.

Inhaber/Inhaberin einer Kartenvorverkaufsstelle; ∼ **collector** n. (on train) Schaffner, der/Schaffnerin, die; (on station) Fahrkartenkontrolleur, der/ -kontrolleurin, die; ∼ **dispenser** n. Kartenautomat, der; (for train etc.) Fahrschein- od. Fahrkartenautomat, der; ∼ **holder** n. Besitzer/Besitzerin einer Eintrittskarte; ∼ **machine** ▶ ∼ DISPENSER; ∼ **office** n. Fahrkartenschalter, der; (for advance booking) Kartenvorverkaufsstelle, die

tickle /'tɪkl/ v.t. & i. kitzeln

ticklish /'tɪklɪʃ/ adj. kitzlig

tidal /'taɪdl/ adj. Gezeiten

'tidal wave n. Flutwelle, die

tiddlywinks /'tɪdlɪwɪŋks/ n. sing. (game) Flohhüpfen, das

tide /taɪd/ ⃞1 n. Tide, die (nordd.); high ∼: Flut, die; low ∼: Ebbe, die; the ∼s die Gezeiten; the ∼ is in/out es ist Flut/Ebbe ⃞2 v.t. ∼ sb. over jmdm. über die Runden helfen (ugs.)

tidiness /'taɪdɪnɪs/ n. Ordentlichkeit, die

tidy /'taɪdɪ/ ⃞1 adj. ordentlich; aufgeräumt ⟨Zimmer, Schreibtisch⟩ ⃞2 v.t. aufräumen; ∼ oneself sich zurechtmachen
■ **tidy 'up** v.i. aufräumen

tie /taɪ/ ⃞1 v.t., tying /'taɪɪŋ/ binden (to an + Akk., into zu); ∼ a knot einen Knoten machen; (Sport) ∼ the match unentschieden spielen ⃞2 v.i., tying (a) (be fastened) it ∼s at the back es wird hinten gebunden (b) (have equal scores) ∼ for second place mit gleicher Punktzahl den zweiten Platz erreichen ⃞3 n. (a) Krawatte, die (b) (bond) Band, das; (restriction) Bindung, die (c) (equality of scores) Punktgleichheit, die (d) (Sport: match) Begegnung, die
■ **tie 'in** v.i. ∼ in with sth. zu etw. passen
■ **tie 'up** v.t. (a) festbinden; ∼ up a parcel ein Paket verschnüren (b) (keep busy) beschäftigen

tier /tɪə(r)/ n. (a) Rang, der (b) (unit) Stufe, die

tiger /'taɪgə(r)/ n. Tiger, der

tiger e'conomy n. Tigerstaat, der

tight /taɪt/ ⃞1 adj. (a) (firm) fest; fest angezogen ⟨Schraube, Mutter⟩; fest sitzend ⟨Deckel⟩ (b) (close-fitting) eng ⟨Kleid, Schuh usw.⟩ (c) (impermeable) ∼ seal/joint dichter Verschluss/dichte Fuge (d) (taut) straff (e) (difficult to negotiate) a ∼ corner eine enge Kurve; be in a ∼ corner (fig.) in der Klemme sein (ugs.) (f) (strict) streng ⟨Kontrolle, Disziplin⟩ (g) (coll.: stingy) knauserig (ugs.) (h) (coll.: drunk) voll (salopp) ⃞2 adv. fest; hold ∼! halt dich fest!

⃞3 n. in pl. (a) (Brit.) [pair of] ∼s Strumpfhose, die (b) (of dancer etc.) Trikothose, die

tighten /'taɪtn/ ⃞1 v.t. (a) [fest] anziehen ⟨Knoten, Schraube⟩; straff ziehen ⟨Seil⟩ (b) verschärfen ⟨Kontrolle⟩ ⃞2 v.i. sich spannen

tight-fisted /taɪt'fɪstɪd/ adj. geizig

'tightrope n. Drahtseil, das

tile /taɪl/ ⃞1 n. (on roof) Ziegel, der; (on floor) Fliese, die; (on wall) Kachel, die ⃞2 v.t. [mit Ziegeln] decken ⟨Dach⟩; fliesen ⟨Fußboden⟩; kacheln ⟨Wand⟩

till¹ /tɪl/ ⃞1 prep. bis; (followed by article + noun) bis zu; not [...] ∼: erst ⃞2 conj. bis

till² n. Kasse, die

'till receipt n. Kassenzettel, der

tilt /tɪlt/ ⃞1 v.i. kippen ⃞2 v.t. kippen; neigen ⟨Kopf⟩ ⃞3 n. (a) Schräglage, die; a 45° ∼: eine Neigung von 45° (b) [at] full ∼: mit voller Wucht

timber /'tɪmbə(r)/ n. [Bau]holz, das

time /taɪm/ ⃞1 n. (a) Zeit, die; in [the course of] ∼, as ∼ goes on/went on mit der Zeit; im Laufe der Zeit; in ∼, with ∼ (sooner or later) mit der Zeit; in [good] ∼ (not late) rechtzeitig; all the or this ∼: die ganze Zeit; (without ceasing) ständig; a short ∼ ago vor kurzem; ∼ off or out freie Zeit; in 'no ∼: im Handumdrehen; in a week's/year's ∼: in einer Woche/einem Jahr; harvest/ Christmas ∼: Ernte-/Weihnachtszeit, die; on ∼ (punctually) pünktlich; ahead of ∼: zu früh ⟨ankommen⟩; vorzeitig ⟨fertig werden⟩; have a good ∼: sich amüsieren; Spaß haben (ugs.); have no ∼ for sb./sth. (fig.) für jmdn./ etw. ist einem seine Zeit zu schade (b) (occasion) Mal, das; for the first ∼: zum ersten Mal; at ∼s gelegentlich; ∼ and again, ∼ after ∼: immer [und immer] wieder; at one ∼, at [one and] the same ∼ (simultaneously) gleichzeitig; one at a ∼: einzeln; two at a ∼: jeweils zwei (c) (point in day etc.) [Uhr]zeit, die; tell the ∼: die Uhr lesen; what ∼ is it?, what is the ∼? wie spät ist es?; by this/that ∼: inzwischen; by the ∼ [that] we arrived bis wir hinkamen; T∼! (Brit.: in pub) Feierabend!; ∼, [ladies and] gentlemen, please! wir machen Feierabend, meine [Damen und] Herren! (d) (multiplication) mal; three ∼s four drei mal vier (e) (Mus.) Takt, der; in ∼: im Takt ⃞2 v.t. (a) zeitlich abstimmen; be well ∼d zur richtigen Zeit kommen (b) (set to operate at correct ∼) einstellen (c) (measure ∼ taken by) stoppen

time: ∼ **bomb** n. Zeitbombe, die; ∼-**consuming** adj. (a) (taking ∼) zeitaufwendig; (b) (wasteful of ∼) zeitraubend; ∼ **lag** n. zeitliche Verzögerung ····⫶

timeless /'taɪmlɪs/ adj. zeitlos

'time limit n. Frist, die

timely /'taɪmlɪ/ adj. rechtzeitig

time: ~**scale** n. Zeitskala, die; ~ **sheet** n. Stundenzettel, der; ~ **switch** n. Zeitschalter, der; ~**table** n. (a) (scheme of work) Zeitplan, der; (Educ.) Stundenplan, der; (b) (Transport) Fahrplan, der; ~ **warp** n. Verwerfung im Raum-Zeit-Kontinuum; ~ **zone** n. Zeitzone, die

timid /'tɪmɪd/ adj. (a) scheu ⟨Tier⟩ (b) zaghaft ⟨Mensch⟩; (shy) schüchtern

timing /'taɪmɪŋ/ n. (a) that was perfect ~! du kommst gerade im richtigen Augenblick! (b) (Theatre, Sport) Timing, das

tin /tɪn/ ① n. (a) (metal) Zinn, das; ~[plate] Weißblech, das (b) (Brit.: for preserving) [Konserven]dose, die ② v.t., **-nn-** (Brit.) zu Konserven verarbeiten

tin 'foil n. Stanniol, das; Alufolie, die

tinge /tɪndʒ/ ① v.t., ~**ing** /'tɪndʒɪŋ/ tönen ② n. [leichte] Färbung; (fig.) Hauch, der

tingle /'tɪŋgl/ v.i. kribbeln

tinker /'tɪŋkə(r)/ ① n. Kesselflicker, der ② v.i. ~ **with** sth. an etw. (Dat.) herumbasteln (ugs.)

tinkle /'tɪŋkl/ ① n. Klingeln, das ② v.i. klingeln

tinned /tɪnd/ adj. (Brit.) Dosen-

tin: ~**-opener** n. (Brit.) Dosenöffner, der; ~**pot** attrib. adj. (derog.) schäbig

tinsel /'tɪnsl/ n. Lametta, das

tint /tɪnt/ ① n. Farbton, der ② v.t. tönen; kolorieren ⟨Zeichnung⟩

tiny /'taɪnɪ/ adj. winzig

tip¹ /tɪp/ n. (end, point) Spitze, die

tip² ① v.i., **-pp-** (lean, fall) kippen; ~ **over** umkippen ② v.t., **-pp-**: (a) (make tilt) kippen (b) (make overturn) umkippen; (Brit.: discharge) kippen (c) voraussagen ⟨Sieger⟩; ~ **sb. to win** auf jmds. Sieg tippen (d) (reward) ~ **sb.** jmdm. Trinkgeld geben ③ n. (a) (money) Trinkgeld, das (b) (special information) Hinweis, der; Tipp, der (ugs.) (c) (Brit.) Müllkippe, die

■ **tip 'off** v.t. ~ sb. off jmdm. einen Hinweis od. (ugs.) Tipp geben

'tip-off n. Hinweis, der

tipsy /'tɪpsɪ/ adj. (coll.) angeheitert; beschwipst (ugs.)

tip: ~**toe** ① v.i. auf Zehenspitzen gehen; ② n. on ~**toe[s]** auf Zehenspitzen; ~**top** adj. tipptopp (ugs.)

tire¹ /'taɪə(r)/ (Amer.) ▸ TYRE

tire² ① v.t. ermüden ② v.i. müde werden; ermüden; ~ **of** sth./ doing sth. einer Sache (Gen.) überdrüssig werden

■ **tire 'out** v.t. erschöpfen; ~ oneself out doing sth. etw. bis zur Erschöpfung tun

tired /'taɪəd/ adj. (a) (weary) müde (b) (fed up) be ~ of sth./doing sth. etw. satt haben/es satt haben, etw. zu tun

tiredness /'taɪədnɪs/ n. Müdigkeit, die

'tireless adj. unermüdlich

tiresome /'taɪəsəm/ adj. (a) (wearisome) mühsam (b) (annoying) lästig

tiring /'taɪərɪŋ/ adj. ermüdend

tissue /'tɪʃuː, 'tɪsjuː/ n. (a) Gewebe, das (b) [paper] ~: Papiertuch, das; (handkerchief) Papiertaschentuch, das (c) ~ [paper] Seidenpapier, das

tit¹ /tɪt/ n. (Ornith.) Meise, die

tit² n. it's ~ for tat wie du mir, so ich dir

'titbit n. (a) (food) Häppchen, das (ugs.) (b) (piece of news) Neuigkeit, die

titchy /'tɪtʃɪ/ adj. (coll.) klitzeklein (ugs.)

titillate /'tɪtɪleɪt/ v.t. erregen

titillation /tɪtɪ'leɪʃn/ n. Kitzel, der

title /'taɪtl/ n. Titel, der

title: ~ **deed** n. (Law) Eigentumsurkunde, die; ~**holder** n. (Sport) Titelhalter, der/ -halterin, die; ~ **page** n. Titelseite, die; ~ **role** n. Titelrolle, die

tittle-tattle /'tɪtltætl/ n. Klatsch, der (ugs.)

'T-junction n. Einmündung, die

to ① /before vowel tʊ, before consonant tə, stressed tuː/ prep. (a) (in the direction of and reaching) zu; (with name of place) nach; **go to work**/**to the theatre** zur Arbeit/ins Theater gehen; **to France** nach Frankreich (b) (as far as) bis zu; **from London to Edinburgh** von London [bis] nach Edinburgh; **increase from 10% to 20%** von 10% auf 20% steigen (c) (introducing relationship or indirect object) **to sb./sth.** jmdm./einer Sache (Dat.); **lend/explain** etc. **sth. to sb.** jmdm. etw. leihen/erklären usw.; **speak to sb.** mit jmdm. sprechen; **that's all there is to it** mehr ist dazu nicht zu sagen; **what's that to you?** was geht dich das an?; **to me** (in my opinion) meiner Meinung nach; **14 miles to the gallon** 14 Meilen auf eine Gallone (d) (until) bis; **to the end** bis zum Ende; **to this day** bis heute; **five [minutes] to eight** fünf [Minuten] vor acht (e) (with infinitive of a verb) zu; (expr. purpose, or after) too um [...] zu; **want to know** wissen wollen; **do sth. to annoy sb.** etw. tun, um jmdn. zu ärgern; **too hot to drink** zu heiß zum Trinken; **he would have phoned but forgot to** er hätte angerufen, aber er vergaß es ② adv. /tuː/ **to and fro** hin und her

toad /təʊd/ n. (also fig. derog.) Kröte, die

'toadstool n. Giftpilz, der

toast /təʊst/ ① n. (a) no pl. Toast, der; **a piece of** ~: eine Scheibe Toast (b) (call to drink) Toast, der; **drink a** ~ **to sb./** sth. auf jmdn./etw. trinken ② v.t. (a) rösten; toasten ⟨Brot⟩

(b) (drink to) trinken auf (+ *Akk.*)

'toaster *n.* Toaster, *der*

'toast rack *n.* Toastständer, *der*

tobacco /təˈbækəʊ/ *n., pl.* ~s Tabak, *der*

tobacconist /təˈbækənɪst/ *n.* Tabak[waren]händler, *der*/-händlerin, *die*

toboggan /təˈbɒɡən/ [1] *n.* Schlitten, *der* [2] *v.i.* Schlitten fahren

tod /tɒd/ *n.* (Brit. coll.) **on one's ~:** [ganz] allein

today /təˈdeɪ/ [1] *n.* heute; **~'s newspaper** die Zeitung von heute [2] *adv.* heute

toddler /ˈtɒdlə(r)/ *n.* ≈ Kleinkind, *das*

to-do /təˈduː/ *n.* Getue, *das* (ugs.)

toe /təʊ/ [1] *n.* Zeh, *der;* Zehe, *die;* (of footwear) Spitze, *die* [2] *v.t.,* ~**ing** (fig.) ~ **the line** *or* (Amer.) **mark** sich einordnen

'toenail *n.* Zeh[en]nagel, *der*

toffee /ˈtɒfɪ/ *n.* Karamell, *der;* (Brit.: piece) Toffee, *das;* Sahnebonbon, *das*

'toffee apple *n.* mit Karamell überzogener Apfel am Stiel

tofu /ˈtəʊfuː/ *n., no indef. art.* Tofu, *der*

together /təˈɡeðə(r)/ *adv.* **(a)** (in or into company) zusammen **(b)** (simultaneously) gleichzeitig **(c)** (one with another) miteinander

toggle /ˈtɒɡl/ [1] *n.* **(a)** (button) Knebelknopf, *der* **(b)** (Comp.) [Kipp]schalter, *der;* Umschalttaste, *die* [2] *v.i.* (Comp.) [hin und her] schalten

toil /tɔɪl/ [1] *v.i.* schwer arbeiten [2] *n.* [harte] Arbeit

toilet /ˈtɔɪlɪt/ *n.* Toilette, *die;* **go to the ~:** auf die Toilette gehen

toilet: ~ **bag** *n.* Kulturbeutel, *der;* ~ **brush** *n.* Klosettbürste, *die;* ~ **paper** *n.* Toilettenpapier, *das*

toiletries /ˈtɔɪlɪtrɪz/ *n. pl.* Körperpflegemittel *Pl.;* Toilettenartikel *Pl.*

toilet: ~ **roll** *n.* Rolle Toilettenpapier; ~ **seat** *n.* Klosettbrille, *die* (ugs.); Toilettensitz, *der;* ~ **tissue** ▸ ~ PAPER; ~ **water** *n.* Toilettenwasser, *das;* Eau de Toilette, *das*

token /ˈtəʊkn/ [1] *n.* **(a)** (voucher) Gutschein, *der* **(b)** (counter, disc) Marke, *die* **(c)** (sign) Zeichen, *das* [2] *attrib. adj.* symbolisch ⟨*Preis*⟩

Tokyo /ˈtəʊkjəʊ/ *pr. n.* Tokio (*das*)

told ▸ TELL

tolerable /ˈtɒlərəbl/ *adj.* **(a)** (endurable) erträglich **(to, for** für) **(b)** (fairly good) leidlich; annehmbar

tolerance /ˈtɒlərəns/ *n.* Toleranz, *die*

tolerant /ˈtɒlərənt/ *adj.* tolerant (**of, towards** gegen[über])

tolerate /ˈtɒləreɪt/ *v.t.* dulden; (bear) ertragen ⟨*Schmerzen*⟩

toleration /tɒləˈreɪʃn/ *n.* Tolerierung, *die* (geh.)

toll¹ /təʊl/ *n.* **(a)** (tax, duty) Gebühr, *die* **(b)** (damage etc.) Aufwand, *der;* **take its ~ of** sth. einen Tribut an etw. (*Dat.*) fordern (fig.)

toll² *v.i.* ⟨*Glocke:*⟩ läuten

toll: ~ **bridge** *n.* gebührenpflichtige Brücke; ~**road** *n.* gebührenpflichtige Straße; Mautstraße, *die* (bes. österr.)

tom /tɒm/ *n.* (cat) Kater, *der*

tomato /təˈmɑːtəʊ/ *n., pl.* ~**es** Tomate, *die*

tomato: ~ **juice** *n.* Tomatensaft, *der;* ~ **ketchup** *n.* Tomatenketschup, *der od. das;* ~ **purée** *n.* Tomatenmark, *das*

tomb /tuːm/ *n.* Grab, *das;* (monument) Grabmal, *das*

'tomboy *n.* Wildfang, *der*

'tombstone *n.* Grabstein, *der*

'tomcat *n.* Kater, *der*

tome /təʊm/ *n.* dicker Band; Wälzer, *der* (ugs.)

tomfoolery /tɒmˈfuːlərɪ/ *n.* Blödsinn, *der* (ugs.)

tomorrow /təˈmɒrəʊ/ [1] *n.* morgen; ~ **morning/afternoon/evening/night** morgen früh *od.* Vormittag/Nachmittag/Abend/ Nacht; **~'s newspaper** die morgige Zeitung [2] *adv.* morgen; **see you ~!** (coll.) bis morgen!; **the day after ~:** übermorgen

ton /tʌn/ *n.* Tonne, *die*

tone /təʊn/ [1] *n.* **(a)** (sound) Klang, *der;* (Teleph.) Ton, *der* **(b)** (style of speaking) Ton, *der* **(c)** (tint, shade) [Farb]ton, *der* **(d)** (fig.: character) **lower/raise the ~ of** sth. das Niveau einer Sache (*Gen.*) senken/ erhöhen; **set the ~:** den Ton angeben [2] *v.t.* tönen; abtönen ⟨*Farbe*⟩

▪ **tone 'down** *v.t.* [ab]dämpfen ⟨*Farbe*⟩; (fig.) mäßigen ⟨*Sprache*⟩

tone: ~-'deaf *adj.* ohne musikalisches Gehör; ~ **dialling** (Teleph.) *n.* Tonwahl, *die*

tongs /tɒŋz/ *n. pl.* [pair of] ~: Zange, *die*

tongue /tʌŋ/ *n.* Zunge, *die;* **bite one's ~** (lit. or fig.) sich auf die Zunge beißen; **find one's ~:** seine Sprache wieder finden; **hold one's ~:** stillschweigen; **he made the remark ~ in cheek** (fig.) er meinte die Bemerkung nicht ernst

tongue: ~-**tied** *adj.* schüchtern; ~-**twister** *n.* Zungenbrecher, *der* (ugs.)

tonic /ˈtɒnɪk/ [1] *n.* **(a)** (Med.) Tonikum, *das* **(b)** (fig.: invigorating influence) Wohltat, *die* (geh.) **(c)** (~ water) Tonic, *das* [2] *attrib. adj.* kräftigend; (fig.) wohltuend ⟨*Wirkung*⟩

'tonic water *n.* Tonic[wasser], *das*

tonight /təˈnaɪt/ [1] *n.* **(a)** (this evening) heute Abend; **~'s performance** die heutige [Abend]vorstellung **(b)** (this or the coming night) heute Nacht ····⟩

② *adv.* (a) (this evening) heute Abend
(b) (during this or the coming night) heute Nacht;
[I'll] see you ∼! bis heute Abend!

tonne /tʌn/ *n.* [metrische] Tonne

tonsil /'tɒnsl/ *n.* [Gaumen]mandel, *die;* have one's ∼s out sich (*Dat.*) die Mandeln herausnehmen lassen

tonsillitis /tɒnsə'laɪtɪs/ *n.* Mandelentzündung, *die*

too /tuː/ *adv.* (a) (excessively) zu; ∼ difficult a task eine zu schwierige Aufgabe
(b) (also) auch
(c) (coll.: very) besonders; not ∼ pleased nicht gerade erfreut

took ▶ TAKE

tool /tuːl/ *n.* (a) Werkzeug, *das;* (garden ∼) Gerät, *das;* [set of] ∼s Werkzeug, *das*
(b) (Comp.) Tool, *das;* Werkzeug, *das*
(c) (fig.: means) [Hilfs]mittel, *das*

tool: ∼**bar** *n.* (Comp.) Werkzeugleiste, *die;* ∼**box** *n.* Werkzeugkasten, *der;* ∼ **kit** *n.* Werkzeug, *das*

toot /tuːt/ ① *v.i.* (on car etc. horn) hupen
② *n.* Tuten, *das*

tooth /tuːθ/ *n., pl.* **teeth** /tiːθ/ (a) Zahn, *der*
(b) (of rake, fork, comb) Zinke, *die;* (of cogwheel, saw) Zahn, *der*

tooth: ∼**ache** *n.* Zahnschmerzen *Pl.;* ∼**brush** *n.* Zahnbürste, *die;* ∼ **decay** *n.* Zahnverfall, *der;* ∼**glass** *n.* Zahnputzglas, *das;* ∼ **mug** *n.* Zahnputzbecher, *der;* ∼**paste** *n.* Zahnpasta, *die;* ∼**pick** *n.* Zahnstocher, *der;* ∼ **powder** *n.* Zahnpulver, *das*

top¹ /tɒp/ ① *n.* (a) (highest part) Spitze, *die;* (of table) Platte, *die;* (∼ end) oberes Ende; (of tree) Wipfel, *der;* (∼ floor) oberstes Stockwerk; (rim of glass) Rand, *der;* on ∼ of one another aufeinander; on ∼ of sth. (fig.: in addition) zusätzlich zu etw.; from ∼ to bottom von oben bis unten; at the ∼: oben; at the ∼ of the building/hill/stairs oben im Gebäude/ [oben] auf dem Hügel/[oben] auf dem Stapel/ oben an der Treppe
(b) (highest rank) Spitze, *die;* ∼ of the table (Sport) Tabellenspitze, *die;* be [at the] ∼ of the class der/die Klassenbeste sein
(c) (upper surface) Oberfläche, *die;* (of cupboard, chest) Oberseite, *die;* on ∼ of sth. [oben] auf etw. (*position: Dat.; direction: Akk.*)
(d) (folding roof) Verdeck, *das*
(e) (upper deck of bus) Oberdeck, *das*
(f) (cap of pen) [Verschluss]kappe, *die*
(g) (upper garment) Oberteil, *das*
(h) (lid) Deckel, *der;* (of bottle) Stöpsel, *der*
② *adj.* oberst...; höchst... ⟨*Ton, Preis*⟩; ∼ end oberes Ende; the ∼ pupil der beste Schüler; ∼ speed Spitzen- *od.* Höchstgeschwindigkeit, *die*
③ *v.t.* (a) (be taller than) überragen
(b) (surpass) übertreffen

■ **top 'up** (Brit. coll.) *v.t.* auffüllen ⟨*Tank, Flasche, Glas*⟩

top² *n.* (toy) Kreisel, *der*

top: ∼**-flight** *attrib. adj.* erstrangig; Spitzen⟨*sportler, -politiker*⟩; ∼ **'hat** *n.* Zylinder[hut], *der;* ∼**-heavy** *adj.* oberlastig

topic /'tɒpɪk/ *n.* Thema, *das*

topical /'tɒpɪkl/ *adj.* aktuell

'topless *adj.* a ∼ dress/swimsuit ein busenfreies Kleid/ein Oben-ohne-Badeanzug; go/bathe ∼: oben ohne gehen/baden

top-level *attrib. adj.* Gipfel⟨*treffen, -konferenz*⟩; ∼**-level negotiations/deals** Verhandlungen/Vereinbarungen auf höchster Ebene

topmost /'tɒpməʊst, 'tɒpməst/ *adj.* oberst...; höchst... ⟨*Gipfel, Note*⟩

top-'notch *adj.* (coll.) fantastisch (ugs.)

topple /'tɒpl/ ① *v.i.* fallen
② *v.t.* stürzen

■ **topple 'down** *v.i.* hinab-/herabfallen

■ **topple 'over** *v.i.* umfallen

top: ∼**-quality** *adj.* [qualitativ] hochwertig; ∼**-ranking** *attrib. adj.* Spitzen⟨*funktionär, -beamter, -politiker, -sportler*⟩; hochrangig ⟨*Offizier*⟩; ∼ **'secret** *adj.* streng geheim; ∼**soil** *n.* Mutterboden, *der*

topsy-turvy /tɒpsɪ'tɜːvɪ/ *adv.* verkehrtrum (ugs.); turn sth. ∼: etw. auf den Kopf stellen (ugs.)

'top-up *n.* (coll.) Auffüllung, *die;* I need a ∼: ich muss mir noch mal nachgießen/ nachgießen lassen

torch /tɔːtʃ/ *n.* (Brit.) Taschenlampe, *die*

'torchlight *n.* Licht der einer Taschenlampe; by ∼light im Schein einer Taschenlampe

tore, torn ▶ TEAR¹ 2, 3

torment ① /'tɔːment/ *n.* Qual, *die*
② /tɔː'ment/ *v.t.* quälen

tornado /tɔː'neɪdəʊ/ *n., pl.* ∼**es** Wirbelsturm, *der;* (in North America) Tornado, *der*

torpedo /tɔː'piːdəʊ/ ① *n., pl.* ∼**es** Torpedo, *der*
② *v.t.* torpedieren

torrent /'tɒrənt/ *n.* reißender Bach; (fig.) Flut, *die*

torrential /tə'renʃl/ *adj.* wolkenbruchartig ⟨*Regen*⟩

torso /'tɔːsəʊ/ *n., pl.* ∼**s** Rumpf, *der;* bare ∼: nackter Oberkörper

tortoise /'tɔːtəs/ *n.* Schildkröte, *die*

tortoiseshell /'tɔːtəsʃel/ *n.* Schildpatt, *das*

tortuous /'tɔːtjʊəs/ *adj.* verschlungen; (fig.) umständlich

torture /'tɔːtʃə(r)/ ① *n.* Folter, *die*
② *v.t.* foltern; (fig.) quälen

Tory /'tɔːrɪ/ (Brit. Polit. coll.) *n.* Tory, *der*

toss /tɒs/ ① *v.t.* (a) (throw upwards) hochwerfen; ∼ a pancake einen Pfannkuchen [durch Hochwerfen] wenden
(b) (throw casually) werfen; schmeißen (ugs.)
(c) ∼ a coin eine Münze werfen

(d) (Cookery: mix) wenden; mischen ⟨*Salat*⟩
② *v.i.* (a) ~ **and turn** sich [schlaflos] im
Bett wälzen
(b) ⟨*Schiff:*⟩ hin und her geworfen werden
(c) (~ coin) eine Münze werfen; ~ **for sth.**
mit einer Münze um etw. losen
③ *n.* (a) ~ **of a coin** Hochwerfen einer
Münze
(b) (throw) Wurf, *der*
(c) **I couldn't give a** ~ (fig. Brit. sl.) es ist mir
scheißegal (salopp)
∎ **toss 'up** *v.i.* eine Münze werfen; ~ **up for**
sth. mit einer Münze um etw. losen

tot¹ /tɒt/ *n.* (coll.) (a) kleines Kind
(b) (of liquor) Gläschen, *das*

tot² (coll.) *v.t.,* -tt-: ~ '**up** zusammenziehen
(ugs.)

total /'təʊtl/ ① *adj.* (a) gesamt;
Gesamt⟨*gewicht, -wert, usw.*⟩
(b) (absolute) völlig *nicht präd.;* **a** ~ **beginner**
ein absoluter Anfänger
② *n.* (number) Gesamtzahl, *die;* (amount)
Gesamtbetrag, *der;* (result of addition) Summe,
die; **a** ~ **of 200** insgesamt 200; **in** ~:
insgesamt
③ *v.t.,* (Brit.) -ll-: (a) addieren,
zusammenzählen ⟨*Zahlen*⟩
(b) (amount to) [insgesamt] betragen

total e'clipse *n.* (Astron.) totale Finsternis

totalitarian /təʊtælɪ'teərɪən/ *adj.* totalitär

'**totally** *adv.* völlig

totter /'tɒtə(r)/ *v.i.* wanken; taumeln

touch /tʌtʃ/ ① *v.t.* (a) berühren
(b) (harm) anrühren
(c) (fig.: rival) ~ **sth.** an etw. (*Akk.*)
heranreichen
(d) (affect emotionally) rühren
② *v.i.* sich berühren; **don't** ~! nicht
anfassen!
③ *n.* (a) Berührung, *die*
(b) *no art.* (faculty) [sense of] ~: Tastsinn,
der
(c) (small amount) **a** ~ **of salt/pepper** etc. eine
Spur Salz/Pfeffer *usw.;* **a** ~ **of irony** etc. ein
Anflug von Ironie *usw.*
(d) (fig.) Detail, *das*
(e) (communication) **be in/out of** ~ [**with sb.**]
[mit jmdm.] Kontakt/keinen Kontakt haben;
get in ~: mit jmdm. Kontakt aufnehmen
∎ **touch 'down** *v.i.* ⟨*Flugzeug:*⟩ landen
∎ '**touch on** *v.t.* (mention) ansprechen
∎ **touch 'up** *v.t.* (improve) ausbessern

'**touch:** ~-**and-go** *adj.* **it is** ~-**and-go**
[**whether...**] es steht auf des Messers
Schneide [, ob...]; ~**down** *n.* (Aeronaut.)
Landung, *die*

'**touching** *adj.* rührend

touch: ~**line** *n.* (Footb., Rugby) Seitenlinie,
die; ~**paper** *n.* Zündpapier, *das;* (on
firework) Papierlunte, *die;* ~**tone** *adj.* a
~-**tone telephone** ein Telefon mit
Mehrfrequenzwahl; ~-**type** *v.i.* blind
schreiben; ~-**typing** *n.* Blindschreiben,
das

touchy /'tʌtʃɪ/ *adj.* empfindlich; heikel
⟨*Thema*⟩

tough /tʌf/ *adj.* (a) fest ⟨*Material, Stoff*⟩;
zäh ⟨*Fleisch; fachspr.: Werkstoff, Metall*⟩;
widerstandsfähig ⟨*Belag, Glas, Haut*⟩;
strapazierfähig ⟨*Kleidung*⟩
(b) (hardy) zäh ⟨*Person*⟩
(c) (difficult) schwierig
(d) (severe, harsh) hart
(e) (coll.) ~ **luck** Pech, *das*

toughen /'tʌfn/ *v.t.* ~ [**up**] abhärten
⟨*Person*⟩; verschärfen ⟨*Gesetz*⟩

toupee, toupet /'tu:peɪ/ *n.* Toupet, *das*

tour /tʊə(r)/ ① *n.* (a) [Rund]reise, *die;* Tour,
die (ugs.)
(b) (Theatre, Sport) Tournee, *die*
(c) (of house etc.) Besichtigung, *die*
(d) ~ [**of duty**] Dienstzeit, *die*
② *v.i.* (a) ~/**go** ~**ing in** *or* **through a**
country eine Reise *od.* (ugs.) Tour durch ein
Land machen
(b) (Theatre, Sport) eine Tournee machen
③ *v.t.* (a) besichtigen ⟨*Stadt, Gebäude*⟩; ~ **a**
country/region eine Reise *od.* (ugs.) Tour
durch ein Land/Gebiet machen
(b) (Theatre, Sport) ~ **a country/the provinces**
eine Tournee durch das Land/die Provinz
machen

tour de force /tʊə də 'fɔːs/ *n., pl.* **tours de**
force /tʊə də 'fɔːs/ Glanzleistung, *die*

'**tour guide** *n.* Reiseführer, *der/*
Reiseführerin, *die;* (book) Reiseführer, *der*
(**to, of** von)

'**touring holiday** *n.* **have a** ~ **in a country**
in den Ferien/im Urlaub durch ein Land
fahren

tourism /'tʊərɪzm/ *n.* (a) Tourismus, *der*
(b) (operation of tours) Touristik, *die*

tourist /'tʊərɪst/ ① *n.* Tourist, *der/*
Touristin, *die*
② *attrib. adj.* Touristen-

tourist: ~ **agency** *n.* Reisebüro, *das;*
~ **attraction** *n.* Touristenattraktion, *die;*
~ **board** *n.* (Brit.) Amt für
Fremdenverkehrswesen; ~ **class** *n.*
Touristenklasse, *die;* ~ **hotel** *n.*
Touristenhotel, *das;* ~ **industry** *n.*
Tourismusindustrie, *die;* ~ **infor'mation**
centre, ~ **office** *ns.*
Fremdenverkehrsbüro, *das;*
Touristeninformation, *die* (ugs.);
~ **season** *n.* Touristensaison, *die;*
~ **trade** ▸ ~ INDUSTRY

'**touristy** /'tʊərɪstɪ/ *adj.* (derog.) auf
Tourismus getrimmt (ugs.); Touristen⟨*stadt,*
-nest, -gegend⟩ (ugs. abwertend)

'**tour leader** *n.* Reiseleiter, *der/*-leiterin,
die

tournament /'tʊənəmənt/ *n.* (Hist.; Sport)
Turnier, *das*

tourniquet /'tʊənɪkeɪ/ *n.* (Med.)
Tourniquet, *das*

'**tour operator** *n.* Reiseveranstalter, *der/*
-veranstalterin, *die*

t

tousle /'taʊzl/ v.t. zerzausen

tout /taʊt/ 1 v.i. ~ **for customers** Kunden anreißen (ugs.) od. werben
2 n. Anreißer, der/Anreißerin, die (ugs.); **ticket** ~: Kartenschwarzhändler, der/ -händlerin, die

tow /təʊ/ 1 v.t. schleppen; ziehen ‹Anhänger, Wasserskiläufer›
2 n. Schleppen, das; **give a car a** ~: einen Wagen schleppen; **on** ~: im Schlepp[tau]
■ **tow a'way** v.t. abschleppen

toward /tə'wɔːd/, **towards** /tə'wɔːdz/ prep. (a) (in direction of) ~ **sb./sth.** auf jmdn./ etw. zu; **turn** ~ **sb.** sich zu jmdm. umdrehen
(b) (in relation to) gegenüber; **feel sth.** ~ **sb.** jmdm. gegenüber etw. empfinden
(c) (for) a **contribution** ~ **sth.** ein Beitrag zu etw.; **proposals** ~ **solving a problem** Vorschläge zur Lösung eines Problems
(d) (near) gegen; ~ **the end of May** [gegen] Ende Mai

'tow bar n. (Motor Veh.) Anhängerkupplung, die

towel /'taʊəl/ n. Handtuch, das

towelling (Amer.: **toweling**) /'taʊəlɪŋ/ n., no indef. art. Frottierware, die

'towel rail n. Handtuchhalter, der

tower /'taʊə(r)/ 1 n. Turm, der
2 v.i. in die Höhe ragen
■ **'tower above** v.t. ~ **above sb./sth.** jmdn./etw. überragen

'tower block n. Hochhaus, das

'towering attrib. adj. hoch aufragend; (fig.) herausragend ‹Leistung›

town /taʊn/ n. Stadt, die; **the** ~ **of Cambridge** die Stadt Cambridge; **in [the]** ~: in der Stadt; **the** ~ (people) die Stadt; **be in/ out of** ~: in der Stadt/nicht in der Stadt sein

town: ~ **'centre** n. Stadtmitte, die; Stadtzentrum, das; ~ **'council** n. (Brit.) Stadtrat, der; ~ **'councillor** n. (Brit.) Stadtrat, der/-rätin, die; ~ **'hall** n. Rathaus, das; ~ **house** n. (residence in ~) Stadthaus, das; (terrace house) Reihenhaus, das

townie /'taʊnɪ/ n. Stadtmensch, der

town: ~ **'planner** n. Stadtplaner, der/ -planerin, die; ~ **'planning** n. Stadtplanung, die

tow: ~**path** n. Leinpfad, der; ~ **rope** n. Abschleppseil, das

toxic /'tɒksɪk/ adj. giftig

toxicity /tɒk'sɪsɪtɪ/ n. Giftigkeit, die

toxic 'waste n. Giftmüll der; ~ **tip** or **dump** Giftmülldeponie, die

toxin /'tɒksɪn/ n. Toxin, das

toy /tɔɪ/ 1 n. Spielzeug, das; ~**s** Spielzeug, das
2 adj. Spielzeug-
3 v.i. ~ **with the idea of doing sth.** mit dem Gedanken spielen, etw. zu tun

toy: ~ **boy** n. (coll.) Gespiele, der (scherzh.); ~**shop** n. Spielwarengeschäft, das

trace /treɪs/ 1 v.t. (a) (copy) durchpausen; abpausen
(b) (zeichnen ‹Linie›
(c) (follow track of) folgen (+ Dat.); verfolgen
(d) (find) finden
2 n. Spur, die

'trace element n. (Chem.) Spurenelement, das

'tracing paper /'treɪsɪŋ peɪpə(r)/ n. Pauspapier, das

track /træk/ 1 n. (a) Spur, die; (of wild animal) Fährte, die; ~**s** (footprints) [Fuß]spuren; (of animal also) Fährte, die; **keep** ~ **of sb./sth.** jmdn./etw. im Auge behalten
(b) (path) Weg, der; (footpath) Pfad, der
(c) (Sport) Bahn, die; **cycling/greyhound** ~: Radrennbahn, die/Windhundrennbahn, die
(d) (Railw.) Gleis, das
(e) (course taken) Route, die; (of rocket, satellite) Bahn, die
2 v.t. ~ **an animal** die Spur/Fährte eines Tieres verfolgen; **the police** ~**ed him [to Paris]** die Polizei folgte seiner Spur [bis nach Paris]

■ **track 'down** v.t. aufspüren

'trackball, 'tracker ball ns. (Comp.) Rollball, der

'track events n. pl. Laufwettbewerbe Pl.

'tracking station n. (Astronaut.) Bahnverfolgungsstation, die

'track: ~**shoe** n. Rennschuh, der; ~**suit** n. Trainingsanzug, der

tract[1] /trækt/ n. (area) Gebiet, das

tract[2] n. (pamphlet) [Flug]schrift, die

tractor /'træktə(r)/ n. Traktor, der

trad /træd/ (Mus. coll.) adj. traditional (Jargon); ~ **jazz** Traditional Jazz, der

trade /treɪd/ 1 n. (a) (line of business) Gewerbe, das; **he's a butcher/lawyer** etc. **by** ~: er ist von Beruf Metzger/Rechtsanwalt usw.
(b) no indef. art (commerce) Handel, der
(c) (craft) Handwerk, das
2 v.i. (buy and sell) Handel treiben
3 v.t. tauschen; austauschen ‹Waren, Grüße›; sich (Dat.) sagen ‹Beleidigungen›; ~ **sth. for sth.** etw. gegen etw. tauschen
■ **trade 'in** v.t. in Zahlung geben
■ **trade 'up** v.i. sich verbessern

trade: ~ **balance** n. Handelsbilanz, die; ~ **deficit** n. passive Handelsbilanz; Handelsbilanzdefizit, das; ~ **'discount** n. Branchenrabatt, der; ~ **fair** n. [Fach]messe, die; ~ **journal** n. Fachzeitschrift, die; ~ **mark** n. Warenzeichen, das; **leave one's** ~ **mark on sth.** (fig.) einer Sache (Dat.) seinen Stempel aufdrücken; ~ **name** n. Fachbezeichnung, die; (proprietary name) Markenname, der; ~ **price** n. Einkaufspreis, der

'trader n. Händler, der/Händlerin, die

trade: ~ **'secret** n. Geschäftsgeheimnis, das; ~**sman** /'treɪdzmən/ n., pl. ~**smen** /'treɪdzmən/ (shopkeeper) [Einzel]händler, der;

(craftsman) Handwerker, *der;* ∼ **'union** *n.* Gewerkschaft, *die; attrib.* Gewerkschafts-; ∼ **'unionist** *n.* Gewerkschaft[l]er, *der*/ Gewerkschaft[l]erin, *die*

trading /'treɪdɪŋ/ *n.* Handel, *der*

trading: ∼ **estate** *n.* (Brit.) Gewerbegebiet, *das;* ∼ **hours** *n. pl.* Geschäftszeit, *die; during/outside* ∼ **hours** während/außerhalb der Geschäftszeit; 'Trading hours: …' „Geschäftszeiten: …"; ∼ **partner** *n.* Handelspartner, *der*

tradition /trə'dɪʃn/ *n.* Tradition, *die*

traditional /trə'dɪʃənl/ *adj.* traditionell; herkömmlich ⟨*Erziehung, Methode*⟩

tra'ditionally *adv.* traditionell

traffic /'træfɪk/ ① *n.* **(a)** *no indef. art.* Verkehr, *der*
(b) (trade) Handel, *der*
② *v.i.,* -ck-: ∼ in sth. mit etw. handeln

traffic: ∼ **calming** *n.* Verkehrsberuhigung, *die;* ∼ **circle** *n.* (Amer.) Kreisverkehr, *der;* ∼ **cone** *n.* Pylon, *der;* Leitkegel, *der;* ∼ **island** *n.* Verkehrsinsel, *die;* ∼ **jam** *n.* [Verkehrs]stau, *der*

trafficker /'træfɪkə(r)/ *n.* Händler, *der*/ Händlerin, *die;* ∼ in drugs: Drogenhändler, *der*/-händlerin, *die*

traffic: ∼ **lights** *n. pl.* [Verkehrs]ampel, *die;* ∼ **police** *n.* Verkehrspolizei, *die;* ∼ **report** *n.* Verkehrsübersicht, *die;* (on radio) Verkehrsservice, *der;* ∼ **sign** *n.* Verkehrszeichen, *das;* ∼ **signals** ▶ ∼ LIGHTS; ∼ **warden** *n.* (Brit.) Hilfspolizist, *der;* (woman) Hilfspolizistin, *die;* Politesse, *die*

tragedy /'trædʒɪdɪ/ *n.* Tragödie, *die*

tragic /'trædʒɪk/ *adj.* tragisch

trail /treɪl/ ① *n.* **(a)** Spur, *die;* ∼ of smoke/ dust Rauch-/Staubfahne, *die*
(b) (Hunting) Spur, *die;* Fährte, *die*
(c) (path) Pfad, *der;* Weg, *der*
② *v.t.* **(a)** (pursue) verfolgen
(b) (drag) ∼ sth. [after *or* behind one] etw. hinter sich (*Dat.*) herziehen
③ *v.i.* **(a)** (be dragged) schleifen
(b) (lag) hinterhertrotten
(c) ⟨*Pflanze:*⟩ kriechen

trailer /'treɪlə(r)/ *n.* **(a)** Anhänger, *der;* (Amer.: caravan) Wohnanhänger, *der*
(b) (Cinemat., Telev.) Trailer, *der*

train /treɪn/ ① *v.t.* **(a)** ausbilden (in in + *Dat.*); erziehen ⟨*Kind*⟩; abrichten ⟨*Hund*⟩; dressieren ⟨*Tier*⟩
(b) (Sport) trainieren
(c) (Hort.) ziehen
② *v.i.* **(a)** eine Ausbildung machen; he is ∼ing as *or* to be a doctor/engineer er macht eine Arzt-/Ingenieursausbildung
(b) (Sport) trainieren
③ *n.* **(a)** (Railw.) Zug, *der;* on the ∼: im Zug
(b) (of skirt etc.) Schleppe, *die*
(c) ∼ of thought Gedankengang, *der*

'train driver *n.* Lokomotivführer, *der*/ -führerin, *die*

trained /treɪnd/ *adj.* ausgebildet ⟨*Arbeiter, Lehrer, Arzt, Stimme*⟩; abgerichtet ⟨*Hund*⟩; dressiert ⟨*Tier*⟩; geschult ⟨*Geist, Auge, Ohr*⟩

trainee /treɪ'ni:/ *n.* Auszubildende, *der*/*die*

'trainer *n.* [Konditions]trainer, *der*/ -trainerin, *die*

'train fare *n.* Fahrpreis, *der*

'training *n.* **(a)** Ausbildung, *die*
(b) (Sport) Training, *das*

training: ∼ **camp** *n.* (Sport) Trainingslager, *das;* ∼ **college** *n.* berufsbildende Schule; ∼ **course** *n.* Lehrgang, *der;* ∼ **scheme** *n.* Ausbildungsprogramm, *das;* ∼ **shoes** *n. pl.* Trainingsschuhe *Pl.*

train: ∼ **journey** *n.* Bahnfahrt, *die;* (long) Bahnreise, *die;* ∼ **service** *n.* Zugverbindung, *die;* ∼ **set** *n.* [Modell]eisenbahn, *die;* ∼**spotting** *n.:* das Aufschreiben von Lokomotivnummern als Hobby; ∼ **station** *n.* (Amer.) Bahnhof, *der*

traipse /treɪps/ *v.i.* (coll.) latschen (salopp)
■ **traipse about, traipse around** *v.i.* rumlatschen (salopp)

trait /treɪt/ *n.* Eigenschaft, *die*

traitor /'treɪtə(r)/ *n.* Verräter, *der*/ Verräterin, *die*

traitorous /'treɪtərəs/ *adj.* verräterisch

trajectory /trə'dʒektərɪ/ *n.* [Flug]bahn, *die*

tram /træm/ *n.* (Brit.) Straßenbahn, *die;* ∼lines Straßenbahnschienen *Pl.*

tramp /træmp/ ① *n.* Landstreicher, *der*/ -streicherin, *die;* (in city) Stadtstreicher, *der*/ -streicherin, *die*
② *v.i.* **(a)** (tread heavily) trampeln
(b) (walk) marschieren

trample /'træmpl/ ① *v.t.* zertrampeln
② *v.i.* trampeln
■ **'trample on** *v.t.* herumtrampeln auf (+ *Dat.*)

trampoline /'træmpəli:n/ *n.* Trampolin, *das*

'tram stop *n.* Straßenbahnhaltestelle, *die*

trance /trɑ:ns/ *n.* Trance, *die;* be in a ∼: in Trance sein

tranquil /'træŋkwɪl/ *adj.* ruhig

tranquillity /træŋ'kwɪlɪtɪ/ Ruhe, *die*

tranquillizer /'træŋkwɪlaɪzə(r)/ *n.* Beruhigungsmittel, *das*

transact /træn'zækt/ *v.t.* ∼ business Geschäfte tätigen

transaction /træn'zækʃn/ *n.* Geschäft, *das;* (financial) Transaktion, *die*

transatlantic /trænsət'læntɪk/ *adj.* transatlantisch

transcend /træn'send/ *v.t.* übersteigen

transcript /'trænskrɪpt/ *n.* Abschrift, *die;* (of trial) Protokoll, *das*

transfer ① /træns'fɜː(r)/ *v.t.,* -rr-: ⋯⟶

(a) (move) verlegen (**to** nach); überweisen ⟨*Geld*⟩ (**to** auf + *Akk.*); übertragen (*Befugnis, Macht*) (**to** *Dat.*)
(b) übereignen ⟨*Gegenstand, Grundbesitz*⟩ (**to** *Dat.*)
(c) versetzen ⟨*Arbeiter, Angestellte*⟩; (Footb.) transferieren
② /træns'fɜː(r)/ *v.i.*, **-rr-:** **(a)** (when travelling) umsteigen
(b) (change job etc.) wechseln
③ /'trænsfɜː(r)/ *n.* **(a)** (moving) Verlegung, *die;* (of powers) Übertragung, *die* (**to** an + *Akk.*); (of money) Überweisung, *die*
(b) (of employee etc.) Versetzung, *die;* (Footb.) Transfer, *der*
(c) (picture) Abziehbild, *das*
transferable /træns'fɜːrəbl/ *adj.* übertragbar

'**transfer:** ~ **fee** *n.* (Footb.) Ablösesumme, *die;* Transfersumme, *die* (fachspr.); ~ **list** *n.* (Footb.) Transferliste, *die*
transform /træns'fɔːm/ *v.t.* verwandeln
transformation /trænsfə'meɪʃn/ *n.* Verwandlung, *die*
trans'former *n.* (Electr.) Transformator, *der*
transfusion /træns'fjuːʒn/ *n.* (Med.) Transfusion, *die*
transient /'trænzɪənt/ *adj.* kurzlebig; vergänglich
transistor /træn'zɪstə(r)/ *n.* Transistor, *der*
transit /'trænsɪt/ *n.* **in** ~**:** auf der Durchreise; ⟨*Waren*⟩ auf dem Transport; **passengers in** ~**:** Transitreisende *Pl.*
transition /træn'sɪʒn, træn'zɪʃn/ *n.* Übergang, *der;* Wechsel, *der*
transitional /træn'zɪʃənl/ *adj.* Übergangs-
transitive /'trænsɪtɪv/ *adj.* (Ling.) transitiv
'**transit lounge** *n.* Transithalle, *die*
transitory /'trænsɪtəri/ *adj.* vergänglich; (fleeting) flüchtig
'**transit passenger** *n.* Transitpassagier, *der*
translate /træns'leɪt/ *v.t.* übersetzen
translation /træns'leɪʃn/ *n.* Übersetzung, *die*
translator /træns'leɪtə(r)/ *n.* Übersetzer, *der/*Übersetzerin, *die*
translucent /træns'luːsənt/ *adj.* durchscheinend
transmission /træns'mɪʃn/ *n.* **(a)** Übertragung, *die*
(b) (Motor Veh.) Antrieb, *der;* (gearbox) Getriebe, *das*
transmit /træns'mɪt/ *v.t.*, **-tt-:** **(a)** (pass on) übersenden; übertragen
(b) durchlassen ⟨*Licht*⟩; leiten ⟨*Wärme*⟩
trans'mitter *n.* Sender, *der*
transparency /træns'pærənsɪ/ *n.* **(a)** Durchsichtigkeit, *die*
(b) (Photog.) Transparent, *das;* (slide) Dia, *das*
transparent /træns'pærənt/ *adj.* durchsichtig

transparently /træns'pærəntlɪ/ *adv.* offenkundig; ~ **obvious** ganz offenkundig
transpire /træn'spaɪə(r)/ *v.i.* sich herausstellen; (coll.: happen) passieren
transplant ① /træns'plɑːnt/ *v.t.* **(a)** verpflanzen ⟨*Organ*⟩
(b) (plant in another place) umpflanzen
② /'trænsplɑːnt/ *n.* (Med.) Transplantation, *die;* Verpflanzung, *die*
transport ① /træns'pɔːt/ *v.t.* transportieren; befördern
② /'trænspɔːt/ *n.* **(a)** Transport, *der;* Beförderung, *die; attrib.* Beförderungs-
(b) (means of conveyance) Verkehrsmittel, *das;* **be without** ~**:** kein [eigenes] Fahrzeug haben
'**transport café** *n.* (Brit.) Fernfahrerlokal, *das*
transpose /træns'pəʊz/ *v.t.* vertauschen; umstellen
transsexual /træns'seksjʊəl/ ① *adj.* transsexuell
② *n.* Transsexuelle, *der/die*
transvestite /træns'vestaɪt/ *n.* Transvestit, *der*
trap /træp/ ① *n.* **(a)** Falle, *die;* **set** *or* **lay a** ~ **for an animal** eine Falle für ein Tier legen *od.* aufstellen; **set** *or* **lay a** ~ **for sb.** (fig.) jmdm. eine Falle stellen; **fall into a/sb.'s** ~ (fig.) in die/jmdm. in die Falle gehen
(b) (sl.: mouth) Klappe, *die* (salopp)
② *v.t.*, **-pp-:** **(a)** [in *od.* mit einer Falle] fangen ⟨*Tier*⟩; (fig.) in eine Falle locken ⟨*Person*⟩; **be** ~**ped** (fig.) in eine Falle gehen/in der Falle sitzen; **be** ~**ped in a cave/by the tide** in einer Höhle festsitzen/von der Flut abgeschnitten sein
(b) (confine) einschließen; einklemmen ⟨*Körperteil*⟩
'**trapdoor** *n.* Falltür, *die*
trapeze /trə'piːz/ *n.* Trapez, *das*
tra'peze artist *n.* Trapezkünstler, *der/* -künstlerin, *die*
trash /træʃ/ *n.* **(a)** (rubbish) Abfall, *der*
(b) (badly made thing) Mist, *der* (ugs.); (bad literature) Schund, *der* (ugs.)
trauma /'trɔːmə/ *n., pl.* ~**ta** /'trɔːmətə/ *or* ~**s** Trauma, *das*
traumatic /trɔː'mætɪk/ *adj.* traumatisch
traumatize /'trɔːmətaɪz/ *v.t.* traumatisieren
travel /'trævl/ ① *n.* Reisen, *das; attrib.* Reise-
② *v.i.*, (Brit.) **-ll-** reisen; (go in vehicle) fahren
③ *v.t.*, (Brit.) **-ll-** zurücklegen ⟨*Strecke, Entfernung*⟩; benutzen ⟨*Weg, Straße*⟩; **we had** ~**led 10 miles** wir waren 10 Meilen gefahren
■ **travel a'bout, travel a'round** *v.i.* umherreisen

travel: ~ **agency** *n.* Reisebüro, *das;* ~ **agent** *n.* Reisebürokaufmann, *der/* -kauffrau, *die;* ~ **brochure** *n.* Reiseprospekt, *der;* ~ **bureau** *n.* Reisebüro, *das*

traveler, traveling (Amer.) ▶ TRAVELL-

'travel insurance n. Reiseversicherung, *die*

traveller /'trævlə(r)/ n. (Brit.) **(a)** Reisende, *der/die*
(b) *in pl.* (gypsies etc.) fahrendes Volk

'traveller's cheque n. Reisescheck, *der*

travelling /'trævlɪŋ/ *attrib. adj.* (Brit.) Wander⟨zirkus, -ausstellung⟩

travelling: ∼ **clock** n. Reisewecker, *der;* ∼ **'salesman** n. Vertreter, *der*

travel: ∼-**sick** *adj.* reisekrank; ∼-**sickness** n. Reisekrankheit, *die;* ∼-**sickness pill** n. Tablette gegen Reisekrankheit

trawler /'trɔːlə(r)/ n. [Fisch]trawler, *der*

tray /treɪ/ n. Tablett, *das;* (for correspondence) Ablagekorb, *der*

treacherous /'tretʃərəs/ *adj.* **(a)** treulos ⟨*Person*⟩
(b) (deceptive) tückisch

treachery /'tretʃərɪ/ n. Verrat, *der*

treacle /'triːkl/ n. (Brit.) Sirup, *der*

tread /tred/ ① n. **(a)** (of tyre, boot, etc.) Lauffläche, *die;* **2 millimetres of** ∼ **on a tyre** 2 Millimeter Profil auf einem Reifen
(b) (sound of walking) Schritt, *der*
② *v.i.,* trod /trɒd/, trodden /'trɒdn/ *or* trod treten (**in/on** in/auf + *Akk.*); (walk) gehen
③ *v.t.* trod, trodden *or* trod treten auf (+ *Akk.*); stampfen ⟨*Weintrauben*⟩

'treadmill n. (lit. or fig.) Tretmühle, *die*

treason /'triːzn/ n. [**high**] ∼: Hochverrat, *der*

treasure /'treʒə(r)/ ① n. Schatz, *der;* Kostbarkeit, *die;* **art** ∼**s** Kunstschätze *Pl.*
② *v.t.* in Ehren halten

treasure: ∼ **house** n. [wahre] Fundgrube; ∼ **hunt** n. Schatzsuche, *die*

treasurer /'treʒərə(r)/ n. Kassenwart, *der/* -wartin, *die*

treasury /'treʒərɪ/ n. **the T**∼: das Finanzministerium

treat /triːt/ ① n. **(a)** [besonderes] Vergnügen
(b) (entertainment) *Vergnügen, für dessen Kosten jmd. anderes aufkommt;* **lay on a special** ∼ **for sb.** jmdm. etwas Besonderes bieten; **it's my** ∼: ich lade ein
② *v.t.* **(a)** behandeln; ∼ **sth. as a joke** etw. als Witz nehmen; ∼ **sth. with contempt** für etw. nur Verachtung haben
(b) (Med.) behandeln; ∼ **sb. for sth.** jmdn. wegen etw. behandeln; (before confirmation of diagnosis) jmdn. auf etw. ⟨*Akk.*⟩ behandeln
(c) klären ⟨*Abwässer*⟩
(d) (provide with at own expense) einladen; ∼ **sb. to sth.** jmdm. etw. spendieren; ∼ **oneself to a new hat** sich (*Dat.*) einen neuen Hut leisten

treatise /'triːtɪs, 'triːtɪz/ n. Abhandlung, *die*

'treatment n. Behandlung, *die*

treaty /'triːtɪ/ n. [Staats]vertrag, *der*

treble /'trebl/ ① *adj.* **(a)** dreifach
(b) (Brit. Mus.) ∼ **voice** Sopranstimme, *die*
② n. **(a)** (∼ quantity) Dreifache, *das*
(b) (Mus.) **he is a** ∼: er singt Sopran
③ *v.t.* verdreifachen
④ *v.i.* sich verdreifachen

'treble clef n. (Mus.) Violinschlüssel, *der*

tree /triː/ n. Baum, *der*

'tree house n. Baumhaus, *das*

'treeless *adj.* baumlos

tree: ∼-**lined** *adj.* von Bäumen gesäumt; ∼ **surgeon** n. Baumchirurg, *der;* ∼ **surgery** n. Baumchirurgie, *die;* ∼-**top** n. [Baum]wipfel, *der;* ∼ **trunk** n. Baumstamm, *der*

trek /trek/ ① *v.i.,* -kk- ziehen (**across** durch)
② n. [schwierige] Reise

trellis /'trelɪs/ n. Gitter, *das;* (for plants) Spalier, *das*

tremble /'trembl/ *v.i.* zittern (**with** vor + *Dat.*)

trembling /'tremblɪŋ/ ① *adj.* zitternd
② n. Zittern, *das*

tremendous /trɪ'mendəs/ *adj.* gewaltig; (coll.: wonderful) großartig

tremor /'tremə(r)/ n. **(a)** Zittern, *das*
(b) [**earth**] ∼: leichtes Erdbeben

trench /trentʃ/ n. Graben, *der;* (Mil.) Schützengraben, *der*

trench 'warfare n. Grabenkrieg, *der*

trend /trend/ n. **(a)** Trend, *der;* **upward** ∼: steigende Tendenz
(b) (fashion) Mode, *die;* [Mode]trend, *der*

trendiness n. (Brit. coll.) modische Art

'trendsetter n. Trendsetter, *der*

'trendy *adj.* (Brit. coll.) modisch; Schickimicki⟨*kneipe*⟩ (ugs.)

trepidation /trepɪ'deɪʃn/ n. Beklommenheit, *die*

trespass /'trespəs/ *v.i.* ∼ **on** unerlaubt betreten ⟨*Grundstück*⟩

'trespasser n. Unbefugte, *der/die*

trial /'traɪəl/ n. **(a)** (Law) [Gerichts]verfahren, *das;* **be on** ∼ [**for murder**] [wegen Mordes] vor Gericht stehen
(b) (testing) Test, *der;* **employ sb. on** ∼: jmdn. probeweise einstellen; [**by**] ∼ **and error** [durch] Ausprobieren
(c) (trouble) Problem, *das*
(d) (Sport) (competition) Prüfung, *die;* (for selection) Testspiel, *das*

trial 'run n. (of car) Testfahrt, *die;* (fig.) Probelauf, *der*

triangle /'traɪæŋgl/ n. **(a)** Dreieck, *das*
(b) (Mus.) Triangel, *der od. das*

triangular /traɪ'æŋgjʊlə(r)/ *adj.* dreieckig

tribal /'traɪbl/ *adj.* Stammes-

tribalism /'traɪbəlɪzm/ n. Tribalismus, *der* (fachspr.)

t

tribe /traɪb/ n. Stamm, der

tribulation /trɪbjʊˈleɪʃn/ n. Kummer, der

tribunal /traɪˈbjuːnl/ n. Schiedsgericht, das

tributary /ˈtrɪbjʊtərɪ/ n. Nebenfluss, der

tribute /ˈtrɪbjuːt/ n. Tribut, der (to an + Akk.); **pay ~ to sb./sth.** jmdm./einer Sache den schuldigen Tribut zollen (geh.)

trice /traɪs/ n. **in a ~:** im Handumdrehen

trick /trɪk/ 1 n. (a) Trick, der; **it was all a ~:** das war [alles] nur Bluff
(b) (feat of skill etc.) Kunststück, das; **that should do the ~** (coll.) damit dürfte es klappen (ugs.)
(c) (knack) **get or find the ~** [of doing sth.] den Dreh finden[, wie man etw. tut]
(d) (prank) Streich, der; **play a ~ on sb.** jmdm. einen Streich spielen
(e) (Cards) Stich, der
2 v.t. täuschen; hereinlegen; **~ sb. out of/ into sth.** jmdm. etw. ablisten
3 adj. **~ photograph** Trickaufnahme, die; **~ question** Fangfrage, die

trickery /ˈtrɪkərɪ/ n. [Hinter]list, die

trickle /ˈtrɪkl/ v.i. rinnen; (in drops) tröpfeln

trickster /ˈtrɪkstə(r)/ n. Schwindler, der/ Schwindlerin, die

'tricky adj. verzwickt (ugs.)

tricycle /ˈtraɪsɪkl/ n. Dreirad, das

tried ▶ TRY 2, 3

trifle /ˈtraɪfl/ n. (a) (Brit. Gastron.) Trifle, das
(b) (thing of slight value) Kleinigkeit, die

trifling /ˈtraɪflɪŋ/ adj. unbedeutend ⟨Angelegenheit⟩; gering ⟨Wert⟩

trigger /ˈtrɪɡə(r)/ 1 n. (a) (of gun) Abzug, der; (of machine) Drücker, der
(b) (fig.) Auslöser, der
2 v.t. **~ [off]** auslösen

trigonometry /trɪɡəˈnɒmɪtrɪ/ n. Trigonometrie, die

trilingual /traɪˈlɪŋɡwəl/ adj. dreisprachig

trill /trɪl/ 1 n. Trillern, das; (Mus.) Triller, der
2 v.i. trillern

trillion /ˈtrɪljən/ n. (million million) Billion, die

trilogy /ˈtrɪlədʒɪ/ n. Trilogie, die

trim /trɪm/ 1 v.t., -mm-: (a) schneiden ⟨Hecke⟩; [nach]schneiden ⟨Haar⟩; beschneiden ⟨Papier, Hecke, Budget⟩
(b) (ornament) besetzen (with mit)
2 adj. proper; gepflegt ⟨Garten⟩
3 n. (a) **be in ~** (healthy) in Form od. fit sein
(b) (cut) Nachschneiden, das

'trimming n. (a) (decorations) Verzierung, die
(b) in pl. (coll.: accompaniments) Beilagen Pl.; **with all the ~s** mit allem Drum und Dran (ugs.)

Trinity /ˈtrɪnɪtɪ/ n. (Theol.) **the [Holy] ~:** die Heilige Dreieinigkeit

trinket /ˈtrɪŋkɪt/ n. kleines, billiges Schmuckstück

trio /ˈtriːəʊ/ n., pl. **~s** Trio, das

trip /trɪp/ 1 n. (a) Reise, die; (shorter) Ausflug, der
(b) (coll.: drug-induced hallucinations) Trip, der
2 v.i., -pp- stolpern (on über + Akk.)
■ **trip 'over** v.t. stolpern über (+ Akk.)
■ **trip 'up** 1 v.i. (a) stolpern
(b) (fig.) einen Fehler machen
2 v.t. (a) stolpern lassen
(b) (fig.) aufs Glatteis führen (fig.)

tripe /traɪp/ n. (a) Kaldaunen Pl.
(b) (coll.: rubbish) Quatsch, der (ugs.)

triple /ˈtrɪpl/ 1 adj. (a) (threefold) dreifach
(b) (three times greater than) **~ the ...:** der/die/ das dreifache ...
2 n. Dreifache, das
3 v.i. sich verdreifachen
4 v.t. verdreifachen

'triple jump n. (Sport) Dreisprung, der

triplet /ˈtrɪplɪt/ n. Drilling, der

triplicate /ˈtrɪplɪkət/ n. **in ~:** in dreifacher Ausfertigung

trip 'mileage recorder n. (Motor Veh.) Tageskilometerzähler, der

tripod /ˈtraɪpɒd/ n. Dreibein, das

'tripper n. (Brit.) Ausflügler, der/ Ausflüglerin, die

'tripwire n. Stolperdraht, der

trite /traɪt/ adj. banal

triumph /ˈtraɪəmf, ˈtraɪʌmf/ 1 n. Triumph, der (over über + Akk.)
2 v.i. triumphieren (over über + Akk.)

triumphant /traɪˈʌmfənt/ adj. (a) siegreich
(b) triumphierend ⟨Blick⟩

trivia /ˈtrɪvɪə/ n. pl. Belanglosigkeiten Pl.

trivial /ˈtrɪvɪəl/ adj. belanglos

triviality /trɪvɪˈælɪtɪ/ n. Belanglosigkeit, die

trivialize /ˈtrɪvɪəlaɪz/ v.t. auf eine belanglose Ebene bringen

trod, trodden ▶ TREAD 2, 3

trolley /ˈtrɒlɪ/ n. (a) (for serving food) Servierwagen, der
(b) [supermarket] **~:** Einkaufswagen, der

trombone /trɒmˈbəʊn/ n. Posaune, die

troop /truːp/ 1 n. (a) in pl. Truppen Pl.
(b) (fig.) Schar, der
2 v.i. **~ in/out** hinein-/hinausströmen

troop: ~ carrier n. Truppentransporter, der; **~ship** n. Truppentransporter, der

trophy /ˈtrəʊfɪ/ n. Trophäe, die

tropic /ˈtrɒpɪk/ n. **the T~s** (Geog.) die Tropen; **the ~ of Cancer/Capricorn** (Astron., Geog.) der Wendekreis des Krebses/ Steinbocks

tropical /ˈtrɒpɪkl/ adj. tropisch; Tropen⟨krankheit, -kleidung⟩

tropical: ~ 'medicine n. Tropenmedizin, die; **~ 'rainforest** n. tropischer Regenwald

trot /trɒt/ 1 n. (coll.) **on the ~:** hintereinander; **be on the ~:** auf Trab sein (ugs.)
2 v.i., -tt- traben

trouble /'trʌbl/ ⟦1⟧ n. (a) Ärger, der; Schwierigkeiten Pl.; **there'll be ~** [if …] es wird Ärger geben, [wenn …]; **what's the ~?** was ist denn?
(b) **engine/brake ~:** Probleme mit dem Motor/der Bremse; **suffer from heart/liver ~:** herz-/leberkrank sein
(c) (inconvenience) Mühe, die; **take a lot of ~:** sich (Dat.) sehr viel Mühe geben; **it's more ~ than it's worth** es lohnt sich nicht
(d) in sing. or pl. (unrest) Unruhen Pl.
⟦2⟧ v.t. (a) (agitate) beunruhigen; **don't let it ~ you** mach dir deswegen keine Sorgen
(b) (inconvenience) stören
⟦3⟧ v.i. (make an effort) sich bemühen

troubled /'trʌbld/ adj. (a) (worried) besorgt
(b) (restless) unruhig

trouble: ~-free adj. problemlos; **~maker** n. Unruhestifter, der/-stifterin, die

troublesome /'trʌblsəm/ adj. schwierig; lästig ⟨Krankheit⟩

trough /trɒf/ n. Trog, der

troupe /truːp/ n. Truppe, die

trouser /'traʊzə/**: ~ leg** n. Hosenbein, das; **~ press** n. Bügelpresse, die; Hosenbügler, der

trousers /'traʊzəz/ n. pl. **[pair of] ~:** Hose, die

'trouser suit n. (Brit.) Hosenanzug, der

trousseau /'truːsəʊ/ n., pl. **~s** or **~x** /'truːsəʊz/ Aussteuer, die

trout /traʊt/ n., pl. same Forelle, die

trout: ~ farm n. Forellenzuchtbetrieb, der; **~-fishing** n. Forellenfang, der

trowel /'traʊəl/ n. Kelle, die; (Hort.) Pflanzkelle, die

truant /'truːənt/ n. **play ~:** [die Schule] schwänzen (ugs.)

truce /truːs/ n. Waffenstillstand, der

truck /trʌk/ n. (a) Last[kraft]wagen, der; Lkw, der
(b) (Brit. Railw.) offener Güterwagen

'truck driver, trucker /'trʌkə(r)/ ns. Lastwagenfahrer, der/-fahrerin, die; (long-distance) Fernfahrer, der/-fahrerin, die

truculent /'trʌkjʊlənt/ adj. aufsässig

trudge /trʌdʒ/ v.i. trotten; (through snow etc.) stapfen

true /truː/ adj., **~r** /'truːə(r)/, **~st** /'truːɪst/ (a) wahr; wahrheitsgetreu ⟨Bericht⟩; richtig ⟨Vorteil⟩; (rightly so called) eigentlich; echt, wahr ⟨Freund⟩; **is it ~ that …?** stimmt es, dass …?; **~ to life** lebensecht
(b) (loyal) treu

truffle /'trʌfl/ n. Trüffel, die od. (ugs.) der

truism /'truːɪzm/ n. Binsenweisheit, die

truly /'truːlɪ/ adv. (a) wirklich
(b) (accurately) zutreffend; **yours ~:** mit freundlichen Grüßen

trump /trʌmp/ ⟦1⟧ n. Trumpf, der
⟦2⟧ v.t. übertrumpfen

'trump card n. (lit. or fig.) Trumpf, der

trumped up /'trʌmpt ʌp/ adj. falsch ⟨Beschuldigung usw.⟩

trumpet /'trʌmpɪt/ n. Trompete, die

'trumpeter n. Trompeter, der/Trompeterin, die

truncheon /'trʌntʃn/ n. Schlagstock, der

trundle /'trʌndl/ v.t. & i. rollen

trunk /trʌŋk/ n. (a) (of elephant etc.) Rüssel, der
(b) (large box) Schrankkoffer, der
(c) (of tree) Stamm, der
(d) (of body) Rumpf, der
(e) (Amer.: of car) Kofferraum, der
(f) in pl. (Brit.) **[swimming] ~s** Badehose, die

truss /trʌs/ n. (Med.) Bruchband, das

trust /trʌst/ ⟦1⟧ n. (a) Vertrauen, das; **place or put one's ~ in sb./sth.** sein Vertrauen auf od. in jmdn./etw. setzen; **take sth. on ~:** etw. einfach glauben
(b) (organization managed by trustees) Treuhandgesellschaft, die; **[charitable] ~:** Stiftung, die; (association of companies) Trust, der
(c) (Law) **hold in ~:** treuhänderisch verwalten
⟦2⟧ v.t. (rely on) trauen (+ Dat.); vertrauen (+ Dat.) ⟨Person⟩; **~ sb. with sth.** jmdm. etw. anvertrauen
⟦3⟧ v.i. (a) **~ to** sich verlassen auf (+ Akk.)
(b) (believe) **~ in sb./sth.** auf jmdn./etw. vertrauen

trustee /trʌ'stiː/ n. Treuhänder, der/Treuhänderin, die

trustful /'trʌstfl/**, 'trusting** adjs. vertrauensvoll

trust: ~ fund n. Treuhandvermögen, das; **~worthy** adj. vertrauenswürdig

truth /truːθ/ n., pl. **~s** /truːðz, truːθs/ Wahrheit, die; **tell the [whole] ~:** die [ganze] Wahrheit sagen

truthful /'truːθfl/ adj. ehrlich

try /traɪ/ ⟦1⟧ n. Versuch, der; **have a ~ at sth./doing sth.** etw. versuchen/versuchen, etw. zu tun; **give it a ~, have a ~:** es versuchen
⟦2⟧ v.t. (a) (attempt) versuchen
(b) (test usefulness of) probieren
(c) (test) auf die Probe stellen ⟨Fähigkeit, Kraft, Geduld⟩
(d) (Law.: take to trial) **~ a case** einen Fall verhandeln; **~ sb. [for sth.]** jmdn. [wegen einer Sache] vor Gericht stellen
⟦3⟧ v.i. es versuchen; **~ hard/harder** sich (Dat.) viel/mehr Mühe geben
■ **try 'on** v.t. anprobieren ⟨Kleidungsstück⟩
■ **try 'out** v.t. ausprobieren

'trying adj. (a) (testing) schwierig
(b) (difficult to endure) anstrengend

tsar /zɑː(r)/ n. (Hist.) Zar, der

'T-shirt n. T-Shirt, das

tub /tʌb/ n. Kübel, der; (for ice cream etc.) Becher, der

tuba /'tjuːbə/ n. (Mus.) Tuba, die

tubby /'tʌbɪ/ *adj.* rundlich

tube /tjuːb/ *n.* (a) (for conveying liquids etc.) Rohr, *das* (b) (small cylinder) Tube, *die;* (for sweets, tablets) Röhrchen, *das* (c) (Anat., Zool.) Röhre, *die* (d) (of TV etc.) Röhre, *die* (e) (Brit. coll.: underground railway) U-Bahn, *die*

tuber /'tjuːbə(r)/ *n.* (Bot.) Knolle, *die*

tuberculosis /tjuːbɜːkjʊ'ləʊsɪs/ *n.* Tuberkulose, *die*

tube: ~ **station** *n.* (Brit. coll.) U-Bahnhof, *der;* ~ **train** *n.* (Brit. coll.) U-bahn-Zug, *der*

tubing /'tjuːbɪŋ/ *n.* Rohre *Pl.*

tubular /'tjuːbjʊlə(r)/ *adj.* röhrenförmig

tuck /tʌk/ ⒈ *v.t.* stecken ⒉ *n.* (in fabric) (for decoration) Biese, *die;* (to tighten) Abnäher, *der*
■ **tuck 'in** ⒈ *v.t.* hineinstecken ⒉ *v.i.* (coll.) zulangen (ugs.)
■ **tuck 'up** *v.t.* (a) hochkrempeln ⟨*Ärmel, Hose*⟩; hochnehmen ⟨*Rock*⟩ (b) (cover snugly) zudecken

Tue., Tues. *abbrs.* = **Tuesday** Di.

Tuesday /'tjuːzdeɪ, 'tjuːzdɪ/ *n.* Dienstag, *der; see also* FRIDAY

tuft /tʌft/ *n.* Büschel, *das*

tug /tʌg/ ⒈ *n.* (a) Ruck, *der;* ~ **of war** Tauziehen, *das* (b) ~ [boat] Schlepper, *der* ⒉ *v.t.,* -gg- ziehen ⒊ *v.i.,* -gg- zerren (at an + *Dat.*)

tuition /tjuː'ɪʃn/ *n.* Unterricht, *der*

tulip /'tjuːlɪp/ *n.* Tulpe, *die*

tumble /'tʌmbl/ ⒈ *v.i.* stürzen; fallen ⒉ *n.* Sturz, *der*

tumble: ~**down** *adj.* verfallen; ~**-drier** *n.* Wäschetrockner, *der;* ~**-dry** *v.t.* im Automaten trocknen

tumbler /'tʌmblə(r)/ *n.* (short) Whiskyglas, *das;* (long) Wasserglas, *das*

tummy /'tʌmɪ/ *n.* (child lang./coll.) Bäuchlein, *das*

tummy: ~ **ache** *n.* (child lang./coll.) Bauchweh, *das;* ~ **button** *n.* (child lang./coll.) Bauchnabel, *der;* ~ **upset** *n.* (child lang./coll.) Magenverstimmung, *die*

tumour (*Brit.; Amer.:* **tumor**) /'tjuːmə(r)/ *n.* Tumor, *der*

tumult /'tjuːmʌlt/ *n.* Tumult, *der*

tuna /'tjuːnə/ *n., pl. same or* ~**s** Thunfisch, *der*

tune /tjuːn/ ⒈ *n.* (a) (melody) Melodie, *die;* change one's ~ (fig.) sein Verhalten ändern; call the ~: den Ton angeben (b) (correct pitch) sing in/out of ~: richtig/ falsch singen; be in/out of ~ ⟨*Instrument:*⟩ richtig stimmt/verstimmt sein ⒉ *v.t.* (a) (Mus.: put in ~) stimmen (b) (Radio, Telev.) einstellen (to auf + *Akk.*) (c) einstellen ⟨*Motor, Vergaser*⟩

tune 'in *v.i.* (Radio, Telev.) ~ **to a station** einen Sender einstellen

tuneful /'tjuːnfl/ *adj.* melodisch

tuner /'tjuːnə(r)/ *n.* (a) (Mus.) Stimmer, *der/* Stimmerin, *die* (b) (radio) Tuner, *der*

tunic /'tjuːnɪk/ *n.* (of soldier) Uniformjacke, *die;* (of schoolgirl) Kittel, *der*

'tuning fork /'tjuːnɪŋfɔːk/ *n.* Stimmgabel, *die*

Tunisia /tjuː'nɪzɪə/ *pr. n.* Tunesien (*das*)

tunnel /'tʌnl/ ⒈ *n.* Tunnel, *der;* (dug by animal) Gang, *der* ⒉ *v.i.,* (Brit.) -ll- einen Tunnel graben

turban /'tɜːbən/ *n.* Turban, *der*

turbine /'tɜːbaɪn/ *n.* Turbine, *die*

turbocharged /'tɜːbəʊtʃɑːdʒd/ *adj.* mit Turbolader *nachgestellt*

turbot /'tɜːbət/ *n.* Steinbutt, *der*

turbulence /'tɜːbjʊləns/ *n.* (a) Aufgewühltheit, *die;* (fig.) Aufruhr, *der* (b) (Phys.) Turbulenz, *die*

turbulent /'tɜːbjʊlənt/ *adj.* (a) aufgewühlt (b) (Phys.) turbulent

turd /tɜːd/ *n.* (coarse) Scheißhaufen, *der* (derb)

tureen /tjʊə'riːn/ *n.* Terrine, *die*

turf /tɜːf/ *n., pl.* ~**s** *or* **turves** /tɜːvz/ (a) *no pl.* Rasen, *der* (b) (segment) Rasenstück, *das*
■ **turf 'out** *v.t.* (coll.) rausschmeißen (ugs.)

Turk /tɜːk/ *n.* Türke, *der*/Türkin, *die*

turkey *n.* Truthahn, *der*/Truthenne, *die;* (esp. as food) Puter, *der*/Pute, *die*

Turkey /'tɜːkɪ/ *pr. n.* die Türkei

Turkish /'tɜːkɪʃ/ ⒈ *adj.* türkisch; **sb. is** ~: jmd. ist Türke/Türkin ⒉ *n.* Türkisch, *das; see also* ENGLISH 2A

turmoil /'tɜːmɔɪl/ *n.* Aufruhr, *der*

turn /tɜːn/ ⒈ *n.* (a) **it is sb.'s** ~ **to do sth.** jmd. ist an der Reihe, etw. zu tun; **it's your** ~ [next] du bist als Nächster/Nächste dran (ugs.) *od.* an der Reihe; **out of** ~: außer der Reihe; (fig.) an der falschen Stelle ⟨*lachen*⟩; **take [it in]** ~**s** sich abwechseln (b) (rotary motion) Drehung, *die* (c) (change of direction) Wende, *die;* **take a** ~ **to the right/left, do** *or* **take a right/left** ~: nach rechts/links abbiegen; (fig.) **take a favourable** ~ sich zum Guten wenden; **the** ~ **of the year/century** die Jahres-/Jahrhundertwende (d) (bend) Kurve, *die;* (corner) Ecke, *die* (e) (short performance) Nummer, *die* (f) (service) **do sb. a good** ~: jmdm. einen guten Dienst erweisen (g) (coll.: fright) **give sb. quite a** ~: jmdm. einen gehörigen Schrecken einjagen (ugs.) ⒉ *v.t.* (a) (make revolve) drehen (b) (reverse) umdrehen; wenden ⟨*Pfannkuchen, Auto, Heu*⟩; ~ **sth. upside down** *or* **on its head** (lit. or fig.) etw. auf den Kopf stellen; ~ **the page** umblättern (c) (give new direction to) drehen, wenden ⟨*Kopf*⟩; ~ **a hose/gun on sb./sth.** einen

Schlauch/ein Gewehr auf jmdn./etw.
richten; ~ **one's attention/mind to sth.** sich/
seine Gedanken einer Sache (*Dat.*)
zuwenden
(d) ~ **sb. loose on sb./sth.** jmdn. auf jmdn./
etw. loslassen
(e) (cause to become) verwandeln; ~ **the lights
[down] low** das Licht dämpfen; ~ **a play/
book into a film** ein Theaterstück/Buch
verfilmen
(f) (shape in lathe) drechseln ‹*Holz*›; drehen
‹*Metall*›
(g) drehen ‹*Pirouette*›; schlagen
‹*Purzelbaum*›
3 *v.i.* **(a)** (revolve) sich drehen
(b) (reverse direction) ‹*Person:*› sich
herumdrehen; ‹*Auto:*› wenden
(c) (take new direction) sich wenden; (~ round)
sich umdrehen; ~ **to the left/right** nach
links/rechts abbiegen
(d) (become) werden; ~ **[in]to sth.** zu etw.
werden; (be transformed) sich in etw. (*Akk.*)
verwandeln
(e) (become sour) ‹*Milch:*› sauer werden
■ **turn a'way** **1** *v.i.* sich abwenden
2 *v.t.* **(a)** (avert) abwenden
(b) (send away) wegschicken
■ **turn 'down** *v.t.* **(a)** herunterschlagen
‹*Kragen*›
(b) niedriger stellen ‹*Heizung*›;
herunterdrehen ‹*Gas*›; leiser stellen ‹*Ton,
Radio, Fernseher*›
(c) (reject) ablehnen; abweisen ‹*Kandidaten
usw.*›
■ **turn 'in** **1** *v.t.* **(a)** nach innen drehen
(b) (hand in) abgeben
2 *v.i.* **(a)** (enter) einbiegen
(b) (coll.: go to bed) in die Falle gehen (salopp)
■ **turn 'off** **1** *v.t.* abschalten; abstellen
‹*Wasser, Gas*›; zudrehen ‹*Wasserhahn*›
2 *v.i.* abbiegen
■ **turn on** *v.t.* **(a)** /-'-/ anschalten; aufdrehen
‹*Wasserhahn, Gas*›
(b) /'--/ (attack) angreifen
■ **turn 'out** **1** *v.t.* **(a)** (expel) hinauswerfen
(ugs.)
(b) (switch off) ausschalten; abdrehen ‹*Gas*›
(c) (produce) produzieren
(d) (Brit.) (empty) ausräumen; leeren; (get rid
of) wegwerfen
2 *v.i.* **(a)** (prove to be) sb./sth. ~s out to be
sth. jmd./etw. stellt sich als jmd./etw.
heraus; **everything ~ed out well/all right in
the end** alles endete gut
(b) (appear) ‹*Fans usw.:*› erscheinen
■ **turn 'over** **1** *v.t.* umdrehen
2 *v.i.* **(a)** (tip over) umkippen; ‹*Boot:*›
kentern; ‹*Auto, Flugzeug:*› sich
überschlagen
(b) (from one side to other) sich umdrehen
(c) (~ a page) umblättern
■ **turn 'round** *v.i.* sich umdrehen
■ **'turn to** *v.t.* (fig.) ~ **to sb.** sich an jmdn.
wenden; ~ **to sb. for help/advice** jmdm.
Hilfe/Rat suchen; ~ **to drink** sich in den
Alkohol flüchten

■ **turn 'up** **1** *v.i.* **(a)** ‹*Person:*› erscheinen
(b) (present itself) auftauchen; ‹*Gelegenheit:*›
sich bieten
2 *v.t.* **(a)** hochschlagen ‹*Kragen*›
(b) lauter stellen ‹*Ton, Radio, Fernseher*›;
aufdrehen ‹*Heizung, Gas*›; heller machen
‹*Licht*›
'turnaround *n.* **(a)** (change) [Kehrt]wende,
die
(b) (of aircraft, ship, vehicle) Abfertigung, *die*
turned-up /'tɜːndʌp/ *adj.* ~ **nose**
Stupsnase, *die* (ugs.)
'turning *n.* Abzweigung, *die*
'turning point *n.* Wendepunkt, *der*
turnip /'tɜːnɪp/ *n.* [weiße] Rübe
turn: ~**out** *n.* (of people) Beteiligung, *die*
(for an + *Dat.*); ~**over** *n.* **(a)** (Commerc.)
Umsatz, *der;* (of stock) Umschlag, *der;* **(b)** (of
staff) Fluktuation, *die;* ~**pike** *n.* (Amer.)
gebührenpflichtige Autobahn; ~**stile** *n.*
Drehkreuz, *das;* ~**table** *n.* Plattenteller,
der; ~**up** *n.* (Brit. Fashion) Aufschlag, *der*
turpentine /'tɜːpntaɪn/ *n.* Terpentin, *das*
turps /tɜːps/ *n.* (coll.) Terpentin, *das* (ugs.)
turquoise /'tɜːkwɔɪz/ **1** *n.* **(a)** Türkis, *der*
(b) (colour) Türkis, *das*
2 *adj.* türkis[farben]
turret /'tʌrɪt/ *n.* Türmchen, *das*
turreted /'tʌrɪtɪd/ *adj.* ‹*Schloss*› mit
Mauertürmchen
turtle /'tɜːtl/ *n.* **(a)** Meeresschildkröte, *die*
(b) (Amer.: freshwater reptile) Wasserschildkröte,
die
'turtleneck *n.* ~**neck pullover** Pullover
mit Stehbund
turves ▸ TURF B
tusk /tʌsk/ *n.* Stoßzahn, *der*
tussle /'tʌsl/ **1** *n.* Gerangel, *das* (ugs.)
2 *v.i.* sich balgen
tutor /'tjuːtə(r)/ *n.* [private] ~:
[Privat]lehrer, *der*/-lehrerin, *die*
tut[-tut] /tʌt('tʌt)/ **1** *int.* na[, na]
2 *v.i.,* **-tt-:** ~ **with disapproval**]
[missbilligend] „na, na!" sagen
tutu /'tuːtuː/ *n.* Tutu, *das*
tuxedo /tʌk'siːdəʊ/ *n., pl.* ~**s** *or* ~**es**
(Amer.) Smoking, *der*
TV /tiː'viː/ *n.* **(a)** Fernsehen, *das*
(b) (television set) Fernseher, *der* (ugs.)
twaddle /'twɒdl/ *n.* Gewäsch, *das* (ugs.)
twang /twæŋ/ **1** *v.t.* zupfen ‹*Saite*›
2 *n.* [nasal] ~: Näseln, *das*
tweed /twiːd/ *n.* Tweed, *der*
tweezers /'twiːzəz/ *n. pl.* [**pair of**] ~:
Pinzette, *die*
twelfth /twelfθ/ **1** *adj.* zwölft...
2 *n.* (fraction) Zwölftel, *das.* See also EIGHTH
twelve /twelv/ **1** *adj.* zwölf
2 *n.* Zwölf, *die.* See also EIGHT
twentieth /'twentɪɪθ/ **1** *adj.* zwanzigst...
2 *n.* (fraction) Zwanzigstel, *das.* See also
EIGHTH

twenty /'twentɪ/ [1] *adj.* zwanzig
[2] *n.* Zwanzig, *die. See also* EIGHT; EIGHTY 2

twice /twaɪs/ *adv.* **(a)** zweimal
(b) (doubly) doppelt

twiddle /'twɪdl/ *v.t.* herumdrehen an
(+ *Dat.*) (ugs.); ~ one's thumbs (lit. or fig.)
Däumchen drehen

twig¹ /twɪg/ *n.* Zweig, *der*

twig² (coll.) [1] *v.t.,* -gg- kapieren (ugs.)
[2] *v.i.,* -gg- es kapieren (ugs.)

twilight /'twaɪlaɪt/ *n.* **(a)** (evening light)
Dämmerlicht, *das*
(b) (period of half-light) Dämmerung, *die*

twin /twɪn/ [1] *attrib. adj.* **(a)** Zwillings-
(b) (forming a pair) Doppel-
[2] *n.* Zwilling, *der*
[3] *v.t.* Bottrop is ~ned with Blackpool
Bottrop und Blackpool sind Partnerstädte

twin 'beds *n. pl.* zwei Einzelbetten *Pl.*

twine /twaɪn/ [1] *n.* Bindfaden, *der*
[2] *v.i.* sich winden (**about, around** um)

twinge /twɪndʒ/ *n.* Stechen, *das;* ~[s] of
conscience (fig.) Gewissensbisse *Pl.*

twinkle /'twɪŋkl/ [1] *v.i.* funkeln (**with** vor
+ *Dat.*)
[2] *n.* Funkeln, *das*

twinkling /'twɪŋklɪŋ/ *n.* in a ~, in the ~ of
an eye im Handumdrehen

'twin town *n.* (Brit.) Partnerstadt, *die*

twirl /twɜːl/ [1] *v.t.* [schnell] drehen
[2] *v.i.* wirbeln (**around** über + *Akk.*)

twist /twɪst/ [1] *v.t.* **(a)** verdrehen ⟨*Worte,
Bedeutung*⟩; ~ one's ankle sich (*Dat.*) den
Knöchel verrenken; ~ sb.'s arm jmdm. den
Arm umdrehen; (fig.) jmdm. [die]
Daumenschrauben anlegen
(b) (rotate) drehen
[2] *v.i.* sich winden
[3] *n.* **(a)** (motion) Drehung, *die*
(b) (unexpected occurrence) überraschende
Wendung

'twisted *adj.* verbogen; (fig.) verdreht (ugs.
abwertend) ⟨*Geist*⟩; verquer ⟨*Humor*⟩

twit /twɪt/ *n.* (Brit. coll.) Trottel, *der* (ugs.)

twitch /twɪtʃ/ [1] *v.i.* ⟨*Mund, Lippe:*⟩ zucken
[2] *n.* Zucken, *das*

twitter /'twɪtə(r)/ [1] *n.* Zwitschern, *das*
[2] *v.i.* zwitschern

two /tuː/ [1] *adj.* zwei
[2] *n.* Zwei, *die. See also* EIGHT

two: ~-bit *adj.* (Amer.) (of poor quality) mies
(ugs.). ~faced /'tuːfeɪst/ *adj.* (fig.) falsch;
~fold *adj., adv.* zweifach; a ~fold increase
ein Anstieg auf das Doppelte; ~lane *adj.*
zweispurig; ~piece [1] *n.* Zweiteiler, *der;*
[2] *adj.* zweiteilig; ~seater /-'--/ *n.*
Zweisitzer, *der;* ~some /'tuːsəm/ *n.* Paar,
das; ~storey *adj.* zweigeschossig;
~tone *adj.* zweifarbig; ~up ~down *n.*
kleines [Reihen]haus; ~way *adj.* **(a)**
zweibahnig (Verkehrsw.); '~way traffic ahead'
„Achtung Gegenverkehr"; **(b)** ~way mirror
Einwegspiegel, *der*

tycoon /taɪ'kuːn/ *n.* Magnat, *der*

tying ▶ TIE 1, 2

type /taɪp/ [1] *n.* **(a)** Art, *die;* (person) Typ,
der; what ~ of car ...? was für ein Auto ...?
(b) (Printing) Drucktype, *die*
[2] *v.t.* [mit der Maschine] schreiben; tippen
(ugs.)
[3] *v.i.* Maschine schreiben
■ **type 'out** *v.t.* [mit der Schreibmaschine]
abschreiben; abtippen (ugs.)

type: ~cast *v.t.* [auf eine bestimmte Rolle]
festlegen; ~face *n.* Schriftbild, *das;*
~script *n.* maschine[n]geschriebene
Fassung; ~setter *n.* [Schrift]setzer, *der/*
-setzerin, *die;* ~setting *n.* [Schrift]setzen,
das; ~writer *n.* Schreibmaschine, *die;*
~written *adj.* maschine[n]geschrieben

typhoid /'taɪfɔɪd/ *n.* ~ [fever] Typhus, *der*

typhoon /taɪ'fuːn/ *n.* Taifun, *der*

typical /'tɪpɪkl/ *adj.* typisch (**of** für)

typify /'tɪpɪfaɪ/ *v.t.* ~ sth. als typisches
Beispiel für etw. dienen

typing /'taɪpɪŋ/ *n.* Maschineschreiben, *das*

'typing error *n.* Tippfehler, *der*

typist /'taɪpɪst/ *n.* Schreibkraft, *die*

typography /taɪ'pɒgrəfɪ/ *n.* Typographie,
die

tyrannical /tɪ'rænɪkl/ *adj.* tyrannisch

tyranny /'tɪrənɪ/ *n.* Tyrannei, *die*

tyrant /'taɪərənt/ *n.* Tyrann, *der*

tyre /'taɪə(r)/ *n.* Reifen, *der*

'tyre pressure *n.* Reifendruck, *der*

tzar *etc.* ▶ TSAR *etc.*

U u

U, u /juː/ *n.* U, u, *das*
'U-bend *n.* U-Rohr, *das*
ubiquitous /juːˈbɪkwɪtəs/ *adj.*
  allgegenwärtig
udder /ˈʌdə(r)/ *n.* Euter, *das*
UFO /ˈjuːfəʊ/ *n., pl.* ~s Ufo, *das*
ugh /ʌh, ʊh, ɜːh/ *int.* bah
ugliness /ˈʌɡlɪnɪs/ *n.* Hässlichkeit, *die*
ugly /ˈʌɡlɪ/ *adj.* (a) hässlich
  (b) (nasty) übel ‹Wunde, Laune usw.›
UHF *abbr.* = **ultra-high frequency**
  UHF
UHT *abbr.* = **ultra heat-treated**
  ultrahoch erhitzt
UK *abbr.* = **United Kingdom**
Ukraine /juːˈkreɪn/ *pr. n.* Ukraine, *die*
Ukrainian /juːˈkreɪnɪən/ **1** *adj.*
  ukrainisch; *sb.* is ~: jmd. ist Ukrainer/
  Ukrainerin
  2 *n.* (a) (person) Ukrainer, *der*/Ukrainerin,
  die
  (b) (language) Ukrainisch, *das; see also*
  ENGLISH 2 A
ulcer /ˈʌlsə(r)/ *n.* Geschwür, *das*
ulterior /ʌlˈtɪərɪə(r)/ *adj.* hintergründig;
  ~ motive Hintergedanke, *der*
ultimate /ˈʌltɪmət/ **1** *attrib. adj.* (a) (final)
  letzt...; (eventual) endgültig ‹Sieg›
  (b) (fundamental) tiefst...
  2 *n.* the ~ in comfort/luxury der Gipfel an
  Bequemlichkeit/Luxus
'ultimately *adv.* (a) (in the end) schließlich
  (b) (in the last analysis) letzten Endes
ultimatum /ʌltɪˈmeɪtəm/ *n., pl.* ~s *or*
  ultimata /ʌltɪˈmeɪtə/ Ultimatum, *das*
ultra'sound *n.* Ultraschall, *der*
ultra'violet *adj.* (Phys.) ultraviolett; UV-
  ‹Lampe, Filter›
umbilical cord /ʌmˈbɪlɪkl kɔːd/ *n.*
  Nabelschnur, *die*
umbrage /ˈʌmbrɪdʒ/ *n.* take ~ [at sth.] [an
  etw. (+ *Dat.*)] Anstoß nehmen
umbrella /ʌmˈbrelə/ *n.* [Regen]schirm, *der*
um'brella stand *n.* Schirmständer, *der*
umpire /ˈʌmpaɪə(r)/ *n.* Schiedsrichter, *der*/
  -richterin, *die*
umpteen /ʌmpˈtiːn/ *adj.* (coll.) zig (ugs.); x
  (ugs.)
unabashed /ʌnəˈbæʃt/ *adj.* ungeniert
unable /ʌnˈeɪbl/ *pred. adj.* be ~ to do sth.
  etw. nicht tun können
unabridged /ʌnəˈbrɪdʒd/ *adj.* ungekürzt
unac'ceptable *adj.* unannehmbar

unaccompanied /ʌnəˈkʌmpənɪd/ *adj.*
  ohne Begleitung *nachgestellt*
unac'countable *adj.* unerklärlich
unaccountably /ʌnəˈkaʊntəblɪ/ *adv.*
  unerklärlicherweise
unac'customed *adj.* ungewohnt; be ~ to
  sth. etw. (*Akk.*) nicht gewöhnt sein
unadulterated /ʌnəˈdʌltəreɪtɪd/ *adj.* (a)
  (pure) unverfälscht
  (b) (utter) völlig
unadventurous /ʌnədˈventʃərəs/ *adj.*
  bieder ‹Person›; ereignislos ‹Leben›
unafraid /ʌnəˈfreɪd/ *adj.* be ~ [of sb./sth.]
  keine Angst [vor jmdm./etw.] haben
unaided /ʌnˈeɪdɪd/ *adj.* ohne fremde Hilfe
unalike /ʌnəˈlaɪk/ *pred. adj.* unähnlich
unambiguous /ʌnæmˈbɪɡjʊəs/ *adj.*
  unzweideutig
unambitious /ʌnæmˈbɪʃəs/ *adj.* ‹Person›
  ohne Ergeiz
unanimity /juːnəˈnɪmɪtɪ/ *n.* Einmütigkeit,
  die
unanimous /juːˈnænɪməs/ *adj.*
  einstimmig; be ~ in doing sth. etw.
  einmütig tun
u'nanimously *adv.* einstimmig
unannounced /ʌnəˈnaʊnst/ *adj.*
  unangemeldet
unappetizing /ʌnˈæpɪtaɪzɪŋ/ *adj.*
  unappetitlich
unarmed /ʌnˈɑːmd/ *adj.* unbewaffnet;
  ~ combat Kampf ohne Waffen
unassuming /ʌnəˈsjuːmɪŋ/ *adj.*
  bescheiden
unattached /ʌnəˈtætʃt/ *adj.* (a) nicht
  befestigt
  (b) (without a partner) ungebunden
unat'tended *adj.* (a) ~ to (not dealt with)
  unerledigt; nicht bedient ‹Kunde›; nicht
  behandelt ‹Patient›
  (b) (not supervised) unbewacht ‹Parkplatz,
  Gepäck›
unat'tractive *adj.* unattraktiv
unauthorized /ʌnˈɔːθəraɪzd/ *adj.*
  unbefugt; no entry for ~ persons Zutritt für
  Unbefugte verboten
una'vailable *adj.* nicht erhältlich ‹Ware›;
  be ~ for comment zur Stellungnahme nicht
  zur Verfügung stehen
una'voidable *adj.* unvermeidlich
unaware /ʌnəˈweə(r)/ *adj.* be ~ of sth.
  sich (*Dat.*) einer Sache (*Gen.*) nicht bewusst
  sein
unawares /ʌnəˈweəz/ *adv.* catch sb. ~:
  jmdn. überraschen

unbalanced /ʌnˈbælənst/ *adj.* **(a)**
unausgewogen
(b) (mentally ∼) unausgeglichen

un'bearable *adj.*, **unbearably**
/ʌnˈbeərəblɪ/ *adv.* unerträglich

unbeatable /ʌnˈbiːˈtəbl/ *adj.* unschlagbar
(ugs.)

un'beaten *adj.* **(a)** ungeschlagen
(b) (not surpassed) unerreicht; ungebrochen
⟨*Rekord*⟩

unbe'lievable *adj.* **(a)** unglaublich
(b) (tremendous) unwahrscheinlich

unbiased, unbiassed /ʌnˈbaɪəst/ *adj.*
unvoreingenommen

unblemished /ʌnˈblemɪʃt/ *adj.* makellos
⟨*Haut, Ruf*⟩

un'block *v.t.* frei machen

un'bolt *v.t.* aufriegeln ⟨*Tür*⟩

unborn /ʌnˈbɔːn, *attrib.* ˈʌnbɔːn/ *adj.*
ungeboren

un'breakable *adj.* unzerbrechlich

unburden /ʌnˈbɜːdn/ *v.t.* ∼ oneself sein
Herz ausschütten

un'button *v.t.* aufknöpfen

uncalled-for /ʌnˈkɔːldfɔː(r)/ *adj.*
unangebracht

uncanny /ʌnˈkænɪ/ *adj.* unheimlich

uncared-for /ʌnˈkeədfɔː(r)/ *adj.*
vernachlässigt

uncaring /ʌnˈkeərɪŋ/ *adj.* gleichgültig

unceasing /ʌnˈsiːsɪŋ/ *adj.* unaufhörlich

unceremonious /ʌnserɪˈməʊnɪəs/ *adj.* **(a)**
(informal) formlos
(b) (abrupt) brüsk

uncere'moniously *adv.* ohne
Umschweife

un'certain *adj.* **(a)** (not sure) be ∼ [whether
...] sich (*Dat.*) nicht sicher sein[, ob ...]
(b) (not clear) ungewiss ⟨*Ergebnis, Zukunft*⟩;
of ∼ age/origin unbestimmten Alters/
unbestimmter Herkunft
(c) (ambiguous) vage; in no ∼ terms ganz
eindeutig

uncertainty /ʌnˈsɜːtntɪ/ *n.* **(a)**
Ungewissheit, *die*
(b) (hesitation) Unsicherheit, *die*

unchanged /ʌnˈtʃeɪndʒd/ *adj.* unverändert

uncharacteristic /ʌnkærɪktəˈrɪstɪk/ *adj.*
uncharakteristisch (of für)

un'charitable *adj.*, **uncharitably**
/ʌnˈtʃærɪtəblɪ/ *adv.* lieblos

un'civil *adj.* unhöflich

uncle /ˈʌŋkl/ *n.* Onkel, *der*

un'comfortable *adj.* **(a)** unbequem
(b) (feeling discomfort) be ∼: sich unbehaglich
fühlen
(c) (uneasy, disconcerting) unangenehm;
peinlich ⟨*Stille*⟩

un'comfortably *adv.* unbequem; be
∼ aware of sth. sich (*Dat.*) einer Sache
peinlich bewusst sein

un'common *adj.* ungewöhnlich

uncompli'mentary *adj.* wenig
schmeichelhaft

uncompromising /ʌnˈkɒmprəmaɪzɪŋ/
adj. kompromisslos

uncon'ditional *adj.* bedingungslos
⟨*Kapitulation*⟩; kategorisch ⟨*Ablehnung*⟩;
⟨*Versprechen*⟩ ohne Vorbehalte

unconfirmed /ʌnkənˈfɜːmd/ *adj.*
unbestätigt

un'conscious ① *adj.* **(a)** (Med.) bewusstlos
(b) (unaware) be ∼ of sth. sich einer Sache
(*Gen.*) nicht bewusst sein
(c) (not intended; Psych.) unbewusst
② *n.* Unbewusste, *das*

un'consciously *adv.* unbewusst

uncontrollable /ʌnkənˈtrəʊləbl/ *adj.*
unkontrollierbar; the child is ∼: das Kind ist
nicht zu bändigen

uncon'ventional *adj.*,
uncon'ventionally *adv.*
unkonventionell

unconvinced /ʌnkənˈvɪnst/ *adj.* nicht
überzeugt; remain ∼: sich nicht überzeugen
lassen

uncooked /ʌnˈkʊkt/ *adj.* roh

unco'operative *adj.* unkooperativ;
(unhelpful) wenig hilfsbereit

uncoordinated /ʌnkəʊˈɔːdɪneɪtɪd/ *adj.*
unkoordiniert

un'cork *v.t.* entkorken

uncouth /ʌnˈkuːθ/ *adj.* ungehobelt ⟨*Person,
Benehmen*⟩; grob ⟨*Bemerkung*⟩

un'cover *v.t.* aufdecken

undaunted /ʌnˈdɔːntɪd/ *adj.* unverzagt

undecided /ʌndɪˈsaɪdɪd/ *adj.* **(a)** (not settled)
nicht entschieden
(b) (hesitant) unentschlossen

undeclared /ʌndɪˈkleəd/ *adj.* ∼ income (for
tax) nicht angegebenes Einkommen

'undelete *v.t.* (Comp.) wiederherstellen

undemanding /ʌndɪˈmɑːndɪŋ/ *adj.*
anspruchslos

unde'niable *adj.*, **undeniably**
/ʌndɪˈnaɪəblɪ/ *adv.* unbestreitbar

under /ˈʌndə(r)/ ① *prep.* **(a)** (underneath,
below) unter (*position:* + *Dat.; motion:*
+ *Akk.*); from ∼ the table/bed unter dem
Tisch/Bett hervor
(b) (undergoing) ∼ treatment in Behandlung;
∼ repair in Reparatur; ∼ construction im
Bau
(c) (in conditions of) unter ⟨*Stress, hohen
Temperaturen usw.*⟩
(d) (subject to) unter (+ *Dat.*); ∼ the terms of
the contract nach den Bestimmungen des
Vertrags
(e) (with the use of) unter (+ *Dat.*); ∼ an
assumed name unter falschem Namen
(f) (less than) unter (+ *Dat.*).
② *adv.* **(a)** (in or to a lower or subordinate position)
darunter

(b) (in/into a state of unconsciousness) be ∼/put sb. ∼: in Narkose liegen/jmdn. in Narkose versetzen

under: ∼**a'chieve** *v.i.* unter dem erreichbaren Leistungsniveau bleiben; ∼**age** *adj.* minderjährig; ∼**carriage** *n.* Fahrwerk, *das;* ∼**clothes** *n. pl.,* ∼**clothing** *n.* ▶ UNDERWEAR; ∼**coat** *n.* (layer of paint) Grundierung, *die;* (paint) Grundierfarbe, *die;* ∼**cover** *adj.* (disguised) getarnt; (secret) verdeckt; ∼**cover agent** Geheimagent, *der;* ∼**current** *n.* Unterströmung, *die;* (fig.) Unterton, *der;* ∼**cut** *v.t.,* ∼**cut** unterbieten; ∼**dog** *n.* (a) (in fight) Unterlegene, *der/die;* **(b)** (fig.) Benachteiligte, *der/die;* ∼**done** *adj.* halb gar; ∼**estimate** /ʌndər'estimeit/ [1] *v.t.* unterschätzen; [2] /ʌndər'estimət/ *n.* Unterschätzung, *die;* ∼'**fed** *adj.* unterernährt; ∼'**foot** *adv.* am Boden; be trampled ∼**foot** mit Füßen zertrampelt werden; ∼'**go** *v.t., forms as* GO 1: durchmachen; ∼**go treatment** sich einer Behandlung unterziehen; ∼**go a change** sich verändern; ∼'**graduate** *n.* ∼**graduate** [student] Student/Studentin vor der ersten Prüfung; ∼**ground** [1] /-'-'-/ *adv.* **(a)** unter der Erde; (Mining) unter Tage; **(b)** (fig.) (in hiding) im Untergrund; (into hiding) in den Untergrund; [2] /'---/ *adj.* unterirdisch ⟨*Höhle, See*⟩; ∼**ground railway** Untergrundbahn, *die;* U-Bahn, *die;* ∼**ground car park** Tiefgarage, *die;* [3] /'---/ *n.* (railway) U-Bahn, *die;* ∼**ground station/train** U-Bahnhof, *der/*U-Bahn-Zug, *der;* ∼**growth** *n.* Unterholz, *das;* ∼**hand,** ∼'**handed** *adj.* **(a)** (secret) heimlich; **(b)** (crafty) hinterhältig; ∼**lay** *n.* Unterlage, *die;* ∼'**lie** *v.t., forms as* LIE²: ∼**lie sth.** (fig.) einer Sache (*Dat.*) zugrunde liegen; ∼**lying cause** eigentliche Ursache, *die;* ∼'**line** *v.t.* unterstreichen

underling /'ʌndəlıŋ/ *n.* Untergebene, *der/die*

under: ∼'**lying** ▶ UNDERLIE; ∼'**mine** *v.t.* **(a)** unterhöhlen; **(b)** (fig.) untergraben; unterminieren ⟨*Autorität*⟩

underneath /ʌndə'ni:θ/ [1] *prep.* unter (*position:* + *Dat.; motion:* + *Akk.*) [2] *adv.* darunter

under: ∼'**nourished** *adj.* unterernährt; ∼'**paid** *adj.* unterbezahlt; ∼**pants** *n. pl.* Unterhose, *die;* ∼**pass** *n.* Unterführung, *die;* ∼'**play** *v.t.* herunterspielen; ∼'**privileged** *adj.* unterprivilegiert; ∼'**rate** *v.t.* unterschätzen; ∼**seal** *n.* Unterbodenschutz, *der;* ∼**signed** /ʌndə'saınd/ *adj.* (esp. Law) the ∼**signed** der/die Unterzeichnete/(*pl.*) die Unterzeichneten (Papierdt.); ∼'**staffed** *adj.* unterbesetzt; be ∼**staffed** an Personalmangel leiden

understand /ʌndə'stænd/ [1] *v.t.,* understood /ʌndə'stʊd/ **(a)** verstehen; make oneself understood sich verständlich machen **(b)** (have heard) gehört haben

(c) (take as implied) it was understood that ...: es wurde allgemein angenommen, dass ... [2] *v.i.,* understood **(a)** verstehen **(b)** (gather, hear) if I ∼ correctly wenn ich mich nicht irre; he is, I ∼, no longer here er ist, wie ich höre, nicht mehr hier

understandable /ʌndə'stændəbl/ *adj.* verständlich

understandably /ʌndə'stændəblı/ *adv.* verständlicherweise

under'standing [1] *adj.* verständnisvoll [2] *n.* **(a)** (agreement) Verständigung, *die;* reach an ∼ with sb. sich mit jmdm. verständigen; on the ∼ that ...: unter der Voraussetzung, dass ... **(b)** (intelligence) Verstand, *der* **(c)** (insight) Verständnis, *das* (of, for für)

under: ∼**statement** *n.* Untertreibung, *die;* ∼**study** *n.* Ersatzspieler, *der/* -spielerin, *die;* ∼'**take** *v.t., forms as* TAKE 1: unternehmen; ∼**take a task** eine Aufgabe übernehmen; ∼**take to do sth.** sich verpflichten, etw. zu tun; ∼**taker** *n.* Leichenbestatter, *der/*-bestatterin, *die;* ∼'**taking** *n.* **(a)** (task) Aufgabe, *die;* **(b)** (pledge) Versprechen, *das;* ∼**tone** *n.* in ∼**tones** *or* an ∼**tone** mit gedämpfter Stimme; ∼**tone of criticism** kritischer Unterton, *der;* ∼**tow** *n.* Unterströmung, *die;* ∼'**value** *v.t.* unterbewerten; ∼**water** [1] /'---/ *attrib. adj.* Unterwasser-; [2] /-'-'-/ *adv.* unter Wasser; ∼**wear** *n.* Unterwäsche, *die;* ∼'**weight** *adj.* untergewichtig; ∼**world** *n.* Unterwelt, *die*

undeserved /ʌndı'zɜ:vd/ *adj.* unverdient

unde'sirable *adj.* unerwünscht; it is ∼ that ...: es ist nicht wünschenswert, dass ...

undeveloped /ʌndı'veləpt/ *adj.* **(a)** (immature) nicht voll ausgebildet **(b)** (not built on) nicht bebaut

undies /'ʌndız/ *n. pl.* (coll.) Unterwäsche, *die*

un'dignified *adj.* blamabel

undisciplined /ʌn'dısıplınd/ *adj.* undiszipliniert

undiscovered /ʌndı'skʌvəd/ *adj.* unentdeckt

undisguised /ʌndıs'gaızd/ *adj.* unverhohlen

undisturbed /ʌndı'stɜ:bd/ *adj.* (not interrupted) ungestört

undo /ʌn'du:/ *v.t.,* undoes /ʌn'dʌz/, undoing /ʌn'du:ıŋ/, undid /ʌn'dıd/, undone /ʌn'dʌn/ (unfasten) aufmachen

un'done *adj.* **(a)** (not accomplished) unerledigt **(b)** (not fastened) offen

undoubted /ʌn'daʊtıd/ *adj.* unzweifelhaft

un'doubtedly *adv.* zweifellos

un'dress [1] *v.t.* ausziehen; get ∼**ed** sich ausziehen [2] *v.i.* sich ausziehen

U

undrinkable /ʌn'drɪŋkəbl/ *adj.* nicht trinkbar; ungenießbar

un'due *attrib. adj.* übertrieben; übermäßig

undulating /'ʌndjʊleɪtɪŋ/ *adj.* Wellen⟨linie⟩; ∼ country sanfte Hügellandschaft

unduly /ʌn'dju:lɪ/ *adv.* übermäßig

undying /ʌn'daɪɪŋ/ *adj.* ewig; unsterblich ⟨Ruhm⟩

unearth /ʌn'ɜ:θ/ *v.t.* (a) ausgraben (b) (fig.: discover) aufdecken

unearthly /ʌn'ɜ:θlɪ/ *adj.* unheimlich; at an ∼ hour in aller Herrgottsfrühe

un'easy *adj.* (a) (anxious) besorgt; he felt ∼: ihm war unbehaglich zumute (b) (restless) unruhig

uneatable /ʌn'i:təbl/ *adj.* ungenießbar

uneco'nomic *adj.* unrentabel

uneco'nomical *adj.* ∼ [to run] unwirtschaftlich

uneducated /ʌn'edjʊkeɪtɪd/ *adj.* ungebildet

unemotional /ʌnɪ'məʊʃənl/ *adj.* emotionslos; nüchtern

unemployed /ʌnɪm'plɔɪd/ ① *adj.* arbeitslos ② *n. pl.* the ∼: die Arbeitslosen *Pl.*

unem'ployment *n.* Arbeitslosigkeit, *die*

unem'ployment benefit *n.* Arbeitslosengeld, *das*

un'ending *adj.* endlos

un'equal *adj.* unterschiedlich; ungleich ⟨Kampf⟩; be ∼ to sth. einer Sache (*Dat.*) nicht gewachsen sein

unequalled (*Amer.:* **unequaled**) /ʌn'i:kwld/ *adj.* unerreicht

une'quivocal *adj.* eindeutig

unerring /ʌn'ɜ:rɪŋ/ *adj.* unfehlbar

un'ethical *adj.* unmoralisch

un'even *adj.* (a) (not smooth) uneben (b) (not uniform) ungleichmäßig (c) (odd) ungerade ⟨Zahl⟩

un'evenly *adv.* ungleichmäßig

uneventful /ʌnɪ'ventfl/ *adj.* ereignislos

unexciting /ʌnɪk'saɪtɪŋ/ *adj.* wenig aufregend; (boring) langweilig

unex'pected *adj.* unerwartet

unexplained /ʌnɪk'spleɪnd/ *adj.* ungeklärt

un'fair *adj.* unfair; ungerecht

un'fairly *adv.* (a) (unjustly) ungerecht; unfair ⟨spielen⟩ (b) (unreasonably) zu Unrecht

un'fairness *n.* Ungerechtigkeit, *die*

un'faithful *adj.* untreu

unfa'miliar *adj.* (a) (strange) unbekannt; ungewohnt ⟨Arbeit⟩ (b) be ∼ with sth. sich mit etw. nicht auskennen

un'fasten *v.t.* (a) öffnen (b) (detach) lösen

un'favourable *adj.* ungünstig

un'favourably *adv.* ungünstig; be ∼ disposed towards sb./sth. jmdm./etw. gegenüber ablehnend eingestellt sein

un'feeling *adj.* gefühllos

unfinished /ʌn'fɪnɪʃt/ *adj.* unvollendet ⟨Werk⟩; unerledigt ⟨Arbeit⟩

un'fit *adj.* (a) ungeeignet (b) (not physically fit) nicht fit (ugs.); ∼ for military service [wehrdienst]untauglich

un'flattering *adj.* wenig schmeichelhaft

un'flinching *adj.* unerschrocken

un'fold ① *v.t.* entfalten; ausbreiten ⟨Zeitung, Landkarte⟩ ② *v.i.* sich entfalten; (develop) sich entwickeln

unfore'seen *adj.* unvorhergesehen

unforgettable /ʌnfə'getəbl/ *adj.* unvergesslich

unforgivable /ʌnfə'gɪvəbl/ *adj.* unverzeihlich

un'fortunate *adj.* unglücklich

un'fortunately *adv.* leider

un'founded *adj.* (fig.) unbegründet

un'freeze *v.t. & i.*, **unfroze** /ʌn'frəʊz/, **unfrozen** /ʌn'frəʊzn/ auftauen

un'friendly *adj.* unfreundlich; feindlich ⟨Staat⟩

unfulfilled /ʌnfʊl'fɪld/ *adj.* unerfüllt ⟨Person⟩

un'furl ① *v.t.* aufrollen; losmachen ⟨Segel⟩ ② *v.i.* sich aufrollen

un'furnished *adj.* unmöbliert

ungainly /ʌn'geɪnlɪ/ *adj.* unbeholfen

ungram'matical *adj.* ungrammatisch

un'grateful *adj.* undankbar

un'happily *adv.* (a) unglücklich (b) (unfortunately) leider

un'happiness *n.* Bekümmertheit, *die*

un'happy *adj.* unglücklich; (not content) unzufrieden (about with); be or feel ∼ about doing sth. Bedenken haben, etw. zu tun

un'harmed *adj.* unbeschädigt; (uninjured) unverletzt

un'healthy *adj.* ungesund

unheard-of /ʌn'hɜ:dɒv/ *adj.* (unknown) [gänzlich] unbekannt; (unprecedented) beispiellos; (outrageous) unerhört

un'helpful *adj.* wenig hilfsbereit ⟨Person⟩; ⟨Bemerkung, Kritik⟩ die einem nicht weiterhilft

un'hook *v.t.* vom Haken nehmen; aufhaken ⟨Kleid⟩

un'hurt *adj.* unverletzt

unhy'gienic *adj.* unhygienisch

unicorn /'ju:nɪkɔ:n/ *n.* Einhorn, *das*

uni'dentified *adj.* nicht identifiziert; ∼ flying object unbekanntes Flugobjekt

unification /ju:nɪfɪ'keɪʃn/ *n.* Einigung, *die*

uniform /'ju:nɪfɔ:m/ ① *adj.* einheitlich; be ∼ in shape/size die gleiche Form/Größe haben

2 *n.* Uniform, *die;* **in/out of** ∼: in/ohne Uniform

uniformity /juːnɪˈfɔːmɪtɪ/ *n.* Einheitlichkeit, *die*

'uniformly *adv.* einheitlich

unify /ˈjuːnɪfaɪ/ *v.t.* einigen

unilateral /juːnɪˈlætərl/ *adj.* einseitig

uni'maginable *adj.* unvorstellbar

uni'maginative *adj.* fantasielos

unim'portant *adj.* unwichtig; bedeutungslos

unimpressed /ʌnɪmˈprest/ *adj.* nicht beeindruckt

unin'habitable *adj.* unbewohnbar

unin'habited *adj.* unbewohnt

un'injured *adj.* unverletzt

uninspired /ʌnɪnˈspaɪəd/ *adj.* einfallslos; **I am/feel** ∼: mir fehlt die Inspiration

uninspiring /ʌnɪnˈspaɪərɪŋ/ *adj.* langweilig

unin'telligent *adj.* nicht intelligent

unin'telligible *adj.* unverständlich

unin'tended *adj.* unbeabsichtigt

unin'tentional *adj.*, **unin'tentionally** *adv.* unabsichtlich

un'interested *adj.* desinteressiert (**in an** + *Dat.*)

un'interesting *adj.* uninteressant

uninterrupted /ʌnɪntəˈrʌptɪd/ *adj.* ununterbrochen

uninvited /ʌnɪmˈvaɪtɪd/ *adj.* ungeladen

union /ˈjuːnɪən/ *n.* (a) (trade ∼) Gewerkschaft, *die* (b) (Polit.) Union, *die*

Union 'Jack *n.* (Brit.) Union Jack, *der*

unique /juːˈniːk/ *adj.* einzigartig

unisex /ˈjuːnɪseks/ *adj.* Unisex⟨*mantel, -kleidung*⟩; ∼ **hairdresser** Damen-und-Herren-Frisör, *der*

unison /ˈjuːnɪsən/ *n.* Unisono, *das;* **in** ∼: einstimmig; **act in** ∼ (fig.) vereint handeln

unit /ˈjuːnɪt/ *n.* (a) (also Mil., Math.) Einheit, *die;* ∼ **of length/monetary** ∼: Längen-/Währungseinheit, *die* (b) (piece of furniture) Element, *das;* **kitchen** ∼: Küchenelement, *das*

unite /juːˈnaɪt/ **1** *v.t.* vereinigen; einen, einigen ⟨*Partei, Mitglieder*⟩ **2** *v.i.* sich vereinigen

u'nited *adj.* (a) (harmonious) einig (b) (combined) gemeinsam

United: ∼ **'Kingdom** *pr. n.* Vereinigtes Königreich [Großbritannien und Nordirland]; ∼ **'Nations** *pr. n. sing.* Vereinte Nationen *Pl.;* ∼ **States [of A'merica]** *pr. n. sing.* Vereinigte Staaten [von Amerika] *Pl.*

unit 'price *n.* Stückpreis, *der*

unity /ˈjuːnɪtɪ/ *n.* Einheit, *die*

universal /juːnɪˈvɜːsl/ *adj.*, **uni'versally** *adv.* allgemein

universe /ˈjuːnɪvɜːs/ *n.* Universum, *das*

university /juːnɪˈvɜːsɪtɪ/ *n.* Universität, *die; attrib.* Universitäts-

uni'versity place *n.* Studienplatz, *der*

un'just *adj.* ungerecht

unjustified /ʌnˈdʒʌstɪfaɪd/ *adj.* ungerechtfertigt

unkempt /ʌnˈkempt/ *adj.* ungepflegt

un'kind *adj.*, **un'kindly** *adv.* unfreundlich

un'kindness *n.* Unfreundlichkeit, *die*

un'known **1** *adj.* unbekannt **2** *adv.* ∼ **to sb.** ohne dass jmd. davon weiß/wusste

un'lawful *adj.* ungesetzlich

unleaded /ʌnˈledɪd/ *adj.* bleifrei ⟨*Benzin*⟩

unless /ənˈles/ *conj.* es sei denn; wenn … nicht

un'like **1** *adj.* nicht ähnlich **2** *prep.* **be** ∼ **sb./sth.** jmdm./einer Sache nicht ähnlich sein; ∼ **him,** …: im Gegensatz zu ihm …

un'likely *adj.* unwahrscheinlich; **be** ∼ **to do sth.** etw. wahrscheinlich nicht tun

un'limited *adj.* unbegrenzt

un'load *v.t.* entladen ⟨*Lastwagen, Waggon*⟩; löschen ⟨*Schiff, Schiffsladung*⟩; ausladen ⟨*Gepäck*⟩

un'lock *v.t.* aufschließen

un'lucky *adj.* (a) unglücklich; (not successful) glücklos; **be [very]** ∼: [großes] Pech haben (b) (bringing bad luck) **an** ∼ **number** eine Unglückszahl; **be** ∼: Unglück bringen

unmanageable /ʌnˈmænɪdʒəbl/ *adj.* widerspenstig ⟨*Kind, Pferd*⟩; unkontrollierbar ⟨*Situation*⟩

un'manned *adj.* unbemannt

un'married *adj.* unverheiratet; ledig

un'mask *v.t.* (fig.) entlarven

unmi'stakable /ʌnmɪˈsteɪkəbl/ *adj.* deutlich; unverwechselbar ⟨*Handschrift, Stimme*⟩

unmistakably /ʌnmɪˈsteɪkəblɪ/ *adv.* unverkennbar

un'mitigated *adj.* vollkommen; **be an** ∼ **disaster** (coll.) eine einzige Katastrophe sein

unmotivated /ʌnˈməʊtɪveɪtɪd/ *adj.* unmotiviert

un'natural *adj.*, **un'naturally** *adv.* unnatürlich; (abnormal) nicht normal

un'necessarily *adv.*, **un'necessary** *adj.* unnötig

unnerve /ʌnˈnɜːv/ *v.t.* entnerven

unnerving /ʌnˈnɜːvɪŋ/ *adj.* entnervend

unnoticed /ʌnˈnəʊtɪst/ *adj.* unbemerkt

unobservant /ʌnəbˈzɜːvənt/ *adj.* unaufmerksam

unobserved /ʌnəbˈzɜːvd/ *adj.* unbeobachtet

u

unob'tainable *adj.* nicht erhältlich; **number** ~ (Teleph.) kein Anschluss unter dieser Nummer

unof'ficial *adj.*, **unof'ficially** *adv.* inoffiziell

un'pack *v.t. & i.* auspacken

un'paid *adj.* unbezahlt; nicht bezahlt; ~ **for** nicht bezahlt

unpalatable /ʌn'pælətəbl/ *adj.* ungenießbar

un'paralleled *adj.* beispiellos

un'pardonable *adj.* unverzeihlich

un'pleasant *adj.*, **un'pleasantly** *adv.* unangenehm

un'pleasantness *n.* (bad feeling) Verstimmung, *die*

un'plug *v.t.*, **-gg-**: ~ **a lamp** den Stecker einer Lampe herausziehen

un'popular *adj.* unbeliebt ⟨*Lehrer, Regierung usw.*⟩; unpopulär ⟨*Maßnahme, Politik*⟩ (with bei)

un'precedented *adj.* beispiellos

unpre'dictable *adj.* unberechenbar

unpre'pared *adj.* unvorbereitet

unprepos'sessing *adj.* wenig attraktiv

unpre'tentious *adj.* einfach ⟨*Wein, Stil, Haus*⟩; bescheiden ⟨*Person*⟩

unprincipled /ʌn'prɪnsɪpld/ *adj.* skrupellos

unprintable /ʌn'prɪntəbl/ *adj.* nicht druckreif

unpro'ductive *adj.* fruchtlos ⟨*Diskussion, Nachforschung*⟩; unproduktiv ⟨*Zeit, Arbeit*⟩

unpro'fessional *adj.* (contrary to standards) standeswidrig

un'profitable *adj.* unrentabel

un'promising *adj.* nicht sehr viel versprechend

unpublished /ʌn'pʌblɪʃt/ *adj.* unveröffentlicht

un'qualified *adj.* (a) unqualifiziert (b) (absolute) uneingeschränkt; voll ⟨*Erfolg*⟩

un'questionable *adj.* unbezweifelbar ⟨*Tatsache*⟩; unbestreitbar ⟨*Recht, Ehrlichkeit*⟩

unquestionably /ʌn'kwestʃənəblɪ/ *adv.* ohne Frage

unquote /ʌn'kwəʊt/ *v.i.* ..., **quote, ..., ~:** ..., Zitat, ..., Ende des Zitats

unravel /ʌn'rævl/ 1 *v.t.*, (Brit.) **-ll-** entwirren; (undo) aufziehen; (fig.) ~ **a mystery/the truth** ein Geheimnis enträtseln/die Wahrheit aufdecken 2 *v.i.*, (Brit.) **-ll-** sich aufziehen

un'real *adj.* unwirklich

unrea'listic *adj.* unrealistisch

un'reasonable *adj.* unvernünftig; übertrieben ⟨*Ansprüche, Forderung, Preis, Kosten*⟩

unrecognizable /ʌn'rekəgnaɪzəbl/ *adj.* be [absolutely *or* quite] ~: [überhaupt] nicht wieder zu erkennen sein

unre'lated *adj.* be ~: nicht miteinander zusammenhängen; (by family) nicht verwandt sein

unrelenting /ʌnrɪ'lentɪŋ/ *adj.* unvermindert, nicht nachlassend ⟨*Hitze, Kälte*⟩

unre'liable *adj.* unzuverlässig

unrequited /ʌnrɪ'kwaɪtɪd/ *adj.* unerwidert

unreservedly /ʌnrɪ'zɜ:vɪdlɪ/ *adv.* uneingeschränkt

unresolved /ʌnrɪ'zɒlvd/ *adj.* (a) (not solved) ungelöst (b) (undecided) be ~: sich [noch] nicht entschieden haben

un'rest *n.* Unruhen *Pl.*

unre'stricted *adj.* unbeschränkt; uneingeschränkt

un'ripe *adj.* unreif

un'rivalled (*Amer.*: **un'rivaled**) *adj.* unübertroffen

un'roll 1 *v.t.* aufrollen 2 *v.i.* sich aufrollen

unromantic /ʌnrə'mæntɪk/ *adj.* unromantisch

unruly /ʌn'ru:lɪ/ *adj.* ungebärdig

un'safe *adj.* nicht sicher; **feel** ~: sich unsicher fühlen

un'said *adj.* ungesagt

un'salted *adj.* ungesalzen

unsatis'factory *adj.* unbefriedigend

unsatisfying /ʌn'sætɪsfaɪɪŋ/ *adj.* unbefriedigend

un'savoury (*Amer.*: **un'savory**) *adj.* unangenehm; zweifelhaft ⟨*Angelegenheit*⟩; unerfreulich ⟨*Einzelheiten*⟩

unscathed /ʌn'skeɪðd/ *adj.* unversehrt

unscented /ʌn'sentɪd/ *adj.* nicht parfümiert ⟨*Seife, Shampoo*⟩

un'screw 1 *v.t.* abschrauben 2 *v.i.* sich abschrauben lassen

un'scrupulous *adj.* skrupellos

unsecured /ʌnsɪ'kjʊəd/ *adj.* (Finance) ohne Sicherheit[en] *nachgestellt*

un'seemly *adj.* unschicklich

unself'conscious *adj.* unbefangen

un'selfish *adj.* selbstlos

un'selfishness *n.* Selbstlosigkeit, *die*

un'settled *adj.* (changeable) wechselhaft; (fig.) ruhelos ⟨*Leben*⟩; unruhig ⟨*Zeit, Land*⟩

un'settling *adj.* störend

unshak[e]able /ʌn'ʃeɪkəbl/ *adj.* unerschütterlich

un'shaven *adj.* unrasiert

un'sightly *adj.* unschön

un'skilled *adj.* ungelernt ⟨*Arbeiter*⟩

un'skimmed *adj.* ~ **milk** Vollmilch, *die*

un'sociable *adj.* ungesellig

unsolved /ʌn'sɒlvd/ *adj.* unaufgeklärt ⟨*Verbrechen*⟩

unso'phisticated *adj.* einfach

un'sound *adj.* **(a)** (diseased) nicht gesund; krank
(b) baufällig ‹*Gebäude*›
(c) (ill-founded) wenig stichhaltig; nicht vertretbar ‹*Ansicht, Methode*›
(d) of ∼ mind unzurechnungsfähig

unspeakable /ʌn'spiːkəbl/ *adj.* unbeschreiblich; (very bad) unsäglich

unspecified /ʌn'spesɪfaɪd/ *adj.* nicht näher bezeichnet

unspoken /ʌn'spəʊkn/ *adj.* ungesagt

un'stable *adj.* nicht stabil; [mentally/ emotionally] ∼: [psychisch] labil

un'steadily *adv.* unsicher

un'steady *adj.* unsicher; wackelig ‹*Leiter, Tisch*›

unstoppable /ʌn'stɒpəbl/ *adj.* unhaltbar ‹*Schuss aufs Fußballtor*›; (fig.) unaufhaltsam

un'stuck *adj.* come ∼: sich lösen; (fig. coll.: fail) ‹*Person:*› baden gehen (ugs.) (over mit)

unsuc'cessful *adj.* erfolglos; be ∼: keinen Erfolg haben

unsuc'cessfully *adv.* erfolglos

un'suitable *adj.* ungeeignet

unsu'specting *adj.* nichtsahnend

un'sweetened *adj.* ungesüßt

unsympa'thetic *adj.* wenig mitfühlend; be ∼: kein Mitgefühl zeigen

untalented /ʌn'tæləntɪd/ *adj.* untalentiert

untenable /ʌn'tenəbl/ *adj.* unhaltbar

unthinkable /ʌn'θɪŋkəbl/ *adj.* unvorstellbar

unthinking /ʌn'θɪŋkɪŋ/ *adj.*, **un'thinkingly** *adv.* gedankenlos

un'tidily *adv.* unordentlich

un'tidiness *n.* ▶ UNTIDY: Ungepflegtheit, *die;* Unaufgeräumtheit, *die*

un'tidy *adj.* ungepflegt ‹*Äußeres, Person, Garten*›; unaufgeräumt ‹*Zimmer*›

un'tie *v.t.*, untying aufknüpfen ‹*Seil, Paket*›; aufbinden ‹*Knoten*›; losbinden ‹*Pferd, Boot*›

until /ən'tɪl/ ⓵ *prep.* bis; ∼ [the] evening bis zum Abend; ∼ then bis dahin; not ∼ [Christmas/the summer] erst [Weihnachten/im Sommer] ⓶ *conj.* bis

un'timely *adj.* **(a)** ungelegen
(b) (premature) vorzeitig

un'tiring *adj.* unermüdlich

un'told *adj.* unbeschreiblich; unermesslich ‹*Reichtümer, Anzahl*›

untoward /ʌntə'wɔːd, ʌn'təʊəd/ *adj.* ungünstig; nothing ∼ happened es gab keine Schwierigkeiten

untranslatable /ʌntræns'leɪtəbl/ *adj.* unübersetzbar

untreated /ʌn'triːtɪd/ *adj.* unbehandelt

un'true *adj.* unwahr; that's ∼: das ist nicht wahr

un'trustworthy *adj.* unzuverlässig

un'truth *n.* Unwahrheit, *die*

un'truthful *adj.* verlogen

un'typical *adj.* untypisch (of für)

unusable /ʌn'juːzəbl/ *adj.* unbrauchbar

unused¹ /ʌn'juːzd/ *adj.* (new, fresh) unbenutzt; (not utilized) ungenutzt

unused² /ʌn'juːst/ *adj.* (unaccustomed) be ∼ to sth./doing sth. etw. (*Akk.*) nicht gewohnt sein/nicht gewohnt sein, etw. zu tun

un'usual *adj.*, **un'usually** *adv.* ungewöhnlich

unvarnished /ʌn'vɑːnɪʃt/ *adj.* unlackiert; (fig.) ungeschminkt ‹*Wahrheit*›

un'veil *v.t.* enthüllen; (fig.) vorstellen ‹*Produkt*›; enthüllen ‹*Plan*›

un'versed *adj.* nicht bewandert (in in + *Dat.*)

un'wanted *adj.* unerwünscht

un'warranted *adj.* ungerechtfertigt

un'welcome *adj.* unwillkommen

un'well *adj.* unwohl; look ∼: nicht wohl *od.* gut aussehen; he feels ∼ (poorly) er fühlt sich nicht wohl

un'wholesome *adj.* (lit. or fig.) ungesund

unwieldy /ʌn'wiːldɪ/ *adj.* sperrig

un'willing *adj.* widerwillig; be ∼ to do sth. etw. nicht tun wollen

un'willingly *adv.* widerwillig

unwind /ʌn'waɪnd/ ⓵ *v.t.*, unwound /ʌn'waʊnd/ abwickeln
⓶ *v.i.*, unwound **(a)** sich abwickeln
(b) (coll.: relax) sich entspannen

un'wise *adj.* unklug

unwitting /ʌn'wɪtɪŋ/ *adj.*, **un'wittingly** *adv.* unwissentlich

un'workable *adj.* undurchführbar ‹*Plan*›

un'worthy *adj.* unwürdig; be ∼ of sth. einer Sache (*Gen.*) nicht würdig sein; be ∼ of sb./sth. ‹*Verhalten:*› einer Person/ Sache (*Gen.*) unwürdig sein

un'wrap *v.t.*, -pp- auswickeln

un'written *adj.* ungeschrieben

un'zip *v.t.*, -pp-: **(a)** ∼ a dress/bag *etc.* den Reißverschluss eines Kleides/einer Tasche *usw.* öffnen
(b) (Comp.) entpacken ‹*Datei*›

up /ʌp/ ⓵ *adv.* **(a)** (to higher place) nach oben; (in lift) aufwärts; the bird flew up to the roof der Vogel flog aufs Dach [hinauf]; up into the air in die Luft [hinauf]; up here/there hier herauf/dort hinauf; higher/a little way up höher/ein kurzes Stück hinauf; come on up! komm [hier/weiter] herauf!
(b) (to upstairs) herauf/hinauf; nach oben
(c) (in higher place, upstairs) oben; up here/there hier/da oben; the next floor up ein Stockwerk höher
(d) (out of bed) be up auf sein
(e) (in price, value, amount) prices have gone up/are up die Preise sind gestiegen; butter is up [by …] Butter ist […] teurer ····⊹

U

(f) (as far as) **up to sth.** bis zu etw.; **up to here/there** bis hier[hin]/bis dorthin

(g) **[not] be/feel up to sth.** (capable of sth.) einer Sache (*Dat.*) [nicht] gewachsen sein/ sich einer Sache (*Dat.*) [nicht] gewachsen fühlen; **[not] be/feel up to doing sth.** [nicht] in der Lage sein/sich [nicht] in der Lage fühlen, etw. zu tun

(h) **be up to sth.** (doing) etw. anstellen (ugs.); **it is [not] up to sb. to do sth.** (sb.'s duty) es ist [nicht] jmds. Sache, etw. zu tun

(i) **be three points/games up** mit drei Punkten/Spielen vorn liegen

(j) **walk up and down** auf und ab gehen

(k) **time is up** die Zeit ist abgelaufen

2 *prep.* herauf/hinauf; **walk up the hill/road** den Berg/die Straße hinaufgehen; **walk up and down the platform** auf dem Bahnsteig auf und ab gehen; **further up the ladder/coast** weiter oben auf der Leiter/an der Küste; **live just up the road** ein Stück weiter oben in der Straße wohnen

3 *adj.* (coll.: amiss) **what's up?** was ist los? (ugs.); **something is up** irgendwas ist los (ugs.)

4 *v.t.*, **-pp-** (coll.: increase) erhöhen

'up-and-coming *adj.* (coll.) aufstrebend

'up-and-up *n.* (coll.) **be on the** ~: auf dem aufsteigenden Ast sein (ugs.)

'upbeat 1 *n.* (Mus.) Auftakt, *der*
2 *adj.* (coll.) (optimistic) optimistisch; (cheerful) fröhlich

'upbringing *n.* Erziehung, *die*

up'date *v.t.* auf den aktuellen Stand bringen

up 'front *adv.* (coll.: as down payment) im Voraus

upgrade 1 /-'-/ *v.t.* **(a)** aufwerten ⟨*Stellung*⟩
(b) (improve) verbessern
(c) (Comp.) aufrüsten, nachrüsten ⟨*Computer*⟩
2 /'--/ *n.* (Comp.) (act of upgrading) Nachrüsten, *die*; Erweiterung, *die*; (upgraded version) erweiterte Version; Upgrade, *der* (fachspr.)

upheaval /ʌp'hi:vl/ *n.* Aufruhr, *der*; (disturbance) Durcheinander, *das*

up'hill 1 *adj.* (fig.) **an** ~ **task/struggle** eine mühselige Aufgabe/ein harter Kampf
2 *adv.* bergauf

uphold *v.t.*, **upheld** unterstützen; wahren ⟨*Tradition*⟩

upholster /ʌp'həʊlstə(r)/ *v.t.* polstern

up'holsterer *n.* Polsterer, *der*/Polsterin, *die*

up'holstery *n.* **(a)** (craft) Polster[er]handwerk, *das*
(b) (padding) Polsterung, *die*

'upkeep *n.* Unterhalt, *der*

up'lifting *adj.* erhebend

up'lighter *n.* Deckenfluter, *der*

up'load *v.t.* (Comp.) hinaufladen ⟨*Datei, Daten*⟩

'upmarket *adj.* exklusiv

upon /ə'pɒn/ *prep.* auf (direction: + *Akk.*; position: + *Dat.*)

upper /'ʌpə(r)/ 1 compar. adj. ober...; Ober⟨*grenze, -lippe, -arm usw.*⟩; ~ **circle** oberer Rang; ~ **class[es]** Oberschicht, *die*; **have/get/gain the** ~ **hand** die Oberhand haben/gewinnen/erhalten
2 *n.* Oberteil, *das*

upper 'deck *n.* Oberdeck, *das*

'uppermost 1 *adj.* oberst...
2 *adv.* ganz oben

'upright *adj.* aufrecht

'uprising *n.* Aufstand, *der*

'uproar *n.* Aufruhr, *der*

up'root *v.t.* [her]ausreißen; ⟨*Sturm:*⟩ entwurzeln

upset 1 /ʌp'set/ *v.t.*, **-tt-**, **upset** **(a)** (overturn) umkippen; (accidentally) umstoßen ⟨*Tasse, Milch usw.*⟩
(b) (distress) erschüttern; (make angry) aufregen; **don't let it** ~ **you** nimm es nicht so schwer
(c) (make ill) **sth.** ~**s sb.** etw. bekommt jmdm. nicht
(d) durcheinander bringen ⟨*Plan*⟩
2 *v.i.*, **-tt-**, **upset** umkippen
3 *adj.* (distressed) bestürzt; (agitated) aufgeregt; **get** ~ **[about/over sth.]** sich [über etw. (*Akk.*)] aufregen
4 /'ʌpset/ *n.* **(a)** (agitation) Aufregung, *die*; (annoyance) Verärgerung, *die*
(b) **stomach** ~: Magenverstimmung, *die*
(c) (upheaval) Aufruhr, *der*

up'setting *adj.* erschütternd; (sad) traurig; (annoying) ärgerlich

'upshot *n.* Ergebnis, *das*

upside 'down 1 *adv.* verkehrt herum; **turn sth.** ~: etw. auf den Kopf stellen
2 *adj.* auf dem Kopf stehend ⟨*Bild*⟩; **be** ~: auf dem Kopf stehen

upstairs 1 /-'-/ *adv.* nach oben ⟨*gehen, kommen*⟩; oben ⟨*sein, wohnen*⟩
2 /'--/ *adj.* im Obergeschoss nachgestellt

'upstart *n.* Emporkömmling, *der*

up'stream *adv.* flussaufwärts

'uptake *n.* **be quick/slow on the** ~ (coll.) schnell begreifen/schwer von Begriff sein (ugs.)

uptight /-'-, '--/ *adj.* (coll.: tense) nervös (**about** wegen)

up to 'date *adj.* **be/keep** ~: auf dem neuesten Stand sein/bleiben; **bring sth.** ~: etw. auf den neuesten Stand bringen

up-to-'date *attrib. adj.* (current) aktuell; (modern) modern

up-to-the-'minute *adj.* hochaktuell

'upturn *n.* Aufschwung, *der* (in *Gen.*)

upturned /'ʌptɜːnd/ *adj.* umgedreht; ~ **nose** Stupsnase, *die*

upward /'ʌpwəd/ 1 *adj.* nach oben gerichtet
2 *adv.* aufwärts ⟨*sich bewegen*⟩; nach oben ⟨*sehen, gehen*⟩

upwards /ˈʌpwədz/ *adv.* (a) ▶ UPWARD 2
(b) ~ of über (+ *Akk.*)

uranium /jʊəˈreɪnɪəm/ *n.* Uran, *das*

Uranus /ˈjʊərənəs, jʊəˈreɪnəs/ *pr. n.*
(Astron.) Uranus, *der*

urban /ˈɜːbn/ *adj.* städtisch; Stadt⟨*gebiet,
-bevölkerung, -planung*⟩

urbane /ɜːˈbeɪn/ *adj.* weltmännisch

urchin /ˈɜːtʃɪn/ *n.* Strolch, *der*

urge /ɜːdʒ/ ① *v.t.* ~ sb. to do sth. jmdn.
drängen, etw. zu tun
② *n.* Trieb, *der*
■ **urge 'on** *v.t.* antreiben; (encourage)
anfeuern

urgency /ˈɜːdʒənsɪ/ *n.* Dringlichkeit, *die*

urgent /ˈɜːdʒənt/ *adj.* dringend; (to be dealt
with immediately) eilig; **be in ~ need of sth.**
etw. dringend brauchen

'urgently *adv.* dringend; (immediately) eilig

urinal /jʊəˈraɪnl/ *n.* [public] ~: [öffentliche]
Herrentoilette; Pissoir, *das*

urinary /ˈjʊərɪnərɪ/ *adj.* Harn-

urinate /ˈjʊərɪneɪt/ *v.i.* urinieren

urine /ˈjʊərɪn/ *n.* Urin, *der;* Harn, *der*

URL *abbr.* (Comp.) = **uniform resource
locator** URL, *der*

urn /ɜːn/ *n.* (a) **tea/coffee ~:** Tee-/
Kaffeemaschine, *die*
(b) (vessel) Urne, *die*

Uruguay /ˈjʊərəgwaɪ/ *pr. n.* Uruguay (*das*)

us /əs, *stressed* ʌs/ *pron.* uns; **it's us** wir
sinds (ugs.)

US *abbr.* = **United States** USA

USA *abbr.* = **United States of
America** USA

usage /ˈjuːzɪdʒ, ˈjuːsɪdʒ/ *n.* (a) Brauch, *der*
(b) (Ling.) Sprachgebrauch, *der*

use ① /juːs/ *n.* (a) Gebrauch, *der;* (of
dictionary, calculator, room) Benutzung, *die;* (of
word, pesticide, spice) Verwendung, *die;* **[not] be
in ~:** [nicht] in Gebrauch sein; **be no longer
in ~:** nicht mehr verwendet werden; **make
~ of sb./sth.** jmdn./etw. gebrauchen/(exploit)
ausnutzen; **make good ~ of,** turn *or* put to
good ~: gut nutzen ⟨*Zeit, Talent, Geld*⟩; **put
sth. to ~:** etw. verwenden
(b) (usefulness) Nutzen, *der;* **is it of [any] ~?**
ist das [irgendwie] von Nutzen?; **be [of] no
~ [to sb.]** [jmdm.] nicht nützen; **it's no
~ [doing that]** es hat keinen Sinn[, das zu
tun]
(c) (purpose) Verwendung, *die;* **have/find a
~ for sth./sb.** für etw./jmdn. Verwendung
haben/finden; **have no/not much ~ for sth./
sb.** etw./jmdn. nicht/kaum brauchen
② /juːz/ *v.t.* (a) benutzen; nutzen
⟨*Gelegenheit*⟩; anwenden ⟨*Gewalt*⟩; in
Anspruch nehmen ⟨*Firma, Dienstleistung*⟩;
nutzen ⟨*Zeit, Gelegenheit*⟩; verwenden
⟨*Kraftstoff, Butter, Wort*⟩
(b) ~d to /juːst tə/ I ~d to live in London
früher habe ich in London gelebt

■ **use 'up** *v.t.* aufbrauchen; verbrauchen
⟨*Geld, Energie*⟩

use-by date /ˈjuːzbaɪ/ *n.* (esp. Brit.)
[Mindest]haltbarkeitsdatum, *das*

used ① *adj.* (a) /juːzd/ gebraucht;
gestempelt ⟨*Briefmarke*⟩; ~ **car**
Gebrauchtwagen, *der*
(b) /juːst/ ~ **to sth.** [an] etw. (*Akk.*) gewöhnt
② /juːst/ ▶ USE 2B

useful /ˈjuːsfl/ *adj.* nützlich; praktisch
⟨*Werkzeug*⟩; hilfreich ⟨*Rat, Idee*⟩

'usefulness *n.* Nützlichkeit, *die*

useless /ˈjuːslɪs/ *adj.* unbrauchbar
⟨*Werkzeug, Rat, Idee*⟩; nutzlos ⟨*Wissen,
Information, Protest, Anstrengung, Kampf*⟩;
zwecklos ⟨*Widerstand, Protest*⟩

user /ˈjuːzə(r)/ *n.* Benutzer, *der*/Benutzerin,
die

user: ~**-friendly** *adj.* benutzerfreundlich;
~ **group** *n.* Benutzergruppe, *die;*
~ **interface** *n.* (Comp.)
Benutzerschnittstelle, *die;* ~ **name** *n.*
(Comp.) Benutzername, *der*

usher /ˈʌʃə(r)/ ① *n.* (in court)
Gerichtsdiener, *der;* (at cinema, church)
Platzanweiser, *der*
② *v.t.* führen
■ **usher 'in** *v.t.* hineinführen; (fig.)
einläuten

usherette /ʌʃəˈret/ *n.* Platzanweiserin, *die*

USSR *abbr.* (Hist.) = **Union of Soviet
Socialist Republics** UdSSR, *die*

usual /ˈjuːʒʊəl/ *adj.* üblich

usually /ˈjuːʒʊəlɪ/ *adv.* gewöhnlich

usurp /juːˈzɜːp/ *v.t.* sich (*Dat.*)
widerrechtlich aneignen

utensil /juːˈtensɪl/ *n.* Utensil, *das;* **writing
~s** Schreibutensilien *Pl.;* **kitchen ~s**
Küchengeräte *Pl.*

uterus /ˈjuːtərəs/ *n.* Gebärmutter, *die*

utilitarian /juːtɪlɪˈteərɪən/ *adj.* funktionell

utility /juːˈtɪlɪtɪ/ *n.* (a) Nutzen, *der*
(b) [public] ~: öffentlicher
Versorgungsbetrieb

u'tility room *n.:* Raum, in dem [größere]
Haushaltsgeräte (z.B. Waschmaschine)
installiert sind

utilize /ˈjuːtɪlaɪz/ *v.t.* nutzen

utmost /ˈʌtməʊst/ ① *adj.* äußerst...;
größt... ⟨*Höflichkeit, Eleganz, Einfachheit,
Geschwindigkeit*⟩
② *n.* Äußerste, *das;* **do** *or* **try one's ~ to do
sth.** mit allen Mitteln versuchen, etw. zu tun

utter¹ /ˈʌtə(r)/ *adj.* völlig; vollkommen;
~ **fool** Vollidiot, *der* (ugs.)

utter² *v.t.* (a) von sich geben ⟨*Schrei,
Seufzer*⟩
(b) (say) sagen

utterance /ˈʌtərəns/ *n.* Worte *Pl.*

'utterly *adv.* völlig; vollkommen; äußerst
⟨*dumm, lächerlich*⟩

u

'**U-turn** *n.* Wende [um 180°]; (fig.)
Kehrtwendung, *die;* **make a** ~: wenden; '**No**
~**s**' „Wenden verboten"

UV *abbr.* = **ultraviolet** UV

Vv

V¹, v /viː/ *n.* V, v, *das*
V² *abbr.* = **volt[s]** V
v. *abbr.* = **versus** gg.
vacancy /'veɪkənsɪ/ *n.* (a) (job) freie Stelle
(b) (room) freies Zimmer; '**vacancies**'
„Zimmer frei"; '**no vacancies**' „belegt"
vacant /'veɪkənt/ *adj.* (a) frei; '**situations**
~' „Stellenangebote" (b) (mentally) leer
vacate /və'keɪt/ *v.t.* räumen
vacation /və'keɪʃn/ *n.* (a) (Brit. Univ.) Ferien
Pl.
(b) (Amer.) ▶ HOLIDAY B
vaccinate /'væksɪneɪt/ *v.t.* impfen
vaccination /væksɪ'neɪʃn/ *n.* Impfung, *die;*
have a ~: geimpft werden
vaccine /'væksiːn/ *n.* Impfstoff, *der*
vacillate /'væsɪleɪt/ *v.i.* schwanken
vacuum /'vækjʊəm/ ① *n.* (a) Vakuum, *das;*
live in a ~: im luftleeren Raum leben
(b) (coll.: ~ cleaner) Staubsauger, *der* (ugs.)
② *v.t. & i.* [staub]saugen
vacuum: ~ **cleaner** *n.* Staubsauger, *der;*
~ **flask** *n.* (Brit.) Thermosflasche, *die;*
~-**packed** *adj.* vakuumverpackt
vagaries /'veɪɡərɪz/ *n. pl.* Launen *Pl.*
vagina /və'dʒaɪnə/ *n.* Scheide, *die*
vagrant /'veɪɡrənt/ *n.* Landstreicher, *der*/
-streicherin, *die;* (in cities) Stadtstreicher, *der*/
-streicherin, *die*
vague /veɪɡ/ *adj.* vage; verschwommen
⟨*Form, Umriss*⟩; (absent-minded)
geistesabwesend; **not have the** ~**st idea** *or*
notion nicht die blasseste *od.* leiseste
Ahnung haben
'**vaguely** *adv.* vage; entfernt ⟨*bekannt sein,*
erinnern an⟩; schwach ⟨*sich erinnern*⟩
vain /veɪn/ *adj.* (a) (conceited) eitel
(b) (useless) leer; vergeblich ⟨*Hoffnung,*
Versuch⟩; **in** ~: vergeblich
'**vainly** *adv.* vergebens
vale /veɪl/ *n.* (arch./poet.) Tal, *das*
valentine /'væləntaɪn/ *n.* ~ [card]
Grußkarte zum Valentinstag; **St. V**~'**s Day**
Valentinstag, *der*
valet /'væleɪ/ *n.* Kammerdiener, *der*
valiant /'vælɪənt/ *adj.,* '**valiantly** *adv.*
tapfer

valid /'vælɪd/ *adj.* (a) (legally acceptable)
gültig; berechtigt ⟨*Anspruch*⟩
(b) (justifiable) stichhaltig ⟨*Argument*⟩; triftig
⟨*Grund*⟩; begründet ⟨*Einwand,*
Entschuldigung⟩
validate /'vælɪdeɪt/ *v.t.* rechtskräftig
machen
validity /və'lɪdɪtɪ/ *n.* Gültigkeit, *die*
valley /'vælɪ/ *n.* Tal, *das*
valour (*Amer.:* **valor**) /'vælə(r)/ *n.*
Tapferkeit, *die*
valuable /'væljʊəbl/ ① *adj.* wertvoll; **be**
~ **to sb.** für jmdn. wertvoll sein
② *n.* ~**s** Wertsachen *Pl.*
valuation /vælju'eɪʃn/ *n.* Schätzung, *die*
value /'væljuː/ ① *n.* Wert, *der;* **be of great/**
little/some/no ~ [**to sb.**] [für jmdn.] von
großem/geringem/einigem/keinerlei Nutzen
sein; **know the** ~ **of sth.** wissen, was etw.
wert ist; **something/nothing of** ~: etwas/
nichts Wertvolles
② *v.t.* schätzen
value added 'tax *n.* Mehrwertsteuer, *die*
valued /'væljuːd/ *adj.* geschätzt
'**value judgement** *n.* Werturteil, *das*
'**valueless** *adj.* wertlos
valuer /'væljʊə(r)/ *n.* Schätzer, *der;* Taxator,
der
valve /vælv/ *n.* (a) Ventil, *das*
(b) (Anat.) Klappe, *die*
vampire /'væmpaɪə(r)/ *n.* Vampir, *der*
van /væn/ *n.* [delivery] ~: Lieferwagen, *der*
vandal /'vændl/ *n.* Rowdy, *der*
vandalism /'vændəlɪzm/ *n.* Wandalismus,
der
vandalize /'vændəlaɪz/ *v.t.* [mutwillig]
beschädigen
vanilla /və'nɪlə/ ① *n.* Vanille, *die*
② *adj.* Vanille-
vanish /'vænɪʃ/ *v.i.* verschwinden
vanity /'vænɪtɪ/ *n.* Eitelkeit, *die*
'**vanity bag** *n.* Kosmetiktäschchen, *das*
vantage point /'vɑːntɪdʒ pɔɪnt/ *n.*
Aussichtspunkt, *der*
vapour (*Brit.;* *Amer.:* **vapor**) /'veɪpə(r)/ *n.*
Dampf, *der*
'**vapour trail** *n.* (Aeronaut.) Kondensstreifen,
der

variable /ˈveərɪəbl/ adj. (a) (alterable) veränderbar; **be ~:** verändert werden können
(b) (inconsistent) unbeständig ⟨Wetter, Wind, Leistung⟩; wechselhaft ⟨Wetter, Launen, Qualität⟩

variance /ˈveərɪəns/ n. **be at ~** [with sth.] [mit etw.] nicht übereinstimmen

variant /ˈveərɪənt/ n. Variante, die

variation /veərɪˈeɪʃn/ n. (a) (varying) Veränderung, die; (difference) Unterschied, der
(b) (variant) Variante, die (of, on Gen.)

varicose vein /ˈværɪkəʊs ˈveɪn/ n. Krampfader, die

varied /ˈveərɪd/ adj. unterschiedlich; abwechslungsreich ⟨Diät, Leben⟩

variety /vəˈraɪətɪ/ n. (a) (diversity) Vielfältigkeit, die; (in diet, routine) Abwechslung, die; **add** or **give ~ to sth.** etw. abwechslungsreicher gestalten
(b) (assortment) Auswahl, die (of an + Dat., von); **for a ~ of reasons** aus verschiedenen Gründen
(c) (Theatre) Varietee, das
(d) (form) Art, die; (of fruit, vegetable) Sorte, die; (cultivated) Züchtung, die

various /ˈveərɪəs/ adj. (a) pred. (different) verschieden; unterschiedlich
(b) attrib. (several) verschiedene; **at ~ times** mehrere Male

'variously adv. unterschiedlich

varnish /ˈvɑːnɪʃ/ ① n. Lasur, die
② v.t. lasieren

vary /ˈveərɪ/ ① v.t. verändern; ändern ⟨Bestimmungen, Programm, Methode, Route⟩; (add variety to) abwechslungsreicher gestalten
② v.i. (become different) sich ändern; ⟨Preis, Qualität:⟩ schwanken; (be different) unterschiedlich sein

'varying adj. wechselnd; (different) unterschiedlich

vase /vɑːz/ n. Vase, die

vast /vɑːst/ adj. (a) (huge) riesig; weit ⟨Fläche, Meer⟩
(b) (coll.: great) enorm; Riesen⟨menge, -summe⟩

'vastly adv. (coll.) enorm; weitaus ⟨besser⟩; weit ⟨überlegen, unterlegen⟩

vat /væt/ n. Bottich, der

VAT /ˈviːerˈtiː, væt/ abbr. = **value added tax** MwSt.

Vatican /ˈvætɪkən/ pr. n. Vatikan, der

vault¹ /vɔːlt, vɒlt/ n. (a) (Archit.) Gewölbe, das
(b) (in bank) Tresorraum, der
(c) (tomb) Gruft, die

vault² ① v.i. sich schwingen
② v.t. sich schwingen über (+ Akk.)
③ n. Sprung, der

VD n. Geschlechtskrankheit, die

VDU abbr. = **visual display unit**

veal /viːl/ n. Kalb[fleisch], das; attrib. Kalbs-

veer /vɪə(r)/ v.i. ⟨Auto:⟩ ausscheren
■ **veer aˈway, veer ˈoff** v.i. ⟨Auto:⟩ ausscheren; ⟨Fahrer, Straße:⟩ abbiegen

veg /vedʒ/ n., pl. same (coll.) Gemüse, das

vegan /ˈviːgən/ ① n. Veganer, der/ Veganerin, die
② adj. vegan

vegetable /ˈvedʒɪtəbl/ n. Gemüse, das; **fresh ~s** frisches Gemüse; attrib. Gemüse⟨suppe, -extrakt, -garten⟩

'vegetable oil n. Pflanzenöl, das

vegetarian /vedʒɪˈteərɪən/ ① n. Vegetarier, der/Vegetarierin, die
② adj. vegetarisch; **sb. is ~:** jmd. ist Vegetarier/Vegetarierin; **eat ~** [food] vegetarisch essen

vegetarianism /vedʒɪˈteərɪənɪzm/ n. Vegetarismus, der

vegetate /ˈvedʒɪteɪt/ v.i. nur noch [dahin]vegetieren

vegetation /vedʒɪˈteɪʃn/ n. Vegetation, die

veggie /ˈvedʒɪ/ (coll.) ① adj. vegetarisch; **~ burger** Bratling, der
② n. Vegetarier, der/Vegetarierin, die

vehement /ˈviːəmənt/ adj., **'vehemently** adv. heftig

vehicle /ˈviːɪkl/ n. (a) Fahrzeug, das
(b) (fig.: medium) Vehikel, das

vehicular /vɪˈhɪkjʊlə(r)/ adj. Fahrzeug-

veil /veɪl/ ① n. Schleier, der
② v.t. verschleiern

veiled /veɪld/ adj. verschleiert; (fig.) versteckt

vein /veɪn/ n. (a) Vene, die; (any blood vessel) Ader, die
(b) (fig.: mood) Stimmung, die; **in a similar ~:** vergleichbarer Art

Velcro ® /ˈvelkrəʊ/ n. Klettverschluss, der Ⓦ

velocity /vɪˈlɒsɪtɪ/ n. Geschwindigkeit, die

velvet /ˈvelvɪt/ ① n. Samt, der
② adj. aus Samt nachgestellt; Samt-

'velvety adj. samtig

vendetta /venˈdetə/ n. Hetzkampagne, die; (feud) Fehde, die

vending machine /ˈvendɪŋ məʃiːn/ n. [Verkaufs]automat, der

vendor /ˈvendə(r)/ n. Verkäufer, der/ Verkäuferin, die

veneer /vɪˈnɪə(r)/ n. Furnier, das

venerable /ˈvenərəbl/ adj. ehrwürdig

venerate /ˈvenəreɪt/ v.t. verehren

veˈnereal disease n. (Med.) Geschlechtskrankheit, die

venetian blind /vɪˈniːʃn blaɪnd/ n. Jalousie, die

Venezuela /venɪˈzweɪlə/ pr. n. Venezuela (das)

V

vengeance /'vendʒəns/ n. (a) Rache, die; take ~ [up]on sb. [for sth.] sich an jmdm. [für etw.] rächen
(b) with a ~ (coll.) gewaltig (ugs.)

Venice /'venɪs/ pr. n. Venedig (das)

venison /'venɪsn, 'venɪzn/ n. Hirsch, der; Hirschfleisch, das; (roe deer) Reh[fleisch], das

venom /'venəm/ n. Gift, das

venomous /'venəməs/ adj. giftig

vent¹ /vent/ 1 n. (a) Öffnung, die
(b) (fig.) Ventil, das (fig.); give ~ to Luft machen (+ Dat.)
2 v.t. (fig.) Luft machen (+ Dat.)

vent² n. (in garment) Schlitz, der

ventilate /'ventɪleɪt/ v.t. belüften

ventilation /ventɪ'leɪʃn/ n. Belüftung, die

ventilator /'ventɪleɪtə(r)/ n. (a) Ventilator, der
(b) (Med.) Beatmungsgerät, das

ventriloquist /ven'trɪləkwɪst/ n. Bauchredner, der/-rednerin, die

venture /'ventʃə(r)/ 1 n. Unternehmung, die
2 v.i. (a) (dare) wagen
(b) (dare to go) sich wagen
3 v.t. wagen
■ **venture 'out** v.i. sich hinauswagen

venue /'venju:/ n. (Sport) [Austragungs]ort, der; (Mus., Theatre) [Veranstaltungs]ort, der; (meeting place) Treffpunkt, der

Venus /'vi:nəs/ pr. n. (Astron.) Venus, die

veranda[h] /və'rændə/ n. Veranda, die

verb /vɜ:b/ n. Verb, das

verbal /'vɜ:bl/ adj., **verbally** /'vɜ:bəlɪ/ adv. (a) (relating to words) sprachlich
(b) (oral[ly]) mündlich

verbatim /və'beɪtɪm/ adj., adv. [wort]wörtlich

verbose /və'bəʊs/ adj. weitschweifig ⟨Roman, Autor⟩; langatmig ⟨Rede, Redner⟩

verdict /'vɜ:dɪkt/ n. Urteil, das; ~ of guilty/ not guilty Schuld-/Freispruch, der; reach a ~: zu einem Urteil kommen

verge /vɜ:dʒ/ n. (a) Rasensaum, der; (on road) Bankette, die
(b) (fig.) be on the ~ of war/tears am Rande des Krieges stehen/den Tränen nahe sein; be on the ~ of doing sth. kurz davor stehen, etw. zu tun
■ **'verge on** v.t. [an]grenzen an (+ Akk.)

verger /'vɜ:dʒə(r)/ n. Küster, der

verifiable /'verɪfaɪəbl/ adj. nachprüfbar

verification /verɪfɪ'keɪʃn/ n. (a) (check) Überprüfung, die
(b) (confirmation) Bestätigung, die

verify /'verɪfaɪ/ v.t. (a) (check) überprüfen
(b) (confirm) bestätigen

veritable /'verɪtəbl/ adj. richtig

vermin /'vɜ:mɪn/ n. Ungeziefer, das

vermouth /'vɜ:məθ/ n. Wermut[wein], der

vernacular /və'nækjʊlə(r)/ n. Landessprache, die

versatile /'vɜ:sətaɪl/ adj. vielseitig; (having many uses) vielseitig verwendbar

versatility /vɜ:sə'tɪlɪtɪ/ n. Vielseitigkeit, die

verse /vɜ:s/ n. (a) (stanza) Strophe, die
(b) (poetry) Lyrik, die; write some ~: einige Verse schreiben; piece of ~: Gedicht, das; written in ~: in Versform
(c) (in Bible) Vers, der

versed /vɜ:st/ adj. be [well] ~ in sth. sich in etw. (Dat.) [gut] auskennen

version /'vɜ:ʃn/ n. Version, die; (in another language) Übersetzung, die; (of vehicle, machine, tool) Modell, das

versus /'vɜ:səs/ prep. gegen

vertebra /'vɜ:tɪbrə/ n., pl. ~e /'vɜ:tɪbri:/ Wirbel, der

vertebrate /'vɜ:tɪbrət/ n. Wirbeltier, das

vertical /'vɜ:tɪkl/ adj. senkrecht; be ~: senkrecht stehen

vertically /'vɜ:tɪkəlɪ/ adv. senkrecht

vertigo /'vɜ:tɪɡəʊ/ n. Schwindel, der

verve /vɜ:v/ n. Schwung, der

very /'verɪ/ 1 attrib. adj. (a) (precise, exact) genau; you're the ~ person I wanted to see genau die/den ich sehen wollte; at the ~ moment when …: im selben Augenblick, als …; at the ~ centre genau in der Mitte; the ~ thing genau das Richtige
(b) (extreme) at the ~ back/front ganz hinten/vorn; at the ~ end/beginning ganz am Ende/Anfang; from the ~ beginning von Anfang an; only a ~ little nur ein ganz kleines bisschen
(c) (mere) bloß ⟨Gedanke⟩
(d) (absolute) absolut ⟨Minimum, Maximum⟩; the ~ most I can offer is …: ich kann allerhöchstens … anbieten; for the ~ last time zum allerletzten Mal
(e) emphat. before their ~ eyes vor ihren Augen
2 adv. (a) (extremely) sehr; it's ~ near es ist ganz in der Nähe; ~ probably höchstwahrscheinlich; not ~ much nicht sehr; ~ little [nur] sehr wenig ⟨verstehen, essen⟩; thank you [~,] ~ much [vielen,] vielen Dank
(b) (absolutely) aller⟨best…, -letzt…, -leichtest…⟩; at the ~ latest allerspätestens
(c) (precisely) the ~ same one genau der-/ die-/dasselbe

vessel /'vesl/ n. (a) (receptacle) Gefäß, das; [drinking] ~: Trinkgefäß, das
(b) (Naut.) Schiff, das

vest /vest/ n. (a) (Brit.) Unterhemd, das
(b) (Amer.: waistcoat) Weste, die
2 v.t. ~ sb. with sth., ~ sth. in sb. jmdm. etw. verleihen

'vested adj. have a ~ interest in sth. ein persönliches Interesse an etw. (Dat.) haben

vestige /'vestɪdʒ/ n. Spur, die; not a ~ of truth kein Fünkchen Wahrheit

vestment /'vestmənt/ *n.* [Priester]gewand, *das*

vestry /'vestrɪ/ *n.* Sakristei, *die*

vet /vet/ **1** *n.* Tierarzt, *der*/-ärztin, *die* **2** *v.t.*, **-tt-** überprüfen

veteran /'vetərən/ *n.* Veteran, *der*/ Veteranin, *die*

veteran 'car *n.* (Brit.) Veteran, *der*

veterinarian /vetərɪ'neərɪən/ *n.* (Amer.) Tierarzt, *der*/-ärztin, *die*

veterinary /'vetərɪnərɪ/ *adj.* tiermedizinisch

veterinary 'surgeon *n.* (Brit.) Tierarzt, *der*/-ärztin, *die*

veto /'viːtəʊ/ **1** *n.*, *pl.* ～es Veto, *das* **2** *v.t.* sein Veto einlegen gegen

vex /veks/ *v.t.* [ver]ärgern; (cause to worry) beunruhigen; **be ～ed with sb.** sich über jmdn. ärgern

vexation /vek'seɪʃn/ *n.* Verärgerung, *die*

vexed /vekst/ *adj.* **(a)** verärgert **(b)** ～ **question** viel diskutierte Frage

VHF *abbr.* = **Very High Frequency** UKW

via /'vaɪə/ *prep.* über (+ *Akk.*) 〈*Ort, Sender, Telefon*〉; durch 〈*Eingang, Schornstein, Person*〉; per 〈*Post*〉

viability /vaɪə'bɪlɪtɪ/ *n.* (feasibility) Realisierbarkeit, *die*

viable /'vaɪəbl/ *adj.* (feasible) realisierbar

viaduct /'vaɪədʌkt/ *n.* Viadukt, *das od. der*

Viagra ® /vaɪ'ægrə/ *n.* Viagra, *das*

vibrant /'vaɪbrənt/ *adj.* lebensprühend 〈*Atmosphäre*〉; lebhaft 〈*Farbe*〉

vibrate /vaɪ'breɪt/ **1** *v.i.* vibrieren; (under strong impact) beben **2** *v.t.* vibrieren lassen

vibration /vaɪ'breɪʃn/ *n.* Vibrieren, *das;* (under strong impact) Beben, *das*

vicar /'vɪkə(r)/ *n.* Pfarrer, *der*

vicarage /'vɪkərɪdʒ/ *n.* Pfarrhaus, *das*

vicarious /vɪ'keərɪəs/ *adj.* nachempfunden

vice¹ /vaɪs/ *n.* Laster, *das*

vice² *n.* (Brit.: tool) Schraubstock, *der*

vice: ～'**chairman** *n.* stellvertretender Vorsitzender; ～'**president** *n.* Vizepräsident, *der*/-präsidentin, *die;* ～ **squad** *n.* Sittenpolizei, *die*

vice versa /vaɪsɪ 'vɜːsə/ *adv.* umgekehrt

vicinity /vɪ'sɪnɪtɪ/ *n.* Umgebung, *die;* **in the** ～ **[of a place]** in der Nähe [eines Ortes]

vicious /'vɪʃəs/ *adj.* **(a)** (malicious) böse; bösartig 〈*Tier*〉 **(b)** (violent) brutal

vicious 'circle *n.* Teufelskreis, *der*

'viciously *adv.* **(a)** (maliciously) boshaft **(b)** (violently) brutal

victim /'vɪktɪm/ *n.* Opfer, *das;* (of sarcasm, abuse) Zielscheibe, *die* (fig.).

victimization /vɪktɪmaɪ'zeɪʃn/ *n.* Schikanierung, *die*

victimize /'vɪktɪmaɪz/ *v.t.* schikanieren

victor /'vɪktə(r)/ *n.* Sieger, *der*/Siegerin, *die*

victorious /vɪk'tɔːrɪəs/ *adj.* siegreich

victory /'vɪktərɪ/ *n.* Sieg, *der* (**over** über + *Akk.*); *attrib.* Sieges-

video /'vɪdɪəʊ/ **1** *adj.* Video- **2** *n.*, *pl.* ～s (～ recorder) Videorekorder, *der;* (～tape, ～ recording) Video, *das* (ugs.) **3** *v.t.* ▶ VIDEOTAPE 2

video: ～ **camera** *n.* Videokamera, *die;* ～ **cas'sette** *n.* Videokassette, *die;* ～ **cas'sette recorder** *n.* Videokassettenrekorder, *der;* ～ **clip** *n.* Videoclip, *der;* ～ **film** *n.* Videofilm, *der;* ～ **game** *n.* Videospiel, *das;* ～ **library** *n.* Videothek, *die;* ～ **machine** *n.* Videogerät, *das;* ～ '**nasty** *n.* Horrorvideo, *das;* ～**on-demand** *n.* Video-on-Demand, *das;* ～ **player** *n.* Video-Player, *der;* ～ **recorder** *n.* Videorekorder, *der;* ～ **recording** *n.* Videoaufnahme, *die;* ～**tape** **1** *n.* Videoband, *das;* **2** *v.t.* [auf Videoband (*Akk.*)] aufnehmen

vie /vaɪ/ *v.i.*, **vying** /'vaɪɪŋ/ ～ **[with sb.] for sth.** [mit jmdm.] um etw. wetteifern

Vienna /vɪ'enə/ **1** *pr. n.* Wien (*das*) **2** *attrib. adj.* Wiener

Viennese /vɪə'niːz/ **1** *adj.* Wiener **2** *n.*, *pl.* same Wiener, *der*/Wienerin, *die*

Vietnam /vɪet'næm/ *pr. n.* Vietnam (*das*)

Vietnamese /vɪetnə'miːz/ **1** *adj.* vietnamesisch; **sb. is ～:** jmd. ist Vietnamese/Vietnamesin **2** *n.*, *pl.* same **(a)** (person) Vietnamese, *der*/ Vietnamesin, *die* **(b)** (language) Vietnamesisch, *das*

view /vjuː/ **1** *n.* **(a)** (range of vision) Sicht, *die;* **be out of/in ～:** nicht zu sehen/zu sehen sein **(b)** (what is seen) Aussicht, *die* **(c)** (picture) Ansicht, *die* **(d)** (opinion) Ansicht, *die;* **what is your ～ or are your ～s on this?** was meinst du dazu?; **hold** *or* **take the ～ that** ...: der Ansicht sein, dass ...; **in my ～:** meiner Ansicht nach **(e)** **be on ～:** besichtigt werden können; **in ～ of sth.** (fig.) angesichts einer Sache; **with a ～ to doing sth.** in der Absicht, etw. zu tun **2** *v.t.* **(a)** (look at) sich (*Dat.*) ansehen **(b)** (consider) betrachten **(c)** (inspect) besichtigen **3** *v.i.* (Telev.) fernsehen

viewdata /'vjuːdeɪtə/ *n.* Bildschirmtextsystem, *das*

'viewer *n.* **(a)** (Telev.) [Fernseh]zuschauer, *der*/-zuschauerin, *die;* **(b)** (for slides) Diabetrachter, *der*

viewfinder *n.* Sucher, *der*

viewing /'vjuːɪŋ/ *n.* (Telev.) Fernsehen, *das;* ～ **figures** Einschaltquoten *Pl.;* **at peak** ～ **time** zur besten Sendezeit

'viewpoint *n.* Standpunkt, *der*

V

vigil /'vɪdʒɪl/ n. Wachen, das; **keep ~:** wachen

vigilance /'vɪdʒɪləns/ n. Wachsamkeit, die

vigilant /'vɪdʒɪlənt/ adj. wachsam

vigilante /vɪdʒɪ'læntɪ/ n. Mitglied einer/der Bürgerwehr

vigor (Amer.) ▶ VIGOUR

vigorous /'vɪɡərəs/ adj. kräftig; heftig ⟨Attacke, Protest⟩; energisch ⟨Versuch, Anstrengung, Leugnen, Maßnahme⟩

'vigorously adv. heftig; kräftig ⟨schrubben, drücken⟩

vigour /'vɪɡə(r)/ n. (Brit.) (of person) Vitalität, die; (of body) Kraft, die; (of protest, attack) Heftigkeit, die

vile /vaɪl/ adj. gemein ⟨Verleumdung⟩; vulgär ⟨Sprache⟩; (repulsive) widerwärtig; (coll.: very unpleasant) scheußlich (ugs.)

villa /'vɪlə/ n. (a) [holiday] ~: Ferienhaus, das
(b) [country] ~: Landhaus, das

village /'vɪlɪdʒ/ n. Dorf, das; attrib. Dorf-

village: ~ 'green n. Dorfwiese, die;
~ 'hall n. Dorfgemeinschaftshaus, das

villager /'vɪlɪdʒə(r)/ n. Dorfbewohner, der/ -bewohnerin, die

villain /'vɪlən/ n. (a) Verbrecher, der
(b) (Theatre) Bösewicht, der

villainous /'vɪlənəs/ adj. gemein

vindicate /'vɪndɪkeɪt/ v.t. (a) (justify) rechtfertigen
(b) (clear) rehabilitieren

vindication /vɪndɪ'keɪʃn/ n. (a) (justification) Rechtfertigung, die
(b) (clearing) Rehabilitierung, die

vindictive /vɪn'dɪktɪv/ adj. nachtragend

vine /vaɪn/ n. Weinrebe, die

vinegar /'vɪnɪɡə(r)/ n. Essig, der

vinegary /'vɪnɪɡərɪ/ adj. sauer

vineyard /'vɪnjɑːd, 'vɪnjəd/ n. Weinberg, der

vintage /'vɪntɪdʒ/ ① n. Jahrgang, der
② adj. erlesen ⟨Wein⟩

vintage 'car n. (Brit.) Oldtimer, der

vintner /'vɪntnə(r)/ n. Weinhändler, der/ -händlerin, die

vinyl /'vaɪnɪl/ n. Vinyl, das

viola /vɪ'əʊlə/ n. Bratsche, die

violate /'vaɪəleɪt/ v.t. (a) verletzen; brechen ⟨Vertrag, Versprechen, Gesetz⟩
(b) (profane, rape) schänden

violation /vaɪə'leɪʃn/ n. ▶ VIOLATE: Verletzung, die; Bruch, der; Schändung, die

violence /'vaɪələns/ n. (a) (force) Heftigkeit, die; (of blow) Wucht, die
(b) (brutality) Gewalt, die; (at public event) Gewalttätigkeiten Pl.; **resort to** or **use ~:** Gewalt anwenden

violent /'vaɪələnt/ adj. gewalttätig; (fig.) heftig; wuchtig ⟨Schlag, Stoß⟩; Gewalt⟨verbrecher, -tat⟩

'violently adv. brutal; (fig.) heftig

violet /'vaɪələt/ ① n. (a) Veilchen, das
(b) (colour) Violett, das
② adj. violett

violin /vaɪə'lɪn/ n. Violine, die; Geige, die

vio'linist n. Geiger, der/Geigerin, die

VIP /viːaɪ'piː/ n. Prominente, der/die; **the ~s** die Prominenz

viper /'vaɪpə(r)/ n. Viper, die

virgin /'vɜːdʒɪn/ ① n. (a) Jungfrau, die
(b) **the [Blessed] V~ [Mary]** die [Heilige] Jungfrau [Maria]
② adj. (unspoiled) unberührt; **~ olive oil** natives Olivenöl

virginity /və'dʒɪnɪtɪ/ n. Unschuld, die

Virgo /'vɜːɡəʊ/ n., pl. **~s** (Astrol., Astron.) die Jungfrau

virile /'vɪraɪl/ adj. männlich

virility /vɪ'rɪlɪtɪ/ n. Männlichkeit, die

virology /vaɪə'rɒlədʒɪ/ n. Virologie, die

virtual /'vɜːtjʊəl/ adj. **a ~ ...:** so gut wie ein/eine ...; **the traffic came to a ~ standstill** der Verkehr kam praktisch zum Stillstand (ugs.)

'virtually adv. so gut wie; praktisch (ugs.)

virtual re'ality n. (Comp.) virtuelle Realität

virtue /'vɜːtjuː/ n. (a) (moral excellence) Tugend, die
(b) (advantage) Vorteil, der
(c) **by ~ of** aufgrund (+ Gen.)

virtuoso /vɜːtjʊ'əʊzəʊ/ n., pl. **virtuosi** /vɜːtjʊ'əʊziː/ or **~s** Virtuose, der/Virtuosin, die

virtuous /'vɜːtjʊəs/ adj. rechtschaffen ⟨Person⟩; tugendhaft ⟨Leben⟩

virulent /'vɪrʊlənt/ adj. (a) (Med.) virulent; stark wirkend ⟨Gift⟩
(b) (fig.) heftig; scharf ⟨Angriff⟩

virus /'vaɪərəs/ n. (a) Virus, das
(b) (Comp.) [Computer]virus, das od. der

visa /'viːzə/ n. Visum, das

vis-à-vis /viːzɑː'viː/ prep. (in relation to) bezüglich (+ Gen.)

viscosity /vɪs'kɒsɪtɪ/ n. Dickflüssigkeit, die

viscount /'vaɪkaʊnt/ n. Viscount, der

viscous /'vɪskəs/ adj. dickflüssig

visibility /vɪzɪ'bɪlɪtɪ/ n. (a) Sichtbarkeit, die
(b) (range of vision) Sicht, die; (Meteorol.) Sichtweite, die

visible /'vɪzɪbl/ adj. sichtbar

'visibly adv. sichtlich

vision /'vɪʒn/ n. (a) (sight) Sehkraft, die
(b) (dream) Vision, die
(c) usu. pl. (imaginings) Fantasien Pl.
(d) (insight, foresight) Weitblick, der

visit /'vɪzɪt/ ① v.t. besuchen; aufsuchen ⟨Arzt⟩
② v.i. einen Besuch/Besuche machen
③ n. Besuch, der; **pay** or **make a ~ to sb., pay sb. a ~:** jmdm. einen Besuch abstatten (geh.)

'visiting: ~ card n. Visitenkarte, die;
~ hours n. pl. Besuchszeiten Pl.

visitor /'vɪzɪtə(r)/ n. Besucher, der/ Besucherin, die; (to hotel) Gast, der; **have ~s/ a ~**: Besuch haben

'visitors' book n. Gästebuch, das; **sign the ~**: sich ins Gästebuch eintragen

visual /'vɪzjʊəl, 'vɪʒjʊəl/ adj. visuell; optisch ‹Eindruck, Darstellung›

visual: ~ aids n. pl. Anschauungsmaterial, das; **~ dis'play unit** n. Bildschirmgerät, das

visualization /vɪzjʊəlaɪ'zeɪʃn/ n. Veranschaulichung, die; (imagining) Sichvorstellen, das

visualize /'vɪzjʊəlaɪz, 'vɪʒjʊəlaɪz/ v.t. (a) (imagine) sich (Dat.) vorstellen; (b) (envisage) voraussehen

'visually adv. bildlich

vital /'vaɪtl/ adj. (a) (essential to life) lebenswichtig; (b) (essential) unbedingt notwendig; (c) (crucial) entscheidend (to für); **it is ~ that you ...**: es ist von entscheidender Bedeutung, dass Sie ...

vitality /vaɪ'tælɪtɪ/ n. Vitalität, die

'vitally adv. **~ important** von allergrößter Wichtigkeit; (crucial) von entscheidender Bedeutung

vitamin /'vɪtəmɪn, 'vaɪtəmɪn/ n. Vitamin, das

vitamin pill n. Vitamintablette, die

vitriolic /vɪtrɪ'ɒlɪk/ adj. ätzend

vivacious /vɪ'veɪʃəs/ adj. lebhaft

vivacity /vɪ'væsɪtɪ/ n. Lebhaftigkeit, die

vivid /'vɪvɪd/ adj. lebhaft ‹Farbe, Erinnerung›; lebendig ‹Schilderung›

'vividly adv. lebendig ‹beschreiben›; **remember sth. ~**: sich lebhaft an etw. (Akk.) erinnern

vixen /'vɪksn/ n. Füchsin, die

vocabulary /və'kæbjʊlərɪ/ n. (a) (list) Vokabelverzeichnis, das; **learn ~**: Vokabeln lernen; (b) (range of language) Wortschatz, der

vocal /'vəʊkl/ adj. (a) (concerned with voice) stimmlich; (b) lautstark ‹Minderheit, Protest›

'vocal cords n. pl. Stimmbänder Pl.

vocalist /'vəʊkəlɪst/ n. Sänger, der/ Sängerin, die

vocation /və'keɪʃn/ n. Berufung, die

vocational /və'keɪʃənl/ adj. berufsbezogen

vocational: ~ college n. Berufsschule, die; **~ guidance** n. Berufsberatung, die; **~ training** n. berufliche Bildung

vociferous /və'sɪfərəs/ adj. laut; lautstark ‹Forderung, Protest›

vodka /'vɒdkə/ n. Wodka, der

vogue /vəʊg/ n. Mode, die; **be in/come into ~**: in Mode sein/kommen

voice /vɔɪs/ ① n. Stimme, die; **in a firm/ loud/soft ~**: mit fester/lauter/sanfter Stimme

② v.t. zum Ausdruck bringen

voice: ~mail n. Voicemail, die; **~over** n. Begleitkommentar, der; **~ recognition** n. (Comp.) Spracherkennung, die

void /vɔɪd/ ① adj. (a) (empty) leer; (b) (invalid) ungültig; (c) **~ of** ohne [jeden/jedes/jede]. ② n. Nichts, das

vol. abbr. = **volume** Bd.

volatile /'vɒlətaɪl/ adj. (a) (Chem.) flüchtig; (b) (fig.) impulsiv; brisant ‹Lage›

volcanic /vɒl'kænɪk/ adj. vulkanisch

volcano /vɒl'keɪnəʊ/ n., pl. **~es** Vulkan, der

vole /vəʊl/ n. Wühlmaus, die

volition /və'lɪʃn/ n. Wille, der; **of one's own ~**: aus eigenem Willen

volley /'vɒlɪ/ n. (a) (of missiles) Salve, die; **a ~ of arrows** ein Hagel von Pfeilen; (b) (Tennis) Volley, der

'volleyball n. Volleyball, der

volt /vəʊlt/ n. Volt, das

voltage /'vəʊltɪdʒ/ n. Spannung, die

voluble /'vɒljʊbl/ adj. redselig

volume /'vɒljuːm/ n. (a) (book) Band, der; (b) (loudness) Lautstärke, die; (of voice) Volumen, das; (c) (space) Rauminhalt, der; (amount of substance) Teil, der

'volume control n. Lautstärkeregler, der

voluntarily /'vɒləntərɪlɪ/ adv., **voluntary** /'vɒləntərɪ/ adj. freiwillig

volunteer /vɒlən'tɪə(r)/ ① n. Freiwillige, der/die. ② v.t. anbieten ‹Hilfe, Dienste›; herausrücken mit ‹Informationen›. ③ v.i. sich [freiwillig] melden; **~ to do** or **~ for the shopping** sich zum Einkaufen bereit erklären

voluptuous /və'lʌptjʊəs/ adj. üppig

vomit /'vɒmɪt/ ① v.t. erbrechen. ② v.i. sich übergeben. ③ n. Erbrochene, das

voodoo /'vuːduː/ n. Wodu, der

voracious /və'reɪʃəs/ adj. gefräßig ‹Person›; unbändig ‹Appetit›

vote /vəʊt/ ① n. (a) (individual ~) Stimme, die; (b) (act of voting) Abstimmung, die; **take a ~ on sth.** über etw. (Akk.) abstimmen; (c) (right to ~) Stimmrecht, das. ② v.i. abstimmen; (in election) wählen; **~ for/ against** stimmen für/gegen; **~ to do sth.** beschließen, etw. zu tun; **~ Labour/ Conservative** etc. Labour/die Konservativen usw. wählen. ③ v.t. **~ sb. Chairman/President** etc. jmdn. zum Vorsitzenden/Präsidenten usw. wählen. ∎ **vote 'in** v.t. wählen

'voter n. Wähler, der/Wählerin, die

'vote-catching n. Stimmenfang, der

V

voting /'vəʊtɪŋ/ *n.* Abstimmen, *das;* (in election) Wählen, *das*

voting: ~ age *n.* Wahlalter, *das;* **~ slip** *n.* Wahlzettel, *der;* Stimmzettel, *der;* **~ system** *n.* Wahlsystem, *das*

vouch /vaʊtʃ/ ① *v.t.* **~ that** ...: sich dafür verbürgen, dass ... ② *v.i.* **~ for sb./sth.** sich für jmdn./etw. verbürgen

'voucher *n.* Gutschein, *der*

vow /vaʊ/ ① *n.* Gelöbnis, *das;* (Relig.) Gelübde, *das* ② *v.t.* geloben

vowel /'vaʊəl/ *n.* Vokal, *der*

voyage /'vɔɪɪdʒ/ ① *n.* Reise, *die;* (sea ~) Seereise, *die;* **outward/homeward ~, ~ out/**

home Hin-/Rückreise, *die;* **a ~ to the moon** ein Mondflug ② *v.i.* (literary) reisen

voyeur /vwɑː'jɜː(r)/ *n.* Voyeur, *der*

voyeurism /vwɑː'jɜːrɪzm/ *n.* Voyeurismus, *der*

vulgar /'vʌlɡə(r)/ *adj.* vulgär; ordinär ⟨Person, Benehmen, Witz⟩

vulgarity /vʌl'ɡærɪtɪ/ *n.* Vulgarität, *die*

vulnerable /'vʌlnərəbl/ *adj.* **(a)** (exposed to danger) angreifbar; **be ~ to sth.** für etw. anfällig sein; **be ~ to attack/in a ~ position** leicht angreifbar sein **(b)** (without protection) schutzlos

vulture /'vʌltʃə(r)/ *n.* Geier, *der*

vying ▶ VIE

Ww

W¹, w /'dʌblju:/ *n.* W, w, *das*

W² *abbr.* = **watt[s]** W

W. *abbr.* **(a)** = **west** W. **(b)** = **western** w.

wad /wɒd/ *n.* **(a)** Knäuel, *das;* (smaller) Pfropfen, *der* **(b)** (of papers) Bündel, *das*

wadding /'wɒdɪŋ/ *n.* Futter, *das*

waddle /'wɒdl/ ① *v.i.* watscheln ② *n.* watschelnder Gang

wade /weɪd/ *v.i.* waten
■ **'wade through** *v.t.* (fig. coll.) durchackern (ugs.) ⟨Buch⟩

wafer /'weɪfə(r)/ *n.* Waffel, *die*

'wafer-thin *adj.* hauchdünn

waffle¹ /'wɒfl/ *n.* (Gastr.) Waffel, *die*

waffle² (Brit. coll.: talk) ① *v.i.* schwafeln (ugs.) ② *n.* Geschwafel, *das* (ugs.)

waft /wɒft, wɑːft/ ① *v.t.* wehen ② *v.i.* ziehen

wag /wæɡ/ ① *v.t.*, **-gg-** ⟨Hund:⟩ wedeln mit ⟨Schwanz⟩; **~ one's finger at sb.** jmdm. mit dem Finger drohen ② *v.i.*, **-gg-** ⟨Schwanz:⟩ wedeln

wage /weɪdʒ/ ① *n. in sing. or pl.* Lohn, *der* ② *v.t.* führen ⟨Krieg⟩

wage: ~ claim *n.* Lohnforderung, *die;* **~ earner** *n.* Lohnempfänger, *der/* -empfängerin, *die;* **be the ~ earner of the family** der Ernährer/die Ernährerin der Familie sein; **~ freeze** *n.* Lohnstopp, *der;* **~ increase** *n.* Lohnerhöhung, *die;* **~ packet** *n.* Lohntüte, *die*

wager /'weɪdʒə(r)/ (dated/formal) ① *n.* Wette, *die;* **lay a ~ on sth.** auf etw. (Akk.) wetten ② *v.t. & i.* wetten

wage: ~ rise *n.* Lohnerhöhung, *die;* **~ scale** *n.* Tarif, *der;* **~ slave** *n.* Lohnsklave, *der*

waggle /'wæɡl/ (coll.) ① *v.t.* **~ its tail** ⟨Hund:⟩ mit dem Schwanz wedeln ② *v.i.* hin und her schlagen

waggon (Brit.), **wagon** /'wæɡən/ *n.* Wagen, *der*

waif /weɪf/ *n.* (child) verlassenes Kind

wail /weɪl/ ① *v.i.* klagen (geh.) (for um); ⟨Kind:⟩ heulen ② *n.* klagender Schrei; **~s** Geheul, *das*

waist /weɪst/ *n.* Taille, *die;* **tight round the ~:** eng in der Taille

'waistband *n.* Gürtelbund, *der;* (of trousers) [Hosen]bund, *der;* (of skirt) [Rock]bund, *der*

waistcoat /'weɪskəʊt/ *n.* (Brit.) Weste, *die*

'waistline *n.* Taille, *die;* **be bad for the ~:** schlecht für die schlanke Linie sein

wait /weɪt/ ① *v.i.* **(a)** warten; **~ [for] an hour** eine Stunde warten; **~ a moment** Moment mal; **keep sb. ~ing, make sb. ~:** jmdn. warten lassen **(b)** **~ at table** servieren ② *v.t.* (await) warten auf (+ Akk.); **~ one's turn** warten, bis man drankommt ③ *n.* **(a)** **after a long/short ~:** nach langer/ kurzer Wartezeit **(b)** **lie in ~ for sb./sth.** jmdm./einer Sache auflauern
■ **wait be'hind** *v.i.* noch dableiben
■ **'wait for** *v.t.* warten auf (+ Akk.); **~ for sb. to do sth.** darauf warten, dass jmd. etw. tut; **~ for the rain to stop** warten, bis der Regen aufhört
■ **'wait on** *v.t.* (serve) bedienen
■ **wait 'up** *v.i.* aufbleiben (for wegen)

'**waiter** *n.* Kellner, *der;* ∼! Herr Ober!
'**waiting:** ∼ **list** *n.* Warteliste, *die;*
∼ **room** *n.* Wartezimmer, *das;* (Railw.)
Warteraum, *der*
waitress /'weɪtrɪs/ *n.* Serviererin, *die;* ∼!
Fräulein! (veralt.)
waive /weɪv/ *v.t.* verzichten auf (+ *Akk.*)
wake¹ /weɪk/ ① *v.i.,* woke /wəʊk/, woken
/'wəʊkn/ aufwachen
② *v.t.,* woke, woken wecken
③ *n.* (by corpse) Totenwache, *die*
■ **wake 'up** ① *v.i.* aufwachen; ∼ up to sth.
(fig.: realize) etw. erkennen
② *v.t.* (a) wecken
(b) (fig.: enliven) wachrütteln
wake² *n.* Kielwasser, *das;* in the ∼ of sth.
(fig.) im Gefolge von etw.
waken /'weɪkn/ ① *v.t.* wecken
② *v.i.* aufwachen
'**wake-up call** (esp. Amer.) ▶ ALARM CALL
Wales /weɪlz/ *pr. n.* Wales (*das*)
walk /wɔːk/ ① *v.i.* (a) laufen; (not run)
gehen; (not drive) zu Fuß gehen; learn to ∼:
laufen lernen
(b) (exercise) gehen
② *v.t.* (a) (lead) führen; ausführen ⟨*Hund*⟩
(b) (accompany) bringen
③ *n.* (a) Spaziergang, *der;* go [out] for *or*
take *or* have a ∼: einen Spaziergang
machen; ten minutes' ∼ from here zehn
Minuten zu Fuß von hier
(b) (gait) Gang, *der*
(c) (path) [Spazier]weg, *der*
■ **walk a'way with** *v.t.* (coll.: win easily)
spielend leicht gewinnen
■ '**walk into** *v.t.* (hit by accident) laufen
gegen ⟨*Pfosten, Laternenpfahl*⟩; ∼ into sb.
mit jmdm. zusammenstoßen; ∼ into a trap
in eine Falle gehen
■ **walk 'off with** *v.t.* sich davonmachen
mit
■ **walk 'out** *v.i.* (a) (leave in protest) aus
Protest den Saal verlassen
(b) (go on strike) in den Streik treten
■ **walk 'out of** *v.t.* (leave in protest) aus
Protest verlassen
■ **walk 'out on** *v.t.* verlassen
'**walker** *n.* (a) Spaziergänger, *der/*
-gängerin, *die;* (rambler) Wanderer, *der/*
Wanderin, *die*
(b) (baby-∼) Laufstuhl, *der*
walkie-talkie /wɔːkɪ'tɔːkɪ/ *n.* Walkie-
Talkie, *das*
'**walking** *n.* [Spazieren]gehen, *das;* at
∼ pace im Schritttempo; be within
∼ distance zu Fuß zu erreichen sein
walking: ∼ **frame** *n.* Gehbock, *der;*
Gehgestell, *das;* ∼ **holiday** *n.*
Wanderurlaub, *der;* ∼ **shoe** *n.*
Wanderschuh, *der;* ∼ **stick** *n.*
Spazierstock, *der;* ∼ **tour** *n.* Wanderung,
die
Walkman ® /'wɔːkmən/ *n., pl.* **Walkmans**
Walkman, *der* ⓌⓏ

walk: ∼**out** *n.* Arbeitsniederlegung, *die;*
∼**over** *n.* (fig.: easy victory) Spaziergang, *der*
(ugs.); ∼**way** *n.* Fußweg, *der;* (over machinery
etc.) Laufsteg, *der*
wall /wɔːl/ *n.* Wand, *die;* (freestanding) Mauer,
die; drive sb. up the ∼ (fig. coll.) jmdn. auf die
Palme bringen (ugs.); go to the ∼ (fig.) an die
Wand gedrückt werden
■ **wall 'up** *v.t.* zumauern
wall: ∼**chart** *n.* Schautafel, *die;*
∼ **cupboard** *n.* Hängeschrank, *der*
wallet /'wɒlɪt/ *n.* Brieftasche, *die*
wall: ∼**flower** *n.* Goldlack, *der;*
∼ **hanging** *n.* Wandbehang, *der;* ∼ **light**
n. Wandlampe, *die*
wallop /'wɒləp/ (coll.) ① *v.t.* schlagen
② *n.* Schlag, *der*
wallow /'wɒləʊ/ *v.i.* (a) sich wälzen
(b) (fig.) schwelgen (in in + *Dat.*)
wall: ∼ **painting** *n.* Wandgemälde, *das;*
∼**paper** ① *n.* (a) Tapete, *die;* (b) (Comp.)
Hintergrund, *der;* (pattern)
Hintergrundmuster, *das;* ② *v.t.* tapezieren;
∼**-to-**∼ *adj.* ∼-to-∼ carpeting
Teppichboden, *der;* ∼ **unit** *n.*
Hängeelement, *das*
walnut /'wɔːlnʌt/ *n.* Walnuss, *die*
walrus /'wɔːlrəs/ *n.* Walross, *das*
waltz /wɔːlts, wɒls/ ① *n.* Walzer, *der*
② *v.i.* Walzer tanzen
wan /wɒn/ *adj.* bleich
wand /wɒnd/ *n.* Stab, *der*
wander /'wɒndə(r)/ ① *v.i.* (go aimlessly)
umherirren; (walk slowly) bummeln
② *v.t.* wandern durch
③ *n.* (coll.) Spaziergang, *der*
■ **wander a'bout** *v.i.* sich herumtreiben
■ **wander 'off** *v.i.* (stray) weggehen
wane /weɪn/ *v.i.* abnehmen
wangle /'wæŋgl/ *v.t.* (coll.) organisieren
(ugs.)
wannabe /'wɒnəbɪ/ *n.* (coll. derog.)
Möchtegern, *der; attrib.* Möchtegern-
want /wɒnt/ ① *v.t.* (a) (desire) wollen; ∼ to
do sth. etw. tun wollen; I ∼ it done by
tonight ich will, dass es bis heute Abend
fertig wird
(b) (require, need) brauchen; 'W∼ed – cook'
„Koch/Köchin gesucht"; you're ∼ed on the
phone du wirst am Telefon verlangt; the
windows ∼ painting die Fenster müssten
gestrichen werden; you ∼ to be [more]
careful du solltest vorsichtig[er] sein
(c) ∼ed [by the police] [polizeilich] gesucht
② *n.* (a) (lack) Mangel, *der* (of an + *Dat.*); for
∼ of sth. aus Mangel an etw. (*Dat.*)
(b) (need) Not, *der*
(c) (desire) Bedürfnis, *das*
■ '**want for** *v.t.* sb. ∼s for nothing *or*
doesn't ∼ for anything jmdm. fehlt es an
nichts
'**wanting** *adj.* be ∼: fehlen; sb./sth. is ∼ in ····⟡

W

sth. jmdm./einer Sache fehlt es an etw.
(*Dat.*); **be found** ~: für unzureichend
befunden werden

wanton /'wɒntən/ *adj.*, **'wantonly** *adv.*
mutwillig

war /wɔː(r)/ *n.* Krieg, *der;* **between the** ~s
zwischen den Weltkriegen; **declare** ~: den
Krieg erklären (**on** *Dat.*); **be at** ~: sich im
Krieg befinden; **make** ~: Krieg führen (**on**
gegen)

warble /'wɔːbl/ *v.t. & i.* trällern

war: ~ **correspondent** *n.*
Kriegsberichterstatter, *der*/
-berichterstatterin, *die;* ~ **crime** *n.*
Kriegsverbrechen, *das;* ~ **criminal** *n.*
Kriegsverbrecher, *der*/-verbrecherin, *die*

ward /wɔːd/ *n.* **(a)** (in hospital) Station, *die;*
she's in W~ 3 sie liegt auf Station 3
(b) (child) Mündel, *das od. die*
(c) (electoral division) Wahlbezirk, *der*
■ **ward 'off** *v.t.* abwehren

'war damage *n.* Kriegsschäden *Pl.*

warden /'wɔːdn/ *n.* **(a)** (of hostel) Heimleiter,
der/-leiterin, *die;* (of youth hostel)
Herbergsvater, *der*/-mutter, *die*
(b) (supervisor) Aufseher, *der*/Aufseherin, *die*

'warder *n.* (Brit.) Wärter, *der*

wardrobe /'wɔːdrəʊb/ *n.* **(a)**
Kleiderschrank, *der*
(b) (clothes) Garderobe, *die*

warehouse /'weəhaʊs/ *n.* Lagerhaus, *das;*
(part of building) Lager, *das*

wares /weəz/ *n. pl.* Ware, *die*

warfare /'wɔːfeə(r)/ *n.* Krieg, *der*

war: ~ **game** *n.* Kriegsspiel, *das;*
~ **grave** *n.* Kriegs- *od.* Soldatengrab, *das;*
~**head** *n.* Sprengkopf, *der*

warily /'weərɪlɪ/ *adv.* vorsichtig; (suspiciously)
misstrauisch

'warlike *adj.* kriegerisch

warm /wɔːm/ ① *adj.* **(a)** warm; **I am [very]**
~: mir ist [sehr] warm
(b) (enthusiastic) herzlich ⟨*Grüße, Dank*⟩
② *v.t.* wärmen; warm machen ⟨*Flüssigkeit*⟩;
~ **one's hands** sich (*Dat.*) die Hände
wärmen
③ *v.i.* ~ **to sb./sth.** (come to like) sich für
jmdn./etw. erwärmen
■ **warm 'up** ① *v.i.* warm werden;
⟨*Sportler:*⟩ sich aufwärmen
② *v.t.* aufwärmen ⟨*Speisen*⟩; erwärmen
⟨*Raum, Zimmer*⟩

warm-blooded /'wɔːmblʌdɪd/ *adj.*
warmblütig;

'war memorial *n.* Kriegerdenkmal, *das*

warm-hearted /'wɔːmhɑːtɪd/ *adj.*
warmherzig ⟨*Person*⟩

'warmly *adv.* **(a)** warm
(b) (fig.) herzlich ⟨*willkommen heißen,
gratulieren, begrüßen, grüßen, danken*⟩

warmonger /'wɔːmʌŋgə(r)/ *n.*
Kriegshetzer, *der*/-hetzerin, *die*

warmth /wɔːmθ/ *n.* **(a)** Wärme, *die*

(b) (fig.) Herzlichkeit, *die*

'warm-up *n.* **have a** ~ (Sport) sich
aufwärmen; ~ **[lap]** (Motor Racing)
Aufwärmrunde, *die*

warn /wɔːn/ *v.t.* **(a)** (inform, give notice)
warnen (**against, of, about** vor + *Dat.*); ~ **sb.
that** ...: jmdn. darauf hinweisen, dass ...;
~ **sb. not to do sth.** jmdn. davor warnen,
etw. zu tun
(b) (admonish) ermahnen; (officially) abmahnen

warning ① *n.* **(a)** (advance notice)
Vorwarnung, *die*
(b) (lesson) **let that be a** ~ **to you** lass dir das
eine Warnung sein
(c) (caution) Verwarnung, *die;* (less official)
Warnung, *die*
② *adj.* Warn⟨*schild, -signal usw.*⟩

'warning triangle *n.* Warndreieck, *das*

warp /wɔːp/ ① *v.i.* sich verbiegen; ⟨*Holz,
Schallplatte:*⟩ sich verziehen
② *v.t.* **(a)** verbiegen
(b) (fig.) **a** ~**ed sense of humour** ein
abartiger Humor

war: ~**path** *n.* **be on the** ~**path** (fig.) in
Rage sein; ~**plane** *n.* Kampfflugzeug, *das*

warrant /'wɒrənt/ ① *n.* (for sb.'s arrest)
Haftbefehl, *der;* **[search]** ~:
Durchsuchungsbefehl, *der*
② *v.t.* **(a)** (justify) rechtfertigen
(b) (guarantee) garantieren

'warranty *n.* Garantie, *die*

warrior /'wɒrɪə(r)/ *n.* (esp. literary) Krieger,
der (geh.)

Warsaw /'wɔːsɔː/ ① *pr. n.* Warschau (*das*)
② *attrib. adj.* Warschauer; ~ **Pact** (Hist.)
Warschauer Pakt

'warship *n.* Kriegsschiff, *das*

wart /wɔːt/ *n.* Warze, *die*

war: ~**time** *n.* **(a)** Kriegszeit, *die;* **in** *or*
during ~: im Krieg; **(b)** *attrib.*
Kriegs⟨*rationierung, -evakuierung usw.*⟩
~**torn** *adj.* kriegsgeschunden

wary /'weərɪ/ *adj.* vorsichtig; (suspicious)
misstrauisch (**of** gegenüber); **be** ~ **of sb./sth.**
sich vor jmdn./etw. in Acht nehmen

'war zone *n.* Kriegsgebiet, *das*

was ▶ BE

wash /wɒʃ/ ① *v.t.* **(a)** waschen; ~ **oneself**
sich waschen; ~ **one's hands/face/hair** sich
(*Dat.*) die Hände/das Gesicht/die Haare
waschen; ~ **the clothes** Wäsche waschen;
~ **the dishes** [Geschirr] spülen; ~ **the floor**
den Fußboden aufwischen
(b) (remove) waschen ⟨*Fleck*⟩ (**out of** aus);
abwaschen ⟨*Schmutz*⟩ (**off** von)
(c) (carry along) spülen
② *v.i.* **(a)** sich waschen
(b) ⟨*Stoff, Kleidungsstück:*⟩ sich waschen
lassen
③ *n.* **(a)** **give sb./sth. a [good]** ~: jmdn./etw.
[gründlich] waschen
(b) (laundering) Wäsche, *die*
(c) (of ship) Sog, *der*

■ **wash 'down** v.t. abspritzen ⟨Auto, Deck, Hof⟩

■ **wash 'off** ① v.t. ~ sth. off etw. abwaschen

② v.i. abgehen; (from fabric etc.) herausgehen

■ **wash 'out** v.t. ausscheuern ⟨Topf⟩; ausspülen ⟨Mund⟩; ~ **dirt/marks out of clothes** Schmutz/Flecken aus Kleidern [her]auswaschen

■ **wash 'up** ① v.t. (Brit.) ~ **the dishes up** das Geschirr spülen

② v.i. abwaschen; spülen

washable /'wɒʃəbl/ adj. waschbar

'washbasin n. Waschbecken, das

washed-'out adj. verwaschen (fig.: exhausted) abgespannt

washed-'up adj. (coll.) kaputt (ugs.)

washer /'wɒʃə(r)/ n. (of tap) Dichtungsring, der

'washing n. Wäsche, die; do the ~: waschen

washing: ~ **machine** n. Waschmaschine, die; ~ **powder** n. Waschpulver, das; ~**'up** n. (Brit.) Abwasch, der; do the ~-up abwaschen; spülen; ~**'up liquid** n. Spülmittel, das

'washtub n. Waschbottich, der

wasn't /'wɒznt/ (coll.) = was not; ▶ BE

wasp n. Wespe, die

waste /weɪst/ ① n. (a) (useless remains) Abfall, der; **kitchen** ~: Küchenabfälle Pl. (b) (extravagant use) Verschwendung, die; **it's a** ~ **of time/money/energy** das ist Zeit-/Geld-/Energieverschwendung

② v.t. (squander) verschwenden; **all his efforts were** ~d all seine Mühe war umsonst; **don't** ~ **my time!** stehlen Sie mir nicht die Zeit!

③ adj. (a) ~ **material** Abfall, der (b) **lay sth.** ~: etw. verwüsten

■ **waste a'way** v.i. immer mehr abmagern

waste: ~**basket** ▶ WASTE-PAPER BASKET; ~ **disposal** n. Abfallbeseitigung, die; ~ **disposal site** n. [Müll]deponie die; ~ **disposal unit** n. Müllzerkleinerer, der

wasteful /'weɪstfl/ adj. (a) (extravagant) verschwenderisch (b) (causing waste) unwirtschaftlich

waste: ~**land** n. Ödland, das; ~ **management** n. Abfallmanagement, das; Müllmanagement, das; ~ **paper** n. Papierabfall, der; ~**'paper basket** n. Papierkorb, der; ~ **pipe** n. Abflussrohr, das; ~ **reduction** n. Abfallverminderung, die; Müllreduzierung, die

watch /wɒtʃ/ ① n. (a) [wrist/pocket] ~: [Armband-/Taschen]uhr, die (b) **keep** ~: Wache halten; **keep [a]** ~ **for sb./sth.** auf jmdn./etw. achten (c) (Naut.) Wache, die

② v.i. ~ **for sb./sth.** auf jmdn./etw. warten

③ v.t. (a) (observe) sich ⟨Dat.⟩ ansehen ⟨Sportveranstaltung, Fernsehsendung⟩;

~ [the] **television** or **TV** fernsehen; ~ **sb. do** or **doing sth.** zusehen, wie jmd. etw. tut; **we are being** ~ed wir werden beobachtet (b) (be careful of, look after) achten auf (+ Akk.)

■ **watch 'out** v.i. (a) (be careful) aufpassen; ~ **out!** Vorsicht! (b) (look out) ~ **out for sb./sth.** auf jmdn./etw. achten

'watchdog n. Wachhund, der; (fig.) [public] ~: [Leiter/Leiterin einer] Aufsichtsbehörde

watchful /'wɒtʃfl/ adj. wachsam

watch: ~**maker** n. Uhrmacher, der/ -macherin, die; ~**man** /'wɒtʃmən/ n., pl. ~**men** /'wɒtʃmən/ Wachmann, der; ~ **strap** n. [Uhr]armband, das; ~**tower** n. Wachturm, der

water /'wɔ:tə(r)/ ① n. (a) Wasser, das (b) **in** pl. (part of the sea etc.) Gewässer Pl.

② v.t. (a) bewässern ⟨Land⟩; wässern ⟨Pflanzen⟩; ~ **the flowers** die Blumen [be]gießen (b) verwässern ⟨Bier usw.⟩ (c) tränken ⟨Tier⟩

③ v.i. ⟨Augen⟩ tränen; **my mouth was** ~ing mir lief das Wasser im Munde zusammen

■ **water 'down** v.t. verwässern

water: ~**bed** n. Wasserbett, das; ~ **birth** n. Unterwassergeburt, die; ~ **biscuit** n. Cracker, der; ~ **bottle** n. Wasserflasche, die; ~ **butt** n. Regentonne, die; ~ **closet** n. Toilette, die; WC, das; Wasserklosett, das (veralt.); ~**colour** n. (a) (paint) Wasserfarbe, die; (b) (picture) Aquarell, das; ~**cress** n. Brunnenkresse, die; ~**fall** n. Wasserfall, der; ~**front** n. Ufer, das; a ~front location eine Gegend am Wasser; ~ **heater** n. Heißwassergerät, das; ~**hole** n. Wasserloch, das

watering: ~ **can** n. Gießkanne, die; ~ **place** n. (for animals) Wasserstelle, die

water: ~ **level** n. Wasserstand, der; ~**lily** n. Seerose, die; ~**line** n. (Naut.) Wasserlinie, die; ~**logged** /'wɔ:təlɒgd/ adj. nass ⟨Boden⟩; aufgeweicht ⟨Sportplatz⟩; ~ **main** n. Hauptwasserleitung, die; ~**mark** n. Wasserzeichen, das; ~**melon** n. Wassermelone, die; ~ **meter** n. Wasseruhr, die; ~ **pipe** n. Wasserrohr, das; ~ **pistol** n. Wasserpistole, die; ~ **polo** n. Wasserball, der; ~**proof** ① adj. wasserdicht; wasserfest ⟨Farbe⟩; ② v.t. wasserdicht machen; imprägnieren ⟨Stoff⟩; ~ **rates** n. pl. the ~ rates die Wassergebühren Pl.; ~**repellent** adj. Wasser abstoßend; ~**resistant** adj. wasserundurchlässig; wasserfest ⟨Farbe⟩; ~**shed** n. (fig.) Wendepunkt, der; ~**ski** ① n. Wasserski, der; ② v.i. Wasserski laufen; ~**skiing** n. Wasserskilaufen, das; ~ **softener** /'sɒfənə(r)/ n. Wasserenthärter, der; ~**soluble** adj. wasserlöslich; ~ **supply** n. Wasserversorgung, die; ~ **table** n. Grundwasserspiegel, der; ~ **tap** n. Wasserhahn, der; ~**tight** adj. wasserdicht; ···:·

W

~ **tower** n. Wasserturm, der; ~**way** n. Wasserstraße, die; ~ **vapour** n. Wasserdampf, der; ~**works** n. sing., pl. same (establishment) Wasserwerk, das; (system) Wasserversorgungssystem, das

'**watery** adj. wässrig

watt /wɒt/ n. Watt, das

wattage /'wɒtɪdʒ/ n. Wattzahl, die

wave /weɪv/ ⓵ n. (a) Welle, die
(b) (gesture) **give sb. a ~:** jmdm. zuwinken; **with a ~ of one's hand** mit einem Winken ⓶ v.i. (a) ⟨Fahne, Flagge, Wimpel:⟩ wehen; ⟨Baum, Gras, Korn:⟩ sich wiegen
(b) (with hand) winken; ~ **at** or **to sb.** jmdm. zuwinken
⓷ v.t. schwenken; schwingen ⟨Schwert⟩; ~ **one's hand at** or **to sb.** jmdm. zuwinken; ~ **goodbye to sb.** jmdm. zum Abschied zuwinken

▪ **wave a'side** v.t. (a) abtun ⟨Zweifel, Einwand⟩
(b) (signal to move) ~ **sb. aside** [jmdm.] abwinken

wave: ~**band** n. Wellenbereich, der; ~**length** n. Wellenlänge, die; **be on the same ~length [as sb.]** (fig.) die gleiche Wellenlänge [wie jmd.] haben

waver /'weɪvə(r)/ v.i. schwanken

wavy /'weɪvɪ/ adj. wellig; ~ **line** Schlangenlinie, die

wax[1] /wæks/ ⓵ n. (a) Wachs, das
(b) (in ear) Schmalz, das
⓶ v.t. wachsen

wax[2] v.i. (a) ⟨Mond:⟩ zunehmen
(b) (become) werden

wax 'crayon n. Wachsmalstift, der

waxed /wækst/ adj. gewachst; ~ **paper** Wachspapier, das

wax: ~**work** n. Wachsfigur, die; ~**works** n. sing., pl. same Wachsfigurenkabinett, das

'**waxy** adj. wachsweich

way /weɪ/ ⓵ n. (a) Weg, der; **ask the** or **one's ~:** nach dem Weg fragen; '**W~ In/Out**' „Ein-/Ausgang"; **by ~ of Switzerland** über die Schweiz; **lead the ~:** vorausgehen; **go out of one's ~:** einen Umweg machen; (fig.) keine Mühe scheuen
(b) (method) Art und Weise, die; **do it this ~:** mach es so
(c) (distance) Stück, das; **it's a long ~ off** or **a long ~ from here** es ist weit weg von hier; **all the ~:** den ganzen Weg
(d) (direction) Richtung, die; **she went this/ that/the other ~:** sie ist in diese/die/die andere Richtung gegangen; **stand sth. the right/wrong ~ up** etw. richtig/falsch herum stellen
(e) (respect) **in [exactly] the same ~:** [ganz] genauso; **in some ~s** in gewisser Hinsicht; **in one ~:** auf eine Art; **in every ~:** in jeder Hinsicht; **in a ~:** auf eine Art
(f) (custom) Art, die
(g) **get** or **have one's [own] ~,** **have it one's [own] ~:** seinen Willen kriegen; **be in sb.'s**

or **the ~:** [jmdm.] im Weg sein; **make ~ for sth.** für etw. Platz machen; (fig.) einer Sache ⟨Dat.⟩ Platz machen; **in a bad ~:** schlecht; **either ~:** so oder so; **by the ~:** übrigens
⓶ adv. weit; ~ **back** (coll.) vor langer Zeit

way: ~**bill** n. Frachtbrief, der; ~'**lay** v.t., forms as LAY[2] 1: (a) (ambush) überfallen; (b) (stop for conversation) abfangen; ~'**out** adj. (coll.) extrem; verrückt; ~**side** n. Wegrand, der; **fall by the ~side** (fig.) auf der Strecke bleiben (ugs.)

wayward /'weɪwəd/ adj. eigenwillig

WC abbr. = **water closet** WC, das

we /wɪ, stressed wiː/ pl. pron. wir

weak /wiːk/ adj. (a) schwach; (easily led) labil ⟨Charakter, Person⟩
(b) dünn ⟨Getränk⟩

weaken /'wiːkn/ ⓵ v.t. schwächen; beeinträchtigen ⟨Augen⟩
⓶ v.i. ⟨Entschlossenheit, Kraft:⟩ nachlassen

weak-kneed /'wiːkniːd/ adj. (fig.) feige

weakling /'wiːklɪŋ/ n. Schwächling, der

'**weakly** adv. schwach

'**weakness** n. Schwäche, die

'**weak-willed** adj. willensschwach

wealth /welθ/ n. (a) (abundance) Fülle, die
(b) (riches, being rich) Reichtum, der

'**wealthy** ⓵ adj. reich
⓶ n. pl. **the ~:** die Reichen Pl.

'**wealth tax** n. Vermögenssteuer, die

wean /wiːn/ v.t. abstillen; ~ **sb. [away] from sth.** (fig.) jmdm. etw. abgewöhnen

weapon /'wepən/ n. Waffe, die

weaponry /'wepənrɪ/ n. Waffen Pl.

wear /weə(r)/ ⓵ n. (a) ~ **[and tear]** Abnutzung, die
(b) (clothes) Kleidung, die
⓶ v.t., **wore** /wɔː(r)/, **worn** /wɔːn/ (a) (have on) tragen ⟨Schmuck, Brille, Kleidung, Perücke⟩; **I haven't a thing to ~:** ich habe überhaupt nichts anzuziehen
(b) (rub) abtragen ⟨Kleidungsstück⟩; abnutzen ⟨Teppich⟩; **a [badly] worn tyre** ein [stark] abgefahrener Reifen
⓷ v.i., **wore**, **worn** (a) ⟨Kleider:⟩ sich durchscheuern; ⟨Absätze:⟩ sich ablaufen; ⟨Teppich:⟩ sich abnutzen
(b) (endure rubbing) halten; ~ **well/badly** sich gut/schlecht tragen

▪ **wear a'way** ⓵ v.t. abschleifen
⓶ v.i. sich abnutzen

▪ **wear 'down** v.t. (fig.) zermürben

▪ **wear 'off** v.i. ⟨Schicht:⟩ abgehen; ⟨Wirkung, Schmerz:⟩ nachlassen

▪ **wear 'out** ⓵ v.t. (a) aufbrauchen; auftragen ⟨Kleidungsstück⟩
(b) (fig.: exhaust) kaputtmachen (ugs.); **be worn out** kaputt sein (ugs.)
⓶ v.i. kaputtgehen (ugs.)

▪ **wear 'through** ⓵ v.i. sich durchscheuern
⓶ v.t. durchscheuern

W

wearable /'weərəbl/ adj. sth. is [not] ~:
man kann etw. [nicht] anziehen

wearer /'weərə(r)/ n. Träger, der/Trägerin,
die

wearily /'wɪərɪlɪ/ adv. müde

wearing /'weərɪŋ/ adj. ermüdend

wearisome /'wɪərɪsəm/ adj. ermüdend

weary /'wɪərɪ/ ① adj. (a) (tired) müde
(b) be ~ of sth. einer Sache (Gen.)
überdrüssig sein
② v.t. be wearied by sth. durch etw.
erschöpft sein
③ v.i. ~ of sth./sb. einer Sache/jmds.
überdrüssig werden

weasel /'wi:zl/ n. Wiesel, das

weather /'weðə(r)/ ① n. Wetter, das;
what's the ~ like? wie ist das Wetter?; in all
~s bei jedem Wetter; he is feeling under the
~ (fig.) er ist [zur Zeit] nicht ganz auf dem
Posten
② v.t. abwettern ⟨Sturm⟩; (fig.) durchstehen
⟨schwere Zeit⟩

weather: ~**beaten** adj. wettergegerbt
⟨Gesicht⟩; verwittert ⟨Felsen, Gebäude⟩;
~ **chart** n. Wetterkarte, die; ~**cock** n.
Wetterhahn, der; ~ **conditions** n. pl.
Witterungsverhältnisse Pl.; ~ **forecast** n.
Wettervorhersage, die

weathering /'weðərɪŋ/ n., no indef. art.
Verwitterung, die

weather: ~**man** n. Meteorologe, der;
~ **map** n. Wetterkarte, die; ~**proof** adj.
wetterfest; ~ **report** n. Wetterbericht, der;
~ **vane** n. Wetterfahne, die

weave¹ /wi:v/ ① n. Bindung, die
② v.t., wove /wəʊv/, woven /'wəʊvn/ (a)
weben; flechten ⟨Korb, Kranz⟩
(b) (fig.) einflechten ⟨Thema usw.⟩ (into in
+ Akk.)

weave² v.i. (take intricate course) sich
schlängeln

'**weaver** n. Weber, der/Weberin, die

web /web/ n. (a) Netz, das; spider's ~:
Spinnennetz, das
(b) the Web (Comp.) das Web (fachspr.); das
Netz

webbed feet /webd 'fi:t/ n. pl.
Schwimmfüße Pl.

Web: ~ **browser** n. (Comp.) Web-Browser,
der; ~ **page** n. (Comp.) Webseite, die; ~
site n. (Comp.) Website, die

we'd /wɪd, stressed wi:d/ (a) = we had;
(b) = we would

Wed. abbr. = **Wednesday** Mi.

wedding /'wedɪŋ/ n. Hochzeit, die

wedding: ~ **anniversary** n.
Hochzeitstag, der; ~ **cake** n.
Hochzeitskuchen, der; ~ **day** n.
Hochzeitstag, der; ~ **dress** n. Brautkleid,
das; ~ **present** n. Hochzeitsgeschenk,
das; ~ **ring** n. Ehering, der

wedge /wedʒ/ ① n. Keil, der

② v.t. verkeilen; ~ a door/window open
eine Tür/ein Fenster festklemmen, damit
sie/es offen bleibt

'**wedge-shaped** adj. keilförmig

wedlock /'wedlɒk/ n. born in/out of ~:
ehelich/unehelich geboren

Wednesday /'wenzdeɪ, 'wenzdɪ/ n.
Mittwoch, der; see also FRIDAY

wee¹ /wi:/ adj. (child lang./Scot.) klein

wee² ▸ WEE-WEE

weed /wi:d/ ① n. ~[s] Unkraut, das
② v.t. jäten
■ **weed 'out** v.t. (fig.) aussieben

'**weedkiller** n. Unkrautvertilgungsmittel,
das

'**weedy** adj. spillerig (ugs.) ⟨Person⟩

week /wi:k/ n. Woche, die; for several ~s
mehrere Wochen lang; once a ~, every ~:
einmal in der Woche; three times a ~:
dreimal in der Woche; a two-~ visit ein
zweiwöchiger Besuch; a ~ today/tomorrow
heute/morgen in einer Woche; a ~ on
Monday, Monday ~: Montag in einer Woche

'**weekday** n. Wochentag, der

weekend /-'-, '--/ n. Wochenende, das; at
the ~: am Wochenende; go away for the ~:
übers Wochenende wegfahren

weekly /'wi:klɪ/ ① adj. wöchentlich;
Wochen⟨zeitung, -zeitschrift, -lohn⟩
② adv. wöchentlich
③ n. (newspaper) Wochenzeitung, die;
(magazine) Wochenzeitschrift, die

weep /wi:p/ v.i. & t., wept /wept/ weinen

weepie /'wi:pɪ/ n. (coll.) Schmachtfetzen,
der (salopp)

weeping 'willow n. Trauerweide, die

weepy /'wi:pɪ/ ① adj. weinerlich
② n. ▸ WEEPIE

'**wee-wee** (coll.) ① n. Pipi, das (ugs.); do a
~: Pipi machen (ugs.)
② v.i. Pipi machen (ugs.)

weigh /weɪ/ v.t. & i. wiegen
■ **weigh 'down** v.t. (fig.: depress)
niederdrücken
■ **weigh 'up** v.t. abwägen

'**weighing machine** n. Waage, die

weight /weɪt/ n. Gewicht, das; what is your
~? wie viel wiegen Sie?; be under/over ~:
zu wenig/zu viel wiegen

'**weighting** n. Zulage, die

'**weightlessness** n. Schwerelosigkeit, die

weight: ~**lifter** n. Gewichtheber, der/
-heberin, die; ~**lifting** n. Gewichtheben,
das ~**train** v.i. mit Hanteln trainieren;
~ **training** n. Hanteltraining, das;
~**watcher** n. Schlankheitsbewusste, der/
die

'**weighty** adj. (a) (heavy) schwer
(b) (important) gewichtig

weir /wɪə(r)/ n. Wehr, das

weird /wɪəd/ adj. (coll.: odd) bizarr

weirdie /'wɪədɪ/ n. (coll.) Freak, der (ugs.)

W

weirdo /'wɪədəʊ/ n., pl. ~s ▶ WEIRDIE

welcome /'welkəm/ [1] int. willkommen; ~ home/to England! willkommen zu Hause/ in England! [2] n. (a) Willkommen, das (b) (reception) Empfang, der [3] v.t. begrüßen [4] adj. (a) willkommen; gefällig ⟨Anblick⟩ (b) pred. you are ~ to take it du kannst es gern nehmen; you're ~: gern geschehen!

welcoming /'welkəmɪŋ/ adj. einladend

weld /weld/ v.t. (join) verschweißen; (repair, make, attach) schweißen ([on] to an + Akk.)

'**welder** n. Schweißer, der/Schweißerin, die

'**welding** n. Schweißen, das

welfare /'welfeə(r)/ n. (a) (health and prosperity) Wohl, das (b) (social work; payments etc.) Sozialhilfe, die; be on ~ (Amer.) Sozialhilfe bekommen

welfare: W~ 'State n. Wohlfahrtsstaat, der; ~ **work** n. Sozialarbeit, die; ~ **worker** n. Sozialarbeiter, der/ -arbeiterin, die

well¹ /wel/ n. (a) Brunnen, der (b) ▶ OIL WELL (c) (stair~) Treppenloch, das

well² [1] int. ~! meine Güte!; ~, let's forget that na ja, lassen wir das; ~, who was it? nun od. und, wer war's?; oh ~[, never mind] na ja[, macht nichts]; ~? na? [2] adv., better /'betə(r)/, best /best/ gut; gründlich ⟨trocknen, schütteln⟩; the business/ patient is doing ~: das Geschäft geht gut/ dem Patienten geht es gut; ~ done! großartig!; he is ~ over forty er ist weit über vierzig; as ~ (in addition) auch; A as ~ as B B und auch [noch] A [3] adj. (in good health) How are you feeling now? – Quite ~, thank you Wie fühlen Sie sich jetzt? – Ganz gut, danke; look ~: gut aussehen; feel ~: sich wohl fühlen; he isn't [very] ~: es geht ihm nicht [sehr] gut; get ~ soon! gute Besserung!; make sb. ~: jmdn. gesund machen

we'll /wɪl, stressed wiːl/ = we will

well: ~**-aimed** adj. gezielt; ~**-balanced** adj. ausgeglichen ⟨Person⟩; ~**-behaved** ▶ BEHAVE 1; ~**-being** n. Wohl, das; ~**-bred** adj. anständig; ~**-built** adj. ⟨Person⟩ mit guter Figur; be ~-built eine gute Figur haben; ~**-chosen** adj. wohlgesetzt ⟨Worte⟩; ~**-connected** adj. ⟨Person⟩ mit guten Beziehungen; ~ **done** adj. (Cookery) durchgebraten; ~**-dressed** adj. gut gekleidet; ~**-educated** adj. gebildet; ~**-fed** adj. wohlgenährt; ~**-founded** adj. [wohl] fundiert; ~**-heeled** adj. (coll.) gut betucht (ugs.)

wellington /'welɪŋtən/ n. ~ [boot] Gummistiefel, der

well: ~**-intentioned** /'welɪntenʃ(ə)nd/ adj. gut gemeint; ~**-known** adj. bekannt; ~ **made** adj. gut [gearbeitet]; ~**-mannered** adj. ⟨Person⟩ mit guten

Manieren; be ~-mannered gute Manieren haben; ~**-meaning** adj. wohlmeinend; be ~-meaning es gut meinen; ~**-meant** adj. gut gemeint; ~ **off** adj. wohlhabend; sb. is ~ off jmdm. geht es [finanziell] gut; ~ **paid** adj. gut bezahlt; ~**-read** /'welred/ adj. belesen; ~**-spoken** adj. sprachlich gewandt; ~**-timed** adj. zeitlich gut gewählt; ~**-to-do** adj. wohlhabend; ~**-tried** adj. bewährt; ~**-wisher** n. Sympathisant, der/Sympathisantin, die

Welsh /welʃ/ [1] adj. walisisch; sb. is ~: jmd. ist Waliser/Waliserin [2] n. (a) (language) Walisisch, das; see also ENGLISH 2A (b) pl. the ~: die Waliser Pl.

Welsh: ~**man** /'welʃmən/ n., pl. ~men /'welʃmən/ Waliser, der; ~ '**rabbit,** ~ **rarebit** /'reəbɪt/ ns. Käsetoast, der

went ▶ GO 1

wept ▶ WEEP

were ▶ BE

we're /wɪə(r)/ = we are; ▶ BE

weren't (coll.) = were not; ▶ BE

west /west/ [1] n. (a) Westen, der; in/ to[wards]/from the ~: im/nach/von Westen; to the ~ of westlich von (b) usu. W~ (Geog., Polit.) Westen, der [2] adj. westlich; West⟨küste, -wind, -grenze, -tor⟩ [3] adv. nach Westen; ~ of westlich von

West: ~ **Ber'lin** pr. n. (Hist.) West-Berlin (das); **w~bound** adj. ⟨Zug, Verkehr usw.⟩ in Richtung Westen; ~ **Country** n. (Brit.) Westengland, das; ~ '**End** n. (Brit.) Westend, das

westerly /'westəlɪ/ adj. westlich; ⟨Wind⟩ aus westlichen Richtungen

western /'westən/ [1] adj. westlich; West⟨grenze, -hälfte, -seite⟩; ~ Germany Westdeutschland, das [2] n. Western, der

Western 'Europe pr. n. Westeuropa (das)

West: ~ '**German** (Hist.) [1] adj. westdeutsch; he/she is ~ German er ist Westdeutscher/sie ist Westdeutsche; [2] n. Westdeutsche, der/die; ~ '**Germany** pr. n. (Hist.) Westdeutschland (das); ~ '**Indian** [1] adj. westindisch; sb. is ~ Indian jmd. ist Westinder/-inderin; [2] n. Westinder, der/ -inderin, die; ~ '**Indies** pr. n. pl. Westindische Inseln Pl.

westward[s] /'westwəd(z)/ adv. westwärts

wet /wet/ [1] adj. (a) nass (b) (rainy) regnerisch; feucht ⟨Klima⟩ (c) frisch ⟨Farbe⟩; '~ paint„ „frisch gestrichen" (d) (coll.: feeble) schlapp (ugs.) [2] v.t., wet or wetted befeuchten [3] n. (a) (moisture) Feuchtigkeit, die (b) in the ~: im Regen

'**wetness** n. Nässe, die

'**wet suit** n. Tauchanzug, der

W

we've /wɪv, *stressed* wiːv/ = **we have**

whack /wæk/ (coll.) **1** *v.t.* hauen (ugs.) **2** *n.* Schlag, *der*

whacked /wækt/ *adj.* (Brit. coll.: tired out) erledigt (ugs.); kaputt (ugs.)

whale /weɪl/ *n.* (a) Wal, *der* (b) (coll.) **we had a ~ of a [good] time** wir haben uns bombig (ugs.) amüsiert

'whalebone *n.* Fischbein, *das*

whaler /'weɪlə(r)/ *n.* Walfänger, *der*

whaling /'weɪlɪŋ/ *n.* Walfang, *die*

wharf /wɔːf/ *n., pl.* **wharves** /wɔːvz/ *or* **~s** Kai, *der*

what /wɒt/ **1** *adj.* welch...; **~ book?** welches Buch?; **~ time does it start?** um wie viel Uhr fängt es an?; **~ kind of man is he?** was für ein Mensch ist er?; **~ a fool you are!** was für ein Dummkopf du doch bist!; **~ cheek/luck!** was für eine Frechheit/ein Glück!; **I will give you ~ help I can** ich werde dir helfen, so gut ich kann **2** *adv.* **~ do I care?** was kümmerts mich?; **~ does it matter?** was machts? **3** *pron.* was; **~?** wie?; was? (ugs.); **~ is your name?** wie heißt du/heißen Sie?; **~ about ...?** (**~ will become of ...?**) was ist mit ...?; **~ about a game of chess?** wie wärs mit einer Partie Schach?; **~'s-his/-her/-its-name** wie heißt er/sie/es noch; **~ for?** wozu?; **~ is it like?** wie ist es?; **so ~?** na und?; **do ~ I tell you** tu, was ich dir sage

whatever /wɒt'evə(r)/ **1** *adj.* **~ problems you have** was für Probleme Sie auch haben; **nothing ~:** absolut nichts **2** *pron.* **do ~ you like** mach, was du willst; **~ happens, ...:** was auch geschieht, ...; **or ~:** oder was auch immer; **~ does he want?** (coll.) was will er nur?

whatsit /'wɒtsɪt/ *n.* (coll.) (thing) Dingsbums, *das* (ugs.); (person) Dingsda, *der* (ugs.)

wheat /wiːt/ *n.* Weizen, *der*

wheedle /'wiːdl/ *v.t.* **~ sb. into doing sth.** jmdm. so lange gut zureden, bis er etw. tut; **~ sth. out of sb.** jmdm. etw. abschwatzen (ugs.)

wheel /wiːl/ **1** *n.* (a) Rad, *das*; **[potter's] ~:** Töpferscheibe, *die* (b) (steering **~**) Lenkrad, *das*; (ship's **~**) Steuerrad, *das*; **at** *or* **behind the ~** (of car) am Steuer **2** *v.t.* (push) schieben **3** *v.i.* (a) (turn round) kehrtmachen (b) (circle) kreisen

wheel: ~barrow *n.* Schubkarre, *die*; **~ brace** *n.* Radschlüssel, *der*; **~chair** *n.* Rollstuhl, *der*; **~ clamp** *n.* Parkkralle, *die*

wheeler-dealer /wiːlə'diːlə(r)/ *n.* Mauschler, *der*/Mauschlerin, *die*; (financial) Geschäftemacher, *der*/-macherin, *die*

'wheelie bin *n.* (Brit. coll.) Müllcontainer, *der* auf Rollen

'wheel reflector *n.* (on bicycle) Speichenreflektor, *der*

wheeze /wiːz/ *v.t.* schnaufen

whelk /welk/ *n.* Wellhornschnecke, *die*

when /wen/ **1** *adv.* wann; **the time ~ ...:** die Zeit, zu der/(with past tense) als ...; **the day ~ ...:** der Tag, an dem/(with past tense) als ... **2** *conj.* (a) (at the time that) als; (with present or future tense) wenn; **~ reading [a newspaper]** beim Lesen [einer Zeitung] (b) (whereas) **why do you go abroad ~ it's cheaper here?** warum fährst du ins Ausland, wo es doch hier billiger ist? **3** *pron.* **by/till ~ ...?;** bis wann ...?; **since ~ ...?** seit wann ...?

whence /wens/ *adv., conj.* (arch./literary) woher

whenever /wen'evə(r)/ **1** *adv.* wann immer; **or ~:** oder wann immer; **~ did he do it?** (coll.) wann hat er es nur getan? **2** *conj.* jedes Mal wenn

where /weə(r)/ **1** *adv.* (a) (position) wo; **~ shall we sit?** wohin wollen wir uns setzen? (b) (to **~**) wohin **2** *conj.* wo **3** *pron.* **near/not far from ~ it happened** nahe der Stelle/nicht weit von der Stelle, wo es passiert ist

whereabouts 1 /weərə'baʊts/ *adv.* (where) wo; (to where) wohin **2** /'weərəbaʊts/ *n., sing. or pl.* (of thing) Verbleib, *der*; (of person) Aufenthalt[sort], *der*

where: ~'as *conj.* während; **he is very quiet, ~as she is an extrovert** er ist sehr ruhig, sie dagegen ist eher extravertiert; **~'by** *adv.* mit dem/der/denen; **~upon** /weərə'pɒn/ *adv.* worauf

wherever /weər'evə(r)/ **1** *adv.* (a) (position) wo immer; **sit ~ you like** setz dich, wohin du magst; **or ~:** oder wo immer (b) (direction) wohin immer; **or ~:** oder wohin immer (c) **~ have you been?** (coll.) wo hast du bloß gesteckt? **2** *conj.* (a) (position) überall [da], wo; **~ possible** wo od. wenn [irgend] möglich (b) (direction) wohin auch; **~ he went** wohin er auch ging

wherewithal /'weəwɪðɔːl/ *n.* (coll.) **the ~:** das nötige Kleingeld (ugs.)

whet /wet/ *v.t.*, **-tt-:** (a) (sharpen) wetzen (b) (fig.) anregen ⟨*Appetit*⟩

whether /'weðə(r)/ *conj.* ob; **I don't know ~ to go [or not]** ich weiß nicht, ob ich gehen soll [oder nicht]

which /wɪtʃ/ **1** *adj.* welch...; **~ one** welcher/welche/welches; **~ ones** welche; **~ way** (how) wie; (in **~** direction) wohin **2** *pron.* (a) *interrog.* welcher/welche/welches; **~ of you?** wer von euch? (b) *rel.* der/die/das; **of ~:** dessen/deren; **after ~:** worauf[hin]

whichever /wɪtʃ'evə(r)/ **1** *adj.* welcher/welche/welches ... auch

2 *pron.* (a) welcher/welche/welches … auch (b) (coll.) ~ could it be? welcher/welche/welches könnte das nur sein?

whiff /wɪf/ *n.* (puff; fig.: trace) Hauch, *der;* (smell) leichter Geruch

while /waɪl/ 1 *n.* Weile, *die;* [for] a ~: eine Weile; a long ~: lange; for a little *or* short ~: eine kleine Weile; [only] a little *or* short ~ ago [erst] kürzlich *od.* vor kurzem; be worth sb.'s ~: sich [für jmdn.] lohnen
2 *conj.* (a) während; (as long as) solange (b) (although) obgleich (c) (whereas) während
■ **while a'way** *v.t.* ~ away the time sich (*Dat.*) die Zeit vertreiben (by, with mit)

whilst /waɪlst/ (Brit.) ▶ WHILE 2

whim /wɪm/ *n.* Laune, *die*

whimper /'wɪmpə(r)/ 1 *n.* ~[s] Wimmern, *das;* (of dog etc.) Winseln, *das*
2 *v.i.* wimmern; ⟨*Hund:*⟩ winseln

whimsical /'wɪmzɪkl/ *adj.* launenhaft; (odd, fanciful) spleenig

whine /waɪn/ 1 *v.i.* (a) heulen; ⟨*Hund:*⟩ jaulen (b) (complain) jammern
2 *n.* (a) Heulen, *das;* (of dog) Jaulen, *das* (b) (complaint) ~[s] Gejammer, *das*

whip /wɪp/ 1 *n.* (a) Peitsche, *die* (b) (Brit. Parl.) Fraktionsgeschäftsführer, *der/* -führerin, *die*
2 *v.t.,* -**pp-:** (a) peitschen (b) (Cookery) schlagen (c) (move quickly) reißen (d) (coll.: steal) klauen (ugs.)
■ **whip 'out** *v.t.* [blitzschnell] herausziehen
■ **whip 'up** *v.t.* (a) (arouse) anheizen (ugs.) (b) (coll.: make quickly) schnell hinzaubern ⟨*Gericht, Essen*⟩

whiplash *n.* ~lash [injury] Peitschenschlagverletzung, *die*

whipped 'cream *n.* Schlagsahne, *die*

'whipping cream *n.* [flüssige] Schlagsahne

'whip-round *n.* (Brit. coll.) Sammlung, *die*

whirl /wɜːl/ 1 *v.t.* [im Kreis] herumwirbeln
2 *v.i.* wirbeln
3 *n.* (a) Wirbeln, *das;* she was *or* her thoughts were in a ~ (fig.) ihr schwirrte der Kopf (b) (bustle) Trubel, *der*
■ **whirl 'round** 1 *v.t.* [im Kreis] herumwirbeln
2 *v.i.* [im Kreis] herumwirbeln; ⟨*Rad, Rotor:*⟩ wirbeln

whirl: ~**pool** *n.* Strudel, *der;* (bathing pool) Whirlpool, *der;* ~**wind** *n.* Wirbelwind, *der*

whirr /wɜː(r)/ 1 *v.i.* surren
2 *n.* Surren, *das*

whisk /wɪsk/ 1 *n.* (Cookery) Schneebesen, *der;* (part of mixer) Rührbesen, *der*
2 *v.t.* (a) (Cookery) [mit dem Schnee-/ Rührbesen] schlagen (b) (convey rapidly) in Windeseile bringen

■ **whisk a'way** *v.t.* (a) (remove suddenly) ~ sth. away [from sb.] [jmdm.] etw. [plötzlich] wegreißen (b) (convey rapidly) in Windeseile wegbringen

whisker /'wɪskə(r)/ *n.* (a) ~s (on man's cheek) Backenbart, *der* (b) (of cat, mouse, rat) Schnurrhaar, *das*

whiskey (Amer., Ir.)**, whisky** /'wɪskɪ/ *n.* Whisky, *der;* (American or Irish) Whiskey, *der*

whisper /'wɪspə(r)/ 1 *v.i.* flüstern; ~ to sb. jmdm. etwas zuflüstern
2 *v.t.* flüstern; ~ sth. to sb. jmdm. etw. zuflüstern
3 *n.* (a) Flüstern, *das;* in a ~, in ~s im Flüsterton (b) (rumour) Gerücht, *das*

whistle /'wɪsl/ 1 *v.i.* pfeifen; ~ at sb. (in disapproval) jmdn. auspfeifen
2 *v.t.* pfeifen
3 *n.* (a) (sound) Pfiff, *der;* (whistling) Pfeifen, *das* (b) (instrument) Pfeife, *die;* blow a/one's ~: pfeifen

whistling 'kettle *n.* Pfeifkessel, *der*

white /waɪt/ 1 *adj.* weiß
2 *n.* (a) (colour) Weiß, *das* (b) (of egg) Eiweiß, *das* (c) W~ (person) Weiße, *der/die*

white: ~ **bread** *n.* Weißbrot, *das;* ~ **cell** *n.* weißes Blutkörperchen; ~ '**coffee** *n.* (Brit.) Kaffee mit Milch; ~'**collar worker** *n.* Angestellte, *der/die;* ~ **corpuscle** ▶ ~ CELL; ~ '**elephant** ▶ ELEPHANT; **W~ House** *pr. n.* (Amer. Polit.) the W~ House das Weiße Haus; ~**knuckle ride** *n.* Fahrt mit äußerstem Nervenkitzel; ~ '**lie** ▶ LIE[1] 1; ~ '**meat** *n.* weißes Fleisch [und Geflügel]

whiten /'waɪtn/ 1 *v.t.* weiß machen; weißen ⟨*Wand, Schuhe*⟩
2 *v.i.* weiß werden

'whiteness *n.* Weiß, *das*

white: **W~ 'Paper** *n.* (Brit.) öffentliches Diskussionspapier über Vorhaben der Regierung; ~ '**sauce** *n.* weiße *od.* helle Soße; ~**wash** 1 *n.* [weiße] Tünche; (fig.) Schönfärberei, *die;* 2 *v.t.* [weiß] tünchen; ~ '**wedding** *n.* Hochzeit, *die* in Weiß; ~ '**wine** *n.* Weißwein, *der*

Whit 'Monday /wɪt/ *n.* Pfingstmontag, *der*

Whitsun /'wɪtsn/ *n.* Pfingsten, *das od. Pl.;* at ~: zu *od.* an Pfingsten

whittle /'wɪtl/**:** ~ **a'way** *v.t.* ~ away sb.'s rights/power jmdm. nach und nach alle Rechte/Macht nehmen; ~ '**down** *v.t.* allmählich reduzieren ⟨*Anzahl, Gewinn*⟩; verkürzen ⟨*Liste*⟩

whiz, whizz /wɪz/ 1 *v.i.,* -**zz-** zischen
2 *n.* Zischen, *das*

'whiz[z]-kid *n.* (coll.) Senkrechtstarter, *der*

who /huː/, stressed huː/ *pron.* (a) *interrog.* wer; (coll.: whom) wen; (coll.: to whom) wem (b) *rel.* der/die/das; *pl.* die; (coll.: whom) den/

die/das; (coll.: to whom) dem/der/denen; anyone/those ~ ...: wer ...; everybody ~ ...: jeder, der ...

whoa /wəʊ/ *int.* brr

who'd /hʊd, *stressed* hu:d/ **(a)** = who had; **(b)** = who would

whoever /hu:'evə(r)/ *pron.* **(a)** wer [immer]
(b) (no matter who) wer ... auch
(c) (coll.) ~ could it be? wer könnte das nur sein?

whole /həʊl/ ① *adj.* ganz; **the ~ lot** [of them] [sie] alle
② *n.* Ganze, *das;* **the ~:** das Ganze; **the ~ of my money/the village/London** mein ganzes Geld/das ganze Dorf/ganz London; **as a ~:** als Ganzes; **on the ~:** im Großen und Ganzen

whole: ~food *n.* Vollwertkost, *die;* **~hearted** /həʊl'hɑːtɪd/ *adj.* herzlich ⟨Dank⟨barkeit⟩⟩; rückhaltlos ⟨Unterstützung⟩; **~meal** *adj.* Vollkorn-; **~ 'milk** *n.* Vollmilch, *die;* **~ note** *n.* (Amer. Mus.) ganze Note; **~ 'number** *n.* ganze Zahl; **~sale** ① *adj.* **(a)** Großhandels-; **(b)** (fig.: on a large scale) massenhaft; Massen-; ② *adv.* **(a)** en gros; **(b)** (fig.: on a large scale) massenweise; **~saler** /'həʊlseɪlə(r)/ *n.* Großhändler, *der/* -händlerin, *die*

wholesome /'həʊlsəm/ *adj.* gesund

who'll /hʊl, *stressed* hu:l/ = who will

wholly /'həʊllɪ/ *adv.* völlig

whom /hu:m/ *pron.* **(a)** interrog. wen; *as indirect object* wem
(b) rel. den/die/das; *pl.* die; *as indirect object* dem/der/dem; *pl.* denen

whooping cough /'hu:pɪŋ kɒf/ *n.* Keuchhusten, *der*

whopper /'wɒpə(r)/ *n.* (coll.) **(a)** Riese, *der* **(b)** (lie) faustdicke Lüge

whopping /'wɒpɪŋ/ *adj.* (coll.) riesig; Riesen- (ugs.); faustdick ⟨Lüge⟩

whore /hɔː(r)/ *n.* Hure, *die*

who's /hu:z/ **(a)** = who is **(b)** = who has

whose /hu:z/ *pron.* **(a)** interrog. wessen; **~ [book] is that?** wem gehört das [Buch]?
(b) rel. dessen/deren/dessen; *pl.* deren

who've /hʊv, *stressed* hu:v/ = who have

why /waɪ/ ① *adv.* **(a)** (for what reason) warum; (for what purpose) wozu; **~ is that?** warum ist das?
(b) (on account of which) **the reason ~ he did it** der Grund, warum er es tat
② *int.* **~, certainly/of course!** aber sicher!

wick /wɪk/ *n.* Docht, *der*

wicked /'wɪkɪd/ *adj.* böse

'wickedness *n.* Bosheit, *die*

wicker /'wɪkə(r)/ *n.* Korbgeflecht, *das; attrib.* Korb⟨waren, -stuhl⟩

'wickerwork *n.* **(a)** (material) Korbgeflecht, *das*

(b) (articles) Korbwaren *Pl.*

wicket /'wɪkɪt/ *n.* (Cricket) Tor, *das*

'wicketkeeper *n.* (Cricket) Torwächter, *der/*-wächterin, *die*

wide /waɪd/ ① *adj.* **(a)** (broad) breit; groß ⟨Abstand, Winkel⟩; **three feet ~:** drei Fuß breit
(b) (extensive) weit; umfassend ⟨Lektüre, Wissen, Kenntnisse⟩; reichhaltig ⟨Auswahl, Sortiment⟩
(c) (off target) **be ~ of sth.** etw. verfehlen
② *adv.* **(a) ~ awake** hellwach
(b) (off target) **shoot ~:** danebenschießen; **go ~:** das Ziel verfehlen

wide: ~-angle 'lens *n.* (Photog.) Weitwinkelobjektiv, *das;* **~-eyed** *adj.* (surprised) mit großen Augen *nachgestellt*

'widely *adv.* **(a)** (over a wide area) weit ⟨verbreitet, gestreut⟩
(b) (by many people) weithin ⟨bekannt, akzeptiert⟩; **a ~ held view** eine weit verbreitete Ansicht
(c) (greatly) erheblich ⟨sich unterscheiden⟩

widen /'waɪdn/ ① *v.t.* verbreitern ② *v.i.* sich verbreitern

wide: ~-open *attrib. adj.,* **~ 'open** *pred. adj.* weit geöffnet ⟨Fenster, Tür⟩; weit aufgerissen ⟨Mund, Augen⟩; **be ~ open** ⟨Fenster, Tür:⟩ weit offen stehen; **~-ranging** /'waɪdreɪndʒɪŋ/ *adj.* weit gehend ⟨Maßnahme, Veränderung⟩; ausführlich ⟨Diskussion, Gespräch⟩; **~ 'screen** *n.* Breitwand, *die;* **~screen television, ~screen TV** *ns.* Breitwandfernsehen, *das;* **~spread** *adj.* weit verbreitet

widow /'wɪdəʊ/ *n.* Witwe, *die*

widowed /'wɪdəʊd/ *adj.* verwitwet

widower /'wɪdəʊə(r)/ *n.* Witwer, *der*

width /wɪdθ/ *n.* Breite, *die;* (of garment) Weite, *die*

wield /wi:ld/ *v.t.* schwingen; (fig.) ausüben ⟨Macht, Einfluss⟩

wife /waɪf/ *n., pl.* **wives** /waɪvz/ Frau, *die*

'wife battering *n.* Misshandlung, *die* der [Ehe]frau

wig /wɪg/ *n.* Perücke, *die*

wiggle /'wɪgl/ (coll.) ① *v.t.* hin und her bewegen ② *v.i.* wackeln

wild /waɪld/ ① *adj.* **(a)** wild lebend ⟨Tier⟩; wild wachsend ⟨Pflanze⟩
(b) wild ⟨Landschaft⟩
(c) (unrestrained) wild ⟨Erregung⟩; **run ~** ⟨Pferd, Hund:⟩ frei herumlaufen; ⟨Kind:⟩ herumtoben; **send** *or* **drive sb. ~:** jmdn. rasend vor Erregung machen
(d) (coll.: very keen) **be ~ about sb./sth.** wild auf jmdn./etw. sein
② *n.* **the ~[s]** die Wildnis; **see an animal in the ~:** ein Tier in freier Wildbahn sehen

wild: ~ **'boar** n. Wildschwein, das;
~ **card** n. wilde Karte; ~**cat** n. Wildkatze,
die

wilderness /'wɪldənɪs/ n. Wildnis, die;
(desert) Wüste, die

wild: ~ **'goose chase** n. (fig.)
aussichtslose Suche; ~**life** n. die Tier- und
Pflanzenwelt; ~**life park/reserve/sanctuary**
Naturpark, der/-reservat, das/-schutzgebiet,
das

'wildly adv. wild; be ~ **excited about sth.**
über etw. (Akk.) ganz aus dem Häuschen
sein (ugs.); ~ **inaccurate** völlig ungenau

wilful /'wɪlfl/ adj., **wilfully** /'wɪlfəlɪ/ adv.
(a) (deliberate[ly]) vorsätzlich
(b) (obstinate[ly]) starrsinnig

will¹ /wɪl/ v. aux., only in: pres. **will,** neg.
(coll.) **won't** /wəʊnt/, past would /wʊd/, neg.
(coll.) **wouldn't** /'wʊdnt/ **He won't help me.
W~/Would you?** Er will mir nicht helfen.
Bist du bereit?; the car won't start das Auto
springt nicht an; ~/**would you pass the salt,
please?** gibst du bitte mal das Salz rüber?/
würdest du bitte mal das Salz rübergeben?;
~ **you be quiet!** willst du wohl ruhig sein!;
he ~ **sit there hour after hour** er pflegt dort
stundenlang zu sitzen; **he '**~ **insist on doing
it** er besteht unbedingt darauf, es zu tun;
~ **you have some more cake?** möchtest od.
willst du noch etwas Kuchen?; **the box**
~ **hold 5 lb. of tea** in die Kiste gehen
5 Pfund Tee; **tomorrow he** ~ **be in Oxford;
morgen ist er in Oxford; I promise I won't do
it again** ich verspreche, ich mach's nicht
noch mal; **if he tried, he would succeed** wenn
er es versuchen würde, würde er es
schaffen; ~ **you please tidy up** würdest du
bitte aufräumen?

will² n. **(a)** (faculty) Wille, der
(b) (Law: testament) Testament, das
(c) (desire) **at** ~: nach Belieben; ~ **to live**
Lebenswille, der; **against one's/sb.'s** ~:
gegen seinen/jmds. Willen

'willing adj. willig; **ready and** ~: bereit; **be**
~ **to do sth.** bereit sein, etw. zu tun

'willingly adv. **(a)** (with pleasure) gern[e]
(b) (voluntarily) freiwillig

'willingness n. Bereitschaft, die

willow /'wɪləʊ/ n. Weide, die

willowy /'wɪləʊɪ/ adj. gertenschlank

'will power n. Willenskraft, die

willy-nilly /wɪlɪ'nɪlɪ/ adv. wohl oder übel
⟨etw. tun müssen⟩

wilt /wɪlt/ v.i. ⟨Pflanze, Blumen:⟩ welk
werden, welken

wily /'waɪlɪ/ adj. listig; gewieft ⟨Person⟩

wimp /wɪmp/ n. (coll.) Schlappschwanz, der
(ugs.)

wimpish /'wɪmpɪʃ/ adj. (coll.) lahm (ugs.)

win /wɪn/ 1 v.t., **-nn-,** won /wʌn/ gewinnen;
bekommen ⟨Stipendium, Vertrag, Recht⟩;
~ **sb. sth.** jmdm. etw. einbringen
2 v.i., **-nn-,** won gewinnen

3 n. Sieg, der; **have a** ~: gewinnen

■ **win 'over, win 'round** v.t. bekehren;
(to one's side) auf seine Seite bringen;
(convince) überzeugen

■ **win 'through** v.i. Erfolg haben

wince /wɪns/ v.i. zusammenzucken (**at** bei)

winch /wɪntʃ/ 1 n. Winde, die
2 v.t. winden; ~ **up** hochwinden

wind¹ /wɪnd/ 1 n. Wind, der; (Med.)
Blähungen Pl.; **get** ~ **of sth.** (fig.) Wind von
etw. bekommen; **be in the** ~ (fig.) in der Luft
liegen; **get/have the** ~ **up** (coll.) Manschetten
(ugs.) kriegen/haben
2 v.t. **the blow** ~**ed him** der Schlag nahm
ihm den Atem

wind² /waɪnd/ 1 v.i., wound /waʊnd/ **(a)**
(curve) sich winden; (move) sich schlängeln
(b) (coil) sich wickeln
2 v.t., wound **(a)** (coil) wickeln; ~ **sth. on
[to] sth.** etw. auf etw. (Akk.) [auf]wickeln
(b) aufziehen ⟨Uhr⟩

■ **wind 'down** v.t. **(a)** herunterdrehen
⟨Autofenster⟩
(b) (fig.: reduce gradually) einschränken

■ **wind 'up** 1 v.t. **(a)** hochdrehen
⟨Autofenster⟩
(b) (coil) aufwickeln
(c) aufziehen ⟨Uhr⟩
(d) (coll.: annoy deliberately) auf die Palme
bringen (ugs.)
(e) beschließen ⟨Debatte⟩
(f) (Finance, Law) auflösen
2 v.i. **(a)** (conclude) schließen
(b) (coll.: end up) ~ **up in prison/hospital** [zum
Schluss] im Gefängnis/Krankenhaus landen
(ugs.)

wind /wɪnd/: ~**-blown** adj. vom Wind
zerzaust ⟨Haar⟩; ~**break** n. Windschutz,
der; ~**breaker** (Amer.), ~**cheater** (Brit.)
ns. Windjacke, die; ~ **chill factor** n.
Wind-chill-Index, der

winded /'wɪndɪd/ adj. **be** ~: außer Atem
sein

winder /'waɪndə(r)/ n. (of watch) Krone, die;
(of clock, toy) Aufziehschraube, die

wind /wɪnd/: ~**fall** n. **(a)** (fruit) ~**falls**
Fallobst, das; **(b)** (fig.) warmer Regen (ugs.);
~**fall tax** (einmalige) Sondersteuer auf
Privatisierungsgewinne; ~ **farm** n.
Windpark, der; ~ **force** n. Windstärke, die;
~ **instrument** n. Blasinstrument, das;
~**mill** n. Windmühle, die

window /'wɪndəʊ/ n. (also Comp.) Fenster,
das; (shop ~) [Schau]fenster, das; **break a** ~:
eine Fensterscheibe zerbrechen

window: ~ **box** n. Blumenkasten, der;
~ **cleaner** n. Fensterputzer, der/-putzerin,
die; ~ **cleaning** n. Fensterputzen, das;
~ **display** n. Schaufensterauslage, die;
~ **dresser** n. Schaufensterdekorateur,
der/-dekorateurin, die; ~ **dressing** n. (fig.)
Schönfärberei, die; ~ **frame** n.
Fensterrahmen, der; ~ **ledge** n. (inside)
Fensterbank, die; (outside) Fenstersims, der

od. das; ~ **pane** n. Fensterscheibe, die;
~ **shopping** n. Schaufensterbummeln,
das; go ~ shopping einen
Schaufensterbummel machen; ~ **sill** n.
(inside) Fensterbank, die; (outside)
Fenstersims, der od. das

wind /wɪnd/: ~**pipe** n. (Anat.) Luftröhre,
die; ~ **power** n. Windkraft, die; ~**proof**
adj. windabweisend; ~**proof jacket**
Windjacke, die; ~**screen**, (Amer.)
~**shield** ns. Windschutzscheibe, die;
~screen/~shield wiper Scheibenwischer,
der; ~screen/~shield washer
Scheibenwaschanlage, die; ~**surfer** n.
Windsurfer, der; ~**surfing** n. Windsurfen,
das; ~**swept** adj. windgepeitscht; vom
Wind zerzaust ⟨Person, Haare⟩; ~ **tunnel**
n. Windkanal, der

windward /'wɪndwəd/ adj. ~ **side**
Windseite, die

'**windy** adj. windig

wine /waɪn/ n. Wein, der

wine: ~ **bar** n. Weinstube, die; ~ **bottle**
n. Weinflasche, die; ~ **cellar** n.
[Wein]keller, das; ~ **cooler** n.
Weinkühler, der; ~**glass** n. Weinglas, das;
~**grower** n. Winzer, der/Winzerin, die;
~**growing** ① n. Weinbau, der; ② adj.
~-growing area Weingegend, die; ~ **list** n.
Weinkarte, die; ~ **merchant** n.
Weinhändler, der/-händlerin, die;
~ merchants (business) Weinhandlung, die;
~ **tasting** /'waɪnteɪstɪŋ/ n. Weinprobe,
die; ~ **vault** n. Weinkeller, der;
~ '**vinegar** n. Weinessig, der

wing /wɪŋ/ n. (a) (Ornith., Archit., Sport) Flügel,
der
(b) (Aeronaut.) Tragfläche, die
(c) (Brit. Motor. Veh.) Kotflügel, der

winged /wɪŋd/ adj. geflügelt

winger /'wɪŋə(r)/ n. (Sport) Außenstürmer,
der/-stürmerin, die

wing: ~ **mirror** n. (Brit. Motor Veh.)
Außenspiegel, der; ~**span** n.
[Flügel]spannweite, die; ~ **tip** n.
Flügelspitze, die

wink /wɪŋk/ ① v.i. (a) blinzeln; (as signal)
zwinkern; ~ at sb. jmdm. zuzwinkern
(b) (flash) blinken
② n. (a) Blinzeln, das; (signal) Zwinkern,
das; give sb. a ~: jmdm. zuzwinkern
(b) not sleep a ~: kein Auge zutun

'**winner** n. Sieger, der/Siegerin, die; (of
competition or prize) Gewinner, der/
Gewinnerin, die

'**winning** adj. (a) attrib. siegreich;
~ number Gewinnzahl, die
(b) (charming) einnehmend; gewinnend
⟨Lächeln⟩

'**winning post** n. Zielpfosten, der

'**winnings** n. pl. Gewinn, der

winter /'wɪntə(r)/ n. Winter, der; in [the] ~:
im Winter

winter '**sports** n. pl. Wintersport, der

wintry /'wɪntrɪ/ adj. winterlich; ~ **shower**
Schneegestöber, das

wipe /waɪp/ ① v.t. (a) abwischen;
[auf]wischen ⟨Fußboden⟩; (dry) abtrocknen;
~ one's mouth/eyes/nose sich (Dat.) den
Mund/die Tränen/die Nase abwischen;
~ one's feet/shoes [sich (Dat.)] die Füße/
Schuhe abtreten
(b) (get rid of) [ab]wischen; ~ one's/sb.'s
tears sich/jmdm. die Tränen abwischen
② n. give sth. a ~: etw. abwischen
■ **wipe** '**down** v.t. abwischen; (dry)
abtrocknen
■ **wipe** '**off** v.t. (a) (remove) wegwischen;
löschen ⟨Bandaufnahme⟩
(b) (pay off) zurückzahlen ⟨Schulden⟩
■ **wipe** '**out** v.t. (a) (remove) wegwischen;
(erase) auslöschen
(b) (cancel) tilgen; zunichte machen ⟨Vorteil,
Gewinn usw.⟩
(c) (destroy) ausrotten ⟨Rasse, Tierart,
Feinde⟩; ausmerzen ⟨Seuche, Korruption⟩
■ **wipe** '**up** v.t. (a) aufwischen
(b) (dry) abtrocknen

'**wiper** n. (Motor Veh.) Wischer, der

wire /'waɪə(r)/ ① n. (a) Draht, der
(b) (Electr., Teleph.) Leitung, die
(c) (coll.: telegram) Telegramm, das
② v.t. (a) (fasten) ~ sth. together etw. mit
Draht verbinden
(b) (Electr.) ~ sth. to sth. etw. an etw. (Akk.)
anschließen; ~ a house in einem Haus die
Stromleitungen legen

wire: ~ '**brush** n. Drahtbürste, die;
~ **cutters** n. pl. Drahtschneider, der

'**wireless** n. (Brit. dated) Radio, das

wire: ~ '**netting** n. Maschendraht, der;
~ **strippers** n. pl. Abisolierzange, die;
~ '**wool** n. Stahlwolle, die

wiring /'waɪərɪŋ/ n. [elektrische] Leitungen
Pl.

wisdom /'wɪzdəm/ n. (a) Weisheit, die
(b) (prudence) Klugheit, die

'**wisdom tooth** n. Weisheitszahn, der

wise /waɪz/ adj. (a) weise; vernünftig
⟨Meinung⟩
(b) (prudent) klug
(c) be none the ~r kein bisschen klüger als
vorher sein

wise: ~**crack** (coll.) n. witzige
Bemerkung; ~ **guy** n. (coll.) Klugscheißer,
der (salopp)

'**wisely** adv. weise; (prudently) klug

wish /wɪʃ/ ① v.t. wünschen; I ~ I was or
were rich I wish it wollte, ich wäre reich; I ~ to
go ich möchte gehen; ~ sb. luck/success
etc. jmdm. Glück/Erfolg usw. wünschen;
~ sb. well jmdm. alles Gute wünschen
② v.i. wünschen; ~ for sth. sich (Dat.) etw.
wünschen
③ n. Wunsch, der; make a ~: sich (Dat.)
etwas wünschen; get or have one's ~:
seinen Wunsch erfüllt bekommen ⋯❖

W

wishful thinking /wɪʃfl 'θɪŋkɪŋ/ n. Wunschdenken, *das*

'wishing well n. Wunschbrunnen, *der*

wishy-washy /'wɪʃɪwɒʃɪ/ adj. labberig (ugs.); (fig.) lasch

wisp /wɪsp/ n. (of straw) Büschel, *das*; ~ of hair Haarsträhne, *die*; ~ of cloud/smoke Wolkenfetzen, *der*/Rauchfahne, *die*

wistful /'wɪstfl/ adj., **'wistfully** adv. wehmütig

wit /wɪt/ n. (a) (humour) Witz, *der*
(b) (intelligence) Geist, *der*; **be at one's ~'s** or **~s' end** sich (*Dat.*) keinen Rat mehr wissen; **be frightened** or **scared out of one's ~s** Todesangst haben; **have/keep one's ~s about one** auf Draht (ugs.) sein/nicht den Kopf verlieren
(c) (person) geistreicher Mensch

witch /wɪtʃ/ n. Hexe, *die*

witch: ~craft n. Hexerei, *die*; ~ **doctor** n. Medizinmann, *der*; **~-hunt** n. Hexenjagd, *die* (**for** auf + *Akk.*)

with /wɪð/ prep. mit; **put sth. ~ sth.** etw. zu etw. stellen/legen; **have nothing to write ~**: nichts zum Schreiben haben; **I'm not '~ you** (coll.) ich komme nicht mit; **tremble ~ fear** vor Angst zittern; **I have no money ~ me** ich habe kein Geld dabei od. bei mir; **sleep ~ the window open** bei offenem Fenster schlafen

with'draw [1] v.t., *forms as* DRAW 1: zurückziehen; abziehen ⟨*Truppen*⟩; **~ sth. from an account** etw. von einem Konto abheben
[2] v.i., *forms as* DRAW 1: sich zurückziehen

withdrawal /wɪð'drɔːəl/ n. (a) Zurücknahme, *die*; (of troops) Abzug, *der*; (of money) Abhebung, *die*
(b) (from drugs) Entzug, *der*; ~ **symptoms** Entzugserscheinungen Pl.

with'drawn adj. (unsociable) verschlossen

wither /'wɪðə(r)/ [1] v.t. verdorren lassen
[2] v.i. [ver]welken
▪ **wither a'way** v.i. dahinwelken (geh.)

withered /'wɪðəd/ adj. verwelkt ⟨*Gras, Pflanze*⟩; verkrüppelt ⟨*Gliedmaße*⟩

withering /'wɪðərɪŋ/ adj. vernichtend ⟨*Blick*⟩

with'hold v.t., *forms as* HOLD²: ~ **sth. from sb.** jmdm. etw. vorenthalten

within /wɪ'ðɪn/ prep. innerhalb; **stay/be ~ the law** auf dem Boden des Gesetzes nicht verlassen; ~ **eight miles of sth.** acht Meilen im Umkreis von etw.

without /wɪ'ðaʊt/ prep. ohne; ~ **doing sth.** ohne etw. zu tun; ~ **his knowing** ohne dass er davon weiß/wusste

with'stand v.t., **withstood** /wɪθ'stʊd/ standhalten (+ *Dat.*); aushalten ⟨*Beanspruchung, hohe Temperaturen*⟩

witness /'wɪtnɪs/ [1] n. Zeuge, *der*/Zeugin, *die* (**of, to** *Gen.*)

[2] v.t. (a) (see) ~ **sth.** Zeuge/Zeugin einer Sache (*Gen.*) sein
(b) bestätigen ⟨*Unterschrift*⟩

'witness box (Brit.), **'witness stand** (Amer.) ns. Zeugenstand, *der*

witticism /'wɪtɪsɪzm/ n. Witzelei, *die*

wittingly /'wɪtɪŋlɪ/ adv. wissentlich

witty /'wɪtɪ/ adj. witzig; geistreich ⟨*Person*⟩

wives pl. of WIFE

wizard /'wɪzəd/ n. Zauberer, *der*

wizardry /'wɪzədrɪ/ n. Zauberei, *die*

wizened /'wɪzənd/ adj. runz[e]lig

wobble /'wɒbl/ v.i. wackeln

wobbly /'wɒblɪ/ adj. wack[e]lig

woe /wəʊ/ n. (arch./literary/joc.) ~[s] Jammer, *der*; ~ **betide you!** wehe dir!

woebegone /'wəʊbɪgɒn/ adj. jammervoll

woeful /'wəʊfl/ adj. (deplorable) beklagenswert; (distressed) jammervoll

wok /wɒk/ n. (Cookery) Wok, *der*

woke, woken ▶ WAKE¹ 1, 2

wolf /wʊlf/ [1] n., pl. **wolves** /wʊlvz/ Wolf, *der*
[2] v.t. ~ **[down]** verschlingen

woman /'wʊmən/ n., pl. **women** /'wɪmɪn/ Frau, *die*; ~ **doctor** Ärztin, *die*; ~ **friend** Freundin, *die*

womanize /'wʊmənaɪz/ v.i. den Frauen nachstellen

womanizer /'wʊmənaɪzə(r)/ n. Schürzenjäger, *der*

'womanly adj. fraulich

womb /wuːm/ n. Gebärmutter, *die*

women pl. of WOMAN

women: ~folk n. pl. Frauen Pl.; **W~'s 'Lib** (coll.), **W~'s Libe'ration** ns. die Frauenbewegung; **~'s movement** n. Frauenbewegung, *die*; **~'s 'prison** n. Frauengefängnis, *das*; **~'s 'refuge** n. Frauenhaus, *das*; **~'s 'rights** n. pl. die Rechte der Frau

won ▶ WIN 1, 2

wonder /'wʌndə(r)/ [1] n. (a) (thing) Wunder, *das*
(b) (feeling) Staunen, *das*
[2] adj. Wunder-
[3] v.i. sich wundern; staunen (**at** über + *Akk.*)
[4] v.t. sich fragen; **I ~ what the time is** wie viel Uhr mag es wohl sein?; **I ~ whether I might open the window** dürfte ich vielleicht das Fenster öffnen?

wonderful /'wʌndəfl/ adj., **wonderfully** /'wʌndəfəlɪ/ adv. wunderbar

wondering /'wʌndərɪŋ/ adj., **wonderingly** /'wʌndərɪŋlɪ/ adv. staunend

won't /wəʊnt/ (coll.) = will not; ▶ WILL¹

woo /wuː/ v.t. (a) (literary: court) ~ **sb.** um jmdn. werben (geh.)
(b) umwerben ⟨*Kunden, Wähler*⟩

wood /wʊd/ n. (a) Holz, *das*; **touch ~** (Brit.), **knock on ~** (Amer.) unberufen!

(b) (trees) Wald, *der*

wood: ~ carving *n.* (object) Holzschnitzerei, *die;* **~craft** *n.* (~work) Holzschnitzerei, *die;* **~cut** *n.* Holzschnitt, *der;* **~cutter** *n.* Holzfäller, *der*

'wooded *adj.* bewaldet

wooden /'wʊdn/ *adj.* **(a)** hölzern; Holz- **(b)** (fig.: stiff) hölzern

wood: ~land /'wʊdlənd/ *n.* Waldland, *das;* **~pecker** *n.* Specht, *der;* **~ pigeon** *n.* Ringeltaube, *die;* **~shed** *n.* Holzschuppen, *der;* **~wind** *n.* the ~wind [section] die Holzbläser *Pl.;* **~wind instrument** Holzblasinstrument, *das;* **~work** *n.* **(a)** (craft) Arbeiten mit Holz; **(b)** (things) Holzarbeit[en *Pl.*]; **~worm** *n.* Holzwurm, *der;* **it's got ~worm** da ist der Holzwurm drin (ugs.)

'woody *adj.* **(a)** (wooded) waldreich **(b)** (consisting of wood) holzig

wool /wʊl/ *n.* Wolle, *die; attrib.* Woll-

woollen (*Amer.:* **woolen**) /'wʊlən/ ⎡1⎤ *adj.* wollen ⎡2⎤ *n.* ~s Wollsachen *Pl.*

'woolly *adj.* **(a)** wollig; Woll⟨pullover, -mütze⟩ **(b)** (confused) verschwommen

woozy /'wuːzɪ/ *adj.* (coll.) **(a)** (dizzy) duselig (ugs.) **(b)** (drunk) angeduselt (salopp)

word /wɜːd/ ⎡1⎤ *n.* Wort, *das;* ~s (of song or actor) Text, *der;* **in other ~s** mit anderen Worten; **~ for ~:** Wort für Wort; **too funny** *etc.* **for ~s** unsagbar komisch *usw.;* **have ~s** einen Wortwechsel haben; **have a ~ [with sb.] about sth.** [mit jmdm.] über etw. (*Akk.*) sprechen; **could I have a ~ [with you]?** kann ich dich mal sprechen?; **say a few ~s** ein paar Worte sprechen; **keep/break one's ~:** sein Wort halten/brechen; **by ~ of mouth** durch mündliche Mitteilung; **send ~ that** ...: Nachricht geben, dass ... ⎡2⎤ *v.t.* formulieren

'wording *n.* Formulierung, *die*

word: ~ order *n.* Wortstellung, *die;* **~play** *n.* Wortspiel, *das;* **~ processing** *n.* Textverarbeitung, *die;* **~ processor** *n.* Textverarbeitungssystem, *das*

wordy /'wɜːdɪ/ *adj.* weitschweifig

wore ▶ WEAR 2, 3

work /wɜːk/ ⎡1⎤ *n.* **(a)** Arbeit, *die;* **at ~** (engaged in ~ing) bei der Arbeit; (fig.: operating) am Werk; (at job) auf der Arbeit; **out of ~:** arbeitslos; **be in ~:** eine Stelle haben; **set to ~** ⟨*Person:*⟩ sich an die Arbeit machen; **go out to ~:** arbeiten gehen **(b)** ~s *sing. or pl.* (factory) Werk, *das* **(c)** ~s *pl.* (~ing parts) Werk, *das;* (operations) Arbeiten *Pl.* **(d)** (thing made or achieved) Werk, *das;* **a ~ of art/literature** ein Kunstwerk/literarisches Werk ⎡2⎤ *v.i.* **(a)** arbeiten

(c) (function effectively) funktionieren; **make the television ~:** den Fernsehapparat in Ordnung bringen **(c)** (have an effect) wirken (**on** auf + *Akk.*) **(d)** **~ loose** sich lockern ⎡3⎤ *v.t.* **(a)** bedienen ⟨*Maschine*⟩; betätigen ⟨*Bremse*⟩ **(b)** (get labour from) arbeiten lassen **(c)** ausbeuten ⟨*Steinbruch, Grube*⟩ **(d)** (cause to go gradually) führen; **~ one's way up/into sth.** sich hocharbeiten/in etw. hineinarbeiten

■ **work 'off** *v.t.* **(a)** (get rid of) loswerden; abreagieren ⟨*Wut*⟩ **(b)** abarbeiten ⟨*Schuld*⟩

■ **'work on** *v.t.* **(a)** ~ **on sth.** an etw. (*Dat.*) arbeiten **(b)** (try to persuade) ~ **on sb.** jmdn. bearbeiten (ugs.)

■ **work 'out** ⎡1⎤ *v.t.* **(a)** (calculate) ausrechnen **(b)** (solve) lösen **(c)** (devise) ausarbeiten ⎡2⎤ *v.i.* **(a)** sth. ~**s out at £2** etw. ergibt 2 Pfund **(b)** (have result) laufen; **things ~ed out [well] in the end** es ist schließlich doch alles gut gegangen

■ **work 'up** ⎡1⎤ *v.t.* (excite) aufpeitschen ⟨*Menge*⟩; **get ~ed up** sich aufregen ⎡2⎤ *v.i.* ~ **up to sth.** ⟨*Musik:*⟩ sich zu etw. steigern; ⟨*Geschichte, Film:*⟩ auf etw. (*Akk.*) zusteuern

workable /'wɜːkəbl/ *adj.* (feasible) durchführbar

workaholic /wɜːkə'hɒlɪk/ *n.* (coll.) arbeitswütiger Mensch

work: ~bench *n.* Werkbank, *die;* **~day** *n.* Werktag, *der*

'worker *n.* Arbeiter, *der*/Arbeiterin, *die*

'worker bee *n.* Arbeiterbiene, *die*

work: ~ ethic *n.* Arbeitsethos, *das;* **~ experience** *n.* (for schoolchildren) Praktikum, *das;* **~force** *n.* Belegschaft, *die;*

'working *adj.* **(a)** (in work) werktätig **(b)** ~ **model** funktionsfähiges Modell

working: ~ 'capital *n.* Betriebskapital, *das;* **~ 'class** *n.* Arbeiterklasse, *die;* **~-class** *adj.* der Arbeiterklasse *nachgestellt;* **sb. is ~-class** jmd. gehört zur Arbeiterklasse; **~ clothes** *n. pl.* Arbeitskleidung, *die;* **~ 'day** *n.* **(a)** (portion of day) Arbeitstag, *der;* **(b)** (day when work is done) Werktag, *der;* **~ 'hours** *n. pl.* Arbeitszeit, *die;* **~ 'knowledge** *n.* ausreichende Kenntnisse (**of** in + *Dat.*); **~ 'mother** *n.* berufstätige Mutter; **~ 'order** *n.* **be in [good] ~ order** betriebsbereit sein; ⟨*Auto:*⟩ fahrbereit sein; **~-'over** *n.* (sl.) Abreibung, *die* (ugs.); **~ 'week** *n.* Arbeitswoche, *die;* **a 35-hour ~ week** eine 35-Stunden-Woche; **~ 'wife** *n.* berufstätige Ehefrau

work: ~load *n.* Arbeitslast, *die;* **~man** ⸱⸱⸱◊

/'wɜːkmən/ n., pl. ~**men** /'wɜːkmən/
Arbeiter, der; ~**manship** /'wɜːkmənʃɪp/ n.
(quality) Kunstfertigkeit, die; ~**out** n.
[Fitness]training, das; ~ **permit** n.
Arbeitserlaubnis, die; ~**sheet** n. (a)
(recording work done) Arbeitszettel, der; (b) (for
student) Formular mit Prüfungsfragen;
~**shop** n. (a) (room) Werkstatt, die; (b)
(building) Werk, das; ~**station** n. (Comp.)
Workstation, die; ~ **table** n. Arbeitstisch,
der; ~**-to-'rule** n. Dienst nach Vorschrift
world /wɜːld/ n. (a) Welt, die; in the ~: auf
der Welt; **the tallest building in the ~:** das
höchste Gebäude der Welt; **all over the ~:** in
od. auf der ganzen Welt
(b) (vast amount) **it will do him a** or **the ~ of**
good es wird ihm unendlich gut tun; **a ~ of**
difference ein weltweiter Unterschied
world: W~ 'Bank n. Weltbank, die;
~ '**champion** n. Weltmeister, der/
-meisterin, die; **W~ 'Cup** n. Worldcup, der;
~**-famous** adj. weltberühmt
'**worldly** adj. weltlich; weltlich eingestellt
⟨Person⟩
worldly 'wise adj. weltklug
world: ~ '**power** n. Weltmacht, die;
~ '**record** n. Weltrekord, der; ~**-record**
holder Weltrekordhalter, der/-halterin, die;
~**-shaking** adj. welterschütternd;
~ **view** n. Weltsicht, die; ~ '**war** n.
Weltkrieg, der; **the First/Second W~ War,**
W~ War I/II der Erste/Zweite Weltkrieg; der
1./2. Weltkrieg; ~**wide** /'--/ adj. weltweit
nicht präd.; **W~ Wide 'Web** n. (Comp.)
World Wide Web, das
worm /wɜːm/ [1] n. Wurm, der
[2] v.t. (a) ~ **oneself into sb.'s favour** sich in
jmds. Gunst (Akk.) schleichen
(b) ~ **sth. out of sb.** etw. aus jmdm.
herausbringen (ugs.)
'**worm-eaten** adj. wurmstichig
worn ▶ WEAR 2, 3
'**worn-out** adj. (a) abgetragen
⟨Kleidungsstück⟩; abgenutzt ⟨Teppich⟩
(b) erschöpft ⟨Person⟩
worried /'wʌrɪd/ adj. besorgt
worry /'wʌrɪ/ [1] v.t. (a) beunruhigen
(b) (bother) stören
[2] v.i. sich (Dat.) Sorgen machen
[3] n. Sorge, die; **sth. is the least of sb.'s**
worries etw. ist jmds. geringste Sorge
'**worrying** adj. (a) (causing worry)
beunruhigend
(b) (full of worry) sorgenvoll ⟨Zeit, Woche⟩
worse /wɜːs/ [1] adj. schlechter; schlimmer
⟨Schmerz, Krankheit, Benehmen⟩
[2] adv. schlechter; schlimmer, schlechter
⟨sich benehmen⟩
[3] n. Schlimmeres
worsen /'wɜːsn/ [1] v.t. verschlechtern
[2] v.i. sich verschlechtern
worship /'wɜːʃɪp/ [1] v.t., (Brit.) -pp-: (a)
anbeten
(b) (idolize) abgöttisch verehren

[2] v.i., (Brit.) -pp- am Gottesdienst teilnehmen
[3] n. (a) Anbetung, die; (service) Gottesdienst,
der
(b) **Your/His W~:** ≈ Euer/seine Ehren
'**worshipper** (Amer.: **worshiper**) n.
Gottesdienstbesucher, der/-besucherin, die
worst /wɜːst/ [1] adj. schlechtest...;
schlimmst... ⟨Schmerz, Krankheit,
Benehmen⟩
[2] adv. am schlechtesten/schlimmsten
[3] n. (a) **the ~:** der/die/das Schlimmste; **get**
or **have the ~ of it** (suffer the most) am meisten
zu leiden haben; **if the ~ comes to the ~:**
wenn es zum Schlimmsten kommt
(b) (poorest in quality) Schlechteste, der/die/das
worsted /'wʊstɪd/ n. Kammgarn, das
worth /wɜːθ/ [1] adj. wert; **it's ~ £80** es ist
80 Pfund wert; **is it ~ hearing/the effort?** ist
es hörenswert/der Mühe wert?; **is it**
~ **doing?** lohnt es sich?; **it isn't ~ it** es lohnt
sich nicht
[2] n. Wert, der; **ten pounds' ~ of petrol**
Benzin für zehn Pfund
'**worthless** adj. (a) (valueless) wertlos
(b) (having bad qualities) nichtswürdig
'**worthwhile** adj. lohnend
worthy /'wɜːðɪ/ adj. würdig
wouldn't /'wʊdnt/ (coll.) = **would not;**
▶ WILL¹
wound¹ /wuːnd/ [1] n. Wunde, die
[2] v.t. verwunden; (fig.) verletzen
wound² ▶ WIND²
wove, woven ▶ WEAVE¹ 2
wrangle /'ræŋgl/ [1] v.i. [sich] streiten
[2] n. Streit, der
wrap /ræp/ [1] v.t., -pp- einwickeln; (fig.)
hüllen; ~**ped** abgepackt ⟨Brot usw.⟩; ~ **sth.**
[a]**round sth.** etw. um etw. wickeln
[2] n. Umschlag[e]tuch, das
■ **wrap 'up** v.t. (a) einwickeln
(b) (conclude) abschließen
(c) **be ~ped up in one's work** in seine Arbeit
völlig versunken sein
'**wrapper** n. (a) **sweet/toffee ~[s]**
Bonbonpapier, das
(b) (of book) Schutzumschlag, der
'**wrapping** n. Verpackung, die
'**wrapping paper** n. (strong) Packpapier,
das; (decorative) Geschenkpapier, das
wrath /rɒθ/ n. Zorn, der
wreak /riːk/ v.t. (a) (cause) anrichten
(b) ~ **vengeance on sb.** an jmdm. Rache
nehmen
wreath /riːθ/ n., pl. **wreaths** /riːðz, riːθs/
Kranz, der
wreck /rek/ [1] n. (a) Wrack, das
(b) (destruction of ship) Schiffbruch, der
[2] v.t. (a) (destroy) ruinieren; zu Schrott
fahren ⟨Auto⟩; **be ~ed** (shipwrecked)
Schiffbruch erleiden
(b) (fig.: ruin) zerstören; ruinieren
⟨Gesundheit, Urlaub⟩

wreckage /'rekɪdʒ/ *n.* Wrackteile *Pl.;* (fig.) Trümmer *Pl.*

wren *n.* Zaunkönig, *der*

wrench /rentʃ/ ⓵ *n.* **(a)** (*esp. Amer.:* spanner) Schraubenschlüssel, *der* **(b)** (violent twist) Verrenkung, *die* **(c)** (fig.) be a great ∼ [for sb.] sehr schmerzhaft für jmdn. sein ⓶ *v.t.* **(a)** reißen; ∼ sth. from sb. jmdm. etw. entreißen **(b)** ∼ one's ankle sich (*Dat.*) den Knöchel verrenken

wrest /rest/ *v.t.* ∼ sth. from sb. jmdm. etw. entreißen

wrestle /'resl/ *v.i.* ringen

wrestler /'reslə(r)/ *n.* Ringer, *der*/ Ringerin, *die*

wrestling /'reslɪŋ/ *n.* Ringen, *das*

wretch /retʃ/ *n.* Kreatur, *die*

wretched /'retʃɪd/ *adj.* **(a)** (miserable) unglücklich **(b)** (coll.: damned) elend **(c)** (very bad) erbärmlich

wriggle /'rɪgl/ ⓵ *v.i.* **(a)** sich winden; ⟨*Fisch:*⟩ zappeln **(b)** (move) sich schlängeln ⓶ *v.t.* ∼ one's way sich schlängeln ⓷ *n.* Windung, *die*

wring /rɪŋ/ *v.t.,* wrung /rʌŋ/ **(a)** wringen; ∼ out auswringen **(b)** ∼ sb.'s hand jmdm. fest die Hand drücken; ∼ the neck of an animal einem Tier den Hals umdrehen **(c)** ∼ sth. from *or* out of sb. (fig.) jmdm. etw. abpressen

wringing 'wet *adj.* tropfnass

wrinkle /'rɪŋkl/ ⓵ *n.* Falte, *die;* (in paper) Knick, *der* ⓶ *v.t.* falten ⓷ *v.i.* sich in Falten legen

wrinkled /'rɪŋkld/ *adjs.* runz[e]lig

wrinkly /'rɪŋklɪ/ ⓵ *adj.* runz[e]lig ⓶ *n.* (coll.) Grufti, *der* (ugs.)

wrist /rɪst/ *n.* Handgelenk, *das*

'wristwatch *n.* Armbanduhr, *die*

writ /rɪt/ *n.* (Law) Verfügung, *die*

write /raɪt/ ⓵ *v.i.,* wrote /rəʊt/, written /'rɪtn/ schreiben; ∼ to sb./a firm jmdm./an eine Firma schreiben ⓶ *v.t.,* wrote, written schreiben; ausschreiben ⟨Scheck⟩; the written language die Schriftsprache; written applications schriftliche Anträge *Pl.*

■ **write 'back** *v.i.* zurückschreiben

■ **write 'down** *v.t.* aufschreiben

■ **write 'off** ⓵ *v.t.* **(a)** abschreiben ⟨*Schulden, Verlust*⟩ **(b)** (destroy) zu Schrott fahren ⓶ *v.i.* ∼ off for sth. etw. [schriftlich] anfordern

'write-off *n.* Totalschaden, *der*

writer /'raɪtə(r)/ *n.* Schriftsteller, *der*/ Schriftstellerin, *die;* (of letter, article) Verfasser, *der*/Verfasserin, *die*

'write-up *n.* (by critic) Kritik, *die*

writhe /raɪð/ *v.i.* sich winden

writing /'raɪtɪŋ/ *n.* **(a)** Schreiben, *das;* put sth. in ∼: etw. schriftlich machen (ugs.) **(b)** (handwriting, something written) Schrift, *die*

'writing paper *n.* Schreibpapier, *das*

written ▶ WRITE

wrong /rɒŋ/ ⓵ *adj.* **(a)** (morally bad) unrecht (geh.); (unfair) ungerecht **(b)** (mistaken) falsch; be ∼ ⟨Person:⟩ sich irren; the clock is ∼: die Uhr geht falsch **(c)** (not suitable) falsch; give the ∼ answer eine falsche Antwort geben; [the] ∼ way round verkehrt herum **(d)** (out of order) nicht in Ordnung; what's ∼? was ist los? ⓶ *adv.* falsch ⓷ *n.* Unrecht, *das;* do ∼: Unrecht tun ⓸ *v.t.* ∼ sb. jmdm. ungerecht behandeln

'wrongdoer *n.* Übeltäter, *der*/-täterin, *die;* Missetäter, *der*/-täterin, *die* (geh.)

'wrongdoing *n.* no indef. art. Missetaten *Pl.* (geh.)

wrongful /'rɒŋfl/ *adj.* **(a)** (unfair) unrecht (geh.) **(b)** (unlawful) rechtswidrig

'wrongfully *adv.* **(a)** (unfairly) unrecht (geh.) ⟨*handeln*⟩; zu Unrecht ⟨*beschuldigen*⟩ **(b)** (unlawfully) rechtswidrig

'wrongly *adv.* **(a)** falsch **(b)** (mistakenly) zu Unrecht **(c)** ▶ WRONGFULLY A

wrote ▶ WRITE

wrought iron /rɔːt 'aɪən/ *n.* Schmiedeeisen, *das; attrib.* schmiedeeisern

wrung ▶ WRING

wry /raɪ/ *adj.,* ∼er *or* wrier /'raɪə(r)/, ∼est *or* wriest /'raɪɪst/ ironisch ⟨Blick⟩; fein ⟨Humor, Witz⟩

WWW *abbr.* = **World Wide Web** WWW

W

Xx

X, x /eks/ *n.* X, x, *das*

xenophobia /zenəˈfəʊbɪə/ *n.*
Fremdenfeindlichkeit, *die*

xenophobic /zenəˈfəʊbɪk/ *adj.*
fremdenfeindlich

Xerox ®, **xerox** /ˈzɪərɒks/ [1] *n.* (copy)
Xerokopie, *die*

[2] **xerox** *v.t.* xerokopieren

Xmas /ˈkrɪsməs, ˈeksməs/ *n.* (coll.)
Weihnachten, *das*

'X-ray [1] *n.* (picture) Röntgenaufnahme, *die*
[2] *v.t.* röntgen; durchleuchten ⟨*Gepäck*⟩

Yy

Y, y /waɪ/ *n.* Y, y, *das*

yacht /jɒt/ *n.* (a) (for racing) Segeljacht, *die*
(b) (for pleasure) Jacht, *die*

'yachting *n.* Segeln, *das*

yachtsman /ˈjɒtsmən/ *n.*, *pl.* **yachtsmen**
/ˈjɒtsmən/ Segler, *der*

yank (coll.) [1] *v.t.* reißen an (+ *Dat.*)
[2] *n.* Reißen, *das*

Yank /jæŋk/ *n.* (Brit. coll.: American) Ami, *der*
(ugs.)

yap /jæp/ *v.i.*, **-pp-** kläffen

yard[1] /jɑːd/ *n.* (measure) Yard, *das*

yard[2] *n.* (a) (attached to building) Hof, *der; in*
the ∼: auf dem Hof
(b) (for storage) Lager, *das*
(c) (Amer: garden) Garten, *der*

'yardstick *n.* (fig.) Maßstab, *der*

yarn /jɑːn/ *n.* (a) (thread) Garn, *das*
(b) (coll.: story) Geschichte, *die*

yawn /jɔːn/ [1] *n.* Gähnen, *das*
[2] *v.i.* gähnen

'yawning *adj.* gähnend

year /jɪə(r)/ *n.* (a) Jahr, *das; for* [many] ∼s
jahrelang; **once a** ∼, **every** ∼: einmal im
Jahr; **a ten-**∼**-old** ein Zehnjähriger/eine
Zehnjährige
(b) (group of students, vintage of wine) Jahrgang,
der

'yearbook *n.* Jahrbuch, *das*

'yearly [1] *adj.* jährlich;
Einjahres⟨*abonnement*⟩
[2] *adv.* jährlich

yearn /jɜːn/ *v.i.* ∼ **for** *or* **after sth./for sb.**
sich nach etw./jmdm. sehnen; ∼ **to do sth.**
sich danach sehnen, etw. zu tun

'yearning *n.* Sehnsucht, *die*

yeast /jiːst/ *n.* Hefe, *die*

yell /jel/ [1] *n.* gellender Schrei

[2] *v.t. & i.* [gellend] schreien

yellow /ˈjeləʊ/ [1] *adj.* gelb
[2] *n.* Gelb, *das*

yellow: ∼ **'card** *n.* (Footb.) gelbe Karte;
∼ **'fever** *n.* Gelbfieber, *das*

yellowish /ˈjeləʊɪʃ/ *adj.* gelblich

Yellow 'Pages *n. pl.* ® gelbe Seiten *Pl.*

yelp /jelp/ [1] *v.i.* jaulen
[2] *n.* Jaulen, *das*

yen /jen/ *n.* (coll.: longing) **sb. has a** ∼ **to do**
sth. es drängt jmdn. danach, etw. zu tun

yes /jes/ [1] *adv.* ja; (in contradiction) doch
[2] *n.*, *pl.* ∼**es** Ja, *das*

'yes-man *n.* (coll. derog.) Jasager, *der*
(abwertend)

yesterday /ˈjestədeɪ, ˈjestədɪ/ [1] *n.*
gestern; **the day before** ∼: vorgestern; ∼**'s**
paper die gestrige Zeitung
[2] *adv.* gestern; **the day before** ∼:
vorgestern

yet /jet/ [1] *adv.* (a) (still) noch; ∼ **again** noch
einmal
(b) (hitherto) bisher; **his best** ∼: sein bisher
bestes
(c) *neg.* **not** [just] ∼: [jetzt] noch nicht
(d) (before all is over) doch noch; **he could win**
∼: er könnte noch gewinnen
(e) *with compar.* (even) noch
(f) (nevertheless) doch
[2] *conj.* doch

yew /juː/ *n.* ∼ [tree] Eibe, *die*

Yiddish /ˈjɪdɪʃ/ [1] *adj.* jiddisch
[2] *n.* Jiddisch, *das; see also* ENGLISH 2A

yield /jiːld/ [1] *v.t.* (give) bringen;
hervorbringen ⟨*Ernte*⟩; abwerfen ⟨*Gewinn*⟩
[2] *v.i.* (a) sich unterwerfen
(b) (give right of way) Vorfahrt gewähren
[3] *n.* Ertrag, *der*

yob /jɒb/ n. (Brit. coll.) Rowdy, der

yobbish /'jɒbɪʃ/ adj. (Brit. coll.) rowdyhaft

yobbo /'jɒbəʊ/ n. pl. ~s ▶ YOB

yodel /'jəʊdl/ v.i. & t., (Brit.) -ll- jodeln

yoga /'jəʊgə/ n. Joga, der od. das

yoghurt, yogurt /'jɒgət/ n. Joghurt, der od. das

yoke /jəʊk/ n. Joch, das

yokel /'jəʊkl/ n. [Bauern]tölpel, der

yolk /jəʊk/ n. Dotter, der od. das; Eigelb, das

yonder /'jɒndə(r)/ (literary) **1** adj. ~ tree jener Baum dort (geh.)
2 adv. dort drüben

Yorkshire 'pudding n. Yorkshirepudding, der

you /jʊ, stressed ju:/ pron. (a) sing./pl. du/ihr; (polite) sing. or pl. Sie; as direct object dich/euch/Sie; as indirect object dir/euch/Ihnen; refl. dich/dir/euch; (polite) sich; **it was** ~: du warst/ihr wart/Sie waren es
(b) (one) man

you'd /jʊd, stressed ju:d/ (a) = you had
(b) = you would

you'll /jʊl, stressed ju:l/ (a) = you will
(b) = you shall

young /jʌŋ/ **1** adj., ~er /'jʌŋgə(r)/, ~est /'jʌŋgɪst/ jung
2 n. pl. (of animals) Junge Pl.; **the** ~ (~ people) die jungen Leute

youngish adj. ziemlich jung

youngster /'jʌŋstə(r)/ n. (a) (child) Kleine, der/die/das
(b) (young person) Jugendliche, der/die

your /jə(r), stressed jʊə(r), jɔ:(r)/ poss. pron. attrib.: sing. dein; pl. euer; (polite) sing. or pl. Ihr

you're /jə(r), stressed jʊə(r), jɔ:(r)/ = you are

yours /jʊəz, jɔ:z/ poss. pron. pred.: sing. deiner/deine/dein[e]s; pl. eurer/eure/eures; (polite) sing. or pl. Ihrer/Ihre/Ihr[e]s; see also HERS

yourself /jə'self, jʊə'self, jɔ:'self/ pron. (a) emphat. selbst
(b) refl. dich/dir/(polite) sich. See also HERSELF

yourselves /jə'selvz, jʊə'selvz, jɔ:'selvz/ pron. (a) emphat. selbst
(b) refl. euch/(polite) sich. See also HERSELF

youth /ju:θ/ n. (a) Jugend, die
(b) pl. ~s /ju:ðz/ (young man) Jugendliche, der

youth: ~ **centre** n. Jugendzentrum, das; ~ **club** n. Jugendklub, der

youthful /'ju:θfl/ adj. jugendlich

'youth hostel n. Jugendherberge, die

you've /jʊv, stressed ju:v/ = you have

yo-yo ® /'jəʊjəʊ/ n., pl. ~s Jo-Jo, das

Yugoslav /'ju:gəslɑ:v/ ▶ YUGOSLAVIAN

Yugoslavia /ju:gə'slɑ:vɪə/ pr. n. Jugoslawien (das); ex-~: Ex-Jugoslawien (das)

Yugoslavian /ju:gə'slɑ:vɪən/ **1** adj. jugoslawisch; **sb. is** ~: jmd. ist Jugoslawe/Jugoslawin
2 n. Jugoslawe, der/Jugoslawin, die

yuk /jʌk/ int. (coll.) bäh

yummy /'jʌmɪ/ (coll.) int. lecker

yuppie /'jʌpɪ/ n. (coll.) Yuppie, der

yuppie 'flu n. (coll.) Yuppie-Grippe, die

Zz

Z, z /zed, (Amer.) zi:/ n. Z, z, das

Zaire /zɑ:'ɪə(r)/ pr. n. Zaire (das)

Zambia /'zæmbɪə/ pr. n. Sambia (das)

zany /'zeɪnɪ/ adj. irre komisch (ugs.); Wahnsinns⟨humor, -komiker⟩

zap /zæp/ (coll.) v.i. -pp- (Telev. coll.) zappen (ugs.)

zapper /'zæpə(r)/ n. (Telev. coll.) Drücker, der (ugs.)

zeal /zi:l/ n. Eifer, der

zealous /'zeləs/ adj. eifrig

zebra /'zebrə, 'zi:brə/ n. Zebra, das

zebra 'crossing n. (Brit.) Zebrastreifen, der

zenith /'zenɪθ/ n. Zenit, der

zero /'zɪərəʊ/ n., pl. ~s Null, die

zero: ~-**rated** adj. ~-rated goods nicht mehrwertsteuerpflichtige Güter; ~ **'tolerance** n. Nulltoleranz, die (for, to, of gegenüber)

zest /zest/ n. (enthusiasm) Begeisterung, die; ~ **for living** Lebenslust, die

zigzag /'zɪgzæg/ **1** adj. zickzackförmig; Zickzack⟨muster, -anordnung⟩
2 n. Zickzacklinie, die

Zimbabwe /zɪm'bɑ:bwɪ/ pr. n. Simbabwe (das)

zinc /zɪŋk/ n. Zink, das

zip /zɪp/ **1** n. Reißverschluss, der ⋯⋅⋅

2 *v.t.*, -pp-: **(a)** ~ [up] sth. den Reißverschluss an etw. (*Dat.*) zuziehen **(b)** (Comp.) ~ [up] packen ⟨*Datei*⟩

'**zip bag** *n.* Tasche, *die* mit Reißverschluss

'**Zip code** *n.* (Amer.) Postleitzahl, *die*

zip fastener ▶ ZIP 1

zipper /'zɪpə(r)/ ▶ ZIP 1

zither /'zɪðə(r)/ *n.* Zither, *die*

zodiac /'zəʊdɪæk/ *n.* Tierkreis, *der;* **sign of the** ~: Tierkreiszeichen, *das*

zombie (*Amer.:* **zombi**) /'zɒmbɪ/ *n.* Zombie, *der*

zone /zəʊn/ *n.* Zone, *die*

zoo /zu:/ *n.* Zoo, *der*

'**zookeeper** *n.* Zoowärter, *der*/-wärterin, *die*

zoological /zu:ə'lɒdʒɪkl/ *adj.* zoologisch

zoologist /zu:'ɒlədʒɪst/ *n.* Zoologe, *der*/ Zoologin, *die*

zoology /zu:'ɒlədʒɪ/ *n.* Zoologie, *die*

zoom /zu:m/ *v.i.* rauschen

■ **zoom 'in on** *v.t.* zoomen auf (+ *Akk.*)

'**zoom lens** *n.* Zoomobjektiv, *das*

zucchini /zʊ'ki:nɪ/ *n.*, *pl. same or* ~**s** (esp. Amer.) Zucchino, *der*

z

German irregular verbs

Irregular and partly irregular verbs are listed alphabetically by infinitive. 1st, 2nd, and 3rd person present and imperative forms are given after the infinitive, and preterite subjunctive forms after the preterite indicative, where they take an umlaut, change *e* to *i*, etc.

Verbs with a raised number in the German-English section of the Dictionary have the same number in this list.

Compound verbs (including verbs with prefixes) are only given if a) they do not take the same forms as the corresponding simple verb, e.g. *befehlen*, or b) there is no corresponding simple verb, e.g. *bewegen*.

An asterisk (*) indicates a verb which is also conjugated regularly.

Infinitive *Infinitiv*	Preterite *Präteritum*	Past Participle *2. Partizip*
abwägen	wog (wöge) ab	abgewogen
backen (du bäckst, er bäckt; *auch:* du backst, er backt)	backte, *älter:* buk (büke)	gebacken
befehlen (du befiehlst, er befiehlt; befiehl!)	befahl (beföhle, befähle)	befohlen
beginnen	begann (begänne, *seltener:* begönne)	begonnen
beißen	biss	gebissen
bergen (du birgst, er birgt; birg!)	barg (bärge)	geborgen
bersten (du birst, er birst; birst!)	barst (bärste)	geborsten
besinnen	besann (besänne)	besonnen
bewegen[2]	bewog (bewöge)	bewogen
biegen	bog (böge)	gebogen
bieten	bot (böte)	geboten
binden	band (bände)	gebunden
bitten	bat (bäte)	gebeten
blasen (du bläst, er bläst)	blies	geblasen
bleiben	blieb	geblieben
bleichen*	blich	geblichen
braten (du brätst, er brät)	briet	gebraten
brechen (du brichst, er bricht; brich!)	brach (bräche)	gebrochen
brennen	brannte (brennte)	gebrannt
bringen	brachte (brächte)	gebracht
denken	dachte (dächte)	gedacht
dreschen (du drischst, er drischt; drisch!)	drosch (drösche)	gedroschen
dringen	drang (dränge)	gedrungen
dürfen (ich darf, du darfst, er darf)	durfte (dürfte)	gedurft
empfehlen (du empfiehlst, er empfiehlt, empfiehl!)	empfahl (empföhle, *seltener:* empfähle)	empfohlen
erklimmen	erklomm (erklömme)	erklommen
erlöschen (du erlischst, er erlischt; erlisch!)	erlosch (erlösche)	erloschen
erschallen*	erscholl (erschölle)	erschollen
erschrecken[1,3] (du erschrickst, er erschrickt; erschrick!)	erschrak (erschäke)	erschrocken
erwägen	erwog (erwöge)	erwogen

Infinitive *Infinitiv*	Preterite *Präteritum*	Past Participle *2. Partizip*
essen (du isst, er isst; iss!)	aß (äße)	gegessen
fahren (du fährst, er fährt)	fuhr (führe)	gefahren
fallen (du fällst, er fällt)	fiel	gefallen
fangen (du fängst, er fängt)	fing	gefangen
fechten (du fichtst, er ficht; ficht!)	focht (föchte)	gefochten
finden	fand (fände)	gefunden
flechten (du flichtst, er flicht; flicht!)	flocht (flöchte)	geflochten
fliegen	flog (flöge)	geflogen
fliehen	floh (flöhe)	geflohen
fließen	floss (flösse)	geflossen
fressen (du frisst, er frisst; friss!)	fraß (fräße)	gefressen
frieren	fror (fröre)	gefroren
gären*	gor (gäre)	gegoren
gebären (*geh.:* du gebierst, sie gebiert; gebier!)	gebar (gebäre)	geboren
geben (du gibst, er gibt; gib!)	gab (gäbe)	gegeben
gedeihen	gedieh	gediehen
gehen	ging	gegangen
gelingen	gelang (gelänge)	gelungen
gelten (du giltst, er gilt; gilt!)	galt (gölte, gälte)	gegolten
genesen	genas (genäse)	genesen
genießen	genoss (genösse)	genossen
geschehen (es geschieht)	geschah (geschähe)	geschehen
gewinnen	gewann (gewönne, gewänne)	gewonnen
gießen	goss (gösse)	gegossen
gleichen	glich	geglichen
gleiten	glitt	geglitten
glimmen	glomm (glömme)	geglommen
graben (du gräbst, er gräbt)	grub (grübe)	gegraben
greifen	griff	gegriffen
haben (du hast, er hat)	hatte (hätte)	gehabt
halten (du hältst, er hält)	hielt	gehalten
hängen[1]	hing	gehangen
hauen	haute, *geh.:* hieb	gehauen
heben	hob (höbe)	gehoben
heißen	hieß	geheißen
helfen (du hilfst, er hilft; hilf!)	half (hülfe, selten: hälfe)	geholfen
kennen	kannte (kennte)	gekannt
klingen	klang (klänge)	geklungen
kneifen	kniff	gekniffen
kommen	kam (käme)	gekommen
können (ich kann, du kannst, er kann)	konnte (könnte)	gekonnt
kriechen	kroch (kröche)	gekrochen
laden[1,2] (du lädst, er lädt)	lud (lüde)	geladen
lassen (du lässt, er lässt)	ließ	gelassen
laufen (du läufst, er läuft)	lief	gelaufen
leiden	litt	gelitten
leihen	lieh	geliehen
lesen[1,2] (du liest, er liest; lies!)	las (läse)	gelesen
liegen	lag (läge)	gelegen
lügen	log (löge)	gelogen
mahlen	mahlte	gemahlen
meiden	mied	gemieden
melken* (du milkst, er milkt; milk!; du melkst, er melkt; melke!)	molk (mölke)	gemolken
messen (du misst, er misst; miss!)	maß (mäße)	gemessen
misslingen	misslang (misslänge)	misslungen

German irregular verbs

● ●

Infinitive Infinitiv	Preterite Präteritum	Past Participle 2. Partizip
mögen (ich mag, du magst, er mag)	mochte (möchte)	gemocht
müssen (ich muss, du musst, er muss)	musste (müsste)	gemusst
nehmen (du nimmst, er nimmt; nimm!)	nahm (nähme)	genommen
nennen	nannte (nennte)	genannt
pfeifen	pfiff	gepfiffen
preisen	pries	gepriesen
quellen (du quillst, er quillt; quill!)	quoll (quölle)	gequollen
raten (du rätst, er rät)	riet	geraten
reiben	rieb	gerieben
reißen	riss	gerissen
reiten	ritt	geritten
rennen	rannte (rennte)	gerannt
riechen	roch (röche)	gerochen
ringen	rang (ränge)	gerungen
rinnen	rann (ränne, *seltener:* rönne)	geronnen
rufen	rief	gerufen
salzen*	salzte	gesalzen
saufen (du säufst, er säuft)	soff (söffe)	gesoffen
saugen*	sog (söge)	gesogen
schaffen*	schuf (schüfe)	geschaffen
schallen*	scholl (schölle)	geschallt
scheiden	schied	geschieden
scheinen	schien	geschienen
scheißen	schiss	geschissen
schelten (du schiltst, er schilt; schilt!)	schalt (schölte)	gescholten
scheren[1]	schor (schöre)	geschoren
schieben	schob (schöbe)	geschoben
schießen	schoss (schösse)	geschossen
schinden	schindete	geschunden
schlafen (du schläfst, er schläft)	schlief	geschlafen
schlagen (du schlägst, er schlägt)	schlug (schlüge)	geschlagen
schleichen	schlich	geschlichen
schleifen[1]	schliff	geschliffen
schließen	schloss (schlösse)	geschlossen
schlingen	schlang (schlänge)	geschlungen
schmeißen	schmiss	geschmissen
schmelzen (du schmilzt, er schmilzt; schmilz!)	schmolz	geschmolzen
schneiden	schnitt	geschnitten
schrecken* (du schrickst, er schrickt; schrick!)	schrak (schräke)	geschreckt
schreiben	schrieb	geschrieben
schreien	schrie	geschrie[e]n
schreiten	schritt	geschritten
schweigen	schwieg	geschwiegen
schwellen (du schwillst, er schwillt; schwill!)	schwoll (schwölle)	geschwollen
schwimmen	schwamm (schwömme, *seltener:* schwämme)	geschwommen
schwinden	schwand (schwände)	geschwunden
schwingen	schwang (schwänge)	geschwungen
schwören	schwor (schwüre)	geschworen
sehen (du siehst, er sieht; sieh[e]!)	sah (sähe)	gesehen
sein (ich bin, du bist, er ist, wir sind, ihr seid, sie sind; sei!)	war (wäre)	gewesen

German irregular verbs

Infinitive / *Infinitiv*	Preterite / *Präteritum*	Past Participle / *2. Partizip*
senden*	sandte (sendete)	gesandt
sieden*	sott (sötte)	gesotten
singen	sang (sänge)	gesungen
sinken	sank (sänke)	gesunken
sitzen	saß (säße)	gesessen
sollen (ich soll, du sollst, er soll)	sollte	gesollt
spalten*	spaltete	gespalten
speien	spie	gespie[e]n
spinnen	spann (spönne, spänne)	gesponnen
sprechen (du sprichst, er spricht; sprich!)	sprach (spräche)	gesprochen
sprießen	spross (sprösse)	gesprossen
springen	sprang	gesprungen
stechen (du stichst, er sticht; stich!)	stach (stäche)	gestochen
stehen	stand (stünde, *auch:* stände)	gestanden
stehlen (du stiehlst, er stiehlt; stiehl!)	stahl (stähle, *seltener:* stöhle)	gestohlen
steigen	stieg	gestiegen
sterben (du stirbst, er stirbt; stirb!)	starb (stürbe)	gestorben
stinken	stank (stänke)	gestunken
stoßen (du stößt, er stößt)	stieß	gestoßen
streichen	strich	gestrichen
streiten	stritt	gestritten
tragen (du trägst, er trägt)	trug (trüge)	getragen
treffen (du triffst, er trifft; triff!)	traf (träfe)	getroffen
treiben	trieb	getrieben
treten (du trittst, er tritt; tritt!)	trat (träte)	getreten
triefen*	troff (tröffe)	getroffen
trinken	trank (tränke)	getrunken
trügen	trog (tröge)	getrogen
tun	tat (täte)	getan
verderben (du verdirbst, er verdirbt; verdirb!)	verdarb (verdürbe)	verdorben
verdrießen	verdross (verdrösse)	verdrossen
vergessen (du vergisst, er vergisst, vergiss!)	vergaß (vergäße)	vergessen
verlieren	verlor (verlöre)	verloren
verschleißen*	verschliss	verschlissen
verzeihen	verzieh	verziehen
wachsen[1] (du wächst, er wächst)	wuchs (wüchse)	gewachsen
waschen (du wäschst, er wäscht)	wusch (wüsche)	gewaschen
weichen	wich	gewichen
weisen	wies	gewiesen
wenden[2]*	wandte (wendete)	gewandt
werben (du wirbst, er wirbt; wirb!)	warb (würbe)	geworben
werden (du wirst, er wird; werde!)	wurde, *dichter.:* ward (würde)	geworden; *als Hilfsv.:* worden
werfen (du wirfst, er wirft; wirf!)	warf (würfe)	geworfen
wiegen[1]	wog (wöge)	gewogen
winden	wand (wände)	gewunden
wissen (ich weiß, du weißt, er weiß)	wusste (wüsste)	gewusst
wollen (ich will, du willst, er will)	wollte	gewollt
wringen	wrang (wränge)	gewrungen
ziehen	zog (zöge)	gezogen
zwingen	zwang (zwänge)	gezwungen

Englische unregelmäßige Verben

Ein Sternchen (*) weist darauf hin, dass die korrekte Form von der jeweiligen Bedeutung abhängt.

Infinitive / Infinitiv	Past Tense / Präteritum	Past Participle / 2. Partizip
arise	arose	arisen
awake	awoke	awoken
be	was *sing.*, were *pl.*	been
bear	bore	borne
beat	beat	beaten
become	became	become
begin	began	begun
bend	bent	bent
bet	bet, betted	bet, betted
bid	*bade, bid	*bidden, bid
bind	bound	bound
bite	bit	bitten
bleed	bled	bled
blow	blew	blown
break	broke	broken
breed	bred	bred
bring	brought	brought
broadcast	broadcast	broadcast
build	built	built
burn	burnt, burned	burnt, burned
burst	burst	burst
bust	bust, busted	bust, busted
buy	bought	bought
cast	cast	cast
catch	caught	caught
choose	chose	chosen
cling	clung	clung
come	came	come
cost	*cost, costed	*cost, costed
creep	crept	crept
cut	cut	cut
deal	dealt	dealt
dig	dug	dug
dive	dived, (*Amer.*) dove	dived
do	did	done
draw	drew	drawn
dream	dreamt, dreamed	dreamt, dreamed
drink	drank	drunk
drive	drove	driven
dwell	dwelt	dwelt
eat	ate	eaten
fall	fell	fallen
feed	fed	fed
feel	felt	felt
fight	fought	fought
find	found	found
flee	fled	fled
fling	flung	flung
floodlight	floodlit	floodlit
fly	flew	flown
forbid	forbade, forbad	forbidden
forecast	forecast, forecasted	forecast, forecasted
foretell	foretold	foretold
forget	forgot	forgotten
forgive	forgave	forgiven
forsake	forsook	forsaken
freeze	froze	frozen
get	got	got, (*Amer.*) gotten
give	gave	given
go	went	gone
grind	ground	ground
grow	grew	grown
hang	*hung, hanged	*hung, hanged
have	had	had
hear	heard	heard
hew	hewed	hewn, hewed
hide	hid	hidden
hit	hit	hit
hold	held	held
hurt	hurt	hurt
keep	kept	kept
kneel	knelt, (*esp. Amer.*) kneeled	knelt, (*esp. Amer.*) kneeled
know	knew	known
lay	laid	laid
lead	led	led
lean	leaned, (*Brit.*) leant	leaned, (*Brit.*) leant
leap	leapt, leaped	leapt, leaped
learn	learnt, learned	learnt, learned
leave	left	left
lend	lent	lent
let	let	let
lie³	lay	lain
light	lit, lighted	lit, lighted
lose	lost	lost
make	made	made
mean	meant	meant
meet	met	met
mow	mowed	mown, mowed
overhang	overhung	overhung

Englische unregelmäßige Verben

Infinitive / *Infinitiv*	Past Tense / *Präteritum*	Past Participle / *2. Partizip*
pay	paid	paid
prove	proved	proved, proven
put	put	put
quit	quitted, (*Amer.*) quit	quitted, (*Amer.*) quit
read /riːd/	read /red/	read /red/
rid	rid	rid
ride	rode	ridden
ring[3]	rang	rung
rise	rose	risen
run	ran	run
saw	sawed	sawn, sawed
say	said	said
see	saw	seen
seek	sought	sought
sell	sold	sold
send	sent	sent
set	set	set
sew	sewed	sewn, sewed
shake	shook	shaken
shear	sheared	shorn, sheared
shed	shed	shed
shine	shone	shone
shit	shitted, shit	shitted, shit
shoe	shod	shod
shoot	shot	shot
show	showed	shown
shrink	shrank	shrunk
shut	shut	shut
sing	sang	sung
sink	sank, sunk	sunk
sit	sat	sat
slay	slew	slain
sleep	slept	slept
slide	slid	slid
sling	slung	slung
slink	slunk	slunk
slit	slit	slit
smell	smelt, smelled	smelt, smelled
sow	sowed	sown, sowed
speak	spoke	spoken
speed	*sped, speeded	*sped, speeded
spell	spelled, (*Brit.*) spelt	spelled, (*Brit.*) spelt
spend	spent	spent
spill	spilt, spilled	spilt, spilled
spin	spun	spun
spit	spat, spit	spat, spit
split	split	split
spoil	spoilt, spoiled	spoilt, spoiled
spread	spread	spread
spring	sprang, (*Amer.*) sprung	sprung
stand	stood	stood
steal	stole	stolen
stick	stuck	stuck
sting	stung	stung
stink	stank, stunk	stunk
strew	strewed	strewed, strewn
stride	strode	stridden
strike	struck	struck
string	strung	strung
strive	strove	striven
sublet	sublet	sublet
swear	swore	sworn
sweep	swept	swept
swell	swelled	swollen, swelled
swim	swam	swum
swing	swung	swung
take	took	taken
teach	taught	taught
tear	tore	torn
tell	told	told
think	thought	thought
thrive	thrived, throve	thrived, thriven
throw	threw	thrown
thrust	thrust	thrust
tread	trod	trodden, trod
understand	understood	understood
undo	undid	undone
wake	woke	woken
wear	wore	worn
weave[1]	wove	woven
weep	wept	wept
wet	wet, wetted	wet, wetted
win	won	won
wind[2] /waɪnd/	wound /waʊnd/	wound /waʊnd/
wring	wrung	wrung
write	wrote	written

Glossary of grammatical terms

Abbreviation A shortened form of a word or phrase: **etc.** = **usw.**

Absolute use The use of a transitive verb without an expressed object, as in: **I didn't** *realize*

Accusative The case of a direct object; some German prepositions take the accusative

Active In the active form the subject of the verb performs the action: **he asked** = **er hat gefragt**

Adjective A word describing a noun: **a** *red* **pencil** = **ein** *roter* **Stift**

Adverb A word that describes or changes the meaning of a verb, an adjective, or another adverb: **she sings** *beautifully* = **sie singt** *schön*

Article The definite article, **the** = **der/die/das**, and indefinite article, **a/an** = **ein/eine/ein**, used in front of a noun

Attributive An adjective or noun is attributive when it is used directly before a noun: **the** *black* **dog** = **der** *schwarze* **Hund;** *farewell* **speech** = **Abschiedsrede**

Auxiliary verb One of the verbs – as German **haben, sein, werden** - used to form the perfect or future tense: **I will help** = **ich** *werde* **helfen**

Cardinal number A whole number representing a quantity: **one/two/three** = **eins/zwei/drei**

Case The form of a noun, pronoun, adjective, or article that shows the part it plays in a sentence; there are four cases in German - nominative, accusative, genitive, and dative

Clause A self-contained section of a sentence that contains a subject and a verb

Collective noun A noun that is singular in form but refers to a group of individual persons or things, e.g. **royalty, grain**

Collocate A word that regularly occurs with another; **Buch** is a typical collocate of the verb **lesen**

Comparative The form of an adjective or adverb that makes it "more": **smaller** = **kleiner, more clearly** = **klarer**

Compound adjective An adjective formed from two or more separate words: **selbstbewusst (selbst + bewusst)** = **self-confident**

Compound noun A noun formed from two or more separate words: **der Flughafen (Flug+ Hafen)** = **airport**

Compound verb A verb formed by adding a prefix to a simple verb; in German, some compound verbs are separable **(an|fangen)**, and some are inseparable **(verlassen)**

Conditional tense A tense of a verb that expresses what might happen if something else occurred: **he would go** = **er würde gehen**

Conjugation Variation of the form of a verb to show tense, person, mood, etc.

Conjunction A word used to join clauses together: **and** = **und, because** = **weil**

Copula A verb, such as **be** or **become**, which links a **subject** and **predicate**

Dative The case of an indirect object; many German prepositions take the dative

Declension The form of a noun, pronoun, or adjective that corresponds to a particular case, number, or gender; some German nouns decline like adjectives, e.g. **Beamte, Taube**

Definite article: the = **der/die/das**

Demonstrative pronoun A pronoun indicating the person or thing referred to; *this* **is my bicycle** = *das* **ist mein Fahrrad**

Direct object The noun or pronoun directly affected by the verb: **he caught** *the* *ball* = **er fing** *den* **Ball**

Direct speech A speaker's actual words or the use of these in writing

Elliptical Having a word or words omitted, especially where the sense can be guessed from the context

Ending Letters added to the stem of verbs, as well as to nouns and adjectives, according to tense, case, etc.

Feminine One of the three noun genders in German: **die Frau** = **the woman**

Future tense The tense of a verb that refers to something that will happen in the future: **I will go** = **ich werde gehen**

Gender One of the three groups of nouns in German: masculine, feminine, or neuter

Genitive The case that shows possession; some prepositions in German take the genitive

Imperative A form of a verb that expresses a command: **go away!** = **geh weg!**

Imperfect tense The tense of a verb that refers to an uncompleted or a habitual action in the past: **I went there every Friday** = ich ging jeden Freitag dorthin

Impersonal verb A verb in English used only with 'it', and in German only with 'es': **it is raining** = es regnet

Indeclinable adjective An adjective that has no inflected forms, as German **klasse, Moskauer**

Indefinite article: a/an = ein/eine/ein

Indefinite pronoun A pronoun that does not identify a specific person or object: **one** = man, something = etwas

Indicative form The form of a verb used when making a statement of fact or asking questions of fact: **he is just coming** = er kommt gleich

Indirect object The noun or pronoun indirectly affected by the verb, at which the direct object is aimed: **I gave** *him* **the book** = ich gab *ihm* das Buch

Indirect speech A report of what someone has said which does not reproduce the exact words

Infinitive The basic part of a verb: **to play** = spielen

Inflect To change the ending or form of a word to show its tense or its grammatical relation to other words: **gehe** and **gehst** are inflected forms of the verb **gehen**

Inseparable verb A verb with a prefix that can never be separated from it: **verstehen, ich verstehe**

Interjection A sound, word, or remark expressing a strong feeling such as anger, fear, or joy: **oh!** = ach!

Interrogative pronoun A pronoun that asks a question: **who?** = wer?

Intransitive verb A verb that does not have a direct object: **he died suddenly** = er ist plötzlich gestorben

Irregular verb A verb that does not follow one of the set patterns and has its own individual forms

Masculine One of the three noun genders in German: **der Mann** = the man, **der Stuhl** = the chair

Modal verb A verb that is used with another verb (not a model) to express permission, obligation, possibility, etc., as German **können, sollen**, English **might, should**

Negative expressing refusal or denial; **there aren't any** = es gibt keine

Neuter One of the three noun genders in German: **das Buch** = the book, **das Kind** = the child

Nominative The case of the subject of a sentence; in sentences with **sein** and **werden** the noun after the verb is in the nominative: **that is my car** = das ist mein Auto

Noun A word that names a person or a thing

Number The state of being either singular or plural

Object The word or words naming the person or thing acted upon by a verb or preposition, as 'Buch' in **er las das Buch** or 'ihm' in **ich traue ihm**

Ordinal number A number that shows a person's or thing's position in a series: **the** *twenty-first* **century** = das *einundzwanzigste* Jahrhundert, **the** *second* **door on the left** = die *zweite* Tür links

Part of speech A grammatical term for the function of a word; noun, verb, adjective, etc., are parts of speech.

Passive In the passive form the subject of the verb experiences the action rather than performs it: **he was asked** = er wurde gefragt

Past participle The part of a verb used to form past tenses: **she had gone, er hat gelogen**

Perfect tense The tense of a verb that refers to a completed action in the past or an action that started in the past and is still going on: **I have already eaten** = ich habe schon gegessen; **I have been reading all day** = ich habe den ganzen Tag gelesen

Person Any of the three groups of personal pronouns and forms taken by verbs; the **first person** (e.g. **I/ich**) refers to the person(s) speaking, the **second person** (e.g. **you/du**) refers to the person(s) spoken to; the **third person** (e.g. **he/er**) refers to the persons spoken about

Personal pronoun A pronoun that refers to a person or thing: **he/she/it** = er/sie/es

Phrasal verb A verb in English combined with a preposition or an adverb to have a particular meaning: **run away** = weglaufen

Phrase A self-contained section of a sentence that does not contain a full verb

Pluperfect tense The tense of a verb that refers to something that happened before a particular point in the past: **als ich ankam,** *war* **er schon losgefahren** = when I arrived, he *had* already *left*

Plural Of nouns etc., referring to more than one: **the trees** = die Bäume

Possessive adjective An adjective that shows possession, belonging to someone or something; **my** = **mein/meine/mein**

Possessive pronoun A pronoun that shows possession, belonging to someone or something: **mine** = **meiner/meine/meins**

Postpositive Placed after the word to which it relates, as **in stock** in the phrase **items in stock**

Predicate The part of a sentence that says something about the **subject**, e.g. **went home** in **John went home**

Predicative An adjective is predicative when it comes after a verb such as **be** or **become** in English, or after **sein** or **werden** in German: **she is beautiful** = **sie ist schön**

Prefix A letter or group of letters added to the beginning of a word to change its meaning; in German, the prefix can move from separable verbs (**an|fangen**), but stays fixed to inseparable verbs (**verlassen**)

Preposition A word that stands in front of a noun or pronoun, relating it to the rest of the sentence; in German prepositions are always followed by a particular case, usually either the accusative or dative, but occasionally the genitive: **with** = **mit (+ dative)**, **for** = **für (+ accusative)**, **because of** = **wegen (+ genitive)**

Present participle The part of a verb that in English ends in –**ing**, and in German adds –**d** to the infinitive: **asking** = **fragend**

Present tense The tense of a verb that refers to something happening now: **I make** = **ich mache**

Pronoun A word that stands instead of a noun: **he** = **er**, **she** = **sie**, **mine** = **meiner/meine/meins**

Proper noun A name of a person, place, institution, etc., in English written with a capital letter at the start; **Germany**, the **Atlantic**, **Karl**, **Europa** are all proper nouns

Reflexive pronoun A pronoun that goes with a reflexive verb: in German **mich, dich, sich, uns, euch, sich**

Reflexive verb A verb whose object is the same as its subject; in German, it is used with a reflexive pronoun: **du sollst dich waschen** = **you should wash yourself**

Regular verb A verb that follows a set pattern in its different forms

Relative pronoun A pronoun that introduces a subordinate clause, relating to a person or thing mentioned in the main clause: **the man** *who* **visited us** = **der Mann,** *der* **uns besucht hat**

Reported Speech Another name for **Indirect speech**

Root The part of a word to which inflections are added; **fahr-** is the root of the verb **fahren**

Sentence A sequence of words, with a subject and a verb, that can stand on their own to make a statement, ask a question, or give a command

Separable verb A verb with a prefix that can be separated from it in some tenses: **anfangen, anzufangen, angefangen**, but **ich fange an, du fingst an**

Singular Of nouns etc., referring to just one: **the tree** = **der Baum**

Stem The part of a verb to which endings are added; **fahr-** is the stem of **fahren**

Subject In a clause or sentence, the noun or pronoun that causes the action of the verb: *he* **caught the ball** = *er* **fing den Ball**

Subjunctive A verb form that is used to express doubt or unlikelihood: **if I were to tell you that …** = **wenn ich dir sagen würde, dass …**

Subordinate clause A clause which adds information to the main clause of a sentence but cannot be used as a sentence by itself

Suffix A letter or group of letters joined to the end of a word to make another word, as –**heit** in **Schönheit**

Superlative The form of an adjective or adverb that makes it "most": **the** *smallest* **house** = **das** *kleinste* **Haus**, **most clearly** = **am klarsten**

Tense The form of a verb that tells when the action takes place: present, future, imperfect, perfect, pluperfect

Transitive verb A verb that is used with a direct object: **she read the book** = **sie las das Buch**

Verb A word or group of words that describes an action: **the children** *are playing* = **die Kinder** *spielen*

Glossar grammatischer Fachausdrücke

abhängiger Satz Von einem übergeordneten Satz (Hauptsatz) abhängiger Satz, der diesen ergänzt und der nur zusammen mit ihm gebraucht werden kann

absoluter Gebrauch Der Gebrauch eines transitiven Verbs ohne Objekt: ich *weiß*

Adjektiv Wort, das ein Substantiv näher bestimmt: ein *roter* Stift = a *red* pencil

Adverb Wort, das ein Verb, ein Adjektiv oder ein anderes Adverb näher bestimmt: sie singt *schön* = she sings *beautifully*

Akkusativ Einer der vier Kasus; im Deutschen stehen u. a. die von transitiven Verben erforderten Objekte im Akkusativ; manche deutschen Präpositionen stehen mit dem Akkusativ

Akkusativobjekt Objekt im Akkusativ: er fing den Ball = **he caught the ball**

Aktiv Form des Verbs in Sätzen, in denen das Subjekt der Träger der Handlung ist: **er hat gefragt = he asked**

Artikel Vor dem Substantiv stehendes, im Deutschen dessen Genus anzeigendes Wort (bestimmter Artikel, **der/die/das** = **the**, und unbestimmter Artikel, **ein, eine, ein** = **a/an)**

attributiv Ein Adjektiv ist attributiv, wenn es unmittelbar vor einem Substantiv steht, das es näher bestimmt: der *schwarze* Hund = the *black* dog

bestimmter Artikel: der/die/das = **the**

Dativ Einer der vier Kasus; im Deutschen stehen manche Objekte im Dativ; viele deutsche Präpositonen stehen mit dem Dativ

Dativobjekt Objekt im Dativ: ich gab *ihm* das Buch = I gave *him* the book

Deklination Die bei bestimmten Wortarten, vor allem bei Substantiv, Pronomen und Adjektiv, vorkommende Veränderung der Form zur Kennzeichnung von Kasus, Numerus und Genus

Demonstrativpronomen Pronomen, das auf eine Person oder eine Sache, von der die Rede ist, hinweist: *das* ist mein Fahrrad = *this* is my bicycle

direkte Rede Wörtliche Wiedergabe einer Äußerung

Eigenname Als Name einer Person, eines Orts, einer Institution usw. verwendetes Substantiv; Eigennamen werden im Englischen und im Deutschen großgeschrieben: **Karl, Europa, Germany, the Atlantic**

Ellipse Auslassung eines Teils einer Äußerung, der aus dem Kontext erschlossen werden kann

Endung Hinten an den Wortstamm angehängter, eine bestimmte Flexionsform kennzeichnender Wortbestandteil

erstes Partizip Im Deutschen mit dem Suffix **-nd**, im Englischen mit **-ing** gebildete Form des Verbs: **fragend** = **asking**

Fall *siehe* Kasus

Femininum Das weibliche Genus: **die Frau** = **the woman, die Bank** = **the bench**

fest zusammengesetztes Verb (Im Deutschen) Verb mit einem in allen Formen fest mit dem Stamm verbundenen Präfix: **verstehen, verstanden, ich verstehe**

flektieren Die Form eines Worts zur Kennzeichnung von Tempus, Kasus usw. verändern; vgl. **Flexion**

Flexion Die bei bestimmten Wortarten vorkommende Veränderung der Form zur Kennzeichnung von Tempus, Kasus usw.

Futur Tempus, das ein Geschehen, eine Handlung oder einen Zustand, ein Sein als zukünftig kennzeichnet: **ich werde gehen** = **I will go**

Genitiv Kasus, in dem häufig (besitzanzeigende oder andere) substantivische Attribute stehen; einige deutsche Präpositionen stehen auch mit dem Genitv

Genus, Geschlecht Eine der drei Klassen, in die im Deutschen die Substantive eingeteilt sind: Maskulinum, Femininum, Neutrum

Hauptsatz Aus Wörtern und gegliederten Wortgruppen zusammengesetzte selbständige sprachliche Einheit, mit der eine Aussage gemacht, eine Frage gestellt oder eine Aufforderung oder dergleichen ausgesprochen wird

Hilfsverb Eines der Verben, mit deren Hilfe zusammengesetzte Zeitformen gebildet werden (z. B. englisch **to have, to be**): she *had* gone, it *was* caught

Imperativ Verbform, die eine Aufforderung, einen Befehl oder dergleichen ausdrückt: **geh weg!** = **go away!**

Indefinitpronomen Pronomen, das eine unbestimmte Person oder Sache bezeichnet: **man** = **one, etwas** = **something**

indeklinables Adjektiv (Im Deutschen) ein Adjektiv, das nur eine Form hat: **klasse, Moskauer**

Indikativ Form des Verbs (Modus), mit der ein Geschehen oder ein Zustand als tatsächlich gegeben gekennzeichnet wird: **sie ist krank** = **she is ill**

indirekte Rede Nicht wörtliche Wiedergabe einer Äußerung

Infinitiv Grundform des Verbs: **spielen** = **to play**

Interjektion Wort, das nicht flektiert werden kann und das besonders dazu dient, Emotionen auszudrücken: **ach** = **oh**

Interrogativpronomen Eine Frage ausdrückendes Pronomen: **wer** = **who**

intransitives Verb Verb, das ohne Akkusativobjekt bzw. ohne direktes Objekt steht: **er ist gestorben** = **he died**

Kardinalzahl Zahlwort, das eine Anzahl angibt: **eins/zwei/drei** = **one/two/three**

Kasus (Fall) Form des Substantivs, Pronomens, Adjektivs und Artikels, die anzeigt, welche Rolle das betreffende Wort im Satz spielt; im Deutschen gibt es vier Kasus/Fälle - Nominativ, Genitiv, Dativ, Akkusativ

Kollektivum Substantiv, dessen Singular mehrere gleichartige Dinge bezeichnet (z. B. Laub, Gebirge)

Kollokator Wort, das regelmäßig mit einem bestimmten anderen Wort zusammen verwendet wird; im Englischen ist z. B. **book** ein typischer Kollokator des Verbs **to read**

Komparativ Form des Adjektivs und des Adverbs, die einen höheren Grad ausdrückt: **kleiner** = **smaller**, **öfter** = **more often**

Konjugation Veränderung der Form eines Verbs zur Kennzeichnung von Tempus, Person, Modus usw.

Konjunktion Wort, das dazu dient, Wörter oder Sätze miteinander zu verbinden: **und** = **and**, **weil** = **because**

Konjunktiv Form des Verbs (Modus), mit der ein Geschehen oder ein Zustand als erwünscht, vorgestellt, möglich, von einem anderen nur behauptet oder dergleichen gekennzeichnet wird: **sie sagte, sie** *sei* **krank** = **she said she was ill**

Maskulinum Das männliche Genus: **der Mann** = **the man**, **der Stuhl** = **the chair**

Modalverb Verb, das nur in Verbindung mit dem Infinitiv eines anderen Verbs gebraucht wird, und durch das z. B. eine Erlaubnis, eine Verpflichtung, eine Möglichkeit usw. ausgedrückt wird; z. B. englisch **might**, **should** und deutsch **können**, **sollen**

nachgestellt Attribute sind nachgestellt, wenn sie hinter dem Wort stehen, zu dem sie gehören: **ein Haus** *am Meer*

Nebensatz Vollständiger, aber von einem übergeordneten Satz abhängiger Satz in der Rolle eines Satzglieds oder eines Attributs

Neutrum Das sächliche Genus: **das Buch** = **the book**, **das Kind** = **the child**

Nominativ Kasus, in dem das Subjekt eines Satzes steht; auch zum Prädikat gehörende Substantive in Sätzen mit **sein** oder **werden** stehen im Nominativ: **das ist mein Auto** = **that is my car**

Numerus Der Numerus gibt an, ob etwas einmal oder mehrmals vorhanden ist; im Deutschen und im Englischen gibt es die Numeri Singular und Plural

Objekt Satzglied, das von einem Verb (neben dem Subjekt) als Ergänzung gefordert wird

Ordinalzahl Zahlwort, mit dem die Stelle angegeben wird, die etwas in einer Reihenfolge hat: **das** *einundzwanzigste* **Jahrhundert** = **the** *twenty-first* **century**, *die zweite* **Tür links** = **the** *second* **door on the left**

Partizip *siehe* **erstes Partizip, zweites Partizip**

Passiv Form des Verbs in Sätzen, in denen das Subjekt nicht der Träger der Handlung ist: **er wurde gefragt** = **he was asked**

Perfekt Tempus, das (im Deutschen) ein Geschehen als in der Vergangenheit abgeschlossen, vollendet kennzeichnet: **ich habe schon gegessen** = **I have already eaten**

Person Bei den Formen des Verbs und bestimmter Pronomina unterscheidet man drei "Personen"; die **erste Person** (z. B. **ich/I**) kennzeichnet die sprechende Person bzw. die sprechenden Personen, die **zweite Person** (z. B. **du/you**) die angesprochene Person bzw. die angesprochenen Personen und die **dritte Person** (z. B. **sie/she**) die Person bzw. Personen, über die etwas ausgesagt wird

Personalpronomen Pronomen, das (anstelle eines Substantivs) eine Person oder Sache bezeichnet: **er/sie/es** = **he/she/it**

Plural Numerus, durch den ausgedrückt wird, dass es sich um mehrere Personen oder Sachen handelt

Plusquamperfekt Tempus, das ein Geschehen, eine Handlung oder einen Zustand, ein Sein als zu einem bestimmten Zeitpunkt in der Vergangenheit schon abgeschlossen kennzeichnet: **als ich ankam,** *war* **er schon** *losgefahren* = **when I arrived, he had already left**

Possessivpronomen Pronomen, das ein Besitzverhältnis oder eine Zugehörigkeit oder dergleichen ausdrückt; im Deutschen unterscheidet man das allein stehend gebrauchte Possessivpronomen (englisch possessive pronoun: **meiner/meine/meins** = **mine**) und das attributiv gebrauchte Possessivpronomen (englisch possessive adjective: **mein/meine/mein** = **my**)

Prädikat Im Kern durch eine Verbform gebildetes Satzglied, durch das ein Geschehen, eine Handlung oder ein Zustand, ein Sein benannt wird und das bestimmte Ergänzungen (z. B. ein direktes Objekt bzw. ein Akkusativobjekt) erfordern kann

prädikativ Ein Adjektiv ist prädikativ, wenn es, wie nach **sein** oder **werden** bzw. **be** oder **become**, zum Prädikat gehört: **sie ist schön** = **she is beautiful**

Präfix Vor den Stamm eines Grundworts gesetztes Wortbildungselement: *zurückkommen, verlassen*

Präposition Nicht flektierbares Wort, das die Beziehung, das Verhältnis zwischen Wörtern und Wortgruppen im Satz kennzeichnet; im Deutschen steht nach einer Präposition stets ein bestimmter Kasus, meist der Akkusativ oder der Dativ, seltener auch der Genitiv; **mit** (+ Dativ) = **with**, **für** (+ Akkusativ) = **for**, **wegen** (+ Genitiv) = **because of**

Präsens Tempus, das ein Geschehen, eine Handlung oder einen Zustand, ein Sein als gegenwärtig kennzeichnet: **ich mache** = **I make**

Präteritum Tempus, das ein Geschehen, eine Handlung oder einen Zustand, ein Sein als vergangen kennzeichnet: **der Wagen** *fuhr* **sehr schnell** = **the car** *went* **very fast**

Pronomen Wort, das anstelle eines Substantivs stehen kann: **sie** = **she**, **du** = **you**, **meiner/meine/meins** = **mine**

reflexives Verb Verb, bei dem Subjekt und Objekt dieselbe Person oder Sache bezeichnen und das Objekt ein Reflexivpronomen ist: **du sollst dich waschen** = **you should wash yourself**

Reflexivpronomen Pronomen, das in Sätzen mit reflexiven Verben als Objekt verwendet wird: im Englischen **myself, yourself, himself, herself, itself, ourselves, yourselves, themselves, oneself**; im Deutschen in der dritten Person **sich** und in allen übrigen Personen dem Personalpronomen gleich

regelmäßiges Verb Verb, bei dem alle Formen nach einem bestimmten Muster von demselben Stamm abgeleitet werden

Relativpronomen Pronomen, mit dem ein Nebensatz (oft ein Attributsatz) eingeleitet wird und das sich auf eine im Hauptsatz genannte Person oder Sache bezieht: **es war der Mann,** *der* **uns besucht hat** = **it was the man** *who* **visited us**

Singular Numerus, durch den ausgedrückt wird, dass es sich um nur eine Person oder Sache handelt: **der Baum** = **the tree**

Stamm Der Teil eines Worts, an den bei der Flexion die Endungen angehängt werden; **fahr-** ist der Stamm des Verbs **fahren,**

Subjekt Satzglied, das diejenige Person oder Sache bezeichnet, von der (in Sätzen im Aktiv) das im Verb ausgedrückte Geschehen ausgeht: *er* **fing den Ball** = *he* **caught the ball**

Substantiv Wort, das eine Person oder eine Sache bezeichnet

Suffix Hinter den Stamm eines Grundworts gesetztes Wortbildungselement, z. B. *-heit* in **Schön***heit*

Superlativ Form des Adjektivs und des Adverbs, die einen höchsten Grad ausdrückt: **das** *kleinste* **Haus** = **the** *smallest* **house, am klarsten** = **most clearly**

Tempus Kategorie des Verbs, die ein Geschehen (unter anderem) als gegenwärtig, vergangen oder zukünftig kennzeichnet; die wichtigsten Tempora des Deutschen sind: Präsens, Perfekt, Präteritum, Plusquamperfekt, Futur

transitives Verb Verb, das mit einem Akkusativobjekt bzw. einem direkten Objekt steht: **ein Buch** *lesen* = *read* **a book**

unbestimmter Artikel: **ein/eine/ein** = **a/an**

unfest zusammengesetztes Verb (Im Deutschen) mit einem Präfix gebildetes Verb, bei dem das Präfix in bestimmten Flexionsformen vom Grundverb getrennt steht: **anfangen, anzufangen, angefangen,** aber: **ich fange an, du fingst an**

unpersönliches Verb Verb, das nur mit dem Subjekt **es** bzw. **it** verwendet wird: **es regnet** = **it is raining**

unregelmäßiges Verb Verb, dessen Formen nicht regelmäßig gebildet werden

Verb Wort, das ein Geschehen, eine Handlung oder ein Sein, einen Zustand bezeichnet: **die Kinder** *spielen* = **the children** *are playing*

verneinend Eine Verneinung ausdrückend: **es gibt keine** = **there aren't any**

Wortart Klasse von Wörtern, die bestimmte gemeinsame grammatische Eigenschaften haben, z. B Substantiv, Verb, Adjektiv

zusammengesetztes Adjektiv Aus mehreren Wörtern gebildetes Adjektiv: **self-confident** = **selbstbewusst**

zusammengesetztes Substantiv Aus mehreren Wörtern gebildetes Substantiv: **airport (air + port)** = **Flughafen**

zusammengesetztes Verb Aus einem Verb und einem weiteren Bestandteil gebildetes Verb; im Deutschen gibt es unfest (z. B. **anfangen**) und fest (z. B. **verlassen**) zusammengesetzte Verben

zweites Partizip Form des Verbs, die zur Bildung der Perfekttempora verwendet wird: **er hat** *gelogen*, **she had** *gone*

Numbers / Zahlen

Cardinal numbers	*Kardinalzahlen*	Ordinal numbers	*Ordinalzahlen*
1 one	1 eins, ein...	1st first	1. erst...
2 two	2 zwei	2nd second	2. zweit...
3 three	3 drei	3rd third	3. dritt...
4 four	4 vier	4th fourth	4. viert...
5 five	5 fünf	5th fifth	5. fünft...
6 six	6 sechs	6th sixth	6. sechst...
7 seven	7 sieben	7th seventh	7. siebt..., siebent...
8 eight	8 acht	8th eighth	8. acht...
9 nine	9 neun	9th ninth	9. neunt...
10 ten	10 zehn	10th tenth	10. zehnt...
11 eleven	11 elf	11th eleventh	11. elft...
12 twelve	12 zwölf	12th twelfth	12. zwölft...
13 thirteen	13 dreizehn	13th thirteenth	13. dreizehnt...
14 fourteen	14 vierzehn	14th fourteenth	14. vierzehnt...
15 fifteen	15 fünfzehn	15th fifteenth	15. fünfzehnt...
16 sixteen	16 sechzehn	16th sixteenth	16. sechzehnt...
17 seventeen	17 siebzehn	17th seventeenth	17. siebzehnt...
18 eighteen	18 achtzehn	18th eighteenth	18. achtzehnt...
19 nineteen	19 neunzehn	19th nineteenth	19. neunzehnt...
20 twenty	20 zwanzig	20th twentieth	20. zwanzigst...
21 twenty-one	21 einundzwanzig	21st twenty-first	21. einundzwanzigst...
30 thirty	30 dreißig	30th thirtieth	30. dreißigst...
40 forty	40 vierzig	40th fortieth	40. vierzigst...
50 fifty	50 fünfzig	50th fiftieth	50. fünfzigst...
60 sixty	60 sechzig	60th sixtieth	60. sechzigst...
70 seventy	70 siebzig	70th seventieth	70. siebzigst...
80 eighty	80 achtzig	80th eightieth	80. achtzigst...
90 ninety	90 neunzig	90th ninetieth	90. neunzigst...
100 one hundred	100 [ein]hundert	100th [one] hundredth	100. [ein]hundertst...
101 one hundred and one	101 [ein]hundert-[und]eins	101st [one] hundred and first	101. [ein]hundert-[und]erst...
1,000 one thousand	1 000 [ein]tausend	1,000th [one] thousandth	1 000. [ein]tausendst...
1,001 one thousand and one	1 001 [ein]tausend-[und]eins	1,001st one thousand and first	1 001. [ein]tausend[und]erst...
10,000 ten thousand	10 000 zehntausend	10,000th ten thousandth	10 000. zehntausendst...
13,438 thirteen thousand, four hundred and thirty-eight	13 438 dreizehntausendvierhundert-[und]achtunddreißig	13,438th thirteen thousand, four hundred and thirty-eighth	13 438. dreizehntausendvierhundert-[und]achtunddreißigst...
100,000 one hundred thousand	100 000 [ein]hunderttausend	100,000th [one] hundred thousandth	100 000. [ein]hunderttausendst...
1,000,000 one million	1 000 000 eine Million	1,000,000th [one] millionth	1 000 000. millionst...
2,000,000 two million	2 000 000 zwei Millionen	2,000,000th two millionth	2 000 000. zweimillionst...
1,000,000,000 one thousand million (Brit.);one billion (Amer.)	1 000 000 000 eine Milliarde	1,000,000,000th [one] thousand millionth (Brit.); one billionth (Amer.)	1 000 000 000. milliardst...

Vulgar fractions and mixed numbers / Brüche (gemeine Brüche) und gemischte Zahlen

in figures in Zahlen	in words	in Worten
$1/2$	a/one half	ein halb
$1/3$	a/one third	ein drittel
$1/4$	a/one quarter	ein viertel
$1/0$	a/one tenth	ein zehntel
$2/3$	two-thirds	zwei drittel
$1/1$	one over one	ein eintel
$4/1$	four over one	vier eintel
m/n	m over n	m n-tel
$x/6$	x over six	x sechstel
$1\,1/2$	one and a half	ein[und]einhalb

Decimal numbers / Dezimalzahlen

written as	geschrieben	spoken as	gesprochen
0.1	0,1	nought point one	null Komma eins
0.015	0,015	nought point nought one five	null Komma null eins fünf
1.40	1,40	one point four o [əʊ]	eins Komma vier null

Weights and Measures / Maße und Gewichte

Weight / Gewichte

1,000 milligrams (mg)	= 1 gram (g)	= 15.43 grains
1 000 Milligramm (mg)	= *1 Gramm (g)*	
1,000 grams	= 1 kilogram (kg)	= 2.205 pounds
1 000 Gramm	= *1 Kilogramm (kg)*	
1,000 kilograms	= 1 tonne (t)	= 19.684 hundredweight
1 000 Kilogramm	= *1 Tonne (t)*	
	1 ounce (oz.)	= 28.35 g
16 ounces	= 1 pound (lb.)	= 0.454 kg
14 pounds	= 1 stone (st.)	= 6.35 kg
112 pounds	= 1 hundredweight	= 50.8 kg
20 hundredweight	= 1 ton (t.)	= 1,016.05 kg

Length / Längenmaße

10 millimetres (mm)	= 1 centimetre (cm)	= 0.394 inch
10 Millimeter (mm)	= *1 Zentimeter (cm)*	
100 centimetres	= 1 metre (m)	= 39.4 inches/1.094 yards
100 Zentimeter	= *1 Meter (m)*	
1,000 metres	= 1 kilometre (km)	= 0.6214 mile/ $5/8$ mile
1 000 Meter	= *1 Kilometer (km)*	
	1 inch (in.)	= 25.4 mm
12 inches	= 1 foot (ft.)	= 30.48 cm
3 feet	= 1 yard (yd.)	= 0.914 m
220 yards	= 1 furlong	= 201.17 m
8 furlongs	= 1 mile (m.)	= 1.609 km
1,760 yards	= 1 mile	= 1.609 km

Square measure / Flächenmaße

100 square metres (sq. m)	= 1 are	= 0.025 acre
100 Quadratmeter (m²)	= *1 Ar (a)*	
100 ares	= 1 hectare (ha)	= 2.471 acres
100 Ar	= *1 Hektar (ha)*	
100 hectares	= 1 square kilometre (sq.km)	= 0.386 square miles
100 hektar	= *1 Quadratkilometer (km²)*	
	1 square inch	= 6.452cm²
144 square inches	= 1 square foot	= 929.03 cm²
9 square feet	= 1 square yard	= 0.836 m²
4,840 square yards	= 1 acre	= 0.405 ha
640 acres	= 1 square mile	= 2.59k²/259 ha

Cubic measure / Raummaße

1 cubic centimetre (cc) .... = 0.06 cubic inches
1 Kubikzentimeter (cm³)

1,000,000 cubic centimetres .... = 1 cubic metre (cu. m) .... = 35.714 cubic feet/
1 000 000 Kubikzentimeter. .... = *1 Kubikmeter (m³)* .... 1.307 cubic yards

                               1 cubic inch .... = 16.4 cm³

1,728 cubic inches .... = 1 cubic foot. .... = 0.028 m³

27 cubic feet .... = 1 cubic yard .... = 0.764 m³

Capacity / Hohlmaße

10 millilitres (ml) .... = 1 centilitre (cl)
10 Milliliter (ml) .... = *1 Zentiliter (cl)*

100 centilitres .... = 1 litre (l) .... = 1.76 pints (2.1 US pints)/
100 Zentiliter .... = *1 Liter (l)* .... 0.22 gallons (0.264 US gallons)

4 gills .... = 1 pint (pt.) (1.201 US pints). ... = 0.568 l

2 pints. .... = 1 quart (qt.) (1.201 US quarts) = 1.136 l

4 quarts .... = 1 gallon (gal) (1.201 US gallons) = 4.546 l